THE COLLINS PAPERBACK SPANISH DICTIONARY

SPANISH · ENGLISH   ENGLISH · SPANISH

HarperCollins*Publishers*

First published in this edition 1989

© William Collins Sons & Co. Ltd. 1989

Latest reprint 1991

ISBN 0 00 433335 7

contributors/colaboradores
Jeremy Butterfield, Mike Gonzalez, Gerry Breslin,
John Forry, Alicia Harland, Val McNulty,
M.ª Ángeles Recio Corral, M.ª José Sanchez Blanco

editorial staff/redacción
Claire Evans   Jane Horwood   Irene Lakhani

Printed in Great Britain by
HarperCollins Manufacturing, Glasgow

ÍNDICE DE MATERIAS

CONTENTS

INTRODUCCIÓN

Para comprender el inglés

Este diccionario, nuevo y completamente puesto al día, pone a disposición del usuario de la lengua una cobertura amplia y a la vez práctica de los usos lingüísticos más corrientes del inglés de hoy, e incluye la terminología necesaria en el dominio empresarial y de la microinformática, así como una numerosa selección de las abreviaturas, siglas y topónimos que suelen aparecer en la prensa. A fin de facilitar la labor del lector, se mencionan también las formas irregulares de los verbos ingleses, con indicaciones que hacen referencia a las formas básicas, donde se encuentra la traducción.

Para expresarse en inglés

A fin de ayudar al lector a expresarse correcta e idiomáticamente en inglés, el diccionario contiene frecuentes indicaciones – a manera de glosas de orientación – que pueden servirle para encontrar la traducción más apropiada en un contexto dado. Todas las palabras de uso más corriente en la lengua reciben tratamiento detallado, en el que se mencionan muchas ilustraciones de sus usos característicos.

Para acompañarle en su trabajo

Nos hemos esmerado en hacer de este nuevo diccionario de Collins una compilación fiable y fácil de utilizar que responda a sus necesidades laborales y de estudio. Nuestra esperanza es que le sirva mucho tiempo como fiel compañero de trabajo en todo lo que le haga falta mientras maneja el inglés como lengua extranjera.

INTRODUCTION

Understanding Spanish

This new and thoroughly up-to-date dictionary provides the user with wide-ranging, practical coverage of current usage, including terminology relevant to business and office automation, and a comprehensive selection of abbreviations, acronyms and geographical names commonly found in the press. You will also find, for ease of consultation, irregular forms of Spanish verbs and nouns with a cross-reference to the basic form where a translation is given.

Self-expression in Spanish

To help you express yourself correctly and idiomatically in Spanish, numerous indications – think of them as signposts – guide you to the most appropriate translation for your context. All the most commonly used words are given detailed treatment, with many examples of typical usage.

A working companion

Much care has been taken to make this new Collins dictionary thoroughly reliable, easy to use and relevant to your work and study. We hope it will become a long-serving companion for all your foreign language needs.

ABREVIATURAS

ABBREVIATIONS

adjetivo, locución adjetiva	**a**	adjective, adjectival phrase
abreviatura	**ab(b)r**	abbreviation
adverbio, locución adverbial	**ad**	adverb, adverbial phrase
administración, lengua administrativa	**ADMIN**	administration
agricultura	**AGR**	agriculture
América Latina	**AM**	Latin America
anatomía	**ANAT**	anatomy
arquitectura	**ARQ, ARCH**	architecture
astrología, astronomía	**ASTRO**	astrology, astronomy
el automóvil	**AUT(O)**	the motor car and motoring
aviación, viajes aéreos	**AVIAT**	flying, air travel
biología	**BIO(L)**	biology
botánica, flores	**BOT**	botany
inglés británico	**Brit**	British English
química	**CHEM**	chemistry
lengua familiar (! vulgar)	**col (!)**	colloquial usage (! particularly offensive)
comercio, finanzas, banca	**COM(M)**	commerce, finance, banking
informática	**COMPUT**	computing
conjunción	**conj**	conjunction
construcción	**CONSTR**	building
compuesto	**cpd**	compound element
cocina	**CULIN**	cookery
economía	**ECON**	economics
electricidad, electrónica	**ELEC**	electricity, electronics
enseñanza, sistema escolar	**ESCOL**	schooling, schools
España	**Esp**	Spain
especialmente	**esp**	especially
exclamación, interjección	**excl**	exclamation, interjection
femenino	**f**	feminine
lengua familiar (! vulgar)	**fam (!)**	colloquial usage (! particularly offensive)
ferrocarril	**FERRO**	railways
uso figurado	**fig**	figurative use
fotografía	**FOTO**	photography
(verbo inglés) del cual la partícula es inseparable	**fus**	(phrasal verb) where the particle is inseparable
generalmente	**gen**	generally
geografía, geología	**GEO**	geography, geology
geometría	**GEOM**	geometry
informática	**INFORM**	computing
invariable	**inv**	invariable
irregular	**irg**	irregular
lo jurídico	**JUR**	law
América Latina	**LAm**	Latin America
gramática, lingüística	**LING**	grammar, linguistics
literatura	**LIT**	literature
masculino	**m**	masculine
matemáticas	**MAT(H)**	mathematics
medicina	**MED**	medical term, medicine
masculino/femenino	**m/f**	masculine/feminine
lo militar, ejército	**MIL**	military matters
música	**MUS**	music

sustantivo, nombre	**n**	noun
navegación, náutica	**NAUT**	sailing, navigation
sustantivo numérico	**num**	numeral noun
complemento	**obj**	(grammatical) object
	o.s.	oneself
peyorativo	**pey, pej**	derogatory, pejorative
fotografía	**PHOT**	photography
fisiología	**PHYSIOL**	physiology
plural	**pl**	plural
política	**POL**	politics
participio de pasado	**pp**	past participle
prefijo	**pref**	prefix
preposición	**prep**	preposition
pronombre	**pron**	pronoun
psicología, psiquiatría	**PSICO, PSYCH**	psychology, psychiatry
tiempo pasado	**pt**	past tense
sustantivo no empleado en el plural	**q**	collective (uncountable) noun, not used in plural
ferrocarril	**RAIL**	railways
religión, lo eclesiástico	**REL**	religion, church service
	sb	somebody
enseñanza, sistema escolar	**SCOL**	schooling, schools
singular	**sg**	singular
España	**Sp**	Spain
	sth	something
subjuntivo	**subjun**	subjunctive
sujeto	**su(b)j**	(grammatical) subject
sufijo	**suff**	suffix
tauromaquia	**TAUR**	bullfighting
también	**tb**	also
técnica, tecnología	**TEC(H)**	technical term, technology
telecomunicaciones	**TELEC, TEL**	telecommunications
televisión	**TV**	television
imprenta, tipografía	**TIP, TYP**	typography, printing
sistema universitario	**UNIV**	universities
inglés norteamericano	**US**	American English
verbo	**vb**	verb
verbo intransitivo	**vi**	intransitive verb
verbo pronominal	**vr**	reflexive verb
verbo transitivo	**vt**	transitive verb
zoología, animales	**ZOOL**	zoology
marca registrada	®	registered trademark
indica un equivalente cultural	≈	introduces a cultural equivalent

SPANISH PRONUNCIATION

CONSONANTS

b	[b, ß]	*b*oda bom*b*a la*b*or	see notes on *v* below
c	[k]	*c*aja	*c* before *a*, *o* or *u* is pronounced as in *c*at
ce, ci	[θe, θi]	*c*ero *c*ielo	*c* before *e* or *i* is pronounced as in *th*in
ch	[tʃ]	*ch*iste	*ch* is pronounced as *ch* in *ch*air
d	[d, ð]	*d*anés ciu*d*ad	at the beginning of a phrase or after *l* or *n*, *d* is pronounced as in English. In any other position it is pronounced like *th* in *th*e
g	[g, ɣ]	*g*afas pa*g*a	*g* before *a*, *o* or *u* is pronounced as in *g*ap, if at the beginning of a phrase or after *n*. In other positions the sound is softened
ge, gi	[xe, xi]	*g*ente *g*irar	*g* before *e* or *i* is pronounced similar to *ch* in Scottish lo*ch*
h		*h*aber	*h* is always silent in Spanish
j	[x]	*j*ugar	*j* is pronounced similar to *ch* in Scottish lo*ch*
ll	[ʎ]	ta*ll*e	*ll* is pronounced like the *lli* in mi*lli*on
ñ	[ɲ]	ni*ñ*o	*ñ* is pronounced like the *ni* in o*ni*on
q	[k]	*q*ue	*q* is pronounced as *k* in *k*ing
r, rr	[r, rr]	quita*r* ga*rr*a	*r* is always pronounced in Spanish, unlike the silent *r* in dance*r*. *rr* is trilled, like a Scottish *r*
s	[s]	quizá*s* i*s*la	*s* is usually pronounced as in pa*ss*, but before *b*, *d*, *g*, *l*, *m* or *n* it is pronounced as in ro*s*e
v	[b, ß]	*v*ía en*v*iar di*v*idir	*v* is pronounced something like *b*. At the beginning of a phrase or after *m* or *n* it is pronounced as *b* in *b*oy. In any other position it is pronounced with the lips in position to pronounce *b* of *b*oy, but not meeting
w	[b, ß, w]	*w*áter *wh*isky	pronounced either like Spanish *b*, or like English *w*
z	[θ]	tena*z*	*z* is pronounced as *th* in *th*in

f, k, l, m, n, p, t and x are pronounced as in English.

In general, we give the pronunciation of each entry in square brackets after the word in question. However, where the entry is composed of two or more unhyphenated words, each of which is given elsewhere in this dictionary, you will find the pronunciation of each word in its alphabetical position.

VOWELS

a	[a]	p*a*ta	not as long as *a* in f*a*r. When followed by a consonant in the same syllable (i.e. in a closed syllable), as in am*a*nte, the *a* is short, as in b*a*t
e	[e]	m*e*	like *e* in th*e*y. In a closed syllable, as in g*e*nte, the *e* is short as in p*e*t
i	[i]	p*i*no	as in m*ea*n or mach*i*ne
o	[o]	l*o*	as in l*o*cal. In a closed syllable, as in c*o*ntrol, the *o* is short as in c*o*t
u	[u]	l*u*nes	as in r*u*le. It is silent after *q*, and in *gue*, *gui*, unless marked *güe*, *güi* e.g. anti*güe*dad, when it is pronounced like *w* in *w*olf

SEMIVOWELS

i, y	[j]	b*i*en *hi*elo *y*unta	pronounced like *y* in *y*es
u	[w]	h*u*evo f*u*ente antig*ü*edad	unstressed *u* between consonant and vowel is pronounced like *w* in *w*ell. See also notes on *u* above

DIPHTHONGS

ai, ay	[ai]	b*ai*le	as *i* in r*i*de
au	[au]	*au*to	as *ou* in sh*ou*t
ei, ey	[ei]	bu*ey*	as *ey* in gr*ey*
eu	[eu]	d*eu*da	both elements pronounced independently [e]+[u]
oi, oy	[oi]	h*oy*	as *oy* in t*oy*

STRESS

The rules of stress in Spanish are as follows:

(a) when a word ends in a vowel or in *n* or *s*, the second last syllable is stressed: pat*a*ta, pat*a*tas, c*o*me, c*o*men

(b) when a word ends in a consonant other than *n* or *s*, the stress falls on the last syllable: par*e*d, habl*a*r

(c) when the rules set out in a and b are not applied, an acute accent appears over the stressed vowel: com*ú*n, geograf*í*a, ingl*é*s

In the phonetic transcription, the symbol ['] precedes the syllable on which the stress falls.

PRONUNCIACIÓN INGLESA

VOCALES Y DIPTONGOS

	Ejemplo inglés	*Ejemplo español/explicación*
[ɑ:]	f*a*ther	Entre *a* de p*a*dre y *o* de n*o*che
[ʌ]	b*u*t, c*o*me	*a* muy breve
[æ]	m*a*n, c*a*t	Se mantienen los labios en la posición de *e* en p*e*na y luego se pronuncia el sonido *a*
[ə]	fath*e*r, *a*go	Sonido indistinto parecido a una *e* u *o* casi mudas
[ə:]	b*i*rd, h*ea*rd	Entre *e* abierta, y *o* cerrada, sonido alargado
[ɛ]	g*e*t, b*e*d	Como en p*e*rro
[ɪ]	*i*t, b*i*g	Más breve que en s*i*
[i:]	t*ea*, s*ee*	Como en f*i*no
[ɔ]	h*o*t, w*a*sh	Como en t*o*rre
[ɔ:]	s*aw*, *a*ll	Como en p*o*r
[u]	p*u*t, b*oo*k	Sonido breve, más cerrado que b*u*rro
[u:]	t*oo*, y*ou*	Sonido largo, como en *u*no
[aɪ]	fl*y*, h*i*gh	Como en fr*ai*le
[au]	h*ow*, h*ou*se	Como en p*au*sa
[ɛə]	th*e*re, b*ea*r	Casi como en v*ea*, pero el sonido *a* se mezcla con el indistinto [ə]
[eɪ]	d*a*y, ob*e*y	*e* cerrada seguida por una *i* débil
[ɪə]	h*e*re, h*ea*r	Como en man*ía*, mezclándose el sonido *a* con el indistinto [ə]
[əu]	g*o*, n*o*te	[ə] seguido por una breve *u*
[ɔɪ]	b*oy*, *oi*l	Como en v*oy*
[uə]	p*oo*r, s*u*re	*u* bastante larga más el sonido indistinto [ə]

CONSONANTES

	Ejemplo inglés	*Ejemplo español/explicación*
[b]	*b*ut	Como en *b*omba, tum*b*a
[d]	men*d*e*d*	Como en con*d*e, an*d*ar
[g]	*g*o, *g*et, bi*g*	Como en *g*rande, *g*ol
[dʒ]	*g*in, *j*u*dg*e	Como en la *ll* andaluza y en *G*eneralitat (catalán)
[ŋ]	si*ng*	Como en ví*n*culo
[h]	*h*ouse, *h*e	Como la jota hispanoamericana
[j]	*y*oung, *y*es	Como en *y*a
[k]	*c*ome, mo*ck*	Como en *c*aña, Es*c*ocia
[r]	*r*ed, t*r*ead	Se pronuncia con la punta de la lengua hacia atrás y sin hacerla vibrar
[s]	*s*and, ye*s*	Como en ca*s*a, *s*esión
[z]	ro*s*e, *z*ebra	Como en de*s*de, mi*s*mo
[ʃ]	*sh*e, ma*ch*ine	Como en *ch*ambre (francés), ro*x*o (portugués)
[tʃ]	*ch*in, ri*ch*	Como en *ch*ocolate
[v]	*v*alley	Con los labios en la posición de la *f* de *f*ondo, pero es sonoro
[w]	*w*ater, *wh*ich	Como en la *u* de h*u*evo, p*u*ede
[ʒ]	vi*s*ion	Como en *j*ournal (francés)
[θ]	*th*ink, my*th*	Como en re*c*eta, *z*apato
[ð]]	*th*is, *th*e	Como en la *d* de habla*d*o, verda*d*

p, f, m, n, l, t iguales que en español
El signo * indica que la r final escrita apenas se pronuncia en inglés británico cuando la palabra siguiente empieza con vocal. El signo ['] indica la sílaba acentuada.

Por regla general, la pronunciación viene dada entre corchetes después de cada entrada léxica. Sin embargo, allí donde la entrada es un compuesto de dos o más palabras separadas, cada una de las cuales es objeto de entrada en alguna otra parte del diccionario, la pronunciación de cada palabra se encontrará en su correspondiente posición alfabética.

SPANISH VERB FORMS

1 Gerund. *2* Imperative. *3* Present. *4* Preterite. *5* Future. *6* Present subjunctive. *7* Imperfect subjunctive. *8* Past participle. *9* Imperfect.
Etc indicates that the irregular root is used for all persons of the tense, e.g. **oír**: *6* oiga, oigas, oigamos, oigáis, oigan.

acertar *2* acierta *3* acierto, aciertas, acierta, aciertan *6* acierte, aciertes, acierte, acierten

acordar *2* acuerda *3* acuerdo, acuerdas, acuerda, acuerdan *6* acuerde, acuerdes, acuerde, acuerden

advertir *1* advirtiendo *2* advierte *3* advierto, adviertes, advierte, advierten *4* advirtió, advirtieron *6* advierta, adviertas, advierta, advirtamos, advirtáis, adviertan *7* advirtiera *etc*

agradecer *3* agradezco *6* agradezca *etc*

aparecer *3* aparezco *6* aparezca *etc*

aprobar *2* aprueba *3* apruebo, apruebas, aprueba, aprueban *6* apruebe, apruebes, apruebe, aprueben

atravesar *2* atraviesa *3* atravieso, atraviesas, atraviesa, atraviesan *6* atraviese, atravieses, atraviese, atraviesen

caber *3* quepo *4* cupe, cupiste, cupo, cupimos, cupisteis, cupieron *5* cabré *etc* *6* quepa *etc* *7* cupiera *etc*

caer *1* cayendo *3* caigo *4* cayó, cayeron *6* caiga *etc* *7* cayera *etc*

calentar *2* calienta *3* caliento, calientas, calienta, calientan *6* caliente, calientes, caliente, calienten

cerrar *2* cierra *3* cierro, cierras, cierra, cierran *6* cierre, cierres, cierre, cierren

COMER *1* comiendo *2* come, comed *3* como, comes, come, comemos, coméis, comen *4* comí, comiste, comió, comimos, comisteis, comieron *5* comeré, comerás, comerá, comeremos, comeréis, comerán *6* coma, comas, coma, comamos, comáis, coman *7* comiera, comieras, comiera, comiéramos, comierais, comieran *8* comido *9* comía, comías, comía, comíamos, comíais, comían

conocer *3* conozco *6* conozca *etc*

contar *2* cuenta *3* cuento, cuentas, cuenta, cuentan *6* cuente, cuentes, cuente, cuenten

costar *2* cuesta *3* cuesto, cuestas, cuesta, cuestan *6* cueste, cuestes, cueste, cuesten

dar *3* doy *4* di, diste, dio, dimos, disteis, dieron *7* diera *etc*

decir *2* di *3* digo *4* dije, dijiste, dijo, dijimos, dijisteis, dijeron *5* diré *etc* *6* diga *etc* *7* dijera *etc* *8* dicho

despertar *2* despierta *3* despierto, despiertas, despierta, despiertan *6* despierte, despiertes, despierte, despierten

divertir *1* divirtiendo *2* divierte *3* divierto, diviertes, divierte, divierten *4* divirtió, divirtieron *6* divierta, diviertas, divierta, divirtamos, divirtáis, diviertan *7* divirtiera *etc*

dormir *1* durmiendo *2* duerme *3* duermo, duermes, duerme, duermen *4* durmió, durmieron *6* duerma, duermas, duerma, durmamos, durmáis, duerman *7* durmiera *etc*

empezar *2* empieza *3* empiezo, empiezas, empieza, empiezan *4* empecé *6* empiece, empieces, empiece, empecemos, empecéis, empiecen

entender *2* entiende *3* entiendo, entiendes, entiende, entienden *6* entienda, entiendas, entienda, entiendan

ESTAR *2* está *3* estoy, estás, está, están *4* estuve, estuviste, estuvo, estuvimos, estuvisteis, estuvieron *6* esté, estés, esté, estén *7* estuviera *etc*

HABER *3* he, has, ha, hemos, han *4* hube, hubiste, hubo, hubimos, hubisteis, hubieron *5* habré *etc* *6* haya *etc* *7* hubiera *etc*

HABLAR *1* hablando *2* habla, hablad *3* hablo, hablas, habla, hablamos, habláis, hablan *4* hablé, hablaste, habló, hablamos, hablasteis, hablaron *5* hablaré, hablarás, hablará, hablaremos, hablaréis, hablarán *6* hable, hables, hable, hablemos, habléis, hablen *7* hablara, hablaras, hablara, habláramos, hablarais, hablaran *8* hablado *9* hablaba, hablabas, hablaba, hablábamos, hablabais, hablaban

hacer *2* haz *3* hago *4* hice, hiciste, hizo, hicimos, hicisteis, hicieron *5* haré *etc* *6* haga *etc* *7* hiciera *etc* *8* hecho

instruir *1* instruyendo *2* instruye *3* instruyo, instruyes, instruye, instruyen *4* instruyó, instruyeron *6* instruya *etc* *7* instruyera *etc*

ir *1* yendo *2* ve *3* voy, vas, va, vamos, vais, van *4* fui, fuiste, fue, fuimos, fuisteis, fueron *6* vaya, vayas, vaya, vayamos, vayáis, vayan *7* fuera *etc* *8* iba, ibas, iba, íbamos, ibais, iban

jugar *2* juega *3* juego, juegas, juega, juegan *4* jugué *6* juegue *etc*

leer *1* leyendo *4* leyó, leyeron *7* leyera *etc*

morir *1* muriendo *2* muere *3* muero, mueres, muere, mueren *4* murió, murieron *6* muera, mueras, muera, muramos, muráis, mueran *7* muriera *etc* *8* muerto

mostrar *2* muestra *3* muestro, muestras, muestra, muestran *6* muestre, muestres, muestre, muestren

mover *2* mueve *3* muevo, mueves, mueve, mueven *6* mueva, muevas, mueva, muevan

negar *2* niega *3* niego, niegas, niega, niegan *4* negué *6* niegue, niegues, niegue, neguemos, neguéis, nieguen

ofrecer *3* ofrezco *6* ofrezca *etc*

oír *1* oyendo *2* oye *3* oigo, oyes, oye, oyen *4* oyó, oyeron *6* oiga *etc* *7* oyera *etc*

oler *2* huele *3* huelo, hueles, huele, huelen *6* huela, huelas, huela, huelan

parecer *3* parezco *6* parezca *etc*

pedir *1* pidiendo *2* pide *3* pido, pides, pide, piden *4* pidió, pidieron *6* pida *etc* *7* pidiera *etc*

pensar *2* piensa *3* pienso, piensas, piensa, piensan *6* piense, pienses, piense, piensen

perder *2* pierde *3* pierdo, pierdes, pierde, pierden *6* pierda, pierdas, pierda, pierdan

poder *1* pudiendo *2* puede *3* puedo, puedes, puede, pueden *4* pude, pudiste, pudo, pudimos, pudisteis, pudieron *5* podré *etc* *6* pueda, puedas, pueda, puedan *7* pudiera *etc*

poner *2* pon *3* pongo *4* puse, pusiste, puso, pusimos, pusisteis, pusieron *5* pondré *etc* *6* ponga *etc* *7* pusiera *etc* *8* puesto

preferir *1* prefiriendo *2* prefiere *3* prefiero, prefieres, prefiere, prefieren *4* prefirió, prefirieron *6* prefiera, prefieras, prefiera, prefiramos, prefiráis, prefieran *7* prefiriera *etc*

querer *2* quiere *3* quiero, quieres, quiere, quieren *4* quise, quisiste, quiso, quisimos, quisisteis, quisieron *5* querré *etc* *6* quiera, quieras, quiera, quieran *7* quisiera *etc*

reír *2* ríe *3* río, ríes, ríe, ríen *4* rio, rieron *6* ría, rías, ría, riamos, riáis, rían *7* riera *etc*

repetir *1* repitiendo *2* repite *3* repito, repites, repite, repiten *4* repitió, repitieron *6* repita *etc* *7* repitiera *etc*

rogar *2* ruega *3* ruego, ruegas, ruega, ruegan *4* rogué *6* ruegue, ruegues, ruegue, roguemos, roguéis, rueguen

saber *3* sé *4* supe, supiste, supo, supimos, supisteis, supieron *5* sabré *etc* *6* sepa *etc* *7* supiera *etc*

salir *2* sal *3* salgo *5* saldré *etc* *6* salga *etc*

seguir *1* siguiendo *2* sigue *3* sigo, sigues, sigue, siguen *4* siguió, siguieron *6* siga *etc* *7* siguiera *etc*

sentar *2* sienta *3* siento, sientas, sienta, sientan *6* siente, sientes, siente, sienten

sentir *1* sintiendo *2* siente *3* siento, sientes, siente, sienten *4* sintió, sintieron *6* sienta, sientas, sienta, sintamos, sintáis, sientan *7* sintiera *etc*

SER *2* sé *3* soy, eres, es, somos, sois, son *4* fui, fuiste, fue, fuimos, fuisteis, fueron *6* sea *etc* *7* fuera *etc* *9* era, eras, era, éramos, erais, eran

servir *1* sirviendo *2* sirve *3* sirvo, sirves, sirve, sirven *4* sirvió, sirvieron *6* sirva *etc* *7* sirviera *etc*

soñar *2* sueña *3* sueño, sueñas, sueña, sueñan *6* sueñe, sueñes, sueñe, sueñen

tener *2* ten *3* tengo, tienes, tiene, tienen *4* tuve, tuviste, tuvo, tuvimos, tuvisteis, tuvieron *5* tendré *etc* *6* tenga *etc* *7* tuviera *etc*

traer *1* trayendo *3* traigo *4* traje, trajiste, trajo, trajimos, trajisteis, trajeron *6* traiga *etc* *7* trajera *etc*

valer *2* val *3* valgo *5* valdré *etc* *6* valga *etc*

venir *2* ven *3* vengo, vienes, viene, vienen *4* vine, viniste, vino, vinimos, vinisteis, vinieron *5* vendré *etc* *6* venga *etc* *7* viniera *etc*

ver *3* veo *6* vea *etc* *9* veía *etc*

vestir *1* vistiendo *2* viste *3* visto, vistes, viste, visten *4* vistió, vistieron *6* vista *etc* *7* vistiera *etc*

VIVIR *1* viviendo *2* vive, vivid *3* vivo, vives, vive, vivimos, vivís, viven *4* viví, viviste, vivió, vivimos, vivisteis, vivieron *5* viviré, vivirás, vivirá, viviremos, viviréis, vivirán *6* viva, vivas, viva, vivamos, viváis, vivan *7* viviera, vivieras, viviera, viviéramos, vivierais, vivieran *8* vivido *9* vivía, vivías, vivía, vivíamos, vivíais, vivían

volver *2* vuelve *3* vuelvo, vuelves, vuelve, vuelven *6* vuelva, vuelvas, vuelva, vuelvan *8* vuelto

VERBOS IRREGULARES EN INGLÉS

present	pt	pp	present	pt	pp
arise (arising)	arose	arisen	feed	fed	fed
awake (awaking)	awoke	awaked	feel	felt	felt
			fight	fought	fought
be (am, is, are; being)	was, were	been	find	found	found
			flee	fled	fled
bear	bore	born(e)	fling	flung	flung
beat	beat	beaten	fly (flies)	flew	flown
become (becoming)	became	become	forbid (forbidding)	forbade	forbidden
befall	befell	befallen	forecast	forecast	forecast
begin (beginning)	began	begun	forget (forgetting)	forgot	forgotten
behold	beheld	beheld	forgive (forgiving)	forgave	forgiven
bend	bent	bent			
beset (besetting)	beset	beset	forsake (forsaking)	forsook	forsaken
bet (betting)	bet (also betted)	bet (also betted)	freeze (freezing)	froze	frozen
bid (bidding)	bid (also bade)	bid (also bidden)	get (getting)	got	got, (US) gotten
bind	bound	bound	give (giving)	gave	given
bite (biting)	bit	bitten	go (goes)	went	gone
bleed	bled	bled	grind	ground	ground
blow	blew	blown	grow	grew	grown
break	broke	broken	hang	hung (also hanged)	hung (also hanged)
breed	bred	bred			
bring	brought	brought	have (has; having)	had	had
build	built	built			
burn	burnt (also burned)	burnt (also burned)	hear	heard	heard
			hide (hiding)	hid	hidden
burst	burst	burst	hit (hitting)	hit	hit
buy	bought	bought	hold	held	held
can	could	(been able)	hurt	hurt	hurt
cast	cast	cast	keep	kept	kept
catch	caught	caught	kneel	knelt (also kneeled)	knelt (also kneeled)
choose (choosing)	chose	chosen			
			know	knew	known
cling	clung	clung	lay	laid	laid
come (coming)	came	come	lead	led	led
cost	cost	cost	lean	leant (also leaned)	leant (also leaned)
creep	crept	crept			
cut (cutting)	cut	cut	leap	leapt (also leaped)	leapt (also leaped)
deal	dealt	dealt			
dig (digging)	dug	dug	learn	learnt (also learned)	learnt (also learned)
do (3rd person: he/she/it/ does)	did	done			
			leave (leaving)	left	left
			lend	lent	lent
draw	drew	drawn	let (letting)	let	let
dream	dreamed (also dreamt)	dreamed (also dreamt)	lie (lying)	lay	lain
			light	lit (also lighted)	lit (also lighted)
drink	drank	drunk	lose (losing)	lost	lost
drive (driving)	drove	driven	make (making)	made	made
dwell	dwelt	dwelt	may	might	—
eat	ate	eaten	mean	meant	meant
fall	fell	fallen	meet	met	met

present	pt	pp	present	pt	pp
mistake (mistaking)	mistook	mistaken	spend	spent	spent
mow	mowed	mown (also mowed)	spill	spilt (also spilled)	spilt (also spilled)
must	(had to)	(had to)	spin (spinning)	spun	spun
pay	paid	paid	spit (spitting)	spat	spat
put (putting)	put	put	split (splitting)	split	split
quit (quitting)	quit (also quitted)	quit (also quitted)	spoil	spoiled (also spoilt)	spoiled (also spoilt)
read	read	read	spread	spread	spread
rend	rent	rent	spring	sprang	sprung
rid (ridding)	rid	rid	stand	stood	stood
ride (riding)	rode	ridden	steal	stole	stolen
ring	rang	rung	stick	stuck	stuck
rise (rising)	rose	risen	sting	stung	stung
run (running)	ran	run	stink	stank	stunk
saw	sawed	sawn	stride (striding)	strode	stridden
say	said	said	strike (striking)	struck	struck (also stricken)
see	saw	seen	strive (striving)	strove	striven
seek	sought	sought	swear	swore	sworn
sell	sold	sold	sweep	swept	swept
send	sent	sent	swell	swelled	swollen (also swelled)
set (setting)	set	set	swim (swimming)	swam	swum
shake (shaking)	shook	shaken	swing	swung	swung
shall	should	—	take (taking)	took	taken
shear	sheared	shorn (also sheared)	teach	taught	taught
shed (shedding)	shed	shed	tear	tore	torn
shine (shining)	shone	shone	tell	told	told
shoot	shot	shot	think	thought	thought
show	showed	shown	throw	threw	thrown
shrink	shrank	shrunk	thrust	thrust	thrust
shut (shutting)	shut	shut	tread	trod	trodden
sing	sang	sung	wake (waking)	woke (also waked)	woken (also waked)
sink	sank	sunk	wear	wore	worn
sit (sitting)	sat	sat	weave (weaving)	wove (also weaved)	woven (also weaved)
slay	slew	slain	wed (wedding)	wedded (also wed)	wedded (also wed)
sleep	slept	slept	weep	wept	wept
slide (sliding)	slid	slid	win (winning)	won	won
sling	slung	slung	wind	wound	wound
slit (slitting)	slit	slit	wring	wrung	wrung
smell	smelt (also smelled)	smelt (also smelled)	write (writing)	wrote	written
sow	sowed	sown (also sowed)			
speak	spoke	spoken			
speed	sped (also speeded)	sped (also speeded)			
spell	spelt (also spelled)	spelt (also spelled)			

NÚMEROS

NUMBERS

uno (un, una)*	1	one
dos	2	two
tres	3	three
cuatro	4	four
cinco	5	five
seis	6	six
siete	7	seven
ocho	8	eight
nueve	9	nine
diez	10	ten
once	11	eleven
doce	12	twelve
trece	13	thirteen
catorce	14	fourteen
quince	15	fifteen
dieciséis	16	sixteen
diecisiete	17	seventeen
dieciocho	18	eighteen
diecinueve	19	nineteen
veinte	20	twenty
veintiuno(-un, -una)*	21	twenty-one
veintidós	22	twenty-two
treinta	30	thirty
treinta y uno(un, una)*	31	thirty-one
treinta y dos	32	thirty-two
cuarenta	40	forty
cincuenta	50	fifty
sesenta	60	sixty
setenta	70	seventy
ochenta	80	eighty
noventa	90	ninety
cien(ciento)**	100	a hundred, one hundred
ciento uno(un, una)*	101	a hundred and one
ciento dos	102	a hundred and two
ciento cincuenta y seis	156	a hundred and fifty-six
doscientos(as)	200	two hundred
trescientos(as)	300	three hundred
quinientos(as)	500	five hundred
mil	1,000	a thousand
mil tres	1,003	a thousand and three
dos mil	2,000	two thousand
un millón	1,000,000	a million

* 'uno' (+ 'veintiuno' etc) agrees in gender (but not number) with its noun: treinta y una personas; the masculine form is shortened to 'un' unless it stands alone: veintiún caballos, veintiuno.

** 'ciento' is used in compound numbers, except when it multiplies: ciento diez, but cien mil. 'Cien' is used before nouns: cien hombres, cien casas.

NÚMEROS   NUMBERS

primero(primer, primera), 1°, $1^{er}/1^a$, 1^{era}	first, 1st
segundo(a), $2^o/2^a$	second, 2nd
tercero(tercer, tercera), 3°, $3^{er}/3^a$, 3^{era}	third, 3rd
cuarto(a), $4^o/4^a$	fourth, 4th
quinto(a)	fifth, 5th
sexto(a)	sixth, 6th
séptimo(a)	seventh
octavo(a)	eighth
noveno(a); nono(a)	ninth
décimo(a)	tenth
undécimo(a)	eleventh
duodécimo(a)	twelfth
decimotercio(a)	thirteenth
decimocuarto(a)	fourteenth
decimoquinto(a)	fifteenth
decimosexto(a)	sixteenth
decimoséptimo(a)	seventeenth
decimoctavo(a)	eighteenth
decimonono(a)	nineteenth
vigésimo(a)	twentieth
vigésimo primero(a)	twenty-first
vigésimo segundo(a)	twenty-second
trigésimo(a)	thirtieth
trigésimo primero(a)	thirty-first
trigésimo segundo(a)	thirty-second
cuadragésimo(a)	fortieth
quincuagésimo(a)	fiftieth
sexagésimo(a)	sixtieth
septuagésimo(a)	seventieth
octogésimo(a)	eightieth
nonagésimo(a)	ninetieth
centésimo(a)	hundredth
centésimo primero(a)	hundred-and-first
milésimo(a)	thousandth

ESPAÑOL - INGLÉS
SPANISH - ENGLISH

A

A, a [a] *nf* (*letra*) A, a; **A de Antonio** A for Andrew (*Brit*) *o* Able (*US*).

a [a] *prep* (*a* + *el* = *al*) (*lugar*) at; (*dirección*) to; (*destino*) to, towards; (*tiempo*) at; (*complemento de objeto*): **quiero ~ mis padres** I love my parents; (*manera*): **hacerlo ~ la fuerza** to do it by force; (*con verbo*): **empezó ~ llover** it started raining; **~ la derecha/izquierda** on the right/left; **al lado de** beside, at the side of; **subir ~ un avión/tren** to board a plane/train; **está ~ 7 km de aquí** it is 7 km (away) from here; **hablar ~ larga distancia** to speak long distance; **~ las cuatro** at four o'clock; **~ eso de las cuatro** at about four o'clock; **¿~ qué hora?** (at) what time?; **~ los 30 años** at 30 years of age; **al día siguiente** the next day; **al poco tiempo** a short time later; **al verlo yo** when I saw it; **ir ~ caballo/pie** to go on horseback/foot; **poco ~ poco** little by little; **de dos ~ tres** from two to three; **ocho horas al día** eight hours a *o* per day; **al año/~ la semana** a year/week later; **~ 50 ptas el kilo** 50 pesetas a kilo; **enseñar ~ leer** to teach to read; **voy ~ llevarlo** I am going to carry it; **cercano ~** near (to); **por miedo ~** out of fear of; **¡~ comer!** let's eat!; **¡~ que llueve!** I bet it's going to rain!; **¿~ qué viene eso?** what's the meaning of this?; **~ ver** let's see.

A. *abr* (*ESCOL*: = *aprobado*) pass.

AA *nfpl abr* = *Aerolíneas Argentinas*.

ab. *abr* (= *abril*) Apr.

abad, esa [a'βað, 'ðesa] *nm/f* abbot/abbess.

abadía [aβa'ðia] *nf* abbey.

abajo [a'βaxo] *ad* (*situación*) (down) below, underneath; (*en edificio*) downstairs; (*dirección*) down, downwards; **~ de** *prep* below, under; **el piso de ~** the downstairs flat; **la parte de ~** the lower part; **¡~ el gobierno!** down with the government!; **cuesta/río ~** downhill/downstream; **de arriba ~** from top to bottom; **el ~ firmante** the undersigned; **más ~** lower *o* further down.

abalance [aβa'lanθe] *etc vb V* **abalanzarse**.

abalanzarse [aβalan'θarse] *vr*: **~ sobre** *o* **contra** to throw o.s. at.

abalorios [aβa'lorjos] *nmpl* (*chucherías*) trinkets.

abanderado [aβande'raðo] *nm* standard bearer.

abandonado, a [aβando'naðo, a] *a* derelict; (*desatendido*) abandoned; (*desierto*) deserted; (*descuidado*) neglected.

abandonar [aβando'nar] *vt* to leave; (*persona*) to abandon, desert; (*cosa*) to abandon, leave behind; (*descuidar*) to neglect; (*renunciar a*) to give up; (*INFORM*) to quit; **~se** *vr*: **~se a** to abandon o.s. to; **~se al alcohol** to take to drink.

abandono [aβan'dono] *nm* (*acto*) desertion, abandonment; (*estado*) abandon, neglect; (*renuncia*) withdrawal, retirement; **ganar por ~** to win by default.

abanicar [aβani'kar] *vt* to fan.

abanico [aβa'niko] *nm* fan; (*NAUT*) derrick; **en ~** fan-shaped.

abanique [aβa'nike] *etc vb V* **abanicar**.

abaratar [aβara'tar] *vt* to lower the price of ♦ *vi*, **~se** *vr* to go *o* come down in price.

abarcar [aβar'kar] *vt* to include, embrace; (*contener*) to comprise; (*AM*) to monopolize; **quien mucho abarca poco aprieta** don't bite off more than you can chew.

abarque [a'βarke] *etc vb V* **abarcar**.

abarrotado, a [aβarro'taðo, a] *a* packed; **~ de** packed *o* bursting with.

abarrote [aβa'rrote] *nm* packing; **~s** *nmpl* (*AM*) groceries, provisions.

abarrotero, a [aβarro'tero, a] *nm/f* (*AM*) grocer.

abastecedor, a [aβasteθe'ðor, a] *a* supplying ♦ *nm/f* supplier.

abastecer [aβaste'θer] *vt* to supply (*de* with).

abastecimiento [aβasteθi'mjento] *nm* supply.

abastezca [aβas'teθka] *etc vb V* **abastecer**.

abasto [a'βasto] *nm* supply; (*abundancia*) abundance; **no dar ~ a algo** not to be able to cope with sth.

abatible [aβa'tiβle] *a*: **asiento ~** tip-up seat.

abatido, a [aβa'tiðo, a] *a* dejected, downcast; **estar muy ~** to be very depressed.

abatimiento [aβati'mjento] *nm* (*depresión*) dejection, depression.

abatir [aβa'tir] *vt* (*muro*) to demolish; (*pájaro*) to shoot *o* bring down; (*fig*) to depress; **~se** *vr* to get depressed; **~se sobre** to swoop *o* pounce on.

abdicación [aβðika'θjon] *nf* abdication.

abdicar [aβði'kar] *vi* to abdicate; ~ **en uno** to abdicate in favour of sb.

abdique [aβ'ðike] *etc vb* V **abdicar**.

abdomen [aβ'ðomen] *nm* abdomen.

abecedario [aβeθe'ðarjo] *nm* alphabet.

abedul [aβe'ðul] *nm* birch.

abeja [a'βexa] *nf* bee; (*fig:* *hormiguita*) hard worker.

abejorro [aβe'xorro] *nm* bumblebee.

aberración [aβerra'θjon] *nf* aberration.

aberrante [aβe'rrante] *a* (*disparatado*) ridiculous.

abertura [aβer'tura] *nf* = **apertura**.

abeto [a'βeto] *nm* fir.

abierto, a [a'βjerto, a] *pp de* **abrir** ♦ *a* open; (*AM*) generous; (*fig:* *carácter*) frank.

abigarrado, a [aβiɣa'rraðo, a] *a* multicoloured; (*fig*) motley.

abismal [aβis'mal] *a* (*fig*) vast, enormous.

abismar [aβis'mar] *vt* to humble, cast down; ~**se** *vr* to sink; (*AM*) to be amazed; ~**se en** (*fig*) to be plunged into.

abismo [a'βismo] *nm* abyss; **de sus ideas a las mías hay un** ~ our views are worlds apart.

abjurar [aβxu'rar] *vt* to abjure, forswear ♦ *vi:* ~ **de** to abjure, forswear.

ablandar [aβlan'dar] *vt* to soften up; (*conmover*) to touch; (*CULIN*) to tenderize ♦ *vi,* ~**se** *vr* to get softer.

abnegación [aβneɣa'θjon] *nf* self-denial.

abnegado, a [aβne'ɣaðo, a] *a* self-sacrificing.

abobado, a [aβo'βaðo, a] *a* silly.

abobamiento [aβoβa'mjento] *nm* (*asombro*) bewilderment.

abocado, a [aβo'kaðo, a] *a:* **verse** ~ **al desastre** to be heading for disaster.

abochornar [aβotʃor'nar] *vt* to embarrass; ~**se** *vr* to get flustered; (*BOT*) to wilt; ~**se de** to get embarrassed about.

abofetear [aβofete'ar] *vt* to slap (in the face).

abogacía [aβoɣa'θia] *nf* legal profession; (*ejercicio*) practice of the law.

abogado, a [aβo'ɣaðo, a] *nm/f* lawyer; (*notario*) solicitor; (*asesor*) counsel; (*en tribunal*) barrister, advocate, attorney (*US*); ~ **defensor** defence lawyer *o* attorney (*US*); ~ **del diablo** devil's advocate.

abogar [aβo'ɣar] *vi:* ~ **por** to plead for; (*fig*) to advocate.

abogue [a'βoɣe] *etc vb* V **abogar**.

abolengo [aβo'lengo] *nm* ancestry, lineage.

abolición [aβoli'θjon] *nf* abolition.

abolir [aβo'lir] *vt* to abolish; (*cancelar*) to cancel.

abolladura [aβoʎa'ðura] *nf* dent.

abollar [aβo'ʎar] *vt* to dent.

abominable [aβomi'naβle] *a* abominable.

abominación [aβomina'θjon] *nf* abomination.

abonado, a [aβo'naðo, a] *a* (*deuda*) paid(-up) ♦ *nm/f* subscriber.

abonar [aβo'nar] *vt* to pay; (*deuda*) to settle; (*terreno*) to fertilize; (*idea*) to endorse; ~**se** *vr* to subscribe; ~ **dinero en una cuenta** to pay money into an account, credit money to an account.

abono [a'βono] *nm* payment; fertilizer; subscription.

abordable [aβor'ðaβle] *a* (*persona*) approachable.

abordar [aβor'ðar] *vt* (*barco*) to board; (*asunto*) to broach; (*individuo*) to approach.

aborigen [aβo'rixen] *nm/f* aborigine.

aborrecer [aβorre'θer] *vt* to hate, loathe.

aborrezca [aβo'rreθka] *etc vb* V **aborrecer**.

abortar [aβor'tar] *vi* (*malparir*) to have a miscarriage; (*deliberadamente*) to have an abortion.

aborto [a'βorto] *nm* miscarriage; abortion.

abotagado, a [aβota'ɣaðo, a] *a* swollen.

abotonar [aβoto'nar] *vt* to button (up), do up.

abovedado, a [aβoβe'ðaðo, a] *a* vaulted, domed.

abr. *abr* (= *abril*) Apr.

abrace [a'βraθe] *etc vb* V **abrazar**.

abrasar [aβra'sar] *vt* to burn (up); (*AGR*) to dry up, parch.

abrazadera [aβraθa'ðera] *nf* bracket.

abrazar [aβra'θar] *vt* to embrace, hug; ~**se** *vr* to embrace, hug each other.

abrazo [a'βraθo] *nm* embrace, hug; **un** ~ (*en carta*) with best wishes.

abrebotellas [aβreβo'teʎas] *nm inv* bottle opener.

abrecartas [aβre'kartas] *nm inv* letter opener.

abrelatas [aβre'latas] *nm inv* tin (*Brit*) *o* can (*US*) opener.

abrevadero [aβreβa'ðero] *nm* watering place.

abreviar [aβre'βjar] *vt* to abbreviate; (*texto*) to abridge; (*plazo*) to reduce ♦ *vi:* **bueno, para** ~ well, to cut a long story short.

abreviatura [aβreβja'tura] *nf* abbreviation.

abridor [aβri'ðor] *nm* (*de botellas*) bottle opener; (*de latas*) tin (*Brit*) *o* can (*US*) opener.

abrigar [aβri'ɣar] *vt* (*proteger*) to shelter; (*suj: ropa*) to keep warm; (*fig*) to cherish; ~**se** *vr* to take shelter, protect o.s (*de* from); (*con ropa*) to cover (o.s.) up; **¡abrígate bien!** wrap up well!

abrigo [a'βriɣo] *nm* (*prenda*) coat, overcoat; (*lugar protegido*) shelter; **al** ~ **de** in the shelter of.

abrigue [a'ßriɣe] *etc vb* V **abrigar**.

abril [a'ßril] *nm* April.

abrillantar [aßriʎan'tar] *vt (pulir)* to polish; *(fig)* to enhance.

abrir [a'ßrir] *vt* to open (up); *(camino etc)* to open up; *(apetito)* to whet; *(lista)* to head ♦ *vi* to open; ~**se** *vr* to open (up); *(extenderse)* to open out; *(cielo)* to clear; ~ **un negocio** to start up a business; **en un** ~ **y cerrar de ojos** in the twinkling of an eye; ~**se paso** to find *o* force a way through.

abrochar [aßro'tʃar] *vt (con botones)* to button (up); *(AM)* to staple; *(zapato, con broche)* to do up; ~**se** *vr*: ~**se los zapatos** to tie one's shoelaces.

abrogación [aßroɣa'θjon] *nf* repeal.

abrogar [aßro'ɣar] *vt* to repeal.

abrumador, a [aßruma'ðor, a] *a (mayoría)* overwhelming.

abrumar [aßru'mar] *vt* to overwhelm; *(sobrecargar)* to weigh down.

abrupto, a [a'ßrupto, a] *a* abrupt; *(empinado)* steep.

absceso [aßs'θeso] *nm* abscess.

absentismo [aßsen'tismo] *nm (de obreros)* absenteeism.

absolución [aßsolu'θjon] *nf (REL)* absolution; *(JUR)* acquittal.

absoluto, a [aßso'luto, a] *a* absolute; *(total)* utter, complete; **en** ~ *ad* not at all.

absolver [aßsol'ßer] *vt* to absolve; *(JUR)* to pardon; (: *acusado)* to acquit.

absorbente [aßsor'ßente] *a* absorbent; *(interesante)* absorbing, interesting; *(exigente)* demanding.

absorber [aßsor'ßer] *vt* to absorb; *(embeber)* to soak up; ~**se** *vr* to become absorbed.

absorción [aßsor'θjon] *nf* absorption; *(COM)* takeover.

absorto, a [aß'sorto, a] *pp de* **absorber** ♦ *a* absorbed, engrossed.

abstemio, a [aßs'temjo, a] *a* teetotal.

abstención [aßsten'θjon] *nf* abstention.

abstendré [aßsten'dre] *etc vb* V **abstenerse**.

abstenerse [aßste'nerse] *vr*: ~ **(de)** to abstain *o* refrain (from).

abstenga [aßs'tenga] *etc vb* V **abstenerse**.

abstinencia [aßsti'nenθja] *nf* abstinence; *(ayuno)* fasting.

abstracción [aßstrak'θjon] *nf* abstraction.

abstracto, a [aß'strakto, a] *a* abstract; **en** ~ in the abstract.

abstraer [aßstra'er] *vt* to abstract; ~**se** *vr* to be *o* become absorbed.

abstraído, a [aßstra'iðo, a] *a* absent-minded.

abstraiga [aßs'traiɣa] *etc*, **abstraje** [aßs'traxe] *etc*, **abstrayendo** [aßstra'jendo] *etc vb* V **abstraer**.

abstuve [aßs'tuße] *etc vb* V **abstenerse**.

absuelto [aß'swelto] *pp de* **absolver**.

absurdo, a [aß'surðo, a] *a* absurd; **lo** ~ **es que** ... the ridiculous thing is that ... ♦ *nm* absurdity.

abuchear [aßutʃe'ar] *vt* to boo.

abucheo [aßu'tʃeo] *nm* booing; **ganarse un** ~ *(TEATRO)* to be booed.

abuela [a'ßwela] *nf* grandmother; **¡cuéntaselo a tu** ~! *(fam!)* do you think I was born yesterday? *(fam)*; **no tener/ necesitar** ~ *(fam)* to be full of o.s./blow one's own trumpet.

abuelita [aßwe'lita] *nf* granny.

abuelo [a'ßwelo] *nm* grandfather; *(antepasado)* ancestor; ~**s** *nmpl* grandparents.

abulense [aßu'lense] *a* of Ávila ♦ *nm/f* native *o* inhabitant of Ávila.

abulia [a'ßulja] *nf* lethargy.

abultado, a [aßul'taðo, a] *a* bulky.

abultar [aßul'tar] *vt* to enlarge; *(aumentar)* to increase; *(fig)* to exaggerate ♦ *vi* to be bulky.

abundancia [aßun'danθja] *nf*: **una** ~ **de** plenty of; **en** ~ in abundance.

abundante [aßun'dante] *a* abundant, plentiful.

abundar [aßun'dar] *vi* to abound, be plentiful; ~ **en una opinión** to share an opinion.

aburguesarse [aßurɣe'sarse] *vr* to become middle-class.

aburrido, a [aßu'rriðo, a] *a (hastiado)* bored; *(que aburre)* boring.

aburrimiento [aßurri'mjento] *nm* boredom, tedium.

aburrir [aßu'rrir] *vt* to bore; ~**se** *vr* to be bored, get bored; ~**se como una almeja** *u* **ostra** to be bored stiff.

abusar [aßu'sar] *vi* to go too far; ~ **de** to abuse.

abusivo, a [aßu'sißo, a] *a (precio)* exorbitant.

abuso [a'ßuso] *nm* abuse; ~ **de confianza** betrayal of trust.

abyecto, a [aß'jekto, a] *a* wretched, abject.

A.C. *abr (= Año de Cristo)* A.D.

a/c *abr (= al cuidado de)* c/o; (= *a cuenta)* on account.

acá [a'ka] *ad (lugar)* here; **pasearse de** ~ **para allá** to walk up and down; **¡vente para** ~! come over here!; **¿de cuándo** ~? since when?

acabado, a [aka'ßaðo, a] *a* finished, complete; *(perfecto)* perfect; *(agotado)* worn out; *(fig)* masterly ♦ *nm* finish.

acabar [aka'ßar] *vt (llevar a su fin)* to finish, complete; *(consumir)* to use up; *(rematar)* to finish off ♦ *vi* to finish, end; *(morir)* to die; ~**se** *vr* to finish, stop;

(*terminarse*) to be over; (*agotarse*) to run out; ~ **con** to put an end to; ~ **mal** to come to a sticky end; **esto acabará conmigo** this will be the end of me; ~ **de llegar** to have just arrived; **acababa de hacerlo** I had just done it; ~ **haciendo** *o* **por hacer algo** to end up (by) doing sth; **¡se acabó!** (*¡basta!*) that's enough!; (*se terminó*) it's all over!; **se me acabó el tabaco** I ran out of cigarettes.

acabóse [aka'ßose] *nm*: **esto es el** ~ this is the limit.

academia [aka'ðemja] *nf* academy.

académico, a [aka'ðemiko, a] *a* academic.

acaecer [akae'θer] *vi* to happen, occur.

acaezca [aka'eθka] *etc vb* V **acaecer**.

acalorado, a [akalo'raðo, a] *a* (*discusión*) heated.

acalorarse [akalo'rarse] *vr* (*fig*) to get heated.

acallar [aka'ʎar] *vt* (*silenciar*) to silence; (*calmar*) to pacify.

acampar [akam'par] *vi* to camp.

acanalado, a [akana'laðo, a] *a* (*hierro*) corrugated.

acanalar [akana'lar] *vt* to groove; (*ondular*) to corrugate.

acantilado [akanti'laðo] *nm* cliff.

acaparador, a [akapara'ðor, a] *nm/f* monopolizer.

acaparar [akapa'rar] *vt* to monopolize; (*acumular*) to hoard.

acaramelado, a [akarame'laðo, a] *a* (*CU-LIN*) toffee-coated; (*fig*) sugary.

acariciar [akari'θjar] *vt* to caress; (*esperanza*) to cherish.

acarrear [akarre'ar] *vt* to transport; (*fig*) to cause, result in; **le acarreó muchos disgustos** it brought him lots of problems.

acaso [a'kaso] *ad* perhaps, maybe ♦ *nm* chance; (**por**) **si** ~ (just) in case.

acatamiento [akata'mjento] *nm* respect; (*de la ley*) observance.

acatar [aka'tar] *vt* to respect; (*ley*) to obey, observe.

acatarrarse [akata'rrarse] *vr* to catch a cold.

acaudalado, a [akauða'laðo, a] *a* well-off.

acaudillar [akauði'ʎar] *vt* to lead, command.

acceder [akθe'ðer] *vi* to accede, agree; ~ **a** (*INFORM*) to access.

accesar [akθe'sar] *vt* to access.

accesible [akθe'sißle] *a* accessible; ~ **a** open to.

accésit, *pl* **accésits** [ak'θesit, ak'θesits] *nm* consolation prize.

acceso [ak'θeso] *nm* access, entry; (*camino*) access road; (*MED*) attack, fit; (*de cólera*) fit; (*POL*) accession; (*INFORM*) access; ~ **aleatorio/directo/secuencial** *o* **en serie**

(*INFORM*) random/direct/sequential *o* serial access; **de** ~ **múltiple** multi-access.

accesorio, a [akθe'sorjo, a] *a* accessory ♦ *nm* accessory; ~**s** *nmpl* (*AUTO*) accessories, extras; (*TEATRO*) props.

accidentado, a [akθiðen'taðo, a] *a* uneven; (*montañoso*) hilly; (*azaroso*) eventful ♦ *nm/f* accident victim.

accidental [akθiðen'tal] *a* accidental; (*empleo*) temporary.

accidentarse [akθiðen'tarse] *vr* to have an accident.

accidente [akθi'ðente] *nm* accident; **por** ~ by chance; ~**s** *nmpl* unevenness *sg*, roughness *sg*.

acción [ak'θjon] *nf* action; (*acto*) action, act; (*TEATRO*) plot; (*COM*) share; (*JUR*) action, lawsuit; **capital en acciones** capital; ~ **liberada/ordinaria/preferente** fully-paid/ordinary/preference share.

accionamiento [akθjona'mjento] *nm* (*de máquina*) operation.

accionar [akθjo'nar] *vt* to work, operate; (*INFORM*) to drive.

accionista [akθjo'nista] *nm/f* shareholder.

acebo [a'θeßo] *nm* holly; (*árbol*) holly tree.

acechanza [aθe'tʃanθa] *nf* = **acecho**.

acechar [aθe'tʃar] *vt* to spy on; (*aguardar*) to lie in wait for.

acecho [a'θetʃo] *nm*: **estar al** ~ **(de)** to lie in wait (for).

acedera [aθe'ðera] *nf* sorrel.

aceitar [aθei'tar] *vt* to oil, lubricate.

aceite [a'θeite] *nm* oil; (*de oliva*) olive oil; ~ **de hígado de bacalao** cod-liver oil.

aceitera [aθei'tera] *nf* oilcan.

aceitoso, a [aθei'toso, a] *a* oily.

aceituna [aθei'tuna] *nf* olive.

aceitunado, a [aθeitu'naðo, a] *a* olive *cpd*; **de tez aceitunada** olive-skinned.

acelerador [aθelera'ðor] *nm* accelerator.

acelerar [aθele'rar] *vt* to accelerate; ~**se** *vr* to hurry.

acelga [a'θelxa] *nf* chard, beet.

acendrado, a [aθen'draðo, a] *a*: **de** ~ **carácter español** typically Spanish.

acendrar [aθen'drar] *vt* to purify.

acento [a'θento] *nm* accent; (*acentuación*) stress; ~ **cerrado** strong *o* thick accent.

acentuar [aθen'twar] *vt* to accent; to stress; (*fig*) to accentuate; (*INFORM*) to highlight.

acepción [aθep'θjon] *nf* meaning.

aceptación [aθepta'θjon] *nf* acceptance; (*aprobación*) approval.

aceptar [aθep'tar] *vt* to accept; to approve.

acequia [a'θekja] *nf* irrigation ditch.

acera [a'θera] *nf* pavement (*Brit*), sidewalk (*US*).

acerado, a [aθe'raðo, a] *a* steel; (*afilado*) sharp; (*fig: duro*) steely; (: *mordaz*) biting.

acerbo, a [a'θerßo, a] *a* bitter; (*fig*) harsh.

acerca [a'θerka]: ~ **de** *ad* about, concerning.

acercar [aθer'kar] *vt* to bring *o* move nearer; ~**se** *vr* to approach, come near.

acerico [aθe'riko] *nm* pincushion.

acero [a'θero] *nm* steel; ~ **inoxidable** stainless steel.

acerque [a'θerke] *etc vb* V **acercar.**

acérrimo, a [a'θerrimo, a] *a* (*partidario*) staunch; (*enemigo*) bitter.

acertado, a [aθer'taðo, a] *a* correct; (*apropiado*) apt; (*sensato*) sensible.

acertar [aθer'tar] *vt* (*blanco*) to hit; (*solución*) to get right; (*adivinar*) to guess ♦ *vi* to get it right, be right; ~ **a** to manage to; ~ **con** to happen *o* hit on.

acertijo [aθer'tixo] *nm* riddle, puzzle.

acervo [a'θerßo] *nm* heap; ~ **común** undivided estate.

aciago, a [a'θjaγo, a] *a* ill-fated, fateful.

acicalar [aθika'lar] *vt* to polish; (*adornar*) to bedeck; ~**se** *vr* to get dressed up.

acicate [aθi'kate] *nm* spur; (*fig*) incentive.

acidez [aθi'ðeθ] *nf* acidity.

ácido, a ['aθiðo, a] *a* sour, acid ♦ *nm* acid; (*fam*: *droga*) LSD.

acierto [a'θjerto] *etc vb* V **acertar** ♦ *nm* success; (*buen paso*) wise move; (*solución*) solution; (*habilidad*) skill, ability; (*al adivinar*) good guess; **fue un** ~ **suyo** it was a sensible choice on his part.

aclamación [aklama'θjon] *nf* acclamation; (*aplausos*) applause.

aclamar [akla'mar] *vt* to acclaim; to applaud.

aclaración [aklara'θjon] *nf* clarification, explanation.

aclarar [akla'rar] *vt* to clarify, explain; (*ropa*) to rinse ♦ *vi* to clear up; ~**se** *vr* (*suj*: *persona*: *explicarse*) to understand; (*fig*: *asunto*) to become clear; ~**se la garganta** to clear one's throat.

aclaratorio, a [aklara'torjo, a] *a* explanatory.

aclimatación [aklimata'θjon] *nf* acclimatization.

aclimatar [aklima'tar] *vt* to acclimatize; ~**se** *vr* to become *o* get acclimatized; ~**se a algo** to get used to sth.

acné [ak'ne] *nm* acne.

acobardar [akoßar'ðar] *vt* to daunt, intimidate; ~**se** *vr* (*atemorizarse*) to be intimidated; (*echarse atrás*): ~**se (ante)** to shrink back (from).

acodarse [ako'ðarse] *vr*: ~ **en** to lean on.

acogedor, a [akoxe'ðor, a] *a* welcoming; (*hospitalario*) hospitable.

acoger [ako'xer] *vt* to welcome; (*abrigar*) to shelter; ~**se** *vr* to take refuge; ~**se a** (*pretexto*) to take refuge in; (*ley*) to resort to.

acogida [ako'xiða] *nf* reception; refuge.

acogollar [akoγo'ʎar] *vt* (*AGR*) to cover up ♦ *vi* to sprout.

acoja [a'koxa] *etc vb* V **acoger.**

acojonante [akoxo'nante] *a* (*Esp fam*) tremendous.

acolchar [akol'tʃar] *vt* to pad; (*fig*) to cushion.

acólito [a'kolito] *nm* (*REL*) acolyte; (*fig*) minion.

acometer [akome'ter] *vt* to attack; (*emprender*) to undertake.

acometida [akome'tiða] *nf* attack, assault.

acomodado, a [akomo'ðaðo, a] *a* (*persona*) well-to-do.

acomodador, a [akomoða'ðor, a] *nm/f* usher(ette).

acomodar [akomo'ðar] *vt* to adjust; (*alojar*) to accommodate; ~**se** *vr* to conform; (*instalarse*) to install o.s.; (*adaptarse*) to adapt o.s.; **¡acomódese a su gusto!** make yourself comfortable!

acomodaticio, a [akomoða'tiθjo, a] *a* (*pey*) accommodating, obliging; (*manejable*) pliable.

acompañamiento [akompaɲa'mjento] *nm* (*MUS*) accompaniment.

acompañante, a [akompa'ɲante, a] *nm/f* companion.

acompañar [akompa'ɲar] *vt* to accompany, go with; (*documentos*) to enclose; **¿quieres que te acompañe?** do you want me to come with you?; ~ **a uno a la puerta** to see sb to the door *o* out; **le acompaño en el sentimiento** please accept my condolences.

acompasar [akompa'sar] *vt* (*MUS*) to mark the rhythm of.

acomplejado, a [akomple'xaðo, a] *a* neurotic.

acomplejar [akomple'xar] *vt* to give a complex to; ~**se** *vr*: ~**se (con)** to get a complex (about).

acondicionado, a [akondiθjo'naðo, a] *a* (*TEC*) in good condition.

acondicionador [akondiθjona'ðor] *nm* conditioner.

acondicionar [akondiθjo'nar] *vt* to get ready, prepare; (*pelo*) to condition.

acongojar [akongo'xar] *vt* to distress, grieve.

aconsejable [akonse'xaßle] *a* advisable.

aconsejar [akonse'xar] *vt* to advise, counsel; ~**se** *vr*: ~**se con** *o* **de** to consult.

acontecer [akonte'θer] *vi* to happen, occur.

acontecimiento [akonteθi'mjento] *nm* event.

acontezca [akon'teθka] *etc vb* V **acontecer.**

acopiar [ako'pjar] *vt* (*recoger*) to gather;

(COM) to buy up.
acopio [a'kopjo] *nm* store, stock.
acoplador [akopla'ðor] *nm*: ~ **acústico** *(IN-FORM)* acoustic coupler.
acoplamiento [akopla'mjento] *nm* coupling, joint.
acoplar [ako'plar] *vt* to fit; *(ELEC)* to connect; *(vagones)* to couple.
acoquinar [akoki'nar] *vt* to scare; ~**se** *vr* to get scared.
acorazado, a [akora'θaðo, a] *a* armour-plated, armoured ◆ *nm* battleship.
acordar [akor'ðar] *vt* *(resolver)* to agree, resolve; *(recordar)* to remind; ~**se** *vr* to agree; ~**se (de algo)** to remember (sth).
acorde [a'korðe] *a* *(MUS)* harmonious; ~ **con** *(medidas etc)* in keeping with ◆ *nm* chord.
acordeón [akorðe'on] *nm* accordion.
acordonado, a [akorðo'naðo, a] *a* *(calle)* cordoned-off.
acorralar [akorra'lar] *vt* to round up, corral; *(fig)* to intimidate.
acortar [akor'tar] *vt* to shorten; *(duración)* to cut short; *(cantidad)* to reduce; ~**se** *vr* to become shorter.
acosar [ako'sar] *vt* to pursue relentlessly; *(fig)* to hound, pester; ~ **a uno a preguntas** to pester sb with questions.
acostar [akos'tar] *vt* *(en cama)* to put to bed; *(en suelo)* to lay down; *(barco)* to bring alongside; ~**se** *vr* to go to bed; to lie down.
acostumbrar [akostum'brar] *vt*: ~ **a uno a algo** to get sb used to sth ◆ *vi*: ~ **(a hacer algo)** to be in the habit (of doing sth); ~**se** *vr*: ~**se a** to get used to.
acotación [akota'θjon] *nf* *(apunte)* marginal note; *(GEO)* elevation mark; *(de límite)* boundary mark; *(TEATRO)* stage direction.
acotar [ako'tar] *vt* *(terreno)* to mark out; *(fig)* to limit; *(caza)* to protect.
ácrata ['akrata] *a, nm/f* anarchist.
acre ['akre] *a* *(sabor)* sharp, bitter; *(olor)* acrid; *(fig)* biting ◆ *nm* acre.
acrecentar [akreθen'tar] *vt* to increase, augment.
acreciente [akre'θjente] *etc vb V* **acrecentar**.
acreditado, a [akreði'taðo, a] *a* *(POL)* accredited; *(COM)*: **una casa acreditada** a reputable firm.
acreditar [akreði'tar] *vt* *(garantizar)* to vouch for, guarantee; *(autorizar)* to authorize; *(dar prueba de)* to prove; *(COM: abonar)* to credit; *(embajador)* to accredit; ~**se** *vr* to become famous; *(demostrar valía)* to prove one's worth; ~**se de** to get a reputation for.
acreedor, a [akree'ðor, a] *a*: ~ **a** worthy of ◆ *nm/f* creditor; ~ **común/diferido/con**

garantía *(COM)* unsecured/deferred/secured creditor.
acribillar [akriβi'ʎar] *vt*: ~ **a balazos** to riddle with bullets.
acrimonia [akri'monja], **acritud** [akri'tuð] *nf* acrimony.
acrobacia [akro'ßaθja] *nf* acrobatics; ~ **aérea** aerobatics.
acróbata [a'kroßata] *nm/f* acrobat.
acta ['akta] *nf* certificate; *(de comisión)* minutes *pl*, record; ~ **de nacimiento/de matrimonio** birth/marriage certificate; ~ **notarial** affidavit; **levantar** ~ *(JUR)* to make a formal statement *o* deposition.
actitud [akti'tuð] *nf* attitude; *(postura)* posture; **adoptar una** ~ **firme** to take a firm stand.
activar [akti'ßar] *vt* to activate; *(acelerar)* to speed up.
actividad [aktißi'ðað] *nf* activity; **estar en plena** ~ to be in full swing.
activo, a [ak'tißo, a] *a* active; *(vivo)* lively ◆ *nm* *(COM)* assets *pl*; ~ **y pasivo** assets and liabilities; ~ **circulante/fijo/inmaterial/invisible** *(COM)* current/fixed/intangible/invisible assets; ~ **realizable** liquid assets; ~**s congelados** *o* **bloqueados** frozen assets; **estar en** ~ *(MIL)* to be on active service.
acto ['akto] *nm* act, action; *(ceremonia)* ceremony; *(TEATRO)* act; **en el** ~ immediately; **hacer** ~ **de presencia** *(asistir)* to attend (formally).
actor [ak'tor] *nm* actor; *(JUR)* plaintiff.
actora [ak'tora] *a*: **parte** ~ prosecution; *(demandante)* plaintiff.
actriz [ak'triθ] *nf* actress.
actuación [aktwa'θjon] *nf* action; *(comportamiento)* conduct, behaviour; *(JUR)* proceedings *pl*; *(desempeño)* performance.
actual [ak'twal] *a* present(-day), current; **el 6 del** ~ the 6th of this month.
actualidad [aktwali'ðað] *nf* present; ~**es** *nfpl* news *sg*; **en la** ~ nowadays, at present; **ser de gran** ~ to be current.
actualice [aktwa'liθe] *etc vb V* **actualizar**.
actualización [aktwaliθa'θjon] *nf* updating, modernization.
actualizar [aktwali'θar] *vt* to update, modernize.
actualmente [aktwal'mente] *ad* at present; *(hoy día)* nowadays.
actuar [ak'twar] *vi* *(obrar)* to work, operate; *(actor)* to act, perform ◆ *vt* to work, operate; ~ **de** to act as.
actuario, a [ak'twarjo] *nm/f* clerk; *(COM)* actuary.
acuarela [akwa'rela] *nf* watercolour.
acuario [a'kwarjo] *nm* aquarium; **A~** *(ASTRO)* Aquarius.

acuartelar [akwarte'lar] *vt* (*MIL*: *alojar*) to quarter.

acuático, a [a'kwatiko, a] *a* aquatic.

acuciar [aku'θjar] *vt* to urge on.

acuclillarse [akukli'ʎarse] *vr* to crouch down.

acuchillar [akutʃi'ʎar] *vt* (*TEC*) to plane (down), smooth.

ACUDE [a'kuðe] *nf abr* = Asociación de Consumidores y Usuarios de España.

acudir [aku'ðir] *vi* to attend, turn up; ~ **a** to turn to; ~ **en ayuda de** to go to the aid of; ~ **a una cita** to keep an appointment; ~ **a una llamada** to answer a call; **no tener a quién** ~ to have nobody to turn to.

acuerdo [a'kwerðo] *etc vb* V **acordar** ◆ *nm* agreement; (*POL*) resolution; ~ **de pago respectivo** (*COM*) knock-for-knock agreement; **A~ general sobre aranceles aduaneros y comercio** (*COM*) General Agreement on Tariffs and Trade; **tomar un** ~ to pass a resolution; **¡de** ~**!** agreed!; **de** ~ **con** (*persona*) in agreement with; (*acción, documento*) in accordance with; **de común** ~ by common consent; **estar de** ~ (*persona*) to agree; **llegar a un** ~ to come to an understanding.

acueste [a'kweste] *etc vb* V **acostar**.

acullá [aku'ʎa] *ad* over there.

acumular [akumu'lar] *vt* to accumulate, collect.

acunar [aku'nar] *vt* to rock (to sleep).

acuñar [aku'ɲar] *vt* (*moneda*) to mint; (*frase*) to coin.

acuoso, a [a'kwoso, a] *a* watery.

acupuntura [akupun'tura] *nf* acupuncture.

acurrucarse [akurru'karse] *vr* to crouch; (*ovillarse*) to curl up.

acurruque [aku'rruke] *etc vb* V **acurrucarse**.

acusación [akusa'θjon] *nf* accusation.

acusado, a [aku'saðo, a] *a* (*JUR*) accused; (*marcado*) marked; (*acento*) strong.

acusar [aku'sar] *vt* to accuse; (*revelar*) to reveal; (*denunciar*) to denounce; (*emoción*) to show; ~ **recibo** to acknowledge receipt; **su rostro acusó extrañeza** his face registered surprise; ~**se** *vr* to confess (*de* to).

acuse [a'kuse] *nm*: ~ **de recibo** acknowledgement of receipt.

acusete [aku'sete] *nm/f*, **acusón, ona** [aku'son, ona] *nm/f* telltale, sneak.

acústico, a [a'kustiko, a] *a* acoustic ◆ *nf* (*de una sala etc*) acoustics *pl*; (*ciencia*) acoustics *sg*.

achacar [atʃa'kar] *vt* to attribute.

achacoso, a [atʃa'koso, a] *a* sickly.

achantar [atʃan'tar] *vt* (*fam*) to scare, frighten; ~**se** *vr* to back down.

achaque [a'tʃake] *etc vb* V **achacar** ◆ *nm* ailment.

achatar [atʃa'tar] *vt* to flatten.

achicar [atʃi'kar] *vt* to reduce; (*humillar*) to humiliate; (*NAUT*) to bale out; ~**se** (*ropa*) to shrink; (*fig*) to humble o.s.

achicoria [atʃi'korja] *nf* chicory.

achicharrar [atʃitʃa'rrar] *vt* to scorch, burn.

achinado, a [atʃi'naðo, a] *a* (*ojos*) slanting.

achique [a'tʃike] *etc vb* V **achicar**.

achuchar [atʃu'tʃar] *vt* to crush.

achuchón [atʃu'tʃon] *nm* shove; **tener un** ~ (*MED*) to be poorly.

ADA ['aða] *nf abr* (*Esp*: = Ayuda del Automovilista*) ≈ AA, RAC (*Brit*), AAA (*US*).

adagio [a'ðaxjo] *nm* adage; (*MUS*) adagio.

adalid [aða'lið] *nm* leader, champion.

adaptación [aðapta'θjon] *nf* adaptation.

adaptador [aðapta'ðor] *nm* (*ELEC*) adapter.

adaptar [aðap'tar] *vt* to adapt; (*acomodar*) to fit; (*convertir*): ~ (**para**) to convert (to).

adecentar [aðeθen'tar] *vt* to tidy up.

adecuado, a [aðe'kwaðo, a] *a* (*apto*) suitable; (*oportuno*) appropriate; **el hombre** ~ **para el puesto** the right man for the job.

adecuar [aðe'kwar] *vt* (*adaptar*) to adapt; (*hacer apto*) to make suitable.

adefesio [aðe'fesjo] *nm* (*fam*): **estaba hecha un** ~ she looked a sight.

a. de J.C. *abr* (= antes de Jesucristo) B.C.

adelantado, a [aðelan'taðo, a] *a* advanced; (*reloj*) fast; **pagar por** ~ to pay in advance.

adelantamiento [aðelanta'mjento] *nm* advance, advancement; (*AUTO*) overtaking.

adelantar [aðelan'tar] *vt* to move forward; (*avanzar*) to advance; (*acelerar*) to speed up; (*AUTO*) to overtake ◆ *vi* (*ir delante*) to go ahead; (*progresar*) to improve; (*tb*: ~**se** *vr*: *tomar la delantera*) to go forward, advance; ~**se a uno** to get ahead of sb; ~**se a los deseos de uno** to anticipate sb's wishes.

adelante [aðe'lante] *ad* forward(s), onward(s), ahead ◆ *excl* come in!; **de hoy en** ~ from now on; **más** ~ later on; (*más allá*) further on.

adelanto [aðe'lanto] *nm* advance; (*mejora*) improvement; (*progreso*) progress; (*dinero*) advance; **los** ~**s de la ciencia** the advances of science.

adelgace [aðel'ɣaθe] *etc vb* V **adelgazar**.

adelgazar [aðelɣa'θar] *vt* to thin (down); (*afilar*) to taper ◆ *vi* to get thin; (*con régimen*) to slim down, lose weight.

ademán [aðe'man] *nm* gesture; **ademanes** *nmpl* manners; **en** ~ **de** as if to.

además [aðe'mas] *ad* besides; (*por otra parte*) moreover; (*también*) also; ~ **de** besides, in addition to.

adentrarse [aðen'trarse] *vr*: ~ **en** to go into, get inside; (*penetrar*) to penetrate (into).

adentro [a'ðentro] *ad* inside, in; **mar** ~ out at sea; **tierra** ~ inland ♦ *nm*: **dijo para sus** ~**s** he said to himself.

adepto, a [a'ðepto, a] *nm/f* supporter.

aderece [aðe'reθe] *etc vb* V **aderezar.**

aderezar [aðere'θar] *vt* (*ensalada*) to dress; (*comida*) to season.

aderezo [aðe'reθo] *nm* dressing; seasoning.

adeudar [aðeu'ðar] *vt* to owe; ~**se** *vr* to run into debt; ~ **una suma en una cuenta** to debit an account with a sum.

a.D.g. *abr* (= *a Dios gracias*) D.G. (thanks be to God).

adherirse [aðe'rirse] *vr*: ~ **a** to adhere to; (*fig*) to follow.

adhesión [aðe'sjon] *nf* adhesion; (*fig*) adherence.

adhesivo, a [aðe'siɓo, a] *a* adhesive ♦ *nm* sticker.

adhiera [a'ðjera] *etc*, **adhiriendo** [aði'rjendo] *etc vb* V **adherirse.**

adición [aði'θjon] *nf* addition.

adicional [aðiθjo'nal] *a* additional; (*INFORM*) add-on.

adicionar [aðiθjo'nar] *vt* to add.

adicto, a [a'ðikto, a] *a*: ~ **a** (*droga etc*) addicted to; (*dedicado*) devoted to ♦ *nm/f* supporter, follower; (*toxicómano etc*) addict.

adiestrar [aðjes'trar] *vt* to train, teach; (*conducir*) to guide, lead; ~**se** *vr* to practise; (*enseñarse*) to train o.s.

adinerado, a [aðine'raðo, a] *a* wealthy.

adiós [a'ðjos] *excl* (*para despedirse*) goodbye!, cheerio!; (*al pasar*) hello!

aditivo [aði'tiɓo] *nm* additive.

adivinanza [aðiɓi'nanθa] *nf* riddle.

adivinar [aðiɓi'nar] *vt* (*profetizar*) to prophesy; (*conjeturar*) to guess.

adivino, a [aði'ɓino, a] *nm/f* fortune-teller.

adj *abr* (= *adjunto*) encl.

adjetivo [aðxe'tiɓo] *nm* adjective.

adjudicación [aðxuðika'θjon] *nf* award; (*COM*) adjudication.

adjudicar [aðxuði'kar] *vt* to award; ~**se** *vr*: ~**se algo** to appropriate sth.

adjudique [aðxu'ðike] *etc vb* V **adjudicar.**

adjuntar [aðxun'tar] *vt* to attach, enclose.

adjunto, a [að'xunto, a] *a* attached, enclosed ♦ *nm/f* assistant.

adminículo [aðmi'nikulo] *nm* gadget.

administración [aðministra'θjon] *nf* administration; (*dirección*) management; ~ **pública** civil service; **A**~ **de Correos** General Post Office.

administrador, a [aðministra'ðor, a] *nm/f* administrator; manager(ess).

administrar [aðminis'trar] *vt* to administer.

administrativo, a [aðministra'tiɓo, a] *a* administrative.

admirable [aðmi'raɓle] *a* admirable.

admiración [aðmira'θjon] *nf* admiration; (*asombro*) wonder; (*LING*) exclamation mark.

admirar [aðmi'rar] *vt* to admire; (*extrañar*) to surprise; ~**se** *vr* to be surprised; **se admiró de saberlo** he was amazed to hear it; **no es de** ~ **que** ... it's not surprising that ...

admisible [aðmi'siɓle] *a* admissible.

admisión [aðmi'sjon] *nf* admission; (*reconocimiento*) acceptance.

admitir [aðmi'tir] *vt* to admit; (*aceptar*) to accept; (*dudas*) to leave room for; **esto no admite demora** this must be dealt with immediately.

admón. *abr* (= *administración*) admin.

admonición [aðmoni'θjon] *nf* warning.

adobar [aðo'ɓar] *vt* (*preparar*) to prepare; (*cocinar*) to season.

adobe [a'ðoɓe] *nm* adobe, sun-dried brick.

adocenado, a [aðoθe'naðo, a] *a* (*fam*) mediocre.

adoctrinar [aðoktri'nar] *vt* to indoctrinate.

adolecer [aðole'θer] *vi*: ~ **de** to suffer from.

adolescente [aðoles'θente] *nm/f* adolescent, teenager ♦ *a* adolescent, teenage.

adolezca [aðo'leθka] *etc vb* V **adolecer.**

adonde [a'ðonde] *conj* (to) where.

adónde [a'ðonde] *ad* = **dónde.**

adondequiera [aðonðe'kjera] *adv* wherever.

adopción [aðop'θjon] *nf* adoption.

adoptar [aðop'tar] *vt* to adopt.

adoptivo, a [aðop'tiɓo, a] *a* (*padres*) adoptive; (*hijo*) adopted.

adoquín [aðo'kin] *nm* paving stone.

adorar [aðo'rar] *vt* to adore.

adormecer [aðorme'θer] *vt* to put to sleep; ~**se** *vr* to become sleepy; (*dormirse*) to fall asleep.

adormezca [aðor'meθka] *etc vb* V **adormecer.**

adormilarse [aðormi'larse] *vr* to doze.

adornar [aðor'nar] *vt* to adorn.

adorno [a'ðorno] *nm* adornment; (*decoración*) decoration.

adosado, a [aðo'saðo, a] *a*: **una casa** ~**a** a semi-detached house.

adquiera [að'kjera] *etc vb* V **adquirir.**

adquirir [aðki'rir] *vt* to acquire, obtain.

adquisición [aðkisi'θjon] *nf* acquisition; (*compra*) purchase.

adrede [a'ðreðe] *ad* on purpose.

Adriático [að'rjatiko] *nm*: **el (Mar)** ~ the Adriatic (Sea).

adscribir [aðskri'ɓir] *vt* to appoint; **estuvo adscrito al servicio de** ... he was attached to ...

adscrito [að'skrito] *pp de* **adscribir.**

aduana [a'ðwana] *nf* customs *pl*; (*impuesto*)

(customs) duty.

aduanero, a [aðwa'nero, a] *a* customs *cpd* ◆ *nm/f* customs officer.

aducir [aðu'θir] *vt* to adduce; (*dar como prueba*) to offer as proof.

adueñarse [aðwe'ɲarse] *vr*: ~ **de** to take possession of.

adulación [aðula'θjon] *nf* flattery.

adular [aðu'lar] *vt* to flatter.

adulterar [aðulte'rar] *vt* to adulterate ◆ *vi* to commit adultery.

adulterio [aðul'terjo] *nm* adultery.

adúltero, a [a'ðultero, a] *a* adulterous ◆ *nm/f* adulterer/adulteress.

adulto, a [a'ðulto, a] *a, nm/f* adult.

adusto, a [a'ðusto, a] *a* stern; (*austero*) austere.

aduzca [a'ðuθka] *etc vb V* **aducir.**

advenedizo, a [aðβene'ðiθo, a] *nm/f* upstart.

advenimiento [aðβeni'mjento] *nm* arrival; (*al trono*) accession.

adverbio [að'βerβjo] *nm* adverb.

adversario, a [aðβer'sarjo, a] *nm/f* adversary.

adversidad [aðβersi'ðað] *nf* adversity; (*contratiempo*) setback.

adverso, a [að'βerso, a] *a* adverse; (*suerte*) bad.

advertencia [aðβer'tenθja] *nf* warning; (*prefacio*) preface, foreword.

advertir [aðβer'tir] *vt* (*observar*) to notice; (*avisar*): ~ **a uno de** to warn sb about *o* of.

Adviento [að'βjento] *nm* Advent.

advierta [að'βjerta] *etc,* **advirtiendo** [aðβir'tjendo] *etc vb V* **advertir.**

adyacente [aðja'θente] *a* adjacent.

AECE [a'eθe] *nf abr = Asociación Española de Cooperación Europea.*

aéreo, a [a'ereo, a] *a* aerial; (*tráfico*) air *cpd.*

aerobic [ae'roβik] *nm* aerobics *sg.*

aerodeslizador [aeroðesliθa'ðor], **aerodeslizante** [aeroðesli'θante] *nm* hovercraft.

aeródromo [ae'roðromo] *nm* aerodrome.

aerograma [aero'ɣrama] *nm* airmail letter.

aeromozo, a [aero'moθo, a] *nm/f* (*AM*) air steward(ess).

aeronáutica [aero'nautika] *nf* aeronautics *sg.*

aeronave [aero'naβe] *nm* spaceship.

aeroplano [aero'plano] *nm* aeroplane.

aeropuerto [aero'pwerto] *nm* airport.

aerosol [aero'sol] *nm* aerosol, spray.

AES *nm abr = Acuerdo Económico y Social.*

a/f *abr* (= *a favor*) in favour.

afabilidad [afaβili'ðað] *nf* affability, pleasantness.

afable [a'faβle] *a* affable, pleasant.

afamado, a [afa'maðo, a] *a* famous.

afán [a'fan] *nm* hard work; (*deseo*) desire; **con** ~ keenly.

afanar [afa'nar] *vt* to harass; (*fam*) to pinch; ~**se** *vr*: ~**se por** to strive to.

afanoso, a [afa'noso, a] *a* (*trabajo*) hard; (*trabajador*) industrious.

AFE ['afe] *nf abr* (= *Asociación de Futbolistas Españoles*) ≈ F.A.

afear [afe'ar] *vt* to disfigure.

afección [afek'θjon] *nf* affection; (*MED*) disease.

afectación [afekta'θjon] *nf* affectation.

afectado, a [afek'taðo, a] *a* affected.

afectar [afek'tar] *vt* to affect, have an effect on; (*AM*: *dañar*) to hurt; **por lo que afecta a esto** as far as this is concerned.

afectísimo, a [afek'tisimo, a] *a* affectionate; ~ **suyo** yours truly.

afectivo, a [afek'tiβo, a] *a* affective.

afecto, a [a'fekto, a] *a*: ~ **a** fond of; (*JUR*) subject to ◆ *nm* affection; **tenerle** ~ **a uno** to be fond of sb.

afectuoso, a [afek'twoso, a] *a* affectionate.

afeitar [afei'tar] *vt* to shave; ~**se** *vr* to shave.

afeminado, a [afemi'naðo, a] *a* effeminate.

aferrado, a [afe'rraðo, a] *a* stubborn.

aferrar [afe'rrar] *vt* to moor; (*fig*) to grasp ◆ *vi* to moor; ~**se a** (*agarrarse*) to cling on; ~**se a un principio** to stick to a principle; ~**se a una esperanza** to cling to a hope.

affmo., a. *abr* (= *afectísimo, a*) Yours.

Afganistán [afɣanis'tan] *nm* Afghanistan.

afgano, a [af'ɣano, a] *a, nm/f* Afghan.

afiance [a'fjanθe] *etc vb V* **afianzar.**

afianzamiento [afjanθa'mjento] *nm* strengthening; security.

afianzar [afjan'θar] *vt* to strengthen, secure; ~**se** *vr* to steady o.s.; (*establecerse*) to become established.

afición [afi'θjon] *nf*: ~ **a** fondness *o* liking for; **la** ~ the fans *pl*; **pinto por** ~ I paint as a hobby.

aficionado, a [afiθjo'naðo, a] *a* keen, enthusiastic; (*no profesional*) amateur ◆ *nm/f* enthusiast, fan; amateur.

aficionar [afiθjo'nar] *vt*: ~ **a uno a algo** to make sb like sth; ~**se** *vr*: ~**se a algo** to grow fond of sth.

afiche [a'fitʃe] *nm* (*AM*) poster.

afierre [a'fjerre] *etc vb V* **aferrar.**

afilado, a [afi'laðo, a] *a* sharp.

afilador [afila'ðor] *nm* (*persona*) knife grinder.

afilalápices [afila'lapiθes] *nm inv* pencil sharpener.

afilar [afi'lar] *vt* to sharpen; ~**se** *vr* (*cara*) to grow thin.

afiliación [afilja'θjon] *nf* (*de sindicatos*) membership.

afiliado, a [afi'ljaðo, a] *a* subsidiary ◆ *nm/f* affiliate.

afiliarse [afi'ljarse] *vr* to affiliate.

afín [a'fin] *a* (*parecido*) similar; (*conexo*) related.

afinar [afi'nar] *vt* (*TEC*) to refine; (*MUS*) to tune ◆ *vi* to play/sing in tune.

afincarse [afin'karse] *vr* to settle.

afinidad [afini'ðað] *nf* affinity; (*parentesco*) relationship; **por ~** by marriage.

afirmación [afirma'θjon] *nf* affirmation.

afirmar [afir'mar] *vt* to affirm, state; (*sostener*) to strengthen; **~se** *vr* (*recuperar el equilibrio*) to steady o.s.; **~se en lo dicho** to stand by what one has said.

afirmativo, a [afirma'tiβo, a] *a* affirmative.

aflicción [aflik'θjon] *nf* affliction; (*dolor*) grief.

afligir [afli'xir] *vt* to afflict; (*apenar*) to distress; **~se** *vr*: **~se (por** *o* **con** *o* **de)** to grieve (about *o* at); **no te aflijas tanto** you must not let it affect you like this.

aflija [a'flixa] *etc vb* V **afligir**.

aflojar [aflo'xar] *vt* to slacken; (*desatar*) to loosen, undo; (*relajar*) to relax ◆ *vi* (*amainar*) to drop; (*bajar*) to go down; **~se** *vr* to relax.

aflorar [aflo'rar] *vi* (*GEO*, *fig*) to come to the surface, emerge.

afluencia [aflu'enθja] *nf* flow.

afluente [aflu'ente] *a* flowing ◆ *nm* (*GEO*) tributary.

afluir [aflu'ir] *vi* to flow.

afluya [a'fluja] *etc*, **afluyendo** [aflu'jendo] *etc vb* V **afluir**.

afmo., a. *abr* (= *afectísimo, a suyo, a*) Yours.

afónico, a [a'foniko, a] *a*: **estar ~** to have a sore throat; to have lost one's voice.

aforar [afo'rar] *vt* (*TEC*) to gauge; (*fig*) to value.

aforo [a'foro] *nm* (*TEC*) gauging; (*de teatro etc*) capacity; **el teatro tiene un ~ de 2.000** the theatre can seat 2,000.

afortunado, a [afortu'naðo, a] *a* fortunate, lucky.

afrancesado, a [afranθe'saðo, a] *a* francophile; (*pey*) Frenchified.

afrenta [a'frenta] *nf* affront, insult; (*deshonra*) dishonour (*Brit*), dishonor (*US*), shame.

afrentoso, a [afren'toso, a] *a* insulting; shameful.

África ['afrika] *nf* Africa; **~ del Sur** South Africa.

africano, a [afri'kano, a] *a, nm/f* African.

afrontar [afron'tar] *vt* to confront; (*poner cara a cara*) to bring face to face.

afuera [a'fwera] *ad* out, outside; **por ~** on the outside; **~s** *nfpl* outskirts.

ag., ag.º *abr* (= *agosto*) Aug.

agachar [aɣa'tʃar] *vt* to bend, bow; **~se** *vr* to stoop, bend.

agalla [a'ɣaʎa] *nf* (*ZOOL*) gill; **~s** *nfpl* (*MED*) tonsillitis *sg*; (*ANAT*) tonsils; **tener ~s** (*fam*) to have guts.

agarradera [aɣarra'ðera] *nf* (*AM*), **agarradero** [aɣarra'ðero] *nm* handle; **~s** *npl* pull *sg*, influence *sg*.

agarrado, a [aɣa'rraðo, a] *a* mean, stingy.

agarrar [aɣa'rrar] *vt* to grasp, grab; (*AM*) to take, catch ◆ *vi* (*planta*) to take root; **~se** *vr* to hold on (tightly); (*meterse uno con otro*) to grapple (with each other); **agarrársela con uno** (*AM*) to pick on sb.

agarrotar [aɣarro'tar] *vt* (*lío*) to tie tightly; (*persona*) to squeeze tightly; (*reo*) to garrotte; **~se** *vr* (*motor*) to seize up; (*MED*) to stiffen.

agasajar [aɣasa'xar] *vt* to treat well, fête.

agazapar [aɣaθa'par] *vt* (*coger*) to grab hold of; **~se** *vr* (*agacharse*) to crouch down.

agencia [a'xenθja] *nf* agency; **~ de créditos/publicidad/viajes** credit/advertising/travel agency; **~ inmobiliaria** estate agent's (office) (*Brit*), real estate office (*US*); **~ de matrimonios** marriage bureau.

agenciar [axen'θjar] *vt* to bring about; **~se** *vr* to look after o.s.; **~se algo** to get hold of sth.

agenda [a'xenda] *nf* diary; **~ telefónica** telephone directory.

agente [a'xente] *nm* agent; (*de policía*) policeman; **~ femenino** policewoman; **~ acreditado** (*COM*) accredited agent; **~ de bolsa** stockbroker; **~ inmobiliario** estate agent (*Brit*), realtor (*US*); **~ de negocios** (*COM*) business agent; **~ de seguros** insurance broker; **~ de viajes** travel agent.

ágil ['axil] *a* agile, nimble.

agilidad [axili'ðað] *nf* agility, nimbleness.

agitación [axita'θjon] *nf* (*de mano etc*) shaking, waving; (*de líquido etc*) stirring; agitation.

agitar [axi'tar] *vt* to wave, shake; (*líquido*) to stir; (*fig*) to stir up, excite; **~se** *vr* to get excited; (*inquietarse*) to get worried *o* upset.

aglomeración [aɣlomera'θjon] *nf*: **~ de tráfico/gente** traffic jam/mass of people.

aglomerar [aɣlome'rar] *vt*, **~se** *vr* to crowd together.

agnóstico, a [aɣ'nostiko, a] *a, nm/f* agnostic.

agobiante [aɣo'βjante] *a* (*calor*) oppressive.

agobiar [aɣo'βjar] *vt* to weigh down; (*oprimir*) to oppress; (*cargar*) to burden; **sentirse agobiado por** to be overwhelmed by.

agobio [a'ɣoβjo] *nm* (*peso*) burden; (*fig*)

oppressiveness.

agolpamiento [aɣolpa'mjento] nm crush.

agolparse [aɣol'parse] vr to crowd together.

agonía [aɣo'nia] nf death throes pl; (fig) agony, anguish.

agonice [aɣo'niθe] etc vb V **agonizar**.

agonizante [aɣoni'θante] a dying.

agonizar [aɣoni'θar] vi (tb: **estar agonizando**) to be dying.

agorero, a [aɣo'rero, a] a ominous ♦ nm/f soothsayer; **ave agorera** bird of ill omen.

agostar [aɣo'star] vt (quemar) to parch; (fig) to wither.

agosto [a'ɣosto] nm August; (fig) harvest; **hacer su** ~ to make one's pile.

agotado, a [aɣo'taðo, a] a (persona) exhausted; (acabado) finished; (COM) sold out; (: libros) out of print; (pila) flat.

agotador, a [aɣota'ðor, a] a exhausting.

agotamiento [aɣota'mjento] nm exhaustion.

agotar [aɣo'tar] vt to exhaust; (consumir) to drain; (recursos) to use up, deplete; ~se vr to be exhausted; (acabarse) to run out; (libro) to go out of print.

agraciado, a [aɣra'θjaðo, a] a (atractivo) attractive; (en sorteo etc) lucky.

agraciar [aɣra'θjar] vt (JUR) to pardon; (con premio) to reward; (hacer más atractivo) to make more attractive.

agradable [aɣra'ðaβle] a pleasant, nice.

agradar [aɣra'ðar] vt, vi to please; ~se vr to like each other.

agradecer [aɣraðeθ'θer] vt to thank; (favor etc) to be grateful for; **le agradecería me enviara ...** I would be grateful if you would send me ...; ~se vr: ¡se agradece! much obliged!

agradecido, a [aɣraðe'θiðo, a] a grateful; ¡muy ~! thanks a lot!

agradecimiento [aɣraðeθi'mjento] nm thanks pl; gratitude.

agradezca [aɣra'ðeθka] etc vb V **agradecer**.

agrado [a'ɣraðo] nm: **ser de tu** etc ~ to be to your etc liking.

agrandar [aɣran'dar] vt to enlarge; (fig) to exaggerate; ~se vr to get bigger.

agrario, a [a'ɣrarjo, a] a agrarian, land cpd; (política) agricultural, farming.

agravante [aɣra'βante] a aggravating ♦ nf complication; **con la** ~ **de que ...** with the further difficulty that ...

agravar [aɣra'βar] vt (pesar sobre) to make heavier; (irritar) to aggravate; ~se vr to worsen, get worse.

agraviar [aɣra'βjar] vt to offend; (ser injusto con) to wrong; ~se vr to take offence.

agravio [a'ɣraβjo] nm offence; wrong; (JUR) grievance.

agraz [a'ɣraθ] nm (uva) sour grape; **en** ~

(fig) immature.

agredir [aɣre'ðir] vt to attack.

agregado [aɣre'ɣaðo] nm aggregate; (persona) attaché; (profesor) assistant professor.

agregar [aɣre'ɣar] vt to gather; (añadir) to add; (persona) to appoint.

agregue [a'ɣreɣe] etc vb V **agregar**.

agresión [aɣre'sjon] nf aggression; (ataque) attack.

agresivo, a [aɣre'siβo, a] a aggressive.

agreste [a'ɣreste] a (rural) rural; (fig) rough.

agriar [a'ɣrjar] vt (fig) to (turn) sour; ~se vr to turn sour.

agrícola [a'ɣrikola] a farming cpd, agricultural.

agricultor, a [aɣrikul'tor, a] nm/f farmer.

agricultura [aɣrikul'tura] nf agriculture, farming.

agridulce [aɣri'ðulθe] a bittersweet; (CULIN) sweet and sour.

agrietarse [aɣrje'tarse] vr to crack; (la piel) to chap.

agrimensor, a [aɣrimen'sor, a] nm/f surveyor.

agrio, a ['aɣrjo, a] a bitter.

agro ['aɣro] nm farming, agriculture.

agronomía [aɣrono'mia] nf agronomy, agriculture.

agrónomo, a [a'ɣronomɔ, a] nm/f agronomist, agricultural expert.

agropecuario, a [aɣrope'kwarjo, a] a farming cpd, agricultural.

agrupación [aɣrupa'θjon] nf group; (acto) grouping.

agrupar [aɣru'par] vt to group; (INFORM) to block; ~se vr (POL) to form a group; (juntarse) to gather.

agua ['aɣwa] nf water; (NAUT) wake; (ARQ) slope of a roof; ~s nfpl (de joya) water sg, sparkle sg; (MED) water sg, urine sg; (NAUT) waters; ~s **abajo/arriba** downstream/upstream; ~ **bendita/destilada/potable** holy/distilled/drinking water; ~ **caliente** hot water; ~ **corriente** running water; ~ **de colonia** eau de cologne; ~ **mineral (con/sin gas)** (fizzy/non-fizzy) mineral water; ~s **jurisdiccionales** territorial waters; ~s **mayores** excrement sg; ~ **pasada no mueve molino** it's no use crying over spilt milk; **estar con el** ~ **al cuello** to be up to one's neck; **venir como** ~ **de mayo** to be a godsend.

aguacate [aɣwa'kate] nm avocado pear.

aguacero [aɣwa'θero] nm (heavy) shower, downpour.

aguachirle [aɣwa'tʃirle] nm (bebida) slops.

aguado, a [a'ɣwaðo, a] a watery, watered down ♦ nf (AGR) watering place; (NAUT) water supply; (ARTE) water-colour.

aguafiestas [aɣwa'fjestas] *nm/f inv* spoilsport.

aguafuerte [aɣwa'fwerte] *nf* etching.

aguamar [aɣwa'mar] *nm* jellyfish.

aguanieve [aɣwa'njeße] *nf* sleet.

aguantable [aɣwan'taßle] *a* bearable, tolerable.

aguantar [aɣwan'tar] *vt* to bear, put up with; (*sostener*) to hold up ♦ *vi* to last; ~**se** *vr* to restrain o.s.; **no sé cómo aguanta** I don't know how he can take it.

aguante [a'ɣwante] *nm* (*paciencia*) patience; (*resistencia*) endurance; (*DEPORTE*) stamina.

aguar [a'ɣwar] *vt* to water down; (*fig*): ~ **la fiesta a uno** to spoil sb's fun.

aguardar [aɣwar'ðar] *vt* to wait for.

aguardentoso, a [aɣwarðen'toso, a] *a* (*pey: voz*) husky, gruff.

aguardiente [aɣwar'ðjente] *nm* brandy, liquor.

aguarrás [aɣwa'rras] *nm* turpentine.

aguce [a'ɣuθe] *etc vb V* **aguzar**.

agudeza [aɣu'ðeθa] *nf* sharpness; (*ingenio*) wit.

agudice [aɣu'ðiθe] *etc vb V* **agudizar**.

agudizar [aɣuði'θar] *vt* to sharpen; (*crisis*) to make worse; ~**se** *vr* to worsen, deteriorate.

agudo, a [a'ɣuðo, a] *a* sharp; (*voz*) high-pitched, piercing; (*dolor, enfermedad*) acute.

agüe ['aɣwe] *etc vb V* **aguar**.

agüero [a'ɣwero] *nm*: **buen/mal** ~ good/bad omen; **ser de buen** ~ to augur well; **pájaro de mal** ~ bird of ill omen.

aguerrido, a [aɣe'rriðo, a] *a* hardened; (*fig*) experienced.

aguijar [aɣi'xar] *vt* to goad; (*incitar*) to urge on ♦ *vi* to hurry along.

aguijón [aɣi'xon] *nm* sting; (*fig*) spur.

aguijonear [aɣixone'ar] *vt* = **aguijar**.

águila ['aɣila] *nf* eagle; (*fig*) genius.

aguileño, a [aɣi'leɲo, a] *a* (*nariz*) aquiline; (*rostro*) sharp-featured.

aguinaldo [aɣi'naldo] *nm* Christmas box.

aguja [a'ɣuxa] *nf* needle; (*de reloj*) hand; (*ARQ*) spire; (*TEC*) firing-pin; ~**s** *nfpl* (*ZOOL*) ribs; (*FERRO*) points.

agujerear [aɣuxere'ar] *vt* to make holes in; (*penetrar*) to pierce.

agujero [aɣu'xero] *nm* hole.

agujetas [aɣu'xetas] *nfpl* stitch *sg*; (*rigidez*) stiffness *sg*.

aguzar [aɣu'θar] *vt* to sharpen; (*fig*) to incite; ~ **el oído** to prick up one's ears.

aherrumbrarse [aerrum'brarse] *vr* to get rusty.

ahí [a'i] *ad* there; (*allá*) over there; **de** ~ **que** so that, with the result that; ~ **llega** here he comes; **por** ~ (*dirección*) that

way; **¡hasta** ~ **hemos llegado!** so it has come to this!; **¡~ va!** (*objeto*) here it comes!; (*individuo*) there he goes!; ~ **donde le ve** as sure as he's standing there.

ahijado, a [ai'xaðo, a] *nm/f* godson/daughter.

ahijar [ai'xar] *vt*: ~ **algo a uno** (*fig*) to attribute sth to sb.

ahínco [a'inko] *nm* earnestness; **con** ~ eagerly.

ahíto, a [a'ito, a] *a*: **estoy** ~ I'm full up.

ahogado, a [ao'ɣaðo, a] *a* (*en agua*) drowned; (*emoción*) pent-up; (*grito*) muffled.

ahogar [ao'ɣar] *vt* (*en agua*) to drown; (*asfixiar*) to suffocate, smother; (*fuego*) to put out; ~**se** *vr* (*en agua*) to drown; (*por asfixia*) to suffocate.

ahogo [a'oɣo] *nm* (*MED*) breathlessness; (*fig*) distress; (*problema económico*) financial difficulty.

ahogue [a'oɣe] *etc vb V* **ahogar**.

ahondar [aon'dar] *vt* to deepen, make deeper; (*fig*) to go deeply into ♦ *vi*: ~ **en** to go deeply into.

ahora [a'ora] *ad* now; (*hace poco*) a moment ago, just now; (*dentro de poco*) in a moment; ~ **voy** I'm coming; ~ **mismo** right now; ~ **bien** now then; **por** ~ for the present.

ahorcado, a [aor'kaðo, a] *nm/f* hanged person.

ahorcar [aor'kar] *vt* to hang; ~**se** *vr* to hang o.s.

ahorita [ao'rita] *ad* (*fam*) right now.

ahorque [a'orke] *etc vb V* **ahorcar**.

ahorrar [ao'rrar] *vt* (*dinero*) to save; (*esfuerzos*) to save, avoid; ~**se** *vr*: ~**se molestias** to save o.s. trouble.

ahorrativo, a [aorra'tißo, a] *a* thrifty.

ahorro [a'orro] *nm* (*acto*) saving; (*frugalidad*) thrift; ~**s** *nmpl* savings.

ahuecar [awe'kar] *vt* to hollow (out); (*voz*) to deepen ♦ *vi*: **¡ahueca!** (*fam*) beat it! (*fam*); ~**se** *vr* to give o.s. airs.

ahueque [a'weke] *etc vb V* **ahuecar**.

ahumar [au'mar] *vt* to smoke, cure; (*llenar de humo*) to fill with smoke ♦ *vi* to smoke; ~**se** *vr* to fill with smoke.

ahuyentar [aujen'tar] *vt* to drive off, frighten off; (*fig*) to dispel.

AI *nf abr* (= *Amnistía Internacional*) Amnesty International.

AINS *nf abr* (*Esp*) = **Administración Institucional Nacional de Sanidad**.

airado, a [ai'raðo, a] *a* angry.

airar [ai'rar] *vt* to anger; ~**se** *vr* to get angry.

aire ['aire] *nm* air; (*viento*) wind; (*corriente*) draught; (*MUS*) tune; ~**s** *nmpl*: **darse** ~**s** to give o.s. airs; **al** ~ **libre** in the open air; ~ **acondicionado** air conditioning; **tener** ~ **de** to look like; **estar de buen/mal** ~ to be in a good/bad mood; **estar en el** ~ (*RADIO*) to be on the air; (*fig*) to be up in the air.

airear [aire'ar] *vt* to ventilate; (*fig*: *asunto*) to air; ~**se** *vr* to take the air.

airoso, a [ai'roso, a] *a* windy; draughty; (*fig*) graceful.

aislado, a [ais'laðo, a] *a* (*remoto*) isolated; (*incomunicado*) cut off; (*ELEC*) insulated.

aislante [ais'lante] *nm* (*ELEC*) insulator.

aislar [ais'lar] *vt* to isolate; (*ELEC*) to insulate; ~**se** *vr* to cut o.s. off.

ajar [a'xar] *vt* to spoil; (*fig*) to abuse; ~**se** *vr* to get crumpled; (*fig*: *piel*) to get wrinkled.

ajardinado, a [axarði'naðo, a] *a* landscaped.

ajedrez [axe'ðreθ] *nm* chess.

ajenjo [a'xenxo] *nm* (*bebida*) absinth(e).

ajeno, a [a'xeno, a] *a* (*que pertenece a otro*) somebody else's; ~ **a** foreign to; ~ **de** free from, devoid of; **por razones ajenas a nuestra voluntad** for reasons beyond our control.

ajetreado, a [axetre'aðo, a] *a* busy.

ajetrearse [axetre'arse] *vr* (*atarearse*) to bustle about; (*fatigarse*) to tire o.s. out.

ajetreo [axe'treo] *nm* bustle.

ají [a'xi] *nm* chili, red pepper; (*salsa*) chili sauce.

ajilimoje [axili'moxe] *nm* sauce of garlic and pepper; ~**s** *nmpl* (*fam*) odds and ends.

ajo ['axo] *nm* garlic; ~ **porro** *o* **puerro** leek; **(tieso) como un** ~ (*fam*) snobbish; **estar en el** ~ to be mixed up in it.

ajorca [a'xorka] *nf* bracelet.

ajuar [a'xwar] *nm* household furnishings *pl*; (*de novia*) trousseau; (*de niño*) layette.

ajustado, a [axus'taðo, a] *a* (*tornillo*) tight; (*cálculo*) right; (*ropa*) tight(-fitting); (*DEPORTE*: *resultado*) close.

ajustar [axus'tar] *vt* (*adaptar*) to adjust; (*encajar*) to fit; (*TEC*) to engage; (*TIP*) to make up; (*apretar*) to tighten; (*concertar*) to agree (on); (*reconciliar*) to reconcile; (*cuenta*) to settle ♦ *vi* to fit.

ajuste [a'xuste] *nm* adjustment; (*COSTURA*) fitting; (*acuerdo*) compromise; (*de cuenta*) settlement; (*INFORM*) patch.

al [al] = **a** + **el**; *V* **a**.

ala ['ala] *nf* wing; (*de sombrero*) brim; (*futbolista*) winger; **andar con el** ~ **caída** to be downcast; **cortar las** ~**s a uno** to clip sb's wings; **dar** ~ **a uno** to encourage sb.

alabanza [ala'Banθa] *nf* praise.

alabar [ala'Bar] *vt* to praise.

alacena [ala'θena] *nf* cupboard (*Brit*), closet (*US*).

alacrán [ala'kran] *nm* scorpion.

ALADI [a'laði] *nf abr* = *Asociación Latinoamericana de Integración*.

alado, a [a'laðo, a] *a* winged.

alambicado, a [alambi'kaðo, a] *a* distilled; (*fig*) affected.

alambicar [alambi'kar] *vt* to distil.

alambique [alam'bike] *etc vb V* **alambicar** ♦ *nm* still.

alambrada [alam'braða] *nf*, **alambrado** [alam'braðo] *nm* wire fence; (*red*) wire netting.

alambre [a'lambre] *nm* wire; ~ **de púas** barbed wire.

alambrista [alam'brista] *nm/f* tightrope walker.

alameda [ala'meða] *nf* (*plantío*) poplar grove; (*lugar de paseo*) avenue, boulevard.

álamo ['alamo] *nm* poplar; ~ **temblón** aspen.

alano [a'lano] *nm* mastiff.

alarde [a'larðe] *nm* show, display; **hacer** ~ **de** to boast of.

alardear [alarðe'ar] *vi* to boast.

alargar [alar'xar] *vt* to lengthen, extend; (*paso*) to hasten; (*brazo*) to stretch out; (*cuerda*) to pay out; (*conversación*) to spin out; ~**se** *vr* to get longer.

alargue [a'larxe] *etc vb V* **alargar**.

alarido [ala'riðo] *nm* shriek.

alarma [a'larma] *nf* alarm; **voz de** ~ warning note; **dar la** ~ to raise the alarm.

alarmante [alar'mante] *a* alarming.

alavés, esa [ala'Bes, esa] *a* of Álava ♦ *nm/f* native *o* inhabitant of Álava.

alazán [ala'θan] *nm* sorrel.

alba ['alBa] *nf* dawn.

albacea [alBa'θea] *nm/f* executor/executrix.

albaceteño, a [alBaθe'teno, a] *a* of Albacete ♦ *nm/f* native *o* inhabitant of Albacete.

albahaca [al'Baka] *nf* (*BOT*) basil.

Albania [al'Banja] *nf* Albania.

albañal [alBa'nal] *nm* drain, sewer.

albañil [alBa'nil] *nm* bricklayer; (*cantero*) mason.

albarán [alBa'ran] *nm* (*COM*) invoice.

albarda [al'Barða] *nf* packsaddle.

albaricoque [alBari'koke] *nm* apricot.

albedrío [alBe'ðrio] *nm*: **libre** ~ free will.

alberca [al'Berka] *nf* reservoir; (*AM*) swimming pool.

albergar [alBer'xar] *vt* to shelter; (*esperanza*) to cherish; ~**se** *vr* (*refugiarse*) to shelter; (*alojarse*) to lodge.

albergue [al'Berxe] *etc vb V* **albergar** ♦ *nm* shelter, refuge; ~ **de juventud** youth hostel.

albis ['alBis] *adv*: **quedarse en** ~ not to have a clue.

albóndiga [al'Bondixa] *nf* meatball.

albor [al'Bor] *nm* whiteness; (*amanecer*) dawn.

alborada [alßo'raða] *nf* dawn; (*diana*) reveille.

alborear [alßore'ar] *vi* to dawn.

albornoz [alßor'noθ] *nm* (*de los árabes*) burnous; (*para el baño*) bathrobe.

alborotadizo, a [alßorota'ðiθo, a] *a* excitable.

alborotar [alßoro'tar] *vi* to make a row ◆ *vt* to agitate, stir up; ~**se** *vr* to get excited; (*mar*) to get rough.

alboroto [alßo'roto] *nm* row, uproar.

alboroce [alßo'roθe] *etc vb* V **alborozar**.

alborozar [alßoro'θar] *vt* to gladden; ~**se** *vr* to rejoice, be overjoyed.

alborozo [alßo'roθo] *nm* joy.

albricias [al'ßriθjas] *nfpl*: ¡~! good news!

álbum, *pl* **álbums** o **álbumes** ['alßum] *nm* album.

albumen [al'ßumen] *nm* egg white, albumen.

alcachofa [alka'tʃofa] *nf* (globe) artichoke; (*TIP*) golf ball; (*de ducha*) shower head.

alcahueta [alka'weta] *nf* procuress.

alcahuete [alka'wete] *nm* pimp.

alcalde, esa [al'kalde, alkal'desa] *nm/f* mayor(ess).

alcaldía [alkal'dia] *nf* mayoralty; (*lugar*) mayor's office.

álcali ['alkali] *nm* (*QUÍMICA*) alkali.

alcance [al'kanθe] *etc vb* V **alcanzar** ◆ *nm* (*MIL*, *RADIO*) range; (*fig*) scope; (*COM*) adverse balance, deficit; **estar al/fuera del** ~ **de uno** to be within/beyond one's reach; (*fig*) to be within one's powers/over one's head; **de gran** ~ (*MIL*) long-range; (*fig*) far-reaching.

alcancía [alkan'θia] *nf* money box.

alcanfor [alkan'for] *nm* camphor.

alcantarilla [alkanta'riʎa] *nf* (*de aguas cloacales*) sewer; (*en la calle*) gutter.

alcanzar [alkan'θar] *vt* (*algo: con la mano, el pie*) to reach; (*alguien: en el camino etc*) to catch up (with); (*autobús*) to catch; (*suj: bala*) to hit, strike ◆ *vi* (*ser suficiente*) to be enough; ~ **a hacer** to manage to do.

alcaparra [alka'parra] *nf* (*BOT*) caper.

alcatraz [alka'traθ] *nm* gannet.

alcázar [al'kaθar] *nm* fortress; (*NAUT*) quarter-deck.

alce ['alθe] *etc vb* V **alzar**.

alcista [al'θista] *a* (*COM*, *ECON*): **mercado** ~ bull market; **la tendencia** ~ the upward trend ◆ *nm* speculator.

alcoba [al'koßa] *nf* bedroom.

alcohol [al'kol] *nm* alcohol; **no bebe** ~ he doesn't drink (alcohol).

alcoholice [alko'liθe] *etc vb* V **alcoholizarse**.

alcohólico, a [al'koliko, a] *a, nm/f* alcoholic.

alcoholímetro [alko'limetro] *nm* Breathalyser ®, drunkometer (*US*).

alcoholismo [alko'lismo] *nm* alcoholism.

alcoholizarse [alkoli'θarse] *vr* to become an alcoholic.

alcornoque [alkor'noke] *nm* cork tree; (*fam*) idiot.

alcotana [alko'tana] *nf* pickaxe; (*DEPORTE*) ice-axe.

alcurnia [al'kurnja] *nf* lineage.

alcuzas [al'kuθas] *nfpl* (*AM*) cruet *sg*.

aldaba [al'daßa] *nf* (door) knocker.

aldea [al'dea] *nf* village.

aldeano, a [alde'ano, a] *a* village *cpd* ◆ *nm/f* villager.

ale ['ale] *excl* come on!, let's go!

aleación [alea'θjon] *nf* alloy.

aleatorio, a [alea'torjo, a] *a* random, contingent; **acceso** ~ (*INFORM*) random access.

aleccionador, a [alekθjona'ðor, a] *a* instructive.

aleccionar [alekθjo'nar] *vt* to instruct; (*adiestrar*) to train.

aledaño, a [ale'ðaɲo, a] *a*: ~ **a** bordering on ◆ *nmpl* outskirts.

alegación [aleɣa'θjon] *nf* allegation.

alegar [ale'ɣar] *vt* (*dificultad etc*) to plead; (*JUR*) to allege ◆ *vi* (*AM*) to argue; ~ **que** ... to give as an excuse that ...

alegato [ale'ɣato] *nm* (*JUR*) allegation; (*escrito*) indictment; (*declaración*) statement; (*AM*) argument.

alegoría [aleɣo'ria] *nf* allegory.

alegrar [ale'ɣrar] *vt* (*causar alegría*) to cheer (up); (*fuego*) to poke; (*fiesta*) to liven up; ~**se** *vr* (*fam*) to get merry o tight; ~**se de** to be glad about.

alegre [a'leɣre] *a* happy, cheerful; (*fam*) merry, tight; (*licencioso*) risqué, blue.

alegría [ale'ɣria] *nf* happiness; merriment; ~ **vital** joie de vivre.

alegrón [ale'ɣron] *nm* (*fig*) sudden joy.

alegue [a'leɣe] *etc vb* V **alegar**.

alejamiento [alexa'mjento] *nm* removal; (*distancia*) remoteness.

alejar [ale'xar] *vt* to move away, remove; (*fig*) to estrange; ~**se** *vr* to move away.

alelado, a [ale'laðo, a] *a* (*bobo*) foolish.

alelar [ale'lar] *vt* to bewilder.

aleluya [ale'luja] *nm* (*canto*) hallelujah.

alemán, ana [ale'man, ana] *a, nm/f* German ◆ *nm* (*lengua*) German.

Alemania [ale'manja] *nf* Germany; ~ **Occidental/Oriental** West/East Germany.

alentador, a [alenta'ðor, a] *a* encouraging.

alentar [alen'tar] *vt* to encourage.

alergia [a'lerxja] *nf* allergy.

alero [a'lero] *nm* (*de tejado*) eaves *pl*; (*de foca, DEPORTE*) flipper; (*AUTO*) mudguard.

alerta [a'lerta] *a inv, nm* alert.

aleta [a'leta] *nf* (*de pez*) fin; (*de ave*) wing;

(*de coche*) mudguard.

aletargar [aletar'ɣar] *vt* to make drowsy; (*entumecer*) to make numb; **~se** *vr* to grow drowsy; to become numb.

aletargue [ale'tarɣe] *etc vb* V **aletargar**.

aletear [alete'ar] *vi* to flutter; (*ave*) to flap its wings; (*individuo*) to wave one's arms.

alevín [ale'ßin] *nm*, **alevino** [ale'ßino] *nm* fry, young fish.

alevosía [aleßo'sia] *nf* treachery.

alfabetización [alfaßetiθa'θjon] *nf*: **campaña de ~** literacy campaign.

alfabeto [alfa'ßeto] *nm* alphabet.

alfajor [alfa'xor] *nm* (*Esp*: *polvorón*) cake eaten at Christmas time.

alfalfa [al'falfa] *nf* alfalfa, lucerne.

alfaque [al'fake] *nm* (*NAUT*) bar, sandbank.

alfar [al'far] *nm* (*taller*) potter's workshop; (*arcilla*) clay.

alfarería [alfare'ria] *nf* pottery; (*tienda*) pottery shop.

alfarero [alfa'rero] *nm* potter.

alféizar [al'feiθar] *nm* window-sill.

alférez [al'fereθ] *nm* (*MIL*) second lieutenant; (*NAUT*) ensign.

alfil [al'fil] *nm* (*AJEDREZ*) bishop.

alfiler [alfi'ler] *nm* pin; (*broche*) clip; (*pinza*) clothes peg; **prendido con ~es** shaky.

alfiletero [alfile'tero] *nm* needle case.

alfombra [al'fombra] *nf* carpet; (*más pequeña*) rug.

alfombrar [alfom'brar] *vt* to carpet.

alfombrilla [alfom'briʎa] *nf* rug, mat.

alforja [al'forxa] *nf* saddlebag.

alforza [al'forθa] *nf* pleat.

algas ['alɣas] *nfpl* seaweed *sg*.

algarabía [alɣara'ßia] *nf* (*fam*) gibberish; (*griterío*) hullabaloo.

algarada [alɣa'raða] *nf* outcry; **hacer** *o* **levantar una ~** to kick up a tremendous fuss.

Algarbe [al'ɣarße] *nm*: **el ~** the Algarve.

algarrobo [alɣa'rroßo] *nm* carob tree.

algazara [alɣa'θara] *nf* din, uproar.

álgebra ['alxeßra] *nf* algebra.

álgido, a ['alxiðo, a] *a* icy; (*momento etc*) crucial, decisive.

algo ['alɣo] *pron* something; (*en frases interrogativas*) anything ♦ *ad* somewhat, rather; **por ~ será** there must be some reason for it; **es ~ difícil** it's a bit awkward.

algodón [alɣo'ðon] *nm* cotton; (*planta*) cotton plant; **~ de azúcar** candy floss (*Brit*), cotton candy (*US*); **~ hidrófilo** cotton wool (*Brit*), absorbent cotton (*US*).

algodonero, a [alɣoðo'nero, a] *a* cotton *cpd* ♦ *nm/f* cotton grower ♦ *nm* cotton plant.

algoritmo [alɣo'ritmo] *nm* algorithm.

alguacil [alɣwa'θil] *nm* bailiff; (*TAUR*) mounted official.

alguien ['alɣjen] *pron* someone, somebody; (*en frases interrogativas*) anybody.

alguno, a [al'ɣuno, a] *a* (*delante de nm*: **algún**) some; (*después de n*): **no tiene talento alguno** he has no talent, he hasn't any talent ♦ *pron* (*alguien*) someone, somebody; **algún que otro libro** some book or other; **algún día iré** I'll go one *o* some day; **sin interés alguno** without the slightest interest; **alguno que otro** an occasional one; **algunos piensan** some (people) think; **alguno de ellos** one of them.

alhaja [a'laxa] *nf* jewel; (*tesoro*) precious object, treasure.

alhelí [ale'li] *nm* wallflower, stock.

aliado, a [a'ljaðo, a] *a* allied.

aliancista [aljan'θista] (*Esp POL*) *a* of Alianza Popular ♦ *nm/f* member/supporter of Alianza Popular.

alianza [a'ljanθa] *nf* (*POL etc*) alliance; (*anillo*) wedding ring.

aliar [a'ljar] *vt* to ally; **~se** *vr* to form an alliance.

alias ['aljas] *ad* alias.

alicaído, a [alika'iðo, a] *a* (*MED*) weak; (*fig*) depressed.

alicantino, a [alikan'tino, a] *a* of Alicante ♦ *nm/f* native *o* inhabitant of Alicante.

alicate(s) [ali'kate(s)] *nm(pl)* pliers *pl*; **~ de uñas** nail clippers.

aliciente [ali'θjente] *nm* incentive; (*atracción*) attraction.

alienación [aljena'θjon] *nf* alienation.

aliento [a'ljento] *etc vb* V **alentar** ♦ *nm* breath; (*respiración*) breathing; **sin ~** breathless; **de un ~** in one breath; (*fig*) in one go.

aligerar [alixe'rar] *vt* to lighten; (*reducir*) to shorten; (*aliviar*) to alleviate; (*mitigar*) to ease.

alijo [a'lixo] *nm* (*NAUT*) unloading; (*contrabando*) smuggled goods.

alimaña [ali'maɲa] *nf* pest.

alimentación [alimenta'θjon] *nf* (*comida*) food; (*acción*) feeding; (*tienda*) grocer's (shop); **~ continua** (*en fotocopiador etc*) stream feed.

alimentador [alimenta'ðor] *nm*: **~ de papel** sheet-feeder.

alimentar [alimen'tar] *vt* to feed; (*nutrir*) to nourish; **~se** *vr*: **~se (de)** to feed (on).

alimenticio, a [alimen'tiθjo, a] *a* food *cpd*; (*nutritivo*) nourishing, nutritious.

alimento [ali'mento] *nm* food; (*nutrición*) nourishment; **~s** *nmpl* (*JUR*) alimony *sg*.

alimón [ali'mon]: **al ~** *ad* jointly, together.

alineación [alinea'θjon] *nf* alignment; (*DEPORTE*) line-up.

alineado, a [aline'aðo, a] *a* (*TIP*): **(no) ~** (un)justified; **~ a la izquierda/derecha**

ranged left/right.

alinear [aline'ar] *vt* to align; *(TIP)* to justify; **~se** *vr* to line up; **~se en** to fall in with.

aliñar [ali'ɲar] *vt (CULIN)* to dress.

aliño [a'liɲo] *nm (CULIN)* dressing.

alisar [ali'sar] *vt* to smooth.

aliso [a'liso] *nm* alder.

alistamiento [alista'mjento] *nm* recruitment.

alistar [alis'tar] *vt* to recruit; **~se** *vr* to enlist; *(inscribirse)* to enrol.

aliviar [ali'βjar] *vt (carga)* to lighten; *(persona)* to relieve; *(dolor)* to relieve, alleviate.

alivio [a'liβjo] *nm* alleviation, relief; **~ de luto** half-mourning.

aljibe [al'xiβe] *nm* cistern.

alma ['alma] *nf* soul; *(persona)* person; *(TEC)* core; **se le cayó el ~ a los pies** he became very disheartened; **entregar el ~** to pass away; **estar con el ~ en la boca** to be scared to death; **lo siento en el ~** I am truly sorry; **tener el ~ en un hilo** to have one's heart in one's mouth; **estar como ~ en pena** to suffer; **ir como ~ que lleva el diablo** to go at breakneck speed.

almacén [alma'θen] *nm (depósito)* warehouse, store; *(MIL)* magazine; *(AM)* shop; **(grandes) almacenes** *nmpl* department store *sg*; **~ depositario** *(COM)* depository.

almacenaje [almaθe'naxe] *nm* storage; **~ secundario** *(INFORM)* backing storage.

almacenamiento [almaθena'mjento] *nm* *(INFORM)* storage; **~ temporal en disco** disk spooling.

almacenar [almaθe'nar] *vt* to store, put in storage; *(INFORM)* to store; *(proveerse)* to stock up with.

almacenero [almaθe'nero] *nm* warehouseman; *(AM)* shopkeeper.

almanaque [alma'nake] *nm* almanac.

almeja [al'mexa] *nf* clam.

almenas [al'menas] *nfpl* battlements.

almendra [al'mendra] *nf* almond.

almendro [al'mendro] *nm* almond tree.

almeriense [alme'rjense] *a* of Almería ♦ *nm/f* native *o* inhabitant of Almería.

almiar [al'mjar] *nm* haystack.

almíbar [al'miβar] *nm* syrup.

almidón [almi'ðon] *nm* starch.

almidonado, a [almiðo'naðo, a] *a* starched.

almidonar [almiðo'nar] *vt* to starch.

almirantazgo [almiran'taθvo] *nm* admiralty.

almirante [almi'rante] *nm* admiral.

almirez [almi'reθ] *nm* mortar.

almizcle [al'miθkle] *nm* musk.

almizclero [almiθ'klero] *nm* musk deer.

almohada [almo'aða] *nf* pillow; *(funda)* pillowcase.

almohadilla [almoa'ðiʎa] *nf* cushion; *(TEC)* pad; *(AM)* pincushion.

almohadillado, a [almoaði'ʎaðo, a] *a (acolchado)* padded.

almohadón [almoa'ðon] *nm* large pillow.

almorcé [almor'θe], **almorcemos** [almor'θemos] *etc vb V* **almorzar.**

almorranas [almo'rranas] *nfpl* piles, haemorrhoids *(Brit)*, hemorrhoids *(US)*.

almorzar [almor'θar] *vt:* **~ una tortilla** to have an omelette for lunch ♦ *vi* to (have) lunch.

almuerce [al'mwerθe] *etc vb V* **almorzar.**

almuerzo [al'mwerθo] *etc vb V* **almorzar** ♦ *nm* lunch.

alocado, a [alo'kaðo, a] *a* crazy.

alojamiento [aloxa'mjento] *nf* lodging(s) *(pl)*; *(viviendas)* housing.

alojar [alo'xar] *vt* to lodge; **~se** *vr:* **~se en** to stay at; *(bala)* to lodge in.

alondra [a'londra] *nf* lark, skylark.

alpargata [alpar'ɣata] *nf* espadrille.

Alpes ['alpes] *nmpl:* **los ~** the Alps.

alpinismo [alpi'nismo] *nm* mountaineering, climbing.

alpinista [alpi'nista] *nm/f* mountaineer, climber.

alpiste [al'piste] *nm (semillas)* birdseed; *(AM fam: dinero)* dough; *(fam: alcohol)* booze.

alquería [alke'ria] *nf* farmhouse.

alquilar [alki'lar] *vt (suj: propietario: inmuebles)* to let, rent (out); *(: coche)* to hire out; *(: TV)* to rent (out); *(suj: alquilador: inmuebles, TV)* to rent; *(: coche)* to hire; **"se alquila casa"** "house to let *(Brit)* o to rent *(US)*" .

alquiler [alki'ler] *nm* renting, letting; hiring; *(arriendo)* rent; hire charge; **de ~** for hire; **~ de automóviles** car hire.

alquimia [al'kimja] *nf* alchemy.

alquitrán [alki'tran] *nm* tar.

alrededor [alreðe'ðor] *ad* around, about; **~es** *nmpl* surroundings; **~ de** *prep* around, about; **mirar a su ~** to look (round) about one.

Alsacia [al'saθja] *nf* Alsace.

alta ['alta] *nf* (certificate of) discharge; **dar a uno de ~** to discharge sb; **darse de ~** *(MIL)* to join, enrol; *(DEPORTE)* to declare o.s. fit.

altanería [altane'ria] *nf* haughtiness, arrogance.

altanero, a [alta'nero, a] *a* haughty, arrogant.

altar [al'tar] *nm* altar.

altavoz [alta'βoθ] *nm* loudspeaker; *(amplificador)* amplifier.

alteración [altera'θjon] *nf* alteration; *(alboroto)* disturbance; **~ del orden público** breach of the peace.

alterar [alte'rar] *vt* to alter; to disturb; ~**se** *vr* (*persona*) to get upset.

altercado [alter'kaðo] *nm* argument.

alternar [alter'nar] *vt* to alternate ◆ *vi*, ~**se** *vr* to alternate; (*turnar*) to take turns; ~ **con** to mix with.

alternativo, a [alterna'tiβo, a] *a* alternative; (*alterno*) alternating ◆ *nf* alternative; (*elección*) choice; **alternativas** *nfpl* ups and downs; **tomar la alternativa** (*TAUR*) to become a fully-qualified bullfighter.

alterno, a [al'terno, a] *a* (*BOT, MAT*) alternate; (*ELEC*) alternating.

alteza [al'teθa] *nf* (*tratamiento*) highness.

altibajos [alti'βaxos] *nmpl* ups and downs.

altillo [al'tiʎo] *nm* (*GEO*) small hill; (*AM*) attic.

altiplanicie [altipla'niθje] *nf*, **altiplano** [alti'plano] *nm* high plateau.

altisonante [altiso'nante] *a* high-flown, high-sounding.

altitud [alti'tuð] *nf* altitude, height; **a una ~ de** at a height of.

altivez [alti'βeθ] *nf* haughtiness, arrogance.

altivo, a [al'tiβo, a] *a* haughty, arrogant.

alto, a ['alto, a] *a* high; (*persona*) tall; (*sonido*) high, sharp; (*noble*) high, lofty; (*GEO, clase*) upper ◆ *nm* halt; (*MUS*) alto; (*GEO*) hill; (*AM*) pile ◆ *ad* (*estar*) high; (*hablar*) loud, loudly ◆ *excl* halt!; **la pared tiene 2 metros de ~** the wall is 2 metres high; **en alta mar** on the high seas; **en voz alta** in a loud voice; **las altas horas de la noche** the small (*Brit*) o wee (*US*) hours; **en lo ~ de** at the top of; **pasar por ~** to overlook; ~**s y bajos** ups and downs; **poner la radio más ~** to turn the radio up; **¡más ~, por favor!** louder, please!

altoparlante [altopar'lante] *nm* (*AM*) loudspeaker.

altramuz [altra'muθ] *nm* lupin.

altura [al'tura] *nf* height; (*NAUT*) depth; (*GEO*) latitude; **la pared tiene 1.80 de ~** the wall is 1 metre 80cm high; **a esta ~ del año** at this time of the year; **estar a la ~ de las circunstancias** to rise to the occasion; **ha sido un partido de gran ~** it has been a terrific match.

alubia [a'luβja] *nf* French bean, kidney bean.

alucinación [aluθina'θjon] *nf* hallucination.

alucinante [aluθi'nante] *a* (*fam: estupendo*) great, super.

alucinar [aluθi'nar] *vi* to hallucinate ◆ *vt* to deceive; (*fascinar*) to fascinate.

alud [a'luð] *nm* avalanche; (*fig*) flood.

aludir [alu'ðir] *vi*: ~ **a** to allude to; **darse por aludido** to take the hint; **no te des por aludido** don't take it personally.

alumbrado [alum'braðo] *nm* lighting.

alumbramiento [alumbra'mjento] *nm* light-

ing; (*MED*) childbirth, delivery.

alumbrar [alum'brar] *vt* to light (up) ◆ *vi* (*iluminar*) to give light; (*MED*) to give birth.

aluminio [alu'minjo] *nm* aluminium (*Brit*), aluminum (*US*).

alumnado [alum'naðo] *nm* (*UNIV*) student body; (*ESCOL*) pupils.

alumno, a [a'lumno, a] *nm/f* pupil, student.

alunice [alu'niθe] *etc vb V* **alunizar**.

alunizar [aluni'θar] *vi* to land on the moon.

alusión [alu'sjon] *nf* allusion.

alusivo, a [alu'siβo, a] *a* allusive.

aluvión [alu'βjon] *nm* (*GEO*) alluvium; (*fig*) flood; ~ **de improperios** torrent of abuse.

alvéolo [al'βeolo] *nm* (*ANAT*) alveolus; (*fig*) network.

alza ['alθa] *nf* rise; (*MIL*) sight; ~**s fijas/graduables** fixed/adjustable sights; **al** *o* **en ~** (*precio*) rising; **jugar al ~** to speculate on a rising *o* bull market; **cotizarse** *o* **estar en ~** to be rising.

alzado, a [al'θaðo, a] *a* (*gen*) raised; (*COM: precio*) fixed; (: *quiebra*) fradulent; **por un tanto ~** for a lump sum ◆ *nf* (*de caballos*) height; (*JUR*) appeal.

alzamiento [alθa'mjento] *nm* (*aumento*) rise, increase; (*acción*) lifting, raising; (*mejor postura*) higher bid; (*rebelión*) rising; (*COM*) fraudulent bankruptcy.

alzar [al'θar] *vt* to lift (up); (*precio, muro*) to raise; (*cuello de abrigo*) to turn up; (*AGR*) to gather in; (*TIP*) to gather; ~**se** *vr* to get up, rise; (*rebelarse*) to revolt; (*COM*) to go fraudulently bankrupt; (*JUR*) to appeal; ~**se con el premio** to carry off the prize.

allá [a'ʎa] *ad* (*lugar*) there; (*por ahí*) over there; (*tiempo*) then; ~ **abajo** down there; **más ~** further on; **más ~ de** beyond; **¡~ tú!** that's your problem!

allanamiento [aʎana'mjento] *nm*: ~ **de morada** housebreaking.

allanar [aʎa'nar] *vt* to flatten, level (out); (*igualar*) to smooth (out); (*fig*) to subdue; (*JUR*) to burgle, break into; ~**se** *vr* to fall down; ~**se a** to submit to, accept.

allegado, a [aʎe'xaðo, a] *a* near, close ◆ *nm/f* relation.

allende [a'ʎende] *ad* on the other side ◆ *prep*: ~ **los mares** beyond the seas.

allí [a'ʎi] *ad* there; ~ **mismo** right there; **por ~** over there; (*por ese camino*) that way.

a.m. *abr* (*AM*: = *ante meridiem*) a.m.

ama ['ama] *nf* lady of the house; (*dueña*) owner; (*institutriz*) governess; (*madre adoptiva*) foster mother; ~ **de casa** housewife; ~ **de cría** *o* **de leche** wet-nurse; ~ **de llaves** housekeeper.

amabilidad [amaβili'ðað] *nf* kindness;

(*simpatía*) niceness.
amabilísimo, a [amaβi'lisimo, a] *a superlativo de* **amable**.
amable [a'maβle] *a* kind; nice.
amaestrado, a [amaes'traðo, a] *a* (*animal*) trained; (: *en circo etc*) performing.
amaestrar [amaes'trar] *vt* to train.
amagar [ama'ɣar] *vt, vi* to threaten.
amago [a'maɣo] *nm* threat; (*gesto*) threatening gesture; (*MED*) symptom.
amague [a'maɣe] *etc vb V* **amagar**.
amainar [amai'nar] *vt* (*NAUT*) to lower, take in; (*fig*) to calm ♦ *vi*, **~se** *vr* to drop, die down; **el viento amaina** the wind is dropping.
amalgama [amal'ɣama] *nf* amalgam.
amalgamar [amalɣa'mar] *vt* to amalgamate; (*combinar*) to combine, mix.
amamantar [amaman'tar] *vt* to suckle, nurse.
amancebarse [amanθe'βarse] *vr* (*pareja*) to live together.
amanecer [amane'θer] *vi* to dawn; (*fig*) to appear, begin to show ♦ *nm* dawn; **el niño amaneció afiebrado** the child woke up with a fever.
amanerado, a [amane'raðo, a] *a* affected.
amanezca [ama'neθka] *etc vb V* **amanecer**.
amansar [aman'sar] *vt* to tame; (*persona*) to subdue; **~se** *vr* (*persona*) to calm down.
amante [a'mante] *a:* **~ de** fond of ♦ *nm/f* lover.
amanuense [ama'nwense] *nm* (*escribiente*) scribe; (*copista*) copyist; (*POL*) secretary.
amañar [ama'ɲar] *vt* (*gen*) to do skilfully; (*pey: resultado*) to alter.
amaño [a'maɲo] *nm* (*habilidad*) skill; **~s** *nmpl* (*TEC*) tools; (*fig*) tricks.
amapola [ama'pola] *nf* poppy.
amar [a'mar] *vt* to love.
amarar [ama'rar] *vi* (*AVIAT*) to land (on the sea).
amargado, a [amar'ɣaðo, a] *a* bitter; embittered.
amargar [amar'ɣar] *vt* to make bitter; (*fig*) to embitter; **~se** *vr* to become embittered.
amargo, a [a'marɣo, a] *a* bitter.
amargor [amar'ɣor] *nm* (*sabor*) bitterness; (*fig*) grief.
amargue [a'marɣe] *etc vb V* **amargar**.
amargura [amar'ɣura] *nf* = **amargor**.
amarillento, a [amari'ʎento, a] *a* yellowish; (*tez*) sallow.
amarillismo [amari'ʎismo] *nm* (*de prensa*) sensationalist journalism.
amarillo, a [ama'riʎo, a] *a, nm* yellow.
amarra [a'marra] *nf* (*NAUT*) mooring line; **~s** *nfpl* (*fig*) protection *sg*; **tener buenas ~s** to have good connections; **soltar ~s** to set off.

amarrar [ama'rrar] *vt* to moor; (*sujetar*) to tie up.
amartillar [amarti'ʎar] *vt* (*fusil*) to cock.
amasar [ama'sar] *vt* to knead; (*mezclar*) to mix, prepare; (*confeccionar*) to concoct.
amasijo [ama'sixo] *nm* kneading; mixing; (*fig*) hotchpotch.
amateur ['amatur] *nm/f* amateur.
amatista [ama'tista] *nf* amethyst.
amazacotado, a [amaθako'taðo, a] *a* (*terreno, arroz etc*) lumpy.
amazona [ama'θona] *nf* horsewoman.
Amazonas [ama'θonas] *nm:* **el (Río)** ~ the Amazon.
ambages [am'baxes] *nmpl:* **sin** ~ in plain language.
ámbar ['ambar] *nm* amber.
Amberes [am'beres] *nm* Antwerp.
ambición [ambi'θjon] *nf* ambition.
ambicionar [ambiθjo'nar] *vt* to aspire to.
ambicioso, a [ambi'θjoso, a] *a* ambitious.
ambidextro, a [ambi'ðekstro, a] *a* ambidextrous.
ambientación [ambjenta'θjon] *nf* (*CINE, LIT etc*) setting; (*RADIO etc*) sound effects.
ambientar [ambjen'tar] *vt* (*gen*) to give an atmosphere to; (*LIT etc*) to set.
ambiente [am'bjente] *nm* (*tb fig*) atmosphere; (*medio*) environment.
ambigüedad [ambixwe'ðað] *nf* ambiguity.
ambigüo, a [am'bixwo, a] *a* ambiguous.
ámbito ['ambito] *nm* (*campo*) field; (*fig*) scope.
ambos, as ['ambos, as] *apl, pron pl* both.
ambulancia [ambu'lanθja] *nf* ambulance.
ambulante [ambu'lante] *a* travelling, itinerant; (*biblioteca*) mobile.
ambulatorio [ambula'torjo] *nm* state health-service clinic.
ameba [a'meβa] *nf* amoeba.
amedrentar [ameðren'tar] *vt* to scare.
amén [a'men] *excl* amen; ~ **de** *prep* besides, in addition to; **en un decir** ~ in the twinkling of an eye; **decir** ~ **a todo** to have no mind of one's own.
amenace [ame'naθe] *etc vb V* **amenazar**.
amenaza [ame'naθa] *nf* threat.
amenazar [amena'θar] *vt* to threaten ♦ *vi:* ~ **con hacer** to threaten to do.
amenguar [amen'ɣwar] *vt* to diminish; (*fig*) to dishonour.
amengüe [a'menɣwe] *etc vb V* **amenguar**.
amenidad [ameni'ðað] *nf* pleasantness.
ameno, a [a'meno, a] *a* pleasant.
América [a'merika] *nf* America; Latin America; ~ **del Norte/del Sur** North/South America; ~ **Central/Latina** Central/Latin America.
americano, a [ameri'kano, a] *a, nm/f* American ♦ *nf* coat, jacket.
americe [ame'riθe] *etc vb V* **amerizar**.

amerizaje [ameri'θaxe] *nm* (*AVIAT*) landing (on the sea).

amerizar [ameri'θar] *vi* (*AVIAT*) to land (on the sea).

ametralladora [ametraʎa'ðora] *nf* machine gun.

amianto [a'mjanto] *nm* asbestos.

amigable [ami'ɣaβle] *a* friendly.

amígdala [a'miɣðala] *nf* tonsil.

amigdalitis [amiɣða'litis] *nf* tonsillitis.

amigo, a [a'miɣo, a] *a* friendly ♦ *nm/f* friend; (*amante*) lover; ~ **de lo ajeno** thief; ~ **corresponsal** penfriend; **hacerse** ~**s** to become friends; **ser** ~ **de** to like, be fond of; **ser muy** ~**s** to be close friends.

amigote [ami'ɣote] *nm* mate (*Brit*), buddy.

amilanar [amila'nar] *vt* to scare; ~**se** *vr* to get scared.

aminorar [amino'rar] *vt* to diminish; (*reducir*) to reduce; ~ **la marcha** to slow down.

amistad [amis'tað] *nf* friendship; ~**es** *nfpl* friends.

amistoso, a [ami'stoso, a] *a* friendly.

amnesia [am'nesja] *nf* amnesia.

amnistía [amnis'tia] *nf* amnesty.

amnistiar [amni'stjar] *vt* to amnesty, grant an amnesty to.

amo ['amo] *nm* owner; (*jefe*) boss.

amodorrarse [amoðo'rrarse] *vr* to get sleepy.

amolar [amo'lar] *vt* to annoy.

amoldar [amol'dar] *vt* to mould; (*adaptar*) to adapt.

amonestación [amonesta'θjon] *nf* warning; **amonestaciones** *nfpl* marriage banns.

amonestar [amone'star] *vt* to warn; to publish the banns of.

amontonar [amonto'nar] *vt* to collect, pile up; ~**se** *vr* (*gente*) to crowd together; (*acumularse*) to pile up; (*datos*) to accumulate; (*desastres*) to come one on top of another.

amor [a'mor] *nm* love; (*amante*) lover; **hacer el** ~ to make love; ~ **interesado** cupboard love; ~ **propio** self-respect; **por (el)** ~ **de Dios** for God's sake; **estar al** ~ **de la lumbre** to be close to the fire.

amoratado, a [amora'taðo, a] *a* purple, blue with cold; (*con cardenales*) bruised.

amordace [amor'ðaθe] *etc vb V* **amordazar**.

amordazar [amorða'θar] *vt* to muzzle; (*fig*) to gag.

amorfo, a [a'morfo, a] *a* amorphous, shapeless.

amorío [amo'rio] *nm* (*fam*) love affair.

amoroso, a [amo'roso, a] *a* affectionate, loving.

amortajar [amorta'xar] *vt* (*fig*) to shroud.

amortice [amor'tiθe] *etc vb V* **amortizar**.

amortiguador [amortiɣwa'ðor] *nm* shock absorber; (*parachoques*) bumper; (*silenciador*) silencer; ~**es** *nmpl* (*AUTO*) suspension *sg*.

amortiguar [amorti'ɣwar] *vt* to deaden; (*ruido*) to muffle; (*color*) to soften.

amortigüe [amor'tiɣwe] *etc vb V* **amortiguar**.

amortización [amortiθa'θjon] *nf* redemption; repayment; (*COM*) capital allowance.

amortizar [amorti'θar] *vt* (*ECON*: *bono*) to redeem; (: *capital*) to write off; (: *préstamo*) to pay off.

amoscarse [amos'karse] *vr* to get cross.

amosque [a'moske] *etc vb V* **amoscarse**.

amotinar [amoti'nar] *vt* to stir up, incite (to riot); ~**se** *vr* to mutiny.

amparar [ampa'rar] *vt* to protect; ~**se** *vr* to seek protection; (*de la lluvia etc*) to shelter.

amparo [am'paro] *nm* help, protection; **al** ~ **de** under the protection of.

amperímetro *nm* ammeter.

amperio [am'perjo] *nm* ampère, amp.

ampliable [am'pljaβle] *a* (*INFORM*) expandable.

ampliación [amplja'θjon] *nf* enlargement; (*extensión*) extension.

ampliar [am'pljar] *vt* to enlarge; to extend.

amplificación [amplifika'θjon] *nf* enlargement.

amplificador [amplifika'ðor] *nm* amplifier.

amplificar [amplifi'kar] *vt* to amplify.

amplifique [ampli'fike] *etc vb V* **amplificar**.

amplio, a ['ampljo, a] *a* spacious; (*falda etc*) full; (*extenso*) extensive; (*ancho*) wide.

amplitud [ampli'tuð] *nf* spaciousness; extent; (*fig*) amplitude; ~ **de miras** broadmindedness; **de gran** ~ far-reaching.

ampolla [am'poʎa] *nf* blister; (*MED*) ampoule.

ampuloso, a [ampu'loso, a] *a* bombastic, pompous.

amputar [ampu'tar] *vt* to cut off, amputate.

amueblar [amwe'βlar] *vt* to furnish.

amurallar [amura'ʎar] *vt* to wall up *o* in.

amusgar [amus'ɣar] *vt* (*orejas*) to lay back; (*ojos*) to screw up.

amusgue [a'musɣe] *etc vb V* **amusgar**.

anacarado, a [anaka'raðo, a] *a* mother-of-pearl *cpd*.

anacardo [ana'karðo] *nm* cashew (nut).

anacronismo [anakro'nismo] *nm* anachronism.

ánade ['anaðe] *nm* duck.

anadear [anaðe'ar] *vi* to waddle.

anales [a'nales] *nmpl* annals.

analfabetismo [analfaβe'tismo] *nm* illiteracy.

analfabeto, a [analfa'βeto, a] *a*, *nm/f* illit-

erate.
analgésico [anal'xesiko] *nm* painkiller, analgesic.
analice [ana'liθe] *etc vb* V **analizar**.
análisis [a'nalisis] *nm inv* analysis; ~ **de costos-beneficios** cost-benefit analysis; ~ **de mercados** market research; ~ **de sangre** blood test.
analista [ana'lista] *nm/f* (*gen*) analyst; (*POL, HISTORIA*) chronicler; ~ **de sistemas** (*INFORM*) systems analyst.
analizar [anali'θar] *vt* to analyse.
analogía [analo'xia] *nf* analogy; **por** ~ **con** on the analogy of.
análogo, a [a'naloɣo, a] *a* analogous, similar.
ananá(s) [ana'na(s)] *nm* pineapple.
anaquel [ana'kel] *nm* shelf.
anaranjado, a [anaran'xaðo, a] *a* orange(-coloured).
anarquía [anar'kia] *nf* anarchy.
anarquismo [anar'kismo] *nm* anarchism.
anarquista [anar'kista] *nm/f* anarchist.
anatematizar [anatemati'θar] *vt* (*REL*) to anathematize; (*fig*) to curse.
anatemice [anate'miθe] *etc vb* V **anatemizar**.
anatomía [anato'mia] *nf* anatomy.
anca ['anka] *nf* rump, haunch; ~**s** *nfpl* (*fam*) behind *sg*; **llevar a uno en** ~**s** to carry sb behind one.
anciano, a [an'θjano, a] *a* old, aged ♦ *nm/f* old man/woman ♦ *nm* elder.
ancla ['ankla] *nf* anchor; **levar** ~**s** to weigh anchor.
ancladero [ankla'ðero] *nm* anchorage.
anclar [an'klar] *vi* to (drop) anchor.
ancho, a ['antʃo, a] *a* wide; (*falda*) full; (*fig*) liberal ♦ *nm* width; (*FERRO*) gauge; **le viene muy** ~ **el cargo** (*fig*) the job is too much for him; **ponerse** ~ to get conceited; **quedarse tan** ~ to go on as if nothing had happened; **estar a sus anchas** to be at one's ease.
anchoa [an'tʃoa] *nf* anchovy.
anchura [an'tʃura] *nf* width; (*extensión*) wideness.
anchuroso, a [antʃu'roso, a] *a* wide.
andadas [an'daðas] *nfpl* (*aventuras*) adventures; **volver a las** ~ to backslide.
andaderas [anda'ðeras] *nfpl* baby-walker *sg*.
andadura [anda'ðura] *nf* gait; (*de caballo*) pace.
Andalucía [andalu'θia] *nf* Andalusia.
andaluz, a [anda'luθ, a] *a, nm/f* Andalusian.
andamio [an'damjo] *nm*, **andamiaje** [anda'mjaxe] *nm* scaffold(ing).
andanada [anda'naða] *nf* (*fig*) reprimand; **soltarle a uno una** ~ to give sb a rocket.

andante [an'dante] *a*: **caballero** ~ knight-errant.
andar [an'dar] *vt* to go, cover, travel ♦ *vi* to go, walk, travel; (*funcionar*) to go, work; (*estar*) to be ♦ *nm* walk, gait, pace; ~**se** *vr* (*irse*) to go away *o* off; ~ **a pie/a caballo/en bicicleta** to go on foot/on horseback/by bicycle; **¡anda!** (*sorpresa*) go on!; **anda en** *o* **por los 40** he's about 40; **¿en qué andas?** what are you up to?; **andamos mal de dinero/tiempo** we're badly off for money/we're short of time; ~**se por las ramas** to beat about the bush; **no** ~**se con rodeos** to call a spade a spade (*fam*); **todo se andará** all in good time; **anda por aquí** it's round here somewhere; ~ **haciendo algo** to be doing sth.
andariego, a [anda'rjeɣo, a] *a* fond of travelling.
andas ['andas] *nfpl* stretcher *sg*.
andén [an'den] *nm* (*FERRO*) platform; (*NAUT*) quayside; (*AM: de la calle*) pavement (*Brit*), sidewalk (*US*).
Andes ['andes] *nmpl*: **los** ~ the Andes.
andino, a [an'dino, a] *a* Andean, of the Andes.
andorga [an'dorɣa] *nf* belly.
Andorra [an'dorra] *nf* Andorra.
andrajo [an'draxo] *nm* rag.
andrajoso, a [andra'xoso, a] *a* ragged.
andurriales [andu'rrjales] *nmpl* out-of-the-way place *sg*, the sticks; **en esos** ~ in that godforsaken spot.
anduve [an'dußε], **anduviera** [andu'ßjera] *etc vb* V **andar**.
anécdota [a'nekðota] *nf* anecdote, story.
anegar [ane'ɣar] *vt* to flood; (*ahogar*) to drown; ~**se** *vr* to drown; (*hundirse*) to sink.
anegue [a'neɣe] *etc vb* V **anegar**.
anejo, a [a'nexo, a] *a* attached ♦ *nm* (*ARQ*) annexe.
anemia [a'nemja] *nf* anaemia.
anestésico [anes'tesiko] *nm* anaesthetic.
anexar [anek'sar] *vt* to annex; (*documento*) to attach; (*INFORM*) to append.
anexión [anek'sjon] *nf*, **anexionamiento** [aneksjona'mjento] *nm* annexation.
anexo, a [a'nekso, a] *a* attached ♦ *nm* annexe.
anfibio, a [an'fißjo, a] *a* amphibious ♦ *nm* amphibian.
anfiteatro [anfite'atro] *nm* amphitheatre; (*TEATRO*) dress circle.
anfitrión, ona [anfi'trjon, ona] *nm/f* host(ess).
ángel ['anxel] *nm* angel; ~ **de la guarda** guardian angel; **tener** ~ to have charm.
Ángeles ['anxeles] *nmpl*: **los** ~ Los Angeles.
angélico, a [an'xeliko, a], **angelical** [anxe-

li'kal] *a* angelic(al).

angina [an'xina] *nf* (*MED*): ~ **de pecho** angina; **tener ~s** to have a sore throat *o* throat infection.

anglicano, a [angli'kano, a] *a, nm/f* Anglican.

Angola [an'gola] *nf* Angola.

angoleño, a [ango'leɲo, a] *a, nm/f* Angolan.

angosto, a [an'gosto, a] *a* narrow.

anguila [an'gila] *nf* eel; **~s** *nfpl* slipway *sg*.

angula [an'gula] *nf* elver, baby eel.

ángulo ['angulo] *nm* angle; (*esquina*) corner; (*curva*) bend.

angustia [an'gustja] *nf* anguish.

angustiar [angus'tjar] *vt* to distress, grieve; **~se** *vr* to be distressed (*por* at, on account of).

anhelante [ane'lante] *a* eager; (*deseoso*) longing.

anhelar [ane'lar] *vt* to be eager for; to long for, desire ♦ *vi* to pant, gasp.

anhelo [a'nelo] *nm* eagerness; desire.

anidar [ani'ðar] *vt* (*acoger*) to take in, shelter ♦ *vi* to nest; (*fig*) to make one's home.

anilina [ani'lina] *nf* aniline.

anillo [a'niʎo] *nm* ring; ~ **de boda** wedding ring; ~ **de compromiso** engagement ring; **venir como** ~ **al dedo** to suit to a tee.

ánima ['anima] *nf* soul; **las ~s** the Angelus (bell) *sg*.

animación [anima'θjon] *nf* liveliness; (*vitalidad*) life; (*actividad*) bustle.

animado, a [ani'maðo, a] *a* (*vivo*) lively; (*vivaz*) animated; (*concurrido*) bustling; (*alegre*) in high spirits; **dibujos ~s** cartoon *sg*.

animador, a [anima'ðor, a] *nm/f* (*TV*) host(ess) ♦ *nf* (*DEPORTE*) cheerleader.

animadversión [animaðßer'sjon] *nf* ill-will, antagonism.

animal [ani'mal] *a* animal; (*fig*) stupid ♦ *nm* animal; (*fig*) fool; (*bestia*) brute.

animalada [anima'laða] *nf* (*gen*) silly thing (to do *o* say); (*ultraje*) disgrace.

animar [ani'mar] *vt* (*BIO*) to animate, give life to; (*fig*) to liven up, brighten up, cheer up; (*estimular*) to stimulate; **~se** *vr* to cheer up, feel encouraged; (*decidirse*) to make up one's mind.

ánimo ['animo] *nm* soul, mind; (*valentía*) courage ♦ *excl* cheer up!; **cobrar** ~ to take heart; **dar ~(s) a** to encourage.

animoso, a [ani'moso, a] *a* brave; (*vivo*) lively.

aniñado, a [ani'ɲaðo, a] *a* (*facción*) childlike; (*carácter*) childish.

aniquilar [aniki'lar] *vt* to annihilate, destroy.

anís [a'nis] *nm* (*grano*) aniseed; (*licor*) anisette.

aniversario [anißer'sarjo] *nm* anniversary.

Ankara [an'kara] *nf* Ankara.

ano ['ano] *nm* anus.

anoche [a'notʃe] *ad* last night; **antes de** ~ the night before last.

anochecer [anotʃe'θer] *vi* to get dark ♦ *nm* nightfall, dark; **al** ~ at nightfall.

anochezca [ano'tʃeθka] *etc vb V* **anochecer.**

anomalía [anoma'lia] *nf* anomaly.

anodino, a [ano'ðino, a] *a* dull, anodyne.

anonimato [anoni'mato] *nm* anonimity.

anónimo, a [a'nonimo, a] *a* anonymous; (*COM*) limited ♦ *nm* (*carta*) anonymous letter; (: *maliciosa*) poison-pen letter.

anormal [anor'mal] *a* abnormal.

anotación [anota'θjon] *nf* note; annotation.

anotar [ano'tar] *vt* to note down; (*comentar*) to annotate.

anquilosado, a [ankilo'saðo, a] *a* (*fig*) stale, out of date.

anquilosamiento [ankilosa'mjento] *nm* (*fig*) paralysis, stagnation.

ansia ['ansja] *nf* anxiety; (*añoranza*) yearning.

ansiar [an'sjar] *vt* to long for.

ansiedad [ansje'ðað] *nf* anxiety.

ansioso, a [an'sjoso, a] *a* anxious; (*anhelante*) eager; ~ **de** *o* **por algo** greedy for sth.

antagónico, a [anta'ɣoniko, a] *a* antagonistic; (*opuesto*) contrasting.

antagonista [antaɣo'nista] *nm/f* antagonist.

antaño [an'taɲo] *ad* long ago.

Antártico [an'tartiko] *nm*: **el** ~ the Antarctic.

Antártida [an'tartiða] *nf* Antarctica.

ante ['ante] *prep* before, in the presence of; (*encarado con*) faced with ♦ *nm* suede; ~ **todo** above all.

anteanoche [antea'notʃe] *ad* the night before last.

anteayer [antea'jer] *ad* the day before yesterday.

antebrazo [ante'ßraθo] *nm* forearm.

antecámara [ante'kamara] *nf* (*ARQ*) anteroom; (*antesala*) waiting room; (*POL*) lobby.

antecedente [anteθe'ðente] *a* previous ♦ *nm*: **~s** *nmpl* (*profesionales*) background *sg*; **~s penales** criminal record; **no tener ~s** to have a clean record; **estar en ~s** to be well-informed; **poner a uno en ~s** to put sb in the picture.

anteceder [anteθe'ðer] *vt* to precede, go before.

antecesor, a [anteθe'sor, a] *nm/f* predecessor.

antedicho, a [ante'ðitʃo, a] *a* aforementioned.

antelación [antela'θjon] *nf*: **con** ~ in advance.

antemano [ante'mano]: **de** ~ *ad* beforehand, in advance.

antena [an'tena] *nf* antenna; *(de televisión etc)* aerial.

anteojeras [anteo'xeras] *nfpl* blinkers *(Brit)*, blinders *(US)*.

anteojo [ante'oxo] *nm* eyeglass; ~**s** *nmpl (esp AM)* glasses, spectacles.

antepasados [antepa'saðos] *nmpl* ancestors.

antepecho [ante'petʃo] *nm* guardrail, parapet; *(repisa)* ledge, sill.

antepondré [antepon'dre] *etc vb* V **anteponer**.

anteponer [antepo'ner] *vt* to place in front; *(fig)* to prefer.

anteponga [ante'ponɣa] *etc vb* V **anteponer**.

anteproyecto [antepro'jekto] *nm* preliminary sketch; *(fig)* blueprint; *(POL)*: ~ **de ley** draft bill.

antepuesto, a [ante'pwesto, a] *pp de* **anteponer**.

antepuse [ante'puse] *etc vb* V **anteponer**.

anterior [ante'rjor] *a* preceding, previous.

anterioridad [anterjori'ðað] *nf*: **con** ~ **a** prior to, before.

anteriormente [anterjor'mente] *ad* previously, before.

antes ['antes] *ad* sooner; *(primero)* first; *(con prioridad)* before; *(hace tiempo)* previously, once; *(más bien)* rather ◆ *prep*: ~ **de** before ◆ *conj*: ~ **(de) que** before; ~ **bien** (but) rather; **dos días** ~ two days before *o* previously; **mucho/poco** ~ long/ shortly before; ~ **muerto que esclavo** better dead than enslaved; **tomo el avión** ~ **que el barco** I take the plane rather than the boat; **cuanto** ~, **lo** ~ **posible** as soon as possible; **cuanto** ~ **mejor** the sooner the better.

antesala [ante'sala] *nf* anteroom.

antiadherente [antiaðe'rente] *a* non-stick.

antiaéreo, a [antia'ereo, a] *a* anti-aircraft.

antialcohólico, a [antial'koliko, a] *a*: **centro** ~ *(MED)* detoxification unit.

antibalas [anti'ßalas] *a inv*: **chaleco** ~ bullet-proof jacket.

antibiótico [anti'ßjotiko] *nm* antibiotic.

anticiclón [antiθi'klon] *nm (METEOROLOGÍA)* anti-cyclone.

anticipación [antiθipa'θjon] *nf* anticipation; **con 10 minutos de** ~ 10 minutes early.

anticipado, a [antiθi'paðo, a] *a* (in) advance; **por** ~ in advance.

anticipar [antiθi'par] *vt* to anticipate; *(adelantar)* to bring forward; *(COM)* to advance; ~**se** *vr*: ~**se a su época** to be ahead of one's time.

anticipo [anti'θipo] *nm (COM)* advance; V *tb* **anticipación**.

anticonceptivo, a [antikonθep'tißo, a] *a, nm* contraceptive; **métodos** ~**s** contraceptive devices.

anticongelante [antikonxe'lante] *nm* antifreeze.

anticonstitucional [antikonstituθjo'nal] *a* unconstitutional.

anticuado, a [anti'kwaðo, a] *a* out-of-date, old-fashioned; *(desusado)* obsolete.

anticuario [anti'kwarjo] *nm* antique dealer.

anticuerpo [anti'kwerpo] *nm (MED)* antibody.

antidemocrático, a [antiðemo'kratiko, a] *a* undemocratic.

antideportivo, a [antiðepor'tißo, a] *a* unsporting.

antideslumbrante [antiðeslum'brante] *a (INFORM)* anti-dazzle.

antídoto [an'tiðoto] *nm* antidote.

antidroga [anti'ðroɣa] *a inv* anti-drug; **brigada** ~ drug squad.

antiestético, a [anties'tetiko, a] *a* unsightly.

antifaz [anti'faθ] *nm* mask; *(velo)* veil.

antigás [anti'gas] *a inv*: **careta** ~ gasmask.

antigualla [anti'ɣwaʎa] *nf* antique; *(reliquia)* relic; ~**s** *nfpl* old things.

antiguamente [antiɣwa'mente] *ad* formerly; *(hace mucho tiempo)* long ago.

antigüedad [antiɣwe'ðað] *nf* antiquity; *(artículo)* antique; *(rango)* seniority.

antiguo, a [an'tiɣwo, a] *a* old, ancient; *(que fue)* former; **a la antigua** in the old-fashioned way.

antihigiénico, a [anti'xjeniko, a] *a* unhygienic.

antihistamínico, a [antista'miniko, a] *a, nm* antihistamine.

antiinflacionista [antinflaθjo'nista] *a* anti-inflationary, counter-inflationary.

antílope [an'tilope] *nm* antelope.

antillano, a [anti'ʎano, a] *a, nm/f* West Indian.

Antillas [an'tiʎas] *nfpl*: **las** ~ the West Indies, the Antilles; **el mar de las** ~ the Caribbean Sea.

antimonopolios [antimono'poljos] *a inv*: **ley** ~ anti-trust law.

antinatural [antinatu'ral] *a* unnatural.

antiparras [anti'parras] *nfpl (fam)* specs.

antipatía [antipa'tia] *nf* antipathy, dislike.

antipático, a [anti'patiko, a] *a* disagreeable, unpleasant.

Antípodas [an'tipoðas] *nfpl*: **las** ~ the antipodes.

antiquísimo, a [anti'kisimo, a] *a* ancient.

antirreglamentario, a [antirreɣlamen-'tarjo, a] *a (gen)* unlawful; *(POL etc)* unconstitutional.

antirrobo [anti'rroβo] *a inv*: (**dispositivo**) ~ (*para casas etc*) burglar alarm; (*para coches*) car alarm.

antisemita [antise'mita] *a* anti-Semitic ♦ *nm/f* anti-Semite.

antiséptico, a [anti'septiko, a] *a, nm* antiseptic.

antítesis [an'titesis] *nf inv* antithesis.

antiterrorista [antiterro'rista] *a* antiterrorist; **la lucha** ~ the fight against terrorism.

antojadizo, a [antoxa'ðiθo, a] *a* capricious.

antojarse [anto'xarse] *vr* (*desear*): **se me antoja comprarlo** I have a mind to buy it; (*pensar*): **se me antoja que** I have a feeling that.

antojo [an'toxo] *nm* caprice, whim; (*rosa*) birthmark; (*lunar*) mole; **hacer a su** ~ to do as one pleases.

antología [antolo'xia] *nf* anthology.

antonomasia [antono'masja] *nf*: **por** ~ par excellence.

antorcha [an'tortʃa] *nf* torch.

antro ['antro] *nm* cavern; ~ **de corrupción** (*fig*) den of iniquity.

antropófago, a [antro'pofaɣo, a] *a, nm/f* cannibal.

antropología [antropolo'xia] *nf* anthropology.

anual [a'nwal] *a* annual.

anualidad [anwali'ðað] *nf* annuity, annual payment; ~ **vitalicia** life annuity.

anuario [a'nwarjo] *nm* yearbook.

anudar [anu'ðar] *vt* to knot, tie; (*unir*) to join; ~**se** *vr* to get tied up; **se me anudó la voz** I got a lump in my throat.

anulación [anula'θjon] *nf* annulment; cancellation; repeal.

anular [anu'lar] *vt* to annul, cancel; (*suscripción*) to cancel; (*ley*) to repeal ♦ *nm* ring finger.

anunciación [anunθja'θjon] *nf* announcement; **A**~ (*REL*) Annunciation.

anunciante [anun'θjante] *nm/f* (*COM*) advertiser.

anunciar [anun'θjar] *vt* to announce; (*proclamar*) to proclaim; (*COM*) to advertise.

anuncio [a'nunθjo] *nm* announcement; (*señal*) sign; (*COM*) advertisement; (*cartel*) poster; (*TEATRO*) bill; ~**s por palabras** classified ads.

anverso [am'berso] *nm* obverse.

anzuelo [an'θwelo] *nm* hook; (*para pescar*) fish hook; **tragar el** ~ to swallow the bait.

añadidura [aɲaði'ðura] *nf* addition, extra; **por** ~ besides, in addition.

añadir [aɲa'ðir] *vt* to add.

añejo, a [a'ɲexo, a] *a* old; (*vino*) vintage; (*jamón*) well-cured.

añicos [a'ɲikos] *nmpl*: **hacer** ~ to smash, shatter; **hacerse** ~ to smash, shatter.

añil [a'ɲil] *nm* (*BOT, color*) indigo.

año ['aɲo] *nm* year; **¡Feliz A**~ **Nuevo!** Happy New Year!; **tener 15** ~**s** to be 15 (years old); **los** ~**s 80** the eighties; ~ **bisiesto/escolar** leap/school year; ~ **fiscal** fiscal *o* tax year; **estar de buen** ~ to be in good shape; **en el** ~ **de la nana** in the year dot; **el** ~ **que viene** next year.

añoranza [aɲo'ranθa] *nf* nostalgia; (*anhelo*) longing.

añoso, a [a'ɲoso, a] *a* ancient, old.

aojar [ao'xar] *vt* to put the evil eye on.

aovado, a [ao'βaðo, a] *a* oval.

aovar [ao'βar] *vi* to lay eggs.

apabullar [apaβu'ʎar] *vt* (*lit, fig*) to crush.

apacentar [apaθen'tar] *vt* to pasture, graze.

apacible [apa'θiβle] *a* gentle, mild.

apaciente [apa'θjente] *etc vb V* **apacentar**.

apaciguar [apaθi'ɣwar] *vt* to pacify, calm (down).

apacigüe [apa'θiɣwe] *etc vb V* **apaciguar**.

apadrinar [apaðri'nar] *vt* to sponsor, support; (*REL*) to act as godfather to.

apagado, a [apa'ɣaðo, a] *a* (*volcán*) extinct; (*color*) dull; (*voz*) quiet; (*sonido*) muted, muffled; (*persona: apático*) listless; **estar** ~ (*fuego, luz*) to be out; (*radio, TV etc*) to be off.

apagar [apa'ɣar] *vt* to put out; (*color*) to tone down; (*sonido*) to silence, muffle; (*sed*) to quench; (*INFORM*) to toggle off; ~**se** *vr* (*luz, fuego*) to go out; (*sonido*) to die away; (*pasión*) to wither; ~ **el sistema** (*INFORM*) to close *o* shut down.

apagón [apa'ɣon] *nm* blackout, power cut.

apague [a'paɣe] *etc vb V* **apagar**.

apalabrar [apala'βrar] *vt* to agree to; (*obrero*) to engage.

Apalaches [apa'latʃes] *nmpl*: (**Montes**) ~ Appalachians.

apalear [apale'ar] *vt* to beat, thrash; (*AGR*) to winnow.

apañar [apa'ɲar] *vt* to pick up; (*asir*) to take hold of, grasp; (*reparar*) to mend, patch up; ~**se** *vr* to manage, get along; **apañárselas por su cuenta** to look after number one (*fam*).

apaño [a'paɲo] *nm* (*COSTURA*) patch; (*maña*) skill; **esto no tiene** ~ there's no answer to this one.

aparador [apara'ðor] *nm* sideboard; (*escaparate*) shop window.

aparato [apa'rato] *nm* apparatus; (*máquina*) machine; (*doméstico*) appliance; (*boato*) ostentation; (*INFORM*) device; ~ **de facsímil** facsimile (machine), fax; ~ **respiratorio** respiratory system; ~**s de mando** (*AVIAT etc*) controls.

aparatoso, a [apara'toso, a] *a* showy, ostentatious.

aparcamiento [aparka'mjento] *nm* car park (*Brit*), parking lot (*US*).

aparcar [apar'kar] *vt, vi* to park.

aparear [apare'ar] *vt* (*objetos*) to pair, match; (*animales*) to mate; ~**se** *vr* to form a pair; to mate.

aparecer [apare'θer] *vi*, ~**se** *vr* to appear; **apareció borracho** he turned up drunk.

aparejado, a [apare'xaðo, a] *a* fit, suitable; **ir** ~ **con** to go hand in hand with; **llevar** *o* **traer** ~ to involve.

aparejar [apare'xar] *vt* to prepare; (*caballo*) to saddle, harness; (*NAUT*) to fit out, rig out.

aparejo [apa'rexo] *nm* preparation; (*de caballo*) harness; (*NAUT*) rigging; (*de poleas*) block and tackle.

aparentar [aparen'tar] *vt* (*edad*) to look; (*fingir*): ~ **tristeza** to pretend to be sad.

aparente [apa'rente] *a* apparent; (*adecuado*) suitable.

aparezca [apa'reθka] *etc vb V* **aparecer**.

aparición [apari'θjon] *nf* appearance; (*de libro*) publication; (*fantasma*) spectre.

apariencia [apa'rjenθja] *nf* (outward) appearance; **en** ~ outwardly, seemingly.

aparque [a'parke] *etc vb V* **aparcar**.

apartado, a [apar'taðo, a] *a* separate; (*lejano*) remote ♦ *nm* (*tipográfico*) paragraph; ~ (**de correos**) post office box.

apartamento [aparta'mento] *nm* apartment, flat (*Brit*).

apartamiento [aparta'mjento] *nm* separation; (*aislamiento*) remoteness; (*AM*) apartment, flat (*Brit*).

apartar [apar'tar] *vt* to separate; (*quitar*) to remove; (*MINERALOGÍA*) to extract; ~**se** *vr* (*separarse*) to separate, part; (*irse*) to move away; (*mantenerse aparte*) to keep away.

aparte [a'parte] *ad* (*separadamente*) separately; (*además*) besides ♦ *prep*: ~ **de** apart from ♦ *nm* (*TEATRO*) aside; (*tipográfico*) new paragraph; "**punto y** ~" "new paragraph".

apasionado, a [apasjo'naðo, a] *a* passionate; (*pey*) biassed, prejudiced ♦ *nm/f* admirer.

apasionar [apasjo'nar] *vt* to arouse passion in; ~**se** *vr* to get excited; **le apasiona el fútbol** she's crazy about football.

apatía [apa'tia] *nf* apathy.

apático, a [a'patiko, a] *a* apathetic.

apátrida [a'patriða] *a* stateless.

Apdo. *nm abr* (= *Apartado (de Correos)*) P.O. Box.

apeadero [apea'ðero] *nm* halt, stopping place.

apearse [ape'arse] *vr* (*jinete*) to dismount; (*bajarse*) to get down *o* out; (*de coche*) to get out, alight; **no** ~ **del burro** to refuse to climb down.

apechugar [apetʃu'ɣar] *vi*: ~ **con algo** to face up to sth.

apechugue [ape'tʃuɣe] *etc vb V* **apechugar**.

apedrear [apeðre'ar] *vt* to stone.

apegarse [ape'ɣarse] *vr*: ~ **a** to become attached to.

apego [a'peɣo] *nm* attachment, devotion.

apegue [a'peɣe] *etc vb V* **apegarse**.

apelación [apela'θjon] *nf* appeal.

apelar [ape'lar] *vi* to appeal; ~ **a** (*fig*) to resort to.

apelativo [apela'tiβo] *nm* (*LING*) appellative; (*AM*) surname.

apelmazado, a [apelma'θaðo, a] *a* compact, solid.

apelotonar [apeloto'nar] *vt* to roll into a ball; ~**se** *vr* (*gente*) to crowd together.

apellidar [apeʎi'ðar] *vt* to call, name; ~**se** *vr*: **se apellida Pérez** her (sur)name's Pérez.

apellido [ape'ʎiðo] *nm* surname.

apenar [ape'nar] *vt* to grieve, trouble; ~**se** *vr* to grieve.

apenas [a'penas] *ad* scarcely, hardly ♦ *conj* as soon as, no sooner.

apéndice [a'pendiθe] *nm* appendix.

apendicitis [apendi'θitis] *nf* appendicitis.

Apeninos [ape'ninos] *nmpl* Apennines.

apercibimiento [aperθiβi'mjento] *nm* (*aviso*) warning.

apercibir [aperθi'βir] *vt* to prepare; (*avisar*) to warn; (*JUR*) to summon; (*AM*) to notice, see; ~**se** *vr* to get ready; ~**se de** to notice.

aperitivo [aperi'tiβo] *nm* (*bebida*) aperitif; (*comida*) appetizer.

apero [a'pero] *nm* (*AGR*) implement; ~**s** *nmpl* farm equipment *sg*.

aperrear [aperre'ar] *vt* to set the dogs on; (*fig*) to plague.

apertura [aper'tura] *nf* (*gen*) opening; (*POL*) openness, liberalization; (*TEATRO etc*) beginning; ~ **de un juicio hipotecario** (*COM*) foreclosure.

aperturismo [apertu'rismo] *nm* (*POL*) (policy of) liberalization.

apesadumbrar [apesaðum'brar] *vt* to grieve, sadden; ~**se** *vr* to distress o.s.

apestar [apes'tar] *vt* to infect ♦ *vi*: ~(**a**) to stink (of).

apestoso, a [apes'toso, a] *a* (*hediondo*) stinking; (*asqueroso*) sickening.

apetecer [apete'θer] *vt*: **¿te apetece una tortilla?** do you fancy an omelette?

apetecible [apete'θiβle] *a* desirable; (*comida*) tempting.

apetezca [ape'teθka] *etc vb V* **apetecer**.

apetito [ape'tito] *nm* appetite.

apetitoso, a [apeti'toso, a] *a* (*gustoso*) appetizing; (*fig*) tempting.

apiadarse [apja'ðarse] *vr*: ~ **de** to take pity on.

ápice ['apiθe] *nm* apex; (*fig*) whit, iota; **ni un ~** not a whit; **no ceder un ~** not to budge an inch.

apicultor, a [apikul'tor, a] *nm/f* beekeeper, apiarist.

apicultura [apikul'tura] *nf* beekeeping.

apiladora [apila'ðora] *nf* (*para máquina impresora*) stacker.

apilar [api'lar] *vt* to pile *o* heap up; **~se** *vr* to pile up.

apiñado, a [api'ɲaðo, a] *a* (*apretado*) packed.

apiñar [api'ɲar] *vt* to crowd; **~se** *vr* to crowd *o* press together.

apio ['apjo] *nm* celery.

apisonadora [apisona'ðora] *nf* (*máquina*) steamroller.

aplacar [apla'kar] *vt* to placate; **~se** *vr* to calm down.

aplace [a'plaθe] *etc vb V* **aplazar**.

aplanamiento [aplana'mjento] *nm* smoothing, levelling.

aplanar [apla'nar] *vt* to smooth, level; (*allanar*) to roll flat, flatten; **~se** *vr* (*edificio*) to collapse; (*persona*) to get discouraged.

aplaque [a'plake] *etc vb V* **aplacar**.

aplastar [aplas'tar] *vt* to squash (flat); (*fig*) to crush.

aplatanarse [aplata'narse] *vr* to get lethargic.

aplaudir [aplau'ðir] *vt* to applaud.

aplauso [a'plauso] *nm* applause; (*fig*) approval, acclaim.

aplazamiento [aplaθa'mjento] *nm* postponement.

aplazar [apla'θar] *vt* to postpone, defer.

aplicación [aplika'θjon] *nf* application; (*esfuerzo*) effort; **aplicaciones de gestión** business applications.

aplicado, a [apli'kaðo, a] *a* diligent, hardworking.

aplicar [apli'kar] *vt* (*gen*) to apply; (*poner en vigor*) to put into effect; (*esfuerzos*) to devote; **~se** *vr* to apply o.s.

aplique [a'plike] *etc vb V* **aplicar** ◆ *nm* wall light *o* lamp.

aplomo [a'plomo] *nm* aplomb, self-assurance.

apocado, a [apo'kaðo, a] *a* timid.

apocamiento [apoka'mjento] *nm* timidity; (*depresión*) depression.

apocarse [apo'karse] *vr* to feel small *o* humiliated.

apocopar [apoko'par] *vt* (*LING*) to shorten.

apodar [apo'ðar] *vt* to nickname.

apoderado [apoðe'raðo] *nm* agent, representative.

apoderar [apoðe'rar] *vt* to authorize, empower; (*JUR*) to grant (a) power of attorney to; **~se** *vr*: **~se de** to take possession of.

apodo [a'poðo] *nm* nickname.

apogeo [apo'xeo] *nm* peak, summit.

apolillado, a [apoli'ʎaðo, a] *a* moth-eaten.

apolillarse [apoli'ʎarse] *vr* to get moth-eaten.

apología [apolo'xia] *nf* eulogy; (*defensa*) defence.

apoltronarse [apoltro'narse] *vr* to get lazy.

apoplejía [apople'xia] *nf* apoplexy, stroke.

apoque [a'poke] *etc vb V* **apocar**.

apoquinar [apoki'nar] *vt* (*fam*) to cough up, fork out.

aporrear [aporre'ar] *vt* to beat (up).

aportación [aporta'θjon] *nf* contribution.

aportar [apor'tar] *vt* to contribute ◆ *vi* to reach port; **~se** *vr* (*AM*) to arrive, come.

aposentar [aposen'tar] *vt* to lodge, put up.

aposento [apo'sento] *nm* lodging; (*habitación*) room.

apósito [a'posito] *nm* (*MED*) dressing.

aposta(s) [a'posta(s)] *ad* on purpose.

apostar [apos'tar] *vt* to bet, stake; (*tropas etc*) to station, post ◆ *vi* to bet.

apostatar [aposta'tar] *vi* (*REL*) to apostatize; (*fig*) to change sides.

apostilla [apos'tiʎa] *nf* note, comment.

apóstol [a'postol] *nm* apostle.

apóstrofo [a'postrofo] *nm* apostrophe.

apostura [apos'tura] *nf* neatness, elegance.

apoteósico, a [apote'osiko, a] *a* tremendous.

apoyar [apo'jar] *vt* to lean, rest; (*fig*) to support, back; **~se** *vr*: **~se en** to lean on.

apoyo [a'pojo] *nm* support, backing.

apreciable [apre'θjaβle] *a* considerable; (*fig*) esteemed.

apreciación [apreθja'θjon] *nf* appreciation; (*COM*) valuation.

apreciar [apre'θjar] *vt* to evaluate, assess; (*COM*) to appreciate, value ◆ *vi* (*ECON*) to appreciate.

aprecio [a'preθjo] *nm* valuation, estimate; (*fig*) appreciation.

aprehender [apreen'der] *vt* to apprehend, detain; (*ver*) to see, observe.

aprehensión [apreen'sjon] *nf* detention, capture.

apremiante [apre'mjante] *a* urgent, pressing.

apremiar [apre'mjar] *vt* to compel, force ◆ *vi* to be urgent, press.

apremio [a'premjo] *nm* urgency; **~ de pago** demand note.

aprender [apren'der] *vt, vi* to learn; **~ a conducir** to learn to drive; **~se** *vr*: **~se algo** to learn sth (off) by heart.

aprendiz, a [apren'diθ, a] *nm/f* apprentice; (*principiante*) learner, trainee; **~ de comercio** business trainee.

aprendizaje [aprendi'θaxe] *nm* apprenticeship.

aprensión [apren'sjon] *nm* apprehension, fear.

aprensivo, a [apren'sißo, a] *a* apprehensive.

apresar [apre'sar] *vt* to seize; (*capturar*) to capture.

aprestar [apres'tar] *vt* to prepare, get ready; (*TEC*) to prime, size; ~**se** *vr* to get ready.

apresto [a'presto] *nm* (*gen*) preparation; (*sustancia*) size.

apresurado, a [apresu'raðo, a] *a* hurried, hasty.

apresuramiento [apresura'mjento] *nm* hurry, haste.

apresurar [apresu'rar] *vt* to hurry, accelerate; ~**se** *vr* to hurry, make haste; **me apresuré a sugerir que ...** I hastily suggested that ...

apretado, a [apre'taðo, a] *a* tight; (*escritura*) cramped.

apretar [apre'tar] *vt* to squeeze, press; (*mano*) to clasp; (*dientes*) to grit; (*TEC*) to tighten; (*presionar*) to press together, pack ♦ *vi* to be too tight; ~**se** *vr* to crowd together; ~ **la mano a uno** to shake sb's hand; ~ **el paso** to quicken one's step.

apretón [apre'ton] *nm* squeeze; ~ **de manos** handshake.

aprieto [a'prjeto] *etc vb* V **apretar** ♦ *nm* squeeze; (*dificultad*) difficulty, jam; **estar en un** ~ to be in a jam; **ayudar a uno a salir de un** ~ to help sb out of trouble.

aprisa [a'prisa] *ad* quickly, hurriedly.

aprisionar [aprisjo'nar] *vt* to imprison.

aprobación [aproßa'θjon] *nf* approval.

aprobado [apro'ßaðo] *nm* (*nota*) pass mark.

aprobar [apro'ßar] *vt* to approve (of); (*examen, materia*) to pass ♦ *vi* to pass.

apropiación [apropja'θjon] *nf* appropriation.

apropiado, a [apro'pjaðo, a] *a* appropriate.

apropiarse [apro'pjarse] *vr*: ~ **de** to appropriate.

aprovechado, a [aproße'tʃaðo, a] *a* industrious, hardworking; (*económico*) thrifty; (*pey*) unscrupulous.

aprovechamiento [aproßetʃa'mjento] *nm* use, exploitation.

aprovechar [aproße'tʃar] *vt* to use; (*explotar*) to exploit; (*experiencia*) to profit from; (*oferta, oportunidad*) to take advantage of ♦ *vi* to progress, improve; ~**se** *vr*: ~**se de** to make use of; (*pey*) to take advantage of; **¡que aproveche!** enjoy your meal!

aprovisionar [aproßisjo'nar] *vt* to supply.

aproximación [aproksima'θjon] *nf* approximation; (*de lotería*) consolation prize.

aproximadamente [aproksimaða'mente] *ad* approximately.

aproximado, a [aproksi'maðo, a] *a* approximate.

aproximar [aproksi'mar] *vt* to bring nearer; ~**se** *vr* to come near, approach.

apruebe [a'prweße] *etc vb* V **aprobar**.

aptitud [apti'tuð] *nf* aptitude; (*capacidad*) ability; ~ **para los negocios** business sense.

apto, a ['apto, a] *a* (*apropiado*) fit, suitable (*para* for, to)*;* (*hábil*) capable; ~**/no** ~ **para menores** (*CINE*) suitable/unsuitable for children.

apuesto, a [a'pwesto, a] *etc vb* V **apostar** ♦ *a* neat, elegant ♦ *nf* bet, wager.

apuntador [apunta'ðor] *nm* prompter.

apuntalar [apunta'lar] *vt* to prop up.

apuntar [apun'tar] *vt* (*con arma*) to aim at; (*con dedo*) to point at *o* to; (*anotar*) to note (down); (*datos*) to record; (*TEATRO*) to prompt; ~**se** *vr* (*DEPORTE: tanto, victoria*) to score; (*ESCOL*) to enrol; ~ **una cantidad en la cuenta de uno** to charge a sum to sb's account; ~**se en un curso** to enrol on a course; **¡yo me apunto!** count me in!

apunte [a'punte] *nm* note; (*TEATRO: voz*) prompt; (: *texto*) prompt book.

apuñalar [apuɲa'lar] *vt* to stab.

apurado, a [apu'raðo, a] *a* needy; (*difícil*) difficult; (*peligroso*) dangerous; (*AM*) hurried, rushed; **estar en una situación apurada** to be in a tight spot; **estar** ~ to be in a hurry.

apurar [apu'rar] *vt* (*agotar*) to drain; (*recursos*) to use up; (*molestar*) to annoy; ~**se** *vr* (*preocuparse*) to worry; (*darse prisa*) to hurry.

apuro [a'puro] *nm* (*aprieto*) fix, jam; (*escasez*) want, hardship; (*vergüenza*) embarrassment; (*AM*) haste, urgency.

aquejado, a [ake'xaðo, a] *a*: ~ **de** (*MED*) afflicted by.

aquejar [ake'xar] *vt* (*afligir*) to distress; **le aqueja una grave enfermedad** he suffers from a serious disease.

aquel, aquella, aquellos, as [a'kel, a'keʎa, a'keʎos, as] *a* that; (*pl*) those.

aquél, aquélla, aquéllos, as [a'kel, a'keʎa, a'keʎos, as] *pron* that (one); (*pl*) those (ones).

aquello [a'keʎo] *pron* that, that business.

aquí [a'ki] *ad* (*lugar*) here; (*tiempo*) now; ~ **arriba** up here; ~ **mismo** right here; ~ **yace** here lies; **de** ~ **a siete días** a week from now.

aquietar [akje'tar] *vt* to quieten (down), calm (down).

Aquisgrán [akis'ɣran] *nm* Aachen, Aix-la-Chapelle.

A.R. *abr* (= *Alteza Real*) R.H.

ara ['ara] *nf* (*altar*) altar; **en** ~**s de** for the sake of.

árabe ['araße] a Arab, Arabian, Arabic ♦ nm/f Arab ♦ nm (LING) Arabic.

Arabia [a'raßja] nf Arabia; ~ **Saudí** o **Saudita** Saudi Arabia.

arábigo, a [a'raßiɣo, a] a Arab, Arabian, Arabic.

arácnido [a'rakniðo] nm arachnid.

arado [a'raðo] nm plough.

aragonés, esa [araɣo'nes, esa] a, nm/f Aragonese ♦ nm (LING) Aragonese.

arancel [aran'θel] nm tariff, duty; ~ **de aduanas** (customs) duty.

arandela [aran'dela] nf (TEC) washer; (chorrera) frill.

araña [a'raɲa] nf (ZOOL) spider; (lámpara) chandelier.

arañar [ara'ɲar] vt to scratch.

arañazo [ara'ɲaθo] nm scratch.

arar [a'rar] vt to plough, till.

araucano, a [arau'kano, a] a, nm/f Araucanian.

arbitraje [arßi'traxe] nm arbitration.

arbitrar [arßi'trar] vt to arbitrate in; (recursos) to bring together; (DEPORTE) to referee ♦ vi to arbitrate.

arbitrariedad [arßitrarje'ðað] nf arbitrariness; (acto) arbitrary act.

arbitrario, a [arßi'trarjo] a arbitrary.

arbitrio [ar'ßitrjo] nm free will; (JUR) adjudication, decision; **dejar al** ~ **de uno** to leave to sb's discretion.

árbitro ['arßitro] nm arbitrator; (DEPORTE) referee; (TENIS) umpire.

árbol ['arßol] nm (BOT) tree; (NAUT) mast; (TEC) axle, shaft.

arbolado, a [arßo'laðo, a] a wooded; (camino) tree-lined ♦ nm woodland.

arboladura [arßola'ðura] nf rigging.

arbolar [arßo'lar] vt to hoist, raise.

arboleda [arßo'leða] nf grove, plantation.

arbusto [ar'ßusto] nm bush, shrub.

arca ['arka] nf chest, box; **A~ de la Alianza** Ark of the Covenant; **A~ de Noé** Noah's Ark.

arcada [ar'kaða] nf arcade; (de puente) arch, span; ~**s** nfpl retching sg.

arcaico, a [ar'kaiko, a] a archaic.

arce ['arθe] nm maple tree.

arcén [ar'θen] nm (de autopista) hard shoulder; (de carretera) verge.

arcilla [ar'θiʎa] nf clay.

arco ['arko] nm arch; (MAT) arc; (MIL, MUS) bow; ~ **iris** rainbow.

arcón [ar'kon] nm large chest.

archiconocido, a [artʃikono'θiðo, a] a extremely well-known.

archipiélago [artʃi'pjelaɣo] nm archipelago.

archisabido, a [artʃisa'ßiðo, a] a extremely well-known.

archivador [artʃißa'ðor] nm filing cabinet;

~ **colgante** suspension file.

archivar [artʃi'ßar] vt to file (away); (INFORM) to archive.

archivo [ar'tʃißo] nm archive(s) (pl); (INFORM) file, archive; **A~ Nacional** Public Record Office; ~**s policíacos** police files; **nombre de** ~ (INFORM) filename; ~ **maestro** (INFORM) master file; ~ **de transacciones** (INFORM) transactions file.

arder [ar'ðer] vt to burn; ~ **sin llama** to smoulder; **estar que arde** (persona) to fume.

ardid [ar'ðið] nm ruse.

ardiente [ar'ðjente] a ardent.

ardilla [ar'ðiʎa] nf squirrel.

ardor [ar'ðor] nm (calor) heat, warmth; (fig) ardour; ~ **de estómago** heartburn.

arduo, a ['arðwo, a] a arduous.

área ['area] nf area; (DEPORTE) penalty area; ~ **de excedentes** (INFORM) overflow area.

ARENA [a'rena] nf abr (El Salvador: POL) = Alianza Republicana Nacionalista.

arena [a'rena] nf sand; (de una lucha) arena.

arenal [are'nal] nm (arena movediza) quicksand.

arenga [a'renga] nf (fam) sermon.

arengar [aren'gar] vt to harangue.

arengue [a'renge] etc vb V **arengar**.

arenillas [are'niʎas] nfpl (MED) stones.

arenisca [are'nisko, a] nf sandstone; (cascajo) grit.

arenoso, a [are'noso, a] a sandy.

arenque [a'renke] nm herring.

arete [a'rete] nm earring.

argamasa [arɣa'masa] nf mortar, plaster.

Argel [ar'xel] n Algiers.

Argelia [ar'xelja] nf Algeria.

argelino, a [arxe'lino, a] a, nm/f Algerian.

Argentina [arxen'tina] nf: **(la)** ~ the Argentine, Argentina.

argentino, a [arxen'tino, a] a Argentinian; (de plata) silvery ♦ nm/f Argentinian.

argolla [ar'ɣoʎa] nf (large) ring.

argot [ar'ɣo] nm, pl **argots** [ar'ɣo, ar'ɣos] slang.

argucia [ar'ɣuθja] nf subtlety, sophistry.

argüir [ar'ɣwir] vt to deduce; (discutir) to argue; (indicar) to indicate, imply; (censurar) to reproach ♦ vi to argue.

argumentación [arɣumenta'θjon] nf (line of) argument.

argumentar [arɣumen'tar] vt, vi to argue.

argumento [arɣu'mento] nm argument; (razonamiento) reasoning; (de novela etc) plot; (CINE, TV) storyline.

arguyendo [arɣu'jendo] etc vb V **argüir**.

aria ['arja] nf aria.

aridez [ari'ðeθ] nf aridity, dryness.

árido, a ['ariðo, a] a arid, dry; ~**s** nmpl

dry goods.
Aries ['arjes] *nm* Aries.
ariete [a'rjete] *nm* battering ram.
ario, a ['arjo, a] *a* Aryan.
arisco, a [a'risko, a] *a* surly; (*insociable*) unsociable.
aristocracia [aristo'kraθja] *nf* aristocracy.
aristócrata [aris'tokrata] *nm/f* aristocrat.
aristocrático, a [aristo'kratiko, a] *a* aristocratic.
aritmética [arit'metika] *nf* arithmetic.
aritmético, a [arit'metiko, a] *a* arithmetic(al) ♦ *nm/f* arithmetician.
arma ['arma] *nf* arm; ~**s** *nfpl* arms; ~ **blanca** blade, knife; (*espada*) sword; ~ **de fuego** firearm; ~**s cortas** small arms; **rendir las** ~**s** to lay down one's arms; **ser de** ~**s tomar** to be somebody to be reckoned with.
armada [ar'maða] *nf* armada; (*flota*) fleet; *V tb* **armado**.
armadillo [arma'ðiʎo] *nm* armadillo.
armado, a [ar'maðo, a] *a* armed; (*TEC*) reinforced.
armador [arma'ðor] *nm* (*NAUT*) shipowner.
armadura [arma'ðura] *nf* (*MIL*) armour; (*TEC*) framework; (*ZOOL*) skeleton; (*FÍSICA*) armature.
armamentista [armamen'tista], **armamentístico, a** [armamen'tistiko, a] *a* arms *cpd*.
armamento [arma'mento] *nm* armament; (*NAUT*) fitting-out.
armar [ar'mar] *vt* (*soldado*) to arm; (*máquina*) to assemble; (*navío*) to fit out; ~**la**, ~ **un lío** to start a row; ~**se** *vr*: ~**se de valor** to summon up one's courage.
armario [ar'marjo] *nm* wardrobe.
armatoste [arma'toste] *nm* (*mueble*) monstrosity; (*máquina*) contraption.
armazón [arma'θon] *nf o m* body, chassis; (*de mueble etc*) frame; (*ARQ*) skeleton.
armería [arme'ria] *nf* (*museo*) military museum; (*tienda*) gunsmith's.
armiño [ar'miɲo] *nm* stoat; (*piel*) ermine.
armisticio [armis'tiθjo] *nm* armistice.
armonía [armo'nia] *nf* harmony.
armónica [ar'monika] *nf* harmonica; *V tb* **armónico**.
armonice [armo'niθe] *etc vb V* **armonizar**.
armónico, a [ar'moniko, a] *a* harmonic.
armonioso, a [armo'njoso, a] *a* harmonious.
armonizar [armoni'θar] *vt* to harmonize; (*diferencias*) to reconcile ♦ *vi* to harmonize; ~ **con** (*fig*) to be in keeping with; (*colores*) to tone in with.
arnés [ar'nes] *nm* armour; **arneses** *nmpl* harness *sg*.
aro ['aro] *nm* ring; (*tejo*) quoit; (*AM: pendiente*) earring; **entrar por el** ~ to give

in.
aroma [a'roma] *nm* aroma.
aromático, a [aro'matiko, a] *a* aromatic.
arpa ['arpa] *nf* harp.
arpegio [ar'pexjo] *nm* (*MUS*) arpeggio.
arpía [ar'pia] *nf* (*fig*) shrew.
arpillera [arpi'ʎera] *nf* sacking, sackcloth.
arpón [ar'pon] *nm* harpoon.
arquear [arke'ar] *vt* to arch, bend; ~**se** *vr* to arch, bend.
arqueo [ar'keo] *nm* (*gen*) arching; (*NAUT*) tonnage.
arqueología [arkeolo'xia] *nf* archaeology.
arqueológico, a [arkeo'loxiko, a] *a* archaeological.
arqueólogo, a [arke'oloɣo, a] *nm/f* archaeologist.
arquero [ar'kero] *nm* archer, bowman.
arquetipo [arke'tipo] *nm* archetype.
arquitecto, a [arki'tekto, a] *nm/f* architect; ~ **paisajista** *o* **de jardines** landscape gardener.
arquitectónico, a [arkitek'toniko, a] *a* architectural.
arquitectura [arkitek'tura] *nf* architecture.
arrabal [arra'βal] *nm* suburb; (*AM*) slum; ~**es** *nmpl* outskirts.
arrabalero, a [arraβa'lero, a] *a* (*fig*) common, coarse.
arracimarse [arraθi'marse] *vr* to cluster together.
arraigado, a [arrai'ɣaðo, a] *a* deep-rooted; (*fig*) established.
arraigar [arrai'ɣar] *vt* to establish ♦ *vi*, ~**se** *vr* to take root; (*persona*) to settle.
arraigo [a'rraiɣo] *nm* (*raíces*) roots *pl*; (*bienes*) property; (*influencia*) hold; **hombre de** ~ man of property.
arraigue [a'rraiɣe] *etc vb V* **arraigar**.
arrancada [arran'kaða] *nf* (*arranque*) sudden start; (*LAm*: *fuga*) sudden dash.
arrancar [arran'kar] *vt* (*sacar*) to extract, pull out; (*arrebatar*) to snatch (away); (*pedazo*) to tear off; (*página*) to rip out; (*suspiro*) to heave; (*AUTO*) to start; (*INFORM*) to boot; (*fig*) to extract; ~ **información a uno** to extract information from sb ♦ *vi* (*AUTO*, *máquina*) to start; (*ponerse en marcha*) to get going; ~ **de** to stem from.
arranque [a'rranke] *etc vb V* **arrancar** ♦ *nm* sudden start; (*AUTO*) start; (*fig*) fit, outburst.
arras ['arras] *nfpl* pledge *sg*, security *sg*.
arrasar [arra'sar] *vt* (*aplanar*) to level, flatten; (*destruir*) to demolish.
arrastrado, a [arras'traðo, a] *a* poor, wretched; (*AM*) servile.
arrastrador [arrastra'ðor] *nm* (*en máquina impresora*) tractor.
arrastrar [arras'trar] *vt* to drag (along);

(fig) to drag down, degrade; *(suj: agua, viento)* to carry away ◆ *vi* to drag, trail on the ground; ~**se** *vr* to crawl; *(fig)* to grovel; **llevar algo arrastrado** to drag sth along.

arrastre [a'rrastre] *nm* drag, dragging; *(DEPORTE)* crawl; **estar para el** ~ *(fig)* to have had it; ~ **de papel por fricción/por tracción** *(en máquina impresora)* friction/tractor feed.

array [a'rrai] *nm* *(INFORM)* array; ~ **empaquetado** *(INFORM)* packed array.

arrayán [arra'jan] *nm* myrtle.

arre ['arre] *excl* gee up!

arrear [arre'ar] *vt* to drive on, urge on ◆ *vi* to hurry along.

arrebañaduras [arreßaɲa'ðuras] *nfpl* leftovers *pl*.

arrebañar [arreßa'ɲar] *vt* *(juntar)* to scrape together.

arrebatado, a [arreßa'taðo, a] *a* rash, impetuous; *(repentino)* sudden, hasty.

arrebatar [arreßa'tar] *vt* to snatch (away), seize; *(fig)* to captivate; ~**se** *vr* to get carried away, get excited.

arrebato [arre'ßato] *nm* fit of rage, fury; *(éxtasis)* rapture; **en un** ~ **de cólera** in an outburst of anger.

arrebol [arre'ßol] *nm* *(colorete)* rouge; ~**es** *nmpl* red clouds.

arrebolar [arreßo'lar] *vt* to redden; ~**se** *vr* *(enrojecer)* to blush.

arrebujar [arreßu'xar] *vt* *(objetos)* to jumble together; ~**se** *vr* to wrap o.s. up.

arreciar [arre'θjar] *vi* to get worse; *(viento)* to get stronger.

arrecife [arre'θife] *nm* reef.

arrechucho [arre'tʃutʃo] *nm* *(MED)* turn.

arredrar [arre'ðrar] *vt* *(hacer retirarse)* to drive back; ~**se** *vr* *(apartarse)* to draw back; ~**se ante algo** to shrink away from sth.

arreglado, a [arre'xlaðo, a] *a* *(ordenado)* neat, orderly; *(moderado)* moderate, reasonable.

arreglar [arre'xlar] *vt* *(poner orden)* to tidy up; *(algo roto)* to fix, repair; *(problema)* to solve; ~**se** *vr* to reach an understanding; **arreglárselas** *(fam)* to get by, manage.

arreglo [a'rrexlo] *nm* settlement; *(orden)* order; *(acuerdo)* agreement; *(MUS)* arrangement, setting; *(INFORM)* array; **con** ~ **a** in accordance with; **llegar a un** ~ to reach a compromise.

arrellanarse [arreʎa'narse] *vr* to sprawl; ~ **en el asiento** to lie back in one's chair.

arremangar [arreman'gar] *vt* to roll up, turn up; ~**se** *vr* to roll up one's sleeves.

arremangue [arre'mange] *etc vb V* **arremangar**.

arremeter [arreme'ter] *vt* to attack, assault; ~ **contra uno** to attack sb.

arremetida [arreme'tiða] *nf* assault.

arremolinarse [arremoli'narse] *vr* to crowd around, mill around; *(corriente)* to swirl, eddy.

arrendador, a [arrenda'ðor, a] *nm/f* landlord/lady.

arrendamiento [arrenda'mjento] *nm* letting; *(el alquilar)* hiring; *(contrato)* lease; *(alquiler)* rent.

arrendar [arren'dar] *vt* to let; to hire; to lease; to rent.

arrendatario, a [arrenda'tarjo, a] *nm/f* tenant.

arreo [a'rreo] *nm* adornment; ~**s** *nmpl* harness *sg*, trappings.

arrepentimiento [arrepenti'mjento] *nm* regret, repentance.

arrepentirse [arrepen'tirse] *vr* to repent; ~ **de (haber hecho) algo** to regret (doing) sth.

arrepienta [arre'pjenta] *etc*, **arrepintiendo** [arrepin'tjendo] *etc vb V* **arrepentirse**.

arrestar [arres'tar] *vt* to arrest; *(encarcelar)* to imprison.

arresto [a'rresto] *nm* arrest; *(MIL)* detention; *(audacia)* boldness, daring; ~ **domiciliario** house arrest.

arriar [a'rrjar] *vt* *(velas)* to haul down; *(bandera)* to lower, strike; *(un cable)* to pay out.

arriate [a'rrjate] *nm* *(BOT)* bed; *(camino)* road.

arriba [a'rriβa] *ad* *(posición)* above, overhead, on top; *(en casa)* upstairs; *(dirección)* up, upwards; ~ **de** above, higher (up) than; ~ **del todo** at the very top; **el piso de** ~ the flat upstairs; **de** ~ **abajo** from top to bottom; *(persona)* from head to foot; **calle** ~ up the street; **lo** ~ **mencionado** the aforementioned; ~ **de 20 pesetas** more than 20 pesetas; **de 10 dólares para** ~ from 10 dollars upwards; **¡**~ **España!** long live Spain!; **¡**~ **las manos!** hands up!

arribar [arri'ßar] *vi* to put into port; *(llegar)* to arrive.

arribista [arri'ßista] *nm/f* parvenu(e), upstart.

arriendo [a'rrjendo] *etc vb V* **arrendar** ◆ *nm* = **arrendamiento**.

arriero [a'rrjero] *nm* muleteer.

arriesgado, a [arrjes'xaðo, a] *a* *(peligroso)* risky; *(audaz)* bold, daring.

arriesgar [arrjes'xar] *vt* to risk; *(poner en peligro)* to endanger; ~**se** *vr* to take a risk.

arriesgue [a'rrjesxe] *etc vb V* **arriesgar**.

arrimar [arri'mar] *vt* *(acercar)* to bring close; *(poner de lado)* to set aside; ~**se** *vr* to come close o closer; ~**se a** to lean on; *(fig)* to keep company with; *(buscar ayuda)* to seek the protection of; **arrímate a mí**

cuddle up to me.

arrinconado, a [arrinko'naðo, a] *a* forgotten, neglected.

arrinconar [arrinko'nar] *vt* to put in a corner; *(fig)* to put on one side; *(abandonar)* to push aside.

arriscado, a [arris'kaðo, a] *a (GEO)* craggy; *(fig)* bold, resolute.

arroba [a'rroßa] *nf (peso)* 25 pounds; **tiene talento por ~s** he has loads *o* bags of talent.

arrobado, a [arro'ßaðo, a] *a* entranced, enchanted.

arrobamiento [arroßa'mjento] *nm* ecstasy.

arrobar [arro'ßar] *vt* to enchant; **~se** *vr* to be enraptured; *(místico)* to go into a trance.

arrodillarse [arroði'ʎarse] *vr* to kneel (down).

arrogancia [arro'ɣanθja] *nf* arrogance.

arrogante [arro'ɣante] *a* arrogant.

arrojar [arro'xar] *vt* to throw, hurl; *(humo)* to emit, give out; *(COM)* to yield, produce; **~se** *vr* to throw *o* hurl o.s.

arrojo [a'rroxo] *nm* daring.

arrollador, a [arroʎa'ðor, a] *a* crushing, overwhelming.

arrollar [arro'ʎar] *vt (enrollar)* to roll up; *(suj: inundación)* to wash away; *(AUTO)* to run over; *(DEPORTE)* to crush.

arropar [arro'par] *vt* to cover (up), wrap up; **~se** *vr* to wrap o.s. up.

arrostrar [arros'trar] *vt* to face (up to); **~se** *vr*: **~se con uno** to face up to sb.

arroyo [a'rrojo] *nm* stream; *(de la calle)* gutter; **poner a uno en el ~** to turn sb onto the streets.

arroz [a'rroθ] *nm* rice; **~ con leche** rice pudding.

arruga [a'rruɣa] *nf* fold; *(de cara)* wrinkle; *(de vestido)* crease.

arrugar [arru'ɣar] *vt* to fold; to wrinkle; to crease; **~se** *vr* to get wrinkled; to get creased.

arrugue [a'rruɣe] *etc vb V* **arrugar**.

arruinar [arrwi'nar] *vt* to ruin, wreck; **~se** *vr* to be ruined.

arrullar [arru'ʎar] *vi* to coo ♦ *vt* to lull to sleep.

arrumaco [arru'mako] *nm (caricia)* caress; *(halago)* piece of flattery.

arrumbar [arrum'bar] *vt (objeto)* to discard; *(individuo)* to silence.

arsenal [arse'nal] *nm* naval dockyard; *(MIL)* arsenal.

arsénico [ar'seniko] *nm* arsenic.

arte ['arte] *nm (gen m en sg y siempre f en pl)* art; *(maña)* skill, guile; **por ~ de magia** (as if) by magic; **no tener ~ ni parte en algo** to have nothing whatsoever to do with sth; **~s** *nfpl* arts; **Bellas A~s** Fine

Art *sg*; **~s y oficios** arts and crafts.

artefacto [arte'fakto] *nm* appliance; *(ARQUEOLOGÍA)* artefact.

arteria [ar'terja] *nf* artery.

artesa [ar'tesa] *nf* trough.

artesanía [artesa'nia] *nf* craftsmanship; *(artículos)* handicrafts *pl*.

artesano, a [arte'sano, a] *nm/f* artisan, craftsman/woman.

ártico, a ['artiko, a] *a* Arctic ♦ *nm*: **el Á~** the Arctic.

articulación [artikula'θjon] *nf* articulation; *(MED, TEC)* joint.

articulado, a [artiku'laðo, a] *a* articulated; jointed.

articular [artiku'lar] *vt* to articulate; to join together.

articulista [artiku'lista] *nm/f* columnist, contributor (to a newspaper).

artículo [ar'tikulo] *nm* article; *(cosa)* thing, article; *(TV)* feature, report; **~ de fondo** leader, editorial; **~s** *nmpl* goods; **~s de marca** *(COM)* proprietary goods.

artífice [ar'tifiθe] *nm* artist, craftsman; *(fig)* architect.

artificial [artifi'θjal] *a* artificial.

artificio [arti'fiθjo] *nm* art, skill; *(artesanía)* craftsmanship; *(astucia)* cunning.

artilugio [arti'luxjo] *nm* gadget.

artillería [artiʎe'ria] *nf* artillery.

artillero [arti'ʎero] *nm* artilleryman, gunner.

artimaña [arti'maɲa] *nf* trap, snare; *(astucia)* cunning.

artista [ar'tista] *nm/f (pintor)* artist, painter; *(TEATRO)* artist, artiste.

artístico, a [ar'tistiko, a] *a* artistic.

artritis [ar'tritis] *nf* arthritis.

arveja [ar'ßexa] *nf (AM)* pea.

Arz. *abr* (= *Arzobispo*) Abp.

arzobispo [arθo'ßispo] *nm* archbishop.

as [as] *nm* ace; **~ del fútbol** star player.

asa ['asa] *nf* handle; *(fig)* lever.

asado [a'saðo] *nm* roast (meat).

asador [asa'ðor] *nm (varilla)* spit; *(aparato)* spit roaster.

asadura(s) [asa'ðura(s)] *nf(pl)* entrails *pl*, offal *sg*; *(CULIN)* chitterlings *pl*.

asaetar [asae'tar] *vt (fig)* to bother.

asalariado, a [asala'rjaðo, a] *a* paid, wage-earning, salaried ♦ *nm/f* wage earner.

asaltador, a [asalta'ðor, a], **asaltante** [asal'tante] *nm/f* assailant.

asaltar [asal'tar] *vt* to attack, assault; *(fig)* to assail.

asalto [a'salto] *nm* attack, assault; *(DEPORTE)* round.

asamblea [asam'blea] *nf* assembly; *(reunión)* meeting.

asar [a'sar] *vt* to roast; **~ al horno/a la parrilla** to bake/grill; **~se** *vr (fig)*: **me aso**

de calor I'm roasting; **aquí se asa uno vivo** it's boiling hot here.

asbesto [as'ßesto] *nm* asbestos.

ascendencia [asθen'denθja] *nf* ancestry; (*AM*) ascendancy; **de ~ francesa** of French origin.

ascender [asθen'der] *vi* (*subir*) to ascend, rise; (*ser promovido*) to gain promotion ♦ *vt* to promote; **~ a** to amount to.

ascendiente [asθen'djente] *nm* influence ♦ *nm/f* ancestor.

ascensión [asθen'sjon] *nf* ascent; **la A~** the Ascension.

ascenso [as'θenso] *nm* ascent; (*promoción*) promotion.

ascensor [asθen'sor] *nm* lift (*Brit*), elevator (*US*).

ascético, a [as'θetiko, a] *a* ascetic.

ascienda [as'θjenda] *etc vb V* **ascender**.

asco ['asko] *nm*: **el ajo me da ~** I hate *o* loathe garlic; **hacer ~s de algo** to turn up one's nose at sth; **estar hecho un ~** to be filthy; **poner a uno de ~** to call sb all sorts of names *o* every name under the sun; **¡qué ~!** how revolting *o* disgusting!

ascua ['askwa] *nf* ember; **arrimar el ~ a su sardina** to look after number one; **estar en ~s** to be on tenterhooks.

aseado, a [ase'aðo, a] *a* clean; (*arreglado*) tidy; (*pulcro*) smart.

asear [ase'ar] *vt* (*lavar*) to wash; (*ordenar*) to tidy (up).

asechanza [ase'tʃanθa] *nf* trap, snare.

asechar [ase'tʃar] *vt* to set a trap for.

asediar [ase'ðjar] *vt* (*MIL*) to besiege, lay siege to; (*fig*) to chase, pester.

asedio [a'seðjo] *nm* siege; (*COM*) run.

asegurado, a [aseɣu'raðo, a] *a* insured.

asegurador, a [aseɣura'ðor, a] *nm/f* insurer.

asegurar [aseɣu'rar] *vt* (*consolidar*) to secure, fasten; (*dar garantía de*) to guarantee; (*preservar*) to safeguard; (*afirmar, dar por cierto*) to assure, affirm; (*tranquilizar*) to reassure; (*tomar un seguro*) to insure; **~se** *vr* to assure o.s., make sure.

asemejarse [aseme'xarse] *vr* to be alike; **~ a** to be like, resemble.

asentado, a [asen'taðo, a] *a* established, settled.

asentar [asen'tar] *vt* (*sentar*) to seat, sit down; (*poner*) to place, establish; (*alisar*) to level, smooth down *o* out; (*anotar*) to note down ♦ *vi* to be suitable, suit.

asentimiento [asenti'mjento] *nm* assent, agreement.

asentir [asen'tir] *vi* to assent, agree.

aseo [a'seo] *nm* cleanliness; **~s** *nmpl* toilet *sg* (*Brit*), restroom *sg* (*US*), cloakroom *sg*.

aséptico, a [a'septiko, a] *a* germ-free, free from infection.

asequible [ase'kißle] *a* (*precio*) reasonable; (*meta*) attainable; (*persona*) approachable.

aserradero [aserra'ðero] *nm* sawmill.

aserrar [ase'rrar] *vt* to saw.

aserrín [ase'rrin] *nm* sawdust.

asesinar [asesi'nar] *vt* to murder; (*POL*) to assassinate.

asesinato [asesi'nato] *nm* murder; assassination.

asesino, a [ase'sino, a] *nm/f* murderer, killer; (*POL*) assassin.

asesor, a [ase'sor, a] *nm/f* adviser, consultant; (*COM*) assessor, consultant; **~ administrativo** management consultant.

asesorar [aseso'rar] *vt* (*JUR*) to advise, give legal advice to; (*COM*) to act as consultant to; **~se** *vr*: **~se con** *o* **de** to take advice from, consult.

asesoría [aseso'ria] *nf* (*cargo*) consultancy; (*oficina*) consultant's office.

asestar [ases'tar] *vt* (*golpe*) to deal; (*arma*) to aim; (*tiro*) to fire.

aseverar [aseße'rar] *vt* to assert.

asfaltado, a [asfal'taðo, a] *a* asphalted ♦ *nm* (*pavimiento*) asphalt.

asfalto [as'falto] *nm* asphalt.

asfixia [as'fiksja] *nf* asphyxia, suffocation.

asfixiar [asfik'sjar] *vt* to asphyxiate, suffocate.

asga ['asɣa] *etc vb V* **asir**.

así [a'si] *ad* (*de esta manera*) in this way, like this, thus; (*aunque*) although; (*tan pronto como*) as soon as; **~ que** so; **~ como** as well as; **~ y todo** even so; **¿no es ~?** isn't it?, didn't you? *etc*; **~ de grande** this big; **¡~ sea!** so be it!; **~ es la vida** such is life, that's life.

Asia ['asja] *nf* Asia.

asiático, a [a'sjatiko, a] *a, nm/f* Asian, Asiatic.

asidero [asi'ðero] *nm* handle.

asiduidad [asiðwi'ðað] *nf* assiduousness.

asiduo, a [a'siðwo, a] *a* assiduous; (*frecuente*) frequent ♦ *nm/f* regular (customer).

asiento [a'sjento] *etc vb V* **asentar, asentir** ♦ *nm* (*mueble*) seat, chair; (*de coche, en tribunal etc*) seat; (*localidad*) seat, place; (*fundamento*) site; **~ delantero/trasero** front/back seat.

asierre [a'sjerre] *etc vb V* **aserrar**.

asignación [asiɣna'θjon] *nf* (*atribución*) assignment; (*reparto*) allocation; (*COM*) allowance; **~ (semanal)** pocket money; **~ de presupuesto** budget appropriation.

asignar [asiɣ'nar] *vt* to assign, allocate.

asignatura [asiɣna'tura] *nf* subject; (*curso*) course.

asilado, a [asi'laðo, a] *nm/f* refugee.

asilo [a'silo] *nm* (*refugio*) asylum, refuge; (*establecimiento*) home, institution; **~**

político political asylum.
asimilación [asimila'θjon] *nf* assimilation.
asimilar [asimi'lar] *vt* to assimilate.
asimismo [asi'mismo] *ad* in the same way, likewise.
asintiendo [asin'tjendo] *etc vb V* **asentir**.
asir [a'sir] *vt* to seize, grasp; ~**se** *vr* to take hold; ~**se a** *o* **de** to seize.
asistencia [asis'tenθja] *nf* presence; (*TEATRO*) audience; (*MED*) attendance; (*ayuda*) assistance; ~ **social** social *o* welfare work.
asistente, a [asis'tente, a] *nm/f* assistant ♦ *nm* (*MIL*) orderly ♦ *nf* daily help; **los** ~**s** those present; ~ **social** social worker.
asistido, a [asis'tiðo, a] *a* (*AUTO*: *dirección*) power-assisted; ~ **por ordenador** computer-assisted.
asistir [asis'tir] *vt* to assist, help ♦ *vi*: ~ **a** to attend, be present at.
asma ['asma] *nf* asthma.
asno ['asno] *nm* donkey; (*fig*) ass.
asociación [asoθja'θjon] *nf* association; (*COM*) partnership.
asociado, a [aso'θjaðo, a] *a* associate ♦ *nm/f* associate; (*COM*) partner.
asociar [aso'θjar] *vt* to associate; ~**se** *vr* to become partners.
asolar [aso'lar] *vt* to destroy.
asolear [asole'ar] *vt* to put in the sun; ~**se** *vr* to sunbathe.
asomar [aso'mar] *vt* to show, stick out ♦ *vi* to appear; ~**se** *vr* to appear, show up; ~ **la cabeza por la ventana** to put one's head out of the window.
asombrar [asom'brar] *vt* to amaze, astonish; ~**se** *vr*: ~**se (de)** (*sorprenderse*) to be amazed (at); (*asustarse*) to be frightened (at).
asombro [a'sombro] *nm* amazement, astonishment.
asombroso, a [asom'broso, a] *a* amazing, astonishing.
asomo [a'somo] *nm* hint, sign; **ni por** ~ by no means.
asonancia [aso'nanθja] *nf* (*LIT*) assonance; (*fig*) connection; **no tener** ~ **con** to bear no relation to.
aspa ['aspa] *nf* (*cruz*) cross; (*de molino*) sail; **en** ~ X-shaped.
aspaviento [aspa'βjento] *nm* exaggerated display of feeling; (*fam*) fuss.
aspecto [as'pekto] *nm* (*apariencia*) look, appearance; (*fig*) aspect; **bajo ese** ~ from that point of view.
aspereza [aspe'reθa] *nf* roughness; (*agrura*) sourness; (*de carácter*) surliness.
áspero, a ['aspero, a] *a* rough; sour; harsh.
aspersión [asper'sjon] *nf* sprinkling; (*AGR*) spraying.
aspiración [aspira'θjon] *nf* breath, inhalation; (*MUS*) short pause; **aspiraciones** *nfpl* aspirations.
aspiradora [aspira'ðora] *nf* vacuum cleaner, Hoover ®.
aspirante [aspi'rante] *nm/f* (*candidato*) candidate; (*DEPORTE*) contender.
aspirar [aspi'rar] *vt* to breathe in ♦ *vi*: ~ **a** to aspire to.
aspirina [aspi'rina] *nf* aspirin.
asquear [aske'ar] *vt* to sicken ♦ *vi* to be sickening; ~**se** *vr* to feel disgusted.
asquerosidad [askerosi'ðað] *nf* (*suciedad*) filth; (*dicho*) obscenity; (*truco*) dirty trick.
asqueroso, a [aske'roso, a] *a* disgusting, sickening.
asta ['asta] *nf* lance; (*arpón*) spear; (*mango*) shaft, handle; (*ZOOL*) horn; **a media** ~ at half mast.
astado, a [as'taðo, a] *a* horned ♦ *nm* bull.
asterisco [aste'risko] *nm* asterisk.
astilla [as'tiʎa] *nf* splinter; (*pedacito*) chip; ~**s** *nfpl* firewood *sg*.
astillarse [asti'ʎarse] *vr* to splinter; (*fig*) to shatter.
astillero [asti'ʎero] *nm* shipyard.
astringente [astrin'xente] *a*, *nm* astringent.
astro ['astro] *nm* star.
astrología [astrolo'xia] *nf* astrology.
astrólogo, a [as'troloɣo, a] *nm/f* astrologer.
astronauta [astro'nauta] *nm/f* astronaut.
astronave [astro'naβe] *nm* spaceship.
astronomía [astrono'mia] *nf* astronomy.
astrónomo, a [as'tronomo, a] *nm/f* astronomer.
astroso, a [as'troso, a] *a* (*desaliñado*) untidy; (*vil*) contemptible.
astucia [as'tuθja] *nf* astuteness; (*destreza*) clever trick.
asturiano, a [astu'rjano, a] *a*, *nm/f* Asturian.
Asturias [as'turjas] *nfpl* Asturias; **Príncipe de** ~ crown prince.
astuto, a [as'tuto, a] *a* astute; (*taimado*) cunning.
asueto [a'sweto] *nm* holiday; (*tiempo libre*) time off; **día de** ~ day off; **tarde de** ~ (*trabajo*) afternoon off; (*ESCOL*) half-holiday.
asumir [asu'mir] *vt* to assume.
asunción [asun'θjon] *nf* assumption.
asunto [a'sunto] *nm* (*tema*) matter, subject; (*negocio*) business; **¡eso es** ~ **mío!** that's my business!; ~**s exteriores** foreign affairs; ~**s a tratar** agenda *sg*.
asustadizo, a [asusta'ðiθo, a] *a* easily frightened.
asustar [asus'tar] *vt* to frighten; ~**se** *vr* to be/become frightened.
atacante [ata'kante] *nm/f* attacker.
atacar [ata'kar] *vt* to attack.

atadura [ata'ðura] *nf* bond, tie.

atajar [ata'xar] *vt* (*gen*) to stop; (*ruta de fuga*) to cut off; (*discurso*) to interrupt ♦ *vi* to take a short cut.

atajo [a'taxo] *nm* short cut; (*DEPORTE*) tackle.

atalaya [ata'laja] *nf* watchtower.

atañer [ata'ɲer] *vi*: ~ **a** to concern; **en lo que atañe a eso** with regard to that.

ataque [a'take] *etc vb V* **atacar** ♦ *nm* attack; ~ **cardíaco** heart attack.

atar [a'tar] *vt* to tie, tie up; ~ **la lengua a uno** (*fig*) to silence sb.

atardecer [atarðe'θer] *vi* to get dark ♦ *nm* evening; (*crepúsculo*) dusk.

atardezca [atar'ðeθka] *etc vb V* **atardecer**.

atareado, a [atare'aðo, a] *a* busy.

atascar [atas'kar] *vt* to clog up; (*obstruir*) to jam; (*fig*) to hinder; ~**se** *vr* to stall; (*cañería*) to get blocked up; (*fig*) to get bogged down; (*en discurso*) to dry up.

atasco [a'tasko] *nm* obstruction; (*AUTO*) traffic jam.

atasque [a'taske] *etc vb V* **atascar**.

ataúd [ata'uð] *nm* coffin.

ataviar [ata'ßjar] *vt* to deck, array; ~**se** *vr* to dress up.

atavío [ata'ßio] *nm* attire, dress; ~**s** *nmpl* finery *sg*.

ateísmo [ate'ismo] *nm* atheism.

atemorice [atemo'riθe] *etc vb V* **atemorizar**.

atemorizar [atemori'θar] *vt* to frighten; scare; ~**se** *vr* to get frightened *o* scared.

Atenas [a'tenas] *nf* Athens.

atención [aten'θjon] *nf* attention; (*bondad*) kindness ♦ *excl* (be) careful!, look out!; **en** ~ **a esto** in view of this.

atender [aten'der] *vt* to attend to, look after; (*TEC*) to service; (*enfermo*) to care for; (*ruego*) to comply with ♦ *vi* to pay attention; ~ **a** to attend to; (*detalles*) to take care of.

atendré [aten'dre] *etc vb V* **atenerse**.

atenerse [ate'nerse] *vr*: ~ **a** to abide by, adhere to.

atenga [a'tenga] *etc vb V* **atenerse**.

ateniense [ate'njense] *a, nm/f* Athenian.

atentado [aten'taðo] *nm* crime, illegal act; (*asalto*) assault; (*terrorista*) attack; ~ **contra la vida de uno** attempt on sb's life; ~ **golpista** (*POL*) attempted coup.

atentamente [atenta'mente] *ad*: **le saluda** ~ Yours faithfully.

atentar [aten'tar] *vi*: ~ **a** *o* **contra** to commit an outrage against.

atento, a [a'tento, a] *a* attentive, observant; (*cortés*) polite, thoughtful; **su atenta (carta)** (*COM*) your letter.

atenuante [ate'nwante] *a*: **circunstancias** ~**s** extenuating *o* mitigating cirumstances

♦ *nmpl*: ~**s** extenuating *o* mitigating circumstances.

atenuar [ate'nwar] *vt* to attenuate; (*disminuir*) to lessen, minimize.

ateo, a [a'teo, a] *a* atheistic ♦ *nm/f* atheist.

aterciopelado, a [aterθjope'laðo, a] *a* velvety.

aterido, a [ate'riðo, a] *a*: ~ **de frío** frozen stiff.

aterrador, a [aterra'ðor, a] *a* frightening.

aterrar [ate'rrar] *vt* to frighten; (*aterrorizar*) to terrify; ~**se** *vr* to be frightened; to be terrified.

aterrice [ate'rriθe] *etc vb V* **aterrizar**.

aterrizar [aterri'θar] *vi* to land.

aterrorice [aterro'riθe] *etc vb V* **aterrorizar**.

aterrorizar [aterrori'θar] *vt* to terrify.

atesorar [ateso'rar] *vt* to hoard, store up.

atestado, a [ates'taðo, a] *a* packed ♦ *nm* (*JUR*) affidavit.

atestar [ates'tar] *vt* to pack, stuff; (*JUR*) to attest, testify to.

atestiguar [atesti'ɣwar] *vt* to testify to, bear witness to.

atestigüe [ates'tiɣwe] *etc vb V* **atestiguar**.

atiborrar [atißo'rrar] *vt* to fill, stuff; ~**se** *vr* to stuff o.s.

atice [a'tiθe] *etc vb V* **atizar**.

ático ['atiko] *nm* attic; ~ **de lujo** penthouse flat.

atienda [a'tjenda] *etc vb V* **atender**.

atildar [atil'dar] *vt* to criticize; (*TIP*) to put a tilde over; ~**se** *vr* to spruce o.s. up.

atinado, a [ati'naðo, a] *a* correct; (*sensato*) sensible.

atinar [ati'nar] *vi* (*acertar*) to be right; ~ **con** *o* **en** (*solución*) to hit upon; ~ **a hacer** to manage to do.

atiplado, a [ati'plaðo, a] *a* (*voz*) high-pitched.

atisbar [atis'ßar] *vt* to spy on; (*echar ojeada*) to peep at.

atizar [ati'θar] *vt* to poke; (*horno etc*) to stoke; (*fig*) to stir up, rouse.

atlántico, a [at'lantiko, a] *a* Atlantic ♦ *nm*: **el (Océano) A~** the Atlantic (Ocean).

atlas ['atlas] *nm* atlas.

atleta [at'leta] *nm/f* athlete.

atlético, a [at'letiko, a] *a* athletic.

atletismo [atle'tismo] *nm* athletics *sg*.

atmósfera [at'mosfera] *nf* atmosphere.

atolondramiento [atolondra'mjento] *nm* bewilderment; (*insensatez*) silliness.

atolladero [atoʎa'ðero] *nm*: **estar en un** ~ to be in a jam.

atollar [ato'ʎar] *vi*, ~**se** *vr* to get stuck; (*fig*) to get into a jam.

atómico, a [a'tomiko, a] *a* atomic.

atomizador [atomiθa'ðor] *nm* atomizer.

átomo ['atomo] *nm* atom.

atónito, a [a'tonito, a] *a* astonished, amazed.

atontado, a [aton'taðo, a] *a* stunned; (*bobo*) silly, daft.

atontar [aton'tar] *vt* to stun; ~**se** *vr* to become confused.

atorar [ato'rar] *vt* to obstruct; ~**se** *vr* (*atragantarse*) to choke.

atormentar [atormen'tar] *vt* to torture; (*molestar*) to torment; (*acosar*) to plague, harass.

atornillar [atorni'ʎar] *vt* to screw on *o* down.

atosigar [atosi'ɣar] *vt* to harass.

atosigue [ato'siɣe] *etc vb* V **atosigar**.

atrabiliario, a [atraβi'ljarjo, a] *a* bad-tempered.

atracadero [atraka'ðero] *nm* pier.

atracador, a [atraka'ðor, a] *nm/f* robber.

atracar [atra'kar] *vt* (*NAUT*) to moor; (*robar*) to hold up, rob ♦ *vi* to moor; ~**se** *vr* (*hartarse*) to stuff o.s.

atracción [atrak'θjon] *nf* attraction.

atraco [a'trako] *nm* holdup, robbery.

atractivo, a [atrak'tiβo, a] *a* attractive ♦ *nm* attraction; (*belleza*) attractiveness.

atraer [atra'er] *vt* to attract; **dejarse ~ por** to be tempted by.

atragantarse [atraɣan'tarse] *vr*: ~ **(con algo)** to choke (on sth); **se me ha atragantado el chico ese/el inglés** I don't take to that boy/English.

atraiga [a'traiɣa] *etc*, **atraje** [a'traxe] *etc vb* V **atraer**.

atrancar [atran'kar] *vt* (*con tranca, barra*) to bar, bolt.

atranque [a'tranke] *etc vb* V **atrancar**.

atrapar [atra'par] *vt* to trap; (*resfriado etc*) to catch.

atraque [a'trake] *etc vb* V **atracar**.

atrás [a'tras] *ad* (*movimiento*) back(wards); (*lugar*) behind; (*tiempo*) previously; **ir hacia ~** to go back(wards); to go to the rear; **estar ~** to be behind *o* at the back.

atrasado, a [atra'saðo, a] *a* slow; (*pago*) overdue, late; (*país*) backward.

atrasar [atra'sar] *vi* to be slow; ~**se** *vr* to remain behind; (*llegar tarde*) to arrive late.

atraso [a'traso] *nm* slowness; lateness, delay; (*de país*) backwardness; ~**s** *nmpl* arrears.

atravesar [atraβe'sar] *vt* (*cruzar*) to cross (over); (*traspasar*) to pierce; (*período*) to go through; (*poner al través*) to lay *o* put across; ~**se** *vr* to come in between; (*intervenir*) to interfere.

atraviese [atra'βjese] *etc vb* V **atravesar**.

atrayendo [atra'jendo] *vb* V **atraer**.

atrayente [atra'jente] *a* attractive.

atreverse [atre'βerse] *vr* to dare; (*insolentarse*) to be insolent.

atrevido, a [atre'βiðo, a] *a* daring; insolent.

atrevimiento [atreβi'mjento] *nm* daring; insolence.

atribución [atriβu'θjon] *nf* (*LIT*) attribution; **atribuciones** *nfpl* (*POL*) functions; (*ADMIN*) responsibilities.

atribuir [atriβu'ir] *vt* to attribute; (*funciones*) to confer.

atribular [atriβu'lar] *vt* to afflict, distress.

atributo [atri'βuto] *nm* attribute.

atribuya [atri'βuja] *etc*, **atribuyendo** [atriβu'jendo] *etc vb* V **atribuir**.

atril [a'tril] *nm* lectern; (*MUS*) music stand.

atrio ['atrjo] *nm* (*REL*) porch.

atrocidad [atroθi'ðað] *nf* atrocity, outrage.

atronador, a [atrona'ðor, a] *a* deafening.

atropellar [atrope'ʎar] *vt* (*derribar*) to knock over *o* down; (*empujar*) to push (aside); (*AUTO*) to run over *o* down; (*agraviar*) to insult; ~**se** *vr* to act hastily.

atropello [atro'peʎo] *nm* (*AUTO*) accident; (*empujón*) push; (*agravio*) wrong; (*atrocidad*) outrage.

atroz [a'troθ] *a* atrocious, awful.

atto., a. *abr* (= *atento, a*) Yours faithfully.

attrezzo [a'treθo] *nm* props *pl*.

atuendo [a'twendo] *nm* attire.

atufar [atu'far] *vt* (*suj: olor*) to overcome; (*molestar*) to irritate; ~**se** *vr* (*fig*) to get cross.

atún [a'tun] *nm* tuna, tunny.

aturdir [atur'ðir] *vt* to stun; (*suj: ruido*) to deafen; (*fig*) to dumbfound, bewilder.

atur(r)ullar [atur(r)u'ʎar] *vt* to bewilder.

atusar [atu'sar] *vt* (*cortar*) to trim; (*alisar*) to smooth (down).

atuve [a'tuβe] *etc vb* V **atenerse**.

audacia [au'ðaθja] *nf* boldness, audacity.

audaz [au'ðaθ] *a* bold, audacious.

audible [au'ðiβle] *a* audible.

audición [auði'θjon] *nf* hearing; (*TEATRO*) audition; ~ **radiofónica** radio concert.

audiencia [au'ðjenθja] *nf* audience; (*JUR*) high court; (*POL*): ~ **pública** public inquiry.

audífono [au'ðifono] *nm* hearing aid.

auditor [auði'tor] *nm* (*JUR*) judge-advocate; (*COM*) auditor.

auditorio [auði'torjo] *nm* audience; (*sala*) auditorium.

auge ['auxe] *nm* boom; (*clímax*) climax; (*ECON*) expansion; **estar en ~** to thrive.

augurar [auɣu'rar] *vt* to predict; (*presagiar*) to portend.

augurio [au'ɣurjo] *nm* omen.

aula ['aula] *nf* classroom.

aullar [au'ʎar] *vi* to howl, yell.

aullido [au'ʎiðo] *nm* howl, yell.

aumentar [aumen'tar] *vt* to increase; (*precios*) to put up; (*producción*) to step up;

(*con microscopio, anteojos*) to magnify ♦ *vi,* ~**se** *vr* to increase, be on the increase.

aumento [au'mento] *nm* increase; rise.

aun [a'un] *ad* even.

aún [a'un] *ad* still, yet.

aunque [a'unke] *conj* though, although, even though.

aúpa [a'upa] *excl* up!, come on! (*fam*): **una función de** ~ a slap-up do; **una paliza de** ~ a good hiding.

aupar [au'par] *vt* (*levantar*) to help up; (*fig*) to praise.

aura ['aura] *nf* (*atmósfera*) aura.

aureola [aure'ola] *nf* halo.

auricular [auriku'lar] *nm* earpiece, receiver; ~**es** *nmpl* headphones.

aurora [au'rora] *nf* dawn; ~ **boreal(is)** northern lights *pl.*

auscultar [auskul'tar] *vt* (*MED: pecho*) to listen to, sound.

ausencia [au'senθja] *nf* absence.

ausentarse [ausen'tarse] *vr* to go away; (*por poco tiempo*) to go out.

ausente [au'sente] *a* absent ♦ *nm/f* (*ESCOL*) absentee; (*JUR*) missing person.

auspicios [aus'piθjos] *nmpl* auspices; (*protección*) protection *sg.*

austeridad [austeri'ðað] *nf* austerity.

austero, a [aus'tero, a] *a* austere.

austral [aus'tral] *a* southern ♦ *nm monetary unit of Argentina.*

Australia [aus'tralja] *nf* Australia.

australiano, a [austra'ljano, a] *a, nm/f* Australian.

Austria ['austrja] *nf* Austria.

austriaco, a [aus'trjako, a], **austríaco, a** [aus'triako, a] *a, nm/f* Austrian.

autenticar [autenti'kar] *vt* to authenticate.

auténtico, a [au'tentiko, a] *a* authentic.

autentique [auten'tike] *etc vb* V **autenticar.**

auto ['auto] *nm* (*coche*) car; (*JUR*) edict, decree; (: *orden*) writ; ~**s** *nmpl* (*JUR*) proceedings; (: *acta*) court record *sg*; ~ **de comparecencia** summons, subpoena; ~ **de ejecución** writ of execution.

autoadhesivo, a [autoaðe'siβo, a] *a* self-adhesive; (*sobre*) self-sealing.

autoalimentación [autoalimenta'θjon] *nf* (*INFORM*): ~ **de hojas** automatic paper feed.

autobiografía [autoβjoɣra'fia] *nf* autobiography.

autobús [auto'βus] *nm* bus (*Brit*), (passenger) bus (*US*).

autocar [auto'kar] *nm* coach; ~ **de línea** inter-city coach.

autocomprobación [autokomproβa'θjon] *nf* (*INFORM*) self-test.

autóctono, a [au'toktono, a] *a* native, indigenous.

autodefensa [autoðe'fensa] *nf* self-defence.

autodeterminación [autoðetermina'θjon] *nf* self-determination.

autodidacto, a [autoði'ðakto, a] *a* self-taught.

autoescuela [autoes'kwela] *nf* driving school.

autofinanciado, a [autofinan'θjaðo, a] *a* self-financing.

autógrafo [au'toɣrafo] *nm* autograph.

automación [automa'θjon] *nf* = **automatización.**

autómata [au'tomata] *nm* automaton.

automatice [automa'tiθe] *etc vb* V **automatizar.**

automático, a [auto'matiko, a] *a* automatic ♦ *nm* press stud.

automatización [automatiθa'θjon] *nf:* ~ **de fábricas** factory automation; ~ **de oficinas** office automation.

automatizar [automati'θar] *vt* to automate.

automotor, triz [automo'tor, 'triz] *a* self-propelled ♦ *nm* diesel train.

automóvil [auto'moβil] *nm* (motor) car (*Brit*), automobile (*US*).

automovilismo [automoβi'lismo] *nm* (*DEPORTE*) (sports) car racing.

automovilista [automoβi'lista] *nm/f* motorist, driver.

automovilístico, a [automoβi'listiko, a] *a* (*industria*) car *cpd.*

autonomía [autono'mia] *nf* autonomy; **Estatuto de A**~ (*Esp*) Devolution Statute.

autonómico, a [auto'nomiko, a] *a* (*Esp POL*) relating to autonomy, autonomous; **gobierno** ~ autonomous government.

autónomo, a [au'tonomo, a] *a* autonomous; (*INFORM*) stand-alone, offline.

autopista [auto'pista] *nf* motorway (*Brit*), freeway (*US*).

autopsia [au'topsja] *nf* autopsy.

autor, a [au'tor, a] *nm/f* author; **los** ~**es del atentado** those responsible for the attack.

autorice [auto'riθe] *etc vb* V **autorizar.**

autoridad [autori'ðað] *nf* authority; ~ **local** local authority.

autoritario, a [autori'tarjo, a] *a* authoritarian.

autorización [autoriθa'θjon] *nf* authorization.

autorizado, a [autori'θaðo, a] *a* authorized; (*aprobado*) approved.

autorizar [autori'θar] *vt* to authorize; to approve.

autorretrato [autorre'trato] *nm* self-portrait.

autoservicio [autoser'βiθjo] *nm* self-service shop *o* store; (*restaurante*) self-service restaurant.

autostop [auto'stop] *nm* hitch-hiking; **hacer**

~ to hitch-hike.

autostopista [autosto'pista] *nm/f* hitchhiker.

autosuficiencia [autosufi'θjenθja] *nf* selfsufficiency.

autovía [auto'ßia] *nf* ≈ A road (*Brit*), state highway (*US*).

auxiliar [auksi'ljar] *vt* to help ◆ *nm/f* assistant.

auxilio [auk'siljo] *nm* assistance, help; **primeros ~s** first aid *sg.*

Av *abr* (= *Avenida*) Av(e).

a/v *abr* (*COM*: = *a vista*) at sight.

aval [a'ßal] *nm* guarantee; (*persona*) guarantor.

avalancha [aßa'lantʃa] *nf* avalanche.

avalar [aßa'lar] *vt* (*COM etc*) to underwrite; (*fig*) to endorse.

avalista [aßa'lista] *nm* (*COM*) endorser.

avance [a'ßanθe] *etc vb* V **avanzar** ◆ *nm* advance; (*pago*) advance payment; (*CINE*) trailer.

avanzado, a [aßan'θaðo, a] *a* advanced; **de edad avanzada, ~ de edad** elderly.

avanzar [aßan'θar] *vt, vi* to advance.

avaricia [aßa'riθja] *nf* avarice, greed.

avaricioso, a [aßari'θjoso, a] *a* avaricious, greedy.

avaro, a [a'ßaro, a] *a* miserly, mean ◆ *nm/f* miser.

avasallar [aßasa'ʎar] *vt* to subdue, subjugate.

avatar [aßa'tar] *nm* change; **~es** ups and downs.

Avda *abr* (= *Avenida*) Av(e).

ave ['aße] *nf* bird; **~ de rapiña** bird of prey.

avecinarse [aßeθi'narse] *vr* (*tormenta, fig*) to approach, be on the way.

avejentar [aßexen'tar] *vt, vi*, **~se** *vr* to age.

avellana [aße'ʎana] *nf* hazelnut.

avellano [aße'ʎano] *nm* hazel tree.

avemaría [aßema'ria] *nm* Hail Mary, Ave Maria.

avena [a'ßena] *nf* oats *pl.*

avendré [aßen'dre] *etc,* **avenga** [a'ßenga] *etc vb* V **avenir.**

avenida [aße'niða] *nf* (*calle*) avenue.

avenir [aße'nir] *vt* to reconcile; **~se** *vr* to come to an agreement, reach a compromise.

aventajado, a [aßenta'xaðo, a] *a* outstanding.

aventajar [aßenta'xar] *vt* (*sobrepasar*) to surpass, outstrip.

aventar [aßen'tar] *vt* to fan, blow; (*grano*) to winnow.

aventón [aßen'ton] *nm* (*AM*) push; **pedir ~** to hitch a lift.

aventura [aßen'tura] *nf* adventure; **~ sentimental** love affair.

aventurado, a [aßentu'raðo, a] *a* risky.

aventurar [aßentu'rar] *vt* to risk; **~se** *vr* to dare; **~se a hacer algo** to venture to do sth.

aventurero, a [aßentu'rero, a] *a* adventurous.

avergoncé [aßerɣon'θe], **avergoncemos** [aßerɣon'θemos] *etc vb* V **avergonzar.**

avergonzar [aßerɣon'θar] *vt* to shame; (*desconcertar*) to embarrass; **~se** *vr* to be ashamed; to be embarrassed.

avergüence [aßer'ɣwenθe] *etc vb* V **avergonzar.**

avería [aße'ria] *nf* (*TEC*) breakdown, fault.

averiado, a [aße'rjaðo, a] *a* broken-down.

averiguación [aßeriɣwa'θjon] *nf* investigation; (*determinación*) ascertainment.

averiguar [aßeri'ɣwar] *vt* to investigate; (*descubrir*) to find out, ascertain.

averigüe [aße'riɣwe] *etc vb* V **averiguar.**

aversión [aßer'sjon] *nf* aversion, dislike; **cobrar ~ a** to take a strong dislike to.

avestruz [aßes'truθ] *nm* ostrich.

aviación [aßja'θjon] *nf* aviation; (*fuerzas aéreas*) air force.

aviado, a [a'ßjaðo, a] *a*: **estar ~** to be in a mess.

aviador, a [aßja'ðor, a] *nm/f* aviator, airman/woman.

aviar [a'ßjar] *vt* to prepare, get ready.

avicultura [aßikul'tura] *nf* poultry farming.

avidez [aßi'ðeθ] *nf* avidity, eagerness.

ávido, a ['aßiðo, a] *a* avid, eager.

aviente [a'ßjente] *etc vb* V **aventar.**

avieso, a [a'ßjeso, a] *a* (*torcido*) distorted; (*perverso*) wicked.

avinagrado, a [aßina'ɣraðo, a] *a* sour, acid.

avinagrarse [aßina'ɣrarse] *vr* to go o turn sour.

avine [a'ßine] *etc vb* V **avenir.**

Aviñón [aßi'ɲon] *nm* Avignon.

avío [a'ßio] *nm* preparation; **~s** *nmpl* gear *sg*, kit *sg.*

avión [a'ßjon] *nm* aeroplane; (*ave*) martin; **~ de reacción** jet (plane); **por ~** (*CORREOS*) by air mail.

avioneta [aßjo'neta] *nf* light aircraft.

avisar [aßi'sar] *vt* (*advertir*) to warn, notify; (*informar*) to tell; (*aconsejar*) to advise, counsel.

aviso [a'ßiso] *nm* warning; (*noticia*) notice; (*COM*) demand note; (*INFORM*) prompt; **~ escrito** notice in writing; **sin previo ~** without warning; **estar sobre ~** to be on the look-out.

avispa [a'ßispa] *nf* wasp.

avispado, a [aßis'paðo, a] *a* sharp, clever.

avispero [aßis'pero] *nm* wasp's nest.

avispón [aßis'pon] *nm* hornet.

avistar [aßis'tar] *vt* to sight, spot.

avitaminosis [aßitami'nosis] *nf inv* vitamin

deficiency.

avituallar [aβitwa'ʎar] vt to supply with food.

avivar [aβi'βar] vt to strengthen, intensify; **~se** vr to revive, acquire new life.

avizor [aβi'θor] a: **estar ojo ~** to be on the alert.

avizorar [aβiθo'rar] vt to spy on.

axila [ak'sila] nf armpit.

axioma [ak'sjoma] nm axiom.

ay [ai] excl (dolor) ow!, ouch!; (aflicción) oh!, oh dear!; **¡~ de mi!** poor me!

aya ['aja] nf governess; (niñera) nanny.

ayer [a'jer] ad, nm yesterday; **antes de ~** the day before yesterday; **~ por la tarde** yesterday afternoon/evening.

ayo ['ajo] nm tutor.

ayote [a'jote] nm (AM) pumpkin.

Ayto. abr = **Ayuntamiento.**

ayuda [a'juða] nf help, assistance; (MED) enema; (AM) laxative ◆ nm page.

ayudante, a [aju'ðante, a] nm/f assistant, helper; (ESCOL) assistant; (MIL) adjutant.

ayudar [aju'ðar] vt to help, assist.

ayunar [aju'nar] vi to fast.

ayunas [a'junas] nfpl: **estar en ~** (no haber comido) to be fasting; (ignorar) to be in the dark.

ayuno [a'juno] nm fasting.

ayuntamiento [ajunta'mjento] nm (consejo) town/city council; (edificio) town/city hall; (cópula) sexual intercourse.

azabache [aθa'βatʃe] nm jet.

azada [a'θaða] nf hoe.

azafata [aθa'fata] nf air hostess (Brit) o stewardess.

azafrán [aθa'fran] nm saffron.

azahar [aθa'ar] nm orange/lemon blossom.

azar [a'θar] nm (casualidad) chance, fate; (desgracia) misfortune, accident; **por ~** by chance; **al ~** at random.

azaroso, a [aθa'roso, a] a (arriesgado) risky; (vida) eventful.

azogue [a'θoɣe] nm mercury.

azor [a'θor] nm goshawk.

azoramiento [aθora'mjento] nm alarm; (confusión) confusion.

azorar [aθo'rar] vt to alarm; **~se** vr to get alarmed.

Azores [a'θores] nfpl: **las (Islas) ~** the Azores.

azotar [aθo'tar] vt to whip, beat; (pegar) to spank.

azotaina [aθo'taina] nf beating.

azote [a'θote] nm (látigo) whip; (latigazo) lash, stroke; (en las nalgas) spank; (calamidad) calamity.

azotea [aθo'tea] nf (flat) roof.

azteca [aθ'teka] a, nm/f Aztec.

azúcar [a'θukar] nm sugar.

azucarado, a [aθuka'raðo, a] a sugary, sweet.

azucarero, a [aθuka'rero, a] a sugar cpd ◆ nm sugar bowl.

azuce [a'θuθe] etc vb V **azuzar.**

azucena [aθu'θena] nf white lily.

azufre [a'θufre] nm sulphur.

azul [a'θul] a, nm blue; **~ celeste/marino** sky/navy blue.

azulejo [aθu'lexo] nm tile.

azulgrana [aθul'ɣrana] a inv of Barcelona Football Club ◆ nm: **los A~** the Barcelona F.C. players o team.

azuzar [aθu'θar] vt to incite, egg on.

B

B, b [be] nf (letra) B, b; **B de Barcelona** B for Benjamin (Brit) o Baker (US).

B.A. abr = **Buenos Aires.**

baba ['baβa] nf spittle, saliva; **se le caía la ~** (fig) he was thrilled to bits.

babear [baβe'ar] vi (echar saliva) to slobber; (niño) to dribble; (fig) to drool, slaver.

babel [ba'βel] nm o f bedlam.

babero [ba'βero] nm bib.

Babia ['baβja] nf: **estar en ~** to be daydreaming.

bable ['baβle] nm Asturian (dialect).

babor [ba'βor] nm port (side); **a ~** to port.

babosa, a [ba'βoso, a] a slobbering; (ZOOL) slimy; (AM) silly.

babucha [ba'βutʃa] nf slipper.

baca ['baka] nf (AUTO) luggage o roof rack.

bacalao [baka'lao] nm cod(fish).

bacanal [baka'nal] nf orgy.

bacilo [ba'θilo] nm bacillus, germ.

bacinica [baθi'nika] nf, **bacinilla** [baθi'niʎa] nf chamber pot.

bacteria [bak'terja] nf bacterium, germ.

báculo ['bakulo] nm stick, staff; (fig) support.

bache ['batʃe] nm pothole, rut; (fig) bad patch.

badajo [ba'ðaxo] nm clapper (of a bell).

bachillerato [batʃiʎe'rato] nm (ESCOL) school-leaving examination (Brit), bachelor's degree (US), baccalaureate (US).

bagaje [ba'ɣaxe] nm baggage; (fig) background.

bagatela [baɣa'tela] nf trinket, trifle.

Bahama [ba'ama]: **las (Islas) ~, las ~s** nfpl the Bahamas.

bahía [ba'ia] nf bay.

bailar [bai'lar] vt, vi to dance.

bailarín, ina [baila'rin, ina] *nm/f* dancer; (*de ballet*) ballet dancer.

baile ['baile] *nm* dance; (*formal*) ball.

baja ['baxa] *nf* drop, fall; (ECON) slump; (MIL) casualty; (*paro*) redundancy; **dar de** ~ (*soldado*) to discharge; (*empleado*) to dismiss, sack; **darse de** ~ (*retirarse*) to drop out; (MED) to go sick; (*dimitir*) to resign; **estar de** ~ (*enfermo*) to be off sick; (BOLSA) to be dropping *o* falling; **jugar a la** ~ (ECON) to speculate on a fall in prices; *V* tb **bajo**.

bajada [ba'xaða] *nf* descent; (*camino*) slope; (*de aguas*) ebb.

bajamar [baxa'mar] *nf* low tide.

bajar [ba'xar] *vi* to go *o* come down; (*temperatura, precios*) to drop, fall ♦ *vt* (*cabeza*) to bow; (*escalera*) to go *o* come down; (*radio etc*) to turn down; (*precio, voz*) to lower; (*llevar abajo*) to take down; ~**se** *vr* (*de vehículo*) to get out; (*de autobús*) to get off; ~ **de** (*coche*) to get out of; (*autobús*) to get off; ~**le los humos a uno** (*fig*) to cut sb down to size.

bajeza [ba'xeθa] *nf* baseness; (*una* ~) vile deed.

bajío [ba'xio] *nm* shoal, sandbank; (AM) lowlands *pl*.

bajista [ba'xista] *nm/f* (MUS) bassist ♦ *a* (BOLSA) bear *cpd*.

bajo, a ['baxo, a] *a* (*terreno*) low(-lying); (*mueble, número, precio*) low; (*piso*) ground; (*de estatura*) small, short; (*color*) pale; (*sonido*) faint, soft, low; (*voz, tono*) deep; (*metal*) base ♦ *ad* (*hablar*) softly, quietly; (*volar*) low ♦ *prep* under, below, underneath ♦ *nm* (MUS) bass; **hablar en voz baja** to whisper; ~ **la lluvia** in the rain.

bajón [ba'xon] *nm* fall, drop.

bajura [ba'xura] *nf*: **pesca de** ~ coastal fishing.

bala ['bala] *nf* bullet.

balacera [bala'θera] *nf* (AM) shoot-out.

balada [ba'laða] *nf* ballad.

baladí [bala'ði] *a* trivial.

baladrón, ona [bala'ðron, ona] *a* boastful.

baladronada [balaðro'naða] *nf* (*dicho*) boast, brag; (*hecho*) piece of bravado.

balance [ba'lanθe] *nm* (COM) balance; (: *libro*) balance sheet; (: *cuenta general*) stocktaking; ~ **de comprobación** trial balance; ~ **consolidado** consolidated balance sheet; **hacer** ~ to take stock.

balancear [balanθe'ar] *vt* to balance ♦ *vi*, ~**se** *vr* to swing (to and fro); (*vacilar*) to hesitate.

balanceo [balan'θeo] *nm* swinging.

balanza [ba'lanθa] *nf* scales *pl*, balance; ~ **comercial** balance of trade; ~ **de pagos/de poder(es)** balance of payments/of power; (ASTRO): **B**~ Libra.

balar [ba'lar] *vi* to bleat.

balaustrada [balaus'traða] *nf* balustrade; (*pasamanos*) banister.

balazo [ba'laθo] *nm* (*tiro*) shot; (*herida*) bullet wound.

balboa [bal'ßoa] *nf* Panamanian currency unit.

balbucear [balßuθe'ar] *vi, vt* to stammer, stutter.

balbuceo [balßu'θeo] *nm* stammering, stuttering.

balbucir [balßu'θir] *vi, vt* to stammer, stutter.

balbuzca [bal'ßuθka] *etc vb V* **balbucir**.

Balcanes [bal'kanes] *nmpl*: **los (Montes)** ~ the Balkans, the Balkan Mountains; **la Península de los** ~ the Balkan Peninsula.

balcón [bal'kon] *nm* balcony.

balda ['balda] *nf* (*estante*) shelf.

baldar [bal'dar] *vt* to cripple; (*agotar*) to exhaust.

balde ['balde] *nm* bucket, pail; **de** ~ *ad* (for) free, for nothing; **en** ~ *ad* in vain.

baldío, a [bal'dio, a] *a* uncultivated; (*terreno*) waste; (*inútil*) vain ♦ *nm* wasteland.

baldosa [bal'dosa] *nf* (*azulejo*) floor tile; (*grande*) flagstone.

balear [bale'ar] *a* Balearic, of the Balearic Islands ♦ *nm/f* native *o* inhabitant of the Balearic Islands.

Baleares [bale'ares] *nfpl*: **las (Islas)** ~ the Balearics, the Balearic Islands.

balido [ba'liðo] *nm* bleat, bleating.

balín [ba'lin] *nm* pellet; **balines** *nmpl* buckshot *sg*.

balística [ba'listika] *nf* ballistics *pl*.

baliza [ba'liθa] *nf* (AVIAT) beacon; (NAUT) buoy.

balneario, a [balne'arjo, a] *a*: **estación balnearia** (bathing) resort ♦ *nm* spa, health resort.

balompié [balom'pje] *nm* football.

balón [ba'lon] *nm* ball.

baloncesto [balon'θesto] *nm* basketball.

balonmano [balon'mano] *nm* handball.

balonvolea [balombo'lea] *nm* volleyball.

balsa ['balsa] *nf* raft; (BOT) balsa wood.

bálsamo ['balsamo] *nm* balsam, balm.

balsón [bal'son] *nm* (AM) swamp, bog.

báltico, a ['baltiko, a] *a* Baltic; **el (Mar) B**~ the Baltic (Sea).

baluarte [ba'lwarte] *nm* bastion, bulwark.

ballena [ba'ʎena] *nf* whale.

ballenero, a [baʎe'nero, a] *a*: **industria ballenera** whaling industry ♦ *nm* (*pescador*) whaler; (*barco*) whaling ship.

ballesta [ba'ʎesta] *nf* crossbow; (AUTO) spring.

ballet, *pl* **ballets** [ba'le, ba'les] *nm* ballet.

bambolear [bambole'ar] *vi*, ~**se** *vr* to swing, sway; (*silla*) to wobble.

bamboleo [bambo'leo] *nm* swinging, swaying; wobbling.

bambú [bam'bu] *nm* bamboo.

banal [ba'nal] *a* banal, trivial.

banana [ba'nana] *nf (AM)* banana.

bananal [bana'nal] *nm (AM)* banana plantation.

banano [ba'nano] *nm (AM)* banana tree.

banasta [ba'nasta] *nf* large basket, hamper.

banca ['banka] *nf (asiento)* bench; *(COM)* banking.

bancario, a [ban'karjo, a] *a* banking *cpd*, bank *cpd*; **giro ~** bank draft.

bancarrota [banka'rrota] *nf* bankruptcy; **declararse en** *o* **hacer ~** to go bankrupt.

banco ['banko] *nm* bench; *(ESCOL)* desk; *(COM)* bank; *(GEO)* stratum; **~ comercial** *o* **mercantil** commercial bank; **~ por acciones** joint-stock bank; **~ de crédito/de ahorros** credit/savings bank; **~ de arena** sandbank; **~ de datos** *(INFORM)* data bank; **~ de hielo** iceberg.

banda ['banda] *nf* band; *(cinta)* ribbon; *(pandilla)* gang; *(MUS)* brass band; *(NAUT)* side, edge; **la B~ Oriental** Uruguay; **~ sonora** soundtrack; **~ transportadora** conveyor belt.

bandada [ban'daða] *nf (de pájaros)* flock; *(de peces)* shoal.

bandeja [ban'dexa] *nf* tray; **~ de entrada/ salida** in-tray/out-tray.

bandera [ban'dera] *nf (de tela)* flag; *(estandarte)* banner; *(INFORM)* marker, flag; **izar la ~** to hoist the flag.

banderilla [bande'riʎa] *nf* banderilla; *(tapa) savoury appetizer (served on a cocktail stick)*.

banderín [bande'rin] *nm* pennant, small flag.

banderola [bande'rola] *nf (MIL)* pennant.

bandido [ban'diðo] *nm* bandit.

bando ['bando] *nm (edicto)* edict, proclamation; *(facción)* faction; **pasar al otro ~** to change sides; **los ~s** *(REL)* the banns.

bandolera [bando'lera] *nf:* **bolsa de ~** shoulder bag.

bandolero [bando'lero] *nm* bandit, brigand.

bandoneón [bandone'on] *nm (AM)* large accordion.

BANESTO [ba'nesto] *nm abr* = *Banco Español de Crédito*.

banquero [ban'kero] *nm* banker.

banqueta [ban'keta] *nf* stool; *(AM: en la calle)* pavement *(Brit)*, sidewalk *(US)*.

banquete [ban'kete] *nm* banquet; *(para convidados)* formal dinner; **~ de boda** wedding breakfast.

banquillo [ban'kiʎo] *nm (JUR)* dock, prisoner's bench; *(banco)* bench; *(para los pies)* footstool.

bañador [baɲa'ðor] *nm* swimming costume *(Brit)*, bathing suit *(US)*.

bañar [ba'ɲar] *vt (niño)* to bath, bathe; *(objeto)* to dip; *(de barniz)* to coat; **~se** *vr (en el mar)* to bathe, swim; *(en la bañera)* to have a bath.

bañero, a [ba'ɲero, a] *nm* lifeguard ♦ *nf* bath(tub).

bañista [ba'ɲista] *nm/f* bather.

baño ['baɲo] *nm (en bañera)* bath; *(en río, mar)* dip, swim; *(cuarto)* bathroom; *(bañera)* bath(tub); *(capa)* coating; **ir a tomar los ~s** to take the waters.

baptista [bap'tista] *nm/f* Baptist.

baqueta [ba'keta] *nf (MUS)* drumstick.

bar [bar] *nm* bar.

barahúnda [bara'unda] *nf* uproar, hubbub.

baraja [ba'raxa] *nf* pack (of cards).

barajar [bara'xar] *vt (naipes)* to shuffle; *(fig)* to jumble up.

baranda [ba'randa], **barandilla** [baran'ðiʎa] *nf* rail, railing.

baratija [bara'tixa] *nf* trinket; *(fig)* trifle; **~s** *nfpl (COM)* cheap goods.

baratillo [bara'tiʎo] *nm (tienda)* junkshop; *(subasta)* bargain sale; *(conjunto de cosas)* second-hand goods *pl*.

barato, a [ba'rato, a] *a* cheap ♦ *ad* cheap, cheaply.

baratura [bara'tura] *nf* cheapness.

baraúnda [bara'unda] *nf* = **barahúnda**.

barba ['barβa] *nf (mentón)* chin; *(pelo)* beard; **tener ~** to be unshaven; **hacer algo en las ~s de uno** to do sth under sb's very nose; **reírse en las ~s de uno** to laugh in sb's face.

barbacoa [barβa'koa] *nf (parrilla)* barbecue; *(carne)* barbecued meat.

barbaridad [barβari'ðað] *nf* barbarity; *(acto)* barbarism; *(atrocidad)* outrage; **una ~ de** *(fam)* loads of; **¡qué ~!** *(fam)* how awful!; **cuesta una ~** *(fam)* it costs a fortune.

barbarie [bar'βarje] *nf*, **barbarismo** [barβa'rismo] *nm* barbarism; *(crueldad)* barbarity.

bárbaro, a ['barβaro, a] *a* barbarous, cruel; *(grosero)* rough, uncouth ♦ *nm/f* barbarian ♦ *ad*: **lo pasamos ~** *(fam)* we had a great time; **¡qué ~!** *(fam)* how marvellous!; **un éxito ~** *(fam)* a terrific success; **es un tipo ~** *(fam)* he's a great bloke.

barbecho [bar'βetʃo] *nm* fallow land.

barbero [bar'βero] *nm* barber, hairdresser.

barbilampiño [barβilam'piɲo] *a* smooth-faced; *(fig)* inexperienced.

barbilla [bar'βiʎa] *nf* chin, tip of the chin.

barbo ['barβo] *nm*: **~ de mar** red mullet.

barbotar [barβo'tar], **barbotear** [barβote'ar] *vt, vi* to mutter, mumble.

barbudo, a [bar'βuðo, a] *a* bearded.

barbullar [barβu'ʎar] *vi* to jabber away.

barca ['barka] *nf* (small) boat; ~ **pesquera** fishing boat; ~ **de pasaje** ferry.

barcaza [bar'kaθa] *nf* barge; ~ **de desembarco** landing craft.

Barcelona [barθe'lona] *nf* Barcelona.

barcelonés, esa [barθelo'nes, esa] *a* of *o* from Barcelona ◆ *nm/f* native *o* inhabitant of Barcelona.

barco ['barko] *nm* boat; (*buque*) ship; (*COM etc*) vessel; ~ **de carga** cargo boat; ~ **de guerra** warship; ~ **de vela** sailing ship; **ir en** ~ to go by boat.

baremo [ba'remo] *nm* scale; (*tabla de cuentas*) ready reckoner.

barítono [ba'ritono] *nm* baritone.

barman ['barman] *nm* barman.

Barna. *abr* = **Barcelona**.

barnice [bar'niθe] *etc vb V* **barnizar**.

barniz [bar'niθ] *nm* varnish; (*en la loza*) glaze; (*fig*) veneer.

barnizar [barni'θar] *vt* to varnish; (*loza*) to glaze.

barómetro [ba'rometro] *nm* barometer.

barquero [bar'kero] *nm* boatman.

barquilla [bar'kiʎa] *nf* (*NAUT*) log.

barquillo [bar'kiʎo] *nm* cone, cornet.

barra ['barra] *nf* bar, rod; (*JUR*) rail; (: *banquillo*) dock; (*de un bar, café*) bar; (*de pan*) French loaf; (*palanca*) lever; ~ **de carmín** *o* **de labios** lipstick; ~ **de espaciado** (*INFORM*) space bar; ~ **inversa** backslash; **no pararse en** ~**s** to stick *o* stop at nothing.

barrabasada [barraβa'saða] *nf* (piece of) mischief.

barraca [ba'rraka] *nf* hut, cabin; (*en Valencia*) thatched farmhouse; (*en feria*) booth.

barracón [barra'kon] *nm* (*caseta*) big hut.

barragana [barra'vana] *nf* concubine.

barranca [ba'rranka] *nf* ravine, gully.

barranco [ba'rranko] *nm* ravine; (*fig*) difficulty.

barrena [ba'rrena] *nf* drill.

barrenar [barre'nar] *vt* to drill (through), bore.

barrendero, a [barren'dero, a] *nm/f* street-sweeper.

barreno [ba'rreno] *nm* large drill.

barreño [ba'rreɲo] *nm* washing-up bowl.

barrer [ba'rrer] *vt* to sweep; (*quitar*) to sweep away; (*MIL, NAUT*) to sweep, rake (with gunfire) ◆ *vi* to sweep up.

barrera [ba'rrera] *nf* barrier; (*MIL*) barricade; (*FERRO*) crossing gate; **poner** ~**s** a to hinder; ~ **arancelaria** (*COM*) tariff barrier; ~ **comercial** (*COM*) trade barrier.

barriada [ba'rrjaða] *nf* quarter, district.

barricada [barri'kaða] *nf* barricade.

barrido [ba'rriðo] *nm*, **barrida** [ba'rriða] *nf* sweep, sweeping.

barriga [ba'rriɣa] *nf* belly; (*panza*) paunch; (*vientre*) guts *pl*; **echar** ~ to get middle-age spread.

barrigón, ona [barri'ɣon, ona], **barrigudo, a** [barri'ɣuðo, a] *a* potbellied.

barril [ba'rril] *nm* barrel, cask; **cerveza de** ~ draught beer.

barrio ['barrjo] *nm* (*vecindad*) area, neighborhood (*US*); (*en las afueras*) suburb; ~**s bajos** poor quarter *sg*; ~ **chino** red-light district.

barriobajero, a [barrjoba'xero, a] *a* (*vulgar*) common.

barro ['barro] *nm* (*lodo*) mud; (*objetos*) earthenware; (*MED*) pimple.

barroco, a [ba'rroko, a] *a* Baroque; (*fig*) elaborate ◆ *nm* Baroque.

barrote [ba'rrote] *nm* (*de ventana etc*) bar.

barruntar [barrun'tar] *vt* (*conjeturar*) to guess; (*presentir*) to suspect.

barrunto [ba'rrunto] *nm* guess; suspicion.

bartola [bar'tola]: **a la** ~ *ad*: **tirarse a la** ~ to take it easy, be lazy.

bártulos ['bartulos] *nmpl* things, belongings.

barullo [ba'ruʎo] *nm* row, uproar.

basa ['basa] *nf* (*ARQ*) base.

basamento [basa'mento] *nm* base, plinth.

basar [ba'sar] *vt* to base; ~**se** *vr*: ~**se en** to be based on.

basca ['baska] *nf* nausea.

báscula ['baskula] *nf* (platform) scales *pl*; ~ **biestable** (*INFORM*) flip-flop, toggle.

bascular [basku'lar] *vt* (*INFORM*) to toggle.

base ['base] *nf* base; **a** ~ **de** on the basis of, based on; (*mediante*) by means of; **a** ~ **de bien** in abundance; ~ **de conocimiento** knowledge base; ~ **de datos** database.

básico, a ['basiko, a] *a* basic.

Basilea [basi'lea] *nf* Basle.

basílica [ba'silika] *nf* basilica.

basilisco [basi'lisko] *nm* (*AM*) iguana; **estar hecho un** ~ to be hopping mad.

bastante [bas'tante] *a* (*suficiente*) enough, sufficient; (*no poco(s)*) quite a lot of ◆ *ad* (*suficientemente*) enough, sufficiently; (*muy*) quite, rather; **es** ~ **alto (como) para alcanzarlo** he's tall enough to reach it.

bastar [bas'tar] *vi* to be enough *o* sufficient; ~**se** *vr* to be self-sufficient; ~ **para** to be enough to; ¡**basta**! (that's) enough!

bastardilla [bastar'ðiʎa] *nf* italics *pl*.

bastardo, a [bas'tarðo, a] *a*, *nm/f* bastard.

bastidor [basti'ðor] *nm* frame; (*de coche*) chassis; (*ARTE*) stretcher; (*TEATRO*) wing; **entre** ~**es** behind the scenes.

basto, a ['basto, a] *a* coarse, rough ◆ *nmpl*: ~**s** (*NAIPES*) clubs.

bastón [bas'ton] *nm* stick, staff; (*para pasear*) walking stick; ~ **de mando** baton.

bastonazo [basto'naθo] *nm* blow with a stick.

basura [ba'sura] *nf* rubbish, refuse (*Brit*), garbage (*US*).

basurero [basu'rero] *nm* (*hombre*) dustman (*Brit*), garbage man (*US*); (*lugar*) rubbish dump; (*cubo*) (rubbish) bin (*Brit*), trash can (*US*).

bata ['bata] *nf* (*gen*) dressing gown; (*cubretodo*) smock, overall; (*MED, TEC etc*) lab(oratory) coat.

batacazo [bata'kaθo] *nm* bump.

batalla [ba'taʎa] *nf* battle; **de ~** for everyday use.

batallar [bata'ʎar] *vi* to fight.

batallón [bata'ʎon] *nm* battalion.

batata [ba'tata] *nf* (*AM: CULIN*) sweet potato.

bate ['bate] *nm* (*DEPORTE*) bat.

bateador [batea'ðor] *nm* batter, batsman.

batería [bate'ria] *nf* battery; (*MUS*) drums *pl*; (*TEATRO*) footlights *pl*; **~ de cocina** kitchen utensils *pl*.

batiburrillo [batiβu'rriʎo] *nm* hotchpotch.

batido, a [ba'tiðo, a] *a* (*camino*) beaten, well-trodden ◆ *nm* (*CULIN*) batter; **~ (de leche)** milk shake ◆ *nf* (*AM*) (police) raid.

batidora [bati'ðora] *nf* beater, mixer; **~ eléctrica** food mixer, blender.

batir [ba'tir] *vt* to beat, strike; (*vencer*) to beat, defeat; (*revolver*) to beat, mix; (*pelo*) to back-comb; **~se** *vr* to fight; **~ palmas** to clap, applaud.

batuta [ba'tuta] *nf* baton; **llevar la ~** (*fig*) to be the boss.

baudio ['bauðjo] *nm* (*INFORM*) baud.

baúl [ba'ul] *nm* trunk; (*AUTO*) boot (*Brit*), trunk (*US*).

bautice [bau'tiθe] *etc vb* V **bautizar**.

bautismo [bau'tismo] *nm* baptism, christening.

bautista [bau'tista] *a, nm/f* Baptist.

bautizar [bauti'θar] *vt* to baptize, christen; (*fam: diluir*) to water down; (*dar apodo*) to dub.

bautizo [bau'tiθo] *nm* baptism, christening.

bávaro, a ['baβaro, a] *a, nm/f* Bavarian.

Baviera [ba'βjera] *nf* Bavaria.

baya ['baja] *nf* berry; V *tb* **bayo**.

bayeta [ba'jeta] *nf* (*trapo*) floorcloth; (*AM: pañal*) nappy (*Brit*), diaper (*US*).

bayo, a ['bajo, a] *a* bay.

bayoneta [bajo'neta] *nf* bayonet.

baza ['baθa] *nf* trick; **meter ~** to butt in.

bazar [ba'θar] *nm* bazaar.

bazofia [ba'θofja] *nf* pigswill (*Brit*), hogwash (*US*); (*libro etc*) trash.

beato, a [be'ato, a] *a* blessed; (*piadoso*) pious.

bebé, pl bebés [be'βe, be'βes] *nm* baby.

bebedero, a [beβe'ðero, a] *nm* (*para animales*) drinking trough.

bebedizo, a [beβe'ðiθo, a] *a* drinkable ◆

nm potion.

bebedor, a [beβe'ðor, a] *a* hard-drinking.

beber [be'βer] *vt, vi* to drink; **~ a sorbos/ tragos** to sip/gulp; **se lo bebió todo** he drank it all up.

bebido, a [be'βiðo, a] *a* drunk ◆ *nf* drink.

beca ['beka] *nf* grant, scholarship.

becado, a [be'kaðo, a] *nm/f*, **becario, a** [be'karjo, a] *nm/f* scholarship holder.

becerro [be'θerro] *nm* yearling calf.

becuadro [be'kwaðro] *nm* (*MUS*) natural sign.

bedel [be'ðel] *nm* porter, janitor.

befarse [be'farse] *vr*: **~ de algo** to scoff at sth.

béisbol ['beisβol] *nm* baseball.

beldad [bel'dað] *nf* beauty.

Belén [be'len] *nm* Bethlehem; **b~** (*de Navidad*) nativity scene, crib.

belga ['belɣa] *a, nm/f* Belgian.

Bélgica ['belxika] *nf* Belgium.

Belgrado [bel'ɣraðo] *nm* Belgrade.

Belice [be'liθe] *nm* Belize.

bélico, a ['beliko, a] *a* (*actitud*) warlike.

belicoso, a [beli'koso, a] *a* (*guerrero*) warlike; (*agresivo*) aggressive, bellicose.

beligerante [belixe'rante] *a* belligerent.

bellaco, a [be'ʎako, a] *a* sly, cunning ◆ *nm* villain, rogue.

belladona [beʎa'ðona] *nf* deadly nightshade.

bellaquería [beʎake'ria] *nf* (*acción*) dirty trick; (*calidad*) wickedness.

belleza [be'ʎeθa] *nf* beauty.

bello, a ['beʎo, a] *a* beautiful, lovely; **Bellas Artes** Fine Art *sg*.

bellota [be'ʎota] *nf* acorn.

bemol [be'mol] *nm* (*MUS*) flat; **esto tiene ~es** (*fam*) this is a tough one.

bencina [ben'θina] *nf* (*AM*) petrol (*Brit*), gas (*US*).

bendecir [bende'θir] *vt* to bless; **~ la mesa** to say grace.

bendición [bendi'θjon] *nf* blessing.

bendiga [ben'diɣa] *etc*, **bendije** [ben'dixe] *etc*, **bendiré** [bendi're] *etc vb* V **bendecir**.

bendito, a [ben'dito, a] *pp de* **bendecir** ◆ *a* (*santo*) blessed; (*agua*) holy; (*afortunado*) lucky; (*feliz*) happy; (*sencillo*) simple ◆ *nm/f* simple soul; **¡~ sea Dios!** thank goodness!; **es un ~** he's sweet; **dormir como un ~** to sleep like a log.

benedictino, a [beneðik'tino, a] *a, nm* Benedictine.

benefactor, a [benefak'tor, a] *nm/f* benefactor/benefactress.

beneficencia [benefi'θenθja] *nf* charity.

beneficiar [benefi'θjar] *vt* to benefit, be of benefit to; **~se** *vr* to benefit, profit.

beneficiario, a [benefi'θjarjo, a] *nm/f* beneficiary; (*de cheque*) payee.

beneficio [bene'fiθjo] *nm* (*bien*) benefit, advantage; (*COM*) profit, gain; **a ~ de** for the benefit of; **en ~ propio** to one's own advantage; **~ bruto/neto** gross/net profit; **~ por acción** earnings *pl* per share.

beneficioso, a [benefi'θjoso, a] *a* beneficial.

benéfico, a [be'nefiko, a] *a* charitable; **sociedad ~a** charity (organisation).

benemérito, a [bene'merito, a] *a* meritorious ◆ *nf*: **la Benemérita** (*Esp*) the Civil Guard.

beneplácito [bene'plaθito] *nm* approval, consent.

benevolencia [beneßo'lenθja] *nf* benevolence, kindness.

benévolo, a [be'neßolo, a] *a* benevolent, kind.

Bengala [ben'gala] *nf* Bengal; **el Golfo de ~** the Bay of Bengal.

bengala [ben'gala] *nf* (*MIL*) flare; (*fuego*) Bengal light; (*materia*) rattan.

bengalí [benga'li] *a, nm/f* Bengali.

benignidad [beniɣni'ðað] *nf* (*afabilidad*) kindness; (*suavidad*) mildness.

benigno, a [be'niɣno, a] *a* kind; (*suave*) mild; (*MED: tumor*) benign, non-malignant.

benjamín [benxa'min] *nm* youngest child.

beodo, a [be'oðo, a] *a* drunk ◆ *nm/f* drunkard.

berberecho [berße'retʃo] *nm* cockle.

berenjena [beren'xena] *nf* aubergine (*Brit*), eggplant (*US*).

berenjenal [berenxe'nal] *nm* (*AGR*) aubergine bed; (*fig*) mess; **en buen ~ nos hemos metido** we've got ourselves into a fine mess.

bergantín [berɣan'tin] *nm* brig(antine).

Berlín [ber'lin] *nm* Berlin.

berlinés, esa [berli'nes, esa] *a* of *o* from Berlin ◆ *nm/f* Berliner.

bermejo, a [ber'mexo, a] *a* red.

bermellón [berme'ʎon] *nm* vermilion.

berrear [berre'ar] *vi* to bellow, low.

berrido [be'rriðo] *nm* bellow(ing).

berrinche [be'rrintʃe] *nm* (*fam*) temper, tantrum.

berro ['berro] *nm* watercress.

berza ['berθa] *nf* cabbage; **~ lombarda** red cabbage.

besamel [besa'mel], **besamela** [besa'mela] *nf* (*CULIN*) white sauce, bechamel sauce.

besar [be'sar] *vt* to kiss; (*fig: tocar*) to graze; **~se** *vr* to kiss (one another).

beso ['beso] *nm* kiss.

bestia ['bestja] *nf* beast, animal; (*fig*) idiot; **~ de carga** beast of burden; **¡~!** you idiot!; **¡no seas ~!** (*bruto*) don't be such a brute!; (*idiota*) don't be such an idiot!

bestial [bes'tjal] *a* bestial; (*fam*) terrific.

bestialidad [bestjali'ðað] *nf* bestiality; (*fam*) stupidity.

besugo [be'suɣo] *nm* sea bream; (*fam*) idiot.

besuguera [besu'ɣera] *nf* (*CULIN*) fish pan.

besuquear [besuke'ar] *vt* to cover with kisses; **~se** *vr* to kiss and cuddle.

bético, a ['betiko, a] *a* Andalusian.

betún [be'tun] *nm* shoe polish; (*QUÍMICA*) bitumen, asphalt.

Bib. *abr* = **Biblioteca**.

biberón [biße'ron] *nm* feeding bottle.

Biblia ['bißlja] *nf* Bible.

bíblico, a ['bißliko, a] *a* biblical.

bibliografía [bißljoɣra'fia] *nf* bibliography.

biblioteca [bißljo'teka] *nf* library; (*estantes*) bookcase, bookshelves *pl*; **~ de consulta** reference library.

bibliotecario, a [bißljote'karjo, a] *nm/f* librarian.

B.I.C. [bik] *nf abr* (= *Brigada de Investigación Criminal*) ≈ CID (*Brit*), FBI (*US*).

bicarbonato [bikarßo'nato] *nm* bicarbonate.

bici ['biθi] *nf* (*fam*) bike.

bicicleta [biθi'kleta] *nf* bicycle, cycle.

bicoca [bi'koka] *nf* (*Esp fam*) cushy job; (*AM: bofetada*) slap.

bicho ['bitʃo] *nm* (*animal*) small animal; (*sabandija*) bug, insect; (*TAUR*) bull; **~ raro** (*fam*) queer fish.

bidé [bi'ðe] *nm* bidet.

bidireccional [bidirekθjo'nal] *a* bidirectional.

bidón [bi'ðon] *nm* (*grande*) drum; (*pequeño*) can.

bien [bjen] *nm* good; (*interés*) advantage, benefit; **hombre de ~** honest man; **el ~ público** the common *o* public good; **~es de capital** (*COM*) capital goods; **~es inmuebles/muebles** real estate *sg*/personal property *sg*; **~es de consumo** consumer goods; **~es de producción** industrial goods; **~es raíces** real estate *sg* ◆ *a:* **de casa** well brought up ◆ *ad* well; (*correctamente*) properly, right; (*oler*) nice; (*muy*) very; **más ~** rather; **hablas ~ (el español)** you speak good Spanish; **estar ~ de salud/dinero** to be well/well off; **estar a ~ con uno** to be on good terms with sb ◆ *excl*: **¡(muy) ~!** well done! ◆ *conj*: **no ~ llovió, bajó la temperatura** no sooner had it rained than the temperature dropped; **~ que** although.

bienal [bje'nal] *a* biennial.

bienaventurado, a [bjenaßentu'raðo, a] *a* (*feliz*) happy; (*afortunado*) fortunate; (*REL*) blessed.

bienestar [bjenes'tar] *nm* well-being; **estado de ~** welfare state.

bienhechor, a [bjene'tʃor, a] *a* beneficent ◆ *nm/f* benefactor/benefactress.

bienio ['bjenjo] *nm* two-year period.
bienvenido, a [bjembe'niðo, a] *a* welcome ◆ *excl* welcome! ◆ *nf* welcome; **dar la bienvenida a uno** to welcome sb.
bifásico, a [bi'fasiko, a] *a* (*ELEC*) two-phase.
bife ['bife] *nm* (*AM*) steak.
bifurcación [bifurka'θjon] *nf* fork; (*FERRO, INFORM*) branch.
bigamia [bi'ɣamja] *nf* bigamy.
bígamo, a ['biɣamo, a] *a* bigamous ◆ *nm/f* bigamist.
bígaro ['biɣaro] *nm* winkle.
bigote [bi'ɣote] *nm* (*tb: ~s*) moustache.
bigotudo, a [biɣo'tuðo, a] *a* with a big moustache.
bigudí [biɣu'ði] *nm* (hair-)curler.
bikini [bi'kini] *nm* bikini; (*CULIN*) toasted cheese and ham sandwich.
bilbaíno, a [bilßa'ino, a] *a* of o from Bilbao ◆ *nm/f* native o inhabitant of Bilbao.
bilingüe [bi'lingwe] *a* bilingual.
bilis ['bilis] *nf inv* bile.
billar [bi'ʎar] *nm* billiards *sg*; (*lugar*) billiard hall; (*galería de atracciones*) amusement arcade; **~ americano** pool.
billete [bi'ʎete] *nm* ticket; (*de banco*) banknote (*Brit*), bill (*US*); (*carta*) note; **~ sencillo, ~ de ida solamente/~ de ida y vuelta** single (*Brit*) o one-way (*US*) ticket/return (*Brit*) o round-trip (*US*) ticket; **sacar (un) ~** to get a ticket; **un ~ de 5 libras** a five-pound note.
billetera [biʎe'tera] *nf*, **billetero** [biʎe'tero] *nm* wallet.
billón [bi'ʎon] *nm* billion.
bimensual [bimen'swal] *a* twice monthly.
bimestral [bimes'tral] *a* bimonthly.
bimestre [bi'mestre] *nm* two-month period.
bimotor [bimo'tor] *a* twin-engined ◆ *nm* twin-engined plane.
binario, a [bi'narjo, a] *a* (*INFORM*) binary.
binóculo [bi'nokulo] *nm* pince-nez.
biografía [bjoɣra'fia] *nf* biography.
biógrafo, a [bi'oɣrafo, a] *nm/f* biographer.
biología [biolo'xia] *nf* biology.
biológico, a [bio'loxiko, a] *a* biological; **guerra biológica** biological warfare.
biólogo, a [bi'oloɣo, a] *nm/f* biologist.
biombo ['bjombo] *nm* (folding) screen.
biopsia [bi'opsja] *nf* biopsy.
bioquímico, a [bio'kimiko, a] *a* biochemical ◆ *nm/f* biochemist ◆ *nf* biochemistry.
bióxido [bi'oksiðo] *nm* dioxide.
bipartidismo [biparti'ðismo] *nm* (*POL*) two-party system.
birlar [bir'lar] *vt* (*fam*) to pinch.
birlibirloque [birlißir'loke] *nm*: **por arte de ~** (as if) by magic.
Birmania [bir'manja] *nf* Burma.
birmano, a [bir'mano, a] *a nm/f* Burmese.

birrete [bi'rrete] *nm* (*JUR*) judge's cap.
bis [bis] *excl* encore! ◆ *ad* (*dos veces*) twice; **viven en el 27 ~** they live at 27a.
bisabuelo, a [bisa'ßwelo, a] *nm/f* great-grandfather/mother; **~s** *nmpl* great-grandparents.
bisagra [bi'saɣra] *nf* hinge.
bisbisar [bisßi'sar], **bisbisear** [bisßise'ar] *vt* to mutter, mumble.
bisbiseo [bisßi'seo] *nm* muttering.
biselar [bise'lar] *vt* to bevel.
bisexual [bisek'swal] *a* bisexual.
bisiesto [bi'sjesto] *a*: **año ~** leap year.
bisnieto, a [bis'njeto, a] *nm/f* great-grandson/daughter; **~s** *nmpl* great-grandchildren.
bisonte [bi'sonte] *nm* bison.
bisoñé [biso'ɲe] *nm* toupée.
bisoño, a [bi'soɲo, a] *a* green, inexperienced.
bistec [bis'tek], **bisté** [bis'te] *nm* steak.
bisturí [bistu'ri] *nm* scalpel.
bisutería [bisute'ria] *nf* imitation o costume jewellery.
bit [bit] *nm* (*INFORM*) bit; **~ de parada** stop bit; **~ de paridad** parity bit.
bitio ['bitjo] *nm* (*INFORM*) bit.
bizantino, a [biθan'tino, a] *a* Byzantine; (*fig*) pointless.
bizarría [biθa'rria] *nf* (*valor*) bravery; (*generosidad*) generosity.
bizarro, a [bi'θarro, a] *a* brave; generous.
bizcar [biθ'kar] *vi* to squint.
bizco, a ['biθko, a] *a* cross-eyed.
bizcocho [biθ'kotʃo] *nm* (*CULIN*) sponge cake.
bizque ['biθke] *etc vb V* **bizcar**.
bizquear [biθke'ar] *vi* to squint.
blanco, a ['blanko, a] *a* white ◆ *nm/f* white man/woman, white ◆ *nm* (*color*) white; (*en texto*) blank; (*MIL, fig*) target ◆ *nf* (*MUS*) minim; **en ~** blank; **cheque en ~** blank cheque; **votar en ~** to spoil one's vote; **quedarse en ~** to be disappointed; **noche en ~** sleepless night; **estar sin ~** to be broke; **ser el ~ de las burlas** to be the butt of jokes.
blancura [blan'kura] *nf* whiteness.
blandengue [blan'denge] *a* (*fam*) soft, weak.
blandir [blan'dir] *vt* to brandish.
blando, a ['blando, a] *a* soft; (*tierno*) tender, gentle; (*carácter*) mild; (*fam*) cowardly ◆ *nm/f* (*POL etc*) soft-liner.
blandura [blan'dura] *nf* softness; tenderness; mildness.
blanquear [blanke'ar] *vt* to whiten; (*fachada*) to whitewash; (*paño*) to bleach ◆ *vi* to turn white.
blanquecino, a [blanke'θino, a] *a* whitish.
blasfemar [blasfe'mar] *vi* to blaspheme;

(fig) to curse.

blasfemia [blas'femja] *nf* blasphemy.

blasfemo, a [blas'femo, a] *a* blasphemous ◆ *nm/f* blasphemer.

blasón [bla'son] *nm* coat of arms; *(fig)* honour.

blasonar [blaso'nar] *vt* to emblazon ◆ *vi* to boast, brag.

bledo ['bleðo] *nm*: **(no) me importa un ~** I couldn't care less.

blindado, a [blin'daðo, a] *a* *(MIL)* armour-plated; *(antibalas)* bulletproof; **coche** *o* *(AM)* **carro ~** armoured car; **puertas blindadas** security doors.

blindaje [blin'daxe] *nm* armour, armour-plating.

bloc, *pl* blocs [blok, blos] *nm* writing pad; *(ESCOL)* jotter; **~ de dibujos** sketch pad.

bloque ['bloke] *nm* *(tb INFORM)* block; *(POL)* bloc; **~ de cilindros** cylinder block.

bloquear [bloke'ar] *vt* *(NAUT etc)* to blockade; *(aislar)* to cut off; *(COM, ECON)* to freeze; **fondos bloqueados** frozen assets.

bloqueo [blo'keo] *nm* blockade; *(COM)* freezing, blocking.

blusa ['blusa] *nf* blouse.

B.° *abr (FINANZAS:* = *banco)* bank; *(COM:* = *beneficiario)* beneficiary.

boato [bo'ato] *nm* show, ostentation.

bobada [bo'ßaða], **bobería** [boße'ria] *nf* foolish action *(o* statement); **decir ~s** to talk nonsense.

bobalicón, ona [boßali'kon, ona] *a* utterly stupid.

bobina [bo'ßina] *nf* *(TEC)* bobbin; *(FOTO)* spool; *(ELEC)* coil, winding.

bobo, a ['boßo, a] *a (tonto)* daft, silly; *(cándido)* naïve ◆ *nm/f* fool, idiot ◆ *nm* *(TEATRO)* clown, funny man.

boca ['boka] *nf* mouth; *(de crustáceo)* pincer; *(de cañón)* muzzle; *(entrada)* mouth, entrance; *(INFORM)* slot; **~s** *nfpl* *(de río)* mouth *sg;* **~ abajo/arriba** face down/up; **a ~ jarro** point-blank; **se me hace la ~ agua** my mouth is watering; **todo salió a pedir de ~** it all turned out perfectly; **en ~ de** *(AM)* according to; **la cosa anda de ~ en ~** the story is going the rounds; **¡cállate la ~!** *(fam)* shut up!; **quedarse con la ~ abierta** to be dumbfounded; **no abrir la ~** to keep quiet; **~ del estómago** pit of the stomach; **~ de metro** tube *(Brit) o* subway *(US)* entrance.

bocacalle [boka'kaλe] *nf* (entrance to a) street; **la primera ~** the first turning *o* street.

bocadillo [boka'ðiλo] *nm* sandwich.

bocado [bo'kaðo] *nm* mouthful, bite; *(de caballo)* bridle; **~ de Adán** Adam's apple.

bocajarro [boka'xarro]: **a ~** *ad* *(MIL)* at point-blank range; **decir algo a ~** to say sth bluntly.

bocanada [boka'naða] *nf* *(de vino)* mouthful, swallow; *(de aire)* gust, puff.

bocazas [bo'kaθas] *nm/f inv* *(fam)* big-mouth.

boceto [bo'θeto] *nm* sketch, outline.

bocina [bo'θina] *nf* *(MUS)* trumpet; *(AUTO)* horn; *(para hablar)* megaphone; **tocar la ~** *(AUTO)* to sound *o* blow one's horn.

bocinazo [boθi'naθo] *nm* *(AUTO)* toot, blast (of the horn).

bocio ['boθjo] *nm* *(MED)* goitre.

bocha ['botʃa] *nf* bowl; **~s** *nfpl* bowls *sg.*

bochinche [bo'tʃintʃe] *nm* *(fam)* uproar.

bochorno [bo'tʃorno] *nm* *(vergüenza)* embarrassment; *(calor)*: **hace ~** it's very muggy.

bochornoso, a [botʃor'noso, a] *a* muggy; embarrassing.

boda ['boða] *nf* *(tb:* **~s)** wedding, marriage; *(fiesta)* wedding reception; **~s de plata/de oro** silver/golden wedding *sg.*

bodega [bo'ðeɣa] *nf* *(de vino)* (wine) cellar; *(bar)* bar; *(restaurante)* restaurant; *(depósito)* storeroom; *(de barco)* hold.

bodegón [boðe'ɣon] *nm* *(ARTE)* still life.

bodrio [bo'ðrio] *nm*: **el libro es un ~** the book is awful *o* rubbish.

B.O.E. ['boe] *nm abr* (= *Boletín Oficial del Estado)* ≈ Hansard.

bofe ['bofe] *nm* *(tb:* **~s:** *de res)* lights *pl;* **echar los ~s** to slave (away).

bofetada [bofe'taða] *nf* slap (in the face); **dar de ~s a uno** to punch sb.

bofetón [bofe'ton] *nm* = **bofetada.**

boga ['boɣa] *nf:* **en ~** in vogue.

bogar [bo'ɣar] *vi (remar)* to row; *(navegar)* to sail.

bogavante [boɣa'ßante] *nm* *(NAUT)* stroke, first rower; *(ZOOL)* lobster.

Bogotá [boɣo'ta] *n* Bogota.

bogotano, a [boɣo'tano, a] *a* of *o* from Bogota ◆ *nm/f* native *o* inhabitant of Bogota.

bogue ['boɣe] *etc vb V* **bogar.**

bohemio, a [bo'emjo, a] *a, nm/f* Bohemian.

boicot, *pl* boicots [boi'ko(t)] *nm* boycott.

boicotear [boikote'ar] *vt* to boycott.

boicoteo [boiko'teo] *nm* boycott.

boina ['boina] *nf* beret.

bola ['bola] *nf* ball; *(canica)* marble; *(NAIPES)* (grand) slam; *(betún)* shoe polish; *(mentira)* tale, story; **~s** *nfpl* *(AM)* bolas; **~ de billar** billiard ball; **~ de nieve** snowball.

bolado [bo'laðo] *nm* *(AM)* deal.

bolchevique [boltʃe'ßike] *a, nm/f* Bolshevik.

boleadoras [bolea'ðoras] *nfpl* *(AM)* bolas *sg.*

bolera [bo'lera] *nf* skittle *o* bowling alley.

boleta [bo'leta] *nf* *(AM: billete)* ticket; (:

permiso) pass, permit.

boletería [bolete'ria] *nf* (*AM*) ticket office.

boletín [bole'tin] *nm* bulletin; (*periódico*) journal, review; ~ **escolar** (*Esp*) school report; ~ **de noticias** news bulletin; ~ **de pedido** application form; ~ **de precios** price list; ~ **de prensa** press release.

boleto [bo'leto] *nm* ticket; ~ **de apuestas** betting slip.

boli ['boli] *nm* biro ®.

boliche [bo'litʃe] *nm* (*bola*) jack; (*juego*) bowls *sg*; (*lugar*) bowling alley; (*AM*: *tienda*) small grocery store.

bólido ['boliðo] *nm* meteorite; (*AUTO*) racing car.

bolígrafo [bo'liɣrafo] *nm* ball-point pen, biro ®.

bolillo [bo'liʎo] *nm* (*COSTURA*) bobbin (for lacemaking).

bolívar [bo'lißar] *nm* monetary unit of *Venezuela*.

Bolivia [bo'lißja] *nf* Bolivia.

boliviano, a [boli'ßjano, a] *a, nm/f* Bolivian.

bolo ['bolo] *nm* skittle; (*píldora*) (large) pill; (**juego de**) ~**s** skittles *sg*.

Bolonia [bo'lonja] *nf* Bologna.

bolsa ['bolsa] *nf* (*cartera*) purse; (*saco*) bag; (*AM*) pocket; (*ANAT*) cavity, sac; (*COM*) stock exchange; (*MINERÍA*) pocket; ~ **de agua caliente** hot water bottle; ~ **de aire** air pocket; ~ **de papel** paper bag; ~ **de plástico** plastic (*o* carrier) bag; **"B~ de la propiedad"** "Property Mart"; ~ **de trabajo** employment bureau; **jugar a la** ~ to play the market.

bolsillo [bol'siʎo] *nm* pocket; (*cartera*) purse; **de** ~ pocket *cpd*; **meterse a uno en el** ~ to get sb eating out of one's hand.

bolsista [bol'sista] *nm/f* stockbroker.

bolso ['bolso] *nm* (*bolsa*) bag; (*de mujer*) handbag.

bollo ['boʎo] *nm* (*pan*) roll; (*dulce*) scone; (*bulto*) bump, lump; (*abolladura*) dent; ~**s** *nmpl* (*AM*) troubles.

bomba ['bomba] *nf* (*MIL*) bomb; (*TEC*) pump; (*AM*: *globo*) balloon; (: *borrachera*) drunkenness ♦ *a* (*fam*): **noticia** ~ bombshell ♦ *ad* (*fam*): **pasarlo** ~ to have a great time; ~ **atómica/de humo/de retardo** atomic/smoke/time bomb; ~ **de gasolina** petrol pump; ~ **de incendios** fire engine.

bombacho, a [bom'batʃo, a] *a* (*AM*) baggy.

bombardear [bombarðe'ar] *vt* to bombard; (*MIL*) to bomb.

bombardeo [bombar'ðeo] *nm* bombardment; bombing.

bombardero [bombar'ðero] *nm* bomber.

bombear [bombe'ar] *vt* (*agua*) to pump

(out *o* up); (*MIL*) to bomb; (*FÚTBOL*) to lob; ~**se** *vr* to warp.

bombero [bom'bero] *nm* fireman; (**cuerpo de**) ~**s** fire brigade.

bombilla [bom'biʎa] *nf* (*Esp*) (light) bulb.

bombín [bom'bin] *nm* bowler hat.

bombo ['bombo] *nm* (*MUS*) bass drum; (*TEC*) drum; (*fam*) exaggerated praise; **hacer algo a** ~ **y platillo** to make a great song and dance about sth; **tengo la cabeza hecha un** ~ I've got a splitting headache.

bombón [bom'bon] *nm* chocolate; (*belleza*) gem.

bombona [bom'bona] *nf*: ~ **de butano** gas cylinder.

bombonería [bombone'ria] *nf* sweetshop.

bonaerense [bonae'rense] *a o* from Buenos Aires ♦ *nm/f* native *o* inhabitant of Buenos Aires.

bonancible [bonan'θißle] *a* (*tiempo*) fair, calm.

bonanza [bo'nanθa] *nf* (*NAUT*) fair weather; (*fig*) bonanza; (*MINERÍA*) rich pocket *o* vein.

bondad [bon'dað] *nf* goodness, kindness; **tenga la** ~ **de** (please) be good enough to.

bondadoso, a [bonda'ðoso, a] *a* good, kind.

boniato [bo'njato] *nm* sweet potato, yam.

bonificación [bonifika'θjon] *nf* (*COM*) allowance, discount; (*pago*) bonus; (*DEPORTE*) extra points *pl*.

bonito, a [bo'nito, a] *a* (*lindo*) pretty; (*agradable*) nice ♦ *ad* (*AM fam*) well ♦ *nm* (*atún*) tuna (fish).

bono ['bono] *nm* voucher; (*FIN*) bond; ~ **de billetes de metro** booklet of metro tickets; ~ **del Tesoro** treasury bill.

bonobús [bono'ßus] *nm* (*Esp*) bus pass.

boquear [boke'ar] *vi* to gasp.

boquerón [boke'ron] *nm* (*pez*) (kind of) anchovy; (*agujero*) large hole.

boquete [bo'kete] *nm* gap, hole.

boquiabierto, a [bokia'ßjerto, a] *a* open-mouthed (in astonishment); **quedar** ~ to be left aghast.

boquilla [bo'kiʎa] *nf* (*para riego*) nozzle; (*para cigarro*) cigarette holder; (*MUS*) mouthpiece.

borbollar [borßo'ʎar], **borbollear** [borßoʎe'ar] *vi* to bubble.

borbollón [borßo'ʎon] *nm* bubbling; **hablar a borbollones** to gabble; **salir a borbollones** (*agua*) to gush out.

borbotar [borßo'tar] *vi* = **borbollar**.

borbotón [borßo'ton] *nm*: **salir a borbotones** to gush out.

borda ['borða] *nf* (*NAUT*) gunwale; **echar** *o* **tirar algo por la** ~ to throw sth overboard.

bordado [bor'ðaðo] *nm* embroidery.

bordar [bor'ðar] *vt* to embroider.

borde ['borðe] *nm* edge, border; (*de camino*

etc) side; (*en la costura*) hem; **al ~ de** (*fig*) on the verge *o* brink of; **ser ~** (*Esp fam*) to be a pain in the neck.

bordear [borðe'ar] *vt* to border.

bordillo [bor'ðiʎo] *nm* kerb (*Brit*), curb (*US*).

bordo ['borðo] *nm* (*NAUT*) side; **a ~ on** board.

Borgoña [bor'ɣoɲa] *nf* Burgundy.

borgoña [bor'ɣoɲa] *nm* burgundy.

borinqueño, a [borin'keɲo, a] *a, nm/f* Puerto Rican.

borla ['borla] *nf* (*gen*) tassel; (*de gorro*) pompon.

borra ['borra] *nf* (*pelusa*) fluff; (*sedimento*) sediment.

borrachera [borra'tʃera] *nf* (*ebriedad*) drunkenness; (*orgía*) spree, binge.

borracho, a [bo'rratʃo, a] *a* drunk ♦ *nm/f* (*que bebe mucho*) drunkard, drunk; (*temporalmente*) drunk, drunk man/woman ♦ *nm* (*CULIN*) cake soaked in liqueur or spirit.

borrador [borra'ðor] *nm* (*escritura*) first draft, rough sketch; (*cuaderno*) scribbling pad; (*goma*) rubber (*Brit*), eraser; (*COM*) daybook; (*para pizarra*) duster; **hacer un nuevo ~ de** (*COM*) to redraft.

borrajear [borraxe'ar] *vt, vi* to scribble.

borrar [bo'rrar] *vt* to erase, rub out; (*tachar*) to delete; (*cinta*) to wipe out; (*INFORM: archivo*) to delete, erase; (*POL etc: eliminar*) to deal with.

borrasca [bo'rraska] *nf* (*METEOROLOGÍA*) storm.

borrascoso, a [borras'koso, a] *a* stormy.

borrego, a [bo'rreɣo, a] *nm/f* lamb; (*oveja*) sheep; (*fig*) simpleton.

borricada [borri'kaða] *nf* foolish action/ statement.

borrico, a [bo'rriko, a] *nm* donkey; (*fig*) stupid man ♦ *nf* she-donkey; (*fig*) stupid woman.

borrón [bo'rron] *nm* (*mancha*) stain; **~ y cuenta nueva** let bygones be bygones.

borroso, a [bo'rroso, a] *a* vague, unclear; (*escritura*) illegible; (*escrito*) smudgy; (*foto*) blurred.

Bósforo ['bosforo] *nm*: **el (Estrecho del) ~** the Bosp(h)orus.

bosque ['boske] *nm* wood; (*grande*) forest.

bosquejar [boske'xar] *vt* to sketch.

bosquejo [bos'kexo] *nm* sketch.

bosta ['bosta] *nf* dung, manure.

bostece [bos'teθe] *etc vb V* **bostezar**.

bostezar [boste'θar] *vi* to yawn.

bostezo [bos'teθo] *nm* yawn.

bota ['bota] *nf* (*calzado*) boot; (*saco*) leather wine bottle; **ponerse las ~s** (*fam*) to strike it rich.

botadura [bota'ðura] *nf* launching.

botánico, a [bo'taniko, a] *a* botanical ♦ *nm/f* botanist ♦ *nf* botany.

botar [bo'tar] *vt* to throw, hurl; (*NAUT*) to launch; (*fam*) to throw out ♦ *vi* to bounce.

botarate [bota'rate] *nm* (*imbécil*) idiot.

bote ['bote] *nm* (*salto*) bounce; (*golpe*) thrust; (*vasija*) tin, can; (*embarcación*) boat; **de ~ en ~** packed, jammed full; **~ salvavidas** lifeboat; **dar un ~** to jump; **dar ~s** (*AUTO etc*) to bump; **~ de la basura** (*AM*) dustbin (*Brit*), trashcan (*US*).

botella [bo'teʎa] *nf* bottle; **~ de vino** (*contenido*) bottle of wine; (*recipiente*) wine bottle.

botellero [bote'ʎero] *nm* wine rack.

botica [bo'tika] *nf* chemist's (shop) (*Brit*), pharmacy.

boticario, a [boti'karjo, a] *nm/f* chemist (*Brit*), pharmacist.

botijo [bo'tixo] *nm* (earthenware) jug; (*tren*) excursion train.

botín [bo'tin] *nm* (*calzado*) half boot; (*polaina*) spat; (*MIL*) booty; (*de ladrón*) loot.

botiquín [boti'kin] *nm* (*armario*) medicine chest; (*portátil*) first-aid kit.

botón [bo'ton] *nm* button; (*BOT*) bud; (*de florete*) tip; **~ de arranque** (*AUTO etc*) starter; **~ de oro** buttercup; **pulsar el ~** to press the button.

botones [bo'tones] *nm inv* bellboy, bellhop (*US*).

botulismo [botu'lismo] *nm* botulism, food poisoning.

bóveda ['boβeða] *nf* (*ARQ*) vault.

bovino, a [bo'βino, a] *a* bovine; (*AGR*): **ganado ~** cattle.

boxeador [boksea'ðor] *nm* boxer.

boxear [bokse'ar] *vi* to box.

boxeo [bok'seo] *nm* boxing.

boya ['boja] *nf* (*NAUT*) buoy; (*flotador*) float.

boyante [bo'jante] *a* (*NAUT*) buoyant; (*feliz*) buoyant; (*próspero*) prosperous.

bozal [bo'θal] *nm* (*de caballo*) halter; (*de perro*) muzzle.

bozo ['boθo] *nm* (*pelusa*) fuzz; (*boca*) mouth.

bracear [braθe'ar] *vi* (*agitar los brazos*) to wave one's arms.

bracero [bra'θero] *nm* labourer; (*en el campo*) farmhand.

bracete [bra'θete]: **de ~** *ad* arm in arm.

braga ['braɣa] *nf* (*cuerda*) sling, rope; (*de bebé*) nappy, diaper (*US*); **~s** *nfpl* (*de mujer*) panties.

braguero [bra'ɣero] *nm* (*MED*) truss.

bragueta [bra'ɣeta] *nf* fly (*Brit*), flies *pl* (*Brit*), zipper (*US*).

braguetazo [braɣe'taθo] *nm* (*AM*) marriage of convenience.

braille [breil] *nm* braille.

bramante [bra'mante] *nm* twine, string.

bramar [bra'mar] *vi* to bellow, roar.
bramido [bra'miðo] *nm* bellow, roar.
branquias ['brankjas] *nfpl* gills.
brasa ['brasa] *nf* live o hot coal; **carne a la** ~ grilled meat.
brasero [bra'sero] *nm* brazier; (*AM*: *chimenea*) fireplace.
Brasil [bra'sil] *nm*: (**el**) ~ Brazil.
brasileño, a [brasi'leɲo, a] *a, nm/f* Brazilian.
brava ['braßa]: **a la** ~ *ad* by force.
bravata [bra'ßata] *nf* boast.
braveza [bra'ßeθa] *nf* (*valor*) bravery; (*ferocidad*) ferocity.
bravío, a [bra'ßio, a] *a* wild; (*feroz*) fierce.
bravo, a ['braßo, a] *a* (*valiente*) brave; (*bueno*) fine, splendid; (*feroz*) ferocious; (*salvaje*) wild; (*mar etc*) rough, stormy; (*CULIN*) hot, spicy ◆ *excl* bravo!
bravucón, ona [braßu'kon, ona] *a* swaggering ◆ *nm/f* braggart.
bravura [bra'ßura] *nf* bravery; ferocity; (*pey*) boast.
braza ['braθa] *nf* fathom; **nadar a la** ~ to swim (the) breast-stroke.
brazada [bra'θaða] *nf* stroke.
brazado [bra'θaðo] *nm* armful.
brazalete [braθa'lete] *nm* (*pulsera*) bracelet; (*banda*) armband.
brazo ['braθo] *nm* arm; (*ZOOL*) foreleg; (*BOT*) limb, branch; ~s *nmpl* (*braceros*) hands, workers; ~ **derecho** (*fig*) right-hand man; **a** ~ **partido** hand-to-hand; **cogidos** *etc* **del** ~ arm in arm; **no dar su** ~ **a torcer** not to give way easily; **huelga de** ~s **caídos** sit-down strike.
brea ['brea] *nf* pitch, tar.
brebaje [bre'ßaxe] *nm* potion.
brécol ['brekol] *nm* broccoli.
brecha ['bretʃa] *nf* breach; (*hoyo vacío*) gap, opening.
brega ['breɣa] *nf* (*lucha*) struggle; (*trabajo*) hard work.
bregar [bre'ɣar] *vi* (*luchar*) to struggle; (*trabajar mucho*) to slog away.
bregue ['breɣe] *etc vb V* **bregar**.
breña ['breɲa] *nf* rough ground.
Bretaña [bre'taɲa] *nf* Brittany.
brete ['brete] *nm* (*cepo*) shackles *pl*; (*fig*) predicament; **estar en un** ~ to be in a jam.
bretón, ona [bre'ton, ona] *a, nm/f* Breton.
breva ['breßa] *nf* (*BOT*) early fig; (*puro*) flat cigar; ¡**no caerá esa** ~! no such luck!
breve ['breße] *a* short, brief; **en** ~ (*pronto*) shortly; (*en pocas palabras*) in short ◆ *nf* (*MUS*) breve.
brevedad [breße'ðað] *nf* brevity, shortness.
breviario [bre'ßjarjo] *nm* (*REL*) breviary.
brezal [bre'θal] *nm* moor(land), heath.
brezo ['breθo] *nm* heather.

bribón, ona [bri'ßon, ona] *a* idle, lazy ◆ *nm/f* (*vagabundo*) vagabond; (*pícaro*) rascal, rogue.
bricolaje [briko'laxe] *nm* do-it-yourself, DIY.
brida ['briða] *nf* bridle, rein; (*TEC*) clamp; **a toda** ~ at top speed.
bridge [britʃ] *nm* (*NAIPES*) bridge.
brigada [bri'ɣaða] *nf* (*unidad*) brigade; (*trabajadores*) squad, gang ◆ *nm* warrant officer.
brigadier [briɣa'ðjer] *nm* brigadier(-general).
brigantino, a [briɣan'tino, a] *a* of o from Corunna ◆ *nm/f* native o inhabitant of Corunna.
brillante [bri'ʎante] *a* brilliant; (*color*) bright; (*joya*) sparkling ◆ *nm* diamond.
brillantez [briʎan'teθ] *nf* (*color etc*) brightness; (*fig*) brilliance.
brillar [bri'ʎar] *vi* (*tb fig*) to shine; (*joyas*) to sparkle; ~ **por su ausencia** to be conspicuous by one's absence.
brillo ['briʎo] *nm* shine; (*brillantez*) brilliance; (*fig*) splendour; **sacar** ~ **a** to polish.
brincar [brin'kar] *vi* to skip about, hop about, jump about; **está que brinca** he's hopping mad.
brinco ['brinko] *nm* jump, leap; **a** ~s by fits and starts; **de un** ~ at one bound.
brindar [brin'dar] *vi*: ~ **a** o **por** to drink (a toast) to ◆ *vt* to offer, present; **le brinda la ocasión de** it offers o affords him the opportunity to; ~**se** *vr*: ~**se a hacer algo** to offer to do sth.
brindis ['brindis] *nm inv* toast; (*TAUR*) (ceremony of) dedication.
brinque ['brinke] *etc vb V* **brincar**.
brío ['brio] *nm* spirit, dash.
brioso, a [bri'oso, a] *a* spirited, dashing.
brisa ['brisa] *nf* breeze.
británico, a [bri'taniko, a] *a* British ◆ *nm/f* Briton, British person; **los** ~s the British.
brizna ['briθna] *nf* (*hebra*) strand, thread; (*de hierba*) blade; (*trozo*) piece; (*AM*) drizzle.
broca ['broka] *nf* (*COSTURA*) bobbin; (*TEC*) drill bit; (*clavo*) tack.
brocado [bro'kaðo] *nm* brocade.
brocal [bro'kal] *nm* rim.
brocha ['brotʃa] *nf* (*large*) paintbrush; ~ **de afeitar** shaving brush; **pintor de** ~ **gorda** painter and decorator; (*fig*) poor painter.
brochazo [bro'tʃaθo] *nm* brush-stroke; **a grandes** ~s (*fig*) in general terms.
broche ['brotʃe] *nm* brooch.
broma ['broma] *nf* joke; (*inocentada*) practical joke; **en** ~ in fun, as a joke; **gastar una** ~ **a uno** to play a joke on sb;

tomar algo a ~ to take sth as a joke.
bromear [brome'ar] *vi* to joke.
bromista [bro'mista] *a* fond of joking ◆ *nm/f* joker, wag.
bromuro [bro'muro] *nm* bromide.
bronca ['broŋka] *nf* row; (*regañada*) ticking-off; **armar una** ~ to kick up a fuss; **echar una** ~ **a uno** to tell sb off.
bronce ['bronθe] *nm* bronze; (*latón*) brass.
bronceado, a [bronθe'aðo, a] *a* bronze *cpd*; (*por el sol*) tanned ◆ *nm* (sun)tan; (*TEC*) bronzing.
bronceador [bronθea'ðor] *nm* suntan lotion.
broncearse [bronθe'arse] *vr* to get a suntan.
bronco, a ['bronko, a] *a* (*manera*) rude, surly; (*voz*) harsh.
bronquios ['bronkjos] *nmpl* bronchial tubes.
bronquitis [bron'kitis] *nf inv* bronchitis.
brotar [bro'tar] *vt* (*tierra*) to produce ◆ *vi* (*BOT*) to sprout; (*aguas*) to gush (forth); (*lágrimas*) to well up; (*MED*) to break out.
brote ['brote] *nm* (*BOT*) shoot; (*MED*, *fig*) outbreak.
broza ['broθa] *nf* (*BOT*) dead leaves *pl*; (*fig*) rubbish.
bruces ['bruθes]: **de** ~ *ad*: **caer** *o* **dar de** ~ to fall headlong, fall flat.
bruja ['bruxa] *nf* witch.
Brujas ['bruxas] *nf* Bruges.
brujería [bruxe'ria] *nf* witchcraft.
brujo ['bruxo] *nm* wizard, magician.
brújula ['bruxula] *nf* compass.
bruma ['bruma] *nf* mist.
brumoso, a [bru'moso, a] *a* misty.
bruñendo [bru'ɲendo] *etc vb* V **bruñir**.
bruñido [bru'ɲiðo] *nm* polish.
bruñir [bru'ɲir] *vt* to polish.
brusco, a ['brusko, a] *a* (*súbito*) sudden; (*áspero*) brusque.
Bruselas [bru'selas] *nf* Brussels.
brusquedad [bruske'ðað] *nf* suddenness; brusqueness.
brutal [bru'tal] *a* brutal.
brutalidad [brutali'ðað] *nf* brutality.
bruto, a ['bruto, a] *a* (*idiota*) stupid; (*bestial*) brutish; (*peso*) gross ◆ *nm* brute; **a la bruta, a lo** ~ roughly; **en** ~ raw, unworked.
Bs.As. *abr* = **Buenos Aires**.
buba ['bußa] *nf* tumour.
bucal [bu'kal] *a* oral; **por vía** ~ orally.
bucanero [buka'nero] *nm* buccaneer.
bucear [buθe'ar] *vi* to dive ◆ *vt* to explore.
buceo [bu'θeo] *nm* diving; (*fig*) investigation.
bucle ['bukle] *nm* curl; (*INFORM*) loop.
buche ['butʃe] *nm* (*de ave*) crop; (*ZOOL*) maw; (*fam*) belly.
budín [bu'ðin] *nm* pudding.

budismo [bu'ðismo] *nm* Buddhism.
buen [bwen] *a* V **bueno**.
buenamente [bwena'mente] *ad* (*fácilmente*) easily; (*voluntariamente*) willingly.
buenaventura [bwenaßen'tura] *nf* (*suerte*) good luck; (*adivinación*) fortune; **decir** *o* **echar la** ~ **a uno** to tell sb's fortune.
bueno, a ['bweno, a], **buen** [bwen] *a* (*amable*) kind; (*MED*) well; **¡buenas!** 'afternoon! (*fam*); **¡buen día!**, **¡buenos días!** good morning!; good afternoon!; hello!; **¡buenas tardes!** good afternoon!; good evening!; **¡buenas noches!** good night!; **los buenos** (*CINE*) the goodies; **¡buen sinvergüenza resultó!** a fine rascal he turned out to be; **el bueno de Manolo** good old Manolo; **fue muy bueno conmigo** he was very good to me; **de buenas a primeras** all of a sudden; **por las buenas o por las malas** by hook or by crook ◆ *excl* right!, all right!; **bueno, ¿y qué?** well, so what?
Buenos Aires [bweno'saires] *nm* Buenos Aires.
buey [bwei] *nm* ox.
búfalo ['bufalo] *nm* buffalo.
bufanda [bu'fanda] *nf* scarf.
bufar [bu'far] *vi* to snort.
bufete [bu'fete] *nm* (*despacho de abogado*) lawyer's office; **establecer su** ~ to set up in legal practice.
buffer ['bufer] *nm* (*INFORM*) buffer.
bufón [bu'fon] *nm* clown.
bufonada [bufo'naða] *nf* (*dicho*) jest; (*hecho*) piece of buffoonery; (*TEATRO*) farce.
buhardilla [buar'ðiʎa] *nf* attic.
búho ['buo] *nm* owl; (*fig*) hermit, recluse.
buhonero [buo'nero] *nm* pedlar.
buitre ['bwitre] *nm* vulture.
bujía [bu'xia] *nf* (*vela*) candle; (*ELEC*) candle (power); (*AUTO*) spark plug.
bula ['bula] *nf* (*papal*) bull.
bulbo ['bulßo] *nm* (*BOT*) bulb.
bulevar [bule'ßar] *nm* boulevard.
Bulgaria [bul'xarja] *nf* Bulgaria.
búlgaro, a ['bulxaro, a] *a*, *nm/f* Bulgarian.
bulo ['bulo] *nm* false rumour.
bulto ['bulto] *nm* (*paquete*) package; (*fardo*) bundle; (*tamaño*) size, bulkiness; (*MED*) swelling, lump; (*silueta*) vague shape; (*estatua*) bust, statue; **hacer** ~ to take up space; **escurrir el** ~ to make o.s. scarce; (*fig*) to dodge the issue.
bulla ['buʎa] *nf* (*ruido*) uproar; (*de gente*) crowd; **armar** *o* **meter** ~ to kick up a row.
bullendo [bu'ʎendo] *etc vb* V **bullir**.
bullicio [bu'ʎiθjo] *nm* (*ruido*) uproar; (*movimiento*) bustle.
bullicioso, a [buʎi'θjoso, a] *a* (*ruidoso*)

noisy, (*calle etc*) busy; (*situación*) turbulent.

bullir [bu'ʎir] *vi* (*hervir*) to boil; (*burbujear*) to bubble; (*mover*) to move, stir; (*insectos*) to swarm; ~ **de** (*fig*) to teem o seethe with.

buñuelo [bu'ɲwelo] *nm* ≈ doughnut, donut (*US*).

BUP [bup] *nm abr* (*Esp* ESCOL:= *Bachillerato Unificado y Polivalente*) *secondary education and leaving certificate for 14-17 age group.*

buque ['buke] *nm* ship, vessel; ~ **de guerra** warship; ~ **mercante** merchant ship; ~ **de vela** sailing ship.

burbuja [bur'ßuxa] *nf* bubble; **hacer** ~**s** to bubble; (*gaseosa*) to fizz.

burbujear [burßuxe'ar] *vi* to bubble.

burdel [bur'ðel] *nm* brothel.

Burdeos [bur'ðeos] *nm* Bordeaux.

burdo, a ['burðo, a] *a* coarse, rough.

burgalés, esa [burɣa'les, esa] *a* of o from Burgos ♦ *nm/f* native o inhabitant of Burgos.

burgués, esa [bur'ɣes, esa] *a* middle-class, bourgeois; **pequeño** ~ lower middle-class; (*POL, pey*) petty bourgeois.

burguesía [burɣe'sia] *nf* middle class, bourgeoisie.

burla ['burla] *nf* (*mofa*) gibe; (*broma*) joke; (*engaño*) trick; **hacer** ~ **de** to make fun of.

burladero [burla'ðero] *nm* (bullfighter's) refuge.

burlador, a [burla'ðor, a] *a* mocking ♦ *nm/f* mocker; (*bromista*) joker ♦ *nm* (*libertino*) seducer.

burlar [bur'lar] *vt* (*engañar*) to deceive; (*seducir*) to seduce ♦ *vi*, ~**se** *vr* to joke; ~**se de** to make fun of.

burlesco, a [bur'lesko, a] *a* burlesque.

burlón, ona [bur'lon, ona] *a* mocking.

buró [bu'ro] *nm* bureau.

burocracia [buro'kraθja] *nf* bureaucracy.

burócrata [bu'rokrata] *nm/f* bureaucrat.

buromática [buro'matika] *nf* office automation.

burrada [bu'rraða] *nf* stupid act; **decir** ~**s** to talk nonsense.

burro, a ['burro, a] *nm/f* (*ZOOL*) donkey; (*fig*) ass, idiot ♦ *a* stupid; **caerse del** ~ to realise one's mistake; **no ver tres en un** ~ to be as blind as a bat.

bursátil [bur'satil] *a* stock-exchange *cpd*.

bus [bus] *nm* bus.

busca ['buska] *nf* search, hunt; **en** ~ **de** in search of.

buscador, a [buska'ðor, a] *nm/f* searcher.

buscapiés [buska'pjes] *nm inv* jumping jack (*Brit*), firecracker (*US*).

buscapleitos [buska'pleitos] *nm/f inv* troublemaker.

buscar [bus'kar] *vt* to look for; (*objeto perdido*) to have a look for; (*beneficio*) to seek; (*enemigo*) to seek out; (*traer*) to bring, fetch; (*provocar*) to provoke; (*INFORM*) to search ♦ *vi* to look, search, seek; **ven a** ~**me a la oficina** come and pick me up at the office; ~**le 3 o 4 pies al gato** to split hairs; "~ **y reemplazar**" (*INFORM*) "search and replace"; **se busca secretaria** secretary wanted; **se la buscó** he asked for it.

buscavidas [buska'ßiðas] *nm/f inv* snooper; (*persona ambiciosa*) go-getter.

buscón, ona [bus'kon, ona] *a* thieving ♦ *nm* petty thief ♦ *nf* whore.

busilis [bu'silis] *nm inv* (*fam*) snag.

busque ['buske] *etc vb V* buscar.

búsqueda ['buskeða] *nf* = busca.

busto ['busto] *nm* (*ANAT, ARTE*) bust.

butaca [bu'taka] *nf* armchair; (*de cine, teatro*) stall, seat.

butano [bu'tano] *nm* butane (gas); **bombona de** ~ gas cylinder.

butifarra [buti'farra] *nf* Catalan sausage.

buzo ['buθo] *nm* diver.

buzón [bu'θon] *nm* (*gen*) letter box; (*en la calle*) pillar box; (*TELEC*) mailbox; **echar al** ~ to post.

byte [bait] *nm* (*INFORM*) byte.

C

C, c [θe, se (*esp AM*)] *nf* (*letra*) C, c; **C de Carmen** C for Charlie.

c. *abr* (= *capítulo*) ch.

C. *abr* (= *centígrado*) C.; (= *compañía*) Co.

c/ *abr* (*COM*: = *cuenta*) a/c.

C/ *abr* (= *calle*) St, Rd.

c.a. *abr* (= *corriente alterna*) A.C.

ca [ka] *excl* not a bit of it!

cabal [ka'ßal] *a* (*exacto*) exact; (*correcto*) right, proper; (*acabado*) finished, complete; ~**es** *nmpl*: **estar en sus** ~**es** to be in one's right mind.

cábala [ka'ßala] *nf* (*REL*) cab(b)ala; (*fig*) cabal, intrigue; ~**s** *nfpl* guess *sg*, supposition *sg*.

cabalgadura [kaßalɣa'ðura] *nf* mount, horse.

cabalgar [kaßal'ɣar] *vt, vi* to ride.

cabalgata [kaßal'ɣata] *nf* procession.

cabalgue [ka'ßalɣe] *etc vb V* cabalgar.

cabalístico, a [kaßa'listiko, a] *a* (*fig*) mysterious.

caballa [ka'βaʎa] *nf* mackerel.
caballeresco, a [kaβaʎe'resko, a] *a* noble, chivalrous.
caballería [kaβaʎe'ria] *nf* mount; (*MIL*) cavalry.
caballeriza [kaβaʎe'riθa] *nf* stable.
caballerizo [kaβaʎe'riθo] *nm* groom, stableman.
caballero [kaβa'ʎero] *nm* gentleman; (*de la orden de caballería*) knight; (*trato directo*) sir; "**C~s**" "Gents".
caballerosidad [kaβaʎerosi'ðað] *nf* chivalry.
caballete [kaβa'ʎete] *nm* (*AGR*) ridge; (*ARTE*) easel.
caballito [kaβa'ʎito] *nm* (*caballo pequeño*) small horse, pony; (*juguete*) rocking horse; **~s** *nmpl* merry-go-round *sg*; **~ de mar** seahorse; **~ del diablo** dragonfly.
caballo [ka'βaʎo] *nm* horse; (*AJEDREZ*) knight; (*NAIPES*) queen; **~ de vapor** *o* **de fuerza** horsepower; **es su ~ de batalla** it's his hobby-horse; **~ blanco** (*COM*) backer.
cabaña [ka'βaɲa] *nf* (*casita*) hut, cabin.
cabaré, cabaret, *pl* **cabarets** [kaβa're, kaβa'res] *nm* cabaret.
cabecear [kaβeθe'ar] *vi* to nod.
cabecera [kaβe'θera] *nf* (*gen*) head; (*de distrito*) chief town; (*de cama*) headboard; (*IMPRENTA*) headline.
cabecilla [kaβe'θiʎa] *nm* ringleader.
cabellera [kaβe'ʎera] *nf* (head of) hair; (*de cometa*) tail.
cabello [ka'βeʎo] *nm* (*tb:* **~s**) hair *sg*.
caber [ka'βer] *vi* (*entrar*) to fit, go; **caben 3 más** there's room for 3 more; **cabe preguntar si...** one might ask whether...; **cabe que venga más tarde** he may come later.
cabestrillo [kaβes'triʎo] *nm* sling.
cabestro [ka'βestro] *nm* halter.
cabeza [ka'βeθa] *nf* head; (*POL*) chief, leader; **caer de ~** to fall head first; **sentar la ~** to settle down; **~ de lectura/escritura** read/write head; **~ impresora** *o* **de impresión** printhead.
cabezada [kaβe'θaða] *nf* (*golpe*) butt; **dar una ~** to nod off.
cabezal [kaβe'θal] *nm*: **~ impresor** print head.
cabezón, ona [kaβe'θon, ona] *a* with a big head; (*vino*) heady; (*obstinado*) obstinate, stubborn.
cabezota [kaβe'θota] *a inv* obstinate, stubborn.
cabezudo, a [kaβe'θuðo, a] *a* with a big head; (*obstinado*) obstinate, stubborn.
cabida [ka'βiða] *nf* space; **dar ~ a** to make room for; **tener ~ para** to have room for.
cabildo [ka'βildo] *nm* (*de iglesia*) chapter; (*POL*) town council.

cabina [ka'βina] *nf* (*de camión*) cabin; **~ telefónica** (tele)phone box (*Brit*) *o* booth.
cabizbajo, a [kaβiθ'βaxo, a] *a* crestfallen, dejected.
cable ['kaβle] *nm* cable; (*de aparato*) lead; **~ aéreo** (*ELEC*) overhead cable; **conectar con ~** (*INFORM*) to hardwire.
cabo ['kaβo] *nm* (*de objeto*) end, extremity; (*MIL*) corporal; (*NAUT*) rope, cable; (*GEO*) cape; (*TEC*) thread; **al ~ de 3 días** after 3 days; **de ~ a rabo** *o* **~** from beginning to end; (*libro: leer*) from cover to cover; **llevar a ~** to carry out; **atar ~s** to tie up the loose ends; (*GEO*): **C~ de Buena Esperanza** Cape of Good Hope; **C~ de Hornos** Cape Horn; **las Islas de C~ Verde** the Cape Verde Islands.
cabra ['kaβra] *nf* goat; **estar como una ~** (*fam*) to be nuts.
cabré [ka'βre] *etc vb V* **caber.**
cabrear [kaβre'ar] *vt* to annoy; **~se** *vr* to fly off the handle.
cabrío [ka'βrio, a] *a* goatish; **macho ~** (he-)goat, billy goat.
cabriola [ka'βrjola] *nf* caper.
cabritilla [kaβri'tiʎa] *nf* kid, kidskin.
cabrito [ka'βrito] *nm* kid.
cabrón [ka'βron] *nm* (*fig: fam!*) bastard (!).
caca ['kaka] *nf* (*palabra de niños*) pooh ◆ *excl:* **no toques, ¡~!** don't touch, it's dirty!
cacahuete [kaka'wete] *nm* (*Esp*) peanut.
cacao [ka'kao] *nm* cocoa; (*BOT*) cacao.
cacarear [kakare'ar] *vi* (*persona*) to boast; (*gallina*) to cackle.
cacatúa [kaka'tua] *nf* cockatoo.
cacereño, a [kaθe'reɲo, a] *a* of *o* from Cáceres ◆ *nm/f* native *o* inhabitant of Cáceres.
cacería [kaθe'ria] *nf* hunt.
cacerola [kaθe'rola] *nf* pan, saucepan.
cacique [ka'θike] *nm* chief, local ruler; (*POL*) local party boss; (*fig*) despot.
caciquismo [kaθi'kismo] *nm* system of dominance by the local boss.
caco ['kako] *nm* pickpocket.
cacofonía [kakofo'nia] *nf* cacophony.
cacto ['kakto] *nm*, **cactus** ['kaktus] *nm inv* cactus.
cacha ['katʃa] *nf* (*mango*) handle; (*nalga*) buttock.
cacharro [ka'tʃarro] *nm* (*vasija*) (earthenware) pot; (*cerámica*) piece of pottery; (*AM fam*) useless object; **~s** *nmpl* pots and pans.
cachear [katʃe'ar] *vt* to search, frisk.
cachemir [katʃe'mir] *nm* cashmere.
cacheo [ka'tʃeo] *nm* searching, frisking.
cachete [ka'tʃete] *nm* (*ANAT*) cheek; (*bofetada*) slap (in the face).
cachimba [ka'tʃimba] *nf* pipe.

cachiporra [katʃi'porra] *nf* truncheon.
cachivache [katʃi'ßatʃe] *nm* piece of junk; ~**s** *nmpl* trash *sg*, junk *sg*.
cacho, a ['katʃo, a] *nm* (small) bit; (*AM*: *cuerno*) horn.
cachondearse [katʃonde'arse] *vr*: ~ **de uno** to tease sb.
cachondeo [katʃon'deo] *nm* (*fam*) farce, joke; (*guasa*) laugh.
cachondo, a [ka'tʃondo, a] *a* (*ZOOL*) on heat; (*persona*) randy, sexy; (*gracioso*) funny.
cachorro, a [ka'tʃorro, a] *nm/f* (*perro*) pup, puppy; (*león*) cub.
cada ['kaða] *a inv* each; (*antes de número*) every; ~ **día** each day, every day; ~ **dos días** every other day; ~ **uno/a** each one, every one; ~ **vez más** more and more; ~ **uno de** ~ **diez** one out of every ten; ¿~ cuánto? how often?
cadalso [ka'ðalso] *nm* scaffold.
cadáver [ka'ðaßer] *nm* (dead) body, corpse.
cadavérico, a [kaða'ßeriko, a] *a* cadaverous; (*pálido*) deathly pale.
cadena [ka'ðena] *nf* chain; (*TV*) channel; **reacción en** ~ chain reaction; **trabajo en** ~ assembly line work; ~ **perpetua** (*JUR*) life imprisonment; ~ **de caracteres** (*INFORM*) character string.
cadencia [ka'ðenθja] *nf* cadence, rhythm.
cadera [ka'ðera] *nf* hip.
cadete [ka'ðete] *nm* cadet.
Cádiz ['kaðiθ] *nm* Cadiz.
caducar [kaðu'kar] *vi* to expire.
caducidad [kaðuθi'ðað] *nf*: **fecha de** ~ expiry date; (*de comida*) sell-by date.
caduco, a [ka'ðuko, a] *a* (*idea etc*) outdated, outmoded; **de hoja caduca** deciduous.
caduque [ka'ðuke] *etc vb V* **caducar**.
C.A.E. *abr* (= *cóbrese al entregar*) COD.
caer [ka'er] *vi*, ~**se** *vr* to fall (down); (*noche, fecha*) to fall; (*pago*) to fall due; (*AM*) to drop in; **dejar** ~ to drop; **estar por** ~ to be due to happen; **me cae bien/mal** I get on well with him/I can't stand him; ~ **en la cuenta** to catch on; **su cumpleaños cae en viernes** her birthday falls on a Friday.
café, pl cafés [ka'fe, ka'fes] *nm* (*bebida, planta*) coffee; (*lugar*) café ♦ *a* (*color*) brown; ~ **con leche** white coffee; ~ **solo, ~ negro** (*AM*) (small) black coffee.
cafeína [kafe'ina] *nf* caffein(e).
cafetal [kafe'tal] *nm* coffee plantation.
cafetera [kafe'tera] *nf V* **cafetero**.
cafetería [kafete'ria] *nf* cafe.
cafetero, a [kafe'tero, a] *a* coffee *cpd* ♦ *nf* coffee pot; **ser muy** ~ to be a coffee addict.
cafre ['kafre] *nm/f*: **como** ~**s** (*fig*) like savages.

cagar [ka'ɣar] (*fam!*) *vt* to shit (*!*); (*fig*) to bungle, mess up ♦ *vi* to have a shit (*!*); ~**se** *vr*: ¡**me cago en diez** (*etc*)! Christ! (*!*).
cague ['kaɣe] *etc vb V* **cagar**.
caído, a [ka'iðo, a] *a* fallen; (*INFORM*) down ♦ *nf* fall; (*declive*) slope; (*disminución*) fall, drop; ~ **del cielo** out of the blue; **a la caída del sol** at sunset; **sufrir una caída** to have a fall.
caiga ['kaiɣa] *etc vb V* **caer**.
caimán [kai'man] *nm* alligator.
Cairo ['kairo] *nm*: **el** ~ Cairo.
caja ['kaxa] *nf* box; (*ataúd*) coffin, casket (*US*); (*para reloj*) case; (*de ascensor*) shaft; (*COM*) cashbox; (*ECON*) fund; (*donde se hacen los pagos*) cashdesk; (*en supermercado*) checkout, till; (*TIP*) case; ~ **de ahorros** savings bank; ~ **de cambios** gearbox; ~ **fuerte, ~ de caudales** safe, strongbox; **ingresar en** ~ to be paid in.
cajero, a [ka'xero, a] *nm/f* cashier; (*en banco*) (bank) teller ♦ *nm*: ~ **automático** cash dispenser, automatic telling machine, A.T.M.
cajetilla [kaxe'tiʎa] *nf* (*de cigarrillos*) packet.
cajista [ka'xista] *nm/f* typesetter.
cajón [ka'xon] *nm* big box; (*de mueble*) drawer.
cal [kal] *nf* lime; **cerrar algo a** ~ **y canto** to shut sth firmly.
cala ['kala] *nf* (*GEO*) cove, inlet; (*de barco*) hold.
calabacín [kalaßa'θin] *nm*, **calabacita** [kalaßa'θita] *nf* (*AM*) (*BOT*) baby marrow, courgette, zucchini (*US*).
calabaza [kala'ßaθa] *nf* (*BOT*) pumpkin; **dar** ~**s a** (*candidato*) to fail.
calabozo [kala'ßoθo] *nm* (*cárcel*) prison; (*celda*) cell.
calado, a [ka'laðo, a] *a* (*prenda*) lace *cpd* ♦ *nm* (*TEC*) fretwork; (*NAUT*) draught ♦ *nf* (*de cigarrillo*) puff; **estar** ~ (**hasta los huesos**) to be soaked (to the skin).
calamar [kala'mar] *nm* squid.
calambre [ka'lambre] *nm* (*tb*: ~**s**) cramp.
calamidad [kalami'ðað] *nf* calamity, disaster; (*persona*): **es una** ~ he's a dead loss.
calamina [kala'mina] *nf* calamine.
cálamo ['kalamo] *nm* (*BOT*) stem; (*MUS*) reed.
calaña [ka'laɲa] *nf* model, pattern; (*fig*) nature, stamp.
calar [ka'lar] *vt* to soak, drench; (*penetrar*) to pierce, penetrate; (*comprender*) to see through; (*vela, red*) to lower; ~**se** *vr* (*AUTO*) to stall; ~**se las gafas** to stick one's glasses on.

calavera [kala'ßera] *nf* skull.
calcañal [kalka'ɲal], **calcañar** [kalka'ɲar], **calcaño** [kal'kaɲo] *nm* heel.
calcar [kal'kar] *vt* (*reproducir*) to trace; (*imitar*) to copy.
calce ['kalθe] *etc vb V* **calzar**.
calceta [kal'θeta] *nf* (knee-length) stocking; **hacer** ~ to knit.
calcetín [kalθe'tin] *nm* sock.
calcinar [kalθi'nar] *vt* to burn, blacken.
calcio ['kalθjo] *nm* calcium.
calco ['kalko] *nm* tracing.
calcomanía [kalkoma'nia] *nf* transfer.
calculadora [kalkula'ðora] *nf* calculator.
calcular [kalku'lar] *vt* (*MAT*) to calculate, compute; ~ **que** ... to reckon that ....
cálculo ['kalkulo] *nm* calculation; (*MED*) (gall)stone; (*MAT*) calculus; ~ **de costo** costing; ~ **diferencial** differential calculus; **obrar con mucho** ~ to act cautiously.
caldear [kalde'ar] *vt* to warm (up), heat (up); (*metales*) to weld.
caldera [kal'dera] *nf* boiler.
calderero [kalde'rero] *nm* boilermaker.
calderilla [kalde'riʎa] *nf* (*moneda*) small change.
caldero [kal'dero] *nm* small boiler.
caldo ['kaldo] *nm* stock; (*consomé*) consommé; ~ **de cultivo** (*BIO*) culture medium; **poner a** ~ **a uno** to tear sb off a strip; **los** ~**s jerezanos** sherries.
calé [ka'le] *a* gipsy *cpd*.
calefacción [kalefak'θjon] *nf* heating; ~ **central** central heating.
calendario [kalen'darjo] *nm* calendar.
calentador [kalenta'ðor] *nm* heater.
calentar [kalen'tar] *vt* to heat (up); (*fam*: *excitar*) to turn on; (*AM*: *enfurecer*) to anger; ~**se** *vr* to heat up, warm up; (*fig*: *discusión etc*) to get heated.
calentura [kalen'tura] *nf* (*MED*) fever, (high) temperature; (*de boca*) mouth sore.
calero, a [ka'lero, a] *a* lime *cpd*.
calibrar [kali'ßrar] *vt* to gauge, measure.
calibre [ka'lißre] *nm* (*de cañón*) calibre, bore; (*diámetro*) diameter; (*fig*) calibre.
calidad [kali'ðað] *nf* quality; **de** ~ quality *cpd*; ~ **de borrador** (*INFORM*) draft quality; ~ **de carta** *o* **de correspondencia** (*INFORM*) letter quality; ~ **texto** (*INFORM*) text quality; **en** ~ **de** in the capacity of.
cálido, a [ka'liðo, a] *a* hot; (*fig*) warm.
caliente [ka'ljente] *etc vb V* **calentar** ♦ *a* hot; (*fig*) fiery; (*disputa*) heated; (*fam*: *cachondo*) randy.
calificación [kalifika'θjon] *nf* qualification; (*de alumno*) grade, mark; ~ **de sobresaliente** first-class mark.
calificar [kalifi'kar] *vt* to qualify; (*alumno*) to grade, mark; ~ **de** to describe as.
calificativo, a [kalifika'tißo] *a* qualifying ♦

nm qualifier, epithet.
califique [kali'fike] *etc vb V* **calificar**.
californiano, a [kalifor'njano, a] *a*, *nm/f* Californian.
calina [ka'lina] *nf* haze.
cáliz ['kaliθ] *nm* (*BOT*) calyx; (*REL*) chalice.
calma ['kalma] *nf* calm; (*pachorra*) slowness; (*COM, ECON*) calm, lull; ~ **chicha** dead calm; ¡~!, ¡**con** ~! take it easy!
calmante [kal'mante] *a* soothing ♦ *nm* sedative, tranquillizer.
calmar [kal'mar] *vt* to calm, calm down; (*dolor*) to relieve ♦ *vi*, ~**se** *vr* (*tempestad*) to abate; (*mente etc*) to become calm.
calmoso, a [kal'moso, a] *a* calm, quiet.
caló [ka'lo] *nm* (*de gitanos*) gipsy language, Romany; (*argot*) slang.
calor [ka'lor] *nm* heat; (~ *agradable*) warmth; **entrar en** ~ to get warm; **tener** ~ to be *o* feel hot.
caloría [kalo'ria] *nf* calorie.
calorífero, a [kalo'rifero, a] *a* heat-producing, heat-giving ♦ *nm* heating system.
calque ['kalke] *etc vb V* **calcar**.
calumnia [ka'lumnja] *nf* slander; (*por escrito*) libel.
calumniar [kalum'njar] *vt* to slander; to libel.
calumnioso, a [kalum'njoso, a] *a* slanderous; libellous.
caluroso, a [kalu'roso, a] *a* hot; (*sin exceso*) warm; (*fig*) enthusiastic.
calva ['kalßa] *nf* bald patch; (*en bosque*) clearing.
calvario [kal'ßarjo] *nm* stations *pl* of the cross; (*fig*) cross, heavy burden.
calvicie [kal'ßiθje] *nf* baldness.
calvo, a ['kalßo, a] *a* bald; (*terreno*) bare, barren; (*tejido*) threadbare ♦ *nm* bald man.
calza ['kalθa] *nf* wedge, chock.
calzado, a [kal'θaðo, a] *a* shod ♦ *nm* footwear ♦ *nf* roadway, highway.
calzador [kalθa'ðor] *nm* shoehorn.
calzar [kal'θar] *vt* (*zapatos etc*) to wear; (*un mueble*) to put a wedge under; (*TEC*: *rueda etc*) to scotch; ~**se** *vr*: ~**se los zapatos** to put on one's shoes; **¿qué (número) calza?** what size do you take?
calzón [kal'θon] *nm* (*tb*: **calzones**) shorts *pl*; (*AM*: *de hombre*) pants; (: *de mujer*) panties.
calzonazos [kalθo'naθos] *nm inv* henpecked husband.
calzoncillos [kalθon'θiʎos] *nmpl* underpants.
callado, a [ka'ʎaðo, a] *a* quiet, silent.
callar [ka'ʎar] *vt* (*asunto delicado*) to keep quiet about, say nothing about; (*omitir*) to pass over in silence; (*persona, oposición*) to

silence ◆ *vi*, **~se** *vr* to keep quiet, be silent; (*dejar de hablar*) to stop talking; **¡calla!**, be quiet!; **¡cállate!**, **¡cállese!** shut up!; **¡cállate la boca!** shut your mouth!

calle ['kaʎe] *nf* street; (*DEPORTE*) lane; ~ **arriba/abajo** up/down the street; ~ **de sentido único** one-way street; **poner a uno (de patitas) en la** ~ to kick sb out.

calleja [ka'ʎexa] *nf* alley, narrow street.

callejear [kaʎexe'ar] *vi* to wander (about) the streets.

callejero, a [kaʎe'xero, a] *a* street *cpd* ◆ *nm* street map.

callejón [kaʎe'xon] *nm* alley, passage; (*GEO*) narrow pass; ~ **sin salida** cul-de-sac; (*fig*) blind alley.

callejuela [kaʎe'xwela] *nf* side-street, alley.

callista [ka'ʎista] *nm/f* chiropodist.

callo ['kaʎo] *nm* callus; (*en el pie*) corn; **~s** *nmpl* (*CULIN*) tripe *sg*.

calloso, a [ka'ʎoso, a] *a* horny, rough.

cama ['kama] *nf* bed; (*GEO*) stratum; ~ **individual/de matrimonio** single/double bed; **guardar** ~ to be ill in bed.

camada [ka'maða] *nf* litter; (*de personas*) gang, band.

camafeo [kama'feo] *nm* cameo.

cámara ['kamara] *nf* (*POL etc*) chamber; (*habitación*) room; (*sala*) hall; (*CINE*) cine camera; (*fotográfica*) camera; ~ **de aire** inner tube; ~ **alta/baja** upper/lower house; ~ **de comercio** chamber of commerce; ~ **de gas** gas chamber; **a** ~ **lenta** in slow motion.

camarada [kama'raða] *nm* comrade, companion.

camaradería [kamaraðe'ria] *nf* comradeship.

camarero, a [kama'rero, a] *nm* waiter ◆ *nf* (*en restaurante*) waitress; (*en casa, hotel*) maid.

camarilla [kama'riʎa] *nf* (*clan*) clique; (*POL*) lobby.

camarín [kama'rin] *nm* (*TEATRO*) dressing room.

camarón [kama'ron] *nm* shrimp.

camarote [kama'rote] *nm* (*NAUT*) cabin.

cambiable [kam'bjaßle] *a* (*variable*) changeable, variable; (*intercambiable*) interchangeable.

cambiante [kam'bjante] *a* variable.

cambiar [kam'bjar] *vt* to change; (*trocar*) to exchange ◆ *vi* to change; **~se** *vr* (*mudarse*) to move; (*de ropa*) to change; **~(se) de ...** to change one's ...; ~ **de idea/de ropa** to change one's mind/clothes.

cambiazo [kam'bjaθo] *nm*: **dar el** ~ **a uno** to swindle sb.

cambio ['kambjo] *nm* change; (*trueque*) exchange; (*COM*) rate of exchange; (*oficina*) bureau of change; (*dinero menudo*) small change; **en** ~ on the other hand; (*en lugar de eso*) instead; ~ **de divisas** (*COM*) foreign exchange; ~ **de línea** (*INFORM*) line feed; ~ **de página** (*INFORM*) form feed; ~ **a término** (*COM*) forward exchange; ~ **de velocidades** gear lever; ~ **de vía** points *pl*.

cambista [kam'bista] *nm* (*COM*) exchange broker.

Camboya [kam'boja] *nf* Cambodia, Kampuchea.

camboyano, a [kambo'jano, a] *a*, *nm/f* Cambodian, Kampuchean.

camelar [kame'lar] *vt* (*con mujer*) to flirt with; (*persuadir*) to cajole.

camelo [ka'melo] *nm*: **me huele a** ~ it smells fishy.

camello [ka'meʎo] *nm* camel; (*fam: traficante*) pusher.

camerino [kame'rino] *nm* (*TEATRO*) dressing room.

camilla [ka'miʎa] *nf* (*MED*) stretcher.

caminante [kami'nante] *nm/f* traveller.

caminar [kami'nar] *vi* (*marchar*) to walk, go; (*viajar*) to travel, journey ◆ *vt* (*recorrer*) to cover, travel.

caminata [kami'nata] *nf* long walk.

camino [ka'mino] *nm* way, road; (*sendero*) track; **a medio** ~ halfway (there); **en el** ~ on the way, en route; ~ **de** on the way to; ~ **particular** private road; ~ **vecinal** country road; **C~s, Canales y Puertos** (*UNIV*) Civil Engineering; **ir por buen** ~ (*fig*) to be on the right track.

camión [ka'mjon] *nm* lorry, truck (*US*); ~ **de bomberos** fire engine.

camionero [kamjo'nero] *nm* lorry *o* truck (*US*) driver, trucker (*esp US*).

camioneta [kamjo'neta] *nf* van, transit ®, light truck.

camisa [ka'misa] *nf* shirt; (*BOT*) skin; ~ **de dormir** nightdress; ~ **de fuerza** straitjacket.

camisería [kamise'ria] *nf* outfitter's (shop).

camiseta [kami'seta] *nf* tee-shirt; (*ropa interior*) vest; (*de deportista*) top.

camisón [kami'son] *nm* nightdress, nightgown.

camomila [kamo'mila] *nf* camomile.

camorra [ka'morra] *nf*: **armar** ~ to kick up a row; **buscar** ~ to look for trouble.

campamento [kampa'mento] *nm* camp.

campana [kam'pana] *nf* bell.

campanada [kampa'naða] *nf* peal.

campanario [kampa'narjo] *nm* belfry.

campanilla [kampa'niʎa] *nf* (*campana*) small bell.

campante [kam'pante] *a*: **siguió tan** ~ he went on as if nothing had happened.

campaña [kam'paɲa] *nf* (*MIL*, *POL*) campaign; **hacer** ~ (**en pro de/contra**) to campaign (for/against); ~ **de venta** sales campaign.

campechano, a [kampe'tʃano, a] *a* open.

campeón, ona [kampe'on, ona] *nm/f* champion.

campeonato [kampeo'nato] *nm* championship.

campesino, a [kampe'sino, a] *a* country *cpd*, rural; (*gente*) peasant *cpd* ◆ *nm/f* countryman/woman; (*agricultor*) farmer.

campestre [kam'pestre] *a* country *cpd*, rural.

camping ['kampin] *nm* camping; (*lugar*) campsite; **ir de** *o* **hacer** ~ to go camping.

campiña [kam'piɲa] *nf* countryside.

campista [kam'pista] *nm/f* camper.

campo ['kampo] *nm* (*fuera de la ciudad*) country, countryside; (*AGR, ELEC, INFORM*) field; (*de fútbol*) pitch; (*de golf*) course; (*MIL*) camp; ~ **de batalla** battlefield; ~ **de minas** minefield; ~ **petrolífero** oilfield; ~ **visual** field of vision; ~ **de concentración/ de internación/de trabajo** concentration/ internment/labour camp.

camposanto [kampo'santo] *nm* cemetery.

CAMPSA ['kampsa] *nf abr* (*Esp COM*)= *Compañía Arrendataria del Monopolio de Petróleos, S.A.*

campus ['kampus] *nm inv* (*UNIV*) campus.

camuflaje [kamu'flaxe] *nm* camouflage.

can [kan] *nm* dog, mutt (*fam*).

cana ['kana] *nf V* **cano.**

Canadá [kana'ða] *nm* Canada.

canadiense [kana'ðjense] *a, nm/f* Canadian ◆ *nf* fur-lined jacket.

canal [ka'nal] *nm* canal; (*GEO*) channel, strait; (*de televisión*) channel; (*de tejado*) gutter; **C~ de la Mancha** English Channel; **C~ de Panamá** Panama Canal.

canalice [kana'liθe] *etc vb V* **canalizar.**

canalizar [kanali'θar] *vt* to channel.

canalón [kana'lon] *nm* (*conducto vertical*) drainpipe; (*del tejado*) gutter; **canalones** *nmpl* (*CULIN*) cannelloni.

canalla [ka'naʎa] *nf* rabble, mob ◆ *nm* swine.

canallada [kana'ʎaða] *nf* (*hecho*) dirty trick.

canapé, *pl* **canapés** [kana'pe, kana'pes] *nm* sofa, settee; (*CULIN*) canapé.

Canarias [ka'narjas] *nfpl*: **las (Islas)** ~ the Canaries, the Canary Isles.

canario, a [ka'narjo, a] *a* of *o* from the Canary Isles ◆ *nm/f* native *o* inhabitant of the Canary Isles ◆ *nm* (*ZOOL*) canary.

canasta [ka'nasta] *nf* (round) basket.

canastilla [kanas'tiʎa] *nf* small basket; (*de niño*) layette.

canasto [ka'nasto] *nm* large basket.

cancela [kan'θela] *nf* (wrought-iron) gate.

cancelación [kanθela'θjon] *nf* cancellation.

cancelar [kanθe'lar] *vt* to cancel; (*una deu-*

da) to write off.

cáncer ['kanθer] *nm* (*MED*) cancer; **C~** (*ASTRO*) Cancer.

canciller [kanθi'ʎer] *nm* chancellor.

canción [kan'θjon] *nf* song; ~ **de cuna** lullaby.

cancionero [kanθjo'nero] *nm* song book.

cancha ['kantʃa] *nf* (*de baloncesto, tenis etc*) court; (*AM: de fútbol*) pitch.

candado [kan'daðo] *nm* padlock.

candela [kan'dela] *nf* candle.

candelabro [kande'laβro] *nm* candelabra.

candelero [kande'lero] *nm* (*para vela*) candlestick; (*de aceite*) oil lamp.

candente [kan'dente] *a* red-hot; (*tema*) burning.

candidato, a [kandi'ðato, a] *nm/f* candidate; (*para puesto*) applicant.

candidatura [kandiða'tura] *nf* candidature.

candidez [kandi'ðeθ] *nf* (*sencillez*) simplicity; (*simpleza*) naiveté.

cándido, a ['kandiðo, a] *a* simple; naive.

candil [kan'dil] *nm* oil lamp.

candilejas [kandi'lexas] *nfpl* (*TEATRO*) footlights.

candor [kan'dor] *nm* (*sinceridad*) frankness; (*inocencia*) innocence.

canela [ka'nela] *nf* cinnamon.

canelo [ka'nelo] *nm*: **hacer el** ~ to act the fool.

cangrejo [kan'grexo] *nm* crab.

canguro [kan'guro] *nm* (*ZOOL*) kangaroo; (*de niños*) baby-sitter; **hacer de** ~ to baby-sit.

caníbal [ka'niβal] *a, nm/f* cannibal.

canica [ka'nika] *nf* marble.

canícula [ka'nikula] *nf* midsummer heat.

caniche [ka'nitʃe] *nm* poodle.

canijo, a [ka'nixo, a] *a* frail, sickly.

canilla [ka'niʎa] *nf* (*TEC*) bobbin.

canino, a [ka'nino, a] *a* canine ◆ *nm* canine (tooth).

canje [kan'xe] *nm* exchange; (*trueque*) swap.

canjear [kanxe'ar] *vt* to exchange; (*trocar*) to swap.

cano, a ['kano, a] *a* grey-haired, white-haired ◆ *nf* (*tb*: **canas**) white *o* grey hair; **tener canas** to be going grey.

canoa [ka'noa] *nf* canoe.

canon ['kanon] *nm* canon; (*pensión*) rent; (*COM*) tax.

canonice [kano'niθe] *etc vb V* **canonizar.**

canónico, a [ka'noniko, a] *a*: **derecho** ~ canon law.

canónigo [ka'noniɣo] *nm* canon.

canonizar [kanoni'θar] *vt* to canonize.

canoro, a [ka'noro, a] *a* melodious.

cansado, a [kan'saðo, a] *a* tired, weary; (*tedioso*) tedious, boring; **estoy** ~ **de hacerlo** I'm sick of doing it.

cansancio [kan'sanθjo] *nm* tiredness, fatigue.

cansar [kan'sar] *vt* (*fatigar*) to tire, tire out; (*aburrir*) to bore; (*fastidiar*) to bother; ~**se** *vr* to tire, get tired; (*aburrirse*) to get bored.

cantabro, a [kantaβro, a] *a, nm/f* Cantabrian.

cantábrico, a [kan'taβriko, a] *a* Cantabrian; **Mar C**~ Bay of Biscay; **(Montes) C**~**s, Cordillera Cantábrica** Cantabrian Mountains.

cantante [kan'tante] *a* singing ♦ *nm/f* singer.

cantaor, a [kanta'or, a] *nm/f* Flamenco singer.

cantar [kan'tar] *vt* to sing ♦ *vi* to sing; (*insecto*) to chirp; (*rechinar*) to squeak; (*fam: criminal*) to squeal ♦ *nm* (*acción*) singing; (*canción*) song; (*poema*) poem; ~ **a uno las cuarenta** to tell sb a few home truths; ~ **a dos voces** to sing a duet.

cántara ['kantara] *nf* large pitcher.

cántaro ['kantaro] *nm* pitcher, jug.

cante ['kante] *nm*: ~ **jondo** flamenco singing.

cantera [kan'tera] *nf* quarry.

cántico ['kantiko] *nm* (*REL*) canticle; (*fig*) song.

cantidad [kanti'ðað] *nf* quantity, amount; (*ECON*) sum ♦ *ad* (*fam*) a lot; ~ **alzada** lump sum; ~ **de** lots of.

cantilena [kanti'lena] *nf* = **cantinela.**

cantimplora [kantim'plora] *nf* (*frasco*) water bottle, canteen.

cantina [kan'tina] *nf* canteen; (*de estación*) buffet.

cantinela [kanti'nela] *nf* ballad, song.

canto ['kanto] *nm* singing; (*canción*) song; (*borde*) edge, rim; (*de un cuchillo*) back; ~ **rodado** boulder.

cantón [kan'ton] *nm* canton.

cantor, a [kan'tor, a] *nm/f* singer.

canturrear [kanturre'ar] *vi* to sing softly.

canuto [ka'nuto] *nm* (*tubo*) small tube; (*fam: droga*) joint.

caña ['kaɲa] *nf* (*BOT: tallo*) stem, stalk; (*carrizo*) reed; (*vaso*) tumbler; (*de cerveza*) glass of beer; (*ANAT*) shinbone; ~ **de azúcar** sugar cane; ~ **de pescar** fishing rod.

cañada [ka'ɲaða] *nf* (*entre dos montañas*) gully, ravine; (*camino*) cattle track.

cáñamo ['kaɲamo] *nm* (*BOT*) hemp.

cañaveral [kaɲaβe'ral] *nm* (*BOT*) reedbed; (*AGR*) sugar-cane field.

caño ['kaɲo] *nm* (*tubo*) tube, pipe; (*de aguas servidas*) sewer; (*MUS*) pipe; (*NAUT*) navigation channel; (*de fuente*) jet.

cañón [ka'ɲon] *nm* (*MIL*) cannon; (*de fusil*) barrel; (*GEO*) canyon, gorge.

cañonazo [kaɲo'naθo] *nm* (*MIL*) gunshot.

cañonera [kaɲo'nera] *nf* (*tb:* **lancha** ~) gunboat.

caoba [ka'oβa] *nf* mahogany.

caos ['kaos] *nm* chaos.

caótico, a [ka'otiko, a] *a* chaotic.

cap. *abr* (= *capítulo*) ch.

capa ['kapa] *nf* cloak, cape; (*CULIN*) coating; (*GEO*) layer, stratum; (*de pintura*) coat; **de** ~ **y espada** cloak-and-dagger; **so** ~ **de** under the pretext of; ~**s sociales** social groups.

capacidad [kapaθi'ðað] *nf* (*medida*) capacity; (*aptitud*) capacity, ability; **una sala con** ~ **para 900** a hall seating 900; ~ **adquisitiva** purchasing power.

capacitación [kapaθita'θjon] *nf* training.

capacitar [kapaθi'tar] *vt*: ~ **a uno para algo** to qualify sb for sth; (*TEC*) to train sb for sth.

capacho [ka'patʃo] *nm* wicker basket.

capar [ka'par] *vt* to castrate, geld.

caparazón [kapara'θon] *nm* (*ZOOL*) shell.

capataz [kapa'taθ] *nm* foreman, chargehand.

capaz [ka'paθ] *a* able, capable; (*amplio*) capacious, roomy.

capcioso, a [kap'θjoso, a] *a* wily, deceitful; **pregunta capciosa** trick question.

capellán [kape'ʎan] *nm* chaplain; (*sacerdote*) priest.

caperuza [kape'ruθa] *nf* hood; (*de bolígrafo*) cap.

capicúa [kapi'kua] *nf* reversible number, *e.g. 1441.*

capilar [kapi'lar] *a* hair *cpd.*

capilla [ka'piʎa] *nf* chapel.

capital [kapi'tal] *a* capital ♦ *nm* (*COM*) capital ♦ *nf* (*ciudad*) capital (city); ~ **activo/en acciones** working/share o equity capital; ~ **arriesgado** venture capital; ~ **autorizado** o **social** authorised capital; ~ **emitido** issued capital; ~ **improductivo** idle money; ~ **invertido** o **utilizado** capital employed; ~ **pagado** paid-up capital ~ **de riesgo** risk capital; ~ **social** equity o share capital; **inversión de** ~**es** capital investment.

capitalice [kapita'liθe] *etc vb V* **capitalizar.**

capitalismo [kapita'lismo] *nm* capitalism.

capitalista [kapita'lista] *a, nm/f* capitalist.

capitalizar [kapitali'θar] *vt* to capitalize.

capitán [kapi'tan] *nm* captain; (*fig*) leader.

capitana [kapi'tana] *nf* flagship.

capitanear [kapitane'ar] *vt* to captain.

capitanía [kapita'nia] *nf* captaincy.

capitel [kapi'tel] *nm* (*ARQ*) capital.

capitolio [kapi'toljo] *nm* capitol.

capitulación [kapitula'θjon] *nf* (*rendición*) capitulation, surrender; (*acuerdo*) agreement, pact; **capitulaciones matrimoniales**

marriage contract *sg*.
capitular [kapitu'lar] *vi* to come to terms, make an agreement; (*MIL*) to surrender.
capítulo [ka'pitulo] *nm* chapter.
capó [ka'po] *nm* (*AUTO*) bonnet (*Brit*), hood (*US*).
capón [ka'pon] *nm* capon.
caporal [kapo'ral] *nm* chief, leader.
capota [ka'pota] *nf* (*de mujer*) bonnet; (*AUTO*) hood (*Brit*), top (*US*).
capote [ka'pote] *nm* (*abrigo: de militar*) greatcoat; (*de torero*) cloak.
Capricornio [kapri'kornjo] *nm* Capricorn.
capricho [ka'pritʃo] *nm* whim, caprice.
caprichoso, a [kapri'tʃoso, a] *a* capricious.
cápsula ['kapsula] *nf* capsule; ~ **espacial** space capsule.
captar [kap'tar] *vt* (*comprender*) to understand; (*RADIO*) to pick up; (*atención, apoyo*) to attract.
captura [kap'tura] *nf* capture; (*JUR*) arrest.
capturar [kaptu'rar] *vt* to capture; (*JUR*) to arrest; (*datos*) to input.
capucha [ka'putʃa] *nf* hood, cowl.
capullo [ka'puʎo] *nm* (*ZOOL*) cocoon; (*BOT*) bud; (*fam*) idiot.
caqui ['kaki] *nm* khaki.
cara ['kara] *nf* (*ANAT, de moneda*) face; (*aspecto*) appearance; (*de disco*) side; (*fig*) boldness; (*descara*) cheek, nerve ♦ *prep*: ~ **a** facing; **de** ~ **a** opposite, facing; **dar la** ~ to face the consequences; **echar algo en** ~ **a uno** to reproach sb for sth; **¿~ o cruz?** heads or tails?; **¡ qué ~ más dura!** what a nerve!; **de una** ~ (*disquete*) single-sided.
carabina [kara'ßina] *nf* carbine, rifle; (*persona*) chaperone.
carabinero [karaßi'nero] *nm* (*de aduana*) customs officer; (*AM*) gendarme.
Caracas [ka'rakas] *nm* Caracas.
caracol [kara'kol] *nm* (*ZOOL*) snail; (*concha*) (sea)shell; **escalera de** ~ spiral staircase.
caracolear [karakole'ar] *vi* (*caballo*) to prance about.
carácter, *pl* **caracteres** [ka'rakter, karak'teres] *nm* character; ~ **de cambio de página** (*INFORM*) form feed character; **caracteres de imprenta** (*TIP*) type(face) *sg*; ~ **libre** (*INFORM*) wildcard character; **tener buen/mal** ~ to be good-natured/bad tempered.
caracterice [karakte'riθe] *etc vb V* **caracterizar**.
característico, a [karakte'ristiko, a] *a* characteristic ♦ *nf* characteristic.
caracterizar [karakteri'θar] *vt* (*distinguir*) to characterize, typify; (*honrar*) to confer (a) distinction on.
caradura [kara'ðura] *nm/f* cheeky person; **es un** ~ he's got a nerve.

carajo [ka'raxo] *nm* (*fam!*): **¡~!** shit!(*!*); **¡qué** ~ **!** what the hell!; **me importa un** ~ I don't give a damn.
caramba [ka'ramba] *excl* well!, good gracious!
carámbano [ka'rambano] *nm* icicle.
carambola [karam'bola] *nf*: **por** ~ by a fluke.
caramelo [kara'melo] *nm* (*dulce*) sweet; (*azúcar fundido*) caramel.
carapacho [kara'patʃo] *nm* shell, carapace.
caraqueño, a [kara'keɲo, a] *a* of *o* from Caracas ♦ *nm/f* native *o* inhabitant of Caracas.
carátula [ka'ratula] *nf* (*máscara*) mask; (*TEATRO*): **la** ~ the stage.
caravana [kara'ßana] *nf* caravan; (*fig*) group; (*de autos*) tailback.
carbón [kar'ßon] *nm* coal; ~ **de leña** charcoal; **papel** ~ carbon paper.
carbonatado, a [karßono'taðo, a] *a* carbonated.
carbonato [karßo'nato] *nm* carbonate; ~ **sódico** sodium carbonate.
carboncillo [karßon'θiʎo] *nm* (*ARTE*) charcoal.
carbonice [karßo'niθe] *etc vb V* **carbonizar**.
carbonilla [karßo'niʎa] *nf* coal dust.
carbonizar [karßoni'θar] *vt* to carbonize; (*quemar*) to char; **quedar carbonizado** (*ELEC*) to be electrocuted.
carbono [kar'ßono] *nm* carbon.
carburador [karßura'ðor] *nm* carburettor.
carburante [karßu'rante] *nm* fuel.
carca ['karka] *a, nm/f inv* reactionary.
carcajada [karka'xaða] *nf* (loud) laugh, guffaw.
cárcel ['karθel] *nf* prison, jail; (*TEC*) clamp.
carcelero, a [karθe'lero, a] *a* prison *cpd* ♦ *nm/f* warder.
carcomer [karko'mer] *vt* to bore into, eat into; (*fig*) to undermine; ~**se** *vr* to become worm-eaten; (*fig*) to decay.
carcomido, a [karko'miðo, a] *a* worm-eaten; (*fig*) rotten.
cardar [kar'ðar] *vt* (*TEC*) to card, comb.
cardenal [karðe'nal] *nm* (*REL*) cardinal; (*MED*) bruise.
cárdeno, a ['karðeno, a] *a* purple; (*lívido*) livid.
cardíaco, a [kar'ðiako, a] *a* cardiac, heart *cpd*.
cardinal [karði'nal] *a* cardinal.
cardiólogo, a [karðj'oloɤo, a] *nm/f* cardiologist.
cardo ['karðo] *nm* thistle.
carear [kare'ar] *vt* to bring face to face; (*comparar*) to compare; ~**se** *vr* to come face to face, meet.
carecer [kare'θer] *vi*: ~ **de** to lack, be in

need of.

carencia [ka'renθja] *nf* lack; (*escasez*) shortage; (*MED*) deficiency.

carente [ka'rente] *a*: ~ **de** lacking in, devoid of.

carestía [kares'tia] *nf* (*escasez*) scarcity, shortage; (*COM*) high cost; **época de** ~ period of shortage.

careta [ka'reta] *nf* mask.

carey [ka'rei] *nm* tortoiseshell.

carezca [ka'reθka] *etc vb V* **carecer**.

carga ['karɣa] *nf* (*peso*, *ELEC*) load; (*de barco*) cargo, freight; (*FINANZAS*) tax, duty; (*MIL*) charge; (*INFORM*) loading; (*obligación, responsabilidad*) duty, obligation; ~ **aérea** (*COM*) air cargo; ~ **útil** (*COM*) payload; **la** ~ **fiscal** the tax burden.

cargadero [karɣa'ðero] *nm* goods platform, loading bay.

cargado, a [kar'ɣaðo, a] *a* loaded; (*ELEC*) live; (*café, té*) strong; (*cielo*) overcast.

cargador, a [karɣa'ðor, a] *nm/f* loader; (*NAUT*) docker ◆ *nm* (*INFORM*): ~ **de discos** disk pack.

cargamento [karɣa'mento] *nm* (*acción*) loading; (*mercancías*) load, cargo.

cargante [kar'ɣante] *a* (*persona*) trying.

cargar [kar'ɣar] *vt* (*barco, arma*) to load; (*ELEC*) to charge; (*impuesto*) to impose; (*COM: algo en cuenta*) to charge, debit; (*MIL: enemigo*) to charge ◆ *vi* (*AUTO*) to load (up); (*inclinarse*) to lean; (*INFORM*) to load, feed in; ~ **con** to pick up, carry away; ~**se** *vr* (*fam: estropear*) to break; (: *matar*) to bump off; (*ELEC*) to become charged.

cargo ['karɣo] *nm* (*COM etc*) charge, debit; (*puesto*) post, office; (*responsabilidad*) duty, obligation; (*fig*) weight, burden; (*JUR*) charge; **altos** ~**s** high-ranking officials; **una cantidad en** ~ **a uno** a sum chargeable to sb; **hacerse** ~ **de** to take charge *o* responsibility for.

cargue ['karɣe] *etc vb V* **cargar**.

carguero [kar'ɣero] *nm* freighter, cargo boat; (*avión*) freight plane.

Caribe [ka'riβe] *nm*: **el** ~ the Caribbean.

caribeño, a [kari'βeɲo, a] *a* Caribbean.

caricatura [karika'tura] *nf* caricature.

caricia [ka'riθja] *nf* caress; (*a animal*) pat, stroke.

caridad [kari'ðað] *nf* charity.

caries ['karjes] *nf inv* (*MED*) tooth decay.

carilla [ka'riʎa] *nf* (*TIP*) page.

cariño [ka'riɲo] *nm* affection, love; (*caricia*) caress; (*en carta*) love ... .

cariñoso, a [kari'ɲoso, a] *a* affectionate.

carioca [ka'rjoka] *a* (*AM*) of *o* from Rio de Janeiro ◆ *nm/f* native *o* inhabitant of Rio de Janeiro.

carisma [ka'risma] *nm* charisma.

caritativo, a [karita'tiβo, a] *a* charitable.

cariz [ka'riθ] *nm*: **tener** *o* **tomar buen/mal** ~ to look good/bad.

carmesí [karme'si] *a, nm* crimson.

carmín [kar'min] *nm* (*color*) carmine; ~ **(de labios)** lipstick.

carnal [kar'nal] *a* carnal; **primo** ~ first cousin.

carnaval [karna'βal] *nm* carnival.

carne ['karne] *nf* flesh; (*CULIN*) meat; ~ **de cañon** cannon fodder; ~ **de cerdo/de cordero/de ternera/de vaca** pork/lamb/veal/beef; ~ **picada** mince; ~ **de gallina** (*fig*) gooseflesh.

carné [kar'ne] *nm* = **carnet**.

carnero [kar'nero] *nm* sheep, ram; (*carne*) mutton.

carnet, *pl* **carnets** [kar'ne, kar'nes] *nm*: ~ **de conducir** driving licence; ~ **de identidad** identity card.

carnicería [karniθe'ria] *nf* butcher's (shop); (*fig: matanza*) carnage, slaughter.

carnicero, a [karni'θero, a] *a* carnivorous ◆ *nm/f* (*tb fig*) butcher ◆ *nm* carnivore.

carnívoro, a [kar'niβoro, a] *a* carnivorous ◆ *nm* carnivore.

carnoso, a [kar'noso, a] *a* beefy, fat.

caro, a ['karo, a] *a* dear; (*COM*) dear, expensive ◆ *ad* dear, dearly; **vender** ~ to sell at a high price.

carpa ['karpa] *nf* (*pez*) carp; (*de circo*) big top; (*AM: de camping*) tent.

carpeta [kar'peta] *nf* folder, file.

carpetazo [karpe'taθo] *nm*: **dar** ~ **a** to shelve.

carpintería [karpinte'ria] *nf* carpentry.

carpintero [karpin'tero] *nm* carpenter; **pajaro** ~ woodpecker.

carraca [ka'rraka] *nf* (*DEPORTE*) rattle.

carraspear [karraspe'ar] *vi* (*aclararse*) to clear one's throat.

carraspera [karras'pera] *nf* hoarseness.

carrera [ka'rrera] *nf* (*acción*) run(ning); (*espacio recorrido*) run; (*certamen*) race; (*trayecto*) course; (*profesión*) career; (*ESCOL, UNIV*) course; (*de taxi*) ride; (*en medias*) ladder; **a la** ~ at (full) speed; **caballo de** ~**(s)** racehorse; ~ **de armamentos** arms race.

carrerilla [karre'riʎa] *nf*: **decir algo de** ~ to reel sth off; **tomar** ~ to get up speed.

carreta [ka'rreta] *nf* wagon, cart.

carrete [ka'rrete] *nm* reel, spool; (*TEC*) coil.

carretera [karre'tera] *nf* (*main*) road, highway; ~ **nacional** ≈ A road (*Brit*), state highway (*US*); ~ **de circunvalación** ring road.

carretilla [karre'tiʎa] *nf* trolley; (*AGR*) (wheel)barrow.

carril [ka'rril] *nm* furrow; (*de autopista*) lane; (*FERRO*) rail.

carrillo [ka'rriʎo] *nm* (*ANAT*) cheek; (*TEC*) pulley.

carrizo [ka'rriθo] *nm* reed.

carro ['karro] *nm* cart, wagon; (*MIL*) tank; (*AM*: *coche*) car; (*TIP*) carriage; ~ **blindado** armoured car.

carrocería [karroθe'ria] *nf* body, bodywork *q* (*Brit*).

carroña [ka'rroɲa] *nf* carrion *q*.

carroza [ka'rroθa] *nf* (*vehículo*) coach ◆ *nm/f* (*fam*) old fogey.

carrusel [karru'sel] *nm* merry-go-round, roundabout.

carta ['karta] *nf* letter; (*CULIN*) menu; (*naipe*) card; (*mapa*) map; (*JUR*) document; ~ **de crédito** credit card; ~ **de crédito documentaria** (*COM*) documentary letter of credit; ~ **de crédito irrevocable** (*COM*) irrevocable letter of credit; ~ **certificada/urgente** registered/special delivery letter; ~ **marítima** chart; ~ **de pedido** (*COM*) order; ~ **verde** (*AUTO*) green card; ~ **de vinos** wine list; **echar una** ~ **al correo** to post a letter; **echar las** ~**s a uno** to tell sb's fortune.

cartabón [karta'ßon] *nm* set square.

cartel [kar'tel] *nm* (*anuncio*) poster, placard; (*ESCOL*) wall chart; (*COM*) cartel.

cartelera [karte'lera] *nf* hoarding, billboard; (*en periódico etc*) listings *pl*, entertainments guide; "**en** ~" "showing".

cartera [kar'tera] *nf* (*de bolsillo*) wallet; (*de colegial, cobrador*) satchel; (*de señora*) handbag; (*para documentos*) briefcase; **ministro sin** ~ (*POL*) minister without portfolio; **ocupa la** ~ **de Agricultura** he is Minister of Agriculture; ~ **de pedidos** (*COM*) order book; **efectos en** ~ (*ECON*) holdings.

carterista [karte'rista] *nm/f* pickpocket.

cartero [kar'tero] *nm* postman.

cartílago [kar'tilaɣo] *nm* cartilage.

cartilla [kar'tiʎa] *nf* (*ESCOL*) primer, first reading book; ~ **de ahorros** bank book.

cartón [kar'ton] *nm* cardboard.

cartucho [kar'tutʃo] *nm* (*MIL*) cartridge; (*bolsita*) paper cone; ~ **de datos** (*INFORM*) data cartridge.

cartulina [kartu'lina] *nf* fine cardboard, card.

CASA ['kasa] *nf abr* (*Esp AVIAT*) = *Construcciones Aeronáuticas S.A.*

casa ['kasa] *nf* house; (*hogar*) home; (*edificio*) building; (*COM*) firm, company; ~ **consistorial** town hall; ~ **de huéspedes** boarding house; ~ **de socorro** first aid post; ~ **de citas** (*fam*) brothel; **ir a** ~ to go home; **salir de** ~ to go out; (*para siempre*) to leave home; **echar la** ~ **por la ventana** (*gastar*) to spare no expense.

casadero, a [kasa'ðero, a] *a* marriageable.

casado, a [ka'saðo, a] *a* married ◆ *nm/f* married man/woman.

casamiento [kasa'mjento] *nm* marriage, wedding.

casar [ka'sar] *vt* to marry; (*JUR*) to quash, annul; ~**se** *vr* to marry, get married; ~**se por lo civil** to have a civil wedding, get married in a registry office (*Brit*) .

cascabel [kaska'ßel] *nm* (*small*) bell; (*ZOOL*) rattlesnake.

cascada [kas'kaða] *nf* waterfall.

cascajo [kas'kaxo] *nm* gravel, stone chippings *pl*.

cascanueces [kaska'nweθes] *nm inv*: **un** ~ a pair of nutcrackers.

cascar [kas'kar] *vt* to split; (*nuez*) to crack ◆ *vi* to chatter; ~**se** *vr* to crack, split, break (open).

cáscara ['kaskara] *nf* (*de huevo, fruta seca*) shell; (*de fruta*) skin; (*de limón*) peel.

cascarón [kaska'ron] *nm* (broken) eggshell.

cascarrabias [kaska'rraßjas] *nm/f inv* (*fam*) hothead.

casco ['kasko] *nm* (*de bombero, soldado*) helmet; (*cráneo*) skull; (*NAUT*: *de barco*) hull; (*ZOOL*: *de caballo*) hoof; (*botella*) empty bottle; (*de ciudad*): **el** ~ **antiguo** the old part; **el** ~ **urbano** the town centre.

caserío [kase'rio] *nm* hamlet, group of houses; (*casa*) country house.

casero, a [ka'sero, a] *a*: **ser muy** ~ (*persona*) to be homeloving; "**comida casera**" "home cooking" ◆ *nm/f* (*propietario*) landlord/lady; (*COM*) house agent.

caserón [kase'ron] *nm* large (ramshackle) house.

caseta [ka'seta] *nf* hut; (*para bañista*) cubicle; (*de feria*) stall.

casete [ka'sete] *nm o f* cassette.

casi ['kasi] *ad* almost; ~ **nunca** hardly ever, almost never; ~ **nada** next to nothing; ~ **te caes** you almost o nearly fell.

casilla [ka'siʎa] *nf* (*casita*) hut, cabin; (*TEATRO*) box office; (*para cartas*) pigeonhole; (*AJEDREZ*) square; **sacar a uno de sus** ~ **s** to drive sb round the bend (*fam*), make sb lose his temper.

casillero [kasi'ʎero] *nm* (set of) pigeonholes.

casino [ka'sino] *nm* club; (*de juego*) casino.

caso ['kaso] *nm* case; (*suceso*) event; **en** ~ **de ...** in case of ...; **el** ~ **es que** the fact is that; **en el mejor de los** ~**s** at best; **en ese** ~ in that case; **en todo** ~ in any case; **en último** ~ as a last resort; **hacer** ~ **a** to pay attention to; **hacer** ~ **omiso de** to fail to mention, pass over; **hacer** o **venir al** ~ to be relevant.

caspa ['kaspa] *nf* dandruff.

Caspio ['kaspjo] *a*: **Mar** ~ Caspian Sea.

casque ['kaske] *etc vb V* **cascar.**

cassette [ka'set] *nf o m* cassette.

casta ['kasta] nf caste; (raza) breed; (linaje) lineage.

castaña [kas'taɲa] nf V **castaño**.

castañetear [kastaɲete'ar] vi (dientes) to chatter.

castaño, a [kas'taɲo, a] a chestnut(-coloured), brown ♦ nm chestnut tree ♦ nf chestnut; (fam: golpe) punch; ~ **de Indias** horse chestnut tree.

castañuelas [kasta'ɲwelas] nfpl castanets.

castellano, a [kaste'ʎano, a] a Castilian; (fam) Spanish ♦ nm/f Castilian; (fam) Spaniard ♦ nm (LING) Castilian, Spanish.

castellonense [kasteʎo'nense] a of o from Castellón de la Plana ♦ nm/f native o inhabitant of Castellón de la Plana.

castidad [kasti'ðað] nf chastity, purity.

castigar [kasti'ɣar] vt to punish; (DEPORTE) to penalize; (afligir) to afflict.

castigo [kas'tiɣo] nm punishment; (DEPORTE) penalty.

castigue [kas'tiɣe] etc vb V **castigar**.

Castilla [kas'tiʎa] nf Castile.

castillo [kas'tiʎo] nm castle.

castizo, a [kas'tiθo, a] a (LING) pure; (de buena casta) purebred, pedigree; (auténtico) genuine.

casto, a ['kasto, a] a chaste, pure.

castor [kas'tor] nm beaver.

castrar [kas'trar] vt to castrate; (gato) to doctor; (BOT) to prune.

castrense [kas'trense] a army cpd, military.

casual [ka'swal] a chance, accidental.

casualidad [kaswali'ðað] nf chance, accident; (combinación de circunstancias) coincidence; **¡qué ~!** what a coincidence!

casualmente [kaswal'mente] ad by chance.

cataclismo [kata'klismo] nm cataclysm.

catador [kata'ðor] nm taster.

catadura [kata'ðura] nf (aspecto) looks pl.

catalán, ana [kata'lan, ana] a, nm/f Catalan ♦ nm (LING) Catalan.

catalizador [kataliθa'ðor] nm catalyst.

catalogar [katalo'ɣar] vt to catalogue; ~ (de) (fig) to classify (as).

catálogo [ka'taloɣo] nm catalogue.

catalogue [kata'loɣe] etc vb V **catalogar**.

Cataluña [kata'luɲa] nf Catalonia.

catar [ka'tar] vt to taste, sample.

catarata [kata'rata] nf (GEO) (water)fall; (MED) cataract.

catarro [ka'tarro] nm catarrh; (constipado) cold.

catástrofe [ka'tastrofe] nf catastrophe.

catecismo [kate'θismo] nm catechism.

cátedra ['kateðra] nf (UNIV) chair, professorship; (ESCOL) principal teacher's post; **sentar ~ sobre un argumento** to take one's stand on an argument.

catedral [kate'ðral] nf cathedral.

catedrático, a [kate'ðratiko, a] nm/f professor; (ESCOL) principal teacher.

categoría [kateɣo'ria] nf category; (rango) rank, standing; (calidad) quality; **de ~** (hotel) top-class; **de baja ~** (oficial) low-ranking; **de segunda ~** second-rate; **no tiene ~** he has no standing.

categórico, a [kate'ɣoriko, a] a categorical.

caterva [ka'terβa] nf throng, crowd.

cateto, a [ka'teto, a] nm/f yokel.

cátodo ['katoðo] nm cathode.

catolicismo [katoli'θismo] nm Catholicism.

católico, a [ka'toliko, a] a, nm/f Catholic.

catorce [ka'torθe] num fourteen.

Cáucaso ['kaukaso] nm Caucasus.

cauce ['kauθe] nm (de río) riverbed; (fig) channel.

caución [kau'θjon] nf bail.

caucionar [kauθjo'nar] vt (JUR) to bail (out), go bail for.

caucho ['kautʃo] nm rubber; (AM: llanta) tyre.

caudal [kau'ðal] nm (de río) volume, flow; (fortuna) wealth; (abundancia) abundance.

caudaloso, a [kauða'loso, a] a (río) large; (persona) wealthy, rich.

caudillo [kau'ðiʎo] nm leader, chief.

caudillaje [kauði'ʎaxe] nm leadership.

causa ['kausa] nf cause; (razón) reason; (JUR) lawsuit, case; **a o por ~ de** because of, on account of.

causar [kau'sar] vt to cause.

cáustico, a ['kaustiko, a] a caustic.

cautela [kau'tela] nf caution, cautiousness.

cauteloso, a [kaute'loso, a] a cautious, wary.

cautivar [kauti'βar] vt to capture; (fig) to captivate.

cautiverio [kauti'βerjo] nm, **cautividad** [kautiβi'ðað] nf captivity.

cautivo, a [kau'tiβo, a] a, nm/f captive.

cauto, a ['kauto, a] a cautious, careful.

cava ['kaβa] nf (bodega) (wine) cellar ♦ nm (vino) champagne-type wine.

cavar [ka'βar] vt to dig; (AGR) to dig over.

caverna [ka'βerna] nf cave, cavern.

cavernoso, a [kaβer'noso, a] a cavernous; (voz) resounding.

cavidad [kaβi'ðað] nf cavity.

cavilación [kaβila'θjon] nf deep thought.

cavilar [kaβi'lar] vt to ponder.

cayado [ka'jaðo] nm (de pastor) crook; (de obispo) crozier.

cayendo [ka'jendo] etc vb V **caer**.

caza ['kaθa] nf (acción: gen) hunting; (: con fusil) shooting; (una ~) hunt, chase; (animales) game; **coto de ~** hunting estate ♦ nm (AVIAT) fighter.

cazador, a [kaθa'ðor, a] nm/f hunter/huntress ♦ nf jacket.

cazaejecutivos [kaθaexeku'tiβos] *nm inv* (*com*) headhunter.

cazar [ka'θar] *vt* to hunt; (*perseguir*) to chase; (*prender*) to catch; ~**las al vuelo** to be pretty sharp.

cazasubmarinos [kaθasuβma'rinos] *nm inv* (*naut*) destroyer; (*aviat*) anti-submarine craft.

cazo ['kaθo] *nm* saucepan.

cazuela [ka'θwela] *nf* (*vasija*) pan; (*guisado*) casserole.

cazurro, a [ka'θurro, a] *a* surly.

CC *nm abr* (*pol*: = *Comité Central*) Central Committee.

c/c. *abr* (*com*: = *cuenta corriente*) current account.

CCI *nf abr* (*com*: = *Cámara de Comercio Internacional*) ICC.

CC.OO. *nfpl abr* = **Comisiones Obreras.**

c/d *abr* (= *en casa de*) c/o; (= *con descuento*) with discount.

CDN *nm abr* (= *Centro Dramático Nacional*) ≈ RADA (*Brit*).

CE *nm abr* (= *Consejo de Europa*) Council of Europe ♦ *nf abr* (= *Comunidad Europea*) EC.

cebada [θe'βaða] *nf* barley.

cebar [θe'βar] *vt* (*animal*) to fatten (up); (*anzuelo*) to bait; (*mil, tec*) to prime; ~**se** *vr*: ~**se en** to vent one's fury on, take it out on.

cebo ['θeβo] *nm* (*para animales*) feed, food; (*para peces, fig*) bait; (*de arma*) charge.

cebolla [θe'βoʎa] *nf* onion.

cebollín [θeβo'ʎin] *nm* spring onion.

cebón, ona [θe'βon, ona] *a* fat, fattened.

cebra ['θeβra] *nf* zebra; **paso de** ~ zebra crossing.

CECA ['θeka] *nf abr* (= *Comunidad Europea del Carbón y del Acero*) ECSC.

ceca ['θeka] *nf*: **andar** *o* **ir de la** ~ **a la Meca** to chase about all over the place.

cecear [θeθe'ar] *vi* to lisp.

ceceo [θe'θeo] *nm* lisp.

cecina [θe'θina] *nf* cured *o* smoked meat.

cedazo [θe'ðaθo] *nm* sieve.

ceder [θe'ðer] *vt* (*entregar*) to hand over; (*renunciar a*) to give up, part with ♦ *vi* (*renunciar*) to give in, yield; (*disminuir*) to diminish, decline; (*romperse*) to give way; (*viento*) to drop; (*fiebre etc*) to abate; "**ceda el paso**" (*auto*) "give way".

cedro ['θeðro] *nm* cedar.

cédula ['θeðula] *nf* certificate, document; ~ **en blanco** blank cheque.

CEE *nf abr* (= *Comunidad Económica Europea*) EEC.

cegar [θe'xar] *vt* to blind; (*tubería etc*) to block up, stop up ♦ *vi* to go blind; ~**se** *vr* to be blinded (*de* by).

cegué [θe'xe] *etc vb V* **cegar.**

ceguemos [θe'xemos] *etc vb V* **cegar.**

ceguera [θe'xera] *nf* blindness.

Ceilán [θei'lan] *nm* Ceylon, Sri Lanka.

ceja ['θexa] *nf* eyebrow; ~**s pobladas** bushy eyebrows; **arquear las** ~**s** to raise one's eyebrows; **fruncir las** ~**s** to frown.

cejar [θe'xar] *vi* (*fig*) to back down; **no** ~ to keep it up, stick at it.

cejijunto, a [θexi'xunto, a] *a* with bushy eyebrows; (*fig*) scowling.

celada [θe'laða] *nf* ambush, trap.

celador, a [θela'ðor, a] *nm/f* (*de edificio*) watchman; (*de museo etc*) attendant; (*de cárcel*) warder.

celda ['θelda] *nf* cell.

celebérrimo, a [θele'βerrimo, a] *a superlativo de* **célebre.**

celebración [θeleβra'θjon] *nf* celebration.

celebrar [θele'βrar] *vt* to celebrate; (*alabar*) to praise ♦ *vi* to be glad; ~**se** *vr* to occur, take place.

célebre ['θeleβre] *a* celebrated, renowned.

celebridad [θeleβri'ðað] *nf* fame; (*persona*) celebrity.

celeridad [θeleri'ðað] *nf*: **con** ~ promptly.

celeste [θe'leste] *a* sky-blue; (*cuerpo etc*) heavenly ♦ *nm* sky blue.

celestial [θeles'tjal] *a* celestial, heavenly.

celibato [θeli'βato] *nm* celibacy.

célibe ['θeliβe] *a, nm/f* celibate.

celo ['θelo] *nm* zeal; (*rel*) fervour; (*pey*) envy; ~**s** *nmpl* jealousy *sg*; **dar** ~**s a uno** to make sb jealous; **tener** ~**s de uno** to be jealous of sb; **en** ~ (*animales*) on heat.

celofán [θelo'fan] *nm* cellophane.

celosía [θelo'sia] *nf* lattice (window).

celoso, a [θe'loso, a] *a* (*envidioso*) jealous; (*trabajador*) zealous; (*desconfiado*) suspicious.

celta ['θelta] *a* Celtic ♦ *nm/f* Celt.

célula ['θelula] *nf* cell.

celular [θelu'lar] *a*: **tejido** ~ cell tissue.

celuloide [θelu'loiðe] *nm* celluloid.

celulosa [θelu'losa] *nf* cellulose.

cementerio [θemen'terjo] *nm* cemetery, graveyard; ~ **de coches** used-car dump.

cemento [θe'mento] *nm* cement; (*hormigón*) concrete; (*am: cola*) glue.

CEN *nm abr* (*Esp*) = *Consejo de Economía Nacional.*

cena ['θena] *nf* evening meal, dinner.

cenagal [θena'xal] *nm* bog, quagmire.

cenar [θe'nar] *vt* to have for dinner, dine on ♦ *vi* to have dinner, dine.

cencerro [θen'θerro] *nm* cowbell; **estar como un** ~ (*fam*) to be round the bend.

cenicero [θeni'θero] *nm* ashtray.

cenit [θe'nit] *nm* zenith.

ceniciento, a [θeni'θjento, a] *a* ash-coloured, ashen.

ceniza [θe'niθa] *nf* ash, ashes *pl*.

censar [θen'sar] *vt* to take a census of.

censo ['θenso] *nm* census; ~ **electoral** electoral roll.

censor [θen'sor] *nm* censor; ~ **de cuentas** (*COM*) auditor; ~ **jurado de cuentas** chartered accountant.

censura [θen'sura] *nf* (*POL*) censorship; (*moral*) censure, criticism.

censurable [θensu'raβle] *a* reprehensible.

censurar [θensu'rar] *vt* (*idea*) to censure; (*cortar: película*) to censor.

centella [θen'teʎa] *nf* spark.

centellear [θenteʎe'ar] *vi* (*metal*) to gleam; (*estrella*) to twinkle; (*fig*) to sparkle.

centelleo [θente'ʎeo] *nm* gleam(ing); twinkling; sparkling.

centenar [θente'nar] *nm* hundred.

centenario, a [θente'narjo, a] *a* one hundred years old ♦ *nm* centenary.

centeno [θen'teno] *nm* rye.

centésimo, a [θen'tesimo, a] *a, nm* hundredth.

centígrado [θen'tiɣraðo] *a* centigrade.

centigramo [θenti'ɣramo] *nm* centigramme.

centilitro [θenti'litro] *nm* centilitre (*Brit*), centiliter (*US*).

centímetro [θen'timetro] *nm* centimetre (*Brit*), centimeter (*US*).

céntimo, a ['θentimo, a] *a* hundredth ♦ *nm* cent.

centinela [θenti'nela] *nm* sentry, guard.

centollo, a [θen'toʎo, a] *nm/f* large (*o* spider) crab.

central [θen'tral] *a* central ♦ *nf* head office; (*TEC*) plant; (*TELEC*) exchange; ~ **nuclear** nuclear power station.

centralice [θentra'liθe] *etc vb V* **centralizar**.

centralita [θentra'lita] *nf* (*TELEC*) switchboard.

centralización [θentraliθa'θjon] *nf* centralization.

centralizar [θentrali'θar] *vt* to centralize.

centrar [θen'trar] *vt* to centre.

céntrico, a ['θentriko, a] *a* central.

centrifugar [θentrifu'ɣar] *vt* (*ropa*) to spin-dry.

centrifugue [θentri'fuɣe] *etc vb V* **centrifugar**.

centrista [θen'trista] *a* centre *cpd*.

centro ['θentro] *nm* centre; ~ **de beneficios** (*COM*) profit centre; ~ **comercial** shopping centre; ~ **de computatión** computer centre; ~ **(de determinación) de costos** (*COM*) cost centre; ~ **delantero** (*DEPORTE*) centre forward; ~ **docente** teaching institution; ~ **juvenil** youth club; ~ **social** community centre; **ser del** ~ (*POL*) to be a moderate.

centroafricano, a [θentroafri'kano, a] *a*:

la República Centroafricana the Central African Republic.

centroamericano, a [θentroameri'kano, a] *a, nm/f* Central American.

centrocampista [θentrokam'pista] *nm/f* (*DEPORTE*) midfielder.

cent(s). *abr* (= *céntimo(s)*) c.

ceñir [θe'ɲir] *vt* (*rodear*) to encircle, surround; (*ajustar*) to fit (tightly); (*apretar*) to tighten; ~**se** *vr*: ~**se algo** to put sth on; ~**se al asunto** to stick to the matter in hand.

ceño ['θeɲo] *nm* frown, scowl; **fruncir el** ~ to frown, knit one's brow.

CEOE *nf abr* (= *Confederación Española de Organizaciones Empresariales*) ≈ CBI (*Brit*).

cepa ['θepa] *nf* (*de vid, fig*) stock; (*BIO*) strain.

CEPAL [θe'pal] *nf abr* (= *Comisión Económica de las Naciones Unidas para la América Latina*) Economic Commission for Latin America.

cepillar [θepi'ʎar] *vt* to brush; (*madera*) to plane (down).

cepillo [θe'piʎo] *nm* brush; (*para madera*) plane; (*REL*) poorbox, alms box.

cepo ['θepo] *nm* (*caza*) trap.

CEPSA ['θepsa] *nf abr* (*COM*) = *Compañía Española de Petróleos, S.A.*

cera ['θera] *nf* wax; ~ **de abejas** beeswax.

cerámica [θe'ramika] *nf* pottery; (*arte*) ceramics *sg*.

ceramista [θera'mista] *nm/f* potter.

cerbatana [θerβa'tana] *nf* blowpipe.

cerca ['θerka] *nf* fence ♦ *ad* near, nearby, close; **por aquí** ~ nearby ♦ *prep*: ~ **de** (*cantidad*) nearly, about; (*distancia*) near, close to ♦ *nmpl*: ~**s** foreground *sg*.

cercado [θer'kaðo] *nm* enclosure.

cercanía [θerka'nia] *nf* nearness, closeness; ~**s** *nfpl* outskirts, suburbs; **tren de** ~**s** commuter *o* local train.

cercano, a [θer'kano, a] *a* close, near; (*pueblo etc*) nearby; **C~ Oriente** Near East.

cercar [θer'kar] *vt* to fence in; (*rodear*) to surround.

cerciorar [θerθjo'rar] *vt* (*asegurar*) to assure; ~**se** *vr* (*descubrir*) to find out (*de* about); (*asegurarse*) to make sure (*de* of).

cerco ['θerko] *nm* (*AGR*) enclosure; (*AM*) fence; (*MIL*) siege.

Cerdeña [θer'ðeɲa] *nf* Sardinia.

cerdo ['θerðo] *nm* pig; **carne de** ~ pork.

cereal [θere'al] *nm* cereal; ~**es** *nmpl* cereals, grain *sg*.

cerebro [θe'reβro] *nm* brain; (*fig*) brains *pl*; **ser un** ~ (*fig*) to be brilliant.

ceremonia [θere'monja] *nf* ceremony; **reunión de** ~ formal meeting; **hablar sin**

~ to speak plainly.
ceremonial [θeremo'njal] *a, nm* ceremonial.
ceremonioso, a [θeremo'njoso, a] *a* ceremonious; (*cumplido*) formal.
cereza [θe'reθa] *nf* cherry.
cerezo [θe'reθo] *nm* cherry tree.
cerilla [θe'riʎa] *nf* (*fósforo*) match.
cerner [θer'ner] *vt* to sift, sieve; ~**se** *vr* to hover.
cernidor [θerni'ðor] *nm* sieve.
cero ['θero] *nm* nothing, zero; (*DEPORTE*) nil; **8 grados bajo** ~ 8 degrees below zero; **a partir de** ~ from scratch.
cerque ['θerke] *etc vb* V **cercar**.
cerrado, a [θe'rraðo, a] *a* closed, shut; (*con llave*) locked; (*tiempo*) cloudy, overcast; (*curva*) sharp; (*acento*) thick, broad; **a puerta cerrada** (*JUR*) in camera.
cerradura [θerra'ðura] *nf* (*acción*) closing; (*mecanismo*) lock.
cerrajería [θerraxe'ria] *nf* locksmith's craft; (*tienda*) locksmith's (shop).
cerrajero, a [θerra'xero, a] *nm/f* locksmith.
cerrar [θe'rrar] *vt* to close, shut; (*paso, carretera*) to close; (*grifo*) to turn off; (*trato, cuenta, negocio*) to close; ~ **con llave** to lock; ~ **el sistema** (*INFORM*) to close *o* shut down the system; ~ **un trato** to strike a bargain ♦ *vi* to close, shut; (*la noche*) to come down; ~**se** *vr* to close, shut; (*herida*) to heal.
cerro ['θerro] *nm* hill; **andar por las** ~**s de Úbeda** to wander from the point, digress.
cerrojo [θe'rroxo] *nm* (*herramienta*) bolt; (*de puerta*) latch.
certamen [θer'tamen] *nm* competition, contest.
certero, a [θer'tero, a] *a* (*gen*) accurate.
certeza [θer'teθa], **certidumbre** [θerti'ðumbre] *nf* certainty.
certificación [θertifika'θjon] *nf* certification; (*JUR*) affidavit.
certificado, a [θertifi'kaðo, a] *a* certified; (*CORREOS*) registered ♦ *nm* certificate.
certificar [θertifi'kar] *vt* (*asegurar, atestar*) to certify.
certifique [θerti'fike] *etc vb* V **certificar**.
cervatillo [θerßa'tiʎo] *nm* fawn.
cervecería [θerßeθe'ria] *nf* (*fábrica*) brewery; (*taberna*) public house.
cerveza [θer'ßeθa] *nf* beer.
cervical [θerßi'kal] *a* cervical.
cerviz [θer'ßiθ] *nf* nape of the neck.
cesación [θesa'θjon] *nf* cessation, suspension.
cesante [θe'sante] *a* redundant ♦ *nm/f* redundant worker.
cesantía [θesan'tia] *nf* (*AM*) unemployment.
cesar [θe'sar] *vi* to cease, stop ♦ *vt* (*en el trabajo*) to lay off; (*funcionario*) to remove

from office.
cese ['θese] *nm* (*de trabajo*) dismissal; (*de pago*) suspension.
cesión [θe'sjon] *nf*: ~ **de bienes** surrender of property.
césped ['θespeð] *nm* grass, lawn.
cesta ['θesta] *nf* basket.
cesto ['θesto] *nm* (large) basket, hamper.
cetrería [θetre'ria] *nf* falconry.
cetrino, a [θe'trino, a] *a* (*tez*) sallow.
cetro ['θetro] *nm* sceptre.
Ceuta [θe'uta] *nf* Ceuta.
ceutí [θeu'ti] *a* of *o* from Ceuta ♦ *nm/f* native *o* inhabitant of Ceuta.
C.F. *nm abr* (= *Club de Fútbol*) F.C.
cfr. *abr* (= *confróntese, compárese*) cf.
cg. *abr* (= *centígramo*) cg.
CGS *nf abr* (*Guatemala, El Salvador*) = *Confederación General de Sindicatos*.
CGT *nf abr* (*Colombia, México, Nicaragua*) = *Confederación General de Trabajadores*; (*Argentina*) = *Confederación General del Trabajo*.
ch... *V bajo la letra* CH, *después de* C.
C.I. *nm abr* = **coeficiente intelectual** *o* **de inteligencia**.
Cía *abr* (= *compañía*) Co.
cianuro [θja'nuro] *nm* cyanide.
ciática [θ'jatika] *nf* sciatica.
cicatrice [θika'triθe] *etc vb* V **cicatrizar**.
cicatriz [θika'triθ] *nf* scar.
cicatrizar [θikatri'θar] *vt* to heal; ~**se** *vr* to heal (up), form a scar.
cíclico, a ['θikliko, a] *a* cyclical.
ciclismo [θi'klismo] *nm* cycling.
ciclista [θi'klista] *nm/f* cyclist.
ciclo ['θiklo] *nm* cycle.
ciclón [θi'klon] *nm* cyclone.
cicuta [θi'kuta] *nf* hemlock.
C.I.D. *nm abr* = *Centro Internacional para el Desarrollo* (*Ginebra*).
ciego, a ['θjeɣo, a] *etc vb* V **cegar** ♦ *a* blind ♦ *nm/f* blind man/woman; **a ciegas** blindly.
ciegue ['θjeɣe] *etc vb* V **cegar**.
cielo ['θjelo] *nm* sky; (*REL*) heaven; (*ARQ*: *tb*: ~ **raso**) ceiling; ¡~**s!** good heavens!; **ver el** ~ **abierto** to see one's chance.
ciempiés [θjem'pjes] *nm inv* centipede.
cien [θjen] *num* V **ciento**.
ciénaga [θ'jenaɣa] *nf* marsh, swamp.
ciencia ['θjenθja] *nf* science; ~**s** *nfpl* science *sg*; **saber algo a** ~ **cierta** to know sth for certain.
ciencia-ficción ['θjenθjafik'θjon] *nf* science fiction.
cieno ['θjeno] *nm* mud, mire.
científico, a [θjen'tifiko, a] *a* scientific ♦ *nm/f* scientist.
ciento ['θjento], **cien** *num* hundred; **pagar al 10 por ciento** to pay at 10 per cent.

cierne ['θjerne] *etc vb* V cerner ♦ *nm*: en ~ in blossom; **en ~(s)** (*fig*) in its infancy.

cierre ['θjerre] *etc vb* V cerrar ♦ *nm* closing, shutting; (*con llave*) locking; (*RADIO*, *TV*) close-down; **~ de cremallera** zip (fastener); **precios de** ~ (*BOLSA*) closing prices; **~ del sistema** (*INFORM*) system shutdown.

cierto, a ['θjerto, a] *a* sure, certain; (*un tal*) a certain; (*correcto*) right, correct; **~ hombre** a certain man; **ciertas personas** certain *o* some people; **sí, es** ~ yes, that's correct; **por** ~ by the way; **lo** ~ **es que ...** the fact is that ...; **estar en lo** ~ to be right.

ciervo ['θjerβo] *nm* (*ZOOL*) deer; (: *macho*) stag.

cierzo ['θjerθo] *nm* north wind.

CIES *nm abr* = *Consejo Interamericano Económico y Social*.

cifra ['θifra] *nf* number, figure; (*cantidad*) number, quantity; (*secreta*) code; **~ global** lump sum; **~ de negocios** (*COM*) turnover; **en ~s redondas** in round figures; **~ de referencia** (*COM*) bench mark; **~ de ventas** (*COM*) sales figures.

cifrado, a [θi'fraðo, a] *a* in code.

cifrar [θi'frar] *vt* to code, write in code; (*resumir*) to abridge; (*calcular*) to reckon.

cigala [θi'ɣala] *nf* Norway lobster.

cigarra [θi'ɣarra] *nf* cicada.

cigarrera [θiɣa'rrera] *nf* cigar case.

cigarrillo [θiɣa'rriʎo] *nm* cigarette.

cigarro [θi'ɣarro] *nm* cigarette; (*puro*) cigar.

cigüeña [θi'ɣweɲa] *nf* stork.

CIJ *nf abr* (= *Corte Internacional de Justicia*) International Court of Justice.

cilíndrico, a [θi'lindriko, a] *a* cylindrical.

cilindro [θi'lindro] *nm* cylinder.

cima ['θima] *nf* (*de montaña*) top, peak; (*de árbol*) top; (*fig*) height.

címbalo ['θimbalo] *nm* cymbal.

cimbrar [θim'brar], **cimbrear** [θimbre'ar] *vt* to brandish; **~se** *vr* to sway.

cimentar [θimen'tar] *vt* to lay the foundations of; (*fig: reforzar*) to strengthen; (: *fundar*) to found.

cimiento [θi'mjento] *etc vb* V cimentar ♦ *nm* foundation.

cinc [θink] *nm* zinc.

cincel [θin'θel] *nm* chisel.

cincelar [θinθe'lar] *vt* to chisel.

cinco ['θinko] *num* five; (*fecha*) fifth; **las ~** five o'clock; **no estar en sus ~** (*fam*) to be off one's rocker.

cincuenta [θin'kwenta] *num* fifty.

cincuentón, ona [θinkwen'ton, ona] *a*, *nm/f* fifty-year old.

cincha ['θintʃa] *nf* girth, saddle strap.

cincho ['θintʃo] *nm* sash, belt.

cine ['θine] *nm* cinema; **el ~ mudo** silent films *pl*; **hacer** ~ to make films.

cineasta [θine'asta] *nm/f* (*director de cine*) film-maker *o* director.

cine-club ['θine'klub] *nm* film club.

cinéfilo, a [θi'nefilo, a] *nm/f* film buff.

cinematográfico, a [θinemato'ɣrafiko, a] *a* cine-, film *cpd*.

cínico, a ['θiniko, a] *a* cynical; (*descarado*) shameless ♦ *nm/f* cynic.

cinismo [θi'nismo] *nm* cynicism.

cinta ['θinta] *nf* band, strip; (*de tela*) ribbon; (*película*) reel; (*de máquina de escribir*) ribbon; (*métrica*) tape measure; (*magnetofónica*) tape; **~ adhesiva** sticky tape; **~ aislante** insulating tape; **~ de carbón** carbon ribbon; **~ magnética** (*INFORM*) magnetic tape; **~ métrica** tape measure; **~ de múltiples impactos** (*en impresora*) multistrike ribbon; **~ de tela** (*para máquina de escribir*) fabric ribbon; **~ transportadora** conveyor belt.

cinto ['θinto] *nm* belt, girdle.

cintura [θin'tura] *nf* waist; (*medida*) waistline.

cinturón [θintu'ron] *nm* belt; (*fig*) belt, zone; **~ salvavidas** lifebelt; **~ de seguridad** safety belt.

ciña ['θiɲa] *etc*, **ciñendo** [θi'ɲendo] *etc vb* V ceñir.

CIP [θip] *nm abr* = *Club Internacional de Prensa (Madrid)*.

ciprés [θi'pres] *nm* cypress (tree).

circo ['θirko] *nm* circus.

circuito [θir'kwito] *nm* circuit; (*DEPORTE*) lap; **TV por ~ cerrado** closed-circuit TV; **~ experimental** (*INFORM*) breadboard; **~ impreso** printed circuit; **~ lógico** (*INFORM*) logical circuit.

circulación [θirkula'θjon] *nf* circulation; (*AUTO*) traffic; "**cerrado a la ~ rodada**" "closed to vehicles".

circular [θirku'lar] *a*, *nf* circular ♦ *vt* to circulate ♦ *vi* to circulate; (*dinero*) to be in circulation; (*AUTO*) to drive; (*autobús*) to run.

círculo ['θirkulo] *nm* circle; (*centro*) clubhouse; (*POL*) political group.

circuncidar [θirkunθi'dar] *vt* to circumcise.

circunciso, a [θirkun'θiso, a] *pp de* circuncidar.

circundante [θirkun'dante] *a* surrounding.

circundar [θirkun'dar] *vt* to surround.

circunferencia [θirkunfe'renθja] *nf* circumference.

circunloquio [θirkun'lokjo] *nm* circumlocution.

circunscribir [θirkunskri'βir] *vt* to circumscribe; **~se** *vr* to be limited.

circunscripción [θirkunskrip'θjon] *nf* division; (*POL*) constituency.

circunscrito [θirkuns'krito] *pp de* circunscribir.

circunspección [θirkunspek'θjon] *nf* circunspection, caution.

circunspecto, a [θirkuns'pekto, a] *a* circumspect, cautious.

circunstancia [θirkuns'tanθja] *nf* circumstance; **~s agravantes/extenuantes** aggravating/extenuating circumstances; **estar a la altura de las ~s** to rise to the occasion.

circunstante [θirkuns'tante] *nm/f* onlooker, bystander.

circunvalación [θirkumbala'θjon] *nf*: **carretera de ~** ring road.

cirio ['θirjo] *nm* (wax) candle.

ciruela [θi'rwela] *nf* plum; **~ pasa** prune.

ciruelo [θi'rwelo] *nm* plum tree.

cirugía [θiru'xia] *nf* surgery; **~ estética** *o* **plástica** plastic surgery.

cirujano [θiru'xano] *nm* surgeon.

cisco ['θisko] *nm*: **armar un ~** to kick up a row; **estar hecho ~** to be a wreck.

cisma ['θisma] *nm* schism; (*POL etc*) split.

cisne ['θisne] *nm* swan; **canto de ~** swan song.

cisterna [θis'terna] *nf* cistern, tank.

cistitis [θis'titis] *nf* cystitis.

cita ['θita] *nf* appointment, meeting; (*de novios*) date; (*referencia*) quotation; **acudir/ faltar a una ~** to turn up for/miss an appointment.

citación [θita'θjon] *nf* (*JUR*) summons *sg*.

citar [θi'tar] *vt* to make an appointment with, arrange to meet; (*JUR*) to summons; (*un autor, texto*) to quote; **~se** *vr*: **~se con uno** to arrange to meet sb; **se citaron en el cine** they arranged to meet at the cinema.

cítara ['θitara] *nf* zither.

cítrico, a ['θitriko, a] *a* citric ◆ *nm*: **~s** citrus fruits.

CiU *nm abr* (*POL*) = **Convergència i Unió**.

ciudad [θju'ðað] *nf* town; (*capital de país etc*) city; **~ universitaria** university campus; **C~ del Cabo** Cape Town; **la C~ Condal** Barcelona.

ciudadanía [θjuðaða'nia] *nf* citizenship.

ciudadano, a [θjuða'ðano, a] *a* civic ◆ *nm/f* citizen.

ciudadrealeño, a [θjuðaðrea'leɲo, a] *a* of *o* from Ciudad Real ◆ *nm/f* native *o* inhabitant of Ciudad Real.

cívico, a ['θiβiko, a] *a* civic; (*fig*) public-spirited.

civil [θi'βil] *a* civil ◆ *nm* (*guardia*) policeman.

civilice [θiβi'liθe] *etc vb V* **civilizar**.

civilización [θiβiliθa'θjon] *nf* civilization.

civilizar [θiβili'θar] *vt* to civilize.

civismo [θi'βismo] *nm* public spirit.

cizaña [θi'θaɲa] *nf* (*fig*) discord; **sembrar ~**

to sow discord.

cl. *abr* (= *centilitro*) cl.

clamar [kla'mar] *vt* to clamour for, cry out for ◆ *vi* to cry out, clamour.

clamor [kla'mor] *nm* (*grito*) cry, shout; (*fig*) clamour, protest.

clamoroso, a [klamo'roso, a] *a* (*éxito etc*) resounding.

clandestinidad [klandestini'ðað] *nf* secrecy.

clandestino, a [klandes'tino, a] *a* clandestine; (*POL*) underground.

clara ['klara] *nf* (*de huevo*) eggwhite.

claraboya [klara'βoja] *nf* skylight.

clarear [klare'ar] *vi* (*el día*) to dawn; (*el cielo*) to clear up, brighten up; **~se** *vr* to be transparent.

clarete [kla'rete] *nm* rosé (wine).

claridad [klari'ðað] *nf* (*del día*) brightness; (*de estilo*) clarity.

clarificar [klarifi'kar] *vt* to clarify.

clarifique [klari'fike] *etc vb V* **clarificar**.

clarín [kla'rin] *nm* bugle.

clarinete [klari'nete] *nm* clarinet.

clarividencia [klariβi'ðenθja] *nf* clairvoyance; (*fig*) far-sightedness.

claro, a ['klaro, a] *a* clear; (*luminoso*) bright; (*color*) light; (*evidente*) clear, evident; (*poco espeso*) thin ◆ *nm* (*en bosque*) clearing ◆ *ad* clearly ◆ *excl* of course!; **hablar ~** (*fig*) to speak plainly; **a las claras** openly; **no sacamos nada en ~** we couldn't get anything definite.

clase ['klase] *nf* class; (*tipo*) kind, sort; (*ESCOL etc*) class; (: *aula*) classroom; **~ alta/media/obrera** upper/middle/working class; **dar ~s** to teach.

clásico, a ['klasiko, a] *a* classical; (*fig*) classic.

clasificable [klasifi'kaβle] *a* classifiable.

clasificación [klasifika'θjon] *nf* classification; (*DEPORTE*) league; (*COM*) ratings *pl*.

clasificador [klasifika'ðor] *nm* filing cabinet.

clasificar [klasifi'kar] *vt* to classify; (*INFORM*) to sort; **~se** *vr* (*DEPORTE*: *torneo*) to qualify.

clasifique [klasi'fike] *etc vb V* **clasificar**.

clasista [kla'sista] *a* (*fam*: *actitud*) snobbish.

claudia ['klauðja] *nf* greengage.

claudicar [klauði'kar] *vi* (*fig*) to back down.

claudique [klau'ðike] *etc vb V* **claudicar**.

claustro ['klaustro] *nm* cloister; (*UNIV*) staff; (*junta*) senate.

cláusula ['klausula] *nf* clause; **~ de exclusión** (*COM*) exclusion clause.

clausura [klau'sura] *nf* closing, closure.

clausurar [klausu'rar] *vt* (*congreso etc*) to close, bring to a close; (*POL etc*) to adjourn; (*cerrar*) to close (down).

clavado, a *a* nailed ♦ *excl* exactly!, precisely!

clavar [kla'ßar] *vt* (*tablas etc*) to nail (together); (*con alfiler*) to pin; (*clavo*) to hammer in; (*cuchillo*) to stick, thrust; (*mirada*) to fix; (*fam: estafar*) to cheat.

clave ['klaße] *nf* key; (*MUS*) clef; ~ **de búsqueda** (*INFORM*) search key; ~ **de clasificación** (*INFORM*) sort key.

clavel [kla'ßel] *nm* carnation.

claveteado [klaßete'aðo] *nm* studding.

clavicémbalo [klaßi'θembalo] *nm* harpsichord.

clavicordio [klaßikor'ðjo] *nm* clavicord.

clavícula [kla'ßikula] *nf* collar bone.

clavija [kla'ßixa] *nf* peg, pin; (*MUS*) peg; (*ELEC*) plug.

clavo ['klaßo] *nm* (*de metal*) nail; (*BOT*) clove; **dar en el** ~ (*fig*) to hit the nail on the head.

claxon ['klakson], *pl* **claxons** *nm* horn; **tocar el** ~ to sound one's horn.

clemencia [kle'menθja] *nf* mercy, clemency.

clemente [kle'mente] *a* merciful, clement.

cleptómano, a [klep'tomano, a] *nm/f* kleptomaniac.

clerical [kleri'kal] *a* clerical.

clérigo ['kleriɣo] *nm* priest, clergyman.

clero ['klero] *nm* clergy.

cliché [kli'tʃe] *nm* cliché; (*TIP*) stencil; (*FOTO*) negative.

cliente, a ['kljente, a] *nm/f* client, customer.

clientela [kljen'tela] *nf* clientele, customers *pl*; (*COM*) goodwill; (*MED*) patients *pl*.

clima ['klima] *nm* climate.

climatizado, a [klimati'θaðo, a] *a* air-conditioned.

clínico, a ['kliniko, a] *a* clinical ♦ *nf* clinic; (*particular*) private hospital.

clip *nm*, *pl* **clips** [klip, klis] paper clip.

cloaca [klo'aka] *nf* sewer, drain.

clorhídrico, a [klo'ridriko, a] *a* hydrochloric.

cloro ['kloro] *nm* chlorine.

cloroformo [kloro'formo] *nm* chloroform.

cloruro [klo'ruro] *nm* chloride; ~ **sódico** sodium chloride.

club, *pl* **clubs** *o* **clubes** [klub, klus, 'klußes] *nm* club; ~ **de jóvenes** youth club.

cm *abr* (= *centímetro*) cm.

CN *nf abr* (= *Carretera Nacional*) ≈ A road.

C.N.T. *nf abr* (*Esp*) = *Confederación Nacional de Trabajo*; (*AM*) = *Confederación Nacional de Trabajadores*.

coacción [koak'θjon] *nf* coercion, compulsion.

coaccionar [koakθjo'nar] *vt* to coerce, compel.

coagular [koaɣu'lar] *vt*, ~**se** *vr* (*sangre*) to clot; (*leche*) to curdle.

coágulo [ko'aɣulo] *nm* clot.

coalición [koali'θjon] *nf* coalition.

coartada [koar'taða] *nf* alibi.

coartar [koar'tar] *vt* to limit, restrict.

coba ['koßa] *nf*: **dar** ~ **a uno** to soft-soap sb.

cobarde [ko'ßarðe] *a* cowardly ♦ *nm/f* coward.

cobardía [koßar'ðia] *nf* cowardice.

cobaya [ko'ßaja] *nf*, **cobayo** [ko'ßajo] *nm* guinea pig.

cobertizo [koßer'tiθo] *nm* shelter.

cobertor [koßer'tor] *nm* bedspread.

cobertura [koßer'tura] *nf* cover; (*COM*) coverage; ~ **de dividendo** (*COM*) dividend cover.

cobija [ko'ßixa] *nf* (*AM*) blanket.

cobijar [koßi'xar] *vt* (*cubrir*) to cover; (*abrigar*) to shelter; ~**se** *vr* to take shelter.

cobijo [ko'ßixo] *nm* shelter.

cobra ['koßra] *nf* cobra.

cobrador, a [koßra'ðor, a] *nm/f* (*de autobús*) conductor/conductress; (*de impuestos, gas*) collector.

cobrar [ko'ßrar] *vt* (*cheque*) to cash; (*sueldo*) to collect, draw; (*objeto*) to recover; (*precio*) to charge; (*deuda*) to collect ♦ *vi* to draw one's pay; ~**se** *vr* to recover, get on well; **cóbrese al entregar** cash on delivery (COD); **a** ~ (*COM*) receivable; **cantidades por** ~ sums due.

cobre ['koßre] *nm* copper; ~**s** *nmpl* brass instruments.

cobrizo, a [ko'ßriθo, a] *a* coppery.

cobro ['koßro] *nm* (*de cheque*) cashing; (*pago*) payment; **presentar al** ~ to cash; *V tb* **llamada**.

coca ['koka] *nf* coca.

Coca-Cola ® ['koka'kola] *nf* Coca-Cola ®.

cocaína [koka'ina] *nf* cocaine.

cocainómano, a [kokai'nomano, a] *nm/f* cocaine addict.

cocción [kok'θjon] *nf* (*CULIN*) cooking; (*el hervir*) boiling.

cocear [koθe'ar] *vi* to kick.

cocer [ko'θer] *vt*, *vi* to cook; (*en agua*) to boil; (*en horno*) to bake.

cocido, a [ko'θiðo, a] *a* boiled ♦ *nm* stew.

cocina [ko'θina] *nf* kitchen; (*aparato*) cooker, stove; (*acto*) cookery; ~ **casera** home cooking; ~ **eléctrica** electric cooker; ~ **francesa** French cuisine; ~ **de gas** gas cooker.

cocinar [koθi'nar] *vt*, *vi* to cook.

cocinero, a [koθi'nero, a] *nm/f* cook.

coco ['koko] *nm* coconut; (*fantasma*) bogeyman; (*fam: cabeza*) nut; **comer el** ~ **a uno** (*fam*) to brainwash sb.

cocodrilo [koko'ðrilo] *nm* crocodile.

cocotero [koko'tero] *nm* coconut palm.

cóctel ['koktel] *nm* (*bebida*) cocktail; (*reunión*) cocktail party.

coctelera [kokte'lera] *nf* cocktail shaker.

coche ['kotʃe] *nm* (*AUTO*) car, automobile (*US*); (*de tren, de caballos*) coach, carriage; (*para niños*) pram (*Brit*), baby carriage (*US*); ~ **de bomberos** fire engine; ~ **celular** Black Maria, prison van; ~ (**comedor**) (*FERRO*) (dining) car; ~ **fúnebre** hearse.

coche-cama ['kotʃe'kama], *pl* **coches-cama** *nm* (*FERRO*) sleeping car, sleeper.

cochera [ko'tʃera] *nf* garage; (*de autobuses, trenes*) depot.

coche-restaurante, *pl* **coches-restaurante** ['kotʃerestau'rante] *nm* (*FERRO*) dining-car, diner.

cochinada [kotʃi'naða] *nf* dirty trick.

cochinillo [kotʃi'niʎo] *nm* piglet, suckling pig.

cochino, a [ko'tʃino, a] *a* filthy, dirty ♦ *nm/f* pig.

cod. *abr* (= *código*) code.

codazo [ko'ðaθo] *nm*: **dar un ~ a uno** to nudge sb.

codear [koðe'ar] *vi* to elbow, jostle; ~**se** *vr*: ~**se con** to rub shoulders with.

códice ['koðiθe] *nm* manuscript, codex.

codicia [ko'ðiθja] *nf* greed; (*fig*) lust.

codiciar [koði'θjar] *vt* to covet.

codicioso, a [koði'θjoso, a] *a* covetous.

codificador [koðifika'ðor] *nm* (*INFORM*) encoder; ~ **digital** digitizer.

código ['koðiɣo] *nm* code; ~ **de barras** (*COM*) bar code; ~ **binario** binary code; ~ **de caracteres** (*INFORM*) character code; ~ **de (la) circulación** highway code; ~ **civil** common law; ~ **de control** (*INFORM*) control code; ~ **máquina** (*INFORM*) machine code; ~ **militar** military law; ~ **de operación** (*INFORM*) operational *o* machine code; ~ **penal** penal code; ~ **de práctica** code of practice.

codillo [ko'ðiʎo] *nm* (*ZOOL*) knee; (*TEC*) elbow (joint).

codo ['koðo] *nm* (*ANAT, de tubo*) elbow; (*ZOOL*) knee; **hablar por los ~s** to talk 19 to the dozen.

codorniz [koðor'niθ] *nf* quail.

coeficiente [koefi'θjente] *nm* (*MAT*) coefficient; (*ECON etc*) rate; ~ **intelectual** *o* **de inteligencia** I.Q.

coerción [koer'θjon] *nf* coercion.

coercitivo, a [koerθi'tiβo, a] *a* coercive.

coetáneo, a [koe'taneo, a] *nm/f*: ~**s** contemporaries.

coexistencia [koeksis'tenθja] *nf* coexistence.

coexistir [koeksis'tir] *vi* to coexist.

cofia ['kofja] *nf* (*de enfermera*) (white) cap.

cofradía [kofra'ðia] *nf* brotherhood, frater-

nity.

cogedor [koxe'ðor] *nm* dustpan.

coger [ko'xer] *vt* (*Esp*) to take (hold of); (*objeto caído*) to pick up; (*frutas*) to pick, harvest; (*resfriado, ladrón, pelota*) to catch; (*AM fam!*) to lay (*!*); ~ **a uno desprevenido** to take sb unawares ♦ *vi*: ~ **por el buen camino** to take the right road; ~**se** *vr* (*el dedo*) to catch; ~**se a algo** to get hold of sth.

cogida [ko'xiða] *nf* gathering, harvesting; (*de peces*) catch; (*TAUR*) goring.

cogollo [ko'ɣoʎo] *nm* (*de lechuga*) heart; (*fig*) core, nucleus.

cogote [ko'ɣote] *nm* back *o* nape of the neck.

cohabitar [koaβi'tar] *vi* to live together, cohabit.

cohecho [ko'etʃo] *nm* (*acción*) bribery; (*soborno*) bribe.

coherencia [koe'renθja] *nf* coherence.

coherente [koe'rente] *a* coherent.

cohesión [koe'sjon] *nm* cohesion.

cohete [ko'ete] *nm* rocket.

cohibido, a [koi'βiðo, a] *a* (*PSICO*) inhibited; (*tímido*) shy; **sentirse ~** to feel embarrassed.

cohibir [koi'βir] *vt* to restrain, restrict; ~**se** *vr* to feel inhibited.

COI *nm abr* (= *Comité Olímpico Internacional*) IOC.

coima ['koima] *nf* (*fam*) bribe.

coincidencia [koinθi'ðenθja] *nf* coincidence.

coincidir [koinθi'ðir] *vi* (*en idea*) to coincide, agree; (*en lugar*) to coincide.

coito ['koito] *nm* intercourse, coitus.

cojear [koxe'ar] *vi* (*persona*) to limp, hobble; (*mueble*) to wobble, rock.

cojera [ko'xera] *nf* lameness; (*andar cojo*) limp.

cojín [ko'xin] *nm* cushion.

cojinete [koxi'nete] *nm* small cushion, pad; (*TEC*) (ball) bearing.

cojo, a ['koxo, a] *etc vb V* **coger** ♦ *a* (*que no puede andar*) lame, crippled; (*mueble*) wobbly ♦ *nm/f* lame person, cripple.

cojón [ko'xon] *nm* (*fam!*) ball (*!*), testicle; **¡cojones!** shit! (*!*).

cojonudo, a [koxo'nuðo, a] *a* (*Esp fam*) great, fantastic.

col [kol] *nf* cabbage; ~**es de Bruselas** Brussels sprouts.

col., col.ª *abr* (= *columna*) col.

cola ['kola] *nf* tail; (*de gente*) queue; (*lugar*) end, last place; (*para pegar*) glue, gum; (*de vestido*) train; **hacer ~** to queue (up).

colaboración [kolaβora'θjon] *nf* (*gen*) collaboration; (*en periódico*) contribution.

colaborador, a [kolaβora'ðor, a] *nm/f* collaborator; contributor.

colaborar [kolaβo'rar] *vi* to collaborate.

colación [kola'θjon] *nf*: **sacar a ~** to bring up.

colado, a [ko'laðo, a] *a (metal)* cast ♦ *nf*: **hacer la colada** to do the washing.

colador [kola'ðor] *nm (de té)* strainer; *(para verduras etc)* colander.

colapso [ko'lapso] *nm* collapse; **~ nervioso** nervous breakdown.

colar [ko'lar] *vt (líquido)* to strain off; *(metal)* to cast ♦ *vi* to ooze, seep (through); **~se** *vr* to jump the queue; *(en mitin)* to sneak in; *(equivocarse)* to slip up; **~se en** to get into without paying; *(en una fiesta)* to gatecrash.

colateral [kolate'ral] *nm* collateral.

colcha ['koltʃa] *nf* bedspread.

colchón [kol'tʃon] *nm* mattress; **~ inflable** inflatable mattress.

colchoneta [koltʃo'neta] *nf (en gimnasio)* mattress.

colear [kole'ar] *vi (perro)* to wag its tail.

colección [kolek'θjon] *nf* collection.

coleccionar [kolekθjo'nar] *vt* to collect.

coleccionista [kolekθjo'nista] *nm/f* collector.

colecta [ko'lekta] *nf* collection.

colectivo, a [kolek'tiβo, a] *a* collective, joint ♦ *nm (AM)* (small) bus.

colector [kolek'tor] *nm* collector; *(sumidero)* sewer.

colega [ko'leɣa] *nm/f* colleague.

colegial, a [kole'xjal, a] *a (ESCOL etc)* school *cpd*, college *cpd* ♦ *nm/f* schoolboy/girl.

colegio [ko'lexjo] *nm* college; *(escuela)* school; *(de abogados etc)* association; **~ de internos** boarding school; **ir al ~** to go to school.

colegir [kole'xir] *vt (juntar)* to collect, gather; *(deducir)* to infer, conclude.

cólera ['kolera] *nf (ira)* anger; **montar en ~** to get angry ♦ *nm (MED)* cholera.

colérico, a [ko'leriko, a] *a* angry, furious.

colesterol [koleste'rol] *nm* cholesterol.

coleta [ko'leta] *nf* pigtail.

coletazo [kole'taθo] *nm*: **dar un ~** *(animal)* to flap its tail; **los últimos ~s** death throes.

colgado, a [kol'ɣaðo, a] *pp de* **colgar** ♦ *a* hanging; *(ahorcado)* hanged; **dejar ~ a uno** to let sb down.

colgajo [kol'ɣaxo] *nm* tatter.

colgante [kol'ɣante] *a* hanging; *V* **puente** ♦ *nm (joya)* pendant.

colgar [kol'ɣar] *vt* to hang (up); *(tender: ropa)* to hang out ♦ *vi* to hang; *(teléfono)* to hang up.

colgué [kol'ɣe], **colguemos** [kol'ɣemos] *etc vb V* **colgar**.

colibrí [koli'βri] *nm* hummingbird.

coliflor [koli'flor] *nf* cauliflower.

coligiendo [koli'xjenðo] *etc vb V* **colegir**.

colija [ko'lixa] *etc vb V* **colegir**.

colilla [ko'liʎa] *nf* cigarette end, butt.

colina [ko'lina] *nf* hill.

colindante [kolin'dante] *a* adjacent, neighbouring.

colindar [kolin'dar] *vi* to adjoin, be adjacent.

colisión [koli'sjon] *nf* collision; **~ de frente** head-on crash.

colitis [ko'litis] *nf inv*: **tener ~** to have diarrhoea.

colmado, a [kol'maðo, a] *a* full ♦ *nm* grocer's shop.

colmar [kol'mar] *vt* to fill to the brim; *(fig)* to fulfil, realize.

colmena [kol'mena] *nf* beehive.

colmillo [kol'miʎo] *nm (diente)* eye tooth; *(de elefante)* tusk; *(de perro)* fang.

colmo ['kolmo] *nm* height, summit; **para ~ de desgracias** to cap it all; **¡eso es ya el ~!** that's beyond a joke!.

colocación [koloka'θjon] *nf (acto)* placing; *(empleo)* job, position; *(situación)* place, position; *(COM)* placement.

colocar [kolo'kar] *vt* to place, put, position; *(poner en empleo)* to find a job for; **~ dinero** to invest money; **~se** *vr* to place o.s.; *(conseguir trabajo)* to find a job.

colofón [kolo'fon] *nm*: **como ~ de las conversaciones** as a sequel to o following the talks.

Colombia [ko'lombja] *nf* Colombia.

colombiano, a [kolom'bjano, a] *a, nm/f* Colombian.

colon ['kolon] *nm* colon.

Colonia [ko'lonja] *nf* Cologne.

colonia [ko'lonja] *nf* colony; *(de casas)* housing estate; *(agua de ~)* cologne; **~ escolar** summer camp (for schoolchildren).

colonice [kolo'niθe] *etc vb V* **colonizar**.

colonización [koloniθa'θjon] *nf* colonization.

colonizador, a [koloniθa'ðor, a] *a* colonizing ♦ *nm/f* colonist, settler.

colonizar [koloni'θar] *vt* to colonize.

colono [ko'lono] *nm (POL)* colonist, settler; *(AGR)* tenant farmer.

coloque [ko'loke] *etc vb V* **colocar**.

coloquio [ko'lokjo] *nm* conversation; *(congreso)* conference; *(INFORM)* handshake.

color [ko'lor] *nm* colour; **a todo ~** in full colour; **verlo todo ~ de rosa** to see everything through rose-coloured spectacles; **le salieron los ~es** she blushed.

colorado, a [kolo'raðo, a] *a (rojo)* red; *(AM: chiste)* rude, blue; **ponerse ~** to blush.

colorante [kolo'rante] *nm* colouring (matter).

colorar [kolo'rar] *vt* to colour; *(teñir)* to dye.

colorear [kolore'ar] *vt* to colour.

colorete [kolo'rete] *nm* blusher.

colorido [kolo'riðo] *nm* colour(ing).

columbrar [kolum'brar] *vt* to glimpse, spy.

columna [ko'lumna] *nf* column; *(pilar)* pillar; *(apoyo)* support; ~ **blindada** (*MIL*) armoured column; ~ **vertebral** spine, spinal column.

columpiar [kolum'pjar] *vt*, ~**se** *vr* to swing.

columpio [ko'lumpjo] *nm* swing.

collar [ko'ʎar] *nm* necklace; *(de perro)* collar.

coma ['koma] *nf* comma ♦ *nm* (*MED*) coma.

comadre [ko'maðre] *nf* (*madrina*) godmother; *(vecina)* neighbour; *(chismosa)* gossip.

comadrear [komaðre'ar] *vi* to gossip.

comadreja [koma'ðrexa] *nf* weasel.

comadrona [koma'ðrona] *nf* midwife.

comandancia [koman'danθja] *nf* command.

comandante [koman'dante] *nm* commandant; *(grado)* major.

comandar [koman'dar] *vt* to command.

comando [ko'mando] *nm* (*MIL*: *mando*) command; (: *grupo*) commando unit; (*INFORM*) command; ~ **de búsqueda** search command.

comarca [ko'marka] *nf* region.

comarcal [komar'kal] *a* local.

comba ['komba] *nf* (*curva*) curve; *(en viga)* warp; *(cuerda)* skipping rope; **saltar a la** ~ to skip.

combar [kom'bar] *vt* to bend, curve.

combate [kom'bate] *nm* fight; *(fig)* battle; **fuera de** ~ out of action.

combatiente [komba'tjente] *nm* combatant.

combatir [komba'tir] *vt* to fight, combat.

combatividad [kombatißi'ðað] *nf* (*actitud*) fighting spirit; *(agresividad)* aggressiveness.

combativo, a [komba'tißo, a] *a* full of fight.

combinación [kombina'θjon] *nf* combination; (*QUÍMICA*) compound; *(bebida)* cocktail; *(plan)* scheme, setup; *(prenda)* slip.

combinar [kombi'nar] *vt* to combine; *(colores)* to match.

combinado, a [kombi'naðo, a] *a*: **plato** ~ main course served with vegetables.

combustible [kombus'tißle] *nm* fuel.

combustión [kombus'tjon] *nf* combustion.

comedia [ko'meðja] *nf* comedy; (*TEATRO*) play, drama; *(fig)* farce.

comediante [kome'ðjante] *nm/f* (comic) actor/actress.

comedido, a [kome'ðiðo, a] *a* moderate.

comedirse [kome'ðirse] *vr* to behave moderately; *(ser cortés)* to be courteous.

comedor, a [kome'ðor, a] *nm/f* *(persona)* glutton ♦ *nm* *(habitación)* dining room; *(restaurante)* restaurant; *(cantina)* canteen.

comencé [komen'θe], **comencemos** [komen'θemos] *etc vb V* **comenzar**.

comensal [komen'sal] *nm/f* fellow guest/ diner.

comentar [komen'tar] *vt* to comment on; *(fam)* to discuss; **comentó que...** he made the comment that....

comentario [komen'tarjo] *nm* comment, remark; (*LIT*) commentary; ~**s** *nmpl* gossip *sg*; **dar lugar a** ~**s** to cause gossip.

comentarista [komenta'rista] *nm/f* commentator.

comenzar [komen'θar] *vt*, *vi* to begin, start, commence; ~ **a hacer algo** to begin o start doing o to do sth.

comer [ko'mer] *vt* to eat; (*DAMAS, AJEDREZ*) to take, capture; *(párrafo etc)* to skip ♦ *vi* to eat; *(almorzar)* to have lunch; ~**se** *vr* to eat up; ~ **el coco a** *(fam)* to brainwash; ¡**a** ~! food's ready!

comerciable [komer'θjaßle] *a* marketable, saleable.

comercial [komer'θjal] *a* commercial; *(relativo al negocio)* business *cpd*.

comerciante [komer'θjante] *nm/f* trader, merchant; *(tendero)* shopkeeper; ~ **exclusivo** (*COM*) sole trader.

comerciar [komer'θjar] *vi* to trade, do business.

comercio [ko'merθjo] *nm* commerce, trade; *(negocio)* business; *(grandes empresas)* big business; *(fig)* dealings *pl*; ~ **autorizado** (*COM*) licensed trade; ~ **exterior** foreign trade.

comestible [komes'tißle] *a* eatable, edible ♦ *nm*: ~**s** food *sg*, foodstuffs; (*COM*) groceries.

cometa [ko'meta] *nm* comet ♦ *nf* kite.

cometer [kome'ter] *vt* to commit.

cometido [kome'tiðo] *nm* *(misión)* task, assignment; *(deber)* commitment.

comezón [kome'θon] *nf* itch, itching.

comicios [ko'miθjos] *nmpl* elections; *(voto)* voting *sg*.

cómico, a ['komiko, a] *a* comic(al) ♦ *nm/f* comedian; *(de teatro)* (comic) actor/ actress.

comida [ko'miða] *etc vb V* **comedirse** ♦ *nf* *(alimento)* food; *(almuerzo, cena)* meal; *(de mediodía)* lunch.

comidilla [komi'ðiʎa] *nf*: **ser la** ~ **de la ciudad** to be the talk of the town.

comience [ko'mjenθe] *etc vb V* **comenzar**.

comienzo [ko'mjenθo] *etc vb V* **comenzar** ♦ *nm* beginning, start; **dar** ~ **a un acto** to begin a ceremony; ~ **del archivo** (*INFORM*) top-of-file.

comilón, ona [komi'lon, ona] *a* greedy ◆ *nf (fam)* blow-out.

comillas [ko'miʎas] *nfpl* quotation marks.

comino [ko'mino] *nm* cumin (seed); **no me importa un ~** I don't give a damn.

comisaría [komisa'ria] *nf* police station, precinct *(US)*; *(MIL)* commissariat.

comisario [komi'sarjo] *nm (MIL etc)* commissary; *(POL)* commissar.

comisión [komi'sjon] *nf (COM: pago)* commission, rake-off *(fam)*; (: *junta*) board; *(encargo)* assignment; **~ mixta/ permanente** joint/standing committee; **Comisiones Obreras** *(Esp)* Workers' Unions.

comisura [komi'sura] *nf:* **~ de los labios** corner of the mouth.

comité, *pl* **comités** *nm* [komi'te, komi'tes] committee; **~ de impresa** works council.

comitiva [komi'tißa] *nf* suite, retinue.

como ['komo] *ad* as; *(tal* ~) like; *(aproximadamente)* about, approximately ◆ *conj (ya que, puesto que)* as, since; *(en seguida que)* as soon as; *(si:* +*subjun)* if; **¡~ no!** of course!; **~ no lo haga hoy** unless he does it today; **~ si** as if; **es tan alto ~ ancho** it is as high as it is wide.

cómo ['komo] *ad* how?, why? ◆ *excl* what?, I beg your pardon? ◆ *nm:* **el ~ y el porqué** the whys and wherefores; **¿~ está Ud?** how are you?; **¿~ no?** why not?; **¿~ son?** what are they like?

cómoda ['komoða] *nf* chest of drawers.

comodidad [komoði'ðað] *nf* comfort; **venga a su ~** come at your convenience.

comodín [komo'ðin] *nm* joker; *(INFORM)* wild card; **símbolo ~** wildcard character.

cómodo, a ['komoðo, a] *a* comfortable; *(práctico, de fácil uso)* convenient.

comoquiera [como'kjera] *conj:* **~ que** (+ *subjun*) in whatever way; **~ que sea eso** however that may be.

comp. *abr* (= *compárese*) cp.

compacto, a [kom'pakto, a] *a* compact.

compadecer [kompaðe'θer] *vt* to pity, be sorry for; **~se** *vr:* **~se de** to pity, be sorry for.

compadezca [kompa'ðeθka] *etc vb V* **compadecer.**

compadre [kom'paðre] *nm (padrino)* godfather; *(amigo)* friend, pal.

compaginar [kompaxi'nar] *vt:* **~ A con B** to bring A into line with B; **~se** *vr:* **~se con** to tally with, square with.

compañerismo [kompaɲe'rismo] *nm* comradeship.

compañero, a [kompa'ɲero, a] *nm/f* companion; *(novio)* boyfriend/girlfriend; **~ de clase** classmate.

compañía [kompa'ɲia] *nf* company; **~ afiliada** associated company; **~ concesionadora** franchiser; **~ (no) cotizable**

(un) listed company; **~ inversionista** investment trust; **hacer ~ a uno** to keep sb company.

comparación [kompara'θjon] *nf* comparison; **en ~ con** in comparison with.

comparar [kompa'rar] *vt* to compare.

comparativo, a [kompara'tißo, a] *a* comparative.

comparecencia [kompare'θenθja] *nf (JUR)* appearance (in court); **orden de ~** summons *sg.*

comparecer [kompare'θer] *vi* to appear (in court).

comparezca [kompa'reθka] *etc vb V* **comparecer.**

comparsa [kom'parsa] *nm/f* extra.

compartimiento [komparti'mjento] *nm (FERRO)* compartment.

compartir [kompar'tir] *vt* to divide (up), share (out).

compás [kom'pas] *nm (MUS)* beat, rhythm; *(MAT)* compasses *pl; (NAUT etc)* compass; **al ~** in time.

compasión [kompa'sjon] *nf* compassion, pity.

compasivo, a [kompa'sißo, a] *a* compassionate.

compatibilidad [kompatißili'ðað] *nf (tb INFORM)* compatibility.

compatible [kompa'tißle] *a* compatible.

compatriota [kompa'trjota] *nm/f* compatriot, fellow countryman/woman.

compendiar [kompen'djar] *vt* to summarize; *(libro)* to abridge.

compendio [kom'pendjo] *nm* summary; abridgement.

compenetración [kompenetra'θjon] *nf (fig)* mutual understanding.

compenetrarse [kompene'trarse] *vr (fig):* **~ (muy) bien** to get on (very) well together.

compensación [kompensa'θjon] *nf* compensation; *(JUR)* damages *pl; (COM)* clearing.

compensar [kompen'sar] *vt* to compensate; *(pérdida)* to make up for.

competencia [kompe'tenθja] *nf (incumbencia)* domain, field; *(COM)* receipt; *(JUR, habilidad)* competence; *(rivalidad)* competition.

competente [kompe'tente] *a (JUR, persona)* competent; *(conveniente)* suitable.

competer [kompe'ter] *vi:* **~ a** to be the responsibility of, fall to.

competición [kompeti'θjon] *nf* competition.

competidor, a [kompeti'ðor, a] *nm/f* competitor.

competir [kompe'tir] *vi* to compete.

compilación [kompila'θjon] *nf* compilation; **tiempo de ~** *(INFORM)* compile time.

compilador [kompila'ðor] *nm* compiler.

compilar [kompi'lar] *vt* to compile.

compita [kom'pita] *etc vb* V **competir**.

complacencia [kompla'θenθja] *nf* (*placer*) pleasure; (*satisfacción*) satisfaction; (*buena voluntad*) willingness.

complacer [kompla'θer] *vt* to please; ~**se** *vr* to be pleased.

complaciente [kompla'θjente] *a* kind, obliging, helpful.

complazca [kom'plaθka] *etc vb* V **complacer**.

complejo, a [kom'plexo, a] *a*, *nm* complex.

complementario, a [komplemen'tarjo, a] *a* complementary.

completar [komple'tar] *vt* to complete.

completo, a [kom'pleto, a] *a* complete; (*perfecto*) perfect; (*lleno*) full ♦ *nm* full complement.

complicado, a [kompli'kaðo, a] *a* complicated; **estar** ~ **en** to be involved in.

complicar [kompli'kar] *vt* to complicate.

cómplice ['kompliθe] *nm/f* accomplice.

complique [kom'plike] *etc vb* V **complicar**.

complot *pl* **complots** [kom'plo(t), kom'plos] *nm* plot; (*conspiración*) conspiracy.

compondré [kompon'dre] *etc vb* V **componer**.

componenda [kompo'nenda] *nf* compromise; (*pey*) shady deal.

componer [kompo'ner] *vt* to make up, put together; (*MUS, LIT, IMPRENTA*) to compose; (*algo roto*) to mend, repair; (*adornar*) to adorn; (*arreglar*) to arrange; (*reconciliar*) to reconcile; ~**se** *vr*: ~**se de** to consist of; **componérselas para hacer algo** to manage to do sth.

componga [kom'ponga] *etc vb* V **componer**.

comportamiento [komporta'mjento] *nm* behaviour, conduct.

comportarse [kompor'tarse] *vr* to behave.

composición [komposi'θjon] *nf* composition.

compositor, a [komposi'tor, a] *nm/f* composer.

compostelano, a [komposte'lano, a] *a* of *o* from Santiago de Compostela ♦ *nm/f* native *o* inhabitant of Santiago de Compostela.

compostura [kompos'tura] *nf* (*reparación*) mending, repair; (*composición*) composition; (*acuerdo*) agreement; (*actitud*) composure.

compota [kom'pota] *nf* compote, preserve.

compra ['kompra] *nf* purchase; ~**s** *nfpl* purchases, shopping *sg*; **hacer la** ~**/ir de** ~**s** to do the/go shopping; ~ **a granel** (*COM*) bulk buying; ~ **proteccionista** (*COM*) support buying.

comprador, a [kompra'ðor, a] *nm/f* buyer, purchaser.

comprar [kom'prar] *vt* to buy, purchase; ~ **deudas** (*COM*) to factor.

compraventa [kompra'βenta] *nf* (*JUR*) contract of sale.

comprender [kompren'der] *vt* to understand; (*incluir*) to comprise, include.

comprensible [kompren'sißle] *a* understandable.

comprensión [kompren'sjon] *nf* understanding; (*totalidad*) comprehensiveness.

comprensivo, a [kompren'sißo, a] *a* comprehensive; (*actitud*) understanding.

compresa [kom'presa] *nf* compress; ~ **higiénica** sanitary towel (*Brit*) *o* napkin (*US*).

compresión [kompre'sjon] *nf* compression.

comprimido, a [kompri'miðo] *a* compressed ♦ *nm* (*MED*) pill, tablet; **en caracteres** ~**s** (*TIP*) condensed.

comprimir [kompri'mir] *vt* to compress; (*fig*) to control; (*INFORM*) to pack.

comprobación [komproßa'θjon] *nf*: ~ **general de cuentas** (*COM*) general audit.

comprobante [kompro'ßante] *nm* proof; (*COM*) voucher; ~ **(de pago)** receipt.

comprobar [kompro'ßar] *vt* to check; (*probar*) to prove; (*TEC*) to check, test.

comprometedor, a [kompromete'ðor, a] *a* compromising.

comprometido, a [komprome'tiðo, a] *a* (*situación*) awkward; (*escritor etc*) committed.

comprometer [komprome'ter] *vt* to compromise; (*exponer*) to endanger; ~**se** *vr* to compromise o.s.; (*involucrarse*) to get involved.

compromiso [kompro'miso] *nm* (*obligación*) obligation; (*cita*) engagement, date; (*cometido*) commitment; (*convenio*) agreement; (*dificultad*) awkward situation; **libre de** ~ (*COM*) without obligation.

comprueba [kom'prweßa] *etc vb* V **comprobar**.

compuerta [kom'pwerta] *nf* (*en canal*) sluice, floodgate; (*INFORM*) gate.

compuesto, a [kom'pwesto, a] *pp de* **componer** ♦ *a*: ~ **de** composed of, made up of ♦ *nm* compound; (*MED*) preparation.

compulsar [kompul'sar] *vt* (*cotejar*) to collate, compare; (*JUR*) to make an attested copy of.

compulsivo, a [kompul'sißo, a] *a* compulsive.

compuse [com'puse] *etc vb* V **componer**.

computador [komputa'ðor] *nm*, **computadora** [komputa'ðora] *nf* computer; ~ **central** mainframe computer; **computador especializado** dedicated computer; ~ **personal** personal computer.

computar [kompu'tar] *vt* to calculate, compute.

cómputo ['komputo] *nm* calculation, computation.

comulgar [komul'ɣar] *vi* to receive communion.

comulgue [ko'mulɣe] *etc vb V* **comulgar**.

común [ko'mun] *a* (*gen*) common; (*corriente*) ordinary; **por lo** ~ generally ♦ *nm*: **el** ~ the community.

comuna [ko'muna] *nf* commune; (*AM*) district.

comunicación [komunika'θjon] *nf* communication; (*informe*) report.

comunicado [komuni'kaðo] *nm* announcement; ~ **de prensa** press release.

comunicar [komuni'kar] *vt* to communicate; (*ARQ*) to connect ♦ *vi* to communicate; to send a report; ~**se** *vr* to communicate; **está comunicando** (*TELEC*) the line's engaged (*Brit*) *o* busy (*US*).

comunicativo, a [komunika'tiβo, a] *a* communicative.

comunidad [komuni'ðað] *nf* community; ~ **de vecinos** residents' association; **C~ Económica Europea (CEE)** European Economic Community (EEC).

comunión [komu'njon] *nf* communion.

comunique [komu'nike] *etc vb V* **comunicar**.

comunismo [komu'nismo] *nm* communism.

comunista [komu'nista] *a, nm/f* communist.

con [kon] *prep* with; (*a pesar de*) in spite of; (*hacia: tb:* **para** ~) towards; ~ **arreglo a** in accordance with; ~ **que** so, and so; ~ **tal que** so long as; ~ **apretar el botón** by pressing the button; ~ **todo, él la quiere mucho** in spite of it all, he loves her dearly.

conato [ko'nato] *nm* attempt; ~ **de robo** attempted robbery.

cóncavo, a ['konkaβo, a] *a* concave.

concebir [konθe'βir] *vt* to conceive; (*imaginar*) to imagine ♦ *vi* to conceive.

conceder [konθe'ðer] *vt* to concede.

concejal, a [konθe'xal, a] *nm/f* town councillor.

concejo [kon'θexo] *nm* council.

concentración [konθentra'θjon] *nf* concentration.

concentrar [konθen'trar] *vt*, ~**se** *vr* to concentrate.

concepción [konθep'θjon] *nf* conception.

concepto [kon'θepto] *nm* concept; **por** ~ **de** as, by way of; **tener buen** ~ **de uno** to think highly of sb; **bajo ningún** ~ under no circumstances.

conceptuar [konθep'twar] *vt* to judge.

concernir [konθer'nir] *vi*: **en lo que concierne a** concerning.

concertar [konθer'tar] *vt* (*MUS*) to harmonize; (*acordar: precio*) to agree; (: *tratado*) to conclude; (*trato*) to arrange, fix up;

(*combinar: esfuerzos*) to coordinate; (*reconciliar: personas*) to reconcile ♦ *vi* to harmonize, be in tune.

concesión [konθe'sjon] *nf* concession; (*COM: fabricación*) licence.

concesionario, a [konθesjo'narjo, a] *nm/f* (*COM*) (licensed) dealer, agent, concessionaire; (: *de venta*) franchisee; (: *de transportes etc*) contractor.

conciencia [kon'θjenθja] *nf* (*moral*) conscience; (*conocimiento*) awareness; **libertad de** ~ freedom of worship; **tener/tomar** ~ **de** to be/become aware of; **tener la** ~ **limpia** *o* **tranquila** to have a clear conscience; **tener plena** ~ **de** to be fully aware of.

concienciar [konθjen'θjar] *vt* to make aware; ~**se** *vr* to become aware.

concienzudo, a [konθjen'θuðo, a] *a* conscientious.

concierne [kon'θjerne] *etc vb V* **concernir**.

concierto [kon'θjerto] *etc vb V* **concertar** ♦ *nm* concert; (*obra*) concerto.

conciliación [konθilja'θjon] *nf* conciliation.

conciliar [konθi'ljar] *vt* to reconcile ♦ *a* (*REL*) of a council; ~ **el sueño** to get to sleep.

concilio [kon'θiljo] *nm* council.

concisión [konθi'sjon] *nf* conciseness.

conciso, a [kon'θiso, a] *a* concise.

conciudadano, a [konθjuða'ðano, a] *nm/f* fellow citizen.

concluir [konklu'ir] *vt* (*acabar*) to conclude; (*inferir*) to infer, deduce ♦ *vi*, ~**se** *vr* to conclude; **todo ha concluido** it's all over.

conclusión [konklu'sjon] *nf* conclusion; **llegar a la** ~ **de que** ... to come to the conclusion that ....

concluya [kon'kluja] *etc vb V* **concluir**.

concluyente [konklu'jente] *a* (*prueba, información*) conclusive.

concordancia [konkor'ðanθja] *nf* agreement.

concordar [konkor'ðar] *vt* to reconcile ♦ *vi* to agree, tally.

concordia [kon'korðja] *nf* harmony.

concretamente [konkreta'mente] *ad* specifically, to be exact.

concretar [konkre'tar] *vt* to make concrete, make more specific; (*problema*) to pinpoint; ~**se** *vr* to become more definite.

concreto, a [kon'kreto, a] *a, nm* (*AM*) concrete; **en** ~ (*en resumen*) to sum up; (*específicamente*) specifically; **no hay nada en** ~ there's nothing definite.

concubina [konku'βina] *nf* concubine.

concuerde [kon'kwerðe] *etc vb V* **concordar**.

concupiscencia [konkupis'θenθja] *nf* (*avancia*) greed; (*lujuria*) lustfulness.

concurrencia [konku'rrenθja] *nf* turnout.

concurrido, a [konku'rriðo, a] *a* (*calle*) busy; (*local, reunión*) crowded.

concurrir [konku'rrir] *vi* (*juntarse: ríos*) to meet, come together; (: *personas*) to gather, meet.

concursante [konkur'sante] *nm* competitor.

concursar [konkur'sar] *vi* to compete.

concurso [kon'kurso] *nm* (*de público*) crowd; (*ESCOL, DEPORTE, competencia*) competition; (*COM*) invitation to tender; (*examen*) open competition; (*TV etc*) quiz; (*ayuda*) help, cooperation.

concha ['kontʃa] *nf* shell.

condado [kon'daðo] *nm* county.

condal [kon'dal] *a*: **la ciudad** ~ Barcelona.

conde ['konde] *nm* count.

condecoración [kondekora'θjon] *nf* (*MIL*) medal, decoration.

condecorar [kondeko'rar] *vt* to decorate.

condena [kon'dena] *nf* sentence; **cumplir una** ~ to serve a sentence.

condenación [kondena'θjon] *nf* condemnation; (*REL*) damnation.

condenado, a [konde'naðo, a] *a* (*JUR*) condemned; (*fam: maldito*) damned ♦ *nm/f* (*JUR*) convicted person.

condenar [konde'nar] *vt* to condemn; (*JUR*) to convict; ~**se** *vr* (*JUR*) to confess (one's guilt); (*REL*) to be damned.

condensar [konden'sar] *vt* to condense.

condesa [kon'desa] *nf* countess.

condescendencia [kondesθen'denθja] *nf* condescension; **aceptar algo por** ~ to accept sth so as not to hurt feelings.

condescender [kondesθen'der] *vi* to acquiesce, comply.

condescienda [kondes'θjenda] *etc vb* V **condescender**.

condición [kondi'θjon] *nf* (*gen*) condition; (*rango*) social class; **condiciones** *nfpl* (*cualidades*) qualities; (*estado*) condition; **a** ~ **de que** ... on condition that ...; **las condiciones del contrato** the terms of the contract; **condiciones de trabajo** working conditions; **condiciones de venta** conditions of sale.

condicionamiento [kondiθjona'mjento] *nm* conditioning.

condicional [kondiθjo'nal] *a* conditional.

condicionar [kondiθjo'nar] *vt* (*acondicionar*) to condition; ~ **algo a algo** to make sth conditional *o* dependent on sth.

condimento [kondi'mento] *nm* seasoning.

condiscípulo, a [kondis'θipulo, a] *nm/f* fellow student.

condolerse [kondo'lerse] *vr* to sympathize.

condominio [kondo'minjo] *nm* (*COM*) joint ownership.

condón [kon'don] *nm* condom.

condonar [kondo'nar] *vt* (*JUR: reo*) to reprieve; (*COM: deuda*) to cancel.

conducente [kondu'θente] *a*: ~ **a** conducive to, leading to.

conducir [kondu'θir] *vt* to take, convey; (*ELEC etc*) to carry; (*AUTO*) to drive; (*negocio*) to manage ♦ *vi* to drive; (*fig*) to lead; ~**se** *vr* to behave.

conducta [kon'dukta] *nf* conduct, behaviour.

conducto [kon'dukto] *nm* pipe, tube; (*fig*) channel; (*ELEC*) lead; **por** ~ **de** through.

conductor, a [konduk'tor, a] *a* leading, guiding ♦ *nm* (*FISICA*) conductor; (*de vehículo*) driver.

conduela [kon'dwela] *etc vb* V **condolerse**.

conduje [kon'duxe] *etc vb* V **conducir**.

conduzca [kon'duθka] *etc vb* V **conducir**.

conectado, a [konek'taðo, a] *a* (*ELEC*) connected, plugged in; (*INFORM*) on-line.

conectar [konek'tar] *vt* to connect (up), plug in; (*INFORM*) to toggle on; ~**se** *vr* (*INFORM*) to log in (on).

conejillo [kone'xiʎo] *nm*: ~ **de Indias** guinea pig.

conejo [ko'nexo] *nm* rabbit.

conexión [konek'sjon] *nf* connection; (*INFORM*) logging in (on).

confabularse [konfaβu'larse] *vr*: ~ **(para hacer algo)** to plot, conspire (to do sth).

confección [konfek'θjon] *nf* (*preparación*) preparation, making-up; (*industria*) clothing industry; (*producto*) article; **de** ~ (*ropa*) off-the-peg.

confeccionar [konfe(k)θjo'nar] *vt* to make (up).

confederación [konfeðera'θjon] *nf* confederation.

conferencia [konfe'renθja] *nf* conference; (*lección*) lecture; (*TELEC*) call; ~ **de cobro revertido** (*TELEC*) reversed-charge (*Brit*) *o* collect (*US*) call; ~ **cumbre** summit (conference).

conferenciante [konferen'θjante] *nm/f* lecturer.

conferir [konfe'rir] *vt* to award.

confesar [konfe'sar] *vt* (*admitir*) to confess, admit; (*error*) to acknowledge; (*crimen*) to own up to.

confesión [konfe'sjon] *nf* confession.

confesionario [konfesjo'narjo] *nm* confessional.

confeso, a [kon'feso, a] *a* (*JUR etc*) self-confessed.

confeti [kon'feti] *nm* confetti.

confiado, a [kon'fjaðo, a] *a* (*crédulo*) trusting; (*seguro*) confident; (*presumido*) conceited, vain.

confianza [kon'fjanθa] *nf* trust; (*aliento, confidencia*) confidence; (*familiaridad*) intimacy, familiarity; (*pey*) vanity, conceit; **margen de** ~ credibility gap; **tener** ~ **con uno** to be on close terms with sb.

confiar [kon'fjar] *vt* to entrust ♦ *vi* (*fiarse*) to trust; (*contar con*) to rely; ~**se** *vr* to put one's trust.

confidencia [konfi'ðenθja] *nf* confidence.

confidencial [konfiðen'θjal] *a* confidential.

confidente [konfi'ðente] *nm/f* confidant/e; (*policial*) informer.

confiera [kon'fjera] *etc vb* V **conferir**.

confiese [kon'fjese] *etc vb* V **confesar**.

configuración [konfiɣura'θjon] *nf* (*tb IN-FORM*) configuration; **la ~ del terreno** the lie of the land; **~ de bits** (*INFORM*) bit pattern.

configurar [konfiɣu'rar] *vt* to shape, form.

confín [kon'fin] *nm* limit; **confines** *nmpl* confines, limits.

confinar [konfi'nar] *vi* to confine; (*desterrar*) to banish.

confiriendo [konfi'rjendo] *etc vb* V **conferir**.

confirmar [konfir'mar] *vt* to confirm; (*JUR etc*) to corroborate; **la excepción confirma la regla** the exception proves the rule.

confiscar [konfis'kar] *vt* to confiscate.

confisque [kon'fiske] *etc vb* V **confiscar**.

confitado, a [konfi'taðo, a] *a*: **fruta confitada** crystallised fruit.

confite [kon'fite] *nm* sweet (*Brit*), candy (*US*).

confitería [konfite'ria] *nf* confectionery; (*tienda*) confectioner's (shop).

confitura [konfi'tura] *nf* jam.

conflagración [konflaɣra'θjon] *nf* conflagration.

conflictivo, a [konflik'tiβo, a] *a* (*asunto, propuesta*) controversial; (*país, situación*) troubled.

conflicto [kon'flikto] *nm* conflict; (*fig*) clash; (: *dificultad*): **estar en un ~** to be in a jam; **~ laboral** labour dispute.

confluir [konflu'ir] *vi* (*ríos etc*) to meet; (*gente*) to gather.

confluya [kon'fluja] *etc vb* V **confluir**.

conformar [konfor'mar] *vt* to shape, form ♦ *vi* to agree; ~**se** *vr* to conform; (*resignarse*) to resign o.s.

conforme [kon'forme] *a* alike, similar; (*de acuerdo*) agreed, in agreement; (*satisfecho*) satisfied ♦ *ad* as ♦ *excl* agreed! ♦ *nm* agreement ♦ *prep*: ~ **a** in accordance with.

conformidad [konformi'ðað] *nf* (*semejanza*) similarity; (*acuerdo*) agreement; (*resignación*) resignation; **de/en ~ con** in accordance with; **dar su ~** to consent.

conformismo [konfor'mismo] *nm* conformism.

conformista [konfor'mista] *nm/f* conformist.

confortable [konfor'taβle] *a* comfortable.

confortar [konfor'tar] *vt* to comfort.

confraternidad [konfraterni'ðað] *nf* brotherhood; **espíritu de ~** feeling of unity.

confrontación [konfronta'θjon] *nf* confrontation.

confrontar [konfron'tar] *vt* to confront; (*dos personas*) to bring face to face; (*cotejar*) to compare ♦ *vi* to border.

confundir [konfun'dir] *vt* (*borrar*) to blur; (*equivocar*) to mistake, confuse; (*mezclar*) to mix; (*turbar*) to confuse; ~**se** *vr* (*hacerse borroso*) to become blurred; (*turbarse*) to get confused; (*equivocarse*) to make a mistake; (*mezclarse*) to mix.

confusión [konfu'sjon] *nf* confusion.

confusionismo [konfusjo'nismo] *nm* confusion, uncertainty.

confuso, a [kon'fuso, a] *a* (*gen*) confused; (*recuerdo*) hazy; (*estilo*) obscure.

congelación [konxela'θjon] *nf* freezing; ~ **de créditos** credit freeze.

congelado, a [konxe'laðo, a] *a* frozen ♦ *nmpl*: ~**s** frozen food(s) (*sg*).

congelador [konxela'ðor], **congeladora** [konxela'ðora] *nf* (*aparato*) freezer, deep freeze.

congelar [konxe'lar] *vt* to freeze; ~**se** *vr* (*sangre, grasa*) to congeal.

congeniar [konxe'njar] *vi* to get on (*Brit*) o along (*US*) (well).

congénito, a [kon'xenito, a] *a* congenital.

congestión [konxes'tjon] *nf* congestion.

congestionado, a [konxestjo'naðo, a] *a* congested.

congestionar [konxestjo'nar] *vt* to congest; ~**se** *vr* to become congested; **se le congestionó la cara** his face became flushed.

conglomeración [konglomera'θjon] *nf* conglomeration.

conglomerado [konglome'raðo] *nm* conglomerate.

Congo ['kongo] *nm*: **el ~** the Congo.

congoja [kon'goxa] *nf* distress, grief.

congraciarse [kongra'θjarse] *vr* to ingratiate o.s.

congratular [kongratu'lar] *vt* to congratulate.

congregación [kongreɣa'θjon] *nf* congregation.

congregar [kongre'ɣar] *vt*, ~**se** *vr* to gather together.

congregue [kon'greɣe] *etc vb* V **congregar**.

congresista [kongre'sista] *nm/f* delegate, congressman/woman.

congreso [kon'greso] *nm* congress; **C~ de los Diputados** (*Esp POL*) ≈ House of Commons (*Brit*), House of Representatives (*US*).

congrio ['kongrjo] *nm* conger (eel).

congruente [kon'grwente], **congruo, a** ['kongrwo, a] *a* congruent, congruous.

conjetura [konxe'tura] *nf* guess; (*COM*) guesstimate.

conjeturar [konxetu'rar] *vt* to guess.

conjugar [konxu'ɣar] *vt* to combine, fit together; (*LING*) to conjugate.

conjugue [kon'xuɣe] *etc vb V* **conjugar**.

conjunción [konxun'θjon] *nf* conjunction.

conjunto, a [kon'xunto, a] *a* joint, united ♦ *nm* whole; (*MUS*) band; (*vestido*) ensemble; (*INFORM*) set; **en ~** as a whole; **~ integrado de programas** (*INFORM*) integrated software suite.

conjura [kon'xura] *nf* plot, conspiracy.

conjurar [konxu'rar] *vt* (*REL*) to exorcise; (*peligro*) to ward off ♦ *vi* to plot.

conjuro [kon'xuro] *nm* spell.

conllevar [konʎe'βar] *vt* to bear; (*implicar*) to imply, involve.

conmemoración [konmemora'θjon] *nf* commemoration.

conmemorar [konmemo'rar] *vt* to commemorate.

conmigo [kon'miɣo] *pron* with me.

conminar [konmi'nar] *vt* to threaten.

conmiseración [konmisera'θjon] *nf* pity, commiseration.

conmoción [konmo'θjon] *nf* shock; (*POL*) disturbance; (*fig*) upheaval; **~ cerebral** (*MED*) concussion.

conmovedor, a [konmoβe'ðor, a] *a* touching, moving; (*emocionante*) exciting.

conmover [konmo'βer] *vt* to shake, disturb; (*fig*) to move; **~se** *vr* (*fig*) to be moved.

conmueva [kon'mweβa] *etc vb V* **conmover**.

conmutación [konmuta'θjon] *nf* (*INFORM*) switching; **~ de mensajes** message switching; **~ por paquetes** packet switching.

conmutador [konmuta'ðor] *nm* switch; (*AM TELEC*) switchboard.

conmutar [konmu'tar] *vt* (*JUR*) to commute.

connivencia [konni'βenθja] *nf*: **estar en ~ con** to be in collusion with.

cono ['kono] *nm* cone.

conocedor, a [konoθe'ðor, a] *a* expert, knowledgeable ♦ *nm/f* expert, connoisseur.

conocer [kono'θer] *vt* to know; (*por primera vez*) to meet, get to know; (*entender*) to know about; (*reconocer*) to recognize; **~se** *vr* (*una persona*) to know o.s.; (*dos personas*) to (get to) know each other; **darse a ~** (*presentarse*) to make o.s. known; **se conoce que ...** (*parece*) apparently ....

conocido, a [kono'θiðo, a] *a* (well-)known ♦ *nm/f* acquaintance.

conocimiento [konoθi'mjento] *nm* knowledge; (*MED*) consciousness; (*NAUT*: *tb*: **~ de embarque**) bill of lading; **~s** *nmpl* (*personas*) acquaintances; (*saber*) knowledge *sg*; **hablar con ~ de causa** to speak from experience; **~ (de embarque) aéreo** (*COM*) air waybill.

conotación [konota'θjon] *nf* connotation.

conozca [ko'noθka] *etc vb V* **conocer**.

conque ['konke] *conj* and so, so then.

conquense [kon'kense] *a* of *o* from Cuenca ♦ *nm/f* native *o* inhabitant of Cuenca.

conquista [kon'kista] *nf* conquest.

conquistador, a [konkista'ðor, a] *a* conquering ♦ *nm* conqueror.

conquistar [konkis'tar] *vt* (*MIL*) to conquer; (*puesto, simpatía*) to win; (*enamorar*) to win the heart of.

consabido, a [konsa'βiðo, a] *a* (*frase etc*) old; (*pey*): **las consabidas excusas** the same old excuses.

consagrado, a [konsa'ɣraðo, a] *a* (*REL*) consecrated; (*actor*) established.

consagrar [konsa'ɣrar] *vt* (*REL*) to consecrate; (*fig*) to devote.

consciente [kons'θjente] *a* conscious; **ser** *o* **estar ~ de** to be aware of.

consecución [konseku'θjon] *nf* acquisition; (*de fin*) attainment.

consecuencia [konse'kwenθja] *nf* consequence, outcome; (*firmeza*) consistency; **de ~ of** importance.

consecuente [konse'kwente] *a* consistent.

consecutivo, a [konseku'tiβo, a] *a* consecutive.

conseguir [konse'ɣir] *vt* to get, obtain; (*sus fines*) to attain.

consejero, a [konse'xero, a] *nm/f* adviser, consultant; (*POL*) councillor; (*COM*) director; (*en comisión*) member.

consejo [kon'sexo] *nm* advice; (*POL*) council; (*COM*) board; **un ~** a piece of advice; **~ de administración** board of directors; **~ de guerra** court-martial; **C~ de Europa** Council of Europe.

consenso [kon'senso] *nm* consensus.

consentido, a [konsen'tiðo, a] *a* (*mimado*) spoiled.

consentimiento [konsenti'mjento] *nm* consent.

consentir [konsen'tir] *vt* (*permitir, tolerar*) to consent to; (*mimar*) to pamper, spoil ♦ *vi* to agree, consent; **~ que uno haga algo** to allow sb to do sth.

conserje [kon'serxe] *nm* caretaker; (*portero*) porter.

conservación [konserβá'θjon] *nf* conservation; (*de alimentos, vida*) preservation.

conservador, a [konserβa'ðor, a] *a* (*POL*) conservative ♦ *nm/f* conservative.

conservadurismo [konserβaðu'rismo] *nm* (*POL etc*) conservatism.

conservante [konser'βante] *nm* preservative.

conservar [konser'βar] *vt* (*gen*) to preserve; (*recursos*) to conserve, keep; (*alimentos, vida*) to preserve; ~**se** *vr* to survive.

conservas [kon'serβas] *nfpl*: ~ **(alimenticias)** tinned *o* canned goods.

conservatorio [konserβa'torjo] *nm* (*MUS*) conservatoire; (*AM*) greenhouse.

considerable [konsiðe'raβle] *a* considerable.

consideración [konsiðera'θjon] *nf* consideration; (*estimación*) respect; **de** ~ important; **tomar en** ~ to take into account.

considerado, a [konsiðe'raðo, a] *a* (*atento*) considerate; (*respetado*) respected.

considerar [konsiðe'rar] *vt* (*gen*) to consider; (*meditar*) to think about; (*tener en cuenta*) to take into account.

consienta [kon'sjenta] *etc vb V* **consentir**.

consigna [kon'siɣna] *nf* (*orden*) order, instruction; (*para equipajes*) left-luggage office.

consignación [konsiɣna'θjon] *nf* consignment; ~ **de créditos** allocation of credits.

consignador [konsiɣna'ðor] *nm* (*COM*) consignor.

consignar [konsiɣ'nar] *vt* (*COM*) to send; (*créditos*) to allocate.

consignatario, a [konsiɣna'tarjo, a] *nm/f* (*COM*) consignee.

consigo [kon'siɣo] *etc vb V* **conseguir** ♦ *pron* (*m*) with him; (*f*) with her; (*usted*) with you; (*reflexivo*) with o.s.

consiguiendo [konsi'ɣjendo] *etc vb V* **conseguir**.

consiguiente [konsi'ɣjente] *a* consequent; **por** ~ and so, therefore, consequently.

consintiendo [konsin'tjendo] *etc vb V* **consentir**.

consistente [konsis'tente] *a* consistent; (*sólido*) solid, firm; (*válido*) sound; ~ **en** consisting of.

consistir [konsis'tir] *vi*: ~ **en** (*componerse de*) to consist of; (*ser resultado de*) to be due to.

consola [kon'sola] *nf* console, control panel; (*mueble*) console table; ~ **de mando** (*INFORM*) control console; ~ **de visualización** visual display console.

consolación [konsola'θjon] *nf* consolation.

consolar [konso'lar] *vt* to console.

consolidar [konsoli'ðar] *vt* to consolidate.

consomé, *pl* **consomés** *nm* [konso'me, konso'mes] consommé, clear soup.

consonancia [konso'nanθja] *nf* harmony; **en** ~ **con** in accordance with.

consonante [konso'nante] *a* consonant, harmonious ♦ *nf* consonant.

consorcio [kon'sorθjo] *nm* (*COM*) consortium, syndicate.

consorte [kon'sorte] *nm/f* consort.

conspicuo, a [kons'pikwo, a] *a* conspicuous.

conspiración [konspira'θjon] *nf* conspiracy.

conspirador, a [konspira'ðor, a] *nm/f* conspirator.

conspirar [konspi'rar] *vi* to conspire.

constancia [kons'tanθja] *nf* (*gen*) constancy; (*certeza*) certainly; **dejar** ~ **de algo** to put sth on record.

constante [kons'tante] *a, nf* constant.

constar [kons'tar] *vi* (*evidenciarse*) to be clear *o* evident; ~ **(en)** to appear (in); ~ **de** to consist of; **hacer** ~ to put on record; **me consta que ...** I have evidence that ...; **que conste que lo hice por ti** believe me, I did it for your own good.

constatar [konsta'tar] *vt* (*controlar*) to check; (*observar*) to note.

constelación [konstela'θjon] *nf* constellation.

consternación [konsterna'θjon] *nf* consternation.

constipado, a [konsti'paðo, a] *a*: **estar** ~ to have a cold ♦ *nm* cold.

constitución [konstitu'θjon] *nf* constitution.

constitucional [konstituθjo'nal] *a* constitutional.

constituir [konstitu'ir] *vt* (*formar, componer*) to constitute, make up; (*fundar, erigir, ordenar*) to constitute, establish; (*ser*) to be; ~**se** *vr* (*POL etc*: *cuerpo*) to be composed; (: *fundarse*) to be established.

constitutivo, a [konstitu'tiβo, a] *a* constitutive, constituent.

constituya [konsti'tuja] *etc vb V* **constituir**.

constituyente [konstitu'jente] *a* constituent.

constreñir [konstre'ɲir] *vt* (*obligar*) to compel, oblige; (*restringir*) to restrict.

constriño [kons'triɲo] *etc*, **constriñendo** [konstri'ɲendo] *etc vb V* **constreñir**.

construcción [konstruk'θjon] *nf* construction, building.

constructor, a [konstruk'tor, a] *nm/f* builder.

construir [konstru'ir] *vt* to build, construct.

construyendo [konstru'jendo] *etc vb V* **construir**.

consuelo [kon'swelo] *etc vb V* **consolar** ♦ *nm* consolation, solace.

consuetudinario, a [konswetuði'narjo, a] *a* customary; **derecho** ~ common law.

cónsul ['konsul] *nm* consul.

consulado [konsu'laðo] *nm* (*sede*) consulate; (*cargo*) consulship.

consulta [kon'sulta] *nf* consultation; (*MED*: *consultorio*) consulting room; (*INFORM*) enquiry; **horas de** ~ surgery hours; **obra de** ~ reference book.

consultar [konsul'tar] *vt* to consult; ~ **un archivo** (*INFORM*) to interrogate a file.

consultor, a [konsul'tor, a] *nm*: ~ **en dirección de empresas** management consultant.

consultorio [konsul'torjo] *nm* (*MED*) surgery.

consumado, a [konsu'maðo, a] *a* perfect; (*bribón*) out-and-out.

consumar [konsu'mar] *vt* to complete, carry out; (*crimen*) to commit; (*sentencia*) to carry out.

consumición [konsumi'θjon] *nf* consumption; (*bebida*) drink; (*comida*) food; ~ **mínima** cover charge.

consumido, a [konsu'miðo, a] *a* (*flaco*) skinny.

consumidor, a [konsumi'ðor, a] *nm/f* consumer.

consumir [konsu'mir] *vt* to consume; ~**se** *vr* to be consumed; (*persona*) to waste away.

consumismo [konsu'mismo] *nm* (*COM*) consumerism.

consumo [kon'sumo] *nm* consumption; **bienes de** ~ consumer goods.

contabilice [kontaβi'liθe] *etc vb* V **contabilizar**.

contabilidad [kontaβili'ðað] *nf* accounting, book-keeping; (*profesión*) accountancy; (*COM*): ~ **analítica** variable costing; ~ **de costos** cost accounting; ~ **de doble partida** double-entry book-keeping; ~ **de gestión** management accounting; ~ **por partida simple** single-entry book-keeping.

contabilizar [kontaβi'liθar] *vt* to enter in the accounts.

contable [kon'taβle] *nm/f* bookkeeper; (*licenciado*) accountant; ~ **de costos** (*COM*) cost accountant.

contacto [kon'takto] *nm* contact; **lentes de** ~ contact lenses; **estar en** ~ **con** to be in touch with.

contado, a [kon'taðo, a] *a*: ~**s** (*escasos*) numbered, scarce, few ♦ *nm*: **al** ~ **for cash**; **pagar al** ~ to pay (in) cash; **precio al** ~ cash price.

contador [konta'ðor] *nm* (*aparato*) meter; (*AM*: *contable*) accountant.

contaduría [kontaðu'ria] *nf* accountant's office.

contagiar [konta'xjar] *vt* (*enfermedad*) to pass on, transmit; (*persona*) to infect; ~**se** *vr* to become infected.

contagio [kon'taxjo] *nm* infection.

contagioso, a [konta'xjoso, a] *a* infectious; (*fig*) catching.

contaminación [kontamina'θjon] *nf* (*gen*) contamination; (*del ambiente etc*) pollution.

contaminar [kontami'nar] *vt* (*gen*) to contaminate; (*aire, agua*) to pollute; (*fig*) to taint.

contante [kon'tante] *a*: **dinero** ~ **(y sonante)** hard cash.

contar [kon'tar] *vt* (*páginas, dinero*) to count; (*anécdota etc*) to tell ♦ *vi* to count; ~**se** *vr* to be counted, figure; ~ **con** to rely on, count on; **sin** ~ not to mention; **le cuento entre mis amigos** I reckon him among my friends.

contemplación [kontempla'θjon] *nf* contemplation; **no andarse con contemplaciones** not to stand on ceremony.

contemplar [kontem'plar] *vt* to contemplate; (*mirar*) to look at.

contemporáneo, a [kontempo'raneo, a] *a*, *nm/f* contemporary.

contemporizar [kontempori'θar] *vi*: ~ **con** to keep in with.

contención [konten'θjon] *nf* (*JUR*) suit; **muro de** ~ retaining wall.

contencioso, a [konten'θjoso, a] *a* (*JUR etc*) contentious ♦ *nm* (*POL*) conflict, dispute.

contender [konten'der] *vi* to contend; (*en un concurso*) to compete.

contendiente [konten'djente] *nm/f* contestant.

contendrá [konten'dra] *etc vb* V **contener**.

contenedor [kontene'ðor] *nm* container.

contenedorización [konteneðoriθa'θjon] *nf* (*COM*) containerization.

contener [konte'ner] *vt* to contain, hold; (*risa etc*) to hold back, contain; ~**se** *vr* to control *o* restrain o.s.

contenga [kon'tenga] *etc vb* V **contener**.

contenido, a [konte'niðo, a] *a* (*moderado*) restrained; (*risa etc*) suppressed ♦ *nm* contents *pl*, content.

contentar [konten'tar] *vt* (*satisfacer*) to satisfy; (*complacer*) to please; (*COM*) to endorse; ~**se** *vr* to be satisfied.

contento, a [kon'tento, a] *a* contented, content; (*alegre*) pleased; (*feliz*) happy.

contestación [kontesta'θjon] *nf* answer, reply; ~ **a la demanda** (*JUR*) defence plea.

contestador [kontesta'ðor] *nm*: ~ **automático** answering machine.

contestar [kontes'tar] *vt* to answer (back), reply; (*JUR*) to corroborate, confirm.

contexto [kon'teksto] *nm* context.

contienda [kon'tjenda] *nf* contest, struggle.

contiene [kon'tjene] *etc vb* V **contener**.

contigo [kon'tiɣo] *pron* with you.

contiguo, a [kon'tiɣwo, a] *a* (*de al lado*) next; (*vecino*) adjacent, adjoining.

continente [konti'nente] *a*, *nm* continent.

contingencia [kontin'xenθja] *nf* contingency; (*riesgo*) risk; (*posibilidad*) eventuality.

contingente [kontin'xente] *a* contingent ♦

nm contingent; (*COM*) quota.

continuación [kontinwa'θjon] *nf* continuation; **a** ~ then, next.

continuar [konti'nwar] *vt* to continue, go on with; (*reanudar*) to resume ♦ *vi* to continue, go on; ~ **hablando** to continue talking *o* to talk.

continuidad [kontinwi'ðað] *nf* continuity.

continuo, a [kon'tinwo, a] *a* (*sin interrupción*) continuous; (*acción perseverante*) continual.

contonearse [kontone'arse] *vr* (*hombre*) to swagger; (*mujer*) to swing her hips.

contorno [kon'torno] *nm* outline; (*GEO*) contour; ~**s** *nmpl* neighbourhood *sg*, surrounding area *sg*.

contorsión [kontor'sjon] *nf* contortion.

contra ['kontra] *prep* against; (*COM: giro*) on ♦ *ad* against ♦ *a*, *nm/f* (*POL fam*) counter-revolutionary ♦ *nm* con ♦ *nf*: **la C~** (**nicaragüense**) the Contras *pl*.

contraalmirante [kontraalmi'rante] *nm* rear admiral.

contraataque [kontraa'take] *nm* counter-attack.

contrabajo [kontra'ßaxo] *nm* double bass.

contrabandista [kontraßan'dista] *nm/f* smuggler.

contrabando [kontra'ßando] *nm* (*acción*) smuggling; (*mercancías*) contraband; ~ **de armas** gun-running.

contracción [kontrak'θjon] *nf* contraction.

contracorriente [kontrako'rrjente] *nf* cross-current.

contrachapado [kontratʃa'paðo] *nm* plywood.

contradecir [kontraðe'θir] *vt* to contradict.

contradicción [kontraðik'θjon] *nf* contradiction; **espíritu de** ~ contrariness.

contradiciendo [kontraði'θjendo] *etc vb V* **contradecir**.

contradictorio, a [kontraðik'torjo, a] *a* contradictory.

contradicho [kontra'ðitʃo] *pp de* **contradecir**.

contradiga [kontra'ðiɣa] *etc*, **contradije** [kontra'ðixe], **contradirá** [kontraði'ra] *etc vb V* **contradecir**.

contraer [kontra'er] *vt* to contract; (*hábito*) to acquire; (*limitar*) to restrict; ~**se** *vr* to contract; (*limitarse*) to limit o.s.

contragolpe [kontra'ɣolpe] *nm* backlash.

contrahaga [kontra'aɣa] *etc*, **contraharé** [kontraa're] *etc vb V* **contrahacer**.

contrahecho, a [kontra'etʃo, a] *pp de* **contrahacer** ♦ *a* fake; (*ANAT*) hunchbacked.

contrahice [kontra'iθe] *etc vb V* **contrahacer**.

contraiga [kon'traiɣa] *etc vb V* **contraer**.

contraindicaciones [kontraindika'θjones] *nfpl* (*MED*) contraindications.

contraje [kon'traxe] *etc vb V* **contraer**.

contraluz [kontra'luθ] *nf* (*FOTO etc*) back lighting; **a** ~ against the light.

contramaestre [kontrama'estre] *nm* foreman.

contraorden [kontra'orðen] *nf* counter-order, countermand.

contrapartida [kontrapar'tiða] *nf* (*COM*) balancing entry; **como** ~ (**de**) in return (for), as *o* in compensation (for).

contrapelo [kontra'pelo]: **a** ~ *ad* the wrong way.

contrapesar [kontrape'sar] *vt* to counterbalance; (*fig*) to offset.

contrapeso [kontra'peso] *nm* counterweight; (*fig*) counterbalance; (*COM*) makeweight.

contrapondré [kontrapon'dre] *etc vb V* **contraponer**.

contraponer [kontrapo'ner] *vt* (*cotejar*) to compare; (*oponer*) to oppose.

contraponga [kontra'ponga] *etc vb V* **contraponer**.

contraproducente [kontraproðu'θente] *a* counterproductive.

contrapuesto [kontra'pwesto] *pp de* **contraponer**.

contrapunto [kontra'punto] *nm* counterpoint.

contrapuse [kontra'puse] *etc vb V* **contraponer**.

contrariar [kontra'rjar] *vt* (*oponerse*) to oppose; (*poner obstáculo*) to impede; (*enfadar*) to vex.

contrariedad [kontrarje'ðað] *nf* (*oposición*) opposition; (*obstáculo*) obstacle, setback; (*disgusto*) vexation, annoyance.

contrario, a [kon'trarjo, a] *a* contrary; (*persona*) opposed; (*sentido, lado*) opposite ♦ *nm/f* enemy, adversary; (*DEPORTE*) opponent; **al** ~, **por el** ~ on the contrary; **de lo** ~ otherwise.

Contrarreforma [kontrarre'forma] *nf* Counter-Reformation.

contrarrestar [kontrarres'tar] *vt* to counteract.

contrarrevolución [kontrarreßolu'θjon] *nf* counter-revolution.

contrasentido [kontrasen'tiðo] *nm* contradiction; **es un** ~ **que él** ... it doesn't make sense for him to ... .

contraseña [kontra'seɲa] *nf* countersign; (*frase*) password.

contrastar [kontras'tar] *vt* to resist ♦ *vi* to contrast.

contraste [kon'traste] *nm* contrast.

contrata [kon'trata] *nf* (*JUR*) written contract; (*empleo*) hiring.

contratar [kontra'tar] *vt* (*firmar un acuerdo para*) to contract for; (*empleados, obreros*) to hire, engage; (*DEPORTE*) to sign up; ~**se**

vr to sign on.

contratiempo [kontra'tjempo] *nm* (*revés*) setback; (*accidente*) mishap; **a ~** (*MUS*) off-beat.

contratista [kontra'tista] *nm/f* contractor.

contrato [kon'trato] *nm* contract; **~ de compraventa** contract of sale; **~ a precio fijo** fixed-price contract; **~ a término** forward contract; **~ de trabajo** contract of employment *o* service.

contravalor [kontraßa'lor] *nm* exchange value.

contravención [kontraßen'θjon] *nf* contravention, violation.

contravendré [kontraßen'dre] *etc*, **contravenga** [kontra'ßenga] *etc vb V* **contravenir**.

contravenir [kontraße'nir] *vi*: **~ a** to contravene, violate.

contraventana [kontraßen'tana] *nf* shutter.

contraviene [kontra'ßjene] *etc*, **contraviniendo** [kontraßi'njendo] *etc vb V* **contravenir**.

contrayendo [kontra'jendo] *vb V* **contraer**.

contribución [kontrißu'θjon] *nf* (*municipal etc*) tax; (*ayuda*) contribution; **exento de contribuciones** tax-free.

contribuir [kontrißu'ir] *vt, vi* to contribute; (*COM*) to pay (in taxes).

contribuyendo [kontrißu'jendo] *etc vb V* **contribuir**.

contribuyente [kontrißu'jente] *nm/f* (*COM*) taxpayer; (*que ayuda*) contributor.

contrincante [kontrin'kante] *nm* opponent, rival.

control [kon'trol] *nm* control; (*inspección*) inspection, check; (*COM*): **~ de calidad** quality control; **~ de cambios** exchange control; **~ de costos** cost control; **~ de créditos** credit control; **~ de existencias** stock control; **~ de precios** price control.

controlador, a [kontrola'ðor, a] *nm/f* controller; **~ aéreo** air-traffic controller.

controlar *vt* to control; to inspect, check; (*COM*) to audit.

controversia [kontro'ßersja] *nf* controversy.

contubernio [kontu'ßernjo] *nm* ring, conspiracy.

contumaz [kontu'maθ] *a* obstinate, stubbornly disobedient.

contundente [kontun'dente] *a* (*prueba*) conclusive; (*fig: argumento*) convincing; **instrumento ~** blunt instrument.

contusión [kontu'sjon] *nf* bruise.

contuve [kon'tuße] *etc vb V* **contener**.

convalecencia [kombale'θenθja] *nf* convalescence.

convalecer [kombale'θer] *vi* to convalesce, get better.

convaleciente [kombale'θjente] *a, nm/f* convalescent.

convalezca [komba'leθka] *etc vb V* **convalecer**.

convalidar [kombali'ðar] *vt* (*título*) to recognize.

convencer [komben'θer] *vt* to convince; (*persuadir*) to persuade.

convencimiento [kombenθi'mjento] *nm* (*acción*) convincing; (*persuasión*) persuasion; (*certidumbre*) conviction; **tener el ~ de que ...** to be convinced that ... .

convención [komben'θjon] *nf* convention.

convendré [komben'dre] *etc*, **convenga** [kom'benga] *etc vb V* **convenir**.

conveniencia [kombe'njenθja] *nf* suitability; (*conformidad*) agreement; (*utilidad, provecho*) usefulness; **~s** *nfpl* conventions; (*COM*) property *sg*; **ser de la ~ de uno** to suit sb.

conveniente [kombe'njente] *a* suitable; (*útil*) useful; (*correcto*) fit, proper; (*aconsejable*) advisable.

convenio [kom'benjo] *nm* agreement, treaty; **~ de nivel crítico** threshold agreement.

convenir [kombe'nir] *vi* (*estar de acuerdo*) to agree; (*ser conveniente*) to suit, be suitable; **"sueldo a ~"** "salary to be agreed"; **conviene recordar que...** it should be remembered that... .

convento [kom'bento] *nm* monastery; (*de monjas*) convent.

convenza [kom'benθa] *etc vb V* **convencer**.

convergencia [komber'xenθja] *nf* convergence.

converger [komber'xer], **convergir** [komber'xir] *vi* to converge; **sus esfuerzos convergen a un fin común** their efforts are directed towards the same objective.

converja [kom'berxa] *etc vb V* **converger**, **convergir**.

conversación [kombersa'θjon] *nf* conversation.

conversar [komber'sar] *vi* to talk, converse.

conversión [komber'sjon] *nf* conversion.

converso, a [kom'berso, a] *nm/f* convert.

convertir [komber'tir] *vt* to convert; (*transformar*) to transform, turn; (*COM*) to (ex)change; **~se** *vr* (*REL*) to convert.

convicción [kombik'θjon] *nf* conviction.

convicto, a [kom'bikto, a] *a* convicted; (*condenado*) condemned.

convidado, a [kombi'ðaðo, a] *nm/f* guest.

convidar [kombi'ðar] *vt* to invite.

conviene [kom'bjene] *etc vb V* **convenir**.

convierta [kom'bjerta] *etc vb V* **convertir**.

convincente [kombin'θente] *a* convincing.

conviniendo [kombi'njendo] *etc vb V* **convenir**.

convirtiendo [kombir'tjendo] *etc vb V* **convertir**.

convite [kom'bite] *nm* invitation; (*banquete*) banquet.

convivencia [kombi'ßenθja] *nf* coexistence, living together.

convivir [kombi'ßir] *vi* to live together; (*POL*) to coexist.

convocar [kombo'kar] *vt* to summon, call (together).

convocatoria [komboka'torja] *nf* summons *sg*; (*anuncio*) notice of meeting; (*ESCOL*) examination session.

convoque [kom'boke] *etc vb V* **convocar**.

convoy [kom'boj] *nm* (*FERRO*) train.

convulsión [kombul'sjon] *nf* convulsion; (*POL etc*) upheaval.

conyugal [konju'xal] *a* conjugal; **vida ~** married life.

cónyuge ['konyuxe] *nm/f* spouse, partner.

coña ['koɲa] *nf*: **tomar algo a ~** (*fam!*) to take sth as a joke.

coñac *pl* **coñacs** ['koɲa(k), 'koɲas] *nm* cognac, brandy.

coñazo [ko'ɲaθo] *nm* (*fam*) pain; **dal el ~** to be a real pain.

coño ['koɲo] (*fam!*) *nm* cunt(!) ◆ *excl* (*enfado*) shit(!); (*sorpresa*) bloody hell(!); **¡qué ~!** what a pain in the arse(!).

cooperación [koopera'θjon] *nf* cooperation.

cooperar [koope'rar] *vi* to cooperate.

cooperativo, a [koopera'tißo, a] *a* cooperative ◆ *nf* cooperative.

coordenada [koorðe'naða] *nf* (*MAT*) coordinate; (*fig*): **~s** *nfpl* guidelines, framework *sg*.

coordinación [koorðina'θjon] *nf* coordination.

coordinador, a [koorðina'ðor, a] *nm/f* coordinator ◆ *nf* coordinating committee.

coordinar [koorði'nar] *vt* to coordinate.

copa ['kopa] *nf* (*tb DEPORTE*) cup; (*vaso*) glass; (*de árbol*) top; (*de sombrero*) crown; **~s** *nfpl* (*NAIPES*) ≈ hearts; **(tomar una) ~** (to have a) drink; **ir de ~s** to go out for a drink.

coparticipación [kopartiθipa'θjon] *nf* (*COM*) co-ownership.

Copenhague [kope'naxe] Copenhagen.

copete [ko'pete] *nm* tuft (of hair); **de alto ~** aristocratic, upper-crust (*fam*).

copia ['kopja] *nf* copy; (*ARTE*) replica; (*COM etc*) duplicate; (*INFORM*): **~ impresa** hard copy; **~ de respaldo** *o* **de seguridad** back-up copy; **hacer ~ de seguridad** to back up; **~ de trabajo** working copy; **~ vaciada** dump.

copiadora [kopja'ðora] *nf* photocopier; **~ al alcohol** spirit duplicator.

copiar [ko'pjar] *vt* to copy; **~ al pie de la letra** to copy word for word.

copioso, a [ko'pjoso, a] *a* copious, plentiful.

copita [ko'pita] *nf* (small) glass; (*GOLF*) tee.

copla ['kopla] *nf* verse; (*canción*) (popular) song.

copo ['kopo] *nm*: **~s de maíz** cornflakes; **~ de nieve** snowflake.

coprocesador [koproθesa'ðor] *nm* (*INFORM*) co-processor.

coproducción [koproðuk'θjon] *nf* (*CINE etc*) joint production.

copropietarios [kopropje'tarjos] *nmpl* (*COM*) joint owners.

cópula ['kopula] *nf* copulation.

copular [kopu'lar] *vi* to copulate.

coqueta [ko'keta] *a* flirtatious, coquettish ◆ *nf* (*mujer*) flirt.

coquetear [kokete'ar] *vi* to flirt.

coraje [ko'raxe] *nm* courage; (*ánimo*) spirit; (*ira*) anger.

coral [ko'ral] *a* choral ◆ *nf* choir ◆ *nm* (*ZOOL*) coral.

Corán [ko'ran] *nm*: **el ~** the Koran.

coraza [ko'raθa] *nf* (*armadura*) armour; (*blindaje*) armour-plating.

corazón [kora'θon] *nm* heart; (*BOT*) core; **corazones** *nmpl* (*NAIPES*) hearts; **de buen ~** kind-hearted; **de todo ~** wholeheartedly; **estar mal del ~** to have heart trouble.

corazonada [koraθo'naða] *nf* impulse; (*presentimiento*) presentiment, hunch.

corbata [kor'ßata] *nf* tie.

corbeta [kor'ßeta] *nf* corvette.

Córcega ['korßexa] *nf* Corsica.

corcel [kor'θel] *nm* steed.

corcovado, a [korko'ßaðo, a] *a* hunchbacked ◆ *nm/f* hunchback.

corchete [kor'tʃete] *nm* catch, clasp; **~s** *nmpl* (*TIP*) square brackets.

corcho ['kortʃo] *nm* cork; (*PESCA*) float.

cordel [kor'ðel] *nm* cord, line.

cordero [kor'ðero] *nm* lamb; (*piel*) lambskin.

cordial [kor'ðjal] *a* cordial ◆ *nm* cordial, tonic.

cordialidad [korðjali'ðað] *nf* warmth, cordiality.

cordillera [korði'ʎera] *nf* range (of mountains).

Córdoba ['korðoßa] *nf* Cordova.

cordobés, esa [korðo'ßes, esa] *a, nm/f* Cordovan.

cordón [kor'ðon] *nm* (*cuerda*) cord, string; (*de zapatos*) lace; (*ELEC*) flex, wire (*US*); (*MIL etc*) cordon.

cordura [kor'ðura] *nf* (*MED*) sanity; (*fig*) good sense.

Corea [ko'rea] *nf* Korea; **~ del Norte/Sur** North/South Korea.

coreano, a [kore'ano, a] *a, nm/f* Korean.

corear [kore'ar] *vt* to chorus.

coreografía [koreogra'fia] *nf* choreography.

corista [ko'rista] *nf* (*TEATRO etc*) chorus girl.

cornada [kor'naða] *nf* (*TAUR etc*) butt, goring.

corneta [kor'neta] *nf* bugle.

cornisa [kor'nisa] *nf* cornice.

Cornualles [kor'nwaʎes] *nm* Cornwall.

cornudo, a [kor'nuðo, a] *a* (*ZOOL*) horned; (*marido*) cuckolded.

coro ['koro] *nm* chorus; (*conjunto de cantores*) choir.

corolario [koro'larjo] *nm* corollary.

corona [ko'rona] *nf* crown; (*de flores*) garland.

coronación [korona'θjon] *nf* coronation.

coronar [koro'nar] *vt* to crown.

coronel [koro'nel] *nm* colonel.

coronilla [koro'niʎa] *nf* (*ANAT*) crown (of the head); **estar hasta la ~ (de)** to be utterly fed up (with).

corporación [korpora'θjon] *nf* corporation.

corporal [korpo'ral] *a* corporal, bodily.

corpulento, a [korpu'lento a] *a* (*persona*) well-built.

corral [ko'rral] *nm* (*patio*) farmyard; (*AGR: de aves*) poultry yard; (*redil*) pen.

correa [ko'rrea] *nf* strap; (*cinturón*) belt; (*de perro*) lead, leash; **~ transportadora** conveyor belt.

correaje [korre'axe] *nm* (*AGR*) harness.

corrección [korrek'θjon] *nf* correction; (*reprensión*) rebuke; (*cortesía*) good manners; (*INFORM*): **~ por líneas** line editing; **~ en pantalla** screen editing; **~ (de pruebas)** (*TIP*) proofreading.

correccional [korrekθjo'nal] *nm* reformatory.

correcto, a [ko'rrekto, a] *a* correct; (*persona*) well-mannered.

corredera [korre'ðera] *nf*: **puerta de ~** sliding door.

corredizo, a [korre'ðiθo, a] *a* (*puerta etc*) sliding; (*nudo*) running.

corredor, a [korre'ðor, a] *a* running; (*rápido*) fast ♦ *nm/f* (*DEPORTE*) runner ♦ *nm* (*pasillo*) corridor; (*balcón corrido*) gallery; (*COM*) agent, broker; (*pasillo*) corridor, passage; **~ de bienes raíces** real-estate broker; **~ de bolsa** stockbroker; **~ de seguros** insurance broker.

corregir [korre'xir] *vt* (*error*) to correct; (*amonestar, reprender*) to rebuke, reprimand; **~se** *vr* to reform.

correo [ko'rreo] *nm* post, mail; (*persona*) courier; **C~s** *nmpl* Post Office *sg*; **~ aéreo** airmail; **~ certificado** registered mail; **~ electrónico** electronic mail; **~ urgente** special delivery; **a vuelta de ~** by return (of post).

correr [ko'rrer] *vt* to run; (*viajar*) to cover, travel; (*riesgo*) to run; (*aventura*) to have; (*cortinas*) to draw; (*cerrojo*) to shoot ♦ *vi* to run; (*líquido*) to run, flow; (*rumor*) to go round; **~se** *vr* to slide, move; (*colores*) to run; (*fam: tener orgasmo*) to come; **echar a ~** to break into a run; **~ con los gastos** to pay the expenses; **eso corre de mi cuenta** I'll take care of that.

correspondencia [korrespon'denθja] *nf* correspondence; (*FERRO*) connection; (*reciprocidad*) return; **~ directa** (*COM*) direct mail.

corresponder [korrespon'der] *vi* to correspond; (*convenir*) to be suitable; (*pertenecer*) to belong; (*tocar*) to concern; (*favor*) to repay; **~se** *vr* (*por escrito*) to correspond; (*amarse*) to love one another; **"a quien corresponda"** "to whom it may concern".

correspondiente [korrespon'djente] *a* corresponding; (*respectivo*) respective.

corresponsal [korrespon'sal] *nm/f* (*newspaper*) correspondent; (*COM*) agent.

corretaje [korre'taxe] *nm* (*COM*) brokerage.

corretear [korrete'ar] *vi* to loiter.

corrido, a [ko'rriðo, a] *a* (*avergonzado*) abashed; (*fluido*) fluent ♦ *nf* run, dash; (*de toros*) bullfight; **de ~** fluently; **3 noches corridas** 3 nights running; **un kilo ~** a good kilo.

corriente [ko'rrjente] *a* (*agua*) running; (*fig*) flowing; (*dinero, cuenta etc*) current; (*común*) ordinary, normal ♦ *nf* current; (*fig: tendencia*) course ♦ *nm* current month; **~ f de aire** draught; **~ eléctrica** electric current; **las ~s modernas del arte** modern trends in art; **estar al ~ de** to be informed about.

corrigiendo [korri'xjendo] *etc vb V* **corregir**.

corrija [ko'rrixa] *etc vb V* **corregir**.

corrillo [ko'rriʎo] *nm* ring, circle (of people); (*fig*) clique.

corro ['korro] *nm* ring, circle (of people); (*baile*) ring-a-ring-a-roses; **la gente hizo ~** the people formed a ring.

corroborar [korroßo'rar] *vt* to corroborate.

corroer [korro'er] *vt* (*tb fig*) to corrode, eat away; (*GEO*) to erode.

corroyendo [korro'jendo] *etc vb V* **corroer**.

corromper [korrom'per] *vt* (*madera*) to rot; (*fig*) to corrupt.

corrompido, a [korrom'piðo, a] *a* corrupt.

corrosivo, a [korro'sißo, a] *a* corrosive.

corrupción [korrup'θjon] *nf* rot, decay; (*fig*) corruption.

corsario [kor'sarjo] *nm* privateer, corsair.

corsé [kor'se] *nm* corset.

corso, a ['korso, a] *a*, *nm/f* Corsican.

cortacésped [korta'θespeð] *nm* lawn mower.

cortado, a [kor'taðo, a] *a* (*con cuchillo*) cut; (*leche*) sour; (*confuso*) confused; (*desconcertado*) embarrassed; (*tímido*) shy ♦ *nm* white coffee (with a little milk).

cortadora [korta'ðora] *nf* cutter, slicer.

cortadura [korta'ðura] *nf* cut.

cortante [kor'tante] *a* (*viento*) biting; (*frío*) bitter.

cortapisa [korta'pisa] *nf* (*restricción*) restriction; (*traba*) snag.

cortar [kor'tar] *vt* to cut; (*suministro*) to cut off; (*un pasaje*) to cut out; (*comunicación*) to cut off ♦ *vi* to cut; ~**se** *vr* (*turbarse*) to become embarrassed; (*leche*) to turn, curdle; ~ **por lo sano** to settle things once and for all; ~**se el pelo** to have one's hair cut.

cortauñas [korta'uɲas] *nm inv* nail clippers *pl*.

corte ['korte] *nm* cut, cutting; (*filo*) edge; (*de tela*) piece, length; (*COSTURA*) tailoring ♦ *nf* (*real*) (royal) court; ~ **y confección** dressmaking; ~ **de corriente** *o* **luz** power cut; **me da** ~ **pedírselo** I'm embarrassed to ask him for it; **¡qué** ~ **le di!** I left him with no comeback!; **C~ Internacional de Justicia** International Court of Justice; **las C~s** the Spanish Parliament *sg*; **hacer la** ~ **a** to woo, court.

cortedad [korte'ðað] *nf* shortness; (*fig*) bashfulness, timidity.

cortejar [korte'xar] *vt* to court.

cortejo [kor'texo] *nm* entourage; ~ **fúnebre** funeral procession, cortège.

cortés [kor'tes] *a* courteous, polite.

cortesano, a [korte'sano, a] *a* courtly.

cortesía [korte'sia] *nf* courtesy.

corteza [kor'teθa] *nf* (*de árbol*) bark; (*de pan*) crust; (*de fruta*) peel, skin; (*de queso*) rind.

cortijo [kor'tixo] *nm* farmhouse.

cortina [kor'tina] *nf* curtain; ~ **de humo** smoke screen.

corto, a ['korto, a] *a* (*breve*) short; (*tímido*) bashful; ~ **de luces** not very bright; ~ **de oído** hard of hearing; ~ **de vista** shortsighted; **estar** ~ **de fondos** to be short of funds.

cortocircuito [kortoθir'kwito] *nm* shortcircuit.

cortometraje [kortome'traxe] *nm* (*CINE*) short.

Coruña [ko'ruɲa] *nf*: **La** ~ Corunna.

coruñés, esa [koru'ɲes, esa] *a* of *o* from Corunna ♦ *nm/f* native *o* inhabitant of Corunna.

corvo, a ['korβo, a] *a* curved; (*nariz*) hooked ♦ *nf* back of knee.

cosa ['kosa] *nf* thing; (*asunto*) affair; ~ **de** about; **eso es** ~ **mía** that's my business; **es poca** ~ it's not important; **¡qué** ~ **más rara!** how strange; **en** ~ **de 10 minutos** in about 10 minutes.

cosaco, a [ko'sako, a] *a, nm/f* Cossack.

coscorrón [kosko'rron] *nm* bump on the head.

cosecha [ko'setʃa] *nf* (*AGR*) harvest; (*acto*) harvesting; (*de vino*) vintage; (*producción*) yield.

cosechadora [kosetʃa'ðora] *nf* combine harvester.

cosechar [kose'tʃar] *vt* to harvest, gather (in).

coser [ko'ser] *vt* to sew; (*MED*) to stitch (up).

cosido [ko'siðo] *nm* sewing.

cosmético, a [kos'metiko, a] *a, nm* cosmetic.

cosmopolita [kosmopo'lita] *a* cosmopolitan.

coso ['koso] *nm* bullring.

cosquillas [kos'kiʎas] *nfpl*: **hacer** ~ to tickle; **tener** ~ to be ticklish.

cosquilleo [koski'ʎeo] *nm* tickling (sensation).

cosquilloso, a [koski'ʎoso, a] *a* ticklish.

costa ['kosta] *nf* (*GEO*) coast; **C~ Brava** Costa Brava; **C~ Cantábrica** Cantabrian Coast; **C~ de Marfil** Ivory Coast; **C~ del Sol** Costa del Sol; **a** ~ (*COM*) at cost; **a** ~ **de** at the expense of; **a toda** ~ at any price.

costado [kos'taðo] *nm* side; **de** ~ (*dormir*) on one's side; **español por los 4** ~**s** Spanish through and through.

costal [kos'tal] *nm* sack.

costalada [kosta'laða] *nf* bad fall.

costar [kos'tar] *vt* (*valer*) to cost; **me cuesta hablarle** I find it hard to talk to him; **¿cuánto cuesta?** how much does it cost?

Costa Rica [kosta'rika] *nf* Costa Rica.

costarricense [kostarri'θense], **costarriqueño, a** [kostarri'keɲo, a] *a, nm/f* Costa Rican.

coste ['koste] *nm* (*COM*): ~ **promedio** average cost; ~**s fijos** fixed costs; *V tb* **costo**.

costear [koste'ar] *vt* to pay for; (*COM etc*) to finance; (*NAUT*) to sail along the coast of; ~**se** *vr* (*negocio*) to pay for itself, cover its costs.

costeño, a [kos'teɲo, a] *a* coastal.

costilla [kos'tiʎa] *nf* rib; (*CULIN*) cutlet.

costo ['kosto] *nm* cost, price; ~ **directo** direct cost; ~ **de expedición** shipping charges; ~ **de sustitución** replacement cost; ~ **unitario** unit cost; ~ **de la vida** cost of living.

costoso, a [kos'toso, a] *a* costly, expensive.

costra ['kostra] *nf* (*corteza*) crust; (*MED*) scab.

costumbre [kos'tumbre] *nf* custom, habit; **como de** ~ as usual.

costura [kos'tura] *nf* sewing, needlework; (*confección*) dressmaking; (*zurcido*) seam.

costurera [kostu'rera] *nf* dressmaker.

costurero [kostu'rero] *nm* sewing box *o* case.

cotejar [kote'xar] *vt* to compare.

cotejo [ko'texo] *nm* comparison.

cotice [ko'tiθe] *etc vb* V **cotizar**.

cotidiano, a [koti'ðjano, a] *a* daily, day to day.

cotilla [ko'tiʎa] *nf* busybody, gossip.

cotillear [kotiʎe'ar] *vi* to gossip.

cotización [kotiθa'θjon] *nf* (*COM*) quotation, price; (*de club*) dues *pl*.

cotizado, a [koti'θaðo, a] *a* (*fig*) highly-prized.

cotizar [koti'θar] *vt* (*COM*) to quote, price; ~**se** *vr* (*fig*) to be highly prized; ~**se a** to sell at, fetch; (*BOLSA*) to stand at, be quoted at.

coto ['koto] *nm* (*terreno cercado*) enclosure; (*de caza*) reserve; (*COM*) price-fixing agreement; **poner** ~ **a** to put a stop to.

cotorra [ko'torra] *nf* (*ZOOL*: *loro*) parrot; (*fam*: *persona*) windbag.

COU [kou] *nm abr* (*Esp* = *Curso de Orientación Universitario*) *one year course leading to final school leaving certificate and university entrance examinations*.

coyote [ko'jote] *nm* coyote, prairie wolf.

coyuntura [kojun'tura] *nf* (*ANAT*) joint; (*fig*) juncture, occasion; **esperar una** ~ **favorable** to await a favourable moment.

coz [koθ] *nf* kick.

CP *nm abr* (= *computador personal*) PC.

C.P. *abr* (*Esp*) = *Caja Postal*.

C.P.A. *nf abr* (= *Caja Postal de Ahorros*) Post Office Savings Bank.

CP/M *nm abr* (= *Programa de control para microprocesadores*) CP/M.

CPN *nm abr* (*Esp*) = *Cuerpo de la Policía Nacional*.

cps *abr* (= *caracteres por segundo*) c.p.s.

crac [krak] *nm* (*ECON*) crash.

cráneo ['kraneo] *nm* skull, cranium.

crápula ['krapula] *nf* drunkenness.

cráter ['krater] *nm* crater.

creación [krea'θjon] *nf* creation.

creador, a [krea'ðor, a] *a* creative ♦ *nm/f* creator.

crear [kre'ar] *vt* to create, make; (*originar*) to originate; (*INFORM*: *archivo*) to create; ~**se** *vr* (*comité etc*) to be set up.

crecer [kre'θer] *vi* to grow; (*precio*) to rise; ~**se** *vr* (*engreírse*) to get cocky.

creces ['kreθes]: **con** ~ *ad* amply, fully.

crecido, a [kre'θiðo, a] *a* (*persona, planta*) full-grown; (*cantidad*) large ♦ *nf* (*de río*) spate, flood.

creciente [kre'θjente] *a* growing; (*cantidad*) increasing; (*luna*) crescent ♦ *nm* crescent.

crecimiento [kreθi'mjento] *nm* growth; (*aumento*) increase; (*COM*) rise.

credenciales [kreðen'θjales] *nfpl* credentials.

crédito ['kreðito] *nm* credit; **a** ~ on credit; **dar** ~ **a** to believe (in); ~ **al consumidor** consumer credit; ~ **rotativo** *o* **renovable** revolving credit.

credo ['kreðo] *nm* creed.

crédulo, a ['kreðulo, a] *a* credulous.

creencia [kre'enθja] *nf* belief.

creer [kre'er] *vt, vi* to think, believe; (*considerar*) to think, consider; ~**se** *vr* to believe o.s. (to be); ~ **en** to believe in; **¡ya lo creo!** I should think so!

creíble [kre'iβle] *a* credible, believable.

creído, a [kre'iðo, a] *a* (*engreído*) conceited.

crema ['krema] *a inv* cream (coloured) ♦ *nf* cream; (*natillas*) custard; **la** ~ **de la sociedad** the cream of society.

cremallera [krema'ʎera] *nf* zip (fastener) (*Brit*), zipper (*US*).

cremoso, a [kre'moso, a] *a* creamy.

crepitar [krepi'tar] *vi* (*fuego*) to crackle.

crepúsculo [kre'puskulo] *nm* twilight, dusk.

crespo, a ['krespo, a] *a* (*pelo*) curly.

crespón [kres'pon] *nm* crêpe.

cresta ['kresta] *nf* (*GEO, ZOOL*) crest.

Creta ['kreta] *nf* Crete.

creyendo [kre'jendo] *etc vb* V **creer**.

creyente [kre'jente] *nm/f* believer.

crezca ['kreθka] *etc vb* V **crecer**.

cría ['kria] *etc vb* V **criar** ♦ *nf* V **crío, a**.

criada [kri'aða] *nf* V **criado, a**.

criadero [kria'ðero] *nm* nursery; (*ZOOL*) breeding place.

criadillas *nfpl* [krja'ðiʎas] *nfpl* (*CULIN*) bull's (*o* sheep's) testicles.

criado, a [kri'aðo, a] *nm* servant ♦ *nf* servant, maid.

criador [kria'ðor] *nm* breeder.

crianza [kri'anθa] *nf* rearing, breeding; (*fig*) breeding; (*MED*) lactation.

criar [kri'ar] *vt* (*amamantar*) to suckle, feed; (*educar*) to bring up; (*producir*) to grow, produce; (*animales*) to breed; ~**se** *vr* to grow (up); ~ **cuervos** to nourish a viper in one's bosom; **Dios los cría y ellos se juntan** birds of a feather flock together.

criatura [kria'tura] *nf* creature; (*niño*) baby, (small) child.

criba ['kriβa] *nf* sieve.

cribar [kri'βar] *vt* to sieve.

crimen ['krimen] *nm* crime; ~ **pasional** crime of passion.

criminal [krimi'nal] *a, nm/f* criminal.

crin [krin] *nf* (*tb*: ~**es**) mane.

crío, a ['krio, a] *nm/f* (*fam*: *chico*) kid ♦ *nf* (*de animales*) rearing, breeding; (*animal*) young.

criollo, a [kri'oʎo, a] *a* (*gen*) Creole; (*AM*) native (to America), national ◆ *nm/f* (*gen*) Creole; (*AM*) native American.

crisis ['krisis] *nf inv* crisis; ~ **nerviosa** nervous breakdown.

crisol [kri'sol] *nm* (*TEC*) crucible; (*fig*) melting pot.

crispar [kris'par] *vt* (*músculo*) to cause to contract; (*nervios*) to set on edge.

cristal [kris'tal] *nm* crystal; (*de ventana*) glass, pane; (*lente*) lens; **de** ~ glass *cpd*; ~ **ahumado/tallado** smoked/cut glass.

cristalería [kristale'ria] *nf* (*tienda*) glassware shop; (*objetos*) glassware.

cristalice [krista'liθe] *etc vb V* **cristalizar**.

cristalino, a [krista'lino, a] *a* crystalline; (*fig*) clear ◆ *nm* lens of the eye.

cristalizar [kristali'θar] *vt, vi* to crystallize.

cristiandad [kristjan'dað] *nf*, **cristianismo** [kristja'nismo] *nm* Christianity.

cristiano, a [kris'tjano, a] *a, nm/f* Christian; **hablar en** ~ to speak proper Spanish; (*fig*) to speak clearly.

Cristo ['kristo] *nm* (*dios*) Christ; (*crucifijo*) crucifix.

Cristóbal [kris'toβal] *nm*: ~ **Colón** Christopher Columbus.

criterio [kri'terjo] *nm* criterion; (*juicio*) judgement; (*enfoque*) attitude, approach; (*punto de vista*) view, opinion; ~ **de clasificación** (*INFORM*) sort criterion.

criticar [kriti'kar] *vt* to criticize.

crítico, a ['kritiko, a] *a* critical ◆ *nm* critic ◆ *nf* criticism; (*TEATRO etc*) review, notice; **la crítica** the critics *pl*.

critique [kri'tike] *etc vb V* **criticar**.

croar [kro'ar] *vi* to croak.

croata [kro'ata] *a, nm/f* Croat(ian).

cromado [kro'maðo] *nm* chromium plating, chrome.

cromo ['kromo] *nm* chrome; (*TIP*) coloured print.

crónico, a ['kroniko, a] *a* chronic ◆ *nf* chronicle, account; (*de periódico*) feature, article.

cronometraje [kronome'traxe] *nm* timing.

cronómetro [kro'nometro] *nm* (*DEPORTE*) stopwatch; (*TEC etc*) chronometer.

croqueta [kro'keta] *nf* croquette, rissole.

croquis ['krokis] *nm inv* sketch.

cruce ['kruθe] *etc vb V* **cruzar** ◆ *nm* crossing; (*de carreteras*) crossroads; (*AUTO etc*) junction, intersection; (*BIO: proceso*) crossbreeding; **luces de** ~ dipped headlights.

crucero [kru'θero] *nm* (*NAUT: barco*) cruise ship; (: *viaje*) cruise.

crucificar [kruθifi'kar] *vt* to crucify; (*fig*) to torment.

crucifijo [kruθi'fixo] *nm* crucifix.

crucifique [kruθi'fike] *etc vb V* **crucificar**.

crucigrama [kruθi'ɣrama] *nm* crossword (puzzle).

crudeza [kru'ðeθa] *nf* (*rigor*) harshness; (*aspereza*) crudeness.

crudo, a ['kruðo, a] *a* raw; (*no maduro*) unripe; (*petróleo*) crude; (*rudo, cruel*) cruel; (*agua*) hard; (*clima etc*) harsh ◆ *nm* crude (oil).

cruel [krwel] *a* cruel.

crueldad [krwel'ðað] *nf* cruelty.

cruento, a ['krwento, a] *a* bloody.

crujido [kru'xiðo] *nm* (*de madera etc*) creak.

crujiente [kru'xjente] *a* (*galleta etc*) crunchy.

crujir [kru'xir] *vi* (*madera etc*) to creak; (*dedos*) to crack; (*dientes*) to grind; (*nieve, arena*) to crunch.

cruz [kruθ] *nf* cross; (*de moneda*) tails *sg*; (*fig*) burden; ~ **gamada** swastika; **C~ Roja** Red Cross.

cruzado, a [kru'θaðo, a] *a* crossed ◆ *nm* crusader ◆ *nf* crusade.

cruzar [kru'θar] *vt* to cross; (*palabras*) to exchange; ~**se** *vr* (*líneas etc*) to cross, intersect; (*personas*) to pass each other; ~**se de brazos** to fold one's arms; (*fig*) not to lift a finger to help; ~**se con uno en la calle** to pass sb in the street.

c.s.f. *abr* (= *costo, seguro y flete*) c.i.f.

CSIC [θe'sik] *nm abr* (*Esp ESCOL*) = *Consejo Superior de Investigaciones Científicas*.

cta, c.ta *nf abr* (= *cuenta*) a/c.

cta. cto. *abr* (= *carta de crédito*) L.C.

cte. *abr* (= *corriente, de los corrientes*) inst.

CTNE *nf abr* (*TELEC*) = *Compañía Telefónica Nacional de España*.

c/u *abr* (= *cada uno*) ea.

cuaco ['kwako] *nm* (*AM*) horse.

cuaderno [kwa'ðerno] *nm* notebook; (*de escuela*) exercise book; (*NAUT*) logbook.

cuadra ['kwaðra] *nf* (*caballeriza*) stable; (*AM*) (city) block.

cuadrado, a [kwa'ðraðo, a] *a* square ◆ *nm* (*MAT*) square.

cuadragésimo, a [kwaðra'xesimo, a] *num* fortieth.

cuadrángulo [kwa'ðrangulo, a] *nm* quadrangle.

cuadrante [kwa'ðrante] *nm* quadrant.

cuadrar [kwa'ðrar] *vt* to square; (*TIP*) to justify ◆ *vi*: ~ **con** (*cuenta*) to square with, tally with; ~**se** *vr* (*soldado*) to stand to attention; ~ **por la derecha/izquierda** to right-/left-justify.

cuadrícula [kwa'ðrikula] *nf* (*TIP etc*) grid, ruled squares.

cuadriculado, a [kwaðriku'laðo, a] *a*: **papel** ~ squared *o* graph paper.

cuadrilátero [kwaðri'latero] *nm* (*DEPORTE*) boxing ring; (*GEOM*) quadrilateral.

cuadrilla [kwa'ðriʎa] *nf* (*amigos*) party, group; (*pandilla*) gang; (*obreros*) team.

cuadro ['kwaðro] *nm* square; (*PINTURA*) painting; (*TEATRO*) scene; (*diagrama*: *tb*: ~ **sinóptico**) chart, table, diagram; (*DEPORTE*, *MED*) team; (*POL*) executive; ~ **de mandos** control panel; **a** ~**s** check *cpd*.

cuadruplicarse [kwaðrupli'karse] *vr* to quadruple.

cuádruplo, a ['kwaðruplo, a], **cuádruple** ['kwaðruple] *a* quadruple.

cuajado, a [kwa'xado, a] *a*: ~ **de** (*fig*) full of ♦ *nf* (*de leche*) curd.

cuajar [kwa'xar] *vt* to thicken; (*leche*) to curdle; (*sangre*) to congeal; (*adornar*) to adorn; (*CULIN*) to set ♦ *vi* (*nieve*) to lie; (*fig*) to become set, become established; (*idea*) to be received, be acceptable; ~**se** *vr* to curdle; to congeal; (*llenarse*) to fill up.

cuajo ['kwaxo] *nm*: **arrancar algo de** ~ to tear sth out by its roots.

cual [kwal] *ad* like, as ♦ *pron*: **el** ~ *etc* which; (*persona: sujeto*) who; (: *objeto*) whom; **lo** ~ (*relativo*) which; **allá cada** ~ every man to his own taste; **son a** ~ **más gandul** each is as idle as the other; **cada** ~ each one ♦ *a* such as; **tal** ~ just as it is.

cuál [kwal] *pron interrogativo* which (one), what.

cualesquier(a) [kwales'kjer(a)] *pl de* **cualquier(a)**.

cualidad [kwali'ðað] *nf* quality.

cualificado, a [kwalifi'kaðo, a] *a* (*obrero*) skilled, qualified.

cualquiera [kwal'kjera], **cualquier** [kwal-'kjer], *pl* **cualesquier(a)** *a* any ♦ *pron* anybody, anyone; (*quienquiera*) whoever; **en cualquier momento** any time; **en cualquier parte** anywhere; **cualquiera que sea** whichever it is; (*persona*) whoever it is.

cuán [kwan] *adv* how.

cuando ['kwando] *ad* when; (*aún si*) if, even if ♦ *conj* (*puesto que*) since ♦ *prep*: **yo,** ~ **niño** ... when I was a child ..., as a child I ...; ~ **no sea así** even if it is not so; ~ **más** at (the) most; ~ **menos** at least; ~ **no** if not, otherwise; **de** ~ **en** ~ from time to time; **ven** ~ **quieras** come when(ever) you like.

cuándo ['kwando] *ad* when; **¿desde** ~**?, ¿de** ~ **acá?** since when?

cuantía [kwan'tia] *nf* (*alcance*) extent; (*importancia*) importance.

cuantioso, a [kwan'tjoso, a] *a* substantial.

cuanto, a ['kwanto, a] *a, pron*: **llévate todo** ~ **quieras** take as much as you like; **en** ~ (*en seguida que*) as soon as; (*ya que*) since, inasmuch as; **en** ~ **a** as for; ~ **más difícil sea** the more difficult it is; ~ **más**

hace (tanto) menos avanza the more he does, the less he progresses; ~**s más invitados vengan tantas más comidas habrá que preparar** the more guests come, the more meals will have to be cooked; ~ **antes** as soon as possible; **unos** ~**s libros** a few books.

cuánto, a ['kwanto, a] *a* (*exclamación*) what a lot of; (*interrogativo*: *sg*) how much?; (: *pl*) how many? ♦ *pron, ad* how; (*interrogativo*: *sg*) how much?; (: *pl*) how many? ♦ *excl*: **¡**~ **me alegro!** I'm so glad!; **¡cuánta gente!** what a lot of people!; **¿**~ **tiempo?** how long?; **¿**~ **cuesta?** how much does it cost?; **¿a** ~**s estamos?** what's the date?; **¿**~ **hay de aquí a Bilbao?** how far is it from here to Bilbao?; **Señor no sé** ~**s** Mr. So-and-So.

cuarenta [kwa'renta] *num* forty.

cuarentena [kwaren'tena] *nf* (*MED etc*) quarantine; (*conjunto*) forty(-odd).

cuarentón, ona [kwaren'ton, ona] *a* fortyyear-old, fortyish ♦ *nm/f* person of about forty.

cuaresma [kwa'resma] *nf* Lent.

cuarta ['kwarta] *nf V* **cuarto**.

cuartear [kwarte'ar] *vt* to quarter; (*dividir*) to divide up; ~**se** *vr* to crack, split.

cuartel [kwar'tel] *nm* (*de ciudad*) quarter, district; (*MIL*) barracks *pl*; ~ **general** headquarters *pl*.

cuartelazo [kwarte'laθo] *nm* coup, military uprising.

cuarteto [kwar'teto] *nm* quartet.

cuartilla [kwar'tiʎa] *nf* (*hoja*) sheet (of paper); ~**s** *nfpl* (*TIP*) copy *sg*.

cuarto, a ['kwarto, a] *a* fourth ♦ *nm* (*MAT*) quarter, fourth; (*habitación*) room ♦ *nf* (*MAT*) quarter, fourth; (*palmo*) span; ~ **de baño** bathroom; ~ **de estar** living room; ~ **de hora** quarter (of an) hour; ~ **de kilo** quarter kilo; **no tener un** ~ to be broke (*fam*).

cuarzo ['kwarθo] *nm* quartz.

cuatrero [kwa'trero] *nm* (*AM*) rustler, stock thief.

cuatro ['kwatro] *num* four; **las** ~ four o'clock; **el** ~ **de octubre** (on) the fourth of October; *V tb* **seis**.

cuatrocientos, as [kwatro'θjentos, as] *num* four hundred; *V tb* **seiscientos**.

Cuba ['kuβa] *nf* Cuba.

cuba ['kuβa] *nf* cask, barrel; **estar como una** ~ (*fam*) to be sloshed.

cubalibre [kuβa'liβre] *nm* (white) rum and coke ®.

cubano, a [ku'βano, a] *a, nm/f* Cuban.

cubata [ku'βata] *nm* = **cubalibre**.

cubertería [kuβerte'ria] *nf* cutlery.

cúbico, a ['kuβiko, a] *a* cubic.

cubierto, a [ku'βjerto, a] *pp de* **cubrir** ♦ *a*

covered; (*cielo*) overcast ◆ *nm* cover; (*en la mesa*) place ◆ *nf* cover, covering; (*neumático*) tyre; (*NAUT*) deck; ~s *nmpl* cutlery *sg*; **a ~ de** covered with *o* in; **precio del ~** cover charge.

cubil [ku'βil] *nm* den.

cubilete [kuβi'lete] *nm* (*en juegos*) cup.

cubito [ku'βito] *nm*: **~ de (la) basura** dustbin; **~ de hielo** ice cube.

cubo ['kuβo] *nm* cube; (*balde*) bucket, tub; (*TEC*) drum.

cubrecama [kuβre'kama] *nm* (*AM*) bedspread.

cubrir [ku'βrir] *vt* to cover; (*vacante*) to fill; (*BIO*) to mate with; (*gastos*) to meet; **~se** *vr* (*cielo*) to become overcast; (*COM*: *gastos*) to be met *o* paid; (: *deuda*) to be covered; **~ las formas** to keep up appearances; **lo cubrieron las aguas** the waters closed over it; **el agua casi me cubría** I was almost out of my depth.

cucaracha [kuka'ratʃa] *nf* cockroach.

cuclillas [ku'kliʎas] *nfpl*: **en ~** squatting.

cuco, a ['kuko, a] *a* pretty; (*astuto*) sharp ◆ *nm* cuckoo.

cucurucho [kuku'rutʃo] *nm* paper cone, cornet.

cuchara [ku'tʃara] *nf* spoon; (*TEC*) scoop.

cucharada [kutʃa'raða] *nf* spoonful; **~ colmada** heaped spoonful.

cucharadita [kutʃara'ðita] *nf* teaspoonful.

cucharita [kutʃa'rita] *nf* teaspoon.

cucharón [kutʃa'ron] *nm* ladle.

cuchichear [kutʃitʃe'ar] *vi* to whisper.

cuchicheo [kutʃi'tʃeo] *nm* whispering.

cuchilla [ku'tʃiʎa] *nf* (large) knife; (*de arma blanca*) blade; **~ de afeitar** razor blade; **pasar a ~** to put to the sword.

cuchillo [ku'tʃiʎo] *nm* knife.

cuchitril [kutʃi'tril] *nm* hovel; (*habitación etc*) pigsty.

cuece ['kweθe] *etc vb V* **cocer**.

cuele ['kwele] *etc vb V* **colar**.

cuelgue ['kwelɣe] *etc vb V* **colgar**.

cuello ['kweʎo] *nm* (*ANAT*) neck; (*de vestido, camisa*) collar.

cuenca ['kwenka] *nf* (*ANAT*) eye socket; (*GEO*: *valle*) bowl, deep valley; (: *fluvial*) basin.

cuenco ['kwenko] *nm* (earthenware) bowl.

cuenta ['kwenta] *etc vb V* **contar** ◆ *nf* (*cálculo*) count, counting; (*en café, restaurante*) bill; (*COM*) account; (*de collar*) bead; (*fig*) account; **a fin de ~s** in the end; **en resumidas ~s** in short; **caer en la ~** to catch on; **dar ~ a uno de sus actos** to account to sb for one's actions; **darse ~ de** to realize; **tener en ~** to bear in mind; **echar ~s** to take stock; **~ de atrás** countdown; **~ corriente/de ahorros/a plazo (fijo)** current/savings/deposit account; **~ de**

asignación appropriation account; **~ de caja** cash account; **~ de capital** capital account; **~ por cobrar** account receivable; **~ de crédito** credit *o* loan account; **~ de gastos e ingresos** income and expenditure account; **~ por pagar** account payable; **abonar una cantidad en ~ a uno** to credit a sum to sb's account; **ajustar** *o* **liquidar una ~** to settle an account; **pasar la ~** to send the bill.

cuentagotas [kwenta'ɣotas] *nm inv* (*MED*) dropper; **a** *o* **con ~** (*fam*, *fig*) drop by drop, bit by bit.

cuentakilómetros [kwentaki'lometros] *nm inv* (*de distancias*) ≈ milometer, clock; (*velocímetro*) speedometer.

cuentista [kwen'tista] *nm/f* gossip; (*LIT*) short-story writer.

cuento ['kwento] *etc vb V* **contar** ◆ *nm* story; (*LIT*) short story; **~ de hadas** fairy story; **es el ~ de nunca acabar** it's an endless business; **eso no viene a ~** that's irrelevant.

cuerda ['kwerða] *nf* rope; (*hilo*) string; (*de reloj*) spring; (*MUS*: *de violín etc*) string; (*MAT*) chord; (*ANAT*) cord; **~ floja** tightrope; **~s vocales** vocal cords; **dar ~ a un reloj** to wind up a clock.

cuerdo, a ['kwerðo, a] *a* sane; (*prudente*) wise, sensible.

cuerno ['kwerno] *nm* (*ZOOL*: *gen*) horn; (: *de ciervo*) antler; **poner los ~s a** (*fam*) to cuckold; **saber a ~ quemado** to leave a nasty taste.

cuero ['kwero] *nm* (*ZOOL*) skin, hide; (*TEC*) leather; **en ~s** stark naked; **~ cabelludo** scalp.

cuerpo ['kwerpo] *nm* body; (*cadáver*) corpse; (*fig*) main part; **~ de bomberos** fire brigade; **~ diplomático** diplomatic corps; **luchar ~ a ~** to fight hand-to-hand; **tomar ~** (*plan etc*) to take shape.

cuervo ['kwerβo] *nm* (*ZOOL*) raven, crow; *V* **criar**.

cuesta ['kwesta] *etc vb V* **costar** ◆ *nf* slope; (*en camino etc*) hill; **~ arriba/abajo** uphill/downhill; **a ~s** on one's back.

cuestión [kwes'tjon] *nf* matter, question, issue; (*riña*) quarrel, dispute; **eso es otra ~** that's another matter.

cuestionar [kwestjo'nar] *vt* to question.

cueva ['kweβa] *nf* cave.

cueza ['kweθa] *etc vb V* **cocer**.

cuidado [kwi'ðaðo] *nm* care, carefulness; (*preocupación*) care, worry ◆ *excl* careful!, look out!; **eso me tiene sin ~** I'm not worried about that.

cuidadoso, a [kwiða'ðoso, a] *a* careful; (*preocupado*) anxious.

cuidar [kwi'ðar] *vt* (*MED*) to care for; (*ocuparse de*) to take care of, look after;

(*detalles*) to pay attention to ♦ *vi*: ~ **de** to take care of, look after; ~**se de hacer algo** to take care to do something.

cuita ['kwita] *nf* (*preocupación*) worry, trouble; (*pena*) grief.

culata [ku'lata] *nf* (*de fusil*) butt.

culatazo [kula'taθo] *nm* kick, recoil.

culebra [ku'leßra] *nf* snake; ~ **de cascabel** rattlesnake.

culebrear [kuleßre'ar] *vi* to wriggle along; (*río*) to meander.

culinario, a [kuli'narjo, a] *a* culinary, cooking *cpd*.

culminación [kulmina'θjon] *nf* culmination.

culminante [kulmi'nante] *a*: **momento** ~ climax, highlight, highspot.

culminar [kulmi'nar] *vi* to culminate.

culo ['kulo] *nm* (*fam*: *asentaderas*) bottom, backside, bum (*Brit*); (: *ano*) arse(hole) (*Brit!*), ass(hole) (*US!*); (*de vaso*) bottom.

culpa ['kulpa] *nf* fault; (*JUR*) guilt; ~**s** *nfpl* sins; **por** ~ **de** through, because of; **tener la** ~ (**de**) to be to blame (for).

culpabilidad [kulpaßili'ðað] *nf* guilt.

culpable [kul'paßle] *a* guilty ♦ *nm/f* culprit; **confesarse** ~ to plead guilty; **declarar** ~ **a uno** to find sb guilty.

culpar [kul'par] *vt* to blame; (*acusar*) to accuse.

cultivadora [kultißa'ðora] *nf* cultivator.

cultivar [kulti'ßar] *vt* to cultivate; (*cosecha*) to raise; (*talento*) to develop.

cultivo [kul'tißo] *nm* (*acto*) cultivation; (*plantas*) crop; (*BIO*) culture.

culto, a ['kulto, a] *a* (*cultivado*) cultivated; (*que tiene cultura*) cultured, educated ♦ *nm* (*homenaje*) worship; (*religión*) cult; (*POL etc*) cult.

cultura [kul'tura] *nf* culture.

culturismo [kultu'rismo] *nm* body building.

cumbre ['kumbre] *nf* summit, top; (*fig*) top, height; **conferencia (en la)** ~ summit (conference).

cumpleaños [kumple'aɲos] *nm inv* birthday.

cumplido, a [kum'pliðo, a] *a* complete, perfect; (*abundante*) plentiful; (*cortés*) courteous ♦ *nm* compliment; **visita de** ~ courtesy call.

cumplidor, a [kumpli'ðor, a] *a* reliable.

cumplimentar [kumplimen'tar] *vt* to congratulate; (*órdenes*) to carry out.

cumplimiento [kumpli'mjento] *nm* (*de un deber*) fulfilment, execution, performance; (*acabamiento*) completion; (*COM*) expiry, end.

cumplir [kum'plir] *vt* (*orden*) to carry out, obey; (*promesa*) to carry out, fulfil; (*condena*) to serve; (*años*) to reach, attain ♦ *vi* (*pago*) to fall due; (*plazo*) to expire; ~**se**

vr (*plazo*) to expire; (*plan etc*) to be fulfilled; (*vaticinio*) to come true; **hoy cumple dieciocho años** he is eighteen today; ~ **con** (*deberes*) to carry out, fulfil.

cúmulo ['kumulo] *nm* (*montón*) heap; (*nube*) cumulus.

cuna ['kuna] *nf* cradle, cot; **canción de** ~ lullaby.

cundir [kun'dir] *vi* (*noticia, rumor, pánico*) to spread; (*rendir*) to go a long way.

cuneta [ku'neta] *nf* ditch.

cuña ['kuɲa] *nf* (*TEC*) wedge; (*COM*) advertising spot; (*MED*) bedpan; **tener** ~**s** to have influence.

cuñado, a [ku'ɲaðo, a] *nm/f* brother/sister-in-law.

cuño ['kuɲo] *nm* (*TEC*) die-stamp; (*fig*) stamp.

cuota ['kwota] *nf* (*parte proporcional*) share; (*cotización*) fee, dues *pl*; ~ **inicial** (*COM*) down payment.

cupo ['kupo] *etc vb V* **caber** ♦ *nm* quota, share; (*COM*): ~ **de importación** import quota; ~ **de ventas** sales quota.

cupón [ku'pon] *nm* coupon.

cúpula ['kupula] *nf* (*ARQ*) dome.

cura ['kura] *nf* (*curación*) cure; (*método curativo*) treatment ♦ *nm* priest; ~ **de emergencia** emergency treatment.

curación [kura'θjon] *nf* cure; (*acción*) curing.

curado, a [ku'raðo, a] *a* (*CULIN*) cured; (*pieles*) tanned.

curar [ku'rar] *vt* (*MED*: *herida*) to treat, dress; (: *enfermo*) to cure; (*CULIN*) to cure, salt; (*cuero*) to tan ♦ *vi*, ~**se** *vr* to get well, recover.

curda ['kurða] (*fam*) *nm* drunk ♦ *nf*: **agarrar una/estar** ~ to get/be sloshed.

curiosear [kurjose'ar] *vt* to glance at, look over ♦ *vi* to look round, wander round; (*explorar*) to poke about.

curiosidad [kurjosi'ðað] *nf* curiosity.

curioso, a [ku'rjoso, a] *a* curious; (*aseado*) neat ♦ *nm/f* bystander, onlooker; ¡**qué** ~! how odd!

curita [ku'rita] *nf* (*AM*) sticking plaster.

currante [ku'rrante] *nm/f* (*fam*) worker.

currar [ku'rrar] *vi* (*fam*), **currelar** [kurre'lar] *vi* (*fam*) to work.

currículo [ku'rrikulo] *nm*, **currículum** [ku'rrikulum] *nm* curriculum vitae.

curro ['kurro] *nm* (*fam*) work, job.

cursar [kur'sar] *vt* (*ESCOL*) to study.

cursi ['kursi] *a* (*fam*) pretentious; (: *amanerado*) affected.

cursilería [kursile'ria] *nf* (*vulgaridad*) bad taste; (*amaneramiento*) affectation.

cursillo [kur'siʎo] *nm* short course.

cursiva [kur'sißa] *nf* italics *pl*.

curso ['kurso] *nm* (*dirección*) course; (*fig*)

progress; (*ESCOL*) school year; (*UNIV*) academic year; **en ~ (año)** current; (*proceso*) going on, under way; **moneda de ~ legal** legal tender.

cursor [kur'sor] *nm* (*INFORM*) cursor; (*TEC*) slide.

curtido, a [kur'tiðo, a] *a* (*cara etc*) weather-beaten; (*fig: persona*) experienced.

curtir [kur'tir] *vt* (*piel*) to tan; (*fig*) to harden.

curvo, a ['kurßo, a] *a* (*gen*) curved; (*torcido*) bent ♦ *nf* (*gen*) curve, bend; **curva de rentabilidad** (*COM*) break-even chart.

cúspide ['kuspiðe] *nf* (*GEO*) summit, peak; (*fig*) top, pinnacle.

custodia [kus'toðja] *nf* (*cuidado*) safekeeping; (*JUR*) custody.

custodiar [kusto'ðjar] *vt* (*conservar*) to keep, take care of; (*vigilar*) to guard.

custodio [kus'toðjo] *nm* guardian, keeper.

cutícula [ku'tikula] *nf* cuticle.

cutis ['kutis] *nm inv* skin, complexion.

cutre ['kutre] *a* (*fam: lugar*) grotty; (: *persona*) naff.

cuyano, a [ku'jano, a] *a*, *nm/f* (*AM: fam*) Argentinian.

cuyo, a ['kujo, a] *pron* (*de quien*) whose; (*de que*) whose, of which; **la señora en cuya casa me hospedé** the lady in whose house I stayed; **el asunto cuyos detalles conoces** the affair the details of which you know; **por ~ motivo** for which reason.

C.V. *abr* (= *caballos de vapor*) H.P.

C y F *abr* (= *costo y flete*) C & F.

CH

Ch, ch [tʃe] *nf* (*letra*) Ch, ch.

chabacano, a [tʃaßa'kano, a] *a* vulgar, coarse.

chabola [tʃa'ßola] *nf* shack; **~s** *nfpl* shanty town *sg*.

chabolismo [tʃaßo'lismo] *nm*: **el problema del ~** the problem of substandard housing, the shanty town problem.

chacal [tʃa'kal] *nm* jackal.

chacarero [tʃaka'rero] *nm* (*AM*) small farmer.

chacra ['tʃakra] *nf* (*AM*) smallholding.

chacha ['tʃatʃa] *nf* (*fam*) maid.

cháchara ['tʃatʃara] *nf* chatter; **estar de ~** to chatter away.

chafar [tʃa'far] *vt* (*aplastar*) to crush, flatten; (*arruinar*) to ruin.

chaflán [tʃa'flan] *nm* (*TEC*) bevel.

chal [tʃal] *nm* shawl.

chalado, a [tʃa'laðo, a] *a* (*fam*) crazy.

chalé, pl chalés [tʃa'le, tʃa'les] *nm* villa, ≈ detached house.

chaleco [tʃa'leko] *nm* waistcoat, vest (*US*); **~ antibala** bulletproof vest; **~ salvavidas** life jacket.

chalet [tʃa'le], *pl* **chalets** [tʃa'les] *nm* = **chalé**.

chalupa [tʃa'lupa] *nf* launch, boat.

chamaco, a [tʃa'mako, a] *nm/f* boy/girl.

chamarra [tʃa'marra] *nf* sheepskin jacket; (*AM: poncho*) blanket.

champán [tʃam'pan] *nm*, **champaña** [tʃam'paɲa] *nm* champagne.

champiñón [tʃampi'ɲon] *nm* mushroom.

champú [tʃam'pu] (*pl* **champúes**, **champús**) *nm* shampoo.

chamuscar [tʃamus'kar] *vt* to scorch, sear, singe.

chamusque [tʃa'muske] *etc vb V* **chamuscar**.

chamusquina [tʃamus'kina] *nf* singeing.

chancla ['tʃankla] *nf* (*AM: zapato viejo*) old shoe.

chancleta [tʃan'kleta] *nf* sandal, slipper.

chancho, a ['tʃantʃo, a] *nm/f* (*AM*) pig.

chanchullo [tʃan'tʃuʎo] *nm* (*fam*) fiddle, wangle.

chandal [tʃan'dal] *nm* tracksuit.

chantaje [tʃan'taxe] *nm* blackmail; **hacer ~ a uno** to blackmail sb.

chanza ['tʃanθa] *nf* joke.

chao [tʃao] *excl* (*fam*) cheerio.

chapa ['tʃapa] *nf* (*de metal*) plate, sheet; (*de madera*) board, panel; (*de botella*) bottle top; (*insignia*) (lapel) badge; (*AM: AUTO*) number (*Brit*) *o* license (*US*) plate; **de 3 ~s** (*madera*) 3-ply.

chapado, a [tʃa'paðo, a] *a* (*metal*) plated; (*muebles etc*) finished.

chaparrón [tʃapa'rron] *nm* downpour, cloudburst.

chapotear [tʃapote'ar] *vt* to sponge down ♦ *vi* (*fam*) to splash about.

chapucero, a [tʃapu'θero, a] *a* rough, crude ♦ *nm/f* bungler.

chapurr(e)ar [tʃapurr(e)'ar] *vt* (*idioma*) to speak badly.

chapuza [tʃa'puθa] *nf* botched job; (*AM: estafa*) trick, swindle.

chapuzón [tʃapu'θon] *nm*: **darse un ~** to go for a dip.

chaqueta [tʃa'keta] *nf* jacket; **cambiar la ~** (*fig*) to change sides.

charca ['tʃarka] *nf* pond, pool.

charco ['tʃarko] *nm* pool, puddle.

charcutería [tʃarkute'ria] *nf* (*tienda*) *shop selling chiefly pork meat products*; (*productos*) cooked pork meats *pl*.

charla ['tʃarla] *nf* talk, chat; (*conferencia*)

lecture.

charlar [tʃar'lar] *vi* to talk, chat.

charlatán, ana [tʃarla'tan, ana] *nm/f* chatterbox; (*estafador*) trickster.

charol [tʃa'rol] *nm* varnish; (*cuero*) patent leather.

charro, a ['tʃarro, a] *a* Salamancan; (*AM*) Mexican; (*ropa*) loud, gaudy; (*AM*: *costumbres*) traditional ◆ *nm/f* Salamancan; Mexican.

chárter ['tʃarter] *a inv*: **vuelo** ~ charter flight.

chascarrillo [tʃaska'rriʎo] *nm* (*fam*) funny story.

chasco ['tʃasko] *nm* (*broma*) trick, joke; (*desengaño*) disappointment.

chasis ['tʃasis] *nm inv* (*AUTO*) chassis; (*FOTO*) plateholder.

chasquear [tʃaske'ar] *vt* (*látigo*) to crack; (*lengua*) to click.

chasquido [tʃas'kiðo] *nm* (*de lengua*) click; (*de látigo*) crack.

chatarra [tʃa'tarra] *nf* scrap (metal).

chato, a ['tʃato, a] *a* flat; (*nariz*) snub ◆ *nm* wine tumbler; **beber unos** ~**s** to have a few drinks.

chauvinismo [tʃoßi'nismo] *nm* chauvinism.

chauvinista [tʃoßi'nista] *a*, *nm/f* chauvinist.

chaval, a [tʃa'ßal, a] *nm/f* kid (*fam*), lad/ lass.

chavo ['tʃaßo] *nm* (*AM*: *fam*) boy, kid.

checo, a *a*, *nm/f* Czech ◆ *nm* (*LING*) Czech.

checo(e)slovaco, a [tʃeko(e)slo'ßako, a] *a*, *nm/f* Czech, Czechoslovak.

Checo(e)slovaquia [tʃeko(e)slo'ßakja] *nf* Czechoslovakia.

chepa ['tʃepa] *nf* hump.

cheque ['tʃeke] *nm* cheque (*Brit*), check (*US*); ~ **abierto/en blanco/cruzado** open/ blank/crossed cheque; ~ **al portador** cheque payable to bearer; ~ **caducado** stale cheque; ~ **de viajero** traveller's cheque.

chequeo [tʃe'keo] *nm* (*MED*) check-up; (*AUTO*) service.

chequera [tʃe'kera] *nf* (*AM*) chequebook (*Brit*), checkbook (*US*).

chévere ['tʃeßere] *a* (*AM*) great, fabulous (*fam*).

chico, a ['tʃiko, a] *a* small, little ◆ *nm/f* child; (*muchacho*) boy; (*muchacha*) girl.

chicano, a [tʃi'kano, a] *a* chicano, Mexican-American.

chicle ['tʃikle] *nm* chewing gum.

chicha ['tʃitʃa] *nf* (*AM*) maize liquor.

chícharo ['tʃitʃaro] *nm* (*AM*) pea.

chicharra [tʃi'tʃarra] *nf* harvest bug, cicada.

chicharrón [tʃitʃa'rron] *nm* (pork) crackling.

chichón [tʃi'tʃon] *nm* bump, lump.

chiflado, a [tʃi'flaðo, a] *a* (*fam*) crazy, round the bend ◆ *nm/f* nutcase.

chiflar [tʃi'flar] *vt* to hiss, boo.

Chile ['tʃile] *nm* Chile.

chile ['tʃile] *nm* chilli, pepper.

chileno, a [tʃi'leno, a] *a*, *nm/f* Chilean.

chillar [tʃi'ʎar] *vi* (*persona*) to yell, scream; (*animal salvaje*) to howl; (*cerdo*) to squeal; (*puerta*) to creak.

chillido [tʃi'ʎiðo] *nm* (*de persona*) yell, scream; (*de animal*) howl; (*de frenos*) screech(ing).

chillón, ona [tʃi'ʎon, ona] *a* (*niño*) noisy; (*color*) loud, gaudy.

chimenea [tʃime'nea] *nf* chimney; (*hogar*) fireplace.

chimpancé, pl chimpancés [tʃimpan'θe, tʃimpan'θes] *nm* chimpanzee.

China ['tʃina] *nf*: (**la**) ~ China.

china ['tʃina] *nf* pebble.

chinchar [tʃin'tʃar] (*fam*) *vt* to pester, annoy; ~**se** *vr* to get cross; ¡**chínchate!** tough!

chinche ['tʃintʃe] *nf* bug; (*TEC*) drawing pin (*Brit*), thumbtack (*US*) ◆ *nm/f* nuisance, pest.

chincheta [tʃin'tʃeta] *nf* drawing pin (*Brit*), thumbtack (*US*).

chingar [tʃin'gar] *vt* (*AM*: *fam!*) to fuck (up)(!) ◆ *vi* (*AM*: *bromear*) to joke; (: *fracasar*) to fail, fall through.

chingue ['tʃinge] *etc vb V* **chingar**.

chino, a ['tʃino, a] *a*, *nm/f* Chinese ◆ *nm* (*LING*) Chinese.

chip [tʃip] *nm* (*INFORM*) chip.

chipirón [tʃipi'ron] *nm* squid.

Chipre ['tʃipre] *nf* Cyprus.

chipriota [tʃi'prjota], **chipriote** [tʃi'prjote] *a* Cypriot, Cyprian ◆ *nm/f* Cypriot.

chiquillada [tʃiki'ʎada] *nf* childish prank.

chiquillo, a [tʃi'kiʎo, a] *nm/f* kid (*fam*), youngster, child.

chiquito, a [tʃi'kito, a] *a* very small, tiny ◆ *nm/f* kid (*fam*).

chirigota [tʃiri'yota] *nf* joke.

chirimbolo [tʃirim'bolo] *nm* thingummyjig (*fam*).

chirimoya [tʃiri'moja] *nf* custard apple.

chiringuito [tʃirin'gito] *nm* refreshment stall *o* stand.

chiripa [tʃi'ripa] *nf* fluke; **por** ~ by chance.

chirona [tʃi'rona], (*AM*) **chirola** [tʃi'rola] *nf* (*fam*) clink, jail.

chirriar [tʃi'rrjar] *vi* (*goznes*) to creak, squeak; (*pájaros*) to chirp, sing.

chirrido [tʃi'rriðo] *nm* creak(ing), squeak(ing); (*de pájaro*) chirp(ing).

chis [tʃis] *excl* sh!

chisme ['tʃisme] *nm* (*habladurías*) piece of gossip; (*fam*: *objeto*) thingummyjig.

chismoso, a [tʃis'moso, a] *a* gossiping ◆ *nm/f* gossip.

chispa ['tʃispa] *nf* spark; (*fig*) sparkle; (*ingenio*) wit; (*fam*) drunkenness.

chispeante [tʃispe'ante] *a* (*tb fig*) sparkling.

chispear [tʃispe'ar] *vi* to spark; (*lloviznar*) to drizzle.

chisporrotear [tʃisporrote'ar] *vi* (*fuego*) to throw out sparks; (*leña*) to crackle; (*aceite*) to hiss, splutter.

chistar [tʃistar] *vi*: **no ~** not to say a word.

chiste ['tʃiste] *nm* joke, funny story; **~ verde** blue joke.

chistoso, a [tʃis'toso, a] *a* (*gracioso*) funny, amusing; (*bromista*) witty.

chistu ['tʃistu] *nm* = **txistu.**

chivarse [tʃi'βarse] *vr* (*fam*) to grass.

chivatazo [tʃiβa'taθo] *nm* (*fam*) tip-off; **dar ~** to inform.

chivo, a ['tʃiβo, a] *nm/f* (billy/nanny-)goat; **~ expiatorio** scapegoat.

chocante [tʃo'kante] *a* startling; (*extraño*) odd; (*ofensivo*) shocking.

chocar [tʃo'kar] *vi* (*coches etc*) to collide, crash; (*MIL, fig*) to clash ◆ *vt* to shock; (*sorprender*) to startle; **~ con** to collide with; (*fig*) to run into, run up against; **¡chócala!** (*fam*) put it there!

chocolate [tʃoko'late] *a* chocolate ◆ *nm* chocolate; (*fam*) dope, marijuana.

chocolatería [tʃokolate'ria] *nf* chocolate factory (*o* shop).

chochear [tʃotʃe'ar] *vi* to dodder, be senile.

chocho, a ['tʃotʃo, a] *a* doddering, senile; (*fig*) soft, doting.

chófer ['tʃofer], **chofer** [tʃo'fer] *nm* driver.

chollo ['tʃoʎo] *nm* (*fam*) bargain, snip.

chopo ['tʃopo] *nm* black poplar.

choque ['tʃoke] *etc vb* V **chocar** ◆ *nm* (*impacto*) impact; (*golpe*) jolt; (*AUTO*) crash; (*fig*) conflict.

chorizo [tʃo'riθo] *nm* hard pork sausage, (*type of*) salami; (*ladrón*) crook.

chorra ['tʃorra] *nf* luck.

chorradas [tʃo'rraðas] *nfpl* (*objetos*) rubbish *sg*, junk *sg*; **decir ~** to talk rubbish *o* nonsense.

chorrear [tʃorre'ar] *vt* to pour ◆ *vi* to gush (out), spout (out); (*gotear*) to drip, trickle.

chorreras [tʃo'rreras] *nfpl* (*COSTURA*) frill *sg*.

chorro ['tʃorro] *nm* jet; (*caudalito*) dribble, trickle; (*fig*) stream; **salir a ~s** to gush forth; **con propulsión a ~** jet-propelled.

chotearse [tʃote'arse] *vr* to joke.

choteo [tʃo'teo] *nm* kidding.

choto [tʃo'to] *nm* (*cabrito*) kid.

chovinismo [tʃoβi'nismo] *nm* = **chauvinismo.**

chovinista [tʃoβi'nista] *a, nm/f* = **chauvinista.**

choza ['tʃoθa] *nf* hut, shack.

chubasco [tʃu'βasko] *nm* squall.

chubasquero [tʃuβas'kero] *nm* oilskins *pl.*

chuchería [tʃutʃe'ria] *nf* trinket.

chucho ['tʃutʃo] *nm* (*ZOOL*) mongrel.

chufa ['tʃufa] *nf* chufa, earth almond, tiger nut; **horchata de ~s** *drink made from chufas.*

chuleta [tʃu'leta] *nf* chop, cutlet; (*ESCOL etc: fam*) crib.

chulo, a ['tʃulo, a] *a* (*encantador*) charming; (*aire*) proud; (*pey*) fresh; (*fam: estupendo*) great, fantastic ◆ *nm* (*pícaro*) rascal; (*madrileño*) working-class Madrilenian; (*rufián: tb:* **~ de putas**) pimp.

chumbera [tʃum'bera] *nf* prickly pear.

chungo, a ['tʃungo, a] (*fam*) *a* lousy ◆ *nf*: **estar de chunga** to be in a merry mood.

chupado, a [tʃu'paðo, a] *a* (*delgado*) skinny, gaunt; **está ~** (*fam*) it's simple, it's dead easy.

chupar [tʃu'par] *vt* to suck; (*absorber*) to absorb; **~se** *vr* to grow thin; **para ~se los dedos** mouthwatering.

chupatintas [tʃupa'tintas] *nm inv* penpusher.

chupete [tʃu'pete] *nm* dummy (*Brit*), pacifier (*US*).

churrasco [tʃu'rrasko] *nm* (*AM*) barbecue, barbecued meat.

churrería [tʃurre'ria] *nf* fritter stall *o* shop.

churrete [tʃu'rrete] *nm* grease spot.

churrigueresco, a [tʃurrige'resko, a] *a* (*ARQ*) baroque; (*fig*) excessively ornate.

churro, a ['tʃurro, a] *a* coarse ◆ *nm* (*CULIN*) (type of) fritter; (*chapuza*) botch, mess.

churruscar [tʃurrus'kar] *vt* to fry crisp.

churrusque [tʃu'rruske] *etc vb* V **churruscar.**

churumbel [tʃurum'bel] *nm* (*fam*) kid.

chus [tʃus] *excl*: **no decir ni ~ ni mus** not to say a word.

chusco, a ['tʃusko, a] *a* funny.

chusma ['tʃusma] *nf* rabble, mob.

chutar [tʃu'tar] *vi* (*DEPORTE*) to shoot (at goal); **esto va que chuta** it's going fine.

chuzo ['tʃuθo] *nm*: **llueve a ~s, llueven ~s de punta** it's raining cats and dogs.

D

D, d [de] *nf* (*letra*) D, d; **D de Dolores** D for David (*Brit*), D for Dog (*US*).

D. *abr* = **Don.**

Da., D.ª *abr* = **Doña.**

dactilar [dakti'lar] *a*: **huellas** ~**es** finger-prints.

dactilógrafo, a [dakti'loʏrafo, a] *nm/f* typist.

dádiva ['daðiβa] *nf* (*donación*) donation; (*regalo*) gift.

dadivoso, a [daði'βoso, a] *a* generous.

dado, a ['daðo, a] *pp de* **dar** ♦ *nm* die; ~**s** *nmpl* dice ♦ *a*: **en un momento** ~ at a certain point; **ser** ~ **a** (**hacer algo**) to be very fond of (doing sth); ~ **que** *conj* given that.

daga ['daʏa] *nf* dagger.

daltónico, a [dal'toniko, a] *a* colour-blind.

daltonismo [dalto'nismo] *nm* colour blindness.

dama ['dama] *nf* (*gen*) lady; (*AJEDREZ*) queen; ~**s** *nfpl* draughts; **primera** ~ (*TEATRO*) leading lady; (*POL*) president's wife, first lady (*US*); ~ **de honor** (*de reina*) lady-in-waiting; (*de novia*) bridesmaid.

damasco [da'masko] *nm* (*tela*) damask.

damnificado, a [damnifi'kaðo, a] *nm/f*: **los** ~**s** the victims.

damnificar [damnifi'kar] *vt* to harm; (*persona*) to injure.

damnifique [damni'fike] *etc* *vb* V **damnificar**.

dance ['danθe] *etc* *vb* V **danzar**.

danés, esa [da'nes, esa] *a* Danish ♦ *nm/f* Dane ♦ *nm* (*LING*) Danish.

Danubio [da'nuβjo] *nm* Danube.

danza ['danθa] *nf* (*gen*) dancing; (*una* ~) dance.

danzar [dan'θar] *vt*, *vi* to dance.

danzarín, ina [danθa'rin, ina] *nm/f* dancer.

dañar [da'ɲar] *vt* (*objeto*) to damage; (*persona*) to hurt; (*estropear*) to spoil; ~**se** *vr* (*objeto*) to get damaged.

dañino, a [da'ɲino, a] *a* harmful.

daño ['daɲo] *nm* (*a un objeto*) damage; (*a una persona*) harm, injury; ~**s y perjuicios** (*JUR*) damages; **hacer** ~ **a** to damage; (*persona*) to hurt, injure; **hacerse** ~ to hurt o.s.

dar [dar] *vt* to give; (*entregar: objeto*) to hand; (*grito*) to let out; (*noticias*) to tell; (*olor*) to give off; (*lección*) to teach; (*TEATRO*) to perform, put on; (*película*) to show; (*COM*) to yield; (*naipes*) to deal; (*la hora*): ~ **las 3** to strike 3 ♦ *vi*: ~ **a** to look out on(to), overlook; ~ **como** *o* **por** to consider, regard as; ~ **con** (*persona etc*) to meet, run into; (*idea*) to hit on; ~ **contra** to knock against, bang into; ~ **en** to strike, hit; ~ **de sí** to give, stretch; ~ **para** to be enough for; ~ **que hablar** to set people talking; ~**se** *vr* (*suceso*) to happen; (*presentarse*) to occur; (*AGR*) to grow; ~**se a** to be given to; ~**se por** to consider o.s.; **dárselas de** to pose as; **se me dan muy**

bien/mal los idiomas I am very good/bad at languages; ~ **de comer/beber a uno** to give sb sth to eat/drink; **¡dale!** go on!; ~**le a uno por hacer algo** to take it into one's head to do sth; **lo mismo da** it makes no difference; **da lo mismo** *o* **qué más da** it's all the same; **me da igual** I don't care; ~ **en el blanco** to hit the mark; **me da asco/miedo** it sickens/frightens me; **me da pena** it makes me sad; ~**se prisa** to hurry (up).

dardo ['darðo] *nm* dart.

dársena ['darsena] *nf* (*NAUT*) dock.

datar [da'tar] *vi*: ~ **de** to date from.

dátil ['datil] *nm* date.

dativo [da'tiβo] *nm* (*LING*) dative.

dato ['dato] *nm* fact, piece of information; (*MAT*) datum; ~**s** *nmpl* (*INFORM*) data; ~**s de entrada/salida** input/output data; ~**s personales** personal particulars.

dcha. *abr* (= *derecha*) r.h.

d. de J. C. *abr* (= *después de Jesucristo*) A.D.

de [de] *prep* (*posesión*) of; (*origen, distancia*) from; **la ciudad** ~ **Madrid** the city of Madrid; **el coche de mi amigo/mis amigos** my friend's car/my friends' car; **el más caro del negocio/mundo** the most expensive in the shop/world; **un libro** ~ **Unamuno** a book by Unamuno; **un chico** ~ **15 años** a 15-year-old boy; **un viaje** ~ **2 días** a two-day journey; **un libro grato** ~ **leer** a nice book to read; **libro** ~ **cocina** cookery book; **el hombre** ~ **largos cabellos** the man with long hair; **guantes** ~ **cuero** leather gloves; **vuelo 507** ~ **Londres** flight 507 from London; **es** ~ **Sevilla** she's from Seville; **estar loco** ~ **alegría** to be overjoyed; ~ **un salto** with one bound; ~ **niño** as a child; **fue a Londres** ~ **profesor** he went to London as a teacher; **una** ~ **dos** one or the other; **3** ~ **cada 4** three out of every four; ~ **día/noche** by day/night; ~ **mañana** in the morning; **vestido** ~ **negro** dressed in black; **más/menos** ~ **3** more/less than 3; ~ **cara a** facing; ~ **ser posible** if possible.

dé [de] *vb* V **dar**.

deambular [deambu'lar] *vi* to stroll, wander.

debajo [de'βaxo] *ad* underneath; ~ **de** below, under; **por** ~ **de** beneath.

debate [de'βate] *nm* debate.

debatir [deβa'tir] *vt* to debate; ~**se** *vr* to struggle.

debe ['deβe] *nm* (*en cuenta*) debit side; ~ **y haber** debit and credit.

deber [de'βer] *nm* duty ♦ *vt* to owe ♦ *vi*: **debe (de)** it must, it should; **debo hacerlo** I must do it; **debe de ir** he should go; ~**se** *vr*: ~**se a** to be owing *o* due to; **¿qué** *o* **cuánto le debo?** how much is it?; ~**es**

nmpl (*ESCOL*) homework *sg*.

debidamente [deβiða'mente] *ad* properly; (*rellenar: documento, solicitud*) duly.

debido, a [de'βiðo, a] *a* proper, due; ~ **a** due to, because of; **en debida forma** duly.

débil ['deβil] *a* weak; (*persona: físicamente*) feeble; (*salud*) poor; (*voz, ruido*) faint; (*luz*) dim.

debilidad [deβili'ðað] *nf* weakness; feebleness; dimness; **tener ~ por uno** to have a soft spot for sb.

debilitar [deβili'tar] *vt* to weaken; ~**se** *vr* to grow weak.

débito ['deβito] *nm* debit; (*deuda*) debt.

debutante [deβu'tante] *nm/f* beginner.

debutar [deβu'tar] *vi* to make one's debut.

década ['dekaða] *nf* decade.

decadencia [deka'ðenθja] *nf* (*estado*) decadence; (*proceso*) decline, decay.

decadente [deka'ðente] *a* decadent.

decaer [deka'er] *vi* (*declinar*) to decline; (*debilitarse*) to weaken; (*salud*) to fail; (*negocio*) to fall off.

decaído, a [deka'iðo, a] *a*: **estar ~** (*persona*) to be down.

decaiga [de'kaiɣa] *etc vb* V **decaer**.

decaimiento [dekai'mjento] *nm* (*declinación*) decline; (*desaliento*) discouragement; (*MED: depresión*) depression.

decanato [deka'nato] *nm* (*cargo*) deanship; (*despacho*) dean's office.

decano, a [de'kano, a] *nm/f* (*UNIV etc*) dean; (*de grupo*) senior member.

decantar [dekan'tar] *vt* (*vino*) to decant.

decapitar [dekapi'tar] *vt* to behead.

decayendo [deka'jendo] *etc vb* V **decaer**.

decena [de'θena] *nf*: **una ~** ten (or so).

decencia [de'θenθja] *nf* (*modestia*) modesty; (*honestidad*) respectability.

decenio [de'θenjo] *nm* decade.

decente [de'θente] *a* (*correcto*) proper; (*honesto*) respectable.

decepción [deθep'θjon] *nf* disappointment.

decepcionante [deθepθjo'nante] *a* disappointing.

decepcionar [deθepθjo'nar] *vt* to disappoint.

decibel [deθi'βel], **decibelio** [deθi'βeljo] *nm* decibel.

decidido, a [deθi'ðiðo, a] *a* decided; (*resuelto*) resolute.

decidir [deθi'ðir] *vt* (*persuadir*) to convince, persuade; (*resolver*) to decide ♦ *vi* to decide; ~**se** *vr*: ~**se a** to make up one's mind to; ~**se por** to decide o settle on, choose.

décimo, a ['deθimo, a] *num* tenth ♦ *nf* (*esp en lotería*) tenth part.

decimoctavo, a [deθimok'taβo, a] *num* eighteenth; V *tb* **sexto**.

decimoséptimo, a [deθimo'septimo, a]

num seventeenth; V *tb* **sexto**.

decimosexto, a [deθimo'seksto, a] *num* sixteenth; V *tb* **sexto**.

decimotercero, a [deθimoter'θero, a], **decimotercio, a** [deθimo'terθjo, a] *num* thirteenth; V *tb* **sexto**.

decir [de'θir] *vt* (*expresar*) to say; (*contar*) to tell; (*hablar*) to speak; (*indicar*) to show; (*revelar*) to reveal; (*fam: nombrar*) to call ♦ *nm* saying; ~**se** *vr*: **se dice** it is said, they say; (*se cuenta*) the story goes; **¿cómo se dice en inglés "cursi"?** what's the English for "cursi"?; ~ **para/entre sí** to say to o.s.; ~ **por** ~ to talk for talking's sake; **dar que** ~ **(a la gente)** to make people talk; **querer** ~ to mean; **es** ~ that is to say, namely; **ni que** ~ **tiene que...** it goes without saying that...; **como quien dice** so to speak; **¡quién lo diría!** would you believe it!; **el qué dirán** gossip; **¡diga!**, **¡dígame!** (*en tienda etc*) can I help you?; (*TELEC*) hullo?; **le dije que fuera más tarde** I told her to go later; **es un** ~ it's just a phrase.

decisión [deθi'sjon] *nf* decision; (*firmeza*) decisiveness; (*voluntad*) determination.

decisivo, a [deθi'siβo, a] *a* decisive.

declamar [dekla'mar] *vt, vi* to declaim; (*versos etc*) to recite.

declaración [deklara'θjon] *nf* (*manifestación*) statement; (*explicación*) explanation; (*JUR: testimonio*) evidence; ~ **de derechos** (*POL*) bill of rights; ~ **de impuestos** (*COM*) tax return; ~ **de ingresos** o **de renta** o **fiscal** (*AM*) income tax return; ~ **jurada** affidavit; **falsa** ~ (*JUR*) misrepresentation.

declarar [dekla'rar] *vt* to declare ♦ *vi* to declare; (*JUR*) to testify; ~**se** *vr* (*opinión*) to make one's opinion known; (*a una chica*) to propose; (*guerra, incendio*) to break out; ~ **culpable/inocente a uno** to find sb guilty/not guilty; ~**se culpable/inocente** to plead guilty/not guilty.

declinación [deklina'θjon] *nf* (*decaimiento*) decline; (*LING*) declension.

declinar [dekli'nar] *vt* (*gen, LING*) to decline; (*JUR*) to reject ♦ *vi* (*el día*) to draw to a close.

declive [de'kliβe] *nm* (*cuesta*) slope; (*inclinación*) incline; (*fig*) decline; (*COM: tb*: ~ **económico**) slump.

decodificador [dekoðifika'ðor] *nm* (*INFORM*) decoder.

decolorarse [dekolo'rarse] *vr* to become discoloured.

decomisar [dekomi'sar] *vt* to seize, confiscate.

decoración [dekora'θjon] *nf* decoration; (*TEATRO*) scenery, set; ~ **de escaparates** window dressing.

decorado [deko'raðo] *nm* (*CINE, TEATRO*)

scenery, set.

decorador, a [dekora'ðor, a] nm/f (de interiores) (interior) decorator; (TEATRO) stage o set designer.

decorar [deko'rar] vt to decorate.

decorativo, a [dekora'tiβo, a] a ornamental, decorative.

decoro [de'koro] nm (respeto) respect; (dignidad) decency; (recato) propriety.

decoroso, a [deko'roso, a] a (decente) decent; (modesto) modest; (digno) proper.

decrecer [dekre'θer] vi to decrease, diminish; (nivel de agua) to go down; (días) to draw in.

decrépito, a [de'krepito, a] a decrepit.

decretar [dekre'tar] vt to decree.

decreto [de'kreto] nm decree; (POL) act.

decreto-ley [dekreto'lei], pl **decretosleyes** nm decree.

decrezca [de'kreθka] etc vb V **decrecer**.

decúbito [de'kuβito] nm (MED): ~ **prono/ supino** prone/supine position.

dedal [de'ðal] nm thimble.

dedalera [deða'lera] nf foxglove.

dédalo ['deðalo] nm (laberinto) labyrinth; (fig) tangle, mess.

dedicación [deðika'θjon] nf dedication; **con ~ exclusiva** o **plena** full-time.

dedicar [deði'kar] vt (libro) to dedicate; (tiempo, dinero) to devote; ~**se** vr: ~**se a** to devote o.s. to (hacer algo doing sth); (carrera, estudio) to go in for, take up; **¿a qué se dedica usted?** what do you do (for a living)?

dedicatoria [deðika'torja] nf (de libro) dedication.

dedillo [de'ðiʎo] nm: **saber algo al ~** to have sth at one's fingertips.

dedique [de'ðike] etc vb V **dedicar**.

dedo ['deðo] nm finger; (de vino etc) drop; ~ **(del pie)** toe; ~ **pulgar** thumb; ~ **índice** index finger; ~ **mayor** o **cordial** middle finger; ~ **anular** ring finger; ~ **meñique** little finger; **contar con los ~s** to count on one's fingers; **comerse los ~s** to get very impatient; **entrar a ~** to get a job by pulling strings; **hacer ~** (fam) to hitch (a lift); **poner el ~ en la llaga** to put one's finger on it; **no tiene dos ~s de frente** he's pretty dim.

deducción [deðuk'θjon] nf deduction.

deducir [deðu'θir] vt (concluir) to deduce, infer; (COM) to deduct.

deduje [de'ðuxe] etc, **dedujera** [deðu'xera] etc, **deduzca** [de'ðuθka] etc vb V **deducir**.

defección [defek'θjon] nf defection, desertion.

defecto [de'fekto] nm defect, flaw; (de cara) imperfection; ~ **de pronunciación** speech defect; **por ~** (INFORM) default; ~ **latente** (COM) latent defect.

defectuoso, a [defek'twoso, a] a defective, faulty.

defender [defen'der] vt to defend; (ideas) to uphold; (causa) to champion; (amigos) to stand up for; ~**se** vr to defend o.s.; ~**se bien** to give a good account of o.s.; **me defiendo en inglés** (fig) I can get by in English.

defendible [defen'diβle] a defensible.

defensa [de'fensa] nf defence; (NAUT) fender ♦ nm (DEPORTE) back; **en ~ propia** in self-defence.

defensivo, a [defen'siβo, a] a defensive ♦ nf: **a la defensiva** on the defensive.

defensor, a [defen'sor, a] a defending ♦ nm/f (abogado ~) defending counsel; (protector) protector; ~ **del pueblo** (Esp) ≈ ombudsman.

deferir [defe'rir] vt (JUR) to refer, delegate ♦ vi: ~ **a** to defer to.

deficiencia [defi'θjenθja] nf deficiency.

deficiente [defi'θjente] a (defectuoso) defective; ~ **en** lacking o deficient in ♦ nm/f: **ser un ~ mental** to be mentally handicapped.

déficit, ~s ['defiθit] nm (COM) deficit; (fig) lack, shortage; ~ **presupuestario** budget deficit.

defienda [de'fjenda] etc vb V **defender**.

defiera [de'fjera] etc vb V **deferir**.

definición [defini'θjon] nf definition; (INFORM: de pantalla) resolution.

definido, a [defi'niðo, a] a (tb LING) definite; **bien ~** well o clearly defined; ~ **por el usuario** (INFORM) user-defined.

definir [defi'nir] vt (determinar) to determine, establish; (decidir, INFORM) to define; (aclarar) to clarify.

definitivo, a [defini'tiβo, a] a (edición, texto) definitive; (fecha) definite; **en definitiva** definitively; (en conclusión) finally; (en resumen) in short.

defiriendo [defi'rjendo] etc vb V **deferir**.

deflacionario, a [deflaθjo'narjo, a], **deflacionista** [deflaθjo'nista] a deflationary.

deflector [deflek'tor] nm (TEC) baffle.

deformación [deforma'θjon] nf (alteración) deformation; (RADIO etc) distortion.

deformar [defor'mar] vt (gen) to deform; ~**se** vr to become deformed.

deforme [de'forme] a (informe) deformed; (feo) ugly; (mal hecho) misshapen.

deformidad [deformi'ðað] nf (forma anormal) deformity; (fig: defecto) (moral) shortcoming.

defraudar [defrau'ðar] vt (decepcionar) to disappoint; (estafar) to cheat; to defraud; ~ **impuestos** to evade tax.

defunción [defun'θjon] nf decease, demise.

degeneración [dexenera'θjon] nf (de las células) degeneration; (moral) degeneracy.

degenerar [dexene'rar] *vi* to degenerate; (*empeorar*) to get worse.

deglutir [deɣlu'tir] *vt, vi* to swallow.

degolladero [deɣoʎa'ðero] *nm* (*ANAT*) throat; (*cadalso*) scaffold; (*matadero*) slaughterhouse.

degollar [deɣo'ʎar] *vt* to slaughter.

degradar [deɣra'ðar] *vt* to debase, degrade; (*INFORM: datos*) to corrupt; ~**se** *vr* to demean o.s.

degüelle [de'ɣweʎe] *etc vb V* **degollar**.

degustación [deɣusta'θjon] *nf* sampling, tasting.

deificar [deifi'kar] *vt* (*persona*) to deify.

deifique [dei'fike] *etc vb V* **deificar**.

dejadez [dexa'ðeθ] *nf* (*negligencia*) neglect; (*descuido*) untidiness, carelessness.

dejado, a [de'xaðo, a] *a* (*desaliñado*) slovenly; (*negligente*) careless; (*indolente*) lazy.

dejar [de'xar] *vt* (*gen*) to leave; (*permitir*) to allow, let; (*abandonar*) to abandon, forsake; (*actividad, empleo*) to give up; (*beneficios*) to produce, yield ♦ *vi*: ~ **de** (*parar*) to stop; ~**se** *vr* (*abandonarse*) to let o.s. go; **no puedo** ~ **de fumar** I can't give up smoking; **no dejes de visitarles** don't fail to visit them; **no dejes de comprar un billete** make sure you buy a ticket; ~ **a un lado** to leave o set aside; ~ **caer** to drop; ~ **entrar/salir** to let in/out; ~ **pasar** to let through; ¡**déjalo**! (*no te preocupes*) don't worry about it; **te dejo en tu casa** I'll drop you off at your place; **deja mucho que desear** it leaves a lot to be desired; ~**se persuadir** to allow o.s. to o let o.s. be persuaded; ¡**déjate de tonterías**! stop messing about!

deje ['dexe] *nm* (trace of) accent.

dejo ['dexo] *nm* (*LING*) accent.

del [del] = **de** + **el**, *ver* **de**.

del. *abr* (*ADMIN*: = *Delegación*) district office.

delantal [delan'tal] *nm* apron.

delante [de'lante] *ad* in front; (*enfrente*) opposite; (*adelante*) ahead ♦ *prep*: ~ **de** in front of, before; **la parte de** ~ the front part; **estando otros** ~ with others present.

delantero, a [delan'tero, a] *a* front; (*patas de animal*) fore ♦ *nm* (*DEPORTE*) forward ♦ *nf* (*de vestido, casa etc*) front part; (*TEATRO*) front row; (*DEPORTE*) forward line; **llevar la delantera (a uno)** to be ahead (of sb).

delatar [dela'tar] *vt* to inform on o against, betray; **los delató a la policía** he reported them to the police.

delator, a [dela'tor, a] *nm/f* informer.

delegación [deleɣa'θjon] *nf* (*acción, delegados*) delegation; (*COM: oficina*) district office, branch; ~ **de poderes** (*POL*) devolu-

tion; ~ **de policía** police station.

delegado, a [dele'ɣaðo, a] *nm/f* delegate; (*COM*) agent.

delegar [dele'ɣar] *vt* to delegate.

delegue [de'leɣe] *etc vb V* **delegar**.

deleitar [delei'tar] *vt* to delight; ~**se** *vr*: ~**se con** o **en** to delight in, take pleasure in.

deleite [de'leite] *nm* delight, pleasure.

deletrear [deletre'ar] *vt* (*tb fig*) to spell (out).

deletreo [dele'treo] *nm* spelling; (*fig*) interpretation, decipherment.

deleznable [deleθ'naβle] *a* (*frágil*) fragile; (*fig: malo*) poor; (*excusa*) feeble.

delfín [del'fin] *nm* dolphin.

delgadez [delɣa'ðeθ] *nf* thinness, slimness.

delgado, a [del'ɣaðo, a] *a* thin; (*persona*) slim, thin; (*tierra*) poor; (*tela etc*) light, delicate ♦ *ad*: **hilar (muy)** ~ (*fig*) to split hairs.

deliberación [deliβera'θjon] *nf* deliberation.

deliberar [deliβe'rar] *vt* to debate, discuss ♦ *vi* to deliberate.

delicadeza [delika'ðeθa] *nf* delicacy; (*refinamiento, sutileza*) refinement.

delicado, a [deli'kaðo, a] *a* delicate; (*sensible*) sensitive; (*rasgos*) dainty; (*gusto*) refined; (*situación: difícil*) tricky; (*: violento*) embarrassing; (*punto, tema*) sore; (*persona: difícil de contentar*) hard to please; (*: sensible*) touchy, hypersensitive; (*: atento*) considerate.

delicia [de'liθja] *nf* delight.

delicioso, a [deli'θjoso, a] *a* (*gracioso*) delightful; (*exquisito*) delicious.

delictivo, a [delik'tiβo, a] *a* criminal *cpd*.

delimitar [delimi'tar] *vt* to delimit.

delincuencia [delin'kwenθja] *nf*: ~ **juvenil** juvenile delinquency; **cifras de la** ~ crime rate.

delincuente [delin'kwente] *nm/f* delinquent; (*criminal*) criminal; ~ **sin antecedentes** first offender; ~ **habitual** hardened criminal.

delineante [deline'ante] *nm/f* draughtsman.

delinear [deline'ar] *vt* to delineate; (*dibujo*) to draw; (*contornos, fig*) to outline; ~ **un proyecto** to outline a project.

delinquir [delin'kir] *vi* to commit an offence.

delirante [deli'rante] *a* delirious.

delirar [deli'rar] *vi* to be delirious, rave; (*fig: desatinar*) to talk nonsense.

delirio [de'lirjo] *nm* (*MED*) delirium; (*palabras insensatas*) ravings *pl*; ~ **de grandeza** megalomania; ~ **de persecución** persecution mania; **con** ~ (*fam*) madly; ¡**fue el** ~! (*fam*) it was great!

delito [de'lito] *nm* (*gen*) crime; (*infracción*) offence.

demacrado, a [dema'kraðo, a] *a* emaciated.

demagogo [dema'ɣoɣo] *nm* demagogue.

demanda [de'manda] *nf* (*pedido, COM*) demand; (*petición*) request; (*pregunta*) inquiry; (*reivindicación*) claim; (*JUR*) action, lawsuit; (*TEATRO*) call; (*ELEC*) load; ~ **de pago** demand for payment; **escribir en** ~ **de ayuda** to write asking for help; **entablar** ~ (*JUR*) to sue; **presentar** ~ **de divorcio** to sue for divorce; ~ **final** final demand; ~ **indirecta** derived demand; ~ **de mercado** market demand.

demandado, a [deman'daðo, a] *nm/f* defendant; (*en divorcio*) respondent.

demandante [deman'dante] *nm/f* claimant; (*JUR*) plaintiff.

demandar [deman'dar] *vt* (*gen*) to demand; (*JUR*) to sue, file a lawsuit against, start proceedings against; ~ **a uno por calumnia/daños y perjuicios** to sue sb for libel/damages.

demarcación [demarka'θjon] *nf* (*de terreno*) demarcation.

demás [de'mas] *a*: **los** ~ **niños** the other children, the remaining children ♦ *pron*: **los/las** ~ the others, the rest (of them); **lo** ~ the rest (of it); **por** ~ moreover; (*en vano*) in vain; **y** ~ etcetera.

demasía [dema'sia] *nf* (*exceso*) excess, surplus; **comer en** ~ to eat to excess.

demasiado, a [dema'sjaðo, a] *a*: ~ **vino** too much wine; ~**s libros** too many books ♦ *ad* (*antes de a, ad*) too; **¡es** ~**!** it's too much!; **es** ~ **pesado para levantar** it is too heavy to lift; ~ **lo sé** I know it only too well; **hace** ~ **calor** it's too hot.

demencia [de'menθja] *nf* (*locura*) madness.

demencial [demen'θjal] *a* crazy.

demente [de'mente] *a* mad, insane ♦ *nm/f* lunatic.

demérito [de'merito] *nm* (*falta*) fault; (*AM*: *depreciación*) depreciation.

democracia [demo'kraθja] *nf* democracy.

demócrata [de'mokrata] *nm/f* democrat.

democratacristiano, a [demokrata-kris'tjano, a], **democristiano, a** [demokris-'tjano, a] *a, nm/f* Christian Democrat.

democrático, a [demo'kratiko, a] *a* democratic.

demográfico, a [demo'ɣrafiko, a] *a* demographic, population *cpd*; **la explosión demográfica** the population explosion.

demoledor, a [demole'ðor, a] *a* (*fig: argumento*) overwhelming; (: *ataque*) shattering.

demoler [demo'ler] *vt* to demolish; (*edificio*) to pull down.

demolición [demoli'θjon] *nf* demolition.

demonio [de'monjo] *nm* devil, demon; **¡~s!** hell!; **¿cómo** ~**s?** how the hell?; **¿qué** ~**s**

será? what the devil can it be?; **¿dónde** ~ **lo habré dejado?** where the devil can I have left it?; **tener el** ~ **en el cuerpo** (*no parar*) to be always on the go.

demora [de'mora] *nf* delay.

demorar [demo'rar] *vt* (*retardar*) to delay, hold back; (*dilatar*) to hold up ♦ *vi* to linger, stay on; ~**se** *vr* to linger, stay on; (*retrasarse*) to take a long time.

demos ['demos] *vb V* **dar**.

demostración [demostra'θjon] *nf* (*gen, MAT*) demonstration; (*de cariño, fuerza*) show; (*de teorema*) proof; (*de amistad*) gesture; (*de cólera, gimnasia*) display; ~ **comercial** commercial exhibition.

demostrar [demos'trar] *vt* (*probar*) to prove; (*mostrar*) to show; (*manifestar*) to demonstrate.

demostrativo, a [demostra'tiβo, a] *a* demonstrative.

demudado, a [demu'ðaðo, a] *a* (*rostro*) pale; (*fig*) upset; **tener el rostro** ~ to look pale.

demudar [demu'ðar] *vt* to change, alter; ~**se** *vr* (*expresión*) to alter; (*perder color*) to change colour.

demuela [de'mwela] *etc vb V* **demoler**.

demuestre [de'mwestre] *etc vb V* **demostrar**.

den [den] *vb V* **dar**.

denegación [deneɣa'θjon] *nf* refusal, denial.

denegar [dene'ɣar] *vt* (*rechazar*) to refuse; (*negar*) to deny; (*JUR*) to reject.

denegué [dene'ɣe], **deneguemos** [dene-'ɣemos] *etc*, **deniego** [de'njeɣo] *etc*, **deniegue** [de'njeɣe] *etc vb V* **denegar**.

denigrante [deni'ɣrante] *a* (*injurioso*) insulting; (*deshonroso*) degrading.

denigrar [deni'ɣrar] *vt* (*desacreditar*) to denigrate; (*injuriar*) to insult.

denodado, a [deno'ðaðo, a] *a* bold, brave.

denominación [denomina'θjon] *nf* (*acto*) naming; (*clase*) denomination; ~ **de origen** (*vino*) guarantee of vintage, ≈ appellation controlée.

denostar [denos'tar] *vt* to insult.

denotar [deno'tar] *vt* (*indicar*) to indicate, denote.

densidad [densi'ðað] *nf* (*FÍSICA*) density; (*fig*) thickness; ~ **de caracteres** (*INFORM*) pitch.

denso, a ['denso, a] *a* (*apretado*) solid; (*espeso, pastoso*) thick; (*fig*) heavy.

dentado, a [den'taðo, a] *a* (*rueda*) cogged; (*filo*) jagged; (*sello*) perforated; (*BOT*) dentate.

dentadura [denta'ðura] *nf* (set of) teeth *pl*; ~ **postiza** false teeth *pl*.

dentellada [dente'ʎaða] *nf* (*mordisco*) bite,

nip; (*señal*) tooth mark; **partir algo a ~s** to sever sth with one's teeth.

dentera [den'tera] *nf* (*sensación desagradable*) the shivers *pl*.

dentición [denti'θjon] *nf* (*acto*) teething; (ANAT) dentition; **estar con la ~** to be teething.

dentífrico, a [den'tifriko, a] *a* dental, tooth *cpd* ◆ *nm* toothpaste; **pasta dentífrica** toothpaste.

dentista [den'tista] *nm/f* dentist.

dentro ['dentro] *ad* inside ◆ *prep*: ~ **de** in, inside, within; **allí ~** in there; **mirar por ~** to look inside; ~ **de lo posible** as far as possible; ~ **de todo** all in all; ~ **de tres meses** within three months.

denuedo [de'nweðo] *nm* boldness, daring.

denuesto [de'nwesto] *nm* insult.

denuncia [de'nunθja] *nf* (*delación*) denunciation; (*acusación*) accusation; (*de accidente*) report; **hacer** o **poner una ~** to report an incident to the police.

denunciable [denun'θjaßle] *a* indictable, punishable.

denunciador, a [denunθja'ðor, a], **denunciante** [denun'θjante] *nm/f* accuser; (*delator*) informer.

denunciar [denun'θjar] *vt* to report; (*delatar*) to inform on o against.

Dep. *abr* (= *Departamento*) Dept.; (= *Depósito*) dep.

deparar [depa'rar] *vt* (*brindar*) to provide o furnish with; (*suj: futuro, destino*) to have in store for; **los placeres que el viaje nos deparó** the pleasures which the trip afforded us.

departamento [departa'mento] *nm* (*sección administrativa*) department, section; (AM: *piso*) flat (*Brit*), apartment (*US*); (*distrito*) department, province; ~ **de envíos** (COM) dispatch department; ~ **de máquinas** (NAUT) engine room.

departir [depar'tir] *vi* to talk, converse.

dependencia [depen'denθja] *nf* dependence; (POL) dependency; (COM) office, section; (*sucursal*) branch office; (ARQ: *cuarto*) room; ~**s** *nfpl* outbuildings.

depender [depen'der] *vi*: ~ **de** to depend on; (*contar con*) to rely on; (*de autoridad*) to be under, be answerable to; **depende** it (all) depends; **no depende de mí** it's not up to me.

dependienta [depen'djenta] *nf* saleswoman, shop assistant.

dependiente [depen'djente] *a* dependent ◆ *nm* salesman, shop assistant.

depilación [depila'θjon] *nf* hair removal.

depilar [depi'lar] *vt* (*con cera: piernas*) to wax; (*cejas*) to pluck.

depilatorio, a [depila'torjo, a] *a* depilatory ◆ *nm* hair remover.

deplorable [deplo'raßle] *a* deplorable.

deplorar [deplo'rar] *vt* to deplore.

depondré [depon'dre] *etc vb* V **deponer**.

deponer [depo'ner] *vt* (*armas*) to lay down; (*rey*) to depose; (*gobernante*) to oust; (*ministro*) to remove from office ◆ *vi* (JUR) to give evidence; (*declarar*) to make a statement.

deponga [de'ponga] *etc vb* V **deponer**.

deportación [deporta'θjon] *nf* deportation.

deportar [depor'tar] *vt* to deport.

deporte [de'porte] *nm* sport.

deportista [depor'tista] *a* sports *cpd* ◆ *nm/f* sportsman/woman.

deportivo, a [depor'tißo, a] *a* (*club, periódico*) sports *cpd* ◆ *nm* sports car.

deposición [deposi'θjon] *nf* (*de funcionario etc*) removal from office; (JUR: *testimonio*) evidence.

depositante [deposi'tante], **depositador, a** [deposita'ðor, a] *nm/f* depositor.

depositar [deposi'tar] *vt* (*dinero*) to deposit; (*mercaderías*) to put away, store; ~**se** *vr* to settle; ~ **la confianza en uno** to place one's trust in sb.

depositario, a [deposi'tarjo, a] *nm/f* trustee; ~ **judicial** official receiver.

depósito [de'posito] *nm* (*gen*) deposit; (*de mercaderías*) warehouse, store; (*de animales, coches*) pound; (*de agua, gasolina etc*) tank; (*en retrete*) cistern; ~ **afianzado** bonded warehouse; ~ **bancario** bank deposit; ~ **de cadáveres** mortuary; ~ **de maderas** timber yard; ~ **de suministro** feeder bin.

depravar [depra'ßar] *vt* to deprave, corrupt; ~**se** *vr* to become depraved.

depreciación [depreθja'θjon] *nf* depreciation.

depreciar [depre'θjar] *vt* to depreciate, reduce the value of; ~**se** *vr* to depreciate, lose value.

depredador, a [depreða'ðor, a] (ZOOL) *a* predatory ◆ *nm* predator.

depredar [depre'ðar] *vt* to pillage.

depresión [depre'sjon] *nf* (*gen, MED*) depression; (*hueco*) hollow; (*en horizonte, camino*) dip; (*merma*) drop; (ECON) slump, recession; ~ **nerviosa** nervous breakdown.

deprimente [depri'mente] *a* depressing.

deprimido, a [depri'miðo, a] *a* depressed.

deprimir [depri'mir] *vt* to depress; ~**se** *vr* (*persona*) to become depressed.

deprisa [de'prisa] *ad* V **prisa**.

depuesto [de'pwesto] *pp de* **deponer**.

depuración [depura'θjon] *nf* purification; (POL) purge; (INFORM) debugging.

depurador [depura'ðor] *nm* purifier.

depurar [depu'rar] *vt* to purify; (*purgar*) to purge; (INFORM) to debug.

depuse [de'puse] *etc vb* V **deponer**.

der., der.º *abr* (= *derecho*) r.

derecha [de'retʃa] *nf* V **derecho, a.**

derechazo [dere'tʃaθo] *nm* (*BOXEO*) right; (*TENIS*) forehand drive; (*TAUR*) *a pass with the cape.*

derechista [dere'tʃista] (*POL*) *a* right-wing ◆ *nm/f* right-winger.

derecho, a [de'retʃo, a] *a* right, right-hand ◆ *nm* (*privilegio*) right; (*título*) claim, title; (*lado*) right(-hand) side; (*leyes*) law ◆ *nf* right(-hand) side ◆ *ad* straight, directly; ~**s** *nmpl* dues; (*profesionales*) fees; (*impuestos*) taxes; (*de autor*) royalties; **la(s) derecha(s)** (*pl*) (*POL*) the Right; ~**s civiles** civil rights; ~**s de muelle** (*COM*) dock dues; ~**s de patente** patent rights; ~**s portuarios** (*COM*) harbour dues; ~ **de propiedad literaria** copyright; ~ **de retención** (*COM*) lien; ~ **de timbre** (*COM*) stamp duty; ~ **de votar** right to vote; ~ **a voto** voting right; **Facultad de D**~ Faculty of Law; **a derechas** rightly, correctly; **de derechas** (*POL*) right-wing; "**reservados todos los** ~**s**" "all rights reserved"; **¡no hay** ~**!** it's not fair!; **tener** ~ **a** to have a right to; **a la derecha** on the right; (*dirección*) to the right.

deriva [de'riβa] *nf*: **ir** *o* **estar a la** ~ to drift, be adrift.

derivación [deriβa'θjon] *nf* derivation.

derivado, a [deri'βaðo, a] *a* derived ◆ *nm* (*LING*) derivative; (*INDUSTRIA, QUÍMICA*) by-product.

derivar [deri'βar] *vt* to derive; (*desviar*) to direct ◆ *vi*, ~**se** *vr* to derive, be derived; ~**(se) de** (*consecuencia*) to spring from.

dermatólogo, a [derma'toloɤo, a] *nm/f* dermatologist.

dérmico, a ['dermiko, a] *a* skin *cpd.*

derogación [deroɤa'θjon] *nf* repeal.

derogar [dero'ɤar] *vt* (*ley*) to repeal; (*contrato*) to revoke.

derogue [de'roɤe] *etc vb* V **derogar.**

derramamiento [derrama'mjento] *nm* (*dispersión*) spilling; (*fig*) squandering; ~ **de sangre** bloodshed.

derramar [derra'mar] *vt* to spill; (*verter*) to pour out; (*esparcir*) to scatter; ~**se** *vr* to pour out; ~ **lágrimas** to weep.

derrame [de'rrame] *nm* (*de líquido*) spilling; (*de sangre*) shedding; (*de tubo etc*) overflow; (*pérdida*) leakage; (*MED*) discharge; (*declive*) slope; ~ **cerebral** brain haemorrhage; ~ **sinovial** water on the knee.

derredor [derre'ðor] *ad*: **al** *o* **en** ~ **de** around, about.

derrengado, a [derren'gaðo, a] *a* (*torcido*) bent; (*cojo*) crippled; **estar** ~ (*fig*) to ache all over; **dejar** ~ **a uno** (*fig*) to wear sb out.

derretido, a [derre'tiðo, a] *a* melted; (*metal*) molten; **estar** ~ **por uno** (*fig*) to be crazy about sb.

derretir [derre'tir] *vt* (*gen*) to melt; (*nieve*) to thaw; (*fig*) to squander; ~**se** *vr* to melt.

derribar [derri'βar] *vt* to knock down; (*construcción*) to demolish; (*persona, gobierno, político*) to bring down.

derribo [de'rriβo] *nm* (*de edificio*) demolition; (*LUCHA*) throw; (*AVIAT*) shooting down; (*POL*) overthrow; ~**s** *nmpl* rubble *sg*, debris *sg.*

derrita [de'rrita] *etc vb* V **derretir.**

derrocar [derro'kar] *vt* (*gobierno*) to bring down, overthrow; (*ministro*) to oust.

derrochador, a [derrotʃa'ðor, a] *a, nm/f* spendthrift.

derrochar [derro'tʃar] *vt* (*dinero, recursos*) to squander; (*energía, salud*) to be bursting with *o* full of.

derroche [de'rrotʃe] *nm* (*despilfarro*) waste, squandering; (*exceso*) extravagance; **con un** ~ **de buen gusto** with a fine display of good taste.

derroque [de'rroke] *etc vb* V **derrocar.**

derrota [de'rrota] *nf* (*NAUT*) course; (*MIL*) defeat, rout; **sufrir una grave** ~ (*fig*) to suffer a grave setback.

derrotar [derro'tar] *vt* (*gen*) to defeat.

derrotero [derro'tero] *nm* (*rumbo*) course; **tomar otro** ~ (*fig*) to adopt a different course.

derrotista [derro'tista] *a, nm/f* defeatist.

derruir [derru'ir] *vt* to demolish, tear down.

derrumbamiento [derrumba'mjento] *nm* (*caída*) plunge; (*demolición*) demolition; (*desplome*) collapse; ~ **de tierra** landslide.

derrumbar [derrum'bar] *vt* to throw down; (*despeñar*) to fling *o* hurl down; (*volcar*) to upset; ~**se** *vr* (*hundirse*) to collapse; (: *techo*) to fall in, cave in; (*fig: esperanzas*) to collapse.

derrumbe [de'rrumbe] *nm* = **derrumbamiento.**

derruyendo [derru'jendo] *etc vb* V **derruir.**

des [des] *vb* V **dar.**

desabastecido, a [desaβaste'θiðo, a] *a*: **estar** ~ **de algo** to be short of *o* out of sth.

desabotonar [desaβoto'nar] *vt* to unbutton, undo ◆ *vi* (*flores*) to blossom; ~**se** *vr* to come undone.

desabrido, a [desa'βriðo, a] *a* (*comida*) insipid, tasteless; (*persona: soso*) dull; (: *antipático*) rude, surly; (*respuesta*) sharp; (*tiempo*) unpleasant.

desabrigado, a [desaβri'ɤaðo, a] *a* (*sin abrigo*) not sufficiently protected; (*fig*) exposed.

desabrigar [desaβri'ɤar] *vt* (*quitar ropa a*) to remove the clothing of; (*descubrir*) to uncover; (*fig*) to deprive of protection; ~**se**

vr: **me desabrigué en la cama** the bedclothes came off.

desabrigue [desa'ßriɣe] *etc vb V* **desabrigar**.

desabrochar [desaßro'tʃar] *vt* (*botones, broches*) to undo, unfasten; **~se** *vr* (*ropa etc*) to come undone.

desacatar [desaka'tar] *vt* (*ley*) to disobey.

desacato [desa'kato] *nm* (*falta de respeto*) disrespect; (*JUR*) contempt.

desacertado, a [desaθer'taðo, a] *a* (*equivocado*) mistaken; (*inoportuno*) unwise.

desacierto [desa'θjerto] *nm* (*error*) mistake, error; (*dicho*) unfortunate remark.

desaconsejable [desakonse'xaßle] *a* inadvisable.

desaconsejado, a [desakonse'xaðo, a] *a* ill-advised.

desaconsejar [desakonse'xar] *vt*: **~ algo a uno** to advise sb against sth.

desacoplar [desako'plar] *vt* (*ELEC*) to disconnect; (*TEC*) to take apart.

desacorde [desa'korðe] *a* (*MUS*) discordant; (*fig*: *opiniones*) conflicting; **estar ~ con algo** to disagree with sth.

desacreditar [desakreði'tar] *vt* (*desprestigiar*) to discredit, bring into disrepute; (*denigrar*) to run down.

desactivar [desakti'ßar] *vt* to deactivate; (*bomba*) to defuse.

desacuerdo [desa'kwerðo] *nm* (*conflicto*) disagreement, discord; (*error*) error, blunder; **en ~** out of keeping.

desafiador, a [desafja'ðor, a], **desafiante** [desa'fjante] *a* (*insolente*) defiant; (*retador*) challenging ◆ *nm/f* challenger.

desafiar [desa'fjar] *vt* (*retar*) to challenge; (*enfrentarse a*) to defy.

desafilado, a [desafi'laðo, a] *a* blunt.

desafinado, a [desafi'naðo, a] *a*: **estar ~** to be out of tune.

desafinarse [desafi'narse] *vr* to go out of tune.

desafío [desa'fio] *nm* (*reto*) challenge; (*combate*) duel; (*resistencia*) defiance.

desaforadamente [desaforaða'mente] *ad*: **gritar ~** to shout one's head off.

desaforado, a [desafo'raðo, a] *a* (*grito*) ear-splitting; (*comportamiento*) outrageous.

desafortunadamente [desafortunaða'mente] *ad* unfortunately.

desafortunado, a [desafortu'naðo, a] *a* (*desgraciado*) unfortunate, unlucky.

desagradable [desaɣra'ðaßle] *a* (*fastidioso, enojoso*) unpleasant; (*irritante*) disagreeable; **ser ~ con uno** to be rude to sb.

desagradar [desaɣra'ðar] *vi* (*disgustar*) to displease; (*molestar*) to bother.

desagradecido, a [desaɣraðe'θiðo, a] *a* ungrateful.

desagrado [desa'ɣraðo] *nm* (*disgusto*) displeasure; (*contrariedad*) dissatisfaction; **con ~** unwillingly.

desagraviar [desaɣra'ßjar] *vt* to make amends to.

desagravio [desa'ɣraßjo] *nm* (*satisfacción*) amends; (*compensación*) compensation.

desagregarse [desaɣre'ɣarse] *vr* to disintegrate.

desagregue [desa'ɣreɣe] *etc vb V* **desagregarse**.

desaguadero [desaɣwa'ðero] *nm* drain.

desagüe [de'saɣwe] *nm* (*de un líquido*) drainage; (*cañería*: *tb*: **tubo de ~**) drainpipe; (*salida*) outlet, drain.

desaguisado, a [desaɣi'saðo, a] *a* illegal ◆ *nm* outrage.

desahogado, a [desao'ɣaðo, a] *a* (*holgado*) comfortable; (*espacioso*) roomy.

desahogar [desao'ɣar] *vt* (*aliviar*) to ease, relieve; (*ira*) to vent; **~se** *vr* (*distenderse*) to relax; (*desfogarse*) to let off steam (*fam*); (*confesarse*) to confess, get sth off one's chest (*fam*).

desahogo [desa'oɣo] *nm* (*alivio*) relief; (*comodidad*) comfort, ease; **vivir con ~** to be comfortably off.

desahogue [desa'oɣe] *etc vb V* **desahogar**.

desahuciado, a [desau'θjaðo, a] *a* hopeless.

desahuciar [desau'θjar] *vt* (*enfermo*) to give up hope for; (*inquilino*) to evict.

desahucio [de'sauθjo] *nm* eviction.

desairado, a [desai'raðo, a] *a* (*menospreciado*) disregarded; (*desgarbado*) shabby; (*sin éxito*) unsuccessful; **quedar ~** to come off badly.

desairar [desai'rar] *vt* (*menospreciar*) to slight, snub; (*cosa*) to disregard; (*COM*) to default on.

desaire [des'aire] *nm* (*menosprecio*) slight; (*falta de garbo*) unattractiveness; **dar** *o* **hacer un ~ a uno** to offend sb; **¿me va usted a hacer ese ~?** I won't take no for an answer!

desajustar [desaxus'tar] *vt* (*desarreglar*) to disarrange; (*desconcertar*) to throw off balance; (*fig*: *planes*) to upset; **~se** *vr* to get out of order; (*aflojarse*) to loosen.

desajuste [desa'xuste] *nm* (*de máquina*) disorder; (*avería*) breakdown; (*situación*) imbalance; (*desacuerdo*) disagreement.

desalentador, a [desalenta'ðor, a] *a* discouraging.

desalentar [desalen'tar] *vt* (*desanimar*) to discourage; **~se** *vr* to get discouraged.

desaliento [desa'ljento] *etc vb V* **desalentar** ◆ *nm* discouragement; (*abatimiento*) depression.

desalineación [desalinea'θjon] *nf* misalignment.

desaliñado, a [desali'ɲaðo, a] *a* (*descuidado*) slovenly; (*raído*) shabby; (*desordenado*) untidy; (*negligente*) careless.

desaliño [desa'liɲo] *nm* (*descuido*) slovenliness; (*negligencia*) carelessness.

desalmado, a [desal'maðo, a] *a* (*cruel*) cruel, heartless.

desalojar [desalo'xar] *vt* (*gen*) to remove, expel; (*expulsar, echar*) to eject; (*abandonar*) to move out of ◆ *vi* to move out; **la policía desalojó el local** the police cleared people out of the place.

desalquilar [desalki'lar] *vt* to vacate, move out; **~se** *vr* to become vacant.

desamarrar [desama'rrar] *vt* to untie; (*NAUT*) to cast off.

desamor [desa'mor] *nm* (*frialdad*) indifference; (*odio*) dislike.

desamparado, a [desampa'raðo, a] *a* (*persona*) helpless; (*lugar: expuesto*) exposed; (*: desierto*) deserted.

desamparar [desampa'rar] *vt* (*abandonar*) to desert, abandon; (*JUR*) to leave defenceless; (*barco*) to abandon.

desamparo [desam'paro] *nm* (*acto*) desertion; (*estado*) helplessness.

desamueblado, a [desamwe'βlaðo, a] *a* unfurnished.

desandar [desan'dar] *vt*: **~ lo andado** *o* **el camino** to retrace one's steps.

desanduve [desan'duβe] *etc*, **desanduviera** [desandu'βjera] *etc vb V* **desandar**.

desangelado, a [desanxe'laðo, a] *a* (*habitación, edificio*) lifeless.

desangrar [desan'grar] *vt* to bleed; (*fig: persona*) to bleed dry; (*lago*) to drain; **~se** *vr* to lose a lot of blood; (*morir*) to bleed to death.

desanimado, a [desani'maðo, a] *a* (*persona*) downhearted; (*espectáculo, fiesta*) dull.

desanimar [desani'mar] *vt* (*desalentar*) to discourage; (*deprimir*) to depress; **~se** *vr* to lose heart.

desánimo [de'sanimo] *nm* despondency; (*abatimiento*) dejection; (*falta de animación*) dullness.

desanudar [desanu'ðar] *vt* to untie; (*fig*) to clear up.

desapacible [desapa'θiβle] *a* unpleasant.

desaparecer [desapare'θer] *vi* to disappear; (*el sol, la luz*) to vanish; (**~ de vista**) to drop out of sight; (*efectos, señales*) to wear off.

desaparecido, a [desapare'θiðo, a] *a* missing; (*especie*) extinct ◆ *nm*: **~s** (*en accidente etc*) people missing.

desaparezca [desapa'reθka] *etc vb V* **desaparecer**.

desaparición [desapari'θjon] *nf* disappearance; (*de especie etc*) extinction.

desapasionado, a [desapasjo'naðo, a] *a* dispassionate, impartial.

desapego [desa'peɣo] *nm* (*frialdad*) coolness; (*distancia*) detachment.

desapercibido, a [desaperθi'βiðo, a] *a* unnoticed; (*desprevenido*) unprepared; **pasar ~** to go unnoticed.

desaplicado, a [desapli'kaðo, a] *a* slack, lazy.

desaprender [desapren'der] *vt* to forget; (*lo aprendido*) to unlearn.

desaprensivo, a [desapren'siβo, a] *a* unscrupulous.

desaprobar [desapro'βar] *vt* (*reprobar*) to disapprove of; (*condenar*) to condemn; (*no consentir*) to reject.

desaprovechado, a [desaproβe'tʃaðo, a] *a* (*oportunidad, tiempo*) wasted; (*estudiante*) slack.

desaprovechar [desaproβe'tʃar] *vt* to waste; (*talento*) not to use to the full ◆ *vi* (*perder terreno*) to lose ground.

desapruebe [desa'prweβe] *etc vb V* **desaprobar**.

desarmar [desar'mar] *vt* (*MIL, fig*) to disarm; (*TEC*) to take apart, dismantle.

desarme [de'sarme] *nm* disarmament.

desarraigado, a [desarrai'ɣaðo, a] *a* (*persona*) without roots, rootless.

desarraigar [desarrai'ɣar] *vt* to uproot; (*fig: costumbre*) to root out; (*: persona*) to banish.

desarraigo [desa'rraiɣo] *nm* uprooting.

desarraigue [desa'rraiɣe] *etc vb V* **desarraigar**.

desarreglado, a [desarre'ɣlaðo, a] *a* (*desordenado*) disorderly, untidy; (*hábitos*) irregular.

desarreglar [desarre'ɣlar] *vt* to mess up; (*desordenar*) to disarrange; (*trastocar*) to upset, disturb.

desarreglo [desa'rreɣlo] *nm* (*de casa, persona*) untidiness; (*desorden*) disorder; (*TEC*) trouble; (*MED*) upset; **viven en el mayor ~** they live in complete chaos.

desarrollado, a [desarro'ʎaðo, a] *a* developed.

desarrollar [desarro'ʎar] *vt* (*gen*) to develop; (*extender*) to unfold; (*teoría*) to explain; **~se** *vr* to develop; (*extenderse*) to open (out); (*film*) to develop; (*fig*) to grow; (*tener lugar*) to take place; **aquí desarrollan un trabajo muy importante** they carry on *o* out very important work here; **la acción se desarrolla en Roma** (*CINE etc*) the scene is set in Rome.

desarrollo [desa'rroʎo] *nm* development; (*de acontecimientos*) unfolding; (*de industria, mercado*) expansion, growth; **país en vías de ~** developing country; **la industria está en pleno ~** industry is expanding steadily.

desarrugar [desarru'ɣar] vt (alisar) to smooth (out); (ropa) to remove the creases from.

desarrugue [desa'rruɣe] etc vb V **desarrugar**.

desarticulado, a [desartiku'laðo, a] a disjointed.

desarticular [desartiku'lar] vt (huesos) to dislocate, put out of joint; (objeto) to take apart; (grupo terrorista etc) to break up.

desaseado, a [desase'aðo, a] a (sucio) dirty; (desaliñado) untidy.

desaseo [desa'seo] nm (suciedad) dirtiness; (desarreglo) untidiness.

desasga [de'sasɣa] etc vb V **desasir**.

desasir [desa'sir] vt to loosen; ~se vr to extricate o.s.; ~se de to let go, give up.

desasosegar [desasose'ɣar] vt (inquietar) to disturb, make uneasy; ~se vr to become uneasy.

desasosegué [desasose'ɣe], **desasoseguemos** [desasose'ɣemos] etc vb V **desasosegar**.

desasosiego [desaso'sjeɣo] etc vb V **desasosegar** ♦ nm (intranquilidad) uneasiness, restlessness; (ansiedad) anxiety; (POL etc) unrest.

desasosiegue [desaso'sjeɣue] etc vb V **desasosegar**.

desastrado, a [desas'traðo, a] a (desaliñado) shabby; (sucio) dirty.

desastre [de'sastre] nm disaster; ¡un ~! how awful!; **la función fue un ~** the show was a shambles.

desastroso, a [desas'troso, a] a disastrous.

desatado, a [desa'taðo, a] a (desligado) untied; (violento) violent, wild.

desatar [desa'tar] vt (nudo) to untie; (paquete) to undo; (perro, odio) to unleash; (misterio) to solve; (separar) to detach; ~se vr (zapatos) to come untied; (tormenta) to break; (perder control de sí) to lose self-control; ~se en injurias to pour out a stream of insults.

desatascar [desatas'kar] vt (cañería) to unblock, clear; (carro) to pull out of the mud; ~ a uno (fig) to get sb out of a jam.

desatasque [desa'taske] etc vb V **desatascar**.

desatención [desaten'θjon] nf (descuido) inattention; (distracción) absent-mindedness.

desatender [desaten'der] vt (no prestar atención a) to disregard; (abandonar) to neglect.

desatento, a [desa'tento, a] a (distraído) inattentive; (descortés) discourteous.

desatienda [desa'tjenda] etc vb V **desatender**.

desatinado, a [desati'naðo, a] a foolish,

silly.

desatino [desa'tino] nm (idiotez) foolishness, folly; (error) blunder; ~s nmpl nonsense sg; ¡qué ~! how silly!, what rubbish!

desatornillar [desatorni'ʎar] vt to unscrew.

desatrancar [desatran'kar] vt (puerta) to unbolt; (cañería) to unblock.

desatranque [desa'tranke] etc vb V **desatrancar**.

desautorice [desauto'riθe] etc vb V **desautorizar**.

desautorizado, a [desautori'θaðo, a] a unauthorized.

desautorizar [desautori'θar] vt (oficial) to deprive of authority; (informe) to deny.

desavendré [desaβen'dre] etc vb V **desavenir**.

desavenencia [desaβe'nenθja] nf (desacuerdo) disagreement; (discrepancia) quarrel.

desavenga [desa'βenga] etc vb V **desavenir**.

desavenido, a [desaβe'niðo, a] a (opuesto) contrary; (reñidos) in disagreement; **ellos están ~s** they are at odds.

desavenir [desaβe'nir] vt (enemistar) to make trouble between; ~se vr to fall out.

desaventajado, a [desaβenta'xaðo, a] a (inferior) inferior; (poco ventajoso) disadvantageous.

desaviene [desa'βjene] etc, **desaviniendo** [desaβi'njendo] etc vb V **desavenir**.

desayunar [desaju'nar] vi, ~se vr to have breakfast ♦ vt to have for breakfast; ~ con café to have coffee for breakfast; ~ con algo (fig) to get the first news of sth.

desayuno [desa'juno] nm breakfast.

desazón [desa'θon] nf (angustia) anxiety; (MED) discomfort; (fig) annoyance.

desazonar [desaθo'nar] vt (fig) to annoy, upset; ~se vr (enojarse) to be annoyed; (preocuparse) to worry, be anxious.

desbancar [desβan'kar] vt (quitar el puesto a) to oust; (suplantar) to supplant (in sb's affections).

desbandada [desβan'daða] nf rush; ~ general mass exodus; **a la ~** in disorder.

desbandarse [desβan'darse] vr (MIL) to disband; (fig) to flee in disorder.

desbanque [des'βanke] etc vb V **desbancar**.

desbarajuste [desβara'xuste] nm confusion, disorder; ¡qué ~! what a mess!

desbaratar [desβara'tar] vt (gen) to mess up; (plan) to spoil; (deshacer, destruir) to ruin ♦ vi to talk nonsense; ~se vr (máquina) to break down; (persona: irritarse) to fly off the handle (fam).

desbarrar [desβa'rrar] vi to talk nonsense.

desbloquear [desβloke'ar] vt (negociaciones, tráfico) to get going again; (COM:

cuenta) to unfreeze.

desbocado, a [desßo'kaðo, a] *a* (*caballo*) runaway; (*herramienta*) worn.

desbocar [desßo'kar] *vt* (*vasija*) to break the rim of; **~se** *vr* (*caballo*) to bolt; (*persona: soltar injurias*) to let out a stream of insults.

desboque [des'ßoke] *etc vb V* **desbocar**.

desbordamiento [desßorða'mjento] *nm* (*de río*) overflowing; (*INFORM*) overflow; (*de cólera*) outburst; (*de entusiasmo*) upsurge.

desbordar [desßor'ðar] *vt* (*sobrepasar*) to go beyond; (*exceder*) to exceed ◆ *vi*, **~se** *vr* (*líquido, río*) to overflow; (*entusiasmo*) to erupt; (*persona: exaltarse*) to get carried away.

desbravar [desßra'ßar] *vt* (*caballo*) to break in; (*animal*) to tame.

descabalgar [deskaßal'ɣar] *vi* to dismount.

descabalgue [deska'ßalɣe] *etc vb V* **descabalgar**.

descabellado, a [deskaße'ʎaðo, a] *a* (*disparatado*) wild, crazy; (*insensato*) preposterous.

descabellar [deskaße'ʎar] *vt* to ruffle; (*TAUR: toro*) to give the coup de grace to.

descabezado, a [deskaße'θaðo, a] *a* (*sin cabeza*) headless; (*insensato*) wild.

descafeinado, a [deskafei'naðo, a] *a* decaffeinated ◆ *nm* decaffeinated coffee.

descalabrar [deskala'ßrar] *vt* to smash; (*persona*) to hit; (: *en la cabeza*) to hit on the head; (*NAUT*) to cripple; (*dañar*) to harm, damage; **~se** *vr* to hurt one's head.

descalabro [deska'laßro] *nm* blow; (*desgracia*) misfortune.

descalce [des'kalθe] *etc vb V* **descalzar**.

descalificar [deskalifi'kar] *vt* to disqualify; (*desacreditar*) to discredit.

descalifique [deskali'fike] *etc vb V* **descalificar**.

descalzar [deskal'θar] *vt* (*zapato*) to take off.

descalzo, a [des'kalθo, a] *a* barefoot(ed); (*fig*) destitute; **estar (con los pies) ~(s)** to be barefooted.

descambiar [deskam'bjar] *vt* to exchange.

descaminado, a [deskami'naðo, a] *a* (*equivocado*) on the wrong road; (*fig*) misguided; **en eso no anda usted muy ~** you're not far wrong there.

descamisado, a [deskami'saðo, a] *a* barechested.

descampado [deskam'paðo] *nm* open space, piece of empty ground; **comer al ~** to eat in the open air.

descansado, a [deskan'saðo, a] *a* (*gen*) rested; (*que tranquiliza*) restful.

descansar [deskan'sar] *vt* (*gen*) to rest; (*apoyar*): **~ (sobre)** to lean (on) ◆ *vi* to

rest, have a rest; (*echarse*) to lie down; (*cadáver, restos*) to lie; **¡que usted descanse!** sleep well!; **~ en** (*argumento*) to be based on.

descansillo [deskan'siʎo] *nm* (*de escalera*) landing.

descanso [des'kanso] *nm* (*reposo*) rest; (*alivio*) relief; (*pausa*) break; (*DEPORTE*) interval, half time; **día de ~** day off; **~ de enfermedad/maternidad** sick/maternity leave; **tomarse unos días de ~** to take a few days' leave *o* rest.

descapitalizado, a [deskapitali'θaðo, a] *a* undercapitalized.

descapotable [deskapo'taßle] *nm* (*tb:* **coche ~**) convertible.

descarado, a [deska'raðo, a] *a* (*sin vergüenza*) shameless; (*insolente*) cheeky.

descarga [des'karɣa] *nf* (*ARQ, ELEC, MIL*) discharge; (*NAUT*) unloading.

descargador [deskarɣa'ðor] *nm* (*de barcos*) docker.

descargar [deskar'ɣar] *vt* to unload; (*golpe*) to let fly; (*arma*) to fire; (*ELEC*) to discharge; (*pila*) to run down; (*conciencia*) to relieve; (*COM*) to take up; (*persona: de una obligación*) to release; (: *de una deuda*) to free; (*JUR*) to clear ◆ *vi* (*río*): **~ (en)** to flow (into); **~se** *vr* to unburden o.s.; **~se de algo** to get rid of sth.

descargo [des'karɣo] *nm* (*de obligación*) release; (*COM: recibo*) receipt; (: *de deuda*) discharge; (*JUR*) evidence; **~ de una acusación** acquittal on a charge.

descargue [des'karɣe] *etc vb V* **descargar**.

descarnado, a [deskar'naðo, a] *a* scrawny; (*fig*) bare; (*estilo*) straightforward.

descaro [des'karo] *nm* nerve.

descarriar [deska'rrjar] *vt* (*descaminar*) to misdirect; (*fig*) to lead astray; **~se** *vr* (*perderse*) to lose one's way; (*separarse*) to stray; (*pervertirse*) to err, go astray.

descarrilamiento [deskarrila'mjento] *nm* (*de tren*) derailment.

descarrilar [deskarri'lar] *vi* to be derailed.

descartable [deskar'taßle] *a* (*INFORM*) temporary.

descartar [deskar'tar] *vt* (*rechazar*) to reject; (*eliminar*) to rule out; **~se** *vr* (*NAIPES*) to discard; **~se de** to shirk.

descascarar [deskaska'rar] *vt* (*naranja, limón*) to peel; (*nueces, huevo duro*) to shell; **~se** *vr* to peel (off).

descascarillado, a [deskaskari'ʎaðo, a] *a* (*paredes*) peeling.

descendencia [desθen'denθja] *nf* (*origen*) origin, descent; (*hijos*) offspring; **morir sin dejar ~** to die without issue.

descendente [desθen'dente] *a* (*cantidad*) diminishing; (*INFORM*) top-down.

descender [desθen'der] *vt* (*bajar: escalera*)

to go down; ◆ *vi* to descend; (*temperatura, nivel*) to fall, drop; (*líquido*) to run; (*cortina etc*) to hang; (*fuerzas, persona*) to fail, get weak; ~ **de** to be descended from.
descendiente [desθen'djente] *nm/f* descendant.
descenso [des'θenso] *nm* descent; (*de temperatura*) drop; (*de producción*) downturn; (*de calidad*) decline; (*MINERÍA*) collapse; (*bajada*) slope; (*fig: decadencia*) decline; (*de empleado etc*) demotion.
descentrado, a [desθen'traðo, a] *a* (*pieza de una máquina*) off-centre; (*rueda*) out of true; (*persona*) bewildered; (*desequilibrado*) unbalanced; (*problema*) out of focus; **todavía está algo** ~ he is still somewhat out of touch.
descentralice [desθentra'liθe] *etc vb V* **descentralizar**.
descentralizar [desθentrali'θar] *vt* to decentralize.
descerrajar [desθerra'xar] *vt* (*puerta*) to break open.
descienda [des'θjenda] *etc vb V* **descender**.
descifrable [desθi'fraβle] *a* (*gen*) decipherable; (*letra*) legible.
descifrar [desθi'frar] *vt* (*escritura*) to decipher; (*mensaje*) to decode; (*problema*) to puzzle out; (*misterio*) to solve.
descocado, a [desko'kaðo, a] *a* (*descarado*) cheeky; (*desvergonzado*) brazen.
descoco [des'koko] *nm* (*descaro*) cheek; (*atrevimiento*) brazenness.
descolgar [deskol'var] *vt* (*bajar*) to take down; (*desde una posición alta*) to lower; (*de una pared etc*) to unhook; (*teléfono*) to pick up; ~**se** *vr* to let o.s. down; ~**se por** (*bajar escurriéndose*) to slip down; (*pared*) to climb down; **dejó el teléfono descolgado** he left the phone off the hook.
descolgué [deskol'ɣe], **descolguemos** [deskol'ɣemos] *etc vb V* **descolgar**.
descolocado, a [deskolo'kaðo, a] *a*: **estar** ~ (*cosa*) to be out of place; (*criada*) to be unemployed.
descolorido, a [deskolo'riðo, a] *a* (*color, tela*) faded; (*pálido*) pale; (*fig: estilo*) colourless.
descollar [desko'ʎar] *vi* (*sobresalir*) to stand out; (*montaña etc*) to rise; **la obra que más descuella de las suyas** his most outstanding work.
descompaginar [deskompaxi'nar] *vt* (*desordenar*) to disarrange, mess up.
descompasado, a [deskompa'saðo, a] *a* (*sin proporción*) out of all proportion; (*excesivo*) excessive; (*hora*) unearthly.
descompondré [deskompon'dre] *etc vb V* **descomponer**.
descompensar [deskompen'sar] *vt* to

unbalance.
descomponer [deskompo'ner] *vt* (*gen, LING, MAT*) to break down; (*desordenar*) to disarrange, disturb; (*materia orgánica*) to rot, decompose; (*TEC*) to put out of order; (*facciones*) to distort; (*estómago etc*) to upset; (*planes*) to mess up; (*persona: molestar*) to upset; (: *irritar*) to annoy; ~**se** *vr* (*corromperse*) to rot, decompose; (*estómago*) to get upset; (*el tiempo*) to change (for the worse); (*TEC*) to break down.
descomponga [deskom'ponga] *etc vb V* **descomponer**.
descomposición [deskomposi'θjon] *nf* (*gen*) breakdown; (*de fruta etc*) decomposition; (*putrefacción*) rotting; (*de cara*) distortion; ~ **de vientre** (*MED*) stomach upset, diarrhoea.
descompostura [deskompos'tura] *nf* (*TEC*) breakdown; (*desorganización*) disorganization; (*desorden*) untidiness.
descompuesto, a [deskom'pwesto, a] *pp de* **descomponer** ◆ *a* (*corrompido*) decomposed; (*roto*) broken.
descompuse [deskom'puse] *etc vb V* **descomponer**.
descomunal [deskomu'nal] *a* (*enorme*) huge; (*fam: excelente*) fantastic.
desconcertado, a [deskonθer'taðo, a] *a* disconcerted, bewildered.
desconcertar [deskonθer'tar] *vt* (*confundir*) to baffle; (*incomodar*) to upset, put out; (*orden*) to disturb; ~**se** *vr* (*turbarse*) to be upset; (*confundirse*) to be bewildered.
desconcierto [deskon'θjerto] *etc vb V* **desconcertar** ◆ *nm* (*gen*) disorder; (*desorientación*) uncertainty; (*inquietud*) uneasiness; (*confusión*) bewilderment.
desconchado, a [deskon'tʃaðo, a] *a* (*pintura*) peeling.
desconchar [deskon'tʃar] *vt* (*pared*) to strip off; (*loza*) to chip off.
desconectado, a [deskonek'taðo, a] *a* (*ELEC*) disconnected, switched off; (*INFORM*) offline; **estar** ~ **de** (*fig*) to have no contact with.
desconectar [deskonek'tar] *vt* to disconnect; (*desenchufar*) to unplug; (*radio, televisión*) to switch off; (*INFORM*) to toggle off.
desconfiado, a [deskon'fjaðo, a] *a* suspicious.
desconfianza [deskon'fjanθa] *nf* distrust.
desconfiar [deskon'fjar] *vi* to be distrustful; ~ **de** (*sospechar*) to mistrust, suspect; (*no tener confianza en*) to have no faith o confidence in; **desconfío de ello** I doubt it; **desconfíe de las imitaciones** (*COM*) beware of imitations.
desconforme [deskon'forme] *a* = **disconforme**.

descongelar [deskonxe'lar] *vt* (*nevera*) to defrost; (*comida*) to thaw; (*AUTO*) to de-ice; (*COM, POL*) to unfreeze.

descongestionar [desconxestjo'nar] *vt* (*cabeza, tráfico*) to clear; (*calle, ciudad*) to relieve congestion in; (*fig: despejar*) to clear.

desconocer [deskono'θer] *vt* (*ignorar*) not to know, be ignorant of; (*no aceptar*) to deny; (*repudiar*) to disown.

desconocido, a [deskono'θiðo, a] *a* unknown; (*que no se conoce*) unfamiliar; (*no reconocido*) unrecognized ♦ *nm/f* stranger; (*recién llegado*) newcomer; **está ~** he is hardly recognizable.

desconocimiento [deskonoθi'mjento] *nm* (*falta de conocimientos*) ignorance; (*repudio*) disregard.

desconozca [desko'noθka] *etc vb V* **desconocer**.

desconsiderado, a [deskonsiðe'raðo, a] *a* inconsiderate; (*insensible*) thoughtless.

desconsolado, a [deskonso'laðo, a] *a* (*afligido*) disconsolate; (*cara*) sad; (*desanimado*) dejected.

desconsolar [deskonso'lar] *vt* to distress; **~se** *vr* to despair.

desconsuelo [deskon'swelo] *etc vb V* **desconsolar** ♦ *nm* (*tristeza*) distress; (*desesperación*) despair.

descontado, a [deskon'taðo, a] *a*: **por ~** of course; **dar por ~ (que)** to take it for granted (that).

descontar [deskon'tar] *vt* (*deducir*) to take away, deduct; (*rebajar*) to discount.

descontento, a [deskon'tento, a] *a* dissatisfied ♦ *nm* dissatisfaction, discontent.

descontrolado, a [deskontro'laðo, a] *a* (*AM*) uncontrolled.

desconvendré [deskomben'dre] *etc*, **desconvenga** [deskom'benga] *etc vb V* **desconvenir**.

desconvenir [deskombe'nir] *vi* (*personas*) to disagree; (*no corresponder*) not to fit; (*no convenir*) to be inconvenient.

desconviene [deskom'bjene] *etc*, **desconviniendo** [deskombi'njendo] *etc vb V* **desconvenir**.

descorazonar [deskoraθo'nar] *vt* to discourage, dishearten; **~se** *vr* to get discouraged, lose heart.

descorchador [deskortʃa'ðor] *nm* corkscrew.

descorchar [deskor'tʃar] *vt* to uncork, open.

descorrer [desko'rrer] *vt* (*cortina, cerrojo*) to draw back; (*velo*) to remove.

descortés [deskor'tes] *a* (*mal educado*) discourteous; (*grosero*) rude.

descortesía [deskorte'sia] *nf* discourtesy; (*grosería*) rudeness.

descoser [desko'ser] *vt* to unstitch; **~se** *vr* to come apart (at the seams); (*fam: descu-*

brir un secreto*) to blurt out a secret; **~se de risa** to split one's sides laughing.

descosido, a [desko'siðo, a] *a* (*costura*) unstitched; (*desordenado*) disjointed ♦ *nm*: **como un ~** (*obrar*) wildly; (*beber, comer*) to excess; (*estudiar*) like mad.

descoyuntar [deskojun'tar] *vt* (*ANAT*) to dislocate; (*hechos*) to twist; **~se** *vr*: **~se un hueso** (*ANAT*) to put a bone out of joint; **~se de risa** (*fam*) to split one's sides laughing; **estar descoyuntado** (*persona*) to be double-jointed.

descrédito [des'kreðito] *nm* discredit; **caer en ~** to fall into disrepute; **ir en ~ de** to be to the discredit of.

descreído, a [deskre'iðo, a] *a* (*incrédulo*) incredulous; (*falto de fe*) unbelieving.

descremado, a [deskre'maðo, a] *a* skimmed.

descremar [deskre'mar] *vt* (*leche*) to skim.

describir [deskri'βir] *vt* to describe.

descripción [deskrip'θjon] *nf* description.

descrito [des'krito] *pp de* **describir**.

descuajar [deskwa'xar] *vt* (*disolver*) to melt; (*planta*) to pull out by the roots; (*extirpar*) to eradicate, wipe out; (*desanimar*) to dishearten.

descuajaringarse [deskwaxarin'garse] *vr* to fall to bits.

descuajaringue [deskwaxa'ringe] *etc vb V* **descuajaringarse**.

descuartice [deskwar'tiθe] *etc vb V* **descuartizar**.

descuartizar [deskwarti'θar] *vt* (*animal*) to carve up, cut up; (*fig: hacer pedazos*) to tear apart.

descubierto, a [desku'βjerto, a] *pp de* **descubrir** ♦ *a* uncovered, bare; (*persona*) bare-headed; (*cielo*) clear; (*coche*) open; (*campo*) treeless ♦ *nm* (*lugar*) open space; (*COM: en el presupuesto*) shortage; (: *bancario*) overdraft; **al ~** in the open; **poner al ~** to lay bare; **quedar al ~** to be exposed; **estar en ~** to be overdrawn.

descubridor, a [desku'βri'ðor, a] *nm/f* discoverer.

descubrimiento [deskuβri'mjento] *nm* (*hallazgo*) discovery; (*de criminal, fraude*) detection; (*revelación*) revelation; (*de secreto etc*) disclosure; (*de estatua etc*) unveiling.

descubrir [desku'βrir] *vt* to discover, find; (*petróleo*) to strike; (*inaugurar*) to unveil; (*vislumbrar*) to detect; (*sacar a luz: crimen*) to bring to light; (*revelar*) to reveal, show; (*poner al descubierto*) to expose to view; (*naipes*) to lay down; (*quitar la tapa de*) to uncover; (*cacerola*) to take the lid off; (*enterarse de: causa, solución*) to find out; (*divisar*) to see, make out; (*delatar*) to give away, betray; **~se** *vr* to reveal o.s.;

(*quitarse sombrero*) to take off one's hat; (*confesar*) to confess; (*fig: salir a luz*) to come out *o* to light.

descuelga [des'kwelɣa] *etc*, **descuelgue** [des'kwelɣe] *etc vb V* **descolgar**.

descuelle [des'kweʎe] *etc vb V* **descollar**.

descuento [des'kwento] *etc vb V* **descontar** ♦ *nm* discount; ~ **del 3%** 3% off; **con** ~ at a discount; ~ **por pago al contado** (*COM*) cash discount; ~ **por volumen de compras** (*COM*) volume discount.

descuidado, a [deskwi'ðaðo, a] *a* (*sin cuidado*) careless; (*desordenado*) untidy; (*olvidadizo*) forgetful; (*dejado*) neglected; (*desprevenido*) unprepared.

descuidar [deskwi'ðar] *vt* (*dejar*) to neglect; (*olvidar*) to overlook ♦ *vi*, ~**se** *vr* (*distraerse*) to be careless; (*estar desaliñado*) to let o.s. go; (*desprevenirse*) to drop one's guard; **¡descuida!** don't worry!

descuidero, a [deskwi'ðero, a] *nm/f* sneak thief.

descuido [des'kwiðo] *nm* (*dejadez*) carelessness; (*olvido*) negligence; (*un* ~) oversight; **al** ~ casually; (*sin cuidado*) carelessly; **al menor** ~ if my *etc* attention wanders for a minute; **con** ~ thoughtlessly; **por** ~ by an oversight.

desde ['desðe] *prep* from; ~ **entonces** since then; **¿**~ **cuándo es esto así?** how long has it been like this?; ~ **lejos** from afar; ~ **ahora en adelante** from now on(wards); ~ **hace 3 días** for 3 days; ~ **luego** of course ♦ *conj*: ~ **que** since; ~ **que puedo recordar** for as long as I can remember.

desdecir [desðe'θir] *vi*: ~ **de** (*no merecer*) to be unworthy of; (*no corresponder*) to clash with; ~**se** *vr*: ~**se de** to go back on.

desdén [des'ðen] *nm* scorn.

desdentado, a [desðen'taðo, a] *a* toothless.

desdeñable [desðe'ɲaβle] *a* contemptible; **nada** ~ far from negligible, considerable.

desdeñar [desðe'ɲar] *vt* (*despreciar*) to scorn.

desdeñoso, a [desðe'ɲoso, a] *a* scornful.

desdibujar [desðiβu'xar] *vt* to blur (the outlines of); ~**se** *vr* to get blurred, fade (away); **el recuerdo se ha desdibujado** the memory has become blurred.

desdiciendo [desði'θjendo] *etc vb V* **desdecir**.

desdichado, a [desði'tʃaðo, a] *a* (*sin suerte*) unlucky; (*infeliz*) unhappy; (*día*) ill-fated ♦ *nm/f* (*pobre desgraciado*) poor devil.

desdicho, a [des'ðitʃo, a] *pp de* **desdecir** ♦ *nf* (*desgracia*) misfortune; (*infelicidad*) unhappiness.

desdiga [des'ðiɣa] *etc*, **desdije** [des'dixe] *etc vb V* **desdecir**.

desdoblado, a [desðo'βlaðo, a] *a* (*persona-lidad*) split.

desdoblar [desðo'βlar] *vt* (*extender*) to spread out; (*desplegar*) to unfold.

deseable [dese'aβle] *a* desirable.

desear [dese'ar] *vt* to want, desire, wish for; **¿qué desea la señora?** (*tienda etc*) what can I do for you, madam?; **estoy deseando que esto termine** I'm longing for this to finish.

desecar [dese'kar] *vt*, **desecarse** *vr* to dry up.

desechable [dese'tʃaβle] *a* (*envase etc*) disposable.

desechar [dese'tʃar] *vt* (*basura*) to throw out *o* away; (*ideas*) to reject, discard; (*miedo*) to cast aside; (*plan*) to drop.

desecho [de'setʃo] *nm* (*desprecio*) contempt; (*lo peor*) dregs *pl*; ~**s** *nmpl* rubbish *sg*, waste *sg*; **de** ~ (*hierro*) scrap; (*producto*) waste; (*ropa*) cast-off.

desembalar [desemba'lar] *vt* to unpack.

desembarace [desemba'raθe] *etc vb V* **desembarazar**.

desembarazado, a [desembara'θaðo, a] *a* (*libre*) clear, free; (*desenvuelto*) free and easy.

desembarazar [desembara'θar] *vt* (*desocupar*) to clear; (*desenredar*) to free; ~**se** *vr*: ~**se de** to free o.s. of, get rid of.

desembarazo [desemba'raθo] *nm* (*acto*) clearing; (*AM: parto*) birth; (*desenfado*) ease.

desembarcadero [desembarka'ðero] *nm* quay.

desembarcar [desembar'kar] *vt* (*personas*) to land; (*mercancías etc*) to unload ♦ *vi*, ~**se** *vr* (*de barco, avión*) to disembark; (*esp AM: de tren, autobús*) to alight.

desembarco [desem'barko] *nm* landing.

desembargar [desembar'ɣar] *vt* (*gen*) to free; (*JUR*) to remove the embargo on.

desembargue [desem'βarɣe] *etc vb V* **desembargar**.

desembarque [desem'barke] *etc vb V* **desembarcar** ♦ *nm* disembarkation; (*de pasajeros*) landing; (*de mercancías*) unloading.

desembocadura [desemboka'ðura] *nf* (*de río*) mouth; (*de calle*) opening.

desembocar [desembo'kar] *vi*: ~ **en** to flow into; (*fig*) to result in.

desemboce [desem'boθe] *etc vb V* **desembozar**.

desembolsar [desembol'sar] *vt* (*pagar*) to pay out; (*gastar*) to lay out.

desembolso [desem'bolso] *nm* payment.

desemboque [desem'boke] *etc vb V* **desembocar**.

desembozar [desembo'θar] *vt* to unmask.

desembragar [desembra'ɣar] *vt* (*TEC*) to disengage; (*embrague*) to release ♦ *vi*

(*AUTO*) to declutch.

desembrague [desem'ßraɣe] *etc vb* V **desembragar.**

desembrollar [desembro'ʎar] *vt* (*madeja*) to unravel; (*asunto, malentendido*) to sort out.

desembuchar [desembu'tʃar] *vt* to disgorge; (*fig*) to come out with ♦ *vi* (*confesar*) to spill the beans (*fam*); **¡desembucha!** out with it!

desemejante [deseme'xante] *a* dissimilar; ~ **de** different from, unlike.

desemejanza [deseme'xanθa] *nf* dissimilarity.

desempacar [desempa'kar] *vt* to unpack.

desempañar [desempa'ɲar] *vt* (*cristal*) to clean, demist.

desempaque [desem'pake] *etc vb* V **desempacar.**

desempaquetar [desempake'tar] *vt* to unpack, unwrap.

desempatar [desempa'tar] *vi* to break a tie; **volvieron a jugar para** ~ they held a play-off.

desempate [desem'pate] *nm* (*FÚTBOL*) play-off; (*TENIS*) tie-break(er).

desempeñar [desempe'ɲar] *vt* (*cargo*) to hold; (*papel*) to play; (*deber, función*) to perform, carry out; (*lo empeñado*) to redeem; ~**se** *vr* to get out of debt; ~ **un papel** (*fig*) to play (a role).

desempeño [desem'peɲo] *nm* occupation; (*de lo empeñado*) redeeming; **de mucho** ~ very capable.

desempleado, a [desemple'aðo, a] *a* unemployed, out of work ♦ *nm/f* unemployed person.

desempleo [desem'pleo] *nm* unemployment.

desempolvar [desempol'ßar] *vt* (*muebles etc*) to dust; (*lo olvidado*) to revive.

desencadenar [desenkaðe'nar] *vt* to unchain; (*ira*) to unleash; (*provocar*) to cause, set off; ~**se** *vr* to break loose; (*tormenta*) to burst; (*guerra*) to break out; **se desencadenó una lucha violenta** a violent struggle ensued.

desencajar [desenka'xar] *vt* (*hueso*) to put out of joint; (*mandíbula*) to dislocate; (*mecanismo, pieza*) to disconnect, disengage.

desencantar [desenkan'tar] *vt* to disillusion, disenchant.

desencanto [desen'kanto] *nm* disillusionment, disenchantment.

desencoger [desenko'xer] *vt* (*extender*) to spread out; (*desdoblar*) to smooth out; ~**se** *vr* to lose one's timidity.

desencoja [desen'koxa] *etc vb* V **desencoger.**

desenchufar [desentʃu'far] *vt* to unplug, disconnect.

desenfadado, a [desenfa'ðaðo, a] *a* (*desenvuelto*) uninhibited; (*descarado*) forward; (*en el vestir*) casual.

desenfado [desen'faðo] *nm* (*libertad*) freedom; (*comportamiento*) free and easy manner; (*descaro*) forwardness; (*desenvoltura*) self-confidence.

desenfocado, a [desenfo'kaðo, a] *a* (*FOTO*) out of focus.

desenfrenado, a [desenfre'naðo, a] *a* (*descontrolado*) uncontrolled; (*inmoderado*) unbridled.

desenfrenarse [desenfre'narse] *vr* (*persona: desmandarse*) to lose all self-control; (*multitud*) to run riot; (*tempestad*) to burst; (*viento*) to rage.

desenfreno [desen'freno] *nm* (*vicio*) wildness; (*falta de control*) lack of self-control; (*de pasiones*) unleashing.

desenganchar [desengan'tʃar] *vt* (*gen*) to unhook; (*FERRO*) to uncouple; (*TEC*) to disengage.

desengañar [desenga'ɲar] *vt* to disillusion; (*abrir los ojos a*) to open the eyes of; ~**se** *vr* to become disillusioned; **¡desengáñate!** don't you believe it!

desengaño [desen'gaɲo] *nm* disillusionment; (*decepción*) disappointment; **sufrir un** ~ **amoroso** to be disappointed in love.

desengrasar [desengra'sar] *vt* to degrease.

desenlace [desen'laθe] *etc vb* V **desenlazar** ♦ *nm* outcome; (*LIT*) ending.

desenlazar [desenla'θar] *vt* (*desatar*) to untie; (*problema*) to solve; (*aclarar: asunto*) to unravel; ~**se** *vr* (*desatarse*) to come undone; (*LIT*) to end.

desenmarañar [desenmara'ɲar] *vt* (*fig*) to unravel.

desenmascarar [desenmaska'rar] *vt* to unmask, expose.

desenredar [desenre'ðar] *vt* to resolve.

desenrollar [desenro'ʎar] *vt* to unroll, unwind.

desenroscar [desenros'kar] *vt* (*tornillo etc*) to unscrew.

desenrosque [desen'roske] *etc vb* V **desenroscar.**

desentenderse [desenten'derse] *vr*: ~ **de** to pretend not to know about; (*apartarse*) to have nothing to do with.

desentendido, a [desenten'diðo, a] *a*: **hacerse el** ~ to pretend not to notice; **se hizo el** ~ he didn't take the hint.

desenterrar [desente'rrar] *vt* to exhume; (*tesoro, fig*) to unearth, dig up.

desentierre [desen'tjerre] *etc vb* V **desenterrar.**

desentonar [desento'nar] *vi* (*MUS*) to sing (*o* play) out of tune; (*no encajar*) to be out of place; (*color*) to clash.

desentorpecer [desentorpe'θer] *vt* (*miembro*) to stretch; (*fam: persona*) to polish up.

desentorpezca [desentor'peθka] *etc vb V* **desentorpecer**.

desentrañar [desentra'ɲar] *vt* (*misterio*) to unravel.

desentrenado, a [desentre'naðo, a] *a* out of training.

desentumecer [desentume'θer] *vt* (*pierna etc*) to stretch; (*DEPORTE*) to loosen up.

desentumezca [desentu'meθka] *etc vb V* **desentumecer**.

desenvainar [desembai'nar] *vt* (*espada*) to draw, unsheathe.

desenvoltura [desembol'tura] *nf* (*libertad, gracia*) ease; (*descaro*) free and easy manner; (*al hablar*) fluency.

desenvolver [desembol'ßer] *vt* (*paquete*) to unwrap; (*fig*) to develop; ~**se** *vr* (*desarrollarse*) to unfold, develop; (*suceder*) to go off; (*prosperar*) to prosper; (*arreglárselas*) to cope.

desenvolvimiento [desembolßi'mjento] *nm* (*desarrollo*) development; (*de idea*) exposition.

desenvuelto, a [desem'bwelto, a] *pp de* **desenvolver** ♦ *a* (*suelto*) easy; (*desenfadado*) confident; (*al hablar*) fluent; (*pey*) forward.

desenvuelva [desem'buelßa] *etc vb V* **desenvolver**.

deseo [de'seo] *nm* desire, wish; ~ **de saber** thirst for knowledge; **buen** ~ good intentions *pl*; **arder en** ~**s de algo** to yearn for sth.

deseoso, a [dese'oso, a] *a*: **estar** ~ **de hacer** to be anxious to do.

deseque [de'seke] *etc vb V* **desecar**.

desequilibrado, a [desekili'ßraðo, a] *a* unbalanced ♦ *nm/f* unbalanced person; ~ **mental** mentally disturbed person.

desequilibrar [desekili'ßrar] *vt* (*mente*) to unbalance; (*objeto*) to throw out of balance; (*persona*) to throw off balance.

desequilibrio [deseki'lißrio] *nm* (*de mente*) unbalance; (*entre cantidades*) imbalance; (*MED*) unbalanced mental condition.

desertar [deser'tar] *vt* (*JUR: derecho de apelación*) to forfeit ♦ *vi* to desert; ~ **de sus deberes** to neglect one's duties.

desértico, a [de'sertiko, a] *a* desert *cpd*; (*vacío*) deserted.

desesperación [desespera'θjon] *nf* desperation, despair; (*irritación*) fury; **es una** ~ it's maddening; **es una** ~ **tener que ...** it's infuriating to have to ... .

desesperado, a [desespe'raðo, a] *a* (*persona: sin esperanza*) desperate; (*caso, situación*) hopeless; (*esfuerzo*) furious ♦ *nm*: **como un** ~ like mad ♦ *nf*: **hacer algo a la**

desesperada to do sth as a last resort *o* in desperation.

desesperance [desespe'ranθe] *etc vb V* **desesperanzar**.

desesperante [desespe'rante] *a* (*exasperante*) infuriating; (*persona*) hopeless.

desesperanzar [desesperan'θar] *vt* to drive to despair; ~**se** *vr* to lose hope, despair.

desesperar [desespe'rar] *vt* to drive to despair; (*exasperar*) to drive to distraction ♦ *vi*: ~ **de** to despair of; ~**se** *vr* to despair, lose hope.

desestabilice [desestaßi'liθe] *etc vb V* **desestabilizar**.

desestabilizar [desestaßili'θar] *vt* to destabilize.

desestimar [desesti'mar] *vt* (*menospreciar*) to have a low opinion of; (*rechazar*) to reject.

desfachatez [desfatʃa'teθ] *nf* (*insolencia*) impudence; (*descaro*) rudeness.

desfalco [des'falko] *nm* embezzlement.

desfallecer [desfaʎe'θer] *vi* (*perder las fuerzas*) to become weak; (*desvanecerse*) to faint.

desfallecido, a [desfaʎe'θiðo, a] *a* (*débil*) weak.

desfallezca [desfa'ʎeθka] *etc vb V* **desfallecer**.

desfasado, a [desfa'saðo, a] *a* (*anticuado*) old-fashioned; (*TEC*) out of phase.

desfasar [desfa'sar] *vt* to phase out.

desfase [des'fase] *nm* (*diferencia*) gap.

desfavorable [desfaßo'raßle] *a* unfavourable.

desfavorecer [desfaßore'θer] *vt* (*sentar mal*) not to suit.

desfavorezca [desfaßo'reθka] *etc vb V* **desfavorecer**.

desfiguración [desfiɣura'θjon] *nf*, **desfiguramiento** [desfiɣura'mjento] *nm* (*de persona*) disfigurement; (*de monumento*) defacement; (*FOTO*) blurring.

desfigurar [desfiɣu'rar] *vt* (*cara*) to disfigure; (*cuerpo*) to deform; (*cuadro, monumento*) to deface; (*FOTO*) to blur; (*sentido*) to twist; (*suceso*) to misrepresent.

desfiladero [desfila'ðero] *nm* gorge, defile.

desfilar [desfi'lar] *vi* to parade; **desfilaron ante el general** they marched past the general.

desfile [des'file] *nm* procession; (*MIL*) parade; ~ **de modelos** fashion show.

desflorar [desflo'rar] *vt* (*mujer*) to deflower; (*arruinar*) to tarnish; (*asunto*) to touch on.

desfogar [desfo'ɣar] *vt* (*fig*) to vent ♦ *vi* (*NAUT: tormenta*) to burst; ~**se** *vr* (*fig*) to let off steam.

desfogue [des'foɣe] *etc vb V* **desfogar**.

desgajar [desɣa'xar] *vt* (*arrancar*) to tear

off; (*romper*) to break off; (*naranja*) to split into segments; ~**se** *vr* to come off.

desgana [desˈɣana] *nf* (*falta de apetito*) loss of appetite; (*renuencia*) unwillingness; **hacer algo a** ~ to do sth unwillingly.

desganado, a [desɣaˈnaðo, a] *a*: **estar** ~ (*sin apetito*) to have no appetite; (*sin entusiasmo*) to have lost interest.

desgañitarse [desɣaɲiˈtarse] *vr* to shout o.s. hoarse.

desgarbado, a [desɣarˈβaðo, a] *a* (*sin gracia*) clumsy, ungainly.

desgarrador, a [desɣarraˈðor, a] *a* heartrending.

desgarrar [desɣaˈrrar] *vt* to tear (up); (*fig*) to shatter.

desgarro [desˈɣarro] *nm* (*en tela*) tear; (*aflicción*) grief; (*descaro*) impudence.

desgastar [desɣasˈtar] *vt* (*deteriorar*) to wear away o down; (*estropear*) to spoil; ~**se** *vr* to get worn out.

desgaste [desˈɣaste] *nm* wear (and tear); (*de roca*) erosion; (*de cuerda*) fraying; (*de metal*) corrosion; ~ **económico** drain on one's resources.

desglosar [desɣloˈsar] *vt* to detach.

desgobernar [desɣoβerˈnar] *vt* (*POL*) to misgovern; (*asunto*) to handle badly; (*ANAT*) to dislocate.

desgobierno [desɣoˈβjerno] *etc vb V* **desgobernar** ◆ *nm* (*POL*) misgovernment, misrule.

desgracia [desˈɣraθja] *nf* misfortune; (*accidente*) accident; (*vergüenza*) disgrace; (*contratiempo*) setback; **por** ~ unfortunately; **en el accidente no hay que lamentar** ~**s personales** there were no casualties in the accident; **caer en** ~ to fall from grace; **tener la** ~ **de** to be unlucky enough to.

desgraciadamente [desɣraθjaðaˈmente] *ad* unfortunately.

desgraciado, a [desɣraˈθjaðo, a] *a* (*sin suerte*) unlucky, unfortunate; (*miserable*) wretched; (*infeliz*) miserable ◆ *nm/f* (*malo*) swine; (*infeliz*) poor creature.

desgraciar [desɣraˈθjar] *vt* (*estropear*) to spoil; (*ofender*) to displease.

desgranar [desɣraˈnar] *vt* (*trigo*) to thresh; (*guisantes*) to shell; ~ **un racimo** to pick the grapes from a bunch; ~ **mentiras** to come out with a string of lies.

desgravación [desɣraβaˈθjon] *nf* (*COM*): ~ **de impuestos** tax relief; ~ **personal** personal allowance.

desgravar [desɣraˈβar] *vt* (*producto*) to reduce the tax o duty on.

desgreñado, a [desɣreˈɲaðo, a] *a* dishevelled.

deshabitado, a [desaβiˈtaðo, a] *a* uninhabited.

deshabitar [desaβiˈtar] *vt* (*casa*) to leave empty; (*despoblar*) to depopulate.

deshacer [desaˈθer] *vt* (*lo hecho*) to undo, unmake; (*proyectos: arruinar*) to spoil; (*casa*) to break up; (*TEC*) to take apart; (*enemigo*) to defeat; (*diluir*) to melt; (*contrato*) to break; (*intriga*) to solve; (*cama*) to strip; (*maleta*) to unpack; (*paquete*) to unwrap; (*nudo*) to untie; (*costura*) to unpick; ~**se** *vr* (*desatarse*) to come undone; (*estropearse*) to be spoiled; (*descomponerse*) to fall to pieces; (*disolverse*) to melt; (*despedazarse*) to come apart o undone; ~**se de** to get rid of; (*COM*) to dump, unload; ~**se en** (*cumplidos, elogios*) to be lavish with; ~**se en lágrimas** to burst into tears; ~**se por algo** to be crazy about sth.

deshaga [deˈsaɣa] *etc*, **desharé** [desaˈre] *etc vb V* **deshacer**.

des(h)arrapado, a [desarraˈpaðo, a] *a* ragged; (**de aspecto**) ~ shabby.

deshecho, a [deˈsetʃo, a] *pp de* **deshacer** ◆ *a* (*lazo, nudo*) undone; (*roto*) smashed; (*despedazado*) in pieces; (*cama*) unmade; (*MED: persona*) weak, emaciated; (: *salud*) broken; **estoy** ~ I'm shattered.

deshelar [deseˈlar] *vt* (*cañería*) to thaw; (*heladera*) to defrost.

desheredar [desereˈðar] *vt* to disinherit.

deshice [deˈsiθe] *etc vb V* **deshacer**.

deshidratación [desiðrataˈθjon] *nf* dehydration.

deshidratar [desiðraˈtar] *vt* to dehydrate.

deshielo [desˈjelo] *etc vb V* **deshelar** ◆ *nm* thaw.

deshilachar [desilaˈtʃar] *vt*, **deshilacharse** *vr* to fray.

deshilar [desiˈlar] *vt* (*tela*) to unravel.

deshilvanado, a [desilβaˈnaðo, a] *a* (*fig*) disjointed, incoherent.

deshinchar [desinˈtʃar] *vt* (*neumático*) to let down; (*herida etc*) to reduce (the swelling of); ~**se** *vr* (*neumático*) to go flat; (*hinchazón*) to go down.

deshojar [desoˈxar] *vt* (*árbol*) to strip the leaves off; (*flor*) to pull the petals off; ~**se** *vr* to lose its leaves *etc*.

deshollinar [desoʎiˈnar] *vt* (*chimenea*) to sweep.

deshonesto, a [desoˈnesto, a] *a* (*no honrado*) dishonest; (*indecente*) indecent.

deshonor [desoˈnor] *nm* dishonour, disgrace; (*un* ~) insult, affront.

deshonra [deˈsonra] *nf* (*deshonor*) dishonour; (*vergüenza*) shame.

deshonrar [desonˈrar] *vt* to dishonour.

deshonroso, a [desonˈroso, a] *a* dishonourable, disgraceful.

deshora [deˈsora]: **a** ~ *ad* at the wrong time; (*llegar*) unexpectedly; (*acostarse*) at some unearthly hour.

deshuesar [deswe'sar] *vt* (*carne*) to bone; (*fruta*) to stone.

desidia [de'siðja] *nf* (*pereza*) idleness.

desierto, a [de'sjerto, a] *a* (*casa, calle, negocio*) deserted; (*paisaje*) bleak ♦ *nm* desert.

designación [desiɣna'θjon] *nf* (*para un cargo*) appointment; (*nombre*) designation.

designar [desiɣ'nar] *vt* (*nombrar*) to designate; (*indicar*) to fix.

designio [de'siɣnjo] *nm* plan; **con el ~ de** with the intention of.

desigual [desi'ɣwal] *a* (*lucha*) unequal; (*diferente*) different; (*terreno*) uneven; (*tratamiento*) unfair; (*cambiadizo: tiempo*) changeable; (: *carácter*) unpredictable.

desigualdad [desiɣwal'ðað] *nf* (ECON, POL) inequality; (*de carácter, tiempo*) unpredictability; (*de escritura*) unevenness; (*de terreno*) roughness.

desilusión [desilu'sjon] *nf* disillusionment; (*decepción*) disappointment.

desilusionar [desilusjo'nar] *vt* to disillusion; (*decepcionar*) to disappoint; **~se** *vr* to become disillusioned.

desinencia [desi'nenθja] *nf* (LING) ending.

desinfectar [desinfek'tar] *vt* to disinfect.

desinfestar [desinfes'tar] *vt* to decontaminate.

desinflación [desinfla'θjon] *nf* (COM) disinflation.

desinflar [desin'flar] *vt* to deflate; **~se** *vr* (*neumático*) to go down *o* flat.

desintegración [desinteɣra'θjon] *nf* disintegration; **~ nuclear** nuclear fission.

desintegrar [desinte'ɣrar] *vt* (*gen*) to disintegrate; (*átomo*) to split; (*grupo*) to break up; **~se** *vr* to disintegrate; to split; to break up.

desinterés [desinte'res] *nm* (*objetividad*) disinterestedness; (*altruismo*) unselfishness.

desinteresado, a [desintere'saðo, a] *a* (*imparcial*) disinterested; (*altruista*) unselfish.

desintoxicar [desintoksi'kar] *vt* to detoxify; **~se** *vr*: **~se de** (*rutina, trabajo*) to get away from.

desintoxique [desintok'sike] *etc vb* V **desintoxicar.**

desistir [desis'tir] *vi* (*renunciar*) to stop, desist; **~ de** (*empresa*) to give up; (*derecho*) to waive.

deslavazado, a [deslaßa'θaðo, a] *a* (*lacio*) limp; (*desteñido*) faded; (*insípido*) colourless; (*incoherente*) disjointed.

desleal [desle'al] *a* (*infiel*) disloyal; (COM: *competencia*) unfair.

deslealtad [desleal'tað] *nf* disloyalty.

desleído, a [desle'iðo, a] *a* weak, woolly.

desleír [desle'ir] *vt* (*líquido*) to dilute; (*sólido*) to dissolve.

deslenguado, a [deslen'gwaðo, a] *a* (*grosero*) foul-mouthed.

deslía [des'lia] *etc vb* V **desleír.**

desliar [des'ljar] *vt* (*desatar*) to untie; (*paquete*) to open; **~se** *vr* to come undone.

deslice [des'liθe] *etc vb* V **deslizar.**

desliendo [desli'endo] *etc vb* V **desleír.**

desligar [desli'ɣar] *vt* (*desatar*) to untie, undo; (*separar*) to separate; **~se** *vr* (*de un compromiso*) to extricate o.s.

desligue [des'liɣe] *etc vb* V **desligar.**

deslindar [deslin'dar] *vt* (*señalar las lindes de*) to mark out, fix the boundaries of; (*fig*) to define.

desliz [des'liθ] *nm* (*fig*) lapse; **~ de lengua** slip of the tongue; **cometer un ~** to slip up.

deslizar [desli'θar] *vt* to slip, slide; **~se** *vr* (*escurrirse: persona*) to slip, slide; (: *coche*) to skid; (*aguas mansas*) to flow gently; (*error*) to creep in; (*tiempo*) to pass; (*persona: irse*) to slip away; **~se en un cuarto** to slip into a room.

deslomar [deslo'mar] *vt* (*romper el lomo de*) to break the back of; (*fig*) to wear out; **~se** *vr* (*fig fam*) to work one's guts out.

deslucido, a [deslu'θiðo, a] *a* dull; (*torpe*) awkward, graceless; (*deslustrado*) tarnished; (*fracasado*) unsuccessful; **quedar ~** to make a poor impression.

deslucir [deslu'θir] *vt* (*deslustrar*) to tarnish; (*estropear*) to spoil, ruin; (*persona*) to discredit; **la lluvia deslució el acto** the rain ruined the ceremony.

deslumbrar [deslum'brar] *vt* (*con la luz*) to dazzle; (*cegar*) to blind; (*impresionar*) to dazzle; (*dejar perplejo a*) to puzzle, confuse.

deslustrar [deslus'trar] *vt* (*vidrio*) to frost; (*quitar lustre a*) to dull; (*reputación*) to sully.

desluzca [des'luθka] *etc vb* V **deslucir.**

desmadrarse [desma'ðrarse] *vr* (*fam*) to run wild.

desmán [des'man] *nm* (*exceso*) outrage; (*abuso de poder*) abuse.

desmandarse [desman'darse] *vr* (*portarse mal*) to behave badly; (*excederse*) to get out of hand; (*caballo*) to bolt.

desmantelar [desmante'lar] *vt* (*deshacer*) to dismantle; (*casa*) to strip; (*organización*) to disband; (MIL) to raze; (*andamio*) to take down; (NAUT) to unrig.

desmaña [des'maɲa] *nf* clumsiness.

desmaquillador [desmakiʎa'ðor] *nm* make-up remover.

desmayado, a [desma'jaðo, a] *a* (*sin sentido*) unconscious; (*carácter*) dull; (*débil*) faint, weak; (*color*) pale.

desmayar [desma'jar] *vi* to lose heart; **~se** *vr* (MED) to faint.

desmayo [des'majo] *nm* (*MED:* *acto*) faint; (*estado*) unconsciousness; (*depresión*) dejection; (*de voz*) faltering; **sufrir un** ~ to have a fainting fit.

desmedido, a [desme'ðiðo, a] *a* excessive; (*ambición*) boundless.

desmedrado, a [desme'ðraðo, a] *a* (*estropeado*) impaired; (*MED*) run down.

desmejorado, a [desmexo'raðo, a] *a*: **está muy desmejorada** (*MED*) she's not looking too well.

desmejorar [desmexo'rar] *vt* (*dañar*) to impair, spoil; (*MED*) to weaken.

desmembración [desmembra'θjon] *nf* dismemberment; (*fig*) break-up.

desmembrar [desmem'brar] *vt* (*MED*) to dismember; (*fig*) to separate.

desmemoriado, a [desmemo'rjaðo, a] *a* forgetful, absent-minded.

desmentir [desmen'tir] *vt* (*contradecir*) to contradict; (*refutar*) to deny; (*rumor*) to scotch ◆ *vi*: ~ **de** to refute; ~**se** *vr* to contradict o.s.

desmenuce [desme'nuθe] *etc vb V* **desmenuzar**.

desmenuzar [desmenu'θar] *vt* (*deshacer*) to crumble; (*carne*) to chop; (*examinar*) to examine closely.

desmerecer [desmere'θer] *vt* to be unworthy of ◆ *vi* (*deteriorarse*) to deteriorate.

desmerezca [desme'reθka] *etc vb V* **desmerecer**.

desmesurado, a [desmesu'raðo, a] *a* (*desmedido*) disproportionate; (*enorme*) enormous; (*ambición*) boundless; (*descarado*) insolent.

desmiembre [des'mjembre] *etc vb V* **desmembrar**.

desmienta [des'mjenta] *etc vb V* **desmentir**.

desmigajar [desmiɣa'xar], **desmigar** [desmi'ɣar] *vt* to crumble.

desmigue [des'miɣe] *etc vb V* **desmigar**.

desmilitarice [desmilita'riθe] *etc vb V* **desmilitarizar**.

desmilitarizar [desmilitari'θar] *vt* to demilitarize.

desmintiendo [desmin'tjendo] *etc vb V* **desmentir**.

desmochar [desmo'tʃar] *vt* (*árbol*) to lop; (*texto*) to cut, hack about.

desmontable [desmon'taßle] *a* (*que se quita*) detachable; (*en compartimientos*) sectional; (*que se puede plegar etc*) collapsible.

desmontar [desmon'tar] *vt* (*deshacer*) to dismantle; (*motor*) to strip down; (*máquina*) to take apart; (*escopeta*) to uncock; (*tienda de campaña*) to take down; (*tierra*) to level; (*quitar los árboles a*) to clear; (*ji-*

nete) to throw ◆ *vi* to dismount.

desmonte [des'monte] *nm* (*de tierra*) levelling; (*de árboles*) clearing; (*terreno*) levelled ground; (*FERRO*) cutting.

desmoralice [desmora'liθe] *etc vb V* **desmoralizar**.

desmoralizador, a [desmoraliθa'ðor, a] *a* demoralizing.

desmoralizar [desmorali'θar] *vt* to demoralize.

desmoronado, a [desmoro'naðo, a] *a* (*casa, edificio*) dilapidated.

desmoronamiento [desmorona'mjento] *nm* (*tb fig*) crumbling.

desmoronar [desmoro'nar] *vt* to wear away, erode; ~**se** *vr* (*edificio, dique*) to fall into disrepair; (*economía*) to decline.

desmovilice [desmoßi'liθe] *etc vb V* **desmovilizar**.

desmovilizar [desmoßili'θar] *vt* to demobilize.

desnacionalización [desnaθjonaliθa'θjon] *nf* denationalization.

desnacionalizado, a [desnaθjonali'θaðo, a] *a* (*industria*) denationalized; (*persona*) stateless.

desnatado, a [desna'taðo, a] *a* skimmed.

desnatar [desna'tar] *vt* (*leche*) to skim; **leche sin** ~ whole milk.

desnaturalice [desnatura'liθe] *etc vb V* **desnaturalizar**.

desnaturalizado, a [desnaturali'θaðo, a] *a* (*persona*) unnatural; **alcohol** ~ methylated spirits.

desnaturalizar [desnaturali'θar] *vt* (*QUÍMICA*) to denature; (*corromper*) to pervert; (*sentido de algo*) to distort; ~**se** *vr* (*perder la nacionalidad*) to give up one's nationality.

desnivel [desni'ßel] *nm* (*de terreno*) unevenness; (*POL*) inequality; (*diferencia*) difference.

desnivelar [desniße'lar] *vt* (*terreno*) to make uneven; (*fig: desequilibrar*) to unbalance; (*balanza*) to tip.

desnuclearizado, a [desnukleari'θaðo, a] *a*: **región desnuclearizada** nuclear-free zone.

desnudar [desnu'ðar] *vt* (*desvestir*) to undress; (*despojar*) to strip; ~**se** *vr* (*desvestirse*) to get undressed.

desnudez [desnu'ðeθ] *nf* (*de persona*) nudity; (*fig*) bareness.

desnudo, a [des'nuðo, a] *a* (*cuerpo*) naked; (*árbol, brazo*) bare; (*paisaje*) flat; (*estilo*) unadorned; (*verdad*) plain ◆ *nm/f* nude; ~ **de** devoid o bereft of; **la retrató al** ~ he painted her in the nude; **poner al** ~ to lay bare.

desnutrición [desnutri'θjon] *nf* malnutrition.

desnutrido, a [desnu'triðo, a] *a* undernourished.

desobedecer [desoβeðe'θer] *vt, vi* to disobey.

desobedezca [desoβe'ðeθka] *etc vb* V **desobedecer.**

desobediencia [desoβe'ðjenθja] *nf* disobedience.

desocupado, a [desocu'paðo, a] *a* at leisure; *(desempleado)* unemployed; *(deshabitado)* empty, vacant.

desocupar [desocu'par] *vt* to vacate; ~**se** *vr (quedar libre)* to be free; **se ha desocupado aquella mesa** that table's free now.

desodorante [desoðo'rante] *nm* deodorant.

desoiga [de'soiɣa] *etc vb* V **desoír.**

desoír [deso'ir] *vt* to ignore, disregard.

desolación [desola'θjon] *nf (de lugar)* desolation; *(fig)* grief.

desolar [deso'lar] *vt* to ruin, lay waste.

desolladero [desoʎa'ðero] *nm* slaughterhouse.

desollar [deso'ʎar] *vt (quitar la piel a)* to skin; *(criticar)*: ~ **vivo a** to criticize unmercifully.

desorbitado, a [desorßi'taðo, a] *a (excesivo)* excessive; *(precio)* exorbitant; **con los ojos** ~**s** pop-eyed.

desorbitar [desorßi'tar] *vt (exagerar)* to exaggerate; *(interpretar mal)* to misinterpret; ~**se** *vr (persona)* to lose one's sense of proportion; *(asunto)* to get out of hand.

desorden [de'sorðen] *nm* confusion; *(de casa, cuarto)* mess; *(político)* disorder; **desórdenes** *nmpl (alborotos)* disturbances; *(excesos)* excesses; **en** ~ *(gente)* in confusion.

desordenado, a [desorðe'naðo, a] *a (habitación, persona)* untidy; *(objetos: revueltos)* in a mess, jumbled; *(conducta)* disorderly.

desordenar [desorðe'nar] *vt (gen)* to disarrange; *(pelo)* to mess up; *(cuarto)* to make a mess in; *(causar confusión a)* to throw into confusion.

desorganice [desorɣa'niθe] *etc vb* V **desorganizar.**

desorganizar [desorɣani'θar] *vt* to disorganize.

desorientar [desorjen'tar] *vt (extraviar)* to mislead; *(confundir, desconcertar)* to confuse; ~**se** *vr (perderse)* to lose one's way.

desovar [deso'ßar] *vi (peces)* to spawn; *(insectos)* to lay eggs.

desoyendo [deso'jendo] *etc vb* V **desoír.**

despabilado, a [despaßi'laðo, a] *a (despierto)* wide-awake; *(fig)* alert, sharp.

despabilar [despaßi'lar] *vt (despertar)* to wake up; *(fig: persona)* to liven up; *(trabajo)* to get through quickly ♦ *vi*, ~**se** *vr* to wake up; *(fig)* to get a move on.

despacio [des'paθjo] *ad (lentamente)* slowly; *(en voz baja)* softly; ¡~! take it easy!

despacito [despa'θito] *ad (fam)* slowly; *(suavemente)* softly.

despachar [despa'tʃar] *vt (negocio)* to do, complete; *(resolver: problema)* to settle; *(correspondencia)* to deal with; *(fam: comida)* to polish off; *(: bebida)* to knock back; *(enviar)* to send, dispatch; *(vender)* to sell, deal in; *(com: cliente)* to attend to; *(billete)* to issue; *(mandar ir)* to send away ♦ *vi (decidirse)* to get things settled; *(apresurarse)* to hurry up; ~**se** *vr* to finish off; *(apresurarse)* to hurry up; ~**se de algo** to get rid of sth; ~**se a su gusto con uno** to give sb a piece of one's mind; **¿quién despacha?** is anybody serving?

despacho [des'patʃo] *nm (oficina)* office; *(: en una casa)* study; *(de paquetes)* dispatch; *(com: venta)* sale (of goods); *(comunicación)* message; ~ **de billetes** *o* **boletos** *(AM)* booking office; ~ **de localidades** box office; **géneros sin** ~ unsaleable goods; **tener buen** ~ to find a ready sale.

despachurrar [despatʃu'rrar] *vt (aplastar)* to crush; *(persona)* to flatten.

despampanante [despampa'nante] *a (fam: chica)* stunning.

desparejado, a [despare'xaðo, a], **desparejo, a** [despa'rexo, a] *a* odd.

desparpajo [despar'paxo] *nm (desenvoltura)* self-confidence; *(pey)* nerve.

desparramar [desparra'mar] *vt (esparcir)* to scatter; *(líquido)* to spill.

despatarrar [despata'rrar] *vt (asombrar)* to amaze; ~**se** *vr (abrir las piernas)* to open one's legs wide; *(caerse)* to tumble; *(fig)* to be flabbergasted.

despavorido, a [despaßo'riðo, a] *a* terrified.

despectivo, a [despek'tißo, a] *a (despreciativo)* derogatory; *(LING)* pejorative.

despechar [despe'tʃar] *vt (provocar ira a)* to enrage; *(fam: destetar)* to wean.

despecho [des'petʃo] *nm* spite; **a** ~ **de** in spite of; **por** ~ out of (sheer) spite.

despedace [despe'ðaθe] *etc vb* V **despedazar.**

despedazar [despeða'θar] *vt* to tear to pieces.

despedida [despe'ðiða] *nf (adiós)* goodbye, farewell; *(antes de viaje)* send-off; *(en carta)* closing formula; *(de obrero)* sacking; *(INFORM)* logout; **cena/función de** ~ farewell dinner/performance; **regalo de** ~ parting gift; ~ **de soltero/soltera** stag/hen party.

despedir [despe'ðir] *vt (visita)* to see off, show out; *(empleado)* to dismiss; *(inquili-*

no) to evict; (*objeto*) to hurl; (*olor etc*) to give out *o* off; ~**se** *vr* (*dejar un empleo*) to give up one's job; (*INFORM*) to log out *o* off; ~**se de** to say goodbye to; **se despidieron** they said goodbye to each other.

despegado, a [despe'ɣaðo, a] *a* (*separado*) detached; (*persona: poco afectuoso*) cold, indifferent ♦ *nm/f*: **es un** ~ he has cut himself off from his family.

despegar [despe'ɣar] *vt* to unstick; (*sobre*) to open ♦ *vi* (*avión*) to take off; (*cohete*) to blast off; ~**se** *vr* to come loose, come unstuck; **sin** ~ **los labios** without uttering a word.

despego [des'peɣo] *nm* detachment.

despegue [des'peɣe] *etc vb* V **despegar** ♦ *nm* takeoff; (*de cohete*) blastoff.

despeinado, a [despei'naðo, a] *a* dishevelled, unkempt.

despeinar [despei'nar] *vt* (*pelo*) to ruffle; **¡me has despeinado todo!** you've completely ruined my hairdo!

despejado, a [despe'xaðo, a] *a* (*lugar*) clear, free; (*cielo*) clear; (*persona*) wideawake, bright.

despejar [despe'xar] *vt* (*gen*) to clear; (*misterio*) to clarify, clear up; (*MAT: incógnita*) to find ♦ *vi* (*el tiempo*) to clear; ~**se** *vr* (*tiempo, cielo*) to clear (up); (*misterio*) to become clearer; (*cabeza*) to clear; **¡despejen!** (*moverse*) move along!; (*salirse*) everybody out!

despeje [des'pexe] *nm* (*DEPORTE*) clearance.

despelotarse [despelo'tarse] *vr* (*fam*) to strip off; (*fig*) to let one's hair down.

despeluce [despe'luθe] *etc vb* V **despeluzar**.

despeluzar [despelu'θar] *vt* (*pelo*) to tousle; ~ **a uno** (*fig*) to horrify sb.

despellejar [despeʎe'xar] *vt* (*animal*) to skin; (*criticar*) to criticize unmercifully; (*fam: arruinar*) to fleece.

despensa [des'pensa] *nf* (*armario*) larder; (*NAUT*) storeroom; (*provisión de comestibles*) stock of food.

despeñadero [despeɲa'ðero] *nm* (*GEO*) cliff, precipice.

despeñar [despe'ɲar] *vt* (*arrojar*) to fling down; ~**se** *vr* to fling o.s. down; (*caer*) to fall headlong.

desperdiciar [desperði'θjar] *vt* (*comida, tiempo*) to waste; (*oportunidad*) to throw away.

desperdicio [desper'ðiθjo] *nm* (*despilfarro*) squandering; (*residuo*) waste; ~**s** *nmpl* (*basura*) rubbish *sg*, refuse *sg*, garbage *sg* (*US*); (*residuos*) waste *sg*; ~**s de cocina** kitchen scraps; **el libro no tiene** ~ the book is excellent from beginning to end.

desperdigar [desperði'ɣar] *vt* (*esparcir*) to

scatter; (*energía*) to dissipate; ~**se** *vr* to scatter.

desperdigue [desper'ðiɣe] *etc vb* V **desperdigar**.

desperece [despe'reθe] *etc vb* V **desperezarse**.

desperezarse [despere'θarse] *vr* to stretch.

desperfecto [desper'fekto] *nm* (*deterioro*) slight damage; (*defecto*) flaw, imperfection.

despertador [desperta'ðor] *nm* alarm clock; ~ **de viaje** travelling clock.

despertar [desper'tar] *vt* (*persona*) to wake up; (*recuerdos*) to revive; (*esperanzas*) to raise; (*sentimiento*) to arouse ♦ *vi*, ~**se** *vr* to awaken, wake up; ~**se a la realidad** to wake up to reality ♦ *nm* awakening.

despiadado, a [despja'ðaðo, a] *a* (*ataque*) merciless; (*persona*) heartless.

despido [des'piðo] *etc vb* V **despedir** ♦ *nm* dismissal, sacking; ~ **improcedente** *o* **injustificado** wrongful dismissal; ~ **injusto** unfair dismissal; ~ **voluntario** voluntary redundancy.

despierto, a [des'pjerto, a] *etc vb* V **despertar** ♦ *a* awake; (*fig*) sharp, alert.

despilfarrado, a [despilfa'rraðo, a] *a* (*malgastador*) wasteful; (*con dinero*) spendthrift ♦ *nm/f* spendthrift.

despilfarrar [despilfa'rrar] *vt* (*gen*) to waste; (*dinero*) to squander.

despilfarro [despil'farro] *nm* (*derroche*) squandering; (*lujo desmedido*) extravagance.

despintar [despin'tar] *vt* (*quitar pintura a*) to take the paint off; (*hechos*) to distort ♦ *vi*: **A no despinta a B** A is in no way inferior to B; ~**se** *vr* (*desteñir*) to fade.

despiojar [despjo'xar] *vt* to delouse.

despistado, a [despis'taðo, a] *a* (*distraído*) vague, absent-minded; (*poco práctico*) unpractical; (*confuso*) confused; (*desorientado*) off the track ♦ *nm/f* (*tipo: distraído*) scatterbrain, absent-minded person.

despistar [despis'tar] *vt* to throw off the track *o* scent; (*fig*) to mislead, confuse; ~**se** *vr* to take the wrong road; (*fig*) to become confused.

despiste [des'piste] *nm* (*AUTO etc*) swerve; (*error*) slip; (*distracción*) absent-mindedness; **tiene un terrible** ~ he's terribly absent-minded.

desplace [des'plaθe] *etc vb* V **desplazar**.

desplante [des'plante] *nm*: **hacer un** ~ **a uno** to be rude to sb.

desplazado, a [despla'θaðo, a] *a* (*pieza*) wrongly placed ♦ *nm/f* (*inadaptado*) misfit; **sentirse un poco** ~ to feel rather out of place.

desplazamiento [desplaθa'mjento] *nm* displacement; (*viaje*) journey; (*de opinión*, *votos*) shift, swing; (*INFORM*) scrolling; ~ **hacia arriba/abajo** (*INFORM*) scroll up/down.

desplazar [despla'θar] *vt* (*gen*) to move; (*FÍSICA, NAUT, TEC*) to displace; (*tropas*) to transfer; (*suplantar*) to take the place of; (*INFORM*) to scroll; ~**se** *vr* (*persona, vehículo*) to travel, go; (*objeto*) to move, shift; (*votos, opinión*) to shift, swing.

desplegar [desple'ɣar] *vt* (*tela, papel*) to unfold, open out; (*bandera*) to unfurl; (*alas*) to spread; (*MIL*) to deploy; (*manifestar*) to display.

desplegué [desple'ɣe], **despleguemos** [desple'ɣemos] *etc vb V* **desplegar**.

despliegue [des'pljeɣe] *etc vb V* **desplegar** ◆ *nm* unfolding, opening; deployment, display.

desplomarse [desplo'marse] *vr* (*edificio, gobierno, persona*) to collapse; (*derrumbarse*) to topple over; (*precios*) to slump; **se ha desplomado el techo** the ceiling has fallen in.

desplumar [desplu'mar] *vt* (*ave*) to pluck; (*fam: estafar*) to fleece.

despoblado, a [despo'βlaðo, a] *a* (*sin habitantes*) uninhabited; (*con pocos habitantes*) depopulated; (*con insuficientes habitantes*) underpopulated ◆ *nm* deserted spot.

despojar [despo'xar] *vt* (*alguien: de sus bienes*) to divest of, deprive of; (*casa*) to strip, leave bare; (*de su cargo*) to strip of; ~**se** *vr* (*desnudarse*) to undress; ~**se de** (*ropa, hojas*) to shed; (*poderes*) to relinquish.

despojo [des'poxo] *nm* (*acto*) plundering; (*objetos*) plunder, loot; ~**s** *nmpl* (*de ave, res*) offal *sg*.

desposado, a [despo'saðo, a] *a, nm/f* newly-wed.

desposar [despo'sar] *vt* (*suj: sacerdote: pareja*) to marry; ~**se** *vr* (*casarse*) to marry, get married.

desposeer [despose'er] *vt* (*despojar*) to dispossess; ~ **a uno de su autoridad** to strip sb of his authority.

desposeído, a [despose'iðo, a] *nm/f*: **los** ~**s** the have-nots.

desposeyendo [despose'jendo] *etc vb V* **desposeer**.

desposorios [despo'sorjos] *nmpl* (*esponsales*) betrothal *sg*; (*boda*) marriage ceremony *sg*.

déspota ['despota] *nm/f* despot.

despotricar [despotri'kar] *vi*: ~ **contra** to moan *o* complain about.

despotrique [despo'trike] *etc vb V* **despotricar**.

despreciable [despre'θjaβle] *a* (*moralmente*) despicable; (*objeto*) worthless; (*cantidad*) negligible.

despreciar [despre'θjar] *vt* (*desdeñar*) to despise, scorn; (*afrentar*) to slight.

despreciativo, a [despreθja'tiβo, a] *a* (*observación, tono*) scornful, contemptuous; (*comentario*) derogatory.

desprecio [des'preθjo] *nm* scorn, contempt; slight.

desprender [despren'der] *vt* (*soltar*) to loosen; (*separar*) to separate; (*desatar*) to unfasten; (*olor*) to give off; ~**se** *vr* (*botón: caerse*) to fall off; (: *abrirse*) to unfasten; (*olor, perfume*) to be given off; ~**se de** to follow from; ~**se de algo** (*ceder*) to give sth up; (*desembarazarse*) to get rid of sth; **se desprende que** it transpires that.

desprendido, a [despren'diðo, a] *a* (*pieza*) loose; (*sin abrochar*) unfastened; (*desinteresado*) disinterested; (*generoso*) generous.

desprendimiento [desprendi'mjento] *nm* (*gen*) loosening; (*generosidad*) disinterestedness; (*indiferencia*) detachment; (*de gas*) leak; (*de tierra, rocas*) landslide.

despreocupado, a [despreoku'paðo, a] *a* (*sin preocupación*) unworried, unconcerned; (*tranquilo*) nonchalant; (*en el vestir*) casual; (*negligente*) careless.

despreocuparse [despreoku'parse] *vr* to be carefree; (*dejar de inquietarse*) to stop worrying; (*ser indiferente*) to be unconcerned; ~ **de** to have no interest in.

desprestigiar [despresti'xjar] *vt* (*criticar*) to run down, disparage; (*desacreditar*) to discredit.

desprestigio [despres'tixjo] *nm* (*denigración*) disparagement; (*impopularidad*) unpopularity.

desprevenido, a [despreβe'niðo, a] *a* (*no preparado*) unprepared, unready; **coger** (*Sp*) *o* **agarrar** (*AM*) **a uno** ~ to catch sb unawares.

desproporción [despropor'θjon] *nf* disproportion, lack of proportion.

desproporcionado, a [desproporθjo'naðo, a] *a* disproportionate, out of proportion.

despropósito [despro'posito] *nm* (*salida de tono*) irrelevant remark; (*disparate*) piece of nonsense.

desprovisto, a [despro'βisto, a] *a*: ~ **de** devoid of; **estar** ~ **de** to lack.

después [des'pwes] *ad* afterwards, later; (*desde entonces*) since (then); (*próximo paso*) next; **poco** ~ soon after; **un año** ~ a year later; ~ **se debatió el tema** next the matter was discussed ◆ *prep*: ~ **de** (*tiempo*) after, since; (*orden*) next (to); ~ **de comer** after lunch; ~ **de corregido el texto** after the text had been corrected; ~ **de esa fecha** (*pasado*) since that date; (*futuro*) from *o* after that date; ~ **de todo** after all; ~ **de verlo** after seeing it, after I *etc* saw it; **mi nombre está** ~ **del tuyo** my name comes next to yours ◆ *conj:* ~ **(de) que** after; ~ **(de) que lo escribí** after *o* since I wrote it, after writing it.

despuntar [despun'tar] *vt (lápiz)* to blunt ◆ *vi (BOT: plantas)* to sprout; (: *flores*) to bud; (*alba*) to break; (*día*) to dawn; (*persona: descollar*) to stand out.

desquiciar [deski'θjar] *vt (puerta)* to take off its hinges; (*descomponer*) to upset; (*persona: turbar*) to disturb; (: *volver loco a*) to unhinge.

desquitarse [deski'tarse] *vr* to obtain satisfaction; (*COM*) to recover a debt; (*fig: vengarse de*) to get one's own back; ~ **de una pérdida** to make up for a loss.

desquite [des'kite] *nm (satisfacción)* satisfaction; (*venganza*) revenge.

Dest. *abr* = **destinatario.**

destacado, a [desta'kaðo, a] *a* outstanding.

destacamento [destaka'mento] *nm (MIL)* detachment.

destacar [desta'kar] *vt (ARTE: hacer resaltar)* to make stand out; (*subrayar*) to emphasize, point up; (*MIL*) to detach, detail; (*INFORM*) to highlight ◆ *vi,* ~**se** *vr (resaltarse)* to stand out; (*persona*) to be outstanding *o* exceptional; **quiero** ~ **que...** I wish to emphasize that...; ~**(se) contra** *o* **en** *o* **sobre** to stand out *o* be outlined against.

destajo [des'taxo] *nm:* **a** ~ (*por pieza*) by the job; (*con afán*) eagerly; **trabajar a** ~ to do piecework; (*fig*) to work one's fingers to the bone.

destapar [desta'par] *vt (botella)* to open; (*cacerola*) to take the lid off; (*descubrir*) to uncover; ~**se** *vr (descubrirse)* to get uncovered; (*revelarse*) to reveal one's true character.

destape [des'tape] *nm* nudity; (*fig*) permissiveness; **el** ~ **español** *the process of liberalization in Spain after Franco's death.*

destaque [des'take] *etc vb V* **destacar.**

destartalado, a [destarta'laðo, a] *a (desordenado)* untidy; (*casa etc: grande*) rambling; (: *ruinoso*) tumbledown.

destellar [deste'ʎar] *vi (diamante)* to sparkle; (*metal*) to glint; (*estrella*) to twinkle.

destello [des'teʎo] *nm (de diamante)* sparkle; (*de metal*) glint; (*de estrella*) twinkle; (*de faro*) signal light; **no tiene un** ~ **de verdad** there's not a grain of truth in it.

destemplado, a [destem'plaðo, a] *a (MUS)* out of tune; (*voz*) harsh; (*MED*) out of sorts; (*METEOROLOGÍA*) unpleasant, nasty.

destemplar [destem'plar] *vt (MUS)* to put out of tune; (*alterar*) to upset; ~**se** *vr (MUS)* to lose its pitch; (*descomponerse*) to

get out of order; (*persona: irritarse*) to get upset; (*MED*) to get out of sorts.

desteñir [deste'ɲir] *vt* to fade ◆ *vi,* ~**se** *vr* to fade; **esta tela no destiñe** this fabric will not run.

desternillarse [desterni'ʎarse] *vr:* ~ **de risa** to split one's sides laughing.

desterrado, a [deste'rraðo, a] *nm/f (exiliado)* exile.

desterrar [deste'rrar] *vt (exilar)* to exile; (*fig*) to banish, dismiss.

destetar [deste'tar] *vt* to wean.

destiempo [des'tjempo]: **a** ~ *ad* at the wrong time.

destierro [des'tjerro] *etc vb V* **desterrar** ◆ *nm* exile; **vivir en el** ~ to live in exile.

destilar [desti'lar] *vt* to distil; (*pus, sangre*) to ooze; (*fig: rebosar*) to exude; (: *revelar*) to reveal ◆ *vi (gotear)* to drip.

destilería [destile'ria] *nf* distillery; ~ **de petróleo** oil refinery.

destinar [desti'nar] *vt (funcionario)* to appoint, assign; (*fondos*) to set aside; **es un libro destinado a los niños** it is a book (intended *o* meant) for children; **una carta que viene destinada a usted** a letter for you, a letter addressed to you.

destinatario, a [destina'tarjo, a] *nm/f* addressee; (*COM*) payee.

destino [des'tino] *nm (suerte)* destiny; (*de viajero*) destination; (*función*) use; (*puesto*) post, placement; ~ **público** public appointment; **salir con** ~ **a** to leave for; **con** ~ **a Londres** (*avión, barco*) (bound) for London; (*carta*) to London.

destiña [des'tiɲa] *etc,* **destiñendo** [desti'ɲendo] *etc vb V* **desteñir.**

destitución [destitu'θjon] *nf* dismissal, removal.

destituir [destitu'ir] *vt (despedir)* to dismiss; (: *ministro, funcionario*) to remove from office.

destituyendo [destitu'jendo] *etc vb V* **destituir.**

destornillador [destorniʎa'ðor] *nm* screwdriver.

destornillar [destorni'ʎar] *vt,* ~**se** *vr (tornillo)* to unscrew.

destrabar [destra'βar] *vt* to untie, unfetter.

destreza [des'treθa] *nf (habilidad)* skill; (*maña*) dexterity.

destripar [destri'par] *vt (animal)* to gut; (*reventar*) to mangle.

destronar [destro'nar] *vt (rey)* to dethrone; (*fig*) to overthrow.

destroncar [destron'kar] *vt (árbol)* to chop off, lop; (*proyectos*) to ruin; (*discurso*) to interrupt.

destronque [des'tronke] *etc vb V* **destroncar.**

destroce [de'stroθe] *etc vb V* **destrozar.**

destrozar [destro'θar] *vt* (*romper*) to smash, break (up); (*estropear*) to ruin; (*nervios*) to shatter; ~ **a uno en una discusión** to crush sb in an argument.

destrozo [des'troθo] *nm* (*acción*) destruction; (*desastre*) smashing; ~**s** *nmpl* (*pedazos*) pieces; (*daños*) havoc *sg*.

destrucción [destruk'θjon] *nf* destruction.

destructor, a [destruk'tor, a] *a* destructive ♦ *nm* (*NAUT*) destroyer.

destruir [destru'ir] *vt* to destroy; (*casa*) to demolish; (*equilibrio*) to upset; (*proyecto*) to spoil; (*esperanzas*) to dash; (*argumento*) to demolish.

destruyendo [destru'jendo] *etc vb V* **destruir.**

desuelle [de'sweʎe] *etc vb V* **desollar.**

desueve [de'sweße] *etc vb V* **desovar.**

desunión [desu'njon] *nf* (*separación*) separation; (*discordia*) disunity.

desunir [desu'nir] *vt* to separate; (*TEC*) to disconnect; (*fig*) to cause a quarrel *o* rift between.

desuso [de'suso] *nm* disuse; **caer en** ~ to fall into disuse, become obsolete; **una expresión caída en** ~ an obsolete expression.

desvaído, a [desßa'iðo, a] *a* (*color*) pale; (*contorno*) blurred.

desvalido, a [desßa'liðo, a] *a* (*desprotegido*) destitute; (*sin fuerzas*) helpless; **niños** ~**s** waifs and strays.

desvalijar [desßali'xar] *vt* (*persona*) to rob; (*casa, tienda*) to burgle; (*coche*) to break into.

desvalorice [desßalo'riθe] *etc vb V* **desvalorizar.**

desvalorizar [desßalori'θar] *vt* to devalue.

desván [des'ßan] *nm* attic.

desvanecer [desßane'θer] *vt* (*disipar*) to dispel; (*recuerdo, temor*) to banish; (*borrar*) to blur; ~**se** *vr* (*humo etc*) to vanish, disappear; (*duda*) to be dispelled; (*color*) to fade; (*recuerdo, sonido*) to fade away; (*MED*) to pass out.

desvanecido, a [desßane'θiðo, a] *a* (*MED*) faint; **caer** ~ to fall in a faint.

desvanecimiento [desßaneθi'mjento] *nm* (*desaparición*) disappearance; (*de dudas*) dispelling; (*de colores*) fading; (*evaporación*) evaporation; (*MED*) fainting fit.

desvanezca [desßa'neθka] *etc vb V* **desvanecer.**

desvariar [desßa'rjar] *vi* (*enfermo*) to be delirious; (*delirar*) to talk nonsense.

desvarío [desßa'rio] *nm* delirium; (*desatino*) absurdity; ~**s** *nmpl* ravings.

desvelar [desße'lar] *vt* to keep awake; ~**se** *vr* (*no poder dormir*) to stay awake; (*vigilar*) to be vigilant *o* watchful; ~**se por algo** (*inquietarse*) to be anxious about sth; (*poner gran cuidado*) to take great care

over sth.

desvelo [des'ßelo] *nm* lack of sleep; (*insomnio*) sleeplessness; (*fig*) vigilance; ~**s** *nmpl* (*preocupación*) anxiety *sg*, effort *sg*.

desvencijado, a [desßenθi'xaðo, a] *a* (*silla*) rickety; (*máquina*) broken-down.

desvencijar [desßenθi'xar] *vt* (*romper*) to break; (*soltar*) to loosen; (*persona: agotar*) to exhaust; ~**se** *vr* to come apart.

desventaja [desßen'taxa] *nf* disadvantage; (*inconveniente*) drawback.

desventajoso, a [desßenta'xoso, a] *a* disadvantageous, unfavourable.

desventura [desßen'tura] *nf* misfortune.

desventurado, a [desßenturaðo, a] *a* (*desgraciado*) unfortunate; (*de poca suerte*) ill-fated.

desvergonzado, a [desßerɣon'θaðo, a] *a* (*sin vergüenza*) shameless; (*descarado*) insolent ♦ *nm/f* shameless person.

desvergüenza [desßer'ɣwenθa] *nf* (*descaro*) shamelessness; (*insolencia*) impudence; (*mala conducta*) effrontery; **esto es una** ~ this is disgraceful; **¡qué** ~**!** what a nerve!

desvestir [desßes'tir] *vt*, **desvestirse** *vr* to undress.

desviación [desßja'θjon] *nf* deviation; (*AUTO*: *rodeo*) diversion, detour; (: *carretera de circunvalación*) ring road (*Brit*), circular route (*US*); ~ **de la circulación** traffic diversion; **es una** ~ **de sus principios** it is a departure from his usual principles.

desviar [des'ßjar] *vt* to turn aside; (*balón, flecha, golpe*) to deflect; (*pregunta*) to parry; (*ojos*) to avert, turn away; (*río*) to alter the course of; (*navío*) to divert, reroute; (*conversación*) to sidetrack; ~**se** *vr* (*apartarse del camino*) to turn aside; (: *barco*) to go off course; (*AUTO*: *dar un rodeo*) to make a detour; ~**se de un tema** to get away from the point.

desvincular [desßinku'lar] *vt* to free, release; ~**se** *vr* (*aislarse*) to be cut off; (*alejarse*) to cut o.s. off.

desvío [des'ßio] *etc vb V* **desviar** ♦ *nm* (*desviación*) detour, diversion; (*fig*) indifference.

desvirtuar [desßir'twar] *vt* (*estropear*) to spoil; (*argumento, razonamiento*) to detract from; (*efecto*) to counteract; (*sentido*) to distort; ~**se** *vr* to spoil.

desvistiendo [desßis'tjendo] *etc vb V* **desvestir.**

desvivirse [desßi'ßirse] *vr*: ~ **por** to long for, crave for; ~ **por los amigos** to do anything for one's friends.

detalladamente [detaʎaða'mente] *ad* (*con detalles*) in detail; (*extensamente*) at great length.

detallar [deta'ʎar] vt to detail; (asunto por asunto) to itemize.

detalle [de'taʎe] nm detail; (fig) gesture, token; **al** ~ in detail; (COM) retail cpd; **comercio al** ~ retail trade; **vender al** ~ to sell retail; **no pierde** ~ he doesn't miss a trick; **me observaba sin perder** ~ he watched my every move; **tiene muchos** ~s she is very considerate.

detallista [deta'ʎista] nm/f retailer ◆ a (meticuloso) meticulous; **comercio** ~ retail trade.

detectar [detek'tar] vt to detect.

detector [detek'tor] nm (NAUT, TEC etc) detector; ~ **de mentiras/de minas** lie/mine detector.

detención [deten'θjon] nf (acción) stopping; (estancamiento) stoppage; (retraso) holdup, delay; (JUR: arresto) arrest; (cuidado) care; ~ **de juego** (DEPORTE) stoppage of play; ~ **ilegal** unlawful detention.

detendré [deten'dre] etc vb V **detener**.

detener [dete'ner] vt (gen) to stop; (JUR: arrestar) to arrest; (: encarcelar) to detain; (objeto) to keep; (retrasar) to hold up, delay; (aliento) to hold; ~**se** vr to stop; ~**se en** (demorarse) to delay over, linger over.

detenga [de'tenga] etc vb V **detener**.

detenidamente [deteniða'mente] ad (minuciosamente) carefully; (extensamente) at great length.

detenido, a [dete'niðo, a] a (arrestado) under arrest; (minucioso) detailed; (examen) thorough; (tímido) timid ◆ nm/f person under arrest, prisoner.

detenimiento [deteni'mjento] nm care; **con** ~ thoroughly.

detentar [deten'tar] vt to hold; (sin derecho: título) to hold unlawfully; (: puesto) to occupy unlawfully.

detergente [deter'xente] a, nm detergent.

deteriorado, a [deterjo'raðo, a] a (estropeado) damaged; (desgastado) worn.

deteriorar [deterjo'rar] vt to spoil, damage; ~**se** vr to deteriorate.

deterioro [dete'rjoro] nm deterioration.

determinación [determina'θjon] nf (empeño) determination; (decisión) decision; (de fecha, precio) settling, fixing.

determinado, a [determi'naðo, a] a (preciso) fixed, set; (LING: artículo) definite; (persona: resuelto) determined; **un día** ~ on a certain day; **no hay ningún tema** ~ there is no particular theme.

determinar [determi'nar] vt (plazo) to fix; (precio) to settle; (daños, impuestos) to assess; (pleito) to decide; (causar) to cause; ~**se** vr to decide; **el reglamento determina que...** the rule lays it down o

states that...; **aquello determinó la caída del gobierno** that brought about the fall of the government; **esto le determinó** this decided him.

detestable [detes'taβle] a (persona) hateful; (acto) detestable.

detestar [detes'tar] vt to detest.

detonar [deto'nar] vi to detonate.

detracción [detrak'θjon] nf (denigración) disparagement.

detractor, a [detrak'tor, a] a disparaging ◆ nm/f detractor.

detrás [de'tras] ad behind; (atrás) at the back ◆ prep: ~ **de** behind; **por** ~ **de uno** (fig) behind sb's back; **salir de** ~ to come out from behind; **por** ~ behind.

detrimento [detri'mento] nm: **en** ~ **de** to the detriment of.

detuve [de'tuβe] etc vb V **detener**.

deuda [de'uða] nf (condición) indebtedness, debt; (cantidad) debt; ~ **a largo plazo** long-term debt; ~ **exterior/pública** foreign/national debt; ~ **incobrable** o **morosa** bad debt; ~s **activas/pasivas** assets/liabilities; **contraer** ~s to get into debt.

deudor, a [deu'ðor, a] nm/f debtor; ~ **hipotecario** mortgager; ~ **moroso** slow payer.

devaluación [deβalwa'θjon] nf devaluation.

devaluar [deβalu'ar] vt to devalue.

devanador [deβana'ðor] nm (carrete) spool, bobbin.

devanar [deβa'nar] vt (hilo) to wind; ~**se** vr: ~**se los sesos** to rack one's brains.

devaneo [deβa'neo] nm (MED) delirium; (desatino) nonsense; (fruslería) idle pursuit; (amorío) flirtation.

devastar [deβas'tar] vt (destruir) to devastate.

devendré [deβen'dre] etc, **devenga** [de'βenga] etc vb V **devenir**.

devengar [deβen'gar] vt (salario: ganar) to earn; (: tener que cobrar) to be due; (intereses) to bring in, accrue, earn.

devengue [de'βenge] etc vb V **devengar**.

devenir [deβe'nir] vi: ~ **en** to become, turn into ◆ nm (movimiento progresivo) process of development; (transformación) transformation.

deviene [de'βjene] etc, **deviniendo** [deβi'njendo] etc vb V **devenir**.

devoción [deβo'θjon] nf devotion; (afición) strong attachment.

devolución [deβolu'θjon] nf (reenvío) return, sending back; (reembolso) repayment; (JUR) devolution.

devolver [deβol'βer] vt (lo extraviado, prestado) to give back; (a su sitio) to put back; (carta al correo) to send back; (COM) to repay, refund; (visita, la palabra) to return; (salud, vista) to restore; (fam:

vomitar) to throw up ◆ *vi* (*fam*) to be sick; ~ **mal por bien** to return ill for good; ~ **la pelota a uno** to give sb tit for tat.

devorar [deβo'rar] *vt* to devour; (*comer ávidamente*) to gobble up; (*fig: fortuna*) to run through; **todo lo devoró el fuego** the fire consumed everything; **le devoran los celos** he is consumed with jealousy.

devoto, a [de'ßoto, a] *a* (*REL: persona*) devout; (: *obra*) devotional; (*amigo*): ~ **(de uno)** devoted (to sb) ◆ *nm/f* admirer; **los ~s** (*REL*) the faithful; **su muy ~** your devoted servant.

devuelto [de'ßwelto], **devuelva** [de'ßwelßa] *etc vb V* **devolver**.

D.F. *abr* (*México*) = *Distrito Federal*.

dg. *abr* (= *decigramo*) dg.

D.G. *abr* = *Dirección General*; (= *Director General*) D.G.

DGS *nf abr* = *Dirección General de Seguridad*; = *Dirección General de Sanidad*.

DGT *nf abr* = *Dirección General de Tráfico*; = *Dirección General de Turismo*.

di [di] *vb V* **dar**; **decir**.

día ['dia] *nm* day; ~ **de asueto** day off; ~ **festivo** holiday; ~ **hábil/inhábil** working/non-working day; ~ **de inocentes** (*28 December*) ≈ All Fools' Day; ~ **lectivo** teaching day; ~ **libre** day off; **D~ de Reyes** Epiphany (*6 January*); **¿qué ~ es?** what's the date?; **estar/poner al** ~ to be/keep up to date; **el** ~ **de hoy/de mañana** today/tomorrow; **el** ~ **menos pensado** when you least expect it; **al** ~ **siguiente** on the following day; **todos los ~s** every day; **un** ~ **sí y otro no** every other day; **vivir al** ~ to live from hand to mouth; **de** ~ by day, in daylight; **del** ~ (*estilos*) fashionable; (*menú*) today's; **de un** ~ **para otro** any day now; **en pleno** ~ in full daylight; **en su** ~ in due time; **¡hasta otro ~!** so long!

diablo ['djaßlo] *nm* (*tb fig*) devil; **pobre** ~ poor devil; **hace un frío de todos los ~s** it's hellishly cold.

diablura [dja'ßlura] *nf* prank; (*travesura*) mischief.

diabólico, a [dja'ßoliko, a] *a* diabolical.

diáfano, a ['djafano, a] *a* (*tela*) diaphanous; (*agua*) crystal-clear.

diafragma [dja'fraɣma] *nm* diaphragm.

diagnosis [djaɣ'nosis] *nf inv*, **diagnóstico** [djaɣ'nostiko] *nm* diagnosis.

diagrama [dja'ɣrama] *nm* diagram; ~ **de barras** (*COM*) bar chart; ~ **de dispersión** (*COM*) scatter diagram; ~ **de flujo** (*INFORM*) flowchart.

dialecto [dja'lekto] *nm* dialect.

dialogar [djalo'ɣar] *vt* to write in dialogue form ◆ *vi* (*conversar*) to have a conversation; ~ **con** (*POL*) to hold talks with.

diálogo ['djaloɣo] *nm* dialogue.

dialogue [dja'loɣe] *etc vb V* **dialogar**.

diamante [dja'mante] *nm* diamond.

diametralmente [djametral'mentre] *ad* diametrically; ~ **opuesto a** diametrically opposed to.

diámetro [di'ametro] *nm* diameter; ~ **de giro** (*AUTO*) turning circle; **faros de gran** ~ wide-angle headlights.

diana ['djana] *nf* (*MIL*) reveille; (*de blanco*) centre, bull's-eye.

diantre ['djantre] *nm*: **¡~!** (*fam*) oh hell!

diapasón ['djapa'son] *nm* (*instrumento*) tuning fork; (*de violín etc*) fingerboard; (*de voz*) tone.

diapositiva [djaposi'tißa] *nf* (*FOTO*) slide, transparency.

diario, a ['djarjo, a] *a* daily ◆ *nm* newspaper; (*libro diario*) diary; (: *COM*) daybook; (*COM: gastos*) daily expenses; ~ **de navegación** (*NAUT*) logbook; ~ **hablado** (*RADIO*) news (bulletin); ~ **de sesiones** parliamentary report; **a** ~ daily; **de** *o* **para** ~ everyday.

diarrea [dja'rrea] *nf* diarrhoea.

diatriba [dja'trißa] *nf* diatribe, tirade.

dibujante [dißu'xante] *nm/f* (*de bosquejos*) sketcher; (*de dibujos animados*) cartoonist; (*de moda*) designer; ~ **de publicidad** commercial artist.

dibujar [dißu'xar] *vt* to draw, sketch; ~**se** *vr* (*emoción*) to show; ~**se contra** to be outlined against.

dibujo [di'ßuxo] *nm* drawing; (*TEC*) design; (*en papel, tela*) pattern; (*en periódico*) cartoon; (*fig*) description; ~**s animados** cartoons; ~ **del natural** drawing from life.

dic., dic.⁰ *abr* (= *diciembre*) Dec.

diccionario [dikθjo'narjo] *nm* dictionary.

diciembre [di'θjembre] *nm* December.

diciendo [di'θjendo] *etc vb V* **decir**.

dictado [dik'taðo] *nm* dictation; **escribir al** ~ to take dictation; **los ~s de la conciencia** (*fig*) the dictates of conscience.

dictador [dikta'ðor] *nm* dictator.

dictadura [dikta'ðura] *nf* dictatorship.

dictáfono ® [dik'tafono] *nm* Dictaphone ®.

dictamen [dik'tamen] *nm* (*opinión*) opinion; (*informe*) report; ~ **contable** auditor's report; ~ **facultativo** (*MED*) medical report.

dictar [dik'tar] *vt* (*carta*) to dictate; (*JUR: sentencia*) to pass; (*decreto*) to issue; (*AM: clase*) to give; (: *conferencia*) to deliver.

dicharachero, a [ditʃara'tʃero, a] *a* talkative ◆ *nm/f* (*ingenioso*) wit; (*parlanchín*) chatterbox.

dicho, a ['ditʃo, a] *pp de* **decir** ◆ *a* (*susodicho*) aforementioned ◆ *nm* saying; (*proverbio*) proverb; (*ocurrencia*) bright remark ◆ *nf* (*buena suerte*) good luck; **mejor** ~ rather; ~ **y hecho** no sooner said than done.

dichoso, a [di'tʃoso, a] *a* (*feliz*) happy; (*afortunado*) lucky; ¡aquel ~ coche! (*fam*) that blessed car!

diecinueve [djeθinu'eβe] *num* nineteen; (*fecha*) nineteenth; *V tb* **seis.**

dieciochesco, a [djeθio'tʃesko, a] *a* eighteenth-century.

dieciocho [djeθi'otʃo] *num* eighteen; (*fecha*) eighteenth; *V tb* **seis.**

dieciséis [djeθi'seis] *num* sixteen; (*fecha*) sixteenth; *V tb* **seis.**

diecisiete [djeθi'sjete] *num* seventeen; (*fecha*) seventeenth; *V tb* **seis.**

diente ['djente] *nm* (ANAT, TEC) tooth; (ZOOL) fang; (: *de elefante*) tusk; (*de ajo*) clove; ~ de león dandelion; ~s postizos false teeth; enseñar los ~s (*fig*) to show one's claws; hablar entre ~s to mutter, mumble; hincar el ~ en (*comida*) to bite into.

diera ['djera] *etc vb V* **dar.**

diéresis [di'eresis] *nf* diaeresis.

dieron ['djeron] *vb V* **dar.**

diesel ['disel] *a*: motor ~ diesel engine.

diestro, a ['djestro, a] *a* (*derecho*) right; (*hábil*) skilful; (: *con las manos*) handy ♦ *nm* (TAUR) matador ♦ *nf* right hand; a ~ y siniestro (*sin método*) wildly.

dieta ['djeta] *nf* diet; ~s *nfpl* expenses; estar a ~ to be on a diet.

dietético, a [dje'tetiko, a] *a* dietetic ♦ *nm/f* dietician.

diez [djeθ] *num* ten; (*fecha*) tenth; hacer las ~ de últimas (NAIPES) to sweep the board; *V tb* **seis.**

difamación [difama'θjon] *nf* slander; libel.

difamar [difa'mar] *vt* (JUR: *hablando*) to slander; (: *por escrito*) to libel.

difamatorio, a [difama'torjo, a] *a* slanderous; libellous.

diferencia [dife'renθja] *nf* difference; a ~ de unlike; hacer ~ entre to make a distinction between; ~ salarial (COM) wage differential.

diferencial [diferen'θjal] *nm* (AUTO) differential.

diferenciar [diferen'θjar] *vt* to differentiate between ♦ *vi* to differ; ~se *vr* to differ, be different; (*distinguirse*) to distinguish o.s.

diferente [dife'rente] *a* different.

diferido [dife'riðo] *nm*: en ~ (TV *etc*) recorded.

diferir [dife'rir] *vt* to defer.

difícil [di'fiθil] *a* difficult; (*tiempos, vida*) hard; (*situación*) delicate; es un hombre ~ he's a difficult man to get on with.

difícilmente [di'fiθilmente] *ad* (*con dificultad*) with difficulty; (*apenas*) hardly.

dificultad [difikul'tað] *nf* difficulty; (*problema*) trouble; (*objeción*) objection.

dificultar [difikul'tar] *vt* (*complicar*) to complicate, make difficult; (*estorbar*) to obstruct; las restricciones dificultan el comercio the restrictions hinder trade.

dificultoso, a [difikul'toso, a] *a* (*difícil*) difficult, hard; (*fam: cara*) odd, ugly; (*persona: exigente*) fussy.

difiera [di'fjera] *etc*, **difiriendo** [difi'rjendo] *etc vb V* **diferir.**

difuminar [difumi'nar] *vt* to blur.

difundir [difun'dir] *vt* (*calor, luz*) to diffuse; (RADIO) to broadcast; ~se *vr* to spread (out); ~ una noticia to spread a piece of news.

difunto, a [di'funto, a] *a* dead, deceased ♦ *nm/f*: el ~ the deceased.

difusión [difu'sjon] *nf* (*de calor, luz*) diffusion; (*de noticia, teoría*) dissemination; (*de programa*) broadcasting; (*programa*) broadcast.

difuso, a [di'fuso, a] *a* (*luz*) diffused; (*conocimientos*) widespread; (*estilo, explicación*) wordy.

diga ['diɣa] *etc vb V* **decir.**

digerir [dixe'rir] *vt* to digest; (*fig*) to absorb; (*reflexionar sobre*) to think over.

digiera [di'xjera] *etc*, **digiriendo** [dixi'rjenðo] *etc vb V* **digerir.**

digital [dixi'tal] *a* (INFORM) digital; (*dactilar*) finger *cpd* ♦ *nf* (BOT) foxglove; (*droga*) digitalis.

digitalizador [dixitaliθa'ðor] *nm* (INFORM) digitizer.

dignarse [diɣ'narse] *vr* to deign to.

dignidad [diɣni'ðað] *nf* dignity; (*honra*) honour; (*rango*) rank; (*persona*) dignitary; herir la ~ de uno to hurt sb's pride.

dignificar [diɣnifi'kar] *vt* to dignify.

dignifique [diɣni'fike] *etc vb V* **dignificar.**

digno, a ['diɣno, a] *a* worthy; (*persona: honesto*) honourable; ~ de elogio praiseworthy; ~ de mención worth mentioning; es ~ de verse it is worth seeing; poco ~ unworthy.

digresión [diɣre'sjon] *nf* digression.

dije ['dixe] *etc*, **dijera** [di'xera] *etc vb V* **decir.**

dilación [dila'θjon] *nf* delay; sin ~ without delay, immediately.

dilapidar [dilapi'ðar] *vt* to squander, waste.

dilatación [dilata'θjon] *nf* (*expansión*) dilation.

dilatado, a [dila'taðo, a] *a* dilated; (*período*) long drawn-out; (*extenso*) extensive.

dilatar [dila'tar] *vt* (*gen*) to dilate; (*prolongar*) to prolong; (*aplazar*) to delay; ~se *vr* (*pupila etc*) to dilate; (*agua*) to expand.

dilema [di'lema] *nm* dilemma.

diligencia [dili'xenθja] *nf* diligence; (*rapidez*) speed; (*ocupación*) errand, job;

(*carruaje*) stagecoach; **~s** *nfpl* (*JUR*) formalities; **~s judiciales** judicial proceedings; **~s previas** inquest *sg*.

diligente [dili'xente] *a* diligent; **poco ~** slack.

dilucidar [diluθi'ðar] *vt* (*aclarar*) to elucidate, clarify; (*misterio*) to clear up.

diluir [dilu'ir] *vt* to dilute; (*aguar*, *fig*) to water down.

diluviar [dilu'βjar] *vi* to pour with rain.

diluvio [di'luβjo] *nm* deluge, flood; **un ~ de cartas** (*fig*) a flood of letters.

diluyendo [dilu'jendo] *etc vb* V **diluir**.

dimanar [dima'nar] *vi*: **~ de** to arise *o* spring from.

dimensión [dimen'sjon] *nf* dimension; **dimensiones** *nfpl* size *sg*; **tomar las dimensiones de** to take the measurements of.

dimes ['dimes] *nmpl*: **andar en ~ y diretes con uno** to bicker *o* squabble with sb.

diminuto, a [dimi'nuto, a] *a* tiny, diminutive.

dimisión [dimi'sjon] *nf* resignation.

dimitir [dimi'tir] *vt* (*cargo*) to give up; (*despedir*) to sack ◆ *vi* to resign.

dimos ['dimos] *vb* V **dar**.

Dinamarca [dina'marka] *nf* Denmark.

dinamarqués, esa [dinamar'kes, esa] *a* Danish ◆ *nm/f* Dane ◆ *nm* (*LING*) Danish.

dinámico, a [di'namiko, a] *a* dynamic ◆ *nf* dynamics *sg*.

dinamita [dina'mita] *nf* dynamite.

dinamitar [dinami'tar] *vt* to dynamite.

dínamo ['dinamo] *nf* dynamo.

dinastía [dinas'tia] *nf* dynasty.

dinerada [dine'raða] *nf*, **dineral** [dine'ral] *nm* fortune.

dinero [di'nero] *nm* money; (**~ en circulación**) currency; **~ caro** (*COM*) dear money; **~ contante (y sonante)** hard cash; **~ de curso legal** legal tender; **~ efectivo** cash, ready cash; **es hombre de ~** he is a man of means; **andar mal de ~** to be short of money; **ganar ~ a espuertas** to make money hand over fist.

dintel [din'tel] *nm* lintel; (*umbral*) threshold.

diñar [di'ɲar] *vt* (*fam*) to give; **~la** to kick the bucket.

dio [djo] *vb* V **dar**.

Dios [djos] *nm* God; **~ mediante** God willing; **a ~ gracias** thank heaven; **a la buena de ~** any old how; **una de ~ es Cristo** an almighty row; **~ los cría y ellos se juntan** birds of a feather flock together; **como ~ manda** as is proper; **¡~ mío!** (oh,) my God!; **¡por ~!** for God's sake!; **¡válgame ~!** bless my soul!

dios [djos] *nm* god.

diosa ['djosa] *nf* goddess.

Dip. *abr* (= *Diputación*) ≈ CC.

diploma [di'ploma] *nm* diploma.

diplomacia [diplo'maθja] *nf* diplomacy; (*fig*) tact.

diplomado, a [diplo'maðo, a] *a* qualified ◆ *nm/f* holder of a diploma; (*UNIV*) graduate.

diplomático, a [diplo'matiko, a] *a* (*cuerpo*) diplomatic; (*que tiene tacto*) tactful ◆ *nm/f* diplomat.

diptongo [dip'tongo] *nm* diphthong.

diputación [diputa'θjon] *nf* deputation; **~ permanente** (*POL*) standing committee; **~ provincial** ≈ county council.

diputado, a [dipu'taðo, a] *nm/f* delegate; (*POL*) ≈ member of parliament (*Brit*), ≈ representative (*US*).

dique ['dike] *nm* dyke; (*rompeolas*) breakwater; **~ de contención** dam.

Dir. *abr* = **dirección**; (= *director*) dir.

diré [di're] *etc vb* V **decir**.

dirección [direk'θjon] *nf* direction; (*fig*: *tendencia*) trend; (*señas*, *tb INFORM*) address; (*AUTO*) steering; (*gerencia*) management; (*de periódico*) editorship; (*en escuela*) headship; (*POL*) leadership; (*junta*) board of directors; (*despacho*) director's/ manager's/headmaster's/editor's office; **~ absoluta** (*INFORM*) absolute address; **~ administrativa** office management; **~ asistida** power-assisted steering; **D~ General de Seguridad/Turismo** State Security/Tourist Office; **~ relativa** (*INFORM*) relative address; **~ única** *o* **prohibida** one-way; **tomar la ~ de una empresa** to take over the running of a company.

direccionamiento [direkθjona'mjento] *nm* (*INFORM*) addressing.

directivo, a [direc'tiβo, a] *a* (*junta*) managing; (*función*) administrative ◆ *nm* (*COM*) manager.

directo, a [di'rekto, a] *a* direct; (*línea*) straight; (*inmediato*) immediate; (*tren*) through; (*TV*) live; **en ~** (*INFORM*) on line; **transmitir en ~** to broadcast live.

director, a [direk'tor, a] *a* leading ◆ *nm/f* director; (*ESCOL*) head (teacher) (*Brit*), principal (*US*); (*gerente*) manager(ess); (*de compañía*) president; (*jefe*) head; (*PRENSA*) editor; (*de prisión*) governor; (*MUS*) conductor; **~ adjunto** assistant manager; **~ de cine** film director; **~ comercial** marketing manager; **~ ejecutivo** executive director; **~ de empresa** company director; **~ general** general manager; **~ gerente** managing director; **~ de sucursal** branch manager.

directorial [direkto'rjal] *a* (*COM*) managing, executive; **clase ~** management.

directorio [direk'torjo] *nm* (*INFORM*) directory.

directrices [direk'triθes] *nfpl* guidelines.

dirigencia [diri'xenθja] *nf* (*POL*) leadership.

dirigente [diri'xente] *a* leading ◆ *nm/f* (*POL*) leader; **los ~s del partido** the party leaders.

dirigible [diri'xiβle] *a* (*AVIAT, NAUT*) steerable ◆ *nm* airship.

dirigir [diri'xir] *vt* to direct; (*acusación*) to level; (*carta*) to address; (*obra de teatro, film*) to produce, direct; (*MUS*) to conduct; (*comercio*) to manage; (*expedición*) to lead; (*sublevación*) to head; (*periódico*) to edit; (*guiar*) to guide; **~se** *vr*: **~se a** to go towards, make one's way towards; (*hablar con*) to speak to; **~se a uno solicitando algo** to apply to sb for sth; "**diríjase a ...**" "apply to ...".

dirigismo [diri'xismo] *nm* management, control; **~ estatal** state control.

dirija [di'rixa] *etc vb* V **dirigir**.

dirimir [diri'mir] *vt* (*contrato, matrimonio*) to dissolve.

discado [dis'kaðo] *nm*: **~ automático** autodial.

discernir [disθer'nir] *vt* to discern ◆ *vi* to distinguish.

discierna [dis'θjerna] *etc vb* V **discernir**.

disciplina [disθi'plina] *nf* discipline.

disciplinar [disθipli'nar] *vt* to discipline; (*enseñar*) to school; (*MIL*) to drill; (*azotar*) to whip.

discípulo, a [dis'θipulo, a] *nm/f* disciple; (*seguidor*) follower; (*ESCOL*) pupil.

disco ['disko] *nm* disc (*Brit*), disk (*US*); (*DEPORTE*) discus; (*TELEC*) dial; (*AUTO: semáforo*) light; (*MUS*) record; (*INFORM*) disk; **~ de arranque** boot disk; **~ compacto** compact disc; **~ de densidad sencilla/doble** single/double density disk; **~ de larga duración** long-playing record (L.P.); **~ flexible** *o* **floppy** floppy disk; **~ de freno** brake disc; **~ maestro** master disk; **~ de reserva** backup disk; **~ rígido** hard disk; **~ de una cara/dos caras** single-/double-sided disk; **~ virtual** ramdisk.

discóbolo [dis'koβolo] *nm* discus thrower.

discográfico, a [disko'γrafiko, a] *a* record *cpd*; **casa discográfica** record company; **sello ~** label.

díscolo, a ['diskolo, a] *a* (*rebelde*) unruly.

disconforme [diskon'forme] *a* differing; **estar ~ (con)** to be in disagreement (with).

discordar [discor'ðar] *vi* (*MUS*) to be out of tune; (*estar en desacuerdo*) to disagree; (*colores, opiniones*) to clash.

discorde [dis'korðe] *a* (*sonido*) discordant; (*opiniones*) clashing.

discordia [dis'korðja] *nf* discord.

discoteca [disko'teka] *nf* disco(theque).

discreción [diskre'θjon] *nf* discretion; (*reserva*) prudence; **¡a ~!** (*MIL*) stand easy!; **añadir azúcar a ~** (*CULIN*) add sugar to taste; **comer a ~** to eat as much as one wishes.

discrecional [diskreθjo'nal] *a* (*facultativo*) discretionary; **parada ~** request stop.

discrepancia [diskre'panθja] *nf* (*diferencia*) discrepancy; (*desacuerdo*) disagreement.

discrepante [diskre'pante] *a* divergent; **hubo varias voces ~s** there were some dissenting voices.

discreto, a [dis'kreto, a] *a* (*diplomático*) discreet; (*sensato*) sensible; (*reservado*) quiet; (*sobrio*) sober; (*mediano*) fair, fairly good; **le daremos un plazo ~** we'll allow him a reasonable time.

discriminación [diskrimina'θjon] *nf* discrimination.

discuerde [dis'kwerðe] *etc vb* V **discordar**.

disculpa [dis'kulpa] *nf* excuse; (*pedir perdón*) apology; **pedir ~s a/por** to apologize to/for.

disculpar [diskul'par] *vt* to excuse, pardon; **~se** *vr* to excuse o.s.; to apologize.

discurrir [disku'rrir] *vt* to contrive, think up ◆ *vi* (*pensar, reflexionar*) to think, meditate; (*recorrer*) to roam, wander; (*río*) to flow; (*el tiempo*) to pass, flow by.

discurso [dis'kurso] *nm* speech; **~ de clausura** closing speech; **pronunciar un ~** to make a speech; **en el ~ del tiempo** with the passage of time.

discusión [disku'sjon] *nf* (*diálogo*) discussion; (*riña*) argument; **tener una ~** to have an argument.

discutible [disku'tiβle] *a* debatable; **de mérito ~** of dubious worth.

discutido, a [disku'tiðo, a] *a* controversial.

discutir [disku'tir] *vt* (*debatir*) to discuss; (*pelear*) to argue about; (*contradecir*) to argue against ◆ *vi* to discuss; (*disputar*) to argue; **~ de política** to argue about politics; **¡no discutas!** don't argue!

disecar [dise'kar] *vt* (*para conservar: animal*) to stuff; (: *planta*) to dry.

diseminar [disemi'nar] *vt* to disseminate, spread.

disentir [disen'tir] *vi* to dissent, disagree.

diseño [di'seɲo] *nm* (*TEC*) design; (*ARTE*) drawing; (*COSTURA*) pattern; **de ~ italiano** Italian-designed; **~ asistido por ordenador** computer-assisted design, CAD.

diseque [di'seke] *etc vb* V **disecar**.

disertar [diser'tar] *vi* to speak.

disfrace [dis'fraθe] *etc vb* V **disfrazar**.

disfraz [dis'fraθ] *nm* (*máscara*) disguise; (*traje*) fancy dress; (*excusa*) pretext; **bajo el ~ de** under the cloak of.

disfrazado, a [disfra'θaðo, a] *a* disguised; **ir ~ de** to masquerade as.

disfrazar [disfra'θar] *vt* to disguise; **~se** *vr* to dress (o.s.) up; **~se de** to disguise o.s. as.

disfrutar [disfru'tar] *vt* to enjoy ♦ *vi* to enjoy o.s.; **¡que disfrutes!** have a good time; ~ **de** to enjoy, possess; ~ **de buena salud** to enjoy good health.

disfrute [dis'frute] *nm* (*goce*) enjoyment; (*aprovechamiento*) use.

disgregar [disɣre'ɣar] *vt* (*desintegrar*) to disintegrate; (*manifestantes*) to disperse; ~**se** *vr* to disintegrate, break up.

disgregue [dis'ɣreɣe] *etc vb* V **disgregar**.

disgustar [disɣus'tar] *vt* (*no gustar*) to displease; (*contrariar, enojar*) to annoy; to upset; ~**se** *vr* to be annoyed; (*dos personas*) to fall out; **estaba muy disgustado con el asunto** he was very upset about the affair.

disgusto [dis'ɣusto] *nm* (*repugnancia*) disgust; (*contrariedad*) annoyance; (*desagrado*) displeasure; (*tristeza*) grief; (*riña*) quarrel; (*avería*) misfortune; **hacer algo a** ~ to do sth unwillingly; **matar a uno a** ~**s** to drive sb to distraction.

disidente [disi'ðente] *nm* dissident.

disienta [di'sjenta] *etc vb* V **disentir**.

disimulado, a [disimu'laðo, a] *a* (*solapado*) furtive, underhand; (*oculto*) covert; **hacerse el** ~ to pretend not to notice.

disimular [disimu'lar] *vt* (*ocultar*) to hide, conceal ♦ *vi* to dissemble.

disimulo [disi'mulo] *nm* (*fingimiento*) dissimulation; **con** ~ cunningly.

disipar [disi'par] *vt* (*duda, temor*) to dispel; (*esperanza*) to destroy; (*fortuna*) to squander; ~**se** *vr* (*nubes*) to vanish; (*dudas*) to be dispelled; (*indisciplinarse*) to dissipate.

diskette [dis'ket] *nm* (*INFORM*) diskette, floppy disk.

dislate [dis'late] *nm* (*absurdo*) absurdity; ~**s** *nmpl* nonsense *sg*.

dislocar [dislo'kar] *vt* (*gen*) to dislocate; (*tobillo*) to sprain.

disloque [dis'loke] *etc vb* V **dislocar** ♦ *nm*: **es el** ~ (*fam*) it's the last straw.

disminución [disminu'θjon] *nf* diminution.

disminuir [disminu'ir] *vt* to decrease, diminish; (*estrechar*) to lessen; (*temperatura*) to lower; (*gastos, raciones*) to cut down; (*dolor*) to relieve; (*autoridad, prestigio*) to weaken; (*entusiasmo*) to damp ♦ *vi* (*días*) to grow shorter; (*precios, temperatura*) to drop, fall; (*velocidad*) to slacken; (*población*) to decrease; (*beneficios, número*) to fall off; (*memoria, vista*) to fail.

disminuyendo [disminu'jendo] *etc vb* V **disminuir**.

disociar [diso'θjar] *vt* to disassociate; ~**se** *vr* to disassociate o.s.

disoluble [diso'lußle] *a* soluble.

disolución [disolu'θjon] *nf* (*acto*) dissolution; (*QUÍMICA*) solution; (*COM*) liquidation;

(*moral*) dissoluteness.

disoluto, a [diso'luto, a] *a* dissolute.

disolver [disol'ßer] *vt* (*gen*) to dissolve; (*manifestación*) to break up; ~**se** *vr* to dissolve; (*COM*) to go into liquidation.

disonar [diso'nar] *vi* (*MUS*) to be out of tune; ~ **con** (*fig*) to be out of keeping with.

dispar [dis'par] *a* (*distinto*) different; (*irregular*) uneven.

disparado, a [dispa'raðo, a] *a*: **entrar** ~ to shoot in; **salir** ~ to shoot out; **ir** ~ to go like mad.

disparador [dispara'ðor] *nm* (*de arma*) trigger; (*FOTO, TEC*) release; ~ **atómico** aerosol; ~ **de bombas** bomb release.

disparar [dispa'rar] *vt*, *vi* to shoot, fire; ~**se** *vr* (*arma de fuego*) to go off; (*persona: marcharse*) to rush off; (*caballo*) to bolt; (*enojarse*) to lose control.

disparatado, a [dispara'taðo, a] *a* crazy.

disparatar [dispara'tar] *vi* (*decir disparates*) to talk nonsense; (*hacer disparates*) to blunder.

disparate [dispa'rate] *nm* (*tontería*) foolish remark; (*error*) blunder; **decir** ~**s** to talk nonsense; **¡qué** ~! how absurd!; **costar un** ~ to cost a hell of a lot.

disparo [dis'paro] *nm* shot; (*acto*) firing; ~**s** *nmpl* shooting *sg*, (exchange of) shots (*sg*); ~ **inicial** (*de cohete*) blastoff.

dispendio [dis'pendjo] *nm* waste.

dispensar [dispen'sar] *vt* to dispense; (*ayuda*) to give; (*honores*) to grant; (*disculpar*) to excuse; **¡usted dispense!** I beg your pardon!; ~ **a uno de hacer algo** to excuse sb from doing sth.

dispensario [dispen'sarjo] *nm* (*clínica*) community clinic; (*de hospital*) outpatients' department.

dispersar [disper'sar] *vt* to disperse; (*manifestación*) to break up; ~**se** *vr* to scatter.

disperso, a [dis'perso, a] *a* scattered.

displicencia [displi'θenθja] *nf* (*mal humor*) peevishness; (*desgana*) lack of enthusiasm.

displicente [disθipli'θente] *a* (*malhumorado*) peevish; (*poco entusiasta*) unenthusiastic.

dispondré [dispon'dre] *etc vb* V **disponer**.

disponer [dispo'ner] *vt* (*arreglar*) to arrange; (*ordenar*) to put in order; (*preparar*) to prepare, get ready ♦ *vi*: ~ **de** to have, own; ~**se** *vr*: ~**se para** to prepare to, prepare for; **la ley dispone que...** the law provides that...; **no puede** ~ **de esos bienes** she cannot dispose of those properties.

disponga [dis'ponga] *etc vb* V **disponer**.

disponibilidad [disponißili'ðað] *nf* availability; ~**es** *nfpl* (*COM*) resources, financial assets.

disponible [dispo'nißle] *a* available;

(*tiempo*) spare; (*dinero*) on hand.

disposición [disposi'θjon] *nf* arrangement, disposition; (*de casa, INFORM*) layout; (*ley*) order; (*cláusula*) provision; (*aptitud*) aptitude; ~ **de ánimo** attitude of mind; **última** ~ last will and testament; **a la** ~ **de** at the disposal of; **a su** ~ at your service.

dispositivo [disposi'tiβo] *nm* device, mechanism; ~ **de alimentación** hopper; ~ **de almacenaje** storage device; ~ **periférico** peripheral (device); ~ **de seguridad** safety catch; (*fig*) security measure.

dispuesto, a [dis'pwesto, a] *pp de* **disponer** ◆ *a* (*arreglado*) arranged; (*preparado*) disposed; (*persona: dinámico*) bright; **estar** ~**/poco** ~ **a hacer algo** to be inclined/ reluctant to do sth.

dispuse [dis'puse] *etc vb* V **disponer**.

disputa [dis'puta] *nf* (*discusión*) dispute, argument; (*controversia*) controversy.

disputar [dispu'tar] *vt* (*discutir*) to dispute, question; (*contender*) to contend for ◆ *vi* to argue.

disquete [dis'kete] *nm* (*INFORM*) diskette, floppy disk.

Dist. *abr* (= *distancia, Distrito*) dist.

distancia [dis'tanθja] *nf* distance; (*de tiempo*) interval; ~ **de parada** braking distance; ~ **del suelo** (*AUTO etc*) height off the ground; **a gran** *o* **a larga** ~ long-distance; **mantenerse a** ~ to keep one's distance; (*fig*) to remain aloof; **guardar las** ~**s** to keep one's distance.

distanciado, a [distan'θjaðo, a] *a* (*remoto*) remote; (*fig: alejado*) far apart; **estamos** ~**s en ideas** our ideas are poles apart.

distanciamiento [distanθja'mjento] *nm* (*acto*) spacing out; (*estado*) remoteness; (*fig*) distance.

distanciar [distan'θjar] *vt* to space out; ~**se** *vr* to become estranged.

distante [dis'tante] *a* distant.

distar [dis'tar] *vi*: **dista 5 kms de aquí** it is 5 kms from here; **¿dista mucho?** is it far?; **dista mucho de la verdad** it's very far from the truth.

diste ['diste], **disteis** ['disteis] *vb* V **dar**.

distensión [disten'sjon] *nf* distension; (*POL*) détente; ~ **muscular** (*MED*) muscular strain.

distinción [distin'θjon] *nf* distinction; (*elegancia*) elegance; (*honor*) honour; **a** ~ **de** unlike; **sin** ~ indiscriminately; **sin** ~ **de edades** irrespective of age.

distinga [dis'tinga] *etc vb* V **distinguir**.

distinguido, a [distin'giðo, a] *a* distinguished; (*famoso*) prominent, well-known; (*elegante*) elegant.

distinguir [distin'gir] *vt* to distinguish; (*divisar*) to make out; (*escoger*) to single out; (*caracterizar*) to mark out; ~**se** *vr* to be

distinguished; (*destacarse*) to distinguish o.s.; **a lo lejos no se distingue** it's not visible from a distance.

distintivo, a [distin'tiβo, a] *a* distinctive; (*signo*) distinguishing ◆ *nm* (*de policía etc*) badge; (*fig*) characteristic.

distinto, a [dis'tinto, a] *a* different; (*claro*) clear; ~**s** several, various.

distorsión [distor'sjon] *nf* (*ANAT*) twisting; (*RADIO etc*) distortion.

distracción [distrak'θjon] *nf* distraction; (*pasatiempo*) hobby, pastime; (*olvido*) absent-mindedness, distraction.

distraer [distra'er] *vt* (*atención*) to distract; (*divertir*) to amuse; (*fondos*) to embezzle ◆ *vi* to be relaxing; ~**se** *vr* (*entretenerse*) to amuse o.s.; (*perder la concentración*) to allow one's attention to wander; ~ **a uno de su pensamiento** to divert sb from his train of thought; **el pescar distrae** fishing is a relaxation.

distraído, a [distra'iðo, a] *a* (*gen*) absentminded; (*desatento*) inattentive; (*entretenido*) amusing ◆ *nm*: **hacerse el** ~ to pretend not to notice; **con aire** ~ idly; **me miró distraída** she gave me a casual glance.

distraiga [dis'traiva] *etc*, **distraje** [dis'traxe] *etc*, **distrajera** [distra'xera] *etc*, **distrayendo** [distra'jendo] *vb* V **distraer**.

distribución [distriβu'θjon] *nf* distribution; (*entrega*) delivery; (*en estadística*) distribution, incidence; (*ARQ*) layout; ~ **de premias** prize giving; **la** ~ **de los impuestos** the incidence of taxes.

distribuidor, a [distriβui'ðor, a] *nm/f* (*persona: gen*) distributor; (: *CORREOS*) sorter; (: *COM*) dealer; **su** ~ **habitual** your regular dealer.

distribuir [distriβu'ir] *vt* to distribute; (*prospectos*) to hand out; (*cartas*) to deliver; (*trabajo*) to allocate; (*premios*) to award; (*dividendos*) to pay; (*peso*) to distribute; (*ARQ*) to plan.

distribuyendo [distriβu'jendo] *etc vb* V **distribuir**.

distrito [dis'trito] *nm* (*sector, territorio*) region; (*barrio*) district; ~ **electoral** constituency; ~ **postal** postal district.

disturbio [dis'turβjo] *nm* disturbance; (*desorden*) riot; **los** ~**s** the troubles.

disuadir [diswa'ðir] *vt* to dissuade.

disuasión [diswa'sjon] *nf* dissuasion; (*MIL*) deterrent; ~ **nuclear** nuclear deterrent.

disuasivo, a [diswa'siβo, a] *a* dissuasive; **arma disuasiva** deterrent.

disuelto [di'swelto] *pp de* **disolver**.

disuelva [di'swelβa] *etc vb* V **disolver**.

disuene [di'swene] *etc vb* V **disonar**.

disyuntiva [disjun'tiβa] *nf* (*dilema*) dilemma.

DIU ['diu] *nm abr* (= *dispositivo intrauterino*) I.U.D.

diurno, a ['djurno, a] *a* day *cpd*, diurnal.

diva ['diβa] *nf* prima donna.

divagar [diβa'ɣar] *vi* (*desviarse*) to digress.

divague [di'βaɣe] *etc vb* V **divagar**.

diván [di'βan] *nm* divan.

divergencia [diβer'xenθja] *nf* divergence.

divergir [diβer'xir] *vi* (*líneas*) to diverge; (*opiniones*) to differ; (*personas*) to disagree.

diverja [di'βerxa] *etc vb* V **divergir**.

diversidad [diβersi'ðað] *nf* diversity, variety.

diversificación [diβersifika'θjon] *nf* (*COM*) diversification.

diversificar [diβersifi'kar] *vt* to diversify.

diversifique [diβersi'fike] *etc vb* V **diversificar**.

diversión [diβer'sjon] *nf* (*gen*) entertainment; (*actividad*) hobby, pastime.

diverso, a [di'βerso, a] *a* diverse; (*diferente*) different ◆ *nm*: ~**s** (*COM*) sundries; ~**s libros** several books.

divertido, a [diβer'tiðo, a] *a* (*chiste*) amusing, funny; (*fiesta etc*) enjoyable; (*película, libro*) entertaining; **está** ~ (*irónico*) this is going to be fun.

divertir [diβer'tir] *vt* (*entretener, recrear*) to amuse, entertain; ~**se** *vr* (*pasarlo bien*) to have a good time; (*distraerse*) to amuse o.s.

dividendo [diβi'ðendo] *nm* (*COM*): ~**s** *nmpl* dividends; ~**s por acción** earnings per share; ~ **definitivo** final dividend.

dividir [diβi'ðir] *vt* ·(*gen*) to divide; (*separar*) to separate; (*distribuir*) to distribute, share out.

divierta [di'βjerta] *etc vb* V **divertir**.

divinidad [diβini'ðað] *nf* (*esencia divina*) divinity; **la D~** God.

divino, a [di'βino, a] *a* divine; (*fig*) lovely.

divirtiendo [diβir'tjendo] *etc vb* V **divertir**.

divisa [di'βisa] *nf* (*emblema, moneda*) emblem, badge; ~**s** *nfpl* currency *sg*; (*COM*) foreign exchange *sg*; **control de** ~**s** exchange control; ~ **de reserva** reserve currency.

divisar [diβi'sar] *vt* to make out, distinguish.

división [diβi'sjon] *nf* division; (*de partido*) split; (*de país*) partition.

divisorio, a [diβi'sorjo, a] *a* (*línea*) dividing; **línea divisoria de las aguas** watershed.

divorciado, a [diβor'θjaðo, a] *a* divorced; (*opinion*) split ◆ *nm/f* divorcé(e).

divorciar [diβor'θjar] *vt* to divorce; ~**se** *vr* to get divorced.

divorcio [di'βorθjo] *nm* divorce; (*fig*) split.

divulgación [diβulɣa'θjon] *nf* (*difusión*) spreading; (*popularización*) popularization.

divulgar [diβul'ɣar] *vt* (*desparramar*) to spread; (*popularizar*) to popularize; (*hacer circular*) to divulge, circulate; ~**se** *vr* (*secreto*) to leak out; (*rumor*) to get about.

divulgue [di'βulɣe] *etc vb* V **divulgar**.

DM *abr* = **decimal**.

dm. *abr* (= *decímetro*) dm.

DNI *nm abr Esp*: = **Documento Nacional de Identidad**.

Dña. *abr* = **Doña**.

dobladillo [doβla'ðiʎo] *nm* (*de vestido*) hem; (*de pantalón: vuelta*) turn-up (*Brit*), cuff (*US*).

doblaje [do'βlaxe] *nm* (*CINE*) dubbing.

doblar [do'βlar] *vt* to double; (*papel*) to fold; (*caño*) to bend; (*la esquina*) to turn, go round; (*film*) to dub ◆ *vi* to turn; (*campana*) to toll; ~**se** *vr* (*plegarse*) to fold (up), crease; (*encorvarse*) to bend.

doble ['doβle] *a* (*gen*) double; (*de dos aspectos*) dual; (*cuerda*) thick; (*fig*) two-faced ◆ *nm* double ◆ *nm/f* (*TEATRO*) double, stand-in; ~**s** *nmpl* (*DEPORTE*) doubles *sg*; ~ **o nada** double or quits; ~ **página** double-page spread; **con** ~ **sentido** with a double meaning; **el** ~ twice the quantity *o* as much; **su sueldo es el** ~ **del mío** his salary is twice (as much as) mine; (*INFORM*): ~ **cara** double-sided; ~ **densidad** double density; ~ **espacio** double spacing.

doblegar [doβle'ɣar] *vt* to fold, crease; ~**se** *vr* to yield.

doblegue [do'βleɣe] *etc vb* V **doblegar**.

doblez [do'βleθ] *nm* (*pliegue*) fold, hem ◆ *nf* (*falsedad*) duplicity.

doc. *abr* (= *docena*) doz.; (= *documento*) doc.

doce ['doθe] *num* twelve; (*fecha*) twelfth; **las** ~ twelve o'clock; *V tb* **seis**.

docena [do'θena] *nf* dozen; **por** ~**s** by the dozen.

docente [do'θente] *a*: **centro/personal** ~ teaching institution/staff.

dócil ['doθil] *a* (*pasivo*) docile; (*manso*) gentle; (*obediente*) obedient.

docto, a ['dokto, a] *a* learned, erudite ◆ *nm/f* scholar.

doctor, a [dok'tor, a] *nm/f* doctor; ~ **en filosofía** Doctor of Philosophy.

doctorado [dokto'raðo] *nm* doctorate.

doctorarse [dokto'rarse] *vr* to get a doctorate.

doctrina [dok'trina] *nf* doctrine, teaching.

documentación [dokumenta'θjon] *nf* documentation; (*de identidad etc*) papers *pl*.

documental [dokumen'tal] *a*, *nm* documentary.

documentar [dokumen'tar] *vt* to document; ~**se** *vr* to gather information.

documento [doku'mento] *nm* (*certificado*) document; (*JUR*) exhibit; ~**s** *nmpl* papers;

~ **justificativo** voucher; ~ **nacional de identidad** national identity card.

dogo ['doɣo] *nm* bulldog.

dólar ['dolar] *nm* dollar.

dolencia [do'lenθja] *nf* (*achaque*) ailment; (*dolor*) ache.

doler [do'ler] *vt, vi* to hurt; (*fig*) to grieve; ~**se** *vr* (*de su situación*) to grieve, feel sorry; (*de las desgracias ajenas*) to sympathize; (*quejarse*) to complain; **me duele el brazo** my arm hurts; **no me duele el dinero** I don't mind about the money; **¡ahí le duele!** you've put your finger on it!

doliente [do'ljente] *a* (*enfermo*) sick; (*dolorido*) aching; (*triste*) sorrowful; **la familia** ~ the bereaved family.

dolor [do'lor] *nm* pain; (*fig*) grief, sorrow; ~ **de cabeza** headache; ~ **de estómago** stomach ache; ~ **de oídos** earache; ~ **sordo** dull ache.

dolorido, a [dolo'riðo, a] *a* (*MED*) sore; **la parte dolorida** the part which hurts.

doloroso, a [dolo'roso, a] *a* (*MED*) painful; (*fig*) distressing.

domar [do'mar] *vt* to tame.

domesticado, a [domesti'kaðo, a] *a* (*amansado*) tame.

domesticar [domesti'kar] *vt* to tame.

doméstico, a [do'mestiko, a] *a* domestic ♦ *nm/f* servant; **economía doméstica** home economy; **gastos** ~**s** household expenses.

domestique [domes'tike] *etc vb* V **domesticar**.

domiciliación [domiθilja'θjon] *nf*: ~ **de pagos** (*COM*) standing order, direct debit.

domiciliar [domiθi'ljar] *vt* to domicile; ~**se** *vr* to take up (one's) residence.

domiciliario, a [domiθi'ljarjo, a] *a*: **arresto** ~ house arrest.

domicilio [domi'θiljo] *nm* home; ~ **particular** private residence; ~ **social** (*COM*) head office, registered office; **servicio a** ~ delivery service; **sin** ~ **fijo** of no fixed abode.

dominante [domi'nante] *a* dominant; (*person*) domineering.

dominar [domi'nar] *vt* (*gen*) to dominate; (*países*) to rule over; (*adversario*) to overpower; (*caballo, nervios, emoción*) to control; (*incendio, epidemia*) to bring under control; (*idiomas*) to be fluent in ♦ *vi* to dominate, prevail; ~**se** *vr* to control o.s.

domingo [do'mingo] *nm* Sunday; **D~ de Ramos** Palm Sunday; **D~ de Resurrección** Easter Sunday; *V tb* **sábado**.

dominguero, a [domin'gero, a] *a* Sunday *cpd*.

dominical [domini'kal] *a* Sunday *cpd*; **periódico** ~ Sunday newspaper.

dominio [do'minjo] *nm* (*tierras*) domain; (*POL*) dominion; (*autoridad*) power, authority; (*supremacía*) supremacy; (*de las pasiones*) grip, hold; (*de idioma*) command; **ser del** ~ **público** to be widely known.

dominó [domi'no] *nm* (*pieza*) domino; (*juego*) dominoes.

dom.º *abr* (= *domingo*) Sun.

don [don] *nm* (*talento*) gift; **D~ Juan Gómez** Mr Juan Gomez *o* Juan Gomez Esq.; **tener** ~ **de gentes** to known how to handle people; ~ **de lenguas** gift for languages; ~ **de mando** (qualities of) leadership; ~ **de palabra** gift of the gab.

donaire [do'naire] *nm* charm.

donante [do'nante] *nm/f* donor; ~ **de sangre** blood donor.

donar [do'nar] *vt* to donate.

donativo [dona'tiβo] *nm* donation.

doncella [don'θeʎa] *nf* (*criada*) maid.

donde ['donde] *ad* where ♦ *prep*: **el coche está allí** ~ **el farol** the car is over there by the lamppost *o* where the lamppost is; **por** ~ through which; **a** ~ to where, to which; **en** ~ where, in which; **es a** ~ **vamos nosotros** that's where we're going.

dónde ['donde] *ad interrogativo* where?; **¿a** ~ **vas?** where are you going (to)?; **¿de** ~ **vienes?** where have you come from?; **¿en** ~**?** where?; **¿por** ~**?** where?, whereabouts?; **¿por** ~ **se va al estadio?** how do you get to the stadium?

dondequiera [donde'kjera] *ad* anywhere ♦ *conj*: ~ **que** wherever; **por** ~ everywhere, all over the place.

donostiarra [donos'tjarra] *a* of *o* from San Sebastián ♦ *nm/f* native *o* inhabitant of San Sebastián.

doña ['doɲa] *nf* *título de mujer que no se traduce*.

dopar [do'par] *vt* to dope, drug.

doquier [do'kjer] *ad*: **por** ~ all over, everywhere.

dorado, a [do'raðo, a] *a* (*color*) golden; (*TEC*) gilt.

dorar [do'rar] *vt* (*TEC*) to gild; (*CULIN*) to brown, cook lightly; ~ **la píldora** to sweeten the pill.

dormilón, ona [dormi'lon, ona] *a* fond of sleeping ♦ *nm/f* sleepyhead.

dormir [dor'mir] *vt*: ~ **la siesta por la tarde** to have an afternoon nap ♦ *vi* to sleep; ~**se** *vr* (*persona, brazo, pierna*) to fall asleep; ~**la** (*fam*) to sleep it off; ~ **la mona** (*fam*) to sleep off a hangover; ~ **como un lirón** *o* **tronco** to sleep like a log; ~ **a pierna suelta** to sleep soundly.

dormitar [dormi'tar] *vi* to doze.

dormitorio [dormi'torjo] *nm* bedroom; ~ **común** dormitory.

dorsal [dor'sal] *a* dorsal ♦ *nm* (*DEPORTE*) number.

dorso ['dorso] *nm* back; **escribir algo al ~** to write sth on the back; **"vease al ~"** "see other side", "please turn over".

DOS *nm abr* (= *sistema operativo de disco*) DOS.

dos [dos] *num* two; (*fecha*) second; **los ~** the two of them, both of them; **cada ~ por tres** every 5 minutes; **de ~ en ~** in twos; **estamos a ~** (*TENIS*) the score is deuce; *V tb* **seis**.

doscientos, as [dos'θjentos, as] *num* two hundred; *V tb* **seiscientos**.

dosel [do'sel] *nm* canopy.

dosificar [dosifi'kar] *vt* (*CULIN, MED, QUÍMICA*) to measure out; (*no derrochar*) to be sparing with.

dosifique [dosi'fike] *etc vb V* **dosificar**.

dosis ['dosis] *nf inv* dose, dosage.

dossier [do'sjer] *nm* dossier, file.

dotación [dota'θjon] *nf* (*acto, dinero*) endowment; (*plantilla*) staff; (*NAUT*) crew; **la ~ es insuficiente** we are under-staffed.

dotado, a [do'taðo, a] *a* gifted; **~ de** (*persona*) endowed with; (*máquina*) equipped with.

dotar [do'tar] *vt* to endow; (*TEC*) to fit; (*barco*) to man; (*oficina*) to staff.

dote ['dote] *nf* (*de novia*) dowry; **~s** *nfpl* (*talentos*) gifts.

doy [doj] *vb V* **dar**.

Dpto. *abr* (= *Departamento*) dept.

Dr(a). *abr* (= *Doctor, Doctora*) Dr.

draga ['draɣa] *nf* dredge.

dragado [dra'ɣaðo] *nm* dredging.

dragar [dra'ɣar] *vt* to dredge; (*minas*) to sweep.

drague ['draɣe] *etc vb V* **dragar**.

drama ['drama] *nm* drama; (*obra*) play.

dramático, a [dra'matiko, a] *a* dramatic ♦ *nm/f* dramatist; (*actor*) actor; **obra dramática** play.

dramaturgo, a [drama'turɣo, a] *nm/f* dramatist, playwright.

dramón [dra'mon] *nm* (*TEATRO*) melodrama; **¡qué ~!** what a scene!

drenaje [dre'naxe] *nm* drainage.

drenar [dre'nar] *vt* to drain.

droga ['droɣa] *nf* drug; (*DEPORTE*) dope; **el problema de la ~** the drug problem.

drogadicto, a [droɣa'ðikto, a] *nm/f* drug addict.

drogar [dro'ɣar] *vt* to drug; (*DEPORTE*) to dope; **~se** *vr* to take drugs.

drogue ['droɣe] *etc vb V* **drogar**.

droguería [droɣe'ria] *nf* ≈ hardware shop (*Brit*) o store (*US*).

Dto., D.to *abr* = **descuento**.

Dtor(a). *abr* (= *Director, Directora*) Dir.

ducado [du'kaðo] *nm* duchy, dukedom.

ducentésimo, a [duθen'tesimo, a] *a* two hundredth; *V tb* **sexto, a**.

dúctil ['duktil] *a* (*metal*) ductile; (*persona*) easily influenced.

ducha ['dutʃa] *nf* (*baño*) shower; (*MED*) douche.

ducharse [du'tʃarse] *vr* to take a shower.

ducho, a ['dutʃo, a] *a*: **~ en** (*experimentado*) experienced in; (*hábil*) skilled at.

duda ['duða] *nf* doubt; **sin ~** no doubt, doubtless; **¡sin ~!** of course!; **no cabe ~** there is no doubt about it; **no le quepa ~** make no mistake about it; **no quiero poner en ~ su conducta** I don't want to call his behaviour into question; **sacar a uno de la ~** to settle sb's doubts; **tengo una ~** I have a query.

dudar [du'ðar] *vt* to doubt ♦ *vi* to doubt, have doubts; **~ acerca de algo** to be uncertain about sth; **dudó en comprarlo** he hesitated to buy it; **dudan que sea verdad** they doubt whether o if it's true.

dudoso, a [du'ðoso, a] *a* (*incierto*) hesitant; (*sospechoso*) doubtful; (*conducta*) dubious.

duelo ['dwelo] *etc vb V* **doler** ♦ *nm* (*combate*) duel; (*luto*) mourning; **batirse en ~** to fight a duel.

duende ['dwende] *nm* imp, goblin; **tiene ~** he's got real soul.

dueño, a ['dweɲo, a] *nm/f* (*propietario*) owner; (*de pensión, taberna*) landlord/lady; (*de casa, perro*) master/mistress; (*empresario*) employer; **ser ~ de sí mismo** to have self-control; (*libre*) to be one's own boss; **eres ~ de hacer como te parezca** you're free to do as you think fit; **hacerse ~ de una situación** to take command of a situation.

duerma ['dwerma] *etc vb V* **dormir**.

duermevela [dwerme'βela] *nf* (*fam*) nap, snooze.

Duero ['dwero] *nm* Douro.

dulce ['dulθe] *a* sweet; (*carácter, clima*) gentle, mild ♦ *ad* gently, softly ♦ *nm* sweet.

dulcificar [dulθifi'kar] *vt* (*fig*) to soften.

dulcifique [dulθi'fike] *etc vb V* **dulcificar**.

dulzura [dul'θura] *nf* sweetness; (*ternura*) gentleness.

Dunquerque [dun'kerke] *nm* Dunkirk.

dúo ['duo] *nm* duet, duo.

duodécimo, a [duo'deθimo, a] *a* twelfth; *V tb* **sexto, a**.

dup., dup.do *abr* (= *duplicado*) duplicated.

dúplex ['dupleks] *nm inv* (*piso*) flat on two floors; (*TELEC*) link-up; (*INFORM*): **~ integral** full duplex.

duplicar [dupli'kar] *vt* (*hacer el doble de*) to duplicate; (*cantidad*) to double; **~se** *vr* to double.

duplique [du'plike] *etc vb V* **duplicar**.

duque ['duke] *nm* duke.

duquesa [du'kesa] *nf* duchess.

duración [dura'θjon] *nf* duration, length; (*de máquina*) life; ~ **media de la vida** average life expectancy; **de larga** ~ (*enfermedad*) lengthy; (*pila*) long-life; (*disco*) long-playing; **de poca** ~ short.

duradero, a [dura'ðero, a] *a* (*tela*) hard-wearing; (*fe, paz*) lasting.

durante [du'rante] *ad* during; ~ **toda la noche** all night long; **habló** ~ **una hora** he spoke for an hour.

durar [du'rar] *vi* (*permanecer*) to last; (*recuerdo*) to remain; (*ropa*) to wear (well).

durazno [du'raθno] *nm* (*AM*: *fruta*) peach; (: *árbol*) peach tree.

durex ['dureks] *nm* (*AM*: *tira adhesiva*) Sellotape ® (*Brit*), Scotch tape ® (*US*).

dureza [du'reθa] *nf* (*cualidad*) hardness; (*de carácter*) toughness.

durmiendo [dur'mjendo] *etc vb V* **dormir**.

durmiente [dur'mjente] *a* sleeping ♦ *nm/f* sleeper.

duro, a ['duro, a] *a* hard; (*carácter*) tough; (*pan*) stale; (*cuello, puerta*) stiff; (*clima, luz*) harsh ♦ *ad* hard ♦ *nm* (*moneda*) five peseta coin; **el sector** ~ **del partido** the hardliners *pl* in the party; **ser** ~ **con uno** to be tough with *o* hard on sb; ~ **de mollera** (*torpe*) dense; ~ **de oído** hard of hearing; **trabajar** ~ to work hard; **estar sin un** ~ to be broke.

E

E, e [e] *nf* (*letra*) E, e; **E de Enrique** E for Edward (*Brit*) *o* Easy (*US*).

E *abr* (= *este*) E.

e [e] *conj* (*delante de* i- *e* hi-, *pero no* hie-) and; *V tb* **y**.

e/ *abr* (*COM*: = *envío*) shpt.

ebanista [eβa'nista] *nm/f* cabinetmaker.

ébano ['eβano] *nm* ebony.

ebrio, a ['eβrjo, a] *a* drunk.

Ebro ['eβro] *nm* Ebro.

ebullición [eβuʎi'θjon] *nf* boiling; **punto de** ~ boiling point.

eccema [ek'θema] *nm* (*MED*) eczema.

eclesiástico, a [ekle'sjastiko, a] *a* ecclesiastical; (*autoridades etc*) church *cpd* ♦ *nm* clergyman.

eclipse [e'klipse] *nm* eclipse.

eco ['eko] *nm* echo; **encontrar un** ~ **en** to produce a response from; **hacerse** ~ **de una opinión** to echo an opinion; **tener** ~ to catch on.

ecología [ekolo'xia] *nf* ecology.

ecológico, a [eko'loxiko, a] *a* ecological.

economato [ekono'mato] *nm* cooperative store.

economía [ekono'mia] *nf* (*sistema*) economy; (*cualidad*) thrift; ~ **dirigida** planned economy; ~ **doméstica** housekeeping; ~ **mixta** mixed economy; ~ **sumergida** black economy; **hacer** ~**s** to economize; ~**s de escala** economies of scale.

economice [ekono'miθe] *etc vb V* **economizar**.

económico, a [eko'nomiko, a] *a* (*barato*) cheap, economical; (*persona*) thrifty; (*COM*: *año etc*) financial; (: *situación*) economic.

economista [ekono'mista] *nm/f* economist.

economizar [ekonomi'θar] *vt* to economize on ♦ *vi* (*ahorrar*) to save up; (*pey*) to be miserly.

ecuador [ekwa'ðor] *nm* equator; **(el) E**~ Ecuador.

ecuánime [e'kwanime] *a* (*carácter*) level-headed; (*estado*) calm.

ecuatorial [ekwato'rjal] *a* equatorial.

ecuatoriano, a [ekwato'rjano, a] *a, nm/f* Ecuador(i)an.

ecuestre [e'kwestre] *a* equestrian.

echar [e'tʃar] *vt* to throw; (*agua, vino*) to pour (out); (*CULIN*) to put in, add; (*dientes*) to cut; (*discurso*) to give; (*empleado*: *despedir*) to fire, sack; (*hojas*) to sprout; (*cartas*) to post; (*humo*) to emit, give out; (*reprimenda*) to deal out; (*cuenta*) to make up; (*freno*) to put on ♦ *vi*: ~ **a correr/llorar** to break into a run/ burst into tears; ~ **a reír** to burst out laughing; ~**se** *vr* to lie down; ~ **abajo** (*gobierno*) to overthrow; (*edificio*) to demolish; ~ **la buenaventura a uno** to tell sb's fortune; ~ **la culpa a** to lay the blame on; ~ **de menos** to miss; ~**se atrás** to throw o.s. back(wards); (*fig*) to go back on what one has said; ~**se una novia** to get o.s. a girlfriend; ~**se una siestecita** to have a nap.

echarpe [e'tʃarpe] *nm* (woman's) stole.

ed. *abr* (= *edición*) ed.

edad [e'ðað] *nf* age; **¿qué** ~ **tienes?** how old are you?; **tiene ocho años de** ~ he is eight (years old); **de** ~ **corta** young; **ser de** ~ **mediana/avanzada** to be middle-aged/getting on; **ser mayor de** ~ to be of age; **llegar a mayor** ~ to come of age; **ser menor de** ~ to be under age; **la E**~ **Media** the Middle Ages.

Edén [e'ðen] *nm* Eden.

edición [eði'θjon] *nf* (*acto*) publication; (*ejemplar*) edition; **"al cerrar la** ~**"** (*TIP*) "stop press".

edicto [e'ðikto] *nm* edict, proclamation.

edificante [eði̯fi'kante] *a* edifying.

edificar [eðifi'kar] *vt* (*ARQ*) to build.

edificio [eði'fiθjo] *nm* building; (*fig*) edifice, structure.

edifique [eði'fike] *etc vb V* **edificar**.

Edimburgo [eðim'burɣo] *nm* Edinburgh.

editar [eði'tar] *vt* (*publicar*) to publish; (*preparar textos, tb INFORM*) to edit.

editor, a [eði'tor, a] *nm/f* (*que publica*) publisher; (*redactor*) editor ♦ *a*: **casa ~a** publishing company.

editorial [eðito'rjal] *a* editorial ♦ *nm* leading article, editorial ♦ *nf* (*tb*: **casa ~**) publishers.

editorialista [eðitorja'lista] *nm/f* leader-writer.

edredón [eðre'ðon] *nm* eiderdown, quilt.

educación [eðuka'θjon] *nf* education; (*crianza*) upbringing; (*modales*) (good) manners *pl*; (*formación*) training; **sin ~** ill-mannered; **¡qué falta de ~!** how rude!

educado, a [eðu'kaðo, a] *a* well-mannered; **mal ~** ill-mannered.

educar [eðu'kar] *vt* to educate; (*criar*) to bring up; (*voz*) to train.

eduque [e'ðuke] *etc vb V* **educar**.

EE.UU. *nmpl abr* (= *Estados Unidos*) USA.

efectista [efek'tista] *a* sensationalist.

efectivamente [efektißa'mente] *ad* (*como respuesta*) exactly, precisely; (*verdaderamente*) really; (*de hecho*) in fact.

efectivo, a [efek'tißo, a] *a* effective; (*real*) actual, real ♦ *nm*: **pagar en ~** to pay (in) cash; **hacer ~ un cheque** to cash a cheque.

efecto [e'fekto] *nm* effect, result; (*objetivo*) purpose, end; **~s** *nmpl* (*personales*) effects; (*bienes*) goods; (*COM*) assets; (*ECON*) bills, securities; **~s de consumo** consumer goods; **~s a cobrar** bills receivable; **~s personales** personal effects; **~ secundarios** (*COM*) spin-off effects; **~s sonoros** sound effects; **hacer o surtir ~** to have the desired effect; **hacer ~** (*impresionar*) to make an impression; **llevar algo a ~** to carry sth out; **en ~** in fact; (*respuesta*) exactly, indeed.

efectuar [efek'twar] *vt* to carry out; (*viaje*) to make.

efervescente [eferßes'θente] *a* (*bebida*) fizzy, bubbly.

eficacia [efi'kaθja] *nf* (*de persona*) efficiency; (*de medicamento etc*) effectiveness.

eficaz [efi'kaθ] *a* (*persona*) efficient; (*acción*) effective.

eficiencia [efi'θjenθja] *nf* efficiency.

eficiente [efi'θjente] *a* efficient.

efigie [e'fixje] *nf* effigy.

efímero, a [e'fimero, a] *a* ephemeral.

efusión [efu'sjon] *nf* outpouring; (*en el trato*) warmth; **con ~** effusively.

efusivo, a [efu'sißo, a] *a* effusive; **mis más efusivas gracias** my warmest thanks.

EGB *nf abr* (*Esp ESCOL*) = *Educación General Básica*.

Egeo [e'xeo] *nm*: **(Mar) ~** Aegean (Sea).

egipcio, a [e'xipθjo, a] *a, nm/f* Egyptian.

Egipto [e'xipto] *nm* Egypt.

egocéntrico, a [eɣo'θentriko, a] *a* self-centred.

egoísmo [eɣo'ismo] *nm* egoism.

egoísta [eɣo'ista] *a* egoistical, selfish ♦ *nm/f* egoist.

egolatra [eɣo'latra] *a* big-headed.

egregio, a [e'ɣrexjo, a] *a* eminent, distinguished.

eh [e] *excl* hey!, hi!

Eire ['eire] *nm* Eire.

ej. *abr* (= *ejemplo*) ex.

eje ['exe] *nm* (*GEO, MAT*) axis; (*POL, fig*) axis, main line; (*de rueda*) axle; (*de máquina*) shaft, spindle.

ejecución [exeku'θjon] *nf* execution; (*cumplimiento*) fulfilment; (*actuación*) performance; (*JUR*: *embargo de deudor*) attachment.

ejecutar [exeku'tar] *vt* to execute, carry out; (*matar*) to execute; (*cumplir*) to fulfil; (*MUS*) to perform; (*JUR*: *embargar*) to attach, distrain; (*deseos*) to fulfil; (*INFORM*) to run.

ejecutivo, a [exeku'tißo, a] *a, nm/f* executive; **el (poder) ~** the Executive (Power).

ejecutor [exeku'tor] *nm* (*tb*: **~ testamentario**) executor.

ejecutoria [exeku'torja] *nf* (*JUR*) final judgment.

ejemplar [exem'plar] *a* exemplary ♦ *nm* example; (*ZOOL*) specimen; (*de libro*) copy; (*de periódico*) number, issue; **~ de regalo** complimentary copy; **sin ~** unprecedented.

ejemplificar [exemplifi'kar] *vt* to exemplify, illustrate.

ejemplifique [exempli'fike] *etc vb V* **ejemplificar**.

ejemplo [e'xemplo] *nm* example; (*caso*) instance; **por ~** for example; **dar ~** to set an example.

ejercer [exer'θer] *vt* to exercise; (*funciones*) to perform; (*negocio*) to manage; (*influencia*) to exert; (*un oficio*) to practise; (*poder*) to wield ♦ *vi*: **~ de** to practise as.

ejercicio [exer'θiθjo] *nm* exercise; (*MIL*) drill; (*COM*) fiscal *o* financial year; (*período*) tenure; **~ acrobático** (*AVIAT*) stunt; **~ comercial** business year; **~s espirituales** (*REL*) retreat *sg*; **hacer ~** to take exercise.

ejercitar [exerθi'tar] *vt* to exercise; (*MIL*) to drill.

ejército [e'xerθito] *nm* army; **~ de**

ocupación army of occupation; ~ **permanente** standing army; **entrar en el** ~ to join the army, join up.

ejerza [e'xerθa] *etc vb V* **ejercer**.

ejote [e'xote] *nm (AM)* green bean.

el [el], *pl* **los** *artículo definido msg* the; **me gusta** ~ **fútbol** I like football; ~ **General Prim** General Prim ◆ *pron demostrativo*: **mi libro y** ~ **de usted** my book and yours; ~ **de Pepe es mejor** Pepe's is better ◆ *pron relativo*: ~ **que** he *etc* who, whoever, the one(s) that; ~ **que compramos no vale** the one we bought is no good.

él [el] *pron (persona)* he; *(cosa)* it; *(después de prep: persona)* him; (: *cosa)* it; **mis libros y los de** ~ my books and his.

elaboración [elaβora'θjon] *nf (producción)* manufacture; ~ **de presupuestos** *(COM)* budgeting.

elaborar [elaβo'rar] *vt (producto)* to make, manufacture; *(preparar)* to prepare; *(madera, metal etc)* to work; *(proyecto etc)* to work on *o* out.

elasticidad [elastiθi'ðað] *nf* elasticity.

elástico, a [e'lastiko, a] *a* elastic; *(flexible)* flexible ◆ *nm* elastic; *(gomita)* elastic band.

elección [elek'θjon] *nf* election; *(selección)* choice, selection; **elecciones parciales** by-election *sg*; **elecciones generales** general election *sg*.

electo, a [e'lekto, a] *a* elect; **el presidente** ~ the president-elect.

electorado [elekto'raðo] *nm* electorate, voters *pl*.

electrice [elek'triθe] *etc vb V* **electrizar**.

electricidad [elektriθi'ðað] *nf* electricity.

electricista [elektri'θista] *nm/f* electrician.

eléctrico, a [e'lektriko, a] *a* electric.

electrizar [elektri'θar] *vt (FERRO, fig)* to electrify.

electro... [elektro] *pref* electro....

electrocución [elektroku'θjon] *nf* electrocution.

electrocutar [elektroku'tar] *vt* to electrocute.

electrodo [elek'troðo] *nm* electrode.

electrodomésticos [elektroðo'mestikos] *nmpl (electrical)* household appliances; *(COM)* white goods.

electroimán [electroi'man] *nm* electromagnet.

electromagnético, a [elektromaɣ'netiko, a] *a* electromagnetic.

electrónico, a [elek'troniko, a] *a* electronic ◆ *nf* electronics *sg*; **proceso** ~ **de datos** *(INFORM)* electronic data processing.

electrotecnia [elektro'teknja] *nf* electrical engineering.

electrotécnico, a [elektro'tekniko, a] *nm/f* electrical engineer.

electrotermo [elektro'termo] *nm* immersion heater.

elefante [ele'fante] *nm* elephant.

elegancia [ele'ɣanθja] *nf* elegance, grace; *(estilo)* stylishness.

elegante [ele'ɣante] *a* elegant, graceful; *(traje etc)* smart, fashionable; *(decoración)* tasteful.

elegía [ele'xia] *nf* elegy.

elegir [ele'xir] *vt (escoger)* to choose, select; *(optar)* to opt for; *(presidente)* to elect.

elemental [elemen'tal] *a (claro, obvio)* elementary; *(fundamental)* elemental, fundamental.

elemento [ele'mento] *nm* element; *(fig)* ingredient; *(AM)* person, individual; *(tipo raro)* odd person; *(de pila)* cell; ~**s** *nmpl* elements, rudiments; **estar en su** ~ to be in one's element; **vino a verle un** ~ someone came to see you.

elenco [e'lenko] *nm* catalogue, list; *(TEATRO)* cast.

elevación [eleβa'θjon] *nf* elevation; *(acto)* raising, lifting; *(de precios)* rise; *(GEO etc)* height, altitude.

elevar [ele'ßar] *vt* to raise, lift (up); *(precio)* to put up; *(producción)* to step up; *(informe etc)* to present; ~**se** *vr (edificio)* to rise; *(precios)* to go up; *(transportarse, enajenarse)* to get carried away; **la cantidad se eleva a** ... the total amounts to ... .

eligiendo [eli'xjenðo] *etc*, **elija** [e'lixa] *etc vb V* **elegir**.

eliminar [elimi'nar] *vt* to eliminate, remove; *(olor, persona)* to get rid of; *(DEPORTE)* to eliminate, knock out.

eliminatoria [elimina'torja] *nf* heat, preliminary (round).

elite [e'lite] *nf* elite.

elocuencia [elo'kwenθja] *nf* eloquence.

elocuente [elo'kwente] *a* eloquent; *(fig)* significant; **un dato** ~ a fact which speaks for itself.

elogiar [elo'xjar] *vt* to praise, eulogize.

elogio [e'loxjo] *nm* praise; **queda por encima de todo** ~ it's beyond praise; **hacer** ~ **de** to sing the praises of.

elote [e'lote] *nm (AM)* corn on the cob.

El Salvador *nm* El Salvador.

eludir [elu'ðir] *vt (evitar)* to avoid, evade; *(escapar)* to escape, elude.

ella ['eʎa] *pron (persona)* she; *(cosa)* it; *(después de prep: persona)* her; (: *cosa)* it; **de** ~ hers.

ellas ['eʎas] *pron V* **ellos**.

ello ['eʎo] *pron neutro* it; **es por** ~ **que** ... that's why ... .

ellos, as ['eʎos, as] *pron personal pl* they; *(después de prep)* them; **de** ~ theirs.

E.M. *abr (MIL:* = *Estado Mayor)* G.S.

Em.ᵃ *abr* = **Eminencia**.

emanar [ema'nar] *vi*: ~ **de** to emanate from, come from; *(derivar de)* to originate in.

emancipar [emanθi'par] *vt* to emancipate; ~**se** *vr* to become emancipated, free o.s.

embadurnar [embaður'nar] *vt* to smear.

embajada [emba'xaða] *nf* embassy.

embajador, a [embaxa'ðor, a] *nm/f* ambassador/ambassadress.

embaladura [embala'ðura] *nf* (*AM*), **embalaje** [emba'laxe] *nm* packing.

embalar [emba'lar] *vt* (*envolver*) to parcel, wrap (up); *(envasar)* to package ◆ *vi* to sprint.

embalsamar [embalsa'mar] *vt* to embalm.

embalsar [embal'sar] *vt* (*río*) to dam (up); *(agua)* to retain.

embalse [em'balse] *nm* (*presa*) dam; *(lago)* reservoir.

embarace [emba'raθe] *etc vb V* **embarazar.**

embarazada [embara'θaða] *af* pregnant ◆ *nf* pregnant woman.

embarazar [embara'θar] *vt* to obstruct, hamper; ~**se** *vr* (*aturdirse*) to become embarrassed; *(confundirse)* to get into a mess.

embarazo [emba'raθo] *nm* (*de mujer*) pregnancy; *(impedimento)* obstacle, obstruction; *(timidez)* embarrassment.

embarazoso, a [embara'θoso, a] *a* (*molesto*) awkward; *(violento)* embarrassing.

embarcación [embarka'θjon] *nf* (*barco*) boat, craft; *(acto)* embarkation; ~ **de arrastre** trawler; ~ **de cabotaje** coasting vessel.

embarcadero [embarka'ðero] *nm* pier, landing stage.

embarcar [embar'kar] *vt* (*cargamento*) to ship, stow; *(persona)* to embark, put on board; *(fig)*: ~ **a uno en una empresa** to involve sb in an undertaking; ~**se** *vr* to embark, go on board; *(marinero)* to sign on.

embargar [embar'ɣar] *vt* (*frenar*) to restrain; *(sentidos)* to overpower; *(JUR)* to seize, impound.

embargo [em'barɣo] *nm* (*JUR*) seizure; *(COM etc)* embargo; **sin** ~ still, however, nonetheless.

embargue [em'barɣe] *etc vb V* **embargar.**

embarque [em'barke] *etc vb V* **embarcar** ◆ *nm* shipment, loading.

embarrancar [embarran'kar] *vt, vi* (*NAUT*) to run aground; *(AUTO etc)* to run into a ditch.

embarranque [emba'rranke] *etc vb V* **embarrancar.**

embarullar [embaru'ʎar] *vt* to make a mess of.

embate [em'bate] *nm* (*de mar, viento*) beating, violence.

embaucador, a [embauka'ðor, a] *nm/f* (*estafador*) trickster; *(impostor)* impostor.

embaucar [embau'kar] *vt* to trick, fool.

embauque [em'bauke] *etc vb V* **embaucar.**

embebecido, a [embeße'θiðo, a] *a* fascinated.

embeber [embe'ßer] *vt* (*absorber*) to absorb, soak up; *(empapar)* to saturate ◆ *vi* to shrink; ~**se** *vr*: ~**se en un libro** to be engrossed *o* absorbed in a book.

embelesado, a [embele'saðo, a] *a* spellbound.

embelesar [embele'sar] *vt* to enchant; ~**se** *vr*: ~**se (con)** to be enchanted (by).

embellecer [embeʎe'θer] *vt* to embellish, beautify.

embellezca [embe'ʎeθka] *etc vb V* **embellecer.**

embestida [embes'tiða] *nf* attack, onslaught; *(carga)* charge.

embestir [embes'tir] *vt* to attack, assault; to charge, attack ◆ *vi* to attack.

embistiendo [embis'tjendo] *etc vb V* **embestir.**

emblandecer [emblande'θer] *vt* to soften; *(fig)* to mollify; ~**se** *vr* to relent.

emblandezca [emblan'deθka] *etc vb V* **emblandecer.**

emblanquecer [emblanke'θer] *vt* to whiten, bleach; ~**se** *vr* to turn white.

emblanquezca [emblan'keθka] *etc vb V* **emblanquecer.**

emblema [em'blema] *nm* emblem.

embobado, a [embo'ßaðo, a] *a* (*atontado*) stunned, bewildered.

embobar [embo'ßar] *vt* (*asombrar*) to amaze; *(fascinar)* to fascinate; ~**se** *vr*: ~**se con** *o* **de** *o* **en** to be amazed at; to be fascinated by.

embocadura [emboka'ðura] *nf* narrow entrance; *(de río)* mouth; *(MUS)* mouthpiece.

embolado [embo'laðo] *nm* (*TEATRO*) bit part, minor role; *(fam)* trick.

embolia [em'bolja] *nf* (*MED*) embolism; ~ **cerebral** clot on the brain.

émbolo ['embolo] *nm* (*AUTO*) piston.

embolsar [embol'sar] *vt* to pocket, put in one's pocket.

emboquillado, a [emboki'ʎaðo, a] *a* (*cigarrillo*) tipped, filter *cpd*.

emborrachar [emborra'tʃar] *vt* to make drunk; ~**se** *vr* to get drunk.

emboscada [embos'kaða] *nf* (*celada*) ambush.

embotar [embo'tar] *vt* to blunt, dull; ~**se** *vr* (*adormecerse*) to go numb.

embotellamiento [emboteʎa'mjento] *nm* (*AUTO*) traffic jam.

embotellar [embote'ʎar] *vt* to bottle; ~**se** *vr* (*circulación*) to get into a jam.

embozo [em'boθo] *nm* muffler, mask; (*de sábana*) turn over.

embragar [embra'ɣar] *vt* (*AUTO, TEC*) to engage; (*partes*) to connect ♦ *vi* to let in the clutch.

embrague [em'braɣe] *etc vb* V **embragar** ♦ *nm* (*tb*: **pedal de** ~) clutch.

embravecer [embraβe'θer] *vt* to enrage, infuriate; ~**se** *vr* to become furious; (*mar*) to get rough; (*tormenta*) to rage.

embravecido, a [embraβe'θiðo, a] *a* (*mar*) rough; (*persona*) furious.

embriagador, a [embrjaɣa'ðor, a] *a* intoxicating.

embriagar [embrja'ɣar] *vt* (*emborrachar*) to make drunk; (*alegrar*) to delight; ~**se** *vr* (*emborracharse*) to get drunk.

embriague [em'brjaɣe] *etc vb* V **embriagar**.

embriaguez [embrja'ɣeθ] *nf* (*borrachera*) drunkenness.

embrión [em'brjon] *nm* embryo.

embrionario, a [embrjo'narjo, a] *a* embryonic.

embrollar [embro'ʎar] *vt* (*asunto*) to confuse, complicate; (*persona*) to involve, embroil; ~**se** *vr* (*confundirse*) to get into a muddle *o* mess.

embrollo [em'broʎo] *nm* (*enredo*) muddle, confusion; (*aprieto*) fix, jam.

embromar [embro'mar] *vt* (*burlarse de*) to tease, make fun of.

embrujado, a [embru'xaðo, a] *a* (*persona*) bewitched; **casa embrujada** haunted house.

embrutecer [embrute'θer] *vt* (*atontar*) to stupefy; ~**se** *vr* to be stupefied.

embrutezca [embru'teθka] *etc vb* V **embrutecer**.

embudo [em'buðo] *nm* funnel.

embuste [em'buste] *nm* trick; (*mentira*) lie; (*hum*) fib.

embustero, a [embus'tero, a] *a* lying, deceitful ♦ *nm/f* (*tramposo*) cheat; (*mentiroso*) liar; (*hum*) fibber.

embutido [embu'tiðo] *nm* (*CULIN*) sausage; (*TEC*) inlay.

embutir [embu'tir] *vt* to insert; (*TEC*) to inlay; (*llenar*) to pack tight, cram.

emergencia [emer'xenθja] *nf* emergency; (*surgimiento*) emergence.

emergente [emer'xente] *a* resultant, consequent; (*nación*) emergent.

emerger [emer'xer] *vi* to emerge, appear.

emeritense [emeri'tense] *a* of *o* from Mérida ♦ *nm/f* native *o* inhabitant of Mérida.

emerja [e'merxa] *etc vb* V **emerger**.

emigración [emiɣra'θjon] *nf* emigration; (*de pájaros*) migration.

emigrado, a [emi'ɣraðo, a] *nm/f* emigrant; (*POL etc*) émigré(e).

emigrante [emi'ɣrante] *a, nm/f* emigrant.

emigrar [emi'ɣrar] *vi* (*personas*) to emigrate; (*pájaros*) to migrate.

eminencia [emi'nenθja] *nf* eminence; (*en títulos*): **Su E~** His Eminence; **Vuestra E~** Your Eminence.

eminente [emi'nente] *a* eminent, distinguished; (*elevado*) high.

emisario [emi'sarjo] *nm* emissary.

emisión [emi'sjon] *nf* (*acto*) emission; (*COM etc*) issue; (*RADIO, TV*: *acto*) broadcasting; (: *programa*) broadcast, programme, program (*US*); ~ **de acciones** (*COM*) share issue; ~ **gratuita de acciones** (*COM*) rights issue; ~ **de valores** (*COM*) flotation.

emisor, a [emi'sor, a] *nm* transmitter ♦ *nf* radio *o* broadcasting station.

emitir [emi'tir] *vt* (*olor etc*) to emit, give off; (*moneda etc*) to issue; (*opinión*) to express; (*voto*) to cast; (*señal*) to send out; (*RADIO*) to broadcast; ~ **una señal sonora** to beep.

emoción [emo'θjon] *nf* emotion; (*excitación*) excitement; (*sentimiento*) feeling; ¡**qué** ~! how exciting!; (*irónico*) what a thrill!

emocionado, a [emoθjo'naðo, a] *a* deeply moved, stirred.

emocionante [emoθjo'nante] *a* (*excitante*) exciting, thrilling.

emocionar [emoθjo'nar] *vt* (*excitar*) to excite, thrill; (*conmover*) to move, touch; (*impresionar*) to impress; ~**se** *vr* to get excited.

emotivo, a [emo'tiβo, a] *a* emotional.

empacar [empa'kar] *vt* (*gen*) to pack; (*en caja*) to bale, crate.

empacharse [empa'tʃarse] *vr* (*MED*) to get indigestion.

empacho [em'patʃo] *nm* (*MED*) indigestion; (*fig*) embarrassment.

empadronamiento [empaðrona'mjento] *nm* census; (*de electores*) electoral register.

empadronarse [empaðro'narse] *vr* (*POL*: *como elector*) to register.

empalagar [empala'ɣar] *vt* (*suj*: *comida*) to cloy; (*hartar*) to pall on ♦ *vi* to pall.

empalagoso, a [empala'ɣoso, a] *a* cloying; (*fig*) tiresome.

empalague [empa'laɣe] *etc vb* V **empalagar**.

empalizada [empali'θaða] *nf* fence; (*MIL*) palisade.

empalmar [empal'mar] *vt* to join, connect ♦ *vi* (*dos caminos*) to meet, join.

empalme [em'palme] *nm* joint, connection; (*de vías*) junction; (*de trenes*) connection.

empanada [empa'naða] *nf* pie, pasty.

empanar [empa'nar] *vt* (*CULIN*) to cook *o* roll in breadcrumbs *o* pastry.

empantanarse [empanta'narse] *vr* to get

swamped; (*fig*) to get bogged down.
empañarse [empa'narse] *vr* (*nublarse*) to get misty, steam up.
empapar [empa'par] *vt* (*mojar*) to soak, saturate; (*absorber*) to soak up, absorb; ~**se** *vr*: ~**se de** to soak up.
empapelar [empape'lar] *vt* (*paredes*) to paper.
empaque [em'pake] *etc vb* V **empacar**.
empaquetar [empake'tar] *vt* to pack, parcel up; (*COM*) to package.
emparedado [empare'ðaðo] *nm* sandwich.
emparejar [empare'xar] *vt* to pair ◆ *vi* to catch up.
emparentar [emparen'tar] *vi*: ~ **con** to marry into.
empariente [empa'rjente] *etc vb* V **emparentar**.
empastar [empas'tar] *vt* (*embadurnar*) to paste; (*diente*) to fill.
empaste [em'paste] *nm* (*de diente*) filling.
empatar [empa'tar] *vi* to draw, tie.
empate [em'pate] *nm* draw, tie; **un ~ a cero** a no-score draw.
empecé [empe'θe], **empecemos** [empe'θemos] *etc vb* V **empezar**.
empecinado, a [empeθi'naðo, a] *a* (*AM*) stubborn.
empedernido, a [empeðer'niðo, a] *a* hard, heartless; (*fijado*) hardened, inveterate; **un fumador ~** a heavy smoker.
empedrado, a [empe'ðraðo, a] *a* paved ◆ *nm* paving.
empedrar [empe'ðrar] *vt* to pave.
empeine [em'peine] *nm* (*de pie, zapato*) instep.
empellón [empe'ʎon] *nm* push, shove; **abrirse paso a empellones** to push *o* shove one's way past *o* through.
empeñado, a [empe'ɲaðo, a] *a* (*persona*) determined; (*objeto*) pawned.
empeñar [empe'ɲar] *vt* (*objeto*) to pawn, pledge; (*persona*) to compel; ~**se** *vr* (*obligarse*) to bind o.s., pledge o.s.; (*endeudarse*) to get into debt; ~**se en hacer** to be set on doing, be determined to do.
empeño [em'peɲo] *nm* (*determinación*) determination; (*cosa prendada*) pledge; **casa de ~s** pawnshop; **con ~** insistently; (*con celo*) eagerly; **tener ~ en hacer algo** to be bent on doing sth.
empeoramiento [empeora'mjento] *nm* worsening.
empeorar [empeo'rar] *vt* to make worse, worsen ◆ *vi* to get worse, deteriorate.
empequeñecer [empekeɲe'θer] *vt* to dwarf; (*fig*) to belittle.
empequeñezca [empeke'ɲeθka] *etc vb* V **empequeñecer**.
emperador [empera'ðor] *nm* emperor.
emperatriz [empera'triθ] *nf* empress.

emperrarse [empe'rrarse] *vr* to get stubborn; ~ **en algo** to persist in sth.
empezar [empe'θar] *vt, vi* to begin, start; **empezó a llover** it started to rain; **bueno, para ~** well, to start with.
empiece [em'pjeθe] *etc vb* V **empezar**.
empiedre [em'pjeðre] *etc vb* V **empedrar**.
empiezo [em'pjeθo] *etc vb* V **empezar**.
empinado, a [empi'naðo, a] *a* steep.
empinar [empi'nar] *vt* to raise; (*botella*) to tip up; ~**se** *vr* (*persona*) to stand on tiptoe; (*animal*) to rear up; (*camino*) to climb steeply; ~ **el codo** to booze (*fam*).
empingorotado, a [empingoro'taðo, a] *a* (*fam*) stuck-up.
empírico, a [em'piriko, a] *a* empirical.
emplace [em'plaθe] *etc vb* V **emplazar**.
emplaste [em'plaste], **emplasto** [em'plasto] *nm* (*MED*) plaster.
emplazamiento [emplaθa'mjento] *nm* site, location; (*JUR*) summons *sg*.
emplazar [empla'θar] *vt* (*ubicar*) to site, place, locate; (*JUR*) to summons; (*convocar*) to summon.
empleado, a [emple'aðo, a] *nm/f* (*gen*) employee; (*de banco etc*) clerk; ~ **público** civil servant.
emplear [emple'ar] *vt* (*usar*) to use, employ; (*dar trabajo a*) to employ; ~**se** *vr* (*conseguir trabajo*) to be employed; (*ocuparse*) to occupy o.s.; ~ **mal el tiempo** to waste time; **¡te está bien empleado!** it serves you right!
empleo [em'pleo] *nm* (*puesto*) job; (*puestos: colectivamente*) employment; (*uso*) use, employment; "**modo de ~**" "instructions for use".
emplumar [emplu'mar] *vt* (*estafar*) to swindle.
empobrecer [empoβre'θer] *vt* to impoverish; ~**se** *vr* to become poor *o* impoverished.
empobrecimiento [empoβreθi'mjento] *nm* impoverishment.
empobrezca [empo'βreθka] *etc vb* V **empobrecer**.
empolvar [empol'βar] *vt* (*cara*) to powder; ~**se** *vr* to powder one's face; (*superficie*) to get dusty.
empollar [empo'ʎar] *vt* to incubate; (*ESCOL fam*) to swot (up) ◆ *vi* (*gallina*) to brood; (*ESCOL fam*) to swot.
empollón, ona [empo'ʎon, ona] *nm/f* (*ESCOL fam*) swot.
emponzoñar [emponθo'ɲar] *vt* (*esp fig*) to poison.
emporio [em'porjo] *nm* emporium, trading centre; (*AM: gran almacén*) department store.
empotrado, a [empo'traðo, a] *a* (*armario etc*) built-in.

empotrar [empo'trar] *vt* to embed; *(armario etc)* to build in.

emprender [empren'der] *vt* to undertake; *(empezar)* to begin, embark on; *(acometer)* to tackle, take on; ~ **marcha a** to set out for.

empreñar [empre'ɲar] *vt* to make pregnant; **~se** *vr* to become pregnant.

empresa [em'presa] *nf* enterprise; *(COM: sociedad)* firm, company; (: *negocio)* business; *(esp TEATRO)* management; ~ **filial** *(COM)* affiliated company; ~ **matriz** *(COM)* parent company.

empresario, a [empre'sarjo, a] *nm/f (COM)* businessman/woman, entrepreneur; *(TEC)* manager; *(MUS: de ópera etc)* impresario; ~ **de pompas fúnebres** undertaker *(Brit)*, mortician *(US)*.

empréstito [em'prestito] *nm* (public) loan; *(COM)* loan capital.

empujar [empu'xar] *vt* to push, shove.

empuje [em'puxe] *nm* thrust; *(presión)* pressure; *(fig)* vigour, drive.

empujón [empu'xon] *nm* push, shove; **abrirse paso a empujones** to shove one's way through.

empuñadura [empuɲa'ðura] *nf (de espada)* hilt; *(de herramienta etc)* handle.

empuñar [empu'ɲar] *vt (asir)* to grasp, take *(firm)* hold of; ~ **las armas** *(fig)* to take up arms.

emulación [emula'θjon] *nf* emulation.

emular [emu'lar] *vt* to emulate; *(rivalizar)* to rival.

émulo, a ['emulo, a] *nm/f* rival, competitor.

en [en] *prep (gen)* in; *(sobre)* on, upon; *(tiempo)* in, on; *(tipo)* by; **meter ~ el bolsillo** to put in *o* into one's pocket; **vivir ~ Toledo** to live in Toledo; ~ **casa** at home; **lo terminó ~ 6 días** he finished it in 6 days; ~ **(el mes de) enero** in (the month of) January; ~ **aquel momento/aquella época** at that moment/that time; ~ **aquel día/aquella ocasión** on that day/that occasion; **ha aumentado ~ un 20 por ciento** it has increased by 20%; ~ **serio** seriously; ~ **fin** well, well then; **ir de puerta ~ puerta** to go from door to door; **(viajar)** ~ **tren** (to travel) by train.

enajenación [enaxena'θjon] *nf*, **enajenamiento** [enaxena'mjento] *nm* alienation; *(fig: distracción)* absent-mindedness; (: *embelesamiento)* rapture, trance; ~ **mental** mental derangement.

enajenar [enaxe'nar] *vt* to alienate; *(fig)* to carry away.

enamorado, a [enamo'raðo, a] *a* in love ◆ *nm/f* lover; **estar ~ (de)** to be in love (with).

enamorar [enamo'rar] *vt* to win the love of; **~se** *vr*: **~se (de)** to fall in love (with).

enano, a [e'nano, a] *a* tiny, dwarf ◆ *nm/f* dwarf; *(pey)* runt.

enarbolar [enarβo'lar] *vt (bandera etc)* to hoist; *(espada etc)* to brandish.

enardecer [enarðe'θer] *vt (pasiones)* to fire, inflame; *(persona)* to fill with enthusiasm; **~se** *vr* to get excited; **~se por** to get enthusiastic about.

enardezca [enar'deθka] *etc vb V* **enardecer**.

encabece [enka'βeθe] *etc vb V* **encabezar**.

encabezado [enkaβe'θaðo] *nm (COM)* header.

encabezamiento [enkaβeθa'mjento] *nm (de carta)* heading; *(COM)* billhead, letterhead; *(de periódico)* headline; *(preámbulo)* foreword, preface; ~ **normal** *(TIP etc)* running head.

encabezar [enkaβe'θar] *vt (movimiento, revolución)* to lead, head; *(lista)* to head; *(carta)* to put a heading to; *(libro)* to entitle.

encadenar [enkaðe'nar] *vt* to chain (together); *(poner grilletes a)* to shackle.

encajar [enka'xar] *vt (ajustar)*: ~ **en** to fit (into); *(meter a la fuerza)* to push in; *(máquina etc)* to house; *(partes)* to join; *(fam: golpe)* to give, deal; *(entrometer)* to insert ◆ *vi* to fit (well); *(fig: corresponder a)* to match; **~se** *vr*: **~se en un sillón** to squeeze into a chair.

encaje [en'kaxe] *nm (labor)* lace.

encajonar [enkaxo'nar] *vt* to box (up), put in a box.

encalar [enka'lar] *vt (pared)* to whitewash.

encallar [enka'ʎar] *vi (NAUT)* to run aground.

encaminado, a [enkaminaðo, a] *a*: **medidas encaminadas a ...** measures designed to *o* aimed at ...

encaminar [enkami'nar] *vt* to direct, send; **~se** *vr*: **~se a** to set out for; ~ **por** *(expedición etc)* to route via.

encandilar [enkandi'lar] *vt* to dazzle; *(persona)* to daze, bewilder.

encanecer [enkane'θer] *vi*, **encanecerse** *vr (pelo)* to go grey.

encanezca [enka'neθka] *etc vb V* **encanecer**.

encantado, a [enkan'taðo, a] *a* delighted; ¡~! how do you do!, pleased to meet you.

encantador, a [enkanta'ðor, a] *a* charming, lovely ◆ *nm/f* magician, enchanter/ enchantress.

encantar [enkan'tar] *vt* to charm, delight; *(cautivar)* to fascinate; *(hechizar)* to bewitch, cast a spell on.

encanto [en'kanto] *nm (magia)* spell, charm; *(fig)* charm, delight; *(expresión de ternura)* sweetheart; **como por ~** as if by magic.

encapotado, a [enkapo'taðo, a] a (cielo) overcast.

encapricharse [enkapritʃarse] vr: **se ha encaprichado con ir** ... he's taken it into his head to go ...; **se ha encaprichado** he's digging his heels in.

encaramar [enkara'mar] vt (subir) to raise, lift up; ~**se** vr (subir) to perch; ~**se a** (árbol etc) to climb.

encararse [enka'rarse] vr: ~ **a** o **con** to confront, come face to face with.

encarcelar [enkarθe'lar] vt to imprison, jail.

encarecer [enkare'θer] vt to put up the price of ◆ vi, ~**se** vr to get dearer.

encarecidamente [enkareθiða'mente] ad earnestly.

encarecimiento [enkareθi'mjento] nm price increase.

encarezca [enka'reθka] etc vb V **encarecer**.

encargado, a [enkar'ɣaðo, a] a in charge ◆ nm/f agent, representative; (responsable) person in charge.

encargar [enkar'ɣar] vt to entrust; (COM) to order; (recomendar) to urge, recommend; ~**se** vr: ~**se de** to look after, take charge of; ~ **algo a uno** to put sb in charge of sth.

encargo [en'karɣo] nm (pedido) assignment, job; (responsabilidad) responsibility; (recomendación) recommendation; (COM) order.

encargue [en'karɣe] etc vb V **encargar**.

encariñarse [enkari'ɲarse] vr: ~ **con** to grow fond of, get attached to.

encarnación [enkarna'θjon] nf incarnation, embodiment.

encarnado, a [enkar'naðo, a] a (color) red; **ponerse** ~ to blush.

encarnar [enkar'nar] vt to personify; (TEATRO: papel) to play ◆ vi (REL etc) to become incarnate.

encarnizado, a [enkarni'θaðo, a] a (lucha) bloody, fierce.

encarrilar [enkarri'lar] vt (tren) to put back on the rails; (fig) to correct, put on the right track.

encasillar [enkasi'ʎar] vt (TEATRO) to typecast; (clasificar: pey) to pigeonhole.

encauce [en'kauθe] etc vb V **encauzar**.

encausar [enkau'sar] vt to prosecute, sue.

encauzar [enkau'θar] vt to channel; (fig) to direct.

encendedor [enθende'ðor] nm lighter.

encender [enθen'der] vt (con fuego) to light; (incendiar) to set fire to; (luz, radio) to put on, switch on; (INFORM) to toggle on, switch on; (avivar: pasiones etc) to inflame; (despertar: entusiasmo) to arouse; (odio) to awaken; ~**se** vr to catch fire; (excitarse) to get excited; (de cólera) to flare up; (el rostro) to blush.

encendidamente [enθendiða'mente] ad passionately.

encendido, a [enθen'diðo, a] a alight; (aparato) (switched) on; (mejillas) glowing; (cara: por el vino etc) flushed; (mirada) passionate ◆ nm (AUTO) ignition; (de faroles) lighting.

encerado, a [enθe'raðo, a] a (suelo) waxed, polished ◆ nm (ESCOL) blackboard; (hule) oilcloth.

encerar [enθe'rar] vt (suelo) to wax, polish.

encerrar [enθe'rrar] vt (confinar) to shut in o up; (con llave) to lock in o up; (comprender, incluir) to include, contain; ~**se** vr to shut o lock o.s. up o in.

encerrona [enθe'rrona] nf trap.

encía [en'θia] nf (ANAT) gum.

enciclopedia [enθiklo'peðja] nf encyclopaedia.

encienda [en'θjenda] etc vb V **encender**.

encierro [en'θjerro] etc vb V **encerrar** ◆ nm shutting in o up; (calabozo) prison; (AGR) pen; (TAUR) penning.

encima [en'θima] ad (sobre) above, over; (además) besides; ~ **de** (en) on, on top of; (sobre) above, over; (además de) besides, on top of; **por** ~ **de** over; ¿**llevas dinero** ~? have you (got) any money on you?; **se me vino** ~ it took me by surprise.

encina [en'θina] nf (holm) oak.

encinta [en'θinta] af pregnant.

enclenque [en'klenke] a weak, sickly.

encoger [enko'xer] vt (gen) to shrink, contract; (fig: asustar) to scare; (: desanimar) to discourage; ~**se** vr to shrink, contract; (fig) to cringe; ~**se de hombros** to shrug one's shoulders.

encoja [en'koxa] etc vb V **encoger**.

encojar [enko'xar] vt to lame; (tullir) to cripple; ~**se** vr to go lame; to become crippled.

encolar [enko'lar] vt (engomar) to glue, paste; (pegar) to stick down.

encolerice [enkole'riθe] etc vb V **encolerizar**.

encolerizar [enkoleri'θar] vt to anger, provoke; ~**se** vr to get angry.

encomendar [enkomen'dar] vt to entrust, commend; ~**se** vr: ~**se a** to put one's trust in.

encomiar [enko'mjar] vt to praise, pay tribute to.

encomienda [enko'mjenda] etc vb V **encomendar** ◆ nf (encargo) charge, commission; (elogio) tribute; ~ **postal** (AM) parcel post.

encomio [en'komjo] nm praise, tribute.

encono [en'kono] nm (rencor) rancour, spite.

encontrado, a [enkon'traðo, a] a (contrario) contrary, conflicting; (hostil) hostile.

encontrar [enkon'trar] vt (hallar) to find; (inesperadamente) to meet, run into; ~se vr to meet (each other); (situarse) to be (situated); (persona) to find o.s., be; (entrar en conflicto) to crash, collide; ~se con to meet; ~se bien (de salud) to feel well; no se encuentra aquí en este momento he's not in at the moment.

encontronazo [enkontro'naθo] nm collision, crash.

encorvar [enkor'βar] vt to curve; (inclinar) to bend (down); ~se vr to bend down, bend over.

encrespado, a [enkres'paðo, a] a (pelo) curly; (mar) rough.

encrespar [enkres'par] vt (cabellos) to curl; (fig) to anger, irritate; ~se vr (el mar) to get rough; (fig) to get cross o irritated.

encrucijada [enkruθi'xaða] nf crossroads sg; (empalme) junction.

encuadernación [enkwaðerna'θjon] nf binding; (taller) binder's.

encuadernador, a [enkwaðerna'ðor, a] nm/f bookbinder.

encuadrar [enkwa'ðrar] vt (retrato) to frame; (ajustar) to fit, insert; (encerrar) to contain.

encubierto [enku'βjerto] pp de **encubrir**.

encubrir [enku'βrir] vt (ocultar) to hide, conceal; (criminal) to harbour, shelter; (ayudar) to be an accomplice in.

encuentro [en'kwentro] etc vb V **encontrar** ♦ nm (de personas) meeting; (AUTO etc) collision, crash; (DEPORTE) match, game; (MIL) encounter.

encuesta [en'kwesta] nf inquiry, investigation; (sondeo) public opinion poll; ~ judicial post mortem.

encumbrado, a [enkum'braðo, a] a eminent, distinguished.

encumbrar [enkum'brar] vt (persona) to exalt; ~se vr (fig) to become conceited.

encharcar [entʃar'kar] vt to swamp, flood; ~se vr to become flooded.

encharque [en'tʃarke] etc vb V **encharcar**.

enchufar [entʃu'far] vt (ELEC) to plug in; (TEC) to connect, fit together; (COM) to merge.

enchufe [en'tʃute] nm (ELEC: clavija) plug; (: toma) socket; (de dos tubos) joint, connection; (fam: influencia) contact, connection; (: puesto) cushy job; ~ de clavija jack plug; tiene un ~ en el ministerio he can pull strings at the ministry.

endeble [en'deβle] a (argumento, excusa, persona) weak.

endemoniado, a [endemo'njaðo, a] a possessed (of the devil); (travieso) devilish.

enderece [ende'reθe] etc vb V **enderezar**.

enderezar [endere'θar] vt (poner derecho) to straighten (out); (: verticalmente) to set upright; (fig) to straighten o sort out; (dirigir) to direct; ~se vr (persona sentada) to sit up straight.

endeudarse [endeu'ðarse] vr to get into debt.

endiablado, a [endja'βlaðo, a] a devilish, diabolical; (hum) mischievous.

endilgar [endil'var] vt (fam): ~ algo a uno to lumber sb with sth; ~ un sermón a uno to give sb a lecture.

endilgue [en'dilve] etc vb V **endilgar**.

endomingarse [endomin'garse] vr to dress up, put on one's best clothes.

endomingue [endo'minge] etc vb V **endomingarse**.

endosante [endo'sante] nm/f endorser.

endosar [endo'sar] vt (cheque etc) to endorse.

endulce [en'dulθe] etc vb V **endulzar**.

endulzar [endul'θar] vt to sweeten; (suavizar) to soften.

endurecer [endure'θer] vt to harden; ~se vr to harden, grow hard.

endurecido, a [endure'θiðo, a] a (duro) hard; (fig) hardy, tough; estar ~ a algo to be hardened o used to sth.

endurezca [endu'reθka] etc vb V **endurecer**.

ene. abr (= enero) Jan.

enemigo, a [ene'mivo, a] a enemy, hostile ♦ nm/f enemy ♦ nf enmity, hostility; ser ~ de (persona) to dislike; (suj: tendencia) to be inimical to.

enemistad [enemis'tað] nf enmity.

enemistar [enemis'tar] vt to make enemies of, cause a rift between; ~se vr to become enemies; (amigos) to fall out.

energético, a [ener'xetiko, a] a: política energética energy policy.

energía [ener'xia] nf (vigor) energy, drive; (TEC, ELEC) energy, power.

enérgico, a [e'nerxiko, a] a (gen) energetic; (ataque) vigorous; (ejercicio) strenuous; (medida) bold; (voz, modales) forceful.

energúmeno, a [ener'vumeno, a] nm/f madman/woman; ponerse como un ~ con uno to get furious with sb.

enero [e'nero] nm January.

enervar [ener'βar] vt (poner nervioso a) to get on sb's nerves.

enésimo, a [e'nesimo, a] a (MAT) nth; por enésima vez (fig) for the umpteenth time.

enfadado, a [enfa'ðaðo, a] a angry, annoyed.

enfadar [enfa'ðar] vt to anger, annoy; ~se vr to get angry o annoyed.

enfado [en'faðo] nm (enojo) anger, annoyance; (disgusto) trouble, bother.

énfasis ['enfasis] *nm* emphasis, stress; **poner ~ en** to stress.

enfático, a [en'fatiko, a] *a* emphatic.

enfatizado, a [enfati'θaðo, a] *a*: **en caracteres ~s** (*INFORM*) emphasized.

enfermar [enfer'mar] *vt* to make ill ◆ *vi* to fall ill, be taken ill; **su actitud me enferma** his attitude makes me sick; **~ del corazón** to develop heart trouble.

enfermedad [enferme'ðað] *nf* illness; **~ venérea** venereal disease.

enfermera [enfer'mera] *nf* V **enfermero**.

enfermería [enferme'ria] *nf* infirmary; (*de colegio etc*) sick bay.

enfermero, a [enfer'mero, a] *nm* (male) nurse ◆ *nf* nurse; **enfermera jefa** matron.

enfermizo, a [enfer'miθo, a] *a* (*persona*) sickly, unhealthy; (*fig*) unhealthy.

enfermo, a [en'fermo, a] *a* ill, sick ◆ *nm/f* invalid, sick person; (*en hospital*) patient.

enfilar [enfi'lar] *vt* (*aguja*) to thread; (*calle*) to go down.

enflaquecer [enflake'θer] *vt* (*adelgazar*) to make thin; (*debilitar*) to weaken.

enflaquezca [enfla'keθka] *etc vb* V **enflaquecer**.

enfocar [enfo'kar] *vt* (*foto etc*) to focus; (*problema etc*) to consider, look at.

enfoque [en'foke] *etc vb* V **enfocar** ◆ *nm* focus; (*acto*) focusing; (*óptica*) approach.

enfrascado, a [enfras'kaðo, a] *a*: **estar ~ en algo** (*fig*) to be wrapped up in sth.

enfrascar [enfras'kar] *vt* to bottle; **~se** *vr*: **~se en un libro** to bury o.s. in a book.

enfrasque [en'fraske] *etc vb* V **enfrascar**.

enfrentamiento [enfrenta'mjento] *nm* confrontation.

enfrentar [enfren'tar] *vt* (*peligro*) to face (up to), confront; (*oponer*) to bring face to face; **~se** *vr* (*dos personas*) to face o confront each other; (*DEPORTE: dos equipos*) to meet; **~se a** o **con** to face up to, confront.

enfrente [en'frente] *ad* opposite; **~ de** *prep* opposite, facing; **la casa de ~** the house opposite, the house across the street.

enfriamiento [enfria'mjento] *nm* chilling, refrigeration; (*MED*) cold, chill.

enfriar [enfri'ar] *vt* (*alimentos*) to cool, chill; (*algo caliente*) to cool down; (*habitación*) to air, freshen; (*entusiasmo*) to dampen; **~se** *vr* to cool down; (*MED*) to catch a chill; (*amistad*) to cool.

enfurecer [enfure'θer] *vt* to enrage, madden; **~se** *vr* to become furious, fly into a rage; (*mar*) to get rough.

enfurezca [enfu'reθka] *etc vb* V **enfurecer**.

engalanar [engala'nar] *vt* (*adornar*) to adorn; (*ciudad*) to decorate; **~se** *vr* to get dressed up.

enganchar [engan'tʃar] *vt* to hook; (*ropa*) to hang up; (*dos vagones*) to hitch up;

(*TEC*) to couple, connect; (*MIL*) to recruit; (*fam: atraer: persona*) to rope into; **~se** *vr* (*MIL*) to enlist, join up; **~se (a)** (*drogas*) to get hooked (on).

enganche [en'gantʃe] *nm* hook; (*TEC*) coupling, connection; (*acto*) hooking (up); (*MIL*) recruitment, enlistment; (*AM: depósito*) deposit.

engañar [enga'ɲar] *vt* to deceive; (*estafar*) to cheat, swindle ◆ *vi*: **las apariencias engañan** appearances are deceptive; **~se** *vr* (*equivocarse*) to be wrong; (*asímismo*) to deceive o kid o.s.; **engaña a su mujer** he's unfaithful to o cheats on his wife.

engaño [en'gaɲo] *nm* deceit; (*estafa*) trick, swindle; (*error*) mistake, misunderstanding; (*ilusión*) delusion.

engañoso, a [enga'ɲoso, a] *a* (*tramposo*) crooked; (*mentiroso*) dishonest, deceitful; (*aspecto*) deceptive; (*consejo*) misleading.

engarce [en'garθe] *etc vb* V **engarzar**.

engarzar [engar'θar] *vt* (*joya*) to set, mount; (*fig*) to link, connect.

engatusar [engatu'sar] *vt* (*fam*) to coax.

engendrar [enxen'drar] *vt* to breed; (*procrear*) to beget; (*fig*) to cause, produce.

engendro [en'xendro] *nm* (*BIO*) foetus; (*fig*) monstrosity; (*idea*) brainchild.

englobar [englo'βar] *vt* (*comprender*) to include, comprise; (*incluir*) to lump together.

engomar [engo'mar] *vt* to glue, stick.

engordar [engor'ðar] *vt* to fatten ◆ *vi* to get fat, put on weight.

engorro [en'gorro] *nm* bother, nuisance.

engorroso, a [engo'rroso, a] *a* bothersome, trying.

engranaje [engra'naxe] *nm* (*AUTO*) gear; (*juego*) gears *pl*.

engrandecer [engrande'θer] *vt* to enlarge, magnify; (*alabar*) to praise, speak highly of; (*exagerar*) to exaggerate.

engrandezca [engran'deθka] *etc vb* V **engrandecer**.

engrasar [engra'sar] *vt* (*TEC: poner grasa*) to grease; (*: lubricar*) to lubricate, oil; (*manchar*) to make greasy.

engrase [en'grase] *nm* greasing, lubrication.

engreído, a [engre'iðo, a] *a* vain, conceited.

engrosar [engro'sar] *vt* (*ensanchar*) to enlarge; (*aumentar*) to increase; (*hinchar*) to swell.

engrudo [en'gruðo] *nm* paste.

engruese [en'grwese] *etc vb* V **engrosar**.

engullir [engu'ʎir] *vt* to gobble, gulp (down).

enhebrar [ene'βrar] *vt* to thread.

enhiesto, a [e'njesto, a] *a* (*derecho*) erect; (*bandera*) raised; (*edificio*) lofty.

enhorabuena [enora'βwena] *excl* congratulations.

enigma [e'niɣma] *nm* enigma; (*problema*) puzzle; (*misterio*) mystery.

enigmático, a [eniɣ'matiko, a] *a* enigmatic.

enjabonar [enxaßo'nar] *vt* to soap; (*barba*) to lather; (*fam: adular*) to soft-soap; (: *regañar*) to tick off.

enjalbegar [enxalße'ɣar] *vt* (*pared*) to whitewash.

enjalbegue [enxal'ßeɣe] *etc vb* V **enjalbegar.**

enjambre [en'xamßre] *nm* swarm.

enjaular [enxau'lar] *vt* to (put in a) cage; (*fam*) to jail, lock up.

enjuagadientes [enxwaɣa'djentes] *nm inv* mouthwash.

enjuagar [enxwa'ɣar] *vt* (*ropa*) to rinse (out).

enjuague [en'xwaɣe] *etc vb* V **enjuagar** ◆ *nm* (*MED*) mouthwash; (*de ropa*) rinse, rinsing.

enjugar [enxu'ɣar] *vt* to wipe (off); (*lágrimas*) to dry; (*déficit*) to wipe out.

enjugue [en'xuɣe] *etc vb* V **enjugar.**

enjuiciar [enxwi'θjar] *vt* (*JUR: procesar*) to prosecute, try; (*fig*) to judge.

enjuto, a [en'xuto, a] *a* dry, dried up; (*fig*) lean, skinny.

enlace [en'laθe] *etc vb* V **enlazar** ◆ *nm* link, connection; (*relación*) relationship; (*tb*: ~ **matrimonial**) marriage; (*de trenes*) connection; ~ **de datos** data link; ~ **sindical** shop steward; ~ **telefónico** telephone linkup.

enlazar [enla'θar] *vt* (*unir con lazos*) to bind together; (*atar*) to tie; (*conectar*) to link, connect; (*AM*) to lasso.

enlodar [enlo'ðar] *vt* to cover in mud; (*fig*: *manchar*) to stain; (: *rebajar*) to debase.

enloquecer [enloke'θer] *vt* to drive mad ◆ *vi*, ~**se** *vr* to go mad.

enloquezca [enlo'keθka] *etc vb* V **enloquecer.**

enlutado, a [enlu'taðo, a] *a* (*persona*) in mourning.

enlutar [enlu'tar] *vt* to dress in mourning; ~**se** *vr* to go into mourning.

enmarañar [enmara'ɲar] *vt* (*enredar*) to tangle up, entangle; (*complicar*) to complicate; (*confundir*) to confuse; ~**se** *vr* (*enredarse*) to become entangled; (*confundirse*) to get confused.

enmarcar [enmar'kar] *vt* (*cuadro*) to frame; (*fig*) to provide a setting for.

enmarque [en'marke] *etc vb* V **enmarcar.**

enmascarar [enmaska'rar] *vt* to mask; (*intenciones*) to disguise; ~**se** *vr* to put on a mask.

enmendar [enmen'dar] *vt* to emend, correct; (*constitución etc*) to amend; (*comportamiento*) to reform; ~**se** *vr* to reform, mend one's ways.

enmienda [en'mjenda] *etc vb* V **enmendar** ◆ *nf* correction; amendment; reform.

enmohecerse [enmoe'θerse] *vr* (*metal*) to rust, go rusty; (*muro, plantas*) to go mouldy.

enmohezca [enmo'eθka] *etc vb* V **enmohecerse.**

enmudecer [enmuðe'θer] *vt* to silence ◆ *vi*, ~**se** *vr* (*perder el habla*) to fall silent; (*guardar silencio*) to remain silent; (*por miedo*) to be struck dumb.

enmudezca [enmu'ðeθka] *etc vb* V **enmudecer.**

ennegrecer [enneɣre'θer] *vt* (*poner negro*) to blacken; (*oscurecer*) to darken; ~**se** *vr* to turn black; (*oscurecerse*) to get dark, darken.

ennegrezca [enne'ɣreθka] *etc vb* V **ennegrecer.**

ennoblecer [ennoße'θer] *vt* to ennoble.

ennoblezca [enno'ßleθka] *etc vb* V **ennoblecer.**

en.º *abr* (= *enero*) Jan.

enojadizo, a [enoxa'ðiθo, a] *a* irritable, short-tempered.

enojar [eno'xar] *vt* (*encolerizar*) to anger; (*disgustar*) to annoy, upset; ~**se** *vr* to get angry; to get annoyed.

enojo [e'noxo] *nm* (*cólera*) anger; (*irritación*) annoyance; ~**s** *nmpl* trials, problems.

enojoso, a [eno'xoso, a] *a* annoying.

enorgullecerse [enorɣuʎe'θerse] *vr* to be proud; ~ **de** to pride o.s. on, be proud of.

enorgullezca [enorɣu'ʎeθka] *etc vb* V **enorgullecerse.**

enorme [e'norme] *a* enormous, huge; (*fig*) monstrous.

enormidad [enormi'ðað] *nf* hugeness, immensity.

enraice [en'raiθe] *etc vb* V **enraizar.**

enraizar [enrai'θar] *vi* to take root.

enrarecido, a [enrare'θiðo, a] *a* rarefied.

enredadera [enreða'ðera] *nf* (*BOT*) creeper, climbing plant.

enredar [enre'ðar] *vt* (*cables, hilos etc*) to tangle (up), entangle; (*situación*) to complicate, confuse; (*meter cizaña*) to sow discord among o between; (*implicar*) to embroil, implicate; ~**se** *vr* to get entangled, get tangled (up); (*situación*) to get complicated; (*persona*) to get embroiled; (*AM*: *fam*) to meddle.

enredo [en'reðo] *nm* (*maraña*) tangle; (*confusión*) mix-up, confusion; (*intriga*) intrigue; (*apuro*) jam; (*amorío*) love affair.

enrejado [enre'xaðo] *nm* grating; (*de ventana*) lattice; (*en jardín*) trellis.

enrevesado, a [enreße'saðo, a] *a* (*asunto*) complicated, involved.

enriquecer [enrike'θer] *vt* to make rich;

(fig) to enrich; ~**se** *vr* to get rich.

enriquezca [enri'keθka] *etc vb* V **enriquecer.**

enrojecer [enroxe'θer] *vt* to redden ♦ *vi,* ~**se** *vr (persona)* to blush.

enrojezca [enro'xeθka] *etc vb* V **enrojecer.**

enrolar [enro'lar] *vt (MIL)* to enlist; *(reclutar)* to recruit; ~**se** *vr (MIL)* to join up; *(afiliarse)* to enrol, sign on.

enrollar [enro'ʎar] *vt* to roll (up), wind (up); ~**se** *vr:* ~**se con uno** to get involved with sb.

enroque [en'roke] *nm (AJEDREZ)* castling.

enroscar [enros'kar] *vt (torcer, doblar)* to twist; *(arrollar)* to coil (round), wind; *(tornillo, rosca)* to screw in; ~**se** *vr* to coil, wind.

enrosque [en'roske] *etc vb* V **enroscar.**

ensalada [ensa'laða] *nf* salad; *(lío)* mix-up.

ensaladilla [ensala'ðiʎa] *nf (tb:* ~ **rusa)** ≈ Russian salad.

ensalce [en'salθe] *etc vb* V **ensalzar.**

ensalzar [ensal'θar] *vt (alabar)* to praise, extol; *(exaltar)* to exalt.

ensamblador [ensambla'ðor] *nm (INFORM)* assembler.

ensambladura [ensambla'ðura] *nf,* **ensamblaje** [ensam'blaxe] *nm* assembly; *(TEC)* joint.

ensamblar [ensam'blar] *vt (montar)* to assemble; *(madera etc)* to join.

ensanchar [ensan'tʃar] *vt (hacer más ancho)* to widen; *(agrandar)* to enlarge, expand; *(COSTURA)* to let out; ~**se** *vr* to get wider, expand; *(pey)* to give o.s. airs.

ensanche [en'santʃe] *nm (de calle)* widening; *(de negocio)* expansion.

ensangrentado, a [ensangren'taðo, a] *a* bloodstained, covered with blood.

ensangrentar [ensangren'tar] *vt* to stain with blood.

ensangriente [ensan'grjente] *etc vb* V **ensangrentar.**

ensañar [ensa'ɲar] *vt* to enrage; ~**se** *vr:* ~**se con** to treat brutally.

ensartar [ensar'tar] *vt (gen)* to string (together); *(carne)* to spit, skewer.

ensayar [ensa'jar] *vt* to test, try (out); *(TEATRO)* to rehearse.

ensayista [ensa'jista] *nm/f* essayist.

ensayo [en'sajo] *nm* test, trial; *(QUÍMICA)* experiment; *(TEATRO)* rehearsal; *(DEPORTE)* try; *(ESCOL, LITERATURA)* essay; **pedido de** ~ *(COM)* trial order; ~ **general** *(TEATRO)* dress rehearsal; *(MUS)* full rehearsal.

ensenada [ense'naða] *nf* inlet, cove.

enseña [en'seɲa] *nf* ensign, standard.

enseñante [ense'ɲante] *nm/f* teacher.

enseñanza [ense'ɲanθa] *nf (educación)* education; *(acción)* teaching; *(doctrina)*

teaching, doctrine; ~ **primaria/secundaria/superior** primary/secondary/higher education.

enseñar [ense'ɲar] *vt (educar)* to teach; *(instruir)* to teach, instruct; *(mostrar, señalar)* to show.

enseres [en'seres] *nmpl* belongings.

ENSIDESA [ensi'ðesa] *abr (Esp COM)* = *Empresa Nacional Siderúrgica, S. A.*

ensillar [ensi'ʎar] *vt* to saddle (up).

ensimismarse [ensimis'marse] *vr (abstraerse)* to become lost in thought; *(estar absorto)* to be lost in thought; *(AM)* to become conceited.

ensordecer [ensorðe'θer] *vt* to deafen ♦ *vi* to go deaf.

ensordezca [ensor'ðeθka] *etc vb* V **ensordecer.**

ensortijado, a [ensorti'xaðo, a] *a (pelo)* curly.

ensuciar [ensu'θjar] *vt (manchar)* to dirty, soil; *(fig)* to defile; ~**se** *vr (mancharse)* to get dirty; *(niño)* to dirty *(o* wet) o.s.

ensueño [en'sweɲo] *nm (sueño)* dream, fantasy; *(ilusión)* illusion; *(soñando despierto)* daydream; **de** ~ dream-like.

entablado [enta'ßlaðo] *nm (piso)* floorboards *pl; (armazón)* boarding.

entablar [enta'ßlar] *vt (recubrir)* to board (up); *(AJEDREZ, DAMAS)* to set up; *(conversación)* to strike up; *(JUR)* to file ♦ *vi* to draw.

entablillar [entaßli'ʎar] *vt (MED)* to (put in a) splint.

entallar [enta'ʎar] *vt (traje)* to tailor ♦ *vi:* **el traje entalla bien** the suit fits well.

ente ['ente] *nm (organización)* body, organization; *(compañía)* company; *(fam: persona)* odd character; *(ser)* being; ~ **público** *(Esp)* state(-owned) body.

entender [enten'der] *vt (comprender)* to understand; *(darse cuenta)* to realize; *(querer decir)* to mean ♦ *vi* to understand; *(creer)* to think, believe ♦ *nm:* **a mi** ~ in my opinion; ~ **de** to know all about; ~ **algo de** to know a little about; ~ **en** to deal with, have to do with; ~**se** *vr (comprenderse)* to be understood; *(2 personas)* to get on together; *(ponerse de acuerdo)* to agree, reach an agreement; **dar a** ~ **que** ... to lead to believe that ...; ~**se mal** to get on badly; **¿entiendes?** (do you) understand?

entendido, a [enten'diðo, a] *a (comprendido)* understood; *(hábil)* skilled; *(inteligente)* knowledgeable ♦ *nm/f (experto)* expert ♦ *excl* agreed!

entendimiento [entendi'mjento] *nm (comprensión)* understanding; *(inteligencia)* mind, intellect; *(juicio)* judgement.

enterado, a [ente'raðo, a] *a* well-informed;

estar ~ de to know about, be aware of; **no darse por ~** to pretend not to understand.
enteramente [entera'mente] *ad* entirely, completely.
enterar [ente'rar] *vt* (*informar*) to inform, tell; **~se** *vr*: **~se de** to find out about.
entereza [ente're0a] *nf* (*totalidad*) entirety; (*fig: carácter*) strength of mind; (*honradez*) integrity.
enternecedor, a [enterne0e'ðor, a] *a* touching.
enternecer [enterne'0er] *vt* (*ablandar*) to soften; (*apiadar*) to touch, move; **~se** *vr* to be touched, be moved.
enternezca [enter'ne0ka] *etc vb V* **enternecer.**
entero, a [en'tero, a] *a* (*total*) whole, entire; (*fig: recto*) honest; (: *firme*) firm, resolute ◆ *nm* (*MAT*) integer; (*COM: punto*) point; (*AM: pago*) payment; **las acciones han subido dos ~s** the shares have gone up two points.
enterrador [enterra'ðor] *nm* gravedigger.
enterrar [ente'rrar] *vt* to bury; (*fig*) to forget.
entibiar [enti'ßjar] *vt* (*enfriar*) to cool; (*calentar*) to warm; **~se** *vr* (*fig*) to cool.
entidad [enti'ðað] *nf* (*empresa*) firm, company; (*organismo*) body; (*sociedad*) society; (*FILOSOFÍA*) entity.
entienda [en'tjenda] *etc vb V* **entender.**
entierro [en'tjerro] *etc vb V* **enterrar** ◆ *nm* (*acción*) burial; (*funeral*) funeral.
entomología [entomolo'xia] *nf* entomology.
entomólogo, a [ento'moloɣo, a] *nm/f* entomologist.
entonación [entona'0jon] *nf* (*LING*) intonation; (*fig*) conceit.
entonar [ento'nar] *vt* (*canción*) to intone; (*colores*) to tone; (*MED*) to tone up ◆ *vi* to be in tune; **~se** *vr* (*engreírse*) to give o.s. airs.
entonces [en'ton0es] *ad* then, at that time; **desde ~** since then; **en aquel ~** at that time; **(pues) ~** and so; **el ~ embajador de España** the then Spanish ambassador.
entornar [entor'nar] *vt* (*puerta, ventana*) to half close, leave ajar; (*los ojos*) to screw up.
entorno [en'torno] *nm* setting, environment; **~ de redes** (*INFORM*) network environment.
entorpecer [entorpe'0er] *vt* (*entendimiento*) to dull; (*impedir*) to obstruct, hinder; (: *tránsito*) to slow down, delay.
entorpezca [entor'pe0ka] *etc vb V* **entorpecer.**
entrado, a [en'traðo, a] *a*: **~ en años** elderly; **(una vez) ~ el verano** in the summer(time), when summer comes ◆ *nf* (*acción*) entry, access; (*sitio*) entrance,

way in; (*principio*) beginning; (*COM*) receipts *pl*, takings *pl*; (*CULIN*) entrée; (*DEPORTE*) innings *sg*; (*TEATRO*) house, audience; (*para el cine etc*) ticket; (*INFORM*) input; (*ECON*): **entradas** *nfpl* income *sg*; **entradas brutas** gross receipts; **entradas y salidas** (*COM*) income and expenditure; **entrada de aire** (*TEC*) air intake *o* inlet; **de entrada** right away; **"entrada gratis"** "admission free"; **entrada de datos vocal** (*INFORM*) voice input; **tiene entradas** he's losing his hair.
entrante [en'trante] *a* next, coming; (*POL*) incoming ◆ *nm* inlet; (*CULIN*) starter; **mes/año ~** next month/year.
entraña [en'trapa] *nf* (*fig: centro*) heart, core; (*raíz*) root; **~s** *nfpl* (*ANAT*) entrails; (*fig*) heart *sg*.
entrañable [entra'paßle] *a* close, intimate.
entrañar [entra'par] *vt* to entail.
entrar [en'trar] *vt* (*introducir*) to bring in; (*persona*) to show in; (*INFORM*) to input ◆ *vi* (*meterse*) to go *o* come in, enter; (*comenzar*): **~ diciendo** to begin by saying; **le entraron ganas de reír** he felt a sudden urge to laugh; **no me entra** I can't get the hang of it.
entre ['entre] *prep* (*dos*) between; (*en medio de*) among(st); (*por*): **se abrieron paso ~ la multitud** they forced their way through the crowd; **~ una cosa y otra** what with one thing and another.
entreabierto [entrea'ßjerto] *pp de* **entreabrir.**
entreabrir [entrea'ßrir] *vt* to half-open, open halfway.
entreacto [entre'akto] *nm* interval.
entrecano, a [entre'kano, a] *a* greying; **ser ~** (*persona*) to be going grey.
entrecejo [entre'0exo] *nm*: **fruncir el ~** to frown.
entrecomillado, a [entrekomi'ʎaðo, a] *a* in inverted commas.
entrecortado, a [entrekor'taðo, a] *a* (*respiración*) laboured, difficult; (*habla*) faltering.
entrecot [entre'ko(t)] *nm* (*CULIN*) sirloin steak.
entrecruce [entre'kru0e] *etc vb V* **entrecruzarse.**
entrecruzarse [entrekru'0arse] *vr* (*BIO*) to interbreed.
entrechocar [entretʃo'kar] *vi* (*dientes*) to chatter.
entrechoque [entre'tʃoke] *etc vb V* **entrechocar.**
entredicho [entre'ðitʃo] *nm* (*JUR*) injunction; **poner en ~** to cast doubt on; **estar en ~** to be in doubt.
entrega [en'treɣa] *nf* (*de mercancías*) delivery; (*de premios*) presentation; (*de novela*

etc) instalment; **"~ a domicilio"** "door-to-door delivery service".

entregar [entre'ɣar] *vt* (*dar*) to hand (over), deliver; (*ejercicios*) to hand in; **~se** *vr* (*rendirse*) to surrender, give in, submit; **~se a** (*dedicarse*) to devote o.s. to; **a ~** (*COM*) to be supplied.

entregue [en'treɣe] *etc vb V* **entregar.**

entrelace [entre'laθe] *etc vb V* **entrelazar.**

entrelazar [entrela'θar] *vt* to entwine.

entremedias [entre'meðjas] *ad* (*en medio*) in between, halfway.

entremeses [entre'meses] *nmpl* hors d'œuvres.

entremeter [entreme'ter] *vt* to insert, put in; **~se** *vr* to meddle, interfere.

entremetido, a [entreme'tiðo, a] *a* meddling, interfering.

entremezclar [entremeθ'klar] *vt*, **~se** *vr* to intermingle.

entrenador, a [entrena'ðor, a] *nm/f* trainer, coach.

entrenamiento [entrena'mjento] *nm* training.

entrenar [entre'nar] *vt* (*DEPORTE*) to train; (*caballo*) to exercise; **~se** *vr* to train.

entrepierna [entre'pjerna] *nf* (*tb:* **~s**) crotch, crutch.

entresacar [entresa'kar] *vt* to pick out, select.

entresaque [entre'sake] *etc vb V* **entresacar.**

entresuelo [entre'swelo] *nm* mezzanine, entresol; (*TEATRO*) dress o first circle.

entretanto [entre'tanto] *ad* meanwhile, meantime.

entretejer [entrete'xer] *vt* to interweave.

entretela [entre'tela] *nf* (*de ropa*) interlining; **~s** *nfpl* heart-strings.

entretendré [entreten'dre] *etc vb V* **entretener.**

entretener [entrete'ner] *vt* (*divertir*) to entertain, amuse; (*detener*) to hold up, delay; (*mantener*) to maintain; **~se** *vr* (*divertirse*) to amuse o.s.; (*retrasarse*) to delay, linger; **no le entretengo más** I won't keep you any longer.

entretenga [entre'tenga] *etc vb V* **entretener.**

entretenido, a [entrete'niðo, a] *a* entertaining, amusing.

entretenimiento [entreteni'mjento] *nm* entertainment, amusement; (*mantenimiento*) upkeep, maintenance.

entretiene [entre'tjene] *etc*, **entretuve** [entre'tuβe] *etc vb V* **entretener.**

entreveía [entreβe'ia] *etc vb V* **entrever.**

entrever [entre'βer] *vt* to glimpse, catch a glimpse of.

entrevista [entre'βista] *nf* interview.

entrevistar [entreβis'tar] *vt* to interview;

~se *vr*: **~se con** to have an interview with, see; **el ministro se entrevistó con el Rey ayer** the minister had an audience with the King yesterday.

entrevisto [entre'βisto] *pp de* **entrever.**

entristecer [entriste'θer] *vt* to sadden, grieve; **~se** *vr* to grow sad.

entristezca [entris'teθka] *etc vb V* **entristecer.**

entrometerse [entrome'terse] *vr*: **~ (en)** to interfere (in o with).

entrometido, a [entrome'tiðo, a] *a* interfering, meddlesome.

entroncar [entron'kar] *vi* to be connected o related.

entronque [en'tronke] *etc vb V* **entroncar.**

entuerto [en'twerto] *nm* wrong, injustice; **~s** *nmpl* (*MED*) afterpains.

entumecer [entume'θer] *vt* to numb, benumb; **~se** *vr* (*por el frío*) to go o become numb.

entumecido, a [entume'θiðo, a] *a* numb, stiff.

entumezca [entu'meθka] *etc vb V* **entumecer.**

enturbiar [entur'βjar] *vt* (*el agua*) to make cloudy; (*fig*) to confuse; **~se** *vr* (*oscurecerse*) to become cloudy; (*fig*) to get confused, become obscure.

entusiasmar [entusjas'mar] *vt* to excite, fill with enthusiasm; (*gustar mucho*) to delight; **~se** *vr*: **~se con** o **por** to get enthusiastic o excited about.

entusiasmo [entu'sjasmo] *nm* enthusiasm; (*excitación*) excitement.

entusiasta [entu'sjasta] *a* enthusiastic ◆ *nm/f* enthusiast.

enumerar [enume'rar] *vt* to enumerate.

enunciación [enunθja'θjon] *nf*, **enunciado** [enun'θjaðo] *nm* enunciation; (*declaración*) declaration, statement.

enunciar [enun'θjar] *vt* to enunciate; to declare, state.

envainar [embai'nar] *vt* to sheathe.

envalentonar [embalento'nar] *vt* to give courage to; **~se** *vr* (*pey: jactarse*) to boast, brag.

envanecer [embane'θer] *vt* to make conceited; **~se** *vr* to grow conceited.

envanezca [emba'neθka] *etc vb V* **envanecer.**

envasar [emba'sar] *vt* (*empaquetar*) to pack, wrap; (*enfrascar*) to bottle; (*enlatar*) to can; (*embolsar*) to pocket.

envase [em'base] *nm* packing, wrapping; bottling; canning; pocketing; (*recipiente*) container; (*paquete*) package; (*botella*) bottle; (*lata*) tin (*Brit*), can.

envejecido, a [embexe'θiðo, a] *a* old, aged; (*de aspecto*) old-looking.

envejecer [embexe'θer] *vt* to make old, age

◆ *vi*, ~**se** *vr* (*volverse viejo*) to grow old; (*parecer viejo*) to age.

envejezca [embe'xeθka] *etc vb* V **envejecer.**

envenenar [embene'nar] *vt* to poison; (*fig*) to embitter.

envergadura [embervaˈðura] *nf* (*expansión*) expanse; (*NAUT*) breadth; (*fig*) scope; **un programa de gran** ~ a wide-ranging programme.

envés [em'bes] *nm* (*de tela*) back, wrong side.

enviado, a [em'bjaðo, a] *nm/f* (*POL*) envoy; ~ **especial** (*de periódico*, *TV*) special correspondent.

enviar [em'bjar] *vt* to send.

enviciar [embi'θjar] *vt* to corrupt ◆ *vi* (*trabajo etc*) to be addictive; ~**se** *vr*: ~**se** (**con** *o* **en**) to get addicted (to).

envidia [em'biðja] *nf* envy; **tener** ~ **a** to envy, be jealous of.

envidiar [embi'ðjar] *vt* (*desear*) to envy; (*tener celos de*) to be jealous of.

envidioso, a [embi'ðjoso, a] *a* envious, jealous.

envío [em'bio] *nm* (*acción*) sending; (*de mercancías*) consignment; (*de dinero*) remittance; (*en barco*) shipment; **gastos de** ~ postage and packing; ~ **contra reembolso** COD shipment.

enviudar [embju'ðar] *vi* to be widowed.

envoltura [embol'tura] *nf* (*cobertura*) cover; (*embalaje*) wrapper, wrapping.

envolver [embol'ßer] *vt* to wrap (up); (*cubrir*) to cover; (*enemigo*) to surround; (*implicar*) to involve, implicate.

envuelto [em'bwelto], **envuelva** [em'bwelßa] *etc vb* V **envolver.**

enyesar [enje'sar] *vt* (*pared*) to plaster; (*MED*) to put in plaster.

enzarzarse [enθar'θarse] *vr*: ~ **en algo** to get mixed up in sth.

E.P.D. *abr* (= *en paz descanse*) R.I.P.

épico, a ['epiko, a] *a* epic ◆ *nf* epic (poetry).

epidemia [epi'ðemja] *nf* epidemic.

epidémico, a [epi'ðemiko, a] *a* epidemic.

epifanía [epifa'nia] *nf* Epiphany.

epilepsia [epi'lepsja] *nf* epilepsy.

epílogo [e'pilovo] *nm* epilogue.

episcopado [episco'paðo] *nm* (*cargo*) bishopric; (*obispos*) bishops *pl* (*collectively*).

episodio [epi'soðjo] *nm* episode; (*suceso*) incident.

epístola [e'pistola] *nf* epistle.

epitafio [epi'tafjo] *nm* epitaph.

época ['epoka] *nf* period, time; (*temporada*) season; (*HISTORIA*) age, epoch; **hacer** ~ to be epoch-making.

equidad [eki'ðað] *nf* equity, fairness.

equilibrar [ekili'ßrar] *vt* to balance.

equilibrio [eki'lißrjo] *nm* balance, equilibrium; ~ **político** balance of power.

equilibrista [ekili'ßrista] *nm/f* (*funámbulo*) tightrope walker; (*acróbata*) acrobat.

equinoccio [eki'nokθjo] *nm* equinox.

equipaje [eki'paxe] *nm* luggage (*Brit*), baggage (*US*); (*avíos*) equipment, kit; ~ **de mano** hand luggage; **hacer el** ~ to pack.

equipar [eki'par] *vt* (*proveer*) to equip.

equiparar [ekipa'rar] *vt* (*igualar*) to put on the same level; (*comparar*) to compare (*con* with); ~**se** *vr*: ~**se con** to be on a level with.

equipo [e'kipo] *nm* (*conjunto de cosas*) equipment; (*DEPORTE*, *grupo*) team; (*de obreros*) shift; (*de máquinas*) plant; (*turbinas etc*) set; ~ **de caza** hunting gear; ~ **físico** (*INFORM*) hardware; ~ **médico** medical team.

equis ['ekis] *nf* (the letter) X.

equitación [ekita'θjon] *nf* (*acto*) riding; (*arte*) horsemanship.

equitativo, a [ekita'tißo, a] *a* equitable, fair.

equivaldré [ekißal'dre] *etc vb* V **equivaler.**

equivalencia [ekißa'lenθja] *nf* equivalence.

equivalente [ekißa'lente] *a*, *nm* equivalent.

equivaler [ekißa'ler] *vi*: ~ **a** to be equivalent *o* equal to; (*en rango*) to rank as.

equivalga [eki'ßalva] *etc vb* V **equivaler.**

equivocación [ekißoka'θjon] *nf* mistake, error; (*malentendido*) misunderstanding.

equivocado, a [ekißo'kaðo, a] *a* wrong, mistaken.

equivocarse [ekißo'karse] *vr* to be wrong, make a mistake; ~ **de camino** to take the wrong road.

equívoco, a [e'kißoko, a] *a* (*dudoso*) suspect; (*ambiguo*) ambiguous ◆ *nm* ambiguity; (*malentendido*) misunderstanding.

equivoque [eki'ßoke] *etc vb* V **equivocar.**

era ['era] *vb* V **ser** ◆ *nf* era, age; (*AGR*) threshing floor.

erais ['erais], **éramos** ['eramos], **eran** ['eran] *vb* V **ser.**

erario [e'rarjo] *nm* exchequer, treasury.

eras ['eras], **eres** ['eres] *vb* V **ser.**

ergonomía [ervono'mia] *nf* ergonomics *sg*, human engineering.

erguir [er'xir] *vt* to raise, lift; (*poner derecho*) to straighten; ~**se** *vr* to straighten up.

erice [e'riθe] *etc vb* V **erizarse.**

erigir [eri'xir] *vt* to erect, build; ~**se** *vr*: ~**se en** to set o.s. up as.

erija [e'rixa] *etc vb* V **erigir.**

erizado, a [eri'θaðo, a] *a* bristly.

erizarse [eri'θarse] *vr* (*pelo: de perro*) to bristle; (: *de persona*) to stand on end.

erizo [e'riθo] *nm* hedgehog; ~ **de mar** sea

urchin.

ermita [er'mita] *nf* hermitage.

ermitaño, a [ermi'taɲo, a] *nm/f* hermit.

erosionar [erosjo'nar] *vt* to erode.

erótico, a [e'rotiko, a] *a* erotic.

erotismo [ero'tismo] *nm* eroticism.

erradicar [erraði'kar] *vt* to eradicate.

erradique [erra'ðike] *etc vb V* **erradicar.**

errado, a [e'rraðo, a] *a* mistaken, wrong.

errante [e'rrante] *a* wandering, errant.

errar [e'rrar] *vi* (*vagar*) to wander, roam; (*equivocarse*) to be mistaken ♦ *vt*: ~ **el camino** to take the wrong road; ~ **el tiro** to miss.

errata [e'rrata] *nf* misprint.

erre ['erre] *nf* (the letter) R; ~ **que** ~ stubbornly.

erróneo, a [e'rroneo, a] *a* (*equivocado*) wrong, mistaken; (*falso*) false, untrue.

error [e'rror] *nm* error, mistake; (*INFORM*) bug; ~ **de imprenta** misprint; ~ **de lectura/escritura** (*INFORM*) read/write error; ~ **sintáctico** syntax error; ~ **judicial** miscarriage of justice.

eructar [eruk'tar] *vt* to belch, burp.

erudición [eruði'θjon] *nf* erudition, learning.

erudito, a [eru'ðito, a] *a* erudite, learned ♦ *nm/f* scholar; **los** ~**s en esta materia** the experts in this field.

erupción [erup'θjon] *nf* eruption; (*MED*) rash; (*de violencia*) outbreak; (*de ira*) outburst.

es [es] *vb V* **ser.**

E/S *abr* (*INFORM*: *entrada/salida*) I/O.

esa ['esa], **esas** ['esas] *a demostrativo V* **ese.**

ésa ['esa], **ésas** ['esas] *pron V* **ése.**

esbelto, a [es'ßelto, a] *a* slim, slender.

esbirro [es'ßirro] *nm* henchman.

esbozar [esßo'θar] *vt* to sketch, outline.

esbozo [es'ßoθo] *nm* sketch, outline.

escabeche [eska'ßetʃe] *nm* brine; (*de aceitunas etc*) pickle; **en** ~ pickled.

escabechina [eskaße'tʃina] *nf* (*batalla*) massacre; **hacer una** ~ (*ESCOL*) to fail a lot of students.

escabroso, a [eska'ßroso, a] *a* (*accidentado*) rough, uneven; (*fig*) tough, difficult; (: *atrevido*) risqué.

escabullirse [eskaßu'ʎirse] *vr* to slip away; (*largarse*) to clear out.

escafandra [eska'fandra] *nf* (*buzo*) diving suit; (~ *espacial*) spacesuit.

escala [es'kala] *nf* (*proporción, MUS*) scale; (*de mano*) ladder; (*AVIAT*) stopover; (*de colores etc*) range; ~ **de tiempo** time scale; ~ **de sueldos** salary scale; **una investigación** ~ **nacional** a nationwide inquiry; **reproducir según** ~ to reproduce to scale; **hacer** ~ **en** to stop off *o* over at.

escalada [eska'laða] *nf* (*de montaña*) climb; (*de pared*) scaling.

escalafón [eskala'fon] *nm* (*escala de salarios*) salary scale, wage scale.

escalar [eska'lar] *vt* to climb, scale ♦ *vi* (*MIL, POL*) to escalate.

escaldar [eskal'dar] *vt* (*quemar*) to scald; (*escarmentar*) to teach a lesson.

escalera [eska'lera] *nf* stairs *pl*, staircase; (*escala*) ladder; (*NAIPES*) run; (*de camión*) tailboard; ~ **mecánica** escalator; ~ **de caracol** spiral staircase; ~ **de incendios** fire escape.

escalfar [eskal'far] *vt* (*huevos*) to poach.

escalinata [eskali'nata] *nf* staircase.

escalofriante [eskalo'frjante] *a* chilling.

escalofrío [eskalo'frio] *nm* (*MED*) chill; ~**s** *nmpl* (*fig*) shivers.

escalón [eska'lon] *nm* step, stair; (*de escalera*) rung; (*fig: paso*) step; (*al éxito*) ladder.

escalonar [eskalo'nar] *vt* to spread out; (*tierra*) to terrace; (*horas de trabajo*) to stagger.

escalope [eska'lope] *nm* (*CULIN*) escalope.

escama [es'kama] *nf* (*de pez, serpiente*) scale; (*de jabón*) flake; (*fig*) resentment.

escamar [eska'mar] *vt* (*pez*) to scale; (*producir recelo*) to make wary.

escamotear [eskamote'ar] *vt* (*fam: robar*) to lift, swipe; (*hacer desaparecer*) to make disappear.

escampar [eskam'par] *vb impersonal* to stop raining.

escanciar [eskan'θjar] *vt* (*vino*) to pour (out).

escandalice [eskanda'liθe] *etc vb V* **escandalizar.**

escandalizar [eskandali'θar] *vt* to scandalize, shock; ~**se** *vr* to be shocked; (*ofenderse*) to be offended.

escándalo [es'kandalo] *nm* scandal; (*alboroto, tumulto*) row, uproar; **armar un** ~ to make a scene; **¡es un** ~! it's outrageous!

escandaloso, a [eskanda'loso, a] *a* scandalous, shocking; (*risa*) hearty; (*niño*) noisy.

Escandinavia [eskandi'naßja] *nf* Scandinavia.

escandinavo, a [eskandi'naßo, a] *a, nm/f* Scandinavian.

escaño [es'kaɲo] *nm* bench; (*POL*) seat.

escapada [eska'paða] *nf* (*huida*) escape, flight; (*deportes*) breakaway; (*viaje*) quick trip.

escapar [eska'par] *vi* (*gen*) to escape, run away; (*DEPORTE*) to break away; ~**se** *vr* to escape, get away; (*agua, gas, noticias*) to leak (out); **se me escapa su nombre** his name escapes me.

escaparate [eskapa'rate] *nm* shop window; (*COM*) showcase.

escapatoria [eskapa'torja] *nf*: **no tener** ~

(fig) to have no way out.

escape [es'kape] *nm* *(huida)* escape; *(de agua, gas)* leak; *(de motor)* exhaust; **salir a ~** to rush out.

escapismo [eska'pismo] *nm* escapism.

escarabajo [eskara'βaxo] *nm* beetle.

escaramuza [eskara'muθa] *nf* skirmish; *(fig)* brush.

escarbar [eskar'βar] *vt* *(gallina)* to scratch; *(fig)* to inquire into, investigate.

escarcha [es'kartʃa] *nf* frost.

escarlata [eskar'lata] *a inv* scarlet.

escarlatina [eskarla'tina] *nf* scarlet fever.

escarmentar [eskarmen'tar] *vt* to punish severely ♦ *vi* to learn one's lesson; ¡**para que escarmientes!** that'll teach you!

escarmiento [eskar'mjento] *etc vb* V **escarmentar** ♦ *nm* *(ejemplo)* lesson; *(castigo)* punishment.

escarnio [es'karnjo] *nm* mockery; *(injuria)* insult.

escarola [eska'rola] *nf* *(BOT)* endive.

escarpado, a [eskar'paðo, a] *a* *(pendiente)* sheer, steep; *(rocas)* craggy.

escasamente [eskasa'mente] *ad* *(insuficientemente)* scantily; *(apenas)* scarcely.

escasear [eskase'ar] *vi* to be scarce.

escasez [eska'seθ] *nf* *(falta)* shortage, scarcity; *(pobreza)* poverty; **vivir con ~** to live on the breadline.

escaso, a [es'kaso, a] *a* *(poco)* scarce; *(raro)* rare; *(ralo)* thin, sparse; *(limitado)* limited; *(recursos)* scanty; *(público)* sparse; *(posibilidad)* slim; *(visibilidad)* poor.

escatimar [eskati'mar] *vt* *(limitar)* to skimp (on), be sparing with; **no ~ esfuerzos (para)** to spare no effort (to).

escayola [eska'jola] *nf* plaster.

escayolar [eskajo'lar] *vt* to put in plaster.

escena [es'θena] *nf* scene; *(decorado)* scenery; *(escenario)* stage; **poner en ~** to put on.

escenario [esθe'narjo] *nm* *(TEATRO)* stage; *(CINE)* set; *(fig)* scene; **el ~ del crimen** the scene of the crime; **el ~ político** the political scene.

escenografía [esθenoɣra'fia] *nf* set o stage design.

escepticismo [esθepti'θismo] *nm* scepticism.

escéptico, a [es'θeptiko, a] *a* sceptical ♦ *nm/f* sceptic.

escindir [esθin'dir] *vt* to split; **~se** *vr* *(facción)* to split off; **~se en** to split into.

escisión [esθi'sjon] *nf* *(MED)* excision; *(fig, POL)* split; **~ nuclear** nuclear fission.

esclarecer [esklare'θer] *vt* *(iluminar)* to light up, illuminate; *(misterio, problema)* to shed light on.

esclarezca [eskla'reθka] *etc vb* V **esclarecer.**

esclavice [eskla'βiθe] *etc vb* V **esclavizar.**

esclavitud [esklaβi'tuð] *nf* slavery.

esclavizar [esklaβi'θar] *vt* to enslave.

esclavo, a [es'klaβo, a] *nm/f* slave.

esclusa [es'klusa] *nf* *(de canal)* lock; *(compuerta)* floodgate.

escoba [es'koβa] *nf* broom; **pasar la ~** to sweep up.

escobazo [esko'βaθo] *nm* *(golpe)* blow with a broom; **echar a uno a ~s** to kick sb out.

escocer [esko'θer] *vi* to burn, sting; **~se** *vr* to chafe, get chafed.

escocés, esa [esko'θes, esa] *a* Scottish; *(whisky)* Scotch ♦ *nm/f* Scotsman/woman, Scot ♦ *nm* *(LING)* Scots *sg*; **tela escocesa** tartan.

Escocia [es'koθja] *nf* Scotland.

escoger [esko'xer] *vt* to choose, pick, select.

escogido, a [esko'xiðo, a] *a* chosen, selected; *(calidad)* choice, select; *(persona)*: **ser muy ~** to be very fussy.

escoja [es'koxa] *etc vb* V **escoger.**

escolar [esko'lar] *a* school *cpd* ♦ *nm/f* schoolboy/girl, pupil.

escolaridad [eskolari'ðað] *nf* schooling; **libro de ~** school record.

escolarización [eskolariθa'θjon] *nf*: **~ obligatoria** compulsory education.

escolarizado, a [eskolari'θaðo, a] *a*, *nm/f*: **los ~s** those in o attending school.

escolta [es'kolta] *nf* escort.

escoltar [eskol'tar] *vt* to escort; *(proteger)* to guard.

escollo [es'koʎo] *nm* *(arrecife)* reef, rock; *(fig)* pitfall.

escombros [es'kombros] *nmpl* *(basura)* rubbish *sg*; *(restos)* debris *sg*.

esconder [eskon'der] *vt* to hide, conceal; **~se** *vr* to hide.

escondidas [eskon'diðas] *nfpl* *(AM)* hide-and-seek *sg*; **a ~** secretly; **hacer algo a ~ de uno** to do sth behind sb's back.

escondite [eskon'dite] *nm* hiding place; *(juego)* hide-and-seek.

escondrijo [eskon'drixo] *nm* hiding-place, hideout.

escopeta [esko'peta] *nf* shotgun; **~ de aire comprimido** air gun.

escoria [es'korja] *nf* *(desecho mineral)* slag; *(fig)* scum, dregs *pl*.

Escorpio [es'korpjo] *nm* *(ASTRO)* Scorpio.

escorpión [eskor'pjon] *nm* scorpion.

escotado, a [esko'taðo, a] *a* low-cut.

escotar [esko'tar] *vt* *(vestido: ajustar)* to cut to fit; *(cuello)* to cut low.

escote [es'kote] *nm* *(de vestido)* low neck; **pagar a ~** to share the expenses.

escotilla [esko'tiʎa] *nf* *(NAUT)* hatchway.

escotillón [eskoti'ʎon] *nm* trapdoor.

escozor [esko'θor] *nm* (*dolor*) sting(ing).

escribano, a [eskri'βano, a], **escribiente** [eskri'βjente] *nm/f* clerk; (*secretario judicial*) court *o* lawyer's clerk.

escribir [eskri'βir] *vt*, *vi* to write; ~ a **máquina** to type; **¿cómo se escribe?** how do you spell it?

escrito, a [es'krito, a] *pp de* **escribir** ◆ *a* written, in writing; (*examen*) written ◆ *nm* (*documento*) document; (*manuscrito*) text, manuscript; **por** ~ in writing.

escritor, a [eskri'tor, a] *nm/f* writer.

escritorio [eskri'torjo] *nm* desk; (*oficina*) office.

escritura [eskri'tura] *nf* (*acción*) writing; (*caligrafía*) (hand)writing; (*JUR*: *documento*) deed; (*COM*) indenture; ~ **de propiedad** title deed; **Sagrada E~** (Holy) Scripture; ~ **social** articles *pl* of association.

escroto [es'kroto] *nm* scrotum.

escrúpulo [es'krupulo] *nm* scruple; (*minuciosidad*) scrupulousness.

escrupuloso, a [eskrupu'loso, a] *a* scrupulous.

escrutar [eskru'tar] *vt* to scrutinize, examine; (*votos*) to count.

escrutinio [eskru'tinjo] *nm* (*examen atento*) scrutiny; (*POL*: *recuento de votos*) count(ing).

escuadra [es'kwaðra] *nf* (*TEC*) square; (*MIL etc*) squad; (*NAUT*) squadron; (*de coches etc*) fleet.

escuadrilla [eskwa'ðriʎa] *nf* (*de aviones*) squadron; (*AM: de obreros*) gang.

escuadrón [eskwa'ðron] *nm* squadron.

escuálido, a [es'kwaliðo, a] *a* skinny, scraggy; (*sucio*) squalid.

escucha [es'kutʃa] *nf* (*acción*) listening ◆ *nm* (*TELEC*: *sistema*) monitor; (*oyente*) listener; **estar a la** ~ to listen in; **estar de** ~ to spy; ~**s telefónicas** (*telephone*) tapping *sg*.

escuchar [esku'tʃar] *vt* to listen to; (*consejo*) to heed ◆ *vi* to listen; ~**se** *vr*: **se escucha muy mal** (*AM TELEC*) it's a very bad line.

escudarse [esku'ðarse] *vr*: ~ **en** (*fig*) to hide behind.

escudería [eskuðe'ria] *nf*: **la** ~ **Ferrari** the Ferrari team.

escudero [esku'ðero] *nm* squire.

escudilla [esku'ðiʎa] *nf* bowl, basin.

escudo [es'kuðo] *nm* shield; ~ **de armas** coat of arms.

escudriñar [eskuðri'ɲar] *vt* (*examinar*) to investigate, scrutinize; (*mirar de lejos*) to scan.

escuece [es'kweθe] *etc vb V* **escocer**.

escuela [es'kwela] *nf* (*tb fig*) school; ~ **normal** teacher training college; ~ **de**

párvulos kindergarten.

escueto, a [es'kweto, a] *a* plain; (*estilo*) simple; (*explicación*) concise.

escueza [es'kweθa] *etc vb V* **escocer**.

escuincle [es'kwinkle] *nm* (*AM fam*) kid.

esculpir [eskul'pir] *vt* to sculpt; (*grabar*) to engrave; (*tallar*) to carve.

escultor, a [eskul'tor, a] *nm/f* sculptor.

escultura [eskul'tura] *nf* sculpture.

escupidera [eskupi'ðera] *nf* spittoon.

escupir [esku'pir] *vt* to spit (out) ◆ *vi* to spit.

escurreplatos [eskurre'platos] *nm inv* plate rack.

escurridizo, a [eskurri'ðiθo, a] *a* slippery.

escurrir [esku'rrir] *vt* (*ropa*) to wring out; (*verduras, platos*) to drain ◆ *vi* (*los líquidos*) to drip; ~**se** *vr* (*secarse*) to drain; (*resbalarse*) to slip, slide; (*escaparse*) to slip away.

ese ['ese] *nf* (the letter) S; **hacer** ~**s** (*carretera*) to zigzag; (*borracho*) to reel about.

ese ['ese], **esa** ['esa], **esos** ['esos], **esas** ['esas] *a demostrativo* (*sg*) that; (*pl*) those.

ése ['ese], **ésa** ['esa], **ésos** ['esos], **ésas** ['esas] *pron* (*sg*) that (one); (*pl*) those (ones); **ése ... éste** ... the former ... the latter ...; **¡no me vengas con ésas!** don't give me any more of that nonsense!

esencia [e'senθja] *nf* essence.

esencial [esen'θjal] *a* essential; (*principal*) chief; **lo** ~ the main thing.

esfera [es'fera] *nf* sphere; (*de reloj*) face; ~ **de acción** scope; ~ **terrestre** globe.

esférico, a [es'feriko, a] *a* spherical.

esfinge [es'finxe] *nf* sphinx.

esforcé [esfor'θe], **esforcemos** [esfor'θemos] *etc vb V* **esforzar**.

esforzado, a [esfor'θaðo, a] *a* (*enérgico*) energetic, vigorous.

esforzarse [esfor'θarse] *vr* to exert o.s., make an effort.

esfuerce [es'fwerθe] *etc vb V* **esforzar**.

esfuerzo [es'fwerθo] *etc vb V* **esforzar** ◆ *nm* effort; **sin** ~ effortlessly.

esfumarse [esfu'marse] *vr* (*apoyo, esperanzas*) to fade away; (*persona*) to vanish.

esgrima [es'ɣrima] *nf* fencing.

esgrimidor [esɣrimi'ðor] *nm* fencer.

esgrimir [esɣri'mir] *vt* (*arma*) to brandish; (*argumento*) to use ◆ *vi* to fence.

esguince [es'ɣinθe] *nm* (*MED*) sprain.

eslabón [esla'βon] *nm* link; ~ **perdido** (*BIO, fig*) missing link.

eslabonar [eslaβo'nar] *vt* to link, connect.

eslavo, a [es'laβo, a] *a* Slav, Slavonic ◆ *nm/f* Slav ◆ *nm* (*LING*) Slavonic.

eslogan [es'loɣan] *nm*, *pl* **eslogans** = **slogan**.

eslora [es'lora] *nf* (*NAUT*) length.

esmaltar [esmal'tar] *vt* to enamel.

esmalte [es'malte] *nm* enamel; ~ **de uñas** nail varnish *o* polish.

esmerado, a [esme'raðo, a] *a* careful, neat.

esmeralda [esme'ralda] *nf* emerald.

esmerarse [esme'rarse] *vr (aplicarse)* to take great pains, exercise great care; *(afanarse)* to work hard; *(hacer lo mejor)* to do one's best.

esmero [es'mero] *nm* (great) care.

esmirriado, a [esmi'rrjaðo, a] *a* puny.

esmoquin [es'mokin] *nm* dinner jacket *(Brit)*, tuxedo *(US)*.

esnob [es'nob] *a inv (persona)* snobbish; *(coche etc)* posh ♦ *nm/f* snob.

esnobismo [esno'ßismo] *nm* snobbery.

eso ['eso] *pron* that, that thing *o* matter; ~ **de su coche** that business about his car; ~ **de ir al cine** all that about going to the cinema; **a** ~ **de las cinco** at about five o'clock; **en** ~ thereupon, at that point; **por** ~ therefore; ~ **es** that's it; **nada de** ~ far from it; **¡**~ **sí que es vida!** now this is really living!; **por** ~ **te lo dije** that's why I told you; **y** ~ **que llovía** in spite of the fact it was raining.

esófago [e'sofaɣo] *nm (ANAT)* oesophagus.

esos ['esos] *a demostrativo V* **ese**.

ésos ['esos] *pron V* **ése**.

esp. *abr* (= *español*) Sp., Span.

espabilar [espaßi'lar] *vt*, **espabilarse** *vr* = **despabilar(se)**.

espaciado [espa'θjaðo] *nm (INFORM)* spacing.

espacial [espa'θjal] *a (del espacio)* space *cpd*.

espaciar [espa'θjar] *vt* to space (out).

espacio [es'paθjo] *nm* space; *(MUS)* interval; *(RADIO, TV)* programme, program *(US)*; **el** ~ space; **ocupar mucho** ~ to take up a lot of room; **a dos** ~**s, a doble** ~ *(TIP)* double-spaced; **por** ~ **de** during, for.

espacioso, a [espa'θjoso, a] *a* spacious, roomy.

espada [es'paða] *nf* sword; ~**s** *nfpl (NAIPES)* spades; **estar entre la** ~ **y la pared** to be between the devil and the deep blue sea ♦ *nm* swordsman; *(TAUR)* matador.

espadachín [espaða'tʃin] *nm (esgrimidor)* skilled swordsman.

espaguetis [espa'ɣetis] *nmpl* spaghetti *sg*.

espalda [es'palda] *nf (gen)* back; *(NATACIÓN)* backstroke; ~**s** *nfpl (hombros)* shoulders; **a** ~**s de uno** behind sb's back; **estar de** ~**s** to have one's back turned; **tenderse de** ~**s** to lie (down) on one's back; **volver la** ~ **a uno** to cold-shoulder sb.

espaldarazo [espalda'raθo] *nm (tb fig)* slap on the back.

espaldilla [espal'ðiʎa] *nf* shoulder blade.

espantadizo, a [espanta'ðiθo, a] *a* timid, easily frightened.

espantajo [espan'taxo] *nm*, **espanta- pájaros** [espanta'paxaros] *nm inv* scarecrow.

espantar [espan'tar] *vt (asustar)* to frighten, scare; *(ahuyentar)* to frighten off; *(asombrar)* to horrify, appal; ~**se** *vr* to get frightened *o* scared; to be appalled.

espanto [es'panto] *nm (susto)* fright; *(terror)* terror; *(asombro)* astonishment; **¡qué** ~**!** how awful!

espantoso, a [espan'toso, a] *a* frightening, terrifying; *(ruido)* dreadful.

España [es'paɲa] *nf* Spain; **la** ~ **de pandereta** touristy Spain.

español, a [espa'ɲol, a] *a* Spanish ♦ *nm/f* Spaniard ♦ *nm (LING)* Spanish.

españolice [espaɲo'liθe] *etc vb V* **españolizar**.

españolizar [espaɲoli'θar] *vt* to make Spanish, Hispanicize; ~**se** *vr* to adopt Spanish ways.

esparadrapo [espara'ðrapo] *nm* (sticking) plaster, Band-Aid ® *(US)*.

esparcido, a [espar'θiðo, a] *a* scattered.

esparcimiento [esparθi'mjento] *nm (dispersión)* spreading; *(derramamiento)* scattering; *(fig)* cheerfulness.

esparcir [espar'θir] *vt* to spread; *(derramar)* to scatter; ~**se** *vr* to spread (out); to scatter; *(divertirse)* to enjoy o.s.

espárrago [es'parraɣo] *nm (tb:* ~**s)** asparagus; **estar hecho un** ~ to be as thin as a rake; **¡vete a freír** ~**s!** *(fam)* go to hell!

espasmo [es'pasmo] *nm* spasm.

esparto [es'parto] *nm* esparto (grass).

esparza [es'parθa] *etc vb V* **esparcir**.

espátula [es'patula] *nf (MED)* spatula; *(ARTE)* palette knife; *(CULIN)* fish slice.

especia [es'peθja] *nf* spice.

especial [espe'θjal] *a* special.

especialidad [espeθjali'ðað] *nf* speciality, specialty *(US)*; *(ESCOL: ramo)* specialism.

especialista [espeθja'lista] *nm/f* specialist; *(CINE)* stuntman/woman.

especializado, a [espeθjali'θaðo, a] *a* specialized; *(obrero)* skilled.

especie [es'peθje] *nf (BIO)* species; *(clase)* kind, sort; **pagar en** ~ to pay in kind.

especificar [espeθifi'kar] *vt* to specify.

específico, a [espe'θifiko, a] *a* specific.

especifique [espeθi'fike] *etc vb V* **especificar**.

espécimen [es'peθimen], *pl* **especímenes** *nm* specimen.

espectáculo [espek'takulo] *nm (gen)* spectacle; *(TEATRO etc)* show; *(función)* performance; **dar un** ~ to make a scene.

espectador, a [espekta'ðor, a] *nm/f* spectator; *(de incidente)* onlooker; **los** ~**es** *(TEA-*

TRO) the audience *sg*.

espectro [es'pektro] *nm* ghost; (*fig*) spectre.

especulación [espekula'θjon] *nf* speculation; ~ **bursátil** speculation on the Stock Market.

especular [espeku'lar] *vt*, *vi* to speculate.

especulativo, a [espekula'tiβo, a] *a* speculative.

espejismo [espe'xismo] *nm* mirage.

espejo [es'pexo] *nm* mirror; (*fig*) model; ~ **retrovisor** rear-view mirror; **mirarse al** ~ to look (at o.s.) in the mirror.

espeluznante [espeluθ'nante] *a* horrifying, hair-raising.

espera [es'pera] *nf* (*pausa, intervalo*) wait; (*JUR: plazo*) respite; **en** ~ **de** waiting for; (*con expectativa*) expecting; **en** ~ **de su contestación** awaiting your reply.

esperance [espe'ranθe] *etc vb V* **esperanzar**.

esperanza [espe'ranθa] *nf* (*confianza*) hope; (*expectativa*) expectation; **hay pocas** ~**s de que venga** there is little prospect of his coming.

esperanzador, a [esperanθa'ðor, a] *a* hopeful, encouraging.

esperanzar [esperan'θar] *vt* to give hope to.

esperar [espe'rar] *vt* (*aguardar*) to wait for; (*tener expectativa de*) to expect; (*desear*) to hope for ♦ *vi* to wait; to expect; to hope; ~**se** *vr*: **como podía** ~**se** as was to be expected; **hacer** ~' **a uno** to keep sb waiting; **ir a** ~ **a uno** to go and meet sb; ~ **un bebé** to be expecting.

esperma [es'perma] *nf* sperm.

esperpento [esper'pento] *nm* (*persona*) sight (*fam*); (*disparate*) (piece of) nonsense.

espesar [espe'sar] *vt* to thicken; ~**se** *vr* to thicken, get thicker.

espeso, a [es'peso, a] *a* thick; (*bosque*) dense; (*nieve*) deep; (*sucio*) dirty.

espesor [espe'sor] *nm* thickness; (*de nieve*) depth.

espesura [espe'sura] *nf* (*bosque*) thicket.

espetar [espe'tar] *vt* (*reto, sermón*) to give.

espía [es'pia] *nm/f* spy.

espiar [espi'ar] *vt* (*observar*) to spy on ♦ *vi*: ~ **para** to spy for.

espiga [es'piɣa] *nf* (*BOT: de trigo etc*) ear; (: *de flores*) spike.

espigado, a [espi'ɣaðo, a] *a* (*BOT*) ripe; (*fig*) tall, slender.

espigón [espi'ɣon] *nm* (*BOT*) ear; (*NAUT*) breakwater.

espina [es'pina] *nf* thorn; (*de pez*) bone; ~ **dorsal** (*ANAT*) spine; **me da mala** ~ I don't like the look of it.

espinaca [espi'naka] *nf* (*tb*: ~**s**) spinach.

espinar [espi'nar] *nm* (*matorral*) thicket.

espinazo [espi'naθo] *nm* spine, backbone.

espinilla [espi'niʎa] *nf* (*ANAT*: *tibia*) shin(bone); (: *en la piel*) blackhead.

espino [es'pino] *nm* hawthorn.

espinoso, a [espi'noso, a] *a* (*planta*) thorny, prickly; (*fig*) bony; (*problema*) knotty.

espionaje [espjo'naxe] *nm* spying, espionage.

espiral [espi'ral] *a, nf* spiral; **la** ~ **inflacionista** the inflationary spiral.

espirar [espi'rar] *vt, vi* to breathe out, exhale.

espiritista [espiri'tista] *a, nm/f* spiritualist.

espíritu [es'piritu] *nm* spirit; (*mente*) mind; (*inteligencia*) intelligence; (*REL*) spirit, soul; **E~ Santo** Holy Ghost; **con** ~ **amplio** with an open mind.

espiritual [espiri'twal] *a* spiritual.

espita [es'pita] *nf* tap (*Brit*), faucet (*US*).

esplendidez [esplendi'ðeθ] *nf* (*abundancia*) lavishness; (*magnificencia*) splendour.

espléndido, a [es'plendiðo, a] *a* (*magnífico*) magnificent, splendid; (*generoso*) generous, lavish.

esplendor [esplen'dor] *nm* splendour.

espliego [es'pljeɣo] *nm* lavender.

espolear [espole'ar] *vt* to spur on.

espoleta [espo'leta] *nf* (*de bomba*) fuse.

espolvorear [espolβore'ar] *vt* to dust, sprinkle.

esponja [es'ponxa] *nf* sponge; (*fig*) sponger.

esponjoso, a [espon'xoso, a] *a* spongy.

esponsales [espon'sales] *nmpl* betrothal *sg*.

espontaneidad [espontanei'ðað] *nf* spontaneity.

espontáneo, a [espon'taneo, a] *a* spontaneous; (*improvisado*) impromptu; (*persona*) natural.

espora [es'pora] *nf* spore.

esporádico, a [espo'raðiko, a] *a* sporadic.

esposa [es'posa] *nf V* **esposo**.

esposar [espo'sar] *vt* to handcuff.

esposo, a [es'poso, a] *nm* husband ♦ *nf* wife; **esposas** *nfpl* handcuffs.

espuela [es'pwela] *nf* spur; (*fam: trago*) one for the road.

espuerta [es'pwerta] *nf* basket, pannier.

espuma [es'puma] *nf* foam; (*de cerveza*) froth, head; (*de jabón*) lather; (*de olas*) surf.

espumarajo [espuma'raxo] *nm* froth, foam; **echar** ~**s (de rabia)** to splutter with rage.

espumoso, a [espu'moso, a] *a* frothy, foamy; (*vino*) sparkling.

esputo [es'puto] *nm* (*saliva*) spit; (*MED*) sputum.

esqueje [es'kexe] *nm* (*BOT*) cutting.

esquela [es'kela] *nf*: ~ **mortuoria** announcement of death.

esqueleto [eske'leto] *nm* skeleton; (*lo*

esencial) bare bones (of a matter); **en ~** unfinished.

esquema [es'kema] *nm* (*diagrama*) diagram; (*dibujo*) plan; (*plan*) scheme; (*FILOSOFÍA*) schema.

esquí [es'ki], *pl* **esquís** *nm* (*objeto*) ski; (*deporte*) skiing; **~ acuático** water-skiing; **hacer ~** to go skiing.

esquiador, a [eskja'ðor, a] *nm/f* skier.

esquiar [es'kjar] *vi* to ski.

esquila [es'kila] *nf* (*campanilla*) small bell; (*encerro*) cowbell.

esquilar [eski'lar] *vt* to shear.

esquimal [eski'mal] *a, nm/f* Eskimo.

esquina [es'kina] *nf* corner; **doblar la ~** to turn the corner.

esquinar [eski'nar] *vi* (*hacer esquina*) to form a corner ◆ *vt* (*madera*) to square (off); **~se** *vr* (*pelearse*) to quarrel.

esquinazo [eski'naθo] *nm*: **dar ~ a uno** to give sb the slip.

esquirla [es'kirla] *nf* splinter.

esquirol [eski'rol] *nm* blackleg.

esquivar [eski'ßar] *vt* to avoid; (*evadir*) to dodge, elude.

esquivo, a [es'kißo, a] *a* (*altanero*) aloof; (*desdeñoso*) scornful, disdainful.

esquizofrenia [eskiθo'frenja] *nf* schizophrenia.

esta ['esta] *a demostrativo V* **este**.

ésta ['esta] *pron V* **éste**.

está [es'ta] *vb V* **estar**.

estabilice [estaßi'liθe] *etc vb V* **estabilizar**.

estabilidad [estaßili'ðað] *nf* stability.

estabilización [estaßiliθa'θjon] *nf* (*COM*) stabilization.

estabilizar [estaßili'θar] *vt* to stabilize; (*fijar*) to make steady; (*precios*) to peg; **~se** *vr* to become stable.

estable [es'taßle] *a* stable.

establecer [estaßle'θer] *vt* to establish; (*fundar*) to set up; (*colonos*) to settle; (*récord*) to set (up); **~se** *vr* to establish o.s.; (*echar raíces*) to settle (down); (*COM*) to start up.

establecimiento [estaßleci'mjento] *nm* establishment; (*fundación*) institution; (*de negocio*) start-up; (*de colonias*) settlement; (*local*) establishment; **~ comercial** business house.

establezca [esta'ßleθka] *etc vb V* **establecer**.

establo [es'taßlo] *nm* (*AGR*) stall; (: *esp AM*) barn.

estaca [es'taka] *nf* stake, post; (*de tienda de campaña*) peg.

estacada [esta'kaða] *nf* (*cerca*) fence, fencing; (*palenque*) stockade; **dejar a uno en la ~** to leave sb in the lurch.

estación [esta'θjon] *nf* station; (*del año*) season; **~ de autobuses/ferrocarril** bus/

railway station; **~ balnearia (de turistas)** seaside resort; **~ de servicio** service station; **~ terminal** terminus; **~ de trabajo** (*COM*) work station; **~ transmisora** transmitter; **~ de visualización** display unit.

estacionamiento [estaθjona'mjento] *nm* (*AUTO*) parking; (*MIL*) stationing.

estacionar [estaθjo'nar] *vt* (*AUTO*) to park; (*MIL*) to station.

estacionario, a [estaθjo'narjo, a] *a* stationary; (*COM: mercado*) slack.

estadio [es'taðjo] *nm* (*fase*) stage, phase; (*DEPORTE*) stadium.

estadista [esta'ðista] *nm* (*POL*) statesman; (*ESTADÍSTICA*) statistician.

estadística [esta'ðistika] *nf* (*una ~*) figure, statistic; (*ciencia*) statistics *sg*.

estado [es'taðo] *nm* (*POL: condición*) state; **~ civil** marital status; **~ de cuenta(s)** bank statement, statement of accounts; **~ de excepción** (*POL*) state of emergency; **~ financiero** (*COM*) financial statement; **~ mayor** (*MIL*) staff; **~ de pérdidas y ganancias** (*COM*) profit and loss statement, operating statement; **E~s Unidos** (**EE.UU.**) United States (of America) (USA); **estar en ~ (de buena esperanza)** to be pregnant.

estadounidense [estaðouni'ðense] *a* United States *cpd*, American ◆ *nm/f* United States citizen, American.

estafa [es'tafa] *nf* swindle, trick; (*COM etc*) racket.

estafar [esta'far] *vt* to swindle, defraud.

estafeta [esta'feta] *nf* (*oficina de correos*) post office; **~ diplomática** diplomatic bag.

estalactita [estalak'tita] *nf* stalactite.

estalagmita [estalav'mita] *nf* stalagmite.

estallar [esta'ʎar] *vi* to burst; (*bomba*) to explode, go off; (*volcán*) to erupt; (*vidrio*) to shatter; (*látigo*) to crack; (*epidemia, guerra, rebelión*) to break out; **~ en llanto** to burst into tears.

estallido [esta'ʎiðo] *nm* explosion; (*de látigo, trueno*) crack; (*fig*) outbreak.

estambre [es'tambre] *nm* (*tela*) worsted; (*BOT*) stamen.

Estambul [estam'bul] *nm* Istanbul.

estamento [esta'mento] *nm* (social) class.

estampa [es'tampa] *nf* (*impresión, imprenta*) print, engraving; (*imagen, figura: de persona*) appearance.

estampado, a [estam'paðo, a] *a* printed ◆ *nm* (*impresión: acción*) printing; (: *efecto*) print; (*marca*) stamping.

estampar [estam'par] *vt* (*imprimir*) to print; (*marcar*) to stamp; (*metal*) to engrave; (*poner sello en*) to stamp; (*fig*) to stamp, imprint.

estampida [estam'piða] *nf* stampede.

estampido [estam'piðo] *nm* bang, report.

estampilla [estam'piʎa] *nf* (*sello de goma*) (rubber) stamp; (*AM*) stamp.

están [es'tan] *vb* V **estar**.

estancado, a [estan'kaðo, a] *a* (*agua*) stagnant.

estancamiento [estanka'mjento] *nm* stagnation.

estancar [estan'kar] *vt* (*aguas*) to hold up, hold back; (*COM*) to monopolize; (*fig*) to block, hold up; **~se** *vr* to stagnate.

estancia [es'tanθja] *nf* (*permanencia*) stay; (*sala*) room; (*AM*) farm, ranch.

estanciero [estan'θjero] *nm* (*AM*) farmer, rancher.

estanco, a [es'tanko, a] *a* watertight ♦ *nm* tobacconist's (shop).

estándar [es'tandar] *a*, *nm* standard.

estandarice [estanda'riθe] *etc* *vb* V **estandarizar**.

estandarizar [estandari'θar] *vt* to standardize.

estandarte [estan'darte] *nm* banner, standard.

estanque [es'tanke] *etc* *vb* V **estancar** ♦ *nm* (*lago*) pool, pond; (*AGR*) reservoir.

estanquero, a [estan'kero, a] *nm/f* tobacconist.

estante [es'tante] *nm* (*armario*) rack, stand; (*biblioteca*) bookcase; (*anaquel*) shelf; (*AM*) prop.

estantería [estante'ria] *nf* shelving, shelves *pl*.

estaño [es'taɲo] *nm* tin.

estar [es'tar] *vi* (*gen*) to be; (*en casa*) to be in; (*ubicarse*) to be found; (*presente*) to be present; **~se** *vr*: **¡éstate quieto!** keep still!; **se está bien aquí** it's nice here; **estamos a 2 de mayo** it is the 2nd May; **¿cómo está usted?** how are you?; **~ enfermo o mal** to be ill; **~ viejo/joven** (*parecerse*) to seem old/young; **¿a cuánto estamos de Madrid?** (*seguido de una preposición*) how far are we from Madrid?; **~ de fiesta o vacaciones** to be on holiday; **las uvas están a 5 pesetas** grapes are at 5 pesetas; **María no está** Maria isn't in; **está fuera** (*de casa*) she's out; (*de ciudad*) she's away; **está de camarero** he's working as a waiter; **estaba de uniforme** he was (dressed) in uniform; **el problema está en que ...** the problem lies in the fact that ...; **no estoy para bromas** I'm not in the mood for jokes *o* joking; **~ por** (*moción*) to be in favour of; (*persona*) to support, back; **está por hacer** it remains to be done; **¿estamos?** are we agreed?; **¡ya está!** that's it!, there you are!; **¡ya está bien!** that's enough!

estarcir [estar'θir] *vt* to stencil.

estarza [es'tarθa] *etc* *vb* V **estarcir**.

estas ['estas] *a demostrativo* V **este**.

éstas ['estas] *pron* V **éste**.

estás [es'tas] *vb* V **estar**.

estatal [esta'tal] *a* state *cpd*.

estático, a [es'tatiko, a] *a* static.

estatua [es'tatwa] *nf* statue.

estatura [esta'tura] *nf* stature, height.

estatutario, a [estatu'tarjo, a] *a* statutory.

estatuto [esta'tuto] *nm* (*JUR*) statute; (*de ciudad*) bye-law; (*de comité*) rule; **~s sociales** (*COM*) articles of association.

este ['este] *a* (*lado*) east; (*dirección*) easterly ♦ *nm* east; **en la parte del ~** in the eastern part.

este ['este], **esta** ['esta], **estos** ['estos], **estas** ['estas] *a demostrativo* (*sg*) this; (*pl*) these.

éste ['este], **ésta** ['esta], **éstos** ['estos], **éstas** ['estas] *pron* (*sg*) this (one); (*pl*) these (ones); **ése ... éste ...** the former ... the latter ....

esté [es'te] *vb* V **estar**.

estela [es'tela] *nf* wake, wash; (*fig*) trail.

estelar [este'lar] *a* (*ASTRO*) stellar; (*TEATRO*) star *cpd*.

estén [es'ten] *vb* V **estar**.

estenografía [estenoɤra'fia] *nf* shorthand.

estentóreo, a [esten'toreo, a] *a* (*sonido*) strident; (*voz*) booming.

estepa [es'tepa] *nf* (*GEO*) steppe.

estera [es'tera] *nf* (*alfombra*) mat; (*tejido*) matting.

estercolero [esterko'lero] *nm* manure heap, dunghill.

estéreo [es'tereo] *a inv*, *nm* stereo.

estereofónico, a [estereo'foniko, a] *a* stereophonic.

estereotipar [estereoti'par] *vt* to stereotype.

estereotipo [estereo'tipo] *nm* stereotype.

estéril [es'teril] *a* sterile, barren; (*fig*) vain, futile.

esterilice [esteri'liθe] *etc* *vb* V **esterilizar**.

esterilizar [esterili'θar] *vt* to sterilize.

esterilla [este'riʎa] *nf* (*alfombrilla*) small mat.

esterlina [ester'lina] *a*: **libra ~** pound sterling.

esternón [ester'non] *nm* breastbone.

estertor [ester'tor] *nm* death rattle.

estés [es'tes] *vb* V **estar**.

esteta [es'teta] *nm/f* aesthete.

esteticienne [esteti'θjen] *nf* beautician.

estético, a [es'tetiko, a] *a* aesthetic ♦ *nf* aesthetics *sg*.

estetoscopio [estetos'kopjo] *nm* stethoscope.

estibador [estiβa'ðor] *nm* stevedore.

estibar [esti'βar] *vt* (*NAUT*) to stow.

estiércol [es'tjerkol] *nm* dung, manure.

estigma [es'tiɤma] *nm* stigma.

estigmatice [estiɤma'tiθe] *etc* *vb* V

estigmatizar.

estigmatizar [estiɣmati'θar] vt to stigmatize.

estilar [esti'lar] vi, ~se vr (estar de moda) to be in fashion; (usarse) to be used.

estilice [esti'liθe] etc vb V **estilizar**.

estilizar [estili'θar] vt to stylize; (TEC) to design.

estilo [es'tilo] nm style; (TEC) stylus; (NATACIÓN) stroke; ~ **de vida** lifestyle; **al ~ de** in the style of; **algo por el ~** something along those lines.

estilográfica [estilo'ɣrafika] nf fountain pen.

estima [es'tima] nf esteem, respect.

estimación [estima'θjon] nf (evaluación) estimation; (aprecio, afecto) esteem, regard.

estimado, a [esti'maðo, a] a esteemed; "E~ Señor" "Dear Sir".

estimador [estima'ðor] nm (COM) estimator.

estimar [esti'mar] vt (evaluar) to estimate; (valorar) to value; (apreciar) to esteem, respect; (pensar, considerar) to think, reckon.

estimulante [estimu'lante] a stimulating ♦ nm stimulant.

estimular [estimu'lar] vt to stimulate; (excitar) to excite; (animar) to encourage.

estímulo [es'timulo] nm stimulus; (ánimo) encouragement; (INFORM) prompt.

estío [es'tio] nm summer.

estipendio [esti'pendjo] nm salary; (COM) stipend.

estipulación [estipula'θjon] nf stipulation, condition.

estipular [estipu'lar] vt to stipulate.

estirado, a [esti'raðo, a] a (tenso) (stretched o drawn) tight; (fig: persona) stiff, pompous; (engreído) stuck-up.

estirar [esti'rar] vt to stretch; (dinero, suma etc) to stretch out; (cuello) to crane; (dinero) to eke out; (discurso) to spin out; ~ **la pata** (fam) to kick the bucket; **~se** vr to stretch.

estirón [esti'ron] nm pull, tug; (crecimiento) spurt, sudden growth; **dar un ~** (niño) to shoot up.

estirpe [es'tirpe] nf stock, lineage.

estival [esti'ßal] a summer cpd.

esto ['esto] pron this, this thing o matter; ~ **de la boda** this business about the wedding; **en ~** at this o that point; **por ~** for this reason.

estocada [esto'kaða] nf (acción) stab; (TAUR) death blow.

Estocolmo [esto'kolmo] nm Stockholm.

estofa [es'tofa] nf: **de baja ~** poor-quality.

estofado [esto'faðo] nm stew.

estofar [esto'far] vt (bordar) to quilt; (CU-
LIN) to stew.

estoico, a [es'toiko, a] a (FILOSOFÍA) stoic(al); (fig) cold, indifferent.

estomacal [estoma'kal] a stomach cpd; **trastorno ~** stomach upset.

estómago [es'tomaɣo] nm stomach; **tener ~** to be thick-skinned.

estoque [es'toke] nm rapier, sword.

estorbar [estor'ßar] vt to hinder, obstruct; (fig) to bother, disturb ♦ vi to be in the way.

estorbo [es'torßo] nm (molestia) bother, nuisance; (obstáculo) hindrance, obstacle.

estornino [estor'nino] nm starling.

estornudar [estornu'ðar] vi to sneeze.

estornudo [estor'nuðo] nm sneeze.

estos ['estos] a demostrativo V **este**.

éstos ['estos] pron V **éste**.

estoy [es'toi] vb V **estar**.

estrabismo [estra'ßismo] nm squint.

estrado [es'traðo] nm (tarima) platform; (MUS) bandstand; **~s** nmpl law courts.

estrafalario, a [estrafa'larjo, a] a odd, eccentric; (desarreglado) slovenly, sloppy.

estrago [es'traɣo] nm ruin, destruction; **hacer ~s en** to wreak havoc among.

estragón [estra'ɣon] nm (CULIN) tarragon.

estrambólico, a [estram'boliko, a] a (AM), **estrambótico, a** [estram'botiko, a] a odd, eccentric.

estrangulación [estrangula'θjon] nf strangulation.

estrangulador, a [estrangula'ðor, a] nm/f strangler ♦ nm (TEC) throttle; (AUTO) choke.

estrangulamiento [estrangula'mjento] nm (AUTO) bottleneck.

estrangular [estrangu'lar] vt (persona) to strangle; (MED) to strangulate.

estraperlista [estraper'lista] nm/f black marketeer.

estraperlo [estra'perlo] nm black market.

estratagema [estrata'xema] nf (MIL) stratagem; (astucia) cunning.

estratega [estra'teɣa] nm/f strategist.

estrategia [estra'texja] nf strategy.

estratégico, a [estra'texiko, a] a strategic.

estratificar [estratifi'kar] vt to stratify.

estratifique [estrati'fike] etc vb V **estratificar**.

estrato [es'trato] nm stratum, layer.

estratosfera [estratos'fera] nf stratosphere.

estrechar [estre'tʃar] vt (reducir) to narrow; (vestido) to take in; (persona) to hug, embrace; **~se** vr (reducirse) to narrow, grow narrow; (2 personas) to embrace; **~ la mano** to shake hands.

estrechez [estre'tʃeθ] nf narrowness; (de ropa) tightness; (intimidad) intimacy; (COM) want o shortage of money; **estrecheces** nfpl financial difficulties.

estrecho, a [es'tretʃo, a] *a* narrow; *(apretado)* tight; *(íntimo)* close, intimate; *(miserable)* mean ◆ *nm* strait; ~ **de miras** narrow-minded; **E~ de Gibraltar** Straits of Gibraltar.

estrella [es'treʎa] *nf* star; ~ **fugaz** shooting star; ~ **de mar** starfish; **tener (buena)/ mala** ~ to be lucky/unlucky.

estrellado, a [estre'ʎaðo, a] *a (forma)* star-shaped; *(cielo)* starry; *(huevos)* fried.

estrellar [estre'ʎar] *vt (hacer añicos)* to smash (to pieces); *(huevos)* to fry; ~**se** *vr* to smash; *(chocarse)* to crash; *(fracasar)* to fail.

estrellato [estre'ʎato] *nm* stardom.

estremecer [estreme'θer] *vt* to shake; ~**se** *vr* to shake, tremble; ~ **de** *(horror)* to shudder with; *(frío)* to shiver with.

estremecimiento [estremeθi'mjento] *nm (temblor)* trembling, shaking.

estremezca [estre'meθka] *etc vb* V **estremecer.**

estrenar [estre'nar] *vt (vestido)* to wear for the first time; *(casa)* to move into; *(película, obra de teatro)* to present for the first time; ~**se** *vr (persona)* to make one's début; *(película)* to have its premiere; *(TEATRO)* to open.

estreno [es'treno] *nm (primer uso)* first use; *(CINE etc)* premiere.

estreñido, a [estre'niðo, a] *a* constipated.

estreñimiento [estreni'mjento] *nm* constipation.

estrépito [es'trepito] *nm* noise, racket; *(fig)* fuss.

estrepitoso, a [estrepi'toso, a] *a* noisy; *(fiesta)* rowdy.

estrés [es'tres] *nm* stress.

estresante [estre'sante] *a* stressful.

estría [es'tria] *nf* groove; ~**s (en el cutis)** stretchmarks.

estribación [estriβa'θjon] *nf (GEO)* spur; **estribaciones** *nfpl* foothills.

estribar [estri'βar] *vi:* ~ **en** to rest on, be supported by; **la dificultad estriba en el texto** the difficulty lies in the text.

estribillo [estri'βiʎo] *nm (LITERATURA)* refrain; *(MUS)* chorus.

estribo [es'triβo] *nm (de jinete)* stirrup; *(de coche, tren)* step; *(de puente)* support; *(GEO)* spur; **perder los** ~**s** to fly off the handle.

estribor [estri'βor] *nm (NAUT)* starboard.

estricnina [estrik'nina] *nf* strychnine.

estricto, a [es'trikto, a] *a (riguroso)* strict; *(severo)* severe.

estridente [estri'ðente] *a (color)* loud; *(voz)* raucous.

estro ['estro] *nm* inspiration.

estrofa [es'trofa] *nf* verse.

estropajo [estro'paxo] *nm* scourer.

estropear [estrope'ar] *vt (arruinar)* to spoil; *(dañar)* to damage ◆ *vi (coche)* to break down; ~**se** *vr (objeto)* to get damaged; *(la piel etc)* to be ruined.

estropicio [estro'piθjo] *nm (rotura)* breakage; *(efectos)* harmful effects *pl.*

estructura [estruk'tura] *nf* structure.

estruendo [es'trwendo] *nm (ruido)* racket, din; *(fig: alboroto)* uproar, turmoil.

estrujar [estru'xar] *vt (apretar)* to squeeze; *(aplastar)* to crush; *(fig)* to drain, bleed.

estuario [es'twarjo] *nm* estuary.

estuche [es'tutʃe] *nm* box, case.

estudiante [estu'ðjante] *nm/f* student.

estudiantil [estuðjan'til] *a inv* student *cpd.*

estudiantina [estuðjan'tina] *nf* student music group.

estudiar [estu'ðjar] *vt* to study; *(propuesta)* to think about *o* over; ~ **para abogado** to study to become a lawyer.

estudio [es'tuðjo] *nm* study; *(encuesta)* research; *(proyecto)* plan; *(piso)* studio flat; *(CINE, ARTE, RADIO)* studio; ~**s** *nmpl* studies; *(erudición)* learning *sg*; **cursar** *o* **hacer** ~**s** to study; ~ **de casos prácticos** case study; ~ **de desplazamientos y tiempos** *(COM)* time and motion study; ~**s de motivación** motivational research *sg*; ~ **del trabajo** *(COM)* work study; ~ **de viabilidad** *(COM)* feasibility study.

estudioso, a [es'tuðjoso, a] *a* studious.

estufa [es'tufa] *nf* heater, fire.

estulticia [estul'tiθja] *nf* foolishness.

estupefaciente [estupefa'θjente] *a, nm* narcotic.

estupefacto, a [estupe'fakto, a] *a* speechless, thunderstruck.

estupendamente [estupenda'mente] *ad (fam):* **estoy** ~ I feel great; **le salió** ~ he did it very well.

estupendo, a [estu'pendo, a] *a* wonderful, terrific; *(fam)* great; ¡~! that's great!, fantastic!

estupidez [estupi'ðeθ] *nf (torpeza)* stupidity; *(acto)* stupid thing (to do); **fue una** ~ **mía** that was a silly thing for me to do *o* say.

estúpido, a [es'tupiðo, a] *a* stupid, silly.

estupor [estu'por] *nm* stupor; *(fig)* astonishment, amazement.

estupro [es'tupro] *nm* rape.

estuve [es'tuβe] *etc,* **estuviera** [estu'βjera] *etc vb* V **estar.**

esvástica [es'βastika] *nf* swastika.

ETA ['eta] *nf abr (POL:* = **Euskadi Ta Askatasuna)** ETA.

etapa [e'tapa] *nf (de viaje)* stage; *(DEPORTE)* leg; *(parada)* stopping place; *(fig)* stage, phase; **por** ~**s** gradually *o* in stages.

etarra [e'tarra] *a* ETA *cpd* ◆ *nm/f* member of ETA.

etc. *abr* (= *etcétera*) etc.

etcétera [et'θetera] *ad* etcetera.

etéreo, a [e'tereo, a] *a* ethereal.

eternice [eter'niθe] *etc vb* V **eternizar**.

eternidad [eterni'ðað] *nf* eternity.

eternizarse [eterni'θarse] *vr*: ~ **en hacer algo** to take ages to do sth.

eterno, a [e'terno, a] *a* eternal, everlasting; *(despectivo)* never-ending.

ético, a ['etiko, a] *a* ethical ♦ *nf* ethics.

etimología [etimolo'xia] *nf* etymology.

etiqueta [eti'keta] *nf* *(modales)* etiquette; *(rótulo)* label, tag; **de** ~ formal.

étnico, a ['etniko, a] *a* ethnic.

eucalipto [euka'lipto] *nm* eucalyptus.

Eucaristía [eukaris'tia] *nf* Eucharist.

eufemismo [eufe'mismo] *nm* euphemism.

euforia [eu'forja] *nf* euphoria.

eufórico, a [eu'foriko, a] *a* euphoric.

eunuco [eu'nuko] *nm* eunuch.

Europa [eu'ropa] *nf* Europe.

europeice [euro'peiθe] *etc vb* V **europeizar**.

europeizar [europei'θar] *vt* to Europeanize; ~**se** *vr* to become Europeanized.

europeo, a [euro'peo, a] *a, nm/f* European.

éuscaro, a ['euskaro, a] *a, nm/f* Basque.

Euskadi [eus'kaði] *nm* the Basque Provinces *pl*.

euskera, eusquera [eus'kera] *nm* (*LING*) Basque.

eutanasia [euta'nasja] *nf* euthanasia.

evacuación [eβakwa'θjon] *nf* evacuation.

evacuar [eβa'kwar] *vt* to evacuate.

evadir [eβa'ðir] *vt* to evade, avoid; ~**se** *vr* to escape.

evaluación [eβalwa'θjon] *nf* evaluation, assessment.

evaluar [eβa'lwar] *vt* to evaluate, assess.

evangélico, a [eβan'xeliko, a] *a* evangelical.

evangelio [eβan'xeljo] *nm* gospel.

evaporación [eβapora'θjon] *nf* evaporation.

evaporar [eβapo'rar] *vt* to evaporate; ~**se** *vr* to vanish.

evasión [eβa'sjon] *nf* escape, flight; *(fig)* evasion; ~ **fiscal** *o* **tributaria** tax evasion.

evasivo, a [eβa'siβo, a] *a* evasive, noncommittal ♦ *nf* *(pretexto)* excuse; **contestar con evasivas** to avoid giving a straight answer.

evento [e'βento] *nm* event; *(eventualidad)* eventuality.

eventual [eβen'twal] *a* possible, conditional *(upon circumstances)*; *(trabajador)* casual, temporary.

Everest [eβe'rest] *nm*: **el (Monte)** ~ (Mount) Everest.

evidencia [eβi'ðenθja] *nf* evidence, proof; **poner en** ~ to make clear; **ponerse en** ~ *(persona)* to show o.s. up.

evidenciar [eβiðen'θjar] *vt* *(hacer patente)* to make evident; *(probar)* to prove, show; ~**se** *vr* to be evident.

evidente [eβi'ðente] *a* obvious, clear, evident.

evitar [eβi'tar] *vt* *(evadir)* to avoid; *(impedir)* to prevent; *(peligro)* to escape; *(molestia)* to save; *(tentación)* to shun; **si puedo** ~**lo** if I can help it.

evocador, a [eβoka'ðor, a] *a* *(sugestivo)* evocative.

evocar [eβo'kar] *vt* to evoke, call forth.

evolución [eβolu'θjon] *nf* *(desarrollo)* evolution, development; *(cambio)* change; *(MIL)* manoeuvre.

evolucionar [eβoluθjo'nar] *vi* to evolve; *(MIL, AVIAT)* to manoeuvre.

evoque [e'βoke] *etc vb* V **evocar**.

ex [eks] *a* ex-; **el** ~ **ministro** the former minister, the ex-minister.

exabrupto [eksa'βrupto] *nm* interjection.

exacción [eksak'θjon] *nf* *(acto)* exaction; *(de impuestos)* demand.

exacerbar [eksaθer'βar] *vt* to irritate, annoy.

exactamente [eksakta'mente] *ad* exactly.

exactitud [eksakti'tuð] *nf* exactness; *(precisión)* accuracy; *(puntualidad)* punctuality.

exacto, a [ek'sakto, a] *a* exact; accurate; punctual; ¡~! exactly!; **eso no es del todo** ~ that's not quite right; **para ser** ~ to be precise.

exageración [eksaxera'θjon] *nf* exaggeration.

exagerado, a [eksaxe'raðo, a] *a* *(relato)* exaggerated; *(precio)* excessive; *(persona)* over-demonstrative; *(gesto)* theatrical.

exagerar [eksaxe'rar] *vt* to exaggerate; *(exceder)* to overdo.

exaltado, a [eksal'taðo, a] *a* *(apasionado)* over-excited, worked up; *(exagerado)* extreme; *(fanático)* hot-headed; *(discurso)* impassioned ♦ *nm/f* *(fanático)* hothead; *(POL)* extremist.

exaltar [eksal'tar] *vt* to exalt, glorify; ~**se** *vr* *(excitarse)* to get excited *o* worked up.

examen [ek'samen] *nm* examination; *(de problema)* consideration; ~ **de** *(encuesta)* inquiry into; ~ **de ingreso** entrance examination; ~ **de conducir** driving test; ~ **eliminatorio** qualifying examination.

examinar [eksami'nar] *vt* to examine; *(poner a prueba)* to test; *(inspeccionar)* to inspect; ~**se** *vr* to be examined, take an examination.

exánime [ek'sanime] *a* lifeless; *(fig)* exhausted.

exasperar [eksaspe'rar] *vt* to exasperate; ~**se** *vr* to get exasperated, lose patience.

Exc.ª *abr* = **Excelencia**.

excarceler [ekskarθe'lar] *vt* to release

(from prison).

excavador, a [ekskaßa'ðor, a] *nm/f* (*persona*) excavator ♦ *nf* (*TEC*) digger.

excavar [ekska'ßar] *vt* to excavate, dig (out).

excedencia [eksθe'ðenθja] *nf* (*MIL*) leave; (*ESCOL*) sabbatical.

excedente [eksθe'ðente] *a, nm* excess, surplus.

exceder [eksθe'ðer] *vt* to exceed, surpass; ~**se** *vr* (*extralimitarse*) to go too far; (*sobrepasarse*) to excel o.s.

excelencia [eksθe'lenθja] *nf* excellence; **E~** Excellency; **por ~** par excellence.

excelente [eksθe'lente] *a* excellent.

excelso, a [eks'θelso, a] *a* lofty, sublime.

excentricidad [eksθentriθi'ðað] *nf* eccentricity.

excéntrico, a [eks'θentriko, a] *a, nm/f* eccentric.

excepción [eksθep'θjon] *nf* exception; **la ~ confirma la regla** the exception proves the rule.

excepcional [eksθepθjo'nal] *a* exceptional.

excepto [eks'θepto] *ad* excepting, except (for).

exceptuar [eksθep'twar] *vt* to except, exclude.

excesivo, a [eksθe'sißo, a] *a* excessive.

exceso [eks'θeso] *nm* excess; (*COM*) surplus; **~ de equipaje/peso** excess luggage/ weight; **~ de velocidad** speeding; **en** *o* **por ~** excessively.

excitación [eksθita'θjon] *nf* (*sensación*) excitement; (*acción*) excitation.

excitado, a [eksθi'taðo, a] *a* excited; (*emociones*) aroused.

excitante [eksθi'tante] *a* exciting; (*MED*) stimulating ♦ *nm* stimulant.

excitar [eksθi'tar] *vt* to excite; (*incitar*) to urge; (*emoción*) to stir up; (*esperanzas*) to raise; (*pasión*) to arouse; ~**se** *vr* to get excited.

exclamación [eksklama'θjon] *nf* exclamation.

exclamar [ekskla'mar] *vi* to exclaim; ~**se** *vr*: ~**se (contra)** to complain (about).

excluir [eksklu'ir] *vt* to exclude; (*dejar fuera*) to shut out; (*solución*) to reject; (*posibilidad*) to rule out.

exclusión [eksklu'sjon] *nf* exclusion.

exclusiva [eksklu'sißa] *nf* V **exclusivo**.

exclusive [eksklu'siße] *prep* exclusive of, not counting.

exclusivo, a [eksklu'sißo, a] *a* exclusive ♦ *nf* (*PRENSA*) exclusive, scoop; (*COM*) sole right *o* agency; **derecho ~** sole *o* exclusive right.

excluyendo [eksklu'jendo] *etc vb* V **excluir**.

Excma., Excmo. *abr* (= *Excelentísima*,

Excelentísimo) *courtesy title*.

excombatiente [ekskomba'tjente] *nm* exserviceman, war veteran (*US*).

excomulgar [ekskomul'ɣar] *vt* (*REL*) to excommunicate.

excomulgue [eksko'mulɣe] *etc vb* V **excomulgar**.

excomunión [ekskomu'njon] *nf* excommunication.

excoriar [eksko'rjar] *vt* to flay, skin.

excremento [ekskre'mento] *nm* excrement.

exculpar [ekskul'par] *vt* to exonerate; (*JUR*) to acquit; ~**se** *vr* to exonerate o.s.

excursión [ekskur'sjon] *nf* excursion, outing; **ir de ~** to go (off) on a trip.

excursionista [ekskursjo'nista] *nm/f* (*turista*) sightseer.

excusa [eks'kusa] *nf* excuse; (*disculpa*) apology; **presentar sus ~s** to excuse o.s.

excusado, a [eksku'saðo, a] *a* unnecessary; (*disculpado*) excused, forgiven.

excusar [eksku'sar] *vt* to excuse; (*evitar*) to avoid, prevent; ~**se** *vr* (*disculparse*) to apologize.

execrable [ekse'kraßle] *a* appalling.

exención [eksen'θjon] *nf* exemption.

exento, a [ek'sento, a] *pp de* **eximir** ♦ *a* exempt.

exequias [ek'sekjas] *nfpl* funeral rites.

exhalación [eksala'θjon] *nf* (*del aire*) exhalation; (*vapor*) fumes *pl*, vapour; (*rayo*) shooting star; **salir como una ~** to shoot out.

exhalar [eksa'lar] *vt* to exhale, breathe out; (*olor etc*) to give off; (*suspiro*) to breathe, heave.

exhaustivo, a [eksaus'tißo, a] *a* exhaustive.

exhausto, a [ek'sausto, a] *a* exhausted, worn-out.

exhibición [eksißi'θjon] *nf* exhibition; (*demostración*) display, show; (*de película*) showing; (*de equipo*) performance.

exhibicionista [eksißiθjo'nista] *a, nm/f* exhibitionist.

exhibir [eksi'ßir] *vt* to exhibit; to display, show; (*cuadros*) to exhibit; (*artículos*) to display; (*pasaporte*) to show; (*película*) to screen; (*mostrar con orgullo*) to show off; ~**se** *vr* (*mostrarse en público*) to show o.s. off; (*fam: indecentemente*) to expose o.s.

exhortación [eksorta'θjon] *nf* exhortation.

exhortar [eksor'tar] *vt*: ~ **a** to exhort to.

exhumar [eksu'mar] *vt* to exhume.

exigencia [eksi'xenθja] *nf* demand, requirement.

exigente [eksi'xente] *a* demanding; (*profesor*) strict; **ser ~ con uno** to be hard on sb.

exigir [eksi'xir] *vt* (*gen*) to demand, require; (*impuestos*) to exact, levy; **~ el pago** to to demand payment.

exiguo, a [ek'siɣwo, a] *a* (*cantidad*) meagre; (*objeto*) tiny.

exija [e'ksixa] *etc vb* V **exigir**.

exiliado, a [eksi'ljaðo, a] *a* exiled, in exile ♦ *nm/f* exile.

exiliar [eksi'ljar] *vt* to exile; ~**se** *vr* to go into exile.

exilio [ek'siljo] *nm* exile.

eximio, a [ek'simjo, a] *a* (*eminente*) distinguished, eminent.

eximir [eksi'mir] *vt* to exempt.

existencia [eksis'tenθja] *nf* existence; ~**s** *nfpl* stock *sg*; ~ **de mercancías** (*COM*) stock-in-trade; **tener en** ~ to have in stock; **amargar la** ~ **a uno** to make sb's life a misery.

existir [eksis'tir] *vi* to exist, be.

éxito ['eksito] *nm* (*resultado*) result, outcome; (*triunfo*) success; (*MUS, TEATRO*) hit; ~ **editorial** bestseller; ~ **rotundo** smash hit; **tener** ~ to be successful.

exitoso, a [eksi'toso, a] *a* successful.

éxodo ['eksoðo] *nm* exodus; **el** ~ **rural** the drift from the land.

ex oficio [ekso'fiθjo] *a, ad* ex officio.

exonerar [eksone'rar] *vt* to exonerate; ~ **de una obligación** to free from an obligation.

exorcice [eksor'θiθe] *etc vb* V **exorcizar**.

exorcismo [eksor'θismo] *nm* exorcism.

exorcizar [eksorθi'θar] *vt* to exorcize.

exótico, a [ek'sotiko, a] *a* exotic.

expandido, a [ekspan'diðo, a] *a*: **en caracteres** ~**s** (*INFORM*) double width.

expandir [ekspan'dir] *vt* to expand; (*COM*) to expand, enlarge; ~**se** *vr* to expand, spread.

expansión [ekspan'sjon] *nf* expansion; (*recreo*) relaxation; **la** ~ **económica** economic growth; **economía en** ~ expanding economy.

expansionar [ekspansjo'nar] *vt* to expand; ~**se** *vr* (*dilatarse*) to expand; (*recrearse*) to relax.

expansivo, a [ekspan'siβo, a] *a* expansive; (*efusivo*) communicative.

expatriado, a [ekspa'trjaðo, a] *nm/f* (*emigrado*) expatriate; (*exiliado*) exile.

expatriarse [ekspa'trjarse] *vr* to emigrate; (*POL*) to go into exile.

expectación [ekspekta'θjon] *nf* (*esperanza*) expectation; (*ilusión*) excitement.

expectativa [ekspekta'tiβa] *nf* (*espera*) expectation; (*perspectiva*) prospect; ~ **de vida** life expectancy; **estar a la** ~ to wait and see (what will happen).

expedición [ekspeði'θjon] *nf* (*excursión*) expedition; **gastos de** ~ shipping charges.

expedientar [ekspeðjen'tar] *vt* to open a file on; (*funcionario*) to discipline, start disciplinary proceedings against.

expediente [ekspe'ðjente] *nm* expedient; (*JUR*: *procedimento*) action, proceedings *pl*; (: *papeles*) dossier, file, record; ~ **judicial** court proceedings *pl*; ~ **académico** (student's) record.

expedir [ekspe'ðir] *vt* (*despachar*) to send, forward; (*pasaporte*) to issue; (*cheque*) to make out.

expedito, a [ekspe'ðito, a] *a* (*libre*) clear, free.

expeler [ekspe'ler] *vt* to expel, eject.

expendedor, a [ekspende'ðor, a] *nm/f* (*vendedor*) dealer; (*TEATRO*) ticket agent ♦ *nm* (*aparato*) (vending) machine; ~ **de cigarrillos** cigarette machine.

expendeduría [ekspendedu'ria] *nf* (*estanco*) tobacconist's (shop) (*Brit*), cigar store (*US*).

expensas [eks'pensas] *nfpl* (*JUR*) costs; **a** ~ **de** at the expense of.

experiencia [ekspe'rjenθja] *nf* experience.

experimentado, a [eksperimen'taðo, a] *a* experienced.

experimentar [eksperimen'tar] *vt* (*en laboratorio*) to experiment with; (*probar*) to test, try out; (*notar, observar*) to experience; (*deterioro, pérdida*) to suffer; (*aumento*) to show; (*sensación*) to feel.

experimento [eksperi'mento] *nm* experiment.

experto, a [eks'perto, a] *a* expert ♦ *nm/f* expert.

expiar [ekspi'ar] *vt* to atone for.

expida [eks'piða] *etc vb* V **expedir**.

expirar [ekspi'rar] *vi* to expire.

explanada [ekspla'naða] *nf* (*paseo*) esplanade; (*a orillas del mar*) promenade.

explayarse [ekspla'jarse] *vr* (*en discurso*) to speak at length; ~ **con uno** to confide in sb.

explicación [eksplika'θjon] *nf* explanation.

explicar [ekspli'kar] *vt* to explain; (*teoría*) to expound; (*UNIV*) to lecture in; ~**se** *vr* to explain (o.s.); **no me lo explico** I can't understand it.

explícito, a [eks'pliθito, a] *a* explicit.

explique [eks'plike] *etc vb* V **explicar**.

exploración [eksplora'θjon] *nf* exploration; (*MIL*) reconnaissance.

explorador, a [eksplora'ðor, a] *nm/f* (*pionero*) explorer; (*MIL*) scout ♦ *nm* (*MED*) probe; (*radar*) (radar) scanner.

explorar [eksplo'rar] *vt* to explore; (*MED*) to probe; (*radar*) to scan.

explosión [eksplo'sjon] *nf* explosion.

explosivo, a [eksplo'siβo, a] *a* explosive.

explotación [eksplota'θjon] *nf* exploitation; (*de planta etc*) running; (*de mina*) working; (*de recurso*) development; ~ **minera** mine; **gastos de** ~ operating costs.

explotar [eksplo'tar] *vt* to exploit; (*planta*)

to run, operate; (*mina*) to work ◆ *vi* (*bomba etc*) to explode, go off.

expondré [ekspon'dre] *etc vb* V **exponer.**

exponer [ekspo'ner] *vt* to expose; (*cuadro*) to display; (*vida*) to risk; (*idea*) to explain; (*teoría*) to expound; (*hechos*) to set out; ~**se** *vr*: ~**se a (hacer) algo** to run the risk of (doing) sth.

exponga [eks'ponga] *etc vb* V **exponer.**

exportación [eksporta'θjon] *nf* (*acción*) export; (*mercancías*) exports *pl*.

exportador, a [eksporta'ðor, a] *a* (*país*) exporting ◆ *nm/f* exporter.

exportar [ekspor'tar] *vt* to export.

exposición [eksposi'θjon] *nf* (*gen*) exposure; (*de arte*) show, exhibition; (*COM*) display; (*feria*) show, fair; (*explicación*) explanation; (*de teoría*) exposition; (*narración*) account, statement.

exprés [eks'pres] *a inv* (*café*) espresso ◆ *nm* (*AM*) express (train).

expresado, a [ekspre'saðo, a] *a* abovementioned.

expresamente [ekspresa'mente] *ad* (*concretamente*) expressly; (*a propósito*) on purpose.

expresar [ekspre'sar] *vt* to express; (*redactar*) to phrase, put; (*emoción*) to show; ~**se** *vr* to express o.s.; (*dato*) to be stated; **como abajo se expresa** as stated below.

expresión [ekspre'sjon] *nf* expression; ~ **familiar** colloquialism.

expresivo, a [ekspre'siβo, a] *a* expressive; (*cariñoso*) affectionate.

expreso, a [eks'preso, a] *a* (*explícito*) express; (*claro*) specific, clear; (*tren*) fast ◆ *nm* (*FERRO*) fast train ◆ *ad*: **mandar** ~ to send by express (delivery).

exprimidor [eksprimi'ðor] *nm* (lemon) squeezer.

exprimir [ekspri'mir] *vt* (*fruta*) to squeeze; (*zumo*) to squeeze out.

ex profeso [ekspro'feso] *ad* (*ADMIN, JUR*) on purpose.

expropiar [ekspro'pjar] *vt* to expropriate.

expuesto, a [eks'pwesto, a] *pp de* **exponer** ◆ *a* exposed; (*cuadro etc*) on show, on display; **según lo** ~ **arriba** according to what has been stated above.

expulsar [ekspul'sar] *vt* (*echar*) to eject, throw out; (*alumno*) to expel; (*despedir*) to sack, fire; (*DEPORTE*) to send off.

expulsión [ekspul'sjon] *nf* expulsion; sending-off.

expuse [eks'puse] *etc vb* V **exponer.**

expurgar [ekspur'ɣar] *vt* to expurgate.

exquisito, a [ekski'sito, a] *a* exquisite; (*comida*) delicious; (*afectado*) affected.

Ext. *abr* (= *Exterior*) ext.; (= *Extensión*) ext.

éxtasis ['ekstasis] *nm* ecstasy.

extemporáneo, a [ekstempo'raneo, a] *a* unseasonal.

extender [eksten'der] *vt* to extend; (*los brazos*) to stretch out, hold out; (*mapa, tela*) to spread (out), open (out); (*mantequilla*) to spread; (*certificado*) to issue; (*cheque, recibo*) to make out; (*documento*) to draw up; ~**se** *vr* to extend; (*terreno*) to stretch o spread (out); (*persona: en el suelo*) to stretch out; (*en el tiempo*) to extend, last; (*costumbre, epidemia*) to spread; (*guerra*) to escalate; ~**se sobre un tema** to enlarge on a subject.

extendido, a [eksten'diðo, a] *a* (*abierto*) spread out, open; (*brazos*) outstretched; (*costumbre etc*) widespread.

extensible [eksten'siβle] *a* extending.

extensión [eksten'sjon] *nf* (*de terreno, mar*) expanse, stretch; (*MUS*) range; (*de conocimientos*) extent; (*de programa*) scope; (*de tiempo*) length, duration; (*TELEC*) extension; ~ **de plazo** (*COM*) extension; **en toda la** ~ **de la palabra** in every sense of the word; **de** ~ (*INFORM*) add-on.

extenso, a [eks'tenso, a] *a* extensive.

extenuar [ekste'nwar] *vt* (*debilitar*) to weaken.

exterior [ekste'rjor] *a* (*de fuera*) external; (*afuera*) outside, exterior; (*apariencia*) outward; (*deuda, relaciones*) foreign ◆ *nm* exterior, outside; (*aspecto*) outward appearance; (*DEPORTE*) wing(er); (*países extranjeros*) abroad; **asuntos** ~**es** foreign affairs; **al** ~ outwardly, on the outside; **en el** ~ abroad; **noticias del** ~ foreign o overseas news.

exteriorice [eksterjo'riθe] *etc vb* V **exteriorizar.**

exteriorizar [eksterjori'θar] *vt* (*emociones*) to show, reveal.

exteriormente [eksterjor'mente] *ad* outwardly.

exterminar [ekstermi'nar] *vt* to exterminate.

exterminio [ekster'minjo] *nm* extermination.

externo, a [eks'terno, a] *a* (*exterior*) external, outside; (*superficial*) outward ◆ *nm/f* day pupil.

extienda [eks'tjenda] *etc vb* V **extender.**

extinción [ekstin'θjon] *nf* extinction.

extinga [eks'tinga] *etc vb* V **extinguir.**

extinguido, a [ekstin'giðo, a] *a* (*animal, volcán*) extinct; (*fuego*) out, extinguished.

extinguir [ekstin'gir] *vt* (*fuego*) to extinguish, put out; (*raza, población*) to wipe out; ~**se** *vr* (*fuego*) to go out; (*BIO*) to die out, become extinct.

extinto, a [eks'tinto, a] *a* extinct.

extintor [ekstin'tor] *nm* (fire) extinguisher.

extirpar [ekstir'par] vt (vicios) to eradicate, stamp out; (MED) to remove (surgically).
extorsión [ekstor'sjon] nf blackmail.
extra ['ekstra] a inv (tiempo) extra; (vino) vintage; (chocolate) good-quality; (gasolina) high-octane ◆ nm/f extra ◆ nm (bono) bonus; (periódico) special edition.
extracción [ekstrak'θjon] nf extraction; (en lotería) draw; (de carbón) mining.
extracto [eks'trakto] nm extract.
extradición [ekstraði'θjon] nf extradition.
extradicionar [ekstraðiθjo'nar], **extraditar** [ekstraði'tar] vt to extradite.
extraer [ekstra'er] vt to extract, take out.
extrafino, a [ekstra'fino, a] a extra-fine; **azúcar** ~ caster sugar.
extraiga [eks'traiɣa] etc, **extraje** [eks'traxe] etc, **extrajera** [ekstra'xera] etc vb V **extraer**.
extralimitarse [ekstralimi'tarse] vr to go too far.
extranjerismo [ekstranxe'rismo] nm foreign word o phrase etc.
extranjero, a [ekstran'xero, a] a foreign ◆ nm/f foreigner ◆ nm foreign lands pl; **en el** ~ abroad.
extrañamiento [ekstraɲa'mjento] nm estrangement.
extrañar [ekstra'ɲar] vt (sorprender) to find strange o odd; (echar de menos) to miss; ~**se** vr (sorprenderse) to be amazed, be surprised; (distanciarse) to become estranged, grow apart; **me extraña** I'm surprised.
extrañeza [ekstra'ɲeθa] nf (rareza) strangeness, oddness; (asombro) amazement, surprise.
extraño, a [eks'traɲo, a] a (extranjero) foreign; (raro, sorprendente) strange, odd.
extraoficial [ekstraofi'θjal] a unofficial, informal.
extraordinario, a [ekstraorði'narjo, a] a extraordinary; (edición, número) special ◆ nm (de periódico) special edition; **horas extraordinaras** overtime sg.
extrarradio [ekstra'rraðjo] nm suburbs pl.
extrasensorial [ekstrasenso'rjal] a: **percepción** ~ extrasensory perception.
extraterrestre [ekstrate'rrestre] a of o from outer space ◆ nm/f creature from outer space.
extravagancia [ekstraβa'ɣanθja] nf oddness; outlandishness; (rareza) peculiarity; ~**s** nfpl (tonterías) nonsense sg.
extravagante [ekstraβa'ɣante] a (excéntrico) eccentric; (estrafalario) outlandish.
extraviado, a [ekstra'βjaðo, a] a lost, missing.
extraviar [ekstra'βjar] vt to mislead, misdirect; (perder) to lose, misplace; ~**se** vr to lose one's way, get lost; (objeto) to go mis-

sing, be mislaid.
extravío [ekstra'βio] nm loss; (fig) misconduct.
extrayendo [ekstra'jendo] vb V **extraer**.
extremado, a [ekstre'maðo, a] a extreme, excessive.
Extremadura [ekstrema'ðura] nf Estremadura.
extremar [ekstre'mar] vt to carry to extremes; ~**se** vr to do one's utmost, make every effort.
extremaunción [ekstremaun'θjon] nf extreme unction, last rites pl.
extremidad [ekstremi'ðað] nf (punta) extremity; (fila) edge; ~**es** nfpl (ANAT) extremities.
extremo, a [eks'tremo, a] a extreme; (más alejado) furthest; (último) last ◆ nm end; (situación) extreme; **E~ Oriente** Far East; **en último** ~ as a last resort; **pasar de un** ~ **a otro** (fig) to go from one extreme to the other; **con** ~ in the extreme; **la extrema derecha** (POL) the far right; ~ **derecho/izquierdo** (DEPORTE) outside right/left.
extrínseco, a [eks'trinseko, a] a extrinsic.
extrovertido, a [ekstroβer'tiðo, a] a extrovert, outgoing ◆ nm/f extrovert.
exuberancia [eksuβe'ranθja] nf exuberance.
exuberante [eksuβe'rante] a exuberant; (fig) luxuriant, lush.
exudar [eksu'ðar] vt, vi to exude.
exultar [eksul'tar] vi: ~ (**en**) to exult (in); (pey) to gloat (over).
exvoto [eks'βoto] nm votive offering.
eyacular [ejaku'lar] vt, vi to ejaculate.

F

F,f ['efe] nf (letra) F, f; **F de Francia** F for Frederick (Brit), F for Fox (US).
f.ª abr (COM: = factura) Inv.
f.a.b. abr (= franco a bordo) f.o.b.
fabada [fa'βaða] nf bean and sausage stew.
fábrica ['faβrika] nf factory; ~ **de moneda** mint; **marca de** ~ trademark; **precio de** ~ factory price.
fabricación [faβrika'θjon] nf (manufactura) manufacture; (producción) production; **de** ~ **casera** home-made; **de** ~ **nacional** home produced; ~ **en serie** mass production.
fabricante [faβri'kante] nm/f manufacturer.
fabricar [faβri'kar] vt (manufacturar) to manufacture, make; (construir) to build; (cuento) to fabricate, devise; ~ **en serie** to

mass-produce.

fabrique [fa'ßrike] *etc vb V* **fabricar.**

fabril [fa'ßril] *a*: **industria** ~ manufacturing industry.

fábula ['faßula] *nf* (*cuento*) fable; (*chisme*) rumour; (*mentira*) fib.

FACA ['faka] *nm abr* (*Esp AVIAT*) = *Futuro Avión de Combate y Ataque.*

facción [fak'θjon] *nf* (*POL*) faction; **facciones** *nfpl* (*del rostro*) features.

faceta [fa'θeta] *nf* facet.

fácil ['faθil] *a* (*simple*) easy; (*sencillo*) simple, straightforward; (*probable*) likely; (*respuesta*) facile; ~ **de usar** (*INFORM*) user-friendly.

facilidad [faθili'ðað] *nf* (*capacidad*) ease; (*sencillez*) simplicity; (*de palabra*) fluency; ~**es** *nfpl* facilities; "~**es de pago**" (*COM*) "credit facilities", "payment terms".

facilitar [faθili'tar] *vt* (*hacer fácil*) to make easy; (*proporcionar*) to provide; (*documento*) to issue; **le agradecería me facilitara** ... I would be grateful if you could let me have ....

fácilmente ['faθilmente] *ad* easily.

facsímil [fak'simil] *nm* (*documento*) facsimile; **enviar por** ~ to fax.

factible [fak'tißle] *a* feasible.

factor [fak'tor] *nm* factor; (*COM*) agent; (*FERRO*) freight clerk.

factoría [fakto'ria] *nf* (*COM*: *agencia*) agency; (: *fábrica*) factory.

factura [fak'tura] *nf* (*cuenta*) bill; (*nota de pago*) invoice; (*hechura*) manufacture; **presentar** ~ **a** to invoice.

facturación [faktura'θjon] *nf* (*COM*) invoicing; (: *ventas*) turnover; ~ **de equipajes** luggage check-in.

facturar [faktu'rar] *vt* (*COM*) to invoice, charge for; (*AVIAT*) to check in; (*equipaje*) to register, check (*US*).

facultad [fakul'tað] *nf* (*aptitud*, *ESCOL etc*) faculty; (*poder*) power.

facultativo, a [fakulta'tißo, a] *a* optional; (*de un oficio*) professional; **prescripción facultativa** medical prescription.

facha ['fatʃa] (*fam*) *nm/f* fascist, right-wing extremist ♦ *nf* (*aspecto*) look; (*cara*) face; **¡qué** ~ **tienes!** you look a sight!

fachada [fa'tʃaða] *nf* (*ARQ*) façade, front; (*TIP*) title page; (*fig*) façade, outward show.

FAD *nm abr* (*Esp*) = *Fondo de Ayuda y Desarrollo.*

faena [fa'ena] *nf* (*trabajo*) work; (*quehacer*) task, job; ~**s domésticas** housework *sg*.

faenar [fae'nar] *vi* to fish.

fagot [fa'yot] *nm* (*MUS*) bassoon.

faisán [fai'san] *nm* pheasant.

faja ['faxa] *nf* (*para la cintura*) sash; (*de mujer*) corset; (*de tierra*) strip.

fajo ['faxo] *nm* (*de papeles*) bundle; (*de*

billetes) role, wad.

falange [fa'lanxe] *nf*: **la F~** (*POL*) the Falange.

falda ['falda] *nf* (*prenda de vestir*) skirt; (*GEO*) foothill; ~ **escocesa** kilt.

fálico, a ['faliko, a] *a* phallic.

falo ['falo] *nm* phallus.

falsear [false'ar] *vt* to falsify; (*firma etc*) to forge ♦ *vi* (*MUS*) to be out of tune.

falsedad [false'ðað] *nf* falseness; (*hipocresía*) hypocrisy; (*mentira*) falsehood.

falsificación [falsifika'θjon] *nf* (*acto*) falsification; (*objeto*) forgery.

falsificar [falsifi'kar] *vt* (*firma etc*) to forge; (*voto etc*) to rig; (*moneda*) to counterfeit.

falsifique [falsi'fike] *etc vb V* **falsificar.**

falso, a ['falso, a] *a* false; (*erróneo*) wrong, mistaken; (*firma*, *documento*) forged; (*documento*, *moneda etc*) fake; **en** ~ falsely; **dar un paso en** ~ to trip; (*fig*) to take a false step.

falta ['falta] *nf* (*defecto*) fault, flaw; (*privación*) lack, want; (*ausencia*) absence; (*carencia*) shortage; (*equivocación*) mistake; (*JUR*) default; (*DEPORTE*) foul; (*TENIS*) fault; ~ **de ortografía** spelling mistake; ~ **de respeto** disrespect; **echar en** ~ to miss; **hacer** ~ **hacer algo** to be necessary to do sth; **me hace** ~ **una pluma** I need a pen; **sin** ~ without fail; **por** ~ **de** through *o* for lack of.

faltar [fal'tar] *vi* (*escasear*) to be lacking, be wanting; (*ausentarse*) to be absent, be missing; **¿falta algo?** is anything missing?; **falta mucho todavía** there's plenty of time yet; **¿falta mucho?** is there long to go?; **faltan 2 horas para llegar** there are 2 hours to go till arrival; ~ **(al respeto) a uno** to be disrespectful to sb; ~ **a una cita** to miss an appointment; ~ **a la verdad** to lie; **¡no faltaba más!** that's the last straw!

falto, a ['falto, a] *a* (*desposeído*) deficient, lacking; (*necesitado*) poor, wretched; **estar** ~ **de** to be short of.

falla ['faʎa] *nf* (*defecto*) fault, flaw.

fallar [fa'ʎar] *vt* (*JUR*) to pronounce sentence on; (*NAIPES*) to trump ♦ *vi* (*memoria*) to fail; (*plan*) to go wrong; (*motor*) to miss; ~ **a uno** to let sb down.

fallecer [faʎe'θer] *vi* to pass away, die.

fallecido, a [faʎe'θiðo, a] *a* late ♦ *nm/f* deceased.

fallecimiento [faʎeθi'mjento] *nm* decease, demise.

fallezca [fa'ʎeθka] *etc vb V* **fallecer.**

fallido, a [fa'ʎiðo, a] *a* vain; (*intento*) frustrated, unsuccessful; (*esperanza*) disappointed.

fallo ['faʎo] *nm* (*JUR*) verdict, ruling; (*decisión*) decision; (*de jurado*) findings; (*fracaso*) failure; (*DEPORTE*) miss; (*INFORM*) bug.

fama ['fama] nf (renombre) fame; (reputación) reputation.

famélico, a [fa'meliko, a] a starving.

familia [fa'milja] nf family; ~ **política** in-laws pl.

familiar [fami'ljar] a (relativo a la familia) family cpd; (conocido, informal) familiar; (estilo) informal; (LING) colloquial ♦ nm/f relative, relation.

familiarice [familja'riθe] etc vb V **familiarizarse**.

familiaridad [familjari'ðað] nf familiarity; (informalidad) homeliness.

familiarizarse [familjari'θarse] vr: ~ **con** to familiarize o.s. with.

famoso, a [fa'moso, a] a (renombrado) famous.

fanático, a [fa'natiko, a] a fanatical ♦ nm/f fanatic; (CINE, DEPORTE etc) fan.

fanatismo [fana'tismo] nm fanaticism.

fanfarrón, ona [fanfa'rron, ona] a boastful; (pey) showy.

fango ['fango] nm mud.

fangoso, a [fan'goso, a] a muddy.

fantasear [fantase'ar] vi to fantasize; ~ **con una idea** to toy with an idea.

fantasía [fanta'sia] nf fantasy, imagination; (MUS) fantasia; (capricho) whim; **joyas de** ~ imitation jewellery sg.

fantasma [fan'tasma] nm (espectro) ghost, apparition; (presumido). show-off.

fantástico, a [fan'tastiko, a] a (irreal, fam) fantastic.

FAO ['fao] nf abr (= Organización de las Naciones Unidas para la Agricultura y la Alimentación) FAO.

fardar [far'ðar] vi to show off; ~ **de** to boast about.

fardo ['farðo] nm bundle; (fig) burden.

farmacéutico, a [farma'θeutiko, a] a pharmaceutical ♦ nm/f chemist (Brit), pharmacist.

farmacia [far'maθja] nf (ciencia) pharmacy; (tienda) chemist's (shop) (Brit), pharmacy, drugstore (US); ~ **de turno** duty chemist.

fármaco ['farmako] nm medicine, drug.

faro ['faro] nm (NAUT: torre) lighthouse; (señal) beacon; (AUTO) headlamp; ~**s antiniebla** fog lamps; ~**s delanteros/traseros** headlights/rear lights.

farol [fa'rol] nm (luz) lantern, lamp; (FERRO) headlamp; (poste) lamppost; **echarse un** ~ (fam) to show off.

farola [fa'rola] nf street lamp (Brit) o light (US), lamppost.

farruco, a [fa'rruko, a] a (fam): **estar** o **ponerse** ~ to get aggressive.

farsa ['farsa] nf (gen) farce.

farsante [far'sante] nm/f fraud, fake.

FASA ['fasa] nf abr (Esp AUTO) = Fábrica de Automóviles, S.A.

fascículo [fas'θikulo] nm (gen) part, instalment (Brit), installment (US).

fascinante [fasθi'nante] a fascinating.

fascinar [fasθi'nar] vt to fascinate; (encantar) to captivate.

fascismo [fas'θismo] nm fascism.

fascista [fas'θista] a, nm/f fascist.

fase ['fase] nf phase.

fastidiar [fasti'ðjar] vt (disgustar) to annoy, bother; (estropear) to spoil; ~**se** vr (disgustarse) to get annoyed o cross; **¡no fastidies!** you're joking!; **¡que se fastidie!** (fam) he'll just have to put up with it!

fastidio [fas'tiðjo] nm (disgusto) annoyance.

fastidioso, a [fasti'ðjoso, a] a (molesto) annoying.

fastuoso, a [fas'twoso, a] a (espléndido) magnificent; (banquete etc) lavish.

fatal [fa'tal] a (gen) fatal; (desgraciado) ill-fated; (fam: malo, pésimo) awful ♦ ad terribly; **lo pasó** ~ he had a terrible time (of it).

fatalidad [fatali'ðað] nf (destino) fate; (mala suerte) misfortune.

fatídico, a [fa'tiðiko, a] a fateful.

fatiga [fa'tiɣa] nf (cansancio) fatigue, weariness; ~**s** nfpl hardships.

fatigar [fati'ɣar] vt to tire, weary; ~**se** vr to get tired.

fatigoso, a [fati'ɣoso, a] a (cansador) tiring.

fatigue [fa'tiɣe] etc vb V **fatigar**.

fatuo, a ['fatwo, a] a (vano) fatuous; (presuntuoso) conceited.

fauces ['fauθes] nfpl (ANAT) gullet sg; (fam) jaws.

fauna ['fauna] nf fauna.

favor [fa'ßor] nm favour (Brit), favor (US); **haga el** ~ **de** ... would you be so good as to ..., kindly ...; **por** ~ please; **a** ~ in favo(u)r; **a** ~ **de** to be in favo(u)r of; (COM) to the order of.

favorable [faßo'raßle] a favourable (Brit), favorable (US); (condiciones etc) advantageous.

favorecer [faßore'θer] vt to favour (Brit), favor (US); (amparar) to help; (vestido etc) to become, flatter; **este peinado le favorece** this hairstyle suits him.

favorezca [faßo'reθka] etc vb V **favorecer**.

favorito, a [faßo'rito, a] a, nm/f favourite (Brit), favorite (US).

faz [faθ] nf face; **la** ~ **de la tierra** the face of the earth.

F.C., f.c. abr = **ferrocarril**.

FE nf abr = Falange Española.

fe [fe] nf (REL) faith; (confianza) belief; (documento) certificate; **de buena** ~ (JUR) bona fide; **prestar** ~ **a** to believe, credit; **actuar con buena/mala** ~ to act in good/bad faith; **dar** ~ **de** to bear witness to; ~

de erratas errata.

fealdad [feal'daθ] *nf* ugliness.

feb., feb.º *abr* (= *febrero*) Feb.

febrero [fe'ßrero] *nm* February.

febril [fe'ßril] *a* feverish; (*movido*) hectic.

fécula ['fekula] *nf* starch.

fecundación [fekunda'θjon] *nf* fertilization; ~ **in vitro** in vitro fertilization, I.V.F.

fecundar [fekun'dar] *vt* (*generar*) to fertilize, make fertile.

fecundidad [fekundi'ðaθ] *nf* fertility; (*fig*) productiveness.

fecundo, a [fe'kundo, a] *a* (*fértil*) fertile; (*fig*) prolific; (*productivo*) productive.

fecha ['fetʃa] *nf* date; ~ **límite** *o* **tope** closing *o* last date; ~ **límite de venta** (*de alimentos*) sell-by date; ~ **de caducidad** (*de alimentos*) sell-by date; (*de contrato*) expiry date; **en** ~ **próxima** soon; **hasta la** ~ to date, so far; ~ **de vencimiento** (*COM*) due date; ~ **de vigencia** (*COM*) effective date.

fechar [fe'tʃar] *vt* to date.

federación [feðera'θjon] *nf* federation.

federal [feðe'ral] *a* federal.

federalismo [feðera'lismo] *nm* federalism.

FEF [fef] *nf abr* = *Federación Española de Fútbol.*

felicidad [feliθi'ðaθ] *nf* (*satisfacción, contento*) happiness; ~**es** *nfpl* best wishes, congratulations.

felicitaciones [feliθita'θjones] *nfpl* congratulations.

felicitar [feliθi'tar] *vt* to congratulate.

feligrés, esa [feli'ɣres, esa] *nm/f* parishioner.

feliz [fe'liθ] *a* (*contento*) happy; (*afortunado*) lucky.

felonía [felo'nia] *nf* felony, crime.

felpa ['felpa] *nf* (*terciopelo*) plush; (*toalla*) towelling.

felpudo [fel'puðo] *nm* doormat.

femenino, a [feme'nino, a] *a* feminine; (*ZOOL etc*) female ♦ *nm* (*LING*) feminine.

feminismo [femi'nismo] *nm* feminism.

feminista [femi'nista] *a, nm/f* feminist.

fenomenal [fenome'nal] *a* phenomenal; (*fam*) great, terrific.

fenómeno [fe'nomeno] *nm* phenomenon; (*fig*) freak, accident ♦ *ad*: **lo pasamos** ~ we had a great time ♦ *excl* great!, marvellous!

feo, a ['feo, a] *a* (*gen*) ugly; (*desagradable*) bad, nasty ♦ *nm* insult; **hacer un** ~ **a uno** to offend sb; **más** ~ **que Picio** as ugly as sin.

féretro ['feretro] *nm* (*ataúd*) coffin; (*sarcófago*) bier.

feria ['ferja] *nf* (*gen*) fair; (*AM: mercado*) market; (*descanso*) holiday, rest day; (*AM: cambio*) small change; ~ **comercial** trade fair; ~ **de muestras** trade show.

feriado, a [fe'rjaðo, a] (*AM*) *a*: **día** ~ (public) holiday ♦ *nm* (public) holiday.

fermentar [fermen'tar] *vi* to ferment.

fermento [fer'mento] *nm* leaven, leavening.

ferocidad [feroθi'ðaθ] *nf* fierceness, ferocity.

ferocísimo, a [fero'θisimo, a] *a superlativo de* **feroz.**

feroz [fe'roθ] *a* (*cruel*) cruel; (*salvaje*) fierce.

férreo, a ['ferreo, a] *a* iron *cpd*; (*TEC*) ferrous; (*fig*) (of) iron.

ferretería [ferrete'ria] *nf* (*tienda*) ironmonger's (shop) (*Brit*), hardware store.

ferrocarril [ferroka'rril] *nm* railway, railroad (*US*); ~ **de vía estrecha/única** narrow-gauge/single-track railway *o* line.

ferroviario, a [ferrovja'rjo, a] *a* rail *cpd*, railway *cpd* (*Brit*), railroad *cpd* (*US*) ♦ *nm*: ~**s** railway (*Brit*) *o* railroad (*US*) workers.

fértil ['fertil] *a* (*productivo*) fertile; (*rico*) rich.

fertilice [ferti'liθe] *etc vb V* **fertilizar.**

fertilidad [fertili'ðaθ] *nf* (*gen*) fertility; (*productividad*) fruitfulness.

fertilizar [fertili'θar] *vt* to fertilize.

fervor [fer'ßor] *nm* fervour (*Brit*), fervor (*US*).

fervoroso, a [ferßo'roso, a] *a* fervent.

festejar [feste'xar] *vt* (*agasajar*) to wine and dine, fête; (*galantear*) to court; (*celebrar*) to celebrate.

festejo [fes'texo] *nm* (*diversión*) entertainment; (*galanteo*) courtship; (*fiesta*) celebration.

festín [fes'tin] *nm* feast, banquet.

festival [festi'ßal] *nm* festival.

festividad [festißi'ðaθ] *nf* festivity.

festivo, a [fes'tißo, a] *a* (*de fiesta*) festive; (*fig*) witty; (*CINE, LIT*) humorous; **día** ~ holiday.

fetiche [fe'titʃe] *nm* fetish.

fetichista [feti'tʃista] *a* fetishistic ♦ *nm/f* fetishist.

fétido, a ['fetiðo, a] *a* (*hediondo*) foul-smelling.

feto ['feto] *nm* foetus; (*fam*) monster.

FF.AA. *nfpl abr* (*MIL*) = **Fuerzas Armadas.**

FF.CC. *nmpl abr* = **Ferrocarriles.**

fiable [fi'aßle] *a* (*persona*) trustworthy; (*máquina*) reliable.

fiado [fi'aðo] *nm*: **comprar al** ~ to buy on credit; **en** ~ on bail.

fiador, a [fia'ðor, a] *nm/f* (*JUR*) surety, guarantor; (*COM*) backer; **salir** ~ **por uno** to stand bail for sb.

fiambre ['fjambre] *a* (*CULIN*) (served) cold ♦ *nm* (*CULIN*) cold meat (*Brit*), cold cut (*US*); (*fam*) corpse, stiff.

fiambrera [fjam'brera] *nf* ≈ lunch box, dinner pail (*US*).

fianza ['fjanθa] *nf* surety; (*JUR*): **libertad bajo** ~ release on bail.

fiar [fi'ar] *vt* (*salir garante de*) to guarantee; (*JUR*) to stand bail o bond (*US*) for; (*vender a crédito*) to sell on credit; (*secreto*) to confide ♦ *vi*: ~ (**de**) to trust (in); **ser de** ~ to be trustworthy; ~**se** *vr*: ~ **de** to trust (in), rely on.

fiasco ['fjasko] *nm* fiasco.

fibra ['fiβra] *nf* fibre (*Brit*), fiber (*US*); (*fig*) vigour (*Brit*), vigor (*US*); ~ **óptica** (*INFORM*) optical fibre (*Brit*) o fiber (*US*).

ficción [fik'θjon] *nf* fiction.

ficticio, a [fik'tiθjo, a] *a* (*imaginario*) fictitious; (*falso*) fabricated.

ficus ['fikus] *nm inv* (*BOT*) rubber plant.

ficha ['fitʃa] *nf* (*TELEC*) token; (*en juegos*) counter, marker; (*en casino*) chip; (*COM*, *ECON*) tally, check (*US*); (*INFORM*) file; (*tarjeta*) (index) card; (*ELEC*) plug; (*en hotel*) registration form; ~ **policíaca** police dossier.

fichaje [fi'tʃaxe] *nm* signing(-up).

fichar [fi'tʃar] *vt* (*archivar*) to file, index; (*DEPORTE*) to sign (up) ♦ *vi* (*deportista*) to sign (up); (*obrero*) to clock in o on; **estar fichado** to have a record.

fichero [fi'tʃero] *nm* card index; (*archivo*) filing cabinet; (*COM*) box file; (*INFORM*) file, archive; (*de policía*) criminal records; ~ **activo** (*INFORM*) active file; ~ **archivado** (*INFORM*) archived file; ~ **indexado** (*IN-FORM*) index file; ~ **de reserva** (*INFORM*) backup file; ~ **de tarjetas** card index; **nombre de** ~ filename.

fidedigno, a [fiðe'ðixno, a] *a* reliable.

fideicomiso [fiðeiko'miso] *nm* (*COM*) trust.

fidelidad [fiðeli'ðað] *nf* (*lealtad*) fidelity, loyalty; (*exactitud: de dato etc*) accuracy; **alta** ~ high fidelity, hi-fi.

fidelísimo, a [fiðe'lisimo, a] *a superlativo de* **fiel**.

fideos [fi'ðeos] *nmpl* noodles.

fiduciario, a [fiðu'θjarjo, a] *nm/f* fiduciary.

fiebre ['fjeβre] *nf* (*MED*) fever; (*fig*) fever, excitement; ~ **amarilla/del heno** yellow/hay fever; ~ **palúdica** malaria; **tener** ~ to have a temperature.

fiel [fjel] *a* (*leal*) faithful, loyal; (*fiable*) reliable; (*exacto*) accurate ♦ *nm* (*aguja*) needle, pointer; **los** ~**es** the faithful.

fieltro ['fjeltro] *nm* felt.

fiera [fjera] *nf* V **fiero**.

fiereza [fje'reθa] *nf* (*ZOOL*) wildness; (*bravura*) fierceness.

fiero, a ['fjero, a] *a* (*cruel*) cruel; (*feroz*) fierce; (*duro*) harsh ♦ *nm/f* (*fig*) fiend ♦ *nf* (*animal feroz*) wild animal o beast; (*fig*) dragon.

fiesta ['fjesta] *nf* party; (*de pueblo*) festival; (*vacaciones: tb:* ~**s**) holiday; ~ **nacional** public o bank holiday; **mañana es** ~ it's a holiday tomorrow; ~ **de guardar** (*REL*) day of obligation.

figura [fi'ɣura] *nf* (*gen*) figure; (*forma, imagen*) shape, form; (*NAIPES*) face card.

figurado, a [fiɣu'raðo, a] *a* figurative.

figurar [fiɣu'rar] *vt* (*representar*) to represent; (*fingir*) to feign ♦ *vi* to figure; ~**se** *vr* (*imaginarse*) to imagine; (*suponer*) to suppose; **ya me lo figuraba** I thought as much.

fijador [fixa'ðor] *nm* (*FOTO etc*) fixative; (*de pelo*) gel.

fijar [fi'xar] *vt* (*gen*) to fix; (*cartel*) to post, put up; (*estampilla*) to affix, stick (on); (*pelo*) to set; (*fig*) to settle (on), decide; ~**se** *vr*: ~**se en** to notice; **¡fíjate!** just imagine!; **¿te fijas?** see what I mean?

fijo, a ['fixo, a] *a* (*gen*) fixed; (*firme*) firm; (*permanente*) permanent; (*trabajo*) steady; (*color*) fast ♦ *ad*: **mirar** ~ to stare.

fila ['fila] *nf* row; (*MIL*) rank; (*cadena*) line; (*MIL*) rank; (*en marcha*) file; ~ **india** single file; **ponerse en** ~ to line up, get into line; **primera** ~ front row.

filántropo, a [fi'lantropo, a] *nm/f* philanthropist.

filarmónico, a [filar'moniko, a] *a*, *nf* philharmonic.

filatelia [fila'telja] *nf* philately, stamp collecting.

filatelista [filate'lista] *nm/f* philatelist, stamp collector.

filete [fi'lete] *nm* (*carne*) fillet steak; (*de cerdo*) tenderloin; (*pescado*) fillet; (*MEC*: *rosca*) thread.

filiación [filja'θjon] *nf* (*POL etc*) affiliation; (*señas*) particulars *pl*; (*MIL, POLICÍA*) records *pl*.

filial [fi'ljal] *a* filial ♦ *nf* subsidiary; (*sucursal*) branch.

filibustero [filiβus'tero] *nm* pirate.

Filipinas [fili'pinas] *nfpl*: **las (Islas)** ~ the Philippines.

filipino, a [fili'pino, a] *a*, *nm/f* Philippine.

film [film], *pl* **films** *nm* film, movie (*US*).

filmación [filma'θjon] *nf* filming, shooting.

filmar [fil'mar] *vt* to film, shoot.

filmoteca [filmo'teka] *nf* film library.

filo ['filo] *nm* (*gen*) edge; **sacar** ~ **a** to sharpen; **al** ~ **del medio día** at about midday; **de doble** ~ double-edged.

filología [filolo'xia] *nf* philology.

filólogo, a [fi'loloɣo, a] *nm/f* philologist.

filón [fi'lon] *nm* (*MINERÍA*) vein, lode; (*fig*) gold mine.

filosofía [filoso'fia] *nf* philosophy.

filosófico, a [filo'sofiko, a] *a* philosophic(al).

filósofo, a [fi'losofo, a] *nm/f* philosopher.

filtración [filtra'θjon] *nf* (*TEC*) filtration; (*INFORM*) sorting; (*fig*: *de fondos*) misappropriation; (*de datos*) leak.

filtrar [fil'trar] *vt*, *vi* to filter, strain; (*información*) to leak; ~**se** *vr* to filter; (*fig*: *dinero*) to dwindle.

filtro ['filtro] *nm* (*TEC, utensilio*) filter.

fin [fin] *nm* end; (*objetivo*) aim, purpose; **a ~ de cuentas** at the end of the day; **al ~ y al cabo** when all's said and done; **a ~ de** in order to; **por ~** finally; **en ~** in short; ~ **de archivo** (*INFORM*) end-of-file; ~ **de semana** weekend; **sin ~** endless(ly).

final [fi'nal] *a* final ♦ *nm* end, conclusion ♦ *nf* (*DEPORTE*) final.

finalice [fina'liθe] *etc vb V* **finalizar**.

finalidad [finali'ðað] *nf* finality; (*propósito*) purpose, aim.

finalista [fina'lista] *nm/f* finalist.

finalizar [finali'θar] *vt* to end, finish ♦ *vi* to end, come to an end; ~ **la sesión** (*INFORM*) to log out *o* off.

financiación [finanθja'θjon] *nf* financing.

financiar [finan'θjar] *vt* to finance.

financiero, a [finan'θjero, a] *a* financial ♦ *nm/f* financier.

finanzas [fi'nanθas] *nfpl* finances.

finca ['finka] *nf* country estate.

fineza [fi'neθa] *nf* (*cualidad*) fineness; (*modales*) refinement.

fingir [fin'xir] *vt* (*simular*) to simulate, feign; (*pretextar*) to sham, fake ♦ *vi* (*aparentar*) to pretend; ~**se** *vr*: ~**se dormido** to pretend to be asleep.

finiquitar [finiki'tar] *vt* (*ECON*: *cuenta*) to settle and close.

Finisterre [finis'terre] *nm*: **el cabo de** ~ Cape Finisterre.

finja ['finxa] *etc vb V* **fingir**.

finlandés, esa [finlan'des, esa] *a* Finnish ♦ *nm/f* Finn ♦ *nm* (*LING*) Finnish.

Finlandia [fin'landja] *nf* Finland.

fino, a ['fino, a] *a* fine; (*delgado*) slender; (*de buenas maneras*) polite, refined; (*inteligente*) shrewd; (*punta*) sharp; (*gusto*) discriminating; (*oído*) sharp; (*jerez*) fino, dry ♦ *nm* (*jerez*) dry sherry.

finura [fi'nura] *nf* (*calidad*) fineness; (*cortesía*) politeness; (*elegancia*) elegance; (*agudeza*) shrewdness.

FIP [fip] *nf abr* (*Esp*) = *Formación Intensiva Profesional*.

firma ['firma] *nf* signature; (*COM*) firm, company.

firmante [fir'mante] *a*, *nm/f* signatory; **los abajo ~s** the undersigned.

firmar [fir'mar] *vt* to sign; ~ **un contrato** (*COM*: *colocarse*) to sign on; **firmado y sellado** signed and sealed.

firme ['firme] *a* firm; (*estable*) stable; (*sóli-do*) solid; (*constante*) steady; (*decidido*) resolute; (*duro*) hard; **¡~s!** (*MIL*) attention!; **oferta en** ~ (*COM*) firm offer ♦ *nm* road (surface).

firmemente [firme'mente] *ad* firmly.

firmeza [fir'meθa] *nf* firmness; (*constancia*) steadiness; (*solidez*) solidity.

fiscal [fis'kal] *a* fiscal ♦ *nm* (*JUR*) ≈ Crown Prosecutor, Procurator Fiscal (*Escocia*), district attorney (*US*).

fiscalice [fiska'liθe] *etc vb V* **fiscalizar**.

fiscalizar [fiskali'θar] *vt* (*controlar*) to control; (*registrar*) to inspect (officially); (*fig*) to criticize.

fisco ['fisko] *nm* (*hacienda*) treasury, exchequer; **declarar algo al** ~ to declare sth for tax purposes.

fisgar [fis'yar] *vt* to pry into.

fisgue ['fisye] *etc vb V* **fisgar**.

físico, a ['fisiko, a] *a* physical ♦ *nm* physique; (*aspecto*) appearance, looks ♦ *nm/f* physicist ♦ *nf* physics *sg*.

fisonomía [fisono'mia] *nf* physiognomy, features *pl*.

fisonomista [fisono'mista] *nm/f*: **ser buen** ~ to have a good memory for faces.

flac(c)idez [fla(k)θi'ðeθ] *nf* softness, flabbiness.

flác(c)ido, a ['fla(k)θiðo, a] *a* flabby.

flaco, a ['flako, a] *a* (*muy delgado*) skinny, thin; (*débil*) weak, feeble.

flagrante [fla'yrante] *a* flagrant.

flamante [fla'mante] *a* (*fam*) brilliant; (: *nuevo*) brand-new.

flamear [flame'ar] *vt* (*CULIN*) to flambé.

flamenco, a [fla'menko, a] *a* (*de Flandes*) Flemish; (*baile*, *música*) gipsy ♦ *nm/f* Fleming; **los ~s** the Flemish ♦ *nm* (*LING*) Flemish; (*baile*, *música*) flamenco.

flan [flan] *nm* creme caramel.

flanco ['flanko] *nm* side; (*MIL*) flank.

Flandes ['flandes] *nm* Flanders.

flanquear [flanke'ar] *vt* to flank; (*MIL*) to outflank.

flaquear [flake'ar] *vi* (*debilitarse*) to weaken; (*persona*) to slack.

flaqueza [fla'keθa] *nf* (*delgadez*) thinness, leanness; (*fig*) weakness.

flaquísimo, a [fla'kisimo, a] *a superlativo de* **flaco**.

flash [flas], *pl* **flashes** [flas] *nm* (*FOTO*) flash.

flato ['flato] *nm*: **el** (*o* **un**) ~ **the** (*o* **a**) stitch.

flauta ['flauta] (*MUS*) *nf* flute ♦ *nm/f* flautist, flute player.

fleco ['fleko] *nm* fringe.

flecha ['fletʃa] *nf* arrow.

flechazo [fle'tʃaθo] *nm* (*acción*) bowshot; (*fam*): **fue un** ~ it was love at first sight.

flema ['flema] *nm* phlegm.

flemático, a [fle'matiko, a] *a* phlegmatic;

(*tono etc*) matter-of-fact.

flemón [fle'mon] *nm* (*MED*) gumboil.

flequillo [fle'kiʎo] *nm* (*pelo*) fringe.

fletar [fle'tar] *vt* (*COM*) to charter; (*embarcar*) to load; (*AUTO*) to lease (-purchase).

flete ['flete] *nm* (*carga*) freight; (*alquiler*) charter; (*precio*) freightage; ~ **debido** (*COM*) freight forward; ~ **sobre compras** (*COM*) freight inward.

flexible [flek'siβle] *a* flexible; (*individuo*) compliant.

flipper ['fliper] *nm* pinball machine.

flirtear [flirte'ar] *vi* to flirt.

FLN *nm abr* (*POL*: *Esp, Perú, Venezuela*) = *Frente de Liberación Nacional*.

flojera [flo'xera] *nf* (*AM*) laziness; **me da** ~ I can't be bothered.

flojo, a ['floxo, a] *a* (*gen*) loose; (*sin fuerzas*) limp; (*débil*) weak; (*viento*) light; (*bebida*) weak; (*trabajo*) poor; (*actitud*) slack; (*precio*) low; (*COM*: *mercado*) dull, slack.

flor [flor] *nf* flower; (*piropo*) compliment; **la ~ y nata de la sociedad** (*fig*) the cream of society; **en la ~ de la vida** in the prime of life; **a ~ de** on the surface of.

florecer [flore'θer] *vi* (*BOT*) to flower, bloom; (*fig*) to flourish.

floreciente [flore'θjente] *a* (*BOT*) in flower, flowering; (*fig*) thriving.

Florencia [flo'renθja] *nf* Florence.

florero [flo'rero] *nm* vase.

florezca [flo'reθka] *etc vb V* **florecer**.

florista [flo'rista] *nm/f* florist.

flota ['flota] *nf* fleet.

flotación [flota'θjon] *nf* (*COM*) flotation.

flotador [flota'ðor] *nm* (*gen*) float; (*para nadar*) rubber ring; (*de cisterna*) ballcock.

flotante [flo'tante] *a* floating; (*INFORM*): **de coma** ~ floating-point.

flotar [flo'tar] *vi* to float.

flote ['flote] *nm*: **a** ~ afloat; **ponerse a** ~ (*fig*) to get back on one's feet.

FLS *nm abr* (*POL*: *Nicaragua*) = *Frente de Liberación Sandinista*.

fluctuación [fluktwa'θjon] *nf* fluctuation.

fluctuante [fluk'twante] *a* fluctuating.

fluctuar [fluk'twar] *vi* (*oscilar*) to fluctuate.

fluidez [flui'ðeθ] *nf* fluidity; (*fig*) fluency.

flúido, a ['flwiðo, a] *a* fluid; (*lenguaje*) fluent; (*estilo*) smooth ◆ *nm* (*líquido*) fluid.

fluir [flu'ir] *vi* to flow.

flujo ['fluxo] *nm* flow; (*POL*) swing; (*NAUT*) rising tide; ~ **y reflujo** ebb and flow; ~ **de sangre** (*MED*) haemorrhage (*Brit*), hemorrhage (*US*); ~ **positivo/negativo de efectivo** (*COM*) positive/negative cash flow.

flujograma [fluxo'xrama] *nm* flowchart.

fluoruro [flwo'ruro] *nm* fluoride.

fluvial [fluβi'al] *a* fluvial, river *cpd*.

fluyendo [flu'jendo] *etc vb V* **fluir**.

F.M. *nf abr* (= *Frecuencia Modulada*) F.M.

FMI *nm abr* (= *Fondo Monetario Internacional*) I.M.F.

F.N. *nf abr* (*Esp POL*) = *Fuerza Nueva* ◆ *nm* = *Frente Nacional*.

FNPT *nm abr* (*Esp*) = *Fondo Nacional de Protección del Trabajo*.

f.º *abr* (= *folio*) fo., fol.

foca ['foka] *nf* seal.

foco ['foko] *nm* focus; (*centro*) focal point; (*fuente*) source; (*de incendio*) seat; (*ELEC*) floodlight; (*TEATRO*) spotlight; (*AM*) (light) bulb.

fofo, a ['fofo, a] *a* (*esponjoso*) soft, spongy; (*músculo*) flabby.

fogata [fo'xata] *nf* (*hoguera*) bonfire.

fogón [fo'xon] *nm* (*de cocina*) ring, burner.

fogoso, a [fo'xoso, a] *a* spirited.

fol. *abr* (= *folio*) fo., fol.

folio ['foljo] *nm* folio; (*hoja*) leaf.

follaje [fo'ʎaxe] *nm* foliage.

follar [fo'ʎar] *vt, vi* (*fam!*) to fuck(!).

folletinesco, a [foʎetin'esko, a] *a* melodramatic.

folleto [fo'ʎeto] *nm* pamphlet; (*COM*) brochure; (*prospecto*) leaflet; (*ESCOL etc*) handout.

follón [fo'ʎon] *nm* (*fam*: *lío*) mess; (: *conmoción*) fuss, rumpus, shindy; **armar un** ~ to kick up a fuss; **se armó un** ~ there was a hell of a row.

fomentar [fomen'tar] *vt* (*MED*) to foment; (*fig*: *promover*) to promote, foster; (*odio etc*) to stir up.

fomento [fo'mento] *nm* (*fig*: *ayuda*) fostering; (*promoción*) promotion.

fonda ['fonda] *nf* inn.

fondear [fonde'ar] *vt* (*NAUT*: *sondear*) to sound; (*barco*) to search.

fondo ['fondo] *nm* (*de caja etc*) bottom; (*medida*) depth; (*de coche, sala*) back; (*ARTE etc*) background; (*reserva*) fund; (*fig*: *carácter*) nature; ~**s** *nmpl* (*COM*) funds, resources; ~ **de amortización** (*COM*) sinking fund; **F~ Monetario Internacional** International Monetary Fund; ~ **del mar** sea bed *o* floor; **una investigación a** ~ a thorough investigation; **en el** ~ at bottom, deep down; **tener buen** ~ to be good natured.

fonética [fo'netika] *nf* phonetics *sg*.

fonógrafo [fo'noxrafo] *nm* (*AM*) gramophone, phonograph (*US*).

fonología [fonolo'xia] *nf* phonology.

fontanería [fontane'ria] *nf* plumbing.

fontanero [fonta'nero] *nm* plumber.

footing ['futin] *nm* jogging; **hacer** ~ to jog.

F.O.P. [fop] *nfpl abr* (*Esp*) = **Fuerzas del Orden Público**.

forajido [fora'xiðo] *nm* outlaw.

foráneo, a [fo'raneo, a] *a* foreign ◆ *nm/f* outsider.

forastero, a [foras'tero, a] *nm/f* stranger.

forcé [for'θe] *vb* V **forzar**.

forcejear [forθexe'ar] *vi* (*luchar*) to struggle.

forcemos [for'θemos] *etc vb* V **forzar**.

forense [fo'rense] *a* forensic ◆ *nm/f* pathologist.

forestal [fores'tal] *a* forest *cpd*.

forjar [for'xar] *vt* to forge; (*formar*) to form.

forma ['forma] *nf* (*figura*) form, shape; (*molde*) mould, pattern; (*MED*) fitness; (*método*) way, means; **estar en** ~ to be fit; ~ **de pago** (*COM*) method of payment; **las** ~**s** the conventions; **de** ~ **que** ... so that ...; **de todas** ~**s** in any case.

formación [forma'θjon] *nf* (*gen*) formation; (*enseñanza*) training; ~ **profesional** vocational training; ~ **fuera del trabajo** off-the-job training; ~ **en el trabajo** *o* **sobre la práctica** on-the-job training.

formal [for'mal] *a* (*gen*) formal; (*fig: persona*) serious; (*: de fiar*) reliable; (*conducta*) steady.

formalice [forma'liθe] *etc vb* V **formalizar**.

formalidad [formali'ðað] *nf* formality; seriousness; reliability; steadiness.

formalizar [formali'θar] *vt* (*JUR*) to formalize; (*plan*) to draw up; (*situación*) to put in order, regularize; ~**se** *vr* (*situación*) to be put in order, be regularized.

formar [for'mar] *vt* (*componer*) to form, shape; (*constituir*) to make up, constitute; (*ESCOL*) to train, educate ◆ *vi* (*MIL*) to fall in; (*DEPORTE*) to line up; ~**se** *vr* (*ESCOL*) to be trained (*o* educated); (*cobrar forma*) to form, take form; (*desarrollarse*) to develop.

formatear [formate'ar] *vt* (*INFORM*) to format.

formateo [forma'teo] *nm* (*INFORM*) formatting.

formato [for'mato] *nm* (*INFORM*): **sin** ~ (*disco, texto*) unformatted; ~ **de registro** record format.

formidable [formi'ðaβle] *a* (*temible*) formidable; (*asombroso*) tremendous.

fórmula ['formula] *nf* formula.

formulario [formu'larjo] *nm* form; ~ **de solicitud/de pedido** (*COM*) application/order form; **llenar un** ~ to fill in a form; ~ **continuo desplegable** (*INFORM*) fanfold paper.

fornicar [forni'kar] *vi* to fornicate.

fornido, a [for'niðo, a] *a* well-built.

fornique [for'nike] *etc vb* V **fornicar**.

foro ['foro] *nm* (*gen*) forum; (*JUR*) court.

forofo, a [fo'rofo, a] *nm/f* fan.

FORPPA ['forpa] *nm abr* (*Esp*) = Fondo de Ordenación y Regulación de Productos y Precios Agrarios.

forrado, a [fo'rraðo, a] *a* (*ropa*) lined; (*fam*) well-heeled.

forrar [fo'rrar] *vt* (*abrigo*) to line; (*libro*) to cover; (*coche*) to upholster; ~**se** *vr* (*fam*) to line one's pockets.

forro ['forro] *nm* (*de cuaderno*) cover; (*costura*) lining; (*de sillón*) upholstery.

fortalecer [fortale'θer] *vt* to strengthen; ~**se** *vr* to fortify o.s.; (*opinión etc*) to become stronger.

fortaleza [forta'leθa] *nf* (*MIL*) fortress, stronghold; (*fuerza*) strength; (*determinación*) resolution.

fortalezca [forta'leθka] *etc vb* V **fortalecer**.

fortificar [fortifi'kar] *vt* to fortify; (*fig*) to strengthen.

fortifique [forti'fike] *etc vb* V **fortificar**.

fortísimo, a [for'tismo, a] *a* superlativo de **fuerte**.

fortuito, a [for'twito, a] *a* accidental, chance *cpd*.

fortuna [for'tuna] *nf* (*suerte*) fortune, (good) luck; (*riqueza*) fortune, wealth.

forzar [for'θar] *vt* (*puerta*) to force (open); (*compeler*) to compel; (*violar*) to rape; (*ojos etc*) to strain.

forzoso, a [for'θoso, a] *a* necessary; (*inevitable*) inescapable; (*obligatorio*) compulsory.

forzudo, a [for'θuðo, a] *a* burly.

fosa ['fosa] *nf* (*sepultura*) grave; (*en tierra*) pit; (*MED*) cavity; ~**s nasales** nostrils.

fosfato [fos'fato] *nm* phosphate.

fósforo ['fosforo] *nm* (*QUIMICA*) phosphorus; (*cerilla*) match.

fósil ['fosil] *a* fossil, fossilized ◆ *nm* fossil.

foso ['foso] *nm* ditch; (*TEATRO*) pit; (*AUTO*): ~ **de reconocimiento** inspection pit.

foto ['foto] *nf* photo, snap(shot); **sacar una** ~ to take a photo *o* picture.

fotocopia [foto'kopja] *nf* photocopy.

fotocopiadora [fotokopja'ðora] *nf* photocopier.

fotocopiar [fotoko'pjar] *vt* to photocopy.

fotoestilo [fotoes'tilo] *nm* (*INFORM*) light pen.

fotografía [fotoɤra'fia] *nf* (*arte*) photography; (*una* ~) photograph.

fotografiar [fotoɤra'fjar] *vt* to photograph.

fotógrafo, a [fo'toɤrafo, a] *nm/f* photographer.

fotómetro [fo'tometro] *nm* (*FOTO*) light meter.

foulard [fu'lar] *nm* head(scarf).

FP *nf abr* (*Esp*: *ESCOL, COM*) = Formación Profesional ◆ *nm abr* (*POL*) = Frente Popular.

FPLP *nm abr* (*POL*: = Frente Popular para la Liberación de Palestina*) PFLP.

Fr. *abr* (= *Fray*) Fr.; (= *franco*) Fr.

frac [frak], *pl* **fracs** *o* **fraques** ['frakes] *nm* dress coat, tails.

fracasar [fraka'sar] *vi* (*gen*) to fail; (*plan etc*) to fall through.

fracaso [fra'kaso] *nm* (*desgracia, revés*) failure; (*de negociaciones etc*) collapse, breakdown.

fracción [frak'θjon] *nf* fraction; (*POL*) faction, splinter group.

fraccionamiento [frakθjona'mjento] *nm* (*AM*) housing estate.

fractura [frak'tura] *nf* fracture, break.

fragancia [fra'ɣanθja] *nf* (*olor*) fragrance, perfume.

fragante [fra'ɣante] *a* fragrant, scented.

fraganti [fra'ɣanti]: **in** ~ *ad*: **coger a uno in** ~ to catch sb red-handed.

frágil ['fraxil] *a* (*débil*) fragile; (*COM*) breakable; (*fig*) frail, delicate.

fragilidad [fraxili'ðað] *nf* fragility; (*de persona*) frailty.

fragmento [fraɣ'mento] *nm* fragment; (*pedazo*) piece; (*de discurso*) excerpt; (*de canción*) snatch.

fragor [fra'ɣor] *nm* (*ruido intenso*) din.

fragua ['fraɣwa] *nf* forge.

fraguar [fra'ɣwar] *vt* to forge; (*fig*) to concoct ♦ *vi* to harden.

fragüe ['fraɣwe] *etc vb* V **fraguar**.

fraile ['fraile] *nm* (*REL*) friar; (: *monje*) monk.

frambuesa [fram'bwesa] *nf* raspberry.

francés, esa [fran'θes, esa] *a* French ♦ *nm/f* Frenchman/woman ♦ *nm* (*LING*) French.

Francia ['franθja] *nf* France.

franco, a ['franko, a] *a* (*cándido*) frank, open; (*COM: exento*) free ♦ *nm* (*moneda*) franc; ~ **de derechos** duty-free; ~ **al costado del buque** (*COM*) free alongside ship; ~ **puesto sobre vagón** (*COM*) free on rail; ~ **a bordo** free on board.

francotirador, a [frankotira'ðor, a] *nm/f* sniper.

franela [fra'nela] *nf* flannel.

franja ['franxa] *nf* fringe; (*de uniforme*) stripe; (*de tierra etc*) strip.

franquear [franke'ar] *vt* (*camino*) to clear; (*carta, paquete postal*) to frank, stamp; (*obstáculo*) to overcome; (*COM etc*) to free, exempt.

franqueo [fran'keo] *nm* postage.

franqueza [fran'keθa] *nf* (*candor*) frankness.

franquicia [fran'kiθja] *nf* exemption; ~ **aduanera** exemption from customs duties.

franquísimo, a [fran'kisimo, a] *a superlativo de* **franco**.

franquista [fran'kista] *a* pro-Franco ♦ *nm/f* supporter of Franco.

frasco ['frasko] *nm* bottle, flask; ~ **al vacio** (*vacuum*) flask.

frase ['frase] *nf* sentence; (*locución*) phrase, expression; ~ **hecha** set phrase; (*despectivo*) cliché.

fraude ['frauðe] *nm* (*cualidad*) dishonesty; (*acto*) fraud, swindle.

fraudulento, a [frauðu'lento, a] *a* fraudulent.

frazada [fra'θaða] *nf* (*AM*) blanket.

frecuencia [fre'kwenθja] *nf* frequency; **con** ~ frequently, often; ~ **de red** (*INFORM*) mains frequency; ~ **del reloj** (*INFORM*) clock speed; ~ **telefónica** voice frequency.

frecuente [fre'kwente] *a* frequent; (*costumbre*) common; (*vicio*) rife.

fregadero [freɣa'ðero] *nm* (kitchen) sink.

fregador, a [freɣa'ðor, a] *nm/f* (*tb*: ~ **de platos**) dishwasher.

fregar [fre'ɣar] *vt* (*frotar*) to scrub; (*platos*) to wash (up); (*AM*) to annoy.

fregona [fre'ɣona] *nf* (*utensilio*) mop; (*pey: sirvienta*) skivvy.

fregué [fre'ɣe], **freguemos** [fre'ɣemos] *etc vb* V **fregar**.

freír [fre'ir] *vt* to fry.

fréjol ['frexol] *nm* = **fríjol**.

frenar [fre'nar] *vt* to brake; (*fig*) to check.

frenazo [fre'naθo] *nm*: **dar un** ~ to brake sharply.

frenesí [frene'si] *nm* frenzy.

frenético, a [fre'netiko, a] *a* frantic; **ponerse** ~ to lose one's head.

freno ['freno] *nm* (*TEC, AUTO*) brake; (*de cabalgadura*) bit; (*fig*) check.

frente ['frente] *nm* (*ARQ, MIL, POL*) front; (*de objeto*) front part ♦ *nf* forehead, brow; ~ **de batalla** battle front; **hacer** ~ **común con uno** to make common cause with sb; ~ **a** in front of; (*en situación opuesta de*) opposite; **chocar de** ~ to crash head-on; **hacer** ~ **a** to face up to.

fresa ['fresa] *nf* (*Esp: fruta*) strawberry; (*de dentista*) drill.

fresco, a ['fresko, a] *a* (*nuevo*) fresh; (*huevo*) newly-laid; (*frío*) cool; (*descarado*) cheeky, bad-mannered ♦ *nm* (*aire*) fresh air; (*ARTE*) fresco ♦ *nm/f* (*fam*) shameless person; (*persona insolente*) impudent person; **tomar el** ~ to get some fresh air; **¡qué** ~! what a cheek!

frescor [fres'kor] *nm* freshness.

frescura [fres'kura] *nf* freshness; (*descaro*) cheek, nerve; (*calma*) calmness.

fresno ['fresno] *nm* ash (tree).

fresón [fre'son] *nm* strawberry.

frialdad [frjal'dað] *nf* (*gen*) coldness; (*indiferencia*) indifference.

fricción [frik'θjon] *nf* (*gen*) friction; (*acto*) rub(bing); (*MED*) massage; (*POL, fig etc*) friction, trouble.

friega ['frjeɣa] *etc*, **friegue** ['frjeɣe] *etc vb* V

fregar.

friendo [fri'endo] *etc vb V* **freír.**

frigidez [frixi'ðeθ] *nf* frigidity.

frígido, a ['frixiðo, a] *a* frigid.

frigorífico, a [friɣo'rifiko, a] *a* refrigerating; **instalación frigorífica** cold-storage plant ♦ *nm* refrigerator; (*camión*) freezer lorry *o* truck (*US*).

frijol [fri'xol], **fríjol** ['frixol] *nm* kidney bean.

frió [fri'o] *vb V* **freír.**

frío, a ['frio, a] *etc vb V* **freír** ♦ *a* cold; (*fig: indiferente*) unmoved, indifferent; (*poco entusiasta*) chilly ♦ *nm* cold(ness); indifference; **¡que ~!** how cold it is!

friolero, a [frjo'lero, a] *a* sensitive to cold.

frito, a ['frito, a] *pp de* **freír** ♦ *a* fried ♦ *nm* fry; **me trae ~ ese hombre** I'm sick and tired of that man; **~s variados** mixed grill.

frívolo, a ['friβolo, a] *a* frivolous.

frondoso, a [fron'doso, a] *a* leafy.

frontera [fron'tera] *nf* frontier; (*línea divisoria*) border; (*zona*) frontier area.

fronterizo, a [fronte'riθo, a] *a* frontier *cpd*; (*contiguo*) bordering.

frontal [fron'tal] *nm*: **choque ~** head-on collision.

frontón [fron'ton] *nm* (*DEPORTE: cancha*) pelota court; (: *juego*) pelota.

frotar [fro'tar] *vt* to rub; (*fósforo*) to strike; **~se** *vr*: **~se las manos** to rub one's hands.

frs. *abr* (= *francos*) fr.

fructífero, a [fruk'tifero, a] *a* productive, fruitful.

frugal [fru'ɣal] *a* frugal.

fruncir [frun'θir] *vt* (*COSTURA*) to gather; (*ceño*) to frown; (*labios*) to purse.

frunza ['frunθa] *etc vb V* **fruncir.**

frustrar [frus'trar] *vt* to frustrate; **~se** *vr* to be frustrated; (*plan etc*) to fail.

fruta ['fruta] *nf* fruit.

frutal [fru'tal] *a* fruit-bearing, fruit *cpd* ♦ *nm*: (*árbol*) **~** fruit tree.

frutería [frute'ria] *nf* fruit shop.

frutero, a [fru'tero, a] *a* fruit *cpd* ♦ *nm/f* fruiterer ♦ *nm* fruit dish *o* bowl.

frutilla [fru'tiʎa] *nf* (*AM*) strawberry.

fruto ['fruto] *nm* (*BOT*) fruit; (*fig: resultado*) result, outcome; **~s secos** ≈ nuts and raisins.

FSLN *nm abr* (*POL: Nicaragua*) = *Frente Sandinista de Liberación Nacional.*

fue [fwe] *vb V* **ser, ir.**

fuego ['fweɣo] *nm* (*gen*) fire; (*CULIN: gas*) burner, ring; (*fig: pasión*) fire, passion; **~s artificiales** *o* **de artificio** fireworks; **prender ~ a** to set fire to; **a ~ lento** on a low flame *o* gas; **¡alto el ~!** cease fire!; **estar entre dos ~s** to be in the crossfire; **¿tienes ~?** have you (got) a light?

fuel-oil [fuel'oil] *nm* paraffin (*Brit*), kerosene (*US*).

fuelle ['fweʎe] *nm* bellows *pl.*

fuente ['fwente] *nf* fountain; (*manantial, fig*) spring; (*origen*) source; (*plato*) large dish; **~ de alimentación** (*INFORM*) power supply; **de ~ desconocida/fidedigna** from an unknown/reliable source.

fuera ['fwera] *etc vb V* **ser, ir** ♦ *ad* out(side); (*en otra parte*) away; (*excepto, salvo*) except, save ♦ *prep*: **~ de** outside; (*fig*) besides; **~ de alcance** out of reach; **~ de combate** out of action; (*boxeo*) knocked out; **~ de sí** beside o.s.; **por ~** (on the) outside; **los de ~** strangers, newcomers; **estar ~** (*en el extranjero*) to be abroad.

fuera-borda [fwera'ßorða] *nm inv* outboard engine *o* motor.

fuerce ['fwerθe] *etc vb V* **forzar.**

fuero ['fwero] *nm* (*carta municipal*) municipal charter; (*leyes locales*) local *o* regional law code; (*privilegio*) privilege; (*autoridad*) jurisdiction; (*fig*): **en mi** *etc* **~ interno** in my *etc* heart of hearts ..., deep down ....

fuerte ['fwerte] *a* strong; (*golpe*) hard; (*ruido*) loud; (*comida*) rich; (*lluvia*) heavy; (*dolor*) intense ♦ *ad* strongly; hard; loud(ly) ♦ *nm* (*MIL*) fort, strongpoint; (*fig*): **el canto no es mi ~** singing is not my strong point.

fuerza ['fwerθa] *etc vb V* **forzar** ♦ *nf* (*fortaleza*) strength; (*TEC, ELEC*) power; (*coacción*) force; (*violencia*) violence; (*MIL: tb:* **~s**) forces *pl*; **~ de arrastre** (*TEC*) pulling power; **~ de brazos** manpower; **~ mayor** force majeure; **~ bruta** brute force; **~s armadas** (**FF.AA.**) armed forces; **~ de Orden Público** (**F.O.P.**) police (forces); **~ vital** vitality; **a ~ de** by (dint of); **cobrar ~s** to recover one's strength; **tener ~s para** to have the strength to; **a la ~** forcibly, by force; **con ~ legal** (*COM*) legally binding; **por ~** of necessity; **~ de voluntad** willpower.

fuga ['fuɣa] *nf* (*huida*) flight, escape; (*de enamorados*) elopement; (*de gas etc*) leak; **~ de cerebros** (*fig*) brain drain.

fugarse [fu'ɣarse] *vr* to flee, escape.

fugaz [fu'ɣaθ] *a* fleeting.

fugitivo, a [fuxi'tiβo, a] *a* fugitive, fleeing ♦ *nm/f* fugitive.

fugue ['fuɣe] *etc vb V* **fugarse.**

fui [fwi] *etc vb V* **ser, ir.**

fulano, a [fu'lano, a] *nm/f* so-and-so, what's-his-name.

fulgor [ful'ɣor] *nm* brilliance.

fulminante [fulmi'nante] *a* (*pólvora*) fulminating; (*fig: mirada*) withering; (*MED*) fulminant; (*fam*) terrific, tremendous.

fumador, a [fuma'ðor, a] *nm/f* smoker; **no ~** non-smoker.

fumar [fu'mar] *vt, vi* to smoke; ~**se** *vr* (*disipar*) to squander; ~ **en pipa** to smoke a pipe.

funámbulo, a [fu'nambulo, a], **funambulista** [funambu'lista] *nm/f* tightrope walker.

función [fun'θjon] *nf* function; (*de puesto*) duties *pl*; (*TEATRO etc*) show; **entrar en funciones** to take up one's duties; ~ **de tarde/de noche** matinée/evening performance.

funcionamiento [funθjona'mjento] *nm* functioning; (*TEC*) working; **en** ~ (*COM*) on stream; **entrar en** ~ to come into operation.

funcionar [funθjo'nar] *vi* (*gen*) to function; (*máquina*) to work; **"no funciona"** "out of order".

funcionario, a [funθjo'narjo, a] *nm/f* official; (*público*) civil servant.

funda ['funda] *nf* (*gen*) cover; (*de almohada*) pillowcase; ~ **protectora del disco** (*INFORM*) disk-jacket.

fundación [funda'θjon] *nf* foundation.

fundado, a [fun'daðo, a] *a* (*justificado*) well-founded.

fundamental [fundamen'tal] *a* fundamental, basic.

fundamentar [fundamen'tar] *vt* (*poner base*) to lay the foundations of; (*establecer*) to found; (*fig*) to base.

fundamento [funda'mento] *nm* (*base*) foundation; (*razón*) grounds; **eso carece de** ~ that is groundless.

fundar [fun'dar] *vt* to found; (*crear*) to set up; (*fig: basar*): ~ **(en)** to base *o* found (on); ~**se** *vr*: ~**se en** to be founded on.

fundición [fundi'θjon] *nf* (*acción*) smelting; (*fábrica*) foundry; (*TIP*) fount (*Brit*), font.

fundir [fun'dir] *vt* (*gen*) to fuse; (*metal*) to smelt, melt down; (*COM*) to merge; (*estatua*) to cast; ~**se** *vr* (*colores etc*) to merge, blend; (*unirse*) to fuse together; (*ELEC: fusible, lámpara etc*) to blow; (*nieve etc*) to melt.

fúnebre ['funeßre] *a* funeral *cpd*, funereal.

funeral [fune'ral] *nm* funeral.

funeraria [fune'rarja] *nf* undertaker's (*Brit*), mortician's (*US*).

funesto, a [fu'nesto, a] *a* ill-fated; (*desastroso*) fatal.

furgón [fur'ɣon] *nm* wagon.

furgoneta [furɣo'neta] *nf* (*AUTO, COM*) (transit) van (*Brit*), pickup (truck) (*US*).

furia ['furja] *nf* (*ira*) fury; (*violencia*) violence.

furibundo, a [furi'ßundo, a] *a* furious.

furioso, a [fu'rjoso, a] *a* (*iracundo*) furious; (*violento*) violent.

furor [fu'ror] *nm* (*cólera*) rage; (*pasión*) frenzy, passion; **hacer** ~ to be a sensation.

furtivo, a [fur'tißo, a] *a* furtive ◆ *nm* poacher.

furúnculo [fu'runkulo] *nm* (*MED*) boil.

fuselaje [fuse'laxe] *nm* fuselage.

fusible [fu'sißle] *nm* fuse.

fusil [fu'sil] *nm* rifle.

fusilamiento [fusila'mjento] *nm* (*JUR*) execution by firing squad.

fusilar [fusi'lar] *vt* to shoot.

fusión [fu'sjon] *nf* (*gen*) melting; (*unión*) fusion; (*COM*) merger, amalgamation.

fusionar [fusjo'nar] *vt* to fuse (together); (*COM*) to merge; ~**se** *vr* (*COM*) to merge, amalgamate.

fusta ['fusta] *nf* (*látigo*) riding crop.

fútbol ['futßol] *nm* football.

futbolín [futßo'lin] *nm* table football.

futbolista [futßo'lista] *nm/f* footballer.

fútil ['futil] *a* trifling.

futilidad [futili'ðað], **futileza** [futi'leθa] *nf* triviality.

futuro, a [fu'turo, a] *a* future ◆ *nm* future; (*LING*) future tense; ~**s** *nmpl* (*COM*) futures.

G

G, g [xe] *nf* (*letra*) G, g; **G de Gerona** G for George.

g/ *abr* = **giro**.

gabacho, a [ga'ßatʃo, a] *a* Pyrenean; (*fam*) Frenchified ◆ *nm/f* Pyrenean villager; (*fam*) Frenchy.

gabán [ga'ßan] *nm* overcoat.

gabardina [gaßar'ðina] *nf* (*tela*) gabardine; (*prenda*) raincoat.

gabinete [gaßi'nete] *nm* (*POL*) cabinet; (*estudio*) study; (*de abogados etc*) office; ~ **de consulta/de lectura** consulting/reading room.

gacel [ga'θel] *nm*, **gacela** [ga'θela] *nf* gazelle.

gaceta [ga'θeta] *nf* gazette.

gacetilla [gaθe'tiʎa] *nf* (*en periódico*) news in brief; (*de personalidades*) gossip column.

gacha ['gatʃa] *nf* mush; ~**s** *nfpl* porridge *sg*.

gacho, a ['gatʃo, a] *a* (*encorvado*) bent down; (*orejas*) drooping.

gaditano, a [gaði'tano, a] *a* of *o* from Cadiz ◆ *nm/f* native *o* inhabitant of Cadiz.

GAE *nm abr* (*Esp MIL*) = **Grupo Aéreo Embarcado**.

gaélico, a [ga'eliko, a] *a* Gaelic ◆ *nm/f* Gael ◆ *nm* (*LING*) Gaelic.

gafar [ga'far] *vt* (*fam: traer mala suerte*) to put a jinx on.

gafas ['gafas] *nfpl* glasses; ~ **oscuras** dark glasses; ~ **de sol** sunglasses.

gafe ['gafe] *a*: **ser** ~ to be jinxed ◆ *nm* (*fam*) jinx.

gaita ['gaita] *nf* flute; (~ *gallega*) bagpipes *pl*; (*dificultad*) bother; (*cosa engorrosa*) tough job.

gajes ['gaxes] *nmpl* (*salario*) pay *sg*; **los** ~ **del oficio** occupational hazards; ~ **y emolumentos** perquisites.

gajo ['gaxo] *nm* (*gen*) bunch; (*de árbol*) bough; (*de naranja*) segment.

gala ['gala] *nf* full dress; (*fig: lo mejor*) cream, flower; ~**s** *nfpl* finery *sg*; **estar de** ~ to be in one's best clothes; **hacer** ~ **de** to display, show off; **tener algo a** ~ to be proud of sth.

galaico, a [ga'laiko, a] *a* Galician.

galán [ga'lan] *nm* lover, gallant; (*hombre atractivo*) ladies' man; (*TEATRO*): **primer** ~ leading man.

galano, a [ga'lano, a] *a* (*elegante*) elegant; (*bien vestido*) smart.

galante [ga'lante] *a* gallant; (*atento*) charming; (*cortés*) polite.

galantear [galante'ar] *vt* (*hacer la corte a*) to court, woo.

galanteo [galan'teo] *nm* (*coqueteo*) flirting; (*de pretendiente*) wooing.

galantería [galante'ria] *nf* (*caballerosidad*) gallantry; (*cumplido*) politeness; (*piropo*) compliment.

galápago [ga'lapaɣo] *nm* (*ZOOL*) freshwater tortoise.

galardonar [galarðo'nar] *vt* (*premiar*) to reward; (*una obra*) to award a prize for.

galaxia [ga'laksja] *nf* galaxy.

galbana [gal'ßana] *nf* (*pereza*) sloth, laziness.

galeote [gale'ote] *nm* galley slave.

galera [ga'lera] *nf* (*nave*) galley; (*carro*) wagon; (*MED*) hospital ward; (*TIP*) galley.

galería [gale'ria] *nf* (*gen*) gallery; (*balcón*) veranda(h); (*de casa*) corridor; (*fam: público*) audience; ~ **secreta** secret passage.

Gales ['gales] *nm*: (**el País de**) ~ Wales.

galés, esa [ga'les, esa] *a* Welsh ◆ *nm/f* Welshman/woman ◆ *nm* (*LING*) Welsh.

galgo, a ['galɣo, a] *nm/f* greyhound.

Galia [ga'lja] *nf* Gaul.

Galicia [ga'liθja] *nf* Galicia.

galicismo [gali'θismo] *nm* gallicism.

Galilea [gali'lea] *nf* Galilee.

galimatías [galima'tias] *nm inv* (*asunto*) rigmarole; (*lenguaje*) gibberish, nonsense.

galo, a ['galo, a] *a* Gallic; (= *francés*) French ◆ *nm/f* Gaul.

galón [ga'lon] *nm* (*COSTURA*) braid; (*MIL*) stripe; (*medida*) gallon.

galopar [galo'par] *vi* to gallop.

galope [ga'lope] *nm* gallop; **al** ~ (*fig*) in great haste; **a** ~ **tendido** at full gallop.

galvanice [galßa'niθe] *etc vb V* **galvanizar**.

galvanizar [galßani'θar] *vt* to galvanize.

gallardía [gaʎar'ðia] *nf* (*galantería*) dash; (*gracia*) gracefulness; (*valor*) bravery; (*elegancia*) elegance; (*nobleza*) nobleness.

gallego, a [ga'ʎeɣo, a] *a* Galician; (*AM pey*) Spanish ◆ *nm/f* Galician; (*AM pey*) Spaniard ◆ *nm* (*LING*) Galician.

galleta [ga'ʎeta] *nf* biscuit; (*fam: bofetada*) whack, slap.

gallina [ga'ʎina] *nf* hen ◆ *nm* (*fam*) coward; ~ **ciega** blind man's buff; ~ **llueca** broody hen.

gallinero [gaʎi'nero] *nm* (*criadero*) henhouse; (*TEATRO*) gods *sg*, top gallery; (*voces*) hubbub.

gallo ['gaʎo] *nm* cock, rooster; (*MUS*) false o wrong note; (*cambio de voz*) break in the voice; **en menos que canta un** ~ in an instant.

gama ['gama] *nf* (*MUS*) scale; (*fig*) range; (*ZOOL*) doe.

gamba ['gamba] *nf* prawn.

gamberrada [gambe'rraða] *nf* act of hooliganism.

gamberro, a [gam'berro, a] *nm/f* hooligan, lout.

gamo ['gamo] *nm* (*ZOOL*) buck.

gamuza [ga'muθa] *nf* chamois; (*bayeta*) duster; (*AM: piel*) suede.

gana ['gana] *nf* (*deseo*) desire, wish; (*apetito*) appetite; (*voluntad*) will; (*añoranza*) longing; **de buena** ~ willingly; **de mala** ~ reluctantly; **me dan** ~**s de** I feel like, I want to; **tener** ~**s de** to feel like; **no me da la (real)** ~ I don't (damned well) want to; **son** ~**s de molestar** they're just trying to be awkward.

ganadería [ganaðe'ria] *nf* (*ganado*) livestock; (*ganado vacuno*) cattle *pl*; (*cría, comercio*) cattle raising.

ganadero, a [gana'ðero, a] *a* stock *cpd* ◆ *nm* stockman.

ganado [ga'naðo] *nm* livestock; ~ **caballar/cabrío** horses *pl*/ goats *pl*; ~ **lanar** u **ovejuno** sheep *pl*; ~ **porcino/vacuno** pigs *pl*/cattle *pl*.

ganador, a [gana'ðor, a] *a* winning ◆ *nm/f* winner; (*ECON*) earner.

ganancia [ga'nanθja] *nf* (*lo ganado*) gain; (*aumento*) increase; (*beneficio*) profit; ~**s** *nfpl* (*ingresos*) earnings; (*beneficios*) profit *sg*, winnings; ~**s y pérdidas** profit and loss; ~ **bruta/líquida** gross/net profit; ~**s de capital** capital gains; **sacar** ~ **de** to draw profit from.

ganapán [gana'pan] *nm* (*obrero casual*) odd-job man; (*individuo tosco*) lout.

ganar [ga'nar] *vt* (*obtener*) to get, obtain; (*sacar ventaja*) to gain; (*COM*) to earn; (*DEPORTE, premio*) to win; (*derrotar*) to beat; (*alcanzar*) to reach; (*MIL: objetivo*) to take; (*apoyo*) to gain, win ♦ *vi* (*DEPORTE*) to win; ~**se** *vr*: ~**se la vida** to earn one's living; **se lo ha ganado** he deserves it; ~ **tiempo** to gain time.

ganchillo [gan'tʃiʎo] *nm* (*para croché*) crochet hook; (*arte*) crochet work.

gancho ['gantʃo] *nm* (*gen*) hook; (*colgador*) hanger; (*pey: revendedor*) tout; (*fam: atractivo*) sex appeal; (*BOXEO: golpe*) hook.

gandul, a [gan'dul, a] *a, nm/f* good-for-nothing.

ganga ['ganga] *nf* (*cosa*) bargain; (*buena situación*) cushy job.

Ganges ['ganxes] *nm*: **el (Río)** ~ the Ganges.

ganglio ['gangljo] *nm* (*ANAT*) ganglion; (*MED*) swelling.

gangrena [gan'grena] *nf* gangrene.

gansada [gan'saða] *nf* (*fam*) stupid thing (to do).

ganso, a ['ganso, a] *nm/f* (*ZOOL*) gander/goose; (*fam*) idiot.

Gante ['gante] *nm* Ghent.

ganzúa [gan'θua] *nf* skeleton key ♦ *nm/f* burglar.

gañán [ga'ɲan] *nm* farmhand, farm labourer.

garabatear [garaβate'ar] *vt* to scribble, scrawl.

garabato [gara'βato] *nm* (*gancho*) hook; (*garfio*) grappling iron; (*escritura*) scrawl, scribble; (*fam*) sex appeal.

garaje [ga'raxe] *nm* garage.

garante [ga'rante] *a* responsible ♦ *nm/f* guarantor.

garantía [garan'tia] *nf* guarantee; (*seguridad*) pledge; (*compromiso*) undertaking; (*JUR: caución*) warranty; **de máxima** ~ absolutely guaranteed; ~ **de trabajo** job security.

garantice [garan'tiθe] *etc vb* V **garantizar**.

garantir [garan'tir], **garantizar** [garanti'θar] *vt* (*hacerse responsable de*) to vouch for; (*asegurar*) to guarantee.

garbanzo [gar'βanθo] *nm* chickpea.

garbeo [gar'βeo] *nm*: **darse un** ~ to go for a walk.

garbo ['garβo] *nm* grace, elegance; (*aire*) jauntiness; (*de mujer*) glamour; **andar con** ~ to walk gracefully.

garboso, a [gar'βoso, a] *a* graceful, elegant.

garfa ['garfa] *nf* claw.

garfio ['garfjo] *nm* grappling iron; (*gancho*) hook; (*ALPINISMO*) climbing iron.

gargajo [gar'ɣaxo] *nm* phlegm, sputum.

garganta [gar'ɣanta] *nf* (*interna*) throat; (*externa, de botella*) neck; (*GEO: barranco*) ravine; (*desfiladero*) narrow pass.

gargantilla [garɣan'tiʎa] *nf* necklace.

gárgara ['garɣara] *nf* gargle, gargling; **hacer** ~**s** to gargle; **¡vete a hacer** ~**s!** (*fam*) go to blazes!

gárgola ['garɣola] *nf* gargoyle.

garita [ga'rita] *nf* cabin, hut; (*MIL*) sentry box; (*puesto de vigilancia*) lookout post.

garito [ga'rito] *nm* (*lugar*) gaming house *o* den.

Garona [ga'rona] *nm*: **el (Río)** ~ the Garonne.

garra ['garra] *nf* (*de gato, TEC*) claw; (*de ave*) talon; (*fam*) hand, paw; (*fig: de canción etc*) bite; **caer en las** ~**s de uno** to fall into sb's clutches.

garrafa [ga'rrafa] *nf* carafe, decanter.

garrafal [garra'fal] *a* enormous, terrific; (*error*) terrible.

garrapata [garra'pata] *nf* (*ZOOL*) tick.

garrido, a [ga'rriðo, a] *a* handsome.

garrotazo [garro'taθo] *nm* blow with a stick *o* club.

garrote [ga'rrote] *nm* (*palo*) stick; (*porra*) club, cudgel; (*suplicio*) garrotte.

garza ['garθa] *nf* heron.

garzo, a ['garθo, a] *a* blue.

gas [gas] *nm* gas; (*vapores*) fumes *pl*; ~**es de escape** exhaust (fumes).

gasa ['gasa] *nf* gauze; (*de pañal*) nappy liner.

gaseoso, a [gase'oso, a] *a* gassy, fizzy ♦ *nf* lemonade, pop (*fam*).

gasoducto [gaso'ðukto] *nm* gas pipeline.

gasoil [ga'soil], **gasóleo** [ga'soleo] *nm* diesel (oil).

gasolina [gaso'lina] *nf* petrol, gas(oline) (*US*).

gasolinera [gasoli'nera] *nf* petrol (*Brit*) *o* gas (*US*) station.

gastado, a [gas'taðo, a] *a* (*ropa*) worn out; (*usado: frase etc*) trite.

gastar [gas'tar] *vt* (*dinero, tiempo*) to spend; (*consumir*) to use (up), consume; (*desperdiciar*) to waste; (*llevar*) to wear; ~**se** *vr* to wear out; (*terminarse*) to run out; (*estropearse*) to waste; ~ **bromas** to crack jokes; **¿qué número gastas?** what size (shoe) do you take?

gasto ['gasto] *nm* (*desembolso*) expenditure, spending; (*cantidad gastada*) outlay, expense; (*consumo, uso*) use; (*desgaste*) waste; ~**s** *nmpl* (*desembolsos*) expenses; (*cargos*) charges, costs; ~ **corriente** (*COM*) revenue expenditure; ~ **fijo** (*COM*) fixed charge; ~**s bancarios** bank charges; ~**s corrientes** running expenses; ~**s de distribución** (*COM*) distribution costs; ~**s ge-**

nerales overheads; **~s de mantenimiento** maintenance expenses; **~s operacionales** operating costs; **~s de tramitación** (*COM*) handling charge *sg*; **~s vencidos** (*COM*) accrued charges; **cubrir ~s** to cover expenses; **meterse en ~s** to incur expense.

gastronomía [gastrono'mia] *nf* gastronomy.

gata ['gata] *nf* (*ZOOL*) she-cat; **andar a ~s** to go on all fours.

gatear [gate'ar] *vi* to go on all fours.

gatillo [ga'tiʎo] *nm* (*de arma de fuego*) trigger; (*de dentista*) forceps.

gato ['gato] *nm* (*ZOOL*) cat; (*TEC*) jack; **~ de Angora** Angora cat; **~ montés** wildcat; **dar a uno ~ por liebre** to take sb in; **aquí hay ~ encerrado** there's something fishy here.

gatuno, a [ga'tuno, a] *a* feline.

gaucho, a ['gautʃo, a] *a*, *nm/f* gaucho.

gaveta [ga'βeta] *nf* drawer.

gavilán [gaβi'lan] *nm* sparrowhawk.

gavilla [ga'βiʎa] *nf* sheaf.

gaviota [ga'βjota] *nf* seagull.

gay [ge] *a*, *nm* gay, homosexual.

gazapo [ga'θapo] *nm* young rabbit.

gaznate [gaθ'nate] *nm* (*pescuezo*) gullet; (*garganta*) windpipe.

gazpacho [gaθ'patʃo] *nm* gazpacho.

gelatina [xela'tina] *nf* jelly; (*polvos etc*) gelatine.

gema ['xema] *nf* gem.

gemelo, a [xe'melo, .a] *a*, *nm/f* twin; **~s** *nmpl* (*de camisa*) cufflinks; **~s de campo** field glasses, binoculars; **~s de teatro** opera glasses.

gemido [xe'miðo] *nm* (*quejido*) moan, groan; (*lamento*) wail, howl.

Géminis ['xeminis] *nm* (*ASTRO*) Gemini.

gemir [xe'mir] *vi* (*quejarse*) to moan, groan; (*animal*) to whine; (*viento*) to howl. Interrupt

gen. *abr* (*LING*) = **género**; **genitivo**.

gendarme [xen'darme] *nm* (*AM*) policeman.

genealogía [xenealo'xia] *nf* genealogy.

generación [xenera'θjon] *nf* generation; **primera/segunda/tercera/cuarta ~** (*INFORM*) first/second/third/fourth generation.

generado, a [xene'raðo, a] *a* (*INFORM*): **~ por ordenador** computer generated.

generador [xenera'ðor] *nm* generator; **~ de programas** (*INFORM*) program generator.

general [xene'ral] *a* general; (*común*) common; (*pey*: *corriente*) rife; (*frecuente*) usual ♦ *nm* general; **~ de brigada/de división** brigadier-/major-general; **por lo** *o* **en ~** in general.

generalice [xenera'liθe] *etc vb V* **generalizar**.

generalidad [xenerali'ðað] *nf* generality.

Generalitat [xenerali'tat] *nf Catalan parliament*.

generalización [xeneraliθa'θjon] *nf* generalization.

generalizar [xenerali'θar] *vt* to generalize; **~se** *vr* to become generalized, spread; (*difundirse*) to become widely known.

generalmente [xeneral'mente] *ad* generally.

generar [xene'rar] *vt* to generate.

genérico, a [xe'neriko, a] *a* generic.

género ['xenero] *nm* (*clase*) kind, sort; (*tipo*) type; (*BIO*) genus; (*LING*) gender; (*COM*) material; **~s** *nmpl* (*productos*) goods; **~ humano** human race; **~ chico** (*zarzuela*) Spanish operetta; **~s de punto** knitwear *sg*.

generosidad [xenerosi'ðað] *nf* generosity.

generoso, a [xene'roso, a] *a* generous.

genial [xe'njal] *a* inspired; (*idea*) brilliant; (*afable*) genial.

genialidad [xenjali'ðað] *nf* (*singularidad*) genius; (*acto genial*) stroke of genius; **es una ~ suya** it's one of his brilliant ideas.

genio ['xenjo] *nm* (*carácter*) nature, disposition; (*humor*) temper; (*facultad creadora*) genius; **mal ~** bad temper; **~ vivo** quick *o* hot temper; **de mal ~** bad-tempered.

genital [xeni'tal] *a* genital ♦ *nm*: **~es** genitals, genital organs.

genocidio [xeno'θiðjo] *nm* genocide.

Génova ['xenoβa] *nf* Genoa.

genovés, esa [xeno'βes, esa] *a*, *nm/f* Genoese.

gente ['xente] *nf* (*personas*) people *pl*; (*raza*) race; (*nación*) nation; (*parientes*) relatives *pl*; **~ bien/baja** upper-class/lower-class people *pl*; **~ menuda** (*niños*) children *pl*; **es buena ~** (*fam*: *esp AM*) he's a good sort.

gentil [xen'til] *a* (*elegante*) graceful; (*encantador*) charming; (*REL*) gentile.

gentileza [xenti'leθa] *nf* grace; charm; (*cortesía*) courtesy; **por ~ de** by courtesy of.

gentilicio, a [xenti'liθjo, a] *a* (*familiar*) family *cpd*.

gentío [xen'tio] *nm* crowd, throng.

gentuza [xen'tuθa] *nf* (*pey*: *plebe*) rabble; (: *chusma*) riffraff.

genuflexión [xenuflek'sjon] *nf* genuflexion.

genuino, a [xe'nwino, a] *a* genuine.

GEO ['xeo] *nmpl abr* (*Esp*: = *Grupos Especiales de Operaciones*) *Special Police Units used in anti-terrorist operations etc*.

geografía [xeoɣra'fia] *nf* geography.

geográfico, a [xeo'ɣrafiko, a] *a* geographic(al).

geología [xeolo'xia] *nf* geology.

geólogo, a [xe'oloɣo, a] *nm/f* geologist.

geometría [xeome'tria] *nf* geometry.

geométrico, a [xeo'metriko, a] *a* geometric(al).

geranio [xe'ranjo] *nm* (*BOT*) geranium.

gerencia [xe'renθja] *nf* management; (*cargo*) post of manager; (*oficina*) manager's office.

gerente [xe'rente] *nm/f* (*supervisor*) manager; (*jefe*) director.

geriatría [xerja'tria] *nf* (*MED*) geriatrics *sg*.

germano, a [xer'mano, a] *a* German, Germanic ♦ *nm/f* German.

germen ['xermen] *nm* germ.

germinar [xermi'nar] *vi* to germinate; (*brotar*) to sprout.

gerundense [xerun'dense] *a* of *o* from Gerona ♦ *nm/f* native *o* inhabitant of Gerona.

gerundio [xe'rundjo] *nm* (*LING*) gerund.

gesticulación [xestikula'θjon] *nf* (*ademán*) gesticulation; (*mueca*) grimace.

gestión [xes'tjon] *nf* management; (*diligencia, acción*) negotiation; **hacer las gestiones preliminares** to do the groundwork; ~ **de cartera** (*COM*) portfolio management; ~ **financiera** (*COM*) financial management; ~ **interna** (*INFORM*) housekeeping; ~ **de personal** personnel management; ~ **de riesgos** (*COM*) risk management.

gestionar [xestjo'nar] *vt* (*lograr*) to try to arrange; (*llevar*) to manage.

gesto ['xesto] *nm* (*mueca*) grimace; (*ademán*) gesture; **hacer ~s** to make faces.

gestor, a [xes'tor, a] *a* managing ♦ *nm/f* manager; (*promotor*) promoter; (*agente*) business agent.

gestoría [xesto'ria] *nf* agency undertaking business with government departments, insurance companies etc.

Gibraltar [xiβral'tar] *nm* Gibraltar.

gibraltareño, a [xiβralta'reɲo, a] *a* of *o* from Gibraltar ♦ *nm/f* native *o* inhabitant of Gibraltar.

gigante [xi'ʋante] *a, nm/f* giant.

gijonés [xixo'nes, esa] *a* of *o* from Gijón ♦ *nm/f* native *o* inhabitant of Gijón.

gilipollas [xili'poʎas] (*fam*) *a inv* daft ♦ *nm/f* berk.

gima ['xima] *etc vb V* **gemir**.

gimnasia [xim'nasja] *nf* gymnastics *pl*; **confundir la ~ con la magnesia** to get things mixed up.

gimnasio [xim'nasjo] *nm* gymnasium, gym.

gimnasta [xim'nasta] *nm/f* gymnast.

gimotear [ximote'ar] *vi* to whine, whimper; (*lloriquear*) to snivel.

Ginebra [xi'neβra] *n* Geneva.

ginebra [xi'neβra] *nf* gin.

ginecológico, a [xineko'loxiko, a] *a* gyn(a)ecological.

ginecólogo, a [xine'koloʋo, a] *nm/f* gyn(a)ecologist.

gira ['xira] *nf* tour, trip.

girado, a [xi'raðo, a] *nm/f* (*COM*) drawee.

girar [xi'rar] *vt* (*dar la vuelta*) to turn (around); (: *rápidamente*) to spin; (*COM*: *giro postal*) to draw; (*comerciar: letra de cambio*) to issue ♦ *vi* to turn (round); (*dar vueltas*) to rotate; (*rápido*) to spin; **la conversación giraba en torno a las elecciones** the conversation centred on the election; ~ **en descubierto** to overdraw.

girasol [xira'sol] *nm* sunflower.

giratorio, a [xira'torjo, a] *a* (*gen*) revolving; (*puente*) swing *cpd*; (*silla*) swivel *cpd*.

giro ['xiro] *nm* (*movimiento*) turn, revolution; (*LING*) expression; (*COM*) draft; (*de sucesos*) trend, course; ~ **bancario** money order, bank giro; ~ **de existencias** (*COM*) stock turnover; ~ **postal** postal order; ~ **a la vista** (*COM*) sight draft.

gis [xis] *nm* (*AM*) chalk.

gitano, a [xi'tano, a] *a, nm/f* gypsy.

glacial [gla'θjal] *a* icy, freezing.

glaciar [gla'θjar] *nm* glacier.

glándula ['glandula] *nf* (*ANAT, BOT*) gland.

glicerina [gliθe'rina] *nf* (*TEC*) glycerin(e).

global [glo'ßal] *a* (*en conjunto*) global; (*completo*) total; (*investigación*) full; (*suma*) lump *cpd*.

globo ['gloßo] *nm* (*esfera*) globe, sphere; (*aeróstato, juguete*) balloon.

glóbulo ['gloßulo] *nm* globule; (*ANAT*) corpuscle; ~ **blanco/rojo** white/red corpuscle.

gloria ['glorja] *nf* glory; (*fig*) delight; (*delicia*) bliss.

glorieta [glo'rjeta] *nf* (*de jardín*) bower, arbour, (*US*) arbor; (*AUTO*) roundabout (*Brit*), traffic circle (*US*); (*plaza redonda*) circus; (*cruce*) junction.

glorificar [glorifi'kar] *vt* (*enaltecer*) to glorify, praise.

glorifique [glori'fike] *etc vb V* **glorificar**.

glorioso, a [glo'rjoso, a] *a* glorious.

glosa ['glosa] *nf* comment; (*explicación*) gloss.

glosar [glo'sar] *vt* (*comentar*) to comment on.

glosario [glo'sarjo] *nm* glossary.

glotón, ona [glo'ton, ona] *a* gluttonous, greedy ♦ *nm/f* glutton.

glotonería [glotone'ria] *nf* gluttony, greed.

glúteo ['gluteo] *nm* (*fam: nalga*) buttock.

gnomo ['nomo] *nm* gnome.

gobernación [goßerna'θjon] *nf* government, governing; (*POL*) Provincial Governor's office.

gobernador, a [goßerna'ðor, a] *a* governing ♦ *nm/f* governor.

gobernanta [goßer'nanta] *nf* (*AM*: niñera) governess.

gobernante [goßer'nante] *a* governing ♦ *nm* ruler, governor ♦ *nf* (*en hotel etc*) housekeeper.

gobernar [goβer'nar] *vt* (*dirigir*) to guide, direct; (*POL*) to rule, govern ♦ *vi* to govern; (*NAUT*) to steer; ~ **mal** to misgovern.

gobierno [go'βjerno] *etc vb V* **gobernar** ♦ *nm* (*POL*) government; (*gestión*) management; (*dirección*) guidance, direction; (*NAUT*) steering; (*puesto*) governorship.

goce ['goθe] *etc vb V* **gozar** ♦ *nm* enjoyment.

godo, a ['goðo, a] *nm/f* Goth; (*AM pey*) Spaniard.

gol [gol] *nm* goal.

gola ['gola] *nf* gullet; (*garganta*) throat.

golear [gole'ar] *vt* (*marcar*) to score a goal against.

golf [golf] *nm* golf.

golfo, a ['golfo, a] *nm/f* (*pilluelo*) street urchin; (*vago*) tramp; (*gorrón*) loafer; (*gamberro*) lout ♦ *nm* (*GEO*) gulf ♦ *nf* (*fam: prostituta*) slut, whore, hooker (*US*).

golondrina [golon'drina] *nf* swallow.

golosina [golo'sina] *nf* titbit; (*dulce*) sweet.

goloso, a [go'loso, a] *a* sweet-toothed; (*fam: glotón*) greedy.

golpe ['golpe] *nm* blow; (*de puño*) punch; (*de mano*) smack; (*de remo*) stroke; (*FÚTBOL*) kick; (*TENIS etc*) hit, shot; (*mala suerte*) misfortune; (*fam: atraco*) job, heist (*US*); (*fig: choque*) clash; **no dar** ~ to be bone idle; **de un** ~ with one blow; **de** ~ suddenly; ~ **(de estado)** coup (d'état); ~ **de gracia** coup de grâce (*tb fig*); ~ **de fortuna/maestro** stroke of luck/genius; **cerrar una puerta de** ~ to slam a door.

golpear [golpe'ar] *vt, vi* to strike, knock; (*asestar*) to beat; (*de puño*) to punch; (*golpetear*) to tap; (*mesa*) to bang.

goma ['goma] *nf* (*caucho*) rubber; (*elástico*) elastic; (*tira*) rubber *o* elastic (*Brit*) band; (*fam: preservativo*) condom; (*droga*) hashish; (*explosivo*) plastic explosive; ~ **(de borrar)** eraser, rubber (*Brit*); ~ **de mascar** chewing gum; ~ **de pegar** gum, glue.

goma-espuma [gomaes'puma] *nf* foam rubber.

gomina [go'mina] *nf* (*AM*) hair gel.

gomita [go'mita] *nf* rubber *o* elastic (*Brit*) band.

góndola ['gondola] *nf* (*barco*) gondola; (*de tren*) goods wagon.

gordo, a ['gorðo, a] *a* (*gen*) fat; (*persona*) plump; (*agua*) hard; (*fam*) enormous ♦ *nm/f* fat man *o* woman; **el (premio)** ~ (*en lotería*) first prize; **¡~!** (*fam*) fatty!

gordura [gor'ðura] *nf* fat; (*corpulencia*) fatness, stoutness.

gorgojo [gor'xoxo] *nm* (*insecto*) grub.

gorgorito [gorɣ'rito] *nm* (*gorjeo*) trill, warble.

gorila [go'rila] *nm* gorilla; (*fam*) tough, thug; (*guardaespaldas*) bodyguard.

gorjear [gorxe'ar] *vi* to twitter, chirp.

gorjeo [gor'xeo] *nm* twittering, chirping.

gorra ['gorra] *nf* (*gen*) cap; (*de niño*) bonnet; (*militar*) bearskin; ~ **de montar/ de paño/de punto/de visera** riding/cloth/ knitted/peaked cap; **andar** *o* **ir** *o* **vivir de** ~ to sponge, scrounge; **entrar de** ~ (*fam*) to gatecrash.

gorrión [go'rrjon] *nm* sparrow.

gorro ['gorro] *nm* cap; (*de niño, mujer*) bonnet; **estoy hasta el** ~ I am fed up.

gorrón, ona [go'rron, ona] *nm* pebble; (*TEC*) pivot ♦ *nm/f* scrounger.

gorronear [gorrone'ar] *vi* (*fam*) to sponge, scrounge.

gota ['gota] *nf* (*gen*) drop; (*de pintura*) blob; (*de sudor*) bead; (*MED*) gout; ~ **a** ~ drop by drop; **caer a** ~**s** to drip.

gotear [gote'ar] *vi* to drip; (*escurrir*) to trickle; (*salirse*) to leak; (*cirio*) to gutter; (*lloviznar*) to drizzle.

gotera [go'tera] *nf* leak.

gótico, a ['gotiko, a] *a* Gothic.

gozar [go'θar] *vi* to enjoy o.s.; ~ **de** (*disfrutar*) to enjoy; (*poseer*) to possess; ~ **de buena salud** to enjoy good health.

gozne ['goθne] *nm* hinge.

gozo ['goθo] *nm* (*alegría*) joy; (*placer*) pleasure; **¡mi** ~ **en el pozo!** that's torn it!, just my luck!

g.p. *nm abr* (= *giro postal*) m.o.

GPI *nm abr* (*Esp POL*) = *Grupo Parlamentario Independiente*.

gr. *abr* (= *gramo(s)*) g.

grabación [graβa'θjon] *nf* recording.

grabado, a [gra'βaðo, a] *a* (*MUS*) recorded; (*en cinta*) taped, on tape ♦ *nm* print, engraving; ~ **al agua fuerte** etching; ~ **al aguatinta** aquatint; ~ **en cobre** copperplate; ~ **en madera** woodcut; ~ **rupestre** rock carving.

grabador, a [graβa'ðor, a] *nm/f* engraver ♦ *nf* tape-recorder; ~**a de cassettes** cassette recorder.

grabar [gra'βar] *vt* to engrave; (*discos, cintas*) to record; (*impresionar*) to impress.

gracejo [gra'θexo] *nm* (*humor*) wit, humour; (*elegancia*) grace.

gracia ['graθja] *nf* (*encanto*) grace, gracefulness; (*REL*) grace; (*chiste*) joke; (*humor*) humour, wit; **¡muchas** ~**s!** thanks very much!; ~**s a** thanks to; **tener** ~ (*chiste etc*) to be funny; **¡qué** ~**!** how funny!; (*irónico*) what a nerve!; **no me hace** ~ I am not keen; **con** ~**s anticipadas/repetidas** thanking you in advance/again; **dar las** ~**s a uno por algo** to thank sb for sth.

grácil ['graθil] *a* (*sutil*) graceful; (*delgado*) slender; (*delicado*) delicate.

gracioso, a [gra'θjoso, a] *a* (*garboso*) graceful; (*chistoso*) funny; (*cómico*) comical; (*agudo*) witty; (*título*) gracious ◆ *nm/f* (*TEATRO*) comic character, fool; **su graciosa Majestad** His/Her Gracious Majesty.

grada ['graða] *nf* (*de escalera*) step; (*de anfiteatro*) tier, row; ~**s** *nfpl* (*de estadio*) terraces.

gradación [graða'θjon] *nf* gradation; (*serie*) graded series.

gradería [graðe'ria] *nf* (*gradas*) (flight of) steps *pl*; (*de anfiteatro*) tiers *pl*, rows *pl*; ~ **cubierta** covered stand.

grado ['graðo] *nm* degree; (*etapa*) stage, step; (*nivel*) rate; (*de parentesco*) order of lineage; (*de aceite, vino*) grade; (*grada*) step; (*ESCOL*) class, year, grade (*US*); (*UNIV*) degree; (*LING*) degree of comparison; (*MIL*) rank; **de buen** ~ willingly; **en sumo** ~, **en** ~ **superlativo** in the highest degree.

graduación [graðwa'θjon] *nf* (*acto*) gradation; (*clasificación*) rating; (*del alcohol*) proof, strength; (*ESCOL*) graduation; (*MIL*) rank; **de alta** ~ high-ranking.

gradual [gra'ðwal] *a* gradual.

graduar [gra'ðwar] *vt* (*gen*) to graduate; (*medir*) to gauge; (*TEC*) to calibrate; (*UNIV*) to confer a degree on; (*MIL*) to commission; ~**se** *vr* to graduate; ~**se la vista** to have one's eyes tested.

grafía [gra'fia] *nf* (*escritura*) writing; (*ortografía*) spelling.

gráfico, a [ˈgrafiko, a] *a* graphic; (*fig: vívido*) vivid, lively ◆ *nm* diagram ◆ *nf* graph; ~ **de barras** (*COM*) bar chart; ~ **de sectores** *o* **de tarta** (*COM*) pie chart; ~**s** *nmpl* (*tb INFORM*) graphics; ~**s empresariales** (*COM*) business graphics.

grafito [gra'fito] *nm* (*TEC*) graphite, black lead.

grafología [grafolo'xia] *nf* graphology.

gragea [gra'xea] *nf* (*MED*) pill; (*caramelo*) dragée.

grajo ['graxo] *nm* rook.

Gral. *abr* (*MIL*: = *General*) Gen.

gramático, a [gra'matiko, a] *nm/f* (*persona*) grammarian ◆ *nf* grammar.

gramo ['gramo] *nm* gramme (*Brit*), gram (*US*).

gran [gran] *a V* **grande**.

grana ['grana] *nf* (*BOT*) seedling; (*color*) scarlet; **ponerse como la** ~ to go as red as a beetroot.

granada [gra'naða] *nf* pomegranate; (*MIL*) grenade; ~ **de mano** hand grenade; ~ **de metralla** shrapnel shell.

granadino, a [grana'ðino, a] *a* of *o* from

Granada ◆ *nm/f* native *o* inhabitant of Granada ◆ *nf* grenadine.

granar [gra'nar] *vi* to seed.

granate [gra'nate] *nm* garnet.

Gran Bretaña [grambre'taɲa] *nf* Great Britain.

Gran Canaria [granka'narja] *nf* Grand Canary.

grancanario, a [grankana'rjano, a] *a* of *o* from Grand Canary ◆ *nm/f* native *o* inhabitant of Grand Canary.

grande ['grande], **gran** *a* (*de tamaño*) big, large; (*alto*) tall; (*distinguido*) great; (*impresionante*) grand ◆ *nm* grandee; **¿cómo es de** ~? how big is it?, what size is it?; **pasarlo en** ~ to have a tremendous time.

grandeza [gran'deθa] *nf* greatness; (*tamaño*) bigness; (*esplendidez*) grandness; (*nobleza*) nobility.

grandioso, a [gran'djoso, a] *a* magnificent, grand.

grandullón, ona [granðu'ʎon, ona] *a* oversized.

granel [gra'nel] *nm* (*montón*) heap; **a** ~ (*COM*) in bulk.

granero [gra'nero] *nm* granary, barn.

granice [gra'niθe] *etc vb V* **granizar**.

granito [gra'nito] *nm* (*AGR*) small grain; (*roca*) granite.

granizada [grani'θaða] *nf* hailstorm; (*fig*) hail; **una** ~ **de balas** a hail of bullets.

granizado [grani'θaðo] *nm* iced drink; ~ **de café** iced coffee.

granizar [grani'θar] *vi* to hail.

granizo [gra'niθo] *nm* hail.

granja ['granxa] *nf* (*gen*) farm; ~ **avícola** chicken *o* poultry farm.

granjear [granxe'ar] *vt* (*cobrar*) to earn; (*ganar*) to win; (*avanzar*) to gain; ~**se** *vr* (*amistad etc*) to gain for o.s.

granjero, a [gran'xero, a] *nm/f* farmer.

grano ['grano] *nm* grain; (*semilla*) seed; (*baya*) berry; (*MED*) pimple, spot; (*partícula*) particle; (*punto*) speck; ~**s** *nmpl* cereals; ~ **de café** coffee bean; **ir al** ~ to get to the point.

granuja [gra'nuxa] *nm* rogue; (*golfillo*) urchin.

grapa ['grapa] *nf* staple; (*TEC*) clamp; (*sujetador*) clip, fastener; (*ARQ*) cramp.

GRAPO ['grapo] *nm abr* (*Esp POL*) = *Grupo de Resistencia Antifascista Primero de Octubre*.

grasa ['grasa] *nf V* **graso**.

grasiento, a [gra'sjento, a] *a* greasy; (*de aceite*) oily; (*mugriento*) filthy.

graso, a ['graso, a] *a* fatty; (*aceitoso*) greasy, oily ◆ *nf* (*gen*) grease; (*de cocina*) fat, lard; (*sebo*) suet; (*mugre*) filth; (*AUTO*) oil; (*lubricante*) grease; ~ **de ballena** blubber; ~ **de pescado** fish oil.

gratificación [gratifika'θjon] *nf (propina)* tip; *(aguinaldo)* gratuity; *(bono)* bonus; *(recompensa)* reward.

gratificar ['gratifi'kar] *vt (dar propina)* to tip; *(premiar)* to reward; **"se gratificará"** "a reward is offered".

gratifique [grati'fike] *etc vb V* **gratificar**.

gratis ['gratis] *ad* free, for nothing.

gratitud [grati'tuð] *nf* gratitude.

grato, a ['grato, a] *a (agradable)* pleasant, agreeable; *(bienvenido)* welcome; **nos es** ~ **informarle que** ... we are pleased to inform you that ....

gratuito, a [gra'twito, a] *a (gratis)* free; *(sin razón)* gratuitous; *(acusación)* unfounded.

grava ['graβa] *nf (guijos)* gravel; *(piedra molida)* crushed stone; *(en carreteras)* road metal.

gravamen [gra'βamen] *nm (carga)* burden; *(impuesto)* tax; **libre de** ~ *(ECON)* free from encumbrances.

gravar [gra'βar] *vt* to burden; *(COM)* to tax; *(ECON)* to assess for tax; ~ **con impuestos** to burden with taxes.

grave ['graβe] *a* heavy; *(fig, MED)* grave, serious; *(importante)* important; *(herida)* severe; *(MUS)* low, deep; *(LING: acento)* grave; **estar** ~ to be seriously ill.

gravedad [graβe'ðað] *nf* gravity; *(fig)* seriousness; *(grandeza)* importance; *(dignidad)* dignity; *(MUS)* depth.

grávido, a ['graβiðo, a] *a (preñada)* pregnant.

gravilla [gra'βiʎa] *nf* gravel.

gravitación [graβita'θjon] *nf* gravitation.

gravitar [graβi'tar] *vi* to gravitate; ~ **sobre** to rest on.

gravoso, a [gra'βoso, a] *a (pesado)* burdensome; *(costoso)* costly.

graznar [graθ'nar] *vi (cuervo)* to squawk; *(pato)* to quack; *(hablar ronco)* to croak.

graznido [graθ'niðo] *nm* squawk; croak.

Grecia ['greθja] *nf* Greece.

gregario, a [gre'γarjo, a] *a* gregarious; **instinto** ~ herd instinct.

gremio ['gremjo] *nm (asociación)* professional association, guild.

greña ['greɲa] *nf (cabellos)* shock of hair; *(maraña)* tangle; **andar a la** ~ to bicker, squabble.

greñudo, a [gre'ɲuðo, a] *a (persona)* dishevelled; *(hair)* tangled.

gresca ['greska] *nf* uproar; *(trifulca)* row.

griego, a ['grjeɣo, a] *a* Greek, Grecian ♦ *nm/f* Greek ♦ *nm (LING)* Greek.

grieta ['grjeta] *nf* crack; *(hendidura)* chink; *(quiebra)* crevice; *(MED)* chap; *(POL)* rift.

grifa ['grifa] *nf (fam: droga)* marijuana.

grifo ['grifo] *nm* tap *(Brit)*, faucet *(US)*; *(AM)* petrol *(Brit)* o gas *(US)* station.

grilletes [gri'ʎetes] *nmpl* fetters, shackles.

grillo ['griʎo] *nm (ZOOL)* cricket; *(BOT)* shoot; ~**s** *nmpl* shackles, irons.

grima ['grima] *nf (horror)* loathing; *(desagrado)* reluctance; *(desazón)* uneasiness; **me da** ~ it makes me sick.

gringo, a ['gringo, a] *(AM) a (pey: extranjero)* foreign; *(: norteamericano)* Yankee; *(idioma)* foreign ♦ *nm/f* foreigner; Yank.

gripe ['gripe] *nf* flu, influenza.

gris [gris] *a* grey.

grisáceo, a [gri'saθeo, a] *a* greyish.

gritar [gri'tar] *vt, vi* to shout, yell; **¡no grites!** stop shouting!

grito ['grito] *nm* shout, yell; *(de horror)* scream; **a** ~ **pelado** at the top of one's voice; **poner el** ~ **en el cielo** to scream blue murder; **es el último** ~ *(de moda)* it's all the rage.

groenlandés, esa [groenlan'des, esa] *a* Greenland *cpd* ♦ *nm/f* Greenlander.

Groenlandia [groen'landja] *nf* Greenland.

grosella [gro'seʎa] *nf* (red)currant; ~ **negra** blackcurrant.

grosería [grose'ria] *nf (actitud)* rudeness; *(comentario)* vulgar comment; *(palabrota)* swearword.

grosero, a [gro'sero, a] *a (poco cortés)* rude, bad-mannered; *(ordinario)* vulgar, crude.

grosor [gro'sor] *nm* thickness.

grotesco, a [gro'tesko, a] *a* grotesque; *(absurdo)* bizarre.

grúa ['grua] *nf (TEC)* crane; *(de petróleo)* derrick; ~ **corrediza** o **móvil/de pescante/puente/de torre** travelling/jib/ overhead/tower crane.

grueso, a ['grweso, a] *a* thick; *(persona)* stout; *(calidad)* coarse ♦ *nm* bulk; *(espesor)* thickness; *(densidad)* density; *(de gente)* main body, mass; **el** ~ **de** the bulk of.

grulla ['gruʎa] *nf (ZOOL)* crane.

grumete [gru'mete] *nm (NAUT)* cabin o ship's boy.

grumo ['grumo] *nm (coágulo)* clot, lump; *(masa)* dollop.

gruñido [gru'ɲiðo] *nm* grunt, growl; *(fig)* grumble.

gruñir [gru'ɲir] *vi (animal)* to grunt, growl; *(fam)* to grumble.

gruñón, ona [gru'ɲon, ona] *a* grumpy ♦ *nm/f* grumbler.

grupa ['grupa] *nf (ZOOL)* rump.

grupo ['grupo] *nm* group; *(TEC)* unit, set; *(de árboles)* cluster; ~ **sanguíneo** blood group.

gruta ['gruta] *nf* grotto.

Gta. *abr (AUTO)* = **Glorieta.**

guadalajareño, a [gwaðalaxa'reɲo, a] *a* of o from Guadalajara ♦ *nm/f* native o inhabitant of Guadalajara.

Guadalquivir [gwaðalki'ßir] *nm*: **el (Río)** ~ the Guadalquivir.

guadaña [gwa'ðaɲa] *nf* scythe.

guadañar [gwaða'ɲar] *vt* to scythe, mow.

Guadiana [gwa'ðjana] *nm*: **el (Río)** ~ the Guadiana.

guagua ['gwaɣwa] *nf* (*AM*, *Canarias*) bus; (*AM*: *criatura*) baby.

guajolote [gwajo'lote] *nm* (*AM*) turkey.

guano ['gwano] *nm* guano.

guantada [gwan'taða] *nf*, **guantazo** [gwan'taθo] *nm* slap.

guante ['gwante] *nm* glove; **se ajusta como un** ~ it fits like a glove; **echar el** ~ **a uno** to catch hold of sb; (*fig*: *policía*) to catch sb.

guapo, a ['gwapo, a] *a* good-looking; (*mujer*) pretty, attractive; (*hombre*) handsome; (*elegante*) smart ◆ *nm* lover, gallant.

guarda ['gwarða] *nm/f* (*persona*) warden, keeper ◆ *nf* (*acto*) guarding; (*custodia*) custody; (*TIP*) flyleaf, endpaper; ~ **forestal** game warden.

guarda(a)gujas [gwarda'ɣuxas] *nm inv* (*FERRO*) switchman.

guardabarros [gwarða'ßarros] *nm inv* mudguard (*Brit*), fender (*US*).

guardabosques [gwarda'ßoskes] *nm inv* gamekeeper.

guardacostas [gwarda'kostas] *nm inv* coastguard vessel.

guardacoches [gwarða'kotʃes] *nm/f inv* (*celador*) parking attendant.

guardador, a [gwarða'ðor, a] *a* protective; (*tacaño*) mean, stingy ◆ *nm/f* guardian, protector.

guardaespaldas [gwardaes'paldas] *nm/f inv* bodyguard.

guardameta [gwarða'meta] *nm* goalkeeper.

guardapolvo [gwarda'polßo] *nm* dust cover; (*prenda de vestir*) overalls *pl*.

guardar [gwar'ðar] *vt* (*gen*) to keep; (*vigilar*) to guard, watch over; (*conservar*) to put away; (*dinero*: *ahorrar*) to save; (*promesa etc*) to keep; (*ley*) to observe; (*rencor*) to bear, harbour; (*INFORM*: *archivo*) to save; ~**se** *vr* (*preservarse*) to protect o.s.; ~**se de algo** (*evitar*) to avoid sth; (*abstenerse*) to refrain from sth; ~**se de hacer algo** to be careful not to do sth; **guardársela a uno** to have it in for sb.

guardarropa [gwarða'rropa] *nm* (*armario*) wardrobe; (*en establecimiento público*) cloakroom.

guardería [gwarðe'ria] *nf* nursery.

guardia ['gwarðja] *nf* (*MIL*) guard; (*cuidado*) care, custody; **estar de** ~ to be on guard; **montar** ~ to mount guard; **la G~ Civil** the Civil Guard; ~ **municipal** o **urbana** municipal police ◆ *nm/f* guard; (*policía*) policeman/woman; **un** ~ **civil** a Civil Guard(sman); **un(a)** ~ **nacional** a policeman/woman; ~ **urbano** traffic policeman.

guardián, ana [gwar'ðjan, ana] *nm/f* (*gen*) guardian, keeper.

guarecer [gware'θer] *vt* (*proteger*) to protect; (*abrigar*) to shelter; ~**se** *vr* to take refuge.

guarezca [gwa're0ka] *etc vb* V **guarecer**.

guarida [gwa'riða] *nf* (*de animal*) den, lair; (*de persona*) haunt, hideout; (*refugio*) refuge.

guarnecer [gwarne'θer] *vt* (*equipar*) to provide; (*adornar*) to adorn; (*TEC*) to reinforce.

guarnezca [gwar'neθka] *etc vb* V **guarnecer**.

guarnición [gwarni'θjon] *nf* (*de vestimenta*) trimming; (*de piedra*) mount; (*CULIN*) garnish; (*arneses*) harness; (*MIL*) garrison.

guarro, a ['gwarro, a] *nm/f* pig; (*fig*) dirty o slovenly person.

guasa ['gwasa] *nf* joke; **con** o **de** ~ jokingly, in fun.

guasón, ona [gwa'son, ona] *a* witty; (*bromista*) joking ◆ *nm/f* wit; joker.

Guatemala [gwate'mala] *nf* Guatemala.

guatemalteco, a [gwatemal'teko, a] *a*, *nm/f* Guatemalan.

guateque [gwa'teke] *nm* (*fiesta*) party, binge.

guayaba [gwa'jaßa] *nf* (*BOT*) guava.

Guayana [gwa'jana] *nf* Guyana, Guaiana.

guyanés, esa [gwaja'nes, esa] *a*, *nm/f* Guyanese.

gubernamental [gußernamen'tal], **gubernativo, a** [gußerna'tißo, a] *a* governmental.

guedeja [ge'ðexa] *nf* long hair.

guerra ['gerra] *nf* war; (*arte*) warfare; (*pelea*) struggle; ~ **atómica/bacteriológica/ nuclear/de guerrillas** atomic/germ/nuclear/ guerrilla warfare; **Primera/Segunda G~ Mundial** First/Second World War; ~ **de precios** (*COM*) price war; ~ **civil/fría** civil/ cold war; ~ **a muerte** fight to the death; **de** ~ military, war *cpd*; **estar en** ~ to be at war; **dar** ~ to be annoying.

guerrear [gerre'ar] *vi* to wage war.

guerrero, a [ge'rrero, a] *a* fighting; (*carácter*) warlike ◆ *nm/f* warrior.

guerrilla [ge'rriʎa] *nf* guerrilla warfare; (*tropas*) guerrilla band o group.

guerrillero, a [gerri'ʎero, a] *nm/f* guerrilla (fighter); (*contra invasor*) partisan.

guía ['gia] *etc vb* V **guiar** ◆ *nm/f* (*persona*) guide ◆ *nf* (*libro*) guidebook; (*manual*) handbook; (*INFORM*) prompt; ~ **de ferrocarriles** railway timetable; ~ **telefónica** telephone directory; ~ **del turista/**

del viajero tourist/traveller's guide.
guiar [gi'ar] *vt* to guide, direct; (*dirigir*) to lead; (*orientar*) to advise; (*AUTO*) to steer; ~**se** *vr*: ~**se por** to be guided by.
guijarro [gi'xarro] *nm* pebble.
guillotina [giʎo'tina] *nf* guillotine.
guinda ['ginda] *nf* morello cherry; (*licor*) cherry liqueur.
guindar [gin'dar] *vt* to hoist; (*fam: robar*) to nick.
guindilla [gin'diʎa] *nf* chilli pepper.
Guinea [gi'nea] *nf* Guinea.
guineo, a [gi'neo, a] *a* Guinea *cpd*, Guinean ◆ *nm/f* Guinean.
guiñapo [gi'ɲapo] *nm* (*harapo*) rag; (*persona*) rogue.
guiñar [gi'ɲar] *vi* to wink.
guiño ['giɲo] *nm* (*parpadeo*) wink; (*muecas*) grimace; **hacer** ~**s a** (*enamorados*) to make eyes at.
guiñol [gi'ɲol] *nm* (*TEATRO*) puppet theatre.
guión [gi'on] *nm* (*LING*) hyphen, dash; (*esquema*) summary, outline; (*CINE*) script.
guionista [gjo'nista] *nm/f* scriptwriter.
guipuzcoano, a [gipuθko'ano, a] *a* of *o* from Guipúzcoa ◆ *nm/f* native *o* inhabitant of Guipúzcoa.
guirigay [giri'gai] *nm* (*griterío*) uproar; (*confusión*) chaos.
guirnalda [gir'nalda] *nf* garland.
guisa ['gisa] *nf*: **a** ~ **de** as, like.
guisado [gi'saðo] *nm* stew.
guisante [gi'sante] *nm* pea.
guisar [gi'sar] *vt, vi* to cook; (*fig*) to arrange.
guiso ['giso] *nm* cooked dish.
guita ['gita] *nf* twine; (*fam: dinero*) dough.
guitarra [gi'tarra] *nf* guitar.
guitarrista [gita'rrista] *nm/f* guitarist.
gula ['gula] *nf* gluttony, greed.
gusano [gu'sano] *nm* maggot, worm; (*de mariposa, polilla*) caterpillar; (*fig*) worm; (*ser despreciable*) creep; ~ **de seda** silkworm.
gustar [gus'tar] *vt* to taste, sample ◆ *vi* to please, be pleasing; ~ **de algo** to like *o* enjoy sth; **me gustan las uvas** I like grapes; **le gusta nadar** she likes *o* enjoys swimming; **¿gusta Ud?** would you like some?; **como Ud guste** as you wish.
gusto ['gusto] *nm* (*sentido, sabor*) taste; (*agrado*) liking; (*placer*) pleasure; **tiene un** ~ **amargo** it has a bitter taste; **tener buen** ~ to have good taste; **sobre** ~**s no hay nada escrito** there's no accounting for tastes; **de buen/mal** ~ in good/bad taste; **sentirse a** ~ to feel at ease; **¡mucho** *o* **tanto** ~ **(en conocerle)!** how do you do?, pleased to meet you; **el** ~ **es mío** the pleasure is mine; **tomar** ~ **a** to take a liking to; **con** ~ willingly, gladly.

gustoso, a [gus'toso, a] *a* (*sabroso*) tasty; (*agradable*) pleasant; (*con voluntad*) willing, glad; **lo hizo** ~ he did it gladly.
gutural [gutu'ral] *a* guttural.

H

H, h ['atʃe] *nf* (*letra*) H, h; **H de Historia** H for Harry (*Brit*) *o* How (*US*).
h. *abr* (= *hora(s)*) h., hr(s).; (= *hacia*) c. ◆ *nmpl abr* (= *habitantes*) pop.
H. *abr* (*QUÍMICA*: = *Hidrógeno*) H; (= *Hectárea(s)*) ha.; (*COM*: = *Haber*) cr.
ha [a] *vb* V **haber**.
Ha. *abr* (= *Hectárea(s)*) ha.
haba ['aβa] *nf* bean; **son** ~**s contadas** it goes without saying; **en todas partes cuecen** ~**s** it's the same (story) the whole world over.
Habana [a'βana] *nf*: **la** ~ Havana.
habanero, a [aβa'nero, a] *a* of *o* from Havana ◆ *nm/f* native *o* inhabitant of Havana ◆ *nf* (*MUS*) habanera.
habano [a'βano] *nm* Havana cigar.
habeas corpus [a'βeas'korpus] *nm* (*LAW*) habeas corpus.
haber [a'βer] *vt* (*LAW etc*): **todos los inventos habidos y por** ~ all inventions present and future; **en el encuentro habido ayer** in the fight which occurred yesterday ◆ *vb auxiliar* (*en tiempos compuestos*) to have; **de** ~**lo sabido** if I had known (it); **lo hubiéramos hecho** we would have done it; **antes de** ~**lo visto** before seeing him; ~ **de** to have to ◆ *vb impersonal*: **hay** there is/are; **hay un hombre/2 hombres en la calle** there is one man/there are two men in the street; **ha habido problemas** there have been problems; **hay sol** it is sunny; **hay que** it is necessary to, one must; **hay que hacerlo** it has to be done; **¿habrá tiempo?** will there be time?; **tomará lo que haya** he'll take whatever there is; **lo que hay es que** ... it's like this, ...; **¿cuánto hay de aquí a Cuzco?** how far is it from here to Cuzco?; **¿qué hay?** how's it going?; **no hay de qué** don't mention it; ~**se** *vr*: **habérselas con uno** (*tener delante*) to be up against sb ◆ *nm* (*ingreso*) income; (*COM: crédito*) credit; (*balance*) credit side; (: *tb*: ~**es**) assets *pl*.
habichuela [aβi'tʃwela] *nf* kidney bean.
hábil ['aβil] *a* (*listo*) clever, smart; (*capaz*) fit, capable; (*experto*) expert; **día** ~ working day.

habilidad [aβili'ðað] *nf* (*gen*) skill, ability; (*inteligencia*) cleverness; (*destreza*) expertness, expertise; (*JUR*) competence; ~ **(para)** fitness (for); **tener ~ manual** to be clever with one's hands.

habilitación [aβilita'θjon] *nf* qualification; (*colocación de muebles*) fitting out; (*financiamiento*) financing; (*oficina*) paymaster's office.

habilitado [aβili'taðo] *nm* paymaster.

habilitar [aβili'tar] *vt* to qualify; (*autorizar*) to authorize; (*capacitar*) to enable; (*dar instrumentos*) to equip; (*financiar*) to finance.

hábilmente [aβil'mente] *ad* skilfully, expertly.

habitable [aβi'taβle] *a* inhabitable.

habitación [aβita'θjon] *nf* (*cuarto*) room; (*casa*) dwelling, abode; (*BIO: morada*) habitat; ~ **sencilla** *o* **individual** single room; ~ **doble** *o* **de matrimonio** double room.

habitante [aβi'tante] *nm/f* inhabitant.

habitar [aβi'tar] *vt* (*residir en*) to inhabit; (*ocupar*) to occupy ♦ *vi* to live.

hábito ['aβito] *nm* habit; **tener el ~ de hacer algo** to be in the habit of doing sth.

habitual [aβi'twal] *a* habitual.

habituar [aβi'twar] *vt* to accustom; ~**se** *vr*: ~**se a** to get used to.

habla ['aβla] *nf* (*capacidad de hablar*) speech; (*idioma*) language; (*dialecto*) dialect; **perder el ~** to become speechless; **de ~ francesa** French-speaking; **estar al ~** to be in contact; (*TELEC*) to be on the line; **¡González al ~!** (*TELEC*) Gonzalez speaking!

hablador, a [aβla'ðor, a] *a* talkative ♦ *nm/ f* chatterbox.

habladuría [aβlaðu'ria] *nf* rumour; ~**s** *nfpl* gossip *sg*.

hablante [a'βlante] *a* speaking ♦ *nm/f* speaker.

hablar [a'βlar] *vt* to speak, talk ♦ *vi* to speak; ~**se** *vr* to speak to each other; ~ **con** to speak to; **¡hable!**, **¡puede ~!** (*TELEC*) you're through!; **de eso ni ~** no way, that's not on; ~ **alto/bajo/claro** to speak loudly/quietly/plainly *o* bluntly; ~ **de** to speak of *o* about; **"se habla inglés"** "English spoken here"; **no se hablan** they are not on speaking terms.

habré [a'βre] *etc vb V* **haber.**

hacedor, a [aθe'ðor, a] *nm/f* maker.

hacendado, a [aθen'daðo, a] *a* propertyowning ♦ *nm* (*terrateniente*) large landowner.

hacendoso, a [aθen'doso, a] *a* industrious, hard-working.

hacer [a'θer] *vt* (*gen*) to make; (*crear*) to create; (*TEC*) to manufacture; (*preparar*) to prepare; (*ejecutar*) to do, execute; (*obligar*) to force, compel; (*dinero*) to earn; (*volver*) to make, turn ♦ *vi* (*comportarse*) to act, behave; (*disimular*) to pretend; (*convenir, ser apto*) to be suitable; ~**se** *vr* (*fabricarse*) to be made, be done; (*volverse*) to become; (*acostumbrarse a*) to get used to; ~ **bien/mal** to act rightly/ wrongly; **hace frío/calor** it's cold/hot; **hace un momento/dos años** a moment/two years ago; **hace poco** a little while ago; **te hacíamos en el Perú** we assumed you were in Peru; **hágale entrar** show him in; ~ **polvo algo** to smash sth to pieces; ~ **polvo a uno** to exhaust sb; ~ **un papel** (*TEATRO*) to play a role *o* part; **¿qué le vamos a ~?** what can we do about it?; **¿qué haces ahí?** what are you up to?; ~ **como que** *o* **como si** to act as though *o* as if; **dar que ~** to cause trouble; ~ **de** to act as; **¿hace?** will it do?; **me hice un traje** I had a suit made; ~**se el sordo** to turn a deaf ear; ~**se el tonto** *o* **el sueco** to act dumb, play the innocent; ~**se a (~) algo** to get used to (doing) sth; ~**se viejo** to grow old; ~**se con algo** to get hold of sth; ~**se a un lado** to stand aside; **se hace tarde** it's getting late; **se me hace imposible trabajar** I'm finding it impossible to work; **no le hace** it doesn't matter.

hacia ['aθja] *prep* (*en dirección de, actitud*) towards; (*cerca de*) near; ~ **arriba/abajo** up(wards)/down(wards); ~ **mediodía** about noon.

hacienda [a'θjenda] *nf* (*propiedad*) property; (*finca*) farm; (*AM*) ranch; ~ **pública** public finance; **(Ministerio de) H**~ Exchequer (*Brit*), Treasury Department (*US*).

hacina [a'θina] *nf* pile, stack.

hacinar [aθi'nar] *vt* to pile (up); (*AGR*) to stack; (*fig*) to overcrowd.

hacha ['atʃa] *nf* axe; (*antorcha*) torch.

hache ['atʃe] *nf* (the letter) H; **llámele usted** ~ call it what you will.

hachís [a'tʃis] *nm* hashish.

hada ['aða] *nf* fairy; ~ **madrina** fairy godmother.

hado ['aðo] *nm* fate, destiny.

haga ['aɣa] *etc vb V* **hacer.**

Haití [ai'ti] *nm* Haiti.

haitiano, a [ai'tjano, a] *a, nm/f* Haitian.

hala ['ala] *excl* (*vamos*) come on!; (*anda*) get on with it!

halagar [ala'ɣar] *vt* (*lisonjear*) to flatter.

halago [a'laɣo] *nm* (*adulación*) flattery.

halague [a'laɣe] *etc vb V* **halagar.**

halagüeño, a [ala'ɣweɲo, a] *a* flattering.

halcón [al'kon] *nm* falcon, hawk.

hálito ['alito] *nm* breath.

halitosis [ali'tosis] *nf* halitosis, bad breath.

halo ['alo] *nm* halo.
halterofilia [altero'filja] *nf* weightlifting.
hallar [a'ʎar] *vt* (*gen*) to find; (*descubrir*) to discover; (*toparse con*) to run into; ~**se** *vr* to be (situated); (*encontrarse*) to find o.s.; **se halla fuera** he is away; **no se halla** he feels out of place.
hallazgo [a'ʎaθɣo] *nm* discovery; (*cosa*) find.
hamaca [a'maka] *nf* hammock.
hambre ['ambre] *nf* hunger; (*carencia*) famine; (*inanición*) starvation; (*fig*) longing; **tener** ~ to be hungry.
hambriento, a [am'brjento, a] *a* hungry, starving ♦ *nm/f* starving person; **los** ~**s** the hungry; ~ **de** hungry o longing for.
Hamburgo [am'burɣo] *nm* Hamburg.
hamburguesa [ambur'ɣesa] *nf* hamburger.
hampa ['ampa] *nf* underworld.
hampón [am'pon] *nm* thug.
han [an] *vb* V **haber**.
haragán, ana [ara'ɣan, ana] *a*, *nm/f* good-for-nothing.
haraganear [araɣane'ar] *vi* to idle, loaf about.
harapiento, a [ara'pjento, a] *a* tattered, in rags.
harapo [a'rapo] *nm* rag.
hardware ['xardwer] *nm* (*INFORM*) hardware.
haré [a're] *etc vb* V **hacer**.
harén [a'ren] *nm* harem.
harina [a'rina] *nf* flour; **eso es** ~ **de otro costal** that's another kettle of fish.
harinero, a [ari'nero, a] *a*, *nm/f* flour merchant.
harinoso, a [ari'noso, a] *a* floury.
hartar [ar'tar] *vt* to satiate, glut; (*fig*) to tire, sicken; ~**se** *vr* (*de comida*) to fill o.s., gorge o.s.; (*cansarse*) to get fed up (*de* with).
hartazgo [ar'taθɣo] *nm* surfeit, glut.
harto, a ['arto, a] *a* (*lleno*) full; (*cansado*) fed up ♦ *ad* (*bastante*) enough; (*muy*) very; **estar** ~ **de** to be fed up with; **¡estoy** ~ **de decírtelo!** I'm sick and tired of telling you (so)!
hartura [ar'tura] *nf* (*exceso*) surfeit; (*abundancia*) abundance; (*satisfacción*) satisfaction.
has [as] *vb* V **haber**.
Has. *abr* (= *Hectáreas*) ha.
hasta ['asta] *ad* even ♦ *prep* (*alcanzando a*) as far as, up/down to; (*de tiempo: a tal hora*) till, until; (: *antes de*) before ♦ *conj:* ~ **que** until; ~ **luego** o **ahora** (*fam*)/**el sábado** see you soon/on Saturday; ~ **la fecha** (up) to date; ~ **nueva orden** until further notice; ~ **en Valencia hiela a veces** even in Valencia it freezes sometimes.
hastiar [as'tjar] *vt* (*gen*) to weary; (*aburrir*)

to bore; ~**se** *vr:* ~**se de** to get fed up with.
hastío [as'tio] *nm* weariness; boredom.
hatajo [a'taxo] *nm:* **un** ~ **de gamberros** a bunch of hooligans.
hatillo [a'tiʎo] *nm* belongings *pl*, kit; (*montón*) bundle, heap.
Hawai [a'wai] *nm* (*tb:* **las Islas** ~) Hawaii.
hawaiano, a [awa'jano, a] *a*, *nm/f* Hawaian.
hay [ai] *vb* V **haber**.
Haya ['aja] *nf:* **la** ~ The Hague.
haya ['aja] *etc vb* V **haber** ♦ *nf* beech tree.
hayal [a'jal] *nm* beech grove.
haz [aθ] *vb* V **hacer** ♦ *nm* bundle, bunch; (*rayo: de luz*) beam ♦ *nf:* ~ **de la tierra** face of the earth.
hazaña [a'θaɲa] *nf* feat, exploit; **sería una** ~ it would be a great achievement.
hazmerreír [aθmerre'ir] *nm inv* laughing stock.
HB *abr* (= *Herri Batasuna*) *Basque political party.*
he [e] *vb* V **haber** ♦ *ad:* ~ **aquí** here is, here are; ~ **aquí por qué ...** that is why ....
hebilla [e'βiʎa] *nf* buckle, clasp.
hebra ['eβra] *nf* thread; (*BOT: fibra*) fibre, grain.
hebreo, a [e'βreo, a] *a*, *nm/f* Hebrew ♦ *nm* (*LING*) Hebrew.
Hébridas ['eβriðas] *nfpl:* **las** ~ the Hebrides.
hectárea [ek'tarea] *nf* hectare.
hechice [e'tʃiθe] *etc vb* V **hechizar**.
hechicera [etʃi'θera] *nf* witch.
hechizar [etʃi'θar] *vt* to cast a spell on, bewitch.
hechizo [e'tʃiθo] *nm* witchcraft, magic; (*acto de magia*) spell, charm.
hecho, a ['etʃo, a] *pp de* **hacer** ♦ *a* complete; (*maduro*) mature; (*COSTURA*) ready-to-wear ♦ *nm* deed, act; (*dato*) fact; (*cuestión*) matter; (*suceso*) event ♦ *excl* agreed!, done!; **¡bien** ~**!** well done!; **de** ~ in fact, as a matter of fact; (*POL etc: a, ad*) de facto; **de** ~ **y de derecho** de facto and de jure; ~ **a la medida** made-to-measure; **a lo** ~**, pecho** it's no use crying over spilt milk.
hechura [e'tʃura] *nf* making, creation; (*producto*) product; (*forma*) form, shape; (*de persona*) build; (*TEC*) craftsmanship.
heder [e'ðer] *vi* to stink, smell; (*fig*) to be unbearable.
hediondez [eðjon'deθ] *nf* stench, stink; (*cosa*) stinking thing.
hediondo, a [e'ðjondo, a] *a* stinking.
hedor [e'ðor] *nm* stench.
helada [e'laða] *nf* frost.
heladera [ela'ðera] *nf* (*AM: refrigerador*) refrigerator.

heladería [elaðe'ria] *nf* ice-cream stall (*o* parlour).

helado, a [e'laðo, a] *a* frozen; (*glacial*) icy; (*fig*) chilly, cold ♦ *nm* ice-cream; **dejar ~ a uno** to dumbfound sb.

helador, a [ela'ðor, a] *a* (*viento etc*) icy, freezing.

helar [e'lar] *vt* to freeze, ice (up); (*dejar atónito*) to amaze; (*desalentar*) to discourage ♦ *vi*, **~se** *vr* to freeze; (*AVIAT, FERRO etc*) to ice (up), freeze up; (*líquido*) to set.

helecho [e'letʃo] *nm* bracken, fern.

helénico, a [e'leniko, a] *a* Hellenic, Greek.

heleno, a [e'leno, a] *nm/f* Hellene, Greek.

hélice ['eliθe] *nf* spiral; (*TEC*) propeller; (*MAT*) helix.

helicóptero [eli'koptero] *nm* helicopter.

helmántico, a [el'mantiko, a] *a* of *o* from Salamanca.

helvético, a [el'ßetiko, a] *a*, *nm/f* Swiss.

hembra ['embra] *nf* (*BOT, ZOOL*) female; (*mujer*) woman; (*TEC*) nut; **un elefante ~** a female elephant.

hemeroteca [emero'teka] *nf* newspaper library.

hemofilia [emo'filja] *nf* haemophilia (*Brit*), hemophilia (*US*).

hemorragia [emo'rraxja] *nf* haemorrhage (*Brit*), hemorrhage (*US*).

hemorroides [emo'rroiðes] *nfpl* haemorrhoids (*Brit*), hemorrhoids (*US*).

hemos ['emos] *vb V* **haber**.

henar [e'nar] *nm* meadow, hayfield.

henchir [en'tʃir] *vt* to fill, stuff; **~se** *vr* (*llenarse de comida*) to stuff o.s. (with food); (*inflarse*) to swell (up).

Hendaya [en'daja] *nf* Hendaye.

hender [en'der] *vt* to cleave, split.

hendidura [endi'ðura] *nf* crack, split; (*GEO*) fissure.

heno ['eno] *nm* hay.

herbario, a [er'ßarjo, a] *a* herbal ♦ *nm* (*colección*) herbarium; (*especialista*) herbalist; (*botánico*) botanist.

herbicida [erßi'θiða] *nm* weedkiller.

heredad [ere'ðað] *nf* landed property; (*granja*) farm.

heredar [ere'ðar] *vt* to inherit.

heredero, a [ere'ðero, a] *nm/f* heir(ess); **~ del trono** heir to the throne.

hereditario, a [ereði'tarjo, a] *a* hereditary.

hereje [e'rexe] *nm/f* heretic.

herejía [ere'xia] *nf* heresy.

herencia [e'renθja] *nf* inheritance; (*fig*) heritage; (*BIO*) heredity.

herético, a [e'retiko, a] *a* heretical.

herido, a [e'riðo, a] *a* injured, wounded; (*fig*) offended ♦ *nm/f* casualty ♦ *nf* wound, injury.

herir [e'rir] *vt* to wound, injure; (*fig*) to offend; (*conmover*) to touch, move.

hermana [er'mana] *nf V* **hermano**.

hermanar [erma'nar] *vt* to match; (*unir*) to join; (*ciudades*) to twin.

hermanastro, a [erma'nastro, a] *nm/f* stepbrother/sister.

hermandad [erman'dað] *nf* brotherhood; (*de mujeres*) sisterhood; (*sindicato etc*) association.

hermano, a [er'mano, a] *a* similar ♦ *nm* brother ♦ *nf* sister; **~ gemelo** twin brother; **~ político** brother-in-law; **~ primo** first cousin; **mis ~s** my brothers, my brothers and sisters; **hermana política** sister-in-law.

hermético, a [er'metiko, a] *a* hermetic; (*fig*) watertight.

hermoso, a [er'moso, a] *a* beautiful, lovely; (*estupendo*) splendid; (*guapo*) handsome.

hermosura [ermo'sura] *nf* beauty; (*de hombre*) handsomeness.

héroe ['eroe] *nm* hero.

heroicidad [eroiθi'ðað] *nf* heroism; (*una ~*) heroic deed.

heroico, a [e'roiko, a] *a* heroic.

heroína [ero'ina] *nf* (*mujer*) heroine; (*droga*) heroin.

heroísmo [ero'ismo] *nm* heroism.

herpes ['erpes] *nmpl o nfpl* (*MED: gen*) herpes *sg*; (: *de la piel*) shingles *sg*.

herradura [erra'ðura] *nf* horseshoe.

herraje [e'rraxe] *nm* (*trabajos*) ironwork.

herramienta [erra'mjenta] *nf* tool.

herrería [erre'ria] *nf* smithy; (*TEC*) forge.

herrero [e'rrero] *nm* blacksmith.

herrumbre [e'rrumbre] *nf* rust.

herrumbroso, a [errum'broso, a] *a* rusty.

hervidero [erßi'ðero] *nm* (*fig*) swarm; (*POL etc*) hotbed.

hervir [er'ßir] *vi* to boil; (*burbujear*) to bubble; (*fig*): **~ de** to teem with; **~ a fuego lento** to simmer.

hervor [er'ßor] *nm* boiling; (*fig*) ardour, fervour.

heterogéneo, a [etero'xeneo, a] *a* heterogeneous.

heterosexual [eterosek'swal] *a*, *nm/f* heterosexual.

hez [eθ] *nf* (*tb*: **heces** *pl*) dregs.

hibernar [ißer'nar] *vi* to hibernate.

hice ['iθe] *etc vb V* **hacer**.

hidalgo, a [i'ðalɣo, a] *a* noble; (*honrado*) honourable (*Brit*), honorable (*US*) ♦ *nm/f* noble(man/woman).

hidratante [iðra'tante] *a*: **crema ~** moisturizing cream, moisturizer.

hidratar [iðra'tar] *vt* to moisturize.

hidrato [i'ðrato] *nm* hydrate; **~ de carbono** carbohydrate.

hidráulico, a [i'ðrauliko, a] *a* hydraulic ♦ *nf* hydraulics *sg*.

hidro... [iðro] *pref* hydro..., water-....
hidroavión [iðroa'ßjon] *nm* seaplane.
hidroeléctrico, a [iðroe'lektriko, a] *a* hydroelectric.
hidrófilo, a [i'ðrofilo, a] *a* absorbent; **algodón** ~ cotton wool (*Brit*), absorbent cotton (*US*).
hidrofobia [iðro'foßja] *nf* hydrophobia, rabies.
hidrófugo, a [i'ðrofuɣo, a] *a* damp-proof.
hidrógeno [i'ðroxeno] *nm* hydrogen.
hieda ['jeða] *etc vb V* **heder.**
hiedra ['jeðra] *nf* ivy.
hiel [jel] *nf* gall, bile; (*fig*) bitterness.
hielo ['jelo] *etc vb V* **helar** ◆ *nm* (*gen*) ice; (*escarcha*) frost; (*fig*) coldness, reserve; **romper el** ~ (*fig*) to break the ice.
hiena ['jena] *nf* (*ZOOL*) hyena.
hiera ['jera] *etc vb V* **herir.**
hierba ['jerßa] *nf* (*pasto*) grass; (*CULIN, MED: planta*) herb; **mala** ~ weed; (*fig*) evil influence.
hierbabuena [jerßa'ßwena] *nf* mint.
hierro ['jerro] *nm* (*metal*) iron; (*objeto*) iron object; ~ **acanalado** corrugated iron; ~ **colado** *o* **fundido** cast iron; **de** ~ iron *cpd.*
hierva ['jerßa] *etc vb V* **hervir.**
hígado ['iɣaðo] *nm* liver; ~**s** *nmpl* (*fig*) guts; **echar los** ~**s** to wear o.s. out.
higiene [i'xjene] *nf* hygiene.
higiénico, a [i'xjeniko, a] *a* hygienic.
higo ['iɣo] *nm* fig; ~ **seco** dried fig; ~ **chumbo** prickly pear; **de** ~**s a brevas** once in a blue moon.
higuera [i'ɣera] *nf* fig tree.
hijastro, a [i'xastro, a] *nm/f* stepson/daughter.
hijo, a ['ixo, a] *nm/f* son/daughter, child; (*uso vocativo*) dear; ~**s** *nmpl* children, sons and daughters; **sin** ~**s** childless; ~/ **hija político/a** son-/daughter-in-law; ~ **pródigo** prodigal son; ~ **de papá/mamá** daddy's/mummy's boy; ~ **de puta** (*fam!*) bastard(!), son of a bitch(!); **cada** ~ **de vecino** any Tom, Dick or Harry.
hilacha [i'latʃa] *nf* ravelled thread; ~ **de acero** steel wool.
hilado, a [i'laðo, a] *a* spun.
hilandero, a [ilan'dero, a] *nm/f* spinner.
hilar [i'lar] *vt* to spin; (*fig*) to reason, infer; ~ **delgado** to split hairs.
hilera [i'lera] *nf* row, file.
hilo ['ilo] *nm* thread; (*BOT*) fibre; (*tela*) linen; (*metal*) wire; (*de agua*) trickle, thin stream; (*de luz*) beam, ray; (*de conversación*) thread, theme; (*de pensamientos*) train; **colgar de un** ~ (*fig*) to hang by a thread; **traje de** ~ linen suit.
hilvanar [ilßa'nar] *vt* (*COSTURA*) to tack (*Brit*), baste (*US*); (*fig*) to do hurriedly.

Himalaya [ima'laja] *nm:* **el** ~, **los Montes** ~ the Himalayas.
himno ['imno] *nm* hymn; ~ **nacional** national anthem.
hincapié [inka'pje] *nm:* **hacer** ~ **en** to emphasize, stress.
hincar [in'kar] *vt* to drive (in), thrust (in); (*diente*) to sink; ~**se** *vr:* ~**se de rodillas** to kneel down.
hincha ['intʃa] *nm/f* (*fam: DEPORTE*) fan.
hinchado, a [in'tʃaðo, a] *a* (*gen*) swollen; (*persona*) pompous.
hinchar [in'tʃar] *vt* (*gen*) to swell; (*inflar*) to blow up, inflate; (*fig*) to exaggerate; ~**se** *vr* (*inflarse*) to swell up; (*fam: llenarse*) to stuff o.s.; (*fig*) to get conceited; ~**se de reír** to have a good laugh.
hinchazón [intʃa'θon] *nf* (*MED*) swelling; (*protuberancia*) bump, lump; (*altivez*) arrogance.
hindú [in'du] *a, nm/f* Hindu.
hinojo [i'noxo] *nm* fennel.
hinque ['inke] *etc vb V* **hincar.**
hipar [i'par] *vi* to hiccup.
hiper... [iper] *pref* hyper....
hiperactivo, a [iperak'tißo, a] *a* hyperactive.
hipermercado [ipermer'kaðo] *nm* hypermarket, superstore.
hipersensible [ipersen'sißle] *a* hypersensitive.
hípico, a ['ipiko, a] *a* horse *cpd*, equine; **club** ~ riding club.
hipnotice [ipno'tiθe] *etc vb V* **hipnotizar.**
hipnotismo [ipno'tismo] *nm* hypnotism.
hipnotizar [ipnoti'θar] *vt* to hypnotize.
hipo ['ipo] *nm* hiccups *pl*; **quitar el** ~ **a uno** to cure sb's hiccups.
hipocondría [ipokon'dria] *nf* hypochondria.
hipocondríaco, a [ipokon'drjako, a] *a, nm/f* hypochondriac.
hipocresía [ipokre'sia] *nf* hypocrisy.
hipócrita [i'pokrita] *a* hypocritical ◆ *nm/f* hypocrite.
hipodérmico, a [ipo'ðermiko, a] *a:* **aguja hipodérmica** hypodermic needle.
hipódromo [i'poðromo] *nm* racetrack.
hipopótamo [ipo'potamo] *nm* hippopotamus.
hipoteca [ipo'teka] *nf* mortgage; **redimir una** ~ to pay off a mortgage.
hipotecario, a [ipote'karjo, a] *a* mortgage *cpd.*
hipótesis [i'potesis] *nf inv* hypothesis; **es una** ~ (**nada más**) that's just a theory.
hipotético, a [ipo'tetiko, a] *a* hypothetic(al).
hiriendo [i'rjendo] *etc vb V* **herir.**
hiriente [i'rjente] *a* offensive, wounding.
hirsuto, a [ir'suto, a] *a* hairy.
hirviendo [ir'ßjendo] *etc vb V* **hervir.**

hisopo [i'sopo] *nm* (*REL*) sprinkler; (*BOT*) hyssop; (*de algodón*) swab.

hispánico, a [is'paniko, a] *a* Hispanic, Spanish.

hispanidad [ispani'ðað] *nf* (*cualidad*) Spanishness; (*POL*) Spanish *o* Hispanic world.

hispanista [ispa'nista] *nm/f* (*UNIV etc*) Hispan(ic)ist.

hispano, a [is'pano, a] *a* Hispanic, Spanish, Hispano- ♦ *nm/f* Spaniard.

Hispanoamérica [ispanoa'merika] *nf* Spanish *o* Latin America.

hispanoamericano, a [ispanoameri'kano, a] *a*, *nm/f* Spanish *o* Latin American.

hispanohablante [ispanoa'βlante], **hispanoparlante** [ispanopar'lante] *a* Spanish-speaking.

histeria [is'terja] *nf* hysteria.

histérico, a [is'teriko, a] *a* hysterical.

histerismo [iste'rismo] *nm* (*MED*) hysteria; (*fig*) hysterics.

histograma [isto'ɣrama] *nm* histogram.

historia [is'torja] *nf* history; (*cuento*) story, tale; ~s *nfpl* (*chismes*) gossip *sg*; **dejarse de** ~s to come to the point; **pasar a la** ~ to go down in history.

historiador, a [istorja'ðor, a] *nm/f* historian.

historial [isto'rjal] *nm* record; (*profesional*) curriculum vitae, c.v., résumé (*US*); (*MED*) case history.

historiar [isto'rjar] *vt* to chronicle, write the history of.

histórico, a [is'toriko, a] *a* historical; (*fig*) historic.

historieta [isto'rjeta] *nf* tale, anecdote; (*dibujos*) comic strip.

histrionismo [istrjo'nismo] *nm* (*TEATRO*) acting; (*fig*) histrionics *pl*.

hito ['ito] *nm* (*fig*) landmark; (*objetivo*) goal, target; (*fig*) milestone.

hizo ['iθo] *vb V* hacer.

Hna(s). *abr* (= *Hermana(s)*) Sr(s).

Hno(s). *abr* (= *Hermano(s)*) Bro(s).

hocico [o'θiko] *nm* snout; (*fig*) grimace.

hockey ['xoki] *nm* hockey; ~ **sobre hielo** ice hockey.

hogar [o'ɣar] *nm* fireplace, hearth; (*casa*) home; (*vida familiar*) home life.

hogareño, a [oɣa'reɲo, a] *a* home *cpd*; (*persona*) home-loving.

hogaza [o'ɣaθa] *nf* (*pan*) large loaf.

hoguera [o'ɣera] *nf* (*gen*) bonfire; (*para herejes*) stake.

hoja ['oxa] *nf* (*gen*) leaf; (*de flor*) petal; (*de hierba*) blade; (*de papel*) sheet; (*página*) page; (*formulario*) form; (*de puerta*) leaf; ~ **de afeitar** razor blade; ~ **de cálculo electrónico** spreadsheet; ~ **de trabajo** (*INFORM*) worksheet; **de** ~ **ancha** broad-leaved; **de** ~ **caduca/perenne** deciduous/evergreen.

hojalata [oxa'lata] *nf* tin(plate).

hojaldre [o'xaldre] *nm* (*CULIN*) puff pastry.

hojarasca [oxa'raska] *nf* (*hojas*) dead *o* fallen leaves *pl*; (*fig*) rubbish.

hojear [oxe'ar] *vt* to leaf through, turn the pages of.

hola ['ola] *excl* hello!

Holanda [o'landa] *nf* Holland.

holandés, esa [olan'des, esa] *a* Dutch ♦ *nm/f* Dutchman/woman; **los holandeses** the Dutch ♦ *nm* (*LING*) Dutch.

holgado, a [ol'ɣaðo, a] *a* loose, baggy; (*rico*) well-to-do.

holganza [ol'ɣanθa] *nf* (*ocio*) leisure; (*diversión*) amusement.

holgar [ol'ɣar] *vi* (*descansar*) to rest; (*sobrar*) to be superfluous; **huelga decir que** it goes without saying that.

holgazán, ana [olɣa'θan, ana] *a* idle, lazy ♦ *nm/f* loafer.

holgazanear [olɣaθane'ar] *vi* to laze *o* loaf around.

holgué [ol'ɣe], **holguemos** [ol'ɣemos] *etc vb V* holgar.

holgura [ol'ɣura] *nf* looseness, bagginess; (*TEC*) play, free movement; (*vida*) comfortable living, luxury.

hollar [o'ʎar] *vt* to tread (on), trample.

hollín [o'ʎin] *nm* soot.

hombre ['ombre] *nm* man; (*raza humana*): **el** ~ man(kind) ♦ *excl*: **¡sí** ~**!** (*claro*) of course!; (*para énfasis*) man, old chap; ~ **de negocios** businessman; ~**-rana** frogman; ~ **de bien** *o* **pro** honest man; ~ **de confianza** right-hand man; ~ **de estado** statesman; **el** ~ **medio** the average man.

hombrera [om'brera] *nf* shoulder strap.

hombro ['ombro] *nm* shoulder; **arrimar el** ~ to lend a hand; **encogerse de** ~**s** to shrug one's shoulders.

hombruno, a [om'bruno, a] *a* mannish.

homenaje [ome'naxe] *nm* (*gen*) homage; (*tributo*) tribute; **un partido** ~ a benefit match.

homicida [omi'θiða] *a* homicidal ♦ *nm/f* murderer.

homicidio [omi'θiðjo] *nm* murder, homicide; (*involuntario*) manslaughter.

homologación [omoloɣa'θjon] *nf* (*de sueldo, condiciones*) parity.

homólogo, a [o'moloɣo, a] *nm/f* counterpart, opposite number.

homónimo [o'monimo] *nm* (*tocayo*) namesake.

homosexual [omosek'swal] *a*, *nm/f* homosexual.

hondo, a ['ondo, a] *a* deep; **lo** ~ the depth(s) (*pl*), the bottom; **con** ~ **pesar** with deep regret.

hondonada [ondo'naða] *nf* hollow, depression; (*cañón*) ravine; (*GEO*) lowland.

hondura [on'dura] *nf* depth, profundity.

Honduras [on'duras] *nf* Honduras.

hondureño, a [ondu're ɲo, a] *a, nm/f* Honduran.

honestidad [onesti'ðað] *nf* purity, chastity; (*decencia*) decency.

honesto, a [o'nesto, a] *a* chaste; decent, honest; (*justo*) just.

hongo ['ongo] *nm* (*BOT: gen*) fungus; (: *comestible*) mushroom; (: *venenoso*) toadstool; (*sombrero*) bowler (hat) (*Brit*), derby (*US*); ~s del pie footrot *sg*, athlete's foot *sg*.

honor [o'nor] *nm* (*gen*) honour (*Brit*), honor US); (*gloria*) glory; ~ profesional professional etiquette; en ~ a la verdad to be fair.

honorable [ono'raßle] *a* honourable (*Brit*), honorable (*US*).

honorario, a [ono'rarjo, a] *a* honorary ◆ *nm*: ~s fees.

honorífico, a [ono'rifiko, a] *a* honourable (*Brit*), honorable (*US*); mención honorífica hono(u)rable mention.

honra ['onra] *nf* (*gen*) honour; (*renombre*) good name; ~s fúnebres funeral rites; tener algo a mucha ~ to be proud of sth.

honradez [onra'ðeθ] *nf* honesty; (*de persona*) integrity.

honrado, a [on'raðo, a] *a* honest, upright.

honrar [on'rar] *vt* to honour; ~se *vr*: ~se con algo/de hacer algo to be honoured by sth/to do sth.

honroso, a [on'roso, a] *a* (*honrado*) honourable; (*respetado*) respectable.

hora ['ora] *nf* hour; (*tiempo*) time; ¿qué ~ es? what time is it?; ¿a qué ~? at what time?; media ~ half an hour; a la ~ de comer/de recreo at lunchtime/at playtime; a primera ~ first thing (in the morning); a última ~ at the last moment; "última ~" "stop press"; noticias de última ~ last-minute news; a altas ~s in the small hours; a la ~ en punto on the dot; ¡a buena ~! about time, too!; en mala ~ unluckily; dar la ~ to strike the hour; poner el reloj en ~ to set one's watch; ~s de oficina/de trabajo office/working hours; ~s de visita visiting times; ~s extras o extraordinarias overtime *sg*; ~s punta rush hours; no ver la ~ de to look forward to; ¡ya era ~! and about time too!

horadar [ora'ðar] *vt* to drill, bore.

horario, a [o'rarjo, a] *a* hourly, hour *cpd* ◆ *nm* timetable; ~ comercial business hours.

horca ['orka] *nf* gallows *sg*; (*AGR*) pitchfork.

horcajadas [orka'xaðas]: a ~ *ad* astride.

horchata [or'tʃata] *nf* cold drink made from tiger nuts and water, tiger nut milk.

horda ['orða] *nf* horde.

horizontal [oriθon'tal] *a* horizontal.

horizonte [ori'θonte] *nm* horizon.

horma ['orma] *nf* mould; ~ (de calzado) last; ~ de sombrero hat block.

hormiga [or'miɣa] *nf* ant; ~s *nfpl* (*MED*) pins and needles.

hormigón [ormi'ɣon] *nm* concrete; ~ armado/pretensado reinforced/prestressed concrete.

hormigueo [ormi'ɣeo] *nm* (*comezón*) itch; (*fig*) uneasiness.

hormona [or'mona] *nf* hormone.

hornada [or'naða] *nf* batch of loaves (*etc*).

hornillo [or'niʎo] *nm* (*cocina*) portable stove.

horno ['orno] *nm* (*CULIN*) oven; (*TEC*) furnace; (*para cerámica*) kiln; ~ microondas microwave (oven); alto ~ blast furnace; ~ crematorio crematorium.

horóscopo [o'roskopo] *nm* horoscope.

horquilla [or'kiʎa] *nf* hairpin; (*AGR*) pitchfork.

horrendo, a [o'rrendo, a] *a* horrendous, frightful.

horrible [o'rriβle] *a* horrible, dreadful.

horripilante [orripi'lante] *a* hair-raising, horrifying.

horripilar [orripi'lar] *vt*: ~ a uno to horrify sb; ~se *vr* to be horrified.

horror [o'rror] *nm* horror, dread; (*atrocidad*) atrocity; ¡qué ~! (*fam*) oh, my God!; estudia horrores he studies a hell of a lot.

horrorice [orro'riθe] *etc vb V* **horrorizar**.

horrorizar [orrori'θar] *vt* to horrify, frighten; ~se *vr* to be horrified.

horroroso, a [orro'roso, a] *a* horrifying, ghastly.

hortaliza [orta'liθa] *nf* vegetable.

hortelano, a [orte'lano, a] *nm/f* (market) gardener.

hortera [or'tera] *a* (*fam*) vulgar, naff.

hortícola [or'tikola] *a* horticultural.

horticultura [ortikul'tura] *nf* horticulture.

hosco, a ['osko, a] *a* dark; (*persona*) sullen, gloomy.

hospedaje [ospe'ðaxe] *nm* (cost of) board and lodging.

hospedar [ospe'ðar] *vt* to put up; ~se *vr*: ~se (con/en) to stay o lodge (with/at).

hospedería [ospeðe'ria] *nf* (*edificio*) inn; (*habitación*) guest room.

hospicio [os'piθjo] *nm* (*para niños*) orphanage.

hospital [ospi'tal] *nm* hospital.

hospitalario, a [ospita'larjo, a] *a* (*acogedor*) hospitable.

hospitalice [ospita'liθe] *etc vb V* **hospitalizar**.

hospitalidad [ospitali'ðað] *nf* hospitality.

hospitalizar [ospitali'θar] *vt* to send o take to hospital, hospitalize.

hosquedad [oske'ðað] *nf* sullenness.

hostal [os'tal] *nm* small hotel.

hostelería [ostele'ria] *nf* hotel business *o* trade.

hostelero, a [oste'lero, a] *nm/f* innkeeper, landlord/lady.

hostia ['ostja] *nf* (REL) host, consecrated wafer; *(fam: golpe)* whack, punch ♦ *excl*: ¡~(s)! *(fam!)* damn!

hostigar [osti'ɣar] *vt* to whip; *(fig)* to harass, pester.

hostigue [os'tiɣe] *etc vb* V **hostigar**.

hostil [os'til] *a* hostile.

hostilidad [ostili'ðað] *nf* hostility.

hotel [o'tel] *nm* hotel.

hotelero, a [ote'lero, a] *a* hotel *cpd* ♦ *nm/f* hotelier.

hoy [oi] *ad* *(este día)* today; *(en la actualidad)* now(adays) ♦ *nm* present time; ~ **(en) día** now(adays); **el día de ~, ~ día** (AM) this very day; **~ por ~** right now; **de ~ en ocho días** a week today; **de ~ en adelante** from now on.

hoya ['oja] *nf* pit; *(sepulcro)* grave; *(GEO)* valley.

hoyo ['ojo] *nm* hole, pit; *(tumba)* grave; *(GOLF)* hole; *(MED)* pockmark.

hoyuelo [oj'welo] *nm* dimple.

hoz [oθ] *nf* sickle.

hube ['uße] *etc vb* V **haber**.

hucha ['utʃa] *nf* money box.

hueco, a ['weko, a] *a* *(vacío)* hollow, empty; *(resonante)* booming; *(sonido)* resonant; *(persona)* conceited; *(estilo)* pompous ♦ *nm* hollow, cavity; *(agujero)* hole; *(de escalera)* well; *(de ascensor)* shaft; *(vacante)* vacancy; ~ **de la mano** hollow of the hand.

huela ['wela] *etc vb* V **oler**.

huelga ['welɣa] *etc vb* V **holgar** ♦ *nf* strike; **declararse en ~** to go on strike, come out on strike; ~ **general** general strike; ~ **de hambre** hunger strike; ~ **oficial** official strike.

huelgue ['welɣe] *etc vb* V **holgar**.

huelguista [wel'ɣista] *nm/f* striker.

huella ['weʎa] *nf* *(acto de pisar, pisada)* tread(ing); *(marca del paso)* footprint, footstep; (: *de animal, máquina)* track; ~ **digital** fingerprint; **sin dejar ~** without leaving a trace.

huérfano, a ['werfano, a] *a* orphan(ed); *(fig)* unprotected ♦ *nm/f* orphan.

huerta ['werta] *nf* market garden *(Brit)*, truck farm *(US)*; *(Murcia, Valencia)* irrigated region.

huerto ['werto] *nm* kitchen garden; *(de árboles frutales)* orchard.

hueso ['weso] *nm* (ANAT) bone; *(de fruta)* stone, pit *(US)*; **sin ~** *(carne)* boned; **estar en los ~s** to be nothing but skin and bone;

ser un ~ *(profesor)* to be terribly strict; **un ~ duro de roer** a hard nut to crack.

huésped, a ['wespeð, a] *nm/f* *(invitado)* guest; *(habitante)* resident; *(anfitrión)* host(ess).

huesudo, a [we'suðo, a] *a* bony, big-boned.

huevera [we'ßera] *nf* eggcup.

huevo ['weßo] *nm* egg; *(fam!)* ball(!), testicle; ~ **duro/escalfado/estrellado** *o* **frito/pasado por agua** hard-boiled/ poached/fried/soft-boiled egg; ~**s revueltos** scrambled eggs; **me costó un ~** *(fam!)* it was hard work; **tener ~s** *(fam!)* to have guts.

huida [u'iða] *nf* escape, flight; ~ **de capitales** *(COM)* flight of capital.

huidizo, a [ui'ðiθo, a] *a* *(tímido)* shy; *(pasajero)* fleeting.

huir [u'ir] *vt* *(escapar)* to flee, escape; *(evadir)* to avoid ♦ *vi* to flee, run away; ~**se** *vr* *(escaparse)* to escape.

hule ['ule] *nm* *(encerado)* oilskin.

hulla ['uʎa] *nf* bituminous coal.

humanice [uma'niθe] *etc vb* V **humanizar**.

humanidad [umani'ðað] *nf* *(género humano)* man(kind); *(cualidad)* humanity; *(fam: gordura)* corpulence.

humanitario, a [umani'tarjo, a] *a* humanitarian; *(benévolo)* humane.

humanizar [umani'θar] *vt* to humanize; ~**se** *vr* to become more human.

humano, a [u'mano, a] *a* *(gen)* human; *(humanitario)* humane ♦ *nm* human; **ser ~** human being.

humareda [uma'reða] *nf* cloud of smoke.

humeante [ume'ante] *a* smoking, smoky.

humedad [ume'ðað] *nf* *(del clima)* humidity; *(de pared etc)* dampness; **a prueba de ~** damp-proof.

humedecer [umeðe'θer] *vt* to moisten, wet; ~**se** *vr* to get wet.

humedezca [ume'ðeθka] *etc vb* V **humedecer**.

húmedo, a ['umeðo, a] *a* *(mojado)* damp, wet; *(tiempo etc)* humid.

humildad [umil'dað] *nf* humility, humbleness.

humilde [u'milde] *a* humble, modest; *(clase etc)* low, modest.

humillación [umiʎa'θjon] *nf* humiliation.

humillante [umi'ʎante] *a* humiliating.

humillar [umi'ʎar] *vt* to humiliate; ~**se** *vr* to humble o.s., grovel.

humo ['umo] *nm* *(de fuego)* smoke; *(gas nocivo)* fumes *pl*; *(vapor)* steam, vapour; ~**s** *nmpl* *(fig)* conceit *sg*; **irse todo en ~** *(fig)* to vanish without trace; **bajar los ~s a uno** to take sb down a peg or two.

humor [u'mor] *nm* *(disposición)* mood, temper; *(lo que divierte)* humour; **de buen/mal ~** in a good/bad mood.

humorado, a [umo'raðo, a] *a*: **bien ~** good-humoured; **mal ~** bad-tempered, cross ♦ *nf* witticism.

humorismo [umo'rismo] *nm* humour.

humorista [umo'rista] *nm/f* comic.

humorístico, a [umo'ristiko, a] *a* funny, humorous.

hundimiento [undi'mjento] *nm* (*gen*) sinking; (*colapso*) collapse.

hundir [un'dir] *vt* to sink; (*edificio, plan*) to ruin, destroy; **~se** *vr* to sink, collapse; (*fig: arruinarse*) to be ruined; (*desaparecer*) to disappear; **se hundió la economía** the economy collapsed; **se hundieron los precios** prices slumped.

húngaro, a ['ungaro, a] *a*, *nm/f* Hungarian ♦ *nm* (*LING*) Hungarian, Magyar.

Hungría [un'gria] *nf* Hungary.

huracán [ura'kan] *nm* hurricane.

huraño, a [u'raɲo, a] *a* shy; (*antisocial*) unsociable.

hurgar [ur'ɣar] *vt* to poke, jab; (*remover*) to stir (up); **~se** *vr*: **~se (las narices)** to pick one's nose.

hurgonear [urɣone'ar] *vt* to poke.

hurgue ['urɣe] *etc vb* V **hurgar**.

hurón [u'ron] *nm* (*ZOOL*) ferret.

huronera [uro'nera] *nf* (*fig*) den.

hurra ['urra] *excl* hurray!, hurrah!

hurtadillas [urta'ðiʎas]: **a ~** *ad* stealthily, on the sly.

hurtar [ur'tar] *vt* to steal; **~se** *vr* to hide, keep out of the way.

hurto ['urto] *nm* theft, stealing; (*lo robado*) (piece of) stolen property, loot.

husmear [usme'ar] *vt* (*oler*) to sniff out, scent; (*fam*) to pry into ♦ *vi* to smell bad.

huso ['uso] *nm* (*TEC*) spindle; (*de torno*) drum.

huy ['ui] *excl* (*dolor*) ow!, ouch!; (*sorpresa*) well!; (*alivio*) phew!

huyendo [u'jendo] *etc vb* V **huir**.

I

I, i [i] *nf* (*letra*) I, i; **I de Inés** I for Isaac (*Brit*) o Item (*US*).

I.A. *abr* = **inteligencia artificial**.

iba ['iβa] *etc vb* V **ir**.

Iberia [i'βerja] *nf* Iberia.

ibérico, a [i'βeriko, a] *a* Iberian; **la Península ibérica** the Iberian Peninsula.

ibero, a [i'βero, a], **íbero, a** ['iβero, a] *a*, *nm/f* Iberian.

iberoamericano, a [iβeroameri'kano, a] *a*,

nm/f Latin American.

íbice ['iβiθe] *nm* ibex.

ibicenco, a [iβi'θenko, a] *a* of o from Ibiza ♦ *nm/f* native o inhabitant of Ibiza.

Ibiza [i'βiθa] *nf* Ibiza.

ice ['iθe] *etc vb* V **izar**.

iceberg [iθe'ber] *nm* iceberg.

ICONA [i'kona] *nm abr* (*Esp*) = *Instituto Nacional para la Conservacion de la Naturaleza*.

ícono ['ikono] *nm* (*tb INFORM*) icon.

iconoclasta [ikono'klasta] *a* iconoclastic ♦ *nm/f* iconoclast.

ictericia [ikte'riθja] *nf* jaundice.

íd. *abr* = **ídem**.

ida ['iða] *nf* going, departure; **~ y vuelta** round trip, return; **~s y venidas** comings and goings.

IDE [iðe] *nf abr* (= *Iniciativa de Defensa Estratégica*) SDI.

idea [i'ðea] *nf* idea; (*impresión*) opinion; (*propósito*) intention; **~ genial** brilliant idea; **a mala ~** out of spite; **no tengo la menor ~** I haven't a clue.

ideal [iðe'al] *a*, *nm* ideal.

idealice [iðea'liθe] *etc vb* V **idealizar**.

idealista [iðea'lista] *a* idealistic ♦ *nm/f* idealist.

idealizar [iðeali'θar] *vt* to idealize.

idear [iðe'ar] *vt* to think up; (*aparato*) to invent; (*viaje*) to plan.

ídem ['iðem] *pron* ditto.

idéntico, a [i'ðentiko, a] *a* identical.

identidad [iðenti'ðað] *nf* identity; **~ corporativa** corporate identity o image.

identificación [iðentifika'θjon] *nf* identification.

identificar [iðentifi'kar] *vt* to identify; **~se** *vr*: **~se con** to identify with.

identifique [iðenti'fike] *etc vb* V **identificar**.

ideología [iðeolo'xia] *nf* ideology.

ideológico, a [iðeo'loxiko, a] *a* ideological.

idílico, a [i'ðiliko, a] *a* idyllic.

idioma [i'ðjoma] *nm* language.

idiomático, a [iðjo'matiko, a] *a* idiomatic.

idiota [i'ðjota] *a* idiotic ♦ *nm/f* idiot.

idiotez [iðjo'teθ] *nf* idiocy.

ídolo ['iðolo] *nm* (*tb fig*) idol.

idoneidad [iðonei'ðað] *nf* suitability; (*capacidad*) aptitude.

idóneo, a [i'ðoneo, a] *a* suitable.

iglesia [i'ɣlesja] *nf* church; **~ parroquial** parish church; **¡con la ~ hemos topado!** now we're really up against it!

ignición [iɣni'θjon] *nf* ignition.

ignominia [iɣno'minja] *nf* ignominy.

ignominioso, a [iɣnomi'njoso, a] *a* ignominious.

ignorado, a [iɣno'raðo, a] *a* unknown; (*dato*) obscure.

ignorancia [iɣno'ranθja] *nf* ignorance; **por** ~ through ignorance.

ignorante [iɣno'rante] *a* ignorant, uninformed ♦ *nm/f* ignoramus.

ignorar [iɣno'rar] *vt* not to know, be ignorant of; (*no hacer caso a*) to ignore; **ignoramos su paradero** we don't know his whereabouts.

ignoto, a [iɣ'noto, a] *a* unknown.

igual [i'ɣwal] *a* equal; (*similar*) like, similar; (*mismo*) (the) same; (*constante*) constant; (*temperatura*) even ♦ *nm/f* equal; **al** ~ **que** *prep, conj* like, just like; ~ **que** the same as; **sin** ~ peerless; **me da** *o* **es** ~ I don't care, it makes no difference; **no tener** ~ to be unrivalled; **son** ~**es** they're the same.

iguala [i'ɣwala] *nf* equalization; (*COM*) agreement.

igualada [iɣwa'laða] *nf* equalizer.

igualar [iɣwa'lar] *vt* (*gen*) to equalize, make equal; (*terreno*) to make even; (*COM*) to agree upon; ~**se** *vr* (*platos de balanza*) to balance out; ~**se (a)** (*equivaler*) to be equal (to).

igualdad [iɣwal'dað] *nf* equality; (*similaridad*) sameness; (*uniformidad*) uniformity; **en** ~ **de condiciones** on an equal basis.

igualmente [iɣwal'mente] *ad* equally; (*también*) also, likewise ♦ *excl* the same to you!

ikurriña [iku'rriɲa] *nf* Basque flag.

ilegal [ile'ɣal] *a* illegal.

ilegitimidad [ilexitimi'ðað] *nf* illegitimacy.

ilegítimo, a [ile'xitimo, a] *a* illegitimate.

ileso, a [i'leso, a] *a* unhurt, unharmed.

ilícito, a [i'liθito, a] *a* illicit.

ilimitado, a [ilimi'taðo, a] *a* unlimited.

Ilma., Ilmo. *abr* (= *Ilustrísima, Ilustrísimo*) *courtesy title.*

ilógico, a [i'loxiko, a] *a* illogical.

iluminación [ilumina'θjon] *nf* illumination; (*alumbrado*) lighting; (*fig*) enlightenment.

iluminar [ilumi'nar] *vt* to illuminate, light (up); (*fig*) to enlighten.

ilusión [ilu'sjon] *nf* illusion; (*quimera*) delusion; (*esperanza*) hope; (*emoción*) excitement, thrill; **hacerse ilusiones** to build up one's hopes; **no te hagas ilusiones** don't build up your hopes *o* get too excited.

ilusionado, a [ilusjo'naðo, a] *a* excited.

ilusionista [ilusjo'nista] *nm/f* conjurer.

iluso, a [i'luso, a] *a* gullible, easily deceived ♦ *nm/f* dreamer, visionary.

ilusorio, a [ilu'sorjo, a] *a* (*de ilusión*) illusory, deceptive; (*esperanza*) vain.

ilustración [ilustra'θjon] *nf* illustration; (*saber*) learning, erudition; **la I**~ the Enlightenment.

ilustrado, a [ilus'traðo, a] *a* illustrated; learned.

ilustrar [ilus'trar] *vt* to illustrate; (*instruir*) to instruct; (*explicar*) to explain, make clear; ~**se** *vr* to acquire knowledge.

ilustre [i'lustre] *a* famous, illustrious.

imagen [i'maxen] *nf* (*gen*) image; (*dibujo, TV*) picture; (*REL*) statue; **ser la viva** ~ **de** to be the spitting *o* living image of; **a su** ~ in one's own image.

imaginación [imaxina'θjon] *nf* imagination; (*fig*) fancy; **ni por** ~ on no account; **no se me pasó por la** ~ **que...** it never even occurred to me that ... .

imaginar [imaxi'nar] *vt* (*gen*) to imagine; (*idear*) to think up; (*suponer*) to suppose; ~**se** *vr* to imagine; **¡imagínate!** just imagine!, just fancy!; **imagínese que...** suppose that ...; **me imagino que sí** I should think so.

imaginario, a [imaxi'narjo, a] *a* imaginary.

imaginativo, a [imaxina'tiβo, a] *a* imaginative ♦ *nf* imagination.

imán [i'man] *nm* magnet.

iman(t)ar [ima'n(t)ar] *vt* to magnetize.

imbécil [im'beθil] *nm/f* imbecile, idiot.

imbecilidad [imbeθili'ðað] *nf* imbecility, stupidity.

imberbe [im'berβe] *a* beardless.

imborrable [imbo'rraβle] *a* indelible; (*inolvidable*) unforgettable.

imbuir [imbu'ir] *vi* to imbue.

imbuyendo [imbu'jendo] *etc vb V* **imbuir**.

imitación [imita'θjon] *nf* imitation; (*parodia*) mimicry; **a** ~ **de** in imitation of; **desconfíe de las imitaciones** (*COM*) beware of copies *o* imitations.

imitador, a [imita'ðor, a] *a* imitative ♦ *nm/f* imitator; (*TEATRO*) mimic.

imitar [imi'tar] *vt* to imitate; (*parodiar, remedar*) to mimic, ape; (*copiar*) to follow.

impaciencia [impa'θjenθja] *nf* impatience.

impacientar [impaθjen'tar] *vt* to make impatient; (*enfadar*) to irritate; ~**se** *vr* to get impatient; (*inquietarse*) to fret.

impaciente [impa'θjente] *a* impatient; (*nervioso*) anxious.

impacto [im'pakto] *nm* impact.

impagado, a [impa'ɣaðo, a] *a* unpaid, still to be paid.

impar [im'par] *a* odd ♦ *nm* odd number.

imparable [impa'raβle] *a* unstoppable.

imparcial [impar'θjal] *a* impartial, fair.

imparcialidad [imparθjali'ðað] *nf* impartiality, fairness.

impartir [impar'tir] *vt* to impart, give.

impasible [impa'siβle] *a* impassive.

impavidez [impaβi'ðeθ] *nf* fearlessness, intrepidness.

impávido, a [im'paβiðo, a] *a* fearless, intrepid.

IMPE ['impe] *nm abr* (*Esp COM*) = *Instituto de la Mediana y Pequeña Empresa.*

impecable [impe'kaßle] a impeccable.

impedido, a [impe'ðiðo, a] a: **estar** ~ to be an invalid ♦ nm/f: **ser un** ~ **físico** to be an invalid.

impedimento [impeði'mento] nm impediment, obstacle.

impedir [impe'ðir] vt (obstruir) to impede, obstruct; (estorbar) to prevent; ~ **el tráfico** to block the traffic.

impeler [impe'ler] vt to drive, propel; (fig) to impel.

impenetrabilidad [impenetraßili'ðað] nf impenetrability.

impenetrable [impene'traßle] a impenetrable; (fig) incomprehensible.

impensable [impen'saßle] a unthinkable.

impepinable [impepi'naßle] a (fam) certain, inevitable.

imperante [impe'rante] a prevailing.

imperar [impe'rar] vi (reinar) to rule, reign; (fig) to prevail, reign; (precio) to be current.

imperativo, a [impera'tißo, a] a (persona) imperious; (urgente, LING) imperative.

imperceptible [imperθep'tißle] a imperceptible.

imperdible [imper'ðißle] nm safety pin.

imperdonable [imperðo'naßle] a unforgivable, inexcusable.

imperecedero, a [impereθe'ðero, a] a undying.

imperfección [imperfek'θjon] nf imperfection; (falla) flaw, fault.

imperfecto, a [imper'fekto, a] a faulty, imperfect ♦ nm (LING) imperfect tense.

imperial [impe'rjal] a imperial.

imperialismo [imperja'lismo] nm imperialism.

imperialista [imperja'lista] a imperialist(ic) ♦ nm/f imperialist.

impericia [impe'riθja] nf (torpeza) unskilfulness; (inexperiencia) inexperience.

imperio [im'perjo] nm empire; (autoridad) rule, authority; (fig) pride, haughtiness; **vale un** ~ (fig) it's worth a fortune.

imperioso, a [impe'rjoso, a] a imperious; (urgente) urgent; (imperativo) imperative.

impermeable [imperme'aßle] a (a prueba de agua) waterproof ♦ nm raincoat, mac (Brit).

impersonal [imperso'nal] a impersonal.

impertérrito, a [imper'territo, a] a undaunted.

impertinencia [imperti'nenθja] nf impertinence.

impertinente [imperti'nente] a impertinent.

imperturbable [impertur'ßaßle] a imperturbable; (sereno) unruffled; (impasible) impassive.

ímpetu ['impetu] nm (impulso) impetus, impulse; (impetuosidad) impetuosity; (violencia) violence.

impetuosidad [impetwosi'ðað] nf impetuousness; (violencia) violence.

impetuoso, a [impe'twoso, a] a impetuous; (río) rushing; (acto) hasty.

impida [im'piða] etc vb V **impedir**.

impío, a [im'pio, a] a impious, ungodly; (cruel) cruel, pitiless.

implacable [impla'kaßle] a implacable, relentless.

implantación [implanta'θjon] nf implantation; (introducción) introduction.

implicar [impli'kar] vt to involve; (entrañar) to imply; **esto no implica que** ... this does not mean that ....

implícito, a [im'pliθito, a] a (tácito) implicit; (sobreentendido) implied.

implique [im'plike] etc vb V **implicar**.

implorar [implo'rar] vt to beg, implore.

impoluto, a [impo'luto, a] a unpolluted, pure.

impondré [impon'dre] etc vb V **imponer**.

imponente [impo'nente] a (impresionante) impressive, imposing; (solemne) grand ♦ nm/f (COM) depositor.

imponer [impo'ner] vt (gen) to impose; (tarea) to set; (exigir) to exact; (miedo) to inspire; (COM) to deposit; ~**se** vr to assert o.s.; (prevalecer) to prevail; (costumbre) to grow up; ~**se un deber** to assume a duty.

imponga [im'ponga] etc vb V **imponer**.

imponible [impo'nißle] a (COM) taxable, subject to tax; (importación) dutiable, subject to duty; **no** ~ tax-free, tax-exempt (US).

impopular [impopu'lar] a unpopular.

importación [importa'θjon] nf (acto) importing; (mercancías) imports pl.

importancia [impor'tanθja] nf importance; (valor) value, significance; (extensión) size, magnitude; **no dar** ~ **a** to consider unimportant; (fig) to make light of; **no tiene** ~ it's nothing.

importante [impor'tante] a important; valuable, significant.

importar [impor'tar] vt (del extranjero) to import; (costar) to amount to; (implicar) to involve ♦ vi to be important, matter; **me importa un bledo** I don't give a damn; **¿le importa que fume?** do you mind if I smoke?; **¿te importa prestármelo?** would you mind lending it to me?; **¿qué importa?** what difference does it make?; **no importa** it doesn't matter; **no le importa** he doesn't care, it doesn't bother him; **"no importa precio"** "cost no object".

importe [im'porte] nm (total) amount; (valor) value.

importunar [importu'nar] vt to bother, pester.

importuno, a [impor'tuno, a] a (inoportuno, molesto) inopportune; (indiscreto) troublesome.

imposibilidad [imposißili'ðað] nf impossibility; **mi ~ para hacerlo** my inability to do it.

imposibilitado, a [imposißili'taðo, a] a: **verse ~ para hacer algo** to be unable to do sth.

imposibilitar [imposißili'tar] vt to make impossible, prevent.

imposible [impo'sißle] a impossible; (insoportable) unbearable, intolerable; **es ~** it's out of the question; **es ~ de predecir** it's impossible to forecast o predict.

imposición [imposi'θjon] nf imposition; (COM) tax; (inversión) deposit; **efectuar una ~** to make a deposit.

impostor, a [impos'tor, a] nm/f impostor.

impostura [impos'tura] nf fraud, imposture.

impotencia [impo'tenθja] nf impotence.

impotente [impo'tente] a impotent.

impracticable [imprakti'kaßle] a (irrealizable) impracticable; (intransitable) impassable.

imprecar [impre'kar] vi to curse.

imprecisión [impreθi'sjon] nf lack of precision, vagueness.

impreciso, a [impre'θiso, a] a imprecise, vague.

impredecible [impreðe'θißle], **impredictible** [impreðik'tißle] a unpredictable.

impregnar [impreɣ'nar] vt to impregnate; (fig) to pervade; **~se** vr to become impregnated.

imprenta [im'prenta] nf (acto) printing; (aparato) press; (casa) printer's; (letra) print.

impreque [im'preke] etc vb V **imprecar**.

imprescindible [impresθin'dißle] a essential, vital.

impresión [impre'sjon] nf impression; (IMPRENTA) printing; (edición) edition; (FOTO) print; (marca) imprint; **~ digital** fingerprint.

impresionable [impresjo'naßle] a (sensible) impressionable.

impresionado, a [impresjo'naðo, a] a impressed; (FOTO) exposed.

impresionante [impresjo'nante] a impressive; (tremendo) tremendous; (maravilloso) great, marvellous.

impresionar [impresjo'nar] vt (conmover) to move; (afectar) to impress, strike; (película fotográfica) to expose; **~se** vr to be impressed; (connoverse) to be moved.

impresionista [impresjo'nista] a impressionist(ic); (ARTE) impressionist ♦ nm/f impressionist.

impreso, a [im'preso, a] pp de **imprimir** ♦ a printed ♦ nm printed paper/book etc; **~s**

nmpl printed matter sg; **~ de solicitud** application form.

impresora [impre'sora] nf (INFORM) printer; **~ de chorro de tinta** ink-jet printer; **~ (por) láser** laser printer; **~ de línea** line printer; **~ de matriz (de agujas)** dotmatrix printer; **~ de rueda** o **de margarita** daisy-wheel printer.

imprevisible [impreßi'sißle] a unforeseeable; (individuo) unpredictable.

imprevisión [impreßi'sjon] nf shortsightedness; (irreflexión) thoughtlessness.

imprevisto, a [impre'ßisto, a] a unforeseen; (inesperado) unexpected ♦ nm: **~s** (dinero) incidentals, unforeseen expenses.

imprimir [impri'mir] vt to stamp; (textos) to print; (INFORM) to output, print out.

improbabilidad [improßaßili'ðað] nf improbability, unlikelihood.

improbable [impro'ßaßle] a improbable; (inverosímil) unlikely.

improcedente [improθe'ðente] a inappropriate; (JUR) inadmissible.

improductivo, a [improðuk'tißo, a] a unproductive.

impronunciable [impronun'θjaßle] a unpronounceable.

improperio [impro'perjo] nm insult; **~s** nmpl abuse sg.

impropiedad [impropje'ðað] nf impropriety (of language).

impropio, a [im'propjo, a] a improper; (inadecuado) inappropriate.

improvisación [improßisa'θjon] nf improvisation.

improvisado, a [improßi'saðo, a] a improvised, impromptu.

improvisar [improßi'sar] vt to improvise; (comida) to rustle up ♦ vi to improvise; (MUS) to extemporize; (TEATRO etc) to ad-lib.

improviso [impro'ßiso] ad **de ~** unexpectedly, suddenly; (MUS etc) impromptu.

imprudencia [impru'ðenθja] nf imprudence; (indiscreción) indiscretion; (descuido) carelessness.

imprudente [impru'ðente] a imprudent; indiscreet.

Impte. abr (= Importe) amt.

impúdico, a [im'puðiko, a] a shameless; (lujurioso) lecherous.

impudor [impu'ðor] nm shamelessness; (lujuria) lechery.

impuesto, a [im'pwesto, a] pp de **imponer** ♦ a imposed ♦ nm tax; (derecho) duty; **anterior al ~** pre-tax; **sujeto a ~** taxable; **~ de lujo** luxury tax; **~ de plusvalía** capital gains tax; **~ sobre la propiedad** property tax; **~ sobre la renta** income tax; **~ sobre la renta de las personas físicas (IRPF)** personal income tax; **~ sobre la**

riqueza wealth tax; ~ **de transferencia de capital** capital transfer tax; ~ **de venta** sales tax; ~ **sobre el valor añadido (IVA)** value added tax (VAT).

impugnar [impuɤ'nar] *vt* to oppose, contest; (*refutar*) to refute, impugn.

impulsar [impul'sar] *vt* = **impeler.**

impulso [im'pulso] *nm* impulse; (*fuerza, empuje*) thrust, drive; (*fig*: *sentimiento*) urge, impulse; **a ~s del miedo** driven on by fear.

impune [im'pune] *a* unpunished.

impunemente [impune'mente] *ad* with impunity.

impureza [impu'reθa] *nf* impurity; (*fig*) lewdness.

impuro, a [im'puro, a] *a* impure; lewd.

impuse [im'puse] *etc vb* V **imponer.**

imputación [imputa'θjon] *nf* imputation.

imputar [impu'tar] *vt*: ~ **a** to attribute to, to impute to.

inabordable [inaβor'ðaβle] *a* unapproachable.

inacabable [inaka'βaβle] *a* (*infinito*) endless; (*interminable*) interminable.

inaccesible [inakθe'siβle] *a* inaccessible; (*fig*: *precio*) beyond one's reach, prohibitive; (*individuo*) aloof.

inacción [inak'θjon] *nf* inactivity.

inaceptable [inaθep'taβle] *a* unacceptable.

inactividad [inaktiβi'ðað] *nf* inactivity; (*COM*) dullness.

inactivo, a [inak'tiβo, a] *a* inactive; (*COM*) dull; (*población*) non-working.

inadaptación [inaðapta'θjon] *nf* maladjustment.

inadaptado, a [inaðap'taðo, a] *a* maladjusted ◆ *nm/f* misfit.

inadecuado, a [inaðe'kwaðo, a] *a* (*insuficiente*) inadequate; (*inapto*) unsuitable.

inadmisible [inaðmi'siβle] *a* inadmissible.

inadvertido, a [inaðβer'tiðo, a] *a* (*no visto*) unnoticed.

inagotable [inaɤo'taβle] *a* inexhaustible.

inaguantable [inaɤwan'taβle] *a* unbearable.

inalcanzable [inalkan'θaβle] *a* unattainable.

inalterable [inalte'raβle] *a* immutable, unchangeable.

inamovible [inamo'βiβle] *a* fixed, immovable; (*TEC*) undetachable.

inanición [inani'θjon] *nf* starvation.

inanimado, a [inani'maðo, a] *a* inanimate.

inánime [i'nanime] *a* lifeless.

inapelable [inape'laβle] *a* (*JUR*) unappealable; (*fig*) irremediable.

inapetencia [inape'tenθja] *nf* lack of appetite.

inaplicable [inapli'kaβle] *a* not applicable.

inapreciable [inapre'θjaβle] *a* invaluable.

inapto, a [i'napto] *a* unsuited.

inarrugable [inarru'ɤaβle] *a* crease-resistant.

inasequible [inase'kiβle] *a* unattainable.

inaudito, a [inau'ðito, a] *a* unheard-of.

inauguración [inauɤura'θjon] *nf* inauguration; (*de exposición*) opening.

inaugurar [inauɤu'rar] *vt* to inaugurate; to open.

I.N.B. *abr* (= *Instituto Nacional de Bachillerato*) ≈ comprehensive school (*Brit*), high school (*US*).

inca ['inka] *nm/f* Inca.

INCAE [in'kae] *nm abr* = *Instituto Centroamericano de Administración de Empresas.*

incaico, a [in'kaiko, a] *a* Inca.

incalculable [inkalku'laβle] *a* incalculable.

incandescente [inkandes'θente] *a* incandescent.

incansable [inkan'saβle] *a* tireless, untiring.

incapacidad [inkapaθi'ðað] *nf* incapacity; (*incompetencia*) incompetence; ~ **física/mental** physical/mental disability.

incapacitar [inkapaθi'tar] *vt* (*inhabilitar*) to incapacitate, handicap; (*descalificar*) to disqualify.

incapaz [inka'paθ] *a* incapable; ~ **de hacer algo** unable to do sth.

incautación [inkauta'θjon] *nf* seizure, confiscation.

incautarse [inkau'tarse] *vr*: ~ **de** to seize, confiscate.

incauto, a [in'kauto, a] *a* (*imprudente*) incautious, unwary.

incendiar [inθen'djar] *vt* to set fire to; (*fig*) to inflame; ~**se** *vr* to catch fire.

incendiario, a [inθen'djarjo, a] *a* incendiary ◆ *nm/f* fire-raiser, arsonist.

incendio [in'θendjo] *nm* fire; ~ **intencionado** arson.

incentivo [inθen'tiβo] *nm* incentive.

incertidumbre [inθerti'ðumbre] *nf* (*inseguridad*) uncertainty; (*duda*) doubt.

incesante [inθe'sante] *a* incessant.

incesto [in'θesto] *nm* incest.

incidencia [inθi'ðenθja] *nf* (*MAT*) incidence; (*fig*) effect.

incidente [inθi'ðente] *nm* incident.

incidir [inθi'ðir] *vi*: ~ **en** (*influir*) to influence; (*afectar*) to affect; ~ **en un error** to be mistaken.

incienso [in'θjenso] *nm* incense.

incierto, a [in'θjerto, a] *a* uncertain.

incineración [inθinera'θjon] *nf* incineration; (*de cadáveres*) cremation.

incinerar [inθine'rar] *vt* to burn; to cremate.

incipiente [inθi'pjente] *a* incipient.

incisión [inθi'sjon] *nf* incision.

incisivo, a [inθi'siβo, a] *a* sharp, cutting; (*fig*) incisive.

inciso [in'θiso] *nm* (*LING*) clause, sentence;

(*coma*) comma; (*JUR*) subsection.

incitante [inθi'tante] *a* (*estimulante*) exciting; (*provocativo*) provocative.

incitar [inθi'tar] *vt* to incite, rouse.

incivil [inθi'ßil] *a* rude, uncivil.

inclemencia [inkle'menθja] *nf* (*severidad*) harshness, severity; (*del tiempo*) inclemency.

inclemente [inkle'mente] *a* harsh, severe; inclement.

inclinación [inklina'θjon] *nf* (*gen*) inclination; (*de tierras*) slope, incline; (*de cabeza*) nod, bow; (*fig*) leaning, bent.

inclinar [inkli'nar] *vt* to incline; (*cabeza*) to nod, bow ♦ *vi* to lean, slope; ~**se** *vr* to bow; (*encorvarse*) to stoop; ~**se a** (*parecerse*) to take after, resemble; ~**se ante** to bow down to; **me inclino a pensar que ...** I'm inclined to think that ... .

incluir [inklu'ir] *vt* to include; (*incorporar*) to incorporate; (*meter*) to enclose; **todo incluido** (*COM*) inclusive, all-in.

inclusive [inklu'siße] *ad* inclusive ♦ *prep* including.

incluso, a [in'kluso, a] *a* included ♦ *ad* inclusively; (*hasta*) even.

incluyendo [inklu'jendo] *etc vb V* **incluir**.

incobrable [inko'ßraßle] *a* irrecoverable; (*deuda*) bad.

incógnita [in'koɣnita] *nf* (*fig*) mystery.

incógnito [in'koɣnito]: **de** ~ *ad* incognito.

incoherencia [inkoe'renθja] *nf* incoherence; (*falta de conexión*) disconnectedness.

incoherente [inkoe'rente] *a* incoherent.

incoloro, a [inko'loro, a] *a* colourless.

incólume [in'kolume] *a* safe; (*indemne*) unhurt, unharmed.

incombustible [inkombus'tißle] *a* (*gen*) fire-resistant; (*telas*) fireproof.

incomestible [inkomes'tißle] *a* inedible.

incomodar [inkomo'ðar] *vt* to inconvenience; (*molestar*) to bother, trouble; (*fastidiar*) to annoy; ~**se** *vr* to put o.s. out; (*fastidiarse*) to get annoyed; **no se incomode** don't bother.

incomodidad [inkomoði'ðað] *nf* inconvenience; (*fastidio, enojo*) annoyance; (*de vivienda*) discomfort.

incómodo, a [in'komoðo, a] *a* (*inconfortable*) uncomfortable; (*molesto*) annoying; (*inconveniente*) inconvenient; **sentirse** ~ to feel ill at ease.

incomparable [inkompa'raßle] *a* incomparable.

incomparecimiento [inkompareci'mjento] *nm* (*JUR etc*) failure to appear.

incompatible [inkompa'tißle] *a* incompatible.

incompetencia [inkompe'tenθja] *nf* incompetence.

incompetente [inkompe'tente] *a* incompetent.

incompleto, a [inkom'pleto, a] *a* incomplete, unfinished.

incomprensible [inkompren'sißle] *a* incomprehensible.

incomunicado, a [inkomuni'kaðo, a] *a* (*aislado*) cut off, isolated; (*confinado*) in solitary confinement.

incomunicar [inkomuni'kar] *vt* (*gen*) to cut off; (*preso*) to put into solitary confinement; ~**se** *vr* (*fam*) to go into one's shell.

incomunique [inkomu'nike] *etc vb V* **incomunicar**.

inconcebible [inkonθe'ßißle] *a* inconceivable.

inconcluso, a [inkon'kluso, a] *a* (*inacabado*) unfinished.

inconcuso, a [inkon'kuso, a] *a* indisputable, undeniable.

incondicional [inkondiθjo'nal] *a* unconditional; (*apoyo*) wholehearted; (*partidario*) staunch.

inconexo, a [inko'nekso, a] *a* unconnected; (*desunido*) disconnected; (*incoherente*) incoherent.

inconfeso, a [inkon'feso, a] *a* unconfessed; **un homosexual** ~ a closet homosexual.

inconfundible [inkonfun'dißle] *a* unmistakable.

incongruente [inkon'grwente] *a* incongruous.

inconmensurable [inkonmensu'raßle] *a* immeasurable, vast.

inconsciencia [inkons'θjenθja] *nf* unconsciousness; (*fig*) thoughtlessness.

inconsciente [inkons'θjente] *a* unconscious; thoughtless; (*ignorante*) unaware; (*involuntario*) unwitting.

inconsecuencia [inkonse'kwenθja] *nf* inconsistency.

inconsecuente [inkonse'kwente] *a* inconsistent.

inconsiderado, a [inkonsiðe'raðo, a] *a* inconsiderate.

inconsistente [inkonsis'tente] *a* inconsistent; (*CULIN*) lumpy; (*endeble*) weak; (*tela*) flimsy.

inconstancia [inkons'tanθja] *nf* inconstancy; (*de tiempo*) changeability; (*capricho*) fickleness.

inconstante [inkons'tante] *a* inconstant; changeable; fickle.

incontable [inkon'taßle] *a* countless, innumerable.

incontestable [inkontes'taßle] *a* unanswerable; (*innegable*) undeniable.

incontinencia [inkonti'nenθja] *nf* incontinence.

incontrolado, a [inkontro'laðo, a] *a* uncontrolled.

incontrovertible [inkontroßer'tißle] *a* undeniable, incontrovertible.

inconveniencia [inkombe'njenθja] *nf* unsuitability, inappropriateness; (*descortesía*) impoliteness.

inconveniente [inkombe'njente] *a* unsuitable; impolite ♦ *nm* obstacle; (*desventaja*) disadvantage; **el ~ es que ...** the trouble is that ...; **no hay ~ en** *o* **para hacer eso** there is no objection to doing that; **no tengo ~** I don't mind.

incorporación [inkorpora'θjon] *nf* incorporation; (*fig*) inclusion.

incorporado, a [inkorpo'raðo, a] *a* (*TEC*) built-in.

incorporar [inkorpo'rar] *vt* to incorporate; (*abarcar*) to embody; (*CULIN*) to mix; **~se** *vr* to sit up; **~se a** to join.

incorrección [inkorrek'θjon] *nf* incorrectness, inaccuracy; (*descortesía*) bad-mannered behaviour.

incorrecto, a [inko'rrekto, a] *a* incorrect, wrong; (*comportamiento*) bad-mannered.

incorregible [inkorre'xiβle] *a* incorrigible.

incorruptible [inkorrup'tiβle] *a* incorruptible.

incorrupto, a [inko'rrupto, a] *a* uncorrupted; (*fig*) pure.

incredulidad [inkreðuli'ðað] *nf* incredulity; (*escepticismo*) scepticism.

incrédulo, a [in'kreðulo, a] *a* incredulous, unbelieving; sceptical.

increíble [inkre'iβle] *a* incredible.

incrementar [inkremen'tar] *vt* (*aumentar*) to increase; (*alzar*) to raise; **~se** *vr* to increase.

incremento [inkre'mento] *nm* increment; (*aumento*) rise, increase; **~ de precio** rise in price.

increpar [inkre'par] *vt* to reprimand.

incriminar [inkrimi'nar] *vt* (*JUR*) to incriminate.

incruento, a [in'krwento, a] *a* bloodless.

incrustar [inkrus'tar] *vt* to incrust; (*piedras: en joya*) to inlay; (*fig*) to graft; (*TEC*) to set.

incubar [inku'βar] *vt* to incubate; (*fig*) to hatch.

incuestionable [inkwestjo'naβle] *a* unchallengeable.

inculcar [inkul'kar] *vt* to inculcate.

inculpar [inkul'par] *vt*: **~ de** (*acusar*) to accuse of; (*achacar, atribuir*) to charge with, blame for.

inculque [in'kulke] *etc vb V* **inculcar**.

inculto, a [in'kulto, a] *a* (*persona*) uneducated, uncultured; (*fig: grosero*) uncouth ♦ *nm/f* ignoramus.

incumbencia [inkum'benθja] *nf* obligation; **no es de mi ~** it is not my field.

incumbir [inkum'bir] *vi*: **~ a** to be incumbent upon; **no me incumbe a mí** it is

no concern of mine.

incumplimiento [inkumpli'mjento] *nm* non-fulfilment; (*COM*) repudiation; **~ de contrato** breach of contract; **por ~** by default.

incurrir [inku'rrir] *vi*: **~ en** to incur; (*crimen*) to commit; **~ en un error** to make a mistake.

indagación [indaɣa'θjon] *nf* investigation; (*búsqueda*) search; (*JUR*) inquest.

indagar [inda'ɣar] *vt* to investigate; to search; (*averiguar*) to ascertain.

indague [in'daɣe] *etc vb V* **indagar**.

indebido, a [inde'βiðo, a] *a* undue; (*dicho*) improper.

indecente [inde'θente] *a* indecent, improper; (*lascivo*) obscene.

indecible [inde'θiβle] *a* unspeakable; (*indescriptible*) indescribable.

indeciso, a [inde'θiso, a] *a* (*por decidir*) undecided; (*vacilante*) hesitant.

indefenso, a [inde'fenso, a] *a* defenceless.

indefinido, a [indefi'niðo, a] *a* indefinite; (*vago*) vague, undefined.

indeleble [inde'leβle] *a* indelible.

indemne [in'demne] *a* (*objeto*) undamaged; (*persona*) unharmed, unhurt.

indemnice [indem'niθe] *etc vb V* **indemnizar**.

indemnización [indemniθa'θjon] *nf* (*acto*) indemnification; (*suma*) indemnity; **~ de cese** redundancy payment; **~ de despido** severance pay; **doble ~** double indemnity.

indemnizar [indemni'θar] *vt* to indemnify; (*compensar*) to compensate.

independencia [indepen'denθja] *nf* independence.

independice [indepen'diθe] *etc vb V* **independizar**.

independiente [indepen'djente] *a* (*libre*) independent; (*autónomo*) self-sufficient; (*INFORM*) stand-alone.

independizar [independi'θar] *vt* to make independent; **~se** *vr* to become independent.

indescifrable [indesθi'fraβle] *a* (*MIL: código*) indecipherable; (*fig: misterio*) impenetrable.

indeterminado, a [indetermi'naðo, a] *a* (*tb LING*) indefinite; (*desconocido*) indeterminate.

India ['indja] *nf*: **la ~** India.

indiano, a [in'djano, a] *a* (Spanish-)American ♦ *nm Spaniard who has made good in America*.

indicación [indika'θjon] *nf* indication; (*dato*) piece of information; (*señal*) sign; (*sugerencia*) suggestion, hint; **indicaciones** *nfpl* (*COM*) instructions.

indicado, a [indi'kaðo, a] *a* (*apto*) right, appropriate.

indicador [indika'ðor] *nm* indicator; (*TEC*)

gauge, meter; (*aguja*) hand, pointer; (*de carretera*) roadsign; ~ **de encendido** (*INFORM*) power-on indicator.

indicar [indi'kar] *vt* (*mostrar*) to indicate, show; (*suj: termómetro etc*) to read, register; (*señalar*) to point to.

indicativo, a [indika'tißo, a] *a* indicative ♦ *nm* (*RADIO*) call sign; ~ **de nacionalidad** (*AUTO*) national identification plate.

índice ['indiθe] *nm* index; (*catálogo*) catalogue; (*ANAT*) index finger, forefinger; ~ **del coste de (la) vida** cost-of-living index; ~ **de crédito** credit rating; ~ **de materias** table of contents; ~ **de natalidad** birth rate; ~ **de precios al por menor (IPM)** (*COM*) retail price index (RPI).

indicio [in'diθjo] *nm* indication, sign; (*en pesquisa etc*) clue; (*INFORM*) marker, mark.

indiferencia [indife'renθja] *nf* indifference; (*apatía*) apathy.

indiferente [indife'rente] *a* indifferent; **me es** ~ it makes no difference to me.

indígena [in'dixena] *a* indigenous, native ♦ *nm/f* native.

indigencia [indi'xenθja] *nf* poverty, need.

indigenista [indixe'nista] (*AM*) *a* pro-Indian ♦ *nm/f* (*estudiante*) student of Indian cultures; (*POL etc*) promoter of Indian cultures.

indigestar [indixes'tar] *vt* to cause indigestion to; ~**se** *vr* to get indigestion.

indigestión [indixes'tjon] *nf* indigestion.

indigesto, a [indi'xesto, a] *a* undigested; (*indigestible*) indigestible; (*fig*) turgid.

indignación [indixna'θjon] *nf* indignation.

indignante [indix'nante] *a* outrageous, infuriating.

indignar [indix'nar] *vt* to anger, make indignant; ~**se** *vr*: ~**se por** to get indignant about.

indigno, a [in'dixno, a] *a* (*despreciable*) low, contemptible; (*inmerecido*) unworthy.

indio, a ['indjo, a] *a*, *nm/f* Indian.

indique [in'dike] *etc vb* V **indicar**.

indirecto, a [indi'rekto, a] *a* indirect ♦ *nf* insinuation, innuendo; (*sugerencia*) hint.

indisciplina [indisθi'plina] *nf* (*gen*) lack of discipline; (*MIL*) insubordination.

indiscreción [indiskre'θjon] *nf* (*imprudencia*) indiscretion; (*irreflexión*) tactlessness; (*acto*) gaffe, faux pas; ..., **si no es** ~ ..., if I may say so.

indiscreto, a [indis'kreto, a] *a* indiscreet.

indisculpable [indiskul'paßle] *a* inexcusable, unforgivable.

indiscutible [indisku'tißle] *a* indisputable, unquestionable.

indispensable [indispen'saßle] *a* indispensable.

indispondré [indispon'dre] *etc vb* V **indisponer**.

indisponer [indispo'ner] *vt* to spoil, upset; (*salud*) to make ill; ~**se** *vr* to fall ill; ~**se con uno** to fall out with sb.

indisponga [indis'ponga] *etc vb* V **indisponer**.

indisposición [indisposi'θjon] *nf* indisposition; (*desgana*) unwillingness.

indispuesto, a [indis'pwesto, a] *pp de* **indisponer** ♦ *a* indisposed; **sentirse** ~ to feel unwell *o* indisposed.

indispuse [indis'puse] *etc vb* V **indisponer**.

indistinto, a [indis'tinto, a] *a* indistinct; (*vago*) vague.

individual [indißi'ðwal] *a* individual; (*habitación*) single ♦ *nm* (*DEPORTE*) singles *sg*.

individuo, a [indi'ßiðwo, a] *a* individual ♦ *nm* individual.

indocumentado, a [indokumen'taðo, a] *a* without identity papers.

Indochina [indo'tʃina] *nf* Indochina.

indoeuropeo, a [indoeuro'peo, a] *a*, *nm/f* Indo-European.

índole ['indole] *nf* (*naturaleza*) nature; (*clase*) sort, kind.

indolencia [indo'lenθja] *nf* indolence, laziness.

indoloro, a [in'doloro, a] *a* painless.

indómito, a [in'domito, a] *a* indomitable.

Indonesia [indo'nesja] *nf* Indonesia.

indonesio, a [indo'nesjo, a] *a*, *nm/f* Indonesian.

inducción [induk'θjon] *nf* (*FILOSOFÍA*, *ELEC*) induction; **por** ~ by induction.

inducir [indu'θir] *vt* to induce; (*inferir*) to infer; (*persuadir*) to persuade; ~ **a uno en el error** to mislead sb.

indudable [indu'ðaßle] *a* undoubted; (*incuestionable*) unquestionable; **es** ~ **que** ... there is no doubt that ... .

indulgencia [indul'xenθja] *nf* indulgence; (*JUR etc*) leniency; **proceder sin** ~ **contra** to proceed ruthlessly against.

indultar [indul'tar] *vt* (*perdonar*) to pardon, reprieve; (*librar de pago*) to exempt.

indulto [in'dulto] *nm* pardon; exemption.

indumentaria [indumen'tarja] *nf* (*ropa*) clothing, dress.

industria [in'dustrja] *nf* industry; (*habilidad*) skill; ~ **agropecuaria** farming and fishing; ~ **pesada** heavy industry; ~ **petrolífera** oil industry.

industrial [indus'trjal] *a* industrial ♦ *nm* industrialist.

INE ['ine] *nm abr* (*Esp*) = *Instituto Nacional de Estadística*.

inédito, a [i'neðito, a] *a* (*libro*) unpublished; (*nuevo*) unheard-of.

inefable [ine'faßle] *a* ineffable, indescribable.

ineficacia [inefi'kaθja] *nf* (*de medida*) ineffectiveness; (*de proceso*) inefficiency.

ineficaz [inefi'kaθ] *a* (*inútil*) ineffective; (*ineficiente*) inefficient.

ineludible [inelu'ðiβle] *a* inescapable, unavoidable.

INEN ['inen] *nm abr* (*México*) = *Instituto Nacional de Energía Nuclear*.

inenarrable [inena'rraβle] *a* inexpressible.

ineptitud [inepti'tuð] *nf* ineptitude, incompetence.

inepto, a [i'nepto, a] *a* inept, incompetent.

inequívoco, a [ine'kiβoko, a] *a* unequivocal; (*inconfundible*) unmistakable.

inercia [i'nerθja] *nf* inertia; (*pasividad*) passivity.

inerme [i'nerme] *a* (*sin armas*) unarmed; (*indefenso*) defenceless.

inerte [i'nerte] *a* inert; (*inmóvil*) motionless.

inesperado, a [inespe'raðo, a] *a* unexpected, unforeseen.

inestable [ines'taβle] *a* unstable.

inevitable [ineβi'taβle] *a* inevitable.

inexactitud [ineksakti'tuð] *nf* inaccuracy.

inexacto, a [inek'sakto, a] *a* inaccurate; (*falso*) untrue.

inexistente [ineksis'tente] *a* non-existent.

inexperiencia [inekspe'rjenθja] *nf* inexperience, lack of experience.

inexperto, a [ineks'perto, a] *a* (*novato*) inexperienced.

inexplicable [inekspli'kaβle] *a* inexplicable.

inexpresable [inekspre'saβle] *a* inexpressible.

inexpresivo, a [inekspre'siβo, a] *a* inexpressive; (*ojos*) dull; (*cara*) wooden.

inexpugnable [inekspuɣ'naβle] *a* (*MIL*) impregnable; (*fig*) firm.

infalible [infa'liβle] *a* infallible; (*indefectible*) certain, sure; (*plan*) foolproof.

infame [in'fame] *a* infamous.

infamia [in'famja] *nf* infamy; (*deshonra*) disgrace.

infancia [in'fanθja] *nf* infancy, childhood; **jardín de la ~** nursery school.

infanta [in'fanta] *nf* (*hija del rey*) infanta princess.

infante [in'fante] *nm* (*hijo del rey*) infante, prince.

infantería [infante'ria] *nf* infantry.

infantil [infan'til] *a* child's, children's; (*pueril, aniñado*) infantile; (*cándido*) childlike.

infarto [in'farto] *nm* (*tb*: **~ de miocardio**) heart attack.

infatigable [infati'ɣaβle] *a* tireless, untiring.

infección [infek'θjon] *nf* infection.

infeccioso, a [infek'θjoso, a] *a* infectious.

infectar [infek'tar] *vt* to infect; **~se** *vr*: **~se (de)** (*tb fig*) to become infected (with).

infecundidad [infekundi'ðað] *nf* (*de tierra*) infertility, barrenness; (*de mujer*) sterility.

infecundo, a [infe'kundo, a] *a* infertile, barren; sterile.

infeliz [infe'liθ] *a* (*desgraciado*) unhappy, wretched; (*inocente*) gullible ♦ *nm/f* (*desgraciado*) wretch; (*inocentón*) simpleton.

inferior [infe'rjor] *a* inferior; (*situación*, *MAT*) lower ♦ *nm/f* inferior, subordinate; **cualquier número ~ a 9** any number less than o under o below 9; **una cantidad ~** a lesser quantity.

inferir [infe'rir] *vt* (*deducir*) to infer, deduce; (*causar*) to cause.

infértil [in'fertil] *a* infertile.

infestar [infes'tar] *vt* to infest.

infidelidad [infiðeli'ðað] *nf* (*gen*) infidelity, unfaithfulness.

infiel [in'fjel] *a* unfaithful, disloyal; (*falso*) inaccurate ♦ *nm/f* infidel, unbeliever.

infiera [in'fjera] *etc vb* V **inferir**.

infierno [in'fjerno] *nm* hell; **¡vete al ~!** go to hell; **está en el quinto ~** it's at the back of beyond.

infiltrar [infil'trar] *vt* to infiltrate; **~se** *vr* to infiltrate, filter; (*líquidos*) to percolate.

ínfimo, a ['infimo, a] *a* (*vil*) vile, mean; (*más bajo*) lowest; (*peor*) worst; (*miserable*) wretched.

infinidad [infini'ðað] *nf* infinity; (*abundancia*) great quantity; **~ de** vast numbers of; **~ de veces** countless times.

infinito, a [infi'nito, a] *a* infinite; (*fig*) boundless ♦ *ad* infinitely ♦ *nm* infinite; (*MAT*) infinity; **hasta lo ~** ad infinitum.

infiriendo [infi'rjendo] *etc vb* V **inferir**.

inflación [infla'θjon] *nf* (*hinchazón*) swelling; (*monetaria*) inflation; (*fig*) conceit.

inflacionario, a [inflaθjo'narjo, a] *a* inflationary.

inflacionismo [inflaθjo'nismo] *nm* (*ECON*) inflation.

inflacionista [inflaθjo'nista] *a* inflationary.

inflamar [infla'mar] *vt* to set on fire; (*MED*, *fig*) to inflame; **~se** *vr* to catch fire; to become inflamed.

inflar [in'flar] *vt* (*hinchar*) to inflate, blow up; (*fig*) to exaggerate; **~se** *vr* to swell (up); (*fig*) to get conceited.

inflexible [inflek'siβle] *a* inflexible; (*fig*) unbending.

infligir [infli'xir] *vt* to inflict.

inflija [in'flixa] *etc vb* V **infligir**.

influencia [in'flwenθja] *nf* influence.

influenciar [influen'θjar] *vt* to influence.

influir [influ'ir] *vt* to influence ♦ *vi* to have influence, carry weight; **~ en o sobre** to influence, affect; (*contribuir a*) to have a hand in.

influjo [in'fluxo] *nm* influence; **~ de capitales** (*ECON etc*) capital influx.

influyendo [influ'jendo] *etc vb* V **influir**.

influyente [influ'jente] *a* influential.

información [informa'θjon] *nf* information; (*noticias*) news *sg*; (*informe*) report; (*INFORM*: *datos*) data; (*JUR*) inquiry; l~ (*oficina*) Information; (*TELEC*) Directory Enquiries (*Brit*), Directory Assistance (*US*); (*mostrador*) Information Desk; **una ~ a** piece of information; **abrir una ~** (*JUR*) to begin proceedings; **~ deportiva** (*en periódico*) sports section.

informal [infor'mal] *a* (*gen*) informal.

informante [infor'mante] *nm/f* informant.

informar [infor'mar] *vt* (*gen*) to inform; (*revelar*) to reveal, make known ♦ *vi* (*JUR*) to plead; (*denunciar*) to inform; (*dar cuenta de*) to report on; **~se** *vr* to find out; **~se de** to inquire into.

informática [infor'matika] *nf* V **informático**.

informatice [informa'tiθe] *etc vb* V **informatizar**.

informático, a [infor'matiko, a] *a* computer *cpd* ♦ *nf* (*TEC*) information technology; computing; (*ESCOL*) computer science *o* studies; **~ de gestión** commercial computing.

informatización [informatiθa'θjon] *nf* computerization.

informatizar [informati'θar] *vt* to computerize.

informe [in'forme] *a* shapeless ♦ *nm* report; (*dictamen*) statement; (*MIL*) briefing; (*JUR*) plea; **~s** *nmpl* information *sg*; (*datos*) data; **~ anual** annual report; **~ del juez** summing-up.

infortunio [infor'tunjo] *nm* misfortune.

infracción [infrak'θjon] *nf* infraction, infringement; (*AUTO*) offence.

infraestructura [infraestruk'tura] *nf* infrastructure.

in fraganti [infra'ɣanti] *ad*: **pillar a uno ~** to catch sb red-handed.

infranqueable [infranke'aßle] *a* impassable; (*fig*) insurmountable.

infrarrojo, a [infra'rroxo, a] *a* infrared.

infringir [infrin'xir] *vt* to infringe, contravene.

infrinja [in'frinxa] *etc vb* V **infringir**.

infructuoso, a [infruk'twoso, a] *a* fruitless, unsuccessful.

infundado, a [infun'daðo, a] *a* groundless, unfounded.

infundir [infun'dir] *vt* to infuse, instil; **~ ánimo a uno** to encourage sb; **~ miedo a uno** to intimidate sb.

infusión [infu'sjon] *nf* infusion; **~ de manzanilla** camomile tea.

Ing. *abr* = **Ingeniero**.

ingeniar [inxe'njar] *vt* to think up, devise; **~se** *vr* to manage; **~se para** to manage to.

ingeniería [inxenje'ria] *nf* engineering; **~ de sistemas** (*INFORM*) systems engineering.

ingeniero, a [inxe'njero, a] *nm/f* engineer; **~ de sonido** sound engineer; **~ de caminos** civil engineer.

ingenio [in'xenjo] *nm* (*talento*) talent; (*agudeza*) wit; (*habilidad*) ingenuity, inventiveness; (*TEC*): **~ azucarero** sugar refinery.

ingenioso, a [inxe'njoso, a] *a* ingenious, clever; (*divertido*) witty.

ingente [in'xente] *a* huge, enormous.

ingenuidad [inxenwi'ðað] *nf* ingenuousness; (*sencillez*) simplicity.

ingenuo, a [in'xenwo, a] *a* ingenuous.

ingerir [inxe'rir] *vt* to ingest; (*tragar*) to swallow; (*consumir*) to consume.

ingiera [in'xjera] *etc*, **ingiriendo** [inxi'rjenðo] *etc vb* V **ingerir**.

Inglaterra [ingla'terra] *nf* England.

ingle ['ingle] *nf* groin.

inglés, esa [in'gles, esa] *a* English ♦ *nm/f* Englishman/woman ♦ *nm* (*LING*) English; **los ingleses** the English.

ingratitud [ingrati'tuð] *nf* ingratitude.

ingrato, a [in'grato, a] *a* ungrateful; (*tarea*) thankless.

ingravidez [ingraßi'ðeθ] *nf* weightlessness.

ingrediente [ingre'ðjente] *nm* ingredient.

ingresar [ingre'sar] *vt* (*dinero*) to deposit ♦ *vi* to come *o* go in; **~ en** (*club*) to join; (*MIL*, *ESCOL*) to enrol in; **~ en el hospital** to go into hospital.

ingreso [in'greso] *nm* (*entrada*) entry; (: *en hospital etc*) admission; (*MIL*, *ESCOL*) enrolment; **~s** *nmpl* (*dinero*) income *sg*; (: *COM*) takings *pl*; **~ gravable** taxable income *sg*; **~s accesorios** fringe benefits; **~s brutos** gross receipts; **~s devengados** earned income *sg*; **~s exentos de impuestos** non-taxable income *sg*; **~s personales disponibles** disposable personal income *sg*.

inhábil [i'naßil] *a* unskilful, clumsy.

inhabitable [inaßi'taßle] *a* uninhabitable.

inhabituado, a [inaßi'twaðo, a] *a* unaccustomed.

inhalador [inala'ðor] *nm* (*MED*) inhaler.

inhalar [ina'lar] *vt* to inhale.

inherente [ine'rente] *a* inherent.

inhibición [inißi'θjon] *nf* inhibition.

inhibir [ini'ßir] *vt* to inhibit; (*REL*) to restrain; **~se** *vr* to keep out.

inhospitalario, a [inospita'larjo, a], **inhóspito, a** [i'nospito, a] *a* inhospitable.

inhumación [inuma'θjon] *nf* burial, interment.

inhumano, a [inu'mano, a] *a* inhuman.

INI ['ini] *nm abr* = **Instituto Nacional de Industria**.

inicial [ini'θjal] *a*, *nf* initial.

inicialice [iniθja'liθe] *etc vb* V **inicializar**.

inicializar [iniθjali'θar] *vt* (*INFORM*) to initialize.

iniciar [ini'θjar] *vt* (*persona*) to initiate;

(*empezar*) to begin, commence; (*conversación*) to start up; ~ **a uno en un secreto** to let sb into a secret; ~ **la sesión** (*INFORM*) to log in *o* on.

iniciativa [iniθja'tiβa] *nf* initiative; (*liderazgo*) leadership; **la ~ privada** private enterprise.

inicuo, a [i'nikwo, a] *a* iniquitous.

inigualado, a [iniɤwa'laðo, a] *a* unequalled.

ininteligible [ininteli'xiβle] *a* unintelligible.

ininterrumpido, a [ininterrum'piðo, a] *a* uninterrupted; (*proceso*) continuous; (*progreso*) steady.

injerencia [inxe'renθja] *nf* interference.

injertar [inxer'tar] *vt* to graft.

injerto [in'xerto] *nm* graft; ~ **de piel** skin graft.

injuria [in'xurja] *nf* (*agravio*, *ofensa*) offence; (*insulto*) insult; ~**s** *nfpl* abuse *sg*.

injuriar [inxu'rjar] *vt* to insult.

injurioso, a [inxu'rjoso, a] *a* offensive; insulting.

injusticia [inxus'tiθja] *nf* injustice, unfairness; **con ~** unjustly.

injusto, a [in'xusto, a] *a* unjust, unfair.

inmaculado, a [inmaku'laðo, a] *a* immaculate, spotless.

inmadurez [inmaðu'reθ] *nf* immaturity.

inmaduro, a [inma'ðuro, a] *a* immature; (*fruta*) unripe.

inmediaciones [inmeðja'θjones] *nfpl* neighbourhood *sg*, environs.

inmediatez [inmeðja'teθ] *nf* immediacy.

inmediato, a [inme'ðjato, a] *a* immediate; (*contiguo*) adjoining; (*rápido*) prompt; (*próximo*) neighbouring, next; **de ~** immediately.

inmejorable [inmexo'raβle] *a* unsurpassable; (*precio*) unbeatable.

inmemorable [inmemo'raβle], **inmemorial** [inmemo'rjal] *a* immemorial.

inmenso, a [in'menso, a] *a* immense, huge.

inmerecido, a [inmere'θiðo, a] *a* undeserved.

inmergir [inmer'xir] *vt* to immerse.

inmersión [inmer'sjon] *nf* immersion; (*buzo*) dive.

inmigración [inmiɤra'θjon] *nf* immigration.

inmigrante [inmi'ɤrante] *a*, *nm/f* immigrant.

inmiscuirse [inmisku'irse] *vr* to interfere, meddle.

inmiscuyendo [inmisku'jendo] *etc vb V* **inmiscuirse**.

inmobiliario, a [inmoβi'ljarjo, a] *a* real-estate *cpd*, property *cpd* ♦ *nf* estate agency.

inmolar [inmo'lar] *vt* to immolate, sacrifice.

inmoral [inmo'ral] *a* immoral.

inmortal [inmor'tal] *a* immortal.

inmortalice [inmorta'liθe] *etc vb V* **in-**

mortalizar.

inmortalizar [inmortali'θar] *vt* to immortalize.

inmotivado, a [inmoti'βaðo, a] *a* motiveless; (*sospecha*) groundless.

inmóvil [in'moβil] *a* immobile.

inmueble [in'mweβle] *a*: **bienes ~s** real estate *sg*, landed property *sg* ♦ *nm* property.

inmundicia [inmun'diθja] *nf* filth.

inmundo, a [in'mundo, a] *a* filthy.

inmunidad [inmuni'ðað] *nf* immunity; (*fisco*) exemption; ~ **diplomática/parlamentaria** diplomatic/parliamentary immunity.

inmutarse [inmu'tarse] *vr*: **siguió sin ~** he carried on unperturbed.

innato, a [in'nato, a] *a* innate.

innecesario, a [inneθe'sarjo, a] *a* unnecessary.

innegable [inne'ɤaβle] *a* undeniable.

innoble [in'noβle] *a* ignoble.

innocuo, a [in'nokwo, a] *a* innocuous, harmless.

innovación [innoβa'θjon] *nf* innovation.

innovador, a [innoβa'ðor, a] *a* innovatory, innovative ♦ *nm/f* innovator.

innovar [inno'βar] *vt* to introduce.

innumerable [innume'raβle], **innúmero, a** [in'numero, a] *a* countless.

inocencia [ino'θenθja] *nf* innocence.

inocentada [inoθen'taða] *nf* practical joke.

inocente [ino'θente] *a* (*ingenuo*) naive, innocent; (*inculpable*) innocent; (*sin malicia*) harmless ♦ *nm/f* simpleton; **día de los (Santos) I~s** ≈ April Fool's Day.

inocuidad [inokwi'ðað] *nf* harmlessness.

inocular [inoku'lar] *vt* to inoculate.

inocuo, a [i'nokwo, a] *a* (*sustancia*) harmless.

inodoro, a [ino'ðoro, a] *a* odourless ♦ *nm* toilet (*Brit*), lavatory (*Brit*), washroom (*US*).

inofensivo, a [inofen'siβo, a] *a* inoffensive.

inolvidable [inolβi'ðaβle] *a* unforgettable.

inoperante [inope'rante] *a* ineffective.

inopinado, a [inopi'naðo, a] *a* ineffective.

inoportuno, a [inopor'tuno, a] *a* untimely; (*molesto*) inconvenient; (*inapropiado*) inappropriate.

inoxidable [inoksi'ðaβle] *a* stainless; **acero ~** stainless steel.

inquebrantable [inkeβran'taβle] *a* unbreakable; (*fig*) unshakeable.

inquiera [in'kjera] *etc vb V* **inquirir**.

inquietante [inkje'tante] *a* worrying.

inquietar [inkje'tar] *vt* to worry, trouble; ~**se** *vr* to worry, get upset.

inquieto, a [in'kjeto, a] *a* anxious, worried; **estar ~ por** to be worried about.

inquietud [inkje'tuð] *nf* anxiety, worry.

inquilino, a [inki'lino, a] *nm/f* tenant;

(*com*) lessee.

inquina [in'kina] *nf* (*aversión*) dislike; (*rencor*) ill will; **tener ~ a uno** to have a grudge against sb.

inquiriendo [inki'rjendo] *etc vb* V **inquirir**.

inquirir [inki'rir] *vt* to enquire into, investigate.

insaciable [insa'θjaβle] *a* insatiable.

insalubre [insa'luβre] *a* unhealthy; (*condiciones*) insanitary.

INSALUD [insa'luð] *nm abr* (*Esp*) = *Instituto Nacional de la Salud*.

insano, a [in'sano, a] *a* (*loco*) insane; (*malsano*) unhealthy.

insatisfacción [insatisfak'θjon] *nf* dissatisfaction.

insatisfecho, a [insatis'fetʃo, a] *a* (*condición*) unsatisfied; (*estado de ánimo*) dissatisfied.

inscribir [inskri'βir] *vt* to inscribe; (*en lista*) to put; (*en censo*) to register; **~se** *vr* to register; (*ESCOL etc*) to enrol.

inscripción [inskrip'θjon] *nf* inscription; (*ESCOL etc*) enrolment; (*en censo*) registration.

inscrito [ins'krito] *pp de* **inscribir**.

insecticida [insekti'θiða] *nm* insecticide.

insecto [in'sekto] *nm* insect.

inseguridad [inseɣuri'ðað] *nf* insecurity.

inseguro, a [inse'ɣuro, a] *a* insecure; (*inconstante*) unsteady; (*incierto*) uncertain.

inseminación [insemina'θjon] *nf:* **~ artificial** artificial insemination (A.I.).

inseminar [insemi'nar] *vt* to inseminate, fertilize.

insensato, a [insen'sato, a] *a* foolish, stupid.

insensibilice [insensiβi'liθe] *etc vb* V **insensibilizar**.

insensibilidad [insensiβili'ðað] *nf* (*gen*) insensitivity; (*dureza de corazón*) callousness.

insensibilizar [insensiβili'θar] *vt* to desensitize; (*MED*) to anaesthetize (*Brit*), anesthetize (*US*); (*eufemismo*) (*knock out o un*)conscious.

insensible [insen'siβle] *a* (*gen*) insensitive; (*movimiento*) imperceptible; (*sin sentido*) numb.

insertar [inser'tar] *vt* to insert.

inservible [inser'βiβle] *a* useless.

insidioso, a [insi'ðjoso, a] *a* insidious.

insigne [in'siɣne] *a* distinguished; (*famoso*) notable.

insignia [in'siɣnja] *nf* (*señal distintivo*) badge; (*estandarte*) flag.

insignificante [insiɣnifi'kante] *a* insignificant.

insinuar [insi'nwar] *vt* to insinuate, imply; **~se** *vr:* **~se con uno** to ingratiate o.s. with sb.

insípido, a [in'sipiðo, a] *a* insipid.

insistencia [insis'tenθja] *nf* insistence.

insistir [insis'tir] *vi* to insist; **~ en algo** to insist on sth; (*enfatizar*) to stress sth.

insobornable [insoβor'naβle] *a* incorruptible.

insolación [insola'θjon] *nf* (*MED*) sunstroke.

insolencia [inso'lenθja] *nf* insolence.

insolente [inso'lente] *a* insolent.

insólito, a [in'solito, a] *a* unusual.

insoluble [inso'luβle] *a* insoluble.

insolvencia [insol'βenθja] *nf* insolvency.

insomne [in'somne] *a* sleepless ♦ *nm/f* insomniac.

insomnio [in'somnjo] *nm* insomnia.

insondable [inson'daβle] *a* bottomless.

insonorización [insonoriθa'θjon] *nf* soundproofing.

insonorizado, a [insonori'θaðo, a] *a* (*cuarto etc*) soundproof.

insoportable [insopor'taβle] *a* unbearable.

insoslayable [insosla'jaβle] *a* unavoidable.

insospechado, a [insospe'tʃaðo, a] *a* (*inesperado*) unexpected.

insostenible [insoste'niβle] *a* untenable.

inspección [inspek'θjon] *nf* inspection, check; **I~** inspectorate.

inspeccionar [inspekθjo'nar] *vt* (*examinar*) to inspect, examine; (*controlar*) to check; (*INFORM*) to peek.

inspector, a [inspek'tor, a] *nm/f* inspector.

inspectorado [inspekto'raðo] *nm* inspectorate.

inspiración [inspira'θjon] *nf* inspiration.

inspirador, a [inspira'ðor, a] *a* inspiring.

inspirar [inspi'rar] *vt* to inspire; (*MED*) to inhale; **~se** *vr:* **~se en** to be inspired by.

instalación [instala'θjon] *nf* (*equipo*) fittings *pl*, equipment; **~ eléctrica** wiring.

instalar [insta'lar] *vt* (*establecer*) to instal; (*erguir*) to set up, erect; **~se** *vr* to establish o.s.; (*en una vivienda*) to move into.

instancia [ins'tanθja] *nf* (*solicitud*) application; (*ruego*) request; (*JUR*) petition; **a ~ de** at the request of; **en última ~** in the last resort.

instantáneo, a [instan'taneo, a] *a* instantaneous ♦ *nf* snap(shot); **café ~** instant coffee.

instante [ins'tante] *nm* instant, moment; **en un ~** in a flash.

instar [ins'tar] *vt* to press, urge.

instaurar [instau'rar] *vt* (*establecer*) to establish, set up.

instigador, a [instiɣa'ðor, a] *nm/f* instigator; **~ de un delito** (*JUR*) accessory before the fact.

instigar [insti'ɣar] *vt* to instigate.

instigue [ins'tiɣe] *etc vb* V **instigar**.

instintivo, a [instin'tiβo, a] *a* instinctive.

instinto [ins'tinto] *nm* instinct; **por ~** instinctively.

institución [institu'θjon] *nf* institution, establishment; ~ **benéfica** charitable foundation.

instituir [institu'ir] *vt* to establish; (*fundar*) to found.

instituto [insti'tuto] *nm* (*gen*) institute; I~ **Nacional de Enseñanza** (*Esp*) ≈ comprehensive (*Brit*) o high (*US*) school; I~ **Nacional de Industria (INI)** (*Esp COM*) ≈ National Enterprise Board (*Brit*) .

institutriz [institu'triθ] *nf* governess.

instituyendo [institu'jendo] *etc vb* V **instituir**.

instrucción [instruk'θjon] *nf* instruction; (*enseñanza*) education, teaching; (*JUR*) proceedings *pl*; (*MIL*) training; (*DEPORTE*) coaching; (*conocimientos*) knowledge; (*INFORM*) statement; **instrucciones para el uso** directions for use; **instrucciones de funcionamiento** operating instructions.

instructivo, a [instruk'tiβo, a] *a* instructive.

instruir [instru'ir] *vt* (*gen*) to instruct; (*enseñar*) to teach, educate; (*JUR*: *proceso*) to prepare, draw up; ~**se** *vr* to learn, teach o.s.

instrumento [instru'mento] *nm* (*gen*, *MUS*) instrument; (*herramienta*) tool, implement; (*COM*) indenture; (*JUR*) legal document; ~ **de percusión/cuerda/viento** percussion/string(ed)/wind instrument.

instruyendo [instru'jendo] *etc vb* V **instruir**.

insubordinarse [insuβorδi'narse] *vr* to rebel.

insuficiencia [insufi'θjenθja] *nf* (*carencia*) lack; (*inadecuación*) inadequacy; ~ **cardíaca/renal** heart/kidney failure.

insuficiente [insufi'θjente] *a* (*gen*) insufficient; (*ESCOL*: *nota*) unsatisfactory.

insufrible [insu'friβle] *a* insufferable.

insular [insu'lar] *a* insular.

insulso, a [in'sulso] *a* insipid; (*fig*) dull.

insultar [insul'tar] *vt* to insult.

insulto [in'sulto] *nm* insult.

insumiso, a [insu'miso, a] *a* (*rebelde*) rebellious.

insuperable [insupe'raβle] *a* (*excelente*) unsurpassable; (*problema etc*) insurmountable.

insurgente [insur'xente] *a, nm/f* insurgent.

insurrección [insurrek'θjon] *nf* insurrection, rebellion.

insustituible [insusti'twiβle] *a* irreplaceable.

intacto, a [in'takto, a] *a* (*sin tocar*) untouched; (*entero*) intact.

intachable [inta'tʃaβle] *a* irreproachable.

integrado, a [inte'yraδo, a] *a* (*INFORM*): **circuito** ~ integrated circuit.

integral [inte'yral] *a* integral; (*completo*) complete; (*TEC*) built-in; **pan** ~ wholemeal bread.

integrante [inte'yrante] *a* integral ◆ *nm/f* member.

integrar [inte'yrar] *vt* to make up, compose; (*MAT*, *fig*) to integrate.

integridad [inteyri'δaδ] *nf* wholeness; (*carácter*, *tb INFORM*) integrity; **en su** ~ completely.

íntegro, a ['inteyro, a] *a* whole, entire; (*texto*) uncut, unabridged; (*honrado*) honest.

intelectual [intelek'twal] *a, nm/f* intellectual.

intelectualidad [intelektwali'δaδ] *nf* intelligentsia, intellectuals *pl*.

inteligencia [inteli'xenθja] *nf* intelligence; (*ingenio*) ability; ~ **artificial** artificial intelligence.

inteligente [inteli'xente] *a* intelligent.

inteligible [inteli'xiβle] *a* intelligible.

intemperancia [intempe'ranθja] *nf* excess, intemperance.

intemperie [intem'perje] *nf*: **a la** ~ outdoors, in the open air.

intempestivo, a [intempes'tiβo, a] *a* untimely.

intención [inten'θjon] *nf* (*gen*) intention, purpose; **con segundas intenciones** maliciously; **con** ~ deliberately.

intencionado, a [intenθjo'naδo, a] *a* deliberate; **bien/mal** ~ well-meaning/ill-disposed, hostile.

intendencia [inten'denθja] *nf* management, administration; (*MIL*: *tb*: **cuerpo de** ~) ≈ service corps.

intensidad [intensi'δaδ] *nf* (*gen*) intensity; (*ELEC*, *TEC*) strength; (*de recuerdo*) vividness; **llover con** ~ to rain hard.

intensificar [intensifi'kar] *vt*, **intensificarse** *vr* to intensify.

intensifique [intensi'fike] *etc vb* V **intensificar**.

intensivo, a [inten'siβo, a] *a* intensive; **curso** ~ crash course.

intenso, a [in'tenso, a] *a* intense; (*impresión*) vivid; (*sentimiento*) profound, deep.

intentar [inten'tar] *vt* (*tratar*) to try, attempt.

intento [in'tento] *nm* (*intención*) intention, purpose; (*tentativa*) attempt.

intentona [inten'tona] *nf* (*POL*) attempted coup.

interaccionar [interakθjo'nar] *vi* (*INFORM*) to interact.

interactivo, a [interak'tiβo, a] *a* (*INFORM*): **computación interactiva** interactive computing.

intercalación [interkala'θjon] *nf* (*INFORM*) merging.

intercalar [interka'lar] *vt* to insert; (*INFORM*: *archivos*, *texto*) to merge.

intercambiable [interkam'bjaßle] *a* interchangeable.

intercambio [inter'kambjo] *nm* (*canje*) exchange; (*trueque*) swap.

interceder [interθe'ðer] *vi* to intercede.

interceptar [interθep'tar] *vt* to intercept, cut off; (*AUTO*) to hold up.

interceptor [interθep'tor] *nm* interceptor; (*TEC*) trap.

intercesión [interθe'sjon] *nf* intercession.

interés [inte'res] *nm* (*gen*, *COM*) interest; (*importancia*) concern; (*parte*) share, part; (*pey*) self-interest; ~ **compuesto** compound interest; ~ **simple** simple interest; **con un** ~ **de 9 por ciento** at an interest of 9%; **dar a** ~ to lend at interest; **tener** ~ **en** (*COM*) to hold a share in; **intereses acumulados** accrued interest *sg*; **intereses por cobrar** interest receivable *sg*; **intereses creados** vested interests; **intereses por pagar** interest payable *sg*.

interesado, a [intere'saðo, a] *a* interested; (*prejuiciado*) prejudiced; (*pey*) mercenary, self-seeking ◆ *nm/f* person concerned; (*firmante*) the undersigned.

interesante [intere'sante] *a* interesting.

interesar [intere'sar] *vt* to interest, be of interest to ◆ *vi* to interest, be of interest; (*importar*) to be important; ~**se** *vr*: ~**se en** *o* **por** to take an interest in; **no me interesan los toros** bullfighting does not appeal to me.

interestatal [interesta'tal] *a* inter-state.

interface [inter'faθe], **interfase** [inter'fase] *nm* (*INFORM*) interface; ~ **hombre/máquina/por menús** man/machine/menu interface.

interferir [interfe'rir] *vt* to interfere with; (*TELEC*) to jam ◆ *vi* to interfere.

interfiera [inter'fjera] *etc*, **interfiriendo** [interfi'rjendo] *etc vb V* **interferir**.

interfono [inter'fono] *nm* intercom.

ínterin ['interin] *ad* meanwhile ◆ *nm* interim; **en el** ~ in the meantime.

interino, a [inte'rino, a] *a* temporary; (*empleado etc*) provisional ◆ *nm/f* temporary holder of a post; (*MED*) locum; (*ESCOL*) supply teacher; (*TEATRO*) stand-in.

interior [inte'rjor] *a* inner, inside; (*COM*) domestic, internal ◆ *nm* interior, inside; (*fig*) soul, mind; (*DEPORTE*) inside-forward; **Ministerio del I~** ≈ Home Office (*Brit*), Ministry of the Interior; **dije para mi** ~ I said to myself.

interjección [interxek'θjon] *nf* interjection.

interlínea [inter'linea] *nf* (*INFORM*) line feed.

interlocutor, a [interloku'tor, a] *nm/f* speaker; (*al teléfono*) person at the other end (of the line); **mi** ~ the person I was speaking to.

intermediario, a [interme'ðjarjo, a] *a* (*mediador*) mediating ◆ *nm/f* intermediary, go-between; (*mediador*) mediator.

intermedio, a [inter'meðjo, a] *a* intermediate; (*tiempo*) intervening ◆ *nm* interval; (*POL*) recess.

interminable [intermi'naßle] *a* endless, interminable.

intermitente [intermi'tente] *a* intermittent ◆ *nm* (*AUTO*) indicator.

internacional [internaθjo'nal] *a* international.

internado [inter'naðo] *nm* boarding school.

internamiento [interna'mjento] *nm* internment.

internar [inter'nar] *vt* to intern; (*en un manicomio*) to commit; ~**se** *vr* (*penetrar*) to penetrate; ~**se en** to go into *o* right inside; ~**se en un estudio** to study a subject in depth.

interno, a [in'terno, a] *a* internal, interior; (*POL etc*) domestic ◆ *nm/f* (*alumno*) boarder.

interpelación [interpela'θjon] *nf* appeal, plea.

interpelar [interpe'lar] *vt* (*rogar*) to implore; (*hablar*) to speak to; (*POL*) to ask for explanations, question formally.

interpondré [interpon'dre] *etc vb V* **interponer**.

interponer [interpo'ner] *vt* to interpose, put in; ~**se** *vr* to intervene.

interponga [inter'ponga] *etc vb V* **interponer**.

interposición [interposi'θjon] *nf* insertion.

interpretación [interpreta'θjon] *nf* interpretation; (*MUS*, *TEATRO*) performance; **mala** ~ misinterpretation.

interpretar [interpre'tar] *vt* to interpret.

intérprete [in'terprete] *nm/f* (*LING*) interpreter, translator; (*MUS*, *TEATRO*) performer, artist(e).

interpuesto [inter'pwesto], **interpuse** [inter'puse] *etc vb V* **interponer**.

interrogación [interroɣa'θjon] *nf* interrogation; (*LING*: *tb*: **signo de** ~) question mark; (*TELEC*) polling.

interrogante [interro'ɣante] *a* questioning ◆ *nm* question mark; (*fig*) question mark, query.

interrogar [interro'ɣar] *vt* to interrogate, question.

interrogatorio [interroɣa'torjo] *nm* interrogation; (*MIL*) debriefing; (*JUR*) examination.

interrogue [inte'rroɣe] *etc vb V* **interrogar**.

interrumpir [interrum'pir] *vt* to interrupt; (*vacaciones*) to cut short; (*servicio*) to cut off; (*tráfico*) to block.

interrupción [interrup'θjon] *nf* interruption.
interruptor [interrup'tor] *nm* (*ELEC*) switch.
intersección [intersek'θjon] *nf* intersection; (*AUTO*) junction.
interurbano, a [interur'βano, a] *a* intercity; (*TELEC*) long-distance.
intervalo [inter'βalo] *nm* interval; (*descanso*) break; **a ~s** at intervals, every now and then.
intervención [interßen'θjon] *nf* supervision; (*COM*) audit(ing); (*MED*) operation; (*TELEC*) tapping; (*participación*) intervention; **~ quirúrgica** surgical operation; **la política de no ~** the policy of nonintervention.
intervencionista [interßenθjo'nista] *a*: **no ~** (*COM*) laissez-faire.
intervendré [interßen'dre] *etc*, **intervenga** [inter'ßenga] *etc vb V* **intervenir**.
intervenir [interße'nir] *vt* (*controlar*) to control, supervise; (*COM*) to audit; (*MED*) to operate on ♦ *vi* (*participar*) to take part, participate; (*mediar*) to intervene.
interventor, a [interßen'tor, a] *nm/f* inspector; (*COM*) auditor.
interviniendo [interßi'njendo] *etc vb V* **intervenir**.
interviú [inter'ßju] *nf* interview.
intestino [intes'tino] *nm* intestine.
inti ['inti] *nm monetary unit of Peru*.
intimar [inti'mar] *vt* to intimate, announce; (*mandar*) to order ♦ *vi*, **~se** *vr* to become friendly.
intimidad [intimi'ðað] *nf* intimacy; (*familiaridad*) familiarity; (*vida privada*) private life; (*JUR*) privacy.
intimidar [intimi'ðar] *vt* to intimidate, scare.
íntimo, a ['intimo, a] *a* intimate; (*pensamientos*) innermost; (*vida*) personal, private; **una boda íntima** a quiet wedding.
intolerable [intole'raßle] *a* intolerable, unbearable.
intoxicación [intoksika'θjon] *nf* poisoning; **~ alimenticia** food poisoning.
intraducible [intraðu'θißle] *a* untranslatable.
intranquilice [intranki'liθe] *etc vb V* **intranquilizarse**.
intranquilizarse [intrankili'θarse] *vr* to get worried *o* anxious.
intranquilo, a [intran'kilo, a] *a* worried.
intranscendente [intransθen'dente] *a* unimportant.
intransferible [intransfe'rißle] *a* not transferable.
intransigente [intransi'xente] *a* intransigent.
intransitable [intransi'taßle] *a* impassable.
intratable [intra'taßle] *a* (*problema*) intractable; (*dificultad*) awkward; (*indivi-*

duo) unsociable.
intrepidez [intrepi'ðeθ] *nf* courage, bravery.
intrépido, a [in'trepiðo, a] *a* intrepid, fearless.
intriga [in'triɣa] *nf* intrigue; (*plan*) plot.
intrigar [intri'ɣar] *vt*, *vi* to intrigue.
intrigue [in'triɣe] *etc vb V* **intrigar**.
intrincado, a [intrin'kaðo, a] *a* intricate.
intrínseco, a [in'trinseko, a] *a* intrinsic.
introducción [introðuk'θjon] *nf* introduction; (*de libro*) foreword; (*INFORM*) input.
introducir [introðu'θir] *vt* (*gen*) to introduce; (*moneda*) to insert; (*INFORM*) to input, enter.
introduje [intro'ðuxe] *etc*, **introduzca** [intro'ðuθka] *etc vb V* **introducir**.
intromisión [intromi'sjon] *nf* interference, meddling.
introvertido, a [introßer'tiðo, a] *a*, *nm/f* introvert.
intruso, a [in'truso, a] *a* intrusive ♦ *nm/f* intruder.
intuición [intwi'θjon] *nf* intuition.
intuir [intu'ir] *vt* to know by intuition, intuit.
intuyendo [intu'jendo] *etc vb V* **intuir**.
inundación [inunda'θjon] *nf* flood(ing).
inundar [inun'dar] *vt* to flood; (*fig*) to swamp, inundate.
inusitado, a [inusi'taðo, a] *a* unusual.
inútil [i'nutil] *a* useless; (*esfuerzo*) vain, fruitless.
inutilice [inuti'liθe] *etc vb V* **inutilizar**.
inutilidad [inutili'ðað] *nf* uselessness.
inutilizar [inutili'θar] *vt* to make unusable, put out of action; (*incapacitar*) to disable; **~se** *vr* to become useless.
invadir [imba'ðir] *vt* to invade.
invalidez [imbali'ðeθ] *nf* (*MED*) disablement; (*JUR*) invalidity.
inválido, a [im'baliðo, a] *a* invalid; (*JUR*) null and void ♦ *nm/f* invalid.
invariable [imba'rjable] *a* invariable.
invasión [imba'sjon] *nf* invasion.
invasor, a [imba'sor, a] *a* invading ♦ *nm/f* invader.
invención [imben'θjon] *nf* invention.
inventar [imben'tar] *vt* to invent.
inventario [imben'tarjo] *nm* inventory; (*COM*) stocktaking.
inventiva [imben'tißa] *nf* inventiveness.
inventor, a [imben'tor, a] *nm/f* inventor.
invernadero [imberna'ðero] *nm* greenhouse.
invernal [imber'nal] *a* wintry, winter *cpd*.
inverosímil [imbero'simil] *a* implausible.
inversión [imber'sjon] *nf* (*COM*) investment; **~ de capitales** capital investment; **inversiones extranjeras** foreign investment *sg*.
inverso, a [im'berso, a] *a* inverse, opposite; **en el orden ~** in reverse order; **a la inver-**

sa inversely, the other way round.

inversor, a [imber'sor, a] *nm/f* (*COM*) investor.

invertido, a [imber'tiðo, a] *a* inverted; (*al revés*) reversed; (*homosexual*) homosexual ♦ *nm/f* homosexual.

invertir [imber'tir] *vt* (*COM*) to invest; (*volcar*) to turn upside down; (*tiempo etc*) to spend.

investigación [imbestiɣa'θjon] *nf* investigation; (*indagación*) inquiry; (*UNIV*) research; ~ **y desarrollo** (*COM*) research and development (R and D); ~ **de los medios de publicidad** media research; ~ **del mercado** market research.

investigador, a [imbestiɣa'ðor, a] *nm/f* investigator; (*UNIVERSIDAD*) research fellow.

investigar [imbesti'ɣar] *vt* to investigate; (*estudiar*) to do research into.

investigue [imbes'tiɣe] *etc vb* V **investigar**.

invicto, a [im'bikto, a] *a* unconquered.

invidente [imbi'ðente] *a* sightless ♦ *nm/f* blind person; **los ~s** the sightless.

invierno [im'bjerno] *nm* winter.

invierta [im'bjerta] *etc vb* V **invertir**.

inviolabilidad [imbjolaßili'ðað] *nf* inviolability; ~ **parlamentaria** parliamentary immunity.

invirtiendo [imbir'tjendo] *etc vb* V **invertir**.

invisible [imbi'sißle] *a* invisible; **exportaciones/importaciones ~s** invisible exports/imports.

invitado, a [imbi'taðo, a] *nm/f* guest.

invitar [imbi'tar] *vt* to invite; (*incitar*) to entice; ~ **a uno a hacer algo** to invite sb to do sth; ~ **a algo** to pay for sth; **nos invitó a cenar fuera** she took us out for dinner; **invito yo** it's on me.

invocar [imbo'kar] *vt* to invoke, call on; (*INFORM*) to call.

involucrar [imbolu'krar] *vt*: ~ **algo en un discurso** to bring something irrelevant into a discussion; ~ **a uno en algo** to involve sb in sth; ~**se** *vr* (*interesarse*) to get involved.

involuntario, a [imbolun'tarjo, a] *a* involuntary; (*ofensa etc*) unintentional.

invoque [im'boke] *etc vb* V **invocar**.

inyección [injek'θjon] *nf* injection.

inyectar [injek'tar] *vt* to inject.

IPC *nm abr* (*Esp*: = *índice de precios al consumo*) CPI.

IPM *nm abr* (= *índice de precios al por menor*) RPI.

ir [ir] *vi* to go; (*viajar*) to travel; (*ropa*) to suit; ~**se** *vr* to go away, leave; (*mano etc*) to slip; ¡**vete!** go away!; ¡**vámonos!** let's go!; ~ **caminando** to walk; ~ **en coche/bicicleta/caballo/a pie** to drive/cycle/ride/walk; ~ **de mal en peor** to go from bad to

worse; ¡**voy!** I'm coming!; ~ **de viaje** to travel, go away; **voy para viejo** I'm getting on; ~ **por/a por algo** to go for/go and get sth; ¡**qué va!** (*no diga*) you don't say!; (¡*no!*) no way!, rubbish! (*Brit*); **esto va de veras** this is serious; ¿**me va bien esto?** (*ropa*) does this suit me?; **eso no va por usted** I wasn't referring to you; **va mucho de A a B** there's a lot of difference between A and B; ¡**vamos!** come on!; **vaya susto que me has dado** what a fright you gave me; **vaya donde vaya, encontrará ...** wherever you go, you will find ... .

ira ['ira] *nf* anger, rage.

iracundo, a [ira'kundo, a] *a* irascible.

Irak [i'rak] *nm* = **Iraq**.

Irán [i'ran] *nm* Iran.

iraní [ira'ni] *a*, *nm/f* Iranian.

Iraq [i'rak] *nm* Iraq.

iraquí [ira'ki] *a*, *nm/f* Iraqui.

irguiendo [ir'ɣjendo] *etc vb* V **erguir**.

iris ['iris] *nm inv* (*arco* ~) rainbow; (*ANAT*) iris.

Irlanda [ir'landa] *nf* Ireland; ~ **del Norte** Northern Ireland, Ulster.

irlandés, esa [irlan'des, esa] *a* Irish ♦ *nm/f* Irishman/woman ♦ *nm* (*LING*) Gaelic, Irish; **los irlandeses** *npl* the Irish.

ironía [iro'nia] *nf* irony.

irónico, a [i'roniko, a] *a* ironic(al).

IRPF *nm abr* (*Esp*) = *impuesto sobre la renta de las personas físicas*.

irrazonable [irraθo'naßle] *a* unreasonable.

irreal [irre'al] *a* unreal.

irrealizable [irreali'θaßle] *a* (*gen*) unrealizable; (*meta*) unrealistic.

irrebatible [irreßa'tißle] *a* irrefutable.

irreconocible [irrekono'θißle] *a* unrecognizable.

irrecuperable [irrekupe'raßle] *a* irrecoverable, irretrievable.

irreembolsable [irreembol'saßle] *a* (*COM*) non-returnable.

irreflexión [irreflek'sjon] *nf* thoughtlessness; (*ímpetu*) rashness.

irregular [irreɣu'lar] *a* irregular; (*situación*) abnormal, anomalous; **margen izquierdo/ derecho** ~ (*texto*) ragged left/right (margin).

irremediable [irreme'ðjaßle] *a* irremediable; (*vicio*) incurable.

irresoluto, a [irreso'luto, a] *a* irresolute, hesitant; (*sin resolver*) unresolved.

irrespetuoso, a [irrespe'twoso, a] *a* disrespectful.

irresponsable [irrespon'saßle] *a* irresponsible.

irreverente [irreße'rente] *a* disrespectful.

irrigar [irri'ɣar] *vt* to irrigate.

irrigue [i'rriɣe] *etc vb* V **irrigar**.

irrisible [irri'sißle] *a* laughable; (*precio*)

absurdly low.

irrisorio, a [irri'sorjo, a] *a* derisory, ridiculous; *(precio)* bargain *cpd*.

irritar [irri'tar] *vt* to irritate, annoy; ~**se** *vr* to get angry, lose one's temper.

irrompible [irrom'piβle] *a* unbreakable.

irrumpir [irrum'pir] *vi*: ~ **en** to burst *o* rush into.

irrupción [irrup'θjon] *nf* irruption; *(invasión)* invasion.

IRTP *nm abr (Esp*: = *impuesto sobre el rendimiento del trabajo personal)* ≈ PAYE.

isla ['isla] *nf (GEO)* island; **I~s Británicas** British Isles; **I~s Filipinas/Malvinas/Canarias** Philippines/Falklands/Canaries.

Islam [is'lam] *nm* Islam.

islámico, a [is'lamiko, a] *a* Islamic.

islandés, esa [islan'des, esa] *a* Icelandic ♦ *nm/f* Icelander ♦ *nm (LING)* Icelandic.

Islandia [is'landja] *nf* Iceland.

isleño, a [is'leɲo, a] *a* island *cpd* ♦ *nm/f* islander.

islote [is'lote] *nm* small island.

isótopo [i'sotopo] *nm* isotope.

Israel [isra'el] *nm* Israel.

israelí [israe'li] *a*, *nm/f* Israeli.

istmo ['istmo] *nm* isthmus; **el I~ de Panamá** the Isthmus of Panama.

Italia [i'talja] *nf* Italy.

italiano, a [ita'ljano, a] *a*, *nm/f* Italian ♦ *nm (LING)* Italian.

italica [i'talika] *nf (INFORM)*: **en ~** in italics.

itinerante [itine'rante] *a* travelling; *(embajador)* roving.

itinerario [itine'rarjo] *nm* itinerary, route.

IVA ['iβa] *nm abr (Esp COM*: = *Impuesto sobre el Valor Añadido)* VAT.

IVP *nm abr* = *Instituto Venezolano de Petroquímica*.

izar [i'θar] *vt* to hoist.

izda, izq.ª *abr* = **izquierda**.

izdo, izq, izq.º *abr* = **izquierdo**.

izquierda [iθ'kjerða] *nf V* **izquierdo**.

izquierdista [iθkjer'ðista] *a* leftist, left-wing ♦ *nm/f* left-winger, leftist.

izquierdo, a [iθ'kjerðo, a] *a* left ♦ *nf* left; *(POL)* left (wing); **a la ~** on the left; **es un cero a la ~** *(fam)* he is a nonentity; **conducción por la ~** left-hand drive.

J

J, j ['xota] *nf (letra)* J, j; **J de José** J for Jack *(Brit) o* Jig *(US)*.

jabalí [xaβa'li] *nm* wild boar.

jabalina [xaβa'lina] *nf* javelin.

jabato, a [xa'βato, a] *a* brave, bold ♦ *nm* young wild boar.

jabón [xa'βon] *nm* soap; *(fam: adulación)* flattery; ~ **de afeitar** shaving soap; ~ **de tocador** toilet soap; **dar ~ a uno** to soft-soap sb.

jabonar [xaβo'nar] *vt* to soap.

jaca ['xaka] *nf* pony.

jacinto [xa'θinto] *nm* hyacinth.

jactancia [xak'tanθja] *nf* boasting, boastfulness.

jactarse [xak'tarse] *vr*: ~ **(de)** to boast *o* brag (about *o* of).

jadear [xaðe'ar] *vi* to pant, gasp for breath.

jadeo [xa'ðeo] *nm* panting, gasping.

jaguar [xa'vwar] *nm* jaguar.

jalar [xa'lar] *vt (AM)* to pull.

jalbegue [xal'βeve] *nm (pintura)* whitewash.

jalea [xa'lea] *nf* jelly.

jaleo [xa'leo] *nm* racket, uproar; **armar un ~** to kick up a racket.

jalón [xa'lon] *nm (AM)* tug.

jalonar [xalo'nar] *vt* to stake out; *(fig)* to mark.

Jamaica [xa'maika] *nf* Jamaica.

jamaicano, a [xamai'kano, a] *a*, *nm/f* Jamaican.

jamás [xa'mas] *ad* never, not ... ever; *(interrogativo)* ever; **¿~ se vio tal cosa?** did you ever see such a thing?

jamón [xa'mon] *nm* ham; ~ **dulce/serrano** boiled/cured ham.

Japón [xa'pon] *nm*: **el ~** Japan.

japonés, esa [xapo'nes, esa] *a*, *nm/f* Japanese ♦ *nm (LING)* Japanese.

jaque ['xake] *nm*: ~ **mate** checkmate.

jaqueca [xa'keka] *nf* (very bad) headache, migraine.

jarabe [xa'raβe] *nm* syrup; ~ **para la tos** cough syrup *o* mixture.

jarana [xa'rana] *nf (juerga)* spree *(fam)*; **andar/ir de ~** to be/go on a spree.

jarcia ['xarθja] *nf (NAUT)* ropes *pl*, rigging.

jardín [xar'ðin] *nm* garden; ~ **botánico** botanical garden; ~ **de (la) infancia** *(Esp) o* **de niños** *(AM) o* **infantil** *(AM)* kindergarten, nursery school.

jardinería [xarðine'ria] *nf* gardening.

jardinero, a [xarði'nero, a] *nm/f* gardener.

jarra ['xarra] *nf* jar; *(jarro)* jug; *(de leche)* churn; *(de cerveza)* mug; **de o en ~s** with arms akimbo.

jarro ['xarro] *nm* jug.

jarrón [xa'rron] *nm* vase; *(ARQUEOLOGÍA)* urn.

jaspeado, a [xaspe'ado, a] *a* mottled, speckled.

jaula ['xaula] *nf* cage; *(embalaje)* crate.

jauría [xau'ria] *nf* pack of hounds.

jazmín [xaθ'min] *nm* jasmine.

J. C. *abr* = **Jesucristo**.

JD *nf abr* (*Esp com*) = *Junta Democrática*.

jefa ['xefa] *nf ver* **jefe**.

jefatura [xefa'tura] *nf* (*liderato*) leadership; (*sede*) central office; **J~ de la aviación civil** ≈ Civil Aviation Authority; **~ de policía** police headquarters *sg*.

jefazo [xe'faθo] *nm* bigwig.

jefe, a ['xefe, a] *nm/f* (*gen*) chief, head; (*patrón*) boss; (*POL*) leader; (*COM*) manager(ess); **~ de camareros** head waiter; **~ de cocina** chef; **~ ejecutivo** (*COM*) chief executive; **~ de estación** stationmaster; **~ de estado** head of state; **~ de oficina** (*COM*) office manager; **~ de producción** (*COM*) production manager; **~ supremo** commander-in-chief; **ser el ~** (*fig*) to be the boss.

JEN [xen] *nf abr Esp*: = *Junta de Energía Nuclear*.

jengibre [xen'xiβre] *nm* ginger.

jeque ['xeke] *nm* sheik(h).

jerarquía [xerar'kia] *nf* (*orden*) hierarchy; (*rango*) rank.

jerárquico, a [xe'rarkiko, a] *a* hierarchic(al).

jerez [xe'reθ] *nm* sherry; **J~ de la Frontera** Jerez.

jerezano, a [xere'θano, a] *a* of *o* from Jerez ◆ *nm/f* native *o* inhabitant of Jerez.

jerga ['xerɣa] *nf* (*tela*) coarse cloth; (*lenguaje*) jargon; **~ informática** computer jargon.

jerigonza [xeri'xonθa] *nf* (*jerga*) jargon, slang; (*galimatías*) nonsense, gibberish.

jeringa [xe'ringa] *nf* syringe; (*AM*) annoyance, bother; **~ de engrase** grease gun.

jeringar [xerin'gar] *vt* (*AM*) to annoy, bother.

jeringue [xe'ringe] *etc vb* V **jeringar**.

jeringuilla [xerin'guiʎa] *nf* hypodermic (syringe).

jeroglífico [xero'ɣlifiko] *nm* hieroglyphic.

jersé [xer'se] *pl* **jersés**, **jersey** [xer'sei], *pl* **jerseys** *nm* jersey, pullover, jumper.

Jerusalén [xerusa'len] *n* Jerusalem.

Jesucristo [xesu'kristo] *nm* Jesus Christ.

jesuita [xe'swita] *a*, *nm* Jesuit.

Jesús [xe'sus] *nm* Jesus; **¡~!** good heavens!; (*al estornudar*) bless you!

jeta ['xeta] *nf* (*ZOOL*) snout; (*fam: cara*) mug; **¡que ~ tienes!** (*fam: insolencia*) you've got a nerve!

jícara ['xikara] *nf* small cup.

jiennense [xjen'nense] *a* of *o* from Jaén ◆ *nm/f* native *o* inhabitant of Jaén.

jilguero [xil'ɣero] *nm* goldfinch.

jinete, a [xi'nete, a] *nm/f* horseman/woman.

jipijapa [xipi'xapa] *nm* (*AM*) straw hat.

jira ['xira] *nf* (*de tela*) strip; (*excursión*) picnic.

jirafa [xi'rafa] *nf* giraffe.

jirón [xi'ron] *nm* rag, shred.

JJ.OO. *nmpl abr* = **Juegos Olímpicos**.

jocosidad [xokosi'ðað] *nf* humour; (*chiste*) joke.

jocoso, a [xo'koso, a] *a* humorous, jocular.

joder [xo'ðer] (*fam!*) *vt* to fuck (*!*), screw (*!*); **~se** *vr* (*fracasar*) to fail; **¡~!** damn it!; **se jodió todo** everything was ruined.

jodido, a [xo'ðiðo, a] *a* (*fam!*: *difícil*) awkward; **estoy ~** I'm knackered *o* buggered (*!*).

jofaina [xo'faina] *nf* washbasin.

jolgorio [xol'ɣorjo] *nm* (*juerga*) fun, revelry.

Jordania [xor'ðanja] *nf* Jordan.

jornada [xor'naða] *nf* (*viaje de un día*) day's journey; (*camino o viaje entero*) journey; (*día de trabajo*) working day; **~ de 8 horas** 8-hour day; **(trabajar a) ~ partida** (to work a) split shift.

jornal [xor'nal] *nm* (day's) wage.

jornalero [xorna'lero] *nm* (day) labourer.

joroba [xo'roβa] *nf* hump.

jorobado, a [xoro'βaðo, a] *a* hunchbacked ◆ *nm/f* hunchback.

jorobar [xoro'βar] *vt* to annoy, pester, bother; **~se** *vr* to get cross; **¡hay que ~se!** to hell with it!; **esto me joroba** I'm fed up with this!

jota ['xota] *nf* letter J; (*danza*) Aragonese dance; (*fam*) jot, iota; **no saber ~** to have no idea.

joven ['xoβen] *a* young ◆ *nm* young man, youth ◆ *nf* young woman, girl.

jovencito, a [xoβen'θito, a] *nm/f* youngster.

jovial [xo'βjal] *a* cheerful, jolly.

jovialidad [xoβjali'ðað] *nf* cheerfulness, jolliness.

joya ['xoja] *nf* jewel, gem; (*fig: persona*) gem; **~s de fantasía** imitation jewellery *sg*.

joyería [xoje'ria] *nf* (*joyas*) jewellery; (*tienda*) jeweller's (shop).

joyero [xo'jero] *nm* (*persona*) jeweller; (*caja*) jewel case.

JSP *nf abr* (*COM*) = *Junta Superior de Precios*.

juanete [xwa'nete] *nm* (*del pie*) bunion.

jubilación [xuβila'θjon] *nf* (*retiro*) retirement.

jubilado, a [xuβi'laðo, a] *a* retired ◆ *nm/f* retired person, pensioner (*Brit*), senior citizen (*esp US*).

jubilar [xuβi'lar] *vt* to pension off, retire; (*fam*) to discard; **~se** *vr* to retire.

jubileo [xuβi'leo] *nm* jubilee.

júbilo ['xuβilo] *nm* joy, rejoicing.

jubiloso, a [xuβi'loso, a] *a* jubilant.

judaísmo [xuða'ismo] *nm* Judaism.
judía [xu'ðia] *nf* V **judío**.
judicatura [xuðika'tura] *nf* (*cargo de juez*) office of judge; (*cuerpo de jueces*) judiciary.
judicial [xuði'θjal] *a* judicial.
judío, a [xu'ðio, a] *a* Jewish ♦ *nm* Jew ♦ *nf* Jewess, Jewish woman; (*CULIN*) bean; **judía blanca** haricot bean; **judía verde** French *o* string bean.
juego ['xweɣo] *etc vb* V **jugar** ♦ *nm* (*gen*) play; (*pasatiempo, partido*) game; (*en casino*) gambling; (*deporte*) sport; (*conjunto*) set; (*herramientas*) kit; ~ **de azar** game of chance; ~ **de café** coffee set; ~ **de caracteres** (*INFORM*) font; ~ **limpio/sucio** fair/foul *o* dirty play; **J~s Olímpicos** Olympic Games; ~ **de programas** (*INFORM*) suite of programs; **fuera de** ~ (*DEPORTE*: *persona*) offside; (: *pelota*) out of play; **por** ~ in fun, for fun.
juegue ['xweɣe] *etc vb* V **jugar**.
juerga ['xwerɣa] *nf* binge; (*fiesta*) party; **ir de** ~ to go out on a binge.
juerguista [xwer'ɣista] *nm/f* reveller.
jueves ['xweßes] *nm inv* Thursday.
juez [xweθ] *nm/f* (*f tb*: **jueza**) judge; (*TENIS*) umpire; ~ **de línea** linesman; ~ **de paz** justice of the peace; ~ **de salida** starter.
jugada [xu'ɣaða] *nf* play; **buena** ~ good move (*o* shot *o* stroke) *etc*.
jugador, a [xuɣa'ðor, a] *nm/f* player; (*en casino*) gambler.
jugar [xu'ɣar] *vt* to play; (*en casino*) to gamble; (*apostar*) to bet ♦ *vi* to play; to gamble; (*COM*) to speculate; ~**se** *vr* to gamble (away); ~**se el todo por el todo** to stake one's all, go for bust; **¿quién juega?** whose move is it?; **¡me la han jugado!** (*fam*) I've been had!
jugarreta [xuɣa'rreta] *nf* (*mala jugada*) bad move; (*trampa*) dirty trick; **hacer una** ~ **a uno** to play a dirty trick on sb.
juglar [xu'ɣlar] *nm* minstrel.
jugo ['xuɣo] *nm* (*BOT, de fruta*) juice; (*fig*) essence, substance; ~ **de naranja** (*esp AM*) orange juice.
jugoso, a [xu'ɣoso, a] *a* juicy; (*fig*) substantial, important.
jugue [xu'ɣe], **juguemos** [xu'ɣemos] *etc vb* V **jugar**.
juguete [xu'ɣete] *nm* toy.
juguetear [xuɣete'ar] *vi* to play.
juguetería [xuɣete'ria] *nf* toyshop.
juguetón, ona [xuɣe'ton, ona] *a* playful.
juicio ['xwiθjo] *nm* judgement; (*sana razón*) sanity, reason; (*opinión*) opinion; (*JUR*: *proceso*) trial; **estar fuera de** ~ to be out of one's mind; **a mi** ~ in my opinion.
juicioso, a [xwi'θjoso, a] *a* wise, sensible.
JUJEM [xu'xem] *nf abr* (*Esp MIL*) = *Junta*

de Jefes del Estado Mayor.
jul. *abr* (= *julio*) Jul.
julio ['xuljo] *nm* July.
jumento, a [xu'mento, a] *nm/f* donkey.
jun. *abr* (= *junio*) Jun.
junco ['xunko] *nm* rush, reed.
jungla ['xungla] *nf* jungle.
junio ['xunjo] *nm* June.
junta ['xunta] *nf* V **junto**.
juntar [xun'tar] *vt* to join, unite; (*maquinaria*) to assemble, put together; (*dinero*) to collect; ~**se** *vr* to join, meet; (*reunirse*: *personas*) to meet, assemble; (*arrimarse*) to approach, draw closer; ~**se con uno** to join sb.
junto, a ['xunto, a] *a* joined; (*unido*) united; (*anexo*) near, close; (*contiguo, próximo*) next, adjacent ♦ *nf* (*asamblea*) meeting, assembly; (*comité, consejo*) board, council, committee; (*MIL, POL*) junta; (*articulación*) joint ♦ *ad*: **todo** ~ all at once ♦ *prep*: ~ **a** near (to), next to; ~**s** together; **junta constitutiva** (*COM*) statutory meeting; **junta directiva** (*COM*) board of management; **junta general extraordinaria** (*COM*) extraordinary general meeting.
juntura [xun'tura] *nf* (*punto de unión*) join, junction; (*articulación*) joint.
jura ['xura] *nf* oath, pledge; ~ **de bandera** (ceremony of taking the) oath of allegiance.
jurado [xu'raðo] *nm* (*JUR*: *individuo*) juror; (: *grupo*) jury; (*de concurso*: *grupo*) panel (of judges); (: *individuo*) member of a panel.
juramentar [xuramen'tar] *vt* to swear in, administer the oath to; ~**se** *vr* to be sworn in, take the oath.
juramento [xura'mento] *nm* oath; (*maldición*) curse, swear; **bajo** ~ on oath; **prestar** ~ to take the oath; **tomar** ~ **a** to swear in, administer the oath to.
jurar [xu'rar] *vt, vi* to swear; ~ **en falso** to commit perjury; **jurárselas a uno** to have it in for sb.
jurídico, a [xu'riðiko, a] *a* legal, juridical.
jurisdicción [xurisðik'θjon] *nf* (*poder, autoridad*) jurisdiction; (*territorio*) district.
jurisprudencia [xurispru'ðenθja] *nf* jurisprudence.
jurista [xu'rista] *nm/f* jurist.
justamente [xusta'mente] *ad* justly, fairly; (*precisamente*) just, exactly.
justicia [xus'tiθja] *nf* justice; (*equidad*) fairness, justice; **de** ~ deservedly.
justiciero, a [xusti'θjero, a] *a* just, righteous.
justificable [xustifi'kaßle] *a* justifiable.
justificación [xustifika'θjon] *nf* justification; ~ **automática** (*INFORM*) automatic justification.

justificado, a [xustifi'kaðo, a] *a* (*TIP*): **(no)**
~ (un)justified.
justificante [xustifi'kante] *nm* voucher.
justificar [xustifi'kar] *vt* (*tb TIP*) to justify;
(*probar*) to verify.
justifique [xusti'fike] *etc vb* V **justificar**.
justo, a ['xusto, a] *a* (*equitativo*) just, fair,
right; (*preciso*) exact, correct; (*ajustado*)
tight ♦ *ad* (*precisamente*) exactly, precisely; (*apenas a tiempo*) just in time; ¡~!
that's it!, correct!; **llegaste muy** ~ you
just made it; **vivir muy** ~ to be hard up.
juvenil [xuße'nil] *a* youthful.
juventud [xußen'tuð] *nf* (*adolescencia*)
youth; (*jóvenes*) young people *pl*.
juzgado [xuθ'yaðo] *nm* tribunal; (*JUR*)
court.
juzgar [xuθ'yar] *vt* to judge; **a** ~ **por** ... to
judge by ..., judging by ...; ~ **mal** to misjudge; **júzguelo usted mismo** see for
yourself.
juzgue ['xuθɤe] *etv vb* V **juzgar**.

K

K, k [ka] *nf* (*letra*) K, k; **K de Kilo** K for
King.
K *abr* (= *1.000*) K; (*INFORM*: = *1.024*) K.
Kampuchea [kampu'tʃea] *nf* Kampuchea.
karate [ka'rate] *nm* karate.
k/c. *abr* (= *kilociclos*) kc.
Kenia ['kenja] *nf* Kenya.
keniata [ke'njata] *a*, *nm/f* Kenyan.
kg. *abr* (= *kilogramo(s)*) kg.
kilate [ki'late] *nm* = **quilate**.
kilo ['kilo] *nm* kilo.
kilobyte [kilo'ßait] *nm* (*INFORM*) kilobyte.
kilogramo [kilo'ɤramo] *nm* kilogramme
(*Brit*), kilogram (*US*).
kilolitro [kilo'litro] *nm* kilolitre (*Brit*), kilo-
liter (*US*).
kilometraje [kilome'traxe] *nm* distance in
kilometres, ≈ mileage.
kilométrico, a [kilo'metriko, a] *a* kilo-
metric; (*fam*) very long; **(billete)** ~
(*FERRO*) mileage ticket.
kilómetro [ki'lometro] *nm* kilometre (*Brit*),
kilometer (*US*).
kiloocteto [kilook'teto] *nm* (*INFORM*) kilobyte.
kilovatio [kilo'ßatjo] *nm* kilowatt.
kiosco ['kjosko] *nm* = **quiosco**.
km *abr* (= *kilómetro(s)*) km.
km/h *abr* (= *kilómetros por hora*) km/h.
knock-out ['nokau], **K.O.** ['kao] *nm* knock-

out; (*golpe*) knockout blow; **dejar** *o* **poner**
a uno ~ to knock sb out.
k.p.h. *abr* (= *kilómetros por hora*) km/h.
k.p.l. *abr* (= *kilómetros por litro*) ≈ m.p.g.
kv *abr* (= *kilovatio*) kw.
kv/h *abr* (= *kilovatios-hora*) kw-h.

L

L, l ['ele] *nf* (*letra*) L, l; **L de Lorenzo** L for
Lucy (*Brit*) *o* Love (*US*).
l. *abr* (= *litro(s)*) l.; (*JUR*) = **ley**; (*LITERA-
TURA*: = *libro*) bk.
L/ *abr* (*COM*) = **letra**.
la [la] *artículo definido fsg* the ♦ *pron* her;
(*usted*) you; (*cosa*) it ♦ *nm* (*MUS*) la; **está**
en ~ **cárcel** he's in jail; ~ **del sombrero**
rojo the woman/girl/one in the red hat.
laberinto [laße'rinto] *nm* labyrinth.
labia ['laßja] *nf* fluency; (*pey*) glibness;
tener mucha ~ to have the gift of the gab.
labial [la'ßjal] *a* labial.
labio ['laßjo] *nm* lip; (*de vasija etc*) edge,
rim; ~ **inferior/superior** lower/upper lip.
labor [la'ßor] *nf* labour; (*AGR*) farm work;
(*tarea*) job, task; (*COSTURA*) needlework,
sewing; (*punto*) knitting; ~ **de equipo**
teamwork; ~ **de ganchillo** crochet.
laborable [laßo'raßle] *a* (*AGR*) workable;
día ~ working day.
laborar [laßo'rar] *vi* to work.
laboratorio [laßora'torjo] *nm* laboratory.
laborioso, a [laßo'rjoso, a] *a* (*persona*)
hard-working; (*trabajo*) tough.
laborista [laßo'rista] (*Brit POL*) *a*: **Partido**
L~ Labour Party ♦ *nm/f* Labour Party
member *o* supporter.
labrado, a [la'ßraðo, a] *a* worked; (*madera*) carved; (*metal*) wrought ♦ *nm*
(*AGR*) cultivated field.
Labrador [laßra'ðor] *nm* Labrador.
labrador, a [la'ßraðor, a] *a*, *nm/f* farmer.
labranza [la'ßranθa] *nf* (*AGR*) cultivation.
labrar [la'ßrar] *vt* (*gen*) to work; (*madera
etc*) to carve; (*fig*) to cause, bring about.
labriego, a [la'ßrjeɤo, a] *nm/f* peasant.
laca ['laka] *nf* lacquer; (*de pelo*) hairspray;
~ **de uñas** nail varnish.
lacayo [la'kajo] *nm* lackey.
lacerar [laθe'rar] *vt* to lacerate.
lacio, a ['laθjo, a] *a* (*pelo*) lank, straight.
lacón [la'kon] *nm* shoulder of pork.
lacónico, a [la'koniko, a] *a* laconic.
lacrar [la'krar] *vt* (*cerrar*) to seal (with sealing wax).

lacre ['lakre] *nm* sealing wax.

lacrimógeno, a [lakri'moxeno, a] *a* (*fig*) sentimental; **gas** ~ tear gas.

lacrimoso, a [lakri'moso, a] *a* tearful.

lactar [lak'tar] *vt, vi* to suckle, breast-feed.

lácteo, a ['lakteo, a] *a*: **productos** ~**s** dairy products.

ladear [laðe'ar] *vt* to tip, tilt ◆ *vi* to tilt; ~**se** *vr* to lean; (*DEPORTE*) to swerve; (*AVIAT*) to bank, turn.

ladera [la'ðera] *nf* slope.

ladino, a [la'ðino, a] *a* cunning.

lado ['laðo] *nm* (*gen*) side; (*fig*) protection; (*MIL*) flank; ~ **izquierdo** left(-hand) side; ~ **a** ~ side by side; **al** ~ **de** beside; **hacerse a un** ~ to stand aside; **poner de** ~ to put on its side; **poner a un** ~ to put aside; **me da de** ~ I don't care; **por un** ~ ..., **por otro** ~ ... on the one hand ..., on the other (hand), ...; **por todos** ~**s** on all sides, all round (*Brit*).

ladrar [la'ðrar] *vi* to bark.

ladrido [la'ðriðo] *nm* bark, barking.

ladrillo [la'ðriʎo] *nm* (*gen*) brick; (*azulejo*) tile.

ladrón, ona [la'ðron, ona] *nm/f* thief.

lagar [la'ɣar] *nm* (wine/oil) press.

lagartija [laɣar'tixa] *nf* (small) lizard, wall lizard.

lagarto [la'ɣarto] *nm* (*ZOOL*) lizard.

lago ['laɣo] *nm* lake.

Lagos ['laɣos] *nm* Lagos.

lágrima ['laɣrima] *nf* tear.

lagrimear [laɣrime'ar] *vi* to weep; (*ojos*) to water.

laguna [la'ɣuna] *nf* (*lago*) lagoon; (*en escrito, conocimientos*) gap.

laico, a ['laiko, a] *a* lay ◆ *nm/f* layman/woman.

lameculos [lame'kulos] *nm/f inv* (*fam*) arselicker(!), crawler.

lamentable [lamen'taßle] *a* lamentable, regrettable; (*miserable*) pitiful.

lamentación [lamenta'θjon] *nf* lamentation; **ahora no sirven lamentaciones** it's no good crying over spilt milk.

lamentar [lamen'tar] *vt* (*sentir*) to regret; (*deplorar*) to lament; ~**se** *vr* to lament; **lo lamento mucho** I'm very sorry.

lamento [la'mento] *nm* lament.

lamer [la'mer] *vt* to lick.

lámina ['lamina] *nf* (*plancha delgada*) sheet; (*para estampar, estampa*) plate; (*grabado*) engraving.

laminar [lami'nar] *vt* (*en libro*) to laminate; (*TEC*) to roll.

lámpara ['lampara] *nf* lamp; ~ **de alcohol/ gas** spirit/gas lamp; ~ **de pie** standard lamp.

lamparilla [lampa'riʎa] *nf* nightlight.

lamparón [lampa'ron] *nm* (*MED*) scrofula;

(*mancha*) (large) grease spot.

lampiño, a [lam'piɲo, a] *a* (*sin pelo*) hairless.

lana ['lana] *nf* wool; (*tela*) woollen (*Brit*) o woolen (*US*) cloth; (**hecho**) **de** ~ wool *cpd*.

lance ['lanθe] *etc vb* V **lanzar** ◆ *nm* (*golpe*) stroke; (*suceso*) event, incident.

lancha ['lantʃa] *nf* launch; ~ **motora** motorboat; ~ **de pesca** fishing boat; ~ **salvavidas/torpedera** lifeboat/torpedo boat; ~ **neumática** rubber dinghy.

Landas ['landas] *nfpl*: **las** ~ Landes *sg*.

lanero, a [la'nero, a] *a* wool *cpd*.

langosta [lan'gosta] *nf* (*insecto*) locust; (*crustáceo*) lobster (: *de río*) crayfish.

langostino [langos'tino] *nm* prawn; (*de agua dulce*) crayfish.

languidecer [langiðe'θer] *vi* to languish.

languidez [langi'ðeθ] *nf* languor.

languidezca [langi'ðeθka] *etc vb* V **languidecer**.

lánguido, a ['langiðo, a] *a* (*gen*) languid; (*sin energía*) listless.

lanilla [la'niʎa] *nf* nap; (*tela*) thin flannel cloth.

lanolina [lano'lina] *nf* lanolin(e).

lanudo, a [la'nuðo, a] *a* woolly, fleecy.

lanza ['lanθa] *nf* (*arma*) lance, spear; **medir** ~**s** to cross swords.

lanzabombas [lanθa'ßombas] *nm inv* (*AVIAT*) bomb release; (*MIL*) mortar.

lanzacohetes [lanθako'etes] *nm inv* rocket launcher.

lanzadera [lanθa'ðera] *nf* shuttle.

lanzallamas [lanθa'ʎamas] *nm inv* flamethrower.

lanzamiento [lanθa'mjento] *nm* (*gen*) throwing; (*NAUT, COM*) launch, launching; ~ **de pesos** putting the shot.

lanzar [lan'θar] *vt* (*gen*) to throw; (*con violencia*) to fling; (*DEPORTE: pelota*) to bowl; (: *US*) to pitch; (*NAUT, COM*) to launch; (*JUR*) to evict; (*grito*) to give, utter; ~**se** *vr* to throw o.s.; (*fig*) to take the plunge; ~**se a** (*fig*) to embark upon.

Lanzarote [lanθa'rote] *nm* Lanzarote.

lanzatorpedos [lanθator'peðos] *nm inv* torpedo tube.

lapa ['lapa] *nf* limpet.

La Paz *nf* La Paz.

lapicero [lapi'θero] *nm* propelling (*Brit*) o mechanical (*US*) pencil; (*AM: bolígrafo*) biro ®.

lápida ['lapiða] *nf* stone; ~ **conmemorativa** memorial stone; ~ **mortuoria** headstone.

lapidar [lapi'ðar] *vt* to stone; (*TEC*) to polish, lap.

lapidario, a [lapi'ðarjo, a] *a, nm* lapidary.

lápiz ['lapiθ] *nm* pencil; ~ **de color** coloured pencil; ~ **de labios** lipstick; ~ **óptico** o **luminoso** light pen.

lapón, ona [la'pon, ona] *a* Lapp ◆ *nm/f* Laplander, Lapp ◆ *nm* (*LING*) Lapp.

Laponia [la'ponja] *nf* Lapland.

lapso ['lapso] *nm* lapse; (*error*) error; ~ **de tiempo** interval of time.

lapsus ['lapsus] *nm inv* error, mistake.

LAR [lar] *nf abr* (*Esp JUR*) = *Ley de Arrendamientos Rústicos*.

largamente [larɣa'mente] *ad* for a long time; (*relatar*) at length.

largar [lar'ɣar] *vt* (*soltar*) to release; (*aflojar*) to loosen; (*lanzar*) to launch; (*fam*) to let fly; (*velas*) to unfurl; (*AM*) to throw; ~**se** *vr* (*fam*) to beat it; ~**se a** (*AM*) to start to.

largo, a ['larɣo, a] *a* (*longitud*) long; (*tiempo*) lengthy; (*persona: alta*) tall; (: *fig*) generous ◆ *nm* length; (*MUS*) largo; **dos años** ~**s** two long years; **a** ~ **plazo** in the long term; **tiene 9 metros de** ~ it is 9 metres long; **a lo** ~ (*posición*) lengthways; **a lo** ~ **de** along; (*tiempo*) all through, throughout; **a la larga** in the long run; **me dio largas con una promesa** she put me off with a promise; **¡~ de aquí!** (*fam*) clear off!

largometraje [larɣome'traxe] *nm* full-length *o* feature film.

largue ['larɣe] *etc vb V* **largar**.

larguero [lar'ɣero] *nm* (*ARQ*) main beam, chief support; (*de puerta*) jamb; (*DEPORTE*) crossbar; (*en cama*) bolster.

largueza [lar'ɣeθa] *nf* generosity.

larguirucho, a [larɣi'rutʃo, a] *a* lanky, gangling.

larguísimo, a [lar'ɣisimo, a] *a superlativo de* **largo**.

largura [lar'ɣura] *nf* length.

laringe [la'rinxe] *nf* larynx.

laringitis [larin'xitis] *nf* laryngitis.

larva ['larβa] *nf* larva.

las [las] *artículo definido fpl* the ◆ *pron* them; ~ **que cantan** the ones/women/girls who sing.

lasca ['laska] *nf* chip of stone.

lascivia [las'θiβja] *nf* lewdness; (*lujuria*) lust; (*fig*) playfulness.

lascivo, a [las'θiβo, a] *a* lewd.

láser ['laser] *nm* laser.

Las Palmas *nf* Las Palmas.

lástima ['lastima] *nf* (*pena*) pity; **dar** ~ to be pitiful; **es una** ~ **que** it's a pity that; **¡qué** ~**!** what a pity!; **estar hecho una** ~ to be a sorry sight.

lastimar [lasti'mar] *vt* (*herir*) to wound; (*ofender*) to offend; ~**se** *vr* to hurt o.s.

lastimero, a [lasti'mero, a] *a* pitiful, pathetic.

lastre ['lastre] *nm* (*TEC*, *NAUT*) ballast; (*fig*) dead weight.

lata ['lata] *nf* (*metal*) tin; (*envase*) tin, can;

(*fam*) nuisance; **en** ~ tinned; **dar (la)** ~ to be a nuisance.

latente [la'tente] *a* latent.

lateral [late'ral] *a* side, lateral ◆ *nm* (*TEATRO*) wings *pl*.

latido [la'tiðo] *nm* (*del corazón*) beat; (*de herida*) throb(bing).

latifundio [lati'fundjo] *nm* large estate.

latifundista [latifun'dista] *nm/f* owner of a large estate.

latigazo [lati'ɣaθo] *nm* (*golpe*) lash; (*sonido*) crack; (*fig: regaño*) dressing-down.

látigo ['latiɣo] *nm* whip.

latiguillo [lati'ɣiʎo] *nm* (*TEATRO*) hamming.

latín [la'tin] *nm* Latin; **saber (mucho)** ~ (*fam*) to be pretty sharp.

latinajo [lati'naxo] *nm* dog Latin; **echar** ~**s** to come out with Latin words.

latino, a [la'tino, a] *a* Latin.

Latinoamérica [latinoa'merika] *nf* Latin America.

latinoamericano, a [latinoameri'kano, a] *a*, *nm/f* Latin American.

latir [la'tir] *vi* (*corazón, pulso*) to beat.

latitud [lati'tuð] *nf* (*GEO*) latitude; (*fig*) breadth, extent.

lato, a ['lato, a] *a* broad.

latón [la'ton] *nm* brass.

latoso, a [la'toso, a] *a* (*molesto*) annoying; (*aburrido*) boring.

latrocinio [latro'θinjo] *nm* robbery.

LAU *nf abr* (*Esp JUR*) = *Ley de Arrendamientos Urbanos*.

laúd [la'uð] *nm* lute.

laudatorio, a [lauða'torjo, a] *a* laudatory.

laudo ['lauðo] *nm* (*JUR*) decision, finding.

laurear [laure'ar] *vt* to honour, reward.

laurel [lau'rel] *nm* (*BOT*) laurel; (*CULIN*) bay.

Lausana [lau'sana] *nf* Lausanne.

lava ['laβa] *nf* lava.

lavable [la'βaβle] *a* washable.

lavabo [la'βaβo] *nm* (*jofaina*) washbasin; (*retrete*) lavatory (*Brit*), toilet (*Brit*), washroom (*US*).

lavadero [laβa'ðero] *nm* laundry.

lavado [la'βaðo] *nm* washing; (*de ropa*) wash, laundry; (*ARTE*) wash; ~ **de cerebro** brainwashing.

lavadora [laβa'ðora] *nf* washing machine.

lavamanos [laβa'manos] *nm inv* washbasin.

lavanda [la'βanda] *nf* lavender.

lavandería [laβande'ria] *nf* laundry; ~ **automática** launderette.

lavaparabrisas [laβapara'βrisas] *nm inv* windscreen washer.

lavaplatos [laβa'platos] *nm inv* dishwasher.

lavar [la'βar] *vt* to wash; (*borrar*) to wipe away; ~**se** *vr* to wash o.s.; ~**se las manos** to wash one's hands; (*fig*) to wash one's hands of it; ~ **y marcar** (*pelo*) to shampoo

and set; ~ **en seco** to dry-clean.

lavativa [laβa'tiβa] nf (MED) enema.

lavavajillas [laβaβa'xiʎas] nm inv dishwasher.

laxante [lak'sante] nm laxative.

laxitud [laksi'tuð] nf laxity, slackness.

lazada [la'θaða] nf bow.

lazarillo [laθa'riʎo] nm: **perro de** ~ guide dog.

lazo ['laθo] nm knot; (lazada) bow; (para animales) lasso; (trampa) snare; (vínculo) tie; ~ **corredizo** slipknot.

LBE nf abr (Esp JUR) = Ley Básica de Empleo.

lb(s) abr = **libra(s)**.

L/C abr (= Letra de Crédito) B/E.

Lda., Ldo. abr = **Licenciado, a.**

le [le] pron (directo) him (o her); (: usted) you; (indirecto) to him (o her o it); (: usted) to you.

leal [le'al] a loyal.

lealtad [leal'tað] nf loyalty.

lebrel [le'βrel] nm greyhound.

lección [lek'θjon] nf lesson; ~ **práctica** object lesson; **dar lecciones** to teach, give lessons; **dar una** ~ **a uno** (fig) to teach sb a lesson.

lector, a [lek'tor, a] nm/f reader; (ESCOL, UNIV) (conversation) assistant ♦ nm: ~ **óptico de caracteres** (INFORM) optical character reader ♦ nf: ~**a de fichas** (INFORM) card reader.

lectura [lek'tura] nf reading; ~ **de marcas sensibles** (INFORM) mark sensing.

leche ['letʃe] nf milk; (fam!) semen, spunk(!); **dar una** ~ **a uno** (fam) to belt sb; **estar de mala** ~ (fam) to be in a foul mood; **tener mala** ~ (fam) to be a nasty piece of work; ~ **condensada/en polvo** condensed/powdered milk; ~ **desnatada** skimmed milk; ~ **de magnesia** milk of magnesia; ¡~! hell!

lechera [le'tʃera] nf V **lechero.**

lechería [letʃe'ria] nf dairy.

lecherita [letʃe'rita] nf milk jug.

lechero, a [le'tʃero, a] a milk cpd ♦ nm milkman ♦ nf (vendedora) milkmaid; (recipiente) milk pan; (para servir) milk churn; (AM) cow.

lecho ['letʃo] nm (cama, de río) bed; (GEO) layer; ~ **mortuorio** deathbed.

lechón [le'tʃon] nm sucking (Brit) o suckling (US) pig.

lechoso, a [le'tʃoso, a] a milky.

lechuga [le'tʃuɣa] nf lettuce.

lechuza [le'tʃuθa] nf (barn) owl.

leer [le'er] vt to read; ~ **entre líneas** to read between the lines.

legación [leɣa'θjon] nf legation.

legado [le'ɣaðo] nm (don) bequest; (herencia) legacy; (enviado) legate.

legajo [le'ɣaxo] nm file, bundle (of papers).

legal [le'ɣal] a legal, lawful; (persona) trustworthy.

legalice [leɣa'liθe] etc vb V **legalizar.**

legalidad [leɣali'ðað] nf legality.

legalizar [leɣali'θar] vt to legalize; (documento) to authenticate.

legaña [le'ɣaɲa] nf sleep (in eyes).

legar [le'ɣar] vt to bequeath, leave.

legatario, a [leɣa'tarjo, a] nm/f legatee.

legendario, a [lexen'darjo, a] a legendary.

legible [le'xiβle] a legible; ~ **por máquina** (INFORM) machine-readable.

legión [le'xjon] nf legion.

legionario, a [lexjo'narjo, a] a legionary ♦ nm legionnaire.

legislación [lexisla'θjon] nf legislation; (leyes) laws pl; ~ **antimonopolio** (COM) anti-trust legislation.

legislar [lexis'lar] vt to legislate.

legislativo, a [lexisla'tiβo, a] a: **(elecciones) legislativas** ≈ general elections.

legitimar [lexiti'mar] vt to legitimize.

legítimo, a [le'xitimo, a] a (genuino) authentic; (legal) legitimate, rightful.

lego, a ['leɣo, a] a (REL) secular; (ignorante) ignorant ♦ nm layman.

legua ['leɣwa] nf league; **se ve (o nota) a la** ~ you can tell (it) a mile off.

legue [le'ɣe] etc vb V **legar.**

leguleyo [leɣu'lejo] nm (pey) petty o shyster (US) lawyer.

legumbres [le'ɣumbres] nfpl pulses.

leído, a [le'iðo, a] a well-read.

lejanía [lexa'nia] nf distance.

lejano, a [le'xano, a] a far-off; (en el tiempo) distant; (fig) remote; **L~ Oriente** Far East.

lejía [le'xia] nf bleach.

lejísimos [le'xisimos] ad a long, long way.

lejos ['lexos] ad far, far away; **a lo** ~ in the distance; **de** o **desde** ~ from afar; **está muy** ~ it's a long way (away); **¿está ~?** is it far?; ~ **de** prep far from.

lelo, a ['lelo, a] a silly ♦ nm/f idiot.

lema ['lema] nm motto; (POL) slogan.

lencería [lenθe'ria] nf (telas) linen, drapery; (ropa interior) lingerie.

lendakari [lenda'kari] nm head of the Basque Autonomous Government.

lengua ['lengwa] nf tongue; ~ **materna** mother tongue; ~ **de tierra** (GEO) spit o tongue of land; **dar a la** ~ to chatter; **morderse la** ~ to hold one's tongue; **sacar la** ~ **a uno** (fig) to cock a snook at sb.

lenguado [len'gwaðo] nm sole.

lenguaje [len'gwaxe] nm language; (forma de hablar) (mode of) speech; ~ **comercial** business language; ~ **ensamblador** o **de alto nivel** (INFORM) high-level language; ~

máquina (*INFORM*) machine language; ~ **original** source language; ~ **periodístico** journalese; ~ **de programación** (*INFORM*) programming language; **en ~ llano** ≈ in plain English.

lenguaraz [lengwa'raθ] *a* talkative; (*pey*) foul-mouthed.

lengüeta [len'gweta] *nf* (*ANAT*) epiglottis; (*de zapatos*, *MUS*) tongue.

lenidad [leni'ðað] *nf* lenience.

Leningrado [lenin'graðo] *nm* Leningrad.

lente ['lente] *nm o nf* lens; (*lupa*) magnifying glass; **~s** *pl* glasses; **~s de contacto** contact lenses.

lenteja [len'texa] *nf* lentil.

lentejuela [lente'xwela] *nf* sequin.

lentilla [len'tiʎa] *nf* contact lens.

lentitud [lenti'tuð] *nf* slowness; **con ~** slowly.

lento, a ['lento, a] *a* slow.

leña ['leɲa] *nf* firewood; **dar ~ a** to thrash; **echar ~ al fuego** to add fuel to the flames.

leñador, a [leɲa'ðor, a] *nm/f* woodcutter.

leño ['leɲo] *nm* (*trozo de árbol*) log; (*madera*) timber; (*fig*) blockhead.

Leo ['leo] *nm* (*ASTRO*) Leo.

león [le'on] *nm* lion; ~ **marino** sea lion.

leonera [leo'nera] *nf* (*jaula*) lion's cage; **parece una ~** it's shockingly dirty.

leonés, esa [leo'nes, esa] *a, nm/f* Leonese ♦ *nm* (*LING*) Leonese.

leonino, a [leo'nino, a] *a* leonine.

leontina [leon'tina] *nf* watch chain.

leopardo [leo'parðo] *nm* leopard.

leotardos [leo'tarðos] *nmpl* tights.

lepra ['lepra] *nf* leprosy.

leproso, a [le'proso, a] *nm/f* leper.

lerdo, a ['lerðo, a] *a* (*lento*) slow; (*patoso*) clumsy.

leridano, a [leri'ðano, a] *a* of *o* from Lérida ♦ *nm/f* native *o* inhabitant of Lérida.

les [les] *pron* (*directo*) them; (: *ustedes*) you; (*indirecto*) to them; (: *ustedes*) to you.

lesbiana [les'ßjana] *nf* lesbian.

lesión [le'sjon] *nf* wound, lesion; (*DEPORTE*) injury.

lesionado, a [lesjo'naðo, a] *a* injured ♦ *nm/f* injured person.

lesionar [lesjo'nar] *vt* (*dañar*) to hurt; (*herir*) to wound; **~se** *vr* to get hurt.

letal [le'tal] *a* lethal.

letanía [leta'nia] *nf* litany; (*retahíla*) long list.

letárgico, a [le'tarxiko, a] *a* lethargic.

letargo [le'tarxo] *nm* lethargy.

Letonia [le'tonja] *nf* Latvia.

letra ['letra] *nf* letter; (*escritura*) handwriting; (*COM*) letter, bill, draft; (*MUS*) lyrics *pl*; **~s** *nfpl* (*UNIV*) arts; ~ **bastardilla/ negrilla** italics *pl*/bold type; ~ **de cambio**

bill of exchange; ~ **de imprenta** print; ~ **inicial/mayúscula/minúscula** initial/capital/ small letter; **lo tomó al pie de la ~** he took it literally; ~ **bancaria** (*COM*) bank draft; ~ **de patente** (*COM*) letters patent *pl*; **escribir 4 ~s a uno** to drop a line to sb.

letrado, a [le'traðo, a] *a* learned; (*fam*) pedantic ♦ *nm/f* lawyer.

letrero [le'trero] *nm* (*cartel*) sign; (*etiqueta*) label.

letrina [le'trina] *nf* latrine.

leucemia [leu'θemja] *nf* leukaemia.

leva ['leßa] *nf* (*NAUT*) weighing anchor; (*MIL*) levy; (*TEC*) lever.

levadizo, a [leßa'ðiθo, a] *a*: **puente ~** drawbridge.

levadura [leßa'ðura] *nf* yeast, leaven; ~ **de cerveza** brewer's yeast.

levantamiento [leßanta'mjento] *nm* raising, lifting; (*rebelión*) revolt, rising; (*GEO*) survey; ~ **de pesos** weightlifting.

levantar [leßan'tar] *vt* (*gen*) to raise; (*del suelo*) to pick up; (*hacia arriba*) to lift (up); (*plan*) to make, draw up; (*mesa*) to clear; (*campamento*) to strike; (*fig*) to cheer up, hearten; **~se** *vr* to get up; (*enderezarse*) to straighten up; (*rebelarse*) to rebel; (*sesión*) to be adjourned; (*niebla*) to lift; (*viento*) to rise; **~se (de la cama)** to get up, get out of bed; ~ **el ánimo** to cheer up.

levante [le'ßante] *nm* east; (*viento*) east wind; **el L~** *region of Spain extending from Castellón to Murcia.*

levantino, a [leßan'tino, a] *a* of *o* from the *Levante* ♦ *nm/f*: **los ~s** the people of the *Levante*.

levar [le'ßar] *vi* to weigh anchor.

leve ['leße] *a* light; (*fig*) trivial; (*mínimo*) slight.

levedad [leße'ðað] *nf* lightness; (*fig*) levity.

levita [le'ßita] *nf* frock coat.

léxico, a ['leksiko, a] *a* lexical ♦ *nm* (*vocabulario*) vocabulary; (*LING*) lexicon.

ley [lei] *nf* (*gen*) law; (*metal*) standard; **decreto-~** decree law; **de buena ~** (*fig*) genuine; **según la ~** in accordance with the law, by law, in law.

leyenda [le'jenda] *nf* legend; (*TIP*) inscription.

leyendo [le'jendo] *etc vb V* **leer.**

liar [li'ar] *vt* to tie (up); (*unir*) to bind; (*envolver*) to wrap (up); (*enredar*) to confuse; (*cigarrillo*) to roll; **~se** *vr* (*fam*) to get involved; (*confundirse*) to get mixed up; **~se a palos** to get involved in a fight.

lib. *abr* (= *libro*) bk.

libanés, esa [lißa'nes, esa] *a, nm/f* Lebanese.

Líbano ['lißano] *nm*: **el ~** the Lebanon.

libar [li'ßar] *vt* to suck.

libelo [li'ßelo] *nm* satire, lampoon; (*JUR*) petition.

libélula [li'ßelula] *nf* dragonfly.

liberación [lißera'θjon] *nf* liberation; (*de la cárcel*) release.

liberado, a [liße'raðo, a] *a* liberated; (*COM*) paid-up, paid-in (*US*).

liberal [liße'ral] *a*, *nm/f* liberal.

liberalidad [lißerali'ðað] *nf* liberality, generosity.

liberar [liße'rar] *vt* to liberate.

libertad [lißer'tað] *nf* liberty, freedom; ~ **de asociación/de culto/de prensa/de comer- cio/de palabra** freedom of association/of worship/of the press/of trade/ of speech; ~ **condicional** probation; ~ **bajo palabra** parole; ~ **bajo fianza** bail; **estar en** ~ to be free; **poner a uno en** ~ to set sb free.

libertador, a [lißerta'ðor, a] *a* liberating ♦ *nm/f* liberator.

libertar [lißer'tar] *vt* (*preso*) to set free; (*de una obligación*) to release; (*eximir*) to exempt.

libertino, a [lißer'tino, a] *a* permissive ♦ *nm/f* permissive person.

Libia ['lißja] *nf* Libya.

libio, a ['lißjo, a] *a*, *nm/f* Libyan.

libra ['lißra] *nf* pound; **L~** (*ASTRO*) Libra; ~ **esterlina** pound sterling.

librador, a [lißra'ðor, a] *nm/f* drawer.

libramiento [lißra'mjento] *nm* rescue; (*COM*) delivery.

libranza [li'ßranθa] *nf* (*COM*) draft; (*letra de cambio*) bill of exchange.

librar [li'ßrar] *vt* (*de peligro*) to save; (*batalla*) to wage, fight; (*de impuestos*) to exempt; (*cheque*) to make out; (*JUR*) to exempt; ~**se** *vr*: ~**se de** to escape from, free o.s. from; **de buena nos hemos librado** we're well out of that.

libre ['lißre] *a* (*gen*) free; (*lugar*) unoccupied; (*tiempo*) spare; (*asiento*) vacant; (*COM*): ~ **a bordo** free on board; ~ **de franqueo** post-free; ~ **de impuestos** free of tax; **tiro** ~ free kick; **los 100 metros** ~ the 100 metres free-style (race); **al aire** ~ in the open air; **¿estás** ~**?** are you free?

librecambio [lißre'kambjo] *nm* free trade.

librecambista [lißrekam'bista] *a* free-trade *cpd* ♦ *nm* free-trader.

librería [lißre'ria] *nf* (*tienda*) bookshop; (*estante*) bookcase; ~ **de ocasión** second-hand bookshop.

librero, a [li'ßrero, a] *nm/f* bookseller.

libreta [li'ßreta] *nf* notebook; (*pan*) one-pound loaf; ~ **de ahorros** savings book.

libro ['lißro] *nm* book; ~ **de actas** minute book; ~ **de bolsillo** paperback; ~ **de cabecera** bedside book; ~ **de caja** (*COM*) cashbook; ~ **de caja auxiliar** (*COM*) petty cash book; ~ **de cocina** cookery book (*Brit*), cookbook (*US*); ~ **de consulta** reference book; ~ **de cuentas** account book; ~ **de cuentos** storybook; ~ **de cheques** cheque (*Brit*) o check (*US*) book; ~ **diario** journal; ~ **de entradas y salidas** (*COM*) daybook; ~ **de honor** visitors' book; ~ **mayor** (*COM*) general ledger; ~ **de reclamaciones** complaints book; ~ **de texto** textbook.

Lic. *abr* = **Licenciado, a.**

licencia [li'θenθja] *nf* (*gen*) licence; (*permiso*) permission; ~ **por enfermedad/con goce de sueldo** sick/paid leave; ~ **de armas/de caza** gun/game licence; ~ **de exportación** (*COM*) export licence; ~ **poética** poetic licence.

licenciado, a [liθen'θjaðo, a] *a* licensed ♦ *nm/f* graduate; **L~ en Filosofía y Letras** Bachelor of Arts.

licenciar [liθen'θjar] *vt* (*empleado*) to dismiss; (*permitir*) to permit, allow; (*soldado*) to discharge; (*estudiante*) to confer a degree upon; ~**se** *vr*: ~**se en letras** to get an arts degree.

licenciatura [liθenθja'tura] *nf* (*título*) degree; (*estudios*) degree course.

licencioso, a [liθen'θjoso, a] *a* licentious.

liceo [li'θeo] *nm* (high) school.

licitación [liθita'θjon] *nf* bidding; (*oferta*) tender, offer.

licitador [liθita'ðor] *nm* bidder; (*AM*) auctioneer.

licitante [liθi'tante] *nm* bidder.

licitar [liθi'tar] *vt* to bid for; (*AM*) to sell by auction ♦ *vi* to bid.

lícito, a ['liθito, a] *a* (*legal*) lawful; (*justo*) fair, just; (*permisible*) permissible.

licor [li'kor] *nm* spirits *pl* (*Brit*), liquor (*US*); (*con hierbas etc*) liqueur.

licuadora [likwa'ðora] *nf* blender.

licuar [li'kwar] *vt* to liquidize.

lid [lið] *nf* combat; (*fig*) controversy.

líder ['liðer] *nm/f* leader.

liderato [liðe'rato] *nm* leadership.

lidia ['liðja] *nf* bullfighting; (*una* ~) bullfight; **toros de** ~ fighting bulls.

lidiar [li'ðjar] *vt*, *vi* to fight.

liebre ['ljeßre] *nf* hare; **dar gato por** ~ to con.

Lieja ['ljexa] *nf* Liège.

lienzo ['ljenθo] *nm* linen; (*ARTE*) canvas; (*ARQ*) wall.

lifting ['liftin] *nm* facelift.

liga ['liɣa] *nf* (*de medias*) garter, suspender; (*confederación*) league; (*AM*: *gomita*) rubber band.

ligadura [liɣa'ðura] *nf* bond, tie; (*MED*, *MUS*) ligature.

ligamento [liɣa'mento] *nm* (*ANAT*) ligament; (*atadura*) tie; (*unión*) bond.

ligar [li'ɣar] *vt* (*atar*) to tie; (*unir*) to join; (*MED*) to bind up; (*MUS*) to slur; (*fam*) to get off with, pick up ♦ *vi* to mix, blend; (*fam*) to get off with sb; (*2 personas*) to get off with one another; ~**se** *vr* (*fig*) to commit o.s.; ~ **con** (*fam*) to get off with, pick up; ~**se a uno** to get off with o pick up sb.

ligereza [lixe'reθa] *nf* lightness; (*rapidez*) swiftness; (*agilidad*) agility; (*superficialidad*) flippancy.

ligero, a [li'xero, a] *a* (*de peso*) light; (*tela*) thin; (*rápido*) swift, quick; (*ágil*) agile, nimble; (*de importancia*) slight; (*de carácter*) flippant, superficial ♦ *ad* quickly, swiftly; **a la ligera** superficially; **juzgar a la ligera** to jump to conclusions.

ligón [li'ɣon] *nm* (*fam*) Romeo.

ligue ['liɣe] *etc vb V* **ligar** ♦ *nm/f* boyfriend/girlfriend ♦ *nm* (*persona*) pick-up.

liguero [li'ɣero] *nm* suspender (*Brit*) o garter (*US*) belt.

lija ['lixa] *nf* (*ZOOL*) dogfish; (**papel de**) ~ sandpaper.

Lila ['lila] *nf* Lille.

lila ['lila] *a inv, nf* lilac ♦ *nm* (*fam*) twit.

lima ['lima] *nf* file; (*BOT*) lime; ~ **de uñas** nail file; **comer como una** ~ to eat like a horse.

limar [li'mar] *vt* to file; (*alisar*) to smooth over; (*fig*) to polish up.

limitación [limita'θjon] *nf* limitation, limit; ~ **de velocidad** speed limit.

limitado, a [limi'taðo, a] *a* limited; **sociedad limitada** (*COM*) limited company.

limitar [limi'tar] *vt* to limit; (*reducir*) to reduce, cut down ♦ *vi*: ~ **con** to border on; ~**se** *vr*: ~**se a** to limit o confine o.s. to.

límite ['limite] *nm* (*gen*) limit; (*fin*) end; (*frontera*) border; **como** ~ at (the) most; (*fecha*) at the latest; **no tener** ~**s** to know no bounds; ~ **de crédito** (*COM*) credit limit; ~ **de página** (*INFORM*) page break; ~ **de velocidad** speed limit.

limítrofe [li'mitrofe] *a* bordering, neighbouring.

limón [li'mon] *nm* lemon ♦ *a*: **amarillo** ~ lemon-yellow.

limonada [limo'naða] *nf* lemonade.

limonero [limo'nero] *nm* lemon tree.

limosna [li'mosna] *nf* alms *pl*; **pedir** ~ to beg; **vivir de** ~ to live on charity.

limpiabotas [limpja'ßotas] *nm/f inv* bootblack (*Brit*), shoeshine boy/girl.

limpiacristales [limpjakris'tales] *nm inv* (*detergente*) window cleaner.

limpiador, a [limpja'ðor, a] *a* cleaning, cleansing ♦ *nm/f* cleaner.

limpiaparabrisas [limpjapara'ßrisas] *nm inv* windscreen (*Brit*) o windshield (*US*) wiper.

limpiar [lim'pjar] *vt* to clean; (*con trapo*) to wipe; (*quitar*) to wipe away; (*zapatos*) to shine, polish; (*casa*) to tidy up; (*fig*) to clean up; (: *purificar*) to cleanse, purify; (*MIL*) to mop up; ~ **en seco** to dry-clean.

limpieza [lim'pjeθa] *nf* (*estado*) cleanliness; (*acto*) cleaning; (: *de las calles*) cleansing; (: *de zapatos*) polishing; (*habilidad*) skill; (*fig*: *POLICÍA*) clean-up; (*pureza*) purity; (*MIL*): **operación de** ~ mopping-up operation; ~ **en seco** dry cleaning.

limpio, a ['limpjo, a] *a* clean; (*moralmente*) pure; (*ordenado*) tidy; (*despejado*) clear; (*COM*) clear, net; (*fam*) honest ♦ *ad*: **jugar** ~ to play fair; **pasar a** (*Esp*) o **en** (*AM*) ~ to make a fair copy; **sacar algo en** ~ to get benefit from sth; ~ **de** free from.

linaje [li'naxe] *nm* lineage, family.

linajudo, a [lina'xuðo, a] *a* highborn, noble.

linaza [li'naθa] *nf* linseed; **aceite de** ~ linseed oil.

lince ['linθe] *nm* lynx; **ser un** ~ (*fig*: *observador*) to be very observant; (: *astuto*) to be shrewd.

linchar [lin'tʃar] *vt* to lynch.

lindante [lin'dante] *a* adjoining; ~ **con** bordering on.

lindar [lin'dar] *vi* to adjoin; ~ **con** to border on; (*ARQ*) to abut on.

linde ['linde] *nm o nf* boundary.

lindero, a [lin'dero, a] *a* adjoining ♦ *nm* boundary.

lindo, a ['lindo, a] *a* pretty, lovely ♦ *ad*: **nos divertimos de lo** ~ we had a marvellous time; **canta muy** ~ (*AM*) he sings beautifully.

línea ['linea] *nf* (*gen, moral, POL etc*) line; (*talle*) figure; (*INFORM*): **en** ~ on-line; **fuera de** ~ off line; ~ **de estado** status line; ~ **de formato** format line; ~ **aérea** airline; ~ **de alto el fuego** ceasefire line; ~ **de fuego** firing line; ~ **de meta** goal line; (*de carrera*) finishing line; ~ **de montaje** assembly line; ~ **dura** (*POL*) hard line; ~ **recta** straight line; **la** ~ **de 1989** (*moda*) the 1989 look.

lineal [line'al] *a* linear; (*INFORM*) on-line.

lingote [lin'gote] *nm* ingot.

lingüista [lin'gwista] *nm/f* linguist.

lingüística [lin'gwistika] *nf* linguistics *sg*.

linimento [lini'mento] *nm* liniment.

lino ['lino] *nm* linen; (*BOT*) flax.

linóleo [li'noleo] *nm* lino, linoleum.

linterna [lin'terna] *nf* lantern, lamp; ~ **eléctrica** o **a pilas** torch (*Brit*), flashlight (*US*).

lío ['lio] *nm* bundle; (*desorden*) muddle, mess; (*fam*: *follón*) fuss; (: *relación amorosa*) affair; **armar un** ~ to make a fuss; **meterse en un** ~ to get into a jam; **tener un** ~ **con uno** to be having an affair

with sb.
liquen ['liken] *nm* lichen.
liquidación [likiða'θjon] *nf* liquidation; (*cuenta*) settlement; **venta de** ~ clearance sale.
liquidar [liki'ðar] *vt* (*QUÍMICA*) to liquefy; (*COM*) to liquidate; (*deudas*) to pay off; (*empresa*) to wind up; ~ **a uno** to bump sb off, rub sb out (*fam*).
líquido, a ['likiðo, a] *a* liquid; (*ganancia*) net ◆ *nm* liquid; (*COM: efectivo*) ready cash *o* money; (: *ganancia*) net amount *o* profit; ~ **imponible** net taxable income.
lira ['lira] *nf* (*MUS*) lyre; (*moneda*) lira.
lírico, a ['liriko, a] *a* lyrical.
lirio ['lirjo] *nm* (*BOT*) iris.
lirismo [li'rismo] *nm* lyricism; (*sentimentalismo*) sentimentality.
lirón [li'ron] *nm* (*ZOOL*) dormouse; (*fig*) sleepyhead.
Lisboa [lis'βoa] *nf* Lisbon.
lisboeta [lisβo'eta] *a* of *o* from Lisbon ◆ *nm/f* native *o* inhabitant of Lisbon.
lisiado, a [li'sjaðo, a] *a* injured ◆ *nm/f* cripple.
lisiar [li'sjar] *vt* to maim; ~**se** *vr* to injure o.s.
liso, a ['liso, a] *a* (*terreno*) flat; (*cabello*) straight; (*superficie*) even; (*tela*) plain; **lisa y llanamente** in plain language, plainly.
lisonja [li'sonxa] *nf* flattery.
lisonjear [lisonxe'ar] *vt* to flatter; (*fig*) to please.
lisonjero, a [lison'xero, a] *a* flattering; (*agradable*) gratifying, pleasing ◆ *nm/f* flatterer.
lista ['lista] *nf* list; (*de alumnos*) school register; (*de libros*) catalogue; (*de correos*) poste restante; (*de platos*) menu; (*de precios*) price list; **pasar** ~ to call the roll; (*ESCOL*) to call the register; ~ **de correos** poste restante; ~ **de direcciones** mailing list; ~ **electoral** electoral roll; ~ **de espera** waiting list; **tela a** ~**s** striped material.
listado, a [lis'taðo, a] *a* striped ◆ *nm* (*COM, INFORM*) listing; ~ **paginado** (*INFORM*) paged listing.
listar [lis'tar] *vt* (*INFORM*) to list.
listo, a ['listo, a] *a* (*perspicaz*) smart, clever; (*preparado*) ready; ~ **para usar** ready-to-use; ¿**estás** ~? are you ready?; **pasarse de** ~ to be too clever by half.
listón [lis'ton] *nm* (*tela*) ribbon; (*de madera, metal*) strip.
litera [li'tera] *nf* (*en barco, tren*) berth; (*en dormitorio*) bunk, bunk bed.
literal [lite'ral] *a* literal.
literario, a [lite'rarjo, a] *a* literary.
literato, a [lite'rato, a] *nm/f* writer.
literatura [litera'tura] *nf* literature.

litigante [liti'ɣante] *nm/f* litigant, claimant.
litigar [liti'ɣar] *vt* to fight ◆ *vi* (*JUR*) to go to law; (*fig*) to dispute, argue.
litigio [li'tixjo] *nm* (*JUR*) lawsuit; (*fig*): **en** ~ **con** in dispute with.
litigue [li'tiɣe] *etc vb V* **litigar**.
litografía [litoɣra'fia] *nf* lithography; (*una* ~) lithograph.
litoral [lito'ral] *a* coastal ◆ *nm* coast, seaboard.
litro ['litro] *nm* litre, liter (*US*).
Lituania [li'twanja] *nf* Lithuania.
liturgia [li'turxja] *nf* liturgy.
liviano, a [li'βjano, a] *a* (*persona*) fickle; (*cosa, objeto*) trivial.
lívido, a ['liβiðo, a] *a* livid.
líving ['liβin] *pl* **lívings** *nm* sitting room.
ll... *V bajo la letra LL, después de L.*
lo [lo] *artículo definido neutro*: ~ **bueno** the good; ~ **mío** what is mine; ~ **difícil es que** ... the difficult thing about it is that ... **no saben** ~ **aburrido que es** they don't know how boring it is; **viste a** ~ **americano** he dresses in the American style ◆ *pron* (*persona*) him; (*cosa*) it; ~ **de** that matter of; ~ **que** what, that which; **toma** ~ **que quieras** take what(ever) you want; ~ **que sea** whatever; ¡**toma** ~ **que he dicho!** I stand by what I said!
loa ['loa] *nf* praise.
loable [lo'aβle] *a* praiseworthy.
LOAPA [lo'apa] *nf abr* (*Esp JUR*) = *Ley Orgánica de Armonización del Proceso Autónomo.*
loar [lo'ar] *vt* to praise.
lobato [lo'βato] *nm* (*ZOOL*) wolf cub.
lobo ['loβo] *nm* wolf; ~ **de mar** (*fig*) sea dog; ~ **marino** seal.
lóbrego, a ['loβreɣo, a] *a* dark; (*fig*) gloomy.
lóbulo ['loβulo] *nm* lobe.
LOC *nm abr* (= *lector óptico de caracteres*) OCR.
locación [loka'θjon] *nf* lease.
local [lo'kal] *a* local ◆ *nm* place, site; (*oficinas*) premises *pl*.
localice [loka'liθe] *etc vb V* **localizar**.
localidad [lokali'ðað] *nf* (*barrio*) locality; (*lugar*) location; (*TEATRO*) seat, ticket.
localizar [lokali'θar] *vt* (*ubicar*) to locate, find; (*encontrar*) to find, track down; (*restringir*) to localize; (*situar*) to place.
loción [lo'θjon] *nf* lotion, wash.
loco, a ['loko, a] *a* mad; (*fig*) wild, mad ◆ *nm/f* lunatic, madman/woman; ~ **de atar**, (*AM*) ~ **rematado** raving mad; **a lo** ~ without rhyme or reason; **ando** ~ **con el examen** the exam is driving me crazy; **estar** ~ **de alegría** to be overjoyed *o* over the moon.
locomoción [lokomo'θjon] *nf* locomotion.

locomotora [lokomo'tora] *nf* engine, locomotive.

locuaz [lo'kwaθ] *a* loquacious, talkative.

locución [loku'θjon] *nf* expression.

locura [lo'kura] *nf* madness; (*acto*) crazy act.

locutor, a [loku'tor, a] *nm/f* (*RADIO*) announcer; (*comentarista*) commentator; (*TV*) newscaster, newsreader.

locutorio [loku'torjo] *nm* (*TELEC*) telephone box *o* booth.

lodo ['loðo] *nm* mud.

logia ['loxja] *nf* (*MIL, de masones*) lodge; (*ARQ*) loggia.

lógico, a ['loxiko, a] *a* logical; (*correcto*) natural; (*razonable*) reasonable ♦ *nm* logician ♦ *nf* logic; **es ~ que** ... it stands to reason that ...; **ser de una lógica aplastante** to be as clear as day.

logística [lo'xistika] *nf* logistics *pl*.

lograr [lo'ɣrar] *vt* (*obtener*) to get, obtain; (*conseguir*) to achieve, attain; **~ hacer** to manage to do; **~ que uno venga** to manage to get sb to come; **~ acceso a** (*INFORM*) to access.

logro ['loɣro] *nm* achievement, success; (*COM*) profit.

logroñés, esa [loɣro'ɲes, esa] *a* of *o* from Logroño ♦ *nm/f* native *o* inhabitant of Logroño.

Loira ['loira] *nm* Loire.

loma ['loma] *nf* hillock, low ridge.

Lombardía [lombar'ðia] *nf* Lombardy.

lombriz [lom'briθ] *nf* (earth)worm.

lomo ['lomo] *nm* (*de animal*) back; (*CULIN: de cerdo*) pork loin; (: *de vaca*) rib steak; (*de libro*) spine.

lona ['lona] *nf* canvas.

loncha ['lontʃa] *nf* = **lonja**.

lonche ['lontʃe] *nm* (*AM*) lunch.

lonchería [lontʃe'ria] *nf* (*AM*) snack bar, diner (*US*).

londinense [londi'nense] *a* London *cpd*, of *o* from London ♦ *nm/f* Londoner.

Londres ['londres] *nm* London.

longaniza [longa'niθa] *nf* pork sausage.

longitud [lonxi'tuð] *nf* length; (*GEO*) longitude; **tener 3 metros de ~** to be 3 metres long; **~ de onda** wavelength; **salto de ~** long jump.

lonja ['lonxa] *nf* slice; (*de tocino*) rasher; (*COM*) market, exchange; **~ de pescado** fish market.

lontananza [lonta'nanθa] *nf* background; **en ~** far away, in the distance.

loor [lo'or] *nm* praise.

Lorena [lo'rena] *nf* Lorraine.

loro ['loro] *nm* parrot.

los [los] *artículo definido mpl* the ♦ *pron* them; (*ustedes*) you; **mis libros y ~ de usted** my books and yours.

losa ['losa] *nf* stone; **~ sepulcral** gravestone.

lote ['lote] *nm* portion, share; (*COM*) lot; (*INFORM*) batch.

lotería [lote'ria] *nf* lottery; (*juego*) lotto; **le tocó la ~** he won a big prize in the lottery; (*fig*) he struck lucky; **~ nacional** national lottery; **~ primitiva** (*Esp*) *type of state-run lottery.*

lotero, a [lo'tero, a] *nm/f* seller of lottery tickets.

Lovaina [lo'βaina] *nf* Louvain.

loza ['loθa] *nf* crockery; **~ fina** china.

lozanía [loθa'nia] *nf* (*lujo*) luxuriance.

lozano, a [lo'θano, a] *a* luxuriant; (*animado*) lively.

lubina [lu'βina] *nf* (*ZOOL*) sea bass.

lubricante [luβri'kante] *a, nm* lubricant.

lubricar [luβri'kar], **lubrificar** [luβrifi'kar] *vt* to lubricate.

lubrifique [luβri'fike] *etc vb V* **lubrificar**.

lubrique [lu'βrike] *etc vb V* **lubricar**.

lucense [lu'θense] *a* of *o* from Lugo ♦ *nm/f* native *o* inhabitant of Lugo.

Lucerna [lu'θerna] *nf* Lucerne.

lucero [lu'θero] *nm* (*ASTRO*) bright star; (*fig*) brilliance; **~ del alba/de la tarde** morning/evening star.

luces ['luθes] *nfpl de* **luz**.

lucidez [luθi'ðeθ] *nf* lucidity.

lucido, a [lu'θiðo, a] *a* (*espléndido*) splendid, brilliant; (*elegante*) elegant; (*exitoso*) successful.

lúcido, a [lu'θiðo, a] *a* lucid.

luciérnaga [lu'θjernaɣa] *nf* glow-worm.

lucimiento [luθi'mjento] *nm* (*brillo*) brilliance; (*éxito*) success.

lucio ['luθjo] *nm* (*ZOOL*) pike.

lucir [lu'θir] *vt* to illuminate, light (up); (*ostentar*) to show off ♦ *vi* (*brillar*) to shine; **~se** *vr* (*irónico*) to make a fool of o.s.; (*ostentarse*) to show off.

lucrativo, a [lukra'tiβo, a] *a* lucrative, profitable; **institución no lucrativa** non profit-making institution.

lucro ['lukro] *nm* profit, gain; **~s y daños** (*COM*) profit and loss *sg*.

luctuoso, a [luk'twoso, a] *a* mournful.

lucha ['lutʃa] *nf* fight, struggle; **~ de clases** class struggle; **~ libre** wrestling.

luchar [lu'tʃar] *vi* to fight.

luego ['lweɣo] *ad* (*después*) next; (*más tarde*) later, afterwards; **desde ~** of course; **¡hasta ~!** see you later!, so long!; **¿y ~?** what next?

lugar [lu'ɣar] *nm* place; (*sitio*) spot; (*pueblo*) village, town; **en ~ de** instead of; **en primer ~** in the first place, firstly; **dar ~ a** to give rise to; **hacer ~** to make room; **fuera de ~** out of place; **tener ~** to take place; **~ común** commonplace; **yo en su ~** if I were him; **no hay ~ para preo-**

cupaciones there is no cause for concern.

lugareño, a [luɣa'reɲo, a] *a* village *cpd* ♦ *nm/f* villager.

lugarteniente [luɣarte'njente] *nm* deputy.

lúgubre ['luɣuβre] *a* mournful.

lujo ['luxo] *nm* luxury; (*fig*) profusion, abundance; **de** ~ luxury *cpd*, de luxe.

lujoso, a [lu'xoso, a] *a* luxurious.

lujuria [lu'xurja] *nf* lust.

lumbre ['lumbre] *nf* (*luz*) light; (*fuego*) fire; **cerca de la** ~ near the fire, at the fireside; **¿tienes** ~**?** (*para cigarro*) have you got a light?

lumbrera [lum'brera] *nf* luminary; (*fig*) leading light.

luminoso, a [lumi'noso, a] *a* luminous, shining; (*idea*) bright, brilliant.

luna ['luna] *nf* moon; (*vidrio: escaparate*) plate glass; (: *de un espejo*) glass; (: *de gafas*) lens; (*fig*) crescent; ~ **creciente/ llena/menguante/nueva** crescent/full/waning/new moon; ~ **de miel** honeymoon; **estar en la** ~ to have one's head in the clouds.

lunar [lu'nar] *a* lunar ♦ *nm* (*ANAT*) mole; **tela a** ~**es** spotted material.

lunes ['lunes] *nm inv* Monday.

luneta [lu'neta] *nf* lens.

lupa ['lupa] *nf* magnifying glass.

lusitano, a [lusi'tano, a], **luso, a** ['luso, a] *a, nm/f* Portuguese.

lustrar [lus'trar] *vt* (*mueble*) to polish; (*zapatos*) to shine.

lustre ['lustre] *nm* polish; (*fig*) lustre; **dar** ~ **a** to polish.

lustro ['lustro] *nm* period of five years.

lustroso, a [lus'troso, a] *a* shining.

luterano, a [lute'rano, a] *a* Lutheran.

luto ['luto] *nm* mourning; (*congoja*) grief, sorrow; **llevar el** *o* **vestirse de** ~ to be in mourning.

luxación [luksa'θjon] *nf* (*MED*) dislocation; **tener una** ~ **de tobillo** to have a dislocated ankle.

Luxemburgo [luksem'burɣo] *nm* Luxembourg.

luz [luθ], *pl* **luces** *nf* (*tb fig*) light; (*fam*) electricity; **dar a** ~ **un niño** to give birth to a child; **sacar a la** ~ to bring to light; **dar la** ~ to switch on the light; **encender** (*Esp*) *o* **prender** (*AM*)**/apagar la** ~ to switch the light on/off; **les cortaron la** ~ their (electricity) supply was cut off; **a la** ~ **de** in the light of; **a todas luces** by any reckoning; **hacer la** ~ **sobre** to shed light on; **tener pocas luces** to be dim *o* stupid; ~ **de la luna/del sol** *o* **solar** moonlight/sunlight; ~ **eléctrica** electric light; ~ **roja/ verde** red/green light; ~ **de cruce** (*AUTO*) dipped headlight; ~ **de freno** brake light; ~ **intermitente/trasera** flashing/rear light;

luces de tráfico traffic lights; **el Siglo de las Luces** the Age of Enlightenment; **traje de luces** bullfighter's costume.

luzca ['luθka] *etc vb V* **lucir.**

LL

Ll, ll ['eʎe] *nf* (*letra*) Ll, ll.

llaga ['ʎaɣa] *nf* wound.

llagar [ʎa'ɣar] *vt* to make sore; (*herir*) to wound.

llague ['ʎaɣe] *etc vb V* **llagar.**

llama ['ʎama] *nf* flame; (*fig*) passion; (*ZOOL*) llama; **en** ~**s** burning, ablaze.

llamada [ʎa'maða] *nf* call; (*a la puerta*) knock; (: *timbre*) ring; ~ **a cobro revertido** reverse-charge call; ~ **al orden** call to order; ~ **a pie de página** reference note; ~ **a procedimiento** (*INFORM*) procedure call; ~ **interurbana** trunk call.

llamamiento [ʎama'mjento] *nm* call; **hacer un** ~ **a uno para que haga algo** to appeal to sb to do sth.

llamar [ʎa'mar] *vt* to call; (*convocar*) to summon; (*invocar*) to invoke; (*atraer con gesto*) to beckon; (*atención*) to attract; (*TELEC: tb*: ~ **por teléfono**) to call, ring up, telephone; (*MIL*) to call up ♦ *vi* (*por teléfono*) to telephone; (*a la puerta*) to knock (*o* ring); (*por señas*) to beckon; ~**se** *vr* to be called, be named; **¿cómo se llama usted?** what's your name?; **¿quién llama?** (*TELEC*) who's calling?, who's that?; **no me llama la atención** (*fam*) I don't fancy it.

llamarada [ʎama'raða] *nf* (*llamas*) blaze; (*rubor*) flush; (*fig*) flare-up.

llamativo, a [ʎama'tiβo, a] *a* showy; (*color*) loud.

llamear [ʎame'ar] *vi* to blaze.

llanamente [ʎana'mente] *ad* (*lisamente*) smoothly; (*sin ostentaciones*) plainly; (*sinceramente*) frankly; *V tb* **liso.**

llaneza [ʎa'neθa] *nf* (*gen*) simplicity; (*honestidad*) straightforwardness, frankness.

llano, a ['ʎano, a] *a* (*superficie*) flat; (*persona*) straightforward; (*estilo*) clear ♦ *nm* plain, flat ground.

llanta ['ʎanta] *nf* (*wheel*) rim; (*AM: tb*: ~ **de goma**) tyre; (: *cámara*) inner (tube).

llanto ['ʎanto] *nm* weeping; (*fig*) lamentation; (*canción*) dirge, lament.

llanura [ʎa'nura] *nf* (*lisura*) flatness, smoothness; (*GEO*) plain.

llave ['ʎaβe] *nf* key; (*de gas, agua*) tap

(*Brit*), faucet (*US*); (*MECÁNICA*) spanner; (*de la luz*) switch; (*MUS*) key; ~ **inglesa** monkey wrench; ~ **maestra** master key; ~ **de contacto** (*AUTO*) ignition key; ~ **de paso** stopcock; **echar** ~ **a** to lock up.

llavero [ʎa'ßero] *nm* keyring.

llavín [ʎa'ßin] *nm* latchkey.

llegada [ʎe'ɣaða] *nf* arrival.

llegar [ʎe'ɣar] *vt* to bring up, bring over ♦ *vi* to arrive; (*bastar*) to be enough; ~**se a** to approach; ~ **a** (*alcanzar*) to reach; to manage to, succeed in; ~ **a saber** to find out; ~ **a ser famoso/el jefe** to become famous/the boss; ~ **a las manos** to come to blows; ~ **a las manos de** to come into the hands of; **no llegues tarde** don't be late; **esta cuerda no llega** this rope isn't long enough.

llegue ['ʎeɣe] *etc vb V* **llegar**.

llenar [ʎe'nar] *vt* to fill; (*superficie*) to cover; (*espacio, tiempo*) to fill, take up; (*formulario*) to fill in *o* out; (*deber*) to fulfil; (*fig*) to heap; ~**se** *vr* to fill (up); ~**se de** (*fam*) to stuff o.s. with.

lleno, a ['ʎeno, a] *a* full, filled; (*repleto*) full up ♦ *nm* (*abundancia*) abundance; (*TEATRO*) full house; **dar de** ~ **contra un muro** to hit a wall head-on.

llevadero, a [ʎeßa'ðero, a] *a* bearable, tolerable.

llevar [ʎe'ßar] *vt* to take; (*ropa*) to wear; (*cargar*) to carry; (*quitar*) to take away; (*en coche*) to drive; (*transportar*) to transport; (*ruta*) to follow, keep to; (*traer: dinero*) to carry; (*suj: camino etc*): ~ **a** to lead to; (*MAT*) to carry; (*aguantar*) to bear; (*negocio*) to conduct, direct; to manage; ~**se** *vr* to carry off, take away; **llevamos dos días aquí** we have been here for two days; **él me lleva 2 años** he's 2 years older than me; ~ **adelante** (*fig*) to carry forward; ~ **por delante a uno** (*en coche etc*) to run sb over; (*fig*) to ride roughshod over sb; ~ **la ventaja** to be winning *o* in the lead; ~ **los libros** (*COM*) to keep the books; **llevo las de perder** I'm likely to lose; **no las lleva todas consigo** he's not all there; **nos llevó a cenar fuera** she took us out for a meal; ~**se a uno por delante** (*atropellar*) to run sb over; ~**se bien** to get on well (together).

llorar [ʎo'rar] *vt* to cry, weep ♦ *vi* to cry, weep; (*ojos*) to water; ~ **a moco tendido** to sob one's heart out; ~ **de risa** to cry with laughter.

lloriquear [ʎorike'ar] *vi* to snivel, whimper.

lloro ['ʎoro] *nm* crying, weeping.

llorón, ona [ʎo'ron, ona] *a* tearful ♦ *nm/f* cry-baby.

lloroso, a [ʎo'roso, a] *a* (*gen*) weeping, tearful; (*triste*) sad, sorrowful.

llover [ʎo'ßer] *vi* to rain; ~ **a cántaros** *o* **a cubos** *o* **a mares** to rain cats and dogs, pour (down); **ser una cosa llovida del cielo** to be a godsend; **llueve sobre mojado** it never rains but it pours.

llovizna [ʎo'ßiθna] *nf* drizzle.

lloviznar [ʎoßiθ'nar] *vi* to drizzle.

llueve ['ʎweße] *etc vb V* **llover**.

lluvia ['ʎußja] *nf* rain; (*cantidad*) rainfall; (*fig: balas etc*) hail, shower; ~ **radioactiva** radioactive fallout; **día de** ~ rainy day; **una** ~ **de regalos** a shower of gifts.

lluvioso, a [ʎu'ßjoso, a] *a* rainy.

M

M, m ['eme] *nf* (*letra*) M, m; **M de Madrid** M for Mike.

M. *abr* (*FERRO*) = **Metro.**

m. *abr* (= *metro(s)*) m; (= *minuto(s)*) min., m; (= *masculino*) m., masc.

M.ª *abr* = **María.**

macabro, a [ma'kaßro, a] *a* macabre.

macaco [ma'kako] *nm* (*ZOOL*) rhesus monkey; (*fam*) runt, squirt.

macana [ma'kana] *nf* (*AM: porra*) club; (: *mentira*) lie, fib; (: *tontería*) piece of nonsense.

macanudo, a [maka'nuðo, a] *a* (*AM fam*) great.

macarra [ma'karra] *nm* (*fam*) thug.

macarrones [maka'rrones] *nmpl* macaroni *sg*.

macedonia [maθe'ðonja] *nf*: ~ **de frutas** fruit salad.

macerar [maθe'rar] *vt* (*CULIN*) to soak, macerate; ~**se** *vr* to soak, soften.

maceta [ma'θeta] *nf* (*de flores*) pot of flowers; (*para plantas*) flowerpot.

macetero [maθe'tero] *nm* flowerpot stand *o* holder.

macilento, a [maθi'lento, a] *a* (*pálido*) pale; (*ojeroso*) haggard.

macizo, a [ma'θiθo, a] *a* (*grande*) massive; (*fuerte, sólido*) solid ♦ *nm* mass, chunk; (*GEO*) massif.

macrobiótico, a [makro'ßjotiko, a] *a* macrobiotic.

macro-comando [makroko'mando] *nm* (*INFORM*) macro (command).

macroeconomía [makroekono'mia] *nf* (*COM*) macroeconomics *sg*.

mácula ['makula] *nf* stain, blemish.

macuto [ma'kuto] *nm* (*MIL*) knapsack.

machacar [matʃa'kar] *vt* to crush, pound;

(moler) to grind (up); *(aplastar)* to mash ♦ *vi (insistir)* to go on, keep on.

machacón, ona [matʃa'kon, ona] *a (pesado)* tiresome; *(insistente)* insistent; *(monótono)* monotonous.

machamartillo [matʃamar'tiʎo]: **a** ~ *ad*: **creer a** ~ *(firmemente)* to believe firmly.

machaque [ma'tʃake] *etc vb V* **machacar.**

machete [ma'tʃete] *nm (AM)* machete, (large) knife.

machismo [ma'tʃismo] *nm* sexism; male chauvinism.

machista [ma'tʃista] *a, nm* sexist; male chauvinist.

macho ['matʃo] *a* male; *(fig)* virile ♦ *nm* male; *(fig)* he-man, tough guy *(US)*; *(TEC: perno)* pin, peg; *(ELEC)* pin, plug; *(COSTURA)* hook.

machucar [matʃu'kar] *vt* to pound.

machuque [ma'tʃuke] *etc vb V* **machucar.**

Madagascar [maðaɣas'kar] *nm* Madagascar.

madeja [ma'ðexa] *nf (de lana)* skein, hank.

madera [ma'ðera] *nf* wood; *(fig)* nature, character; *(: aptitud)* aptitude; **una** ~ **a** piece of wood; ~ **contrachapada** *o* **laminada** plywood; **tiene buena** ~ he's made of solid stuff; **tiene** ~ **de futbolista** he's got the makings of a footballer.

maderaje [maðe'raxe], **maderamen** [maðe'ramen] *nm* timber; *(trabajo)* woodwork, timbering.

maderero [maðe'rero] *nm* timber merchant.

madero [ma'ðero] *nm* beam; *(fig)* ship.

madrastra [ma'ðrastra] *nf* stepmother.

madre ['maðre] *a* mother *cpd*; *(AM)* tremendous ♦ *nf* mother; *(de vino etc)* dregs *pl*; ~ **adoptiva/política/soltera** foster mother/mother-in-law/unmarried mother; **sin** ~ motherless; **¡**~ **mía!** oh dear!; **¡tu** ~**!** *(fam!)* fuck off! *(!)*; **salirse de** ~ *(río)* to burst its banks; *(persona)* to lose all self-control.

madreperla [maðre'perla] *nf* mother-of-pearl.

madreselva [maðre'selβa] *nf* honeysuckle.

Madrid [ma'ðrið] *n* Madrid.

madriguera [maðri'ɣera] *nf* burrow.

madrileño, a [maðri'leɲo, a] *a* of *o* from Madrid ♦ *nm/f* native *o* inhabitant of Madrid.

Madriles [ma'ðriles] *nmpl*: **Los** ~ *(fam)* Madrid *sg*.

madrina [ma'ðrina] *nf* godmother; *(ARQ)* prop, shore; *(TEC)* brace; ~ **de boda** bridesmaid.

madroño [ma'ðroɲo] *nm (BOT)* strawberry tree, arbutus.

madrugada [maðru'ɣaða] *nf* early morning, small hours; *(alba)* dawn, daybreak; **a las**

4 de la ~ at 4 o'clock in the morning.

madrugador, a [maðruɣa'ðor, a] *a* early-rising.

madrugar [maðru'ɣar] *vi* to get up early; *(fig)* to get a head start.

madrugue [ma'ðruɣe] *etc vb V* **madrugar.**

madurar [maðu'rar] *vt, vi (fruta)* to ripen; *(fig)* to mature.

madurez [maðu'reθ] *nf* ripeness; *(fig)* maturity.

maduro, a [ma'ðuro, a] *a* ripe; *(fig)* mature; **poco** ~ unripe.

MAE *nm abr (Esp POL)* = **Ministerio de Asuntos Exteriores.**

maestra [ma'estra] *nf V* **maestro.**

maestría [maes'tria] *nf* mastery; *(habilidad)* skill, expertise.

maestro, a [ma'estro, a] *a* masterly; *(perito)* skilled, expert; *(principal)* main; *(educado)* trained ♦ *nm/f* master/mistress; *(profesor)* teacher ♦ *nm (autoridad)* authority; *(MUS)* maestro; *(AM)* skilled workman; ~ **albañil** master mason; ~ **de obras** foreman.

mafioso [ma'fjoso] *nm (AM)* gangster.

Magallanes [maɣa'ʎanes] *nm*: **Estrecho de** ~ Strait of Magellan.

magia ['maxja] *nf* magic.

mágico, a ['maxiko, a] *a* magic(al) ♦ *nm/f* magician.

magisterio [maxis'terjo] *nm (enseñanza)* teaching; *(profesión)* teaching profession; *(maestros)* teachers *pl*.

magistrado [maxis'traðo] *nm* magistrate.

magistral [maxis'tral] *a* magisterial; *(fig)* masterly.

magistratura [maxistra'tura] *nf* magistracy; **M**~ **del Trabajo** *(Esp)* ≈ Industrial Tribunal.

magnánimo, a [maɣ'nanimo, a] *a* magnanimous.

magnate [maɣ'nate] *nm* magnate, tycoon; ~ **de la prensa** press baron.

magnesio [maɣ'nesjo] *nm (QUÍMICA)* magnesium.

magnetice [maɣne'tiθe] *etc vb V* **magnetizar.**

magnético, a [maɣ'netiko, a] *a* magnetic.

magnetizar [maɣneti'θar] *vt* to magnetize.

magnetofón [maɣneto'fon], **magnetófono** [maɣne'tofono] *nm* tape recorder.

magnetofónico, a [maɣneto'foniko, a] *a*: **cinta magnetofónica** recording tape.

magnicidio [maɣni'θiðjo] *nm* assassination *(of an important person)*.

magnífico, a [maɣ'nifiko, a] *a* splendid, magnificent.

magnitud [maɣni'tuð] *nf* magnitude.

mago, a ['maɣo, a] *nm/f* magician, wizard; **los Reyes M**~**s** the Magi, the Three Wise Men.

magrear [maɤre'ar] *vt* (*fam*) to touch up.

magrez [maɤ'reθ] *nf* leanness.

magro, a ['maɤro, a] *a* (*persona*) thin, lean; (*carne*) lean.

maguey [ma'ɤei] *nm* (*AM BOT*) agave.

magulladura [maɤuʎa'ðura] *nf* bruise.

magullar [maɤu'ʎar] *vt* (*amoratar*) to bruise; (*dañar*) to damage; (*fam*: *golpear*) to bash, beat.

Maguncia [ma'ɤunθja] *nf* Mainz.

mahometano, a [maome'tano, a] *a* Mohammedan.

mahonesa [mao'nesa] *nf* = **mayonesa**.

maicena [mai'θena] *nf* cornflour, corn starch (*US*).

maillot [ma'jot] *nm* swimming costume; (*DEPORTE*) vest.

maitre ['metre] *nm* head waiter.

maíz [ma'iθ] *nm* maize (*Brit*), corn (*US*); sweet corn.

majadero, a [maxa'ðero, a] *a* silly, stupid.

majar [ma'xar] *vt* to crush, grind.

majareta [maxa'reta] *a* (*fam*) cracked, potty.

majestad [maxes'tað] *nf* majesty; **Su M~** His/Her Majesty; (**Vuestra**) **M~** Your Majesty.

majestuoso, a [maxes'twoso, a] *a* majestic.

majo, a ['maxo, a] *a* nice; (*guapo*) attractive, good-looking; (*elegante*) smart.

mal [mal] *ad* badly; (*equivocadamente*) wrongly; (*con dificultad*) with difficulty ♦ *a* = **malo, a** ♦ *nm* evil; (*desgracia*) misfortune; (*daño*) harm, damage; (*MED*) illness ♦ *conj*: ~ **que le pese** whether he likes it or not; **me entendió** ~ he misunderstood me; **hablar** ~ **de uno** to speak ill of sb; **huele** ~ it smells bad; **ir de** ~ **en peor** to go from bad to worse; **oigo/veo** ~ I can't hear/see very well; **si** ~ **no recuerdo** if my memory serves me right; **¡menos** ~! just as well!; ~ **que bien** rightly or wrongly; **no hay** ~ **que por bien no venga** every cloud has a silver lining; ~ **de ojo** evil eye.

mala ['mala] *nf V* **malo**.

malabarismo [malaβa'rismo] *nm* juggling.

malabarista [malaβa'rista] *nm/f* juggler.

malaconsejado, a [malakonse'xaðo, a] *a* ill-advised.

malacostumbrado, a [malakostum'braðo, a] *a* (*consentido*) spoiled.

malacostumbrar [malakostum'brar] *vt*: ~ **a uno** to get sb into bad habits.

malagueño, a [mala'ɤeɲo, a] *a* of *o* from Málaga ♦ native *o* inhabitant of Málaga.

malaria [ma'larja] *nf* malaria.

Malasia [ma'lasja] *nf* Malaysia.

malavenido, a [malaβe'niðo, a] *a* incompatible.

malayo, a [ma'lajo, a] *a* Malay(an) ♦ *nm/f* Malay ♦ *nm* (*LING*) Malay ♦ *excl*: **¡malaya!** (*AM*) damn!

malcarado, a [malka'raðo, a] *a* ugly, grim-faced.

malcriado, a [mal'krjaðo, a] *a* (*consentido*) spoiled.

malcriar [mal'krjar] *vt* to spoil, pamper.

maldad [mal'dað] *nf* evil, wickedness.

maldecir [malde'θir] *vt* to curse ♦ *vi*: ~ **de** to speak ill of.

maldiciendo [maldi'θjendo] *etc vb V* **maldecir**.

maldición [maldi'θjon] *nf* curse; **¡~!** curse it!, damn!

maldiga [mal'diɤa] *etc*, **maldije** [mal'dixe] *etc*, **maldiré** [maldi're] *etc vb V* **maldecir**.

maldito, a [mal'dito, a] *a* (*condenado*) damned; (*perverso*) wicked ♦ *nm*: **el** ~ the devil; **¡~ sea!** damn it!; **no le hace** ~ **(el) caso** he doesn't take a blind bit of notice.

maleable [male'aßle] *a* malleable.

maleante [male'ante] *a* wicked ♦ *nm/f* criminal, crook.

malecón [male'kon] *nm* pier, jetty.

maledicencia [maleði'θenθja] *nf* slander, scandal.

maleducado, a [maleðu'kaðo, a] *a* bad-mannered, rude.

maleficio [male'fiθjo] *nm* curse, spell.

malentendido [malenten'diðo] *nm* misunderstanding.

malestar [males'tar] *nm* (*gen*) discomfort; (*enfermedad*) indisposition; (*fig*: *inquietud*) uneasiness; (*POL*) unrest; **siento un** ~ **en el estómago** my stomach is upset.

maleta [ma'leta] *nf* case, suitcase; (*AUTO*) boot (*Brit*), trunk (*US*); **hacer la** ~ to pack.

maletera [male'tera] *nf* (*AM AUTO*) boot (*Brit*), trunk (*US*).

maletero [male'tero] *nm* (*AUTO*) boot (*Brit*), trunk (*US*); (*persona*) porter.

maletín [male'tin] *nm* small case, bag; (*portafolio*) briefcase.

malevolencia [maleβo'lenθja] *nf* malice, spite.

malévolo, a [ma'leßolo, a] *a* malicious, spiteful.

maleza [ma'leθa] *nf* (*hierbas malas*) weeds *pl*; (*arbustos*) thicket.

malgache [mal'ɤatʃe] *a* of *o* from Madagascar ♦ *nm/f* native *o* inhabitant of Madagascar.

malgastar [malɤas'tar] *vt* (*tiempo, dinero*) to waste; (*recursos*) to squander; (*salud*) to ruin.

malhechor, a [male'tʃor, a] *nm/f* delinquent; (*criminal*) criminal.

malhumorado, a [malumo'raðo, a] *a* bad-tempered.

malicia [ma'liθja] *nf* (*maldad*) wickedness; (*astucia*) slyness, guile; (*mala intención*) malice, spite; (*carácter travieso*) mischievousness.

malicioso, a [mali'θjoso, a] *a* wicked, evil; sly, crafty; malicious, spiteful; mischievous.

malignidad [maliɣni'ðað] *nf* (*MED*) malignancy; (*malicia*) malice.

maligno, a [ma'liɣno, a] *a* evil; (*dañino*) pernicious, harmful; (*malévolo*) malicious; (*MED*) malignant ♦ *nm*: **el ~** the devil.

malintencionado, a [malintenθjo'naðo, a] *a* (*comentario*) hostile; (*persona*) malicious.

malnutrido, a [malnu'triðo, a] *a* undernourished.

malo, a ['malo, a] *a* (**mal** *before nmsg*) bad; (*calidad*) poor; (*falso*) false; (*espantoso*) dreadful; (*niño*) naughty ♦ *nm/f* villain ♦ *nm* (*CINE fam*) bad guy ♦ *nf* spell of bad luck; **estar ~** to be ill; **andar a malas con uno** to be on bad terms with sb; **estar de malas** (*mal humor*) to be in a bad mood; **lo ~ es que** ... the trouble is that ....

malograr [malo'ɣrar] *vt* to spoil; (*plan*) to upset; (*ocasión*) to waste; **~se** *vr* (*plan etc*) to fail, come to grief; (*persona*) to die before one's time.

maloliente [malo'ljente] *a* stinking, smelly.

malparado, a [malpa'raðo, a] *a*: **salir ~** to come off badly.

malparir [malpa'rir] *vi* to have a miscarriage.

malpensado, a [malpen'saðo, a] *a* evilminded.

malquerencia [malke'renθja] *nf* dislike.

malquistar [malkis'tar] *vt*: **~ a dos personas** to cause a rift between two people; **~se** *vr* to fall out.

malsano, a [mal'sano, a] *a* unhealthy.

malsonante [malso'nante] *a* (*palabra*) nasty, rude.

Malta ['malta] *nf* Malta.

malteada [malte'aða] *nf* (*AM*) milk shake.

maltés, esa [mal'tes, esa] *a, nm/f* Maltese.

maltraer [maltra'er] *vt* (*abusar*) to insult, abuse; (*maltratar*) to ill-treat.

maltratar [maltra'tar] *vt* to ill-treat, mistreat.

maltrecho, a [mal'tretʃo, a] *a* battered, damaged.

malva ['malβa] *nf* mallow; **~ loca** hollyhock; (**de color de**) **~** mauve.

malvado, a [mal'βaðo, a] *a* evil, villainous.

malvavisco [malβa'βisko] *nm* marshmallow.

malvender [malβen'der] *vt* to sell off cheap *o* at a loss.

malversación [malβersa'θjon] *nf* embezzle-

ment, misappropriation.

malversar [malβer'sar] *vt* to embezzle, misappropriate.

Malvinas [mal'βinas] *nfpl*: **Islas ~** Falkland Islands.

malla ['maʎa] *nf* (*de una red*) mesh; (*red*) network; (*de baño*) swimsuit; (*de ballet, gimnasia*) leotard; **~s** *nfpl* tights; **~ de alambre** wire mesh.

Mallorca [ma'ʎorka] *nf* Majorca.

mallorquín, ina [maʎor'kin, ina] *a, nm/f* Majorcan ♦ *nm* (*LING*) Majorcan.

mama ['mama], *pl* **mamás** *nf* (*de animal*) teat; (*de mujer*) breast.

mamá [ma'ma] *nf* (*fam*) mum, mummy.

mamar [ma'mar] *vt* (*pecho*) to suck; (*fig*) to absorb, assimilate ♦ *vi* to suck; **dar de ~** to (breast-)feed; (*animal*) to suckle.

mamarracho [mama'rratʃo] *nm* sight, mess.

mamífero, a [ma'mifero, a] *a* mammalian, mammal *cpd* ♦ *nm* mammal.

mamón, ona [ma'mon, ona] *a* small, baby *cpd* ♦ *nm/f* small baby; (*fam*) idiot, berk.

mamotreto [mamo'treto] *nm* hefty volume; (*fam*) whacking great thing.

mampara [mam'para] *nf* (*entre habitaciones*) partition; (*biombo*) screen.

mamporro [mam'porro] *nm* (*fam*): **dar un ~ a** to clout.

mampostería [mamposte'ria] *nf* masonry.

mamut [ma'mut] *nm* mammoth.

maná [ma'na] *nm* manna.

manada [ma'naða] *nf* (*ZOOL*) herd; (: *de leones*) pride; (: *de lobos*) pack; **llegaron en ~s** (*fam*) they came in droves.

Managua [ma'naɣwa] *n* Managua.

manantial [manan'tjal] *nm* spring; (*fuente*) fountain; (*fig*) source.

manar [ma'nar] *vt* to run with, flow with ♦ *vi* to run, flow; (*abundar*) to abound.

manaza [ma'naθa] *nf* big hand ♦ *a, nm/f inv*: **~s: ser un ~s** to be clumsy.

mancebo [man'θeβo] *nm* (*joven*) young man.

mancilla [man'θiʎa] *nf* stain, blemish.

mancillar [manθi'ʎar] *vt* to stain, sully.

manco, a ['manko, a] *a* one-armed; onehanded; (*fig*) defective, faulty; **no ser ~** to be useful *o* active.

mancomunar [mankomu'nar] *vt* to unite, bring together; (*recursos*) to pool; (*JUR*) to make jointly responsible.

mancomunidad [mankomuni'ðað] *nf* union, association; (*comunidad*) community; (*JUR*) joint responsibility.

mancha ['mantʃa] *nf* stain, mark; (*de tinta*) blot; (*de vegetación*) patch; (*imperfección*) stain, blemish, blot; (*boceto*) sketch, outline; **la M~** La Mancha.

manchado, a [man'tʃaðo, a] *a* (*sucio*)

dirty; (*animal*) spotted; (*ave*) speckled; (*tinta*) smudged.

manchar [man'tʃar] *vt* to stain, mark; (*ZOOL*) to patch; (*ensuciar*) to soil, dirty; ~**se** *vr* to get dirty; (*fig*) to dirty one's hands.

manchego, a [man'tʃeɣo, a] *a* of *o* from La Mancha ♦ *nm/f* native *o* inhabitant of La Mancha.

mandadero [manda'ðero] *nm* messenger.

mandado [man'daðo] *nm* (*orden*) order; (*recado*) commission, errand.

mandamás [manda'mas] *a nm/f inv* boss; **ser un** ~ to be very bossy.

mandamiento [manda'mjento] *nm* (*orden*) order, command; (*REL*) commandment; ~ **judicial** warrant.

mandar [man'dar] *vt* (*ordenar*) to order; (*dirigir*) to lead, command; (*país*) to rule over; (*enviar*) to send; (*pedir*) to order, ask for ♦ *vi* to be in charge; (*pey*) to be bossy; **¿mande?** pardon?, excuse me? (*US*); **¿manda usted algo más?** is there anything else?; ~ **a uno a paseo** *o* **a la porra** to tell sb to go to hell; **se lo mandaremos por correo** we'll post it to you; ~ **hacer un traje** to have a suit made.

mandarín [manda'rin] *nm* petty bureaucrat.

mandarina [manda'rina] *nf* (*fruta*) tangerine, mandarin (orange).

mandatario, a [manda'tarjo, a] *nm/f* (*representante*) agent; **primer** ~ head of state.

mandato [man'dato] *nm* (*orden*) order; (*POL*: *período*) term of office; (: *territorio*) mandate; (*INFORM*) command; ~ **judicial** (search) warrant.

mandíbula [man'diβula] *nf* jaw.

mandil [man'dil] *nm* (*delantal*) apron.

mando ['mando] *nm* (*MIL*) command; (*de país*) rule; (*el primer lugar*) lead; (*POL*) term of office; (*TEC*) control; ~ **a la izquierda** left-hand drive; **los altos** ~**s** the high command *sg*; ~ **por botón** push-button control; **al** ~ **de** in charge of; **tomar el** ~ to take the lead.

mandolina [mando'lina] *nf* mandolin(e).

mandón, ona [man'don, ona] *a* bossy, domineering.

manecilla [mane'θiʎa] *nf* (*TEC*) pointer; (*de reloj*) hand.

manejable [mane'xaβle] *a* manageable; (*fácil de usar*) handy.

manejar [mane'xar] *vt* to manage; (*máquina*) to work, operate; (*caballo etc*) to handle; (*casa*) to run, manage; (*AM AUTO*) to drive; *"*~ **con cuidado***"* "handle with care" ♦ *vi* (*AM AUTO*) to drive; ~**se** *vr* (*comportarse*) to act, behave; (*arreglárselas*) to manage.

manejo [ma'nexo] *nm* management; han-

dling; running; driving; (*facilidad de trato*) ease, confidence; (*de idioma*) command; ~**s** *nmpl* intrigues; **tengo** ~ **del francés** I have a good command of French.

manera [ma'nera] *nf* way, manner, fashion; (*ARTE, LITERATURA etc*: *estilo*) manner, style; ~**s** *nfpl* (*modales*) manners; **su** ~ **de ser** the way he is; (*aire*) his manner; **de mala** ~ (*fam*) badly, unwillingly; **de ninguna** ~ no way, by no means; **de otra** ~ otherwise; **de todas** ~**s** at any rate; **en gran** ~ to a large extent; **sobre** ~ exceedingly; **a mi** ~ **de ver** in my view; **no hay** ~ **de persuadirle** there's no way of convincing him.

manga ['manga] *nf* (*de camisa*) sleeve; (*de riego*) hose; **de** ~ **corta/larga** short-/long-sleeved; **andar** ~ **por hombro** (*desorden*) to be topsy-turvy; **tener** ~ **ancha** to be easy-going.

mangante [man'gante] *a* (*descarado*) brazen ♦ *nm* (*mendigo*) beggar.

mangar [man'gar] *vt* (*unir*) to plug in; (*fam: birlar*) to pinch, nick, swipe; (*mendigar*) to beg.

mango ['mango] *nm* handle; (*BOT*) mango; ~ **de escoba** broomstick.

mangonear [mangone'ar] *vt* to boss about ♦ *vi* to be bossy.

mangue ['mange] *etc vb V* **mangar**.

manguera [man'gera] *nf* (*de riego*) hose; (*tubo*) pipe; ~ **de incendios** fire hose.

maní(s) [ma'ni] *nm, pl* **maníes** *o* **manises** (*AM*: *cacahuete*) peanut; (: *planta*) groundnut plant.

manía [ma'nia] *nf* (*MED*) mania; (*fig*: *moda*) rage, craze; (*disgusto*) dislike; (*malicia*) spite; **tiene** ~**s** she's a bit fussy; **tener** ~ **a uno** to dislike sb.

maníaco, a [ma'niako, a] *a* maniac(al) ♦ *nm/f* maniac.

maniatar [manja'tar] *vt* to tie the hands of.

maniático, a [ma'njatiko, a] *a* maniac(al); (*loco*) crazy; (*tiquismiquis*) fussy ♦ *nm/f* maniac.

manicomio [mani'komjo] *nm* mental hospital (*Brit*), insane asylum (*US*).

manicuro, a [mani'kuro, a] *nm/f* manicurist ♦ *nf* manicure.

manido, a [ma'niðo, a] *a* (*tema etc*) trite, stale.

manifestación [manifesta'θjon] *nf* (*declaración*) statement, declaration; (*demostración*) show, display; (*POL*) demonstration.

manifestante [manifes'tante] *nm/f* demonstrator.

manifestar [manifes'tar] *vt* to show, manifest; (*declarar*) to state, declare; ~**se** *vr* to show, become apparent; (*POL*: *desfilar*) to demonstrate; (: *reunirse*) to hold a mass meeting.

manifiesto, a [mani'fjesto, a] *etc vb* V **manifestar** ♦ *a* clear, manifest ♦ *nm* manifesto; (*ANAT, NAUT*) manifest; **poner algo de** ~ (*aclarar*) to make sth clear; (*revelar*) to reveal sth; **quedar** ~ to be plain *o* clear.

manija [ma'nixa] *nf* handle.

manilla [ma'niʎa] *nf* (*de reloj*) hand; ~**s** (**de hierro**) *nfpl* handcuffs.

manillar [mani'ʎar] *nm* handlebars *pl.*

maniobra [ma'njoßra] *nf* manœuvring; (*maneja*) handling; (*fig: movimiento*) manœuvre, move; (: *estratagema*) trick, stratagem; ~**s** *nfpl* manœuvres.

maniobrar [manio'ßrar] *vt* to manœuvre; (*manejar*) to handle ♦ *vi* to manœuvre.

manipulación [manipula'θjon] *nf* manipulation; (*COM*) handling.

manipular [manipu'lar] *vt* to manipulate; (*manejar*) to handle.

maniquí [mani'ki] *nm/f* model ♦ *nm* dummy.

manirroto, a [mani'rroto, a] *a* lavish, extravagant ♦ *nm/f* spendthrift.

manita [ma'nita] *nf* little hand; ~**s de plata** artistic hands.

manitas [ma'nitas] *a inv* good with one's hands ♦ *nm/f inv*: **ser un** ~ to be very good with one's hands.

manito [ma'nito] *nm* (*AM: en conversación*) mate (*fam*), chum.

manivela [mani'ßela] *nf* crank.

manjar [man'xar] *nm* (tasty) dish.

mano ['mano] *nf* hand; (*ZOOL*) foot, paw; (*de pintura*) coat; (*serie*) lot, series; **a** ~ by hand; **a** ~ **derecha/izquierda** on (*o* to) the right(-hand side)/left(-hand side); **hecho a** ~ handmade; **a** ~**s llenas** lavishly, generously; **de primera** ~ (at) first hand; **de segunda** ~ (at) second hand; **robo a** ~ **armada** armed robbery; **Pedro es mi** ~ **derecha** Pedro is my right-hand man; ~ **de obra** labour, manpower; ~ **de santo** sure remedy; **darse la(s)** ~**(s)** to shake hands; **echar una** ~ to lend a hand; **echar una** ~ **a** to lay hands on; **echar** ~ **de** to make use of; **estrechar la** ~ **a uno** to shake sb's hand; **traer** *o* **llevar algo entre** ~**s** to deal *o* be busy with sth; **está en tus** ~**s** it's up to you; **se le fue la** ~ his hand slipped; (*fig*) he went too far; **¡~s a la obra!** to work!

manojo [ma'noxo] *nm* handful, bunch; ~ **de llaves** bunch of keys.

manómetro [ma'nometro] *nm* (pressure) gauge.

manopla [ma'nopla] *nf* (*paño*) flannel; ~**s** *nfpl* mittens.

manoseado, a [manose'aðo, a] *a* well-worn.

manosear [manose'ar] *vt* (*tocar*) to handle, touch; (*desordenar*) to mess up, rumple;

(*insistir en*) to overwork; (*acariciar*) to caress, fondle; (*pey: persona*) to feel *o* touch up.

manotazo [mano'taθo] *nm* slap, smack.

mansalva [man'salßa]: **a** ~ *ad* indiscriminately.

mansedumbre [manse'ðumbre] *nf* gentleness, meekness; (*de animal*) tameness.

mansión [man'sjon] *nf* mansion.

manso, a ['manso, a] *a* gentle, mild; (*animal*) tame.

manta ['manta] *nf* blanket; (*AM*) poncho.

manteca [man'teka] *nf* fat; (*AM*) butter; ~ **de cacahuete/cacao** peanut/cocoa butter; ~ **de cerdo** lard.

mantecado [mante'kaðo] *nm* (*AM*) ice cream.

mantecoso, a [mante'koso, a] *a* fat, greasy; **queso** ~ soft cheese.

mantel [man'tel] *nm* tablecloth.

mantelería [mantele'ria] *nf* table linen.

mantendré [manten'dre] *etc vb* V **mantener.**

mantener [mante'ner] *vt* to support, maintain; (*alimentar*) to sustain; (*conservar*) to keep; (*TEC*) to maintain, service; ~**se** *vr* (*seguir de pie*) to be still standing; (*no ceder*) to hold one's ground; (*subsistir*) to sustain o.s., keep going; ~ **algo en equilibrio** to keep sth balanced; ~**se a distancia** to keep one's distance; ~**se firme** to hold one's ground.

mantenga [man'tenga] *etc vb* V **mantener.**

mantenimiento [manteni'mjento] *nm* maintenance; sustenance; (*sustento*) support.

mantequería [manteke'ria] *nf* (*ultramarinos*) grocer's (shop).

mantequilla [mante'kiʎa] *nf* butter.

mantilla [man'tiʎa] *nf* mantilla; ~**s** *nfpl* baby clothes; **estar en** ~**s** (*persona*) to be terribly innocent; (*proyecto*) to be in its infancy.

manto ['manto] *nm* (*capa*) cloak; (*de ceremonia*) robe, gown.

mantón [man'ton] *nm* shawl.

mantuve [man'tuße] *etc vb* V **mantener.**

manual [ma'nwal] *a* manual ♦ *nm* manual, handbook; **habilidad** ~ manual skill.

manufactura [manufak'tura] *nf* manufacture; (*fábrica*) factory.

manuscrito, a [manus'krito, a] *a* hand-written ♦ *nm* manuscript.

manutención [manuten'θjon] *nf* maintenance; (*sustento*) support.

manzana [man'θana] *nf* apple; (*ARQ*) block; ~ **de la discordia** (*fig*) bone of contention.

manzanal [manθa'nal] *nm* apple orchard.

manzanilla [manθa'niʎa] *nf* (*planta*) camomile; (*infusión*) camomile tea; (*vino*) manzanilla.

manzano [man'θano] *nm* apple tree.

maña ['maɲa] *nf* (*gen*) skill, dexterity; (*pey*) guile; (*costumbre*) habit; (*una ~*) trick, knack; **con ~** craftily.

mañana [ma'ɲana] *ad* tomorrow ◆ *nm* future ◆ *nf* morning; **de** *o* **por la ~** in the morning; **¡hasta ~!** see you tomorrow!; **pasado ~** the day after tomorrow; **~ por la ~** tomorrow morning.

mañanero, a [maɲa'nero, a] *a* early-rising.

mañoso, a [ma'ɲoso, a] *a* (*hábil*) skilful; (*astuto*) smart, clever.

mapa ['mapa] *nm* map.

maqueta [ma'keta] *nf* (scale) model.

maquiavélico, a [makja'βeliko, a] *a* Machiavellian.

maquillador, a [makiʎa'ðor, a] *nm/f* (*TEATRO etc*) make-up artist.

maquillaje [maki'ʎaxe] *nm* make-up; (*acto*) making up.

maquillar [maki'ʎar] *vt* to make up; **~se** *vr* to put on (some) make-up.

máquina ['makina] *nf* machine; (*de tren*) locomotive, engine; (*FOTO*) camera; (*AM: coche*) car; (*fig*) machinery; (: *proyecto*) plan, project; **a toda ~** at full speed; **escrito a ~** typewritten; **~ de escribir** typewriter; **~ de coser/lavar** sewing/washing machine; **~ de facsímil** facsimile (machine), fax; **~ de franqueo** franking machine; **~ tragaperras** fruit machine; (*COM*) slot machine.

maquinación [makina'θjon] *nf* machination, plot.

maquinal [maki'nal] *a* (*fig*) mechanical, automatic.

maquinar [maki'nar] *vt, vi* to plot.

maquinaria [maki'narja] *nf* (*máquinas*) machinery; (*mecanismo*) mechanism, works *pl*.

maquinilla [maki'niʎa] *nf* small machine; (*torno*) winch; **~ de afeitar** razor; **~ eléctrica** electric razor.

maquinista [maki'nista] *nm* (*FERRO*) engine driver (*Brit*), engineer (*US*); (*TEC*) operator; (*NAUT*) engineer.

mar [mar] *nm* sea; **~ de fondo** groundswell; **~ llena** high tide; **~ adentro** *o* **afuera** out at sea; **en alta ~** on the high seas; **por ~** by sea *o* boat; **hacerse a la ~** to put to sea; **a ~es** in abundance; **un ~ de** lots of; **es la ~ de guapa** she is ever so pretty; **el M~ Negro/Báltico** the Black/Baltic Sea; **el M~ Muerto/Rojo** the Dead/Red Sea; **el M~ del Norte** the North Sea.

mar. *abr* (= *marzo*) Mar.

maraña [ma'raɲa] *nf* (*maleza*) thicket; (*confusión*) tangle.

maravilla [mara'βiʎa] *nf* marvel, wonder; (*BOT*) marigold; **hacer ~s** to work wonders; **a (las mil) ~s** wonderfully well.

maravillar [maraβi'ʎar] *vt* to astonish, amaze; **~se** *vr* to be astonished, be amazed.

maravilloso, a [maraβi'ʎoso, a] *a* wonderful, marvellous.

marbellí [marβe'ʎi] *a* of *o* from Marbella ◆ *nm/f* native *o* inhabitant of Marbella.

marca ['marka] *nf* mark; (*sello*) stamp; (*COM*) make, brand; (*de ganado*) brand; (: *acto*) branding; (*NAUT*) seamark; (: *boya*) marker; (*DEPORTE*) record; **de ~** excellent, outstanding; **~ de fábrica** trademark; **~ propia** own brand; **~ registrada** registered trademark.

marcación [marka'θjon] *nf* (*TELEC*): **~ automática** autodial.

marcado, a [mar'kaðo, a] *a* marked, strong.

marcador [marka'ðor] *nm* marker; (*rotulador*) marker (pen); (*de libro*) bookmark; (*DEPORTE*) scoreboard; (: *persona*) scorer.

marcar [mar'kar] *vt* to mark; (*número de teléfono*) to dial; (*gol*) to score; (*números*) to record, keep a tally of; (*el pelo*) to set; (*suj: termómetro*) to register; (*tarea*) to assign; (*COM*) to put a price on ◆ *vi* (*DEPORTE*) to score; (*TELEC*) to dial; **mi reloj marca las 2** it's 2 o'clock by my watch; **~ el compás** (*MUS*) to keep time.

marcial [mar'θjal] *a* martial, military.

marciano, a [mar'θjano, a] *a* Martian, of *o* from Mars.

marco ['marko] *nm* frame; (*DEPORTE*) goalposts *pl*; (*moneda*) mark; (*fig*) setting; (*contexto*) framework; **~ de chimenea** mantelpiece.

marcha ['martʃa] *nf* march; (*DEPORTE*) walk; (*TEC*) running, working; (*AUTO*) gear; (*velocidad*) speed; (*fig*) progress; (*dirección*) course; **dar ~ atrás** to reverse, put into reverse; **estar en ~** to be under way, be in motion; **hacer algo sobre la ~** to do sth as you *etc* go along; **poner en ~** to put into gear; **ponerse en ~** to start, get going; **a ~s forzadas** (*fig*) with all speed; **¡en ~!** (*MIL*) forward march!; (*fig*) let's go!; **"~ moderada"** (*AUTO*) "drive slowly"; **que tiene** *o* **de mucha ~** (*fam*) very lively.

marchante, a [mar'tʃante, a] *nm/f* dealer, merchant.

marchar [mar'tʃar] *vi* (*ir*) to go; (*funcionar*) to work, go; (*fig*) to go, proceed; **~se** *vr* to go (away), leave; **todo marcha bien** everything is going well.

marchitar [martʃi'tar] *vt* to wither, dry up; **~se** *vr* (*BOT*) to wither; (*fig*) to fade away.

marchito, a [mar'tʃito, a] *a* withered, faded; (*fig*) in decline.

marchoso, a [mar'tʃoso, a] *a* (*fam: animado*) lively; (: *moderno*) modern.

marea [ma'rea] *nf* tide; (*llovizna*) drizzle; ~ **alta/baja** high/low tide; ~ **negra** oil slick.

mareado, a [mare'aðo, a] *a*: **estar** ~ (*con náuseas*) to feel sick; (*aturdido*) to feel dizzy.

marear [mare'ar] *vt* (*fig: irritar*) to annoy, upset; (*MED*): ~ **a uno** to make sb feel sick; ~**se** *vr* (*tener náuseas*) to feel sick; (*desvanecerse*) to feel faint; (*aturdirse*) to feel dizzy; (*fam: emborracharse*) to get tipsy.

marejada [mare'xaða] *nf* (*NAUT*) swell, heavy sea.

maremágnum [mare'maɣnum], **maremagno** [mare'maɣno] *nm* (*fig*) ocean, abundance.

maremoto [mare'moto] *nm* tidal wave.

mareo [ma'reo] *nm* (*náusea*) sick feeling; (*aturdimiento*) dizziness; (*fam: lata*) nuisance.

marfil [mar'fil] *nm* ivory.

margarina [marɣa'rina] *nf* margarine.

margarita [marɣa'rita] *nf* (*BOT*) daisy; (**rueda**) ~ (*en máquina impresora*) daisy wheel.

margen ['marxen] *nm* (*borde*) edge, border; (*fig*) margin, space; ~ **de beneficio** *o* **de ganancia** profit margin; ~ **comercial** mark-up; ~ **de confianza** credibility gap ♦ *nf* (*de río etc*) bank; **dar** ~ **para** to give an opportunity for; **dejar a uno al** ~ to leave sb out (in the cold); **mantenerse al** ~ to keep out (of things); **al** ~ **de lo que digas** despite what you say.

marginado, a [marxi'naðo, a] *nm/f* outcast.

marginar [marxi'nar] *vt* to exclude.

marica [ma'rika] *nm* (*fam*) sissy; (*homosexual*) queer.

Maricastaña [marikas'taɲa] *nf*: **en los días** *o* **en tiempos de** ~ way back, in the good old days.

maricón [mari'kon] *nm* (*fam*) queer.

marido [ma'riðo] *nm* husband.

mariguana [mari'ywana], **marijuana** [mari'xwana] *nf* marijuana, cannabis.

marimacho [mari'matʃo] *nf* (*fam*) mannish woman.

marimorena [marimo'rena] *nf* fuss, row; **armar una** ~ to kick up a row.

marina [ma'rina] *nf* navy; ~ **mercante** merchant navy.

marinero, a [mari'nero, a] *a* sea *cpd*; (*barco*) seaworthy ♦ *nm* sailor, seaman.

marino, a [ma'rino, a] *a* sea *cpd*, marine ♦ *nm* sailor; ~ **de agua dulce/de cubierta/ de primera** landlubber/deckhand/able seaman.

marioneta [marjo'neta] *nf* puppet.

mariposa [mari'posa] *nf* butterfly.

mariposear [maripose'ar] *vi* (*revolotear*) to flutter about; (*ser inconstante*) to be fickle;

(*coquetear*) to flirt.

mariquita [mari'kita] *nm* (*fam*) sissy; (*homosexual*) queer ♦ *nf* (*ZOOL*) ladybird (*Brit*), ladybug (*US*).

mariscos [ma'riskos] *nmpl* shellfish *sg*, seafood *sg*.

marisma [ma'risma] *nf* marsh, swamp.

marisquería [mariske'ria] *nf* shellfish bar, seafood restaurant.

marítimo, a [ma'ritimo, a] *a* sea *cpd*, maritime.

marmita [mar'mita] *nf* pot.

mármol ['marmol] *nm* marble.

marmóreo, a [mar'moreo, a] *a* marble.

marmota [mar'mota] *nf* (*ZOOL*) marmot; (*fig*) sleepyhead.

maroma [ma'roma] *nf* rope.

marque ['marke] *etc vb* V **marcar**.

marqués, esa [mar'kes, esa] *nm/f* marquis/marchioness.

marquesina [marke'sina] *nf* (*de parada*) bus-shelter.

marquetería [markete'ria] *nf* marquetry, inlaid work.

marrano, a [ma'rrano, a] *a* filthy, dirty ♦ *nm* (*ZOOL*) pig; (*malo*) swine; (*sucio*) dirty pig.

marrar [ma'rrar] *vi* to miss; (*fig*) to miss the mark.

marras ['marras]: **de** ~ *ad*: **es el problema de** ~ it's the same old problem.

marrón [ma'rron] *a* brown.

marroquí [marro'ki] *a*, *nm/f* Moroccan ♦ *nm* Morocco (leather).

Marruecos [ma'rrwekos] *nm* Morocco.

marta ['marta] *nf* (*animal*) (pine) marten; (*piel*) sable.

Martes ['martes] *nm inv* Mars.

martes ['martes] *nm inv* Tuesday; ~ **de carnaval** Shrove Tuesday.

martillar [marti'ʎar], **martillear** [martiʎe'ar] *vt* to hammer.

martilleo [marti'ʎeo] *nm* hammering.

martillo [mar'tiʎo] *nm* hammer; (*de presidente de asamblea, comité*) gavel; ~ **neumático** pneumatic drill (*Brit*), jackhammer (*US*).

Martinica [marti'nika] *nf* Martinique.

mártir ['martir] *nm/f* martyr.

martirice [marti'riθe] *etc vb* V **martirizar**.

martirio [mar'tirjo] *nm* martyrdom; (*fig*) torture, torment.

martirizar [martiri'θar] *vt* (*REL*) to martyr; (*fig*) to torture, torment.

marxismo [mark'sismo] *nm* Marxism.

marxista [mark'sista] *a nm/f* Marxist.

marzo ['marθo] *nm* March.

mas [mas] *conj* but.

más [mas] *a*, *ad* (*comparativo*) more; (*superlativo*) most; (*otro*) another, more ♦ *conj* and, plus; **A es** ~ **difícil que B** A is more difficult o harder than B; **cada vez ~ difícil** more and more difficult, harder and harder; **es ~ de medianoche** it's after midnight; **el libro ~ leído del año** the most widely-read book of the year; **un kilómetro ~** one more kilometre; **él es el ~ inteligente** he is the most intelligent (one); **¡qué perro ~ feo!** what an ugly dog!; **~ de 6** more than 6; **~ que/~ de lo que pensaba** more than he thought; **~ bien** rather; **así no ~** (*AM*) just like that; **es ~** furthermore; **de ~ extra**; **estar de ~** to be unnecessary; **¡qué ~ da!** what does it matter?; **~ o menos** more or less; **a las 8 a ~ tardar** at 8 o'clock at the latest; **~ vale tarde que nunca** better late than never; **no ~ se fue se acordó** (*AM*) no sooner had she left than she remembered.

masa ['masa] *nf* (*mezcla*) dough; (*volumen*) volume, mass; (*FÍSICA*) mass; **en ~** en masse; **las ~s** (*POL*) the masses.

masacrar [masa'krar] *vt* to massacre.

masacre [ma'sakre] *nf* massacre.

masaje [ma'saxe] *nm* massage; **dar ~ a** to massage.

masajista [masa'xista] *nm/f* masseur/masseuse.

mascar [mas'kar] *vt, vi* to chew; (*fig*) to mumble, mutter.

máscara ['maskara] *nf* (*tb INFORM*) mask ◆ *nm/f* masked person; **~ antigás** gas mask.

mascarada [maska'raða] *nf* masquerade.

mascarilla [maska'riʎa] *nf* mask; (*vaciado*) deathmask; (*maquillaje*) face pack.

mascarón [maska'ron] *nm* large mask; **~ de proa** figurehead.

masculino, a [masku'lino, a] *a* masculine; (*BIO*) male ◆ *nm* (*LING*) masculine.

mascullar [masku'ʎar] *vt* to mumble, mutter.

masilla [ma'siʎa] *nf* putty.

masivo, a [ma'siβo, a] *a* (*en masa*) mass.

masón [ma'son] *nm* (free)mason.

masonería [masone'ria] *nf* (free)masonry.

masoquista [maso'kista] *a* masochistic ◆ *nm/f* masochist.

masque ['maske] *etc vb* V **mascar**.

masticar [masti'kar] *vt* to chew; (*fig*) to ponder over.

mástil ['mastil] *nm* (*de navío*) mast; (*de guitarra*) neck.

mastín [mas'tin] *nm* mastiff.

mastique [mas'tike] *etc vb* V **masticar**.

masturbación [masturβa'θjon] *nf* masturbation.

masturbarse [mastur'βarse] *vr* to masturbate.

Mat. *abr* = **Matemáticas**.

mata ['mata] *nf* (*arbusto*) bush, shrub; (*de hierbas*) tuft; (*campo*) field; (*manojo*) tuft, blade; **~s** *nfpl* scrub *sg*; **~ de pelo** mop of

hair; **a salto de ~** (*día a día*) from day to day; (*al azar*) haphazardly.

matadero [mata'ðero] *nm* slaughterhouse, abattoir.

matador, a [mata'ðor, a] *a* killing ◆ *nm/f* killer ◆ *nm* (*TAUR*) matador, bullfighter.

matamoscas [mata'moskas] *nm inv* (*palo*) fly swat.

matanza [ma'tanθa] *nf* slaughter.

matar [ma'tar] *vt* to kill; (*tiempo, pelota*) to kill ◆ *vi* to kill; **~se** *vr* (*suicidarse*) to kill o.s., commit suicide; (*morir*) to be o get killed; (*gastarse*) to wear o.s. out; **~ el hambre** to stave off hunger; **~ a uno a disgustos** make sb's life a misery; **~las callando** to go about things slyly; **~se trabajando** to kill o.s. with work; **~se por hacer algo** to struggle to do sth.

matarife [mata'rife] *nm* slaughterman.

matasellos [mata'seʎos] *nm inv* postmark.

matasanos [mata'sanos] *nm inv* quack.

mate ['mate] *a* (*sin brillo: color*) dull, matt ◆ *nm* (*en ajedrez*) (check)mate; (*AM: hierba*) maté; (: *vasija*) gourd.

matemático, a [mate'matiko, a] *a* mathematical ◆ *nm/f* mathematician ◆ **matemáticas** *nfpl* mathematics *sg*.

materia [ma'terja] *nf* (*gen*) matter; (*TEC*) material; (*ESCOL*) subject; **en ~ de** on the subject of; (*en cuanto a*) as regards; **~ prima** raw material; **entrar en ~** to get down to business.

material [mate'rjal] *a* material; (*dolor*) physical; (*real*) real; (*literal*) literal ◆ *nm* material; (*TEC*) equipment; **~ de construcción** building material; **~es de derribo** rubble *sg*.

materialismo [materja'lismo] *nm* materialism.

materialista [materja'lista] *a* materialist(ic).

materialmente [materjal'mente] *ad* materially; (*fig*) absolutely.

maternal [mater'nal] *a* motherly, maternal.

maternidad [materni'ðað] *nf* motherhood, maternity.

materno, a [ma'terno, a] *a* maternal; (*lengua*) mother *cpd*.

matice [ma'tiθe] *etc vb* V **matizar**.

matinal [mati'nal] *a* morning *cpd*.

matiz [ma'tiθ] *nm* shade; (*de sentido*) shade, nuance; (*ironía etc*) touch.

matizar [mati'θar] *vt* (*variar*) to vary; (*ARTE*) to blend; **~ de** to tinge with.

matón [ma'ton] *nm* bully.

matorral [mato'rral] *nm* thicket.

matraca [ma'traka] *nf* rattle; (*fam*) nuisance.

matraz [ma'traθ] *nm* (*QUÍMICA*) flask.

matriarcado [matrjar'kaðo] *nm* matriarchy.

matrícula [ma'trikula] *nf* (*registro*) register; (*ESCOL*: *inscripción*) registration; (*AUTO*) registration number; (: *placa*) number plate.

matricular [matriku'lar] *vt* to register, enrol.

matrimonial [matrimo'njal] *a* matrimonial.

matrimonio [matri'monjo] *nm* (*pareja*) (married) couple; (*acto*) marriage; ~ **civil/clandestino** civil/secret marriage; **contraer ~ (con)** to marry.

matriz [ma'triθ] *nf* (*ANAT*) womb; (*TEC*) mould; (*MAT*) matrix; **casa ~** (*COM*) head office.

matrona [ma'trona] *nf* (*persona de edad*) matron.

matutino, a [matu'tino, a] *a* morning *cpd*.

maula ['maula] *a* (*persona*) good-for-nothing ♦ *nm/f* (*vago*) idler, slacker ♦ *nf* (*persona*) dead loss (*fam*).

maullar [mau'ʎar] *vi* to mew, miaow.

maullido [mau'ʎiðo] *nm* mew(ing), miaow (-ing).

Mauricio [mau'riθjo] *nm* Mauritius.

Mauritania [mauri'tanja] *nf* Mauritania.

mausoleo [mauso'leo] *nm* mausoleum.

maxilar [maksi'lar] *nm* jaw(bone).

máxima ['maksima] *nf* V **máximo.**

máxime ['maksime] *ad* especially.

máximo, a ['maksimo, a] *a* maximum; (*más alto*) highest; (*más grande*) greatest ♦ *nm* maximum ♦ *nf* maxim; **como ~** at most; **al ~** to the utmost.

mayo ['majo] *nm* May.

mayonesa [majo'nesa] *nf* mayonnaise.

mayor [ma'jor] *a* main, chief; (*adulto*) grown-up, adult; (*JUR*) of age; (*de edad avanzada*) elderly; (*MUS*) major; (*comparativo: de tamaño*) bigger; (: *de edad*) older; (*superlativo: de tamaño*) biggest; (*tb: fig*) greatest; (: *de edad*) oldest ♦ *nm* chief, boss; (*adulto*) adult; **al por ~** wholesale; **~ de edad** adult; *V tb* **mayores.**

mayores [ma'jores] *nmpl* grown-ups; **llegar a ~es** to get out of hand.

mayoral [majo'ral] *nm* foreman.

mayordomo [major'ðomo] *nm* butler.

mayoría [majo'ria] *nf* majority, greater part; **en la ~ de los casos** in most cases; **en su ~** on the whole.

mayorista [majo'rista] *nm/f* wholesaler.

mayoritario, a [majori'tarjo, a] *a* majority *cpd*; **gobierno ~** majority government.

mayúsculo, a [ma'juskulo, a] *a* (*fig*) big, tremendous ♦ *nf* capital (letter); **mayúsculas** *nfpl* capitals; (*TIP*) upper case *sg*.

maza ['maθa] *nf* (*arma*) mace; (*DEPORTE*) bat; (*POLO*) stick.

mazacote [maθa'kote] *nm* hard mass; (*CULIN*) dry doughy food; (*ARTE, LITERATURA*

etc) mess, hotchpotch.

mazapán [maθa'pan] *nm* marzipan.

mazmorra [maθ'morra] *nf* dungeon.

mazo ['maθo] *nm* (*martillo*) mallet; (*de mortero*) pestle; (*de flores*) bunch; (*DEPORTE*) bat.

mazorca [ma'θorka] *nf* (*BOT*) spike; (*de maíz*) cob, ear.

MCAC *nm abr* = *Mercado Común de la América Central.*

MCI *nm abr* = *Mercado Común Iberoamericano.*

me [me] *pron* (*directo*) me; (*indirecto*) (to) me; (*reflexivo*) (to) myself; **¡dámelo!** give it to me!; **~ lo compró** (*de mí*) he bought it from me; (*para mí*) he bought it for me.

mear [me'ar] (*fam*) *vt* to piss on (*!*) ♦ *vi* to pee, have a piss (*!*); **~se** *vr* to wet o.s.

Meca ['meka] *nf*: **La ~** Mecca.

mecánica [me'kanika] *nf* V **mecánico.**

mecanice [meka'niθe] *etc vb* V **mecanizar.**

mecánico, a [me'kaniko, a] *a* mechanical; (*repetitivo*) repetitive ♦ *nm/f* mechanic ♦ *nf* (*estudio*) mechanics *sg*; (*mecanismo*) mechanism.

mecanismo [meka'nismo] *nm* mechanism; (*engranaje*) gear.

mecanizar [mekani'θar] *vt* to mechanize.

mecanografía [mekanoɣra'fia] *nf* typewriting.

mecanografiado, a [mekanoɣra'fjaðo, a] *a* typewritten ♦ *nm* typescript.

mecanógrafo, a [meka'noɣrafo, a] *nm/f* (*copy*) typist.

mecate [me'kate] *nm* (*AM*) rope.

mecedora [meθe'ðora] *nf* rocking chair.

mecenas [me'θenas] *nm inv* patron.

mecenazgo [meθe'naɣo] *nm* patronage.

mecer [me'θer] *vt* (*cuna*) to rock; **~se** *vr* to rock; (*rama*) to sway.

mecha ['metʃa] *nf* (*de vela*) wick; (*de bomba*) fuse; **a toda ~** at full speed; **ponerse ~s** to streak one's hair.

mechero [me'tʃero] *nm* (cigarette) lighter.

mechón [me'tʃon] *nm* (*gen*) tuft; (*manojo*) bundle; (*de pelo*) lock.

medalla [me'ðaʎa] *nf* medal.

media ['meðja] *nf* V **medio.**

mediado, a [me'ðjaðo, a] *a* half-full; (*trabajo*) half-completed; **a ~s de** in the middle of, halfway through.

medianamente [meðjana'mente] *ad* (*moderadamente*) moderately, fairly; (*regularmente*) moderately well.

mediano, a [me'ðjano, a] *a* (*regular*) medium, average; (*mediocre*) mediocre; (**de tamaño**) ~ medium-sized.

medianoche [meðja'notʃe] *nf* midnight.

mediante [me'ðjante] *ad* by (means of), through.

mediar [me'ðjar] *vi* (*tiempo*) to elapse; (*interceder*) to mediate, intervene; (*existir*) to exist; **media el hecho de que** ... there is the fact that ....

medicación [meðika'θjon] *nf* medication, treatment.

medicamento [meðika'mento] *nm* medicine, drug.

medicina [meði'θina] *nf* medicine.

medición [meði'θjon] *nf* measurement.

médico, a ['meðiko, a] *a* medical ◆ *nm/f* doctor; ~ **de cabecera** family doctor; ~ **pediatra** paediatrician; ~ **residente** house physician, intern (*US*).

medida [me'ðiða] *nf* measure; (*medición*) measurement; (*de camisa, zapato etc*) size, fitting; (*prudencia*) moderation, prudence; **en cierta/gran** ~ up to a point/to a great extent; **un traje a la** ~ made-to-measure suit; ~ **de cuello** collar size; **a** ~ **de** in proportion to; (*de acuerdo con*) in keeping with; **con** ~ with restraint; **sin** ~ immoderately; **a** ~ **que** ... (at the same time) as ...; **tomar** ~**s** to take steps.

medio, a ['meðjo, a] *a* half (a); (*punto*) mid, middle; (*promedio*) average ◆ *ad* half ◆ *nm* (*centro*) middle, centre; (*promedio*) average; (*método*) means, way; (*ambiente*) environment ◆ *nf* ~**s panti** tights; **a** ~**s** barely; **pagar a** ~**s** to share the cost; (*prenda de vestir*) stocking, (*AM*) sock; (*promedio*) average; **media hora** half an hour; ~ **litro** half a litre; **las tres y media** half past three; **M**~ **Oriente** Middle East; **a** ~ **camino** halfway (there); ~ **dormido** half asleep; **a** ~ **terminar** half finished; **en** ~ in the middle; (*entre*) in between; **por** ~ **de** by (means of), through; **en los** ~**s financieros** in financial circles; **encontrarse en su** ~ to be in one's element; ~ **circulante** (*COM*) money supply; *V tb* **medios**.

mediocre [me'ðjokre] *a* middling, average; (*pey*) mediocre.

mediocridad [meðjokri'ðað] *nf* middling quality; (*pey*) mediocrity.

mediodía [meðjo'ðia] *nm* midday, noon.

mediopensionista [meðjopensjo'nista] *nm/f* day boy/girl.

medios ['meðjos] *nmpl* means, resources.

medir [me'ðir] *vt* (*gen*) to measure ◆ *vi* to measure; ~**se** *vr* (*moderarse*) to be moderate, act with restraint; **¿cuánto mides?** — **mido 1.50 m** how tall are you? — I am 1.50 m tall.

meditar [meði'tar] *vt* to ponder, think over, meditate on; (*planear*) to think out ◆ *vi* to ponder, think, meditate.

mediterráneo, a [meðite'rraneo, a] *a* Mediterranean ◆ *nm*: **el (mar) M**~ the Mediterranean (Sea).

medrar [me'ðrar] *vi* to increase, grow; (*mejorar*) to improve; (*prosperar*) to prosper, thrive; (*animal, planta etc*) to grow.

medroso, a [me'ðroso, a] *a* fearful, timid.

médula ['meðula] *nf* (*ANAT*) marrow; (*BOT*) pith; ~ **espinal** spinal cord; **hasta la** ~ (*fig*) to the core.

medusa [me'ðusa] *nf* (*Esp*) jellyfish.

megabyte ['meɣaßait] *nm* (*INFORM*) megabyte.

megáfono [me'ɣafono] *nm* public address system.

megalomanía [meɣaloma'nia] *nf* megalomania.

megalómano, a [meɣa'lomano, a] *nm/f* megalomaniac.

megaocteto [meɣaok'teto] *nm* (*INFORM*) megabyte.

mejicano, a [mexi'kano, a] *a, nm/f* Mexican.

Méjico ['mexiko] *nm* Mexico.

mejilla [me'xiʎa] *nf* cheek.

mejillón [mexi'ʎon] *nm* mussel.

mejor [me'xor] *a, ad* (*comparativo*) better; (*superlativo*) best; **lo** ~ the best thing; **lo** ~ **de la vida** the prime of life; **a lo** ~ probably; (*quizá*) maybe; ~ **dicho** rather; **tanto** ~ so much the better; **es el** ~ **de todos** he's the best of all.

mejora [me'xora] *nf*, **mejoramiento** [mexora'mjento] *nm* improvement.

mejorar [mexo'rar] *vt* to improve, make better ◆ *vi*, ~**se** *vr* to improve, get better; (*COM*) to do well, prosper; ~ **a** to be better than; **los negocios mejoran** business is picking up.

mejoría [mexo'ria] *nf* improvement; (*restablecimiento*) recovery.

melancólico, a [melan'koliko, a] *a* (*triste*) sad, melancholy; (*soñador*) dreamy.

melena [me'lena] *nf* (*de persona*) long hair; (*ZOOL*) mane.

melillense [meli'ʎense] *a* of o from Melilla ◆ *nm/f* native o inhabitant of Melilla.

melocotón [meloko'ton] *nm* (*Esp*) peach.

melodía [melo'ðia] *nf* melody; (*aire*) tune.

melodrama [melo'ðrama] *nm* melodrama.

melodramático, a [meloðra'matiko, a] *a* melodramatic.

melón [me'lon] *nm* melon.

melopea [melo'pea] *nf* (*fam*): **tener una** ~ to be sloshed.

meloso, a [me'loso, a] *a* honeyed, sweet; (*empalagoso*) sickly, cloying; (*voz*) sweet; (*zalamero*) smooth.

mella ['meʎa] *nf* (*rotura*) notch, nick; **hacer** ~ (*fig*) to make an impression.

mellizo, a [me'ʎiθo, a] *a, nm/f* twin ◆ *nm* (*AM*): ~**s** cufflinks.

membrete [mem'brete] *nm* letterhead.

membrillo [mem'briʎo] *nm* quince; **carne**

de ~ quince jelly.

memo, a ['memo, a] *a* silly, stupid ◆ *nm/f* idiot.

memorable [memo'raßle] *a* memorable.

memorándum [memo'randum] *nm* (*libro*) notebook; (*comunicación*) memorandum.

memoria [me'morja] *nf* (*gen*) memory; (*artículo*) (learned) paper; **~s** *nfpl* (*de autor*) memoirs; **~ anual** annual report; **aprender algo de ~** to learn sth by heart; **si tengo buena ~** if my memory serves me right; **venir a la ~** to come to mind; (*INFORM*): **~ de acceso aleatorio** random access memory, RAM; **~ auxiliar** backing storage; **~ fija** read-only memory, ROM; **~ fija programable** programmable memory; **~ del teclado** keyboard memory.

memorice [memo'riθe] *etc vb* V **memorizar.**

memorizar [memori'θar] *vt* to memorize.

menaje [me'naxe] *nm* (*muebles*) furniture; (*utensilios domésticos*) household equipment; **~ de cocina** kitchenware.

mencionar [menθjo'nar] *vt* to mention; (*nombrar*) to name; **sin ~ ...** let alone ....

mendicidad [mendiθi'ðað] *nf* begging.

mendigar [mendi'ɣar] *vt* to beg (for).

mendigo, a [men'diɣo, a] *nm/f* beggar.

mendigue [men'diɣe] *etc vb* V **mendigar.**

mendrugo [men'druɣo] *nm* crust.

menear [mene'ar] *vt* to move; (*cola*) to wag; (*cadera*) to swing; (*fig*) to handle; **~se** *vr* to shake; (*balancearse*) to sway; (*moverse*) to move; (*fig*) to get a move on.

menester [menes'ter] *nm* (*necesidad*) necessity; **~es** *nmpl* (*deberes*) duties; **es ~ hacer algo** it is necessary to do sth, sth must be done.

menestra [me'nestra] *nf*: **~ de verduras** vegetable stew.

mengano, a [men'gano, a] *nm/f* Mr (*o* Mrs *o* Miss) So-and-so.

mengua ['mengwa] *nf* (*disminución*) decrease; (*falta*) lack; (*pobreza*) poverty; (*fig*) discredit; **en ~ de** to the detriment of.

menguante [men'gwante] *a* decreasing, diminishing; (*luna*) waning; (*marea*) ebb *cpd.*

menguar [men'gwar] *vt* to lessen, diminish; (*fig*) to discredit ◆ *vi* to diminish, decrease; (*fig*) to decline.

mengüe ['mengwe] *etc vb* V **menguar.**

menopausia [meno'pausja] *nf* menopause.

menor [me'nor] *a* (*más pequeño: comparativo*) smaller; (*número*) less, lesser; (*: superlativo*) smallest; (*número*) least; (*más joven: comparativo*) younger; (*: superlativo*) youngest; (*MUS*) minor ◆ *nm/f* (*joven*) young person, juvenile; **Juanito es ~ que Pepe** Juanito is younger than Pepe; **ella es la ~ de todas** she is the youngest of all; **no tengo la ~ idea** I haven't the faintest idea; **al por ~** retail; **~ de edad** under age.

Menorca [me'norka] *nf* Minorca.

menoría [meno'ria] *n* (*AM COM*): **a ~** retail.

menorquín, ina [menor'kin, ina] *a, nm/f* Minorcan.

menos ['menos] *a* (*comparativo: sg*) less; (*: pl*) fewer; (*superlativo: sg*) least; (*: pl*) fewest ◆ *ad* (*comparativo*) less; (*superlativo*) least ◆ *conj, prep* except ◆ *nm* (*MAT*) minus; **~ de lo que piensas** less than you think; **es el ~ inteligente de los 4** he is the least intelligent of the 4; **eso es lo de ~** that's the least of it; **es lo ~ que puedo hacer** it's the least I can do; **lo ~ posible** as little as possible; **a ~ que** unless; **~ de 5** less than 5; **hay 7 de ~** we're 7 short; **no es rico, ni mucho ~** he's far from being rich; **ir o venir a ~** to come down in the world; **al o por lo ~** at least; **¡~ mal!** just as well!; **¡todo ~ eso!** anything but that!; **¿qué ~?** (*fam*) what else did you expect?; **las 7 ~ 20** (*hora*) 20 to 7.

menoscabar [menoska'ßar] *vt* (*estropear*) to damage, harm; (*fig*) to discredit.

menospreciar [menospre'θjar] *vt* to underrate, undervalue; (*despreciar*) to scorn, despise.

menosprecio [menos'preθjo] *nm* underrating, undervaluation; scorn, contempt.

mensaje [men'saxe] *nm* message; **~ de error** (*INFORM*) error message.

mensajero, a [mensa'xero, a] *nm/f* messenger.

menstruación [menstrwa'θjon] *nf* menstruation.

menstruar [mens'trwar] *vi* to menstruate.

mensual [men'swal] *a* monthly; **100 ptas ~es** 100 ptas. a month.

mensualidad [menswali'ðað] *nf* (*salario*) monthly salary; (*COM*) monthly payment *o* instalment.

menta ['menta] *nf* mint.

mentado, a [men'taðo, a] *a* (*mencionado*) aforementioned; (*famoso*) well-known.

mental [men'tal] *a* mental.

mentalidad [mentali'ðað] *nf* mentality, way of thinking.

mentar [men'tar] *vt* to mention, name.

mente ['mente] *nf* mind; (*inteligencia*) intelligence; **no tengo en ~ hacer eso** it is not my intention to do that.

mentecato, a [mente'kato, a] *a* silly, stupid ◆ *nm/f* fool, idiot.

mentir [men'tir] *vi* to lie; **¡miento!** sorry, I'm wrong!

mentira [men'tira] *nf* (*una ~*) lie; (*acto*) lying; (*invención*) fiction; **~ piadosa** white lie; **una ~ como una casa** a whopping great lie (*fam*); **parece ~ que** ... it seems incredible that ..., I can't believe that ....

mentiroso, a [menti'roso, a] *a* lying; (*falso*) deceptive ◆ *nm/f* liar.

mentís [men'tis] *nm inv* denial; **dar el ~ a** to deny.

mentón [men'ton] *nm* chin.

menú [me'nu] *nm* (*tb* INFORM) menu; (*en restaurante*) set meal; **guiado por ~** (IN-FORM) menu-driven.

menudear [menuðe'ar] *vt* (*repetir*) to repeat frequently ◆ *vi* (*ser frecuente*) to be frequent; (*detallar*) to go into great detail.

menudencia [menu'ðenθja] *nf* (*bagatela*) trifle; **~s** *nfpl* odds and ends.

menudillos [menu'ðiʎos] *nmpl* giblets.

menudo, a [me'nuðo, a] *a* (*pequeño*) small, tiny; (*sin importancia*) petty, insignificant; **¡~ negocio!** (*fam*) some deal!; **a ~** often, frequently.

meñique [me'ɲike] *nm* little finger.

meollo [me'oʎo] *nm* (*fig*) essence, core.

mequetrefe [meke'trefe] *nm* good-for-nothing, whippersnapper.

mercader [merka'ðer] *nm* merchant.

mercadería [merkaðe'ria] *nf* commodity; **~s** *nfpl* goods, merchandise *sg*.

mercado [mer'kaðo] *nm* market; **~ en baja** falling market; **M~ Común** Common Market; **~ de demanda/de oferta** seller's/buyer's market; **~ laboral** labour market; **~ objetivo** target market; **~ de productos básicos** commodity market; **~ de valores** stock market; **~ exterior/interior** *o* **nacional/libre** overseas/home/free market.

mercancía [merkan'θia] *nf* commodity; **~s** *nfpl* goods, merchandise *sg*; **~s en depósito** bonded goods; **~s perecederas** perishable goods.

mercancías [merkan'θias] *nm inv* goods train, freight train (*US*).

mercantil [merkan'til] *a* mercantile, commercial.

mercenario, a [merθe'narjo, a] *a, nm* mercenary.

mercería [merθe'ria] *nf* (*artículos*) haberdashery (*Brit*), notions *pl* (*US*); (*tienda*) haberdasher's shop (*Brit*), drapery (*Brit*), notions store (*US*).

mercurio [mer'kurjo] *nm* mercury.

merecedor, a [mereθe'ðor, a] *a* deserving; **~ de confianza** trustworthy.

merecer [mere'θer] *vt* to deserve, merit ◆ *vi* to be deserving, be worthy; **merece la pena** it's worthwhile.

merecido, a [mere'θiðo, a] *a* (well) deserved; **llevarse su ~** to get one's deserts.

merendar [meren'dar] *vt* to have for tea ◆ *vi* to have tea; (*en el campo*) to have a picnic.

merendero [meren'dero] *nm* (*café*) tea-room; (*en el campo*) picnic spot.

merengue [me'renge] *nm* meringue.

merezca [me'reθka] *etc vb* V **merecer**.

meridiano [meri'ðjano] *nm* (ASTRO, GEO) meridian; **la explicación es de una claridad meridiana** the explanation is as clear as day.

meridional [meriðjo'nal] *a* Southern ◆ *nm/f* Southerner.

merienda [me'rjenda] *etc vb* V **merendar** ◆ *nf* (light) tea, afternoon snack; (*de campo*) picnic; **~ de negros** free-for-all.

mérito ['merito] *nm* merit; (*valor*) worth, value; **hacer ~s** to make a good impression; **restar ~ a** to detract from.

meritorio, a [meri'torjo, a] *a* deserving.

merluza [mer'luθa] *nf* hake; **coger una ~** (*fam*) to get sozzled.

merma ['merma] *nf* decrease; (*pérdida*) wastage.

mermar [mer'mar] *vt* to reduce, lessen ◆ *vi* to decrease, dwindle.

mermelada [merme'laða] *nf* jam; **~ de naranja** marmalade.

mero, a ['mero, a] *a* mere, simple; (*AM fam*) very ◆ *nm* (ZOOL) grouper.

merodear [meroðe'ar] *vi* (MIL) to maraud; (*de noche*) to prowl (about); (*curiosear*) to snoop around.

mes [mes] *nm* month; (*salario*) month's pay; **el ~ corriente** this *o* the current month.

mesa ['mesa] *nf* table; (*de trabajo*) desk; (COM) counter; (*en mitin*) platform; (GEO) plateau; (ARQ) landing; **~ de noche/de tijera/de operaciones** *u* **operatoria** bedside/folding/operating table; **~ redonda** (*reunión*) round table; **~ digitalizadora** (IN-FORM) graph pad; **~ directiva** board; **~ y cama** bed and board; **poner/quitar la ~** to lay/clear the table.

mesarse [me'sarse] *vr*: **~ el pelo** *o* **los cabellos** to tear one's hair.

mesera [me'sera] *nf* (AM) waitress.

mesero [me'sero] *nm* (AM) waiter.

meseta [me'seta] *nf* (GEO) meseta, tableland; (ARQ) landing.

mesilla [me'siʎa], **mesita** [me'sita] *nf*: **~ de noche** bedside table.

mesón [me'son] *nm* inn.

mestizo, a [mes'tiθo, a] *a* half-caste, of mixed race; (ZOOL) crossbred ◆ *nm/f* half-caste.

mesura [me'sura] *nf* (*calma*) calm; (*moderación*) moderation, restraint; (*cortesía*) courtesy.

mesurar [mesu'rar] *vt* (*contener*) to restrain; **~se** *vr* to restrain o.s.

meta ['meta] *nf* goal; (*de carrera*) finish; (*fig*) goal, aim, objective.

metafísico, a [meta'fisiko, a] *a* metaphysical ◆ *nf* metaphysics *sg*.

metafórico, a [meta'foriko, a] *a* metaphorical.

metáfora [me'tafora] *nf* metaphor.

metal [me'tal] *nm* (*materia*) metal; (*MUS*) brass.

metálico, a [me'taliko, a] *a* metallic; (*de metal*) metal ◆ *nm* (*dinero contante*) cash.

metalurgia [meta'lurxja] *nf* metallurgy.

metalúrgico, a [meta'lurxiko, a] *a* metallurgic(al); **industria** ~**a** engineering industry.

metamorfosear [metamorfose'ar] *vt*: ~ (**en**) to metamorphose *o* transform (into).

metamorfosis [metamor'fosis] *nf inv* metamorphosis, transformation.

metedura [mete'ðura] *nf*: ~ **de pata** (*fam*) blunder.

meteoro [mete'oro] *nm* meteor.

meteorólogo, a [meteo'roloɣo, a] *nm/f* meteorologist; (*RADIO, TV*) weather reporter.

meter [me'ter] *vt* (*colocar*) to put, place; (*introducir*) to put in, insert; (*involucrar*) to involve; (*causar*) to make, cause; ~**se** *vr*: ~**se en** to go into, enter; (*fig*) to interfere in, meddle in; ~**se a** to start; ~**se a escritor** to become a writer; ~**se con uno** to provoke sb, pick a quarrel with sb; ~ **prisa a uno** to hurry sb up.

meticuloso, a [metiku'loso, a] *a* meticulous, thorough.

metido, a [me'tiðo, a] *a*: **estar muy ~ en un asunto** to be deeply involved in a matter; ~ **en años** elderly; ~ **en carne** plump.

metódico, a [me'toðiko, a] *a* methodical.

metodismo [meto'ðismo] *nm* Methodism.

método ['metoðo] *nm* method.

metomentodo [metomen'toðo] *nm inv* meddler, busybody.

metraje [me'traxe] *nm* (*CINE*) length; **cinta de largo/corto** ~ full-length film/short.

metralleta [metra'ʎeta] *nf* sub-machine-gun.

métrico, a ['metriko, a] *a* metric; **cinta métrica** tape measure.

metro ['metro] *nm* metre; (*tren: tb:* **metropolitano**) underground (*Brit*), subway (*US*); (*instrumento*) rule; ~ **cuadrado/cúbico** square/cubic metre.

mexicano, a [mexi'kano, a] *a, nm/f* (*AM*) Mexican.

México ['mexiko] *nm* (*AM*) Mexico; **Ciudad de** ~ Mexico City.

meza ['meθa] *etc vb* V **mecer**.

mezcla ['meθkla] *nf* mixture; (*fig*) blend.

mezclar [meθ'klar] *vt* to mix (up); (*armonizar*) to blend; (*combinar*) to merge; ~**se** *vr* to mix, mingle; ~ **en** to get mixed up in, get involved in.

mezcolanza [meθko'lanθa] *nf* hotchpotch, jumble.

mezquindad [meθkin'daθ] *nf* (*cicatería*) meanness; (*miras estrechas*) pettiness; (*acto*) mean action.

mezquino, a [meθ'kino, a] *a* (*cicatero*) mean ◆ *nm/f* (*avaro*) mean person; (*miserable*) petty individual.

mezquita [meθ'kita] *nf* mosque.

MF *abr* (= *Modulación de Frecuencia*) FM.

mg. *abr* (= *miligramo(s)*) mg.

mi [mi] *a posesivo* my ◆ *nm* (*MUS*) E.

mí [mi] *pron* me, myself; **¿y a ~ qué?** so what?

miaja ['mjaxa] *nf* crumb; **ni una ~** (*fig*) not the least little bit.

micro ['mikro] *nm* (*RADIO*) mike, microphone; (*AM*) minibus.

microbio [mi'kroβjo] *nm* microbe.

microbús [mikro'βus] *nm* minibus.

microcomputador [mikrokomputa'ðor] *nm*, **microcomputadora** [mikrokomputa'ðora] *nf* micro(computer).

microchip [mikro'tʃip] *nm* microchip.

microeconomía [mikroekono'mia] *nf* microeconomics *sg*.

microficha [mikro'fitʃa] *nf* microfiche.

micrófono [mi'krofono] *nm* microphone.

microinformática [mikroinfor'matika] *nf* microcomputing.

micrómetro [mi'krometro] *nm* micrometer.

microonda [mikro'onda] *nf* microwave; **horno ~s** microwave oven.

microordenador [mikroordena'ðor] *nm* microcomputer.

micropastilla [mikropas'tiʎa], **microplaqueta** [mikropla'keta] *nf* (*INFORM*) chip, wafer.

microplaquita [mikropla'kita] *nf*: ~ **de silicio** silicon chip.

microprocesador [mikroprocesa'ðor] *nm* microprocessor.

microprograma [mikropro'ɣrama] *nm* (*INFORM*) firmware.

microscopio [mikros'kopjo] *nm* microscope.

midiendo [mi'ðjendo] *etc vb* V **medir**.

MIE *nm abr* (*Esp*) = *Ministerio de Industria y Energía*.

miedo ['mjeðo] *nm* fear; (*nerviosismo*) apprehension, nervousness; **meter ~ a** to scare, frighten; **tener ~ to be afraid; de ~** wonderful, marvellous; **¡qué ~!** (*fam*) how awful!; **me da ~** it scares me; **hace un frío de ~** (*fam*) it's terribly cold.

miedoso, a [mje'ðoso, a] *a* fearful, timid.

miel [mjel] *nf* honey; **no hay ~ sin hiel** there's no rose without a thorn.

miembro ['mjembro] *nm* limb; (*socio*) member; (*de institución*) fellow; ~ **viril** penis.

mientes ['mjentes] *etc vb* V **mentar; mentir**

♦ *nfpl*: **no parar ~ en** to pay no attention to; **traer a las ~** to recall.

mientras ['mjɛntras] *conj* while; (*duración*) as long as ♦ *ad* meanwhile; **~ (que)** whereas; **~ tanto** meanwhile; **~ más tiene, más quiere** the more he has, the more he wants.

miérc. *abr* (= *miércoles*) Wed.

miércoles ['mjɛrkoles] *nm inv* Wednesday; **~ de ceniza** Ash Wednesday.

mierda ['mjɛrða] *nf* (*fam!*) shit (*!*), crap (*!*); (*fig*) filth, dirt; **¡vete a la ~!** go to hell!

mies [mjes] *nf* (ripe) corn, wheat, grain.

miga ['miɣa] *nf* crumb; (*fig*: *meollo*) essence; **hacer buenas ~s** (*fam*) to get on well; **esto tiene su ~** there's more to this than meets the eye.

migración [miɣra'θjon] *nf* migration.

mil [mil] *num* thousand; **dos ~ libras** two thousand pounds.

milagro [mi'laɣro] *nm* miracle; **hacer ~s** (*fig*) to work wonders.

milagroso, a [mila'ɣroso, a] *a* miraculous.

Milán [mi'lan] *nm* Milan.

milenario, a [mile'narjo, a] *a* millennial; (*fig*) very ancient.

milenio [mi'lenjo] *nm* millennium.

milésimo, a [mi'lesimo, a] *num* thousandth.

mili ['mili] *nf*: **hacer la ~** (*fam*) to do one's military service.

milicia [mi'liθja] *nf* (*MIL*) militia; (*servicio militar*) military service.

milímetro [mi'limetro] *nm* millimetre (*Brit*), millimeter (*US*).

militante [mili'tante] *a* militant.

militar [mili'tar] *a* military ♦ *nm/f* soldier ♦ *vi* to serve in the army; (*fig*) to militate, fight.

milla ['miʎa] *nf* mile; **~ marina** nautical mile.

millar [mi'ʎar] *num* thousand; **a ~es** in thousands.

millón [mi'ʎon] *num* million.

millonario, a [miʎo'narjo, a] *nm/f* millionaire.

millonésimo, a [miʎo'nesimo, a] *num* millionth.

mimado, a [mi'maðo, a] *a* spoiled.

mimar [mi'mar] *vt* to spoil, pamper.

mimbre ['mimbre] *nm* wicker; **de ~** wicker *cpd*, wickerwork.

mímica ['mimika] *nf* (*para comunicarse*) sign language; (*imitación*) mimicry.

mimetismo [mime'tismo] *nm* mimicry.

mimo ['mimo] *nm* (*caricia*) caress; (*de niño*) spoiling; (*TEATRO*) mime; (*: actor*) mime artist.

mina ['mina] *nf* mine; (*pozo*) shaft; (*de lápiz*) lead refill; **hullera** *o* **~ de carbón** coalmine.

minar [mi'nar] *vt* to mine; (*fig*) to undermine.

mineral [mine'ral] *a* mineral ♦ *nm* (*GEO*) mineral; (*mena*) ore.

minería [mine'ria] *nf* mining.

minero, a [mi'nero, a] *a* mining *cpd* ♦ *nm/f* miner.

miniatura [minja'tura] *a inv, nf* miniature.

minicomputador [minikomputa'ðor] *nm* minicomputer.

minidisco [mini'ðisko] *nm* diskette.

minifalda [mini'falda] *nf* miniskirt.

minifundio [mini'fundjo] *nm* smallholding, small farm.

mínimo, a ['minimo, a] *a* minimum; (*insignificante*) minimal ♦ *nm* minimum; **precio/salario ~** minimum price/wage; **lo ~ que pueden hacer** the least they can do.

minino, a [mi'nino, a] *nm/f* (*fam*) puss, pussy.

ministerio [minis'terjo] *nm* ministry (*Brit*), department (*US*); **M~ de Asuntos Exteriores** Foreign Office (*Brit*), State Department (*US*); **M~ del Comercio e Industria** Department of Trade and Industry; **M~ de (la) Gobernación** *o* **del Interior** ≈ Home Office (*Brit*), Ministry of the Interior; **M~ de Hacienda** Treasury (*Brit*), Treasury Department (*US*).

ministro, a [mi'nistro, a] *nm/f* minister, secretary (*esp US*); **M~ de Hacienda** Chancellor of the Exchequer, Secretary of the Treasury (*US*); **M~ de (la) Gobernación** *o* **del Interior** ≈ Home Secretary (*Brit*), Secretary of the Interior (*US*).

minoría [mino'ria] *nf* minority.

mintiendo [min'tjendo] *etc vb* V **mentir**.

minucia [mi'nuθja] *nf* (*detalle insignificante*) trifle; (*bagatela*) mere nothing.

minuciosidad [minuθjosi'ðað] *nf* (*meticulosidad*) thoroughness, meticulousness.

minucioso, a [minu'θjoso, a] *a* thorough, meticulous; (*prolijo*) very detailed.

minúsculo, a [mi'nuskulo, a] *a* tiny, minute ♦ *nf* small letter; **minúsculas** *nfpl* (*TIP*) lower case *sg*.

minusvalía [minusβa'lia] *nf* physical handicap; (*COM*) depreciation, capital loss.

minusválido, a [minus'βaliðo, a] *a* (*physically*) handicapped *o* disabled ♦ *nm/f* disabled person.

minuta [mi'nuta] *nf* (*de comida*) menu; (*de abogado etc*) fee.

minutero [minu'tero] *nm* minute hand.

minuto [mi'nuto] *nm* minute.

Miño ['miɲo] *nm*: **el (río) ~** the Miño.

mío, a ['mio, a] *a, pron*: **el ~** mine; **un amigo ~** a friend of mine; **lo ~** what is mine; **los ~s** my people, my relations.

miope ['mjope] *a* short-sighted.

miopía [mjo'pia] *nf* near- *o* short-sightedness.

MIR [mir] *nm abr* (*POL*) = *Movimiento de Izquierda Revolucionaria*; (*Esp MED*) *Médico Interno y Residente*.

mira ['mira] *nf* (*de arma*) sight(s) (*pl*); (*fig*) aim, intention; **de amplias/estrechas ~s** broad-/narrow-minded.

mirada [mi'raða] *nf* look, glance; (*expresión*) look, expression; **~ de soslayo** sidelong glance; **~ fija** stare, gaze; **~ perdida** distant look; **echar una ~ a** to glance at; **levantar/bajar la ~** to look up/down; **resistir la ~ de uno** to stare sb out.

mirado, a [mi'raðo, a] *a* (*sensato*) sensible; (*considerado*) considerate; **bien/mal ~** well/not well thought of.

mirador [mira'ðor] *nm* viewpoint, vantage point.

miramiento [mira'mjento] *nm* (*consideración*) considerateness; **tratar sin ~ a uno** to ride roughshod over sb.

mirar [mi'rar] *vt* to look at; (*observar*) to watch; (*considerar*) to consider, think over; (*vigilar, cuidar*) to watch, look after ♦ *vi* to look; (*ARQ*) to face; **~se** *vr* (*dos personas*) to look at each other; **~ algo/a uno de reojo** *o* **de través** to look askance at sth/sb; **~ algo/a uno por encima del hombro** to look down on sth/sb; **~ bien/mal** to think highly of/have a poor opinion of; **~ fijamente** to stare *o* gaze at; **~ por** (*fig*) to look after; **~ por la ventana** to look out of the window; **~se al espejo** to look at o.s. in the mirror; **~se a los ojos** to look into each other's eyes.

mirilla [mi'riʎa] *nf* (*agujero*) spyhole, peephole.

mirlo ['mirlo] *nm* blackbird.

misa ['misa] *nf* mass; **~ del gallo** midnight mass (*on Christmas Eve*); **~ de difuntos** requiem mass; **como en ~** in dead silence; **estos datos van a ~** (*fig*) these facts are utterly trustworthy.

misántropo [mi'santropo] *nm* misanthrope, misanthropist.

miscelánea [misθe'lanea] *nf* miscellany.

miserable [mise'raßle] *a* (*avaro*) mean, stingy; (*nimio*) miserable, paltry; (*lugar*) squalid; (*fam*) vile, despicable ♦ *nm/f* (*malvado*) rogue.

miseria [mi'serja] *nf* misery; (*pobreza*) poverty; (*tacañería*) meanness, stinginess; (*condiciones*) squalor; **una ~** a pittance.

misericordia [miseri'korðja] *nf* (*compasión*) compassion, pity; (*perdón*) forgiveness, mercy.

misil [mi'sil] *nm* missile.

misión [mi'sjon] *nf* mission; (*tarea*) job, duty; (*POL*) assignment; **misiones** *nfpl* (*REL*) overseas missions.

misionero, a [misjo'nero, a] *nm/f* missionary.

mismamente [misma'mente] *ad* (*fam*: *sólo*) only, just.

mismísimo, a [mis'misimo, a] *a* *superlativo* selfsame, very (same).

mismo, a ['mismo, a] *a* (*semejante*) same; (*después de pronombre*) -self; (*para énfasis*) very ♦ *ad*: **aquí/ayer/hoy ~** right here/only yesterday/this very day; **ahora ~** right now ♦ *conj*: **lo ~ que** just like, just as; **por lo ~** for the same reason; **el ~ traje** the same suit; **en ese ~ momento** at that very moment; **vino el ~ Ministro** the Minister himself came; **yo ~ lo vi** I saw it myself; **lo hizo por si ~** he did it by himself; **lo ~ the same** (thing); **da lo ~** it's all the same; **quedamos en las mismas** we're no further forward.

misógino [mi'soxino] *nm* misogynist.

miss [mis] *nf* beauty queen.

misterio [mis'terjo] *nm* mystery; (*lo secreto*) secrecy.

misterioso, a [miste'rjoso, a] *a* mysterious; (*inexplicable*) puzzling.

misticismo [misti'θismo] *nm* mysticism.

místico, a ['mistiko, a] *a* mystic(al) ♦ *nm/f* mystic ♦ *nf* mysticism.

mitad [mi'tað] *nf* (*medio*) half; (*centro*) middle; **~ (y) ~** half-and-half; (*fig*) yes and no; **a ~ de precio** (at) half-price; **en** *o* **a ~ del camino** halfway along the road; **cortar por la ~** to cut through the middle.

mítico, a ['mitiko, a] *a* mythical.

mitigar [miti'ɣar] *vt* to mitigate; (*dolor*) to relieve; (*sed*) to quench; (*ira*) to appease; (*preocupación*) to allay; (*soledad*) to alleviate.

mitigue [mi'tiɣe] *etc vb* V **mitigar**.

mitin ['mitin] *nm* (*esp POL*) meeting.

mito ['mito] *nm* myth.

mitología [mitolo'xia] *nf* mythology.

mitológico, a [mito'loxiko, a] *a* mythological.

mixto, a ['miksto, a] *a* mixed; (*comité*) joint.

ml. *abr* (= *mililitro*) ml.

MLN *nm abr* (*POL*) = *Movimiento de Liberación Nacional*.

mm. *abr* (= *milímetro*) mm.

m/n *abr* (*ECON*) = *moneda nacional*.

M.º *abr* (*POL*: = *Ministerio*) Min.

m/o *abr* (*COM*) = *mi orden*.

mobiliario [moßi'ljarjo] *nm* furniture.

mocedad [moθe'ðað] *nf* youth.

moción [mo'θjon] *nf* motion; **~ compuesta** (*POL*) composite motion.

moco ['moko] *nm* mucus; **limpiarse los ~s** to blow one's nose; **no es ~ de pavo** it's no trifle.

mocoso, a [mo'koso, a] *a* snivelling; (*fig*)

ill-bred ♦ *nm/f* (*fam*) brat.

mochila [mo't∫ila] *nf* rucksack (*Brit*), backpack.

moda ['moða] *nf* fashion; (*estilo*) style; **de o a la ~** in fashion, fashionable; **pasado de ~** out of fashion; **vestido a la última ~** trendily dressed.

modal [mo'ðal] *a* modal ♦ *nm*: **~es** *nmpl* manners.

modalidad [moðali'ðað] *nf* (*clase*) kind, variety; (*manera*) way; (*INFORM*) mode; **~ de texto** (*INFORM*) text mode.

modelar [moðe'lar] *vt* to model.

modelo [mo'ðelo] *a inv* model ♦ *nm/f* model ♦ *nm* (*patrón*) pattern; (*norma*) standard.

módem ['moðem] *nm* (*INFORM*) modem.

moderado, a [moðe'raðo, a] *a* moderate.

moderar [moðe'rar] *vt* to moderate; (*violencia*) to restrain, control; (*velocidad*) to reduce; **~se** *vr* to restrain o.s., control o.s.

modernice [moðer'niθe] *etc vb* V **modernizar.**

modernizar [moðerni'θar] *vt* to modernize; (*INFORM*) to upgrade.

moderno, a [mo'ðerno, a] *a* modern; (*actual*) present-day; (*equipo etc*) up-to-date.

modestia [mo'ðestja] *nf* modesty.

modesto, a [mo'ðesto, a] *a* modest.

módico, a ['moðiko, a] *a* moderate, reasonable.

modificar [moðifi'kar] *vt* to modify.

modifique [moði'fike] *etc vb* V **modificar.**

modismo [mo'ðismo] *nm* idiom.

modisto, a [mo'ðisto, a] *nm/f* dressmaker.

modo ['moðo] *nm* (*manera, forma*) way, manner; (*INFORM, MUS*) mode; (*LING*) mood; **~s** *nmpl* manners; "**~ de empleo**" "instructions for use"; **~ de gobierno** form of government; **a ~ de** like; **de este ~** in this way; **de ningún ~** in no way; **de todos ~s** at any rate; **de un ~ u otro** (in) one way or another.

modorra [mo'ðorra] *nf* drowsiness.

modoso, a [mo'ðoso, a] *a* (*educado*) quiet, well-mannered.

modulación [moðula'θjon] *nf* modulation; **~ de frecuencia** (*RADIO*) frequency modulation, FM.

mofarse [mo'farse] *vr*: **~ de** to mock, scoff at.

moflete [mo'flete] *nm* fat cheek, chubby cheek.

mogollón [moɣo'ʎon] (*fam*) *nm*: **~ de discos** *etc* loads of records *etc* ♦ *ad*: **un ~ a** hell of a lot.

mohín [mo'in] *nm* (*mueca*) (wry) face; (*pucheros*) pout.

mohíno, a [mo'ino, a] *a* (*triste*) gloomy, depressed; (*enojado*) sulky.

moho ['moo] *nm* (*BOT*) mould, mildew; (*en metal*) rust.

mohoso, a [mo'oso, a] *a* mouldy; rusty.

mojado, a [mo'xaðo, a] *a* wet; (*húmedo*) damp; (*empapado*) drenched.

mojar [mo'xar] *vt* to wet; (*humedecer*) to damp(en), moisten; (*calar*) to soak; **~se** *vr* to get wet; **~ el pan en el café** to dip o dunk one's bread in one's coffee.

mojigato, a [moxi'ɣato, a] *a* (*hipócrita*) hypocritical; (*santurrón*) sanctimonious; (*gazmoño*) prudish ♦ *nm/f* hypocrite; sanctimonious person; prude.

mojón [mo'xon] *nm* (*hito*) landmark; (*en un camino*) signpost; (**~ kilométrico**) milestone.

mol. *abr* (= *molécula*) mol.

molar [mo'lar] *nm* molar ♦ *vt* (*fam*): **lo que más me mola es** ... what I'm really into is ...; **¿te mola un pitillo?** do you fancy a smoke?

molde ['molde] *nm* mould; (*vaciado*) cast; (*de costura*) pattern; (*fig*) model.

moldear [molde'ar] *vt* to mould; (*en yeso etc*) to cast.

mole ['mole] *nf* mass, bulk; (*edificio*) pile.

moler [mo'ler] *vt* to grind, crush; (*pulverizar*) to pound; (*trigo etc*) to mill; (*cansar*) to tire out, exhaust; **~ a uno a palos** to give sb a beating.

molestar [moles'tar] *vt* to bother; (*fastidiar*) to annoy; (*incomodar*) to inconvenience, put out; (*perturbar*) to trouble, upset ♦ *vi* to be a nuisance; **~se** *vr* to bother; (*incomodarse*) to go to a lot of trouble; (*ofenderse*) to take offence; **¿le molesta el ruido?** do you mind the noise?; **siento ~le** I'm sorry to trouble you.

molestia [mo'lestja] *nf* bother, trouble; (*incomodidad*) inconvenience; (*MED*) discomfort; **no es ninguna ~** it's no trouble at all.

molesto, a [mo'lesto, a] *a* (*que fastidia*) annoying; (*incómodo*) inconvenient; (*inquieto*) uncomfortable, ill at ease; (*enfadado*) annoyed; **estar ~** (*MED*) to be in some discomfort; **estar ~ con uno** (*fig*) to be cross with sb; **me sentí ~** I felt embarrassed.

molido, a [mo'liðo, a] *a* (*machacado*) ground; (*pulverizado*) powdered; **estar ~** (*fig*) to be exhausted o dead beat.

molinero [moli'nero] *nm* miller.

molinillo [moli'niʎo] *nm* hand mill; **~ de carne/café** mincer/coffee grinder.

molino [mo'lino] *nm* (*edificio*) mill; (*máquina*) grinder.

Molucas [mo'lukas] *nfpl*: **las (Islas) ~** the Moluccas, the Molucca Islands.

molusco [mo'lusko] *nm* mollusc.

mollera [mo'ʎera] *nf* (*ANAT*) crown of the head; (*fam: seso*) brains *pl*; **duro de ~**

(*estúpido*) thick.

momentáneo, a [momen'taneo, a] *a* momentary.

momento [mo'mento] *nm* (*gen*) moment; (*TEC*) momentum; **de ~** at the moment, for the moment; **por el ~** for the time being.

momia ['momja] *nf* mummy.

mona ['mona] *nf* V **mono**.

Mónaco ['monako] *nm* Monaco.

monada [mo'naða] *nf* (*de niño*) charming habit; (*cosa primorosa*) lovely thing; (*chica*) pretty girl; **¡qué ~!** isn't it cute?

monaguillo [mona'ɣiʎo] *nm* altar boy.

monarca [mo'narka] *nm/f* monarch, ruler.

monarquía [monar'kia] *nf* monarchy.

monárquico, a [mo'narkiko, a] *nm/f* royalist, monarchist.

monasterio [monas'terjo] *nm* monastery.

monda ['monda] *nf* (*poda*) pruning; (: *de árbol*) lopping; (: *de fruta*) peeling; (*cáscara*) skin; **¡es la ~!** (*fam*: *fantástico*) it's great!; (: *el colmo*) it's the limit!; (: *persona*: *gracioso*) he's a knockout!

mondadientes [monda'ðjentes] *nm inv* toothpick.

mondar [mon'dar] *vt* (*limpiar*) to clean; (*pelar*) to peel; **~se** *vr*: **~se de risa** (*fam*) to split one's sides laughing.

moneda [mo'neða] *nf* (*tipo de dinero*) currency, money; (*pieza*) coin; **una ~ de 5 pesetas** a 5 peseta coin; **~ de curso legal** tender; **~ extranjera** foreign exchange; **es ~ corriente** (*fig*) it's common knowledge.

monedero [mone'ðero] *nm* purse.

monegasco, a [mone'ɣasko, a] *a* of o from Monaco, Monegasque ♦ *nm/f* Monegasque.

monetario, a [mone'tarjo, a] *a* monetary, financial.

monetarista [moneta'rista] *a*, *nm/f* monetarist.

monitor [moni'tor] *nm* (*INFORM*) monitor; **~ en color** colour monitor; **~ fósfor verde** green screen.

monja ['monxa] *nf* nun.

monje ['monxe] *nm* monk.

mono, a ['mono, a] *a* (*bonito*) lovely, pretty; (*gracioso*) nice, charming ♦ *nm/f* monkey, ape ♦ *nm* dungarees *pl*; (*overoles*) overalls *pl*; **una chica muy mona** a very pretty girl; **dormir la ~** to sleep it off.

monolingüe [mono'lingwe] *a* monolingual.

monólogo [mo'noloɣo] *nm* monologue.

monopatín [monopa'tin] *nm* skateboard.

monopolice [monopo'liθe] *etc* *vb* V **monopolizar**.

monopolio [mono'poljo] *nm* monopoly; **~ total** absolute monopoly.

monopolista [monopo'lista] *a*, *nm/f* monopolist.

monopolizar [monopoli'θar] *vt* to monopolize.

monosílabo, a [mono'silaßo, a] *a* monosyllabic ♦ *nm* monosyllable.

monotonía [monoto'nia] *nf* (*sonido*) monotone; (*fig*) monotony.

monótono, a [mo'notono, a] *a* monotonous.

mono-usuario, a [monou'swarjo, a] *a* (*INFORM*) single-user.

monóxido [mo'noksiðo] *nm* monoxide; **~ de carbono** carbon monoxide.

Mons. *abr* (*REL*) = **Monseñor.**

monseñor [monse'ɲor] *nm* monsignor.

monserga [mon'serɣa] *nf* (*lenguaje confuso*) gibberish; (*tonterías*) drivel.

monstruo ['monstrwo] *nm* monster ♦ *a inv* fantastic.

monstruoso, a [mons'trwoso, a] *a* monstrous.

monta ['monta] *nf* total, sum; **de poca ~** unimportant, of little account.

montacargas [monta'karɣas] *nm inv* service lift (*Brit*), freight elevator (*US*).

montador [monta'ðor] *nm* (*para montar*) mounting block; (*profesión*) fitter; (*CINE*) film editor.

montaje [mon'taxe] *nm* assembly; (*organización*) fitting up; (*TEATRO*) décor; (*CINE*) montage.

montante [mon'tante] *nm* (*poste*) upright; (*soporte*) stanchion; (*ARQ*: *de puerta*) transom; (: *de ventana*) mullion; (*suma*) amount, total.

montaña [mon'taɲa] *nf* (*monte*) mountain; (*sierra*) mountains *pl*, mountainous area; (*AM*: *selva*) forest; **~ rusa** roller coaster.

montañero, a [monta'ɲero, a] *a* mountain *cpd* ♦ *nm/f* mountaineer, climber.

montañés, esa [monta'ɲes, esa] *a* mountain *cpd*; (*de Santander*) of o from the Santander region ♦ *nm/f* highlander; native o inhabitant of the Santander region.

montañismo [monta'ɲismo] *nm* mountaineering, climbing.

montañoso, a [monta'ɲoso, a] *a* mountainous.

montar [mon'tar] *vt* (*subir a*) to mount, get on; (*caballo etc*) to ride; (*TEC*) to assemble, put together; (*negocio*) to set up; (*colocar*) to lift on to; (*CINE*: *película*) to edit; (*TEATRO*: *obra*) to stage, put on; (*CULIN*: *batir*) to whip, beat ♦ *vi* to mount, get on; (*sobresalir*) to overlap; **~ en cólera** to get angry; **~ un número** o **numerito** to make a scene; **tanto monta** it makes no odds.

montaraz [monta'raθ] *a* mountain *cpd*, highland *cpd*; (*pey*) uncivilized.

monte ['monte] *nm* (*montaña*) mountain; (*bosque*) woodland; (*área sin cultivar*) wild area, wild country; **~ de piedad** pawnshop; **~ alto** forest; **~ bajo** scrub(land).

montera [mon'tera] *nf* (*sombrero*) cloth cap; (*de torero*) bullfighter's hat.

monto ['monto] *nm* total, amount.

montón [mon'ton] *nm* heap, pile; **un ~ de** (*fig*) heaps of, lots of; **a montones** by the score, galore.

montura [mon'tura] *nf* (*cabalgadura*) mount; (*silla*) saddle; (*arreos*) harness; (*de joya*) mounting; (*de gafas*) frame.

monumento [monu'mento] *nm* monument; (*de conmemoración*) memorial.

monzón [mon'θon] *nm* monsoon.

moña ['moɲa] *nf* hair ribbon.

moño ['moɲo] *nm* (*de pelo*) bun; **estar hasta el ~** (*fam*) to be fed up to the back teeth.

MOPU ['mopu] *nm abr* (*Esp*) = *Ministerio de Obras Públicas y Urbanismo.*

moqueta [mo'keta] *nf* fitted carpet.

moquillo [mo'kiʎo] *nm* (*enfermedad*) distemper.

mora ['mora] *nf* (*BOT*) mulberry; (: *zarzamora*) blackberry; (*COM*): **en ~** in arrears.

morado, a [mo'raðo, a] *a* purple, violet ◆ *nm* bruise ◆ *nf* (*casa*) dwelling, abode; **pasarlas moradas** to have a tough time of it.

moral [mo'ral] *a* moral ◆ *nf* (*ética*) ethics *pl*; (*moralidad*) morals *pl*, morality; (*ánimo*) morale; **tener baja la ~** to be in low spirits.

moraleja [mora'lexa] *nf* moral.

moralice [mora'liθe] *etc vb* V **moralizar.**

moralidad [morali'ðað] *nf* morals *pl*, morality.

moralizar [morali'θar] *vt* to moralize.

morar [mo'rar] *vi* to live, dwell.

moratoria [mora'torja] *nf* moratorium.

morbosidad [morβosi'ðað] *nf* morbidity.

morboso, a [mor'βoso, a] *a* morbid.

morcilla [mor'θiʎa] *nf* blood sausage, ≈ black pudding (*Brit*).

mordaz [mor'ðaθ] *a* (*crítica*) biting, scathing.

mordaza [mor'ðaθa] *nf* (*para la boca*) gag; (*TEC*) clamp.

morder [mor'ðer] *vt* to bite; (*mordisquear*) to nibble; (*fig: consumir*) to eat away, eat into ◆ *vi*, **~se** *vr* to bite; **está que muerde** he's hopping mad; **~se la lengua** to hold one's tongue.

mordiscar [morðis'kar] *vt* to nibble at; (*con fuerza*) to gnaw at; (*pinchar*) to nip.

mordisco [mor'ðisko] *nm* bite.

mordisque [mor'ðiske] *etc vb* V **mordiscar.**

mordisquear [morðiske'ar] *vt* = **mordiscar.**

moreno, a [mo'reno, a] *a* (*color*) (dark) brown; (*de tez*) dark; (*de pelo ~*) darkhaired; (*negro*) black ◆ *nm/f* (*de tez*)

dark-skinned man/woman; (*de pelo*) darkhaired man/woman.

moretón [more'ton] *nm* (*fam*) bruise.

morfina [mor'fina] *nf* morphine.

morfinómano, a [morfi'nomano, a] *a* addicted to hard drugs ◆ *nm/f* drug addict.

moribundo, a [mori'βundo, a] *a* dying ◆ *nm/f* dying person.

morir [mo'rir] *vi* to die; (*fuego*) to die down; (*luz*) to go out; **~se** *vr* to die; (*fig*) to be dying; (*FERRO etc: vías*) to end; (*calle*) to come out; **fue muerto a tiros/en un accidente** he was shot (dead)/was killed in an accident; **~ de frío/hambre** to die of cold/starve to death; **¡me muero de hambre!** (*fig*) I'm starving!; **~se por algo** to be dying for sth; **~se por uno** to be crazy about sb.

moro, a ['moro, a] *a* Moorish ◆ *nm/f* Moor; **¡hay ~s en la costa!** watch out!

moroso, a [mo'roso, a] *a* (*lento*) slow ◆ *nm* (*COM*) bad debtor, defaulter; **deudor ~** (*COM*) slow payer.

morral [mo'rral] *nm* haversack.

morro ['morro] *nm* (*ZOOL*) snout, nose; (*AUTO, AVIAT*) nose; (*fam: labio*) (thick) lip; **beber a ~** to drink from the bottle; **caer de ~** to nosedive; **estar de ~s (con uno)** to be in a bad mood (with sb); **tener ~** to have a nerve.

morrocotudo, a [morroko'tuðo, a] *a* (*fam*) (*fantástico*) smashing; (*riña, golpe*) tremendous; (*fuerte*) strong; (*pesado*) heavy; (*difícil*) awkward.

morsa ['morsa] *nf* walrus.

mortaja [mor'taxa] *nf* shroud; (*TEC*) mortise; (*AM*) cigarette paper.

mortal [mor'tal] *a* mortal; (*golpe*) deadly.

mortalidad [mortali'ðað], **mortandad** [mortan'dað] *nf* mortality.

mortecino, a [morte'θino, a] *a* (*débil*) weak; (*luz*) dim; (*color*) dull.

mortero [mor'tero] *nm* mortar.

mortífero, a [mor'tifero, a] *a* deadly, lethal.

mortificar [mortifi'kar] *vt* to mortify; (*atormentar*) to torment.

mortifique [morti'fike] *etc vb* V **mortificar.**

mortuorio, a [mor'tworjo, a] *a* mortuary, death *cpd*.

Mosa ['mosa] *nm*: **el (Río) ~** the Meuse.

mosca ['moska] *nf* fly; **por si las ~s** just in case; **estar ~** (*desconfiar*) to smell a rat; **tener la ~ en** *o* **detrás de la oreja** to be wary.

moscovita [mosko'βita] *a* Muscovite, Moscow *cpd* ◆ *nm/f* Muscovite.

Moscú [mos'ku] *nm* Moscow.

mosquearse [moske'arse] *vr* (*fam: enfadarse*) to get cross; (: *ofenderse*) to take offence.

mosquitero [moski'tero] *nm* mosquito net.
mosquito [mos'kito] *nm* mosquito.
mostaza [mos'taθa] *nf* mustard.
mosto ['mosto] *nm* unfermented grape juice.
mostrador [mostra'ðor] *nm* (*de tienda*) counter; (*de café*) bar.
mostrar [mos'trar] *vt* to show; (*exhibir*) to display, exhibit; (*explicar*) to explain; ~**se** *vr*: ~**se amable** to be kind; to prove to be kind; **no se muestra muy inteligente** he doesn't seem (to be) very intelligent; ~ **en pantalla** (*INFORM*) to display.
mota ['mota] *nf* speck, tiny piece; (*en diseño*) dot.
mote ['mote] *nm* (*apodo*) nickname.
motín [mo'tin] *nm* (*del pueblo*) revolt, rising; (*del ejército*) mutiny.
motivar [moti'ßar] *vt* (*causar*) to cause, motivate; (*explicar*) to explain, justify.
motivo [mo'tißo] *nm* motive, reason; (*ARTE, MUS*) motif; **con ~ de** (*debido a*) because of; (*en ocasión de*) on the occasion of; (*con el fin de*) in order to; **sin ~** for no reason at all.
moto ['moto], *nf*, **motocicleta** [motoθi'kleta] *nf* motorbike (*Brit*), motorcycle.
motor, a [mo'tor, a] *a* (*TEC*) motive; (*ANAT*) motor ♦ *nm* motor, engine; ~ **a chorro** *o* **de reacción/de explosión** jet engine/internal combustion engine ♦ *nf* motorboat.
motorismo [moto'rismo] *nm* motorcycling.
motorizado, a [motori'θaðo, a] *a* motorized.
motosierra [moto'sjerra] *nf* mechanical saw.
movedizo, a [moße'ðiθo, a] *a* (*inseguro*) unsteady; (*fig*) unsettled, changeable; (*persona*) fickle.
mover [mo'ßer] *vt* to move; (*cambiar de lugar*) to shift; (*cabeza: para negar*) to shake; (: *para asentir*) to nod; (*accionar*) to drive; (*fig*) to cause, provoke; ~**se** *vr* to move; (*mar*) to get rough; (*viento*) to rise; (*fig: apurarse*) to get a move on; (: *transformarse*) to be on the move.
movible [mo'ßißle] *a* (*no fijo*) movable; (*móvil*) mobile; (*cambiadizo*) changeable.
movido, a [mo'ßiðo, a] *a* (*FOTO*) blurred; (*persona: activo*) active; (*mar*) rough; (*día*) hectic ♦ *nf* move; **la movida madrileña** the Madrid scene.
móvil ['moßil] *a* mobile; (*pieza de máquina*) moving; (*mueble*) movable ♦ *nm* motive.
movilice [moßi'liθe] *etc vb V* **movilizar**.
movilidad [moßili'ðað] *nf* mobility.
movilizar [moßili'θar] *vt* to mobilize.
movimiento [moßi'mjento] *nm* (*gen, LITERATURA, POL*) movement; (*TEC*) motion; (*actividad*) activity; (*MUS*) tempo; **el M~**

the Falangist Movement; ~ **de bloques** (*INFORM*) block move; ~ **de mercancías** (*COM*) turnover, volume of business; ~ **obrero/sindical** workers'/trade union movement; ~ **sísmico** earth tremor.
Mozambique [moθam'bike] *nm* Mozambique.
mozambiqueño, a [moθambi'keɲo, a] *a, nm/f* Mozambican.
mozo, a ['moθo, a] *a* (*joven*) young; (*soltero*) single, unmarried ♦ *nm/f* (*joven*) youth, young man/girl; (*camarero*) waiter; (*camarera*) waitress; ~ **de estación** porter.
MPAIAC [emepa'jak] *nm abr* (*Esp POL*) = *Movimiento para la Autodeterminación y la Independencia del Archipiélago Canario*.
mucama [mu'kama] *nf* (*AM*) maid.
muchacho, a [mu'tʃatʃo, a] *nm/f* (*niño*) boy/girl; (*criado*) servant/servant *o* maid.
muchedumbre [mutʃe'ðumbre] *nf* crowd.
muchísimo, a [mu'tʃisimo, a] *a* (*superlativo de* **mucho**) lots and lots of, ever so much ♦ *ad* ever so much.
mucho, a ['mutʃo, a] *a* (*sg*) a lot of; (*gen en frase negativa o interrogativa*) much; (*pl*) many, a lot of, lots of ♦ *ad* (*en cantidad*) a lot, a great deal, much; (*del tiempo*) long; (*muy*) very ♦ *pron*: **tengo ~ que hacer** I have a lot to do; ~**s dicen que** a lot of people say that; **como ~** at (the) most; **ni con ~** not nearly; **ni ~ menos** far from it; **por ~ que** however much; **me alegro/lo siento ~** I'm very glad/sorry.
muda ['muða] *nf* (*de ropa*) change of clothing; (*ZOOL*) moult; (*de serpiente*) slough.
mudanza [mu'ðanθa] *nf* (*cambio*) change; (*de casa*) move; **estar de** ~ to be moving.
mudar [mu'ðar] *vt* to change; (*ZOOL*) to shed ♦ *vi* to change; ~**se** *vr* (*la ropa*) to change; ~**se de casa** to move house.
mudo, a ['muðo, a] *a* dumb; (*callado, película*) silent; (*LING: letra*) mute; (: *consonante*) voiceless; **quedarse ~ (de)** (*fig*) to be dumb with; **quedarse ~ de asombro** to be speechless.
mueble ['mweßle] *nm* piece of furniture; ~**s** *nmpl* furniture *sg*.
mueble-bar [mweßle'ßar] *nm* cocktail cabinet.
mueca ['mweka] *nf* face, grimace; **hacer ~s a** to make faces at.
muela ['mwela] *etc vb V* **moler** ♦ *nf* (*diente*) tooth; (: *de atrás*) molar; (*de molino*) millstone; (*de afilar*) grindstone; ~ **del juicio** wisdom tooth.
muelle ['mweʎe] *a* (*blando*) soft; (*fig*) soft, easy ♦ *nm* spring; (*NAUT*) wharf; (*malecón*) jetty.
muera ['mwera] *etc vb V* **morir**.
muerda ['mwerða] *etc vb V* **morder**.

muermo ['mwermo] *nm* (*fam*) wimp.

muerte ['mwerte] *nf* death; (*homicidio*) murder; **dar ~ a** to kill; **de mala ~** (*fam*) lousy, rotten; **es la ~** (*fam*) it's deadly boring.

muerto, a ['mwerto, a] *pp de* **morir** ♦ *a* dead; (*color*) dull ♦ *nm/f* dead man/woman; (*difunto*) deceased; (*cadáver*) corpse; **cargar con el ~** (*fam*) to carry the can; **echar el ~ a uno** to pass the buck; **hacer el ~** (*nadando*) to float; **estar ~ de cansancio** to be dead tired.

muestra ['mwestra] *etc vb V* **mostrar** ♦ *nf* (*señal*) indication, sign; (*demostración*) demonstration; (*prueba*) proof; (*estadística*) sample; (*modelo*) model, pattern; (*testimonio*) token; **dar ~s de** to show signs of; **~ al azar** (*COM*) random sample.

muestrario [mwes'trarjo] *nm* collection of samples; (*exposición*) showcase.

muestreo [mwes'treo] *nm* sample, sampling.

mueva [mweβa] *etc vb V* **mover**.

mugir [mu'xir] *vi* (*vaca*) to moo.

mugre ['muɣre] *nf* dirt, filth, muck.

mugriento, a [mu'ɣrjento, a] *a* dirty, filthy mucky.

muja ['muxa] *etc vb V* **mugir**.

mujer [mu'xer] *nf* woman; (*esposa*) wife.

mujeriego [muxe'rjeɣo] *nm* womaniser.

mula ['mula] *nf* mule.

muladar [mula'ðar] *nm* dungheap, dunghill.

mulato, a [mu'lato, a] *a*, *nm/f* mulatto.

muleta [mu'leta] *nf* (*para andar*) crutch; (*TAUR*) *stick with red cape attached*.

muletilla [mule'tiʎa] *nf* (*palabra*) pet word, tag; (*de cómico*) catch phrase.

multa ['multa] *nf* fine; **echar o poner una ~ a** to fine.

multar [mul'tar] *vt* to fine; (*DEPORTE*) to penalize.

multiacceso [multjak'θeso] *a* (*INFORM*) multi-access.

multicopista [multiko'pista] *nm* duplicator.

multinacional [multinaθjo'nal] *a*, *nf* multinational.

múltiple ['multiple] *a* multiple; (*pl*) many, numerous; **de tarea ~** (*INFORM*) multitasking; **de usuario ~** (*INFORM*) multi-user.

multiplicar [multipli'kar] *vt* (*MAT*) to multiply; (*fig*) to increase; **~se** *vr* (*BIO*) to multiply; (*fig*) to be everywhere at once.

multiplique [multi'plike] *etc vb V* **multiplicar**.

multitud [multi'tuð] *nf* (*muchedumbre*) crowd; **~ de** lots of.

multitudinario, a [multituði'narjo, a] *a* (*numeroso*) multitudinous; (*de masa*) mass *cpd*.

mullido, a [mu'ʎiðo, a] *a* (*cama*) soft; (*hierba*) soft, springy.

mundanal [munda'nal] *a* worldly; **lejos del ~ ruido** far from the madding crowd.

mundano, a [mun'dano, a] *a* worldly; (*de moda*) fashionable.

mundial [mun'djal] *a* world-wide, universal; (*guerra, récord*) world *cpd*.

mundialmente [mundjal'mente] *ad* worldwide; **~ famoso** world-famous.

mundo ['mundo] *nm* world; (*ámbito*) world, circle; **el otro ~** the next world; **el ~ del espectáculo** show business; **todo el ~** everybody; **tener ~** to be experienced, know one's way around; **el ~ es un pañuelo** it's a small world; **no es nada del otro ~** it's nothing special; **se le cayó el ~ (encima)** his world fell apart.

munición [muni'θjon] *nf* (*MIL*: *provisiones*) stores *pl*, supplies *pl*; (: *de armas*) ammunition.

municipal [muniθi'pal] *a* (*elección*) municipal; (*concejo*) town *cpd*, local; (*piscina etc*) public ♦ *nm* (*guardia*) policeman.

municipio [muni'θipjo] *nm* (*ayuntamiento*) town council, corporation; (*territorio administrativo*) town, municipality.

Munich ['munitʃ] *nm* Munich.

muniqués, esa [muni'kes, esa] *a* of *o* from Munich ♦ *nm/f* native *o* inhabitant of Munich.

muñeca [mu'ɲeka] *nf* (*ANAT*) wrist; (*juguete*) doll.

muñeco [mu'ɲeko] *nm* (*figura*) figure; (*marioneta*) puppet; (*fig*) puppet, pawn; (*niño*) pretty little boy; **~ de nieve** snowman.

muñón [mu'ɲon] *nm* (*ANAT*) stump.

mural [mu'ral] *a* mural, wall *cpd* ♦ *nm* mural.

muralla [mu'raʎa] *nf* (city) wall(s) (*pl*).

murciano, a [mur'θjano, a] *a* of *o* from Murcia ♦ *nm/f* native *o* inhabitant of Murcia.

murciélago [mur'θjelaɣo] *nm* bat.

murga ['murɣa] *nf* (*banda*) band of street musicians; **dar la ~** to be a nuisance.

murmullo [mur'muʎo] *nm* murmur(ing); (*cuchicheo*) whispering; (*de arroyo*) murmur, rippling; (*de hojas, viento*) rustle, rustling; (*ruido confuso*) hum(ming).

murmuración [murmura'θjon] *nf* gossip; (*críticas*) backbiting.

murmurador, a [murmura'ðor, a] *a* gossiping; (*criticón*) backbiting ♦ *nm/f* gossip; backbiter.

murmurar [murmu'rar] *vi* to murmur, whisper; (*criticar*) to criticize; (*cotillear*) to gossip.

muro ['muro] *nm* wall; **~ de contención** retaining wall.

musaraña [musa'raɲa] *nf* (*ZOOL*) shrew; (*insecto*) creepy-crawly; **pensar en las ~s**

to daydream.
muscular [musku'lar] *a* muscular.
músculo ['muskulo] *nm* muscle.
museo [mu'seo] *nm* museum; ~ **de arte** *o* **de pintura** art gallery; ~ **de cera** waxworks.
musgo ['musɣo] *nm* moss.
músico, a ['musiko, a] *a* musical ◆ *nm/f* musician ◆ *nf* music; **irse con la música a otra parte** to clear off.
musitar [musi'tar] *vt, vi* to mutter, mumble.
muslo ['muslo] *nm* thigh; (*de pollo*) leg, drumstick.
mustio, a ['mustjo, a] *a* (*persona*) depressed, gloomy; (*planta*) faded, withered.
musulmán, ana [musul'man, ana] *nm/f* Moslem, Muslim.
mutación [muta'θjon] *nf* (*BIO*) mutation; (: *cambio*) (sudden) change.
mutilar [muti'lar] *vt* to mutilate; (*a una persona*) to maim.
mutis ['mutis] *nm inv* (*TEATRO*) exit; **hacer** ~ (*TEATRO*: *retirarse*) to exit, go off; (*fig*) to say nothing.
mutualidad [mutwali'ðað] *nf* (*reciprocidad*) mutual character; (*asociación*) friendly *o* benefit (*US*) society.
mutuamente [mutwa'mente] *ad* mutually.
mutuo, a ['mutwo, a] *a* mutual.
muy [mwi] *ad* very; (*demasiado*) too; **M~ Señor mío** Dear Sir; ~ **bien** (*de acuerdo*) all right; ~ **de noche** very late at night; **eso es** ~ **de él** that's just like him; **eso es** ~ **español** that's typically Spanish.

N

N, n ['ene] *nf* (*letra*) N, n; **N de Navarra** N for Nellie (*Brit*) *o* Nan (*US*).
N *abr* (= *norte*) N.
N. *abr* (= *noviembre*) Nov.
n. *abr* (*LING*: = *nombre*) n; (= *nacido*) b.
n/ *abr* = **nuestro, a.**
nabo ['naβo] *nm* turnip.
nácar ['nakar] *nm* mother-of-pearl.
nacer [na'θer] *vi* to be born; (*huevo*) to hatch; (*vegetal*) to sprout; (*río*) to rise; (*fig*) to begin, originate, have its origins; **nació para poeta** he was born to be a poet; **nadie nace enseñado** we all have to learn; **nació una sospecha en su mente** a suspicion formed in her mind.
nacido, a [na'θiðo, a] *a* born; **recién** ~ newborn.
naciente [na'θjente] *a* new, emerging; (*sol*)

rising.
nacimiento [naθi'mjento] *nm* birth; (*fig*) birth, origin; (*de Navidad*) Nativity; (*linaje*) descent, family; (*de río*) source; **ciego de** ~ blind from birth.
nación [na'θjon] *nf* nation; (*pueblo*) people; **Naciones Unidas** United Nations.
nacional [naθjo'nal] *a* national; (*COM, ECON*) domestic, home *cpd*.
nacionalice [naθjona'liθe] *etc vb V* **nacionalizar.**
nacionalismo [naθjona'lismo] *nm* nationalism.
nacionalista [naθjona'lista] *a, nm/f* nationalist.
nacionalizar [naθjonali'θar] *vt* to nationalize; ~**se** *vr* (*persona*) to become naturalized.
nada ['naða] *pron* nothing ◆ *ad* not at all, in no way ◆ *nf* nothingness; **no decir** ~ to say nothing, not to say anything; **de** ~ don't mention it; ~ **de eso** nothing of the kind; **antes de** ~ right away; **como si** ~ as if it didn't matter; **no ha sido** ~ it's nothing; **la** ~ the void.
nadador, a [naða'ðor, a] *nm/f* swimmer.
nadar [na'ðar] *vi* to swim; ~ **en la abundancia** (*fig*) to be rolling in money.
nadie ['naðje] *pron* nobody, no-one; ~ **habló** nobody spoke; **no había** ~ there was nobody there, there wasn't anybody there; **es un don** ~ he's a nobody *o* nonentity.
nado ['naðo] **a** ~ *ad*: **pasar a** ~ to swim across.
nafta ['nafta] *nf* (*AM*) petrol (*Brit*), gas(oline) (*US*).
naftalina [nafta'lina] *nf*: **bolas de** ~ mothballs.
naipe ['naipe] *nm* (playing) card; ~**s** *nmpl* cards.
nal. *abr* (= *nacional*) nat.
nalgas ['nalɣas] *nfpl* buttocks.
Namibia [na'miβja] *nf* Namibia.
nana ['nana] *nf* lullaby.
Nápoles ['napoles] *nf* Naples.
napolitano, a [napoli'tano, a] *a* of *o* from Naples, Neapolitan ◆ *nm/f* Neapolitan.
naranja [na'ranxa] *a inv, nf* orange; **media** ~ (*fam*) better half; **¡~s de la China!** nonsense!
naranjada [naran'xaða] *nf* orangeade.
naranjo [na'ranxo] *nm* orange tree.
Narbona [nar'βona] *nf* Narbonne.
narciso [nar'θiso] *nm* narcissus.
narcotice [narko'tiθe] *etc vb V* **narcotizar.**
narcótico, a [nar'kotiko, a] *a, nm* narcotic.
narcotizar [narkoti'θar] *vt* to drug.
narcotraficante [narkotrafi'kante] *nm/f* narcotics *o* drug trafficker.
narcotráfico [narko'trafiko] *nm* narcotics *o* drug trafficking.

nardo ['narðo] *nm* lily.

narices [na'riθes] *nfpl V* **nariz**.

narigón, ona, [nari'ɣon, ona] **narigudo, a** [nari'ɣuðo, a] *a* big-nosed.

nariz [na'riθ] *nf* nose; **narices** *nfpl* nostrils; **¡narices!** (*fam*) rubbish!; **delante de las narices de uno** under one's (very) nose; **estar hasta las narices** to be completely fed up; **meter las narices en algo** to poke one's nose into sth.

narración [narra'θjon] *nf* narration.

narrador, a [narra'ðor, a] *nm/f* narrator.

narrar [na'rrar] *vt* to narrate, recount.

narrativo, a [narra'tiβo, a] *a* narrative ◆ *nf* narrative, story.

nasal [na'sal] *a* nasal.

N.ª S.ʳª *abr = Nuestra Señora*.

nata ['nata] *nf* cream (*tb fig*); (*en leche cocida etc*) skin; ~ **batida** whipped cream.

natación [nata'θjon] *nf* swimming.

natal [na'tal] *a* natal; (*país*) native; **ciudad** ~ home town.

natalicio [nata'liθjo] *nm* birthday.

natalidad [natali'ðað] *nf* birth rate.

natillas [na'tiʎas] *nfpl* (*egg*) custard *sg*.

natividad [natiβi'ðað] *nf* nativity.

nativo, a [na'tiβo, a] *a*, *nm/f* native.

nato, a ['nato, a] *a* born; **un músico** ~ a born musician.

natural [natu'ral] *a* natural; (*fruta etc*) fresh ◆ *nm/f* native ◆ *nm* disposition, temperament; **buen** ~ good nature; **fruta al** ~ fruit in its own juice.

naturaleza [natura'leθa] *nf* nature; (*género*) nature, kind; ~ **muerta** still life.

naturalice [natura'liθe] *etc vb V* **naturalizarse**.

naturalidad [naturali'ðað] *nf* naturalness.

naturalización [naturaliθa'θjon] *nf* naturalization.

naturalizarse [naturali'θarse] *vr* to become naturalized; (*aclimatarse*) to become acclimatized.

naturalmente [natural'mente] *ad* naturally; **¡~!** of course!

naufragar [naufra'ɣar] *vi* (*barco*) to sink; (*gente*) to be shipwrecked; (*fig*) to fail.

naufragio [nau'fraxjo] *nm* shipwreck.

náufrago, a ['naufraɣo, a] *nm/f* castaway, shipwrecked person.

naufrague [nau'fraɣe] *etc vb V* **naufragar**.

náusea ['nausea] *nf* nausea; **me da** ~**s** it makes me feel sick.

nauseabundo, a [nausea'βundo, a] *a* nauseating, sickening.

náutico, a ['nautiko, a] *a* nautical; **club** ~ sailing *o* yacht club ◆ *nf* navigation, seamanship.

navaja [na'βaxa] *nf* (*cortaplumas*) clasp knife (*Brit*), penknife; ~ **(de afeitar)** razor.

Navarra [na'βarra] *nf* Navarre.

navarro, a [na'βarro, a] *a* of *o* from Navarre, Navarrese ◆ *nm/f* Navarrese ◆ *nm* (*LING*) Navarrese.

nave ['naβe] *nf* (*barco*) ship, vessel; (*ARQ*) nave; ~ **espacial** spaceship; **quemar las** ~**s** to burn one's boats.

navegación [naβeɣa'θjon] *nf* navigation; (*viaje*) sea journey; ~ **aérea** air traffic; ~ **costera** coastal shipping; ~ **fluvial** river navigation.

navegante [naβe'ɣante] *nm/f* navigator.

navegar [naβe'ɣar] *vi* (*barco*) to sail; (*avión*) to fly ◆ *vt* to sail; to fly; (*dirigir el rumbo de*) to navigate.

navegue [na'βeɣe] *etc vb V* **navegar**.

navidad [naβi'ðað] *nf* Christmas; ~**es** *nfpl* Christmas time *sg*; **día de** ~ Christmas Day; **por** ~**es** at Christmas (time); **¡felices** ~**es!** Merry Christmas.

navideño, a [naβi'ðeɲo, a] *a* Christmas *cpd*.

navío [na'βio] *nm* ship.

nazi ['naθi] *a*, *nm/f* Nazi.

n/cta *abr = nuestra cuenta*.

N. de la R. *abr* (= *nota de la redacción*) editor's note.

N. de la T./del T. *abr* (= *nota de la traductora/del traductor*) translator's note.

NE *abr* (= *nor(d)este*) NE.

neblina [ne'βlina] *nf* mist.

nebuloso, a [neβu'loso, a] *a* foggy; (*calinoso*) misty; (*indefinido*) nebulous, vague ◆ *nf* nebula.

necedad [neθe'ðað] *nf* foolishness; (*una* ~) foolish act.

necesario, a [neθe'sarjo, a] *a* necessary; **si fuera** *o* **fuese** ~ if need(s) be.

neceser [neθe'ser] *nm* vanity case; (*bolsa grande*) holdall.

necesidad [neθesi'ðað] *nf* need; (*lo inevitable*) necessity; (*miseria*) poverty, need; **en caso de** ~ in case of need *o* emergency; **hacer sus** ~**es** to relieve o.s.

necesitado, a [neθesi'taðo, a] *a* needy, poor; ~ **de** in need of.

necesitar [neθesi'tar] *vt* to need, require ◆ *vi:* ~ **de** to have need of; ~**se** *vr* to be needed; (*anuncios*) **"necesítase coche"** "car wanted".

necio, a ['neθjo, a] *a* foolish ◆ *nm/f* fool.

necrología [nekrolo'xia] *nf* obituary.

necrópolis [ne'kropolis] *nf inv* cemetery.

nectarina [nekta'rina] *nf* nectarine.

neerlandés, esa [neerlan'des, esa] *a* Dutch ◆ *nm/f* Dutchman/woman ◆ *nm* (*LING*) Dutch; **los neerlandeses** the Dutch.

nefando, a [ne'fando, a] *a* unspeakable.

nefasto, a [ne'fasto, a] *a* ill-fated, unlucky.

negación [neɣa'θjon] *nf* negation; (*LING*) negative; (*rechazo*) refusal, denial.

negado, a [ne'ɣaðo, a] *a:* ~ **para** inept at,

unfitted for.

negar [ne'ɣar] vt (renegar, rechazar) to refuse; (prohibir) to refuse, deny; (desmentir) to deny; ~se vr: ~se a hacer algo to refuse to do sth.

negativo, a [neɣa'tiβo, a] a negative ♦ nm (FOTO) negative; (MAT) minus ♦ nf (gen) negative; (rechazo) refusal, denial; negativa rotunda flat refusal.

negligencia [neɣli'xenθja] nf negligence.

negligente [neɣli'xente] a negligent.

negociable [neɣo'θjaβle] a (COM) negotiable.

negociado [neɣo'θjaðo] nm department, section.

negociante [neɣo'θjante] nm/f businessman/woman.

negociar [neɣo'θjar] vt, vi to negotiate; ~ en to deal in, trade in.

negocio [ne'ɣoθjo] nm (COM) business; (asunto) affair, business; (operación comercial) deal, transaction; (AM) firm; (lugar) place of business; los ~s business sg; hacer ~ to do business; el ~ del libro the book trade; ~ autorizado licensed trade; hombre de ~s businessman; ~ sucio shady deal; hacer un buen ~ to pull off a profitable deal; ¡mal ~! it looks bad!

negra ['neɣra] nf V negro ♦ nf (MUS) crotchet.

negrita [ne'ɣrita] nf (TIP) bold face; en ~ in bold (type).

negro, a ['neɣro, a] a black; (suerte) awful, atrocious; (humor etc) sad; (lúgubre) gloomy ♦ nm (color) black ♦ nm/f Negro/Negress, black ♦ nf (MUS) crotchet; ~ como la boca del lobo pitch-black; estoy ~ con esto I'm getting desperate about it; ponerse ~ (fam) to get cross.

negrura [ne'ɣrura] nf blackness.

negué [ne'ɣe], **neguemos** [ne'ɣemos] etc vb V negar.

nene, a ['nene, a] nm/f baby, small child.

nenúfar [ne'nufar] nm water lily.

neologismo [neolo'xismo] nm neologism.

neoyorquino, a [neojor'kino, a] a New York cpd ♦ nm/f New Yorker.

neozelandés, esa [neoθelan'des, esa] a New Zealand cpd ♦ nm/f New Zealander.

nepotismo [nepo'tismo] nm nepotism.

nervio ['nerβjo] nm (ANAT) nerve; (: tendón) tendon; (fig) vigour; (TEC) rib; crispar los ~s a uno, poner los ~s de punta a uno to get on sb's nerves.

nerviosismo [nerβjo'sismo] nm nervousness, nerves pl.

nervioso, a [ner'βjoso, a] a nervous; (sensible) nervy, highly-strung; (impaciento) restless; ¡no te pongas ~! take it easy!

nervudo, a [ner'βuðo, a] a tough; (mano) sinewy.

neto, a ['neto, a] a clear; (limpio) clean; (COM) net.

neumático, a [neu'matiko, a] a pneumatic ♦ nm (Esp) tyre (Brit), tire (US); ~ de recambio spare tyre.

neumonía [neumo'nia] nf pneumonia.

neuralgia [neu'ralxja] nf neuralgia.

neurastenia [neuras'tenja] nf neurasthenia; (fig) excitability.

neurasténico, a [neuras'teniko, a] a neurasthenic; excitable.

neurólogo, a [neu'roloɣo, a] nm/f neurologist.

neurosis [neu'rosis] nf inv neurosis.

neurótico, a [neu'rotiko, a] a, nm/f neurotic.

neutral [neu'tral] a neutral.

neutralice [neutra'liθe] etc vb V neutralizar.

neutralizar [neutrali'θar] vt to neutralize; (contrarrestar) to counteract.

neutro, a ['neutro, a] a (BIO, LING) neuter.

neutrón [neu'tron] nm neutron.

nevado, a [ne'βaðo, a] a snow-covered; (montaña) snow-capped; (fig) snowy, snow-white ♦ nf snowstorm; (caída de nieve) snowfall.

nevar [ne'βar] vi to snow ♦ vt (fig) to whiten.

nevera [ne'βera] nf (Esp) refrigerator (Brit), icebox (US).

nevería [neβe'ria] nf (AM) ice cream parlour.

nevisca [ne'βiska] nf flurry of snow.

nexo ['nekso] nm link, connection.

n/f abr (COM) = nuestro favor.

ni [ni] conj nor, neither; (tb: ~ siquiera) not even; ~ que not even if; ~ blanco ~ negro neither white nor black; ~ el uno ~ el otro neither one nor the other.

Nicaragua [nika'raɣwa] nf Nicaragua.

nicaragüense [nikara'ɣwense] a, nm/f Nicaraguan.

nicotina [niko'tina] nf nicotine.

nicho ['nitʃo] nm niche.

nido ['niðo] nm nest; (fig) hiding place; ~ de ladrones den of thieves.

niebla ['njeβla] nf fog; (neblina) mist; hay ~ it is foggy.

niego ['njeɣo] etc, niegue ['njeɣe] etc vb V negar.

nieto, a ['njeto, a] nm/f grandson/daughter; ~s nmpl grandchildren.

nieve ['njeβe] etc vb V nevar ♦ nf snow; (AM) ice cream; copo de ~ snowflake.

Nigeria [ni'xerja] nf Nigeria.

nigeriano, a [nixe'rjano, a] a, nm/f Nigerian.

nigromancia [niɣro'manθja] nf necromancy, black magic.

nihilista [nii'lista] a nihilistic ♦ nm nihilist.

Nilo ['nilo] *nm*: **el (Río)** ~ the Nile.

nimbo ['nimbo] *nm* (*aureola*) halo; (*nube*) nimbus.

nimiedad [nimje'ðað] *nf* small-mindedness; (*trivialidad*) triviality; (*una* ~) trifle, tiny detail.

nimio, a ['nimjo, a] *a* trivial, insignificant.

ninfa ['ninfa] *nf* nymph.

ninfómana [nin'fomana] *nf* nymphomaniac.

ninguno, a [nin'guno, a] *a* (**ningún** *delante de nmsg*) no ◆ *pron* (*nadie*) nobody; (*ni uno*) none, not one; (*ni uno ni otro*) neither; **de ninguna manera** by no means, not at all; **no voy a ninguna parte** I'm not going anywhere.

niña ['nina] *nf* V **niño**.

niñera [ni'nera] *nf* nursemaid, nanny.

niñería [nine'ria] *nf* childish act.

niñez [ni'neθ] *nf* childhood; (*infancia*) infancy.

niño, a ['nino, a] *a* (*joven*) young; (*inmaduro*) immature ◆ *nm* (*chico*) boy, child ◆ *nf* girl, child; (*ANAT*) pupil; **los** ~**s** the children; ~ **bien** Hooray Henry; ~ **expósito** foundling; ~ **de pecho** babe-in-arms; ~ **prodigio** child prodigy; **de** ~ as a child; **ser el** ~ **mimado de uno** to be sb's pet; **ser la niña de los ojos de uno** to be the apple of sb's eye.

nipón, ona [ni'pon, ona] *a, nm/f* Japanese; **los nipones** the Japanese.

níquel ['nikel] *nm* nickel.

niquelar [nike'lar] *vt* (*TEC*) to nickel-plate.

níspero ['nispero] *nm* medlar.

nitidez [niti'ðeθ] *nf* (*claridad*) clarity; (: *de atmósfera*) brightness; (: *de imagen*) sharpness.

nítido, a ['nitiðo, a] *a* bright; (*fig*) pure; (*imagen*) clear, sharp.

nitrato [ni'trato] *nm* nitrate.

nitrógeno [ni'troxeno] *nm* nitrogen.

nitroglicerina [nitroɣliθe'rina] *nf* nitroglycerine.

nivel [ni'ßel] *nm* (*GEO*) level; (*norma*) level, standard; (*altura*) height; ~ **de aceite** oil level; ~ **de aire** spirit level; ~ **de vida** standard of living; **al** ~ **de** on a level with, at the same height as; (*fig*) on a par with; **a 900m sobre el** ~ **del mar** at 900m above sea level.

nivelado, a [niße'laðo, a] *a* level, flat; (*TEC*) flush.

nivelar [niße'lar] *vt* to level out; (*fig*) to even up; (*COM*) to balance.

Niza ['niθa] *nf* Nice.

n/l. *abr* (*COM*) = *nuestra letra*.

NNE *abr* (= *nornordeste*) NNE.

NNO *abr* (= *nornoroeste*) NNW.

NN. UU. *nfpl abr* (= *Naciones Unidas*) UN *sg*.

NO *abr* (= *noroeste*) NW.

no [no] *ad* no; (*con verbo*) not ◆ *excl* no!; ~ **tengo nada** I don't have anything, I have nothing; ~ **es el mío** it's not mine; **ahora** ~ not now; *¿*~ **lo sabes?** don't you know?; ~ **mucho** not much; ~ **bien termine, lo entregaré** as soon as I finish I'll hand it over; **¡a que** ~ **lo sabes!** I bet you don't know!; **¡cómo** ~**!** of course!; **pacto de** ~ **agresión** non-aggression pact; **los países** ~ **alineados** the non-aligned countries; **el** ~ **va más** the ultimate; **la** ~ **intervención** non-intervention.

N.° *abr* (= *número*) No.

n/o *abr* (*COM*) = *nuestra orden*.

noble ['noßle] *a, nm/f* noble; **los** ~**s** the nobility *sg*.

nobleza [no'ßleθa] *nf* nobility.

noción [no'θjon] *nf* notion; **nociones** *nfpl* elements, rudiments.

nocivo, a [no'θißo, a] *a* harmful.

noctambulismo [noktambu'lismo] *nm* sleepwalking.

noctámbulo, a [nok'tambulo, a] *nm/f* sleepwalker.

nocturno, a [nok'turno, a] *a* (*de la noche*) nocturnal, night *cpd*; (*de la tarde*) evening *cpd* ◆ *nm* nocturne.

noche ['notʃe] *nf* night, night-time; (*la tarde*) evening; (*fig*) darkness; **de** ~, **por la** ~ at night; **ayer por la** ~ last night; **esta** ~ tonight; **(en) toda la** ~ all night; **hacer** ~ **en un sitio** to spend the night in a place; **se hace de** ~ it's getting dark.

Nochebuena [notʃe'ßwena] *nf* Christmas Eve.

Nochevieja [notʃe'ßjexa] *nf* New Year's Eve.

nodriza [no'ðriθa] *nf* wet nurse; **buque** *o* **nave** ~ supply ship.

Noé [no'e] *nm* Noah.

nogal [no'ɣal] *nm* walnut tree; (*madera*) walnut.

nómada ['nomaða] *a* nomadic ◆ *nm/f* nomad.

nomás [no'mas] *ad*: (*AM: gen*) just; (: *tan sólo*) only.

nombramiento [nombra'mjento] *nm* naming; (*a un empleo*) appointment; (*POL etc*) nomination; (*MIL*) commission.

nombrar [nom'brar] *vt* (*gen*) to name; (*mencionar*) to mention; (*designar*) to appoint, nominate; (*MIL*) to commission.

nombre ['nombre] *nm* name; (*sustantivo*) noun; (*fama*) renown; ~ **y apellidos** name in full; ~ **común/propio** common/proper noun; ~ **de pila/de soltera** Christian/maiden name; ~ **de fichero** (*INFORM*) file name; **en** ~ **de** in the name of, on behalf of; **sin** ~ nameless; **su conducta no tiene** ~ his behaviour is utterly despicable.

nomenclatura [nomenkla'tura] *nf* nomenclature.

nomeolvides [nomeol'ßiðes] *nm inv* forget-me-not.

nómina ['nomina] *nf* (*lista*) list; (*COM*: *tb*: ~s) payroll.

nominal [nomi'nal] *a* nominal; (*valor*) face *cpd*; (*LING*) noun *cpd*, substantival.

nominar [nomi'nar] *vt* to nominate.

nominativo, a [nomina'tißo, a] *a* (*LING*) nominative; (*COM*): **un cheque ~ a X** a cheque made out to X.

non [non] *a* odd, uneven ♦ *nm* odd number; **pares y ~es** odds and evens.

nonagésimo, a [nona'xesimo, a] *num* ninetieth.

nono, a ['nono, a] *num* ninth.

nordeste [nor'ðeste] *a* north-east, north-eastern, north-easterly ♦ *nm* north-east; (*viento*) north-east wind, north-easterly.

nórdico, a ['norðiko, a] *a* (*del norte*) northern, northerly; (*escandinavo*) Nordic, Norse ♦ *nm/f* northerner; (*escandinavo*) Norseman/woman ♦ *nm* (*LING*) Norse.

noreste [no'reste] *a, nm* = **nordeste**.

noria ['norja] *nf* (*AGR*) waterwheel; (*de carnaval*) big (*Brit*) o Ferris (*US*) wheel.

norma ['norma] *nf* standard, norm, rule; (*patrón*) pattern; (*método*) method.

normal [nor'mal] *a* (*corriente*) normal; (*habitual*) usual, natural; (*TEC*) standard; **Escuela N~** teacher training college; (**gasolina**) ~ two-star petrol.

normalice [norma'liθe] *etc vb V* **normalizar**.

normalidad [normali'ðað] *nf* normality; **restablecer la ~** to restore order.

normalización [normaliθa'θjon] *nf* (*COM*) standardization.

normalizar [normali'θar] *vt* (*reglamentar*) to normalize; (*COM, TEC*) to standardize; **~se** *vr* to return to normal.

Normandía [norman'dia] *nf* Normandy.

normando, a [nor'mando, a] *a, nm/f* Norman.

normativo, a [norma'tißo, a] *a*: **es ~ en todos los coches nuevos** it is standard in all new cars.

noroeste [noro'este] *a* north-west, northwestern, north-westerly ♦ *nm* north-west; (*viento*) north-west wind, north-westerly.

norte ['norte] *a* north, northern, northerly ♦ *nm* north; (*fig*) guide.

Norteamérica [nortea'merika] *nf* North America.

norteamericano, a [norteameri'kano, a] *a, nm/f* (North) American.

norteño, a [nor'teɲo, a] *a* northern ♦ *nm/f* northerner.

Noruega [no'rweɣa] *nf* Norway.

noruego, a [no'rweɣo, a] *a, nm/f* Norwegian ♦ *nm* (*LING*) Norwegian.

nos [nos] *pron* (*directo*) us; (*indirecto*) (to) us; (*reflexivo*) (to) ourselves; (*recíproco*) (to) each other; ~ **levantamos a las 7** we get up at 7.

nosotros, as [no'sotros, as] *pron* (*sujeto*) we; (*después de prep*) us; ~ (**mismos**) ourselves.

nostalgia [nos'talxja] *nf* nostalgia, homesickness.

nostálgico, a [nos'talxiko, a] *a* nostalgic, homesick.

nota ['nota] *nf* note; (*ESCOL*) mark; (*de fin de año*) report; (*UNIV etc*) footnote; (*COM*) account; ~ **de aviso** advice note; ~ **de crédito/débito** credit/debit note; ~ **de gastos** expenses claim; ~ **de sociedad** gossip column; **tomar ~s** to take notes.

notable [no'taßle] *a* noteworthy, notable; (*ESCOL etc*) outstanding ♦ *nm/f* notable.

notar [no'tar] *vt* to notice, note; (*percibir*) to feel; (*ver*) to see; **~se** *vr* to be obvious; **se nota que ...** one observes that ....

notaría [nota'ria] *nf* (*profesión*) profession of notary; (*despacho*) notary's office.

notarial [nota'rjal] *a* (*estilo*) legal; **acta ~** affidavit.

notario [no'tarjo] *nm* notary; (*abogado*) solicitor.

noticia [no'tiθja] *nf* (*información*) piece of news; (*TV etc*) news item; **las ~s** the news *sg*; **según nuestras ~s** according to our information; **tener ~s de uno** to hear from sb.

noticiar [noti'θjar] *vt* to notify.

noticiario [noti'θjarjo] *nm* (*CINE*) newsreel; (*TV*) news bulletin.

noticiero [noti'θjero] *nm* newspaper, gazette; (*AM: also:* ~ **telediario**) news bulletin.

notificación [notifika'θjon] *nf* notification.

notificar [notifi'kar] *vt* to notify, inform.

notifique [noti'fike] *etc vb V* **notificar**.

notoriedad [notorje'ðað] *nf* fame, renown.

notorio, a [no'torjo, a] *a* (*público*) wellknown; (*evidente*) obvious.

nov. *abr* (= *noviembre*) Nov.

novatada [noßa'taða] *nf* (*burla*) teasing, hazing (*US*); **pagar la ~** to learn the hard way.

novato, a [no'ßato, a] *a* inexperienced ♦ *nm/f* beginner, novice.

novecientos, as [noße'θjentos, as] *num* nine hundred.

novedad [noße'ðað] *nf* (*calidad de nuevo*) newness, novelty; (*noticia*) piece of news; (*cambio*) change, (new) development; (*sorpresa*) surprise; **~es** *nfpl* (*noticia*) latest (news) *sg*.

novedoso, a [noße'ðoso, a] *a* novel.

novel [no'ßel] *a* new; (*inexperto*) inexperienced ♦ *nm/f* beginner.

novela [no'ßela] *nf* novel; ~ **policíaca** detective story.

novelero, a [noße'lero, a] *a* highly imaginative.

novelesco, a [noße'lesko, a] *a* fictional; (*romántico*) romantic; (*fantástico*) fantastic.

novelista [noße'lista] *nm/f* novelist.

novelística [noße'listika] *nf*: **la** ~ fiction, the novel.

noveno, a [no'ßeno, a] *num* ninth.

noventa [no'ßenta] *num* ninety.

novia ['noßja] *nf V* **novio**.

noviazgo [no'ßjaɣo] *nm* engagement.

novicio, a [no'ßiθjo, a] *nm/f* novice.

noviembre [no'ßjembre] *nm* November.

novilla [no'ßiʎa] *nf* heifer.

novillada [noßi'ʎaða] *nf* (*TAUR*) bullfight *with young bulls*.

novillero [noßi'ʎero] *nm* novice bullfighter.

novillo [no'ßiʎo] *nm* young bull, bullock; **hacer** ~**s** (*fam*) to play truant (*Brit*) *o* hooky (*US*).

novio, a ['noßjo, a] *nm/f* boyfriend/ girlfriend; (*prometido*) fiancé/fiancée; (*recién casado*) bridegroom/bride; **los** ~**s** the newly-weds.

novísimo, a [no'ßisimo, a] *a superlativo de* **nuevo, a**.

NPI *nm abr* (*INFORM*: = *número personal de identificación*) PIN.

N. S. *abr* = *Nuestro Señor*.

ntra., ntro. *abr* = **nuestra, nuestro**.

NU *nfpl abr* (= *Naciones Unidas*) UN.

nubarrón [nußa'rron] *nm* storm cloud.

nube ['nuße] *nf* cloud; (*MED*: *ocular*) cloud, film; (*fig*) mass; **una** ~ **de críticas** a storm of criticism; **los precios están por las** ~**s** prices are sky-high; **estar en las** ~**s** to be away with the fairies.

nublado, a [nu'ßlaðo, a] *a* cloudy ◆ *nm* storm cloud.

nublar [nu'ßlar] *vt* (*oscurecer*) to darken; (*confundir*) to cloud; ~**se** *vr* to cloud over.

nuca ['nuka] *nf* nape of the neck.

nuclear [nukle'ar] *a* nuclear.

nuclearizado, a [nukleari'θaðo, a] *a*: **países** ~**s** countries possessing nuclear weapons.

núcleo ['nukleo] *nm* (*centro*) core; (*FÍSICA*) nucleus.

nudillo [nu'ðiʎo] *nm* knuckle.

nudo ['nuðo] *nm* knot; (*unión*) bond; (*de problema*) crux; (*FERRO*) junction; (*fig*) lump; ~ **corredizo** slipknot; **con un** ~ **en la garganta** with a lump in one's throat.

nudoso, a [nu'ðoso, a] *a* knotty; (*tronco*) gnarled; (*bastón*) knobbly.

nueces ['nweθes] *nfpl de* **nuez**.

nuera ['nwera] *nf* daughter-in-law.

nuestro, a ['nwestro, a] *a posesivo* our ◆

pron ours; ~ **padre** our father; **un amigo** ~ a friend of ours; **es el** ~ it's ours; **los** ~**s** our people; (*DEPORTE*) our *o* the local team *o* side.

nueva ['nweßa] *nf V* **nuevo**.

Nueva Escocia *nf* Nova Scotia.

nuevamente [nweßa'mente] *ad* (*otra vez*) again; (*de nuevo*) anew.

Nueva York [-'jork] *nf* New York.

Nueva Zeland(i)a [-θe'land(j)a] *nf* New Zealand.

nueve ['nweße] *num* nine.

nuevo, a ['nweßo, a] *a* (*gen*) new ◆ *nf* piece of news; **¿qué hay de** ~**?** (*fam*) what's new?; **de** ~ again.

Nuevo Méjico *nm* New Mexico.

nuez [nweθ], *pl* **nueces** *nf* (*del nogal*) walnut; (*fruto*) nut; ~ **de Adán** Adam's apple; ~ **moscada** nutmeg.

nulidad [nuli'ðað] *nf* (*incapacidad*) incompetence; (*abolición*) nullity; (*individuo*) nonentity; **es una** ~ he's a dead loss.

nulo, a ['nulo, a] *a* (*inepto, torpe*) useless; (*inválido*) (null and) void; (*DEPORTE*) drawn, tied.

núm. *abr* (= *número*) no.

numen ['numen] *nm* inspiration.

numeración [numera'θjon] *nf* (*cifras*) numbers *pl*; (*arábiga, romana etc*) numerals *pl*; ~ **de línea** (*INFORM*) line numbering.

numeral [nume'ral] *nm* numeral.

numerar [nume'rar] *vt* to number; ~**se** *vr* (*MIL etc*) to number off.

numerario, a [nume'rarjo, a] *a* numerary; **profesor** ~ permanent *o* tenured member of teaching staff ◆ *nm* hard cash.

numérico, a [nu'meriko, a] *a* numerical.

número ['numero] *nm* (*gen*) number; (*tamaño: de zapato*) size; (*ejemplar: de diario*) number, issue; (*TEATRO etc*) turn, act, number; **sin** ~ numberless, unnumbered; ~ **binario** (*INFORM*) binary number; ~ **de matrícula/de teléfono** registration/telephone number; ~ **personal de identificación** (*INFORM etc*) personal identification number; ~ **de serie** (*COM*) serial number; ~ **atrasado** back number.

numeroso, a [nume'roso, a] *a* numerous; **familia numerosa** large family.

nunca ['nunka] *ad* (*jamás*) never; (*con verbo negativo*) ever; ~ **lo pensé** I never thought it; **no viene** ~ he never comes; ~ **más** never again.

nuncio ['nunθjo] *nm* (*REL*) nuncio.

nupcias ['nupθjas] *nfpl* wedding *sg*, nuptials.

nutria ['nutrja] *nf* otter.

nutrición [nutri'θjon] *nf* nutrition.

nutrido, a [nu'triðo, a] *a* (*alimentado*) nourished; (*fig: grande*) large; (*abundante*) abundant; **mal** ~ undernourished; ~ **de**

full of.
nutrir [nu'trir] *vt* to feed, nourish; (*fig*) to feed, strengthen.
nutritivo, a [nutri'tiβo, a] *a* nourishing, nutritious.
nylon [ni'lon] *nm* nylon.

Ñ

Ñ , ñ ['eɲe] *nf* (*letra*) Ñ , ñ.
ñato, a ['ɲato, a] *a* (*AM*) snub-nosed.
ñoñería [ɲoɲe'ria], **ñoñez** [ɲo'ɲeθ] *nf* insipidness.
ñoño, a ['ɲoɲo, a] *a* (*AM: tonto*) silly, stupid; (*soso*) insipid; (*persona: débil*) spineless.
ñoquis ['ɲokis] *nmpl* (*CULIN*) gnocchi.

O

O, o [o] *nf* (*letra*) O, o; **O de Oviedo** O for Oliver (*Brit*) *o* Oboe (*US*).
O *abr* (= *oeste*) W.
o [o] *conj* or; **~ ... ~** either ... or; **~ sea** that is.
o/ *nm* (*COM*: = *orden*) o.
OACI *nf abr* (= *Organización de la Aviación Civil Internacional*) ICAO.
oasis [o'asis] *nm inv* oasis.
obcecado, a [oβθe'kaðo, a] *a* blind; (*terco*) stubborn.
obcecarse [oβθe'karse] *vr* to be obstinate; **~ en hacer** to insist on doing.
obceque [oβ'θeke] *etc vb V* **obcecarse**.
obedecer [oβeðe'θer] *vt* to obey; **~ a** (*MED etc*) to yield to; (*fig*) **~ a ...**, **~ al hecho de que ...** to be due to ..., arise from ....
obedezca [oβe'ðeθka] *etc vb V* **obedecer**.
obediencia [oβe'ðjenθja] *nf* obedience.
obediente [oβe'ðjente] *a* obedient.
obertura [oβer'tura] *nf* overture.
obesidad [oβesi'ðað] *nf* obesity.
obeso, a [o'βeso, a] *a* obese.
óbice ['oβiθe] *nm* obstacle, impediment.
obispado [oβis'paðo] *nm* bishopric.
obispo [o'βispo] *nm* bishop.
óbito ['oβito] *nm* demise.
objeción [oβxe'θjon] *nf* objection; **hacer**

una **~**, **poner objeciones** to raise objections, object.
objetante [oβxe'tante] *nm/f* objector; (*POL*) heckler.
objetar [oβxe'tar] *vt, vi* to object.
objetivo, a [oβxe'tiβo, a] *a* objective ◆ *nm* objective; (*fig*) aim; (*FOTO*) lens.
objeto [oβ'xeto] *nm* (*cosa*) object; (*fin*) aim.
objetor, a [oβxe'tor, a] *nm/f* objector; **~ de conciencia** conscientious objector.
oblea [o'βlea] *nf* (*REL, fig*) wafer; (*INFORM*) chip, wafer.
oblicuo, a [o'βlikwo, a] *a* oblique; (*mirada*) sidelong.
obligación [oβliɣa'θjon] *nf* obligation; (*COM*) bond, debenture.
obligar [oβli'ɣar] *vt* to force; **~se** *vr*: **~se a** to commit o.s. to.
obligatorio, a [oβliɣa'torjo, a] *a* compulsory, obligatory.
obligue [o'βliɣe] *etc vb V* **obligar**.
oboe [o'βoe] *nm* oboe; (*músico*) oboist.
Ob.ᵖᵒ *abr* (= *Obispo*) Bp.
obra ['oβra] *nf* work; (*hechura*) piece of work; (*ARQ*) construction, building; (*libro*) book; (*MUS*) opus; (*TEATRO*) play; **~ de arte** work of art; **~ maestra** masterpiece; **~ de consulta** reference book; **~s completas** complete works; **~ benéfica** charity; **"~s"** (*en carretera*) "men at work"; **~s públicas** public works; **por ~ de** thanks to (the efforts of); **~s son amores y no buenas razones** actions speak louder than words.
obrar [o'βrar] *vt* to work; (*tener efecto*) to have an effect on ◆ *vi* to act, behave; (*tener efecto*) to have an effect; **la carta obra en su poder** the letter is in his/her possession.
obr. cit. *abr* (= *obra citada*) op. cit.
obrero, a [o'βrero, a] *a* working; (*movimiento*) labour *cpd*; **clase obrera** working class ◆ *nm/f* (*gen*) worker; (*sin oficio*) labourer.
obscenidad [oβsθeni'ðað] *nf* obscenity.
obsceno, a [oβs'θeno, a] *a* obscene.
obscu... = **oscu...**
obsequiar [oβse'kjar] *vt* (*ofrecer*) to present; (*agasajar*) to make a fuss of, lavish attention on.
obsequio [oβ'sekjo] *nm* (*regalo*) gift; (*cortesía*) courtesy, attention.
obsequioso, a [oβse'kjoso, a] *a* attentive.
observación [oβserßa'θjon] *nf* observation; (*reflexión*) remark; (*objeción*) objection.
observador, a [oβserßa'ðor, a] *a* observant ◆ *nm/f* observer.
observancia [oβser'ßanθja] *nf* observance.
observar [oβser'ßar] *vt* to observe; (*notar*) to notice; (*leyes*) to observe, respect; (*re-*

glas) to abide by.

observatorio [oßserßa'torjo] *nm* observatory; ~ **del tiempo** weather station.

obsesión [oßse'sjon] *nf* obsession.

obsesionar [oßsesjo'nar] *vt* to obsess.

obsolescencia [oßsoles'θenθja] *nf*: ~ **incorporada** (*COM*) built-in obsolescence.

obstaculice [oßstaku'liθe] *etc vb V* **obstaculizar**.

obstaculizar [oßstakuli'θar] *vt* (*dificultar*) to hinder, hamper.

obstáculo [oßs'takulo] *nm* (*gen*) obstacle; (*impedimento*) hindrance, drawback.

obstante [oßs'tante]: **no** ~ *ad* nevertheless; (*de todos modos*) all the same ♦ *prep* in spite of.

obstetricia [oßste'triθja] *nf* obstetrics *sg*.

obstétrico, a [oßs'tetriko, a] *a* obstetric ♦ *nm/f* obstetrician.

obstinado, a [oßsti'naðo, a] *a* (*gen*) obstinate; (*terco*) stubborn.

obstinarse [oßsti'narse] *vr* to dig one's heels in; ~ **en** to persist in.

obstrucción [oßstruk'θjon] *nf* obstruction.

obstruir [oßstru'ir] *vt* to obstruct; (*bloquear*) to block; (*estorbar*) to hinder.

obstruyendo [oßstru'jendo] *etc vb V* **obstruir**.

obtención [oßten'θjon] *nf* (*COM*) procurement.

obtendré [oßten'dre] *etc vb V* **obtener**.

obtener [oßte'ner] *vt* (*conseguir*) to obtain; (*ganar*) to gain.

obtenga [oß'tenga] *etc vb V* **obtener**.

obturación [oßtura'θjon] *nf* plugging, stopping; (*FOTO*): **velocidad de** ~ shutter speed.

obturador [oßtura'ðor] *nm* (*FOTO*) shutter.

obtuso, a [oß'tuso, a] *a* (*filo*) blunt; (*MAT, fig*) obtuse.

obtuve [oß'tuße] *etc vb V* **obtener**.

obús [o'ßus] *nm* (*MIL*) shell.

obviar [oß'ßjar] *vt* to obviate, remove.

obvio, a ['oßßjo, a] *a* obvious.

ocasión [oka'sjon] *nf* (*oportunidad*) opportunity, chance; (*momento*) occasion, time; (*causa*) cause; **de** ~ secondhand; **con** ~ **de** on the occasion of; **en algunas ocasiones** sometimes; **aprovechar la** ~ to seize one's opportunity.

ocasionar [okasjo'nar] *vt* to cause.

ocaso [o'kaso] *nm* sunset; (*fig*) decline.

occidental [okθiðen'tal] *a* western ♦ *nm/f* westerner ♦ *nm* west.

occidente [okθi'ðente] *nm* west; **el O**~ the West.

occiso, a [ok'θiso, a] *nm/f*: **el** ~ (*AM*) the deceased; (*de asesinato*) the victim.

océano [o'θeano] *nm* ocean; **el** ~ **Índico** the Indian Ocean.

O.C.D.E. *nf abr* (= *Organización de*

Cooperación y Desarrollo Económicos) OECD.

OCI ['oθi] *nf abr* (*POL*: *Venezuela, Perú*) = *Oficina Central de Información*.

ocio ['oθjo] *nm* (*tiempo*) leisure; (*pey*) idleness; **"guía del** ~**"** "what's on".

ociosidad [oθjosi'ðað] *nf* idleness.

ocioso, a [o'θjoso, a] *a* (*inactivo*) idle; (*inútil*) useless.

oct. *abr* (= *octubre*) Oct.

octanaje [okta'naxe] *nm*: **de alto** ~ high octane.

octano [ok'tano] *nm* octane.

octavilla [okta'ßiʎa] *nm* leaflet, pamphlet.

octavo, a [ok'taßo, a] *num* eighth.

octeto [ok'teto] *nm* (*INFORM*) byte.

octogenario, a [oktoxe'narjo, a] *a, nm/f* octogenarian.

octubre [ok'tußre] *nm* October.

OCU ['oku] *nf abr* (*Esp*: = *Organización de Consumidores y Usuarios*) ≈ Consumers' Association.

ocular [oku'lar] *a* ocular, eye *cpd*; **testigo** ~ eyewitness.

oculista [oku'lista] *nm/f* oculist.

ocultar [okul'tar] *vt* (*esconder*) to hide; (*callar*) to conceal; (*disfrazar*) to screen; ~**se** *vr* to hide (o.s.); ~**se a la vista** to keep out of sight.

oculto, a [o'kulto, a] *a* hidden; (*fig*) secret.

ocupación [okupa'θjon] *nf* occupation; (*tenencia*) occupancy.

ocupado, a [oku'paðo, a] *a* (*persona*) busy; (*plaza*) occupied, taken; (*teléfono*) engaged; **¿está ocupada la silla?** is that seat taken?

ocupar [oku'par] *vt* (*gen*) to occupy; (*puesto*) to hold, fill; (*individuo*) to engage; (*obreros*) to employ; (*confiscar*) to seize; ~**se** *vr*: ~**se de o en** to concern o.s. with; (*cuidar*) to look after; ~**se de lo suyo** to mind one's own business.

ocurrencia [oku'rrenθja] *nf* (*ocasión*) occurrence; (*agudeza*) witticism.

ocurrir [oku'rrir] *vi* to happen; ~**se** *vr*: **se me ocurrió que** ... it occurred to me that ...; **¿se te ocurre algo?** can you think of *o* come up with anything? **¿qué ocurre?** what's going on?

ochenta [o't∫enta] *num* eighty.

ocho ['ot∫o] *num* eight; (*fecha*) eighth; ~ **días** a week.

oda ['oða] *nf* ode.

ODECA [o'ðeka] *nf abr* = *Organización de Estados Centroamericanos*.

odiar [o'ðjar] *vt* to hate.

odio ['oðjo] *nm* (*gen*) hate, hatred; (*disgusto*) dislike.

odioso, a [o'ðjoso, a] *a* (*gen*) hateful; (*malo*) nasty.

odontología [oðontolo'xia] *nf* dentistry,

dental surgery.

odontólogo, a [oðon'toloɣo, a] *nm/f* dentist, dental surgeon.

odre ['oðre] *nm* wineskin.

O.E.A. *nf abr* (= *Organización de Estados Americanos*) O.A.S.

OECE *nf abr* (= *Organización Europea de Cooperación Económica*) OEEC.

OELA [o'ela] *nf abr* = *Organización de Estados Latinoamericanos.*

oeste [o'este] *nm* west; **una película del ~** a western.

ofender [ofen'der] *vt* (*agraviar*) to offend; (*insultar*) to insult; **~se** *vr* to take offence.

ofensa [o'fensa] *nf* offence; (*insulto*) slight.

ofensivo, a [ofen'siβo, a] *a* (*insultante*) insulting; (*MIL*) offensive ♦ *nf* offensive.

ofensor, a [ofen'sor, a] *a* offending ♦ *nm/f* offender.

oferta [o'ferta] *nf* offer; (*propuesta*) proposal; (*para contrato*) bid, tender; **la ~ y la demanda** supply and demand; **artículos en ~** goods on offer; **~ excedentaria** (*COM*) excess supply; **~ monetaria** money supply; **~ pública de compra** (*COM*) takeover bid; **~s de trabajo** (*en periódicos*) situations vacant column.

oficial [ofi'θjal] *a* official ♦ *nm* official; (*MIL*) officer.

oficialista [ofiθja'lista] *a* (*AM*) (pro-)government; **el candidato ~** the governing party's candidate.

oficiar [ofi'θjar] *vt* to inform officially ♦ *vi* (*REL*) to officiate.

oficina [ofi'θina] *nf* office; **~ de colocación** employment agency; **~ de información** information bureau; **~ de objetos perdidos** lost property office (*Brit*), lost-and-found department (*US*); **~ de turismo** tourist office.

oficinista [ofiθi'nista] *nm/f* clerk; **los ~s** white-collar workers.

oficio [o'fiθjo] *nm* (*profesión*) profession; (*puesto*) post; (*REL*) service; (*función*) function; (*comunicado*) official letter; **ser del ~** to be an old hand; **tener mucho ~** to have a lot of experience; **~ de difuntos** funeral service; **de ~** officially.

oficioso, a [ofi'θjoso, a] *a* (*pey*) officious; (*no oficial*) unofficial, informal.

ofimática [ofi'matika] *nf* office automation.

ofrecer [ofre'θer] *vt* (*dar*) to offer; (*proponer*) to propose; **~se** *vr* (*persona*) to offer o.s., volunteer; (*situación*) to present itself; **¿qué se le ofrece?, ¿se le ofrece algo?** what can I do for you?, can I get you anything?

ofrecimiento [ofreθi'mjento] *nm* offer, offering.

ofrendar [ofren'dar] *vt* to offer, contribute.

ofrezca [o'freθka] *etc vb V* **ofrecer.**

oftalmología [oftalmolo'xia] *nf* ophthalmology.

oftalmólogo, a [oftal'moloɣo, a] *nm/f* ophthalmologist.

ofuscación [ofuska'θjon] *nf*, **ofuscamiento** [ofuska'mjento] *nm* (*fig*) bewilderment.

ofuscar [ofus'kar] *vt* (*confundir*) to bewilder; (*enceguecer*) to dazzle, blind.

ofusque [o'fuske] *etc vb V* **ofuscar.**

ogro ['oɣro] *nm* ogre.

OIC *nf abr* = *Organización Interamericana del Café*; (*COM*) = *Organización Internacional del Comercio.*

oída [o'iða] *nf*: **de ~s** by hearsay.

oído [o'iðo] *nm* (*ANAT, MUS*) ear; (*sentido*) hearing; **~ interno** inner ear; **de ~** by ear; **apenas pude dar crédito a mis ~s** I could scarcely believe my ears; **hacer ~s sordos a** to turn a deaf ear to.

OIEA *nm abr* (= *Organismo International de Energía Atómica*) IAEA.

oiga ['oiɣa] *etc vb V* **oír.**

OIR [o'ir] *nf abr* (= *Organización Internacional para los Refugiados*) IRO.

oír [o'ir] *vt* (*gen*) to hear; (*atender a*) to listen to; **¡oye!** (*sorpresa*) I say!, say! (*US*); **¡oiga!** (*TELEC*) hullo?; **~ misa** to attend mass; **como quien oye llover** without paying (the slightest) attention.

O.I.T. *nf abr* (= *Organización Internacional del Trabajo*) ILO.

ojal [o'xal] *nm* buttonhole.

ojalá [oxa'la] *excl* if only (it were so)!, some hope! ♦ *conj* if only...!, would that...!; **~ que venga hoy** I hope he comes today; **¡~ pudiera!** I wish I could!

ojeada [oxe'aða] *nf* glance; **echar una ~ a** to take a quick look at.

ojera [o'xera] *nf*: **tener ~s** to have bags under one's eyes.

ojeriza [oxe'riθa] *nf* ill-will; **tener ~ a** to have a grudge against, have it in for.

ojeroso, a [oxe'roso, a] *a* haggard.

ojete [o'xete] *nm* eye(let).

ojo ['oxo] *nm* eye; (*de puente*) span; (*de cerradura*) keyhole ♦ *excl* careful!; **tener ~ a** to have an eye for; **~s saltones** bulging *o* goggle eyes; **~ de buey** porthole; **~ por ~** an eye for an eye; **en un abrir y cerrar de ~s** in the twinkling of an eye; **a ~s vistas** openly; (*crecer etc*) before one's (very) eyes; **a ~ (de buen cubero)** roughly; **~s que no ven, corazón que no siente** out of sight, out of mind; **ser el ~ derecho de uno** (*fig*) to be the apple of sb's eye.

ola ['ola] *nf* wave; **~ de calor/frío** heatwave/cold spell; **la nueva ~** the latest fashion; (*CINE, MUS*) (the) new wave.

OLADE [o'laðe] *nf abr* = *Organización Latinoamericana de Energía.*

olé [o'le] *excl* bravo!, olé!

oleada [ole'aða] *nf* big wave, swell; (*fig*) wave.

oleaje [ole'axe] *nm* swell.

óleo ['oleo] *nm* oil.

oleoducto [oleo'ðukto] *nm* (oil) pipeline.

oler [o'ler] *vt* (*gen*) to smell; (*inquirir*) to pry into; (*fig*: *sospechar*) to sniff out ♦ *vi* to smell; ~ **a** to smell of; **huele mal** it smells bad, it stinks.

olfatear [olfate'ar] *vt* to smell; (*fig*: *sospechar*) to sniff out; (*inquirir*) to pry into.

olfato [ol'fato] *nm* sense of smell.

oligarquía [oliɣar'kia] *nf* oligarchy.

olimpíada [olim'piaða] *nf*: **las O~s** the Olympics.

olímpico, a [o'limpiko, a] *a* Olympian; (*deportes*) Olympic.

oliva [o'lißa] *nf* (*aceituna*) olive; **aceite de** ~ olive oil.

olivar [oli'ßar] *nm* olive grove *o* plantation.

olivo [o'lißo] *nm* olive tree.

olmo ['olmo] *nm* elm (tree).

olor [o'lor] *nm* smell.

oloroso, a [olo'roso, a] *a* scented.

OLP *nf* *abr* (= *Organización para la Liberación de Palestina*) PLO.

olvidadizo, a [olßiða'ðiθo, a] *a* (*desmemoriado*) forgetful; (*distraído*) absent-minded.

olvidar [olßi'ðar] *vt* to forget; (*omitir*) to omit; (*abandonar*) to leave behind; ~**se** *vr* (*fig*) to forget o.s.; **se me olvidó** I forgot.

olvido [ol'ßiðo] *nm* oblivion; (*acto*) oversight; (*descuido*) slip; **caer en el** ~ to fall into oblivion.

olla ['oʎa] *nf* pan; (*para hervir agua*) kettle; (*comida*) stew; ~ **a presión** pressure cooker.

O.M. *abr* (*POL*) = *Orden Ministerial*.

ombligo [om'bliɣo] *nm* navel.

OMI *nf* *abr* (= *Organización Marítima Internacional*) IMO.

ominoso, a [omi'noso, a] *a* ominous.

omisión [omi'sjon] *nf* (*abstención*) omission; (*descuido*) neglect.

omiso, a [o'miso, a] *a*: **hacer caso** ~ **de** to ignore, pass over.

omitir [omi'tir] *vt* to leave *o* miss out, omit.

omnipotente [omnipo'tente] *a* omnipotent.

omnipresente [omnipre'sente] *a* omnipresent.

omnívoro, a [om'nißoro, a] *a* omnivorous.

omóplato [o'moplato] *nm* shoulder blade.

OMS *nf* *abr* (= *Organización Mundial de la Salud*) WHO.

ONCE ['onθe] *nf* *abr* (= *Organización Nacional de Ciegos Españoles*) charity for the blind.

once ['onθe] *num* eleven ♦ *nm* (*AM*): ~**s** tea break *sg*.

onda ['onda] *nf* wave; ~ **corta/larga/media** short/long/medium wave; ~**s acústicas/**

hertzianas acoustic/Hertzian waves; ~ **sonora** sound wave.

ondear [onde'ar] *vi* to wave; (*tener ondas*) to be wavy; (*agua*) to ripple; ~**se** *vr* to swing, sway.

ondulación [ondula'θjon] *nf* undulation.

ondulado, a [ondu'laðo, a] *a* wavy ♦ *nm* wave.

ondulante [ondu'lante] *a* undulating.

ondular [ondu'lar] *vt* (*el pelo*) to wave ♦ *vi*, ~**se** *vr* to undulate.

oneroso, a [one'roso, a] *a* onerous.

onomástico, a [ono'mastiko, a] *a*: **fiesta onomástica** saint's day ♦ *nm* saint's day.

ONU ['onu] *nf* *abr* V **Organización de las Naciones Unidas**.

onubense [onu'ßense] *a* of *o* from Huelva ♦ *nm/f* native *o* inhabitant of Huelva.

ONUDI [o'nuði] *nf* *abr* (= *Organización de las Naciones Unidas para el Desarrollo Industrial*) UNIDO (*United Nations Industrial Development Organization*).

onza ['onθa] *nf* ounce.

O.P. *nfpl* *abr* = **obras públicas**; (*COM*) = *Oficina Principal*.

opaco, a [o'pako, a] *a* opaque; (*fig*) dull.

ópalo ['opalo] *nm* opal.

opción [op'θjon] *nf* (*gen*) option; (*derecho*) right, option; **no hay** ~ there is no alternative.

O.P.E.P. [o'pep] *nf* *abr* (= *Organización de Países Exportadores de Petróleo*) OPEC.

ópera ['opera] *nf* opera; ~ **bufa** *o* **cómica** comic opera.

operación [opera'θjon] *nf* (*gen*) operation; (*COM*) transaction, deal; ~ **"llave en manos"** (*INFORM*) turnkey operation; ~ **a plazo** (*COM*) forward transaction; **operaciones accesorias** (*INFORM*) housekeeping; **operaciones a término** (*COM*) futures.

operador, a [opera'ðor, a] *nm/f* operator; (*CINE*: *proyección*) projectionist; (: *rodaje*) cameraman.

operante [ope'rante] *a* operating.

operar [ope'rar] *vt* (*producir*) to produce, bring about; (*MED*) to operate on ♦ *vi* (*COM*) to operate, deal; ~**se** *vr* to occur; (*MED*) to have an operation; **se han operado grandes cambios** great changes have been made *o* have taken place.

operario, a [ope'rarjo, a] *nm/f* operative.

opereta [ope'reta] *nf* operetta.

opinar [opi'nar] *vt* (*estimar*) to think ♦ *vi* (*enjuiciar*) to give one's opinion; ~ **bien de** to think well of, have a good opinion of.

opinión [opi'njon] *nf* (*creencia*) belief; (*criterio*) opinion; **la** ~ **pública** public opinion.

opio ['opjo] *nm* opium.

opíparo, a [o'piparo, a] *a* sumptuous.

opondré [opon'dre] *etc vb* V **oponer**.

oponente [opo'nente] *nm/f* opponent.

oponer [opo'ner] *vt* (*resistencia*) to put up, offer; (*negativa*) to raise; ~**se** *vr* (*objetar*) to object; (*estar frente a frente*) to be opposed; (*dos personas*) to oppose each other; ~ **A a B** to set A against B; **me opongo a pensar que** ... I refuse to believe *o* think that ....

oponga [o'ponga] *etc vb* V **oponer**.

Oporto [o'porto] *nm* Oporto.

oportunidad [oportuni'ðað] *nf* (*ocasión*) opportunity; (*posibilidad*) chance.

oportunismo [oportu'nismo] *nm* opportunism.

oportunista [oportu'nista] *nm/f* opportunist; (*infección*) opportunistic.

oportuno, a [opor'tuno, a] *a* (*en su tiempo*) opportune, timely; (*respuesta*) suitable; **en el momento** ~ at the right moment.

oposición [oposi'θjon] *nf* opposition; **oposiciones** *nfpl* public examinations; **ganar un puesto por oposiciones** to win a post by public competitive examination; **hacer oposiciones a, presentarse a unas oposiciones a** to sit a competitive examination for.

opositor, a [oposi'tor, a] *nm/f* (*adversario*) opponent; (*concurrente*) competitor.

opresión [opre'sjon] *nf* oppression.

opresivo, a [opre'sißo, a] *a* oppressive.

opresor, a [opre'sor, a] *nm/f* oppressor.

oprimir [opri'mir] *vt* to squeeze; (*asir*) to grasp; (*pulsar*) to press; (*fig*) to oppress.

oprobio [o'proßjo] *nm* (*infamia*) ignominy; (*descrédito*) shame.

optar [op'tar] *vi* (*elegir*) to choose; ~ **a** *o* **por** to opt for.

optativo, a [opta'tißo, a] *a* optional.

óptico, a ['optiko, a] *a* optic(al) ◆ *nm/f* optician ◆ *nf* optics *sg*; (*fig*) viewpoint.

optimismo [opti'mismo] *nm* optimism.

optimista [opti'mista] *nm/f* optimist.

óptimo, a ['optimo, a] *a* (*el mejor*) very best.

opuesto, a [o'pwesto, a] *pp de* **oponer** ◆ *a* (*contrario*) opposite; (*antagónico*) opposing.

opulencia [opu'lenθja] *nf* opulence.

opulento, a [opu'lento, a] *a* opulent.

opuse [o'puse] *etc vb* V **oponer**.

ORA ['ora] *abr* (*Esp*: = *Ordenación de la Regulación del Aparcamiento*) parking regulations.

ora ['ora] *ad*: ~ **tú** ~ **yo** now you, now me.

oración [ora'θjon] *nf* (*discurso*) speech; (*REL*) prayer; (*LING*) sentence.

oráculo [o'rakulo] *nm* oracle.

orador, a [ora'ðor, a] *nm/f* orator; (*conferenciante*) speaker.

oral [o'ral] *a* oral; **por vía** ~ (*MED*) orally.

orangután [orangu'tan] *nm* orang-utan.

orar [o'rar] *vi* (*REL*) to pray.

oratoria [ora'torja] *nf* oratory.

orbe ['orße] *nm* orb, sphere; (*fig*) world; **en todo el** ~ all over the globe.

órbita ['orßita] *nf* orbit; (*ANAT*: *ocular*) (eye-)socket.

orden ['orðen] *nm* (*gen*) order; (*INFORM*) command; ~ **público** public order, law and order; (*números*) **del** ~ **de** about; **de primer** ~ first-rate; **en** ~ **de prioridad** in order of priority ◆ *nf* (*gen*) order; ~ **bancaria** banker's order; ~ **de compra** (*COM*) purchase order; ~ **del día** agenda; **eso ahora está a la** ~ **del día** that is now the order of the day; **a la** ~ **de usted** at your service; **dar la** ~ **de hacer algo** to give the order to do sth.

ordenación [orðena'θjon] *nf* (*estado*) order; (*acto*) ordering; (*REL*) ordination.

ordenado, a [orðe'naðo, a] *a* (*metódico*) methodical; (*arreglado*) orderly.

ordenador [orðena'ðor] *nm* computer; ~ **central** mainframe computer; ~ **de gestión** business computer; ~ **de sobremesa** desktop computer.

ordenanza [orðe'nanθa] *nf* ordinance; ~**s municipales** by-laws ◆ *nm* (*COM etc*) messenger; (*MIL*) orderly; (*bedel*) porter.

ordenar [orðe'nar] *vt* (*mandar*) to order; (*poner orden*) to put in order, arrange; ~**se** *vr* (*REL*) to be ordained.

ordeñadora [orðeɲa'ðora] *nf* milking machine.

ordeñar [orðe'ɲar] *vt* to milk.

ordinariez [orðina'rjeθ] *nf* (*cualidad*) coarseness, vulgarity; (*una* ~) coarse remark *o* joke *etc*.

ordinario, a [orði'narjo, a] *a* (*común*) ordinary, usual; (*vulgar*) vulgar, common.

ordinograma [orðino'γrama] *nm* flowchart.

orear [ore'ar] *vt* to air; ~**se** *vr* (*ropa*) to air.

orégano [o'reγano] *nm* oregano.

oreja [o'rexa] *nf* ear; (*MECÁNICA*) lug, flange.

orensano, a [oren'sano, a] *a* of *o* from Orense ◆ *nm/f* native *o* inhabitant of Orense.

orfanato [orfa'nato] *nm*, **orfanatorio** [orfana'torjo] *nm* orphanage.

orfandad [orfan'dað] *nf* orphanhood.

orfebre [or'feßre] *nm* gold-/silversmith.

orfebrería [orfeßre'ria] *nf* gold/silver work.

orfelinato [orfeli'nato] *nm* orphanage.

orfeón [orfe'on] *nm* (*MUS*) choral society.

organice [orγa'niθe] *etc vb* V **organizar**.

orgánico, a [or'γaniko, a] *a* organic.

organigrama [orγani'γrama] *nm* flow chart; (*de organización*) organization chart.

organillo [orγa'niʎo] *nm* barrel organ.

organismo [orγa'nismo] *nm* (*BIO*) organism; (*POL*) organization; **O~ Internacional de Energía Atómica** International Atomic Energy Agency.

organista [orɣa'nista] *nm/f* organist.

organización [orɣaniθa'θjon] *nf* organization; **O~ de las Naciones Unidas (ONU)** United Nations Organization **O~ del Tratado del Atlántico Norte (OTAN)** North Atlantic Treaty Organization (NATO).

organizador, a [orɣaniθa'ðor, a] *a* organizing; **el comité** ~ the organizing committee ♦ *nm/f* organizer.

organizar [orɣani'θar] *vt* to organize.

órgano ['orɣano] *nm* organ.

orgasmo [or'ɣasmo] *nm* orgasm.

orgía [or'xia] *nf* orgy.

orgullo [or'ɣuʎo] *nm* (*altanería*) pride; (*autorespeto*) self-respect.

orgulloso, a [orɣu'ʎoso, a] *a* (*gen*) proud; (*altanero*) haughty.

orientación [orjenta'θjon] *nf* (*posición*) position; (*dirección*) direction; ~ **profesional** occupational guidance.

oriental [orjen'tal] *a* oriental; (*región etc*) eastern ♦ *nm/f* oriental.

orientar [orjen'tar] *vt* (*situar*) to orientate; (*señalar*) to point; (*dirigir*) to direct; (*guiar*) to guide; ~**se** *vr* to get one's bearings; (*decidirse*) to decide on a course of action.

oriente [o'rjente] *nm* east; **el O~** the East, the Orient; **Cercano/Medio/Lejano O~** Near/ Middle/Far East.

orificio [ori'fiθjo] *nm* orifice.

origen [o'rixen] *nm* origin; (*nacimiento*) lineage, birth; **dar ~ a** to cause, give rise to.

original [orixi'nal] *a* (*nuevo*) original; (*extraño*) odd, strange ♦ *nm* original; (*TIP*) manuscript; (*TEC*) master (copy).

originalidad [orixinali'ðað] *nf* originality.

originar [orixi'nar] *vt* to originate; ~**se** *vr* to originate.

originario, a [orixi'narjo, a] *a* (*nativo*) native; (*primordial*) original; **ser ~ de** to originate from; **país** ~ country of origin.

orilla [o'riʎa] *nf* (*borde*) border; (*de río*) bank; (*de bosque, tela*) edge; (*de mar*) shore; **a ~s de** on the banks of.

orillar [ori'ʎar] *vt* (*bordear*) to skirt, go round; (*COSTURA*) to edge; (*resolver*) to wind up; (*tocar: asunto*) to touch briefly on; (*dificultad*) to avoid.

orín [o'rin] *nm* rust.

orina [o'rina] *nf* urine.

orinal [ori'nal] *nm* (chamber) pot.

orinar [ori'nar] *vi* to urinate; ~**se** *vr* to wet o.s.

orines [o'rines] *nmpl* urine *sg*.

oriundo, a [o'rjundo, a] *a*: ~ **de** native of.

orla ['orla] *nf* edge, border; (*ESCOL*) graduation photograph.

ornamentar [ornamen'tar] *vt* (*adornar, ataviar*) to adorn; (*revestir*) to bedeck.

ornamento [orna'mento] *nm* ornament.

ornar [or'nar] *vt* to adorn.

ornitología [ornitolo'xia] *nf* ornithology, bird watching.

ornitólogo, a [orni'toloɣo, a] *nm/f* ornithologist.

oro ['oro] *nm* gold; ~ **en barras** gold ingots; **de** ~ gold, golden; **no es** ~ **todo lo que reluce** all that glitters is not gold; **hacerse de** ~ to make a fortune; *V tb* **oros.**

orondo, a [o'rondo, a] *a* (*vasija*) rounded; (*individuo*) smug, self-satisfied.

oropel [oro'pel] *nm* tinsel.

oros ['oros] *nmpl* (*NAIPES*) hearts.

orquesta [or'kesta] *nf* orchestra; ~ **de cámara/sinfónica** chamber/symphony orchestra; ~ **de jazz** jazz band.

orquídea [or'kiðea] *nf* orchid.

ortiga [or'tiɣa] *nf* nettle.

ortodoxo, a [orto'ðokso, a] *a* orthodox.

ortografía [ortoɣra'fia] *nf* spelling.

ortopedia [orto'peðja] *nf* orthopaedics *sg*.

oruga [o'ruɣa] *nf* caterpillar.

orujo [o'ruxo] *nm* type of strong grape liqueur made from grape pressings.

orzuelo [or'θwelo] *nm* (*MED*) stye.

os [os] *pron* (*gen*) you; (*a vosotros*) (to) you; (*reflexivo*) (to) yourselves; (*mutuo*) (to) each other; **vosotros** ~ **laváis** you wash yourselves; **¡callar~!** (*fam*) shut up!

osa ['osa] *nf* (she-)bear; **O~ Mayor/Menor** Great/Little Bear, Ursa Major/Minor.

osadía [osa'ðia] *nf* daring; (*descaro*) impudence.

osamenta [osa'menta] *nf* skeleton.

osar [o'sar] *vi* to dare.

oscense [os'θense] *a* of o from Huesca ♦ *nm/f* native o inhabitant of Huesca.

oscilación [osθila'θjon] *nf* (*movimiento*) oscillation; (*fluctuación*) fluctuation; (*vacilación*) hesitation; (*columpio*) swinging, movement to and fro.

oscilar [osθi'lar] *vi* to oscillate; to fluctuate; to hesitate.

ósculo ['oskulo] *nm* kiss.

oscurecer [oskure'θer] *vt* to darken ♦ *vi* to grow dark; ~**se** *vr* to grow o get dark.

oscurezca [osku'reθka] *etc vb V* **oscurecer.**

oscuridad [oskuri'ðað] *nf* obscurity; (*tinieblas*) darkness.

oscuro, a [os'kuro, a] *a* dark; (*fig*) obscure; (*indefinido*) confused; (*cielo*) overcast, cloudy; (*futuro etc*) uncertain; **a oscuras** in the dark.

óseo, a ['oseo, a] *a* bony; (*MED etc*) bone *cpd*.

oso ['oso] *nm* bear; ~ **blanco/gris/pardo** polar/grizzly/brown bear; ~ **de peluche** teddy bear; ~ **hormiguero** anteater; **hacer**

el ~ to play the fool.
Ostende [os'tende] *nm* Ostend.
ostensible [osten'siβle] *a* obvious.
ostensiblemente [ostensiβle'mente] *ad* perceptibly, visibly.
ostentación [ostenta'θjon] *nf* (*gen*) ostentation; (*acto*) display.
ostentar [osten'tar] *vt* (*gen*) to show; (*pey*) to flaunt, show off; (*poseer*) to have, possess.
ostentoso, a [osten'toso, a] *a* ostentatious, showy.
osteópata [oste'opata] *nm/f* osteopath.
ostra ['ostra] *nf* oyster ♦ *excl:* ¡~s! (*fam*) sugar!
ostracismo [ostra'θismo] *nm* ostracism.
OTAN ['otan] *nf abr V* **Organización del Tratado del Atlántico Norte.**
OTASE [o'tase] *nf abr* (= *Organización del Tratado del Sudeste Asiático*) SEATO.
otear [ote'ar] *vt* to observe; (*fig*) to look into.
otero [o'tero] *nm* low hill, hillock.
otitis [o'titis] *nf* earache.
otoñal [oto'ɲal] *a* autumnal.
otoño [o'toɲo] *nm* autumn, fall (*US*).
otorgamiento [otorɣa'mjento] *nm* conferring, granting; (*JUR*) execution.
otorgar [otor'ɣar] *vt* (*conceder*) to concede; (*dar*) to grant; (*poderes*) to confer; (*premio*) to award.
otorgue [o'torɣe] *etc vb V* **otorgar.**
otorrinolaringólogo, a [otorrinolarin'goloɣo, a] *nm/f* (*MED: tb:* **otorrino**) ear, nose and throat specialist.
otro, a ['otro, a] *a* (*sg*) another; (*pl*) other ♦ *pron* another one; ~s others; **otra cosa** something else; **de otra manera** otherwise; **en ~ tiempo** formerly, once; ¡otra! (*TEATRO*) encore!; **otra parte** elsewhere; **otra vez** again; **ni uno ni ~** neither one nor the other; ~ **tanto** the same again; ~ **dijo que** ... somebody else said that ...
otrora [o'trora] *ad* formerly; **el ~ señor del país** the one-time ruler of the country.
OUA *nf abr* (= *Organización de la Unidad Africana*) OAU.
ovación [oβa'θjon] *nf* ovation.
ovacionar [oβaθjo'nar] *vt* to cheer.
oval [o'βal], **ovalado, a** [oβa'laðo, a] *a* oval.
óvalo ['oβalo] *nm* oval.
oveja [o'βexa] *nf* sheep; ~ **negra** (*fig*) black sheep (of the family).
overol [oβe'rol] *nm* (*AM*) overalls *pl*.
ovetense [oβe'tense] *a* of *o* from Oviedo ♦ *nm/f* native *o* inhabitant of Oviedo.
ovillo [o'βiʎo] *nm* (*de lana*) ball; (*fig*) tangle; **hacerse un ~** to curl up (into a ball).
OVNI ['oβni] *nm abr* (= *objeto volante no identificado*) UFO.

ovulación [oβula'θjon] *nf* ovulation.
óvulo ['oβulo] *nm* ovum.
oxidación [oksiða'θjon] *nf* rusting.
oxidar [oksi'ðar] *vt* to rust; ~**se** *vr* to go rusty; (*TEC*) to oxidize.
óxido ['oksiðo] *nm* oxide.
oxigenado, a [oksixe'naðo, a] *a* (*QUÍMICA*) oxygenated; (*pelo*) bleached.
oxigenar [oksixe'nar] *vt* to oxygenate; ~**se** *vr* to become oxygenated; (*fam*) to get some fresh air.
oxígeno [ok'sixeno] *nm* oxygen.
oyendo [o'jendo] *etc vb V* **oír.**
oyente [o'jente] *nm/f* listener, hearer; (*ESCOL*) unregistered *o* occasional student.
ozono [o'θono] *nm* ozone.

P

P, p [pe] *nf* (*letra*) P, p; **P de París** P for Peter.
P *abr* (*REL:* = *padre*) Fr.; = **papa.**
p. *abr* (= *página*) p.
p.a. *abr* = **por autorización.**
pabellón [paβe'ʎon] *nm* bell tent; (*ARQ*) pavilion; (*de hospital etc*) block, section; (*bandera*) flag; ~ **de conveniencia** (*COM*) flag of convenience; ~ **de la oreja** outer ear.
pábilo ['paβilo] *nm* wick.
pábulo ['paβulo] *nm* food; **dar ~ a** to feed, encourage.
PAC *nf abr* (= *Política Agrícola Común*) CAP.
pacense [pa'θense] *a* of *o* from Badajoz ♦ *nm/f* native *o* inhabitant of Badajoz.
paceño, a [pa'θeɲo, a] *a* of *o* from La Paz ♦ *nm/f* native *o* inhabitant of La Paz.
pacer [pa'θer] *vi* to graze ♦ *vt* to graze on.
paciencia [pa'θjenθja] *nf* patience; ¡~! be patient!; ¡~ **y barajar!** don't give up!; **perder la ~** to lose one's temper.
paciente [pa'θjente] *a, nm/f* patient.
pacificación [paθifika'θjon] *nf* pacification.
pacificar [paθifi'kar] *vt* to pacify; (*tranquilizar*) to calm.
pacífico, a [pa'θifiko, a] *a* peaceful; (*persona*) peace-loving; (*existencia*) pacific; **el (Océano) P~** the Pacific (Ocean).
pacifique [paθi'fike] *etc vb V* **pacificar.**
pacifismo [paθi'fismo] *nm* pacifism.
pacifista [paθi'fista] *nm/f* pacifist.
pacotilla [pako'tiʎa] *nf* trash; **de ~** shoddy.
pactar [pak'tar] *vt* to agree to, agree on ♦ *vi* to come to an agreement.

pacto ['pakto] *nm* (*tratado*) pact; (*acuerdo*) agreement.

pachá [pa'tʃa] *nm*: **vivir como un** ~ to live like a king.

pachorra [pa'tʃorra] *nf* (*indolencia*) slowness; (*tranquilidad*) calmness.

pachucho, a [pa'tʃutʃo, a] *a* (*fruta*) overripe; (*persona*) off-colour, poorly.

padecer [paðe'θer] *vt* (*sufrir*) to suffer; (*soportar*) to endure, put up with; (*ser víctima de*) to be a victim of ♦ *vi*: ~ **de** to suffer from.

padecimiento [paðeθi'mjento] *nm* suffering.

padezca [pa'ðeθka] *etc vb* V **padecer**.

padrastro [pa'ðrastro] *nm* stepfather.

padre ['paðre] *nm* father ♦ *a* (*fam*): **un éxito** ~ a tremendous success; ~**s** *nmpl* parents; ~ **espiritual** confessor; **P**~ **Nuestro** Lord's Prayer; ~ **político** father-in-law; **García** ~ García senior; **¡tu** ~**!** (*fam!*) up yours! (*!*).

padrino [pa'ðrino] *nm* godfather; (*fig*) sponsor, patron; ~**s** *nmpl* godparents; ~ **de boda** best man.

padrón [pa'ðron] *nm* (*censo*) census, roll; (*de socios*) register.

paella [pa'eʎa] *nf* paella, *dish of rice with meat, shellfish etc*.

paga ['paɣa] *nf* (*dinero pagado*) payment; (*sueldo*) pay, wages *pl*.

pagadero, a [paɣa'ðero, a] *a* payable; ~ **a la entrega/a plazos** payable on delivery/in instalments.

pagano, a [pa'ɣano, a] *a, nm/f* pagan, heathen.

pagar [pa'ɣar] *vt* (*gen*) to pay; (*las compras, crimen*) to pay for; (*deuda*) to pay (off); (*fig: favor*) to repay ♦ *vi* to pay; ~**se** *vr*: ~**se con algo** to be content with sth; **¡me las pagarás!** I'll get you for this!

pagaré [paɣa're] *nm* I.O.U.

página ['paxina] *nf* page.

paginación [paxina'θjon] *nf* (*INFORM, TIP*) pagination.

paginar [paxi'nar] *vt* (*INFORM, TIP*) to paginate.

pág(s). *abr* (= *página(s)*) p(p).

pago ['paɣo] *nm* (*dinero*) payment; (*fig*) return; ~ **anticipado/a cuenta/a la entrega/ en especie/inicial** advance payment/ payment on account/cash on delivery/ payment in kind/down payment; ~ **a título gracioso** ex gratia payment; **en** ~ **de** in return for.

pague ['paɣe] *etc vb* V **pagar**.

país [pa'is] *nm* (*gen*) country; (*región*) land; **los Países Bajos** the Low Countries; **el P**~ **Vasco** the Basque Country.

paisaje [pai'saxe] *nm* countryside, landscape; (*vista*) scenery.

paisano, a [pai'sano, a] *a* of the same country ♦ *nm/f* (*compatriota*) fellow countryman/woman; **vestir de** ~ (*soldado*) to be in civilian clothes; (*guardia*) to be in plain clothes.

paja ['paxa] *nf* straw; (*fig*) trash, rubbish; (*en libro, ensayo*) padding, waffle; **riñeron por un quítame allá esas** ~**s** they quarrelled over a trifle.

pajarita [paxa'rita] *nf* bow tie.

pájaro ['paxaro] *nm* bird; (*fam: astuto*) clever fellow; **tener la cabeza a** ~**s** to be featherbrained.

pajita [pa'xita] *nf* (drinking) straw.

pajizo, a [pa'xiθo, a] *a* (*de paja*) straw *cpd*; (*techo*) thatched; (*color*) straw-coloured.

pakistaní [pakista'ni] *a, nm/f* Pakistani.

pala ['pala] *nf* (*de mango largo*) spade; (*de mango corto*) shovel; (*raqueta etc*) bat; (: *de tenis*) racquet; (*CULIN*) slice; ~ **matamoscas** fly swat.

palabra [pa'laβra] *nf* (*gen, promesa*) word; (*facultad*) (power of) speech; (*derecho de hablar*) right to speak; **faltar a su** ~ to go back on one's word; **quedarse con la** ~ **en la boca** to stop short; (*en reunión, comité etc*) **tomar la** ~ to speak, take the floor; **pedir la** ~ to ask to be allowed to speak; **tener la** ~ to have the floor; **no encuentro** ~**s para expresarme** words fail me.

palabrota [pala'βrota] *nf* swearword.

palacio [pa'laθjo] *nm* palace; (*mansión*) mansion, large house; ~ **de justicia** courthouse; ~ **municipal** town/city hall.

palada [pa'laða] *nf* shovelful, spadeful; (*de remo*) stroke.

paladar [pala'ðar] *nm* palate.

paladear [palaðe'ar] *vt* to taste.

palanca [pa'lanka] *nf* lever; (*fig*) pull, influence; ~ **de cambio** (*AUTO*) gear lever, gearshift (*US*); ~ **de freno** (*AUTO*) brake lever; ~ **de gobierno** *o* **de control** (*INFORM*) joystick.

palangana [palan'gana] *nf* washbasin.

palco ['palko] *nm* box.

palenque [pa'lenke] *nm* (*cerca*) stockade, fence; (*área*) arena, enclosure; (*de gallos*) pit.

palentino, a [palen'tino, a] *a* of *o* from Palencia ♦ *nm/f* native *o* inhabitant of Palencia.

paleolítico, a [paleo'litiko, a] *a* paleolithic.

paleontología [paleontolo'xia] *nf* paleontology.

Palestina [pales'tina] *nf* Palestine.

palestino, a [pales'tino, a] *a, nm/f* Palestinian.

paletización [paletiθa'θjon] *nf* palletization.

paleto, a [pa'leto, a] *nm/f* yokel, hick (*US*) ♦ *nf* (*pala*) small shovel; (*ARTE*) palette; (*ANAT*) shoulder blade; (*AM*) ice lolly.

paliar [pa'ljar] *vt* (*mitigar*) to mitigate; (*disfrazar*) to conceal.

paliativo [palja'tiβo] *nm* palliative.

palidecer [paliðe'θer] *vi* to turn pale.

palidez [pali'ðeθ] *nf* paleness.

palidezca [pali'ðeθka] *etc vb* V **palidecer**.

pálido, a ['paliðo, a] *a* pale.

palillo [pa'liʎo] *nm* small stick; (*para dientes*) toothpick; **~s (chinos)** chopsticks; **estar hecho un ~** to be as thin as a rake.

palique [pa'like] *nm*: **estar de ~** (*fam*) to have a chat.

paliza [pa'liθa] *nf* beating, thrashing; **dar** *o* **propinar** (*fam*) **una ~ a uno** to give sb a thrashing.

palma ['palma] *nf* (*ANAT*) palm; (*árbol*) palm tree; **batir** *o* **dar ~s** to clap, applaud; **llevarse la ~** to triumph, win.

palmada [pal'maða] *nf* slap; **~s** *nfpl* clapping *sg*, applause *sg*.

Palma de Mallorca *nf* Palma.

palmar [pal'mar] *vi* (*tb*: **~la**) to die, kick the bucket.

palmear [palme'ar] *vi* to clap.

palmero, a [pal'mero, a] *a* of the island of Palma ♦ *nm/f* native *o* inhabitant of the island of Palma ♦ *nm* (*AM*), *nf* palm tree.

palmo ['palmo] *nm* (*medida*) span; (*fig*) small amount; **~ a ~** inch by inch.

palmotear [palmote'ar] *vi* to clap, applaud.

palmoteo [palmo'teo] *nm* clapping, applause.

palo ['palo] *nm* stick; (*poste*) post, pole; (*mango*) handle, shaft; (*golpe*) blow, hit; (*de golf*) club; (*de béisbol*) bat; (*NAUT*) mast; (*NAIPES*) suit; **vermut a ~ seco** straight vermouth; **de tal ~ tal astilla** like father like son.

paloma [pa'loma] *nf* dove, pigeon; **~ mensajera** carrier *o* homing pigeon.

palomilla [palo'miʎa] *nf* moth; (*TEC*: *tuerca*) wing nut; (*soporte*) bracket.

palomitas [palo'mitas] *nfpl* popcorn *sg*.

palpable [pal'paβle] *a* palpable; (*fig*) tangible.

palpar [pal'par] *vt* to touch, feel.

palpitación [palpita'θjon] *nf* palpitation.

palpitante [palpi'tante] *a* palpitating; (*fig*) burning.

palpitar [palpi'tar] *vi* to palpitate; (*latir*) to beat.

palta ['palta] *nf* (*AM*) avocado.

palúdico, a [pa'luðiko, a] *a* marshy.

paludismo [palu'ðismo] *nm* malaria.

palurdo, a [pa'lurðo, a] *a* coarse, uncouth ♦ *nm/f* yokel, hick (*US*).

pampa ['pampa] *nf* (*AM*) pampa(s), prairie.

pamplinas [pam'plinas] *nfpl* nonsense *sg*.

pamplonés, esa [pamplo'nes, esa], **pamplonica** [pamplo'nika] *a* of *o* from Pamplona ♦ *nm/f* native *o* inhabitant of Pamplona.

pan [pan] *nm* bread; (*una barra*) loaf; **~ de molde** sliced loaf; **~ integral** wholemeal bread; **~ rallado** breadcrumbs *pl*; **eso es ~ comido** it's a cinch; **llamar al ~ ~ y al vino vino** to call a spade a spade.

pana ['pana] *nf* corduroy.

panadería [panaðe'ria] *nf* baker's (shop).

panadero, a [pana'ðero, a] *nm/f* baker.

panal [pa'nal] *nm* honeycomb.

Panamá [pana'ma] *nm* Panama.

panameño, a [pana'meɲo, a] *a* Panamanian.

pancarta [pan'karta] *nf* placard, banner.

pancho, a ['pantʃo, a] *a*: **estar tan ~** to remain perfectly calm.

panda ['panda] *nm* panda ♦ *nf* gang.

pandereta [pande'reta] *nf* tambourine.

pandilla [pan'diʎa] *nf* set, group; (*de criminales*) gang; (*pey*) clique.

pando, a ['pando, a] *a* sagging.

panel [pa'nel] *nm* panel; **~ acústico** acoustic screen.

panera [pa'nera] *nf* bread basket.

panfleto [pan'fleto] *nm* (*POL etc*) pamphlet; (*AM*) lampoon.

pánico ['paniko] *nm* panic.

panorama [pano'rama] *nm* panorama; (*vista*) view.

pantalón [panta'lon] *nm*, **pantalones** [panta'lones] *nmpl* trousers *pl*, pants *pl* (*US*); **pantalones vaqueros** jeans *pl*.

pantalla [pan'taʎa] *nf* (*de cine*) screen; (*cubre-luz*) lampshade; (*INFORM*) screen, display; **servir de ~ a** to be a blind for; **~ de cristal líquido** liquid crystal display; **~ táctil** touch-sensitive screen; **~ de ayuda** help screen; **~ plana** plane screen.

pantano [pan'tano] *nm* (*ciénaga*) marsh, swamp; (*depósito: de agua*) reservoir; (*fig*) jam, fix, difficulty.

pantera [pan'tera] *nf* panther.

pantomima [panto'mima] *nf* pantomime.

pantorrilla [panto'rriʎa] *nf* calf (of the leg).

pantufla [pan'tufla] *nf* slipper.

panza ['panθa] *nf* belly, paunch.

panzón, ona [pan'θon, ona], **panzudo, a** [pan'θuðo, a] *a* fat, potbellied.

pañal [pa'ɲal] *nm* nappy, diaper (*US*); **estar todavía en ~es** to be still wet behind the ears.

pañería [paɲe'ria] *nf* (*artículos*) drapery; (*tienda*) draper's (shop), dry-goods store (*US*).

pañero, a [pa'ɲero, a] *nm/f* draper.

paño ['paɲo] *nm* (*tela*) cloth; (*pedazo de tela*) (piece of) cloth; (*trapo*) duster, rag; **~ de cocina** dishcloth; **~ higiénico** sanitary towel; **~s menores** underclothes; **~s calientes** (*fig*) half-measures; **no andarse con ~s calientes** to pull no punches.

pañuelo [pa'ɲwelo] *nm* handkerchief, hanky

(fam); *(para la cabeza)* (head)scarf.

papa ['papa] *nf (AM)* potato ♦ *nm*: **el P~** the Pope.

papá [pa'pa] *nm, pl* **papás** *(fam)* dad, daddy, pop *(US)*; **~s** *nmpl* parents; **hijo de ~** Hooray Henry *(fam)*.

papagayo [papa'ɣajo] *nm* parrot.

papanatas [papa'natas] *nm inv (fam)* sucker, simpleton.

paparrucha [papa'rrutʃa] *nf (tontería)* piece of nonsense.

papaya [pa'paja] *nf* papaya.

papel [pa'pel] *nm (gen)* paper; *(hoja de papel)* sheet of paper; *(TEATRO)* part, role; **~es** *nmpl* identification papers; **~ de calco/carbón/de cartas** tracing paper/ carbon paper/stationery; **~ contínuo** *(INFORM)* continuous stationery; **~ de envolver/de empapelar** brown paper, wrapping paper/wallpaper; **~ de aluminio/higiénico** tinfoil/toilet paper; **~ del** *o* **de pagos al Estado** government bonds *pl*; **~ de lija** sandpaper; **~ moneda** paper money; **~ plegado (en abanico** *o* **en acordeón)** fanfold paper; **~ secante** blotting paper; **~ térmico** thermal paper.

papeleo [pape'leo] *nm* red tape.

papelera [pape'lera] *nf (cesto)* wastepaper basket; *(escritorio)* desk.

papelería [papele'ria] *nf (tienda)* stationer's (shop).

papeleta [pape'leta] *nf (pedazo de papel)* slip *o* bit of paper; *(POL)* ballot paper; *(ESCOL)* report; **¡vaya ~!** this is a tough one!

paperas [pa'peras] *nfpl* mumps *sg*.

papilla [pa'piʎa] *nf (de bebé)* baby food; *(pey)* mush; **estar hecho ~** to be dog-tired.

paquete [pa'kete] *nm (caja)* packet; *(bulto)* parcel; *(AM fam)* nuisance, bore; *(INFORM)* package *(of software)*; *(vacaciones)* package tour; **~ de aplicaciones** *(INFORM)* applications package; **~ integrado** *(INFORM)* integrated package; **~ de gestión integrado** combined management suite; **~s postales** parcel post *sg*.

paquistaní [pakista'ni] = **pakistaní**.

par [par] *a (igual)* like, equal; equal; *(MAT)* even ♦ *nm* equal; *(de guantes)* pair; *(de veces)* couple; *(dignidad)* peer; *(GOLF, COM)* par ♦ *nf* par; **~es o nones** odds or evens; **abrir de ~ en ~** to open wide; **a la ~** par; **sobre/bajo la ~** above/below par.

para ['para] *prep (gen)* for; **no es ~ comer** it's not for eating; **decir ~ sí** to say to o.s.; **¿~ qué lo quieres?** what do you want it for?; **se casaron ~ separarse otra vez** they married only to separate again; **~ entonces** by then *o* that time; **lo tendré ~ mañana** I'll have it for tomorrow; **ir ~ casa** to go home, head for home; **~**

profesor es muy estúpido he's very stupid for a teacher; **¿quién es usted ~ gritar así?** who are you to shout like that?; **tengo bastante ~ vivir** I have enough to live on.

parabellum [paraβe'lum] *nm* (automatic) pistol.

parabién [para'βjen] *nm* congratulations *pl*.

parábola [pa'raβola] *nf* parable; *(MAT)* parabola.

parabrisas [para'βrisas] *nm inv* windscreen, windshield *(US)*.

paracaídas [paraka'iðas] *nm inv* parachute.

paracaidista [parakai'ðista] *nm/f* parachutist; *(MIL)* paratrooper.

parachoques [para'tʃokes] *nm inv* bumper, fender *(US)*; shock absorber.

parada [pa'raða] *nf* V **parado**.

paradero [para'ðero] *nm* stopping-place; *(situación)* whereabouts.

parado, a [pa'raðo, a] *a (persona)* motionless, standing still; *(fábrica)* closed, at a standstill; *(coche)* stopped; *(de pie)* standing (up); *(sin empleo)* unemployed, idle; *(confuso)* confused ♦ *nf (gen)* stop; *(acto)* stopping; *(de industria)* shutdown, stoppage; *(lugar)* stopping-place; **salir bien ~** to come off well; **parada de autobús** bus stop; **parada discrecional** request stop; **parada en seco** sudden stop; **parada de taxis** taxi rank.

paradoja [para'ðoxa] *nf* paradox.

paradójico, a [para'ðoxiko, a] *a* paradoxical.

parador [para'ðor] *nm* (luxury) hotel.

parafrasear [parafrase'ar] *vt* to paraphrase.

paráfrasis [pa'rafrasis] *nf inv* paraphrase.

paraguas [pa'raɣwas] *nm inv* umbrella.

Paraguay [para'ɣwai] *nm*: **el ~** Paraguay.

paraguayo, a [para'ɣwajo, a] *a, nm/f* Paraguayan.

paraíso [para'iso] *nm* paradise, heaven; **~ fiscal** *(COM)* tax haven.

paraje [pa'raxe] *nm* place, spot.

paralelo, a [para'lelo, a] *a, nm* parallel; **en ~** *(ELEC, INFORM)* (in) parallel.

paralice [para'liθe] *etc vb* V **paralizar**.

parálisis [pa'ralisis] *nf inv* paralysis; **~ cerebral** cerebral palsy; **~ progresiva** creeping paralysis.

paralítico, a [para'litiko, a] *a, nm/f* paralytic.

paralizar [parali'θar] *vt* to paralyse; **~se** *vr* to become paralysed; *(fig)* to come to a standstill.

parámetro [pa'rametro] *nm* parameter.

paramilitar [paramili'tar] *a* paramilitary.

páramo ['paramo] *nm* bleak plateau.

parangón [paran'gon] *nm*: **sin ~** incomparable.

paraninfo [para'ninfo] *nm (ESCOL)* assembly hall.

paranoico, a [para'noiko, a] *a, nm/f* paranoid.

parapetarse [parape'tarse] *vr* to shelter.

parapléjico, a [para'plexiko, a] *a, nm/f* paraplegic.

parar [pa'rar] *vt* to stop; (*progreso etc*) to check, halt; (*golpe*) to ward off ◆ *vi* to stop; (*hospedarse*) to stay, put up; ~**se** *vr* to stop; (*AM*) to stand up; **no** ~ **de hacer algo** to keep on doing sth; **ha parado de llover** it has stopped raining; **van a** ~ **en la comisaría** they're going to end up in the police station; **no sabemos en qué va a** ~ **todo esto** we don't know where all this is going to end; ~**se a hacer algo** to stop to do sth; ~**se en** to pay attention to.

pararrayos [para'rrajos] *nm inv* lightning conductor.

parásito, a [pa'rasito, a] *nm/f* parasite.

parasol [para'sol] *nm* parasol, sunshade.

parcela [par'θela] *nf* plot, piece of ground, smallholding.

parcial [par'θjal] *a* (*pago*) part-; (*eclipse*) partial; (*juez*) prejudiced, biased.

parcialidad [parθjali'ðað] *nf* (*prejuicio*) prejudice, bias.

parco, a ['parko, a] *a* (*frugal*) sparing; (*moderado*) moderate.

parche ['partʃe] *nm* patch.

pardo, a ['parðo, a] *a* (*color*) brown; (*cielo*) overcast; (*voz*) flat, dull.

parear [pare'ar] *vt* (*juntar, hacer par*) to match, put together; (*calcetines*) to put into pairs; (*BIO*) to mate, pair.

parecer [pare'θer] *nm* (*opinión*) opinion, view; (*aspecto*) looks *pl* ◆ *vi* (*tener apariencia*) to seem, look; (*asemejarse*) to look like, seem like; (*aparecer, llegar*) to appear; ~**se** *vr* to look alike, resemble each other; ~**se a** to look like, resemble; **al** ~ apparently; **me parece que** I think (that), it seems to me that.

parecido, a [pare'θiðo, a] *a* similar ◆ *nm* similarity, likeness, resemblance; ~ **a** like, similar to; **bien** ~ good-looking, nice-looking.

pared [pa'reð] *nf* wall; ~ **divisoria/medianera** dividing/party wall; **subirse por las** ~**es** (*fam*) to go up the wall.

paredón [pare'ðon] *nm*: **llevar a uno al** ~ to put sb up against a wall, shoot sb.

parejo, a [pa'rexo, a] *a* (*igual*) equal; (*liso*) smooth, even ◆ *nf* (*dos*) pair; (: *de personas*) couple; (*el otro*: *de un par*) other one (of a pair); (: *persona*) partner; (*Guardias*) Civil Guard patrol.

parentela [paren'tela] *nf* relations *pl*.

parentesco [paren'tesko] *nm* relationship.

paréntesis [pa'rentesis] *nm inv* parenthesis; (*digresión*) digression; (*en escrito*) bracket.

parezca [pa'reθka] *etc vb V* **parecer**.

parida [pa'riða] *nf*: ~ **mental** (*fam*) dumb idea.

pariente, a [pa'rjente, a] *nm/f* relative, relation.

parihuela [pari'wela] *nf* stretcher.

paripé [pari'pe] *nm*: **hacer el** ~ to put on an act.

parir [pa'rir] *vt* to give birth to ◆ *vi* (*mujer*) to give birth, have a baby; (*yegua*) to foal; (*vaca*) to calve.

París [pa'ris] *nm* Paris.

parisiense [pari'sjense], **parisiano, a** [pari'sjano, a] *a, nm/f* Parisian.

parking ['parkin] *nm* car park, parking lot (*US*).

parlamentar [parlamen'tar] *vi* (*negociar*) to parley.

parlamentario, a [parlamen'tarjo, a] *a* parliamentary ◆ *nm/f* member of parliament.

parlamento [parla'mento] *nm* (*POL*) parliament; (*JUR*) speech.

parlanchín, ina [parlan'tʃin, ina] *a* loose-tongued, indiscreet ◆ *nm/f* chatterbox.

parlotear [parlote'ar] *vi* to chatter, prattle.

parloteo [parlo'teo] *nm* chatter, prattle.

parné [par'ne] *nm* (*fam: dinero*) dough.

paro ['paro] *nm* (*huelga*) stoppage (of work), strike; (*desempleo*) unemployment; **subsidio de** ~ unemployment benefit; **hay** ~ **en la industria** work in the industry is at a standstill; ~ **del sistema** (*INFORM*) system shutdown.

parodia [pa'roðja] *nf* parody.

parodiar [paro'ðjar] *vt* to parody.

parpadear [parpaðe'ar] *vi* (*los ojos*) to blink; (*luz*) to flicker.

parpadeo [parpa'ðeo] *nm* (*de ojos*) blinking, winking; (*de luz*) flickering.

párpado [par'paðo] *nm* eyelid.

parque ['parke] *nm* (*lugar verde*) park; ~ **de atracciones/de bomberos/zoológico** fairground/fire station/zoo.

parquímetro [par'kimetro] *nm* parking meter.

párrafo ['parrafo] *nm* paragraph; **echar un** ~ (*fam*) to have a chat.

parranda [pa'rranda] *nf* (*fam*) spree, binge.

parrilla [pa'rriʎa] *nf* (*CULIN*) grill; (*de coche*) grille; (**carne de**) ~ barbecue.

parrillada [parri'ʎaða] *nf* barbecue.

párroco ['parroko] *nm* parish priest.

parroquia [pa'rrokja] *nf* parish; (*iglesia*) parish church; (*COM*) clientele, customers *pl*.

parroquiano, a [parro'kjano, a] *nm/f* parishioner; client, customer.

parsimonia [parsi'monja] *nf* (*frugalidad*) sparingness; (*calma*) deliberateness; **con** ~ calmly.

parte ['parte] *nm* message; (*informe*) re-

port; ~ **meteorológico** weather forecast ◆
nf part; (*lado, cara*) side; (*de reparto*)
share; (*JUR*) party; **en alguna ~ de
Europa** somewhere in Europe; **en cualquier
~** anywhere; **por ahí no se va a ninguna
~** that leads nowhere; (*fig*) this is getting
us nowhere; **en gran ~** to a large extent;
la mayor ~ de los españoles most Span-
iards; **de algún tiempo a esta ~** for some
time past; **de ~ de uno** on sb's behalf; **¿de
~ de quién?** (*TELEC*) who is speaking?;
por ~ de on the part of; **yo por mi ~** I for
my part; **por una ~ ... por otra ~** on the
one hand, ... on the other (hand); **dar ~ a
uno** to report to sb; **tomar ~** to take part.

partera [par'tera] *nf* midwife.

parterre [par'terre] *nm* (*de flores*) (flower)bed.

partición [parti'θjon] *nf* division, sharing-
out; (*POL*) partition.

participación [partiθipa'θjon] *nf* (*acto*)
participation, taking part; (*parte*) share;
(*COM*) share, stock (*US*); (*de lotería*)
shared prize; (*aviso*) notice, notification; **~
en los beneficios** profit-sharing; **~
minoritaria** minority interest.

participante [partiθi'pante] *nm/f* participant.

participar [partiθ'par] *vt* to notify, inform ◆
vi to take part, participate; **~ en una empresa** (*COM*) to invest in an enterprise; **le
participo que** ... I have to tell you that ....

partícipe [par'tiθipe] *nm/f* participant;
hacer ~ a uno de algo to inform sb of sth.

participio [parti'θipjo] *nm* participle; **~ de
pasado/presente** past/present participle.

partícula [par'tikula] *nf* particle.

particular [partiku'lar] *a* (*especial*)
particular, special; (*individual, personal*)
private, personal ◆ *nm* (*punto, asunto*)
particular, point; (*individuo*) individual;
tiene coche ~ he has a car of his own; **no
dijo mucho sobre el ~** he didn't say much
about the matter.

particularice [partikula'riθe] *etc vb V* **particularizar**.

particularidad [partikulari'ðað] *nf* peculiarity; **tiene la ~ de que** ... one of its special
features is (that) ....

particularizar [partikulari'θar] *vt* to
distinguish; (*especificar*) to specify; (*detallar*) to give details about.

partida [par'tiða] *nf* (*salida*) departure;
(*COM*) entry, item; (*juego*) game; (*grupo,
bando*) band, group; **mala ~** dirty trick; **~
de nacimiento/matrimonio/defunción**
birth/ marriage/death certificate; **echar una
~** to have a game.

partidario, a [parti'ðarjo, a] *a* partisan ◆
nm/f (*DEPORTE*) supporter; (*POL*) partisan.

partidismo [parti'ðismo] *nm* (*JUR*) partisan-

ship, bias; (*POL*) party politics.

partido [par'tiðo] *nm* (*POL*) party; (*encuentro*) game, match; (*apoyo*) support; (*equipo*) team; **~ amistoso** (*DEPORTE*) friendly
(game); **~ de fútbol** football match; **sacar
~ de** to profit from, benefit from; **tomar ~**
to take sides.

partir [par'tir] *vt* (*dividir*) to split, divide;
(*compartir, distribuir*) to share (out), distribute; (*romper*) to break open, split open;
(*rebanada*) to cut (off) ◆ *vi* (*tomar camino*) to set off, set out; (*comenzar*) to start
(off *o* out); **~se** *vr* to crack *o* split *o* break
(in two *etc*); **a ~ de** (starting) from; **~se
de risa** to split one's sides (laughing).

parto ['parto] *nm* birth, delivery; (*fig*) product, creation; **estar de ~** to be in labour.

parvulario [parβu'larjo] *nm* nursery school,
kindergarten.

párvulo, a ['parβulo, a] *nm/f* infant.

pasa ['pasa] *nf V* **paso**.

pasada [pa'saða] *nf V* **pasado**.

pasadizo [pasa'ðiθo] *nm* (*pasillo*) passage,
corridor; (*callejuela*) alley.

pasado, a [pa'saðo, a] *a* past; (*malo: comida, fruta*) bad; (*muy cocido*) overdone;
(*anticuado*) out of date ◆ *nm* past; (*LING*)
past (tense) ◆ *nf* passing, passage; (*acción
de pulir*) rub, polish; **~ mañana** the day
after tomorrow; **el mes ~** last month; **~s
dos días** after two days; **lo ~, ~** let bygones be bygones; **~ de moda** old-
fashioned; **~ por agua** (*huevo*) boiled; **de
pasada** in passing, incidentally; **una mala
pasada** a dirty trick.

pasador [pasa'ðor] *nm* (*gen*) bolt; (*de pelo*)
pin, grip, slide.

pasaje [pa'saxe] *nm* (*gen*) passage; (*pago
de viaje*) fare; (*los pasajeros*) passengers
pl; (*pasillo*) passageway.

pasajero, a [pasa'xero, a] *a* passing; (*ave*)
migratory ◆ *nm/f* passenger; (*viajero*)
traveller.

pasamanos [pasa'manos] *nm inv* rail,
handrail; (*de escalera*) banister.

pasamontañas [pasamon'taɲas] *nm inv*
balaclava (helmet).

pasaporte [pasa'porte] *nm* passport.

pasar [pa'sar] *vt* (*gen*) to pass; (*tiempo*) to
spend; (*durezas*) to suffer, endure; (*noticia*) to give, pass on; (*película*) to show;
(*persona*) to take, conduct; (*río*) to cross;
(*barrera*) to pass through; (*falta*) to overlook, tolerate; (*contrincante*) to surpass, do
better than; (*coche*) to overtake; (*contrabando*) to smuggle (in/out); (*enfermedad*)
to give, infect with ◆ *vi* (*gen*) to pass, go;
(*terminarse*) to be over; (*ocurrir*) to happen; **~se** *vr* (*efectos*) to pass, be over;
(*flores*) to fade; (*comida*) to go bad, go off;
(*fig*) to overdo it, go too far *o* over the top;

~ de to go beyond, exceed; **¡pase!** come in!; **nos hicieron ~** they showed us in; **~ por** to fetch; **~ por alto** to skip; **~ por una crisis** to go through a crisis; **se hace ~ por médico** he passes himself off as a doctor; **~lo bien/bomba** o **de maravilla** to have a good/great time; **~se al enemigo** to go over to the enemy; **~se de la raya** to go too far; **¡no te pases!** don't try me!; **se me pasó** I forgot; **se me pasó el turno** I missed my turn; **no se le pasa nada** nothing escapes him, he misses nothing; **ya se te pasará** you'll get over it; **¿qué pasa?** what's happening?, what's going on?, what's up?; **¡cómo pasa el tiempo!** time just flies!; **pase lo que pase** come what may; **el autobús pasa por nuestra casa** the bus goes past our house.

pasarela [pasa'rela] *nf* footbridge; *(en barco)* gangway.

pasatiempo [pasa'tjempo] *nm* pastime, hobby; *(distracción)* amusement.

Pascua, pascua ['paskwa] *nf*: **~ (de Resurrección)** Easter; **~ de Navidad** Christmas; **~s** *nfpl* Christmas time; **¡felices ~s!** Merry Christmas; **de ~s a Ramos** once in a blue moon; **hacer la ~ a** *(fam)* to annoy, bug.

pase ['pase] *nm* pass; *(CINE)* performance, showing; *(COM)* permit; *(JUR)* licence.

pasear [pase'ar] *vt* to take for a walk; *(exhibir)* to parade, show off ♦ *vi*, **~se** *vr* to walk, go for a walk; **~ en coche** to go for a drive.

paseo [pa'seo] *nm* *(avenida)* avenue; *(distancia corta)* short walk; **~ marítimo** promenade; **dar un ~** to go for a walk; **mandar a uno a ~** to tell sb to go to blazes; **¡vete a ~!** get lost!

pasillo [pa'siʎo] *nm* passage, corridor.

pasión [pa'sjon] *nf* passion.

pasional [pasjo'nal] *a* passionate; **crimen ~** crime of passion.

pasivo, a [pa'siβo, a] *a* passive; *(inactivo)* inactive ♦ *nm* *(COM)* liabilities *pl*, debts *pl*; *(de cuenta)* debit side; **~ circulante** current liabilities.

pasma ['pasma] *nm* *(fam)* cop.

pasmado, a [pas'maðo, a] *a* *(asombrado)* astonished; *(atontado)* bewildered.

pasmar [pas'mar] *vt* *(asombrar)* to amaze, astonish; **~se** *vr* to be amazed o astonished.

pasmo ['pasmo] *nm* amazement, astonishment; *(fig)* wonder, marvel.

pasmoso, a [pas'moso, a] *a* amazing, astonishing.

paso, a ['paso, a] *a* dried ♦ *nm* *(gen, de baile)* step; *(modo de andar)* walk; *(huella)* footprint; *(rapidez)* speed, pace, rate; *(camino accesible)* way through,

passage; *(cruce)* crossing; *(pasaje)* passing, passage; *(GEO)* pass; *(estrecho)* strait; *(fig)* step, measure; *(apuro)* difficulty ♦ *nf* raisin; **pasa de Corinto/de Esmirna** currant/sultana; **~ a ~** step by step; **a ese ~** *(fig)* at that rate; **salir al ~ de** o **a** to waylay; **salir del ~** to get out of trouble; **dar un ~ en falso** to trip; *(fig)* to take a false step; **estar de ~** to be passing through; **~ atrás** step backwards; *(fig)* backward step; **~ elevado/subterráneo** flyover/subway, underpass *(US)*; **prohibido el ~** no entry; **ceda el ~** give way.

pasota [pa'sota] *a, nm/f* *(fam)* ≈ dropout; **ser un (tipo) ~** to be a bit of a dropout; *(ser indiferente)* not to care about anything.

pasotismo [paso'tismo] *nm* underground o alternative culture.

pasta ['pasta] *nf* *(gen)* paste; *(CULIN: masa)* dough; (: *de bizcochos etc)* pastry; *(fam)* money, dough; *(encuadernación)* hardback; **~s** *nfpl* *(bizcochos)* pastries, small cakes; *(fideos, espaguetis etc)* noodles, spaghetti *sg etc*; **~ de dientes** o **dentífrica** toothpaste; **~ de madera** wood pulp.

pastar [pas'tar] *vt, vi* to graze.

pastel [pas'tel] *nm* *(dulce)* cake; *(de carne)* pie; *(ARTE)* pastel; *(fig)* plot; **~es** *nmpl* pastry *sg*, confectionery *sg*.

pastelería [pastele'ria] *nf* cake shop, pastry shop.

pasteurizado, a [pasteuri'θaðo, a] *a* pasteurized.

pastilla [pas'tiʎa] *nf* *(de jabón, chocolate)* cake, bar; *(píldora)* tablet, pill.

pastizal [pasti'θal] *nm* pasture.

pasto ['pasto] *nm* *(hierba)* grass; *(lugar)* pasture, field; *(fig)* food, nourishment.

pastor, a [pas'tor, a] *nm/f* shepherd(ess) ♦ *nm* clergyman, pastor; *(ZOOL)* sheepdog; **~ alemán** Alsatian.

pastoso, a [pas'toso, a] *a* *(material)* doughy, pasty; *(lengua)* furry; *(voz)* mellow.

pat. *abr* (= *patente*) pat.

pata ['pata] *nf* *(pierna)* leg; *(pie)* foot; *(de muebles)* leg; **~s arriba** upside down; **a cuatro ~s** on all fours; **meter la ~** to put one's foot in it; **~ de cabra** *(TEC)* crowbar; **~s de gallo** crow's feet; **tener buena/mala ~** to be lucky/unlucky.

patada [pa'taða] *nf* stamp; *(puntapié)* kick; **a ~s** in abundance; *(trato)* roughly; **echar a uno a ~s** to kick sb out.

patalear [patale'ar] *vi* to stamp one's feet.

pataleo [pata'leo] *nm* stamping.

patán [pa'tan] *nm* rustic, yokel.

patata [pa'tata] *nf* potato; **~s fritas** o **a la española** chips, French fries; **~s a la inglesa** crisps; **ni ~** *(fam)* nothing at all; **no**

entendió ni ~ he didn't understand a single word.

patear [pate'ar] *vt* (*pisar*) to stamp on, trample (on); (*pegar con el pie*) to kick ◆ *vi* to stamp (with rage), stamp one's foot.

patentar [paten'tar] *vt* to patent.

patente [pa'tente] *a* obvious, evident; (*COM*) patent ◆ *nf* patent.

paternal [pater'nal] *a* fatherly, paternal.

paternalista [paterna'lista] *a* (*tono, actitud etc*) patronizing.

paternidad [paterni'ðað] *nf* fatherhood, parenthood; (*JUR*) paternity.

paterno, a [pa'terno, a] *a* paternal.

patético, a [pa'tetiko, a] *a* pathetic, moving.

patíbulo [pa'tiβulo] *nm* scaffold, gallows.

patillas [pa'tiʎas] *nfpl* sideburns.

patín [pa'tin] *nm* skate; (*de tobogán*) runner; ~ **de hielo** ice skate; ~ **de ruedas** roller skate.

patinaje [pati'naxe] *nm* skating.

patinar [pati'nar] *vi* to skate; (*resbalarse*) to skid, slip; (*fam*) to slip up, blunder.

patinazo [pati'naθo] *nm* (*AUTO*) skid; **dar un** ~ (*fam*) to blunder.

patio [' patjo] *nm* (*de casa*) patio, courtyard; ~ **de recreo** playground.

pato [' pato] *nm* duck; **pagar el** ~ (*fam*) to take the blame, carry the can.

patológico, a [pato'loxiko, a] *a* pathological.

patoso, a [pa'toso, a] *a* awkward, clumsy.

patraña [pa'traɲa] *nf* story, fib.

patria [' patrja] *nf* native land, mother country; ~ **chica** home town.

patrimonio [patri'monjo] *nm* inheritance; (*fig*) heritage; (*COM*) net worth.

patriota [pa'trjota] *nm/f* patriot.

patriotero, a [patrjo'tero, a] *a* chauvinistic.

patriótico, a [patri'otiko, a] *a* patriotic.

patriotismo [patrjo'tismo] *nm* patriotism.

patrocinar [patroθi'nar] *vt* to sponsor; (*apoyar*) to back, support.

patrocinio [patro'θinjo] *nm* sponsorship; backing, support.

patrón, ona [pa'tron, ona] *nm/f* (*jefe*) boss, chief, master/mistress; (*propietario*) landlord/lady; (*REL*) patron saint ◆ *nm* (*COSTURA*) pattern; (*TEC*) standard; ~ **oro** gold standard.

patronal [patro'nal] *a*: **la clase** ~ management; **cierre** ~ lockout.

patronato [patro'nato] *nm* sponsorship; (*acto*) patronage; (*COM*) employers' association; (*fundación*) trust; **el** ~ **de turismo** the tourist board.

patrulla [pa'truʎa] *nf* patrol.

patrullar [patru'ʎar] *vi* to patrol.

paulatino, a [paula'tino, a] *a* gradual, slow.

paupérrimo, a [pau'perrimo, a] *a* very poor, poverty-stricken.

pausa [' pausa] *nf* pause; (*intervalo*) break; (*interrupción*) interruption; (*TEC*: *en videograbadora*) hold; **con** ~ slowly.

pausado, a [pau'saðo, a] *a* slow, deliberate.

pauta [' pauta] *nf* line, guide line.

pavimento [paβi'mento] *nm* (*ARQ*) flooring.

pavo [' paβo] *nm* turkey; (*necio*) silly thing, idiot; ~ **real** peacock; ¡no **seas** ~! don't be silly!

pavonearse [paβone'arse] *vr* to swagger, show off.

pavor [pa'βor] *nm* dread, terror.

payasada [paja'saða] *nf* ridiculous thing (to do); ~**s** *nfpl* clowning *sg*.

payaso, a [pa'jaso, a] *nm/f* clown.

payo, a [' pajo, a] *a, nm/f* non-gipsy.

paz [paθ] *nf* peace; (*tranquilidad*) peacefulness, tranquillity; **dejar a uno en** ~ to leave sb alone *o* in peace; **hacer las paces** to make peace; (*fig*) to make up; ¡haya ~! stop it!

pazca [' paθka] *etc vb V* **pacer.**

PC *nm abr* (*POL*: = *Partido Comunista*) CP.

P.C.E. *nm abr* = *Partido Comunista Español.*

PCL *nf abr* (= *pantalla de cristal líquido*) LCD.

PCUS [pe'kus] *nm abr* (= *Partido Comunista de la Unión Soviética*) Soviet Communist Party.

P.D. *abr* (= *posdata*) P.S.

PDC *nm abr* (*POL*) = *Partido Demócrata Cristiano.*

pdo. *abr* (= *pasado*) ult.

peaje [pe'axe] *nm* toll; **autopista de** ~ toll motorway, turnpike (*US*).

peatón [pea'ton] *nm* pedestrian; **paso de peatones** pedestrian crossing, crosswalk (*US*).

peca [' peka] *nf* freckle.

pecado [pe'kaðo] *nm* sin.

pecador, a [peka'ðor, a] *a* sinful ◆ *nm/f* sinner.

pecaminoso, a [pekami'noso, a] *a* sinful.

pecar [pe'kar] *vi* (*REL*) to sin; (*fig*): ~ **de generoso** to be too generous.

peculiar [peku'ljar] *a* special, peculiar; (*característico*) typical, characteristic.

peculiaridad [pekuljari'ðað] *nf* peculiarity; special feature, characteristic.

pecho [' petʃo] *nm* (*ANAT*) chest; (*de mujer*) breast(s) (*pl*), bosom; (*corazón*) heart, breast; (*valor*) courage, spirit; **dar el** ~ **a** to breast-feed; **tomar algo a** ~ to take sth to heart; **no le cabía en el** ~ he was bursting with happiness.

pechuga [pe'tʃuɣa] *nf* breast (of chicken *etc*).

pedagogo [peða'ɣoɣo] *nm* pedagogue,

teacher.

pedal [pe'ðal] *nm* pedal; ~ **de embrague** clutch (pedal); ~ **de freno** footbrake.

pedalear [peðale'ar] *vi* to pedal.

pedante [pe'ðante] *a* pedantic ♦ *nm/f* pedant.

pedantería [peðante'ria] *nf* pedantry.

pedazo [pe'ðaθo] *nm* piece, bit; **hacerse ~s** to fall to pieces; (*romperse*) to smash, shatter; **un ~ de pan** a scrap of bread; (*fig*) a terribly nice person.

pedernal [peðer'nal] *nm* flint.

pedestre [pe'ðestre] *a* pedestrian; **carrera ~** foot race.

pediatra [pe'ðjatra] *nm/f* paediatrician (*Brit*), pediatrician (*US*).

pediatría [peðja'tria] *nf* paediatrics *sg* (*Brit*), pediatrics *sg* (*US*).

pedicuro, a [peði'kuro, a] *nm/f* chiropodist (*Brit*), podiatrist (*US*).

pedido [pe'ðiðo] *nm* (*COM*: *mandado*) order; (*petición*) request; **~s en cartera** (*COM*) backlog.

pedir [pe'ðir] *vt* to ask for, request; (*comida, COM*: *mandar*) to order; (*exigir*: *precio*) to ask; (*necesitar*) to need, demand, require ♦ *vi* to ask; ~ **prestado** to borrow; ~ **disculpas** to apologize; **me pidió que cerrara la puerta** he asked me to shut the door; **¿cuánto piden por el coche?** how much are they asking for the car?

pedo ['peðo] (*fam*) *a inv*: **estar ~** to be pissed (*!*) ♦ *nm* fart (*!*).

pedrea [pe'ðrea] *nf* (*granizada*) hailstorm; (*de lotería*) minor prizes.

pedrisco [pe'ðrisko] *nm* (*granizo*) hail; (*granizada*) hailstorm.

Pedro ['peðro] *nm* Peter; **entrar como ~ por su casa** to come in as if one owned the place.

pega ['peɣa] *nf* (*dificultad*) snag; **de ~** false, dud; **poner ~s** to raise objections.

pegadizo, a [peɣa'ðiθo, a] *a* (*canción etc*) catchy.

pegajoso, a [peɣa'xoso, a] *a* sticky, adhesive.

pegamento [peɣa'mento] *nm* gum.

pegar [pe'ɣar] *vt* (*papel, sellos*) to stick (on); (*con cola*) to glue; (*cartel*) to post, stick up; (*coser*) to sew (on); (*unir*: *partes*) to join, fix together; (*MED*) to give, infect with; (*dar*: *golpe*) to give, deal ♦ *vi* (*adherirse*) to stick, adhere; (*ir juntos*: *colores*) to match, go together; (*golpear*) to hit; (*quemar*: *el sol*) to strike hot, burn (*fig*); **~se** *vr* (*gen*) to stick; (*dos personas*) to hit each other, fight; **~le a algo** to be a great one for sth; ~ **un grito** to let out a yell; ~ **un salto** to jump (with fright); ~ **fuego** to catch fire; ~ **en** to touch; **~se un tiro** to shoot o.s.; **no pega** that doesn't

seem right; **ese sombrero no pega con el abrigo** that hat doesn't go with the coat.

pegatina [peɣa'tina] *nf* (*POL etc*) sticker.

pegote [pe'ɣote] *nm* (*fig*) patch, ugly mend; **tirarse ~s** (*fam*) to come on strong.

pegue ['peɣe] *etc vb* V **pegar**.

peinado [pei'naðo] *nm* (*en peluquería*) hairdo; (*estilo*) hair style.

peinar [pei'nar] *vt* to comb sb's hair; (*hacer estilo*) to style; **~se** *vr* to comb one's hair.

peine ['peine] *nm* comb.

peineta [pei'neta] *nf* ornamental comb.

p.ej. *abr* (= *por ejemplo*) e.g.

Pekín [pe'kin] *n* Peking.

pela ['pela] *nf* (*Esp fam*) peseta; *V tb* **pelas**.

pelado, a [pe'laðo, a] *a* (*cabeza*) shorn; (*fruta*) peeled; (*campo, fig*) bare; (*AM fam*: *sin dinero*) broke.

pelaje [pe'laxe] *nm* (*ZOOL*) fur, coat; (*fig*) appearance.

pelambre [pe'lambre] *nm* long hair, mop.

pelar [pe'lar] *vt* (*fruta, patatas*) to peel; (*cortar el pelo a*) to cut the hair of; (*quitar la piel*: *animal*) to skin; (*ave*) to pluck; (*habas etc*) to shell; **~se** *vr* (*la piel*) to peel off; **corre que se las pela** (*fam*) he runs like nobody's business.

pelas ['pelas] *nfpl* (*Esp fam*) dough.

peldaño [pel'daɲo] *nm* step; (*de escalera portátil*) rung.

pelea [pe'lea] *nf* (*lucha*) fight; (*discusión*) quarrel, row.

peleado, a [pele'aðo, a] *a*: **estar ~ (con uno)** to have fallen out (with sb).

pelear [pele'ar] *vi* to fight; **~se** *vr* to fight; (*reñirse*) to fall out, quarrel.

pelele [pe'lele] *nm* (*figura*) guy, dummy; (*fig*) puppet.

peletería [pelete'ria] *nf* furrier's, fur shop.

pelícano [pe'likano] *nm* pelican.

pelicorto, a [peli'korto, a] *a* short-haired.

película [pe'likula] *nf* (*CINE*) film, movie (*US*); (*cobertura ligera*) film, thin covering; (*FOTO*: *rollo*) roll *o* reel of film; ~ **de dibujos (animados)** cartoon film; ~ **muda** silent film; **de ~** (*fam*) astonishing, out of this world.

peligro [pe'liɣro] *nm* danger; (*riesgo*) risk; "~ **de muerte**" "danger"; **correr ~ de** to be in danger of; **con ~ de la vida** at the risk of one's life.

peligrosidad [peliɣrosi'ðað] *nf* danger, riskiness.

peligroso, a [peli'ɣroso, a] *a* dangerous; risky.

pelirrojo, a [peli'rroxo, a] *a* red-haired, red-headed.

pelma ['pelma] *nm/f*, **pelmazo** [pel'maθo] *nm* (*fam*) pest.

pelo ['pelo] *nm* (*cabellos*) hair; (*de barba, bigote*) whisker; (*de animal*: *pellejo*) fur, coat; (*de perro etc*) hair, coat; (*de ave*) down; (*de tejido*) nap; (*TEC*) fibre; **a ~ bareheaded**; (*desnudo*) naked; **al ~** just right; **venir al ~** to be exactly what one needs; **por los ~s** by the skin of one's teeth; **escaparse por un ~** to have a close shave; **se me pusieron los ~s de punta** my hair stood on end; **no tener ~s en la lengua** to be outspoken, not mince words; **tomar el ~ a uno** to pull sb's leg.

pelón, ona [pe'lon, ona] *a* hairless, bald.

pelota [pe'lota] *nf* ball; (*fam: cabeza*) nut (*fam*); **en ~(s)** stark naked; **~ vasca** pelota; **devolver la ~ a uno** (*fig*) to turn the tables on sb; **hacer la ~ (a uno)** to creep (to sb).

pelotón [pelo'ton] *nm* (*MIL*) squad, detachment.

peluca [pe'luka] *nf* wig.

peluche [pe'lutʃe] *nm*: **muñeco de ~** soft toy.

peludo, a [pe'luðo, a] *a* hairy, shaggy.

peluquería [peluke'ria] *nf* hairdresser's; (*para hombres*) barber's (shop).

peluquero, a [pelu'kero, a] *nm/f* hairdresser; barber.

peluquín [pelu'kin] *nm* toupée.

pelusa [pe'lusa] *nf* (*BOT*) down; (*COSTURA*) fluff.

pellejo [pe'ʎexo] *nm* (*de animal*) skin, hide; **salvar el ~** to save one's skin.

pellizcar [peʎiθ'kar] *vt* to pinch, nip.

pellizco [pe'ʎiθko] *nm* (*gen*) pinch.

pellizque [pe'ʎiθke] *etc vb* V **pellizcar**.

PEMEX [pe'meks] *nm abr* = *Petróleos Mejicanos*.

PEN [pen] *nm abr* (*Esp*) = *Plan Energético Nacional*.

pena ['pena] *nf* (*congoja*) grief, sadness; (*remordimiento*) regret; (*dificultad*) trouble; (*dolor*) pain; (*JUR*) sentence; (*DEPORTE*) penalty; **merecer** *o* **valer la ~** to be worthwhile; **a duras ~s** with great difficulty; **so ~ de** on pain of; **~ capital** capital punishment; **~ de muerte** death penalty; **~ pecuniaria** fine; **¡qué ~!** what a shame *o* pity!

penal [pe'nal] *a* penal ♦ *nm* (*cárcel*) prison.

penalidad [penali'ðað] *nf* (*problema, dificultad*) trouble, hardship; (*JUR*) penalty, punishment.

penalty [pe'nalti] *nm* (*DEPORTE*) penalty.

penar [pe'nar] *vt* to penalize; (*castigar*) to punish ♦ *vi* to suffer.

pender [pen'der] *vi* (*colgar*) to hang; (*JUR*) to be pending.

pendiente [pen'djente] *a* pending, unsettled ♦ *nm* earring ♦ *nf* hill, slope; **tener una asignatura ~** to have to resit a subject.

pendón [pen'don] *nm* banner, standard.

pene ['pene] *nm* penis.

penene [pe'nene] *nm/f* = **PNN**.

penetración [penetra'θjon] *nf* (*acto*) penetration; (*agudeza*) sharpness, insight.

penetrante [pene'trante] *a* (*herida*) deep; (*persona, arma*) sharp; (*sonido*) penetrating, piercing; (*mirada*) searching; (*viento, ironía*) biting.

penetrar [pene'trar] *vt* to penetrate, pierce; (*entender*) to grasp ♦ *vi* to penetrate, go in; (*líquido*) to soak in; (*emoción*) to pierce.

penicilina [peniθi'lina] *nf* penicillin.

península [pe'ninsula] *nf* peninsula; **P~ Ibérica** Iberian Peninsula.

peninsular [peninsu'lar] *a* peninsular.

penique [pe'nike] *nm* penny; **~s** *nmpl* pence.

penitencia [peni'tenθja] *nf* (*remordimiento*) penitence; (*castigo*) penance; **en ~** as a penance.

penitencial [peniten'θjal] *a* penitential.

penitenciaría [penitenθja'ria] *nf* prison, penitentiary.

penitenciario, a [peniten'θjarjo, a] *a* prison cpd.

penoso, a [pe'noso, a] *a* laborious, difficult.

pensado, a [pen'saðo, a] *a*: **bien/mal ~** well intentioned/cynical; **en el momento menos ~** when least expected.

pensador, a [pensa'ðor, a] *nm/f* thinker.

pensamiento [pensa'mjento] *nm* (*gen*) thought; (*mente*) mind; (*idea*) idea; (*BOT*) pansy; **no le pasó por el ~** it never occurred to him.

pensar [pen'sar] *vt* to think; (*considerar*) to think over, think out; (*proponerse*) to intend, plan, propose; (*imaginarse*) to think up, invent ♦ *vi* to think; **~ en** to think of *o* about; (*anhelar*) to aim at, aspire to; **dar que ~ a uno** to give sb food for thought.

pensativo, a [pensa'tiβo, a] *a* thoughtful, pensive.

pensión [pen'sjon] *nf* (*casa*) boarding house, guest house; (*dinero*) pension; (*cama y comida*) board and lodging; **~ de jubilación** retirement pension; **~ escalada** graduated pension; **~ completa** full board.

pensionista [pensjo'nista] *nm/f* (*jubilado*) (old-age) pensioner; (*quien vive en pensión*) lodger; (*ESCOL*) boarder.

pentágono [pen'taɣono] *nm* pentagon: **el P~** (*US*) the Pentagon.

pentagrama [penta'ɣrama] *nm* (*MUS*) stave, staff.

penúltimo, a [pe'nultimo, a] *a* penultimate, second last.

penumbra [pe'numbra] *nf* half-light, semi-darkness.

penuria [pe'nurja] *nf* shortage, want.

peña ['pena] *nf* (*roca*) rock; (*cuesta*) cliff, crag; (*grupo*) group, circle; (*DEPORTE*) supporters' club; (*AM: club*) folk club.

peñasco [pe'ɲasko] *nm* large rock, boulder.

peñón [pe'ɲon] *nm* crag; **el P~** the Rock (of Gibraltar).

peón [pe'on] *nm* labourer; (*AM*) farm labourer, farmhand; (*TEC*) spindle, shaft; (*AJEDREZ*) pawn.

peor [pe'or] *a* (*comparativo*) worse; (*superlativo*) worst ◆ *ad* worse; worst; **de mal en ~** from bad to worse; **tanto ~** so much the worse; **A es ~ que B** A is worse than B; **Z es el ~ de todos** Z is the worst of all.

pepinillo [pepi'niʎo] *nm* gherkin.

pepino [pe'pino] *nm* cucumber; **(no) me importa un ~** I don't care two hoots.

pepita [pe'pita] *nf* (*BOT*) pip; (*MINERÍA*) nugget.

pepito [pe'pito] *nm* meat sandwich.

peque ['peke] *etc vb* V **pecar.**

pequeñez [peke'ɲeθ] *nf* smallness, littleness; (*trivialidad*) trifle, triviality.

pequeño, a [pe'keɲo, a] *a* small, little; (*cifra*) small, low; (*bajo*) short; **~ burgués** lower middle-class.

pequinés, esa [peki'nes, esa] *a*, *nm/f* Pekinese.

pera ['pera] *a inv* classy; **niño ~** spoiled upper-class brat ◆ *nf* pear; **eso es pedir ~s al olmo** that's asking the impossible.

peral [pe'ral] *nm* pear tree.

percance [per'kanθe] *nm* setback, misfortune.

percatarse [perka'tarse] *vr*: **~ de** to notice, take note of.

percebe [per'θeβe] *nm* (*ZOOL*) barnacle; (*fam*) idiot.

percepción [perθep'θjon] *nf* (*vista*) perception; (*idea*) notion, idea; (*COM*) collection.

perceptible [perθep'tiβle] *a* perceptible, noticeable; (*COM*) payable, receivable.

percibir [perθi'βir] *vt* to perceive, notice; (*ver*) to see; (*peligro etc*) to sense; (*COM*) to earn, receive, get.

percusión [perku'sjon] *nf* percussion.

percusor [perku'sor], **percutor** [perku'tor] *nm* (*TEC*) hammer; (*de arma*) firing pin.

percha ['pertʃa] *nf* (*poste*) pole, support; (*gancho*) peg; (*de abrigos*) coat stand; (*colgador*) coat hanger; (*de ave*) perch.

perchero [per'tʃero] *nm* clothes rack.

perdedor, a [perðe'ðor, a] *a* losing ◆ *nm/f* loser.

perder [per'ðer] *vt* to lose; (*tiempo, palabras*) to waste; (*oportunidad*) to lose, miss; (*tren*) to miss ◆ *vi* to lose; **~se** *vr* (*extraviarse*) to get lost; (*desaparecer*) to disappear, be lost to view; (*arruinarse*) to be ruined; **echar a ~** (*comida*) to spoil, ruin; (*oportunidad*) to waste; **tener buen ~** to be a good loser; **¡no te lo pierdas!** don't miss it!; **he perdido la costumbre** I have got

out of the habit.

perdición [perði'θjon] *nf* perdition; (*fig*) ruin.

pérdida ['perðiða] *nf* loss; (*de tiempo*) waste; (*COM*) net loss; **~s** *nfpl* (*COM*) losses; **¡no tiene ~!** you can't go wrong!; **~ contable** (*COM*) book loss.

perdido, a [per'ðiðo, a] *a* lost; **estar ~ por** to be crazy about; **es un caso ~** he is a hopeless case.

perdiz [per'ðiθ] *nf* partridge.

perdón [per'ðon] *nm* (*disculpa*) pardon, forgiveness; (*clemencia*) mercy; **¡~!** sorry!, I beg your pardon!; **con ~** if I may, if you don't mind.

perdonar [perðo'nar] *vt* to pardon, forgive; (*la vida*) to spare; (*excusar*) to exempt, excuse ◆ *vi* to pardon, forgive; **¡perdone (usted)!** sorry!, I beg your pardon!; **perdone, pero me parece que ...** excuse me, but I think ...

perdurable [perðu'raβle] *a* lasting; (*eterno*) everlasting.

perdurar [perðu'rar] *vi* (*resistir*) to last, endure; (*seguir existiendo*) to stand, still exist.

perecer [pere'θer] *vi* to perish, die.

peregrinación [pereɣrina'θjon] *nf* (*REL*) pilgrimage.

peregrino, a [pere'ɣrino] *a* (*extraño*) strange; (*singular*) rare ◆ *nm/f* pilgrim.

perejil [pere'xil] *nm* parsley.

perenne [pe'renne] *a* everlasting, perennial.

perentorio, a [peren'torjo, a] *a* (*urgente*) urgent; (*terminante*) peremptory; (*fijo*) set, fixed.

pereza [pe'reθa] *nf* (*flojera*) laziness; (*lentitud*) sloth, slowness.

perezca [pe'reθka] *etc vb* V **perecer.**

perezoso, a [pere'θoso, a] *a* lazy; slow, sluggish.

perfección [perfek'θjon] *nf* perfection; **a la ~** to perfection.

perfeccionar [perfekθjo'nar] *vt* to perfect; (*acabar*) to complete, finish.

perfecto, a [per'fekto, a] *a* perfect ◆ *nm* (*LING*) perfect (tense).

perfidia [per'fiðja] *nf* perfidy, treachery.

pérfido, a ['perfiðo, a] *a* perfidious, treacherous.

perfil [per'fil] *nm* (*parte lateral*) profile; (*silueta*) silhouette, outline; (*TEC*) (cross) section; **~es** *nmpl* features; (*fig*) social graces; **~ del cliente** (*COM*) customer profile; **en ~** from the side, in profile.

perfilado, a [perfi'laðo, a] *a* (*bien formado*) well-shaped; (*largo: cara*) long.

perfilar [perfi'lar] *vt* (*trazar*) to outline; (*dar carácter a*) to shape, give character to; **~se** *vr* to be silhouetted (*en* against); **el proyecto se va perfilando** the project is taking shape.

perforación [perfora'θjon] *nf* perforation; (*con taladro*) drilling.

perforadora [perfora'ðora] *nf* drill; ~ **de fichas** card-punch.

perforar [perfo'rar] *vt* to perforate; (*agujero*) to drill, bore; (*papel*) to punch a hole in ♦ *vi* to drill, bore.

perfumado, a [perfu'maðo, a] *a* scented, perfumed.

perfumar [perfu'mar] *vt* to scent, perfume.

perfume [per'fume] *nm* perfume, scent.

pergamino [perɣa'mino] *nm* parchment.

pericia [pe'riθja] *nf* skill, expertise.

periferia [peri'ferja] *nf* periphery; (*de ciudad*) outskirts *pl*.

periférico, a [peri'feriko, a] *a* peripheral ♦ *nm* (*INFORM*) peripheral; (*AUTO*) ring road; **barrio** ~ outlying district.

perímetro [pe'rimetro] *nm* perimeter.

periódico, a [pe'rjoðiko, a] *a* periodic(al) ♦ *nm* (news)paper; ~ **dominical** Sunday (news)paper.

periodismo [perjo'ðismo] *nm* journalism.

periodista [perjo'ðista] *nm/f* journalist.

periodístico, a [perjo'ðistiko, a] *a* journalistic.

periodo [pe'rjoðo], **período** [pe'rioðo] *nm* period; ~ **contable** (*COM*) accounting period.

peripuesto, a [peri'pwesto, a] *a* dressed up; **tan** ~ all dressed up (to the nines).

perito, a [pe'rito, a] *a* (*experto*) expert; (*diestro*) skilled, skilful ♦ *nm/f* expert; skilled worker; (*técnico*) technician.

perjudicar [perxuði'kar] *vt* (*gen*) to damage, harm; (*fig*) to prejudice.

perjudicial [perxuði'θjal] *a* damaging, harmful; (*en detrimento*) detrimental.

perjudique [perxu'ðike] *etc vb V* **perjudicar.**

perjuicio [per'xwiθjo] *nm* damage, harm; **en/sin** ~ **de** to the detriment of/without prejudice to.

perjurar [perxu'rar] *vi* to commit perjury.

perla ['perla] *nf* pearl; **me viene de** ~**s** it suits me fine.

permanecer [permane'θer] *vi* (*quedarse*) to stay, remain; (*seguir*) to continue to be.

permanencia [perma'nenθja] *nf* (*duración*) permanence; (*estancia*) stay.

permanente [perma'nente] *a* (*que queda*) permanent; (*constante*) constant; (*comisión etc*) standing ♦ *nf* perm; **hacerse una** ~ to have one's hair permed.

permanezca [perma'neθka] *etc vb V* **permanecer.**

permisible [permi'siβle] *a* permissible, allowable.

permiso [per'miso] *nm* permission; (*licencia*) permit, licence (*Brit*), license

(*US*); **con** ~ excuse me; **estar de** ~ (*MIL*) to be on leave; ~ **de conducir** *o* **conductor** driving licence (*Brit*), driver's license (*US*); ~ **de exportación/importación** export/import licence.

permitir [permi'tir] *vt* to permit, allow; ~**se** *vr*: ~**se algo** to allow o.s. sth; **no me puedo** ~ **ese lujo** I can't afford that; **¿me permite?** may I?; **si lo permite el tiempo** weather permitting.

permuta [per'muta] *nf* exchange.

permutar [permu'tar] *vt* to switch, exchange; ~ **destinos con uno** to swap *o* exchange jobs with sb.

pernicioso, a [perni'θjoso, a] *a* (*maligno, MED*) pernicious; (*persona*) wicked.

perno ['perno] *nm* bolt.

pernoctar [pernok'tar] *vi* to stay for the night.

pero ['pero] *conj* but; (*aún*) yet ♦ *nm* (*defecto*) flaw, defect; (*reparo*) objection; **¡no hay** ~ **que valga!** there are no buts about it.

perogrullada [peroɣru'ʎaða] *nf* platitude, truism.

perol [pe'rol] *nm*, **perola** [pe'rola] *nf* pan.

peronista [pero'nista] *a, nm/f* Peronist.

perorar [pero'rar] *vi* to make a speech.

perorata [pero'rata] *nf* long-winded speech.

perpendicular [perpendiku'lar] *a* perpendicular; **el camino es** ~ **al río** the road is at right angles to the river.

perpetrar [perpe'trar] *vt* to perpetrate.

perpetuamente [perpetwa'mente] *ad* perpetually.

perpetuar [perpe'twar] *vt* to perpetuate.

perpetuo, a [per'petwo, a] *a* perpetual; (*JUR etc: condena*) life *cpd*.

Perpiñán [perpi'ɲan] *nm* Perpignan.

perplejo, a [per'plexo, a] *a* perplexed, bewildered.

perra ['perra] *nf* bitch; (*fam: dinero*) money; (: *manía*) mania, crazy idea; (: *rabieta*) tantrum; **estar sin una** ~ to be flat broke.

perrera [pe'rrera] *nf* kennel.

perro ['perro] *nm* dog; ~ **caliente** hot dog; "~ **peligroso**" "beware of the dog''; **ser** ~ **viejo** to be an old hand; **tiempo de** ~**s** filthy weather; ~ **que ladra no muerde** his bark is worse than his bite.

persa ['persa] *a, nm/f* Persian ♦ *nm* (*LING*) Persian.

persecución [perseku'θjon] *nf* pursuit, hunt, chase; (*REL, POL*) persecution.

perseguir [perse'ɣir] *vt* to pursue, hunt; (*cortejar*) to chase after; (*molestar*) to pester, annoy; (*REL, POL*) to persecute; (*JUR*) to prosecute.

perseverante [perseβe'rante] *a* persevering, persistent.

perseverar [perseve'rar] *vi* to persevere, persist; ~ **en** to persevere in, persist with.

persiana [per'sjana] *nf* (Venetian) blind.

persiga [per'siɣa] *etc vb* V **perseguir**.

persignarse [persiɣ'narse] *vr* to cross o.s.

persiguiendo [persi'ɣjenðo] *etc vb* V **perseguir**.

persistente [persis'tente] *a* persistant.

persistir [persis'tir] *vi* to persist.

persona [per'sona] *nf* person; **10** ~**s** 10 people; **tercera** ~ third party; (*LING*) third person; **en** ~ in person *o* the flesh; **por** ~ a head; **es buena** ~ he's a good sort.

personaje [perso'naxe] *nm* important person, celebrity; (*TEATRO*) character.

personal [perso'nal] *a* (*particular*) personal; (*para una persona*) single, for one person ♦ *nm* (*plantilla*) personnel, staff; (*NAUT*) crew; (*fam: gente*) people.

personalidad [personali'ðað] *nf* personality; (*JUR*) status.

personarse [perso'narse] *vr* to appear in person; ~ **en** to present o.s. at, report to.

personificar [personifi'kar] *vt* to personify.

personifique [personi'fike] *etc vb* V **personificar**.

perspectiva [perspek'tiβa] *nf* perspective; (*vista, panorama*) view, panorama; (*posibilidad futura*) outlook, prospect; **tener algo en** ~ to have sth in view.

perspicacia [perspi'kaθja] *nf* discernment, perspicacity.

perspicaz [perspi'kaθ] *a* shrewd.

persuadir [perswa'ðir] *vt* (*gen*) to persuade; (*convencer*) to convince; ~**se** *vr* to become convinced.

persuasión [perswa'sjon] *nf* (*acto*) persuasion; (*convicción*) conviction.

persuasivo, a [perwa'siβo, a] *a* persuasive; convincing.

pertenecer [pertene'θer] *vi*: ~ **a** to belong to; (*fig*) to concern.

perteneciente [pertene'θjente] *a*: ~ **a** belonging to.

pertenencia [perte'nenθja] *nf* ownership; ~**s** *nfpl* possessions, property *sg*.

pertenezca [perte'neθka] *etc vb* V **pertenecer**.

pértiga ['pertiɣa] *nf* pole; **salto de** ~ pole vault.

pertinaz [perti'naθ] *a* (*persistente*) persistent; (*terco*) obstinate.

pertinente [perti'nente] *a* relevant, pertinent; (*apropiado*) appropriate; ~ **a** concerning, relevant to.

pertrechar [pertre'tʃar] *vt* (*gen*) to supply; (*MIL*) to supply with ammunition and stores; ~**se** *vr*: ~**se de algo** to provide o.s. with sth.

pertrechos [per'tretʃos] *nmpl* (*gen*) implements; (*MIL*) supplies and stores.

perturbación [perturβa'θjon] *nf* (*POL*) disturbance; (*MED*) upset, disturbance; ~ **del orden público** breach of the peace.

perturbador, a [perturβa'ðor, a] *a* (*que perturba*) perturbing, disturbing; (*subversivo*) subversive.

perturbar [pertur'βar] *vt* (*el orden*) to disturb; (*MED*) to upset, disturb; (*mentalmente*) to perturb.

Perú [pe'ru] *nm*: **el** ~ Peru.

peruano, a [pe'rwano, a] *a, nm/f* Peruvian.

perversión [perβer'sjon] *nf* perversion.

perverso, a [per'βerso, a] *a* perverse; (*depravado*) depraved.

pervertido, a [perβer'tiðo, a] *a* perverted ♦ *nm/f* pervert.

pervertir [perβer'tir] *vt* to pervert, corrupt.

pervierta [per'βjerta] *etc*, **pervirtiendo** [perβir'tjendo] *etc vb* V **pervertir**.

pesa ['pesa] *nf* weight; (*DEPORTE*) shot.

pesadez [pesa'ðeθ] *nf* (*calidad de pesado*) heaviness; (*lentitud*) slowness; (*aburrimiento*) tediousness; **es una** ~ **tener que ...** it's a bind having to ...

pesadilla [pesa'ðiʎa] *nf* nightmare, bad dream; (*fig*) worry, obsession.

pesado, a [pe'saðo, a] *a* (*gen*) heavy; (*lento*) slow; (*difícil, duro*) tough, hard; (*aburrido*) tedious, boring; (*bochornoso*) sultry ♦ *nm/f* bore; **tener el estómago** ~ to feel bloated; **¡no seas** ~**!** come off it!

pesadumbre [pesa'ðumbre] *nf* grief, sorrow.

pésame ['pesame] *nm* expression of condolence, message of sympathy; **dar el** ~ to express one's condolences.

pesar [pe'sar] *vt* to weigh; (*fig*) to weigh heavily on; (*afligir*) to grieve ♦ *vi* to weigh; (*ser pesado*) to weigh a lot, be heavy; (*fig: opinión*) to carry weight ♦ *nm* (*sentimiento*) regret; (*pena*) grief, sorrow; **a** ~ **de (que)** in spite of, despite; **no me pesa haberlo hecho** I'm not sorry I did it.

pesca ['peska] *nf* (*acto*) fishing; (*cantidad de pescado*) catch; ~ **de altura/en bajura** deep sea/coastal fishing; **ir de** ~ to go fishing.

pescadería [peskaðe'ria] *nf* fish shop, fishmonger's.

pescadilla [peska'ðiʎa] *nf* whiting.

pescado [pes'kaðo] *nm* fish.

pescador, a [peska'ðor, a] *nm/f* fisherman/woman.

pescar [pes'kar] *vt* (*coger*) to catch; (*tratar de coger*) to fish for; (*fam: lograr*) to get hold of, land; (*conseguir: trabajo*) to manage to get; (*sorprender*) to catch unawares ♦ *vi* to fish, go fishing.

pescuezo [pes'kweθo] *nm* neck.

pese ['pese] *prep*: ~ **a** despite, in spite of.

pesebre [pe'seβre] *nm* manger.

peseta [pe'seta] *nf* peseta.

pesetero, a [pese'tero, a] *a* money-grubbing.

pesimista [pesi'mista] *a* pessimistic ◆ *nm/f* pessimist.

pésimo, a ['pesimo, a] *a* abominable, vile.

peso ['peso] *nm* weight; (*balanza*) scales *pl*; (*AM COM*) *monetary unit*; (*moneda*) peso; (*DEPORTE*) shot; ~ **bruto/neto** gross/net weight; **de poco** ~ light(weight); **levantamiento de** ~**s** weightlifting; **vender a** ~ to sell by weight; **argumento de** ~ weighty argument; **eso cae de su** ~ that goes without saying.

pesque ['peske] *etc vb V* **pescar**.

pesquero, a [pes'kero, a] *a* fishing *cpd*.

pesquisa [pes'kisa] *nf* inquiry, investigation.

pestaña [pes'taɲa] *nf* (*ANAT*) eyelash; (*borde*) rim.

pestañear [pestaɲe'ar] *vi* to blink.

peste ['peste] *nf* plague; (*fig*) nuisance; (*mal olor*) stink, stench; ~ **negra** Black Death; **echar** ~**s** to swear, fume.

pesticida [pesti'θiða] *nm* pesticide.

pestilencia [pesti'lenθja] *nf* (*mal olor*) stink, stench.

pestillo [pes'tiʎo] *nm* bolt, latch; (*cerrojo*) catch; (*picaporte*) (door) handle.

petaca [pe'taka] *nf* (*de cigarrillos*) cigarette case; (*de pipa*) tobacco pouch; (*AM: maleta*) suitcase.

pétalo ['petalo] *nm* petal.

petardo [pe'tarðo] *nm* firework, firecracker.

petición [peti'θjon] *nf* (*pedido*) request, plea; (*memorial*) petition; (*JUR*) plea; **a** ~ **de** at the request of; ~ **de aumento de salarios** wage demand *o* claim.

petirrojo [peti'rroxo] *nm* robin.

peto ['peto] *nm* (*corpiño*) bodice; (*TAUR*) horse's padding.

pétreo, a ['petreo, a] *a* stony, rocky.

petrificar [petrifi'kar] *vt* to petrify.

petrifique [petri'fike] *etc vb V* **petrificar**.

petrodólar [petro'ðolar] *nm* petrodollar.

petróleo [pe'troleo] *nm* oil, petroleum.

petrolero, a [petro'lero, a] *a* petroleum *cpd* ◆ *nm* (*COM*) oil man; (*buque*) (oil) tanker.

petulancia [petu'lanθja] *nf* (*insolencia*) vanity, opinionated nature.

peyorativo, a [pejora'tiβo, a] *a* pejorative.

pez [peθ] *nm* fish; ~ **de colores** goldfish; ~ **espada** swordfish; **estar como el** ~ **en el agua** to feel completely at home.

pezón [pe'θon] *nm* teat, nipple.

pezuña [pe'θuɲa] *nf* hoof.

piadoso, a [pja'ðoso, a] *a* (*devoto*) pious, devout; (*misericordioso*) kind, merciful.

Piamonte [pja'monte] *nm* Piedmont.

pianista [pja'nista] *nm/f* pianist.

piano ['pjano] *nm* piano; ~ **de cola** grand piano.

piar [pjar] *vi* to cheep.

piara ['pjara] *nf* (*manada*) herd, drove.

PIB *nm abr* (*Esp COM*: = *Producto Interno Bruto*) GDP.

pibe, a ['piβe, a] *nm/f* (*AM*) boy/girl, kid, child.

pica ['pika] *nf* (*MIL*) pike; (*TAUR*) goad; **poner una** ~ **en Flandes** to bring off something difficult.

picadero [pika'ðero] *nm* riding school.

picadillo [pika'ðiʎo] *nm* mince, minced meat.

picado, a [pi'kaðo, a] *a* pricked, punctured; (*mar*) choppy; (*diente*) bad; (*tabaco*) cut; (*enfadado*) cross.

picador [pika'ðor] *nm* (*TAUR*) picador; (*minero*) faceworker.

picadura [pika'ðura] *nf* (*pinchazo*) puncture; (*de abeja*) sting; (*de mosquito*) bite; (*tabaco picado*) cut tobacco.

picante [pi'kante] *a* (*comida, sabor*) hot; (*comentario*) racy, spicy.

picaporte [pika'porte] *nm* (*tirador*) handle; (*pestillo*) latch.

picar [pi'kar] *vt* (*agujerear, perforar*) to prick, puncture; (*billete*) to punch, clip; (*abeja*) to sting; (*mosquito, serpiente*) to bite; (*persona*) to nibble (at); (*incitar*) to incite, goad; (*dañar, irritar*) to annoy, bother; (*quemar: lengua*) to burn, sting ◆ *vi* (*pez*) to bite, take the bait; (*el sol*) to burn, scorch; (*abeja, MED*) to sting; (*mosquito*) to bite; ~**se** *vr* (*agriarse*) to turn sour, go off; (*mar*) to get choppy; (*ofenderse*) to take offence; **me pican los ojos** my eyes sting; **me pica el brazo** my arm itches.

picardía [pikar'ðia] *nf* villainy; (*astucia*) slyness, craftiness; (*una* ~) dirty trick; (*palabra*) rude/bad word *o* expression.

picaresco, a [pika'resko, a] *a* (*travieso*) roguish, rascally; (*LIT*) picaresque.

pícaro, a ['pikaro, a] *a* (*malicioso*) villainous; (*travieso*) mischievous ◆ *nm* (*astuto*) sly sort; (*sinvergüenza*) rascal, scoundrel.

picazón [pika'θon] *nf* (*comezón*) itch; (*ardor*) sting(ing feeling); (*remordimiento*) pang of conscience.

pico ['piko] *nm* (*de ave*) beak; (*punto agudo*) peak, sharp point; (*TEC*) pick, pickaxe; (*GEO*) peak, summit; (*labia*) talkativeness; **no abrir el** ~ to keep quiet; ~ **parásito** (*ELEC*) spike; **y** ~ and a bit; **son las 3 y** ~ it's just after 3; **tiene 50 libros y** ~ he has 50-odd books; **me costó un** ~ it cost me quite a bit.

picor [pi'kor] *nm* itch; (*ardor*) sting(ing feeling).

picota [pi'kota] *nf* pillory; **poner a uno en la** ~ (*fig*) to ridicule sb.

picotada [piko'taða] *nf*, **picotazo**

[piko'taθo] *nm* (*de pájaro*) peck; (*de insecto*) sting, bite.

picotear [pikote'ar] *vt* to peck ◆ *vi* to nibble, pick.

pictórico, a [pik'toriko, a] *a* pictorial; **tiene dotes pictóricas** she has a talent for painting.

picudo, a [pi'kuðo, a] *a* pointed, with a point.

pichón, ona [pi'tʃon, ona] *nm/f* (*paloma*) young pigeon; (*apelativo*) darling, dearest.

pidiendo [pi'ðjendo] *etc vb* V **pedir**.

pie [pje] (*pl* ~**s**) *nm* (*gen*, *MAT*) foot; (*de cama*, *página*, *escalera*) foot, bottom; (*TEATRO*) cue; (*fig*: *motivo*) motive, basis; (: *fundamento*) foothold; ~**s planos** flat feet; **ir a** ~ to go on foot, walk; **estar de** ~ to be standing (up); **ponerse de** ~ to stand up; **al** ~ **de la letra** (*citar*) literally, verbatim; (*copiar*) exactly, word for word; **de** ~**s a cabeza** from head to foot; **en** ~ **de guerra** on a war footing; **sin** ~**s ni cabeza** pointless, absurd; **dar** ~ **a** to give cause for; **no dar** ~ **con bola** to be no good at anything; **saber de qué** ~ **cojea uno** to know sb's weak spots.

piedad [pje'ðað] *nf* (*lástima*) pity, compassion; (*clemencia*) mercy; (*devoción*) piety, devotion; **tener** ~ **de** to take pity on.

piedra ['pjeðra] *nf* stone; (*roca*) rock; (*de mechero*) flint; (*METEOROLOGÍA*) hailstone; **primera** ~ foundation stone; ~ **de afilar** grindstone; ~ **arenisca/caliza** sand-/limestone.

piel [pjel] *nf* (*ANAT*) skin; (*ZOOL*) skin, hide; (*de oso*) fur; (*cuero*) leather; (*BOT*) skin, peel ◆ *nm/f*: ~ **roja** redskin.

pienso ['pjenso] *etc vb* V **pensar** ◆ *nm* (*AGR*) feed.

pierda ['pjerða] *etc vb* V **perder**.

pierna ['pjerna] *nf* leg; **en** ~**s** bare-legged.

pieza ['pjeθa] *nf* piece; (*habitación*) room; (*MUS*) piece, composition; (*TEATRO*) work, play; ~ **de recambio** o **repuesto** spare (part), extra (*US*); ~ **de ropa** article of clothing; **quedarse de una** ~ to be dumbfounded.

pigmeo, a [piɣ'meo, a] *a*, *nm/f* pigmy.

pija ['pixa] *nf* V **pijo, a**.

pijama [pi'xama] *nm* pyjamas *pl*.

pijo, a ['pixo, a] *nm/f* (*fam*) upper-class twit.

pijotada [pixo'taða] *nf* nuisance.

pila ['pila] *nf* (*ELEC*) battery; (*montón*) heap, pile; (*fuente*) sink; (*REL*: *tb*: ~ **bautismal**) font; **nombre de** ~ Christian o first name; **tengo una** ~ **de cosas que hacer** (*fam*) I have heaps o stacks of things to do; ~ **de discos** (*INFORM*) disk pack.

pilar [pi'lar] *nm* pillar; (*de puente*) pier; (*fig*) prop, mainstay.

píldora ['pildora] *nf* pill; **la** ~ (**anticonceptiva**) the pill; **tragarse la** ~ to be taken in.

pileta [pi'leta] *nf* basin, bowl; (*AM*) swimming pool.

pilón [pi'lon] *nm* pillar, post; (*ELEC*) pylon; (*bebedero*) drinking trough; (*de fuente*) basin.

piloto [pi'loto] *nm* pilot; (*AUTO*) rear light, tail light; (*conductor*) driver ◆ *a inv*: **planta** ~ pilot plant; **luz** ~ side light.

piltrafa [pil'trafa] *nf* (*carne*) poor quality meat; (*fig*) worthless object; (: *individuo*) wretch.

pillaje [pi'ʎaxe] *nm* pillage, plunder.

pillar [pi'ʎar] *vt* (*fam*: *coger*) to catch; (: *agarrar*) to grasp, seize; (: *entender*) to grasp, catch on to; (*suj*: *coche etc*) to run over; ~ **un resfriado** (*fam*) to catch a cold.

pillo, a ['piʎo, a] *a* villainous; (*astuto*) sly, crafty ◆ *nm/f* rascal, rogue, scoundrel.

pimentón [pimen'ton] *nm* (*polvo*) paprika.

pimienta [pi'mjenta] *nf* pepper.

pimiento [pi'mjento] *nm* pepper, pimiento.

pimpante [pim'pante] *a* (*encantador*) charming; (*tb*: **tan** ~) smug, self-satisfied.

PIN *nm abr* (*Esp COM*: = *Producto Interior Neto*) net domestic product.

pinacoteca [pinako'teka] *nf* art gallery.

pinar [pi'nar] *nm* pinewood.

pincel [pin'θel] *nm* paintbrush.

pincelada [pinθe'laða] *nf* brushstroke; **última** ~ (*fig*) finishing touch.

pinchar [pin'tʃar] *vt* (*perforar*) to prick, pierce; (*neumático*) to puncture; (*incitar*) to prod; ~**se** *vr* (*con droga*) to inject o.s.; (*neumático*) to burst, puncture; **no** ~ **ni cortar** (*fam*) to cut no ice; **tener un neumático pinchado** to have a puncture o a flat tyre.

pinchazo [pin'tʃaθo] *nm* (*perforación*) prick; (*de llanta*) puncture, flat (*US*).

pinche ['pintʃe] *nm* (*de cocina*) kitchen boy, scullion.

pinchito [pin'tʃito] *nm* shish kebab.

pincho ['pintʃo] *nm* point; (*aguijón*) spike; (*CULIN*) savoury (snack); ~ **moruno** shish kebab; ~ **de tortilla** small slice of omelette.

pingüe ['pingwe] *a* (*grasoso*) greasy; (*cosecha*) bumper *cpd*; (*negocio*) lucrative.

pingüino [pin'gwino] *nm* penguin.

pino ['pino] *nm* pine (tree); **vivir en el quinto** ~ to live at the back of beyond.

pinta ['pinta] *nf* spot; (*gota*) spot, drop; (*aspecto*) appearance, look(s) (*pl*); (*medida*) pint; **tener buena** ~ to look good, look well; **por la** ~ by the look of it.

pintadas [pin'taðas] *nfpl* political graffiti.

pintado, a [pin'taðo, a] *a* spotted; (*de muchos colores*) colourful; **me sienta que ni**

~, **viene que ni** ~ it suits me a treat.

pintar [pin'tar] *vt* to paint ◆ *vi* to paint; (*fam*) to count, be important; ~**se** *vr* to put on make-up; **pintárselas solo para hacer algo** to manage to do sth by o.s.; **no pinta nada** (*fam*) he has no say.

pintor, a [pin'tor, a] *nm/f* painter; ~ **de brocha gorda** house painter; (*fig*) bad painter.

pintoresco, a [pinto'resko, a] *a* picturesque.

pintura [pin'tura] *nf* painting; ~ **a la acuarela** watercolour; ~ **al óleo** oil painting; ~ **rupestre** cave painting.

pinza ['pinθa] *nf* (*ZOOL*) claw; (*para colgar ropa*) clothes peg, clothespin (*US*); (*TEC*) pincers *pl*; ~**s** *nfpl* (*para depilar*) tweezers.

piña ['pina] *nf* (*fruto del pino*) pine cone; (*fruta*) pineapple; (*fig*) group.

piñón [pi'non] *nm* (*BOT*) pine nut; (*TEC*) pinion.

PIO *nm abr* (*Esp*: = *Patronato de Igualdad de Oportunidades*) ≈ Equal Opportunities Board.

pío, a ['pio, a] *a* (*devoto*) pious, devout; (*misericordioso*) merciful ◆ *nm*: **no decir ni** ~ not to breathe a word.

piojo ['pjoxo] *nm* louse.

piojoso, a [pjo'xoso, a] *a* lousy; (*sucio*) dirty.

piolet [pjo'le], *pl* ~**s** [-s] *nm* ice axe.

pionero, a [pjo'nero, a] *a* pioneering ◆ *nm/f* pioneer.

pipa ['pipa] *nf* pipe; (*BOT*) seed, pip.

pipí [pi'pi] *nm* (*fam*): **hacer** ~ to have a wee(-wee).

pipiolo [pi'pjolo] *nm* youngster; (*novato*) novice, greenhorn.

pique ['pike] *etc vb V* **picar** ◆ *nm* (*resentimiento*) pique, resentment; (*rivalidad*) rivalry, competition; **irse a** ~ to sink; (*familia*) to be ruined; **tener un** ~ **con uno** to have a grudge against sb.

piqueta [pi'keta] *nf* pick(axe).

piquete [pi'kete] *nm* (*agujerito*) small hole; (*MIL*) squad, party; (*de obreros*) picket; ~ **secundario** secondary picket.

pirado, a [pi'raðo, a] *a* (*fam*) round the bend.

piragua [pi'raɣwa] *nf* canoe.

piragüismo [pira'ɣwismo] *nm* (*DEPORTE*) canoeing.

pirámide [pi'ramiðe] *nf* pyramid.

pirarse [pi'rarse] *vr*: ~**(las)** (*largarse*) to beat it (*fam*); (*ESCOL*) to cut class.

pirata [pi'rata] *a*: **edición/disco** ~ pirate edition/bootleg record ◆ *nm* pirate; (*INFORM*) hacker.

pirenaico, a [pire'naiko, a] *a* Pyrenean.

Pirineo(s) [piri'neo(s)] *nm(pl)* Pyrenees *pl*.

piropo [pi'ropo] *nm* compliment, (piece of)

flattery; **echar** ~**s a** to make flirtatious remarks to.

pirulí [piru'li] *nm* toffee apple; (*AM*) lollipop.

pisada [pi'saða] *nf* (*paso*) footstep; (*huella*) footprint.

pisar [pi'sar] *vt* (*caminar sobre*) to walk on, tread on; (*apretar con el pie*) to press; (*fig*) to trample on, walk all over ◆ *vi* to tread, step, walk; ~ **el acelerador** to step on the accelerator; ~ **fuerte** (*fig*) to act determinedly.

piscina [pis'θina] *nf* swimming pool.

Piscis ['pisθis] *nm* (*ASTRO*) Pisces.

piso ['piso] *nm* (*suelo, de edificio*) floor; (*apartamento*) flat, apartment; **primer** ~ (*Esp*) first *o* second (*US*) floor; (*AM*) ground *o* first (*US*) floor.

pisotear [pisote'ar] *vt* to trample (on *o* underfoot); (*fig: humillar*) to trample on.

pisotón [piso'ton] *nm* (*con el pie*) stamp.

pista ['pista] *nf* track, trail; (*indicio*) clue; (*INFORM*) track; ~ **de auditoría** (*COM*) audit trail; ~ **de aterrizaje** runway; ~ **de baile** dance floor; ~ **de tenis** tennis court; ~ **de hielo** ice rink; **estar sobre la** ~ **de uno** to be on sb's trail.

pistola [pis'tola] *nf* pistol; (*TEC*) spray-gun.

pistolero, a [pisto'lero, a] *nm/f* gunman, gangster ◆ *nf* holster.

pistón [pis'ton] *nm* (*TEC*) piston; (*MUS*) key.

pitar [pi'tar] *vt* (*hacer sonar*) to blow; (*partido*) to referee; (*rechiflar*) to whistle at, boo; (*actor, obra*) to hiss ◆ *vi* to whistle; (*AUTO*) to sound *o* toot one's horn; (*AM*) to smoke; **salir pitando** to beat it.

pitido [pi'tiðo] *nm* whistle.

pitillo [pi'tiʎo] *nm* cigarette.

pito ['pito] *nm* whistle; (*de coche*) horn; (*cigarrillo*) cigarette; (*fam: de marijuana*) joint; (*fam!*) prick (*!*); **me importa un** ~ I don't care two hoots.

pitón [pi'ton] *nm* (*ZOOL*) python.

pitonisa [pito'nisa] *nf* fortune-teller.

pitorrearse [pitorre'arse] *vr*: ~ **de** to scoff at, make fun of.

pitorreo [pito'rreo] *nm* joke, laugh; **estar de** ~ to be in a joking mood.

píxel ['piksel] *nm* (*INFORM*) pixel.

pizarra [pi'θarra] *nf* (*piedra*) slate; (*encerado*) blackboard.

pizca ['piθka] *nf* pinch, spot; (*fig*) spot, speck, trace; **ni** ~ not a bit.

placa ['plaka] *nf* plate; (*MED*) dental plate; (*distintivo*) badge; ~ **de matrícula** number plate; ~ **madre** (*INFORM*) mother board.

placentero, a [plaθen'tero, a] *a* pleasant, agreeable.

placer [pla'θer] *nm* pleasure; **a** ~ at one's pleasure.

plácido, a ['plaθiðo, a] *a* placid.

plaga ['plaɣa] *nf* pest; (*MED*) plague; (*fig*) swarm.

plagar [pla'ɣar] *vt* to infest, plague; (*llenar*) to fill; **plagado de** riddled with; **han plagado la ciudad de carteles** they have plastered the town with posters.

plagio ['plaxjo] *nm* plagiarism.

plague ['plaɣe] *etc vb* V **plagar**.

plan [plan] *nm* (*esquema, proyecto*) plan; (*idea, intento*) idea, intention; (*de curso*) programme; ~ **cotizable de jubilación** contributory pension scheme; ~ **de estudios** curriculum, syllabus; ~ **de incentivos** (*COM*) incentive scheme; **tener** ~ (*fam*) to have a date; **tener un** ~ (*fam*) to have an affair; **en** ~ **cachondeo** for a laugh; **en** ~ **económico** (*fam*) on the cheap; **vamos en** ~ **de turismo** we're going as tourists; **si te pones en ese** ~ ... if that's your attitude ...

plana ['plana] *nf* V **plano**.

plancha ['plantʃa] *nf* (*para planchar*) iron; (*rótulo*) plate, sheet; (*NAUT*) gangway; (*CULIN*) grill; **pescado a la** ~ grilled fish.

planchado, a [plan'tʃaðo, a] *a* (*ropa*) ironed; (*traje*) pressed ♦ *nm* ironing.

planchar [plan'tʃar] *vt* to iron ♦ *vi* to do the ironing.

planeador [planea'ðor] *nm* glider.

planear [plane'ar] *vt* to plan ♦ *vi* to glide.

planeta [pla'neta] *nm* planet.

planetario, a [plane'tarjo, a] *a* planetary ♦ *nm* planetarium.

planicie [pla'niθje] *nf* plain.

planificación [planifika'θjon] *nf* planning; ~ **corporativa** (*COM*) corporate planning; ~ **familiar** family planning; **diagrama de** ~ (*COM*) planner.

plano, a ['plano, a] *a* flat, level, even; (*liso*) smooth ♦ *nm* (*MAT, TEC, AVIAT*) plane; (*FOTO*) shot; (*ARQ*) plan; (*GEO*) map; (*de ciudad*) map, street plan ♦ *nf* sheet of paper, page; (*TEC*) trowel **primer** ~ close-up; **caer de** ~ to fall flat; **rechazar algo de** ~ to turn sth down flat; **le daba el sol de** ~ (*fig*) the sun shone directly on it; **en primera plana** on the front page; **plana mayor** staff.

planta ['planta] *nf* (*BOT, TEC*) plant; (*ANAT*) sole of the foot, foot; (*AM: personal*) permanent staff; ~ **baja** ground floor.

plantación [planta'θjon] *nf* (*AGR*) plantation; (*acto*) planting.

plantar [plan'tar] *vt* (*BOT*) to plant; (*puesto*) to put in; (*levantar*) to erect, set up; ~**se** *vr* to stand firm; ~ **a uno en la calle** to chuck sb out; **dejar plantado a uno** (*fam*) to stand sb up; ~**se en** to reach, get to.

plantear [plante'ar] *vt* (*problema*) to pose; (*dificultad*) to raise; **se lo plantearé** I'll put it to him.

plantel [plan'tel] *nm* (*fig*) group, set.

plantilla [plan'tiʎa] *nf* (*de zapato*) insole; (*personal*) personnel; **ser de** ~ to be on the staff.

plantío [plan'tio] *nm* (*acto*) planting; (*lugar*) plot, bed, patch.

plantón [plan'ton] *nm* (*MIL*) guard, sentry; (*fam*) long wait; **dar (un)** ~ **a uno** to stand sb up.

plañir [pla'ɲir] *vi* to mourn.

plasmar [plas'mar] *vt* (*dar forma*) to mould, shape; (*representar*) to represent ♦ *vi*: ~ **en** to take the form of.

plasta ['plasta] *nf* soft mass, lump; (*desastre*) botch, mess.

plasticidad [plastiθi'ðað] *nf* (*fig*) expressiveness.

plasticina [plasti'θina], (*AM*) **plastilina** [plasti'lina] *nf* Plasticine ®.

plástico, a ['plastiko, a] *a* plastic ♦ *nf* (art of) sculpture, modelling ♦ *nm* plastic.

plastificar [plastifi'kar] *vt* (*documento*) to laminate.

plastifique [plasti'fike] *etc vb* V **plastificar**.

plata ['plata] *nf* (*metal*) silver; (*cosas hechas de plata*) silverware; (*AM*) cash, dough (*fam*); **hablar en** ~ to speak bluntly *o* frankly.

plataforma [plata'forma] *nf* platform; ~ **de lanzamiento/perforación** launch(ing) pad/ drilling rig.

plátano ['platano] *nm* (*fruta*) banana; (*árbol*) plane tree.

platea [pla'tea] *nf* (*TEATRO*) pit.

plateado, a [plate'aðo, a] *a* silver; (*TEC*) silver-plated.

platense [pla'tense] (*fam*) = **ríoplatense**.

plática ['platika] *nf* talk, chat; (*REL*) sermon.

platicar [plati'kar] *vi* to talk, chat.

platillo [pla'tiʎo] *nm* saucer; (*de limosnas*) collecting bowl; ~**s** *nmpl* cymbals; ~ **volador** *o* **volante** flying saucer; **pasar el** ~ to pass the hat round.

platino [pla'tino] *nm* platinum; ~**s** *nmpl* (*AUTO*) (contact) points.

platique [pla'tike] *etc vb* V **platicar**.

plato ['plato] *nm* plate, dish; (*parte de comida*) course; (*guiso*) dish; ~ **sopero** fruit/soup dish; **pagar los** ~**s rotos** (*fam*) to carry the can (*fam*).

playa ['plaja] *nf* beach; (*costa*) seaside; ~ **de estacionamiento** (*AM*) car park.

playera [pla'jera] *nf* (*AM: camiseta*) T-shirt; ~**s** *nfpl* canvas shoes; (*TENIS*) tennis shoes.

plaza ['plaθa] *nf* square; (*mercado*) market(place); (*sitio*) room, space; (*en vehículo*) seat, place; (*colocación*) post, job; ~ **de abastos** food market; ~ **mayor** main square; ~ **de toros** bullring; **hacer la** ~ to do the daily shopping; **reservar una** ~ to reserve a seat; **el hotel tiene 100** ~**s** the hotel has 100 beds.

plazca ['plaθka] *etc vb* V **placer**.

plazo ['plaθo] *nm* (*lapso de tiempo*) time, period, term; (*fecha de vencimiento*) expiry date; (*pago parcial*) instalment; **a corto/largo** ~ short-/long-term; **comprar a** ~**s** to buy on hire purchase, pay for in instalments; **nos dan un** ~ **de 8 días** they allow us a week.

plazoleta [plaθo'leta], **plazuela** [pla'θwela] *nf* small square.

pleamar [plea'mar] *nf* high tide.

plebe ['pleβe] *nf*: **la** ~ the common people *pl*, the masses *pl*; (*pey*) the plebs *pl*.

plebeyo, a [ple'βejo, a] *a* plebeian; (*pey*) coarse, common.

plebiscito [pleβis'θito] *nm* plebiscite.

pleca ['pleka] *nf* (*INFORM*) backslash.

plegable [ple'ɣaβle] *a* pliable; (*silla*) folding.

plegar [ple'ɣar] *vt* (*doblar*) to fold, bend; (*COSTURA*) to pleat; ~**se** *vr* to yield, submit.

plegaria [ple'ɣarja] *nf* (*oración*) prayer.

plegué, [ple'ɣe] **pleguemos** [ple'ɣemos] *etc vb* V **plegar**.

pleitear [pleite'ar] *vi* (*JUR*) to plead, conduct a lawsuit; (*litigar*) to go to law.

pleito ['pleito] *nm* (*JUR*) lawsuit, case; (*fig*) dispute, feud; ~**s** *nmpl* litigation *sg*; **entablar** ~ to bring an action *o* a lawsuit; **poner** ~ to sue.

plenario, a [ple'narjo, a] *a* plenary, full.

plenilunio [pleni'lunjo] *nm* full moon.

plenitud [pleni'tuð] *nf* plenitude, fullness; (*abundancia*) abundance.

pleno, a ['pleno, a] *a* full; (*completo*) complete ♦ *nm* plenum; **en** ~ as a whole; (*por unanimidad*) unanimously; **en** ~ **día** in broad daylight; **en** ~ **verano** at the height of summer; **en plena cara** full in the face.

pleuresía [pleure'sia] *nf* pleurisy.

plexiglás [pleksi'ɣlas] *nm* acrylic.

plica ['plika] *nf* sealed envelope *o* document; (*en un concurso*) sealed entry.

pliego ['pljeɣo] *etc vb* V **plegar** ♦ *nm* (*hoja*) sheet (of paper); (*carta*) sealed letter/document; ~ **de condiciones** details *pl*, specifications *pl*.

pliegue ['pljeɣe] *etc vb* V **plegar** ♦ *nm* fold, crease; (*de vestido*) pleat.

plisado [pli'saðo] *nm* pleating.

plomero [plo'mero] *nm* plumber.

plomizo, a [plo'miθo, a] *a* leaden, lead-coloured.

plomo ['plomo] *nm* (*metal*) lead; (*ELEC*) fuse; **caer a** ~ to fall heavily *o* flat.

pluma ['pluma] *nf* (*ZOOL*) feather; ~ **estilográfica,** ~ **fuente** (*AM*) fountain pen.

plumazo [plu'maθo] *nm* (*lit, fig*) stroke of the pen.

plumero [plu'mero] *nm* (*quitapolvos*) feather duster; **ya te veo el** ~ I know what you're up to.

plumón [plu'mon] *nm* (*AM*: *fino*) felt-tip pen; (*: ancho*) marker.

plural [plu'ral] *a* plural ♦ *nm*: **en** ~ in the plural.

pluralidad [plurali'ðað] *nf* plurality; **una** ~ **de votos** a majority of votes.

pluriempleo [pluriem'pleo] *nm* moonlighting.

plus [plus] *nm* bonus.

plusmarquista [plusmar'kista] *nm/f* (*DEPORTE*) record holder.

plusvalía [plusßa'lia] *nf* (*mayor valor*) appreciation, added value; (*COM*) goodwill.

plutocracia [pluto'kraθja] *nf* plutocracy.

PM *nf abr* (*MIL*: = *Policía Militar*) MP.

p.m. *abr* (= *post meridiem*) p.m.; (= *por minuto*) per minute.

PMA *nm abr* (= *Programa Mundial de Alimentos*) World Food Programme.

pmo. *abr* (= *próximo*) prox.

PN *nf abr* (*MIL*: = *Policía Naval*) Naval Police.

PNB *nm abr* (*Esp COM*: = *producto nacional bruto*) GNP.

P.N.D. *nm abr* (*ESCOL*: = *personal no docente*) non-teaching staff.

PNN *nm/f abr* (= *profesor no numerario*) untenured teacher; (*Esp COM*: = *producto nacional neto*) net national product.

PNUD *nm abr* (= *Programa de las Naciones Unidas para el Desarrollo*) United Nations Development Programme.

PNV *nm abr* (*Esp POL*) = *Partido Nacional Vasco*.

P.º *abr* (= *Paseo*) Av(e).

p.o. *abr* = **por orden**.

población [poßla'θjon] *nf* population; (*pueblo, ciudad*) town, city; ~ **activa** working population.

poblado, a [po'ßlaðo, a] *a* inhabited; (*barba*) thick; (*cejas*) bushy ♦ *nm* (*aldea*) village; (*pueblo*) (small) town; ~ **de** (*lleno*) filled with; **densamente** ~ densely populated.

poblador, a [poßla'ðor, a] *nm/f* settler, colonist.

poblar [po'ßlar] *vt* (*colonizar*) to colonize; (*fundar*) to found; (*habitar*) to inhabit; ~**se** *vr*: ~**se de** to fill up with; (*irse cubriendo*) to become covered with.

pobre ['poßre] *a* poor ♦ *nm/f* poor person; (*mendigo*) beggar; **los** ~**s** the poor; ¡~! poor thing!; ~ **diablo** (*fig*) poor wretch *o* devil.

pobreza [po'ßreθa] *nf* poverty.

pocilga [po'θilɣa] *nf* pigsty.

pócima ['poθima], **poción** [po'θjon] *nf* potion; (*brebaje*) concoction, nasty drink.

pocito [po'sito] *nf* (*AM*) coffee cup.

poco, a ['poko, a] *a* little; (*escaso*) slight, scanty; ~**s** few ♦ *ad* (*no mucho*) little, not much ♦ *nm*: **un** ~ a little, a bit; **tener a uno en** ~ to think little *o* not think much of sb; **por** ~ almost, nearly; ~ **a** ~ little by little, gradually; **a** ~ **de hacer** shortly after doing; **dentro de** ~ (+ *presente o futuro*) shortly; (+ *pasado*) soon after; **hace** ~ a short time ago, not long ago; ~ **más o menos** more or less.

pocho, a ['potʃo, a] *a* (*flor, color*) faded, discoloured; (*persona*) pale; (*fruta*) over-ripe; (*deprimido*) depressed.

poda ['poða] *nf* (*acto*) pruning; (*temporada*) pruning season.

podar [po'ðar] *vt* to prune.

podenco [po'ðenko] *nm* hound.

poder [po'ðer] *vi* can; (*sujeto: persona*) to be able to, can; (*permiso*) can, may; (*posibilidad, hipótesis*) may ♦ *nm* (*gen, JUR, POL*) power; (*autoridad*) authority; **¡puede!** who knows!, maybe!; **puede que sea así** it may be, maybe; **¿se puede?** may I come in?; **¿puedes con eso?** can you manage that?; **el dinero puede mucho** money talks; **A le puede a B** (*fam*) A is more than a match for B; **a más no** ~ to the utmost; **no** ~ **menos de hacer algo** not to be able to help doing sth; **no** ~ **más** to have had enough; ~ **adquisitivo** purchasing power; ~ **ejecutivo/legislativo** executive/legislative power; **estar en el** ~, **ocupar el** ~ to be in power; **por** ~**(es)** by proxy.

poderío [poðe'rio] *nm* power; (*autoridad*) authority.

poderoso, a [poðe'roso, a] *a* powerful.

podré [po'ðre] *etc vb V* **poder**.

podrido, a [po'ðriðo, a] *a* rotten, bad; (*fig*) rotten, corrupt.

podrir [po'ðrir] = **pudrir**.

poema [po'ema] *nm* poem.

poesía [poe'sia] *nf* poetry.

poeta [po'eta] *nm* poet.

poético, a [po'etiko, a] *a* poetic(al).

poetisa [poe'tisa] *nf* (woman) poet.

póker ['poker] *nm* poker.

polaco, a [po'lako, a] *a* Polish ♦ *nm/f* Pole ♦ *nm* (*LING*) Polish.

polar [po'lar] *a* polar.

polarice [pola'riθe] *etc vb V* **polarizar**.

polaridad [polari'ðað] *nf* polarity.

polarizar [polari'θar] *vt* to polarize.

polea [po'lea] *nf* pulley.

polémica [po'lemika] *nf* polemics *sg*; (*una* ~) controversy.

polemice [pole'miθe] *etc vb V* **polemizar**.

polémico, a [po'lemiko, a] *a* polemic(al).

polemizar [polemi'θar] *vi* to indulge in a polemic, argue.

polen ['polen] *nm* pollen.

poli ['poli] *nm* (*fam*) cop (*fam*) ♦ *nf*: **la** ~ the cops *pl* (*fam*).

policía [poli'θia] *nm/f* policeman/woman ♦ *nf* police.

policíaco, a [poli'θiako, a] *a* police *cpd*; **novela policíaca** detective story.

polietileno [polieti'leno] *nm* polythene (*Brit*), polyethylene (*US*).

polifacético, a [polifa'θetiko, a] *a* (*persona, talento*) many-sided, versatile.

poligamia [poli'ɣamja] *nf* polygamy.

polígamo, a [po'liɣamo, a] *a* polygamous ♦ *nm* polygamist.

polígono [po'liɣono] *nm* (*MAT*) polygon; (*solar*) building lot; (*zona*) area; (*unidad vecina*) housing estate; ~ **industrial** industrial estate.

polilla [po'liʎa] *nf* moth.

Polinesia [poli'nesja] *nf* Polynesia.

polinesio, a [poli'nesjo, a] *a*, *nm/f* Polynesian.

polio ['poljo] *nf* polio.

Polisario [poli'sarjo] *nm abr* (*POL*: *tb*: **Frente** ~) = *Frente Político de Liberación del Sáhara y Río de Oro*.

politécnico [poli'tekniko] *nm* polytechnic.

político, a [po'litiko, a] *a* political; (*discreto*) tactful; (*pariente*) in-law ♦ *nm/f* politician ♦ *nf* politics *sg*; (*económica, agraria*) policy; **padre** ~ father-in-law; **política exterior/de ingresos y precios** foreign/prices and incomes policy.

politicastro [politi'kastro] *nm* (*pey*) politician, politico.

póliza ['poliθa] *nf* certificate, voucher; (*impuesto*) tax *o* fiscal stamp; ~ **de seguro(s)** insurance policy.

polizón [poli'θon] *nm* (*AVIAT, NAUT*) stowaway.

polo ['polo] *nm* (*GEO, ELEC*) pole; (*helado*) iced lolly; (*DEPORTE*) polo; (*suéter*) polo-neck; **P~ Norte/Sur** North/South Pole; **esto es el** ~ **opuesto de lo que dijo antes** this is the exact opposite of what he said before.

Polonia [po'lonja] *nf* Poland.

poltrona [pol'trona] *nf* reclining chair, easy chair.

polución [polu'θjon] *nf* pollution; ~ **ambiental** environmental pollution.

polvera [pol'ßera] *nf* powder compact.

polvo ['polßo] *nm* dust; (*QUÍMICA, CULIN, MED*) powder; (*fam!*) screw(!); **en** ~ powdered; ~ **de talco** talcum powder; **estar hecho** ~ to be worn out *o* exhausted; **hacer algo** ~ to smash sth; **hacer** ~ **a uno** to shatter sb; *V tb* **polvos**.

pólvora ['polßora] *nf* gunpowder; (*fuegos artificiales*) fireworks *pl*; **propagarse como la** ~ (*noticia*) to spread like wildfire.

polvorosa [polɓoˈrosa] a (fam): **poner pies en ~** to beat it.

polvoriento, a [polɓoˈrjento, a] a (superficie) dusty; (sustancia) powdery.

polvos [ˈpolɓos] nmpl powder sg.

pollera [poˈʎera] nf (criadero) hencoop; (AM) skirt, overskirt.

pollería [poʎeˈria] nf poulterer's (shop).

pollo [ˈpoʎo] nm chicken; (joven) young man; (señorito) playboy; **~ asado** roast chicken.

pomada [poˈmaða] nf pomade.

pomelo [poˈmelo] nm grapefruit.

pómez [ˈpomeθ] nf: **piedra ~** pumice stone.

pompa [ˈpompa] nf (burbuja) bubble; (bomba) pump; (esplendor) pomp, splendour; **~s funebres** funeral sg.

pomposo, a [pomˈposo, a] a splendid, magnificent; (pey) pompous.

pómulo [ˈpomulo] nm cheekbone.

ponche [ˈpontʃe] nm punch.

poncho [ˈpontʃo] nm (AM) poncho, cape.

ponderar [pondeˈrar] vt (considerar) to weigh up, consider; (elogiar) to praise highly, speak in praise of.

pondré [ponˈdre] etc vb V **poner**.

ponencia [poˈnenθja] nf (exposición) (learned) paper, communication; (informe) report.

poner [poˈner] vt (gen) to put; (colocar) to place, set; (ropa) to put on; (problema, la mesa) to set; (telegrama) to send; (TELEC) to connect; (RADIO, TV) to switch on, turn on; (tienda) to open, set up; (nombre) to give; (añadir) to add; (TEATRO, CINE) to put on; (+ adjetivo) to make, turn; (suponer) to suppose ♦ vi (ave) to lay (eggs); **~se** vr to put o place o.s.; (ropa) to put on; (+ adjetivo) to turn, get, become; (el sol) to set; **~ al tanto** to keep informed; **~ algo en duda** to cast doubt on sth; **~ de relieve** (INFORM) to highlight; **póngame con el Señor X** get me Mr X, put me through to Mr X; **¡no te pongas así!** don't be like that!; **~se cómodo** to make o.s. comfortable; **~se delante** (estorbar) to get in the way; **~se a bien con uno** to get on good terms with sb; **~se rojo** to blush; **~se a** to begin to; **~se en** (lugar) to get to, arrive at.

ponga [ˈponga] etc vb V **poner**.

poniente [poˈnjente] nm west.

p.º n.º abr (= peso neto) nt. wt.

pontevedrés, esa [ponteɓeˈðres, esa] a of o from Pontevedra ♦ nm/f native o inhabitant of Pontevedra.

pontificado [pontifiˈkaðo] nm papacy, pontificate.

pontífice [ponˈtifiθe] nm pope, pontiff; **el Sumo P~** His Holiness the Pope.

pontón [ponˈton] nm pontoon.

ponzoña [ponˈθoɲa] nf poison, venom.

ponzoñoso, a [ponθoˈɲoso, a] a poisonous, venomous.

popa [ˈpopa] nf stern; **a ~** astern, abaft; **de ~ a proa** fore and aft.

popular [popuˈlar] a popular; (del pueblo) of the people.

popularice [popolaˈriθe] etc vb V **popularizarse**.

popularidad [populariˈðað] nf popularity.

popularizarse [populariˈθarse] vr to become popular.

poquísimo, a [poˈkisimo, a] a (superlativo de poco) very little; (pl) very few; (casi nada) hardly any.

poquito [poˈkito] nm: **un ~** a little bit ♦ ad a little, a bit; **a ~s** bit by bit.

por [por] prep (+ infin: para) so as to; (a favor de, hacia) for; (a causa de) out of, because of, from; (según) according to; (por agencia de) by; (a cambio de) for, in exchange for; (en lugar de) instead of, in place of; (durante) for; **10 ~ 10 son 100** 10 times 10 are 100; **será ~ poco tiempo** it won't be for long; **~ correo/avión** by post/ plane; **~ centenares** by the hundred; **(el) 10 ~ ciento** 10 per cent; **~ orden** in order; **ir a Bilbao ~ Santander** to go to Bilbao via Santander; **pasar ~ Madrid** to pass through Madrid; **camina ~ la izquierda** walk on the left; **~ todo el país** throughout the country; **entra ~ delante/detrás** come/ go in by the front/back (door); **~ la calle** along the street; **~ la mañana** in the morning; **~ la noche** at night; **$2 ~ hora** $2 an hour; **~ allí** over there; **está ~ el norte** it's somewhere in the north; **~ mucho que quisiera, no puedo** much as I would like to, I can't; **te doy éste ~ aquél** I'll swap you this one for that one; **¿~ qué?** why?; **~ (lo) tanto** so, therefore; **~ cierto** (seguro) certainly; (a propósito) by the way; **~ ejemplo** for example; **~ favor** please; **~ fuera/dentro** outside/inside; **~ mí ...** so far as I'm concerned ...; **hazlo ~ mí** do it for my sake; **~ si (acaso)** just in case; **~ sí mismo** o **sólo** by o.s.

porcelana [porθeˈlana] nf porcelain; (china) china.

porcentaje [porθenˈtaxe] nm percentage; **~ de actividad** (INFORM) hit rate.

porción [porˈθjon] nf (parte) portion, share; (cantidad) quantity, amount.

porche [ˈportʃe] nm (de una plaza) arcade; (de casa) porch.

pordiosear [porðjoseˈar] vi to beg.

pordiosero, a [porðjoˈsero, a] nm/f beggar.

porfía [porˈfia] nf persistence; (terquedad) obstinacy.

porfiado, a [porˈfjaðo, a] a persistent; obstinate.

porfiar [por'fjar] *vi* to persist, insist; *(disputar)* to argue stubbornly.

pormenor [porme'nor] *nm* detail, particular.

pormenorice [pormeno'riθe] *etc vb* V **pormenorizar**.

pormenorizar [pormenori'θar] *vt* to (set out in) detail ◆ *vi* to go into detail.

pornografía [pornoɣra'fia] *nf* pornography.

poro ['poro] *nm* pore.

poroso, a [po'roso, a] *a* porous.

poroto [po'roto] *nm (AM)* kidney bean.

porque ['porke] *conj (a causa de)* because; *(ya que)* since; ~ **sí** because I feel like it.

porqué [por'ke] *nm* reason, cause.

porquería [porke'ria] *nf (suciedad)* filth, muck, dirt; *(acción)* dirty trick; *(objeto)* small thing, trifle; *(fig)* rubbish.

porqueriza [porke'riθa] *nf* pigsty.

porra ['porra] *nf (arma)* stick, club; *(cachiporra)* truncheon; ¡~**s!** bother!; ¡**vete a la** ~! go to blazes!

porrazo [po'rraθo] *nm (golpe)* blow; *(caída)* bump; **de un** ~ in one go.

porrón [po'rron] *nm glass wine jar with a long spout.*

port ['por(t)] *nm (INFORM)* port.

portada [por'taða] *nf (TIP)* title page; (: *de revista)* cover.

portador, a [porta'ðor, a] *nm/f* carrier, bearer; *(COM)* bearer, payee.

portaequipajes [portaeki'paxes] *nm inv* boot *(Brit)*, trunk *(US)*; *(baca)* luggage rack.

portafolio [porta'foljo] *nm*: ~ **de inversiones** *(COM)* investment portfolio.

portal [por'tal] *nm (entrada)* vestibule, hall; *(pórtico)* porch, doorway; *(puerta de entrada)* main door; *(DEPORTE)* goal; ~**es** *nmpl* arcade *sg*.

portaligas [porta'liɣas] *nm inv* suspender belt.

portamaletas [portama'letas] *nm inv* roof rack.

portamonedas [portamo'neðas] *nm inv* purse.

portar [por'tar] *vt* to carry, bear; ~**se** *vr* to behave, conduct o.s.; ~**se mal** to misbehave; **se portó muy bien conmigo** he treated me very well.

portátil [por'tatil] *a* portable.

portaviones [porta'ßjones] *nm inv* aircraft carrier.

portavoz [porta'ßoθ] *nm/f* spokesman/woman.

portazo [por'taθo] *nm*: **dar un** ~ to slam the door.

porte ['porte] *nm (COM)* transport; *(precio)* transport charges *pl*; *(CORREOS)* postage; ~ **debido** *(COM)* carriage forward; ~ **pagado** *(COM)* carriage paid, post-paid.

portento [por'tento] *nm* marvel, wonder.

portentoso, a [porten'toso, a] *a* marvellous, extraordinary.

porteño, a [por'teɲo, a] *a* of *o* from Buenos Aires ◆ *nm/f* native *o* inhabitant of Buenos Aires.

portería [porte'ria] *nf (oficina)* porter's office; *(gol)* goal.

portero, a [por'tero, a] *nm/f* porter; *(conserje)* caretaker; *(DEPORTE)* goalkeeper.

pórtico ['portiko] *nm (porche)* portico, porch; *(fig)* gateway; *(arcada)* arcade.

portilla [por'tiʎa] *nf*, **portillo** [por'tiʎo] *nm* gate.

portorriqueño, a [portorri'keɲo, a] *a, nm/f* Puerto Rican.

portuario, a [por'twarjo] *a (del puerto)* port *cpd*, harbour *cpd*; *(del muelle)* dock *cpd*; **trabajador** ~ docker.

Portugal [portu'ɣal] *nm* Portugal.

portugués, esa [portu'ɣes, esa] *a, nm/f* Portuguese ◆ *nm (LING)* Portuguese.

porvenir [porße'nir] *nm* future.

pos [pos] **en** ~ **de**: *prep* after, in pursuit of.

posada [po'saða] *nf (refugio)* shelter, lodging; *(mesón)* guest house; **dar** ~ **a** to give shelter to, take in.

posaderas [posa'ðeras] *nfpl* backside *sg*, buttocks.

posar [po'sar] *vt (en el suelo)* to lay down, put down; *(la mano)* to place, put gently ◆ *vi* to sit, pose; ~**se** *vr* to settle; *(pájaro)* to perch; *(avión)* to land, come down.

posdata [pos'ðata] *nf* postscript.

pose ['pose] *nf (ARTE, afectación)* pose.

poseedor, a [pose'ðor, a] *nm/f* owner, possessor; *(de récord, puesto)* holder.

poseer [pose'er] *vt* to have, possess, own; *(ventaja)* to enjoy; *(récord, puesto)* to hold.

poseído, a [pose'iðo, a] *a* possessed; **estar muy** ~ **de** to be very vain about.

posesión [pose'sjon] *nf* possession; **tomar** ~ **(de)** to take over.

posesionarse [posesjo'narse] *vr*: ~ **de** to take possession of, take over.

posesivo, a [pose'sißo, a] *a* possessive.

poseyendo [pose'jendo] *etc vb* V **poseer**.

posibilidad [posißili'ðað] *nf* possibility; *(oportunidad)* chance.

posibilitar [posißili'tar] *vt* to make possible, permit; *(hacer factible)* to make feasible.

posible [po'sißle] *a* possible; *(factible)* feasible ◆ *nm*: ~**s** means; *(bienes)* funds, assets; **de ser** ~ if possible; **en** *o* **dentro de lo** ~ as far as possible; **lo antes** ~ as quickly as possible.

posición [posi'θjon] *nf (gen)* position; *(rango social)* status.

positivo, a [posi'tißo, a] *a* positive ◆ *nf (FOTO)* print.

poso ['poso] *nm* sediment.

posponer [pospo'ner] *vt* to put behind *o* below; (*aplazar*) to postpone.

posponga [pos'ponga] *etc*, **pospuesto** [pos'pwesto], **pospuse** [pos'puse] *etc vb V* **posponer**.

posta ['posta] *nf* (*de caballos*) relay, team; **a ~** on purpose, deliberately.

postal [pos'tal] *a* postal ♦ *nf* postcard.

poste ['poste] *nm* (*de telégrafos*) post, pole; (*columna*) pillar.

postergar [poster'ɣar] *vt* (*esp AM*) to put off, postpone, delay.

postergue [pos'terɣe] *etc vb V* **postergar**.

posteridad [posteri'ðað] *nf* posterity.

posterior [poste'rjor] *a* back, rear; (*siguiente*) following, subsequent; (*más tarde*) later; **ser ~ a** to be later than.

posterioridad [posterjori'ðað] *nf*: **con ~** later, subsequently.

postgraduado, a [postɣra'ðwaðo, a] *a*, *nm/f* postgraduate.

pos(t)guerra [pos(t)'ɣerra] *nf* postwar period; **en la ~** after the war.

postigo [pos'tiɣo] *nm* (*portillo*) postern; (*contraventana*) shutter.

postín [pos'tin] *nm* (*fam*) elegance; **de ~** posh; **darse ~** to show off.

postizo, a [pos'tiθo, a] *a* false, artificial; (*sonrisa*) false, phoney ♦ *nm* hairpiece.

postor, a [pos'tor, a] *nm/f* bidder; **mejor ~** highest bidder.

postrado, a [pos'traðo, a] *a* prostrate.

postrar [pos'trar] *vt* (*derribar*) to cast down, overthrow; (*humillar*) to humble; (*MED*) to weaken, exhaust.

postre ['postre] *nm* sweet, dessert ♦ *nf*: **a la ~** in the end, when all is said and done; **para ~** (*fam*) to crown it all; **llegar a los ~s** (*fig*) to come too late.

postrero, a [pos'trero, a] *a* (*delante de nmsg*: **postrer**: *último*) last; (: *que viene detrás*) rear.

postrimerías [postrime'rias] *nfpl* final stages.

postulado [postu'laðo] *nm* postulate.

postulante [postu'lante] *nm/f* petitioner; (*REL*) postulant.

póstumo, a ['postumo, a] *a* posthumous.

postura [pos'tura] *nf* (*del cuerpo*) posture, position; (*fig*) attitude, position.

post-venta [post'ßenta] *a* (*COM*) after-sales.

potable [po'taßle] *a* drinkable.

potaje [po'taxe] *nm* thick vegetable soup.

pote ['pote] *nm* pot, jar.

potencia [po'tenθja] *nf* power; (*capacidad*) capacity; **~ (en caballos)** horsepower; **en ~** potential, in the making; **las grandes ~s** the great powers.

potencial [poten'θjal] *a, nm* potential.

potenciar [poten'θjar] *vt* (*promover*) to promote; (*fortalecer*) to boost.

potente [po'tente] *a* powerful.

potestad [potes'tað] *nf* authority; **patria ~** paternal authority.

potosí [poto'si] *nm* fortune; **cuesta un ~** it costs the earth.

potra ['potra] *nf* (*ZOOL*) filly; **tener ~** to be lucky.

potro ['potro] *nm* (*ZOOL*) colt; (*DEPORTE*) vaulting horse.

pozo ['poθo] *nm* well; (*de río*) deep pool; (*de mina*) shaft; **~ negro** cesspool; **ser un ~ de ciencia** (*fig*) to be deeply learned.

PP *abr* (= *por poderes*) pp; (= *porte pagado*) carriage paid.

p.p.m. *abr* (= *palabras por minuto*) wpm.

práctica ['praktika] *nf V* **práctico**.

practicable [prakti'kaßle] *a* practicable; (*camino*) passable, usable.

practicante [prakti'kante] *nm/f* (*MED*: *ayudante de doctor*) medical assistant; (: *enfermero*) nurse; (*quien practica algo*) practitioner ♦ *a* practising.

practicar [prakti'kar] *vt* to practise; (*deporte*) to go in for, play; (*ejecutar*) to carry out, perform.

práctico, a ['praktiko, a] *a* (*gen*) practical; (*conveniente*) handy; (*instruído*: *persona*) skilled, expert ♦ *nf* practice; (*método*) method; (*arte, capacidad*) skill; **en la práctica** in practice.

practique [prak'tike] *etc vb V* **practicar**.

pradera [pra'ðera] *nf* meadow; (*de Canadá*) prairie.

prado ['praðo] *nm* (*campo*) meadow, field; (*pastizal*) pasture.

Praga ['praɣa] *nf* Prague.

pragmático, a [praɣ'matiko, a] *a* pragmatic.

preámbulo [pre'ambulo] *nm* preamble, introduction; **decir algo sin ~s** to say sth without beating about the bush.

precalentar [prekalen'tar] *vt* to preheat.

precaliente [preka'ljente] *etc vb V* **precalentar**.

precario, a [pre'karjo, a] *a* precarious.

precaución [prekau'θjon] *nf* (*medida preventiva*) preventive measure, precaution; (*prudencia*) caution, wariness.

precaver [preka'ßer] *vt* to guard against; (*impedir*) to forestall; **~se** *vr*: **~se de** *o* **contra algo** to (be on one's) guard against sth.

precavido, a [preka'ßiðo, a] *a* cautious, wary.

precedencia [preθe'ðenθja] *nf* precedence; (*prioridad*) priority; (*superioridad*) greater importance, superiority.

precedente [preθe'ðente] *a* preceding; (*anterior*) former ♦ *nm* precedent; **sin ~(s)** unprecedented; **establecer** *o* **sentar un ~** to establish *o* set a precedent.

preceder [preθe'ðer] *vt, vi* to precede, go/ come before.

precepto [pre'θepto] *nm* precept.

preceptor [preθep'tor] *nm* (*maestro*) teacher; (: *particular*) tutor.

preciado, a [pre'θjaðo, a] *a* (*estimado*) esteemed, valuable.

preciar [pre'θjar] *vt* to esteem, value; ~se *vr* to boast; ~se de to pride o.s. on.

precinto [pre'θinto] *nm* (*COM*: *tb*: ~ de garantía) seal.

precio ['preθjo] *nm* (*de mercado*) price; (*costo*) cost; (*valor*) value, worth; (*de viaje*) fare; ~ de coste *o* de cobertura cost price; ~ al contado cash price; ~ al detalle *o* al por menor retail price; ~ al detallista trade price; ~ de entrega inmediata spot price; ~ de oferta offer price; ~ de oportunidad bargain price; ~ de salida upset price; ~ tope top price; ~ unitario unit price; no tener ~ (*fig*) to be priceless; "no importa ~" "cost no object".

preciosidad [preθjosi'ðað] *nf* (*valor*) (high) value, (great) worth; (*encanto*) charm; (*cosa bonita*) beautiful thing; es una ~ it's lovely, it's really beautiful.

precioso, a [pre'θjoso, a] *a* precious; (*de mucho valor*) valuable; (*fam*) lovely, beautiful.

precipicio [preθi'piθjo] *nm* cliff, precipice; (*fig*) abyss.

precipitación [preθipita'θjon] *nf* (*prisa*) haste; (*lluvia*) rainfall; (*QUÍMICA*) precipitation.

precipitado, a [preθipi'taðo, a] *a* hasty, rash; (*salida*) hasty, sudden ♦ *nm* (*QUÍMICA*) precipitate.

precipitar [preθipi'tar] *vt* (*arrojar*) to hurl, throw; (*apresurar*) to hasten; (*acelerar*) to speed up, accelerate; (*QUÍMICA*) to precipitate; ~se *vr* to throw o.s.; (*apresurarse*) to rush; (*actuar sin pensar*) to act rashly; ~se hacia to rush towards.

precisado, a [preθi'saðo, a] *a*: verse ~ a hacer algo to be obliged to do sth.

precisamente [preθisa'mente] *ad* precisely; (*justo*) precisely, exactly, just; ~ por eso for that very reason; ~ fue él quien lo dijo as a matter of fact he said it; no es eso ~ it's not really that.

precisar [preθi'sar] *vt* (*necesitar*) to need, require; (*fijar*) to determine exactly, fix; (*especificar*) to specify; (*señalar*) to pinpoint.

precisión [preθi'sjon] *nf* (*exactitud*) precision.

preciso, a [pre'θiso, a] *a* (*exacto*) precise; (*necesario*) necessary, essential; (*estilo, lenguaje*) concise; es ~ que lo hagas you must do it.

precocidad [prekoθi'ðað] *nf* precociousness, precocity.

preconcebido, a [prekonθe'ßiðo, a] *a* preconceived.

preconice [preko'niθe] etc *vb* V **preconizar**.

preconizar [prekoni'θar] *vt* (*aconsejar*) to advise; (*prever*) to foresee.

precoz [pre'koθ] *a* (*persona*) precocious; (*calvicie*) premature.

precursor, a [prekur'sor, a] *nm/f* precursor.

predecir [preðe'θir] *vt* to predict, foretell, forecast.

predestinado, a [preðesti'naðo, a] *a* predestined.

predeterminar [preðetermi'nar] *vt* to predetermine.

prédica ['preðika] *nf* sermon.

predicador, a [preðika'ðor, a] *nm/f* preacher.

predicar [preði'kar] *vt, vi* to preach.

predicción [preðik'θjon] *nf* prediction; (*pronóstico*) forecast; ~ del tiempo weather forecast(ing).

predicho [pre'ðitʃo], **prediga** [pre'ðiɣa] etc, **predije** [pre'ðixe] etc *vb* V **predecir**.

predilecto, a [preði'lekto, a] *a* favourite.

predio ['preðjo] *nm* property, estate.

predique [pre'ðike] etc *vb* V **predicar**.

prediré [preði're] etc *vb* V **predecir**.

predispondré [preðispon'dre] etc *vb* V **predisponer**.

predisponer [preðispo'ner] *vt* to predispose; (*pey*) to prejudice.

predisponga [preðis'ponga] etc *vb* V **predisponer**.

predisposición [preðisposi'θjon] *nf* predisposition, inclination; prejudice, bias; (*MED*) tendency.

predispuesto [preðis'pwesto], **predispuse** [preðis'puse] etc *vb* V **predisponer**.

predominante [preðomi'nante] *a* predominant; (*preponderante*) prevailing; (*interés*) controlling.

predominar [preðomi'nar] *vt* to dominate ♦ *vi* to predominate; (*prevalecer*) to prevail.

predominio [preðo'minjo] *nm* predominance; prevalence.

preescolar [preesko'lar] *a* preschool.

preestreno [prees'treno] *nm* preview, press view.

prefabricado, a [prefaßri'kaðo, a] *a* prefabricated.

prefacio [pre'faθjo] *nm* preface.

preferencia [prefe'renθja] *nf* preference; de ~ preferably, for preference; localidad de ~ reserved seat.

preferible [prefe'rißle] *a* preferable.

preferir [prefe'rir] *vt* to prefer.

prefiera [pre'fjera] etc *vb* V **preferir**.

prefijo [pre'fixo] *nm* prefix.

prefiriendo [prefi'rjendo] *etc vb* V **preferir**.

pregón [pre'ɣon] *nm* proclamation, announcement.

pregonar [preɣo'nar] *vt* to proclaim, announce; *(mercancía)* to hawk.

pregonero [preɣo'nero] *nm* town crier.

pregunta [pre'ɣunta] *nf* question; ~ **capciosa** catch question; **hacer una** ~ to ask a question.

preguntar [preɣun'tar] *vt* to ask; *(cuestionar)* to question ♦ *vi* to ask; ~**se** *vr* to wonder; ~ **por uno** to ask for sb; ~ **por la salud de uno** to ask after sb's health.

preguntón, ona [preɣun'ton, ona] *a* inquisitive.

prehistórico, a [preis'toriko, a] *a* prehistoric.

prejuicio [pre'xwiθjo] *nm* prejudgement; *(preconcepción)* preconception; *(pey)* prejudice, bias.

prejuzgar [prexuθ'ɣar] *vt* *(predisponer)* to prejudge.

prejuzgue [pre'xuθɣe] *etc vb* V **prejuzgar**.

preliminar [prelimi'nar] *a, nm* preliminary.

preludio [pre'luðjo] *nm* *(MUS, fig)* prelude.

prematuro, a [prema'turo, a] *a* premature.

premeditación [premeðita'θjon] *nf* premeditation.

premeditado, a [premeði'taðo, a] *a* premeditated, deliberate; *(intencionado)* wilful.

premeditar [premeði'tar] *vt* to premeditate.

premiar [pre'mjar] *vt* to reward; *(en un concurso)* to give·a prize to.

premio ['premjo] *nm* reward; prize; *(COM)* premium; ~ **gordo** first prize.

premonición [premoni'θjon] *nf* premonition.

premura [pre'mura] *nf* *(prisa)* haste, urgency.

prenatal [prena'tal] *a* antenatal, prenatal.

prenda ['prenda] *nf* *(ropa)* garment, article of clothing; *(garantía)* pledge; *(fam)* darling!; ~**s** *nfpl* talents, gifts; **dejar algo en** ~ to pawn sth; **no soltar** ~ to give nothing away; *(fig)* not to say a word.

prendar [pren'dar] *vt* to captivate, enchant; ~**se de algo** to fall in love with sth.

prendedor [prende'ðor] *nm* brooch.

prender [pren'der] *vt* *(captar)* to catch, capture; *(detener)* to arrest; *(coser)* to pin, attach; *(sujetar)* to fasten ♦ *vi* to catch; *(arraigar)* to take root; ~**se** *vr* *(encenderse)* to catch fire.

prendido, a [pren'diðo, a] *a* *(AM: luz etc)* on.

prensa ['prensa] *nf* press; **la P~** the press; **tener mala** ~ to have o get a bad press; **la** ~ **nacional** the national press.

prensar [pren'sar] *vt* to press.

preñado, a [pre'ɲaðo, a] *a* *(mujer)* pregnant; ~ **de** pregnant with, full of.

preñez [pre'ɲeθ] *nf* pregnancy.

preocupación [preokupa'θjon] *nf* worry, concern; *(ansiedad)* anxiety.

preocupado, a [preoku'paðo, a] *a* worried, concerned; anxious.

preocupar [preoku'par] *vt* to worry; ~**se** *vr* to worry; ~**se de algo** *(hacerse cargo)* to take care of sth; ~**se por algo** to worry about sth.

preparación [prepara'θjon] *nf* *(acto)* preparation; *(estado)* preparedness, readiness; *(entrenamiento)* training.

preparado, a [prepa'raðo, a] *a* *(dispuesto)* prepared; *(CULIN)* ready (to serve) ♦ *nm* *(MED)* preparation; ¡~**s, listos, ya!** ready, steady, go!

preparar [prepa'rar] *vt* *(disponer)* to prepare, get ready; *(TEC: tratar)* to prepare, process, treat; *(entrenar)* to teach, train; ~**se** *vr*: ~**se a** *o* **para hacer algo** to prepare *o* get ready to do sth.

preparativo, a [prepara'tiβo] *a* preparatory, preliminary ♦ *nm*: ~**s** preparations.

preparatoria [prepara'torja] *n* *(AM)* sixth form college *(Brit)*, senior high school *(US)*.

prerrogativa [prerroɣa'tiβa] *nf* prerogative, privilege.

presa ['presa] *nf* *(cosa apresada)* catch; *(víctima)* victim; *(de animal)* prey; *(de agua)* dam; **hacer** ~ **en** to clutch (on to), seize; **ser** ~ **de** *(fig)* to be a prey to.

presagiar [presa'xjar] *vt* to threaten.

presagio [pre'saxjo] *nm* omen.

presbítero [pres'βitero] *nm* priest.

prescindir [presθin'dir] *vi*: ~ **de** *(privarse de)* to do without, go without; *(descartar)* to dispense with; **no podemos** ~ **de él** we can't manage without him.

prescribir [preskri'βir] *vt* to prescribe.

prescripción [preskrip'θjon] *nf* prescription; ~ **facultativa** medical prescription.

prescrito [pres'krito] *pp de* **prescribir**.

preseleccionar [preselekθjo'nar] *vt* *(DEPORTE)* to seed.

presencia [pre'senθja] *nf* presence; **en** ~ **de** in the presence of.

presencial [presen'θjal] *a*: **testigo** ~ eyewitness.

presenciar [presen'θjar] *vt* to be present at; *(asistir a)* to attend; *(ver)* to see, witness.

presentación [presenta'θjon] *nf* presentation; *(introducción)* introduction.

presentador, a [presenta'ðor, a] *nm/f* compère.

presentar [presen'tar] *vt* to present; *(ofrecer)* to offer; *(mostrar)* to show, display; *(renuncia)* to tender; *(moción)* to propose; *(a una persona)* to introduce; ~**se** *vr* (*llegar inesperadamente*) to appear, turn up; (*ofrecerse: como candidato*) to run, stand; (*aparecer*) to show, appear; (*solicitar empleo*) to apply; ~ **al cobro** (*COM*) to present for payment; ~**se a la policía** to report to the police.

presente [pre'sente] *a* present ♦ *nm* present; (*LING*) present (tense); (*regalo*) gift; **los** ~**s** those present; **hacer** ~ to state, declare; **tener** ~ to remember, bear in mind; **la carta** ~, **la** ~ this letter.

presentimiento [presenti'mjento] *nm* premonition, presentiment.

presentir [presen'tir] *vt* to have a premonition of.

preservación [preserßa'θjon] *nf* protection, preservation.

preservar [preser'ßar] *vt* to protect, preserve.

preservativo [preserßa'tißo] *nm* sheath, condom.

presidencia [presi'ðenθja] *nf* presidency; (*de comité*) chairmanship; **ocupar la** ~ to preside, be in *o* take the chair.

presidente [presi'ðente] *nm/f* president; chairman/woman; (*en parlamento*) speaker; (*JUR*) presiding magistrate.

presidiario [presi'ðjarjo] *nm* convict.

presidio [pre'siðjo] *nm* prison, penitentiary.

presidir [presi'ðir] *vt* (*dirigir*) to preside at, preside over; (: *comité*) to take the chair at; (*dominar*) to dominate, rule ♦ *vi* to preside; to take the chair.

presienta [pre'sjenta] *etc*, **presintiendo** [presin'tjendo] *etc vb* V **presentir**.

presión [pre'sjon] *nf* pressure; ~ **arterial** *o* **sanguínea** blood pressure; **a** ~ under pressure.

presionar [presjo'nar] *vt* to press; (*botón*) to push, press; (*fig*) to press, put pressure on ♦ *vi*: ~ **para** *o* **por** to press for.

preso, a ['preso, a] *a*: **estar** ~ **de terror** *o* **pánico** to be panic-stricken ♦ *nm/f* prisoner; **tomar** *o* **llevar** ~ **a uno** to arrest sb, take sb prisoner.

prestación [presta'θjon] *nf* (*aportación*) lending; (*INFORM*) capability; ~ **de juramento** oath-taking; ~ **personal** obligatory service.

prestado, a [pres'taðo, a] *a* on loan; **dar algo** ~ to lend sth; **pedir** ~ to borrow.

prestamista [presta'mista] *nm/f* moneylender.

préstamo ['prestamo] *nm* loan; ~ **con garantía** loan against collateral; ~ **hipotecario** mortgage.

prestar [pres'tar] *vt* to lend, loan; (*atención*) to pay; (*ayuda*) to give; (*servicio*) to do, render; (*juramento*) to take, swear; ~**se** *vr* (*ofrecerse*) to offer *o* volunteer.

prestatario, a [presta'tarjo, a] *nm/f*

borrower.

presteza [pres'teθa] *nf* speed, promptness.

prestidigitador [prestiðixita'ðor] *nm* conjurer.

prestigio [pres'tixjo] *nm* prestige; (*reputación*) face; (*renombre*) good name.

prestigioso, a [presti'xjoso, a] *a* (*honorable*) prestigious; (*famoso, renombrado*) renowned, famous.

presto, a ['presto, a] *a* (*rápido*) quick, prompt; (*dispuesto*) ready ♦ *ad* at once, right away.

presumido, a [presu'miðo, a] *a* conceited.

presumir [presu'mir] *vt* to presume ♦ *vi* (*tener aires*) to be conceited; **según cabe** ~ as may be presumed, presumably; ~ **de listo** to think o.s. very smart.

presunción [presun'θjon] *nf* presumption; (*sospecha*) suspicion; (*vanidad*) conceit.

presunto, a [pre'sunto, a] *a* (*supuesto*) supposed, presumed; (*así llamado*) so-called.

presuntuoso, a [presun'twoso, a] *a* conceited, presumptuous.

presupondré [presupon'dre] *etc vb* V **presuponer**.

presuponer [presupo'ner] *vt* to presuppose.

presuponga [presu'ponga] *etc vb* V **presuponer**.

presupuestar [presupwes'tar] *vi* to budget ♦ *vt*: ~ **algo** to budget for sth.

presupuestario, a [presupwes'tarjo, a] *a* (*FINANZAS*) budgetary, budget *cpd*.

presupuesto [presu'pwesto] *pp de* **presuponer** ♦ *nm* (*FINANZAS*) budget; (*estimación: de costo*) estimate; **asignación de** ~ (*COM*) budget appropriation.

presupuse [presu'puse] *etc vb* V **presuponer**.

presuroso, a [presu'roso, a] *a* (*rápido*) quick, speedy; (*que tiene prisa*) hasty.

pretencioso, a [preten'θjoso, a] *a* pretentious.

pretender [preten'der] *vt* (*intentar*) to try to, seek to; (*reivindicar*) to claim; (*buscar*) to seek, try for; (*cortejar*) to woo, court; ~ **que** to expect that; **¿qué pretende usted?** what are you after?

pretendiente [preten'djente] *nm/f* (*candidato*) candidate, applicant; (*amante*) suitor.

pretensión [preten'sjon] *nf* (*aspiración*) aspiration; (*reivindicación*) claim; (*orgullo*) pretension.

pretérito, a [pre'terito, a] *a* (*LING*) past; (*fig*) past, former.

pretextar [preteks'tar] *vt* to plead, use as an excuse.

pretexto [pre'teksto] *nm* pretext; (*excusa*) excuse; **so** ~ **de** under pretext of.

pretil [pre'til] *nm* (*valla*) parapet; (*baran-*

da) handrail.

prevalecer [preßale'θer] *vi* to prevail.

prevaleciente [preßale'θjente] *a* prevailing, prevalent.

prevalezca [preßa'leθka] *etc vb V* **prevalecer.**

prevención [preßen'θjon] *nf* (*preparación*) preparation; (*estado*) preparedness, readiness; (*medida*) prevention; (*previsión*) foresight, forethought; (*precaución*) precaution.

prevendré [preßen'dre] *etc*, **prevenga** [pre'ßenga] *etc vb V* **prevenir.**

prevenido, a [preße'niðo, a] *a* prepared, ready; (*cauteloso*) cautious; **estar** ~ (*preparado*) to be ready; **ser** ~ (*cuidadoso*) to be cautious; **hombre** ~ **vale por dos** forewarned is forearmed.

prevenir [preße'nir] *vt* (*impedir*) to prevent; (*prever*) to foresee, anticipate; (*predisponer*) to prejudice, bias; (*avisar*) to warn; (*preparar*) to prepare, get ready; ~**se** *vr* to get ready, prepare; ~**se contra** to take precautions against.

preventivo, a [preßen'tißo, a] *a* preventive, precautionary.

prever [pre'ßer] *vt* to foresee; (*anticipar*) to anticipate.

previniendo [preßi'njendo] *etc vb V* **prevenir.**

previo, a ['preßjo, a] *a* (*anterior*) previous, prior ♦ *prep*: ~ **acuerdo de los otros** subject to the agreement of the others; ~ **pago de los derechos** on payment of the fees.

previsible [preßi'sißle] *a* foreseeable.

previsión [preßi'sjon] *nf* (*perspicacia*) foresight; (*predicción*) forecast; (*prudencia*) caution; ~ **de ventas** (*COM*) sales forecast.

previsor, a [preßi'sor, a] *a* (*precavido*) farsighted; (*prudente*) thoughtful.

previsto [pre'ßisto] *pp de* **prever.**

prieto, a ['prjeto, a] *a* (*oscuro*) dark; (*fig*) mean; (*comprimido*) tight, compressed.

prima ['prima] *nf V* **primo.**

primacía [prima'θia] *nf* primacy.

primar [pri'mar] *vi* (*tener primacía*) to occupy first place; ~ **sobre** to have priority over.

primario, a [pri'marjo, a] *a* primary.

primavera [prima'ßera] *nf* (*temporada*) spring; (*período*) springtime.

primaveral [primaße'ral] *a* spring *cpd*, springlike.

primero, a [pri'mero, a] *a* (*delante de nmsg*: **primer**) first; (*fig*) prime; (*anterior*) former; (*básico*) fundamental ♦ *ad* first; (*más bien*) sooner, rather ♦ *nf* (*AUTO*) first gear; (*FERRO*) first class; **de primera** (*fam*) first-class, first-rate; **de buenas a primeras** suddenly; **primera dama** (*TEATRO*) leading lady.

primicias [primi'θjas] *nfpl* first fruits (*tb fig*).

primitivo, a [primi'tißo, a] *a* primitive; (*original*) original; (*COM*: *acción*) ordinary.

primo, a ['primo, a] *a* (*MAT*) prime ♦ *nm/f* cousin; (*fam*) fool, dupe ♦ *nf* (*COM*) bonus; (*seguro*) premium; (*a la exportación*) subsidy; ~ **hermano** first cousin; **materias primas** raw materials; **hacer el** ~ to be taken for a ride.

primogénito, a [primo'xenito, a] *a* firstborn.

primordial [primor'ðjal] *a* basic, fundamental.

primoroso, a [primo'roso, a] *a* exquisite, fine.

princesa [prin'θesa] *nf* princess.

principado [prinθi'paðo] *nm* principality.

principal [prinθi'pal] *a* principal, main; (*más destacado*) foremost; (*piso*) first, second (*US*); (*INFORM*) foreground ♦ *nm* (*jefe*) chief, principal.

príncipe ['prinθipe] *nm* prince; ~ **heredero** crown prince; ~ **de gales** (*tela*) check.

principiante [prinθi'pjante] *nm/f* beginner; (*novato*) novice.

principiar [prinθi'pjar] *vt* to begin.

principio [prin'θipjo] *nm* (*comienzo*) beginning, start; (*origen*) origin; (*base*) rudiment, basic idea; (*moral*) principle; **a** ~**s de** at the beginning of; **desde el** ~ from the first; **en un** ~ at first.

pringar [prin'gar] *vt* (*CULIN*: *pan*) to dip; (*ensuciar*) to dirty; ~**se** *vr* to get splashed *o* soiled; ~ **a uno en un asunto** (*fam*) to involve sb in a matter.

pringoso, a [prin'goso, a] *a* greasy; (*pegajoso*) sticky.

pringue ['pringe] *etc vb V* **pringar** ♦ *nm* (*grasa*) grease, fat, dripping.

prioridad [priori'ðað] *nf* priority; (*AUTO*) right of way.

prioritario, a [priori'tarjo, a] *a* (*INFORM*) foreground.

prisa ['prisa] *nf* (*apresuramiento*) hurry, haste; (*rapidez*) speed; (*urgencia*) (sense of) urgency; **correr** ~ to be urgent; **darse** ~ to hurry up; **estar de** *o* **tener** ~ to be in a hurry.

prisión [pri'sjon] *nf* (*cárcel*) prison; (*período de cárcel*) imprisonment.

prisionero, a [prisjo'nero, a] *nm/f* prisoner.

prismáticos [pris'matikos] *nmpl* binoculars.

privación [prißa'θjon] *nf* deprivation; (*falta*) want, privation; **privaciones** *nfpl* hardships, privations.

privado, a [pri'ßaðo, a] *a* (*particular*) private; (*POL*: *favorito*) favourite (*Brit*), favorite (*US*); **en** ~ privately, in private; "~ **y confidencial**" "private and confidential".

privar [pri'ßar] *vt* to deprive; ~**se** *vr*: ~**se**

de (*abstenerse*) to deprive o.s. of; (*renunciar*) to give up.

privativo, a [priβa'tiβo, a] *a* exclusive.

privilegiado, a [priβile'xjaðo, a] *a* privileged; (*memoria*) very good ♦ *nm/f* (*afortunado*) privileged person.

privilegiar [priβile'xjar] *vt* to grant a privilege to; (*favorecer*) to favour.

privilegio [priβi'lexjo] *nm* privilege; (*concesión*) concession.

pro [pro] *nm o nf* profit, advantage ♦ *prep*: **asociación ~ ciegos** association for the blind ♦ *pref*: **~ soviético/americano** pro-Soviet/-American; **en ~ de** on behalf of, for; **los ~s y los contras** the pros and cons.

proa ['proa] *nf* (*NAUT*) bow, prow.

probabilidad [proβaβili'ðað] *nf* probability, likelihood; (*oportunidad*, *posibilidad*) chance, prospect.

probable [pro'βaβle] *a* probable, likely; **es ~ que** + *subjun* it is probable *o* likely that; **es ~ que no venga** he probably won't come.

probador [proβa'ðor] *nm* (*persona*) taster (*of wine etc*); (*en una tienda*) fitting room.

probar [pro'βar] *vt* (*demostrar*) to prove; (*someter a prueba*) to test, try out; (*ropa*) to try on; (*comida*) to taste ♦ *vi* to try; **~se** *vr*: **~se un traje** to try on a suit.

probeta [pro'βeta] *nf* test tube.

problema [pro'βlema] *nm* problem.

procaz [pro'kaθ] *a* insolent, impudent.

procedencia [proθe'ðenθja] *nf* (*principio*) source, origin; (*lugar de salida*) point of departure.

procedente [proθe'ðente] *a* (*razonable*) reasonable; (*conforme a derecho*) proper, fitting; **~ de** coming from, originating in.

proceder [proθe'ðer] *vi* (*avanzar*) to proceed; (*actuar*) to act; (*ser correcto*) to be right (and proper), be fitting ♦ *nm* (*comportamiento*) behaviour, conduct; **no procede obrar así** it is not right to act like that; **~ de** to come from, originate in.

procedimiento [proθeði'mjento] *nm* procedure; (*proceso*) process; (*método*) means, method; (*trámite*) proceedings.

prócer ['proθer] *nm* (*persona eminente*) worthy; (*líder*) great man, leader.

procesado, a [proθe'saðo, a] *nm/f* accused (person).

procesador [proθesa'ðor] *nm*: **~ de textos** (*INFORM*) word processor.

procesamiento [proθesa'mjento] *nm* (*INFORM*) processing; **~ de datos** data processing; **~ por lotes** batch processing; **~ solapado** multiprogramming; **~ de textos** word processing.

procesar [proθe'sar] *vt* to try, put on trial; (*INFORM*) to process.

procesión [proθe'sjon] *nf* procession; **la ~ va por dentro** he keeps his troubles to himself.

proceso [pro'θeso] *nm* process; (*JUR*) trial; (*lapso*) course (of time); (*INFORM*): **~ (automático) de datos** (automatic) data processing; **~ no prioritario** background process; **~ por pasadas** batch processing; **~ en tiempo real** real-time programming.

proclama [pro'klama] *nf* (*acto*) proclamation; (*cartel*) poster.

proclamar [prokla'mar] *vt* to proclaim.

proclive [pro'kliβe] *a*: **~ (a)** inclined *o* prone (to).

procreación [prokrea'θjon] *nf* procreation.

procrear [prokre'ar] *vt*, *vi* to procreate.

procurador, a [prokura'ðor, a] *nm/f* attorney, solicitor.

procurar [proku'rar] *vt* (*intentar*) to try, endeavour; (*conseguir*) to get, obtain; (*asegurar*) to secure; (*producir*) to produce.

prodigio [pro'ðixjo] *nm* prodigy; (*milagro*) wonder, marvel.

prodigioso, a [proði'xjoso, a] *a* prodigious, marvellous.

pródigo, a ['proðiyo, a] *a* (*rico*) rich, productive; **hijo ~** prodigal son.

producción [proðuk'θjon] *nf* production; (*suma de productos*) output; (*producto*) product; **~ en serie** mass production.

producir [proðu'θir] *vt* to produce; (*generar*) to cause, bring about; (*impresión*) to give; (*COM*: *interés*) to bear; **~se** *vr* (*gen*) to come about, happen; (*hacerse*) to be produced, be made; (*estallar*) to break out; (*accidente*) to take place.

productividad [proðuktiβi'ðað] *nf* productivity.

productivo, a [proðuk'tiβo, a] *a* productive; (*provechoso*) profitable.

producto [pro'ðukto] *nm* (*resultado*) product; (*producción*) production; **~ alimenticio** foodstuff; **~ (nacional) bruto** gross (national) product; **~ interno bruto** gross domestic product.

productor, a [proðuk'tor, a] *a* productive, producing ♦ *nm/f* producer.

produje [pro'ðuxe], **produjera** [proðu'xera], **produzca** [pro'ðuθka] *etc vb V* **producir**.

proeza [pro'eθa] *nf* exploit, feat.

profanar [profa'nar] *vt* to desecrate, profane.

profano, a [pro'fano, a] *a* profane ♦ *nm/f* (*inexperto*) layman/woman; **soy ~ en música** I don't know anything about music.

profecía [profe'θia] *nf* prophecy.

proferir [profe'rir] *vt* (*palabra*, *sonido*) to utter; (*injuria*) to hurl, let fly.

profesar [profe'sar] *vt* (*declarar*) to profess; (*practicar*) to practise.

profesiograma [profesjo'ɣrama] *nm* job

specification.

profesión [profe'sjon] *nf* profession; (*confesión*) avowal; **abogado de ~, de ~ abogado** a lawyer by profession.

profesional [profesjo'nal] *a* professional.

profesor, a [profe'sor, a] *nm/f* teacher; (*instructor*) instructor; (~ *de universidad*) lecturer; ~ **adjunto** assistant lecturer, associate professor (*US*).

profesorado [profeso'raðo] *nm* (*profesión*) teaching profession; (*cuerpo*) teaching staff, faculty (*US*); (*cargo*) professorship.

profeta [pro'feta] *nm/f* prophet.

profetice [profe'tiθe] *etc vb* V **profetizar**.

profetizar [profeti'θar] *vt, vi* to prophesy.

profiera [pro'fjera] *etc*, **profiriendo** [profi'rjendo] *etc vb* V **proferir**.

profilaxis [profi'laksis] *nf inv* prevention.

prófugo, a ['profuɣo, a] *nm/f* fugitive; (*desertor*) deserter.

profundice [profun'diθe] *etc vb* V **profundizar**.

profundidad [profundi'ðað] *nf* depth; **tener una ~ de 30 cm** to be 30 cm deep.

profundizar [profundi'θar] *vt* (*fig*) to go deeply into, study in depth.

profundo, a [pro'fundo, a] *a* deep; (*misterio, pensador*) profound; **poco ~** shallow.

profusión [profu'sjon] *nf* (*abundancia*) profusion; (*prodigalidad*) wealth.

progenie [pro'xenje] *nf* offspring.

progenitor [proxeni'tor] *nm* ancestor; ~**es** *nmpl* (*fam*) parents.

programa [pro'ɣrama] *nm* programme; (*INFORM*) program; ~ **de estudios** curriculum, syllabus; ~ **verificador de ortografía** (*INFORM*) spelling checker.

programación [proɣrama'θjon] *nf* (*INFORM*) programming; ~ **estructurada** structured programming.

programador, a [proɣrama'ðor, a] *nm/f* (computer) programmer; ~ **de aplicaciones** applications programmer.

programar [proɣra'mar] *vt* (*INFORM*) to programme.

programería [proɣrame'ria] *nf* (*INFORM*): ~ **fija** firmware.

progresar [proɣre'sar] *vi* to progress, make progress.

progresista [proɣre'sista] *a, nm/f* progressive.

progresivo, a [proɣre'siβo, a] *a* progressive; (*gradual*) gradual; (*continuo*) continuous.

progreso [pro'ɣreso] *nm* (*tb*: ~**s**) progress; **hacer ~s** to progress, advance.

prohibición [proiβi'θjon] *nf* prohibition, ban; **levantar la ~ de** to remove the ban on.

prohibir [proi'βir] *vt* to prohibit, ban, forbid; **se prohíbe fumar** no smoking.

prohibitivo, a [proiβi'tiβo, a] *a* prohibitive.

prójimo, a ['proximo, a] *nm* fellow man ♦ *nm/f* (*vecino*) neighbour.

prole ['prole] *nf* (*descendencia*) offspring.

proletariado [proleta'rjaðo] *nm* proletariat.

proletario, a [prole'tarjo, a] *a, nm/f* proletarian.

proliferación [prolifera'θjon] *nf* proliferation; ~ **de armas nucleares** spread of nuclear arms.

proliferar [prolife'rar] *vi* to proliferate.

prolífico, a [pro'lifiko, a] *a* prolific.

prolijo, a [pro'lixo, a] *a* long-winded, tedious.

prólogo ['proloɣo] *nm* prologue; (*preámbulo*) preface, introduction.

prolongación [prolonga'θjon] *nf* extension.

prolongado, a [prolon'gaðo, a] *a* (*largo*) long; (*alargado*) lengthy.

prolongar [prolon'gar] *vt* (*gen*) to extend; (*en el tiempo*) to prolong; (*calle, tubo*) to make longer, extend; ~**se** *vr* (*alargarse*) to extend, go on.

prolongue [pro'longe] *etc vb* V **prolongar**.

prom. *abr* (= *promedio*) av.

promedio [pro'meðjo] *nm* average; (*de distancia*) middle, mid-point.

promesa [pro'mesa] *nf* promise ♦ *a*: **jugador** ~ promising player; **faltar a una** ~ to break a promise.

prometer [prome'ter] *vt* to promise ♦ *vi* to show promise; ~**se** *vr* (*dos personas*) to get engaged.

prometido, a [prome'tiðo, a] *a* promised; engaged ♦ *nm/f* fiancé/fiancée.

prominente [promi'nente] *a* prominent.

promiscuidad [promiskwi'ðað] *nf* promiscuity.

promiscuo, a [pro'miskwo, a] *a* promiscuous.

promoción [promo'θjon] *nf* promotion; (*año*) class, year; ~ **por correspondencia directa** (*COM*) direct mailshot; ~ **de ventas** sales promotion *o* drive.

promocionar [promoθjo'nar] *vt* (*COM*: *dar publicidad*) to promote.

promotor [promo'tor] *nm* promoter; (*instigador*) instigator.

promover [promo'βer] *vt* to promote; (*causar*) to cause; (*juicio*) to bring; (*motín*) to instigate, stir up.

promueva [pro'mweβa] *etc vb* V **promover**.

promulgar [promul'ɣar] *vt* to promulgate; (*fig*) to proclaim.

promulgue [pro'mulɣe] *etc vb* V **promulgar**.

pronombre [pro'nombre] *nm* pronoun.

pronosticar [pronosti'kar] *vt* to predict, foretell, forecast.

pronóstico [pro'nostiko] *nm* prediction,

forecast; (*profecía*) omen; (*MED*: *diagnósti-co*) prognosis; **de ~ leve** slight, not serious; **~ del tiempo** weather forecast.

pronostique [pronos'tike] *etc vb* V **pronosticar**.

prontitud [pronti'tuð] *nf* speed, quickness.

pronto, a ['pronto, a] *a* (*rápido*) prompt, quick; (*preparado*) ready ◆ *ad* quickly, promptly; (*en seguida*) at once, right away; (*dentro de poco*) soon; (*temprano*) early ◆ *nm* urge, sudden feeling; **tener ~s de enojo** to be quick-tempered; **al ~** at first; **de ~** suddenly; **¡hasta ~!** see you soon!; **lo más ~ posible** as soon as possible; **por lo ~** meanwhile, for the present; **tan ~ como** as soon as.

pronunciación [pronunθja'θjon] *nf* pronunciation.

pronunciado, a [pronun'θjaðo, a] *a* (*marcado*) pronounced; (*curva etc*) sharp; (*facciones*) marked.

pronunciamiento [pronunθja'mjento] *nm* (*rebelión*) insurrection.

pronunciar [pronun'θjar] *vt* to pronounce; (*discurso*) to make, deliver; (*JUR*: *sentencia*) to pass, pronounce; **~se** *vr* to revolt, rise, rebel; (*declararse*) to declare o.s.; **~se sobre** to pronounce on.

propagación [propaɣa'θjon] *nf* propagation; (*difusión*) spread(ing).

propaganda [propa'ɣanda] *nf* (*política*) propaganda; (*comercial*) advertising; **hacer ~ de** (*COM*) to advertise.

propagar [propa'ɣar] *vt* to propagate; (*difundir*) to spread, disseminate; **~se** *vr* (*BIO*) to propagate; (*fig*) to spread.

propague [pro'paɣe] *etc vb* V **propagar**.

propalar [propa'lar] *vt* (*divulgar*) to divulge; (*publicar*) to publish an account of.

propasarse [propa'sarse] *vr* (*excederse*) to go too far; (*sexualmente*) to take liberties.

propensión [propen'sjon] *nf* inclination, propensity.

propenso, a [pro'penso, a] *a*: **~ a** prone *o* inclined to; **ser ~ a hacer algo** to be inclined *o* have a tendency to do sth.

propiamente [propja'mente] *ad* properly; (*realmente*) really, exactly; **~ dicho** real, true.

propicio, a [pro'piθjo, a] *a* favourable, propitious.

propiedad [propje'ðað] *nf* property; (*posesión*) possession, ownership; (*conveniencia*) suitability; (*exactitud*) accuracy; **~ particular** private property; **~ pública** (*COM*) public ownership; **ceder algo a uno en ~** to transfer to sb the full rights over sth.

propietario, a [propje'tarjo, a] *nm/f* owner, proprietor.

propina [pro'pina] *nf* tip; **dar algo de ~** to

give something extra.

propinar [propi'nar] *vt* (*golpe*) to strike; (*azotes*) to give.

propio, a ['propjo, a] *a* own, of one's own; (*característico*) characteristic, typical; (*conveniente*) proper; (*mismo*) selfsame, very; **el ~ ministro** the minister himself; **¿tienes casa propia?** have you a house of your own?; **eso es muy ~ de él** that's just like him; **tiene un olor muy ~** it has a smell of its own.

propondré [propon'dre] *etc vb* V **proponer**.

proponente [propo'nente] *nm* proposer, mover.

proponer [propo'ner] *vt* to propose, put forward; (*candidato*) to propose, nominate; (*problema*) to pose; **~se** *vr* to propose, plan, intend.

proponga [pro'ponga] *etc vb* V **proponer**.

proporción [propor'θjon] *nf* proportion; (*MAT*) ratio; (*razón, porcentaje*) rate; **proporciones** *nfpl* dimensions; (*fig*) size *sg*; **en ~ con** in proportion to.

proporcionado, a [proporθjo'naðo, a] *a* proportionate; (*regular*) medium, middling; (*justo*) just right; **bien ~** well-proportioned.

proporcionar [proporθjo'nar] *vt* (*dar*) to give, supply, provide; **esto le proporciona una renta anual de ...** this brings him in a yearly income of ...

proposición [proposi'θjon] *nf* proposition; (*propuesta*) proposal.

propósito [pro'posito] *nm* (*intención*) purpose; (*intento*) aim, intention ◆ *ad*: **a ~** by the way, incidentally; **a ~ de** about, with regard to.

propuesto, a [pro'pwesto, a] *pp de* **proponer** ◆ *nf* proposal.

propulsar [propul'sar] *vt* to drive, propel; (*fig*) to promote, encourage.

propulsión [propul'sjon] *nf* propulsion; **~ a chorro** *o* **por reacción** jet propulsion.

propuse [pro'puse] *etc vb* V **proponer**.

prorrata [pro'rrata] *nf* (*porción*) share, quota, prorate (*US*) ◆ *ad* (*COM*) pro rata.

prorratear [prorrate'ar] *vt* (*dividir*) to share out, prorate (*US*).

prórroga ['prorroɣa] *nf* (*gen*) extension; (*JUR*) stay; (*COM*) deferment.

prorrogable [prorro'ɣaβle] *a* which can be extended.

prorrogar [prorro'ɣar] *vt* (*período*) to extend; (*decisión*) to defer, postpone.

prorrogue [pro'rroɣe] *etc vb* V **prorrogar**.

prorrumpir [prorrum'pir] *vi* to burst forth, break out; **~ en gritos** to start shouting; **~ en lágrimas** to burst into tears.

prosa ['prosa] *nf* prose.

proscribir [proskri'βir] *vt* to prohibit, ban;

proscripción [proskrip'θjon] *nf* prohibition, ban; banishment; proscription.

proscrito, a [pros'krito, a] *pp de* **proscribir** ♦ *a* (*prohibido*) banned; (*desterrado*) outlawed ♦ *nm/f* (*exilado*) exile; (*bandido*) outlaw.

prosecución [proseku'θjon] *nf* continuation; (*persecución*) pursuit.

proseguir [prose'ɣir] *vt* to continue, carry on, proceed with; (*investigación, estudio*) to pursue ♦ *vi* to continue, go on.

prosiga [pro'siɣa] *etc*, **prosiguiendo** [prosi'ɣjenðo] *etc vb* V **proseguir**.

prosista [pro'sista] *nm/f* (*escritor*) prose writer.

prospección [prospek'θjon] *nf* exploration; (*del petróleo, del oro*) prospecting.

prospecto [pros'pekto] *nm* prospectus; (*folleto*) leaflet, sheet of instructions.

prosperar [prospe'rar] *vi* to prosper, thrive, flourish.

prosperidad [prosperi'ðað] *nf* prosperity; (*éxito*) success.

próspero, a ['prospero, a] *a* prosperous, thriving, flourishing; (*que tiene éxito*) successful.

prostíbulo [pros'tiβulo] *nm* brothel.

prostitución [prostitu'θjon] *nf* prostitution.

prostituir [prosti'twir] *vt* to prostitute; ~**se** *vr* to prostitute o.s., become a prostitute.

prostituta [prosti'tuta] *nf* prostitute.

prostituyendo [prostitu'jendo] *etc vb* V **prostituir**.

protagonice [protaɣo'niθe] *etc vb* V **protagonizar**.

protagonista [protaɣo'nista] *nm/f* protagonist; (*LIT*: *personaje*) main character, hero(ine).

protagonizar [protaɣoni'θar] *vt* to head, take the chief role in.

protección [protek'θjon] *nf* protection.

proteccionismo [protekθjo'nismo] *nm* (*COM*) protectionism.

protector, a [protek'tor, a] *a* protective, protecting; (*tono*) patronizing ♦ *nm/f* protector; (*bienhechor*) patron; (*de la tradición*) guardian.

proteger [prote'xer] *vt* to protect; ~ **contra grabación** *o* **contra escritura** (*INFORM*) to write-protect.

protegido, a [prote'xiðo, a] *nm/f* protégé/protégée.

proteína [prote'ina] *nf* protein.

proteja [pro'texa] *etc vb* V **proteger**.

protesta [pro'testa] *nf* protest; (*declaración*) protestation.

protestante [protes'tante] *a* Protestant.

protestar [protes'tar] *vt* to protest, declare; (*fe*) to protest ♦ *vi* to protest; (*objetar*) to object; **cheque protestado por falta de fondos** cheque referred to drawer.

protocolo [proto'kolo] *nm* protocol; **sin ~s** (*formalismo*) informal(ly), without formalities.

prototipo [proto'tipo] *nm* prototype; (*ideal*) model.

prov. *abr* (= *provincia*) prov.

provecho [pro'βetʃo] *nm* advantage, benefit; (*FINANZAS*) profit; **¡buen ~!** bon appétit!; **en ~ de** to the benefit of; **sacar ~ de** to benefit from, profit by.

provechoso, a [proβe'tʃoso, a] *a* (*ventajoso*) advantageous; (*beneficioso*) beneficial, useful; (*FINANZAS*: *lucrativo*) profitable.

proveedor, a [proβee'ðor, a] *nm/f* (*abastecedor*) supplier; (*distribuidor*) dealer.

proveer [proβe'er] *vt* to provide, supply; (*preparar*) to provide, get ready; (*vacante*) to fill; (*negocio*) to transact, dispatch ♦ *vi*: ~ **a** to provide for; ~**se** *vr*: ~**se de** to provide o.s. with.

provendré [proβen'dre] *etc*, **provenga** [pro'βenɡa] *etc vb* V **provenir**.

provenir [proβe'nir] *vi*: ~ **de** to come from, stem from.

Provenza [pro'βenθa] *nf* Provence.

proverbial [proβer'βjal] *a* proverbial; (*fig*) notorious.

proverbio [pro'βerβjo] *nm* proverb.

proveyendo [proβe'jendo] *etc vb* V **proveer**.

providencia [proβi'ðenθja] *nf* providence; (*previsión*) foresight; ~**s** *nfpl* measures, steps.

provincia [pro'βinθja] *nf* province; **un pueblo de ~(s)** a country town.

provinciano, a [proβin'θjano, a] *a* provincial; (*del campo*) country *cpd*.

proviniendo [proβi'njendo] *etc vb* V **provenir**.

provisión [proβi'sjon] *nf* provision; (*abastecimiento*) provision, supply; (*medida*) measure, step.

provisional [proβisjo'nal] *a* provisional.

provisto, a [pro'βisto, a] *a*: ~ **de** provided *o* supplied with; (*que tiene*) having, possessing.

provocación [proβoka'θjon] *nf* provocation.

provocador, a [proβoka'ðor, a] *a* provocative, provoking.

provocar [proβo'kar] *vt* to provoke; (*alentar*) to tempt, invite; (*causar*) to bring about, lead to; (*promover*) to promote; (*estimular*) to rouse, stir, stimulate; (*protesta, explosión*) to cause, spark off; (*AM*): **¿te provoca un café?** would you like a coffee?

provocativo, a [proβoka'tiβo, a] *a* provocative.

provoque [pro'βoke] *etc vb* V **provocar**.

proxeneta [prokse'neta] *nm/f* go-between; (*de prostitutas*) pimp/procuress.

próximamente [proksima'mente] *ad* shortly, soon.

proximidad [proksimi'ðað] *nf* closeness, proximity.

próximo, a ['proksimo, a] *a* near, close; (*vecino*) neighbouring; (*el que viene*) next; **en fecha próxima** at an early date; **el mes ~** next month.

proyección [projek'θjon] *nf* projection; (*CINE*) showing; (*diapositiva*) slide, transparency; (*influencia*) influence; **el tiempo de ~ es de 35 minutos** the film runs for 35 minutes.

proyectar [projek'tar] *vt* (*objeto*) to hurl, throw; (*luz*) to cast, shed; (*CINE*) to screen, show; (*planear*) to plan.

proyectil [projek'til] *nm* projectile, missile; **~ (tele)dirigido** guided missile.

proyecto [pro'jekto] *nm* plan; (*idea*) project; (*estimación de costo*) detailed estimate; **tener algo en ~** to be planning sth; **~ de ley** (*POL*) bill.

proyector [projek'tor] *nm* (*CINE*) projector.

prudencia [pru'ðenθja] *nf* (*sabiduría*) wisdom, prudence; (*cautela*) care.

prudente [pru'ðente] *a* sensible, wise, prudent; (*cauteloso*) careful.

prueba ['prweßa] *etc vb* **V** probar ♦ *nf* proof; (*ensayo*) test, trial; (*cantidad*) taste, sample; (*saboreo*) testing, sampling; (*de ropa*) fitting; (*DEPORTE*) event; **a ~ on** trial; (*COM*) on approval; **a ~ de** proof against; **a ~ de agua/fuego** waterproof/ fireproof; **~ de capacitación** (*COM*) proficiency test; **~ de fuego** (*fig*) acid test; **~ de vallas** hurdles; **someter a ~** to put to the test; **¿tiene usted ~ de ello?** can you prove it?, do you have proof?

prurito [pru'rito] *nm* itch; (*de bebé*) nappy rash; (*anhelo*) urge.

PS *nm abr* (*POL*) = *Partido Socialista.*

psico... [siko] *pref* psycho...

psicoanálisis [sikoa'nalisis] *nm* psychoanalysis.

psicoanalista [sikoana'lista] *nm/f* psychoanalyst.

psicología [sikolo'xia] *nf* psychology.

psicológico, a [siko'loxiko, a] *a* psychological.

psicólogo, a [si'kolovo, a] *nm/f* psychologist.

psicópata [si'kopata] *nm/f* psychopath.

psicosis [si'kosis] *nf inv* psychosis.

psicoterapia [sikote'rapja] *nf* psychotherapy.

psiquiatra [si'kjatra] *nm/f* psychiatrist.

psiquiátrico, a [si'kjatriko, a] *a* psychiatric.

psíquico, a ['sikiko, a] *a* psychic(al).

PSOE [pe'soe] *nm abr* = *Partido Socialista Obrero Español.*

Pta. *abr* (*GEO*: = *Punta*) Pt.

pta(s). *abr* = **peseta(s).**

ptmo. *abr* (*COM*) = **préstamo.**

pts. *abr* = **pesetas.**

púa ['pua] *nf* sharp point; (*para guitarra*) plectrum; **alambre de ~s** barbed wire.

púber, a ['pußer, a] *a*, *nm/f* adolescent.

pubertad [pußer'tað] *nf* puberty.

publicación [pußlika'θjon] *nf* publication.

publicar [pußli'kar] *vt* (*editar*) to publish; (*hacer público*) to publicize; (*divulgar*) to make public, divulge.

publicidad [pußliθi'ðað] *nf* publicity; (*COM*) advertising; **dar ~ a** to publicize, give publicity to; **~ gráfica** display advertising; **~ en el punto de venta** point-of-sale advertising.

publicitar [pußliθi'tar] *vt* to publicize.

publicitario, a [pußliθi'tarjo, a] *a* publicity *cpd*; advertising *cpd*.

público, a ['pußliko, a] *a* public ♦ *nm* public; (*TEATRO etc*) audience; (*DEPORTE*) spectators *pl*, crowd; (*restaurantes etc*) clients *pl*; **el gran ~** the general public; **hacer ~** to publish; (*difundir*) to disclose; **~ objetivo** (*COM*) target audience.

publique [pu'ßlike] *etc vb* **V** publicar.

pucherazo [putʃe'raθo] *nm* (*fraude*) electoral fiddle; **dar ~** to rig an election.

puchero [pu'tʃero] *nm* (*CULIN*: *olla*) cooking pot; (: *guiso*) stew; **hacer ~s** to pout.

pudibundo, a [puði'ßundo, a] *a* bashful.

púdico, a ['puðiko, a] *a* modest; (*pudibundo*) bashful.

pudiendo [pu'ðjendo] *etc vb* **V** poder.

pudiente [pu'ðjente] *a* (*opulento*) wealthy; (*poderoso*) powerful.

pudín [pu'ðin] *nm* pudding.

pudor [pu'ðor] *nm* modesty; (*vergüenza*) (sense of) shame.

pudoroso, a [puðo'roso, a] *a* (*modesto*) modest; (*casto*) chaste.

pudrir [pu'ðrir] *vt* to rot; (*fam*) to upset, annoy; **~se** *vr* to rot, decay; (*fig*) to rot, languish.

pueblerino, a [pweßle'rino, a] *a* (*lugareño*) small-town *cpd*; (*persona*) rustic, provincial ♦ *nm/f* (*aldeano*) country person.

pueblo ['pweßlo] *etc vb* **V** poblar ♦ *nm* people; (*nación*) nation; (*aldea*) village; (*plebe*) common people; (*población pequeña*) small town, country town.

pueda ['pweða] *etc vb* **V** poder.

puente ['pwente] *nm* (*gen*) bridge; (*NAUT*: *tb*: **~ de mando**) bridge; (: *cubierta*) deck; **~ aéreo** airlift; **~ colgante** suspension bridge; **~ levadizo** drawbridge; **hacer (el) ~** (*fam*) to take a long weekend.

puerco, a ['pwerko, a] *a* (*sucio*) dirty,

filthy; (*obsceno*) disgusting ♦ *nm/f* pig/sow.

pueril [pwe'ril] *a* childish.

puerro ['pwerro] *nm* leek.

puerta ['pwerta] *nf* door; (*de jardín*) gate; (*portal*) doorway; (*fig*) gateway; (*gol*) goal; (*INFORM*) port; **a ~ cerrada** behind closed doors; **~ corredera/giratoria** sliding/swing *o* revolving door; **~ principal/trasera** *o* **de servicio** front/back door; **~ (de transmisión en) paralelo/serie** (*INFORM*) parallel/serial port; **tomar la ~** (*fam*) to leave.

puerto ['pwerto] *nm* (*tb INFORM*) port; (*de mar*) seaport; (*paso*) pass; (*fig*) haven, refuge; **llegar a ~** (*fig*) to get over a difficulty.

Puerto Rico [pwerto'riko] *nm* Puerto Rico.

puertorriqueño, a [pwertorri'keɲo, a] *a*, *nm/f* Puerto Rican.

pues [pwes] *ad* (*entonces*) then; (¡*entonces!*) well, well then; (*así que*) so ♦ *conj* (*porque*) since; **~ ... no sé** well ... I don't know.

puesto, a ['pwesto, a] *pp de* **poner** ♦ *a* dressed ♦ *nm* (*lugar, posición*) place; (*trabajo*) post, job; (*MIL*) stall; (*COM*) stall; (*quiosco*) kiosk ♦ *conj*: **~ que** since, as ♦ *nf* (*apuesta*) bet, stake; **~ de mercado** market stall; **~ de policía** police station; **~ de socorro** first aid post; **puesta en escena** staging; **puesta en marcha** starting; **puesta del sol** sunset; **puesta a cero** (*INFORM*) reset.

pugna ['puɣna] *nf* battle, conflict.

pugnar [puɣ'nar] *vi* (*luchar*) to struggle, fight; (*pelear*) to fight.

puja ['puxa] *nf* (*esfuerzo*) attempt; (*en una subasta*) bid.

pujante [pu'xante] *a* strong, vigorous.

pujar [pu'xar] *vt* (*precio*) to raise, push up ♦ *vi* (*en licitación*) to bid, bid up; (*fig: esforzarse*) to struggle, strain.

pulcro, a ['pulkro, a] *a* neat, tidy.

pulga ['pulɣa] *nf* flea; **tener malas ~s** to be short-tempered.

pulgada [pul'ɣaða] *nf* inch.

pulgar [pul'ɣar] *nm* thumb.

pulgón [pul'ɣon] *nm* plant louse, greenfly.

pulir [pu'lir] *vt* to polish; (*alisar*) to smooth; (*fig*) to polish up, touch up.

pulmón [pul'mon] *nm* lung; **a pleno ~** (*respirar*) deeply; (*gritar*) at the top of one's voice; **~ de acero** iron lung.

pulmonía [pulmo'nia] *nf* pneumonia.

pulpa ['pulpa] *nf* pulp; (*de fruta*) flesh, soft part.

pulpería [pulpe'ria] *nf* (*AM*) small grocery store.

púlpito ['pulpito] *nm* pulpit.

pulpo ['pulpo] *nm* octopus.

pulsación [pulsa'θjon] *nf* beat, pulsation;

(*ANAT*) throb(bing); (*en máquina de escribir*) tap; (*de pianista, mecanógrafo*) touch; **~ (de una tecla)** (*INFORM*) keystroke; **~ doble** (*INFORM*) strikeover.

pulsador [pulsa'ðor] *nm* button, push button.

pulsar [pul'sar] *vt* (*tecla*) to touch, tap; (*MUS*) to play; (*botón*) to press, push ♦ *vi* to pulsate; (*latir*) to beat, throb.

pulsera [pul'sera] *nf* bracelet; **reloj de ~** wristwatch.

pulso ['pulso] *nm* (*MED*) pulse; **hacer algo a ~** to do sth unaided *o* by one's own efforts.

pulular [pulu'lar] *vi* (*estar plagado*): **~ (de)** to swarm (with).

pulverice [pulβe'riθe] *etc vb V* **pulverizar**.

pulverizador [pulβeriθa'ðor] *nm* spray, spray gun.

pulverizar [pulβeri'θar] *vt* to pulverize; (*líquido*) to spray.

pulla ['puʎa] *nf* cutting remark.

puna ['puna] *nf* (*AM MED*) mountain sickness.

punce ['punθe] *etc vb V* **punzar**.

punción [pun'θjon] *nf* (*MED*) puncture.

pundonor [pundo'nor] *nm* (*dignidad*) self-respect.

punición [puni'θjon] *nf* punishment.

punitivo, a [puni'tiβo, a] *a* punitive.

punta ['punta] *nf* point, tip; (*extremidad*) end; (*promontorio*) headland; (*COSTURA*) corner; (*TEC*) small nail; (*fig*) touch, trace; **horas ~s** peak hours, rush hours; **sacar ~ a** to sharpen; **de ~** on end; **de ~ a** from one end to the other; **estar de ~** to be edgy; **ir de ~ en blanco** to be all dressed up to the nines; **tener algo en la ~ de la lengua** to have sth on the tip of one's tongue; **se le pusieron los pelos de ~** her hair stood on end.

puntada [pun'taða] *nf* (*COSTURA*) stitch.

puntal [pun'tal] *nm* prop, support.

puntapié [punta'pje], *pl* **puntapiés** *nm* kick; **echar a uno a ~s** to kick sb out.

punteado, a [punte'aðo, a] *a* (*moteado*) dotted; (*diseño*) of dots ♦ *nm* (*MUS*) twang.

puntear [punte'ar] *vt* to tick, mark; (*MUS*) to pluck.

puntería [punte'ria] *nf* (*de arma*) aim, aiming; (*destreza*) marksmanship.

puntero, a [pun'tero, a] *a* leading ♦ *nm* (*señal, INFORM*) pointer; (*dirigente*) leader.

puntiagudo, a [puntja'ɣuðo, a] *a* sharp, pointed.

puntilla [pun'tiʎa] *nf* (*TEC*) tack, braid; (*COSTURA*) lace edging; **(andar) de ~s** (to walk) on tiptoe.

puntilloso, a [punti'ʎoso, a] *a* (*pundonoroso*) punctilious; (*susceptible*) touchy.

punto ['punto] *nm* (*gen*) point; (*señal diminuta*) spot, dot; (*lugar*) spot, place; (*mo-*

mento) point, moment; (*en un examen*) mark; (*tema*) item; (*COSTURA*) stitch; (*INFORM*: *impresora*) pitch; (: *pantalla*) pixel; **a ~** ready; **estar a ~ de** to be on the point of *o* about to; **llegar a ~** to come just at the right moment; **al ~** at once; **en ~** on the dot; **estar en su ~** (*CULIN*) to be done to a turn; **hasta cierto ~** to some extent; **hacer ~** to knit; **poner un motor en ~** to tune an engine; **~ de partida/de congelación/de fusión** starting/freezing/melting point; **~ de vista** point of view, viewpoint; **~ muerto** dead centre; (*AUTO*) neutral (gear); **~s a tratar** matters to be discussed, agenda *sg*; **~ final** full stop; **dos ~s** colon; **~ y coma** semicolon; **~ de interrogación** question mark; **~s suspensivos** suspension points; **~ de equilibrio/de pedido** (*COM*) breakeven/reorder point; **~ inicial** *o* **de partida** (*INFORM*) home; **~ de referencia/de venta** (*COM*) benchmark point/point-of-sale.

puntuación [puntwa'θjon] *nf* punctuation; (*puntos: en examen*) mark(s) (*pl*); (: *DEPORTE*) score.

puntual [pun'twal] *a* (*a tiempo*) punctual; (*cálculo*) exact, accurate; (*informe*) reliable.

puntualice [puntwa'liθe] *etc vb V* **puntualizar**.

puntualidad [puntwali'ðað] *nf* punctuality; exactness, accuracy; reliability.

puntualizar [puntwali'θar] *vt* to fix, specify.

puntuar [pun'twar] *vt* (*LING*, *TIP*) to punctuate; (*examen*) to mark ♦ *vi* (*DEPORTE*) to score, count.

punzada [pun'θaða] *nf* (*puntura*) prick; (*MED*) stitch; (*dolor*) twinge (of pain).

punzante [pun'θante] *a* (*dolor*) shooting, sharp; (*herramienta*) sharp; (*comentario*) biting.

punzar [pun'θar] *vt* to prick, pierce ♦ *vi* to shoot, stab.

punzón [pun'θon] *nm* (*TEC*) punch.

puñado [pu'ɲaðo] *nm* handful (*tb fig*); **a ~s** by handfuls.

puñal [pu'ɲal] *nm* dagger.

puñalada [puɲa'laða] *nf* stab.

puñeta [pu'ɲeta] *nf*: ¡**~!**, ¡**qué ~(s)!** (*fam!*) hell!; **mandar a uno a hacer ~s** (*fam*) to tell sb to go to hell.

puñetazo [puɲe'taθo] *nm* punch.

puño ['puɲo] *nm* (*ANAT*) fist; (*cantidad*) fistful, handful; (*COSTURA*) cuff; (*de herramienta*) handle; **como un ~** (*verdad*) obvious; (*palpable*) tangible, visible; **de ~ y letra del poeta** in the poet's own handwriting.

pupila [pu'pila] *nf* (*ANAT*) pupil.

pupitre [pu'pitre] *nm* desk.

puré [pu're], *pl* **purés** *nm* puree; (*sopa*)

(thick) soup; **~ de patatas** mashed potatoes; **estar hecho ~** (*fig*) to be knackered.

pureza [pu'reθa] *nf* purity.

purga ['purɣa] *nf* purge.

purgante [pur'ɣante] *a*, *nm* purgative.

purgar [pur'ɣar] *vt* to purge; (*POL*: *depurar*) to purge, liquidate; **~se** *vr* (*MED*) to take a purge.

purgatorio [purɣa'torjo] *nm* purgatory.

purgue ['purɣe] *etc vb V* **purgar**.

purificar [purifi'kar] *vt* to purify; (*refinar*) to refine.

purifique [puri'fike] *etc vb V* **purificar**.

puritano, a [puri'tano, a] *a* (*actitud*) puritanical; (*iglesia, tradición*) puritan ♦ *nm/f* puritan.

puro, a ['puro, a] *a* pure; (*depurado*) unadulterated; (*oro*) solid; (*cielo*) clear; (*verdad*) simple, plain ♦ *ad*: **de ~ cansado** out of sheer tiredness ♦ *nm* cigar; **por pura casualidad** by sheer chance.

púrpura ['purpura] *nf* purple.

purpúreo, a [pur'pureo, a] *a* purple.

pus [pus] *nm* pus.

puse ['puse] *etc vb V* **poner**.

pústula ['pustula] *nf* pimple, sore.

puta ['puta] *nf* whore, prostitute.

putañear [putaɲe'ar], **putear** [pute'ar] *vi* to go whoring.

putería [pute'ria] *nf* (*prostitución*) prostitution; (*prostíbulo*) brothel.

putrefacción [putrefak'θjon] *nf* rotting, putrefaction.

pútrido, a ['putriðo, a] *a* rotten.

PVP *abr* (*Esp*: = *Precio Venta al Público*) ≈ RRP.

Q

Q, q [ku] *nf* (*letra*) Q, q; **Q de Querido** Q for Queen.

q.e.g.e. *abr* (= *que en gloria esté*) R.I.P.

q.e.p.d. *abr* (= *que en paz descanse*) R.I.P.

q.e.s.m. *abr* (= *que estrecha su mano*) *courtesy formula*.

qm. *abr* = **quintal(es) métrico(s)**.

qts. *abr* = **quilates**.

que [ke] *pron* (*sujeto: individuo*) who, that; (: *cosa*) which, that; (*complemento: individuo*) whom, that; (: *cosa*) which, that ♦ *conj* that; **el momento en ~ llegó** the moment he arrived; **lo ~ digo** what I say; **dar ~ hablar** to give cause to talk, cause talk; ¡**~ entre!** send him in!; **le ruego ~ se calle** I'm asking you to keep quiet; ¡**~ sí!**

yes!; **te digo ~ sí** I'm telling you, I assure you; **el ~ + subjun** the fact that ...; **ya o por ~** for, since, because; **yo ~ tú** if I were you; **siguió toca ~ toca** he kept on playing.

qué [ke] a what?, which? ♦ pron what?; **¡~ divertido/asco!** how funny/revolting!; **¡~ día más espléndido!** what a glorious day!; **¿~ edad tienes?** how old are you?; **¿de ~ me hablas?** what are you saying to me?; **¿~ tal?** how are you?, how are things?; **¿~ hay (de nuevo)?** what's new?; **¿~ más?** anything else?

quebrada [ke'βraða] nf V **quebrado**.

quebradero [keβra'ðero] nm: **~ de cabeza** headache, worry.

quebradizo, a [keβra'ðiθo, a] a fragile; (persona) frail.

quebrado, a [ke'βraðo, a] a (roto) broken; (terreno) rough, uneven ♦ nm/f bankrupt ♦ nm (MAT) fraction ♦ nf ravine; **~ rehabilitado** discharged bankrupt.

quebradura [keβra'ðura] nf (fisura) fissure; (MED) rupture.

quebrantadura [keβranta'ðura] nf, **quebrantamiento** [keβranta'mjento] nm (acto) breaking; (de ley) violation; (estado) exhaustion.

quebrantar [keβran'tar] vt (infringir) to violate, transgress; **~se** vr (persona) to fail in health.

quebranto [ke'βranto] nm damage, harm; (decaimiento) exhaustion; (dolor) grief, pain.

quebrar [ke'βrar] vt to break, smash ♦ vi to go bankrupt; **~se** vr to break, get broken; (MED) to be ruptured.

queda ['keða] nf: **(toque de) ~** curfew.

quedar [ke'ðar] vi to stay, remain; (encontrarse) to be; (restar) to remain, be left; **~se** vr to remain, stay (behind); **~ en** (acordar) to agree on/to; (acabar siendo) to end up as; **~ por hacer** to be still to be done; **~ ciego/mudo** to be left blind/dumb; **no te queda bien ese vestido** that dress doesn't suit you; **quedamos a las seis** we agreed to meet at six; **eso queda muy lejos** that's a long way (away); **nos quedan 12 kms para llegar al pueblo** there are still 12 kms before we get to the village; **no queda otra** there's no alternative; **~se (con) algo** to keep sth; **~se con uno** (fam) to swindle sb; **~se en nada** to come to nothing o nought; **~se sin** to run out of.

quedo, a ['keðo, a] a still ♦ ad softly, gently.

quehacer [kea'θer] nm task, job; **~es (domésticos)** household chores.

queja ['kexa] nf complaint.

quejarse [ke'xarse] vr (enfermo) to moan,

groan; (protestar) to complain; **~ de que** ... to complain (about the fact) that ...

quejica [ke'xika] a grumpy, complaining ♦ nm/f grumbler, whinger.

quejido [ke'xiðo] nm moan.

quejoso, a [ke'xoso, a] a complaining.

quema ['kema] nf fire; (combustión) burning.

quemado, a [ke'maðo, a] a burnt; (irritado) annoyed.

quemadura [kema'ðura] nf burn, scald; (de sol) sunburn; (de fusible) blow-out.

quemar [ke'mar] vt to burn; (fig: malgastar) to burn up, squander; (COM: precios) to slash, cut; (fastidiar) to annoy, bug ♦ vi to be burning hot; **~se** vr (consumirse) to burn (up); (del sol) to get sunburnt.

quemarropa [kema'rropa]: **a ~** ad point-blank.

quemazón [kema'θon] nf burn; (calor) intense heat; (sensación) itch.

quena ['kena] nf (AM) Indian flute.

quepo ['kepo] etc vb V **caber**.

querella [ke'reʎa] nf (JUR) charge; (disputa) dispute.

querencia [ke'renθja] nf (ZOOL) homing instinct; (fig) homesickness.

querer [ke'rer] vt, vi (desear) to want, wish; (amar) to love; **~ hacer algo** to want to do sth; **como quien no quiere la cosa** offhandedly; **sin ~** unintentionally; **¿quiere abrir la ventana?** would you mind opening the window?; **no quiso** he refused; **~ bien a uno** to be fond of sb.

querido, a [ke'riðo, a] a dear ♦ nm/f darling; (amante) lover; **nuestra querida patria** our beloved country.

querré [ke'rre] etc vb V **querer**.

quesería [kese'ria] nf dairy; (fábrica) cheese factory.

quesero, a [ke'sero, a] a: **la industria quesera** the cheese industry ♦ nm/f cheesemaker ♦ nf cheese dish.

queso ['keso] nm cheese; **~ rallado** grated cheese; **~ crema** cream cheese; **dárselas con ~ a uno** (fam) to take sb in.

quetzal [ket'sal] nm monetary unit of Guatemala.

quicio ['kiθjo] nm hinge; **estar fuera de ~** to be beside o.s.; **sacar a uno de ~** to drive sb up the wall.

quid [kið] nm gist, crux; **dar en el ~** to hit the nail on the head.

quiebra ['kjeβra] nf break, split; (COM) bankruptcy; (ECON) slump.

quiebro ['kjeβro] etc vb V **quebrar** ♦ nm (del cuerpo) swerve.

quien [kjen] pron relativo (suj) who; (complemento) whom; (indefinido): **~ dice eso es tonto** whoever says that is a fool; **hay**

~ **piensa que** there are those who think that; **no hay ~ lo haga** no-one will do it; ~ **más, ~ menos tiene sus problemas** everybody has problems.

quién [kjen] *pron interrogativo* who; *(complemento)* whom; *¿~ es?* who is it?, who's there?; *(TELEC)* who's calling?

quienquiera [kjen'kjera] *(pl* **quienesquiera)** *pron* whoever.

quiera ['kjera] *etc vb* V **querer**.

quieto, a ['kjeto, a] *a* still; *(carácter)* placid; *¡estáte ~!* keep still!

quietud [kje'tuð] *nf* stillness.

quijada [ki'xaða] *nf* jaw, jawbone.

quijote [ki'xote] *nm* dreamer; **Don Q~** Don Quixote.

quil. *abr* = **quilates.**

quilate [ki'late] *nm* carat.

quilo... ['kilo] = **kilo...**

quilla ['kiʎa] *nf* keel.

quimera [ki'mera] *nf (sueño)* pipe dream.

quimérico, a [ki'meriko, a] *a* fantastic.

químico, a ['kimiko, a] *a* chemical ♦ *nm/f* chemist ♦ *nf* chemistry.

quincallería [kinkaʎe'ria] *nf* ironmonger's (shop), hardware store *(US)*.

quince ['kinθe] *num* fifteen; ~ **días** a fortnight.

quinceañero, a [kinθea'ɲero, a] *a* fifteen-year-old; *(adolescente)* teenage ♦ *nm/f* fifteen-year-old; *(adolescente)* teenager.

quincena [kin'θena] *nf* fortnight; *(pago)* fortnightly pay.

quincenal [kinθe'nal] *a* fortnightly.

quincuagésimo, a [kinkwa'xesimo, a] *num* fiftieth.

quiniela [ki'njela] *nf* football pools *pl;* ~**s** *nfpl* pools coupon *sg.*

quinientos, as [ki'njentos, as] *num* five hundred.

quinina [ki'nina] *nf* quinine.

quinqué [kin'ke] *nm* oil lamp.

quinquenal [kinke'nal] *a* five-year *cpd.*

quinqui ['kinki] *nm* delinquent.

quinta ['kinta] *nf* V **quinto.**

quintaesencia [kintae'senθja] *nf* quintessence.

quintal [kin'tal] *nm (Castilla: peso)* = 46kg; ~ **métrico** = 100kg.

quinto, a ['kinto, a] *a* fifth ♦ *nm (MIL)* conscript, draftee ♦ *nf* country house; *(MIL)* call-up, draft.

quintuplo, a [kin'tuplo, a] *a* quintuple, five-fold.

quiosco ['kjosko] *nm (de música)* bandstand; *(de periódicos)* news stand.

quirófano [ki'rofano] *nm* operating theatre.

quiromancia [kiro'manθja] *nf* palmistry.

quirúrgico, a [ki'rurxiko, a] *a* surgical.

quise ['kise] *etc vb* V **querer.**

quisque ['kiske] *pron fam:* **cada** *o* **todo** ~ (absolutely) everyone.

quisquilloso [kiski'ʎoso, a] *a (susceptible)* touchy; *(meticuloso)* pernickety.

quiste ['kiste] *nm* cyst.

quitaesmalte [kitaes'malte] *nm* nail polish remover.

quitamanchas [kita'mantʃas] *nm inv* stain remover.

quitanieves [kita'njeßes] *nm inv* snowplough *(Brit)*, snowplow *(US)*.

quitar [ki'tar] *vt* to remove, take away; *(ropa)* to take off; *(dolor)* to relieve; *(vida)* to take; *(valor)* to reduce; *(hurtar)* to remove, steal ♦ *vi:* **¡quita de ahí!** get away!; ~**se** *vr* to withdraw; *(mancha)* to come off *o* out; *(ropa)* to take off; **me quita mucho tiempo** it takes up a lot of my time; **el café me quita el sueño** coffee stops me sleeping; ~ **de en medio a uno** to get rid of sb; ~**se algo de encima** to get rid of sth; ~**se del tabaco** to give up smoking; **se quitó el sombrero** he took off his hat.

quitasol [kita'sol] *nm* sunshade *(Brit)*, parasol.

quite ['kite] *nm (esgrima)* parry; *(evasión)* dodge; **estar al** ~ to be ready to go to sb's aid.

Quito ['kito] *n* Quito.

quizá(s) [ki'θa(s)] *ad* perhaps, maybe.

quórum ['kworum] *nm, pl* **quórums** ['kworum] quorum.

R

R, r ['erre] *nf (letra)* R, r; **R de Ramón** R for Robert *(Brit) o* Roger *(US)*.

R. *abr* = **Remite, Remitente.**

rábano ['raßano] *nm* radish; **me importa un** ~ I don't give a damn.

rabia ['raßja] *nf (MED)* rabies *sg;* *(fig: ira)* fury, rage; **¡qué ~!** isn't it infuriating!; **me da** ~ it maddens me; **tener** ~ **a uno** to have a grudge against sb.

rabiar [ra'ßjar] *vi* to have rabies; to rage, be furious; ~ **por algo** to long for sth.

rabieta [ra'ßjeta] *nf* tantrum, fit of temper.

rabino [ra'ßino] *nm* rabbi.

rabioso, a [ra'ßjoso, a] *a* rabid; *(fig)* furious.

rabo ['raßo] *nm* tail.

racanear [rakane'ar] *vi (fam)* to skive.

rácano ['rakano] *nm (fam)* slacker, skiver.

racial [ra'θjal] *a* racial, race *cpd.*

racimo [ra'θimo] *nm* bunch.

raciocinio [raθjo'θinjo] *nm* reason; (*razonamiento*) reasoning.

ración [ra'θjon] *nf* portion; **raciones** *nfpl* rations.

racional [raθjo'nal] *a* (*razonable*) reasonable; (*lógico*) rational.

racionalice [raθjona'liθe] *etc vb* V **racionalizar.**

racionalizar [raθjonali'θar] *vt* to rationalize; (*COM*) to streamline.

racionamiento [raθjona'mjento] *nm* (*COM*) rationing.

racionar [raθjo'nar] *vt* to ration (out).

racismo [ra'θismo] *nm* racialism, racism.

racista [ra'θista] *a*, *nm/f* racist.

racha ['ratʃa] *nf* gust of wind; (*serie*) string, series; **buena/mala** ~ spell of good/bad luck.

radar [ra'ðar] *nm* radar.

radiación [raðja'θjon] *nf* radiation; (*TELEC*) broadcasting.

radiactividad [raðjaktiβi'ðað] *nf* radioactivity.

radiado, a [ra'ðjaðo, a] *a* radio *cpd*, broadcast.

radiador [raðja'ðor] *nm* radiator.

radiante [ra'ðjante] *a* radiant.

radiar [ra'ðjar] *vt* to radiate; (*TELEC*) to broadcast; (*MED*) to give radiotherapy to.

radical [raði'kal] *a*, *nm/f* radical ♦ *nm* (*LING*) root; (*MAT*) square-root sign.

radicar [raði'kar] *vi* to take root; ~ **en** to lie *o* consist in; ~**se** *vr* to establish o.s., put down (one's) roots.

radio ['raðjo] *nf* radio; (*aparato*) radio (set) ♦ *nm* (*MAT*) radius; (*QUÍMICA*) radium; ~ **de acción** extent of one's authority, sphere of influence.

radioactivo, a [raðjoak'tiβo, a] *a* radioactive.

radiodifusión [raðjodifu'sjon] *nf* broadcasting.

radioemisora [raðjoemi'sora] *nf* transmitter, radio station.

radiofónico, a [raðjo'foniko, a] *a* radio *cpd*.

radiografía [raðjoɣra'fia] *nf* X-ray.

radiólogo, a [ra'ðjoloɣo, a] *nm/f* radiologist.

radioterapia [raðjote'rapja] *nf* radiotherapy.

radioyente [raðjo'jente] *nm/f* listener.

radique [ra'ðike] *etc vb* V **radicar.**

RAE *nf abr* = *Real Academia Española.*

ráfaga ['rafaɣa] *nf* gust; (*de luz*) flash; (*de tiros*) burst.

raído, a [ra'iðo, a] *a* (*ropa*) threadbare; (*persona*) shabby.

raigambre [rai'ɣambre] *nf* (*BOT*) roots *pl*; (*fig*) tradition.

raíz [ra'iθ] (*pl* **raíces**) *nf* root; ~ **cuadrada** square root; **a** ~ **de** as a result of; (*después de*) immediately after.

raja ['raxa] *nf* (*de melón etc*) slice; (*hendedura*) slit, split; (*grieta*) crack.

rajar [ra'xar] *vt* to split; (*fam*) to slash; ~**se** *vr* to split, crack; ~**se de** to back out of.

rajatabla [raxa'taβla]: **a** ~ *ad* (*estrictamente*) strictly, to the letter.

ralea [ra'lea] *nf* (*pey*) kind, sort.

ralenti [ra'lenti] *nm* (*TV etc*) slow motion; (*AUTO*) neutral; **al** ~ in slow motion; (*AUTO*) ticking over.

ralo, a ['ralo, a] *a* thin, sparse.

rallador [raʎa'ðor] *nm* grater.

rallar [ra'ʎar] *vt* to grate.

RAM [ram] *nf abr* (= *random access memory*) RAM.

rama ['rama] *nf* bough, branch; **andarse por las** ~**s** (*fig*, *fam*) to beat about the bush.

ramaje [ra'maxe] *nm* branches *pl*, foliage.

ramal [ra'mal] *nm* (*de cuerda*) strand; (*FERRO*) branch line; (*AUTO*) branch (road).

rambla ['rambla] *nf* (*avenida*) avenue.

ramera [ra'mera] *nf* whore, hooker (*US*).

ramificación [ramifika'θjon] *nf* ramification.

ramificarse [ramifi'karse] *vr* to branch out.

ramifique [rami'fike] *etc vb* V **ramificarse.**

ramillete [rami'ʎete] *nm* bouquet; (*fig*) select group.

ramo ['ramo] *nm* branch, twig; (*sección*) department, section; (*sector*) field, sector.

rampa ['rampa] *nf* ramp.

ramplón, ona [ram'plon, ona] *a* uncouth, coarse.

rana ['rana] *nf* frog; **salto de** ~ leapfrog; **cuando las** ~**s críen pelos** when pigs fly.

rancio, a ['ranθjo, a] *a* (*comestibles*) stale, rancid; (*vino*) aged, mellow; (*fig*) ancient.

ranchero [ran'tʃero] *nm* (*AM*) rancher; (*pequeño propietario*) smallholder.

rancho ['rantʃo] *nm* grub (*fam*); (*AM*: *grande*) ranch; (: *pequeño*) small farm.

rango ['rango] *nm* rank; (*prestigio*) standing.

ranura [ra'nura] *nf* groove; (*de teléfono etc*) slot; ~ **de expansión** (*INFORM*) expansion slot.

rapacidad [rapaθi'ðað] *nf* rapacity.

rapapolvo [rapa'polβo] *nm*: **echar un** ~ **a uno** to give sb a ticking off.

rapar [ra'par] *vt* to shave; (*los cabellos*) to crop.

rapaz [ra'paθ] *a* (*ZOOL*) predatory ♦ *nm/f* (*f*: **rapaza**) young boy/girl.

rape ['rape] *nm* quick shave; (*pez*) angler (fish); **al** ~ cropped.

rapé [ra'pe] *nm* snuff.

rapidez [rapi'ðeθ] *nf* speed, rapidity.

rápido, a ['rapiðo, a] *a* fast, quick ♦ *ad* quickly ♦ *nm* (*FERRO*) express; ~**s** *nmpl* rapids.

rapiña [ra'piɲa] *nm* robbery; **ave de** ~ bird of prey.

raptar [rap'tar] *vt* to kidnap.

rapto ['rapto] *nm* kidnapping; (*impulso*) sudden impulse; (*éxtasis*) ecstasy, rapture.

raqueta [ra'keta] *nf* racquet.

raquítico, a [ra'kitiko, a] *a* stunted; (*fig*) poor, inadequate.

raquitismo [raki'tismo] *nm* rickets *sg*.

rareza [ra'reθa] *nf* rarity; (*fig*) eccentricity.

raro, a ['raro, a] *a* (*poco común*) rare; (*extraño*) odd, strange; (*excepcional*) remarkable; **¡qué** ~**!** how (very) odd!; **¡(qué) cosa más rara!** how strange!

ras [ras] *nm*: **a** ~ **de** level with; **a** ~ **de tierra** at ground level.

rasar [ra'sar] *vt* to level.

rascacielos [raska'θjelos] *nm inv* skyscraper.

rascar [ras'kar] *vt* (*con las uñas etc*) to scratch; (*raspar*) to scrape; ~**se** *vr* to scratch (o.s.).

rasgar [ras'ɣar] *vt* to tear, rip (up).

rasgo ['rasɣo] *nm* (*con pluma*) stroke; ~**s** *nmpl* features, characteristics; **a grandes** ~**s** in outline, broadly.

rasguear [rasɣe'ar] *vt* (*MUS*) to strum.

rasgue ['rasɣe] *etc vb* V **rasgar**.

rasguñar [rasɣu'ɲar] *vt* to scratch; (*bosquejar*) to sketch.

rasguño [ras'ɣuɲo] *nm* scratch.

raso, a ['raso, a] *a* (*liso*) flat, level; (*a baja altura*) very low ♦ *nm* satin; (*campo llano*) flat country; **cielo** ~ clear sky; **al** ~ in the open.

raspador [raspa'ðor] *nm* scraper.

raspadura [raspa'ðura] *nf* (*acto*) scrape, scraping; (*marca*) scratch; ~**s** *nfpl* scrapings.

raspar [ras'par] *vt* to scrape; (*arañar*) to scratch; (*limar*) to file ♦ *vi* (*manos*) to be rough; (*vino*) to be sharp, have a rough taste.

rasque ['raske] *etc vb* V **rascar**.

rastra ['rastra] *nf*: **a** ~**s** by dragging; (*fig*) unwillingly.

rastreador [rastrea'ðor] *nm* tracker; ~ **de minas** minesweeper.

rastrear [rastre'ar] *vt* (*seguir*) to track; (*minas*) to sweep.

rastrero, a [ras'trero, a] *a* (*BOT, ZOOL*) creeping; (*fig*) despicable, mean.

rastrillar [rastri'ʎar] *vt* to rake.

rastrillo [ras'triʎo] *nm* rake.

rastro ['rastro] *nm* (*AGR*) rake; (*pista*) track, trail; (*vestigio*) trace; **el R~** the Madrid fleamarket; **perder el** ~ to lose the scent; **desaparecer sin** ~ to vanish without trace.

rastrojo [ras'troxo] *nm* stubble.

rasurador [rasura'ðor] *nm*, (*AM*)

rasuradora [rasura'ðora] *nf* electric shaver *o* razor.

rasurarse [rasu'rarse] *vr* to shave.

rata ['rata] *nf* rat.

ratear [rate'ar] *vt* (*robar*) to steal.

ratero, a [ra'tero, a] *a* light-fingered ♦ *nm/f* pickpocket; (*AM: de casas*) burglar.

ratificar [ratifi'kar] *vt* to ratify.

ratifique [rati'fike] *etc vb* V **ratificar**.

rato ['rato] *nm* while, short time; **a** ~**s** from time to time; **al poco** ~ shortly after, soon afterwards; ~**s libres** *o* **de ocio** leisure *sg*, spare *o* free time *sg*; **hay para** ~ there's still a long way to go; **pasar el** ~ to kill time; **pasar un buen/mal** ~ to have a good/rough time.

ratón [ra'ton] *nm* (*tb INFORM*) mouse.

ratonera [rato'nera] *nf* mousetrap.

RAU *nf abr* (= *República Árabe Unida*) UAR.

raudal [rau'ðal] *nm* torrent; **a** ~**es** in abundance; **entrar a** ~**es** to pour in.

raudo, a ['rauðo, a] *a* (*rápido*) swift; (*precipitado*) rushing.

raya ['raja] *nf* line; (*marca*) scratch; (*en tela*) stripe; (*TIP*) hyphen; (*de pelo*) parting; (*límite*) boundary; (*pez*) ray; **a** ~**s** striped; **pasarse de la** ~ to overstep the mark, go too far; **tener a** ~ to keep in check.

rayado, a [ra'jaðo, a] *a* (*papel*) ruled; (*tela, diseño*) striped.

rayar [ra'jar] *vt* to line; to scratch; (*subrayar*) to underline ♦ *vi*: ~ **en** *o* **con** to border on; **al** ~ **el alba** at first light.

rayo ['rajo] *nm* (*del sol*) ray, beam; (*de luz*) shaft; (*en una tormenta*) (flash of) lightning; ~ **solar** *o* **de sol** sunbeam; ~**s infrarrojos** infrared rays; ~**s X** X-rays; **como un** ~ like a shot; **la noticia cayó como un** ~ the news was a bombshell; **pasar como un** ~ to flash past.

raza ['raθa] *nf* race; (*de animal*) breed; ~ **humana** human race; **de pura** ~ (*caballo*) thoroughbred; (*perro etc*) pedigree.

razón [ra'θon] *nf* reason; (*justicia*) right, justice; (*razonamiento*) reasoning; (*motivo*) reason, motive; (*proporción*) rate; (*MAT*) ratio; **a** ~ **de 10 cada día** at the rate of 10 a day; **"~: ..."** "inquiries to ..."; **en** ~ **de** with regard to; **perder la** ~ to go out of one's mind; **dar** ~ **a uno** to agree that sb is right; **dar** ~ **de** to give an account of, report on; **tener/no tener** ~ to be right/wrong; ~ **directa/inversa** direct/inverse proportion; ~ **de ser** raison d'être.

razonable [raθo'naβle] *a* reasonable; (*justo, moderado*) fair.

razonado, a [raθo'naðo, a] *a* (*COM: cuenta etc*) itemized.

razonamiento [raθona'mjento] *nm* (*juicio*)

judgement; (*argumento*) reasoning.
razonar [raθo'nar] *vt*, *vi* to reason, argue.
RDA *nf* = **República Democrática Alemana**.
Rdo. *abr* (*REL*: = *Reverendo*) Rev.
reabierto [rea'ßjerto] *pp de* **reabrir**.
reabrir [rea'ßrir] *vt*, ~**se** *vr* to reopen.
reacción [reak'θjon] *nf* reaction; **avión a** ~ jet plane; ~ **en cadena** chain reaction.
reaccionar [reakθjo'nar] *vi* to react.
reaccionario, a [reakθjo'narjo, a] *a* reactionary.
reacio, a [re'aθjo, a] *a* stubborn; **ser** *o* **estar** ~ **a** to be opposed to.
reactor [reak'tor] *nm* reactor; (*avión*) jet plane; ~ **nuclear** nuclear reactor.
readaptación [reaðapta'θjon] *nf*: ~ **profesional** industrial retraining.
reafirmar [reafir'mar] *vt* to reaffirm.
reagrupar [reaɣru'par] *vt* to regroup.
reajustar [reaxus'tar] *vt* (*INFORM*) to reset.
reajuste [rea'xuste] *nm* readjustment; ~ **salarial** wage increase; ~ **de plantilla** rationalization.
real [re'al] *a* real; (*del rey*, *fig*) royal; (*espléndido*) grand ◆ *nm* (*de feria*) fairground.
realce [re'alθe] *etc vb V* **realzar** ◆ *nm* (*TEC*) embossing; (*lustre*, *fig*) splendour (*Brit*), splendor (*US*); (*ARTE*) highlight; **poner de** ~ to emphasize.
realeza [rea'leθa] *nf* royalty.
realice [rea'liθe] *etc vb V* **realizar**.
realidad [reali'ðað] *nf* reality; (*verdad*) truth; **en** ~ in fact.
realista [rea'lista] *nm/f* realist.
realización [realiθa'θjon] *nf* fulfilment, realization; (*COM*) selling up (*Brit*), conversion into money (*US*); ~ **de plusvalías** profit-taking.
realizador, a [realiθa'ðor, a] *nm/f* (*TV etc*) producer.
realizar [reali'θar] *vt* (*objetivo*) to achieve; (*plan*) to carry out; (*viaje*) to make, undertake; (*COM*) to realize; ~**se** *vr* to come about, come true; ~**se como persona** to fulfil one's aims in life.
realmente [real'mente] *ad* really.
realquilar [realki'lar] *vt* (*subarrendar*) to sublet; (*alquilar de nuevo*) to relet.
realzar [real'θar] *vt* (*TEC*) to raise; (*embellecer*) to enhance; (*acentuar*) to highlight.
reanimar [reani'mar] *vt* to revive; (*alentar*) to encourage; ~**se** *vr* to revive.
reanudar [reanu'ðar] *vt* (*renovar*) to renew; (*historia*, *viaje*) to resume.
reaparición [reapari'θjon] *nf* reappearance; (*vuelta*) return.
reapertura [reaper'tura] *nf* reopening.
rearme [re'arme] *nm* rearmament.

rebaja [re'ßaxa] *nf* reduction, lowering; (*COM*) discount; "**grandes** ~**s**" "big reductions", "sale".
rebajar [reßa'xar] *vt* (*bajar*) to lower; (*reducir*) to reduce; (*precio*) to cut; (*disminuir*) to lessen; (*humillar*) to humble; ~**se** *vr*: ~**se a hacer algo** to stoop to doing sth.
rebanada [reßa'naða] *nf* slice.
rebaño [re'ßaɲo] *nm* herd; (*de ovejas*) flock.
rebasar [reßa'sar] *vt* (*tb*: ~ **de**) to exceed; (*AUTO*) to overtake.
rebatir [reßa'tir] *vt* to refute; (*rebajar*) to reduce; (*ataque*) to repel.
rebato [re'ßato] *nm* alarm; (*ataque*) surprise attack; **llamar** *o* **tocar a** ~ (*fig*) to sound the alarm.
rebeca [re'ßeka] *nf* cardigan.
rebelarse [reße'larse] *vr* to rebel, revolt.
rebelde [re'ßelde] *a* rebellious; (*niño*) unruly ◆ *nm/f* rebel; **ser** ~ **a** to be in revolt against, rebel against.
rebeldía [reßel'dia] *nf* rebelliousness; (*desobediencia*) disobedience; (*JUR*) default.
rebelión [reße'ljon] *nf* rebellion.
reblandecer [reßlande'θer] *vt* to soften.
reblandezca [reßlan'deθka] *etc vb V* **reblandecer**.
reboce [re'ßoθe] *etc vb V* **rebozar**.
rebosante [reßo'sante] *a*: ~ **de** (*fig*) brimming *o* overflowing with.
rebosar [reßo'sar] *vi* to overflow; (*abundar*) to abound, be plentiful; ~ **de salud** to be bursting *o* brimming with health.
rebotar [reßo'tar] *vt* to bounce; (*rechazar*) to repel.
rebote [re'ßote] *nm* rebound; **de** ~ on the rebound.
rebozado, a [reßo'θaðo, a] *a* (*CULIN*) fried in batter *o* breadcrumbs *o* flour.
rebozar [reßo'θar] *vt* to wrap up; (*CULIN*) to fry in batter *etc*.
rebuscado, a [reßus'kaðo, a] *a* affected.
rebuznar [reßuθ'nar] *vi* to bray.
recabar [reka'ßar] *vt* (*obtener*) to manage to get; ~ **fondos** to collect money.
recadero [reka'ðero] *nm* messenger.
recado [re'kaðo] *nm* message; **dejar/tomar un** ~ (*TELEC*) to leave/take a message.
recaer [reka'er] *vi* to relapse; ~ **en** to fall to *o* on; (*criminal etc*) to fall back into, relapse into; (*premio*) to go to.
recaída [reka'iða] *nf* relapse.
recaiga [re'kaixa] *etc vb V* **recaer**.
recalcar [rekal'kar] *vt* (*fig*) to stress, emphasize.
recalcitrante [rekalθi'trante] *a* recalcitrant.
recalentar [rekalen'tar] *vt* (*comida*) to warm up, reheat; (*demasiado*) to overheat; ~**se** *vr* to overheat, get too hot.
recaliente [reka'ljente] *etc vb V* **recalentar**.

recalque [re'kalke] *etc vb* V **recalcar**.

recámara [re'kamara] *nf* side room; (*AM*) bedroom.

recambio [re'kambjo] *nm* spare; (*de pluma*) refill; **piezas de** ~ spares.

recapacitar [rekapaθi'tar] *vi* to reflect.

recargado, a [rekar'ɣaðo, a] *a* overloaded; (*exagerado*) over-elaborate.

recargar [rekar'ɣar] *vt* to overload; (*batería*) to recharge.

recargo [re'karɣo] *nm* surcharge; (*aumento*) increase.

recargue [re'karɣe] *etc vb* V **recargar**.

recatado, a [reka'taðo, a] *a* (*modesto*) modest, demure; (*prudente*) cautious.

recato [re'kato] *nm* (*modestia*) modesty, demureness; (*cautela*) caution.

recaudación [rekauða'θjon] *nf* (*acción*) collection; (*cantidad*) takings *pl*; (*en deporte*) gate; (*oficina*) tax office.

recaudador, a [rekauða'ðor, a] *nm/f* tax collector.

recaudar [rekau'ðar] *vt* to collect.

recaudo [re'kauðo] *nm* (*impuestos*) collection; (*JUR*) surety; **estar a buen** ~ to be in safekeeping; **poner algo a buen** ~ to put sth in a safe place.

recayendo [reka'jendo] *etc vb* V **recaer**.

rece ['reθe] *etc vb* V **rezar**.

recelar [reθe'lar] *vt:* ~ **que** (*sospechar*) to suspect that; (*temer*) to fear that ◆ *vi:* ~(**se**) **de** to distrust.

recelo [re'θelo] *nm* distrust, suspicion.

receloso, a [reθe'loso, a] *a* distrustful, suspicious.

recepción [reθep'θjon] *nf* reception; (*acto de recibir*) receipt.

recepcionista [reθepθjo'nista] *nm/f* receptionist.

receptáculo [reθep'takulo] *nm* receptacle.

receptivo, a [reθep'tiβo, a] *a* receptive.

receptor, a [reθep'tor, a] *nm/f* recipient ◆ *nm* (*TELEC*) receiver; **descolgar el** ~ to pick up the receiver.

recesión [reθe'sjon] *nf* (*COM*) recession.

receta [re'θeta] *nf* (*CULIN*) recipe; (*MED*) prescription.

recetar [reθe'tar] *vt* to prescribe.

recibidor [reθiβi'ðor] *nm* entrance hall.

recibimiento [reθiβi'mjento] *nm* reception, welcome.

recibir [reθi'βir] *vt* to receive; (*dar la bienvenida*) to welcome; (*salir al encuentro de*) to go and meet ◆ *vi* to entertain; ~**se** *vr:* ~**se de** to qualify as.

recibo [re'θiβo] *nm* receipt; **acusar** ~ **de** to acknowledge receipt of.

recién [re'θjen] *ad* recently, newly; (*AM*) just, recently; ~ **casado** newly-wed; **el** ~ **llegado** the newcomer; **el** ~ **nacido** the newborn child.

reciente [re'θjente] *a* recent; (*fresco*) fresh.

recientemente [reθjente'mente] *ad* recently.

recinto [re'θinto] *nm* enclosure; (*área*) area, place.

recio, a ['reθjo, a] *a* strong, tough; (*voz*) loud ◆ *ad* hard; loud(ly).

recipiente [reθi'pjente] *nm* (*objeto*) container, receptacle; (*persona*) recipient.

reciprocidad [reθiproθi'ðað] *nf* reciprocity.

recíproco, a [re'θiproko, a] *a* reciprocal.

recital [reθi'tal] *nm* (*MUS*) recital; (*LIT*) reading.

recitar [reθi'tar] *vt* to recite.

reclamación [reklama'θjon] *nf* claim, demand; (*queja*) complaint; ~ **salarial** pay claim.

reclamar [rekla'mar] *vt* to claim, demand ◆ *vi:* ~ **contra** to complain about; ~ **a uno en justicia** to take sb to court.

reclamo [re'klamo] *nm* (*anuncio*) advertisement; (*tentación*) attraction.

reclinar [rekli'nar] *vt* to recline, lean; ~**se** *vr* to lean back.

recluir [reklu'ir] *vt* to intern, confine.

reclusión [reklu'sjon] *nf* (*prisión*) prison; (*refugio*) seclusion; ~ **perpetua** life imprisonment.

recluso, a [re'kluso, a] *a* imprisoned; **población reclusa** prison population ◆ *nm/f* (*solitario*) recluse; (*JUR*) prisoner.

recluta [re'kluta] *nm/f* recruit ◆ *nf* recruitment.

reclutamiento [rekluta'mjento] *nm* recruitment.

recluyendo [reklu'jendo] *etc vb* V **recluir**.

recobrar [reko'βrar] *vt* (*recuperar*) to recover; (*rescatar*) to get back; (*ciudad*) to recapture; (*tiempo*) to make up (for); ~**se** *vr* to recover.

recodo [re'koðo] *nm* (*de río, camino*) bend.

recogedor, a [rekoxe'ðor, a] *nm/f* picker, harvester.

recoger [reko'xer] *vt* to collect; (*AGR*) to harvest; (*fruta*) to pick; (*levantar*) to pick up; (*juntar*) to gather; (*pasar a buscar*) to come for, get; (*dar asilo*) to give shelter to; (*faldas*) to gather up; (*mangas*) to roll up; (*pelo*) to put up; ~**se** *vr* (*retirarse*) to retire; **me recogieron en la estación** they picked me up at the station.

recogido, a [reko'xiðo, a] *a* (*lugar*) quiet, secluded; (*pequeño*) small ◆ *nf* (*CORREOS*) collection; (*AGR*) harvest; **recogida de datos** (*INFORM*) data capture.

recogimiento [rekoxi'mjento] *nm* collection; (*AGR*) harvesting.

recoja [re'koxa] *etc vb* V **recoger**.

recolección [rekolek'θjon] *nf* (*AGR*) harvesting; (*colecta*) collection.

recomendable [rekomen'daβle] *a* recommendable; **poco** ~ inadvisable.

recomendación [rekomenda'θjon] *nf (sugerencia)* suggestion, recommendation; *(referencia)* reference; **carta de** ~ **para** letter of introduction to.

recomendar [rekomen'dar] *vt* to suggest, recommend; *(confiar)* to entrust.

recomencé [rekomen'θe], **recomencemos** [rekomen'θemos] *etc vb* V **recomenzar**.

recomenzar [rekomen'θar] *vt, vi* to begin again, recommence.

recomience [reko'mjenθe] *etc vb* V **recomenzar**.

recomiende [reko'mjende] *etc vb* V **recomendar**.

recomienzo [reko'mjenθo] *etc vb* V **recomenzar**.

recompensa [rekom'pensa] *nf* reward, recompense; *(compensación)*: ~ **(de una pérdida)** compensation (for a loss); **como** *o* **en** ~ **por** in return for.

recompensar [rekompen'sar] *vt* to reward, recompense.

recompondré [rekompon'dre] *etc vb* V **recomponer**.

recomponer [rekompo'ner] *vt* to mend; *(INFORM: texto)* to reformat.

recomponga [rekom'ponga] *etc*, **recompuesto** [rekom'pwesto], **recompuse** [rekom'puse] *etc vb* V **recomponer**.

reconciliación [rekonθilja'θjon] *nf* reconciliation.

reconciliar [rekonθi'ljar] *vt* to reconcile; ~**se** *vr* to become reconciled.

recóndito, a [re'kondito, a] *a (lugar)* hidden, secret.

reconfortar [rekonfor'tar] *vt* to comfort.

reconocer [rekono'θer] *vt* to recognize; ~ **los hechos** to face the facts.

reconocido, a [rekono'θiðo, a] *a* recognized; *(agradecido)* grateful.

reconocimiento [rekonoθi'mjento] *nm* recognition; *(registro)* search; *(inspección)* examination; *(gratitud)* gratitude; *(confesión)* admission; ~ **óptico de caracteres** *(INFORM)* optical character recognition; ~ **de la voz** *(INFORM)* speech recognition.

reconozca [reko'noθka] *etc vb* V **reconocer**.

reconquista [rekon'kista] *nf* reconquest.

reconquistar [rekonkis'tar] *vt (MIL)* to reconquer; *(fig)* to recover, win back.

reconstituyente [rekonstitu'jente] *nm* tonic.

reconstruir [rekonstru'ir] *vt* to reconstruct.

reconstruyendo [rekonstru'jendo] *etc vb* V **reconstruir**.

reconversión [rekomber'sjon] *nf* restructuring, reorganization; *(tb:* ~ **industrial)** rationalization.

recopilación [rekopila'θjon] *nf (resumen)*

summary; *(compilación)* compilation.

recopilar [rekopi'lar] *vt* to compile.

récord ['rekorð] *a inv* record; **cifras** ~ record figures ◆ *nm, pl* **records, récords** ['rekorð] record; **batir el** ~ to break the record.

recordar [rekor'ðar] *vt (acordarse de)* to remember; *(traer a la memoria)* to recall; *(acordar a otro)* to remind ◆ *vi* to remember; **recuérdale que me debe 5 dólares** remind him that he owes me 5 dollars; **que yo recuerde** as far as I can remember; **creo** ~, **si mal no recuerdo** if my memory serves me right.

recorrer [reko'rrer] *vt (país)* to cross, travel through; *(distancia)* to cover; *(registrar)* to search; *(repasar)* to look over.

recorrido [reko'rriðo] *nm* run, journey; **tren de largo** ~ main-line *o* inter-city *(Brit)* train.

recortado, a [rekor'taðo, a] *a* uneven, irregular.

recortar [rekor'tar] *vt (papel)* to cut out; *(el pelo)* to trim; *(dibujar)* to draw in outline; ~**se** *vr* to stand out, be silhouetted.

recorte [re'korte] *nm (acción, de prensa)* cutting; *(de telas, chapas)* trimming.

recostado, a [rekos'taðo, a] *a* leaning; **estar** ~ to be lying down.

recostar [rekos'tar] *vt* to lean; ~**se** *vr* to lie down.

recoveco [reko'ßeko] *nm (de camino, río etc)* bend; *(en casa)* cubbyhole.

recreación [rekrea'θjon] *nf* recreation.

recrear [rekre'ar] *vt (entretener)* to entertain; *(volver a crear)* to recreate.

recreativo, a [rekrea'tißo, a] *a* recreational.

recreo [re'kreo] *nm* recreation; *(ESCOL)* break, playtime.

recriminar [rekrimi'nar] *vt* to reproach ◆ *vi* to recriminate; ~**se** *vr* to reproach each other.

recrudecer [rekruðe'θer] *vt, vi*, **recrudecerse** *vr* to worsen.

recrudecimiento [rekruðeθi'mjento] *nm* upsurge.

recrudezca [recru'ðeθka] *etc vb* V **recrudecer**.

recta ['rekta] *nf* V **recto**.

rectángulo, a [rek'tangulo, a] *a* rectangular ◆ *nm* rectangle.

rectificable [rektifi'kaßle] *a* rectifiable; **fácilmente** ~ easily rectified.

rectificación [rektifika'θjon] *nf* correction.

rectificar [rektifi'kar] *vt* to rectify; *(volverse recto)* to straighten ◆ *vi* to correct o.s.

rectifique [rekti'fike] *etc vb* V **rectificar**.

rectitud [rekti'tuð] *nf* straightness; *(fig)* rectitude.

recto, a ['rekto, a] *a* straight; *(persona)*

honest, upright; (*estricto*) strict; (*juez*) fair; (*juicio*) sound ◆ *nm* rectum; (*ATLETISMO*) straight ◆ *nf* straight line; **en el sentido ~ de la palabra** in the proper sense of the word; **recta final** *o* **de llegada** home straight.

rector, a [rek'tor, a] *a* governing ◆ *nm/f* head, chief; (*ESCOL*) rector, president (*US*).

rectorado [rekto'raðo] *nm* (*cargo*) rectorship, presidency (*US*); (*oficina*) rector's office.

recuadro [re'kwaðro] *nm* box; (*TIP*) inset.

recuento [re'kwento] *nm* inventory; **hacer el ~ de** to count *o* reckon up.

recuerdo [re'kwerðo] *etc vb V* **recordar** ◆ *nm* souvenir; **~s** *nmpl* memories; **¡~s a tu madre!** give my regards to your mother!; **"R~ de Mallorca"** "a present from Majorca"; **contar los ~s** to reminisce.

recueste [re'kweste] *etc vb V* **recostar**.

recular [reku'lar] *vi* to back down.

recuperable [rekupe'raßle] *a* recoverable.

recuperación [rekupera'θjon] *nf* recovery; **~ de datos** (*INFORM*) data retrieval.

recuperar [rekupe'rar] *vt* to recover; (*tiempo*) to make up; (*INFORM*) to retrieve; **~se** *vr* to recuperate.

recurrir [reku'rrir] *vi* (*JUR*) to appeal; **~ a** to resort to; (*persona*) to turn to.

recurso [re'kurso] *nm* resort; (*medio*) means *pl*, resource; (*JUR*) appeal; **como último ~** as a last resort; **~s económicos** economic resources; **~s naturales** natural resources.

recusar [reku'sar] *vt* to reject, refuse.

rechace [re'tʃaθe] *etc vb V* **rechazar**.

rechazar [retʃa'θar] *vt* to repel, drive back; (*idea*) to reject; (*oferta*) to turn down.

rechazo [re'tʃaθo] *nm* (*de fusil*) recoil; (*rebote*) rebound; (*negación*) rebuff.

rechifla [re'tʃifla] *nf* hissing, booing; (*fig*) derision.

rechinar [retʃi'nar] *vi* to creak; (*dientes*) to grind; (*máquina*) to clank, clatter; (*metal seco*) to grate; (*motor*) to hum.

rechistar [retʃis'tar] *vi*: **sin ~** without complaint.

rechoncho, a [re'tʃontʃo, a] *a* (*fam*) stocky, thickset (*Brit*), heavy-set (*US*).

red [reð] *nf* net, mesh; (*FERRO, INFORM*) network; (*ELEC, de agua*) mains, supply system; (*de tiendas*) chain; (*trampa*) trap; **estar conectado con la ~** to be connected to the mains; **~ local** (*INFORM*) local area network; **~ de transmisión** (*INFORM*) data network.

redacción [reðak'θjon] *nf* (*acción*) writing; (*ESCOL*) essay, composition; (*limpieza de texto*) editing; (*personal*) editorial staff.

redactar [reðak'tar] *vt* to draw up, draft; (*periódico, INFORM*) to edit.

redactor, a [reðak'tor, a] *nm/f* writer; (*en periódico*) editor.

redada [re'ðaða] *nf* (*PESCA*) cast, throw; (*fig*) catch; **~ policial** police raid, round-up.

redención [reðen'θjon] *nf* redemption.

redentor, a [reðen'tor, a] *a* redeeming ◆ *nm/f* (*COM*) redeemer.

redescubierto [reðesku'ßjerto] *pp de* **redescubrir**.

redescubrir [reðesku'ßrir] *vt* to rediscover.

redesignar [reðesiɣ'nar] *vt* (*INFORM*) to rename.

redicho, a [re'ðitʃo, a] *a* affected.

redil [re'ðil] *nm* sheepfold.

redimir [reði'mir] *vt* to redeem; (*rehén*) to ransom.

redistribución [reðistrißu'θjon] *nf* (*COM*) redeployment.

rédito ['reðito] *nm* interest, yield.

redoblar [reðo'ßlar] *vt* to redouble ◆ *vi* (*tambor*) to play a roll on the drums.

redoble [re'ðoßle] *nm* (*MUS*) drumroll, drumbeat; (*de trueno*) roll.

redomado, a [reðo'maðo, a] *a* (*astuto*) sly, crafty; (*perfecto*) utter.

redonda [re'ðonda] *nf V* **redondo**.

redondear [reðonde'ar] *vt* to round, round off; (*cifra*) to round up.

redondel [reðon'del] *nm* (*círculo*) circle; (*TAUR*) bullring, arena; (*AUTO*) roundabout.

redondo, a [re'ðondo, a] *a* (*circular*) round; (*completo*) complete ◆ *nf*: **a la redonda** around, round about; **en muchas millas a la redonda** for many miles around; **rehusar en ~** to give a flat refusal.

reducción [reðuk'θjon] *nf* reduction; **~ del activo** (*COM*) divestment; **~ de precios** (*COM*) price-cutting.

reducido, a [reðu'θiðo, a] *a* reduced; (*limitado*) limited; (*pequeño*) small; **quedar ~ a** to be reduced to.

reducir [reðu'θir] *vt* to reduce, limit; (*someter*) to bring under control; **~se** *vr* to diminish; (*MAT*) **~ a** to reduce (to), convert (into); **~ las millas a kilómetros** to convert miles into kilometres; **~se a** (*fig*) to come *o* boil down to.

reduje [re'ðuxe] *etc vb V* **reducir**.

redundancia [reðun'danθja] *nf* redundancy.

reduzca [re'ðuθka] *etc vb V* **reducir**.

reembolsable [re(e)mbol'saßle] *a* (*COM*) redeemable, refundable.

reembolsar [re(e)mbol'sar] *vt* (*persona*) to reimburse; (*dinero*) to repay, pay back; (*depósito*) to refund.

reembolso [re(e)m'bolso] *nm* reimbursement; refund; **enviar algo contra ~** to send sth cash on delivery; **contra ~ del flete** freight forward; **~ fiscal** tax rebate.

reemplace [re(e)m'plaθe] *etc vb V* **reemplazar**.

reemplazar [re(e)mpla'θar] vt to replace.

reemplazo [re(e)m'plaθo] nm replacement; **de ~** (MIL) reserve.

reexportación [re(e)ksporta'θjon] nf (COM) re-export.

reexportar [re(e)kspor'tar] vt (COM) to re-export.

REF nm abr (Esp ECON) = Régimen Económico Fiscal.

Ref.ª abr (= referencia) ref.

referencia [refe'renθja] nf reference; **con ~ a** with reference to; **hacer ~ a** to refer o allude to; **~ comercial** (COM) trade reference.

referéndum [refe'rendum], pl **referéndums** nm referendum.

referente [refe'rente] a: **~ a** concerning, relating to.

referir [refe'rir] vt (contar) to tell, recount; (relacionar) to refer, relate; **~se** vr: **~se a** to refer to; **~ al lector a un apéndice** to refer the reader to an appendix; **~ a** (COM) to convert into; **por lo que se refiere a eso** as for that, as regards that.

refiera [re'fjera] etc vb V **referir**.

refilón [refi'lon]: **de ~** ad obliquely; **mirar a uno de ~** to look out of the corner of one's eye at sb.

refinado, a [refi'naðo, a] a refined.

refinamiento [refina'mjento] nm refinement; **~ por pasos** (INFORM) stepwise refinement.

refinar [refi'nar] vt to refine.

refinería [refine'ria] nf refinery.

refiriendo [refi'rjendo] etc vb V **referir**.

reflector [reflek'tor] nm reflector; (ELEC) spotlight; (AVIAT, MIL) searchlight.

reflejar [refle'xar] vt to reflect; **~se** vr to be reflected.

reflejo, a [re'flexo, a] a reflected; (movimiento) reflex ♦ nm reflection; (ANAT) reflex; (en el pelo): **~s** nmpl highlights; **tiene el pelo castaño con ~s rubios** she has chestnut hair with blond streaks.

reflexión [reflek'sjon] nf reflection.

reflexionar [refleksjo'nar] vt to reflect on ♦ vi to reflect; (detenerse) to pause (to think); **¡reflexione!** you think it over!

reflexivo, a [reflek'siβo, a] a thoughtful; (LING) reflexive.

refluir [reflu'ir] vi to flow back.

reflujo [re'fluxo] nm ebb.

refluyendo [reflu'jendo] etc vb V **refluir**.

reforcé [refor'θe], **reforcemos** [refor'θemos] etc vb V **reforzar**.

reforma [re'forma] nf reform; (ARQ etc) repair; **~ agraria** agrarian reform.

reformar [refor'mar] vt to reform; (modificar) to change, alter; (texto) to revise; (ARQ) to repair; **~se** vr to mend one's ways.

reformatear [reformate'ar] vt (INFORM: disco) to reformat.

reformatorio [reforma'torjo] nm reformatory; **~ de menores** remand home.

reforzamiento [reforθa'mjento] nm reinforcement.

reforzar [refor'θar] vt to strengthen; (ARQ) to reinforce; (fig) to encourage.

refractario, a [refrak'tarjo, a] a (TEC) heat-resistant; **ser ~ a una reforma** to resist o be opposed to a reform.

refrán [re'fran] nm proverb, saying.

refregar [refre'xar] vt to scrub.

refregué [refre'xe], **refreguemos** [refre'xemos] etc vb V **refregar**.

refrenar [refre'nar] vt to check, restrain.

refrendar [refren'dar] vt (firma) to endorse, countersign; (ley) to approve.

refrescante [refres'kante] a refreshing, cooling.

refrescar [refres'kar] vt to refresh ♦ vi to cool down; **~se** vr to get cooler; (tomar aire fresco) to go out for a breath of fresh air; (beber) to have a drink.

refresco [re'fresko] nm soft drink, cool drink; **"~s"** "refreshments".

refresque [re'freske] etc vb V **refrescar**.

refriega [re'frjexa] etc vb V **refregar** ♦ nf scuffle, brawl.

refriegue [re'frjexe] etc vb V **refregar**.

refrigeración [refrixera'θjon] nf refrigeration; (de casa) air-conditioning.

refrigerado, a [refrixe'raðo, a] a cooled; (sala) air-conditioned.

refrigerador [refrixera'ðor] nm, (AM) **refrigeradora** [refrixera'ðora] nf refrigerator, icebox (US).

refrigerar [refrixe'rar] vt to refrigerate; (sala) to air-condition.

refuerce [re'fwerθe] etc vb V **reforzar**.

refuerzo [re'fwerθo] etc vb V **reforzar** ♦ nm reinforcement; (TEC) support.

refugiado, a [refu'xjaðo, a] nm/f refugee.

refugiarse [refu'xjarse] vr to take refuge, shelter.

refugio [re'fuxjo] nm refuge; (protección) shelter; (AUTO) street o traffic island; **~ alpino** o **de montaña** mountain hut; **~ subterráneo** (MIL) underground shelter.

refulgencia [reful'xenθja] nf brilliance.

refulgir [reful'xir] vi to shine, be dazzling.

refulja [re'fulxa] etc vb V **refulgir**.

refundir [refun'dir] vt to recast; (escrito etc) to adapt, rewrite.

refunfuñar [refunfu'ɲar] vi to grunt, growl; (quejarse) to grumble.

refunfuñón, ona [refunfu'ɲon, ona] (fam) a grumpy ♦ nm/f grouch.

refutación [refuta'θjon] nf refutation.

refutar [refu'tar] vt to refute.

regadera [reɣa'ðera] nf watering can; **estar**

como una ~ (*fam*) to be as mad as a hatter.

regadío [reɣa'ðio] *nm* irrigated land.

regalado, a [reɣa'laðo, a] *a* comfortable, luxurious; (*gratis*) free, for nothing; **lo tuvo** ~ it was handed to him on a plate.

regalar [reɣa'lar] *vt* (*dar*) to give (as a present); (*entregar*) to give away; (*mimar*) to pamper, make a fuss of; **~se** *vr* to treat o.s. to.

regalía [reɣa'lia] *nf* privilege, prerogative; (*COM*) bonus; (*de autor*) royalty.

regaliz [reɣa'liθ] *nm* liquorice.

regalo [re'ɣalo] *nm* (*obsequio*) gift, present; (*gusto*) pleasure; (*comodidad*) comfort.

regalón, ona [reɣa'lon, ona] *a* spoiled, pampered.

regañadientes [reɣaɲa'ðjentes]: **a ~** *ad* reluctantly.

regañar [reɣa'ɲar] *vt* to scold ♦ *vi* to grumble; (*dos personas*) to fall out, quarrel.

regaño [re'ɣaɲo] *nm* scolding, telling-off; (*queja*) grumble.

regañón, ona [reɣa'ɲon, ona] *a* nagging.

regar [re'ɣar] *vt* to water, irrigate; (*fig*) to scatter, sprinkle.

regata [re'ɣata] *nf* (*NAUT*) race.

regatear [reɣate'ar] *vt* (*COM*) to bargain over; (*escatimar*) to be mean with ♦ *vi* to bargain, haggle; (*DEPORTE*) to dribble; **no ~ esfuerzo** to spare no effort.

regateo [reɣa'teo] *nm* bargaining; (*DEPORTE*) dribbling; (*del cuerpo*) swerve, dodge.

regazo [re'ɣaθo] *nm* lap.

regeneración [rexenera'θjon] *nf* regeneration.

regenerar [rexene'rar] *vt* to regenerate.

regentar [rexen'tar] *vt* to direct, manage; (*puesto*) to hold in an acting capacity; (*negocio*) to be in charge of.

regente, a [re'xente, a] *a* (*príncipe*) regent; (*director*) managing ♦ *nm* (*COM*) manager; (*POL*) regent.

régimen ['reximen] *pl* **regímenes** [re'ximenes] *nm* regime; (*reinado*) rule; (*MED*) diet; (*reglas*) (set of) rules; (*manera de vivir*) lifestyle; **estar a ~** to be on a diet.

regimiento [rexi'mjento] *nm* regiment.

regio, a ['rexjo, a] *a* royal, regal; (*fig*: *suntuoso*) splendid; (*AM fam*) great, terrific.

región [re'xjon] *nf* region; (*área*) area.

regional [rexjo'nal] *a* regional.

regir [re'xir] *vt* to govern, rule; (*dirigir*) to manage, run; (*ECON, JUR, LING*) to govern ♦ *vi* to apply, be in force.

registrador [rexistra'ðor] *nm* registrar, recorder.

registrar [rexis'trar] *vt* (*buscar*) to search; (*en cajón*) to look through; (*inspeccionar*) to inspect; (*anotar*) to register, record; (*INFORM, MUS*) to record; **~se** *vr* to register; (*ocurrir*) to happen.

registro [re'xistro] *nm* (*acto*) registration; (*MUS, libro*) register; (*lista*) list, record; (*INFORM*) record; (*inspección*) inspection, search; ~ **civil** registry office; ~ **electoral** voting register; ~ **de la propiedad** land registry (office).

regla ['reɣla] *nf* (*ley*) rule, regulation; (*de medir*) ruler, rule; (*MED*: *período*) period; (~ **científica**) law, principle; **no hay ~ sin excepción** every rule has its exception.

reglamentación [reɣlamenta'θjon] *nf* (*acto*) regulation; (*lista*) rules *pl*.

reglamentar [reɣlamen'tar] *vt* to regulate.

reglamentario, a [reɣlamen'tarjo, a] *a* statutory; **en la forma reglamentaria** in the properly established way.

reglamento [reɣla'mento] *nm* rules *pl*, regulations *pl*; ~ **del tráfico** highway code.

reglar [re'ɣlar] *vt* (*acciones*) to regulate; **~se** *vr*: **~se por** to be guided by.

regocijarse [reɣoθi'xarse] *vr*: ~ **de** *o* **por** to rejoice at, be glad about.

regocijo [reɣo'θixo] *nm* joy, happiness.

regodearse [reɣoðe'arse] *vr* to be glad, be delighted; (*pey*): ~ **con** *o* **en** to gloat over.

regodeo [reɣo'ðeo] *nm* delight; (*pey*) perverse pleasure.

regresar [reɣre'sar] *vi* to come/go back, return.

regresivo, a [reɣre'siβo, a] *a* backward; (*fig*) regressive.

regreso [re'ɣreso] *nm* return; **estar de ~** to be back, be home.

regué [re'ɣe], **reguemos** [re'ɣemos] *etc vb V* **regar**.

reguero [re'ɣero] *nm* (*de sangre*) trickle; (*de humo*) trail.

regulación [reɣula'θjon] *nf* regulation; (*TEC*) adjustment; (*control*) control; ~ **del tráfico** traffic control.

regulador [reɣula'ðor] *nm* (*TEC*) regulator; (*de radio etc*) knob, control.

regular [reɣu'lar] *a* regular; (*normal*) normal, usual; (*común*) ordinary; (*organizado*) regular, orderly; (*mediano*) average; (*fam*) not bad, so-so ♦ *ad*: **estar ~** to be so-so *o* alright ♦ *vt* (*controlar*) to control, regulate; (*TEC*) to adjust; **por lo ~** as a rule.

regularice [reɣula'riθe] *etc vb V* **regularizar**.

regularidad [reɣulari'ðað] *nf* regularity; **con ~** regularly.

regularizar [reɣulari'θar] *vt* to regularize.

regusto [re'ɣusto] *nm* aftertaste.

rehabilitación [reaβilita'θjon] *nf* rehabilitation; (*ARQ*) restoration.

rehabilitar [reaβili'tar] *vt* to rehabilitate;

(*ARQ*) to restore; (*reintegrar*) to reinstate.
rehacer [rea'θer] *vt* (*reparar*) to mend, repair; (*volver a hacer*) to redo, repeat; ~**se** *vr* (*MED*) to recover.
rehaga [re'aɣa] *etc*, **reharé** [rea're] *etc*, **rehaz** [re'aθ], **rehecho** [re'etʃo] *vb* V **rehacer**.
rehén [re'en] *nm* hostage.
rehice [re'iθe] *etc*, **rehizo** [re'iθo] *vb* V **rehacer**.
rehuir [reu'ir] *vt* to avoid, shun.
rehusar [reu'sar] *vt*, *vi* to refuse.
rehuyendo [reu'jendo] *etc vb* V **rehuir**.
reina ['reina] *nf* queen.
reinado [rei'naðo] *nm* reign.
reinante [rei'nante] *a* (*fig*) prevailing.
reinar [rei'nar] *vi* to reign; (*fig: prevalecer*) to prevail, be general.
reincidir [reinθi'ðir] *vi* to relapse; (*criminal*) to repeat an offence.
reincorporarse [reinkorpo'rarse] *vr*: ~ **a** to rejoin.
reinicializar [reiniθjali'θar] *vt* (*INFORM*) to reset.
reino ['reino] *nm* kingdom; **el R~ Unido** the United Kingdom.
reintegración [reinteɣra'θjon] *nf* (*COM*) reinstatement.
reintegrar [reinte'ɣrar] *vt* (*reconstituir*) to reconstruct; (*persona*) to reinstate; (*dinero*) to refund, pay back; ~**se** *vr*: ~**se a** to return to.
reintegro [rein'teɣro] *nm* refund, reimbursement; (*en banco*) withdrawal.
reír [re'ir] *vi*, **reírse** *vr* to laugh; ~**se de** to laugh at.
reiterar [reite'rar] *vt* to reiterate; (*repetir*) to repeat.
reivindicación [reißindika'θjon] *nf* (*demanda*) claim, demand; (*justificación*) vindication.
reivindicar [reißindi'kar] *vt* to claim.
reivindique [reißin'dike] *etc vb* V **reivindicar**.
reja ['rexa] *nf* (*de ventana*) grille, bars *pl*; (*en la calle*) grating.
rejamos [re'xamos] *etc vb* V **regir**.
rejilla [re'xiʎa] *nf* grating, grille; (*muebles*) wickerwork; (*de ventilación*) vent; (*de coche etc*) luggage rack.
rejuvenecer [rexußene'θer] *vt*, *vi* to rejuvenate.
rejuvenezca [rexuße'neθka] *etc vb* V **rejuvenecer**.
relación [rela'θjon] *nf* relation, relationship; (*MAT*) ratio; (*lista*) list; (*narración*) report; ~ **costo-efectivo** *o* **costo-rendimiento** (*COM*) cost-effectiveness; **relaciones** *nfpl* (*enchufes*) influential friends, connections; **relaciones carnales** sexual relations; **relaciones comerciales** business connec-

tions; **relaciones empresariales/humanas** industrial/human relations; **relaciones laborales/públicas** labour/public relations; **con ~ a, en ~ con** in relation to; **estar en** *o* **tener buenas relaciones con** to be on good terms with.
relacionar [relaθjo'nar] *vt* to relate, connect; ~**se** *vr* to be connected *o* linked.
relajación [relaxa'θjon] *nf* relaxation.
relajado, a [rela'xaðo, a] *a* (*disoluto*) loose; (*cómodo*) relaxed; (*MED*) ruptured.
relajante [rela'xante] *a* relaxing; (*MED*) sedative.
relajar [rela'xar] *vt*, **relajarse** *vr* to relax.
relamerse [rela'merse] *vr* to lick one's lips.
relamido, a [rela'miðo, a] *a* (*pulcro*) overdressed; (*afectado*) affected.
relámpago [re'lampaɣo] *nm* flash of lightning ♦ *a* lightning *cpd*; **como un** ~ as quick as lightning, in a flash; **visita/huelga** ~ lightning visit/strike.
relampaguear [relampaɣe'ar] *vi* to flash.
relatar [rela'tar] *vt* to tell, relate.
relativo, a [rela'tißo, a] *a* relative; **en lo** ~ **a** concerning.
relato [re'lato] *nm* (*narración*) story, tale.
relegar [rele'ɣar] *vt* to relegate; ~ **algo al olvido** to banish sth from one's mind.
relegue [re'leɣe] *etc vb* V **relegar**.
relevante [rele'ßante] *a* eminent, outstanding.
relevar [rele'ßar] *vt* (*sustituir*) to relieve; ~**se** *vr* to relay; ~ **a uno de un cargo** to relieve sb of his post.
relevo [re'leßo] *nm* relief; **carrera de** ~**s** relay race; ~ **con cinta** (*INFORM*) tape relay; **coger** *o* **tomar el** ~ to take over, stand in.
relieve [re'ljeße] *nm* (*ARTE, TEC*) relief; (*fig*) prominence, importance; **bajo** ~ bas-relief; **un personaje de** ~ an important man; **dar** ~ **a** to highlight.
religión [reli'xjon] *nf* religion.
religioso, a [reli'xjoso, a] *a* religious ♦ *nm/f* monk/nun.
relinchar [relin'tʃar] *vi* to neigh.
relincho [re'lintʃo] *nm* neigh; (*acto*) neighing.
reliquia [re'likja] *nf* relic; ~ **de familia** heirloom.
reloj [re'lo(x)] *nm* clock; ~ **de pie** grandfather clock; ~ **(de pulsera)** wristwatch; ~ **de sol** sundial; ~ **despertador** alarm (clock); **como un** ~ like clockwork; **contra (el)** ~ against the clock.
relojería [reloxe'ria] (*tienda*) watchmaker's (shop); **aparato de** ~ clockwork; **bomba de** ~ time bomb.
relojero, a [relo'xero, a] *nm/f* clockmaker; watchmaker.
reluciente [relu'θjente] *a* brilliant, shining.
relucir [relu'θir] *vi* to shine; (*fig*) to excel;

sacar algo a ~ to show sth off.
relumbrante [relum'brante] *a* dazzling.
relumbrar [relum'brar] *vi* to dazzle, shine brilliantly.
reluzca [re'luθka] *etc vb* V **relucir**.
rellano [re'ʎano] *nm* (*ARQ*) landing.
rellenar [reʎe'nar] *vt* (*llenar*) to fill up; (*CULIN*) to stuff; (*COSTURA*) to pad; (*formulario etc*) to fill in *o* out.
relleno, a [re'ʎeno, a] *a* full up; (*CULIN*) stuffed ♦ *nm* stuffing; (*de tapicería*) padding.
remachar [rema'tʃar] *vt* to rivet; (*fig*) to hammer home, drive home.
remache [re'matʃe] *nm* rivet.
remanente [rema'nente] *nm* remainder; (*COM*) balance; (*de producto*) surplus.
remanso [re'manso] *nm* pool.
remar [re'mar] *vi* to row.
rematado, a [rema'taðo, a] *a* complete, utter; **es un loco** ~ he's a raving lunatic.
rematar [rema'tar] *vt* to finish off; (*animal*) to put out of its misery; (*COM*) to sell off cheap ♦ *vi* to end, finish off; (*DEPORTE*) to shoot.
remate [re'mate] *nm* end, finish; (*punta*) tip; (*DEPORTE*) shot; (*ARQ*) top; (*COM*) auction sale; **de** *o* **para** ~ to crown it all (*Brit*), to top it off.
remediable [reme'ðjaßle] *a*: **fácilmente** ~ easily remedied.
remediar [reme'ðjar] *vt* (*gen*) to remedy; (*subsanar*) to make good, repair; (*evitar*) to avoid; **sin poder** ~**lo** without being able to prevent it.
remedio [re'meðjo] *nm* remedy; (*JUR*) recourse, remedy; **poner** ~ **a** to correct, stop; **no tener más** ~ to have no alternative; **¡qué** ~**!** there's no other way; **como último** ~ as a last resort; **sin** ~ inevitable; (*MED*) hopeless.
remedo [re'meðo] *nm* imitation; (*pey*) parody.
remendar [remen'dar] *vt* to repair; (*con parche*) to patch; (*fig*) to correct.
remesa [re'mesa] *nf* remittance; (*COM*) shipment.
remiendo [re'mjendo] *etc vb* V **remendar** ♦ *nm* mend; (*con parche*) patch; (*cosido*) darn; (*fig*) correction.
remilgado, a [remil'ɣaðo, a] *a* prim; (*afectado*) affected.
remilgo [re'milɣo] *nm* primness; (*afectación*) affectation.
reminiscencia [reminis'θenθja] *nf* reminiscence.
remirar [remi'rar] *vt* (*volver a mirar*) to look at again; (*examinar*) to look hard at.
remisión [remi'sjon] *nf* (*acto*) sending, shipment; (*REL*) forgiveness, remission; **sin** ~ hopelessly.

remiso, a [re'miso, a] *a* remiss.
remite [re'mite] *nm* (*en sobre*) name and address of sender.
remitente [remi'tente] *nm/f* (*CORREOS*) sender.
remitir [remi'tir] *vt* to remit, send ♦ *vi* to slacken.
remo ['remo] *nm* (*de barco*) oar; (*DEPORTE*) rowing; **cruzar un río a** ~ to row across a river.
remoce [re'moθe] *etc vb* V **remozar**.
remodelación [remodela'θjon] *nf* (*POL*): ~ **del gobierno** cabinet reshuffle.
remojar [remo'xar] *vt* to steep, soak; (*galleta etc*) to dip, dunk; (*fam*) to celebrate with a drink.
remojo [re'moxo] *nm* steeping, soaking; (*por la lluvia*) drenching, soaking; **dejar la ropa en** ~ to leave clothes to soak.
remojón [remo'xon] *nm* soaking; **darse un** ~ (*fam*) to go (in) for a dip.
remolacha [remo'latʃa] *nf* beet, beetroot (*Brit*).
remolcador [remolka'ðor] *nm* (*NAUT*) tug; (*AUTO*) breakdown lorry.
remolcar [remol'kar] *vt* to tow.
remolino [remo'lino] *nm* eddy; (*de agua*) whirlpool; (*de viento*) whirlwind; (*de gente*) crowd.
remolón, ona [remo'lon, ona] *a* lazy ♦ *nm/f* slacker, shirker.
remolque [re'molke] *etc vb* V **remolcar** ♦ *nm* tow, towing; (*cuerda*) towrope; **llevar a** ~ to tow.
remontar [remon'tar] *vt* to mend; (*obstáculo*) to negotiate, get over; ~**se** *vr* to soar; ~**se a** (*COM*) to amount to; (*en tiempo*) to go back to, date from; ~ **el vuelo** to soar.
rémora ['remora] *nf* hindrance.
remorder [remor'ðer] *vt* to distress, disturb.
remordimiento [remorði'mjento] *nm* remorse.
remotamente [remota'mente] *ad* vaguely.
remoto, a [re'moto, a] *a* remote.
remover [remo'ßer] *vt* to stir; (*tierra*) to turn over; (*objetos*) to move round.
remozar [remo'θar] *vt* (*ARQ*) to refurbish; (*fig*) to brighten *o* polish up.
remuerda [re'mwerða] *etc vb* V **remorder**.
remueva [re'mweßa] *etc vb* V **remover**.
remuneración [remunera'θjon] *nf* remuneration.
remunerado, a [remune'raðo, a] *a*: **trabajo bien/mal** ~ well-/badly-paid job.
remunerar [remune'rar] *vt* to remunerate; (*premiar*) to reward.
renacer [rena'θer] *vi* to be reborn; (*fig*) to revive.
renacimiento [renaθi'mjento] *nm* rebirth; **el R**~ the Renaissance.

renacuajo [rena'kwaxo] *nm* (*zool*) tadpole.

renal [re'nal] *a* renal, kidney *cpd*.

Renania [re'nanja] *nf* Rhineland.

renazca [re'naθka] *etc vb* V **renacer**.

rencilla [ren'θiʎa] *nf* quarrel; **~s** *nfpl* bickering *sg*.

rencor [ren'kor] *nm* rancour, bitterness; (*resentimiento*) ill feeling, resentment; **guardar ~ a** to have a grudge against.

rencoroso, a [renko'roso, a] *a* spiteful.

rendición [rendi'θjon] *nf* surrender.

rendido, a [ren'diðo, a] *a* (*sumiso*) submissive; (*agotado*) worn-out, exhausted; (*enamorado*) devoted.

rendija [ren'dixa] *nf* (*hendedura*) crack; (*abertura*) aperture; (*fig*) rift, split; (*JUR*) loophole.

rendimiento [rendi'mjento] *nm* (*producción*) output; (*COM*) yield, profit(s) (*pl*); (*TEC, COM*) efficiency; **~ de capital** (*COM*) return on capital.

rendir [ren'dir] *vt* (*vencer*) to defeat; (*producir*) to produce; (*dar beneficio*) to yield; (*agotar*) to exhaust ♦ *vi* to pay; (*COM*) to yield, produce; **~se** *vr* (*someterse*) to surrender; (*ceder*) to yield; (*cansarse*) to wear o.s. out; **~ homenaje** *o* **culto a** to pay homage to; **el negocio no rinde** the business doesn't pay.

renegado, a [rene'ɣaðo, a] *a*, *nm/f* renegade.

renegar [rene'ɣar] *vt* (*negar*) to deny vigorously ♦ *vi* (*blasfemar*) to blaspheme; **~ de** (*renunciar*) to renounce; (*quejarse*) to complain about.

renegué [rene'ɣe], **reneguemos** [rene'ɣemos] *etc vb* V **renegar**.

RENFE ['renfe] *nf abr Esp*: = Red Nacional de Ferrocarriles Españoles.

renglón [ren'glon] *nm* (*línea*) line; (*COM*) item, article; **a ~ seguido** immediately after.

reniego [re'njeɣo] *etc*, **reniegue** [re'njeɣe] *etc vb* V **renegar**.

reno ['reno] *nm* reindeer.

renombrado, a [renom'braðo, a] *a* renowned.

renombre [re'nombre] *nm* renown.

renovación [renoßa'θjon] *nf* (*de contrato*) renewal; (*ARQ*) renovation.

renovar [reno'ßar] *vt* to renew; (*ARQ*) to renovate; (*sala*) to redecorate.

renquear [renke'ar] *vi* to limp; (*fam*) to get along, scrape by.

renta ['renta] *nf* (*ingresos*) income; (*beneficio*) profit; (*alquiler*) rent; **política de ~s** incomes policy; **~ gravable** *o* **imponible** taxable income; **~ nacional (bruta)** (gross) national income; **~ no salarial** unearned income; **~ sobre el terreno** (*COM*) ground rent; **vivir de sus ~s** to live on one's pri-

vate income; **~ vitalicia** annuity.

rentable [ren'taßle] *a* profitable; **no ~** unprofitable.

rentar [ren'tar] *vt* to produce, yield.

rentista [ren'tista] *nm/f* (*accionista*) shareholder (*Brit*), stockholder (*US*).

renuencia [re'nwenθja] *nf* reluctance.

renuente [re'nwente] *a* reluctant.

renueve [re'nweße] *etc vb* V **renovar**.

renuncia [re'nunθja] *nf* resignation.

renunciar [renun'θjar] *vt* to renounce, give up ♦ *vi* to resign; **~ a hacer algo** to give up doing sth.

reñido, a [re'ɲiðo, a] *a* (*batalla*) bitter, hard-fought; **estar ~ con uno** to be on bad terms with sb; **está ~ con su familia** he has fallen out with his family.

reñir [re'ɲir] *vt* (*regañar*) to scold ♦ *vi* (*estar peleado*) to quarrel, fall out; (*combatir*) to fight.

reo ['reo] *nm/f* culprit, offender; (*JUR*) accused.

reojo [re'oxo]: **de ~** *ad* out of the corner of one's eye.

reorganice [reorɣa'niθe] *etc vb* V **reorganizar**.

reorganizar [reorɣani'θar] *vt* to reorganize.

Rep *abr* = **República**.

reparación [repara'θjon] *nf* (*acto*) mending, repairing; (*TEC*) repair; (*fig*) amends, reparation; **"reparaciones en el acto"** "repairs while you wait".

reparar [repa'rar] *vt* to repair; (*fig*) to make amends for; (*suerte*) to retrieve; (*observar*) to observe ♦ *vi*: **~ en** (*darse cuenta de*) to notice; (*poner atención en*) to pay attention to; **sin ~ en los gastos** regardless of the cost.

reparo [re'paro] *nm* (*advertencia*) observation; (*duda*) doubt; (*dificultad*) difficulty; (*escrúpulo*) scruple, qualm; **poner ~s (a)** to raise objections (to); (*criticar*) to criticize; **no tuvo ~ en hacerlo** he did not hesitate to do it.

repartición [reparti'θjon] *nf* distribution; (*división*) division.

repartidor, a [reparti'ðor, a] *nm/f* distributor; **~ de leche** milkman.

repartir [repar'tir] *vt* to distribute, share out; (*COM, CORREOS*) to deliver; (*MIL*) to partition; (*libros*) to give out; (*comida*) to serve out; (*naipes*) to deal.

reparto [re'parto] *nm* distribution; (*COM, CORREOS*) delivery; (*TEATRO, CINE*) cast; (*AM: urbanización*) housing estate (*Brit*), real estate development (*US*); **"~ a domicilio"** "home delivery service".

repasar [repa'sar] *vt* (*ESCOL*) to revise; (*MECÁNICA*) to check, overhaul; (*COSTURA*) to mend.

repaso [re'paso] *nm* revision; (*MECÁNICA*)

overhaul, checkup; (*COSTURA*) mending; ~ **general** servicing, general overhaul; **curso de** ~ refresher course.

repatriar [repa'trjar] *vt* to repatriate; ~**se** *vr* to return home.

repelente [repe'lente] *a* repellent, repulsive.

repeler [repe'ler] *vt* to repel; (*idea, oferta*) to reject.

repensar [repen'sar] *vt* to reconsider.

repente [re'pente] *nm* sudden movement; (*fig*) impulse; **de** ~ suddenly; ~ **de ira** fit of anger.

repentice [repen'tiθe] *etc vb V* **repentizar**.

repentino, a [repen'tino, a] *a* sudden; (*imprevisto*) unexpected.

repentizar [repenti'θar] *vi* (*MUS*) to sight-read.

repercusión [reperku'sjon] *nf* repercussion; **de amplia** *o* **ancha** ~ far-reaching.

repercutir [reperku'tir] *vi* (*objeto*) to rebound; (*sonido*) to echo; ~ **en** (*fig*) to have repercussions *o* effects on.

repertorio [reper'torjo] *nm* list; (*TEATRO*) repertoire.

repetición [repeti'θjon] *nf* repetition.

repetido, a [repe'tiðo, a] *a* repeated; **repetidas veces** repeatedly.

repetir [repe'tir] *vt* to repeat; (*plato*) to have a second helping of; (*TEATRO*) to give as an encore, sing *etc* again ♦ *vi* to repeat; (*sabor*) to come back; ~**se** *vr* to repeat o.s.; (*suceso*) to recur.

repetitivo, a [repeti'tiβo, a] *a* repetitive, repetitious.

repicar [repi'kar] *vi* (*campanas*) to ring (out).

repiense [re'pjense] *etc vb V* **repensar**.

repique [re'pike] *etc vb V* **repicar** ♦ *nm* pealing, ringing.

repiqueteo [repike'teo] *nm* pealing; (*de tambor*) drumming.

repisa [re'pisa] *nf* ledge, shelf; ~ **de chimenea** mantelpiece; ~ **de ventana** windowsill.

repitiendo [repi'tjendo] *etc vb V* **repetir**.

replegarse [reple'varse] *vr* to fall back, retreat.

replegué [reple'xe], **repleguemos** [reple'xemos] *etc vb V* **replegarse**.

repleto, a [re'pleto, a] *a* replete, full up; ~ **de** filled *o* crammed with.

réplica ['replika] *nf* answer; (*ARTE*) replica; **derecho de** ~ right of *o* to reply.

replicar [repli'kar] *vi* to answer; (*objetar*) to argue, answer back.

repliego [re'pljexo] *etc vb V* **replegarse**.

repliegue [re'pljexe] *etc vb V* **replegarse** ♦ *nm* (*MIL*) withdrawal.

replique [re'plike] *etc vb V* **replicar**.

repoblación [repoβla'θjon] *nf* repopulation; (*de río*) restocking; ~ **forestal** reafforesta-

tion.

repoblar [repo'βlar] *vt* to repopulate; to restock.

repollo [re'poλo] *nm* cabbage.

repondré [repon'dre] *etc vb V* **reponer**.

reponer [repo'ner] *vt* to replace, put back; (*máquina*) to re-set; (*TEATRO*) to revive; ~**se** *vr* to recover; ~ **que** to reply that.

reponga [re'ponga] *etc vb V* **reponer**.

reportaje [repor'taxe] *nm* report, article; ~ **gráfico** illustrated report.

reportar [repor'tar] *vt* (*traer*) to bring, carry; (*conseguir*) to obtain; (*fig*) to check; ~**se** *vr* (*contenerse*) to control o.s.; (*calmarse*) to calm down; **la cosa no le reportó sino disgustos** the affair brought him nothing but trouble.

reportero, a [repor'tero, a] *nm/f* reporter; ~ **gráfico/a** news photographer.

reposacabezas [reposaka'βeθas] *nm inv* headrest.

reposado, a [repo'saðo, a] *a* (*descansado*) restful; (*tranquilo*) calm.

reposar [repo'sar] *vi* to rest, repose; (*muerto*) to lie, rest.

reposición [reposi'θjon] *nf* replacement; (*CINE*) second showing; (*TEATRO*) revival.

reposo [re'poso] *nm* rest.

repostar [repos'tar] *vt* to replenish; (*AUTO*) to fill up (with petrol *o* gasoline).

repostería [reposte'ria] *nf* (*arte*) confectionery, pastry-making; (*tienda*) confectioner's (shop).

repostero, a [repos'tero, a] *nm/f* confectioner.

reprender [repren'der] *vt* to reprimand; (*niño*) to scold.

reprensión [repren'sjon] *nf* rebuke, reprimand; (*de niño*) telling-off, scolding.

represa [re'presa] *nf* dam; (*lago artificial*) lake, pool.

represalia [repre'salja] *nf* reprisal; **tomar** ~**s** to take reprisals, retaliate.

representación [representa'θjon] *nf* representation; (*TEATRO*) performance; **en** ~ **de** representing; **por** ~ by proxy; ~ **visual** (*INFORM*) display.

representante [represen'tante] *nm/f* (*POL, COM*) representative; (*TEATRO*) performer.

representar [represen'tar] *vt* to represent; (*significar*) to mean; (*TEATRO*) to perform; (*edad*) to look; ~**se** *vr* to imagine; **tal acto representaría la guerra** such an act would mean war.

representativo, a [representa'tiβo, a] *a* representative.

represión [repre'sjon] *nf* repression.

reprimenda [repri'menda] *nf* reprimand, rebuke.

reprimir [repri'mir] *vt* to repress; ~**se** *vr*: ~**se de hacer algo** to stop o.s. from doing sth.

reprobación [reproβa'θjon] *nf* reproval; (*culpa*) blame.

reprobar [repro'βar] *vt* to censure, reprove.

réprobo, a ['reproβo, a] *nm/f* reprobate.

reprochar [repro'tʃar] *vt* to reproach; (*censurar*) to condemn, censure.

reproche [re'protʃe] *nm* reproach.

reproducción [reproðuk'θjon] *nf* reproduction.

reproducir [reproðu'θir] *vt* to reproduce; ~**se** *vr* to breed; (*situación*) to recur.

reproductor, a [reproðuk'tor, a] *a* reproductive.

reproduje [repro'ðuxe], **reprodujera** [reproðu'xera] *etc,* **reproduzca** [repro'duθka] *etc vb V* **reproducir.**

repruebe [re'prweβe] *etc vb V* **reprobar.**

reptar [rep'tar] *vi* to creep, crawl.

reptil [rep'til] *nm* reptile.

república [re'puβlika] *nf* republic; **R~ Dominicana** Dominican Republic; **R~ Democrática Alemana (RDA)** German Democratic Republic; **R~ Federal Alemana (RFA)** Federal Republic of Germany; **R~ Árabe Unida** United Arab Republic.

republicano, a [repuβli'kano, a] *a, nm/f* republican.

repudiar [repu'ðjar] *vt* to repudiate; (*fe*) to renounce.

repudio [re'puðjo] *nm* repudiation.

repueble [re'pweβle] *etc vb V* **repoblar.**

repuesto [re'pwesto] *pp de* **reponer** ♦ *nm* (*pieza de recambio*) spare (part); (*abastecimiento*) supply; **rueda de ~** spare wheel; **y llevamos otro de ~** and we have another as a spare *o* in reserve.

repugnancia [repuɣ'nanθja] *nf* repugnance.

repugnante [repuɣ'nante] *a* repugnant, repulsive.

repugnar [repuɣ'nar] *vt* to disgust ♦ *vi,* ~**se** *vr* (*contradecirse*) to contradict each other; (*dar asco*) to be disgusting.

repulsa [re'pulsa] *nf* rebuff.

repulsión [repul'sjon] *nf* repulsion, aversion.

repulsivo, a [repul'siβo, a] *a* repulsive.

repuse [re'puse] *etc vb V* **reponer.**

reputación [reputa'θjon] *nf* reputation.

reputar [repu'tar] *vt* to consider, deem.

requemado, a [reke'maðo, a] *a* (*quemado*) scorched; (*bronceado*) tanned.

requemar [reke'mar] *vt* (*quemar*) to scorch; (*secar*) to parch; (*CULIN*) to overdo, burn; (*la lengua*) to burn, sting.

requerimiento [rekeri'mjento] *nm* request; (*demanda*) demand; (*JUR*) summons.

requerir [reke'rir] *vt* (*pedir*) to ask, request; (*exigir*) to require; (*ordenar*) to call for; (*llamar*) to send for, summon.

requesón [reke'son] *nm* cottage cheese.

requete... [rekete] *pref* extremely.

requiebro [re'kjeβro] *nm* (*piropo*) compliment, flirtatious remark.

réquiem ['rekjem] *nm* requiem.

requiera [re'kjera] *etc,* **requiriendo** [reki'rjendo] *etc vb V* **requerir.**

requisa [re'kisa] *nf* (*inspección*) survey, inspection; (*MIL*) requisition.

requisar [reki'sar] *vt* (*MIL*) to requisition; (*confiscar*) to seize, confiscate.

requisito [reki'sito] *nm* requirement, requisite; ~ **previo** prerequisite; **tener los ~s para un cargo** to have the essential qualifications for a post.

res [res] *nf* beast, animal.

resabio [re'saβjo] *nm* (*maña*) vice, bad habit; (*dejo*) (unpleasant) aftertaste.

resaca [re'saka] *nf* (*en el mar*) undertow, undercurrent; (*fig*) backlash; (*fam*) hangover.

resaltar [resal'tar] *vi* to project, stick out; (*fig*) to stand out.

resarcir [resar'θir] *vt* to compensate; (*pagar*) to repay; ~**se** *vr* to make up for; ~ **a uno de una pérdida** to compensate sb for a loss; ~ **a uno de una cantidad** to repay sb a sum.

resarza [re'sarθa] *etc vb V* **resarcir.**

resbaladizo, a [resβala'ðiθo, a] *a* slippery.

resbalar [resβa'lar] *vi,* **resbalarse** *vr* to slip, slide; (*fig*) to slip (up); **le resbalaban las lágrimas por las mejillas** tears were trickling down his cheeks.

resbalón [resβa'lon] *nm* (*acción*) slip; (*deslizamiento*) slide; (*fig*) slip.

rescatar [reska'tar] *vt* (*salvar*) to save, rescue; (*objeto*) to get back, recover; (*cautivos*) to ransom.

rescate [res'kate] *nm* rescue; (*objeto*) recovery; **pagar un ~** to pay a ransom.

rescindir [resθin'dir] *vt* (*contrato*) to annul, rescind.

rescisión [resθi'sjon] *nf* cancellation.

rescoldo [res'koldo] *nm* embers *pl*.

resecar [rese'kar] *vt* to dry off, dry thoroughly; (*MED*) to cut out, remove; ~**se** *vr* to dry up.

reseco, a [re'seko, a] *a* very dry; (*fig*) skinny.

resentido, a [resen'tiðo, a] *a* resentful; **es un ~** he's bitter.

resentimiento [resenti'mjento] *nm* resentment, bitterness.

resentirse [resen'tirse] *vr* (*debilitarse: persona*) to suffer; ~ **con** to resent; ~ **de** (*consecuencias*) to feel the effects of.

reseña [re'seɲa] *nf* (*cuenta*) account; (*informe*) report; (*LIT*) review.

reseñar [rese'ɲar] *vt* to describe; (*LIT*) to review.

reseque [re'seke] *etc vb V* **resecar.**

reserva [re'serβa] *nf* reserve; (*reservación*) reservation; **a ~ de que ... unless ...; con toda ~** in strictest confidence; **de ~** spare; **tener algo de ~** to have sth in reserve; **~ de indios** Indian reservation; (*COM*): **~ para amortización** depreciation allowance; **~ de caja** *o* **en efectivo** cash reserves; **~s del Estado** government stock; **~s en oro** gold reserves.

reservado, a [reser'βaðo, a] *a* reserved; (*retraído*) cold, distant ♦ *nm* private room; (*FERRO*) reserved compartment.

reservar [reser'βar] *vt* (*guardar*) to keep; (*FERRO, TEATRO etc*) to reserve, book; **~se** *vr* to save o.s.; (*callar*) to keep to o.s.; **~ con exceso** to overbook.

resfriado [res'friaðo] *nm* cold.

resfriarse [res'friarse] *vr* to cool off; (*MED*) to catch (a) cold.

resguardar [resɣwar'ðar] *vt* to protect, shield; **~se** *vr*: **~se de** to guard against.

resguardo [res'ɣwarðo] *nm* defence; (*vale*) voucher; (*recibo*) receipt, slip.

residencia [resi'ðenθja] *nf* residence; (*UNIV*) hall of residence; **~ para ancianos** *o* **jubilados** rest home.

residencial [resiðen'θjal] *a* residential ♦ *nf* (*urbanización*) housing estate (*Brit*), real estate development (*US*).

residente [resi'ðente] *a, nm/f* resident.

residir [resi'ðir] *vi* to reside, live; **~ en** to reside *o* lie in; (*consistir en*) to consist of.

residual [resi'ðwal] *a* residual; **aguas ~es** sewage.

residuo [re'siðwo] *nm* residue; **~s atmosféricos** *o* **radiactivos** fallout *sg*.

resienta [re'sjenta] *etc vb V* **resentir**.

resignación [resiɣna'θjon] *nf* resignation.

resignarse [resiɣ'narse] *vr*: **~ a** *o* **con** to resign o.s. to, be resigned to.

resina [re'sina] *nf* resin.

resintiendo [resin'tjendo] *etc vb V* **resentir**.

resistencia [resis'tenθja] *nf* (*dureza*) endurance, strength; (*oposición, ELEC*) resistance; **la R~** (*MIL*) the Resistance.

resistente [resis'tente] *a* strong, hardy; (*TEC*) resistant; **~ al calor** heat-resistant.

resistir [resis'tir] *vt* (*soportar*) to bear; (*oponerse a*) to resist, oppose; (*aguantar*) to put up with ♦ *vi* to resist; (*aguantar*) to last, endure; **~se** *vr*: **~se a** to refuse to, resist; **no puedo ~ este frío** I can't bear *o* stand this cold; **me resisto a creerlo** I refuse to believe it; **se le resiste la química** chemistry escapes her.

resol [re'sol] *nm* glare of the sun.

resolución [resolu'θjon] *nf* resolution; (*decisión*) decision; (*moción*) motion; **~ judicial** legal ruling; **tomar una ~** to take a decision.

resoluto, a [reso'luto, a] *a* resolute.

resolver [resol'βer] *vt* to resolve; (*solucionar*) to solve, resolve; (*decidir*) to decide, settle; **~se** *vr* to make up one's mind.

resollar [reso'ʎar] *vi* to breathe noisily, wheeze.

resonancia [reso'nanθja] *nf* (*del sonido*) resonance; (*repercusión*) repercussion; (*fig*) wide effect, impact.

resonante [reso'nante] *a* resonant, resounding; (*fig*) tremendous.

resonar [reso'nar] *vi* to ring, echo.

resoplar [reso'plar] *vi* to snort; (*por cansancio*) to puff.

resoplido [reso'pliðo] *nm* heavy breathing.

resorte [re'sorte] *nm* spring; (*fig*) lever.

respaldar [respal'dar] *vt* to back (up), support; (*INFORM*) to back up; **~se** *vr* to lean back; **~se con** *o* **en** (*fig*) to take one's stand on.

respaldo [res'paldo] *nm* (*de sillón*) back; (*fig*) support, backing.

respectivo, a [respek'tiβo, a] *a* respective; **en lo ~ a** with regard to.

respecto [res'pekto] *nm*: **al ~** on this matter; **con ~ a, ~ de** with regard to, in relation to.

respetable [respe'taβle] *a* respectable.

respetar [respe'tar] *vt* to respect.

respeto [res'peto] *nm* respect; (*acatamiento*) deference; **~s** *nmpl* respects; **por ~ a** out of consideration for; **presentar sus ~s a** to pay one's respects to.

respetuoso, a [respe'twoso, a] *a* respectful.

respingar [respin'gar] *vi* to shy.

respingo [res'pingo] *nm* start, jump.

respingue [res'pinge] *etc vb V* **respingar**.

respiración [respira'θjon] *nf* breathing; (*MED*) respiration; (*ventilación*) ventilation.

respirar [respi'rar] *vt, vi* to breathe; **no dejar ~ a uno** to keep on at sb; **estuvo escuchándole sin ~** he listened to him in complete silence.

respiratorio, a [respira'torjo, a] *a* respiratory.

respiro [res'piro] *nm* breathing; (*fig: descanso*) respite, rest; (*COM*) period of grace.

resplandecer [resplande'θer] *vi* to shine.

resplandeciente [resplande'θjente] *a* resplendent, shining.

resplandezca [resplan'deθka] *etc vb V* **resplandecer**.

resplandor [resplan'dor] *nm* brilliance, brightness; (*del fuego*) blaze.

responder [respon'der] *vt* to answer ♦ *vi* to answer; (*fig*) to respond; (*pey*) to answer back; (*corresponder*) to correspond; **~ a** (*situación etc*) to respond to; **~ a una pregunta** to answer a question; **~ a una**

descripción to fit a description; ~ **de** *o* **por** to answer for.

respondón, ona [respon'don, ona] *a* cheeky.

responsabilice [responsaβi'liθe] *etc vb* V **responsabilizarse.**

responsabilidad [responsaβili'ðað] *nf* responsibility; **bajo mi** ~ on my authority; ~ **ilimitada** (*COM*) unlimited liability.

responsabilizarse [responsaβili'θarse] *vr* to make o.s. responsible, take charge.

responsable [respon'sable] *a* responsible; **la persona** ~ the person in charge; **hacerse** ~ **de algo** to assume responsibility for sth.

respuesta [res'pwesta] *nf* answer, reply; (*reacción*) response.

resquebrajar [reskeßra'xar] *vt*, **resquebrajarse** *vr* to crack, split.

resquemor [reske'mor] *nm* resentment.

resquicio [res'kiθjo] *nm* chink; (*hendedura*) crack.

resta ['resta] *nf* (*MAT*) remainder.

restablecer [restaßle'θer] *vt* to re-establish, restore; ~**se** *vr* to recover.

restablecimiento [restaßleθi'mjento] *nm* re-establishment; (*restauración*) restoration; (*MED*) recovery.

restablezca [resta'ßleθka] *etc vb* V **restablecer.**

restallar [resta'ʎar] *vi* to crack.

restante [res'tante] *a* remaining; **lo** ~ the remainder; **los** ~**s** the rest, those left (over).

restar [res'tar] *vt* (*MAT*) to subtract; (*descontar*) to deduct; (*fig*) to take away ♦ *vi* to remain, be left.

restauración [restaura'θjon] *nf* restoration.

restaurador, a [restaura'ðor, a] *nm/f* (*persona*) restorer.

restaurante [restau'rante] *nm* restaurant.

restaurar [restau'rar] *vt* to restore.

restitución [restitu'θjon] *nf* return, restitution.

restituir [restitu'ir] *vt* (*devolver*) to return, give back; (*rehabilitar*) to restore.

restituyendo [restitu'jendo] *etc vb* V **restituir.**

resto ['resto] *nm* (*residuo*) rest, remainder; (*apuesta*) stake; ~**s** *nmpl* remains; (*CULIN*) leftovers, scraps; ~**s mortales** mortal remains.

restregar [restre'ɣar] *vt* to scrub, rub.

restregué [restre'ɣe], **restreguemos** [restre'ɣemos] *etc vb* V **restregar.**

restricción [restrik'θjon] *nf* restriction; **sin** ~ **de** without restrictions on *o* as to; **hablar sin restricciones** to talk freely.

restrictivo, a [restrik'tißo, a] *a* restrictive.

restriego [res'trjeɣo] *etc*, **restriegue** [res'trjeɣe] *etc vb* V **restregar.**

restringir [restrin'xir] *vt* to restrict, limit.

restrinja [res'trinxa] *etc vb* V **restringir.**

resucitar [resuθi'tar] *vt*, *vi* to resuscitate, revive.

resuelto, a [re'swelto, a] *pp de* **resolver** ♦ *a* resolute, determined; **estar** ~ **a algo** to be set on sth; **estar** ~ **a hacer algo** to be determined to do sth.

resuelva [re'swelßa] *etc vb* V **resolver.**

resuello [re'sweʎo] *etc vb* V **resollar** ♦ *nm* (*aliento*) breath.

resuene [re'swene] *etc vb* V **resonar.**

resulta [re'sulta] *nf* result; **de** ~**s de** as a result of.

resultado [resul'taðo] *nm* result; (*conclusión*) outcome; ~**s** *nmpl* (*INFORM*) output *sg*; **dar** ~ to produce results.

resultante [resul'tante] *a* resulting, resultant.

resultar [resul'tar] *vi* (*ser*) to be; (*llegar a ser*) to turn out to be; (*salir bien*) to turn out well; (*seguir*) to ensue; ~ **a** (*COM*) to amount to; ~ **de** to stem from; ~ **en** to result in, produce; **resulta que** ... (*por consecuencia*) it follows that ...; (*parece que*) it seems that ...; **el conductor resultó muerto** the driver was killed; **no resultó** it didn't work *o* come off; **me resulta difícil hacerlo** it's difficult for me to do it.

resumen [re'sumen] *nm* summary, résumé; **en** ~ in short.

resumir [resu'mir] *vt* to sum up; (*condensar*) to summarize; (*cortar*) to abridge, cut down; (*condensar*) to summarize; ~**se** *vr*: **la situación se resume en pocas palabras** the situation can be summed up in a few words.

resurgir [resur'xir] *vi* (*reaparecer*) to reappear.

resurrección [resurrek'θjon] *nf* resurrection.

retablo [re'taßlo] *nm* altarpiece.

retaguardia [reta'ɣwarðja] *nf* rearguard.

retahíla [reta'ila] *nf* series, string; (*de injurias*) volley, stream.

retal [re'tal] *nm* remnant.

retar [re'tar] *vt* (*gen*) to challenge; (*desafiar*) to defy, dare.

retardar [retar'ðar] *vt* (*demorar*) to delay; (*hacer más lento*) to slow down; (*retener*) to hold back.

retardo [re'tarðo] *nm* delay.

retazo [re'taθo] *nm* snippet (*Brit*), fragment.

RETD *nf abr* (*Esp TELEC*) = **Red Especial de Transmisión de Datos.**

rete... ['rete] *pref* very, extremely.

retención [reten'θjon] *nf* retention; (*de pago*) deduction; ~ **de llamadas** (*TELEC*) hold facility.

retendré [reten'dre] *etc vb* V **retener.**

retener [rete'ner] *vt* (*guardar*) to retain, keep; (*intereses*) to withhold.

retenga [re'tenga] *etc vb V* **retener**.

reticencia [reti'θenθja] *nf* (*sugerencia*) insinuation, (malevolent) suggestion; (*engaño*) half-truth.

reticente [reti'θente] *a* (*insinuador*) insinuating; (*engañoso*) deceptive.

retiene [re'tjene] *etc vb V* **retener**.

retina [re'tina] *nf* retina.

retintín [retin'tin] *nm* jangle, jingle; **decir algo con** ~ to say sth sarcastically.

retirado, a [reti'raðo, a] *a* (*lugar*) remote; (*vida*) quiet; (*jubilado*) retired ◆ *nf* (*MIL*) retreat; (*de dinero*) withdrawal; (*de embajador*) recall; (*refugio*) safe place; **batirse en retirada** to retreat.

retirante [reti'rante] *a*: **ser** ~ **a hacer algo** to be reluctant to do sth.

retirar [reti'rar] *vt* to withdraw; (*la mano*) to draw back; (*quitar*) to remove; (*dinero*) to take out, withdraw; (*jubilar*) to retire, pension off; **~se** *vr* to retreat, withdraw; (*jubilarse*) to retire; (*acostarse*) to retire, go to bed.

retiro [re'tiro] *nm* retreat; (*jubilación, tb DEPORTE*) retirement; (*pago*) pension; (*lugar*) quiet place.

reto ['reto] *nm* dare, challenge.

retocar [reto'kar] *vt* to touch up, retouch.

retoce [re'toθe] *etc vb V* **retozar**.

retoño [re'toɲo] *nm* sprout, shoot; (*fig*) offspring, child.

retoque [re'toke] *etc vb V* **retocar** ◆ *nm* retouching.

retorcer [retor'θer] *vt* to twist; (*argumento*) to turn, twist; (*manos, lavado*) to wring; **~se** *vr* to become twisted; (*persona*) to writhe; **~se de dolor** to writhe in *o* squirm with pain.

retorcimiento [retorθi'mjento] *nm* twist, twisting; (*fig*) deviousness.

retórico, a [re'toriko, a] *a* rhetorical; (*pey*) affected, windy ◆ *nf* rhetoric; (*pey*) affectedness.

retornar [retor'nar] *vt* to return, give back ◆ *vi* to return, go/come back.

retorno [re'torno] *nm* return; ~ **del carro** (*INFORM, TIP*) carriage return; ~ **del carro automático** (*INFORM*) wordwrap, word wraparound.

retortero [retor'tero] *nm*: **andar al** ~ to bustle about, have heaps of things to do; **andar al** ~ **por uno** to be madly in love with sb.

retortijón [retorti'xon] *nm* twist, twisting; ~ **de tripas** stomach cramp.

retorzamos [retor'θamos] *etc vb V* **retorcer**.

retozar [reto'θar] *vi* (*juguetear*) to frolic, romp; (*saltar*) to gambol.

retozón, ona [reto'θon, ona] *a* playful.

retracción [retrak'θjon] *nf* retraction.

retractarse [retrak'tarse] *vr* to retract; **me retracto** I take that back.

retraerse [retra'erse] *vr* to retreat, withdraw.

retraído, a [retra'iðo, a] *a* shy, retiring.

retraiga [re'traixa] *etc vb V* **retraerse**.

retraimiento [retrai'mjento] *nm* retirement; (*timidez*) shyness.

retraje [re'traxe] *etc*, **retrajera** [retra'xera] *etc vb V* **retraerse**.

retransmisión [retransmi'sjon] *nf* repeat (broadcast).

retransmitir [retransmi'tir] *vt* (*mensaje*) to relay; (*TV etc*) to repeat, retransmit; (: *en vivo*) to broadcast live.

retrasado, a [retra'saðo, a] *a* late; (*MED*) mentally retarded; (*país etc*) backward, underdeveloped; **estar** ~ (*reloj*) to be slow; (*persona, industria*) to be *o* lag behind.

retrasar [retra'sar] *vt* (*demorar*) to postpone, put off; (*retardar*) to slow down ◆ *vi*, **~se** *vr* (*atrasarse*) to be late; (*reloj*) to be slow; (*producción*) to fall (away); (*quedarse atrás*) to lag behind.

retraso [re'traso] *nm* (*demora*) delay; (*lentitud*) slowness; (*tardanza*) lateness; (*atraso*) backwardness; **~s** *nmpl* (*COM*) arrears; (*deudas*) deficit *sg*, debts; **llegar con** ~ to arrive late; **llegar con 25 minutos de** ~ to be 25 minutes late; **llevo un** ~ **de 6 semanas** I'm 6 weeks behind (with my work *etc*); ~ **mental** mental deficiency.

retratar [retra'tar] *vt* (*ARTE*) to paint the portrait of; (*fotografiar*) to photograph; (*fig*) to depict, describe; **~se** *vr* to have one's portrait painted; to have one's photograph taken.

retratista [retra'tista] *nm/f* (*pintura*) (portrait) painter; (*FOTO*) photographer.

retrato [re'trato] *nm* portrait; (*FOTO*) photograph; (*descripción*) portrayal, depiction; (*fig*) likeness; **ser el vivo** ~ **de** to be the spitting image of.

retrato-robot [re'tratoroˈβo(t)], *pl* **retratos-robot** *nm* identikit picture.

retrayendo [retra'jendo] *etc vb V* **retraerse**.

retreta [re'treta] *nf* retreat.

retrete [re'trete] *nm* toilet.

retribución [retriβu'θjon] *nf* (*recompensa*) reward; (*pago*) pay, payment.

retribuir [retriβu'ir] *vt* (*recompensar*) to reward; (*pagar*) to pay.

retribuyendo [retriβu'jendo] *etc vb V* **retribuir**.

retro... [retro] *pref* retro....

retroactivo, a [retroak'tiβo, a] *a* retroactive, retrospective; **dar efecto** ~ **a**

un pago to backdate a payment.

retroalimentación [retroalimenta'θjon] *nf* (*INFORM*) feedback.

retroceder [retroθe'ðer] *vi* (*echarse atrás*) to move back(wards); (*fig*) to back down; **no ~** to stand firm; **la policía hizo ~ a la multitud** the police forced the crowd back.

retroceso [retro'θeso] *nm* backward movement; (*MED*) relapse; (*COM*) recession, depression; (*fig*) backing down.

retrógrado, a [re'troɣraðo, a] *a* retrograde, retrogressive; (*POL*) reactionary.

retropropulsión [retropropul'sjon] *nf* jet propulsion.

retrospectivo, a [retrospek'tiβo, a] *a* retrospective; **mirada retrospectiva** backward glance.

retrovisor [retroβi'sor] *nm* rear-view mirror.

retuerce [re'twerθe] *etc*, **retuerza** [re'twerθa] *etc vb V* **retorcer**.

retumbante [retum'bante] *a* resounding.

retumbar [retum'bar] *vi* to echo, resound; (*continuamente*) to reverberate.

retuve [re'tuβe] *etc vb V* **retener**.

reuma ['reuma] *nm* rheumatism.

reumático, a [reu'matiko, a] *a* rheumatic.

reumatismo [reuma'tismo] *nm* rheumatism.

reunificar [reunifi'kar] *vt* to reunify.

reunifique [reuni'fike] *etc vb V* **reunificar**.

reunión [reu'njon] *nf* (*asamblea*) meeting; (*fiesta*) party; **~ en la cumbre** summit meeting; **~ de ventas** (*COM*) sales meeting.

reunir [reu'nir] *vt* (*juntar*) to reunite, join (together); (*recoger*) to gather (together); (*personas*) to bring o get together; (*cualidades*) to combine; **~se** *vr* (*personas: en asamblea*) to meet, gather; **reunió a sus amigos para discutirlo** he got his friends together to talk it over.

reválida [re'βaliða] *nf* (*ESCOL*) final examination.

revalidar [reβali'ðar] *vt* (*ratificar*) to confirm, ratify.

revalorar [reβalo'rar] *vt* to revalue, reassess.

revalor(iz)ación [reβalor(iθ)a'θjon] *nf* revaluation; (*ECON*) reassessment.

revancha [re'βantʃa] *nf* revenge; (*DEPORTE*) return match; (*BOXEO*) return fight.

revelación [reβela'θjon] *nf* revelation.

revelado [reβe'laðo] *nm* developing.

revelador, a [reβela'ðor, a] *a* revealing.

revelar [reβe'lar] *vt* to reveal; (*secreto*) to disclose; (*mostrar*) to show; (*FOTO*) to develop.

revendedor, a [reβende'ðor, a] *nm/f* retailer; (*pey*) ticket tout.

revendré [reβen'dre] *etc*, **revenga** [re'βenga] *etc vb V* **revenirse**.

revenirse [reβe'nirse] *vr* to shrink; (*comida*) to go bad o off; (*vino*) to sour; (*CULIN*) to get tough.

reventa [re'βenta] *nf* resale; (*especulación*) speculation; (*de entradas*) touting.

reventar [reβen'tar] *vt* to burst, explode; (*molestar*) to annoy, rile ◆ *vi*, **~se** *vr* (*estallar*) to burst, explode; **me revienta tener que ponérmelo** I hate having to wear it; **~ de** (*fig*) to be bursting with; **~ por** to be bursting to.

reventón [reβen'ton] *nm* (*AUTO*) blow-out (*Brit*), flat (*US*).

reverberación [reβerβera'θjon] *nf* reverberation.

reverberar [reβerβe'rar] *vi* (*luz*) to play, be reflected; (*superficie*) to shimmer; (*nieve*) to glare; (*sonido*) to reverberate.

reverbero [reβer'βero] *nm* play; shimmer, shine; glare; reverberation.

reverencia [reβe'renθja] *nf* reverence; (*inclinación*) bow.

reverenciar [reβeren'θjar] *vt* to revere.

reverendo, a [reβe'rendo, a] *a* reverend; (*fam*) big, awful; **un ~ imbécil** an awful idiot.

reverente [reβe'rente] *a* reverent.

reverso [re'βerso] *nm* back, other side; (*de moneda*) reverse.

revertir [reβer'tir] *vi* to revert; **~ en beneficio de** to be to the advantage of; **~ en perjuicio de** to be to the detriment of.

revés [re'βes] *nm* back, wrong side; (*fig*) reverse, setback; (*DEPORTE*) backhand; **al ~** the wrong way round; (*de arriba abajo*) upside down; (*ropa*) inside out; **y al ~** and vice versa; **volver algo al ~** to turn sth round; (*ropa*) to turn sth inside out; **los reveses de la fortuna** the blows of fate.

revestir [reβes'tir] *vt* (*poner*) to put on; (*cubrir*) to cover, coat; (*cualidad*) to have, possess; **~se** *vr* (*REL*) to put on one's vestments; (*ponerse*) to put on; **~ con** o **de** to arm o.s. with; **el acto revestía gran solemnidad** the ceremony had great dignity.

reviejo, a [re'βjexo, a] *a* very old, ancient.

reviene [re'βjene] *etc vb V* **revenirse**.

reviente [re'βjente] *etc vb V* **reventar**.

revierta [re'βjerta] *etc vb V* **revertir**.

reviniendo [reβi'njendo] *etc vb V* **revenirse**.

revirtiendo [reβir'tjendo] *etc vb V* **revertir**.

revisar [reβi'sar] *vt* (*examinar*) to check; (*texto etc*) to revise; (*JUR*) to review.

revisión [reβi'sjon] *nf* revision; **~ aduanera** customs inspection; **~ de cuentas** audit.

revisor, a [reβi'sor, a] *nm/f* inspector; (*FERRO*) ticket collector; **~ de cuentas**

auditor.

revista [re'ßista] *etc vb V* **revestir** ◆ *nf* magazine, review; (*sección*) section, page; (*TEATRO*) revue; (*inspección*) inspection; ~ **literaria** literary review; ~ **de libros** book reviews (page); **pasar** ~ **a** to review, inspect.

revivir [reßi'ßir] *vt* (*recordar*) to revive memories of ◆ *vi* to revive.

revocación [reßoka'θjon] *nf* repeal.

revocar [reßo'kar] *vt* (*decisión*) to revoke; (*ARQ*) to plaster.

revolcar [reßol'kar] *vt* to knock down, send flying; ~**se** *vr* to roll about.

revolcón [reßol'kon] *nm* tumble.

revolotear [reßolote'ar] *vi* to flutter.

revoloteo [reßolo'teo] *nm* fluttering.

revolqué [reßol'ke], **revolquemos** [reßol'kemos] *etc vb V* **revolcar**.

revoltijo [reßol'tixo] *nm* mess, jumble.

revoltoso, a [reßol'toso, a] *a* (*travieso*) naughty, unruly.

revolución [reßolu'θjon] *nf* revolution.

revolucionar [reßoluθjo'nar] *vt* to revolutionize.

revolucionario, a [reßoluθjo'narjo, a] *a*, *nm/f* revolutionary.

revolver [reßol'ßer] *vt* (*desordenar*) to disturb, mess up; (*agitar*) to shake; (*líquido*) to stir; (*mover*) to move about; (*POL*) to stir up ◆ *vi*: ~ **en** to go through, rummage (about) in; ~**se** *vr* (*en cama*) to toss and turn; (*METEOROLOGÍA*) to break, turn stormy; ~**se contra** to turn on *o* against; **han revuelto toda la casa** they've turned the whole house upside down.

revólver [re'ßolßer] *nm* revolver.

revoque [re'ßoke] *etc vb V* **revocar**.

revuelco [re'ßwelko] *etc vb V* **revolcar**.

revuelo [re'ßwelo] *nm* fluttering; (*fig*) commotion; **armar** *o* **levantar un gran** ~ to cause a great stir.

revuelque [re'ßwelke] *etc vb V* **revolcar**.

revuelto, a [re'ßwelto, a] *pp de* **revolver** ◆ *a* (*mezclado*) mixed-up, in disorder; (*mar*) rough; (*tiempo*) unsettled ◆ *nf* (*motín*) revolt; (*agitación*) commotion; **todo estaba** ~ everything was in disorder *o* was topsy-turvy.

revuelva [re'ßwelßa] *etc vb V* **revolver**.

rey [rei] *nm* king; **los R**~**es** the King and Queen.

reyerta [re'jerta] *nf* quarrel, brawl.

rezagado, a [reθa'γaðo, a] *a*: **quedar** ~ to be left behind; (*estar retrasado*) to be late, be behind ◆ *nm/f* straggler.

rezagar [reθa'γar] *vt* (*dejar atrás*) to leave behind; (*retrasar*) to delay, postpone; ~**se** *vr* (*atrasarse*) to fall behind.

rezague [re'θaxe] *etc vb V* **rezagar**.

rezar [re'θar] *vi* to pray; ~ **con** (*fam*) to concern, have to do with.

rezo ['reθo] *nm* prayer.

rezongar [reθon'gar] *vi* to grumble; (*murmurar*) to mutter; (*refunfuñar*) to growl.

rezongue [re'θonge] *etc vb V* **rezongar**.

rezumar [reθu'mar] *vt* to ooze ◆ *vi* to leak; ~**se** *vr* to leak out.

RFA *nf abr* = **República Federal Alemana**.

ría ['ria] *nf* estuary.

riada [ri'aða] *nf* flood.

ribera [ri'ßera] *nf* (*de río*) bank; (: *área*) riverside.

ribete [ri'ßete] *nm* (*de vestido*) border; (*fig*) addition.

ribetear [rißete'ar] *vt* to edge, border.

rice ['riθe] *etc vb V* **rizar**.

ricino [ri'θino] *nm*: **aceite de** ~ castor oil.

rico, a ['riko, a] *a* (*adinerado*) rich, wealthy; (*lujoso*) luxurious; (*comida*) delicious; (*niño*) lovely, cute ◆ *nm/f* rich person; **nuevo** ~ nouveau riche.

rictus ['riktus] *nm* (*mueca*) sneer, grin; ~ **de amargura** bitter smile.

ridiculez [riðiku'leθ] *nf* absurdity.

ridiculice [riðiku'liθe] *etc vb V* **ridiculizar**.

ridiculizar [riðikuli'θar] *vt* to ridicule.

ridículo, a [ri'ðikulo, a] *a* ridiculous; **hacer el** ~ to make a fool of o.s.; **poner a uno en** ~ to make a fool of sb; **ponerse en** ~ to make a fool *o* laughing-stock of o.s.

riego ['rjeγo] *etc vb V* **regar** ◆ *nm* (*aspersión*) watering; (*irrigación*) irrigation.

riegue ['rjeγe] *etc vb V* **regar**.

riel [rjel] *nm* rail.

rienda ['rjenda] *nf* rein; (*fig*) restraint, moderating influence; **dar** ~ **suelta a** to give free rein to; **llevar las** ~**s** to be in charge.

riendo ['rjendo] *vb V* **reír**.

riesgo ['rjesγo] *nm* risk; **seguro a** *o* **contra todo** ~ comprehensive insurance; ~ **para la salud** health hazard; **correr el** ~ **de** to run the risk of.

Rif [rif] *nm* Rif(f).

rifa ['rifa] *nf* (*lotería*) raffle.

rifar [ri'far] *vt* to raffle.

rifeño, a [ri'feɲo, a] *a* of the Rif(f), Rif(f)ian ◆ *nm/f* Rif(f)ian, Rif(f).

rifle ['rifle] *nm* rifle.

rigidez [rixi'ðeθ] *nf* rigidity, stiffness; (*fig*) strictness.

rígido, a ['rixiðo, a] *a* rigid, stiff; (*moralmente*) strict, inflexible; (*cara*) wooden, expressionless.

rigiendo [ri'xjendo] *etc vb V* **regir**.

rigor [ri'γor] *nm* strictness, rigour; (*dureza*) toughness; (*inclemencia*) harshness; (*meticulosidad*) accuracy; **el** ~ **del verano** the hottest part of the summer; **con todo** ~ **científico** with scientific precision; **de** ~ de rigueur, essential; **después de los saludos**

de ~ after the inevitable greetings.

riguroso, a [riɣu'roso, a] *a* rigorous; (*METEOROLOGÍA*) harsh; (*severo*) severe.

rija ['rixa] *etc vb V* **regir** ♦ *nf* quarrel.

rima ['rima] *nf* rhyme; ~**s** *nfpl* verse *sg*; ~ **imperfecta** assonance; ~ **rimando** (*fam*) merrily.

rimar [ri'mar] *vi* to rhyme.

rimbombante [rimbom'bante] *a* (*fig*) pompous.

rímel, rímmel ['rimel] *nm* mascara.

rimero [ri'mero] *nm* stack, pile.

Rin [rin] *nm* Rhine.

rincón [rin'kon] *nm* corner (*inside*).

rindiendo [rin'djendo] *etc vb V* **rendir**.

rinoceronte [rinoθe'ronte] *nm* rhinoceros.

riña ['riɲa] *nf* (*disputa*) argument; (*pelea*) brawl.

riñendo [ri'ɲendo] *etc vb V* **reñir**.

riñón [ri'ɲon] *nm* kidney; **me costó un** ~ (*fam*) it cost me an arm and a leg; **tener riñones** to have guts.

rió [ri'o] *vb V* **reír**.

río ['rio] *etc vb V* **reír** ♦ *nm* river; (*fig*) torrent, stream; ~ **abajo/arriba** downstream/upstream; **cuando el** ~ **suena, agua lleva** there's no smoke without fire.

Río de Janeiro ['rioðexa'neiro] *nm* Rio de Janeiro.

Río de la Plata ['rioðela'plata] *nm* Rio de la Plata, River Plate.

Rioja [ri'oxa] *nf*: **La** ~ La Rioja ♦ *nm*: **r~** rioja wine.

riojano, a [rjo'xano, a] *a, nm/f* Riojan.

rioplatense [riopla'tense] *a* of *o* from the River Plate region ♦ *nm/f* native *o* inhabitant of the River Plate region.

riqueza [ri'keθa] *nf* wealth, riches *pl*; (*cualidad*) richness.

risa ['risa] *nf* laughter; (*una* ~) laugh; **¡qué** ~**!** what a laugh!; **caerse** *o* **morirse de** ~ to split one's sides laughing, die laughing; **tomar algo a** ~ to laugh sth off.

risco ['risko] *nm* crag, cliff.

risible [ri'siβle] *a* ludicrous, laughable.

risotada [riso'taða] *nf* guffaw, loud laugh.

ristra ['ristra] *nf* string.

ristre ['ristre] *nm*: **en** ~ at the ready.

risueño, a [ri'sweɲo, a] *a* (*sonriente*) smiling; (*contento*) cheerful.

ritmo ['ritmo] *nm* rhythm; **a** ~ **lento** slowly; **trabajar a** ~ **lento** to go slow.

rito ['rito] *nm* rite.

ritual [ri'twal] *a, nm* ritual.

rival [ri'βal] *a, nm/f* rival.

rivalice [riβa'liθe] *etc vb V* **rivalizar**.

rivalidad [riβali'ðað] *nf* rivalry, competition.

rivalizar [riβali'θar] *vi*: ~ **con** to rival, compete with.

rizado, a [ri'θaðo, a] *a* (*pelo*) curly; (*superficie*) ridged; (*terreno*) undulating; (*mar*)

choppy ♦ *nm* curls *pl*.

rizar [ri'θar] *vt* to curl; ~**se** *vr* (*el pelo*) to curl; (*agua*) to ripple; (*el mar*) to become choppy.

rizo ['riθo] *nm* curl; (*agua*) ripple.

Rma. *abr* (= *Reverendísima*) courtesy title.

Rmo. *abr* (= *Reverendísimo*) Rt. Rev.

RNE *nf abr* = *Radio Nacional de España*.

R. O. *abr* (=*Real Orden*) royal order.

robar [ro'βar] *vt* to rob; (*objeto*) to steal; (*casa etc*) to break into; (*NAIPES*) to draw; (*atención*) to steal, capture; (*paciencia*) to exhaust.

roble ['roβle] *nm* oak.

robledal [roβle'ðal], **robledo** [ro'βleðo] *nm* oakwood.

robo ['roβo] *nm* robbery, theft; (*objeto robado*) stolen article *o* goods *pl*; **¡esto es un** ~**!** this is daylight robbery!

robot [ro'βo(t)], *pl* **robots** *a*, *nm* robot.

robótica [ro'βotika] *nf* robotics *sg*.

robustecer [roβuste'θer] *vt* to strengthen.

robustezca [roβus'teθka] *etc vb V* **robustecer**.

robusto, a [ro'βusto, a] *a* robust, strong.

ROC *abr* (*INFORM*: = *reconocimiento óptico de caracteres*) OCR.

roca ['roka] *nf* rock; **la R~** the Rock (of Gibraltar).

roce ['roθe] *etc vb V* **rozar** ♦ *nm* rub, rubbing; (*caricia*) brush; (*TEC*) friction; (*en la piel*) graze; **tener** ~ **con** to have a brush with.

rociar [ro'θjar] *vt* to sprinkle, spray.

rocín [ro'θin] *nm* nag, hack.

rocío [ro'θio] *nm* dew.

rocoso, a [ro'koso, a] *a* rocky.

rodado, a [ro'ðaðo, a] *a* (*con ruedas*) wheeled ♦ *nf* rut.

rodaja [ro'ðaxa] *nf* (*raja*) slice.

rodaje [ro'ðaxe] *nm* (*CINE*) shooting, filming; (*AUTO*): **en** ~ running in.

Ródano ['roðano] *nm* Rhône.

rodar [ro'ðar] *vt* (*vehículo*) to wheel (along); (*escalera*) to roll down; (*viajar por*) to travel (over) ♦ *vi* to roll; (*coche*) to go, run; (*CINE*) to shoot, film; (*persona*) to move about (from place to place), drift; **echarlo todo a** ~ (*fig*) to mess it all up.

Rodas ['roðas] *nf* Rhodes.

rodear [roðe'ar] *vt* to surround ♦ *vi* to go round; ~**se** *vr*: ~**se de amigos** to surround o.s. with friends.

rodeo [ro'ðeo] *nm* (*ruta indirecta*) long way round, roundabout way; (*desvío*) detour; (*evasión*) evasion; (*AM*) rodeo; **dejarse de** ~**s** to talk straight; **hablar sin** ~**s** to come to the point, speak plainly.

rodilla [ro'ðiʎa] *nf* knee; **de** ~**s** kneeling.

rodillo [ro'ðiʎo] *nm* roller; (*CULIN*) rolling-pin; (*en máquina de escribir, impresora*)

platen.
rododendro [roðo'ðendro] *nm* rhododendron.
roedor, a [roe'ðor, a] *a* gnawing ♦ *nm* rodent.
roer [ro'er] *vt* (*masticar*) to gnaw; (*corroer*,
fig) to corrode.
rogar [ro'ɣar] *vt* (*pedir*) to beg, ask for ♦ *vi*
(*suplicar*) to beg, plead; ~**se** *vr*: **se ruega
no fumar** please do not smoke; ~ **que** +
subjun to ask to ...; **ruegue a este señor
que nos deje en paz** please ask this gentleman to leave us alone; **no se hace de** ~ he
doesn't have to be asked twice.
rogué [ro'ɣe], **roguemos** [ro'ɣemos] *etc vb*
V **rogar**.
rojizo, a [ro'xiθo, a] *a* reddish.
rojo, a ['roxo, a] *a* red ♦ *nm* red (colour);
(*POL*) red; **ponerse** ~ to turn red, blush; **al**
~ **vivo** red-hot.
rol [rol] *nm* list, roll; (*AM: papel*) role.
rollizo, a [ro'ʎiθo, a] *a* (*objeto*) cylindrical;
(*persona*) plump.
rollo, a ['roʎo, a] *a* (*fam*) boring, tedious ♦
nm roll; (*de cuerda*) coil; (*madera*) log;
(*fam*) bore; (*discurso*) boring speech; **¡qué**
~**!** what a carry-on!; **la conferencia fue un**
~ the lecture was a big drag.
ROM [rom] *nf abr* (= *memoria de sólo
lectura*) ROM.
Roma ['roma] *nf* Rome; **por todas partes
se va a** ~ all roads lead to Rome.
romance [ro'manθe] *nm* (*LING*) Romance
language; (*LIT*) ballad; **hablar en** ~ to
speak plainly.
romano, a [ro'mano, a] *a* Roman, of Rome
♦ *nm/f* Roman.
romanticismo [romanti'θismo] *nm* romanticism.
romántico, a [ro'mantiko, a] *a* romantic.
romería [rome'ria] *nf* (*REL*) pilgrimage;
(*excursión*) trip, outing.
romero, a [ro'mero, a] *nm/f* pilgrim ♦ *nm*
rosemary.
romo, a ['romo, a] *a* blunt; (*fig*) dull.
rompecabezas [rompeka'βeθas] *nm inv*
riddle, puzzle; (*juego*) jigsaw (puzzle).
rompehuelgas [rompe'welɣas] *nm inv*
strikebreaker, blackleg (*Brit*).
rompeolas [rompe'olas] *nm inv* breakwater.
romper [rom'per] *vt* to break; (*hacer pedazos*) to smash; (*papel, tela etc*) to tear,
rip; (*relaciones*) to break off ♦ *vi* (*olas*) to
break; (*sol, diente*) to break through; ~ **un
contrato** to break a contract; ~ **a** to start
(suddenly) to; ~ **a llorar** to burst into
tears; ~ **con uno** to fall out with sb; **ha
roto con su novio** she has broken up with
her fiancé.
rompimiento [rompi'mjento] *nm* (*acto*)

breaking; (*fig*) break; (*quiebra*) crack; ~
de relaciones breaking off of relations.
ron [ron] *nm* rum.
roncar [ron'kar] *vi* (*al dormir*) to snore;
(*animal*) to roar.
ronco, a ['ronko, a] *a* (*afónico*) hoarse;
(*áspero*) raucous.
ronda ['ronda] *nf* (*de bebidas etc*) round;
(*patrulla*) patrol; (*de naipes*) hand, game;
ir de ~ to do one's round.
rondar [ron'dar] *vt* to patrol; (*a una persona*) to hang round; (*molestar*) to harass;
(*a una chica*) to court ♦ *vi* to patrol; (*fig*)
to prowl round; (*MUS*) to go serenading.
rondeño, a [ron'deɲo, a] *a* of *o* from
Ronda ♦ *nm/f* native *o* inhabitant of Ronda.
ronque ['ronke] *etc vb* V **roncar**.
ronquera [ron'kera] *nf* hoarseness.
ronquido [ron'kiðo] *nm* snore, snoring.
ronronear [ronrone'ar] *vi* to purr.
ronroneo [ronro'neo] *nm* purr.
roña ['roɲa] *nf* (*veterinaria*) mange;
(*mugre*) dirt, grime; (*óxido*) rust.
roñoso, a [ro'ɲoso, a] *a* (*mugriento*) filthy;
(*tacaño*) mean.
ropa ['ropa] *nf* clothes *pl*, clothing; ~ **blanca**
linen; ~ **de cama** bed linen; ~ **interior**
underwear; ~ **lavada** *o* **para lavar** washing; ~ **planchada** ironing; ~ **sucia** dirty
clothes *pl*, washing; ~ **usada** secondhand
clothes.
ropaje [ro'paxe] *nm* gown, robes *pl*.
ropavejero, a [ropaβe'xero, a] *nm/f*
second-hand clothes dealer.
ropero [ro'pero] *nm* linen cupboard;
(*guardarropa*) wardrobe.
roque ['roke] *nm* (*AJEDREZ*) rook, castle;
estar ~ to be fast asleep.
rosa ['rosa] *a inv* pink ♦ *nf* rose; (*ANAT*) red
birthmark; ~ **de los vientos** the compass;
estar como una ~ to feel as fresh as a daisy; (*color*) **de** ~ pink.
rosado, a [ro'saðo, a] *a* pink ♦ *nm* rosé.
rosal [ro'sal] *nm* rosebush.
rosaleda [rosa'leða] *nf* rose bed *o* garden.
rosario [ro'sarjo] *nm* (*REL*) rosary; (*fig:
serie*) string; **rezar el** ~ to say the rosary.
rosbif [ros'βif] *nm* roast beef.
rosca ['roska] *nf* (*de tornillo*) thread; (*de
humo*) coil, spiral; (*pan, postre*) ring-
shaped roll/pastry; **hacer la** ~ **a uno** (*fam*)
to suck up to sb; **pasarse de** ~ (*fig*) to go
too far.
Rosellón [rose'ʎon] *nm* Roussillon.
rosetón [rose'ton] *nm* rosette; (*ARQ*) rose
window.
rosquilla [ros'kiʎa] *nf* small ring-shaped
cake; (*de humo*) ring.
rostro ['rostro] *nm* (*cara*) face; (*fig*) cheek.
rotación [rota'θjon] *nf* rotation; ~ **de
cultivos** crop rotation.

rotativo, a [rota'tiβo, a] *a* rotary ♦ *nm* newspaper.

roto, a ['roto, a] *pp de* **romper** ♦ *a* broken; *(en pedazos)* smashed; *(tela, papel)* torn; *(vida)* shattered ♦ *nm (en vestido)* hole, tear.

rótula ['rotula] *nf* kneecap; *(TEC)* ball-and-socket joint.

rotulador [rotula'ðor] *nm* felt-tip pen.

rotular [rotu'lar] *vt (carta, documento)* to head, entitle; *(objeto)* to label.

rótulo ['rotulo] *nm (título)* heading, title; *(etiqueta)* label; *(letrero)* sign.

rotundo, a [ro'tundo, a] *a* round; *(enfático)* emphatic.

rotura [ro'tura] *nf (rompimiento)* breaking; *(MED)* fracture.

roturar [rotu'rar] *vt* to plough.

rozado, a [ro'θaðo, a] *a* worn.

rozadura [roθa'ðura] *nf* abrasion, graze.

rozar [ro'θar] *vt (frotar)* to rub; *(ensuciar)* to dirty; *(MED)* to graze; *(tocar ligeramente)* to shave, skim; *(fig)* to touch *o* border on; **~se** *vr* to rub (together); **~ con** *(fam)* to rub shoulders with.

Rte. *abr* = **remite, remitente.**

RTVE *nf abr (TV)* = *Radiotelevisión Española.*

Ruán [ru'an] *nm* Rouen.

rubéola [ru'βeola] *nf* German measles, rubella.

rubí [ru'βi] *nm* ruby; *(de reloj)* jewel.

rubio, a ['ruβjo, a] *a* fair-haired, blond(e) ♦ *nm/f* blond/blonde; **tabaco ~** Virginia tobacco; **(cerveza) rubia** lager.

rubor [ru'βor] *nm (sonrojo)* blush; *(timidez)* bashfulness.

ruborice [ruβo'riθe] *etc vb V* **ruborizarse.**

ruborizarse [ruβori'θarse] *vr* to blush.

ruboroso, a [ruβo'roso, a] *a* blushing.

rúbrica ['ruβrika] *nf (título)* title, heading; *(de la firma)* flourish; **bajo la ~ de** under the heading of.

rubricar [ruβri'kar] *vt (firmar)* to sign with a flourish; *(concluir)* to sign and seal.

rubrique [ru'βrike] *etc vb V* **rubricar.**

rudeza [ru'ðeθa] *nf (tosquedad)* coarseness; *(sencillez)* simplicity.

rudimentario, a [ruðimen'tarjo, a] *a* rudimentary, basic.

rudo, a ['ruðo, a] *a (sin pulir)* unpolished; *(grosero)* coarse; *(violento)* violent; *(sencillo)* simple.

rueda ['rweða] *nf* wheel; *(círculo)* ring, circle; *(rodaja)* slice, round; *(en impresora etc)* sprocket; **~ delantera/trasera/de repuesto** front/back/spare wheel; **~ impresora** *(INFORM)* print wheel; **~ de prensa** press conference.

ruedo ['rweðo] *etc vb V* **rodar** ♦ *nm (contorno)* edge, border; *(de vestido)* hem;

(círculo) circle; *(TAUR)* arena, bullring; *(esterilla)* (round) mat.

ruego ['rweɣo] *etc vb V* **rogar** ♦ *nm* request; **a ~ de** at the request of; **"~s y preguntas"** "question and answer session".

ruegue ['rweɣe] *etc vb V* **rogar.**

rufián [ru'fjan] *nm* scoundrel.

rugby ['ruɣβi] *nm* rugby.

rugido [ru'xiðo] *nm* roar.

rugir [ru'xir] *vi* to roar; *(toro)* to bellow; *(estómago)* to rumble.

rugoso, a [ru'ɣoso, a] *a (arrugado)* wrinkled; *(áspero)* rough; *(desigual)* ridged.

ruibarbo [rwi'βarβo] *nm* rhubarb.

ruido ['rwiðo] *nm (sonido)* noise; *(sonido)* sound; *(alboroto)* racket, row; *(escándalo)* commotion, rumpus; **~ de fondo** background noise; **hacer** *o* **meter ~** to cause a stir.

ruidoso, a [rwi'ðoso, a] *a* noisy, loud; *(fig)* sensational.

ruin [rwin] *a* contemptible, mean.

ruina ['rwina] *nf* ruin; *(colapso)* collapse; *(de persona)* ruin, downfall; **estar hecho una ~** to be a wreck; **la empresa le llevó a la ~** the venture ruined him (financially).

ruindad [rwin'dað] *nf* lowness, meanness; *(acto)* low *o* mean act.

ruinoso, a [rwi'noso, a] *a* ruinous; *(destartalado)* dilapidated, tumbledown; *(COM)* disastrous.

ruiseñor [rwise'ɲor] *nm* nightingale.

ruja ['ruxa] *etc vb V* **rugir.**

rula ['rula], **ruleta** [ru'leta] *nf* roulette.

rulo ['rulo] *nm (para el pelo)* curler.

rulota [ru'lota] *nf* caravan *(Brit)*, trailer *(US)*.

Rumania [ru'manja] *nf* Rumania.

rumano, a [ru'mano, a] *a, nm/f* Rumanian.

rumba ['rumba] *nf* rumba.

rumbo ['rumbo] *nm (ruta)* route, direction; *(ángulo de dirección)* course, bearing; *(fig)* course of events; **con ~ a** in the direction of; **ir con ~ a** to be heading for; *(NAUT)* to be bound for.

rumboso, a [rum'boso, a] *a (generoso)* generous.

rumiante [ru'mjante] *nm* ruminant.

rumiar [ru'mjar] *vt* to chew; *(fig)* to chew over ♦ *vi* to chew the cud.

rumor [ru'mor] *nm (ruido sordo)* low sound; *(murmuración)* murmur, buzz.

rumorearse [rumore'arse] *vr:* **se rumorea que** it is rumoured that.

rumoroso, a [rumo'roso, a] *a* full of sounds; *(arroyo)* murmuring.

runrún [run'run] *nm (voces)* murmur, sound of voices; *(fig)* rumour; *(de una máquina)* whirr.

rupestre [ru'pestre] *a* rock *cpd*; **pintura ~**

cave painting.

ruptura [rup'tura] *nf* (*gen*) rupture; (*disputa*) split; (*de contrato*) breach; (*de relaciones*) breaking-off.

rural [ru'ral] *a* rural.

Rusia ['rusja] *nf* Russia.

ruso, a ['ruso, a] *a*, *nm/f* Russian ♦ *nm* (*LING*) Russian.

rústico, a ['rustiko, a] *a* rustic; (*ordinario*) coarse, uncouth ♦ *nm/f* yokel ♦ *nf*: **libro en rústica** paperback (book).

ruta ['ruta] *nf* route.

rutina [ru'tina] *nf* routine; ~ **diaria** daily routine; **por** ~ as a matter of course.

rutinario, a [ruti'narjo, a] *a* routine.

S

S, s ['ese] *nf* S, s; **S de Sábado** S for Sugar.

S *abr* (= *san, santo, a*) St.; (= *sur*) S.

s. *abr* (= *siglo*) c.; (= *siguiente*) foll.

s/ *abr* (*COM*) = **su(s)**.

S.ª *abr* (= *Sierra*) Mts.

S.A. *abr* (= *Sociedad Anónima*) Ltd., Inc. (*US*); (= *Su Alteza*) H.H.

sáb. *abr* (= *sábado*) Sun.

sábado ['saβaðo] *nm* Saturday; (*de los judíos*) Sabbath; **del** ~ **en ocho días** a week on Saturday; **un** ~ **sí y otro no, cada dos** ~**s** every other Saturday.

sabana [sa'βana] *nf* savannah.

sábana ['saβana] *nf* sheet; **se le pegan las** ~**s** he can't get up in the morning.

sabandija [saβan'dixa] *nf* (*bicho*) bug; (*fig*) louse.

sabañón [saβa'ɲon] *nm* chilblain.

sabático, a [sa'βatiko, a] *a* (*REL, UNIV*) sabbatical.

sabelotodo [saβelo'toðo] *nm/f inv* know-all.

saber [sa'βer] *vt* to know; (*llegar a conocer*) to find out, learn; (*tener capacidad de*) to know how to ♦ *vi*: ~ **a** to taste of, taste like ♦ *nm* knowledge, learning; ~**se** *vr*: **se sabe que ...** it is known that ...; **no se sabe** nobody knows; **a** ~ namely; **¿sabes conducir/nadar?** can you drive/swim?; **¿sabes francés?** do you *o* can you speak French?; ~ **de memoria** to know by heart; **lo sé** I know; **hacer** ~ to inform, let know; **que yo sepa** as far as I know; **vete** *o* **anda a** ~ your guess is as good as mine; **¿sabe?** (*fam*) you know (what I mean)?; **le sabe mal que otro la saque a bailar** it upsets him that anybody else should ask her to dance.

sabido, a [sa'βiðo, a] *a* (*consabido*) well-known; **como es** ~ as we all know.

sabiduría [saβiðu'ria] *nf* (*conocimientos*) wisdom; (*instrucción*) learning; ~ **popular** folklore.

sabiendas [sa'βjendas]: **a** ~ *ad* knowingly; **a** ~ **de que ...** knowing full well that ....

sabihondo, a [sa'βjondo, a] *a*, *nm/f* know-all, know-it-all (*US*).

sabio, a ['saβjo, a] *a* (*docto*) learned; (*prudente*) wise, sensible.

sablazo [sa'βlaθo] *nm* (*herida*) sword wound; (*fam*) sponging; **dar un** ~ **a uno** to tap sb for money.

sabor [sa'βor] *nm* taste, flavour; (*fig*) flavour; **sin** ~ flavourless.

saborear [saβore'ar] *vt* to taste, savour; (*fig*) to relish.

sabotaje [saβo'taxe] *nm* sabotage.

saboteador, a [saβotea'ðor, a] *nm/f* saboteur.

sabotear [saβote'ar] *vt* to sabotage.

Saboya [sa'βoja] *nf* Savoy.

sabré [sa'βre] *etc vb* V **saber**.

sabroso, a [sa'βroso, a] *a* tasty; (*fig fam*) racy, salty.

saca ['saka] *nf* big sack; ~ **de correo(s)** mailbag; (*COM*) withdrawal.

sacacorchos [saka'kortʃos] *nm inv* corkscrew.

sacapuntas [saka'puntas] *nm inv* pencil sharpener.

sacar [sa'kar] *vt* to take out; (*fig: extraer*) to get (out); (*quitar*) to remove, get out; (*hacer salir*) to bring out; (*fondos: de cuenta*) to draw out, withdraw; (*obtener: legado etc*) to get; (*demostrar*) to show; (*conclusión*) to draw; (*novela etc*) to publish, bring out; (*ropa*) to take off; (*obra*) to make; (*premio*) to receive; (*entradas*) to get; (*TENIS*) to serve; (*FÚTBOL*) to put into play; ~ **adelante** (*niño*) to bring up; ~ **a uno a bailar** to dance with sb; ~ **a uno de sí** to infuriate sb; ~ **una foto** to take a photo; ~ **la lengua** to stick out one's tongue; ~ **buenas/malas notas** to get good/bad marks.

sacarina [saka'rina] *nf* saccharin(e).

sacerdote [saθer'ðote] *nm* priest.

saciar [sa'θjar] *vt* (*hartar*) to satiate; (*fig*) to satisfy; ~**se** *vr* (*fig*) to be satisfied.

saciedad [saθje'ðað] *nf* satiety; **hasta la** ~ (*comer*) one's fill; (*repetir*) ad nauseam.

saco ['sako] *nm* bag; (*grande*) sack; (*su contenido*) bagful; (*AM: chaqueta*) jacket; ~ **de dormir** sleeping bag.

sacramento [sakra'mento] *nm* sacrament.

sacrificar [sakrifi'kar] *vt* to sacrifice; (*animal*) to slaughter; (*perro etc*) to put to sleep; ~**se** *vr* to sacrifice o.s.

sacrificio [sakri'fiθjo] *nm* sacrifice.

sacrifique [sakri'fike] *etc vb V* **sacrificar**.
sacrilegio [sakri'lexjo] *nm* sacrilege.
sacrílego, a [sa'krileɣo, a] *a* sacrilegious.
sacristán [sakris'tan] *nm* verger.
sacristía [sakris'tia] *nf* sacristy.
sacro, a ['sakro, a] *a* sacred.
sacudida [saku'ðiða] *nf* (*agitación*) shake, shaking; (*sacudimiento*) jolt, bump; (*fig*) violent change; (*POL etc*) upheaval; ~ **eléctrica** electric shock.
sacudir [saku'ðir] *vt* to shake; (*golpear*) to hit; (*ala*) to flap; (*alfombra*) to beat; ~ **a uno** (*fam*) to belt sb.
sádico, a ['saðiko, a] *a* sadistic ♦ *nm/f* sadist.
sadismo [sa'ðismo] *nm* sadism.
saeta [sa'eta] *nf* (*flecha*) arrow; (*MUS*) sacred song in flamenco style.
sagacidad [saɣaθi'ðað] *nf* shrewdness, cleverness.
sagaz [sa'ɣaθ] *a* shrewd, clever.
sagitario [saxi'tarjo] *nm* (*ASTRO*) Sagittarius.
sagrado, a [sa'ɣraðo, a] *a* sacred, holy.
Sáhara ['saara] *nm*: **el** ~ the Sahara (desert).
saharaui [saxa'rawi] *a* Saharan ♦ *nm/f* native *o* inhabitant of the Sahara.
sajón, ona [sa'xon, 'xona] *a, nm/f* Saxon.
Sajonia [sa'xonja] *nf* Saxony.
sal [sal] *vb ver* **salir** ♦ *nf* salt; (*gracia*) wit; (*encanto*) charm; ~**es de baño** bath salts; ~ **gorda** *o* **de cocina** kitchen *o* cooking salt.
sala ['sala] *nf* (*cuarto grande*) large room; (~ **de estar**) living room; (*TEATRO*) house, auditorium; (*de hospital*) ward; ~ **de apelación** court; ~ **de conferencias** lecture hall; ~ **de espera** waiting room; ~ **de embarque** departure lounge; ~ **de estar** living room; ~ **de fiestas** function room; ~ **de juntas** (*COM*) boardroom.
salado, a [sa'laðo, a] *a* salty; (*fig*) witty, amusing; **agua salada** salt water.
salar [sa'lar] *vt* to salt, add salt to.
salarial [sala'rjal] *a* (*aumento*, *revisión*) wage *cpd*, salary *cpd*, pay *cpd*.
salario [sa'larjo] *nm* wage, pay.
salchicha [sal'tʃitʃa] *nf* (pork) sausage.
salchichón [saltʃi'tʃon] *nm* (salami-type) sausage.
saldar [sal'dar] *vt* to pay; (*vender*) to sell off; (*fig*) to settle, resolve.
saldo ['saldo] *nm* (*pago*) settlement; (*de una cuenta*) balance; (*lo restante*) remnant(s) (*pl*), remainder; (*liquidación*) sale; (*COM*): ~ **anterior** balance brought forward; ~ **acreedor/deudor** *o* **pasivo** credit/debit balance; ~ **final** final balance.
saldré [sal'dre] *etc vb V* **salir**.
salero [sa'lero] *nm* salt cellar; (*ingenio*)

wit; (*encanto*) charm.
salga ['salɣa] *etc vb V* **salir**.
salida [sa'liða] *nf* (*puerta etc*) exit, way out; (*acto*) leaving, going out; (*de tren*, *AVIAT*) departure; (*COM*, *TEC*) output, production; (*fig*) way out; (*resultado*) outcome; (*COM*: *oportunidad*) opening; (*GEO*, *válvula*) outlet; (*de gas*) escape; (*ocurrencia*) joke; **calle sin** ~ cul-de-sac; **a la** ~ **del teatro** after the theatre; **dar la** ~ (*DEPORTE*) to give the starting signal; ~ **de incendios** fire escape; ~ **impresa** (*INFORM*) hard copy; **no hay** ~ there's no way out of it; **no tenemos otra** ~ we have no option; **tener** ~**s** to be witty.
saliente [sa'ljente] *a* (*ARQ*) projecting; (*sol*) rising; (*fig*) outstanding.
salina [sa'lina] *nf* salt mine; ~**s** *nfpl* saltworks *sg*.
salir [sa'lir] *vi* to come/go out; (*resultar*) to turn out; (*partir*) to leave, depart; (*aparecer*) to appear; (*sobresalir*) to project, jut out; (*mancha*) to come out *o* off; (*disco*) to be released; (*número de lotería*, *planta*) to come up; (*pelo*) to grow; (*diente*) to come through; (*INFORM*) to quit, exit; ~**se** *vr* (*vasija*) to leak; (*animal*) to escape, get out; ~ **con** to go out with; ~ **a la superficie** to come to the surface; ~ **bien/mal** to turn out well/badly; ~ **caro/barato** to work out expensive/cheap; ~ **ganando** to come out on top; ~ **perdiendo** to lose out; **sale a su padre** he takes after his father; ~**se de la carretera** to leave the road; ~**se de la vía** to jump the rails; ~**se con la suya** to get one's own way.
saliva [sa'liβa] *nf* saliva.
salmantino, a [salman'tino, a] *a* of *o* from Salamanca ♦ *nm/f* native *o* inhabitant of Salamanca.
salmo ['salmo] *nm* psalm.
salmón [sal'mon] *nm* salmon.
salmonete [salmo'nete] *nm* red mullet.
salmuera [sal'mwera] *nf* pickle, brine.
salón [sa'lon] *nm* (*de casa*) living-room, lounge; (*muebles*) lounge suite; ~ **de belleza** beauty parlour; ~ **de baile** dance hall; ~ **de sesiones** assembly hall.
salpicadero [salpika'ðero] *nm* (*AUTO*) dashboard.
salpicar [salpi'kar] *vt* (*de barro*, *pintura*) to splash; (*rociar*) to sprinkle, spatter; (*esparcir*) to scatter.
salpicón [salpi'kon] *nm* (*acto*) splashing; (*CULIN*) meat *o* fish salad.
salpimentar [salpimen'tar] *vt* (*CULIN*) to season.
salpique [sal'pike] *etc vb V* **salpicar**.
salsa ['salsa] *nf* sauce; (*con carne asada*) gravy; (*fig*) spice; ~ **mayonesa** mayonnaise; **estar en su** ~ (*fam*) to be in

one's element.

saltado, a [sal'taðo, a] *a* (*desprendido*) missing; (*ojos*) bulging.

saltamontes [salta'montes] *nm inv* grasshopper.

saltar [sal'tar] *vt* to jump (over), leap (over); (*dejar de lado*) to skip, miss out ♦ *vi* to jump, leap; (*pelota*) to bounce; (*al aire*) to fly up; (*quebrarse*) to break; (*al agua*) to dive; (*fig*) to explode, blow up; (*botón*) to come off; (*corcho*) to pop out; ~**se** *vr* (*omitir*) to skip, miss; **salta a la vista** it's obvious; ~**se todas las reglas** to break all the rules.

salteado, a [salte'aðo, a] *a* (*CULIN*) sauté(ed).

salteador [saltea'ðor] *nm* (*tb*: ~ **de caminos**) highwayman.

saltear [salte'ar] *vt* (*robar*) to rob (in a holdup); (*asaltar*) to assault, attack; (*CULIN*) to sauté.

saltimbanqui [saltim'banki] *nm/f* acrobat.

salto ['salto] *nm* jump, leap; (*al agua*) dive; **a** ~**s** by jumping; ~ **de agua** waterfall; ~ **de altura** high jump; ~ **de cama** negligee; ~ **mortal** somersault; (*INFORM*): ~ **de línea** line feed; ~ **de línea automático** wordwrap; ~ **de página** formfeed.

saltón, ona [sal'ton, ona] *a* (*ojos*) bulging, popping; (*dientes*) protruding.

salubre [sa'luβre] *a* healthy, salubrious.

salud [sa'luð] *nf* health; **estar bien/mal de** ~ to be in good/poor health; **¡(a su)** ~**!** cheers!, good health!; **beber a la** ~ **de** to drink (to) the health of.

saludable [salu'ðaβle] *a* (*de buena salud*) healthy; (*provechoso*) good, beneficial.

saludar [salu'ðar] *vt* to greet; (*MIL*) to salute; **ir a** ~ **a uno** to drop in to see sb; **salude de mi parte a X** give my regards to X; **le saluda atentamente** (*en carta*) yours faithfully.

saludo [sa'luðo] *nm* greeting; ~**s** (*en carta*) best wishes, regards; **un** ~ **afectuoso** *o* **cordial** yours sincerely.

salva ['salβa] *nf* (*MIL*) salvo; **una** ~ **de aplausos** thunderous applause.

salvación [salβa'θjon] *nf* salvation; (*rescate*) rescue.

salvado [sal'βaðo] *nm* bran.

salvador [salβa'ðor] *nm* rescuer, saviour; **el S~** the Saviour; **El S~** El Salvador; **San S~** San Salvador.

salvadoreño, a [salβaðo'reɲo, a] *a, nm/f* Salvdoran, Salvadorian.

salvaguardar [salβaɣwar'ðar] *vt* to safeguard; (*INFORM*) to back up, make a backup copy of.

salvajada [salβa'xaða] *nf* savage deed, atrocity.

salvaje [sal'βaxe] *a* wild; (*tribu*) savage.

salvajismo [salβa'xismo] *nm* savagery.

salvamento [salβa'mento] *nm* (*acción*) rescue; (*de naufragio*) salvage; ~ **y socorrismo** life-saving.

salvar [sal'βar] *vt* (*rescatar*) to save, rescue; (*resolver*) to overcome, resolve; (*cubrir distancias*) to cover, travel; (*hacer excepción*) to except, exclude; (*un barco*) to salvage; ~**se** *vr* to save o.s., escape; **¡sálvese el que pueda!** every man for himself!

salvavidas [salβa'βiðas] *a inv*: **bote/ chaleco/cinturón** ~ lifeboat/lifejacket/lifebelt.

salvedad [salβe'ðað] *nf* reservation, qualification; **con la** ~ **de que** ... with the proviso that ....

salvia ['salβja] *nf* sage.

salvo, a ['salβo, a] *a* safe ♦ *prep* except (for), save; ~ **error u omisión** (*COM*) errors and omissions excepted; **a** ~ out of danger; ~ **que** unless.

salvoconducto [salβokon'dukto] *nm* safeconduct.

san [san] *nm* (*apócope de santo*) saint; ~ **Juan** St. John.

sanar [sa'nar] *vt* (*herida*) to heal; (*persona*) to cure ♦ *vi* (*persona*) to get well, recover; (*herida*) to heal.

sanatorio [sana'torjo] *nm* sanatorium.

sanción [san'θjon] *nf* sanction.

sancionar [sanθjo'nar] *vt* to sanction.

sandalia [san'dalja] *nf* sandal.

sándalo ['sandalo] *nm* sandal (wood).

sandez [san'deθ] *nf* (*cualidad*) foolishness; (*acción*) stupid thing; **decir sandeces** to talk nonsense.

sandía [san'dia] *nf* watermelon.

sandwich ['sandwitʃ], *pl* **sandwichs** *o* **sandwiches** *nm* sandwich.

saneamiento [sanea'mjento] *nm* sanitation.

sanear [sane'ar] *vt* to drain; (*indemnizar*) to compensate; (*ECON*) to reorganize.

sangrante [san'grante] *a* (*herida*) bleeding; (*fig*) flagrant.

sangrar [san'grar] *vt, vi* to bleed; (*texto*) to indent.

sangre ['sangre] *nf* blood; ~ **fría** sangfroid; **a** ~ **fría** in cold blood.

sangría [san'gria] *nf* (*MED*) bleeding; (*CULIN*) sangria, *sweetened drink of red wine with fruit*, ≈ fruit cup.

sangriento, a [san'grjento, a] *a* bloody.

sanguijuela [sangi'xwela] *nf* (*ZOOL, fig*) leech.

sanguinario, a [sangi'narjo, a] *a* bloodthirsty.

sanguíneo, a [san'gineo, a] *a* blood *cpd*.

sanguinolento, a [sangino'lento, a] *a* (*que echa sangre*) bleeding; (*manchado*) bloodstained; (*ojos*) bloodshot.

sanidad [sani'ðað] nf sanitation; (calidad de sano) health, healthiness; ~ **pública** public health (department).

sanitario, a [sani'tarjo, a] a sanitary; (de la salud) health cpd ◆ nm: ~**s** toilets (Brit), restroom sg (US).

San Marino [sanma'rino] nm: **(La República de)** ~ San Marino.

sano, a ['sano, a] a healthy; (sin daños) sound; (comida) wholesome; (entero) whole, intact; ~ **y salvo** safe and sound.

santanderino, a [santande'rino, a] a of o from Santander ◆ nm/f native o inhabitant of Santander.

Santiago [san'tjaɣo] nm: ~ **(de Chile)** Santiago.

santiamén [santja'men] nm: **en un** ~ in no time at all.

santidad [santi'ðað] nf holiness, sanctity.

santificar [santifi'kar] vt to sanctify, make holy.

santifique [santi'fike] etc vb V **santificar**.

santiguarse [santi'ɣwarse] vr to make the sign of the cross.

santigüe [san'tiɣwe] etc vb V **santiguarse**.

santo, a ['santo, a] a holy; (fig) wonderful, miraculous ◆ nm/f saint ◆ nm saint's day; **hacer su santa voluntad** to do as one jolly well pleases; **¿a** ~ **de qué ...?** why on earth ...?; **se le fue el** ~ **al cielo** he forgot what he was about to say; ~ **y seña** password.

santuario [san'twarjo] nm sanctuary, shrine.

saña ['saɲa] nf rage, fury.

sapo ['sapo] nm toad.

saque ['sake] etc vb V **sacar** ◆ nm (TENIS) service, serve; (FÚTBOL) throw-in; ~ **inicial** kick-off; ~ **de esquina** corner (kick); **tener buen** ~ to eat heartily.

saquear [sake'ar] vt (MIL) to sack; (robar) to loot, plunder; (fig) to ransack.

saqueo [sa'keo] nm sacking; looting, plundering; ransacking.

sarampión [saram'pjon] nm measles sg.

sarape [sa'rape] nm (AM) blanket.

sarcasmo [sar'kasmo] nm sarcasm.

sarcástico, a [sar'kastiko, a] a sarcastic.

sardina [sar'ðina] nf sardine.

sardo, a ['sarðo, a] a, nm/f Sardinian.

sardónico, a [sar'ðoniko, a] a sardonic; (irónico) ironical, sarcastic.

sargento [sar'xento] nm sergeant.

SARL abr (= Sociedad Anónima de Responsabilidad Limitada) Ltd., plc.

sarna ['sarna] nf itch; (MED) scabies.

sarpullido [sarpu'ʎiðo] nm (MED) rash.

sarro ['sarro] nm deposit; (en dientes) tartar.

sarta ['sarta] nf, **sartal** [sar'tal] nm (fig): **una** ~ **de mentiras** a pack of lies.

sartén [sar'ten] nf frying pan; **tener la** ~

por el mango to rule the roost.

sastre ['sastre] nm tailor.

sastrería [sastre'ria] nf (arte) tailoring; (tienda) tailor's (shop).

Satanás [sata'nas] nm Satan.

satélite [sa'telite] nm satellite.

satinado, a [sati'naðo, a] a glossy ◆ nm gloss, shine.

sátira ['satira] nf satire.

satírico, a [sa'tiriko, a] a satiric(al).

sátiro ['satiro] nm (MITOLOGÍA) satyr; (fig) sex maniac.

satisfacción [satisfak'θjon] nf satisfaction.

satisfacer [satisfa'θer] vt to satisfy; (gastos) to meet; (deuda) to pay; (COM: letra de cambio) to honour (Brit), honor (US); (pérdida) to make good; ~**se** vr to satisfy o.s., be satisfied; (vengarse) to take revenge.

satisfaga [satis'faɣa] etc, **satisfaré** [satisfa're] etc vb V **satisfacer**.

satisfecho, a [satis'fetʃo, a] pp de **satisfacer** ◆ a satisfied; (contento) content(ed), happy; (tb: ~ **de sí mismo**) self-satisfied, smug.

satisfice [satis'fiθe] etc vb V **satisfacer**.

saturar [satu'rar] vt to saturate.

sauce ['sauθe] nm willow; ~ **llorón** weeping willow.

saúco [sa'uko] nm (BOT) elder.

sauna ['sauna] nf sauna.

savia ['saβja] nf sap.

saxofón [sakso'fon] nm saxophone.

saya ['saja] nf (falda) skirt; (enagua) petticoat.

sayo ['sajo] nm smock.

sazón [sa'θon] nf (de fruta) ripeness; **a la** ~ then, at that time.

sazonado, a [saθo'naðo, a] a (fruta) ripe; (CULIN) flavoured, seasoned.

sazonar [saθo'nar] vt to ripen; (CULIN) to flavour, season.

s/c abr (COM: = su casa) your firm; (: = su cuenta) your account.

Scotch [es'kotʃ] nm (AM) adhesive tape.

Sdo. abr (COM: = Saldo) bal.

SE abr (= sudeste) SE.

se [se] pron reflexivo oneself; (sg: m) himself; (: f) herself; (: de una cosa) itself; (: de usted) yourself; (pl) themselves; (: de ustedes) yourselves; (recíproco) each other, one another; ~ **mira en el espejo** he looks at himself in the mirror; **¡siénte~!** sit down; ~ **ayudan** they help each other; ~ **miraron (el uno al otro)** they looked at one another; ~ **compró hace 3 años** it was bought 3 years ago; **en esa parte** ~ **habla francés** in that area French is spoken o people speak French; **"**~ **vende coche"** "car for sale"; ~ **lo daré** I'll give it to him/her/you; **él** ~ **ha**

comprado un sombrero he has bought himself a hat.

sé [se] *vb V* **saber, ser**.

sea ['sea] *etc vb V* **ser**.

SEAT ['seat] *nf abr = Sociedad Española de Automóviles de Turismo*.

sebo ['seβo] *nm* fat, grease.

Sec. *abr* (= *Secretario*) Sec.

seca ['seka] *nf V* **seco**.

secado [se'kaðo] *nm* drying; ~ **a mano** blow-dry.

secador [seka'ðor] *nm*: ~ **para el pelo** hair-dryer.

secadora [seka'ðora] *nf* tumble dryer; ~ **centrífuga** spin-dryer.

secano [se'kano] *nm* (*AGR*: *tb*: **tierra de** ~) dry land *o* region; **cultivo de** ~ dry farming.

secante [se'kante] *a* (*viento*) drying ◆ *nm* blotting paper.

secar [se'kar] *vt* to dry; (*superficie*) to wipe dry; (*frente, suelo*) to mop; (*líquido*) to mop up; (*tinta*) to blot; ~**se** *vr* to dry (off); (*río, planta*) to dry up.

sección [sek'θjon] *nf* section; (*COM*) department; ~ **deportiva** (*en periódico*) sports page(s).

seco, a ['seko, a] *a* dry; (*fruta*) dried; (*persona*: *magro*) thin, skinny; (*carácter*) cold; (*antipático*) disagreeable; (*respuesta*) sharp, curt ◆ *nf* dry season; **habrá pan a secas** there will be just bread; **decir algo a secas** to say sth curtly; **parar en** ~ to stop dead.

secreción [sekre'θjon] *nf* secretion.

secretaría [sekreta'ria] *nf* secretariat; (*oficina*) secretary's office.

secretariado [sekreta'rjaðo] *nm* (*oficina*) secretariat; (*cargo*) secretaryship; (*curso*) secretarial course.

secretario, a [sekre'tarjo, a] *nm/f* secretary; ~ **adjunto** (*COM*) assistant secretary.

secreto, a [se'kreto, a] *a* secret; (*información*) confidential; (*persona*) secretive ◆ *nm* secret; (*calidad*) secrecy.

secta ['sekta] *nf* sect.

sectario, a [sek'tarjo, a] *a* sectarian.

sector [sek'tor] *nm* sector (*tb INFORM*); (*de opinión*) section; (*fig*: *campo*) area, field; ~ **privado/público** (*COM, ECON*) private/public sector.

secuela [se'kwela] *nf* consequence.

secuencia [se'kwenθja] *nf* sequence.

secuestrar [sekwes'trar] *vt* to kidnap; (*avión*) to hijack; (*bienes*) to seize, confiscate.

secuestro [se'kwestro] *nm* kidnapping; hijack; seizure, confiscation.

secular [seku'lar] *a* secular.

secundar [sekun'dar] *vt* to second, support.

secundario, a [sekun'darjo, a] *a* second-

ary; (*carretera*) side *cpd*; (*INFORM*) background *cpd*.

sed [seð] *nf* thirst; (*fig*) thirst, craving; **tener** ~ to be thirsty.

seda ['seða] *nf* silk.

sedal [se'ðal] *nm* fishing line.

sedante [se'ðante] *nm* sedative.

sede ['seðe] *nf* (*de gobierno*) seat; (*de compañía*) headquarters *pl*, head office; **Santa S**~ Holy See.

SEDIC [se'ðik] *nf abr = Sociedad Española de Documentación e Información Científica*.

sedición [seði'θjon] *nf* sedition.

sediento, a [se'ðjento, a] *a* thirsty.

sedimentar [seðimen'tar] *vt* to deposit; ~**se** *vr* to settle.

sedimento [seði'mento] *nm* sediment.

sedoso, a [se'ðoso, a] *a* silky, silken.

seducción [seðuk'θjon] *nf* seduction.

seducir [seðu'θir] *vt* to seduce; (*sobornar*) to bribe; (*cautivar*) to charm, fascinate; (*atraer*) to attract.

seductor, a [seðuk'tor, a] *a* seductive; charming, fascinating; attractive; (*engañoso*) deceptive, misleading ◆ *nm/f* seducer.

seduje [se'ðuxe] *etc*, **seduzca** [se'ðuθka] *etc vb V* **seducir**.

sefardí [sefar'ði], **sefardita** [sefar'ðita] *a* Sephardi(c) ◆ *nm/f* Sephardi.

segador, a [seɣa'ðor, a] *nm/f* (*persona*) harvester ◆ *nf* (*TEC*) mower, reaper.

segadora-trilladora [seɣa'ðoratriʎa'ðora] *nf* combine harvester.

segar [se'ɣar] *vt* (*mies*) to reap, cut; (*hierba*) to mow, cut; (*esperanzas*) to ruin.

seglar [se'ɣlar] *a* secular, lay.

segoviano, a [seɣo'βjano, a] *a* of *o* from Segovia ◆ *nm/f* native *o* inhabitant of Segovia.

segregación [seɣreɣa'θjon] *nf* segregation; ~ **racial** racial segregation.

segregar [seɣre'ɣar] *vt* to segregate, separate.

segregue [se'ɣreɣe] *etc vb V* **segregar**.

seguidamente [seɣiða'mente] *ad* (*sin parar*) without a break; (*inmediatamente después*) immediately after.

seguido, a [se'ɣiðo, a] *a* (*continuo*) continuous, unbroken; (*recto*) straight ◆ *ad* (*directo*) straight (on); (*después*) after; (*AM*: *a menudo*) often ◆ *nf*: **en seguida** at once, right away; **5 días** ~**s** 5 days running, 5 days in a row; **en seguida termino** I've nearly finished, I shan't be long now.

segué [se'ɣe], **seguemos** [se'ɣemos] *etc vb V* **segar**.

seguimiento [seɣi'mjento] *nm* chase, pursuit; (*continuación*) continuation.

seguir [se'ɣir] *vt* to follow; (*venir después*) to follow on, come after; (*proseguir*) to continue; (*perseguir*) to chase, pursue; (*indicio*) to follow up; (*mujer*) to court ◆ *vi* (*gen*) to follow; (*continuar*) to continue, carry *o* go on; ~se *vr* to follow; **a** ~ to be continued; **sigo sin comprender** I still don't understand; **sigue lloviendo** it's still raining; **sigue** (*en carta*) P.T.O.; (*en libro, TV*) continued; "**hágase** ~" "please forward".

según [se'ɣun] *prep* according to ◆ *ad*: ~ **(y conforme)** it all depends ◆ *conj* as; ~ **esté el tiempo** depending on the weather; ~ **me consta** as far as I know; **está** ~ **lo dejaste** it is just as you left it.

segundo, a [se'ɣundo, a] *a* second; (*en discurso*) secondly ◆ *nm* (*gen, medida de tiempo*) second; (*piso*) second floor ◆ *nf* (*sentido*) second meaning; ~ **(de a bordo)** (*NAUT*) first mate; **segunda (clase)** (*FERRO*) second class; **segunda (marcha)** (*AUTO*) second (gear); **de segunda mano** second hand.

seguramente [seɣura'mente] *ad* surely; (*con certeza*) for sure, with certainty; (*probablemente*) probably; **¿lo va a comprar?** — ~ is he going to buy it? — I should think so.

seguridad [seɣuri'ðað] *nf* safety; (*del estado, de casa etc*) security; (*certidumbre*) certainty; (*confianza*) confidence; (*estabilidad*) stability; ~ **social** social security; ~ **contra incendios** fire precautions; ~ **en sí mismo** (self-)confidence.

seguro, a [se'ɣuro, a] *a* (*cierto*) sure, certain; (*fiel*) trustworthy; (*libre de peligro*) safe; (*bien defendido, firme*) secure; (*datos etc*) reliable; (*fecha*) firm ◆ *ad* for sure, certainly ◆ *nm* (*dispositivo*) safety device; (*de cerradura*) tumbler; (*de arma*) safety catch; (*COM*) insurance; ~ **contra accidentes/incendios** fire/accident insurance; ~ **contra terceros/a todo riesgo** third party/comprehensive insurance; ~ **dotal con beneficios** with-profits endowment assurance; **S**~ **de Enfermedad** ≈ National Insurance; ~ **marítimo** marine insurance; ~ **mixto** endowment assurance; ~ **temporal** term insurance; ~ **de vida** life insurance.

seis [seis] *num* six; ~ **mil** six thousand; **tiene** ~ **años** she is six (years old); **unos** ~ about six; **hoy es el** ~ today is the sixth.

seiscientos, as [seis'θjentos, as] *num* six hundred.

seísmo [se'ismo] *nm* tremor, earthquake.

selección [selek'θjon] *nf* selection; ~ **múltiple** multiple choice; ~ **nacional** (*DEPORTE*) national team.

seleccionador, a [selekθjona'ðor, a] *nm/f* (*DEPORTE*) selector.

seleccionar [selekθjo'nar] *vt* to pick, choose, select.

selectividad [selektiβi'ðað] *nf* (*UNIV*) entrance examination.

selecto, a [se'lekto, a] *a* select, choice; (*escogido*) selected.

selva ['selβa] *nf* (*bosque*) forest, woods *pl*; (*jungla*) jungle; **la S**~ **Negra** the Black Forest.

selvático, a [sel'βatiko, a] *a* woodland *cpd*; (*BOT*) wild.

sellado, a [se'ʎaðo, a] *a* (*documento oficial*) sealed; (*pasaporte*) stamped.

sellar [se'ʎar] *vt* (*documento oficial*) to seal; (*pasaporte, visado*) to stamp; (*marcar*) to brand; (*pacto, labios*) to seal.

sello ['seʎo] *nm* stamp; (*precinto*) seal; (*fig: tb:* ~ **distintivo**) hallmark; ~ **fiscal** revenue stamp; ~**s de prima** (*COM*) trading stamps.

semáforo [se'maforo] *nm* (*AUTO*) traffic lights *pl*; (*FERRO*) signal.

semana [se'mana] *nf* week; ~ **inglesa** 5-day (working) week; ~ **laboral** working week; **S**~ **Santa** Holy Week; **entre** ~ during the week.

semanal [sema'nal] *a* weekly.

semanario [sema'narjo] *nm* weekly (magazine).

semántica [se'mantika] *nf* semantics *sg*.

semblante [sem'blante] *nm* face; (*fig*) look.

semblanza [sem'blanθa] *nf* biographical sketch, profile.

sembrar [sem'brar] *vt* to sow; (*objetos*) to sprinkle, scatter about; (*noticias etc*) to spread.

semejante [seme'xante] *a* (*parecido*) similar; (*tal*) such; ~**s** alike, similar ◆ *nm* fellow man, fellow creature; **son muy** ~**s** they are very much alike; **nunca hizo cosa** ~ he never did such a *o* any such thing.

semejanza [seme'xanθa] *nf* similarity, resemblance; **a** ~ **de** like, as.

semejar [seme'xar] *vi* to seem like, resemble; ~**se** *vr* to look alike, be similar.

semen ['semen] *nm* semen.

semental [semen'tal] *nm* (*macho*) stud.

sementera [semen'tera] *nf* (*acto*) sowing; (*temporada*) seedtime; (*tierra*) sown land.

semestral [semes'tral] *a* half-yearly, biannual.

semestre [se'mestre] *nm* period of six months; (*US UNIV*) semester; (*COM*) half-yearly payment.

semicírculo [semi'θirkulo] *nm* semicircle.

semiconductor [semikonduk'tor] *nm* semiconductor.

semiconsciente [semikons'θjente] *a* semiconscious.

semifinal [semifi'nal] *nf* semifinal.

semilla [se'miʎa] *nf* seed.

semillero [semi'ʎero] *nm* (*AGR* *etc*) seedbed; (*fig*) hotbed.

seminario [semi'narjo] *nm* (*REL*) seminary; (*ESCOL*) seminar.

semiseco [semi'seko] *nm* medium-dry.

semita [se'mita] *a* Semitic ◆ *nm/f* Semite.

sémola ['semola] *nf* semolina.

sempiterno, a [sempi'terno, a] *a* everlasting.

Sena ['sena] *nm*: **el ~** the (river) Seine.

senado [se'naðo] *nm* senate.

senador, a [sena'ðor, a] *nm/f* senator.

sencillez [senθi'ʎeθ] *nf* simplicity; (*de persona*) naturalness.

sencillo, a [sen'θiʎo, a] *a* simple; (*carácter*) natural, unaffected; (*billete*) single.

senda ['senda] *nf*, **sendero** [sen'dero] *nm* path, track.

sendos, as ['sendos, as] *apl*: **les dio ~ golpes** he hit both of them.

senil [se'nil] *a* senile.

seno ['seno] *nm* (*ANAT*) bosom, bust; (*fig*) bosom; **~s** *nmpl* breasts; **~ materno** womb.

sensación [sensa'θjon] *nf* sensation; (*sentido*) sense; (*sentimiento*) feeling; **causar** *o* **hacer ~** to cause a sensation.

sensacional [sensaθjo'nal] *a* sensational.

sensato, a [sen'sato, a] *a* sensible.

sensible [sen'sible] *a* sensitive; (*apreciable*) perceptible, appreciable; (*pérdida*) considerable.

sensiblero, a [sensi'ßlero, a] *a* sentimental, slushy.

sensitivo, a [sensi'tißo, a], **sensorial** [senso'rjal] *a* sense *cpd*.

sensor [sen'sor] *nm*: **~ de fin de papel** paper out sensor.

sensual [sen'swal] *a* sensual.

sentado, a [sen'taðo, a] *a* (*establecido*) settled; (*carácter*) sensible ◆ *nf* sitting; (*protesta*) sit-down, sit-in; **dar por ~** to take for granted, assume; **dejar algo ~** to establish sth firmly; **estar ~** to sit, be sitting (down).

sentar [sen'tar] *vt* to sit, seat; (*fig*) to establish ◆ *vi* (*vestido*) to suit; (*alimento*): **~ bien/mal a** to agree/disagree with; **~se** *vr* (*persona*) to sit, sit down; (*el tiempo*) to settle (down); (*los depósitos*) to settle; **¡siéntese!** (do) sit down, take a seat.

sentencia [sen'tenθja] *nf* (*máxima*) maxim, saying; (*JUR*) sentence; (*INFORM*) statement; **~ de muerte** death sentence.

sentenciar [senten'θjar] *vt* to sentence.

sentido, a [sen'tiðo, a] *a* (*pérdida*) regrettable; (*carácter*) sensitive ◆ *nm* sense; (*sentimiento*) feeling; (*significado*) sense, meaning; (*dirección*) direction; **mi más ~ pésame** my deepest sympathy; **~ del humor** sense of humour; **~ común**

common sense; **en el buen ~ de la palabra** in the best sense of the word; **sin ~** meaningless; **tener ~** to make sense; **~ único** one-way (street).

sentimental [sentimen'tal] *a* sentimental; **vida ~** love life.

sentimiento, [senti'mjento] *nm* (*emoción*) feeling, emotion; (*sentido*) sense; (*pesar*) regret, sorrow.

sentir [sen'tir] *vt* to feel; (*percibir*) to perceive, sense; (*lamentar*) to regret, be sorry for; (*música etc*) to have a feeling for ◆ *vi* to feel; (*lamentarse*) to feel sorry ◆ *nm* opinion, judgement; **~se** *vr* to feel; **lo siento** I'm sorry; **~se bien/mal** to feel well/ill; **~se como en su casa** to feel at home.

seña ['seɲa] *nf* sign; (*MIL*) password; **~s** *nfpl* address *sg*; **~s personales** personal description *sg*; **por más ~s** moreover; **dar ~s de** to show signs of.

señal [se'ɲal] *nf* sign; (*síntoma*) symptom; (*indicio*) indication; (*FERRO, TELEC*) signal; (*marca*) mark; (*COM*) deposit; (*INFORM*) marker, mark; **en ~ de** as a token of, as a sign of; **dar ~es de** to show signs of; **~ de auxilio/de peligro** distress/danger signal; **~ de llamada** ringing tone; **~ para marcar** dialling tone.

señalado, a [seɲa'laðo, a] *a* (*persona*) distinguished; (*pey*) notorious.

señalar [seɲa'lar] *vt* to mark; (*indicar*) to point out, indicate; (*significar*) to denote; (*referirse a*) to allude to; (*fijar*) to fix, settle; (*pey*) to criticize.

señalice [seɲa'liθe] *etc vb* V **señalizar**.

señalización [seɲaliθa'θjon] *nf* signposting; signals *pl*.

señalizar [seɲali'θar] *vt* (*AUT*) to put up road signs on; (*FERRO*) to put signals on; (*AUT: ruta*): **está bien señalizada** it's well signposted.

señas ['seɲas] *nfpl* V **seña**.

señor, a [se'ɲor, a] *a* (*fam*) lordly ◆ *nm* (*hombre*) man; (*caballero*) gentleman; (*dueño*) owner, master; (*trato: antes de nombre propio*) Mr; (: *hablando directamente*) sir ◆ *nf* (*dama*) lady; (*trato: antes de nombre propio*) Mrs; (: *hablando directamente*) madam; (*esposa*) wife; **los ~es González** Mr and Mrs González; **S~ Don Jacinto Benavente** (*en sobre*) Mr J. Benavente, J. Benavente Esq.; **S~ Director ...** (*de periódico*) Dear Sir ...; **~ juez** my lord, your worship (*US*); **Muy ~ mío** Dear Sir; **Muy ~es nuestros** Dear Sirs; **Nuestro S~** (*REL*) Our Lord; **¿está la señora?** is the lady of the house in?; **la señora de Smith** Mrs Smith; **Nuestra Señora** (*REL*) Our Lady.

señoría [seɲo'ria] *nf* rule; **su** *o* **vuestra S~** your *o* his/her lordship/ladyship.

señorío [seɲo'rio] *nm* manor; *(fig)* rule.

señorita [seɲo'rita] *nf (gen)* Miss; *(mujer joven)* young lady; *(maestra)* schoolteacher.

señorito [seɲo'rito] *nm* young gentleman; *(lenguaje de criados)* master; *(pey)* toff.

señuelo [se'ɲwelo] *nm* decoy.

Sep. *abr* (= *septiembre*) Sept.

sepa ['sepa] *etc vb* V **saber**.

separable [sepa'raßle] *a* separable; *(TEC)* detachable.

separación [separa'θjon] *nf* separation; *(división)* division; *(distancia)* gap, distance; ~ **de bienes** division of property.

separado, a [sepa'raðo, a] *a* separate; *(TEC)* detached; **vive ~ de su mujer** he is separated from his wife; **por ~** separately.

separador [separa'ðor] *nm (INFORM)* delimiter.

separadora [separa'ðora] *nf:* ~ **de hojas** burster.

separar [sepa'rar] *vt* to separate; *(silla de la mesa)* to move away; *(TEC: pieza)* to detach; *(persona: de un cargo)* to remove, dismiss; *(dividir)* to divide; **~se** *vr (parte)* to come away; *(partes)* to come apart; *(persona)* to leave, go away; *(matrimonio)* to separate.

separatismo [separa'tismo] *nm (POL)* separatism.

sepelio [se'peljo] *nm* burial, interment.

sepia ['sepja] *nf* cuttlefish.

Sept. *abr* (= *septiembre*) Sept.

septentrional [septentrjo'nal] *a* north *cpd*, northern.

septiembre [sep'tjembre] *nm* September.

séptimo, a ['septimo, a] *a, nm* seventh.

septuagésimo, a [septwa'xesimo, a] *a* seventieth.

sepulcral [sepul'kral] *a* sepulchral; *(fig)* gloomy, dismal.

sepulcro [se'pulkro] *nm* tomb, grave, sepulchre.

sepultar [sepul'tar] *vt* to bury; *(en accidente)* to trap; **quedaban sepultados en la caverna** they were trapped in the cave.

sepultura [sepul'tura] *nf (acto)* burial; *(tumba)* grave, tomb; **dar ~ a** to bury; **recibir ~** to be buried.

sepulturero, a [sepultu'rero, a] *nm/f* gravedigger.

seque ['seke] *etc vb* V **secar**.

sequedad [seke'ðað] *nf* dryness; *(fig)* brusqueness, curtness.

sequía [se'kia] *nf* drought.

séquito ['sekito] *nm (de rey etc)* retinue; *(POL)* followers *pl*.

ser [ser] *vi (gen)* to be; *(devenir)* to become ♦ *nm* being; ~ **de** *(origen)* to be from, come from; *(hecho de)* to be (made) of; *(pertenecer a)* to belong to; ¿**qué será de mí?** what will become of me?; **soy ingeniero** I'm an engineer; **soy yo** it's me; **es la una** it is one o'clock; **es de esperar que** it is to be hoped that; **era de ver** you should have seen it; **a no ~ que** unless; **de no ~ así** if it were not so, were it not so; **o sea** that is to say; **sea como sea** be that as it may; ~ **vivo** living creature.

serenarse [sere'narse] *vr* to calm down; *(mar)* to grow calm; *(tiempo)* to clear up.

sereno, a [se'reno, a] *a (persona)* calm, unruffled; *(el tiempo)* fine, settled; *(ambiente)* calm, peaceful ♦ *nm* night watchman.

serial [se'rjal] *nm* serial.

serie ['serje] *nf* series; *(cadena)* sequence, succession; *(TV etc)* serial; *(de inyecciones)* course; **fuera de ~** out of order; *(fig)* special, out of the ordinary; **fabricación en ~** mass production; *(INFORM)*: **interface/impresora en ~** serial interface/printer.

seriedad [serje'ðað] *nf* seriousness; *(formalidad)* reliability; *(de crisis)* gravity, seriousness.

serio, a ['serjo, a] *a* serious; reliable, dependable; grave, serious; **poco ~** *(actitud)* undignified; *(carácter)* unreliable; **en ~** seriously.

sermón [ser'mon] *nm (REL)* sermon.

sermonear [sermone'ar] *vt (fam)* to lecture ♦ *vi* to sermonize.

serpentear [serpente'ar] *vi* to wriggle; *(camino, río)* to wind, snake.

serpentina [serpen'tina] *nf* streamer.

serpiente [ser'pjente] *nf* snake; ~ **boa** boa constrictor; ~ **de cascabel** rattlesnake.

serranía [serra'nia] *nf* mountainous area.

serrano, a [se'rrano, a] *a* highland *cpd*, hill *cpd* ♦ *nm/f* highlander.

serrar [se'rrar] *vt* to saw.

serrín [se'rrin] *nm* sawdust.

serrucho [se'rrutʃo] *nm* handsaw.

Servia ['serßja] *nf* Serbia.

servicial [serßi'θjal] *a* helpful, obliging.

servicio [ser'ßiθjo] *nm* service; *(CULIN etc)* set; **~s** *nmpl* toilet(s) *(pl)*; **estar de ~** to be on duty; ~ **aduanero** *o* **de aduana** customs service; ~ **a domicilio** home delivery service; ~ **incluido** *(en hotel etc)* service charge included; ~ **militar** military service; ~ **público** *(COM)* public utility.

servidor, a [serßi'ðor, a] *nm/f* servant; **su seguro** ~ **(s.s.s.)** yours faithfully; **un** ~ *(el que habla o escribe)* your humble servant.

servidumbre [serßi'ðumbre] *nf (sujeción)* servitude; *(criados)* servants *pl*, staff.

servil [ser'ßil] *a* servile.

servilleta [serßi'ʎeta] *nf* serviette, napkin.

servilletero [serßiʎe'tero] *nm* napkin ring.

servir [ser'ßir] *vt* to serve; (*comida*) to serve out *o* up; (*TENIS etc*) to serve ◆ *vi* to serve; (*camarero*) to serve, wait; (*tener utilidad*) to be of use, be useful; **~se** *vr* to serve *o* help o.s.; **¿en qué puedo ~le?** how can I help you?; **~ vino a uno** to pour out wine for sb; **~ de guía** to act *o* serve as a guide; **no sirve para nada** it's no use at all; **~se de algo** to make use of sth, use sth; **sírvase pasar** please come in.

sesenta [se'senta] *num* sixty.

sesentón, ona [sesen'ton, ona] *a, nm/f* sixty-year-old.

sesgado, a [ses'ɣaðo, a] *a* slanted, slanting.

sesgo ['sesɣo] *nm* slant; (*fig*) slant, twist.

sesión [se'sjon] *nf* (*POL*) session, sitting; (*CINE*) showing; (*TEATRO*) performance; **abrir/levantar la** ~ to open/close *o* adjourn the meeting; **la segunda** ~ the second house.

seso ['seso] *nm* brain; (*fig*) intelligence; **~s** *nmpl* (*CULIN*) brains; **devanarse los ~s** to rack one's brains.

sesudo, a [se'suðo, a] *a* sensible, wise.

Set. *abr* (= *setiembre*) Sept.

seta ['seta] *nf* mushroom; ~ **venenosa** toadstool.

setecientos, as [sete'θjentos, as] *num* seven hundred.

setenta [se'tenta] *num* seventy.

setiembre [se'tjembre] *nm* = **septiembre**.

seto ['seto] *nm* fence; ~ **vivo** hedge.

seudo... [seuðo] *pref* pseudo....

seudónimo [seu'ðonimo] *nm* pseudonym.

Seúl [se'ul] *nm* Seoul.

s.e.u.o. *abr* (= *salvo error u omisión*) E & O E.

severidad [seßeri'ðað] *nf* severity.

severo, a [se'ßero, a] *a* severe; (*disciplina*) strict; (*frío*) bitter.

Sevilla [se'ßiʎa] *nf* Seville.

sevillano, a [seßi'ʎano, a] *a* of *o* from Seville ◆ *nm/f* native *o* inhabitant of Seville.

sexagenario, a [seksaxe'narjo, a] *a* sixty-year-old ◆ *nm/f* person in his/her sixties.

sexagésimo, a [seksa'xesimo, a] *num* sixtieth.

sexo ['sekso] *nm* sex; **el** ~ **femenino/ masculino** the female/male sex.

sexto, a ['seksto, a] *num* sixth; **Juan S~** John the Sixth.

sexual [sek'swal] *a* sexual; **vida** ~ sex life.

s.f. *abr* (= *sin fecha*) no date.

s/f *abr* (*COM*: = *su favor*) your favour.

sgte(s). *abr* (= *siguiente(s)*) foll.

si [si] *conj* if; (*en pregunta indirecta*) if, whether; ~ ... ~ ... whether ... or ...; **me pregunto** ~ ... I wonder if *o* whether ...; ~ **no** if not, otherwise; **¡~ fuera verdad!** if only it were true!

sí [si] *ad* yes ◆ *nm* consent ◆ *pron* (*uso impersonal*) oneself; (*sg: m*) himself; (*: f*) herself; (*: de cosa*) itself; (*: de usted*) yourself; (*pl*) themselves; (*: de ustedes*) yourselves; (*: recíproco*) each other; **él no quiere pero yo** ~ he doesn't want to but I do; **ella** ~ **vendrá** she will certainly come, she is sure to come; **claro que** ~ of course; **creo que** ~ I think so; **porque** ~ because that's the way it is; (*porque lo digo yo*) because I say so; **¡~ que lo es!** I'll say it is!; **¡eso** ~ **que no!** never; **se ríe de** ~ **misma** she laughs at herself; **cambiaron una mirada entre** ~ they gave each other a look; **de por** ~ in itself.

siamés, esa [sja'mes, esa] *a, nm/f* Siamese.

Sicilia [si'θilja] *nf* Sicily.

siciliano, a [siθi'ljano, a] *a, nm/f* Sicilian ◆ *nm* (*LING*) Sicilian.

SIDA ['siða] *nm abr* (= *síndrome de inmunodeficiencia adquirida*) AIDS.

siderurgia [siðe'rurxja] *nf* iron and steel industry.

siderúrgico, a [siðe'rurxico, a] *a* iron and steel *cpd*.

sidra ['siðra] *nf* cider.

siega ['sjeɣa] *etc vb V* **segar** ◆ *nf* (*cosechar*) reaping; (*segar*) mowing; (*época*) harvest (time).

siegue ['sjeɣe] *etc vb V* **segar**.

siembra ['sjembra] *etc vb V* **sembrar** ◆ *nf* sowing.

siempre ['sjempre] *ad* always; (*todo el tiempo*) all the time ◆ *conj*: ~ **que** ... (+ *indic*) whenever ...; (+ *subjun*) provided that ...; **es lo de** ~ it's the same old story; **como** ~ as usual; **para** ~ forever.

sien [sjen] *nf* (*ANAT*) temple.

siento ['sjento] *etc vb V* **sentar, sentir**.

sierra ['sjerra] *etc vb V* **serrar** ◆ *nf* (*TEC*) saw; (*GEO*) mountain range; **S~ Leona** Sierra Leone.

siervo, a ['sjerßo, a] *nm/f* slave.

siesta ['sjesta] *nf* siesta, nap; **dormir la** *o* **echarse una** *o* **tomar una** ~ to have an afternoon nap *o* a doze.

siete ['sjete] *num* seven.

sífilis ['sifilis] *nf* syphilis.

sifón [si'fon] *nm* syphon; **whisky con** ~ whisky and soda.

siga ['siɣa] *etc vb V* **seguir**.

sigilo [si'xilo] *nm* secrecy; (*discreción*) discretion.

sigla ['siɣla] *nf* initial, abbreviation.

siglo ['siɣlo] *nm* century; (*fig*) age; **S~ de las Luces** Age of Enlightenment; **S~ de Oro** Golden Age.

significación [siɣnifika'θjon] *nf* significance.

significado [siɣnifi'kaðo] *nm* significance; (*de palabra etc*) meaning.

significar [siɣnifi'kar] *vt* to mean, signify;

(*notificar*) to make known, express.
significativo, a [siɣnifika'tiβo, a] *a* significant.
signifique [siɣni'fike] *etc vb* V **significar.**
signo ['siɣno] *nm* sign; ~ **de admiración** *o* **exclamación** exclamation mark; ~ **igual** equals sign; ~ **de interrogación** question mark; ~ **de más/de menos** plus/minus sign; ~**s de puntuación** punctuation marks.
siguiendo [si'ɣjendo] *etc vb* V **seguir.**
siguiente [si'ɣjente] *a* following; (*próximo*) next.
sílaba ['silaβa] *nf* syllable.
silbar [sil'βar] *vt, vi* to whistle; (*silbato*) to blow; (*TEATRO etc*) to hiss.
silbato [sil'βato] *nm* (*instrumento*) whistle.
silbido [sil'βiðo], **silbo** ['silβo] *nm* whistle, whistling; (*abucheo*) hiss.
silenciador [silenθja'ðor] *nm* silencer.
silenciar [silen'θjar] *vt* (*persona*) to silence; (*escándalo*) to hush up.
silencio [si'lenθjo] *nm* silence, quiet; **en el** ~ **más absoluto** in dead silence; **guardar** ~ to keep silent.
silencioso, a [silen'θjoso, a] *a* silent, quiet.
sílfide ['silfiðe] *nf* sylph.
silicio [si'liθjo] *nm* silicon.
silueta [si'lweta] *nf* silhouette; (*de edificio*) outline; (*figura*) figure.
silvestre [sil'βestre] *a* (*BOT*) wild; (*fig*) rustic, rural.
silla ['siʎa] *nf* (*asiento*) chair; (*tb*: ~ **de montar**) saddle; ~ **de ruedas** wheelchair.
sillería [siʎe'ria] *nf* (*asientos*) chairs *pl*, set of chairs; (*REL*) choir stalls *pl*; (*taller*) chairmaker's workshop.
sillón [si'ʎon] *nm* armchair, easy chair.
sima ['sima] *nf* abyss, chasm.
simbolice [simbo'liθe] *etc vb* V **simbolizar.**
simbólico, a [sim'boliko, a] *a* symbolic(al).
simbolizar [simboli'θar] *vt* to symbolize.
símbolo ['simbolo] *nm* symbol; ~ **gráfico** (*INFORM*) icon.
simetría [sime'tria] *nf* symmetry.
simiente [si'mjente] *nf* seed.
similar [simi'lar] *a* similar.
similitud [simili'tuð] *nf* similarity, resemblance.
simio ['simjo] *nm* ape.
simpatía [simpa'tia] *nf* liking; (*afecto*) affection; (*amabilidad*) kindness; (*de ambiente*) friendliness; (*de persona, lugar*) charm, attractiveness; (*solidaridad*) mutual support, solidarity; **tener** ~ **a** to like; **la famosa** ~ **andaluza** that well-known Andalusian charm.
simpatice [simpa'tiθe] *etc vb* V **simpatizar.**
simpático, a [sim'patiko, a] *a* nice, pleasant; (*bondadoso*) kind; **no le hemos caído muy** ~**s** she didn't much take to us.

simpatiquísimo, a [simpati'kisimo, a] *a* (*superl de* **simpático**) ever so nice; ever so kind.
simpatizante [simpati'θante] *nm/f* sympathizer.
simpatizar [simpati'θar] *vi*: ~ **con** to get on well with.
simple ['simple] *a* simple; (*elemental*) simple, easy; (*mero*) mere; (*puro*) pure, sheer ♦ *nm/f* simpleton; **un** ~ **soldado** an ordinary soldier.
simpleza [sim'pleθa] *nf* simpleness; (*necedad*) silly thing.
simplicidad [simpliθi'ðað] *nf* simplicity.
simplificar [simplifi'kar] *vt* to simplify.
simplifique [simpli'fike] *etc vb* V **simplificar.**
simplón, ona [sim'plon, ona] *a* simple, gullible ♦ *nm/f* simple soul.
simposio [sim'posjo] *nm* symposium.
simulacro [simu'lakro] *nm* (*apariencia*) semblance; (*fingimiento*) sham.
simular [simu'lar] *vt* to simulate; (*fingir*) to feign, sham.
simultanear [simultane'ar] *vt*: ~ **dos cosas** to do two things simultaneously.
simultáneo, a [simul'taneo, a] *a* simultaneous.
sin [sin] *prep* without; (*a no ser por*) but for ♦ *conj*: ~ **que** (+ *subjun*) without; ~ **decir nada** without a word; ~ **verlo yo** without my seeing it; **platos** ~ **lavar** unwashed *o* dirty dishes; **la ropa está** ~ **lavar** the clothes are unwashed; ~ **que lo sepa él** without his knowing; ~ **embargo** however.
sinagoga [sina'ɣoɣa] *nf* synagogue.
Sinaí [sina'i] *nm*: **El** ~ Sinai, the Sinai Peninsula; **el Monte** ~ Mount Sinai.
sinceridad [sinθeri'ðað] *nf* sincerity.
sincero, a [sin'θero, a] *a* sincere; (*persona*) genuine; (*opinión*) frank; (*felicitaciones*) heartfelt.
síncope ['sinkope] *nm* (*desmayo*) blackout; ~ **cardíaco** (*MED*) heart failure.
sincronice [sinkro'niθe] *etc vb* V **sincronizar.**
sincronizar [sinkroni'θar] *vt* to synchronize.
sindical [sindi'kal] *a* union *cpd*, trade-union *cpd*.
sindicalista [sindika'lista] *a* trade-union *cpd* ♦ *nm/f* trade unionist.
sindicar [sindi'kar] *vt* (*obreros*) to organize, unionize; ~**se** *vr* (*obrero*) to join a union.
sindicato [sindi'kato] *nm* (*de trabajadores*) trade(s) *o* labor (*US*) union; (*de negociantes*) syndicate.
sindique [sin'dike] *etc vb* V **sindicar.**
sinfín [sin'fin] *nm*: **un** ~ **de** a great many, no end of.
sinfonía [sinfo'nia] *nf* symphony.
Singapur [singa'pur] *nm* Singapore.

singular [singu'lar] *a* singular; *(fig)* outstanding, exceptional; *(pey)* peculiar, odd ◆ *nm* (*LING*) singular; **en** ~ in the singular.

singularice [singula'riθe] *etc vb V* **singularizar**.

singularidad [singulari'ðað] *nf* singularity, peculiarity.

singularizar [singulari'θar] *vt* to single out; ~**se** *vr* to distinguish o.s., stand out.

siniestro, a [si'njestro, a] *a* left; *(fig)* sinister ◆ *nm* (*accidente*) accident; (*desastre*) natural disaster.

sinnúmero [sin'numero] *nm* = **sinfín**.

sino ['sino] *nm* fate, destiny ◆ *conj* (*pero*) but; *(salvo)* except, save; **no son 8** ~ **9** there are not 8 but 9; **todos** ~ **él** all except him.

sinónimo, a [si'nonimo, a] *a* synonymous ◆ *nm* synonym.

sinrazón [sinra'θon] *nf* wrong, injustice.

sinsabor [sinsa'ßor] *nm* (*molestia*) trouble; *(dolor)* sorrow; *(preocupación)* uneasiness.

síntesis ['sintesis] *nf inv* synthesis.

sintetice [sinte'tiθe] *etc vb V* **sintetizar**.

sintético, a [sin'tetiko, a] *a* synthetic.

sintetizador [sintetiθa'ðor] *nm* synthesizer.

sintetizar [sinteti'θar] *vt* to synthesize.

sintiendo [sin'tjendo] *etc vb V* **sentir**.

síntoma ['sintoma] *nm* symptom.

sintonía [sinto'nia] *nf* (*RADIO*) tuning; *(melodía)* signature tune.

sintonice [sinto'niθe] *etc vb V* **sintonizar**.

sintonizador [sintoniθa'ðor] *nm* (*RADIO*) tuner.

sintonizar [sintoni'θar] *vt* (*RADIO*) to tune (in) to, pick up.

sinuoso, a [si'nwoso, a] *a* (*camino*) winding; *(rumbo)* devious.

sinvergüenza [simber'ɣwenθa] *nm/f* rogue, scoundrel.

sionismo [sjo'nismo] *nm* Zionism.

siquiera [si'kjera] *conj* even if, even though ◆ *ad* at least; **ni** ~ not even.

sirena [si'rena] *nf* siren, mermaid; *(bocina)* siren, hooter.

Siria ['sirja] *nf* Syria.

sirio, a ['sirjo, a] *a, nm/f* Syrian.

sirviendo [sir'ßjendo] *etc vb V* **servir**.

sirviente, a [sir'ßjénte, a] *nm/f* servant.

sisa ['sisa] *nf* petty theft; (*COSTURA*) dart; (*sobaquera*) armhole.

sisar [si'sar] *vt* (*robar*) to thieve; (*COSTURA*) to take in.

sisear [sise'ar] *vt, vi* to hiss.

sismógrafo [sis'moɣrafo] *nm* seismograph.

sistema [sis'tema] *nm* system; *(método)* method; ~ **impositivo** *o* **tributario** taxation, tax system; ~ **pedagógico** educational system; ~ **de alerta inmediata** early-warning system; ~ **binario** (*INFORM*)

binary system; ~ **experto** expert system; ~ **de facturación** (*COM*) invoicing system; ~ **de fondo fijo** (*COM*) imprest system; ~ **de lógica compartida** (*INFORM*) shared logic system; ~ **métrico** metric system; ~ **operativo (en disco)** (*INFORM*) (disk-based) operating system.

sistemático, a [siste'matiko, a] *a* systematic.

sitiar [si'tjar] *vt* to besiege, lay siege to.

sitio ['sitjo] *nm* (*lugar*) place; (*espacio*) room, space; (*MIL*) siege; **¿hay** ~**?** is there any room?; **hay** ~ **de sobra** there's plenty of room.

situación [sitwa'θjon] *nf* situation, position; *(estatus)* position, standing.

situado, a [si'twaðo, a] *a* situated, placed; **estar** ~ (*COM*) to be financially secure.

situar [si'twar] *vt* to place, put; (*edificio*) to locate, situate.

S.L. *abr* (*COM*: = *Sociedad Limitada*) Ltd.

slip [es'lip], *pl* **slips** *nm* pants *pl*, briefs *pl*.

slot [es'lot], *pl* **slots** *nm*: ~ **de expansión** expansion slot.

S.M. *abr* (= *Su Majestad*) HM.

smoking [(e)'smokin] (*pl* ~**s**) *nm* dinner jacket (*Brit*), tuxedo (*US*).

s/n *abr* (= *sin número*) no number.

snob [es'nob] = **esnob**.

SO *abr* (= *suroeste*) SW.

so [so] *excl* whoa!; **¡**~ **burro!** you idiot! ◆ *prep* under.

s/o *abr* (*COM*: = *su orden*) your order.

sobaco [so'ßako] *nm* armpit.

sobado, a [so'ßaðo, a] *a* (*ropa*) worn; *(arrugado)* crumpled; *(libro)* well-thumbed; (*CULIN*: *masa*) short.

sobar [so'ßar] *vt* (*tela*) to finger; (*ropa*) to rumple, mess up; (*músculos*) to rub, massage.

soberanía [soßera'nia] *nf* sovereignty.

soberano, a [soße'rano, a] *a* sovereign; *(fig)* supreme ◆ *nm/f* sovereign; **los** ~**s** the king and queen.

soberbio, a [so'ßerßjo, a] *a* (*orgulloso*) proud; *(altivo)* haughty, arrogant; *(fig)* magnificent, superb ◆ *nf* pride; haughtiness, arrogance; magnificence.

sobornar [soßor'nar] *vt* to bribe.

soborno [so'ßorno] *nm* (*un* ~) bribe; (*el* ~) bribery.

sobra ['soßra] *nf* excess, surplus; ~**s** *nfpl* left-overs, scraps; **de** ~ surplus, extra; **lo sé de** ~ I'm only too aware of it; **tengo de** ~ I've more than enough.

sobradamente [soßraða'mente] *ad* amply; *(saber)* only too well.

sobrado, a [so'ßraðo, a] *a* (*más que suficiente*) more than enough; *(superfluo)* excessive ◆ *ad* too, exceedingly; **sobradas veces** repeatedly.

sobrante [so'ßrante] *a* remaining, extra ◆ *nm* surplus, remainder.

sobrar [so'ßrar] *vt* to exceed, surpass ◆ *vi* (*tener de más*) to be more than enough; (*quedar*) to remain, be left (over).

sobrasada [soßra'saða] *nf* ≈ sausage spread.

sobre ['soßre] *prep* (*gen*) on; (*encima*) on (top of); (*por encima de, arriba de*) over, above; (*más que*) more than; (*además*) in addition to, besides; (*alrededor de*) about; (*porcentaje*) in, out of; (*tema*) about, on ◆ *nm* envelope; ~ **todo** above all; **3** ~ **100** 3 in a 100, 3 out of every 100; **un libro** ~ **Tirso** a book about Tirso; ~ **de ventanilla** window envelope.

sobrecama [soßre'kama] *nf* bedspread.

sobrecapitalice [soßrekapita'liθe] *etc vb V* **sobrecapitalizar**.

sobrecapitalizar [soßrekapitali'θar] *vi* to overcapitalize.

sobrecargar [soßrekar'ɣar] *vt* (*camión*) to overload; (*com*) to surcharge.

sobrecargue [soßre'karɣe] *etc vb V* **sobrecargar**.

sobrecoger [soßreko'xer] *vt* (*sobresaltar*) to startle; (*asustar*) to scare; ~**se** *vr* (*sobresaltarse*) to be startled; (*asustarse*) to get scared; (*quedar impresionado*): ~**se** (**de**) to be overawed (by).

sobrecoja [soßre'koxa] *etc vb V* **sobrecoger**.

sobredosis [soßre'ðosis] *nf inv* overdose.

sobre(e)ntender [soßre(e)nten'der] *vt* to understand; (*adivinar*) to deduce, infer; ~**se** *vr*: **se sobre(e)ntiende que** ... it is implied that ....

sobreescribir [soßreeskri'ßir] *vt* (*inform*) to overwrite.

sobre(e)stimar [soßre(e)sti'mar] *vt* to overestimate.

sobregiro [soßre'xiro] *nm* (*com*) overdraft.

sobrehumano, a [soßreu'mano, a] *a* superhuman.

sobreimprimir [soßreimpri'mir] *vt* (*com*) to merge.

sobrellevar [soßreʎe'ßar] *vt* (*fig*) to bear, endure.

sobremesa [soßre'mesa] *nf* (*después de comer*) sitting on after a meal; (*inform*) desktop; **conversación de** ~ table talk.

sobremodo [soßre'moðo] *ad* very much, enormously.

sobrenatural [soßrenatu'ral] *a* supernatural.

sobrenombre [soßre'nombre] *nm* nickname.

sobrepasar [soßrepa'sar] *vt* to exceed, surpass.

sobrepondré [soßrepon'dre] *etc vb V* **sobreponer**.

sobreponer [soßrepo'ner] *vt* (*poner encima*) to put on top; (*añadir*) to add; ~**se** *vr*: ~**se a** to overcome.

sobreponga [soßre'ponga] *etc vb V* **sobreponer**.

sobreprima [soßre'prima] *nf* (*com*) loading.

sobreproducción [soßreproðuk'θjon] *nf* overproduction.

sobrepuesto [soßre'pwesto], **sobrepuse** [soßre'puse] *etc vb V* **sobreponer**.

sobresaldré [soßresal'dre] *etc*, **sobresalga** [soßre'salɣa] *etc vb V* **sobresalir**.

sobresaliente [soßresa'ljente] *a* projecting; (*fig*) outstanding, excellent; (*univ etc*) first class ◆ *nm* (*univ etc*) first class (mark), distinction.

sobresalir [soßresa'lir] *vi* to project, jut out; (*fig*) to stand out, excel.

sobresaltar [soßresal'tar] *vt* (*asustar*) to scare, frighten; (*sobrecoger*) to startle.

sobresalto [soßre'salto] *nm* (*movimiento*) start; (*susto*) scare; (*turbación*) sudden shock.

sobreseer [soßrese'er] *vt*: ~ **una causa** (*jur*) to stop a case.

sobrestadía [soßresta'ðia] *nf* (*com*) demurrage.

sobretensión [soßreten'sjon] *nf* (*elec*): ~ **transitoria** surge.

sobretodo [soßre'toðo] *nm* overcoat.

sobrevendré [soßreßen'dre] *etc*, **sobrevenga** [soßre'ßenga] *etc vb V* **sobrevenir**.

sobrevenir [soßreße'nir] *vi* (*ocurrir*) to happen (unexpectedly); (*resultar*) to follow, ensue.

sobreviene [soßre'ßjene] *etc*, **sobrevine** [soßre'ßine] *etc vb V* **sobrevenir**.

sobreviviente [soßreßi'ßjente] *a* surviving ◆ *nm/f* survivor.

sobrevivir [soßreßi'ßir] *vi* to survive; (*persona*) to outlive; (*objeto etc*) to outlast.

sobrevolar [soßreßo'lar] *vt* to fly over.

sobrevuele [soßre'ßwele] *etc vb V* **sobrevolar**.

sobriedad [soßrje'ðað] *nf* sobriety, soberness; (*moderación*) moderation, restraint.

sobrino, a [so'ßrino, a] *nm/f* nephew/niece.

sobrio, a ['soßrjo, a] *a* (*moderado*) moderate, restrained.

socarrón, ona [soka'rron, ona] *a* (*sarcástico*) sarcastic, ironic(al).

socavar [soka'ßar] *vt* to undermine; (*excavar*) to dig underneath *o* below.

socavón [soka'ßon] *nm* (*en mina*) gallery; (*hueco*) hollow; (*en la calle*) hole.

sociable [so'θjaßle] *a* (*persona*) sociable, friendly; (*animal*) social.

social [so'θjal] *a* social; (*com*) company *cpd*.

socialdemócrata [soθjalde'mokrata] *nm/f*

social democrat.

socialdemocrático, a [soθjaldemo'kratiko, a] a social-democratic.

socialice [soθja'liθe] etc vb V **socializar**.

socialista [soθja'lista] a, nm/f socialist.

socializar [soθjali'θar] vt to socialize.

sociedad [soθje'ðað] nf society; (COM) company; ~ **de ahorro y préstamo** savings and loan society; ~ **anónima (S.A.)** limited company (Ltd) (Brit), incorporated company (Inc) (US); ~ **de beneficiencia** friendly society (Brit), benefit association (US); ~ **de cartera** investment trust; ~ **comanditaria** (COM) co-ownership; ~ **conjunta** (COM) joint venture; ~ **inmobiliaria** building society (Brit), savings and loan (society) (US); ~ **de responsabilidad limitada** (COM) private limited company.

socio, a ['soθjo, a] nm/f (miembro) member; (COM) partner; ~ **activo** active partner; ~ **capitalista** o **comanditario** sleeping o silent (US) partner.

socioeconómico, a [soθjoeko'nomiko, a] a socio-economic.

sociología [soθjolo'xia] nf sociology.

sociólogo, a [so'θjoloɣo, a] nm/f sociologist.

socorrer [soko'rrer] vt to help.

socorrido, a [soko'rriðo, a] a (tienda) well-stocked; (útil) handy; (persona) helpful.

socorrista [soko'rrista] nm/f first aider; (en piscina, playa) lifeguard.

socorro [so'korro] nm (ayuda) help, aid; (MIL) relief; ¡~! help!

soda ['soða] nf (sosa) soda; (bebida) soda (water).

soez [so'eθ] a dirty, obscene.

sofá [so'fa] nm sofa, settee.

sofá-cama [so'fakama] nm studio couch, sofa bed.

Sofia ['sofja] nf Sofia.

sofisticación [sofistika'θjon] nf sophistication.

sofocado, a [sofo'kaðo, a] a: **estar** ~ (fig) to be out of breath; (ahogarse) to feel stifled.

sofocar [sofo'kar] vt to suffocate; (apagar) to smother, put out; ~**se** vr to suffocate; (fig) to blush, feel embarrassed.

sofoco [so'foko] nm suffocation; (azoro) embarrassment.

sofocón [sofo'kon] nm: **llevarse** o **pasar un** ~ to have a sudden shock.

sofreír [sofre'ir] vt to fry lightly.

sofría [so'fria] etc, **sofriendo** [so'frjendo] etc, **sofrito** [so'frito] vb V **sofreír**.

soft(ware) ['sof(wer)] nm (INFORM) software.

soga ['soɣa] nf rope.

sois [sois] vb V **ser**.

soja ['soxa] nf soya.

sojuzgar [soxuθ'ɣar] vt to subdue, rule despotically.

sojuzgue [so'xuθɣe] etc vb V **sojuzgar**.

sol [sol] nm sun; (luz) sunshine, sunlight; ~ **naciente/poniente** rising/setting sun; **tomar el** ~ to sunbathe; **hace** ~ it is sunny.

solace [so'laθe] etc vb V **solazar**.

solamente [sola'mente] ad only, just.

solapa [so'lapa] nf (de chaqueta) lapel; (de libro) jacket.

solapado, a [sola'paðo, a] a sly, underhand.

solar [so'lar] a solar, sun cpd ♦ nm (terreno) plot (of ground); (local) undeveloped site.

solaz [so'laθ] nm recreation, relaxation.

solazar [sola'θar] vt (divertir) to amuse; ~**se** vr to enjoy o.s., relax.

soldada [sol'daða] nf pay.

soldado [sol'daðo] nm soldier; ~ **raso** private.

soldador [solda'ðor] nm soldering iron; (persona) welder.

soldar [sol'dar] vt to solder, weld; (unir) to join, unite.

soleado, a [sole'aðo, a] a sunny.

soledad [sole'ðað] nf solitude; (estado infeliz) loneliness.

solemne [so'lemne] a solemn; (tontería) utter; (error) complete.

solemnidad [solemni'ðað] nf solemnity.

soler [so'ler] vi to be in the habit of, be accustomed to; **suele salir a las ocho** she usually goes out at 8 o'clock; **solíamos ir todos los años** we used to go every year.

solera [so'lera] nf (tradición) tradition; **vino de** ~ vintage wine.

solicitar [soliθi'tar] vt (permiso) to ask for, seek; (puesto) to apply for; (votos) to canvass for; (atención) to attract; (persona) to pursue, chase after.

solícito, a [so'liθito, a] a (diligente) diligent; (cuidadoso) careful.

solicitud [soliθi'tuð] nf (calidad) great care; (petición) request; (a un puesto) application.

solidaridad [soliðari'ðað] nf solidarity; **por** ~ **con** (POL etc) out of o in solidarity with.

solidario, a [soli'ðarjo, a] a (participación) joint, common; (compromiso) mutually binding; **hacerse** ~ **de** to declare one's solidarity with.

solidez [soli'ðeθ] nf solidity.

sólido, a ['soliðo, a] a solid; (TEC) solidly made; (bien construido) well built.

soliloquio [soli'lokjo] nm soliloquy.

solista [so'lista] nm/f soloist.

solitario, a [soli'tarjo, a] a (persona) lonely, solitary; (lugar) lonely, desolate ♦ nm/f (*reclusa*) recluse; (*en la sociedad*) loner ◆ *nm* solitaire ◆ *nf* tapeworm.

soliviantar [soliβjan'tar] *vt* to stir up, rouse (to revolt); (*enojar*) to anger; (*sacar de quicio*) to exasperate.

solo, a ['solo, a] *a* (*único*) single, sole; (*sin compañía*) alone; (*MUS*) solo; (*solitario*) lonely; **hay una sola dificultad** there is just one difficulty; **a solas** alone, by o.s.

sólo ['solo] *ad* only, just; (*exclusivamente*) solely; **tan** ~ only just.

solomillo [solo'miʎo] *nm* sirloin.

soltar [sol'tar] *vt* (*dejar ir*) to let go of; (*desprender*) to unfasten, loosen; (*librar*) to release, set free; (*amarras*) to cast off; (*AUTO: freno etc*) to release; (*suspiro*) to heave; (*risa etc*) to let out; ~**se** *vr* (*desanudarse*) to come undone; (*desprenderse*) to come off; (*adquirir destreza*) to become expert; (*en idioma*) to become fluent.

soltero, a [sol'tero, a] *a* single, unmarried ◆ *nm* bachelor ◆ *nf* single woman, spinster.

solterón [solte'ron] *nm* confirmed bachelor.

solterona [solte'rona] *nf* spinster, maiden lady; (*pey*) old maid.

soltura [sol'tura] *nf* looseness, slackness; (*de los miembros*) agility, ease of movement; (*en el hablar*) fluency, ease.

soluble [so'luβle] *a* (*QUÍMICA*) soluble; (*problema*) solvable; ~ **en agua** soluble in water.

solución [solu'θjon] *nf* solution; ~ **de continuidad** break in continuity.

solucionar [soluθjo'nar] *vt* (*problema*) to solve; (*asunto*) to settle, resolve.

solvencia [sol'βenθja] *nf* (*COM: estado*) solvency; (: *acción*) settlement, payment.

solventar [solβen'tar] *vt* (*pagar*) to settle, pay; (*resolver*) to resolve.

solvente [sol'βente] *a* solvent, free of debt.

solloce [so'ʎoθe] *etc vb V* **sollozar**.

sollozar [soʎo'θar] *vi* to sob.

sollozo [so'ʎoθo] *nm* sob.

Somalia [so'malja] *nf* Somalia.

sombra ['sombra] *nf* shadow; (*como protección*) shade; ~**s** *nfpl* darkness *sg*, shadows; **sin** ~ **de duda** without a shadow of doubt; **tener buena/mala** ~ (*suerte*) to be lucky/unlucky; (*carácter*) to be likeable/disagreeable.

sombrero [som'brero] *nm* hat; ~ **hongo** bowler (hat), derby (*US*); ~ **de copa** *o* **de pelo** (*AM*) top hat.

sombrilla [som'briʎa] *nf* parasol, sunshade.

sombrío, a [som'brio, a] *a* (*oscuro*) shady; (*fig*) sombre, sad; (*persona*) gloomy.

somero, a [so'mero, a] *a* superficial.

someter [some'ter] *vt* (*país*) to conquer; (*persona*) to subject to one's will; (*informe*) to present, submit; ~**se** *vr* to give

in, yield, submit; ~**se a** to submit to; ~**se a una operación** to undergo an operation.

sometimiento [someti'mjento] *nm* (*estado*) submission; (*acción*) presentation.

somier [so'mjer], *pl* **somiers** *nm* spring mattress.

somnífero [som'nifero] *nm* sleeping pill *o* tablet.

somnolencia [somno'lenθja] *nf* sleepiness, drowsiness.

somos ['somos] *vb V* **ser**.

son [son] *vb V* **ser** ◆ *nm* sound; **en** ~ **de broma** as a joke.

sonado, a [so'naðo, a] *a* (*comentado*) talked-of; (*famoso*) famous; (*COM: pey*) hyped(-up).

sonajero [sona'xero] *nm* (baby's) rattle.

sonambulismo [sonambu'lismo] *nm* sleepwalking.

sonámbulo, a [so'nambulo, a] *nm/f* sleepwalker.

sonar [so'nar] *vt* (*campana*) to ring; (*trompeta, sirena*) to blow ◆ *vi* to sound; (*hacer ruido*) to make a noise; (*LING*) to be sounded, be pronounced; (*ser conocido*) to sound familiar; (*campana*) to ring; (*reloj*) to strike, chime; ~**se** *vr:* ~**se (la nariz)** to blow one's nose; **es un nombre que suena** it's a name that's in the news; **me suena ese nombre** that name rings a bell.

sonda ['sonda] *nf* (*NAUT*) sounding; (*TEC*) bore, drill; (*MED*) probe.

sondear [sonde'ar] *vt* to sound; to bore (into), drill; to probe, sound; (*fig*) to sound out.

sondeo [son'deo] *nm* sounding; boring, drilling; (*encuesta*) poll, enquiry; ~ **de la opinión pública** public opinion poll.

sónico, a ['soniko, a] *a* sonic, sound *cpd*.

sonido [so'niðo] *nm* sound.

sonoro, a [so'noro, a] *a* sonorous; (*resonante*) loud, resonant; (*LING*) voiced; **efectos** ~**s** sound effects.

sonreír [sonre'ir] *vi*, **sonreírse** *vr* to smile.

sonría [son'ria] *etc*, **sonriendo** [son'rjendo] *etc vb V* **sonreír**.

sonriente [son'rjente] *a* smiling.

sonrisa [son'risa] *nf* smile.

sonrojar [sonro'xar] *vt:* ~ **a uno** to make sb blush; ~**se** *vr:* ~**se (de)** to blush (at).

sonrojo [son'roxo] *nm* blush.

sonsacar [sonsa'kar] *vt* to wheedle, coax; ~ **a uno** to pump sb for information.

sonsaque [son'sake] *etc vb V* **sonsacar**.

sonsonete [sonso'nete] *nm* (*golpecitos*) tap(ping); (*voz monótona*) monotonous delivery, singsong (voice).

soñador, a [soɲa'ðor, a] *nm/f* dreamer.

soñar [so'ɲar] *vt*, *vi* to dream; ~ **con** to dream about *o* of; **soñé contigo anoche** I dreamed about you last night.

soñoliento, a [soɲo'ljento, a] *a* sleepy, drowsy.

sopa ['sopa] *nf* soup; ~ **de fideos** noodle soup.

sopero, a [so'pero, a] *a* (*plato, cuchara*) soup *cpd* ♦ *nm* soup plate ♦ *nf* soup tureen.

sopesar [sope'sar] *vt* to try the weight of; (*fig*) to weigh up.

sopetón [sope'ton] *nm*: **de** ~ suddenly, unexpectedly.

soplar [so'plar] *vt* (*polvo*) to blow away, blow off; (*inflar*) to blow up; (*vela*) to blow out; (*ayudar a recordar*) to prompt; (*birlar*) to nick; (*delatar*) to split on ♦ *vi* to blow; (*delatar*) to squeal; (*beber*) to booze, bend the elbow.

soplete [so'plete] *nm* blowlamp; ~ **soldador** welding torch.

soplo ['soplo] *nm* blow, puff; (*de viento*) puff, gust.

soplón, ona [so'plon, ona] *nm/f* (*fam: chismoso*) telltale; (: *de policía*) informer, grass.

soponcio [so'ponθjo] *nm* dizzy spell.

sopor [so'por] *nm* drowsiness.

soporífero, a [sopo'rifero, a] *a* sleep-inducing; (*fig*) soporific ♦ *nm* sleeping pill.

soportable [sopor'taβle] *a* bearable.

soportar [sopor'tar] *vt* to bear, carry; (*fig*) to bear, put up with.

soporte [so'porte] *nm* support; (*fig*) pillar, support; (*INFORM*) medium; ~ **de entrada/ salida** input/output medium.

soprano [so'prano] *nf* soprano.

sor [sor] *nf*: **S~ María** Sister Mary.

sorber [sor'βer] *vt* (*chupar*) to sip; (*inhalar*) to sniff, inhale; (*absorber*) to soak up, absorb.

sorbete [sor'βete] *nm* sherbet.

sorbo ['sorβo] *nm* (*trago*) gulp, swallow; (*chupada*) sip; **beber a** ~**s** to sip.

sordera [sor'ðera] *nf* deafness.

sórdido, a ['sorðiðo, a] *a* dirty, squalid.

sordo, a ['sorðo, a] *a* (*persona*) deaf; (*ruido*) dull; (*LING*) voiceless ♦ *nm/f* deaf person; **quedarse** ~ to go deaf.

sordomudo, a [sorðo'muðo, a] *a* deaf and dumb ♦ *nm/f* deaf-mute.

soriano, a [so'rjano, a] *a* of *o* from Soria ♦ *nm/f* native *o* inhabitant of Soria.

sorna ['sorna] *nf* (*malicia*) slyness; (*tono burlón*) sarcastic tone.

soroche [so'rotʃe] *nm* (*AM MED*) mountain sickness.

sorprendente [sorpren'dente] *a* surprising.

sorprender [sorpren'der] *vt* to surprise; (*asombrar*) to amaze; (*sobresaltar*) to startle; (*coger desprevenido*) to catch unawares; ~**se** *vr*: ~**se** (**de**) to be surprised *o* amazed (at).

sorpresa [sor'presa] *nf* surprise.

sorpresivo, a [sorpre'siβo, a] *a* (*AM*) surprising; (*imprevisto*) sudden.

sortear [sorte'ar] *vt* to draw lots for; (*rifar*) to raffle; (*dificultad*) to dodge, avoid.

sorteo [sor'teo] *nm* (*en lotería*) draw; (*rifa*) raffle.

sortija [sor'tixa] *nf* ring; (*rizo*) ringlet, curl.

sortilegio [sorti'lexjo] *nm* (*hechicería*) sorcery; (*hechizo*) spell.

sosegado, a [sose'xaðo, a] *a* quiet, calm.

sosegar [sose'xar] *vt* to quieten, calm; (*el ánimo*) to reassure ♦ *vi* to rest.

sosegué [sose'xe], **soseguemos** [sose-'xemos] *etc vb* V **sosegar**.

sosiego [so'sjexo] *etc vb* V **sosegar** ♦ *nm* quiet(ness), calm(ness).

sosiegue [so'sjexe] *etc vb* V **sosegar**.

soslayo [sos'lajo]: **de** ~ *ad* obliquely, sideways; **mirar de** ~ to look out of the corner of one's eye (at).

soso, a ['soso, a] *a* (*CULIN*) tasteless; (*fig*) dull, uninteresting.

sospecha [sos'petʃa] *nf* suspicion.

sospechar [sospe'tʃar] *vt* to suspect ♦ *vi*: ~ **de** to be suspicious of.

sospechoso, a [sospe'tʃoso, a] *a* suspicious; (*testimonio, opinión*) suspect ♦ *nm/f* suspect.

sostén [sos'ten] *nm* (*apoyo*) support; (*sujetador*) bra; (*alimentación*) sustenance, food.

sostendré [sosten'dre] *etc vb* V **sostener**.

sostener [soste'ner] *vt* to support; (*mantener*) to keep up, maintain; (*alimentar*) to sustain, keep going; ~**se** *vr* to support o.s.; (*seguir*) to continue, remain.

sostenga [sos'tenga] *etc vb* V **sostener**.

sostenido, a [soste'niðo, a] *a* continuous, sustained; (*prolongado*) prolonged; (*MUS*) sharp ♦ *nm* (*MUS*) sharp.

sostuve [sos'tuβe] *etc vb* V **sostener**.

sotana [so'tana] *nf* (*REL*) cassock.

sótano ['sotano] *nm* basement.

sotavento [sota'βento] *nm* (*NAUT*) lee, leeward.

soterrar [sote'rrar] *vt* to bury; (*esconder*) to hide away.

sotierre [so'tjerre] *etc vb* V **soterrar**.

soviético, a [so'βjetiko, a] *a*, *nm/f* Soviet; **los** ~**s** the Soviets, the Russians.

soy [soi] *vb* V **ser**.

spooling [es'pulin] *nm* (*INFORM*) spooling.

sport [es'por(t)] *nm* sport.

spot [es'pot], *pl* **spot** *nm* (*publicitario*) ad.

Sr. *abr* (= *Señor*) Mr.

Sra. *abr* (= *Señora*) Mrs.

S.R.C. *abr* (= *se ruega contestación*) R.S.V.P.

Sres., Srs. *abr* (= *Señores*) Messrs.

Sri Lanka [sri'lanka] *nm* Sri Lanka.

Srta. *abr* = **Señorita.**

SS *abr* (= *Santos, Santas*) SS.

S.S. *abr* (*REL*: = *Su Santidad*) H.H.

ss. *abr* (= *siguientes*) foll.

Sta. *abr* (= *Santa*) St; (= *Señorita*) Miss.

stárter [es'tarter] *nm* (*AUTO*) self-starter, starting motor.

status ['status, es'tatus] *nm inv* status.

Sto. *abr* (= *Santo*) St.

su [su] *pron* (*de él*) his; (*de ella*) her; (*de una cosa*) its; (*de ellos, ellas*) their; (*de usted, ustedes*) your.

suave ['swaße] *a* gentle; (*superficie*) smooth; (*trabajo*) easy; (*música, voz*) soft, sweet; (*clima, sabor*) mild.

suavice [swa'ßiθe] *etc vb* V **suavizar.**

suavidad [swaßi'ðað] *nf* gentleness; (*de superficie*) smoothness; (*de música*) softness, sweetness.

suavizar [swaßi'θar] *vt* to soften; (*quitar la aspereza*) to smooth (out); (*pendiente*) to ease; (*colores*) to tone down; (*carácter*) to mellow; (*dureza*) to temper.

subalimentado, a [sußalimen'taðo, a] *a* undernourished.

subalterno, a [sußal'terno, a] *a* (*importancia*) secondary; (*personal*) minor, auxiliary ◆ *nm* subordinate.

subarrendar [sußarren'dar] *vt* (*COM*) to lease back.

subarriendo [sußa'rrjendo] *nm* (*COM*) leaseback.

subasta [su'ßasta] *nf* auction; **poner en** *o* **sacar a pública** ~ to put up for public auction; ~ **a la rebaja** Dutch auction.

subastador, a [sußasta'ðor, a] *nm/f* auctioneer.

subastar [sußas'tar] *vt* to auction (off).

subcampeón, ona [sußkampe'on, ona] *nm/f* runner-up.

subconsciente [sußkons'θjente] *a* subconscious.

subcontratar [sußkontra'tar] *vt* (*COM*) to subcontract.

subcontrato [sußkon'trato] *nm* (*COM*) subcontract.

subdesarrollado, a [sußðesarro'ʎaðo, a] *a* underdeveloped.

subdesarrollo [sußðesa'rroʎo] *nm* underdevelopment.

subdirector, a [sußðirek'tor, a] *nm/f* assistant *o* deputy manager.

subdirectorio [sußðirek'torjo] *nm* (*INFORM*) subdirectory.

súbdito, a ['sußðito, a] *nm/f* subject.

subdividir [sußðißi'ðir] *vt* to subdivide.

subempleo [sußem'pleo] *nm* underemployment.

subestimar [sußesti'mar] *vt* to underestimate, underrate.

subido, a [su'ßiðo, a] *a* (*color*) bright, strong; (*precio*) high ◆ *nf* (*de montaña etc*) ascent, climb; (*de precio*) rise, increase; (*pendiente*) slope, hill.

subíndice [su'ßindiθe] *nm* (*INFORM, TIP*) subscript.

subir [su'ßir] *vt* (*objeto*) to raise, lift up; (*cuesta, calle*) to go up; (*colina, montaña*) to climb; (*precio*) to raise, put up; (*empleado etc*) to promote ◆ *vi* to go/come up; (*a un coche*) to get in; (*a un autobús, tren*) to get on; (*precio*) to rise, go up; (*en el empleo*) to be promoted; (*río, marea*) to rise; ~**se** *vr* to get up, climb; ~**se a un coche** to get in(to) a car.

súbito, a ['sußito, a] *a* (*repentino*) sudden; (*imprevisto*) unexpected.

subjetivo, a [sußxe'tißo, a] *a* subjective.

subjuntivo [sußxun'tißo] *nm* subjunctive (mood).

sublevación [sußleßa'θjon] *nf* revolt, rising.

sublevar [sußle'ßar] *vt* to rouse to revolt; ~**se** *vr* to revolt, rise.

sublimar [sußli'mar] *vt* (*persona*) to exalt; (*deseos etc*) to sublimate.

sublime [su'ßlime] *a* sublime.

submarino, a [sußma'rino, a] *a* underwater ◆ *nm* submarine.

subnormal [sußnor'mal] *a* subnormal ◆ *nm/f* subnormal person.

suboficial [sußofi'θjal] *nm* non-commissioned officer.

subordinado, a [sußorði'naðo, a] *a, nm/f* subordinate.

subproducto [sußpro'ðukto] *nm* by-product.

subrayado [sußra'jaðo] *nm* underlining.

subrayar [sußra'jar] *vt* to underline; (*recalcar*) to underline, emphasize.

subrepticio, a [sußrep'tiθjo, a] *a* surreptitious.

subrutina [sußru'tina] *nf* (*INFORM*) subroutine.

subsanar [sußsa'nar] *vt* (*reparar*) to make good; (*perdonar*) to excuse; (*sobreponerse a*) to overcome.

subscribir [sußskri'ßir] *vt* = **suscribir.**

subscrito [sußs'krito] *pp de* **subscribir.**

subsecretario, a [sußsekre'tarjo, a] *nm/f* undersecretary, assistant secretary.

subsidiario, a [sußsi'ðjarjo, a] *a* subsidiary.

subsidio [sußsi'ðjo] *nm* (*ayuda*) aid, financial help; (*subvención*) subsidy, grant; (*de enfermedad, paro etc*) benefit, allowance.

subsistencia [sußsis'tenθja] *nf* subsistence.

subsistir [sußsis'tir] *vi* to subsist; (*vivir*) to live; (*sobrevivir*) to survive, endure.

subsuelo [sußʼswelo] *nm* subsoil.

subterfugio [sußter'fuxjo] *nm* subterfuge.

subterráneo, a [sußte'rraneo, a] *a* underground, subterranean ◆ *nm* underpass, underground passage; (*AM*) underground railway, subway (*US*).

subtítulo [suß'titulo] *nm* subtitle, subheading.

suburbano, a [sußur'ßano, a] *a* suburban.

suburbio [su'ßurßjo] *nm* (*barrio*) slum quarter; (*afueras*) suburbs *pl.*

subvención [sußßen'θjon] *nf* subsidy, subvention, grant; ~ **estatal** state subsidy *o* support; ~ **para la inversión** (*COM*) investment grant.

subvencionar [sußßenθjo'nar] *vt* to subsidize.

subversión [sußßer'sjon] *nf* subversion.

subversivo, a [sußßer'sißo, a] *a* subversive.

subyacente [sußja'θente] *a* underlying.

subyugar [sußju'xar] *vt* (*país*) to subjugate, subdue; (*enemigo*) to overpower; (*voluntad*) to dominate.

subyugue [sub'juxe] *etc vb V* **subyugar**.

succión [suk'θjon] *nf* suction.

succionar [sukθjo'nar] *vt* (*sorber*) to suck; (*TEC*) to absorb, soak up.

sucedáneo, a [suθe'ðaneo, a] *a* substitute ♦ *nm* substitute (food).

suceder [suθe'ðer] *vi* to happen; ~ **a** (*seguir*) to succeed, follow; **lo que sucede es que** ... the fact is that ...; ~ **al trono** to succeed to the throne.

sucesión [suθe'sjon] *nf* succession; (*serie*) sequence, series; (*hijos*) issue, offspring.

sucesivamente [suθesißa'mente] *ad:* **y así** ~ and so on.

sucesivo, a [suθe'sißo, a] *a* successive, following; **en lo** ~ in future, from now on.

suceso [su'θeso] *nm* (*hecho*) event, happening; (*incidente*) incident.

sucesor, a [suθe'sor, a] *nm/f* successor; (*heredero*) heir/heiress.

suciedad [suθje'ðað] *nf* (*estado*) dirtiness; (*mugre*) dirt, filth.

sucinto, a [su'θinto, a] *a* (*conciso*) succinct, concise.

sucio, a [su'θjo, a] *a* dirty; (*mugriento*) grimy; (*manchado*) grubby; (*borroso*) smudged; (*conciencia*) bad; (*conducta*) vile; (*táctica*) dirty, unfair.

Sucre ['sukre] *n* Sucre.

suculento, a [suku'lento, a] *a* (*sabroso*) tasty; (*jugoso*) succulent.

sucumbir [sukum'bir] *vi* to succumb.

sucursal [sukur'sal] *nf* branch (office); (*filial*) subsidiary.

Sudáfrica [su'ðafrika] *nf* South Africa.

sudafricano, a [suðafri'kano, a] *a, nm/f* South African.

Sudamérica [suða'merika] *nf* South America.

sudamericano, a [suðameri'kano, a] *a, nm/f* South American.

sudanés, esa [suða'nes, esa] *a, nm/f* Sudanese.

sudar [su'ðar] *vt, vi* to sweat; (*BOT*) to ooze, give out *o* off.

sudeste [su'ðeste] *a* south-east(ern); (*rumbo, viento*) south-easterly ♦ *nm* south-east; (*viento*) south-east wind.

sudoeste [suðo'este] *a* south-west(ern); (*rumbo, viento*) south-westerly ♦ *nm* south-west; (*viento*) south-west wind.

sudor [su'ðor] *nm* sweat.

sudoroso, a [suðo'roso, a] *a* sweaty, sweating.

Suecia ['sweθja] *nf* Sweden.

sueco, a ['sweko, a] *a* Swedish ♦ *nm/f* Swede ♦ *nm* (*LING*) Swedish; **hacerse el** ~ to pretend not to hear *o* understand.

suegro, a ['swexro, a] *nm/f* father-/mother-in-law; **los** ~**s** one's in-laws.

suela ['swela] *nf* (*de zapato, tb pescado*) sole.

sueldo ['sweldo] *etc vb V* **soldar** ♦ *nm* pay, wage(s) (*pl*).

suelo ['swelo] *etc vb V* **soler** ♦ *nm* (*tierra*) ground; (*de casa*) floor.

suelto, a ['swelto, a] *etc vb V* **soltar** ♦ *a* loose; (*libre*) free; (*separado*) detached; (*ágil*) quick, agile; (*corriente*) fluent, flowing ♦ *nm* (*loose*) change, small change; **está muy** ~ **en inglés** he is very good at *o* fluent in English.

suene ['swene] *etc vb V* **sonar**.

sueño ['sweɲo] *etc vb V* **soñar** ♦ *nm* sleep; (*somnolencia*) sleepiness, drowsiness; (*lo soñado, fig*) dream; ~ **pesado** *o* **profundo** deep *o* heavy sleep; **tener** ~ to be sleepy.

suero ['swero] *nm* (*MED*) serum; (*de leche*) whey.

suerte ['swerte] *nf* (*fortuna*) luck; (*azar*) chance; (*destino*) fate, destiny; (*condición*) lot; (*género*) sort, kind; **lo echaron a** ~**s** they drew lots *o* tossed up for it; **tener** ~ to be lucky; **de otra** ~ otherwise, if not; **de** ~ **que** so that, in such a way that.

suéter ['sweter], *pl* **suéters** *nm* sweater.

suficiencia [sufi'θjenθja] *nf* (*cabida*) sufficiency; (*idoneidad*) suitability; (*aptitud*) adequacy.

suficiente [sufi'θjente] *a* enough, sufficient.

sufijo [su'fixo] *nm* suffix.

sufragar [sufra'xar] *vt* (*ayudar*) to help; (*gastos*) to meet; (*proyecto*) to pay for.

sufragio [su'fraxjo] *nm* (*voto*) vote; (*derecho de voto*) suffrage.

sufrague [su'fraxe] *etc vb V* **sufragar**.

sufrido, a [su'friðo, a] *a* (*de carácter fuerte*) tough; (*paciente*) long-suffering; (*tela*) hard-wearing; (*color*) that does not show the dirt; (*marido*) complaisant.

sufrimiento [sufri'mjento] *nm* suffering.

sufrir [su'frir] *vt* (*padecer*) to suffer; (*soportar*) to bear, stand, put up with; (*apoyar*) to hold up, support ♦ *vi* to suffer.

sugerencia [suxe'renθja] *nf* suggestion.

sugerir [suxe'rir] *vt* to suggest; (*sutilmente*) to hint; (*idea: incitar*) to prompt.

sugestión [suxes'tjon] *nf* suggestion; (*sutil*) hint; (*poder*) hypnotic power.

sugestionar [suxestjo'nar] *vt* to influence.

sugestivo, a [suxes'tiβo, a] *a* stimulating; (*atractivo*) attractive; (*fascinante*) fascinating.

sugiera [su'xjera] *etc*, **sugiriendo** [suxi'rjendo] *etc vb* V **sugerir**.

suicida [sui'θiða] *a* suicidal ♦ *nm/f* suicidal person; (*muerto*) suicide, person who has committed suicide.

suicidarse [suiθi'ðarse] *vr* to commit suicide, kill o.s.

suicidio [sui'θiðjo] *nm* suicide.

Suiza ['swiθa] *nf* Switzerland.

suizo, a ['swiθo, a] *a, nm/f* Swiss ♦ *nm* sugared bun.

sujeción [suxe'θjon] *nf* subjection.

sujetador [suxeta'ðor] *nm* fastener, clip; (*prenda femenina*) bra, brassiere.

sujetapapeles [suxetapa'peles] *nm inv* paper clip.

sujetar [suxe'tar] *vt* (*fijar*) to fasten; (*detener*) to hold down; (*fig*) to subject, subjugate; (*pelo etc*) to keep *o* hold in place; (*papeles*) to fasten together; ~**se** *vr* to subject o.s.

sujeto, a [su'xeto, a] *a* fastened, secure ♦ *nm* subject; (*individuo*) individual; (*fam: tipo*) fellow, character, type, guy (*US*); ~ **a** subject to.

sulfurar [sulfu'rar] *vt* (*TEC*) to sulphurate; (*sacar de quicio*) to annoy; ~**se** *vr* (*enojarse*) to get riled, see red, blow up.

sulfuro [sul'furo] *nm* sulphide.

suma ['suma] *nf* (*cantidad*) total, sum; (*de dinero*) sum; (*acto*) adding (up), addition; **en** ~ in short; ~ **y sigue** (*COM*) carry forward.

sumador [suma'ðor] *nm* (*INFORM*) adder.

sumamente [suma'mente] *ad* extremely, exceedingly.

sumar [su'mar] *vt* to add (up); (*reunir*) to collect, gather ♦ *vi* to add up.

sumario, a [su'marjo, a] *a* brief, concise ♦ *nm* summary.

sumergir [sumer'xir] *vt* to submerge; (*hundir*) to sink; (*bañar*) to immerse, dip; ~**se** *vr* (*hundirse*) to sink beneath the surface.

sumerja [su'merxa] *etc vb* V **sumergir**.

sumidero [sumi'ðero] *nm* drain, sewer; (*TEC*) sump.

suministrador, a [suministra'ðor, a] *nm/f* supplier.

suministrar [suminis'trar] *vt* to supply, provide.

suministro [sumi'nistro] *nm* supply; (*acto*) supplying, providing.

sumir [su'mir] *vt* to sink, submerge; (*fig*) to plunge; ~**se** *vr* (*objeto*) to sink; ~**se en el estudio** to become absorbed in one's studies.

sumisión [sumi'sjon] *nf* (*acto*) submission; (*calidad*) submissiveness, docility.

sumiso, a [su'miso, a] *a* submissive, docile.

súmmum ['sumum] *nm inv* (*fig*) height.

sumo, a ['sumo, a] *a* great, extreme; (*mayor*) highest, supreme; **a lo** ~ at most.

suntuoso, a [sun'twoso, a] *a* sumptuous, magnificent; (*lujoso*) lavish.

sup. *abr* (= *superior*) sup.

supe ['supe] *etc vb* V **saber**.

supeditar [supeði'tar] *vt* to subordinate; (*sojuzgar*) to subdue; (*oprimir*) to oppress; ~**se** *vr:* ~**se a** to subject o.s. to.

super... [super] *pref* super..., over....

súper ['super] *a* (*fam*) super, great.

superable [supe'raβle] *a* (*dificultad*) surmountable; (*tarea*) that can be performed.

superar [supe'rar] *vt* (*sobreponerse a*) to overcome; (*rebasar*) to surpass, do better than; (*pasar*) to go beyond; (*marca, récord*) to break; (*etapa: dejar atrás*) to get past; ~**se** *vr* to excel o.s.

superávit [supe'raβit], *pl* **superávits** *nm* surplus.

superchería [supertʃe'ria] *nf* fraud, trick, swindle.

superficial [superfi'θjal] *a* superficial; (*medida*) surface *cpd*.

superficie [super'fiθje] *nf* surface; (*área*) area.

superfluo, a [su'perflwo, a] *a* superfluous.

superíndice [supe'rindiθe] *nm* (*INFORM, TIP*) superscript.

superintendente [superinten'dente] *nm/f* supervisor, superintendent.

superior [supe'rjor] *a* (*piso, clase*) upper; (*temperatura, número, nivel*) higher; (*mejor: calidad, producto*) superior, better ♦ *nm/f* superior.

superiora [supe'rjora] *nf* (*REL*) mother superior.

superioridad [superjori'ðað] *nf* superiority.

supermercado [supermer'kaðo] *nm* supermarket.

superpoblación [superpoβla'θjon] *nf* overpopulation; (*congestionamiento*) overcrowding.

superponer [superpo'ner] *vt* (*INFORM*) to overstrike.

superposición [superposi'θjon] *nf* (*en impresora*) overstrike.

superpotencia [superpo'tenθja] *nf* superpower, great power.

superproducción [superproðuk'θjon] *nf* overproduction.

supersónico, a [super'soniko, a] *a* supersonic.

superstición [supersti'θjon] *nf* superstition.

supersticioso, a [supersti'θjoso, a] *a* superstitious.

supervisar [superßi'sar] *vt* to supervise; (*COM*) to superintend.

supervisor, a [superßi'sor, a] *nm/f* supervisor.

supervivencia [superßi'ßenθja] *nf* survival.

suplantar [suplan'tar] *vt* (*persona*) to supplant; (*hacerse pasar por otro*) to take the place of.

suplementario, a [suplemen'tarjo, a] *a* supplementary.

suplemento [suple'mento] *nm* supplement.

suplencia [su'plenθja] *nf* substitution, replacement; (*etapa*) period during which one deputizes *etc*.

suplente [su'plente] *a* substitute; (*disponible*) reserve ♦ *nm/f* substitute.

supletorio, a [suple'torjo, a] *a* supplementary; (*adicional*) extra ♦ *nm* supplement; **mesa supletoria** spare table.

súplica ['suplika] *nf* request; (*REL*) supplication; (*JUR*: *instancia*) petition; ~s *nfpl* entreaties.

suplicar [supli'kar] *vt* (*cosa*) to beg (for), plead for; (*persona*) to beg, plead with; (*JUR*) to appeal to, petition.

suplicio [su'pliθjo] *nm* torture; (*tormento*) torment; (*emoción*) anguish; (*experiencia penosa*) ordeal.

suplique [su'plike] *etc vb V* **suplicar**.

suplir [su'plir] *vt* (*compensar*) to make good, make up for; (*reemplazar*) to replace, substitute ♦ *vi*: ~ **a** to take the place of, substitute for.

supo ['supo] *etc vb V* **saber**.

supondré [supon'dre] *etc vb V* **suponer**.

suponer [supo'ner] *vt* to suppose; (*significar*) to mean; (*acarrear*) to involve ♦ *vi* to count, have authority; **era de ~ que ...** it was to be expected that ....

suponga [su'ponga] *etc vb V* **suponer**.

suposición [suposi'θjon] *nf* supposition.

supremacía [suprema'θia] *nf* supremacy.

supremo, a [su'premo, a] *a* supreme.

supresión [supre'sjon] *nf* suppression; (*de derecho*) abolition; (*de dificultad*) removal; (*de palabra etc*) deletion; (*de restricción*) cancellation, lifting.

suprimir [supri'mir] *vt* to suppress; (*derecho, costumbre*) to abolish; (*dificultad*) to remove; (*palabra etc, INFORM*) to delete; (*restricción*) to cancel, lift.

supuestamente [supwesta'mente] *ad* supposedly.

supuesto, a [su'pwesto, a] *pp de* **suponer** ♦ *a* (*hipotético*) supposed; (*falso*) false ♦ *nm* assumption, hypothesis ♦ *conj*: ~ **que** since; **dar por ~ algo** to take sth for granted; **por ~** of course.

supuse [su'puse] *etc vb V* **suponer**.

sur [sur] *a* southern; (*rumbo*) southerly ♦ *nm* south; (*viento*) south wind.

Suráfrica [su'rafrika] *etc* = **Sudáfrica** *etc*.

Suramérica [sura'merika] *etc* = **Sudamérica** *etc*.

surcar [sur'kar] *vt* to plough; (*superficie*) to cut, score.

surco ['surko] *nm* (*en metal, disco*) groove; (*AGR*) furrow.

surcoreano, a [surkore'ano, a] *a*, *nm/f* South Korean.

sureño, a [su'reɲo, a] *a* southern ♦ *nm/f* southerner.

sureste [su'reste] = **sudeste**.

surgir [sur'xir] *vi* to arise, emerge; (*dificultad*) to come up, crop up.

surja ['surxa] *etc vb V* **surgir**.

suroeste [suro'este] = **sudoeste**.

surque ['surke] *etc vb V* **surcar**.

surrealismo [surrea'lismo] *nm* surrealism.

surrealista [surrea'lista] *a*, *nm/f* surrealist.

surtido, a [sur'tiðo, a] *a* mixed, assorted ♦ *nm* (*selección*) selection, assortment; (*abastecimiento*) supply, stock.

surtidor [surti'ðor] *nm* (*chorro*) jet, spout; (*fuente*) fountain; ~ **de gasolina** petrol (*Brit*) *o* gas (*US*) pump.

surtir [sur'tir] *vt* to supply, provide; (*efecto*) to have, produce ♦ *vi* to spout, spurt; ~**se** *vr*: ~**se de** to provide o.s. with.

susceptible [susθep'tiβle] *a* susceptible; (*sensible*) sensitive; ~ **de** capable of.

suscitar [susθi'tar] *vt* to cause, provoke; (*discusión*) to start; (*duda, problema*) to raise; (*interés, sospechas*) to arouse.

suscribir [suskri'βir] *vt* (*firmar*) to sign; (*respaldar*) to subscribe to, endorse; (*COM*: *acciones*) to take out an option on; ~**se** *vr* to subscribe; ~ **a uno a una revista** to take out a subscription to a journal for sb.

suscripción [suskrip'θjon] *nf* subscription.

suscrito, a [sus'krito, a] *pp de* **suscribir** ♦ *a*: ~ **en exceso** oversubscribed.

susodicho, a [suso'ditʃo, a] *a* abovementioned.

suspender [suspen'der] *vt* (*objeto*) to hang (up), suspend; (*trabajo*) to stop, suspend; (*ESCOL*) to fail.

suspensión [suspen'sjon] *nf* suspension; (*fig*) stoppage, suspension; (*JUR*) stay; ~ **de fuego** *o* **de hostilidades** ceasefire, cessation of hostilities; ~ **de pagos** suspension of payments.

supensivo, a [suspen'siβo, a] *a*: **puntos ~s** dots, suspension points.

suspenso, a [sus'penso, a] *a* hanging, suspended; (*ESCOL*) failed ◆ *nm* (*ESCOL*) fail(ure); **quedar** *o* **estar en** ~ to be pending.
suspicacia [suspi'kaθja] *nf* suspicion, mistrust.
suspicaz [suspi'kaθ] *a* suspicious, distrustful.
suspirar [suspi'rar] *vi* to sigh.
suspiro [sus'piro] *nm* sigh.
sustancia [sus'tanθja] *nf* substance; ~ **gris** (*ANAT*) grey matter; **sin** ~ lacking in substance, shallow.
sustantivo, a [sustan'tiβo, a] *a* substantive; (*LING*) substantival, noun *cpd* ◆ *nm* noun, substantive.
sustentar [susten'tar] *vt* (*alimentar*) to sustain, nourish; (*objeto*) to hold up, support; (*idea, teoría*) to maintain, uphold; (*fig*) to sustain, keep going.
sustento [sus'tento] *nm* support; (*alimento*) sustenance, food.
sustituir [sustitu'ir] *vt* to substitute, replace.
sustituto, a [susti'tuto, a] *nm/f* substitute, replacement.
sustituyendo [sustitu'jendo] *etc vb* V **sustituir**.
susto ['susto] *nm* fright, scare; **dar un** ~ **a uno** to give sb a fright; **darse** *o* **pegarse un** ~ (*fam*) to get a fright.
sustraer [sustra'er] *vt* to remove, take away; (*MAT*) to subtract.
sustraiga [sus'traiχa] *etc*, **sustraje** [sus'traxe] *etc*, **sustrajera** [sustra'xera] *etc vb* V **sustraer**.
sustrato [sus'trato] *nm* substratum.
sustrayendo [sustra'jendo] *etc vb* V **sustraer**.
susurrar [susu'rrar] *vi* to whisper.
susurro [su'surro] *nm* whisper.
sutil [su'til] *a* (*aroma*) subtle; (*tenue*) thin; (*hilo, hebra*) fine; (*olor*) delicate; (*brisa*) gentle; (*diferencia*) fine, subtle; (*inteligencia*) sharp, keen.
sutileza [suti'leθa] *nf* subtlety; (*delgadez*) thinness; (*delicadeza*) delicacy; (*agudeza*) keenness.
sutura [su'tura] *nf* suture.
suturar [sutu'rar] *vt* to suture; (*juntar con puntos*) to stitch.
suyo, a ['sujo, a] *a* (*con artículo o después del verbo* ser: *de él*) his; (: *de ella*) hers; (: *de ellos, ellas*) theirs; (: *de usted, ustedes*) yours; (*después de un nombre*: *de él*) of his; (: *de ella*) of hers; (: *de ellos, ellas*) of theirs; (: *de usted, ustedes*) of yours; **lo** ~ (what is) his; (*su parte*) his share, what he deserves; **los** ~**s** (*familia*) one's family *o* relations; (*partidarios*) one's own people *o* supporters; ~ **afectísimo** (*en carta*) yours faithfully *o* sincerely; **de** ~ in itself; **eso es muy** ~ that's just like him; **hacer de las suyas** to get up to one's old tricks; **ir a la suya, ir a lo** ~ to go one's own way; **salirse con la suya** to get one's way.

T

T, t [te] *nf* (*letra*) T, t; **T de Tarragona** T for Tommy.
t *abr* = **tonelada**.
T. *abr* (= *Telefón, Telégrafo*) tel.; (*COM*) = **Tarifa; Tasa**.
t. *abr* (= *tomo(s)*) vol(s).
Tabacalera [taβaka'lera] *nf* Spanish state tobacco monopoly.
tabaco [ta'βako] *nm* tobacco; (*fam*) cigarettes *pl*.
tabaquería [tabake'ria] *nf* tobacconist's (*Brit*), cigar store (*US*).
tabarra [ta'βarra] *nf* (*fam*) nuisance; **dar la** ~ to be a pain in the neck.
taberna [ta'βerna] *nf* bar.
tabernero, a [taβer'nero, a] *nm/f* (*encargado*) publican; (*camarero*) barman/barmaid.
tabique [ta'βike] *nm* (*pared*) thin wall; (*para dividir*) partition.
tabla ['taβla] *nf* (*de madera*) plank; (*estante*) shelf; (*de anuncios*) board; (*lista, catálogo*) list; (*mostrador*) counter; (*de vestido*) pleat; (*ARTE*) panel; ~**s** *nfpl* (*TAUR, TEATRO*) boards; **hacer** ~**s** to draw; ~ **de consulta** (*INFORM*) lookup table.
tablado [ta'βlaðo] *nm* (*plataforma*) platform; (*suelo*) plank floor; (*TEATRO*) stage.
tablero [ta'βlero] *nm* (*de madera*) plank, board; (*pizarra*) blackboard; (*de ajedrez, damas*) board; (*AUTO*) dashboard; ~ **de gráficos** (*INFORM*) graph pad.
tableta [ta'βleta] *nf* (*MED*) tablet; (*de chocolate*) bar.
tablilla [ta'βliʎa] *nf* small board; (*MED*) splint.
tablón [ta'βlon] *nm* (*de suelo*) plank; (*de techo*) beam; (*de anuncios*) notice board.
tabú [ta'βu] *nm* taboo.
tabulación [taβula'θjon] *nf* (*INFORM*) tab(bing).
tabulador [taβula'ðor] *nm* (*INFORM, TIP*) tab.
tabuladora [taβula'ðora] *nf*: ~ **eléctrica** electric accounting machine.
tabular [taβu'lar] *vt* to tabulate; (*INFORM*) to tab.
taburete [taβu'rete] *nm* stool.

tacaño, a [ta'kaɲo, a] *a* (*avaro*) mean; (*astuto*) crafty.

tácito, a ['taθito, a] *a* tacit; (*acuerdo*) unspoken; (*LING*) understood; (*ley*) unwritten.

taciturno, a [taθi'turno, a] *a* (*callado*) silent; (*malhumorado*) sullen.

taco ['tako] *nm* (*BILLAR*) cue; (*libro de billetes*) book; (*manojo de billetes*) wad; (*AM*) heel; (*tarugo*) peg; (*fam: bocado*) snack; (: *palabrota*) swear word; (: *trago de vino*) swig; (*Méjico*) filled tortilla; **armarse** *o* **hacerse un ~** to get into a mess.

tacógrafo [ta'koɣrafo] *nm* (*COM*) tachograph.

tacón [ta'kon] *nm* heel; **de ~ alto** high-heeled.

taconear [takone'ar] *vi* (*dar golpecitos*) to tap with one's heels; (*MIL etc*) to click one's heels.

taconeo [tako'neo] *nm* (heel) tapping. *o* clicking.

táctico, a ['taktiko, a] *a* tactical ♦ *nf* tactics *pl*.

tacto ['takto] *nm* touch; (*acción*) touching; (*fig*) tact.

tacha ['tatʃa] *nf* (*defecto*) flaw, defect; (*TEC*) stud; **poner ~ a** to find fault with; **sin ~** flawless.

tachar [ta'tʃar] *vt* (*borrar*) to cross out; (*corregir*) to correct; (*criticar*) to criticize; **~ de** to accuse of.

tachón [ta'tʃon] *nm* erasure; (*tachadura*) crossing-out; (*TEC*) ornamental stud; (*COSTURA*) trimming.

tachuela [ta'tʃwela] *nf* (*clavo*) tack.

tafetán [tafe'tan] *nm* taffeta; **tafetanes** *nmpl* (*fam*) frills; **~ adhesivo** *o* **inglés** sticking plaster.

tafilete [tafi'lete] *nm* morocco leather.

tahona [ta'ona] *nf* (*panadería*) bakery; (*molino*) flourmill.

tahur [ta'ur] *nm* gambler; (*pey*) cheat.

tailandés, esa [tailan'des, esa] *a, nm/f* Thai ♦ *nm* (*LING*) Thai.

Tailandia [tai'landja] *nf* Thailand.

taimado, a [tai'maðo, a] *a* (*astuto*) sly; (*resentido*) sullen.

taita ['taita] *nm* dad, daddy.

taja ['taxa] *nf* (*corte*) cut; (*repartición*) division.

tajada [ta'xaða] *nf* slice; (*fam*) rake-off; **sacar ~** to get one's share.

tajadera [taxa'ðera] *nf* (*instrumento*) chopper; (*madera*) chopping block.

tajante [ta'xante] *a* sharp; (*negativa*) emphatic; **es una persona ~** he's an emphatic person.

tajar [ta'xar] *vt* to cut, slice.

Tajo ['taxo] *nm* Tagus.

tajo ['taxo] *nm* (*corte*) cut; (*filo*) cutting edge; (*GEO*) cleft.

tal [tal] *a* such; **un ~ García** a man called García; **~ vez** perhaps ♦ *pron* (*persona*) someone, such a one; (*cosa*) something, such a thing; **~ como** such as; **~ para cual** tit for tat; (*dos iguales*) two of a kind; **hablábamos de que si ~ si cual** we were talking about this, that and the other ♦ *ad*: **~ como** (*igual*) just as; **~ cual** (*como es*) just as it is; **~ el padre, cual el hijo** like father, like son; **¿qué ~?** how are things?; **¿qué ~ te gusta?** how do you like it? ♦ *conj*: **con ~ (de) que** provided that.

tala ['tala] *nf* (*de árboles*) tree felling.

taladradora [talaðra'ðora] *nf* drill; **~ neumática** pneumatic drill.

taladrar [tala'ðrar] *vt* to drill; (*fig: suj: ruido*) to pierce.

taladro [ta'laðro] *nm* (*gen*) drill; (*hoyo*) drill hole; **~ neumático** pneumatic drill.

talante [ta'lante] *nm* (*humor*) mood; (*voluntad*) will, willingness.

talar [ta'lar] *vt* to fell, cut down; (*fig*) to devastate.

talco ['talko] *nm* (*polvos*) talcum powder; (*MINERALOGÍA*) talc.

talega [ta'leɣa[*nf* sack.

talego [ta'leɣo] *nm* sack; **tener ~** (*fam*) to have money.

talento [ta'lento] *nm* talent; (*capacidad*) ability; (*don*) gift.

TALGO, Talgo ['talgo] *nm abr* (*FERRO* = *tren articulado ligero Goicoechea-Oriol*) high-speed train.

talidomida [taliðo'miða] *nm* thalidomide.

talismán [talis'man] *nm* talisman.

talmente [tal'mente] *ad* (*de esta forma*) in such a way; (*hasta tal punto*) to such an extent; (*exactamente*) exactly.

talón [ta'lon] *nm* (*gen*) heel; (*COM*) counterfoil; (*TEC*) rim.

talonario [talo'narjo] *nm* (*de cheques*) cheque book; (*de billetes*) book of tickets; (*de recibos*) receipt book.

talla ['taʎa] *nf* (*estatura, fig, MED*) height, stature; (*de ropa*) size, fitting; (*palo*) measuring rod; (*ARTE: de madera*)) carving; (*de piedra*) sculpture.

tallado, a [ta'ʎaðo, a] *a* carved ♦ *nm* (*de madera*) carving; (*de piedra*) sculpture.

tallar [ta'ʎar] *vt* (*trabajar*) to work, carve; (*grabar*) to engrave; (*medir*) to measure; (*repartir*) to deal ♦ *vi* to deal.

tallarín [taʎa'rin] *nm* noodle.

talle ['taʎe] *nm* (*ANAT*) waist; (*medida*) size; (*física*) build; (: *de mujer*) figure; (*fig*) appearance; **de ~ esbelto** with a slim figure.

taller [ta'ʎer] *nm* (*TEC*) workshop; (*fábrica*) factory; (*AUTO*) garage; (*de artista*) studio.

tallo ['taʎo] *nm* (*de planta*) stem; (*de hierba*) blade; (*brote*) shoot; (*col*) cabbage; (*CULIN*) candied peel.

tamaño, a [ta'maɲo, a] *a* (*tan grande*) such a big; (*tan pequeño*) such a small ♦ *nm* size; **de ~ natural** full-size; **¿de qué ~ es?** what size is it?

tamarindo [tama'rindo] *nm* tamarind.

tambaleante [tambale'ante] *a* (*persona*) staggering; (*mueble*) wobbly; (*vehículo*) swaying.

tambalearse [tambale'arse] *vr* (*persona*) to stagger; (*mueble*) to wobble; (*vehículo*) to sway.

también [tam'bjen] *ad* (*igualmente*) also, too, as well; (*además*) besides; **estoy cansado — yo ~** I'm tired — so am I *o* me too.

tambor [tam'bor] *nm* drum; (*ANAT*) eardrum; **~ del freno** brake drum; **~ magnético** (*INFORM*) magnetic drum.

tamboril [tambo'ril] *nm* small drum.

tamborilear [tamborile'ar] *vi* (*MUS*) to drum; (*con los dedos*) to drum with one's fingers.

tamborilero [tambori'lero] *nm* drummer.

Támesis [ta'mesis] *nm* Thames.

tamice [ta'miθe] *etc vb V* **tamizar**.

tamiz [ta'miθ] *nm* sieve.

tamizar [tami'θar] *vt* to sieve.

tampoco [tam'poko] *ad* nor, neither; **yo ~ lo compré** I didn't buy it either.

tampón [tam'pon] *nm* plug; (*MED*) tampon.

tan [tan] *ad* so; **~ es así que** so much so that; **¡qué cosa ~ rara!** how strange!; **no es una idea ~ buena** it is not such a good idea.

tanda ['tanda] *nf* (*gen*) series; (*de inyecciones*) course; (*juego*) set; (*turno*) shift; (*grupo*) gang.

tándem ['tandem] *nm* tandem; (*POL*) duo.

tangente [tan'xente] *nf* tangent; **salirse por la ~** to go off at a tangent.

Tánger ['tanxer] *n* Tangier.

tangerino, a [tanxe'rino, a] *a* *o* from Tangier ♦ *nm/f* native *o* inhabitant of Tangier.

tangible [tan'xißle] *a* tangible.

tanino [ta'nino] *nm* tannin.

tanque ['tanke] *nm* (*gen*) tank; (*AUTO, NAUT*) tanker.

tantear [tante'ar] *vt* (*calcular*) to reckon (up); (*medir*) to take the measure of; (*probar*) to test, try out; (*tomar la medida: persona*) to take the measurements of; (*considerar*) to weigh up ♦ *vi* (*DEPORTE*) to score.

tanteo [tan'teo] *nm* (*cálculo*) (rough) calculation; (*prueba*) test, trial; (*DEPORTE*) scoring; (*adivinanzas*) guesswork; **al ~** by trial and error.

tantísimo, a [tan'tisimo, a] *a* so much; **~s** so many.

tanto, a ['tanto, a] *a* (*cantidad*) so much, as much; **~s** so many, as many; **20 y ~s** 20-odd ♦ *ad* (*cantidad*) so much, as much; (*tiempo*) so long, as long; **~ tú como yo** both you and I; **~ como eso** it's not as bad as that; **~ más ... cuanto que** it's all the more ... because; **~ mejor/peor** so much the better/the worse; **~ si viene como si va** whether he comes or whether he goes; **~ es así que** so much so that; **por ~, por lo ~** therefore; **me he vuelto ronco de** *o* **con ~ hablar** I have become hoarse with so much talking ♦ *conj*: **con ~ que** provided (that); **en ~ que** while; **hasta ~ (que)** until such time as ♦ *nm* (*suma*) certain amount; (*proporción*) so much; (*punto*) point; (*gol*) goal; **~ alzado** agreed price; **~ por ciento** percentage; **al ~** up to date; **estar al ~ de los acontecimientos** to be fully abreast of events; **un ~ perezoso** somewhat lazy; **al ~ de que** because of the fact that ♦ *pron*: **cada uno paga ~** each one pays so much; **uno de ~s** one of many; **a ~s de agosto** on such and such a day in August; **entre ~** meanwhile.

tañer [ta'ɲer] *vt* (*MUS*) to play; (*campana*) to ring.

T/año *abr* = toneladas por año.

tapa ['tapa] *nf* (*de caja, olla*) lid; (*de botella*) top; (*de libro*) cover; (*comida*) snack.

tapacubos [tapa'kußos] *nm inv* hub cap.

tapadera [tapa'ðera] *nf* lid, cover.

tapado [ta'paðo] *nm* (*AM: abrigo*) coat.

tapar [ta'par] *vt* (*cubrir*) to cover; (*envolver*) to wrap *o* cover up; (*la vista*) to obstruct; (*persona, falta*) to conceal; (*AM*) to fill; **~se** *vr* to wrap o.s. up.

tapete [ta'pete] *nm* table cover; **estar sobre el ~** (*fig*) to be under discussion.

tapia ['tapja] *nf* (garden) wall.

tapiar [ta'pjar] *vt* to wall in.

tapice [ta'piθe] *etc vb V* **tapizar**.

tapicería [tapiθe'ria] *nf* tapestry; (*para muebles*) upholstery; (*tienda*) upholsterer's (shop).

tapicero, a [tapi'θero, a] *nm/f* (*de muebles*) upholsterer.

tapiz [ta'piθ] *nm* (*alfombra*) carpet; (*tela tejida*) tapestry.

tapizar [tapi'θar] *vt* (*pared*) to wallpaper; (*suelo*) to carpet; (*muebles*) to upholster.

tapón [ta'pon] *nm* (*corcho*) stopper; (*TEC*) plug; (*MED*) tampon; **~ de rosca** *o* **de tuerca** screw-top.

taponar [tapo'nar] *vt* (*botella*) to cork; (*tubería*) to block.

taponazo [tapo'naθo] *nm* (*de tapón*) pop.

tapujo [ta'puxo] *nm* (*embozo*) muffler; (*engaño*) deceit; **sin ~s** honestly.

taquigrafía [takiɣra'fia] *nf* shorthand.

taquígrafo, a [ta'kiɣrafo, a] *nm/f* shorthand writer.

taquilla [ta'kiʎa] *nf* (*de estación etc*) booking office; (*de teatro*) box office; (*suma recogida*) takings *pl*; (*archivador*) filing cabinet.

taquillero, a [taki'ʎero, a] *a:* **función taquillera** box office success ♦ *nm/f* ticket clerk.

taquímetro [ta'kimetro] *nm* speedometer; (*de control*) tachymeter.

tara ['tara] *nf* (*defecto*) defect; (*COM*) tare.

tarado, a [ta'raðo, a] *a* (*COM*) defective, imperfect; (*idiota*) stupid; (*loco*) crazy, nuts ♦ *nm/f* idiot, cretin.

tarántula [ta'rantula] *nf* tarantula.

tararear [tarare'ar] *vi* to hum.

tardanza [tar'ðanθa] *nf* (*demora*) delay; (*lentitud*) slowness.

tardar [tar'ðar] *vi* (*tomar tiempo*) to take a long time; (*llegar tarde*) to be late; (*demorar*) to delay; **¿tarda mucho el tren?** does the train take long?; **a más ~** at the (very) latest; **~ en hacer algo** to be slow *o* take a long time to do sth; **no tardes en venir** come soon, come before long.

tarde ['tarðe] *ad* (*hora*) late; (*fuera de tiempo*) too late ♦ *nf* (*de día*) afternoon; (*de noche*) evening; **~ o temprano** sooner or later; **de ~ en ~** from time to time; **¡buenas ~s!** (*de día*) good afternoon!; (*de noche*) good evening!; **a *o* por la ~** in the afternoon; in the evening.

tardío, a [tar'ðio, a] *a* (*retrasado*) late; (*lento*) slow (to arrive).

tardo, a ['tarðo, a] *a* (*lento*) slow; (*torpe*) dull; **~ de oído** hard of hearing.

tarea [ta'rea] *nf* task; **~s** *nfpl* (*ESCOL*) homework *sg*; **~ de ocasión** chore.

tarifa [ta'rifa] *nf* (*lista de precios*) price list; (*COM*) tariff; **~ básica** basic rate; **~ completa** all-in cost; **~ a destajo** piece rate; **~ doble** double time.

tarima [ta'rima] *nf* (*plataforma*) platform; (*taburete*) stool; (*litera*) bunk.

tarjeta [tar'xeta] *nf* card; **~ postal/de crédito/de Navidad** postcard/credit card/Christmas card; **~ de circuitos** (*INFORM*) circuit board; **~ comercial** (*COM*) calling card; **~ dinero** cash card; **~ gráficos** (*INFORM*) graphics card; **~ de multifunción** (*INFORM*) multiplication card.

tarraconense [tarrako'nense] *a* of *o* from Tarragona ♦ *nm/f* native *o* inhabitant of Tarragona.

tarro ['tarro] *nm* jar, pot.

tarta ['tarta] *nf* (*pastel*) cake; (*torta*) tart.

tartajear [tartaxe'ar] *vi* to stammer.

tartamudear [tartamuðe'ar] *vi* to stutter, stammer.

tartamudo, a [tarta'muðo, a] *a* stuttering,

stammering ♦ *nm/f* stutterer, stammerer.

tartárico, a [tar'tariko, a] *a:* **ácido ~** tartaric acid.

tártaro ['tartaro] *a, nm* Tartar ♦ *nm* (*QUIMICA*) tartar.

tarugo, a [ta'ruɣo, a] *a* stupid ♦ *nm* (*de madera*) lump.

tarumba [ta'rumba] *a* (*confuso*) confused.

tasa ['tasa] *nf* (*precio*) (fixed) price, rate; (*valoración*) valuation; (*medida, norma*) measure, standard; **~ básica** (*COM*) basic rate; **~ de cambio** exchange rate; **de ~ cero** (*COM*) zero-rated; **~ de crecimiento** growth rate; **~ de interés/de nacimiento** rate of interest/birth rate; **~ de rendimiento** (*COM*) rate of return.

tasación [tasa'θjon] *nf* assessment, valuation; (*fig*) appraisal.

tasador, a [tasa'ðor, a] *nm/f* valuer; (*COM: de impuestos*) assessor.

tasajo [ta'saxo] *nm* dried beef.

tasar [ta'sar] *vt* (*arreglar el precio*) to fix a price for; (*valorar*) to value, assess; (*limitar*) to limit.

tasca ['taska] *nf* (*fam*) pub.

tata ['tata] *nm* (*fam*) dad(dy) ♦ *nf* (*niñera*) nanny, maid.

tatarabuelo, a [tatara'ßwelo, a] *nm/f* great-great-grandfather/mother; **los ~s** one's great-great-grandparents.

tatuaje [ta'twaxe] *nm* (*dibujo*) tattoo; (*acto*) tattooing.

tatuar [ta'twar] *vt* to tattoo.

taumaturgo [tauma'turɣo] *nm* miracle-worker.

taurino, a [tau'rino, a] *a* bullfighting *cpd*.

Tauro ['tauro] *nm* Taurus.

tauromaquia [tauro'makja] *nf* (art of) bullfighting.

tautología [tautolo'xia] *nf* tautology.

taxativo, a [taksa'tißo, a] *a* (*restringido*) limited; (*sentido*) specific.

taxi ['taksi] *nm* taxi.

taxidermia [taksi'ðermja] *nf* taxidermy.

taxímetro [tak'simetro] *nm* taximeter.

taxista [tak'sista] *nm/f* taxi driver.

taza ['taθa] *nf* cup; (*de retrete*) bowl; **~ para café** coffee cup.

tazón [ta'θon] *nm* mug, large cup; (*escudilla*) basin.

TCI *nf abr* (= *tarjeta de circuito impreso*) PCB.

te [te] *pron* (*complemento de objeto*) you; (*complemento indirecto*) (to) you; (*reflexivo*) (to) yourself; **¿~ duele mucho el brazo?** does your arm hurt a lot?; **~ equivocas** you're wrong; **¡cálma~!** calm yourself!

té [te], *pl* **tés** *nm* tea; (*reunión*) tea party.

tea ['tea] *nf* (*antorcha*) torch.

teatral [tea'tral] *a* theatre *cpd*; (*fig*) theatrical.

teatro [te'atro] *nm* theatre; (*LITERATURA*) plays *pl*, drama; **el ~** (*carrera*) the theatre, acting; **~ de aficionados/de variedades** amateur/variety theatre, vaudeville theater (*US*); **hacer ~** (*fig*) to make a fuss.

tebeo [te'βeo] *nm* children's comic.

tecla ['tekla] *nf* (*INFORM, MUS, TIP*) key; (*INFORM*): **~ de anulación/de borrar** cancel/delete key; **~ de control/de edición** control/edit key; **~ con flecha** arrow key; **~ programable** user-defined key; **~ de retorno/de tabulación** return/tab key; **~ del cursor** cursor key; **~s de control direccional del cursor** cursor control keys.

teclado [te'klaðo] *nm* keyboard (*tb INFORM*); **~ numérico** (*INFORM*) numeric keypad.

teclear [tekle'ar] *vi* to strum; (*fam*) to drum ♦ *vt* (*INFORM*) to key (in), type in, keyboard.

tecleo [te'kleo] *nm* (*MUS: sonido*) strumming; (: *forma de tocar*) fingering; (*fam*) drumming.

tecnicismo [tekni'θismo] *nm* (*carácter técnico*) technical nature; (*LING*) technical term.

técnico, a ['tekniko, a] *a* technical ♦ *nm* technician; (*experto*) expert ♦ *nf* (*procedimientos*) technique; (*arte, oficio*) craft.

tecnócrata [tek'nokrata] *nm/f* technocrat.

tecnología [teknolo'xia] *nf* technology; **~ de estado sólido** (*INFORM*) solid-state technology; **~ de la información** information technology.

tecnológico, a [tekno'loxiko, a] *a* technological.

tecnólogo, a [tek'nologo, a] *nm/f* technologist.

techado [te'tʃaðo] *nm* (*techo*) roof; **bajo ~** under cover.

techo ['tetʃo] *nm* (*externo*) roof; (*interno*) ceiling.

techumbre [te'tʃumbre] *nf* roof.

tedio ['teðjo] *nm* (*aburrimiento*) boredom; (*apatía*) apathy; (*fastidio*) depression.

tedioso, a [te'ðjoso, a] *a* boring; (*cansado*) wearisome, tedious.

Teherán [tee'ran] *nm* Teheran.

teja ['texa] *nf* (*azulejo*) tile; (*BOT*) lime (tree).

tejado [te'xaðo] *nm* (tiled) roof.

tejano, a [te'xano, a] *a, nm/f* Texan ♦ *nmpl*: **~s** (*vaqueros*) jeans.

Tejas ['texas] *nm* Texas.

tejemaneje [texema'nexe] *nm* (*actividad*) bustle; (*lío*) fuss, to-do; (*intriga*) intrigue.

tejer [te'xer] *vt* to weave; (*tela de araña*) to spin; (*AM*) to knit; (*fig*) to fabricate ♦ *vi*: **~ y destejer** to chop and change.

tejido [te'xiðo] *nm* fabric; (*estofa, tela*) (knitted) material; (*ANAT*) tissue; (*textura*) texture.

tejo ['texo] *nm* (*BOT*) yew (tree).

tel. *abr* (= *teléfono*) tel.

tela ['tela] *nf* (*material*) material; (*de fruta, en líquido*) skin; (*del ojo*) film; **hay ~ para rato** there's lots to talk about; **poner en ~ de juicio** to (call in) question; **~ de araña** cobweb, spider's web.

telar [te'lar] *nm* (*máquina*) loom; (*de teatro*) gridiron; **~es** *nmpl* textile mill *sg*.

telaraña [tela'raɲa] *nf* cobweb, spider's web.

tele ['tele] *nf* (*fam*) TV.

tele... [tele] *pref* tele...

telecargar [telekar'ɣar] *vt* (*INFORM*) to download.

telecompras [tele'kompras] *nfpl* teleshopping *sg*.

telecomunicación [telekomunika'θjon] *nf* telecommunication.

telecontrol [telekon'trol] *nm* remote control.

telecopiadora [telekopja'ðora] *nf*: **~ facsímil** fax copier.

telediario [tele'ðjarjo] *nm* television news.

teledifusión [teleðifu'sjon] *nf* (*television*) broadcast.

teledirigido, a [teleðiri'xiðo, a] *a* remote-controlled.

teléf. *abr* (= *teléfono*) tel.

teleférico [tele'feriko] *nm* (*tren*) cablerailway; (*de esquí*) ski-lift.

telefilm [tele'film], **telefilme** [tele'filme] *nm* TV film.

telefonazo [telefo'naθo] *nm* (*fam*) telephone call; **te daré un ~** I'll give you a ring.

telefonear [telefone'ar] *vi* to telephone.

telefónicamente [tele'fonikamente] *ad* by (tele)phone.

telefónico, a [tele'foniko, a] *a* telephone *cpd* ♦ *nf*: **Telefónica** (*Esp*) Spanish national telephone company, ≈ British Telecom.

telefonista [telefo'nista] *nm/f* telephonist.

teléfono [te'lefono] *nm* telephone; **está hablando por ~** he's on the phone.

telefoto [tele'foto] *nf* telephoto.

telegrafía [teleɣra'fia] *nf* telegraphy.

telégrafo [te'leɣrafo] *nm* telegraph; (*fam: persona*) telegraph boy.

telegrama [tele'ɣrama] *nm* telegram.

teleimpresor [teleimpre'sor] *nm* teleprinter.

telemática [tele'matika] *nf* telematics *sg*.

telémetro [te'lemetro] *nm* rangefinder.

telenovela [teleno'βela] *nf* soap (opera).

teleobjetivo [teleobxe'tiβo] *nm* telephoto lens.

telepático, a [tele'patiko, a] a telepathic.
teleproceso [telepro'θeso] nm teleprocessing.
telescópico, a [tele'skopiko, a] a telescopic.
telescopio [tele'skopjo] nm telescope.
telesilla [tele'siʎa] nm chairlift.
telespectador, a [telespekta'ðor, a] nm/f viewer.
telesquí [teles'ki] nm ski-lift.
teletex(to) [tele'teks(to)] nm teletext.
teletipista [teleti'pista] nm/f teletypist.
teletipo [tele'tipo] nm teletype(writer).
teletratamiento [teletrata'mjento] nm teleprocessing.
televidente [teleßi'ðente] nm/f viewer.
televisar [teleßi'sar] vt to televise.
televisión [teleßi'sjon] nf television; ~ **en color** colour television.
televisivo, a [teleßi'sißo, a] a television cpd.
televisor [teleßi'sor] nm television set.
télex ['teleks] nm telex; **máquina** ~ telex (machine); **enviar por** ~ to telex.
telón [te'lon] nm (asunto) curtain; ~ **de boca/seguridad** front/safety curtain; ~ **de acero** (POL) iron curtain; ~ **de fondo** backcloth, background.
tema ['tema] nm (asunto) subject, topic; (MUS) theme; ~**s de actualidad** current affairs ◆ nf (obsesión) obsession; (manía) ill-will; **tener** ~ **a uno** to have a grudge against sb.
temario [te'marjo] nm (ESCOL) set of topics; (de una conferencia) agenda.
temático, a [te'matiko, a] a thematic.
tembladera [tembla'ðera] nf shaking; (AM) quagmire.
temblar [tem'blar] vi to shake, tremble; (de frío) to shiver.
tembleque [tem'bleke] a shaking ◆ nm shaking.
temblón, ona [tem'blon, ona] a shaking.
temblor [tem'blor] nm trembling; (AM: de tierra) earthquake.
tembloroso, a [temblo'roso, a] a trembling.
temer [te'mer] vt to fear ◆ vi to be afraid; **temo que Juan llegue tarde** I am afraid Juan may be late.
temerario, a [teme'rarjo, a] a (imprudente) rash; (descuidado) reckless; (arbitrario) hasty.
temeridad [temeri'ðað] nf (imprudencia) rashness; (audacia) boldness.
temeroso, a [teme'roso, a] a (miedoso) fearful; (que inspira temor) frightful.
temible [te'mißle] a fearsome.
temor [te'mor] nm (miedo) fear; (duda) suspicion.
tempano ['tempano] nm (MUS) kettledrum;

~ **de hielo** ice floe.
temperamento [tempera'mento] nm temperament; **tener** ~ to be temperamental.
temperar [tempe'rar] vt to temper, moderate.
temperatura [tempera'tura] nf temperature.
tempestad [tempes'tað] nf storm; ~ **en un vaso de agua** (fig) storm in a teacup.
tempestuoso, a [tempes'twoso, a] a stormy.
templado, a [tem'plaðo, a] a (moderado) moderate; (: en el comer) frugal; (: en el beber) abstemious; (agua) lukewarm; (clima) mild; (MUS) in tune, well-tuned.
templanza [tem'planθa] nf moderation; (en el beber) abstemiousness; (del clima) mildness.
templar [tem'plar] vt (moderar) to moderate; (furia) to restrain; (calor) to reduce; (solución) to dilute; (afinar) to tune (up); (acero) to temper ◆ vi to moderate; ~**se** vr to be restrained.
temple ['temple] nm (humor) mood; (coraje) courage; (ajuste) tempering; (afinación) tuning; (pintura) tempera.
templo ['templo] nm (iglesia) church; (pagano etc) temple; ~ **metodista** Methodist chapel.
temporada [tempo'raða] nf time, period; (estación, social, DEPORTE) season; **en plena** ~ at the height of the season.
temporal [tempo'ral] a (no permanente) temporary; (REL) temporal ◆ nm storm.
tempranero, a [tempra'nero, a] a (BOT) early; (persona) early-rising.
temprano, a [tem'prano, a] a early ◆ ad early; (demasiado pronto) too soon, too early; **lo más** ~ **posible** as soon as possible.
ten [ten] vb V tener.
tenacidad [tenaθi'ðað] nf (gen) tenacity; (dureza) toughness; (terquedad) stubbornness.
tenacillas [tena'θiʎas] nfpl (gen) tongs; (para el pelo) curling tongs; (MED) forceps.
tenaz [te'naθ] a (material) tough; (persona) tenacious; (pegajoso) sticky; (terco) stubborn.
tenaza(s) [te'naθa(s)] nf(pl) (MED) forceps; (TEC) pliers; (ZOOL) pincers.
tendal [ten'dal] nm awning.
tendedero [tende'ðero] nm (para ropa) drying-place; (cuerda) clothes line.
tendencia [ten'denθja] nf tendency; (proceso) trend; ~ **imperante** prevailing tendency; ~ **del mercado** run of the market; **tener** ~ **a** to tend o have a tendency to.
tendenciosidad [tendenθjosi'ðað] nf ten-

dentiousness.

tendencioso, a [tenden'θjoso, a] *a* tendentious.

tender [ten'der] *vt* (*extender*) to spread out; (*ropa*) to hang out; (*vía férrea, cable*) to lay; (*cuerda*) to stretch; (*trampa*) to set ◆ *vi* to tend; ~**se** *vr* to lie down; (*fig: dejarse llevar*) to let o.s. go; (: *dejar ir*) to let things go; ~ **la cama/la mesa** (*AM*) to make the bed/lay the table.

ténder ['tender] *nm* (*FERRO*) tender.

tenderete [tende'rete] *nm* (*puesto*) stall; (*carretilla*) barrow; (*exposición*) display of goods.

tendero, a [ten'dero, a] *nm/f* shopkeeper.

tendido, a [ten'diðo, a] *a* (*acostado*) lying down, flat; (*colgado*) hanging ◆ *nm* (*ropa*) washing; (*TAUR*) front rows *pl* of seats; (*colocación*) laying; (*ARQ: enyesado*) coat of plaster; **a galope** ~ flat out.

tendón [ten'don] *nm* tendon.

tendré [ten'dre] *etc vb* V **tener**.

tenducho [ten'dutʃo] *nm* small dirty shop.

tenebroso, a [tene'ßroso, a] *a* (*oscuro*) dark; (*fig*) gloomy; (*siniestro*) sinister.

tenedor [tene'ðor] *nm* (*CULIN*) fork; (*poseedor*) holder; ~ **de libros** book-keeper; ~ **de acciones** shareholder; ~ **de póliza** policyholder.

teneduría [teneðu'ria] *nf* keeping; ~ **de libros** book-keeping.

tenencia [te'nenθja] *nf* (*de casa*) tenancy; (*de oficio*) tenure; (*de propiedad*) possession; ~ **asegurada** security of tenure; ~ **ilícita de armas** illegal possession of weapons.

tener [te'ner] *vt* (*poseer*) to have; (*en la mano*) to hold; (*suj: recipiente*) to hold, contain; (*considerar*) to consider; ~**se** *vr* (*erguirse*) to stand; (*fig*) to control o.s.; ~ **suerte** to be lucky; ~ **permiso** to have permission; **tiene 10 años** he is 10 years old; **¿cuántos años tienes?** how old are you?; ~ **sed/hambre/frío/calor** to be thirsty/hungry/cold/hot; ~ **ganas de** to want to; ~ **celos** to be jealous; ~ **cuidado** to be careful; ~ **razón** to be right; ~ **un metro de ancho/de largo** to be one metre wide/long; ~ **a bien** to see fit to; ~ **en cuenta** to bear in mind, take into account; ~ **a menos** to consider it beneath o.s.; ~ **a uno en más (estima)** to think all the more of sb; ~ **a uno por...** to think sb...; ~ **por seguro que** to be sure that; ~ **presente** to remember, bear in mind; ~ **que** (*obligación*) to have to; **tiene que ser así** it has to be this way; **nos tiene preparada una sorpresa** he has prepared a surprise for us; **¿qué tiene?** what's the matter with him?; **¿ésas tenemos?** what's all this?; **tiene un mes de muerto** he has been dead for a

month; ~**se por** (*considerarse*) to consider o.s.

tenería [tene'ria] *nf* tannery.

tenga ['tenga] *etc vb* V **tener**.

tenia ['tenja] *nf* tapeworm.

teniente [te'njente] *nm* lieutenant; ~ **coronel** lieutenant colonel.

tenis ['tenis] *nm* tennis; ~ **de mesa** table tennis.

tenista [te'nista] *nm/f* tennis player.

tenor [te'nor] *nm* (*tono*) tone; (*sentido*) meaning; (*MUS*) tenor; **a** ~ **de** on the lines of.

tenorio [te'norjo] *nm* (*fam*) ladykiller, Don Juan.

tensar [ten'sar] *vt* to tauten; (*arco*) to draw.

tensión [ten'sjon] *nf* tension; (*TEC*) stress; (*MED*): ~ **arterial** blood pressure; ~ **nerviosa** nervous strain; **tener la** ~ **alta** to have high blood pressure.

tenso, a ['tenso, a] *a* tense; (*relaciones*) strained.

tentación [tenta'θjon] *nf* temptation.

tentáculo [ten'takulo] *nm* tentacle.

tentador, a [tenta'ðor, a] *a* tempting ◆ *nm/f* tempter/temptress.

tentar [ten'tar] *vt* (*tocar*) to touch, feel; (*seducir*) to tempt; (*atraer*) to attract; (*probar*) to try (out); (*MED*) to probe; ~ **hacer algo** to try to do sth.

tentativa [tenta'tißa] *nf* attempt; ~ **de asesinato** attempted murder.

tentempié [tentem'pje] *nm* (*fam*) snack.

tenue ['tenwe] *a* (*delgado*) thin, slender; (*alambre*) fine; (*insustancial*) tenuous; (*sonido*) faint; (*neblina*) light; (*lazo, vínculo*) slight.

tenuidad [tenwi'ðað] *nf* thinness; (*de tela*) fineness; (*de relaciones*) tenuousness; (*ligereza*) lightness; (*sencillez*) simplicity.

teñir [te'ɲir] *vt* to dye; (*fig*) to tinge; ~**se el pelo** to dye one's hair.

teología [teolo'xia] *nf* theology.

teólogo, a [te'oloɣo, a] *nm/f* theologist, theologian.

teorema [teo'rema] *nm* theorem.

teoría [teo'ria] *nf* theory; **en** ~ in theory.

teóricamente [teo'rikamente] *ad* theoretically.

teorice [teo'riθe] *etc vb* V **teorizar**.

teórico, a [te'oriko, a] *a* theoretic(al) ◆ *nm/f* theoretician, theorist.

teorizar [teori'θar] *vi* to theorize.

TER [ter] *nm abr* (*FERRO*) = **tren español rápido**.

terapeuta [tera'peuta] *nm/f* therapist.

terapéutico, a [tera'peutiko, a] *a* therapeutic(al) ◆ *nf* therapeutics *sg*.

terapia [te'rapja] *nf* therapy; ~ **laboral** occupational therapy.

tercer [ter'θer] *a* V **tercero**.

tercería [terθe'ria] *nf* (*mediación*) mediation; (*arbitraje*) arbitration.

tercermundista [terθermun'dista] *a* Third World *cpd*.

tercero, a [ter'θero, a] *a* third (*delante de nmsg*: **tercer**) ♦ *nm* (*árbitro*) mediator; (*JUR*) third party.

terceto [ter'θeto] *nm* trio.

terciado, a [ter'θjaðo, a] *a* slanting; **azúcar** ~ brown sugar.

terciar [ter'θjar] *vt* (*MAT*) to divide into three; (*inclinarse*) to slope; (*llevar*) to wear across one's chest ♦ *vi* (*participar*) to take part; (*hacer de árbitro*) to mediate; ~**se** *vr* to arise.

terciario, a [ter'θjarjo, a] *a* tertiary.

tercio ['terθjo] *nm* third.

terciopelo [terθjo'pelo] *nm* velvet.

terco, a ['terko, a] *a* obstinate, stubborn; (*material*) tough.

tergiversación [terxiβersa'θjon] *nf* (*deformación*) distortion; (*evasivas*) prevarication.

tergiversar [terxiβer'sar] *vt* to distort ♦ *vi* to prevaricate.

termal [ter'mal] *a* thermal.

termas ['termas] *nfpl* hot springs.

térmico, a ['termiko, a] *a* thermic, thermal, heat *cpd*.

terminación [termina'θjon] *nf* (*final*) end; (*conclusión*) conclusion, ending.

terminal [termi'nal] *a* terminal ♦ *nm* (*ELEC, INFORM*) terminal; ~ **conversacional** interactive terminal; ~ **de pantalla** visual display unit ♦ *nf* (*AVIAT, FERRO*) terminal.

terminante [termi'nante] *a* (*final*) final, definitive; (*tajante*) categorical.

terminar [termi'nar] *vt* (*completar*) to complete, finish; (*concluir*) to end ♦ *vi* (*llegar a su fin*) to end; (*parar*) to stop; (*acabar*) to finish; ~**se** *vr* to come to an end; ~ **por hacer algo** to end up (by) doing sth.

término ['termino] *nm* end, conclusion; (*parada*) terminus; (*límite*) boundary; (*en discusión*) point; (*LING, COM*) term; ~ **medio** average; (*fig*) middle way; **en otros** ~**s** in other words; **en último** ~ (*a fin de cuentas*) in the last analysis; (*como último recurso*) as a last resort; **en** ~**s de** in terms of; **según los** ~**s del contrato** according to the terms of the contract.

terminología [terminolo'xia] *nf* terminology.

termodinámico, a [termoði'namiko, a] *a* thermodynamic ♦ *nf* thermodynamics *sg*.

termoimpresora [termoimpre'sora] *nf* thermal printer.

termómetro [ter'mometro] *nm* thermometer.

termonuclear [termonukle'ar] *a* thermonuclear.

Termo(s) ® ['termo(s)] *nm* Thermos ® (flask).

termostato [termos'tato] *nm* thermostat.

ternero, a [ter'nero, a] *nm/f* (*animal*) calf ♦ *nf* (*carne*) veal.

terneza [ter'neθa] *nf* tenderness.

ternilla [ter'niʎa] *nf* gristle; (*cartílago*) cartilage.

terno ['terno] *nm* (*traje*) three-piece suit; (*conjunto*) set of three.

ternura [ter'nura] *nf* (*trato*) tenderness; (*palabra*) endearment; (*cariño*) fondness.

terquedad [terke'ðað] *nf* obstinacy; (*dureza*) harshness.

terrado [te'rraðo] *nm* terrace.

Terranova [terra'noβa] *nf* Newfoundland.

terraplén [terra'plen] *nm* (*AGR*) terrace; (*FERRO*) embankment; (*MIL*) rampart; (*cuesta*) slope.

terrateniente [terrate'njente] *nm* landowner.

terraza [te'rraθa] *nf* (*balcón*) balcony; (*techo*) flat roof; (*AGR*) terrace.

terremoto [terre'moto] *nm* earthquake.

terrenal [terre'nal] *a* earthly.

terreno, a [te'rreno, a] *a* (*de la tierra*) earthly, worldly ♦ *nm* (*tierra*) land; (*parcela*) plot; (*suelo*) soil; (*fig*) field; **un** ~ **a piece of land**; **sobre el** ~ **on the spot**; **ceder/perder** ~ to give/lose ground; **preparar el** ~ **(a)** (*fig*) to pave the way (for).

terrero, a [te'rrero, a] *a* (*de la tierra*) earthy; (*vuelo*) low; (*fig*) humble.

terrestre [te'rrestre] *a* terrestrial; (*ruta*) land *cpd*.

terrible [te'rriβle] *a* (*espantoso*) terrible; (*aterrador*) dreadful; (*tremendo*) awful.

territorio [terri'torjo] *nm* territory; ~ **bajo mandato** mandated territory.

terrón [te'rron] *nm* (*de azúcar*) lump; (*de tierra*) clod, lump; **terrones** *nmpl* land *sg*.

terror [te'rror] *nm* terror.

terrorífico, a [terro'rifiko, a] *a* terrifying.

terrorismo [terro'rismo] *nm* terrorism.

terrorista [terro'rista] *a, nm/f* terrorist.

terroso, a [te'rroso, a] *a* earthy.

terruño [te'rruɲo] *nm* (*pedazo*) clod; (*parcela*) plot; (*fig*) native soil; **apego al** ~ attachment to one's native soil.

terso, a ['terso, a] *a* (*liso*) smooth; (*pulido*) polished; (*fig: estilo*) flowing.

tersura [ter'sura] *nf* smoothness; (*brillo*) shine.

tertulia [ter'tulja] *nf* (*reunión informal*) social gathering; (*grupo*) group, circle; (*sala*) clubroom; ~ **literaria** literary circle.

tesar [te'sar] *vt* to tighten up.

tesina [te'sina] *nf* dissertation.

tesis ['tesis] *nf inv* thesis.

tesón [te'son] *nm* (*firmeza*) firmness; (*tena-*

cidad) tenacity.

tesorería [tesore'ria] *nf* treasurership.

tesorero, a [teso'rero, a] *nm/f* treasurer.

tesoro [te'soro] *nm* treasure; **T~ público** (*POL*) Exchequer.

testaferro [testa'ferro] *nm* figurehead.

testamentaría [testamenta'ria] *nf* execution of a will.

testamentario, a [testamen'tarjo, a] *a* testamentary ♦ *nm/f* executor/executrix.

testamento [testa'mento] *nm* will.

testar [tes'tar] *vi* to make a will.

testarada [testa'raða] *nf*, **testarazo** [testa-'raθo] *nm*: **darse un(a) ~** (*fam*) to bump one's head.

testarudo, a [testa'ruðo, a] *a* stubborn.

testero, a [tes'tero, a] *nm/f* (*gen*) front ♦ *nm* (*ARQ*) front wall.

testes ['testes] *nmpl* testes.

testículo [tes'tikulo] *nm* testicle.

testificar [testifi'kar] *vt* to testify; (*fig*) to attest ♦ *vi* to give evidence.

testifique [testi'fike] *etc vb V* **testificar**.

testigo [tes'tiɣo] *nm/f* witness; **~ de cargo/descargo** witness for the prosecution/defence; **~ ocular** eye witness; **poner a uno por ~** to cite sb as a witness.

testimoniar [testimo'njar] *vt* to testify to; (*fig*) to show.

testimonio [testi'monjo] *nm* testimony; **en ~ de** as a token *o* mark of; **falso ~** perjured evidence, false witness.

teta ['teta] *nf* (*de biberón*) teat; (*ANAT*) nipple; (*fam*) breast; (*fam!*) tit (*!*).

tétanos ['tetanos] *nm* tetanus.

tetera [te'tera] *nf* teapot; **~ eléctrica** (electric) kettle.

tetilla [te'tiʎa] *nf* (*ANAT*) nipple; (*de biberón*) teat.

tétrico, a ['tetriko, a] *a* gloomy, dismal.

textil [teks'til] *a* textile; **~es** *nmpl* textiles.

texto ['teksto] *nm* text.

textual [teks'twal] *a* textual; **palabras ~es** exact words.

textura [teks'tura] *nf* (*de tejido*) texture; (*de mineral*) structure.

tez [teθ] *nf* (*cutis*) complexion; (*color*) colouring.

tfno. *abr* (= *teléfono*) tel.

ti [ti] *pron* you; (*reflexivo*) yourself.

tía ['tia] *nf* (*pariente*) aunt; (*mujer cualquiera*) girl, bird (*col*); (*fam: pej: vieja*) old bag; (: *prostituta*) whore.

Tibet [ti'ßet] *nm*: **El ~** Tibet.

tibetano, a [tiße'tano, a] *a, nm/f* Tibetan ♦ *nm* (*LING*) Tibetan.

tibia ['tißja] *nf* tibia.

tibieza [ti'ßjeθa] *nf* (*temperatura*) tepidness; (*fig*) coolness.

tibio, a ['tißjo, a] *a* lukewarm, tepid.

tiburón [tißu'ron] *nm* shark.

tic [tik] *nm* (*ruido*) click; (*de reloj*) tick; **~ nervioso** (*MED*) nervous tic.

tico, a ['tiko, a] *a, nm/f* (*AM fam*) Costa Rican.

tictac [tik'tak] *nm* (*de reloj*) tick tock.

tiemble ['tjemble] *etc vb V* **temblar**.

tiempo ['tjempo] *nm* (*gen*) time; (*época, período*) age, period; (*METEOROLOGÍA*) weather; (*LING*) tense; (*edad*) age; (*de juego*) half; **a ~** in time; **a un** *o* **al mismo ~** at the same time; **al poco ~** very soon (after); **andando el ~** in due course; **cada cierto ~** every so often; **con ~** in time; **con el ~** eventually; **de ~ en ~** from time to time; **en mis ~s** in my time; **en los buenos ~s** in the good old days; **hace buen/mal ~** the weather is fine/bad; **estar a ~ to be** in time; **hace ~** some time ago; **hacer ~** to while away the time; **¿qué ~ tiene?** how old is he?; **motor de 2 ~s** two-stroke engine; **~ compartido** (*INFORM*) time sharing; **~ de ejecución** (*INFORM*) run time; **~ inactivo** (*COM*) downtime; **~ libre** spare time; **~ de paro** (*COM*) idle time; **a ~ partido** (*trabajar*) part-time; **~ preferencial** (*COM*) prime time; **en ~ real** (*INFORM*) real time.

tienda ['tjenda] *etc vb V* **tender** ♦ *nf* shop; (*más grande*) store; (*NAUT*) awning; **~ de campaña** tent.

tiene ['tjene] *etc vb V* **tener**.

tienta ['tjenta] *nf* (*MED*) probe; (*fig*) tact; **andar a ~s** to grope one's way along.

tiento ['tjento] *etc vb V* **tentar** ♦ *nm* (*tacto*) touch; (*precaución*) wariness; (*pulso*) steady hand; (*ZOOL*) feeler, tentacle.

tierno, a ['tjerno, a] *a* (*blando, dulce*) tender; (*fresco*) fresh.

tierra ['tjerra] *nf* earth; (*suelo*) soil; (*mundo*) world; (*país*) country, land; (*ELEC*) earth, ground (*US*); **~ adentro** inland; **~ natal** native land; **echar ~ a un asunto** to hush an affair up; **no es de estas ~s** he's not from these parts; **la T~ Santa** the Holy Land.

tieso, a ['tjeso, a] *etc vb V* **tesar** ♦ *a* (*rígido*) rigid; (*duro*) stiff; (*fig: testarudo*) stubborn; (*fam: orgulloso*) conceited ♦ *ad* strongly.

tiesto ['tjesto] *nm* flowerpot; (*pedazo*) piece of pottery.

tiesura [tje'sura] *nf* rigidity; (*fig*) stubbornness; (*fam*) conceit.

tifo ['tifo] *nm* typhus; **~ de América** yellow fever; **~ asiático** cholera.

tifoidea [tifoi'ðea] *nf* typhoid.

tifón [ti'fon] *nm* (*huracán*) typhoon; (*de mar*) tidal wave.

tifus ['tifus] *nm* typhus; **~ icteroides** yellow fever.

tigre ['tiɣre] *nm* tiger; (*AM*) jaguar.

tijera [ti'xera] *nf* (*AM*) (*una* ~) (pair of) scissors; (*ZOOL*) claw; (*persona*) gossip; **de** ~ folding; **~s** *nfpl* scissors; (*para plantas*) shears; **unas** ~**s** a pair of scissors.

tijeretear [tixerete'ar] *vt* to snip ♦ *vi* (*fig*) to meddle.

tila ['tila] *nf* (*BOT*) lime tree; (*CULIN*) lime flower tea.

tildar [til'dar] *vt*: ~ **de** to brand as.

tilde ['tilde] *nf* (*defecto*) defect; (*trivialidad*) triviality; (*TIP*) tilde.

tilín [ti'lin] *nm* tinkle.

tilo ['tilo] *nm* lime tree.

timador, a [tima'ðor, a] *nm/f* swindler.

timar [ti'mar] *vt* (*robar*) to steal; (*estafar*) to swindle; (*persona*) to con; **~se** *vr* (*fam*) to make eyes (*con uno* at sb).

timbal [tim'bal] *nm* small drum.

timbrar [tim'brar] *vt* to stamp; (*sellar*) to seal; (*carta*) to postmark.

timbrazo [tim'braθo] *nm* ring; **dar un** ~ to ring the bell.

timbre ['timbre] *nm* (*sello*) stamp; (*campanilla*) bell; (*tono*) timbre; (*COM*) stamp duty.

timidez [timi'ðeθ] *nf* shyness.

tímido, a ['timiðo, a] *a* shy, timid.

timo ['timo] *nm* swindle; **dar un** ~ **a uno** to swindle sb.

timón [ti'mon] *nm* helm, rudder; **coger el** ~ (*fig*) to take charge.

timonel [timo'nel] *nm* helmsman.

timorato, a [timo'rato, a] *a* God-fearing; (*mojigato*) sanctimonious.

tímpano ['timpano] *nm* (*ANAT*) eardrum; (*MUS*) small drum.

tina ['tina] *nf* tub; (*baño*) bath(tub).

tinaja [ti'naxa] *nf* large earthern jar.

tinerfeño, a [tiner'feɲo, a] *a* of *o* from Tenerife ♦ *nm/f* native *o* inhabitant of Tenerife.

tinglado [tin'glaðo] *nm* (*cobertizo*) shed; (*fig: truco*) trick; (*intriga*) intrigue; **armar un** ~ to lay a plot.

tinieblas [ti'njeβlas] *nfpl* darkness *sg*; (*sombras*) shadows; **estamos en** ~ **sobre sus proyectos** (*fig*) we are in the dark about his plans.

tino ['tino] *nm* (*habilidad*) skill; (*MIL*) marksmanship; (*juicio*) insight; (*moderación*) moderation; **sin** ~ immoderately; **coger el** ~ to get the feel *o* hang of it.

tinta ['tinta] *nf* ink; (*TEC*) dye; (*ARTE*) colour; ~ **china** Indian ink; ~**s** *nfpl* (*fig*) shades; **medias** ~**s** (*fig*) half measures; **saber algo de buena** ~ to have sth on good authority.

tinte ['tinte] *nm* (*acto*) dyeing; (*fig*) tinge; (*barniz*) veneer.

tinterillo [tinte'riʎo] *nm* penpusher.

tintero [tin'tero] *nm* inkwell; **se le quedó en el** ~ he clean forgot about it.

tintinear [tintine'ar] *vt* to tinkle.

tinto, a ['tinto, a] *a* (*teñido*) dyed: (*manchado*) stained ♦ *nm* red wine.

tintorera [tinto'rera] *nf* shark.

tintorería [tintore'ria] *nf* dry cleaner's.

tintorero [tinto'rero] *nm* dry cleaner('s).

tintura [tin'tura] *nf* (*acto*) dyeing; (*QUÍMICA*) dye; (*farmacéutico*) tincture.

tiña ['tiɲa] *etc vb V* **teñir** ♦ *nf* (*MED*) ringworm.

tío ['tio] *nm* (*pariente*) uncle; (*fam: viejo*) old fellow; (: *individuo*) bloke, chap, guy (*US*).

tiovivo [tio'βiβo] *nm* roundabout.

típico, a ['tipiko, a] *a* typical; (*pintoresco*) picturesque.

tiple ['tiple] *nm* soprano (voice) ♦ *nf* soprano.

tipo ['tipo] *nm* (*clase*) type, kind; (*norma*) norm; (*patrón*) pattern; (*fam: hombre*) fellow, bloke, guy (*US*); (*ANAT*) build; (: *de mujer*) figure; (*IMPRENTA*) type; ~ **bancario/de descuento** bank/discount rate; ~ **de interés** interest rate; ~ **de interés vigente** (*COM*) standard rate; ~ **de cambio** exchange rate; ~ **base** (*COM*) base rate; ~ **a término** (*COM*) forward rate; **dos** ~**s sospechosos** two suspicious characters; ~ **de letra** (*INFORM, TIP*) typeface; ~ **de datos** (*INFORM*) data type.

tipografía [tipoɣra'fia] *nf* (*tipo*) printing; (*lugar*) printing press.

tipográfico, a [tipo'ɣrafiko, a] *a* printing.

tipógrafo, a [ti'poɣrafo, a] *nm/f* printer.

tique(t) ['tike], *pl* ~**s** ['tikes] *nm* ticket; (*en tienda*) cash slip.

tiquismiquis [tikis'mikis] *nm* fussy person ♦ *nmpl* (*querellas*) squabbling *sg*; (*escrúpulos*) silly scruples.

tira ['tira] *nf* strip; (*fig*) abundance ♦ *nm*: ~ **y afloja** give and take; (*cautela*) caution; **la** ~ **de** ... (*fam*) lots of ....

tirabuzón [tiraβu'θon] *nm* corkscrew; (*rizo*) curl.

tiradero [tira'ðero] *nm* (*AM*) rubbish dump.

tirado, a [ti'raðo, a] *a* (*barato*) dirt-cheap; (*fam: fácil*) very easy ♦ *nf* (*acto*) cast, throw; (*distancia*) distance; (*serie*) series; (*TIP*) printing, edition; **de una tirada** at one go; **está** ~ (*fam*) it's a cinch.

tirador, a [tira'ðor, a] *nm/f* (*persona*) shooter ♦ *nm* (*mango*) handle; (*ELEC*) flex; ~ **certero** sniper.

tiranía [tira'nia] *nf* tyranny.

tirano, a [ti'rano, a] *a* tyrannical ♦ *nm/f* tyrant.

tirante [ti'rante] *a* (*cuerda*) tight, taut; (*relaciones*) strained ♦ *nm* (*ARQ*) brace;

(*TEC*) stay; (*correa*) shoulder strap; ~**s** *nmpl* braces, suspenders (*US*).

tirantez [tiran'teθ] *nf* tightness; (*fig*) tension.

tirar [ti'rar] *vt* to throw; (*volcar*) to upset; (*derribar*) to knock down *o* over; (*tiro*) to fire; (*cohete*) to launch; (*bomba*) to drop; (*edificio*) to pull down; (*desechar*) to throw out *o* away; (*disipar*) to squander; (*imprimir*) to print; (*dar: golpe*) to deal ◆ *vi* (*disparar*) to shoot; (*jalar*) to pull; (*fig*) to draw; (*interesar*) to appeal; (*fam: andar*) to go; (*tender a, buscar realizar*) to tend to; (*DEPORTE*) to shoot; ~**se** *vr* to throw o.s.; (*fig*) to demean o.s.; (*fam !*) to screw (*!*); ~ **abajo** to bring down, destroy; **tira más a su padre** he takes more after his father; ~ **de algo** to pull *o* tug (on) sth; **ir tirando** to manage; ~ **a la derecha** to turn *o* go right; **a todo** ~ at the most.

tirita [ti'rita] *nf* (sticking) plaster, bandaid (*US*).

tiritar [tiri'tar] *vi* to shiver.

tiritona [tiri'tona] *nf* shivering (fit).

tiro ['tiro] *nm* (*lanzamiento*) throw; (*disparo*) shot; (*tiroteo*) shooting; (*DEPORTE*) shot; (*TENIS, GOLF*) drive; (*alcance*) range; (*de escalera*) flight (of stairs); (*golpe*) blow; (*engaño*) hoax; ~ **al blanco** target practice; **caballo de** ~ cart-horse; **andar de** ~**s largos** to be all dressed up; **al** ~ (*AM*) at once; **se pegó un** ~ he shot himself; **le salió el** ~ **por la culata** backfired on him.

Tirol [ti'rol] *nm*: **El** ~ the Tyrol.

tirolés, esa [tiro'les, esa] *a, nm/f* Tyrolean.

tirón [ti'ron] *nm* (*sacudida*) pull, tug; **de un** ~ in one go; **dar un** ~ **a** to pull at, tug at.

tirotear [tirote'ar] *vt* to shoot at; ~**se** *vr* to exchange shots.

tiroteo [tiro'teo] *nm* exchange of shots, shooting; (*escaramuza*) skirmish.

tirria ['tirrja] *nf*: **tener una** ~ **a uno** to have a grudge against sb.

tísico, a ['tisiko, a] *a, nm/f* consumptive.

tisis ['tisis] *nf* consumption, tuberculosis.

tít. *abr* = **título.**

títere ['titere] *nm* puppet; **no dejar** ~ **con cabeza** to turn everything upside-down.

titilar [titi'lar] *vi* (*luz, estrella*) to twinkle; (*parpado*) to flutter.

titiritero, a [titiri'tero, a] *nm/f* (*acróbata*) acrobat; (*malabarista*) juggler.

titubeante [tituβe'ante] *a* (*inestable*) shaky, tottering; (*farfullante*) stammering; (*dudoso*) hesitant.

titubear [tituβe'ar] *vi* to stagger; (*tartamudear*) to stammer; (*vacilar*) to hesitate.

titubeo [titu'βeo] *nm* staggering; stammering; hesitation.

titulado, a [titu'laðo, a] *a* (*libro*) entitled;

(*persona*) titled.

titular [titu'lar] *a* titular ◆ *nm/f* (*de oficina*) occupant; (*de pasaporte*) holder ◆ *nm* headline ◆ *vt* to title; ~**se** *vr* to be entitled.

título ['titulo] *nm* (*gen*) title; (*de diario*) headline; (*certificado*) professional qualification; (*universitario*) university degree; (*COM*) bond; (*fig*) right; ~**s** *nmpl* qualifications; **a** ~ **de** by way of; (*en calidad de*) in the capacity of; **a** ~ **de curiosidad** as a matter of interest; ~ **de propiedad** title deed; ~**s convertibles de interés fijo** (*COM*) convertible loan stock *sg*.

tiza ['tiθa] *nf* chalk; **una** ~ a piece of chalk.

tizna ['tiθna] *nf* grime.

tiznar [tiθ'nar] *vt* to blacken; (*manchar*) to smudge, stain; (*fig*) to tarnish.

tizón [ti'θon], **tizo** ['tiθo] *nm* brand; (*fig*) stain.

Tm. *abr* = **tonelada(s) métrica(s).**

toalla [to'aʎa] *nf* towel.

tobillo [to'βiʎo] *nm* ankle.

tobogán [toβo'van] *nm* toboggan; (*montaña rusa*) switchback; (*resbaladilla*) chute, slide.

toca ['toka] *nf* headdress.

tocadiscos [toka'ðiskos] *nm inv* record player.

tocado, a [to'kaðo, a] *a* (*fruta etc*) rotten; ◆ *nm* headdress; **estar** ~ **de la cabeza** (*fam*) to be weak in the head.

tocador [toka'ðor] *nm* (*mueble*) dressing table; (*cuarto*) boudoir; (*neceser*) toilet case; (*fam*) ladies' room.

tocante [to'kante]: ~ **a** *prep* with regard to; **en lo** ~ **a** as for, so far as concerns.

tocar [to'kar] *vt* to touch; (*sentir*) to feel; (*con la mano*) to handle; (*MUS*) to play; (*campana*) to ring; (*tambor*) to beat; (*trompeta*) to blow; (*topar con*) to run into, strike; (*referirse a*) to allude to; (*ser emparentado con*) to be related to ◆ *vi* (*a la puerta*) to knock (on *o* at the door); (*ser de turno*) to fall to, be the turn of; (*ser hora*) to be due; (*atañer*) to concern; ~**se** *vr* (*cubrirse la cabeza*) to cover one's head; (*tener contacto*) to touch (each other); ~**le a uno** to fall to sb's lot; ~ **en** (*NAUT*) to call at; **por lo que a mí me toca** as far as I am concerned; **esto toca en la locura** this verges on madness.

tocayo, a [to'kajo, a] *nm/f* namesake.

tocino [to'θino] *nm* (*bacon*) fat; ~ **de panceta** bacon.

todavía [toða'βia] *ad* (*aun*) even; (*aún*) still, yet; ~ **más** *yet o* still more; ~ **no** not yet; ~ **en 1970** as late as 1970; **está lloviendo** ~ it's still raining.

todo, a ['toðo, a] *a* all; (*cada*) every; (*entero*) whole; (*sentido negativo*): **en** ~ **el día lo he visto** I haven't seen him all day;

todas las semanas/~s los martes every week/Tuesday ♦ *ad* all, completely ♦ *nm* everything ♦ *pron*: ~s/todas everyone; a toda velocidad at full speed; estaba ~ ojos he was all eyes; puede ser ~ lo honesto que quiera he can be as honest as he likes; en un ~ as a whole; corriendo y ~, no llegaron a tiempo even though they ran, they still didn't arrive in time; ante ~ above all; a pesar de ~ even so, in spite of everything; con ~ still, even so; del ~ completely; después de ~ after all; sobre ~ (*especialmente*) after all; (*en primer lugar*) above all.

todopoderoso, a [toðopoðeˈroso, a] *a* all powerful; (*REL*) almighty.

toga [ˈtoɣa] *nf* toga; (*ESCOL*) gown.

Tokio [ˈtokjo] *n* Tokyo.

toldo [ˈtoldo] *nm* (*para el sol*) sunshade; (*tienda*) marquee; (*fig*) pride.

tole [ˈtole] *nm* (*fam*) commotion.

toledano, a [toleˈðano, a] *a* of *o* from Toledo ♦ *nm/f* native *o* inhabitant of Toledo.

tolerable [toleˈraßle] *a* tolerable.

tolerancia [toleˈranθja] *nf* tolerance.

tolerante [toleˈrante] *a* tolerant; (*fig*) open-minded.

tolerar [toleˈrar] *vt* to tolerate; (*resistir*) to endure.

Tolón [toˈlon] *nm* Toulon.

tolvanera [tolßaˈnera] *nf* dust cloud.

toma [ˈtoma] *nf* (*gen*) taking; (*MED*) dose; (*ELEC*) *tb*: ~ de corriente socket; (*MEC*) inlet; ~ de posesión (*por presidente*) taking up office; ~ de tierra (*AVIAT*) landing.

tomadura [tomaˈðura] *nf*: ~ de pelo hoax.

tomar [toˈmar] *vt* (*gen, CINE, FOTO, TV*) to take; (*actitud*) to adopt; (*aspecto*) to take on; (*notas*) to take down; (*beber*) to drink ♦ *vi* to take; (*AM*) to drink; ~se *vr* to take; ~se por to consider o.s. to be; ¡toma! here you are!; ~ asiento to sit down; ~ a uno por loco to think sb mad; ~ a bien/a mal to take well/badly; ~ en serio to take seriously; ~ el pelo a uno to pull sb's leg; ~la con uno to pick a quarrel with sb; ~ por escrito to write down; toma y daca give and take.

tomate [toˈmate] *nm* tomato.

tomatera [tomaˈtera] *nf* tomato plant.

tomavistas [tomaˈßistas] *nm inv* movie camera.

tomillo [toˈmiʎo] *nm* thyme.

tomo [ˈtomo] *nm* (*libro*) volume; (*fig*) importance.

ton [ton] *abr* = **tonelada** ♦ *nm*: sin ~ ni son without rhyme or reason.

tonada [toˈnaða] *nf* tune.

tonalidad [tonaliˈðað] *nf* tone.

tonel [toˈnel] *nm* barrel.

tonelada [toneˈlaða] *nf* ton; ~ métrica metric ton.

tonelaje [toneˈlaxe] *nm* tonnage.

tonelero [toneˈlero] *nm* cooper.

tónico, a [ˈtoniko, a] *a* tonic ♦ *nm* (*MED*) tonic ♦ *nf* (*MUS*) tonic; (*fig*) keynote.

tonificador, a [tonifikaˈðor, a], **tonificante** [tonifiˈkante] *a* invigorating, stimulating.

tonificar [tonifiˈkar] *vt* to tone up.

tonifique [toniˈfike] *etc vb V* tonificar.

tonillo [toˈniʎo] *nm* monotonous voice.

tono [ˈtono] *nm* (*MUS*) tone; (*altura*) pitch; (*color*) shade; fuera de ~ inappropriate; ~ de marcar (*TELEC*) dialling tone; darse ~ to put on airs.

tontear [tonteˈar] *vi* (*fam*) to fool about; (*enamorados*) to flirt.

tontería [tonteˈria] *nf* (*estupidez*) foolishness; (*una* ~) silly thing; ~s *nfpl* rubbish *sg*, nonsense *sg*.

tonto, a [ˈtonto, a] *a* stupid; (*ridículo*) silly ♦ *nm/f* fool; (*payaso*) clown; a tontas y a locas anyhow; hacer(se) el ~ to act the fool.

topacio [toˈpaθjo] *nm* topaz.

topar [toˈpar] *vt* (*tropezar*) to bump into; (*encontrar*) to find, come across; (*cabra etc*) to butt ♦ *vi*: ~ contra *o* en to run into; ~ con to run up against; el problema topa en eso that's where the problem lies.

tope [ˈtope] *a* maximum ♦ *nm* (*fin*) end; (*límite*) limit; (*riña*) quarrel; (*FERRO*) buffer; (*AUTO*) bumper; al ~ end to end; fecha ~ closing date; precio ~ top price; sueldo ~ maximum salary; ~ de tabulación tab stop.

tópico, a [ˈtopiko, a] *a* topical; (*MED*) local ♦ *nm* platitude, cliché; de uso ~ for external application.

topo [ˈtopo] *nm* (*ZOOL*) mole; (*fig*) blunderer.

topografía [topoɣraˈfia] *nf* topography.

topógrafo, a [toˈpoɣrafo, a] *nm/f* topographer; (*agrimensor*) surveyor.

toponimia [topoˈnimja] *nf* place names *pl*; (*estudio*) study of place names.

toque [ˈtoke] *etc vb V* tocar ♦ *nm* touch; (*MUS*) beat; (*de campana*) ring, chime; (*MIL*) bugle call; (*fig*) crux; dar un ~ a to test; dar el último ~ a to put the final touch to; ~ de queda curfew.

toquetear [toketeˈar] *vt* to handle; (*fam!*) to touch up.

toquilla [toˈkiʎa] *nf* (*chal*) shawl.

torbellino [torbeˈʎino] *nm* whirlwind; (*fig*) whirl.

torcedura [torθeˈðura] *nf* twist; (*MED*) sprain.

torcer [torˈθer] *vt* to twist; (*la esquina*) to turn; (*MED*) to sprain; (*cuerda*) to plait; (*ropa, manos*) to wring; (*persona*) to corrupt; (*sentido*) to distort ♦ *vi* (*cambiar* *de dirección*) to turn; ~**se** *vr* to twist; (*doblar*) to bend; (*desviarse*) to go astray; (*fracasar*) to go wrong; ~ **el gesto** to scowl; ~**se un pie** to twist one's foot; **el coche torció a la derecha** the car turned right.

torcido, a [tor'θiðo, a] *a* twisted; (*fig*) crooked ♦ *nm* curl.

tordo, a ['torðo, a] *a* dappled ♦ *nm* thrush.

torear [tore'ar] *vt* (*fig: evadir*) to dodge; (*toro*) to fight ♦ *vi* to fight bulls.

toreo [to'reo] *nm* bullfighting.

torero, a [to'rero, a] *nm/f* bullfighter.

toril [to'ril] *nm* bullpen.

tormenta [tor'menta] *nf* storm; (*fig: confusión*) turmoil.

tormento [tor'mento] *nm* torture; (*fig*) anguish.

tormentoso, a [tormen'toso, a] *a* stormy.

tornar [tor'nar] *vt* (*devolver*) to return, give back; (*transformar*) to transform ♦ *vi* to go back; ~**se** *vr* (*ponerse*) to become; (*volver*) to return.

tornasol [torna'sol] *nm* (*BOT*) sunflower; **papel de** ~ litmus paper.

tornasolado, a [tornaso'laðo, a] *a* (*brillante*) iridescent; (*reluciente*) shimmering.

torneo [tor'neo] *nm* tournament.

tornero, a [tor'nero, a] *nm/f* machinist.

tornillo [tor'niʎo] *nm* screw; **apretar los** ~**s a uno** to apply pressure on sb; **le falta un** ~ (*fam*) he's got a screw loose.

torniquete [torni'kete] *nm* (*puerta*) turnstile; (*MED*) tourniquet.

torno ['torno] *nm* (*TEC: grúa*) winch; (: *de carpintero*) lathe; (*tambor*) drum; ~ **de banco** vice, vise (*US*); **en** ~ **(a)** round, about.

toro ['toro] *nm* bull; (*fam*) he-man; **los** ~**s** bullfighting *sg*.

toronja [to'ronxa] *nf* (*AM*) grapefruit.

torpe ['torpe] *a* (*poco hábil*) clumsy, awkward; (*movimiento*) sluggish; (*necio*) dim; (*lento*) slow; (*indecente*) crude; (*no honrado*) dishonest.

torpedo [tor'peðo] *nm* torpedo.

torpemente [torpe'mente] *ad* (*sin destreza*) clumsily; (*lentamente*) slowly.

torpeza [tor'peθa] *nf* (*falta de agilidad*) clumsiness; (*lentitud*) slowness; (*rigidez*) stiffness; (*error*) mistake; (*crudeza*) obscenity.

torre ['torre] *nf* tower; (*de petróleo*) derrick; (*de electricidad*) pylon; (*AJEDREZ*) rook; (*AVIAT, MIL, NAUT*) turret.

torrencial [torren'θjal] *a* torrential.

torrente [to'rrente] *nm* torrent.

tórrido, a ['torriðo, a] *a* torrid.

torrija [to'rrixa] *nf* fried bread; ~**s** French toast *sg*.

torsión [tor'sjon] *nf* twisting.

torso ['torso] *nm* torso.

torta ['torta] *nf* cake; (*fam*) slap; **no entendió ni** ~ he didn't understand a word of it.

tortazo [tor'taθo] *nm* (*bofetada*) slap; (*de coche*) crash.

tortícolis [tor'tikolis] *nm inv* stiff neck.

tortilla [tor'tiʎa] *nf* omelette; (*AM*) maize pancake; ~ **francesa/española** plain/potato omelette; **cambiar** *o* **volver la** ~ **a uno** to turn the tables on sb.

tortillera [torti'ʎera] *nf* (*fam!*) lesbian.

tórtola ['tortola] *nf* turtledove.

tortuga [tor'tuɣa] *nf* tortoise; ~ **marina** turtle.

tortuoso, a [tor'twoso, a] *a* winding.

tortura [tor'tura] *nf* torture.

torturar [tortu'rar] *vt* to torture.

torvo, a ['torßo, a] *a* grim, fierce.

torzamos [tor'θamos] *etc vb V* **torcer**.

tos [tos] *nf inv* cough; ~ **ferina** whooping cough.

Toscana [tos'kana] *nf*: **La** ~ Tuscany.

tosco, a ['tosko, a] *a* coarse.

toser [to'ser] *vi* to cough; **no hay quien le tosa** he's in a class by himself.

tostado, a [tos'taðo, a] *a* toasted; (*por el sol*) dark brown; (*piel*) tanned ♦ *nf* tan; (*pan*) piece of toast; **tostadas** *nfpl* toast *sg*.

tostador [tosta'ðor] *nm* toaster.

tostar [tos'tar] *vt* to toast; (*café*) to roast; (*al sol*) to tan; ~**se** *vr* to get brown.

total [to'tal] *a* total ♦ *ad* in short; (*al fin y al cabo*) when all is said and done ♦ *nm* total; **en** ~ in all; ~ **que** to cut a long story short; ~ **de comprobación** (*INFORM*) hash total; ~ **debe/haber** (*COM*) debit/assets total.

totalidad [totali'ðað] *nf* whole.

totalitario, a [totali'tarjo, a] *a* totalitarian.

tóxico, a ['toksiko, a] *a* toxic ♦ *nm* poison.

toxicómano, a [toksi'komano, a] *a* addicted to drugs ♦ *nm/f* drug addict.

tozudo, a [to'θuðo, a] *a* obstinate.

traba ['traßa] *nf* bond, tie; (*cadena*) fetter; **poner** ~**s a** to restrain.

trabajador, a [traßaxa'ðor, a] *nm/f* worker ♦ *a* hard-working.

trabajar [traßa'xar] *vt* to work; (*arar*) to till; (*empeñarse en*) to work at; (*empujar: persona*) to push; (*convencer*) to persuade ♦ *vi* to work; (*esforzarse*) to strive; **¡a** ~**!** let's get to work!; ~ **por hacer algo** to strive to do sth.

trabajo [tra'ßaxo] *nm* work; (*tarea*) task; (*POL*) labour; (*fig*) effort; **tomarse el** ~ **de** to take the trouble to; ~ **por turno/a destajo** shift work/piecework; ~ **en proceso** (*COM*) work-in-progress.

trabajoso, a [traßa'xoso, a] *a* hard; (*MED*)

pale.

trabalenguas [traβa'lengwas] *nm inv* tongue twister.

trabar [tra'ßar] *vt* (*juntar*) to join, unite; (*atar*) to tie down, fetter; (*agarrar*) to seize; (*amistad*) to strike up; ~**se** *vr* to become entangled; (*reñir*) to squabble; **se le traba la lengua** he gets tongue-tied.

trabazón [traßa'θon] *nf* (*TEC*) joining, assembly; (*fig*) bond, link.

trabucar [traßu'kar] *vt* (*confundir*) to confuse, mix up; (*palabras*) to misplace.

trabuque [tra'ßuke] *etc vb* V **trabucar**.

tracción [trak'θjon] *nf* traction; ~ **delantera/trasera** front-wheel/rear-wheel drive.

trace ['traθe] *etc vb* V **trazar**.

tractor [trak'tor] *nm* tractor.

trad. *abr* (= *traducido*) trans.

tradición [traði'θjon] *nf* tradition.

tradicional [traðiθjo'nal] *a* traditional.

traducción [traðuk'θjon] *nf* translation; ~ **asistida por ordenador** computer-assisted translation.

traducible [traðu'θißle] *a* translatable.

traducir [traðu'θir] *vt* to translate; ~**se** *vr*: ~**se en** (*fig*) to entail, result in.

traductor, a [traðuk'tor, a] *nm/f* translator.

traduzca [tra'ðuθka] *etc vb* V **traducir**.

traer [tra'er] *vt* to bring; (*llevar*) to carry; (*ropa*) to wear; (*incluir*) to carry; (*fig*) to cause; ~**se** *vr*: ~**se algo** to be up to sth; ~**se bien/mal** to dress well/badly; **traérselas** to be annoying; ~ **consigo** to involve, entail; **es un problema que se las trae** it's a difficult problem.

traficante [trafi'kante] *nm/f* trader, dealer.

traficar [trafi'kar] *vi* to trade; ~ **con** (*pey*) to deal illegally in.

tráfico ['trafiko] *nm* (*COM*) trade; (*AUTO*) traffic.

trafique [tra'fike] *etc vb* V **traficar**.

tragaderas [traɣa'ðeras] *nfpl* (*garganta*) throat *sg*, gullet *sg*; (*credulidad*) gullibility *sg*.

tragaluz [traɣa'luθ] *nm* skylight.

tragamonedas [traɣamo'neðas] *nm inv*, **tragaperras** [traɣa'perras] *nm inv* slot machine.

tragar [tra'ɣar] *vt* to swallow; (*devorar*) to devour, bolt down; ~**se** *vr* to swallow; (*tierra*) to absorb, soak up; **no le puedo** ~ (*persona*) I can't stand him.

tragedia [tra'xeðja] *nf* tragedy.

trágico, a ['traxiko, a] *a* tragic.

trago ['traɣo] *nm* (*líquido*) drink; (*comido de golpe*) gulp; (*fam: de bebida*) swig; (*desgracia*) blow; ~ **amargo** (*fig*) hard time.

trague ['traɣe] *etc vb* V **tragar**.

traición [trai'θjon] *nf* treachery; (*JUR*) treason; (*una* ~) act of treachery.

traicionar [traiθjo'nar] *vt* to betray.

traicionero, a [traiθjo'nero, a] = **traidor, a**.

traída [tra'iða] *nf* carrying; ~ **de aguas** water supply.

traidor, a [trai'ðor, a] *a* treacherous ♦ *nm/f* traitor.

traiga ['traiɣa] *etc vb* V **traer**.

traje ['traxe] *etc vb* V **traer** ♦ *nm* (*gen*) dress; (*de hombre*) suit; (~ *típico*) costume; (*fig*) garb; ~ **de baño** swimsuit; ~ **de luces** bullfighter's costume; ~ **hecho a la medida** made-to-measure suit.

trajera [tra'xera] *etc vb* V **traer**.

trajín [tra'xin] *nm* haulage; (*fam: movimiento*) bustle; **trajines** *nmpl* goings-on.

trajinar [traxi'nar] *vt* (*llevar*) to carry, transport ♦ *vi* (*moverse*) to bustle about; (*viajar*) to travel around.

trama ['trama] *nf* (*fig*) link; (: *intriga*) plot; (*de tejido*) weft.

tramar [tra'mar] *vt* to plot; (*TEC*) to weave; ~**se** *vr* (*fig*): **algo se está tramando** there's something going on.

tramitar [trami'tar] *vt* (*asunto*) to transact; (*negociar*) to negotiate; (*manejar*) to handle.

trámite ['tramite] *nm* (*paso*) step; (*JUR*) transaction; ~**s** *nmpl* (*burocracia*) paperwork *sg*, procedures; (*JUR*) proceedings.

tramo ['tramo] *nm* (*de tierra*) plot; (*de escalera*) flight; (*de vía*) section.

tramoya [tra'moja] *nf* (*TEATRO*) piece of stage machinery; (*fig*) trick.

tramoyista [tramo'jista] *nm/f* scene shifter; (*fig*) trickster.

trampa ['trampa] *nf* trap; (*en el suelo*) trapdoor; (*prestidigitación*) conjuring trick; (*engaño*) trick; (*fam*) fiddle; (*de pantalón*) fly; **caer en la** ~ to fall into the trap; **hacer** ~**s** (*hacer juegos de manos*) to juggle, conjure; (*trampear*) to cheat.

trampear [trampe'ar] *vt, vi* to cheat.

trampilla [tram'piʎa] *nf* trap, hatchway.

trampista [tram'pista] *nm/f* = **tramposo**.

trampolín [trampo'lin] *nm* trampoline; (*de piscina etc*) diving board.

tramposo, a [tram'poso, a] *a* crooked, cheating ♦ *nm/f* crook, cheat.

tranca ['tranka] *nf* (*palo*) stick; (*viga*) beam; (*de puerta, ventana*) bar; (*borrachera*) binge; **a** ~**s y barrancas** with great difficulty.

trancar [tran'kar] *vt* to bar ♦ *vi* to stride along.

trancazo [tran'kaθo] *nm* (*golpe*) blow.

trance ['tranθe] *nm* (*momento difícil*) difficult moment; (*situación crítica*) critical situation; (*estado hipnotizado*) trance; **estar en** ~ **de muerte** to be at death's door.

tranco ['tranko] *nm* stride.

tranque ['tranke] *etc vb* V **trancar**.

tranquilice [tranki'liθe] *etc vb* V **tranquilizar**.

tranquilidad [trankili'ðað] *nf* (*calma*) calmness, stillness; (*paz*) peacefulness.

tranquilizador, a [trankiliθa'ðor, a] *a* (*música*) soothing; (*hecho*) reassuring.

tranquilizar [trankili'θar] *vt* (*calmar*) to calm (down); (*asegurar*) to reassure.

tranquilo, a [tran'kilo, a] *a* (*calmado*) calm; (*apacible*) peaceful; (*mar*) calm; (*mente*) untroubled.

Trans. *abr* (*COM*) = **transferencia**.

transacción [transak'θjon] *nf* transaction.

transar [tran'sar] *vi* = **transigir**.

transbordador [transßorða'ðor] *nm* ferry.

transbordar [transßor'ðar] *vt* to transfer; ~**se** *vr* to change.

transbordo [trans'ßorðo] *nm* transfer; **hacer** ~ to change (trains).

transcurrir [transku'rrir] *vi* (*tiempo*) to pass; (*hecho*) to turn out.

transcurso [trans'kurso] *nm* passing, lapse; **en el** ~ **de 8 días** in the course of a week.

transeúnte [transe'unte] *a* transient ♦ *nm/f* passer-by.

transferencia [transfe'renθja] *nf* transference; (*COM*) transfer; ~ **bancaria** banker's order; ~ **de crédito** (*COM*) credit transfer; ~ **electrónica de fondos** (*COM*) electronic funds transfer.

transferir [transfe'rir] *vt* to transfer; (*aplazar*) to postpone.

transfiera [trans'fjera] *etc vb* V **transferir**.

transfigurar [transfiɣu'rar] *vt* to transfigure.

transfiriendo [transfi'rjendo] *etc vb* V **transferir**.

transformador [transforma'ðor] *nm* transformer.

transformar [transfor'mar] *vt* to transform; (*convertir*) to convert.

tránsfuga ['transfuɣa] *nm/f* (*MIL*) deserter; (*POL*) turncoat.

transgresión [transɣre'sjon] *nf* transgression.

transición [transi'θjon] *nf* transition; **período de** ~ transitional period.

transido, a [tran'siðo, a] *a* overcome; ~ **de angustia** beset with anxiety; ~ **de dolor** racked with pain.

transigir [transi'xir] *vi* to compromise; (*ceder*) to make concessions.

transija [tran'sixa] *etc vb* V **transigir**.

Transilvania [transil'ßanja] *nf* Transylvania.

transistor [transis'tor] *nm* transistor.

transitable [transi'taßle] *a* (*camino*) passable.

transitar [transi'tar] *vi* to go (from place to place).

tránsito ['transito] *nm* transit; (*AUTO*) traffic; (*parada*) stop; **horas de máximo** ~ rush hours; "**se prohíbe el** ~" "no thoroughfare."

transitorio, a [transi'torjo, a] *a* transitory.

transmisión [transmi'sjon] *nf* (*RADIO, TV*) transmission, broadcast(ing); (*transferencia*) transfer; ~ **en circuito** hookup; ~ **en directo/exterior** live/outside broadcast; ~ **de datos (en paralelo/en serie)** (*INFORM*) (parallel/serial) data transfer *o* transmission; **plena/media** ~ **bidireccional** (*INFORM*) full/half duplex.

transmitir [transmi'tir] *vt* to transmit; (*RADIO, TV*) to broadcast; (*enfermedad*) to give, pass on.

transparencia [transpa'renθja] *nf* transparency; (*claridad*) clearness, clarity; (*foto*) slide.

transparentar [transparen'tar] *vt* to reveal ♦ *vi* to be transparent.

transparente [transpa'rente] *a* transparent; (*aire*) clear; (*ligero*) diaphanous ♦ *nm* curtain.

transpirar [transpi'rar] *vi* to perspire; (*fig*) to transpire.

transpondré [transpon'dre] *etc vb* V **transponer**.

transponer [transpo'ner] *vt* to transpose; (*cambiar de sitio*) to move about ♦ *vi* (*desaparecer*) to disappear; (*ir más allá*) to go beyond; ~**se** *vr* to change places; (*ocultarse*) to hide; (*sol*) to go down.

transponga [trans'ponga] *etc vb* V **transponer**.

transportación [transporta'θjon] *nf* transportation.

transportador [transporta'ðor] *nm* (*MECÁNICA*): ~ **de correa** belt conveyor.

transportar [transpor'tar] *vt* to transport; (*llevar*) to carry.

transporte [trans'porte] *nm* transport; (*COM*) haulage; **Ministerio de T~s** Ministry of Transport.

transpuesto [trans'pwesto], **transpuse** [trans'puse] *etc vb* V **transponer**.

transversal [transßer'sal] *a* transverse, cross ♦ *nf* (*tb*: **calle** ~) cross street.

transversalmente [transßersal'mente] *ad* obliquely.

tranvía [tram'bia] *nm* tram, streetcar (*US*).

trapecio [tra'peθjo] *nm* trapeze.

trapecista [trape'θista] *nm/f* trapeze artist.

trapero, a [tra'pero, a] *nm/f* ragman.

trapicheos [trapi'tʃeos] *nmpl* (*fam*) schemes, fiddles.

trapisonda [trapi'sonda] *nf* (*jaleo*) row; (*estafa*) swindle.

trapo ['trapo] *nm* (*tela*) rag; (*de cocina*) cloth; ~**s** *nmpl* (*fam: de mujer*) clothes, dresses; **a todo** ~ under full sail; **soltar el** ~ (*llorar*) to burst into tears.

tráquea ['trakea] *nf* trachea, windpipe.

traqueteo [trake'teo] *nm* (*crujido*) crack; (*golpeteo*) rattling.

tras [tras] *prep* (*detrás*) behind; (*después*) after; ~ **de** besides; **día** ~ **día** day after day; **uno** ~ **otro** one after the other.

trascendencia [trasθen'denθja] *nf* (*importancia*) importance; (*filosofía*) transcendence.

trascendental [trasθenden'tal] *a* important; transcendental.

trascender [trasθen'der] *vi* (*oler*) to smell; (*noticias*) to come out, leak out; (*eventos, sentimientos*) to spread, have a wide effect; ~ **a** (*afectar*) to reach, have an effect on; (*oler a*) to smack of; **en su novela todo trasciende a romanticismo** everything in his novel smacks of romanticism.

trascienda [tras'θjenda] *etc vb V* **trascender.**

trasegar [trase'ɣar] *vt* (*mover*) to move about; (*vino*) to decant.

trasegué [trase'ɣe], **traseguemos** [trase'ɣemos] *etc vb V* **trasegar.**

trasero, a [tra'sero, a] *a* back, rear ♦ *nm* (*ANAT*) bottom; ~**s** *nmpl* ancestors.

trasfondo [tras'fondo] *nm* background.

trasgo ['trasɣo] *nm* (*duende*) goblin.

trasgredir [trasɣre'ðir] *vt* to contravene.

trashumante [trasu'mante] *a* migrating.

trasiego [tra'sjeɣo] *etc vb V* **trasegar** ♦ *nm* (*cambiar de sitio*) move, switch; (*de vino*) decanting; (*trastorno*) upset.

trasiegue [tra'sjeɣe] *etc vb V* **trasegar.**

trasladar [trasla'ðar] *vt* to move; (*persona*) to transfer; (*postergar*) to postpone; (*copiar*) to copy; (*interpretar*) to interpret; ~**se** *vr* (*irse*) to go; (*mudarse*) to move; ~**se a otro puesto** to move to a new job.

traslado [tras'laðo] *nm* move; (*mudanza*) move, removal; (*de persona*) transfer; (*copia*) copy; ~ **de bloque** (*INFORM*) block move, cut-and-paste.

traslucir [traslu'θir] *vt* to show; ~**se** *vr* to be translucent; (*fig*) to be revealed.

trasluz [tras'luθ] *nm* reflected light; **al** ~ against *o* up to the light.

trasluzca [tras'luθka] *etc vb V* **traslucir.**

trasmano [tras'mano]: **a** ~ *ad* (*fuera de alcance*) out of reach; (*apartado*) out of the way.

trasnochador, a [trasnotʃa'ðor, a] *a* given to staying up late ♦ *nm/f* (*fig*) night bird.

trasnochar [trasno'tʃar] *vi* (*acostarse tarde*) to stay up late; (*no dormir*) to have a sleepless night; (*pasar la noche*) to stay the night.

traspasar [traspa'sar] *vt* (*bala*) to pierce, go through; (*propiedad*) to sell, transfer;

(*calle*) to cross over; (*límites*) to go beyond; (*ley*) to break; **"traspaso negocio"** "business for sale".

traspaso [tras'paso] *nm* transfer; (*fig*) anguish.

traspié [tras'pje], *pl* **traspiés** *nm* (*caída*) stumble; (*tropezón*) trip; (*fig*) blunder.

trasplantar [trasplan'tar] *vt* to transplant.

traste ['traste] *nm* (*MUS*) fret; **dar al** ~ **con algo** to ruin sth; **ir al** ~ to fall through.

trastero [tras'tero] *nm* lumber room.

trastienda [tras'tjenda] *nf* backshop; **obtener algo por la** ~ to get sth by underhand means.

trasto ['trasto] *nm* (*mueble*) piece of furniture; (*tarro viejo*) old pot; (*pey: cosa*) piece of junk; (: *persona*) dead loss; ~**s** *nmpl* (*TEATRO*) scenery *sg*; **tirar los** ~**s a la cabeza** to have a blazing row.

trastornado, a [trastor'naðo, a] *a* (*loco*) mad; (*agitado*) crazy.

trastornar [trastor'nar] *vt* to overturn, upset; (*fig: ideas*) to confuse; (: *nervios*) to shatter; (: *persona*) to drive crazy; ~**se** *vr* (*plan*) to fall through.

trastorno [tras'torno] *nm* (*acto*) overturning; (*confusión*) confusion; (*POL*) disturbance, upheaval; (*MED*) upset; ~ **estomacal** stomach upset; ~ **mental** mental disorder, breakdown.

trasunto [tra'sunto] *nm* copy.

tratable [tra'taβle] *a* friendly.

tratado [tra'taðo] *nm* (*POL*) treaty; (*COM*) agreement; (*LITERATURA*) treatise.

tratamiento [trata'mjento] *nm* treatment; (*TEC*) processing; (*de problema*) handling; ~ **de datos** (*INFORM*) data processing; ~ **de gráficos** (*INFORM*) graphics; ~ **de márgenes** margin settings; ~ **de textos** (*INFORM*) word processing; ~ **por lotes** (*INFORM*) batch processing; ~ **de tú** familiar address.

tratante [tra'tante] *nm/f* dealer, merchandizer.

tratar [tra'tar] *vt* (*ocuparse de*) to treat; (*manejar, TEC*) to handle; (*INFORM*) to process; (*MED*) to treat; (*dirigirse a: persona*) to address ♦ *vi*: ~ **de** (*hablar sobre*) to deal with, be about; (*intentar*) to try to; ~ **con** (*COM*) to trade in; (*negociar*) to negotiate with; (*tener contactos*) to have dealings with; ~**se** *vr* to treat each other; **se trata de la nueva piscina** it's about the new pool; **¿de qué se trata?** what's it about?

trato ['trato] *nm* dealings *pl*; (*relaciones*) relationship; (*comportamiento*) manner; (*COM, JUR*) agreement, contract; (*título*) (form of) address; **de** ~ **agradable** pleasant; **de fácil** ~ easy to get on with; ~ **equitativo** fair deal; **¡** ~ **hecho!** it's a deal!; **malos** ~s ill-treatment *sg.*

trauma ['trauma] *nm* trauma.

traumático, a [trau'matiko, a] *a* traumatic.

través [tra'ßes] *nm* (*contratiempo*) reverse; **al** ~ across, crossways; **a** ~ **de** across; (*sobre*) over; (*por*) through; **de** ~ across; (*de lado*) sideways.

travesaño [traße'saɲo] *nm* (*ARQ*) cross-beam; (*DEPORTE*) crossbar.

travesía [traße'sia] *nf* (*calle*) cross-street; (*NAUT*) crossing.

travesura [traße'sura] *nf* (*broma*) prank; (*ingenio*) wit.

travieso, a [tra'ßjeso, a] *a* (*niño*) naughty; (*adulto*) restless; (*ingenioso*) witty ◆ *nf* crossing; (*ARQ*) crossbeam.

trayecto [tra'jekto] *nm* (*ruta*) road, way; (*viaje*) journey; (*tramo*) stretch; (*curso*) course; **final del** ~ end of the line.

trayectoria [trajek'torja] *nf* trajectory; (*desarrollo*) development, path; **la** ~ **actual del partido** the party's present line.

trayendo [tra'jendo] *etc vb* V **traer.**

traza ['traθa] *nf* (*ARQ*) plan, design; (*aspecto*) looks *pl*; (*señal*) sign; (*engaño*) trick; (*habilidad*) skill; (*INFORM*) trace.

trazado, a [tra'θaðo, a] *a*: **bien** ~ shapely, well-formed ◆ *nm* (*ARQ*) plan, design; (*fig*) outline; (*de carretera etc*) line, route.

trazador [traθa'ðor] *nm* plotter; ~ **plano** flatbed plotter.

trazar [tra'θar] *vt* (*ARQ*) to plan; (*ARTE*) to sketch; (*fig*) to trace; (*itinerario: hacer*) to plot; (*plan*) to follow.

trazo ['traθo] *nm* (*línea*) line; (*bosquejo*) sketch; ~s *nmpl* (*de cara*) lines, features.

TRB *abr* = toneladas de registro bruto.

trébol ['treßol] *nm* (*BOT*) clover; ~es *nmpl* (*NAIPES*) clubs.

trece ['treθe] *num* thirteen; **estar en sus** ~ to stand firm.

trecho ['tretʃo] *nm* (*distancia*) distance; (*de tiempo*) while; (*fam*) piece; **de** ~ **en** ~ at intervals.

tregua ['treɣwa] *nf* (*MIL*) truce; (*fig*) lull; **sin** ~ without respite.

treinta ['treinta] *num* thirty.

treintena [trein'tena] *nf* (about) thirty.

tremendo, a [tre'mendo, a] *a* (*terrible*) terrible; (*imponente: cosa*) imposing; (*fam: fabuloso*) tremendous; (*divertido*) entertaining.

trémulo, a ['tremulo, a] *a* quivering; (*luz*) flickering.

tren [tren] *nm* (*FERRO*) train; ~ **de aterrizaje** undercarriage; ~ **directo/ expreso/(de) mercancías/de pasajeros/ suplementario** through/fast/goods *o* freight/ passenger/relief train; ~ **de vida** way of life.

trence ['trenθe] *etc vb* V **trenzar.**

trenza ['trenθa] *nf* (*de pelo*) plait.

trenzar [tren'θar] *vt* (*el pelo*) to plait ◆ *vi* (*en baile*) to weave in and out; ~**se** *vr* (*AM*) to become involved.

trepa ['trepa] *nf* (*subida*) climb; (*ardid*) trick.

trepador(a) [trepa'ðor, a] *nm/f* (*fam*): **ser un(a)** ~ to be on the make ◆ *nf* (*BOT*) climber.

trepar [tre'par] *vt, vi* to climb; (*TEC*) to drill.

trepidación [trepiða'θjon] *nf* shaking, vibration.

trepidar [trepi'ðar] *vi* to shake, vibrate.

tres [tres] *num* three; (*fecha*) third; **las** ~ three o'clock.

trescientos, as [tres'θjentos, as] *num* three hundred.

tresillo [tre'siʎo] *nm* three-piece suite; (*MUS*) triplet.

treta ['treta] *nf* (*COM etc*) gimmick; (*fig*) trick.

tri... [tri] *pref* tri..., three-....

tríada ['triaða] *nf* triad.

triángulo [tri'angulo] *nm* triangle.

tribu ['trißu] *nf* tribe.

tribuna [tri'ßuna] *nf* (*plataforma*) platform; (*DEPORTE*) stand; (*fig*) public speaking; ~ **de la prensa** press box; ~ **del acusado** (*JUR*) dock; ~ **del jurado** jury box.

tribunal [trißu'nal] *nm* (*juicio*) court; (*comisión, fig*) tribunal; (*ESCOL: examinadores*) board of examiners; **T~ Supremo** High Court, (*US*) Supreme Court; **T~ de Justicia de las Comunidades Europeas** European Court of Justice.

tributar [trißu'tar] *vt* to pay; (*las gracias*) to give; (*cariño*) to show.

tributario, a [trißu'tarjo, a] *a* (*GEO, POL*) tributary *cpd*; (*ECON*) tax *cpd*, taxation *cpd* ◆ *nm* (*GEO*) tributary ◆ *nm/f* (*COM*) taxpayer; **sistema** ~ tax system.

tributo [tri'ßuto] *nm* (*COM*) tax.

trice ['triθe] *etc vb* V **trizar.**

tricornio [tri'kornjo] *nm* three-cornered hat.

tricotar [triko'tar] *vi* to knit.

tridimensional [triðimensjo'nal] *a* three-dimensional.

trienal [trje'nal] *a* three-year.

trigal [tri'ɣal] *nm* wheat field.

trigésimo, a [tri'xesimo, a] *num* thirtieth.

trigo ['triɣo] *nm* wheat; ~s *nmpl* wheat field(s) (*pl*).

trigueño, a [tri'ɣeɲo, a] *a* (*pelo*) corn-coloured; (*piel*) olive-skinned.

trilogía [trilo'xia] *nf* triology.

trillado, a [tri'ʎaðo, a] *a* threshed; (*fig*) trite, hackneyed.

trilladora [triʎa'ðora] *nf* threshing machine.

trillar [tri'ʎar] *vt* (*AGR*) to thresh; (*fig*) to frequent.

trillizos, as [tri'ʎiθos, as] *nmpl/nfpl* triplets.
trimestral [trimes'tral] *a* quarterly; (*ESCOL*) termly.
trimestre [tri'mestre] *nm* (*ESCOL*) term; (*COM*) quarter, financial period; (: *pago*) quarterly payment.
trinar [tri'nar] *vi* (*MUS*) to trill; (*ave*) to sing, warble; **está que trina** he's hopping mad.
trincar [trin'kar] *vt* (*atar*) to tie up; (*NAUT*) to lash; (*agarrar*) to pinion.
trinchante [trin'tʃante] *nm* (*para cortar carne*) carving knife; (*tenedor*) meat fork.
trinchar [trin'tʃar] *vt* to carve.
trinchera [trin'tʃera] *nf* (*fosa*) trench; (*para vía*) cutting; (*impermeable*) trench-coat.
trineo [tri'neo] *nm* sledge.
trinidad [trini'ðað] *nf* trio; (*REL*): **la T~** the Trinity.
trino ['trino] *nm* trill.
trinque ['trinke] *etc vb V* **trincar.**
trinquete [trin'kete] *nm* (*TEC*) pawl; (*NAUT*) foremast.
tripa ['tripa] *nf* (*ANAT*) intestine; (*fig, fam*) belly; **~s** *nfpl* (*anat*) insides; (*CULIN*) tripe *sg*; **tener mucha ~** to be fat; **me duelen las ~s** I have a stomach ache.
tripartito, a [tripar'tito, a] *a* tripartite.
triple ['triple] *a* triple; (*tres veces*) threefold.
triplicado, a [tripli'kaðo, a] *a*: **por ~** in triplicate.
Trípoli ['tripoli] *nm* Tripoli.
tríptico ['triptiko] *nm* (*ARTE*) triptych; (*documento*) three-part document.
tripulación [tripula'θjon] *nf* crew.
tripulante [tripu'lante] *nm/f* crewman/woman.
tripular [tripu'lar] *vt* (*barco*) to man; (*AUTO*) to drive.
triquiñuela [triki'ɲwela] *nf* trick.
tris [tris] *nm* crack; **en un ~** in an instant; **estar en un ~ de hacer algo** to be within an inch of doing sth.
triste ['triste] *a* (*afligido*) sad; (*sombrío*) melancholy, gloomy; (*desolado*) desolate; (*lamentable*) sorry, miserable; (*viejo*) old; (*único*) single; **no queda sino un ~ penique** there's just one miserable penny left.
tristeza [tris'teθa] *nf* (*aflicción*) sadness; (*melancolía*) melancholy; (*de lugar*) desolation; (*pena*) misery.
tristón, ona [tris'ton, ona] *a* sad, downhearted.
trituradora [tritura'ðora] *nf* shredder.
triturar [tritu'rar] *vt* (*moler*) to grind; (*mascar*) to chew; (*documentos*) to shred.
triunfador, a [triunfa'ðor, a] *a* triumphant; (*ganador*) winning ♦ *nm/f* winner.
triunfante [triun'fante] *a* triumphant; (*ga-*

nador) winning.
triunfar [triun'far] *vi* (*tener éxito*) to triumph; (*ganar*) to win; (*NAIPES*) to be trumps; **triunfan corazones** hearts are trumps; **~ en la vida** to succeed in life.
triunfo [tri'unfo] *nm* triumph; (*NAIPES*) trump.
trivial [tri'βjal] *a* trivial.
trivialice [triβja'liθe] *etc vb V* **trivializar.**
trivializar [triβjali'θar] *vt* to minimize, play down.
triza ['triθa] *nf* bit, piece; **hacer algo ~s** to smash sth to bits; (*papel*) to tear sth to shreds.
trizar [tri'θar] *vt* to smash to bits.
trocar [tro'kar] *vt* (*COM*) to exchange; (*dinero, de lugar*) to change; (*palabras*) to exchange; (*confundir*) to confuse; (*vomitar*) to vomit; **~se** *vr* (*confundirse*) to get mixed up; (*transformarse*): **~se (en)** to change (into).
trocha ['trotʃa] *nf* (*sendero*) by-path; (*atajo*) short cut.
troche ['trotʃe]: **a ~ y moche** *ad* helter-skelter, pell-mell.
trofeo [tro'feo] *nm* (*premio*) trophy; (*éxito*) success.
tromba ['tromba] *nf* whirlwind; **~ de agua** cloudburst.
trombón [trom'bon] *nm* trombone.
trombosis [trom'bosis] *nf inv* thrombosis.
trompa ['trompa] *nf* (*MUS*) horn; (*de elefante*) trunk; (*trompo*) humming top; (*hocico*) snout; (*ANAT*) tube, duct ♦ *nm* (*MUS*) horn player; **~ de Falopio** Fallopian tube; **cogerse una ~** (*fam*) to get tight.
trompada [trom'paða] *nf*, **trompazo** [trom'paθo] *nm* (*choque*) bump, bang; (*puñetazo*) punch.
trompeta [trom'peta] *nf* trumpet; (*clarín*) bugle ♦ *nm* trumpeter.
trompo ['trompo] *nm* spinning top.
trompón [trom'pon] *nm* bump.
tronado, a [tro'naðo, a] *a* broken-down.
tronar [tro'nar] *vt* (*AM*) to shoot ♦ *vi* to thunder; (*fig*) to rage; (*fam*) to go broke.
tronco ['tronko] *nm* (*de árbol, ANAT*) trunk; (*de planta*) stem; **estar hecho un ~** to be sound asleep.
tronchar [tron'tʃar] *vt* (*árbol*) to chop down; (*fig: vida*) to cut short; (*esperanza*) to shatter; (*persona*) to tire out; **~se** *vr* to fall down; **~se de risa** to split one's sides with laughter.
tronera [tro'nera] *nf* (*MIL*) loophole; (*ARQ*) small window.
trono ['trono] *nm* throne.
tropa ['tropa] *nf* (*MIL*) troop; (*soldados*) soldiers *pl*; (*soldados rasos*) ranks *pl*; (*gentío*) mob.
tropecé [trope'θe], **tropecemos** [trope-

'θemos] *etc vb V* **tropezar**.

tropel [tro'pel] *nm* (*muchedumbre*) crowd; (*prisa*) rush; (*montón*) throng; **acudir** *etc* **en** ~ to come *etc* in a mad rush.

tropelía [trope'lia] *nm* outrage.

tropezar [trope'θar] *vi* to trip, stumble; (*fig*) to slip up; ~**se** *vr* (*dos personas*) to run into each other; ~ **con** (*encontrar*) to run into; (*topar con*) to bump into.

tropezón [trope'θon] *nm* trip; (*fig*) blunder; (*traspié*): **dar un** ~ to trip.

tropical [tropi'kal] *a* tropical.

trópico ['tropiko] *nm* tropic.

tropiece [tro'pjeθe] *etc vb V* **tropezar**.

tropiezo [tro'pjeθo] *etc vb V* **tropezar** ◆ *nm* (*error*) slip, blunder; (*desgracia*) misfortune; (*revés*) setback; (*obstáculo*) snag; (*discusión*) quarrel.

troqué [tro'ke], **troquemos** [tro'kemos] *etc vb V* **trocar**.

trotamundos [trota'mundos] *nm inv* globetrotter.

trotar [tro'tar] *vi* to trot; (*viajar*) to travel about.

trote ['trote] *nm* trot; (*fam*) travelling; **de mucho** ~ hard-wearing.

Troya ['troja] *nf* Troy; **aquí fue** ~ now there's nothing but ruins.

trozo ['troθo] *nm* bit, piece; (*LITERATURA*, *MUS*) passage; **a** ~**s** in bits.

truco ['truko] *nm* (*habilidad*) knack; (*engaño*) trick; (*CINE*) trick effect *o* photography; ~**s** *nmpl* billiards *sg*; ~ **publicitario** advertising gimmick.

trucha ['trutʃa] *nf* (*pez*) trout; (*TEC*) crane.

trueco ['trweko] *etc vb V* **trocar**.

trueno ['trweno] *etc vb V* **tronar** ◆ *nm* (*gen*) thunder; (*estampido*) boom; (*de arma*) bang.

trueque ['trweke] *etc vb V* **trocar** ◆ *nm* exchange; (*COM*) barter.

trufa ['trufa] *nf* (*BOT*) truffle; (*fig: fam*) fib.

truhán, ana [tru'an, ana] *nm/f* rogue.

trulla ['truʎa] *nf* (*disturbio*) commotion; (*ruido*) noise; (*multitud*) crowd.

truncado, a [trun'kaðo, a] *a* truncated.

truncar [trun'kar] *vt* (*cortar*) to truncate; (*la vida etc*) to cut short; (*el desarrollo*) to stunt.

trunque ['trunke] *etc vb V* **truncar**.

tu [tu] *a* your.

tú [tu] *pron* you.

tubérculo [tu'ßerkulo] *nm* (*BOT*) tuber.

tuberculosis [tußerku'losis] *nf inv* tuberculosis.

tubería [tuße'ria] *nf* pipes *pl*, piping; (*conducto*) pipeline.

tubo ['tußo] *nm* tube, pipe; ~ **de desagüe** drainpipe; ~ **de ensayo** test-tube; ~ **de escape** exhaust (pipe); ~ **digestivo** alimentary canal.

tuerca ['twerka] *nf* (*TEC*) nut.

tuerce ['twerθe] *etc vb V* **torcer**.

tuerto, a ['twerto, a] *a* (*torcido*) twisted; (*ciego*) blind in one eye ◆ *nm/f* one-eyed person ◆ *nm* (*ofensa*) wrong; **a tuertas** upside-down.

tuerza ['twerθa] *etc vb V* **torcer**.

tueste ['tweste] *etc vb V* **tostar**.

tuétano ['twetano] *nm* (*ANAT*: *médula*) marrow; (*BOT*) pith; **hasta los** ~**s** through and through, utterly.

tufo ['tufo] *nm* vapour; (*fig: pey*) stench.

tugurio [tu'vurjo] *nm* slum.

tul [tul] *nm* tulle.

tulipán [tuli'pan] *nm* tulip.

tullido, a [tu'ʎiðo, a] *a* crippled; (*cansado*) exhausted.

tumba ['tumba] *nf* (*sepultura*) tomb; (*sacudida*) shake; (*voltereta*) somersault; **ser (como) una** ~ to keep one's mouth shut.

tumbar [tum'bar] *vt* to knock down; (*doblar*) to knock over; (*fam: suj: olor*) to overpower ◆ *vi* to fall down; ~**se** *vr* (*echarse*) to lie down; (*extenderse*) to stretch out.

tumbo ['tumbo] *nm* (*caída*) fall; (*de vehículo*) jolt; (*momento crítico*) critical moment.

tumefacción [tumefak'θjon] *nf* swelling.

tumido, a [tu'miðo, a] *a* swollen.

tumor [tu'mor] *nm* tumour.

tumulto [tu'multo] *nm* turmoil; (*POL*: *motín*) riot.

tuna ['tuna] *nf V* **tuno**.

tunante [tu'nante] *a* rascally ◆ *nm* rogue, villain; ¡~! you villain!

tunda ['tunda] *nf* (*de tela*) shearing; (*golpeo*) beating.

tundir [tun'dir] *vt* (*tela*) to shear; (*hierba*) to mow; (*fig*) to exhaust; (*fam: golpear*) to beat.

tunecino, a [tune'θino, a] *a, nm/f* Tunisian.

túnel ['tunel] *nm* tunnel.

Túnez ['tuneθ] *nm* Tunis.

túnica ['tunika] *nf* tunic; (*vestido largo*) long dress; (*ANAT, BOT*) tunic.

Tunisia [tu'niθja] *nf* Tunisia.

tuno, a ['tuno, a] *nm/f* (*fam*) rogue ◆ *nf* (*BOT*) prickly pear; (*MUS*) student music group.

tuntún [tun'tun]: **al** ~ *ad* thoughtlessly.

tupido, a [tu'piðo, a] *a* (*denso*) dense; (*fig: torpe*) dim; (*tela*) close-woven.

turba ['turßa] *nf* (*combustible*) turf; (*muchedumbre*) crowd.

turbación [turßa'θjon] *nf* (*molestia*) disturbance; (*preocupación*) worry.

turbado, a [tur'ßaðo, a] *a* (*molesto*) disturbed; (*preocupado*) worried.

turbante [tur'ßante] *nm* turban.

turbar [tur'ßar] *vt* (*molestar*) to disturb;

(*incomodar*) to upset; ~**se** *vr* to be disturbed.

turbina [tur'ßina] *nf* turbine.

turbio, a ['turßjo, a] *a* (*agua etc*) cloudy; (*vista*) dim, blurred; (*tema*) unclear, confused; (*negocio*) shady ♦ *ad* indistinctly.

turbión [tur'ßjon] *nf* downpour; (*fig*) shower, hail.

turbohélice [turßo'eliθe] *nm* turboprop.

turbulencia [turßu'lenθja] *nf* turbulence; (*fig*) restlessness.

turbulento, a [turßu'lento, a] *a* turbulent; (*fig*: *intranquilo*) restless; (: *ruidoso*) noisy.

turco, a ['turko, a] *a* Turkish ♦ *nm/f* Turk ♦ *nm* (*LING*) Turkish.

Turena [tu'rena] *nf* Touraine.

turgente [tur'xente], **túrgido, a** ['turxiðo, a] *a* (*hinchado*) turgid, swollen.

Turín [tu'rin] *nm* Turin.

turismo [tu'rismo] *nm* tourism; (*coche*) saloon car; **hacer** ~ to go travelling (abroad).

turista [tu'rista] *nm/f* tourist; (*vacacionista*) holidaymaker (*Brit*), vacationer (*US*).

turístico, a [tu'ristiko, a] *a* tourist *cpd*.

turnar [tur'nar] *vi*, **turnarse** *vr* to take (it in) turns.

turno ['turno] *nm* (*oportunidad, orden de prioridad*) opportunity; (*DEPORTE etc*) turn; **es su** ~ it's his turn (next); ~ **de día/de noche** (*INDUSTRIA*) day/night shift.

turolense [turo'lense] *a* of *o* from Teruel ♦ *nm/f* native *o* inhabitant of Teruel.

turquesa [tur'kesa] *nf* turquoise.

Turquía [tur'kia] *nf* Turkey.

turrón [tu'rron] *nm* (*dulce*) nougat; (*fam*) sinecure, cushy job *o* number.

tutear [tute'ar] *vt* to address as familiar "tú"; ~**se** *vr* to be on familiar terms.

tutela [tu'tela] *nf* (*legal*) guardianship; (*instrucción*) guidance; **estar bajo la** ~ **de** (*fig*) to be under the protection of.

tutelar [tute'lar] *a* tutelary ♦ *vt* to protect.

tutor, a [tu'tor, a] *nm/f* (*legal*) guardian; (*ESCOL*) tutor; ~ **de curso** form master/mistress.

tuve ['tuße] *etc vb* V **tener**.

tuyo, a ['tujo, a] *a* yours, of yours ♦ *pron* yours; **los** ~**s** (*fam*) your relations, your family.

TVE *nf abr* = *Televisión Española*.

U

U, u [u] *nf* (*letra*) U, u; **viraje en U** U-turn; **U de Ulises** U for Uncle.

u [u] *conj* or.

UAR [war] *nfpl abr* (*Esp*) = *Unidades Antiterroristas Rurales*.

ubérrimo, a [u'ßerrimo, a] *a* very rich, fertile.

ubicación [ußika'θjon] *nf* place, position, location.

ubicar [ußi'kar] *vt* to place, situate; (: *fig*) to install in a post; (*esp AM*: *encontrar*) to find; ~**se** *vr* to lie, be located.

ubicuo, a [u'ßikwo, a] *a* ubiquitous.

ubique [u'ßike] *etc vb* V **ubicar**.

ubre ['ußre] *nf* udder.

Ucrania [u'kranja] *nf* Ukraine.

ucraniano, a [ukra'njano, a] *a, nm/f* Ukrainian.

Ud(s) *abr* = **usted(es)**.

UEP *nf abr* = *Unión Europea de Pagos*.

uf [uf] *excl* (*cansancio*) phew!; (*repugnancia*) ugh!

ufanarse [ufa'narse] *vr* to boast; ~ **de** to pride o.s. on.

ufano, a [u'fano, a] *a* (*arrogante*) arrogant; (*presumido*) conceited.

UGT *nf abr* V **Unión General de Trabajadores**.

ujier [u'xjer] *nm* usher; (*portero*) doorkeeper.

úlcera ['ulθera] *nf* ulcer.

ulcerar [ulθe'rar] *vt* to make sore; ~**se** *vr* to ulcerate.

ULE ['ule] *nf abr* (*POL*) = *Unión Liberal Europea*.

ulterior [ulte'rjor] *a* (*más allá*) farther, further; (*subsecuente, siguiente*) subsequent.

ulteriormente [ulterjor'mente] *ad* later, subsequently.

últimamente ['ultimamente] *ad* (*recientemente*) lately, recently; (*finalmente*) finally; (*como último recurso*) as a last resort.

ultimar [ulti'mar] *vt* to finish; (*finalizar*) to finalize; (*AM*: *rematar*) to finish off.

ultimátum [ulti'matum] *nm, pl* **ultimátums** ultimatum.

último, a ['ultimo, a] *a* last; (*más reciente*) latest, most recent; (*más bajo*) bottom; (*más alto*) top; (*fig*) final, extreme; **en las últimas** on one's last legs; **por** ~ finally.

ultra ['ultra] a ultra ♦ nm/f extreme right-winger.

ultrajar [ultra'xar] vt (escandalizar) to outrage; (insultar) to insult, abuse.

ultraje [ul'traxe] nm outrage; insult.

ultramar [ultra'mar] nm: **de** o **en** ~ abroad, overseas; **los países de** ~ the overseas countries.

ultramarino, a [ultrama'rino, a] a overseas, foreign ♦ nmpl: ~**s** groceries; **tienda de** ~**s** grocer's (shop).

ultranza [ul'tranθa]: **a** ~ ad to the death; (a todo trance) at all costs; (completo) outright; (POL etc) out-and-out, extreme; **un nacionalista a** ~ a rabid nationalist.

ultrarrojo, a [ultra'rroxo, a] a = **infrarrojo, a.**

ultrasónico, a [ultra'soniko, a] a ultrasonic.

ultratumba [ultra'tumba] nf: **la vida de** ~ the next life; **una voz de** ~ a ghostly voice.

ultravioleta [ultraβjo'leta] a inv ultraviolet.

ulular [ulu'lar] vi to howl; (búho) to hoot.

umbral [um'bral] nm (gen) threshold; ~ **de rentabilidad** (COM) break-even point.

umbroso, a [um'broso, a], **umbrío, a** [um'brio, a] a shady.

un, una [un, 'una] artículo indefinido a ♦ num one; V **uno.**

unánime [u'nanime] a unanimous.

unanimidad [unanimi'ðað] nf unanimity; **por** ~ unanimously.

unción [un'θjon] nf anointing.

uncir [un'θir] vt to yoke.

undécimo, a [un'deθimo, a] a, nm/f eleventh.

undular [undu'lar] vi V **ondular.**

UNED [u'ned] nf abr (Esp UNIV: = Universidad Nacional de Enseñanza a Distancia) ≈ Open University (Brit).

ungir [un'xir] vt to rub with ointment; (REL) to anoint.

ungüento [un'gwento] nm ointment; (fig) salve, balm.

únicamente ['unikamente] ad solely; (solamente) only.

unicidad [uniθi'ðað] nf uniqueness.

único, a ['uniko, a] a only; (solo) sole, single; (sin par) unique; **hijo** ~ only child.

unidad [uni'ðað] nf unity; (TEC) unit; ~ **móvil** (TV) mobile unit; (INFORM): ~ **central** system unit, central processing unit; ~ **de control** control unit; ~ **de disco** disk drive; ~ **de entrada/salida** input/output device; ~ **de información** data item; ~ **periférica** peripheral device; ~ **de presentación visual** o **de visualización** visual display unit; ~ **procesadora central** central processing unit.

unido, a [u'niðo, a] a joined, linked; (fig) united.

unificar [unifi'kar] vt to unite, unify.

unifique [uni'fike] etc vb V **unificar.**

uniformado, a [unifor'maðo, a] a uniformed, in uniform.

uniformar [unifor'mar] vt to make uniform; (TEC) to standardize.

uniforme [uni'forme] a uniform, equal; (superficie) even ♦ nm uniform.

uniformidad [uniformi'ðað] nf uniformity; (llaneza) levelness, evenness.

unilateral [unilate'ral] a unilateral.

unión [u'njon] nf (gen) union; (acto) uniting, joining; (calidad) unity; (TEC) joint; (fig) closeness, togetherness; **en** ~ **con** (together) with, accompanied by; ~ **aduanera** customs union; **U~ General de Trabajadores (UGT)** (Esp) Socialist Union Confederation; **la U~ Soviética** the Soviet Union; **punto de** ~ (TEC) junction.

unir [u'nir] vt (juntar) to join, unite; (atar) to tie, fasten; (combinar) to combine ♦ vi (ingredientes) to mix well; ~**se** vr to join together, unite; (empresas) to merge; **les une una fuerte simpatía** they are bound by (a) strong affection; ~**se en matrimonio** to marry.

unísono [u'nisono] nm: **al** ~ in unison.

unitario, a [uni'tarjo, a] a unitary; (REL) Unitarian ♦ nm/f (REL) Unitarian.

universal [uniβer'sal] a universal; (mundial) world cpd; **historia** ~ world history.

universidad [uniβersi'ðað] nf university; ~ **laboral** polytechnic, poly.

universitario, a [uniβersi'tarjo, a] a university cpd ♦ nm/f (profesor) lecturer; (estudiante) (university) student.

universo [uni'βerso] nm universe.

unja ['unxa] etc vb V **ungir.**

uno, a ['uno, a] num one ♦ a one; (idéntico) one and the same ♦ pron one; (alguien) someone, somebody; **es todo** ~, **es** ~ **y lo mismo** it's all one, it's all the same; ~**s (cuantos)** some, a few; ~**s 80 dólares** about 80 dollars; ~ **mismo** oneself; ~ **a** ~, ~ **por** ~ one by one; **cada** ~ each o every one; ~**(s) a otro(s)** each other, one another; **estar en** ~ to be at one; **una de dos** either one thing or the other; ~ **que otro** some, a few; ~**s y otros** all of them; ~ **y otro** both.

untar [un'tar] vt (gen) to rub; (engrasar) to grease, oil; (MED) to rub (with ointment); (fig) to bribe; ~**se** vr (fig) to be crooked; ~ **el pan con mantequilla** to spread butter on one's bread.

unto ['unto] nm animal fat; (MED) ointment.

unza ['unθa] etc vb V **uncir.**

uña ['uɲa] nf (ANAT) nail; (del pie) toenail; (garra) claw; (casco) hoof; (arrancaclavos) claw; **ser** ~ **y carne** to be as thick as thieves; **enseñar** o **mostrar** o **sacar las** ~s to show one's claws.

UOE nf abr (Esp MIL) = Unidad de Operaciones Especiales.

UPA nf abr = Unión Panamericana.

UPC nf abr (= unidad procesadora central) CPU.

UPV nf abr (= unidad de presentación visual) VDU.

Urales [u'rales] nmpl (tb: **Montes** ~) Urals.

uranio [u'ranjo] nm uranium.

urbanidad [urßani'ðað] nf courtesy, politeness.

urbanismo [urßa'nismo] nm town planning.

urbanista [urßa'nista] nm/f town planner.

urbanización [urßaniθa'θjon] nf (colonia, barrio) estate, housing scheme.

urbano, a [ur'ßano, a] a (de ciudad) urban, town cpd; (cortés) courteous, polite.

urbe ['urße] nf large city, metropolis.

urdimbre [ur'ðimbre] nf (de tejido) warp; (intriga) intrigue.

urdir [ur'ðir] vt to warp; (fig) to plot, contrive.

urgencia [ur'xenθja] nf urgency; (prisa) haste, rush; **salida de** ~ emergency exit; **servicios de** ~ emergency services.

urgente [ur'xente] a urgent; (insistente) insistent; **carta** ~ registered (Brit) o special delivery (US) letter.

urgir [ur'xir] vi to be urgent; **me urge** I'm in a hurry for it; **me urge terminarlo** I must finish it as soon as I can.

urinario, a [uri'narjo, a] a urinary ◆ nm urinal, public lavatory, comfort station (US).

urja ['urxa] etc vb V **urgir**.

urna ['urna] nf urn; (POL) ballot box; **acudir a las** ~s (fig: persona) to (go and) vote; (: gobierno) to go to the country.

urólogo, a [u'roloɣo, a] nm/f urologist.

urraca [u'rraka] nf magpie.

URSS nf abr (= Unión de Repúblicas Socialistas Soviéticas) USSR.

Uruguay [uru'ɣwai] nm: **El** ~ Uruguay.

uruguayo, a [uru'ɣwajo, a] a, nm/f Uruguayan.

usado, a [u'saðo, a] a (gen) used; (ropa etc) worn; **muy** ~ worn out.

usanza [u'sanθa] nf custom, usage.

usar [u'sar] vt to use; (ropa) to wear; (tener costumbre) to be in the habit of ◆ vi: ~ **de** to make use of; **~se** vr to be used; (ropa) to be worn o in fashion.

uso ['uso] nm use; (MECÁNICA etc) wear; (costumbre) usage, custom; (moda) fashion; **al** ~ in keeping with custom; **al** ~ **de** in the style of; **de** ~ **externo** (MED) for external application; **estar en el** ~ **de la palabra** to be speaking, have the floor; ~ **y desgaste** (COM) wear and tear.

usted [us'teð] pron (sg: abr **Ud** o **Vd**: formal) you sg; **~es** (pl: abr **Uds** o **Vds**: formal) you pl; (AM: formal y fam) you pl.

usual [u'swal] a usual.

usuario, a [usw'arjo, a] nm/f user; ~ **final** (COM) end user.

usufructo [usu'frukto] nm use; ~ **vitalicio (de)** life interest (in).

usura [u'sura] nf usury.

usurero, a [usu'rero, a] nm/f usurer.

usurpar [usur'par] vt to usurp.

utensilio [uten'siljo] nm tool; (CULIN) utensil.

útero ['utero] nm uterus, womb.

útil ['util] a useful; (servible) usable, serviceable ◆ nm tool; **día** ~ working day, weekday; **es muy** ~ **tenerlo aquí cerca** it's very handy having it here close by.

utilice [uti'liθe] etc vb V **utilizar**.

utilidad [utili'ðað] nf usefulness, utility; (COM) profit; **~es líquidas** net profit sg.

utilitario [utili'tarjo] nm (INFORM) utility.

utilizar [utili'θar] vt to use, utilize; (explotar) to harness.

utopía [uto'pia] nf Utopia.

utópico, a [u'topiko, a] a Utopian.

uva ['ußa] nf grape; ~ **pasa** raisin; ~ **de Corinto** currant; **estar de mala** ~ to be in a bad mood.

uve ['uße] nf name of the letter V; **en forma de** ~ V-shaped; ~ **doble** name of the letter W.

UVI ['ußi] nf abr (Esp MED: = unidad de vigilancia intensiva) ICU.

V

V, v ['uße] nf (letra) V, v; **V de Valencia** V for Victor.

V. abr (= visto) approved, passed.

v. abr (= voltio) v.; (= véase) v.; (= verso) v.

va [ba] vb V **ir**.

V.A. abr = Vuestra Alteza.

vaca ['baka] nf (animal) cow; (carne) beef; (cuero) cowhide; **~s flacas/gordas** (fig) bad/good times.

vacaciones [baka'θjones] nfpl holiday(s); **estar/irse** o **marcharse de** ~ to be/go (away) on holiday.

vacante [ba'kante] a vacant, empty ◆ nf vacancy.

vacar [ba'kar] vi to fall vacant; ~ **a** o **en** to engage in.

vaciado, a [ba'θjaðo, a] a (hecho en molde)

cast in a mould; (*hueco*) hollow ♦ *nm* cast, mould(ing).

vaciar [ba'θjar] *vt* to empty (out); (*ahuecar*) to hollow out; (*moldear*) to cast; (*INFORM*) to dump ♦ *vi* (*río*) to flow (*en* into); ~**se** *vr* to empty; (*fig*) to blab, spill the beans.

vaciedad [baθje'ðað] *nf* emptiness.

vacilación [baθila'θjon] *nf* hesitation.

vacilante [baθi'lante] *a* unsteady; (*habla*) faltering; (*luz*) flickering; (*fig*) hesitant.

vacilar [baθi'lar] *vi* to be unsteady; to falter; to flicker; to hesitate, waver; (*persona*) to stagger, stumble; (*memoria*) to fail.

vacío, a [ba'θio, a] *a* empty; (*puesto*) vacant; (*desocupado*) idle; (*vano*) vain; (*charla etc*) light, superficial ♦ *nm* emptiness; (*FÍSICA*) vacuum; (*un* ~) (empty) space; **hacer el** ~ **a uno** to send sb to Coventry.

vacuna [ba'kuna] *nf* vaccine.

vacunar [baku'nar] *vt* to vaccinate; ~**se** *vr* to get vaccinated.

vacuno, a [ba'kuno, a] *a* bovine.

vacuo, a ['bakwo, a] *a* empty.

vadear [baðe'ar] *vt* to ford; (*problema*) to overcome; (*persona*) to sound out.

vado ['baðo] *nm* ford; (*solución*) solution; (*descanso*) respite.

vagabundear [baɣabunde'ar] *vi* (*andar sin rumbo*) to wander, roam; (*ser vago*) to be a tramp *o* bum (*US*).

vagabundo, a [baɣa'βundo, a] *a* wandering; (*pey*) vagrant ♦ *nm/f* (*errante*) wanderer; (*vago*) tramp, bum (*US*).

vagamente [baɣa'mente] *ad* vaguely.

vagancia [ba'ɣanθja] *nf* vagrancy.

vagar [ba'ɣar] *vi* to wander; (*pasear*) to saunter up and down; (*no hacer nada*) to idle ♦ *nm* leisure.

vagido [ba'xiðo] *nm* wail.

vagina [ba'xina] *nf* vagina.

vago, a ['baɣo, a] *a* vague; (*perezoso*) lazy; (*ambulante*) wandering ♦ *nm/f* (*vagabundo*) tramp, bum (*US*); (*flojo*) lazybones *sg*, idler.

vagón [ba'ɣon] *nm* (*de pasajeros*) carriage; (*de mercancías*) wagon; ~ **cama/restaurante** sleeping/dining car.

vague ['baɣe] *etc vb V* **vagar**.

vaguedad [baɣe'ðað] *nf* vagueness.

vahído [ba'iðo] *nm* dizzy spell.

vaho ['bao] *nm* (*vapor*) vapour, steam; (*olor*) smell; (*respiración*) breath; ~**s** *nmpl* (*MED*) inhalation *sg*.

vaina ['baina] *nf* sheath.

vainilla [bai'niʎa] *nf* vanilla.

vainita [bai'nita] *nf* (*AM*) green *o* French bean.

vais [bais] *vb V* **ir**.

vaivén [bai'βen] *nm* to-and-fro movement;

(*de tránsito*) coming and going; **vaivenes** *nmpl* (*fig*) ups and downs.

vajilla [ba'xiʎa] *nf* crockery, dishes *pl*; (*una* ~) service; ~ **de porcelana** chinaware.

val [bal], **valdré** [bal'dre] *etc vb V* **valer**.

vale ['bale] *nm* voucher; (*recibo*) receipt; (*pagaré*) I.O.U.; ~ **de regalo** gift voucher *o* token.

valedero, a [bale'ðero, a] *a* valid.

valenciano, a [balen'θjano, a] *a*, *nm/f* Valencian ♦ *nm* (*LING*) Valencian.

valentía [balen'tia] *nf* courage, bravery; (*pey*) boastfulness; (*acción*) heroic deed.

valentísimo, a [balen'tisimo, a] *a* (*superl de* **valiente**) very brave, courageous.

valentón, ona [balen'ton, ona] *a* blustering.

valer [ba'ler] *vt* to be worth; (*MAT*) to equal; (*costar*) to cost; (*amparar*) to aid, protect ♦ *vi* (*ser útil*) to be useful; (*ser válido*) to be valid; ~**se** *vr* to defend o.s. ♦ *nm* worth, value; ~ **la pena** to be worthwhile; ¿**vale?** O.K.?; ¡**vale!** (¡*basta!*) that'll do!; ¡**eso no vale!** that doesn't count!; **no vale nada** it's no good; (*mercancía*) it's worthless; (*argumento*) it's no use; **no vale para nada** he's no good at all; ~**se de** to make use of, take advantage of; ~**se por sí mismo** to help *o* manage by o.s.

valga ['balɣa] *etc vb V* **valer**.

valía [ba'lia] *nf* worth; **de gran** ~ (*objeto*) very valuable.

validar [bali'ðar] *vt* to validate; (*POL*) to ratify.

validez [bali'ðeθ] *nf* validity; **dar** ~ **a** to validate.

válido, a ['baliðo, a] *a* valid.

valiente [ba'ljente] *a* brave, valiant; (*audaz*) bold; (*pey*) boastful; (*con ironía*) fine, wonderful ♦ *nm/f* brave man/woman.

valija [ba'lixa] *nf* case; (*AM*) suitcase; (*mochila*) satchel; (*CORREOS*) mailbag; ~ **diplomática** diplomatic bag.

valioso, a [ba'ljoso, a] *a* valuable; (*rico*) wealthy.

valor [ba'lor] *nm* value, worth; (*precio*) price; (*valentía*) valour, courage; (*importancia*) importance; (*cara*) nerve, cheek (*fam*); **sin** ~ worthless; ~ **adquisitivo** *o* **de compra** purchasing power; **dar** ~ **a** to attach importance to; **quitar** ~ **a** to minimize the importance of; (*COM*); ~ **según balance** book value; ~ **comercial** *o* **de mercado** market value; ~ **contable/desglosado** asset/break-up value; ~ **de escasez** scarcity value; ~ **intrínseco** intrinsic value; ~ **a la par** par value; ~ **neto** net worth; ~ **de rescate/de sustitución** surrender/replacement value; *V tb* **valores**.

valoración [balora'θjon] *nf* valuation.

valorar [balo'rar] *vt* to value; (*tasar*) to

price; (fig) to assess.
valores [ba'lores] nmpl (COM) securities; ~ **en cartera** o **habidos** investments.
vals [bals] nm waltz.
válvula ['balßula] nf valve.
valla ['baʎa] nf fence; (DEPORTE) hurdle; (fig) barrier.
vallar [ba'ʎar] vt to fence in.
valle ['baʎe] nm valley, vale.
vallisoletano, a [baʎisole'tano, a] a of o from Valladolid ♦ nm/f native o inhabitant of Valladolid.
vamos ['bamos] vb V **ir**.
vampiro, iresa [bam'piro, i'resa] nm/f vampire ♦ nf (CINE) vamp, femme fatale.
van [ban] vb V **ir**.
vanagloriarse [banaɣlo'rjarse] vr to boast.
vandalismo [banda'lismo] nm vandalism.
vándalo, a ['bandalo, a] nm/f vandal.
vanguardia [ban'gwardja] nf vanguard; **de ~** (ARTE) avant-garde; **estar en** o **ir a la ~ de** (fig) to be in the forefront of.
vanidad [bani'ðað] nf vanity; (inutilidad) futility; (irrealidad) unreality.
vanidoso, a [bani'ðoso, a] a vain, conceited.
vano, a ['bano, a] a (irreal) unreal; (irracional) unreasonable; (inútil) vain, useless; (persona) vain, conceited; (frívolo) frivolous.
vapor [ba'por] nm vapour; (vaho) steam; (de gas) fumes pl; (neblina) mist; **~es** nmpl (MED) hysterics; **al ~** (CULIN) steamed.
vaporice [bapo'riθe] etc vb V **vaporizar**.
vaporizador [baporiθa'ðor] nm (perfume etc) spray.
vaporizar [bapori'θar] vt to vaporize; (perfume) to spray.
vaporoso, a [bapo'roso, a] a (vaporous; (vahoso) steamy; (tela) light, airy.
vaque ['bake] etc vb V **vacar**.
vaquería [bake'ria] nf dairy.
vaquero, a [ba'kero, a] a cattle cpd ♦ nm cowboy; **~s** nmpl jeans.
vaquilla [ba'kiʎa] nf heifer.
vara ['bara] nf stick, pole; (TEC) rod; **~ mágica** magic wand.
varado, a [ba'raðo, a] a (NAUT) stranded; **estar ~** to be aground.
varar [ba'rar] vt to beach ♦ vi, **~se** vr to be beached.
varear [bare'ar] vt to hit, beat; (frutas) to knock down (with poles).
variable [ba'rjaßle] a, nf variable (tb INFORM).
variación [barja'θjon] nf variation; **sin ~** unchanged.
variante [ba'rjante] a variant ♦ nf (alternativa) alternative; (AUTO) bypass.
variar [ba'rjar] vt (cambiar) to change;

(poner variedad) to vary; (modificar) to modify; (cambiar de posición) to switch around ♦ vi to vary; **~ de** to differ from; **~ de opinión** to change one's mind; **para ~** just for a change.
variedad [barje'ðað] nf variety.
varilla [ba'riʎa] nf stick; (BOT) twig; (TEC) rod; (de rueda) spoke; **~ mágica** magic wand.
vario, a ['barjo, a] a (variado) varied; (multicolor) motley; (cambiable) changeable; **~s** various, several.
varón [ba'ron] nm male, man.
varonil [baro'nil] a manly.
Varsovia [bar'soßja] nf Warsaw.
vas [bas] vb V **ir**.
vasco, a ['basko, a], **vascongado, a** [baskon'gaðo, a] a, nm/f Basque ♦ nm (LING) Basque ♦ nfpl: **las Vascongadas** the Basque Country sg o Provinces.
vascuence [bas'kwenθe] nm (LING) Basque.
vaselina [base'lina] nf Vaseline ®.
vasija [ba'sixa] nf (earthenware) vessel.
vaso ['baso] nm glass, tumbler; (ANAT) vessel; (cantidad) glass(ful); **~ de vino** glass of wine; **~ para vino** wineglass.
vástago ['bastaɣo] nm (BOT) shoot; (TEC) rod; (fig) offspring.
vasto, a ['basto, a] a vast, huge.
váter ['bater] nm lavatory, W.C.
Vaticano [bati'kano] nm: **el ~** the Vatican; **la Ciudad del ~** the Vatican City.
vaticinar [batiθi'nar] vt to prophesy, predict.
vaticinio [bati'θinjo] nm prophecy.
vatio ['batjo] nm (ELEC) watt.
vaya ['baja] etc vb V **ir**.
Vda. abr = **viuda**.
Vd(s) abr = **usted(es)**.
ve [be] vb V **ir**, **ver**.
vea ['bea] etc vb V **ver**.
vecindad [beθin'dað] nf, **vecindario** [beθin'darjo] nm neighbourhood; (habitantes) residents pl.
vecinal [beθi'nal] a (camino, impuesto etc) local.
vecino, a [be'θino, a] a neighbouring ♦ nm/f neighbour; (residente) resident; **somos ~s** we live next door to one another.
veda ['beða] nf prohibition; (temporada) close season.
vedado [be'ðaðo] nm preserve.
vedar [be'ðar] vt (prohibir) to ban, prohibit; (idea, plan) to veto; (impedir) to stop, prevent.
vedette [be'ðet] nf (TEATRO, CINE) star(let).
vega ['beɣa] nf fertile plain o valley.
vegetación [bexeta'θjon] nf vegetation.
vegetal [bexe'tal] a, nm vegetable.
vehemencia [bee'menθja] nf (insistencia) vehemence; (pasión) passion; (fervor) fervour; (violencia) violence.

vehemente [bee'mente] *a* vehement; passionate; fervent; violent.

vehículo [be'ikulo] *nm* vehicle; *(MED)* carrier; ~ **de servicio público** public service vehicle; ~ **espacial** spacecraft.

veinte ['beinte] *num* twenty; *(orden, fecha)* twentieth; **el siglo** ~ the twentieth century.

veintena [bein'tena] *nf:* **una** ~ (about) twenty, a score.

vejación [bexa'θjon] *nf* vexation; *(humillación)* humiliation.

vejamen [be'xamen] *nm* satire.

vejar [be'xar] *vt (irritar)* to annoy, vex; *(humillar)* to humiliate.

vejez [be'xeθ] *nf* old age.

vejiga [be'xiɣa] *nf (ANAT)* bladder.

vela ['bela] *nf (de cera)* candle; *(NAUT)* sail; *(insomnio)* sleeplessness; *(vigilia)* vigil; *(MIL)* sentry duty; *(fam)* snot; **a toda** ~ *(NAUT)* under full sail; **estar a dos** ~**s** *(fam)* to be skint; **pasar la noche en** ~ to have a sleepless night.

velado, a [be'laðo, a] *a* veiled; *(sonido)* muffled; *(FOTO)* blurred ♦ *nf* soirée.

velador [bela'ðor] *nm* watchman; *(candelero)* candlestick.

velar [be'lar] *vt (vigilar)* to keep watch over; *(cubrir)* to veil ♦ *vi* to stay awake; ~ **por** to watch over, look after.

velatorio [bela'torjo] *nm (funeral)* wake.

veleidad [belei'ðað] *nf (ligereza)* fickleness; *(capricho)* whim.

velero [be'lero] *nm (NAUT)* sailing ship; *(AVIAT)* glider.

veleta [be'leta] *nm/f* fickle person ♦ *nf* weather vane.

veliz [be'liθ] *nm (AM)* suitcase.

velo ['belo] *nm* veil; ~ **de paladar** *(ANAT)* soft palate.

velocidad [beloθi'ðað] *nf* speed; *(TEC)* rate, pace, velocity; *(MECÁNICA, AUTO)* gear; **¿a qué** ~**?** how fast?; **de alta** ~ high-speed; **cobrar** ~ to pick up *o* gather speed; **meter la segunda** ~ to change into second gear; ~ **máxima de impresión** *(INFORM)* maximum print speed.

velocímetro [belo'θimetro] *nm* speedometer.

velódromo [be'loðromo] *nm* cycle track.

veloz [be'loθ] *a* fast, swift.

vello ['beʎo] *nm* down, fuzz.

vellón [be'ʎon] *nm* fleece.

velloso, a [be'ʎoso, a] *a* fuzzy.

velludo, a [be'ʎuðo, a] *a* shaggy ♦ *nm* plush, velvet.

ven [ben] *vb* V **venir**.

vena ['bena] *nf* vein; *(fig)* vein, disposition; *(GEO)* seam, vein.

venablo [be'naβlo] *nm* javelin.

venado [be'naðo] *nm* deer; *(CULIN)* venison.

venal [be'nal] *a (ANAT)* venous; *(pey)* venal.

venalidad [benali'ðað] *nf* venality.

vencedor, a [benθe'ðor, a] *a* victorious ♦ *nm/f* victor, winner.

vencer [ben'θer] *vt (dominar)* to defeat, beat; *(derrotar)* to vanquish; *(superar, controlar)* to overcome, master ♦ *vi (triunfar)* to win (through), triumph; *(pago)* to fall due; *(plazo)* to expire; **dejarse** ~ to yield, give in.

vencido, a [ben'θiðo, a] *a (derrotado)* defeated, beaten; *(COM)* payable, due ♦ *ad:* **pagar** ~ to pay in arrears; **le pagan por meses** ~**s** he is paid at the end of the month; **darse por** ~ to give up.

vencimiento [benθi'mjento] *nm* collapse; *(COM: plazo)* expiration; **a su** ~ when it falls due.

venda ['benda] *nf* bandage.

vendaje [ben'daxe] *nm* bandage, dressing.

vendar [ben'dar] *vt* to bandage; ~ **los ojos** to blindfold.

vendaval [benda'βal] *nm (viento)* gale; *(huracán)* hurricane.

vendedor, a [bende'ðor, a] *nm/f* seller; ~ **ambulante** hawker, pedlar *(Brit)*, peddler *(US)*.

vender [ben'der] *vt* to sell; *(comerciar)* to market; *(traicionar)* to sell out, betray; ~**se** *vr* to be sold; ~ **al contado/al por mayor/al por menor/a plazos** to sell for cash/wholesale/retail/on credit; **"se vende"** "for sale"; **"véndese coche"** "car for sale"; ~ **al descubierto** to sell short.

vendimia [ben'dimja] *nf* grape harvest; **la** ~ **de 1973** the 1973 vintage.

vendré [ben'dre] *etc vb* V **venir**.

Venecia [be'neθja] *nf* Venice.

veneciano, a [bene'θjano, a] *a, nm/f* Venetian.

veneno [be'neno] *nm* poison, venom.

venenoso, a [bene'noso, a] *a* poisonous.

venerable [bene'raβle] *a* venerable.

veneración [benera'θjon] *nf* veneration.

venerar [bene'rar] *vt (reconocer)* to venerate; *(adorar)* to worship.

venéreo, a [be'nereo, a] *a* venereal.

venero [be'nero] *nm (veta)* seam, lode; *(fuente)* spring.

venezolano, a [beneθo'lano, a] *a, nm/f* Venezuelan.

Venezuela [bene'θwela] *nf* Venezuela.

venga ['benga] *etc vb* V **venir**.

vengador, a [benga'ðor, a] *a* avenging ♦ *nm/f* avenger.

venganza [ben'ganθa] *nf* vengeance, revenge.

vengar [ben'gar] *vt* to avenge; ~**se** *vr* to take revenge.

vengativo, a [benga'tiβo, a] *a (persona)* vindictive.

vengue ['benge] *etc vb* V **vengar**.
venia ['benja] *nf* (*perdón*) pardon; (*permiso*) consent; **con su** ~ by your leave.
venial [be'njal] *a* venial.
venida [be'niða] *nf* (*llegada*) arrival; (*regreso*) return; (*fig*) rashness.
venidero, a [beni'ðero, a] *a* coming, future; **en lo** ~ in (the) future.
venir [be'nir] *vi* to come; (*llegar*) to arrive; (*ocurrir*) to happen; ~**se** *vr*: ~**se abajo** to collapse; ~ **a menos** (*persona*) to lose status; (*empresa*) to go downhill; ~ **bien** to be suitable, come just right; (*ropa, gusto*) to suit; ~ **mal** to be unsuitable *o* inconvenient, come awkwardly; **el año que viene** next year; **¡ven acá!** come (over) here!; **¡venga!** (*fam*) come on!
venta ['benta] *nf* (*COM*) sale; (*posada*) inn; ~ **a plazos** hire purchase; ~ **al contado/al por mayor/al por menor** *o* **al detalle** cash sale/wholesale/retail; ~ **a domicilio** door-to-door selling; ~ **y arrendamiento al vendedor** sale and lease back; ~ **de liquidación** clearance sale; **estar de** *o* **en** ~ to be (up) for sale *o* on the market; ~**s brutas** gross sales; ~**s a término** forward sales.
ventaja [ben'taxa] *nf* advantage; **llevar la** ~ (*en carrera*) to be leading *o* ahead.
ventajoso, a [benta'xoso, a] *a* advantageous.
ventana [ben'tana] *nf* window; ~ **de guillotina/galería** sash/bay window; ~ **de la nariz** nostril.
ventanilla [venta'niʎa] *nf* (*de taquilla, tb INFORM*) window.
ventear [bente'ar] *vt* (*ropa*) to hang out to dry; (*oler*) to sniff ◆ *vi* (*investigar*) to investigate; (*soplar*) to blow; ~**se** *vr* (*romperse*) to crack; (*ANAT*) to break wind.
ventilación [bentila'θjon] *nf* ventilation; (*corriente*) draught; (*fig*) airing.
ventilador [bentila'ðor] *nm* ventilator; (*eléctrico*) fan.
ventilar [benti'lar] *vt* to ventilate; (*a secar*) to put out to dry; (*fig*) to air, discuss.
ventisca [ben'tiska] *nf*, **ventisquero** [bentis'kero] *nm* blizzard; (*nieve amontonada*) snowdrift.
ventolera [bento'lera] *nf* (*ráfaga*) gust of wind; (*idea*) whim, wild idea; **le dio la** ~ **de comprarlo** he had a sudden notion to buy it.
ventosear [bentose'ar] *vi* to break wind.
ventoso, a [ben'toso, a] *a* windy.
ventrículo [ben'trikulo] *nm* ventricle.
ventrílocuo, a [ben'trilokwo, a] *nm/f* ventriloquist.
ventriloquia [bentri'lokja] *nf* ventriloquism.
ventura [ben'tura] *nf* (*felicidad*) happiness; (*buena suerte*) luck; (*destino*) fortune; **a la** (**buena**) ~ at random.

venturoso, a [bentu'roso, a] *a* happy; (*afortunado*) lucky, fortunate.
venza ['benθa] *etc vb* V **vencer**.
ver [ber] *vt, vi* to see; (*mirar*) to look at, watch; (*investigar*) to look into; (*entender*) to see, understand; ~**se** *vr* (*encontrarse*) to meet; (*dejarse* ~) to be seen; (*hallarse: en un apuro*) to find o.s., be ◆ *nm* looks *pl*, appearance; **a** ~ let's see; **a** ~ **si** ... I wonder if ...; **por lo que veo** apparently; **dejarse** ~ to become apparent; **no tener nada que** ~ **con** to have nothing to do with; **a mi modo de** ~ as I see it; **merece** ~**se** it's worth seeing; **no lo veo** I can't see it; **¡nos vemos!** see you (later)!; **¡habráse visto!** did you ever! (*fam*); **ya se ve que** ... it is obvious that ...; **si te vi no me acuerdo** they *etc* just don't want to know.
vera ['bera] *nf* edge, verge; (*de río*) bank; **a la** ~ **de** near, next to.
veracidad [beraθi'ðað] *nf* truthfulness.
veraneante [berane'ante] *nm/f* holiday-maker, (summer) vacationer (*US*).
veranear [berane'ar] *vi* to spend the summer.
veraneo [bera'neo] *nm*: **estar de** ~ to be away on (one's summer) holiday; **lugar de** ~ holiday resort.
veraniego, a [bera'njeɣo, a] *a* summer *cpd*.
verano [be'rano] *nm* summer.
veras ['beras] *nfpl* truth *sg*; **de** ~ really, truly; **esto va de** ~ this is serious.
veraz [be'raθ] *a* truthful.
verbal [ber'βal] *a* verbal; (*mensaje etc*) oral.
verbena [ber'βena] *nf* street party.
verbigracia [berβi'ɣraθja] *ad* for example.
verbo ['berβo] *nm* verb.
verborragia [berβo'rraxja], **verborrea** [berβo'rrea] *nf* verbosity, verbal diarrhoea.
verboso, a [ber'βoso, a] *a* verbose.
verdad [ber'ðað] *nf* (*lo verídico*) truth; (*fiabilidad*) reliability ◆ *ad* really; **¿~?, ¿no es** ~**?** isn't it?, aren't you?, don't you? *etc*; **de** ~ *a* real, proper; **a decir** ~, **no quiero** to tell (you) the truth, I don't want to; **la pura** ~ the plain truth.
verdaderamente [berðaðera'mente] *ad* really, indeed, truly.
verdadero, a [berða'ðero, a] *a* (*veraz*) true, truthful; (*fiable*) reliable; (*fig*) real.
verde ['berðe] *a* green; (*fruta etc*) green, unripe; (*chiste etc*) blue, smutty, dirty ◆ *nm* green; **viejo** ~ dirty old man; **poner** ~ **a uno** to give sb a dressing-down.
verdear [berðe'ar], **verdecer** [berðe'θer] *vi* to turn green.
verdezca [ber'ðeθka] *etc vb* V **verdecer**.
verdor [ber'ðor] *nm* (*lo verde*) greenness;

(*BOT*) verdure; (*fig*) youthful vigour.

verdugo [ber'ðuɣo] *nm* executioner; (*BOT*) shoot; (*cardenal*) weal.

verdulero, a [berðu'lero, a] *nm/f* greengrocer.

verdura [ber'ðura] *nf* greenness; ~s *nfpl* (*CULIN*) greens.

vereda [be'reða] *nf* path; (*AM*) pavement, sidewalk (*US*); **meter a uno en** ~ to bring sb into line.

veredicto [bere'ðikto] *nm* verdict.

vergonzoso, a [berɣon'θoso, a] *a* shameful; (*tímido*) timid, bashful.

vergüenza [ber'ɣwenθa] *nf* shame, sense of shame; (*timidez*) bashfulness; (*pudor*) modesty; **tener** ~ to be ashamed; **me da** ~ **decírselo** I feel too shy *o* it embarrasses me to tell him; **¡qué** ~**!** (*de situación*) what a disgrace!; (*a persona*) shame on you!

vericueto [beri'kweto] *nm* rough track.

verídico, a [be'riðiko, a] *a* true, truthful.

verificar [berifi'kar] *vt* to check; (*corroborar*) to verify (*tb INFORM*); (*testamento*) to prove; (*llevar a cabo*) to carry out; ~**se** *vr* to occur, happen; (*mitin etc*) to be held; (*profecía etc*) to come *o* prove true.

verifique [beri'fike] *etc vb* V **verificar**.

verja ['berxa] *nf* iron gate; (*cerca*) railing(s) (*pl*); (*rejado*) grating.

vermut [ber'mu], *pl* **vermuts** *nm* vermouth.

verosímil [bero'simil] *a* likely, probable; (*relato*) credible.

verosimilitud [berosimili'tuð] *nf* likeliness, probability.

verruga [be'rruɣa] *nf* wart.

versado, a [ber'saðo, a] *a*: ~ **en** versed in.

Versalles [ber'saʎes] *nm* Versailles.

versar [ber'sar] *vi* to go round, turn; ~ **sobre** to deal with, be about.

versátil [ber'satil] *a* versatile.

versículo [ber'sikulo] *nm* (*REL*) verse.

versión [ber'sjon] *nf* version; (*traducción*) translation.

verso ['berso] *nm* (*gen*) verse; **un** ~ a line of poetry; ~ **libre/suelto** free/blank verse.

vértebra ['berteßra] *nf* vertebra.

vertebral [berte'ßral] *a* vertebral; **columna** ~ spine.

verter [ber'ter] *vt* (*vaciar*) to empty, pour (out); (*tirar*) to dump ♦ *vi* to flow.

vertical [berti'kal] *a* vertical; (*postura, piano etc*) upright ♦ *nf* vertical.

vértice ['bertiθe] *nm* vertex, apex.

vertiente [ber'tjente] *nf* slope.

vertiginoso, a [bertixi'noso, a] *a* giddy, dizzy.

vértigo ['bertiɣo] *nm* vertigo; (*mareo*) dizziness; (*actividad*) intense activity; **de** ~ (*fam: velocidad*) giddy; (: *ruido*) tremendous; (: *talento*) fantastic.

vesícula [be'sikula] *nf* blister; ~ **biliar** gall bladder.

vespertino, a [besper'tino, a] *a* evening *cpd*.

vestíbulo [bes'tißulo] *nm* hall; (*de teatro*) foyer.

vestido [bes'tiðo] *nm* (*ropa*) clothes *pl*, clothing; (*de mujer*) dress, frock.

vestigio [bes'tixjo] *nm* (*trazo*) trace; (*señal*) sign; ~**s** *nmpl* remains.

vestimenta [besti'menta] *nf* clothing.

vestir [bes'tir] *vt* (*poner: ropa*) to put on; (*llevar: ropa*) to wear; (*cubrir: ropa*) to clothe, cover; (*pagar: la ropa*) to clothe, pay for the clothing of; (*sastre*) to make clothes for ♦ *vi* (*ponerse: ropa*) to dress; (*verse bien*) to look good; ~**se** *vr* to get dressed, dress o.s.; **traje de** ~ (*formal*) formal suit; **estar vestido de** to be dressed *o* clad in; (*como disfraz*) to be dressed as.

vestuario [bes'twarjo] *nm* clothes *pl*, wardrobe; (*TEATRO: para actores*) dressing room; (: *para público*) cloakroom; (*DEPORTE*) changing room.

Vesubio [be'sußjo] *nm* Vesuvius.

veta ['beta] *nf* (*vena*) vein, seam; (*raya*) streak; (*de madera*) grain.

vetar [be'tar] *vt* to veto.

veterano, a [bete'rano, a] *a, nm/f* veteran.

veterinario, a [beteri'narjo, a] *nm/f* vet(erinary surgeon) ♦ *nf* veterinary science.

veto ['beto] *nm* veto.

vetusto, a [be'tusto, a] *a* ancient.

vez [beθ] *nf* time; (*turno*) turn; **a la** ~ **que** at the same time as; **a su** ~ in its turn; **cada** ~ **más/menos** more and more/less and less; **una** ~ once; **dos veces** twice; **de una** ~ in one go; **de una** ~ **para siempre** once and for all; **en** ~ **de** instead of; **a veces** sometimes; **otra** ~ again; **una y otra** ~ repeatedly; **pocas veces** seldom; **de** ~ **en cuando** from time to time; **7 veces 9** 7 times 9; **hacer las veces de** to stand in for; **tal** ~ perhaps; **¿lo viste alguna** ~**?** did you ever see it?; **¿cuántas veces?** how often?; **érase una** ~ once upon a time (there was).

v. g., v. gr. *abr* (= *verbigracia*) viz.

vía ['bia] *nf* (*calle*) road; (*ruta*) track, route; (*FERRO*) line; (*fig*) way; (*ANAT*) passage, tube ♦ *prep* via, by way of; **por** ~ **bucal** orally; **por** ~ **judicial** by legal means; **por** ~ **oficial** through official channels; **por** ~ **de** by way of; **en** ~**s de** in the process of; **un país en** ~**s de desarrollo** a developing country; ~ **aérea** airway; **V**~ **Láctea** Milky Way; ~ **pública** public highway *o* thoroughfare; ~ **única** one-way street; **el tren está en la** ~ **8** the train is (standing) at platform 8.

viable ['bjaßle] *a* (*COM*) viable; (*plan etc*) feasible.

viaducto [bja'ðukto] *nm* viaduct.

viajante [bja'xante] *nm* commercial traveller, traveling salesman (*US*).

viajar [bja'xar] *vi* to travel, journey.

viaje ['bjaxe] *nm* journey; (*gira*) tour; (*NAUT*) voyage; (*COM: carga*) load; **los ~s** travel *sg*; **estar de ~** to be on a journey; **~ de ida y vuelta** round trip; **~ de novios** honeymoon.

viajero, a [bja'xero, a] *a* travelling (*Brit*), traveling (*US*); (*ZOOL*) migratory ♦ *nm/f* (*quien viaja*) traveller; (*pasajero*) passenger.

vial [bjal] *a* road *cpd*, traffic *cpd*.

vianda ['bjanda] *nf* (*tb*: **~s**) food.

viáticos ['bjatikos] *nmpl* (*COM*) travelling (*Brit*) *o* traveling (*US*) expenses.

víbora ['bißora] *nf* viper.

vibración [bißra'θjon] *nf* vibration.

vibrador [bißra'ðor] *nm* vibrator.

vibrante [bi'ßrante] *a* vibrant, vibrating.

vibrar [bi'ßrar] *vt* to vibrate ♦ *vi* to vibrate; (*pulsar*) to throb, beat, pulsate.

vicario [bi'karjo] *nm* curate.

vicecónsul [biθe'konsul] *nm* vice-consul.

vicegerente [biθexe'rente] *nm/f* assistant manager.

vicepresidente [biθepresi'ðente] *nm/f* vice president; (*de comité etc*) vice-chairman.

viceversa [biθe'ßersa] *ad* vice versa.

viciado, a [bi'θjaðo, a] *a* (*corrompido*) corrupt; (*contaminado*) foul, contaminated.

viciar [bi'θjar] *vt* (*pervertir*) to pervert; (*adulterar*) to adulterate; (*falsificar*) to falsify; (*JUR*) to nullify; (*estropear*) to spoil; (*sentido*) to twist; **~se** *vr* to become corrupted; (*aire, agua*) to be(come) polluted.

vicio ['biθjo] *nm* (*libertinaje*) vice; (*mala costumbre*) bad habit; (*mimo*) spoiling; (*alabeo*) warp, warping; **de** *o* **por ~** out of sheer habit.

vicioso, a [bi'θjoso, a] *a* (*muy malo*) vicious; (*corrompido*) depraved; (*mimado*) spoiled ♦ *nm/f* depraved person; (*adicto*) addict.

vicisitud [biθisi'tuð] *nf* vicissitude.

víctima ['biktima] *nf* victim; (*de accidente etc*) casualty.

victoria [bik'torja] *nf* victory.

victorioso, a [bikto'rjoso, a] *a* victorious.

vicuña [bi'kuɲa] *nf* vicuna.

vid [bið] *nf* vine.

vida ['biða] *nf* life; (*duración*) lifetime; (*modo de vivir*) way of life; **¡~!, ¡~ mía!** (*saludo cariñoso*) my love!; **de por ~** for life; **de ~ airada** *o* **libre** loose-living; **en la/mi ~** never; **estar con ~** to be still alive; **ganarse la ~** to earn one's living;

¡esto es ~! this is the life!; **le va la ~ en esto** his life depends on it.

vídeo ['biðeo] *nm* video; (*aparato*) video (recorder); **cinta de ~** videotape; **película de ~** videofilm; **grabar en ~** to record, (video)tape; **~ compuesto/inverso** (*INFORM*) composite/reverse video.

videoconferencia [biðeokonfe'renθja] *nf* video-conference.

videodatos [biðeo'ðatos] *nmpl* (*COM*) viewdata.

videojuego [biðeo'xwexo] *nm* video game.

videotex [biðeo'teks] *nm* teletext ®.

vidriero, a [bi'ðrjero, a] *nm/f* glazier ♦ *nf* (*ventana*) stained-glass window; (*AM: de tienda*) shop window; (*puerta*) glass door.

vidrio ['biðrjo] *nm* glass; **~ cilindrado/ inastillable** plate/splinter-proof glass.

vidrioso, a [bi'ðrjoso, a] *a* glassy; (*frágil*) fragile, brittle; (*resbaladizo*) slippery.

viejo, a ['bjexo, a] *a* old ♦ *nm/f* old man/ woman; **mi ~/vieja** (*fam*) my old man/ woman; **hacerse** *o* **ponerse ~** to grow *o* get old.

Viena ['bjena] *nf* Vienna.

viene ['bjene] *etc vb V* **venir**.

vienés, esa [bje'nes, esa] *a, nm/f* Viennese.

viento ['bjento] *nm* wind; (*olfato*) scent; **contra ~ y marea** at all costs; **ir ~ en popa** to go splendidly; (*negocio*) to prosper.

vientre ['bjentre] *nm* belly; (*matriz*) womb; **~s** *nmpl* bowels; **hacer de ~** to have a movement of the bowels.

vier. *abr* (= *viernes*) Fri.

viernes ['bjernes] *nm inv* Friday; **V~ Santo** Good Friday.

vierta ['bjerta] *etc vb V* **verter**.

Vietnam [bjet'nam] *nm*: **el ~** Vietnam.

vietnamita [bjetna'mita] *a, nm/f* Vietnamese.

viga ['bixa] *nf* beam, rafter; (*de metal*) girder.

vigencia [bi'xenθja] *nf* validity; (*de contrato etc*) term, life; **estar/entrar en ~** to be in/ come into effect *o* force.

vigente [bi'xente] *a* valid, in force; (*imperante*) prevailing.

vigésimo, a [bi'xesimo, a] *num* twentieth.

vigía [bi'xia] *nm* look-out ♦ *nf* (*atalaya*) watchtower; (*acción*) watching.

vigilancia [bixi'lanθja] *nf* vigilance.

vigilante [bixi'lante] *a* vigilant ♦ *nm* caretaker; (*en cárcel*) warder; (*en almacén*) shopwalker (*Brit*), floor-walker (*US*); **~ de noche** *o* **nocturno** night watchman.

vigilar [bixi'lar] *vt* to watch over; (*cuidar*) to look after, keep an eye on ♦ *vi* to be vigilant; (*hacer guardia*) to keep watch.

vigilia [vi'xilja] *nf* wakefulness; (*REL*) fast; **comer de ~** to fast.

vigor [bi'ɣor] *nm* vigour, vitality; **en ~** in force; **entrar/poner en ~** to take/put into effect.

vigoroso, a [biɣo'roso, a] *a* vigorous.

vil [bil] *a* vile, low.

vileza [bi'leθa] *nf* vileness; (*acto*) base deed.

vilipendiar [bilipen'djar] *vt* to vilify, revile.

vilo ['bilo]: **en ~** *ad* in the air, suspended; (*fig*) on tenterhooks, in suspense; **estar** *o* **quedar en ~** to be left in suspense.

villa ['biʎa] *nf* (*pueblo*) small town; (*municipalidad*) municipality; **la V~** (*Esp*) Madrid; **~ miseria** shanty town.

villorrio [bi'ʎorrjo] *nm* one-horse town, dump; (*AM: barrio pobre*) shanty town.

vinagre [bi'naɣre] *nm* vinegar.

vinagrera [bina'ɣrera] *nf* vinegar bottle; **~s** *nfpl* cruet stand *sg*.

vinagreta [bina'ɣreta] *nf* French dressing.

vinatería [binate'ria] *nf* wine shop.

vinatero, a [bina'tero, a] *a* wine *cpd* ♦ *nm* wine merchant.

vinculación [binkula'θjon] *nf* (*lazo*) link, bond; (*acción*) linking.

vincular [binku'lar] *vt* to link, bind.

vínculo ['binkulo] *nm* link, bond.

vindicar [bindi'kar] *vt* to vindicate; (*vengar*) to avenge; (*JUR*) to claim.

vindique [bin'dike] *etc vb V* **vindicar**.

vinícola [bi'nikola] *a* (*industria*) wine *cpd*; (*región*) wine-growing *cpd*.

vinicultura [binikul'tura] *nf* wine growing.

vino ['bino] *etc vb V* **venir** ♦ *nm* wine; **~ de solera/seco/tinto** vintage/dry/red wine; **~ de Jerez** sherry; **~ de Oporto** port (wine).

viña ['biɲa] *nf*, **viñedo** [bi'ɲeðo] *nm* vineyard.

violación [bjola'θjon] *nf* violation; (*JUR*) offence, infringement; (*estupro*): **~ (sexual)** rape; **~ de contrato** (*COM*) breach of contract.

violar [bjo'lar] *vt* to violate; (*JUR*) to infringe; (*cometer estupro*) to rape.

violencia [bjo'lenθja] *nf* (*fuerza*) violence, force; (*embarazo*) embarrassment; (*acto injusto*) unjust act.

violentar [bjolen'tar] *vt* to force; (*casa*) to break into; (*agredir*) to assault; (*violar*) to violate.

violento, a [bjo'lento, a] *a* violent; (*furioso*) furious; (*situación*) embarrassing; (*acto*) forced, unnatural; (*difícil*) awkward; **me es muy ~** it goes against the grain with me.

violeta [bjo'leta] *nf* violet.

violín [bjo'lin] *nm* violin.

violón [bjo'lon] *nm* double bass.

violoncelo [bjolon'θelo] *nm* cello.

virador [bira'ðor] *nm* (*para fotocopiadora*) toner.

viraje [bi'raxe] *nm* turn; (*de vehículo*) swerve; (*de carretera*) bend; (*fig*) change of direction.

virar [bi'rar] *vi* to turn; to swerve; to change direction.

virgen ['birxen] *a* virgin; (*cinta*) blank ♦ *nm/f* virgin; **la Santísima V~** (*REL*) the Blessed Virgin.

Virgo ['birɣo] *nm* Virgo.

viril [bi'ril] *a* virile.

virilidad [birili'ðað] *nf* virility.

virrey [bi'rrei] *nm* viceroy.

virtual [bir'twal] *a* (*real*) virtual; (*en potencia*) potential.

virtud [bir'tuð] *nf* virtue; **en ~ de** by virtue of.

virtuoso, a [bir'twoso, a] *a* virtuous ♦ *nm/f* virtuoso.

viruela [bi'rwela] *nf* smallpox; **~s** *nfpl* pockmarks; **~s locas** chickenpox *sg*.

virulento, a [biru'lento, a] *a* virulent.

virus ['birus] *nm inv* virus.

viruta [bi'ruta] *nf* wood *o* metal shaving.

vis [bis] *nf*: **~ cómica** sense of humour.

visa ['bisa] *nf* (*AM*), **visado** [bi'saðo] *nm* visa; **~ de permanencia** residence permit.

visar [bi'sar] *vt* (*pasaporte*) to visa; (*documento*) to endorse.

viscoso, a [bis'koso, a] *a* viscous.

visera [bi'sera] *nf* visor.

visibilidad [bisißili'ðað] *nf* visibility.

visible [bi'sißle] *a* visible; (*fig*) obvious; **exportaciones/importaciones ~s** (*COM*) visible exports/imports.

visillo [bi'siʎo] *nm* lace curtain.

visión [bi'sjon] *nf* (*ANAT*) vision, (eye)sight; (*fantasía*) vision, fantasy; (*panorama*) view; **ver visiones** to see *o* be seeing things.

visionario, a [bisjo'narjo, a] *a* (*que prevé*) visionary; (*alucinado*) deluded ♦ *nm/f* visionary; (*chalado*) lunatic.

visita [bi'sita] *nf* call, visit; (*persona*) visitor; **horas/tarjeta de ~** visiting hours/card; **~ de cortesía/de cumplido/de despedida** courtesy/formal/farewell visit; **hacer una ~** to pay a visit; **ir de ~** to go visiting.

visitar [bisi'tar] *vt* to visit, call on; (*inspeccionar*) to inspect.

vislumbrar [bislum'brar] *vt* to glimpse, catch a glimpse of.

vislumbre [bis'lumbre] *nf* glimpse; (*centelleo*) gleam; (*idea vaga*) glimmer.

viso ['biso] *nm* (*de metal*) glint, gleam; (*de tela*) sheen; (*aspecto*) appearance; **hay un ~ de verdad en esto** there is an element of truth in this.

visón [bi'son] *nm* mink.

visor [bi'sor] *nm* (*FOTO*) viewfinder.

víspera ['bispera] *nf* eve, day before; **la ~** *o* **en ~s de** on the eve of.

vista ['bista] *nf* sight, vision; (*capacidad de ver*) (eye)sight; (*mirada*) look(s) (*pl*); (*FOTO etc*) view; (*JUR*) hearing ♦ *nm* customs officer; **a primera ~** at first glance; **~ general** overview; **fijar** *o* **clavar la ~ en** to stare at; **hacer la ~ gorda** to turn a blind eye; **volver la ~** to look back; **está a la ~ que** it's obvious that; **a la ~** (*COM*) at sight; **en ~ de** in view of; **en ~ de que** in view of the fact that; **¡hasta la ~!** so long!, see you!; **con ~s a** with a view to; *V tb* **visto, a.**

vistazo [bis'taθo] *nm* glance; **dar** *o* **echar un ~ a** to glance at.

visto, a ['bisto, a] *etc vb* *V* **vestir** ♦ *pp de* **ver** ♦ *a* seen; (*considerado*) considered ♦ *nm*: **~ bueno** approval; "**~ bueno**" "approved"; **por lo ~** evidently; **dar el ~ bueno a algo** to give sth the go-ahead; **está ~ que** it's clear that; **está bien/mal ~** it's acceptable/unacceptable; **está muy ~** it is very common; **estaba ~** it had to be; **~ que** *conj* since, considering that.

vistoso, a [bis'toso, a] *a* colourful; (*alegre*) gay; (*pey*) gaudy.

visualice [biswa'liθe] *etc vb* *V* **visualizar.**

visualizador [biswaliθa'ðor] *nm* (*INFORM*) display screen, VDU.

visualizar [biswali'θar] *vt* (*imaginarse*) to visualize; (*INFORM*) to display.

vital [bi'tal] *a* life *cpd*, living *cpd*; (*fig*) vital; (*persona*) lively, vivacious.

vitalicio, a [bita'liθjo, a] *a* for life.

vitamina [bita'mina] *nf* vitamin.

vitaminado, a [bitami'naðo, a] *a* with added vitamins.

vitamínico, a [bita'miniko, a] *a* vitamin *cpd*; **complejos ~s** vitamin compounds.

viticultor, a [bitikul'tor, a] *nm/f* vine grower.

viticultura [bitikul'tura] *nf* vine growing.

vitorear [bitore'ar] *vt* to cheer, acclaim.

vitoriano, a [bito'rjano, a] *a* of *o* from Vitoria ♦ *nm/f* native *o* inhabitant of Vitoria.

vítreo, a ['bitreo, a] *a* vitreous.

vitrina [bi'trina] *nf* glass case; (*en casa*) display cabinet.

vituperar [bitupe'rar] *vt* to condemn.

vituperio [bitu'perjo] *nm* (*condena*) condemnation; (*censura*) censure; (*insulto*) insult.

viudo, a ['bjuðo, a] *a* widowed ♦ *nm* widower ♦ *nf* widow.

viudez [bju'ðeθ] *nf* widowhood.

vivacidad [biβaθi'ðað] *nf* (*vigor*) vigour; (*vida*) vivacity.

vivamente [biβa'mente] *ad* in lively fashion; (*descripción etc*) vividly; (*protesta*) sharply; (*emoción*) acutely.

vivaracho, a [biβa'ratʃo, a] *a* jaunty, lively; (*ojos*) bright, twinkling.

vivaz [bi'βaθ] *a* (*que dura*) enduring; (*vigoroso*) vigorous; (*vivo*) lively.

víveres ['biβeres] *nmpl* provisions.

vivero [bi'βero] *nm* (*HORTICULTURA*) nursery; (*para peces*) fishpond; (: *COM*) fish farm.

viveza [bi'βeθa] *nf* liveliness; (*agudeza*) sharpness.

vividor, a [biβi'ðor, a] *a* (*pey*) opportunistic ♦ *nm* (*aprovechado*) hustler.

vivienda [bi'βjenda] *nf* (*alojamiento*) housing; (*morada*) dwelling; **~s protegidas ~** council housing *sg* (*Brit*), public housing *sg* (*US*).

viviente [bi'βjente] *a* living.

vivificar [biβifi'kar] *vt* to give life to.

vivifique [biβi'fike] *etc vb* *V* **vivificar.**

vivir [bi'βir] *vt* (*experimentar*) to live *o* go through ♦ *vi* (*gen*, *COM*): **~ (de)** to live (by, off, on) ♦ *nm* life, living; **¡viva!** hurray!; **¡viva el rey!** long live the king!

vivo, a ['biβo, a] *a* living, live, alive; (*fig*) vivid; (*movimiento*) quick; (*color*) bright; (*protesta etc*) strong; (*astuto*) smart, clever; **en ~** (*TV etc*) live; **llegar a lo ~** to cut to the quick.

vizcaíno, a [biθka'ino, a] *a*, *nm/f* Biscayan.

Vizcaya [biθ'kaja] *nf* Biscay; **el Golfo de ~** the Bay of Biscay.

V.M. *abr* = **Vuestra Majestad.**

V.ºB.º *abr* = **visto bueno.**

vocablo [bo'kaβlo] *nm* (*palabra*) word; (*término*) term.

vocabulario [bokaβu'larjo] *nm* vocabulary, word list.

vocación [boka'θjon] *nf* vocation.

vocacional [bokaθjo'nal] *nf* (*AM*) ≈ technical college.

vocal [bo'kal] *a* vocal ♦ *nm/f* member (of a committee *etc*) ♦ *nm* non-executive director ♦ *nf* vowel.

vocalice [boka'liθe] *etc vb* *V* **vocalizar.**

vocalizar [bokali'θar] *vt* to vocalize.

vocear [boθe'ar] *vt* (*para vender*) to cry; (*aclamar*) to acclaim; (*fig*) to proclaim ♦ *vi* to yell.

vocería [boθe'ria] *nf*, **vocerío** [boθe'rio] *nm* shouting; (*escándalo*) hullabaloo.

vocero [bo'θero] *nm/f* spokesman/woman.

vociferar [boθife'rar] *vt* to shout; (*jactarse*) to proclaim boastfully ♦ *vi* to yell.

vocinglero, a [boθin'glero, a] *a* vociferous; (*gárrulo*) garrulous; (*fig*) blatant.

vodevil [boðe'βil] *nm* music hall, variety, (*US*) vaudeville.

vodka ['boðka] *nm* vodka.

vol *abr* = **volumen.**

volado, a [bo'laðo, a] *a*: **estar ~** (*fam*) to be worried; (: *AM*) to be crazy.

volador, a [bola'ðor, a] *a* flying.

voladura [bola'ðura] *nf* blowing up, demolition; (*MINERÍA*) blasting.

volandas [boˈlandas]: **en ~** *ad* in *o* through the air; (*fig*) swiftly.

volante [boˈlante] *a* flying ♦ *nm* (*de máquina, coche*) steering wheel; (*de reloj*) balance; (*nota*) note; **ir al ~** to be at the wheel, be driving.

volar [boˈlar] *vt* (*demolir*) to blow up, demolish ♦ *vi* to fly; (*fig: correr*) to rush, hurry; (*fam: desaparecer*) to disappear; **voy volando** I must dash; **¡cómo vuela el tiempo!** how time flies!

volátil [boˈlatil] *a* volatile; (*fig*) changeable.

volcán [bolˈkan] *nm* volcano.

volcánico, a [bolˈkaniko, a] *a* volcanic.

volcar [bolˈkar] *vt* to upset, overturn; (*tumbar, derribar*) to knock over; (*vaciar*) to empty out ♦ *vi* to overturn; **~se** *vr* to tip over; (*barco*) to capsize.

voleibol [boleiˈβol] *nm* volleyball.

voleo [boˈleo] *nm* volley; **a(l) ~** haphazardly; **de un ~** quickly.

Volga [ˈbolɣa] *nm* Volga.

volición [boliˈθjon] *nf* volition.

volqué [bolˈke], **volquemos** [bolˈkemos] *etc vb V* **volcar.**

volquete [bolˈkete] *nm* dumper, dump truck (*US*).

voltaje [bolˈtaxe] *nm* voltage.

volteador, a [boltea'ðor, a] *nm/f* acrobat.

voltear [bolteˈar] *vt* to turn over; (*volcar*) to turn upside down; (*doblar*) to peal ♦ *vi* to roll over.

voltereta [bolteˈreta] *nf* somersault; **~ sobre las manos** handspring; **~ lateral** cartwheel.

voltio [ˈboltjo] *nm* volt.

voluble [boˈluβle] *a* fickle.

volumen [boˈlumen] *nm* volume; **~ monetario** money supply; **~ de negocios** turnover; **bajar el ~** to turn down the volume; **poner la radio a todo ~** to turn the radio up full.

voluminoso, a [bolumiˈnoso, a] *a* voluminous; (*enorme*) massive.

voluntad [bolunˈtað] *nf* will, willpower; (*deseo*) desire, wish; (*afecto*) fondness; **a ~** at will; (*cantidad*) as much as one likes; **buena ~** goodwill; **mala ~** ill will, malice; **por causas ajenas a mi ~** for reasons beyond my control.

voluntario, a [bolunˈtarjo, a] *a* voluntary ♦ *nm/f* volunteer.

voluntarioso, a [boluntaˈrjoso, a] *a* headstrong.

voluptuoso, a [bolupˈtwoso, a] *a* voluptuous.

volver [bolˈβer] *vt* to turn; (*boca abajo*) to turn (over); (*voltear*) to turn round, turn upside down; (*poner al revés*) to turn inside out; (*devolver*) to return; (*transfor-*

mar) to change, transform; (*manga*) to roll up ♦ *vi* to return, go/come back; **~se** *vr* to turn round; (*llegar a ser*) to become; **~ la espalda** to turn one's back; **~ bien por mal** to return good for evil; **~ a hacer** to do again; **~ en sí** to come to *o* round, regain consciousness; **~ la vista atrás** to look back; **~ loco a uno** to drive sb mad; **~se loco** to go mad.

vomitar [bomiˈtar] *vt, vi* to vomit.

vómito [ˈbomito] *nm* (*acto*) vomiting; (*resultado*) vomit.

vorágine [boˈraxine] *nf* whirlpool; (*fig*) maelstrom.

voraz [boˈraθ] *a* voracious; (*fig*) fierce.

vórtice [ˈbortiθe] *nm* whirlpool; (*de aire*) whirlwind.

vos [bos] *pron* (*AM*) you.

voseo [boˈseo] *nm* (*AM*) addressing a person as "vos", *familiar usage*.

Vosgos [ˈbosɣos] *nmpl* Vosges.

vosotros, as [boˈsotros, as] *pron* you *pl*; (*reflexivo*) yourselves; **entre ~** among yourselves.

votación [botaˈθjon] *nf* (*acto*) voting; (*voto*) vote; **~ a mano alzada** show of hands; **someter algo a ~** to put sth to the vote.

votar [boˈtar] *vt* (*POL: partido etc*) to vote for; (*proyecto: aprobar*) to pass; (*REL*) to vow ♦ *vi* to vote.

voto [ˈboto] *nm* vote; (*promesa*) vow; (*maldición*) oath, curse; **~s** *nmpl* (good) wishes; **~ de bloque/de grupo** block/card vote; **~ de censura/de (des)confianza/de gracias** vote of censure/(no) confidence/thanks; **dar su ~** to cast one's vote.

voy [boi] *vb V* **ir.**

voz [boθ] *nf* voice; (*grito*) shout; (*chisme*) rumour; (*LING: palabra*) word; (: *forma*) voice; **dar voces** to shout, yell; **llamar a uno a voces** to shout to sb; **llevar la ~ cantante** (*fig*) to be the boss; **tener la ~ tomada** to be hoarse; **tener ~ y voto** to have the right to speak; **a media ~** in a low voice; **a ~ en cuello** *o* **en grito** at the top of one's voice; **de viva ~** verbally; **en ~ alta** aloud; **~ de mando** command.

vozarrón [boθaˈrron] *nm* booming voice.

vra., vro. *abr* = **vuestra, vuestro.**

Vto. *abr* (*COM*) = **vencimiento.**

vuelco [ˈbwelko] *etc vb V* **volcar** ♦ *nm* spill, overturning; (*fig*) collapse; **mi corazón dio un ~** my heart missed a beat.

vuelo [ˈbwelo] *etc vb V* **volar** ♦ *nm* flight; (*encaje*) lace, frill; (*de falda etc*) loose part; (*fig*) importance; **de altos ~s** (*fig: plan*) grandiose; (: *persona*) ambitious; **alzar el ~** to take flight; (*fig*) to dash off; **coger al ~** to catch in flight; **~ en picado** dive; **~ libre** hang-gliding; **~ regular**

scheduled flight; **falda de mucho** ~ full *o* wide skirt.

vuelque ['bwelke] *etc vb V* **volcar.**

vuelta ['bwelta] *nf* turn; (*curva*) bend, curve; (*regreso*) return; (*revolución*) revolution; (*paseo*) stroll; (*circuito*) lap; (*de papel, tela*) reverse; (*de pantalón*) turn-up (*Brit*), cuff (*US*); (*dinero*) change; ~ **a empezar** back to square one; ~ **al mundo** world trip; **V**~ **de Francia** Tour de France; ~ **cerrada** hairpin bend; **a la** ~ (*Esp*) on one's return; **a la** ~ **de la esquina, a la** ~ (*AM*) round the corner; **a** ~ **de correo** by return of post; **dar** ~**s** to turn, revolve; **dar** ~**s a una idea** to turn over an idea (in one's mind); **dar una** ~ to go for a walk; **dar media** ~ (*AUTO*) to do a U-turn; (*fam*) to beat it; **estar de** ~ (*fam*) to be back; **poner a uno de** ~ **y media** to heap abuse on sb; **no tiene** ~ **de hoja** there's no alternative.

vuelto ['bwelto] *pp de* **volver.**

vuelva ['bwelßa] *etc vb V* **volver.**

vuestro, a ['bwestro, a] *a* your; (*después de n*) of yours ♦ *pron*: **el** ~**/la vuestra/los** ~**s/las vuestras** yours; **lo** ~ (what is) yours; **un amigo** ~ a friend of yours; **una idea vuestra** an idea of yours.

vulgar [bul'ɤar] *a* (*ordinario*) vulgar; (*común*) common.

vulgarice [bulɤa'riθe] *etc vb V* **vulgarizar.**

vulgaridad [bulɤari'ðað] *nf* commonness; (*acto*) vulgarity; (*expresión*) coarse expression; ~**es** *nfpl* banalities.

vulgarismo [bulɤa'rismo] *nm* popular form of a word.

vulgarizar [bulɤari'θar] *vt* to popularize.

vulgo ['bulɤo] *nm* common people.

vulnerable [bulne'raßle] *a* vulnerable.

vulnerar [bulne'rar] *vt* to harm, damage; (*derechos*) to interfere with; (*JUR, COM*) to violate.

vulpino, a [bul'pino, a] *a* vulpine; (*fig*) foxy.

W

W, w ['ußße'doßle, (*AM*) 'doßleße] *nf* (*letra*) W, w; **W de Washington** W for William.

wáter ['bater] *nm* lavatory.

wátman ['watman] *a inv* (*fam*) cool.

whisky ['wiski] *nm* whisky.

Winchester ['wintʃester] *nm* (*INFORM*): **disco** ~ Winchester disk.

X

X, x ['ekis] *nf* (*letra*) X, x; **X de Xiquena** X for Xmas.

xenofobia [kseno'foßja] *nf* xenophobia.

xilófono [ksi'lofono] *nm* xylophone.

Y

Y, y [i'ɤrjeɤa] *nf* (*letra*) Y, y; **Y de Yegua** Y for Yellow (*Brit*) *o* Yoke (*US*).

y [i] *conj* and.

ya [ja] *ad* (*gen*) already; (*ahora*) now; (*en seguida*) at once; (*pronto*) soon ♦ *excl* all right!; (*por supuesto*) of course! ♦ *conj* (*ahora que*) now that; ~ **no** not any more, no longer; ~ **lo sé** I know; ~ **dice que sí,** ~ **dice que no** first he says yes, then he says no; ¡~, ~! yes, yes!; (*con impaciencia*) all right!, O.K.!; ¡~ **voy!** (*enfático: no se suele traducir*) coming!; ~ **que** since.

yacer [ja'θer] *vi* to lie.

yacimiento [jaθi'mjento] *nm* bed, deposit; ~ **petrolífero** oilfield.

Yakarta [ja'karta] *nf* Jakarta.

yanqui ['janki] *a* Yankee ♦ *nm/f* Yank, Yankee.

yate ['jate] *nm* yacht.

yazca ['jaθka] *etc vb V* **yacer.**

yedra ['jeðra] *nf* ivy.

yegua ['jeɤwa] *nf* mare.

yema ['jema] *nf* (*del huevo*) yoke; (*BOT*) leaf bud; (*fig*) best part; ~ **del dedo** fingertip.

Yemen ['jemen] *nm*: **el** ~ **del Norte** Yemen; **el** ~ **del Sur** Southern Yemen.

yemení [jeme'ni] *a, nm/f* Yemeni.

yendo ['jendo] *vb V* **ir.**

yerba ['jerßa] *nf* = **hierba.**

yerga ['jerɤa] *etc*, **yergue** ['jerɤe] *etc vb V* **erguir.**

yermo, a ['jermo, a] *a* barren; (*de gente*) uninhabited ♦ *nm* waste land.

yerno ['jerno] *nm* son-in-law.

yerre ['jerre] *etc vb V* **errar.**

yerto, a ['jerto, a] *a* stiff.

yesca ['jeska] *nf* tinder.

yeso ['jeso] *nm* (*GEO*) gypsum; (*ARQ*) plaster.

yo ['jo] *pron personal* I; **soy** ~ it's me, it is I; ~ **que tú/usted** if I were you.

yodo ['joðo] *nm* iodine.

yoga ['joɣa] *nm* yoga.

yogur(t) [jo'ɣur(t)] *nm* yogurt.

yogurtera [joɣur'tera] *nf* yogurt maker.

yugo ['juɣo] *nm* yoke.

Yugoslavia [juɣos'laßja] *nf* Yugoslavia.

yugoslavo, a [juɣos'laßo, a] *a* Yugoslavian ◆ *nm/f* Yugoslav.

yugular [juɣu'lar] *a* jugular.

yunque ['junke] *nm* anvil.

yunta ['junta] *nf* yoke.

yuntero [jun'tero] *nm* ploughman.

yute ['jute] *nm* jute.

yuxtapondré [jukstapond're] *etc vb* V **yuxtaponer**.

yuxtaponer [jukstapo'ner] *vt* to juxtapose.

yuxtaponga [juksta'ponga] *etc vb* V **yuxtaponer**.

yuxtaposición [jukstaposi'θjon] *nf* juxtaposition.

yuxtapuesto [juksta'pwesto], **yuxtapuse** [juksta'puse] *etc vb* V **yuxtaponer**.

Z

Z, z ['θeta, (*esp AM*) 'seta] *nf* (*letra*) Z, z; **Z de Zaragoza** Z for Zebra.

zafar [θa'far] *vt* (*soltar*) to untie; (*superficie*) to clear; ~**se** *vr* (*escaparse*) to escape; (*ocultarse*) to hide o.s. away; (*TEC*) to slip off; ~**se de** (*persona*) to get away from.

zafio, a ['θafjo, a] *a* coarse.

zafiro [θa'firo] *nm* sapphire.

zaga ['θaɣa] *nf* rear; **a la** ~ behind, in the rear.

zagal [θa'ɣal] *nm* boy, lad.

zagala [θa'ɣala] *nf* girl, lass.

zaguán [θa'ɣwan] *nm* hallway.

zahareño, a [θaa'reɲo, a] *a* (*salvaje*) wild; (*arisco*) unsociable.

zaherir [θae'rir] *vt* (*criticar*) to criticize; (*fig: herir*) to wound.

zahiera *etc*, **zahiriendo** [θa'jera, θai'rjendo] *etc vb* V **zaherir**.

zahorí [θao'ri] *nm* clairvoyant.

zaino, a ['θaino, a] *a* (*color de caballo*) chestnut; (*pérfido*) treacherous; (*animal*) vicious.

zalamería [θalame'ria] *nf* flattery.

zalamero, a [θala'mero, a] *a* flattering; (*relamido*) suave.

zamarra [θa'marra] *nf* (*piel*) sheepskin; (*saco*) sheepskin jacket.

Zambeze [θam'beθe] *nm* Zambezi.

zambo, a ['θambo, a] *a* knock-kneed ◆ *nm/f* (*AM*) half-breed (*of Negro and Indian parentage*); (*mulato*) mulatto ◆ *nf* samba.

zambra ['θambra] *nf* gypsy dance.

zambullida [θambu'ʎiða] *nf* dive, plunge.

zambullirse [θambu'ʎirse] *vr* to dive; (*ocultarse*) to hide o.s.

zamorano, a [θamo'rano, a] *a* of o from Zamora ◆ *nm/f* native o inhabitant of Zamora.

zampar [θam'par] *vt* (*esconder*) to hide o put away (hurriedly); (*comer*) to gobble; (*arrojar*) to hurl ◆ *vi* to eat voraciously; ~**se** *vr* (*chocar*) to bump; (*fig*) to gatecrash.

zanahoria [θana'orja] *nf* carrot.

zancada [θan'kaða] *nf* stride.

zancadilla [θanka'ðiʎa] *nf* trip; (*fig*) stratagem; **echar la** ~ **a uno** to trip sb up.

zancajo [θan'kaxo] *nm* (*ANAT*) heel; (*fig*) dwarf.

zanco ['θanko] *nm* stilt.

zancudo, a [θan'kuðo, a] *a* long-legged ◆ *nm* (*AM*) mosquito.

zángano ['θangano] *nm* drone; (*holgazán*) idler, slacker.

zanja ['θanxa] *nf* (*fosa*) ditch; (*tumba*) grave.

zanjar [θan'xar] *vt* (*fosa*) to ditch, trench; (*problema*) to surmount; (*conflicto*) to resolve.

zapapico [θapa'piko] *nm* pick, pickaxe.

zapata [θa'pata] *nf* half-boot; (*MECÁNICA*) shoe.

zapateado [θapate'aðo] *nm* (*flamenco*) tap dance.

zapatear [θapate'ar] *vt* (*tocar*) to tap with one's foot; (*patear*) to kick; (*fam*) to illtreat ◆ *vi* to tap with one's feet.

zapatería [θapate'ria] *nf* (*oficio*) shoemaking; (*tienda*) shoe-shop; (*fábrica*) shoe factory.

zapatero, a [θapa'tero, a] *nm/f* shoemaker; ~ **remendón** cobbler.

zapatilla [θapa'tiʎa] *nf* slipper; (*TEC*) washer; (*para deporte*) training shoe.

zapato [θa'pato] *nm* shoe.

zar [θar] *nm* tsar, czar.

zarabanda [θara'ßanda] *nf* saraband; (*fig*) whirl.

Zaragoza [θara'ɣoθa] *nf* Saragossa.

zaragozano, a [θaraɣo'θano, a] *a* of o from Saragossa ◆ *nm/f* native o inhabitant of Saragossa.

zaranda [θa'randa] *nf* sieve.

zarandear [θarande'ar] *vt* to sieve; (*fam*) to shake vigorously.

zarcillo [θar'θiʎo] *nm* earring.

zarpa ['θarpa] *nf* (*garra*) claw, paw; **echar la ~ a** to claw at; (*fam*) to grab.

zarpar [θar'par] *vi* to weigh anchor.

zarza ['θarθa] *nf* (*BOT*) bramble.

zarzal [θar'θal] *nm* (*matorral*) bramble patch.

zarzamora [θarθa'mora] *nf* blackberry.

zarzuela [θar'θwela] *nf* Spanish light opera.

zigzag [θiɣ'θaɣ] *a* zigzag.

zigzaguear [θiɣθaɣe'ar] *vi* to zigzag.

zinc [θink] *nm* zinc.

zócalo ['θokalo] *nm* (*ARQ*) plinth, base; (*de pared*) skirting board.

zona ['θona] *nf* zone; **~ fronteriza** border area; **~ del dólar** (*COM*) dollar area; **~ de fomento** *o* **de desarrollo** development area.

zoología [θoolo'xia] *nf* zoology.

zoológico, a [θoo'loxiko, a] *a* zoological ◆ *nm* (*tb*: **parque ~**) zoo.

zoólogo, a [θo'oloɣo, a] *nm/f* zoologist.

zoom [θum] *nm* zoom lens.

zopenco, a [θo'penko, a] (*fam*) *a* dull, stupid ◆ *nm/f* clot, nitwit.

zopilote [θopi'lote] *nm* (*AM*) buzzard.

zoquete [θo'kete] *nm* (*madera*) block; (*pan*) crust; (*fam*) blockhead.

zorro, a ['θorro, a] *a* crafty ◆ *nm/f* fox/ vixen ◆ *nf* (*fam*) whore, tart, hooker (*US*).

zote ['θote] (*fam*) *a* dim, stupid ◆ *nm/f* dimwit.

zozobra [θo'θoβra] *nf* (*fig*) anxiety.

zozobrar [θoθo'βrar] *vi* (*hundirse*) to capsize; (*fig*) to fail.

zueco ['θweko] *nm* clog.

zulo ['θulo] *nm* (*de armas*) cache.

zumbar [θum'bar] *vt* (*burlar*) to tease; (*golpear*) to hit ◆ *vi* to buzz; (*fam*) to be very close; **~se** *vr*: **~se de** to tease; **me zumban los oídos** I have a buzzing *o* ringing in my ears.

zumbido [θum'biðo] *nm* buzzing; (*fam*) punch; **~ de oídos** buzzing *o* ringing in the ears.

zumo ['θumo] *nm* juice; (*ganancia*) profit; **~ de naranja** (fresh) orange juice.

zurcir [θur'θir] *vt* (*coser*) to darn; (*fig*) to put together; **¡que las zurzan!** to blazes with them!

zurdo, a ['θurðo, a] *a* (*mano*) left; (*persona*) left-handed.

zurrar [θu'rrar] *vt* (*TEC*) to dress; (*fam*: *pegar duro*) to wallop; (: *aplastar*) to flatten; (: *criticar*) to criticize harshly.

zurriagazo [θurrja'ɣaθo] *nm* lash, stroke; (*desgracia*) stroke of bad luck.

zurriago [θu'rrjaɣo] *nm* whip, lash.

zurrón [θu'rron] *nm* pouch.

zurza ['θurθa] *etc vb* V **zurcir**.

zutano, a [θu'tano, a] *nm/f* so-and-so.

ENGLISH - SPANISH
INGLÉS - ESPAÑOL

A

A, a [eɪ] *n* (*letter*) A, a; (*scol: mark*) ≈ sobresaliente; (*mus*): **A** la *m*; **A for Andrew**, (*US*) **A for Able** A de Antonio; **A road** *n* (*Brit AUT*) ≈ carretera nacional; **A shares** *npl* (*Brit STOCK EXCHANGE*) acciones *fpl* de clase A.

a, an [eɪ, ə, æn, ən, n] *indefinite article* un(a); **an apple** una manzana; **a mirror** un espejo; **he's a doctor** es médico; **3 a day/ week** 3 por día/semana; **10 km an hour** 10 km por hora; **50p a kilo** 50 peniques el kilo; **3 times a month** 3 veces al mes; **I haven't got a car** no tengo coche.

a. *abbr* = **acre**.

AA *n abbr* (*Brit*: = *Automobile Association*) ≈ RACE *m* (*Sp*); (= *Alcoholics Anonymous*; (*US*: = *Associate in/of Arts*) título universitario; (= *anti-aircraft*) A.A.

AAA *n abbr* (= *American Automobile Association*) ≈ RACE *m* (*Sp*); ['θri:'eɪz] (*Brit*: = *Amateur Athletics Association*) asociación de atletismo amateur.

AAUP *n abbr* (= *American Association of University Professors*) asociación de profesores universitarios.

AB *abbr* (*Brit*) = **able-bodied seaman**; (*Canada*) = **Alberta**.

aback [ə'bæk] *ad*: **to be taken ~** quedar desconcertado.

abandon [ə'bændən] *vt* abandonar; (*renounce*) renunciar a ◆ *n* abandono; (*wild behaviour*): **with ~** sin reparos; **to ~ ship** abandonar el barco.

abandoned [ə'bændənd] *a* (*child, house etc*) abandonado; (*unrestrained: manner*) desinhibido.

abase [ə'beɪs] *vt*: **to ~ o.s. (so far as to do ...)** rebajarse (hasta el punto de hacer ...).

abashed [ə'bæʃt] *a* avergonzado.

abate [ə'beɪt] *vi* moderarse; (*lessen*) disminuir; (*calm down*) calmarse.

abatement [ə'beɪtmənt] *n* (*of pollution, noise*) disminución *f*.

abattoir ['æbətwɑ:*] *n* (*Brit*) matadero *m*.

abbey ['æbɪ] *n* abadía *f*.

abbot ['æbət] *n* abad *m*.

abbreviate [ə'bri:vɪeɪt] *vt* abreviar.

abbreviation [əbri:vɪ'eɪʃən] *n* (*short form*) abreviatura; (*act*) abreviación *f*.

ABC *n abbr* (= *American Broadcasting Company*) cadena de televisión.

abdicate ['æbdɪkeɪt] *vt, vi* abdicar.

abdication [æbdɪ'keɪʃən] *n* abdicación *f*.

abdomen ['æbdəmən] *n* abdomen *m*.

abdominal [æb'dɔmɪnl] *a* abdominal.

abduct [æb'dʌkt] *vt* raptar, secuestrar.

abduction [æb'dʌkʃən] *n* rapto, secuestro.

Aberdonian [æbə'dəunɪən] *a* de Aberdeen ◆ *n* nativo/a *or* habitante *m/f* de Aberdeen.

aberration [æbə'reɪʃən] *n* aberración *f*; **in a moment of mental ~** en un momento de enajenación mental.

abet [ə'bɛt] *vt see* **aid**.

abeyance [ə'beɪəns] *n*: **in ~** (*law*) en desuso; (*matter*) en suspenso.

abhor [əb'hɔ:*] *vt* aborrecer, abominar (de).

abhorrent [əb'hɔrənt] *a* aborrecible, detestable.

abide [ə'baɪd] *vt*: **I can't ~ it/him** no lo/le puedo ver; **to ~ by** *vt fus* atenerse a.

ability [ə'bɪlɪtɪ] *n* habilidad *f*, capacidad *f*; (*talent*) talento; **to the best of my ~** lo mejor que pueda *or* sepa.

abject ['æbdʒɛkt] *a* (*poverty*) miserable; (*apology*) rastrero; (*coward*) vil.

ablaze [ə'bleɪz] *a* en llamas, ardiendo.

able ['eɪbl] *a* capaz; (*skilled*) hábil; **to be ~ to do sth** poder hacer algo.

able-bodied ['eɪbl'bɔdɪd] *a* sano; **~ seaman** marinero de primera.

ably ['eɪblɪ] *ad* hábilmente.

ABM *n abbr* = **anti-ballistic missile**.

abnormal [æb'nɔ:məl] *a* anormal.

abnormality [æbnɔ:'mælɪtɪ] *n* (*condition*) anormalidad *f*; (*instance*) anomalía.

aboard [ə'bɔ:d] *ad* a bordo ◆ *prep* a bordo de; **~ the train** en el tren.

abode [ə'bəud] *n* (*old*) morada; (*LAW*) domicilio; **of no fixed ~** sin domicilio fijo.

abolish [ə'bɔlɪʃ] *vt* suprimir, abolir.

abolition [æbəu'lɪʃən] *n* supresión *f*, abolición *f*.

abominable [ə'bɔmɪnəbl] *a* abominable.

aborigine [æbə'rɪdʒɪnɪ] *n* aborigen *m/f*.

abort [ə'bɔ:t] *vt* abortar; (*COMPUT*) abandonar ◆ *vi* (*COMPUT*) abandonar.

abortion [ə'bɔ:ʃən] *n* aborto (provocado); **to have an ~** abortar.

abortive [ə'bɔ:tɪv] *a* fracasado.

abound [ə'baund] *vi*: **to ~ (in *or* with)** abundar (de *or* en).

about [ə'baut] *prep* (*subject*) acerca de, sobre; (*place*) alrededor de, por ◆ *ad* más o menos, aproximadamente; **do something ~ it!** ¡haz algo!; **to walk ~ the town**

andar por la ciudad; ~ **a hundred/ thousand** etc unos cien/mil etc; **it takes ~ 10 hours** es cosa de 10 horas más o menos; **it's just ~ finished** está casi terminado; **at ~ 2 o'clock** a eso de las 2; **they left it all lying ~** lo dejaron todo por todas partes; **is Paul ~?** ¿está por aquí Paul?; **to be ~ to** estar a punto de; **I'm not ~ to do all that for nothing** no pienso hacer todo eso gratis; **what** or **how ~ doing this?** ¿qué tal si hacemos esto?; **to run ~** correr por todas partes or de aquí para allá; **to walk ~** pasearse, ir y venir; **it's the other way ~** está al revés.

about face, about turn n (MIL, fig) media vuelta.

above [ə'bʌv] ad encima, por encima, arriba ◆ prep encima de; **mentioned ~** susodicho; **~ all** sobre todo; **he's not ~ a bit of blackmail** es capaz hasta de hacer chantaje.

above board a legítimo.

above-mentioned [əbʌv'mɛnʃnd] a susodicho.

abrasion [ə'breɪʒən] n (on skin) abrasión f.

abrasive [ə'breɪzɪv] a abrasivo.

abreast [ə'brɛst] ad de frente; **to keep ~ of** mantenerse al corriente de.

abridge [ə'brɪdʒ] vt abreviar.

abroad [ə'brɔːd] ad (to be) en el extranjero; (to go) al extranjero; **there is a rumour ~ that ...** corre el rumor de que ...

abrupt [ə'brʌpt] a (sudden: departure) repentino; (manner) brusco.

abruptly [ə'brʌptlɪ] ad (leave) repentinamente; (speak) bruscamente.

abscess ['æbsɪs] n absceso.

abscond [əb'skɔnd] vi fugarse.

absence ['æbsəns] n ausencia; **in the ~ of** (person) en ausencia de; (thing) a falta de.

absent ['æbsənt] a ausente; **~ without leave (AWOL)** ausente sin permiso.

absentee [æbsən'tiː] n ausente m/f.

absenteeism [æbsən'tiːɪzəm] n absentismo.

absent-minded [æbsənt'maɪndɪd] a distraído.

absolute ['æbsəluːt] a absoluto; **~ monopoly** monopolio total.

absolutely [æbsə'luːtlɪ] ad totalmente; **oh yes, ~!** ¡claro or por supuesto que sí!

absolution [æbsə'luːʃən] n (REL) absolución f.

absolve [əb'zɔlv] vt: **to ~ sb (from)** absolver a alguien (de).

absorb [əb'zɔːb] vt absorber; **to be ~ed in a book** estar absorto en un libro.

absorbent [əb'zɔːbənt] a absorbente.

absorbent cotton n (US) algodón m hidrófilo.

absorbing [əb'zɔːbɪŋ] a absorbente; (book etc) interesantísimo.

absorption [əb'zɔːpʃən] n absorción f.

abstain [əb'steɪn] vi: **to ~ (from)** abstenerse (de).

abstemious [əb'stiːmɪəs] a abstemio.

abstention [əb'stɛnʃən] n abstención f.

abstinence ['æbstɪnəns] n abstinencia.

abstract ['æbstrækt] a abstracto.

abstruse [æb'struːs] a oscuro.

absurd [əb'sɔːd] a absurdo.

absurdity [əb'sɔːdɪtɪ] n absurdo.

ABTA ['æbtə] n abbr = Association of British Travel Agents.

abundance [ə'bʌndəns] n abundancia.

abundant [ə'bʌndənt] a abundante.

abuse [ə'bjuːs] n (insults) improperios mpl, injurias fpl; (misuse) abuso ◆ vt [ə'bjuːz] (ill-treat) maltratar; (take advantage of) abusar de; **open to ~** sujeto al abuso.

abusive [ə'bjuːsɪv] a ofensivo.

abysmal [ə'bɪzməl] a pésimo; (ignorance) supino.

abyss [ə'bɪs] n abismo.

AC abbr (= alternating current) corriente f alterna ◆ n abbr (US) = athletic club.

a/c abbr (BANKING etc) = account, account current.

academic [ækə'dɛmɪk] a académico, universitario; (pej: issue) puramente teórico ◆ n estudioso/a; profesor(a) m/f universitario/a; **~ year** (UNIV) año académico.

academy [ə'kædəmɪ] n (learned body) academia; (school) instituto, colegio; **~ of music** conservatorio.

ACAS ['eɪkæs] n abbr (Brit: = Advisory, Conciliation and Arbitration Service) ≈ Instituto de Mediación, Arbitraje y Conciliación.

accede [æk'siːd] vi: **to ~ to** acceder a.

accelerate [æk'sɛləreɪt] vt acelerar ◆ vi acelerarse.

acceleration [æksɛlə'reɪʃən] n aceleración f.

accelerator [æk'sɛləreɪtə*] n (Brit) acelerador m.

accent ['æksɛnt] n acento.

accentuate [æk'sɛntjueɪt] vt (syllable) acentuar; (need, difference etc) recalcar, subrayar.

accept [ək'sɛpt] vt aceptar; (approve) aprobar; (concede) admitir.

acceptable [ək'sɛptəbl] a aceptable; admisible.

acceptance [ək'sɛptəns] n aceptación f; aprobación f; **to meet with general ~** tener acogida general.

access ['æksɛs] n acceso ◆ vt (COMPUT: retrieve) obtener información de; (: store) dar información a; **the burglars gained ~ through a window** los ladrones lograron entrar por una ventana; **to have ~ to** tener acceso a.

accessible [æk'sɛsəbl] a accesible.

accession [æk'sɛʃən] n (of monarch) subida, ascenso; (addition) adquisición f.

accessory [æk'sɛsərɪ] *n* accesorio; **toilet accessories** artículos *mpl* de tocador.

access road *n* carretera de acceso; *(to motorway)* carril *m* de acceso.

access time *n* (*COMPUT*) tiempo de acceso.

accident ['æksɪdənt] *n* accidente *m*; *(chance)* casualidad *f*; **by ~** *(unintentionally)* sin querer; *(by coincidence)* por casualidad; **~s at work** accidentes *mpl* de trabajo; **to meet with** *or* **to have an ~** tener *or* sufrir un accidente.

accidental [æksɪ'dɛntl] *a* accidental, fortuito.

accidentally [æksɪ'dɛntəlɪ] *ad* sin querer; por casualidad.

accident insurance *n* seguro contra accidentes.

accident-prone ['æksɪdənt'prəun] *a* propenso a los accidentes.

acclaim [ə'kleɪm] *vt* aclamar, aplaudir ◆ *n* aclamación *f*, aplausos *mpl.*

acclamation [æklə'meɪʃən] *n* *(approval)* aclamación *f*; *(applause)* aplausos *mpl*; **by ~** por aclamación.

acclimatize [ə'klaɪmətaɪz], *(US)* **acclimate** [ə'klaɪmət] *vt*: **to become ~d** aclimatarse.

accolade ['ækəuleɪd] *n* *(prize)* premio; *(praise)* alabanzas *fpl*, homenaje *m.*

accommodate [ə'kɔmədeɪt] *vt* alojar, hospedar; *(oblige, help)* complacer; **this car ~s 4 people comfortably** en este coche caben 4 personas cómodamente.

accommodating [ə'kɔmədeɪtɪŋ] *a* servicial, complaciente.

accommodation *n*, *(US)* **accommodations** *npl* [əkɔmə'deɪʃən(z)] alojamiento; **"~ to let"** "se alquilan habitaciones"; **seating ~** asientos *mpl.*

accompaniment [ə'kʌmpənɪmənt] *n* acompañamiento.

accompanist [ə'kʌmpənɪst] *n* (*MUS*) acompañante *m/f.*

accompany [ə'kʌmpənɪ] *vt* acompañar.

accomplice [ə'kʌmplɪs] *n* cómplice *m/f.*

accomplish [ə'kʌmplɪʃ] *vt* *(finish)* acabar; *(aim)* realizar; *(task)* llevar a cabo.

accomplished [ə'kʌmplɪʃt] *a* experto, hábil.

accomplishment [ə'kʌmplɪʃmənt] *n* *(ending)* conclusión *f*; *(bringing about)* realización *f*; *(skill)* talento.

accord [ə'kɔːd] *n* acuerdo ◆ *vt* conceder; **of his own ~** espontáneamente; **with one ~** de *or* por común acuerdo.

accordance [ə'kɔːdəns] *n*: **in ~ with** de acuerdo con.

according [ə'kɔːdɪŋ]: **~ to** *prep* según; *(in accordance with)* conforme a; **it went ~ to plan** salió según lo previsto.

accordingly [ə'kɔːdɪŋlɪ] *ad* *(thus)* por consiguiente.

accordion [ə'kɔːdɪən] *n* acordeón *m.*

accordionist [ə'kɔːdɪənɪst] *n* acordeonista *m/f.*

accost [ə'kɔst] *vt* abordar, dirigirse a.

account [ə'kaunt] *n* (*COMM*) cuenta, factura; *(report)* informe *m*; **~s** *npl* (*COMM*) cuentas *fpl*; **"~ payee only"** "únicamente en cuenta del beneficiario"; **your ~ is still outstanding** su cuenta está todavía pendiente; **of little ~** de poca importancia; **on ~** a cuenta; **to buy sth on ~** comprar algo a cuenta; **on no ~** de ninguna manera; **on ~ of** a causa de, por motivo de; **to take into ~, take ~ of** tener en cuenta; **to keep an ~ of** llevar la cuenta de; **to bring sb to ~ for sth/for having done sth** pedirle cuentas a uno por algo/por haber hecho algo.

account for *vt fus* *(explain)* explicar; **all the children were ~ed for** no faltaba ningún niño.

accountability [əkauntə'bɪlɪtɪ] *n* responsabilidad *f.*

accountable [ə'kauntəbl] *a* responsable.

accountancy [ə'kauntənsɪ] *n* contabilidad *f.*

accountant [ə'kauntənt] *n* contable *m/f*, contador(a) *m/f.*

accounting [ə'kauntɪŋ] *n* contabilidad *f.*

accounting period *n* período contable, ejercicio financiero.

account number *n* *(at bank etc)* número de cuenta.

account payable *n* cuenta por pagar.

account receivable *n* cuenta por cobrar.

accoutrements [ə'kuːtrəmənts] *npl* equipo, equipaje *m.*

accredited [ə'krɛdɪtɪd] *a* *(agent etc)* autorizado, acreditado.

accretion [ə'kriːʃən] *n* acumulación *f.*

accrue [ə'kruː] *vi* *(mount up)* aumentarse; *(interest)* acumularse; **to ~ to** corresponder a; **~d charges** gastos *mpl* vencidos; **~d interest** interés *m* acumulado.

accumulate [ə'kjuːmjuleɪt] *vt* acumular ◆ *vi* acumularse.

accumulation [əkjuːmju'leɪʃən] *n* acumulación *f.*

accuracy ['ækjurəsɪ] *n* exactitud *f*, precisión *f.*

accurate ['ækjurɪt] *a* *(number)* exacto; *(answer)* acertado; *(shot)* certero.

accurately ['ækjurɪtlɪ] *ad* *(count, shoot, answer)* con precisión.

accursed [ə'kəːst] *a* maldito.

accusation [ækju'zeɪʃən] *n* acusación *f.*

accusative [ə'kjuːzətɪv] *n* acusativo.

accuse [ə'kjuːz] *vt* acusar; *(blame)* echar la culpa a.

accused [ə'kjuːzd] *n* acusado/a.

accustom [ə'kʌstəm] *vt* acostumbrar; **to ~ o.s. to sth** acostumbrarse a algo.

accustomed [ə'kʌstəmd] *a*: **~ to** acostumbrado a.

AC/DC *abbr* = *alternating current/direct current.*

ACE [eıs] *n abbr* = *American Council on Education.*

ace [eıs] *n* as *m*.

acerbic [ə'sə:bık] *a* acerbo; (*fig*) mordaz.

acetate ['æsıteıt] *n* acetato.

ache [eık] *n* dolor *m* ♦ *vi* doler; (*yearn*): to ~ to do sth suspirar por hacer algo; **I've got stomach** ~ *or* (*US*) **a stomach** ~ tengo dolor de estómago, me duele el estómago; **my head** ~s me duele la cabeza.

achieve [ə'tʃi:v] *vt* (*reach*) alcanzar; (*realize*) realizar; (*victory*, *success*) lograr, conseguir.

achievement [ə'tʃi:vmənt] *n* (*completion*) realización *f*; (*success*) éxito.

acid ['æsıd] *a* ácido; (*bitter*) agrio ♦ *n* ácido.

acidity [ə'sıdıtı] *n* acidez *f*; (*MED*) acedía.

acid rain *n* lluvia ácida.

acknowledge [ək'nɔlıdʒ] *vt* (*letter: also*: ~ **receipt of**) acusar recibo de; (*fact*) reconocer.

acknowledgement [ək'nɔlıdʒmənt] *n* acuse *m* de recibo; reconocimiento; ~s (*in book*) agradecimientos *mpl*.

ACLU *n abbr* (= *American Civil Liberties Union*) unión americana por libertades civiles.

acme ['ækmı] *n* colmo, cima.

acne ['æknı] *n* acné *m*.

acorn ['eıkɔ:n] *n* bellota.

acoustic [ə'ku:stık] *a* acústico.

acoustic coupler [-'kʌplə*] *n* (*COMPUT*) acoplador *m* acústico.

acoustics [ə'ku:stıks] *n*, *npl* acústica *sg*.

acoustic screen *n* panel *m* acústico.

acquaint [ə'kweınt] *vt*: **to** ~ **sb with sth** (*inform*) poner a uno al corriente de algo; **to be** ~**ed with** (*person*) conocer; (*fact*) estar al corriente de.

acquaintance [ə'kweıntəns] *n* conocimiento; (*person*) conocido/a; **to make sb's** ~ conocer a uno.

acquiesce [ækwı'ɛs] *vi* (*agree*): **to** ~ (**in**) consentir (en), conformarse (con).

acquire [ə'kwaıə*] *vt* adquirir.

acquired [ə'kwaıəd] *a* adquirido; **an** ~ **taste** un gusto adquirido.

acquisition [ækwı'zıʃən] *n* adquisición *f*.

acquisitive [ə'kwızıtıv] *a* codicioso.

acquit [ə'kwıt] *vt* absolver, exculpar; **to** ~ **o.s. well** salir con éxito.

acquittal [ə'kwıtl] *n* absolución *f*, exculpación *f*.

acre ['eıkə*] *n* acre *m*.

acreage ['eıkərıdʒ] *n* extensión *f*.

acrid ['ækrıd] *a* (*smell*) acre; (*fig*) mordaz, sarcástico.

acrimonious [ækrı'məunıəs] *a* (*remark*) mordaz; (*argument*) reñido.

acrobat ['ækrəbæt] *n* acróbata *m/f*.

acrobatic [ækrə'bætık] *a* acrobático.

acrobatics [ækrə'bætıks] *npl* acrobacias *fpl*.

acronym ['ækrənım] *n* siglas *fpl*.

across [ə'krɔs] *prep* (*on the other side of*) al otro lado de; (*crosswise*) a través de ♦ *ad* de un lado a otro, de una parte a otra; a través, al través; **to run/swim** ~ atravesar corriendo/nadando; ~ **from** enfrente de; **the lake is 12 km** ~ el lago tiene 12 km de ancho; **to get sth** ~ **to sb** (*fig*) hacer comprender algo a uno.

acrylic [ə'krılık] *a* acrílico.

ACT *n abbr* (= *American College Test*) examen que se hace al término de los estudios secundarios.

act [ækt] *n* acto, acción *f*; (*THEATRE*) acto; (*in music-hall etc*) número; (*LAW*) decreto, ley *f* ♦ *vi* (*behave*) comportarse; (*THEATRE*) actuar; (*pretend*) fingir; (*take action*) tomar medidas ♦ *vt* (*part*) hacer, representar; ~ **of God** fuerza mayor; **it's only an** ~ es cuento; **to catch sb in the** ~ coger a uno en flagrante *or* con las manos en la masa; **to** ~ **Hamlet** hacer el papel de Hamlet; **to** ~ **as** actuar *or* hacer de; ~**ing in my capacity as chairman, I ...** en mi calidad de presidente, yo ...; **it** ~**s as a deterrent** sirve para disuadir; **he's only** ~**ing** está fingiendo nada más.

act on *vt*: **to** ~ **on sth** actuar *or* obrar sobre algo.

act out *vt* (*event*) representar; (*fantasies*) realizar.

acting ['æktıŋ] *a* suplente ♦ *n*: **to do some** ~ hacer algo de teatro; **he is the** ~ **manager** es el gerente en funciones.

action ['ækʃən] *n* acción *f*, acto; (*MIL*) acción *f*; (*LAW*) proceso, demanda; **to put a plan into** ~ poner un plan en acción *or* en marcha; **killed in** ~ (*MIL*) muerto en acto de servicio *or* en combate; **out of** ~ (*person*) fuera de combate; (*thing*) averiado, descompuesto; **to take** ~ tomar medidas; **to bring an** ~ **against sb** entablar *or* presentar demanda contra uno.

action replay *n* (*TV*) repetición *f*.

activate ['æktıveıt] *vt* activar.

active ['æktıv] *a* activo, enérgico; (*volcano*) en actividad; **to play an** ~ **part in** colaborar activamente en; ~ **file** (*COMPUT*) fichero activo.

active duty (AD) *n* (*US MIL*) servicio activo.

actively ['æktıvlı] *ad* (*participate*) activamente; (*discourage*, *dislike*) enérgicamente.

active partner *n* (*COMM*) socio activo.

activist ['æktıvıst] *n* activista *m/f*.

activity [æk'tıvıtı] *n* actividad *f*.

actor ['æktə*] *n* actor *m*.

actress ['æktrıs] *n* actriz *f*.

ACTT *n abbr* (*Brit*: = *Association of Cinematographic, Television and Allied Technicians*) sindicato de técnicos de cine y televisión.

actual ['æktjuəl] *a* verdadero, real.

actually ['æktjuəlɪ] *ad* realmente, en realidad.

actuary ['æktjuərɪ] *n* (*COMM*) actuario/a (de seguros).

actuate ['æktjueɪt] *vt* mover, impulsar.

acumen ['ækjumən] *n* perspicacia; **business** ~ talento para los negocios.

acupuncture ['ækjupʌŋktʃə*] *n* acupuntura.

acute [ə'kjuːt] *a* agudo.

acutely [ə'kjuːtlɪ] *ad* profundamente, extremadamente.

AD *ad abbr* (= *Anno Domini*) A.C. ◆ *n abbr* (*US MIL*) see **active duty**.

ad [æd] *n abbr* = **advertisement**.

adage ['ædɪdʒ] *n* refrán *m*, adagio.

Adam ['ædəm] *n* Adán; ~'s **apple** *n* nuez *f* de la garganta.

adamant ['ædəmənt] *a* firme, inflexible.

adapt [ə'dæpt] *vt* adaptar; (*reconcile*) acomodar ◆ *vi*: **to** ~ (**to**) adaptarse (a), ajustarse (a).

adaptability [ədæptə'bɪlɪtɪ] *n* (*of person, device etc*) adaptabilidad *f*.

adaptable [ə'dæptəbl] *a* (*device*) adaptable; (*person*) acomodadizo, que se adapta.

adaptation [ædæp'teɪʃən] *n* adaptación *f*.

adapter, adaptor [ə'dæptə*] *n* (*ELEC*) adaptador *m*.

ADC *n abbr* (*MIL*) = *aide-de-camp*; (*US*: = *Aid to Dependent Children*) *ayuda para niños dependientes*.

add [æd] *vt* añadir, agregar; (*figures: also*: ~ **up**) sumar ◆ *vi*: **to** ~ **to** (*increase*) aumentar, acrecentar.

add on *vt* añadir.

add up *vt* (*figures*) sumar ◆ *vi* (*fig*): **it doesn't** ~ **up** no tiene sentido; **it doesn't** ~ **up to much** es poca cosa, no tiene gran *or* mucha importancia.

addendum [ə'dɛndəm] *n* apéndice *m*.

adder ['ædə*] *n* víbora.

addict ['ædɪkt] *n* (*to drugs etc*) adicto/a; (*enthusiast*) aficionado/a, entusiasta *m/f*; **heroin** ~ heroinómano/a.

addicted [ə'dɪktɪd] *a*: **to be** ~ **to** ser adicto a; ser aficionado a.

addiction [ə'dɪkʃən] *n* (*dependence*) hábito morboso; (*enthusiasm*) afición *f*.

addictive [ə'dɪktɪv] *a* que causa adicción.

adding machine ['ædɪŋ-] *n* calculadora.

Addis Ababa ['ædɪs'æbəbə] *n* Addis Abeba *m*.

addition [ə'dɪʃən] *n* (*adding up*) adición *f*; (*thing added*) añadidura, añadido; **in** ~ además, por añadidura; **in** ~ **to** además de.

additional [ə'dɪʃənl] *a* adicional.

additive ['ædɪtɪv] *n* aditivo.

addled ['ædld] *a* (*Brit: rotten*) podrido; (: *fig*) confuso.

address [ə'drɛs] *n* dirección *f*, señas *fpl*; (*speech*) discurso; (*COMPUT*) dirección *f* ◆

vt (*letter*) dirigir; (*speak to*) dirigirse a, dirigir la palabra a; **form of** ~ tratamiento; **absolute/relative** ~ (*COMPUT*) dirección *f* absoluta/relativa; **to** ~ **o.s. to sth** (*issue, problem*) abordar.

addressee [ædrɛ'siː] *n* destinatario/a.

Aden ['eɪdn] *n* Adén *m*.

adenoids ['ædɪnɔɪdz] *npl* vegetaciones *fpl* adenoideas.

adept ['ædɛpt] *a*: ~ **at** experto *or* hábil en.

adequacy ['ædɪkwəsɪ] *n* idoneidad *f*.

adequate ['ædɪkwɪt] *a* (*satisfactory*) adecuado; (*enough*) suficiente; **to feel** ~ **to a task** sentirse con fuerzas para una tarea.

adequately ['ædɪkwɪtlɪ] *ad* adecuadamente.

adhere [əd'hɪə*] *vi*: **to** ~ **to** pegarse a; (*fig*: *abide by*) observar.

adherent [əd'hɪərənt] *n* partidario/a.

adhesion [əd'hiːʒən] *n* adherencia.

adhesive [əd'hiːzɪv] *a, n* adhesivo.

adhesive tape *n* (*Brit*) cinta adhesiva; (*US*: *MED*) esparadrapo.

ad hoc [æd'hɔk] *a* (*decision*) ad hoc; (*committee*) formado con fines específicos ◆ *ad* con fines específicos.

adieu [ə'djuː] *excl* ¡vaya con Dios!

ad inf ['æd'ɪnf] *ad* hasta el infinito.

adjacent [ə'dʒeɪsənt] *a*: ~ **to** contiguo a, inmediato a.

adjective ['ædʒektɪv] *n* adjetivo.

adjoin [ə'dʒɔɪn] *vt* estar contiguo a; (*land*) lindar con.

adjoining [ə'dʒɔɪnɪŋ] *a* contiguo, vecino.

adjourn [ə'dʒəːn] *vt* aplazar; (*session*) suspender, levantar; (*US*: *end*) terminar ◆ *vi* suspenderse; **the meeting has been** ~**ed till next week** se ha levantado la sesión hasta la semana que viene; **they** ~**ed to the pub** (*col*) pasaron al bar.

adjournment [ə'dʒəːnmənt] *n* (*period*) suspensión *f*; (*postponement*) aplazamiento.

Adjt. *abbr* = **adjutant**.

adjudicate [ə'dʒuːdɪkeɪt] *vi* sentenciar; (*contest*) hacer de árbitro en, juzgar; (*claim*) decidir.

adjudication [ədʒuːdɪ'keɪʃən] *n* adjudicación *f*.

adjudicator [ə'dʒuːdɪkeɪtə*] *n* juez *m*, árbitro.

adjust [ə'dʒʌst] *vt* (*change*) modificar; (*arrange*) arreglar; (*machine*) ajustar ◆ *vi*: **to** ~ (**to**) adaptarse (a).

adjustable [ə'dʒʌstəbl] *a* ajustable.

adjuster [ə'dʒʌstə*] *n* see **loss**.

adjustment [ə'dʒʌstmənt] *n* modificación *f*; arreglo; (*of prices, wages*) ajuste *m*.

adjutant ['ædʒətənt] *n* ayudante *m*.

ad-lib [æd'lɪb] *vt, vi* improvisar ◆ *ad*: **ad lib** a voluntad, a discreción.

adman ['ædmæn] *n* (*col*) publicista *m*.

admin ['ædmɪn] *n abbr* (*col*) = **administration**.

administer [əd'mɪnɪstə*] *vt* proporcionar;

(*justice*) administrar.

administration [ædmɪnɪ'streɪʃən] *n* administración *f*; (*government*) gobierno; **the A~** (*US*) la Administración.

administrative [əd'mɪnɪstrətɪv] *a* administrativo.

administrator [əd'mɪnɪstreɪtə*] *n* administrador(a) *m/f*.

admirable ['ædmərəbl] *a* admirable.

admiral ['ædmərəl] *n* almirante *m*.

Admiralty ['ædmərəltɪ] *n* (*Brit*) Ministerio de Marina, Almirantazgo.

admiration [ædmə'reɪʃən] *n* admiración *f*.

admire [əd'maɪə*] *vt* admirar.

admirer [əd'maɪərə*] *n* admirador(a) *m/f*; (*suitor*) pretendiente *m*.

admission [əd'mɪʃən] *n* (*exhibition, night-club*) entrada; (*enrolment*) ingreso; (*confession*) confesión *f*; "~ **free**" "entrada gratis *or* libre"; **by his own ~** él mismo reconoce que.

admit [əd'mɪt] *vt* dejar entrar, dar entrada a; (*permit*) admitir; (*acknowledge*) reconocer; "**this ticket ~s two**" "entrada para 2 personas"; **children not ~ted** se prohíbe la entrada a (los) menores de edad; **I must ~ that** ... debo reconocer que ...

admit of *vt fus* admitir, permitir.

admit to *vt fus* confesarse culpable de.

admittance [əd'mɪtəns] *n* entrada; "**no ~**" "se prohíbe la entrada", "prohibida la entrada".

admittedly [əd'mɪtədlɪ] *ad* de acuerdo que.

admonish [əd'mɒnɪʃ] *vt* amonestar; (*advise*) aconsejar.

ad nauseam [æd'nɔːsɪæm] *ad* hasta el cansancio.

ado [ə'duː] *n*: **without (any) more ~** sin más (ni más).

adolescence [ædəu'lɛsns] *n* adolescencia.

adolescent [ædəu'lɛsnt] *a*, *n* adolescente *m/f*.

adopt [ə'dɒpt] *vt* adoptar.

adopted [ə'dɒptɪd] *a* adoptivo.

adoption [ə'dɒpʃən] *n* adopción *f*.

adoptive [ə'dɒptɪv] *a* adoptivo.

adorable [ə'dɔːrəbl] *a* adorable.

adoration [ædə'reɪʃən] *n* adoración *f*.

adore [ə'dɔː*] *vt* adorar.

adoring [ə'dɔːrɪŋ] *a* cariñoso.

adorn [ə'dɔːn] *vt* adornar.

adornment [ə'dɔːnmənt] *n* adorno.

ADP *n abbr see* **automatic data processing.**

adrenalin [ə'drɛnəlɪn] *n* adrenalina.

Adriatic [eɪdrɪ'ætɪk] *n*: **the ~ (Sea)** el (Mar) Adriático.

adrift [ə'drɪft] *ad* a la deriva; **to come ~** (*boat*) ir a la deriva, soltarse; (*wire, rope etc*) soltarse.

adroit [ə'drɔɪt] *a* diestro.

ADT *abbr* (*US*: = *Atlantic Daylight Time*) hora de verano de Nueva York.

adulation [ædju'leɪʃən] *n* adulación *f*.

adult ['ædʌlt] *n* adulto/a ◆ *a*: **~ education** educación *f* para adultos.

adulterate [ə'dʌltəreɪt] *vt* adulterar.

adultery [ə'dʌltərɪ] *n* adulterio.

adulthood ['ædʌlthud] *n* edad *f* adulta.

advance [əd'vɑːns] *n* adelanto, progreso; (*money*) anticipo, préstamo; (*MIL*) avance *m* ◆ *vt* avanzar, adelantar; (*money*) anticipar ◆ *vi* avanzar, adelantarse; **in ~** por adelantado; **to make ~s to sb** (*gen*) ponerse en contacto con uno; (*amorously*) insinuarse a uno.

advanced *a* avanzado; (*SCOL: studies*) adelantado; **~ in years** entrado en años.

advancement [əd'vɑːnsmənt] *n* progreso; (*in rank*) ascenso.

advance notice *n* previo aviso.

advance payment *n* (*part sum*) anticipo.

advantage [əd'vɑːntɪdʒ] *n* (*also TENNIS*) ventaja; **to take ~ of** aprovecharse de; **it's to our ~** es ventajoso para nosotros.

advantageous [ædvən'teɪdʒəs] *a* ventajoso, provechoso.

advent ['ædvənt] *n* advenimiento; **A~** Adviento.

adventure [əd'vɛntʃə*] *n* aventura.

adventurous [əd'vɛntʃərəs] *a* aventurero.

adverb ['ædvɜːb] *n* adverbio.

adversary ['ædvəsərɪ] *n* adversario, contrario.

adverse ['ædvɜːs] *a* adverso, contrario; **~ to** adverso a.

adversity [əd'vɜːsɪtɪ] *n* infortunio.

advert ['ædvɜːt] *n abbr* (*Brit*) = **advertisement.**

advertise ['ædvətaɪz] *vi* hacer propaganda; (*in newspaper etc*) poner un anuncio; **to ~ for** (*staff*) buscar por medio de anuncios ◆ *vt* anunciar.

advertisement [əd'vɜːtɪsmənt] *n* (*COMM*) anuncio.

advertiser ['ædvətaɪzə*] *n* anunciante *m/f*.

advertising ['ædvətaɪzɪŋ] *n* publicidad *f*, propaganda; anuncios *mpl*.

advertising agency *n* agencia de publicidad.

advertising campaign *n* campaña de publicidad.

advice [əd'vaɪs] *n* consejo, consejos *mpl*; (*notification*) aviso; **a piece of ~** un consejo; **to take legal ~** consultar a un abogado; **to ask (sb) for ~** pedir consejo (a uno).

advice note *n* (*Brit*) nota de aviso.

advisable [əd'vaɪzəbl] *a* aconsejable, conveniente.

advise [əd'vaɪz] *vt* aconsejar; **to ~ sb of sth** (*inform*) informar a uno de algo; **to ~ sb against sth/doing sth** desaconsejar algo a uno/aconsejar a uno que no haga algo; **you will be well/ill ~d to go** deberías/no deberías ir.

advisedly [əd'vaɪzɪdlɪ] *ad* (*deliberately*) deliberadamente.

adviser [əd'vaɪzə*] *n* consejero/a; *(business adviser)* asesor(a) *m/f*.

advisory [ad'vaɪzərɪ] *a* consultivo; **in an ~ capacity** como asesor.

advocate ['ædvəkeɪt] *vt (argue for)* abogar por; *(give support to)* ser partidario de ♦ *n* ['ædvəkɪt] abogado/a.

advt. *abbr* = **advertisement**.

AEA *n abbr (Brit: = Atomic Energy Authority)* consejo de energía nuclear.

AEC *n abbr (US: = Atomic Energy Commission)* consejo de energía nuclear.

Aegean [iː'dʒiːən] *n:* **the ~ (Sea)** el Mar Egeo.

aegis ['iːdʒɪs] *n:* **under the ~ of** bajo la tutela de.

aeon ['iːən] *n* eón *m*.

aerial ['ɛərɪəl] *n* antena ♦ *a* aéreo.

aero- ['ɛərəu] *pref* aero-.

aerobatics [ɛərəu'bætɪks] *npl* acrobacia aérea.

aerobics [ɛə'rəubɪks] *nsg* aerobic *m*, aerobismo *(LAm)*.

aerodrome ['ɛərədrəum] *n (Brit)* aeródromo.

aerodynamic [ɛərəudaɪ'næmɪk] *a* aerodinámico.

aeronautics [ɛərəu'nɔːtɪks] *nsg* aeronáutica.

aeroplane ['ɛərəpleɪn] *n (Brit)* avión *m*.

aerosol ['ɛərəsɔl] *n* aerosol *m*.

aerospace industry ['ɛərəuspeɪs-] *n* industria aerospacial.

aesthetic [iːs'θɛtɪk] *a* estético.

aesthetics [iːs'θɛtɪks] *npl* estética.

AEU *n abbr (Brit: = Amalgamated Engineering Union)* sindicato mixto de ingeniería.

a.f. *abbr* = **audiofrequency**.

afar [ə'faː*] *ad* lejos; **from ~** desde lejos.

AFB *n abbr (US)* = **Air Force Base**.

AFDC *n abbr (US: = Aid to Families with Dependent Children)* ayuda a familias con hijos menores.

affable ['æfəbl] *a* afable.

affair [ə'fɛə*] *n* asunto; *(also:* **love ~**) relación *f* amorosa; **~s** *(business)* negocios *mpl*; **the Watergate ~** el asunto (de) Watergate.

affect [ə'fɛkt] *vt* afectar, influir en; *(move)* conmover.

affectation [æfɛk'teɪʃən] *n* afectación *f*.

affected [ə'fɛktɪd] *a* afectado.

affection [ə'fɛkʃən] *n* afecto, cariño.

affectionate [ə'fɛkʃənɪt] *a* afectuoso, cariñoso.

affectionately [ə'fɛkʃənɪtlɪ] *ad* afectuosamente.

affidavit [æfɪ'deɪvɪt] *n (LAW)* declaración *f* jurada.

affiliated [ə'fɪlɪeɪtɪd] *a* afiliado; **~ company** empresa *or* compañía filial *or* subsidiaria.

affinity [ə'fɪnɪtɪ] *n* afinidad *f*.

affirm [ə'fɜːm] *vt* afirmar.

affirmation [æfə'meɪʃən] *n* afirmación *f*.

affirmative [ə'fɜːmətɪv] *a* afirmativo.

affix [ə'fɪks] *vt (signature)* estampar; *(stamp)* pegar.

afflict [ə'flɪkt] *vt* afligir.

affliction [ə'flɪkʃən] *n* enfermedad *f*, aflicción *f*.

affluence ['æfluəns] *n* opulencia, riqueza.

affluent ['æfluənt] *a* adinerado, acaudalado; **the ~ society** la sociedad de consumo.

afford [ə'fɔːd] *vt (provide)* dar, proporcionar; **can we ~ it/to buy it?** ¿tenemos bastante dinero para comprarlo?; **can we ~ a car?** ¿tenemos dinero para comprarnos un coche?

affray [ə'freɪ] *n* refriega, reyerta.

affront [ə'frʌnt] *n* afrenta, ofensa.

affronted [ə'frʌntɪd] *a* ofendido.

Afghan ['æfgæn] *a, n* afgano/a *m/f*.

Afghanistan [æf'gænɪstæn] *n* Afganistán *m*.

afield [ə'fiːld] *ad:* **far ~** muy lejos.

AFL-CIO *n abbr (US: = American Federation of Labor and Congress of Industrial Organizations)* confederación sindicalista.

afloat [ə'fləut] *ad (floating)* a flote; *(at sea)* en el mar.

afoot [ə'fut] *ad:* **there is something ~** algo se está tramando.

aforesaid [ə'fɔːsɛd] *a* antedicho, susodicho; *(COMM)* mencionado anteriormente.

afraid [ə'freɪd] *a:* **to be ~ of** *(person)* tener miedo a; *(thing)* tener miedo de; **to be ~ to** tener miedo de, temer; **I am ~ that** me temo que; **I'm ~ so** ¡me temo que sí!, ¡lo siento, pero es así!; **I'm ~ not** me temo que no.

afresh [ə'frɛʃ] *ad* de nuevo, otra vez.

Africa ['æfrɪkə] *n* África.

African ['æfrɪkən] *a, n* africano/a *m/f*.

Afrikaans [æfrɪ'kaːns] *n* afrikaans *m*.

Afrikaner [æfrɪ'kaːnə*] *n* afrikánder *m/f*.

Afro-American ['æfrəuə'mɛrɪkən] *a, n* afroamericano/a *m/f*.

AFT *n abbr (= American Federation of Teachers)* sindicato de profesores.

aft [aːft] *ad (to be)* en popa; *(to go)* a popa.

after ['aːftə*] *prep (time)* después de; *(place, order)* detrás de, tras ♦ *ad* después ♦ *conj* después (de) que; **what/who are you ~?** ¿qué/a quién busca usted?; **the police are ~ him** la policía le está buscando; **~ having done/he left** después de haber hecho/después de que se marchó; **~ dinner** después de cenar *or* comer; **the day ~ tomorrow** pasado mañana; **to ask ~ sb** preguntar por uno; **~ all** después de todo, al fin y al cabo; **~ you!** ¡pase usted!; **quarter ~ two** *(US)* las 2 y cuarto.

afterbirth ['aːftəbɜːθ] *n* secundinas *fpl*.

aftercare ['aːftəkɛə*] *n (MED)* asistencia postoperatoria.

after-effects [ˈɑːftərɪfɛkts] *npl* consecuencias *fpl*, efectos *mpl*.

afterlife [ˈɑːftəlaɪf] *n* vida eterna.

aftermath [ˈɑːftəmɑːθ] *n* consecuencias *fpl*, resultados *mpl*.

afternoon [ɑːftəˈnuːn] *n* tarde *f*; **good ~!** ¡buenas tardes!

afters [ˈɑːftəz] *n* (*col: dessert*) postre *m*.

after-sales service [ɑːftəˈseɪlz-] *n* (*Brit COMM: for car, washing machine etc*) servicio de asistencia pos-venta.

after-shave (lotion) [ˈɑːftəʃeɪv-] *n* aftershave *m*.

aftershock [ˈɑːftəʃɔk] *n* (*of earthquake*) réplica.

afterthought [ˈɑːftəθɔːt] *n* ocurrencia (tardía).

afterwards [ˈɑːftəwədz] *ad* después, más tarde.

again [əˈgɛn] *ad* otra vez, de nuevo; **to do sth ~** volver a hacer algo; **~ and ~** una y otra vez; **now and ~** de vez en cuando.

against [əˈgɛnst] *prep* (*opposed*) en contra de; (*close to*) contra, junto a; **I was leaning ~ the desk** estaba apoyado contra el escritorio; (**as**) **~** en contraste con.

age [eɪdʒ] *n* edad *f*; (*old ~*) vejez *f*; (*period*) época ♦ *vi* envejecer(se) ♦ *vt* envejecer; **what ~ is he?** ¿qué edad *or* cuántos años tiene?; **he is 20 years of ~** tiene 20 años; **under ~** menor de edad; **to come of ~** llegar a la mayoría de edad; **it's been ~s since I saw you** hace siglos que no te veo.

aged [eɪdʒd] *a*: **~ 10** de 10 años de edad; **the ~** [ˈeɪdʒɪd] *npl* los ancianos.

age group *n*: **to be in the same ~** tener la misma edad; **the 40 to 50 ~** el grupo de 40 a 50 años.

ageless [ˈeɪdʒlɪs] *a* (*eternal*) eterno; (*ever young*) siempre joven.

age limit *n* edad *f* tope.

agency [ˈeɪdʒənsɪ] *n* agencia; **through or by the ~ of** por medio de.

agenda [əˈdʒɛndə] *n* orden *m* del día; **on the ~** (*COMM*) en el orden del día.

agent [ˈeɪdʒənt] *n* (*gen*) agente *m/f*; (*representative*) representante *m/f*, delegado/a.

aggravate [ˈægrəveɪt] *vt* agravar; (*annoy*) irritar, exasperar.

aggravating [ˈægrəveɪtɪŋ] *a* molesto.

aggravation [ægrəˈveɪʃən] *n* agravación *f*.

aggregate [ˈægrɪgɪt] *n* (*whole*) conjunto; (*collection*) agregado.

aggression [əˈgrɛʃən] *n* agresión *f*.

aggressive [əˈgrɛsɪv] *a* agresivo; (*vigorous*) enérgico.

aggressiveness [əˈgrɛsɪvnɪs] *n* agresividad *f*.

aggrieved [əˈgriːvd] *a* ofendido, agraviado.

aghast [əˈgɑːst] *a* horrorizado.

agile [ˈædʒaɪl] *a* ágil.

agitate [ˈædʒɪteɪt] *vt* (*shake*) agitar; (*trou-*

ble) inquietar; **to ~ for** hacer una campaña en pro de *or* en favor de.

agitated [ˈædʒɪteɪtɪd] *a* agitado.

agitator [ˈædʒɪteɪtə*] *n* agitador(a) *m/f*.

AGM *n abbr see* **annual general meeting**.

agnostic [ægˈnɔstɪk] *a*, *n* agnóstico/a *m/f*.

ago [əˈgəu] *ad*: **2 days ~** hace 2 días; **not long ~** hace poco; **how long ~?** ¿hace cuánto tiempo?; **as long ~ as 1960** ya en 1960.

agog [əˈgɔg] *a* (*anxious*) ansiado; (*excited*): (**all**) **~ (for)** (todo) emocionado (por).

agonize [ˈægənaɪz] *vi*: **to ~ (over)** atormentarse (por).

agonized [ˈægənaɪzd] *a* angustioso.

agonizing [ˈægənaɪzɪŋ] *a* (*pain*) atroz; (*suspense*) angustioso.

agony [ˈægənɪ] *n* (*pain*) dolor *m* agudo; (*distress*) angustia; **to be in ~** retorcerse de dolor.

agony column *n* consultorio sentimental.

agree [əˈgriː] *vt* (*price*) acordar, quedar en ♦ *vi* (*statements etc*) coincidir, concordar; **to ~ (with)** (*person*) estar de acuerdo (con), ponerse de acuerdo (con); **to ~ to do sth** aceptar hacer; **to ~ to sth** consentir en algo; **to ~ that** (*admit*) estar de acuerdo en que; **it was ~d that ...** se acordó que ...; **garlic doesn't ~ with me** el ajo no me sienta bien.

agreeable [əˈgriːəbl] *a* agradable; (*person*) simpático; (*willing*) de acuerdo, conforme.

agreeably [əˈgriːəblɪ] *ad* agradablemente.

agreed [əˈgriːd] *a* (*time, place*) convenido.

agreement [əˈgriːmənt] *n* acuerdo; (*COMM*) contrato; **in ~** de acuerdo, conforme; **by mutual ~** de común acuerdo.

agricultural [ægrɪˈkʌltʃərəl] *a* agrícola.

agriculture [ˈægrɪkʌltʃə*] *n* agricultura.

aground [əˈgraund] *ad*: **to run ~** encallar, embarrancar.

ahead [əˈhɛd] *ad* delante; **~ of** delante de; (*fig: schedule etc*) antes de; **~ of time** antes de la hora; **to be ~ of sb** (*fig*) llevar la ventaja *or* delantera a uno; **go right or straight ~** siga adelante; **they were (right) ~ of us** iban (justo) delante de nosotros.

ahoy [əˈhɔɪ] *excl* ¡oiga!

AI *n abbr* = *Amnesty International*; (*COMPUT*) = **artificial intelligence**.

AIB *n abbr* (*Brit: = Accident Investigation Bureau*) oficina de investigación de accidentes.

AID *n abbr* (= *artificial insemination by donor*) inseminación artificial por donante; (*US: = Agency for International Development*) Agencia Internacional para el Desarrollo.

aid [eɪd] *n* ayuda, auxilio ♦ *vt* ayudar, auxiliar; **in ~ of** a beneficio de; **with the ~ of** con la ayuda de; **to ~ and abet** (*LAW*) ser cómplice.

aide [eɪd] *n* (*POL*) ayudante *m/f*.

AIDS [eɪdz] n abbr (= acquired immune deficiency syndrome) SIDA m.
AIH abbr (= artificial insemination by husband) inseminación artificial por esposo.
ailing ['eɪlɪŋ] a (person, economy) enfermizo.
ailment ['eɪlmənt] n enfermedad f, achaque m.
aim [eɪm] vt (gun, camera) apuntar; (missile, remark) dirigir; (blow) asestar ♦ vi (also: **take** ~) apuntar ♦ n puntería; (objective) propósito, meta; **to** ~ **at** (objective) aspirar a, pretender; **to** ~ **to do** tener la intención de hacer.
aimless ['eɪmlɪs] a sin propósito, sin objeto.
aimlessly ['eɪmlɪslɪ] ad a la ventura, a la deriva.
ain't [eɪnt] (col) = **am not; aren't; isn't**.
air [ɛə*] n aire m; (appearance) aspecto ♦ vt (room) ventilar; (clothes, bed, grievances, ideas) airear; (views) hacer público ♦ cpd aéreo; **to throw sth into the** ~ (ball etc) lanzar algo al aire; **by** ~ (travel) en avión; **to be on the** ~ (RADIO, TV: programme) estarse emitiendo; (: station) estar emitiendo.
air base n (MIL) base f aérea.
air bed n (Brit) colchón m neumático.
airborne ['ɛəbɔːn] a (in the air) en el aire; (MIL) aerotransportado; **as soon as the plane was** ~ tan pronto como el avión estuvo en el aire.
air cargo n carga aérea.
air-conditioned ['ɛəkən'dɪʃənd] a climatizado.
air conditioning [-kən'dɪʃənɪŋ] n aire m acondicionado.
air-cooled ['ɛəkuːld] a refrigerado por aire.
aircraft ['ɛəkrɑːft] n, pl inv avión m.
aircraft carrier n porta(a)viones m inv.
air cushion n cojín m de aire; (AVIAT) colchón m de aire.
airfield ['ɛəfiːld] n campo de aviación.
Air Force n fuerzas aéreas fpl, aviación f.
air freight n flete m por avión.
air freshener n ambientador m.
air gun n escopeta de aire comprimido.
air hostess (Brit) n azafata.
airily ['ɛərɪlɪ] ad muy a la ligera.
airing ['ɛərɪŋ] n: **to give an** ~ **to** (linen) airear; (room) ventilar; (fig: ideas etc) airear, someter a discusión.
air letter n (Brit) carta aérea.
airlift ['ɛəlɪft] n puente m aéreo.
airline ['ɛəlaɪn] n línea aérea.
airliner ['ɛəlaɪnə*] n avión m de pasajeros.
airlock ['ɛəlɔk] n (in pipe) esclusa de aire.
airmail ['ɛəmeɪl] n: **by** ~ por avión.
air mattress n colchón m neumático.
airplane ['ɛəpleɪn] n (US) avión m.
airport ['ɛəpɔːt] n aeropuerto.
air raid n ataque m aéreo.
airsick ['ɛəsɪk] a: **to be** ~ marearse (en

avión).
airstrip ['ɛəstrɪp] n pista de aterrizaje.
air terminal n terminal f.
airtight ['ɛətaɪt] a hermético.
air traffic control n control m de tráfico aéreo.
air traffic controller n controlador(a) m/f aéreo/a.
air waybill n conocimiento (de embarque) aéreo.
airy ['ɛərɪ] a (room) bien ventilado; (manners) ligero.
aisle [aɪl] n (of church) nave f lateral, pasadizo; (of theatre, plane) pasillo.
ajar [ə'dʒɑː*] a entreabierto.
AK abbr (US POST) = Alaska.
aka abbr (= also known as) alias.
akin [ə'kɪn] a: ~ **to** parecido a.
AL abbr (US POST) = Alabama.
ALA n abbr = American Library Association.
alabaster ['æləbɑːstə*] n alabastro.
à la carte [ælæ'kɑːt] ad a la carta.
alacrity [ə'lækrɪtɪ] n: **with** ~ con la mayor prontitud.
alarm [ə'lɑːm] n alarma; (anxiety) inquietud f ♦ vt asustar, inquietar.
alarm clock n despertador m.
alarming [ə'lɑːmɪŋ] a alarmante.
alarmist [ə'lɑːmɪst] n alarmista m/f.
alas [ə'læs] ad desgraciadamente ♦ excl ¡ay de mí!
Alaska [ə'læskə] n Alaska.
Albania [æl'beɪnɪə] n Albania.
Albanian [æl'beɪnɪən] a albanés/esa ♦ n albanés/esa m/f; (LING) albanés m.
albeit [ɔːl'biːɪt] conj (although) aunque.
album ['ælbəm] n álbum m; (L.P.) elepé m.
albumen ['ælbjumɪn] n albumen m.
alchemy ['ælkɪmɪ] n alquimia.
alcohol ['ælkəhɔl] n alcohol m.
alcoholic [ælkə'hɔlɪk] a, n alcohólico/a m/f.
alcoholism ['ælkəhɔlɪzəm] n alcoholismo.
alcove ['ælkəuv] n nicho, hueco.
Ald. abbr = alderman.
alderman ['ɔːldəmən] n concejal m.
ale [eɪl] n cerveza.
alert [ə'lɜːt] a alerta inv; (sharp) despierto, despabilado ♦ n alerta m, alarma ♦ vt poner sobre aviso; **to** ~ **sb (to sth)** poner sobre aviso or alertar a uno (de algo); **to** ~ **sb to the dangers of sth** poner sobre aviso or alertar a uno de los peligros de algo; **to be on the** ~ estar alerta or sobre aviso.
alertness [ə'lɜːtnɪs] n vigilancia.
Aleutian Islands [ə'luːʃən-] npl Islas fpl Aleutianas.
Alexandria [ælɪg'zɑːndrɪə] n Alejandría.
alfresco [æl'freskəu] a, ad al aire libre.
algebra ['ældʒɪbrə] n álgebra.
Algeria [æl'dʒɪərɪə] n Argelia.
Algerian [æl'dʒɪərɪən] a, n argelino/a m/f.

Algiers [æl'dʒɪəz] n Argel m.
algorithm ['ælgərɪðəm] n algoritmo.
alias ['eɪlɪəs] ad alias, conocido por ◆ n alias m.
alibi ['ælɪbaɪ] n coartada.
alien ['eɪlɪən] n (foreigner) extranjero/a ◆ a: ~ **to** ajeno a.
alienate ['eɪlɪəneɪt] vt enajenar, alejar.
alienation [eɪlɪə'neɪʃən] n enajenación f.
alight [ə'laɪt] a ardiendo ◆ vi apearse, bajar.
align [ə'laɪn] vt alinear.
alignment [ə'laɪnmənt] n alineación f; **the desks are out of** ~ los pupitres no están bien alineados.
alike [ə'laɪk] a semejantes, iguales ◆ ad igualmente, del mismo modo; **to look** ~ parecerse.
alimony ['ælɪmənɪ] n (LAW) manutención f.
alive [ə'laɪv] a (gen) vivo; (lively) activo.
alkali ['ælkəlaɪ] n álcali m.
all [ɔːl] a todo; (pl) todos(as) ◆ pron todo; (pl) todos(as) ◆ ad completamente, del todo; ~ **day** todo el día; **for** ~ **their efforts** a pesar de sus esfuerzos; ~/**alone** solito, completamente solo; **at** ~: **anything at** ~ lo que sea; **not at** ~ (in answer to thanks) de nada; **I'm not at** ~ **tired** no estoy nada cansado; ~ **but** casi; ~ **the time/his life** todo el tiempo/toda su vida; ~ **the more/ the better** tanto más/mejor; ~ **five** todos los cinco; ~ **of them** todos (ellos); ~ **of us went** fuimos todos; **is that** ~? ¿nada más?, ¿es (eso) todo?; (in shop) ¿algo más?; **not as hard as** ~ **that** no tan difícil; **to be/feel** ~ **in** estar rendido; ~ **in** ~ con todo, total.
allay [ə'leɪ] vt (fears) aquietar; (pain) aliviar.
all clear n (after attack etc) fin m de la alerta; (fig) luz f verde.
allegation [ælɪ'geɪʃən] n alegato.
allege [ə'ledʒ] vt pretender; **he is** ~**d to have said** ... se afirma que él dijo ....
alleged [ə'ledʒd] a supuesto, presunto.
allegedly [ə'ledʒɪdlɪ] ad supuestamente, según se afirma.
allegiance [ə'liːdʒəns] n lealtad f.
allegory ['ælɪgərɪ] n alegoría.
all-embracing ['ɔːləm'breɪsɪŋ] a universal.
allergic [ə'lɜːdʒɪk] a: ~ **to** alérgico a.
allergy ['ælədʒɪ] n alergia.
alleviate [ə'liːvɪeɪt] vt aliviar.
alleviation [əliːvɪ'eɪʃən] n alivio.
alley ['ælɪ] n (street) callejuela; (in garden) paseo.
alliance [ə'laɪəns] n alianza.
allied ['ælaɪd] a aliado; (related) relacionado.
alligator ['ælɪgeɪtə*] n caimán m.
all-important ['ɔːlɪm'pɔːtənt] a de suma importancia.
all-in ['ɔːlɪn] a (Brit) (also ad: charge) todo

incluido.
all-in wrestling n lucha libre.
alliteration [əlɪtə'reɪʃən] n aliteración f.
all-night ['ɔːl'naɪt] a (café) abierto toda la noche; (party) que dura toda la noche.
allocate ['æləkeɪt] vt (share out) repartir; (devote) asignar.
allocation [ælə'keɪʃən] n (of money) ración f, cuota; (distribution) reparto.
allot [ə'lɔt] vt asignar; **in the** ~**ted time** en el tiempo asignado.
allotment [ə'lɔtmənt] n ración f; (garden) parcela.
all-out ['ɔːlaut] a (effort etc) supremo ◆ ad: **all out** con todas las fuerzas.
allow [ə'lau] vt (permit) permitir, dejar; (a claim) admitir; (sum to spend, time estimated) dar, conceder; (concede): **to** ~ **that** reconocer que; **to** ~ **sb to do** permitir a alguien hacer; **smoking is not** ~**ed** prohibido or se prohíbe fumar; **he is** ~**ed to** ... se le permite ...; **we must** ~ **3 days for the journey** debemos dejar 3 días para el viaje.
allow for vt fus tener en cuenta.
allowance [ə'lauəns] n concesión f; (payment) subvención f, pensión f; (discount) descuento, rebaja; **to make** ~**s for** (person) disculpar a; (thing: take into account) tener en cuenta.
alloy ['ælɔɪ] n (mix) mezcla.
all right ad (feel, work) bien; (as answer) ¡conforme!, ¡está bien!
all-round ['ɔːl'raund] a completo; (view) amplio.
all-rounder ['ɔːl'raundə*] n: **to be a good** ~ ser una persona que hace de todo.
allspice ['ɔːlspaɪs] n pimienta inglesa or de Jamaica.
all-time ['ɔːl'taɪm] a (record) de todos los tiempos.
allude [ə'luːd] vi: **to** ~ **to** aludir a.
alluring [ə'ljuərɪŋ] a seductor(a), atractivo.
allusion [ə'luːʒən] n referencia, alusión f.
ally n ['ælaɪ] aliado/a ◆ vt [ə'laɪ]: **to** ~ **o.s. with** aliarse con.
almanac ['ɔːlmənæk] n almanaque m.
almighty [ɔːl'maɪtɪ] a todopoderoso.
almond ['ɑːmənd] n (fruit) almendra; (tree) almendro.
almost ['ɔːlməust] ad casi; **he** ~ **fell** por poco or casi se cae.
alms [ɑːmz] npl limosna sg.
aloft [ə'lɔft] ad arriba.
alone [ə'ləun] a solo ◆ ad sólo, solamente; **to leave sb** ~ dejar a uno en paz; **to leave sth** ~ no tocar algo, dejar algo sin tocar; **let** ~ ... sin hablar de ...
along [ə'lɔŋ] prep a lo largo de, por ◆ ad: **is he coming** ~ **with us?** ¿viene con nosotros?; **he was limping** ~ iba cojeando; ~ **with** junto con; **all** ~ (all the time) desde el principio.

alongside [ə'lɒŋ'saɪd] *prep* al lado de ◆ *ad* (*NAUT*) de costado; **we brought our boat** ~ atracamos nuestro barco.

aloof [ə'lu:f] *a* reservado ◆ *ad*: **to stand** ~ mantenerse a distancia.

aloud [ə'laud] *ad* en voz alta.

alphabet ['ælfəbɛt] *n* alfabeto.

alphabetical [ælfə'bɛtɪkəl] *a* alfabético; **in** ~ **order** por orden alfabético.

alphanumeric ['ælfənju:'mɛrɪk] *a* alfanumérico.

alpine ['ælpaɪn] *a* alpino, alpestre.

Alps [ælps] *npl*: **the** ~ los Alpes.

already [ɔ:l'rɛdɪ] *ad* ya.

alright ['ɔ:l'raɪt] *ad* (*Brit*) = **all right**.

Alsatian [æl'seɪʃən] *n* (*dog*) pastor *m* alemán.

also ['ɔ:lsəu] *ad* también, además.

altar ['ɔltə*] *n* altar *m*.

alter ['ɔltə*] *vt* cambiar, modificar ◆ *vi* cambiarse, modificarse.

alteration [ɔltə'reɪʃən] *n* cambio, modificación *f*; alteración *f*; ~**s** *npl* (*ARCH*) reformas *fpl*; (*SEWING*) arreglos *mpl*; **timetable subject to** ~ el horario puede cambiar.

alternate [ɔl'tə:nɪt] *a* alterno ◆ *vi* ['ɔltəneɪt]: **to** ~ **(with)** alternar (con); **on** ~ **days** un día sí y otro no.

alternately [ɔl'tə:nɪtlɪ] *ad* alternativamente, por turno.

alternating ['ɔltəneɪtɪŋ] *a* (*current*) alterno.

alternative [ɔl'tə:nətɪv] *a* alternativo ◆ *n* alternativa.

alternatively [ɔl'tə:nətɪvlɪ] *ad*: ~ **one could ...** por otra parte se podría....

alternator ['ɔltəneɪtə*] *n* (*AUT*) alternador *m*.

although [ɔ:l'ðəu] *conj* aunque, si bien.

altitude ['æltɪtju:d] *n* altitud *f*, altura.

alto ['æltəu] *n* (*female*) contralto *f*; (*male*) alto.

altogether [ɔ:ltə'gɛðə*] *ad* completamente, del todo; (*on the whole, in all*) en total, en conjunto; **how much is that** ~? ¿cuánto es todo *or* en total?

altruistic [æltru'ɪstɪk] *a* altruista.

aluminium [ælju'mɪnɪəm], (*US*) **aluminum** [ə'lu:mɪnəm] *n* aluminio.

always ['ɔ:lweɪz] *ad* siempre.

AM *abbr* = amplitude modulation.

am [æm] *vb see* **be**.

a.m. *ad abbr* (= *ante meridiem*) de la mañana.

AMA *n abbr* = *American Medical Association*.

amalgam [ə'mælgəm] *n* amalgama.

amalgamate [ə'mælgəmeɪt] *vi* amalgamarse ◆ *vt* amalgamar.

amalgamation [əmælgə'meɪʃən] *n* (*COMM*) fusión *f*.

amass [ə'mæs] *vt* amontonar, acumular.

amateur ['æmətə*] *n* aficionado/a, amateur *m/f*; ~ **dramatics** dramas *mpl* presentados por aficionados, representación *f* de aficionados.

amateurish ['æmətərɪʃ] *a* (*pej*) torpe, inexperto.

amaze [ə'meɪz] *vt* asombrar, pasmar; **to be** ~**d (at)** asombrarse (de).

amazement [ə'meɪzmənt] *n* asombro, sorpresa; **to my** ~ para mi sorpresa.

amazing [ə'meɪzɪŋ] *a* extraordinario, asombroso; (*bargain, offer*) increíble.

amazingly [ə'meɪzɪŋlɪ] *ad* extraordinariamente.

Amazon ['æməzən] *n* (*GEO*) Amazonas *m*; (*MYTHOLOGY*) amazona ◆ *cpd*: **the** ~ **basin/jungle** la cuenca/selva del Amazonas.

Amazonian [æmə'zəunɪən] *a* amazónico.

ambassador [æm'bæsədə*] *n* embajador(a) *m/f*.

amber ['æmbə*] *n* ámbar *m*; **at** ~ (*Brit AUT*) en el amarillo.

ambidextrous [æmbɪ'dɛkstrəs] *a* ambidextro.

ambience ['æmbɪəns] *n* ambiente *m*.

ambiguity [æmbɪ'gjuɪtɪ] *n* ambigüedad *f*; (*of meaning*) doble sentido.

ambiguous [æm'bɪgjuəs] *a* ambiguo.

ambition [æm'bɪʃən] *n* ambición *f*; **to achieve one's** ~ realizar su ambición.

ambitious [æm'bɪʃəs] *a* ambicioso; (*plan*) grandioso.

ambivalent [æm'bɪvələnt] *a* ambivalente; (*pej*) equívoco.

amble ['æmbl] *vi* (*gen*: ~ **along**) deambular, andar sin prisa.

ambulance ['æmbjuləns] *n* ambulancia.

ambulanceman/woman ['æmbjulənsmən/wumən] *n* ambulanciero/a.

ambush ['æmbuʃ] *n* emboscada ◆ *vt* tender una emboscada a; (*fig*) coger (*Sp*) *or* agarrar (*LAm*) por sorpresa.

ameba [ə'mi:bə] *n* (*US*) = **amoeba**.

ameliorate [ə'mi:lɪəreɪt] *vt* mejorar.

amelioration [əmi:lɪə'reɪʃən] *n* mejora.

amen [ɑ:'mɛn] *excl* amén.

amenable [ə'mi:nəbl] *a*: ~ **to** (*advice etc*) sensible a.

amend [ə'mɛnd] *vt* (*law, text*) enmendar; **to make** ~**s** (*apologize*) enmendarlo, dar cumplida satisfacción.

amendment [ə'mɛndmənt] *n* enmienda.

amenities [ə'mi:nɪtɪz] *npl* comodidades *fpl*.

amenity [ə'mi:nɪtɪ] *n* servicio.

America [ə'mɛrɪkə] *n* América del Norte.

American [ə'mɛrɪkən] *a, n* norteamericano/a *m/f*, estadounidense *m/f*.

americanize [ə'mɛrɪkənaɪz] *vt* americanizar.

amethyst ['æmɪθɪst] *n* amatista.

Amex ['æmɛks] *n abbr* = *American Stock Exchange*.

amiable ['eɪmɪəbl] *a* (*kind*) amable, simpático.

amicable ['æmɪkəbl] *a* amistoso, amigable.
amid(st) [ə'mɪd(st)] *prep* entre, en medio de.
amiss [ə'mɪs] *ad*: **to take sth ~** tomar algo a mal; **there's something ~** pasa algo.
ammo ['æməu] *n abbr (col)* = **ammunition**.
ammonia [ə'məunɪə] *n* amoníaco.
ammunition [æmju'nɪʃən] *n* municiones *fpl*; *(fig)* argumentos *mpl*.
ammunition dump *n* depósito de municiones.
amnesia [æm'niːzɪə] *n* amnesia.
amnesty ['æmnɪstɪ] *n* amnistía; **to grant an ~ to** amnistiar (a).
amoeba, *(US)* **ameba** [ə'miːbə] *n* amiba.
amok [ə'mɔk] *ad*: **to run ~** enloquecerse, desbocarse.
among(st) [ə'mʌŋ(st)] *prep* entre, en medio de.
amoral [æ'mɔrəl] *a* amoral.
amorous ['æmərəs] *a* cariñoso.
amorphous [ə'mɔːfəs] *a* amorfo.
amortization [əmɔːtaɪ'zeɪʃən] *n* amortización *f*.
amount [ə'maunt] *n (gen)* cantidad *f*; *(of bill etc)* suma, importe *m* ♦ *vi*: **to ~ to** *(total)* sumar; *(be same as)* equivaler a, significar; **this ~s to a refusal** esto equivale a una negativa; **the total ~** *(of money)* la suma total.
amp(ère) ['æmp(ɛə*)] *n* amperio; **a 13 amp plug** un enchufe de 13 amperios.
ampersand ['æmpəsænd] *n* signo &, ''y'' comercial.
amphibian [æm'fɪbɪən] *n* anfibio.
amphibious [æm'fɪbɪəs] *a* anfibio.
amphitheatre, *(US)* **amphitheater** ['æmfɪθɪətə*] *n* anfiteatro.
ample ['æmpl] *a (spacious)* amplio; *(abundant)* abundante; **to have ~ time** tener tiempo de sobra.
amplifier ['æmplɪfaɪə*] *n* amplificador *m*.
amplify ['æmplɪfaɪ] *vt* amplificar, aumentar; *(explain)* explicar.
amply ['æmplɪ] *ad* ampliamente.
ampoule, *(US)* **ampule** ['æmpuːl] *n (MED)* ampolla.
amputate ['æmpjuteɪt] *vt* amputar.
Amsterdam ['æmstədæm] *n* Amsterdam *m*.
amt *abbr* = **amount**.
amuck [ə'mʌk] *ad* = **amok**.
amuse [ə'mjuːz] *vt* divertir; *(distract)* distraer, entretener; **to ~ o.s. with sth/by doing sth** distraerse con algo/haciendo algo; **he was ~d at the joke** le divirtió el chiste.
amusement [ə'mjuːzmənt] *n* diversión *f*; *(pastime)* pasatiempo; *(laughter)* risa; **much to my ~** con gran regocijo mío.
amusement arcade *n* mini-casino.
amusing [ə'mjuːzɪŋ] *a* divertido.
an [æn, ən, n] *indefinite article see* **a**.

ANA *n abbr* = *American Newspaper Association; American Nurses Association.*
anachronism [ə'nækrənɪzəm] *n* anacronismo.
anaemia [ə'niːmɪə] *n* anemia.
anaemic [ə'niːmɪk] *a* anémico; *(fig)* soso, insípido.
anaesthetic [ænɪs'θetɪk] *n* anestesia; **local/general ~** anestesia local/general.
anaesthetist [æ'niːsθɪtɪst] *n* anestesista *m/f*.
anagram ['ænəgræm] *n* anagrama *m*.
analgesic [ænæl'dʒiːsɪk] *a*, *n* analgésico.
analogous [ə'næləgəs] *a* análogo.
analog(ue) ['ænəlɔg] *a (computer, watch)* analógico.
analogy [ə'nælədʒɪ] *n* analogía; **to draw an ~ between** señalar la analogía entre.
analyse ['ænəlaɪz] *vt (Brit)* analizar.
analysis, *pl* **analyses** [ə'næləsɪs, -siːz] *n* análisis *m inv*.
analyst ['ænəlɪst] *n (political ~, psycho~)* analista *m/f*.
analytic(al) [ænə'lɪtɪk(əl)] *a* analítico.
analyze ['ænəlaɪz] *vt (US)* = **analyse**.
anarchist ['ænəkɪst] *a*, *n* anarquista *m/f*.
anarchy ['ænəkɪ] *n* anarquía, desorden *m*.
anathema [ə'næθɪmə] *n*: **that is ~ to him** eso es pecado para él.
anatomical [ænə'tɔmɪkəl] *a* anatómico.
anatomy [ə'nætəmɪ] *n* anatomía.
ANC *n abbr* = *African National Congress.*
ancestor ['ænsɪstə*] *n* antepasado.
ancestral [æn'sestrəl] *a* ancestral.
ancestry ['ænsɪstrɪ] *n* ascendencia, abolengo.
anchor ['æŋkə*] *n* ancla, áncora ♦ *vi (also:* **to drop ~)** anclar ♦ *vt (fig)* sujetar, afianzar; **to weigh ~** levar anclas.
anchorage ['æŋkərɪdʒ] *n* ancladero.
anchovy ['æntʃəvɪ] *n* anchoa.
ancient ['eɪnʃənt] *a* antiguo; **~ monument** monumento histórico.
ancillary [æn'sɪlərɪ] *a (worker, staff)* auxiliar.
and [ænd] *conj* y; *(before i, hi)* e; **~ so on** etcétera; **try ~ come** procure *or* intente venir; **better ~ better** cada vez mejor.
Andalusia [ændə'luːzɪə] *n* Andalucía.
Andes ['ændiːz] *npl*: **the ~** los Andes.
anecdote ['ænɪkdəut] *n* anécdota.
anemia [ə'niːmɪə] *n (US)* = **anaemia**.
anemic [ə'niːmɪk] *a (US)* = **anaemic**.
anemone [ə'nemənɪ] *n (BOT)* anémone *f*; **sea ~** anémona.
anesthetic [ænɪs'θetɪk] *a*, *n (US)* = **anaesthetic**.
anesthetist [æ'niːsθɪtɪst] *n (US)* = **anaesthetist**.
anew [ə'njuː] *ad* de nuevo, otra vez.
angel ['eɪndʒəl] *n* ángel *m*.
angelic [æn'dʒelɪk] *a* angélico.
anger ['æŋgə*] *n* ira, enfado, cólera ♦ *vt*

enojar, enfurecer.

angina [æn'dʒaɪnə] *n* angina (del pecho).

angle ['æŋgl] *n* ángulo; **from their** ~ desde su punto de vista.

angler ['æŋglə*] *n* pescador(a) *m/f* (de caña).

Anglican ['æŋglɪkən] *a, n* anglicano/a.

anglicize ['æŋglɪsaɪz] *vt* dar forma inglesa a.

angling ['æŋglɪŋ] *n* pesca con caña.

Anglo- [æŋgləʊ] *pref* anglo... .

Angola [æŋ'gəʊlə] *n* Angola.

Angolan [æŋ'gəʊlən] *a, n* angoleño/a *m/f*.

angrily ['æŋgrɪlɪ] *ad* enojado, enfadado.

angry ['æŋgrɪ] *a* enfadado, enojado; **to be** ~ **with sb/at sth** estar enfadado con alguien/ por algo; **to get** ~ enfadarse, enojarse.

anguish ['æŋgwɪʃ] *n* (*physical*) tormentos *mpl*; (*mental*) angustia.

angular ['æŋgjʊlə*] *a* (*shape*) angular; (*features*) anguloso.

animal ['ænɪməl] *n* animal *m*, bestia ◆ *a* animal.

animate ['ænɪmeɪt] *vt* (*enliven*) animar; (*encourage*) estimular, alentar ◆ ['ænɪmɪt] *a* vivo.

animated ['ænɪmeɪtɪd] *a* vivo.

animation [ænɪ'meɪʃən] *n* animación *f*.

animosity [ænɪ'mɒsɪtɪ] *n* animosidad *f*, rencor *m*.

aniseed ['ænɪsiːd] *n* anís *m*.

Ankara ['æŋkərə] *n* Ankara.

ankle ['æŋkl] *n* tobillo *m*.

ankle sock *n* calcetín *m*.

annex ['ænɛks] *n* (*also*: *Brit*: **annexe**) (*building*) edificio anexo ◆ *vt* [æ'nɛks] (*territory*) anexar.

annihilate [ə'naɪəleɪt] *vt* aniquilar.

anniversary [ænɪ'vɜːsərɪ] *n* aniversario.

annotate ['ænəʊteɪt] *vt* anotar.

announce [ə'naʊns] *vt* (*gen*) anunciar; (*inform*) comunicar; **he ~d that he wasn't going** declaró que no iba.

announcement [ə'naʊnsmənt] *n* (*gen*) anuncio; (*declaration*) declaración *f*; **I'd like to make an** ~ quisiera anunciar algo.

announcer [ə'naʊnsə*] *n* (*RADIO, TV*) locutor(a) *m/f*.

annoy [ə'nɔɪ] *vt* molestar, fastidiar, irritar; **to be ~ed (at sth/with sb)** estar enfadado *or* molesto (por algo/con uno); **don't get ~ed!** ¡no se enfade!

annoyance [ə'nɔɪəns] *n* enojo; (*thing*) molestia.

annoying [ə'nɔɪɪŋ] *a* molesto, fastidioso; (*person*) pesado.

annual ['ænjʊəl] *a* anual ◆ *n* (*BOT*) anual *m*; (*book*) anuario.

annual general meeting (AGM) *n* junta general anual.

annually ['ænjʊəlɪ] *ad* anualmente, cada año.

annual report *n* informe *m or* memoria

anual.

annuity [ə'njuːɪtɪ] *n* renta *or* pensión *f* vitalicia.

annul [ə'nʌl] *vt* anular; (*law*) revocar.

annulment [ə'nʌlmənt] *n* anulación *f*.

annum ['ænəm] *n see* **per annum**.

Annunciation [ənʌnsɪ'eɪʃən] *n* Anunciación *f*.

anode ['ænəʊd] *n* ánodo.

anoint [ə'nɔɪnt] *vt* untar.

anomalous [ə'nɒmələs] *a* anómalo.

anomaly [ə'nɒməlɪ] *n* anomalía.

anon. [ə'nɒn] *abbr* = **anonymous**.

anonymity [ænə'nɪmɪtɪ] *n* anonimato.

anonymous [ə'nɒnɪməs] *a* anónimo; **to remain** ~ quedar en el anonimato.

anorak ['ænəræk] *n* anorak *m*.

anorexia [ænə'rɛksɪə] *n* (*MED*) anorexia.

another [ə'nʌðə*] *a*: ~ **book** (*one more*) otro libro; (*a different one*) un libro distinto; ~ **beer?** ¿(quieres) otra cerveza?; **in** ~ **5 years** en cinco años más ◆ *pron* otro; *see also* **one**.

ANSI *n abbr* (= *American National Standards Institute*) *instituto de normas*.

answer ['ɑːnsə*] *n* contestación *f*, respuesta; (*to problem*) solución *f* ◆ *vi* contestar, responder ◆ *vt* (*reply to*) contestar a, responder a; (*problem*) resolver; **to** ~ **the phone** contestar el teléfono; **in** ~ **to your letter** contestando *or* en contestación a su carta; **to** ~ **the bell** *or* **the door** acudir a la puerta.

answer back *vi* replicar, ser respondón/ona.

answer for *vt fus* responder de *or* por.

answer to *vt fus* (*description*) corresponder a.

answerable ['ɑːnsərəbl] *a*: ~ **to sb for sth** responsable ante uno de algo.

answering machine ['ɑːnsərɪŋ-] *n* contestador *m* automático.

ant [ænt] *n* hormiga.

ANTA *n abbr* = *American National Theatre and Academy*.

antagonism [æn'tægənɪzəm] *n* hostilidad *f*.

antagonist [æn'tægənɪst] *n* antagonista *m/f*, adversario/a.

antagonistic [æntægə'nɪstɪk] *a* antagónico; (*opposed*) contrario, opuesto.

antagonize [æn'tægənaɪz] *vt* provocar.

Antarctic [ænt'ɑːktɪk] *a* antártico ◆ *n*: **the** ~ el Antártico.

Antarctica [æn'tɑːktɪkə] *n* Antártida.

Antarctic Circle *n* Círculo Polar Antártico.

Antarctic Ocean *n* Océano Antártico.

ante ['æntɪ] *n*: **to up the** ~ subir la puesta.

ante... ['æntɪ] *pref* ante...

anteater ['æntiːtə*] *n* oso hormiguero.

antecedent [æntɪ'siːdənt] *n* antecedente *m*.

antechamber ['æntɪtʃeɪmbə*] *n* antecámara.

antelope ['æntɪləup] *n* antílope *m*.
antenatal [æntɪ'neɪtl] *a* antenatal, prenatal.
antenatal clinic *n* clínica prenatal.
antenna [æn'tɛnə], *pl* ~**e** [-niː] *n* antena.
anteroom ['æntɪrum] *n* antesala.
anthem ['ænθəm] *n*: **national** ~ himno nacional.
anthology [æn'θɒlədʒɪ] *n* antología.
anthropologist [ænθrə'pɒlədʒɪst] *n* antropólogo/a.
anthropology [ænθrə'pɒlədʒɪ] *n* antropología.
anti... [æntɪ] *pref* anti....
anti-aircraft ['æntɪ'ɛəkrɑːft] *a* antiaéreo.
antiballistic [æntɪbə'lɪstɪk] *a* antibalístico.
antibiotic [æntɪbaɪ'ɒtɪk] *a*, *n* antibiótico.
antibody ['æntɪbɒdɪ] *n* anticuerpo.
anticipate [æn'tɪsɪpeɪt] *vt* (*foresee*) prever; (*expect*) esperar, contar con; (*forestall*) anticiparse a, adelantarse a; **this is worse than I** ~**d** esto es peor de lo que esperaba; **as** ~**d** según se esperaba.
anticipation [æntɪsɪ'peɪʃən] *n* previsión *f*; esperanza; anticipación *f*.
anticlimax [æntɪ'klaɪmæks] *n* decepción *f*.
anticlockwise [æntɪ'klɒkwaɪz] *ad* en dirección contraria a la de las agujas del reloj.
antics ['æntɪks] *npl* payasadas *fpl*; (*of child*) travesuras *fpl*.
anticyclone [æntɪ'saɪkləun] *n* anticiclón *m*.
antidote ['æntɪdəut] *n* antídoto.
antifreeze ['æntɪfriːz] *n* anticongelante *m*.
antihistamine [æntɪ'hɪstəmiːn] *n* antihistamínico.
Antilles [æn'tɪliːz] *npl*: **the** ~ las Antillas.
antipathy [æn'tɪpəθɪ] *n* (*between people*) antipatía; (*to person, thing*) aversión *f*.
Antipodean [æntɪpə'diːən] *a* antípoda.
Antipodes [æn'tɪpədiːz] *npl*: **the** ~ las Antípodas.
antiquarian [æntɪ'kwɛərɪən] *n* anticuario/a.
antiquated ['æntɪkweɪtɪd] *a* anticuado.
antique [æn'tiːk] *n* antigüedad *f* ♦ *a* antiguo.
antique dealer *n* anticuario/a.
antique shop *n* tienda de antigüedades.
antiquity [æn'tɪkwɪtɪ] *n* antigüedad *f*.
anti-Semitic ['æntɪsɪ'mɪtɪk] *a* antisemita.
anti-Semitism [æntɪ'sɛmɪtɪzəm] *n* antisemitismo.
antiseptic [æntɪ'sɛptɪk] *a*, *n* antiséptico.
antisocial [æntɪ'səuʃəl] *a* antisocial.
antitank ['æntɪ'tæŋk] *a* antitanque.
antithesis, *pl* **antitheses** [æn'tɪθɪsɪs, -siːz] *n* antítesis *f inv*.
antitrust ['æntɪ'trʌst] *a*: ~ **legislation** legislación *f* antimonopolio.
antlers ['æntləz] *npl* cornamenta.
anus ['eɪnəs] *n* ano.
anvil ['ænvɪl] *n* yunque *m*.
anxiety [æg'zaɪətɪ] *n* (*worry*) inquietud *f*; (*eagerness*) ansia, anhelo.

anxious ['æŋkʃəs] *a* (*worried*) inquieto; (*keen*) deseoso; **I'm very** ~ **about you** me tienes muy preocupado.
anxiously ['æŋkʃəslɪ] *ad* con inquietud, de manera angustiada.
any ['ɛnɪ] *a* (*in negative and interrogative sentences* = *some*) algún, alguna; (*negative sense*) ningún, ninguna; (*no matter which*) cualquier(a); (*each and every*) todo; **I haven't** ~ **money/books** no tengo dinero/libros; **have you** ~ **butter/children/ money?** ¿tiene mantequilla/hijos/dinero?; **at** ~ **moment** en cualquier momento; ~ **day now** cualquier día de éstos; **in** ~ **case**, **at** ~ **rate** de todas formas, de todas maneras ♦ *pron* alguno; ninguno; (*anybody*) cualquiera; (*in negative and interrogative sentences*): **I haven't** ~ no tengo ninguno; **have you got** ~? ¿tiene algunos?; **can** ~ **of you sing?** ¿alguno de ustedes sabe cantar? ♦ *ad* (*in negative sentences*) nada; (*in interrogative and conditional constructions*) algo; **I can't hear him** ~ **more** no le oigo más; **do you want** ~ **more soup?** ¿quiere más sopa?
anybody ['ɛnɪbɒdɪ] *pron* cualquiera, cualquier persona; (*in interrogative sentences*) alguien; (*in negative sentences*): **I don't see** ~ no veo a nadie.
anyhow ['ɛnɪhau] *ad* de todos modos, de todas maneras; (*carelessly*) de cualquier manera; (*haphazardly*) de cualquier modo; **I shall go** ~ iré de todas maneras.
anyone ['ɛnɪwʌn] = **anybody**.
anyplace ['ɛnɪpleɪs] *ad* (*US*) = **anywhere**.
anything ['ɛnɪθɪŋ] *pron* (*see* **anybody**) cualquier cosa; (*in interrogative sentences*) algo; (*in negative sentences*) nada; (*everything*) todo; ~ **else?** ¿algo más?; **it can cost** ~ **between £15 and £20** puede costar entre 15 y 20 libras.
anytime ['ɛnɪtaɪm] *ad* (*at any moment*) en cualquier momento, de un momento a otro; (*whenever*) no importa cuándo, cuando quiera.
anyway ['ɛnɪweɪ] *ad* de todas maneras; de cualquier modo.
anywhere ['ɛnɪwɛə*] *ad* (*see* **anybody**) dondequiera; (*interrogative*) en algún sitio; (*negative sense*) en ningún sitio; (*everywhere*) en *or* por todas partes; **I don't see him** ~ no le veo en ningún sitio; ~ **in the world** en cualquier parte del mundo.
Anzac ['ænzæk] *n abbr* (= *Australia-New Zealand Army Corps*) soldado del cuerpo *Anzac*.
apace [ə'peɪs] *ad* aprisa.
apart [ə'pɑːt] *ad* aparte, separadamente; **10 miles** ~ separados por 10 millas; **to take** ~ desmontar; ~ **from** *prep* aparte de.
apartheid [ə'pɑːteɪt] *n* apartheid *m*.
apartment [ə'pɑːtmənt] *n* (*US*) piso, departamento (*LAm*), apartamento; (*room*)

cuarto.

apartment block *or* **building** (*US*) bloque *m* de pisos.

apathetic [æpə'θetɪk] *a* apático, indiferente.

apathy ['æpəθɪ] *n* apatía, indiferencia.

APB *n abbr* (*US*: = *all points bulletin*) expresión usada por la policía que significa "descubrir y aprehender al sospechoso".

ape [eɪp] *n* mono ♦ *vt* imitar, remedar.

Apennines ['æpənaɪnz] *npl*: **the ~** los Apeninos *mpl*.

aperitif [ə'perɪtiːf] *n* aperitivo.

aperture ['æpətʃjuə*] *n* rendija, resquicio; (*PHOT*) abertura.

APEX ['eɪpɛks] *n abbr* (*Brit*) = *Association of Professional, Executive, Clerical and Computer Staff*; (*AVIAT* = *advance purchase excursion*) APEX *m*.

apex ['eɪpɛks] *n* ápice *m*; (*fig*) cumbre *f*.

aphid ['eɪfɪd] *n* áfido.

aphorism ['æfərɪzəm] *n* aforismo.

aphrodisiac [æfrəu'dɪzɪæk] *a*, *n* afrodisíaco.

API *n abbr* = *American Press Institute*.

apiece [ə'piːs] *ad* cada uno.

aplomb [ə'plɔm] *n* aplomo, confianza.

APO *n abbr* (*US*: = *Army Post Office*) servicio postal del ejército.

Apocalypse [ə'pɔkəlɪps] *n* Apocalipsis *m*.

apocryphal [ə'pɔkrɪfəl] *a* apócrifo.

apolitical [eɪpə'lɪtɪkl] *a* apolítico.

apologetic [əpɔlə'dʒetɪk] *a* (*look*, *remark*) de disculpa.

apologetically [əpɔlə'dʒetɪkəlɪ] *ad* con aire de disculpa, excusándose, disculpándose.

apologize [ə'pɔlədʒaɪz] *vi*: **to ~ (for sth to sb)** disculparse (con alguien de algo).

apology [ə'pɔlədʒɪ] *n* disculpa, excusa; **please accept my apologies** le ruego me disculpe.

apoplectic [æpə'plɛktɪk] *a* (*MED*) apoplético; (*col*): **~ with rage** furioso.

apoplexy ['æpəplɛksɪ] *n* apoplegía.

apostle [ə'pɔsl] *n* apóstol *m/f*.

apostrophe [ə'pɔstrəfɪ] *n* apóstrofe *m*.

appal [ə'pɔːl] *vt* horrorizar, espantar.

Appalachian Mountains [æpə'leɪʃən-] *npl*: **the ~** los Montes Apalaches.

appalling [ə'pɔːlɪŋ] *a* espantoso; (*awful*) pésimo; **she's an ~ cook** es una cocinera malísima.

apparatus [æpə'reɪtəs] *n* aparato; (*in gymnasium*) aparatos *mpl*.

apparel [ə'pærl] *n* (*US*) indumentaria.

apparent [ə'pærənt] *a* aparente; (*obvious*) manifiesto, claro; **it is ~ that** está claro que.

apparently [ə'pærəntlɪ] *ad* por lo visto, al parecer.

apparition [æpə'rɪʃən] *n* aparición *f*; (*ghost*) fantasma *m*.

appeal [ə'piːl] *vi* (*LAW*) apelar ♦ *n* (*LAW*) apelación *f*; (*request*) llamamiento; (*plea*) súplica; (*charm*) atractivo, encanto; **to ~**

for suplicar, reclamar; **to ~ to** (*subj*: *person*) rogar a, suplicar a; (*subj*: *thing*) atraer, interesar; **to ~ to sb for mercy** rogarle misericordia a alguien; **it doesn't ~ to me** no me atrae, no me llama la atención; **right of ~** derecho de apelación.

appealing [ə'piːlɪŋ] *a* (*nice*) atractivo; (*touching*) conmovedor(a), emocionante.

appear [ə'pɪə*] *vi* aparecer, presentarse; (*LAW*) comparecer; (*publication*) salir (a luz), publicarse; (*seem*) parecer; **it would ~ that** parecería que.

appearance [ə'pɪərəns] *n* aparición *f*; (*look*, *aspect*) apariencia, aspecto; **to keep up ~s** salvar las apariencias; **to all ~s** al parecer.

appease [ə'piːz] *vt* (*pacify*) apaciguar; (*satisfy*) satisfacer.

appeasement [ə'piːzmənt] *n* (*POL*) entreguismo.

append [ə'pɛnd] *vt* (*COMPUT*) anexionar (al final).

appendage [ə'pɛndɪdʒ] *n* añadidura.

appendicitis [əpɛndɪ'saɪtɪs] *n* apendicitis *f*.

appendix, *pl* **appendices** [ə'pɛndɪks, -dɪsɪz] *n* apéndice *m*; **to have one's ~ out** operarse de apendicitis.

appetite ['æpɪtaɪt] *n* apetito; (*fig*) deseo, anhelo; **that walk has given me an ~** ese paseo me ha dado apetito.

appetizer ['æpɪtaɪzə*] *n* (*drink*) aperitivo; (*food*) tapas *fpl* (*Sp*).

appetizing ['æpɪtaɪzɪŋ] *a* apetitoso.

applaud [ə'plɔːd] *vt*, *vi* aplaudir.

applause [ə'plɔːz] *n* aplausos *mpl*.

apple ['æpl] *n* manzana.

apple tree *n* manzano.

appliance [ə'plaɪəns] *n* aparato; **electrical ~s** electrodomésticos *mpl*.

applicable [ə'plɪkəbl] *a* aplicable, pertinente; **the law is ~ from January** la ley es aplicable *or* se pone en vigor desde enero; **to be ~ to** referirse a.

applicant ['æplɪkənt] *n* candidato/a; solicitante *m/f*.

application [æplɪ'keɪʃən] *n* aplicación *f*; (*for a job*, *a grant etc*) solicitud *f*, petición *f*.

application form *n* solicitud *f*.

applications package *n* (*COMPUT*) paquete *m* de programas de aplicación.

applied [ə'plaɪd] *a* (*science*, *art*) aplicado.

apply [ə'plaɪ] *vt*: **to ~ (to)** aplicar (a); (*fig*) emplear (para) ♦ *vi*: **to ~** (*ask*) dirigirse a; (*be suitable for*) ser aplicable a; (*be relevant to*) tener que ver con; **to ~ for** (*permit*, *grant*, *job*) solicitar; **to ~ the brakes** aplicar los frenos; **to ~ o.s. to** aplicarse a, dedicarse a.

appoint [ə'pɔɪnt] *vt* (*to post*) nombrar; (*date*, *place*) fijar, señalar.

appointee [əpɔɪn'tiː] *n* persona nombrada.

appointment [ə'pɔɪntmənt] *n* (*engage-*

ment) cita; (*date*) compromiso; (*act*) nombramiento; (*post*) puesto; **to make an ~ (with)** (*doctor*) pedir hora (con); (*friend*) citarse (con); **"~s (vacant)"** "ofertas de trabajo"; **by ~** por medio de cita.

apportion [ə'pɔːʃən] *vt* repartir.

appraisal [ə'preɪzl] *n* apreciación *f*.

appraise [ə'preɪz] *vt* (*value*) tasar, valorar; (*situation etc*) evaluar.

appreciable [ə'priːʃəbl] *a* sensible.

appreciate [ə'priːʃɪeɪt] *vt* (*like*) apreciar, tener en mucho; (*be grateful for*) agradecer; (*be aware of*) comprender ◆ *vi* (*COMM*) aumentar(se) en valor; **I ~d your help** agradecí tu ayuda.

appreciation [əpriːʃɪ'eɪʃən] *n* aprecio; reconocimiento, agradecimiento; aumento en valor.

appreciative [ə'priːʃɪətɪv] *a* apreciativo, agradecido.

apprehend [æprɪ'hend] *vt* percibir; (*arrest*) detener.

apprehension [æprɪ'henʃən] *n* (*fear*) aprensión *f*.

apprehensive [æprɪ'hensɪv] *a* aprensivo.

apprentice [ə'prentɪs] *n* aprendiz(a) *m/f* ◆ *vt*: **to be ~d to** estar de aprendiz con.

apprenticeship [ə'prentɪsʃɪp] *n* aprendizaje *m*; **to serve one's ~** hacer el aprendizaje.

appro. ['æprəʊ] *abbr* (*Brit COMM*: *col*) = **approval.**

approach [ə'prəʊtʃ] *vi* acercarse ◆ *vt* acercarse a; (*be approximate*) aproximarse a; (*ask, apply to*) dirigirse a ◆ *n* acercamiento; aproximación *f*; (*access*) acceso; (*proposal*) proposición *f*; **to ~ sb about sth** hablar con uno sobre algo.

approachable [ə'prəʊtʃəbl] *a* (*person*) abordable; (*place*) accesible.

approach road *n* vía de acceso.

approbation [æprə'beɪʃən] *n* aprobación *f*.

appropriate [ə'prəʊprɪɪt] *a* apropiado, conveniente ◆ *vt* [-rɪeɪt] (*take*) apropiarse de; (*allot*): **to ~ sth for** destinar algo a; **~ for or to** apropiado para; **it would not be ~ for me to comment** no estaría bien or sería pertinente que yo diera mi opinión.

appropriation [əprəʊprɪ'eɪʃən] *n* asignación *f*.

appropriation account *n* cuenta de asignación.

approval [ə'pruːvəl] *n* aprobación *f*, visto bueno; **on ~** (*COMM*) a prueba; **to meet with sb's ~** obtener la aprobación de uno.

approve [ə'pruːv] *vt* aprobar.

approve of *vt fus* aprobar.

approved school *n* (*Brit*) correccional *m*.

approx. *abbr* (= *approximately*) aprox.

approximate [ə'prɔksɪmɪt] *a* aproximado.

approximately [ə'prɔksɪmɪtlɪ] *ad* aproximadamente, más o menos.

approximation [əprɔksɪ'meɪʃən] *n* aproximación *f*.

Apr. *abbr* (= *April*) abr.

apr *n abbr* (= *annual percentage rate*) tasa de interés anual.

apricot ['eɪprɪkɔt] *n* albaricoque *m* (*Sp*), damasco (*LAm*).

April ['eɪprəl] *n* abril *m*; **~ Fool's Day** *n* (*1 April*) ≈ día *m* de los Inocentes (*28 December*).

apron ['eɪprən] *n* delantal *m*; (*AVIAT*) pista.

apse [æps] *n* (*ARCH*) ábside *m*.

APT *n abbr* (*Brit*) = *advanced passenger train*.

Apt. *abbr* = **apartment.**

apt [æpt] *a* (*to the point*) acertado, oportuno; (*appropriate*) apropiado; **~ to do** (*likely*) propenso a hacer.

aptitude ['æptɪtjuːd] *n* aptitud *f*, capacidad *f*.

aptitude test *n* prueba de aptitud.

aptly ['æptlɪ] *a* aptamente, acertadamente.

aqualung ['ækwəlʌŋ] *n* escafandra autónoma.

aquarium [ə'kwɛərɪəm] *n* acuario.

Aquarius [ə'kwɛərɪəs] *n* Acuario.

aquatic [ə'kwætɪk] *a* acuático.

aqueduct ['ækwɪdʌkt] *n* acueducto.

AR *abbr* (*US POST*) = *Arkansas.*

ARA *n abbr* (*Brit*) = *Associate of the Royal Academy.*

Arab ['ærəb] *a*, *n* árabe *m/f*.

Arabia [ə'reɪbɪə] *n* Arabia.

Arabian [ə'reɪbɪən] *a* árabe, arábigo.

Arabian Desert *n* Desierto Arábigo.

Arabian Sea *n* Mar *m* de Omán.

Arabic ['ærəbɪk] *a* (*language, manuscripts*) árabe, arábigo ◆ *n* árabe *m*; **~ numerals** numeración *f* arábiga.

arable ['ærəbl] *a* cultivable.

Aragon ['ærəgən] *n* Aragón *m*.

ARAM *n abbr* (*Brit*) = *Associate of the Royal Academy of Music.*

arbiter ['ɑːbɪtə*] *n* árbitro.

arbitrary ['ɑːbɪtrərɪ] *a* arbitrario.

arbitrate ['ɑːbɪtreɪt] *vi* arbitrar.

arbitration [ɑːbɪ'treɪʃən] *n* arbitraje *m*; **the dispute went to ~** el conflicto laboral fue sometido al arbitraje.

arbitrator ['ɑːbɪtreɪtə*] *n* árbitro.

ARC *n abbr* = *American Red Cross.*

arc [ɑːk] *n* arco.

arcade [ɑː'keɪd] *n* (*ARCH*) arcada; (*round a square*) soportales *mpl*; (*shopping ~*) galería comercial.

arch [ɑːtʃ] *n* arco; (*vault*) bóveda; (*of foot*) arco del pie ◆ *vt* arquear.

archaeological [ɑːkɪə'lɔdʒɪkl] *a* arqueológico.

archaeologist [ɑːkɪ'ɔlədʒɪst] *n* arqueólogo/a.

archaeology [ɑːkɪ'ɔlədʒɪ] *n* arqueología.

archaic [ɑː'keɪɪk] *a* arcaico.

archangel ['ɑ:keɪndʒəl] n arcángel m.
archbishop [ɑ:tʃ'bɪʃəp] n arzobispo.
arched [ɑ:tʃt] a abovedado.
arch-enemy ['ɑ:tʃ'ɛnəmɪ] n enemigo jurado.
archeology etc [ɑ:kɪ'ɔlədʒɪ] (US) = **archaeology** etc.
archer ['ɑ:tʃə*] n arquero/a.
archery ['ɑ:tʃərɪ] n tiro al arco.
archetypal ['ɑ:kɪtaɪpəl] a arquetípico.
archetype ['ɑ:kɪtaɪp] n arquetipo.
archipelago [ɑ:kɪ'pelɪɡəu] n archipiélago.
architect ['ɑ:kɪtekt] n arquitecto/a.
architectural [ɑ:kɪ'tektʃərəl] a arquitectónico.
architecture ['ɑ:kɪtektʃə*] n arquitectura.
archive ['ɑ:kaɪv] n (also COMPUT) archivo.
archive file n (COMPUT) fichero archivado.
archives ['ɑ:kaɪvz] npl archivo sg.
archivist ['ɑ:kɪvɪst] n archivero/a.
archway ['ɑ:tʃweɪ] n arco, arcada.
ARCM n abbr (Brit) = Associate of the Royal College of Music.
Arctic ['ɑ:ktɪk] a ártico ◆ n: **the ~** el Ártico.
Arctic Circle n Círculo Polar Ártico.
Arctic Ocean n Océano Glacial Ártico.
ARD n abbr (US MED) = acute respiratory disease.
ardent ['ɑ:dənt] a (desire) ardiente; (supporter, lover) apasionado.
ardour, (US) **ardor** ['ɑ:də*] n ardor m, pasión f.
arduous ['ɑ:djuəs] a (gen) arduo; (journey) penoso.
are [ɑ:*] vb see **be.**
area ['ɛərɪə] n área; (MATH etc) superficie f, extensión f; (zone) región f, zona; **the London ~** la zona de Londres.
area code n (US TEL) prefijo.
arena [ə'ri:nə] n arena; (of circus) pista; (for bullfight) plaza, ruedo.
aren't [ɑ:nt] = **are not.**
Argentina [ɑ:dʒən'ti:nə] n Argentina.
Argentinian [ɑ:dʒən'tɪnɪən] a, n argentino/a m/f.
arguable ['ɑ:ɡjuəbl] a: **it is ~ whether ...** es dudoso que + subjun.
arguably ['ɑ:ɡjuəblɪ] ad: **it is ~ ...** es discutiblemente ...
argue ['ɑ:ɡju:] vt (debate: case, matter) mantener, argüir ◆ vi (quarrel) discutir; (reason) razonar, argumentar; **to ~ that** sostener que; **to ~ about sth (with sb)** pelearse (con uno) por algo.
argument ['ɑ:ɡjumənt] n (reasons) argumento; (quarrel) discusión f; (debate) debate m, disputa; **~ for/against** argumento en pro/contra de.
argumentative [ɑ:ɡju'mentətɪv] a discutidor(a).
aria ['ɑ:rɪə] n (MUS) aria.
ARIBA n abbr (Brit) = Associate of the

Royal Institute of British Architects.
arid ['ærɪd] a árido.
aridity [ə'rɪdɪtɪ] n aridez f.
Aries ['ɛərɪz] n Aries m.
arise [ə'raɪz], pt **arose,** pp **arisen** [ə'rɪzn] vi (rise up) levantarse, alzarse; (emerge) surgir, presentarse; **to ~ from** derivar de; **should the need ~** si fuera necesario.
aristocracy [ærɪs'tɔkrəsɪ] n aristocracia.
aristocrat ['ærɪstəkræt] n aristócrata m/f.
aristocratic [ərɪstə'krætɪk] a aristocrático.
arithmetic [ə'rɪθmətɪk] n aritmética.
arithmetical [ærɪθ'metɪkl] a aritmético.
Ark [ɑ:k] n: **Noah's ~** el Arca f de Noé.
arm [ɑ:m] n (ANAT) brazo ◆ vt armar; **~ in ~** cogidos del brazo; see also **arms.**
armaments ['ɑ:məmənts] npl (weapons) armamentos mpl.
armchair ['ɑ:mtʃɛə*] n sillón m.
armed [ɑ:md] a armado; **the ~ forces** las fuerzas armadas.
armed robbery n robo a mano armada.
Armenia [ɑ:'mi:nɪə] n Armenia.
Armenian [ɑ:'mi:nɪən] a armenio ◆ n armenio/a; (LING) armenio.
armful ['ɑ:mful] n brazado, brazada.
armistice ['ɑ:mɪstɪs] n armisticio.
armour, (US) **armor** ['ɑ:mə*] n armadura.
armo(u)red car n coche m or carro (LAm) blindado.
armo(u)ry ['ɑ:mərɪ] n arsenal m.
armpit ['ɑ:mpɪt] n sobaco, axila.
armrest ['ɑ:mrest] n apoyabrazos m inv, brazo.
arms [ɑ:mz] npl (weapons) armas fpl; (HERALDRY) escudo sg.
arms control n control m de armamentos.
arms race n carrera de armamentos.
army ['ɑ:mɪ] n ejército.
aroma [ə'rəumə] n aroma m, fragancia.
aromatic [ærə'mætɪk] a aromático, fragante.
arose [ə'rəuz] pt of **arise.**
around [ə'raund] ad alrededor; (in the area) a la redonda ◆ prep alrededor de.
arouse [ə'rauz] vt despertar.
arrange [ə'reɪndʒ] vt arreglar, ordenar; (programme) organizar ◆ vi: **we have ~d for a taxi to pick you up** hemos hecho los arreglos para que le recoja un taxi; **to ~ to do sth** quedar en hacer algo; **it was ~d that ...** se quedó en que ...
arrangement [ə'reɪndʒmənt] n arreglo; (agreement) acuerdo; **~s** npl (plans) planes mpl, medidas fpl; (preparations) preparativos mpl; **to come to an ~ (with sb)** llegar a un acuerdo (con uno); **by ~** a convenir; **I'll make ~s for you to be met** haré los preparativos para que le estén esperando.
array [ə'reɪ] n (COMPUT) arreglo, array m; **~ of** (things) serie f de; (people) conjunto de.

arrears [ə'rɪəz] *npl* atrasos *mpl*; **in ~** (*COMM*) en mora; **to be in ~ with one's rent** estar retrasado en el pago del alquiler.

arrest [ə'rɛst] *vt* detener; (*sb's attention*) llamar ◆ *n* detención *f*; **under ~** detenido.

arresting [ə'rɛstɪŋ] *a* (*fig*) llamativo.

arrival [ə'raɪvəl] *n* llegada; **new ~** recién llegado/a.

arrive [ə'raɪv] *vi* llegar.

arrogance ['ærəgəns] *n* arrogancia.

arrogant ['ærəgənt] *a* arrogante.

arrow ['ærəu] *n* flecha.

arse [ɑːs] *n* (*Brit col!*) culo, trasero.

arsenal ['ɑːsɪnl] *n* arsenal *m*.

arsenic ['ɑːsnɪk] *n* arsénico.

arson ['ɑːsn] *n* incendio premeditado.

art [ɑːt] *n* arte *m*; (*skill*) destreza; (*technique*) técnica; **A~s** *npl* (*SCOL*) Letras *fpl*; **work of ~** obra de arte.

artefact ['ɑːtɪfækt] *n* artefacto.

arterial [ɑː'tɪərɪəl] *a* (*ANAT*) arterial; (*road etc*) principal.

artery ['ɑːtərɪ] *n* (*MED*, *road etc*) arteria.

artful ['ɑːtful] *a* (*cunning: person, trick*) mañoso.

art gallery *n* pinacoteca; (*COMM*) galería de arte.

arthritis [ɑː'θraɪtɪs] *n* artritis *f*.

artichoke ['ɑːtɪtʃəuk] *n* alcachofa; **Jerusalem ~** aguaturma.

article ['ɑːtɪkl] *n* artículo, objeto, cosa; (*in newspaper*) artículo; (*Brit LAW: training*): **~s** *npl* contrato *sg* de aprendizaje; **~s of clothing** prendas *fpl* de vestir.

articles of association *npl* (*COMM*) estatutos *mpl* sociales, escritura social.

articulate *a* [ɑː'tɪkjulɪt] (*speech*) claro; (*person*) que se expresa bien ◆ *vi* [ɑː'tɪkjuleɪt] articular.

articulated lorry *n* (*Brit*) trailer *m*.

artifice ['ɑːtɪfɪs] *n* artificio, truco.

artificial [ɑːtɪ'fɪʃəl] *a* artificial; (*teeth etc*) postizo.

artificial insemination *n* inseminación *f* artificial.

artificial intelligence (A.I.) *n* inteligencia artificial (I.A.).

artificial respiration *n* respiración *f* artificial.

artillery [ɑː'tɪlərɪ] *n* artillería.

artisan ['ɑːtɪzæn] *n* artesano/a.

artist ['ɑːtɪst] *n* artista *m/f*; (*MUS*) intérprete *m/f*.

artistic [ɑː'tɪstɪk] *a* artístico.

artistry ['ɑːtɪstrɪ] *n* arte *m*, habilidad *f* (artística).

artless ['ɑːtlɪs] *a* (*innocent*) natural, sencillo; (*clumsy*) torpe.

art school *n* escuela de bellas artes.

arty ['ɑːtɪ] *a* artistoide.

ARV *n abbr* (= *American Revised Version*) traducción americana de la Biblia.

AS *n abbr* (*US UNIV*: = *Associate in/of Science*) título universitario ◆ *abbr* (*US POST*) = *American Samoa*.

as [æz, əz] *conj* (*cause*) como, ya que; (*time: moment*) como, cuando; (: *duration*) mientras; (*manner*) como, lo mismo que, tal como; (*in the capacity of*) como; **~ big ~** tan grande como; **twice ~ big ~** dos veces más grande que; **much ~ I like them, ...** por mucho que me gusten, ...; **~ the years went by** con el paso de los años; **~ she said** como ella dijo; **~ a present** de *or* como regalo; **~ if** *or* **though** como si; **~ for** *or* **to that** en cuanto a eso, en lo que a eso se refiere; **~ or so long ~** *conj* mientras (que); **~ much/many ~** tanto(s)... como; **~ soon ~** *conj* tan pronto como; **~ such** *ad* como tal; **~ well** *ad* también, además; **~ well ~** *conj* tanto como; *see also* **such**.

ASA *n abbr* (= *American Standards Association*) instituto de normas; (*Brit*: = *Advertising Standards Authority*) departamento de control de la publicidad; (: = *Amateur Swimming Association*) federación amateur de natación.

a.s.a.p. *abbr* (= *as soon as possible*) cuanto antes, lo más pronto posible.

asbestos [æz'bɛstəs] *n* asbesto, amianto.

ascend [ə'sɛnd] *vt* subir.

ascendancy [ə'sɛndənsɪ] *n* ascendiente *m*, dominio.

ascendant [ə'sɛndənt] *n*: **to be in the ~** estar en auge, ir ganando predominio.

Ascension [ə'sɛnʃən] *n*: **the ~** la Ascensión.

Ascension Island *n* Isla Ascensión.

ascent [ə'sɛnt] *n* subida; (*slope*) cuesta, pendiente *f*; (*of plane*) ascenso.

ascertain [æsə'teɪn] *vt* averiguar.

ascetic [ə'sɛtɪk] *a* ascético.

asceticism [ə'sɛtɪsɪzəm] *n* ascetismo.

ASCII ['æskiː] *n abbr* (= *American Standard Code for Information Interchange*) ASCII.

ascribe [ə'skraɪb] *vt*: **to ~ sth to** atribuir algo a.

ASCU *n abbr* (*US*) = *Association of State Colleges and Universities*.

ASE *n abbr* = *American Stock Exchange*.

ASH [æʃ] *n abbr* (*Brit*: = *Action on Smoking and Health*) organización anti-tabaco.

ash [æʃ] *n* ceniza; (*tree*) fresno.

ashamed [ə'ʃeɪmd] *a* avergonzado; **to be ~ of** avergonzarse de.

ashcan ['æʃkæn] *n* (*US*) cubo *or* bote *m* (*LAm*) de la basura.

ashen ['æʃn] *a* pálido.

ashore [ə'ʃɔː*] *ad* en tierra.

ashtray ['æʃtreɪ] *n* cenicero.

Ash Wednesday *n* miércoles *m* de ceniza.

Asia ['eɪʃə] *n* Asia.

Asian ['eɪʃən], **Asiatic** [eɪsɪ'ætɪk] *a*, *n* asiático/a *m/f*.

aside [ə'saɪd] *ad* a un lado ◆ *n* aparte *m*; ~ **from** *prep* (*as well as*) aparte *or* además de.

ask [ɑːsk] *vt* (*question*) preguntar; (*demand*) pedir; (*invite*) invitar ◆ *vi*: **to ~ about sth** preguntar acerca de algo; **to ~ sb sth/to do sth** preguntar algo a uno/ pedir a uno que haga algo; **to ~ sb about sth** preguntar algo a uno; **to ~ (sb) a question** hacer una pregunta (a uno); **to ~ sb the time** preguntar la hora a uno; **to ~ sb out to dinner** invitar a cenar a uno.

ask after *vt fus* preguntar por.

ask for *vt fus* pedir; **it's just ~ing for trouble** *or* **for it** es buscarse problemas.

askance [ə'skɑːns] *ad*: **to look ~ at sb** mirar con recelo a uno.

askew [ə'skjuː] *ad* sesgado, ladeado.

asking price *n* (*COMM*) precio inicial.

asleep [ə'sliːp] *a* dormido; **to fall ~** dormirse, quedarse dormido.

ASLEF ['æzlɛf] *n abbr* (*Brit*: = *Associated Society of Locomotive Engineers and Firemen*) *sindicato de ferrocarrileros*.

asp [æsp] *n* áspid *m*.

asparagus [əs'pærəgəs] *n* espárragos *mpl*.

ASPCA *n abbr* = *American Society for the Prevention of Cruelty to Animals*.

aspect ['æspɛkt] *n* aspecto, apariencia; (*direction in which a building etc faces*) orientación *f*.

aspersions [əs'pɔːʃənz] *npl*: **to cast ~ on** difamar a, calumniar a.

asphalt ['æsfælt] *n* asfalto.

asphyxiate [æs'fɪksɪeɪt] *vt* asfixiar.

asphyxiation [aesfɪksɪ'eɪʃən] *n* asfixia.

aspirate ['æspəreɪt] *vt* aspirar ◆ *a* ['æspərɪt] aspirado.

aspirations [æspə'reɪʃənz] *npl* anhelo *sg*, deseo *sg*; (*ambition*) ambición *f*.

aspire [əs'paɪə*] *vi*: **to ~ to** aspirar a, ambicionar.

aspirin ['æsprɪn] *n* aspirina.

ass [æs] *n* asno, burro; (*col*) imbécil *m/f*; (*US col!*) culo, trasero.

assailant [ə'seɪlənt] *n* asaltador(a) *m/f*, agresor(a) *m/f*.

assassin [ə'sæsɪn] *n* asesino/a.

assassinate [ə'sæsɪneɪt] *vt* asesinar.

assassination [ə'sæsɪ'neɪʃən] *n* asesinato.

assault [ə'sɔːlt] *n* (*gen*: *attack*) asalto ◆ *vt* asaltar, atacar; (*sexually*) violar.

assemble [ə'sɛmbl] *vt* reunir, juntar; (*TECH*) montar ◆ *vi* reunirse, juntarse.

assembler [ə'sɛmblə*] *n* (*COMPUT*) ensamblador *m*.

assembly [ə'sɛmblɪ] *n* (*meeting*) reunión *f*, asamblea; (*construction*) montaje *m*.

assembly language *n* (*COMPUT*) lenguaje *m* ensamblador.

assembly line *n* cadena de montaje.

assent [ə'sɛnt] *n* asentimiento, aprobación *f* ◆ *vi* consentir, asentir; **to ~ (to sth)** consentir (en algo).

assert [ə'sɔːt] *vt* afirmar; (*insist on*) hacer valer; **to ~ o.s.** imponerse.

assertion [ə'sɔːʃən] *n* afirmación *f*.

assertive [ə'sɔːtɪv] *a* enérgico, agresivo, perentorio.

assess [ə'sɛs] *vt* valorar, calcular; (*tax, damages*) fijar; (*property etc*: *for tax*) gravar.

assessment [ə'sɛsmənt] *n* valoración *f*; gravamen *m*; (*judgment*): **~ (of)** juicio (sobre).

assessor [ə'sɛsə*] *n* asesor(a) *m/f*; (*of tax*) tasador(a) *m/f*.

asset ['æsɛt] *n* posesión *f*; (*quality*) ventaja; **~s** *npl* (*funds*) activo *sg*, fondos *mpl*.

asset-stripping ['æsɛt'strɪpɪŋ] *n* (*COMM*) acaparamiento de activos.

assiduous [ə'sɪdjuəs] *a* asiduo.

assign [ə'saɪn] *vt* (*date*) fijar; (*task*) asignar; (*resources*) destinar; (*property*) traspasar.

assignment [ə'saɪnmənt] *n* asignación *f*; (*task*) tarea.

assimilate [ə'sɪmɪleɪt] *vt* asimilar.

assimilation [əsɪmɪ'leɪʃən] *n* asimilación *f*.

assist [ə'sɪst] *vt* ayudar.

assistance [ə'sɪstəns] *n* ayuda, auxilio.

assistant [ə'sɪstənt] *n* ayudante *m/f*; (*Brit*: *also*: **shop ~**) dependiente/a *m/f*.

assistant manager *n* subdirector(a) *m/f*.

assizes [ə'saɪzɪz] *npl* sesión *f* de un tribunal.

associate [ə'səuʃɪɪt] *a* asociado ◆ *n* socio/a, colega *m/f*; (*in crime*) cómplice *m/f*; (*member*) miembro/a ◆ *vb* [ə'səuʃɪeɪt] *vt* asociar; (*ideas*) relacionar ◆ *vi*: **to ~ with sb** tratar con alguien; **~ director** subdirector/a *m/f*; **~d company** compañía afiliada.

association [əsəusɪ'eɪʃən] *n* asociación *f*; (*COMM*) sociedad *f*; **in ~ with** en asociación con.

association football *n* (*Brit*) fútbol *m*.

assorted [ə'sɔːtɪd] *a* surtido, variado; **in ~ sizes** en distintos tamaños.

assortment [ə'sɔːtmənt] *n* surtido.

Asst. *abbr* = **Assistant**.

assuage [ə'sweɪdʒ] *vt* mitigar.

assume [ə'sjuːm] *vt* (*suppose*) suponer; (*responsibilities etc*) asumir; (*attitude, name*) adoptar, tomar.

assumed name *n* nombre *m* falso.

assumption [ə'sʌmpʃən] *n* (*supposition*) suposición *f*, presunción *f*; (*act*) asunción *f*; **on the ~ that** suponiendo que.

assurance [ə'ʃuərəns] *n* garantía, promesa; (*confidence*) confianza, aplomo; (*Brit*: *insurance*) seguro; **I can give you no ~s** no puedo hacerle ninguna promesa.

assure [ə'ʃuə*] *vt* asegurar.

assuredly [ə'ʃuərɪdlɪ] *ad* seguramente, indudablemente.

AST *n abbr* (= *Atlantic Standard Time*)

hora oficial del este del Canadá.
asterisk ['æstərɪsk] *n* asterisco.
astern [ə'stəːn] *ad* a popa.
asteroid ['æstərɔɪd] *n* asteroide *m*.
asthma ['æsmə] *n* asma.
asthmatic [æs'mætɪk] *a*, *n* asmático/a *m/f*.
astigmatism [ə'stɪgmətɪzəm] *n* astigmatismo.
astir [ə'stəː*] *ad* en acción.
ASTMS ['æstəmz] *n abbr* (*Brit*: = *Association of Scientific, Technical and Managerial Staffs*) sindicato de personal científico, técnico y directivo.
astonish [ə'stɔnɪʃ] *vt* asombrar, pasmar.
astonishing [ə'stɔnɪʃɪŋ] *a* asombroso, pasmoso; **I find it ~ that ...** me asombra *or* pasma que ...
astonishingly [ə'stɔnɪʃɪŋlɪ] *ad* increíblemente, asombrosamente.
astonishment [ə'stɔnɪʃmənt] *n* asombro, sorpresa; **to my ~** con gran sorpresa mía.
astound [ə'staund] *vt* asombrar, pasmar.
astounding [ə'staundɪŋ] *a* asombroso.
astray [ə'streɪ] *ad*: **to go ~** extraviarse; **to lead ~** llevar por mal camino; **to go ~ in one's calculations** equivocarse en sus cálculos.
astride [ə'straɪd] *prep* a caballo *or* horcajadas sobre.
astringent [əs'trɪndʒənt] *a*, *n* astringente *m*.
astrologer [əs'trɔlədʒə*] *n* astrólogo/a.
astrology [əs'trɔlədʒɪ] *n* astrología.
astronaut ['æstrənɔːt] *n* astronauta *m/f*.
astronomer [əs'trɔnəmə*] *n* astrónomo/a.
astronomical [æstrə'nɔmɪkəl] *a* astronómico.
astronomy [aes'trɔnəmɪ] *n* astronomía.
astrophysics ['æstrəu'fɪzɪks] *n* astrofísica.
astute [əs'tjuːt] *a* astuto.
asunder [ə'sʌndə*] *ad*: **to tear ~** hacer pedazos.
ASV *n abbr* (= *American Standard Version*) traducción americana de la Biblia.
asylum [ə'saɪləm] *n* (*refuge*) asilo; (*hospital*) manicomio; **to seek political ~** pedir asilo político.
asymmetric(al) [eɪsɪ'mɛtrɪk(l)] *a* asimétrico.
at [æt] *prep* en, a; **~ the top** en la cumbre; **~ the baker's** en la panadería; **~ 4 o'clock** a las cuatro; **~ £1 a kilo** a una libra el kilo; **~ night** de noche; **~ a stroke** de un golpe; **two ~ a time** de dos en dos; **~ times** a veces; **~ full speed** a toda velocidad.
ate [ɛt, eɪt] *pt of* **eat**.
atheism ['eɪθɪɪzəm] *n* ateísmo.
atheist ['eɪθɪɪst] *n* ateo/a.
Athenian [ə'θiːnɪən] *a*, *n* ateniense *m/f*.
Athens ['æθɪnz] *n* Atenas *f*.
athlete ['æθliːt] *n* atleta *m/f*.
athletic [æθ'lɛtɪk] *a* atlético.

athletics [æθ'lɛtɪks] *n* atletismo.
Atlantic [ət'læntɪk] *a* atlántico ♦ *n*: **the ~ (Ocean)** el (Océano) Atlántico.
atlas ['ætləs] *n* atlas *m*.
Atlas Mountains *npl*: **the ~** el Atlas.
A.T.M. *n abbr* (= *Automatic Telling Machine*) cajero automático.
atmosphere ['ætməsfɪə*] *n* (*air*) atmósfera; (*fig*) ambiente *m*.
atoll ['ætɔl] *n* atolón *m*.
atom ['ætəm] *n* átomo.
atomic [ə'tɔmɪk] *a* atómico.
atom(ic) bomb *n* bomba atómica.
atomic power *n* energía atómica.
atomizer ['ætəmaɪzə*] *n* atomizador *m*.
atone [ə'təun] *vi*: **to ~ for** expiar.
atonement [ə'təunmənt] *n* expiación *f*.
ATP *n abbr* (= *Association of Tennis Professionals*) sindicato de jugadores de tenis profesionales.
atrocious [ə'trəuʃəs] *a* (*very bad*) atroz; (*fig*) horrible, infame.
atrocity [ə'trɔsɪtɪ] *n* atrocidad *f*.
atrophy ['ætrəfɪ] *n* atrofia ♦ *vi* atrofiarse.
attach [ə'tætʃ] *vt* sujetar; (*stick*) pegar; (*document, letter*) adjuntar; **to be ~ed to sb/sth** (*to like*) tener cariño a uno/algo; **the ~ed letter** la carta adjunta.
attaché [ə'tæʃeɪ] *n* agregado/a.
attaché case *n* (*Brit*) maletín *m*.
attachment [ə'tætʃmənt] *n* (*tool*) accesorio; (*love*): **~ (to)** apego (a).
attack [ə'tæk] *vt* (*MIL*) atacar; (*criminal*) agredir, asaltar; (*task etc*) emprender ♦ *n* ataque *m*, asalto; (*on sb's life*) atentado; **heart ~** infarto (de miocardio).
attacker [ə'tækə*] *n* agresor(a) *m/f*, asaltante *m/f*.
attain [ə'teɪn] *vt* (*also*: **~ to**) alcanzar; (*achieve*) lograr, conseguir.
attainments [ə'teɪnmənts] *npl* (*skill*) talento *sg*.
attempt [ə'tɛmpt] *n* tentativa, intento; (*attack*) atentado ♦ *vt* intentar, tratar de; **he made no ~ to help** ni siquiera procuró ayudar.
attempted [ə'tɛmptɪd] *a*: **~ murder/burglary/suicide** tentativa *or* intento de asesinato/robo/suicidio.
attend [ə'tɛnd] *vt* asistir a; (*patient*) atender.
attend to *vt fus* (*needs, affairs etc*) ocuparse de; (*speech etc*) prestar atención a; (*customer*) atender a.
attendance [ə'tɛndəns] *n* asistencia, presencia; (*people present*) concurrencia.
attendant [ə'tɛndənt] *n* sirviente/a *m/f*, mozo/a; (*THEATRE*) acomodador(a) *m/f* ♦ *a* concomitante.
attention [ə'tɛnʃən] *n* atención *f* ♦ *excl* (*MIL*) ¡firme(s)!; **for the ~ of** (*ADMIN*) atención...; **it has come to my ~ that ...** me he enterado de que ...

attentive [ə'tɛntɪv] a atento; (polite) cortés.
attenuate [ə'tɛnjueɪt] vt atenuar.
attest [ə'tɛst] vi: **to ~ to** dar fe de.
attic ['ætɪk] n desván m.
attitude ['ætɪtjuːd] n (gen) actitud f; (disposition) disposición f.
attorney [ə'tɔːnɪ] n (US: lawyer) abogado/a; (having proxy) apoderado.
Attorney General n (Brit) ≈ Presidente m del Consejo del Poder Judicial (Sp); (US) ≈ ministro de justicia.
attract [ə'trækt] vt atraer; (attention) llamar.
attraction [ə'trækʃən] n (gen) encanto; (PHYSICS) atracción f; (fig: towards sth) atractivo.
attractive [ə'træktɪv] a atractivo.
attribute ['ætrɪbjuːt] n atributo ◆ vt [ə'trɪbjuːt]: **to ~ sth to** atribuir algo a; (accuse) achacar algo a.
attrition [ə'trɪʃən] n: **war of ~** guerra de agotamiento.
Atty. Gen abbr = **Attorney General**.
ATV n abbr (Brit: = Associated Television) cadena de televisión británica; (= all terrain vehicle) vehículo todo terreno.
aubergine ['əubəʒiːn] n (Brit) berenjena.
auburn ['ɔːbən] a color castaño rojizo.
auction ['ɔːkʃən] n (also: **sale by ~**) subasta ◆ vt subastar.
auctioneer [ɔːkʃə'nɪə*] n subastador(a) m/f.
auction room n sala de subastas.
audacious [ɔː'deɪʃəs] a (bold) audaz, osado; (impudent) atrevido, descarado.
audacity [ɔː'dæsɪtɪ] n audacia, atrevimiento; (pej) descaro.
audible ['ɔːdɪbl] a audible, que se puede oír.
audience ['ɔːdɪəns] n auditorio; (gathering) público; (interview) audiencia.
audio-typist ['ɔːdɪəu'taɪpɪst] n mecanógrafo/a de dictáfono.
audiovisual [ɔːdɪəu'vɪzjuəl] a audiovisual.
audiovisual aid n ayuda audiovisual.
audit ['ɔːdɪt] vt revisar, intervenir.
audition [ɔː'dɪʃən] n audición f ◆ vi: **to ~ for the part of** hacer una audición para el papel de.
auditor ['ɔːdɪtə*] n interventor(a) m/f, censor(a) m/f de cuentas.
auditorium [ɔːdɪ'tɔːrɪəm] n auditorio.
AUEW n abbr (Brit: = Allied Union of Engineering Workers) sindicato mixto de trabajadores de ingeniería.
Aug. abbr (= August) ag.
augment [ɔːg'mɛnt] vt aumentar ◆ vi aumentarse.
augur ['ɔːgə*] vi: **it ~s well** es de buen agüero.
August ['ɔːgəst] n agosto.
august [ɔː'gʌst] a augusto.
aunt [ɑːnt] n tía.
auntie, aunty ['ɑːntɪ] n diminutive of **aunt**.
au pair ['əu'pɛə*] n (also: ~ **girl**) au pair f.
aura ['ɔːrə] n aura; (atmosphere) ambiente m.
auspices ['ɔːspɪsɪz] npl: **under the ~ of** bajo los auspicios de.
auspicious [ɔːs'pɪʃəs] a propicio, de buen augurio.
austere [ɔs'tɪə*] a austero; (manner) adusto.
austerity [ɔ'stɛrɪtɪ] n austeridad f.
Australasia [ɔːstrə'leɪzɪə] n Australasia.
Australia [ɔs'treɪlɪə] n Australia.
Australian [ɔs'treɪlɪən] a, n australiano/a m/f.
Austria ['ɔstrɪə] n Austria.
Austrian ['ɔstrɪən] a, n austríaco/a m/f.
AUT n abbr (Brit: = Association of University Teachers) sindicato de profesores de universidad.
authentic [ɔː'θɛntɪk] a auténtico.
authenticate [ɔː'θɛntɪkeɪt] vt compulsar.
authenticity [ɔːθɛn'tɪsɪtɪ] n autenticidad f.
author ['ɔːθə] n autor(a) m/f.
authoritarian [ɔːθɔrɪ'tɛərɪən] a autoritario.
authoritative [ɔː'θɔrɪtətɪv] a autorizado; (manner) autoritario.
authority [ɔː'θɔrɪtɪ] n autoridad f; **the authorities** npl las autoridades; **to have ~ to do sth** tener autoridad para hacer algo.
authorization [ɔːθərai'zeɪʃən] n autorización f.
authorize ['ɔːθəraɪz] vt autorizar.
authorized capital n (COMM) capital m autorizado or social.
autistic [ɔː'tɪstɪk] a autístico.
auto ['ɔːtəu] n (US) coche m, carro (LAm), automóvil m.
autobiographical [ɔːtəbaɪə'græfɪkəl] a autobiográfico.
autobiography [ɔːtəbaɪ'ɔgrəfɪ] n autobiografía.
autocratic [ɔːtə'krætɪk] a autocrático.
autograph ['ɔːtəgrɑːf] n autógrafo ◆ vt firmar; (photo etc) dedicar.
automat ['ɔːtəmæt] n (US) restaurán m or restaurante m de autoservicio.
automate ['ɔːtəmeɪt] vt automatizar.
automated ['ɔːtəmeɪtɪd] a automatizado.
automatic [ɔːtə'mætɪk] a automático ◆ n (gun) pistola automática; (washing machine) lavadora.
automatically [ɔːtə'mætɪklɪ] ad automáticamente.
automatic data processing (ADP) n proceso automático de datos.
automation [ɔːtə'meɪʃən] n automatización f.
automaton, pl automata [ɔː'tɔmətən, -tə] n autómata.
automobile ['ɔːtəməbiːl] n (US) coche m, carro (LAm), automóvil m.
autonomous [ɔː'tɔnəməs] a autónomo.

autonomy [ɔː'tɔnəmɪ] *n* autonomía.
autopsy ['ɔːtɔpsɪ] *n* autopsia.
autumn ['ɔːtəm] *n* otoño.
auxiliary [ɔːg'zɪlɪərɪ] *a* auxiliar.
AV *n abbr* (= *Authorized Version*) *traducción inglesa de la Biblia* ♦ *abbr* = **audiovisual**.
Av. *abbr* (= *avenue*) Av., Avda.
avail [ə'veɪl] *vt*: **to** ~ **o.s. of** aprovechar(se) de, valerse de ♦ *n*: **to no** ~ en vano, sin resultado.
availability [əveɪlə'bɪlɪtɪ] *n* disponibilidad *f*.
available [ə'veɪləbl] *a* disponible; (*obtainable*) asequible; **to make sth** ~ **to sb** poner algo a la disposición de uno; **is the manager** ~? ¿está libre el gerente?
avalanche ['ævəlɑːnʃ] *n* alud *m*, avalancha.
avant-garde ['ævæŋ'gɑːd] *a* de vanguardia.
avarice ['ævərɪs] *n* avaricia.
avaricious [æve'rɪʃəs] *a* avaro.
avdp. *abbr* = *avoirdupois*.
Ave. *abbr* (= *avenue*) Av., Avda.
avenge [ə'vendʒ] *vt* vengar.
avenue ['ævənjuː] *n* avenida; (*fig*) camino.
average ['ævərɪdʒ] *n* promedio, término medio ♦ *a* (*mean*) medio, de término medio; (*ordinary*) regular, corriente ♦ *vt* calcular el promedio de, prorratear; **on** ~ por regla general.
average out *vi*: **to** ~ **out at** salir a un promedio de.
averse [ə'vəːs] *a*: **to be** ~ **to sth/doing** sentir aversión *or* antipatía por algo/por hacer.
aversion [ə'vəːʃən] *n* aversión *f*, repugnancia.
avert [ə'vəːt] *vt* prevenir; (*blow*) desviar; (*one's eyes*) apartar.
aviary ['eɪvɪərɪ] *n* pajarera.
aviation [eɪvɪ'eɪʃən] *n* aviación *f*.
aviator ['eɪvɪeɪtə*] *n* aviador(a) *m/f*.
avid ['ævɪd] *a* ávido, ansioso.
avidly ['ævɪdlɪ] *ad* ávidamente, con avidez.
avocado [ævə'kɑːdəu] *n* (*also*: *Brit*: ~ **pear**) aguacate *m*, palta (*LAm*).
avoid [ə'vɔɪd] *vt* evitar, eludir.
avoidable [ə'vɔɪdəbl] *a* evitable, eludible.
avoidance [ə'vɔɪdəns] *n* evasión *f*.
avow [ə'vau] *vt* prometer.
avowal [ə'vauəl] *n* promesa, voto.
avowed [ə'vaud] *a* declarado.
AVP *n abbr* (*US*) = *assistant vice-president*.
avuncular [ə'vʌŋkjulə*] *a* como de tío.
AWACS ['eɪwæks] *n abbr* (= *airborne warning and control system*) AWACS *m*.
await [ə'weɪt] *vt* esperar, aguardar; **long** ~**ed** largamente esperado.
awake [ə'weɪk] *a* despierto ♦ (*vb*: *pt* **awoke**, *pp* **awoken** *or* **awaked**) *vt* despertar ♦ *vi* despertarse; **to be** ~ estar despierto.
awakening [ə'weɪknɪŋ] *n* despertar *m*.
award [ə'wɔːd] *n* (*prize*) premio; (*medal*)

condecoración *f*; (*LAW*) fallo, sentencia; (*act*) concesión *f* ♦ *vt* (*prize*) otorgar, conceder; (*LAW*: *damages*) adjudicar.
aware [ə'wɛə*] *a* consciente; (*awake*) despierto; (*informed*) enterado; **to become** ~ **of** darse cuenta de, enterarse de; **I am fully** ~ **that** sé muy bien que.
awareness [ə'wɛənɪs] *n* conciencia, conocimiento.
awash [ə'wɔʃ] *a* inundado.
away [ə'weɪ] *ad* (*gen*) fuera; (*far* ~) lejos; **two kilometres** ~ a dos kilómetros de distancia; **two hours** ~ **by car** a dos horas en coche; **the holiday was two weeks** ~ faltaban dos semanas para las vacaciones; ~ **from** lejos de, fuera de; **he's** ~ **for a week** estará ausente una semana; **he's** ~ **in Milan** está en Milán; **to take** ~ llevar(se); **to** **work/pedal** ~ seguir trabajando/pedaleando; **to fade** ~ desvanecerse; (*sound*) apagarse.
away game *n* (*SPORT*) partido de fuera.
awe [ɔː] *n* pavor *m*, respeto, temor *m* reverencial.
awe-inspiring ['ɔːɪnspaɪərɪŋ], **awesome** ['ɔːsəm] *a* imponente, pasmoso.
awestruck ['ɔːstrʌk] *a* pasmado.
awful ['ɔːfəl] *a* terrible, pasmoso; **an** ~ **lot of** (*people*, *cars*, *dogs*) la mar de, muchísimos.
awfully ['ɔːfəlɪ] *ad* (*very*) terriblemente.
awhile [ə'waɪl] *ad* (durante) un rato, algún tiempo.
awkward ['ɔːkwəd] *a* (*clumsy*) desmañado, torpe; (*shape*) incómodo; (*difficult*: *question*) difícil; (*problem*) complicado; (*embarrassing*) delicado.
awkwardness ['ɔːkwədnɪs] *n* (*clumsiness*) torpeza; (*of situation*) lo delicado.
awl [ɔːl] *n* lezna, subilla.
awning ['ɔːnɪŋ] *n* (*of shop*) toldo; (*of window etc*) marquesina.
awoke [ə'wəuk], **awoken** [ə'wəukən] *pt*, *pp* *of* **awake**.
AWOL ['eɪwɔl] *abbr* (*MIL*) *see* **absent without leave**.
awry [ə'raɪ] *ad*: **to be** ~ estar descolocado *or* atravesado; **to go** ~ salir mal, fracasar.
axe, (*US*) **ax** [æks] *n* hacha ♦ *vt* (*employee*) despedir; (*project etc*) cortar; (*jobs*) reducir; **to have an** ~ **to grind** (*fig*) tener un interés creado *or* algún fin interesado.
axes ['æksiːz] *npl of* **axis**.
axiom ['æksɪəm] *n* axioma *m*.
axiomatic [æksɪə'mætɪk] *a* axiomático.
axis, *pl* **axes** ['æksɪs, -siːz] *n* eje *m*.
axle ['æksl] *n* eje *m*, árbol *m*.
ay(e) [aɪ] *excl* (*yes*) sí; **the ayes** *npl* los que votan a favor.
AYH *n abbr* = *American Youth Hostels*.
AZ *abbr* (*US POST*) = *Arizona*.
azalea [ə'zeɪlɪə] *n* azalea.
Azores [ə'zɔːz] *npl*: **the** ~ las (Islas) Azo-

res.
Aztec ['æztɛk] *a, n* azteca *m/f.*
azure ['eɪʒə*] *a* celeste.

B

B, b [biː] *n (letter)* B, b *f;* (*SCOL: mark*) N; (*MUS*) si *m;* **B for Benjamin,** (*US*) **B for Baker** B de Barcelona; **B road** (*Brit AUT*) ≈ carretera secundaria.
b. *abbr* = **born.**
BA *n abbr* = *British Academy;* (*SCOL*) = **Bachelor of Arts.**
babble ['bæbl] *vi* barbullar.
babe [beɪb] *n* criatura.
baboon [bə'buːn] *n* mandril *m.*
baby ['beɪbɪ] *n* bebé *m/f.*
baby carriage *n* (*US*) cochecito.
babyish ['beɪbɪɪʃ] *a* infantil.
baby-minder ['beɪbɪ'maɪndə*] *n persona que cuida a los niños mientras la madre trabaja.*
baby-sit ['beɪbɪsɪt] *vi* hacer de canguro.
baby-sitter ['beɪbɪsɪtə*] *n* canguro/a.
bachelor ['bætʃələ*] *n* soltero; **B~ of Arts/ Science (BA/BSc)** licenciado/a en Filosofía y Letras/Ciencias.
back [bæk] *n (of person)* espalda; (*of animal*) lomo; (*of hand*) dorso; (*as opposed to front*) parte *f* de atrás; (*of room, car, etc*) fondo; (*of chair*) respaldo; (*of page*) reverso; (*FOOTBALL*) defensa *m;* **to have one's ~ to the wall** (*fig*) estar entre la espada y la pared; **to break the ~ of a job** hacer lo más difícil de un trabajo; **~ to front** al revés; **at the ~ of my mind was the thought that ...** en el fondo tenía la idea de que ... ♦ *vt (candidate: also:* **~ up**) respaldar, apoyar; (*horse: at races*) apostar a; (*car*) dar marcha atrás a *or* con ♦ *vi (car etc)* dar marcha atrás ♦ *a (in compounds)* de atrás; **~ seats/wheels** (*AUT*) asientos *mpl*/ruedas *fpl* de atrás; **~ garden/room** jardín *m*/habitación *f* de atrás; **~ payments** pagos *mpl* con efecto retroactivo; **~ rent** renta atrasada; **to take a ~ seat** (*fig*) pasar a segundo plano ♦ *ad (not forward)* (hacia) atrás; **he's ~** (*returned*) está de vuelta, ha vuelto; **he ran ~** volvió corriendo; **throw the ball ~** (*restitution*) devuelve la pelota; **can I have it ~?** ¿me lo devuelve?; **he called ~** (*again*) llamó de nuevo; **~ and forth** el uno al otro, entre sí; **as far ~ as the 13th century** ya en el siglo XIII; **when will you be ~?** ¿cuándo volverá?
back down *vi* echarse atrás.

back on to *vt fus:* **the house ~s on to the golf course** por atrás la casa da al campo de golf.
back out *vi (of promise)* volverse atrás.
back up *vt (support: person)* apoyar, respaldar; (: *theory*) defender; (*car*) dar marcha atrás a; (*COMPUT*) hacer una copia preventiva *or* de reserva de.
backache ['bækeɪk] *n* dolor *m* de espalda.
backbencher ['bæk'bɛntʃə*] *n (Brit) miembro/a del parlamento sin portafolio.*
backbiting ['bækbaɪtɪŋ] *n* murmuración *f.*
backbone ['bækbəʊn] *n* columna vertebral; **the ~ of the organization** el pilar de la organización.
backchat ['bæktʃæt] *n* réplicas *fpl.*
backcloth ['bækklɒθ] *n* telón *m* de fondo.
backcomb ['bækkəʊm] *vt* cardar.
backdate [bæk'deɪt] *vt (letter)* poner fecha atrasada a; **~d pay rise** alza de sueldo con efecto retroactivo.
backdrop ['bækdrɒp] *n* = **backcloth.**
backer ['bækə*] *n* partidario/a; (*COMM*) promotor(a) *m/f.*
backfire [bæk'faɪə*] *vi* (*AUT*) petardear; (*plans*) fallar, salir mal.
backgammon ['bækgæmən] *n* backgammon *m.*
background ['bækgraʊnd] *n* fondo; (*of events*) antecedentes *mpl;* (*basic knowledge*) bases *fpl;* (*experience*) conocimientos *mpl,* educación *f* ♦ *cpd (noise, music)* de fondo; (*COMPUT*) secundario; **~ reading** lectura de fondo, preparación *f;* **~ family** ~ origen *m,* antecedentes *mpl.*
backhand ['bækhænd] *n* (*TENNIS: also:* **~ stroke**) revés *m.*
backhanded ['bæk'hændɪd] *a (fig)* ambiguo, equívoco.
backhander ['bæk'hændə*] *n (Brit: bribe)* soborno.
backing ['bækɪŋ] *n (fig)* apoyo, respaldo; (*COMM*) respaldo financiero; (*MUS*) acompañamiento.
backlash ['bæklæʃ] *n* reacción *f,* resaca.
backlog ['bæklɒg] *n:* **~ of work** atrasos *mpl.*
back number *n (of magazine etc)* número atrasado.
backpack ['bækpæk] *n* mochila.
backpacker ['bækpækə*] *n* mochilero/a.
back pay *n* pago atrasado.
backpedal ['bækpɛdl] *vi (fig)* volverse/ echarse atrás.
backside ['bæksaɪd] *n (col)* trasero, culo.
backslash ['bækslæʃ] *n* pleca, barra inversa.
backslide ['bækslaɪd] *vi* reincidir, recaer.
backspace ['bækspeɪs] *vi (in typing)* retroceder.
backstage [bæk'steɪdʒ] *ad* entre bastidores.
back-street ['bækstriːt] *a* de barrio; **~ abortionist** abortista *m/f* ilegal.

backstroke ['bækstrəuk] *n* braza de espaldas.
backtrack ['bæktræk] *vi* (*fig*) = **backpedal**.
backup ['bækʌp] *a* (*train, plane*) suplementario; (*COMPUT: disk, file*) de reserva ♦ *n* (*support*) apoyo; (*also:* ~ **file**) copia preventiva *or* de reserva; (*US: congestion*) embotellamiento, acumulación *f*.
back-up lights *npl* (*US*) luces *fpl* de marcha atrás.
backward ['bækwəd] *a* (*movement*) hacia atrás; (*person, country*) atrasado; (*shy*) tímido.
backwardness ['bækwədnɪs] *n* atraso.
backwards ['bækwədz] *ad* (*move, go*) hacia atrás; (*read a list*) al revés; (*fall*) de espaldas; **to know sth ~** *or* (*US*) ~ **and forwards** (*col*) saberse algo al dedillo.
backwater ['bækwɔːtə*] *n* (*fig*) lugar *m* atrasado *or* apartado.
backyard [bæk'jɑːd] *n* traspatio.
bacon ['beɪkən] *n* tocino, beicon *m*.
bacteria [bæk'tɪərɪə] *npl* bacteria *sg*.
bacteriology [bæktɪərɪ'ɔlədʒɪ] *n* bacteriología.
bad [bæd] *a* malo; (*serious*) grave; (*meat, food*) podrido, pasado; **his ~ leg** su pierna lisiada; **to go ~** pasarse; **to have a ~ time of it** pasarlo mal; **I feel ~ about it** (*guilty*) tengo remordimientos; **~ debt** (*COMM*) cuenta incobrable; **in ~ faith** de mala fe.
bade [bæd, beɪd] *pt of* **bid**.
badge [bædʒ] *n* insignia; (*metal ~*) chapa, placa; (*stick-on*) pegatina.
badger ['bædʒə*] *n* tejón *m*.
badly ['bædlɪ] *ad* (*work, dress etc*) mal; **~ wounded** gravemente herido; **he needs it ~** le hace gran falta; **to be ~ off (for money)** andar mal de dinero; **things are going ~** las cosas van muy mal.
bad-mannered ['bæd'mænəd] *a* grosero, mal educado.
badminton ['bædmɪntən] *n* bádminton *m*.
bad-tempered ['bæd'tempəd] *a* de mal genio *or* carácter; (*temporary*) de mal humor.
baffle ['bæfl] *vt* desconcertar, confundir.
baffling ['bæflɪŋ] *a* incomprensible.
bag [bæg] *n* bolsa, saco; (*handbag*) bolso; (*satchel*) mochila; (*case*) maleta; (*of hunter*) caza ♦ *vt* (*col: take*) coger (*Sp*), agarrar (*LAm*), pescar; **~s of** (*col: lots of*) un montón de; **to pack one's ~s** hacer las maletas.
bagful ['bægful] *n* saco (lleno).
baggage ['bægɪdʒ] *n* equipaje *m*.
baggage claim *n* reclamación *f* de equipajes.
baggy ['bægɪ] *a* (*trousers*) con rodilleras.
Baghdad [bæg'dæd] *n* Bagdad *m*.
bagpipes ['bægpaɪps] *npl* gaita *sg*.
bag-snatcher ['bægsnætʃə*] *n* (*Brit*)

ladrón/ona *m/f* de bolsos.
bag-snatching ['bægsnætʃɪŋ] *n* (*Brit*) tirón *m* (de bolsos).
Bahamas [bə'hɑːməz] *npl*: **the ~** las Islas Bahama.
Bahrain [bɑː'reɪn] *n* Bahrein *m*.
bail [beɪl] *n* fianza ♦ *vt* (*prisoner: also:* **grant ~ to**) poner en libertad bajo fianza; (*boat: also:* ~ **out**) achicar; **on ~** (*prisoner*) bajo fianza; **to be released on ~** ser puesto en libertad bajo fianza; **to ~ sb out** obtener la libertad de uno bajo fianza; *see also* **bale**.
bailiff ['beɪlɪf] *n* alguacil *m*.
bait [beɪt] *n* cebo ♦ *vt* cebar.
bake [beɪk] *vt* cocer (al horno) ♦ *vi* (*cook*) cocerse; (*be hot*) hacer un calor terrible.
baked beans *npl* judías *fpl* en salsa de tomate.
baker ['beɪkə*] *n* panadero/a.
baker's dozen *n* docena del fraile.
bakery ['beɪkərɪ] *n* (*for bread*) panadería; (*for cakes*) pastelería.
baking ['beɪkɪŋ] *n* (*act*) amasar *m*; (*batch*) hornada.
baking powder *n* levadura (en polvo).
baking tin *n* tortera.
balaclava [bælə'klɑːvə] *n* (*also:* ~ **helmet**) pasamontañas *m inv*.
balance ['bæləns] *n* equilibrio; (*COMM: sum*) balance *m*; (*remainder*) resto; (*scales*) balanza ♦ *vt* equilibrar; (*budget*) nivelar; (*account*) saldar; (*compensate*) contrapesar; **~ of trade/payments** balanza de comercio/pagos; **~ carried forward** balance *m* pasado a cuenta nueva; **~ brought forward** saldo de hoja anterior; **to ~ the books** hacer el balance.
balanced ['bælənst] *a* (*personality, diet*) equilibrado.
balance sheet *n* balance *m*.
balcony ['bælkənɪ] *n* (*open*) balcón *m*; (*closed*) galería.
bald [bɔːld] *a* calvo; (*tyre*) liso.
baldness ['bɔːldnɪs] *n* calvicie *f*.
bale [beɪl] *n* (*AGR*) paca, fardo.
bale out *vi* (*of a plane*) lanzarse en paracaídas ♦ *vt* (*NAUT: water*) sacar; (*: boat*) achicar; **to ~ sb out of a difficulty** sacar a uno de un problema.
Balearic Islands [bælɪ'ærɪk-] *npl*: **the ~** las Islas Baleares.
baleful ['beɪlful] *a* (*look*) triste; (*sinister*) funesto, siniestro.
balk [bɔːk] *vi*: **to ~ (at)** resistirse (a); (*horse*) plantarse (ante).
Balkan ['bɔːlkən] *a* balcánico ♦ *n*: **the ~s** los Balcanes.
ball [bɔːl] *n* (*sphere*) bola; (*football*) balón *m*; (*for tennis, golf etc*) pelota; (*dance*) baile *m;* **to be on the ~** (*fig: competent*) estar enterado; (*: alert*) ser despabilado; **to play ~ (with sb)** jugar a la pelota (con

uno); (*fig*) cooperar; **to start the ~ rolling**
(*fig*) empezar; **the ~ is in your court** (*fig*)
le toca a usted.
ballad ['bæləd] *n* balada, romance *m*.
ballast ['bæləst] *n* lastre *m*.
ball bearing *n* cojinete *m* de bolas.
ballcock ['bɔːlkɔk] *n* llave *f* de bola *or* de
flotador.
ballerina [bælə'riːnə] *n* bailarina.
ballet ['bæleɪ] *n* ballet *m*.
ballet dancer *n* bailarín/ina *m/f* (de
ballet).
ballistic [bə'lɪstɪk] *a* balístico; **intercontinental ~ missile** misil *m* balístico intercontinental.
ballistics [bə'lɪstɪks] *n* balística.
balloon [bə'luːn] *n* globo; (*in comic strip*)
globo, bocadillo ♦ *vi* dispararse.
balloonist [bə'luːnɪst] *n* ascensionista *m/f*.
ballot ['bælət] *n* votación *f*.
ballot box *n* urna (electoral).
ballot paper *n* papeleta.
ballpark ['bɔːlpɑːk] *n* (*US*) estadio de béisbol.
ball-point pen ['bɔːlpɔɪnt-] *n* bolígrafo.
ballroom ['bɔːlrum] *n* salón *m* de baile.
balm [bɑːm] *n* (*also fig*) bálsamo.
balmy ['bɑːmɪ] *a* (*breeze*, *air*) suave, fragante; (*col*) = **barmy.**
BALPA ['bælpə] *n abbr* (= *British Airline
Pilots' Association*) *sindicato de pilotos de
líneas aéreas.*
balsa ['bɔːlsə] *n* (madera de) balsa.
Baltic ['bɔːltɪk] *a* báltico ♦ *n*: **the ~ (Sea)**
el (Mar) Báltico.
balustrade ['bæləstreɪd] *n* barandilla.
bamboo [bæm'buː] *n* bambú *m*.
bamboozle [bæm'buːzl] *vt* (*col*) embaucar,
engatusar.
ban [bæn] *n* prohibición *f*, proscripción *f* ♦
vt prohibir, proscribir; (*exclude*) excluir;
he was ~ned from driving le prohibieron
conducir.
banal [bə'nɑːl] *a* banal, vulgar.
banana [bə'nɑːnə] *n* plátano, banana
(*LAm*).
band [bænd] *n* (*group*) banda; (*gang*)
pandilla; (*strip*) faja, tira; (: *circular*)
anillo; (*at a dance*) orquesta; (*MIL*) banda.
band together *vi* juntarse, asociarse.
bandage ['bændɪdʒ] *n* venda, vendaje *m* ♦
vt vendar.
bandaid ® ['bændeɪd] *n* (*US*) tirita.
bandit ['bændɪt] *n* bandido; **one-armed ~**
máquina tragaperras.
bandstand ['bændstænd] *n* quiosco.
bandwagon ['bændwægən] *n*: **to jump on
the ~** (*fig*) subirse al carro.
bandy ['bændɪ] *vt* (*jokes*, *insults*) cambiar.
bandy-legged ['bændɪ'legd] *a* estevado.
bane [beɪn] *n*: **it** (*or* **he** *etc*) **is the ~ of my
life** me amarga la vida.
bang [bæŋ] *n* estallido; (*of door*) portazo;

(*blow*) golpe *m* ♦ *vt* hacer estallar; (*door*)
cerrar de golpe ♦ *vi* estallar ♦ *ad*: **to be
~ on time** (*col*) llegar en punto; **to ~ into**
sth chocar con algo, golpearse contra algo;
see also **bangs.**
banger ['bæŋə*] *n* (*Brit*: *car*: *also*: **old ~**)
armatoste *m*, cacharro; (*Brit col*: *sausage*)
salchicha; (*firework*) petardo.
Bangkok [bæŋ'kɔk] *n* Bangkok *m*.
Bangladesh [bæŋglə'deʃ] *n* Bangladesh *f*.
bangle ['bæŋgl] *n* ajorca.
bangs [bæŋz] *npl* (*US*) flequillo *sg*.
banish ['bænɪʃ] *vt* desterrar.
banister(s) ['bænɪstə(z)] *n*(*pl*) pasamanos
m inv.
banjo, *pl* **~es** *or* **~s** ['bændʒəu] *n* banjo.
bank [bæŋk] *n* (*COMM*) banco; (*of river*,
lake) ribera, orilla; (*of earth*) terraplén *m*
♦ *vi* (*AVIAT*) ladearse; (*COMM*): **to ~ with**
tener la cuenta con.
bank on *vt fus* contar con.
bank account *n* cuenta de banco.
bank card *n* = **banker's card.**
bank charges *npl* comisión *fsg*.
bank draft *n* giro bancario.
banker ['bæŋkə*] *n* banquero; **~'s card**
(*Brit*) tarjeta bancaria; **~'s order** orden *f*
bancaria.
bank giro *n* giro bancario.
Bank holiday *n* (*Brit*) día *m* festivo.
banking ['bæŋkɪŋ] *n* banca.
bank loan *n* empréstito.
bank manager *n* director(a) *m/f* local del
banco.
banknote ['bæŋknəut] *n* billete *m* de banco.
bank rate *n* tipo de interés bancario.
bankrupt ['bæŋkrʌpt] *n* quebrado/a ♦ *a*
quebrado, insolvente; **to go ~** hacer
bancarrota; **to be ~** estar en quiebra.
bankruptcy ['bæŋkrʌptsɪ] *n* quiebra,
bancarrota.
bank statement *n* extracto de cuenta.
banner ['bænə*] *n* bandera; (*in demonstration*) pancarta.
banns [bænz] *npl* amonestaciones *fpl*.
banquet ['bæŋkwɪt] *n* banquete *m*.
banter ['bæntə*] *n* guasa, chungas *fpl*.
BAOR *n abbr* (= *British Army of the
Rhine*) *fuerzas británicas en Alemania.*
baptism ['bæptɪzəm] *n* bautismo; (*act*) bautizo.
baptize [bæp'taɪz] *vt* bautizar.
bar [bɑː*] *n* barra; (*on door*) tranca; (*of
window*, *cage*) reja; (*of soap*) pastilla; (*fig*:
hindrance) obstáculo; (*prohibition*) proscripción *f*; (*pub*) bar *m*; (*counter*: *in pub*)
mostrador *m*; (*MUS*) barra ♦ *vt* (*road*) obstruir; (*window*, *door*) atrancar; (*person*)
excluir; (*activity*) prohibir; **behind ~s**
entre rejas; **the B~** (*LAW*: *profession*) la
abogacía; (: *people*) el cuerpo de abogra-
dos; **~ none** sin excepción.
Barbados [bɑː'beɪdɔs] *n* Barbados *m*.

barbarian [bɑː'bɛərɪən] n bárbaro/a.
barbaric [bɑː'bærɪk] a bárbaro.
barbarity [bɑː'bærɪtɪ] n barbaridad f.
barbarous ['bɑːbərəs] a bárbaro.
barbecue ['bɑːbɪkjuː] n barbacoa.
barbed wire ['bɑːbd-] n alambre m de púas.
barber ['bɑːbə*] n peluquero, barbero.
barbiturate [bɑː'bɪtjurɪt] n barbitúrico.
Barcelona [bɑːsɪ'ləunə] n Barcelona.
bar chart n gráfico de barras.
bar code n código de barras.
bare [bɛə*] a desnudo; (head) descubierto ◆ vt desnudar; **to ~ one's teeth** enseñar los dientes.
bareback ['bɛəbæk] ad sin silla.
barefaced ['bɛəfeɪst] a descarado.
barefoot ['bɛəfut] a, ad descalzo.
bareheaded [bɛə'hɛdɪd] a descubierto, sin sombrero.
barely ['bɛəlɪ] ad apenas.
bareness ['bɛənɪs] n desnudez f.
Barents Sea ['bærənts-] n: **the ~** el Mar de Barents.
bargain ['bɑːgɪn] n pacto, negocio; (good buy) ganga ◆ vi negociar; (haggle) regatear; **into the ~** además, por añadidura.
  bargain for vt fus (col): **he got more than he ~ed for** le resultó peor de lo que esperaba.
bargaining ['bɑːgənɪŋ] n negociación f; regateo; **~ table** mesa de negociaciones.
barge [bɑːdʒ] n barcaza.
  barge in vi irrumpir; (conversation) entrometerse.
  barge into vt fus dar contra.
baritone ['bærɪtəun] n barítono.
barium meal ['bɛərɪəm-] n (MED) comida de bario.
bark [bɑːk] n (of tree) corteza; (of dog) ladrido ◆ vi ladrar.
barley ['bɑːlɪ] n cebada.
barley sugar n azúcar m cande.
barmaid ['bɑːmeɪd] n camarera.
barman ['bɑːmən] n camarero, barman m.
barmy ['bɑːmɪ] a (col) chiflado, lelo.
barn [bɑːn] n granero; (for animals) cuadra.
barnacle ['bɑːnəkl] n percebe m.
barometer [bə'rɒmɪtə*] n barómetro.
baron ['bærən] n barón m; (fig) magnate m; **the press ~s** los magnates de la prensa.
baroness ['bærənɪs] n baronesa.
baroque [bə'rɔk] a barroco.
barracks ['bærəks] npl cuartel msg.
barrage ['bærɑːʒ] n (MIL) descarga, bombardeo; (dam) presa; (fig: of criticism etc) lluvia, aluvión m; **a ~ of questions** una lluvia de preguntas.
barrel ['bærəl] n tonel m, barril m; (of gun) cañón m.
barren ['bærən] a estéril.

barricade [bærɪ'keɪd] n barricada ◆ vt cerrar con barricadas.
barrier ['bærɪə*] n barrera; (crash ~) barrera.
barrier cream n crema protectora.
barring ['bɑːrɪŋ] prep excepto, salvo.
barrister ['bærɪstə*] n (Brit) abogado/a.
barrow ['bærəu] n (cart) carretilla (de mano).
barstool ['bɑːstuːl] n taburete m (de bar).
Bart. abbr (Brit) = baronet.
bartender ['bɑːtɛndə*] n (US) camarero, barman m.
barter ['bɑːtə*] vt: **to ~ sth for sth** trocar algo por algo.
base [beɪs] n base f ◆ vt: **to ~ sth on** basar or fundar algo en ◆ a bajo, infame; **to ~ at** (troops) estacionar en; **I'm ~d in London** (work) trabajo en Londres.
baseball ['beɪsbɔːl] n béisbol m.
base camp n campamento base.
Basel ['bɑːzəl] n Basilea.
baseless ['beɪslɪs] a infundado.
basement ['beɪsmənt] n sótano.
base rate n tipo base.
bases ['beɪsiːz] npl of **basis**; ['beɪsɪz] npl of **base**.
bash [bæʃ] n: **I'll have a ~ (at it)** lo intentaré ◆ vt (col) golpear.
  bash up vt (col: car) estrellar; (: person) aporrear, vapulear.
bashful ['bæʃful] a tímido, vergonzoso.
bashing ['bæʃɪŋ] n (col) tunda; **to go Paki-/queer-~** ir a dar una paliza a los paquistaníes/a los maricas.
BASIC ['beɪsɪk] n BASIC m.
basic ['beɪsɪk] a (salary etc) básico; (elementary: principles) fundamental.
basically ['beɪsɪklɪ] ad fundamentalmente, en el fondo.
basic rate n (of tax) base f mínima imponible.
basil ['bæzl] n albahaca.
basin ['beɪsn] n (vessel) cuenco, tazón m; (GEO) cuenca; (also: **wash~**) palangana, jofaina.
basis ['beɪsɪs], pl **-ses** [-siːz] n base f; **on the ~ of what you've said** a base de lo que has dicho.
bask [bɑːsk] vi: **to ~ in the sun** tomar el sol.
basket ['bɑːskɪt] n cesta, cesto; (with handle) canasta.
basketball ['bɑːskɪtbɔːl] n baloncesto.
basketball player n jugador(a) m/f de baloncesto.
basketwork ['bɑːskɪtwəːk] n cestería.
Basle [bɑːl] n Basilea.
Basque [bæsk] a, n vasco/a m/f.
Basque Country n Euskadi m, País m Vasco.
bass [beɪs] n (MUS) contrabajo.
bass clef n clave f de fa.

bassoon [bə'suːn] *n* bajón *m*.

bastard ['bɑːstəd] *n* bastardo/a; (*col!*) hijo de puta (*!*).

baste [beɪst] *vt* (*CULIN*) pringar.

bastion ['bæstɪən] *n* bastión *m*, baluarte *m*.

BASW *n abbr* (= *British Association of Social Workers*) sindicato de asistentes sociales.

bat [bæt] *n* (*ZOOL*) murciélago; (*for ball games*) palo; (*for cricket, baseball*) bate *m*; (*Brit: for table tennis*) pala; **he didn't ~ an eyelid** ni pestañeó, ni se inmutó.

batch [bætʃ] *n* (*of bread*) hornada; (*of goods, work*) lote *m*; (*of applicants, letters*) montón *m*.

batch processing *n* (*COMPUT*) proceso por lotes.

bated ['beɪtɪd] *a*: **with ~ breath** sin respirar.

bath [bɑːθ, *pl* bɑːðz] *n* (*action*) baño; (*~tub*) baño, bañera, tina (*LAm*) ♦ *vt* bañar; **to have a ~** bañarse, tomar un baño; *see also* **baths**.

bathchair ['bɑːθtʃɛə*] *n* silla de ruedas.

bathe [beɪð] *vi* bañarse; (*US*) tomar un baño ♦ *vt* (*wound etc*) lavar; (*US*) bañar, dar un baño a.

bather ['beɪðə*] *n* bañista *m/f*.

bathing ['beɪðɪŋ] *n* el bañarse.

bathing cap *n* gorro de baño.

bathing costume, (*US*) **bathing suit** *n* traje *m* de baño.

bathing trunks *npl* bañador *m*.

bathmat ['bɑːθmæt] *n* estera de baño.

bathrobe ['bɑːθrəub] *n* (*man's*) batín *m*; (*woman's*) bata.

bathroom ['bɑːθrum] *n* (cuarto de) baño.

baths [bɑːðz] *npl* piscina *sg*.

bath towel *n* toalla de baño.

bathtub ['bɑːθtʌb] *n* bañera.

batman ['bætmən] *n* (*Brit*) ordenanza *m*.

baton ['bætən] *n* (*MUS*) batuta.

battalion [bə'tælɪən] *n* batallón *m*.

batten ['bætn] *n* (*CARPENTRY*) listón *m*; (*NAUT*) junquillo, sable *m*.

batten down *vt* (*NAUT*): **to ~ down the hatches** atrancar las escotillas.

batter ['bætə*] *vt* apalear, azotar ♦ *n* batido.

battered ['bætəd] *a* (*hat, pan*) estropeado.

battery ['bætərɪ] *n* batería; (*of torch*) pila.

battery charger *n* cargador *m* de baterías.

battery farming *n* cría intensiva.

battle ['bætl] *n* batalla; (*fig*) lucha ♦ *vi* luchar; **that's half the ~** (*col*) ya hay medio camino andado; **to fight a losing ~** (*fig*) ir perdiendo poco a poco.

battlefield ['bætlfiːld] *n* campo *m* de batalla.

battlements ['bætlmənts] *npl* almenas *fpl*.

battleship ['bætlʃɪp] *n* acorazado.

batty ['bætɪ] *a* chalado.

bauble ['bɔːbl] *n* chuchería.

baud [bɔːd] *n* (*COMPUT*) baudio.

baud rate *n* (*COMPUT*) velocidad *f* (de transmisión) en baudios.

bauxite ['bɔːksaɪt] *n* bauxita.

Bavaria [bə'vɛərɪə] *n* Baviera.

Bavarian [bə'vɛərɪən] *a, n* baviero/a *m/f*.

bawdy ['bɔːdɪ] *a* indecente; (*joke*) verde.

bawl [bɔːl] *vi* chillar, gritar.

bay [beɪ] *n* (*GEO*) bahía; (*for parking*) parking *m*, estacionamiento; (*loading ~*) patio de carga; (*BOT*) laurel *m* ♦ *vi* aullar; **to hold sb at ~** mantener a alguien a raya.

bay leaf *n* (hoja de) laurel *m*.

bayonet ['beɪənɪt] *n* bayoneta.

bay window *n* ventana salediza.

bazaar [bə'zɑː*] *n* bazar *m*.

bazooka [bə'zuːkə] *n* bazuca.

BB *n abbr* (*Brit*: = *Boys' Brigade*) organización juvenil para chicos.

B. & B. *n abbr* (= *bed and breakfast*) cama y desayuno.

BBB *n abbr* (*US*: = *Better Business Bureau*) organismo para la defensa del consumidor.

BBC *n abbr* (= *British Broadcasting Corporation*) cadena de radio y televisión estatal británica.

BBE *n abbr* (*US*: = *Benevolent and Protective Order of Elks*) organización benéfica.

BC *ad abbr* (= *before Christ*) a. de J.C. ♦ *abbr* (*Canada*) = *British Columbia*.

BCG *n abbr* (= *Bacillus Calmette-Guérin*) vacuna de la tuberculosis.

BD *n abbr* (= *Bachelor of Divinity*) Licenciado/a en Teología.

B/D *abbr* = **bank draft**.

BDS *n abbr* (= *Bachelor of Dental Surgery*) título universitario.

be, *pt* **was, were**, *pp* **been** [biː, wɔz, wɔː*, biːn] *vi* (*of state*) ser; (*of place, temporary condition*) estar; **I am English** soy inglés; **I am tired** estoy cansado; **how are you?** ¿cómo está usted?; **who is it?** ¿quién es?; **it's only me** (*emphatic*) soy yo; **it is raining** está lloviendo; **I am warm** tengo calor; **it is cold** hace frío; **how much is it?** ¿cuánto es or cuesta?; **he is four (years old)** tiene cuatro años; **2 and 2 are 4** dos más dos son cuatro; **it's 8 o'clock** son las 8; **where have you been?** ¿dónde has estado?, ¿de dónde vienes? ♦ *aux vb*: **what are you doing?** ¿qué estás haciendo?; **I've been waiting for her for two hours** le he estado esperando durante dos horas; **to ~ killed** ser matado; **he is nowhere to ~ found** no se le ve en ninguna parte; **the car is to ~ sold** el coche está de venta; **he was to have come yesterday** debía de haber venido ayer; **am I to understand that ...?** ¿debo entender que ...?; **if I were you** yo que tú.

B/E *abbr* = **bill of exchange**.

beach [biːtʃ] *n* playa ♦ *vt* varar.

beach buggy [-bʌgɪ] *n* buggy *m*.
beachcomber ['biːtʃkəumə*] *n* raquero/a.
beachwear ['biːtʃwɛə*] *n* ropa de playa.
beacon ['biːkən] *n* (*lighthouse*) faro; (*marker*) guía; (*radio* ~) radiofaro.
bead [biːd] *n* cuenta, abalorio; (*of dew, sweat*) gota; ~s *npl* (*necklace*) collar *m*.
beady ['biːdɪ] *a* (*eyes*) pequeño y brillante.
beagle ['biːgl] *n* sabueso pequeño.
beak [biːk] *n* pico.
beaker ['biːkə*] *n* jarra.
beam [biːm] *n* (ARCH) viga, travesaño; (*of light*) rayo, haz *m* de luz; (*RADIO*) rayo ◆ *vi* brillar; (*smile*) sonreír; **to drive on full** *or* **main** ~ conducir con luz de carretera.
beaming ['biːmɪŋ] *a* (*sun, smile*) radiante.
bean [biːn] *n* judía; **runner/broad** ~ habichuela/haba; **coffee** ~ grano de café.
beanshoots ['biːnʃuːts] *npl*, **beansprouts** ['biːnsprauts] *npl* brotes *mpl* de soja.
bear [bɛə*] *n* oso; (*STOCK EXCHANGE*) bajista *m* ◆ (*vb*: *pt* **bore**, *pp* **borne**) *vt* (*weight etc*) llevar; (*cost*) pagar; (*responsibility*) tener; (*traces, signs*) mostrar; (*produce*: *fruit*) dar; (*COMM*: *interest*) devengar; (*endure*) soportar, aguantar; (*stand up to*) resistir a; (*children*) parir ◆ *vi*: **to** ~ **right/left** torcer a la derecha/izquierda; **I can't** ~ **him** no le puedo ver, no lo soporto; **to bring pressure to** ~ **on sb** ejercer presión sobre uno.
bear on *vt fus* tener que ver con, referirse a.
bear out *vt fus* (*suspicions*) corroborar, confirmar; (*person*) llevar.
bear up *vi* (*cheer up*) animarse; **he bore up well under the strain** resistió bien la presión.
bear with *vt fus* (*sb's moods, temper*) tener paciencia con.
bearable ['bɛərəbl] *a* soportable, aguantable.
beard [bɪəd] *n* barba.
bearded ['bɪədɪd] *a* barbado.
bearer ['bɛərə*] *n* (*of news, cheque*) portador(a) *m/f*; (*of passport*) titular *m/f*.
bearing ['bɛərɪŋ] *n* porte *m*, comportamiento; (*connection*) relación *f*; (**ball**) ~**s** *npl* cojinetes *mpl* a bolas; **to take a** ~ marcarse; **to find one's** ~**s** orientarse.
bearskin ['bɛəskɪn] *n* (MIL) gorro militar (*de piel de oso*).
beast [biːst] *n* bestia; (*col*) bruto, salvaje *m*.
beastly ['biːstlɪ] *a* bestial; (*awful*) horrible.
beat [biːt] *n* (*of heart*) latido; (MUS) ritmo, compás *m*; (*of policeman*) ronda ◆ (*vb*: *pt* **beat**, *pp* **beaten**) *vt* (*hit*) golpear; (*eggs*) batir; (*defeat*) vencer, derrotar; (*better*) sobrepasar; (*drum*) tocar; (*rhythm*) marcar ◆ *vi* (*heart*) latir; **off the** ~**en track** aislado; **to** ~ **about the bush** ir por rodeos; **to** ~ **it** largarse; **that** ~**s every-**

thing! (*col*) ¡eso es el colmo!; **to** ~ **on a door** dar golpes en una puerta.
beat down *vt* (*door*) derribar a golpes; (*price*) conseguir rebajar, regatear; (*seller*) hacer rebajar ◆ *vi* (*rain*) llover a cántaros; (*sun*) caer de plomo.
beat off *vt* rechazar.
beat up *vt* (*col*: *person*) dar una paliza a.
beater ['biːtə*] *n* (*for eggs, cream*) batidora.
beating ['biːtɪŋ] *n* golpeo; (*defeat*) derrota; **to take a** ~ salir derrotado.
beat-up ['biːtʌp] *a* (*col*) estropeado.
beautiful ['bjuːtɪful] *a* hermoso, bello.
beautifully ['bjuːtɪfəlɪ] *ad* maravillosamente.
beautify ['bjuːtɪfaɪ] *vt* embellecer.
beauty ['bjuːtɪ] *n* belleza, hermosura; (*concept, person*) belleza; **the** ~ **of it is that ...** lo mejor de esto es que ....
beauty contest *n* concurso de belleza.
beauty queen *n* reina de la belleza.
beauty salon *n* salón *m* de belleza.
beauty spot *n* lunar *m* postizo; (*Brit*: *TOURISM*) lugar *m* pintoresco.
beaver ['biːvə*] *n* castor *m*.
becalmed [bɪ'kɑːmd] *a* encalmado.
became [bɪ'keɪm] *pt of* **become**.
because [bɪ'kɔz] *conj* porque; ~ **of** *prep* debido a, a causa de.
beck [bɛk] *n*: **to be at the** ~ **and call of** estar a disposición de.
beckon ['bɛkən] *vt* (*also*: ~ **to**) llamar con señas.
become [bɪ'kʌm] (*irg*: *like* **come**) *vi* (+ *noun*) hacerse, llegar a ser; (+ *adj*) ponerse, volverse ◆ *vt* (*suit*) favorecer, sentar bien a; **to** ~ **fat** engordarse; **to** ~ **angry** enfadarse; **it became known that ...** se descubrió que ....
becoming [bɪ'kʌmɪŋ] *a* (*behaviour*) decoroso; (*clothes*) favorecedor(a).
becquerel [bɛkə'rɛl] *n* becquerelio.
BEd *n abbr* (= *Bachelor of Education*) título universitario.
bed [bɛd] *n* cama; (*of flowers*) macizo; (*of sea, lake*) fondo; (*of coal, clay*) capa; **to go to** ~ acostarse.
bed down *vi* acostarse.
bed and breakfast (B. & B.) *n* (*place*) pensión *f*; (*terms*) cama y desayuno.
bedbug ['bɛdbʌg] *n* chinche *f*.
bedclothes ['bɛdkləuðz] *npl* ropa de cama.
bedding ['bɛdɪŋ] *n* ropa de cama.
bedeck [bɪ'dɛk] *vt* engalanar, adornar.
bedevil [bɪ'dɛvl] *vt* (*dog*) acosar; (*trouble*) fastidiar.
bedfellow ['bɛdfɛləu] *n*: **they are strange** ~**s** (*fig*) son extraños compañeros de cama.
bedlam ['bɛdləm] *n* confusión *f*.
bedpan ['bɛdpæn] *n* bacinilla (*de cama*).
bedraggled [bɪ'drægld] *a* mojado, desastra-

do.

bedridden ['bɛdrɪdn] *a* postrado (en cama).

bedrock ['bɛdrɔk] *n* (*GEO*) roca firme; (*fig*) fondo de la cuestión.

bedroom ['bɛdrum] *n* dormitorio, alcoba.

Beds *abbr* (*Brit*) = Bedfordshire.

bedside ['bɛdsaɪd] *n*: **at sb's ~** a la cabecera de alguien.

bedside lamp *n* lámpara de noche.

bedsit(ter) ['bɛdsɪt(ə*)] *n* (*Brit*) estudio, suite *m* (*LAm*).

bedspread ['bɛdsprɛd] *n* sobrecama *m*, colcha.

bedtime ['bɛdtaɪm] *n* hora de acostarse: **it's ~** es hora de acostarse *or* de irse a la cama.

bee [biː] *n* abeja; **to have a ~ in one's bonnet (about sth)** tener una idea fija (de algo).

beech [biːtʃ] *n* haya.

beef [biːf] *n* carne *f* de vaca; **roast ~** rosbif *m*.

beef up *vt* (*col*) reforzar.

beefburger ['biːfbəːgə*] *n* hamburguesa.

beefeater ['biːfiːtə*] *n* alabardero de la Torre de Londres.

beehive ['biːhaɪv] *n* colmena.

beeline ['biːlaɪn] *n*: **to make a ~ for** ir derecho a.

been [biːn] *pp of* be.

beer [bɪə*] *n* cerveza.

beer can *n* bote *m or* lata de cerveza.

beet [biːt] *n* (*US*) remolacha.

beetle ['biːtl] *n* escarabajo.

beetroot ['biːtruːt] *n* (*Brit*) remolacha.

befall [bɪ'fɔːl] *vi* (*vt*) (*irg: like* **fall**) acontecer (a).

befit [bɪ'fɪt] *vt* convenir a, corresponder a.

before [bɪ'fɔː*] *prep* (*of time*) antes de; (*of space*) delante de ♦ *conj* antes (de) que ♦ *ad* (*time*) antes, anteriormente; (*space*) delante, adelante; **~ going** antes de marcharse; **~ she goes** antes de que se vaya; **the week ~** la semana anterior; **I've never seen it ~** no lo he visto nunca.

beforehand [bɪ'fɔːhænd] *ad* de antemano, con anticipación.

befriend [bɪ'frɛnd] *vt* ofrecer amistad a, ayudar.

befuddled [bɪ'fʌdld] *a* aturdido, atontado.

beg [bɛg] *vi* pedir limosna ♦ *vt* pedir, rogar; (*entreat*) suplicar; **I ~ your pardon** (*apologising*) perdóname; (*not hearing*) ¿perdón?

began [bɪ'gæn] *pt of* **begin**.

beggar ['bɛgə*] *n* mendigo/a.

begin, *pt* **began**, *pp* **begun** [bɪ'gɪn, -gæn, -gʌn] *vt, vi* empezar, comenzar; **to ~ doing** *or* **to do sth** empezar a hacer algo; **I can't ~ to thank you** no encuentro palabras para agradecerle; **to ~ with, I'd like to know** ... en primer lugar, quisiera saber ...; **~ning from Monday** a partir del lunes.

beginner [bɪ'gɪnə*] *n* principiante *m/f*.

beginning [bɪ'gɪnɪŋ] *n* principio, comienzo; **right from the ~** desde el principio.

begrudge [bɪ'grʌdʒ] *vt*: **to ~ sb sth** tenerle envidia a alguien por algo.

beguile [bɪ'gaɪl] *vt* (*enchant*) seducir.

beguiling [bɪ'gaɪlɪŋ] *a* seductor(a), atractivo.

begun [bɪ'gʌn] *pp of* **begin**.

behalf [bɪ'hɑːf] *n*: **on ~ of**, (*US*) **in ~ of** en nombre de, por.

behave [bɪ'heɪv] *vi* (*person*) portarse, comportarse; (*thing*) funcionar; (*well: also*: **~ o.s.**) portarse bien.

behaviour, (*US*) **behavior** [bɪ'heɪvjə*] *n* comportamiento, conducta.

behead [bɪ'hɛd] *vt* decapitar, descabezar.

beheld [bɪ'hɛld] *pt, pp of* **behold**.

behind [bɪ'haɪnd] *prep* detrás de ♦ *ad* detrás, por detrás, atrás ♦ *n* trasero; **to be ~ (schedule)** ir retrasado; **~ the scenes** (*fig*) entre bastidores; **we're ~ them in technology** (*fig*) les quedamos atrás en tecnología; **to leave sth ~** olvidar *or* dejarse algo; **to be ~ with sth** estar atrasado en algo; **to be ~ with payments (on sth)** estar atrasado en el pago (de algo).

behold [bɪ'həuld] (*irg: like* **hold**) *vt* contemplar.

beige [beɪʒ] *a* color beige.

being ['biːɪŋ] *n* ser *m*; **to come into ~** nacer, aparecer.

Beirut [beɪ'ruːt] *n* Beirut *m*.

belated [bɪ'leɪtɪd] *a* atrasado, tardío.

belch [bɛltʃ] *vi* eructar ♦ *vt* (*also*: **~ out**: *smoke etc*) arrojar.

beleaguered [bɪ'liːgəd] *a* (*city, fig*) asediado; (*army*) asediado.

Belfast ['bɛlfɑːst] *n* Belfast *m*.

belfry ['bɛlfrɪ] *n* campanario.

Belgian ['bɛldʒən] *a, n* belga *m/f*.

Belgium ['bɛldʒəm] *n* Bélgica.

Belgrade [bɛl'greɪd] *n* Belgrado.

belie [bɪ'laɪ] *vt* (*give false impression of*) desmentir, contradecir.

belief [bɪ'liːf] *n* (*opinion*) opinión *f*; (*trust, faith*) fe *f*; (*acceptance as true*) creencia; **it's beyond ~** es increíble; **in the ~ that** en la creencia de que.

believable [bɪ'liːvəbl] *a* creíble.

believe [bɪ'liːv] *vt, vi* creer; **to ~ (that)** creer (que); **to ~ in** (*God, ghosts*) creer en; (*method*) ser partidario de; **he is ~d to be abroad** se cree que está en el extranjero; **I don't ~ in corporal punishment** no soy partidario del castigo corporal.

believer [bɪ'liːvə*] *n* (*in idea, activity*) partidario/a; (*REL*) creyente *m/f*, fiel *m/f*.

belittle [bɪ'lɪtl] *vt* minimizar, despreciar.

Belize [be'liːz] *n* Belice *f*.

bell [bɛl] *n* campana; (*small*) campanilla; (*on door*) timbre *m*; (*animal's*) cencerro; (*on toy etc*) cascabel *m*; **that rings a ~**

(*fig*) eso me suena.

bellboy ['bɛlbɔɪ] *n*, (*US*) **bellhop** ['bɛlhɔp] *n* botones *m inv*.

belligerent [bɪ'lɪdʒərənt] *a* (*at war*) beligerante; (*fig*) agresivo.

bellow ['bɛləu] *vi* bramar; (*person*) rugir ♦ *vt* (*orders*) gritar, vociferar.

bellows ['bɛləuz] *npl* fuelle *msg*.

bell push *n* pulsador *m* de timbre.

belly ['bɛlɪ] *n* barriga, panza.

bellyache ['bɛlɪeɪk] *n* dolor *m* de barriga *or* de tripa ♦ *vi* (*col*) quejarse.

belong [bɪ'lɔŋ] *vi*: **to ~ to** pertenecer a; (*club etc*) ser socio de; **this book ~s here** este libro va aquí.

belongings [bɪ'lɔŋɪŋz] *npl*: **personal ~** pertenencias *fpl*.

beloved [bɪ'lʌvɪd] *a*, *n* querido/a *m/f*, amado/a *m/f*.

below [bɪ'ləu] *prep* bajo, debajo de ♦ *ad* abajo, (por) debajo; **see ~** véase más abajo.

belt [bɛlt] *n* cinturón *m*; (*TECH*) correa, cinta ♦ *vt* (*thrash*) golpear con correa; **industrial ~** zona industrial.

belt out *vt* (*song*) cantar a voz en grito *or* a grito pelado.

belt up *vi* (*AUT*) ponerse el cinturón de seguridad; (*fig*, *col*) cerrar el pico.

beltway ['bɛltweɪ] *n* (*US AUT*) carretera de circunvalación.

bemoan [bɪ'məun] *vt* lamentar.

bemused [bɪ'mju:zd] *a* aturdido, confuso.

bench [bɛntʃ] *n* banco; **the B~** (*LAW*) el tribunal; (*people*) la judicatura.

bench mark *n* punto de referencia.

bend [bɛnd] *vb* (*pt*, *pp* **bent** [bɛnt]) *vt* doblar, inclinar; (*leg*, *arm*) torcer ♦ *vi* inclinarse; (*road*) curvarse ♦ *n* (*Brit*: *in road*, *river*) recodo; (*in pipe*) codo; *see also* **bends**.

bend down *vi* inclinarse, doblarse.

bend over *vi* inclinarse.

bends [bɛndz] *npl* (*MED*) apoplejía por cambios bruscos de presión.

beneath [bɪ'ni:θ] *prep* bajo, debajo de; (*unworthy of*) indigno de ♦ *ad* abajo, (por) debajo.

benefactor ['bɛnɪfæktə*] *n* bienhechor *m*.

benefactress ['bɛnɪfæktrɪs] *n* bienhechora.

beneficial [bɛnɪ'fɪʃəl] *a*: **~ to** beneficioso para.

beneficiary [bɛnɪ'fɪʃərɪ] *n* (*LAW*) beneficiario/a.

benefit ['bɛnɪfɪt] *n* beneficio, provecho; (*allowance of money*) subsidio ♦ *vt* beneficiar ♦ *vi*: **he'll ~ from it** le sacará provecho; **unemployment ~** subsidio de paro.

Benelux ['bɛnɪlʌks] *n* Benelux *m*.

benevolence [bɪ'nɛvələns] *n* benevolencia.

benevolent [bɪ'nɛvələnt] *a* benévolo.

BEng *n abbr* (= *Bachelor of Engineering*) *título universitario*.

benign [bɪ'naɪn] *a* (*person*, *MED*) benigno; (*smile*) afable.

bent [bɛnt] *pt*, *pp of* **bend** ♦ *n* inclinación *f* ♦ *a* (*wire*, *pipe*) doblado, torcido; **to be ~ on** estar empeñado en.

bequeath [bɪ'kwi:ð] *vt* legar.

bequest [bɪ'kwɛst] *n* legado.

bereaved [bɪ'ri:vd] *a* afligido ♦ *n*: **the ~** los afligidos *mpl*.

bereavement [bɪ'ri:vmənt] *n* aflicción *f*.

beret ['bɛreɪ] *n* boina.

Bering Sea ['bɛərɪŋ-] *n*: **the ~** el Mar de Bering.

Berks *abbr* (*Brit*) = *Berkshire*.

Berlin [bə:'lɪn] *n* Berlín *m*; **East/West ~** Berlín del Este/Oeste.

berm [bə:m] *n* (*US AUT*) arcén *m*.

Bermuda [bə:'mju:də] *n* las (Islas) Bermudas.

Bermuda shorts *npl* pantalones *mpl* bermudas.

Bern [bə:n] *n* Berna.

berry ['bɛrɪ] *n* baya.

berserk [bə'sə:k] *a*: **to go ~** perder los estribos.

berth [bə:θ] *n* (*bed*) litera; (*cabin*) camarote *m*; (*for ship*) amarradero ♦ *vi* atracar, amarrar; **to give sb a wide ~** (*fig*) evitarle el encuentro a uno.

beseech [bɪ'si:tʃ], *pt*, *pp* **besought** [bɪ'si:tʃ, -'sɔ:t] *vt* suplicar.

beset, *pt*, *pp* **beset** [bɪ'sɛt] *vt* (*person*) acosar ♦ *a*: **a policy ~ with dangers** una política rodeada de peligros.

besetting [bɪ'sɛtɪŋ] *a*: **his ~ sin** su pecado dominante.

beside [bɪ'saɪd] *prep* junto a, al lado de; (*compared with*) comparado con; **to be ~ o.s. with anger** estar fuera de sí; **that's ~ the point** eso no tiene nada que ver con el asunto.

besides [bɪ'saɪdz] *ad* además ♦ *prep* (*as well as*) además de; (*except*) excepto.

besiege [bɪ'si:dʒ] *vt* (*town*) sitiar; (*fig*) asediar.

besmirch [bɪ'smə:tʃ] *vt* (*fig*) manchar, mancillar.

besotted [bɪ'sɔtɪd] *a*: **~ with** encaprichado *or* encalabrinado con.

bespoke [bɪ'spəuk] *a* (*garment*) hecho a la medida; **~ tailor** sastre *m* que confecciona a la medida.

best [bɛst] *a* (el/la) mejor ♦ *ad* (lo) mejor; **the ~ part of** (*quantity*) la mayor parte de; **at ~** en el mejor de los casos; **to make the ~ of sth** sacar el mejor partido de algo; **to do one's ~** hacer todo lo posible; **to the ~ of my knowledge** que yo sepa; **to the ~ of my ability** como mejor puedo; **the ~ thing to do is ...** lo mejor (que se puede hacer) es ...; **he's not exactly patient at the ~ of times** no se puede decir que tiene paciencia en las mejores circunstancias.

bestial ['bɛstɪəl] *a* bestial.

best man *n* padrino de boda.

bestow [bɪ'stəu] *vt* otorgar; (*honour, praise*) dispensar; **to ~ sth on sb** conceder *or* dar algo a uno.

bestseller ['bɛst'sɛlə*] *n* éxito de librería, best-seller *m*.

bet [bɛt] *n* apuesta ♦ *vt, vi* (*pt, pp* **bet** *or* **betted**) apostar (*on* a); **it's a safe ~** (*fig*) es cosa segura.

Bethlehem ['bɛθlɪhɛm] *n* Belén *m*.

betray [bɪ'treɪ] *vt* traicionar; (*inform on*) delatar.

betrayal [bɪ'treɪəl] *n* traición *f*.

better ['bɛtə*] *a* mejor ♦ *ad* mejor ♦ *vt* mejorar; (*record etc*) superar ♦ *n*: **to get the ~ of sb** quedar por encima de uno; **you had ~ do it** más vale que lo hagas; **he thought ~ of it** cambió de parecer; **to get ~** mejorar(se); (*MED*) reponerse; **that's ~!** ¡eso es!; **I had ~ go** tengo que marcharme; **a change for the ~** una mejora; **~ off** *a* más acomodado.

betting ['bɛtɪŋ] *n* juego, el apostar.

betting shop *n* (*Brit*) agencia de apuestas.

between [bɪ'twi:n] *prep* entre ♦ *ad* (*time*) mientras tanto; (*place*) en medio; **the road ~ here and London** la carretera de aquí a Londres; **we only had 5 ~ us** teníamos sólo 5 entre nosotros.

bevel ['bɛvəl] *n* (*also*: **~ edge**) filo biselado.

beverage ['bɛvərɪdʒ] *n* bebida.

bevy ['bɛvɪ] *n*: **a ~ of** una bandada de.

bewail [bɪ'weɪl] *vt* lamentar.

beware [bɪ'wɛə*] *vi*: **to ~ (of)** tener cuidado (con) ♦ *excl* ¡cuidado!

bewildered [bɪ'wɪldəd] *a* aturdido, perplejo.

bewildering [bɪ'wɪldərɪŋ] *a* desconcertante.

bewitching [bɪ'wɪtʃɪŋ] *a* hechicero, encantador(a).

beyond [bɪ'jɔnd] *prep* más allá de; (*exceeding*) además de, fuera de; (*above*) superior a ♦ *ad* más allá, más lejos; **~ doubt** fuera de toda duda; **~ repair** irreparable.

b/f *abbr* (= *brought forward*) saldo anterior.

BFPO *n abbr* (= *British Forces Post Office*) servicio postal del ejército.

bhp *n abbr* (= *brake horsepower*) caballo indicado al freno.

bi ... [baɪ] *pref* bi ....

biannual [baɪ'ænjuəl] *a* semestral.

bias ['baɪəs] *n* (*prejudice*) prejuicio, pasión *f*; (*preference*) predisposición *f*.

bias(s)ed ['baɪəst] *a* parcial; **to be ~ against** tener perjuicios contra.

bib [bɪb] *n* babero.

Bible ['baɪbl] *n* Biblia.

biblical ['bɪblɪkəl] *a* bíblico.

bibliography [bɪblɪ'ɔgrəfɪ] *n* bibliografía.

bicarbonate of soda [baɪ'kɑːbənɪt-] *n* bicarbonato de soda.

bicentenary [baɪsɛn'tiːnərɪ], (*US*) **bicentennial** [baɪsɛn'tɛnɪəl] *n* bicentenario.

biceps ['baɪsɛps] *n* bíceps *m*.

bicker ['bɪkə*] *vi* reñir.

bickering ['bɪkərɪŋ] *n* riñas *fpl*, altercados *mpl*.

bicycle ['baɪsɪkl] *n* bicicleta.

bicycle path *n* camino para ciclistas.

bicycle pump *n* bomba de bicicleta.

bid [bɪd] *n* (*at auction*) oferta, postura; (*attempt*) tentativa, conato ♦ *vi* (*pt, pp* **bid**) hacer una oferta ♦ *vt* (*pt* **bade** [bæd], *pp* **bidden** ['bɪdn]) mandar, ordenar; **to ~ sb good day** dar a uno los buenos días.

bidder *n*: **the highest ~** el mejor postor.

bidding ['bɪdɪŋ] *n* (*at auction*) ofertas *fpl*; (*order*) orden *f*, mandato.

bide [baɪd] *vt*: **to ~ one's time** esperar el momento adecuado.

bidet ['biːdeɪ] *n* bidet *m*.

bidirectional ['baɪdɪ'rɛkʃənl] *a* bidireccional.

biennial [baɪ'ɛnɪəl] *a, n* bienal *f*.

bier [bɪə*] *n* féretro.

bifocals [baɪ'fəuklz] *npl* gafas *fpl or* anteojos *mpl* (*LAm*) bifocales.

big [bɪg] *a* grande; **~ business** gran negocio; **to do things in a ~ way** hacer las cosas en grande.

bigamy ['bɪgəmɪ] *n* bigamia.

big dipper [-'dɪpə*] *n* montaña rusa.

big end *n* (*AUT*) cabeza de biela.

bigheaded ['bɪg'hɛdɪd] *a* engreído.

bigot ['bɪgət] *n* fanático/a, intolerante *m/f*.

bigoted ['bɪgətɪd] *a* fanático, intolerante.

bigotry ['bɪgətrɪ] *n* fanatismo, intolerancia.

big toe *n* dedo gordo (del pie).

big top *n* (*circus*) circo; (*main tent*) tienda principal.

big wheel *n* (*at fair*) noria.

bigwig ['bɪgwɪg] *n* (*col*) pez *m* gordo.

bike [baɪk] *n* bici *f*.

bikini [bɪ'kiːnɪ] *n* bikini *m*.

bilateral [baɪ'lætərl] *a* (*agreement*) bilateral.

bile [baɪl] *n* bilis *f*.

bilge [bɪldʒ] *n* (*water*) agua de pantoque.

bilingual [baɪ'lɪŋgwəl] *a* bilingüe.

bilious ['bɪlɪəs] *a* bilioso (*also fig*).

bill [bɪl] *n* (*gen*) cuenta; (*invoice*) factura; (*POL*) proyecto de ley; (*US: banknote*) billete *m*; (*of bird*) pico; (*notice*) cartel *m*; (*THEATRE*) programa *m* ♦ *vt* extender *or* pasar la factura a; **may I have the ~ please?** ¿puede traerme la cuenta, por favor?; **~ of exchange** letra de cambio; **~ of lading** conocimiento de embarque; **~ of sale** escritura de venta; **"post no ~s"** "prohibido fijar carteles".

billboard ['bɪlbɔːd] *n* (*US*) cartelera.

billet ['bɪlɪt] *n* alojamiento ♦ *vt*: **to ~ sb**

(on sb) alojar a uno (con uno).

billfold ['bɪlfəuld] n (US) cartera.

billiards ['bɪljədz] n billar m.

billion ['bɪljən] n (Brit) billón m; (US) mil millones.

billow ['bɪləu] n (of smoke) nube f; (of sail) ondulación f ◆ vi (smoke) salir en nubes; (sail) ondear, ondular.

billowy ['bɪləuɪ] a (smoke) que asciende en forma de nube.

billy ['bɪlɪ] n (US) porra.

billy goat n macho cabrío.

bin [bɪn] n (gen) cubo or bote m (LAm) de la basura; **litter~** n (Brit) papelera.

binary ['baɪnərɪ] a (MATH) binario; ~ **code** código binario; ~ **system** sistema m binario.

bind, pt, pp **bound** [baɪnd, baund] vt atar, liar; (wound) vendar; (book) encuadernar; (oblige) obligar.

   bind over vt (LAW) obligar a comparecer ante el juez.

   bind up vt (wound) vendar; **to be bound up in** (work, research etc) estar absorto en; **to be bound up with** (person) estar estrechamente ligado con.

binder ['baɪndə*] n (file) carpeta.

binding ['baɪndɪŋ] a (contract) obligatorio.

binge [bɪndʒ] n borrachera, juerga; **to go on a** ~ ir de juerga.

bingo ['bɪŋgəu] n bingo m.

binoculars [bɪ'nɔkjuləz] npl prismáticos mpl.

biochemistry [baɪə'kemɪstrɪ] n bioquímica.

biodegradable ['baɪəudɪ'greɪdəbl] a biodegradable.

biographer [baɪ'ɔgrəfə*] n biógrafo/a.

biographical [baɪə'græfɪkəl] a biográfico.

biography [baɪ'ɔgrəfɪ] n biografía.

biological [baɪə'lɔdʒɪkəl] a biológico.

biologist [baɪ'ɔlədʒɪst] n biólogo/a.

biology [baɪ'ɔlədʒɪ] n biología.

biophysics ['baɪəu'fɪzɪks] nsg biofísica.

biopsy ['baɪɔpsɪ] n biopsia.

biotechnology ['baɪəutek'nɔlədʒɪ] n biotecnología.

biped ['baɪped] n bípedo.

birch [bəːtʃ] n abedul m; (cane) vara.

bird [bəːd] n ave f, pájaro; (Brit col: girl) chica.

birdcage ['bəːdkeɪdʒ] n jaula.

bird's-eye view ['bəːdzaɪ-] n vista de pájaro.

bird watcher n ornitólogo/a.

Biro ['baɪrəu] n ® bolígrafo.

birth [bəːθ] n nacimiento; (MED) parto; **to give** ~ **to** parir, dar a luz a; (fig) dar origen a.

birth certificate n partida de nacimiento.

birth control n control m de natalidad; (methods) métodos mpl anticonceptivos.

birthday ['bəːθdeɪ] n cumpleaños m inv.

birthplace ['bəːθpleɪs] n lugar m de nacimiento.

birth rate n (tasa de) natalidad f.

Biscay ['bɪskeɪ] n: **the Bay of** ~ el Mar Cantábrico, el golfo de Vizcaya.

biscuit ['bɪskɪt] n (Brit) galleta.

bisect [baɪ'sekt] vt (also MATH) bisecar.

bishop ['bɪʃəp] n obispo; (CHESS) alfil m.

bit [bɪt] pt of **bite** ◆ n trozo, pedazo, pedacito; (COMPUT) bit m, bitio; (for horse) freno, bocado; **a** ~ **of** un poco de; **a** ~ **mad** algo loco; ~ **by** ~ poco a poco; **to come to** ~**s** (break) hacerse pedazos; **to do one's** ~ aportar su granito de arena; **bring all your** ~**s and pieces** trae todas tus cosas.

bitch [bɪtʃ] n (dog) perra; (col!) zorra (!).

bite [baɪt] vt, vi (pt **bit** [bɪt], pp **bitten** ['bɪtn]) morder; (insect etc) picar ◆ n (wound: of dog, snake etc) mordedura; (of insect) picadura; (mouthful) bocado; **to** ~ **one's nails** comerse las uñas; **let's have a** ~ **(to eat)** comamos algo.

biting ['baɪtɪŋ] a (wind) que traspasa los huesos; (criticism) mordaz.

bit part n (THEATRE) papel m secundario.

bitten ['bɪtn] pp of **bite**.

bitter ['bɪtə*] n a amargo; (wind, criticism) cortante, penetrante; (icy: weather) glacial; (battle) encarnizado ◆ n (Brit: beer) cerveza típica británica a base de lúpulos.

bitterly ['bɪtəlɪ] ad (disappoint, complain, weep) desconsoladamente; (oppose, criticise) implacablemente; (jealous) agriamente; **it's** ~ **cold** hace un frío glacial.

bitterness ['bɪtənɪs] n amargura; (anger) rencor m.

bitty ['bɪtɪ] a deshilvanado.

bitumen ['bɪtjumɪn] n betún m.

bivouac ['bɪvuæk] n vivac m, vivaque m.

bizarre [bɪ'zaː*] a raro, estrafalario.

bk abbr = **bank, book**.

BL n abbr (= Bachelor of Law(s), Bachelor of Letters) título universitario; (US: = Bachelor of Literature) título universitario.

bl abbr = **bill of lading**.

blab [blæb] vi chismear, soplar ◆ vt (also: ~ **out**) revelar, contar.

black [blæk] a (colour) negro; (dark) oscuro ◆ n (colour) color m negro; (person): **B~** negro/a ◆ vt (shoes) lustrar; (Brit: INDUSTRY) boicotear; **to give sb a** ~ **eye** ponerle a uno el ojo morado; ~ **coffee** café m solo; **there it is in** ~ **and white** (fig) ahí está bien claro; **to be in the** ~ (in credit) tener saldo positivo; ~ **and blue** a amoratado.

   black out vi (faint) desmayarse.

black belt n (SPORT) cinturón m negro; (US: area) zona negra.

blackberry ['blækbərɪ] n zarzamora.

blackbird ['blækbəːd] n mirlo.

blackboard ['blækbɔːd] n pizarra.

black box n (AVIAT) registrador m de vuelo, caja negra.

Black Country n (Brit): **the** ~ región industrial de los Midlands (de Inglaterra).

blackcurrant ['blæk'kʌrənt] n grosella negra.

black economy n economía sumergida.

blacken ['blækən] vt ennegrecer; (fig) denigrar.

Black Forest n: **the** ~ la Selva Negra.

blackguard ['blæɡɑːd] n canalla m, pillo.

black ice n hielo invisible en la carretera.

blackjack ['blækdʒæk] n (US) veintiuna.

blackleg ['blæklɛɡ] n (Brit) esquirol m, rompehuelgas m inv.

blacklist ['blæklɪst] n lista negra ♦ vt poner en la lista negra.

blackmail ['blækmeɪl] n chantaje m ♦ vt chantajear.

blackmailer ['blækmeɪlə*] n chantajista m/f.

black market n mercado negro, estraperlo.

blackness ['blæknɪs] n negrura.

blackout ['blækaut] n (TV, ELEC) apagón m; (fainting) desmayo, pérdida de conocimiento.

Black Sea n: **the** ~ el Mar Negro.

black sheep n oveja negra.

blacksmith ['blæksmɪθ] n herrero.

black spot n (AUT) lugar m peligroso.

bladder ['blædə*] n vejiga.

blade [bleɪd] n hoja; (cutting edge) filo; **a** ~ **of grass** una brizna de hierba.

blame [bleɪm] n culpa ♦ vt: **to** ~ **sb for sth** echar a uno la culpa de algo; **to be to** ~ **(for)** tener la culpa (de); **I'm not to** ~ yo no tengo la culpa; **and I don't** ~ **him** y lo comprendo perfectamente.

blameless ['bleɪmlɪs] a (person) inocente.

blanch [blɑːntʃ] vi (person) palidecer; (CULIN) blanquear.

bland [blænd] a suave; (taste) soso.

blank [blæŋk] a en blanco; (shot) sin bala; (look) sin expresión ♦ n blanco, espacio en blanco; cartucho sin bala or de fogueo; **to draw a** ~ (fig) no conseguir nada.

blank cheque, (US) **blank check** n cheque m en blanco.

blanket ['blæŋkɪt] n manta ♦ a (statement, agreement) comprensivo, general; **to give** ~ **cover** (subj: insurance policy) dar póliza a todo riesgo.

blankly ['blæŋklɪ] ad: **she looked at me** ~ me miró sin comprender.

blare [blɛə*] vi (brass band, horns, radio) resonar.

blasé ['blɑːzeɪ] a hastiado.

blaspheme [blæs'fiːm] vi blasfemar.

blasphemous ['blæsfɪməs] a blasfemo.

blasphemy ['blæsfɪmɪ] n blasfemia.

blast [blɑːst] n (of wind) ráfaga, soplo; (of whistle) toque m; (of explosive) carga explosiva; (force) choque m ♦ vt (blow up) volar; (blow open) abrir con carga explosi-

va ♦ excl (Brit col) ¡maldito sea!; **(at) full** ~ (also fig) a toda marcha.

blast off vi (spacecraft etc) despegar.

blast furnace n alto horno.

blast-off ['blɑːstɔf] n (SPACE) lanzamiento.

blatant ['bleɪtənt] a descarado.

blatantly ['bleɪtəntlɪ] ad: **it's** ~ **obvious** está clarísimo.

blather ['blæðə*] vi decir tonterías.

blaze [bleɪz] n (fire) fuego; (flames) llamarada; (glow: of fire, sun etc) resplandor m; (fig) arranque m ♦ vi (fire) arder en llamas; (fig) brillar ♦ vt: **to** ~ **a trail** (fig) abrir (un) camino; **in a** ~ **of publicity** bajo los focos de la publicidad.

blazer ['bleɪzə*] n chaqueta de uniforme de colegial o de socio de club.

bleach [bliːtʃ] n (also: **household** ~) lejía ♦ vt (linen) blanquear.

bleached [bliːtʃt] a (hair) teñido de rubio; (clothes) decolorado.

bleachers ['bliːtʃez] npl (US SPORT) gradas fpl al sol.

bleak [bliːk] a (countryside) desierto; (landscape) desolado, desierto; (weather) desapacible; (smile) triste; (prospect, future) poco prometedor(a).

bleary-eyed ['blɪərɪ'aɪd] a: **to be** ~ tener ojos de cansado.

bleat [bliːt] vi balar.

bleed, pt, pp **bled** [bliːd, blɛd] vt sangrar; (brakes, radiator) desaguar ♦ vi sangrar.

bleeding ['bliːdɪŋ] a sangrante.

bleeper ['bliːpə*] n (of doctor etc) busca m.

blemish ['blɛmɪʃ] n mancha, tacha.

blench [blɛntʃ] vi (shrink back) acobardarse; (grow pale) palidecer.

blend [blɛnd] n mezcla ♦ vt mezclar ♦ vi (colours etc) combinarse, mezclarse.

blender ['blɛndə*] n (CULIN) licuadora.

bless, pt, pp **blessed** or **blest** [blɛs, blɛst] vt bendecir.

blessed ['blɛsɪd] a (REL: holy) santo, bendito; (: happy) dichoso; **every** ~ **day** cada santo día.

blessing ['blɛsɪŋ] n bendición f; (advantage) beneficio, ventaja; **to count one's** ~**s** agradecer lo que se tiene; **it was a** ~ **in disguise** no hay mal que por bien no venga.

blew [bluː] pt of **blow**.

blight [blaɪt] vt (hopes etc) frustrar, arruinar.

blimey ['blaɪmɪ] excl (Brit col) ¡caray!

blind [blaɪnd] a ciego ♦ n (for window) persiana ♦ vt cegar; (dazzle) deslumbrar.

blind alley n callejón m sin salida.

blind corner n (Brit) esquina escondida.

blinders ['blaɪndəz] npl (US) anteojeras fpl.

blindfold ['blaɪndfəuld] n venda ♦ a, ad con los ojos vendados ♦ vt vendar los ojos a.

blindly ['blaɪndlɪ] ad a ciegas, ciegamente.

blindness ['blaɪndnɪs] n ceguera.

blind spot n mácula.

blink [blɪŋk] *vi* parpadear, pestañear; (*light*) oscilar; **to be on the ~** (*col*) estar estropeado.

blinkers ['blɪŋkəz] *npl* (*esp Brit*) anteojeras *fpl*.

blinking ['blɪŋkɪŋ] *a* (*col*): **this ~**... este condenado... .

bliss [blɪs] *n* felicidad *f*.

blissful ['blɪsful] *a* dichoso; **in ~ ignorance** feliz en la ignorancia.

blissfully ['blɪsfulɪ] *ad* (*sigh, smile*) con felicidad; **~ happy** sumamente feliz.

blister ['blɪstə*] *n* (*on skin, paint*) ampolla ♦ *vi* ampollarse.

blistering ['blɪstərɪŋ] *a* (*heat*) abrasador(a).

blithely ['blaɪðlɪ] *ad* alegremente, despreocupadamente.

blithering ['blɪðərɪŋ] *a* (*col*): **this ~ idiot** este tonto perdido.

BLit(t) *n abbr* (= *Bachelor of Literature*) título universitario.

blitz [blɪts] *n* bombardeo aéreo; **to have a ~ on sth** (*fig*) tener una campaña de algo.

blizzard ['blɪzəd] *n* ventisca.

BLM *n abbr* (*US*) = *Bureau of Land Management*.

bloated ['bləʊtɪd] *a* hinchado.

blob [blɔb] *n* (*drop*) gota; (*stain, spot*) mancha.

bloc [blɔk] *n* (*POL*) bloque *m*.

block [blɔk] *n* bloque *m* (*also COMPUT*); (*in pipes*) obstáculo; (*of buildings*) manzana ♦ *vt* (*gen*) obstruir, cerrar; (*progress*) estorbar; (*COMPUT*) agrupar; **~ of flats** (*Brit*) bloque *m* de pisos; **mental ~** amnesia temporal; **~ and tackle** (*TECH*) polea con aparejo; **3 ~s from here** a 3 manzanas *or* cuadras (*LAm*) de aquí.

  block up *vt* tapar, obstruir; (*pipe*) atascar.

blockade [blɔ'keɪd] *n* bloqueo ♦ *vt* bloquear.

blockage ['blɔkɪdʒ] *n* estorbo, obstrucción *f*.

block booking *n* reserva en grupo.

blockbuster ['blɔkbʌstə*] *n* (*book*) bestseller *m*; (*film*) éxito de público.

block capitals *npl* mayúsculas *fpl*.

block letters *npl* letras *fpl* de molde.

block release *n* (*Brit*) período de trabajo pagado para efectuar estudios superiores.

block vote *n* (*Brit*) voto por delegación.

bloke [bləʊk] *n* (*Brit col*) tipo, tío.

blond(e) [blɔnd] *a, n* rubio/a *m/f*.

blood [blʌd] *n* sangre *f*; **new ~** (*fig*) gente *f* nueva.

blood donor *n* donador(a) *m/f* de sangre.

blood group *n* grupo sanguíneo.

bloodhound ['blʌdhaund] *n* sabueso.

bloodless ['blʌdlɪs] *a* (*pale*) exangüe; (*revolt etc*) sin derramamiento de sangre, incruento.

bloodletting ['blʌdletɪŋ] *n* (*MED*) sangría; (*fig*) sangría, carnicería.

blood poisoning *n* envenenamiento de la sangre.

blood pressure *n* tensión *f* sanguínea; **to have high/low ~** tener la tensión alta/baja.

bloodshed ['blʌdʃed] *n* derramamiento de sangre.

bloodshot ['blʌdʃɔt] *a* inyectado en sangre.

bloodstained ['blʌdsteɪnd] *a* manchado de sangre.

bloodstream ['blʌdstriːm] *n* corriente *f* sanguínea.

blood test *n* análisis *m* de sangre.

bloodthirsty ['blʌdθɜːstɪ] *a* sanguinario.

blood transfusion *n* transfusión *f* de sangre.

blood vessel *n* vaso sanguíneo.

bloody ['blʌdɪ] *a* sangriento; (*Brit col!*): **this ~**... este condenado *or* puñetero... (*!*) ♦ *ad* (*Brit col!*): **~ strong/good** terriblemente fuerte/bueno.

bloody-minded ['blʌdɪ'maɪndɪd] *a* (*Brit col*) malintencionado.

bloom [bluːm] *n* floración *f*; **in ~** en flor ♦ *vi* florecer.

blooming ['bluːmɪŋ] *a* (*col*): **this ~**... este condenado... .

blossom ['blɔsəm] *n* flor *f* ♦ *vi* florecer; (*fig*) desarrollarse; **to ~ into** (*fig*) desarrollarse en.

blot [blɔt] *n* borrón *m* ♦ *vt* (*dry*) secar; (*stain*) manchar; **to ~ out** *vt* (*view*) tapar; (*memories*) borrar; **to be a ~ on the landscape** estropear el paisaje; **to ~ one's copy book** (*fig*) manchar su reputación.

blotchy ['blɔtʃɪ] *a* (*complexion*) lleno de manchas.

blotter ['blɔtə*] *n* secante *m*.

blotting paper ['blɔtɪŋ-] *n* papel *m* secante.

blouse [blauz] *n* blusa.

blow [bləʊ] *n* golpe *m* ♦ *vb* (*pt* **blew,** *pp* **blown** [bluː, bləʊn]) *vi* soplar; (*fuse*) fundirse ♦ *vt* (*glass*) soplar; (*fuse*) quemar; (*instrument*) tocar; **to come to ~s** llegar a golpes; **to ~ one's nose** sonarse.

  blow away *vt* llevarse, arrancar.

  blow down *vt* derribar.

  blow off *vt* arrebatar.

  blow out *vt* apagar ♦ *vi* apagarse; (*tyre*) reventar.

  blow over *vi* amainar.

  blow up *vi* estallar ♦ *vt* volar; (*tyre*) inflar; (*PHOT*) ampliar.

blow-dry ['bləʊdraɪ] *n* secado con secador de mano ♦ *vt* secar con secador de mano.

blowlamp ['bləʊlæmp] *n* (*Brit*) soplete *m*, lámpara de soldar.

blow-out ['bləʊaut] *n* (*of tyre*) pinchazo; (*col: big meal*) banquete *m*, festín *m*.

blowtorch ['bləʊtɔːtʃ] *n* = **blowlamp.**

blow-up ['bləʊʌp] *n* (*COMM*) ampliación *f*.

blowzy ['blauzɪ] *a* (*Brit*) dejado, desaliñado.

BLS *n abbr* (*US*) = *Bureau of Labor Statis-*

tics.
blubber ['blʌbə*] n grasa de ballena ♦ _vi_ (_pej_) lloriquear.
bludgeon ['blʌdʒən] _vt:_ **to ~ sb into doing sth** coaccionar a uno a hacer algo.
blue [bluː] _a_ azul; **~ film/joke** film/chiste verde; **once in a ~ moon** de higos a brevas; **to come out of the ~** (_fig_) ser completamente inesperado; _see also_ **blues.**
blue baby n niño azul _or_ cianótico.
bluebell ['bluːbɛl] n campanilla, campánula azul.
blue-blooded [bluː'blʌdɪd] _a_ de sangre azul.
bluebottle ['bluːbɔtl] n moscarda, mosca azul.
blue cheese n queso de pasta verde.
blue-chip ['bluːtʃɪp] n: **~ investment** inversión _f_ asegurada.
blue-collar worker ['bluːkɔlə*-] n manual _m/f._
blue jeans _npl_ tejanos _mpl_, vaqueros _mpl._
blueprint ['bluːprɪnt] n proyecto; **~ (for)** (_fig_) anteproyecto (de).
blues [bluːz] _npl:_ **the ~** (_MUS_) el blues; **to have the ~** estar triste.
bluff [blʌf] _vi_ hacer un bluff, farolear ♦ _n_ bluff _m_, farol _m_; (_GEO_) precipicio, despeñadero; **to call sb's ~** coger a uno en un renuncio.
bluish ['bluːɪʃ] _a_ azulado.
blunder ['blʌndə*] n patinazo, metedura de pata ♦ _vi_ cometer un error, meter la pata; **to ~ into sb/sth** tropezar con uno/algo.
blunt [blʌnt] _a_ (_knife_) desafilado; (_person_) franco, directo ♦ _vt_ embotar, desafilar; **this pencil is ~** este lápiz está despuntado; **~ instrument** (_LAW_) instrumento contundente.
bluntly ['blʌntlɪ] _ad_ (_speak_) francamente, de modo terminante.
bluntness ['blʌntnɪs] n (_of person_) franqueza, brusquedad _f._
blur [blə*] n aspecto borroso ♦ _vt_ (_vision_) enturbiar; (_memory_) empañar.
blurb [bləːb] n propaganda.
blurred [bləːd] _a_ borroso.
blurt [bləːt]: **to ~ out** _vt_ (_say_) descolgarse con, dejar escapar.
blush [blʌʃ] _vi_ ruborizarse, ponerse colorado ♦ _n_ rubor _m._
blusher ['blʌʃə*] n colorete _m._
bluster ['blʌstə*] n fanfarronada, bravata ♦ _vi_ fanfarronear, amenazar.
blustering ['blʌstərɪŋ] _a_ (_person_) fanfarrón/ona.
blustery ['blʌstərɪ] _a_ (_weather_) tempestuoso, tormentoso.
Blvd _abbr_ = _boulevard._
BM n _abbr_ = _British Museum;_ (_UNIV_: = _Bachelor of Medicine_) título universitario.
BMA n _abbr_ = _British Medical Association._
BMJ n _abbr_ = _British Medical Journal._

BMus n _abbr_ (= _Bachelor of Music_) título universitario.
BO n _abbr_ (_col_: = _body odour_) olor _m_ a sudor; (_US_) = **box office.**
boa ['bəuə] n boa.
boar [bɔː*] n verraco, cerdo.
board [bɔːd] n tabla, tablero; (_on wall_) tablón _m_; (_for chess etc_) tablero; (_committee_) junta, consejo; (_in firm_) mesa _or_ junta directiva; (_NAUT, AVIAT_): **on ~ a** bordo ♦ _vt_ (_ship_) embarcarse en; (_train_) subir a; **full ~** (_Brit_) pensión _f_ completa; **half ~** (_Brit_) media pensión; **~ and lodging** casa y comida; **to go by the ~** (_fig_) ser abandonado _or_ olvidado; **above ~** (_fig_) legítimo; **across the ~** (_fig: ad_) en todos los niveles; (: _a_) general.
board up _vt_ (_door_) tapiar.
boarder ['bɔːdə*] n huésped(a) _m/f_; (_SCOL_) interno/a.
board game n juego de tablero.
boarding card ['bɔːdɪŋ-] n (_Brit_: _AVIAT, NAUT_) tarjeta de embarque.
boarding house ['bɔːdɪŋ-] n casa de huéspedes.
boarding pass ['bɔːdɪŋ-] n (_US_) = **boarding card.**
boarding school ['bɔːdɪŋ-] n internado.
board meeting n reunión _f_ de la junta directiva.
board room n sala de juntas.
boardwalk ['bɔːdwɔːk] n (_US_) paseo entablado.
boast [bəust] _vi:_ **to ~ (about _or_ of)** alardear (de) ♦ _vt_ ostentar ♦ _n_ alarde _m_, baladronada.
boastful ['bəustfəl] _a_ presumido, jactancioso.
boastfulness ['bəustfulnɪs] n fanfarronería.
boat [bəut] n barco, buque _m_; (_small_) barca, bote _m_; **to go by ~** ir en barco.
boater ['bəutə*] n (_hat_) canotié _m._
boating ['bəutɪŋ] n canotaje _m._
boatman ['bəutmən] n barquero.
boatswain ['bəusn] n contramaestre _m._
bob [bɔb] _vi_ (_boat, cork on water: also:_ **~ up and down**) menearse, balancearse ♦ _n_ (_Brit col_) = **shilling.**
bob up _vi_ (re)aparecer de repente.
bobbin ['bɔbɪn] n (_of sewing machine_) carrete _m_, bobina.
bobby ['bɔbɪ] n (_Brit col_) poli _m/f._
bobsleigh ['bɔbsleɪ] n bob _m._
bode [bəud] _vi:_ **to ~ well/ill (for)** ser de buen/mal agüero (para).
bodice ['bɔdɪs] n corpiño.
-bodied ['bɔdɪd] _a suff_ de cuerpo ....
bodily ['bɔdɪlɪ] _a_ (_comfort, needs_) corporal; (_pain_) corpóreo ♦ _ad_ (_in person_) en persona; (_carry_) corporalmente; (_lift_) en peso.
body ['bɔdɪ] n cuerpo; (_corpse_) cadáver _m_; (_of car_) caja, carrocería; (_fig: organization_) organización _f_; (: _public ~_) organis-

mo; (: *quantity*) masa; (: *of speech, document*) parte *f* principal; (: *of speech, document*) parte *f* principal; ~ directiva;
in a ~ todos juntos, en masa.
body-building ['bɔdɪ'bɪldɪŋ] *n* culturismo.
bodyguard ['bɔdɪgɑːd] *n* guardaespaldas *m inv*.
bodywork ['bɔdɪwəːk] *n* carrocería.
boffin ['bɔfɪn] *n* (*Brit*) científico/a.
bog [bɔg] *n* pantano, ciénaga ♦ *vt:* **to get ~ged down** (*fig*) empantanarse, atascarse.
boggle ['bɔgl] *vi:* **the mind ~s!** ¡no puedo creerlo!
Bogotá [bəugə'tɑː] *n* Bogotá.
bogus ['bəugəs] *a* falso, fraudulento; (*person*) fingido.
Bohemia [bə'hiːmɪə] *n* Bohemia.
Bohemian [bə'hiːmɪən] *a, n* bohemio/a *m/f*.
boil [bɔɪl] *vt* cocer; (*eggs*) pasar por agua ♦ *vi* hervir ♦ *n* (*MED*) furúnculo, divieso; **to bring to the ~** calentar hasta que hiervan; **to come to the** (*Brit*) *or* **a** (*US*) **~** comenzar a hervir; **~ed egg** huevo pasado por agua; **~ed potatoes** patatas *fpl or* papas *fpl* (*LAm*) hervidas.
boil down *vi* (*fig*): **to ~ down to** reducirse a.
boil over *vi* (*liquid*) rebosar; (*anger, resentment*) llegar al colmo.
boiler ['bɔɪlə*] *n* caldera.
boiler suit *n* (*Brit*) mono.
boiling ['bɔɪlɪŋ] *a:* **I'm ~** (**hot**) (*col*) estoy asado.
boiling point *n* punto de ebullición *f*.
boisterous ['bɔɪstərəs] *a* (*noisy*) bullicioso; (*excitable*) exuberante; (*crowd*) tumultuoso.
bold [bəuld] *a* (*brave*) valiente, audaz; (*pej*) descarado; (*outline*) grueso; (*colour*) vivo; **~ type** (*TYP*) negrita.
boldly ['bəuldlɪ] *ad* atrevidamente.
boldness ['bəuldnɪs] *n* valor *m*, audacia; (*cheek*) descaro.
Bolivia [bə'lɪvɪə] *n* Bolivia.
Bolivian [bə'lɪvɪən] *a, n* boliviano/a *m/f*.
bollard ['bɔləd] *n* (*Brit AUT*) poste *m*.
bolster ['bəulstə*] *n* travesero, cabezal *m*.
bolster up *vt* reforzar; (*fig*) alentar.
bolt [bəult] *n* (*lock*) cerrojo; (*with nut*) perno, tornillo ♦ *ad:* **~ upright** rígido, erguido ♦ *vt* (*door*) echar el cerrojo a; (*food*) engullir ♦ *vi* fugarse; (*horse*) desbocarse.
bomb [bɔm] *n* bomba ♦ *vt* bombardear.
bombard [bɔm'bɑːd] *vt* bombardear; (*fig*) asediar.
bombardment [bɔm'bɑːdmənt] *n* bombardeo.
bombastic [bɔm'bæstɪk] *a* rimbombante; (*person*) farolero.
bomb disposal *n* desmontaje *m* de explosivos.
bomb disposal expert *n* experto/a en desactivar bombas.

bomber ['bɔmə*] *n* (*AVIAT*) bombardero; (*terrorist*) persona que pone bombas.
bombing ['bɔmɪŋ] *n* bombardeo.
bombshell ['bɔmʃɛl] *n* obús *m*, granada; (*fig*) bomba.
bomb site *n* lugar *m* donde estalló una bomba.
bona fide ['bəunə'faɪdɪ] *a* genuino, auténtico.
bonanza [bə'nænzə] *n* bonanza.
bond [bɔnd] *n* (*binding promise*) fianza; (*FINANCE*) bono; (*link*) vínculo, lazo; **in ~** (*COMM*) en depósito bajo fianza.
bondage ['bɔndɪdʒ] *n* esclavitud *f*.
bonded goods ['bɔndɪd-] *npl* mercancías *fpl* en depósito de aduanas.
bonded warehouse ['bɔndɪd-] *n* depósito de aduanas.
bone [bəun] *n* hueso; (*of fish*) espina ♦ *vt* deshuesar; quitar las espinas a; **~ of contention** manzana de la discordia.
bone china *n* porcelana fina.
bone-dry ['bəun'draɪ] *a* completamente seco.
bone idle *a* gandul.
boner ['bəunə*] *n* (*US col*) plancha, patochada.
bonfire ['bɔnfaɪə*] *n* hoguera, fogata.
Bonn [bɔn] *n* Bonn *m*.
bonnet ['bɔnɪt] *n* gorra; (*Brit: of car*) capó *m*.
bonny ['bɔnɪ] *a* (*esp Scottish*) bonito, hermoso, lindo.
bonus ['bəunəs] *n* (*at Christmas etc*) paga extraordinaria; (*merit award*) sobrepaga, prima.
bony ['bəunɪ] *a* (*arm, face, MED: tissue*) huesudo; (*meat*) lleno de huesos; (*fish*) lleno de espinas; (*thin: person*) flaco, delgado.
boo [buː] *vt* abuchear, rechiflar.
boob [buːb] *n* (*col: mistake*) disparate *m*, sandez *f*; (: *breast*) teta.
booby prize ['buːbɪ-] *n* premio al último.
booby trap ['buːbɪ-] *n* (*MIL etc*) trampa explosiva.
book [buk] *n* libro; (*notebook*) libreta; (*of stamps etc*) librito; **~s** (*COMM*) cuentas *fpl*, contabilidad *f* ♦ *vt* (*ticket, seat, room*) reservar; (*driver*) fichar; (*FOOTBALL*) amonestar; **to keep the ~s** llevar las cuentas *or* los libros; **by the ~** según las reglas; **to throw the ~ at sb** echar un rapapolvo a uno.
book in *vi* (*at hotel*) registrarse.
book up *vt:* **all seats are ~ed up** todas las plazas están reservadas; **the hotel is ~ed up** el hotel está lleno.
bookable ['bukəbl] *a:* **seats are ~** los asientos se pueden reservar (de antemano).
bookcase ['bukkeɪs] *n* librería, estante *m* para libros.
booking office ['bukɪŋ-] *n* (*Brit: RAIL*)

despacho de billetes *or* boletos (*LAm*); (: *THEATRE*) taquilla, boletería (*LAm*).

book-keeping ['buk'ki:pɪŋ] *n* contabilidad *f*.

booklet ['buklɪt] *n* folleto.

bookmaker ['bukmeɪkə*] *n* corredor *m* de apuestas.

bookseller ['buksɛlə*] *n* librero/a.

bookshop ['bukʃɔp] *n* librería.

bookstall ['bukstɔːl] *n* quiosco de libros.

book store *n* = bookshop.

book token *n* vale *m* para libros.

book value *n* (*COMM*) valor *m* contable.

bookworm ['bukwɔːm] *n* (*fig*) ratón/ona *m/f* de biblioteca.

boom [buːm] *n* (*noise*) trueno, estampido; (*in prices etc*) alza rápida; (*ECON*) boom *m*, auge *m* ♦ *vi* (*cannon*) hacer gran estruendo, retumbar; (*ECON*) estar en alza.

boom town *n* ciudad *f* beneficiaria del auge.

boomerang ['buːməræŋ] *n* bumerang *m* (*also fig*) ♦ *vi*: to ~ on sb (*fig*) ser contraproducente para uno.

boon [buːn] *n* favor *m*, beneficio.

boorish ['buərɪʃ] *a* grosero.

boost [buːst] *n* estímulo, empuje *m* ♦ *vt* estimular, empujar; (*increase: sales, production*) aumentar; to give a ~ to (*morale*) levantar; it gave a ~ to his confidence le dio confianza en sí mismo.

booster ['buːstə*] *n* (*MED*) reinyección *f*; (*TV*) repetidor *m*; (*ELEC*) elevador *m* de tensión; (*also: ~ rocket*) cohete *m*.

boot [buːt] *n* bota; (*ankle ~*) borceguí *m*; (*Brit: of car*) maleta, maletero ♦ *vt* dar un puntapié a; (*COMPUT*) arrancar; to ~ (*in addition*) además, por añadidura; to give sb the ~ (*col*) despedir a uno, poner a uno en la calle.

booth [buːð] *n* (*at fair*) barraca; (*telephone ~, voting ~*) cabina.

bootleg ['buːtlɛg] *a* de contrabando; ~ record disco de contrabando.

booty ['buːtɪ] *n* botín *m*.

booze [buːz] (*col*) *n* bebida, trago ♦ *vi* emborracharse.

boozer ['buːzə*] *n* (*col: person*) bebedor(a) *m/f*; (: *Brit: pub*) bar *m*.

border ['bɔːdə*] *n* borde *m*, margen *m*; (*of a country*) frontera ♦ *a* fronterizo; the B~s *región fronteriza entre Escocia e Inglaterra*.

border on *vt fus* lindar con; (*fig*) rayar en.

borderline ['bɔːdəlaɪn] *n* (*fig*) frontera.

bore [bɔː*] *pt of* bear ♦ *vt* (*hole*) taladrar; (*person*) aburrir ♦ *n* (*person*) pelmazo, pesado; (*of gun*) calibre *m*.

bored [bɔːd] *a* aburrido; he's ~ to tears *or* to death *or* stiff está aburrido como una ostra, está muerto de aburrimiento.

boredom ['bɔːdəm] *n* aburrimiento.

boring ['bɔːrɪŋ] *a* aburrido.

born [bɔːn] *a*: to be ~ nacer; I was ~ in 1960 nací en 1960.

borne [bɔːn] *pp of* bear.

Borneo ['bɔːnɪəu] *n* Borneo.

borough ['bʌrə] *n* municipio.

borrow ['bɔrəu] *vt*: to ~ sth (from sb) tomar algo prestado (a alguien); may I ~ your car? ¿me prestas tu coche?

borrower ['bɔrəuə*] *n* prestatario/a.

borrowing ['bɔrəuɪŋ] *n* préstamos *mpl*.

borstal ['bɔːstl] *n* (*Brit*) reformatorio (de menores).

bosom ['buzəm] *n* pecho; (*fig*) seno; ~ friend *n* amigo/a *or* íntimo/a del alma.

boss [bɔs] *n* jefe/a *m/f*; (*employer*) patrón/ona *m/f*; (*political etc*) cacique *m* ♦ *vt* (*also*: ~ about *or* around) mangonear; stop ~ing everyone about! ¡deja de dar órdenes *or* de mangonear a todos!

bossy ['bɔsɪ] *a* mandón/ona.

bosun ['bəusn] *n* contramaestre *m*.

botanical [bə'tænɪkl] *a* botánico.

botanist ['bɔtənɪst] *n* botanista *m/f*.

botany ['bɔtənɪ] *n* botánica.

botch [bɔtʃ] *vt* (*also*: ~ up) arruinar, estropear.

both [bəuθ] *a*, *pron* ambos/as, los/las dos; ~ of us went, we ~ went fuimos los dos, ambos fuimos ♦ *ad*: ~ A and B tanto A como B.

bother ['bɔðə*] *vt* (*worry*) preocupar; (*disturb*) molestar, fastidiar ♦ *vi* (*gen*: ~ o.s.) molestarse ♦ *n*: what a ~! ¡qué lata! ♦ *excl* ¡maldita sea!, ¡caramba!; I'm sorry to ~ you perdona que te moleste; to ~ doing tomarse la molestia de hacer; please don't ~ no te molestes.

Botswana [bɔt'swɑːnə] *n* Botswana.

bottle ['bɔtl] *n* botella; (*small*) frasco; (*baby's*) biberón *m* ♦ *vt* embotellar; ~ of wine/milk botella de vino/de leche; wine/milk ~ botella de vino/de leche.

bottle up *vt* (*fig*) contener.

bottleneck ['bɔtlnɛk] *n* embotellamiento.

bottle-opener ['bɔtləupnə*] *n* abrebotellas *m inv*.

bottom ['bɔtəm] *n* (*of box, sea*) fondo; (*buttocks*) trasero, culo; (*of page, mountain, tree*) pie *m*; (*of list*) final *m* ♦ *a* (*lowest*) más bajo; (*last*) último; to get to the ~ of sth (*fig*) llegar al fondo de algo.

bottomless ['bɔtəmlɪs] *a* sin fondo, insondable.

bough [bau] *n* rama.

bought [bɔːt] *pt, pp of* buy.

bouillon cube ['buːjɔn-] *n* (*US*) cubito de caldo.

boulder ['bəuldə*] *n* canto rodado.

bounce [bauns] *vi* (*ball*) (re)botar; (*cheque*) ser rechazado ♦ *vt* (re)botar ♦ *n* (*rebound*) (re)bote *m*; he's got plenty of ~ (*fig*) tiene mucha energía.

bouncer ['baʊnsə*] n (col) matón m.
bound [baʊnd] pt, pp of **bind** ♦ n (leap) salto; (gen pl: limit) límite m ♦ vi (leap) saltar ♦ a: ~ **by** rodeado de; **to be** ~ **to do sth** (obliged) tener el deber de hacer algo; **he's** ~ **to come** es seguro que vendrá; **"out of** ~**s to the public"** "prohibido el paso"; ~ **for** con destino a.
boundary ['baʊndrɪ] n límite m, lindero.
boundless ['baʊndlɪs] a ilimitado.
bountiful ['baʊntɪful] a (person) liberal, generoso; (God) bondadoso; (supply) abundante.
bounty ['baʊntɪ] n (generosity) generosidad f; (reward) prima.
bounty hunter n cazarrecompensas m inv.
bouquet ['bʊkeɪ] n (of flowers) ramo, ramillete m; (of wine) aroma m.
bourbon ['bʊəbən] n (US: also: ~ **whiskey**) whisky m americano, bourbon m.
bourgeois ['bʊəʒwɑː] a, n burgués/esa m/f.
bout [baʊt] n (of malaria etc) ataque m; (BOXING etc) combate m, encuentro.
boutique [buː'tiːk] n boutique f, tienda de ropa.
bow [bəʊ] n (knot) lazo; (weapon, MUS) arco; [baʊ] (of the head) reverencia; (NAUT: also: ~**s**) proa ♦ vi [baʊ] inclinarse, hacer una reverencia; (yield): **to** ~ **to** or **before** ceder ante, someterse a; **to** ~ **to the inevitable** resignarse a lo inevitable.
bowels ['baʊəlz] npl intestinos mpl, vientre m.
bowl [bəʊl] n tazón m, cuenco; (for washing) palangana, jofaina; (ball) bola; (US: stadium) estadio ♦ vi (CRICKET) arrojar la pelota; see also **bowls**.
bow-legged ['bəʊ'legɪd] a estevado.
bowler ['bəʊlə*] n (CRICKET) lanzador m (de la pelota); (Brit: also: ~ **hat**) hongo, bombín m.
bowling ['bəʊlɪŋ] n (game) bochas fpl, bolos mpl.
bowling alley n bolera.
bowling green n pista para bochas.
bowls [bəʊlz] n juego de las bochas, bolos mpl.
bow tie ['bəʊ-] n corbata de lazo, pajarita.
box [bɒks] n (also: **cardboard** ~) caja, cajón m; (for jewels) estuche m; (for money) cofre m; (crate) cofre m, arca; (THEATRE) palco ♦ vt encajonar ♦ vi (SPORT) boxear.
boxer ['bɒksə*] n (person) boxeador m; (dog) bóxer m.
box file n fichero.
boxing ['bɒksɪŋ] n (SPORT) boxeo.
Boxing Day n (Brit) Día de San Esteban, 26 de diciembre.
boxing gloves npl guantes mpl de boxeo.
boxing ring n ring m, cuadrilátero.
box number n (for advertisements) apartado.

box office n taquilla, boletería (LAm).
boxroom ['bɒksrum] n trastero.
boy [bɔɪ] n (young) niño; (older) muchacho.
boycott ['bɔɪkɒt] n boicot m ♦ vt boicotear.
boyfriend ['bɔɪfrend] n novio.
boyish ['bɔɪɪʃ] a muchachil.
boy scout n boy scout m.
Bp abbr = **bishop**.
BR abbr see **British Rail**.
bra [brɑː] n sostén m, sujetador m.
brace [breɪs] n refuerzo, abrazadera; (Brit: on teeth) corrector m; (tool) berbiquí m ♦ vt asegurar, reforzar; **to** ~ **o.s. (for)** (fig) prepararse (para); see also **braces**.
bracelet ['breɪslɪt] n pulsera, brazalete m.
braces ['breɪsɪz] npl (Brit) tirantes mpl; (US: on teeth) corrector m.
bracing ['breɪsɪŋ] a vigorizante, tónico.
bracken ['brækən] n helecho.
bracket ['brækɪt] n (TECH) soporte m, puntal m; (group) clase f, categoría; (also: **brace** ~) soporte m, abrazadera; (also: **round** ~) paréntesis m inv; (gen: **square** ~) corchete m ♦ vt (fig: also: ~ **together**) agrupar; **income** ~ nivel m económico; **in** ~**s** entre paréntesis.
brackish ['brækɪʃ] a (water) salobre.
brag [bræg] vi jactarse.
braid [breɪd] n (trimming) galón m; (of hair) trenza.
Braille [breɪl] n Braille m.
brain [breɪn] n cerebro; ~**s** npl sesos mpl; **she's got** ~**s** es muy lista.
brainchild ['breɪntʃaɪld] n parto del ingenio.
brainless ['breɪnlɪs] a estúpido, insensato.
brainstorm ['breɪnstɔːm] n (fig) ataque m de locura, frenesí m; (US: brainwave) idea luminosa or genial, inspiración f.
brainstorming ['breɪnstɔːmɪŋ] n discusión intensiva para solucionar problemas.
brainwash ['breɪnwɒʃ] vt lavar el cerebro a.
brainwave ['breɪnweɪv] n idea luminosa or genial, inspiración f.
brainy ['breɪnɪ] a muy listo or inteligente.
braise [breɪz] vt cocer a fuego lento.
brake [breɪk] n (on vehicle) freno ♦ vt, vi frenar.
brake drum n tambor m de freno.
brake fluid n líquido de frenos.
brake light n luz f de frenado.
brake pedal n pedal m de freno.
bramble ['bræmbl] n (fruit) zarza.
bran [bræn] n salvado.
branch [brɑːntʃ] n rama; (fig) ramo; (COMM) sucursal f ♦ vi ramificarse; (fig) extenderse.
branch out vi ramificarse.
branch line n (RAIL) ramal m, línea secundaria.
branch manager n director(a) m/f de sucursal.
brand [brænd] n marca; (iron) hierro de

marcar ♦ *vt* (*cattle*) marcar con hierro candente.
brandish ['brændɪʃ] *vt* blandir.
brand name *n* marca.
brand-new ['brænd'njuː] *a* flamante, completamente nuevo.
brandy ['brændɪ] *n* coñac *m*, brandy *m*.
brash [bræʃ] *a* (*rough*) tosco; (*cheeky*) descarado.
Brasilia [brəˈzɪlɪə] *n* Brasilia.
brass [brɑːs] *n* latón *m*; **the ~** (*MUS*) los cobres.
brass band *n* banda de metal.
brassière ['bræsɪə*] *n* sostén *m*, sujetador *m*.
brass tacks *npl*: **to get down to ~** ir al grano.
brat [bræt] *n* (*pej*) mocoso/a.
bravado [brəˈvɑːdəu] *n* fanfarronería.
brave [breɪv] *a* valiente, valeroso ♦ *n* guerrero indio ♦ *vt* (*challenge*) desafiar; (*resist*) aguantar.
bravely ['breɪvlɪ] *ad* valientemente, con valor.
bravery ['breɪvərɪ] *n* valor *m*, valentía.
bravo [brɑːˈvəu] *excl* ¡bravo!, ¡olé!
brawl [brɔːl] *n* pendencia, reyerta ♦ *vi* pelearse.
brawn [brɔːn] *n* fuerza muscular; (*meat*) carne *f* en gelatina.
brawny ['brɔːnɪ] *a* fornido, musculoso.
bray [breɪ] *n* rebuzno ♦ *vi* rebuznar.
brazen ['breɪzn] *a* descarado, cínico ♦ *vt*: **to ~ it out** echarle cara al asunto.
brazier ['breɪzɪə*] *n* brasero.
Brazil [brəˈzɪl] *n* (el) Brasil.
Brazilian [brəˈzɪlɪən] *a*, *n* brasileño/a *m/f*.
breach [briːtʃ] *vt* abrir brecha en ♦ *n* (*gap*) brecha; (*estrangement*) ruptura; (*breaking*): **~ of confidence** abuso de confianza; **~ of contract** infracción *f* de contrato; **~ of the peace** perturbación *f* del órden público; **in ~ of** por incumplimiento *or* infracción de.
bread [brɛd] *n* pan *m*; (*col: money*) pasta, plata (*LAm*); **~ and butter** *n* pan con mantequilla; (*fig*) pan (de cada día) ♦ *a* común y corriente; **to earn one's daily ~** ganarse el pan; **to know which side one's ~ is buttered (on)** saber dónde aprieta el zapato.
breadbin ['brɛdbɪn] *n* panera.
breadboard ['brɛdbɔːd] *n* (*COMPUT*) circuito experimental.
breadbox ['brɛdbɔks] *n* (*US*) panera.
breadcrumbs ['brɛdkrʌmz] *npl* migajas *fpl*; (*CULIN*) pan *msg* molido.
breadline ['brɛdlaɪn] *n*: **on the ~** en la miseria.
breadth [brɛtθ] *n* anchura; (*fig*) amplitud *f*.
breadwinner ['brɛdwɪnə*] *n* sostén *m* de la familia.
break [breɪk] *vb* (*pt* **broke** [brəuk], *pp*

broken ['brəukən]) *vt* (*gen*) romper; (*promise*) no cumplir; (*fall*) amortiguar; (*journey*) interrumpir; (*law*) violar, infringir; (*record*) batir; (*news*) comunicar ♦ *vi* romperse, quebrarse; (*storm*) estallar; (*weather*) cambiar ♦ *n* (*gap*) abertura; (*crack*) grieta; (*fracture*) fractura; (*in relations*) ruptura; (*rest*) descanso; (*time*) intervalo; (: *at school*) (período de) recreo; (*holiday*) vacaciones *fpl*; (*chance*) oportunidad *f*; (*escape*) evasión *f*, fuga; **to ~ with sb** (*fig*) romper con uno; **to ~ even** *vi* cubrir los gastos; **to ~ free** *or* **loose** *vi* escaparse; **lucky ~** (*col*) chiripa, racha de buena suerte; **to have** *or* **take a ~** (*few minutes*) descansar; **without a ~** sin descanso *or* descansar.
break down *vt* (*door etc*) echar abajo, derribar; (*resistance*) vencer, acabar con; (*figures*, *data*) analizar, descomponer; (*undermine*) acabar con ♦ *vi* estropearse; (*MED*) sufrir un colapso; (*AUT*) averiarse; (*person*) romper a llorar.
break in *vt* (*horse etc*) domar ♦ *vi* (*burglar*) forzar una entrada.
break into *vt fus* (*house*) forzar.
break off *vi* (*speaker*) pararse, detenerse; (*branch*) partir ♦ *vt* (*talks*) suspender; (*engagement*) romper.
break open *vt* (*door etc*) abrir por la fuerza, forzar.
break out *vi* estallar; **to ~ out in spots** salir a uno granos.
break through *vi*: **the sun broke through** el sol salió ♦ *vt fus* (*defences*, *barrier*) abrirse paso por; (*crowd*) abrirse paso por.
break up *vi* (*partnership*) disolverse; (*friends*) romper ♦ *vt* (*rocks*, *ice etc*) partir; (*crowd*) disolver.
breakable ['breɪkəbl] *a* quebradizo ♦ *n*: **~s** cosas *fpl* frágiles.
breakage ['breɪkɪdʒ] *n* rotura; **to pay for ~s** pagar por los objetos rotos.
breakaway ['breɪkəweɪ] *a* (*group etc*) disidente.
break-dancing ['breɪkdɑːnsɪŋ] *n* break *m*.
breakdown ['breɪkdaun] *n* (*AUT*) avería; (*in communications*) interrupción *f*; (*MED*: *also*: **nervous ~**) colapso, crisis *f* nerviosa; (*of figures*) desglose *m*.
breakdown van *n* (*Brit*) (camión *m*) grúa.
breaker ['breɪkə*] *n* rompiente *m*, ola grande.
breakeven ['breɪkˈiːvn] *cpd*: **~ chart** gráfico del punto de equilibrio; **~ point** punto de break-even *or* de equilibrio.
breakfast ['brɛkfəst] *n* desayuno.
breakfast cereal *n* cereales *mpl* para el desayuno.
break-in ['breɪkɪn] *n* robo con allanamiento de morada.

breaking and entering ['breɪkɪŋ-ənd'ɛntərɪŋ] n (LAW) violación f de domicilio, allanamiento de morada.

breaking point ['breɪkɪŋ-] n punto de ruptura.

breakthrough ['breɪkθruː] n ruptura; (fig) avance m, adelanto.

break-up ['breɪkʌp] n (of partnership, marriage) disolución f.

break-up value n (COMM) valor m de liquidación.

breakwater ['breɪkwɔːtə*] n rompeolas m inv.

breast [brɛst] n (of woman) pecho, seno; (chest) pecho; (of bird) pechuga.

breast-feed ['brɛstfiːd] vt, vi (irg: like feed) amamantar, criar a los pechos.

breaststroke ['brɛststrəuk] n braza de pecho.

breath [brɛθ] n aliento, respiración f; out of ~ sin aliento, sofocado; to go out for a ~ of air salir a tomar el fresco.

Breathalyser ® ['brɛθəlaɪzə*] n (Brit) alcoholímetro m; ~ test n prueba de alcoholemia.

breathe [briːð] vt, vi respirar; (noisily) resollar; I won't ~ a word about it no diré ni una palabra acerca de ello.

breathe in vt, vi aspirar.

breathe out vt, vi espirar.

breather ['briːðə*] n respiro.

breathing ['briːðɪŋ] n respiración f.

breathing space n (fig) respiro, pausa.

breathless ['brɛθlɪs] a sin aliento, jadeante; (with excitement) pasmado.

breathtaking ['brɛθteɪkɪŋ] a imponente, pasmoso.

-bred [brɛd] suff: to be well/ill~ estar bien/mal criado.

breed [briːd] vb (pt, pp bred [brɛd]) vt criar; (fig: hate, suspicion) crear, engendrar ♦ vi reproducirse, procrear ♦ n raza, casta.

breeder ['briːdə*] n (person) criador(a) m/f; (PHYSICS: also: ~ reactor) reactor m.

breeding ['briːdɪŋ] n (of person) educación f.

breeze [briːz] n brisa.

breezeblock ['briːzblɔk] n (Brit) bovedilla.

breezy ['briːzɪ] a de mucho viento, ventoso; (person) despreocupado.

Breton ['brɛtən] a bretón/ona ♦ n bretón/ona m/f; (LING) bretón m.

brevity ['brɛvɪtɪ] n brevedad f.

brew [bruː] vt (tea) hacer; (beer) elaborar; (plot) tramar ♦ vi hacerse; elaborarse; tramarse; (storm) amenazar.

brewer ['bruːə*] n cervecero, fabricante m de cerveza.

brewery ['bruːərɪ] n fábrica de cerveza.

briar ['braɪə*] n (thorny bush) zarza; (wild rose) escaramujo, rosa silvestre.

bribe [braɪb] n soborno ♦ vt sobornar, cohechar; to ~ sb to do sth sobornar a uno para que haga algo.

bribery ['braɪbərɪ] n soborno, cohecho.

bric-a-brac ['brɪkəbræk] n inv baratijas fpl.

brick [brɪk] n ladrillo.

bricklayer ['brɪkleɪə*] n albañil m.

brickwork ['brɪkwəːk] n enladrillado.

brickworks ['brɪkwəːks] n ladrillar m.

bridal ['braɪdl] a nupcial.

bride [braɪd] n novia.

bridegroom ['braɪdgruːm] n novio.

bridesmaid ['braɪdzmeɪd] n dama de honor.

bridge [brɪdʒ] n puente m; (NAUT) puente m de mando; (of nose) caballete m; (CARDS) bridge m ♦ vt (river) tender un puente sobre.

bridgehead ['brɪdʒhɛd] n cabeza de puente.

bridging loan ['brɪdʒɪŋ-] n crédito provisional.

bridle ['braɪdl] n brida, freno ♦ vt poner la brida a; (fig) reprimir, refrenar ♦ vi (in anger etc) picarse.

bridle path n camino de herradura.

brief [briːf] a breve, corto ♦ n (LAW) escrito ♦ vt (inform) informar; (instruct) dar instrucciones a; in ~ ... en resumen ...; to ~ sb (about sth) informar a uno (sobre algo).

briefcase ['briːfkeɪs] n cartera, portafolio (LAm).

briefing ['briːfɪŋ] n (PRESS) informe m.

briefly ad (smile, glance) brevemente; (explain, say) brevemente, en pocas palabras.

briefs [briːfs] npl (for men) calzoncillos mpl; (for women) bragas fpl.

Brig. abbr = **brigadier**.

brigade [brɪ'geɪd] n (MIL) brigada.

brigadier [brɪgə'dɪə*] n general m de brigada.

bright [braɪt] a claro; (room) luminoso; (day) de sol; (person: clever) listo, inteligente; (: lively) alegre, animado; (colour) vivo; to look on the ~ side mirar el lado bueno.

brighten ['braɪtn] (also: ~ up) vt (room) hacer más alegre ♦ vi (weather) despejarse; (person) animarse, alegrarse.

brilliance ['brɪljəns] n brillo, brillantez f; (fig: of person) inteligencia.

brilliant ['brɪljənt] a (light, idea, person, success) brillante; (clever) genial.

brilliantly ['brɪljəntlɪ] ad brillantemente.

brim [brɪm] n borde m; (of hat) ala.

brimful ['brɪm'ful] a lleno hasta el borde; (fig) rebosante.

brine [braɪn] n (CULIN) salmuera.

bring, pt, pp **brought** [brɪŋ, brɔːt] vt (thing) traer; (person) conducir; to ~ sth to an end terminar con algo; I can't ~ myself to sack him no soy capaz de echarle.

bring about vt ocasionar, producir.

bring back vt volver a traer; (return) devolver.

bring down *vt* bajar; (*price*) rebajar.
bring forward *vt* adelantar; (*BOOK-KEEPING*) pasar a otra cuenta.
bring in *vt* (*harvest*) recoger; (*person*) hacer entrar *or* pasar; (*object*) traer; (*POL: bill, law*) presentar; (*LAW: verdict*) pronunciar; (*produce: income*) producir, rendir.
bring off *vt* (*task, plan*) lograr, conseguir; (*deal*) cerrar.
bring out *vt* (*object*) sacar; (*new product*) sacar; (*book*) publicar.
bring round *vt* (*unconscious person*) hacer volver en sí; (*convince*) convencer.
bring up *vt* (*person*) educar, criar; (*carry up*) subir; (*question*) sacar a colación; (*food: vomit*) devolver, vomitar.
brink [brɪŋk] *n* borde *m*; **on the ~ of doing sth** a punto de hacer algo; **she was on the ~ of tears** estaba a punto de llorar.
brisk [brɪsk] *a* (*walk*) enérgico, vigoroso; (*speedy*) rápido; (*wind*) fresco; (*trade*) activo, animado; (*abrupt*) brusco; **business is ~** el negocio va bien *or* a paso activo.
brisket ['brɪskɪt] *n* carne *f* de vaca para asar.
bristle ['brɪsl] *n* cerda ♦ *vi* erizarse.
bristly ['brɪslɪ] *a* (*beard, hair*) erizado; **to have a ~ chin** tener la barba crecida.
Brit [brɪt] *n* *abbr* (*col*: = *British person*) británico/a.
Britain ['brɪtən] *n* (*also*: **Great ~**) Gran Bretaña.
British ['brɪtɪʃ] *a* británico; **the ~** *npl* los británicos; **the ~ Isles** *npl* las Islas Británicas.
British Rail (BR) *n* ≈ RENFE *f* (*Sp*).
Briton ['brɪtən] *n* británico/a.
brittle ['brɪtl] *a* quebradizo, frágil.
Br(o). *abbr* (*REL*) = **brother**.
broach [brəutʃ] *vt* (*subject*) abordar.
broad [brɔːd] *a* ancho, amplio; (*accent*) cerrado ♦ *n* (*US col*) tía; **in ~ daylight** en pleno día; **the ~ outlines** las líneas generales.
broad bean *n* haba.
broadcast ['brɔːdkɑːst] *n* emisión *f* ♦ *vb* (*pt, pp* **broadcast**) *vt* (*RADIO*) emitir; (*TV*) transmitir ♦ *vi* emitir; transmitir.
broadcasting ['brɔːdkɑːstɪŋ] *n* radiodifusión *f*, difusión *f*.
broadcasting station *n* emisora.
broaden ['brɔːdn] *vt* ensanchar ♦ *vi* ensancharse.
broadly ['brɔːdlɪ] *ad* en general.
broad-minded ['brɔːd'maɪndɪd] *a* tolerante, liberal.
brocade [brə'keɪd] *n* brocado.
broccoli ['brɔkəlɪ] *n* (*BOT*) brécol *m*; (*CULIN*) bróculi *m*.
brochure ['brəufjuə*] *n* folleto.
brogue [brəug] *n* (*accent*) acento regional; (*shoe*) (*tipo de*) *zapato de cuero grueso*.

broil [brɔɪl] *vt* (*US*) asar a la parrilla.
broiler ['brɔɪlə*] *n* (*fowl*) pollo (para asar).
broke [brəuk] *pt of* **break** ♦ *a* (*col*) pelado, sin una perra; **to go ~** quebrar.
broken ['brəukən] *pp of* **break** ♦ *a* (*stick*) roto; (*fig: marriage*) quebrado; (: *promise, vow*) violado; **~ leg** pierna rota; **in ~ English** en un inglés imperfecto.
broken-down ['brəukn'daun] *a* (*car*) averiado; (*machine*) estropeado; (*house*) destartalado.
broken-hearted ['brəukn'hɑːtɪd] *a* con el corazón partido.
broker ['brəukə*] *n* agente *m/f*, bolsista *m/f*.
brokerage ['brəukərɪdʒ] *n* corretaje *m*.
brolly ['brɔlɪ] *n* (*Brit col*) paraguas *m inv*.
bronchitis [brɔŋ'kaɪtɪs] *n* bronquitis *f*.
bronze [brɔnz] *n* bronce *m*.
bronzed [brɔnzd] *a* bronceado.
brooch [brəutʃ] *n* prendedor *m*.
brood [bruːd] *n* camada, cría; (*children*) progenie *f* ♦ *vi* (*hen*) empollar; **to ~ over** dejarse obsesionar por.
broody ['bruːdɪ] *a* (*fig*) triste, melancólico.
brook [bruk] *n* arroyo.
broom [brum] *n* escoba; (*BOT*) retama.
broomstick ['brumstɪk] *n* palo de escoba.
Bros. *abbr* (*COMM*: = *Brothers*) Hnos.
broth [brɔθ] *n* caldo.
brothel ['brɔθl] *n* burdel *m*.
brother ['brʌðə*] *n* hermano.
brotherhood ['brʌðəhud] *n* hermandad *f*.
brother-in-law ['brʌðərɪn'lɔː] *n* cuñado.
brotherly ['brʌðəlɪ] *a* fraternal.
brought [brɔːt] *pt, pp of* **bring**.
brow [brau] *n* (*forehead*) frente *f*; (*of hill*) cumbre *f*.
browbeat ['braubiːt] *vt* (*irg: like* **beat**) intimidar.
brown [braun] *a* moreno; (*hair*) castaño; (*tanned*) bronceado ♦ *n* (*colour*) color *m* moreno *or* pardo ♦ *vt* (*tan*) broncear; (*CULIN*) dorar; **to go ~** (*person*) broncearse; (*leaves*) dorarse.
brown bread *n* pan *m* moreno.
brownie ['braunɪ] *n* niña exploradora.
brown paper *n* papel *m* de estraza.
brown rice *n* arroz *m* moreno.
brown sugar *n* azúcar *m* terciado.
browse [brauz] *vi* (*animal*) pacer; (*among books*) hojear libros; **to ~ through a book** hojear un libro.
bruise [bruːz] *n* (*on person*) cardenal *m*, hematoma *m* ♦ *vt* (*leg etc*) magullar; (*fig: feelings*) herir.
Brum [brʌm] *n* *abbr*, **Brummagem** ['brʌmədʒəm] *n* (*col*) = *Birmingham*.
Brummie ['brʌmɪ] *n* (*col*) habitante *m/f* de Birmingham.
brunch [brʌntʃ] *n* desayuno-almuerzo.
brunette [bruː'net] *n* morena.
brunt [brʌnt] *n*: **to bear the ~ of** llevar el peso de.

brush [brʌʃ] n cepillo; (large) escoba; (for painting, shaving etc) brocha; (artist's) pincel m; (BOT) maleza ♦ vt cepillar; (gen: ~ past, ~ against) rozar al pasar; **to have a ~ with the police** tener un roce con la policía.
brush aside vt rechazar, no hacer caso a.
brush up vt (knowledge) repasar, refrescar.
brushed [brʌʃt] a (nylon, denim etc) afelpado; (TECH: steel, chrome etc) cepillado.
brushwood ['brʌʃwud] n (bushes) maleza; (sticks) leña.
brusque [bru:sk] a (person, manner) brusco; (tone) áspero.
Brussels ['brʌslz] n Bruselas.
Brussels sprout n col f de Bruselas.
brutal ['bru:tl] a brutal.
brutality [bru:'tælɪtɪ] n brutalidad f.
brute [bru:t] n bruto; (person) bestia ♦ a: **by ~ force** a fuerza bruta.
brutish ['bru:tɪʃ] a brutal.
BS n abbr (US: = Bachelor of Science) título universitario.
bs abbr = **bill of sale.**
BSA n abbr = Boy Scouts of America.
BSc abbr = **Bachelor of Science.**
BSI n abbr (= British Standards Institution) institución británica de normalización.
BST n abbr (= British Summer Time) hora de verano del Reino Unido.
Bt. abbr (Brit) = baronet.
btu n abbr (= British thermal unit) ≈ 1054.2 joules.
bubble ['bʌbl] n burbuja; (in paint) ampolla ♦ vi burbujear, borbotar.
bubble bath n espuma para el baño.
bubble gum n chicle m de globo.
Bucharest [bu:kə'rɛst] n Bucarest m.
buck [bʌk] n macho; (US col) dólar m ♦ vi corcovear; **to pass the ~ (to sb)** echar (a uno) el muerto.
buck up vi (cheer up) animarse, cobrar ánimo ♦ vt: **to ~ one's ideas up** poner más empeño.
bucket ['bʌkɪt] n cubo, balde m ♦ vi: **the rain is ~ing (down)** (col) está lloviendo a cántaros.
buckle ['bʌkl] n hebilla ♦ vt abrochar con hebilla ♦ vi torcerse, combarse.
buckle down vi poner empeño.
Bucks [bʌks] abbr (Brit) = Buckinghamshire.
bud [bʌd] n brote m, yema; (of flower) capullo ♦ vi brotar, echar brotes.
Budapest [bju:də'pɛst] n Budapest m.
Buddhism ['budɪzm] n Budismo.
Buddhist ['budɪst] a, n budista m/f.
budding ['bʌdɪŋ] a en ciernes, en embrión.
buddy ['bʌdɪ] n (US) compañero, compinche m.
budge [bʌdʒ] vt mover; (fig) hacer ceder ♦

vi moverse.
budgerigar ['bʌdʒərɪgɑ:*] n periquito.
budget ['bʌdʒɪt] n presupuesto ♦ vi: **to ~ for sth** presupuestar algo; **I'm on a tight ~** no puedo gastar mucho; **she works out her ~ every month** planea su presupuesto todos los meses.
budgie ['bʌdʒɪ] n = **budgerigar.**
Buenos Aires ['bweɪnɔs'aɪrɪz] n Buenos Aires m.
buff [bʌf] a (colour) color m de ante ♦ n (enthusiast) entusiasta m/f.
buffalo ['bʌfələu], pl ~ or **buffaloes** n (Brit) búfalo; (US: bison) bisonte m.
buffer ['bʌfə*] n amortiguador m; (COMPUT) memoria intermedia, buffer m.
buffering ['bʌfərɪŋ] n (COMPUT) almacenamiento en memoria intermedia.
buffet ['bufeɪ] n (Brit: bar) bar m, cafetería; (food) buffet m ♦ vt ['bʌfɪt] (strike) abofetear; (wind etc) golpear.
buffet car n (Brit RAIL) coche-comedor m.
buffet lunch n buffet m (almuerzo).
buffoon [bə'fu:n] n bufón m.
bug [bʌg] n (insect) chinche m; (: gen) bicho, sabandija; (germ) microbio, bacilo; (spy device) micrófono oculto; (COMPUT) fallo, error m ♦ vt (annoy) fastidiar; (room) poner un micrófono oculto en; (phone) pinchar; **I've got the travel ~** (fig) me encanta viajar; **it really ~s me** me fastidia or molesta mucho.
bugbear ['bʌgbɛə*] n pesadilla.
bugle ['bju:gl] n corneta, clarín m.
build [bɪld] n (of person) talle m, tipo ♦ vt (pt, pp built [bɪlt]) construir, edificar.
build on vt fus (fig) basar en.
build up vt (MED) fortalecer; (stocks) acumular; (establish: business) fomentar, desarrollar; (: reputation) crear(se); (increase: production) aumentar; **don't ~ your hopes up too soon** no te hagas demasiadas ilusiones.
builder ['bɪldə*] n constructor(a) m/f; (contractor) contratista m/f.
building ['bɪldɪŋ] n (act of) construcción f; (habitation, offices) edificio.
building contractor n contratista m/f de obras.
building industry n construcción f.
building site n solar m (Sp), obra (LAm).
building society n (Brit) sociedad f inmobiliaria, cooperativa de construcciones. /
building trade n = **building industry.**
build-up ['bɪldʌp] n (publicity): **to give sb/sth a good ~** hacer mucha propaganda de uno/algo.
built [bɪlt] pt, pp of **build.**
built-in ['bɪlt'ɪn] a (cupboard) empotrado; (device) interior, incorporado; **~ obsolescence** obsolescencia incorporada.
built-up ['bɪltʌp] a (area) urbanizado.
bulb [bʌlb] n (BOT) bulbo; (ELEC) bombilla,

foco (*LAm*).

bulbous ['bʌlbəs] *a* bulboso.

Bulgaria [bʌl'geərɪə] *n* Bulgaria.

Bulgarian [bʌl'geərɪən] *a* búlgaro ♦ *n* búlgaro/a; (*LING*) búlgaro.

bulge [bʌldʒ] *n* bombeo, pandeo; (*in birth rate, sales*) alza, aumento ♦ *vi* bombearse, pandearse; (*pocket etc*) hacer bulto.

bulk [bʌlk] *n* (*mass*) bulto, volumen *m*; (*major part*) grueso; **in ~** (*COMM*) a granel; **the ~ of** la mayor parte de; **to buy in ~** comprar en grandes cantidades.

bulk buying *n* compra a granel.

bulkhead ['bʌlkhed] *n* mamparo.

bulky ['bʌlkɪ] *a* voluminoso, abultado.

bull [bul] *n* toro; (*STOCK EXCHANGE*) alcista *m/f* de bolsa; (*REL*) bula.

bulldog ['buldɔg] *n* dogo.

bulldoze ['buldəuz] *vt* mover con; **I was ~d into doing it** (*fig col*) me obligaron a hacerlo.

bulldozer ['buldəuzə*] *n* buldózer *m*, motoniveladora.

bullet ['bulɪt] *n* bala; **~ wound** balazo.

bulletin ['bulɪtɪn] *n* anuncio, parte *m*.

bulletin board *n* (*US*) tablón *m* de anuncios; (*COMPUT*) tablero de noticias.

bulletproof ['bulɪtpruːf] *a* a prueba de balas; **~ vest** chaleco anti-balas.

bullfight ['bulfaɪt] *n* corrida de toros.

bullfighter ['bulfaɪtə*] *n* torero.

bullfighting ['bulfaɪtɪŋ] *n* los toros *mpl*, el toreo; (*art of ~*) tauromaquia.

bullion ['buljən] *n* oro *or* plata en barras.

bullock ['bulək] *n* novillo.

bullring ['bulrɪŋ] *n* plaza de toros.

bull's-eye ['bulzaɪ] *n* centro del blanco.

bully ['bulɪ] *n* valentón *m*, matón *m* ♦ *vt* intimidar, tiranizar.

bum [bʌm] *n* (*Brit: col: backside*) culo; (: *tramp*) vagabundo; (*col: esp US: idler*) holgazán/ana *m/f*, flojo/a.

bumble ['bʌmbl] *vi* (*walk unsteadily*) andar de forma vacilante; (*fig*) farfullar, trastabillar.

bumblebee ['bʌmblbiː] *n* abejorro.

bumbling ['bʌmblɪŋ] *n* divagación *f*.

bumf [bʌmf] *n* (*col: forms etc*) papeleo.

bump [bʌmp] *n* (*blow*) tope *m*, choque *m*; (*jolt*) sacudida; (*noise*) choque *m*, topetón *m*; (*on road etc*) bache *m*; (*on head*) chichón *m* ♦ *vt* (*strike*) chocar contra, topetar ♦ *vi* dar sacudidas.

bump into *vt fus* chocar contra, tropezar con; (*person*) topar con; (*col: meet*) tropezar con, toparse con.

bumper ['bʌmpə*] *n* (*Brit*) parachoques *m inv* ♦ *a*: **~ crop/harvest** cosecha abundante.

bumper cars *npl* (*US*) coches *mpl* de choque.

bumph [bʌmf] *n* = **bumf**.

bumptious ['bʌmpʃəs] *a* engreído, presuntuoso.

bumpy ['bʌmpɪ] *a* (*road*) lleno de baches; (*journey, flight*) agitado.

bun [bʌn] *n* (*Brit: cake*) pastel *m*; (*US: bread*) bollo; (*of hair*) moño.

bunch [bʌntʃ] *n* (*of flowers*) ramo; (*of keys*) manojo; (*of bananas*) piña; (*of people*) grupo; (*pej*) pandilla.

bundle ['bʌndl] *n* (*gen*) bulto, fardo; (*of sticks*) haz *m*; (*of papers*) legajo ♦ *vt* (*also*: **~ up**) atar, envolver; **to ~ sth/sb into** meter algo/a uno precipitadamente en.

bun fight *n* (*Brit col: tea party*) merienda; (: *function*) fiesta oficial.

bung [bʌŋ] *n* tapón *m*, bitoque *m* ♦ *vt* (*throw: also*: **~ into**) arrojar; (*also*: **~ up**: *pipe, hole*) tapar; **my nose is ~ed up** (*col*) tengo la nariz atascada *or* constipada.

bungalow ['bʌŋgələu] *n* bungalow *m*, chalé *m*.

bungle ['bʌŋgl] *vt* chapucear.

bunion ['bʌnjən] *n* juanete *m*.

bunk [bʌŋk] *n* litera; **~ beds** *npl* literas *fpl*.

bunker ['bʌŋkə*] *n* (*coal store*) carbonera; (*MIL*) refugio; (*GOLF*) bunker *m*.

bunny ['bʌnɪ] *n* (*also*: **~ rabbit**) conejito.

Bunsen burner ['bʌnsn-] *n* mechero Bunsen.

bunting ['bʌntɪŋ] *n* empavesada, banderas *fpl*.

buoy [bɔɪ] *n* boya.

buoy up *vt* mantener a flote; (*fig*) animar.

buoyancy ['bɔɪənsɪ] *n* (*of ship*) capacidad *f* para flotar.

buoyant ['bɔɪənt] *a* (*carefree*) boyante, optimista; (*COMM: market, prices etc*) sostenido.

BUPA ['buːpə] *n abbr* (= *British United Provident Association*) seguro médico privado.

burden ['bɜːdn] *n* carga ♦ *vt* cargar; **to be a ~ to sb** ser una carga para uno.

bureau, *pl* **~x** ['bjuərəu, -z] *n* (*Brit: writing desk*) escritorio, buró *m*; (*US: chest of drawers*) cómoda; (*office*) oficina, agencia.

bureaucracy [bjuə'rɔkrəsɪ] *n* burocracia.

bureaucrat ['bjuərəkræt] *n* burócrata *m/f*.

bureaucratic [bjuərə'krætɪk] *a* burocrático.

burgeon ['bɜːdʒən] *vi* (*develop rapidly*) crecer, incrementarse; (*trade etc*) florecer.

burglar ['bɜːglə*] *n* ladrón/ona *m/f*.

burglarize ['bɜːgləraɪz] *vt* (*US*) robar (con allanamiento).

burglar alarm *n* alarma *f* de ladrones.

burglary ['bɜːglərɪ] *n* robo con allanamiento, robo de una casa.

burgle ['bɜːgl] *vt* robar (con allanamiento).

Burgundy ['bɜːgəndɪ] *n* Borgoña.

burial ['berɪəl] *n* entierro.

burial ground *n* cementerio.

burlap ['bɜːlæp] *n* arpillera.

burlesque [bɜː'lesk] *n* parodia.

burly ['bɜːlɪ] *a* fornido, membrudo.
Burma ['bɜːmə] *n* Birmania.
Burmese [bɜː'miːz] *a* birmano ◆ *n* (*pl inv*) birmano/a; (*LING*) birmano.
burn [bɜːn] *vb* (*pt, pp* **burned** *or* **burnt** [bɜːnt]) *vt* (*house*) incendiar ◆ *vi* quemarse, arder; incendiarse; (*sting*) escocer ◆ *n* (*MED*) quemadura; **the cigarette ~t a hole in her dress** se ha quemado el vestido con el cigarrillo; **I've ~t myself!** ¡me he quemado!
burn down *vt* incendiar.
burn out *vt* (*subj: writer etc*): **to ~ o.s. out** agotarse.
burner ['bɜːnə*] *n* (*gas*) quemador *m*.
burning ['bɜːnɪŋ] *a* ardiente; (*building, forest*) en llamas.
burp [bɜːp] (*col*) *n* eructo ◆ *vi* eructar.
burrow ['bʌrəu] *n* madriguera ◆ *vt* hacer una madriguera.
bursar ['bɜːsə*] *n* tesorero; (*Brit: student*) becario/a.
bursary ['bɜːsərɪ] *n* (*Brit*) beca.
burst [bɜːst] *vb* (*pt, pp* **burst**) *vt* (*balloon, pipe*) reventar; (*banks etc*) romper ◆ *vi* reventarse; romperse; (*tyre*) pincharse; (*bomb*) estallar ◆ *n* (*explosion*) estallido; (*also*: **~ pipe**) reventón *m*; **the river has ~ its banks** el río se ha desbordado; **to ~ into flames** estallar en llamas; **to ~ out laughing** soltar la carcajada; **to ~ into tears** deshacerse en lágrimas; **to be ~ing with** reventar de; **a ~ of energy** una explosión de energía; **a ~ of applause** una salva de aplausos; **a ~ of speed** una escapada; **to ~ open** *vi* abrirse de golpe.
burst into *vt fus* (*room etc*) irrumpir en.
bury ['bɛrɪ] *vt* enterrar; (*body*) enterrar, sepultar; **to ~ the hatchet** echar pelillos a la mar.
bus [bʌs] *n* autobús *m*.
bush [buʃ] *n* arbusto; (*scrub land*) monte *m*; **to beat about the ~** andar(se) con rodeos.
bushel ['buʃl] *n* (*measure: Brit*) = 36,36 litros; (: *US*) = 35,24 litros.
bushy ['buʃɪ] *a* (*beard, eyebrows*) poblado; (*hair*) espeso; (*fur*) tupido.
busily ['bɪzɪlɪ] *ad* afanosamente.
business ['bɪznɪs] *n* (*matter, affair*) asunto; (*trading*) comercio, negocios *mpl*; (*firm*) empresa, casa; (*occupation*) oficio; **to be away on ~** estar en viaje de negocios; **it's my ~ to...** me toca *or* corresponde...; **it's none of my ~** yo no tengo nada que ver; **he means ~** habla en serio; **he's in the insurance ~** se dedica a los seguros; **I'm here on ~** estoy aquí por mi trabajo; **to do ~ with sb** hacer negocios con uno.
business address *n* dirección *f* comercial.
business card *n* tarjeta de visita.
businesslike ['bɪznɪslaɪk] *a* (*company*) serio; (*person*) eficiente.
businessman ['bɪznɪsmən] *n* hombre *m* de negocios.
business trip *n* viaje *m* de negocios.
businesswoman ['bɪznɪswumən] *n* mujer *f* de negocios.
busker ['bʌskə*] *n* (*Brit*) músico/a ambulante.
bus route *n* recorrido del autobús.
bus station *n* estación *f or* terminal *f* de autobuses.
bus-stop ['bʌsstɔp] *n* parada de autobús.
bust [bʌst] *n* (*ANAT*) pecho ◆ *a* (*col: broken*) roto, estropeado ◆ *vt* (*col: POLICE: arrest*) detener; **to go ~** quebrarse.
bustle ['bʌsl] *n* bullicio, movimiento ◆ *vi* menearse, apresurarse.
bustling ['bʌslɪŋ] *a* (*town*) animado, bullicioso.
bust-up ['bʌstʌp] *n* (*col*) riña.
busy ['bɪzɪ] *a* ocupado, atareado; (*shop, street*) concurrido, animado ◆ *vt*: **to ~ o.s. with** ocuparse en; **he's a ~ man** (*normally*) es un hombre muy ocupado; (*temporarily*) está muy ocupado; **the line's ~** (*esp US*) está comunicando.
busybody ['bɪzɪbɔdɪ] *n* entrometido/a.
busy signal *n* (*US TEL*) señal *f* de comunicando.
but [bʌt] *conj* pero ◆ *prep* excepto, menos; **nothing ~** nada más que; **~ for** a no ser por, si no fuera por; **all ~ finished** casi terminado; **no one ~ him** nadie sino él; **the last ~ one** el penúltimo.
butane ['bjuːteɪn] *n* (*also*: **~ gas**) (*gas m*) butano.
butcher ['butʃə*] *n* carnicero/a ◆ *vt* hacer una carnicería con; (*cattle etc for meat*) matar; **~'s (shop)** carnicería.
butler ['bʌtlə*] *n* mayordomo.
butt [bʌt] *n* (*cask*) tonel *m*; (*for rain*) tina; (*thick end*) cabo, extremo; (*of gun*) culata; (*of cigarette*) colilla; (*Brit fig: target*) blanco ◆ *vt* dar cabezadas contra, topetar.
butt in *vi* (*interrupt*) interrumpir.
butter ['bʌtə*] *n* mantequilla ◆ *vt* untar con mantequilla.
butter bean *n* judía blanca.
buttercup ['bʌtəkʌp] *n* ranúnculo.
butterfingers ['bʌtəfɪŋɡəz] *n* (*col*) torpe *m/f*.
butterfly ['bʌtəflaɪ] *n* mariposa; (*SWIMMING: also*: **~ stroke**) (braza de) mariposa.
buttocks ['bʌtəks] *npl* nalgas *fpl*.
button ['bʌtn] *n* botón *m* ◆ *vt* (*also*: **~ up**) abotonar, abrochar ◆ *vi* abrocharse.
buttonhole ['bʌtnhəul] *n* ojal *m*; (*flower*) flor *f* que se lleva en el ojal ◆ *vt* obligar a escuchar.
buttress ['bʌtrɪs] *n* contrafuerte *m*; (*fig*) apoyo, sostén *m*.
buxom ['bʌksəm] *a* (*woman*) frescachona.
buy [baɪ] *vb* (*pt, pp* **bought** [bɔːt]) *vt* com-

prar ◆ *n* compra; **to ~ sb sth/sth from sb** comprarle algo a uno; **to ~ sb a drink** invitar a uno a tomar algo; **a good/bad ~** una buena/mala compra.
buy back *vt* volver a comprar.
buy in *vt* proveerse *or* abastecerse de.
buy into *vt fus* comprar acciones en.
buy off *vt* (*col*: *bribe*) sobornar.
buy out *vt* (*partner*) comprar la parte de.
buyer ['baɪə*] *n* comprador(a) *m/f*; **~'s market** mercado favorable al comprador.
buzz [bʌz] *n* zumbido; (*col*: *phone call*) llamada (por teléfono) ◆ *vt* (*call on intercom*) llamar; (*with buzzer*) hacer sonar; (*AVIAT*: *plane, building*) pasar rozando ◆ *vi* zumbar; **my head is ~ing** me zumba la cabeza.
buzz off *vi* (*Brit col*) largarse.
buzzard ['bʌzəd] *n* águila ratonera.
buzzer ['bʌzə*] *n* timbre *m*.
buzz word *n* palabra que está de moda.
by [baɪ] *prep* por; (*beside*) junto a, cerca de; (*according to*) según, de acuerdo con; (*before*): **~ 4 o'clock** para las cuatro ◆ *ad* **see pass, go** *etc*; **~ bus/car** en autobús/coche; **paid ~ the hour** pagado por horas; **~ the kilo/metre** por kilo/metro; **~ night/day** de noche/día; **~ saving hard, he...** ahorrando mucho, (él)...; **(all) ~ oneself** (completamente) solo; **~ this time tomorrow** mañana a estas horas; **~ the way** a propósito, por cierto; **~ and large** en general; **~ and ~** luego, más tarde; **killed ~ lightning** muerto por relámpago; **to pay ~ cheque** pagar con cheque; **a room 3 metres ~ 4** una habitación de 3 metros por 4; **a painting ~ Picasso** un cuadro por Picasso; **surrounded ~ enemies** rodeado de enemigos; **it missed me ~ inches** por un pelo, no me tocó.
bye(-bye) ['baɪ('baɪ)] *excl* adiós, hasta luego.
by(e)-law ['baɪlɔ:] *n* ordenanza municipal.
by-election ['baɪɪlɛkʃən] *n* (*Brit*) elección *f* parcial.
bygone ['baɪgɔn] *a* pasado, del pasado ◆ *n*: **let ~s be ~s** lo pasado, pasado está.
bypass ['baɪpɑ:s] *n* carretera de circunvalación; (*MED*) (operación *f* de) by-pass *m* ◆ *vt* evitar.
by-product ['baɪprɔdʌkt] *n* subproducto, derivado.
bystander ['baɪstændə*] *n* espectador(a) *m/f*.
byte [baɪt] *n* (*COMPUT*) byte *m*, octeto.
byway ['baɪweɪ] *n* camino poco frecuentado.
byword ['baɪwə:d] *n*: **to be a ~ for** ser conocidísimo por.
by-your-leave ['baɪjɔ:'li:v] *n*: **without so much as a ~** sin decir nada, sin dar ningún tipo de explicación.

C

C, c [si:] *n* (*letter*) C, c *f*; (*MUS*): **C** do *m*; **C for Charlie** C de Carmen.
C *abbr* (= *Celsius, centigrade*) C.
c *abbr* (= *century*) S.; (= *circa*) hacia; (*US etc*) = **cent(s)**.
CA *n abbr* = **Central America**; (*Brit*) = **chartered accountant**; (*US POST*) = *California*.
ca. *abbr* (= *circa*) c.
c/a *abbr* = **capital account, credit account, current account**.
CAA *n abbr* (*Brit*: = *Civil Aviation Authority*) *organismo de control y desarrollo de la aviación civil*.
CAB *n abbr* (*Brit*: = *Citizens' Advice Bureau*) ≈ Servicio de Información Ciudadana.
cab [kæb] *n* taxi *m*; (*of truck*) cabina.
cabaret ['kæbəreɪ] *n* cabaret *m*.
cabbage ['kæbɪdʒ] *n* col *f*, berza.
cabin ['kæbɪn] *n* cabaña; (*on ship*) camarote *m*.
cabin cruiser *n* yate *m* de motor.
cabinet ['kæbɪnɪt] *n* (*POL*) consejo de ministros; (*furniture*) armario; (*also*: **display ~**) vitrina.
cabinet-maker ['kæbɪnɪt'meɪkə*] *n* ebanista *m*.
cabinet minister *n* ministro/a (del gabinete).
cable ['keɪbl] *n* cable *m* ◆ *vt* cablegrafiar.
cable-car ['keɪblkɑ:*] *n* teleférico.
cablegram ['keɪblgræm] *n* telegrama *m*.
cable television *n* televisión *f* por cable.
cache [kæʃ] *n* (*drugs*) alijo; (*arms*) zulo.
cackle ['kækl] *vi* cacarear.
cactus, pl cacti ['kæktəs, -taɪ] *n* cacto.
CAD *n abbr* (= *computer-aided design*) diseño asistido por ordenador.
caddie, caddy ['kædɪ] *n* (*GOLF*) cadi *m*.
cadence ['keɪdəns] *n* ritmo; (*MUS*) cadencia.
cadet [kə'dɛt] *n* (*MIL*) cadete *m*; **police ~** cadete *m* de policía.
cadge [kædʒ] *vt* gorronear.
cadger ['kædʒə*] *n* gorrón/ona *m/f*.
cadre ['kædrɪ] *n* cuadro.
Caesarean, (US) Cesarean [si:'zɛərɪən] *a*: **~ (section)** cesárea.
CAF *abbr* (*Brit*: = *cost and freight*) C y F.
café ['kæfeɪ] *n* café *m*.
cafeteria [kæfɪ'tɪərɪə] *n* café *m*.
caffein(e) ['kæfi:n] *n* cafeína.
cage [keɪdʒ] *n* jaula ◆ *vt* enjaular.

cagey ['keɪdʒɪ] *a* (*col*) cauteloso, reservado.
cagoule [kə'guːl] *n* chubasquero.
CAI *n abbr* (= *computer-aided instruction*) enseñanza asistida por ordenador.
Cairo ['kaɪərəu] *n* el Cairo.
cajole [kə'dʒəul] *vt* engatusar.
cake [keɪk] *n* pastel *m*; (*of soap*) pastilla; **he wants to have his ~ and eat it** (*fig*) quiere estar en misa y repicando; **it's a piece of ~** (*col*) es pan comido.
caked [keɪkt] *a*: **~ with** cubierto de.
cake shop *n* pastelería.
calamine ['kæləmaɪn] *n* calamina.
calamitous [kə'læmɪtəs] *a* calamitoso.
calamity [kə'læmɪtɪ] *n* calamidad *f*.
calcium ['kælsɪəm] *n* calcio.
calculate ['kælkjuleɪt] *vt* (*estimate*: *chances, effect*) calcular.
calculate on *vt fus*: **to ~ on sth/on doing sth** contar con algo/con hacer algo.
calculated ['kælkjuleɪtɪd] *a*: **a ~ risk** un riesgo calculado.
calculating ['kælkjuleɪtɪŋ] *a* (*scheming*) calculador(a).
calculation [kælkju'leɪʃən] *n* cálculo, cómputo.
calculator ['kælkjuleɪtə*] *n* calculadora.
calculus ['kælkjuləs] *n* cálculo.
calendar ['kæləndə*] *n* calendario; **~ month/year** *n* mes *m*/año civil.
calf, *pl* **calves** [kɑːf, kɑːvz] *n* (*of cow*) ternero, becerro; (*of other animals*) cría; (*also:* **~skin**) piel *f* de becerro; (*ANAT*) pantorrilla.
caliber ['kælɪbə*] *n* (*US*) = **calibre.**
calibrate ['kælɪbreɪt] *vt* (*gun etc*) calibrar; (*scale of measuring instrument*) graduar.
calibre, (*US*) **caliber** ['kælɪbə*] *n* calibre *m*.
calico ['kælɪkəu] *n* calicó *m*.
California [kælɪ'fɔːnɪə] *n* California.
calipers ['kælɪpəz] *npl* (*US*) = **callipers.**
call [kɔːl] *vt* (*gen, also TEL*) llamar; (*announce*: *flight*) anunciar; (*meeting, strike*) convocar ♦ *vi* (*shout*) llamar; (*telephone*) llamar (por teléfono), telefonear (*esp LAm*); (*visit: also:* **~ in, ~ round**) hacer una visita ♦ *n* (*shout, TEL*) llamada; (*of bird*) canto; (*appeal*) llamamiento; (*summons: for flight etc*) llamada; (*fig: lure*) llamada; **to be ~ed** (*person, object*) llamarse; **to ~ sb names** poner verde a uno; **let's ~ it a day** (*col*) ¡dejémoslo!, ¡ya está bien!; **who is ~ing?** ¿de parte de quién?; **London ~ing** (*RADIO*) aquí Londres; **on ~** (*nurse, doctor etc*) de guardia; **please give me a ~ at 7** despiérteme *or* llámeme a las 7, por favor; **long-distance ~** conferencia (interurbana); **to make a ~** llamar por teléfono; **port of ~** puerto de escala; **to pay a ~ on sb** pasar a ver a uno; **there's not much ~ for these items** estos artículos no tienen mucha demanda.
call at *vt fus* (*ship*) hacer escala en, tocar en; (*train*) parar en.
call back *vi* (*return*) volver; (*TEL*) volver a llamar.
call for *vt fus* (*demand*) pedir, exigir; (*fetch*) venir por.
call in *vt* (*doctor, expert, police*) llamar a.
call off *vt* suspender; (*cancel*) cancelar; (*deal*) anular; **the strike was ~ed off** se abandonó la huelga.
call on *vt fus* (*visit*) visitar; (*turn to*) acudir a.
call out *vi* gritar, dar voces ♦ *vt* (*doctor*) hacer salir; (*police, troops*) hacer intervenir.
call up *vt* (*MIL*) llamar al servicio militar.
callbox ['kɔːlbɔks] *n* (*Brit*) cabina telefónica.
caller ['kɔːlə] *n* visita *f*; (*TEL*) usuario/a; **hold the line, ~!** ¡no cuelgue!
call girl *n* prostituta.
call-in ['kɔːlɪn] *n* (*US*) *programa en que toma parte el público por teléfono.*
calling ['kɔːlɪŋ] *n* vocación *f*, profesión *f*.
calling card *n* tarjeta de visita.
callipers, (*US*) **calipers** ['kælɪpəz] *npl* (*MED*) soporte *m* ortopédico; (*MATH*) calibrador *m*.
callous ['kæləs] *a* insensible, cruel.
callousness ['kæləsnɪs] *n* crueldad *f*.
callow ['kæləu] *a* inexperto, novato.
calm [kɑːm] *a* tranquilo; (*sea*) liso, en calma ♦ *n* calma, tranquilidad *f* ♦ *vt* calmar, tranquilizar.
calm down *vi* calmarse, tranquilizarse ♦ *vt* calmar, tranquilizar.
calmly ['kɑːmlɪ] *ad* tranquilamente, con calma.
calmness ['kɑːmnɪs] *n* calma.
Calor gas ® ['kælə*-] *n* butano.
calorie ['kælərɪ] *n* caloría; **low-~ product** producto bajo en calorías.
calve [kɑːv] *vi* parir.
calves [kɑːvz] *npl of* **calf.**
CAM *n abbr* (= *computer-aided manufacturing*) producción *f* asistida por ordenador.
camber ['kæmbə*] *n* (*of road*) combadura, comba.
Cambodia [kæm'bəudjə] *n* Camboya.
Cambodian [kæm'bəudjən] *a*, *n* camboyano/a *m/f*.
Cambs *abbr* (*Brit*) = *Cambridgeshire.*
came [keɪm] *pt of* **come.**
camel ['kæməl] *n* camello.
cameo ['kæmɪəu] *n* camafeo.
camera ['kæmərə] *n* máquina fotográfica; (*CINEMA, TV*) cámara; (*movie ~*) cámara, tomavistas *m inv*; **in ~** en secreto.
cameraman ['kæmərəmən] *n* cámara *m*.
Cameroon, Cameroun [kæmeˈruːn] *n* Camerón *m*.
camomile tea ['kæməmaɪl-] *n* manzanilla.

camouflage ['kæməflɑːʒ] *n* camuflaje *m* ♦ *vt* camuflar.

camp [kæmp] *n* campo, campamento ♦ *vi* acampar ♦ *a* afectado, afeminado; **to go ~ing** ir de *or* hacer camping.

campaign [kæm'peɪn] *n* (*MIL, POL etc*) campaña ♦ *vi*: **to ~ (for/against)** hacer campaña (a favor de/en contra de).

campaigner [kæm'peɪnə*] *n*: **~ for** partidario/a de; **~ against** persona que hace campaña contra.

campbed ['kæmpbɛd] *n* (*Brit*) cama de campaña.

camper ['kæmpə*] *n* campista *m/f*; (*vehicle*) caravana.

camping ['kæmpɪŋ] *n* camping *m*.

campsite ['kæmpsaɪt] *n* camping *m*.

campus ['kæmpəs] *n* ciudad *f* universitaria.

camshaft ['kæmʃɑːft] *n* árbol *m* de levas.

can [kæn] *auxiliary vb see next headword* ♦ *n* (*of oil, water*) bidón *m*; (*tin*) lata, bote *m* ♦ *vt* enlatar; (*preserve*) conservar en lata; **a ~ of beer** una lata *or* un bote de cerveza; **to carry the ~** (*col*) pagar el pato.

can [kæn] *n, vt see previous headword* ♦ *auxiliary vb* (*pt* **could** [kud]) poder; (*know how to*) saber; **~ I use your telephone?** ¿puedo usar su teléfono?; **could I have a word with you?** ¿podría hablar contigo un momento?; **they could have forgotten** puede que se hayan olvidado; **I ~'t see you** no te puedo ver; **~ you hear me?** (*not translated*) ¿me oyes?; **I ~ swim** sé nadar.

Canada ['kænədə] *n* el Canadá.

Canadian [kə'neɪdɪən] *a, n* canadiense *m/f*.

canal [kə'næl] *n* canal *m*.

canary [kə'nɛərɪ] *n* canario.

Canary Islands, Canaries [kə'nɛərɪz] *npl* las (Islas) Canarias.

Canberra ['kænbərə] *n* Canberra.

cancel ['kænsəl] *vt* cancelar; (*train*) suprimir; (*appointment, cheque*) anular; (*cross out*) tachar, borrar.

cancel out *vt* (*MATH*) anular; (*fig*) contrarrestar; **they ~ each other out** se anulan mutuamente.

cancellation [kænsə'leɪʃən] *n* cancelación *f*; supresión *f*.

cancer ['kænsə*] *n* cáncer *m*; **C~** (*ASTRO*) Cáncer *m*.

cancerous ['kænsərəs] *a* canceroso.

cancer patient *n* enfermo/a *m/f* de cáncer.

cancer research *n* investigación *f* del cáncer.

C and F *abbr* (= *cost and freight*) C y F.

candid ['kændɪd] *a* franco, abierto.

candidacy ['kændɪdəsɪ] *n* candidatura.

candidate ['kændɪdeɪt] *n* candidato/a.

candidature ['kændɪdətʃə*] *n* (*Brit*) = **candidacy**.

candidly ['kændɪdlɪ] *ad* francamente, con franqueza.

candle ['kændl] *n* vela, (*in church*) cirio.

candle holder *n see* **candlestick**.

candlelight ['kændllaɪt] *n*: **by ~** a la luz de una vela.

candlestick ['kændlstɪk] *n* (*also*: **candle holder**: *single*) candelero; (: *low*) palmatoria; (*bigger, ornate*) candelabro.

candour, (*US*) **candor** ['kændə*] *n* franqueza.

candy ['kændɪ] *n* azúcar *m* cande; (*US*) caramelo ♦ *vt* (*fruit*) escarchar.

candy-floss ['kændɪflɔs] *n* (*Brit*) algodón *m* (azucarado).

cane [keɪn] *n* (*BOT*) caña; (*for baskets, chairs etc*) mimbre *m*; (*stick*) vara, palmeta; (: *for walking*) bastón *m* ♦ *vt* (*Brit SCOL*) castigar (con palmeta).

canine ['kænaɪn] *a* canino.

canister ['kænɪstə*] *n* bote *m*, lata.

cannabis ['kænəbɪs] *n* marijuana.

canned [kænd] *a* en lata, de lata; (*col*: *music*) grabado; (: *drunk*) borracho.

cannibal ['kænɪbəl] *n* caníbal *m/f*.

cannibalism ['kænɪbəlɪzəm] *n* canibalismo.

cannon, *pl* **~** *or* **~s** ['kænən] *n* cañón *m*.

cannonball ['kænənbɔːl] *n* bala (de cañón).

cannon fodder *n* carne *f* de cañón.

cannot ['kænɔt] = **can not**.

canny ['kænɪ] *a* astuto.

canoe [kə'nuː] *n* canoa; (*SPORT*) piragua.

canoeing [kə'nuːɪŋ] *n* (*SPORT*) piragüismo.

canoeist [kə'nuːɪst] *n* piragüista *m/f*.

canon ['kænən] *n* (*clergyman*) canónigo; (*standard*) canon *m*.

canonize ['kænənaɪz] *vt* canonizar.

can opener *n* abrelatas *m inv*.

canopy ['kænəpɪ] *n* dosel *m*, toldo.

can't [kænt] = **can not**.

Cantab. *abbr* (*Brit*: = *cantabrigiensis*) = *of Cambridge*.

cantankerous [kæn'tæŋkərəs] *a* arisco, malhumorado.

canteen [kæn'tiːn] *n* (*eating place*) cantina; (*Brit*: *of cutlery*) juego.

canter ['kæntə*] *n* medio galope ♦ *vi* ir a medio galope.

cantilever ['kæntɪliːvə*] *n* viga voladiza.

canvas ['kænvəs] *n* (*material*) lona; (*painting*) lienzo; (*NAUT*) velas *fpl*; **under ~** (*camping*) bajo lona.

canvass ['kænvəs] *vt* (*POL*: *district*) hacer campaña en; (: *person*) solicitar votos de; (*COMM*: *district*) sondear el mercado en; (: *citizens, opinions*) sondear.

canvasser ['kænvəsə*] *n* (*POL*) representante *m/f* electoral; (*COMM*) corredor(a) *m/f*.

canyon ['kænjən] *n* cañón *m*.

CAP *n abbr* (= *Common Agricultural Policy*) PAC *f*.

cap [kæp] *n* (*hat*) gorra; (*for swimming*) gorro de baño; (*of pen*) capuchón *m*; (*of bottle*) tapa, cápsula; (*contraceptive*) diafragma *m* ♦ *vt* (*outdo*) superar; (*Brit* *sport*) seleccionar (para el equipo nacional); **and to ~ it all, he ...** y para colmo, él ....

capability [keɪpə'bɪlɪtɪ] *n* capacidad *f*.

capable ['keɪpəbl] *a* capaz.

capacious [kə'peɪʃəs] *a* amplio.

capacity [kə'pæsɪtɪ] *n* capacidad *f*; (*position*) calidad *f*; **filled to ~** lleno a reventar; **this work is beyond my ~** este trabajo es superior a mí; **in an advisory ~** como asesor.

cape [keɪp] *n* capa; (*GEO*) cabo.

Cape of Good Hope *n* Cabo de Buena Esperanza.

caper ['keɪpə*] *n* (*CULIN*: *also*: **~s**) alcaparra; (*prank*) travesura.

Cape Town *n* El Cabo.

capital ['kæpɪtl] *n* (*also*: **~ city**) capital *f*; (*money*) capital *m*; (*also*: **~ letter**) mayúscula.

capital account *n* cuenta de capital.

capital allowance *n* desgravación *f* sobre bienes del capital.

capital assets *n* activo fijo.

capital expenditure *n* inversión *f* de capital.

capital gains tax *n* impuesto sobre las ganancias de capital.

capital goods *npl* bienes *mpl* de capital.

capital-intensive [kæpɪtlɪn'tensɪv] *a* de utilización intensiva de capital.

capital investment *n* inversión *f* de capital.

capitalism ['kæpɪtəlɪzəm] *n* capitalismo.

capitalist ['kæpɪtəlɪst] *a*, *n* capitalista *m/f*.

capitalize ['kæpɪtəlaɪz] *vt* (*COMM*: *provide with capital*) aprovechar.

capitalize on *vt fus* (*fig*) sacar provecho de, aprovechar.

capital punishment *n* pena de muerte.

capital transfer tax *n* impuesto sobre transferencia de capital.

capitulate [kə'pɪtjuleɪt] *vi* capitular, rendirse.

capitulation [kəpɪtju'leɪʃən] *n* capitulación *f*, rendición *f*.

capricious [kə'prɪʃəs] *a* caprichoso.

Capricorn ['kæprɪkɔːn] *n* Capricornio.

caps [kæps] *abbr* (= *capital letters*) may.

capsize [kæp'saɪz] *vt* volcar, hacer zozobrar ♦ *vi* volcarse, zozobrar.

capstan ['kæpstən] *n* cabrestante *m*.

capsule ['kæpsjuːl] *n* cápsula.

Capt. *abbr* = **Captain**.

captain ['kæptɪn] *n* capitán *m* ♦ *vt* capitanear, ser el capitán de.

caption ['kæpʃən] *n* (*heading*) título; (*to picture*) leyenda.

captivate ['kæptɪveɪt] *vt* cautivar, encantar.

captive ['kæptɪv] *a*, *n* cautivo/a *m/f*.

captivity [kæp'tɪvɪtɪ] *n* cautiverio.

captor ['kæptə*] *n* (*lawful*) apresador(a) *m/f*; (*unlawful*) secuestrador(a) *m/f*.

capture ['kæptʃə*] *vt* prender, apresar; (*place*) tomar; (*attention*) captar, llamar ♦ *n* apresamiento; toma; (*data* ~) formulación *f* de datos.

car [kɑ:*] *n* coche *m*, carro (*LAm*), automóvil *m*; (*US RAIL*) vagón *m*; **by ~** en coche.

Caracas [kə'rækəs] *n* Caracas *m*.

carafe [kə'ræf] *n* garrafa.

caramel ['kærəməl] *n* caramelo.

carat ['kærət] *n* quilate *m*; **18-~ gold** oro de 18 quilates.

caravan ['kærəvæn] *n* (*Brit*) caravana, ruló *f*; (*of camels*) caravana.

caravan site *n* (*Brit*) camping *m* para caravanas.

caraway ['kærəweɪ] *n*: **~ seed** carvi *m*.

carbohydrates [kɑ:bəu'haɪdreɪts] *npl* (*foods*) hidratos *mpl* de carbono.

carbolic [kɑ:'bɔlɪk] *a*: **~ acid** ácido carbónico.

carbon ['kɑ:bən] *n* carbono.

carbonated ['kɑ:bəneɪtɪd] *a* (*drink*) con gas *or* burbujas.

carbon copy *n* copia al carbón.

carbon dioxide *n* bióxido de carbono.

carbon monoxide *n* monóxido de carbono.

carbon paper *n* papel *m* carbón.

carbon ribbon *n* cinta de carbón.

carburettor, (*US*) **carburetor** [kɑ:bju'retə*] *n* carburador *m*.

carcass ['kɑ:kəs] *n* cadáver *m* de animal.

carcinogenic [kɑ:sɪnə'dʒɛnɪk] *a* cancerígeno.

card [kɑ:d] *n* (*thin cardboard*) cartulina; (*playing* ~) carta, naipe *m*; (*visiting* ~, *post~ etc*) tarjeta; **membership ~** carnet *m*; **to play ~s** jugar a las cartas *or* los naipes.

cardamom ['kɑ:dəməm] *n* cardamomo.

cardboard ['kɑ:dbɔ:d] *n* cartón *m*, cartulina.

cardboard box *n* caja de cartón.

card-carrying member ['kɑ:dkærɪŋ-] *n* miembro con carnet.

card game *n* juego de naipes.

cardiac ['kɑ:dɪæk] *a* cardíaco.

cardigan ['kɑ:dɪgən] *n* rebeca.

cardinal ['kɑ:dɪnl] *a* cardinal ♦ *n* cardenal *m*.

cardinal number *n* número cardinal.

card index *n* fichero.

Cards *abbr* (*Brit*) = *Cardiganshire*.

cardsharp ['kɑ:dʃɑ:p] *n* fullero/a.

card vote *n* voto por delegación.

CARE [kɛə*] *n* *abbr* (= *Cooperative for American Relief Everywhere*) sociedad benéfica.

care [kɛə*] *n* cuidado; (*worry*) inquietud *f*; (*charge*) cargo, custodia ♦ *vi*: **to ~ about** preocuparse por; **~ of (c/o)** en casa de, al cuidado de; (: *on letter*) para (entregar a); **in sb's ~** a cargo de uno; **the child has**

been taken into ~ pusieron al niño bajo custodia del gobierno; **"with ~"** "¡frágil!"; **to take ~ to** cuidarse de, tener cuidado de; **to take ~ of** *vt* cuidar; (*details, arrangements*) encargarse de; **I don't ~** no me importa; **I couldn't ~ less** eso me trae sin cuidado.
care for *vt fus* cuidar; (*like*) querer.
careen [kə'riːn] *vi* (*ship*) inclinarse, escorar ♦ *vt* carenar.
career [kə'rɪə*] *n* carrera; (*occupation*) profesión *f* ♦ *vi* (*also*: ~ **along**) correr a toda velocidad.
career girl *n* chica de carrera.
careers officer *n* consejero/a de orientación profesional.
carefree ['kɛəfriː] *a* despreocupado.
careful ['kɛəful] *a* cuidadoso; (*cautious*) cauteloso; **(be) ~!** ¡tenga cuidado!; **he's very ~ with his money** es muy tacaño.
carefully ['kɛəfəlɪ] *ad* con cuidado, cuidadosamente.
careless ['kɛəlɪs] *a* descuidado; (*heedless*) poco atento.
carelessly ['kɛəlɪslɪ] *ad* sin cuidado, a la ligera.
carelessness ['kɛəlɪsnɪs] *n* descuido, falta de atención.
caress [kə'rɛs] *n* caricia ♦ *vt* acariciar.
caretaker ['kɛəteɪkə*] *n* portero/a, conserje *m/f*.
caretaker government *n* gobierno provisional.
car-ferry ['kɑːfɛrɪ] *n* transbordador *m* para coches.
cargo, *pl* ~**es** ['kɑːgəu] *n* cargamento, carga.
cargo boat *n* buque *m* de carga.
cargo plane *n* avión *m* de carga.
car hire *n* alquiler *m* de coche.
Caribbean [kærɪ'biːən] *a* caribe; **the ~ (Sea)** el (Mar) Caribe.
caricature ['kærɪkətjuə*] *n* caricatura.
caring ['kɛərɪŋ] *a* humanitario.
carnage ['kɑːnɪdʒ] *n* matanza, carnicería.
carnal ['kɑːnl] *a* carnal.
carnation [kɑː'neɪʃən] *n* clavel *m*.
carnival ['kɑːnɪvəl] *n* carnaval *m*; (*US*) parque *m* de atracciones.
carnivore ['kɑːnɪvɔː*] *n* carnívoro/a.
carnivorous [kɑː'nɪvrəs] *a* carnívoro.
carol ['kærəl] *n*: **(Christmas)** ~ villancico.
carouse [kə'rauz] *vi* estar de juerga.
carousel [kærə'sɛl] *n* (*US*) tiovivo, caballitos *mpl*.
carp [kɑːp] *n* (*fish*) carpa.
carp at *or* **about** *vt fus* quejarse de.
car park *n* (*Brit*) aparcamiento, parking *m*.
carpenter ['kɑːpɪntə*] *n* carpintero.
carpentry ['kɑːpɪntrɪ] *n* carpintería.
carpet ['kɑːpɪt] *n* alfombra ♦ *vt* alfombrar; **fitted ~** moqueta.
carpet slippers *npl* zapatillas *fpl*.

carpet sweeper [-'swiːpə*] *n* escoba mecánica.
carping ['kɑːpɪŋ] *a* (*critical*) criticón/ona.
carriage ['kærɪdʒ] *n* coche *m*; (*Brit RAIL*) vagón *m*; (*for goods*) transporte *m*; (*of typewriter*) carro; (*bearing*) porte *m*; ~ **forward** porte *m* debido; ~ **free** franco de porte; ~ **paid** porte pagado; ~ **inwards/outwards** gastos *mpl* de transporte a cargo del comprador/vendedor.
carriage return *n* (*on typewriter etc*) tecla de regreso.
carriageway ['kærɪdʒweɪ] *n* (*Brit: part of road*) carretera; **dual ~** carretera de doble calzada.
carrier ['kærɪə*] *n* trajinista *m/f*; (*company*) empresa de transportes.
carrier bag *n* (*Brit*) bolsa de papel *or* plástico.
carrier pigeon *n* paloma mensajera.
carrion ['kærɪən] *n* carroña.
carrot ['kærət] *n* zanahoria.
carry ['kærɪ] *vt* (*subj: person*) llevar; (*transport*) transportar; (*a motion, bill*) aprobar; (*involve: responsibilities etc*) entrañar, implicar; (*COMM: stock*) tener en existencia; (: *interest*) llevar; (*MATH: figure*) llevarse ♦ *vi* (*sound*) oírse; **to get carried away** (*fig*) entusiasmarse; **this loan carries 10% interest** este empréstito devenga un interés del 10 por ciento.
carry forward *vt* (*MATH, COMM*) pasar a la página/columna siguiente.
carry on *vi* (*continue*) seguir (adelante), continuar; (*fam: complain*) quejarse, protestar ♦ *vt* proseguir, continuar.
carry out *vt* (*orders*) cumplir; (*investigation*) llevar a cabo, realizar.
carrycot ['kærɪkɔt] *n* (*Brit*) cuna portátil.
carry-on ['kærɪ'ɔn] *n* (*col: fuss*) lío; (: *annoying behaviour*) jaleo.
cart [kɑːt] *n* carro, carreta ♦ *vt* llevar (en carro).
carte blanche ['kɑːt'blɒnʃ] *n*: **to give sb ~** dar carta blanca a uno.
cartel [kɑː'tɛl] *n* (*COMM*) cartel *m*.
cartilage ['kɑːtɪlɪdʒ] *n* cartílago.
cartographer [kɑː'tɔgrəfə*] *n* cartógrafo/a.
carton ['kɑːtən] *n* (*box*) caja (de cartón); (*of yogurt*) pote *m*.
cartoon [kɑː'tuːn] *n* (*PRESS*) caricatura; (*comic strip*) tira cómica; (*film*) dibujos *mpl* animados.
cartoonist [kɑː'tuːnɪst] *n* dibujante *m/f* de historietas.
cartridge ['kɑːtrɪdʒ] *n* cartucho.
cartwheel ['kɑːtwiːl] *n*: **to turn a ~** dar una voltereta lateral.
carve [kɑːv] *vt* (*meat*) trinchar; (*wood, stone*) cincelar, esculpir; (*on tree*) grabar.
carve up *vt* dividir, repartir; (*meat*) trinchar.
carving ['kɑːvɪŋ] *n* (*in wood etc*) escultura,

(obra de) talla.

carving knife n trinchante m.

car wash n lavado de coches.

Casablanca [kæsə'blæŋkə] n Casablanca.

cascade [kæs'keɪd] n salto de agua, cascada; (fig) chorro ♦ vi caer a chorros.

case [keɪs] n (container) caja; (MED) caso; (for jewels etc) estuche m; (LAW) causa, proceso; (Brit: also: **suit**~) maleta; **lower/upper** ~ (TYP) caja baja/alta; **in** ~ **of** en caso de; **in any** ~ en todo caso; **just in** ~ por si acaso; **to have a good** ~ tener buenos argumentos; **there's a strong** ~ **for reform** hay buenos fundamentos para exigir una reforma.

case-hardened ['keɪshɑːdnd] a insensible.

case history n (MED) historial m médico, historia clínica.

case study n estudio de casos prácticos.

cash [kæʃ] n (col: money) (dinero) efectivo, dinero contante ♦ vt cobrar, hacer efectivo; **to pay (in)** ~ pagar al contado; ~ **on delivery (COD)** cóbrese al entregar; ~ **with order** pedido con pago inmediato; **to be short of** ~ estar pelado, estar sin blanca.

cash in vt (insurance policy etc) cobrar ♦ vi: **to** ~ **in on sth** sacar partido or aprovecharse de algo.

cash account n cuenta de caja.

cashbook ['kæʃbuk] n libro de caja.

cash box n alcancía.

cash card n tarjeta f dinero.

cash desk n (Brit) caja.

cash discount n descuento por pago al contado.

cash dispenser n cajero automático.

cashew [kæ'ʃuː] n (also: ~ **nut**) anacardo.

cash flow n flujo de fondos, cash-flow m, corriente f de efectivos.

cashier [kæ'ʃɪə*] n cajero/a ♦ vt (MIL) destituir, expulsar.

cashmere ['kæʃmɪə*] n casimir m, cachemira.

cash payment n pago al contado.

cash price n precio al contado.

cash register n caja.

cash reserves npl reserva en efectivo.

cash sale n venta al contado.

casing ['keɪsɪŋ] n revestimiento.

casino [kə'siːnəu] n casino.

cask [kɑːsk] n tonel m, barril m.

casket ['kɑːskɪt] n cofre m, estuche m; (US: coffin) ataúd m.

Caspian Sea ['kæspɪən-] n: **the** ~ el Mar Caspio.

casserole ['kæsərəul] n (food, pot) cazuela.

cassette [kæ'sɛt] n cassette m.

cassette deck n platina a cassette.

cassette player, cassette recorder n cassette m.

cassock ['kæsək] n sotana.

cast [kɑːst] vb (pt, pp **cast**) vt (throw) echar, arrojar, lanzar; (skin) mudar, per-

der; (metal) fundir; (THEATRE): **to** ~ **sb as Othello** dar a uno el papel de Otelo ♦ vi (FISHING) lanzar ♦ n (THEATRE) reparto; (mould) forma, molde m; (also: **plaster** ~) vaciado; **to** ~ **loose** soltar; **to** ~ **one's vote** votar.

cast aside vt (reject) descartar, desechar.

cast away vt desechar.

cast down vt derribar.

cast off vi (NAUT) desamarrar; (KNITTING) cerrar los puntos ♦ vt (KNITTING) cerrar; **to** ~ **sb off** abandonar a uno, desentenderse de uno.

cast on vt (KNITTING) montar.

castanets [kæstə'nɛts] npl castañuelas fpl.

castaway ['kɑːstəwəi] n náufrago/a.

caste [kɑːst] n casta.

caster sugar ['kɑːstə*-] n (Brit) azúcar m extrafino.

Castile [kæs'tiːl] n Castilla.

casting vote ['kɑːstɪŋ-] n (Brit) voto decisivo.

cast iron n hierro fundido or colado ♦ a (fig: alibi, excuse) inquebrantable; (will) férreo.

castle ['kɑːsl] n castillo; (CHESS) torre f.

castor ['kɑːstə*] n (wheel) ruedecilla.

castor oil n aceite m de ricino.

castrate [kæs'treɪt] vt castrar.

casual ['kæʒjul] a (by chance) fortuito; (irregular: work etc) eventual, temporero; (unconcerned) despreocupado; (informal: clothes) de sport.

casually ['kæʒjulɪ] ad por casualidad; de manera despreocupada.

casualty ['kæʒjultɪ] n víctima, herido; (dead) muerto; (MIL) baja; **heavy casualties** grandes pérdidas fpl.

casualty ward n urgencias fpl.

cat [kæt] n gato.

catacombs ['kætəkuːmz] npl catacumbas fpl.

Catalan ['kætəlæn] a, n catalán/ana m/f.

catalogue, (US) catalog ['kætələg] n catálogo ♦ vt catalogar.

Catalonia [kætə'ləunɪə] n Cataluña.

catalyst ['kætəlɪst] n catalizador m.

catapult ['kætəpʌlt] n tirador m.

cataract ['kætərækt] n (also MED) catarata.

catarrh [kə'tɑː*] n catarro.

catastrophe [kə'tæstrəfɪ] n catástrofe f.

catastrophic [kætə'strɔfɪk] a catastrófico.

catcall ['kætkɔːl] n (at meeting etc) rechifla, silbido.

catch [kætʃ] vb (pt, pp **caught** [kɔːt]) vt coger (Sp), agarrar (LAm); (arrest) detener; (grasp) asir; (breath) suspender; (person: by surprise) sorprender; (attract: attention) ganar; (MED) contagiarse de, coger; (also: ~ **up**) alcanzar ♦ vi (fire) encenderse; (in branches etc) enredarse ♦ n (fish etc) pesca; (act of catching) cogida;

(*trick*) trampa; (*of lock*) pestillo, cerradura; **to ~ fire** encenderse; **to ~ sight of** divisar.
catch on *vi* (*understand*) caer en la cuenta; (*grow popular*) tener éxito, cuajar.
catch out *vt* (*fig: with trick question*) hundir.
catch up *vi* (*fig*) ponerse al día.
catching ['kætʃɪŋ] *a* (*MED*) contagioso.
catchment area ['kætʃmənt-] *n* (*Brit*) zona de captación.
catch phrase *n* lema *m*, slogan *m*.
catch-22 ['kætʃtwɛntɪ'tuː] *n*: **it's a ~ situation** es un callejón sin salida, es un círculo vicioso.
catchy ['kætʃɪ] *a* (*tune*) pegadizo.
catechism ['kætɪkɪzəm] *n* (*REL*) catequismo.
categoric(al) [kætɪ'gɔrɪk(əl)] *a* categórico, terminante.
categorically [kætɪ'gɔrɪkəlɪ] *ad* categóricamente, terminantemente.
categorize ['kætɪgəraɪz] *vt* clasificar.
category ['kætɪgɔrɪ] *n* categoría, clase *f*.
cater ['keɪtə*] *vi*: **to ~ for** (*Brit*) abastecer a; (*needs*) atender a; (*consumers*) proveer a.
caterer ['keɪtərə*] *n* abastecedor(a) *m/f*, proveedor(a) *m/f*.
catering ['keɪtərɪŋ] *n* (*trade*) (ramo de la) alimentación *f*.
caterpillar ['kætəpɪlə*] *n* oruga, gusano.
caterpillar track *n* rodado de oruga.
cathedral [kə'θiːdrəl] *n* catedral *f*.
cathode-ray tube ['kæθəʊdreɪ'tjuːb] *n* tubo de rayos catódicos.
catholic ['kæθəlɪk] *a* católico; **C~** *a*, *n* (*REL*) católico/a *m/f*.
cat's-eye ['kætsaɪ] *n* (*Brit AUT*) catafoto.
catsup ['kætsəp] *n* (*US*) catsup *m*.
cattle ['kætl] *npl* ganado *sg*.
catty ['kætɪ] *a* malicioso, rencoroso.
Caucasian [kɔː'keɪzɪən] *a*, *n* caucásico/a *m/f*.
Caucasus ['kɔːkəsəs] *n* Cáucaso.
caucus ['kɔːkəs] *n* (*POL: local committee*) comité *m* local; (: *US: to elect candidates*) comité *m* electoral; (: *group*) camarilla política.
caught [kɔːt] *pt, pp of* **catch**.
cauliflower ['kɔlɪflaʊə*] *n* coliflor *f*.
cause [kɔːz] *n* causa, motivo, razón *f* ◆ *vt* causar; (*provoke*) provocar; **to ~ sth to be done** hacer hacer algo; **to ~ sb to do sth** hacer que uno haga algo.
causeway ['kɔːzweɪ] *n* (*road*) carretera elevada; (*embankment*) terraplén *m*.
caustic ['kɔːstɪk] *a* cáustico; (*fig*) mordaz.
cauterize ['kɔːtəraɪz] *vt* cauterizar.
caution ['kɔːʃən] *n* cautela, prudencia; (*warning*) advertencia, amonestación *f* ◆ *vt* amonestar.
cautious ['kɔːʃəs] *a* cauteloso, prudente,

precavido.
cautiously ['kɔːʃəslɪ] *ad* con cautela.
cautiousness ['kɔːʃəsnɪs] *n* cautela.
cavalcade [kævəl'keɪd] *n* cabalgata.
cavalier [kævə'lɪə*] *n* (*knight*) caballero ◆ *a* (*pej: offhand: person, attitude*) arrogante, desdeñoso.
cavalry ['kævəlrɪ] *n* caballería.
cave [keɪv] *n* cueva, caverna ◆ *vi*: **to go caving** ir en una expedición espeleológica.
cave in *vi* (*roof etc*) derrumbarse, hundirse.
caveman ['keɪvmæn] *n* cavernícola *m*, troglodita *m*.
cavern ['kævən] *n* caverna.
cavernous ['kævənəs] *a* (*cheeks, eyes*) hundido.
caviar(e) ['kævɪɑː*] *n* caviar *m*.
cavity ['kævɪtɪ] *n* hueco, cavidad *f*.
cavity wall insulation *n* aislamiento térmico.
cavort [kə'vɔːt] *vi* dar cabrioladas.
cayenne [keɪ'ɛn] *n*: **~ pepper** pimentón *m*.
CB *n abbr* (= *Citizens' Band (Radio)*) banda ciudadana; (*Brit*: = *Companion of (the Order of) the Bath*) título de nobleza.
CBC *n abbr* (= *Canadian Broadcasting Corporation*) cadena de radio y televisión.
CBE *n abbr* (= *Companion of (the Order of) the British Empire*) título de nobleza.
CBI *n abbr* (= *Confederation of British Industry*) ≈ C.E.O.E. (*Sp*).
CBS *n abbr* (*US*: = *Columbia Broadcasting System*) cadena de radio y televisión.
CC *abbr* (*Brit*) = *County Council*.
cc *abbr* (= *cubic centimetres*) c³; (*on letter etc*) = **carbon copy**.
CCA *n abbr* (*US*: = *Circuit Court of Appeals*) tribunal de apelación itinerante.
CCU *n abbr* (*US*: = *coronary care unit*) unidad *f* de cuidados cardiológicos.
CD *n abbr* = **compact disc**; (*MIL*) = *Civil Defence (Corps)* (*Brit*), *Civil Defense* (*US*) ◆ *abbr* (*Brit*: = *Corps Diplomatique*) CD.
CDC *n abbr* (*US*) = *center for disease control*.
Cdr. *abbr* = **Commander**.
CDT *n abbr* (*US*: = *Central Daylight Time*) hora de verano del centro.
cease [siːs] *vt* cesar.
ceasefire ['siːsfaɪə*] *n* alto *m* el fuego.
ceaseless ['siːslɪs] *a* incesante.
ceaselessly ['siːslɪslɪ] *ad* sin cesar.
CED *n abbr* (*US*) = *Committee for Economic Development*.
cedar ['siːdə*] *n* cedro.
cede [siːd] *vt* ceder.
CEEB *n abbr* (*US*: = *College Entry Examination Board*) tribunal para las pruebas de acceso a la universidad.
ceiling ['siːlɪŋ] *n* techo; (*fig: upper limit*) límite *m*, tope *m*.
celebrate ['sɛlɪbreɪt] *vt* celebrar; (*have a*

party) festejar ◆ *vi* divertirse.
celebrated ['sɛlɪbreɪtɪd] *a* célebre.
celebration [sɛlɪ'breɪʃən] *n* fiesta, celebración *f*.
celebrity [sɪ'lɛbrɪtɪ] *n* celebridad *f*.
celeriac [sə'lɛrɪæk] *n* apio-nabo.
celery ['sɛlərɪ] *n* apio.
celestial [sɪ'lɛstɪəl] *a* (*of sky*) celeste; (*divine*) celestial.
celibacy ['sɛlɪbəsɪ] *n* celibato.
cell [sɛl] *n* celda; (*BIOL*) célula; (*ELEC*) elemento.
cellar ['sɛlə*] *n* sótano; (*for wine*) bodega.
'cellist ['tʃɛlɪst] *n* violoncelista *m/f*.
'cello ['tʃɛləu] *n* violoncelo.
cellophane ['sɛləfeɪn] *n* celofán *m*.
cellular ['sɛljulə*] *a* celular.
celluloid ['sɛljulɔɪd] *n* celuloide *m*.
cellulose ['sɛljuləus] *n* celulosa.
Celsius ['sɛlsɪəs] *a* centígrado.
Celt [kɛlt, sɛlt] *n* celta *m/f*.
Celtic ['kɛltɪk, 'sɛltɪk] *a* celta, céltico ◆ *n* (*LING*) céltico.
cement [sə'mɛnt] *n* cemento ◆ *vt* cementar; (*fig*) cimentar, fortalecer.
cement mixer *n* hormigonera.
cemetery ['sɛmɪtrɪ] *n* cementerio.
cenotaph ['sɛnətɑːf] *n* cenotafio.
censor ['sɛnsə*] *n* censor *m* ◆ *vt* (*cut*) censurar.
censorship ['sɛnsəʃɪp] *n* censura.
censure ['sɛnʃə*] *vt* censurar.
census ['sɛnsəs] *n* censo.
cent [sɛnt] *n* (*US: coin*) centavo, céntimo; *see also* **per**.
centenary [sɛn'tiːnərɪ], (*US*) **centennial** [sɛn'tɛnɪəl] *n* centenario.
center ['sɛntə*] *n* (*US*) = **centre**.
centigrade ['sɛntɪgreɪd] *a* centígrado.
centilitre, (*US*) **centiliter** ['sɛntɪliːtə*] *n* centilitro.
centimetre, (*US*) **centimeter** ['sɛntɪmiːtə*] *n* centímetro.
centipede ['sɛntɪpiːd] *n* ciempiés *m inv*.
central ['sɛntrəl] *a* central; (*of house etc*) céntrico.
Central African Republic *n* República Centroafricana.
Central America *n* Centroamérica.
Central American *a, n* centroamericano/a *m/f*.
central heating *n* calefacción *f* central.
centralize ['sɛntrəlaɪz] *vt* centralizar.
central processing unit (CPU) *n* (*COMPUT*) unidad *f* procesadora central.
central reservation *n* (*Brit AUT*) mediana.
centre, (*US*) **center** ['sɛntə*] *n* centro ◆ *vt* centrar; **to ~ (on)** (*concentrate*) concentrar (en).
centrefold, (*US*) **centerfold** ['sɛntəfəuld] *n* página central plegable.
centre-forward ['sɛntə'fɔːwəd] *n* (*SPORT*)

delantero centro.
centre-half ['sɛntə'hɑːf] *n* (*SPORT*) medio centro.
centrepiece, (*US*) **centerpiece** ['sɛntəpiːs] *n* punto central.
centre spread *n* (*Brit*) páginas *fpl* centrales.
centrifuge ['sɛntrɪfjuːdʒ] *n* centrifugadora.
century ['sɛntjurɪ] *n* siglo; **20th ~** siglo veinte; **in the twentieth ~** en el siglo veinte.
CEO *n abbr* (*US*) = **chief executive officer**.
ceramic [sɪ'ræmɪk] *a* cerámico.
ceramics [sɪ'ræmɪks] *n* cerámica.
cereal ['sɪːrɪəl] *n* cereal *m*.
cerebral ['sɛrɪbrəl] *a* cerebral; (*person*) intelectual.
ceremonial [sɛrɪ'məunɪəl] *n* ceremonial.
ceremony ['sɛrɪmənɪ] *n* ceremonia; **to stand on ~** hacer ceremonias, estar de cumplido.
cert [sɜːt] *n* (*Brit col*): **it's a dead ~** ¡eso está hecho!, ¡es cosa segura!
certain ['sɜːtən] *a* seguro; (*correct*) cierto; (*person*) seguro; (*a particular*) cierto; **for ~** a ciencia cierta.
certainly ['sɜːtənlɪ] *ad* desde luego, por supuesto.
certainty ['sɜːtəntɪ] *n* certeza, certidumbre *f*, seguridad *f*.
certificate [sə'tɪfɪkɪt] *n* certificado.
certified ['sɜːtɪfaɪd] *a*: **~ mail** (*US*) correo certificado.
certified public accountant (CPA) *n* (*US*) contable *m/f* diplomado/a.
certify ['sɜːtɪfaɪ] *vt* certificar.
cervical ['sɜːvɪkl] *a*: **~ cancer** cáncer *m* cervical; **~ smear** citología.
cervix ['sɜːvɪks] *n* cerviz *f*.
Cesarean [sɪ'zɛərɪən] *a, n* (*US*) = **Caesarean**.
cessation [sə'seɪʃən] *n* cese *m*, suspensión *f*.
cesspit ['sɛspɪt] *n* pozo negro.
CET *n abbr* (= *Central European Time*) hora de Europa central.
Ceylon [sɪ'lɔn] *n* Ceilán *m*.
cf. *abbr* (= *compare*) cfr.
c/f *abbr* (*COMM*) = *carried forward*.
CG *n abbr* (*US*) = **coastguard**.
cg *abbr* (= *centigram*) cg.
CH *n abbr* (*Brit*: = *Companion of Honour*) título de nobleza.
ch *abbr* (*Brit*: = *central heating*) cal. cen.
ch. *abbr* (= *chapter*) cap.
Chad [tʃæd] *n* Chad *m*.
chafe [tʃeɪf] *vt* (*rub*) rozar; (*irritate*) irritar; **to ~ (against)** (*fig*) irritarse or enojarse (con).
chaffinch ['tʃæfɪntʃ] *n* pinzón *m* (vulgar).
chagrin ['ʃægrɪn] *n* (*annoyance*) disgusto; (*disappointment*) desazón *f*.

chain [tʃeɪn] n cadena ♦ vt (also: ~ up) encadenar.
chain reaction n reacción f en cadena.
chain-smoke ['tʃeɪnsməuk] vi fumar un cigarrillo tras otro.
chain store n tienda de una cadena, ≈ gran almacén.
chair [tʃeə*] n silla; (armchair) sillón m; (of university) cátedra ♦ vt (meeting) presidir; **the ~** (US: electric ~) la silla eléctrica; **please take a ~** siéntese or tome asiento, por favor.
chairlift ['tʃeəlɪft] n telesilla m.
chairman ['tʃeəmən] n presidente m.
chairperson ['tʃeəpə:sn] n presidente/a m/f.
chairwoman ['tʃeəwumən] n presidenta.
chalet ['ʃæleɪ] n chalet m.
chalice ['tʃælɪs] n cáliz m.
chalk [tʃɔ:k] n (GEO) creta; (for writing) tiza, gis m (LAm).
  chalk up vt apuntar; (fig: success) apuntarse; (: victory) obtener.
challenge ['tʃælɪndʒ] n desafío, reto ♦ vt desafiar, retar; (statement, right) poner en duda; **to ~ sb to do sth** retar a uno a que haga algo.
challenger ['tʃælɪndʒə*] n (SPORT) contrincante m/f.
challenging ['tʃælɪndʒɪŋ] a desafiante; (tone) de desafío.
chamber ['tʃeɪmbə*] n cámara, sala; **~ of commerce** cámara de comercio.
chambermaid ['tʃeɪmbəmeɪd] n camarera.
chamber music n música de cámara.
chamberpot ['tʃeɪmbəpɔt] n orinal m.
chameleon [kə'mi:lɪən] n camaleón m.
chamois ['ʃæmwɑ:] n gamuza.
champagne [ʃæm'peɪn] n champaña m, champán m.
champion ['tʃæmpɪən] n campeón/ona m/f; (of cause) defensor(a) m/f, paladín m/f ♦ vt defender, apoyar.
championship ['tʃæmpɪənʃɪp] n campeonato.
chance [tʃɑ:ns] n (coincidence) casualidad f; (luck) suerte f; (fate) azar m; (opportunity) ocasión f, oportunidad f; (likelihood) posibilidad f; (risk) riesgo ♦ vt arriesgar, probar ♦ a fortuito, casual; **to ~ it** arriesgarse, intentarlo; **to take a ~** arriesgarse; **by ~** por casualidad; **it's the ~ of a lifetime** es la oportunidad de su vida; **the ~s are that ...** lo más probable or factible es que ...; **to ~ to do sth** (happen) hacer algo por casualidad.
  chance (up)on vt fus (person) encontrar por casualidad; (thing) tropezar(se) con.
chancel ['tʃɑ:nsəl] n coro y presbiterio.
chancellor ['tʃɑ:nsələ*] n canciller m; **C~ of the Exchequer** (Brit) Ministro de Hacienda.
chancy ['tʃɑ:nsɪ] a (col) arriesgado.

chandelier [ʃændə'lɪə*] n araña (de luces).
change [tʃeɪndʒ] vt cambiar; (replace) reemplazar; (gear) cambiar de; (clothes, house) mudarse de; (exchange) trocar; (transform) transformar ♦ vi cambiar(se); (trains) hacer transbordo; (be transformed): **to ~ into** transformarse en ♦ n cambio; (alteration) modificación f, transformación f; (coins) suelto; (money returned) vuelta; **to ~ one's mind** cambiar de opinión or idea; **to ~ gear** (AUT) cambiar de marcha; **she ~d into an old skirt** se puso una falda vieja; **for a ~** para variar; **can you give me ~ for £1?** ¿tiene cambio de una libra?; **keep the ~** quédese con la vuelta.
changeable ['tʃeɪndʒəbl] a (weather) cambiable; (person) variable.
changeless ['tʃeɪndʒlɪs] a inmutable.
change machine n máquina de cambio.
changeover ['tʃeɪndʒəuvə*] n (to new system) cambio.
changing ['tʃeɪndʒɪŋ] a cambiante.
changing room n (Brit) vestuario.
channel ['tʃænl] n (TV) canal m; (of river) cauce m; (of sea) estrecho; (groove, fig: medium) conducto, medio ♦ vt (river etc) encauzar; **to ~ into** (fig: interest, energies) encauzar a, dirigir a; **the (English) C~** el Canal (de la Mancha); **the C~ Islands** las Islas Normandas fpl; **~s of communication** canales mpl de comunicación; **green/red ~** (CUSTOMS) pasillo verde/rojo.
chant [tʃɑ:nt] n canto; (of crowd) gritos mpl, cantos mpl ♦ vt cantar; **the demonstrators ~ed their disapproval** los manifestantes gritaron su desaprobación.
chaos ['keɪɔs] n caos m.
chaotic [keɪ'ɔtɪk] a caótico, desordenado.
chap [tʃæp] n (Brit col: man) tío, tipo; **old ~** amigo (mío).
chapel ['tʃæpəl] n capilla.
chaperone ['ʃæpərəun] n carabina.
chaplain ['tʃæplɪn] n capellán m.
chapped [tʃæpt] a agrietado.
chapter ['tʃæptə*] n capítulo.
char [tʃɑ:*] vt (burn) carbonizar, chamuscar ♦ n (Brit) = **charlady**.
character ['kærɪktə*] n carácter m, naturaleza, índole f; (in novel, film) personaje m; (role) papel m; (COMPUT) carácter m; **a person of good ~** una persona de buena reputación.
character code n código de caracteres.
characteristic [kærɪktə'rɪstɪk] a característico ♦ n característica.
characterize ['kærɪktəraɪz] vt caracterizar.
charade [ʃə'rɑ:d] n charada.
charcoal ['tʃɑ:kəul] n carbón m vegetal; (ART) carboncillo.
charge [tʃɑ:dʒ] n carga; (LAW) cargo, acusación f; (cost) precio, coste m; (respon-

sibility) cargo; (*task*) encargo ♦ *vt* (*LAW*) acusar (*with* de); (*gun, battery, MIL*: *enemy*) cargar; (*price*) pedir; (*customer*) cobrar; (*sb with task*) encargar ♦ *vi* precipitarse; (*make pay*) cobrar; ~**s** *npl*: **bank** ~**s** comisiones *fpl* bancarias; **extra** ~ recargo, suplemento; **free of** ~ gratis; **to reverse the** ~**s** (*Brit TEL*) revertir el cobro; **to take** ~ **of** hacerse cargo de, encargarse de; **to be in** ~ **of** estar encargado de; **how much do you** ~? ¿cuánto cobra usted?; **to** ~ **an expense (up)** *or* **to sb's account** cargar algo a cuenta de alguien; ~ **it to my account** póngalo *or* cárguelo a mi cuenta.

charge account *n* (*US*) cuenta personal.

charge card *n* tarjeta de cuenta.

chargé d'affaires ['ʃɑːʒeɪdæ'fɛə*] *n* encargado de negocios.

chargehand ['tʃɑːdʒhænd] *n* capataz *m*.

charger ['tʃɑːdʒə*] *n* (*also*: **battery** ~) cargador *m* de baterías; (*old*: *warhorse*) caballo de batalla.

charisma [kæ'rɪzmə] *n* carisma *m*.

charitable ['tʃærɪtəbl] *a* caritativo.

charity ['tʃærɪtɪ] *n* (*gen*) caridad *f*; (*organization*) sociedad *f* benéfica.

chariot ['tʃærɪət] *n* carro.

charlady ['tʃɑːleɪdɪ] *n* (*Brit*) mujer *f* de la limpieza.

charlatan ['ʃɑːlətən] *n* farsante *m/f*.

charm [tʃɑːm] *n* encanto, atractivo; (*spell*) hechizo; (*object*) amuleto ♦ *vt* encantar; hechizar.

charm bracelet *n* pulsera amuleto.

charming ['tʃɑːmɪŋ] *a* encantador(a); (*person*) simpático.

chart [tʃɑːt] *n* (*table*) cuadro; (*graph*) gráfica; (*map*) carta de navegación; (*weather* ~) mapa *m* meteorológico ♦ *vt* (*course*) trazar; (*sales, progress*) hacer una gráfica de; **to be in the** ~**s** (*record, pop group*) figurar entre los discos que más se venden.

charter ['tʃɑːtə*] *vt* (*plane*) alquilar; (*ship*) fletar ♦ *n* (*document*) carta; **on** ~ en alquiler, alquilado.

chartered accountant (CA) *n* (*Brit*) contable *m/f* diplomado/a.

charter flight *n* vuelo chárter.

charwoman ['tʃɑːwumən] *n* = **charlady**.

chase [tʃeɪs] *vt* (*pursue*) perseguir; (*hunt*) cazar ♦ *n* persecución *f*; caza; **to** ~ **after** correr tras.

chase up *vt* (*information*) recoger; **to** ~ **sb up about sth** recordar algo a uno.

chasm ['kæzəm] *n* abismo.

chassis ['ʃæsɪ] *n* chasis *m*.

chaste [tʃeɪst] *a* casto.

chastened ['tʃeɪsənd] *a* escarmentado.

chastening ['tʃeɪsnɪŋ] *a* aleccionador(a).

chastity ['tʃæstɪtɪ] *n* castidad *f*.

chat [tʃæt] *vi* (*also*: **have a** ~) charlar ♦ *n* charla.

chat up *vt* (*col*: *girl*) enrollarse con.

chat show *n* (*Brit*) programa *m* de entrevistas.

chattel ['tʃætl] *n* bien *m* mueble.

chatter ['tʃætə*] *vi* (*person*) charlar; (*teeth*) castañetear ♦ *n* (*of birds*) parloteo; (*of people*) charla, cháchara.

chatterbox ['tʃætəbɔks] *n* parlanchín/ina *m/f*.

chatty ['tʃætɪ] *a* (*style*) familiar; (*person*) hablador(a).

chauffeur ['ʃəufə*] *n* chófer *m*.

chauvinist ['ʃəuvɪnɪst] *n* (*male* ~) machista *m*; (*nationalist*) chovinista *m/f*, patriotero/a *m/f*.

ChE *abbr* = *chemical engineer*.

cheap [tʃiːp] *a* barato; (*joke*) de mal gusto; (*poor quality*) de mala calidad; (*reduced*: *ticket*) económico, (: *fare*) barato ♦ *ad* barato.

cheapen ['tʃiːpn] *vt* rebajar el precio de, abaratar.

cheaply ['tʃiːplɪ] *ad* barato, a bajo precio.

cheat [tʃiːt] *vi* (*in exam*) hacer trampa ♦ *vt* estafar, timar ♦ *n* trampa; estafa; (*person*) tramposo/a; **he's been** ~**ing on his wife** ha estado engañando a su esposa.

cheating ['tʃiːtɪŋ] *n* trampa, fraude *m*.

check [tʃɛk] *vt* (*examine*) controlar; (*facts*) comprobar; (*count*) contar; (*halt*) parar, detener; (*restrain*) refrenar, restringir ♦ *vi*: **to** ~ **with sb** consultar con uno; (*official etc*) informarse por ♦ *n* (*inspection*) control *m*, inspección *f*; (*curb*) freno; (*bill*) nota, cuenta; (*US*) = **cheque**; (*pattern*: *gen pl*) cuadro ♦ *a* (*also*: ~**ed**: *pattern, cloth*) a cuadros; **to keep a** ~ **on sth/sb** controlar algo/a uno.

check in *vi* (*in hotel, airport*) registrarse ♦ *vt* (*luggage*) facturar.

check out *vi* (*of hotel*) desocupar su cuarto ♦ *vt* (*investigate*: *story*) verificar; (: *person*) hacer investigaciones sobre.

check up *vi*: **to** ~ **up on sth** comprobar algo; **to** ~ **up on sb** investigar a alguien.

checkbook ['tʃɛkbuk] *n* (*US*) = **chequebook**.

checkered ['tʃɛkəd] *a* (*US*) = **chequered**.

checkers ['tʃɛkəz] *n* (*US*) juego de damas.

check-in ['tʃɛkɪn] *n* (*also*: ~ **desk**: *at airport*) mostrador de embarque.

checking account ['tʃɛkɪŋ-] *n* (*US*) cuenta corriente.

checklist ['tʃɛklɪst] *n* lista.

checkmate ['tʃɛkmeɪt] *n* jaque *m* mate.

checkout ['tʃɛkaut] *n* (*in supermarket*) caja.

checkpoint ['tʃɛkpɔɪnt] *n* (punto de) control *m*.

checkroom ['tʃɛkrum] *n* (*US*) consigna.

checkup ['tʃɛkʌp] *n* (*MED*) reconocimiento general; (*of machine*) repaso.

cheek [tʃiːk] *n* mejilla; (*impudence*) descaro.

cheekbone ['tʃiːkbəun] *n* pómulo.

cheeky ['tʃiːkɪ] *a* fresco, descarado.

cheep [tʃiːp] *n* (*of bird*) pío ◆ *vi* piar, gorjear.

cheer [tʃɪə*] *vt* vitorear, aplaudir; (*gladden*) alegrar, animar ◆ *vi* aplaudir, dar vivas ◆ *n* viva *m*; ~**s** *npl* aplausos *mpl*; ~**s!** ¡salud!

cheer on *vt* (*person etc*) animar con aplausos *or* gritos.

cheer up *vi* animarse ◆ *vt* alegrar, animar.

cheerful ['tʃɪəful] *a* alegre.

cheerfulness ['tʃɪəfulnɪs] *n* alegría.

cheering ['tʃɪərɪŋ] *n* aplausos *mpl*, vítores *mpl*.

cheerio [tʃɪərɪ'əu] *excl* (*Brit*) ¡hasta luego!

cheerless ['tʃɪəlɪs] *a* triste, sombrío.

cheese [tʃiːz] *n* queso.

cheeseboard ['tʃiːzbɔːd] *n* plato de quesos.

cheesecake ['tʃiːzkeɪk] *n* pastel *m* de queso.

cheetah ['tʃiːtə] *n* leopardo cazador.

chef [ʃɛf] *n* jefe/a *m/f* de cocina.

chemical ['kɛmɪkəl] *a* químico ◆ *n* producto químico.

chemist ['kɛmɪst] *n* (*Brit: pharmacist*) farmacéutico/a; (*scientist*) químico/a; ~**'s** (**shop**) *n* (*Brit*) farmacia.

chemistry ['kɛmɪstrɪ] *n* química.

cheque, (*US*) **check** [tʃɛk] *n* (*Brit*) cheque *m*; **to pay by** ~ pagar con cheque.

chequebook, (*US*) **checkbook** ['tʃɛkbuk] *n* talonario (de cheques).

cheque card *n* (*Brit*) tarjeta de cheque.

chequered, (*US*) **checkered** ['tʃɛkəd] *a* (*fig*) accidentado; (*pattern*) de cuadros.

cherish ['tʃɛrɪʃ] *vt* (*love*) querer, apreciar; (*protect*) cuidar; (*hope etc*) abrigar.

cheroot [ʃə'ruːt] *n* puro (*cortado en los dos extremos*).

cherry ['tʃɛrɪ] *n* cereza.

Ches *abbr* (*Brit*) = Cheshire.

chess [tʃɛs] *n* ajedrez *m*.

chessboard ['tʃɛsbɔːd] *n* tablero (de ajedrez).

chessman ['tʃɛsmən] *n* pieza, trebejo.

chest [tʃɛst] *n* (*ANAT*) pecho; (*box*) cofre *m*, cajón *m*; **to get sth off one's** ~ (*col*) desahogarse; ~ **of drawers** *n* cómoda.

chest measurement *n* talla (*de chaqueta etc*).

chestnut ['tʃɛsnʌt] *n* castaña; (*also*: ~ **tree**) castaño; (*colour*) castaño ◆ *a* (color) castaño *inv*.

chew [tʃuː] *vt* mascar, masticar.

chewing gum ['tʃuːɪŋ-] *n* chicle *m*.

chic [ʃiːk] *a* elegante.

chicanery [ʃɪ'keɪnərɪ] *n* embustes *mpl*, sofismas *mpl*.

chick [tʃɪk] *n* pollito, polluelo; (*US col*) chica.

chicken ['tʃɪkɪn] *n* gallina, pollo; (*food*) pollo; (*col: coward*) gallina *m/f*.

chicken out *vi* (*col*) rajarse, amedrentarse, retirarse miedoso; **to** ~ **out of doing sth** acobardarse de hacer algo.

chickenpox ['tʃɪkɪnpɔks] *n* varicela.

chickpea ['tʃɪkpiː] *n* garbanzo.

chicory ['tʃɪkərɪ] *n* (*for coffee*) achicoria; (*salad*) escarola.

chide [tʃaɪd] *vt*: **to** ~ **sb for sth** reprender *or* regañar a uno por algo.

chief [tʃiːf] *n* jefe/a *m/f* ◆ *a* principal; **C**~ **of Staff** (*MIL*) jefe *m* del estado mayor.

chief executive, (*US*) **chief executive officer** *n* director *m* general.

chiefly ['tʃiːflɪ] *ad* principalmente.

chieftain ['tʃiːftən] *n* jefe *m*, cacique *m*.

chiffon ['ʃɪfɔn] *n* gasa.

chilblain ['tʃɪlbleɪn] *n* sabañón *m*.

child, *pl* ~**ren** [tʃaɪld, 'tʃɪldrən] *n* niño/a; (*offspring*) hijo/a.

childbirth ['tʃaɪldbəːθ] *n* parto.

childhood ['tʃaɪldhud] *n* niñez *f*, infancia.

childish ['tʃaɪldɪʃ] *a* pueril, aniñado.

childless ['tʃaɪldlɪs] *a* sin hijos.

childlike ['tʃaɪldlaɪk] *a* de niño, infantil.

child minder *n* (*Brit*) niñera.

child's play *n* (*fig*): **this is** ~ esto es coser y cantar.

Chile ['tʃɪlɪ] *n* Chile *m*.

Chilean ['tʃɪlɪən] *a, n* chileno/a *m/f*.

chill [tʃɪl] *n* frío; (*MED*) resfriado ◆ *a* frío ◆ *vt* enfriar; (*CULIN*) congelar.

chil(l)i ['tʃɪlɪ] *n* (*Brit*) chile *m*, ají *m* (*LAm*).

chilly ['tʃɪlɪ] *a* frío.

chime [tʃaɪm] *n* repique *m*, campanada ◆ *vi* repicar, sonar.

chimney ['tʃɪmnɪ] *n* chimenea.

chimney sweep *n* deshollinador *m*.

chimpanzee [tʃɪmpæn'ziː] *n* chimpancé *m*.

chin [tʃɪn] *n* mentón *m*, barbilla.

China ['tʃaɪnə] *n* China.

china ['tʃaɪnə] *n* porcelana; (*crockery*) loza.

Chinese [tʃaɪ'niːz] *a* chino ◆ *n* (*pl inv*) chino/a; (*LING*) chino.

chink [tʃɪŋk] *n* (*opening*) grieta, hendedura; (*noise*) tintineo.

chintz [tʃɪnts] *n* cretona.

chip [tʃɪp] *n* (*gen pl: CULIN: Brit*) patata *or* papa (*LAm*) frita; (: *US: also*: **potato** ~) patata *or* papa frita; (*of wood*) astilla; (*of glass, stone*) lasca; (*in gambling*) ficha; (*COMPUT*) chip *m* ◆ *vt* (*cup, plate*) desconchar; **when the** ~**s are down** (*fig*) en el momento de la verdad.

chip in *vi* (*col: interrupt*) interrumpir; (: *contribute*) compartir los gastos.

chipboard ['tʃɪpbɔːd] *n* madera aglomerada.

chipmunk ['tʃɪpmʌŋk] *n* ardilla listada.

chiropodist [kɪ'rɔpədɪst] *n* (*Brit*) pedicuro/a.

chiropody [kɪ'rɔpədɪ] *n* pedicura.

chirp [tʃə:p] *vi* gorjear, piar; (*cricket*) chirriar ◆ *n* (*of cricket*) chirrido.
chirpy ['tʃə:pɪ] *a* alegre, animado.
chisel ['tʃɪzl] *n* (*for wood*) formón *m*; (*for stone*) cincel *m*.
chit [tʃɪt] *n* nota.
chitchat ['tʃɪttʃæt] *n* chismes *mpl*, habladurías *fpl*.
chivalrous ['ʃɪvəlrəs] *a* caballeroso.
chivalry ['ʃɪvəlrɪ] *n* caballerosidad *f*.
chives [tʃaɪvz] *npl* cebollinos *mpl*.
chloride ['klɔ:raɪd] *n* cloruro.
chlorinate ['klɔ:rɪneɪt] *vt* clorinar.
chlorine ['klɔ:ri:n] *n* cloro.
chock-a-block ['tʃɔkə'blɔk], **chock-full** [tʃɔk'ful] *a* atestado.
chocolate ['tʃɔklɪt] *n* chocolate *m*.
choice [tʃɔɪs] *n* elección *f*, selección *f*; (*preference*) preferencia ◆ *a* escogido; **I did it by** *or* **from ~** lo hice de buena gana; **a wide ~** un gran surtido, una gran variedad.
choir ['kwaɪə*] *n* coro.
choirboy ['kwaɪəbɔɪ] *n* corista *m*.
choke [tʃəuk] *vi* sofocarse; (*on food*) atragantarse ◆ *vt* ahogar, sofocar; (*block*) obstruir ◆ *n* (*AUT*) estárter *m*.
choker ['tʃəukə*] *n* (*necklace*) gargantilla.
cholera ['kɔlərə] *n* cólera *m*.
cholesterol [kɔ'lestərəl] *n* colesterol *m*.
choose, *pt* **chose**, *pp* **chosen** [tʃu:z, tʃəuz, 'tʃəuzn] *vt* escoger, elegir; (*team*) seleccionar; **to ~ between** elegir *or* escoger entre; **to ~ from** elegir de entre.
choosy ['tʃu:zɪ] *a* remilgado.
chop [tʃɔp] *vt* (*wood*) cortar, tajar; (*CULIN*: *also*: **~ up**) picar ◆ *n* golpe *m* cortante; (*CULIN*) chuleta; **~s** *npl* (*jaws*) boca *sg*, labios *mpl*; **to get the ~** (*col*: *project*) ser cortado; (: *person*: *be sacked*) ser despedido.
chopper ['tʃɔpə*] *n* (*helicopter*) helicóptero.
choppy ['tʃɔpɪ] *a* (*sea*) picado, agitado.
chopsticks ['tʃɔpstɪks] *npl* palillos *mpl*.
choral ['kɔ:rəl] *a* coral.
chord [kɔ:d] *n* (*MUS*) acorde *m*.
chore [tʃɔ:*] *n* faena, tarea; (*routine task*) trabajo rutinario.
choreographer [kɔrɪ'ɔgrəfə*] *n* coreógrafo/a.
chorister ['kɔrɪstə*] *n* corista *m/f*; (*US*) director(a) *m/f* de un coro.
chortle ['tʃɔ:tl] *vi* reír entre dientes.
chorus ['kɔ:rəs] *n* coro; (*repeated part of song*) estribillo.
chose [tʃəuz] *pt of* **choose**.
chosen ['tʃəuzn] *pp of* **choose**.
chow [tʃau] *n* (*dog*) perro chino.
chowder ['tʃaudə*] *n* (*esp US*) sopa de pescado.
Christ [kraɪst] *n* Cristo.
christen ['krɪsn] *vt* bautizar.
christening ['krɪsnɪŋ] *n* bautizo.

Christian ['krɪstɪən] *a*, *n* cristiano/a *m/f*.
Christianity [krɪstɪ'ænɪtɪ] *n* cristianismo.
Christian name *n* nombre *m* de pila.
Christmas ['krɪsməs] *n* Navidad *f*; **Merry ~!** ¡Felices Navidades!, ¡Felices Pascuas!
Christmas card *n* crismas *m inv*, tarjeta de Navidad.
Christmas Day *n* día *m* de Navidad.
Christmas Eve *n* Nochebuena.
Christmas Island *n* Isla Christmas.
Christmas tree *n* árbol *m* de Navidad.
chrome [krəum] *n* = **chromium plating**.
chromium ['krəumɪəm] *n* cromo; (*also*: **~ plating**) cromado.
chromosome ['krəuməsəum] *n* cromosoma *m*.
chronic ['krɔnɪk] *a* crónico; (*fig*: *liar, smoker*) empedernido.
chronicle ['krɔnɪkl] *n* crónica.
chronological [krɔnə'lɔdʒɪkəl] *a* cronológico.
chrysalis ['krɪsəlɪs] *n* (*BIO*) crisálida.
chrysanthemum [krɪ'sænθəməm] *n* crisantemo.
chubby ['tʃʌbɪ] *a* rechoncho.
chuck [tʃʌk] *vt* lanzar, arrojar; **to ~ (up** *or* **in)** *vt* (*Brit*: *job*) abandonar; (: *person*) dejar plantado.
chuckle ['tʃʌkl] *vi* reírse entre dientes.
chug [tʃʌg] *vi* (*also*: **~ along**: *train*) ir despacio, ir tirando.
chum [tʃʌm] *n* compinche *m/f*, compañero/a.
chump [tʃʌmp] *n* (*col*) tonto/a, estúpido/a.
chunk [tʃʌŋk] *n* pedazo, trozo.
chunky ['tʃʌŋkɪ] *a* (*furniture etc*) achaparrado; (*person*) fornido; (*knitwear*) de lana espesa, gruesa.
church [tʃə:tʃ] *n* iglesia; **the C~ of England** la Iglesia Anglicana.
churchyard ['tʃə:tʃjɑ:d] *n* camposanto.
churlish ['tʃə:lɪʃ] *a* grosero; (*miserly*) tacaño.
churn [tʃə:n] *n* (*for butter*) mantequera; (*for milk*) lechera.
churn out *vt* producir en serie.
chute [ʃu:t] *n* (*also*: **rubbish ~**) vertedero; (*Brit*: *children's slide*) tobogán *m*.
chutney ['tʃʌtnɪ] *n* salsa picante.
CIA *n abbr* (*US*: = *Central Intelligence Agency*) CIA *f*, Agencia Central de Inteligencia.
cicada [sɪ'kɑ:də] *n* cigarra.
CID *n abbr* (*Brit*: = *Criminal Investigation Department*) ≈ B.I.C. *f* (*Sp*).
cider ['saɪdə*] *n* sidra.
C.I.F. *abbr* (= *cost, insurance and freight*) C.I.F.
cigar [sɪ'gɑ:*] *n* puro.
cigarette [sɪgə'ret] *n* cigarrillo, pitillo.
cigarette case *n* pitillera.
cigarette end *n* colilla.
cigarette holder *n* boquilla.
C-in-C *abbr* = **commander-in-chief**.

cinch [sɪntʃ] n (sure thing) cosa segura.
Cinderella [sɪndə'relə] n Cenicienta.
cinders ['sɪndəz] npl cenizas fpl.
cine-camera ['sɪnɪ'kæmərə] n (Brit) cámara cinematográfica.
cine-film ['sɪnɪfɪlm] n (Brit) película de cine.
cinema ['sɪnəmə] n cine m.
cinnamon ['sɪnəmən] n canela.
cipher ['saɪfə*] n cifra; **in ~** en clave.
circle ['sə:kl] n círculo; (in theatre) anfiteatro ♦ vi dar vueltas ♦ vt (surround) rodear, cercar; (move round) dar la vuelta a.
circuit ['sə:kɪt] n circuito; (track) pista; (lap) vuelta.
circuit board n tarjeta de circuitos impresos.
circuitous [sə:'kjuːtəs] a indirecto.
circular ['sə:kjulə*] a circular ♦ n circular f; (as advertisement) panfleto.
circulate ['sə:kjuleɪt] vi circular; (person: socially) alternar, circular ♦ vt poner en circulación.
circulation [sə:kju'leɪʃən] n circulación f; (of newspaper etc) tirada.
circumcise ['sə:kəmsaɪz] vt circuncidar.
circumference [sə'kʌmfərəns] n circunferencia.
circumscribe ['sə:kəmskraɪb] vt circunscribir.
circumspect ['sə:kəmspekt] a circunspecto, prudente.
circumstances ['sə:kəmstənsɪz] npl circunstancias fpl; (financial condition) situación f económica; **in the ~** en or dadas las circunstancias; **under no ~** de ninguna manera, bajo ningún concepto.
circumstantial [sə:kəm'stænʃəl] a detallado; **~ evidence** prueba indiciaria.
circumvent ['sə:kəmvent] vt (rule etc) burlar.
circus ['sə:kəs] n circo; (also: **C~**: in place names) Plaza.
cissy ['sɪsɪ] n mariquita m.
cistern ['sɪstən] n tanque m, depósito (in toilet) cisterna.
citation [saɪ'teɪʃən] n cita; (LAW) citación f; (MIL) mención f.
cite [saɪt] vt citar.
citizen ['sɪtɪzn] n (POL) ciudadano/a; (of city) habitante m/f.
citizenship ['sɪtɪznʃɪp] n ciudadanía.
citric ['sɪtrɪk] a: **~ acid** ácido cítrico.
citrus fruits ['sɪtrəs-] npl agrios mpl.
city ['sɪtɪ] n ciudad f; **the C~** centro financiero de Londres.
city centre n centro de la ciudad.
civic ['sɪvɪk] a cívico, municipal.
civic centre n (Brit) centro público.
civil ['sɪvɪl] a civil; (polite) atento, cortés/esa; (well-bred) educado.
civil defence n protección f civil.
civil engineer n ingeniero/a de caminos.

civil engineering n ingeniería de caminos.
civilian [sɪ'vɪlɪən] a civil (no militar) ♦ n civil m/f, paisano/a.
civilization [sɪvɪlaɪ'zeɪʃən] n civilización f.
civilized ['sɪvɪlaɪzd] a civilizado.
civil law n derecho civil.
civil rights npl derechos mpl civiles.
civil servant n funcionario/a del Estado.
Civil Service n administración f pública.
civil war n guerra civil.
cl abbr (= centilitre) cl.
clad [klæd] a: **~ (in)** vestido (de).
claim [kleɪm] vt exigir, reclamar; (rights etc) reivindicar; (assert) pretender ♦ vi (for insurance) reclamar ♦ n (for expenses) reclamación f; (LAW) demanda; (pretension) pretensión f; **to put in a ~ for** sth presentar una demanda por algo.
claimant ['kleɪmənt] n (ADMIN, LAW) demandante m/f.
claim form n solicitud f.
clairvoyant [klɛə'vɔɪənt] n clarividente m/f.
clam [klæm] n almeja.
clam up vi (col) cerrar el pico.
clamber ['klæmbə*] vi trepar.
clammy ['klæmɪ] a (cold) frío y húmedo; (sticky) pegajoso.
clamour, (US) **clamor** ['klæmə*] n (noise) clamor m, clamoreo; (protest) reclamación f, protesta ♦ vi: **to ~ for** sth clamar por algo, pedir algo a voces.
clamp [klæmp] n abrazadera, grapa ♦ vt afianzar (con abrazadera).
clamp down on vt fus (subj: government, police) reforzar la lucha contra.
clan [klæn] n clan m.
clandestine [klæn'destɪn] a clandestino.
clang [klæŋ] n estruendo ♦ vi sonar, hacer estruendo.
clansman ['klænzmən] n miembro del clan.
clap [klæp] vi aplaudir ♦ vt (hands) batir ♦ n (of hands) palmada; **to ~ one's hands** dar palmadas, batir las palmas; **a ~ of thunder** un trueno.
clapping ['klæpɪŋ] n aplausos mpl.
claret ['klærət] n vino tinto (de Burdeos).
clarification [klærɪfɪ'keɪʃən] n aclaración f.
clarify ['klærɪfaɪ] vt aclarar.
clarinet [klærɪ'net] n clarinete m.
clarity ['klærɪtɪ] n claridad f.
clash [klæʃ] n estruendo; (fig) choque m ♦ vi (meet) encontrarse; (battle) chocar; (disagree) estar en desacuerdo; (dates, events) coincidir.
clasp [klɑːsp] n broche m; (on jewels) cierre m ♦ vt abrochar; (hand) apretar; (embrace) abrazar.
class [klɑːs] n (gen) clase f; (group, category) clase f, categoría ♦ cpd clasista, de clase ♦ vt clasificar.
class-conscious ['klɑːs'kɒnʃəs] a clasista, con conciencia de clase.

classic ['klæsɪk] *a* clásico ◆ *n* (*work*) obra clásica; **~s** *npl* (*UNIV*) clásicas *fpl*.
classical ['klæsɪkəl] *a* clásico; **~ music** música clásica.
classification [klæsɪfɪ'keɪʃən] *n* clasificación *f*.
classified ['klæsɪfaɪd] *a* (*information*) reservado.
classified advertisement *n* anuncio por palabras.
classify ['klæsɪfaɪ] *vt* clasificar.
classmate ['klɑːsmeɪt] *n* compañero/a de clase.
classroom ['klɑːsrum] *n* aula.
classy ['klɑːsɪ] *a* (*col*) elegante, con estilo.
clatter ['klætə*] *n* ruido, estruendo; (*of hooves*) trápala ◆ *vi* hacer ruido *or* estruendo.
clause [klɔːz] *n* cláusula; (*LING*) oración *f*.
claustrophobia [klɔːstrə'fəubɪə] *n* claustrofobia.
claw [klɔː] *n* (*of cat*) uña; (*of bird of prey*) garra; (*of lobster*) pinza; (*TECH*) garfio ◆ *vi*: **to ~ at** arañar; (*tear*) desgarrar.
clay [kleɪ] *n* arcilla.
clean [kliːn] *a* limpio; (*clear*) neto, bien definido ◆ *vt* limpiar ◆ *ad*: **he ~ forgot** lo olvidó por completo; **to come ~** (*col: admit guilt*) confesarlo todo; **to have a ~ driving licence** tener el carnet de conducir sin sanciones; **to ~ one's teeth** lavarse los dientes.
clean off *vt* limpiar.
clean out *vt* limpiar (a fondo).
clean up *vt* limpiar, asear ◆ *vi* (*fig: make profit*): **to ~ up on** sacar provecho de.
clean-cut ['kliːn'kʌt] *a* (*person*) de buen parecer; (*clear*) nítido.
cleaner ['kliːnə*] *n* (*woman*) mujer *f* de la limpieza; (*also:* **dry ~**) tintorero/a.
cleaning ['kliːnɪŋ] *n* limpieza.
cleaning lady *n* señora de la limpieza, asistenta.
cleanliness ['klɛnlɪnɪs] *n* limpieza.
clean-shaven ['kliːn'ʃeɪvn] *a* sin barba, lampiño.
cleanse [klɛnz] *vt* limpiar.
cleanser ['klɛnzə*] *n* detergente *m*; (*cosmetic*) loción *f or* crema limpiadora.
cleansing department ['klɛnzɪŋ-] *n* (*Brit*) departamento de limpieza.
clear [klɪə*] *a* claro; (*road, way*) libre; (*profit*) neto; (*majority*) absoluto ◆ *vt* (*space*) despejar, limpiar; (*LAW: suspect*) absolver; (*obstacle*) salvar, saltar por encima de; (*debt*) liquidar; (*cheque*) pasar por un banco, aceptar; (*site, woodland*) desmontar ◆ *vi* (*fog etc*) despejarse ◆ *n*: **to be in the ~** (*out of debt*) estar libre de deudas; (*out of suspicion*) quedar fuera de toda sospecha; (*out of danger*) estar fuera de peligro ◆ *ad*: **~ of** a distancia de; **to**

make o.s. ~ explicarse claramente; **to make it ~ to sb that ...** hacer entender a uno que ...; **I have a ~ day tomorrow** mañana tengo el día libre; **to keep ~ of sth/ sb** evitar algo/a uno; **to ~ a profit of ...** sacar una ganancia de ...; **to ~ the table** recoger *or* levantar la mesa.
clear off *vi* (*col: leave*) marcharse.
clear up *vt* limpiar; (*mystery*) aclarar, resolver.
clearance ['klɪərəns] *n* (*removal*) despeje *m*; (*permission*) acreditación *f*.
clear-cut ['klɪə'kʌt] *a* bien definido, nítido.
clearing ['klɪərɪŋ] *n* (*in wood*) claro.
clearing bank *n* (*Brit*) banco central.
clearing house *n* (*COMM*) cámara de compensación.
clearly ['klɪəlɪ] *ad* claramente.
clearway ['klɪəweɪ] *n* (*Brit*) carretera donde no se puede aparcar.
cleaver ['kliːvə] *n* cuchilla (de carnicero).
clef [klɛf] *n* (*MUS*) clave *f*.
cleft [klɛft] *n* (*in rock*) grieta, hendedura.
clemency ['klɛmənsɪ] *n* clemencia.
clement ['klɛmənt] *a* (*weather*) clemente, benigno.
clench [klɛntʃ] *vt* apretar, cerrar.
clergy ['klɜːdʒɪ] *n* clero.
clergyman ['klɜːdʒɪmən] *n* clérigo.
clerical ['klɛrɪkəl] *a* de oficina; (*REL*) clerical; (*error*) de copia.
clerk [klɑːk, (*US*) klɜːrk] *n* oficinista *m/f*; (*US*) dependiente/a *m/f*, vendedor(a) *m/f*; **C~ of the Court** secretario forense.
clever ['klɛvə*] *a* (*mentally*) inteligente, listo; (*skilful*) hábil; (*device, arrangement*) ingenioso.
clew [kluː] *n* (*US*) = **clue**.
cliché ['kliːʃeɪ] *n* cliché *m*, frase *f* hecha.
click [klɪk] *vt* (*tongue*) chasquear; (*heels*) taconear.
client ['klaɪənt] *n* cliente *m/f*.
clientele [kliːɑːn'tɛl] *n* clientela.
cliff [klɪf] *n* acantilado.
cliffhanger ['klɪfhæŋə*] *n* (*TV, fig*) película etc de suspense.
climactic [klaɪ'mæktɪk] *a* culminante.
climate ['klaɪmɪt] *n* clima *m*; (*fig*) ambiente *m*.
climax ['klaɪmæks] *n* colmo, punto culminante; (*of play etc*) nudo, clímax *m*; (*sexual ~*) orgasmo.
climb [klaɪm] *vi* subir, trepar; (*plane*) elevarse, remontar el vuelo ◆ *vt* (*stairs*) subir; (*tree*) trepar a; (*mountain*) escalar ◆ *n* subida; **to ~ over a wall** franquear *or* salvar una tapia.
climb down *vi* (*fig*) volverse atrás.
climbdown ['klaɪmdaun] *n* vuelta atrás.
climber ['klaɪmə*] *n* alpinista *m/f*, montañista *m/f*, andinista *m/f* (*LAm*).
climbing ['klaɪmɪŋ] *n* alpinismo, andinismo (*LAm*).

clinch [klɪntʃ] *vt* (*deal*) cerrar; (*argument*) remachar.

cling, *pt, pp* **clung** [klɪŋ, klʌŋ] *vi*: **to ~** (**to**) agarrarse (a); (*clothes*) pegarse (a).

clinic ['klɪnɪk] *n* clínica.

clinical ['klɪnɪkl] *a* clínico; (*fig*) frío, impasible.

clink [klɪŋk] *vi* tintinar.

clip [klɪp] *n* (*for hair*) horquilla; (*also*: **paper ~**) sujetapapeles *m inv*, clip *m*; (*clamp*) grapa ♦ *vt* (*cut*) cortar; (*hedge*) podar; (*also*: **~ together**) unir.

clippers ['klɪpəz] *npl* (*for gardening*) tijeras *fpl*; (*for hair*) maquinilla *sg*; (*for nails*) cortauñas *m inv*.

clipping ['klɪpɪŋ] *n* (*from newspaper*) recorte *m*.

clique [kli:k] *n* camarilla.

cloak [kləuk] *n* capa, manto ♦ *vt* (*fig*) encubrir, disimular.

cloakroom ['kləukrum] *n* guardarropa *m*; (*Brit*: *WC*) lavabo, aseos *mpl*, baño (*LAm*).

clobber ['klɔbə*] *n* (*col*) bártulos *mpl*, trastos *mpl* ♦ *vt* dar una paliza a.

clock [klɔk] *n* reloj *m*; (*in taxi*) taxímetro; **to work against the ~** trabajar contra reloj; **around the ~** las veinticuatro horas; **to sleep round the ~** dormir un día entero; **30,000 on the ~** (*AUT*) treinta mil millas en el cuentakilómetros.

clock in, clock on *vi* fichar, picar.

clock off, clock out *vi* fichar *or* picar la salida.

clock up *vt* acumular.

clockwise ['klɔkwaɪz] *ad* en el sentido de las agujas del reloj.

clockwork ['klɔkwə:k] *n* aparato de relojería ♦ *a* (*toy, train*) de cuerda.

clog [klɔg] *n* zueco, chanclo ♦ *vt* atascar ♦ *vi* atascarse.

cloister ['klɔɪstə*] *n* claustro.

clone [kləun] *n* clon *m*.

close *a, ad and derivatives* [kləus] *a* cercano, próximo; (*near*): **~** (**to**) cerca (de); (*print, weave*) tupido, compacto; (*friend*) íntimo; (*connection*) estrecho; (*examination*) detallado, minucioso; (*weather*) bochornoso; (*atmosphere*) sofocante; (*room*) mal ventilado ♦ *ad* cerca; **~ by, ~ at hand,** *a, ad* muy cerca; **~ to** *prep* cerca de; **to have a ~ shave** (*fig*) escaparse por un pelo; **how ~ is Edinburgh to Glasgow?** ¿qué distancia hay de Edimburgo a Glasgow?; **at ~ quarters** de cerca ♦ *vb and derivatives* [kləuz] *vt* (*shut*) cerrar; (*end*) concluir, terminar; (*bargain, deal*) cerrar ♦ *vi* (*shop etc*) cerrarse; (*end*) concluirse, terminarse ♦ *n* (*end*) fin *m*, final *m*, conclusión *f*; **to bring sth to a ~** terminar algo.

close down *vi* cerrarse definitivamente.

close in *vi* (*hunters*) acercarse rodeando, rodear; (*evening, night, fog*) caer;

cerrarse; **to ~ in on sb** rodear *or* cercar a uno; **the days are closing in** los días son cada vez más cortos.

close off *vt* (*area*) cerrar al tráfico *or* al público.

closed [kləuzd] *a* (*shop etc*) cerrado.

closed-circuit ['kləuzd'sə:kɪt] *a*: **~ television** televisión *f* por circuito cerrado.

closed shop *n* taller *m* gremial.

close-knit ['kləus'nɪt] *a* (*fig*) muy unido.

closely ['kləuslɪ] *ad* (*study*) con detalle; (*listen*) con atención; (*watch*: *person, events*) de cerca; **we are ~ related** somos parientes cercanos; **a ~ guarded secret** un secreto rigurosamente guardado.

closet ['klɔzɪt] *n* (*cupboard*) armario.

close-up ['kləusʌp] *n* primer plano.

closing ['kləuzɪŋ] *a* (*stages, remarks*) último, final; **~ price** (*STOCK EXCHANGE*) precio de cierre.

closure ['kləuʒə*] *n* cierre *m*.

clot [klɔt] *n* (*gen*: *blood*) ~) embolia; (*col*: *idiot*) imbécil *m/f* ♦ *vi* (*blood*) coagularse.

cloth [klɔθ] *n* (*material*) tela, paño; (*table* ~) mantel *m*; (*rag*) trapo.

clothe [kləuð] *vt* vestir; (*fig*) revestir.

clothes [kləuðz] *npl* ropa *sg*; **to put one's ~ on** vestirse, ponerse la ropa; **to take one's ~ off** desvestirse, desnudarse.

clothes brush *n* cepillo (para la ropa).

clothes line *n* cuerda (para tender la ropa).

clothes peg, (*US*) **clothes pin** *n* pinza.

clothing ['kləuðɪŋ] *n* = **clothes**.

clotted cream ['klɔtɪd-] *n* nata muy espesa.

cloud [klaud] *n* nube *f*; (*storm* ~) nubarrón *m*; (*of dust, smoke, gas*) nube *f* ♦ *vt*: (*liquid*) enturbiar; **every ~ has a silver lining** no hay mal que por bien no venga; **to ~ the issue** empañar el problema.

cloud over *vi* (*also fig*) nublarse.

cloudburst ['klaudbə:st] *n* chaparrón *m*.

cloud-cuckoo-land ['klaud'kuku:'lænd] *n* Babia.

cloudy ['klaudɪ] *a* nublado, nubloso; (*liquid*) turbio.

clout [klaut] *n* (*fig*) influencia ♦ *vt* dar un tortazo a.

clove [kləuv] *n* clavo; **~ of garlic** diente *m* de ajo.

clover ['kləuvə*] *n* trébol *m*.

clown [klaun] *n* payaso ♦ *vi* (*also*: **~ about, ~ around**) hacer el payaso.

cloying ['klɔɪɪŋ] *a* (*taste*) empalagoso.

club [klʌb] *n* (*society*) club *m*; (*weapon*) porra, cachiporra; (*also*: **golf ~**) palo ♦ *vt* aporrear ♦ *vi*: **to ~ together** (*join forces*) unir fuerzas; **~s** *npl* (*CARDS*) tréboles *mpl*.

club car *n* (*US RAIL*) coche *m* salón.

clubhouse ['klʌbhaus] *n* local social, sobre todo en clubs deportivos.

cluck [klʌk] *vi* cloquear.

clue [klu:] n pista; (in crosswords) indicación f; **I haven't a ~** no tengo ni idea.
clued up, (US) **clued in** [klu:d-] a (col) al tanto, al corriente.
clueless ['klu:lɪs] a (col) desorientado.
clump [klʌmp] n (of trees) grupo.
clumsy ['klʌmzɪ] a (person) torpe, desmañado; (tool) difícil de manejar.
clung [klʌŋ] pt, pp of **cling**.
cluster ['klʌstə*] n grupo; (BOT) racimo ◆ vi agruparse, apiñarse.
clutch [klʌtʃ] n (AUT) embrague m; (pedal) pedal m de embrague; **to fall into sb's ~es** caer en las garras de alguien ◆ vt asir; agarrar.
clutter ['klʌtə*] vt (also: ~ **up**) atestar, llenar desordenadamente ◆ n desorden m, confusión f.
CM abbr (US POST) = North Mariana Islands.
cm abbr (= centimetre) cm.
CNAA n abbr (Brit: = Council for National Academic Awards) organismo no universitario que otorga diplomas.
CND n abbr (= Campaign for Nuclear Disarmament) plataforma pro desarme nuclear.
CO n abbr = **commanding officer**; (Brit) = Commonwealth Office ◆ abbr (US POST) = Colorado.
Co. abbr = **county**; = **company**.
c/o abbr (= care of) c/a, a/c.
coach [kəutʃ] n (bus) autocar m (Sp), autobús m; (horse-drawn) coche m; (of train) vagón m, coche m; (SPORT) entrenador(a) m/f, instructor(a) m/f ◆ vt (SPORT) entrenar; (student) preparar, enseñar.
coach trip n excursión f en autocar.
coagulate [kəu'ægjuleɪt] vi coagularse.
coal [kəul] n carbón m.
coal face n frente m de carbón.
coalfield ['kəulfi:ld] n yacimiento de carbón.
coalition [kəuə'lɪʃən] n coalición f.
coal man, coal merchant n carbonero.
coalmine ['kəulmaɪn] n mina de carbón.
coalminer ['kəulmaɪnə*] n minero (de carbón).
coalmining ['kəulmaɪnɪŋ] n minería (de carbón).
coarse [kɔ:s] a basto, burdo; (vulgar) grosero, ordinario.
coast [kəust] n costa, litoral m ◆ vi (AUT) ir en punto muerto.
coastal ['kəustl] a costero, costanero.
coaster ['kəustə*] n buque m costero, barco de cabotaje.
coastguard ['kəustgɑ:d] n guardacostas m inv.
coastline ['kəustlaɪn] n litoral m.
coat [kəut] n (jacket) chaqueta; (overcoat) abrigo; (of animal) pelo, lana; (of paint) mano f, capa ◆ vt cubrir, revestir.
coat of arms n escudo de armas.

coat hanger n percha, gancha (LAm).
coating ['kəutɪŋ] n capa, baño.
co-author ['kəu'ɔ:θə*] n coautor(a) m/f.
coax [kəuks] vt engatusar.
cob [kɔb] n see **corn**.
cobbler ['kɔblə*] n zapatero (remendón).
cobbles ['kɔblz], **cobblestones** ['kɔblstəunz] npl adoquines mpl.
COBOL ['kəubɔl] n COBOL m.
cobra ['kəubrə] n cobra.
cobweb ['kɔbwɛb] n telaraña.
cocaine [kə'keɪn] n cocaína.
cock [kɔk] n (rooster) gallo; (male bird) macho ◆ vt (gun) amartillar.
cock-a-hoop [kɔkə'hu:p] a: **to be ~** estar más contento que unas pascuas.
cockatoo [kɔkə'tu:] n cacatúa.
cockerel ['kɔkərl] n gallito.
cock-eyed ['kɔkaɪd] a bizco; (fig: crooked) torcido; (: idea) disparatado.
cockle ['kɔkl] n berberecho.
cockney ['kɔknɪ] n habitante m/f de ciertos barrios de Londres.
cockpit ['kɔkpɪt] n (in aircraft) cabina.
cockroach ['kɔkrəutʃ] n cucaracha.
cocktail ['kɔkteɪl] n combinado, cóctel m; **prawn ~** cóctel m de gambas.
cocktail cabinet n mueble-bar m.
cocktail party n cocktail m, cóctel m.
cocktail shaker [-ʃeɪkə*] n coctelera.
cocoa ['kəukəu] n cacao; (drink) chocolate m.
coconut ['kəukənʌt] n coco.
cocoon [kə'ku:n] n capullo.
cod [kɔd] n bacalao.
COD abbr see **cash on delivery, collect on delivery** (US).
code [kəud] n código; (cipher) clave f; (TEL) prefijo; **~ of behaviour** código de conducta; **~ of practice** código profesional.
codeine ['kəudi:n] n codeína.
codicil ['kɔdɪsɪl] n codicilo.
codify ['kəudɪfaɪ] vt codificar.
cod-liver oil ['kɔdlɪvə*-] n aceite m de hígado de bacalao.
co-driver ['kəu'draɪvə*] n (in race) copiloto m/f; (of lorry) segundo conductor m.
co-ed ['kəuɛd] a abbr = **coeducational** ◆ n abbr (US: = female student) alumna de una universidad mixta; (Brit: school) colegio mixto.
coeducational [kəuɛdju'keɪʃənl] a mixto.
coerce [kəu'ɔ:s] vt forzar, coaccionar.
coercion [kəu'ɔ:ʃən] n coacción f.
coexistence ['kəuɪg'zɪstəns] n coexistencia.
C. of C. n abbr = **chamber of commerce**.
C of E abbr = **Church of England**.
coffee ['kɔfɪ] n café m; **white ~,** (US) **~ with cream** café con leche.
coffee bar n (Brit) cafetería.
coffee bean n grano de café.
coffee break n descanso (para tomar café).

coffee cup n taza de café.
coffeepot ['kɔfɪpɔt] n cafetera.
coffee table n mesita (para servir el café).
coffin ['kɔfɪn] n ataúd m.
C of I abbr = Church of Ireland.
C of S abbr = Church of Scotland.
cog [kɔg] n diente m.
cogent ['kəudʒənt] a lógico, convincente.
cognac ['kɔnjæk] n coñac m.
cogwheel ['kɔgwiːl] n rueda dentada.
cohabit [kəu'hæbɪt] vi (formal): **to ~ (with sb)** cohabitar (con uno).
coherent [kəu'hɪərənt] a coherente.
cohesion [kəu'hiːʒən] n cohesión f.
cohesive [kəu'hiːsɪv] a (fig) cohesivo, unido.
COHSE ['kəuzɪ] n abbr (Brit: = Confederation of Health Service Employees) sindicato de trabajadores de salud.
COI n abbr (Brit: = Central Office of Information) servicio de información gubernamental.
coil [kɔɪl] n rollo; (rope) aduja; (of smoke) espiral f; (AUT, ELEC) bobina, carrete m; (contraceptive) espiral f ◆ vt enrollar, arrollar.
coin [kɔɪn] n moneda ◆ vt acuñar; (word) inventar, idear.
coinage ['kɔɪnɪdʒ] n moneda.
coin-box ['kɔɪnbɔks] n (Brit) caja recaudadora.
coincide [kəuɪn'saɪd] vi coincidir; (agree) estar de acuerdo.
coincidence [kəu'ɪnsɪdəns] n casualidad f.
coin-operated ['kɔɪn'ɔpəreɪtɪd] a (machine) de meter moneda.
Coke ® [kəuk] n Coca Cola ® f.
coke [kəuk] n (coal) coque m.
Col. abbr (= colonel) col.
COLA n abbr (US: = cost-of-living adjustment) reajuste salarial de acuerdo con el costo de la vida.
colander ['kɔləndə*] n colador m, escurridor m.
cold [kəuld] a frío ◆ n frío; (MED) resfriado; **it's ~** hace frío; **to be ~** tener frío; **to catch a ~** coger un catarro, resfriarse, acatarrarse; **in ~ blood** a sangre fría; **the room's getting ~** está empezando a hacer frío en la habitación; **to give sb the ~ shoulder** tratar a uno con frialdad.
cold-blooded ['kəuld'blʌdɪd] a (ZOOL) de sangre fría.
cold cream n crema.
coldly ['kəuldlɪ] a fríamente.
cold sore n herpes m labial.
coleslaw ['kəulslɔː] n ensalada de col.
colic ['kɔlɪk] n cólico.
collaborate [kə'læbəreɪt] vi colaborar.
collaboration [kəlæbə'reɪʃən] n colaboración f; (POL) colaboracionismo.
collaborator [kə'læbəreɪtə*] n colaborador(a) m/f; (POL) colaboracionista m/f.

collage [kɔ'lɑːʒ] n collage m.
collagen ['kɔlədʒən] n colágeno.
collapse [kə'læps] vi (gen) hundirse, derrumbarse; (MED) sufrir un colapso ◆ n (gen) hundimiento; (MED) colapso; (of government) caída; (of plans, scheme, business) ruina, fracaso.
collapsible [kə'læpsəbl] a plegable.
collar ['kɔlə*] n (of coat, shirt) cuello; (for dog, TECH) collar m ◆ vt (col: person, object) abordar, acorralar.
collarbone ['kɔləbəun] n clavícula.
collate [kɔ'leɪt] vt cotejar.
collateral [kɔ'lætərəl] n (COMM) garantía colateral.
collation [kə'leɪʃən] n colación f.
colleague ['kɔliːg] n colega m/f.
collect [kə'lekt] vt reunir; (as a hobby) coleccionar; (Brit: call and pick up) recoger; (wages) cobrar; (debts) recaudar; (donations, subscriptions) colectar ◆ vi reunirse; coleccionar ◆ ad: **to call ~** (US TEL) llamar a cobro revertido; **to ~ one's thoughts** reponerse, recobrar el dominio de sí mismo; **~ on delivery (COD)** (US) entrega contra reembolso.
collection [kə'lekʃən] n colección f; (of fares, wages) cobro; (of post) recogida.
collective [kə'lektɪv] a colectivo.
collective bargaining n negociación f del convenio colectivo.
collector [kə'lektə*] n coleccionista m/f; (of taxes etc) recaudador(a) m/f; **~'s item** or **piece** pieza de coleccionista.
college ['kɔlɪdʒ] n colegio; (of technology, agriculture etc) escuela.
collide [kə'laɪd] vi chocar.
collie ['kɔlɪ] n (dog) collie m.
colliery ['kɔlɪərɪ] n (Brit) mina de carbón.
collision [kə'lɪʒən] n choque m; **to be on a ~ course** (also fig) ir rumbo al desastre.
colloquial [kə'ləukwɪəl] a familiar, coloquial.
collusion [kə'luːʒən] n confabulación f, connivencia; **in ~ with** en connivencia con.
cologne [kə'ləun] n (also: **eau de ~**) (agua de) colonia.
Colombia [kə'lɔmbɪə] n Colombia.
Colombian [kə'lɔmbɪən] a, n colombiano/a m/f.
colon ['kəulən] n (sign) dos puntos; (MED) colón m.
colonel ['kɔːnl] n coronel m.
colonial [kə'ləunɪəl] a colonial.
colonize ['kɔlənaɪz] vt colonizar.
colonnade [kɔlə'neɪd] n columnata.
colony ['kɔlənɪ] n colonia.
color ['kʌlə*] etc (US) = **colour**.
Colorado beetle [kɔlə'rɑːdəu-] n escarabajo de la patata.
colossal [kə'lɔsl] a colosal.
colour, (US) color ['kʌlə*] n color m ◆ vt color(e)ar; (with crayons) color(e)ar (al

pastel); (dye) teñir ◆ vi (blush) sonrojarse; ~s npl (of party, club) colores mpl.
colo(u)r bar n segregación f racial.
colo(u)r-blind ['kʌləblaɪnd] a daltoniano.
colo(u)red ['kʌləd] a de color; (photo) en color; (of race) de color.
colo(u)r film n película en color.
colo(u)rful ['kʌləful] a lleno de color; (person) excéntrico.
colo(u)ring ['kʌlərɪŋ] n (complexion) colorido, color; (substance) colorante m.
colo(u)rless ['kʌləlɪs] a incoloro, sin color.
colo(u)r scheme n combinación f de colores.
colour supplement n (Brit press) suplemento semanal or dominical.
colo(u)r television n televisión f en color.
colt [kəult] n potro.
column ['kɔləm] n columna; (fashion ~, sports ~ etc) sección f; **the editorial** ~ el editorial, el artículo de fondo.
columnist ['kɔləmnɪst] n columnista m/f.
coma ['kəumə] n coma m.
comb [kəum] n peine m; (ornamental) peineta ◆ vt (hair) peinar; (area) registrar a fondo.
combat ['kɔmbæt] n combate m ◆ vt combatir.
combination [kɔmbɪ'neɪʃən] n (gen) combinación f.
combination lock n cerradura de combinación.
combine [kəm'baɪn] vt combinar; (qualities) reunir ◆ vi combinarse ◆ n ['kɔmbaɪn] (econ) cartel m; **a ~d effort** un esfuerzo conjunto.
combine (harvester) n cosechadora.
combo ['kɔmbəu] n (jazz etc) conjunto.
combustion [kəm'bʌstʃən] n combustión f.
come [kʌm], pt **came**, pp **come** vi venir; **to** ~ **undone** desatarse; **to** ~ **loose** aflojarse; ~ **with me** ven conmigo; **we've just** ~ **from Seville** acabamos de llegar de Sevilla; **coming!** ¡voy!; **if it** ~**s to it** llegado el caso.
come about vi suceder, ocurrir.
come across vt fus (person) topar con; (thing) dar con ◆ vi: **to** ~ **across well/badly** caer bien/mal.
come away vi marcharse; (become detached) desprenderse.
come back vi volver; (reply): **can I** ~ **back to you on that one?** ¡volvamos sobre ese punto!
come by vt fus (acquire) conseguir.
come down vi bajar; (buildings) derrumbarse; (: be demolished) ser derribado.
come forward vi presentarse.
come from vt fus ser de.
come in vi entrar; (train) llegar; (fashion) ponerse de moda.
come in for vt fus (criticism etc) merecer.

come into vt fus (money) heredar.
come off vi (button) soltarse, desprenderse; (succeed) salir bien.
come on vi (pupil, work, project) desarrollarse; (lights) encenderse; ~ **on!** ¡vamos!
come out vi salir; (book) aparecer; (be revealed) salir a luz; (strike) declararse en huelga; **to** ~ **out for/against** declararse por/en contra de.
come over vt fus: **I don't know what's** ~ **over him!** ¡no sé lo que le pasa!
come round vi (after faint, operation) volver en sí.
come through vi (survive) sobrevivir; (telephone call): **the call came through** recibimos la llamada.
come to vi volver en sí; (total) sumar; **how much does it** ~ **to?** ¿cuánto es en total?, ¿a cuánto asciende?
come under vt fus (heading) entrar en; (influence) estar bajo.
come up vi subir; (sun) salir; (problem) surgir.
come up against vt fus (resistance, difficulties) tropezar con.
come up to vt fus llegar hasta; **the film didn't** ~ **up to our expectations** la película no fue tan buena como esperábamos.
come up with vt fus (idea) sugerir, proponer.
come upon vt fus dar or topar con.
comeback ['kʌmbæk] n (reaction) reacción f; (response) réplica; **to make a** ~ (theatre) volver a las tablas.
Comecon ['kɔmɪkɔn] n abbr (= Council for Mutual Economic Aid) COMECON m.
comedian [kə'miːdɪən] n cómico.
comedienne [kəmiːdɪ'en] n cómica.
comedown ['kʌmdaun] n revés m, bajón m.
comedy ['kɔmɪdɪ] n comedia.
comet ['kɔmɪt] n cometa m.
comeuppance [kʌm'ʌpəns] n: **to get one's** ~ llevar su merecido.
comfort ['kʌmfət] n comodidad f, confort m; (well-being) bienestar m; (solace) consuelo; (relief) alivio ◆ vt consolar; see also **comforts**.
comfortable ['kʌmfətəbl] a cómodo; (income) adecuado; (majority) suficiente; **I don't feel very** ~ **about it** la cosa me trae algo preocupado.
comfortably ['kʌmfətəblɪ] ad (sit) cómodamente; (live) holgadamente.
comforter ['kʌmfətə*] n (US: pacifier) chupete m; (: bed cover) colcha.
comforts ['kʌmfəts] npl comodidades fpl.
comfort station n (US) servicios mpl.
comic ['kɔmɪk] a (also: ~al) cómico, gracioso ◆ n (magazine) tebeo; (for adults) cómic m.

comic strip n tira cómica.
coming ['kʌmɪŋ] n venida, llegada ♦ a que viene; (next) próximo; (future) venidero; ~(s) and going(s) n(pl) ir y venir m, ajetreo; in the ~ weeks en las próximas semanas.
Comintern ['komɪntəːn] n Comintern f.
comma ['kɔmə] n coma.
command [kə'mɑːnd] n orden f, mandato; (MIL: authority) mando; (mastery) dominio; (COMPUT) orden f, comando ♦ vt (troops) mandar; (give orders to) mandar, ordenar; (be able to get) disponer de; (deserve) merecer; to have at one's ~ (money, resources etc) tener disponible or a su disposición; to have/take ~ of estar al/asumir el mando de.
commandeer [kɔmən'dɪə*] vt requisar.
commander [kə'mɑːndə*] n (MIL) comandante m/f, jefe/a m/f.
commanding [kə'mɑːndɪŋ] a (appearance) imponente; (voice, tone) imperativo; (lead, position) abrumador(a), dominante.
commanding officer n comandante m.
commandment [kə'mɑːndmənt] n (REL) mandamiento.
command module n módulo de comando.
commando [kə'mɑːndəu] n comando.
commemorate [kə'mɛməreɪt] vt conmemorar.
commemoration [kəmɛmə'reɪʃən] n conmemoración f.
commemorative [kə'mɛmərətɪv] a conmemorativo.
commence [kə'mɛns] vt, vi comenzar, empezar.
commend [kə'mɛnd] vt (praise) elogiar, alabar; (recommend) recomendar; (entrust) encomendar.
commendable [kə'mɛndəbl] a encomiable; it is ~ that ... está muy bien que ...
commendation [kɔmɛn'deɪʃən] n (for bravery etc) elogio, encomio; recomendación f.
commensurate [kə'mɛnʃərɪt] a: ~ with en proporción a, que corresponde a.
comment ['kɔmɛnt] n comentario ♦ vt: to ~ that comentar or observar que ♦ vi: to ~ (on) comentar, hacer comentarios (sobre); "no ~" "no tengo nada que decir".
commentary ['kɔməntərɪ] n comentario.
commentator ['kɔməntɛɪtə*] n comentarista m/f.
commerce ['kɔməːs] n comercio.
commercial [kə'məːʃəl] a comercial ♦ n (TV: also: ~ break) anuncio.
commercial bank n banco comercial.
commercialism [kə'məːʃəlɪzəm] n materialismo.
commercialize [kə'məːʃəlaɪz] vt comercializar.

commercial television n televisión f comercial.
commercial vehicle n vehículo comercial.
commiserate [kə'mɪzəreɪt] vi: to ~ with compadecerse de, condolerse de.
commission [kə'mɪʃən] n (committee, fee, order for work of art etc) comisión f; (act) perpetración f ♦ vt (MIL) nombrar; (work of art) encargar; out of ~ (machine) fuera de servicio; ~ of inquiry comisión f investigadora; I get 10% ~ me dan el diez por ciento de comisión; to ~ sb to do sth encargar a uno que haga algo; to ~ sth from sb (painting etc) encargar algo a uno.
commissionaire [kəmɪʃə'nɛə*] n (Brit) portero.
commissioner [kə'mɪʃənə*] n comisario; (POLICE) comisario m de policía.
commit [kə'mɪt] vt (act) cometer; (to sb's care) entregar; to ~ o.s. (to do) comprometerse (a hacer); to ~ suicide suicidarse; to ~ sb for trial remitir a uno al tribunal.
commitment [kə'mɪtmənt] n compromiso.
committed [kə'mɪtɪd] a (writer, politician etc) comprometido.
committee [kə'mɪtɪ] n comité m; to be on a ~ ser miembro/a de un comité.
committee meeting n reunión f del comité.
commodious [kə'məudɪəs] a grande, espacioso.
commodity [kə'mɔdɪtɪ] n mercancía.
commodity exchange n bolsa de productos or de mercancías.
commodity market n mercado de productos básicos.
commodore ['kɔmədɔː*] n comodoro.
common ['kɔmən] a (gen) común; (pej) ordinario ♦ n campo común; in ~ en común; in ~ use de uso corriente.
commoner ['kɔmənə*] n plebeyo/a.
common law n ley f consuetudinaria.
common-law ['kɔmənlɔː] a: ~ wife esposa de hecho.
commonly ['kɔmənlɪ] ad comúnmente.
Common Market n Mercado Común.
commonplace ['kɔmənpleɪs] a de lo más común.
commonroom ['kɔmənrum] n sala común.
Commons ['kɔmənz] npl (Brit POL): the ~ (la Cámara de) los Comunes.
common sense n sentido común.
Commonwealth ['kɔmənwɛlθ] n: the ~ la Mancomunidad (Británica).
commotion [kə'məuʃən] n tumulto, confusión f.
communal ['kɔmjuːnl] a comunal.
commune ['kɔmjuːn] n (group) comuna ♦ vi [kə'mjuːn]: to ~ with comulgar or conversar con.
communicate [kə'mjuːnɪkeɪt] vt comunicar

◆ *vi*: **to ~ (with)** comunicarse (con).
communication [kəmju:nɪ'keɪʃən] *n* comunicación *f*.
communication cord *n* (*Brit*) timbre *m* de alarma.
communications network *n* red *f* de comunicaciones.
communications satellite *n* satélite *m* de comunicaciones.
communicative [kə'mju:nɪkətɪv] *a* comunicativo.
communion [kə'mju:nɪən] *n* (*also*: **Holy C~**) comunión *f*.
communiqué [kə'mju:nɪkeɪ] *n* comunicado, parte *m*.
communism ['kɔmjunɪzəm] *n* comunismo.
communist ['kɔmjunɪst] *a*, *n* comunista *m/f*.
community [kə'mju:nɪtɪ] *n* comunidad *f*; (*large group*) colectividad *f*; (*local*) vecindario.
community centre *n* centro social.
community chest *n* (*US*) arca comunitaria, fondo común.
community health centre *n* centro médico, dispensario público.
community spirit *n* civismo.
commutation ticket [kɔmju'teɪʃən-] *n* (*US*) billete *m* de abono.
commute [kə'mju:t] *vi* *viajar a diario de la casa al trabajo* ◆ *vt* conmutar.
commuter [kə'mju:tə*] *n* persona (que ... *see vi*).
compact [kəm'pækt] *a* compacto; (*style*) conciso; (*packed*) apretado ◆ *n* ['kɔmpækt] (*pact*) pacto; (*also*: **powder ~**) polvera.
compact disc *n* compact disc *m*.
companion [kəm'pænɪən] *n* compañero/a.
companionship [kəm'pænjənʃɪp] *n* compañerismo.
companionway [kəm'pænjənweɪ] *n* (*NAUT*) escalera de cámara.
company ['kʌmpənɪ] *n* (*gen*) compañía; (*COMM*) sociedad *f*, compañía; **to keep sb ~** acompañar a uno; **Smith and C~** Smith y Compañía.
company car *n* coche *m* de la compañía.
company director *n* director(a) *m/f* de empresa.
company secretary *n* (*Brit*) secretario/a de compañía.
comparable ['kɔmpərəbl] *a* comparable.
comparative [kəm'pærətɪv] *a* (*freedom, luxury, cost*) relativo.
comparatively [kəm'pærətɪvlɪ] *ad* (*relatively*) relativamente.
compare [kəm'pɛə*] *vt* comparar; (*set side by side*) cotejar ◆ *vi*: **to ~ (with)** compararse (con); **~d with** *or* **to** comparado con *or* a; **how do the prices ~?** ¿cómo se comparan los precios?
comparison [kəm'pærɪsn] *n* comparación *f*; cotejo; **in ~ (with)** en comparación (con).

compartment [kəm'pɑ:tmənt] *n* (*also* *RAIL*) departamento.
compass ['kʌmpəs] *n* brújula; **~es** *npl* compás *m*; **within the ~ of** al alcance de.
compassion [kəm'pæʃən] *n* compasión *f*.
compassionate [kəm'pæʃənɪt] *a* compasivo; **on ~ grounds** por compasión.
compatibility [kəmpætɪ'bɪlɪtɪ] *n* compatibilidad *f*.
compatible [kəm'pætɪbl] *a* compatible.
compel [kəm'pel] *vt* obligar.
compelling [kəm'pelɪŋ] *a* (*fig*: *argument*) convincente.
compendium [kəm'pendɪəm] *n* compendio.
compensate ['kɔmpənseɪt] *vt* compensar ◆ *vi*: **to ~ for** compensar.
compensation [kɔmpən'seɪʃən] *n* (*for loss*) indemnización *f*.
compère ['kɔmpɛə*] *n* presentador(a) *m/f*.
compete [kəm'pi:t] *vi* (*take part*) tomar parte, concurrir; (*vie with*) competir, hacer competencia.
competence ['kɔmpɪtəns] *n* capacidad *f*, aptitud *f*.
competent ['kɔmpɪtənt] *a* competente, capaz.
competition [kɔmpɪ'tɪʃən] *n* (*contest*) concurso; (*ECON*, *rivalry*) competencia; **in ~ with** en competencia con.
competitive [kəm'petɪtɪv] *a* (*ECON*, *SPORT*) competitivo; (*spirit*) competidor(a), de competencia.
competitor [kəm'petɪtə*] *n* (*rival*) competidor(a) *m/f*, contrincante *m/f*; (*participant*) concursante *m/f*.
compile [kəm'paɪl] *vt* recopilar.
complacency [kəm'pleɪsnsɪ] *n* autosatisfacción *f*.
complacent [kəm'pleɪsənt] *a* autocomplaciente.
complain [kəm'pleɪn] *vi* (*gen*) quejarse; (*COMM*) reclamar.
complaint [kəm'pleɪnt] *n* (*gen*) queja; reclamación *f*; (*LAW*) demanda, querella; (*MED*) enfermedad *f*.
complement ['kɔmplɪmənt] *n* complemento; (*esp ship's crew*) dotación *f* ◆ *vt* ['kɔmplɪment] (*enhance*) complementar.
complementary [kɔmplɪ'mentərɪ] *a* complementario.
complete [kəm'pli:t] *a* (*full*) completo; (*finished*) acabado ◆ *vt* (*fulfil*) completar; (*finish*) acabar; (*a form*) rellenar; **it's a ~ disaster** es un desastre total.
completely [kəm'pli:tlɪ] *ad* completamente.
completion [kəm'pli:ʃən] *n* (*gen*) conclusión *f*, terminación *f*; **to be nearing ~** estar por *or* para terminarse; **on ~ of contract** cuando se realice el contrato.
complex ['kɔmpleks] *a* complejo ◆ *n* (*gen*) complejo.
complexion [kəm'plekʃən] *n* (*of face*) tez *f*, cutis *m*; (*fig*) aspecto.

complexity [kəm'plɛksɪtɪ] *n* complejidad *f*.
compliance [kəm'plaɪəns] *n* (*submission*) sumisión *f*; (*agreement*) conformidad *f*; **in ~ with** de acuerdo con.
compliant [kəm'plaɪənt] *a* sumiso; conforme.
complicate ['kɒmplɪkeɪt] *vt* complicar.
complicated ['kɒmplɪkeɪtɪd] *a* complicado.
complication [kɒmplɪ'keɪʃən] *n* complicación *f*.
complicity [kəm'plɪsɪtɪ] *n* complicidad *f*.
compliment ['kɒmplɪmənt] *n* (*formal*) cumplido; (*flirtation*) piropo ♦ *vt* felicitar; **~s** *npl* saludos *mpl*; **to pay sb a ~** (*formal*) hacer cumplidos a alguien; (*flirt*) piropear, echar piropos a alguien; **~ sb** (**on sth/on doing sth**) felicitar a uno (por algo/ por haber hecho algo).
complimentary [kɒmplɪ'mɛntərɪ] *a* lisonjero; (*free*) de favor.
compliments slip *n* saluda *m*.
comply [kəm'plaɪ] *vi*: **to ~ with** cumplir con.
component [kəm'pəʊnənt] *a* componente ♦ *n* (*TECH*) pieza.
compose [kəm'pəʊz] *vt* componer; **to be ~d of** componerse de, constar de; **to ~ o.s.** tranquilizarse.
composed [kəm'pəʊzd] *a* sosegado.
composer [kəm'pəʊzə*] *n* (*MUS*) compositor(a) *m/f*.
composite ['kɒmpəzɪt] *a* compuesto; **~ motion** (*COMM*) moción *f* compuesta.
composition [kɒmpə'zɪʃən] *n* composición *f*.
compositor [kəm'pɒzɪtə*] *n* (*TYP*) cajista *m/f*.
compos mentis ['kɒmpəs'mɛntɪs] *a*: **to be ~** estar en su sano juicio.
compost ['kɒmpɒst] *n* abono.
compost heap *n* montón *de basura vegetal para abono*.
composure [kəm'pəʊʒə*] *n* serenidad *f*, calma.
compound ['kɒmpaʊnd] *n* (*CHEM*) compuesto; (*LING*) palabra compuesta; (*enclosure*) recinto ♦ *a* (*gen*) compuesto; (*fracture*) complicado ♦ *vt* [kəm'paʊnd] (*fig: problem, difficulty*) agravar.
comprehend [kɒmprɪ'hɛnd] *vt* comprender.
comprehension [kɒmprɪ'hɛnʃən] *n* comprensión *f*.
comprehensive [kɒmprɪ'hɛnsɪv] *a* (*broad*) extenso; (*general*) de conjunto; **~ (school)** *n centro estatal de enseñanza secundaria*; ≈ Instituto Nacional de Bachillerato (*Sp*).
comprehensive insurance policy *n* seguro a todo riesgo.
compress [kəm'prɛs] *vt* comprimir ♦ *n* ['kɒmprɛs] (*MED*) compresa.
compression [kəm'prɛʃən] *n* compresión *f*.
comprise [kəm'praɪz] *vt* (*also*: **be ~d of**) comprender, constar de.

compromise ['kɒmprəmaɪz] *n* (*agreement*) arreglo ♦ *vt* comprometer ♦ *vi* transigir ♦ *cpd* (*decision, solution*) de término medio.
compulsion [kəm'pʌlʃən] *n* obligación *f*; **under ~** a la fuerza, por obligación.
compulsive [kəm'pʌlsɪv] *a* compulsivo.
compulsory [kəm'pʌlsərɪ] *a* obligatorio.
compulsory purchase *n* adquisición *f* forzosa.
compunction [kəm'pʌŋkʃən] *n* escrúpulo; **to have no ~ about doing sth** no tener escrúpulos acerca de hacer algo.
computer [kəm'pju:tə*] *n* ordenador *m*, computador *m*, computadora.
computerize [kəm'pju:təraɪz] *vt* (*data*) computerizar; (*system*) informatizar.
computer language *n* lenguaje *m* de computadora.
computer peripheral *n* periférico.
computer program *n* programa *m* informático.
computer programmer *n* programador(a) *m/f*.
computer programming *n* programación *f*.
computer science *n* informática.
computing [kəm'pju:tɪŋ] *n* (*activity*) informática.
comrade ['kɒmrɪd] *n* compañero/a.
comradeship ['kɒmrɪdʃɪp] *n* camaradería, compañerismo.
comsat ['kɒmsæt] *n abbr* = **communications satellite**.
con [kɒn] *vt* estafar ♦ *n* estafa; **to ~ sb into doing sth** (*col*) convencer a uno por engaño de que haga algo.
concave ['kɒn'keɪv] *a* cóncavo.
conceal [kən'si:l] *vt* ocultar; (*thoughts etc*) disimular.
concede [kən'si:d] *vt* conceder ♦ *vi* ceder, darse por vencido.
conceit [kən'si:t] *n* presunción *f*.
conceited [kən'si:tɪd] *a* presumido.
conceivable [kən'si:vəbl] *a* concebible; **it is ~ that ...** es posible que ....
conceivably [kən'si:vəblɪ] *ad*: **he may ~ be right** es posible que tenga razón.
conceive [kən'si:v] *vt, vi* concebir; **to ~ of sth/of doing sth** imaginar algo/imaginarse haciendo algo.
concentrate ['kɒnsəntreɪt] *vi* concentrarse ♦ *vt* concentrar.
concentration [kɒnsən'treɪʃən] *n* concentración *f*.
concentration camp *n* campo de concentración.
concentric [kən'sɛntrɪk] *a* concéntrico.
concept ['kɒnsɛpt] *n* concepto.
conception [kən'sɛpʃən] *n* (*idea*) concepto, idea; (*BIOL*) concepción *f*.
concern [kən'sɜːn] *n* (*matter*) asunto; (*COMM*) empresa; (*anxiety*) preocupación *f* ♦ *vt* tener que ver con; **to be ~ed (about)**

interesarse (por), preocuparse (por); **to be ~ed with** tratar de; **"to whom it may ~"** "a quien corresponda"; **the department ~ed** (*under discussion*) el departamento en cuestión; (*relevant*) el departamento competente; **as far as I am ~ed** en cuanto a mí, por lo que a mí se refiere.

concerning [kən'sɜːnɪŋ] *prep* sobre, acerca de.

concert ['kɒnsət] *n* concierto.

concerted [kən'sɜːtəd] *a* (*efforts etc*) concertado.

concert hall *n* sala de conciertos.

concertina [kɒnsə'tiːnə] *n* concertina.

concerto [kən'tʃɜːtəu] *n* concierto.

concession [kən'sɛʃən] *n* concesión *f*; **tax ~** privilegio fiscal.

concessionaire [kənsɛʃə'nɛə*] *n* concesionario/a.

concessionary [kən'sɛʃənərɪ] *a* (*ticket, fare*) concesionario.

conciliation [kənsɪlɪ'eɪʃən] *n* conciliación *f*.

conciliatory [kən'sɪlɪətrɪ] *a* conciliador(a).

concise [kən'saɪs] *a* conciso.

conclave ['kɒnkleɪv] *n* cónclave *m*.

conclude [kən'kluːd] *vt* (*finish*) concluir; (*treaty etc*) firmar; (*agreement*) llegar a; (*decide*): **to ~ that** ... llegar a la conclusión de que ... ♦ *vi* (*events*) terminarse.

conclusion [kən'kluːʒən] *n* conclusión *f*; **to come to the ~ that** llegar a la conclusión de que.

conclusive [kən'kluːsɪv] *a* decisivo, concluyente.

conclusively [kən'kluːsɪvlɪ] *ad* concluyentemente.

concoct [kən'kɒkt] *vt* (*gen*) confeccionar; (*plot*) tramar.

concoction [kən'kɒkʃən] *n* (*food, drink*) confección *f*.

concord ['kɒŋkɔːd] *n* (*harmony*) concordia; (*treaty*) acuerdo.

concourse ['kɒŋkɔːs] *n* (*hall*) vestíbulo.

concrete ['kɒŋkriːt] *n* hormigón *m* ♦ *a* concreto.

concrete mixer *n* hormigonera.

concur [kən'kɜː*] *vi* estar de acuerdo, asentir.

concurrently [kən'kʌrntlɪ] *ad* al mismo tiempo.

concussion [kən'kʌʃən] *n* conmoción *f* cerebral.

condemn [kən'dɛm] *vt* condenar.

condemnation [kɒndɛm'neɪʃən] *n* (*gen*) condena; (*blame*) censura.

condensation [kɒndɛn'seɪʃən] *n* condensación *f*.

condense [kən'dɛns] *vi* condensarse ♦ *vt* condensar, abreviar.

condensed milk *n* leche *f* condensada.

condescend [kɒndɪ'sɛnd] *vi* condescender, dignarse; **to ~ to do sth** dignarse hacer algo.

condescending [kɒndɪ'sɛndɪŋ] *a* condescendiente.

condition [kən'dɪʃən] *n* condición *f*; (*disease*) enfermedad *f* ♦ *vt* condicionar; **on ~ that** a condición (de) que; **weather ~s** condiciones atmosféricas; **in good/poor ~** en buenas/malas condiciones; **~s of sale** condiciones de venta.

conditional [kən'dɪʃənl] *a* condicional.

conditioned reflex [kən'dɪʃənd-] *n* reflejo condicionado.

conditioner [kən'dɪʃənə*] *n* (*for hair*) acondicionador *m*.

condolences [kən'dəulənsɪz] *npl* pésame *msg*.

condom ['kɒndəm] *n* condón *m*.

condominium [kɒndə'mɪnɪəm] *n* (*US*) condominio.

condone [kən'dəun] *vt* condonar.

conducive [kən'djuːsɪv] *a*: **~ to** conducente a.

conduct ['kɒndʌkt] *n* conducta, comportamiento ♦ *vt* [kən'dʌkt] (*lead*) conducir; (*manage*) llevar, dirigir; (*MUS*) dirigir ♦ *vi* (*MUS*) llevar la batuta; **to ~ o.s.** comportarse.

conducted tour *n* (*Brit*) visita acompañada.

conductor [kən'dʌktə*] *n* (*of orchestra*) director(a) *m/f*; (*US: on train*) revisor(a) *m/f*; (*on bus*) cobrador *m*; (*ELEC*) conductor *m*.

conductress [kən'dʌktrɪs] *n* (*on bus*) cobradora.

cone [kəun] *n* cono; (*pine ~*) piña; (*for ice-cream*) barquillo.

confectioner [kən'fɛkʃənə*] *n* (*of cakes*) pastelero/a; (*of sweets*) confitero/a; **~'s (shop)** *n* pastelería; confitería.

confectionery [kən'fɛkʃənrɪ] *n* pasteles *mpl*; dulces *mpl*.

confederate [kən'fɛdrɪt] *a* confederado ♦ *n* (*pej*) cómplice *m/f*; (*US: HISTORY*) confederado/a.

confederation [kənfɛdə'reɪʃən] *n* confederación *f*.

confer [kən'fɜː*] *vt* otorgar (*on* a) ♦ *vi* conferenciar; **to ~ (with sb about sth)** consultar (con uno sobre algo).

conference ['kɒnfərns] *n* (*meeting*) reunión *f*; (*convention*) congreso; **to be in ~** estar en una reunión.

conference room *n* sala de conferencias.

confess [kən'fɛs] *vt* confesar ♦ *vi* confesarse.

confession [kən'fɛʃən] *n* confesión *f*.

confessional [kən'fɛʃənl] *n* confesionario.

confessor [kən'fɛsə*] *n* confesor *m*.

confetti [kən'fɛtɪ] *n* confeti *m*.

confide [kən'faɪd] *vi*: **to ~ in** confiar en.

confidence ['kɒnfɪdns] *n* (*gen, also:* **self-~**) confianza; (*secret*) confidencia; **in ~** (*speak, write*) en confianza; **to have**

(every) ~ that estar seguro *or* confiado de que; **motion of no ~** moción *f* de censura; **to tell sb sth in strict ~** decir algo a uno en absoluta confianza.

confidence trick *n* timo.

confident ['kɔnfɪdənt] *a* seguro de sí mismo.

confidential [kɔnfɪ'dɛnʃəl] *a* confidencial; *(secretary)* de confianza.

confidentiality [kɔnfɪdɛnʃɪ'ælɪtɪ] *n* confidencialidad *f*.

configuration [kənfɪgju'reɪʃən] *n* *(also COMPUT)* configuración *f*.

confine [kən'faɪn] *vt* *(limit)* limitar; *(shut up)* encerrar; **to ~ o.s. to doing sth** limitarse a hacer algo.

confined [kən'faɪnd] *a* *(space)* reducido.

confinement [kən'faɪnmənt] *n* *(prison)* prisión *f*; *(MED)* parto.

confines ['kɔnfaɪnz] *npl* confines *mpl*.

confirm [kən'fɜːm] *vt* confirmar.

confirmation [kɔnfə'meɪʃən] *n* confirmación *f*.

confirmed [kən'fɜːmd] *a* empedernido.

confiscate ['kɔnfɪskeɪt] *vt* confiscar.

confiscation [kɔnfɪs'keɪʃən] *n* incautación *f*.

conflagration [kɔnflə'greɪʃən] *n* conflagración *f*.

conflict ['kɔnflɪkt] *n* conflicto ◆ *vi* [kən'flɪkt] *(opinions)* chocar.

conflicting [kən'flɪktɪŋ] *a* *(reports, evidence, opinions)* contradictorio.

conform [kən'fɔːm] *vi* conformarse; **to ~ to** ajustarse a.

conformist [kən'fɔːmɪst] *n* conformista *m/f*.

confound [kən'faʊnd] *vt* confundir; *(amaze)* pasmar.

confounded [kən'faʊndɪd] *a* condenado.

confront [kən'frʌnt] *vt* *(problems)* hacer frente a; *(enemy, danger)* enfrentarse con.

confrontation [kɔnfrən'teɪʃən] *n* enfrentamiento.

confuse [kən'fjuːz] *vt* *(perplex)* aturdir, desconcertar; *(mix up)* confundir.

confused [kən'fjuːzd] *a* confuso; *(person)* perplejo; **to get ~** desorientarse, aturdirse.

confusing [kən'fjuːzɪŋ] *a* confuso.

confusion [kən'fjuːʒən] *n* confusión *f*.

congeal [kən'dʒiːl] *vi* coagularse.

congenial [kən'dʒiːnɪəl] *a* agradable.

congenital [kən'dʒɛnɪtl] *a* congénito.

congested [kən'dʒɛstɪd] *a* *(gen)* atestado; *(telephone lines)* ocupado.

congestion [kən'dʒɛstʃən] *n* congestión *f*.

conglomerate [kən'glɔmərət] *n* *(COMM, GEO)* conglomerado.

conglomeration [kənglɔmə'reɪʃən] *n* conglomeración *f*.

Congo ['kɔŋgəʊ] *n* *(state)* Congo.

congratulate [kən'grætjuleɪt] *vt* felicitar.

congratulations [kəngrætju'leɪʃənz] *npl*: **(on)** felicitaciones *fpl* (por); **~!** ¡enhorabuena!, ¡felicidades!

congregate ['kɔŋgrɪgeɪt] *vi* congregarse.

congregation [kɔŋgrɪ'geɪʃən] *n* *(in church)* fieles *mpl*.

congress ['kɔŋgrɛs] *n* congreso.

congressman ['kɔŋgrɛsmən] *n* *(US)* diputado.

congresswoman ['kɔŋgrɛswumən] *n* *(US)* diputada.

conical ['kɔnɪkl] *a* cónico.

conifer ['kɔnɪfə*] *n* conífera.

coniferous [kə'nɪfərəs] *a* *(forest)* conífero.

conjecture [kən'dʒɛktʃə*] *n* conjetura.

conjugal ['kɔndʒugl] *a* conyugal.

conjugate ['kɔndʒugeɪt] *vt* conjugar.

conjunction [kən'dʒʌŋkʃən] *n* conjunción *f*; **in ~ with** junto con.

conjunctivitis [kəndʒʌŋktɪ'vaɪtɪs] *n* conjunctivitis *f*.

conjure ['kʌndʒə*] *vi* hacer juegos de manos.

conjure up *vt* *(ghost, spirit)* hacer aparecer; *(memories)* evocar.

conjurer ['kʌndʒərə*] *n* ilusionista *m/f*.

conjuring trick ['kʌndʒərɪŋ-] *n* ilusionismo, juego de manos.

conker ['kɔŋkə*] *n* *(Brit)* castaño de Indias.

conk out [kɔŋk-] *vi* *(col)* descomponerse.

con man *n* timador *m*.

connect [kə'nɛkt] *vt* juntar, unir; *(ELEC)* conectar; *(fig)* relacionar, asociar ◆ *vi*: **to ~ with** *(train)* enlazar con; **to be ~ed with** *(associated)* estar relacionado con; *(related)* estar emparentado con; **I am trying to ~ you** *(TEL)* estoy intentando comunicarle.

connection [kə'nɛkʃən] *n* juntura, unión *f*; *(ELEC)* conexión *f*; *(RAIL)* enlace *m*; *(TEL)* comunicación *f*; *(fig)* relación *f*; **what is the ~ between them?** ¿qué relación hay entre ellos?; **in ~ with** con respeto a, en relación a; **she has many business ~s** tiene muchos contactos profesionales; **to miss/make a ~** perder/coger el enlace.

connive [kə'naɪv] *vi*: **to ~ at** hacer la vista gorda a.

connoisseur [kɔnɪ'sɜː*] *n* experto/a, entendido/a.

connotation [kɔnə'teɪʃən] *n* connotación *f*.

conquer ['kɔŋkə*] *vt* *(territory)* conquistar; *(enemy, feelings)* vencer.

conqueror ['kɔŋkərə*] *n* conquistador(a) *m/f*.

conquest ['kɔŋkwɛst] *n* conquista.

cons [kɔnz] *npl see* **convenience, pro**.

conscience ['kɔnʃəns] *n* conciencia; **in all ~** en conciencia.

conscientious [kɔnʃɪ'ɛnʃəs] *a* concienzudo; *(objection)* de conciencia.

conscientious objector *n* objetor *m* de conciencia.

conscious ['kɔnʃəs] *a* consciente; *(deliberate: insult, error)* premeditado, intencionado; **to become** ~ **of sth/that** darse cuenta de algo/de que.

consciousness ['kɒnʃəsnɪs] n conciencia; (MED) conocimiento.

conscript ['kɒnskrɪpt] n recluta m/f.

conscription [kən'skrɪpʃən] n servicio militar (obligatorio).

consecrate ['kɒnsɪkreɪt] vt consagrar.

consecutive [kən'sekjutɪv] a consecutivo; **on 3** ~ **occasions** en 3 ocasiones consecutivas.

consensus [kən'sensəs] n consenso; **the** ~ **of opinion** el consenso general.

consent [kən'sent] n consentimiento ♦ vi: **to** ~ **to** consentir en; **by common** ~ de común acuerdo.

consequence ['kɒnsɪkwəns] n consecuencia; **in** ~ por consiguiente.

consequently ['kɒnsɪkwəntlɪ] ad por consiguiente.

conservation [kɒnsə'veɪʃən] n conservación f; (of nature) preservación f.

conservationist [kɒnsə'veɪʃnɪst] n conservacionista m/f.

conservative [kən'sə:vətɪv] a conservador(a); (cautious) cauteloso; **C~** a, n (Brit POL) conservador(a) m/f.

conservatory [kən'sə:vətrɪ] n (greenhouse) invernadero.

conserve [kən'sə:v] vt conservar ♦ n conserva.

consider [kən'sɪdə*] vt considerar; (take into account) tomar en cuenta; (study) estudiar, examinar; **to** ~ **doing sth** pensar en (la posibilidad de) hacer algo; **all things** ~**ed** pensándolo bien; ~ **yourself lucky** ¡date por satisfecho!

considerable [kən'sɪdərəbl] a considerable.

considerably [kən'sɪdərəblɪ] ad bastante, considerablemente.

considerate [kən'sɪdərɪt] a considerado.

consideration [kənsɪdə'reɪʃən] n consideración f; (reward) retribución f; **to be under** ~ estar sobre el tapete; **my first** ~ **is my family** mi primera consideración es mi familia.

considering [kən'sɪdərɪŋ] prep: ~ **(that)** teniendo en cuenta (que).

consign [kən'saɪn] vt consignar.

consignee [kɒnsaɪ'ni:] n consignatario/a.

consignment [kən'saɪnmənt] n envío.

consignment note n (COMM) talón m de expedición.

consignor [kən'saɪnə*] n remitente m/f.

consist [kən'sɪst] vi: **to** ~ **of** consistir en.

consistency [kən'sɪstənsɪ] n (of person etc) consecuencia; (thickness) consistencia.

consistent [kən'sɪstənt] a (person, argument) consecuente; (results) constante.

consolation [kɒnsə'leɪʃən] n consuelo.

console [kən'səul] vt consolar ♦ n ['kɒnsəul] (control panel) consola.

consolidate [kən'sɒlɪdeɪt] vt consolidar.

consols ['kɒnsɒlz] npl (Brit STOCK EXCHANGE) valores mpl consolidados.

consommé [kən'sɒmeɪ] n consomé m, caldo.

consonant ['kɒnsənənt] n consonante f.

consort ['kɒnsɔ:t] n consorte m/f ♦ vi [kən'sɔ:t]: **to** ~ **with sb** (often pej) asociarse con uno; **prince** ~ príncipe m consorte.

consortium [kən'sɔ:tɪəm] n consorcio.

conspicuous [kən'spɪkjuəs] a (visible) visible; (garish etc) llamativo; (outstanding) notable; **to make o.s.** ~ llamar la atención.

conspiracy [kən'spɪrəsɪ] n conjura, complot m.

conspiratorial [kənspɪrə'tɔ:rɪəl] a de conspirador.

conspire [kən'spaɪə*] vi conspirar.

constable ['kʌnstəbl] n (Brit) policía m/f; **chief** ~ ≈ jefe m/f de policía.

constabulary [kən'stæbjulərɪ] n ≈ policía.

constancy ['kɒnstənsɪ] n constancia; fidelidad f.

constant ['kɒnstənt] a (gen) constante; (loyal) leal, fiel.

constantly ['kɒnstəntlɪ] ad constantemente.

constellation [kɒnstə'leɪʃən] n constelación f.

consternation [kɒnstə'neɪʃən] n consternación f.

constipated ['kɒnstɪpeɪtəd] a estreñido.

constipation [kɒnstɪ'peɪʃən] n estreñimiento.

constituency [kən'stɪtjuənsɪ] n (POL) distrito electoral; (people) electorado.

constituency party n partido local.

constituent [kən'stɪtjuənt] n (POL) elector(a) m/f; (part) componente m.

constitute ['kɒnstɪtju:t] vt constituir.

constitution [kɒnstɪ'tju:ʃən] n constitución f.

constitutional [kɒnstɪ'tju:ʃənl] a constitucional.

constrain [kən'streɪn] vt obligar.

constrained [kən'streɪnd] a: **to feel** ~ **to** ... sentirse en la necesidad de ....

constraint [kən'streɪnt] n (force) fuerza; (limit) restricción f; (restraint) reserva; (embarrassment) cohibición f.

constrict [kən'strɪkt] vt apretar, estrechar.

constriction [kən'strɪkʃən] n constricción f.

construct [kən'strʌkt] vt construir.

construction [kən'strʌkʃən] n construcción f; (fig: interpretation) interpretación f; **under** ~ en construcción.

construction industry n industria de la construcción.

constructive [kən'strʌktɪv] a constructivo.

construe [kən'stru:] vt interpretar.

consul ['kɒnsl] n cónsul m/f.

consulate ['kɒnsjulɪt] n consulado.

consult [kən'sʌlt] vt, vi consultar; **to** ~ **sb**

(about sth) consultar a uno (sobre algo).
consultancy [kən'sʌltənsɪ] *n* consultorio.
consultant [kən'sʌltənt] *n* (*Brit MED*) especialista *m/f*; (*other specialist*) asesor(a) *m/f*.
consultation [kɔnsəl'teɪʃən] *n* consulta; **in ~ with** en consultación con.
consulting room *n* (*Brit*) consultorio.
consume [kən'sjuːm] *vt* (*eat*) comerse; (*drink*) beberse; (*fire etc*, *COMM*) consumir.
consumer [kən'sjuːmə*] *n* (*of electricity*, *gas etc*) consumidor(a) *m/f*.
consumer association *n* asociación *f* de consumidores.
consumer credit *n* crédito al consumidor.
consumer durables *npl* bienes *mpl* de consumo duraderos.
consumer goods *npl* bienes *mpl* de consumo.
consumerism [kən'sjuːmərɪzəm] *n* consumismo.
consumer society *n* sociedad *f* de consumo.
consummate ['kɔnsʌmeɪt] *vt* consumar.
consumption [kən'sʌmpʃən] *n* consumo; (*MED*) tisis *f*; **not fit for human ~** no apto para el consumo humano.
cont. *abbr* (= *continued*) sigue.
contact ['kɔntækt] *n* contacto; (*person*) enchufe *m* ♦ *vt* ponerse en contacto con; **~ lenses** *npl* lentes *fpl* de contacto; **to be in ~ with sb/sth** estar en contacto con uno/ algo; **business ~s** contactos comerciales.
contagious [kən'teɪdʒəs] *a* contagioso.
contain [kən'teɪn] *vt* contener; **to ~ o.s.** contenerse.
container [kən'teɪnə*] *n* recipiente *m*; (*for shipping etc*) contenedor *m*.
containerization [kən'teɪnəraɪ'zeɪʃən] *n* contenerización *f*.
containerize [kən'teɪnəraɪz] *vt* transportar en contenedores.
contaminate [kən'tæmɪneɪt] *vt* contaminar.
contamination [kəntæmɪ'neɪʃən] *n* contaminación *f*.
cont'd *abbr* (= *continued*) sigue.
contemplate ['kɔntəmpleɪt] *vt* (*gen*) contemplar; (*reflect upon*) considerar; (*intend*) pensar.
contemplation [kɔntəm'pleɪʃən] *n* contemplación *f*.
contemporary [kən'tɛmpərərɪ] *a*, *n* (*of the same age*) contemporáneo/a *m/f*.
contempt [kən'tɛmpt] *n* desprecio; **~ of court** (*LAW*) desacato (a los tribunales *or* a la justicia).
contemptible [kən'tɛmptɪbl] *a* despreciable, desdeñable.
contemptuous [kən'tɛmptjuəs] *a* desdeñoso.
contend [kən'tɛnd] *vt* (*argue*) afirmar ♦ *vi* (*struggle*) luchar; **he has a lot to ~ with** tiene muchos problemas que enfrentar.

contender [kən'tɛndə*] *n* (*SPORT*) contendiente *m/f*.
content [kən'tɛnt] *a* (*happy*) contento; (*satisfied*) satisfecho ♦ *vt* contentar; satisfacer ♦ *n* ['kɔntɛnt] contenido; **~s** *npl* contenido *msg*; (**table of**) **~s** índice *m* de materias; **to ~ o.s. with sth/with doing sth** contentarse *or* darse por contento con algo/ con hacer algo.
contented [kən'tɛntɪd] *a* contento; satisfecho.
contentedly [kən'tɛntɪdlɪ] *ad* con aire satisfecho.
contention [kən'tɛnʃən] *n* discusión *f*; (*belief*) argumento; **bone of ~** manzana de la discordia.
contentious [kən'tɛnʃəs] *a* discutible.
contentment [kən'tɛntmənt] *n* contento.
contest ['kɔntɛst] *n* contienda; (*competition*) concurso ♦ *vt* [kən'tɛst] (*dispute*) impugnar; (*LAW*) disputar, litigar; (*POL: election*, *seat*) presentarse como candidato/a en.
contestant [kən'tɛstənt] *n* concursante *m/f*; (*in fight*) contendiente *m/f*.
context ['kɔntɛkst] *n* contexto; **in/out of ~** en/fuera de contexto.
continent ['kɔntɪnənt] *n* continente *m*; **the C~** (*Brit*) el continente europeo; **on the C~** en el continente europeo.
continental [kɔntɪ'nɛntl] *a* continental.
continental breakfast *n* desayuno estilo europeo.
continental quilt *n* (*Brit*) edredón *m*.
contingency [kən'tɪndʒənsɪ] *n* contingencia.
contingent [kən'tɪndʒənt] *n* (*group*) grupo.
continual [kən'tɪnjuəl] *a* continuo.
continually [kən'tɪnjuəlɪ] *ad* constantemente.
continuation [kəntɪnju'eɪʃən] *n* prolongación *f*; (*after interruption*) reanudación *f*.
continue [kən'tɪnjuː] *vi*, *vt* seguir, continuar; **~d on page 10** sigue en la página 10.
continuity [kɔntɪ'njuɪtɪ] *n* (*also CINEMA*) continuidad *f*.
continuity girl *n* (*CINEMA*) secretaria de continuidad.
continuous [kən'tɪnjuəs] *a* continuo; **~ performance** (*CINEMA*) sesión *f* continua; **~ stationery** papel *m* continuo.
continuously [kən'tɪnjuəslɪ] *ad* (*repeatedly*) continuamente; (*uninterruptedly*) constantemente.
contort [kən'tɔːt] *vt* retorcer.
contortion [kən'tɔːʃən] *n* (*movement*) contorsión *f*.
contortionist [kən'tɔːʃənɪst] *n* contorsionista *m/f*.
contour ['kɔntuə*] *n* contorno; (*also:* **~ line**) curva de nivel.
contraband ['kɔntrəbænd] *n* contrabando ♦ *a* de contrabando.

contraception [kɔntrə'sɛpʃən] *n* contracepción *f*.

contraceptive [kɔntrə'sɛptɪv] *a, n* anticonceptivo.

contract ['kɔntrækt] *n* contrato ♦ *cpd* ['kɔntrækt] (*price, date*) contratado, de contrato; (*work*) de contrato ♦ *vb* [kən'trækt] *vi* (*COMM*): **to** ~ **to do sth** comprometerse por contrato a hacer algo; (*become smaller*) contraerse, encogerse ♦ *vt* contraer; **to be under** ~ **to do sth** estar bajo contrato para hacer algo; ~ **of employment** *or* **of service** contrato de trabajo.

contract in *vi* tomar parte.

contract out *vi*: **to** ~ **out (of)** optar por no tomar parte (en); **to** ~ **out of a pension scheme** optar por no tomar parte en un plan de jubilación.

contraction [kən'trækʃən] *n* contracción *f*.

contractor [kən'træktə*] *n* contratista *m/f*.

contractual [kən'træktjuəl] *a* contractual.

contradict [kɔntrə'dɪkt] *vt* (*declare to be wrong*) desmentir; (*be contrary to*) contradecir.

contradiction [kɔntrə'dɪkʃən] *n* contradicción *f*; **to be in** ~ **with** no estar de acuerdo con.

contradictory [kɔntrə'dɪktərɪ] *a* (*statements*) contradictorio; **to be** ~ **to** ser contradictorio a.

contralto [kən'træltəu] *n* contralto *f*.

contraption [kən'træpʃən] *n* (*pej*) artilugio *m*.

contrary ['kɔntrərɪ] *a* (*opposite, different*) contrario; [kən'trɛərɪ] (*perverse*) terco ♦ *n*: **on the** ~ al contrario; **unless you hear to the** ~ a no ser que le digan lo contrario; ~ **to what we thought** en contra de lo que pensábamos.

contrast ['kɔntrɑːst] *n* contraste *m* ♦ *vt* [kən'trɑːst] comparar; **in** ~ **to** *or* **with** a diferencia de.

contrasting [kən'trɑːstɪŋ] *a* (*opinion*) opuesto; (*colour*) que hace contraste.

contravene [kɔntrə'viːn] *vt* infringir.

contravention [kɔntrə'vɛnʃən] *n*: ~ **(of)** contravención *f* (de).

contribute [kən'trɪbjuːt] *vi* contribuir ♦ *vt*: **to** ~ **to** (*gen*) contribuir a; (*newspaper*) escribir para; (*discussion*) intervenir en.

contribution [kɔntrɪ'bjuːʃən] *n* (*money*) contribución *f*; (*to debate*) intervención *f*; (*to journal*) colaboración *f*.

contributor [kən'trɪbjuːtə*] *n* (*to newspaper*) colaborador(a) *m/f*.

contributory [kən'trɪbjutərɪ] *a* (*cause*) contribuyente; **it was a** ~ **factor in ...** fue un factor contribuyente en ....

contributory pension scheme *n* plan *m* cotizable de jubilación.

contrivance [kən'traɪvəns] *n* (*machine, device*) aparato, dispositivo.

contrive [kən'traɪv] *vt* (*invent*) idear ♦ *vi*:

to ~ **to do** lograr hacer.

control [kən'trəul] *vt* controlar; (*traffic etc*) dirigir; (*machinery*) manejar; (*temper*) dominar; (*disease, fire*) dominar, controlar ♦ *n* (*command*) control *m*; (*of car*) conducción *f*; (*check*) freno; ~**s** *npl* mando *sg*; **to** ~ **o.s.** controlarse, dominarse; **everything is under** ~ todo está bajo control; **to be in** ~ **of** tener el mando de; **the car went out of** ~ el coche se descontroló.

control group *n* (*MED, PSYCH etc*) grupo de control.

control key *n* (*COMPUT*) tecla de control.

controlled economy *n* economía dirigida.

controller [kən'trəulə*] *n* controlador(a) *m/f*.

controlling interest [kən'trəulɪŋ-] *n* interés *m* mayoritario.

control panel *n* (*on aircraft, ship, TV etc*) tablero de instrumentos.

control point *n* (*puesto de*) control *m*.

control room *n* (*NAUT, MIL*) sala de mandos; (*RADIO, TV*) sala de control.

control tower *n* (*AVIAT*) torre *f* de control.

control unit *n* (*COMPUT*) unidad *f* de control.

controversial [kɔntrə'vəːʃl] *a* polémico.

controversy ['kɔntrəvəːsɪ] *n* polémica.

conurbation [kɔnəː'beɪʃən] *n* urbanización *f*.

convalesce [kɔnvə'lɛs] *vi* convalecer.

convalescence [kɔnvə'lɛsns] *n* convalecencia.

convalescent [kɔnvə'lɛsnt] *a, n* convaleciente *m/f*.

convector [kən'vɛktə*] *n* calentador *m* de convección.

convene [kən'viːn] *vt* (*meeting*) convocar ♦ *vi* reunirse.

convenience [kən'viːnɪəns] *n* (*comfort*) comodidad *f*; (*advantage*) ventaja; **at your earliest** ~ (*COMM*) cuando *or* tan pronto como le sea conveniente; **all modern** ~**s**, (*Brit*) **all mod cons** todo confort.

convenience foods *npl* platos *mpl* preparados.

convenient [kən'viːnɪənt] *a* (*useful*) útil; (*place, time*) conveniente; **if it is** ~ **for you** si le conviene.

conveniently [kən'viːnɪəntlɪ] *ad* (*happen*) oportunamente; (*situated*) convenientemente.

convent ['kɔnvənt] *n* convento.

convent school *n* colegio de monjas.

convention [kən'vɛnʃən] *n* convención *f*; (*meeting*) asamblea.

conventional [kən'vɛnʃənl] *a* convencional.

converge [kən'vəːdʒ] *vi* converger.

conversant [kən'vəːsnt] *a*: **to be** ~ **with** estar al tanto de.

conversation [kɔnvə'seɪʃən] *n* conversación

f.

conversational [kɔnvə'seɪʃənl] a (familiar) familiar; (talkative) locuaz; ~ **mode** (COMPUT) modo de conversación.

converse ['kɔnvə:s] n inversa ◆ vi [kən'və:s] conversar; **to** ~ **(with sb about sth)** conversar, platicar (con uno de algo).

conversely [kɔn'və:slı] ad a la inversa.

conversion [kən'və:ʃən] n conversión f; (house ~) reforma, remodelación f.

conversion table n tabla de conversión.

convert [kən'və:t] vt (REL, COMM) convertir; (alter) transformar ◆ n ['kɔnvə:t] converso/a.

convertible [kən'və:təbl] a convertible ◆ n descapotable m; ~ **loan stock** títulos mpl convertibles de interés fijo.

convex ['kɔn'vɛks] a convexo.

convey [kən'veɪ] vt llevar; (thanks) comunicar; (idea) expresar.

conveyance [kən'veɪəns] n (of goods) transporte m; (vehicle) vehículo, medio de transporte.

conveyancing [kən'veɪənsɪŋ] n (LAW) preparación f de escrituras de traspaso.

conveyor belt [kən'veɪə*-] n cinta transportadora.

convict [kən'vɪkt] vt (gen) condenar; (find guilty) declarar culpable a ◆ n ['kɔnvɪkt] presidiario/a.

conviction [kən'vɪkʃən] n condena; (belief) creencia, convicción f.

convince [kən'vɪns] vt convencer; **to** ~ **sb (of sth/that)** convencer a uno (de algo/de que).

convinced [kən'vɪnst] a: ~ **of/that** convencido de/de que.

convincing [kən'vɪnsɪŋ] a convincente.

convincingly [kən'vɪnsɪŋlɪ] ad convincentemente.

convivial [kən'vɪvɪəl] a (person) sociable; (atmosphere) alegre.

convoluted ['kɔnvəluːtɪd] a (argument etc) enrevesado; (shape) enrollado, enroscado.

convoy ['kɔnvɔɪ] n convoy m.

convulse [kən'vʌls] vt convulsionar; **to be** ~**d with laughter** dislocarse de risa.

convulsion [kən'vʌlʃən] n convulsión f.

coo [kuː] vi arrullar.

cook [kuk] vt cocinar; (stew etc) guisar; (meal) preparar, cocinar ◆ vi cocer; (person) cocinar ◆ n cocinero/a.

cook up vt (col: excuse, story) inventar.

cookbook ['kukbuk] n libro de cocina.

cooker ['kukə*] n cocina f.

cookery ['kukərɪ] n (dishes) cocina; (art) arte m culinario.

cookery book n (Brit) = **cookbook.**

cookie ['kukɪ] n (US) galleta.

cooking ['kukɪŋ] n cocina ◆ cpd (apples) para cocinar; (utensils, salt, foil) de cocina.

cooking chocolate n chocolate m

fondant.

cookout ['kukaut] n (US) comida al aire libre.

cool [kuːl] a fresco; (not hot) tibio; (not afraid) tranquilo; (unfriendly) frío ◆ vt enfriar ◆ vi enfriarse; **it is** ~ (weather) hace fresco; **to keep sth** ~ or **in a** ~ **place** conservar algo fresco or en un sitio fresco.

cool down vi enfriarse; (fig: person, situation) calmarse.

cool box, (US) **cooler** ['kuːlə*] n nevera portátil.

cooling-off period [kuːlɪŋ'ɔf-] n (INDUSTRY) plazo para que se entablen negociaciones.

cooling tower n torre f de refrigeración.

coolly ['kuːlɪ] ad (calmly) con tranquilidad; (audaciously) descaradamente; (unenthusiastically) fríamente, con frialdad.

coolness ['kuːlnɪs] n frescura; tranquilidad f; (hostility) frialdad f; (indifference) falta de entusiasmo.

coop [kuːp] n gallinero ◆ vt: **to** ~ **up** (fig) encerrar.

co-op ['kəuɔp] n abbr (= Cooperative (Society)) cooperativa.

cooperate [kəu'ɔpəreɪt] vi cooperar, colaborar; **will he** ~? ¿querrá cooperar?

cooperation [kəuɔpə'reɪʃən] n cooperación f, colaboración f.

cooperative [kəu'ɔpərətɪv] a cooperativo ◆ n cooperativa.

co-opt [kəu'ɔpt] vt: **to** ~ **sb into sth** cooptar a uno a algo.

coordinate [kəu'ɔːdɪneɪt] vt coordinar ◆ n [kəu'ɔːdɪnət] (MATH) coordenada; ~**s** npl (clothes) coordinados mpl.

coordination [kəuɔːdɪ'neɪʃən] n coordinación f.

coot [kuːt] n focha f (común).

co-ownership [kəu'əunəʃɪp] n co-propiedad f.

cop [kɔp] n (col) poli m, tira m (LAm).

cope [kəup] vi: **to** ~ **with** poder con; (problem) hacer frente a.

Copenhagen [kəupən'heɪgən] n Copenhague m.

copier ['kɔpɪə*] n (photo~) fotocopiadora, multicopista.

co-pilot ['kəu'paɪlət] n copiloto/a.

copious ['kəupɪəs] a copioso, abundante.

copper ['kɔpə*] n (metal) cobre m; (col: policeman) poli m, tira m (LAm); ~**s** npl perras fpl.

coppice ['kɔpɪs], **copse** [kɔps] n bosquecillo.

copulate ['kɔpjuleɪt] vi copularse.

copulation [kɔpju'leɪʃən] n cópula.

copy ['kɔpɪ] n copia; (of book etc) ejemplar m; (material: for printing) copia ◆ vt copiar (also COMPUT); (imitate) copiar, imitar; **to make good** ~ (fig) ser una noticia de interés; **rough** ~ borrador m; **fair** ~ co-

pia en limpio.
copy out vt copiar.
copycat ['kɔpɪkæt] n (pej) copión/ona m/f.
copyright ['kɔpɪraɪt] n derechos mpl de autor.
copy typist n mecanógrafo/a.
coral ['kɔrəl] n coral m.
coral reef n arrecife m (de coral).
Coral Sea n: **the** ~ el Mar del Coral.
cord [kɔːd] n cuerda; (ELEC) cable m; (fabric) pana; ~**s** npl (trousers) pantalones mpl de pana.
cordial ['kɔːdɪəl] a afectuoso ♦ n cordial m.
cordless ['kɔːdlɪs] a sin cordón.
cordon ['kɔːdn] n cordón m.
cordon off vt acordonar.
Cordova ['kɔːdəvə] n Córdoba.
corduroy ['kɔːdərɔɪ] n pana.
CORE [kɔː*] n abbr (US) = Congress of Racial Equality.
core [kɔː*] n (of earth, nuclear reactor) centro, núcleo; (of fruit) corazón m; (of problem etc) corazón m, meollo ♦ vt quitar el corazón de.
Corfu [kɔː'fuː] n Corfú m.
coriander [kɔrɪ'ændə*] n culantro, cilantro.
cork [kɔːk] n corcho; (tree) alcornoque m.
corkage ['kɔːkɪdʒ] n precio que se cobra en un restaurante por una botella de vino traída de fuera.
corked [kɔːkt] a (wine) con sabor a corcho.
corkscrew ['kɔːkskruː] n sacacorchos m inv.
cormorant ['kɔːmərnt] n cormorán m grande.
Corn abbr (Brit) = Cornwall.
corn [kɔːn] n (Brit: wheat) trigo; (US: maize) maíz m; (on foot) callo; ~ **on the cob** (CULIN) maíz en la mazorca.
cornea ['kɔːnɪə] n córnea.
corned beef [kɔːnd-] n carne f acecinada.
corner ['kɔːnə*] n ángulo; (outside) esquina; (inside) rincón m; (in road) curva; (FOOTBALL) córner m, saque m de esquina ♦ vt (trap) arrinconar; (COMM) acaparar ♦ vi (in car) tomar las curvas; **to cut** ~**s** atajar.
corner flag n (FOOTBALL) banderola de esquina.
corner kick n (FOOTBALL) córner m, saque m de esquina.
cornerstone ['kɔːnəstəun] n piedra angular.
cornet ['kɔːnɪt] n (MUS) corneta; (Brit: of ice-cream) barquillo.
cornflakes ['kɔːnfleɪks] npl copos mpl de maíz, cornflakes mpl.
cornflour ['kɔːnflauə*] n (Brit) harina de maíz.
cornice ['kɔːnɪs] n cornisa.
Cornish ['kɔːnɪʃ] a de Cornualles.
corn oil n aceite m de maíz.
cornstarch ['kɔːnstɑːtʃ] n (US) =

cornflour.
cornucopia [kɔːnju'kəupɪə] n cornucopia.
Cornwall ['kɔːnwəl] n Cornualles m.
corny ['kɔːnɪ] a (col) gastado.
corollary [kə'rɔlərɪ] n corolario.
coronary ['kɔrənərɪ] n: ~ **(thrombosis)** infarto.
coronation [kɔrə'neɪʃən] n coronación f.
coroner ['kɔrənə*] n juez m (de instrucción).
coronet ['kɔrənɪt] n corona.
Corp. abbr = **corporation.**
corporal ['kɔːpərl] n cabo ♦ a: ~ **punishment** castigo corporal.
corporate ['kɔːpərɪt] a corporativo.
corporate identity, corporate image n (of organization) identidad f corporativa.
corporation [kɔːpə'reɪʃən] n (of town) ayuntamiento; (COMM) corporación f.
corps [kɔː*], pl **corps** [kɔːz] n cuerpo; **press** ~ gabinete m de prensa.
corpse [kɔːps] n cadáver m.
corpulent ['kɔːpjulənt] a corpulento/a.
Corpus Christi ['kɔːpəs'krɪstɪ] n Corpus m.
corpuscle ['kɔːpʌsl] n corpúsculo.
corral [kə'rɑːl] n corral m.
correct [kə'rekt] a (accurate) justo, exacto; (proper) correcto ♦ vt corregir; (exam) calificar; **you are** ~ tiene razón.
correction [kə'rekʃən] n rectificación f; (erasure) tachadura.
correlate ['kɔrɪleɪt] vi: **to** ~ **with** tener correlación con.
correlation [kɔrɪ'leɪʃən] n correlación f.
correspond [kɔrɪs'pɔnd] vi (write) escribirse; (be equal to) corresponder.
correspondence [kɔrɪs'pɔndəns] n correspondencia.
correspondence column n (sección f de) cartas fpl al director.
correspondence course n curso por correspondencia.
correspondent [kɔrɪs'pɔndənt] n corresponsal m/f.
corresponding [kɔrɪs'pɔndɪŋ] a correspondiente.
corridor ['kɔrɪdɔː*] n pasillo.
corroborate [kə'rɔbəreɪt] vt corroborar.
corroboration [kərɔbə'reɪʃən] n corroboración f, confirmación f.
corrode [kə'rəud] vt corroer ♦ vi corroerse.
corrosion [kə'rəuʒən] n corrosión f.
corrosive [kə'rəusɪv] a corrosivo.
corrugated ['kɔrəgeɪtɪd] a ondulado.
corrugated cardboard n cartón m ondulado.
corrugated iron n chapa ondulada.
corrupt [kə'rʌpt] a corrompido; (person) corrupto ♦ vt corromper; (bribe) sobornar; (data) degradar; ~ **practices** (dishonesty, bribery) corrupción f.
corruption [kə'rʌpʃən] n corrupción f; (of data) alteración f.

corset ['kɔːsɪt] n faja.
Corsica ['kɔːsɪkə] n Córcega.
Corsican ['kɔːsɪkən] a, n corso/a m/f.
cortège [kɔːˈteɪʒ] n cortejo, desfile m.
cortisone ['kɔːtɪzəun] n cortisona.
c.o.s. abbr (= cash on shipment) pago al embarcar.
cosh [kɔʃ] n (Brit) cachiporra.
cosignatory ['kəuˈsɪgnətərɪ] n cosignatario/ a.
cosine ['kəusaɪn] n coseno.
cosiness ['kəuzɪnɪs] n comodidad f; (atmosphere) lo holgado.
cos lettuce [kɔs-] n lechuga cos.
cosmetic [kɔzˈmetɪk] n cosmético ◆ a (also fig) cosmético; (surgery) estético.
cosmic ['kɔzmɪk] a cósmico.
cosmonaut ['kɔzmənɔːt] n cosmonauta m/f.
cosmopolitan [kɔzməˈpɔlɪtn] a cosmopolita.
cosmos ['kɔzmɔs] n cosmos m.
cosset ['kɔsɪt] vt mimar.
cost [kɔst] n (gen) coste m, costo; (price) precio; ~s npl (LAW) costas fpl ◆ vb (pt, pp cost) vi costar, valer ◆ vt preparar el presupuesto de; **how much does it ~?** ¿cuánto cuesta?, ¿cuánto vale?; **what will it ~ to have it repaired?** ¿cuánto costará repararlo?; **the ~ of living** el coste or costo de la vida; **at all ~s** cueste lo que cueste.
cost accountant n contable m de costos.
co-star ['kəustɑː*] n colega m/f de reparto.
Costa Rica ['kɔstəˈriːkə] n Costa Rica.
Costa Rican ['kɔstəˈriːkən] a, n costarriqueño/a m/f.
cost centre n centro (de determinación) de costos.
cost control n control m de costos.
cost-effective [kɔstɪˈfektɪv] a (COMM) beneficioso, rentable.
cost-effectiveness ['kɔstɪˈfektɪvnɪs] n relación f costo-eficacia or costo-rendimiento.
costing ['kɔstɪŋ] n cálculo de costos.
costly ['kɔstlɪ] a (expensive) costoso.
cost-of-living [kɔstəvˈlɪvɪŋ] a: ~ **allowance** n plus m de carestía de vida; ~ **index** n índice m del costo or coste de vida.
cost price n (Brit) precio de coste.
costume ['kɔstjuːm] n traje m; (Brit: also: swimming ~) traje de baño.
costume jewellery n bisutería.
cosy, (US) **cozy** ['kəuzɪ] a cómodo; (room, atmosphere) acogedor(a).
cot [kɔt] n (Brit: child's) cuna; (US: folding bed) cama plegable.
Cotswolds ['kɔtswəuldz] npl región de colinas del suroeste inglés.
cottage ['kɔtɪdʒ] n casita de campo.
cottage cheese n requesón m.
cottage industry n industria casera.
cottage pie n pastel m de carne cubierta de puré de patatas.

cotton ['kɔtn] n algodón m; (thread) hilo.
cotton on vi (col): **to ~ on (to sth)** caer en la cuenta (de algo).
cotton candy n (US) algodón m (azucarado).
cotton wool n (Brit) algodón m (hidrófilo).
couch [kautʃ] n sofá m; (in doctor's surgery) camilla.
couchette [kuːˈʃet] n litera.
cough [kɔf] vi toser ◆ n tos f.
cough up vt escupir.
cough drop n pastilla para la tos.
cough mixture n jarabe m para la tos.
could [kud] pt of **can**.
couldn't ['kudnt] = **could not**.
council ['kaunsl] n consejo; **city** or **town ~** consejo municipal; **C~ of Europe** Consejo de Europa.
council estate n (Brit) urbanización f de viviendas municipales de alquiler.
council house n (Brit) vivienda municipal de alquiler.
councillor ['kaunslə*] n concejal m/f.
counsel ['kaunsl] n (advice) consejo; (lawyer) abogado/a ◆ vt aconsejar; ~ **for the defence/the prosecution** abogado/a defensor(a)/fiscal; **to ~ sth/sb to do sth** aconsejar algo/a uno que haga algo.
counsellor, (US) **counselor** ['kaunslə*] n consejero/a; (US LAW) abogado/a.
count [kaunt] vt (gen) contar; (include) incluir ◆ vi contar ◆ n cuenta; (of votes) escrutinio; (nobleman) conde m; (sum) total m, suma; **to ~ the cost of** calcular el costo de; **not ~ing the children** niños aparte; **10 ~ing him** diez incluyéndolo a él, diez con él; ~ **yourself lucky** date por satisfecho; **that doesn't ~!** ¡eso no vale!; **to ~ (up) to 10** contar hasta diez; **it ~s for very little** cuenta poco; **to keep ~ of sth** llevar la cuenta de algo.
count on vt fus contar con; **to ~ on doing sth** contar con hacer algo.
count up vt contar.
countdown ['kauntdaun] n cuenta atrás.
countenance ['kauntɪnəns] n semblante m, rostro ◆ vt (tolerate) aprobar, tolerar.
counter ['kauntə*] n (in shop) mostrador m; (position: in post office, bank) ventanilla; (in games) ficha; (TECH) contador m ◆ vt contrarrestar; (blow) parar; (attack) contestar a ◆ ad: ~ **to** contrario a; **to buy under the ~** (fig) comprar de estraperlo or bajo mano; **to ~ sth with sth/by doing sth** contestar algo con algo/haciendo algo.
counteract ['kauntər'ækt] vt contrarrestar.
counterattack ['kauntərə'tæk] n contraataque m ◆ vi contraatacar.
counterbalance ['kauntə'bæləns] n contrapeso.
counter-clockwise ['kauntə'klɔkwaɪz] ad en sentido contrario al de las agujas del re-

loj.

counter-espionage ['kauntər'ɛspɪənɑːʒ] *n* contraespionaje *m*.

counterfeit ['kauntəfɪt] *n* falsificación *f*, simulación *f* ◆ *vt* falsificar ◆ *a* falso, falsificado.

counterfoil ['kauntəfɔɪl] *n* (*Brit*) talón *m*.

counterintelligence ['kauntərɪn'tɛlɪdʒəns] *n* contraespionaje *m*.

countermand ['kauntəmɑːnd] *vt* revocar, cancelar.

counter-measure ['kauntəmɛʒə*] *n* contramedida.

counteroffensive ['kauntərə'fɛnsɪv] *n* contraofensiva.

counterpane ['kauntəpeɪn] *n* colcha.

counterpart ['kauntəpɑːt] *n* (*of person*) homólogo/a.

counter-productive [kauntəprə'dʌktɪv] *a* contraproducente.

counterproposal ['kauntəprə'pəuzl] *n* contrapropuesta.

countersign ['kauntəsaɪn] *vt* ratificar, refrendar.

countess ['kauntɪs] *n* condesa.

countless ['kauntlɪs] *a* innumerable.

countrified ['kʌntrɪfaɪd] *a* rústico.

country ['kʌntrɪ] *n* país *m*; (*native land*) patria; (*as opposed to town*) campo; (*region*) región *f*, tierra; **in the ~** en el campo; **mountainous ~** región *f* montañosa.

country and western (music) *n* música country.

country dancing *n* (*Brit*) baile *m* regional.

country house *n* casa de campo.

countryman ['kʌntrɪmən] *n* (*national*) compatriota *m*; (*rural*) campesino, paisano.

countryside ['kʌntrɪsaɪd] *n* campo.

country-wide ['kʌntrɪ'waɪd] *a* nacional.

county ['kauntɪ] *n* condado.

county town *n* cabeza de partido.

coup, ~**s** [kuː, -z] *n* golpe *m*; (*triumph*) éxito; (*also:* ~ **d'état**) golpe de estado.

coupé ['kuːpeɪ] *n* cupé *m*.

couple ['kʌpl] *n* (*of things*) par *m*; (*of people*) pareja; (*married* ~) matrimonio ◆ *vt* (*ideas, names*) unir, juntar; (*machinery*) acoplar; **a ~ of** un par de.

couplet ['kʌplɪt] *n* pareado.

coupling ['kʌplɪŋ] *n* (*RAIL*) enganche *m*.

coupon ['kuːpɔn] *n* cupón *m*; (*pools* ~) boleto de quiniela.

courage ['kʌrɪdʒ] *n* valor *m*, valentía.

courageous [kə'reɪdʒəs] *a* valiente.

courgette [kuə'ʒɛt] *n* (*Brit*) calabacín *m*.

courier ['kurɪə*] *n* mensajero/a; (*diplomatic*) correo; (*for tourists*) guía *m/f* (de turismo).

course [kɔːs] *n* (*direction*) dirección *f*; (*of river, SCOL*) curso; (*of ship*) rumbo; (*fig*) proceder *m*; (*GOLF*) campo; (*part of meal*) plato; **of** ~ **ad** desde luego, naturalmente; **of** ~! ¡claro!; **(no) of** ~ **not!** ¡claro que no!, ¡por supuesto que no!; **in due** ~ en el momento oportuno; **in the** ~ **of the next few days** durante los próximos días; **we have no other** ~ **but to ...** no tenemos más remedio que ...; **there are 2** ~**s open to us** se nos ofrecen dos posibilidades; **the best** ~ **would be to ...** lo mejor sería ...; ~ **of treatment** (*MED*) tratamiento.

court [kɔːt] *n* (*royal*) corte *m*; (*LAW*) tribunal *m*, juzgado; (*TENNIS*) pista, cancha ◆ *vt* (*woman*) cortejar a; (*fig: favour, popularity*) solicitar, buscar; (*: death, disaster, danger etc*) buscar; **to take to** ~ demandar; ~ **of appeal** tribunal *m* de apelación.

courteous ['kəːtɪəs] *a* cortés.

courtesan [kɔːtɪ'zæn] *n* cortesana.

courtesy ['kəːtəsɪ] *n* cortesía; **by** ~ **of** (por) cortesía de.

courtesy coach *n* (*Brit*) autocar or autobús de cortesía (*al aeropuerto etc*).

courtesy light *n* (*AUT*) luz *f* interior.

court-house ['kɔːthaus] *n* (*US*) palacio de justicia.

courtier ['kɔːtɪə*] *n* cortesano.

court martial, *pl* **courts martial** ['kɔːt'mɑːʃəl] *n* consejo de guerra ◆ *vt* someter a consejo de guerra.

courtroom ['kɔːtrum] *n* sala de justicia.

court shoe *n* zapato de mujer de estilo clásico.

courtyard ['kɔːtjɑːd] *n* patio.

cousin ['kʌzn] *n* primo/a; **first** ~ primo/a carnal.

cove [kəuv] *n* cala, ensenada.

covenant ['kʌvənənt] *n* convenio ◆ *vt*: **to** ~ **£20 per year to a charity** concertar el pago de veinte libras anuales a una sociedad benéfica.

Coventry ['kɔvəntrɪ] *n*: **to send sb to** ~ (*fig*) hacer el vacío a uno.

cover ['kʌvə*] *vt* cubrir; (*with lid*) tapar; (*chairs etc*) revestir; (*distance*) cubrir, recorrer; (*include*) abarcar; (*protect*) abrigar; (*journalist*) investigar; (*issues*) tratar ◆ *n* cubierta; (*lid*) tapa; (*for chair etc*) funda; (*for bed*) cobertor *m*; (*envelope*) sobre *m*; (*for book*) forro; (*of magazine*) portada; (*shelter*) abrigo; (*insurance*) cobertura; **to take** ~ (*shelter*) protegerse, resguardarse; **under** ~ (*indoors*) bajo techo; **under** ~ **of darkness** al amparo de la oscuridad; **under separate** ~ (*COMM*) por separado; **£10 will** ~ **everything** con diez libras cubriremos todos los gastos.

cover up *vt* (*child, object*) cubrir completamente, tapar; (*fig: hide: truth, facts*) ocultar; **to** ~ **up for sb** (*fig*) encubrir a uno.

coverage ['kʌvərɪdʒ] *n* alcance *m*; (*in*

media) reportaje *m*; (*INSURANCE*) cobertura.

coveralls ['kʌvərɔːlz] *npl* (*US*) mono *sg*.

cover charge *n* precio del cubierto.

covering ['kʌvərɪŋ] *n* cubierta, envoltura.

covering letter, (*US*) **cover letter** *n* carta de explicación.

cover note *n* (*INSURANCE*) póliza provisional.

cover price *n* precio de cubierta.

covert ['kəuvət] *a* (*secret*) secreto, encubierto; (*dissembled*) furtivo.

cover-up ['kʌvərʌp] *n* encubrimiento.

covet ['kʌvɪt] *vt* codiciar.

covetous ['kʌvɪtəs] *a* codicioso.

cow [kau] *n* vaca ♦ *vt* intimidar.

coward ['kauəd] *n* cobarde *m/f*.

cowardice ['kauədɪs] *n* cobardía.

cowardly ['kauədlɪ] *a* cobarde.

cowboy ['kaubɔɪ] *n* vaquero.

cower ['kauə*] *vi* encogerse (de miedo).

co-worker ['kəuwəːkə*] *n* colaborador(a) *m/f*.

cowshed ['kauʃed] *n* establo.

cowslip ['kauslɪp] *n* (*BOT*) primavera, prímula.

coxswain ['kɔksn] *n* (*abbr*: **cox**) timonel *m*.

coy [kɔɪ] *a* tímido.

coyote [kɔɪ'əutɪ] *n* coyote *m*.

cozy ['kəuzɪ] *a* (*US*) = **cosy**.

CP *n abbr* (= *Communist Party*) PC *m*.

cp. *abbr* (= *compare*) cfr.

c/p *abbr* (*Brit*) = **carriage paid**.

CPA *n abbr* (*US*) = **certified public accountant**.

CPI *n abbr* (= *Consumer Price Index*) IPC *m*.

Cpl. *abbr* (*MIL*) = **corporal**.

CP/M *n abbr* (= *Central Program for Microprocessors*) CP/M *m*.

c.p.s. *abbr* (= *characters per second*) c.p.s.

CPSA *n abbr* (*Brit*: = *Civil and Public Services Association*) sindicato de funcionarios.

CPU *n abbr* = **central processing unit**.

cr. *abbr* = **credit, creditor**.

crab [kræb] *n* cangrejo.

crab apple *n* manzana silvestre.

crack [kræk] *n* grieta; (*noise*) crujido; (: *of whip*) chasquido; (*joke*) chiste *m*; (*drug*) cocaína dura; (*col: attempt*): **to have a ~ at sth** intentar algo ♦ *vt* agrietar, romper; (*nut*) cascar; (*safe*) forzar; (*whip etc*) chasquear; (*knuckles*) crujir; (*joke*) contar; (*case: solve*) resolver; (*code*) descifrar ♦ *a* (*athlete*) de primera clase; **to ~ jokes** (*col*) contar chistes *or* cuentos.

crack down on *vt fus* reprimir fuertemente, adoptar medidas severas contra.

crack up *vi* sufrir una crisis nerviosa.

crackdown ['krækdaun] *n*: **~ (on)** (*on crime*) campaña (contra); (*on spending*)

reducción *f* (en).

cracker ['krækə*] *n* (*biscuit*) crácker *m*; (*Christmas ~*) sorpresa (navideña).

crackle ['krækl] *vi* crepitar.

crackling ['kræklɪŋ] *n* (*on radio, telephone*) interferencia; (*of fire*) crepitación *f*; (*of leaves etc*) crujido; (*of pork*) chicharrón *m*.

cradle ['kreɪdl] *n* cuna ♦ *vt* (*child*) mecer, acunar; (*object*) abrazar.

craft [krɑːft] *n* (*skill*) arte *m*; (*trade*) oficio; (*cunning*) astucia; (*boat*) barco.

craftsman ['krɑːftsmən] *n* artesano.

craftsmanship ['krɑːftsmənʃɪp] *n* artesanía.

crafty ['krɑːftɪ] *a* astuto.

crag [kræg] *n* peñasco.

craggy ['krægɪ] *a* escarpado.

cram [kræm] *vt* (*fill*): **to ~ sth with** llenar algo (a reventar) de; (*put*): **to ~ sth into** meter algo a la fuerza en ♦ *vi* (*for exams*) empollar.

crammed [kræmd] *a* atestado.

cramp [kræmp] *n* (*MED*) calambre *m*; (*TECH*) grapa ♦ *vt* (*limit*) poner trabas a.

cramped [kræmpt] *a* apretado, estrecho.

crampon ['kræmpən] *n* crampón *m*.

cranberry ['krænbərɪ] *n* arándano agrio.

crane [kreɪn] *n* (*TECH*) grúa; (*bird*) grulla ♦ *vt, vi*: **to ~ forward**, **to ~ one's neck** estirar el cuello, inclinarse estirando el cuello.

cranium ['kreɪnɪəm] *n* cráneo.

crank [kræŋk] *n* manivela; (*person*) chiflado/a.

crankshaft ['kræŋkʃɑːft] *n* cigüeñal *m*.

cranky ['kræŋkɪ] *a* (*eccentric*) maniático; (*bad-tempered*) irritable.

cranny ['krænɪ] *n see* **nook**.

crap [kræp] *n* (*col!*) mierda (!).

craps [kræps] *n* (*US*) dados *mpl*.

crash [kræʃ] *n* (*noise*) estrépito; (*of cars etc*) choque *m*; (*of plane*) accidente *m* de aviación; (*of business*) quiebra; (*STOCK EXCHANGE*) crac *m* ♦ *vt* (*plane*) estrellar ♦ *vi* (*plane*) estrellarse; (*two cars*) chocar; (*fall noisily*) caer con estrépito; **he ~ed the car into a wall** estrelló el coche contra una pared *or* tapia.

crash barrier *n* (*AUT*) barrera de protección.

crash course *n* curso acelerado.

crash helmet *n* casco (protector).

crash landing *n* aterrizaje *m* forzado.

crass [kræs] *a* grosero, maleducado.

crate [kreɪt] *n* cajón *m* de embalaje; (*col*) armatoste *m*.

crater ['kreɪtə*] *n* cráter *m*.

cravat(e) [krə'væt] *n* pañuelo.

crave [kreɪv] *vt, vi*: **to ~ (for)** ansiar, anhelar.

craving ['kreɪvɪŋ] *n* (*for food, cigarettes, etc*) antojo.

crawl [krɔːl] *vi* (*drag o.s.*) arrastrarse;

(*child*) andar a gatas, gatear; (*vehicle*) avanzar (lentamente); (*col*): **to ~ to sb** dar coba a uno, hacerle la pelota a uno ◆ *n* (*SWIMMING*) crol *m*.

crayfish ['kreɪfɪʃ] *n*, *pl inv* (*freshwater*) cangrejo de río; (*saltwater*) cigala.

crayon ['kreɪən] *n* lápiz *m* de color.

craze [kreɪz] *n* manía; (*fashion*) moda.

crazed [kreɪzd] *a* (*look*, *person*) loco, demente; (*pottery*, *glaze*) agrietado, cuarteado.

crazy ['kreɪzɪ] *a* (*person*) loco; (*idea*) disparatado; **to go ~** volverse loco; **to be ~ about sb/sth** (*col*) estar loco por uno/algo.

crazy paving *n* pavimento de baldosas *irregulares*.

creak [kriːk] *vi* crujir; (*hinge etc*) chirriar, rechinar.

cream [kriːm] *n* (*of milk*) nata, crema; (*lotion*) crema; (*fig*) flor *f* y nata ◆ *a* (*colour*) color *m* crema; **whipped ~** nata batida.

cream off *vt* (*fig*) (*best talents*, *part of profits*) separar lo mejor de.

cream cake *n* pastel *m* de nata.

cream cheese *n* queso crema.

creamery ['kriːmərɪ] *n* (*shop*) quesería; (*factory*) central *f* lechera.

creamy ['kriːmɪ] *a* cremoso.

crease [kriːs] *n* (*fold*) pliegue *m*; (*in trousers*) raya; (*wrinkle*) arruga ◆ *vt* (*fold*) doblar, plegar; (*wrinkle*) arrugar ◆ *vi* (*wrinkle up*) arrugarse.

crease-resistant ['kriːsrɪzɪstənt] *a* inarrugable.

create [kriː'eɪt] *vt* (*also COMPUT*) crear; (*impression*) dar; (*fuss*, *noise*) hacer.

creation [kriː'eɪʃən] *n* creación *f*.

creative [kriː'eɪtɪv] *a* creador(a).

creativity [kriːeɪ'tɪvɪtɪ] *n* creatividad *f*.

creator [kriː'eɪtə*] *n* creador(a) *m/f*.

creature ['kriːtʃə*] *n* (*animal*) animal *m*, bicho; (*living thing*) criatura.

crèche, creche [krɛʃ] *n* (*Brit*) guardería (infantil).

credence ['kriːdəns] *n*: **to lend** or **give ~ to** creer en, dar crédito a.

credentials [krɪ'dɛnʃlz] *npl* credenciales *fpl*; (*letters of reference*) referencias *fpl*.

credibility [krɛdɪ'bɪlɪtɪ] *n* credibilidad *f*.

credible ['krɛdɪbl] *a* creíble; (*witness*, *source*) de integridad.

credit ['krɛdɪt] *n* (*gen*) crédito; (*merit*) honor *m*, mérito; (*UNIV*: *esp US*) curso de valor *f* ◆ *vt* (*COMM*) abonar; (*believe*) creer, prestar fe a ◆ *a* crediticio; **to be in ~** (*person*, *bank account*) tener saldo a favor; **on ~** a crédito; (*col*) al fiado; **he's a ~ to his family** hace honor a su familia; **to ~ sb with** (*fig*) reconocer a uno el mérito de; *see also* **credits**.

creditable ['krɛdɪtəbl] *a* estimable, digno de elogio.

credit account *n* cuenta de crédito.

credit agency *n* agencia de informes comerciales.

credit balance *n* saldo acreedor.

credit card *n* tarjeta de crédito.

credit control *n* control *m* de créditos.

credit facilities *npl* facilidades *fpl* de crédito.

credit limit *n* límite *m* de crédito.

credit note *n* nota de crédito.

creditor ['krɛdɪtə*] *n* acreedor(a) *m/f*.

credits ['krɛdɪts] *npl* (*CINEMA*) títulos *mpl*, rótulos *mpl* de crédito.

credit transfer *n* transferencia de crédito.

creditworthy ['krɛdɪtwəːðɪ] *a* solvente.

credulity [krɪ'djuːlɪtɪ] *n* credulidad *f*.

creed [kriːd] *n* credo.

creek [kriːk] *n* cala, ensenada; (*US*) riachuelo.

creel [kriːl] *n* nasa.

creep, pt, pp crept [kriːp, krɛpt] *vi* (*animal*) deslizarse; (*plant*) trepar; **to ~ up on sb** acercarse sigilosamente a uno; (*fig*: *old age etc*) acercarse ◆ *n* (*col*): **he's a ~** ¡qué lameculos es!; **it gives me the ~s** me da escalofríos.

creeper ['kriːpə*] *n* enredadera.

creepers ['kriːpəz] *npl* (*US*: *for baby*) pelele *msg*.

creepy ['kriːpɪ] *a* (*frightening*) horripilante.

creepy-crawly ['kriːpɪ'krɔːlɪ] *n* (*col*) bicho.

cremate [krɪ'meɪt] *vt* incinerar.

cremation [krɪ'meɪʃən] *n* incineración *f*.

crematorium, *pl* crematoria [krɛmə-'tɔːrɪəm, -'tɔːrɪə] *n* crematorio.

creosote ['krɪəsəʊt] *n* creosota.

crêpe [kreɪp] *n* (*fabric*) crespón *m*; (*also*: **~ rubber**) crep(é) *m*.

crêpe bandage *n* (*Brit*) venda elástica.

crêpe paper *n* papel *m* crep(é).

crêpe sole *n* (*on shoes*) suela de crep(é).

crept [krɛpt] *pt*, *pp of* **creep**.

crescent ['krɛsnt] *n* media luna; (*street*) calle *f* (*en forma de semicírculo*).

cress [krɛs] *n* berro.

crest [krɛst] *n* (*of bird*) cresta; (*of hill*) cima, cumbre *f*; (*of helmet*) cimera; (*of coat of arms*) blasón *m*.

crestfallen ['krɛstfɔːlən] *a* alicaído.

Crete [kriːt] *n* Creta.

cretin ['krɛtɪn] *n* cretino/a.

crevasse [krɪ'væs] *n* grieta.

crevice ['krɛvɪs] *n* grieta, hendedura.

crew [kruː] *n* (*of ship etc*) tripulación *f*; (*CINEMA etc*) equipo; (*gang*) pandilla, banda; (*MIL*) dotación *f*.

crew-cut ['kruːkʌt] *n* corte *m* al rape.

crew-neck ['kruːnɛk] *n* cuello plano.

crib [krɪb] *n* pesebre *m* ◆ *vt* (*col*) plagiar.

crick [krɪk] *n*: **~ in the neck** tortícolis *m inv*.

cricket ['krɪkɪt] *n* (*insect*) grillo; (*game*) críquet *m*.

cricketer ['krɪkɪtə*] jugador *m* de críquet.

crime [kraɪm] n crimen m; (less serious) delito.

crime wave n ola de crímenes or delitos.

criminal ['krɪmɪnl] n criminal m/f, delincuente m/f ◆ a criminal; (law) penal.

Criminal Investigation Department (CID) n ≈ Brigada de Investigación Criminal (B.I.C. f) (Sp).

crimp [krɪmp] vt (hair) rizar.

crimson ['krɪmzn] a carmesí.

cringe [krɪndʒ] vi agacharse, encogerse.

crinkle ['krɪŋkl] vt arrugar.

crinkly ['krɪŋklɪ] a (hair) rizado, crespo.

cripple ['krɪpl] n lisiado/a, cojo/a ◆ vt lisiar, mutilar; (ship, plane) inutilizar; (production, exports) paralizar; ~d with arthritis paralizado por la artritis.

crippling ['krɪplɪŋ] a (injury etc) debilitador(a); (prices, taxes) devastador(a).

crisis, pl **crises** ['kraɪsɪs, -siːz] n crisis f.

crisp [krɪsp] a fresco; (cooked) tostado; (manner) seco.

crisps [krɪsps] npl (Brit) patatas fpl fritas.

crisscross ['krɪskrɒs] a entrelazado, entrecruzado ◆ vt entrecruzar(se).

criterion, pl **criteria** [kraɪˈtɪərɪən, -ˈtɪərɪə] n criterio.

critic ['krɪtɪk] n crítico/a.

critical ['krɪtɪkl] a (gen) crítico; (illness) grave; **to be ~ of sb/sth** criticar a uno/ algo.

critically ['krɪtɪklɪ] ad (speak etc) en tono crítico; (ill) gravemente.

criticism ['krɪtɪsɪzm] n crítica.

criticize ['krɪtɪsaɪz] vt criticar.

critique [krɪˈtiːk] n crítica.

croak [krəʊk] vi (frog) croar; (raven) graznar ◆ n graznido.

crochet ['krəʊʃeɪ] n ganchillo.

crock [krɒk] n cántaro, tarro; (col: person: also: **old ~**) carcamal m/f, viejete/a m/f; (: car etc) cacharro.

crockery ['krɒkərɪ] n (plates, cups etc) loza, vajilla.

crocodile ['krɒkədaɪl] n cocodrilo.

crocus ['krəʊkəs] n azafrán m.

croft [krɒft] n granja pequeña.

crofter ['krɒftə*] n pequeño granjero.

croissant ['krwasɑ̃] n croissant m, medialuna.

crone [krəʊn] n arpía, bruja.

crony ['krəʊnɪ] n compinche m/f.

crook [kruk] n (fam) ladrón/ona m/f; (of shepherd) cayado; (of arm) pliegue m.

crooked ['krukɪd] a torcido; (path) tortuoso; (fam) sucio.

crop [krɒp] n (produce) cultivo; (amount produced) cosecha; (riding ~) látigo de montar; (of bird) buche m ◆ vt cortar, recortar; (cut: hair) cortar al rape; (subj: animals: grass) pacer.

crop up vi surgir, presentarse.

crop spraying [-'spreɪɪŋ] n fumigación f de los cultivos.

croquet ['krəʊkeɪ] n croquet m.

croquette [krəˈkɛt] n croqueta.

cross [krɒs] n cruz f ◆ vt (street etc) cruzar, atravesar; (thwart: person) contrariar, ir contra ◆ vi: **the boat ~es from Santander to Plymouth** el barco hace la travesía de Santander a Plymouth ◆ a de mal humor, enojado; **it's a ~ between geography and sociology** es una mezcla de geografía y sociología; **to ~ o.s.** santiguarse; **they've got their lines ~ed** (fig) hay un malentendido entre ellos; **to be/get ~ with sb (about sth)** estar enfadado/ enfadarse con uno (por algo).

cross out vt tachar.

cross over vi cruzar.

crossbar ['krɒsbɑː*] n travesaño.

cross-Channel ferry ['krɒsˈtʃænl-] n transbordador m que cruza el Canal de la Mancha.

cross-check ['krɒstʃɛk] n verificación f ◆ vt verificar.

cross-country (race) ['krɒsˈkʌntrɪ-] n carrera a campo traviesa, cross m.

cross-examination ['krɒsɪɡzæmɪˈneɪʃən] n repregunta, interrogatorio.

cross-examine ['krɒsɪɡˈzæmɪn] vt interrogar.

cross-eyed ['krɒsaɪd] a bizco.

crossfire ['krɒsfaɪə*] n fuego cruzado.

crossing ['krɒsɪŋ] n (road) cruce m; (rail) paso a nivel; (sea passage) travesía; (also: **pedestrian ~**) paso para peatones.

crossing guard n (US) persona encargada de ayudar a los niños a cruzar la calle.

cross purposes npl: **to be at ~ with sb** tener un malentendido con uno.

cross-reference ['krɒsˈrɛfrəns] n referencia, remisión f.

crossroads ['krɒsrəʊdz] nsg cruce m, encrucijada.

cross section n corte m transversal; (of population) muestra (representativa).

crosswalk ['krɒswɔːk] n (US) paso de peatones.

crosswind ['krɒswɪnd] n viento de costado.

crossword ['krɒswɜːd] n crucigrama m.

crotch [krɒtʃ] n (of garment) entrepierna.

crotchet ['krɒtʃɪt] n (Brit mus) negra.

crotchety ['krɒtʃɪtɪ] a (person) arisco.

crouch [krautʃ] vi agacharse, acurrucarse.

croup [kruːp] n (med) crup m.

croupier ['kruːpɪə] n crupier m/f.

crouton ['kruːtɒn] n cubito de pan frito.

crow [krəʊ] n (bird) cuervo; (of cock) canto, cacareo ◆ vi (cock) cantar; (fig) jactarse.

crowbar ['krəʊbɑː*] n palanca.

crowd [kraud] n muchedumbre f; (sport) público; (common herd) vulgo ◆ vt (gather) amontonar; (fill) llenar ◆ vi (gather) reunirse; (*pile up*) amontonarse; ~s **of people** gran cantidad de gente.

crowded ['kraudɪd] *a* (*full*) atestado; (*well-attended*) concurrido.

crowd scene *n* (*CINEMA, THEATRE*) escena con muchos comparsas.

crown [kraun] *n* corona; (*of head*) coronilla; (*of hat*) copa; (*of hill*) cumbre *f* ◆ *vt* (*also tooth*) coronar; **and to ~ it all** ... (*fig*) y para colmo *or* remate ....

crown court *n* (*LAW*) tribunal *m* superior.

crowning ['kraunɪŋ] *a* (*achievement, glory*) máximo.

crown jewels *npl* joyas *fpl* reales.

crown prince *n* príncipe *m* heredero.

crow's feet ['krəuzfiːt] *npl* patas *fpl* de gallo.

crucial ['kruːʃl] *a* decisivo; **his approval is ~ to the success of the project** su aprobación es crucial para el éxito del proyecto.

crucifix ['kruːsɪfɪks] *n* crucifijo.

crucifixion [kruːsɪ'fɪkʃən] *n* crucifixión *f*.

crucify ['kruːsɪfaɪ] *vt* crucificar; (*fig*) martirizar.

crude [kruːd] *a* (*materials*) bruto; (*fig: basic*) tosco; (: *vulgar*) ordinario.

crude (oil) *n* petróleo crudo.

cruel ['kruəl] *a* cruel.

cruelty ['kruəltɪ] *n* crueldad *f*.

cruet ['kruːɪt] *n* vinagreras *fpl*.

cruise [kruːz] *n* crucero ◆ *vi* (*ship*) hacer un crucero; (*car*) ir a velocidad de crucero.

cruise missile *n* misil *m* de crucero.

cruiser ['kruːzə*] *n* crucero.

cruising speed ['kruːzɪŋ-] *n* velocidad *f* de crucero.

crumb [krʌm] *n* miga, migaja.

crumble ['krʌmbl] *vt* desmenuzar ◆ *vi* (*gen*) desmenuzarse; (*building*) desmoronarse.

crumbly ['krʌmblɪ] *a* desmenuzable.

crummy ['krʌmɪ] *a* (*col: poor quality*) pésimo, cutre (*Sp*); (: *unwell*) fatal.

crumpet ['krʌmpɪt] *n* ≈ bollo para tostar.

crumple ['krʌmpl] *vt* (*paper*) estrujar; (*material*) arrugar.

crunch [krʌntʃ] *vt* (*with teeth*) ronzar; (*underfoot*) hacer crujir ◆ *n* (*fig*) crisis *f inv*.

crunchy ['krʌntʃɪ] *a* crujiente.

crusade [kruː'seɪd] *n* cruzada ◆ *vi*: **to ~ for/against** (*fig*) hacer una campaña en pro de/en contra de.

crusader [kruː'seɪdə*] *n* (*fig*) paladín *m/f*, campeón/ona *m/f*.

crush [krʌʃ] *n* (*crowd*) aglomeración *f* ◆ *vt* (*gen*) aplastar; (*paper*) estrujar; (*cloth*) arrugar; (*grind, break up: garlic, ice*) picar; (*fruit*) exprimir; (*grapes*) exprimir, prensar; **to have a ~ on sb** estar enamorado de uno.

crush barrier *n* barrera antimotín *or* de seguridad.

crushing ['krʌʃɪŋ] *a* aplastante; (*burden*) agobiador(a).

crust [krʌst] *n* corteza.

crustacean [krʌs'teɪʃən] *n* crustáceo.

crusty ['krʌstɪ] *a* (*loaf*) de corteza dura.

crutch [krʌtʃ] *n* (*MED*) muleta; (*support*) apoyo.

crux [krʌks] *n* lo esencial.

cry [kraɪ] *vi* llorar; (*shout: also*: ~ **out**) gritar ◆ *n* grito; (*of animal*) aullido; (*weep*): **she had a good ~** lloró a lágrima viva; **what are you ~ing about?** ¿por qué lloras?; **to ~ for help** pedir socorro a voces; **it's a far ~ from** ... (*fig*) dista mucho de ....

cry off *vi* retirarse.

crypt [krɪpt] *n* cripta.

cryptic ['krɪptɪk] *a* enigmático, secreto.

crystal ['krɪstl] *n* cristal *m*.

crystal-clear ['krɪstl'klɪə*] *a* claro como el agua; (*fig*) cristalino.

crystallize ['krɪstəlaɪz] *vt* (*fig*) cristalizar ◆ *vi* cristalizarse; ~**d fruits** frutas *fpl* escarchadas.

CSA *n abbr* = *Confederate States of America*.

CSC *n abbr* (= *Civil Service Commission*) comisión *f* de reclutamiento de funcionarios.

CSE *n abbr* (*Brit:* = *Certificate of Secondary Education*) ≈ BUP *m*.

CSEU *n abbr* (*Brit:* = *Confederation of Shipbuilding and Engineering Unions*) sindicato de trabajadores de la construcción naval.

CS gas *n* (*Brit*) gas *m* lacrimógeno.

CST *n abbr* (*US:* = *Central Standard Time*) huso horario.

CT *abbr* (*US POST*) = *Connecticut*.

ct *abbr* = **carat**.

cu. *abbr* = **cubic**.

cub [kʌb] *n* cachorro; (*also*: ~ **scout**) niño explorador.

Cuba ['kjuːbə] *n* Cuba.

Cuban ['kjuːbən] *a, n* cubano/a *m/f*.

cubbyhole ['kʌbɪhəul] *n* chiribitil *m*.

cube [kjuːb] *n* cubo; (*of sugar*) terrón *m* ◆ *vt* (*MATH*) cubicar.

cube root *n* raíz *f* cúbica.

cubic ['kjuːbɪk] *a* cúbico; ~ **capacity** (*AUT*) capacidad *f* cúbica.

cubicle ['kjuːbɪkl] *n* (*at pool*) caseta; (*for bed*) cubículo.

cubism ['kjuːbɪzəm] *n* cubismo.

cuckoo ['kuku:] *n* cuco.

cuckoo clock *n* cucú *m*.

cucumber ['kjuːkʌmbə*] *n* pepino.

cuddle ['kʌdl] *vt* abrazar ◆ *vi* abrazarse.

cuddly ['kʌdlɪ] *a* mimoso.

cudgel ['kʌdʒəl] *vt*: **to ~ one's brains** devanarse los sesos.

cue [kjuː] *n* (*snooker* ~) taco; (*THEATRE etc*) entrada.

cuff [kʌf] *n* (*Brit: of shirt, coat etc*) puño;

(*US*: *of trousers*) vuelta; (*blow*) bofetada ♦ *vt* bofetear; **off the ~** *ad* improvisado.

cufflinks ['kʌflɪŋks] *npl* gemelos *mpl*.

cu. in. *abbr* = *cubic inches*.

cuisine [kwɪ'ziːn] *n* cocina.

cul-de-sac ['kʌldəsæk] *n* callejón *m* sin salida.

culinary ['kʌlɪnərɪ] *a* culinario.

cull [kʌl] *vt* (*select*) entresacar; (*kill selectively*: *animals*) matar selectivamente ♦ *n* matanza selectiva; **seal ~** matanza selectiva de focas.

culminate ['kʌlmɪneɪt] *vi*: **to ~ in** terminar en.

culmination [kʌlmɪ'neɪʃən] *n* culminación *f*, colmo.

culottes [kuː'lɒts] *npl* falda *f* pantalón.

culpable ['kʌlpəbl] *a* culpable.

culprit ['kʌlprɪt] *n* culpable *m/f*, delincuente *m/f*.

cult [kʌlt] *n* culto; **a ~ figure** un ídolo.

cultivate ['kʌltɪveɪt] *vt* (*also fig*) cultivar.

cultivated ['kʌltɪveɪtɪd] *a* culto.

cultivation [kʌltɪ'veɪʃən] *n* cultivo; (*fig*) cultura.

cultural ['kʌltʃərəl] *a* cultural.

culture ['kʌltʃə*] *n* (*also fig*) cultura.

cultured ['kʌltʃəd] *a* culto.

cumbersome ['kʌmbəsəm] *a* de mucho bulto, voluminoso.

cumin ['kʌmɪn] *n* (*spice*) comino.

cummerbund ['kʌməbʌnd] *n* faja, fajín *m*.

cumulative ['kjuːmjulətɪv] *a* cumulativo.

cunning ['kʌnɪŋ] *n* astucia ♦ *a* astuto; (*clever*: *device*, *idea*) ingenioso.

cup [kʌp] *n* taza; (*prize*, *event*) copa; **a ~ of tea** una taza de té.

cupboard ['kʌbəd] *n* armario; (*kitchen*) alacena.

cup final *n* (*FOOTBALL*) final *f* de copa.

cupful ['kʌpful] *n* taza.

Cupid ['kjuː'pɪd] *n* Cupido.

cupola ['kjuːpələ] *n* cúpula.

cup-tie ['kʌptaɪ] *n* (*Brit*) partido de copa.

cur [kə:*] *n* perro de mala raza; (*person*) canalla *m*.

curable ['kjuərəbl] *a* curable.

curate ['kjuərɪt] *n* cura *m*.

curator [kjuə'reɪtə*] *n* conservador(a) *m/f*.

curb [kə:b] *vt* refrenar, limitar ♦ *n* freno; (*US*: *kerb*) bordillo.

curd cheese [kə:d-] *n* requesón *m*.

curdle ['kə:dl] *vi* cuajarse.

curds [kə:dz] *npl* requesón *msg*.

cure [kjuə*] *vt* curar ♦ *n* cura, curación *f*; **to be ~d of sth** curarse de algo; **to take a ~** tomar una medicina, hacer una cura.

cure-all ['kjuərɔ:l] *n* (*also fig*) panacea.

curfew ['kə:fjuː] *n* toque *m* de queda.

curio ['kjuərɪəu] *n* curiosidad *f*.

curiosity [kjuərɪ'ɒsɪtɪ] *n* curiosidad *f*.

curious ['kjuərɪəs] *a* curioso; **I'm ~ about him** me intriga.

curiously ['kjuərɪəslɪ] *ad* curiosamente; **~ enough, ...** aunque parezca extraño ....

curl [kə:l] *n* rizo; (*of smoke etc*) espiral *f*, voluta ♦ *vt* (*hair*) rizar; (*paper*) arrollar; (*lip*) fruncir ♦ *vi* rizarse; arrollarse.

curl up *vi* arrollarse; (*person*) hacerse un ovillo; (*fam*) morirse de risa.

curler ['kə:lə*] *n* bigudí *m*.

curlew ['kə:luː] *n* zarapito.

curling tongs, (*US*) **curling irons** ['kə:lɪŋ-] *npl* tenacillas *fpl*.

curly ['kə:lɪ] *a* rizado.

currant ['kʌrnt] *n* pasa; (*black*, *red*) grosella.

currency ['kʌrnsɪ] *n* moneda; **to gain ~** (*fig*) difundirse.

current ['kʌrnt] *n* corriente *f* ♦ *a* corriente, actual; (*tendency*, *price*, *event*) corriente; **direct/alternating ~** corriente directa/ alterna; **the ~ issue of a magazine** el número corriente de una revista; **in ~ use** de uso corriente.

current account *n* (*Brit*) cuenta corriente.

current affairs *npl* actualidades *fpl*.

current assets *npl* (*COMM*) activo disponible.

current liabilities *npl* (*COMM*) pasivo circulante.

currently ['kʌrntlɪ] *ad* actualmente.

curriculum, *pl* **~s** *or* **curricula** [kə'rɪkjuləm, -lə] *n* plan *m* de estudios.

curriculum vitae (CV) [-'viːtaɪ] *n* currículum *m*.

curry ['kʌrɪ] *n* curry *m* ♦ *vt*: **to ~ favour with** buscar favores con.

curry powder *n* curry *m* en polvo.

curse [kə:s] *vi* echar pestes ♦ *vt* maldecir ♦ *n* maldición *f*; (*swearword*) palabrota.

cursor ['kə:sə*] *n* (*COMPUT*) cursor *m*.

cursory ['kə:sərɪ] *a* rápido, superficial.

curt [kə:t] *a* corto, seco.

curtail [kə:'teɪl] *vt* (*cut short*) acortar; (*restrict*) restringir.

curtain ['kə:tn] *n* cortina; (*THEATRE*) telón *m*; **to draw the ~s** (*together*) cerrar las cortinas; (*apart*) abrir las cortinas.

curtain call *n* (*THEATRE*) llamada a escena.

curtain ring *n* anilla.

curts(e)y ['kə:tsɪ] *n* reverencia ♦ *vi* hacer una reverencia.

curvature ['kə:vətʃə*] *n* curvatura.

curve [kə:v] *n* curva ♦ *vt* encorvar, torcer ♦ *vi* encorvarse, torcerse; (*road*) hacer curva.

curved [kə:vd] *a* curvo, encorvado.

cushion ['kuʃən] *n* cojín *m*; (*SNOOKER*) banda ♦ *vt* (*seat*) acolchar; (*shock*) amortiguar.

cushy ['kuʃɪ] *a* (*col*): **a ~ job** un chollo; **to have a ~ time** tener la vida arreglada.

custard ['kʌstəd] *n* (*for pouring*) natillas

fpl.

custard powder *n* polvo para natillas.
custodian [kʌs'təudɪən] *n* custodio *m/f;* *(of museum etc)* conservador(a) *m/f.*
custody ['kʌstədɪ] *n* custodia; **to take sb into** ~ detener a uno; **in the** ~ **of** al cuidado *or* cargo de.
custom ['kʌstəm] *n* costumbre *f;* (*COMM*) clientela; *see also* **customs.**
customary ['kʌstəmərɪ] *a* acostumbrado; **it is** ~ **to do ...** es la costumbre hacer ....
custom-built ['kʌstəm'bɪlt] *a* = **custommade.**
customer ['kʌstəmə*] *n* cliente *m/f;* **he's an awkward** ~ *(col)* es un tipo difícil.
customer profile *n* perfil *m* del cliente.
customized ['kʌstəmaɪzd] *a* *(car etc)* hecho a encargo.
custom-made ['kʌstəm'meɪd] *a* hecho a la medida.
customs ['kʌstəmz] *npl* aduana *sg;* **to go through (the)** ~ pasar la aduana.
Customs and Excise *n* (*Brit*) Aduanas *fpl* y Arbitrios.
customs duty *n* derechos *mpl* de aduana.
customs officer *n* aduanero/a.
cut [kʌt] *vb* (*pt, pp* **cut**) *vt* cortar; *(price)* rebajar; *(record)* grabar; *(reduce)* reducir; *(col: avoid: class, lecture)* fumarse, faltar a ♦ *vi* cortar; *(intersect)* cruzarse ♦ *n* corte *m;* *(in skin)* cortadura; *(with sword)* tajo; *(of knife)* cuchillada; *(in salary etc)* rebaja; *(slice of meat)* tajada; **to** ~ **one's finger** cortarse un dedo; **to get one's hair** ~ cortarse el pelo; **to** ~ **sb dead** negar el saludo, cortarle a uno; **it** ~**s both ways** *(fig)* tiene doble filo; **to** ~ **a tooth** echar un diente; **power** ~ (*Brit*) apagón *m.*
cut back *vt* *(plants)* podar; *(production, expenditure)* reducir.
cut down *vt* *(tree)* cortar, derribar; *(consumption, expenses)* reducir; **to** ~ **sb down to size** *(fig)* bajarle los humos a uno.
cut in *vi:* **to** ~ **in (on)** *(interrupt: conversation)* interrumpir, intervenir (en); *(AUT)* cerrar el paso (a).
cut off *vt* cortar; *(fig)* aislar; *(troops)* cercar; **we've been** ~ **off** (*TEL*) nos han cortado la comunicación.
cut out *vt* *(shape)* recortar; *(delete)* suprimir.
cut up *vt* cortar (en pedazos); *(chop: food)* trinchar, cortar.
cut-and-dried ['kʌtən'draɪd] *a* (*also:* **cut-and-dry**) arreglado de antemano, seguro.
cutback ['kʌtbæk] *n* reducción *f.*
cute [kju:t] *a* lindo; *(shrewd)* listo.
cuticle ['kju:tɪkl] *n* cutícula.
cutlery ['kʌtlərɪ] *n* cubiertos *mpl.*
cutlet ['kʌtlɪt] *n* chuleta.
cutoff ['kʌtɔf] *n* (*also:* ~ **point**) límite *m.*
cutout ['kʌtaut] *n* *(cardboard* ~) recortable

m.
cut-price ['kʌt'praɪs], (*US*) **cut-rate** ['kʌt'reɪt] *a* a precio reducido.
cutthroat ['kʌtθrəut] *n* asesino/a ♦ *a* feroz; ~ **competition** competencia encarnizada *or* despiadada.
cutting ['kʌtɪŋ] *a* *(gen)* cortante; *(remark)* mordaz ♦ *n* (*Brit: from newspaper*) recorte *m;* (: *RAIL*) desmonte *m;* (*CINEMA*) desglose *m.*
CV *n abbr see* **curriculum vitae.**
C & W *n abbr* = **country and western** (music).
cwo *abbr* (*COMM*) = **cash with order.**
cwt. *abbr* = **hundredweight(s).**
cyanide ['saɪənaɪd] *n* cianuro.
cybernetics [saɪbə'nɛtɪks] *nsg* cibernética.
cyclamen ['sɪkləmən] *n* ciclamen *m.*
cycle ['saɪkl] *n* ciclo; *(bicycle)* bicicleta ♦ *vi* ir en bicicleta.
cycle race *n* carrera ciclista.
cycle rack *n* soporte *m* para bicicletas.
cycling ['saɪklɪŋ] *n* ciclismo.
cycling holiday *n* vacaciones *fpl* en bicicleta.
cyclist ['saɪklɪst] *n* ciclista *m/f.*
cyclone ['saɪkləun] *n* ciclón *m.*
cygnet ['sɪgnɪt] *n* pollo de cisne.
cylinder ['sɪlɪndə*] *n* cilindro.
cylinder block *n* bloque *m* de cilindros.
cylinder capacity *n* cilindrada.
cylinder head *n* culata de cilindro.
cylinder-head gasket *n* junta de culata.
cymbals ['sɪmblz] *npl* platillos *mpl.*
cynic ['sɪnɪk] *n* cínico/a.
cynical ['sɪnɪkl] *a* cínico.
cynicism ['sɪnɪsɪzəm] *n* cinismo.
CYO *n abbr* (*US*) = *Catholic Youth Organization.*
cypress ['saɪprɪs] *n* ciprés *m.*
Cypriot ['sɪprɪət] *a, n* chipriota *m/f.*
Cyprus ['saɪprəs] *n* Chipre *f.*
cyst [sɪst] *n* quiste *m.*
cystitis [sɪs'taɪtɪs] *n* cistitis *f.*
CZ *n abbr* (*US:* = *Central Zone*) zona del Canal de Panamá.
czar [zɑ:*] *n* zar *m.*
czarina [zɑ:'ri:nə] *n* zarina.
Czech [tʃɛk] *a* checo ♦ *n* checo/a; (*LING*) checo.
Czechoslovak [tʃɛkə'sləuvæk] *a, n* = **Czechoslovakian.**
Czechoslovakia [tʃɛkəslə'vækɪə] *n* Checoslovaquia.
Czechoslovakian [tʃɛkəslə'vækɪən] *a, n* checo/a *m/f.*

D

D, d [diː] *n* (*letter*) D, d; (*MUS*): **D** re *m*; **D for David**, (*US*) **D for Dog** D de Dolores.
D *abbr* (*US POL*) = **democrat(ic)**.
d *abbr* (*Brit: old*) = **penny**.
d. *abbr* = **died**.
DA *n abbr* (*US*) = **district attorney**.
dab [dæb] *vt:* **to ~ ointment onto a wound** aplicar pomada sobre una herida; **to ~ with paint** cubrir ligeramente de pintura ◆ *n* (*light stroke*) toque *m*; (*small amount*) pizca.
dabble ['dæbl] *vi:* **to ~ in** hacer por afición.
Dacca ['dækə] *n* Dacca.
dachshund ['dækshund] *n* perro tejonero.
Dacron ® ['deɪkrɔn] *n* (*US*) terylene *m*.
dad [dæd], **daddy** ['dædɪ] *n* papá *m*.
daddy-long-legs [dædɪ'lɔŋlegz] *n* típula.
daffodil ['dæfədɪl] *n* narciso.
daft [dɑːft] *a* chiflado.
dagger ['dægə*] *n* puñal *m*, daga; **to look ~s at sb** apuñalar a uno con la mirada.
dahlia ['deɪljə] *n* dalia.
daily ['deɪlɪ] *a* diario, cotidiano ◆ *n* (*paper*) diario; (*domestic help*) asistenta ◆ *ad* todos los días, cada día; **twice ~** dos veces al día.
dainty ['deɪntɪ] *a* delicado; (*tasteful*) elegante.
dairy ['dɛərɪ] *n* (*shop*) lechería; (*on farm*) vaquería ◆ *a* (*cow etc*) lechero.
dairy cow *n* vaca lechera.
dairy farm *n* vaquería.
dairy produce *n* productos *mpl* lácteos.
dais ['deɪs] *n* estrado.
daisy ['deɪzɪ] *n* margarita.
daisy wheel *n* (*on printer*) (rueda) margarita.
daisy-wheel printer *n* impresora de margarita.
Dakar ['dækə*] *n* Dakar *m*.
dale [deɪl] *n* valle *m*.
dally ['dælɪ] *vi* entretenerse.
dalmatian [dæl'meɪʃən] *n* (*dog*) (perro) dálmata *m*.
dam [dæm] *n* presa; (*reservoir*) embalse ◆ *vt* represar.
damage ['dæmɪdʒ] *n* daño; (*fig*) perjuicio; (*to machine*) avería ◆ *vt* dañar; perjudicar; averiar; **~ to property** daños materiales.
damages ['dæmɪdʒɪz] *npl* (*LAW*) daños y perjuicios; **to pay £5000 in ~** pagar £5000 por daños y perjuicios.
damaging ['dæmɪdʒɪŋ] *a:* **~ (to)** perjudicial

(a).
Damascus [də'mɑːskəs] *n* Damasco.
dame [deɪm] *n* (*title*) dama; (*US col*) tía; (*THEATRE*) vieja.
damn [dæm] *vt* condenar; (*curse*) maldecir ◆ *n* (*col*): **I don't give a ~** me importa un pito ◆ *a* (*col: also:* **~ed**) maldito; **~ (it)!** ¡maldito sea!
damnable ['dæmnəbl] *a* (*col: behaviour*) detestable; (: *weather*) horrible.
damnation [dæm'neɪʃən] *n* (*REL*) condenación *f* ◆ *excl* (*col*) ¡maldición!, ¡maldito sea!
damning ['dæmɪŋ] *a* (*evidence*) irrecusable.
damp [dæmp] *a* húmedo, mojado ◆ *n* humedad *f* ◆ *vt* (*also:* **~en**) (*cloth, rag*) mojar; (*enthusiasm*) enfriar.
dampcourse ['dæmpkɔːs] *n* aislante *m* hidrófugo.
damper ['dæmpə*] *n* (*MUS*) sordina; (*of fire*) regulador *m* de tiro; **to put a ~ on things** estropearlo todo.
dampness ['dæmpnɪs] *n* humedad *f*.
damson ['dæmzən] *n* ciruela damascena.
dance [dɑːns] *n* baile *m* ◆ *vi* bailar; **to ~ about** saltar.
dance hall *n* salón *m* de baile.
dancer ['dɑːnsə*] *n* bailador(a) *m/f*; (*professional*) bailarín/ina *m/f*.
dancing ['dɑːnsɪŋ] *n* baile *m*.
D and C *n abbr* (*MED:* = *dilation and curettage*) raspado.
dandelion ['dændɪlaɪən] *n* diente *m* de león.
dandruff ['dændrəf] *n* caspa.
dandy ['dændɪ] *n* dandi *m* ◆ *a* (*US col*) estupendo.
Dane [deɪn] *n* danés/esa *m/f*.
danger ['deɪndʒə*] *n* peligro; (*risk*) riesgo; **~!** (*on sign*) ¡peligro de muerte!; **to be in ~ of** correr riesgo de; **out of ~** fuera de peligro.
danger list *n* (*MED*): **to be on the ~** estar grave.
dangerous ['deɪndʒərəs] *a* peligroso.
dangerously ['deɪndʒərəslɪ] *ad* peligrosamente; **~ ill** muy enfermo.
danger zone *n* área *or* zona de peligro.
dangle ['dæŋgl] *vt* colgar ◆ *vi* pender, estar colgado.
Danish ['deɪnɪʃ] *a* danés/esa ◆ *n* (*LING*) danés *m*.
Danish pastry *n* pasta de almendra.
dank [dæŋk] *a* húmedo y malsano.
Danube ['dænjuːb] *n* Danubio.
dapper ['dæpə*] *a* pulcro, apuesto.
Dardanelles [dɑːdə'nelz] *npl* Dardanelos *mpl*.
dare [dɛə*] *vt:* **to ~ sb to do** desafiar a uno a hacer ◆ *vi:* **to ~ (to) do sth** atreverse a hacer algo; **I ~ say** (*I suppose*) puede ser, a lo mejor; **I ~ say he'll turn up** puede ser que *or* quizás venga; **I ~n't tell him** no me atrevo a decírselo.

daredevil ['dɛədɛvl] *n* temerario/a, atrevido/a.

Dar-es-Salaam ['dɑːrɛssə'lɑːm] *n* Dar es Salaam *m*.

daring ['dɛərɪŋ] *a* (*person*) osado; (*plan, escape*) atrevido ♦ *n* atrevimiento, osadía.

dark [dɑːk] *a* oscuro; (*hair, complexion*) moreno; (*fig: cheerless*) triste, sombrío ♦ *n* (*gen*) oscuridad *f*; (*night*) tinieblas *fpl*; ~ **chocolate** chocolate *m* amargo; **it is/is getting** ~ es de noche/se está poniendo oscuro; **in the** ~ **about** (*fig*) en ignorancia de; **after** ~ después del anochecer.

darken ['dɑːkn] *vt* oscurecer; (*colour*) hacer más oscuro ♦ *vi* oscurecerse; (*cloud over*) anublarse.

dark glasses *npl* gafas *fpl* negras.

darkly ['dɑːklɪ] *ad* (*gloomily*) tristemente; (*sinisterly*) siniestramente.

darkness ['dɑːknɪs] *n* (*in room*) oscuridad *f*; (*night*) tinieblas *fpl*.

darkroom ['dɑːkrum] *n* cuarto oscuro.

darling ['dɑːlɪŋ] *a, n* querido/a *m/f*.

darn [dɑːn] *vt* zurcir.

dart [dɑːt] *n* dardo; (*in sewing*) sisa ♦ *vi* precipitarse; **to** ~ **away/along** *vi* salir/marchar disparado.

dartboard ['dɑːtbɔːd] *n* diana.

darts [dɑːts] *n* dardos *mpl*.

dash [dæʃ] *n* (*small quantity: of liquid*) gota, chorrito; (: *of solid*) pizca; (*sign*) guión *m*; (: *long*) raya ♦ *vt* (*break*) romper, estrellar; (*hopes*) defraudar ♦ *vi* precipitarse, ir de prisa; **a** ~ **of soda** un poco *or* chorrito de sifón *or* soda.

dash away, dash off *vi* marcharse apresuradamente.

dashboard ['dæʃbɔːd] *n* (*AUT*) tablero de instrumentos.

dashing ['dæʃɪŋ] *a* gallardo.

dastardly ['dæstədlɪ] *ad* ruin, vil.

data ['deɪtə] *npl* datos *mpl*.

database ['deɪtəbeɪs] *n* base *f* de datos.

data capture *n* recogida de datos.

data link *n* enlace *m* de datos.

data processing *n* proceso de datos.

data transmission *n* transmisión *f* de datos.

date [deɪt] *n* (*day*) fecha; (*with friend*) cita; (*fruit*) dátil *m* ♦ *vt* fechar; (*col: girl etc*) salir con; **what's the** ~ **today?** ¿qué fecha es hoy?; ~ **of birth** fecha de nacimiento; **closing** ~ fecha tope; **to** ~ *ad* hasta la fecha; **out of** ~ pasado de moda; **up to** ~ moderno; **puesto al día; to bring up to** ~ (*correspondence, information*) poner al día; (*method*) actualizar; **to bring sb up to** ~ poner a uno al corriente; **letter** ~**d 5th July** *or* (*US*) **July 5th** carta fechada el 5 de julio.

dated ['deɪtɪd] *a* anticuado.

date stamp *n* matasellos *m inv*; (*on fresh foods*) sello de fecha.

dative ['deɪtɪv] *n* dativo.

daub [dɔːb] *vt* embadurnar.

daughter ['dɔːtə*] *n* hija.

daughter-in-law ['dɔːtərɪnlɔː] *n* nuera, hija política.

daunting ['dɔːntɪŋ] *a* desalentador(a).

davenport ['dævnpɔːt] *n* escritorio; (*US: sofa*) sofá *m*.

dawdle ['dɔːdl] *vi* (*waste time*) perder el tiempo; (*go slowly*) andar muy despacio; **to** ~ **over one's work** trabajar muy despacio.

dawn [dɔːn] *n* alba, amanecer *m* ♦ *vi* amanecer; (*fig*): **it** ~**ed on him that...** cayó en la cuenta de que...; **at** ~ al amanecer; **from** ~ **to dusk** de sol a sol.

dawn chorus *n* canto de los pájaros al amanecer.

day [deɪ] *n* día *m*; (*working* ~) jornada; **the** ~ **before** el día anterior; **the** ~ **after tomorrow** pasado mañana; **the** ~ **before yesterday** anteayer, antes de ayer; **the** ~ **after, the following** ~ el día siguiente; **by** ~ de día; ~ **by** ~ día por día; **(on) the** ~ **that ...** el día que ...; **to work an 8-hour** ~ trabajar 8 horas diarias *or* al día; **he works 8 hours a** ~ trabaja 8 horas al día; **paid by the** ~ pagado por día; **these** ~**s, in the present** ~ hoy en día.

daybook ['deɪbuk] *n* (*Brit*) diario *or* libro de entradas y salidas.

daybreak ['deɪbreɪk] *n* amanecer *m*.

daydream ['deɪdriːm] *n* ensueño ♦ *vi* soñar despierto.

daylight ['deɪlaɪt] *n* luz *f* (del día).

Daylight Saving Time *n* (*US*) hora de verano.

day-release course [deɪrɪ'liːs-] *n* curso de un día a la semana.

day return (ticket) *n* (*Brit*) billete *m* de ida y vuelta (en un día).

day shift *n* turno de día.

daytime ['deɪtaɪm] *n* día *m*.

day-to-day ['deɪtə'deɪ] *a* cotidiano, diario; (*expenses*) diario; **on a** ~ **basis** día por día.

day trip *n* excursión *f* (de un día).

day tripper *n* excursionista *m/f*.

daze [deɪz] *vt* (*stun*) aturdir ♦ *n*: **in a** ~ aturdido.

dazed [deɪzd] *a* aturdido.

dazzle ['dæzl] *vt* deslumbrar.

dazzling ['dæzlɪŋ] *a* (*light, smile*) deslumbrante; (*colour*) fuerte.

DBS *n abbr* (= *direct broadcasting by satellite*) transmisión por satélite.

DC *abbr* (*ELEC*) = **direct current**; (*US POST*) = District of Columbia.

DD *n abbr* (= *Doctor of Divinity*) título universitario.

dd. *abbr* (*COMM*) = *delivered*.

D/D *abbr* = *direct debit*.

D-day ['diːdeɪ] *n* (*fig*) día *m* clave.

DDS n abbr (US: = Doctor of Dental Science; Doctor of Dental Surgery) títulos universitarios.

DDT n abbr (= dichlorodiphenyltrichloroethane) DDT m.

DE abbr (US POST) = Delaware.

DEA n abbr (US: = Drug Enforcement Administration) brigada especial dedicada a la lucha contra el tráfico de estupefacientes.

deacon ['di:kən] n diácono.

dead [dɛd] a muerto; (limb) dormido; (battery) agotado ◆ ad totalmente; (exactly) justo; **he was ~ on arrival** ingresó cadáver; **to shoot sb ~** matar a uno a tiros; **~ tired** muerto (de cansancio); **to stop ~** parar en seco; **the line has gone ~** (TEL) se ha cortado la línea; **the ~** npl los muertos.

deaden ['dɛdn] vt (blow, sound) amortiguar; (pain) calmar, aliviar.

dead end n callejón m sin salida.

dead-end ['dɛdɛnd] a: **a ~ job** un trabajo sin porvenir.

dead heat n (SPORT) empate m.

deadline ['dɛdlaɪn] n fecha or hora tope; **to work to a ~** trabajar con una fecha tope.

deadlock ['dɛdlɔk] n punto muerto.

dead loss n (col): **to be a ~** (person) ser un inútil; (thing) ser una birria.

deadly ['dɛdlɪ] a mortal, fatal; **~ dull** aburridísimo.

deadly nightshade [-'naɪtʃeɪd] n belladona.

deadpan ['dɛdpæn] a sin expresión.

Dead Sea n: **the ~** el Mar Muerto.

dead season n (TOURISM) temporada baja.

deaf [dɛf] a sordo; **to turn a ~ ear to sth** hacerse el sordo ante algo.

deaf-aid ['dɛfeɪd] n audífono.

deaf-and-dumb ['dɛfən'dʌm] a (person) sordomudo; (alphabet) para sordomudos.

deafen ['dɛfn] vt ensordecer.

deafening ['dɛfnɪŋ] a ensordecedor(a).

deaf-mute ['dɛfmju:t] n sordomudo/a.

deafness ['dɛfnɪs] n sordera.

deal [di:l] n (agreement) pacto, convenio; (business) negocio, transacción f; (CARDS) reparto ◆ vt (pt, pp **dealt**) (gen) dar; **a great ~ (of)** bastante, mucho; **it's a ~!** (col) ¡trato hecho!, ¡de acuerdo!; **to do a ~ with sb** hacer un trato con uno; **he got a bad/fair ~ from them** le trataron mal/bien.

deal in vt fus tratar en, comerciar en.

deal with vt fus (people) tratar con; (problem) ocuparse de; (subject) tratar de.

dealer ['di:lə*] n comerciante m/f; (CARDS) mano f.

dealership ['di:ləʃɪp] n concesionario.

dealings ['di:lɪŋz] npl (COMM) transacciones fpl; (relations) relaciones fpl.

dealt [dɛlt] pt, pp of **deal**.

dean [di:n] n (REL) deán m; (SCOL) decano/a.

dear [dɪə*] a querido; (expensive) caro ◆ n: **my ~** mi querido/a; **~ me!** ¡Dios mío!; **D~ Sir/Madam** (in letter) Muy señor mío, Estimado señor/Estimada señora; **D~ Mr/Mrs X** Estimado/a señor(a) X.

dearly ['dɪəlɪ] ad (love) mucho; (pay) caro.

dearth [də:θ] n (of food, resources, money) escasez f.

death [dɛθ] n muerte f.

deathbed ['dɛθbɛd] n lecho de muerte.

death certificate n partida de defunción.

death duties npl (Brit) derechos mpl de sucesión.

deathly ['dɛθlɪ] a mortal; (silence) profundo.

death penalty n pena de muerte.

death rate n tasa de mortalidad.

death sentence n condena a muerte.

deathtrap ['dɛθtræp] n lugar m (o vehículo etc) peligroso.

deb [dɛb] n abbr (col) = **debutante**.

debacle [deɪ'bɑ:kl] n desastre m, catastrofe f.

debar [dɪ'bɑ:*] vt: **to ~ sb from doing** prohibir a uno hacer.

debase [dɪ'beɪs] vt degradar.

debatable [dɪ'beɪtəbl] a discutible; **it is ~ whether ...** es discutible si ... .

debate [dɪ'beɪt] n debate m ◆ vt discutir.

debauched [dɪ'bɔ:tʃt] a vicioso.

debauchery [dɪ'bɔ:tʃərɪ] n libertinaje m.

debenture [dɪ'bɛntʃə*] n (COMM) bono, obligación f.

debenture capital n capital m hipotecario.

debilitate [dɪ'bɪlɪteɪt] vt debilitar.

debilitating [dɪ'bɪlɪteɪtɪŋ] a (illness etc) debilitante.

debit ['dɛbɪt] n debe m ◆ vt: **to ~ a sum to sb** or **to sb's account** cargar una suma en cuenta a uno.

debit balance n saldo deudor or pasivo.

debit note n nota de débito or cargo.

debonair [dɛbə'nɛə*] a jovial, cortés/esa.

debrief [di:'bri:f] vt hacer dar parte.

debriefing [di:'bri:fɪŋ] n relación f (de un informe).

debris ['dɛbri:] n escombros mpl.

debt [dɛt] n deuda; **to be in ~** tener deudas; **~s of £5000** deudas de cinco mil libras; **bad ~** deuda incobrable.

debt collector n cobrador(a) m/f de deudas.

debtor ['dɛtə*] n deudor(a) m/f.

debug [di:'bʌg] vt (COMPUT) depurar.

debunk [di:'bʌŋk] vt (col: theory) desprestigiar, desacreditar; (: claim) desacreditar; (: person, institution) desenmascarar.

début ['deɪbju:] n presentación f.

debutante ['dɛbjutænt] n debutante f.

Dec. abbr (= December) dic.

decade ['dɛkeɪd] n decenio.
decadence ['dɛkədəns] n decadencia.
decadent ['dɛkədənt] a decadente.
decaffeinated [diːˈkæfɪneɪtɪd] a descafeinado.
decamp [dɪˈkæmp] vi (col) escaparse, largarse, rajarse (LAm).
decant [dɪˈkænt] vt decantar.
decanter [dɪˈkæntə*] n garrafa.
decay [dɪˈkeɪ] n (fig) decadencia; (of building) desmoronamiento; (of tooth) caries f inv ◆ vi (rot) pudrirse; (fig) decaer.
decease [dɪˈsiːs] n fallecimiento ◆ vi fallecer.
deceased [dɪˈsiːst] a difunto.
deceit [dɪˈsiːt] n engaño.
deceitful [dɪˈsiːtful] a engañoso.
deceive [dɪˈsiːv] vt engañar.
decelerate [diːˈsɛləreɪt] vt moderar la marcha de ◆ vi decelerar.
December [dɪˈsɛmbə*] n diciembre m.
decency ['diːsənsɪ] n decencia.
decent ['diːsənt] a (proper) decente; (person) amable, bueno.
decently ['diːsəntlɪ] ad (respectably) decentemente; (kindly) amablemente.
decentralization [diːsɛntrəlaɪˈzeɪʃən] n descentralización f.
decentralize [diːˈsɛntrəlaɪz] vt descentralizar.
deception [dɪˈsɛpʃən] n engaño.
deceptive [dɪˈsɛptɪv] a engañoso.
decibel ['dɛsɪbɛl] n decibel(io) m.
decide [dɪˈsaɪd] vt (person) decidir; (question, argument) resolver ◆ vi: **to ~ to do/that** decidir hacer/que; **to ~ on sth** decidir por algo; **to ~ against doing sth** decidir en contra de hacer algo.
decided [dɪˈsaɪdɪd] a (resolute) decidido; (clear, definite) indudable.
decidedly [dɪˈsaɪdɪdlɪ] ad decididamente.
deciding [dɪˈsaɪdɪŋ] a decisivo.
deciduous [dɪˈsɪdjuəs] a de hoja caduca.
decimal ['dɛsɪməl] a decimal ◆ n decimal f; **to 3 ~ places** con 3 cifras decimales.
decimalize ['dɛsɪməlaɪz] vt convertir al sistema decimal.
decimal point n coma decimal.
decimal system n sistema m métrico.
decimate ['dɛsɪmeɪt] vt diezmar.
decipher [dɪˈsaɪfə*] vt descifrar.
decision [dɪˈsɪʒən] n decisión f; **to make a ~** tomar una decisión.
decisive [dɪˈsaɪsɪv] a (influence) decisivo; (manner, person) decidido; (reply) tajante.
deck [dɛk] n (NAUT) cubierta; (of bus) piso; (of cards) baraja; **cassette ~** platina; **to go up on ~** subir a (la) cubierta; **below ~** en la bodega.
deckchair ['dɛktʃɛə*] n tumbona.
deckhand ['dɛkhænd] n marinero de cubierta.
declaration [dɛkləˈreɪʃən] n declaración f.

declare [dɪˈklɛə*] vt (gen) declarar.
declassify [diːˈklæsɪfaɪ] vt permitir la publicación de.
decline [dɪˈklaɪn] n decaimiento, decadencia; (lessening) disminución f ◆ vt rehusar ◆ vi decaer; disminuir; **~ in living standards** disminución f del nivel de vida; **to ~ to do sth** negarse a hacer algo.
declutch [diːˈklʌtʃ] vi desembragar.
decode [diːˈkəud] vt descifrar.
decoder [diːˈkəudə*] n (COMPUT) decodificador m.
decompose [diːkəmˈpəuz] vi descomponerse.
decomposition [diːkɔmpəˈzɪʃən] n descomposición f.
decompression [diːkəmˈprɛʃən] n descompresión f.
decompression chamber n cámara de descompresión.
decongestant [diːkənˈdʒɛstənt] n descongestionante.
decontaminate [diːkənˈtæmɪneɪt] vt descontaminar.
decontrol [diːkənˈtrəul] vt (trade) quitar controles a; (prices) descongelar.
décor ['deɪkɔː*] n decoración f; (THEATRE) decorado.
decorate ['dɛkəreɪt] vt (paint) pintar; (paper) empapelar; (adorn): **to ~ (with)** adornar (de), decorar (de).
decoration [dɛkəˈreɪʃən] n adorno; (act) decoración f; (medal) condecoración f.
decorative ['dɛkərətɪv] a decorativo.
decorator ['dɛkəreɪtə*] n (workman) pintor m decorador.
decorum [dɪˈkɔːrəm] n decoro.
decoy ['diːkɔɪ] n señuelo; **police ~** trampa or señuelo policial.
decrease ['diːkriːs] n disminución f ◆ (vb: [dɪˈkriːs]) vt disminuir, reducir ◆ vi reducirse; **to be on the ~** ir disminuyendo.
decreasing [dɪˈkriːsɪŋ] a decreciente.
decree [dɪˈkriː] n decreto ◆ vt: **to ~ (that)** decretar (que); **~ absolute/nisi** sentencia absoluta/provisional de divorcio.
decrepit [dɪˈkrɛpɪt] a (person) decrépito; (building) ruinoso.
decry [dɪˈkraɪ] vt criticar, censurar.
dedicate ['dɛdɪkeɪt] vt dedicar.
dedicated ['dɛdɪkeɪtɪd] a dedicado; (COMPUT) especializado; **~ word processor** procesador m de textos especializado or dedicado.
dedication [dɛdɪˈkeɪʃən] n (devotion) dedicación f; (in book) dedicatoria.
deduce [dɪˈdjuːs] vt deducir.
deduct [dɪˈdʌkt] vt restar; (from wage etc) descontar.
deduction [dɪˈdʌkʃən] n (amount deducted) descuento; (conclusion) deducción f, conclusión f.
deed [diːd] n hecho, acto; (feat) hazaña;

(*LAW*) escritura; ~ **of covenant** escritura de contrato.

deem [di:m] *vt* (*formal*) juzgar, considerar; **to ~ it wise to do** considerar prudente hacer.

deep [di:p] *a* profundo; (*voice*) bajo; (*breath*) profundo, a pleno pulmón ♦ *ad*: **the spectators stood 20 ~** los espectadores se formaron de 20 en fondo; **to be 4 metres ~** tener 4 metros de profundo.

deepen ['di:pn] *vt* ahondar, profundizar ♦ *vi* (*darkness*) intensificarse.

deep-freeze ['di:p'fri:z] *n* congeladora.

deep-fry ['di:p'fraı] *vt* freír en aceite abundante.

deeply ['di:plı] *ad* (*breathe*) a pleno pulmón; (*interested, moved, grateful*) profundamente, hondamente; **to regret sth ~** sentir algo profundamente.

deep-rooted ['di:p'ru:tıd] *a* (*prejudice, habit*) profundamente arraigado; (*affection*) profundo.

deep-sea ['di:p'si:] *a*: **~ diver** buzo; **~ diving** buceo de altura.

deep-seated ['di:p'si:tıd] *a* (*beliefs*) (profundamente) arraigado.

deep-set ['di:pset] *a* (*eyes*) hundido.

deer [dıə*] *n, pl inv* ciervo.

deerstalker ['dıəstɔ:kə*] *n* (*hat*) gorro de cazador.

deface [dı'feıs] *vt* desfigurar, mutilar.

defamation [defə'meıʃən] *n* difamación *f*.

defamatory [dı'fæmətrı] *a* difamatorio.

default [dı'fɔ:lt] *vi* faltar al pago; (*sport*) dejar de presentarse ♦ *n* (*comput*) defecto; **by ~** (*LAW*) en rebeldía; (*sport*) por incomparecencia; **to ~ on a debt** dejar de pagar una deuda.

defaulter [dı'fɔ:ltə*] *n* (*in debt*) moroso/a.

default option *n* (*comput*) opción *f* por defecto.

defeat [dı'fi:t] *n* derrota ♦ *vt* derrotar, vencer; (*fig: efforts*) frustrar.

defeatism [dı'fi:tızəm] *n* derrotismo.

defeatist [dı'fi:tıst] *a, n* derrotista *m/f*.

defect ['di:fekt] *n* defecto ♦ *vi* [dı'fekt]: **to ~ to the enemy** pasarse al enemigo; **physical ~** defecto físico; **mental ~** deficiencia mental.

defective [dı'fektıv] *a* (*gen*) defectuoso; (*person*) anormal.

defector [dı'fektə*] *n* defector(a) *m/f*.

defence, (*US*) **defense** [dı'fens] *n* defensa; **the Ministry of D~** el Ministerio de Defensa; **witness for the ~** testigo de descargo.

defenceless [dı'fenslıs] *a* indefenso.

defence spending *n* gasto militar.

defend [dı'fend] *vt* defender; (*decision, action*) defender; (*opinion*) mantener.

defendant [dı'fendənt] *n* acusado/a; (*in civil case*) demandado/a.

defender [dı'fendə*] *n* defensor(a) *m/f*.

defending champion [dı'fendıŋ-] *n* (*sport*) campeón/ona *m/f* titular.

defending counsel *n* (*LAW*) abogado defensor.

defense [dı'fens] *n* (*US*) = **defence.**

defensive [dı'fensıv] *a* defensivo ♦ *n* defensiva; **on the ~** a la defensiva.

defer [dı'fə:*] *vt* (*postpone*) aplazar; **to ~ to** diferir a; (*submit*): **to ~ to sb/sb's opinion** conformarse con uno/someterse al juicio de uno.

deference ['defərəns] *n* deferencia, respeto; **out of** *or* **in ~ to** por respeto a.

deferential [defə'renʃəl] *a* respetuoso.

deferred [dı'fə:d] *a*: **~ creditor** acreedor *m* diferido.

defiance [dı'faıəns] *n* desafío; **in ~ of** en contra de.

defiant [dı'faıənt] *a* (*insolent*) insolente; (*challenging*) retador(a).

defiantly [dı'faıəntlı] *ad* con aire de desafío.

deficiency [dı'fıʃənsı] *n* (*lack*) falta; (*comm*) déficit *m*; (*defect*) defecto.

deficient [dı'fıʃənt] *a* (*lacking*) insuficiente; (*incomplete*) incompleto; (*defective*) defectuoso; (*mentally*) anormal; **~ in** deficiente en.

deficit ['defısıt] *n* déficit *m*.

defile [dı'faıl] *vt* manchar; (*violate*) violar.

define [dı'faın] *vt* (*also comput*) definir.

definite ['defınıt] *a* (*fixed*) determinado; (*clear, obvious*) claro; **he was ~ about it** no dejó lugar a dudas (sobre ello).

definitely ['defınıtlı] *ad*: **he's ~ mad** no cabe duda de que está loco.

definition [defı'nıʃən] *n* definición *f*.

definitive [dı'fınıtıv] *a* definitivo.

deflate [di:'fleıt] *vt* (*gen*) desinflar; (*pompous person*) quitar *or* rebajar los humos a; (*econ*) deflacionar.

deflation [di:'fleıʃən] *n* (*econ*) deflación *f*.

deflationary [di:'fleıʃənrı] *a* (*econ*) deflacionario.

deflect [dı'flekt] *vt* desviar.

defog [di:'fɔg] *vt* desempañar.

defogger [di:fɔgə*] *n* (*US aut*) dispositivo antivaho.

deform [dı'fɔ:m] *vt* deformar.

deformed [dı'fɔ:md] *a* deformado.

deformity [dı'fɔ:mıtı] *n* deformación *f*.

defraud [dı'frɔ:d] *vt* estafar; **to ~ sb of sth** estafar algo a uno.

defray [dı'freı] *vt*: **to ~ sb's expenses** reembolsar a uno los gastos.

defrost [di:'frɔst] *vt* (*frozen food, fridge*) descongelar.

defroster [di:'frɔstə*] *n* (*US*) eliminador *m* de vaho.

deft [deft] *a* diestro, hábil.

defunct [dı'fʌŋkt] *a* difunto; (*organization etc*) ya desaparecido.

defuse [di:'fju:z] *vt* desarmar; (*situation*) calmar, apaciguar.

defy [dɪ'faɪ] *vt* (*resist*) oponerse a; (*challenge*) desafiar; (*order*) contravenir.

degenerate [dɪ'dʒɛnəreɪt] *vi* degenerar ♦ *a* [dɪ'dʒɛnərɪt] degenerado.

degradation [dɛgrə'deɪʃən] *n* degradación *f*.

degrade [dɪ'greɪd] *vt* degradar.

degrading [dɪ'greɪdɪŋ] *a* degradante.

degree [dɪ'griː] *n* grado; (*scol*) título; **10 ~s below freezing** 10 grados bajo cero; **to have a ~ in maths** tener una licenciatura en matemáticas; **by ~s** (*gradually*) poco a poco, por etapas; **to some ~**, **to a certain ~** hasta cierto punto; **a considerable ~ of risk** un gran riesgo.

dehydrated [diːhaɪ'dreɪtɪd] *a* deshidratado; (*milk*) en polvo.

dehydration [diːhaɪ'dreɪʃən] *n* deshidratación *f*.

de-ice [diː'aɪs] *vt* (*windscreen*) deshelar.

de-icer [diː'aɪsə*] *n* deshelador *m*.

deign [deɪn] *vi*: **to ~ to do** dignarse hacer.

deity ['diːɪtɪ] *n* deidad *f*, divinidad *f*.

dejected [dɪ'dʒɛktɪd] *a* abatido, desanimado.

dejection [dɪ'dʒɛkʃən] *n* abatimiento.

del. *abbr* = **delete**.

delay [dɪ'leɪ] *vt* demorar, aplazar; (*person*) entretener; (*train*) retrasar; (*payment*) aplazar ♦ *vi* tardar ♦ *n* demora, retraso; **without ~** en seguida, sin tardar.

delayed-action [dɪleɪd'ækʃən] *a* (*bomb etc*) de acción retardada.

delectable [dɪ'lɛktəbl] *a* (*person*) encantador(a); (*food*) delicioso.

delegate ['dɛlɪgɪt] *n* delegado/a ♦ *vt* ['dɛlɪgeɪt] delegar; **to ~ sth to sb/sb to do sth** delegar algo en uno/en uno para hacer algo.

delegation [dɛlɪ'geɪʃən] *n* (*of work etc*) delegación *f*.

delete [dɪ'liːt] *vt* suprimir, tachar; (*comput*) suprimir, borrar.

Delhi ['dɛlɪ] *n* Delhi *m*.

deliberate [dɪ'lɪbərɪt] *a* (*intentional*) intencionado; (*slow*) pausado, lento ♦ *vi* [dɪ'lɪbəreɪt] deliberar.

deliberately [dɪ'lɪbərɪtlɪ] *ad* (*on purpose*) a propósito; (*slowly*) pausadamente.

deliberation [dɪlɪbə'reɪʃən] *n* (*consideration*) reflexión *f*; (*discussion*) deliberación *f*, discusión *f*.

delicacy ['dɛlɪkəsɪ] *n* delicadeza; (*choice food*) golosina.

delicate ['dɛlɪkɪt] *a* (*gen*) delicado; (*fragile*) frágil.

delicately ['dɛlɪkɪtlɪ] *ad* con delicadeza, delicadamente; (*act*, *express*) con discreción.

delicatessen [dɛlɪkə'tɛsn] *n* tienda especializada en comida exótica.

delicious [dɪ'lɪʃəs] *a* delicioso, rico.

delight [dɪ'laɪt] *n* (*feeling*) placer *m*, deleite *m*; (*object*) encanto, delicia ♦ *vt* encantar,

deleitar; **to take ~ in** deleitarse en.

delighted [dɪ'laɪtɪd] *a*: **~ (at** or **with/to do)** encantado (con/de hacer); **to be ~ that** estar encantado de que; **I'd be ~** con mucho *or* todo gusto.

delightful [dɪ'laɪtful] *a* encantador(a), delicioso.

delimit [diː'lɪmɪt] *vt* delimitar.

delineate [dɪ'lɪnɪeɪt] *vt* delinear.

delinquency [dɪ'lɪŋkwənsɪ] *n* delincuencia.

delinquent [dɪ'lɪŋkwənt] *a*, *n* delincuente *m/f*.

delirious [dɪ'lɪrɪəs] *a* (*med*, *fig*) delirante; **to be ~** delirar, desvariar.

delirium [dɪ'lɪrɪəm] *n* delirio.

deliver [dɪ'lɪvə*] *vt* (*distribute*) repartir; (*hand over*) entregar; (*message*) comunicar; (*speech*) pronunciar; (*blow*) lanzar, dar; (*med*) asistir al parto de.

deliverance [dɪ'lɪvrəns] *n* liberación *f*.

delivery [dɪ'lɪvərɪ] *n* reparto; entrega; (*of speaker*) modo de expresarse; (*med*) parto, alumbramiento; **to take ~ of** recibir.

delivery note *n* nota de entrega.

delivery van *n* furgoneta de reparto.

delta ['dɛltə] *n* delta *m*.

delude [dɪ'luːd] *vt* engañar.

deluge ['dɛljuːdʒ] *n* diluvio ♦ *vt* (*fig*): **to ~ (with)** inundar (de).

delusion [dɪ'luːʒən] *n* ilusión *f*, engaño.

de luxe [də'lʌks] *a* de lujo.

delve [dɛlv] *vi*: **to ~ into** hurgar en.

Dem. *abbr* (*US POL*) = **democrat(ic)**.

demand [dɪ'mɑːnd] *vt* (*gen*) exigir; (*rights*) reclamar; (*need*) requerir ♦ *n* (*gen*) exigencia; (*claim*) reclamación *f*; (*ECON*) demanda; **to ~ sth (from** or **of sb)** exigir algo (a uno); **to be in ~** ser muy solicitado; **on ~** a solicitud.

demanding [dɪ'mɑːndɪŋ] *a* (*boss*) exigente; (*work*) absorbente.

demarcation [diːmɑː'keɪʃən] *n* demarcación *f*.

demarcation dispute *n* conflicto por definición *or* demarcación del trabajo.

demean [dɪ'miːn] *vt*: **to ~ o.s.** rebajarse.

demeanour, (*US*) **demeanor** [dɪ'miːnə*] *n* porte *m*, conducta, comportamiento.

demented [dɪ'mɛntɪd] *a* demente.

demi- ['dɛmɪ] *pref* semi..., medio....

demilitarize [diː'mɪlɪtəraɪz] *vt* desmilitarizar.

demise [dɪ'maɪz] *n* (*death*) fallecimiento.

demist [diː'mɪst] *vt* (*AUT*) eliminar el vaho de.

demister [diː'mɪstə*] *n* (*AUT*) eliminador *m* de vaho.

demo ['dɛməʊ] *n abbr* (*col*: = *demonstration*) manifestación *f*.

demobilization [diː'məʊbɪlaɪ'zeɪʃən] *n* desmovilización *f*.

democracy [dɪ'mɔkrəsɪ] *n* democracia.

democrat ['dɛməkræt] *n* demócrata *m/f*.

democratic [dɛmə'krætɪk] a democrático.
demography [dɪ'mɒɡrəfɪ] n demografía.
demolish [dɪ'mɒlɪʃ] vt derribar, demoler.
demolition [dɛmə'lɪʃən] n derribo, demolición f.
demon ['diːmən] n (evil spirit) demonio ♦ cpd temible.
demonstrate ['dɛmənstreɪt] vt demostrar ♦ vi manifestarse; **to ~ (for/against)** manifestarse (a favor de/en contra de).
demonstration [dɛmən'streɪʃən] n (POL) manifestación f; (proof) prueba, demostración f; **to hold a ~** (POL) hacer una manifestación.
demonstrative [dɪ'mɒnstrətɪv] a (person) expresivo; (LING) demostrativo.
demonstrator [dɛmən'streɪtə*] n (POL) manifestante m/f.
demoralize [dɪ'mɒrəlaɪz] vt desmoralizar.
demote [dɪ'məut] vt degradar.
demotion [dɪ'məuʃən] n degradación f; (COMM) descenso.
demur [dɪ'mə:*] vi: **to ~ (at)** hacer objeciones (a), vacilar (ante) ♦ n: **without ~** sin objeción.
demure [dɪ'mjuə*] a recatado.
demurrage [dɪ'mʌrɪdʒ] n sobrestadía.
den [dɛn] n (of animal) guarida; (study) estudio.
denationalization [diːnæʃnəlaɪ'zeɪʃən] n desnacionalización f.
denationalize [diː'næʃnəlaɪz] vt desnacionalizar.
denatured alcohol [diː'neɪtʃəd-] n (US) alcohol m desnaturalizado.
denial [dɪ'naɪəl] n (refusal) negativa; (of report etc) denegación f.
denier ['dɛnɪə*] n denier m.
denim ['dɛnɪm] n tela vaquera; see also **denims**.
denim jacket n chaqueta vaquera, saco vaquero (LAm).
denims ['dɛnɪms] npl vaqueros mpl.
denizen ['dɛnɪzn] n (inhabitant) habitante m/f; (foreigner) residente m/f extranjero/a.
Denmark ['dɛnmɑːk] n Dinamarca.
denomination [dɪnɒmɪ'neɪʃən] n valor m; (REL) confesión f.
denominator [dɪ'nɒmɪneɪtə*] n denominador m.
denote [dɪ'nəut] vt indicar, significar.
denounce [dɪ'nauns] vt denunciar.
dense [dɛns] a (thick) espeso; (: foliage etc) tupido; (stupid) torpe.
densely [dɛnslɪ] ad: **~ populated** con una alta densidad de población.
density ['dɛnsɪtɪ] n densidad f; **single/double-~ disk** n disco de densidad sencilla/de doble densidad.
dent [dɛnt] n abolladura ♦ vt (also: **make a ~ in**) abollar.
dental ['dɛntl] a dental.
dental surgeon n odontólogo/a.

dentifrice ['dɛntɪfrɪs] n dentífrico.
dentist ['dɛntɪst] n dentista m/f; **~'s surgery** (Brit) consultorio dental.
dentistry ['dɛntɪstrɪ] n odontología.
dentures ['dɛntʃəz] npl dentadura sg (postiza).
denude [dɪ'njuːd] vt: **to ~ of** despojar de.
denunciation [dɪnʌnsɪ'eɪʃən] n denuncia, denunciación f.
deny [dɪ'naɪ] vt negar; (charge) rechazar; (report) desmentir; **to ~ o.s.** privarse (de); **he denies having said it** niega haberlo dicho.
deodorant [diː'əudərənt] n desodorante m.
depart [dɪ'pɑːt] vi irse, marcharse; (train) salir; **to ~ from** (fig: differ from) apartarse de.
departed [dɪ'pɑːtɪd] a (bygone: days, glory) pasado; (dead) difunto.
department [dɪ'pɑːtmənt] n (COMM) sección f; (SCOL) departamento; (POL) ministerio; **that's not my ~** (fig) no tiene que ver conmigo; **D~ of State** (US) Ministerio de Asuntos Exteriores.
departmental [diːpɑːt'mɛntl] a (dispute) departamental; (meeting) departamental, de departamento; **~ manager** jefe/a m/f de sección or de departamento or de servicio.
department store n gran almacén m.
departure [dɪ'pɑːtʃə*] n partida, ida; (of train) salida; **a new ~** un nuevo rumbo.
departure lounge n (at airport) sala de embarque.
depend [dɪ'pɛnd] vi: **to ~ (up)on** (be dependent upon) depender de; (rely on) contar con; **it ~s** depende, según; **~ing on the result** según el resultado.
dependable [dɪ'pɛndəbl] a (person) formal, serio.
dependant [dɪ'pɛndənt] n dependiente m/f.
dependence [dɪ'pɛndəns] n dependencia.
dependent [dɪ'pɛndənt] a: **to be ~ (on)** depender (de) ♦ n = **dependant**.
depict [dɪ'pɪkt] vt (in picture) pintar; (describe) representar.
depilatory [dɪ'pɪlətrɪ] n (also: **~ cream**) depilatorio.
depleted [dɪ'pliːtɪd] a reducido.
deplorable [dɪ'plɔːrəbl] a deplorable.
deplore [dɪ'plɔː*] vt deplorar.
deploy [dɪ'plɔɪ] vt desplegar.
depopulate [diː'pɒpjuleɪt] vt despoblar.
depopulation ['diːpɒpju'leɪʃən] n despoblación f.
deport [dɪ'pɔːt] vt deportar.
deportation [diːpɔː'teɪʃən] n deportación f.
deportation order n orden f de expulsión.
deportment [dɪ'pɔːtmənt] n comportamiento.
depose [dɪ'pəuz] vt deponer.
deposit [dɪ'pɒzɪt] n depósito; (CHEM) sedimento; (of ore, oil) yacimiento ♦ vt (gen)

depositar; **to put down a ~ of £50** dejar un depósito de 50 libras.

deposit account n (Brit) cuenta de ahorros.

depositor [dɪ'pɒzɪtə*] n depositante m/f, cuentacorrentista m/f.

depository [dɪ'pɒzɪtərɪ] n almacén m depositario.

depot ['dɛpəu] n (storehouse) depósito; (for vehicles) parque m.

deprave [dɪ'preɪv] vt depravar.

depraved [dɪ'preɪvd] a depravado, vicioso.

depravity [dɪ'prævɪtɪ] n depravación f, vicio.

deprecate ['dɛprɪkeɪt] vt desaprobar, lamentar.

deprecating ['dɛprɪkeɪtɪŋ] a (disapproving) de desaprobación; (apologetic): **a ~ smile** una sonrisa de disculpa.

depreciate [dɪ'priːʃɪeɪt] vi depreciarse, perder valor.

depreciation [dɪpriːʃɪ'eɪʃən] n depreciación f.

depress [dɪ'prɛs] vt deprimir; (press down) apretar.

depressant [dɪ'prɛsnt] n (MED) calmante m, sedante m.

depressed [dɪ'prɛst] a deprimido; (COMM: market, economy) deprimido; (area) deprimido (económicamente); **to get ~** deprimirse.

depressing [dɪ'prɛsɪŋ] a deprimente.

depression [dɪ'prɛʃən] n depresión f; **the economy is in a state of ~** la economía está deprimida.

deprivation [dɛprɪ'veɪʃən] n privación f; (loss) pérdida.

deprive [dɪ'praɪv] vt: **to ~ sb of** privar a uno de.

deprived [dɪ'praɪvd] a necesitado.

dept. abbr (= department) dto.

depth [dɛpθ] n profundidad f; **at a ~ of 3 metres** a 3 metros de profundidad; **to be out of one's ~** (swimmer) perder pie; (fig) estar perdido; **to study sth in ~** estudiar algo a fondo; **in the ~s of** en lo más hondo de.

depth charge n carga de profundidad.

deputation [dɛpju'teɪʃən] n delegación f.

deputize ['dɛpjutaɪz] vi: **to ~ for sb** suplir a uno.

deputy ['dɛpjutɪ] a: **~ head** subdirector(a) m/f ◆ n sustituto/a, suplente m/f; (POL) diputado/a; (agent) representante m/f.

deputy leader n (POL) vicepresidente/a m/f.

derail [dɪ'reɪl] vt: **to be ~ed** descarrilarse.

derailment [dɪ'reɪlmənt] n descarrilamiento.

deranged [dɪ'reɪndʒd] a trastornado.

derby ['dɜːbɪ] n (US) hongo.

Derbys abbr (Brit) = Derbyshire.

deregulate [diː'rɛgjuleɪt] vt des-

reglamentar.

deregulation [diːrɛgju'leɪʃən] n desreglamentación f.

derelict ['dɛrɪlɪkt] a abandonado.

deride [dɪ'raɪd] vt ridiculizar, mofarse de.

derision [dɪ'rɪʒən] n irrisión f, mofas fpl.

derisive [dɪ'raɪsɪv] a burlón/ona.

derisory [dɪ'raɪzərɪ] a (sum) irrisorio; (laughter, person) burlón/ona, irónico.

derivation [dɛrɪ'veɪʃən] n derivación f.

derivative [dɪ'rɪvətɪv] n derivado ◆ a (work) poco original.

derive [dɪ'raɪv] vt derivar ◆ vi: **to ~ from** derivarse de.

derived [dɪ'raɪvd] a derivado.

dermatitis [dɜːmə'taɪtɪs] n dermatitis f.

dermatology [dɜːmə'tɒlədʒɪ] n dermatología.

derogatory [dɪ'rɒgətərɪ] a despectivo.

derrick ['dɛrɪk] n torre f de perforación.

derv [dɜːv] n (Brit) gasoil m.

DES n abbr (Brit: = Department of Education and Science) ministerio de educación y ciencia.

descend [dɪ'sɛnd] vt, vi descender, bajar; **to ~ from** descender de; **in ~ing order of importance** por orden descendiente de importancia.

descend on vt fus (subj: enemy, angry person) caer sobre; (: misfortune) sobrevenir; (fig: gloom, silence) invadir; **visitors ~ed (up)on us** las visitas nos invadieron.

descendant [dɪ'sɛndənt] n descendiente m/f.

descent [dɪ'sɛnt] n descenso; (GEO) pendiente f, declive m; (origin) descendencia.

describe [dɪs'kraɪb] vt describir.

description [dɪs'krɪpʃən] n descripción f; (sort) clase f, género; **of every ~** de toda clase.

descriptive [dɪs'krɪptɪv] a descriptivo.

desecrate ['dɛsɪkreɪt] vt profanar.

desegregation [diːsɛgrɪ'geɪʃən] n desegregación f.

desert ['dɛzət] n desierto ◆ vb [dɪ'zɜːt] vt abandonar, desamparar ◆ vi (MIL) desertar; see also **deserts**.

deserter [dɪ'zɜːtə*] n desertor(a) m/f.

desertion [dɪ'zɜːʃən] n deserción f.

desert island n isla desierta.

deserts [dɪ'zɜːts] npl: **to get one's just ~** llevarse su merecido.

deserve [dɪ'zɜːv] vt merecer, ser digno de.

deservedly [dɪ'zɜːvɪdlɪ] ad con razón.

deserving [dɪ'zɜːvɪŋ] a (person) digno; (action, cause) meritorio.

desiccated ['dɛsɪkeɪtɪd] a desecado.

design [dɪ'zaɪn] n (sketch) bosquejo; (of dress, car) diseño; (pattern) dibujo ◆ vt (gen) diseñar; **industrial ~** diseño industrial; **to have ~s on sb** tener la(s) mira(s) puesta(s) en uno; **to be ~ed for sb/sth**

estar hecho para uno/algo.

designate ['dezɪgneɪt] *vt* (*appoint*) nombrar; (*destine*) designar ♦ *a* ['dezɪgnɪt] designado.

designation [dezɪg'neɪʃən] *n* (*appointment*) nombramiento; (*name*) denominación *f*.

designer [dɪ'zaɪnə*] *n* diseñador(a) *m/f*; (*fashion* ~) modisto/a.

desirability [dɪzaɪərə'bɪlɪtɪ] *n* ventaja, atractivo.

desirable [dɪ'zaɪərəbl] *a* (*proper*) deseable; (*attractive*) atractivo; **it is ~ that** es conveniente que.

desire [dɪ'zaɪə*] *n* deseo ♦ *vt* desear; **to ~ sth/to do sth/that** desear algo/hacer algo/que.

desirous [dɪ'zaɪərəs] *a*: **to be ~ of** desear.

desist [dɪ'zɪst] *vi*: **to ~ (from)** desistir (de).

desk [desk] *n* (*in office*) escritorio; (*for pupil*) pupitre *m*; (*in hotel, at airport*) recepción *f*; (*Brit: in shop, restaurant*) caja.

desk-top publishing ['desktɔp-] *n* autoedición *f*.

desolate ['desəlɪt] *a* (*place*) desierto; (*person*) afligido.

desolation [desə'leɪʃən] *n* (*of place*) desolación *f*; (*of person*) aflicción *f*.

despair [dɪs'peə*] *n* desesperación *f* ♦ *vi*: **to ~ of** desesperarse de; **in ~** desesperado.

despatch [dɪs'pætʃ] *n, vt* = **dispatch**.

desperate ['despərɪt] *a* desesperado; (*fugitive*) peligroso; (*measures*) extremo; **we are getting ~** nos estamos desesperando.

desperately ['despərɪtlɪ] *ad* desesperadamente; (*very*) terriblemente, gravemente; **~ ill** gravemente enfermo.

desperation [despə'reɪʃən] *n* desesperación *f*; **in ~** desesperado.

despicable [dɪs'pɪkəbl] *a* vil, despreciable.

despise [dɪs'paɪz] *vt* despreciar.

despite [dɪs'paɪt] *prep* a pesar de, pese a.

despondent [dɪs'pɔndənt] *a* deprimido, abatido.

despot ['despɔt] *n* déspota *m/f*.

dessert [dɪ'zə:t] *n* postre *m*.

dessertspoon [dɪ'zə:tspu:n] *n* cuchara (de postre).

destabilize [di:'steɪbɪlaɪz] *vt* desestabilizar.

destination [destɪ'neɪʃən] *n* destino.

destine ['destɪn] *vt* destinar.

destined ['destɪnd] *a*: **~ for London** con destino a Londres.

destiny ['destɪnɪ] *n* destino.

destitute ['destɪtju:t] *a* desamparado, indigente.

destitution [destɪ'tju:ʃən] *n* indigencia, miseria.

destroy [dɪs'trɔɪ] *vt* destruir; (*finish*) acabar con.

destroyer [dɪs'trɔɪə*] *n* (*NAUT*) destructor *m*.

destruction [dɪs'trʌkʃən] *n* destrucción *f*; (*fig*) ruina.

destructive [dɪs'trʌktɪv] *a* destructivo, destructor(a).

desultory ['desəltərɪ] *a* (*reading*) poco metódico; (*conversation*) inconexo; (*contact*) intermitente.

detach [dɪ'tætʃ] *vt* separar; (*unstick*) despegar.

detachable [dɪ'tætʃəbl] *a* separable; (*TECH*) desmontable.

detached [dɪ'tætʃt] *a* (*attitude*) objetivo, imparcial.

detached house *n* chalé *m*, chalet *m*.

detachment [dɪ'tætʃmənt] *n* separación *f*; (*MIL*) destacamento; (*fig*) objetividad *f*, imparcialidad *f*.

detail ['di:teɪl] *n* detalle *m*; (*MIL*) destacamento ♦ *vt* detallar; (*MIL*) destacar; **in ~** detalladamente; **to go into ~(s)** entrar en detalles.

detailed ['di:teɪld] *a* detallado.

detain [dɪ'teɪn] *vt* retener; (*in captivity*) detener.

detainee [di:teɪ'ni:] *n* detenido/a.

detect [dɪ'tekt] *vt* (*gen*) descubrir; (*MED, POLICE*) identificar; (*MIL, RADAR, TECH*) detectar.

detection [dɪ'tekʃən] *n* descubrimiento; identificación *f*; **crime ~** investigación *f*; **to escape ~** (*criminal*) escaparse sin ser descubierto; (*mistake*) pasar inadvertido.

detective [dɪ'tektɪv] *n* detective *m*.

detective story *n* novela policíaca.

detector [dɪ'tektə*] *n* detector *m*.

détente [deɪ'tɑ:nt] *n* distensión *f*, detente *f*.

detention [dɪ'tenʃən] *n* detención *f*, arresto.

deter [dɪ'tə:*] *vt* (*dissuade*) disuadir; (*prevent*) impedir; **to ~ sb from doing sth** disuadir a uno de que haga algo.

detergent [dɪ'tə:dʒənt] *n* detergente *m*.

deteriorate [dɪ'tɪərɪəreɪt] *vi* deteriorarse.

deterioration [dɪtɪərɪə'reɪʃən] *n* deterioro.

determination [dɪtə:mɪ'neɪʃən] *n* resolución *f*.

determine [dɪ'tə:mɪn] *vt* determinar; **to ~ to do sth** decidir hacer algo.

determined [dɪ'tə:mɪnd] *a*: **to be ~ to do sth** estar decidido *or* resuelto a hacer algo; **a ~ effort** un esfuerzo concentrado.

deterrence [dɪ'terns] *n* disuasión *f*.

deterrent [dɪ'terənt] *n* fuerza de disuasión; **to act as a ~** servir para prevenir.

detest [dɪ'test] *vt* aborrecer.

detestable [dɪ'testəbl] *a* aborrecible.

dethrone [di:'θrəun] *vt* destronar.

detonate ['detəneɪt] *vi* estallar ♦ *vt* hacer detonar.

detonator ['detəneɪtə*] *n* detonador *m*, fulminante *m*.

detour ['di:tuə*] *n* (*gen, US AUT: diversion*) desvío ♦ *vt* (*US: traffic*) desviar; **to make a ~** dar un rodeo.

detract [dɪ'trækt] *vt*: **to ~ from** quitar mérito a, desvirtuar.

detractor [dɪ'træktə*] n detractor(a) m/f.
detriment ['detrɪmənt] n: **to the ~ of** en perjuicio de; **without ~ to** sin detrimento or perjuicio a.
detrimental [detrɪ'mentl] a perjudicial.
deuce [djuːs] n (*TENNIS*) cuarenta iguales.
devaluation [dɪvælju'eɪʃən] n devaluación f.
devalue [dɪ'væljuː] vt devaluar.
devastate ['devəsteɪt] vt devastar; **he was ~d by the news** las noticias le dejaron desolado.
devastating ['devəsteɪtɪŋ] a devastador(a); (*fig*) arrollador(a).
devastation [devəs'teɪʃən] n devastación f, ruina.
develop [dɪ'veləp] vt desarrollar; (*PHOT*) revelar; (*disease*) coger; (*habit*) adquirir ♦ vi desarrollarse; (*advance*) progresar; **this land is to be ~ed** se va a construir en este terreno; **to ~ a taste for sth** tomar gusto a algo; **to ~ into** transformarse or convertirse en.
developer [dɪ'veləpə*] n (*property ~*) especulador(a) m/f en construcción.
developing country n país m en (vías de) desarrollo.
development [dɪ'veləpmənt] n desarrollo; (*advance*) progreso; (*of affair, case*) desenvolvimiento; (*of land*) urbanización f.
development area n zona de fomento or desarrollo.
deviant ['diːvɪənt] a anómalo, pervertido.
deviate ['diːvɪeɪt] vi: **to ~ (from)** desviarse (de).
deviation [diːvɪ'eɪʃən] n desviación f.
device [dɪ'vaɪs] n (*scheme*) estratagema, recurso; (*apparatus*) aparato, mecanismo; (*explosive ~*) artefacto explosivo.
devil ['devl] n diablo, demonio.
devilish ['devlɪʃ] a diabólico.
devil-may-care ['devlmeɪ'kɛə*] a despreocupado.
devious ['diːvɪəs] a intricado, enrevesado; (*person*) taimado.
devise [dɪ'vaɪz] vt idear, inventar.
devoid [dɪ'vɔɪd] a: **~ of** desprovisto de.
devolution [diːvə'luːʃən] n (*POL*) descentralización f.
devolve [dɪ'vɔlv] vi: **to ~ (up)on** recaer sobre.
devote [dɪ'vəut] vt: **to ~ sth to** dedicar algo a.
devoted [dɪ'vəutɪd] a (*loyal*) leal, fiel; **the book is ~ to politics** el libro trata de la política.
devotee [devəu'tiː] n devoto/a.
devotion [dɪ'vəuʃən] n dedicación f; (*REL*) devoción f.
devour [dɪ'vauə*] vt devorar.
devout [dɪ'vaut] a devoto.
dew [djuː] n rocío.
dexterity [deks'terɪtɪ] n destreza.
dext(e)rous ['dekstrəs] a (*skilful*) diestro,

hábil; (*movement*) ágil.
dg abbr (= decigram) dg.
diabetes [daɪə'biːtiːz] n diabetes f.
diabetic [daɪə'betɪk] n diabético/a ♦ a diabético; (*chocolate, jam*) para diabéticos.
diabolical [daɪə'bɔlɪkəl] a diabólico; (*col: dreadful*) horrendo, horroroso.
diagnose ['daɪəgnəuz] vt diagnosticar.
diagnosis, pl **diagnoses** [daɪəg'nəusɪs, -siːz] n diagnóstico.
diagonal [daɪ'ægənl] a diagonal ♦ n diagonal f.
diagram ['daɪəgræm] n diagrama m, esquema m.
dial ['daɪəl] n esfera, cuadrante m, cara (*LAm*); (*of phone*) disco ♦ vt (*number*) marcar; **to ~ a wrong number** equivocarse de número; **can I ~ London direct?** ¿puedo marcar Londres directamente?
dial. abbr = **dialect.**
dial code n (*US*) prefijo.
dial tone n (*US*) señal f or tono de marcar.
dialect ['daɪəlekt] n dialecto.
dialling code ['daɪəlɪŋ-] n (*Brit*) prefijo.
dialling tone n (*Brit*) señal f or tono de marcar.
dialogue ['daɪəlɔg] n diálogo.
dialysis [daɪ'ælɪsɪs] n diálisis f.
diameter [daɪ'æmɪtə*] n diámetro.
diametrically [daɪə'metrɪklɪ] ad: **~ opposed (to)** diametralmente opuesto (a).
diamond ['daɪəmənd] n diamante m; **~s** npl (*CARDS*) diamantes mpl.
diamond ring n anillo or sortija de diamantes.
diaper ['daɪəpə*] n (*US*) pañal m.
diaphragm ['daɪəfræm] n diafragma m.
diarrhoea, (*US*) **diarrhea** [daɪə'riːə] n diarrea.
diary ['daɪərɪ] n (*daily account*) diario; (*book*) agenda; **to keep a ~** escribir un diario.
diatribe ['daɪətraɪb] n: **~ (against)** diatriba (contra).
dice [daɪs] n, pl inv dados mpl ♦ vt (*CULIN*) cortar en cuadritos.
dicey ['daɪsɪ] a (*col*): **it's a bit ~** (*risky*) es un poco arriesgado; (*doubtful*) es un poco dudoso.
dichotomy [daɪ'kɔtəmɪ] n dicotomía.
Dictaphone ® ['dɪktəfəun] n dictáfono ®.
dictate [dɪk'teɪt] vt dictar ♦ n ['dɪkteɪt] dictado.
dictate to vt fus (*person*) dar órdenes a; **I won't be ~d to** no estoy a las órdenes de nadie.
dictation [dɪk'teɪʃən] n (*to secretary etc*) dictado; **at ~ speed** para tomar al dictado.
dictator [dɪk'teɪtə*] n dictador m.
dictatorship [dɪk'teɪtəʃɪp] n dictadura.
diction ['dɪkʃən] n dicción f.
dictionary ['dɪkʃənrɪ] n diccionario.
did [dɪd] pt of **do.**

didactic [daɪ'dæktɪk] a didáctico.

diddle ['dɪdl] vt estafar, timar.

didn't ['dɪdənt] = **did not**.

die [daɪ] vi morir; **to ~ (of** or **from)** morirse (de); **to be dying** morirse, estarse muriendo; **to be dying for sth/to do sth** morirse por algo/de ganas de hacer algo.

die away vi (sound, light) perderse.

die down vi (gen) apagarse; (wind) amainar.

die out vi desaparecer, extinguirse.

diehard ['daɪhɑːd] n intransigente m/f.

diesel ['diːzl] n diesel m.

diesel engine n motor m diesel.

diesel fuel, diesel oil n gas-oil m.

diet ['daɪət] n dieta; (restricted food) régimen m ♦ vi (also: **be on a ~**) estar a dieta, hacer régimen; **to live on a ~ of** alimentarse de.

dietician [daɪə'tɪʃən] n dietético/a m/f.

differ ['dɪfə*] vi (be different) ser distinto, diferenciarse; (disagree) discrepar.

difference ['dɪfrəns] n diferencia; (quarrel) desacuerdo; **it makes no ~ to me** me da igual or lo mismo; **to settle one's ~s** arreglarse.

different ['dɪfrənt] a diferente, distinto.

differential [dɪfə'renʃəl] n diferencial f.

differentiate [dɪfə'renʃɪeɪt] vt distinguir ♦ vi diferenciarse; **to ~ between** distinguir entre.

differently ['dɪfrəntlɪ] ad de otro modo, en forma distinta.

difficult ['dɪfɪkəlt] a difícil; **~ to understand** difícil de entender.

difficulty ['dɪfɪkəltɪ] n dificultad f; **to have difficulties with** (police, landlord etc) tener problemas con; **to be in ~** tener dificultad.

diffidence ['dɪfɪdəns] n timidez f, falta de confianza en sí mismo.

diffident ['dɪfɪdənt] a tímido.

diffuse [dɪ'fjuːs] a difuso ♦ vt [dɪ'fjuːz] difundir.

dig [dɪg] vt (pt, pp **dug** [dʌg]) (hole) cavar; (ground) remover; (coal) extraer; (nails etc) hincar ♦ n (prod) empujón m; (archaeological) excavación f; (remark) indirecta; **to ~ into** (savings) consumir; **to ~ into one's pockets for sth** hurgar en el bolsillo por algo; **to ~ one's nails into** clavar las uñas en; see also **digs**.

dig in vi (also: **~ o.s. in**: MIL) atrincherarse; (col: eat) hincar los dientes ♦ vt (compost) añadir al suelo; (knife, claw) clavar; **to ~ in one's heels** (fig) mantenerse en sus trece.

dig out vt (hole) excavar; (survivors, car from snow) sacar.

dig up vt desenterrar; (plant) desarraigar.

digest [daɪ'dʒest] vt (food) digerir; (facts) asimilar ♦ n ['daɪdʒest] resumen m.

digestible [daɪ'dʒestəbl] a digerible.

digestion [dɪ'dʒestʃən] n digestión f.

digestive [daɪ'dʒestɪv] a (juices, system) digestivo.

digit ['dɪdʒɪt] n (number) dígito; (finger) dedo.

digital ['dɪdʒɪtl] a digital.

digital computer n ordenador m digital.

dignified ['dɪgnɪfaɪd] a grave, solemne; (action) decoroso.

dignify ['dɪgnɪfaɪ] vt dignificar.

dignitary ['dɪgnɪtərɪ] n dignatario/a.

dignity ['dɪgnɪtɪ] n dignidad f.

digress [daɪ'gres] vi: **to ~ from** apartarse de.

digression [daɪ'greʃən] n digresión f.

digs [dɪgz] npl (Brit: col) pensión f, alojamiento.

dike [daɪk] n = **dyke**.

dilapidated [dɪ'læpɪdeɪtɪd] a desmoronado, ruinoso.

dilate [daɪ'leɪt] vt dilatar ♦ vi dilatarse.

dilatory ['dɪlətərɪ] a (person) lento; (action) dilatorio.

dilemma [daɪ'lemə] n dilema m; **to be in a ~** estar en un dilema.

dilettante [dɪlɪ'tæntɪ] n diletante m/f.

diligence ['dɪlɪdʒəns] n diligencia.

diligent ['dɪlɪdʒənt] a diligente.

dill [dɪl] n eneldo.

dilly-dally ['dɪlɪ'dælɪ] vi (hesitate) vacilar; (dawdle) entretenerse.

dilute [daɪ'luːt] vt diluir.

dim [dɪm] a (light) débil; (sight) turbio; (outline) indistinto; (stupid) lerdo; (room) oscuro ♦ vt (light) bajar; **to take a ~ view of sth** tener una pobre opinión de algo.

dime [daɪm] n (US) moneda de diez centavos.

dimension [dɪ'menʃən] n dimensión f.

-dimensional [dɪ'menʃənl] a suf: **two~** de dos dimensiones.

dimensions [dɪ'menʃənz] npl dimensiones fpl.

diminish [dɪ'mɪnɪʃ] vt, vi disminuir.

diminished [dɪ'mɪnɪʃt] a: **~ responsibility** (LAW) responsabilidad f disminuida.

diminutive [dɪ'mɪnjutɪv] a diminuto ♦ n (LING) diminutivo.

dimly ['dɪmlɪ] ad débilmente; (not clearly) indistintamente.

dimmer ['dɪmə*] n (US AUT) interruptor m.

dimple ['dɪmpl] n hoyuelo.

dimwitted ['dɪm'wɪtɪd] a (col) lerdo, de pocas luces.

din [dɪn] n estruendo, estrépito ♦ vt: **to ~ sth into sb** (col) meter algo en la cabeza a uno.

dine [daɪn] vi cenar.

diner ['daɪnə*] n (person: in restaurant) comensal m/f; (Brit RAIL) = **dining car**; (US) restaurante económico.

dinghy ['dɪŋgɪ] n bote m; (also: **rubber ~**)

lancha (neumática).

dingy ['dɪndʒɪ] *a* (*room*) sombrío; (*dirty*) sucio; (*dull*) deslucido.

dining car ['daɪnɪŋ-] *n* (*Brit*) coche-comedor *m*.

dining room ['daɪnɪŋ-] *n* comedor *m*.

dinner ['dɪnə*] *n* (*evening meal*) cena; (*lunch*) comida; (*public*) cena, banquete *m*; ~'s **ready!** ¡la cena está servida!

dinner jacket *n* smoking *m*.

dinner party *n* cena.

dinner time *n* hora de cenar *or* comer.

dinosaur ['daɪnəsɔː*] *n* dinosaurio.

dint [dɪnt] *n*: **by ~ of (doing) sth** a fuerza de (hacer) algo.

diocese ['daɪəsɪs] *n* diócesis *f*.

dioxide [daɪ'ɔksaɪd] *n* bióxido; **carbon ~** bióxido de carbono.

Dip. *abbr* (*Brit*) = **diploma.**

dip [dɪp] *n* (*slope*) pendiente *f*; (*in sea*) baño ♦ *vt* (*in water*) mojar; (*ladle etc*) meter; (*Brit AUT*): **to ~ one's lights** poner luces de cruce ♦ *vi* inclinarse hacia abajo.

diphtheria [dɪf'θɪərɪə] *n* difteria.

diphthong ['dɪfθɒŋ] *n* diptongo.

diploma [dɪ'pləumə] *n* diploma *m*.

diplomacy [dɪ'pləuməsɪ] *n* diplomacia.

diplomat ['dɪpləmæt] *n* diplomático/a *m/f*.

diplomatic [dɪplə'mætɪk] *a* diplomático; **to break off ~ relations** romper las relaciones diplomáticas.

diplomatic corps *n* cuerpo diplomático.

dipstick ['dɪpstɪk] *n* (*AUT*) varilla de nivel (del aceite).

dipswitch ['dɪpswɪtʃ] *n* (*Brit AUT*) interruptor *m*.

dire [daɪə*] *a* calamitoso.

direct [daɪ'rɛkt] *a* (*gen*) directo; (*manner, person*) franco ♦ *vt* dirigir; **can you ~ me to...?** ¿puede indicarme dónde está...?; **to ~ sb to do sth** mandar a uno hacer algo.

direct access *n* (*COMPUT*) acceso directo.

direct cost *n* costo directo.

direct current *n* corriente *f* continua.

direct debit *n* domiciliación *f* bancaria de recibos.

direction [dɪ'rɛkʃən] *n* dirección *f*; **sense of ~** sentido de orientación; **~s** *npl* (*advice*) órdenes *fpl*, instrucciones *fpl*; (*to a place*) señas *fpl*; **in the ~ of** hacia, en dirección a; **~s for use** modo de empleo; **to ask for ~s** preguntar el camino.

directional [dɪ'rɛkʃənl] *a* direccional.

directive [daɪ'rɛktɪv] *n* orden *f*, instrucción *f*; **a government ~** una orden del gobierno.

direct labour *n* mano *f* de obra directa.

directly [dɪ'rɛktlɪ] *ad* (*in straight line*) directamente; (*at once*) en seguida.

direct mail *n* correspondencia directa.

direct mailshot *n* (*Brit*) promoción *f* por correspondencia directa.

directness [dɪ'rɛktnɪs] *n* (*of person, speech*) franqueza.

director [dɪ'rɛktə*] *n* director(a) *m/f*; **managing ~** director(a) *m/f* gerente.

Director of Public Prosecutions *n* ≈ fiscal *m/f* oficial *or* gubernamental.

directory [dɪ'rɛktərɪ] *n* (*TEL*) guía (telefónica); (*street ~*) callejero; (*trade ~*) directorio de comercio; (*COMPUT*) directorio.

directory enquiries, (*US*) **directory assistance** *n* (*service*) (servicio de) información *f*.

dirt [dɜːt] *n* suciedad *f*.

dirt-cheap ['dɜːt'tʃiːp] *a* baratísimo.

dirt road *n* (*US*) camino sin firme.

dirty ['dɜːtɪ] *a* sucio; (*joke*) verde, colorado (*LAm*) ♦ *vt* ensuciar; (*stain*) manchar.

dirty trick *n* juego sucio.

disability [dɪsə'bɪlɪtɪ] *n* incapacidad *f*.

disability allowance *n* pensión *f* de invalidez.

disable [dɪs'eɪbl] *vt* (*subj: illness, accident*) dejar incapacitado; (*tank, gun*) inutilizar; (*LAW: disqualify*) incapacitar.

disabled [dɪs'eɪbld] *a* minusválido.

disabuse [dɪsə'bjuːz] *vt*: **I ~d him of that idea** le saqué de esa idea.

disadvantage [dɪsəd'vɑːntɪdʒ] *n* desventaja, inconveniente *m*.

disadvantaged [dɪsəd'vɑːntɪdʒd] *a* (*person*) desventajado.

disadvantageous [dɪsædvən'teɪdʒəs] *a* desventajoso.

disaffected [dɪsə'fɛktɪd] *a* descontento; **to be ~ (to o towards)** estar descontento (de).

disaffection [dɪsə'fɛkʃən] *n* desafecto, descontento.

disagree [dɪsə'griː] *vi* (*differ*) discrepar; **to ~ (with)** no estar de acuerdo (con); **I ~ with you** no estoy de acuerdo contigo.

disagreeable [dɪsə'griːəbl] *a* desagradable.

disagreement [dɪsə'griːmənt] *n* (*gen*) desacuerdo; (*quarrel*) riña; **to have a ~ with sb** estar en desacuerdo con uno.

disallow ['dɪsə'lau] *vt* (*goal*) anular; (*claim*) rechazar.

disappear [dɪsə'pɪə*] *vi* desaparecer.

disappearance [dɪsə'pɪərəns] *n* desaparición *f*.

disappoint [dɪsə'pɔɪnt] *vt* decepcionar; (*hopes*) defraudar.

disappointed [dɪsə'pɔɪntɪd] *a* decepcionado.

disappointing [dɪsə'pɔɪntɪŋ] *a* decepcionante.

disappointment [dɪsə'pɔɪntmənt] *n* decepción *f*.

disapproval [dɪsə'pruːvəl] *n* desaprobación *f*.

disapprove [dɪsə'pruːv] *vi*: **to ~ of** desaprobar.

disapproving [dɪsə'pruːvɪŋ] *a* de desaprobación, desaprobador(a).

disarm [dɪs'ɑːm] *vt* desarmar.

disarmament [dɪs'ɑːməmənt] n desarme m.

disarmament talks npl conversaciones fpl de or sobre desarme.

disarming [dɪs'ɑːmɪŋ] a (smile) que desarma, encantador(a).

disarray [dɪsə'reɪ] n: in ~ (troops) desorganizado; (thoughts) confuso; (hair, clothes) desarreglado; **to throw into** ~ provocar el caos en.

disaster [dɪ'zɑːstə*] n desastre m.

disaster area n zona de desastre.

disastrous [dɪ'zɑːstrəs] a desastroso.

disband [dɪs'bænd] vt disolver ◆ vi desbandarse.

disbelief [dɪsbə'liːf] n incredulidad f; **in** ~ con incredulidad.

disbelieve ['dɪsbə'liːv] vt (person, story) poner en duda, no creer.

disc [dɪsk] n disco; (COMPUT) = **disk**.

disc. abbr (COMM) = **discount**.

discard [dɪs'kɑːd] vt (old things) tirar; (fig) descartar.

discern [dɪ'sɜːn] vt percibir, discernir; (understand) comprender.

discernible [dɪ'sɜːnəbl] a perceptible.

discerning [dɪ'sɜːnɪŋ] a perspicaz.

discharge [dɪs'tʃɑːdʒ] vt (task, duty) cumplir; (ship etc) descargar; (patient) dar de alta; (employee) despedir; (soldier) licenciar; (defendant) poner en libertad; (settle: debt) saldar ◆ n ['dɪstʃɑːdʒ] (ELEC) descarga; (vaginal ~) emisión f vaginal; (dismissal) despedida; (of duty) desempeño; (of debt) pago, descargo; (of gas, chemicals) escape m; **~d bankrupt** quebrado/a rehabilitado/a.

disciple [dɪ'saɪpl] n discípulo/a.

disciplinary ['dɪsɪplɪnərɪ] a: **to take** ~ **action against sb** disciplinar a uno.

discipline ['dɪsɪplɪn] n disciplina ◆ vt disciplinar; **to** ~ **o.s. to do sth** disciplinarse or obligarse a hacer algo.

disc jockey (DJ) n pinchadiscos m/f inv.

disclaim [dɪs'kleɪm] vt negar.

disclaimer [dɪs'kleɪmə*] n rectificación f; **to issue a** ~ hacer una rectificación.

disclose [dɪs'kləuz] vt revelar.

disclosure [dɪs'kləuʒə*] n revelación f.

disco ['dɪskəu] n abbr = **discothèque**.

discolouration, (US) **discoloration** [dɪskʌlə'reɪʃən] n descoloramiento.

discolo(u)red [dɪs'kʌləd] a descolorado.

discomfort [dɪs'kʌmfət] n incomodidad f; (unease) inquietud f; (physical) malestar m.

disconcert [dɪskən'sɜːt] vt desconcertar.

disconnect [dɪskə'nɛkt] vt (gen) separar; (ELEC etc) desconectar; (supply) cortar (el suministro) a.

disconsolate [dɪs'kɒnsəlɪt] a desconsolado.

discontent [dɪskən'tɛnt] n descontento.

discontented [dɪskən'tɛntɪd] a descontento.

discontinue [dɪskən'tɪnjuː] vt interrumpir; (payments) suspender.

discord ['dɪskɔːd] n discordia; (MUS) disonancia.

discordant [dɪs'kɔːdənt] a disonante.

discothèque ['dɪskəutɛk] n discoteca.

discount ['dɪskaunt] n descuento ◆ vt [dɪs'kaunt] descontar; (report etc) descartar; **at a** ~ con descuento; ~ **for cash** descuento por pago en efectivo; **to give sb a** ~ **on sth** hacer un descuento a uno en algo.

discount house n (FINANCE) banco de descuento; (COMM: also: **discount store**) ≈ tienda de descuentos.

discount rate n (COMM) tipo de descuento.

discount store n ≈ tienda de descuentos.

discourage [dɪs'kʌrɪdʒ] vt desalentar; (oppose) oponerse a; (dissuade, deter) desanimar, disuadir.

discouragement [dɪs'kʌrɪdʒmənt] n (dissuasion) disuasión f; (depression) desánimo, desaliento; **to act as a** ~ **to** servir para disuadir.

discouraging [dɪs'kʌrɪdʒɪŋ] a desalentador(a).

discourteous [dɪs'kɜːtɪəs] a descortés.

discover [dɪs'kʌvə*] vt descubrir.

discovery [dɪs'kʌvərɪ] n descubrimiento.

discredit [dɪs'krɛdɪt] vt desacreditar.

discreet [dɪ'skriːt] a (tactful) discreto; (careful) circunspecto, prudente.

discreetly [dɪ'skriːtlɪ] ad discretamente.

discrepancy [dɪ'skrɛpənsɪ] n (difference) diferencia; (disagreement) discrepancia.

discretion [dɪ'skrɛʃən] n (tact) discreción f; (care) prudencia, circunspección f; **use your own** ~ haz lo que creas oportuno.

discretionary [dɪ'skrɛʃənrɪ] a (powers) discrecional.

discriminate [dɪ'skrɪmɪneɪt] vi: **to** ~ **between** distinguir entre; **to** ~ **against** discriminar contra.

discriminating [dɪ'skrɪmɪneɪtɪŋ] a entendido.

discrimination [dɪskrɪmɪ'neɪʃən] n (discernment) perspicacia; (bias) discriminación f; **racial/sexual** ~ discriminación racial/sexual.

discus ['dɪskəs] n disco.

discuss [dɪ'skʌs] vt (gen) discutir; (a theme) tratar.

discussion [dɪ'skʌʃən] n discusión f; **under** ~ en discusión.

disdain [dɪs'deɪn] n desdén m ◆ vt desdeñar.

disease [dɪ'ziːz] n enfermedad f.

diseased [dɪ'ziːzd] a enfermo.

disembark [dɪsɪm'bɑːk] vt, vi desembarcar.

disembarkation [dɪsɛmbɑː'keɪʃən] n desembarque m.

disenchanted [dɪsɪn'tʃɑːntɪd] a: ~ **(with)** desilusionado (con).

disenfranchise ['dısın'fræntʃaız] vt privar del derecho al voto; (COMM) privar de franquicias.

disengage [dısın'geıdʒ] vt soltar; **to ~ the clutch** (AUT) desembragar.

disentangle [dısın'tæŋgl] vt desenredar.

disfavour, (US) **disfavor** [dıs'feıvə*] n desaprobación f.

disfigure [dıs'fıgə*] vt desfigurar.

disgorge [dıs'gɔːdʒ] vt verter.

disgrace [dıs'greıs] n ignominia; (downfall) caída; (shame) vergüenza, escándalo ♦ vt deshonrar.

disgraceful [dıs'greısful] a vergonzoso; (behaviour) escandaloso.

disgruntled [dıs'grʌntld] a disgustado, descontento.

disguise [dıs'gaız] n disfraz m ♦ vt disfrazar; (voice) disimular; (feelings etc) ocultar; **in ~** disfrazado; **to ~ o.s. as** disfrazarse de; **there's no disguising the fact that** ... no puede ocultarse el hecho de que....

disgust [dıs'gʌst] n repugnancia ♦ vt repugnar, dar asco a.

disgusting [dıs'gʌstıŋ] a repugnante, asqueroso.

dish [dıʃ] n (gen) plato; **to do** or **wash the ~es** fregar los platos.

dish out vt (money, exam papers) repartir; (food) servir; (advice) dar.

dish up vt servir.

dishcloth ['dıʃklɔθ] n paño de cocina, bayeta.

dishearten [dıs'hɑːtn] vt desalentar.

dishevelled, (US) **disheveled** [dı'ʃevəld] a (hair) despeinado; (clothes, appearance) desarreglado.

dishonest [dıs'ɔnıst] a (person) poco honrado, tramposo; (means) fraudulento.

dishonesty [dıs'ɔnıstı] n falta de honradez.

dishonour, (US) **dishonor** [dıs'ɔnə*] n deshonra.

dishono(u)rable [dıs'ɔnərəbl] a deshonroso.

dish soap n (US) lavavajillas m inv.

dishtowel ['dıʃtauəl] n (US) trapo de fregar.

dishwasher ['dıʃwɔʃə*] n lavaplatos m inv; (person) friegaplatos m/f inv.

disillusion [dısı'luːʒən] vt desilusionar; **to become ~ed (with)** quedar desilusionado (con).

disillusionment [dısı'luːʒənmənt] n desilusión f.

disincentive [dısın'sentıv] n desincentivo; **to act as a ~ (to)** actuar de freno (a); **to be a ~ to** ser un freno a.

disinclined ['dısın'klaınd] a: **to be ~ to do sth** estar poco dispuesto a hacer algo.

disinfect [dısın'fekt] vt desinfectar.

disinfectant [dısın'fektənt] n desinfectante m.

disinflation [dısın'fleıʃən] n desinflación f.

disingenuous [dısın'dʒenjuəs] a poco sincero, doble.

disinherit [dısın'herıt] vt desheredar.

disintegrate [dıs'ıntıgreıt] vi disgregarse, desintegrarse.

disinterested [dıs'ıntrəstıd] a desinteresado.

disjointed [dıs'dʒɔıntıd] a inconexo.

disk [dısk] n (COMPUT) disco, disquete m; **single-/double-sided ~** disco de una cara/ dos caras.

disk drive n disc drive m.

diskette [dıs'ket] n diskette m, disquete m, disco flexible.

disk operating system (DOS) n sistema m operativo de discos (DOS).

dislike [dıs'laık] n antipatía, aversión f ♦ vt tener antipatía a; **to take a ~ to sb/sth** cogerle or agarrarle (LAm) antipatía a uno/algo; **I ~ the idea** no me gusta la idea.

dislocate ['dısləkeıt] vt dislocar; **he ~d his shoulder** se dislocó el hombro.

dislodge [dıs'lɔdʒ] vt sacar; (enemy) desalojar.

disloyal [dıs'lɔıəl] a desleal.

dismal ['dızml] a (dark) sombrío; (depressing) triste; (very bad) fatal.

dismantle [dıs'mæntl] vt desmontar, desarmar.

dismay [dıs'meı] n consternación f ♦ vt consternar; **much to my ~** para gran consternación mía.

dismiss [dıs'mıs] vt (worker) despedir; (official) destituir; (idea, LAW) rechazar; (possibility) descartar ♦ vi (MIL) romper filas.

dismissal [dıs'mısl] n despedida; destitución f.

dismount [dıs'maunt] vi apearse; (rider) desmontar.

disobedience [dısə'biːdıəns] n desobediencia.

disobedient [dısə'biːdıənt] a desobediente.

disobey [dısə'beı] vt desobedecer; (rule) infringir.

disorder [dıs'ɔːdə*] n desorden m; (rioting) disturbio; (MED) trastorno; (disease) enfermedad f; **civil ~** desorden m civil.

disorderly [dıs'ɔːdəlı] a (untidy) desordenado; (meeting) alborotado; **~ conduct** (LAW) conducta escandalosa.

disorganized [dıs'ɔːgənaızd] a desorganizado.

disorientated [dıs'ɔːrıenteıtəd] a desorientado.

disown [dıs'əun] vt desconocer.

disparaging [dıs'pærıdʒıŋ] a despreciativo; **to be ~ about sth/sb** menospreciar algo/a uno.

disparate ['dıspərıt] a dispar.

disparity [dıs'pærıtı] n disparidad f.

dispassionate [dıs'pæʃənıt] a (unbiased)

imparcial; (*unemotional*) desapasionado.

dispatch [dɪs'pætʃ] *vt* enviar; (*kill*) despachar; (*deal with*: *business*) despachar ♦ *n* (*sending*) envío; (*speed*) prontitud *f*; (*PRESS*) informe *m*; (*MIL*) parte *m*.

dispatch department *n* (*COMM*) departamento de envíos.

dispatch rider *n* (*MIL*) correo.

dispel [dɪs'pɛl] *vt* disipar, dispersar.

dispensary [dɪs'pɛnsərɪ] *n* dispensario, farmacia.

dispensation [dɪspɛn'seɪʃən] *n* (*REL*) dispensa.

dispense [dɪs'pɛns] *vt* dispensar, repartir; (*medicine*) preparar.

dispense with *vt fus* (*make unnecessary*) prescindir de.

dispenser [dɪs'pɛnsə*] *n* (*container*) distribuidor *m* automático.

dispensing chemist [dɪs'pɛnsɪŋ-] *n* (*Brit*) farmacia.

dispersal [dɪs'pəːsl] *n* dispersión *f*.

disperse [dɪs'pəːs] *vt* dispersar ♦ *vi* dispersarse.

dispirited [dɪ'spɪrɪtɪd] *a* desanimado, desalentado.

displace [dɪs'pleɪs] *vt* (*person*) desplazar; (*replace*) reemplazar.

displaced person *n* (*POL*) desplazado/a.

displacement [dɪs'pleɪsmənt] *n* cambio de sitio.

display [dɪs'pleɪ] *n* (*exhibition*) exposición *f*; (*COMPUT*) visualización *f*; (*MIL*) desfile *m*; (*of feeling*) manifestación *f*; (*pej*) aparato, pompa ♦ *vt* exponer; manifestar; (*ostentatiously*) lucir; **on** ~ (*exhibits*) expuesto, exhibido; (*goods*) en el escaparate.

display advertising *n* publicidad *f* gráfica.

displease [dɪs'pliːz] *vt* (*offend*) ofender; (*annoy*) fastidiar; ~**d with** disgustado con.

displeasure [dɪs'plɛʒə*] *n* disgusto.

disposable [dɪs'pəuzəbl] *a* (*not reusable*) desechable; ~ **personal income** ingresos *mpl* personales disponibles.

disposable nappy *n* paño desechable.

disposal [dɪs'pəuzl] *n* (*sale*) venta; (*of house*) traspaso; (*by giving away*) donación *f*; (*arrangement*) colocación *f*; (*of rubbish*) destrucción *f*; **at one's** ~ a la disposición de uno; **to put sth at sb's** ~ poner algo a disposición de uno.

disposed [dɪs'pəuzd] *a*: ~ **to do** dispuesto a hacer.

dispose of [dɪs'pəuz] *vt fus* (*time*, *money*) disponer de; (*unwanted goods*) deshacerse de; (*COMM*: *sell*) traspasar, vender; (*throw away*) tirar.

disposition [dɪspə'zɪʃən] *n* disposición *f*; (*temperament*) carácter *m*.

dispossess ['dɪspə'zɛs] *vt*: **to** ~ **sb (of)** desposeer a uno (de).

disproportion [dɪsprə'pɔːʃən] *n* despro-

porción *f*.

disproportionate [dɪsprə'pɔːʃənət] *a* desproporcionado.

disprove [dɪs'pruːv] *vt* refutar.

dispute [dɪs'pjuːt] *n* disputa; (*verbal*) discusión *f*; (*also*: **industrial** ~) conflicto (laboral) ♦ *vt* (*argue*) disputar; (*question*) cuestionar; **to be in** *or* **under** ~ (*matter*) estar en cuestión; (*territory*) estar en disputa.

disqualification [dɪskwɔlɪfɪ'keɪʃən] *n* inhabilitación *f*; (*SPORT*, *from driving*) descalificación *f*.

disqualify [dɪs'kwɔlɪfaɪ] *vt* (*SPORT*) descalificar; **to** ~ **sb for sth/from doing sth** incapacitar a uno para algo/hacer algo.

disquiet [dɪs'kwaɪət] *n* preocupación *f*, inquietud *f*.

disquieting [dɪs'kwaɪətɪŋ] *a* inquietante.

disregard [dɪsrɪ'gɑːd] *vt* desatender; (*ignore*) no hacer caso de ♦ *n* (*indifference*: *to feelings*, *danger*, *money*): ~ (**for**) indiferencia (a); ~ (**of**) (*non-observance*: *of law*, *rules*) violación *f* (de).

disrepair [dɪsrɪ'pɛə*] *n*: **to fall into** ~ (*building*) desmoronarse; (*street*) deteriorarse.

disreputable [dɪs'rɛpjutəbl] *a* (*person*, *area*) de mala fama; (*behaviour*) vergonzoso.

disrepute ['dɪsrɪ'pjuːt] *n* descrédito, ignominia; **to bring into** ~ desacreditar.

disrespectful [dɪsrɪ'spɛktful] *a* irrespetuoso.

disrupt [dɪs'rʌpt] *vt* (*meeting*, *public transport*, *conversation*) interrumpir; (*plans*) desbaratar, alternar, trastornar.

disruption [dɪs'rʌpʃən] *n* trastorno; desbaratamiento; interrupción *f*.

disruptive [dɪs'rʌptɪv] *a* (*influence*) disruptivo; (*strike action*) perjudicial.

dissatisfaction [dɪssætɪs'fækʃən] *n* disgusto, descontento.

dissatisfied [dɪs'sætɪsfaɪd] *a* insatisfecho.

dissect [dɪ'sɛkt] *vt* (*also fig*) disecar.

disseminate [dɪ'sɛmɪneɪt] *vt* divulgar, difundir.

dissent [dɪ'sɛnt] *n* disensión *f*.

dissenter [dɪ'sɛntə*] *n* (*REL*, *POL etc*) disidente *m/f*.

dissertation [dɪsə'teɪʃən] *n* (*UNIV*) tesina.

disservice [dɪs'səːvɪs] *n*: **to do sb a** ~ perjudicar a alguien.

dissident ['dɪsɪdnt] *a*, *n* disidente *m/f*.

dissimilar [dɪ'sɪmɪlə*] *a* distinto.

dissipate ['dɪsɪpeɪt] *vt* disipar; (*waste*) desperdiciar.

dissipated ['dɪsɪpeɪtɪd] *a* disoluto.

dissipation [dɪsɪ'peɪʃən] *n* disipación *f*; (*moral*) libertinaje *m*, vicio; (*waste*) derroche *m*.

dissociate [dɪ'səuʃɪeɪt] *vt* disociar; **to** ~ **o.s. from** disociarse de.

dissolute ['dɪsəluːt] *a* disoluto.

dissolution [dɪsə'luːʃən] n (of organization, marriage, POL) disolución f.

dissolve [dɪ'zɔlv] vt (gen, COMM) disolver ◆ vi disolverse.

dissuade [dɪ'sweɪd] vt: **to ~ sb (from)** disuadir a uno (de).

distaff ['dɪstæf] n: **~ side** lado materno.

distance ['dɪstns] n distancia; **in the ~ a** lo lejos; **what ~ is it to London?** ¿qué distancia hay de aquí a Londres?; **it's within walking ~** se puede ir andando.

distant ['dɪstnt] a lejano; (manner) reservado, frío.

distaste [dɪs'teɪst] n repugnancia.

distasteful [dɪs'teɪstful] a repugnante, desagradable.

Dist. Atty. abbr (US) = **district attorney.**

distemper [dɪs'tɛmpə*] n (of dogs) moquillo.

distend [dɪ'stɛnd] vt dilatar, hinchar ◆ vi dilatarse, hincharse.

distended [dɪ'stɛndɪd] a (stomach) hinchado.

distil, (US) **distill** [dɪs'tɪl] vt destilar.

distillery [dɪs'tɪlərɪ] n destilería.

distinct [dɪs'tɪŋkt] a (different) distinto; (clear) claro; (unmistakeable) inequívoco; **as ~ from** a diferencia de.

distinction [dɪs'tɪŋkʃən] n distinción f; (in exam) sobresaliente m; **a writer of ~** un escritor destacado; **to draw a ~ between** hacer una distinción entre.

distinctive [dɪs'tɪŋktɪv] a distintivo.

distinctly [dɪs'tɪŋktlɪ] ad claramente.

distinguish [dɪs'tɪŋgwɪʃ] vt distinguir; **to ~ (between)** distinguir (entre).

distinguished [dɪs'tɪŋgwɪʃt] a (eminent) distinguido; (career) eminente; (refined) distinguido, de categoría.

distinguishing [dɪs'tɪŋgwɪʃɪŋ] a (feature) distintivo.

distort [dɪs'tɔːt] vt torcer, retorcer; (account, news) desvirtuar, deformar.

distortion [dɪs'tɔːʃən] n deformación f; (of sound) distorsión f; (of truth etc) torcimiento; (of facts) falseamiento.

distract [dɪs'trækt] vt distraer.

distracted [dɪs'træktɪd] a distraído.

distracting [dɪs'træktɪŋ] a que distrae la atención, molesto.

distraction [dɪs'trækʃən] n distracción f; (confusion) aturdimiento; (amusement) diversión f; **to drive sb to ~** (distress, anxiety) volver loco a uno.

distraught [dɪs'trɔːt] a turbado, enloquecido.

distress [dɪs'trɛs] n (anguish) angustia; (want) miseria; (pain) dolor m; (danger) peligro ◆ vt afligir; (pain) doler; **in ~** (ship etc) en peligro.

distressing [dɪs'trɛsɪŋ] a angustioso; doloroso.

distress signal n señal f de socorro.

distribute [dɪs'trɪbjuːt] vt (gen) distribuir; (share out) repartir.

distribution [dɪstrɪ'bjuːʃən] n distribución f.

distribution cost n gastos mpl de distribución.

distributor [dɪs'trɪbjutə*] n (AUT) distribuidor m; (COMM) distribuidora.

district ['dɪstrɪkt] n (of country) zona, región f; (of town) barrio; (ADMIN) comarca.

district attorney n (US) fiscal m/f.

district council n municipio.

district manager n representante m/f regional.

district nurse n (Brit) enfermera que atiende a pacientes a domicilio.

distrust [dɪs'trʌst] n desconfianza ◆ vt desconfiar de.

distrustful [dɪs'trʌstful] a desconfiado.

disturb [dɪs'tɜːb] vt (person: bother, interrupt) molestar; (meeting) interrumpir; (disorganize) desordenar; **sorry to ~ you** perdone la molestia.

disturbance [dɪs'tɜːbəns] n (political etc) disturbio; (violence) alboroto; (of mind) trastorno; **to cause a ~** causar alboroto; **~ of the peace** alteración f del orden público.

disturbed [dɪs'tɜːbd] a (worried, upset) preocupado, angustiado; **to be emotionally/mentally ~** tener problemas emocionales/ ser un trastornado mental.

disturbing [dɪs'tɜːbɪŋ] a inquietante, perturbador(a).

disuse [dɪs'juːs] n: **to fall into ~** caer en desuso.

disused [dɪs'juːzd] a abandonado.

ditch [dɪtʃ] n zanja; (irrigation ~) acequia ◆ vt (col) deshacerse de.

dither ['dɪðə*] vi vacilar.

ditto ['dɪtəu] ad ídem, lo mismo.

divan [dɪ'væn] n diván m.

divan bed n cama turca.

dive [daɪv] n (from board) salto; (underwater) buceo; (of submarine) sumersión f; (AVIAT) picada ◆ vi saltar; bucear; sumergirse; picar.

diver ['daɪvə*] n (SPORT) saltador(a) m/f; (underwater) buzo.

diverge [daɪ'vɜːdʒ] vi divergir.

divergent [daɪ'vɜːdʒənt] a divergente.

diverse [daɪ'vɜːs] a diversos/as, varios/as.

diversification [daɪvə:sɪfɪ'keɪʃən] n diversificación f.

diversify [daɪ'vɜːsɪfaɪ] vt diversificar.

diversion [daɪ'vɜːʃən] n (Brit AUT) desviación f; (distraction, MIL) diversión f.

diversity [daɪ'vɜːsɪtɪ] n diversidad f.

divert [daɪ'vɜːt] vt (Brit: train, plane, traffic) desviar; (amuse) divertir.

divest [daɪ'vɛst] vt: **to ~ sb of sth** despojar a alguien de algo.

divide [dɪ'vaɪd] vt dividir; (separate) separar ◆ vi dividirse; (road) bifurcarse; **to ~ (between, among)** repartir or dividir (entre); **40 ~d by 5** 40 dividido por 5.

divide out *vt*: **to ~ out (between, among)** (*sweets, tasks etc*) repartir (entre).

divided [dɪ'vaɪdɪd] *a* (*country, couple*) dividido, separado; (*opinions*) en desacuerdo.

divided highway *n* (*US*) carretera de doble calzada.

dividend ['dɪvɪdɛnd] *n* dividendo; (*fig*) beneficio.

dividend cover *n* cobertura de dividendo.

dividers [dɪ'vaɪdəz] *npl* compás *m* de puntas.

divine [dɪ'vaɪn] *a* divino ◆ *vt* (*future*) vaticinar; (*truth*) alumbrar; (*water, metal*) adivinar.

diving ['daɪvɪŋ] *n* (*SPORT*) salto; (*underwater*) buceo.

diving board *n* trampolín *m*.

diving suit *n* escafandra.

divinity [dɪ'vɪnɪtɪ] *n* divinidad *f*; (*SCOL*) teología.

divisible [dɪ'vɪzɪbl] *a* divisible.

division [dɪ'vɪʒən] *n* (*also Brit* FOOTBALL) división *f*; (*sharing out*) repartimiento; (*Brit* POL) votación *f*; **~ of labour** división *f* del trabajo.

divisive [dɪ'vaɪsɪv] *a* divisivo.

divorce [dɪ'vɔːs] *n* divorcio ◆ *vt* divorciarse de.

divorced [dɪ'vɔːst] *a* divorciado.

divorcee [dɪvɔː'siː] *n* divorciado/a.

divulge [daɪ'vʌldʒ] *vt* divulgar, revelar.

D.I.Y. *a, n abbr* (*Brit*) = **do-it-yourself**.

dizziness ['dɪzɪnɪs] *n* vértigo.

dizzy ['dɪzɪ] *a* (*person*) mareado; (*height*) vertiginoso; **to feel ~** marearse; **I feel ~** estoy mareado.

DJ *n abbr see* **disc jockey.**

Djakarta [dʒə'kɑːtə] *n* Yakarta.

DJIA *n abbr* (*US* STOCK EXCHANGE) = *Dow Jones Industrial Average.*

dl *abbr* (= *decilitre(s)*) dl.

DLit(t) *abbr* (= *Doctor of Literature, Doctor of Letters*) título universitario.

DLO *n abbr* (= *dead-letter office*) oficina de Correos que se encarga de las cartas que no llegan a su destino.

dm *abbr* (= *decimetre(s)*) dm.

DMus *abbr* (= *Doctor of Music*) título universitario.

DMZ *n abbr* (= *demilitarized zone*) zona desmilitarizada.

DNA *n abbr* = (*deoxyribonucleic acid*) ADN *m*.

do [duː] *vb* (*pt* **did,** *pp* **done** [dɪd, dʌn]) *vt, vi* (*gen*) hacer; (*speed*) ir a; (*visit: city, museum*) visitar, recorrer; (*THEATRE*) representar ◆ *n* (*col: party*) fiesta, guateque *m*; (: *formal gathering*) reunión *f*, ceremonia; **the ~s and don'ts** las reglas del juego; **he didn't laugh** no se rió; **she swims better than I ~** nada mejor que yo; **he**

laughed, didn't he? se rió ¿no?; **that will ~!** ¡basta!; **to make ~ with** contentarse con; **~ you agree?** ¿está usted de acuerdo?; **I don't understand** no entiendo; **~ you speak English?** ¿habla (usted) inglés?; **you speak better than I ~** tu hablas mejor que yo; **so does he** él también; **DO come!** ¡venga, por favor!; **I DO wish I could ...** ojalá que pudiera ...; **but I DO like it!** pero, sí que *or* por supuesto que me gusta!; **what does he ~ for a living?** ¿a qué se dedica?; **what can I ~ for you?** (*in shop*) ¿en qué puedo servirle?; **to ~ one's hair** (*comb*) peinarse; (*style*) arreglarse el pelo; **I'm going to ~ the washing-up/washing** voy a fregar los platos/lavar la ropa; **we've done 200 km already** llevamos 200 km de viaje ya; **I'll ~ all I can** haré todo lo que pueda; **how ~ you like your steak done?** ¿cómo te gusta el filete? — bien hecho; **will it ~?** ¿sirve?, ¿conviene?; **to ~ sb out of sth** pisar algo a uno; **to ~ well** prosperar, tener éxito; **he's ~ing well/badly at school** va bien/mal en la escuela; **it doesn't ~ to upset her** cuidado en ofenderle; **that'll ~!** (*in annoyance*) ¡basta ya!; **to ~ without sth** prescindir de algo; **what has that got to ~ with it?** ¿qué tiene que ver eso?; **what have you done with my slippers?** ¿qué has hecho con mis zapatillas?

do away with *vt fus* (*kill*) asesinar; (*suppress*) suprimir.

do for *vt fus* (*col: clean for*) llevar la casa a.

do up *vt* (*laces*) liar, atar; (*room*) renovar; **to ~ o.s. up** maquillarse.

do with *vt fus* (*with can, could: need*) no venirle mal; **I could ~ with some help/a drink** no me vendría mal un poco de ayuda/una bebida.

do. *abbr* = **ditto.**

DOA *abbr* = *dead on arrival.*

d.o.b. *abbr* = **date of birth.**

docile ['dəusaɪl] *a* dócil.

dock [dɔk] *n* (*NAUT: wharf*) dársena, muelle *m*; (*LAW*) banquillo (de los acusados); **~s** *npl* muelles *mpl*, puerto *sg* ◆ *vi* (*enter ~*) atracar el muelle ◆ *vt* (*pay etc*) descontar.

dock dues *npl* derechos *mpl* de muelle.

docker ['dɔkə*] *n* trabajador *m* portuario, estibador *m*.

docket ['dɔkɪt] *n* (*on parcel etc*) etiqueta.

dockyard ['dɔkjɑːd] *n* astillero.

doctor ['dɔktə*] *n* médico *m*; (*Ph.D. etc*) doctor(a) *m/f* ◆ *vt* (*fig*) arreglar, falsificar; (*drink etc*) adulterar.

doctorate ['dɔktərɪt] *n* doctorado.

Doctor of Philosophy (Ph.D.) *n* Doctor *m* (en Filosofía y Letras).

doctrinaire [dɔktrɪ'neə*] *a* doctrinario.

doctrine ['dɔktrɪn] *n* doctrina.

document ['dɔkjumənt] *n* documento ◆ *vt*

documentar.

documentary [dɔkju'mɛntərɪ] *a* documental ◆ *n* documental *m*.

documentation [dɔkjumɛn'teɪʃən] *n* documentación *f*.

DOD *n abbr* (*US*: = *Department of Defense*) Ministerio de Defensa.

doddering ['dɔdərɪŋ] *a*, **doddery** ['dɔdərɪ] *a* chocho.

Dodecanese (Islands) [dəudɪkə'niːz-] *n*(*pl*) Dodecaneso *sg*.

dodge [dɔdʒ] *n* (*of body*) regate *m*; (*fig*) truco ◆ *vt* (*gen*) evadir; (*blow*) esquivar ◆ *vi* esquivarse, escabullirse; (*sport*) hacer una finta; **to ~ out of the way** echarse a un lado; **to ~ through the traffic** regatear por el tráfico.

dodgems ['dɔdʒəmz] *npl* (*Brit*) coches *mpl* de choque.

DOE *n abbr* (*Brit*) = **Department of the Environment**; (*US*) = *Department of Energy*.

doe [dəu] *n* (*deer*) cierva, gama; (*rabbit*) coneja.

does [dʌz] *vb see* **do**.

doesn't ['dʌznt] = **does not**.

dog [dɔg] *n* perro ◆ *vt* seguir (de cerca); (*fig*: *memory etc*) perseguir; **to go to the ~s** (*person*) echarse a perder; (*nation etc*) ir a la ruina.

dog biscuit *n* galleta de perro.

dog collar *n* collar *m* de perro; (*fig*) cuello de cura.

dog-eared ['dɔgɪəd] *a* sobado.

dogfish ['dɔgfɪʃ] *n* cazón *m*, perro marino.

dog food *n* comida para perros.

dogged ['dɔgɪd] *a* tenaz, obstinado.

dogma ['dɔgmə] *n* dogma *m*.

dogmatic [dɔg'mætɪk] *a* dogmático.

do-gooder [du:'gudə*] *n* (*col pej*): **to be a ~** ser una persona bien intencionada *or* un filantropista.

dogsbody ['dɔgzbɔdɪ] *n* (*Brit*) burro de carga.

doing ['duɪŋ] *n*: **this is your ~** esto es obra tuya.

doings ['duɪŋz] *npl* (*events*) sucesos *mpl*; (*acts*) hechos *mpl*.

do-it-yourself [du:ɪtjɔː'sɛlf] *n* bricolaje *m*.

doldrums ['dɔldrəmz] *npl*: **to be in the ~** (*person*) estar abatido; (*business*) estar estancado.

dole [dəul] *n* (*Brit*: *payment*) subsidio de paro; **on the ~** parado.

dole out *vt* repartir.

doleful ['dəulful] *a* triste, lúgubre.

doll [dɔl] *n* muñeca.

doll up *vt*: **to ~ o.s. up** ataviarse.

dollar ['dɔlə*] *n* dólar *m*.

dollar area *n* zona del dólar.

dolphin ['dɔlfɪn] *n* delfín *m*.

domain [də'meɪn] *n* (*fig*) campo, competencia; (*land*) dominios *mpl*.

dome [dəum] *n* (*arch*) cúpula; (*shape*) bóveda.

domestic [də'mɛstɪk] *a* (*animal, duty*) doméstico; (*flight, news, policy*) nacional.

domesticated [də'mɛstɪkeɪtɪd] *a* domesticado; (*person*: *home-loving*) casero, hogareño.

domesticity [dəumɛs'tɪsɪtɪ] *n* vida casera.

domestic servant *n* sirviente/a *m/f*.

domicile ['dɔmɪsaɪl] *n* domicilio.

dominant ['dɔmɪnənt] *a* dominante.

dominate ['dɔmɪneɪt] *vt* dominar.

domination [dɔmɪ'neɪʃən] *n* dominación *f*.

domineering [dɔmɪ'nɪərɪŋ] *a* dominante.

Dominican Republic [də'mɪnɪkən-] *n* República Dominicana.

dominion [də'mɪnɪən] *n* dominio.

domino, *pl* **~es** ['dɔmɪnəu] *n* ficha de dominó.

dominoes ['dɔmɪnəuz] *n* (*game*) dominó.

don [dɔn] *n* (*Brit*) catedrático/a.

donate [də'neɪt] *vt* donar.

donation [də'neɪʃən] *n* donativo.

done [dʌn] *pp of* **do**.

donkey ['dɔŋkɪ] *n* burro.

donkey-work ['dɔŋkɪwəːk] *n* (*Brit col*) trabajo pesado.

donor ['dəunə*] *n* donante *m/f*.

don't [dəunt] = **do not**.

donut ['dəunʌt] *n* (*US*) = **doughnut**.

doodle ['du:dl] *n* garabato ◆ *vi* pintar dibujitos *or* garabatos.

doom [du:m] *n* (*fate*) suerte *f*; (*death*) muerte *f* ◆ *vt*: **to be ~ed to failure** ser condenado al fracaso.

doomsday ['du:mzdeɪ] *n* día *m* del juicio final.

door [dɔː*] *n* puerta; (*of car*) portezuela; (*entry*) entrada; **from ~ to ~** de puerta en puerta.

doorbell ['dɔːbɛl] *n* timbre *m*.

door handle *n* tirador *m*; (*of car*) manija.

door knocker *n* aldaba.

doorman ['dɔːmən] *n* (*in hotel*) portero.

doormat ['dɔːmæt] *n* felpudo, estera.

doorstep ['dɔːstɛp] *n* peldaño.

door-to-door ['dɔːtə'dɔː*] *a*: **~ selling** venta a domicilio.

doorway ['dɔːweɪ] *n* entrada, puerta; **in the ~** en la puerta.

dope [dəup] *n* (*col*: *person*) imbécil *m/f*; (: *information*) información *f*, informes *mpl* ◆ *vt* (*horse etc*) drogar.

dopey ['dəupɪ] *a* atontado.

dormant ['dɔːmənt] *a* inactivo; (*latent*) latente.

dormer ['dɔːmə*] *n* (*also*: **~ window**) buhardilla.

dormitory ['dɔːmɪtrɪ] *n* (*Brit*) dormitorio; (*US*: *hall of residence*) residencia, colegio mayor.

dormouse, *pl* **dormice** ['dɔːmaus, -maɪs] *n* lirón *m*.

Dors *abbr* (*Brit*) = *Dorset*.

DOS *n abbr see* **disk operating system.**

dosage ['dəusɪdʒ] *n* (*on medicine bottle*) dosis *f inv*, dosificación *f*.

dose [dəus] *n* (*of medicine*) dosis *f inv*; **a ~ of flu** un ataque de gripe ♦ *vt*: **to ~ o.s. with** tomar una buena dosis de.

doss house ['dɔs-] *n* (*Brit*) pensión *f* de mala muerte.

dossier ['dɔsɪeɪ] *n*: **~ (on)** expediente *m* (sobre).

DOT *n abbr* (*US*: = *Department of Transportation*) ≈ *Ministerio de Transportes, Turismo y Comunicaciones* (*Sp*).

dot [dɔt] *n* punto; **~ted with** salpicado de; **on the ~** en punto.

dot command *n* (*COMPUT*) instrucción *f* (precedida) de punto.

dote [dəut]: **to ~ on** *vt fus* adorar, idolatrar.

dot-matrix printer [dɔt'meɪtrɪks-] *n* impresora matricial *or* de matriz.

dotted line ['dɔtɪd-] *n* línea de puntos; **to sign on the ~** firmar.

dotty ['dɔtɪ] *a* (*col*) disparatado, chiflado.

double ['dʌbl] *a* doble ♦ *ad* (*twice*): **to cost ~** costar el doble ♦ *n* (*gen*) doble *m* ♦ *vt* doblar; (*efforts*) redoblar ♦ *vi* doblarse; (*have two uses etc*): **to ~ as** hacer las veces de; **~ five two six (5526)** (*TELEC*) cinco cinco dos seis; **spelt with a ~ "s"** escrito con dos "eses"; **on the ~,** (*Brit*) **at the ~** corriendo.

double back *vi* (*person*) volver sobre sus pasos.

double up *vi* (*bend over*) doblarse; (*share bedroom*) compartir.

double bass *n* contrabajo.

double bed *n* cama matrimonial.

double bend *n* (*Brit*) doble curva.

double-breasted ['dʌbl'brestɪd] *a* cruzado.

double-check ['dʌbltʃek] *vt, vi* revisar de nuevo.

double cream *n* nata enriquecida.

doublecross ['dʌbl'krɔs] *vt* (*trick*) engañar; (*betray*) traicionar.

doubledecker ['dʌbl'dekə*] *n* autobús *m* de dos pisos.

double glazing *n* (*Brit*) doble acristalamiento.

double indemnity *n* doble indemnización *f.*

double-page ['dʌblpeɪdʒ] *a*: **~ spread** doble página.

double room *n* cuarto para dos.

doubles ['dʌblz] *n* (*TENNIS*) juego de dobles.

double time *n* tarifa doble.

doubly ['dʌblɪ] *ad* doblemente.

doubt [daut] *n* duda ♦ *vt* dudar; (*suspect*) dudar de; **to ~ that** dudar que; **there is no ~ that** no cabe duda de que; **without (a) ~** sin duda (alguna); **beyond ~** fuera de duda; **I ~ it very much** lo dudo mucho.

doubtful ['dautful] *a* dudoso; (*person*)

sospechoso; **to be ~ about sth** tener dudas sobre algo; **I'm a bit ~** no estoy convencido.

doubtless ['dautlɪs] *ad* sin duda.

dough [dəu] *n* masa, pasta; (*col: money*) pasta.

doughnut ['dəunʌt] *n* buñuelo.

douse [daus] *vt* (*drench: with water*) mojar; (*extinguish: flames*) apagar.

dove [dʌv] *n* paloma.

Dover ['dəuvə*] *n* Dover.

dovetail ['dʌvteɪl] *vi* (*fig*) encajar.

dowager ['dauɪdʒə*] *n*: **~ duchess** duquesa viuda.

dowdy ['daudɪ] *a* desaliñado; (*inelegant*) poco elegante.

Dow Jones Index ['daudʒəunz-] *n* (*US*) índice *m* Dow-Jones.

down [daun] *n* (*fluff*) pelusa; (*feathers*) plumón *m*, flojel *m*; (*hill*) loma ♦ *ad* (*~wards*) abajo, hacia abajo; (*on the ground*) por/en tierra ♦ *prep* abajo ♦ *vt* (*col: drink*) beberse, tragar(se); **~ with X!** ¡abajo X!; **~ there** allí abajo; **~ here** aquí abajo; **I'll be ~ in a minute** ahora bajo; **England is two goals ~** Inglaterra está perdiendo por dos tantos; **I've been ~ with flu** he estado con gripe; **the price of meat is ~** ha bajado el precio de la carne; **I've got it ~ in my diary** lo he apuntado en mi agenda; **to pay £2 ~** dejar £2 de depósito; **he went ~ the hill** fue cuesta abajo; **~ under** (*in Australia etc*) en Australia/Nueva Zelanda; **to ~ tools** (*fig*) declararse en huelga.

down-and-out ['daunəndaut] *n* (*tramp*) vagabundo/a.

down-at-heel ['daunət'hi:l] *a* venido a menos; (*appearance*) desaliñado.

downbeat ['daunbi:t] *n* (*MUS*) compás *m* ♦ *a* (*gloomy*) pesimista.

downcast ['daunkɑ:st] *a* abatido.

downer ['daunə*] *n* (*col: drug*) tranquilizante; **to be on a ~** estar pasando un mal bache.

downfall ['daunfɔ:l] *n* caída, ruina.

downgrade [daun'greɪd] *vt* (*job*) degradar; (*hotel*) bajar de categoría a.

downhearted [daun'hɑ:tɪd] *a* desanimado.

downhill [daun'hɪl] *ad*: **to go ~** ir cuesta abajo; (*business*) estar en declive.

download ['daunləud] *vt* (*COMPUT*) transferir, telecargar.

down-market ['daun'mɑ:kɪt] *a* para la sección popular del mercado.

down payment *n* entrada, pago al contado.

downplay ['daunpleɪ] *vt* (*US*) quitar importancia a.

downpour ['daunpɔ:] *n* aguacero.

downright ['daunraɪt] *a* (*nonsense, lie*) manifiesto; (*refusal*) terminante.

downstairs [daun'steəz] *ad* (*below*) (en la

casa de) abajo; (*motion*) escaleras abajo; **to come** (*or* **go**) ~ bajar la escalera.

downstream [daun'striːm] *ad* aguas *or* río abajo.

downtime ['dauntaɪm] *n* (*COMM*) tiempo inactivo.

down-to-earth [dauntu'ɜːθ] *a* práctico.

downtown [daun'taun] *ad* en el centro de la ciudad.

downtrodden ['dauntrɔdn] *a* oprimido.

downward ['daunwəd] *ad* hacia abajo ♦ *a*: **a** ~ **trend** una tendencia descendente.

downward(s) ['daunwəd(z)] *ad* hacia abajo; **face** ~**s** (*person*) boca abajo; (*object*) cara abajo.

dowry ['daurɪ] *n* dote *f*.

doz. *abbr* = **dozen**.

doze [dəuz] *vi* dormitar.

doze off *vi* quedarse medio dormido.

dozen ['dʌzn] *n* docena; **a** ~ **books** una docena de libros; ~**s of** cantidad de; ~**s of times** cantidad de veces; **80p a** ~ 80 peniques la docena.

DPh., D. Phil. *n abbr* (= *Doctor of Philosophy*) título universitario.

DPP *n abbr* (*Brit*) = **Director of Public Prosecutions**.

DPT *n abbr* (= *diphtheria, pertussis, tetanus*) vacuna trivalente.

DPW *n abbr* (*US*: = *Department of Public Works*) ≈ *Ministerio de Obras Públicas y Urbanismo* (*Sp*).

Dr, Dr. *abbr* (= *doctor*) Dr.

Dr. *abbr* (*in street names*) = **Drive**.

dr *abbr* (*COMM*) = **debtor**.

drab [dræb] *a* gris, monótono.

draft [drɑːft] *n* (*first copy: of document, report*) borrador *m*; (*COMM*) giro; (*US*: *call-up*) quinta ♦ *vt* (*write roughly*) hacer un borrador de; *see also* **draught**.

draftsman ['drɑːftsmən] *etc* (*US*) = **draughtsman** *etc*.

drag [dræg] *vt* arrastrar; (*river*) dragar, rastrear ♦ *vi* arrastrarse por el suelo ♦ *n* (*AVIAT*: *resistance*) resistencia aerodinámica; (*col*) lata; (*women's clothing*): **in** ~ vestido de travesti.

drag away *vt*: **to** ~ **away (from)** quitar arrastrando.

drag on *vi* ser interminable.

dragnet ['drægnɛt] *n* (*NAUT*) rastra; (*fig*) emboscada.

dragon ['drægən] *n* dragón *m*.

dragonfly ['drægənflaɪ] *n* libélula.

dragoon [drə'guːn] *n* (*cavalryman*) dragón *m* ♦ *vt*: **to** ~ **sb into doing sth** forzar a uno a hacer algo.

drain [dreɪn] *n* desaguadero; (*in street*) sumidero; (~ *cover*) rejilla del sumidero ♦ *vt* (*land, marshes*) desaguar; (*MED*) drenar; (*reservoir*) desecar; (*fig*) agotar ♦ *vi* escurrirse; **to be a** ~ **on** agotar; **to feel** ~**ed (of energy)** (*fig*) sentirse agotado.

drainage ['dreɪnɪdʒ] *n* (*act*) desagüe *m*; (*MED, AGR*) drenaje *m*; (*sewage*) alcantarillado.

draining board ['dreɪnɪŋ-], (*US*) **drainboard** ['dreɪnbɔːd] *n* escurridera, escurridor *m*.

drainpipe ['dreɪnpaɪp] *n* tubo de desagüe.

drake [dreɪk] *n* pato (macho).

dram [dræm] *n* (*drink*) traguito, copita.

drama ['drɑːmə] *n* (*art*) teatro; (*play*) drama *m*.

dramatic [drə'mætɪk] *a* dramático.

dramatist ['dræmətɪst] *n* dramaturgo/a.

dramatize ['dræmətaɪz] *vt* (*events etc*) dramatizar; (*adapt: novel: for TV, cinema*) adaptar.

drank [dræŋk] *pt of* **drink**.

drape [dreɪp] *vt* cubrir.

draper ['dreɪpə*] *n* (*Brit*) pañero.

drapes [dreɪps] *npl* (*US*) cortinas *fpl*.

drastic ['dræstɪk] *a* (*measure, reduction*) severo; (*change*) radical.

draught, (*US*) **draft** [drɑːft] *n* (*of air*) corriente *f* de aire; (*drink*) trago; (*NAUT*) calado; **on** ~ (*beer*) de barril.

draughtboard ['drɑːftbɔːd] (*Brit*) *n* tablero de damas.

draughts [drɑːfts] *n* (*Brit*) juego de damas.

draughtsman, (*US*) **draftsman** ['drɑːftsmən] *n* proyectista *m*, delineante *m*.

draughtsmanship, (*US*) **draftsmanship** ['drɑːftsmənʃɪp] *n* (*drawing*) dibujo lineal; (*skill*) habilidad *f* para el dibujo.

draw [drɔː] *vb* (*pt* **drew**, *pp* **drawn** [druː, drɔːn]) *vt* (*pull*) tirar; (*take out*) sacar; (*attract*) atraer; (*picture*) dibujar; (*money*) retirar; (*formulate: conclusion*): **to** ~ **(from)** sacar (de); (*comparison, distinction*): **to** ~ **(between)** hacer (entre) ♦ *vi* (*SPORT*) empatar ♦ *n* (*SPORT*) empate *m*; (*lottery*) sorteo; (*attraction*) atracción *f*; **to** ~ **near** *vi* acercarse.

draw back *vi*: **to** ~ **back (from)** echarse atrás (de).

draw in *vi* (*car*) aparcar; (*train*) entrar en la estación.

draw on *vt* (*resources*) utilizar, servirse de; (*imagination, person*) recurrir a.

draw out *vi* (*lengthen*) alargarse.

draw up *vi* (*stop*) pararse ♦ *vt* (*document*) redactar; (*plans*) trazar.

drawback ['drɔːbæk] *n* inconveniente *m*, desventaja.

drawbridge ['drɔːbrɪdʒ] *n* puente *m* levadizo.

drawee [drɔː'iː] *n* girado.

drawer [drɔː*] *n* cajón *m*; (*of cheque*) librador(a) *m/f*.

drawing ['drɔːɪŋ] *n* dibujo.

drawing board *n* tablero (de dibujante).

drawing pin *n* (*Brit*) chinche *m*.

drawing room *n* salón *m*.

drawl [drɔːl] *n* habla lenta y cansina.

drawn [drɔːn] *pp of* **draw** ◆ *a* (*haggard: with tiredness*) ojeroso; (: *with pain*) macilento.

drawstring ['drɔːstrɪŋ] *n* apretadera.

dread [drɛd] *n* pavor *m*, terror *m* ◆ *vt* temer, tener miedo *or* pavor a.

dreadful ['drɛdful] *a* espantoso; **I feel ~!** (*ill*) ¡me siento fatal *or* malísimo!; (*ashamed*) ¡qué vergüenza!

dream [driːm] *n* sueño ◆ *vt*, *vi* (*pt*, *pp* **dreamed** *or* **dreamt** [drɛmt]) soñar; **to have a ~ about sb/sth** soñar con uno/algo; **sweet ~s!** ¡que sueñes con los ángeles!

dream up *vt* (*reason, excuse*) inventar; (*plan, idea*) idear.

dreamer ['driːmə*] *n* soñador(a) *m/f*.

dream world *n* mundo imaginario.

dreamy ['driːmɪ] *a* (*person*) soñador(a), distraído; (*music*) de sueño.

dreary ['drɪərɪ] *a* monótono, aburrido.

dredge [drɛdʒ] *vt* dragar.

dredge up *vt* sacar con draga; (*fig: unpleasant facts*) pescar, sacar a luz.

dredger ['drɛdʒə*] *n* (*ship, machine*) draga; (*CULIN*) espolvoreador *m*.

dregs [drɛgz] *npl* heces *fpl*.

drench [drɛntʃ] *vt* empapar; **~ed to the skin** calado hasta los huesos.

dress [drɛs] *n* vestido; (*clothing*) ropa ◆ *vt* vestir; (*wound*) vendar; (*CULIN*) aliñar; (*shop window*) decorar, arreglar ◆ *vi* vestirse; **to ~ o.s.**, **get ~ed** vestirse; **she ~es very well** se viste muy bien.

dress up *vi* vestirse de etiqueta; (*in fancy dress*) disfrazarse.

dress circle *n* (*Brit*) principal *m*.

dress designer *n* modisto/a.

dresser ['drɛsə*] *n* (*furniture*) aparador *m*; (: *US*) cómoda con espejo; (*THEATRE*) camarero/a.

dressing ['drɛsɪŋ] *n* (*MED*) vendaje *m*; (*CULIN*) aliño.

dressing gown *n* (*Brit*) bata.

dressing room *n* (*THEATRE*) camarín *m*; (*SPORT*) vestidor *m*.

dressing table *n* tocador *m*.

dressmaker ['drɛsmeɪkə*] *n* modista, costurera.

dressmaking ['drɛsmeɪkɪŋ] *n* costura.

dress rehearsal *n* ensayo general.

dress shirt *n* camisa de frac.

dressy ['drɛsɪ] *a* (*col*) elegante.

drew [druː] *pt of* **draw**.

dribble ['drɪbl] *vi* gotear, caer gota a gota; (*baby*) babear ◆ *vt* (*ball*) driblar, regatear.

dried [draɪd] *a* (*gen*) seco; (*fruit*) paso; (*milk*) en polvo.

drier ['draɪə*] *n* = **dryer**.

drift [drɪft] *n* (*of current etc*) velocidad *f*; (*of sand*) montón *m*; (*of snow*) ventisquero; (*meaning*) significado ◆ *vi* (*boat*) ir a la deriva; (*sand, snow*) amontonarse; **to**

catch sb's ~ seguirle la corriente a uno; **to let things ~** dejar las cosas como están; **to ~ apart** (*friends*) seguir su camino; (*lovers*) disgustarse, romper.

drifter ['drɪftə*] *n* vagabundo/a.

driftwood ['drɪftwud] *n* madera de deriva.

drill [drɪl] *n* taladro; (*bit*) broca; (*of dentist*) fresa; (*for mining etc*) perforadora, barrena; (*MIL*) instrucción *f* ◆ *vt* perforar, taladrar; (*soldiers*) ejercitar; (*pupils: in grammar*) dar práctica en gramática a ◆ *vi* (*for oil*) perforar.

drilling ['drɪlɪŋ] *n* (*for oil*) perforación *f*.

drilling rig *n* (*on land*) torre *f* de perforación; (*at sea*) plataforma de perforación.

drily ['draɪlɪ] *ad* secamente.

drink [drɪŋk] *n* bebida ◆ *vt*, *vi* (*pt* **drank**, *pp* **drunk**) beber; **to have a ~** tomar algo; **to mar una copa** *or* un trago; **a ~ of water** un trago de agua; **to invite sb for ~s** invitar a uno a tomar unas copas; **there's food and ~ in the kitchen** hay de comer y de beber en la cocina; **would you like something to ~?** ¿quieres beber *or* tomar algo?

drink in *vt* (*subj: person: fresh air*) respirar; (*story, sight*) beberse.

drinkable ['drɪŋkəbl] *a* (*not poisonous*) potable; (*palatable*) aguantable.

drinker ['drɪŋkə*] *n* bebedor(a) *m/f*.

drinking ['drɪŋkɪŋ] *n* (*drunkenness*) beber *m*.

drinking fountain *n* fuente *f*.

drinking water *n* agua potable.

drip [drɪp] *n* (*act*) goteo; (*one* ~) gota; (*MED*) gota a gota *m*; (*sound: of water etc*) goteo; (*col: spineless person*) soso/a ◆ *vi* gotear, caer gota a gota.

drip-dry ['drɪp'draɪ] *a* (*shirt*) de lava y pon.

dripping ['drɪpɪŋ] *n* (*animal fat*) pringue *m* ◆ *a*: **~ wet** calado.

drive [draɪv] *n* paseo (en coche); (*journey*) viaje *m* (en coche); (*also*: **~way**) entrada; (*street*) calle; (*energy*) energía, vigor *m*; (*PSYCH*) impulso; (*SPORT*) ataque *m*; (*COMPUT: also*: **disk ~**) disc drive *m* ◆ *vb* (*pt* **drove**, *pp* **driven** [drəuv, 'drɪvn]) *vt* (*car*) conducir, manejar (*LAm*); (*nail*) clavar; (*push*) empujar; (*TECH: motor*) impulsar ◆ *vi* (*AUT: at controls*) conducir; (: *travel*) pasearse en coche; **to go for a ~** dar una vuelta en coche; **it's 3 hours' ~ from London** es un viaje de 3 horas desde Londres; **left-/right-hand ~** conducción *f* a la izquierda/derecha; **front-/rear-wheel ~** tracción *f* delantera/trasera; **sales ~** promoción *f* de ventas; **to ~ sb mad** volverle loco a uno; **to ~ sb to (do) sth** empujar a uno a (hacer) algo; **he ~s a taxi** es taxista; **he ~s a Mercedes** tiene un Mercedes; **can you ~?** ¿sabes conducir *or* (*LAm*) manejar?; **to ~ at 50 km an hour** ir a 50km por hora.

drive at *vt fus* (*fig: intend, mean*) querer

decir, insinuar.

drive on *vi* no parar, seguir adelante ♦ *vt* (*incite, encourage*) empujar.

drive-in ['draɪvɪn] *a* (*esp US*): ~ **cinema** autocinema *m*.

drivel ['drɪvl] *n* (*col*) tonterías *fpl*.

driven ['drɪvn] *pp of* **drive**.

driver ['draɪvə*] *n* conductor(a) *m/f*; (*of taxi, bus*) chofer *m*.

driver's license *n* (*US*) carnet *m or* permiso de conducir.

driveway ['draɪvweɪ] *n* entrada.

driving ['draɪvɪŋ] *n* conducir *m*, manejar *m* (*LAm*) ♦ *a* (*force*) impulsor(a).

driving instructor *n* instructor *m/f* de conducción.

driving lesson *n* clase *f* de conducción.

driving licence *n* (*Brit*) carnet *m or* permiso de conducir.

driving mirror *n* retrovisor *m*.

driving school *n* autoescuela.

driving test *n* examen *m* de conducción.

drizzle ['drɪzl] *n* llovizna ♦ *vi* lloviznar.

droll [drəul] *a* gracioso.

dromedary ['drɔmɪdərɪ] *n* dromedario.

drone [drəun] *vi* (*bee, aircraft, engine*) zumbar; (*also*: ~ **on**) murmurar sin interrupción ♦ *n* zumbido; (*male bee*) zángano.

drool [druːl] *vi* babear; **to** ~ **over sb/sth** caérsele la baba por uno/algo.

droop [druːp] *vi* (*fig*) decaer, desanimarse.

drop [drɔp] *n* (*of water*) gota; (*fall*: *in price*) bajada; (: *in salary*) disminución *f* ♦ *vt* (*allow to fall*) dejar caer; (*voice, eyes, price*) bajar; (*set down from car*) dejar ♦ *vi* (*price, temperature*) bajar; (*wind*) calmarse, amainar; (*numbers, attendance*) disminuir; ~**s** *npl* (*MED*) gotas *fpl*; **cough** ~**s** pastillas *fpl* para la tos; **a** ~ **of 10%** una bajada del 10 por ciento; **to** ~ **anchor** echar el ancla; **to** ~ **sb a line** mandar unas líneas a uno.

drop in *vi* (*col*: *visit*): **to** ~ **in (on)** pasar por casa (de).

drop off *vi* (*sleep*) dormirse ♦ *vt* (*passenger*) bajar, dejar.

drop out *vi* (*withdraw*) retirarse.

droplet ['drɔplɪt] *n* gotita.

dropout ['drɔpaut] *n* (*from society*) marginado/a; (*from university*) estudiante *m/f* que ha abandonado el curso.

dropper ['drɔpə*] *n* (*MED*) cuentagotas *m inv*.

droppings ['drɔpɪŋz] *npl* excremento *sg*.

dross [drɔs] *n* (*coal, fig*) escoria.

drought [draut] *n* sequía.

drove [drəuv] *pt of* **drive**.

drown [draun] *vt* (*also*: ~ **out**: *sound*) ahogar ♦ *vi* ahogarse.

drowse [drauz] *vi* estar medio dormido.

drowsy ['drauzı] *a* soñoliento; **to be** ~ tener sueño.

drudge [drʌdʒ] *n* esclavo del trabajo.

drudgery ['drʌdʒərı] *n* trabajo pesado *or* monótono.

drug [drʌg] *n* (*MED*) medicamento, droga; (*narcotic*) droga ♦ *vt* drogar; **he's on** ~**s** se droga.

drug addict *n* drogadicto/a.

druggist ['drʌgɪst] *n* (*US*) farmacéutico/a.

drug peddler *n* vendedor(a) *m/f* de narcóticos.

drugstore ['drʌgstɔ:*] *n* (*US*) farmacia.

drug trafficker *n* narcotraficante *m/f*.

drum [drʌm] *n* tambor *m*; (*large*) bombo; (*for oil, petrol*) bidón *m* ♦ *vi* tocar el tambor; (*with fingers*) tamborilear ♦ *vt*: **to** ~ **one's fingers on the table** tamborilear con los dedos sobre la mesa; ~**s** *npl* batería *sg*.

drum up *vt* (*enthusiasm, support*) movilizar, fomentar.

drummer ['drʌmə*] *n* tambor *m*.

drumstick ['drʌmstɪk] *n* (*MUS*) palillo; (*chicken leg*) muslo (de pollo).

drunk [drʌŋk] *pp of* **drink** ♦ *a* borracho ♦ *n* (*also*: ~**ard**) borracho/a; **to get** ~ emborracharse.

drunken ['drʌŋkən] *a* borracho.

drunkenness ['drʌŋkənnıs] *n* embriaguez *f*.

dry [draɪ] *a* seco; (*day*) sin lluvia; (*climate*) árido, seco; (*humour*) agudo; (*uninteresting*: *lecture*) aburrido, pesado ♦ *vt* secar; (*tears*) enjugarse ♦ *vi* secarse; **on** ~ **land** en tierra firme; **to** ~ **one's hands/hair/ eyes** secarse las manos/el pelo/las lágrimas.

dry up *vi* (*supply, imagination etc*) agotarse; (*in speech*) atascarse.

dry-clean ['draɪ'kliːn] *vt* limpiar *or* lavar en seco; "~ **only**" (*on label*) "limpieza *or* lavado en seco (sólo)".

dry-cleaner's ['draɪ'kliːnəz] *n* tintorería.

dry-cleaning ['draɪ'kliːnıŋ] *n* lavado en seco.

dry dock *n* (*NAUT*) dique *m* seco.

dryer ['draɪə*] *n* (*for hair*) secador *m*; (*for clothes*) secadora.

dry goods *npl* (*COMM*) mercería *sg*.

dry goods store *n* (*US*) mercería.

dry ice *n* nieve *f* carbónica.

dryness ['draɪnıs] *n* sequedad *f*.

dry rot *n* putrefacción *f* seca.

dry run *n* (*fig*) ensayo.

dry ski slope *n* pista artificial de esquí.

DSc *n abbr* (= *Doctor of Science*) título universitario.

DST *n abbr* (*US*: = *Daylight Saving Time*) hora de verano.

DT *n abbr* (*COMPUT*) = **data transmission**.

DTI *n abbr* (*Brit*) = *Department of Trade and Industry*.

DT's *n abbr* (*col*: = *delirium tremens*) delirium *m* tremens.

dual ['djuəl] *a* doble.

dual carriageway n (Brit) carretera de doble calzada.
dual-control ['djuəlkən'trəul] a de doble mando.
dual nationality n doble nacionalidad f.
dual-purpose ['djuəl'pə:pəs] a de doble uso.
dubbed [dʌbd] a (CINEMA) doblado.
dubious ['dju:bɪəs] a indeciso; (reputation, company) dudoso; (character) sospechoso; **I'm very ~ about it** tengo mis grandes dudas sobre ello.
Dublin ['dʌblɪn] n Dublín.
Dubliner ['dʌblɪnə*] n dublinés/esa m/f.
duchess ['dʌtʃɪs] n duquesa.
duck [dʌk] n pato ♦ vi agacharse ♦ vt (plunge in water) zambullir.
duckling ['dʌklɪŋ] n patito.
duct [dʌkt] n conducto, canal m.
dud [dʌd] n (shell) obús m que no estalla; (object, tool): **it's a ~** es una filfa ♦ a: **~ cheque** (Brit) cheque m sin fondos.
due [dju:] a (proper) debido; (fitting) conveniente, oportuno ♦ ad: **~ north** derecho al norte; **~s** npl (for club, union) cuota sg; (in harbour) derechos mpl; **in ~ course** a su debido tiempo; **~ to** debido a; **to be ~ to** deberse a; **the train is ~ to arrive at 8.00** el tren debe llegar a las ocho; **the rent's ~ on the 30th** hay que pagar el alquiler el día 30; **I am ~ 6 days' leave** se me debe 6 días de vacaciones; **she is ~ back tomorrow** ella debe volver mañana.
due date n fecha de vencimiento.
duel ['djuəl] n duelo.
duet [dju:'ɛt] n dúo.
duff [dʌf] a sin valor.
duffel bag ['dʌfl-] n especie de talega que se cuelga al hombro.
duffel coat ['dʌfl-] n trenca.
dug [dʌg] pt, pp of **dig**.
duke [dju:k] n duque m.
dull [dʌl] a (light) apagado; (stupid) torpe; (boring) pesado; (sound, pain) sordo; (weather, day) gris ♦ vt (pain, grief) aliviar; (mind, senses) entorpecer.
duly ['dju:lɪ] ad debidamente; (on time) a su debido tiempo.
dumb [dʌm] a mudo; (stupid) estúpido; **to be struck ~** (fig) quedar boquiabierto.
dumbbell ['dʌmbɛl] n (SPORT) pesa.
dumbfounded [dʌm'faundɪd] a pasmado.
dummy ['dʌmɪ] n (tailor's model) maniquí m; (Brit: for baby) chupete m ♦ a falso, postizo; **~ run** ensayo.
dump [dʌmp] n (heap) montón m de basura; (place) basurero, vaciadero; (col) casucha; (MIL) depósito; (COMPUT) copia vaciada ♦ vt (put down) dejar; (get rid of) deshacerse de; (COMPUT) vaciar; (COMM: goods) inundar el mercado de; **to be (down) in the ~s** (col) tener murria, estar deprimido.

dumping ['dʌmpɪŋ] n (ECON) dumping m; (of rubbish): **"no ~"** "prohibido verter basura".
dumpling ['dʌmplɪŋ] n bola de masa hervida.
dumpy ['dʌmpɪ] a regordete/a.
dunce [dʌns] n zopenco.
dune [dju:n] n duna.
dung [dʌŋ] n estiércol m.
dungarees [dʌŋgə'ri:z] npl mono sg.
dungeon ['dʌndʒən] n calabozo.
dunk [dʌŋk] vt mojar.
duo ['dju:əu] n (gen, MUS) dúo.
duodenal [dju:ə'di:nl] a (ulcer) de duodeno.
duodenum [dju:ə'di:nəm] n duodeno.
dupe [dju:p] n (victim) víctima ♦ vt engañar.
duplex ['dju:plɛks] n (US: also: **~ apartment**) dúplex m.
duplicate ['dju:plɪkət] n duplicado; (copy of letter etc) copia ♦ a (copy) duplicado ♦ vt ['dju:plɪkeɪt] duplicar; (on machine) multicopiar; **in ~** por duplicado.
duplicate key n duplicado de una llave.
duplicating machine ['dju:plɪkeɪtɪŋ-], **duplicator** ['dju:plɪkeɪtə*] n multicopista m.
duplicity [dju:'plɪsɪtɪ] n doblez f, duplicidad f.
Dur abbr (Brit) = Durham.
durability [djuərə'bɪlɪtɪ] n durabilidad f.
durable ['djuərəbl] a duradero.
duration [djuə'reɪʃən] n duración f.
duress [djuə'rɛs] n: **under ~** por compulsión.
Durex ® ['djuərɛks] n (Brit) preservativo.
during ['djuərɪŋ] prep durante.
dusk [dʌsk] n crepúsculo, anochecer m.
dusky ['dʌskɪ] a oscuro; (complexion) moreno.
dust [dʌst] n polvo ♦ vt (furniture) desempolvar; (cake etc): **to ~ with** espolvorear de.
dust off vt (also fig) desempolvar, quitar el polvo de.
dustbin ['dʌstbɪn] n (Brit) cubo de la basura, balde m (LAm).
dustbin liner n bolsa de basura.
duster ['dʌstə*] n paño, trapo; (feather ~) plumero.
dust jacket n sobrecubierta.
dustman ['dʌstmən] n (Brit) basurero.
dustpan ['dʌstpæn] n cogedor m.
dust storm n vendaval m de polvo.
dusty ['dʌstɪ] a polvoriento.
Dutch [dʌtʃ] a holandés/esa ♦ n (LING) holandés m ♦ ad: **to go ~** pagar cada uno lo suyo; **the ~** npl los holandeses.
Dutch auction n subasta a la rebaja.
Dutchman ['dʌtʃmən], **Dutchwoman** ['dʌtʃwumən] n holandés/esa m/f.
dutiful ['dju:tɪful] a (child) obediente; (husband) sumiso; (employee) cumplido.

duty ['djuːtɪ] n deber m; (tax) derechos mpl de aduana; (MED: in hospital) servicio, guardia; **on** ~ de servicio; (at night etc) de guardia; **off** ~ libre (de servicio); **to make it one's** ~ **to do sth** encargarse de hacer algo sin falta; **to pay** ~ **on sth** pagar los derechos sobre algo.

duty-free [djuːtɪ'friː] a libre de derechos de aduana; ~ **shop** tienda libre de impuestos.

duty officer n (MIL etc) oficial m/f de servicio.

duvet ['duːveɪ] n (Brit) edredón m.

DV abbr (= Deo volente) Dios mediante.

DVLC n abbr (Brit: = Driver and Vehicle Licensing Centre) servicio que expide los carnets de conducir y las matrículas.

DVM n abbr (US: = Doctor of Veterinary Medicine) título universitario.

dwarf [dwɔːf], pl **dwarves** [dwɔːvz] n enano ◆ vt empequeñecer.

dwell [dwel], pt, pp **dwelt** [dwelt] vi morar.

dwell on vt fus explayarse en.

dweller ['dwelə*] n habitante m; **city** ~ habitante m de la ciudad.

dwelling ['dwelɪŋ] n vivienda.

dwelt [dwelt] pt, pp of **dwell**.

dwindle ['dwɪndl] vi menguar, disminuir.

dwindling ['dwɪndlɪŋ] a (strength, interest) menguante; (resources, supplies) disminuyente.

dye [daɪ] n tinte m ◆ vt teñir; **hair** ~ tinte m para el pelo.

dying ['daɪɪŋ] a moribundo, agonizante; (moments) final; (words) último.

dyke [daɪk] n (Brit) dique m; (channel) arroyo, acequia; (causeway) calzada.

dynamic [daɪ'næmɪk] a dinámico.

dynamics [daɪ'næmɪks] n or npl dinámica sg.

dynamite ['daɪnəmaɪt] n dinamita ◆ vt dinamitar.

dynamo ['daɪnəməu] n dinamo f.

dynasty ['dɪnəstɪ] n dinastía.

dysentery ['dɪsɪntrɪ] n disentería.

dyslexic [dɪs'leksɪk] a, n disléxico/a m/f.

dyspepsia [dɪs'pepsɪə] n dispepsia.

dystrophy ['dɪstrəfɪ] n distrofia; **muscular** ~ distrofia muscular.

E

E, e [iː] n (letter) E, e f; (MUS) mi m; **E for Edward**, (US) **E for Easy** E de Enrique.

E abbr (= east) E.

E111 n abbr (also: **form** ~) impreso E111.

ea. abbr = **each**.

E.A. abbr (US: = educational age) nivel

escolar.

each [iːtʃ] a cada inv ◆ pron cada uno; ~ **other** el uno al otro; **they hate** ~ **other** se odian (entre ellos or mutuamente); ~ **day** cada día; **they have 2 books** ~ tienen 2 libros por persona; **they cost £5** ~ cuestan cinco libras cada uno; ~ **of us** cada uno de nosotros.

eager ['iːgə*] a (gen) impaciente; (hopeful) ilusionado; (keen) entusiasmado; (: pupil) apasionado; **to be** ~ **to do sth** tener muchas ganas de hacer algo, impacientarse por hacer algo; **to be** ~ **for** ansiar, anhelar.

eagerly ['iːgəlɪ] ad con impaciencia; con ilusión; con entusiasmo.

eagerness ['iːgənɪs] n impaciencia; ilusión f; entusiasmo.

eagle ['iːgl] n águila f.

E and OE abbr = **errors and omissions excepted.**

ear [ɪə*] n oreja; (sense of hearing) oído; (of corn) espiga; **up to the** ~**s in debt** abrumado de deudas.

earache ['ɪəreɪk] n dolor m de oídos.

eardrum ['ɪədrʌm] n tímpano.

earl [əːl] n conde m.

early ['əːlɪ] ad (gen) temprano; (ahead of time) con tiempo, con anticipación ◆ a (gen) temprano; (reply) pronto; (man) primitivo; (first: Christians, settlers) primero; **to have an** ~ **night** acostarse temprano; **in the** ~ **or** ~ **in the spring/19th century** a principios de primavera/del siglo diecinueve; **you're** ~! ¡has llegado temprano or pronto!; ~ **in the morning/afternoon** a primeras horas de la mañana/tarde; **she's in her** ~ **forties** tiene poco más de cuarenta años; **at your earliest convenience** (COMM) con la mayor brevedad posible; **I can't come any earlier** no puedo llegar antes.

early retirement n jubilación f anticipada.

early warning system n sistema m de alerta inmediata.

earmark ['ɪəmɑːk] vt: **to** ~ **for** reservar para, destinar a.

earn [əːn] vt (gen) ganar; (interest) devengar; (praise) merecerse; **to** ~ **one's living** ganarse la vida.

earned income n renta del trabajo.

earnest ['əːnɪst] a serio, formal ◆ n (also: ~ **money**) anticipo, señal f; **in** ~ ad en serio.

earnings ['əːnɪŋz] npl (personal) sueldo sg, ingresos mpl; (of company etc) ganancias fpl.

earphones ['ɪəfəunz] npl auriculares mpl.

earplugs ['ɪəplʌgz] npl tapones mpl para los oídos.

earring ['ɪərɪŋ] n pendiente m, arete m.

earshot ['ɪəʃɔt] n: **out of/within** ~ fuera

del/al alcance del oído.

earth [ə:θ] n (gen) tierra; (Brit: ELEC) cable m de toma de tierra ◆ vt (Brit: ELEC) conectar a tierra.

earthenware ['ə:θnwɛə*] n loza (de barro).

earthly ['ə:θlı] a terrenal, mundano; ~ **paradise** paraíso terrenal; **there is no** ~ **reason to think** ... no existe razón para pensar ....

earthquake ['ə:θkweık] n terremoto.

earthworm ['ə:θwə:m] n lombriz f.

earthy ['ə:θı] a (fig: uncomplicated) sencillo; (: coarse) grosero.

earwig ['ıəwıg] n tijereta.

ease [i:z] n facilidad f; (comfort) comodidad f ◆ vt (task) facilitar; (pain) aliviar; (loosen) soltar; (relieve: pressure, tension) aflojar; (weight) aligerar; (help pass): **to** ~ **sth in/out** meter/sacar algo con cuidado ◆ vi (situation) relajarse; **with** ~ con facilidad; **to feel at** ~/**ill at** ~ sentirse a gusto/a disgusto; **at** ~! (MIL) ¡descansen!

ease off, ease up vi (work, business) aflojar; (person) relajarse.

easel ['i:zl] n caballete m.

easily ['i:zılı] ad fácilmente.

easiness ['i:zınıs] n facilidad f; (of manners) soltura.

east [i:st] n este m, oriente m ◆ a del este, oriental ◆ ad al este, hacia el este; **the E**~ el Oriente; (POL) el Este.

Easter ['i:stə*] n Pascua (de Resurrección).

Easter egg n huevo de Pascua.

Easter holidays npl Semana Santa sg.

Easter Island n Isla de Pascua.

easterly ['i:stəlı] a (to the east) al este; (from the east) del este.

Easter Monday n lunes m de Pascua.

eastern ['i:stən] a del este, oriental; **E**~ **Europe** Europa del Este; **the E**~ **bloc** (POL) el bloque del Este.

Easter Sunday n Domingo de Resurrección.

East Germany n Alemania Oriental.

eastward(s) ['i:stwəd(z)] ad hacia el este.

easy ['i:zı] a fácil; (simple) sencillo; (life) holgado, cómodo; (relaxed) natural ◆ ad: **to take it** or **things** ~ (not worry) no preocuparse; (go slowly) tomarlo con calma; (rest) descansar; **payment on** ~ **terms** (COMM) pago a plazos; **I'm** ~ (col) me da igual, no me importa; **easier said than done** del dicho al hecho hay buen trecho.

easy chair n sillón m.

easy-going ['i:zı'gəuıŋ] a acomodadizo.

eat, **pt ate, **pp** eaten** [i:t, eıt, 'i:tn] vt comer.

eat away vt (subj: sea) desgastar; (: acid) corroer.

eat into, eat away at vt fus corroer.

eat out vi comer fuera.

eat up vt (meal etc) comerse; **it** ~**s up electricity** devora la electricidad.

eatable ['i:təbl] a comestible.

eau de Cologne [əudəkə'ləun] n (agua de) Colonia.

eaves [i:vz] npl alero sg.

eavesdrop ['i:vzdrɔp] vi: **to** ~ **(on sb)** escuchar a escondidas (a uno).

ebb [ɛb] n reflujo ◆ vi bajar; (fig: also: ~ away) decaer; ~ **and flow** el flujo y reflujo; **to be at a low** ~ (fig: person) estar decaído; (: business) ir lento.

ebb tide n marea menguante.

ebony ['ɛbənı] n ébano.

ebullient [ı'bʌlıənt] a entusiasta, animado.

EC n abbr (= European Community) CE f.

eccentric [ık'sɛntrık] a, n excéntrico/a.

ecclesiastical [ıkli:zı'æstıkəl] a eclesiástico.

ECG n abbr (= electrocardiogram) E.C. m.

ECGD n abbr (= Export Credits Guarantee Department) servicio de garantía financiera a la exportación.

echo, **~es ['ɛkəu] n eco m ◆ vt (sound) repetir ◆ vi resonar, hacer eco.

éclair ['eıklɛə*] n relámpago, petisú m.

eclipse [ı'klıps] n eclipse m ◆ vt eclipsar.

ECM n abbr (US: = European Common Market) MCE m.

ecologist [ı'kɔlədʒıst] n ecologista m/f; (scientist) ecólogo/a m/f.

ecology [ı'kɔlədʒı] n ecología.

economic [i:kə'nɔmık] a (profitable: price) económico; (: business etc) rentable.

economical [i:kə'nɔmıkl] a económico.

economically [i:kə'nɔmıklı] ad económicamente.

economics [i:kə'nɔmıks] n economía ◆ npl (financial aspects) finanzas fpl.

economic warfare n guerra económica.

economist [ı'kɔnəmıst] n economista m/f.

economize [ı'kɔnəmaız] vi economizar, ahorrar.

economy [ı'kɔnəmı] n economía; **economies of scale** economías fpl de escala.

economy class n (AVIAT etc) clase f turista.

economy size n tamaño familiar.

ECSC n abbr (= European Coal & Steel Community) CECA f.

ecstasy ['ɛkstəsı] n éxtasis m inv.

ecstatic [ɛks'tætık] a extático.

ECT n abbr see **electroconvulsive therapy.**

ECU n abbr (= European Currency Unit) ECU m.

Ecuador ['ɛkwədɔ:*] n Ecuador m.

Ecuador(i)an [ɛkwə'dɔ:r(ı)ən] a, n ecuatoriano/a m/f.

ecumenical [i:kju'mɛnıkl] a ecuménico.

eczema ['ɛksımə] n eczema m.

eddy ['ɛdı] n remolino.

Eden ['i:dn] n Edén m.

edge [ɛdʒ] n (of knife etc) filo; (of object) borde m; (of lake etc) orilla ◆ vt (SEWING) ribetear ◆ *vi*: **to** ~ **past** pasar con dificultad; **on** ~ (*fig*) = **edgy**; **to** ~ **away from** alejarse poco a poco de; **to** ~ **forward** avanzar poco a poco; **to** ~ **up** subir lentamente.

edgeways ['edʒweɪz] *ad*: **he couldn't get a word in** ~ no pudo meter baza.

edging ['edʒɪŋ] *n* (*SEWING*) ribete *m*; (*of path*) borde *m*.

edgy ['edʒɪ] *a* nervioso, inquieto.

edible ['edɪbl] *a* comestible.

edict ['iːdɪkt] *n* edicto.

edifice ['edɪfɪs] *n* edificio.

edifying ['edɪfaɪɪŋ] *a* edificante.

Edinburgh ['edɪnbərə] *n* Edimburgo.

edit ['edɪt] *vt* (*be editor of*) dirigir; (*rewrite*) redactar; (*cut*) cortar; (*COMPUT*) editar.

edition [ɪ'dɪʃən] *n* (*gen*) edición *f*; (*number printed*) tirada.

editor ['edɪtə*] *n* (*of newspaper*) director(a) *m/f*; (*of book*) redactor(a) *m/f*; (*film* ~) montador(a) *m/f*.

editorial [edɪ'tɔːrɪəl] *a* editorial ◆ *n* editorial *m*; ~ **staff** redacción *f*.

EDP *n abbr* (= *electronic data processing*) TED *m*.

EDT *n abbr* (*US*: = *Eastern Daylight Time*) hora de verano de Nueva York.

educate ['edjukeɪt] *vt* (*gen*) educar; (*instruct*) instruir.

education [edju'keɪʃən] *n* educación *f*; (*schooling*) enseñanza; (*SCOL*: *subject etc*) pedagogía; **primary/secondary** ~ primera/segunda enseñanza.

educational [edju'keɪʃənl] *a* (*policy etc*) educacional; (*teaching*) docente; (*instructive*) educativo; ~ **technology** tecnología educacional.

Edwardian [ed'wɔːdɪən] *a* eduardiano.

E.E. *abbr* = **electrical engineer**.

EEC *n abbr* (= *European Economic Community*) CEE *f*.

EEG *n abbr see* **electroencephalogram**.

eel [iːl] *n* anguila.

EENT *n abbr* (*US MED*) = *eye, ear, nose and throat*.

EEOC *n abbr* (*US*: = *Equal Employment Opportunities Commission*) comisión que investiga discriminación racial o sexual en el empleo.

eerie ['ɪərɪ] *a* (*sound, experience*) espeluznante.

EET *n abbr* (= *Eastern European Time*) hora de Europa oriental.

efface [ɪ'feɪs] *vt* borrar.

effect [ɪ'fekt] *n* efecto ◆ *vt* efectuar, llevar a cabo; ~**s** *npl* (*property*) efectos *mpl*; **to take** ~ (*law*) entrar en vigor *or* vigencia; (*drug*) surtir efecto; **in** ~ en realidad; **to have an** ~ **on sb/sth** hacerle efecto a uno/afectar algo; **to put into** ~ (*plan*) llevar a la práctica; **his letter is to the** ~ **that**... su

carta especifica que....

effective [ɪ'fektɪv] *a* (*gen*) eficaz; (*striking*: *display, outfit*) impresionante; (*real*) efectivo; **to become** ~ (*LAW*) entrar en vigor; ~ **date** fecha de vigencia.

effectively [ɪ'fektɪvlɪ] *ad* (*efficiently*) eficazmente; (*strikingly*) de manera impresionante; (*in reality*) en efecto.

effectiveness [ɪ'fektɪvnɪs] *n* eficacia.

effeminate [ɪ'femɪnɪt] *a* afeminado.

effervescent [efə'vesnt] *a* efervescente.

efficacy ['efɪkəsɪ] *n* eficacia.

efficiency [ɪ'fɪʃənsɪ] *n* (*gen*) eficiencia; (*of machine*) rendimiento.

efficient [ɪ'fɪʃənt] *a* eficiente; (*remedy, product, system*) eficaz; (*machine, car*) de buen rendimiento.

effigy ['efɪdʒɪ] *n* efigie *f*.

effluent ['efluənt] *n* desperdicios *mpl* fluviales.

effort ['efət] *n* esfuerzo; **to make an** ~ **to do sth** esforzarse por hacer algo.

effortless ['efətlɪs] *a* sin ningún esfuerzo.

effrontery [ɪ'frʌntərɪ] *n* descaro.

effusive [ɪ'fjuːsɪv] *a* (*person, welcome, letter*) efusivo; (*thanks, apologies*) expansivo.

EFL *n abbr* (*SCOL*) = *English as a foreign language*.

EFTA ['eftə] *n abbr* (= *European Free Trade Association*) AELC *f*.

e.g. *ad abbr* (= *exempli gratia*) p.ej.

egg [eg] *n* huevo; **hard-boiled/soft-boiled/poached** ~ huevo duro/pasado por agua/escalfado; **scrambled** ~**s** huevos revueltos.

egg on *vt* incitar.

eggcup ['egkʌp] *n* huevera.

eggnog ['egnɔg] *n* ponche *m* de huevo.

eggplant ['egplɑːnt] *n* (*esp US*) berenjena.

eggshell ['egʃel] *n* cáscara de huevo.

egg white *n* clara de huevo.

egg yolk *n* yema de huevo.

ego ['iːgəu] *n* ego.

egotism ['egəutɪzəm] *n* egoísmo.

egotist ['egəutɪst] *n* egoísta *m/f*.

Egypt ['iːdʒɪpt] *n* Egipto.

Egyptian [ɪ'dʒɪpʃən] *a, n* egipcio/a *m/f*.

eiderdown ['aɪdədaun] *n* edredón *m*.

eight [eɪt] *num* ocho.

eighteen [eɪ'tiːn] *num* diez y ocho, dieciocho.

eighth [eɪtθ] *num* octavo.

eighty ['eɪtɪ] *num* ochenta.

Eire ['eərə] *n* Eire *m*.

EIS *n abbr* (= *Educational Institute of Scotland*) sindicato de profesores escoceses.

either ['aɪðə*] *a* cualquiera de los dos ...; (*both, each*) cada ◆ *pron*: ~ (**of them**) cualquiera (de los dos) ◆ *ad* tampoco ◆ *conj*: ~ **yes or no** o sí o no; **on** ~ **side** en ambos lados; **I don't like** ~ no me gusta ninguno de los dos; **no, I don't** ~ no, yo tampoco.

eject [ɪ'dʒɛkt] vt echar; (tenant) desahuciar ♦ vi eyectarse.

ejector seat [ɪ'dʒɛktə-] n asiento proyectable.

eke [iːk]: **to ~ out** vt (money) hacer que llegue.

EKG n abbr (US) see **electrocardiogram**.

el [ɛl] n abbr (US col) = **elevated railroad**.

elaborate a [ɪ'læbərɪt] (design) elaborado; (pattern) intrincado ♦ vb [ɪ'læbəreɪt] vt elaborar ♦ vi explicarse con muchos detalles.

elaborately [ɪ'læbərɪtlɪ] ad de manera complicada; (decorated) profusamente.

elaboration [ɪlæbə'reɪʃən] n elaboración f.

elapse [ɪ'læps] vi transcurrir.

elastic [ɪ'læstɪk] a, n elástico.

elastic band n (Brit) gomita.

elated [ɪ'leɪtɪd] a: **to be ~** regocijarse.

elation [ɪ'leɪʃən] n regocijo.

elbow ['ɛlbəu] n codo ♦ vt: **to ~ one's way through the crowd** abrirse paso a codazos por la muchedumbre.

elder ['ɛldə*] a mayor ♦ n (tree) saúco; (person) mayor; (of tribe) anciano.

elderly ['ɛldəlɪ] a de edad, mayor ♦ npl: **the ~** la gente mayor, los ancianos.

eldest ['ɛldɪst] a, n el/la mayor.

elect [ɪ'lɛkt] vt elegir; (choose): **to ~ to do** optar por hacer ♦ a: **the president ~** el presidente electo.

election [ɪ'lɛkʃən] n elección f; **to hold an ~** convocar elecciones.

election campaign n campaña electoral.

electioneering [ɪlɛkʃə'nɪərɪŋ] n campaña electoral.

elector [ɪ'lɛktə*] n elector(a) m/f.

electoral [ɪ'lɛktərəl] a electoral.

electoral college n colegio electoral.

electoral roll n censo electoral.

electorate [ɪ'lɛktərɪt] n electorado.

electric [ɪ'lɛktrɪk] a eléctrico.

electrical [ɪ'lɛktrɪkl] a eléctrico.

electrical engineer n ingeniero/a electricista.

electrical failure n fallo eléctrico.

electric blanket n manta eléctrica.

electric chair n silla eléctrica.

electric cooker n cocina eléctrica.

electric current n corriente f eléctrica.

electric fire n estufa eléctrica.

electrician [ɪlɛk'trɪʃən] n electricista m/f.

electricity [ɪlɛk'trɪsɪtɪ] n electricidad f; **to switch on/off the ~** conectar/desconectar la electricidad.

electricity board n (Brit) compañía eléctrica (estatal).

electric light n luz f eléctrica.

electric shock n choque m eléctrico.

electrification [ɪlɛktrɪfɪ'keɪʃən] n electrificación f.

electrify [ɪ'lɛktrɪfaɪ] vt (RAIL) electrificar; (fig: audience) electrizar.

electro... [ɪ'lɛktrəu] pref electro....

electrocardiogram (ECG, (US) EKG) [ɪ'lɛktrə'kɑːdɪəgræm] n electrocardiograma m.

electrocardiograph [ɪ'lɛktrəu'kɑːdɪəgræf] n electrocardiógrafo.

electro-convulsive therapy (ECT) [ɪ'lɛktrəkən'vʌlsɪv-] n electroterapia.

electrocute [ɪ'lɛktrəukjuːt] vt electrocutar.

electrode [ɪ'lɛktrəud] n electrodo.

electroencephalogram (EEG) [ɪ'lɛktrəuen'sɛfələgræm] n electroencefalograma m.

electrolysis [ɪlɛk'trɔlɪsɪs] n electrólisis f inv.

electromagnetic [ɪ'lɛktrəmæg'nɛtɪk] a electromagnético.

electron [ɪ'lɛktrɔn] n electrón m.

electronic [ɪlɛk'trɔnɪk] a electrónico.

electronic data processing (EDP) n tratamiento electrónico de datos.

electronic mail n correo electrónico.

electronics [ɪlɛk'trɔnɪks] n electrónica.

electron microscope n microscopio electrónico.

electroplated [ɪ'lɛktrə'pleɪtɪd] a galvanizado.

electrotherapy [ɪ'lɛktrə'θɛrəpɪ] n electroterapia.

elegance ['ɛlɪgəns] n elegancia.

elegant ['ɛlɪgənt] a elegante.

elegy ['ɛlɪdʒɪ] n elegía.

element ['ɛlɪmənt] n (gen) elemento; (of heater, kettle etc) resistencia.

elementary [ɛlɪ'mɛntərɪ] a elemental; (primitive) rudimentario; (school, education) primario.

elephant ['ɛlɪfənt] n elefante m.

elevate ['ɛlɪveɪt] vt (gen) elevar; (in rank) ascender.

elevated railroad n (US) ferrocarril m urbano elevado.

elevation [ɛlɪ'veɪʃən] n elevación f; (rank) ascenso; (height) altura.

elevator ['ɛlɪveɪtə*] n (US) ascensor m.

eleven [ɪ'lɛvn] num once.

elevenses [ɪ'lɛvnzɪz] npl (Brit) ≈ café m de media mañana.

eleventh [ɪ'lɛvnθ] a undécimo; **at the ~ hour** (fig) a última hora.

elf, pl **elves** [ɛlf, ɛlvz] n duende m.

elicit [ɪ'lɪsɪt] vt: **to ~ sth (from sb)** sacar(le) algo (a uno).

eligible ['ɛlɪdʒəbl] a elegible; **to be ~ for a pension** llenar los requisitos para una pensión.

eliminate [ɪ'lɪmɪneɪt] vt eliminar; (score out) suprimir; (a suspect, possibility) descartar.

elimination [ɪlɪmɪ'neɪʃən] n eliminación f; supresión f; **by process of ~** por proceso de eliminación.

elite [eɪ'liːt] n élite f.

elitist [eɪ'liːtɪst] a (pej) elitista.

elixir [ɪ'lɪksɪə*] n elixir m.
Elizabethan [ɪlɪzə'biːθən] a isabelino.
elm [ɛlm] n olmo.
elocution [ɛlə'kjuːʃən] n elocución f.
elongated ['iːlɔŋgeɪtɪd] a alargado, estirado.
elope [ɪ'ləup] vi fugarse para casarse.
elopement [ɪ'ləupmənt] n fuga.
eloquence ['ɛləkwəns] n elocuencia.
eloquent ['ɛləkwənt] a elocuente.
else [ɛls] ad: **or ~** si no; **something ~** otra cosa; **somewhere ~** en otra parte; **everywhere ~** en todas partes menos aquí; **everyone ~** todos los demás; **nothing ~** nada más; **is there anything ~ I can do?** ¿puedo hacer algo más?; **where ~?** ¿dónde más?, ¿en qué otra parte?; **there was little ~ to do** apenas quedaba otra cosa que hacer; **nobody ~ spoke** no habló nadie más.
elsewhere [ɛls'wɛə*] ad (be) en otra parte; (go) a otra parte.
ELT n abbr (SCOL) = English Language Teaching.
elucidate [ɪ'luːsɪdeɪt] vt aclarar, elucidar.
elude [ɪ'luːd] vt eludir; (blow, pursuer) esquivar.
elusive [ɪ'luːsɪv] a esquivo; (answer) difícil de encontrar; **he is very ~** no es fácil encontrarlo.
elves [ɛlvz] npl of elf.
emaciated [ɪ'meɪsɪeɪtɪd] a demacrado.
emanate ['ɛməneɪt] vi emanar, proceder.
emancipate [ɪ'mænsɪpeɪt] vt emancipar.
emancipated [ɪ'mænsɪpeɪtɪd] a liberado.
emancipation [ɪmænsɪ'peɪʃən] n emancipación f, liberación f.
emasculate [ɪ'mæskjuleɪt] vt castrar; (fig) incapacitar, debilitar.
embalm [ɪm'baːm] vt embalsamar.
embankment [ɪm'bæŋkmənt] n (of railway) terraplén m; (riverside) dique m.
embargo, pl **~es** [ɪm'baːgəu] n prohibición f; (COMM, NAUT) embargo; **to put an ~ on sth** embargar algo.
embark [ɪm'baːk] vi embarcarse ◆ vt embarcar; **to ~ on** (journey) comenzar, iniciar; (fig) emprender, lanzarse a.
embarkation [ɛmbaː'keɪʃən] n (people) embarco; (goods) embarque m.
embarkation card n tarjeta de embarque.
embarrass [ɪm'bærəs] vt avergonzar; (financially etc) poner en un aprieto.
embarrassed [ɪm'bærəst] a azorado; **to be ~** sentirse azorado or violento.
embarrassing [ɪm'bærəsɪŋ] a (situation) violento; (question) embarazoso.
embarrassment [ɪm'bærəsmənt] n desconcierto, azoramiento; (financial) apuros mpl.
embassy ['ɛmbəsɪ] n embajada; **the Spanish E~** la embajada española.
embed [ɪm'bɛd] vt (jewel) empotrar; (teeth

etc) clavar.
embellish [ɪm'bɛlɪʃ] vt embellecer; (fig: story, truth) adornar.
embers ['ɛmbəz] npl rescoldo sg, ascua sg.
embezzle [ɪm'bɛzl] vt desfalcar, malversar.
embezzlement [ɪm'bɛzlmənt] n desfalco, malversación f.
embezzler [ɪm'bɛzlə*] n malversador(a) m/f.
embitter [ɪm'bɪtə*] vt (person) amargar; (relationship) envenenar.
embittered [ɪm'bɪtəd] a resentido, amargado.
emblem ['ɛmbləm] n emblema m.
embody [ɪm'bɔdɪ] vt (spirit) encarnar; (ideas) expresar.
embolden [ɪm'bəuldən] vt envalentonar; (TYP) poner en negrita.
embolism ['ɛmbəlɪzəm] n embolia.
emboss [ɪm'bɔs] vt estampar en relieve; (metal, leather) repujar.
embossed [ɪm'bɔst] a realzado; **~ with ...** con ... en relieve.
embrace [ɪm'breɪs] vt abrazar, dar un abrazo a; (include) abarcar; (adopt: idea) adherirse a ◆ vi abrazarse ◆ n abrazo.
embroider [ɪm'brɔɪdə*] vt bordar; (fig: story) adornar, embellecer.
embroidery [ɪm'brɔɪdərɪ] n bordado.
embroil [ɪm'brɔɪl] vt: **to become ~ed (in sth)** enredarse (en algo).
embryo ['ɛmbrɪəu] n (also fig) embrión m.
emend [ɪ'mɛnd] vt (text) enmendar.
emerald ['ɛmərəld] n esmeralda.
emerge [ɪ'məːdʒ] vi (gen) salir; (arise) surgir; **it ~s that** resulta que.
emergence [ɪ'məːdʒəns] n (of nation) salida, surgimiento.
emergency [ɪ'məːdʒənsɪ] n (event) emergencia; (crisis) crisis f inv; **in an ~** en caso de urgencia; **(to declare a) state of ~** (declarar) estado de emergencia or de excepción.
emergency cord n (US) timbre m de alarma.
emergency exit n salida de emergencia.
emergency landing n aterrizaje m forzoso.
emergency lane n (US) andén m, arcén m.
emergency meeting n reunión f extraordinaria.
emergency service n servicio de urgencia or emergencia.
emergency stop n (AUT) parada en seco.
emergent [ɪ'məːdʒənt] a (nation) en vías de desarrollo.
emery board ['ɛmərɪ-] n lima de uñas.
emetic [ɪ'mɛtɪk] n emético.
emigrant ['ɛmɪgrənt] n emigrante m/f.
emigrate ['ɛmɪgreɪt] vi emigrar.
emigration [ɛmɪ'greɪʃən] n emigración f.
émigré ['ɛmɪgreɪ] n emigrado/a.

eminence ['ɛmɪnəns] *n* eminencia; **to gain** *or* **win** ~ ganarse fama.

eminent ['ɛmɪnənt] *a* eminente.

eminently ['ɛmɪnəntlɪ] *ad* eminentemente.

emirate ['ɛmɪrɪt] *n* emirato.

emission [ɪ'mɪʃən] *n* emisión *f*.

emit [ɪ'mɪt] *vt* emitir; (*smoke*) arrojar; (*smell*) despedir; (*sound*) producir.

emolument [ɪ'mɔljumənt] *n* (*often pl*: *formal*) honorario.

emotion [ɪ'məuʃən] *n* emoción *f*.

emotional [ɪ'məuʃənl] *a* (*person*) sentimental; (*scene*) conmovedor(a), emocionante.

emotionally [ɪ'məuʃnəlɪ] *ad* (*behave, speak*) con emoción; (*be involved*) sentimentalmente.

emotive [ɪ'məutɪv] *a* emotivo.

empathy ['ɛmpəθɪ] *n* empatía; **to feel** ~ **with sb** sentir empatía por uno.

emperor ['ɛmpərə*] *n* emperador *m*.

emphasis, *pl* **emphases** ['ɛmfəsɪs, -siːz] *n* énfasis *m inv*; **to lay** *or* **place** ~ **on sth** (*fig*) hacer hincapié en algo; **the** ~ **is on sport** se da mayor importancia al deporte.

emphasize ['ɛmfəsaɪz] *vt* (*word, point*) subrayar, recalcar; (*feature*) hacer resaltar.

emphatic [ɛm'fætɪk] *a* (*condemnation, denial*) enfático.

emphatically [ɛm'fætɪklɪ] *ad* con énfasis.

emphysema [ɛmfɪ'siːmə] *n* (MED) enfisema *m*.

empire ['ɛmpaɪə*] *n* imperio.

empirical [ɛm'pɪrɪkl] *a* empírico.

employ [ɪm'plɔɪ] *vt* (*give job to*) emplear; (*make use of*: *thing, method*) emplear, usar; **he's** ~**ed in a bank** está empleado en un banco.

employee [ɪmplɔɪ'iː] *n* empleado/a.

employer [ɪm'plɔɪə*] *n* patrón/ona *m/f*; (*businessman*) empresario/a.

employment [ɪm'plɔɪmənt] *n* (*gen*) empleo; (*work*) trabajo; **full** ~ pleno empleo; **without** ~ sin empleo; **to find** ~ encontrar trabajo; **place of** ~ lugar *m* de empleo.

employment agency *n* agencia de colocaciones.

employment exchange *n* bolsa de trabajo.

empower [ɪm'pauə*] *vt*: **to** ~ **sb to do sth** autorizar a uno para hacer algo.

empress ['ɛmprɪs] *n* emperatriz *f*.

emptiness ['ɛmptɪnɪs] *n* (*gen*) vacío; (*of life etc*) vaciedad *f*.

empty ['ɛmptɪ] *a* vacío; (*street, area*) desierto; (*house*) desocupado; (*threat*) vano ♦ *n* (*bottle*) envase *m* ♦ *vt* vaciar; (*place*) dejar vacío ♦ *vi* vaciarse; (*house*) quedar desocupado; (*place*) quedar desierto; **to** ~ **into** (*river*) desembocar en.

empty-handed ['ɛmptɪ'hændɪd] *a* con las manos vacías.

empty-headed ['ɛmptɪ'hɛdɪd] *a* casqui-

vano.

EMS *n abbr* (= *European Monetary System*) SME *m*.

EMT *n abbr* = *emergency medical technician*.

emulate ['ɛmjuleɪt] *vt* emular.

emulsion [ɪ'mʌlʃən] *n* emulsión *f*.

enable [ɪ'neɪbl] *vt*: **to** ~ **sb to do sth** (*allow*) permitir a uno hacer algo; (*prepare*) capacitar a uno para hacer algo.

enact [ɪn'ækt] *vt* (*law*) promulgar; (*play, scene*) representar; (*role*) hacer.

enamel [ɪ'næməl] *n* esmalte *m*.

enamel paint *n* esmalte *m*.

enamoured [ɪ'næməd] *a*: **to be** ~ **of** (*person*) estar enamorado de; (*activity etc*) tener gran afición a; (*idea*) aferrarse a.

encampment [ɪn'kæmpmənt] *n* campamento.

encase [ɪn'keɪs] *vt*: **to** ~ **in** (*contain*) encajar; (*cover*) cubrir.

encased [ɪn'keɪst] *a*: ~ **in** (*covered*) revestido de.

encash [ɪn'kæʃ] *vt* (*Brit*) cobrar.

enchant [ɪn'tʃɑːnt] *vt* encantar.

enchanting [ɪn'tʃɑːntɪŋ] *a* encantador(a).

encircle [ɪn'səːkl] *vt* (*gen*) rodear; (*waist*) ceñir.

encl. *abbr* (= *enclosed*) adj.

enclave ['ɛnkleɪv] *n* enclave *m*.

enclose [ɪn'kləuz] *vt* (*land*) cercar; (*with letter etc*) adjuntar; (*in receptacle*): **to** ~ (**with**) encerrar (con); **please find** ~**d** le mandamos adjunto.

enclosure [ɪn'kləuʒə*] *n* cercado, recinto; (COMM) carta adjunta.

encoder [ɪn'kəudə*] *n* (COMPUT) codificador *m*.

encompass [ɪn'kʌmpəs] *vt* abarcar.

encore [ɔŋ'kɔː*] *excl* ¡otra!, ¡bis! ♦ *n* bis *m*.

encounter [ɪn'kauntə*] *n* encuentro ♦ *vt* encontrar, encontrarse con; (*difficulty*) tropezar con.

encourage [ɪn'kʌrɪdʒ] *vt* alentar, animar; (*growth*) estimular; **to** ~ **sb** (**to do sth**) animar a uno (a hacer algo).

encouragement [ɪn'kʌrɪdʒmənt] *n* estímulo; (*of industry*) fomento.

encouraging [ɪn'kʌrɪdʒɪŋ] *a* alentador(a).

encroach [ɪn'krəutʃ] *vi*: **to** ~ (**up)on** (*gen*) invadir; (*time*) adueñarse de.

encrust [ɪn'krʌst] *vt* incrustar.

encrusted [ɪn'krʌstəd] *a*: ~ **with** incrustado de.

encumber [ɪn'kʌmbə*] *vt*: **to be** ~**ed with** (*carry*) estar cargado de; (*debts*) estar gravado de.

encyclop(a)edia [ɛnsaɪkləu'piːdɪə] *n* enciclopedia.

end [ɛnd] *n* (*gen, also aim*) fin *m*; (*of table*) extremo; (*of line, rope etc*) cabo; (*of pointed object*) punta; (*of town*) barrio; (*of street) final *m*; (*SPORT*) lado ♦ *vt* terminar, acabar; (*also*: **bring to an ~**, **put an ~ to**) acabar con ♦ *vi* terminar, acabar; **to ~ (with)** terminar (con); **in the ~** al fin, por fin, finalmente; **to be at an ~** llegar al final; **at the ~ of the day** (*fig*) al fin y al cabo, a fin de cuentas; **to this ~**, **with this ~ in view** con este propósito; **from ~ to ~** de punta a punta; **on ~** (*object*) de punta, de cabeza; **to stand on ~** (*hair*) erizarse; **for hours on ~** hora tras hora.

end up *vi*: **to ~ up in** terminar en; (*place*) ir a parar en.

endanger [ɪn'deɪndʒə*] *vt* poner en peligro; **an ~ed species** (*of animal*) una especie en peligro de extinción.

endear [ɪn'dɪə*] *vt*: **to ~ o.s. to sb** ganarse la simpatía de uno.

endearing [ɪn'dɪərɪŋ] *a* simpático, atractivo.

endearment [ɪn'dɪərmənt] *n* cariño, palabra cariñosa; **to whisper ~s** decir unas palabras cariñosas al oído; **term of ~** nombre *m* cariñoso.

endeavour, (*US*) **endeavor** [ɪn'devə*] *n* esfuerzo; (*attempt*) tentativa ♦ *vi*: **to ~ to do** esforzarse por hacer; (*try*) procurar hacer.

endemic [ɛn'demɪk] *a* (*poverty, disease*) endémico.

ending ['endɪŋ] *n* fin *m*, conclusión *f*; (*of book*) desenlace *m*; (*LING*) terminación *f*.

endive ['endaɪv] *n* (*curly*) escarola; (*smooth, flat*) endibia.

endless ['endlɪs] *a* interminable, inacabable; (*possibilities*) infinito.

endorse [ɪn'dɔːs] *vt* (*cheque*) endosar; (*approve*) aprobar.

endorsee [ɪndɔː'siː] *n* portador(a) *m/f* de un efecto.

endorsement [ɪn'dɔːsmənt] *n* (*approval*) aprobación *f*; (*signature*) endoso; (*Brit: on driving licence*) anotación *f* de una sanción.

endorser [ɪn'dɔːsə*] *n* avalista *m/f*.

endow [ɪn'dau] *vt* (*provide with money*) dotar; (*found*) fundar; **to be ~ed with** (*fig*) estar dotado de.

endowment [ɪn'daumənt] *n* (*amount*) donación *f*.

endowment assurance *n* seguro mixto.

end product *n* (*INDUSTRY*) producto final; (*fig*) resultado.

end result *n* resultado.

endurable [ɪn'djuərəbl] *a* soportable, tolerable.

endurance [ɪn'djuərəns] *n* resistencia.

endurance test *n* prueba de resistencia.

endure [ɪn'djuə*] *vt* (*bear*) aguantar, soportar; (*resist*) resistir ♦ *vi* (*last*) durar; (*resist*) resistir.

enduring [ɪn'djuərɪŋ] *a* duradero.

end user *n* (*COMPUT*) usuario final.

enema ['enɪmə] *n* (*MED*) enema.

enemy ['enəmɪ] *a*, *n* enemigo/a *m/f*; **to make an ~ of sb** enemistarse con uno.

energetic [enə'dʒetɪk] *a* enérgico.

energy ['enədʒɪ] *n* energía.

energy crisis *n* crisis *f* energética.

energy-saving ['enədʒɪseɪvɪŋ] *a* (*policy*) para ahorrar energía; (*device*) que ahorra energía ♦ *n* ahorro de energía.

enervating ['enəveɪtɪŋ] *a* deprimente.

enforce [ɪn'fɔːs] *vt* (*LAW*) hacer cumplir.

enforced [ɪn'fɔːst] *a* forzoso, forzado.

enfranchise [ɪn'fræntʃaɪz] *vt* (*give vote to*) conceder el derecho de voto a; (*set free*) emancipar.

engage [ɪn'geɪdʒ] *vt* (*attention*) llamar; (*in conversation*) abordar; (*worker, lawyer*) contratar; (*clutch*) embragar ♦ *vi* (*TECH*) engranar; **to ~ in** dedicarse a, ocuparse en; **to ~ sb in conversation** entablar conversación con uno.

engaged [ɪn'geɪdʒd] *a* (*Brit: busy, in use*) ocupado; (*betrothed*) prometido; **to get ~** prometerse; **he is ~ in research** se dedica a la investigación.

engaged tone *n* (*Brit TEL*) señal *f* de comunicando.

engagement [ɪn'geɪdʒmənt] *n* (*appointment*) compromiso, cita; (*battle*) combate *m*; (*to marry*) compromiso; (*period*) noviazgo; **I have a previous ~** ya tengo un compromiso.

engagement ring *n* anillo de pedida.

engaging [ɪn'geɪdʒɪŋ] *a* atractivo, simpático.

engender [ɪn'dʒendə*] *vt* engendrar.

engine ['endʒɪn] *n* (*AUT*) motor *m*; (*RAIL*) locomotora.

engine driver *n* (*Brit: of train*) maquinista *m/f*.

engineer [endʒɪ'nɪə*] *n* (*also for domestic appliances*) ingeniero/a; (*US RAIL*) maquinista *m/f*; **civil/mechanical ~** ingeniero/a de caminos, canales y puertos/industrial.

engineering [endʒɪ'nɪərɪŋ] *n* ingeniería ♦ *cpd* (*works, factory, worker etc*) de ingeniería.

engine failure, **engine trouble** *n* avería del motor.

England ['ɪŋglənd] *n* Inglaterra.

English ['ɪŋglɪʃ] *a* inglés/esa ♦ *n* (*LING*) el inglés; **the ~** *npl* los ingleses.

English Channel *n*: **the ~** el Canal de la Mancha.

Englishman ['ɪŋglɪʃmən], **Englishwoman** ['ɪŋglɪʃwumən] *n* inglés/esa *m/f*.

English-speaker ['ɪŋglɪʃspiːkə*] *n* persona de habla inglesa.

English-speaking ['ɪŋglɪʃspiːkɪŋ] *a* de habla inglesa.

engraving [ɪn'greɪvɪŋ] *n* grabado.

engrossed [ɪn'grəust] *a*: **~ in** absorto en.

engulf [ɪn'gʌlf] *vt* sumergir, hundir.

enhance [ɪn'hɑːns] *vt* (*gen*) aumentar;

(*beauty*) realzar; (*position, reputation*) mejorar.

enigma [ɪ'nɪgmə] *n* enigma *m*.

enigmatic [ɛnɪg'mætɪk] *a* enigmático.

enjoy [ɪn'dʒɔɪ] *vt* (*have: health, fortune*) disfrutar de, gozar de; (*food*) comer con gusto; **I ~ doing...** me gusta hacer...; **to ~ o.s.** divertirse, pasarlo bien.

enjoyable [ɪn'dʒɔɪəbl] *a* (*pleasant*) agradable; (*amusing*) divertido.

enjoyment [ɪn'dʒɔɪmənt] *n* (*use*) disfrute *m*; (*joy*) placer *m*.

enlarge [ɪn'lɑːdʒ] *vt* aumentar; (*broaden*) extender; (*PHOT*) ampliar ◆ *vi*: **to ~ on** (*subject*) tratar con más detalles.

enlarged [ɪn'lɑːdʒd] *a* (*edition*) aumentado; (*MED: organ, gland*) dilatado.

enlargement [ɪn'lɑːdʒmənt] *n* (*PHOT*) ampliación *f*.

enlighten [ɪn'laɪtn] *vt* (*inform*) informar.

enlightened [ɪn'laɪtnd] *a* iluminado; (*tolerant*) comprensivo.

enlightening [ɪn'laɪtnɪŋ] *a* informativo.

Enlightenment [ɪn'laɪtnmənt] *n* (*HISTORY*): **the ~** la Ilustración, el Siglo de las Luces.

enlist [ɪn'lɪst] *vt* alistar; (*support*) conseguir ◆ *vi* alistarse; **~ed man** (*US: MIL*) soldado raso.

enliven [ɪn'laɪvn] *vt* (*people*) animar; (*events*) avivar, animar.

enmity ['ɛnmɪtɪ] *n* enemistad *f*.

ennoble [ɪ'nəubl] *vt* ennoblecer.

enormity [ɪ'nɔːmɪtɪ] *n* enormidad *f*.

enormous [ɪ'nɔːməs] *a* enorme.

enough [ɪ'nʌf] *a*: **~ time/books** bastante tiempo/bastantes libros ◆ *n*: **have you got ~?** ¿tiene usted bastante? ◆ *ad*: **big ~** bastante grande; **he has not worked ~** no ha trabajado bastante; (**that's**) **~!** ¡basta ya!, ¡ya está bien!; **that's ~, thanks** con eso basta, gracias; **will 5 be ~?** ¿bastará con 5?; **I've had ~** estoy harto; **he was kind ~ to lend me the money** tuvo la bondad *or* amabilidad de prestarme el dinero; ... **which, funnily ~ ... ...** lo que, por extraño que parezca... .

enquire [ɪn'kwaɪə*] *vt*, *vi* = **inquire**.

enrage [ɪn'reɪdʒ] *vt* enfurecer.

enrich [ɪn'rɪtʃ] *vt* enriquecer.

enrol, (*US*) **enroll** [ɪn'rəul] *vt* (*members*) inscribir; (*SCOL*) matricular ◆ *vi* inscribirse; (*SCOL*) matricularse.

enrol(l)ment [ɪn'rəulmənt] *n* inscripción *f*; matriculación *f*.

en route [ɔn'ruːt] *ad* durante el viaje; **~ for/from/to** camino de/de/a.

ensconce [ɪn'skɔns] *vt*: **to ~ o.s.** instalarse cómodamente, acomodarse.

ensemble [ɔn'sɔmbl] *n* (*MUS*) conjunto *m*.

enshrine [ɪn'ʃraɪn] *vt* encerrar, englobar.

ensign [ɪn'ensaɪn] *n* (*flag*) bandera; (*NAUT*) alférez *m*.

enslave [ɪn'sleɪv] *vt* esclavizar.

ensue [ɪn'sjuː] *vi* seguirse; (*result*) resultar.

ensuing [ɪn'sjuːɪŋ] *a* (*subsequent*) siguiente; (*resulting*) consiguiente.

ensure [ɪn'ʃuə*] *vt* asegurar.

ENT *n abbr* (= *Ear, Nose and Throat*) otorrinolaringología.

entail [ɪn'teɪl] *vt* (*imply*) suponer; (*result in*) acarrear.

entangle [ɪn'tæŋgl] *vt* (*thread etc*) enredar, enmarañar; **to become ~d in sth** (*fig*) enmarañarse en algo.

entanglement [ɪn'tæŋglmənt] *n* enredo.

enter ['ɛntə*] *vt* (*room*) entrar en; (*club*) hacerse socio de; (*army, profession*) alistarse en; (*sb for a competition*) inscribir; (*write down*) anotar, apuntar; (*COMPUT*) introducir ◆ *vi* entrar; **to ~ for** *vt fus* presentarse para; **to ~ into** *vt fus* (*relations*) establecer; (*plans*) formar parte de; (*debate*) tomar parte en; (*negotiations*) entablar; (*agreement*) llegar a, firmar; **to ~ (up)on** *vt fus* (*career*) emprender.

enteritis [ɛntə'raɪtɪs] *n* enteritis *f*.

enterprise ['ɛntəpraɪz] *n* empresa; (*spirit*) iniciativa; **free ~** la libre empresa; **private ~** la iniciativa privada.

enterprising ['ɛntəpraɪzɪŋ] *a* emprendedor(a).

entertain [ɛntə'teɪn] *vt* (*amuse*) divertir; (*receive: guest*) recibir (en casa); (*idea*) abrigar.

entertainer [ɛntə'teɪnə*] *n* artista *m/f*.

entertaining [ɛntə'teɪnɪŋ] *a* divertido, entretenido ◆ *n*: **to do a lot of ~** dar muchas fiestas, tener muchos invitados.

entertainment [ɛntə'teɪnmənt] *n* (*amusement*) diversión *f*; (*show*) espectáculo *m*; (*party*) fiesta.

entertainment allowance *n* (*COMM*) gastos *mpl* de representación.

enthralled [ɪn'θrɔːld] *a* cautivado.

enthralling [ɪn'θrɔːlɪŋ] *a* cautivador(a).

enthuse [ɪn'θuːz] *vi*: **to ~ about** *or* **over** entusiasmarse por.

enthusiasm [ɪn'θuːzɪæzəm] *n* entusiasmo.

enthusiast [ɪn'θuːzɪæst] *n* entusiasta *m/f*.

enthusiastic [ɪnθuːzɪ'æstɪk] *a* entusiasta; **to be ~ about sb/sth** estar entusiasmado con uno/algo.

entice [ɪn'taɪs] *vt* tentar; (*seduce*) seducir.

entire [ɪn'taɪə*] *a* entero.

entirely [ɪn'taɪəlɪ] *ad* totalmente.

entirety [ɪn'taɪərətɪ] *n*: **in its ~** en su totalidad.

entitle [ɪn'taɪtl] *vt*: **to ~ sb to sth** dar a uno derecho a algo.

entitled [ɪn'taɪtld] *a* (*book*) que se titula; **to be ~ to sth/to do sth** tener derecho a algo/a hacer algo.

entity ['ɛntɪtɪ] *n* entidad *f*.

entourage [ɔntu'rɑːʒ] *n* séquito.

entrails ['ɛntreɪlz] *npl* entrañas *fpl*; (*US*) asadura *sg*, menudos *mpl*.

entrance ['ɛntrəns] *n* entrada ♦ *vt* [ɪn'trɑːns] encantar, hechizar; **to gain ~ to** (*university etc*) ingresar en.

entrance examination *n* (*to school*) examen *m* de ingreso.

entrance fee *n* cuota.

entrance ramp *n* (*US AUT*) rampa de acceso.

entrancing [ɪn'trɑːnsɪŋ] *a* encantador(a).

entrant ['ɛntrənt] *n* (*in race, competition*) participante *m/f*; (*in exam*) candidato/a.

entreat [ɛn'triːt] *vt* rogar, suplicar.

entrenched [ɛn'trɛntʃd] *a*: **~ interests** intereses *mpl* creados.

entrepreneur [ɔntrəprə'nəː*] *n* empresario/a, capitalista *m/f*.

entrepreneurial [ɔntrəprə'nəːrɪəl] *a* empresarial.

entrust [ɪn'trʌst] *vt*: **to ~ sth to sb** confiar algo a uno.

entry ['ɛntrɪ] *n* entrada; (*permission to enter*) acceso; (*in register, diary, ship's log*) apunte *m*; (*in account book, ledger, list*) partida; **no ~** prohibido el paso; (*AUT*) dirección prohibida; **single/double ~ bookkeeping** contabilidad *f* simple/por partida doble.

entry form *n* boleto de inscripción.

entry phone *n* (*Brit*) portero automático.

enumerate [ɪ'njuːməreɪt] *vt* enumerar.

enunciate [ɪ'nʌnsɪeɪt] *vt* pronunciar; (*principle etc*) enunciar.

envelop [ɪn'vɛləp] *vt* envolver.

envelope ['ɛnvələup] *n* sobre *m*.

enviable ['ɛnvɪəbl] *a* envidiable.

envious ['ɛnvɪəs] *a* envidioso; (*look*) de envidia.

environment [ɪn'vaɪərnmənt] *n* medio ambiente; **Department of the E~** ministerio del medio ambiente.

environmental [ɪnvaɪərn'mɛntl] *a* ambiental; **~ studies** (*in school etc*) ecología *sg*.

environmentalist [ɪnvaɪərn'mɛntlɪst] *n* ecologista *m/f*.

envisage [ɪn'vɪzɪdʒ] *vt* (*foresee*) prever; (*imagine*) concebir.

envision [ɪn'vɪʒən] *vt* imaginar.

envoy ['ɛnvɔɪ] *n* enviado.

envy ['ɛnvɪ] *n* envidia ♦ *vt* tener envidia a; **to ~ sb sth** envidiar algo a uno.

enzyme ['ɛnzaɪm] *n* enzima *f*.

EPA *n abbr* (*US*: = *Environmental Protection Agency*) *Agencia del Medio Ambiente*.

ephemeral [ɪ'fɛmərl] *a* efímero.

epic ['ɛpɪk] *n* épica ♦ *a* épico.

epicentre, (*US*) **epicenter** ['ɛpɪsɛntə*] *n* epicentro.

epidemic [ɛpɪ'dɛmɪk] *n* epidemia.

epigram ['ɛpɪgræm] *n* epigrama *m*.

epilepsy ['ɛpɪlɛpsɪ] *n* epilepsia.

epileptic [ɛpɪ'lɛptɪk] *a*, *n* epiléptico/a *m/f*.

epilogue ['ɛpɪlɔg] *n* epílogo.

episcopal [ɪ'pɪskəpl] *a* episcopal.

episode ['ɛpɪsəud] *n* episodio.

epistle [ɪ'pɪsl] *n* epístola.

epitaph ['ɛpɪtɑːf] *n* epitafio.

epithet ['ɛpɪθɛt] *n* epíteto.

epitome [ɪ'pɪtəmɪ] *n* epítome *m*.

epitomize [ɪ'pɪtəmaɪz] *vt* epitomar, resumir.

epoch ['iːpɔk] *n* época.

eponymous [ɪ'pɔnɪməs] *a* epónimo.

equable ['ɛkwəbl] *a* (*climate*) estable; (*character*) ecuánime.

equal ['iːkwl] *a* (*gen*) igual; (*treatment*) equitativo ♦ *n* igual *m/f* ♦ *vt* ser igual a; (*fig*) igualar; **to be ~ to** (*task*) estar a la altura de; **the E~ Opportunities Commission** (*Brit*) comisión para la igualdad de la mujer en el trabajo.

equality [iː'kwɔlɪtɪ] *n* igualdad *f*.

equalize ['iːkwəlaɪz] *vt*, *vi* igualar; (*SPORT*) empatar.

equalizer ['iːkwəlaɪzə*] *n* igualada.

equally ['iːkwəlɪ] *ad* igualmente; (*share etc*) a partes iguales; **they are ~ clever** son iguales de inteligente.

equals sign *n* signo de igualdad.

equanimity [ɛkwə'nɪmɪtɪ] *n* ecuanimidad *f*.

equate [ɪ'kweɪt] *vt*: **to ~ sth with** equiparar algo con.

equation [ɪ'kweɪʒən] *n* (*MATH*) ecuación *f*.

equator [ɪ'kweɪtə*] *n* ecuador *m*.

equatorial [ɛkwə'tɔːrɪəl] *a* ecuatorial.

Equatorial Guinea *n* Guinea Ecuatorial.

equestrian [ɪ'kwɛstrɪən] *a* ecuestre ♦ *n* caballista *m/f*, jinete/a *m/f*.

equilibrium [iːkwɪ'lɪbrɪəm] *n* equilibrio.

equinox ['iːkwɪnɔks] *n* equinoccio.

equip [ɪ'kwɪp] *vt* (*gen*) equipar; (*person*) proveer; **~ped with** (*machinery etc*) provisto de; **to be well ~ped** estar bien equipado; **he is well ~ped for the job** tiene las dotes necesarias para este puesto.

equipment [ɪ'kwɪpmənt] *n* equipo; (*tools*) avíos *mpl*.

equitable ['ɛkwɪtəbl] *a* equitativo.

equities ['ɛkwɪtɪz] *npl* (*Brit COMM*) derechos *mpl* sobre *or* en el activo.

equity ['ɛkwɪtɪ] *n* (*fairness*) equidad *f*; (*ECON*: *of debtor*) valor *m* líquido.

equity capital *n* capital *m* social *or* en acciones.

equivalent [ɪ'kwɪvəlnt] *a*, *n* equivalente *m*; **to be ~ to** equivaler a.

equivocal [ɪ'kwɪvəkl] *a* equívoco.

equivocate [ɪ'kwɪvəkeɪt] *vi* ser evasivo.

equivocation [ɪkwɪvə'keɪʃən] *n* evasión *f*, vacilación *f*.

ER *abbr* (*Brit*: = *Elizabeth Regina*) *la reina Isabel*.

ERA *n abbr* (*US POL*: = *Equal Rights Amendment*) *enmienda sobre la igualdad de derechos de la mujer*.

era ['ɪərə] *n* era, época.

eradicate [ɪ'rædɪkeɪt] *vt* erradicar, extirpar.
erase [ɪ'reɪz] *vt* (*also* COMPUT) borrar.
eraser [ɪ'reɪzə*] *n* goma de borrar.
erect [ɪ'rɛkt] *a* erguido ◆ *vt* erigir, levantar; (*assemble*) montar.
erection [ɪ'rɛkʃən] *n* (*of building*) construcción *f*; (*of machinery*) montaje *m*; (*structure*) edificio; (MED) erección *f*.
ergonomics [ɔ:gə'nɔmɪks] *n* ergonomía.
ERISA *n abbr* (US: = *Employee Retirement Income Security Act*) *ley que regula pensiones de jubilados*.
ermine ['ɔːmɪn] *n* armiño.
ERNIE ['ɔːnɪ] *n abbr* (*Brit*: = *Electronic Random Number Indicating Equipment*) *ordenador utilizado para sortear los bonos premiados*.
erode [ɪ'rəud] *vt* (GEO) erosionar; (*metal*) corroer, desgastar.
erosion [ɪ'rəuʒən] *n* erosión *f*; desgaste *m*.
erotic [ɪ'rɔtɪk] *a* erótico.
eroticism [ɪ'rɔtɪsɪzm] *n* erotismo.
err [ɔ:*] *vi* equivocarse; (REL) pecar.
errand ['ɛrnd] *n* recado, mandado (*LAm*); **to run ~s** hacer recados; **~ of mercy** acto caritativo.
errand boy *n* recadero.
erratic [ɪ'rætɪk] *a* variable; (*results etc*) desigual, poco uniforme.
erroneous [ɪ'rəunɪəs] *a* erróneo.
error ['ɛrə*] *n* error *m*, equivocación *f*; **typing/spelling ~** error *m* de mecanografía/ortografía; **in ~** por equivocación; **~s and omissions excepted** salvo error u omisión.
error message *n* (COMPUT) mensaje *m* de error.
erstwhile ['ɔːstwaɪl] *a* antiguo, previo.
erudite ['ɛrudaɪt] *a* erudito.
erudition [ɛru'dɪʃən] *n* erudición *f*.
erupt [ɪ'rʌpt] *vi* entrar en erupción; (MED) hacer erupción; (*fig*) estallar.
eruption [ɪ'rʌpʃən] *n* erupción *f*; (*fig*: *of anger, violence*)) explosión *f*, estallido.
ESA *n abbr* (= *European Space Agency*) Agencia Espacial Europea.
escalate ['ɛskəleɪt] *vi* extenderse, intensificarse; (*costs*) aumentar vertiginosamente.
escalation clause [ɛskə'leɪʃən-] *n* cláusula de reajuste de los precios.
escalator ['ɛskəleɪtə*] *n* escalera móvil.
escapade [ɛskə'peɪd] *n* travesura.
escape [ɪ'skeɪp] *n* (*gen*) fuga; (*from duties*) escapatoria; (*from chase*) evasión *f* ◆ *vi* (*gen*) escaparse; (*flee*) huir, evadirse; (*leak*) fugarse ◆ *vt* evitar, eludir; (*consequences*) escapar a; **to ~ from** (*place*) escaparse de; (*person*) escaparse a; (*clutches*) librarse de; **to ~ to** (*another place, freedom, safety*) huirse a; **to ~ notice** pasar desapercibido.
escape artist *n* escapólogo/a.

escape clause *n* (*fig*: *in agreement*) cláusula de excepción.
escape hatch *n* (*in submarine, space rocket*) escotilla de salvamento.
escape key *n* (COMPUT) tecla de escape.
escape route *n* ruta de escape.
escapism [ɪ'skeɪpɪzəm] *n* escapismo.
escapist [ɪ'skeɪpɪst] *a, n* escapista *m/f*.
escapologist [ɛskə'pɔlədʒɪst] *n* (*Brit*) = **escape artist**.
escarpment [ɪ'skɑːpmənt] *n* escarpa.
eschew [ɪs'tʃuː] *vt* evitar, abstenerse de.
escort ['ɛskɔːt] *n* acompañante *m/f*; (MIL) escolta; (NAUT) convoy *m* ◆ *vt* [ɪ'skɔːt] acompañar; (MIL, NAUT) escoltar.
escort agency *n* servicio de azafatas.
Eskimo ['ɛskɪməu] *a* esquimal ◆ *n* esquimal *m/f*; (LING) esquimal *m*.
ESL *n abbr* (SCOL) = *English as a Second Language*.
esophagus [iː'sɔfəgəs] *n* (US) = **oesophagus**.
esoteric [ɛsəu'tɛrɪk] *a* esotérico.
ESP *n abbr see* **extrasensory perception.**
esp. *abbr* = **especially.**
especially [ɪ'spɛʃlɪ] *ad* (*gen*) especialmente; (*above all*) sobre todo; (*particularly*) en particular.
espionage ['ɛspɪɒnɑːʒ] *n* espionaje *m*.
esplanade [ɛsplə'neɪd] *n* (*by sea*) paseo marítimo.
espouse [ɪ'spauz] *vt* adherirse a.
Esq. *abbr* (= *Esquire*) D.
Esquire [ɪ'skwaɪə*] *n*: J. Brown, **~** Sr. D. J. Brown.
essay ['ɛseɪ] *n* (SCOL) ensayo.
essayist ['ɛseɪɪst] *n* ensayista *m/f*.
essence ['ɛsns] *n* esencia; **in ~** en lo esencial; **speed is of the ~** es esencial hacerlo con la mayor prontitud.
essential [ɪ'sɛnʃl] *a* (*necessary*) imprescindible; (*basic*) esencial ◆ *n* (*often pl*) lo esencial; **it is ~ that** es imprescindible que.
essentially [ɪ'sɛnʃlɪ] *ad* esencialmente.
EST *n abbr* (US: = *Eastern Standard Time*) *hora de invierno de Nueva York.*
est. *abbr* (= *established*) fundado; (= *estimated*) aprox.
establish [ɪ'stæblɪʃ] *vt* establecer; (*prove: fact, identity*) comprobar, verificar; (*prove*) demostrar; (*relations*) entablar.
established [ɪ'stæblɪʃt] *a* (*business*) de buena reputación; (*staff*) de plantilla.
establishment [ɪ'stæblɪʃmənt] *n* (*also business*) establecimiento; **the E~** la clase dirigente; **a teaching ~** un centro de enseñanza.
estate [ɪ'steɪt] *n* (*land*) finca, hacienda; (*property*) propiedad *f*; (*inheritance*) herencia; (POL) estado; **housing ~** (*Brit*) urbanización *f*; **industrial ~** polígono industrial.

estate agency n (Brit) agencia inmobiliaria.

estate agent n (Brit) agente m/f inmobiliario/a.

estate car n (Brit) furgoneta.

esteem [ɪs'tiːm] n: **to hold sb in high** ~ estimar en mucho a uno ♦ vt estimar.

esthetic [iːs'θetɪk] a (US) = **aesthetic**.

estimate ['estɪmət] n estimación f, apreciación f; (assessment) tasa, cálculo; (COMM) presupuesto ♦ vt ['estɪmeɪt] estimar; tasar, calcular; **to give sb an** ~ **of** presentar a uno un presupuesto de; **at a rough** ~ haciendo un cálculo aproximado; **to** ~ **for** (COMM) hacer un presupuesto de.

estimation [estɪ'meɪʃən] n opinión f, juicio; (esteem) aprecio; **in my** ~ según mis cálculos.

estimator ['estɪmeɪtə*] n estimador(a) m/f.

Estonia [ɛ'stəunɪə] n Estonia.

estranged [ɪ'streɪndʒd] a separado.

estrangement [ɪ'streɪndʒmənt] n alejamiento, distanciamiento.

estrogen ['iːstrəudʒən] n (US) = **oestrogen**.

estuary ['estjuərɪ] n estuario, ría.

et al. abbr (= et alii: and others) et al.

etc abbr (= et cetera) etc.

etch [etʃ] vt grabar al aguafuerte.

etching ['etʃɪŋ] n aguafuerte m or f.

ETD n abbr (= estimated time of departure).

eternal [ɪ'təːnl] a eterno.

eternity [ɪ'təːnɪtɪ] n eternidad f.

ether ['iːθə*] n éter m.

ethereal [ɪ'θɪərɪəl] a etéreo.

ethical ['εθɪkl] a ético; (honest) honrado.

ethics ['εθɪks] n ética ♦ npl moralidad f.

Ethiopia [iːθɪ'əupɪə] n Etiopía.

Ethiopian [iːθɪ'əupɪən] a, n etíope m/f.

ethnic ['εθnɪk] a étnico.

ethos ['iːθɔs] n (of culture, group) sistema m de valores.

etiquette ['etɪket] n etiqueta.

ETU n abbr (= Electrical Trades Union) sindicato de electricistas.

ETV n abbr (US: = Educational Television) televisión f escolar.

etymology [etɪ'mɔlədʒɪ] n etimología.

eucalyptus [juːkə'lɪptəs] n eucalipto.

Eucharist ['juːkərɪst] n Eucaristía.

eulogy ['juːlədʒɪ] n elogio, encomio.

eunuch ['juːnək] n eunuco.

euphemism ['juːfəmɪzm] n eufemismo.

euphemistic [juːfə'mɪstɪk] a eufemístico.

euphoria [juː'fɔːrɪə] n euforia.

Eurasia [juə'reɪʃə] n Eurasia.

Eurasian [juə'reɪʃən] a, n eurasiático/a m/f.

Euratom [juə'rætəm] n abbr (= European Atomic Energy Commission) Euratom m.

Eurocheque ['juərəutʃek] n Eurocheque m.

Eurocrat ['juərəukræt] n eurócrata m/f.

Eurodollar ['juərəudɔlə*] n eurodólar m.

Europe ['juərəp] n Europa.

European [juərə'piːən] a, n europeo/a m/f.

European Court of Justice n Tribunal m de Justicia de las Comunidades Europeas.

European Economic Community n Comunidad f Económica Europea.

euthanasia [juːθə'neɪzɪə] n eutanasia.

evacuate [ɪ'vækjueɪt] vt desocupar.

evacuation [ɪvækju'eɪʃən] n evacuación f.

evade [ɪ'veɪd] vt evadir, eludir.

evaluate [ɪ'væljueɪt] vt evaluar; (value) tasar; (evidence) interpretar.

evangelical [iːvæn'dʒelɪkəl] a evangélico.

evangelist [ɪ'vændʒəlɪst] n evangelista m; (preacher) evangelizador(a) m/f.

evaporate [ɪ'væpəreɪt] vi evaporarse; (fig) desvanecerse ♦ vt evaporar.

evaporated milk [ɪ'væpəreɪtɪd-] n leche f evaporada.

evaporation [ɪvæpə'reɪʃən] n evaporación f.

evasion [ɪ'veɪʒən] n evasiva, evasión f.

evasive [ɪ'veɪsɪv] a evasivo.

eve [iːv] n: **on the** ~ **of** en vísperas de.

even ['iːvn] a (level) llano; (smooth) liso; (speed, temperature) uniforme; (number) par; (SPORT) igual(es) ♦ ad hasta, incluso; ~ **if**, ~ **though** aunque + subjun; ~ **more** aun más; ~ **so** aun así; **not** ~ ni siquiera; ~ **he was there** hasta él estuvo allí; ~ **on Sundays** incluso los domingos; ~ **faster** aún más rápido; **to break** ~ cubrir los gastos; **to get** ~ **with sb** ajustar cuentas con uno; **to** ~ **out** vi nivelarse.

evening ['iːvnɪŋ] n tarde f; (dusk) atardecer m; (night) noche f; **in the** ~ por la tarde; **this** ~ esta tarde or noche; **tomorrow/yesterday** ~ mañana/ayer por la tarde or noche.

evening class n clase f nocturna.

evening dress n (man's) traje m de etiqueta; (woman's) traje m de noche.

evenly ['iːvnlɪ] ad (distribute, space, spread) con igualdad, igualmente; (divide) equitativamente.

evensong ['iːvnsɔŋ] n vísperas fpl.

event [ɪ'vent] n suceso, acontecimiento; (SPORT) prueba; **in the** ~ **of** en caso de; **in the** ~ en realidad; **in the course of** ~s en el curso de los acontecimientos; **at all** ~s, **in any** ~ pase lo que pase.

eventful [ɪ'ventful] a accidentado; (game etc) lleno de emoción.

eventing [ɪ'ventɪŋ] n (HORSERIDING) competición f.

eventual [ɪ'ventʃuəl] a final.

eventuality [ɪventʃu'ælɪtɪ] n eventualidad f.

eventually [ɪ'ventʃuəlɪ] ad (finally) finalmente; (in time) a la larga.

ever ['evə*] ad nunca, jamás; (at all times) siempre; **for** ~ (para) siempre; **the best** ~ lo nunca visto; **did you** ~ **meet him?** ¿llegaste a conocerle?; **have you** ~ **been there?** ¿has estado allí alguna vez?; **have**

you ~ **seen** it? ¿lo ha visto usted alguna vez?; **better than** ~ mejor que nunca; **thank you** ~ **so much** muchísimas gracias; **yours** ~ (in letters) un abrazo de; ~ **since** ad desde entonces ♦ conj después de que.

Everest ['ɛvərɪst] n (also: **Mount** ~) Everest m.

evergreen ['ɛvəgriːn] n árbol m de hoja perenne.

everlasting [ɛvə'lɑːstɪŋ] a eterno, perpetuo.

every ['ɛvrɪ] a (each) cada; (all) todo; ~ **day** cada día; ~ **other car** cada dos coches; ~ **now and then** de vez en cuando; **I have** ~ **confidence in him** confío completamente en él.

everybody ['ɛvrɪbɔdɪ] pron todos pl, todo el mundo; ~ **knows about it** todo el mundo lo sabe; ~ **else** todos los demás.

everyday ['ɛvrɪdeɪ] a (daily: use, occurrence, experience) diario, cotidiano; (usual: expression) corriente; (common) vulgar; (routine) rutinario.

everyone ['ɛvrɪwʌn] = **everybody**.

everything ['ɛvrɪθɪŋ] pron todo; ~ **is ready** todo está dispuesto; **he did** ~ **possible** hizo todo lo posible.

everywhere ['ɛvrɪwɛə*] ad (be) en todas partes; (go) a or por todas partes; ~ **you go you meet...** en todas partes encontrarás....

evict [ɪ'vɪkt] vt desahuciar.

eviction [ɪ'vɪkʃən] n desahucio.

eviction notice n orden f de desahucio or desalojo (LAm).

evidence ['ɛvɪdəns] n (proof) prueba; (of witness) testimonio; (facts) datos mpl, hechos mpl; **to give** ~ prestar declaración, dar testimonio.

evident ['ɛvɪdənt] a evidente, manifiesto.

evidently ['ɛvɪdəntlɪ] ad naturalmente.

evil ['iːvl] a malo; (influence) funesto; (smell) horrible ♦ n mal m, maldad f.

evildoer ['iːvlduːə*] n malhechor(a) m/f.

evince [ɪ'vɪns] vt mostrar, dar señales de.

evocative [ɪ'vɔkətɪv] a sugestivo, evocador(a).

evoke [ɪ'vəuk] vt evocar; (admiration) provocar.

evolution [iːvə'luːʃən] n evolución f, desarrollo.

evolve [ɪ'vɔlv] vt desarrollar ♦ vi evolucionar, desarrollarse.

ewe [juː] n oveja.

ex- [ɛks] pref (former: husband, president etc) ex-; (out of): **the price** ~ **works** precio de fábrica.

exacerbate [ɛk'sæsəbeɪt] vt (pain, disease) exacerbar; (fig: relations, situation) empeorar.

exact [ɪg'zækt] a exacto ♦ vt: **to** ~ **sth (from)** exigir algo (de).

exacting [ɪg'zæktɪŋ] a exigente; (condi-

tions) arduo.

exactitude [ɪg'zæktɪtjuːd] n exactitud f.

exactly [ɪg'zæktlɪ] ad exactamente; (time) en punto; ~**!** ¡exactamente!

exactness [ɪg'zæktnɪs] n exactitud f.

exaggerate [ɪg'zædʒəreɪt] vt, vi exagerar.

exaggerated [ɪg'zædʒəreɪtɪd] a exagerado.

exaggeration [ɪgzædʒə'reɪʃən] n exageración f.

exalt [ɪg'zɔːlt] vt (praise) ensalzar; (elevate) elevar, exaltar.

exalted [ɪg'zɔːltɪd] a (position) exaltado; (elated) excitado.

exam [ɪg'zæm] n abbr (SCOL) = **examination**.

examination [ɪgzæmɪ'neɪʃən] n (gen) examen m; (LAW) interrogación f; (inquiry) investigación f; **to take** or **sit an** ~ hacer un examen; **the matter is under** ~ se está examinando el asunto.

examine [ɪg'zæmɪn] vt (gen) examinar; (inspect: machine, premises) inspeccionar; (SCOL, LAW: person) interrogar; (at customs: luggage, passport) registrar; (MED) hacer un reconocimiento médico de.

examiner [ɪg'zæmɪnə*] n inspector(a) m/f.

example [ɪg'zɑːmpl] n ejemplo; **for** ~ por ejemplo; **to set a good/bad** ~ dar buen/mal ejemplo.

exasperate [ɪg'zɑːspəreɪt] vt exasperar, irritar; ~**d by** or **at** or **with** exasperado por or con.

exasperating [ɪg'zɑːspəreɪtɪŋ] a irritante.

exasperation [ɪgzɑːspə'reɪʃən] n exasperación f, irritación f.

excavate ['ɛkskəveɪt] vt excavar.

excavation [ɛkskə'veɪʃən] n excavación f.

excavator ['ɛkskəveɪtə*] n excavadora.

exceed [ɪk'siːd] vt exceder; (number) pasar de; (speed limit) sobrepasar; (limits) rebasar; (powers) excederse en; (hopes) superar.

exceedingly [ɪk'siːdɪŋlɪ] ad sumamente, sobremanera.

excel [ɪk'sɛl] vi sobresalir; **to** ~ **o.s.** lucirse.

excellence ['ɛksələns] n excelencia.

Excellency ['ɛksələnsɪ] n: **His** ~ Su Excelencia.

excellent ['ɛksələnt] a excelente.

except [ɪk'sɛpt] prep (also: ~ **for**, ~**ing**) excepto, salvo ♦ vt exceptuar, excluir; ~ **if/when** excepto si/cuando; ~ **that** salvo que.

exception [ɪk'sɛpʃən] n excepción f; **to take** ~ **to** ofenderse por; **with the** ~ **of** a excepción de; **to make an** ~ hacer una excepción.

exceptional [ɪk'sɛpʃənl] a excepcional.

excerpt ['ɛksəːpt] n extracto.

excess [ɪk'sɛs] n exceso; **in** ~ **of** superior a; see also **excesses**.

excess baggage n exceso de equipaje.

excesses npl excesos mpl.

excess fare n suplemento.

excessive [ɪk'sɛsɪv] a excesivo.
excess supply n oferta excedentaria.
excess weight n exceso de peso.
exchange [ɪks'tʃeɪndʒ] n cambio; (of goods) canje m; (of ideas) intercambio; (also: **telephone** ~) central f (telefónica) ◆ vt: **to** ~ **(for)** cambiar (por); **in** ~ **for** a cambio de; **foreign** ~ (COMM) divisas fpl.
exchange control n control m de cambios.
exchange rate n tipo de cambio.
exchequer [ɪks'tʃɛkə*] n: **the** ~ (Brit) la Hacienda del Fisco.
excisable [ɛk'saɪzəbl] a taxable.
excise ['ɛksaɪz] n impuestos mpl sobre el comercio exterior.
excitable [ɪk'saɪtəbl] a exaltado.
excite [ɪk'saɪt] vt (stimulate) estimular; (anger) provocar; (move) entusiasmar; **to get** ~**d** emocionarse.
excitement [ɪk'saɪtmənt] n emoción f.
exciting [ɪk'saɪtɪŋ] a emocionante.
excl. abbr = **excluding, exclusive (of).**
exclaim [ɪk'skleɪm] vi exclamar.
exclamation [ɛksklə'meɪʃən] n exclamación f.
exclamation mark n punto de admiración.
exclude [ɪk'sklu:d] vt excluir; (except) exceptuar.
excluding [ɪks'klu:dɪŋ] prep: ~ **VAT** IVA no incluido.
exclusion [ɪk'sklu:ʒən] n exclusión f; **to the** ~ **of** con exclusión de.
exclusion clause n cláusula de exclusión.
exclusive [ɪk'sklu:sɪv] a exclusivo; (club, district) selecto; ~ **of tax** excluyendo impuestos; ~ **of postage/service** franqueo/servicio no incluido; **from 1st to 13th March** ~ del 1 al 13 de marzo exclusive.
exclusively [ɪk'sklu:sɪvlɪ] ad únicamente.
excommunicate [ɛkskə'mju:nɪkeɪt] vt excomulgar.
excrement ['ɛkskrəmənt] n excremento.
excrete [ɪk'skri:t] vi excretar.
excruciating [ɪk'skru:ʃɪeɪtɪŋ] a (pain) agudísimo, atroz.
excursion [ɪk'skɜ:ʃən] n excursión f.
excursion ticket n billete m de excursión.
excusable [ɪk'skju:səbl] a perdonable.
excuse n [ɪk'skju:s] disculpa, excusa; (evasion) pretexto ◆ vt [ɪk'skju:z] disculpar, perdonar; (justify) justificar; **to make** ~**s for sb** presentar disculpas por uno; **to** ~ **sb from doing sth** dispensar a uno de hacer algo; **to** ~ **o.s. (for (doing) sth)** pedir disculpas a uno (por (hacer) algo); ~ **me!** ¡perdón!; **if you will** ~ **me** con su permiso.
ex-directory ['ɛksdɪ'rɛktərɪ] a (Brit): ~ **(phone) number** número que no consta en la guía.
execrable ['ɛksɪkrəbl] a execrable, abominable; (manners) detestable.

execute ['ɛksɪkju:t] vt (plan) realizar; (order) cumplir; (person) ajusticiar, ejecutar.
execution [ɛksɪ'kju:ʃən] n realización f; cumplimiento; ejecución f.
executioner [ɛksɪ'kju:ʃənə*] n verdugo.
executive [ɪg'zɛkjutɪv] n (COMM) ejecutivo; (POL) poder m ejecutivo ◆ a (secretary, car, plane) ejecutivo; (offices, suite) de los ejecutivos; (position, job, duties) de ejecutivo.
executive director n director(a) m/f ejecutivo/a.
executor [ɪg'zɛkjutə*] n albacea m, testamentario.
exemplary [ɪg'zɛmplərɪ] a ejemplar.
exemplify [ɪg'zɛmplɪfaɪ] vt ejemplificar.
exempt [ɪg'zɛmpt] a: ~ **from** exento de ◆ vt: **to** ~ **sb from** eximir a uno de.
exemption [ɪg'zɛmpʃən] n exención f; (immunity) inmunidad f.
exercise ['ɛksəsaɪz] n ejercicio ◆ vt ejercer; (right) valerse de; (dog) llevar de paseo ◆ vi hacer ejercicio(s).
exercise book n cuaderno.
exert [ɪg'zɜ:t] vt ejercer; (strength, force) emplear; **to** ~ **o.s.** esforzarse.
exertion [ɪg'zɜ:ʃən] n esfuerzo.
exfoliant [ɛks'fəulɪənt] n exfoliante m.
ex gratia ['ɛks'greɪʃə] a: ~ **payment** pago a título gracioso.
exhale [ɛks'heɪl] vt despedir ◆ vi espirar, exhalar.
exhaust [ɪg'zɔ:st] n (pipe) escape m; (fumes) gases mpl de escape ◆ vt agotar; **to** ~ **o.s.** agotarse.
exhausted [ɪg'zɔ:stɪd] a agotado.
exhausting [ɪg'zɔ:stɪŋ] a: **an** ~ **journey/day** un viaje/día agotador.
exhaustion [ɪg'zɔ:stʃən] n agotamiento; **nervous** ~ postración f nerviosa.
exhaustive [ɪg'zɔ:stɪv] a exhaustivo.
exhibit [ɪg'zɪbɪt] n (ART) obra expuesta; (LAW) objeto expuesto ◆ vt (show: emotions) manifestar; (: courage, skill) demostrar; (paintings) exponer.
exhibition [ɛksɪ'bɪʃən] n exposición f.
exhibitionist [ɛksɪ'bɪʃənɪst] n exhibicionista m/f.
exhibitor [ɪg'zɪbɪtə*] n expositor(a) m/f.
exhilarating [ɪg'zɪləreɪtɪŋ] a estimulante, tónico.
exhilaration [ɪgzɪlə'reɪʃən] n júbilo.
exhort [ɪg'zɔ:t] vt exhortar.
exile ['ɛksaɪl] n exilio; (person) exiliado/a ◆ vt desterrar, exiliar.
exist [ɪg'zɪst] vi existir.
existence [ɪg'zɪstəns] n existencia.
existentialism [ɛgzɪs'tɛnʃəlɪzəm] n existencialismo.
existing [ɪg'zɪstɪŋ] a existente, actual.
exit ['ɛksɪt] n salida ◆ vi (THEATRE) hacer mutis; (COMPUT) salir (al sistema).
exit ramp n (US AUT) vía de acceso.

exit visa *n* visado de salida.

exodus ['ɛksədəs] *n* éxodo.

ex officio ['ɛksə'fɪʃɪəu] *a, ad* ex oficio.

exonerate [ɪg'zɔnəreɪt] *vt*: **to ~ from** exculpar de.

exorbitant [ɪg'zɔːbɪtənt] *a (price, demands)* exorbitante, excesivo.

exorcize ['ɛksɔːsaɪz] *vt* exorcizar.

exotic [ɪg'zɔtɪk] *a* exótico.

expand [ɪk'spænd] *vt* ampliar; *(number)* aumentar ♦ *vi (trade etc)* expandirse; *(gas, metal)* dilatarse; **to ~ on** *(notes, story etc)* ampliar.

expanse [ɪk'spæns] *n* extensión *f*.

expansion [ɪk'spænʃən] *n* ampliación *f*; aumento; *(of trade)* expansión *f*.

expansionism [ɪk'spænʃənɪzəm] *n* expansionismo.

expansionist [ɪk'spænʃənɪst] *a* expansionista.

expatriate [ɛks'pætrɪət] *n* expatriado/a.

expect [ɪk'spɛkt] *vt (gen)* esperar; *(count on) (suppose)* suponer ♦ *vi*: **to be ~ing** estar encinta; **to ~ to do sth** esperar hacer algo; **as ~ed** como era de esperar; **I ~ so** supongo que sí.

expectancy [ɪk'spɛktənsɪ] *n (anticipation)* esperanza; **life ~** esperanza de vida.

expectantly [ɪk'spɛktəntlɪ] *ad (look, listen)* con expectación.

expectant mother [ɪk'spɛktənt-] *n* futura madre *f*.

expectation [ɛkspɛk'teɪʃən] *n* esperanza, expectativa; **in ~ of** en espera de; **against** *or* **contrary to all ~(s)** en contra de todas las previsiones; **to come** *or* **live up to sb's ~s** resultar tan bueno como se esperaba; **to fall short of sb's ~s** no cumplir las esperanzas de uno, decepcionar a uno.

expedience [ɪk'spiːdɪəns], **expediency** [ɪk'spiːdɪənsɪ] *n* conveniencia.

expedient [ɪk'spiːdɪənt] *a* conveniente, oportuno ♦ *n* recurso, expediente *m*.

expedite ['ɛkspɪdaɪt] *vt (speed up)* acelerar; *(: progress)* facilitar.

expedition [ɛkspə'dɪʃən] *n* expedición *f*.

expeditionary force [ɛkspə'dɪʃnrɪ-] *n* cuerpo expedicionario.

expel [ɪk'spɛl] *vt* arrojar; *(scol)* expulsar.

expend [ɪk'spɛnd] *vt* gastar; *(use up)* consumir.

expendable [ɪk'spɛndəbl] *a* prescindible.

expenditure [ɪk'spɛndɪtʃə*] *n* gastos *mpl*, desembolso; *(of time, effort)* gasto.

expense [ɪk'spɛns] *n* gasto, gastos *mpl*; *(high cost)* costa; **~s** *npl (COMM)* gastos *mpl*; **at the ~ of** a costa de; **to meet the ~ of** hacer frente a los gastos de.

expense account *n* cuenta de gastos.

expensive [ɪk'spɛnsɪv] *a* caro, costoso.

experience [ɪk'spɪərɪəns] *n* experiencia ♦ *vt* experimentar; *(suffer)* sufrir; **to learn by ~** aprender por experiencia.

experienced [ɪk'spɪərɪənst] *a* experimentado.

experiment [ɪk'spɛrɪmənt] *n* experimento ♦ *vi* hacer experimentos; **to perform** *or* **carry out an ~** realizar un experimento; **as an ~** como experimento; **to ~ with a new vaccine** experimentar con una vacuna nueva.

experimental [ɪkspɛrɪ'mɛntl] *a* experimental; **the process is still at the ~ stage** el proceso está todavía en prueba.

expert ['ɛkspəːt] *a* experto, perito ♦ *n* experto/a, perito/a; *(specialist)* especialista *m/f*; **~ witness** *(LAW)* testigo pericial; **~ in** *or* **at doing sth** experto *or* perito en hacer algo; **an ~ on sth** un experto en algo.

expertise [ɛkspəː'tiːz] *n* pericia.

expiration [ɛkspɪ'reɪʃən] *n (gen)* expiración *f*, vencimiento.

expire [ɪk'spaɪə*] *vi (gen)* caducar, vencerse.

expiry [ɪk'spaɪərɪ] *n* vencimiento.

explain [ɪk'spleɪn] *vt* explicar; *(mystery)* aclarar.

explain away *vt* justificar.

explanation [ɛksplə'neɪʃən] *n* explicación *f*; aclaración *f*; **to find an ~ for sth** encontrarle una explicación a algo.

explanatory [ɪk'splænətrɪ] *a* explicativo; aclaratorio.

explicable [ɪk'splɪkəbl] *a* explicable.

explicit [ɪk'splɪsɪt] *a* explícito.

explicitly [ɪk'splɪsɪtlɪ] *ad* explícitamente.

explode [ɪk'spləud] *vi* estallar, explotar; *(with anger)* reventar ♦ *vt* volar, explotar; *(fig: theory)* desacreditar, refutar; **to ~ a myth** demoler un mito.

exploit ['ɛksplɔɪt] *n* hazaña ♦ *vt* [ɪk'splɔɪt] explotar.

exploitation [ɛksplɔɪ'teɪʃən] *n* explotación *f*.

exploration [ɛksplə'reɪʃən] *n* exploración *f*.

exploratory [ɪk'splɔrətrɪ] *a (fig: talks)* exploratorio, preliminar.

explore [ɪk'splɔː*] *vt* explorar; *(fig)* examinar, sondear.

explorer [ɪk'splɔːrə*] *n* explorador(a) *m/f*.

explosion [ɪk'spləuʒən] *n* explosión *f*.

explosive [ɪk'spləusɪv] *a, n* explosivo.

exponent [ɪk'spəunənt] *n* partidario/a, intérprete *m/f*.

export *vt* [ɛks'pɔːt] exportar ♦ *n* ['ɛkspɔːt] exportación *f* ♦ *cpd* de exportación.

exportation [ɛkspɔː'teɪʃən] *n* exportación *f*.

export drive *n* campaña de exportación.

exporter [ɛk'spɔːtə*] *n* exportador(a) *m/f*.

export licence *n* licencia de exportación.

export manager *n* gerente *m/f* de exportación.

export trade *n* comercio exterior.

expose [ɪk'spəuz] *vt* exponer; *(unmask)* desenmascarar.

exposé [ɪk'spəuzeɪ] *n* relevación *f*.

exposed [ɪk'spəuzd] *a* expuesto; *(land, house)* desprotegido; *(ELEC: wire)* al aire; *(pipe, beam)* al descubierto.
exposition [ɛkspə'zɪʃən] *n* exposición *f*.
exposure [ɪk'spəuʒə*] *n* exposición *f*; *(PHOT: speed)* velocidad *f* de obturación (: *shot)* fotografía; **to die from** ~ *(MED)* morir de frío.
exposure meter *n* fotómetro.
expound [ɪk'spaund] *vt* exponer; *(theory, text)* comentar; *(one's views)* explicar.
express [ɪk'sprɛs] *a* *(definite)* expreso, explícito; *(Brit: letter etc)* urgente ♦ *n* *(train)* rápido ♦ *ad* *(send)* por correo extraordinario ♦ *vt* expresar; *(squeeze)* exprimir; **to send sth** ~ enviar algo por correo urgente; **to** ~ **o.s.** expresarse.
expression [ɪk'sprɛʃən] *n* expresión *f*.
expressionism [ɪk'sprɛʃənɪzm] *n* expresionismo.
expressive [ɪk'sprɛsɪv] *a* expresivo.
expressly [ɪk'sprɛslɪ] *ad* expresamente.
expressway [ɪk'sprɛsweɪ] *n* (*US: urban motorway)* autopista.
expropriate [ɛks'prəuprɪeɪt] *vt* expropiar.
expulsion [ɪk'spʌlʃən] *n* expulsión *f*.
expurgate ['ɛkspəgeɪt] *vt* expurgar.
exquisite [ɛk'skwɪzɪt] *a* exquisito.
exquisitely [ɛk'skwɪzɪtlɪ] *a* exquisitamente.
ex-serviceman ['ɛks'sə:vɪsmən] *n* excombatiente *m*.
ext. *abbr* (*TEL)* = **extension**.
extemporize [ɪk'stɛmpəraɪz] *vi* improvisar.
extend [ɪk'stɛnd] *vt* *(visit, street)* prolongar; *(building)* ensanchar; *(thanks, friendship etc)* extender; *(COMM: credit)* prorrogar, alargar; *(deadline)* prorrogar ♦ *vi* *(land)* extenderse; **the contract** ~**s to/ for** ... el contrato se prolonga hasta/por ....
extension [ɪk'stɛnʃən] *n* extensión *f*; *(building)* ampliación *f*; *(TEL: line)* línea derivada; (: *telephone)* extensión *f*; *(of deadline)* prórroga; ~ **3718** extensión 3718.
extension cable *n* *(ELEC)* extensión *f*.
extensive [ɪk'stɛnsɪv] *a* *(gen)* extenso; *(damage)* importante; *(knowledge)* amplio.
extensively [ɪk'stɛnsɪvlɪ] *ad* *(altered, damaged etc)* extensamente; **he's travelled** ~ ha viajado por muchos países.
extent [ɪk'stɛnt] *n* *(breadth)* extensión *f*; *(scope: of knowledge, activities)* alcance *m*; *(degree: of damage, loss)* grado; **to some** ~ hasta cierto punto; **to a certain** ~ hasta cierto punto; **to a large** ~ en gran parte; **to the** ~ **of...** hasta el punto de...; **to such an** ~ **that...** hasta tal punto que...; **to what** ~**?** ¿hasta qué punto?; **debts to the** ~ **of £5000** deudas por la cantidad de £5000.
extenuating [ɪk'stɛnjueɪtɪŋ] *a*: ~ **circumstances** circunstancias *fpl* atenuantes.
exterior [ɛk'stɪərɪə*] *a* exterior, externo ♦ *n* exterior *m*.

exterminate [ɪk'stə:mɪneɪt] *vt* exterminar.
extermination [ɪkstə:mɪ'neɪʃən] *n* exterminación *f*.
external [ɛk'stə:nl] *a* externo, exterior ♦ *n*: **the** ~**s** las apariencias; ~ **affairs** asuntos *mpl* exteriores; **for** ~ **use only** (*MED)* para uso tópico.
externally [ɛk'stə:nəlɪ] *ad* por fuera.
extinct [ɪk'stɪŋkt] *a* *(volcano)* extinguido; *(race)* extinto.
extinction [ɪk'stɪŋkʃən] *n* extinción *f*.
extinguish [ɪk'stɪŋgwɪʃ] *vt* extinguir, apagar.
extinguisher [ɪk'stɪŋgwɪʃə*] *n* extintor *m*.
extol, (US) extoll [ɪk'stəul] *vt* *(merits, virtues)* ensalzar, alabar; *(person)* alabar, elogiar.
extort [ɪk'stɔ:t] *vt* sacar a la fuerza.
extortion [ɪk'stɔ:ʃən] *n* exacción *f*.
extortionate [ɪk'stɔ:ʃnət] *a* excesivo, exorbitante.
extra ['ɛkstrə] *a* adicional ♦ *ad* *(in addition)* de más ♦ *n* *(addition)* extra *m*, suplemento; *(THEATRE)* extra *m/f*, comparsa *m/f*; *(newspaper)* edición *f* extraordinaria; **wine will cost** ~ el vino no está incluido (en el precio); ~ **large sizes** tamaños grandes; *see also* **extras.**
extra... ['ɛkstrə] *pref* extra... .
extract *vt* [ɪk'strækt] sacar; *(tooth)* extraer; *(confession)* arrancar, obtener ♦ *n* ['ɛkstrækt] extracto.
extraction [ɪk'strækʃən] *n* extracción *f*; *(origin)* origen *m*.
extracurricular [ɛkstrəkə'rɪkjulə*] *a* *(SCOL)* extraescolar, extra-académico.
extradite ['ɛkstrədaɪt] *vt* extraditar.
extradition [ɛkstrə'dɪʃən] *n* extradición *f*.
extramarital [ɛkstrə'mærɪtl] *a* extramatrimonial.
extramural [ɛkstrə'mjuərl] *a* extraescolar.
extraneous [ɪk'streɪnɪəs] *a* extraño, ajeno.
extraordinary [ɪk'strɔ:dnrɪ] *a* extraordinario; *(odd)* raro; **the** ~ **thing is that** ... la cosa más extraordinaria es que ....
extraordinary general meeting *n* junta general extraordinaria.
extrapolation [ɪkstræpə'leɪʃən] *n* extrapolación *f*.
extras *npl* *(additional expense)* extras *mpl*.
extrasensory perception (ESP) ['ɛkstrə'sɛnsərɪ-] *n* percepción *f* extrasensorial.
extra time *n* *(FOOTBALL)* prórroga.
extravagance [ɪk'strævəgəns] *n* *(excessive spending)* derroche *m*; *(thing bought)* extravagancia.
extravagant [ɪk'strævəgənt] *a* *(lavish)* pródigo; *(wasteful)* derrochador(a); *(price)* exorbitante; *(praise)* excesivo.
extreme [ɪk'stri:m] *a* extremo; *(poverty etc)* extremado; *(case)* excepcional ♦ *n* extremo; **the** ~ **left/right** *(POL)* la extrema

izquierda/derecha; ~s **of temperature** temperaturas extremas.

extremely [ɪkstriːmlɪ] *ad* sumamente, extremadamente.

extremist [ɪkstriːmɪst] *a, n* extremista *m/f*.

extremity [ɪkˈstrɛmətɪ] *n* extremidad *f*, punta; (*need*) apuro, necesidad *f*; **extremities** *npl* (*hands and feet*) extremidades *fpl*.

extricate [ˈɛkstrɪkeɪt] *vt*: **to ~ o.s. from** librarse de.

extrovert [ˈɛkstrəvɔːt] *n* extrovertido/a.

exuberance [ɪgˈzjuːbərns] *n* exuberancia.

exuberant [ɪgˈzjuːbərnt] *a* (*person*) eufórico; (*style*) exuberante.

exude [ɪgˈzjuːd] *vt* rezumar, sudar.

exult [ɪgˈzʌlt] *vi* regocijarse.

exultant [ɪgˈzʌltənt] *a* (*person, smile*) regocijado, jubiloso; (*shout, expression*) jubiloso.

exultation [ɛgzʌlˈteɪʃən] *n* regocijo, júbilo; **in ~** en exultación.

eye [aɪ] *n* ojo ♦ *vt* mirar de soslayo, ojear; **to keep an ~ on** vigilar; **as far as the ~ can see** hasta donde alcanza la vista; **with an ~ to doing sth** con vistas *or* miras a hacer algo; **to have an ~ for sth** tener mucha vista *or* buen ojo para algo; **there's more to this than meets the ~** esto tiene su miga.

eyeball [ˈaɪbɔːl] *n* globo del ojo.

eyebath [ˈaɪbɑːθ] *n* baño para ojos.

eyebrow [ˈaɪbrau] *n* ceja.

eyebrow pencil *n* lápiz *m* de cejas.

eye-catching [ˈaɪkætʃɪŋ] *a* llamativo.

eye cup *n* (*US*) = **eyebath**.

eyedrops [ˈaɪdrɔps] *npl* gotas *fpl* para los ojos.

eyelash [ˈaɪlæʃ] *n* pestaña.

eyelet [ˈaɪlɪt] *n* ojete *m*.

eye-level [ˈaɪlɛvl] *a* a la altura de los ojos.

eyelid [ˈaɪlɪd] *n* párpado.

eyeliner [ˈaɪlaɪnə*] *n* lápiz *m* de ojos.

eye-opener [ˈaɪəupnə*] *n* revelación *f*, gran sorpresa.

eyeshadow [ˈaɪʃædəu] *n* sombreador *m* de ojos.

eyesight [ˈaɪsaɪt] *n* vista.

eyesore [ˈaɪsɔː*] *n* monstruosidad *f*.

eyestrain [ˈaɪstreɪn] *n*: **to get ~** cansar la vista *or* los ojos.

eyetooth, *pl* **eyeteeth** [ˈaɪtuːθ, -tiːθ] *n* colmillo; **to give one's eyeteeth for sth/to do sth** (*col, fig*) dar un ojo de la cara por algo/por hacer algo.

eyewash [ˈaɪwɔʃ] *n* (*fig*) disparates *mpl*, tonterías *fpl*.

eye witness *n* testigo *m/f* presencial.

eyrie [ˈɪərɪ] *n* aguilera.

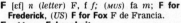

F

F [ɛf] *n* (*letter*) F, f *f*; (*mus*) fa *m*; **F for Frederick,** (*US*) **F for Fox** F de Francia.

F. *abbr* = **Fahrenheit.**

FA *n abbr* (*Brit*: = *Football Association*) ≈ AFE *f* (*Sp*).

FAA *n abbr* (*US*) = *Federal Aviation Administration*.

fable [ˈfeɪbl] *n* fábula.

fabric [ˈfæbrɪk] *n* tejido, tela.

fabricate [ˈfæbrɪkeɪt] *vt* fabricar; (*fig*) inventar.

fabrication [fæbrɪˈkeɪʃən] *n* fabricación *f*; (*fig*) invención *f*.

fabric ribbon *n* (*for typewriter*) cinta de tela.

fabulous [ˈfæbjuləs] *a* fabuloso.

façade [fəˈsɑːd] *n* fachada.

face [feɪs] *n* (*ANAT*) cara, rostro; (*of clock*) esfera, cara (*LAm*); (*side, surface*) superficie *f* ♦ *vt* (*subj: person*) encararse con; (: *building*) dar a; **~ down** (*person, card*) boca abajo; **to lose ~** desprestigiarse; **to save ~** salvar las apariencias; **to make** *or* **pull a ~** hacer muecas; **in the ~ of** (*difficulties etc*) en vista de, ante; **on the ~ of it** a primera vista; **~ to ~** cara a cara; **to ~ the fact that ...** reconocer que ... .

face up to *vt fus* hacer frente a, arrostrar.

face cloth *n* (*Brit*) manopla.

face cream *n* crema (de belleza).

faceless [ˈfeɪslɪs] *a* (*fig*) anónimo.

face lift *n* estirado facial.

face powder *n* polvos *mpl* para la cara.

face-saving [ˈfeɪsseɪvɪŋ] *a* para salvar las apariencias.

facet [ˈfæsɪt] *n* faceta.

facetious [fəˈsiːʃəs] *a* chistoso.

facetiously [fəˈsiːʃəslɪ] *ad* chistosamente.

face value *n* (*of stamp*) valor *m* nominal; **to take sth at ~** (*fig*) tomar algo en sentido literal, aceptar las apariencias de algo.

facial [ˈfeɪʃəl] *a* de la cara ♦ *n* (*also*: **beauty ~**) tratamiento facial, limpieza.

facile [ˈfæsaɪl] *a* superficial.

facilitate [fəˈsɪlɪteɪt] *vt* facilitar.

facility [fəˈsɪlɪtɪ] *n* facilidad *f*; **facilities** *npl* facilidades *fpl*; **credit ~** facilidades de crédito.

facing [ˈfeɪsɪŋ] *prep* frente a ♦ *a* de enfrente.

facsimile [fækˈsɪmɪlɪ] *n* (*document*) facsímil(e) *m*; (*machine*) telefax *m*.

fact [fækt] n hecho; **in** ~ en realidad; **to know for a** ~ **that** ... saber a ciencia cierta que ... .

fact-finding ['fæktfaɪndɪŋ] a: **a** ~ **tour/mission** un viaje/una misión de reconocimiento.

faction ['fækʃən] n facción f.

factor ['fæktə*] n factor m; (COMM: person) agente m/f comisionado/a ♦ vi (COMM) comprar deudas; **safety** ~ factor de seguridad.

factory ['fæktərɪ] n fábrica.

factory farming n cría industrial.

factory ship n buque m factoría.

factual ['fæktjuəl] a basado en los hechos.

faculty ['fækəltɪ] n facultad f; (US: teaching staff) personal m docente.

fad [fæd] n novedad f, moda.

fade [feɪd] vi desteñirse; (sound, hope) desvanecerse; (light) apagarse; (flower) marchitarse.

fade away vi (sound) apagarse.

fade in vt (TV, CINEMA) fundir; (RADIO: sound) mezclar ♦ vi (TV, CINEMA) fundirse; (RADIO) oírse por encima.

fade out vt (TV, CINEMA) desvanecer; (RADIO) apagar, disminuir el volumen de ♦ vi (TV, CINEMA) desvanecerse; (RADIO) apagarse, dejarse de oír.

faded ['feɪdɪd] a (clothes, colour) descolorado; (flower) marchito.

faeces, (US) **feces** ['fiːsiːz] npl excremento sg, heces fpl.

fag [fæg] n (Brit col: cigarette) pitillo (Sp), cigarro; (US col: homosexual) maricón m.

fag end n (Brit col) colilla.

fagged [fægd] a (Brit col: exhausted) rendido, agotado.

Fahrenheit ['fɑːrənhaɪt] n Fahrenheit m.

fail [feɪl] vt (candidate) suspender; (exam) no aprobar; (subj: memory etc) fallar a ♦ vi suspender; (be unsuccessful) fracasar; (strength, brakes, engine) fallar; **to** ~ **to do sth** (neglect) dejar de hacer algo; (be unable) no poder hacer algo; **without** ~ sin falta; **words** ~ **me!** ¡no sé qué decir!

failing ['feɪlɪŋ] n falta, defecto ♦ prep a falta de; ~ **that** de no ser posible eso.

failsafe ['feɪlseɪf] a (device etc) seguro contra todo riesgo.

failure ['feɪljə*] n fracaso; (person) fracasado/a (mechanical etc) fallo; (in exam) suspenso; (of crops) pérdida, destrucción f; **it was a complete** ~ fue un fracaso total.

faint [feɪnt] a débil; (smell, breeze, trace) tenue, apenas perceptible; (recollection) vago; (mark) apenas visible ♦ n desmayo ♦ vi desmayarse; **to feel** ~ estar mareado, marearse.

faint-hearted ['feɪnt'hɑːtɪd] a apocado.

faintly ['feɪntlɪ] ad débilmente; (vaguely) vagamente.

faintness ['feɪntnɪs] n debilidad f; vaguedad f.

fair [fɛə*] a justo; (hair, person) rubio; (weather) bueno; (good enough) suficiente; (sizeable) considerable ♦ ad: **to play** ~ jugar limpio ♦ n feria; (Brit: funfair) parque m de atracciones; **it's not** ~! ¡no es justo!, ¡no hay derecho!; ~ **copy** copia en limpio; ~ **play** juego limpio; **a** ~ **amount of** bastante; ~ **wear and tear** desgaste m natural; **trade** ~ feria de muestras.

fair-haired [fɛə'hɛəd] a (person) rubio.

fairly ['fɛəlɪ] ad (justly) con justicia; (equally) equitativamente; (quite) bastante; **I'm** ~ **sure** estoy bastante seguro.

fairness ['fɛənɪs] n justicia; (impartiality) imparcialidad f; **in all** ~ a decir verdad.

fairy ['fɛərɪ] n hada.

fairy godmother n hada madrina.

fairyland ['fɛərɪlænd] n el país de ensueño.

fairy lights npl bombillas fpl de colorines.

fairy tale n cuento de hadas.

faith [feɪθ] n fe f; (trust) confianza; (sect) religión f; **to have** ~ **in sb/sth** fiarse de uno/algo.

faithful ['feɪθful] a fiel.

faithfully ['feɪθfulɪ] ad fielmente; **yours** ~ (Brit: in letters) le saluda atentamente.

faith healer n curador(a) m/f por fe.

fake [feɪk] n (painting etc) falsificación f; (person) impostor(a) m/f ♦ a falso ♦ vt fingir; (painting etc) falsificar.

falcon ['fɔːlkən] n halcón m.

Falkland Islands ['fɔːlklənd-] npl Islas fpl Malvinas.

fall [fɔːl] n caída; (US) otoño; (decrease) disminución f ♦ vi, pt **fell**, pp **fallen** ['fɔːlən] caer(se); (price) bajar; ~**s** npl (waterfall) cascada sg, salto sg de agua; **a** ~ **of earth** un desprendimiento de tierra; **a** ~ **of snow** una nevada; **to** ~ **flat** vi (on one's face) caerse (boca abajo); (joke, story) no hacer gracia; **to** ~ **short of sb's expectations** decepcionar a uno; **to** ~ **in love (with sb/sth)** enamorarse (de uno/algo).

fall apart vi despedazarse.

fall back vi retroceder.

fall back on vt fus (remedy etc) recurrir a; **to have sth to** ~ **back on** tener algo a que recurrir.

fall behind vi quedarse atrás; (fig: with payments) retrasarse.

fall down vi (person) caerse; (building, hopes) derrumbarse.

fall for vt fus (trick) tragar; (person) enamorarse de.

fall in vi (roof) hundirse; (MIL) alinearse.

fall in with vt fus: **to** ~ **in with sb's plans** acomodarse con los planes de uno.

fall off vi caerse; (diminish) disminuir.

fall out vi (friends etc) reñir; (MIL) romper filas.

fall over vi caer(se).

fall through vi (plan, project) fracasar.

fallacy ['fæləsɪ] n error m.

fallback position ['fɔːlbæk-] n posición f de repliegue.

fallen [fɔːlən] pp of **fall**.

fallible ['fæləbl] a falible.

falling ['fɔːlɪŋ] a: ~ **market** mercado en baja.

falling-off ['fɔːlɪŋ'ɔf] n (reduction) disminución f.

Fallopian tube [fə'ləupɪən-] n (ANAT) trompa de Falopio.

fallout ['fɔːlaut] n lluvia radioactiva.

fallout shelter n refugio antinuclear.

fallow ['fæləu] a (land, field) en barbecho.

false [fɔːls] a (gen) falso; (teeth etc) postizo; (disloyal) desleal, traidor(a); **under** ~ **pretences** con engaños

false alarm n falsa alarma.

falsehood ['fɔːlshud] n (lie) mentira; (falseness) falsedad f.

falsely ['fɔːlslɪ] ad falsamente.

false teeth npl (Brit) dentadura sg postiza.

falsify ['fɔːlsɪfaɪ] vt falsificar; (figures) contrahacer.

falter ['fɔːltə*] vi vacilar.

fame [feɪm] n fama.

familiar [fə'mɪlɪə*] a familiar; (well-known) conocido; (tone) de confianza; **to be** ~ **with** (subject) estar enterado de; **to make o.s.** ~ **with** familiarizarse con; **to be on** ~ **terms with** conocer bien.

familiarity [fəmɪlɪ'ærɪtɪ] n familiaridad f.

familiarize [fə'mɪlɪəraɪz] vr: **to** ~ **o.s. with** familiarizarse con.

family ['fæmɪlɪ] n familia.

family allowance n pensión f familiar.

family business n negocio familiar.

family credit n (Brit) subsidio que se paga a las familias con bajo nivel de ingresos.

family doctor n médico/a de cabecera.

family life n vida doméstica or familiar.

family planning n planificación f familiar.

family planning clinic n clínica de planificación familiar.

family tree n árbol m genealógico.

famine ['fæmɪn] n hambre f, hambruna.

famished ['fæmɪʃt] a hambriento; **I'm** ~! (col) ¡estoy muerto de hambre!, ¡tengo un hambre canina!

famous ['feɪməs] a famoso, célebre.

famously ['feɪməslɪ] ad (get on) estupendamente.

fan [fæn] n abanico; (ELEC) ventilador m; (person) aficionado/a; (SPORT) hincha m/f ◆ vt abanicar; (fire, quarrel) atizar.

fan out vi desparramarse.

fanatic [fə'nætɪk] n fanático/a.

fanatical [fə'nætɪkəl] a fanático.

fan belt n correa de ventilador.

fancied ['fænsɪd] a imaginario.

fanciful ['fænsɪful] a (gen) fantástico; (im-aginary) fantasioso.

fancy ['fænsɪ] n (whim) capricho, antojo; (imagination) imaginación f ◆ a (luxury) de lujo; (price) exorbitado ◆ vt (feel like, want) tener ganas de; (imagine) imaginarse, figurarse; **to take a** ~ **to sb** tomar cariño a uno; **when the** ~ **takes him** cuando se le antoja; **it took** or **caught my** ~ me cayó en gracia; **to** ~ **that...** imaginarse que...; **he fancies her** le gusta (ella) mucho.

fancy dress n disfraz m.

fancy-dress ball ['fænsɪdrɛs-] n baile m de disfraces.

fancy goods n artículos mpl de fantasía.

fanfare ['fænfeə*] n fanfarria (de trompeta).

fanfold paper ['fænfəuld-] n papel m plegado en abanico or en acordeón.

fang [fæŋ] n colmillo.

fan heater n soplador m de aire caliente.

fanlight ['fænlaɪt] n (montante m en) abanico.

fantasize ['fæntəsaɪz] vi fantasear, hacerse ilusiones.

fantastic [fæn'tæstɪk] a fantástico.

FAO n abbr (= Food and Agriculture Organization) OAA f.

FAQ abbr (= free alongside quay) franco sobre muelle.

fantasy ['fæntəzɪ] n fantasía.

far [fɑː*] a (distant) lejano ◆ ad lejos; **the** ~ **left/right** (POL) la extrema izquierda/derecha; ~ **away**, ~ **off** (a lo) lejos; ~ **better** mucho mejor; ~ **from** lejos de; **by** ~ con mucho; **it's by** ~ **the best** es con mucho el mejor; **go as** ~ **as the farm** vaya hasta la granja; **is it** ~ **to London?** ¿a cuánto está Londres?; **it's not** ~ **(from here)** no está lejos (de aquí); **as** ~ **as I know** que yo sepa; **how** ~ **have you got with your work?** ¿hasta dónde has llegado en tu trabajo?

faraway ['fɑːrəweɪ] a remoto; (voice) distraído; (look) ausente, perdido.

farce [fɑːs] n farsa.

farcical ['fɑːsɪkəl] a absurdo.

fare [feə*] n (on trains, buses) precio (del billete); (in taxi: cost) tarifa; (: passenger) pasajero; (food) comida; **half/full** ~ medio pasaje m/pasaje m completo.

Far East n: **the** ~ el Extremo or Lejano Oriente.

farewell [feə'wel] excl, n adiós m.

far-fetched [fɑː'fetʃt] a inverosímil.

farm [fɑːm] n granja, finca, estancia (LAm) ◆ vt cultivar.

farm out vt (work): **to** ~ **out (to sb)** mandar hacer fuera (a uno).

farmer ['fɑːmə*] n granjero, estanciero (LAm).

farmhand ['fɑːmhænd] n peón m.

farmhouse ['fɑːmhaus] n granja, casa de hacienda (LAm).

farming ['fɑːmɪŋ] n (gen) agricultura; (tilling) cultivo; **sheep** ~ cría de ovejas.
farm labourer n = **farmhand**.
farmland ['fɑːmlænd] n tierra de cultivo.
farm produce n productos mpl agrícolas.
farm worker n = **farmhand**.
farmyard ['fɑːmjɑːd] n corral m.
Faroe Islands ['fɛərəu-], **Faroes** ['fɛərəuz] npl: **the** ~ las Islas Feroe.
far-reaching [fɑːˈriːtʃɪŋ] a (reform, effect) de gran alcance.
far-sighted [fɑːˈsaɪtɪd] a previsor(a).
fart [fɑːt] (col!) n pedo(!) ♦ vi tirarse un pedo(!).
farther ['fɑːðə*] ad más lejos, más allá ♦ a más lejano.
farthest ['fɑːðɪst] superlative of **far**.
FAS abbr (= free alongside ship) franco al costado del buque.
fascinate ['fæsɪneɪt] vt fascinar.
fascinating ['fæsɪneɪtɪŋ] a fascinante.
fascination [fæsɪˈneɪʃən] n fascinación f.
fascism ['fæʃɪzəm] n fascismo.
fascist ['fæʃɪst] a, n fascista m/f.
fashion ['fæʃən] n moda; (manner) manera ♦ vt formar; **in** ~ a la moda; **out of** ~ pasado de moda; **in the Greek** ~ a la griega, al estilo griego; **after a** ~ (finish, manage etc) en cierto modo.
fashionable ['fæʃnəbl] a de moda; (writer) de moda, popular; **it is** ~ **to do** ... está de moda hacer ....
fashion designer n modisto/a.
fashion show n desfile m de modelos.
fast [fɑːst] a (also phot: film) rápido; (dye, colour) sólido; (clock): **to be** ~ estar adelantado ♦ ad rápidamente, de prisa; (stuck, held) firmemente ♦ n ayuno ♦ vi ayunar; ~ **asleep** profundamente dormido; **in the** ~ **lane** (aut) en el carril de adelantamiento; **my watch is 5 minutes** ~ mi reloj está adelantado 5 minutos; **as** ~ **as I** etc **can** lo más rápido posible; **to make a boat** ~ amarrar una barca.
fasten ['fɑːsn] vt asegurar, sujetar; (coat, belt) abrochar ♦ vi cerrarse.
fasten (up)on vt fus (idea) aferrarse a.
fastener ['fɑːsnə*] n cierre m; (of door etc) cerrojo; (Brit: zip ~) cremallera.
fastening ['fɑːsnɪŋ] n = **fastener**.
fast food n comida rápida, platos mpl preparados.
fastidious [fæsˈtɪdɪəs] a (fussy) delicado; (demanding) exigente.
fat [fæt] a gordo; (meat) con mucha grasa; (greasy) grasiento ♦ n grasa; (on person) carnes fpl; (lard) manteca; **to live off the** ~ **of the land** vivir a cuerpo de rey.
fatal ['feɪtl] a (mistake) fatal; (injury) mortal; (consequence) funesto.
fatalism ['feɪtəlɪzəm] n fatalismo.
fatality [fəˈtælɪtɪ] n (road death etc) víctima f.

fatally ['feɪtəlɪ] ad: ~ **injured** herido a muerte.
fate [feɪt] n destino, sino.
fated ['feɪtɪd] a predestinado.
fateful ['feɪtful] a fatídico.
father ['fɑːðə*] n padre m.
Father Christmas n Papá m Noel.
fatherhood ['fɑːðəhud] n paternidad f.
father-in-law ['fɑːðərɪnlɔː] n suegro.
fatherland ['fɑːðəlænd] n patria.
fatherly ['fɑːðəlɪ] a paternal.
fathom ['fæðəm] n braza ♦ vt (unravel) desentrañar; (understand) concebir.
fatigue [fəˈtiːg] n fatiga, cansancio; **metal** ~ fatiga del metal.
fatness ['fætnɪs] n gordura.
fatten ['fætn] vt, vi engordar; **chocolate is** ~**ing** el chocolate engorda.
fatty ['fætɪ] a (food) graso ♦ n (fam) gordito/a, gordinflón/ona m/f.
fatuous ['fætjuəs] a fatuo, necio.
faucet ['fɔːsɪt] n (US) grifo, llave f (LAm).
fault [fɔːlt] n (blame) culpa; (defect: in character) defecto; (in manufacture) desperfecto; (geo) falla ♦ vt criticar; **it's my** ~ es culpa mía; **to find** ~ **with** criticar, poner peros a; **at** ~ culpable.
faultless ['fɔːltlɪs] a (action) intachable; (person) sin defectos.
faulty ['fɔːltɪ] a defectuoso.
fauna ['fɔːnə] n fauna.
faux pas ['fəuˈpɑː] n plancha.
favour, (US) **favor** ['feɪvə*] n favor m; (approval) aprobación f ♦ vt (proposition) estar a favor de, aprobar; (person etc) favorecer; (assist) ser propicio a; **to ask a** ~ **of** pedir un favor a; **to do sb a** ~ hacer un favor a uno; **to find** ~ **with sb** (subj: person) caerle bien a uno; (: suggestion) tener buena acogida por parte de uno; **in** ~ **of** a favor de; **to be in** ~ **of sth/of doing sth** ser partidario or estar a favor de algo/de hacer algo.
favo(u)rable ['feɪvərəbl] a favorable.
favo(u)rably ['feɪvərəblɪ] ad favorablemente.
favo(u)rite ['feɪvərɪt] a, n favorito, preferido.
favo(u)ritism ['feɪvərɪtɪzəm] n favoritismo.
fawn [fɔːn] n cervato ♦ a (also: ~-coloured) color de cervato, leonado ♦ vi: **to** ~ **(up)on** adular.
fax [fæks] n (document) facsímil(e) m; (machine) telefax m ♦ vt mandar or enviar por telefax.
FBI n abbr (US: = Federal Bureau of Investigation) ≈ BIC f (Sp).
FCC n abbr (US) = Federal Communications Commission.
FCO n abbr (Brit: = Foreign and Commonwealth Office) ≈ Min. de AA. EE.
FD n abbr (US) = **fire department**.
FDA n abbr (US: = Food and Drug Admin-

istration) oficina que se ocupa del control de los productos alimentarios y farmacéuticos.

fear [fɪə*] *n* miedo, temor *m* ♦ *vt* temer; **for ~ of** por temor a; **~ of heights** vértigo; **to ~ for/that** temer por/que.

fearful ['fɪəful] *a* temeroso, miedoso; *(awful)* terrible; **to be ~ of** *(frightened)* tener miedo de.

fearfully ['fɪəfulɪ] *ad (timidly)* con miedo; *(col: very)* terriblemente.

fearless ['fɪəlɪs] *a (gen)* sin miedo *or* temor; *(bold)* audaz.

fearlessly ['fɪəlɪslɪ] *ad* temerariamente.

fearlessness ['fɪəlɪsnɪs] *n* temeridad *f*.

fearsome ['fɪəsəm] *a (opponent)* temible; *(sight)* espantoso.

feasibility [fi:zə'bɪlɪtɪ] *n* factibilidad *f*, viabilidad *f*.

feasibility study *n* estudio de factibilidad.

feasible ['fi:zəbl] *a* factible.

feast [fi:st] *n* banquete *m*; *(REL: also: ~ day)* fiesta ♦ *vi* banquetear.

feat [fi:t] *n* hazaña.

feather ['fɛðə*] *n* pluma ♦ *vt*: **to ~ one's nest** *(fig)* hacer su agosto, sacar tajada ♦ *cpd (mattress, bed, pillow)* de plumas.

feather-weight ['fɛðəweɪt] *n (BOXING)* peso pluma.

feature ['fi:tʃə*] *n (gen)* característica; *(ANAT)* rasgo; *(article)* artículo de fondo ♦ *vt (subj: film)* presentar ♦ *vi* figurar; **~s** *npl (of face)* facciones *fpl*; **a (special) ~ on sth/sb** un artículo de fondo sobre algo/uno; **it ~d prominently in** ... tuvo un papel destacado en ....

feature film *n* largometraje *m*.

Feb. *abbr* (= *February*) feb.

February ['fɛbruərɪ] *n* febrero.

feces ['fi:si:z] *npl (US)* = **faeces**.

feckless ['fɛklɪs] *a* irresponsable, irreflexivo.

Fed *abbr (US)* = **federal, federation**.

fed [fɛd] *pt, pp of* **feed**.

Fed. [fɛd] *n abbr (US col)* = *Federal Reserve Board*.

federal ['fɛdərəl] *a* federal.

Federal Republic of Germany *n* República Federal de Alemania.

federation [fɛdə'reɪʃən] *n* federación *f*.

fed-up [fɛd'ʌp] *a*: **to be ~ (with)** estar harto (de).

fee [fi:] *n (professional)* derechos *mpl*, honorarios *mpl*; *(of school)* matrícula; *(entrance ~, membership ~)* cuota; **for a small ~** por poco dinero.

feeble ['fi:bl] *a* débil.

feeble-minded [fi:bl'maɪndɪd] *a* imbécil.

feed [fi:d] *n (gen, of baby)* comida; *(of animal)* pienso; *(on printer)* dispositivo de alimentación ♦ *vt (pt, pp fed) (gen)* alimentar; *(Brit: baby: breastfeed)* dar el pecho a; *(animal)* dar de comer a ♦ *vi (baby,*

animal) comer.

feed back *vt (results)* pasar.

feed in *vt (COMPUT)* introducir.

feed into *vt (data, information)* suministrar a; **to ~ sth into a machine** introducir algo en una máquina.

feed on *vt fus* alimentarse de.

feedback ['fi:dbæk] *n (from person)* reacción *f*; *(TEC)* feedback *m*.

feeder ['fi:də*] *n (bib)* babero.

feeding bottle ['fi:dɪŋ-] *n (Brit)* biberón *m*.

feel [fi:l] *n (sensation)* sensación *f*; *(sense of touch)* tacto ♦ *vt (pt, pp felt)* tocar; *(cold, pain etc)* sentir; *(think, believe)* creer; **to get the ~ of sth** *(fig)* acostumbrarse a algo; **to ~ hungry/cold** tener hambre/frío; **to ~ lonely/better** sentirse solo/mejor; **I don't ~ well** no me siento bien; **it ~s soft** es suave al tacto; **it ~s colder out here** se siente más frío aquí fuera; **to ~ like** *(want)* tener ganas de; **I'm still ~ing my way** *(fig)* aún me voy orientando; **I ~ that you ought to do it** creo que debes hacerlo; **to ~ about** *or* **around** *vi* tantear.

feeler ['fi:lə*] *n (of insect)* antena; **to put out ~s** *(fig)* sondear.

feeling ['fi:lɪŋ] *n (physical)* sensación *f*; *(foreboding)* presentimiento; *(impression)* impresión *f*; *(emotion)* sentimiento; **what are your ~s about the matter?** ¿qué opinas tú del asunto?; **to hurt sb's ~s** ofenderle a uno; **~s ran high about it** causó mucha controversia; **I got the ~ that** ... me dio la impresión de que ...; **there was a general ~ that** ... la opinión general fue que ....

feet [fi:t] *npl of* **foot**.

feign [feɪn] *vt* fingir.

feigned [feɪnd] *a* fingido.

feline ['fi:laɪn] *a* felino.

fell [fɛl] *pt of* **fall** ♦ *vt (tree)* talar ♦ *a*: **with one ~ blow** con un golpe feroz; **at one ~ swoop** de un solo golpe ♦ *n (Brit: mountain)* montaña; *(: moorland)*: **the ~s** los páramos.

fellow ['fɛləu] *n* tipo, tío *(Sp)*; *(of learned society)* socio/a; *(UNIV)* miembro de la junta de gobierno de un colegio ♦ *cpd*: **~ students** compañeros/as *m/fpl* de curso, condiscípulos/as *m/fpl*.

fellow citizen *n* conciudadano/a.

fellow countryman *n* compatriota *m*.

fellow feeling *n* compañerismo.

fellow men *npl* semejantes *mpl*.

fellowship ['fɛləuʃɪp] *n* compañerismo; *(grant)* beca.

fellow traveller *n* compañero/a de viaje; *(POL: with communists)* simpatizante *m/f*.

fellow worker *n* colega *m/f*.

felon ['fɛlən] *n* criminal *m/f*.

felony ['fɛlənɪ] *n* crimen *m*.

felt [fɛlt] *pt, pp of* **feel** ♦ *n* fieltro.

felt-tip pen ['felttɪp-] n rotulador m.
female ['fi:meɪl] n (woman) mujer f; (zool) hembra ♦ a femenino.
feminine ['femɪnɪn] a femenino.
femininity [femɪ'nɪnɪtɪ] n feminidad f.
feminism ['femɪnɪzəm] n feminismo.
feminist ['femɪnɪst] n feminista.
fence [fens] n valla, cerca; (racing) valla ♦ vt (also: ~ in) cercar ♦ vi hacer esgrima; **to sit on the ~** (fig) nadar entre dos aguas.
  fence in vt cercar.
  fence off vt separar con cerca.
fencing ['fensɪŋ] n esgrima.
fend [fend] vi: **to ~ for o.s.** valerse por sí mismo.
  fend off vt (attack, attacker) rechazar, repeler; (blow) desviar; (awkward question) evadir.
fender ['fendə*] n guardafuego; (US: aut) parachoques m inv; (: rail) trompa.
fennel ['fenl] n hinojo.
Fens [fenz] npl (Brit): **the ~** las tierras bajas de Norfolk (antiguamente zona de marismas).
ferment vi [fə'ment] fermentar ♦ n ['fɔ:ment] (fig) agitación f.
fermentation [fɔ:men'teɪʃən] n fermentación f.
fern [fɔ:n] n helecho.
ferocious [fə'rəʊʃəs] a feroz.
ferociously [fə'rəʊʃəslɪ] ad ferozmente, con ferocidad.
ferocity [fə'rɔsɪtɪ] n ferocidad f.
ferret ['ferɪt] n hurón m.
  ferret about, ferret around vi buscar.
  ferret out vt (secret, truth) desentrañar.
ferry ['ferɪ] n (small) barca (de pasaje), balsa; (large: also: ~boat) transbordador m, ferry m ♦ vt transportar; **to ~ sth/sb across** or **over** transportar algo/a uno a la otra orilla; **to ~ sb to and fro** llevar a uno de un lado para otro.
ferryman ['ferɪmən] n barquero.
fertile ['fɔ:taɪl] a fértil; (biol) fecundo.
fertility [fə'tɪlɪtɪ] n fertilidad f; fecundidad f.
fertility drug n medicamento contra la infertilidad.
fertilization [fɔ:tɪlaɪ'zeɪʃən] ad fertilización f.
fertilize ['fɔ:tɪlaɪz] vt fertilizar; (biol) fecundar; (agr) abonar.
fertilizer ['fɔ:tɪlaɪzə*] n abono, fertilizante m.
fervent ['fɔ:vənt] a (admirer) entusiasta; (hope) ferviente.
fervour, (US) **fervor** ['fɔ:və*] n fervor m, ardor m.
fester ['festə*] vi ulcerarse.
festival ['festɪvəl] n (rel) fiesta; (art, mus) festival m.
festive ['festɪv] a festivo; **the ~ season**

(Brit: Christmas) las Navidades.
festivities [fes'tɪvɪtɪz] npl fiestas fpl.
festoon [fes'tu:n] vt: **to ~ with** festonear or engalanar de.
fetch [fetʃ] vt ir a buscar; (Brit: sell for) venderse por; **how much did it ~?** ¿por cuánto se vendió?
  fetch up vi ir a parar.
fetching ['fetʃɪŋ] a atractivo.
fête [feɪt] n fiesta.
fetid ['fetɪd] a fétido.
fetish ['fetɪʃ] n fetiche m.
fetter ['fetə*] vt (person) encadenar, poner en grillos; (horse) trabar; (fig) poner trabas a.
fetters ['fetəz] npl grillos mpl.
fettle ['fetl] n: **in fine ~** en buenas condiciones.
fetus ['fi:təs] n (US) = **foetus.**
feud [fju:d] n (hostility) enemistad f; (quarrel) disputa; **a family ~** una pelea familiar.
feudal ['fju:dl] a feudal.
feudalism ['fju:dəlɪzəm] n feudalismo.
fever ['fi:və*] n fiebre f; **he has a ~** tiene fiebre.
feverish ['fi:vərɪʃ] a febril.
feverishly ['fi:vərɪʃlɪ] ad febrilmente.
few [fju:] a (not many) pocos; (some) algunos, unos ♦ pron algunos; **a ~** a unos pocos; **~ people** poca gente; **a good ~**, **quite a ~** bastantes; **in** or **over the next ~ days** en los próximos días; **every ~ weeks** cada 2 o 3 semanas; **a ~ more days** unos días más.
fewer ['fju:ə*] a menos.
fewest ['fju:ɪst] a los/las menos.
FFA n abbr = Future Farmers of America.
FH abbr (Brit) = **fire hydrant.**
FHA n abbr (US: = Federal Housing Association) oficina federal de la vivienda.
fiancé [fɪ'ɑ:ŋseɪ] n novio, prometido.
fiancée [fɪ'ɑ:ŋseɪ] n novia, prometida.
fiasco [fɪ'æskəʊ] n fiasco.
fib [fɪb] n mentirilla ♦ vi decir mentirillas.
fibre, (US) **fiber** ['faɪbə*] n fibra.
fibreboard, (US) **fiberboard** ['faɪbəbɔ:d] n fibra vulcanizada.
fibreglass, (US) **fiberglass** ['faɪbəglɑ:s] n fibra de vidrio.
fibrositis [faɪbrə'saɪtɪs] n fibrositis f inv.
FICA n abbr (US) = Federal Insurance Contributions Act.
fickle ['fɪkl] a inconstante.
fiction ['fɪkʃən] n (gen) ficción f.
fictional ['fɪkʃənl] a novelesco.
fictionalize ['fɪkʃənəlaɪz] vt novelar.
fictitious [fɪk'tɪʃəs] a ficticio.
fiddle ['fɪdl] n (mus) violín m; (cheating) trampa ♦ vt (Brit: accounts) falsificar; **tax ~** evasión f fiscal; **to work a ~** hacer trampa.
  fiddle with vt fus jugar con.

fiddler ['fɪdlə*] n violinista m/f.
fiddly ['fɪdlɪ] a (task) delicado, mañoso; (object) cargado.
fidelity [fɪ'dɛlɪtɪ] n fidelidad f.
fidget ['fɪdʒɪt] vi inquietarse.
fidgety ['fɪdʒɪtɪ] a nervioso.
fiduciary [fɪ'duːʃɪərɪ] n fiduciario/a.
field [fiːld] n (gen, COMPUT) campo; (fig) campo, esfera; (SPORT) campo, cancha (LAm); (competitors) competidores mpl ♦ cpd: **to have a ~ day** (fig) sacar el máximo provecho; **to lead the ~** (SPORT, COMM) llevar la delantera; **to give sth a year's trial in the ~** (fig) sacar algo al mercado a prueba por un año; **my particular ~** mi especialidad.
field glasses npl gemelos mpl.
field marshal n mariscal m.
fieldwork ['fiːldwəːk] n (ARCHAEOLOGY, GEO) trabajo de campo.
fiend [fiːnd] n demonio.
fiendish ['fiːndɪʃ] a diabólico.
fierce [fɪəs] a feroz; (wind, attack) violento; (heat) intenso; (fighting, enemy) encarnizado.
fiercely ['fɪəslɪ] ad con ferocidad; violentamente; intensamente; encarnizadamente.
fierceness ['fɪəsnɪs] n ferocidad f; violencia; intensidad f; encarnizamiento.
fiery ['faɪərɪ] a (burning) ardiente; (temperament) apasionado.
FIFA ['fiːfə] n abbr (= Fédération Internationale de Football Association) FIFA f.
fifteen [fɪf'tiːn] num quince.
fifth [fɪfθ] num quinto.
fiftieth ['fɪftɪθ] num quincuagésimo.
fifty ['fɪftɪ] num cincuenta; **the fifties** los años cincuenta; **to be in one's fifties** andar por los cincuenta.
fifty-fifty ['fɪftɪ'fɪftɪ] a: **to go ~ with sb** ir a medias con uno ♦ ad: **we have a ~ chance of success** tenemos un cincuenta por ciento de posibilidades de tener éxito.
fig [fɪg] n higo.
fight [faɪt] n (gen) pelea; (MIL) combate m; (struggle) lucha ♦ vb (pt, pp **fought**) vt luchar contra; (cancer, alcoholism) combatir; (LAW): **to ~ a case** defenderse; (quarrel): **to ~ (with sb)** pelear (con uno) ♦ vi pelear, luchar; (fig): **to ~ (for/against)** luchar por/contra.
fight back vi defenderse; (after illness) recuperarse ♦ vt (tears) contener.
fight down vt (anger, anxiety, urge) reprimir.
fight off vt (attack, attacker) rechazar; (disease, sleep, urge) luchar contra.
fight out vt: **to ~ it out** luchar hasta resolverlo.
fighter ['faɪtə*] n combatiente m/f; (fig) luchador(a) m/f; (plane) caza m.
fighter-bomber ['faɪtəbɔmə*] n cazabombardero.

fighter pilot n piloto de caza.
fighting ['faɪtɪŋ] n (gen) el luchar; (battle) combate m; (in streets) disturbios mpl.
figment ['fɪgmənt] n: **a ~ of the imagination** una quimera.
figurative ['fɪgjʊrətɪv] a (meaning) figurado; (ART) figurativo.
figure ['fɪgə*] n (DRAWING, GEOM) figura, dibujo; (number, cipher) cifra; (person) figura; (body, outline) talle m, tipo ♦ vt (esp US: think, calculate) calcular, imaginarse ♦ vi (appear) figurar; (esp US: make sense) ser lógico; **~ of speech** (LING) figura retórica; **public ~** personaje m.
figure on vt fus (US) contar con.
figure out vt (understand) comprender.
figurehead ['fɪgəhɛd] n (fig) testaferro.
figure skating n patinaje m de figuras.
Fiji (Islands) ['fiːdʒiː-] n(pl) (Islas fpl de) Fiji fpl.
filament ['fɪləmənt] n (ELEC) filamento.
filch [fɪltʃ] vt (col: steal) hurtar, robar.
file [faɪl] n (tool) lima; (for nails) lima de uñas; (dossier) expediente m; (folder) carpeta; (in cabinet) archivo; (COMPUT) fichero; (row) fila ♦ vt limar; (papers) clasificar; (LAW: claim) presentar; (store) archivar; **to open/close a ~** (COMPUT) abrir/cerrar un fichero; **to ~ in/out** vi entrar/salir en fila; **to ~ a suit against sb** entablar pleito contra uno; **to ~ past** desfilar ante.
file name n (COMPUT) nombre m de fichero.
filibuster ['fɪlɪbʌstə*] (esp US: POL) n filibustero/a ♦ vi ser un(a) filibustero/a.
filing ['faɪlɪŋ] n: **to do the ~** llevar los archivos.
filing cabinet n fichero, archivo.
filing clerk n oficinista m/f.
fill [fɪl] vt llenar; (tooth) empastar; (vacancy) cubrir ♦ n: **to eat one's ~** llenarse; **we've already ~ed that vacancy** ya hemos cubierto esa vacante; **~ed with admiration (for)** lleno de admiración (por).
fill in vt rellenar; (details, report) completar; **to ~ sb in on sth** (col) poner a uno al corriente or al día sobre algo.
fill out vt (form, receipt) rellenar.
fill up vt llenar (hasta el borde) ♦ vi (AUT) poner gasolina.
fillet ['fɪlɪt] n filete m.
fillet steak n filete m de ternera.
filling ['fɪlɪŋ] n (CULIN) relleno; (for tooth) empaste m.
filling station n estación f de servicio.
fillip ['fɪlɪp] n estímulo.
filly ['fɪlɪ] n potra.
film [fɪlm] n película ♦ vt (scene) filmar ♦ vi rodar (una película).
film script n guión m.
film star n astro, estrella de cine.
filmstrip ['fɪlmstrɪp] n tira de película.

film studio n estudio de cine.
filter ['fɪltə*] n filtro ◆ vt filtrar.
filter in, filter through vi filtrarse.
filter coffee n café m (molido) para filtrar.
filter lane n (Brit) carril m de selección.
filter-tipped ['fɪltətɪpt] a con filtro.
filth [fɪlθ] n suciedad f.
filthy ['fɪlθɪ] a sucio; (language) obsceno.
fin [fɪn] n (gen) aleta.
final ['faɪnl] a (last) final, último; (definitive) definitivo, terminante ◆ n (Brit: SPORT) final f; ~s npl (SCOL) examen m de fin de curso; (US: SPORT) final f; ~ **demand** (on invoice etc) último aviso; ~ **dividend** dividendo final.
finale [fɪ'nɑːlɪ] n final m.
finalist ['faɪnəlɪst] n (SPORT) finalista m/f.
finality [faɪ'nælɪtɪ] n finalidad f; **with an air of** ~ en tono resuelto, de modo terminante.
finalize ['faɪnəlaɪz] vt concluir, completar.
finally ['faɪnəlɪ] ad (lastly) por último, finalmente; (eventually) por fin; (irrevocably) de modo definitivo; (once and for all) definitivamente.
finance [faɪ'næns] n (money, funds) fondos mpl; ~s npl finanzas fpl ◆ cpd (page, section, company) financiero ◆ vt financiar.
financial [faɪ'nænʃəl] a financiero.
financially [faɪ'nænʃəlɪ] ad económicamente.
financial management n gestión f financiera.
financial statement n estado financiero.
financial year n ejercicio (financiero).
financier [faɪ'nænsɪə*] n financiero/a.
find [faɪnd] vt (pt, pp found [faund]) (gen) encontrar, hallar; (come upon) descubrir ◆ n hallazgo; descubrimiento; **to** ~ **sb guilty** (LAW) declarar culpable a uno; **to** ~ **(some) difficulty in doing sth** encontrar dificultad en hacer algo.
find out vt averiguar; (truth, secret) descubrir ◆ vi: **to** ~ **out about** enterarse de.
findings ['faɪndɪŋz] npl (LAW) veredicto sg, fallo sg; (of report) recomendaciones fpl.
fine [faɪn] a (delicate) fino; (beautiful) hermoso ◆ ad (well) bien ◆ n (LAW) multa ◆ vt (LAW) multar; **the weather is** ~ hace buen tiempo; **he's** ~ está muy bien; **you're doing** ~ lo estás haciendo muy bien; **to cut it** ~ (of time, money) calcular muy justo; **to get a** ~ **for (doing) sth** recibir una multa por (hacer) algo.
fine arts npl bellas artes fpl.
finely ['faɪnlɪ] ad (splendidly) con elegancia; (chop) en trozos pequeños, fino; (adjust) con precisión.
fineness ['faɪnnɪs] n (of cloth) finura; (of idea) sutilidad f.
finery ['faɪnərɪ] n adornos mpl.
finesse [fɪ'nɛs] n sutileza.
fine-tooth comb ['faɪntuː-θ-] n: **to go**

through sth with a ~ revisar algo a fondo.
finger ['fɪŋgə*] n dedo ◆ vt (touch) manosear; (MUS) puntear; **little/index** ~ (dedo) meñique m/índice m.
fingernail ['fɪŋgəneɪl] n uña.
fingerprint ['fɪŋgəprɪnt] n huella dactilar ◆ vt tomar las huellas dactilares de.
fingertip ['fɪŋgətɪp] n yema del dedo; **to have sth at one's** ~s saberse algo al dedillo.
finicky ['fɪnɪkɪ] a (fussy) delicado.
finish ['fɪnɪʃ] n (end) fin m; (SPORT) meta; (polish etc) acabado ◆ vt, vi terminar; **to** ~ **doing sth** acabar de hacer algo; **to** ~ **first/second/third** (SPORT) llegar el primero/segundo/tercero; **I've** ~ed **with the paper** he terminado con el periódico; **she's** ~ed **with him** ha roto or acabado con él.
finish off vt acabar, terminar; (kill) rematar.
finish up vt acabar, terminar ◆ vi ir a parar, terminar.
finished ['fɪnɪʃt] a (product) acabado; (performance) pulido; (col: tired) rendido, hecho polvo.
finishing ['fɪnɪʃɪŋ] a: ~ **touches** toque m final.
finishing line n línea de llegada or meta.
finishing school n academia para señoritas.
finite ['faɪnaɪt] a finito.
Finland ['fɪnlənd] n Finlandia.
Finn [fɪn] n finlandés/esa m/f.
Finnish ['fɪnɪʃ] a finlandés/esa ◆ n (LING) finlandés m.
fiord [fjɔːd] n fiordo.
fir [fəː*] n abeto.
fire ['faɪə*] n fuego; (accidental, damaging) incendio ◆ vt (gun) disparar; (set fire to) incendiar; (excite) exaltar; (interest) despertar; (dismiss) despedir ◆ vi encenderse; (AUT: subj: engine) encender; **electric/gas** ~ estufa eléctrica/de gas; **on** ~ ardiendo, en llamas; **to be on** ~ estar ardiendo; **to catch** ~ encenderse; **to set** ~ **to sth, set sth on** ~ prender fuego a algo; **insured against** ~ asegurado contra incendios; **to be/come under** ~ estar/caer bajo fuego.
fire alarm n alarma de incendios.
firearm ['faɪərɑːm] n arma de fuego.
fire brigade, (US) **fire department** n (cuerpo de) bomberos mpl.
fire drill n simulacro de incendio.
fire engine n coche m de bomberos.
fire escape n escalera de incendios.
fire extinguisher n extintor m (de fuego).
fireguard ['faɪəgɑːd] n pantalla guardallama.
fire hazard n = **fire risk**.
fire hydrant n boca de incendios.
fire insurance n seguro contra incendios.
fireman ['faɪəmən] n bombero.

fireplace ['faɪəpleɪs] *n* chimenea.
fireplug ['faɪəplʌg] *n* (*US*) boca de incendios.
fire practice *n* = **fire drill**.
fireproof ['faɪəpruːf] *a* a prueba de fuego; (*material*) incombustible.
fire regulations *npl* reglamentos *mpl* contra incendios.
fire risk *n* peligro de incendio.
firescreen ['faɪəskriːn] *n* pantalla refractaria.
fireside ['faɪəsaɪd] *n*: **by the ~** al lado de la chimenea.
fire station *n* parque *m* de bomberos.
firewood ['faɪəwud] *n* leña.
fireworks ['faɪəwɔːks] *npl* fuegos *mpl* artificiales.
firing ['faɪərɪŋ] *n* (*MIL*) disparos *mpl*, tiroteo.
firing line *n* línea de fuego; **to be in the ~** (*fig: liable to be criticised*) estar en la línea de fuego.
firing squad *n* pelotón *m* de ejecución.
firm [fəːm] *a* firme; (*offer, decision*) en firme ♦ *n* firma, empresa; **to be a ~ believer in sth** ser un partidario convencido de algo; **to stand ~** *or* **take a ~ stand over sth** (*fig*) mantenerse firme ante algo.
firmly ['fəːmlɪ] *ad* firmemente.
firmness ['fəːmnɪs] *n* firmeza.
first [fəːst] *a* primero ♦ *ad* (*before others*) primero; (*when listing reasons etc*) en primer lugar, primeramente ♦ *n* (*person: in race*) primero/a; (*AUT: also:* **~ gear**) primera; **at ~** al principio; **~ of all** ante todo; **the ~ of January** el uno *or* primero de enero; **in the ~ instance** en primer lugar; **I'll do it ~ thing tomorrow** lo haré mañana a primera hora; **for the ~ time** por primera vez; **head ~** de cabeza; **from the (very) ~** desde el principio.
first aid *n* primera ayuda, primeros auxilios *mpl*.
first aid kit *n* botiquín *m*.
first aid post, (*US*) **first aid station** *n* puesto de auxilio.
first-class ['fəːstklɑːs] *a* de primera clase; **~ ticket** (*RAIL etc*) billete *m* *or* boleto (*LAm*) de primera clase; **~ mail** correo de primera.
first-hand [fəːst'hænd] *a* de primera mano.
first lady *n* (*esp US*) primera dama.
firstly ['fəːstlɪ] *ad* en primer lugar.
first name *n* nombre *m* de pila.
first night *n* estreno.
first-rate [fəːst'reɪt] *a* de primera clase.
fir tree *n* abeto.
FIS *n* *abbr* (*Brit*: = *Family Income Supplement*) *ayuda estatal familiar*.
fiscal ['fɪskəl] *a* fiscal; **~ year** año fiscal, ejercicio.
fish [fɪʃ] *n, pl inv* pez *m*; (*food*) pescado ♦ *vt, vi* pescar; **to go ~ing** ir de pesca.
fish out *vt* (*from water, box etc*) sacar.

fishbone ['fɪʃbəun] *n* espina.
fisherman ['fɪʃəmən] *n* pescador *m*.
fishery ['fɪʃərɪ] *n* pesquería.
fish factory *n* fábrica de elaboración de pescado.
fish farm *n* piscifactoría.
fish fingers *npl* (*Brit*) croquetas *fpl* de pescado.
fishing boat ['fɪʃɪŋ-] *n* barca de pesca.
fishing industry *n* industria pesquera.
fishing line *n* sedal *m*.
fishing net *n* red *f* de pesca.
fishing rod *n* caña (de pescar).
fishing tackle *n* aparejo (de pescar).
fish market *n* mercado de pescado.
fishmonger ['fɪʃmʌŋgə*] *n* (*Brit*) pescadero/a.
fishmonger's (shop) *n* (*Brit*) pescadería.
fishseller ['fɪʃselə*] *n* (*US*) = **fishmonger**.
fish slice *n* paleta para pescado.
fish sticks *npl* (*US*) = **fish fingers**.
fishstore ['fɪʃstɔː*] *n* (*US*) = **fishmonger's (shop)**.
fishy ['fɪʃɪ] *a* (*fig*) sospechoso.
fission ['fɪʃən] *n* fisión *f*; **atomic/nuclear ~** fisión *f* atómica/nuclear.
fissure ['fɪʃə*] *n* fisura.
fist [fɪst] *n* puño.
fistfight ['fɪstfaɪt] *n* lucha a puñetazos.
fit [fɪt] *a* (*MED, SPORT*) en (buena) forma; (*proper*) adecuado, apropiado ♦ *vt* (*subj: clothes*) sentar bien a; (*try on: clothes*) probar; (*match: facts*) cuadrar *or* corresponder *or* coincidir con; (*description*) estar de acuerdo con; (*accommodate*) ajustar, adaptar ♦ *vi* (*clothes*) entallar; (*in space, gap*) caber; (*facts*) coincidir ♦ *n* (*MED*) ataque *m*; (*outburst*) arranque *m*; **~ to** apto para; **~ for** apropiado para; **do as you think** *or* **see ~** haz lo que te parezca (mejor); **to keep ~** mantenerse en forma; **to be ~ for work** (*after illness*) estar apto para trabajar; **~ of coughing** acceso de tos; **~ of anger/enthusiasm** arranque de cólera/entusiasmo; **to have** *or* **suffer a ~** tener un ataque *or* acceso; **this dress is a good ~** este vestido me sienta bien; **by ~s and starts** a rachas.
fit in *vi* (*gen*) encajarse; (*fig: person*) llevarse bien (con todos) ♦ *vt* (*object*) acomodar; (*fig: appointment, visitor*) incluir; **to ~ in with sb's plans** acomodarse a los planes de uno.
fit out *vt* (*Brit: also:* **fit up**) equipar.
fitful ['fɪtful] *a* espasmódico, intermitente.
fitfully ['fɪtfəlɪ] *ad* irregularmente; **to sleep ~** dormir inquieto.
fitment ['fɪtmənt] *n* mueble *m*.
fitness ['fɪtnɪs] *n* (*MED*) salud *f*; (*of remark*) conveniencia.
fitted carpet ['fɪtɪd-] *n* moqueta.
fitted cupboards ['fɪtɪd-] *npl* armarios *mpl* empotrados.

fitted kitchen ['fɪtɪd-] n cocina amueblada.
fitter ['fɪtə*] n ajustador(a) m/f.
fitting ['fɪtɪŋ] a apropiado ♦ n (of dress) prueba; see also **fittings**.
fitting room n (in shop) probador m.
fittings ['fɪtɪŋz] npl instalaciones fpl.
five [faɪv] num cinco; **she is ~ (years old)** tiene cinco años (de edad); **it costs ~ pounds** cuesta cinco libras; **it's ~ (o'clock)** son las cinco.
five-day week ['faɪvdeɪ] n semana inglesa.
fiver ['faɪvə*] n (col: Brit) billete m de cinco libras; (: US) billete m de cinco dólares.
fix [fɪks] vt (secure) fijar, asegurar; (mend) arreglar; (make ready: meal, drink) preparar ♦ n: **to be in a ~** estar en un aprieto; **to ~ sth in one's mind** fijar algo en la memoria; **the fight was a ~** (col) hubo tongo en la lucha.
fix on vt (decide on) fijar.
fix up vt (arrange: date, meeting) arreglar; **to ~ sb up with sth** proveer a uno de algo.
fixation [fɪk'seɪʃən] n (PSYCH, fig) obsesión f.
fixative ['fɪksətɪv] n fijador m.
fixed [fɪkst] a (prices etc) fijo; **how are you ~ for money?** (col) ¿qué tal andas de dinero?
fixed assets npl activo sg fijo.
fixed charge n gasto fijo.
fixed-price contract ['fɪkstpraɪs-] n contrato a precio fijo.
fixture ['fɪkstʃə*] n (SPORT) encuentro; **~s** npl instalaciones fpl fijas.
fizz [fɪz] vi burbujear.
fizzle out ['fɪzl-] vi apagarse; (enthusiasm, interest) morirse; (plan) fracasar.
fizzy ['fɪzɪ] a (drink) gaseoso.
fjord [fjɔːd] n = **fiord**.
FL (US POST) = Florida.
flabbergasted ['flæbəgɑːstɪd] a pasmado.
flabby ['flæbɪ] a flojo (de carnes); (skin) fofo.
flag [flæg] n bandera; (stone) losa ♦ vi decaer; **~ of convenience** pabellón m de conveniencia.
flag down vt: **to ~ sb down** hacer señas a uno para que se pare.
flagpole ['flægpəul] n asta de bandera.
flagrant ['fleɪɡrənt] a flagrante.
flagship ['flægʃɪp] n buque m insignia or almirante.
flagstone ['flægstəun] n losa.
flag stop n (US) parada a petición.
flair [flɛə*] n aptitud f especial.
flak [flæk] n (MIL) fuego antiaéreo; (col: criticism) lluvia de críticas.
flake [fleɪk] n (of rust, paint) escama; (of snow, soap powder) copo ♦ vi (also: ~ off) (paint) desconcharse; (skin) descamarse.
flaky ['fleɪkɪ] a (paintwork) desconchado; (skin) escamoso.

flaky pastry n (CULIN) hojaldre m.
flamboyant [flæm'bɔɪənt] a (dress) vistoso; (person) extravagante.
flame [fleɪm] n llama; **to burst into ~s** incendiarse; **old ~** (col) antiguo amor m/f.
flamingo [flə'mɪŋɡəu] n flamenco.
flammable ['flæməbl] a inflamable.
flan [flæn] n (Brit) tarta.
flank [flæŋk] n flanco; (of person) costado ♦ vt flanquear.
flannel ['flænl] n (Brit: also: **face ~**) manopla; (fabric) franela; **~s** npl pantalones mpl de franela.
flannelette [flænə'lɛt] n franela de algodón.
flap [flæp] n (of pocket, envelope) solapa; (of table) hoja (plegadiza); (wing movement) aletazo; (AVIAT) flap m ♦ vt (wings) aletear ♦ vi (sail, flag) ondear.
flapjack ['flæpdʒæk] n (US: pancake) torta, (LAm) panqueque m.
flare [flɛə*] n llamarada; (MIL) bengala; (in skirt etc) vuelo.
flare up vi encenderse; (fig: person) encolerizarse; (: revolt) estallar.
flash [flæʃ] n relámpago; (also: **news ~**) noticias fpl de última hora; (PHOT) flash m; (US: torch) linterna ♦ vt (light, headlights) encender y apagar; (torch) encender ♦ vi brillar; **in a ~** en un santiamén; **~ of inspiration** ráfaga de inspiración; **to ~ sth about** (fig, col: flaunt) ostentar algo, presumir con algo; **he ~ed by** or **past** pasó como un rayo.
flashback ['flæʃbæk] n flashback m.
flashbulb ['flæʃbʌlb] n bombilla fusible.
flash card n (SCOL) tarjeta, carta.
flash cube n cubo m de flash.
flasher ['flæʃə*] n exhibicionista m.
flashlight ['flæʃlaɪt] n (US: torch) linterna.
flashpoint ['flæʃpɔɪnt] n punto de inflamación; (fig) punto de inflamación.
flashy ['flæʃɪ] a (pej) ostentoso.
flask [flɑːsk] n frasco; (also: **vacuum ~**) termo(s) m.
flat [flæt] a llano; (smooth) liso; (tyre) desinflado; (battery) descargado; (beer) muerto; (MUS: instrument) desafinado ♦ n (Brit: apartment) piso (Sp), departamento (LAm), apartamento (AUT) pinchazo; (MUS) bemol m; **(to work) ~ out** (trabajar) a toda mecha; **~ rate of pay** sueldo fijo.
flatfooted [flæt'futɪd] a de pies planos.
flatly ['flætlɪ] ad terminantemente, de plano.
flatmate ['flætmeɪt] n compañero/a de piso.
flatness ['flætnɪs] n (of land) llanura, lo llano.
flatten ['flætn] vt (also: **~ out**) allanar; (smooth out) alisar; (house, city) arrasar.
flatter ['flætə*] vt adular, halagar; (show to advantage) favorecer.
flatterer ['flætərə*] n adulador(a) m/f.
flattering ['flætərɪŋ] a halagüeño; (clothes

etc) que favorece, favorecedor(a).

flattery ['flætərı] *n* adulación *f.*

flatulence ['flætjuləns] *n* flatulencia.

flaunt [flɔːnt] *vt* ostentar, lucir.

flavour, *(US)* **flavor** ['fleɪvə*] *n* sabor *m*, gusto ♦ *vt* sazonar, condimentar; **strawberry ~ed** con sabor a fresa.

flavo(u)ring ['fleɪvərɪŋ] *n (in product)* aromatizante *m.*

flaw [flɔː] *n* defecto.

flawless ['flɔːlɪs] *a* intachable.

flax [flæks] *n* lino.

flaxen ['flæksən] *a* rubio.

flea [fliː] *n* pulga.

flea market *n* rastro, mercadillo.

fleck [flɛk] *n (mark, mud, paint)* mota; *(colour, pattern)* punto; *(of dust)* partícula ♦ *vt (with blood, mud etc)* salpicar; **brown ~ed with white** marrón con puntos blancos.

fledg(e)ling ['flɛdʒlɪŋ] *n (fig)* novato/a, principiante *m/f.*

flee [fliː], *pt, pp* **fled** [flɛd] *vt* huir de, abandonar ♦ *vi* huir, fugarse.

fleece [fliːs] *n* vellón *m*; *(wool)* lana ♦ *vt (col)* pelar.

fleecy ['fliːsɪ] *a (blanket)* lanoso, lanudo; *(cloud)* aborregado.

fleet [fliːt] *n* flota; *(of cars, lorries etc)* escuadra.

fleeting ['fliːtɪŋ] *a* fugaz.

Flemish ['flɛmɪʃ] *a* flamenco ♦ *n (LING)* flamenco; **the ~** los flamencos.

flesh [flɛʃ] *n* carne *f*; *(of fruit)* pulpa; **of ~ and blood** de carne y hueso.

flesh wound *n* herida superficial.

flew [fluː] *pt of* **fly**.

flex [flɛks] *n* cordón *m* ♦ *vt (muscles)* tensar.

flexibility [flɛksɪˈbɪlɪtɪ] *n* flexibilidad *f.*

flexible ['flɛksəbl] *a (gen, disk)* flexible; **~ working hours** horario *sg* flexible.

flexitime ['flɛksɪtaɪm] *n* horario flexible.

flick [flɪk] *n* golpecito; *(with finger)* capirotazo; *(Brit: col: film)* película ♦ *vt* dar un golpecito a.

flick off *vt* quitar con el dedo.

flick through *vt fus* hojear.

flicker ['flɪkə*] *vi (light)* parpadear; *(flame)* vacilar ♦ *n* parpadeo.

flick knife *n* navaja de muelle.

flier ['flaɪə*] *n* aviador(a) *m/f.*

flies [flaɪz] *npl of* **fly**.

flight [flaɪt] *n* vuelo; *(escape)* huida, fuga; *(also: ~ of steps)* tramo (de escaleras); **to take ~** huir, darse a la fuga; **to put to ~** ahuyentar; **how long does the ~ take?** ¿cuánto dura el vuelo?

flight attendant *n (US) (male)* camarero; *(female)* azafata.

flight deck *n (AVIAT)* cabina de mandos.

flight recorder *n* registrador *m* de vuelo.

flighty ['flaɪtɪ] *a* frívolo; caprichoso.

flimsy ['flɪmzɪ] *a (thin)* muy ligero; *(excuse)* flojo.

flinch [flɪntʃ] *vi* encogerse.

fling [flɪŋ] *vt (pt, pp* **flung** [flʌŋ]) arrojar ♦ *n (love affair)* aventura amorosa.

flint [flɪnt] *n* pedernal *m*; *(in lighter)* piedra.

flip [flɪp] *vt*: **to ~ a coin** echar a cara o cruz.

flip over *vt* dar la vuelta a.

flip through *vt fus (book, records)* hojear, repasar.

flippancy ['flɪpənsɪ] *n* ligereza.

flippant ['flɪpənt] *a* poco serio.

flipper ['flɪpə*] *n (of seal etc, for swimming)* aleta.

flip side *n (of record)* cara B.

flirt [flɜːt] *vi* coquetear, flirtear ♦ *n* coqueta *f.*

flirtation [flɜːˈteɪʃən] *n* coqueteo, flirteo.

flit [flɪt] *vi* revolotear.

float [fləut] *n* flotador *m*; *(in procession)* carroza; *(sum of money)* reserva ♦ *vi (also COMM: currency)* flotar; *(bather)* hacer la plancha ♦ *vt (gen)* hacer flotar; *(company)* lanzar; **to ~ an idea** propagar una idea.

floating ['fləutɪŋ] *a*: **~ vote** voto indeciso; **~ voter** votante *m/f* indeciso/a.

flock [flɔk] *n (of sheep)* rebaño; *(of birds)* bandada; *(of people)* multitud *f.*

floe [fləu] *n*: **ice ~** témpano de hielo.

flog [flɔg] *vt* azotar; *(col)* vender.

flood [flʌd] *n* inundación *f*; *(of words, tears etc)* torrente *m* ♦ *vt (also AUT: carburettor)* inundar; **to ~ the market** *(COMM)* inundar el mercado.

flooding ['flʌdɪŋ] *n* inundación *f.*

floodlight ['flʌdlaɪt] *n* foco ♦ *vt (irg: like light)* iluminar con focos.

floodlit ['flʌdlɪt] *pt, pp of* **floodlight** ♦ *a* iluminado.

flood tide *n* pleamar *f.*

floor [flɔː*] *n* suelo; *(storey)* piso; *(of sea, valley)* fondo; *(dance ~)* pista ♦ *vt (fig: baffle)* dejar sin respuesta, confundir; *(: silence)* dejar sin réplica posible; **ground ~**, *(US)* **first ~** planta baja; **first ~**, *(US)* **second ~** primer piso; **top ~** último piso; **to have the ~** *(speaker)* tener la palabra.

floorboard ['flɔːbɔːd] *n* tabla.

flooring ['flɔːrɪŋ] *n* suelo; *(material)* solería.

floor lamp *n (US)* lámpara de pie.

floor show *n* cabaret *m.*

floorwalker ['flɔːwɔːkə*] *n (US COMM)* vigilante *m/f.*

flop [flɔp] *n* fracaso ♦ *vi (fail)* fracasar.

floppy ['flɔpɪ] *a* flojo ♦ *n* = **floppy disk.**

floppy disk *n (COMPUT)* floppy *m*, floppy-disk *m*, disco flexible.

flora ['flɔːrə] *n* flora.

floral ['flɔːrl] *a* floral.

Florence ['flɔrəns] *n* Florencia.

Florentine ['flɔrəntaɪn] *a, n* florentino/a *m/f*.
florid ['flɔrɪd] *a* (*style*) florido.
florist ['flɔrɪst] *n* florista *m/f*; ~'s (**shop**) *n* florería.
flotation [fləu'teɪʃən] *n* (*of shares*) emisión *f*; (*of company*) lanzamiento.
flounce [flauns] *n* volante *m*.
  flounce in *vi* entrar con gesto exagerado.
  flounce out *vi* salir enfadado.
flounder ['flaundə*] *vi* tropezar ♦ *n* (*ZOOL*) platija.
flour ['flauə*] *n* harina.
flourish ['flʌrɪʃ] *vi* florecer ♦ *n* ademán *m*, movimiento (ostentoso).
flourishing ['flʌrɪʃɪŋ] *a* floreciente.
flout [flaut] *vt* burlarse de; (*order*) no hacer caso de, hacer caso omiso de.
flow [fləu] *n* (*movement*) flujo; (*direction*) curso; (*of river, tide, also ELEC*) corriente *f* ♦ *vi* correr, fluir.
flow chart *n* organigrama *m*.
flow diagram *n* organigrama *m*.
flower ['flauə*] *n* flor *f* ♦ *vi* florecer; in ~ en flor.
flower bed *n* macizo.
flowerpot ['flauəpɔt] *n* tiesto.
flowery ['flauərɪ] *a* florido.
flowing ['fləuɪŋ] *a* (*hair, clothes*) suelto; (*style*) fluido.
flown [fləun] *pp of* **fly**.
flu [fluː] *n* gripe *f*.
fluctuate ['flʌktjueɪt] *vi* fluctuar.
fluctuation [flʌktju'eɪʃən] *n* fluctuación *f*.
flue [fluː] *n* humero.
fluency ['fluːənsɪ] *n* fluidez *f*.
fluent ['fluːənt] *a* (*speech*) elocuente; **he speaks ~ French, he's ~ in French** domina el francés.
fluently ['fluːəntlɪ] *ad* con fluidez.
fluff [flʌf] *n* pelusa.
fluffy ['flʌfɪ] *a* velloso.
fluid ['fluːɪd] *a, n* fluido, líquido; (*in diet*) líquido.
fluke [fluːk] *n* (*col*) chiripa.
flummox ['flʌməks] *vt* desconcertar.
flung [flʌŋ] *pt, pp of* **fling**.
flunky ['flʌŋkɪ] *n* lacayo.
fluorescent [fluə'rɛsnt] *a* fluorescente.
fluoride ['fluəraɪd] *n* fluoruro.
fluoride toothpaste *n* pasta de dientes con flúor.
flurry ['flʌrɪ] *n* (*of snow*) temporal *m;* (*haste*) agitación *f;* ~ **of activity** frenesí *m* de actividad.
flush [flʌʃ] *n* (*on face*) rubor *m;* (*fig: of youth, beauty*) resplandor *m* ♦ *vt* limpiar con agua; (*also:* ~ **out**) (*game, birds*) levantar; (*fig: criminal*) poner al descubierto ♦ *vi* ruborizarse ♦ *a:* ~ **with** a ras de; **to ~ the toilet** hacer funcionar el WC; **hot ~es** (*MED*) sofocos *mpl*.
flushed [flʌʃt] *a* ruborizado.
fluster ['flʌstə*] *n* aturdimiento ♦ *vt*

aturdir.
flustered ['flʌstəd] *a* aturdido.
flute [fluːt] *n* flauta.
flutter ['flʌtə*] *n* (*of wings*) revoloteo, aleteo; (*fam: bet*) apuesta ♦ *vi* revolotear; **to be in a ~** estar nervioso.
flux [flʌks] *n* flujo; **in a state of ~** cambiando continuamente.
fly [flaɪ] *n* (*insect*) mosca; (*on trousers: also:* **flies**) bragueta ♦ *vb* (*pt* **flew,** *pp* **flown**) *vt* (*plane*) pilot(e)ar; (*cargo*) transportar (en avión); (*distances*) recorrer (en avión) ♦ *vi* volar; (*passengers*) ir en avión; (*escape*) evadirse; (*flag*) ondear.
fly away *vi* (*bird, insect*) volarse.
fly in *vi* (*person*) llegar en avión; (*plane*) aterrizar; **he flew in from Bilbao** llegó en avión desde Bilbao.
fly off *vi* volarse.
fly out *vi* irse en avión.
fly-fishing ['flaɪfɪʃɪŋ] *n* pesca con mosca.
flying ['flaɪɪŋ] *n* (*activity*) (el) volar ♦ *a:* ~ **visit** visita relámpago; **with ~ colours** con lucimiento.
flying buttress *n* arbotante *m*.
flying saucer *n* platillo volante.
flying start *n:* **to get off to a ~** empezar con buen pie.
flyleaf, *pl* **flyleaves** ['flaɪliːf, -liːvz] *n* (hoja de) guarda.
flyover ['flaɪəuvə*] *n* (*Brit: bridge*) paso superior *or* a desnivel.
flypast ['flaɪpɑːst] *n* desfile *m* aéreo.
flysheet ['flaɪʃiːt] *n* (*for tent*) doble techo.
flyswatter ['flaɪswɔtə*] *n* matamoscas *m inv.*
flywheel ['flaɪwiːl] *n* volante *m* mecánico.
FM *abbr* (*Brit MIL*) = **field marshal;** (*RADIO:* = *frequency modulation*) FM.
FMB *n abbr* (*US*) = *Federal Maritime Board.*
FMCS *n abbr* (*US:* = *Federal Mediation and Conciliation Services*) organismo de conciliación en conflictos laborales.
FO *n abbr* (*Brit:* = *Foreign Office*) ≈ Min. de AA. EE.
foal [fəul] *n* potro.
foam [fəum] *n* espuma ♦ *vi* echar espuma.
foam rubber *n* espuma de caucho.
FOB *abbr* (= *free on board*) f.a.b.
fob [fɔb] *n* (*also:* **watch ~**) leontina ♦ *vt:* **to ~ sb off with sth** deshacerse de uno con algo.
foc *abbr* (*Brit:* = *free of charge*) gratis.
focal ['fəukəl] *a* focal; ~ **point** punto focal; (*fig*) centro de atención.
focus ['fəukəs] (*pl:* **~es**) *n* foco ♦ *vt* (*field glasses etc*) enfocar ♦ *vi:* **to ~ (on)** enfocar (a); (*issue etc*) centrarse en; **in/out of ~** enfocado/desenfocado.
fodder ['fɔdə*] *n* pienso.
FOE *n abbr* (= *Friends of the Earth*) Amigos *mpl* de la Tierra; (*US:* = *Fraternal*

Order of Eagles) organización benéfica.
foe [fəu] n enemigo.
foetus, (US) fetus ['fiːtəs] n feto.
fog [fɔg] n niebla.
fogbound ['fɔgbaund] a inmovilizado por la niebla.
foggy ['fɔgɪ] a: **it's ~** hay niebla, está brumoso.
fog lamp, (US) fog light n (AUT) faro antiniebla.
foible ['fɔɪbl] n manía.
foil [fɔɪl] vt frustrar ♦ n hoja; (kitchen ~) papel m (de) aluminio; (FENCING) florete m.
foist [fɔɪst] vt: **to ~ sth on sb** colarle algo a uno.
fold [fəuld] n (bend, crease) pliegue m; (AGR) redil m ♦ vt doblar; (map etc) plegar; **to ~ one's arms** cruzarse de brazos.
fold up vi plegarse, doblarse; (business) quebrar.
folder ['fəuldə*] n (for papers) carpeta; (binder) carpeta de anillas; (brochure) folleto.
folding ['fəuldɪŋ] a (chair, bed) plegable.
foliage ['fəulɪɪdʒ] n follaje m.
folio ['fəulɪəu] n folio.
folk [fəuk] npl gente f ♦ a popular, folklórico; **~s** npl familia, parientes mpl.
folklore ['fəuklɔː*] n folklore m.
folk music n música folk(lórica).
folk singer n cantante m/f de canciones folklóricas.
folk song n canción f popular or folklórica.
follow ['fɔləu] vt seguir ♦ vi seguir; (result) resultar; **he ~ed suit** hizo lo mismo; **to ~ sb's advice** seguir el consejo de uno; **I don't quite ~ you** no le sigo (la pista); **to ~ in sb's footsteps** seguirle los pasos a uno; **it doesn't ~ that ...** no se puede concluir que ....
follow on vi seguir; (continue): **to ~ on from** continuar.
follow out vt (implement: idea, plan) realizar, llevar a cabo.
follow through vt llevar hasta el fin ♦ vi (SPORT) dar el remate.
follow up vt (letter, offer) responder a; (case) investigar.
follower ['fɔləuə*] n seguidor(a) m/f; (POL) partidario/a.
following ['fɔləuɪŋ] a siguiente ♦ n afición f, partidarios mpl.
follow-up ['fɔləuʌp] n seguimiento.
follow-up letter n carta recordatoria.
folly ['fɔlɪ] n locura.
fond [fɔnd] a (loving) cariñoso; **to be ~ of sb** tener cariño a uno; **she's ~ of swimming** tiene afición a la natación, a ella le gusta nadar.
fondle ['fɔndl] vt acariciar.
fondly ['fɔndlɪ] ad (lovingly) con cariño; **he ~ believed that ...** creía inocentemente

que ....
fondness ['fɔndnɪs] n (for things) afición f; (for people) cariño.
font [fɔnt] n pila bautismal.
food [fuːd] n comida.
food mixer n batidora.
food poisoning n botulismo.
food processor n robot m de cocina.
foodstuffs ['fuːdstʌfs] npl comestibles mpl.
fool [fuːl] n tonto/a; (CULIN) puré m de frutas con nata ♦ vt engañar; **to make a ~ of o.s.** ponerse en ridículo; **you can't ~ me** a mí no me engañas.
fool about, fool around vi bromear; (waste time) perder el tiempo.
foolhardy ['fuːlhɑːdɪ] a temerario.
foolish ['fuːlɪʃ] a tonto; (careless) imprudente.
foolishly ['fuːlɪʃlɪ] ad tontamente, neciamente.
foolproof ['fuːlpruːf] a (plan etc) infalible.
foolscap ['fuːlskæp] n papel m folio.
foot [fut], pl **feet** n (gen, also: of page, stairs etc) pie m; (measure) pie m (= 304 mm); (of animal, table) pata ♦ vt (bill) pagar; **on ~** a pie; **to find one's feet** acostumbrarse; **to put one's ~ down** (say no) plantarse; (AUT) pisar el acelerador.
footage ['futɪdʒ] n (CINEMA) imágenes fpl.
foot-and-mouth (disease) [futənd-'mauθ-] n fiebre f aftosa.
football ['futbɔːl] n balón m; (game: Brit) fútbol m; (: US) fútbol m americano.
footballer ['futbɔːlə*] n (Brit) = **football player**.
football match n partido de fútbol.
football player n futbolista m/f, jugador(a) m/f de fútbol.
footbrake ['futbreɪk] n freno de pie.
footbridge ['futbrɪdʒ] n puente m para peatones.
foothills ['futhɪlz] npl estribaciones fpl.
foothold ['futhəuld] n pie m firme.
footing ['futɪŋ] n (fig) posición f; **to lose one's ~** perder el pie; **on an equal ~** en pie de igualdad.
footlights ['futlaɪts] npl candilejas fpl.
footman ['futmən] n lacayo.
footnote ['futnəut] n nota (de pie de página).
footpath ['futpɑːθ] n sendero.
footprint ['futprɪnt] n huella, pisada.
footrest ['futrest] n apoyapiés m inv.
footsore ['futsɔː*] a con los pies doloridos.
footstep ['futstɛp] n paso.
footwear ['futwɛə*] n calzado.
FOR abbr (= free on rail) franco (puesto vagón.
for [fɔː*] prep (gen) para; (as, in exchange for, because of) por; (during) durante; (in spite of) a pesar de ♦ conj pues, ya que; **it was sold ~ 100 pesetas** se vendió por 100 pesetas; **what ~?** ¿para qué?; **what's this**

button ~**?** ¿para qué sirve este botón?; **he was away** ~ **2 years** estuvo fuera 2 años; **I haven't seen him** ~ **3 days** hace 3 días que no le veo; **he went** ~ **the paper** fue a buscar el periódico; **the train** ~ **London** el tren de Londres; **is this** ~ **me?** ¿es para mí esto?; **it's time** ~ **lunch** es la hora de comer; **G** ~ **George** G de Gerona.

forage ['fɔrɪdʒ] *n* forraje *m*.

foray ['fɔreɪ] *n* incursión *f*.

forbid, *pt* **forbad(e)**, *pp* **forbidden** [fə'bɪd, -'bæd, -'bɪdn] *vt* prohibir; **to** ~ **sb to do sth** prohibir a uno hacer algo.

forbidding [fə'bɪdɪŋ] *a* (*landscape*) inhóspito; (*severe*) severo.

force [fɔːs] *n* fuerza ♦ *vt* forzar; **to** ~ **o.s. to do** hacer un esfuerzo por hacer; **the F~s** *npl* (*Brit*) las Fuerzas Armadas; **sales** ~ (*COMM*) personal *m* de ventas; **a** ~ **5 wind** un viento fuerza 5; **to join** ~**s** unir fuerzas; **in** ~ (*law etc*) en vigor; **to** ~ **sb to do sth** obligar a uno a hacer algo.

force back *vt* (*crowd, enemy*) hacer retroceder; (*tears*) reprimir.

force down *vt* (*food*) comer sin gusto.

forced [fɔːst] *a* (*smile*) forzado; (*landing*) forzoso.

force-feed ['fɔːsfiːd] *vt* (*animal, prisoner*) alimentar a la fuerza.

forceful ['fɔːsful] *a* enérgico.

forcemeat ['fɔːsmiːt] *n* (*CULIN*) relleno.

forceps ['fɔːseps] *npl* fórceps *m inv*.

forcible ['fɔːsəbl] *a* (*violent*) a la fuerza; (*telling*) convincente.

forcibly ['fɔːsəblɪ] *ad* a la fuerza.

ford [fɔːd] *n* vado ♦ *vt* vadear.

fore [fɔː*] *n*: **to bring to the** ~ sacar a la luz pública; **to come to the** ~ hacerse notar.

forearm ['fɔːrɑːm] *n* antebrazo.

forebear ['fɔːbɛə*] *n* antepasado.

foreboding [fɔː'bəudɪŋ] *n* presentimiento.

forecast ['fɔːkɑːst] *n* pronóstico ♦ *vt* (*irg: like cast*) pronosticar; **weather** ~ previsión *f* meteorológica.

foreclose [fɔː'kləuz] *vt* (*LAW: also:* ~ **on**) extinguir el derecho de redimir.

foreclosure [fɔː'kləuʒə*] *n* apertura de un juicio hipotecario.

forecourt ['fɔːkɔːt] *n* (*of garage*) patio.

forefathers ['fɔːfɑːðəz] *npl* antepasados *mpl*.

forefinger ['fɔːfɪŋgə*] *n* (dedo) índice *m*.

forefront ['fɔːfrʌnt] *n*: **in the** ~ **of** en la vanguardia de.

forego, *pt* **forewent**, *pp* **foregone** [fɔː'gəu, -'wɛnt, -'gɔn] *vt* = **forgo**.

foregoing ['fɔːgəuɪŋ] *a* anterior, precedente.

foregone ['fɔːgɔn] *pp of* **forego** ♦ *a*: **it's a** ~ **conclusion** es una conclusión inevitable.

foreground ['fɔːgraund] *n* primer plano.

forehand ['fɔːhænd] *n* (*TENNIS*) golpe *m* de-

recho *or* directo.

forehead ['fɔrɪd] *n* frente *f*.

foreign ['fɔrɪn] *a* extranjero; (*trade*) exterior.

foreign currency *n* divisas *fpl*.

foreigner ['fɔrɪnə*] *n* extranjero/a.

foreign exchange *n* (*system*) cambio de divisas; (*money*) divisas *fpl*, moneda extranjera.

foreign investment *n* inversión *f* en el extranjero; (*money, stock*) inversiones *fpl* extranjeras.

Foreign Office *n* Ministerio de Asuntos Exteriores.

Foreign Secretary *n* (*Brit*) Ministro de Asuntos Exteriores.

foreleg ['fɔːlɛg] *n* pata delantera.

foreman ['fɔːmən] *n* capataz *m*; (*in construction*) maestro de obras; (*LAW: of jury*) presidente *m/f*.

foremost ['fɔːməust] *a* principal ♦ *ad*: **first and** ~ ante todo, antes que nada.

forename ['fɔːneɪm] *n* nombre *m* (de pila).

forensic [fə'rɛnsɪk] *a* forense; ~ **scientist** forense *m/f*.

forerunner ['fɔːrʌnə*] *n* precursor(a) *m/f*.

foresee, *pt* **foresaw**, *pp* **foreseen** [fɔː'siː, -'sɔː, -'siːn] *vt* prever.

foreseeable [fɔː'siːəbl] *a* previsible.

foreshadow [fɔː'ʃædəu] *vt* prefigurar, anunciar.

foreshore ['fɔːʃɔː*] *n* playa.

foreshorten [fɔː'ʃɔːtn] *vt* (*figure, scene*) escorzar.

foresight ['fɔːsaɪt] *n* previsión *f*.

foreskin ['fɔːskɪn] *n* (*ANAT*) prepucio.

forest ['fɔrɪst] *n* bosque *m*.

forestall [fɔː'stɔːl] *vt* prevenir.

forestry ['fɔrɪstrɪ] *n* silvicultura.

foretaste ['fɔːteɪst] *n* anticipo.

foretell, *pt*, *pp* **foretold** [fɔː'tɛl, -'təuld] *vt* predecir, pronosticar.

forethought ['fɔːθɔːt] *n* previsión *f*.

forever [fə'rɛvə*] *ad* para siempre.

forewarn [fɔː'wɔːn] *vt* avisar, advertir.

forewent [fɔː'wɛnt] *pt of* **forego**.

foreword ['fɔːwəːd] *n* prefacio.

forfeit ['fɔːfɪt] *n* (*in game*) prenda ♦ *vt* perder (derecho a).

forgave [fə'geɪv] *pt of* **forgive**.

forge [fɔːdʒ] *n* fragua; (*smithy*) herrería ♦ *vt* (*signature*: *Brit*: *money*) falsificar; (*metal*) forjar.

forge ahead *vi* avanzar constantemente.

forger ['fɔːdʒə*] *n* falsificador(a) *m/f*.

forgery ['fɔːdʒərɪ] *n* falsificación *f*.

forget, *pt* **forgot**, *pp* **forgotten** [fə'gɛt, -'gɔt, -'gɔtn] *vt* olvidar ♦ *vi* olvidarse.

forgetful [fə'gɛtful] *a* olvidadizo.

forget-me-not [fə'gɛtmɪnɔt] *n* nomeolvides *f inv*.

forgive, *pt* **forgave**, *pp* **forgiven** [fə'gɪv, -'geɪv, -'gɪvn] *vt* perdonar; **to** ~ **sb for**

sth/for doing sth perdonar algo a uno/a uno por haber hecho algo.

forgiveness [fə'gɪvnɪs] *n* perdón *m*.

forgiving [fə'gɪvɪŋ] *a* compasivo.

forgo, *pt* **forwent**, *pp* **forgone** [fɔː'gəu, -'wɛnt, -'gɔn] *vt* (*give up*) renunciar a; (*go without*) privarse de.

forgot [fə'gɔt] *pt of* **forget**.

forgotten [fə'gɔtn] *pp of* **forget**.

fork [fɔːk] *n* (*for eating*) tenedor *m*; (*for gardening*) horca; (*of roads*) bifurcación *f*; (*in tree*) horcadura ♦ *vi* (*road*) bifurcarse.

fork out *vt* (*col: pay*) desembolsar.

forked [fɔːkt] *a* (*lightning*) en zigzag.

fork-lift truck ['fɔːklɪft-] *n* máquina elevadora.

forlorn [fə'lɔːn] *a* (*person*) triste, melancólico; (*deserted: cottage*) abandonado; (*desperate: attempt*) desesperado.

form [fɔːm] *n* forma; (*Brit scol*) clase *f*; (*document*) formulario ♦ *vt* formar; **in the ~ of** en forma de; **in top ~** en plena forma; **to be in good ~** (*sport, fig*) estar en plena forma; **to ~ part of sth** formar parte de algo; **to ~ a circle/a queue** hacer una curva/una cola.

formal ['fɔːməl] *a* (*offer, receipt*) por escrito; (*person etc*) correcto; (*occasion, dinner*) ceremonioso; **~ dress** traje *m* de vestir; (*evening dress*) traje *m* de etiqueta.

formalities [fɔː'mælɪtɪz] *npl* formalidades *fpl*.

formality [fɔː'mælɪtɪ] *n* ceremonia.

formalize ['fɔːməlaɪz] *vt* formalizar.

formally ['fɔːməlɪ] *ad* oficialmente.

format ['fɔːmæt] *n* formato ♦ *vt* (*COMPUT*) formatear.

formation [fɔː'meɪʃən] *n* formación *f*.

formative ['fɔːmətɪv] *a* (*years*) formativo.

format line *n* (*COMPUT*) línea de formato.

former ['fɔːmə*] *a* anterior; (*earlier*) antiguo; (*ex*) ex; **the ~ ... the latter ...** aquél ... éste ...; **the ~ president** el antiguo *or* ex presidente.

formerly ['fɔːməlɪ] *ad* antiguamente.

form feed *n* (*on printer*) salto de página.

Formica ® [fɔː'maɪkə] *n* Formica ®.

formidable ['fɔːmɪdəbl] *a* formidable.

formula ['fɔːmjulə] *n* fórmula; **F~ One** (*AUT*) Fórmula Uno.

formulate ['fɔːmjuleɪt] *vt* formular.

fornicate ['fɔːnɪkeɪt] *vi* fornicar.

forsake, *pt* **forsook**, *pp* **forsaken** [fə'seɪk, -'suk, -'seɪkən] *vt* (*gen*) abandonar; (*plan*) renunciar a.

fort [fɔːt] *n* fuerte *m*; **to hold the ~** (*fig*) quedarse a cargo.

forte ['fɔːtɪ] *n* fuerte *m*.

forth [fɔːθ] *ad*: **back and ~** de acá para allá; **and so ~** y así sucesivamente.

forthcoming [fɔːθ'kʌmɪŋ] *a* próximo, venidero; (*character*) comunicativo.

forthright ['fɔːθraɪt] *a* franco.

forthwith ['fɔːθ'wɪθ] *ad* en el acto, acto seguido.

fortification [fɔːtɪfɪ'keɪʃən] *n* fortificación *f*.

fortified wine ['fɔːtɪfaɪd-] *n* vino encabezado.

fortify ['fɔːtɪfaɪ] *vt* fortalecer.

fortitude ['fɔːtɪtjuːd] *n* fortaleza.

fortnight ['fɔːtnaɪt] *n* (*Brit*) quincena; **it's a ~ since ...** hace quince días que ....

fortnightly ['fɔːtnaɪtlɪ] *a* quincenal ♦ *ad* quincenalmente.

FORTRAN ['fɔːtræn] *n* FORTRAN *m*.

fortress ['fɔːtrɪs] *n* fortaleza.

fortuitous [fɔː'tjuːɪtəs] *a* fortuito.

fortunate ['fɔːtʃənɪt] *a*: **it is ~ that...** (es una) suerte que....

fortunately ['fɔːtʃənɪtlɪ] *ad* afortunadamente.

fortune ['fɔːtʃən] *n* suerte *f*; (*wealth*) fortuna; **to make a ~** hacer un dineral.

fortuneteller ['fɔːtʃəntɛlə*] *n* adivino/a.

forty ['fɔːtɪ] *num* cuarenta.

forum ['fɔːrəm] *n* (*also fig*) foro.

forward ['fɔːwəd] *a* (*movement, position*) avanzado; (*front*) delantero; (*not shy*) atrevido ♦ *n* (*sport*) delantero ♦ *vt* (*letter*) remitir; (*career*) promocionar; **to move ~** avanzar; **"please ~"** "remítase al destinatario".

forward contract *n* contrato a término.

forward exchange *n* cambio a término.

forward planning *n* planificación *f* por anticipado.

forward rate *n* tipo a término.

forward(s) ['fɔːwəd(z)] *ad* (hacia) adelante.

forward sales *npl* ventas *fpl* a término.

forwent [fɔː'wɛnt] *pt of* **forgo**.

fossil ['fɔsl] *n* fósil *m*; **~ fuel** hidrocarburo.

foster ['fɔstə*] *vt* fomentar.

foster brother *n* hermano de leche.

foster child *n* hijo/a adoptivo/a.

foster mother *n* madre *f* adoptiva.

fought [fɔːt] *pt, pp of* **fight**.

foul [faul] *a* (*gen*) sucio, puerco; (*weather, smell etc*) asqueroso ♦ *n* (*FOOTBALL*) falta ♦ *vt* (*dirty*) ensuciar; (*block*) atascar; (*entangle: anchor, propeller*) atascar, enredarse en; (*football player*) cometer una falta contra.

foul play *n* (*SPORT*) mala jugada; (*LAW*) muerte *f* violenta.

found [faund] *pt, pp of* **find** ♦ *vt* (*establish*) fundar.

foundation [faun'deɪʃən] *n* (*act*) fundación *f*; (*basis*) base *f*; (*also:* **~ cream**) crema base.

foundations [faun'deɪʃənz] *npl* (*of building*) cimientos *mpl*; **to lay the ~** poner los cimientos.

foundation stone *n*: **to lay the ~** poner la primera piedra.

founder ['faundə*] *n* fundador(a) *m/f* ♦ *vi* hundirse.

founding ['faundɪŋ] a: ~ **fathers** (esp US) fundadores mpl, próceres mpl; ~ **member** miembro fundador.

foundry ['faundrɪ] n fundición f.

fountain ['fauntɪn] n fuente f.

fountain pen n (pluma) estilográfica, (LAm) plumafuente f.

four [fɔː*] num cuatro; **on all** ~s a gatas.

four-footed [fɔː'futɪd] a cuadrúpedo.

four-poster ['fɔː'pəustə*] n (also: ~ **bed**) cama de columnas.

foursome ['fɔːsəm] n grupo de cuatro personas.

fourteen ['fɔː'tiːn] num catorce.

fourteenth [fɔː'tiːnθ] num decimocuarto.

fourth [fɔːθ] num cuarto ♦ n (AUT: also: ~ **gear**) cuarta (velocidad).

four-wheel drive ['fɔː'wiːl-] n tracción f a las cuatro ruedas.

fowl [faul] n ave f (de corral).

fox [fɔks] n zorro ♦ vt confundir.

fox fur n piel f de zorro.

foxglove ['fɔksɡlʌv] n (BOT) dedalera.

fox-hunting ['fɔkshʌntɪŋ] n caza de zorros.

foxtrot ['fɔkstrɔt] n fox m.

foyer ['fɔɪeɪ] n vestíbulo.

FP n abbr (Brit) = former pupil; (US) = fireplug.

FPA n abbr (Brit: = Family Planning Association) asociación de planificación familiar.

Fr. abbr (REL) (= Father) P.; (= friar) Fr.

fr. abbr (= franc) f.

fracas ['fræka:] n gresca, refriega.

fraction ['frækʃən] n fracción f.

fractionally ['frækʃnəlɪ] ad ligeramente.

fractious ['frækʃəs] a (person, mood) malhumorado.

fracture ['fræktʃə*] n fractura ♦ vt fracturar.

fragile ['frædʒaɪl] a frágil.

fragment ['frægmənt] n fragmento.

fragmentary [fræg'mɛntərɪ] a fragmentario.

fragrance ['freɪɡrəns] n fragancia.

fragrant ['freɪɡrənt] a fragante, oloroso.

frail [freɪl] a (fragile) frágil, quebradizo; (weak) delicado.

frame [freɪm] n (TECH) armazón f; (of picture, door etc) marco; (of spectacles: also: ~s) montura ♦ vt encuadrar; (picture) enmarcar; (reply) formular; **to** ~ **sb** (col) inculpar por engaños a uno.

frame of mind n estado de ánimo.

framework ['freɪmwəːk] n marco.

France [frɑːns] n Francia.

franchise ['fræntʃaɪz] n (POL) derecho de votar, sufragio; (COMM) licencia, concesión f.

franchisee [fræntʃaɪ'ziː] n concesionario/a.

franchiser ['fræntʃaɪzə*] n compañía concesionaria.

frank [fræŋk] a franco ♦ vt (Brit: letter)

franquear.

frankfurter ['fræŋkfəːtə*] n salchicha de Frankfurt.

frankincense ['fræŋkɪnsɛns] n incienso.

franking machine ['fræŋkɪŋ-] n máquina de franqueo.

frankly ['fræŋklɪ] ad francamente.

frankness ['fræŋknɪs] n franqueza.

frantic ['fræntɪk] a (desperate: need, desire) desesperado; (: search) frenético; (: person) desquiciado.

fraternal [frə'təːnl] a fraterno.

fraternity [frə'təːnɪtɪ] n (club) fraternidad f; (US) club m de estudiantes; (guild) cofradía.

fraternization [frætənaɪ'zeɪʃən] n fraternización f.

fraternize ['frætənaɪz] vi confraternizar.

fraud [frɔːd] n fraude m; (person) impostor(a) m/f.

fraudulent ['frɔːdjulənt] a fraudulento.

fraught [frɔːt] a (tense) tenso; ~ **with** cargado de.

fray [freɪ] n combate m, lucha, refriega ♦ vi deshilacharse; **tempers were** ~ed el ambiente se ponía tenso.

FRB n abbr (US) = Federal Reserve Board.

FRCM n abbr (Brit) = Fellow of the Royal College of Music.

FRCO n abbr (Brit) = Fellow of the Royal College of Organists.

FRCP n abbr (Brit) = Fellow of the Royal College of Physicians.

FRCS n abbr (Brit) = Fellow of the Royal College of Surgeons.

freak [friːk] n (person) fenómeno; (event) suceso anormal; (col: enthusiast) adicto/a ♦ a (storm, conditions) anormal; **health** ~ (col) maniático/a en cuestión de salud.

freak out vi (col: on drugs) tener un viaje.

freakish ['friːkɪʃ] a (result, appearance) inesperado, extravagante; (weather) cambiadizo.

freckle ['frɛkl] n peca.

freckled ['frɛkld] a pecoso, lleno de pecas.

free [friː] a (person: at liberty) libre; (not fixed) suelto; (gratis) gratuito; (unoccupied) desocupado; (liberal) generoso ♦ vt (prisoner etc) poner en libertad; (jammed object) soltar; **to give sb a** ~ **hand** darle campo libre a uno; ~ **and easy** despreocupado; **is this seat** ~? ¿está libre este asiento?; ~ **of tax** libre de impuestos; **admission** ~ entrada libre; ~ **(of charge)**, **for** ~ ad gratis.

freebie ['friːbɪ] n (col): **it's a** ~ es gratis.

freedom ['friːdəm] n libertad f; ~ **of association** libertad f de asociación.

freedom fighter n guerrillero/a.

free enterprise n libre empresa.

free-for-all ['friːfərɔːl] n riña general.

free gift *n* prima.
freehold ['fri:həuld] *n* feudo franco alodio.
free kick *n* tiro libre.
freelance ['fri:lɑːns] *a, ad* por cuenta propia; ~ **work** trabajo independiente.
freely ['fri:lɪ] *ad* libremente; (*liberally*) generosamente.
freemason ['fri:meɪsn] *n* francmasón *m*.
freemasonry ['fri:meɪsnrɪ] *n* (franc)masonería.
freepost ['fri:pəust] *n* porte *m* pagado.
free-range ['fri:'reɪndʒ] *a* (*hen, eggs*) de granja.
free sample *n* muestra gratuita.
freesia ['fri:ʒə] *n* fresia.
free speech *n* libertad *f* de expresión.
free trade *n* libre comercio.
freeway ['fri:weɪ] *n* (*US*) autopista.
freewheel [fri:'wi:l] *vi* ir en punto muerto.
freewheeling [fri:'wi:lɪŋ] *a* libre, espontáneo; (*careless*) irresponsable.
free will *n* libre albedrío; **of one's own** ~ por su propia voluntad.
freeze [fri:z] *vb* (*pt* **froze**, *pp* **frozen** [frəuz, frəuzn]) *vi* helarse, congelarse ♦ *vt* helar; (*prices, food, salaries*) congelar ♦ *n* helada; congelación *f*.
freeze over *vi* (*lake, river*) helarse, congelarse; (*window, windscreen*) cubrirse de escarcha.
freeze up *vi* helarse, congelarse.
freeze-dried ['fri:zdraɪd] *a* liofilizado.
freezer ['fri:zə*] *n* congelador *m*, congeladora (*LAm*).
freezing ['fri:zɪŋ] *a* helado.
freezing point *n* punto de congelación; **3 degrees below** ~ tres grados bajo cero.
freight [freɪt] *n* (*goods*) carga; (*money charged*) flete *m*; ~ **forward** contra reembolso del flete, flete debido; ~ **inward** flete sobre compras.
freight car *n* vagón *m* de mercancías.
freighter ['freɪtə*] *n* nave *f* de mercancías.
freight forwarder [-'fɔːwədə*] *n* agente *m* expedidor.
freight train *n* (*US*) tren *m* de mercancías.
French [frentʃ] *a* francés/esa ♦ *n* (*LING*) francés *m*; **the** ~ *npl* los franceses.
French bean *n* judía verde.
French Canadian *a, n* francocanadiense *m/f*.
French dressing *n* (*CULIN*) vinagreta.
French fried (potatoes), (*US*) **French fries** *npl* patatas *fpl* *or* papas *fpl* (*LAm*) fritas.
French Guiana [-gaɪˈænə] *n* la Guayana Francesa.
Frenchman ['frentʃmən] *n* francés *m*.
French Riviera *n*: **the** ~ la Riviera, la Costa Azul.
French window *n* puertaventana.
Frenchwoman ['frentʃwumən] *n* francesa.

frenetic [frə'netɪk] *a* frenético.
frenzy ['frenzɪ] *n* frenesí *m*.
frequency ['fri:kwənsɪ] *n* frecuencia.
frequency modulation (FM) *n* frecuencia modulada.
frequent *a* ['fri:kwənt] frecuente ♦ *vt* [frɪ'kwent] frecuentar.
frequently ['fri:kwəntlɪ] *ad* frecuentemente, a menudo.
fresco ['freskəu] *n* fresco.
fresh [freʃ] *a* (*gen*) fresco; (*new*) nuevo; (*water*) dulce; **to make a** ~ **start** empezar de nuevo.
freshen ['freʃən] *vi* (*wind, air*) soplar más recio.
freshen up *vi* (*person*) refrescarse.
freshener ['freʃnə*] *n*: **air** ~ ambientador *m*; **skin** ~ tónico.
fresher ['freʃə*] *n* (*Brit SCOL*: *col*) estudiante *m/f* de primer año.
freshly ['freʃlɪ] *ad*: ~ **painted/arrived** recién pintado/llegado.
freshman ['freʃmən] *n* (*US*: *SCOL*) = **fresher**.
freshness ['freʃnɪs] *n* frescura.
freshwater ['freʃwɔːtə*] *a* (*fish*) de agua dulce.
fret [fret] *vi* inquietarse.
fretful ['fretful] *a* (*child*) quejumbroso.
Freudian ['frɔɪdɪən] *a* freudiano; ~ **slip** lapsus *m*.
FRG *n* *abbr* (= *Federal Republic of Germany*) RFA *f*.
Fri. *abbr* (= *Friday*) vier.
friar ['fraɪə*] *n* fraile *m*; (*before name*) fray.
friction ['frɪkʃən] *n* fricción *f*.
friction feed *n* (*on printer*) avance *m* por fricción.
Friday ['fraɪdɪ] *n* viernes *m inv*.
fridge [frɪdʒ] *n* (*Brit*) nevera, frigo, refrigeradora (*LAm*).
fried [fraɪd] *pt, pp* *of* **fry** ♦ *a*: ~ **egg** huevo frito, (*LAm*) huevo estrellado.
friend [frend] *n* amigo/a.
friendliness ['frendlɪnɪs] *n* simpatía.
friendly ['frendlɪ] *a* simpático.
friendly society *n* sociedad *f* de beneficiencia.
friendship ['frendʃɪp] *n* amistad *f*.
frieze [fri:z] *n* friso.
frigate ['frɪgɪt] *n* fragata.
fright [fraɪt] *n* susto; **to take** ~ asustarse.
frighten ['fraɪtn] *vt* asustar.
frighten away, frighten off *vt* (*birds, children etc*) espantar, ahuyentar.
frightened ['fraɪtnd] *a* asustado.
frightening ['fraɪtnɪŋ] *a* espantoso.
frightful ['fraɪtful] *a* espantoso, horrible.
frightfully ['fraɪtfulɪ] *ad* terriblemente; **I'm** ~ **sorry** lo siento muchísimo.
frigid ['frɪdʒɪd] *a* (*MED*) frígido, frío.
frigidity [frɪ'dʒɪdɪtɪ] *n* frialdad *f*; (*MED*) frigidez *f*.

frill [frɪl] *n* volante *m;* **without** ~s (*fig*) sin adornos.

fringe [frɪndʒ] *n* (*Brit*: *of hair*) flequillo; (*edge*: *of forest etc*) borde *m*, margen *m*.

fringe benefits *npl* ventajas *fpl* complementarias.

fringe theatre *n* teatro experimental.

frisk [frɪsk] *vt* cachear, registrar.

frisky ['frɪskɪ] *a* juguetón/ona.

fritter ['frɪtə*] *n* buñuelo.

fritter away *vt* desperdiciar.

frivolity [frɪ'vɔlɪtɪ] *n* frivolidad *f*.

frivolous ['frɪvələs] *a* frívolo.

frizzy ['frɪzɪ] *a* rizado.

fro [frəu] *see* **to**.

frock [frɔk] *n* vestido.

frog [frɔg] *n* rana; **to have a** ~ **in one's throat** tener carraspera.

frogman ['frɔgmən] *n* hombre-rana *m*.

frogmarch ['frɔgmɑːtʃ] *vt*: **to** ~ **sb in/out** hacer entrar/salir a uno a la fuerza.

frolic ['frɔlɪk] *vi* juguetear.

from [frɔm] *prep* de; **where is he** ~? ¿de dónde es?; **where has he come** ~? ¿de dónde ha venido?; **a telephone call** ~ **Mr Smith** una llamada de parte del Sr. Smith; **prices range** ~ **£10 to £50** los precios varían entre 10 y 50 libras; **(as)** ~ **Friday** a partir del viernes; ~ **what he says** por lo que dice.

frond [frɔnd] *n* fronda.

front [frʌnt] *n* (*foremost part*) parte *f* delantera; (*of house*) fachada; (*promenade*: *also*: **sea** ~) paseo marítimo; (*MIL, POL, METEOROLOGY*) frente *m*; (*fig*: *appearances*) apariencias *fpl* ♦ *a* (*wheel, leg*) delantero; (*row, line*) primero ♦ *vi*: **to** ~ **onto sth** dar a algo; **in** ~ **(of)** delante (de).

frontage ['frʌntɪdʒ] *n* (*of building*) fachada.

frontal ['frʌntl] *a* frontal.

front bench *n* (*Brit POL*) los dirigentes del partido del gobierno o de la oposición.

front desk *n* (*US*) recepción *f*.

front door *n* puerta principal.

frontier ['frʌntɪə*] *n* frontera.

frontispiece ['frʌntɪspiːs] *n* portada.

front page *n* primera plana.

front room *n* (*Brit*) salón *m*, sala.

front runner *n* favorito/a.

front-wheel drive ['frʌntwiːl-] *n* tracción *f* delantera.

frost [frɔst] *n* (*gen*) helada; (*also*: **hoar**~) escarcha ♦ *vt* (*US CULIN*) escarchar.

frostbite ['frɔstbaɪt] *n* congelación *f*.

frosted ['frɔstɪd] *a* (*glass*) deslustrado; (*esp US*: *cake*) escarchado.

frosting ['frɔstɪŋ] *n* (*esp US*: *icing*) escarcha.

frosty ['frɔstɪ] *a* (*surface*) cubierto de escarcha; (*welcome etc*) glacial.

froth [frɔθ] *n* espuma.

frothy ['frɔθɪ] *a* espumoso.

frown [fraun] *vi* fruncir el ceño ♦ *n*: **with a** ~ frunciendo el entrecejo.

frown on *vt fus* desaprobar.

froze [frəuz] *pt of* **freeze**.

frozen ['frəuzn] *pp of* **freeze** ♦ *a* (*food*) congelado; (*COMM*): ~ **assets** activos *mpl* congelados *or* bloqueados.

FRS *n* (*Brit*: = *Fellow of the Royal Society*) miembro de la principal asociación de investigación científica; (*US*: = *Federal Reserve System*) banco central de los EE. UU.

frugal ['fruːgəl] *a* (*person*) frugal.

fruit [fruːt] *n* (*pl inv*) fruta.

fruiterer ['fruːtərə*] *n* frutero/a; ~'s **(shop)** frutería.

fruitful ['fruːtful] *a* provechoso.

fruition [fruː'ɪʃən] *n*: **to come to** ~ realizarse.

fruit juice *n* zumo *or* jugo (*LAm*) de fruta.

fruitless ['fruːtlɪs] *a* (*fig*) infructuoso, inútil.

fruit machine *n* (*Brit*) máquina tragaperras.

fruit salad *n* macedonia *or* ensalada (*LAm*) de frutas.

frump [frʌmp] *n* espantajo, adefesio.

frustrate [frʌs'treɪt] *vt* frustrar.

frustrated [frʌs'treɪtɪd] *a* frustrado.

frustrating [frʌs'treɪtɪŋ] *a* (*job, day*) frustrante.

frustration [frʌs'treɪʃən] *n* frustración *f*.

fry, *pt, pp* **fried** [fraɪ, -d] *vt* freír ♦ *n*: **small** ~ gente *f* menuda.

frying pan ['fraɪɪŋ-] *n* sartén *f*.

FT *n abbr* (*Brit*: = *Financial Times*) periódico financiero; **the** ~ **index** el índice de valores del Financial Times.

ft. *abbr* = **foot, feet**.

FTC *n abbr* (*US*) = *Federal Trade Commission*.

fuchsia ['fjuːʃə] *n* fucsia.

fuck [fʌk] (*col!*) *vt* joder (*Sp!*), coger (*LAm!*) ♦ *vi* joder (*Sp!*), coger (*LAm!*); ~ **off!** ¡vete a la mierda! (*!*).

fuddled ['fʌdld] *a* (*muddled*) confuso, aturdido; (*col*: *tipsy*) borracho.

fuddy-duddy ['fʌdɪdʌdɪ] (*pej*) *n* carcamal *m*, carroza *m/f* ♦ *a* chapado a la antigua.

fudge [fʌdʒ] *n* (*CULIN*) caramelo blando ♦ *vt* (*issue, problem*) rehuir, esquivar.

fuel [fjuəl] *n* (*for heating*) combustible *m*; (*coal*) carbón *m*; (*wood*) leña; (*for engine*) carburante *m* ♦ *vt* (*furnace etc*) alimentar; (*aircraft, ship etc*) repostar.

fuel oil *n* fuel oil *m*.

fuel pump *n* (*AUT*) surtidor *m* de gasolina.

fuel tank *n* depósito de combustible.

fug [fʌg] *n* aire *m* viciado.

fugitive ['fjuːdʒɪtɪv] *n* (*from prison*) fugitivo/a.

fulfil, (*US*) **fulfill** [ful'fɪl] *vt* (*function*) cumplir con; (*condition*) satisfacer; (*wish, desire*) realizar.

fulfilled [ful'fɪld] *a* (*person*) satisfecho.

fulfil(l)ment [ful'fɪlmənt] *n* satisfacción *f*; realización *f*.

full [ful] *a* lleno; (*fig*) pleno; (*complete*) completo; (*information*) detallado; (*price*) íntegro, sin descuento ◆ *ad*: ~ **well** perfectamente; **we're** ~ **up for July** estamos completos para julio; **I'm** ~ **(up)** no puedo más; ~ **employment** pleno empleo; ~ **name** nombre *m* y apellidos; **a** ~ **two hours** dos horas completas; **at** ~ **speed** a máxima velocidad; **in** ~ (*reproduce, quote*) íntegramente; **to write sth in** ~ escribir algo por extenso; **to pay in** ~ pagar la deuda entera.

fullback ['fulbæk] *n* (*FOOTBALL*) defensa *m*; (*RUGBY*) zaguero.

full-blooded ['ful'blʌdɪd] *a* (*vigorous*: *attack*) vigoroso; (*pure*) puro.

full-cream ['ful'kri:m] *a*: ~ **milk** leche *f* cremosa.

full-fledged ['fulfledʒd] *a* (*US*) = **fully-fledged**.

full-grown ['ful'grəun] *a* maduro.

full-length ['ful'leŋgθ] *a* (*portrait*) de cuerpo entero; (*film*) de largometraje.

full moon *n* luna llena, plenilunio.

fullness ['fulnɪs] *n* plenitud *f*, amplitud *f*.

full-scale ['fulskeɪl] *a* (*attack, war, search, retreat*) en gran escala; (*plan, model*) de tamaño natural.

full stop *n* punto.

full-time ['fultaɪm] *a* (*work*) de tiempo completo ◆ *ad*: **to work** ~ trabajar a tiempo completo.

fully ['fulɪ] *ad* completamente; (*at least*) al menos.

fully-fledged ['fulɪ'fledʒd], (*US*) **full-fledged** *a* (*teacher, barrister*) diplomado; (*bird*) con todas sus plumas, capaz de volar; (*fig*) con pleno derecho.

fully-paid ['fulɪpeɪd] *a*: ~ **share** acción *f* liberada.

fulsome ['fulsəm] *a* (*pej*: *praise, gratitude*) excesivo, exagerado; (: *manner*) obsequioso.

fumble with ['fʌmbl-] *vt fus* manosear.

fume [fju:m] *vi* humear, echar humo.

fumes [fju:mz] *npl* humo *sg*, gases *mpl*.

fumigate ['fju:mɪgeɪt] *vt* fumigar.

fun [fʌn] *n* (*amusement*) diversión *f*; (*joy*) alegría; **to have** ~ divertirse; **for** ~ en broma; **to make** ~ **of** burlarse de.

function ['fʌŋkʃən] *n* función *f* ◆ *vi* funcionar; **to** ~ **as** hacer (las veces) de.

functional ['fʌŋkʃənl] *a* funcional.

function key *n* (*COMPUT*) tecla de función.

fund [fʌnd] *n* fondo; (*reserve*) reserva; ~**s** *npl* fondos *mpl*.

fundamental [fʌndə'mentl] *a* fundamental ◆ *n*: ~**s** fundamentos *mpl*.

fundamentalist [fʌndə'mentəlɪst] *n* fundamentalista *m/f*.

fundamentally [fʌndə'mentəlɪ] *ad* funda-mentalmente.

fund-raising ['fʌndreɪzɪŋ] *n* recaudación *f* de fondos.

funeral ['fju:nərəl] *n* (*burial*) entierro; (*ceremony*) funerales *mpl*.

funeral director *n* director *m* de pompas fúnebres.

funeral parlour *n* (*Brit*) funeraria.

funeral service *n* misa de difuntos.

funereal [fju:'nɪərɪəl] *a* fúnebre, funéreo.

funfair ['fʌnfɛə*] *n* (*Brit*) parque *m* de atracciones.

fungus, *pl* **fungi** ['fʌŋgəs, -gaɪ] *n* hongo.

funicular [fju:'nɪkjulə*] *a* (*also:* ~ **railway**) funicular *m*.

funnel ['fʌnl] *n* embudo; (*of ship*) chimenea.

funnily ['fʌnɪlɪ] *ad* de modo divertido, graciosamente; (*oddly*) de una manera rara; ~ **enough** aunque parezca extraño.

funny ['fʌnɪ] *a* gracioso, divertido; (*strange*) curioso, raro.

funny bone *n* hueso de la alegría.

fur [fə:*] *n* piel *f*; (*Brit*: *on tongue etc*) sarro.

fur coat *n* abrigo de pieles.

furious ['fjuərɪəs] *a* furioso; (*effort, argument*) violento; **to be** ~ **with sb** estar furioso con uno.

furiously ['fjuərɪəslɪ] *ad* con furia.

furl [fə:l] *vt* (*sail*) aferrar.

furlong ['fə:lɔŋ] *n* octava parte de una milla.

furlough ['fə:ləu] *n* (*MIL, US*) permiso.

furnace ['fə:nɪs] *n* horno.

furnish ['fə:nɪʃ] *vt* amueblar; (*supply*) suministrar; (*information*) facilitar.

furnished ['fə:nɪʃt] *a*: ~ **flat** *or* (*US*) **apartment** piso amueblado.

furnishings ['fə:nɪʃɪŋz] *npl* muebles *mpl*.

furniture ['fə:nɪtʃə*] *n* muebles *mpl*; **piece of** ~ mueble *m*.

furniture polish *n* cera de lustrar.

furore [fjuə'rɔ:rɪ] *n* (*protests*) escándalo.

furrier ['fʌrɪə*] *n* peletero/a.

furrow ['fʌrəu] *n* surco ◆ *vt* (*forehead*) arrugar.

furry ['fə:rɪ] *a* (*toy*) peludo.

further ['fə:ðə*] *a* (*new*) nuevo, adicional; (*place*) más lejano ◆ *ad* más lejos; (*more*) más; (*moreover*) además ◆ *vt* promover, adelantar; **how much** ~ **is it?** ¿a qué distancia queda?; ~ **to your letter of** ... (*COMM*) con referencia a su carta de ...; **to** ~ **one's interests** fomentar sus intereses.

further education *n* educación *f* superior.

furthermore [fə:ðə'mɔ:*] *ad* además.

furthermost ['fə:ðəməust] *a* más lejano.

furthest ['fə:ðɪst] *superlative of* **far**.

furtive ['fə:tɪv] *a* furtivo.

furtively ['fʌ:tɪvlɪ] *ad* furtivamente, a escondidas.

fury ['fjuərɪ] *n* furia.

fuse, (*US*) **fuze** [fju:z] *n* fusible *m*; (*for bomb etc*) mecha ♦ *vt* (*metal*) fundir; (*fig*) fusionar ♦ *vi* fundirse; fusionarse; (*Brit*: *ELEC*): **to** ~ **the lights** fundir los plomos; **a** ~ **has blown** se ha fundido un fusible.
fuse box *n* caja de fusibles.
fuselage ['fju:zəlɑ:ʒ] *n* fuselaje *m*.
fuse wire *n* hilo fusible.
fusillade [fju:zɪ'leɪd] *n* descarga cerrada; (*fig*) lluvia.
fusion ['fju:ʒən] *n* fusión *f*.
fuss [fʌs] *n* (*noise*) bulla; (*dispute*) lío; (*complaining*) protesta ♦ *vi* preocuparse (por pequeñeces) ♦ *vt* (*person*) molestar; **to make a** ~ armar un lío *or* jaleo.
fuss over *vt fus* (*person*) consentir (a).
fussy ['fʌsɪ] *a* (*person*) exigente; **I'm not** ~ (*col*) me da igual.
futile ['fju:taɪl] *a* vano.
futility [fju:'tɪlɪtɪ] *n* inutilidad *f*.
future ['fju:tʃə*] *a* (*gen*) futuro; (*coming*) venidero ♦ *n* futuro, porvenir; **in** ~ de ahora en adelante.
futures ['fju:tʃəz] *npl* (*COMM*) operaciones *fpl* a término.
futuristic [fju:tʃə'rɪstɪk] *a* futurístico.
fuze [fju:z] (*US*) = **fuse**.
fuzzy ['fʌzɪ] *a* (*PHOT*) borroso; (*hair*) muy rizado.
fwd. *abbr* = **forward**.
fwy *abbr* (*US*) = **freeway**.
FY *abbr* = **fiscal year**.
FYI *abbr* = *for your information*.

G

G, g [dʒi:] *n* (*letter*) G, g *f*; **G** (*MUS*) sol *m*; **G for George** G de Gerona.
G *n abbr* (*Brit SCOL*: = *good*) N; (*US CINE-MA*: = *general audience*) todos los públicos.
g. *abbr* (= *gram*(*s*), *gravity*) g.
GA *abbr* (*US POST*) = *Georgia*.
gab [gæb] *n*: **to have the gift of the** ~ (*col*) tener mucha labia.
gabble ['gæbl] *vi* hablar atropelladamente; (*gossip*) cotorrear.
gaberdine [gæbə'di:n] *n* gabardina.
gable ['geɪbl] *n* aguilón *m*.
Gabon [gə'bɔn] *n* Gabón *m*.
gad about [gæd-] *vi* (*col*) moverse mucho.
gadget ['gædʒɪt] *n* aparato.
gadgetry ['gædʒɪtrɪ] *n* chismes *mpl*.
Gaelic ['geɪlɪk] *a*, *n* (*LING*) gaélico.
gaffe [gæf] *n* plancha, patinazo, metedura de pata.
gag [gæg] *n* (*on mouth*) mordaza; (*joke*) chiste *m* ♦ *vt* amordazar.

gaga ['gɑ:gɑ:] *a*: **to go** ~ (*senile*) chochear; (*ecstatic*) cáersele a uno la baba.
gage [geɪdʒ] *n* (*US*) = **gauge**.
gaiety ['geɪtɪ] *n* alegría.
gaily ['geɪlɪ] *ad* alegremente.
gain [geɪn] *n* ganancia ♦ *vt* ganar ♦ *vi* (*watch*) adelantarse; **to** ~ **by sth** sacar provecho de algo; **to** ~ **ground** ganar terreno; **to** ~ **3 lbs (in weight)** engordar 3 libras.
gain (up)on *vt fus* ganar terreno a.
gainful ['geɪnful] *a* (*employment*) remunerado.
gait [geɪt] *n* (modo de) andar *m*.
gala ['gɑ:lə] *n* fiesta; **swimming** ~ gala de natación.
Galapagos Islands [gə'læpəgəs-] *npl*: **the** ~ las Islas Galápagos.
galaxy ['gæləksɪ] *n* galaxia.
gale [geɪl] *n* (*wind*) vendaval *m*; ~ **force 10** vendaval de fuerza 10.
gall [gɔ:l] *n* (*ANAT*) bilis *f*, hiel *f*; (*fig*: *impudence*) descaro, caradura ♦ *vt* molestar.
gal(l). *abbr* = **gallon(s)**.
gallant ['gælənt] *a* valiente; (*towards ladies*) atento.
gallantry ['gæləntrɪ] *n* valor *m*, valentía; (*courtesy*) cortesía.
gall bladder *n* vesícula biliar.
galleon ['gælɪən] *n* galeón *m*.
gallery ['gælərɪ] *n* (*also THEATRE*) galería; (*for spectators*) tribuna; (*also*: **art** ~: *state-owned*) pinacoteca *or* galería de arte; (: *private*) colección *f* de cuadros).
galley ['gælɪ] *n* (*ship's kitchen*) cocina; (*ship*) galera.
galley proof *n* (*TYP*) prueba de galera, galerada.
Gallic ['gælɪk] *a* galo, galicano.
gallon ['gæln] *n* galón *m* (= *8 pints*; *Brit* = *4,546 litros*, *US* = *3,785 litros*).
gallop ['gæləp] *n* galope *m* ♦ *vi* galopar; ~**ing inflation** inflación *f* galopante.
gallows ['gæləuz] *n* horca.
gallstone ['gɔ:lstəun] *n* cálculo biliario.
galore [gə'lɔ:*] *ad* en cantidad, en abundancia.
galvanize ['gælvənaɪz] *vt* (*metal*) galvanizar; (*fig*): **to** ~ **sb into action** animar a uno para que haga algo.
Gambia ['gæmbɪə] *n* Gambia.
gambit ['gæmbɪt] *n* (*fig*): **opening** ~ estrategia inicial.
gamble ['gæmbl] *n* (*risk*) riesgo; (*bet*) apuesta ♦ *vt*: **to** ~ **on** apostar a; (*fig*) confiar en que ♦ *vi* jugar; (*COMM*) especular; **to** ~ **on the Stock Exchange** jugar a la bolsa.
gambler ['gæmblə*] *n* jugador(a) *m/f*.
gambling ['gæmblɪŋ] *n* el juego.
gambol ['gæmbl] *vi* brincar, juguetear.
game [geɪm] *n* (*gen*) juego; (*match*) partido; (*of cards*) partida; (*HUNTING*) caza ♦ *a*

valiente; *(ready)*: **to be ~ for anything** atreverse a todo; **~s** *(SCOL)* el deporte; **big ~** caza mayor.

game bird *n* ave *f* de caza.

gamekeeper ['geɪmkiːpə*] *n* guardabosques *m inv*.

gamely ['geɪmlɪ] *ad* bravamente.

game reserve *n* coto de caza.

gamesmanship ['geɪmzmənʃɪp] *n* habilidad *f*.

gammon ['gæmən] *n (bacon)* tocino ahumado; *(ham)* jamón *m* ahumado.

gamut ['gæmət] *n (MUS)* gama; **to run the (whole) ~ of emotions** *(fig)* pasar por toda la gama de emociones.

gander ['gændə*] *n* ganso.

gang [gæŋ] *n* pandilla; *(of workmen)* brigada ♦ *vi*: **to ~ up on sb** conspirar contra uno.

Ganges ['gændʒiːz] *n*: **the ~** el Ganges.

gangling ['gæŋglɪŋ] *a* larguirucho.

gangplank ['gæŋplæŋk] *n* plancha.

gangrene ['gæŋgriːn] *n* gangrena.

gangster ['gæŋstə*] *n* gángster *m*.

gangway ['gæŋweɪ] *n (Brit: in theatre, bus etc)* pasillo; *(on ship)* pasarela.

gantry ['gæntrɪ] *n (for crane, railway signal)* pórtico; *(for rocket)* torre *f* de lanzamiento.

GAO *n abbr (US: = General Accounting Office) tribunal de cuentas.*

gaol [dʒeɪl] *n, vt (Brit)* = **jail.**

gap [gæp] *n* vacío, hueco *(LAm)*; *(in trees, traffic)* claro; *(in time)* intervalo.

gape [geɪp] *vi* mirar boquiabierto.

gaping ['geɪpɪŋ] *a (hole)* muy abierto.

garage ['gærɑːʒ] *n* garaje *m*.

garb [gɑːb] *n* atuendo.

garbage ['gɑːbɪdʒ] *n (US)* basura; *(nonsense)* tonterías *fpl*; *(fig: film, book etc)* basura.

garbage can *n (US)* cubo *or* balde *m or* bote *m (LAm)* de la basura.

garbage disposal unit *n* triturador *m* (de basura).

garbage man *n* basurero.

garbled ['gɑːbld] *a (account, explanation)* confuso.

garden ['gɑːdn] *n* jardín *m*; **~s** *npl (public)* parque *m*, jardines *mpl*; *(private)* huertos *mpl*.

garden centre *n* viveros *mpl*.

gardener ['gɑːdnə*] *n* jardinero/a.

gardening ['gɑːdnɪŋ] *n* jardinería.

garden party *n* recepción *f* al aire libre.

gargle ['gɑːgl] *vi* hacer gárgaras, gargarear *(LAm)*.

gargoyle ['gɑːgɔɪl] *n* gárgola.

garish ['gɛərɪʃ] *a* chillón/ona.

garland ['gɑːlənd] *n* guirnalda.

garlic ['gɑːlɪk] *n* ajo.

garment ['gɑːmənt] *n* prenda (de vestir).

garner ['gɑːnə*] *vt* acumular.

garnish ['gɑːnɪʃ] *vt* adornar; *(CULIN)* aderezar.

garret ['gærɪt] *n* desván *m*, guardilla.

garrison ['gærɪsn] *n* guarnición *f* ♦ *vt* guarnecer.

garrulous ['gærjuləs] *a* charlatán/ana.

garter ['gɑːtə*] *n (US)* liga.

garter belt *n (US)* portaligas *m inv*.

gas [gæs] *n* gas *m*; *(US: gasoline)* gasolina ♦ *vt* asfixiar con gas; **Calor ~** ® *(gas m* de) butano.

gas chamber *n* cámara de gas.

Gascony ['gæskənɪ] *n* Gascuña.

gas cooker *n (Brit)* cocina de gas.

gas cylinder *n* bombona de gas.

gaseous ['gæsɪəs] *a* gaseoso.

gas fire *n* estufa de gas.

gas pedal *n (esp US)* acelerador *m*.

gash [gæʃ] *n* raja; *(on face)* cuchillada ♦ *vt* rajar; *(with knife)* acuchillar.

gasket ['gæskɪt] *n (AUT)* junta de culata.

gas mask *n* careta antigás.

gas meter *n* contador *m* de gas.

gasoline ['gæsəliːn] *n (US)* gasolina.

gasp [gɑːsp] *n* grito sofocado ♦ *vi (pant)* jadear.

gasp out *vt (say)* decir con voz entrecortada.

gas ring *n* hornillo de gas.

gas station *n (US)* gasolinera.

gas stove *n* cocina de gas.

gassy ['gæsɪ] *a* gaseoso.

gas tank *n (US AUT)* depósito (de gasolina).

gas tap *n* llave *f* del gas.

gastric ['gæstrɪk] *a* gástrico.

gastric ulcer *n* úlcera gástrica.

gastroenteritis ['gæstrəuɛntə'raɪtɪs] *n* gastroenteritis *f*.

gasworks ['gæswəːks] *nsg or npl* fábrica de gas.

gate [geɪt] *n (also at airport)* puerta; *(RAIL: at level crossing)* barrera; *(of castle, town)* reja, puerta.

gateau, *pl* **~x** ['gætəu, z] *n* torta, pastel *m*.

gatecrash ['geɪtkræʃ] *vt* colarse en.

gatecrasher ['geɪtkræʃə*] *n* advenedizo/a, intruso/a.

gateway ['geɪtweɪ] *n* puerta.

gather ['gæðə*] *vt (flowers, fruit)* coger *(Sp)*, recoger *(LAm)*; *(assemble)* reunir; *(pick up)* recoger; *(SEWING)* fruncir; *(understand)* entender ♦ *vi (assemble)* reunirse; *(dust)* acumularse; *(clouds)* cerrarse; **to ~ speed** ganar velocidad; **to ~ (from/that)** tener entendido (por/que); **as far as I can ~** por lo que tengo entendido.

gathering ['gæðərɪŋ] *n* reunión *f*, asamblea.

GATT [gæt] *n abbr (= General Agreement on Tariffs and Trade)* GATT *m*.

gauche [gəuʃ] *a* torpe.

gaudy ['gɔːdɪ] *a* chillón/ona.

gauge, (US) **gage** [geɪdʒ] n calibre m; (RAIL) entrevía; (instrument) indicador m ♦ vt medir; (fig: sb's capabilities, character) estimar, juzgar; **petrol** ~ indicador m del nivel de gasolina; **to** ~ **the right moment** elegir el momento (oportuno).

Gaul [gɔːl] n Galia.

gaunt [gɔːnt] a descarnado; (grim, desolate) desolado.

gauntlet ['gɔːntlɪt] n (fig): **to run the** ~ **of sth** desafiar algo; **to throw down the** ~ arrojar el guante.

gauze [gɔːz] n gasa.

gave [geɪv] pt of **give.**

gawk [gɔːk] vi papar moscas.

gawky ['gɔːkɪ] a desgarbado.

gay [geɪ] a (person) alegre; (colour) vivo; (homosexual) gay.

gaze [geɪz] n mirada fija ♦ vi: **to** ~ **at sth** mirar algo fijamente.

gazelle [gə'zɛl] n gacela.

gazette [gə'zɛt] n (newspaper) gaceta; (official publication) boletín m oficial.

gazetteer [gæzə'tɪə*] n diccionario geográfico.

gazumping [gə'zʌmpɪŋ] n (Brit) la subida del precio de una casa una vez que ya ha sido apalabrado.

GB abbr (= Great Britain) G.B.

GBH n abbr (Brit LAW: col) = **grievous bodily harm.**

GC n abbr (Brit: = George Cross) distinción honorífica.

GCE n abbr (Brit: = General Certificate of Education) ≈ certificado de BUP (Sp) or bachillerato.

GCHQ n abbr (Brit: = Government Communications Headquarters) centro de intercepción de las telecomunicaciones internacionales.

GCSE n abbr (Brit: = General Certificate of Secondary Education) ≈ certificado de BUP (Sp) or bachillerato.

Gdns. abbr (= gardens) jdns.

GDP n abbr (= gross domestic product) PIB m.

GDR n abbr (= German Democratic Republic) RDA f.

gear [gɪə*] n equipo, herramientas fpl; (TECH) engranaje m; (AUT) velocidad f, marcha ♦ vt (fig: adapt): **to** ~ **sth to** adaptar or ajustar algo a; **top** or (US) **high/low** ~ cuarta/primera velocidad; **in** ~ en marcha; **our service is** ~**ed to meet the needs of the disabled** nuestro servicio está destinado a responder a las necesidades de los minusválidos.

gear up vi hacer preparativos.

gear box n caja de cambios.

gear lever, (US) **gear shift** n palanca de cambio.

gear wheel n rueda dentada.

GED n abbr (US SCOL) = general educa-

tional development.

geese [giːs] npl of **goose.**

Geiger counter ['gaɪgə-] n contador m Geiger.

gel [dʒɛl] n gel m.

gelatin(e) ['dʒɛlətiːn] n gelatina.

gelignite ['dʒɛlɪgnaɪt] n gelignita.

gem [dʒɛm] n joya.

Gemini ['dʒɛmɪnaɪ] n Géminis m.

gen ['dʒɛn] n (Brit col): **to give sb the** ~ **on sth** poner a uno al corriente de algo.

Gen. abbr (MIL: = General) Gen., Gral.

gen. abbr (= general) grl.; = **generally.**

gender ['dʒɛndə*] n género.

gene [dʒiːn] n gen(e) m.

genealogy [dʒiːnɪ'ælədʒɪ] n genealogía.

general ['dʒɛnərl] n general m ♦ a general; **in** ~ en general; ~ **audit** comprobación f general de cuentas; **the** ~ **public** el gran público.

general anaesthetic, (US) **general anesthetic** n anestesia general.

general delivery n (US) lista de correos.

general election n elecciones fpl generales.

generalization [dʒɛnrəlaɪ'zeɪʃən] n generalización f.

generalize ['dʒɛnrəlaɪz] vi generalizar.

generally ['dʒɛnrəlɪ] ad generalmente, en general.

general manager n director(a) m/f general.

general practitioner (GP) n médico/a general.

general strike n huelga general.

generate ['dʒɛnəreɪt] vt (ELEC) generar; (fig) producir.

generation [dʒɛnə'reɪʃən] n (of electricity etc) generación f; **first/second/third/fourth** ~ (of computer) primera/segunda/tercera/cuarta generación.

generator ['dʒɛnəreɪtə*] n generador m.

generic [dʒɪ'nɛrɪk] a genérico.

generosity [dʒɛnə'rɒsɪtɪ] n generosidad f.

generous ['dʒɛnərəs] a generoso; (copious) abundante.

generously ['dʒɛnərəslɪ] ad generosamente; abundantemente.

genesis ['dʒɛnɪsɪs] n génesis f.

genetic [dʒɪ'nɛtɪk] a genético; ~ **engineering** selección f genética.

genetics [dʒɪ'nɛtɪks] n genética.

Geneva [dʒɪ'niːvə] n Ginebra.

genial ['dʒiːnɪəl] a afable, simpático.

genitals ['dʒɛnɪtlz] npl (órganos mpl) genitales mpl.

genitive ['dʒɛnɪtɪv] n genitivo.

genius ['dʒiːnɪəs] n genio.

Genoa ['dʒɛnəuə] n Génova.

genocide ['dʒɛnəusaɪd] n genocidio.

gent [dʒɛnt] n abbr (Brit col) = **gentleman.**

genteel [dʒɛn'tiːl] a fino, elegante.

Gentile ['dʒɛntaɪl] *n* gentil *m/f*.

gentle ['dʒɛntl] *a* (*sweet*) amable, dulce; (*touch etc*) ligero, suave.

gentleman ['dʒɛntlmən] *n* señor *m*; (*well-bred man*) caballero; ~'s **agreement** acuerdo entre caballeros.

gentlemanly ['dʒɛntlmənlɪ] *a* caballeroso, cortés.

gentleness ['dʒɛntlnɪs] *n* dulzura; (*of touch*) suavidad *f*.

gently ['dʒɛntlɪ] *ad* suavemente.

gentrification [dʒɛntrɪfɪ'keɪʃən] *n* aburguesamiento.

gentry ['dʒɛntrɪ] *npl* aristocracia *sg*.

gents [dʒɛnts] *n* aseos *mpl* (de caballeros).

genuine ['dʒɛnjuɪn] *a* auténtico; (*person*) sincero.

genuinely ['dʒɛnjuɪnlɪ] *ad* sinceramente.

geographer [dʒɪ'ɒgrəfə*] geógrafo/a.

geographic(al) [dʒɪə'græfɪk(l)] *a* geográfico.

geography [dʒɪ'ɒgrəfɪ] *n* geografía.

geological [dʒɪə'lɒdʒɪkl] *a* geológico.

geologist [dʒɪ'ɒlədʒɪst] *n* geólogo/a.

geology [dʒɪ'ɒlədʒɪ] *n* geología.

geometric(al) [dʒɪə'mɛtrɪk(l)] *a* geométrico.

geometry [dʒɪ'ɒmətrɪ] *n* geometría.

Geordie ['dʒɔːdɪ] *n* habitante *m/f* de Tyneside.

geranium [dʒɪ'reɪnjəm] *n* geranio.

geriatric [dʒɛrɪ'ætrɪk] *a, n* geriátrico/a *m/f*.

germ [dʒɜːm] *n* (*microbe*) microbio, bacteria; (*seed, fig*) germen *m*.

German ['dʒɜːmən] *a* alemán/ana ◆ *n* alemán/ana *m/f*; (*LING*) alemán *m*.

German Democratic Republic *n* República Democrática Alemana.

German measles *n* rubéola.

German Shepherd *n* (*dog*) pastor *m* alemán.

Germany ['dʒɜːmənɪ] *n* Alemania; **East/ West** ~ Alemania Oriental *or* Democrática/Occidental *or* Federal.

germination [dʒɜːmɪ'neɪʃən] *n* germinación *f*.

germ warfare *n* guerra bacteriológica.

gesticulate [dʒɛs'tɪkjuleɪt] *vi* gesticular.

gesticulation [dʒɛstɪkju'leɪʃən] *n* gesticulación *f*.

gesture ['dʒɛstjə*] *n* gesto; **as a** ~ **of friendship** en señal de amistad.

get, *pt, pp* **got**, (*US*) *pp* **gotten** [gɛt, gɔt, 'gɔtn] *vt* (*obtain*) obtener; (*receive*) recibir; (*achieve*) conseguir; (*find*) encontrar; (*catch*) coger (*Sp*), agarrar (*LAm*); (*fetch*) traer, ir a buscar; (*take, move*) llevar; (*understand*) entender; (*col: annoy*) molestar; (: *thrill*) chiflar ◆ *vi* (*become*) hacerse, volverse; **to** ~ **old** hacerse viejo, envejecer; **to** ~ **to** (*place*) llegar a; **he got under the fence** pasó por debajo de la barrera; **to** ~ **ready/washed** prepararse/

lavarse; **to** ~ **sb to do sth** hacer que uno haga algo; **I've got to do it** tengo que hacerlo; **to** ~ **sth for sb** conseguir algo para uno; **to** ~ **sth out of sth** sacar algo de algo; **to** ~ **sth done** (*do*) hacer algo; (*have done*) mandar hacer algo; **to** ~ **sth/ sb ready** preparar algo/a uno; **to** ~ **one's hair cut** pelarse; ~ **me Mr. Jones, please** (*TEL*) póngame *or* (*LAm*) comuníqueme con el Sr. Jones, por favor; **can I** ~ **you a drink?** ¿quieres algo de beber?; **you've got to tell the police** tienes que denunciarlo a la policía; **to** ~ **used to sth** acostumbrarse a algo; **let's** ~ **going** *or* **started** vámonos.

get about *vi* salir mucho; (*travel*) viajar mucho; (*news*) divulgarse.

get across *vt* (*message, meaning*) lograr comunicar ◆ *vi*: **to** ~ **across to sb** lograr hacer que uno comprenda.

get along *vi* (*agree*) entenderse; (*depart*) marcharse; (*manage*) = **get by**.

get around = **get round**.

get at *vt fus* (*attack*) atacar; (*reach*) llegar a; (*the truth*) descubrir; **what are you** ~**ting at?** ¿qué insinúas?

get away *vi* marcharse; (*on holiday*) irse de vacaciones; (*escape*) escaparse.

get away with *vt fus* hacer impunemente.

get back *vi* (*return*) volver ◆ *vt* recobrar.

get back at *vt fus* (*col*): **to** ~ **back at sb (for sth)** vengarse de uno (por algo).

get by *vi* (*pass*) lograr pasar; (*manage*) **I can** ~ **by in Dutch** me defiendo en holandés.

get down *vi* bajarse ◆ *vt* (*object*) bajar; (*depress*) deprimir.

get down to *vt fus* (*work*) ponerse a (hacer); **to** ~ **down to business** ponerse a trabajar en serio.

get in *vi* (*train*) llegar; (*arrive home*) volver a casa, regresar ◆ *vt* (*bring in: harvest*) recoger; (: *coal, shopping, supplies*) comprar, traer; (*insert*) lograr meter en.

get into *vt fus* (*vehicle*) subir a; (*house*) entrar en; (*clothes*) ponerse.

get off *vi* (*from train etc*) bajar; (*depart: person, car*) marcharse ◆ *vt* (*send off*) mandar; (*have as leave: day, time*) tener libre ◆ *vt fus* (*train, bus*) bajar de; **to** ~ **off to a good start** (*fig*) empezar muy bien *or* con buen pie.

get on *vi* (*in exam etc*) tener éxito; (*agree*) entenderse ◆ *vt fus* (*horse*) subir; **how are you** ~**ting on?** ¿qué tal estás?, ¿cómo te va? (*LAm*).

get on to *vt fus* (*deal with*) ocuparse de; (*col: contact: on phone etc*) hablar con.

get out *vi* salir; (*of vehicle*) bajar; (*news*) saberse; (*news etc*) difundirse ◆ *vt* (*take out: money from bank etc*) sacar.

get out of vt fus (duty etc) escaparse de ♦ vt (extract: confession, words) sacar de; (gain from: pleasure, benefit) ganar de.

get over vt fus (illness) recobrarse de ♦ vt (communicate: idea etc) comunicar; **let's ~ it over (with)** acabemos de una vez.

get round vt fus rodear; (fig: person) engatusar a ♦ vi: **to ~ round to doing sth** llegar a hacer algo.

get through vt fus (finish: work) acabar con; (: book) terminar, acabar ♦ vi (TEL) lograr comunicarse.

get through to vt fus (TEL) comunicar con.

get together vi reunirse.

get up vi (rise) levantarse ♦ vt fus levantar; **to ~ up enthusiasm for sth** cobrar entusiasmo por algo.

get up to vt fus (reach) llegar a; (prank etc) hacer.

getaway ['gɛtəweɪ] n fuga, escape m.

getaway car n: **the thieves' ~** el coche en que los ladrones huyeron.

get-together ['gɛttəgɛðə*] n reunión f; (party) fiesta.

get-up ['gɛtʌp] n (Brit col: outfit) atavío, atuendo.

get-well card [gɛt'wɛl-] n tarjeta que se envía a uno que está enfermo deseándole que se mejore.

geyser ['giːzə*] n (water heater) calentador m de agua; (GEO) géiser m.

Ghana ['gɑːnə] n Ghana.

Ghanaian [gɑː'neɪən] a, n ghaneano/a m/f.

ghastly ['gɑːstlɪ] a horrible; (pale) pálido.

gherkin ['gəːkɪn] n pepinillo.

ghetto ['gɛtəʊ] n ghetto.

ghost [gəʊst] n fantasma m ♦ vt (book) escribir por otro.

ghostly ['gəʊstlɪ] a fantasmal.

ghost story n cuento de fantasmas.

ghostwriter ['gəʊstraɪtə*] n negro/a.

ghoul [guːl] n demonio necrófago.

GHQ n abbr (MIL: = general headquarters) E.M.

GI n abbr (US col: = government issue) soldado del ejército norteamericano.

giant ['dʒaɪənt] n gigante m/f ♦ a gigantesco, gigante; **~ (size) packet** paquete m (de tamaño) gigante or familiar.

gibber ['dʒɪbə*] vi (monkey) farfullar; (idiot) hablar de una manera ininteligible.

gibberish ['dʒɪbərɪʃ] n galimatías m.

gibe [dʒaɪb] n mofa.

giblets ['dʒɪblɪts] npl menudillos mpl.

Gibraltar [dʒɪ'brɔːltə*] n Gibraltar m.

giddiness ['gɪdɪnɪs] n vértigo.

giddy ['gɪdɪ] a (dizzy) mareado; (height, speed) vertiginoso; **it makes me ~** me marea; **I feel ~** me siento mareado.

gift [gɪft] n (gen) regalo; (COMM: also: **free ~**) obsequio; (ability) talento; **to have a ~ for sth** tener talento para algo.

gifted ['gɪftɪd] a dotado.

gift token, gift voucher n vale-regalo m.

gig [gɪg] n (col: concert) función f.

gigantic [dʒaɪ'gæntɪk] a gigantesco.

giggle ['gɪgl] vi reírse tontamente ♦ n risilla.

GIGO ['gaɪgəʊ] abbr (COMPUT: col) = garbage in, garbage out.

gill [dʒɪl] n (measure) = 0.25 pints (Brit = 0.148 l, US = 0.118 l).

gills [gɪlz] npl (of fish) branquias fpl, agallas fpl.

gilt [gɪlt] a, n dorado.

gilt-edged ['gɪltɛdʒd] a (COMM: stocks, securities) de máxima garantía.

gimlet ['gɪmlɪt] n barrena de mano.

gimmick ['gɪmɪk] n truco; **sales ~** truco de promoción.

gimmicky ['gɪmɪkɪ] a truquero.

gin [dʒɪn] n (liquor) ginebra.

ginger ['dʒɪndʒə*] n jengibre m.

ginger ale, ginger beer n (Brit) gaseosa de jengibre.

gingerbread ['dʒɪndʒəbrɛd] n pan m de jengibre.

ginger-haired [dʒɪndʒə'hɛəd] a pelirrojo.

gingerly ['dʒɪndʒəlɪ] ad con pies de plomo.

gipsy ['dʒɪpsɪ] n gitano/a.

giraffe [dʒɪ'rɑːf] n jirafa.

girder ['gəːdə*] n viga.

girdle ['gəːdl] n (corset) faja ♦ vt ceñir.

girl [gəːl] n (small) niña; (young woman) chica, joven f, muchacha; **an English ~** una (chica) inglesa.

girlfriend ['gəːlfrɛnd] n (of girl) amiga; (of boy) novia.

Girl Guide n exploradora.

girlish ['gəːlɪʃ] a de niña.

Girl Scout n (US) = Girl Guide.

giro ['dʒaɪrəʊ] n (Brit: bank ~) giro bancario; (post office ~) giro postal.

girth [gəːθ] n circunferencia; (of saddle) cincha.

gist [dʒɪst] n lo esencial.

give [gɪv] vb (pt **gave**, pp **given** [geɪv, 'gɪvn]) vt dar; (deliver) entregar; (as gift) regalar ♦ vi (break) romperse; (stretch: fabric) dar de sí; **to ~ sb sth, ~ sth to sb** dar algo a uno; **how much did you ~ for it?** ¿cuánto pagaste por él?; **12 o'clock, ~ or take a few minutes** más o menos las doce; **~ them my regards** mándales saludos de mi parte; **I can ~ you 10 minutes** le puedo conceder 10 minutos; **to ~ way** (Brit AUT) ceder el paso; **to ~ way to despair** ceder a la desesperación.

give away vt (give free) regalar; (betray) traicionar; (disclose) revelar.

give back vt devolver.

give in vi ceder ♦ vt entregar.

give off vt despedir.

give out vt distribuir ♦ vi (be exhausted: *supplies*) agotarse; (*fail: engine*) averiarse; (*strength*) fallar.

give up *vi* rendirse, darse por vencido ◆ *vt* renunciar a; **to ~ up smoking** dejar de fumar; **to ~ o.s. up** entregarse.

give-and-take ['gɪvənd'teɪk] *n* (*col*) toma y daca *m*.

giveaway ['gɪvəweɪ] *n* (*col*): **her expression was a ~** su expresión la delataba; **the exam was a ~!** ¡el examen estaba tirado! ◆ *cpd*: **~ prices** precios *mpl* de ragalo.

given ['gɪvn] *pp of* **give** ◆ *a* (*fixed: time, amount*) determinado, fijo ◆ *conj*: **~ (that)** ... dado (que) ...; **~ the circumstances ...** dadas las circunstancias.

glacial ['gleɪsɪəl] *a* glacial.

glacier ['glæsɪə*] *n* glaciar *m*.

glad [glæd] *a* contento; **to be ~ about sth/ that** alegrarse de algo/de que; **I was ~ of his help** agradecí su ayuda.

gladden ['glædn] *vt* alegrar.

glade [gleɪd] *n* claro.

gladiator ['glædɪeɪtə*] *n* gladiador *m*.

gladioli [glædɪ'əʊlaɪ] *npl* gladíolos *mpl*.

gladly ['glædlɪ] *ad* con mucho gusto.

glamorous ['glæmərəs] *a* encantador(a), atractivo.

glamour ['glæmə*] *n* encanto, atractivo, hechizo.

glance [glɑːns] *n* ojeada, mirada ◆ *vi*: **to ~ at** echar una ojeada a.

glance off *vt fus* (*bullet*) rebotar en.

glancing ['glɑːnsɪŋ] *a* (*blow*) oblicuo.

gland [glænd] *n* glándula.

glandular ['glændjʊlə*] *a*: **~ fever** fiebre *f* glandular.

glare [glɛə*] *n* deslumbramiento, brillo ◆ *vi* deslumbrar; **to ~ at** mirar ferozmente a.

glaring ['glɛərɪŋ] *a* (*mistake*) manifiesto.

glass [glɑːs] *n* vidrio, cristal *m*; (*for drinking*) vaso; (*: with stem*) copa; (*also:* **looking ~**) espejo.

glass-blowing ['glɑːsbləʊɪŋ] *n* soplado de vidrio.

glasses ['glɑːsəs] *npl* gafas *fpl*, anteojos *mpl* (*LAm*).

glass fibre, (*US*) **glass fiber** *n* fibra de vidrio.

glasshouse ['glɑːshaʊs] *n* invernadero.

glassware ['glɑːswɛə*] *n* cristalería.

glassy ['glɑːsɪ] *a* (*eyes*) vidrioso.

Glaswegian [glæs'wiːdʒən] *a* de Glasgow ◆ *n* nativo/a (*or* habitante *m/f*) de Glasgow.

glaze [gleɪz] *vt* (*window*) poner cristales a; (*pottery*) barnizar; (*CULIN*) glasear ◆ *n* barniz *m*; (*CULIN*) vidriado.

glazed [gleɪzd] *a* (*eye*) vidrioso; (*pottery*) barnizado.

glazier ['gleɪzɪə*] *n* vidriero/a.

GLC *n abbr* (*Brit: old:* = *Greater London Council*) ayuntamiento del Gran Londres.

gleam [gliːm] *n* destello ◆ *vi* brillar; **a ~ of hope** un rayo de esperanza.

gleaming ['gliːmɪŋ] *a* reluciente.

glean [gliːn] *vt* (*gather: information*) recoger.

glee [gliː] *n* alegría, regocijo.

gleeful ['gliːfʊl] *a* alegre.

glen [glɛn] *n* cañada.

glib [glɪb] *a* (*person*) de mucha labia; (*comment*) fácil.

glibly ['glɪblɪ] *ad* (*explain*) con mucha labia.

glide [glaɪd] *vi* deslizarse; (*AVIAT, birds*) planear.

glider ['glaɪdə*] *n* (*AVIAT*) planeador *m*.

gliding ['glaɪdɪŋ] *n* (*AVIAT*) vuelo sin motor.

glimmer ['glɪmə*] *n* luz *f* tenue.

glimpse [glɪmps] *n* vislumbre *m* ◆ *vt* vislumbrar, entrever; **to catch a ~ of** vislumbrar.

glint [glɪnt] *n* destello; (*in the eye*) chispa ◆ *vi* centellear.

glisten ['glɪsn] *vi* relucir, brillar.

glitter ['glɪtə*] *vi* relucir, brillar ◆ *n* brillo.

glittering ['glɪtərɪŋ] *a* reluciente, brillante.

glitz [glɪts] *n* (*col*) brillo, resplandor *m*.

gloat [gləʊt] *vi*: **to ~ over** (*money*) recrearse en; (*sb's misfortune*) saborear.

global ['gləʊbl] *a* (*world-wide*) mundial; (*comprehensive*) global.

globe [gləʊb] *n* globo, esfera.

globetrotter ['gləʊbtrɔtə*] *n* trotamundos *m inv*.

globule ['glɔbjuːl] *n* glóbulo.

gloom [gluːm] *n* tinieblas *fpl*, oscuridad *f*; (*sadness*) tristeza, melancolía.

gloomily ['gluːmɪlɪ] *ad* tristemente; de moda pesimista.

gloomy ['gluːmɪ] *a* (*dark*) oscuro; (*sad*) triste; (*pessimistic*) pesimista; **to feel ~** sentirse pesimista.

glorification [glɔːrɪfɪ'keɪʃən] *n* glorificación *f*.

glorify ['glɔːrɪfaɪ] *vt* glorificar; (*God*) alabar, ensalzar.

glorious ['glɔːrɪəs] *a* glorioso.

glory ['glɔːrɪ] *n* gloria.

glory hole *n* (*col*) trastero.

Glos *abbr* (*Brit*) = *Gloucestershire*.

gloss [glɔs] *n* (*shine*) brillo; (*also:* **~ paint**) pintura de aceite.

gloss over *vt fus* encubrir.

glossary ['glɔsərɪ] *n* glosario.

glossy ['glɔsɪ] *a* lustroso.

glove [glʌv] *n* guante *m*.

glove compartment *n* (*AUT*) guantera.

glow [gləʊ] *vi* (*shine*) brillar ◆ *n* brillo.

glower ['glaʊə*] *vi*: **to ~ at** mirar con ceño.

glowing ['gləʊɪŋ] *a* (*fire*) vivo; (*complexion*) encendido; (*fig: report, description*) entusiasta.

glow-worm ['gləʊwəːm] *n* luciérnaga.

glucose ['gluːkəʊs] *n* glucosa.

glue [gluː] *n* goma (de pegar), cemento (*LAm*) ◆ *vt* pegar.

glue-sniffing ['gluːsnıfıŋ] *n* inhalación *f* del vapor del cemento.

glum [glʌm] *a* (*mood*) abatido; (*person, tone*) melancólico.

glut [glʌt] *n* superabundancia.

glutinous ['gluːtınəs] *a* glutinoso.

glutton ['glʌtn] *n* glotón/ona *m/f*; ~ **for punishment** masoquista *m/f*.

gluttony ['glʌtənı] *n* gula, glotonería.

glycerin(e) ['glısəriːn] *n* glicerina.

gm *abbr* (= *gram*) g.

GMAT *n abbr* (*US*: = *Graduate Management Admissions Test*) examen de admisión en el segundo ciclo de la enseñanza superior.

GMT *abbr* (= *Greenwich Mean Time*) GMT.

GMWU *n abbr* (*Brit*: = *General and Municipal Workers' Union*) sindicato de trabajadores municipales.

gnarled [naːld] *a* nudoso.

gnash [næʃ] *vt*: **to ~ one's teeth** rechinar los dientes.

gnat [næt] *n* mosquito.

gnaw [nɔː] *vt* roer.

gnome [nəum] *n* gnomo.

GNP *n abbr* (= *gross national product*) PNB *m*.

go [gəu] *vb* (*pt* **went**, *pp* **gone** [wɛnt, gɔn]) *vi* ir; (*travel*) viajar; (*depart*) irse, marcharse; (*work*) funcionar, marchar; (*be sold*) venderse; (*time*) pasar; (*become*) ponerse; (*break etc*) estropearse, romperse; (*fit, suit*): **to ~ with** hacer juego con ♦ *n* (*pl* ~**es**): **to have a ~ (at)** probar suerte (con); **to be on the ~** no parar; **whose ~ is it?** ¿a quién le toca?; **to ~ by car/on foot** ir en coche/a pie; **he's ~ing to do it** va a hacerlo; **to ~ for a walk** ir de paseo; **to ~ dancing** ir a bailar; **to ~ looking for sth/sb** ir a buscar algo/a uno; **to make sth ~, get sth ~ing** poner algo en marcha; **my voice has gone** he perdido la voz; **the cake is all gone** se acabó la torta; **the money will ~ towards our holiday** el dinero será un aporte para las vacaciones; **how did it ~?** ¿qué tal salió *or* resultó?, ¿cómo ha ido?; **the meeting went well** la reunión salió bien; **to ~ and see sb, ~ to see sb** ir a ver a uno; **to ~ to sleep** dormirse; **I'll take whatever is ~ing** acepto lo que haya; **... to ~** (*US: food*) ... para llevar; **to ~ round the back** pasar por detrás.

go about *vi* (*rumour*) propagarse; (*also*: ~ **round**: *wander about*) andar (de un sitio para otro) ♦ *vt fus*: **how do I ~ about this?** ¿cómo me las arreglo para hacer esto?; **to ~ about one's business** ocuparse en sus asuntos.

go after *vt fus* (*pursue*) perseguir; (*job, record etc*) andar tras.

go against *vt fus* (*be unfavourable to*: *results*) ir en contra de; (*be contrary to*: *principles*) ser contrario a.

go ahead *vi* seguir adelante.

go along *vi* ir ♦ *vt fus* bordear.

go along with *vt fus* (*accompany*) acompañar; (*agree with*: *idea*) estar de acuerdo con.

go around *vi* = **go round**.

go away *vi* irse, marcharse.

go back *vi* volver.

go back on *vt fus* (*promise*) faltar a.

go by *vi* (*years, time*) pasar ♦ *vt fus* guiarse por.

go down *vi* bajar; (*ship*) hundirse; (*sun*) ponerse ♦ *vt fus* bajar por; **that should ~ down well with him** eso le va a gustar.

go for *vt fus* (*fetch*) ir por; (*like*) gustar; (*attack*) atacar.

go in *vi* entrar.

go in for *vt fus* (*competition*) presentarse a.

go into *vt fus* entrar en; (*investigate*) investigar; (*embark on*) dedicarse a.

go off *vi* irse, marcharse; (*food*) pasarse; (*lights etc*) apagarse; (*explode*) estallar; (*event*) realizarse ♦ *vt fus* dejar de gustar; **the party went off well** la fiesta salió bien.

go on *vi* (*continue*) seguir, continuar; (*lights*) encenderse; (*happen*) pasar, ocurrir; (*be guided by: evidence etc*) partir de; **to ~ on doing sth** seguir haciendo algo; **what's ~ing on here?** ¿qué pasa aquí?

go on at *vt fus* (*nag*) reñir.

go out *vi* salir; (*fire, light*) apagarse; (*ebb: tide*) bajar, menguar; **to ~ out with sb** salir con uno.

go over *vi* (*ship*) zozobrar ♦ *vt fus* (*check*) revisar; **to ~ over sth in one's mind** repasar algo mentalmente.

go round *vi* (*circulate*: *news, rumour*) correr; (*suffice*) alcanzar, bastar; (*revolve*) girar, dar vueltas; (*visit*): **to ~ round (to sb's)** pasar a ver (a uno); **to ~ round (by)** (*make a detour*) dar la vuelta (por).

go through *vt fus* (*town etc*) atravesar; (*search through*) revisar; (*perform: ceremony*) realizar; (*examine: list, book*) repasar.

go through with *vt fus* (*plan, crime*) llevar a cabo; **I couldn't ~ through with it** no pude llevarlo a cabo.

go together *vi* (*harmonize: people etc*) entenderse.

go under *vi* (*sink: ship, person*) hundirse; (*fig: business, firm*) quebrar.

go up *vi* subir; **to ~ up in flames** estallar en llamas.

go without *vt fus* pasarse sin.

goad [gəud] *vt* aguijonear.

go-ahead ['gəuəhɛd] *a* emprendedor(a) ♦ *n* luz *f* verde; **to give sth/sb the ~** autorizar algo/a uno.

goal [gəul] n meta; (score) gol m.

goalkeeper ['gəulkiːpə*] n portero.

goal post n poste m (de la portería).

goat [gəut] n cabra f.

gobble ['gɔbl] vt (also: ~ **down**, ~ **up**) engullirse.

go-between ['gəubɪtwiːn] n medianero/a, intermediario/a.

Gobi Desert ['gəubɪ-] n Desierto de Gobi.

goblet ['gɔblɪt] n copa.

goblin ['gɔblɪn] n duende m.

go-cart ['gəukɑːt] n = **go-kart**.

god [gɔd] n dios m; **G~** n Dios m.

godchild ['gɔdtʃaɪld] n ahijado/a.

goddess ['gɔdɪs] n diosa.

godfather ['gɔdfɑːðə*] n padrino.

god-forsaken ['gɔdfəseɪkən] a olvidado de Dios.

godmother ['gɔdmʌðə*] n madrina.

godparents ['gɔdpɛərənts] npl: **the** ~ los padrinos.

godsend ['gɔdsɛnd] n don m del cielo.

godson ['gɔdsʌn] n ahijado.

goes [gəuz] vb see **go**.

go-getter ['gəugɛtə*] n ambicioso/a.

goggle ['gɔgl] vi: **to** ~ **(at)** mirar con ojos desorbitados.

goggles ['gɔglz] npl (AUT) anteojos mpl; (diver's) gafas fpl submarinas.

going ['gəuɪŋ] n (conditions) estado del terreno ♦ a: **the** ~ **rate** la tarifa corriente or en vigor; **it was slow** ~ íbamos a paso lento.

goings-on ['gəuɪŋz'ɔn] npl (col) tejemanejes mpl.

go-kart ['gəukɑːt] n kart m.

gold [gəuld] n oro ♦ a (reserves) de oro.

golden ['gəuldn] a (made of gold) de oro; (~ in colour) dorado.

Golden Age n Siglo de Oro.

golden handshake n gratificación f al fin del servicio.

golden rule n regla de oro.

goldfish ['gəuldfɪʃ] n pez m de colores.

gold leaf n oro en hojas, pan m de oro.

gold medal n (SPORT) medalla de oro.

goldmine ['gəuldmaɪn] n mina de oro.

gold-plated ['gəuld'pleɪtɪd] a chapado en oro.

goldsmith ['gəuldsmɪθ] n orfebre m/f.

gold standard n patrón m oro.

golf [gɔlf] n golf m.

golf ball n (for game) pelota de golf; (on typewriter) esfera impresora.

golf club n club m de golf; (stick) palo (de golf).

golf course n campo de golf.

golfer ['gɔlfə*] n jugador(a) m/f de golf.

gondola ['gɔndələ] n góndola.

gondolier [gɔndə'lɪə*] n gondolero.

gone [gɔn] pp of **go**.

gong [gɔŋ] n gong m.

gonorrhea [gɔnə'rɪə] n gonorrea.

good [gud] a bueno; (kind) bueno, amable; (well-behaved) educado ♦ n bien m, provecho; ~! ¡qué bien!; **to be** ~ **at** tener aptitud para; **to be** ~ **for** servir para; **it's** ~ **for you** te hace bien; **would you be** ~ **enough to...?** ¿podría hacerme el favor de...?, ¿sería tan amable de...?; **that's very** ~ **of you** es usted muy amable; **to feel** ~ sentirse bien; **it's** ~ **to see you** me alegro de verte; **a** ~ **deal (of)** mucho; **a** ~ **many** muchos; **to make** ~ reparar; **it's no** ~ **complaining** no vale la pena (de) quejarse; **is this any** ~? (will it do?) ¿sirve esto?; (what's it like?) ¿qué tal es esto?; **it's a** ~ **thing you were there** menos mal que tú estabas allí; **for** ~ (for ever) para siempre, definitivamente; ~ **morning/afternoon** ¡buenos días/buenas tardes!; ~ **evening!** ¡buenas noches!; ~ **night!** ¡buenas noches!; **he's up to no** ~ está tramitando algo; **for the common** ~ para el bien común; see also **goods**.

goodbye [gud'baɪ] excl ¡adiós!; **to say** ~ **(to)** (person) despedirse (de).

good faith n buena fe f.

good-for-nothing ['gudfənʌθɪŋ] n gandul(a) m/f, vago/a.

Good Friday n Viernes m Santo.

good-humoured ['gud'hjuːməd] a (person) afable, de buen humor; (remark, joke) bien intencionado.

good-looking ['gud'lukɪŋ] a guapo.

good-natured ['gud'neɪtʃəd] a (person) amable, simpático; (discussion) de tono amistoso.

goodness ['gudnɪs] n (of person) bondad f; **for** ~ **sake!** ¡por Dios!; ~ **gracious!** ¡Dios mío!

goods [gudz] npl bienes mpl; (COMM etc) géneros mpl, mercancías fpl, artículos mpl; **all his** ~ **and chattels** todos sus bienes.

goods train n (Brit) tren m de mercancías.

goodwill [gud'wɪl] n buena voluntad f; (COMM) crédito, clientela.

goody-goody ['gudɪgudɪ] n (pej) santurrón/ona m/f.

goose, pl **geese** [guːs, giːs] n ganso, oca.

gooseberry ['guzbərɪ] n grosella espinosa.

gooseflesh ['guːsfleʃ] n, **goosepimples** ['guːspɪmplz] npl carne f de gallina.

goose step n (MIL) paso de ganso.

GOP n abbr (US POL: col = Grand Old Party) Partido Republicano.

gore [gɔː*] vt cornear ♦ n sangre f.

gorge [gɔːdʒ] n barranco ♦ vr: **to** ~ **o.s. (on)** atracarse (de).

gorgeous ['gɔːdʒəs] a magnífico, maravilloso.

gorilla [gə'rɪlə] n gorila m.

gormless ['gɔːmlɪs] a (col) torpe; (stronger) imbécil.

gorse [gɔːs] n aulaga.

gory ['gɔːrɪ] a sangriento.

go-slow ['gəu'sləu] n (Brit) huelga de manos caídas.

gospel ['gɔspl] n evangelio.

gossamer ['gɔsəmə*] n gasa sutil.

gossip ['gɔsɪp] n (scandal) chismorreo, chismes mpl; (chat) charla; (scandalmonger) chismoso/a; (talker) hablador(a) m/f ◆ vi chismear; **a piece of ~** un chisme, un cotilleo.

gossip column n notas fpl de sociedad, páginas fpl sociales.

got [gɔt] pt, pp of **get**.

Gothic ['gɔθɪk] a gótico.

gotten ['gɔtn] (US) pp of **get**.

gouge [gaudʒ] vt (also: ~ **out**: hole etc) excavar; (: initials) grabar; **to ~ sb's eyes out** sacar or arrancar los ojos a uno.

goulash ['guːlæʃ] n g(o)ulash m.

gourd [guəd] n calabaza.

gourmet ['guəmeɪ] n gastrónomo/a m/f.

gout [gaut] n gota.

govern ['gʌvən] vt (gen) gobernar; (dominate) dominar.

governess ['gʌvənɪs] n institutriz f.

governing ['gʌvənɪŋ] a (POL) de gobierno, gubernamental; **~ body** consejo de administración.

government ['gʌvnmənt] n gobierno; **local ~** administración f local.

governmental [gʌvn'mentl] a gubernamental.

government stock n reservas fpl del Estado.

governor ['gʌvənə*] n gobernador(a) m/f; (of jail) director(a) m/f.

Govt. abbr (= Government) gobno.

gown [gaun] n traje m; (of teacher; Brit: of judge) toga.

GP n abbr see **general practitioner**.

GPO n abbr (Brit: old) = General Post Office; (US) = Government Printing Office.

gr. abbr (COMM: = gross) bto.

grab [græb] vt coger (Sp) or agarrar (LAm), arrebatar; **to ~ at** tratar de coger or agarrar.

grace [greɪs] n (REL) gracia; (gracefulness) elegancia, gracia; (graciousness) cortesía, gracia ◆ vt (favour) honrar; (adorn) adornar; **5 days' ~** un plazo de 5 días; **to say ~** bendecir la mesa; **his sense of humour is his saving ~** su sentido del humor es su mérito.

graceful ['greɪsful] a elegante, gracioso.

gracious ['greɪʃəs] a amable ◆ excl: **good ~!** ¡Dios mío!

grade [greɪd] n (quality) clase f, calidad f; (in hierarchy) grado; (US: SCOL) curso (: gradient) pendiente f, cuesta ◆ vt clasificar; **to make the ~** (fig) llegar al or alcanzar el nivel necesario.

grade crossing n (US) paso a nivel.

grade school n (US) escuela primaria.

gradient ['greɪdɪənt] n pendiente f.

gradual ['grædjuəl] a paulatino.

gradually ['grædjuəlɪ] ad paulatinamente.

graduate n ['grædjuɪt] graduado/a, licenciado/a; (US: SCOL) bachiller m/f ◆ vi ['grædjueɪt] graduarse, licenciarse.

graduated pension ['grædjueɪtɪd-] n pensión f escalonada.

graduation [grædju'eɪʃən] n graduación f; (US SCOL) entrega del bachillerato.

graffiti [grə'fiːtɪ] npl pintada sg.

graft [grɑːft] n (AGR, MED) injerto; (bribery) corrupción f ◆ vt injertar; **hard ~** (col) trabajo duro.

grain [greɪn] n (single particle) grano; (no pl: cereals) cereales mpl; (US: corn) trigo; (in wood) fibra.

gram [græm] n (US) gramo.

grammar ['græmə*] n gramática.

grammar school n (Brit) ≈ instituto (de segunda enseñanza), liceo (Sp).

grammatical [grə'mætɪkl] a gramatical.

gramme [græm] n = **gram**.

gramophone ['græməfəun] n (Brit) tocadiscos m inv.

granary ['grænərɪ] n granero, troj f.

grand [grænd] a magnífico, imponente ◆ n (US: col) mil dólares mpl.

grandchildren ['græntʃɪldrən] npl nietos mpl.

granddad ['grændæd] n yayo, abuelito.

granddaughter ['grændɔːtə*] n nieta.

grandeur ['grændjə*] n magnificencia, lo grandioso; (of occasion, scenery etc) lo imponente; (of style) lo elevado.

grandfather ['grænfɑːðə*] n abuelo.

grandiose ['grændɪəuz] a grandioso; (pej) pomposo.

grand jury n (US) jurado de acusación.

grandma ['grænmɑː] n yaya, abuelita.

grandmother ['grænmʌðə*] n abuela.

grandpa ['grænpɑː] n = **granddad**.

grandparents ['grændpeərənts] npl abuelos mpl.

grand piano n piano de cola.

Grand Prix ['grɑ̃ː'priː] n (AUT) Grand Prix m.

grandson ['grænsʌn] n nieto.

grandstand ['grændstænd] n (SPORT) tribuna.

grand total n suma total, total m.

granite ['grænɪt] n granito.

granny ['grænɪ] n abuelita, yaya.

grant [grɑːnt] vt (concede) conceder; (admit): **to ~ (that)** reconocer (que) ◆ n (SCOL) beca; **to take sth for ~ed** dar algo por sentado.

granulated sugar ['grænjuleɪtɪd-] n (Brit) azúcar m blanquilla or granulada.

granule ['grænjuːl] n gránulo.

grape [greɪp] n uva; **sour ~s** (fig) envidia sg; **a bunch of ~s** un racimo de uvas.

grapefruit ['greɪpfruːt] n pomelo, toronja

(*LAm*).

grape juice *n* zumo (*Sp*) *or* jugo (*LAm*) de uva.

grapevine ['greɪpvaɪn] *n* vid *f*, parra; **I heard it on the ~** (*fig*) me enteré, me lo contaron.

graph [grɑːf] *n* gráfica.

graphic ['græfɪk] *a* gráfico.

graphic designer *n* diseñador(a) *m/f* gráfico/a.

graphics ['græfɪks] *n* (*art*, *process*) artes *fpl* gráficas ♦ *npl* (*drawings*: *also* COMPUT) gráficos *mpl*.

graphite ['græfaɪt] *n* grafito.

graph paper *n* papel *m* cuadriculado.

grapple ['græpl] *vi*: **to ~ with a problem** enfrentar un problema.

grappling iron ['græplɪŋ-] *n* (*NAUT*) rezón *m*.

grasp [grɑːsp] *vt* agarrar, asir; (*understand*) comprender ♦ *n* (*grip*) asimiento; (*reach*) alcance *m*; (*understanding*) comprensión *f*; **to have a good ~ of** (*subject*) dominar.

grasp at *vt fus* (*rope etc*) tratar de asir; (*fig*: *opportunity*) aprovechar.

grasping ['grɑːspɪŋ] *a* avaro.

grass [grɑːs] *n* hierba; (*lawn*) césped *m*; (*pasture*) pasto; (*col*: *informer*) delator(a) *m/f*, denunciador(a) *m/f*.

grasshopper ['grɑːshɔpə*] *n* saltamontes *m inv*.

grassland ['grɑːslænd] *n* pradera, pampa (*LAm*)

grass roots *a* popular ♦ *npl* (*POL*) base *fsg* popular.

grass snake *n* culebra.

grassy ['grɑːsɪ] *a* cubierto de hierba.

grate [greɪt] *n* parrilla ♦ *vi* chirriar ♦ *vt* (*CULIN*) rallar.

grateful ['greɪtful] *a* agradecido.

gratefully ['greɪtfəlɪ] *ad* con agradecimiento.

grater ['greɪtə*] *n* rallador *m*.

gratification [grætɪfɪ'keɪʃən] *n* satisfacción *f*.

gratify ['grætɪfaɪ] *vt* complacer; (*whim*) satisfacer.

gratifying ['grætɪfaɪɪŋ] *a* grato.

grating ['greɪtɪŋ] *n* (*iron bars*) rejilla ♦ *a* (*noise*) áspero.

gratitude ['grætɪtjuːd] *n* agradecimiento.

gratuitous [grə'tjuːɪtəs] *a* gratuito, caprichoso.

gratuity [grə'tjuːɪtɪ] *n* gratificación *f*.

grave [greɪv] *n* tumba ♦ *a* serio, grave.

gravedigger ['greɪvdɪgə*] *n* sepulturero.

gravel ['grævl] *n* grava.

gravely ['greɪvlɪ] *ad* seriamente; **~ ill** muy grave.

gravestone ['greɪvstəun] *n* lápida.

graveyard ['greɪvjɑːd] *n* cementerio, camposanto.

gravitate ['grævɪteɪt] *vi* gravitar.

gravitation [grævɪ'teɪʃən] *n* gravitación *f*.

gravity ['grævɪtɪ] *n* gravedad *f*; (*seriousness*) seriedad *f*.

gravy ['greɪvɪ] *n* salsa de carne.

gravy boat *n* salsera.

gravy train *n* (*esp US*: *col*): **to get on the ~** coger un chollo.

gray [greɪ] *a* = **grey**.

graze [greɪz] *vi* pacer ♦ *vt* (*touch lightly*) rozar; (*scrape*) raspar ♦ *n* (*MED*) abrasión *f*.

grazing ['greɪzɪŋ] *n* (*for livestock*) pastoreo.

grease [griːs] *n* (*fat*) grasa; (*lubricant*) lubricante *m* ♦ *vt* engrasar; **to ~ the skids** (*US*: *fig*) engrasar el mecanismo.

grease gun *n* engrasadora a presión.

greasepaint ['griːspeɪnt] *n* maquillaje *m*.

greaseproof ['griːspruːf] *a* a prueba de grasa; (*Brit*: *paper*) apergaminado.

greasy ['griːsɪ] *a* (*hands*, *clothes*) grasiento; (*road*, *surface*) resbaladizo.

great [greɪt] *a* grande; (*col*) magnífico, estupendo; (*pain*, *heat*) intenso; **we had a ~ time** lo pasamos muy bien; **they're ~ friends** son íntimos *or* muy amigos; **the ~ thing is that** ... lo importante es que ...; **it was ~!** ¡fue estupendo!

Great Barrier Reef *n* Gran Barrera de Coral.

Great Britain *n* Gran Bretaña.

greater ['greɪtə*] *a* mayor; **G~ London** el Gran Londres.

greatest ['greɪtɪst] *a* el/la mayor.

great-grandchild, *pl* **-children** [greɪt-'grændtʃaɪld, 'tʃɪldrən] *n* bisnieto/a.

great-grandfather [greɪt'grændfɑːðə*] *n* bisabuelo.

great-grandmother [greɪt'grændmʌðə*] *n* bisabuela.

Great Lakes *npl*: **the ~** los Grandes Lagos.

greatly ['greɪtlɪ] *ad* sumamente, mucho, muy.

greatness ['greɪtnɪs] *n* grandeza.

Greece [griːs] *n* Grecia.

greed [griːd] *n* (*also*: **~iness**) codicia, avaricia; (*for food*) gula.

greedily ['griːdɪlɪ] *ad* con avidez.

greedy ['griːdɪ] *a* avaro; (*for food*) glotón/ona.

Greek [griːk] *a* griego ♦ *n* griego/a; (*LING*) griego; **ancient/modern ~** griego antiguo/moderno.

green [griːn] *a* verde; (*inexperienced*) novato ♦ *n* verde *m*; (*stretch of grass*) césped *m*; (*of golf course*) campo, "green" *m*; **~s** *npl* verduras *fpl*; **to have ~ fingers** (*fig*) tener habilidad para la jardinería.

green belt *n* zona verde.

green card *n* (*AUT*) carta verde.

greenery ['griːnərɪ] *n* verdura, plantas *fpl* verdes.

greenfly ['gri:nflaɪ] n pulgón m.

greengage ['gri:ngeɪdʒ] n claudia.

greengrocer ['gri:ngrəusə*] n (Brit) verdulero/a.

greenhouse ['gri:nhaus] n invernadero.

greenish ['gri:nɪʃ] a verdoso.

Greenland ['gri:nlənd] n Groenlandia.

Greenlander ['gri:nləndə*] n groenlandés/esa m/f.

green light n luz f verde.

green pepper n pimiento verde.

greet [gri:t] vt saludar; (welcome) dar la bienvenida a.

greeting ['gri:tɪŋ] n (gen) saludo; (welcome) bienvenida; ~s recuerdos mpl, saludos mpl; **season's** ~s Felices Pascuas.

greeting(s) card n tarjeta de felicitación.

gregarious [grə'gɛərɪəs] a gregario.

grenade [grə'neɪd] n (also: **hand** ~) granada.

grew [gru:] pt of **grow**.

grey [greɪ] a gris; **to go** ~ salirle canas.

grey-haired [greɪ'hɛəd] a canoso.

greyhound ['greɪhaund] n galgo.

grid [grɪd] n reja; (ELEC) red f.

griddle ['grɪdl] n (esp US) plancha.

gridiron ['grɪdaɪən] n (CULIN) parrilla.

grief [gri:f] n dolor m, pena; **to come to** ~ (plan) fracasar, ir al traste; (person) acabar mal, desgraciarse.

grievance ['gri:vəns] n (cause for complaint) motivo de queja, agravio.

grieve [gri:v] vi afligirse, acongojarse ◆ vt dar pena a; **to** ~ **for** llorar por; **to** ~ **for sb** (dead person) llorar la pérdida de uno.

grievous ['gri:vəs] a grave; (loss) cruel; ~ **bodily harm** (LAW) daños mpl corporales graves.

grill [grɪl] n (on cooker) parrilla ◆ vt (Brit) asar a la parrilla; (question) interrogar; ~**ed meat** carne f (asada) a la parrilla or plancha.

grille [grɪl] n reja.

grim [grɪm] a (place) sombrío; (person) ceñudo.

grimace [grɪ'meɪs] n mueca ◆ vi hacer muecas.

grime [graɪm] n mugre f.

grimly ['grɪmlɪ] ad (say) sombríamente.

grimy ['graɪmɪ] a mugriento.

grin [grɪn] n sonrisa abierta ◆ vi: **to** ~ **(at)** sonreír abiertamente (a).

grind [graɪnd] vb (pt, pp **ground** [graund]) vt (coffee, pepper etc) moler; (US: meat) picar; (make sharp) afilar; (polish: gem, lens) esmerilar ◆ vi (car gears) rechinar ◆ n: **the daily** ~ (col) la rutina diaria; **to** ~ **one's teeth** hacer rechinar los dientes; **to** ~ **to a halt** (vehicle) pararse con gran estruendo de frenos; (fig: talks, scheme) pararse en seco; (work, production) interrumpirse.

grinder ['graɪndə*] n (machine: for coffee)

molinillo.

grindstone ['graɪndstəun] n: **to keep one's nose to the** ~ batir el yunque.

grip [grɪp] n (hold) asimiento; (of hands) apretón m; (handle) asidero; (of racquet etc) mango; (understanding) comprensión f ◆ vt agarrar; **to get to** ~s **with** enfrentarse con; **to lose one's** ~ írsele de las manos; (fig) perder el control.

gripe [graɪp] n (col: complaint) queja ◆ vi (col: complain): **to** ~ **(about)** quejarse (de); ~s npl retortijones mpl.

gripping ['grɪpɪŋ] a absorbente.

grisly ['grɪzlɪ] a horripilante, horrible.

gristle ['grɪsl] n cartílago.

grit [grɪt] n gravilla; (courage) valor m ◆ vt (road) poner gravilla en; **I've got a piece of** ~ **in my eye** tengo una arenilla en el ojo; **to** ~ **one's teeth** apretar los dientes.

grits [grɪts] npl (US) maíz msg a medio moler.

grizzle ['grɪzl] vi (cry) lloriquear.

grizzly ['grɪzlɪ] n (also: ~ **bear**) oso pardo.

groan [grəun] n gemido, quejido ◆ vi gemir, quejarse.

grocer ['grəusə*] n tendero (de ultramarinos); ~'s **(shop)** n tienda de ultramarinos or de abarrotes (LAm).

groceries ['grəusərɪz] npl comestibles mpl.

grocery ['grəusərɪ] n (shop) tienda de ultramarinos.

grog [grɒg] n (Brit) grog m.

groggy ['grɒgɪ] a atontado.

groin [grɔɪn] n ingle f.

groom [gru:m] n mozo/a de cuadra; (also: **bride**~) novio ◆ vt (horse) almohazar; **well**-~**ed** acicalado.

groove [gru:v] n ranura, surco.

grope [grəup] vi ir a tientas; **to** ~ **for** buscar a tientas.

grosgrain ['grəugreɪn] n grogrén m, cordellate m.

gross [grəus] a grueso; (COMM) bruto ◆ vt (COMM) recaudar en bruto.

gross domestic product (GDP) n producto interno bruto (PIB).

gross income n ingresos mpl brutos.

grossly ['grəuslɪ] ad (greatly) enormemente.

gross national product (GNP) n producto nacional bruto (PNB).

gross profit n beneficios mpl brutos.

gross sales npl ventas fpl brutas.

grotesque [grəu'tɛsk] a grotesco.

grotto ['grɒtəu] n gruta.

grotty ['grɒtɪ] a asqueroso.

grouch [grautʃ] (col) vi refunfuñar ◆ n (col: person) refunfuñón/ona m/f.

ground [graund] pt, pp of **grind** ◆ n suelo, tierra; (SPORT) campo, terreno; (reason: gen pl) causa, razón f; (US: also: ~ **wire**) tierra ◆ vt (plane) mantener en tierra; (US: ELEC) conectar con tierra ◆ vi (ship)

varar, encallar ◆ *a* (*coffee etc*) molido; ~**s**
npl (*of coffee etc*) poso *sg*; (*gardens etc*)
jardines *mpl*, parque *m*; **on the** ~ en el
suelo; **common** ~ terreno común; **to
gain/lose** ~ ganar/perder terreno; **to the**
~ al suelo; **below** ~ debajo de la tierra,
bajo tierra; **he covered a lot of** ~ **in his
lecture** abarcó mucho en la clase.
ground cloth *n* (*US*) = **groundsheet.**
ground control *n* (*AVIAT*, *SPACE*) control
m desde tierra.
ground floor *n* (*Brit*) planta baja.
grounding ['graundɪŋ] *n* (*in education*) conocimientos *mpl* básicos.
groundkeeper ['graundkiːpə*] *n* =
groundsman.
groundless ['graundlɪs] *a* infundado, sin
fundamento.
groundnut ['graundnʌt] *n* cacahuete *m*.
ground rent *n* renta sobre el terreno.
groundsheet ['graundʃiːt] (*Brit*) *n* tela impermeable.
groundsman ['graundzmən], (*US*)
groundskeeper ['graundzkiːpə*] *n* (*SPORT*)
encargado de pista de deportes.
ground staff *n* personal *m* de tierra.
ground swell *n* mar *m* or *f* de fondo; (*fig*)
marejada.
ground-to-ground ['grauntə'graund] *a*: ~
missile proyectil *m* tierra-tierra.
groundwork ['graundwəːk] *n* preparación
f.
group [gruːp] *n* grupo; (*MUS*: *pop* ~)
conjunto, grupo ◆ (*vb*: *also*: ~ **together**)
vt agrupar ◆ *vi* agruparse.
grouse [graus] *n* (*pl inv*) (*bird*) urogallo ◆
vi (*complain*) quejarse.
grove [grəuv] *n* arboleda.
grovel ['grɔvl] *vi* (*fig*) arrastrarse.
grow, *pt* **grew**, *pp* **grown** [grəu, gruː,
grəun] *vi* crecer; (*increase*) aumentarse;
(*expand*) desarrollarse; (*become*) volverse;
to ~ **rich/weak** enriquecerse/debilitarse ◆
vt cultivar; (*hair*, *beard*) dejar crecer; **to**
~ **tired of waiting** cansarse de esperar.
grow apart *vi* (*fig*) alejarse uno del otro.
grow away from *vt fus* (*fig*) alejarse
de.
grow on *vt fus*: **that painting is** ~**ing
on me** ese cuadro me gusta cada vez más.
grow out of *vt fus* (*clothes*): **I've
grown out of this shirt** esta camisa se me
queda pequeña; (*habit*) perder.
grow up *vi* crecer, hacerse hombre/
mujer.
grower ['grəuə*] *n* (*AGR*) cultivador(a) *m/f*,
productor(a) *m/f*.
growing ['grəuɪŋ] *a* creciente; ~ **pains**
(*also fig*) dificultades *fpl* de desarrollo.
growl [graul] *vi* gruñir.
grown [grəun] *pp of* **grow.**
grown-up [grəun'ʌp] *n* adulto/a, mayor *m/f*.
growth [grəuθ] *n* crecimiento, desarrollo;

(*what has grown*) brote *m*; (*MED*) tumor
m.
growth rate *n* tasa de crecimiento.
GRSM *n abbr* (*Brit*) = *Graduate of the
Royal Schools of Music.*
grub [grʌb] *n* gusano; (*col*: *food*) comida.
grubby ['grʌbɪ] *a* sucio, mugriento.
grudge [grʌdʒ] *n* rencor ◆ *vt*: **to** ~ **sb sth**
dar algo a uno de mala gana; **to bear sb a**
~ guardar rencor a uno; **he** ~**s** (*giving*)
the money da el dinero de mala gana.
grudgingly ['grʌdʒɪŋlɪ] *ad* de mala gana.
gruelling, (*US*) **grueling** ['gruəlɪŋ] *a* penoso, duro.
gruesome ['gruːsəm] *a* horrible.
gruff [grʌf] *a* (*voice*) ronco; (*manner*) brusco.
grumble ['grʌmbl] *vi* refunfuñar, quejarse.
grumpy ['grʌmpɪ] *a* gruñón/ona.
grunt [grʌnt] *vi* gruñir ◆ *n* gruñido.
G-string ['dʒiːstrɪŋ] *n* taparrabo.
GSUSA *n abbr* = *Girl Scouts of the United
States of America.*
GT *abbr* (*AUT*: = *gran turismo*) GT.
GU *abbr* (*US POST*) = *Guam.*
guarantee [gærən'tiː] *n* garantía ◆ *vt* garantizar; **he can't** ~ (**that**) **he'll come** no
está seguro de poder venir.
guarantor [gærən'tɔː*] *n* garante *m/f*, fia-
dor(a) *m/f*.
guard [gɑːd] *n* guardia; (*Brit RAIL*) jefe *m*
de tren; (*safety device*: *on machine*) salva-
guardia, resguardo; (*protection*) protección
f; (*fire*~) pantalla; (*mud*~) guardabarros
m inv ◆ *vt* guardar; **to** ~ (**against** *or*
from) proteger (de); **to be on one's** ~
(*fig*) estar en guardia.
guard against *vi*: **to** ~ **against doing
sth** guardarse de hacer algo.
guard dog *n* perro guardián.
guarded ['gɑːdɪd] *a* (*fig*) cauteloso.
guardian ['gɑːdɪən] *n* guardián/ana *m/f*; (*of
minor*) tutor(a) *m/f*.
guardrail ['gɑːdreɪl] *n* pretil *m*.
guard's van *n* (*Brit RAIL*) furgón *m*.
Guatemala [gwɑːtə'mɑːlə] *n* Guatemala.
Guatemalan [gwɑːtə'mɑːlən] *a*, *n*
guatemalteco/a *m/f*.
Guernsey ['gəːnzɪ] *n* Guernsey *m*.
guerrilla [gə'rɪlə] *n* guerrillero/a.
guerrilla warfare *n* guerra de guerrillas.
guess [ges] *vi*, *vt* (*gen*) adivinar; (*suppose*)
suponer ◆ *n* suposición *f*, conjetura; **I** ~
you're right (*esp US*) supongo que tienes
razón; **to keep sb** ~**ing** mantener a uno a
la expectativa; **to take** *or* **have a** ~ tratar
de adivinar; **my** ~ **is that** ... yo creo
que ...
guesstimate ['gestɪmɪt] *n* conjetura.
guesswork ['geswəːk] *n* conjeturas *fpl*; **I
got the answer by** ~ acerté a ojo de buen
cubero.
guest [gest] *n* invitado/a; (*in hotel*)

huésped(a) m/f; **be my** ~ (col) estás en tu casa.

guest-house ['gɛsthaus] n casa de huéspedes, pensión f.

guest room n cuarto de huéspedes.

guffaw [gʌ'fɔː] n carcajada ♦ vi reírse a carcajadas.

guidance ['gaɪdəns] n (gen) dirección f; (advice) consejos mpl; **marriage/vocational** ~ orientación f matrimonial/profesional.

guide [gaɪd] n (person) guía m/f; (book, fig) guía f; (also: **girl** ~) exploradora ♦ vt guiar; **to be** ~**d by sb/sth** dejarse guiar por uno/algo.

guidebook ['gaɪdbuk] n guía.

guided missile ['gaɪdɪd-] n misil m teledirigido.

guide dog n perro guía.

guidelines ['gaɪdlaɪnz] npl (fig) directiva sg.

guild [gɪld] n gremio.

guildhall ['gɪldhɔːl] n (Brit) ayuntamiento.

guile [gaɪl] n astucia.

guileless ['gaɪllɪs] a cándido.

guillotine ['gɪlətiːn] n guillotina.

guilt [gɪlt] n culpabilidad f.

guilty ['gɪltɪ] a culpable; **to feel** ~ **(about)** sentirse culpable (por); **to plead** ~/**not** ~ declararse culpable/inocente.

Guinea ['gɪnɪ] n: **Republic of** ~ República de Guinea.

guinea ['gɪnɪ] n (Brit: old) guinea (= 21 chelines: en la actualidad ya no se usa esta moneda).

guinea pig n cobayo.

guise [gaɪz] n: **in** or **under the** ~ **of** bajo capa de.

guitar [gɪ'tɑː*] n guitarra.

guitarist [gɪ'tɑːrɪst] n guitarrista m/f.

gulch [gʌltʃ] n (US) barranco.

gulf [gʌlf] n golfo; (abyss) abismo.

Gulf States npl: **the** ~ los países del Golfo.

Gulf Stream n: **the** ~ la Corriente del Golfo.

gull [gʌl] n gaviota.

gullet ['gʌlɪt] n esófago.

gullibility [gʌlɪ'bɪlɪtɪ] n credulidad f.

gullible ['gʌlɪbl] a crédulo.

gully ['gʌlɪ] n barranco.

gulp [gʌlp] vi tragar saliva ♦ vt (also: ~ **down**) tragarse ♦ n (of liquid) trago, sorbo; (of food) bocado; **in** or **at one** ~ de un trago.

gum [gʌm] n (ANAT) encía; (glue) goma, cemento (LAm); (sweet) caramelo de goma; (also: **chewing-**~) chicle m ♦ vt pegar con goma.

gum up vt: **to** ~ **up the works** (col) meter un palo en la rueda.

gumboots ['gʌmbuːts] npl (Brit) botas fpl de goma.

gumption ['gʌmpʃən] n (col) iniciativa.

gum tree n árbol m gomero.

gun [gʌn] n (small) pistola, revólver m; (shotgun) escopeta; (rifle) fusil m; (cannon) cañón m ♦ vt (also: ~ **down**) asesinar; **to stick to one's** ~**s** (fig) mantenerse firme, aferrarse.

gunboat ['gʌnbəut] n cañonero.

gun dog n perro de caza.

gunfire ['gʌnfaɪə*] n disparos mpl.

gung-ho [gʌŋ'həu] a (col) fogoso.

gunk [gʌŋk] n (col) sustancia pegajosa or viscosa.

gunman ['gʌnmən] n pistolero.

gunner ['gʌnə*] n artillero.

gunpoint ['gʌnpɔɪnt] n: **at** ~ a mano armada.

gunpowder ['gʌnpaudə*] n pólvora.

gunrunner ['gʌnrʌnə*] n traficante m/f de armas.

gunrunning ['gʌnrʌnɪŋ] n contrabando de armas.

gunshot ['gʌnʃɔt] n escopetazo.

gunsmith ['gʌnsmɪθ] n armero.

gurgle ['gəːgl] vi gorgotear.

guru ['guːruː] n guru m.

gush [gʌʃ] vi chorrear; (fig) deshacerse en efusiones.

gusset ['gʌsɪt] n (in tights, pants) escudete m.

gust [gʌst] n (of wind) ráfaga.

gusto ['gʌstəu] n entusiasmo.

gut [gʌt] n intestino; (MUS etc) cuerda de tripa ♦ vt (poultry, fish) destripar; (building): **the blaze** ~**ted the entire building** el fuego destruyó el edificio entero.

gut reaction n reacción f instintiva.

guts [gʌts] npl (courage) valor m; (col: innards: of people, animals) tripas fpl; **to hate sb's** ~ echar a uno (a muerte).

gutter ['gʌtə*] n (of roof) canalón m; (in street) arroyo.

guttural ['gʌtərl] a gutural.

guy [gaɪ] n (also: ~**rope**) cuerda; (col: man) tío (Sp), tipo.

Guyana [gaɪ'ænə] n Guayana.

guzzle ['gʌzl] vi tragar ♦ vt engullir.

gym [dʒɪm] n (also: **gymnasium**) gimnasio; (also: **gymnastics**) gimnasia.

gymkhana [dʒɪm'kɑːnə] n gincana.

gymnast ['dʒɪmnæst] n gimnasta m/f.

gymnastics [dʒɪm'næstɪks] n gimnasia.

gym shoes npl zapatillas fpl deportivas.

gym slip n (Brit) túnica de colegiala.

gynaecologist, (US) **gynecologist** [gaɪnɪ'kɔlədʒɪst] n ginecólogo/a.

gynaecology, (US) **gynecology** [gaɪnə'kɔlədʒɪ] n ginecología.

gypsy ['dʒɪpsɪ] n = **gipsy**.

gyrate [dʒaɪ'reɪt] vi girar.

gyroscope ['dʒaɪrəskəup] n giroscopio.

H

H, h [eɪtʃ] *n* (*letter*) H, h *f*; **H for Harry**, (*US*) **H for How** H de Historia.

habeas corpus ['heɪbɪəs'kɔ:pəs] *n* (*LAW*) hábeas corpus *m*.

haberdashery ['hæbə'dæʃərɪ] *n* (*Brit*) mercería; (*US: men's clothing*) prendas *fpl* de caballero.

habit ['hæbɪt] *n* hábito, costumbre *f*; **to get out of/into the ~ of doing sth** perder la costumbre de/acostumbrarse a hacer algo.

habitable ['hæbɪtəbl] *a* habitable.

habitat ['hæbɪtæt] *n* hábitat *m*.

habitation [hæbɪ'teɪʃən] *n* habitación *f*.

habitual [hə'bɪtjuəl] *a* acostumbrado, habitual; (*drinker, liar*) empedernido.

habitually [hə'bɪtjuəlɪ] *ad* por costumbre.

hack [hæk] *vt* (*cut*) cortar; (*slice*) tajar ♦ *n* corte *m*; (*axe blow*) hachazo; (*pej: writer*) escritor(a) *m/f* a sueldo; (*old horse*) jamelgo.

hacker ['hækə*] *n* (*COMPUT*) pirata *m* informático.

hackles ['hæklz] *npl*: **to make sb's ~ rise** (*fig*) poner los pelos de punta a uno.

hackney cab ['hæknɪ-] *n* coche *m* de alquiler.

hackneyed ['hæknɪd] *a* trillado, gastado.

had [hæd] *pt, pp of* **have**.

haddock, *pl* ~ *or* ~**s** ['hædək] *n especie de merluza*.

hadn't ['hædnt] = **had not**.

haematology, (*US*) **hematology** ['hi:mə'tɔlədʒɪ] *n* hematología.

haemoglobin, (*US*) **hemoglobin** ['hi:mə'gləubɪn] *n* hemoglobina.

haemophilia, (*US*) **hemophilia** ['hi:mə'fɪlɪə] *n* hemofilia.

haemorrhage, (*US*) **hemorrhage** ['hemərɪdʒ] *n* hemorragia.

haemorrhoids, (*US*) **hemorrhoids** ['hemərɔɪdz] *npl* hemorroides *fpl*, almorranas *fpl*.

hag [hæg] *n* (*ugly*) vieja fea, tarasca; (*nasty*) bruja; (*witch*) hechicera.

haggard ['hægəd] *a* ojeroso.

haggis ['hægɪs] *n* (*Scottish*) estómago de cordero relleno.

haggle ['hægl] *vi* (*argue*) discutir; (*bargain*) regatear.

haggling ['hæglɪŋ] *n* regateo.

Hague [heɪg] *n*: **The ~** La Haya.

hail [heɪl] *n* (*weather*) granizo ♦ *vt* saludar; (*call*) llamar a ♦ *vi* granizar ♦ *vt*: **to ~ (as)** aclamar (como), celebrar (como); **he**

~s from Scotland es natural de Escocia.

hailstone ['heɪlstəun] *n* (piedra de) granizo.

hailstorm ['heɪlstɔ:m] *n* granizada.

hair [heə*] *n* (*gen*) pelo, cabellos *mpl*; (*one* ~) pelo, cabello; (*head of* ~) pelo, cabellera; (*on legs etc*) vello; **to do one's ~** arreglarse el pelo; **grey ~** canas *fpl*.

hairbrush ['heəbrʌʃ] *n* cepillo (para el pelo).

haircut ['heəkʌt] *n* corte *m* (de pelo).

hairdo ['heədu:] *n* peinado.

hairdresser ['heədresə*] *n* peluquero/a; **~'s** peluquería.

hair-dryer ['heədraɪə*] *n* secador *m* de pelo.

-haired [heəd] *a suff*: **fair/long~** de pelo rubio *or* güero/de pelo largo.

hairgrip ['heəgrɪp] *n* horquilla.

hairline ['heəlaɪn] *n* nacimiento del pelo.

hairline fracture *n* fractura fina.

hairnet ['heənet] *n* redecilla.

hair oil *n* brillantina.

hairpiece ['heəpi:s] *n* trenza postiza.

hairpin ['heəpɪn] *n* horquilla.

hairpin bend, (*US*) **hairpin curve** *n* curva de horquilla.

hair-raising ['heəreɪzɪŋ] *a* espeluznante.

hair remover *n* depilatorio.

hair's breadth *n*: **by a ~** por un pelo.

hair spray *n* laca.

hairstyle ['heəstaɪl] *n* peinado.

hairy ['heərɪ] *a* peludo, velludo.

Haiti ['heɪtɪ] *n* Haití *m*.

hake [heɪk] *n* merluza.

halcyon ['hælsɪən] *a* feliz.

hale [heɪl] *a*: **~ and hearty** robusto.

half [hɑ:f] *n* (*pl* **halves** [hɑ:vz]) mitad *f*; (*SPORT: of match*) tiempo; (: *of ground*) campo ♦ *a* medio ♦ *ad* medio, a medias; **~-an-hour** media hora; **two and a ~** dos y media; **~ a dozen** media docena; **~ a pound** media libra, ≈ 250 gr.; **to cut sth in ~** cortar algo por la mitad; **to go halves (with sb)** ir a medias (con uno); **~empty/closed** medio vacío/entreabierto; **~ asleep** medio dormido; **~ past 3** las 3 y media.

half-back ['hɑ:fbæk] *n* (*SPORT*) medio.

half-baked ['hɑ:f'beɪkt] *a* (*col: idea, scheme*) mal concebido *or* pensado.

half-breed ['hɑ:fbri:d] *n* = **half-caste**.

half-brother ['hɑ:fbrʌðə*] *n* medio hermano.

half-caste ['hɑ:fkɑ:st] *n* mestizo/a.

half-hearted ['hɑ:f'hɑ:tɪd] *a* indiferente, poco entusiasta.

half-hour [hɑ:f'auə*] *n* media hora.

half-mast ['hɑ:f'mɑ:st] *n*: **at ~** (*flag*) a media asta.

halfpenny ['heɪpnɪ] *n* medio penique *m*.

half-price ['hɑ:f'praɪs] *a* a mitad de precio.

half term *n* (*Brit SCOL*) vacaciones de mediados del trimestre.

half-time [hɑ:f'taɪm] *n* descanso.

halfway ['hɑ:f'weɪ] *ad* a medio camino; **to**

meet sb ~ (fig) llegar a un acuerdo con uno.

half-yearly [haːfˈjɪəlɪ] ad semestralmente ♦ a semestral.

halibut [ˈhælɪbət] n, pl inv halibut m.

halitosis [hælɪˈtəʊsɪs] n halitosis f.

hall [hɔːl] n (for concerts) sala; (entrance way) entrada, vestíbulo.

hallmark [ˈhɔːlmɑːk] n (mark) contraste m; (seal) sello.

hallo [həˈləʊ] excl = **hello**.

hall of residence n (Brit) colegio mayor.

Hallowe'en [hæləʊˈiːn] n víspera de Todos los Santos.

hallucination [həluːsɪˈneɪʃən] n alucinación f.

hallway [ˈhɔːlweɪ] n vestíbulo.

halo [ˈheɪləʊ] n (of saint) aureola.

halt [hɔːlt] n (stop) alto, parada; (RAIL) apeadero ♦ vt parar ♦ vi pararse; (process) interrumpirse; **to call a ~ (to sth)** (fig) poner fin (a algo).

halter [ˈhɔːltə*] n (for horse) cabestro.

halterneck [ˈhɔːltənɛk] a de espalda escotada.

halve [hɑːv] vt partir por la mitad.

halves [hɑːvz] pl of **half**.

ham [hæm] n jamón m (cocido); (col: also: **radio ~**) radioaficionado/a m/f; (: also: **~ actor**) comicastro.

hamburger [ˈhæmbɜːgə*] n hamburguesa.

ham-fisted [ˈhæmˈfɪstɪd] a torpe, desmañado.

hamlet [ˈhæmlɪt] n aldea.

hammer [ˈhæmə*] n martillo ♦ vt (nail) clavar; **to ~ a point home to sb** remacharle un punto a uno.

hammer out vt (metal) forjar a martillo; (fig: solution, agreement) elaborar con trabajos.

hammock [ˈhæmək] n hamaca.

hamper [ˈhæmpə*] vt estorbar ♦ n cesto.

hamster [ˈhæmstə*] n hámster m.

hand [hænd] n mano f; (of clock) aguja; (writing) letra; (worker) obrero; (measurement: of horse) palmo ♦ vt (give) dar, pasar; (deliver) entregar; **to give sb a ~** echar una mano a uno, ayudar a uno; **to force sb's ~** forzarle la mano a uno; **at ~** a la mano; **in ~** entre manos; **we have the matter in ~** tenemos el asunto entre manos; **to have in one's ~** (knife, victory) tener en la mano; **to have a free ~** tener carta blanca; **on ~** (person, services) a mano, al alcance; **to ~** (information etc) a mano; **on the one ~ ..., on the other ~ ...** por una parte ... por otra (parte) ....

hand down vt pasar, bajar; (tradition) transmitir; (heirloom) dejar en herencia; (US: sentence, verdict) imponer.

hand in vt entregar.

hand out vt (leaflets, advice) repartir, distribuir.

hand over vt (deliver) entregar; (surrender) ceder.

hand round vt (Brit: information, papers) pasar (de mano en mano); (: chocolates etc) ofrecer.

handbag [ˈhændbæg] n bolso, cartera (LAm).

handball [ˈhændbɔːl] n balonmano.

handbasin [ˈhændbeɪsn] n lavabo.

handbook [ˈhændbʊk] n manual m.

handbrake [ˈhændbreɪk] n freno de mano.

hand cream n crema para las manos.

handcuffs [ˈhændkʌfs] npl esposas fpl.

handful [ˈhændfʊl] n puñado.

handicap [ˈhændɪkæp] n desventaja; (SPORT) hándicap m ♦ vt estorbar.

handicapped [ˈhændɪkæpt] a: **to be mentally ~** ser deficiente m/f (mental); **to be physically ~** ser minusválido/a (físico/a).

handicraft [ˈhændɪkrɑːft] n artesanía.

handiwork [ˈhændɪwɔːk] n manualidad(es) f(pl); (fig) obra; **this looks like his ~** (pej) es obra de él, parece.

handkerchief [ˈhæŋkətʃɪf] n pañuelo.

handle [ˈhændl] n (of door etc) manija; (of cup etc) asa; (of knife etc) mango; (for winding) manivela ♦ vt (touch) tocar; (deal with) encargarse de; (treat: people) manejar; **"~ with care"** "(manéjese) con cuidado"; **to fly off the ~** perder los estribos.

handlebar(s) [ˈhændlbɑː(z)] n(pl) manillar msg.

handling charges [ˈhændlɪŋ-] npl gastos mpl de tramitación.

hand-luggage [ˈhændlʌgɪdʒ] n equipaje m de mano.

handmade [ˈhændmeɪd] a hecho a mano.

handout [ˈhændaʊt] n (distribution) repartición f; (charity) limosna; (leaflet) folleto, octavilla; (press ~) nota.

hand-picked [ˈhændˈpɪkt] a (produce) escogido a mano; (staff etc) seleccionado cuidadosamente.

handrail [ˈhændreɪl] n (on staircase etc) pasamanos m inv, barandilla.

handshake [ˈhændʃeɪk] n apretón m de manos; (COMPUT) coloquio.

handsome [ˈhænsəm] a guapo.

hands-on [ˈhændzˈɒn] a: **~ experience** (COMPUT) experiencia práctica.

handstand [ˈhændstænd] n voltereta, salto mortal.

hand-to-mouth [ˈhændtəˈmaʊθ] a (existence) precario.

handwriting [ˈhændraɪtɪŋ] n letra.

handwritten [ˈhændrɪtn] a escrito a mano, manuscrito.

handy [ˈhændɪ] a (close at hand) a la mano; (useful: machine, tool etc) práctico; (skilful) hábil, diestro; **to come in ~** venir bien.

handyman [ˈhændɪmæn] n manitas m inv.

hang, *pt, pp* **hung** [hæŋ, hʌŋ] *vt* colgar; (*head*) bajar; (*criminal: pt, pp* **hanged**) ahorcar; **to get the ~ of sth** (*col*) lograr dominar algo.

hang about *vi* haraganear.

hang back *vi* (*hesitate*): **to ~ back (from doing)** vacilar (ante hacer).

hang on *vi* (*wait*) esperar ◆ *vt fus* (*depend on: decision etc*) depender de; **to ~ on to** (*keep hold of*) agarrarse *or* aferrarse a; (*keep*) guardar, quedarse con.

hang out *vt* (*washing*) tender, colgar ◆ *vi* (*col: live*) vivir, radicarse; **to ~ out of sth** colgar fuera de algo.

hang together *vi* (*cohere: argument etc*) sostenerse.

hang up *vt* (*coat*) colgar ◆ *vi* (*TEL*) colgar; **to ~ up on sb** colgarle a uno.

hangar ['hæŋə*] *n* hangar *m*.

hangdog ['hæŋdɔg] *a* (*guilty: look, expression*) avergonzado.

hanger ['hæŋə*] *n* percha.

hanger-on [hæŋər'ɔn] *n* parásito.

hang-gliding ['hæŋglaɪdɪŋ] *n* vuelo libre.

hanging ['hæŋɪŋ] *n* (*execution*) ejecución *f* (en la horca).

hangman ['hæŋmən] *n* verdugo.

hangover ['hæŋəuvə*] *n* (*after drinking*) resaca.

hang-up ['hæŋʌp] *n* complejo.

hanker ['hæŋkə*] *vi*: **to ~ after** (*miss*) echar de menos; (*long for*) añorar.

hankie, hanky ['hæŋkɪ] *n abbr* = **handkerchief.**

Hants *abbr* (*Brit*) = Hampshire.

haphazard [hæp'hæzəd] *a* fortuito.

hapless ['hæplɪs] *a* desventurado.

happen ['hæpən] *vi* suceder, ocurrir; (*take place*) tener lugar, realizarse; **as it ~s** da la casualidad de que; **what's ~ing?** ¿qué pasa?

happen (up)on *vt fus* tropezar *or* dar con.

happening ['hæpnɪŋ] *n* suceso, acontecimiento.

happily ['hæpɪlɪ] *ad* (*luckily*) afortunadamente; (*cheerfully*) alegremente.

happiness ['hæpɪnɪs] *n* (*contentment*) felicidad *f*; (*joy*) alegría.

happy ['hæpɪ] *a* feliz; (*cheerful*) alegre; **to be ~ (with)** estar contento (con); **yes, I'd be ~ to** sí, con mucho gusto; **H~ Christmas/New Year!** ¡Feliz Navidad!/ ¡Feliz Año Nuevo!; **~ birthday!** ¡felicidades!, ¡feliz cumpleaños!

happy-go-lucky ['hæpɪgəu'lʌkɪ] *a* despreocupado.

harangue [hə'ræŋ] *vt* arengar.

harass ['hærəs] *vt* acosar, hostigar.

harrassed ['hærəst] *a* agobiado, presionado.

harassment ['hærəsmənt] *n* persecución *f*; (*worry*) preocupación *f*.

harbour, (*US*) **harbor** ['hɑːbə*] *n* puerto ◆ *vt* (*hope etc*) abrigar; (*hide*) dar abrigo a; (*retain: grudge etc*) guardar.

harbo(u)r dues *npl* derechos *mpl* portuarios.

hard [hɑːd] *a* duro; (*difficult*) difícil; (*person*) severo ◆ *ad* (*work*) mucho, duro; (*think*) profundamente; **to ~ at/ sth** clavar los ojos en alguien/algo; **to try ~** esforzarse; **no ~ feelings!** ¡sin rencor(es)!; **to be ~ of hearing** ser duro de oído; **to be ~ done by** ser tratado injustamente; **to be ~ on sb** ser muy duro con uno; **I find it ~ to believe that ...** me cuesta trabajo creer que ....

hard-and-fast ['hɑːdən'fɑːst] *a* rígido, definitivo.

hardback ['hɑːdbæk] *n* libro de tapas duras.

hard cash *n* dinero contante.

hard copy *n* (*COMPUT*) copia impresa.

hard-core ['hɑːd'kɔː*] *a* (*pornography*) duro; (*supporters*) incondicional.

hard court *n* (*TENNIS*) cancha (de tenis) de cemento.

hard disk *n* (*COMPUT*) disco duro *or* rígido.

harden ['hɑːdn] *vt* endurecer; (*steel*) templar; (*fig*) curtir; (: *determination*) fortalecer ◆ *vi* (*substance*) endurecerse.

hardened ['hɑːdnd] *a* (*criminal*) empedernido; **to be ~ to sth** estar acostumbrado a algo.

hard-headed ['hɑːd'hɛdɪd] *a* poco sentimental, realista.

hard-hearted ['hɑːd'hɑːtɪd] *a* duro de corazón.

hard labour *n* trabajos *mpl* forzados.

hardliner [hɑːd'laɪnə*] *n* partidario/a de la línea dura.

hardly ['hɑːdlɪ] *ad* (*scarcely*) apenas; **that can ~ be true** eso difícilmente puede ser cierto; **~ ever** casi nunca; **I can ~ believe it** apenas me lo puedo creer.

hardness ['hɑːdnɪs] *n* dureza.

hard sell *n* publicidad *f* agresiva; **~ techniques** técnicas *fpl* agresivas de venta.

hardship ['hɑːdʃɪp] *n* (*troubles*) penas *fpl*; (*financial*) apuro.

hard shoulder *n* (*AUT*) andén *m*, arcén *m*.

hard-up [hɑːd'ʌp] *a* (*col*) sin un duro (*Sp*) *or* plata (*LAm*).

hardware ['hɑːdwɛə*] *n* ferretería; (*COMPUT*) hardware *m*.

hardware shop *n* ferretería.

hard-wearing [hɑːd'wɛərɪŋ] *a* resistente, duradero; (*shoes*) resistente.

hard-working [hɑːd'wəːkɪŋ] *a* trabajador(a).

hardy ['hɑːdɪ] *a* fuerte; (*plant*) resistente.

hare [hɛə*] *n* liebre *f*.

hare-brained ['hɛəbreɪnd] *a* casquivano.

harelip ['hɛəlɪp] *n* labio leporino.

harem [hɑː'riːm] *n* harén *m*.

haricot (bean) ['hærɪkəu-] *n* alubia.

hark back [hɑːk-] *vi*: **to ~ back to** (*former*

days, earlier occasion) recordar.

harm [haːm] *n* daño, mal *m* ◆ *vt (person)* hacer daño a; *(health, interests)* perjudicar; *(thing)* dañar; **out of ~'s way** a salvo; **there's no ~ in trying** nada se pierde con intentar.

harmful ['haːmful] *a (gen)* dañino; *(reputation)* perjudicial.

harmless ['haːmlɪs] *a (person)* inofensivo; *(drugs)* inocuo.

harmonica [haːˈmɒnɪkə] *n* armónica.

harmonious [haːˈməʊnɪəs] *a* armonioso.

harmonize ['haːmənaɪz] *vt, vi* armonizar.

harmony ['haːmənɪ] *n* armonía.

harness ['haːnɪs] *n* arreos *mpl* ◆ *vt (horse)* enjaezar; *(resources)* aprovechar.

harp [haːp] *n* arpa ◆ *vi:* **to ~ on (about)** machacar (con).

harpoon [haːˈpuːn] *n* arpón *m*.

harrow ['hærəʊ] *n* grada ◆ *vt* gradar.

harrowing ['hærəʊɪŋ] *a* angustioso.

harry ['hærɪ] *vt (MIL)* acosar; *(person)* hostigar.

harsh [haːʃ] *a (cruel)* duro, cruel; *(severe)* severo; *(words)* hosco; *(colour)* chillón/ona; *(contrast)* violento.

harshly ['haːʃlɪ] *ad (say)* con aspereza; *(treat)* con mucha dureza.

harshness ['haːʃnɪs] *n* dureza.

harvest ['haːvɪst] *n* cosecha; *(of grapes)* vendimia ◆ *vt, vi* cosechar.

harvester ['haːvɪstə*] *n (machine)* cosechadora; *(person)* segador(a) *m/f;* **combine ~** segadora trilladora.

has [hæz] *vb see* **have**.

has-been ['hæzbiːn] *n (col: person)* persona acabada; *(: thing)* vieja gloria.

hash [hæʃ] *n (CULIN)* picadillo; *(fig: mess)* lío.

hashish ['hæʃɪʃ] *n* hachís *m*, hachich *m*.

hasn't ['hæznt] = **has not**.

hassle ['hæsl] *n (col)* lío, problema ◆ *vt* molestar.

haste [heɪst] *n* prisa.

hasten ['heɪsn] *vt* acelerar ◆ *vi* darse prisa; **I ~ to add that...** me apresuro a añadir que ....

hastily ['heɪstɪlɪ] *ad* de prisa.

hasty ['heɪstɪ] *a* apresurado.

hat [hæt] *n* sombrero.

hatbox ['hætbɒks] *n* sombrerera.

hatch [hætʃ] *n (NAUT: also:* **~way**) escotilla ◆ *vi* salir del cascarón ◆ *vt* incubar; *(fig: scheme, plot)* idear, tramar.

hatchback ['hætʃbæk] *n (AUT)* tres *or* cinco puertas *m*.

hatchet ['hætʃɪt] *n* hacha.

hate [heɪt] *vt* odiar, aborrecer ◆ *n* odio; **I ~ to trouble you, but ...** siento *or* lamento molestarle, pero ....

hateful ['heɪtful] *a* odioso.

hatred ['heɪtrɪd] *n* odio.

hat trick *n:* **to score a ~** *(Brit SPORT)*

marcar tres tantos *(or* triunfos) seguidos.

haughtily ['hɔːtɪlɪ] *ad* con arrogancia.

haughty ['hɔːtɪ] *a* altanero, arrogante.

haul [hɔːl] *vt* tirar; *(by lorry)* transportar ◆ *n (of fish)* redada; *(of stolen goods etc)* botín *m*.

haulage ['hɔːlɪdʒ] *n (Brit)* transporte *m*; *(costs)* gastos *mpl* de transporte.

haulage contractor *n (firm)* empresa de transportes; *(person)* transportista *m/f*.

haulier ['hɔːlɪə*], *(US)* **hauler** ['hɔːlə*] *n* transportista *m/f*.

haunch [hɔːntʃ] *n* anca; *(of meat)* pierna.

haunt [hɔːnt] *vt (subj: ghost)* aparecer en; *(frequent)* frecuentar; *(obsess)* obsesionar ◆ *n* guarida.

haunted ['hɔːntɪd] *a (castle etc)* embrujado; *(look)* de angustia.

haunting ['hɔːntɪŋ] *a (sight, music)* evocativo.

Havana [həˈvɑːnə] *n* la Havana.

have, *pt, pp* **had** [hæv, hæd] *vt (gen)* tener; *(possess)* poseer; *(meal, shower)* tomar ◆ *auxiliary vb:* **to ~ arrived** haber llegado; **to ~ eaten** haber comido; **to ~ breakfast/ lunch/dinner** tomar el desayuno/el almuerzo/la cena; **I'll ~ a coffee** tomaré un café; **to ~ an operation** operarse; **to ~ a party** dar una fiesta; **she has to do it** tiene que hacerlo; **to ~ a cold/flu** estar constipado/con gripe; **I had better leave** más vale que me marche; **I won't ~ it** no lo tolero; **let me ~ a try** déjame que lo intente; **rumour has it (that)** ... corre la voz de que ...; **he has gone** se ha ido; **to ~ it out with sb** ajustar cuentas con uno; **to ~ a baby** parir, dar a luz; *see also* **haves**.

have in *vt:* **to ~ it in for sb** *(col)* tenerla tomada con uno.

have on *vt:* **~ you anything on tomorrow?** ¿tienes compromiso para mañana?; **I don't ~ any money on me** no llevo dinero; **to ~ sb on** *(Brit col)* tomarle el pelo a uno.

haven ['heɪvn] *n* puerto; *(fig)* refugio.

haven't ['hævnt] = **have not**.

haversack ['hævəsæk] *n* mochila.

haves [hævz] *npl:* **the ~ and the have-nots** los ricos y los pobres.

havoc ['hævək] *n* estragos *mpl*.

Hawaii [həˈwaɪiː] *n (Islas fpl)* Hawai *m*.

Hawaiian [həˈwaɪjən] *a, n* hawaiano/a *m/f*.

hawk [hɔːk] *n* halcón *m* ◆ *vt (goods for sale)* pregonar.

hawthorn ['hɔːθɔːn] *n* espino.

hay [heɪ] *n* heno.

hay fever *n* fiebre *f* del heno.

haystack ['heɪstæk] *n* almiar *m*.

haywire ['heɪwaɪə*] *a (col):* **to go ~** *(person)* volverse loco; *(plan)* embrollarse.

hazard ['hæzəd] *n* riesgo; *(danger)* peligro ◆ *vt (remark)* aventurar; *(one's life)* arriesgar; **to be a health ~** ser peligroso para la salud; **to ~ a guess** atreverse a hacer una respuesta.

hazardous ['hæzədəs] *a* (*dangerous*) peligroso; (*risky*) arriesgado.

hazard warning lights *npl* (*AUT*) señales *fpl* de emergencia.

haze [heɪz] *n* neblina.

hazel ['heɪzl] *n* (*tree*) avellano ♦ *a* (*eyes*) color *m* de avellano.

hazelnut ['heɪzlnʌt] *n* avellana.

hazy ['heɪzɪ] *a* brumoso; (*idea*) vago.

H-bomb ['eɪtʃbɔm] *n* bomba H.

h & c *abbr* (*Brit*) = *hot and cold (water)*.

HE *abbr* = **high explosive**; (*REL, DIPLOMA-CY*: = *His (or Her) Excellency*) S. Exc.ª.

he [hiː] *pron* él; **~ who...** él que..., quien... .

head [hɛd] *n* cabeza; (*leader*) jefe/a *m/f*; (*COMPUT*) cabeza (grabadora) ♦ *vt* (*list*) encabezar; (*group*) capitanear; **~s (or tails)** cara (o cruz); **~ first** de cabeza; **~ over heels** patas arriba; **~ over heels in love** perdidamente enamorado; **on your ~ be it!** ¡allá tú!; **they went over my ~ to the manager** fueron directamente al gerente sin hacerme caso; **it was above** *or* **over their ~s** no alcanzaron a entenderlo; **to come to a ~** (*fig: situation etc*) llegar a un punto crítico; **to have a ~ for business** tener talento para los negocios; **to have no ~ for heights** no resistir las alturas; **to lose/keep one's ~** perder la cabeza/mantener la calma; **to sit at the ~ of the table** sentarse a la cabecera; **to ~ the ball** cabecear (la pelota).

head for *vt fus* dirigirse a.

head off *vt* (*threat, danger*) desviar.

headache ['hɛdeɪk] *n* dolor *m* de cabeza; **to have a ~** tener dolor de cabeza.

headdress ['hɛddrɛs] *n* (*of bride, Indian*) tocado.

header ['hɛdə*] *n* (*Brit col: FOOTBALL*) cabezazo; (: *fall*) caída de cabeza.

headhunter ['hɛdhʌntə*] *n* (*fig*) cazaejecutivos *m inv*.

heading ['hɛdɪŋ] *n* título.

headlamp ['hɛdlæmp] *n* (*Brit*) = **headlight**.

headland ['hɛdlənd] *n* promontorio.

headlight ['hɛdlaɪt] *n* faro.

headline ['hɛdlaɪn] *n* titular *m*.

headlong ['hɛdlɔŋ] *ad* (*fall*) de cabeza; (*rush*) precipitadamente.

headmaster/mistress [hɛd'mɑːstə*/mɪstrɪs] *n* director(a) *m/f* (de escuela).

head office *n* oficina central, central *f*.

head-on [hɛd'ɔn] *a* (*collision*) de frente.

headphones ['hɛdfəunz] *npl* auriculares *mpl*.

headquarters (HQ) ['hɛdkwɔːtəz] *npl* sede *f* central; (*MIL*) cuartel *m* general.

head-rest ['hɛdrɛst] *n* reposa-cabezas *m inv*.

headroom ['hɛdrum] *n* (*in car*) altura interior; (*under bridge*) (límite *m* de) altura.

headscarf ['hɛdskɑːf] *n* pañuelo.

headset ['hɛdsɛt] *n* casco auricular.

headstone ['hɛdstəun] *n* lápida mortuoria.

headstrong ['hɛdstrɔŋ] *a* testarudo.

head waiter *n* maître *m*.

headway ['hɛdweɪ] *n*: **to make ~** (*fig*) hacer progresos.

headwind ['hɛdwɪnd] *n* viento contrario.

heady ['hɛdɪ] *a* (*experience, period*) apasionante; (*wine*) cabezón.

heal [hiːl] *vt* curar ♦ *vi* cicatrizarse.

health [hɛlθ] *n* salud *f*.

health centre *n* ambulatorio, centro médico.

health food(s) *n(pl)* alimentos *mpl* orgánicos.

health hazard *n* riesgo para la salud.

Health Service *n* (*Brit*) servicio de salud pública, ≈ Insalud *m* (*Sp*).

healthy ['hɛlθɪ] *a* (*gen*) sano; (*economy, bank balance*) saludable.

heap [hiːp] *n* montón *m* ♦ *vt* amontonar; (*plate*) colmar; **~s (of)** (*col: lots*) montones (de); **to ~ favours/praise/gifts** *etc* **on sb** colmar a uno de favores/elogios/regalos *etc*.

hear, *pt, pp* **heard** [hɪə*, hɜːd] *vt* oír; (*perceive*) sentir; (*listen to*) escuchar; (*lecture*) asistir a; (*LAW: case*) ver ♦ *vi* oír; **to ~ about** oír hablar de; **to ~ from sb** tener noticias de alguien; **I've never heard of that book** nunca he oído de ese libro.

hear out *vt*: **to ~ sb out** dejar que uno termine de hablar.

hearing ['hɪərɪŋ] *n* (*sense*) oído; (*LAW*) vista; **to give sb a ~** dar a uno la oportunidad de hablar, escuchar a uno.

hearing aid *n* audífono.

hearsay ['hɪəseɪ] *n* rumores *mpl*, habladillas *fpl*.

hearse [hɜːs] *n* coche *m* fúnebre.

heart [hɑːt] *n* corazón *m*; **~s** *npl* (*CARDS*) corazones *mpl*; **at ~** en el fondo; **by ~** (*learn, know*) de memoria; **to have a weak ~** tener el corazón débil; **to set one's ~ on sth/on doing sth** anhelar algo/hacer algo; **I did not have the ~ to tell her** no tuve valor para decírselo; **to take ~** cobrar ánimos; **the ~ of the matter** lo esencial *or* el meollo del asunto.

heart attack *n* infarto de miocardio.

heartbeat ['hɑːtbiːt] *n* latido (del corazón).

heartbreak ['hɑːtbreɪk] *n* angustia, congoja.

heartbreaking ['hɑːtbreɪkɪŋ] *a* desgarrador(a).

heartbroken ['hɑːtbrəukən] *a*: **she was ~ about it** le partió el corazón.

heartburn ['hɑːtbɜːn] *n* acedía.

-hearted ['hɑːtɪd] *a suff*: **a kind~ person** una persona bondadosa.

heartening ['hɑːtnɪŋ] a alentador(a).
heart failure n (MED) fallo de corazón, colapso cardíaco.
heartfelt ['hɑːtfɛlt] a (cordial) cordial; (deeply felt) más sentido.
hearth [hɑːθ] n (gen) hogar m; (fireplace) chimenea.
heartily ['hɑːtɪlɪ] ad sinceramente, cordialmente; (laugh) a carcajadas; (eat) con buen apetito; **to be ~ sick of** estar completamente harto de.
heartland ['hɑːtlænd] n zona interior or central; (fig) corazón m.
heartless ['hɑːtlɪs] a cruel.
heart-to-heart ['hɑːttə'hɑːt] n (also: ~ **talk**) conversación f íntima.
heart transplant n transplante m de corazón.
hearty ['hɑːtɪ] a cordial.
heat [hiːt] n (gen) calor m; (SPORT: also: **qualifying** ~) prueba eliminatoria; (ZOOL): **in** or **on** ~ en celo ♦ vt calentar.
heat up vi (gen) calentarse.
heated ['hiːtɪd] a caliente; (fig) acalorado.
heater ['hiːtə*] n calentador m.
heath [hiːθ] n (Brit) brezal m.
heathen ['hiːðn] a, n pagano/a m/f.
heather ['hɛðə*] n brezo.
heating ['hiːtɪŋ] n calefacción f.
heat-resistant ['hiːtrɪzɪstənt] a refractario.
heatstroke ['hiːtstrəuk] n insolación f.
heatwave ['hiːtweɪv] n ola de calor.
heave [hiːv] vt (pull) tirar; (push) empujar con esfuerzo; (lift) levantar (con esfuerzo) ♦ vi (water) subir y bajar ♦ n tirón m; empujón m; (effort) esfuerzo; (throw) echada; **to ~ a sigh** dar or echar un suspiro, suspirar.
heave to vi (NAUT) ponerse al pairo.
heaven ['hɛvn] n cielo; (REL) paraíso; **thank ~!** ¡gracias a Dios!; **for ~'s sake!** (pleading) ¡por el amor de Dios!, ¡por lo que más quiera!; (protesting) ¡por Dios!
heavenly ['hɛvnlɪ] a celestial; (REL) divino.
heavenly body n cuerpo celeste.
heavily ['hɛvɪlɪ] ad pesadamente; (drink, smoke) con exceso; (sleep, sigh) profundamente.
heavy ['hɛvɪ] a pesado; (work) duro; (sea, rain, meal) fuerte; (drinker, smoker) gran; (eater) comilón/ona.
heavy-duty ['hɛvɪ'djuːtɪ] a resistente.
heavy goods vehicle (HGV) n (Brit) vehículo pesado.
heavy-handed ['hɛvɪ'hændɪd] a (clumsy, tactless) torpe.
heavy industry n industria pesada.
heavy user n consumidor m intensivo.
heavyweight ['hɛvɪweɪt] n (SPORT) peso pesado.
Hebrew ['hiːbruː] a, n (LING) hebreo.
Hebrides ['hɛbrɪdiːz] npl: **the ~** las Hébridas.

heckle ['hɛkl] vt interrumpir.
heckler ['hɛklə*] n el/la que interrumpe a un orador.
hectare ['hɛktɑː*] n (Brit) hectárea.
hectic ['hɛktɪk] a agitado; (busy) ocupado.
hector ['hɛktə*] vt intimidar con bravatas.
he'd [hiːd] = **he would**; **he had.**
hedge [hɛdʒ] n seto ♦ vt cercar (con un seto) ♦ vi contestar con evasivas; **as a ~ against inflation** como protección contra la inflación; **to ~ one's bets** (fig) cubrirse.
hedgehog ['hɛdʒhɔg] n erizo.
hedgerow ['hɛdʒrəu] n seto vivo.
hedonism ['hiːdənɪzəm] n hedonismo.
heed [hiːd] vt (also: **take ~ of**) (pay attention) hacer caso de; (bear in mind) tener en cuenta; **to pay (no) ~ to, take (no) ~ of** (no) hacer caso a, (no) tener en cuenta.
heedless ['hiːdlɪs] a desatento.
heel [hiːl] n talón m ♦ vt (shoe) poner tacón a; **to take to one's ~s** (col) echar a correr; **to bring to ~** meter en cintura.
hefty ['hɛftɪ] a (person) fornido; (piece) grande; (price) gordo.
heifer ['hɛfə*] n novilla, ternera.
height [haɪt] n (of person) talle m; (of building) altura; (high ground) cerro; (altitude) altitud f; **what ~ are you?** ¿cuánto mides?; **of average ~** de estatura mediana; **to be afraid of ~s** tener miedo a las alturas; **it's the ~ of fashion** es el último grito en moda.
heighten ['haɪtn] vt elevar; (fig) aumentar.
heinous ['heɪnəs] a atroz, nefasto.
heir [ɛə*] n heredero.
heir apparent n presunto heredero.
heiress ['ɛərɛs] n heredera.
heirloom ['ɛəluːm] n reliquia de familia.
heist [haɪst] n (col: hold-up) atraco armado.
held [hɛld] pt, pp of **hold.**
helicopter ['hɛlɪkɔptə*] n helicóptero.
heliport ['hɛlɪpɔːt] n (AVIAT) helipuerto.
helium ['hiːlɪəm] n helio.
hell [hɛl] n infierno; **oh ~!** (col) ¡demonios!, ¡caramba!
he'll [hiːl] = **he will, he shall.**
hellish ['hɛlɪʃ] a infernal; (col) horrible.
hello [hə'ləu] excl ¡hola!; (surprise) ¡caramba!
helm [hɛlm] n (NAUT) timón m.
helmet ['hɛlmɪt] n casco.
helmsman ['hɛlmzmən] n timonel m.
help [hɛlp] n ayuda; (charwoman) criada, asistenta ♦ vt ayudar; ~! ¡socorro!; **with the ~ of** con la ayuda de; **can I ~ you?** (in shop) ¿qué desea?; **to be of ~ to sb** servir a uno; **to ~ sb (to) do sth** echarle una mano or ayudar a uno a hacer algo; ~ **yourself** sírvete; **he can't ~ it** no es culpa suya.
helper ['hɛlpə*] n ayudante m/f.
helpful ['hɛlpful] a útil; (person) servicial.
helping ['hɛlpɪŋ] n ración f.

helpless ['hɛlplɪs] a (incapable) incapaz; (defenceless) indefenso.

Helsinki ['hɛlsɪŋkɪ] n Helsinki m.

helter-skelter ['hɛltə'skɛltə*] n (in funfair) tobogán m.

hem [hɛm] n dobladillo ♦ vt poner or coser el dobladillo a.
   hem in vt cercar; **to feel ~med in** (fig) sentirse acosado.

he-man ['hiːmæn] n macho.

hematology [hiːmə'tɔlədʒɪ] n (US) = **haematology**.

hemisphere ['hɛmɪsfɪə*] n hemisferio.

hemline ['hɛmlaɪn] n bajo (del vestido).

hemlock ['hɛmlɔk] n cicuta.

hemoglobin ['hiːmə'gləubɪn] n (US) = **haemoglobin**.

hemophilia [hiːmə'fɪlɪə] n (US) = **haemophilia**.

hemorrhage ['hɛmərɪdʒ] n (US) = **haemorrhage**.

hemorrhoids ['hɛmərɔɪdz] npl (US) = **haemorrhoids**.

hemp [hɛmp] n cáñamo.

hen [hɛn] n gallina; (female bird) hembra.

hence [hɛns] ad (therefore) por lo tanto; **2 years ~** de aquí a 2 años.

henceforth [hɛns'fɔːθ] ad de hoy en adelante.

henchman ['hɛntʃmən] n (pej) secuaz m.

henna ['hɛnə] n alheña.

hen party n (col) reunión f de mujeres.

henpecked ['hɛnpɛkt] a: **to be ~** ser un calzonazos.

hepatitis [hɛpə'taɪtɪs] n hepatitis f inv.

her [həː*] pron (direct) la; (indirect) le; (stressed, after prep) ella ♦ a su; see also **me, my**.

herald ['hɛrəld] n (forerunner) precursor(a) m/f ♦ vt anunciar.

heraldic [hɛ'rældɪk] a heráldico.

heraldry ['hɛrəldrɪ] n heráldica.

herb [həːb] n hierba.

herbaceous [həː'beɪʃəs] a herbáceo.

herbal ['həːbl] a herbario.

herbicide ['həːbɪsaɪd] n herbicida m.

herd [həːd] n rebaño; (of wild animals, swine) piara ♦ vt (drive, gather: animals) llevar en manada; (: people) reunir.
   herd together vt agrupar, reunir ♦ vi apiñarse, agruparse.

here [hɪə*] ad aquí; **~!** (present) ¡presente!; **~ is/are** aquí está/están; **~ she is** aquí está; **come ~!** ¡ven aquí or acá!; **~ and there** aquí y allá.

hereabouts ['hɪərə'bauts] ad por aquí (cerca).

hereafter [hɪər'ɑːftə*] ad en el futuro ♦ n: **the ~** el más allá.

hereby [hɪə'baɪ] ad (in letter) por la presente.

hereditary [hɪ'rɛdɪtrɪ] a hereditario.

heredity [hɪ'rɛdɪtɪ] n herencia.

heresy ['hɛrəsɪ] n herejía.

heretic ['hɛrətɪk] n hereje m/f.

heretical [hɪ'rɛtɪkəl] a herético.

herewith [hɪə'wɪð] ad: **I send you ~ ...** le mando adjunto ....

heritage ['hɛrɪtɪdʒ] n (gen) herencia; (fig) patrimonio; **our national ~** nuestro patrimonio nacional.

hermetically [həː'mɛtɪkəlɪ] ad: **~ sealed** cerrado or tapado herméticamente.

hermit ['həːmɪt] n ermitaño/a.

hernia ['həːnɪə] n hernia.

hero, pl ~es ['hɪərəu] n héroe m; (in book, film) protagonista m.

heroic [hɪ'rəuɪk] a heroico.

heroin ['hɛrəuɪn] n heroína.

heroin addict n heroinómano/a, adicto/a a la heroína.

heroine ['hɛrəuɪn] n heroína; (in book, film) protagonista.

heroism ['hɛrəuɪzm] n heroísmo.

heron ['hɛrən] n garza.

hero worship n adulación f.

herring ['hɛrɪŋ] n arenque m.

hers [həːz] pron (el) suyo/(la) suya etc; **a friend of ~** un amigo suyo; **this is ~** esto es suyo or de ella; see also **mine**.

herself [həː'sɛlf] pron (reflexive) se; (emphatic) ella misma; (after prep) sí (misma); see also **oneself**.

Herts abbr (Brit) = **Hertfordshire**.

he's [hiːz] = **he is; he has**.

hesitant ['hɛzɪtənt] a vacilante; **to be ~ about doing sth** no decidirse a hacer algo.

hesitate ['hɛzɪteɪt] vi vacilar; **don't ~ to ask (me)** no vaciles en or no dejes de pedírmelo.

hesitation [hɛzɪ'teɪʃən] n indecisión f; **I have no ~ in saying (that) ...** no tengo el menor reparo en afirmar que ....

hessian ['hɛsɪən] n arpillera.

heterogeneous ['hɛtərə'dʒiːnɪəs] a heterogéneo.

heterosexual [hɛtərəu'sɛksjuəl] a, n heterosexual m/f.

het up [hɛt'ʌp] a (col) agitado, nervioso.

HEW n abbr (US: = Department of Health, Education and Welfare) ministerio de sanidad, educación y bienestar público.

hew [hjuː] vt cortar (con hacha).

hex [hɛks] (US) n maleficio, mal m de ojo ♦ vt embrujar.

hexagon ['hɛksəgən] n (h)exágono.

hexagonal [hɛk'sægənl] a hexagonal.

hey [heɪ] excl ¡oye!

heyday ['heɪdeɪ] n: **the ~ of** el apogeo de.

HF n abbr = high frequency.

HGV n abbr see heavy goods vehicle.

HI abbr (US POST) = Hawaii.

hi [haɪ] excl ¡hola!

hiatus [haɪ'eɪtəs] n vacío, interrupción f; (LING) hiato.

hibernate ['haɪbəneɪt] vi invernar.

hibernation [haɪbə'neɪʃən] n hibernación f.
hiccough, hiccup ['hɪkʌp] vi hipar; ~s
npl hipo sg.
hid [hɪd] pt of hide.
hidden ['hɪdn] pp of hide ♦ a: **there are no
~ extras** no hay gastos extra.
hide [haɪd] n (skin) piel f ♦ vb (pt hid, pp
hidden [hɪd, 'hɪdn]) vt esconder, ocultar;
(feelings, truth) encubrir, ocultar ♦ vi: **to
~ (from sb)** esconderse or ocultarse (de
uno).
hide-and-seek ['haɪdən'siːk] n escondite m.
hideaway ['haɪdəweɪ] n escondite m.
hideous ['hɪdɪəs] a horrible.
hideously ['hɪdɪəslɪ] ad horriblemente.
hide-out ['haɪdaʊt] n escondite m, refugio.
hiding ['haɪdɪŋ] n (beating) paliza; **to be in
~** (concealed) estar escondido.
hiding place n escondrijo.
hierarchy ['haɪərɑːkɪ] n jerarquía.
hieroglyphic [haɪərə'glɪfɪk] a jeroglífico ♦
n: ~s jeroglíficos mpl.
hi-fi ['haɪfaɪ] abbr (= high fidelity) n estéreo,
hifi m ♦ a de alta fidelidad.
higgledy-piggledy ['hɪgldɪ'pɪgldɪ] ad en
desorden.
high [haɪ] a alto; (speed, number) grande;
(price) elevado; (wind) fuerte; (voice)
agudo; (col: on drugs) drogado; (: on
drink) borracho; (CULIN: meat, game) manido; (: spoilt) estropeado ♦ ad alto, a
gran altura ♦ n: **exports have reached a
new ~** las exportaciones han alcanzado niveles inusitados; **it is 20 m ~** tiene 20 m de
altura; **~ in the air** en las alturas; **to pay
a ~ price for sth** pagar algo muy caro.
highball ['haɪbɔːl] n (US: drink) whisky m
soda.
highboy ['haɪbɔɪ] n (US) cómoda alta.
highbrow ['haɪbraʊ] a culto.
highchair ['haɪtʃɛə*] n silla alta.
high-class ['haɪ'klɑːs] a (neighbourhood) de
alta sociedad; (hotel) de lujo; (person) distinguido, de categoría; (food) de alta categoría.
high court n (LAW) tribunal m supremo.
higher ['haɪə*] a (form of life, study etc) superior ♦ ad más alto.
higher education n educación f or enseñanza superior.
high explosive n explosivo de gran potencia.
high finance n altas finanzas fpl.
high-flier [haɪ'flaɪə*] n ambicioso/a.
high-handed [haɪ'hændɪd] a despótico.
high-heeled [haɪ'hiːld] a de tacón alto.
highjack ['haɪdʒæk] = hijack.
high jump n (SPORT) salto de altura.
highlands ['haɪləndz] npl tierras fpl altas;
the H~ (in Scotland) las tierras altas de
Escocia.
high-level ['haɪlevl] a (talks etc) de alto nivel; **~ language** (COMPUT) lenguaje m de

alto nivel.
highlight ['haɪlaɪt] n (fig: of event) punto
culminante ♦ vt subrayar.
highly ['haɪlɪ] ad sumamente; **~ paid** muy
bien pagado; **to speak ~ of** hablar muy
bien de.
highly-strung ['haɪlɪ'strʌŋ] a hipertenso.
High Mass n misa mayor.
highness ['haɪnɪs] n altura; **Her or His H~**
Su Alteza.
high-pitched [haɪ'pɪtʃt] a agudo.
high-powered ['haɪ'paʊəd] a (engine) de
gran potencia; (fig: person) importante.
high-pressure ['haɪprɛʃə*] a de alta presión; (fig: salesman etc) enérgico.
high-rise block ['haɪraɪz-] n torre f de pisos.
high school n centro de enseñanza secundaria; ≈ Instituto Nacional de Bachillerato (Sp).
high season n (Brit) temporada alta.
high-speed ['haɪspiːd] a de alta velocidad.
high-spirited [haɪ'spɪrɪtɪd] a animado.
high spirits npl ánimos mpl.
high street n (Brit) calle f mayor.
high tide n marea alta.
highway ['haɪweɪ] n carretera.
Highway Code n (Brit) código de la
circulación.
highwayman ['haɪweɪmən] n salteador m
de caminos.
hijack ['haɪdʒæk] vt secuestrar ♦ n (also:
~ing) secuestro.
hijacker ['haɪdʒækə*] n secuestrador(a) m/f.
hike [haɪk] vi (go walking) ir de excursión
(de pie); (tramp) caminar ♦ n caminata;
(col: in prices etc) aumento.
hike up vt (raise) aumentar.
hiker ['haɪkə*] n excursionista m/f.
hilarious [hɪ'lɛərɪəs] a divertidísimo.
hilarity [hɪ'lærɪtɪ] n (laughter) risas fpl,
carcajadas fpl.
hill [hɪl] n colina; (high) montaña; (slope)
cuesta.
hillbilly ['hɪlbɪlɪ] n (US) rústico/a montañés/
esa; (pej) palurdo/a.
hillock ['hɪlək] n montecillo, altozano.
hillside ['hɪlsaɪd] n ladera.
hilltop ['hɪltɔp] n cumbre f.
hilly ['hɪlɪ] a montañoso; (uneven) accidentado.
hilt [hɪlt] n (of sword) empuñadura; **to the
~** (fig: support) incondicionalmente; **to be
in debt up to the ~** estar agobiado de deudas.
him [hɪm] pron (direct) le, lo; (indirect) le;
(stressed, after prep) él; see also me.
Himalayas [hɪmə'leɪəz] npl: **the ~** los
montes Himalaya, el Himalaya.
himself [hɪm'sɛlf] pron (reflexive) se; (emphatic) él mismo; (after prep) sí (mismo);
see also oneself.
hind [haɪnd] a posterior ♦ n cierva.

hinder ['hɪndə*] vt estorbar, impedir.
hindquarters ['haɪndkwɔːtəz] npl (ZOOL) cuartos mpl traseros.
hindrance ['hɪndrəns] n estorbo, obstáculo.
hindsight ['haɪndsaɪt] n percepción f tardía or retrospectiva; **with the benefit of** ~ con la perspectiva del tiempo transcurrido.
Hindu ['hɪnduː] n hindú m/f.
hinge [hɪndʒ] n bisagra, gozne m ♦ vi (fig): **to** ~ **on** depender de.
hint [hɪnt] n indirecta; (advice) consejo ♦ vt: **to** ~ **that** insinuar que ♦ vi: **to** ~ **at** referirse indirectamente a; **to drop a** ~ soltar or tirar una indirecta; **give me a** ~ dame una pista.
hip [hɪp] n cadera; (BOT) escaramujo.
hip flask n frasco.
hippie ['hɪpɪ] n hippie m/f, jipi m/f.
hip pocket n bolsillo de atrás.
hippopotamus, pl ~es or hippopotami [hɪpə'pɒtəməs, -'pɒtəmaɪ] hipopótamo.
hippy ['hɪpɪ] n = **hippie**.
hire ['haɪə*] vt (Brit: car, equipment) alquilar; (worker) contratar ♦ n alquiler m; **for** ~ se alquila; (taxi) libre; **on** ~ de alquiler.
hire out vt alquilar, arrendar.
hire(d) car n (Brit) coche m de alquiler.
hire purchase (H.P.) n (Brit) compra a plazos; **to buy sth on** ~ comprar algo a plazos or en abonos.
his [hɪz] pron (el) suyo/(la) suya etc ♦ a su; **this is** ~ esto es suyo or de él; see also **my, mine.**
Hispanic [hɪs'pænɪk] a hispánico.
hiss [hɪs] vi silbar; (in protest) sisear ♦ n silbido; siseo.
histogram ['hɪstəgræm] n histograma m.
historian [hɪ'stɔːrɪən] n historiador(a) m/f.
historic(al) [hɪ'stɔrɪk(l)] a histórico.
history ['hɪstərɪ] n historia; **there's a long** ~ **of that illness in his family** esa enfermedad corre en su familia.
histrionics [hɪstrɪ'ɒnɪks] npl histrionismo.
hit [hɪt] vt (pt, pp hit) (strike) golpear, pegar; (reach: target) alcanzar; (collide with: car) chocar contra; (fig: affect) afectar ♦ n golpe m; (success) éxito; **to** ~ **the headlines** salir en primera plana; **to** ~ **the road** (col) largarse; **to** ~ **it off with sb** llevarse bien con uno.
hit back vi defenderse; (fig) devolver golpe por golpe.
hit out at vt fus asestar un golpe a; (fig) atacar.
hit (up)on vt fus (answer) dar con; (solution) hallar, encontrar.
hit-and-run driver ['hɪtən'rʌn-] n conductor(a) que atropella y huye.
hitch [hɪtʃ] vt (fasten) atar, amarrar; (also: ~ up) remangar ♦ n (difficulty) dificultad f; **to** ~ **a lift** hacer autostop; **technical** ~ problema m técnico.

hitch up vt (horse, cart) enganchar, uncir.
hitch-hike ['hɪtʃhaɪk] vi hacer autostop.
hitch-hiker ['hɪtʃhaɪkə*] n autostopista m/f.
hi-tech [haɪ'tɛk] a de alta tecnología.
hitherto ['hɪðə'tuː] ad hasta ahora, hasta aquí.
hitman ['hɪtmæn] n asesino a sueldo.
hit-or-miss ['hɪtə'mɪs] a: **it's** ~ **whether** ... está a la buena de Dios si ... .
hit parade n: **the** ~ los cuarenta principales.
hive [haɪv] n colmena; **the shop was a** ~ **of activity** (fig) la tienda era una colmena humana.
hive off vt (col: separate) separar; (: privatize) privatizar.
hl abbr (= hectolitre) hl.
HM abbr (= His (or Her) Majesty) S.M.
HMG abbr = His (or Her) Majesty's Government.
HMI n abbr (Brit SCOL) = His (or Her) Majesty's Inspector.
HMO n abbr (US: = health maintenance organization) seguro médico global.
HMS abbr = His (or Her) Majesty's Ship.
HMSO n abbr (= His (or Her) Majesty's Stationery Office) distribuidor oficial de las publicaciones del gobierno del Reino Unido.
HNC n abbr (Brit: = Higher National Certificate) título académico.
HND n abbr (Brit: = Higher National Diploma) título académico.
hoard [hɔːd] n (treasure) tesoro; (stockpile) provisión f ♦ vt acumular.
hoarding ['hɔːdɪŋ] n (for posters) cartelera.
hoarfrost ['hɔːfrɒst] n escarcha.
hoarse [hɔːs] a ronco.
hoax [həʊks] n trampa.
hob [hɒb] n quemador m.
hobble ['hɒbl] vi cojear.
hobby ['hɒbɪ] n pasatiempo, afición f.
hobby-horse ['hɒbɪhɔːs] n (fig) tema, manía.
hobnob ['hɒbnɒb] vi: **to** ~ **(with)** alternar (con).
hobo ['həʊbəʊ] n (US) vagabundo.
hock [hɒk] n (of animal, CULIN) corvejón m; (col: **to be in** ~ (person) estar empeñado or endeudado; (object) estar empeñado.
hockey ['hɒkɪ] n hockey m.
hocus-pocus [həʊkəs'pəʊkəs] n (trickery) juego de manos; (words: of magician) jerigonza.
hodge-podge ['hɒdʒpɒdʒ] n (US) = **hotchpotch.**
hoe [həʊ] n azadón m ♦ vt azadonar.
hog [hɒg] n cerdo, puerco ♦ vt (fig) acaparar; **to go the whole** ~ echar el todo por el todo.
hoist [hɔɪst] n (crane) grúa ♦ vt levantar, alzar.
hold [həʊld] vb (pt, pp held [hɛld]) vt tener;

(*contain*) contener; (*keep back*) retener; (*believe*) sostener; (*take ~ of*) coger (*Sp*), agarrar (*LAm*); (*take weight*) soportar; (*meeting*) celebrar ♦ *vi* (*withstand pressure*) resistir; (*be valid*) valer; (*stick*) pegarse ♦ *n* (*grasp*) asimiento; (*fig*) dominio; (*WRESTLING*) presa; (*NAUT*) bodega; ~ **the line!** (*TEL*) ¡no cuelgue!; **to ~ one's own** (*fig*) defenderse; **to ~ office** (*POL*) ocupar un cargo; **to ~ firm** *or* **fast** mantenerse firme; **he ~s the view that ...** opina *or* es su opinión que ...; **to ~ sb responsible for sth** culpar *or* echarle la culpa a uno de algo; **where can I get ~ of ...?** ¿dónde puedo encontrar (a) ...?; **to catch** *or* **get (a) ~ of** agarrarse *or* asirse de.

hold back *vt* retener; (*secret*) ocultar; **to ~ sb back from doing sth** impedir a uno hacer algo, impedir que uno haga algo.

hold down *vt* (*person*) sujetar; (*job*) mantener.

hold forth *vi* perorar.

hold off *vt* (*enemy*) rechazar ♦ *vi*: **if the rain ~s off** si no llueve.

hold on *vi* agarrarse bien; (*wait*) esperar.

hold on to *vt fus* agarrarse a; (*keep*) guardar.

hold out *vt* ofrecer ♦ *vi* (*resist*) resistir; **to ~ out (against)** resistir (a), sobrevivir.

hold over *vt* (*meeting etc*) aplazar.

hold up *vt* (*raise*) levantar; (*support*) apoyar; (*delay*) retrasar; (: *traffic*) demorar; (*rob*: *bank*) asaltar, atracar.

holdall ['həʊldɔ:l] *n* (*Brit*) bolsa.

holder ['həʊldə*] *n* (*of ticket, record*) poseedor(a) *m/f*; (*of passport, post, office, title etc*) titular *m/f*.

holding ['həʊldɪŋ] *n* (*share*) interés *m*.

holding company *n* holding *m*.

holdup ['həʊldʌp] *n* (*robbery*) atraco; (*delay*) retraso; (*Brit*: *in traffic*) embotellamiento.

hole [həʊl] *n* agujero ♦ *vt* agujerear; **~ in the heart** (*MED*) boquete *m* en el corazón; **to pick ~s in** (*fig*) encontrar defectos en; **the ship was ~d** se abrió una vía de agua en el barco.

hole up *vi* esconderse.

holiday ['hɔlədɪ] *n* vacaciones *fpl*; (*day off*) (día *m* de) fiesta, día *m* feriado; (*from work*) día *m* de asueto; **on ~** de vacaciones; **to be on ~** estar de vacaciones.

holiday camp *n* colonia *or* centro vacacional; (*for children*) colonia veraniega infantil.

holidaymaker ['hɔlədɪmeɪkə*] *n* (*Brit*) turista *m/f*.

holiday pay *n* paga de las vacaciones.

holiday resort *n* centro turístico.

holiday season *n* temporada de las vacaciones; **the ~ is from ... to ...** la época de vacaciones es de ... a ... .

holiness ['həʊlɪnɪs] *n* santidad *f*.

Holland ['hɔlənd] *n* Holanda.

hollow ['hɔləʊ] *a* hueco; (*fig*) vacío; (*eyes*) hundido; (*sound*) sordo ♦ *n* (*gen*) hueco; (*in ground*) hoyo ♦ *vt*: **to ~ out** ahuecar.

holly ['hɔlɪ] *n* acebo.

hollyhock ['hɔlɪhɔk] *n* malva loca.

holocaust ['hɔləkɔ:st] *n* holocausto.

holster ['həʊlstə*] *n* pistolera.

holy ['həʊlɪ] *a* (*gen*) santo, sagrado; (*water*) bendito; **the H~ Father** el Santo Padre.

Holy Communion *n* Sagrada Comunión *f*.

Holy Ghost, Holy Spirit *n* Espíritu *m* Santo.

homage ['hɔmɪdʒ] *n* homenaje *m*; **to pay ~ to** rendir homenaje a.

home [həʊm] *n* casa; (*country*) patria; (*institution*) asilo; (*COMPUT*) punto inicial *or* de partida ♦ *a* (*domestic*) casero, de casa; (*ECON, POL*) nacional; (*SPORT*: *team*) de casa; (: *match, win*) en casa ♦ *ad* (*direction*) a casa; **at ~** en casa; **to go/come ~** ir/volver a casa; **make yourself at ~** ¡estás en tu casa!; **it's near my ~** está cerca de mi casa.

home in on *vt fus* (*missiles*) dirigirse hacia.

home address *n* domicilio.

home-brew [həʊm'bru:] *n* cerveza *etc* casera.

homecoming ['həʊmkʌmɪŋ] *n* regreso (al hogar).

home computer *n* ordenador *m* doméstico.

Home Counties *npl* los alrededores de Londres.

home economics *n* economía doméstica.

home-grown ['həʊmgrəʊn] *a* de cosecha propia.

home key *n* (*COMPUT*) tecla home.

homeland ['həʊmlænd] *n* tierra natal.

homeless ['həʊmlɪs] *a* sin hogar, sin casa ♦ *npl*: **the ~** las personas sin hogar.

home loan *n* préstamo para la vivienda.

homely ['həʊmlɪ] *a* (*domestic*) casero; (*simple*) sencillo.

home-made [həʊm'meɪd] *a* hecho en casa.

Home Office *n* (*Brit*) Ministerio del Interior.

homeopathy [həʊmɪ'ɔpəθɪ] *etc* (*US*) = **homoeopathy** *etc*.

home rule *n* autonomía.

Home Secretary *n* (*Brit*) Ministro del Interior.

homesick ['həʊmsɪk] *a*: **to be ~** tener morriña, tener nostalgia.

homestead ['həʊmsted] *n* hacienda.

home town *n* ciudad *f* natal.

homeward ['həʊmwəd] *a* (*journey*) de vuelta.

homeward(s) ['həʊmwəd(z)] *ad* hacia casa.

homework ['həʊmwɜ:k] *n* deberes *mpl*.

homicidal [hɔmɪ'saɪdl] a homicida.
homicide ['hɔmɪsaɪd] n (US) homicidio.
homily ['hɔmɪlɪ] n homilía.
homing ['həʊmɪŋ] a (device, missile) buscador(a), cazador(a); ~ **pigeon** paloma mensajera.
homoeopath, (US) **homeopath** ['həʊmɪəʊpæθ] n homeópata m/f.
homoeopathic, (US) **homeopathic** [həʊmɪəʊ'pæθɪk] a homeopático.
homoeopathy, (US) **homeopathy** [həʊmɪ'ɔpəθɪ] n homeopatía.
homogeneous [hɔmə'dʒiːnɪəs] a homogéneo.
homogenize [hə'mɔdʒənaɪz] vt homogeneizar.
homosexual [hɔməʊ'sɛksjʊəl] a, n homosexual m/f.
Hon. abbr (= honourable, honorary) en títulos.
Honduras [hɔn'djʊərəs] n Honduras fpl.
hone [həʊn] vt (sharpen) afilar; (fig) perfeccionar.
honest ['ɔnɪst] a honrado; (sincere) franco, sincero; **to be quite** ~ **with you** ... para serte franco ....
honestly ['ɔnɪstlɪ] ad honradamente; francamente.
honesty ['ɔnɪstɪ] n honradez f.
honey ['hʌnɪ] n miel f; (US col) guapa, linda.
honeycomb ['hʌnɪkəʊm] n panal m; (fig) laberinto.
honeymoon ['hʌnɪmuːn] n luna de miel.
honeysuckle ['hʌnɪsʌkl] n madreselva.
Hong Kong ['hɔŋ'kɔŋ] n Hong-Kong m.
honk [hɔŋk] vi (AUT) tocar la bocina.
Honolulu [hɔnə'luːluː] n Honolulú m.
honorary ['ɔnərərɪ] a no remunerado; (duty, title) honorario.
honour, (US) **honor** ['ɔnə*] vt honrar ◆ n honor m, honra; **in** ~ **of** en honor de; **it's a great** ~ es un gran honor.
hono(u)rable ['ɔnərəbl] a honrado, honorable.
hono(u)r-bound ['ɔnə'baʊnd] a moralmente obligado.
hono(u)rs degree n (UNIV) título de licenciado de categoría superior.
Hons. abbr (UNIV) = **hono(u)rs degree.**
hood [hʊd] n capucha; (Brit AUT) capota; (US AUT) capó m; (US col) matón m.
hooded ['hʊdɪd] a (robber) encapuchado.
hoodlum ['huːdləm] n matón m.
hoodwink ['hʊdwɪŋk] vt (Brit) timar.
hoof, pl ~**s** or **hooves** [huːf, huːvz] n pezuña.
hook [hʊk] n gancho; (on dress) corchete m, broche m; (for fishing) anzuelo ◆ vt enganchar; ~**s and eyes** corchetes mpl, macho y hembra m; **by** ~ **or by crook** por las buenas o por las malas; **to be** ~**ed on** (col) ser adicto a; **to be** ~**ed on drugs**

estar colgado.
hook up vt (RADIO, TV) transmitir en cadena.
hooligan ['huːlɪgən] n gamberro.
hooliganism ['huːlɪgənɪzəm] n gamberrismo.
hoop [huːp] n aro.
hoot [huːt] vi (Brit AUT) tocar la bocina; (siren) sonar la sirena; (owl) ulular ◆ n bocinazo, toque m de sirena; **to** ~ **with laughter** morirse de risa.
hooter ['huːtə*] n (Brit AUT) bocina; (NAUT) sirena; (factory ~) silbato.
hoover ® ['huːvə*] (Brit) n aspiradora ◆ vt pasar la aspiradora por.
hooves [huːvz] pl of **hoof.**
hop [hɔp] vi saltar, brincar; (on one foot) saltar con un pie ◆ n salto, brinco; see also **hops.**
hope [həʊp] vt, vi esperar ◆ n esperanza; **I** ~ **so/not** espero que sí/no.
hopeful ['həʊpful] a (person) optimista; (situation) prometedor(a); **I'm** ~ **that she'll manage to come** confío en que podrá venir.
hopefully ['həʊpfulɪ] ad con optimismo, con esperanza.
hopeless ['həʊplɪs] a desesperado.
hopelessly ['həʊplɪslɪ] ad (live etc) sin esperanzas; **I'm** ~ **confused/lost** estoy totalmente despistado/perdido.
hopper ['hɔpə*] n (chute) tolva.
hops [hɔps] npl lúpulo sg.
horde [hɔːd] n horda.
horizon [hə'raɪzn] n horizonte m.
horizontal [hɔrɪ'zɔntl] a horizontal.
hormone ['hɔːməʊn] n hormona.
horn [hɔːn] n cuerno; (MUS: also: **French** ~) trompa; (AUT) bocina, claxón m (LAm).
horned [hɔːnd] a con cuernos.
hornet ['hɔːnɪt] n avispón m.
horny ['hɔːnɪ] a (material) córneo; (hands) calloso; (US col) cachondo.
horoscope ['hɔrəskəʊp] n horóscopo.
horrendous [hə'rɛndəs] a horrendo.
horrible ['hɔrɪbl] a horrible.
horribly ['hɔrɪblɪ] ad horriblemente.
horrid ['hɔrɪd] a horrible, horroroso.
horridly ['hɔrɪdlɪ] ad (behave) tremendamente mal.
horrific [hə'rɪfɪk] a (accident) horroroso; (film) horripilante.
horrify ['hɔrɪfaɪ] vt horrorizar.
horrifying ['hɔrɪfaɪɪŋ] a horroroso.
horror ['hɔrə*] n horror m.
horror film n película de horror.
horror-struck ['hɔrəstrʌk], **horror-stricken** ['hɔrəstrɪkn] a horrorizado.
hors d'œuvre [ɔː'dəːvrə] n entremeses mpl.
horse [hɔːs] n caballo.
horseback ['hɔːsbæk] n: **on** ~ a caballo.
horsebox ['hɔːsbɔks] n camión m para ca-

ballerías.

horse chestnut n (tree) castaño de Indias.

horsedrawn ['hɔːsdrɔːn] a de tracción animal.

horsefly ['hɔːsflaɪ] n tábano.

horseman ['hɔːsmən] n jinete m.

horsemanship ['hɔːsmənʃɪp] n equitación f, manejo del caballo.

horseplay ['hɔːspleɪ] n payasadas fpl.

horsepower (hp) ['hɔːspauə*] n caballo (de fuerza), potencia en caballos.

horse-racing ['hɔːsreɪsɪŋ] n carreras fpl de caballos.

horseradish ['hɔːsrædɪʃ] n rábano picante.

horseshoe ['hɔːsʃuː] n herradura.

horse show n concurso hípico.

horse-trader ['hɔːstreɪdə*] n chalán/ana m/f.

horse trials npl = horse show.

horsewhip ['hɔːswɪp] vt azotar.

horsewoman ['hɔːswumən] n jineta, caballista.

horsey ['hɔːsɪ] a (col: person) aficionado a los caballos.

horticulture ['hɔːtɪkʌltʃə*] n horticultura.

hose [həuz] n (also: ~pipe) manga.

hose down vt regar con manguera.

hosiery ['həuzɪərɪ] n calcetería.

hospice ['hɔspɪs] n hospicio.

hospitable ['hɔspɪtəbl] a hospitalario.

hospital ['hɔspɪtl] n hospital m.

hospitality [hɔspɪ'tælɪtɪ] n hospitalidad f.

hospitalize ['hɔspɪtəlaɪz] vt hospitalizar.

host [həust] n anfitrión m; (TV, RADIO) presentador(a) m/f; (of inn etc) mesonero; (REL) hostia; (large number): **a ~ of** multitud de.

hostage ['hɔstɪdʒ] n rehén m.

hostel ['hɔstl] n hostal m; (for students, nurses etc) residencia; (also: **youth ~**) albergue m juvenil; (for homeless people) hospicio.

hostelling ['hɔstlɪŋ] n: **to go (youth) ~** viajar de alberguista.

hostess ['həustɪs] n anfitriona; (Brit: air ~) azafata; (in night-club) señorita de compañía.

hostile ['hɔstaɪl] a hostil.

hostility [hɔ'stɪlɪtɪ] n hostilidad f.

hot [hɔt] a caliente; (weather) caluroso, de calor; (as opposed to only warm) muy caliente; (spicy) picante; (fig) ardiente, acalorado; **to be ~** (person) tener calor; (object) estar caliente; (weather) hacer calor.

hot up vi (col: situation) ponerse difícil or apurado; (: party) animarse ♦ vt (col: pace) apretar; (: engine) aumentar la potencia de.

hot air n (col) palabras fpl huecas.

hot-air balloon [hɔt'ɛə-] n (AVIAT) globo de aire caliente.

hotbed ['hɔtbɛd] n (fig) semillero.

hot-blooded [hɔt'blʌdɪd] a impetuoso.

hotchpotch ['hɔtʃpɔtʃ] n mezcolanza.

hot dog n perro caliente.

hotel [həu'tɛl] n hotel m.

hotelier [həu'tɛlɪə*] n hotelero.

hotel industry n industria hotelera.

hotel room n habitación f.

hotfoot ['hɔtfut] ad a toda prisa.

hotheaded [hɔt'hɛdɪd] a exaltado.

hothouse ['hɔthaus] n invernadero.

hot line n (POL) teléfono rojo, línea directa.

hotly ['hɔtlɪ] ad con pasión, apasionadamente.

hotplate ['hɔtpleɪt] n (on cooker) hornillo.

hotpot ['hɔtpɔt] n (Brit CULIN) estofado.

hot seat n primera fila.

hot spot n (trouble spot) punto caliente; (night club etc) lugar m popular.

hot spring n terma, fuente f de aguas termales.

hot-tempered ['hɔt'tɛmpəd] a de mal genio or carácter.

hot-water bottle [hɔt'wɔːtə-] n bolsa de agua caliente.

hound [haund] vt acosar ♦ n perro de caza.

hour ['auə*] n hora; **at 30 miles an ~** a 30 millas por hora; **lunch ~** la hora del almuerzo or de comer; **to pay sb by the ~** pagar a uno por hora.

hourly ['auəlɪ] a (de) cada hora; (rate) por hora ♦ ad cada hora.

house n [haus] (pl ~s ['hauzɪz]) (also firm) casa; (POL) cámara; (THEATRE) sala ♦ vt [hauz] (person) alojar; **at/to my ~** en/a mi casa; **on the ~** (fig) la casa invita.

house arrest n arresto domiciliario.

houseboat ['hausbəut] n casa flotante.

housebound ['hausbaund] a confinado en casa.

housebreaking ['hausbreɪkɪŋ] n allanamiento de morada.

house-broken ['hausbrəukən] a (US) = **house-trained**.

housecoat ['hauskəut] n bata.

household ['haushəuld] n familia.

householder ['haushəuldə*] n propietario/a; (head of house) cabeza de familia, jefe m de familia.

househunting ['haushʌntɪŋ] n: **to go ~** ir buscando casa.

housekeeper ['hauskiːpə*] n ama de llaves.

housekeeping ['hauskiːpɪŋ] n (work) trabajos mpl domésticos; (COMPUT) gestión f interna; (also: ~ **money**) dinero para gastos domésticos.

houseman ['hausmən] n (Brit MED) médico recién titulado que vive en el hospital.

house plant n planta de interior.

house-proud ['hauspraud] a preocupado por el embellecimiento de la casa.

house-to-house ['haustə'haus] a (collection) de casa en casa; (search) casa por casa.

house-trained ['haustreɪnd] *a* (*Brit*: *animal*) domesticado.

house-warming ['hauswɔːmɪŋ] *n* (*also*: ~ **party**) fiesta de estreno de una casa.

housewife ['hauswaɪf] *n* ama de casa.

housework ['hauswɜːk] *n* faenas *fpl* (de la casa).

housing ['hauzɪŋ] *n* (*act*) alojamiento; (*houses*) viviendas *fpl* ♦ *cpd* (*problem*, *shortage*) de (la) vivienda.

housing association *n* asociación *f* de la vivienda.

housing conditions *npl* condiciones *fpl* de habitabilidad.

housing development, (*Brit*) **housing estate** *n* urbanización *f*.

hovel ['hɔvl] *n* casucha.

hover ['hɔvə*] *vi* flotar (en el aire); (*helicopter*) cernerse; **to** ~ **on the brink of disaster** estar en el borde mismo del desastre.

hovercraft ['hɔvəkrɑːft] *n* aerodeslizador *m*.

hoverport ['hɔvəpɔːt] *n* puerto de aerodeslizadores.

how [hau] *ad* cómo; ~ **are you?** ¿cómo está usted?, ¿cómo estás?; ~ **do you do?** ¿cómo está usted?, ¿qué tal estás?; ~ **far is it to ...?** ¿qué distancia hay de aquí a ...?; ~ **long have you been here?** ¿cuánto tiempo hace que estás aquí?; ~ **lovely!** ¡qué bonito!; ~ **many/much?** ¿cuántos/cuánto?; ~ **old are you?** ¿cuántos años tienes?; ~ **is school?** ¿qué tal la escuela?; ~ **about a drink?** ¿te gustaría algo de beber?, ¿qué te parece una copa?

however [hau'ɛvə*] *ad* de cualquier manera; (+ *adjective*) por muy ... que; (*in questions*) cómo ♦ *conj* sin embargo, no obstante.

howitzer ['hauɪtsə*] *n* (*MIL*) obús *m*.

howl [haul] *n* aullido ♦ *vi* aullar.

howler ['haulə*] *n* plancha, falta garrafal.

HP *n abbr see* **hire purchase**.

hp *abbr see* **horsepower**.

HQ *n abbr see* **headquarters**.

HR *n abbr* (*US*) = *House of Representatives*.

HRH *abbr* (= *His* (*or Her*) *Royal Highness*) S.A.R.

hr(s) *abbr* (= *hour*(*s*)) hr.

HS *abbr* (*US*) = **high school**.

HST *abbr* (*US*: = *Hawaiian Standard Time*) hora de Hawai.

hub [hʌb] *n* (*of wheel*) centro *m*.

hubbub ['hʌbʌb] *n* barahúnda, barullo.

hubcap ['hʌbkæp] *n* tapacubos *m inv*.

HUD *n abbr* (*US*: = *Department of Housing and Urban Development*) ministerio de la vivienda y urbanismo.

huddle ['hʌdl] *vi*: **to** ~ **together** amontonarse.

hue [hjuː] *n* color *m*, matiz *m*; ~ **and cry** *n* alarma.

huff [hʌf] *n*: **in a** ~ enojado.

hug [hʌg] *vt* abrazar ♦ *n* abrazo.

huge [hjuːdʒ] *a* enorme.

hulk [hʌlk] *n* (*ship*) barco viejo; (*person*, *building etc*) mole *f*.

hulking ['hʌlkɪŋ] *a* pesado.

hull [hʌl] *n* (*of ship*) casco.

hullabaloo ['hʌləbə'luː] *n* (*col*: *noise*) algarabía, jaleo.

hullo [hə'ləu] *excl* = **hello**.

hum [hʌm] *vt* tararear, canturrear ♦ *vi* tararear, canturrear; (*insect*) zumbar ♦ *n* (*also ELEC*) zumbido; (*of traffic, machines*) zumbido, ronroneo; (*of voices etc*) murmullo.

human ['hjuːmən] *a* humano ♦ *n* (*also*: ~ **being**) ser *m* humano.

humane [hjuː'meɪn] *a* humano, humanitario.

humanism ['hjuːmənɪzəm] *n* humanismo.

humanitarian [hjuːmænɪ'tɛərɪən] *a* humanitario.

humanity [hjuː'mænɪtɪ] *n* humanidad *f*.

humanly ['hjuːmənlɪ] *ad* humanamente.

humanoid ['hjuːmənɔɪd] *a*, *n* humanoide *m/f*.

human relations *npl* relaciones *fpl* humanas.

humble ['hʌmbl] *a* humilde ♦ *vt* humillar.

humbly ['hʌmblɪ] *ad* humildemente.

humbug ['hʌmbʌg] *n* tonterías *fpl*; (*Brit*: *sweet*) caramelo de menta.

humdrum ['hʌmdrʌm] *a* (*boring*) monótono, aburrido; (*routine*) rutinario.

humid ['hjuːmɪd] *a* húmedo.

humidifier [hjuː'mɪdɪfaɪə*] *n* humedecedor *m*.

humidity [hjuː'mɪdɪtɪ] *n* humedad *f*.

humiliate [hjuː'mɪlɪeɪt] *vt* humillar.

humiliation [hjuːmɪlɪ'eɪʃən] *n* humillación *f*.

humility [hjuː'mɪlɪtɪ] *n* humildad *f*.

humorist ['hjuːmərɪst] *n* humorista *m/f*.

humorous ['hjuːmərəs] *a* gracioso, divertido.

humour, (*US*) **humor** ['hjuːmə*] *n* humorismo, sentido del humor; (*mood*) humor *m* ♦ *vt* (*person*) complacer; **sense of** ~ sentido del humor; **to be in a good/bad** ~ estar de buen/mal humor.

humo(u)rless ['hjuːməlɪs] *a* arisco.

hump [hʌmp] *n* (*in ground*) montículo; (*camel's*) giba.

humus ['hjuːməs] *n* (*BIO*) humus *m*.

hunch [hʌntʃ] *n* (*premonition*) presentimiento; **I have a** ~ **that** tengo una corazonada *or* un presentimiento de que.

hunchback ['hʌntʃbæk] *n* joroba *m/f*.

hunched [hʌntʃt] *a* jorobado.

hundred ['hʌndrəd] *num* ciento; (*before n*) cien; **about a** ~ **people** unas cien personas, alrededor de cien personas; ~**s of** centenares de; ~**s of people** centenares de personas; **I'm a** ~ **per cent sure** estoy completamente seguro.

hundredweight ['hʌndrədweɪt] n (Brit) = 50.8 kg; 112 lb; (US) = 45.3 kg; 100 lb.

hung [hʌŋ] pt, pp of **hang**.

Hungarian [hʌŋ'gɛərɪən] a, n húngaro/a m/f ♦ n (LING) húngaro.

Hungary ['hʌŋgərɪ] n Hungría.

hunger ['hʌŋgə*] n hambre f ♦ vi: **to ~ for** (fig) tener hambre de, anhelar.

hunger strike n huelga de hambre.

hungrily ['hʌŋgrəlɪ] ad ávidamente, con ganas.

hungry ['hʌŋgrɪ] a hambriento; **to be ~** tener hambre; **~ for** (fig) sediento de.

hunk [hʌŋk] n (of bread etc) trozo, pedazo.

hunt [hʌnt] vt (seek) buscar; (SPORT) cazar ♦ vi cazar ♦ n caza, cacería.

hunt down vt acorralar, seguir la pista a.

hunter ['hʌntə*] n cazador(a) m/f; (horse) caballo de caza.

hunting ['hʌntɪŋ] n caza.

hurdle ['hə:dl] n (SPORT) valla; (fig) obstáculo.

hurl [hə:l] vt lanzar, arrojar.

hurrah [hu'rɑ:], **hurray** [hu'reɪ] n ¡viva!, ¡vítor!

hurricane ['hʌrɪkən] n huracán m.

hurried ['hʌrɪd] a (fast) apresurado; (rushed) hecho de prisa.

hurriedly ['hʌrɪdlɪ] ad con prisa, apresuradamente.

hurry ['hʌrɪ] n prisa ♦ vb (also: **~ up**) vi apresurarse, darse prisa ♦ vt (person) dar prisa a; (work) apresurar, hacer de prisa; **to be in a ~** tener prisa; **to ~ back/home** darse prisa para volver/volver a casa.

hurry along vi pasar de prisa.

hurry away, **hurry off** vi irse corriendo.

hurry on vi: **to ~ on to say** apresurarse a decir.

hurry up vi darse prisa.

hurt [hə:t] vb (pt, pp **hurt**) vt hacer daño a; (business, interests etc) perjudicar ♦ vi doler ♦ a lastimado; **I ~ my arm** me lastimé el brazo; **where does it ~?** ¿dónde te duele?

hurtful ['hə:tful] a (remark etc) dañoso.

hurtle ['hə:tl] vi: **to ~ past** pasar como un rayo.

husband ['hʌzbənd] n marido.

hush [hʌʃ] n silencio ♦ vt hacer callar; (cover up) encubrir; **~!** ¡chitón!, ¡cállate!

hush up vt (fact) encubrir, callar.

hushed [hʌʃt] a (voice) bajo.

hush-hush [hʌʃ'hʌʃ] a (col) muy secreto.

husk [hʌsk] n (of wheat) cáscara.

husky ['hʌskɪ] a ronco; (burly) fornido ♦ n perro esquimal.

hustings ['hʌstɪŋz] npl (POL) mítin msg preelectoral.

hustle ['hʌsl] vt (push) empujar; (hurry) dar prisa a ♦ n bullicio, actividad f febril;

~ and bustle n vaivén m.

hut [hʌt] n cabaña; (shed) cobertizo.

hutch [hʌtʃ] n conejera.

hyacinth ['haɪəsɪnθ] n jacinto.

hybrid ['haɪbrɪd] a, n híbrido.

hydrant ['haɪdrənt] n (also: **fire ~**) boca de incendios.

hydraulic [haɪ'drɔ:lɪk] a hidráulico.

hydraulics [haɪ'drɔ:lɪks] n hidráulica.

hydrochloric ['haɪdrəu'klɔrɪk] a: **~ acid** ácido clorhídrico.

hydroelectric [haɪdrəuɪ'lɛktrɪk] a hidroeléctrico.

hydrofoil ['haɪdrəfɔɪl] n aerodeslizador m.

hydrogen ['haɪdrədʒən] n hidrógeno.

hydrogen bomb n bomba de hidrógeno.

hydrophobia [haɪdrə'fəubɪə] n hidrofobia.

hydroplane ['haɪdrəpleɪn] n hidroplano, hidroavión m.

hyena [haɪ'i:nə] n hiena.

hygiene ['haɪdʒi:n] n higiene f.

hygienic [haɪ'dʒi:nɪk] a higiénico.

hymn [hɪm] n himno.

hype [haɪp] n (col) bombardeo publicitario, superchería.

hyperactive [haɪpər'æktɪv] a hiperactivo.

hypermarket ['haɪpəmɑ:kɪt] n hipermercado.

hypertension ['haɪpə'tɛnʃən] n hipertensión f.

hyphen ['haɪfn] n guión m.

hypnosis [hɪp'nəusɪs] n hipnosis f.

hypnotic [hɪp'nɔtɪk] a hipnótico.

hypnotism ['hɪpnətɪzəm] n hipnotismo.

hypnotist ['hɪpnətɪst] hipnotista m/f.

hypnotize ['hɪpnətaɪz] vt hipnotizar.

hypoallergenic ['haɪpəuælə'dʒɛnɪk] a hipoalérgeno.

hypochondriac [haɪpəu'kɔndrɪæk] n hipocondríaco/a.

hypocrisy [hɪ'pɔkrɪsɪ] n hipocresía.

hypocrite ['hɪpəkrɪt] n hipócrita m/f.

hypocritical [hɪpə'krɪtɪkl] a hipócrita.

hypodermic [haɪpə'də:mɪk] a hipodérmico ♦ n (syringe) aguja hipodérmica.

hypothermia [haɪpəu'θə:mɪə] n hipotermia.

hypothesis [haɪ'pɔθɪsɪs, pl **hypotheses** -si:z] n hipótesis f inv.

hypothetical [haɪpə'θɛtɪkl] a hipotético.

hysterectomy [hɪstə'rɛktəmɪ] n histerectomía.

hysteria [hɪ'stɪərɪə] n histeria.

hysterical [hɪ'stɛrɪkl] a histérico.

hysterics [hɪ'stɛrɪks] npl histeria sg, histerismo sg; **to have ~** ponerse histérico.

Hz abbr (= Hertz) Hz.

I

I, i [aɪ] *n* (*letter*) I, i *f*; **I for Isaac,** (*US*) **I for Item** I de Inés, I de Israel.
I [aɪ] *pron* yo ♦ *abbr* = **island, isle.**
IA *abbr* (*US POST*) = *Iowa.*
IAEA *n abbr see* **International Atomic Energy Agency.**
IBA *n abbr* (*Brit*: = *Independent Broadcasting Authority*) *entidad que controla los medios privados de televisión y radio.*
Iberian [aɪˈbɪərɪən] *a* ibero, ibérico.
Iberian Peninsula *n*: **the ~** la Península Ibérica.
IBEW *n abbr* (*US*: = *International Brotherhood of Electrical Workers*) *sindicato internacional de electricistas.*
ib(id). *abbr* (= *ibidem*: *from the same source*) ibídem.
i/c *abbr* (*Brit*) = **in charge.**
ICBM *n abbr* = **intercontinental ballistic missile.**
ICC *n abbr* (= *International Chamber of Commerce*) CCI *f*; (*US*) = *Interstate Commerce Commission.*
ice [aɪs] *n* hielo ♦ *vt* (*cake*) alcorzar ♦ *vi* (*also*: **~ over, ~ up**) helarse; **to keep sth on ~** (*fig*: *plan, project*) tener algo en reserva.
ice age *n* período glaciar.
ice axe *n* piqueta (de alpinista).
iceberg [ˈaɪsbəːg] *n* iceberg *m*; **the tip of the ~** (*also fig*) lo de menos.
icebox [ˈaɪsbɒks] *n* (*Brit*) congelador *m*; (*US*) nevera, refrigeradora (*LAm*).
icebreaker [ˈaɪsbreɪkə*] *n* rompehielos *m inv.*
ice bucket *n* cubo para el hielo.
ice-cold [aɪsˈkəuld] *a* helado.
ice cream *n* helado.
ice-cream soda *n* soda mezclada con helado.
ice cube *n* cubito de hielo.
iced [aɪst] *a* (*drink*) con hielo; (*cake*) escarchado.
ice hockey *n* hockey *m* sobre hielo.
Iceland [ˈaɪslənd] *n* Islandia.
Icelander [ˈaɪsləndə*] *n* islandés/esa *m/f.*
Icelandic [aɪsˈlændɪk] *a* islandés/esa ♦ *n* (*LING*) islandés *m.*
ice lolly *n* (*Brit*) polo helado.
ice pick *n* piolet *m.*
ice rink *n* pista de hielo.
ice-skate [ˈaɪsskeɪt] *n* patín *m* de hielo ♦ *vi* patinar sobre hielo.
ice-skating [ˈaɪsskeɪtɪŋ] *n* patinaje *m* sobre hielo.

icicle [ˈaɪsɪkl] *n* carámbano.
icing [ˈaɪsɪŋ] *n* (*CULIN*) alcorza; (*AVIAT etc*) formación *f* de hielo.
icing sugar *n* (*Brit*) azúcar *m* glas(eado).
ICJ *n abbr see* **International Court of Justice.**
icon [ˈaɪkɔn] *n* ícono; (*COMPUT*) símbolo gráfico.
ICR *n abbr* (*US*) = *Institute for Cancer Research.*
ICU *n abbr* (= *intensive care unit*) UVI *f.*
icy [ˈaɪsɪ] *a* (*road*) helado; (*fig*) glacial.
ID *abbr* (*US POST*) = *Idaho.*
I'd [aɪd] = **I would, I had.**
ID card *n* (= *identity card*) DNI *m.*
IDD *n abbr* (*Brit TEL*: = *international direct dialling*) *servicio automático internacional.*
idea [aɪˈdɪə] *n* idea; **good ~!** ¡buena idea!; **to have an ~ that ...** tener la impresión de que ...; **I haven't the least ~** no tengo ni (la más remota) idea.
ideal [aɪˈdɪəl] *n* ideal *m* ♦ *a* ideal.
idealism [aɪˈdɪəlɪzəm] *n* idealismo.
idealist [aɪˈdɪəlɪst] *n* idealista *m/f.*
ideally [aɪˈdɪəlɪ] *ad* perfectamente; **~, the book should have ...** idealmente, el libro debería tener ....
identical [aɪˈdɛntɪkl] *a* idéntico.
identification [aɪdɛntɪfɪˈkeɪʃən] *n* identificación *f*; **means of ~** documentos *mpl* personales.
identify [aɪˈdɛntɪfaɪ] *vt* identificar ♦ *vi*: **to ~ with** identificarse con.
Identikit ® [aɪˈdɛntɪkɪt] *n*: **~ (picture)** retrato-robot *m.*
identity [aɪˈdɛntɪtɪ] *n* identidad *f.*
identity card *n* carnet *m* de identidad.
identity papers *npl* documentos *mpl* (de identidad), documentación *fsg.*
identity parade *n* identificación *f* de acusados.
ideological [aɪdɪəˈlɔdʒɪkəl] *a* ideológico.
ideology [aɪdɪˈɔlədʒɪ] *n* ideología.
idiocy [ˈɪdɪəsɪ] *n* idiotez *f*; (*stupid act*) estupidez *f.*
idiom [ˈɪdɪəm] *n* modismo; (*style of speaking*) lenguaje *m.*
idiomatic [ɪdɪəˈmætɪk] *a* idiomático.
idiosyncrasy [ɪdɪəuˈsɪŋkrəsɪ] *n* idiosincrasia.
idiot [ˈɪdɪət] *n* (*gen*) idiota *m/f*; (*fool*) tonto/a.
idiotic [ɪdɪˈɔtɪk] *a* idiota; tonto.
idle [ˈaɪdl] *a* (*lazy*) holgazán/ana; (*unemployed*) parado, desocupado; (*talk*) frívolo ♦ *vi* (*machine*) funcionar or marchar en vacío; **~ capacity** (*COMM*) capacidad *f* sin utilizar; **~ money** (*COMM*) capital *m* improductivo; **~ time** (*COMM*) tiempo de paro.
idle away *vt*: **to ~ away one's time** malgastar *or* desperdiciar el tiempo.

idleness ['aɪdlnɪs] *n* holgazanería; paro, desocupación *f*.
idler ['aɪdlə*] *n* holgazán/ana *m/f*, vago/a.
idol ['aɪdl] *n* ídolo.
idolize ['aɪdəlaɪz] *vt* idolatrar.
idyllic [ɪ'dɪlɪk] *a* idílico.
i.e. *abbr* (= *id est: that is*) esto es.
if [ɪf] *conj* si ◆ *n*: **there are a lot of** ~s **and buts** hay muchas dudas sin resolver; **(even)** ~ aunque, si bien; **I'd be pleased** ~ **you could do it** yo estaría contento si pudieras hacerlo; ~ **necessary** si resultase necesario; ~ **only** si solamente; **as** ~ como si.
igloo ['ɪgluː] *n* iglú *m*.
ignite [ɪg'naɪt] *vt* (*set fire to*) encender ◆ *vi* encenderse.
ignition [ɪg'nɪʃən] *n* (*AUT*) encendido; **to switch on/off the** ~ arrancar/apagar el motor.
ignition key *n* (*AUT*) llave *f* de contacto.
ignoble [ɪg'nəubl] *a* innoble, vil.
ignominious [ɪgnə'mɪnɪəs] *a* ignominioso, vergonzoso.
ignoramus [ɪgnə'reɪməs] *n* ignorante *m/f*, inculto/a.
ignorance ['ɪgnərəns] *n* ignorancia; **to keep sb in** ~ **of sth** ocultarle algo a uno.
ignorant ['ɪgnərənt] *a* ignorante; **to be** ~ **of** (*subject*) desconocer; (*events*) ignorar.
ignore [ɪg'nɔː*] *vt* (*person*) no hacer caso de; (*fact*) pasar por alto.
ikon ['aɪkɔn] *n* = **icon.**
IL *abbr* (*US POST*) = *Illinois*.
ILA *n abbr* (*US*: = *International Longshoremen's Association*) sindicato internacional de trabajadores portuarios.
ILEA ['ɪlɪə] *n abbr* (*Brit*: = *Inner London Education Authority*) organismo que controla la enseñanza en la ciudad de Londres.
ILGWU *n abbr* (*US*: = *International Ladies' Garment Workers Union*) sindicato de empleados del ramo de las prendas de vestir femeninas.
ill [ɪl] *a* enfermo, malo ◆ *n* mal *m*; (*fig*) infortunio ◆ *ad* mal; **to take** *or* **be taken** ~ caer *or* ponerse enfermo; **to feel** ~ **(with)** encontrarse mal (de); **to speak/think** ~ **of sb** hablar/pensar mal de uno; *see also* **ills.**
I'll [aɪl] = **I will, I shall.**
ill-advised [ɪləd'vaɪzd] *a* poco recomendable; **he was** ~ **to go** se equivocaba al ir.
ill-at-ease [ɪlət'iːz] *a* incómodo.
ill-considered [ɪlkən'sɪdəd] *a* (*plan*) poco pensado.
ill-disposed [ɪldɪs'pəuzd] *a*: **to be** ~ **towards sb/sth** estar maldispuesto hacia uno/algo.
illegal [ɪ'liːgl] *a* ilegal.
illegible [ɪ'lɛdʒɪbl] *a* ilegible.
illegitimate [ɪlɪ'dʒɪtɪmət] *a* ilegítimo.
ill-fated [ɪl'feɪtɪd] *a* malogrado.
ill-favoured, (*US*) **ill-favored** [ɪl'feɪvəd] *a*

mal parecido.
ill feeling *n* rencor *m*.
ill-gotten ['ɪlgɔtn] *a* (*gains etc*) mal adquirido.
illicit [ɪ'lɪsɪt] *a* ilícito.
ill-informed [ɪlɪn'fɔːmd] *a* (*judgement*) erróneo; (*person*) mal informado.
illiterate [ɪ'lɪtərət] *a* analfabeto.
ill-mannered [ɪl'mænəd] *a* mal educado.
illness ['ɪlnɪs] *n* enfermedad *f*.
illogical [ɪ'lɔdʒɪkl] *a* ilógico.
ills [ɪlz] *npl* males *mpl*.
ill-suited [ɪl'suːtɪd] *a* (*couple*) incompatible; **he is** ~ **to the job** no es la persona indicada para el trabajo.
ill-timed [ɪl'taɪmd] *a* inoportuno.
ill-treat [ɪl'triːt] *vt* maltratar.
ill-treatment [ɪl'triːtmənt] *n* malos tratos *mpl*.
illuminate [ɪ'luːmɪneɪt] *vt* (*room, street*) iluminar, alumbrar; (*subject*) aclarar; ~**d sign** letrero luminoso.
illuminating [ɪ'luːmɪneɪtɪŋ] *a* revelador(a).
illumination [ɪluːmɪ'neɪʃən] *n* alumbrado; ~**s** *npl* luminarias *fpl*, luces *fpl*.
illusion [ɪ'luːʒən] *n* ilusión *f*; **to be under the** ~ **that...** estar convencido de que ....
illusive [ɪ'luːsɪv], **illusory** [ɪ'luːsərɪ] *a* ilusorio.
illustrate ['ɪləstreɪt] *vt* ilustrar.
illustration [ɪlə'streɪʃən] *n* (*example*) ejemplo, ilustración *f*; (*in book*) lámina.
illustrator ['ɪləstreɪtə*] *n* ilustrador(a) *m/f*.
illustrious [ɪ'lʌstrɪəs] *a* ilustre.
ill will *n* rencor *m*.
ILO *n abbr* (= *International Labour Organization*) OIT *f*.
ILWU *n abbr* (*US*: = *International Longshoremen's and Warehousemen's Union*) sindicato internacional de trabajadores portuarios y almacenistas.
I'm [aɪm] = **I am.**
image ['ɪmɪdʒ] *n* imagen *f*.
imagery ['ɪmɪdʒərɪ] *n* imágenes *fpl*.
imaginable [ɪ'mædʒɪnəbl] *a* imaginable.
imaginary [ɪ'mædʒɪnərɪ] *a* imaginario.
imagination [ɪmædʒɪ'neɪʃən] *n* imaginación *f*; (*inventiveness*) inventiva; (*illusion*) fantasía.
imaginative [ɪ'mædʒɪnətɪv] *a* imaginativo.
imagine [ɪ'mædʒɪn] *vt* imaginarse; (*suppose*) suponer.
imbalance [ɪm'bæləns] *n* desequilibrio.
imbecile ['ɪmbəsiːl] *n* imbécil *m/f*.
imbue [ɪm'bjuː] *vt*: **to** ~ **sth with** imbuir algo de.
IMF *n abbr see* **International Monetary Fund.**
imitate ['ɪmɪteɪt] *vt* imitar.
imitation [ɪmɪ'teɪʃən] *n* imitación *f*; (*copy*) copia; (*pej*) remedo.
imitator ['ɪmɪteɪtə*] *n* imitador(a) *m/f*.
immaculate [ɪ'mækjulət] *a* perfectamente

limpio; (*REL*) inmaculado.

immaterial [ɪməˈtɪərɪəl] *a* incorpóreo; **it is ~ whether...** no importa si... .

immature [ɪməˈtjuə*] *a* (*person*) inmaduro; (*of one's youth*) joven.

immaturity [ɪməˈtjuərɪtɪ] *n* inmadurez *f*.

immeasurable [ɪˈmɛʒrəbl] *a* inconmensurable.

immediacy [ɪˈmiːdɪəsɪ] *n* urgencia, proximidad *f*.

immediate [ɪˈmiːdɪət] *a* inmediato; (*pressing*) urgente, apremiante; **in the ~ future** en el futuro próximo.

immediately [ɪˈmiːdɪətlɪ] *ad* (*at once*) en seguida; **~ next to** muy junto a.

immense [ɪˈmɛns] *a* inmenso, enorme.

immensely [ɪˈmɛnslɪ] *ad* enormemente.

immensity [ɪˈmɛnsɪtɪ] *n* (*of size, difference*) inmensidad *f*; (*of problem*) enormidad *f*.

immerse [ɪˈmɜːs] *vt* (*submerge*) sumergir; **to be ~d in** (*fig*) estar absorto en.

immersion heater [ɪˈmɜːʃən-] *n* (*Brit*) calentador *m* de inmersión.

immigrant [ˈɪmɪɡrənt] *n* inmigrante *m/f*.

immigrate [ˈɪmɪɡreɪt] *vi* inmigrar.

immigration [ɪmɪˈɡreɪʃən] *n* inmigración *f*.

immigration authorities *npl* servicio *sg* de inmigración.

immigration laws *npl* leyes *fpl* inmigratorias.

imminent [ˈɪmɪnənt] *a* inminente.

immobile [ɪˈməubaɪl] *a* inmóvil.

immobilize [ɪˈməubɪlaɪz] *vt* inmovilizar.

immoderate [ɪˈmɔdərɪt] *a* (*person*) desmesurado; (*opinion, reaction, demand*) excesivo.

immodest [ɪˈmɔdɪst] *a* (*indecent*) desvergonzado, impúdico; (*boasting*) jactancioso.

immoral [ɪˈmɔrl] *a* inmoral.

immorality [ɪməˈrælɪtɪ] *n* inmoralidad *f*.

immortal [ɪˈmɔːtl] *a* inmortal.

immortality [ɪmɔːˈtælɪtɪ] *n* inmortalidad *f*.

immortalize [ɪˈmɔːtlaɪz] *vt* inmortalizar.

immovable [ɪˈmuːvəbl] *a* (*object*) imposible de mover; (*person*) inconmovible.

immune [ɪˈmjuːn] *a*: **~ (to)** inmune (contra).

immunity [ɪˈmjuːnɪtɪ] *n* (*MED, of diplomat*) inmunidad *f*; (*COMM*) exención *f*.

immunization [ɪmjunaɪˈzeɪʃən] *n* inmunización *f*.

immunize [ˈɪmjunaɪz] *vt* inmunizar.

imp [ɪmp] *n* (*small devil, also fig: child*) diablillo.

impact [ˈɪmpækt] *n* (*gen*) impacto.

impair [ɪmˈpɛə*] *vt* perjudicar.

impale [ɪmˈpeɪl] *vt* (*with sword*) atravesar.

impart [ɪmˈpɑːt] *vt* comunicar; (*make known*) participar; (*bestow*) otorgar.

impartial [ɪmˈpɑːʃl] *a* imparcial.

impartiality [ɪmpɑːʃɪˈælɪtɪ] *n* imparcialidad *f*.

impassable [ɪmˈpɑːsəbl] *a* (*barrier*) infranqueable; (*river, road*) intransitable.

impasse [ɪmˈpɑːs] *n* callejón *m* sin salida; **to reach an ~** alcanzar un punto muerto.

impassioned [ɪmˈpæʃənd] *a* apasionado, exaltado.

impassive [ɪmˈpæsɪv] *a* impasible.

impatience [ɪmˈpeɪʃəns] *n* impaciencia.

impatient [ɪmˈpeɪʃənt] *a* impaciente; **to get** *or* **grow ~** impacientarse.

impatiently [ɪmˈpeɪʃəntlɪ] *ad* con impaciencia.

impeachment [ɪmˈpiːtʃmənt] *n* denuncia, acusación *f*.

impeccable [ɪmˈpɛkəbl] *a* impecable.

impecunious [ɪmpɪˈkjuːnɪəs] *a* sin dinero.

impede [ɪmˈpiːd] *vt* estorbar, dificultar.

impediment [ɪmˈpedɪmənt] *n* obstáculo, estorbo; (*also*: **speech ~**) defecto (del habla).

impel [ɪmˈpɛl] *vt* (*force*): **to ~ sb (to do sth)** obligar a uno (a hacer algo).

impending [ɪmˈpendɪŋ] *a* (*near*) próximo.

impenetrable [ɪmˈpenɪtrəbl] *a* (*jungle, fortress*) impenetrable; (*unfathomable*) insondable.

imperative [ɪmˈperətɪv] *a* (*tone*) imperioso; (*necessary*) imprescindible ♦ *n* (*LING*) imperativo.

imperceptible [ɪmpəˈsɛptɪbl] *a* imperceptible, insensible.

imperfect [ɪmˈpɜːfɪkt] *a* imperfecto; (*goods etc*) defectuoso.

imperfection [ɪmpəˈfɛkʃən] *n* (*blemish*) desperfecto; (*fault, flaw*) defecto.

imperial [ɪmˈpɪərɪəl] *a* imperial.

imperialism [ɪmˈpɪərɪəlɪzəm] *n* imperialismo.

imperil [ɪmˈperɪl] *vt* poner en peligro.

imperious [ɪmˈpɪərɪəs] *a* señorial, apremiante.

impersonal [ɪmˈpɜːsənl] *a* impersonal.

impersonate [ɪmˈpɜːsəneɪt] *vt* hacerse pasar por.

impersonation [ɪmpəːsəˈneɪʃən] *n* imitación *f*.

impersonator [ɪmˈpɜːsəneɪtə*] *n* (*THEATRE etc*) imitador(a) *m/f*.

impertinence [ɪmˈpɜːtɪnəns] *n* descaro.

impertinent [ɪmˈpɜːtɪnənt] *a* impertinente, insolente.

imperturbable [ɪmpəˈtɜːbəbl] *a* imperturbable, impasible.

impervious [ɪmˈpɜːvɪəs] *a* impermeable; (*fig*): **~ to** insensible a.

impetuous [ɪmˈpetjuəs] *a* impetuoso.

impetus [ˈɪmpətəs] *n* ímpetu *m*; (*fig*) impulso.

impinge [ɪmˈpɪndʒ]: **to ~ on** *vt fus* (*affect*) afectar a.

impish [ˈɪmpɪʃ] *a* travieso.

implacable [ɪmˈplækəbl] *a* implacable.

implant [ɪmˈplɑːnt] *vt* (*MED*) injertar, im-

plantar; (*fig*: *idea, principle*) inculcar.
implausible [ɪm'plɔːzɪbl] *a* implausible.
implement *n* ['ɪmplɪmənt] instrumento, herramienta ◆ *vt* ['ɪmplɪmɛnt] hacer efectivo; (*carry out*) realizar.
implicate ['ɪmplɪkeɪt] *vt* (*compromise*) comprometer; (*involve*) enredar; **to ~ sb in sth** comprometer a uno en algo.
implication [ɪmplɪ'keɪʃən] *n* consecuencia; **by ~** indirectamente.
implicit [ɪm'plɪsɪt] *a* (*gen*) implícito; (*complete*) absoluto.
implicitly [ɪm'plɪsɪtlɪ] *ad* implícitamente.
implore [ɪm'plɔː*] *vt* (*person*) suplicar.
imploring [ɪm'plɔːrɪŋ] *a* de súplica.
imply [ɪm'plaɪ] *vt* (*involve*) implicar; (*mean*) significar; (*hint*) dar a entender.
impolite [ɪmpə'laɪt] *a* mal educado.
impolitic [ɪm'pɔlɪtɪk] *a* poco político.
imponderable [ɪm'pɔndərəbl] *a* imponderable.
import *vt* [ɪm'pɔːt] importar ◆ *n* ['ɪmpɔːt] (*comm*) importación *f*; (*meaning*) significado, sentido ◆ *cpd* (*duty, licence etc*) de importación.
importance [ɪm'pɔːtəns] *n* importancia; **to be of great/little ~** tener mucha/poca importancia.
important [ɪm'pɔːtənt] *a* importante; **it's not ~** no importa, no tiene importancia; **it is ~ that** es importante que.
importantly [ɪm'pɔːtəntlɪ] *ad* (*pej*) dándose importancia; **but, more ~ ...** pero, lo más importante es ....
import duty *n* derechos *mpl* de importación.
imported [ɪm'pɔːtɪd] *a* importado.
importer [ɪm'pɔːtə*] *n* importador(a) *m/f*.
import licence (*US*) **import license** *n* licencia de importación.
impose [ɪm'pəuz] *vt* imponer ◆ *vi*: **to ~ on sb** abusar de uno.
imposing [ɪm'pəuzɪŋ] *a* imponente, impresionante.
imposition [ɪmpə'zɪʃn] *n* (*of tax etc*) imposición *f*; **to be an ~** (*on person*) molestar.
impossibility [ɪmpɔsə'bɪlɪtɪ] *n* imposibilidad *f*.
impossible [ɪm'pɔsɪbl] *a* imposible; (*person*) insoportable; **it is ~ for me to leave now** me es imposible salir ahora.
impossibly [ɪm'pɔsɪblɪ] *ad* imposiblemente.
impostor [ɪm'pɔstə*] *n* impostor(a) *m/f*.
impotence ['ɪmpətəns] *n* impotencia.
impotent ['ɪmpətənt] *a* impotente.
impound [ɪm'paund] *vt* embargar.
impoverished [ɪm'pɔvərɪʃt] *a* necesitado; (*land*) agotado.
impracticable [ɪm'præktɪkəbl] *a* no factible, irrealizable.
impractical [ɪm'præktɪkl] *a* (*person*) poco práctico.
imprecise [ɪmprɪ'saɪs] *a* impreciso.

impregnable [ɪm'prɛgnəbl] *a* invulnerable; (*castle*) inexpugnable.
impregnate ['ɪmprɛgneɪt] *vt* (*gen*) impregnar; (*soak*) empapar; (*fertilize*) fecundar.
impresario [ɪmprɪ'sɑːrɪəu] *n* empresario/a.
impress [ɪm'prɛs] *vt* impresionar; (*mark*) estampar ◆ *vi* hacer buena impresión; **to ~ sth on sb** convencer a uno de la importancia de algo.
impression [ɪm'prɛʃən] *n* impresión *f*; (*footprint etc*) huella; (*print run*) edición *f*; **to be under the ~ that** tener la impresión de que; **to make a good/bad ~ on sb** causar buena/mala impresión a uno.
impressionable [ɪm'prɛʃnəbl] *a* impresionable.
impressionist [ɪm'prɛʃənɪst] *n* impresionista *m/f*.
impressive [ɪm'prɛsɪv] *a* impresionante.
imprint ['ɪmprɪnt] *n* (*publishing*) pie *m* de imprenta; (*fig*) sello.
imprison [ɪm'prɪzn] *vt* encarcelar.
imprisonment [ɪm'prɪznmənt] *n* encarcelamiento; (*term of ~*) cárcel *f*; **life ~** cadena perpetua.
improbable [ɪm'prɔbəbl] *a* improbable, inverosímil.
impromptu [ɪm'prɔmptjuː] *a* improvisado ◆ *ad* de improviso.
improper [ɪm'prɔpə*] *a* (*incorrect*) impropio; (*unseemly*) indecoroso; (*indecent*) indecente.
impropriety [ɪmprə'praɪətɪ] *n* falta de decoro; (*indecency*) indecencia; (*of language*) impropiedad *f*.
improve [ɪm'pruːv] *vt* mejorar; (*foreign language*) perfeccionar ◆ *vi* mejorarse; (*pupils*) hacer progresos.
improve (up)on *vt fus* (*offer*) mejorar.
improvement [ɪm'pruːvmənt] *n* mejoramiento; perfección *f*; progreso; **to make ~s to** mejorar.
improvise ['ɪmprəvaɪz] *vt, vi* improvisar.
imprudence [ɪm'pruːdns] *n* imprudencia.
imprudent [ɪm'pruːdnt] *a* imprudente.
impudent ['ɪmpjudnt] *a* descarado, insolente.
impugn [ɪm'pjuːn] *vt* impugnar.
impulse ['ɪmpʌls] *n* impulso; **to act on ~** obrar sin reflexión.
impulse buying *n* compra impulsiva.
impulsive [ɪm'pʌlsɪv] *a* irreflexivo.
impunity [ɪm'pjuːnɪtɪ] *n*: **with ~** impunemente.
impure [ɪm'pjuə*] *a* (*adulterated*) adulterado; (*morally*) impuro.
impurity [ɪm'pjuərɪtɪ] *n* impureza.
IN *abbr* (*US post*) = Indiana.
in [ɪn] *prep* en; (*within*) dentro de; (*with time: during, within*): **~ 2 days** en 2 días; (: *after*): **~ 2 weeks** dentro de 2 semanas; (*with town, country*): **it's ~ France** está en

Francia ◆ *ad* dentro, adentro; *(fashionable)* de moda; **is he ~?** ¿está en casa?; ~ **the United States** en los Estados Unidos; ~ **1986** en 1986; ~ **May** en mayo; ~ **spring/autumn** en primavera/otoño; ~ **the morning** por la mañana; ~ **the country** en el campo; ~ **the distance** a lo lejos; ~ **town** en el centro (de la ciudad); ~ **the sun** al sol, bajo el sol; ~ **the rain** bajo la lluvia; ~ **French** en francés; ~ **writing** por escrito; ~ **person** en persona; ~ **here/there** aquí/allí (dentro); **1 ~ 10** uno sobre 10, uno de cada 10; ~ **hundreds** por centenares; **the best pupil** ~ **the class** el mejor alumno de la clase; **written** ~ **pencil** escrito con lápiz; **to pay** ~ **dollars** pagar en dólares; **a rise** ~ **prices** un aumento de precios; **once** ~ **a hundred years** una vez al siglo; ~ **saying this** al decir esto; **their party is** ~ su partido ha llegado al poder; **to be** ~ **teaching/publishing** dedicarse a la enseñanza/la publicación de libros; ~ **that** ya que; ~ **all** en total; **to ask sb** ~ invitar a uno a entrar; **to run/limp** ~ entrar corriendo/cojeando; **the ~s and outs** los pormenores.

in., ins *abbr* = **inch(es).**
inability [ɪnə'bɪlɪtɪ] *n* incapacidad *f*; ~ **to pay** incapacidad de pagar.
inaccessible [ɪnək'sɛsɪbl] *a* inaccesible.
inaccuracy [ɪn'ækjurəsɪ] *n* inexactitud *f*.
inaccurate [ɪn'ækjurət] *a* inexacto, incorrecto.
inaction [ɪn'ækʃən] *n* inacción *f*.
inactive [ɪn'æktɪv] *a* inactivo.
inactivity [ɪnæk'tɪvɪtɪ] *n* inactividad *f*.
inadequacy [ɪn'ædɪkwəsɪ] *n* insuficiencia; incapacidad *f*.
inadequate [ɪn'ædɪkwət] *a* (*insufficient*) insuficiente; (*unsuitable*) inadecuado; (*person*) incapaz.
inadmissible [ɪnəd'mɪsəbl] *a* improcedente, inadmisible.
inadvertent [ɪnəd'vəːtənt] *a* descuidado, involuntario.
inadvertently [ɪnəd'vəːtntlɪ] *ad* por descuido.
inadvisable [ɪnəd'vaɪzəbl] *a* poco aconsejable.
inane [ɪ'neɪn] *a* necio, fatuo.
inanimate [ɪn'ænɪmət] *a* inanimado.
inapplicable [ɪn'æplɪkəbl] *a* inaplicable.
inappropriate [ɪnə'prəuprɪət] *a* inadecuado.
inapt [ɪn'æpt] *a* impropio.
inaptitude [ɪn'æptɪtjuːd] *n* incapacidad *f*.
inarticulate [ɪnɑː'tɪkjulət] *a* (*person*) incapaz de expresarse; (*speech*) mal pronunciado.
inartistic [ɪnɑː'tɪstɪk] *a* antiestético.
inasmuch as [ɪnəz'mʌtʃ-] *ad* puesto que, ya que.
inattention [ɪnə'tɛnʃən] desatención *f*.
inattentive [ɪnə'tɛntɪv] *a* distraído.

inaudible [ɪn'ɔːdɪbl] *a* inaudible.
inaugural [ɪ'nɔːgjurəl] *a* (*speech*) de apertura.
inaugurate [ɪ'nɔːgjureɪt] *vt* inaugurar.
inauguration [ɪnɔːgju'reɪʃən] *n* ceremonia de apertura.
inauspicious [ɪnɔːs'pɪʃəs] *a* poco propicio, inoportuno.
in-between [ɪnbɪ'twiːn] *a* intermedio.
inborn [ɪn'bɔːn] *a* (*feeling*) innato.
inbred [ɪn'brɛd] *a* innato; (*family*) consanguíneo.
inbreeding [ɪn'briːdɪŋ] *n* endogamia.
Inc. *abbr* = **incorporated.**
Inca ['ɪŋkə] *a* (*also:* ~**n**) incaico, de los incas ◆ *n* inca *m/f*.
incalculable [ɪn'kælkjuləbl] *a* incalculable.
incapability [ɪnkeɪpə'bɪlɪtɪ] *n* incapacidad *f*.
incapable [ɪn'keɪpəbl] *a*: ~ **(of doing sth)** incapaz (de hacer algo).
incapacitate [ɪnkə'pæsɪteɪt] *vt*: **to** ~ **sb** incapacitar a uno.
incapacitated [ɪnkə'pæsɪteɪtɪd] *a* incapacitado.
incapacity [ɪnkə'pæsɪtɪ] *n* (*inability*) incapacidad *f*.
incarcerate [ɪn'kɑːsəreɪt] *vt* encarcelar.
incarnate *a* [ɪn'kɑːnɪt] en persona ◆ *vt* ['ɪnkɑːneɪt] encarnar.
incarnation [ɪnkɑː'neɪʃən] *n* encarnación *f*.
incendiary [ɪn'sɛndɪərɪ] *a* incendiario ◆ *n* (*bomb*) bomba incendiaria.
incense *n* ['ɪnsɛns] incienso ◆ *vt* [ɪn'sɛns] (*anger*) indignar, encolerizar.
incentive [ɪn'sɛntɪv] *n* incentivo, estímulo.
incentive bonus *n* incentivo de bonificación extra.
incentive scheme *n* plan *m* de incentivos.
inception [ɪn'sɛpʃən] *n* comienzo, principio.
incessant [ɪn'sɛsnt] *a* incesante, continuo.
incessantly [ɪn'sɛsəntlɪ] *ad* constantemente.
incest ['ɪnsɛst] *n* incesto.
inch [ɪntʃ] *n* pulgada; **to be within an** ~ **of** estar a dos dedos de; **he didn't give an** ~ no dio concesión alguna; **a few ~es** unas pulgadas.
inch forward *vi* avanzar palmo a palmo.
incidence ['ɪnsɪdns] *n* (*of crime, disease*) incidencia.
incident ['ɪnsɪdnt] *n* incidente *m*; (*in book*) episodio.
incidental [ɪnsɪ'dɛntl] *a* circunstancial, accesorio; (*unplanned*) fortuito; ~ **to** relacionado con; ~ **expenses** gastos *mpl* imprevistos.
incidentally [ɪnsɪ'dɛntəlɪ] *ad* (*by the way*) a propósito.
incidental music *n* música de fondo.
incinerate [ɪn'sɪnəreɪt] *vt* incinerar, quemar.
incinerator [ɪn'sɪnəreɪtə*] *n* incinerador *m*.
incipient [ɪn'sɪpɪənt] *a* incipiente.

incision [ɪn'sɪʒən] n incisión f.
incisive [ɪn'saɪsɪv] a (mind) penetrante; (remark etc) incisivo.
incisor [ɪn'saɪzə*] n incisivo.
incite [ɪn'saɪt] vt provocar.
incl. abbr = including, inclusive (of).
inclement [ɪn'klɛmənt] a inclemente.
inclination [ɪnklɪ'neɪʃən] n (tendency) tendencia, inclinación f.
incline n ['ɪnklaɪn] pendiente f, cuesta ♦ vb [ɪn'klaɪn] vt (slope) inclinar; (head) poner de lado ♦ vi inclinarse; **to be ~d to** (tend) ser propenso a; (be willing) estar dispuesto a.
include [ɪn'kluːd] vt incluir, comprender; (in letter) adjuntar; **the tip is/is not ~d** la propina está/no está incluida.
including [ɪn'kluːdɪŋ] prep incluso, inclusive; **~ tip** propina incluida.
inclusion [ɪn'kluːʒən] n inclusión f.
inclusive [ɪn'kluːsɪv] a inclusivo ♦ ad inclusive; **~ of tax** incluidos los impuestos; **$50, ~ of all surcharges** 50 dólares, incluidos todos los sobreimpuestos.
incognito [ɪnkɔg'niːtəʊ] ad de incógnito.
incoherent [ɪnkəʊ'hɪərənt] a incoherente.
income ['ɪnkʌm] n (personal) ingresos mpl; (from property etc) renta; (profit) rédito; **gross/net ~** ingresos mpl brutos/netos; **~ and expenditure account** cuenta de gastos e ingresos.
income bracket n categoría económica.
income support n (Brit) subsidio estatal para personas con un nivel de ingresos muy bajo.
income tax n impuesto sobre la renta.
income tax inspector n inspector(a) m/f fiscal.
income tax return n registro fiscal.
incoming ['ɪnkʌmɪŋ] a (passengers) de llegada; (government, tenant) entrante; **~ flight** vuelo entrante.
incommunicado ['ɪnkəmjuːnɪ'kɑːdəʊ] a: **to hold sb ~** mantener incomunicado a uno.
incomparable [ɪn'kɔmpərəbl] a incomparable, sin par.
incompatible [ɪnkəm'pætɪbl] a incompatible.
incompetence [ɪn'kɔmpɪtəns] n incompetencia.
incompetent [ɪn'kɔmpɪtənt] a incompetente.
incomplete [ɪnkəm'pliːt] a incompleto; (unfinished) sin terminar.
incomprehensible [ɪnkɔmprɪ'hɛnsɪbl] a incomprensible.
inconceivable [ɪnkən'siːvəbl] a inconcebible.
inconclusive [ɪnkən'kluːsɪv] a sin resultado (definitivo); (argument) poco convincente.
incongruity [ɪnkɔŋ'gruːɪtɪ] n incongruencia.
incongruous [ɪn'kɔŋgruəs] a discordante.
inconsequential [ɪnkɔnsɪ'kwɛnʃl] a in-

transcendente.
inconsiderable [ɪnkən'sɪdərəbl] a insignificante.
inconsiderate [ɪnkən'sɪdərət] a desconsiderado; **how ~ of him!** ¡qué falta de consideración (de su parte)!
inconsistency [ɪnkən'sɪstənsɪ] n inconsecuencia; (of actions etc) incompatibilidad f, falta de lógica; (of work) carácter m desigual, inconsistencia; (of statement etc) contradicción f, anomalía.
inconsistent [ɪnkən'sɪstnt] a inconsecuente; **~ with** que no concuerda con.
inconsolable [ɪnkən'səʊləbl] a inconsolable.
inconspicuous [ɪnkən'spɪkjuəs] a (discreet) discreto; (person) que llama poco la atención.
inconstancy [ɪn'kɔnstənsɪ] n inconstancia.
inconstant [ɪn'kɔnstənt] a inconstante.
incontinence [ɪn'kɔntɪnəns] n incontinencia.
incontinent [ɪn'kɔntɪnənt] a incontinente.
incontrovertible [ɪnkɔntrə'vəːtəbl] a incontrovertible.
inconvenience [ɪnkən'viːnjəns] n (gen) inconvenientes mpl; (trouble) molestia, incomodidad f ♦ vt incomodar; **to put sb to great ~** causar mucha molestia a uno; **don't ~ yourself** no te molestes.
inconvenient [ɪnkən'viːnjənt] a incómodo, poco práctico; (time, place) inoportuno; **that time is very ~ for me** esa hora me es muy inconveniente.
incorporate [ɪn'kɔːpəreɪt] vt incorporar; (contain) comprender; (add) agregar.
incorporated [ɪn'kɔːpəreɪtɪd] a: **~ company** (US: abbr **Inc.**) ≈ Sociedad f Anónima (S.A.).
incorrect [ɪnkə'rɛkt] a incorrecto.
incorrigible [ɪn'kɔrɪdʒəbl] a incorregible.
incorruptible [ɪnkə'rʌptɪbl] a incorruptible.
increase n ['ɪnkriːs] aumento ♦ vb [ɪn'kriːs] vi aumentarse; (grow) crecer; (price) subir ♦ vt aumentar; **an ~ of 5%** un aumento de 5%; **to be on the ~** estar or ir en aumento.
increasing [ɪn'kriːsɪŋ] a (number) creciente, que va en aumento.
increasingly [ɪn'kriːsɪŋlɪ] ad de más en más, cada vez más.
incredible [ɪn'krɛdɪbl] a increíble.
incredibly [ɪn'krɛdɪblɪ] ad increíblemente.
incredulity [ɪnkrɪ'djuːlɪtɪ] n incredulidad f.
incredulous [ɪn'krɛdjuləs] a incrédulo.
increment ['ɪnkrɪmənt] n aumento, incremento.
incriminate [ɪn'krɪmɪneɪt] vt incriminar.
incriminating [ɪn'krɪmɪneɪtɪŋ] a incriminador(a).
incrust [ɪn'krʌst] vt = encrust.
incubate ['ɪnkjubeɪt] vt (eggs) incubar, empollar ♦ vi (egg, disease) incubar.
incubation [ɪnkju'beɪʃən] n incubación f.

incubation period *n* período de incubación.

incubator ['ɪnkjubeɪtə*] *n* incubadora.

inculcate ['ɪnkʌlkeɪt] *vt*: **to ~ sth in sb** inculcar algo en uno.

incumbent [ɪn'kʌmbənt] *n* ocupante *m/f* ♦ *a*: **it is ~ on him to...** le incumbe... .

incur [ɪn'kə:*] *vt (expenses)* incurrir en; *(loss)* sufrir.

incurable [ɪn'kjuərəbl] *a* incurable.

incursion [ɪn'kə:ʃən] *n* incursión *f*.

indebted [ɪn'detɪd] *a*: **to be ~ to sb** estar agradecido a uno.

indecency [ɪn'di:snsɪ] *n* indecencia.

indecent [ɪn'di:snt] *a* indecente.

indecent assault *n (Brit)* atentado contra el pudor.

indecent exposure *n* exhibicionismo.

indecipherable [ɪndɪ'saɪfərəbl] *a* indescifrable.

indecision [ɪndɪ'sɪʒən] *n* indecisión *f*.

indecisive [ɪndɪ'saɪsɪv] *a* indeciso; *(discussion)* no resuelto, inconcluyente.

indeed [ɪn'di:d] *ad* efectivamente, en realidad; **yes ~!** ¡claro que sí!

indefatigable [ɪndɪ'fætɪgəbl] *a* incansable, infatigable.

indefensible [ɪndɪ'fensəbl] *a (conduct)* injustificable.

indefinable [ɪndɪ'faɪnəbl] *a* indefinible.

indefinite [ɪn'defɪnɪt] *a* indefinido; *(uncertain)* incierto.

indefinitely [ɪn'defɪnɪtlɪ] *ad (wait)* indefinidamente.

indelible [ɪn'delɪbl] *a* imborrable.

indelicate [ɪn'delɪkɪt] *a (tactless)* indiscreto, inoportuno; *(not polite)* indelicado.

indemnify [ɪn'demnɪfaɪ] *vt* indemnizar, resarcir.

indemnity [ɪn'demnɪtɪ] *n (insurance)* indemnidad *f*; *(compensation)* indemnización *f*.

indent [ɪn'dent] *vt (text)* sangrar.

indentation [ɪnden'teɪʃən] *n* mella; *(TYP)* sangría.

indenture [ɪn'dentʃə*] *n* escritura, instrumento.

independence [ɪndɪ'pendns] *n* independencia.

independent [ɪndɪ'pendənt] *a* independiente; **to become ~** independizarse.

indescribable [ɪndɪ'skraɪbəbl] *a* indescriptible.

indestructible [ɪndɪs'trʌktəbl] *a* indestructible.

indeterminate [ɪndɪ'tə:mɪnɪt] *a* indeterminado.

index ['ɪndeks] *n (pl: ~es: in book)* índice *m*; (: *in library etc)* catálogo; *(pl:* **indices** ['ɪndɪsi:z]: *ratio, sign)* exponente *m*.

index card *n* ficha.

index finger *n* índice *m*.

index-linked ['ɪndeks'lɪŋkt], *(US)* indexed ['ɪndekst] *a* indexado.

India ['ɪndɪə] *n* la India.

Indian ['ɪndɪən] *a, n* indio/a *m/f*; *(American ~)* indio/a *m/f* de América, amerindio/a *m/f*; **Red ~** piel roja *m/f*.

Indian Ocean *n*: **the ~** el Océano Índico, el Mar de las Indias.

Indian summer *n (fig)* veranillo de San Martín.

india rubber *n* caucho.

indicate ['ɪndɪkeɪt] *vt* indicar ♦ *vi (Brit AUT)*: **to ~ left/right** indicar a la izquierda/a la derecha.

indication [ɪndɪ'keɪʃən] *n* indicio, señal *f*.

indicative [ɪn'dɪkətɪv] *a*: **to be ~ of sth** indicar algo ♦ *n (LING)* indicativo.

indicator ['ɪndɪkeɪtə*] *n (gen)* indicador *m*.

indices ['ɪndɪsi:z] *npl of* **index**.

indict [ɪn'daɪt] *vt* acusar.

indictable [ɪn'daɪtəbl] *a*: **~ offence** delito procesable.

indictment [ɪn'daɪtmənt] *n* acusación *f*.

indifference [ɪn'dɪfrəns] *n* indiferencia.

indifferent [ɪn'dɪfrənt] *a* indiferente; *(poor)* regular.

indigenous [ɪn'dɪdʒɪnəs] *a* indígena.

indigestible [ɪndɪ'dʒestɪbl] *a* indigesto.

indigestion [ɪndɪ'dʒestʃən] *n* indigestión *f*.

indignant [ɪn'dɪgnənt] *a*: **to be ~ about sth** indignarse por algo.

indignation [ɪndɪg'neɪʃən] *n* indignación *f*.

indignity [ɪn'dɪgnɪtɪ] *n* indignidad *f*.

indigo ['ɪndɪgəu] *a (colour)* de color añil ♦ *n* añil *m*.

indirect [ɪndɪ'rekt] *a* indirecto.

indirectly [ɪndɪ'rektlɪ] *ad* indirectamente.

indiscernible [ɪndɪ'sə:nəbl] *a* imperceptible.

indiscreet [ɪndɪ'skri:t] *a* indiscreto, imprudente.

indiscretion [ɪndɪ'skreʃən] *n* indiscreción *f*, imprudencia.

indiscriminate [ɪndɪ'skrɪmɪnət] *a* indiscriminado.

indispensable [ɪndɪ'spensəbl] *a* indispensable, imprescindible.

indisposed [ɪndɪ'spəuzd] *a (unwell)* indispuesto.

indisposition [ɪndɪspə'zɪʃən] *n* indisposición *f*.

indisputable [ɪndɪ'spju:təbl] *a* incontestable.

indistinct [ɪndɪ'stɪŋkt] *a* indistinto.

indistinguishable [ɪndɪ'stɪŋgwɪʃəbl] *a* indistinguible.

individual [ɪndɪ'vɪdjuəl] *n* individuo ♦ *a* individual; *(personal)* personal; *(for/of one only)* particular.

individualist [ɪndɪ'vɪdjuəlɪst] *n* individualista *m/f*.

individuality [ɪndɪvɪdju'ælɪtɪ] *n* individualidad *f*.

individually [ɪndɪ'vɪdjuəlɪ] *ad* indivi-

dualmente; particularmente.
indivisible [ɪndɪ'vɪzəbl] *a* indivisible.
Indo-China ['ɪndəu'tʃaɪnə] *n* Indochina.
indoctrinate [ɪn'dɔktrɪneɪt] *vt* adoctrinar.
indoctrination [ɪndɔktrɪ'neɪʃən] *n* adoctrinamiento.
indolence ['ɪndələns] *n* indolencia.
indolent ['ɪndələnt] *a* indolente, perezoso.
Indonesia [ɪndə'niːzɪə] *n* Indonesia.
Indonesian [ɪndə'niːzɪən] *a, n* indonesio/a *m/f*.
indoor ['ɪndɔː*] *a* (*swimming pool*) cubierto; (*plant*) de interior; (*sport*) bajo cubierta.
indoors [ɪn'dɔːz] *ad* dentro; (*at home*) en casa.
indubitable [ɪn'djuːbɪtəbl] *a* indudable.
indubitably [ɪn'djuːbɪtəblɪ] *ad* indudablemente.
induce [ɪn'djuːs] *vt* inducir, persuadir; (*bring about*) producir; **to ~ sb to do sth** persuadir a uno a que haga algo.
inducement [ɪn'djuːsmənt] *n* (*incentive*) incentivo, aliciente *m*.
induct [ɪn'dʌkt] *vt* iniciar; (*in job, rank, position*) instalar.
induction [ɪn'dʌkʃən] *n* (*MED*: *of birth*) inducción *f*.
induction course *n* (*Brit*) curso de inducción.
indulge [ɪn'dʌldʒ] *vt* (*whim*) satisfacer; (*person*) complacer; (*child*) mimar ◆ *vi*: **to ~ in** darse el gusto de.
indulgence [ɪn'dʌldʒəns] *n* vicio.
indulgent [ɪn'dʌldʒənt] *a* indulgente.
industrial [ɪn'dʌstrɪəl] *a* industrial.
industrial action *n* huelga.
industrial estate *n* (*Brit*) polígono *or* zona (*LAm*) industrial.
industrial goods *npl* bienes *mpl* de producción.
industrialist [ɪn'dʌstrɪəlɪst] *n* industrial *m/f*.
industrialize [ɪn'dʌstrɪəlaɪz] *vt* industrializar.
industrial park *n* (*US*) = **industrial estate**.
industrial relations *npl* relaciones *fpl* empresariales.
industrial tribunal *n* magistratura del trabajo, tribunal *m* laboral.
industrial unrest *n* (*Brit*) agitación *f* obrera.
industrious [ɪn'dʌstrɪəs] *a* (*gen*) trabajador(a); (*student*) aplicado.
industry ['ɪndəstrɪ] *n* industria; (*diligence*) aplicación *f*.
inebriated [ɪ'niːbrɪeɪtɪd] *a* borracho.
inedible [ɪn'ɛdɪbl] *a* incomestible, incomible; (*plant etc*) no comestible.
ineffective [ɪnɪ'fɛktɪv], **ineffectual** [ɪnɪ'fɛktʃuəl] *a* ineficaz, inútil.
inefficiency [ɪnɪ'fɪʃənsɪ] *n* ineficacia.
inefficient [ɪnɪ'fɪʃənt] *a* ineficaz, ineficiente.

inelegant [ɪn'ɛlɪgənt] *a* poco elegante.
ineligible [ɪn'ɛlɪdʒɪbl] *a* inelegible.
inept [ɪ'nɛpt] *a* incompetente, incapaz.
ineptitude [ɪ'nɛptɪtjuːd] *n* incapacidad *f*, ineptitud *f*.
inequality [ɪnɪ'kwɒlɪtɪ] *n* desigualdad *f*.
inequitable [ɪn'ɛkwɪtəbl] *a* injusto.
ineradicable [ɪnɪ'rædɪkəbl] *a* inextirpable.
inert [ɪ'nɜːt] *a* inerte, inactivo; (*immobile*) inmóvil.
inertia [ɪ'nɜːʃə] *n* inercia; (*laziness*) pereza.
inertia-reel seat-belt [ɪ'nɜːʃə'riːl-] *n* cinturón *m* de seguridad de inercia.
inescapable [ɪnɪ'skeɪpəbl] *a* ineludible, inevitable.
inessential [ɪnɪ'sɛnʃl] *a* no esencial.
inestimable [ɪn'ɛstɪməbl] *a* inestimable.
inevitability [ɪnɛvɪtə'bɪlɪtɪ] *n* inevitabilidad *f*.
inevitable [ɪn'ɛvɪtəbl] *a* inevitable; (*necessary*) forzoso.
inevitably [ɪn'ɛvɪtəblɪ] *ad* inevitablemente; **as ~ happens** ... como siempre pasa ....
inexact [ɪnɪg'zækt] *a* inexacto.
inexcusable [ɪnɪks'kjuːzəbl] *a* imperdonable.
inexhaustible [ɪnɪg'zɔːstɪbl] *a* inagotable.
inexorable [ɪn'ɛksərəbl] *a* inexorable, implacable.
inexpensive [ɪnɪk'spɛnsɪv] *a* económico.
inexperience [ɪnɪk'spɪərɪəns] *n* falta de experiencia.
inexperienced [ɪnɪk'spɪərɪənst] *a* inexperto; **to be ~ in sth** no tener experiencia en algo.
inexplicable [ɪnɪk'splɪkəbl] *a* inexplicable.
inexpressible [ɪnɪk'sprɛsəbl] *a* inexpresable.
inextricable [ɪnɪks'trɪkəbl] *a* inseparable.
inextricably [ɪnɪks'trɪkəblɪ] *ad* indisolublemente.
infallibility [ɪnfælə'bɪlɪtɪ] *n* infalibilidad *f*.
infallible [ɪn'fælɪbl] *a* infalible.
infamous ['ɪnfəməs] *a* infame.
infamy ['ɪnfəmɪ] *n* infamia.
infancy ['ɪnfənsɪ] *n* infancia.
infant ['ɪnfənt] *n* niño/a.
infantile ['ɪnfəntaɪl] *a* infantil; (*pej*) aniñado.
infant mortality *n* mortandad *f* infantil.
infantry ['ɪnfəntrɪ] *n* infantería.
infantryman ['ɪnfəntrɪmən] *n* soldado de infantería.
infant school *n* (*Brit*) escuela de párvulos.
infatuated [ɪn'fætjueɪtɪd] *a*: **~ with** (*in love*) loco por; **to become ~** (**with sb**) enamorarse, encapricharse (con uno).
infatuation [ɪnfætju'eɪʃən] *n* enamoramiento.
infect [ɪn'fɛkt] *vt* (*wound*) infectar; (*person*) contagiar; (*fig: pej*) corromper; **~ed with** (*illness*) contagiado de; **to become ~ed**

(*wound*) infectarse.
infectio [ɪnˈfɛkʃən] *n* infección *f*; (*fig*) contagio.
infectious [ɪnˈfɛkʃəs] *a* contagioso; (*also fig*) infeccioso.
infer [ɪnˈfəː*] *vt* deducir, inferir; **to ~ (from)** inferir (de), deducir (de).
inference [ˈɪnfərəns] *n* deducción *f*, inferencia.
inferior [ɪnˈfɪərɪə*] *a, n* inferior *m/f*; **to feel ~** sentirse inferior.
inferiority [ɪnfɪərɪˈɔrətɪ] *n* inferioridad *f*.
inferiority complex *n* complejo de inferioridad.
infernal [ɪnˈfəːnl] *a* infernal.
inferno [ɪnˈfəːnəu] *n* infierno; (*fig*) hoguera.
infertile [ɪnˈfəːtaɪl] *a* estéril; (*person*) infecundo.
infertility [ɪnfəːˈtɪlɪtɪ] *n* esterilidad *f*; infecundidad *f*.
infest [ɪnˈfɛst] *vt* infestar.
infested [ɪnˈfɛstɪd] *a*: **~ (with)** plagado (de).
infidel [ˈɪnfɪdəl] *n* infiel *m/f*.
infidelity [ɪnfɪˈdɛlɪtɪ] *n* infidelidad *f*.
in-fighting [ˈɪnfaɪtɪŋ] *n* (*fig*) lucha(s) *f(pl)* interna(s).
infiltrate [ˈɪnfɪltreɪt] *vt* (*troops etc*) infiltrarse en ◆ *vi* infiltrarse.
infinite [ˈɪnfɪnɪt] *a* infinito; **an ~ amount of money/time** un sinfín de dinero/tiempo.
infinitely [ˈɪnfɪnɪtlɪ] *ad* infinitamente.
infinitesimal [ɪnfɪnɪˈtɛsɪməl] *a* infinitésimo.
infinitive [ɪnˈfɪnɪtɪv] *n* infinitivo.
infinity [ɪnˈfɪnɪtɪ] *n* (*also* MATH) infinito; (*an ~*) infinidad *f*.
infirm [ɪnˈfəːm] *a* enfermo, débil.
infirmary [ɪnˈfəːmərɪ] *n* hospital *m*.
infirmity [ɪnˈfəːmɪtɪ] *n* debilidad *f*; (*illness*) enfermedad *f*, achaque *m*.
inflame [ɪnˈfleɪm] *vt* inflamar.
inflamed [ɪnˈfleɪmd] *a*: **to become ~** inflamarse.
inflammable [ɪnˈflæməbl] *a* (*Brit*) inflamable; (*situation etc*) explosivo.
inflammation [ɪnfləˈmeɪʃən] *n* inflamación *f*.
inflammatory [ɪnˈflæmətərɪ] *a* (*speech*) incendiario.
inflatable [ɪnˈfleɪtəbl] *a* inflable.
inflate [ɪnˈfleɪt] *vt* (*tyre, balloon*) inflar; (*fig*) hinchar.
inflated [ɪnˈfleɪtɪd] *a* (*tyre etc*) inflado; (*price, self-esteem etc*) exagerado.
inflation [ɪnˈfleɪʃən] *n* (ECON) inflación *f*.
inflationary [ɪnˈfleɪʃnərɪ] *a* inflacionario.
inflationary spiral *n* espiral *f* inflacionista.
inflexible [ɪnˈflɛksɪbl] *a* inflexible.
inflict [ɪnˈflɪkt] *vt*: **to ~ on** infligir en; (*tax etc*) imponer a.
infliction [ɪnˈflɪkʃən] *n* imposición *f*.
in-flight [ˈɪnflaɪt] *a* durante el vuelo.

inflow [ˈɪnfləu] *n* afluencia.
influence [ˈɪnfluəns] *n* influencia ◆ *vt* influir en, influenciar; (*persuade*) sugestionar; **under the ~ of alcohol** en estado de embriaguez.
influential [ɪnfluˈɛnʃl] *a* influyente.
influenza [ɪnfluˈɛnzə] *n* gripe *f*.
influx [ˈɪnflʌks] *n* afluencia.
inform [ɪnˈfɔːm] *vt*: **to ~ sb of sth** informar a uno sobre *or* de algo; (*warn*) avisar a uno de algo; (*communicate*) comunicar algo a uno ◆ *vi* : **to ~ on sb** delatar a uno.
informal [ɪnˈfɔːml] *a* (*manner, tone*) desenfadado; (*dress, interview, occasion*) informal.
informality [ɪnfɔːˈmælɪtɪ] *n* falta de ceremonia; (*intimacy*) intimidad *f*; (*familiarity*) familiaridad *f*; (*ease*) afabilidad *f*.
informally [ɪnˈfɔːməlɪ] *ad* sin ceremonia; (*invite*) informalmente.
informant [ɪnˈfɔːmənt] *n* informante *m/f*.
informatics [ɪnfɔːˈmætɪks] *n* informática.
information [ɪnfəˈmeɪʃən] *n* información *f*; (*news*) noticias *fpl*; (*knowledge*) conocimientos *mpl*; (LAW) delación *f*; **a piece of ~** un dato; **for your ~** para que se informe usted, para su información.
information bureau *n* oficina de informaciones.
information processing *n* procesamiento de datos.
information retrieval *n* recuperación *f* de la información.
information science *n* gestión *f* de la información.
information technology *n* informática.
informative [ɪnˈfɔːmətɪv] *a* informativo.
informed [ɪnˈfɔːmd] *a* (*observer*) informado, al corriente; **an ~ guess** una opinión bien fundamentada.
informer [ɪnˈfɔːmə*] *n* delator(a) *m/f*; (*also*: **police ~**) soplón/ona *m/f*.
infra dig [ˈɪnfrəˈdɪg] *a abbr* (*col*: = *infra dignitatem*) denigrante.
infra-red [ɪnfrəˈrɛd] *a* infrarrojo.
infrastructure [ˈɪnfrəstrʌktʃə*] *n* (*of system etc*, ECON) infraestructura.
infrequent [ɪnˈfriːkwənt] *a* infrecuente.
infringe [ɪnˈfrɪndʒ] *vt* infringir, violar ◆ *vi*: **to ~ on** abusar de.
infringement [ɪnˈfrɪndʒmənt] *n* infracción *f*; (*of rights*) usurpación *f*; (SPORT) falta.
infuriate [ɪnˈfjuərɪeɪt] *vt*: **to become ~d** ponerse furioso.
infuriating [ɪnˈfjuərɪeɪtɪŋ] *a*: **I find it ~** me saca de quicio.
infuse [ɪnˈfjuːz] *vt* (*with courage, enthusiasm*): **to ~ sb with sth** infundir a uno con algo.
infusion [ɪnˈfjuːʒən] *n* (*tea etc*) infusión *f*.
ingenious [ɪnˈdʒiːnjəs] *a* ingenioso.
ingenuity [ɪndʒɪˈnjuːɪtɪ] *n* ingeniosidad *f*.

ingenuous [ɪn'dʒɛnjuəs] *a* ingenuo.

ingot ['ɪŋgət] *n* lingote *m*, barra.

ingrained [ɪn'greɪnd] *a* arraigado.

ingratiate [ɪn'greɪʃɪeɪt] *vt*: **to ~ o.s. with** congraciarse con.

ingratiating [ɪn'greɪʃɪeɪtɪŋ] *a* (*smile*, *speech*) insinuante; (*person*) zalamero, congraciador(a).

ingratitude [ɪn'grætɪtjuːd] *n* ingratitud *f*.

ingredient [ɪn'griːdɪənt] *n* ingrediente *m*.

ingrowing ['ɪngrəʊɪŋ] *a*: **~ (toe)nail** uña encarnada.

inhabit [ɪn'hæbɪt] *vt* vivir en; (*occupy*) ocupar.

inhabitable [ɪn'hæbɪtəbl] *a* habitable.

inhabitant [ɪn'hæbɪtənt] *n* habitante *m/f*.

inhale [ɪn'heɪl] *vt* inhalar ♦ *vi* (*in smoking*) tragar.

inherent [ɪn'hɪərənt] *a*: **~ in** *or* **to** inherente a.

inherently [ɪn'hɪərəntlɪ] *a* esencialmente.

inherit [ɪn'hɛrɪt] *vt* heredar.

inheritance [ɪn'hɛrɪtəns] *n* herencia; (*fig*) patrimonio.

inhibit [ɪn'hɪbɪt] *vt* inhibir, impedir; **to ~ sb from doing sth** impedir a uno hacer algo.

inhibited [ɪn'hɪbɪtɪd] *a* (*person*) cohibido.

inhibition [ɪnhɪ'bɪʃən] *n* cohibición *f*.

inhospitable [ɪnhɔs'pɪtəbl] *a* (*person*) inhospitalario; (*place*) inhóspito.

inhuman [ɪn'hjuːmən] *a* inhumano.

inhumane [ɪnhjuː'meɪn] *a* inhumano.

inimitable [ɪ'nɪmɪtəbl] *a* inimitable.

iniquity [ɪ'nɪkwɪtɪ] *n* iniquidad *f*; (*injustice*) injusticia.

initial [ɪ'nɪʃl] *a* inicial; (*first*) primero ♦ *n* inicial *f* ♦ *vt* firmar con las iniciales; **~s** *npl* iniciales *fpl*; (*abbreviation*) siglas *fpl*.

initialize [ɪ'nɪʃəlaɪz] *vt* (*COMPUT*) inicializar.

initially [ɪ'nɪʃəlɪ] *ad* al principio.

initiate [ɪ'nɪʃɪeɪt] *vt* (*start*) iniciar; **to ~ sb into a secret** iniciar a uno en un secreto; **to ~ proceedings against sb** (*LAW*) entablar una demanda contra uno.

initiation [ɪnɪʃɪ'eɪʃən] *n* (*into secret etc*) iniciación *f*; (*beginning*) comienzo.

initiative [ɪ'nɪʃətɪv] *n* iniciativa; **to take the ~** tomar la iniciativa.

inject [ɪn'dʒɛkt] *vt* inyectar; (*money*, *enthusiasm*) aportar.

injection [ɪn'dʒɛkʃən] *n* inyección *f*; **to have an ~** hacerse inyectar.

injudicious [ɪndʒuː'dɪʃəs] *a* imprudente, indiscreto.

injunction [ɪn'dʒʌŋkʃən] *n* entredicho, interdicto.

injure ['ɪndʒə*] *vt* herir; (*hurt*) lastimar; (*fig: reputation etc*) perjudicar; (*feelings*) herir; **to ~ o.s** hacerse daño, lastimarse.

injured ['ɪndʒəd] *a* (*also fig*) herido; **~ party** (*LAW*) parte *f* perjudicada.

injurious [ɪn'dʒuərɪəs] *a*: **~ (to)** perjudicial (a).

injury ['ɪndʒərɪ] *n* herida, lesión *f*; (*wrong*) perjuicio, daño; **to escape without ~** salir ileso.

injury time *n* (*SPORT*) descuento.

injustice [ɪn'dʒʌstɪs] *n* injusticia; **you do me an ~** usted es injusto conmigo.

ink [ɪŋk] *n* tinta.

ink-jet printer ['ɪŋkdʒɛt-] *n* impresora de chorro de tinta.

inkling ['ɪŋklɪŋ] *n* sospecha; (*idea*) idea.

inkpad ['ɪŋkpæd] *n* almohadilla.

inlaid ['ɪnleɪd] *a* (*wood*) taraceado; (*tiles*) entarimado.

inland *a* ['ɪnlənd] interior; (*town*) del interior ♦ *ad* [ɪn'lænd] tierra adentro.

Inland Revenue *n* (*Brit*) Hacienda.

in-laws ['ɪnlɔːz] *npl* suegros *mpl*.

inlet ['ɪnlɛt] *n* (*GEO*) ensenada, cala; (*TECH*) admisión *f*, entrada.

inmate ['ɪnmeɪt] *n* (*in prison*) preso/a, presidiario/a; (*in asylum*) internado/a.

inmost ['ɪnməʊst] *a* más íntimo, más secreto.

inn [ɪn] *n* posada, mesón *m*.

innards ['ɪnədz] *npl* (*col*) tripas *fpl*.

innate [ɪ'neɪt] *a* innato.

inner ['ɪnə*] *a* interior, interno.

inner city *n* barrios deprimidos del centro de una ciudad.

innermost ['ɪnəməʊst] *a* más íntimo, más secreto.

inner tube *n* (*of tyre*) cámara, llanta (*LAm*).

innings ['ɪnɪŋz] *n* (*CRICKET*) entrada, turno.

innocence ['ɪnəsns] *n* inocencia.

innocent ['ɪnəsnt] *a* inocente.

innocuous [ɪ'nɔkjuəs] *a* inocuo.

innovation [ɪnəʊ'veɪʃən] *n* novedad *f*.

innuendo, **~es** [ɪnjʊ'ɛndəʊ] *n* indirecta.

innumerable [ɪ'njuːmrəbl] *a* innumerable.

inoculate [ɪ'nɔkjuleɪt] *vt*: **to ~ sb with sth/against sth** inocular *or* vacunar a uno con algo/contra algo.

inoculation [ɪnɔkju'leɪʃən] *n* inoculación *f*.

inoffensive [ɪnə'fɛnsɪv] *a* inofensivo.

inopportune [ɪn'ɔpətjuːn] *a* inoportuno.

inordinate [ɪ'nɔːdɪnət] *a* excesivo, desmesurado.

inordinately [ɪ'nɔːdɪnətlɪ] *ad* excesivamente, desmesuradamente.

inorganic [ɪnɔː'gaenɪk] *a* inorgánico.

in-patient ['ɪnpeɪʃənt] *n* paciente *m/f* interno/a.

input ['ɪnput] *n* (*ELEC*) entrada; (*COMPUT*) entrada de datos ♦ *vt* (*COMPUT*) introducir, entrar.

inquest ['ɪnkwɛst] *n* (*coroner's*) encuesta judicial.

inquire [ɪn'kwaɪə*] *vi* preguntar ♦ *vt*: **to ~ when/where/whether** preguntar cuándo/dónde/si; **to ~ about** (*person*) preguntar por; (*fact*) informarse de.

inquire into vt fus: **to ~ into sth** investigar or indagar algo.

inquiring [ɪn'kwaɪərɪŋ] a (mind) penetrante; (look) interrogativo.

inquiry [ɪn'kwaɪərɪ] n pregunta; (LAW) investigación f, pesquisa; (commission) comisión f investigadora; **to hold an ~ into sth** montar una investigación sobre algo.

inquiry desk n mesa de informes.

inquiry office n (Brit) oficina de informaciones.

inquisition [ɪnkwɪ'zɪʃən] n inquisición f.

inquisitive [ɪn'kwɪzɪtɪv] a (mind) inquisitivo; (person) fisgón/ona.

inroad ['ɪnrəud] n incursión f; (fig) invasión f; **to make ~s into** (time) ocupar parte de; (savings, supplies) agotar parte de.

insane [ɪn'seɪn] a loco; (MED) demente.

insanitary [ɪn'sænɪtərɪ] a insalubre.

insanity [ɪn'sænɪtɪ] n demencia, locura.

insatiable [ɪn'seɪʃəbl] a insaciable.

inscribe [ɪn'skraɪb] vt inscribir; (book etc): **to ~ (to sb)** dedicar (a uno).

inscription [ɪn'skrɪpʃən] n (gen) inscripción f; (in book) dedicatoria.

inscrutable [ɪn'skruːtəbl] a inescrutable, insondable.

inseam measurement ['ɪnsiːm-] n (US) = **inside leg measurement**.

insect ['ɪnsɛkt] n insecto.

insect bite n picadura.

insecticide [ɪn'sɛktɪsaɪd] n insecticida m.

insect repellent n loción f contra los insectos.

insecure [ɪnsɪ'kjuə*] a inseguro.

insecurity [ɪnsɪ'kjuərɪtɪ] n inseguridad f.

insemination [ɪnsɛmɪ'neɪʃn] n: **artificial ~** inseminación f artificial.

insensible [ɪn'sɛnsɪbl] a inconsciente; (unconscious) sin conocimiento.

insensitive [ɪn'sɛnsɪtɪv] a insensible.

insensitivity [ɪnsɛnsɪ'tɪvɪtɪ] n insensibilidad f.

inseparable [ɪn'sɛprəbl] a inseparable; **they were ~ friends** los unía una estrecha amistad.

insert vt [ɪn'səːt] (into sth) introducir; (COMPUT) insertar ♦ n ['ɪnsəːt] encarte m.

insertion [ɪn'səːʃən] n inserción f.

in-service [ɪn'səːvɪs] a (training, course) en el trabajo, a cargo de la empresa.

inshore [ɪn'ʃɔː*] a: **~ fishing** pesca f costera ♦ ad (fish) a lo largo de la costa; (move) hacia la orilla.

inside ['ɪn'saɪd] n interior m; (lining) forro; (of road: Brit) lado izquierdo; (: US, Europe etc) lado derecho ♦ a interior, interno; (information) confidencial ♦ ad (within) (por) dentro; (with movement) hacia dentro; (fam: in prison) en la cárcel ♦ prep dentro de; (of time): **~ 10 minutes** en menos de 10 minutos; **~s** npl (col) tripas fpl; **~ out** ad (turn) al revés; (know) a

fondo.

inside forward n (SPORT) interior m.

inside information n información f confidencial.

inside lane n (AUT: in Britain) carril m izquierdo; (: in US, Europe) carril m derecho.

inside leg measurement n medida de pernera.

insider [ɪn'saɪdə*] n enterado/a.

insider dealing n delito de iniciados.

inside story n historia íntima.

insidious [ɪn'sɪdɪəs] a insidioso.

insight ['ɪnsaɪt] n perspicacia, percepción f; **to gain** or **get an ~ into sth** formarse una idea de algo.

insignia [ɪn'sɪgnɪə] npl insignias fpl.

insignificant [ɪnsɪg'nɪfɪknt] a insignificante.

insincere [ɪnsɪn'sɪə*] a poco sincero.

insincerity [ɪnsɪn'sɛrɪtɪ] n falta de sinceridad, doblez f.

insinuate [ɪn'sɪnjueɪt] vt insinuar.

insinuation [ɪnsɪnju'eɪʃən] n insinuación f.

insipid [ɪn'sɪpɪd] a soso, insulso.

insist [ɪn'sɪst] vi insistir; **to ~ on doing** empeñarse en hacer; **to ~ that** insistir en que; (claim) exigir que.

insistence [ɪn'sɪstəns] n insistencia; (stubbornness) empeño.

insistent [ɪn'sɪstənt] a insistente; empeñado.

insole ['ɪnsəul] n plantilla.

insolence ['ɪnsələns] n insolencia, descaro.

insolent ['ɪnsələnt] a insolente, descarado.

insoluble [ɪn'sɔljubl] a insoluble.

insolvency [ɪn'sɔlvənsɪ] n insolvencia.

insolvent [ɪn'sɔlvənt] a insolvente.

insomnia [ɪn'sɔmnɪə] n insomnio.

insomniac [ɪn'sɔmnɪæk] n insomne m/f.

inspect [ɪn'spɛkt] vt inspeccionar, examinar; (troops) pasar revista a.

inspection [ɪn'spɛkʃən] n inspección f, examen m.

inspector [ɪn'spɛktə*] n inspector(a) m/f; (Brit: on buses, trains) revisor(a) m/f.

inspiration [ɪnspə'reɪʃən] n inspiración f.

inspire [ɪn'spaɪə*] vt inspirar; **to ~ sb (to do sth)** inspirar a uno (a hacer algo).

inspired [ɪn'spaɪəd] a (writer, book etc) inspirado, genial, iluminado; **in an ~ moment** en un momento de inspiración.

inspiring [ɪn'spaɪərɪŋ] a inspirador(a).

inst. abbr (Brit COMM: = instant, of the present month) cte.

instability [ɪnstə'bɪlɪtɪ] n inestabilidad f.

install [ɪn'stɔːl] vt instalar.

installation [ɪnstə'leɪʃən] n instalación f.

installment plan n (US) compra a plazos.

instalment, (US) **installment** [ɪn'stɔːlmənt] n plazo; (of story) entrega; (of TV serial etc) capítulo; **in ~s** (pay, receive) a plazos; **to pay in ~s** pagar a plazos or por abonos.

instance ['ɪnstəns] n ejemplo, caso; **for** ~ por ejemplo; **in the first** ~ en primer lugar; **in that** ~ en ese caso.

instant ['ɪnstənt] n instante m, momento ♦ a inmediato; (coffee) instantáneo.

instantaneous [ɪnstən'teɪnɪəs] a instantáneo.

instantly ['ɪnstəntlɪ] ad en seguida.

instant replay n (US TV) repetición f de jugada.

instead [ɪn'stɛd] ad en cambio; ~ **of** en lugar de, en vez de.

instep ['ɪnstɛp] n empeine m.

instigate ['ɪnstɪɡeɪt] vt (rebellion, strike, crime) instigar; (new ideas etc) fomentar.

instigation [ɪnstɪ'ɡeɪʃən] n instigación f; **at sb's** ~ a instigación de uno.

instil [ɪn'stɪl] vt: **to** ~ **into** inculcar a.

instinct ['ɪnstɪŋkt] n instinto.

instinctive [ɪn'stɪŋktɪv] a instintivo.

instinctively [ɪn'stɪŋktɪvlɪ] ad por instinto.

institute ['ɪnstɪtjuːt] n instituto; (professional body) colegio ♦ vt (begin) iniciar, empezar; (proceedings) entablar.

institution [ɪnstɪ'tjuːʃən] n institución f; (beginning) iniciación f; (MED: home) asilo; (asylum) manicomio; (custom) costumbre f arraigada.

institutional [ɪnstɪ'tjuːʃənl] a institutional.

instruct [ɪn'strʌkt] vt: **to** ~ **sb in sth** instruir a uno en or sobre algo; **to** ~ **sb to do sth** dar instrucciones a uno de hacer algo.

instruction [ɪn'strʌkʃən] n (teaching) instrucción f; ~**s** npl órdenes fpl; ~**s (for use)** modo sg de empleo.

instruction book n manual m.

instructive [ɪn'strʌktɪv] a instructivo.

instructor [ɪn'strʌktə*] n instructor(a) m/f.

instrument ['ɪnstrəmənt] n instrumento.

instrumental [ɪnstrə'mɛntl] a (MUS) instrumental; **to be** ~ **in** ser (el) artífice de; **to be** ~ **in sth/in doing sth** ser responsable de algo/de hacer algo.

instrumentalist [ɪnstrə'mɛntəlɪst] n instrumentalista m/f.

instrument panel n tablero (de instrumentos).

insubordinate [ɪnsə'bɔːdənɪt] a insubordinado.

insubordination [ɪnsəbɔːdə'neɪʃən] n insubordinación f.

insufferable [ɪn'sʌfrəbl] a insoportable.

insufficient [ɪnsə'fɪʃənt] a insuficiente.

insufficiently [ɪnsə'fɪʃəntlɪ] ad insuficientemente.

insular ['ɪnsjulə*] a insular; (outlook) estrecho de miras.

insularity [ɪnsju'lærɪtɪ] n insularidad f.

insulate ['ɪnsjuleɪt] vt aislar.

insulating tape ['ɪnsjuleɪtɪŋ-] n cinta aislante.

insulation [ɪnsju'leɪʃən] n aislamiento.

insulator ['ɪnsjuleɪtə*] n aistante m.

insulin ['ɪnsjulɪn] n insulina.

insult n ['ɪnsʌlt] insulto; (offence) ofensa ♦ vt [ɪn'sʌlt] insultar; ofender.

insulting [ɪn'sʌltɪŋ] a insultante; ofensivo.

insuperable [ɪn'sjuːprəbl] a insuperable.

insurance [ɪn'ʃuərəns] n seguro; **fire/life** ~ seguro sobre la vida/contra incendios; **to take out** ~ **(against)** hacerse un seguro (contra).

insurance agent n agente m/f de seguros.

insurance broker n corredor(a) m/f or agente m/f de seguros.

insurance policy n póliza (de seguros).

insurance premium n prima de seguros.

insure [ɪn'ʃuə*] vt asegurar; **to** ~ **sb** or **sb's life** asegurar la vida de uno; **to** ~ **(against)** asegurar (contra); **to be** ~**d for £5000** tener un seguro de 5000 libras.

insured [ɪn'ʃuəd] n: **the** ~ el/la asegurado/a.

insurer [ɪn'ʃuərə*] n asegurador(a).

insurgent [ɪn'sɔːdʒənt] a, n insurgente m/f, insurrecto/a m/f.

insurmountable [ɪnsə'mauntəbl] a insuperable.

insurrection [ɪnsə'rɛkʃən] n insurrección f.

intact [ɪn'tækt] a íntegro; (untouched) intacto.

intake ['ɪnteɪk] n (TECH) entrada, toma; (: pipe) tubo de admisión; (of food) ingestión f; (Brit SCOL): **an** ~ **of 200 a year** 200 matriculados al año.

intangible [ɪn'tændʒɪbl] a intangible.

integer ['ɪntɪdʒə*] n (número) entero.

integral ['ɪntɪɡrəl] a (whole) íntegro; (part) integrante.

integrate ['ɪntɪɡreɪt] vt integrar ♦ vi integrarse.

integrated circuit ['ɪntɪɡreɪtɪd-] n (COMPUT) circuito integrado.

integration [ɪntɪ'ɡreɪʃən] n integración f; **racial** ~ integración de razas.

integrity [ɪn'tɛɡrɪtɪ] n honradez f, rectitud f; (COMPUT) integridad f.

intellect ['ɪntəlɛkt] n intelecto.

intellectual [ɪntə'lɛktjuəl] a, n intelectual m/f.

intelligence [ɪn'tɛlɪdʒəns] n inteligencia.

intelligence quotient (IQ) n cociente m de inteligencia.

Intelligence Service n Servicio de Inteligencia.

intelligence test n prueba de inteligencia.

intelligent [ɪn'tɛlɪdʒənt] a inteligente.

intelligently [ɪn'tɛlɪdʒəntlɪ] ad inteligentemente.

intelligentsia [ɪntɛlɪ'dʒɛntsɪə] n intelectualidad f.

intelligible [ɪn'tɛlɪdʒɪbl] a inteligible, comprensible.

intemperate [ɪn'tɛmpərət] a inmoderado.

intend [ɪn'tɛnd] vt (gift etc): **to** ~ **sth for** destinar algo a; **to** ~ **to do sth** tener intención de *or* pensar hacer algo.

intended [ɪn'tɛndɪd] *a* (*effect*) deseado.

intense [ɪn'tɛns] *a* intenso; (*person*) nervioso.

intensely [ɪn'tɛnslɪ] *ad* intensamente; (*very*) sumamente.

intensify [ɪn'tɛnsɪfaɪ] *vt* intensificar; (*increase*) aumentar.

intensity [ɪn'tɛnsɪtɪ] *n* (*gen*) intensidad *f*.

intensive [ɪn'tɛnsɪv] *a* intensivo.

intensive care *n*: **to be in** ~ estar bajo cuidados intensivos; ~ **unit** *n* unidad *f* de vigilancia intensiva.

intensively [ɪn'tɛnsɪvlɪ] *ad* intensivamente.

intent [ɪn'tɛnt] *n* propósito ◆ *a* (*absorbed*) absorto; (*attentive*) atento; **to all** ~**s and purposes** prácticamente; **to be** ~ **on doing sth** estar resuelto *or* decidido a hacer algo.

intention [ɪn'tɛnʃən] *n* intención *f*, propósito.

intentional [ɪn'tɛnʃənl] *a* deliberado.

intentionally [ɪn'tɛnʃnəlɪ] *ad* a propósito.

intently [ɪn'tɛntlɪ] *ad* atentamente, fijamente.

inter [ɪn'tə:*] *vt* enterrar.

inter- ['ɪntə*] *pref* inter-.

interact [ɪntər'ækt] *vi* influirse mutuamente.

interaction [ɪntər'ækʃən] *n* interacción *f*, acción *f* recíproca.

interactive [ɪntər'æktɪv] *a* (*also COMPUT*) interactivo.

intercede [ɪntə'si:d] *vi*: **to** ~ (**with**) interceder (con); **to** ~ **with sb/on behalf of sb** interceder con uno/en nombre de uno.

intercept [ɪntə'sɛpt] *vt* interceptar; (*stop*) detener.

interception [ɪntə'sɛpʃən] *n* interceptación *f*; detención *f*.

interchange *n* ['ɪntətʃeɪndʒ] intercambio; (*on motorway*) intersección *f* ◆ *vt* [ɪntə'tʃeɪndʒ] intercambiar.

interchangeable [ɪntə'tʃeɪndʒəbl] *a* intercambiable.

intercity [ɪntə'sɪtɪ] *a*: ~ (**train**) (tren *m*) interurbano.

intercom ['ɪntəkɔm] *n* interfono.

interconnect [ɪntəkə'nɛkt] *vi* (*rooms*) conectarse.

intercontinental ['ɪntəkɔntɪ'nɛntl] *a* intercontinental.

intercourse ['ɪntəkɔ:s] *n* (*sexual* ~) relaciones *fpl* sexuales, contacto sexual; (*social*) trato.

interdependence [ɪntədɪ'pɛndəns] *n* interdependencia.

interdependent [ɪntədɪ'pɛndənt] *a* interdependiente.

interest ['ɪntrɪst] *n* (*also COMM*) interés *m* ◆ *vt* interesar; **compound/simple** ~ interés compuesto/simple; **business** ~**s** negocios *mpl*; **British** ~**s in the Middle East** los intereses británicos en el Medio Oriente.

interested ['ɪntrɪstɪd] *a* interesado; **to be** ~ **in** interesarse por.

interest-free ['ɪntrɪst'fri:] *a* libre *or* franco de interés.

interesting ['ɪntrɪstɪŋ] *a* interesante.

interest rate *n* tipo *or* tasa de interés.

interface ['ɪntəfeɪs] *n* (*COMPUT*) junción *f*, interface *m*.

interfere [ɪntə'fɪə*] *vi*: **to** ~ **in** (*quarrel*, *other people's business*) entrometerse en; **to** ~ **with** (*hinder*) estorbar; (*damage*) estropear; (*radio*) interferir con.

interference [ɪntə'fɪərəns] *n* (*gen*) intromisión *f*; (*RADIO*, *TV*) interferencia.

interfering [ɪntə'fɪərɪŋ] *a* entrometido.

interim ['ɪntərɪm] *a*: ~ **dividend** dividendo parcial ◆ *n*: **in the** ~ en el ínterin.

interior [ɪn'tɪərɪə*] *n* interior *m* ◆ *a* interior.

interior decorator, interior designer *n* interiorista *m/f*.

interjection [ɪntə'dʒɛkʃən] *n* interyección *f*.

interlock [ɪntə'lɔk] *vi* entrelazarse; (*wheels etc*) endentarse.

interloper ['ɪntələupə*] *n* intruso/a.

interlude ['ɪntəlu:d] *n* intervalo; (*rest*) descanso; (*THEATRE*) intermedio.

intermarriage [ɪntə'mærɪdʒ] *n* endogamia.

intermarry [ɪntə'mærɪ] *vi* casarse (entre parientes).

intermediary [ɪntə'mi:dɪərɪ] *n* intermediario/a.

intermediate [ɪntə'mi:dɪət] *a* intermedio.

interminable [ɪn'tə:mɪnəbl] *a* inacabable.

intermission [ɪntə'mɪʃən] *n* (*THEATRE*) descanso.

intermittent [ɪntə'mɪtnt] *a* intermitente.

intermittently [ɪntə'mɪtntlɪ] *ad* intermitentemente.

intern *vt* [ɪn'tə:n] internar; (*enclose*) encerrar ◆ *n* ['ɪntə:n] (*US*) interno/a.

internal [ɪn'tə:nl] *a* interno, interior; ~ **injuries** heridas *fpl or* lesiones *fpl* internas.

internally [ɪn'tə:nəlɪ] *ad* interiormente; "**not to be taken** ~" "uso externo".

Internal Revenue Service (IRS) *n* (*US*) Hacienda.

international [ɪntə'næʃənl] *a* internacional; ~ (**game**) partido internacional; ~ (**player**) jugador(a) *m/f* internacional.

International Atomic Energy Agency (IAEA) *n* Organismo Internacional de Energía Atómica.

International Chamber of Commerce (ICC) *n* Cámara de Comercio Internacional (CCI *f*).

International Court of Justice (ICJ) *n* Corte *f* Internacional de Justicia (CIJ *f*).

international date line *n* línea de cambio de fecha.

internationally [ɪntə'næʃnəlɪ] *ad* internacionalmente.

International Monetary Fund (IMF) *n*

Fondo Monetario Internacional (FMI *m*).

internecine [ɪntə'niːsaɪn] *a* internecino.

internee [ɪntəː'niː] *n* internado/a.

internment [ɪn'təːnmənt] *n* internamiento.

interplanetary [ɪntə'plænɪtərɪ] *a* interplanetario.

interplay ['ɪntəpleɪ] *n* interacción *f*.

Interpol ['ɪntəpɔl] *n* Interpol *f*.

interpret [ɪn'təːprɪt] *vt* interpretar; (*translate*) traducir; (*understand*) entender ♦ *vi* hacer de intérprete.

interpretation [ɪntəːprɪ'teɪʃən] *n* interpretación *f*; traducción *f*; entendimiento.

interpreter [ɪn'təːprɪtə*] *n* intérprete *m/f*.

interrelated [ɪntərɪ'leɪtɪd] *a* interrelacionado.

interrogate [ɪn'terəʊgeɪt] *vt* interrogar.

interrogation [ɪnterəʊ'geɪʃən] *n* interrogatorio.

interrogative [ɪntə'rɔgətɪv] *a* interrogativo.

interrupt [ɪntə'rʌpt] *vt, vi* interrumpir.

interruption [ɪntə'rʌpʃən] *n* interrupción *f*.

intersect [ɪntə'sɛkt] *vt* cruzar ♦ *vi* (*roads*) cruzarse.

intersection [ɪntə'sɛkʃən] *n* intersección *f*; (*of roads*) cruce *m*.

intersperse [ɪntə'spəːs] *vt*: **to ~ with** salpicar de.

intertwine [ɪntə'twaɪn] *vt* entrelazar ♦ *vi* entrelazarse.

interval ['ɪntəvl] *n* intervalo; (*Brit*: THEATRE, SPORT) descanso; **at ~s** a ratos, de vez en cuando; **sunny ~s** (METEOROLOGY) claros *mpl*.

intervene [ɪntə'viːn] *vi* intervenir; (*take part*) participar; (*occur*) sobrevenir.

intervening [ɪntə'viːnɪŋ] *a* intermedio.

intervention [ɪntə'vɛnʃən] *n* intervención *f*.

interview ['ɪntəvjuː] *n* (RADIO, TV *etc*) entrevista ♦ *vt* entrevistarse con.

interviewee [ɪntəvjuː'iː] *n* entrevistado/a.

interviewer ['ɪntəvjuːə*] *n* entrevistador(a) *m/f*.

intestate [ɪn'tɛsteɪt] *a* intestado.

intestinal [ɪn'tɛstɪnl] *a* intestinal.

intestine [ɪn'tɛstɪn] *n*: **large/small ~** intestino grueso/delgado.

intimacy ['ɪntɪməsɪ] *n* intimidad *f*; (*relations*) relaciones *fpl* íntimas.

intimate *a* ['ɪntɪmət] íntimo; (*friendship*) estrecho; (*knowledge*) profundo ♦ *vt* ['ɪntɪmeɪt] (*announce*) dar a entender.

intimately ['ɪntɪmətlɪ] *ad* íntimamente.

intimidate [ɪn'tɪmɪdeɪt] *vt* intimidar, amedrentar.

intimidation [ɪntɪmɪ'deɪʃən] *n* intimidación *f*.

into ['ɪntuː] *prep* (*gen*) en; (*towards*) a; (*inside*) hacia el interior de; **~ 3 pieces/French** en 3 pedazos/al francés; **to change pounds ~ dollars** cambiar libras por dólares.

intolerable [ɪn'tɔlərəbl] *a* intolerable, insoportable.

intolerance [ɪn'tɔlərəns] *n* intolerancia.

intolerant [ɪn'tɔlərənt] *a*: **~ (of)** intolerante (con *or* para).

intonation [ɪntəʊ'neɪʃən] *n* entonación *f*.

intoxicate [ɪn'tɔksɪkeɪt] *vt* embriagar.

intoxicated [ɪn'tɔksɪkeɪtɪd] *a* embriagado.

intoxication [ɪntɔksɪ'keɪʃən] *n* embriaguez *f*.

intractable [ɪn'træktəbl] *a* (*person*) intratable; (*problem*) insoluble; (*illness*) incurable.

intransigence [ɪn'trænsɪdʒəns] *n* intransigencia.

intransigent [ɪn'trænsɪdʒənt] *a* intransigente.

intransitive [ɪn'trænsɪtɪv] *a* intransitivo.

intravenous [ɪntrə'viːnəs] *a* intravenoso.

in-tray ['ɪntreɪ] *n* bandeja de entrada.

intrepid [ɪn'trɛpɪd] *a* intrépido.

intricacy ['ɪntrɪkəsɪ] *n* complejidad *f*.

intricate ['ɪntrɪkət] *a* intrincado; (*plot, problem*) complejo.

intrigue [ɪn'triːg] *n* intriga ♦ *vt* fascinar ♦ *vi* andar en intrigas.

intriguing [ɪn'triːgɪŋ] *a* fascinante.

intrinsic [ɪn'trɪnsɪk] *a* intrínseco.

introduce [ɪntrə'djuːs] *vt* introducir, meter; **to ~ sb (to sb)** presentar uno (a otro); **to ~ sb to** (*pastime, technique*) introducir a uno a; **may I ~ ...?** permítame presentarle a ....

introduction [ɪntrə'dʌkʃən] *n* introducción *f*; (*of person*) presentación *f*; **a letter of ~** una carta de recomendación.

introductory [ɪntrə'dʌktərɪ] *a* introductorio; **an ~ offer** una oferta introductoria; **~ remarks** comentarios *mpl* introductorios.

introspection [ɪntrəʊ'spɛkʃən] *n* introspección *f*.

introspective [ɪntrəʊ'spɛktɪv] *a* introspectivo.

introvert ['ɪntrəʊvəːt] *a, n* introvertido/a *m/f*.

intrude [ɪn'truːd] *vi* (*person*) entrometerse; **to ~ on** estorbar.

intruder [ɪn'truːdə*] *n* intruso/a.

intrusion [ɪn'truːʒən] *n* invasión *f*.

intrusive [ɪn'truːsɪv] *a* intruso.

intuition [ɪntjuː'ɪʃən] *n* intuición *f*.

intuitive [ɪn'tjuːɪtɪv] *a* intuitivo.

intuitively [ɪn'tjuːɪtɪvlɪ] *ad* por intuición, intuitivamente.

inundate ['ɪnʌndeɪt] *vt*: **to ~ with** inundar de.

inure [ɪn'juə*] *vt*: **to ~ (to)** acostumbrar *or* habituar (a).

invade [ɪn'veɪd] *vt* invadir.

invader [ɪn'veɪdə*] *n* invasor(a) *m/f*.

invalid *n* ['ɪnvəlɪd] minusválido/a ♦ *a* [ɪn'vælɪd] (*not valid*) inválido, nulo.

invalidate [ɪn'vælɪdeɪt] *vt* invalidar, anular.

invalid chair *n* sillón *m* para inválidos.

invaluable [ɪn'væljuəbl] *a* inestimable.
invariable [ɪn'vɛərɪəbl] *a* invariable.
invariably [ɪn'vɛərɪəblɪ] *ad* sin excepción, siempre; **she is ~ late** siempre llega tarde.
invasion [ɪn'veɪʒən] *n* invasión *f*.
invective [ɪn'vɛktɪv] *n* invectiva.
inveigle [ɪn'viːgl] *vt*: **to ~ sb into (doing) sth** embaucar *or* engatusar a uno para (que haga) algo.
invent [ɪn'vɛnt] *vt* inventar.
invention [ɪn'vɛnʃən] *n* invento; (*inventiveness*) inventiva; (*lie*) ficción *f*, mentira.
inventive [ɪn'vɛntɪv] *a* inventivo.
inventiveness [ɪn'vɛntɪvnɪs] *n* ingenio, inventiva.
inventor [ɪn'vɛntə*] *n* inventor(a) *m/f*.
inventory ['ɪnvəntrɪ] *n* inventario.
inventory control *n* control *m* del inventario.
inverse [ɪn'vɜːs] *a, n* inverso; **in ~ proportion (to)** en proporción inversa (a).
inversely [ɪn'vɜːslɪ] *ad* a la inversa.
invert [ɪn'vɜːt] *vt* invertir.
invertebrate [ɪn'vɜːtɪbrət] *n* invertebrado.
inverted commas [ɪn'vɜːtɪd] *npl* (*Brit*) comillas *fpl*.
invest [ɪn'vɛst] *vt* invertir; (*fig: time, effort*) dedicar ♦ *vi* invertir; **to ~ sb with sth** investir a uno con algo.
investigate [ɪn'vɛstɪgeɪt] *vt* investigar; (*study*) estudiar, examinar.
investigation [ɪnvɛstɪ'geɪʃən] *n* investigación *f*, pesquisa; examen *m*.
investigative journalism [ɪn'vɛstɪgətɪv-] *n* periodismo investigador.
investigator [ɪn'vɛstɪgeɪtə*] *n* investigador(a) *m/f*; **private ~** investigador(a) *m/f* privado/a.
investiture [ɪn'vɛstɪtʃə*] *n* investidura.
investment [ɪn'vɛstmənt] *n* inversión *f*.
investment grant *n* subvención *f* para la inversión.
investment income *n* ingresos *mpl* procedentes de inversiones.
investment portfolio *n* portafolio de inversiones.
investment trust *n* compañía inversionista, sociedad *f* de cartera.
investor [ɪn'vɛstə*] *n* inversionista *m/f*.
inveterate [ɪn'vɛtərət] *a* empedernido.
invidious [ɪn'vɪdɪəs] *a* odioso.
invigilate [ɪn'vɪdʒɪleɪt] *vt, vi* (*in exam*) vigilar.
invigilator [ɪn'vɪdʒɪleɪtə*] *n* celador(a) *m/f*.
invigorating [ɪn'vɪgəreɪtɪŋ] *a* vigorizante.
invincible [ɪn'vɪnsɪbl] *a* invencible.
inviolate [ɪn'vaɪələt] *a* inviolado.
invisible [ɪn'vɪzɪbl] *a* invisible.
invisible assets *npl* activo invisible.
invisible ink *n* tinta simpática.
invisible mending *n* puntada invisible.
invitation [ɪnvɪ'teɪʃən] *n* invitación *f*; **at sb's ~** a invitación de uno; **by ~ only** sola-

mente por invitación.
invite [ɪn'vaɪt] *vt* invitar; (*opinions etc*) solicitar, pedir; (*trouble*) buscarse; **to ~ sb (to do)** invitar a uno (a hacer); **to ~ sb to dinner** invitar a uno a cenar.
invite out *vt* invitar a salir.
invite over *vt* invitar a casa.
inviting [ɪn'vaɪtɪŋ] *a* atractivo; (*look*) provocativo; (*food*) apetitoso.
invoice ['ɪnvɔɪs] *n* factura ♦ *vt* facturar; **to ~ sb for goods** facturar a uno por mercancías.
invoicing ['ɪnvɔɪsɪŋ] *n* facturación *f*.
invoke [ɪn'vəuk] *vt* invocar; (*aid*) pedir; (*law*) recurrir a.
involuntary [ɪn'vɔləntrɪ] *a* involuntario.
involve [ɪn'vɔlv] *vt* (*entail*) suponer, implicar; **to ~ sb (in)** comprometer a uno (con).
involved [ɪn'vɔlvd] *a* complicado; **to be/ become ~ in sth** estar comprometido *or* involucrado/involucrarse en algo.
involvement [ɪn'vɔlvmənt] *n* (*gen*) enredo; (*obligation*) compromiso; (*difficulty*) apuro.
invulnerable [ɪn'vʌlnərəbl] *a* invulnerable.
inward ['ɪnwəd] *a* (*movement*) interior, interno; (*thought, feeling*) íntimo.
inwardly ['ɪnwədlɪ] *ad* (*feel, think etc*) para sí, para dentro.
inward(s) ['ɪnwəd(z)] *ad* hacia dentro.
I/O *abbr* (*COMPUT* = *input/output*) E/S; **~ error** error *m* de E/S.
IOC *n abbr* (= *International Olympic Committee*) COI *m*.
iodine ['aɪəudiːn] *n* yodo.
ion ['aɪən] *n* ion *m*.
Ionian Sea [aɪ'əunɪən-] *n*: **the ~** el Mar Jónico.
iota [aɪ'əutə] *n* (*fig*) jota, ápice *m*.
IOU *n abbr* (= *I owe you*) pagaré *m*.
IOW *abbr* (*Brit*) = *Isle of Wight*.
IPA *n abbr* = *International Phonetic Alphabet*.
IQ *n abbr* (= *intelligence quotient*) C.I. *m*.
IRA *n abbr* (= *Irish Republican Army*) IRA *m*; (*US*) = *individual retirement account*.
Iran [ɪ'rɑːn] *n* Irán *m*.
Iranian [ɪ'reɪnɪən] *a* iraní ♦ *n* iraní *m/f*; (*LING*) iraní *m*.
Iraq [ɪ'rɑːk] *n* Irak *m*.
Iraqi [ɪ'rɑːkɪ] *a, n* irakí *m/f*.
irascible [ɪ'ræsɪbl] *a* irascible.
irate [aɪ'reɪt] *a* enojado, airado.
Ireland ['aɪələnd] *n* Irlanda; **Republic of ~** República de Irlanda.
iris, ~es ['aɪrɪs, -ɪz] *n* (*ANAT*) iris *m*; (*BOT*) lirio.
Irish ['aɪrɪʃ] *a* irlandés/esa ♦ *n* (*LING*) irlandés *m*; **the ~** *npl* los irlandeses.
Irishman ['aɪrɪʃmən] *n* irlandés *m*.
Irish Sea *n*: **the ~** el Mar de Irlanda.
Irishwoman ['aɪrɪʃwumən] *n* irlandesa.
irk [əːk] *vt* fastidiar.

irksome ['ɔːksəm] a fastidioso.
IRN n abbr (= Independent Radio News) servicio de noticias en las cadenas de radio privadas.
IRO n abbr (US) = International Refugee Organization.
iron ['aɪən] n hierro; (for clothes) plancha ♦ a de hierro ♦ vt (clothes) planchar; ~s npl (chains) grillos mpl.
iron out vt (crease) quitar; (fig) allanar.
Iron Curtain n: the ~ el Telón de Acero.
iron foundry n fundición f, fundidora.
ironic(al) [aɪ'rɔnɪk(l)] a irónico.
ironically [aɪ'rɔnɪklɪ] ad irónicamente.
ironing ['aɪənɪŋ] n (act) planchado; (ironed clothes) ropa planchada; (to be ironed) ropa por planchar.
ironing board n tabla de planchar.
iron lung n (MED) pulmón m de acero.
ironmonger ['aɪənmʌŋgə*] n (Brit) ferretero/a; ~'s (shop) ferretería, quincallería.
iron ore n mineral m de hierro.
ironworks ['aɪənwɔːks] n fundición f.
irony ['aɪrənɪ] n ironía; the ~ of it is that... lo irónico es que... .
irrational [ɪ'ræʃənl] a irracional.
irreconcilable [ɪrekən'saɪləbl] a inconciliable; (enemies) irreconciliable.
irredeemable [ɪrɪ'diːməbl] a irredimible.
irrefutable [ɪrɪ'fjuːtəbl] a irrefutable.
irregular [ɪ'regjulə*] a irregular; (surface) desigual.
irregularity [ɪregju'lærɪtɪ] n irregularidad f; desigualdad f.
irrelevance [ɪ'reləvəns] n impertinencia.
irrelevant [ɪ'reləvənt] a fuera de lugar, inoportuno.
irreligious [ɪrɪ'lɪdʒəs] a irreligioso.
irreparable [ɪ'reprəbl] a irreparable.
irreplaceable [ɪrɪ'pleɪsəbl] a irremplazable.
irrepressible [ɪrɪ'presəbl] a incontenible.
irreproachable [ɪrɪ'prəutʃəbl] a irreprochable.
irresistible [ɪrɪ'zɪstɪbl] a irresistible.
irresolute [ɪ'rezəluːt] a indeciso.
irrespective [ɪrɪ'spektɪv]: ~ of prep sin tener en cuenta, no importa.
irresponsibility [ɪrɪspɔnsɪ'bɪlɪtɪ] n irresponsabilidad f.
irresponsible [ɪrɪ'spɔnsɪbl] a (act) irresponsable; (person) poco serio.
irretrievable [ɪrɪ'triːvəbl] a (object) irrecuperable; (loss, damage) irremediable, irreparable.
irretrievably [ɪrɪ'triːvəblɪ] ad irremisiblemente.
irreverence [ɪ'revərns] n irreverencia.
irreverent [ɪ'revərnt] a irreverente, irrespetuoso.
irrevocable [ɪ'revəkəbl] a irrevocable.
irrigate ['ɪrɪgeɪt] vt regar.
irrigation [ɪrɪ'geɪʃən] n riego.

irritability [ɪrɪtə'bɪlɪtɪ] n irritabilidad f.
irritable ['ɪrɪtəbl] a (person: temperament) de (mal) carácter; (: mood) de mal humor.
irritant ['ɪrɪtənt] n agente m irritante.
irritate ['ɪrɪteɪt] vt fastidiar; (MED) picar.
irritating ['ɪrɪteɪtɪŋ] a fastidioso.
irritation [ɪrɪ'teɪʃən] n fastidio; picazón f, picor m.
IRS n abbr (US) see Internal Revenue Service.
is [ɪz] vb see be.
ISBN n abbr (= International Standard Book Number) ISBN m.
Islam ['ɪzlaːm] n Islam m.
island ['aɪlənd] n isla; (also: traffic ~) isleta.
islander ['aɪləndə*] n isleño/a.
isle [aɪl] n isla.
isn't ['ɪznt] = is not.
isobar ['aɪsəubaː*] n isobara.
isolate ['aɪsəleɪt] vt aislar.
isolated ['aɪsəleɪtɪd] a aislado.
isolation [aɪsə'leɪʃən] n aislamiento.
isolationism [aɪsə'leɪʃənɪzəm] n aislacionismo.
isolation ward n pabellón m de aislamiento.
isotope ['aɪsəutəup] n isótopo.
Israel ['ɪzreɪl] n Israel m.
Israeli [ɪz'reɪlɪ] a, n israelí m/f.
issue ['ɪsjuː] n cuestión f, asunto; (outcome) resultado; (of banknotes etc) emisión f; (of newspaper etc) número; (offspring) sucesión f, descendencia ♦ vt (rations, equipment) distribuir, repartir; (orders) dar; (certificate, passport) expedir; (decree) promulgar; (magazine) publicar; (cheques) extender; (banknotes, stamps) emitir ♦ vi: to ~ (from) derivar (de), brotar (de); at ~ en cuestión; to take ~ with sb (over) estar en desacuerdo con uno (sobre); to avoid the ~ andar con rodeos; to confuse or obscure the ~ confundir las cosas; to make an ~ of sth hacer hincapié en algo; to ~ sth to sb, ~ sb with sth entregar algo a uno.
Istanbul [ɪstæn'buːl] n Estambul m.
isthmus ['ɪsməs] n istmo.
IT n abbr = information technology.
it [ɪt] pron (subject) él/ella; (direct object) lo/la; (indirect object) le; (impersonal) ello; (after prep) él/ella/ello; of/from ~ de él; about ~ sobre él; out of ~ desde él; in ~ en él; to ~ a él; at ~ en/a él; in front of/behind ~ delante de/detrás de él; above ~, over ~ por encima de él, sobre él; below ~, under ~ debajo de él; ~'s 6 o'clock son las seis; ~'s 2 hours on the train son dos horas en el tren; ~'s raining llueve, está lloviendo; where is ~? ¿dónde está?; what is ~? ¿qué pasa?; who is ~? ¿quién es?; ~'s me soy yo; he's proud of

~ le enorgullece; **he agreed to** ~ está de acuerdo (con ello).

ITA *n abbr* (*Brit:* = *initial teaching alphabet*) *alfabeto parcialmente fonético, ayuda para enseñar lectura.*

Italian [ɪ'tæljən] *a, n* italiano/a *m/f* ◆ *n* (*LING*) italiano.

italic [ɪ'tælɪk] *a* cursivo; ~**s** *npl* cursiva *sg.*

Italy ['ɪtəlɪ] *n* Italia.

itch [ɪtʃ] *n* picazón *f*; (*fig*) prurito ◆ *vi* (*person*) sentir *or* tener comezón; (*part of body*) picar; **to be** ~**ing to do sth** rabiar por hacer algo.

itching ['ɪtʃɪŋ] *n* picazón *f*, comezón *f.*

itchy ['ɪtʃɪ] *a:* **to be** ~ picar.

it'd ['ɪtd] = **it would, it had.**

item ['aɪtəm] *n* artículo; (*on agenda*) asunto (a tratar); (*in programme*) número; (*also:* **news** ~) noticia; ~**s of clothing** prendas *fpl* de vestir.

itemize ['aɪtəmaɪz] *vt* detallar.

itinerant [ɪ'tɪnərənt] *a* ambulante.

itinerary [aɪ'tɪnərərɪ] *n* itinerario.

it'll ['ɪtl] = **it will, it shall.**

ITN *n abbr* (*Brit:* = *Independent Television News*) *servicio de noticias en las cadenas privadas de televisión.*

its [ɪts] *a* su.

it's [ɪts] = **it is, it has.**

itself [ɪt'sɛlf] *pron* (*reflexive*) sí mismo/a; (*emphatic*) él mismo/ella misma.

ITV *n abbr* (*Brit:* = *Independent Television*) *cadena de televisión comercial independiente del Estado.*

IUD *n abbr* (= *intra-uterine device*) DIU *m.*

I've [aɪv] = **I have.**

ivory ['aɪvərɪ] *n* marfil *m.*

Ivory Coast *n:* **the** ~ la Costa de Marfil.

ivory tower *n* (*fig*) torre *f* de marfil.

ivy ['aɪvɪ] *n* hiedra.

Ivy League *n* (*US*) *grupo de famosos colegios en el noreste de los Estados Unidos.*

J

J, j [dʒeɪ] *n* (*letter*) J, j *f*; **J for Jack,** (*US*) **J for Jig** J de José.

JA *n abbr* = **judge advocate.**

J/A *abbr* = **joint account.**

jab [dʒæb] *vt* (*elbow*) dar un codazo a; (*punch*) dar un golpe rápido a ◆ *vi:* **to** ~ **at** intentar golpear a; **to** ~ **sth into sth** clavar algo en algo ◆ *n* codazo; golpe *m* (rápido); (*MED col*) pinchazo.

jabber ['dʒæbə*] *vt, vi* farfullar.

jack [dʒæk] *n* (*AUT*) gato; (*BOWLS*) boliche

m; (*CARDS*) sota.

jack in *vt* (*col*) dejar.

jack up *vt* (*AUT*) alzar con gato.

jackal ['dʒækl] *n* (*ZOOL*) chacal *m.*

jackass ['dʒækæs] *n* (*also fig*) asno, burro.

jackdaw ['dʒækdɔː] *n* grajo/a, chova.

jacket ['dʒækɪt] *n* chaqueta, americana; (*of boiler etc*) camisa; (*of book*) sobrecubierta.

jack-in-the-box ['dʒækɪnðəbɔks] *n* caja sorpresa, caja de resorte.

jack-knife ['dʒæknaɪf] *vi* colear.

jack-of-all-trades [d'ʒækəv'ɔːltreɪdz] *n* factótum *m.*

jack plug *n* (*ELEC*) enchufe *m* de clavija.

jackpot ['dʒækpɔt] *n* premio gordo.

jacuzzi ® [dʒə'kuːzɪ] *n* jacuzzi *m* ®.

jade [dʒeɪd] *n* (*stone*) jade *m.*

jaded ['dʒeɪdɪd] *a* (*tired*) cansado; (*fed up*) hastiado.

jagged ['dʒægɪd] *a* dentado.

jaguar ['dʒægjuə*] *n* jaguar *m.*

jail [dʒeɪl] *n* cárcel *f* ◆ *vt* encarcelar.

jailbird ['dʒeɪlbɜːd] *n* presidiario/a *or* preso/ a reincidente.

jailer ['dʒeɪlə*] *n* carcelero/a.

jalopy [dʒə'lɔpɪ] *n* (*col*) cacharro, armatoste *m.*

jam [dʒæm] *n* mermelada; (*also:* **traffic** ~) embotellamiento; (*difficulty*) apuro ◆ *vt* (*passage etc*) obstruir; (*mechanism, drawer etc*) atascar; (*RADIO*) interferir ◆ *vi* atascarse, trabarse; **to get sb out of a** ~ sacar a uno del paso *or* de un apuro; **to** ~ **sth into sth** meter algo a la fuerza en algo; **the telephone lines are** ~**med** las líneas están ocupadas.

Jamaica [dʒə'meɪkə] *n* Jamaica.

Jamaican [dʒə'meɪkən] *a, n* jamaicano/a *m/f.*

jamb [dʒæm] *n* jamba.

jamboree [dʒæmbə'riː] *n* congreso de niños exploradores.

jam-packed [dʒæm'pækt] *a:* ~ **(with)** atestado (de).

jam session *n* concierto improvisado de jazz/rock *etc.*

Jan. *abbr* (= *January*) ene.

jangle ['dʒæŋgl] *vi* sonar (de manera) discordante.

janitor ['dʒænɪtə*] *n* (*caretaker*) portero, conserje *m.*

January ['dʒænjuərɪ] *n* enero.

Japan [dʒə'pæn] *n* (el) Japón.

Japanese [dʒæpə'niːz] *a* japonés/esa ◆ *n* (*pl inv*) japonés/esa *m/f*; (*LING*) japonés *m.*

jar [dʒɑː*] *n* (*glass: large*) jarra; (: *small*) tarro ◆ *vi* (*sound*) chirriar; (*colours*) desentonar.

jargon ['dʒɑːgən] *n* jerga.

jarring ['dʒɑːrɪŋ] *a* (*sound, colour*) discordante, desafinado, chocante.

Jas. *abbr* = *James*.
jasmin(e) ['dʒæzmin] *n* jazmín *m*.
jaundice ['dʒɔːndɪs] *n* ictericia.
jaundiced ['dʒɔːndɪst] *a* (*fig*: *embittered*) amargado; (: *disillusioned*) desilusionado.
jaunt [dʒɔːnt] *n* excursión *f*.
jaunty ['dʒɔːntɪ] *a* alegre, desenvuelto.
Java ['dʒɑːvə] *n* Java.
javelin ['dʒævlɪn] *n* jabalina.
jaw [dʒɔː] *n* mandíbula; ~**s** *npl* (*TECH*: *of vice etc*) mordaza *sg*.
jawbone ['dʒɔːbəun] *n* mandíbula, quijada.
jay [dʒeɪ] *n* (*ZOOL*) arrendajo.
jaywalker ['dʒeɪwɔːkə*] *n* peatón/ona *m/f* imprudente.
jazz [dʒæz] *n* jazz *m*.
jazz up *vt* (*liven up*) animar, avivar.
jazz band *n* orquesta de jazz.
jazzy ['dʒæzɪ] *a* de colores llamativos.
JCS *n abbr* (*US*) = *Joint Chiefs of Staff*.
JD *n abbr* (*US*: = *Doctor of Laws*) *título universitario*; (: = *Justice Department*) Ministerio de Justicia.
jealous ['dʒɛləs] *a* (*gen*) celoso; (*envious*) envidioso; **to be** ~ tener celos.
jealously ['dʒɛləslɪ] *ad* (*enviously*) envidiosamente; (*watchfully*) vigilantemente, celosamente.
jealousy ['dʒɛləsɪ] *n* celos *mpl*; envidia.
jeans [dʒiːnz] *npl* (pantalones *mpl*) vaqueros *mpl or* tejanos *mpl*.
jeep [dʒiːp] *n* jeep *m*.
jeer [dʒɪə*] *vi*: **to** ~ **(at)** (*boo*) abuchear; (*mock*) mofarse (de).
jeering ['dʒɪərɪŋ] *a* (*crowd*) insolente, ofensivo ♦ *n* protestas *fpl*, burlas *fpl*.
jelly ['dʒɛlɪ] *n* jalea, gelatina.
jellyfish ['dʒɛlɪfɪʃ] *n* medusa.
jemmy ['dʒɛmɪ] *n* palanqueta.
jeopardize ['dʒɛpədaɪz] *vt* arriesgar, poner en peligro.
jeopardy ['dʒɛpədɪ] *n*: **to be in** ~ estar en peligro.
jerk [dʒəːk] *n* (*jolt*) sacudida; (*wrench*) tirón *m*; (*US col*) pesado/a ♦ *vt* dar una sacudida a; tirar bruscamente de ♦ *vi* (*vehicle*) traquetear.
jerkin ['dʒəːkɪn] *n* chaleco.
jerky ['dʒəːkɪ] *a* espasmódico.
jerry-built ['dʒɛrɪbɪlt] *a* mal construido.
jerry can ['dʒɛrɪ-] *n* bidón *m*.
Jersey ['dʒəːzɪ] *n* Jersey *m*.
jersey ['dʒəːzɪ] *n* jersey *m*; (*fabric*) tejido de punto.
Jerusalem [dʒəˈruːsləm] *n* Jerusalén *m*.
jest [dʒɛst] *n* broma.
jester ['dʒɛstə*] *n* bufón *m*.
Jesus ['dʒiːzəs] *n* Jesús *m*; ~ **Christ** Jesucristo.
jet [dʒɛt] *n* (*of gas, liquid*) chorro; (*AVIAT*) avión *m* a reacción.
jet-black ['dʒɛt'blæk] *a* negro como el azabache.

jet engine *n* motor *m* a reacción.
jet lag *n* desorientación *f* después de un largo vuelo.
jetsam ['dʒɛtsəm] *n* echazón *f*.
jettison ['dʒɛtɪsn] *vt* desechar.
jetty ['dʒɛtɪ] *n* muelle *m*, embarcadero.
Jew [dʒuː] *n* judío.
jewel ['dʒuːəl] *n* joya; (*in watch*) rubí *m*.
jeweller, (*US*) **jeweler** ['dʒuːələ*] *n* joyero/a; ~**'s (shop)** joyería.
jewellery, (*US*) **jewelry** ['dʒuːəlrɪ] *n* joyas *fpl*, alhajas *fpl*.
Jewess ['dʒuːɪs] *n* judía.
Jewish ['dʒuːɪʃ] *a* judío.
JFK *n abbr* (*US*) = *John Fitzgerald Kennedy International Airport*.
jib [dʒɪb] *vi* (*horse*) plantarse; **to** ~ **at doing sth** resistirse a hacer algo.
jibe [dʒaɪb] *n* mofa.
jiffy ['dʒɪfɪ] *n* (*col*): **in a** ~ en un santiamén.
jig [dʒɪg] *n* (*dance, tune*) giga.
jigsaw ['dʒɪgsɔː] *n* (*also*: ~ **puzzle**) rompecabezas *m inv*; (*tool*) sierra de vaivén.
jilt [dʒɪlt] *vt* dejar plantado a.
jingle ['dʒɪŋgl] *n* (*advert*) musiquilla ♦ *vi* tintinear.
jingoism ['dʒɪŋgəʊɪzəm] *n* patriotería, jingoísmo.
jinx [dʒɪŋks] *n*: **there's a** ~ **on it** está gafado.
jitters ['dʒɪtəz] *npl* (*col*): **to get the** ~ ponerse nervioso.
jittery ['dʒɪtərɪ] *a* (*col*) muy inquieto, nervioso.
jiujitsu [dʒuːˈdʒɪtsuː] *n* ju-jitsu *m*.
job [dʒɔb] *n* trabajo; (*task*) tarea; (*duty*) deber *m*; (*post*) empleo; (*fam*: *difficulty*) dificultad *f*; **it's a good** ~ **that...** menos mal que...; **just the** ~**!** ¡estupendo!; **a part-time/full-time** ~ un trabajo de medio tiempo/tiempo completo; **that's not my** ~ eso no me incumbe *or* toca a mí; **he's only doing his** ~ está cumpliendo nada más.
job centre *n* (*Brit*) oficina estatal de colocaciones.
job creation scheme *n* plan *m* de creación de puestos de trabajo.
job description *n* descripción *f* del puesto de trabajo.
jobless ['dʒɔblɪs] *a* sin trabajo.
job lot *n* lote *m* de mercancías, saldo.
job satisfaction *n* satisfacción *f* en el trabajo.
job security *n* garantía de trabajo.
job specification *n* especificación *f* del trabajo, profesiograma *m*.
jockey ['dʒɔkɪ] *n* jockey *m/f* ♦ *vi*: **to** ~ **for position** maniobrar para conseguir una posición.
jockey box *n* (*US AUT*) guantera.
jocular ['dʒɔkjulə*] *a* (*humorous*) gracioso; (*merry*) alegre.
jodhpurs ['dʒɔdpəːz] *npl* pantalón *msg* de

montar.

jog [dʒɔg] *vt* empujar (ligeramente) ♦ *vi* (*run*) hacer footing; **to ~ along** ir tirando; **to ~ sb's memory** refrescar la memoria a uno.

jogger ['dʒɔgə*] *n* corredor(a) *m/f.*

jogging ['dʒɔgɪŋ] *n* footing *m.*

john [dʒɔn] *n* (*US col*) wáter *m.*

join [dʒɔɪn] *vt* (*things*) juntar, unir; (*become member of: club*) hacerse socio de; (*POL: party*) afiliarse a; (*meet: people*) reunirse con; (*fig*) juntarse con ♦ *vi* (*roads*) empalmar; (*rivers*) confluir ♦ *n* juntura; **will you ~ us for dinner?** ¿nos acompañas a cenar?; **I'll ~ you later** te encontraré luego; **to ~ forces (with)** aliarse (con).

join in *vi* tomar parte, participar ♦ *vt fus* tomar parte *or* participar en.

join up *vi* unirse; (*MIL*) alistarse.

joiner ['dʒɔɪnə*] *n* carpintero/a.

joinery ['dʒɔɪnərɪ] *n* carpintería.

joint [dʒɔɪnt] *n* (*TECH*) junta, unión *f*; (*ANAT*) articulación *f*; (*Brit CULIN*) pieza de carne (para asar); (*col: place*) garito ♦ *a* (*common*) común; (*combined*) combinado; (*responsibility*) compartido; (*committee*) mixto.

joint account *n* (*with bank etc*) cuenta común.

jointly ['dʒɔɪntlɪ] *ad* (*gen*) en común; (*collectively*) colectivamente; (*together*) conjuntamente.

joint owners *npl* copropietarios *mpl.*

joint ownership *n* copropiedad *f*, propiedad *f* común.

joint-stock bank ['dʒɔɪntstɔk-] *n* banco por acciones.

joint-stock company ['dʒɔɪntstɔk-] *n* sociedad *f* anónima.

joint venture *n* sociedad *f* conjunta.

joist [dʒɔɪst] *n* viga.

joke [dʒəuk] *n* chiste *m*; (*also:* **practical ~**) broma ♦ *vi* bromear; **to play a ~ on** gastar una broma a.

joker ['dʒəukə*] *n* chistoso/a, bromista *m/f*; (*CARDS*) comodín *m.*

joking ['dʒəukɪŋ] *n* bromas *fpl.*

jokingly ['dʒəukɪŋlɪ] *ad* en broma.

jollity ['dʒɔlɪtɪ] *n* alegría.

jolly ['dʒɔlɪ] *a* (*merry*) alegre; (*enjoyable*) divertido ♦ *ad* (*col*) muy, terriblemente ♦ *vt*: **to ~ sb along** animar *or* darle ánimos a uno; **~ good!** ¡estupendo!

jolt [dʒəult] *n* (*shake*) sacudida; (*blow*) golpe *m*; (*shock*) susto ♦ *vt* sacudir; asustar.

Jordan ['dʒɔːdən] *n* (*country*) Jordania; (*river*) Jordán *m.*

joss stick [dʒɔs-] *n* pebete *m.*

jostle ['dʒɔsl] *vt* dar empellones a, codear.

jot [dʒɔt] *n*: **not one ~** ni jota, ni pizca.

jot down *vt* apuntar.

jotter ['dʒɔtə*] *n* (*Brit*) bloc *m.*

journal ['dʒəːnl] *n* (*paper*) periódico; (*magazine*) revista; (*diary*) diario.

journalese [dʒəːnə'liːz] *n* (*pej*) lenguaje *m* periodístico.

journalism ['dʒəːnəlɪzəm] *n* periodismo.

journalist ['dʒəːnəlɪst] *n* periodista *m/f*, reportero/a.

journey ['dʒəːnɪ] *n* viaje *m*; (*distance covered*) trayecto ♦ *vi* viajar; **return ~** viaje de regreso; **a 5-hour ~** un viaje de 5 horas.

jovial ['dʒəuvɪəl] *a* risueño, alegre.

jowl [dʒaul] *n* quijada.

joy [dʒɔɪ] *n* alegría.

joyful ['dʒɔɪful] *a* alegre.

joyfully ['dʒɔɪfulɪ] *ad* alegremente.

joyous ['dʒɔɪəs] *a* alegre.

joy ride *n* (*illegal*) paseo en coche robado.

joystick ['dʒɔɪstɪk] *n* (*AVIAT*) palanca de mando; (*COMPUT*) palanca de control.

JP *n abbr see* **Justice of the Peace.**

Jr. *abbr* = **junior.**

JTPA *n abbr* (*US*: = *Job Training Partnership Act*) programa gubernamental de formación profesional.

jubilant ['dʒuːbɪlnt] *a* jubiloso.

jubilation [dʒuːbɪ'leɪʃən] *n* júbilo.

jubilee ['dʒuːbɪliː] *n* aniversario; **silver ~** vigésimo quinto aniversario.

judge [dʒʌdʒ] *n* juez *m/f* ♦ *vt* juzgar; (*estimate*) considerar; (: *weight, size etc*) calcular ♦ *vi*: **judging** *or* **to ~ by his expression** a juzgar por su expresión; **as far as I can ~** por lo que puedo entender, a mi entender; **I ~d it necessary to inform him** lo consideré necesario informarle.

judge advocate *n* (*MIL*) auditor *m* de guerra.

judg(e)ment ['dʒʌdʒmənt] *n* juicio; (*punishment*) sentencia, fallo; **to pass ~ (on)** (*LAW*) pronunciar *or* dictar sentencia (sobre); (*fig*) emitir un juicio crítico *or* dictaminar (sobre); **in my ~** a mi criterio.

judicial [dʒuː'dɪʃl] *a* judicial.

judiciary [dʒuː'dɪʃɪərɪ] *n* poder *m* judicial, magistratura.

judicious [dʒuː'dɪʃəs] *a* juicioso.

judo ['dʒuːdəu] *n* judo.

jug [dʒʌg] *n* jarro.

jugged hare [dʒʌgd-] *n* (*Brit*) liebre *f* en estofado.

juggernaut ['dʒʌgənɔːt] *n* (*Brit: huge truck*) camionazo *m.*

juggle ['dʒʌgl] *vi* hacer juegos malabares.

juggler ['dʒʌglə*] *n* malabarista *m/f.*

Jugoslav ['juːgəuslɑːv] *etc* = **Yugoslav** *etc.*

jugular ['dʒʌgjulə*] *a*: **~ vein** vena yugular.

juice [dʒuːs] *n* zumo, jugo (*esp LAm*); (*of meat*) jugo; (*col: petrol*): **we've run out of ~** se nos acabó la gasolina.

juiciness ['dʒuːsɪnɪs] *n* jugosidad *f.*

juicy ['dʒuːsɪ] *a* jugoso.

jujitsu [dʒuː'dʒɪtsuː] n = **juijitsu**.
jukebox ['dʒuːkbɔks] n tocadiscos m inv tragaperras.
Jul. abbr (= July) jul.
July [dʒuː'laɪ] n julio; **the first of** ~ el primero de julio; **during** ~ en el mes de julio; **in** ~ **of next year** en julio del año que viene.
jumble ['dʒʌmbl] n revoltijo ♦ vt (also: ~ **together, ~ up**: mix up) revolver; (: disarrange) mezclar.
jumble sale n (Brit) venta de objetos usados con fines benéficos.
jumbo (jet) ['dʒʌmbəu-] n jumbo.
jump [dʒʌmp] vi saltar, dar saltos; (start) asustarse, sobresaltarse; (increase) aumentar ♦ vt saltar ♦ n salto; (fence) obstáculo; (increase) aumento; **to** ~ **the queue** (Brit) colarse.
jump about vi dar saltos, brincar.
jump at vt fus (fig) apresurarse a aprovechar; **he** ~**ed at the offer** se apresuró a aceptar la oferta.
jump down vi bajar de un salto, saltar a tierra.
jump up vi levantarse de un salto.
jumped-up ['dʒʌmptʌp] a (pej) engreído.
jumper ['dʒʌmpə*] n (Brit: pullover) suéter m, jersey m; (US: pinafore dress) mandil m; (sport) saltador(a) m/f.
jump leads, (US) **jumper cables** npl cables mpl puente de batería.
jump suit n mono.
jumpy ['dʒʌmpɪ] a nervioso.
Jun. abbr = **junior**; (= June) jun.
junction ['dʒʌŋkʃən] n (Brit: of roads) cruce m; (rail) empalme m.
juncture ['dʒʌŋktʃə*] n: **at this** ~ en este momento, en esta coyuntura.
June [dʒuːn] n junio.
jungle ['dʒʌŋgl] n selva, jungla.
junior ['dʒuːnɪə*] a (in age) menor, más joven; (competition) juvenil; (position) subalterno ♦ n menor m/f, joven m/f; **he's** ~ **to me** es menor que yo.
junior executive n ejecutivo/a subalterno/a.
junior high school n (US) instituto de enseñanza media.
junior school n (Brit) escuela primaria.
junk [dʒʌŋk] n (cheap goods) baratijas fpl; (lumber) trastos mpl viejos; (rubbish) basura; (ship) junco ♦ vt (esp US) desechar.
junk dealer n vendedor(a) m/f de objetos usados.
junket ['dʒʌŋkɪt] n (culin) dulce de leche cuajada; (Brit col): **to go on a** ~, **go** ~**ing** viajar a costo ajeno or del erario público.
junk foods npl alimentos preparados y envasados de escaso valor nutritivo.
junkie ['dʒʌŋkɪ] n (col) yonqui m/f, heroinómano/a.

junk room n trastero.
junk shop n tienda de objetos usados.
junta ['dʒʌntə] n junta militar.
Jupiter ['dʒuːpɪtə*] n (mythology, astro) Júpiter m.
jurisdiction [dʒuərɪs'dɪkʃən] n jurisdicción f; **it falls** or **comes within/outside our** ~ es/no es de nuestra competencia.
jurisprudence [dʒuərɪs'pruːdəns] n jurisprudencia.
juror ['dʒuərə*] n jurado.
jury ['dʒuərɪ] n jurado.
jury box n tribuna del jurado.
juryman ['dʒuərɪmən] n miembro del jurado.
just [dʒʌst] a justo ♦ ad (exactly) exactamente; (only) sólo, solamente; **he's** ~ **done it/left** acaba de hacerlo/irse; **I've** ~ **seen him** acabo de verle; ~ **right** perfecto, perfectamente; ~ **two o'clock** las dos en punto; **she's** ~ **as clever as you** es tan lista como tú; ~ **as well that...** menos mal que...; **it's** ~ **as well you didn't go** menos mal que no fuiste; **it's** ~ **as good (as)** es igual (que), es tan bueno (como); ~ **as he was leaving** en el momento en que se marchaba; **we were** ~ **going** ya nos íbamos; **I was** ~ **about to phone** estaba a punto de llamar; ~ **before/enough** justo antes/lo suficiente; ~ **here** aquí mismo; **he** ~ **missed** falló por poco; ~ **listen to this** escucha esto un momento; ~ **ask someone the way** simplemente pregúntale a uno por dónde se va; **not** ~ **now** ahora no.
justice ['dʒʌstɪs] n justicia; **this photo doesn't do you** ~ esta foto no te favorece.
Justice of the Peace (JP) n juez m/f de paz.
justifiable [dʒʌstɪ'faɪəbl] a justificable, justificado.
justifiably [dʒʌstɪ'faɪəblɪ] ad justificadamente, con razón.
justification [dʒʌstɪfɪ'keɪʃən] n justificación f.
justify ['dʒʌstɪfaɪ] vt justificar; (text) alinear, justificar; **to be justified in doing sth** tener motivo para or razón al hacer algo.
justly ['dʒʌstlɪ] ad (gen) justamente; (with reason) con razón.
justness ['dʒʌstnɪs] n justicia.
jut [dʒʌt] vi (also: ~ **out**) sobresalir.
jute [dʒuːt] n yute m.
juvenile ['dʒuːvənaɪl] a juvenil; (court) de menores ♦ n joven m/f, menor m/f de edad.
juvenile delinquency n delincuencia juvenil.
juvenile delinquent n delincuente m/f juvenil.
juxtapose ['dʒʌkstəpəuz] vt yuxtaponer.
juxtaposition ['dʒʌkstəpə'zɪʃən] n yuxtaposición f.

K

K, k [keɪ] *n* (*letter*) K, k *f*; **K for King** K de
Kilo.
K *abbr* (= *one thousand*) K; (= *kilobyte*) K;
(*Brit*: = *Knight*) *caballero de una orden.*
kaftan ['kæftæn] *n* caftán *m*.
Kalahari Desert [kælə'hɑːrɪ-] *n* desierto de
Kalahari.
kale [keɪl] *n* col *f* rizada.
kaleidoscope [kə'laɪdəskəup] *n* calidosco-
pio.
Kampala [kæm'pɑːlə] *n* Kampala.
Kampuchea [kæmpu'tʃɪə] *n* Kampuchea.
kangaroo [kæŋgə'ruː] *n* canguro.
kaput [kə'put] *a* (*col*) roto, estropeado.
karate [kə'rɑːtɪ] *n* karate *m*.
Kashmir [kæʃ'mɪə*] *n* Cachemira.
kayak ['kaɪæk] *n* kayak *m*.
KC *n abbr* (*Brit LAW*: = *King's Counsel*)
título concedido a determinados abogados.
kd *abbr* (*US*: = *knocked down*) desmontado.
kebab [kə'bæb] *n* pincho moruno, brocheta.
keel [kiːl] *n* quilla; **on an even** ~ (*fig*) en
equilibrio.
keel over *vi* (*NAUT*) zozobrar, volcarse;
(*person*) desplomarse.
keen [kiːn] *a* (*interest, desire*) grande, vivo;
(*eye, intelligence*) agudo; (*competition*) intenso; (*edge*) afilado; (*Brit: eager*)
entusiasta; **to be** ~ **to do** *or* **on doing sth**
tener muchas ganas de hacer algo; **to be** ~
on sth/sb interesarse por algo/uno; **I'm not**
~ **on going** no tengo ganas de ir.
keenly ['kiːnlɪ] *ad* (*enthusiastically*) con entusiasmo; (*acutely*) vivamente; (*intensely*)
intensamente.
keenness ['kiːnnɪs] *n* (*eagerness*) entusiasmo, interés *m*.
keep [kiːp] *vb* (*pt, pp* **kept** [kept]) *vt* (*retain, preserve*) guardar; (*hold back*) quedarse con; (*shop*) ser propietario de; (*feed:
family etc*) mantener; (*promise*) cumplir;
(*chickens, bees etc*) criar ♦ *vi* (*food*)
conservarse; (*remain*) seguir, continuar ♦
n (*of castle*) torreón *m*; (*food etc*) comida,
subsistencia; **to** ~ **doing sth** seguir haciendo algo; **to** ~ **sb from doing sth** impedir a uno hacer algo; **to** ~ **sth from
happening** impedir que algo ocurra; **to** ~
sb happy hacer a uno feliz; **to** ~ **sb waiting** hacer esperar a uno; **to** ~ **a place tidy**
mantener un lugar limpio; **to** ~ **sth to o.s.**
guardar algo para sí mismo; **to** ~ **time**
(*clock*) mantener la hora exacta; ~ **the
change** quédese con la vuelta; **to** ~ **an**

appointment guardar cita; **to** ~ **a record**
or **note of sth** tomar nota de *or* apuntar
algo; *see also* **keeps**.
keep away *vt*: **to** ~ **sth/sb away from
sb** mantener algo/a uno aparte de uno ♦
vi: **to** ~ **away (from)** mantenerse aparte
(de).
keep back *vt* (*crowd, tears, money*)
contener, reprimir; (*conceal: information*):
to ~ **sth back from sb** ocultar algo a uno
♦ *vi* hacerse a un lado.
keep down *vt* (*control: prices, spending*) controlar; (*retain: food*) retener ♦ *vi*
seguir agachado, no levantar la cabeza.
keep in *vt* (*invalid, child*) impedir que
salga, no dejar salir; (*SCOL*) castigar (a
quedarse en el colegio) ♦ *vi* (*col*): **to** ~ **in
with sb** congraciarse con uno.
keep off *vt* (*dog, person*) mantener a distancia ♦ *vi* evitar; ~ **your hands off!** ¡no
toques!; "~ **off the grass**" "prohibido pisar el césped".
keep on *vi* seguir, continuar.
keep out *vi* (*stay out*) permanecer fuera; "~ **out**" "prohibida la entrada".
keep up *vt* mantener, conservar ♦ *vi* no
retrasarse; (*fig: in comprehension*) seguir
(la corriente); **to** ~ **up with** (*pace*) ir al
paso de; (*level*) mantenerse a la altura de;
to ~ **up with sb** seguir el ritmo a uno;
(*fig*) seguir a uno.
keeper ['kiːpə*] *n* guardián/ana *m/f*.
keep-fit [kiːp'fɪt] *n* gimnasia (para mantenerse en forma).
keeping ['kiːpɪŋ] *n* (*care*) cuidado; **in** ~
with de acuerdo con.
keeps [kiːps] *n*: **for** ~ (*col*) para siempre.
keepsake ['kiːpseɪk] *n* recuerdo.
keg [keg] *n* barrilete *m*, barril *m*.
kennel ['kɛnl] *n* perrera; ~**s** *npl* perreras
fpl.
Kenya ['kiːnjə] *n* Kenia.
Kenyan ['kiːnjən] *a, n* keniano/a *m/f*.
kept [kept] *pt, pp* de **keep**.
kerb [kəːb] *n* (*Brit*) bordillo.
kernel ['kəːnl] *n* (*nut*) fruta; (*fig*) meollo.
kerosene ['kɛrəsiːn] *n* keroseno.
kestrel ['kɛstrəl] *n* cernícalo.
ketchup ['kɛtʃəp] *n* salsa de tomate, catsup
m.
kettle ['kɛtl] *n* hervidor *m*, olla.
kettle drum *n* (*MUS*) timbal *m*.
key [kiː] *n* (*gen*) llave *f*; (*MUS*) tono; (*of
piano, typewriter*) tecla; (*on map*) clave *f*
♦ *cpd* (*vital: position, industry etc*) clave
♦ *vt* (*also*: ~ **in**) teclear.
keyboard ['kiːbɔːd] *n* teclado ♦ *vt* (*text*) teclear.
keyed up [kiːd-] *a* (*person*) nervioso; **to be
(all)** ~ estar nervioso or emocionado.
keyhole ['kiːhəul] *n* ojo (de la cerradura).
key man *n* hombre *m* clave.
keynote ['kiːnəut] *n* (*MUS*) tónica; (*fig*) idea

fundamental.

keynote speech *n* discurso de apertura.

keypad ['ki:pæd] *n* teclado numérico.

keyring ['ki:rɪŋ] *n* llavero.

keystone ['ki:stəʊn] *n* piedra clave.

keystroke ['ki:strəʊk] *n* pulsación *f* (de una tecla).

kg *abbr* (= *kilogram*) kg.

KGB *n abbr* KGB *f*.

khaki ['kɑːkɪ] *n* caqui.

kibbutz, ~im [kɪ'buts, -ɪm] *n* kibutz *m*.

kick [kɪk] *vt* (*person*) dar una patada a; (*ball*) dar un puntapié a ◆ *vi* (*horse*) dar coces ◆ *n* patada; puntapié *m*; (*of rifle*) culetazo; (*col*: *thrill*): **he does it for ~s** lo hace por pura diversión.

   kick around *vt* (*idea*) dar vueltas a; (*person*) tratar a patadas a.

   kick off *vi* (*SPORT*) hacer el saque inicial.

kick-start ['kɪkstɑːt] *n* (*also*: ~**er**) (pedal *m* de) arranque *m*.

kid [kɪd] *n* (*col*: *child*) chiquillo/a; (*animal*) cabrito; (*leather*) cabritilla ◆ *vi* (*col*) bromear.

kidnap ['kɪdnæp] *vt* secuestrar.

kidnapper ['kɪdnæpə*] *n* secuestrador(a) *m/f*.

kidnapping ['kɪdnæpɪŋ] *n* secuestro.

kidney ['kɪdnɪ] *n* riñón *m*.

kidney bean *n* judía, alubia.

kidney machine *n* riñón *m* artificial.

Kilimanjaro [kɪlɪmæn'dʒɑːrəʊ] *n* Kilimanjaro.

kill [kɪl] *vt* matar; (*murder*) asesinar; (*fig*: *story*) suprimir; (: *rumour*) acabar con ◆ *n* matanza; **to ~ time** matar el tiempo.

   kill off *vt* exterminar, terminar con; (*fig*) echar por tierra.

killer ['kɪlə*] *n* asesino/a.

killing ['kɪlɪŋ] *n* (*one*) asesinato; (*several*) matanza; (*COMM*): **to make a ~** tener un gran éxito financiero.

killjoy ['kɪldʒɔɪ] *n* (*Brit*) aguafiestas *m/f inv*.

kiln [kɪln] *n* horno.

kilo ['ki:ləʊ] *n* (*abbr*: = *kilogram(me)*) kilo.

kilobyte ['kɪləʊbaɪt] *n* (*COMPUT*) kilobyte *m*, kiloocteto.

kilogram(me) ['kɪləʊgræm] *n* kilogramo.

kilometre, (*US*) kilometer ['kɪləmi:tə*] *n* kilómetro.

kilowatt ['kɪləʊwɔt] *n* kilovatio.

kilt [kɪlt] *n* falda escocesa.

kilter ['kɪltə*] *n*: **out of ~** desbaratado.

kimono [kɪ'məʊnəʊ] *n* quimono.

kin [kɪn] *n* parientes *mpl*.

kind [kaɪnd] *a* (*treatment*) bueno, cariñoso; (*person, act, word*) amable, atento ◆ *n* clase *f*, especie *f*; (*species*) género; **in ~** (*COMM*) en especie; **a ~ of** una especie de; **to be two of a ~** ser tal para cual; **would you be ~ enough to ...?, would you be so ~ as to ...?** ¿me hace el favor de ...?; **it's very ~ of you (to do)** le agradezco mucho (el que haya hecho).

kindergarten ['kɪndəgɑːtn] *n* jardín *m* de infantes.

kind-hearted [kaɪnd'hɑːtɪd] *a* bondadoso, de buen corazón.

kindle ['kɪndl] *vt* encender.

kindliness ['kaɪndlɪnəs] *n* bondad *f*, amabilidad *f*.

kindling ['kɪndlɪŋ] *n* leña (menuda).

kindly ['kaɪndlɪ] *a* bondadoso; (*gentle*) cariñoso ◆ *ad* bondadosamente, amablemente; **will you ~...** sea usted tan amable de... .

kindness ['kaɪndnɪs] *n* bondad *f*, amabilidad *f*.

kindred ['kɪndrɪd] *n* familia, parientes *mpl* ◆ *a*: ~ **spirits** almas *fpl* gemelas.

kinetic [kɪ'netɪk] *a* cinético.

king [kɪŋ] *n* rey *m*.

kingdom ['kɪŋdəm] *n* reino.

kingfisher ['kɪŋfɪʃə*] *n* martín *m* pescador.

kingpin ['kɪŋpɪn] *n* (*TECH*) perno real *or* pinzote; (*fig*) persona clave.

king-size(d) ['kɪŋsaɪz(d)] *a* de tamaño gigante; (*cigarette*) extra largo.

kink [kɪŋk] *n* (*in rope etc*) enroscadura; (*in hair*) rizo; (*fig*: *emotional, psychological*) trauma *m*, manía.

kinky ['kɪŋkɪ] *a* (*pej*) perverso.

kinship ['kɪnʃɪp] *n* parentesco, afinidad *f*.

kinsman ['kɪnzmən] *n* pariente *m*.

kinswoman ['kɪnzwumən] *n* parienta.

kiosk ['ki:ɒsk] *n* quiosco; (*Brit TEL*) cabina; **newspaper ~** quiosco, kiosco.

kipper ['kɪpə*] *n* arenque *m* ahumado.

kiss [kɪs] *n* beso ◆ *vt* besar; ~ **of life** (*artificial respiration*) respiración *f* artificial; **to ~ sb goodbye** dar un beso de despedida a uno; **to ~ (each other)** besarse.

kit [kɪt] *n* avíos *mpl*; (*equipment*) equipo; (*set of tools etc*) (caja de) herramientas *fpl*; (*assembly ~*) juego de armar; **tool ~** juego *or* estuche *m* de herramientas.

   kit out *vt* equipar.

kitbag ['kɪtbæg] *n* (*MIL*) petate *m*.

kitchen ['kɪtʃɪn] *n* cocina.

kitchen garden *n* huerto.

kitchen sink *n* fregadero.

kitchen unit *n* mueble *m* de cocina.

kitchenware ['kɪtʃɪnwɛə*] *n* batería de cocina.

kite [kaɪt] *n* (*toy*) cometa.

kith [kɪθ] *n*: ~ **and kin** parientes *mpl* y allegados.

kitten ['kɪtn] *n* gatito/a.

kitty ['kɪtɪ] *n* (*pool of money*) fondo común; (*CARDS*) puesta.

KKK *n abbr* (*US*) = *Ku Klux Klan*.

kleptomaniac [klɛptəʊ'meɪniæk] *n* cleptómano/a.

km *abbr* (= *kilometre*) km.

km/h *abbr* (= *kilometres per hour*) km/h.

knack [næk] *n*: **to have the ~ of doing sth**

tener el don de hacer algo.
knapsack ['næpsæk] n mochila.
knead [niːd] vt amasar.
knee [niː] n rodilla.
kneecap ['niːkæp] n rótula.
knee-deep ['niː'diːp] a: **the water was** ~ el agua llegaba hasta la rodilla.
kneel, pt, pp **knelt** [niːl, nɛlt] vi (also: ~ **down**) arrodillarse.
kneepad ['niːpæd] n rodillera.
knell [nɛl] n toque m de difuntos.
knelt [nɛlt] pt, pp of **kneel**.
knew [njuː] pt of **know**.
knickers ['nɪkəz] npl (Brit) bragas fpl.
knick-knack ['nɪknæk] n chuchería, baratija.
knife [naɪf] (pl **knives**) n cuchillo ◆ vt acuchillar; ~, **fork and spoon** cubiertos mpl.
knight [naɪt] n caballero; (CHESS) caballo.
knighthood ['naɪthud] n (title): **to get a** ~ recibir el título de Sir.
knit [nɪt] vt tejer, tricotar; (brows) fruncir; (fig): **to** ~ **together** unir, juntar ◆ vi tejer, tricotar; (bones) soldarse.
knitted ['nɪtɪd] a tejido.
knitting ['nɪtɪŋ] n labor f de punto.
knitting machine n máquina de calcetar or tricotar.
knitting needle, (US) **knit pin** n aguja de tejer.
knitting pattern n patrón m para tricotar.
knitwear ['nɪtwɛə*] n prendas fpl de punto.
knives [naɪvz] pl of **knife**.
knob [nɔb] n (of door) tirador m; (of stick) puño; (lump) bulto; (fig): **a** ~ **of butter** (Brit) un pedazo de mantequilla.
knobbly ['nɔblɪ], (US) **knobby** ['nɔbɪ] a (wood, surface) nudoso; (knee) huesudo.
knock [nɔk] vt (strike) golpear; (bump into) chocar contra; (fig: col) criticar ◆ vi (at door etc): **to** ~ **at/on** llamar a ◆ n golpe m; (on door) llamada; **he** ~**ed at the door** llamó a la puerta.
knock down vt (pedestrian) atropellar; (price) rebajar.
knock off vi (col: finish) salir del trabajo ◆ vt (col: steal) birlar; (strike off) quitar; (fig: from price, record): **to** ~ **off £10** rebajar en £10.
knock out vt dejar sin sentido; (BOXING) poner fuera de combate, dejar K.O.; (stop) estropear, dejar fuera de servicio.
knock over vt (object) derribar, tirar; (pedestrian) atropellar.
knockdown ['nɔkdaun] a (price) de regalo.
knocker ['nɔkə*] n (on door) aldaba.
knock-for-knock ['nɔkfə'nɔk] a (Brit): ~ **agreement** acuerdo de pago respectivo.
knocking ['nɔkɪŋ] n golpes mpl, golpeteo.
knock-kneed [nɔk'niːd] a patizambo.
knockout ['nɔkaut] n (BOXING) K.O. m, knockout m.

knock-up ['nɔkʌp] n (TENNIS) peloteo.
knot [nɔt] n (gen) nudo ◆ vt anudar; **to tie a** ~ anudar, atar.
knotted ['nɔtɪd] a anudado.
knotty ['nɔtɪ] a (fig) complicado.
know [nəu] vb (pt **knew**, pp **known** [njuː, nəun]) vt (gen) saber; (person, author, place) conocer ◆ vi: **as far as I** ~ ... que yo sepa ...; **yes, I** ~ sí, ya lo sé; **I don't** ~ no lo sé; **to** ~ **how to do** saber hacer; **to** ~ **how to swim** saber nadar; **to** ~ **about** or **of sb/sth** saber de uno/algo; **to get to** ~ **sth** enterarse de algo; **I** ~ **nothing about it** no sé nada de eso; **I don't** ~ **him** no lo or le conozco; **to** ~ **right from wrong** saber distinguir el bien del mal.
know-all ['nəuɔːl] n (Brit pej) sabelotodo m/f inv, sabihondo/a.
know-how ['nəuhau] n conocimientos mpl.
knowing ['nəuɪŋ] a (look etc) de complicidad.
knowingly ['nəuɪŋlɪ] ad (purposely) adrede; (smile, look) con complicidad.
know-it-all ['nəuɪtɔːl] n (US) = **know-all**.
knowledge ['nɔlɪdʒ] n (gen) conocimiento; (learning) saber m, conocimientos mpl; **to have no** ~ **of** no saber nada de; **with my** ~ con mis conocimientos, sabiéndolo; **to (the best of) my** ~ a mi entender, que yo sepa; **not to my** ~ que yo sepa, no; **it is common** ~ **that** ... es del dominio público que ...; **it has come to my** ~ **that** ... me he enterado de que ...; **to have a working** ~ **of Spanish** manejárselas con el español.
knowledgeable ['nɔlɪdʒəbl] a entendido, erudito.
known [nəun] pp of **know** ◆ a (thief, facts) conocido; (expert) reconocido.
knuckle ['nʌkl] n nudillo.
knuckle under vi someterse.
knuckleduster ['nʌkldʌstə*] n puño de hierro.
KO abbr n (= knockout) K.O. m ◆ vt (= knock out) dejar K.O.
koala [kəu'ɑːlə] n (also: ~ **bear**) koala m.
kook [kuːk] n (US col) majareta m/f, excéntrico/a.
Koran [kɔ'rɑːn] n Corán m.
Korea [kə'rɪə] n Corea; **North/South** ~ Corea del Norte/Sur.
Korean [kə'rɪən] a, n coreano/a m/f.
kosher ['kəuʃə*] a autorizado por la ley judía.
kowtow ['kau'tau] vi: **to** ~ **to sb** humillarse ante uno.
KS abbr (US POST) = **Kansas**.
Kt abbr (Brit: = Knight) caballero de una orden.
Kuala Lumpur ['kwɑːlə'lumpuə*] n Kuala Lumpur m.
kudos ['kjuːdɔs] n gloria, méritos mpl.
Kuwait [ku'weɪt] n Kuwait m.
Kuwaiti [ku'weɪtɪ] a, n Kuwaití m/f.

kW *abbr* (= *kilowatt*) Kv.
KY *abbr* (*US POST*) = *Kentucky*.

L

L, l [ɛl] *n* (*letter*) L, l *f*; **L for Lucy**, (*US*) **L for Love** L de Lorenzo.
L *abbr* (*on maps etc*) = **lake**; **large**; (= *left*) izq.; (*Brit AUT*: = *learner*) L.
l. *abbr* = **litre**.
LA *n abbr* (*US*) = *Los Angeles* ♦ *abbr* (*US POST*) = *Louisiana*.
lab [læb] *n abbr* = **laboratory**.
label ['leɪbl] *n* etiqueta; (*brand: of record*) sello (discográfico) ♦ *vt* poner etiqueta a.
labor *etc* ['leɪbə*] (*US*) = **labour**.
laboratory [lə'bɔrətərɪ] *n* laboratorio.
Labor Day *n* (*US*) día *m* del trabajador.
laborious [lə'bɔːrɪəs] *a* penoso.
laboriously [lə'bɔːrɪəslɪ] *ad* penosamente.
labor union *n* (*US*) sindicato.
labor unrest *n* (*US*) conflictividad *f* laboral.
Labour ['leɪbə*] *n* (*Brit POL*: *also*: **the ~ Party**) el partido laborista, los laboristas.
labour, (*US*) **labor** ['leɪbə*] *n* (*task*) trabajo; (~ *force*) mano *f* de obra; (*workers*) trabajadores *mpl*; (*MED*) (dolores *mpl* de) parto ♦ *vi*: **to ~ (at)** trabajar (en) ♦ *vt* insistir en; **hard ~** trabajos *mpl* forzados; **to be in ~** estar de parto.
labo(u)r cost *n* costo de la mano de obra.
labo(u)r dispute *n* conflicto laboral.
labo(u)red ['leɪbəd] *a* (*breathing*) fatigoso; (*style*) forzado, pesado.
labo(u)rer ['leɪbərə*] *n* peón *m*; (*on farm*) peón *m*, obrero; (*day ~*) jornalero.
labo(u)r force *n* mano *f* de obra.
labo(u)r-intensive [leɪbərɪn'tɛnsɪv] *a* intensivo en mano de obra.
labo(u)r relations *npl* relaciones *fpl* laborales.
labo(u)r-saving ['leɪbəseɪvɪŋ] *a* que ahorra trabajo.
laburnum [lə'bəːnəm] *n* codeso.
labyrinth ['læbɪrɪnθ] *n* laberinto.
lace [leɪs] *n* encaje *m*; (*of shoe etc*) cordón *m* ♦ *vt* (*shoes: also*: ~ **up**); (*drink: fortify with spirits*) echar licor a.
lacemaking ['leɪsmeɪkɪŋ] *n* obra de encaje.
lacerate ['læsəreɪt] *vt* lacerar.
laceration [læsə'reɪʃən] *n* laceración *f*.
lace-up ['leɪsʌp] *a* (*shoes etc*) con cordones.
lack [læk] *n* (*absence*) falta, carencia; (*scarcity*) escasez *f* ♦ *vt* faltarle a uno, carecer de; **through** *or* **for ~ of** por falta de; **to be ~ing** faltar, no haber.

lackadaisical [lækə'deɪzɪkl] *a* (*careless*) descuidado; (*indifferent*) indiferente.
lackey ['lækɪ] *n* (*also fig*) lacayo.
lacklustre, (*US*) **lackluster** ['læklʌstə*] *a* (*surface*) deslustrado, deslucido; (*style*) inexpresivo; (*eyes*) apagado.
laconic [lə'kɔnɪk] *a* lacónico.
lacquer ['lækə*] *n* laca; **hair ~** laca para el pelo.
lacrosse [lə'krɔs] *n* lacrosse *f*.
lacy ['leɪsɪ] *a* (*like lace*) parecido al encaje.
lad [læd] *n* muchacho, chico; (*in stable etc*) mozo.
ladder ['lædə*] *n* escalera (de mano); (*Brit: in tights*) carrera ♦ *vt* (*Brit: tights*) hacer una carrera en.
laden ['leɪdn] *a*: ~ **(with)** cargado (de); **fully ~** (*truck, ship*) cargado hasta el tope.
ladle ['leɪdl] *n* cucharón *m*.
lady ['leɪdɪ] *n* señora; (*distinguished, noble*) dama; **young ~** señorita; **the ladies' (room)** los servicios de señoras.
ladybird ['leɪdɪbəːd], (*US*) **ladybug** ['leɪdɪbʌg] *n* mariquita.
lady doctor *n* médica, doctora.
lady-in-waiting ['leɪdɪɪn'weɪtɪŋ] *n* dama de honor.
ladykiller ['leɪdɪkɪlə*] *n* ladrón *m* de corazones.
ladylike ['leɪdɪlaɪk] *a* fino.
Ladyship ['leɪdɪʃɪp] *n*: **your ~** su Señoría.
lag [læg] *vi* (*also*: ~ **behind**) retrasarse, quedarse atrás ♦ *vt* (*pipes*) revestir.
lager ['lɑːgə*] *n* cerveza (rubia).
lagging ['lægɪŋ] *n* revestimiento.
lagoon [lə'guːn] *n* laguna.
Lagos ['leɪgɔs] *n* Lagos *m*.
laid [leɪd] *pt, pp* of **lay**.
laid-back [leɪd'bæk] *a* (*col*) tranquilo, relajado.
laid up *a*: **to be ~** (*person*) tener que guardar cama.
lain [leɪn] *pp* of **lie**.
lair [lɛə*] *n* guarida.
laissez-faire [leseɪ'fɛə*] *n* laissez-faire *m*.
laity ['leɪtɪ] *n* laicado.
lake [leɪk] *n* lago.
Lake District *n* (*Brit*): **the ~** el País de los Lagos.
lamb [læm] *n* cordero; (*meat*) carne *f* de cordero.
lamb chop *n* chuleta de cordero.
lambswool ['læmzwʊl] *n* lana de cordero.
lame [leɪm] *a* cojo; (*weak*) débil, poco convincente; ~ **duck** (*fig: person*) inútil *m/f*; (: *firm*) empresa en quiebra.
lamely ['leɪmlɪ] *ad* (*fig*) sin convicción.
lament [lə'mɛnt] *n* lamento ♦ *vt* lamentarse de.
lamentable ['læməntəbl] *a* lamentable.
lamentation [læmən'teɪʃən] *n* lamento.
laminated ['læmɪneɪtɪd] *a* laminado.
lamp [læmp] *n* lámpara.

lamplight ['læmplaɪt] n: **by** ~ a la luz de la lámpara.

lampoon [læm'pu:n] vt satirizar.

lamppost ['læmppəust] n (Brit) (poste m de) farol m.

lampshade ['læmpʃeɪd] n pantalla.

lance [lɑ:ns] n lanza ♦ vt (MED) abrir con lanceta.

lance corporal n (Brit) soldado de primera clase.

lancet ['lɑ:nsɪt] n (MED) lanceta.

Lancs [læŋks] abbr (Brit) = Lancashire.

land [lænd] n tierra; (country) país m; (piece of ~) terreno; (estate) tierras fpl, finca; (AGR) campo ♦ vi (from ship) desembarcar; (AVIAT) aterrizar; (fig: fall) caer ♦ vt (obtain) conseguir; (passengers, goods) desembarcar; **to go/travel by** ~ ir/viajar por tierra; **to own** ~ ser dueño de tierras; **to** ~ **on one's feet** caer de pie; (fig: to be lucky) salir adelante.
  land up vi: **to** ~ **up in/at** ir a parar a/en.

landed ['lændɪd] a: ~ **gentry** terratenientes mpl.

landing ['lændɪŋ] n desembarco; aterrizaje m; (of staircase) rellano.

landing card n tarjeta de desembarque.

landing craft n barca de desembarco.

landing gear n (AVIAT) tren m de aterrizaje.

landing stage n (Brit) desembarcadero.

landing strip n pista de aterrizaje.

landlady ['lændleɪdɪ] n (of boarding house) patrona; (owner) dueña.

landlocked ['lændlɔkt] a cercado de tierra.

landlord ['lændlɔ:d] n propietario; (of pub etc) patrón m.

landlubber ['lændlʌbə*] n marinero de agua dulce.

landmark ['lændmɑ:k] n lugar m conocido; **to be a** ~ (fig) hacer época.

landowner ['lændəunə*] n terrateniente m/f.

landscape ['lænskeɪp] n paisaje m.

landscape architecture n arquitectura paisajista.

landscaped ['lænskeɪpt] a reformado artísticamente.

landscape gardener n diseñador(a) m/f de paisajes.

landscape gardening n jardinería paisajista.

landscape painting n (ART) paisaje m.

landslide ['lændslaɪd] n (GEO) corrimiento de tierras; (fig: POL) victoria arrolladora.

lane [leɪn] n (in country) camino; (in town) callejón m; (AUT) carril m; (in race) calle f; (for air or sea traffic) ruta; **shipping** ~ ruta marina.

language ['læŋgwɪdʒ] n lenguaje m; (national tongue) idioma m, lengua; **bad** ~ palabrotas fpl.

language laboratory n laboratorio de idiomas.

language studies npl estudios mpl filológicos.

languid ['læŋgwɪd] a lánguido.

languish ['læŋgwɪʃ] vi languidecer.

languor ['læŋgə*] n languidez f.

languorous ['læŋgərəs] a lánguido.

lank [læŋk] a (hair) lacio.

lanky ['læŋkɪ] a larguirucho.

lanolin(e) ['lænəlɪn] n lanolina.

lantern ['læntn] n linterna, farol m.

lanyard ['lænjed] n acollador m.

Laos [laus] n Laos m.

lap [læp] n (of track) vuelta; (of body): **to sit on sb's** ~ sentarse en las rodillas de uno ♦ vt (also: ~ **up**) beber a lengüetadas ♦ vi (waves) chapotear.
  lap up vt beber a lengüetadas; (fig: compliments, attention) disfrutar; (lies etc) tragarse.

La Paz [læ'pæz] n La Paz.

lapdog ['læpdɔg] n perro faldero.

lapel [lə'pɛl] n solapa.

Lapland ['læplænd] n Laponia.

Laplander ['læplændə*] n lapón/ona m/f.

lapse [læps] n (fault) error m, fallo; (moral) desliz m ♦ vi (expire) caducar; (morally) cometer un desliz; (time) pasar, transcurrir; **to** ~ **into bad habits** volver a las andadas; ~ **of time** lapso, período; **a** ~ **of memory** un fallo de memoria.

larceny ['lɑ:sənɪ] n latrocinio.

lard [lɑ:d] n manteca (de cerdo).

larder ['lɑ:də*] n despensa.

large [lɑ:dʒ] a grande ♦ ad: **by and** ~ en general, en términos generales; **at** ~ (free) en libertad; (generally) en general; **to make** ~**(r)** hacer mayor or más extenso; **a** ~ **number of people** una gran cantidad de personas; **on a** ~ **scale** en gran escala.

largely ['lɑ:dʒlɪ] ad en gran parte.

large-scale ['lɑ:dʒ'skeɪl] a (map, drawing) en gran escala; (reforms, business activities) importante.

largesse [lɑ:'ʒɛs] n generosidad f.

lark [lɑ:k] n (bird) alondra; (joke) broma.
  lark about vi bromear, hacer el tonto.

larva, pl **larvae** ['lɑ:və, -i:] n larva.

laryngitis [lærɪn'dʒaɪtɪs] n laringitis f.

larynx ['lærɪŋks] n laringe f.

lascivious [lə'sɪvɪəs] a lascivo.

laser ['leɪzə*] n láser m.

laser beam n rayo láser.

laser printer n impresora (por) láser.

lash [læʃ] n latigazo; (punishment) azote m; (also: **eyelash**) pestaña ♦ vt azotar; (tie) atar.
  lash down vt sujetar con cuerdas ♦ vi (rain) caer a trombas.
  lash out vi (col: spend) gastar a la loca; **to** ~ **out at** or **against sb** lanzar invectivas

contra uno.
lashing ['læʃɪŋ] *n* (*beating*) azotaina, flagelación *f;* ~s of (*col*) montones *mpl* de.
lass [læs] *n* chica.
lassitude ['læsɪtjuːd] *n* lasitud *f.*
lasso [læ'suː] *n* lazo ◆ *vt* coger con lazo.
last [lɑːst] *a* (*gen*) último; (*final*) último, final ◆ *ad* por último ◆ *vi* (*endure*) durar; (*continue*) continuar, seguir; ~ **night** anoche; ~ **week** la semana pasada; **at** ~ por fin; ~ **but one** penúltimo; ~ **time** la última vez; **it** ~**s (for) 2 hours** dura dos horas.
last-ditch ['lɑːst'dɪtʃ] *a* (*attempt*) de último recurso, último, desesperado.
lasting ['lɑːstɪŋ] *a* duradero.
lastly ['lɑːstlɪ] *ad* por último, finalmente.
last-minute ['lɑːstmɪnɪt] *a* de última hora.
latch [lætʃ] *n* picaporte *m,* pestillo.
latch on to *vt fus* (*cling to*: *person*) pegarse a; (: *idea*) agarrarse de.
latchkey ['lætʃkiː] *n* llavín *m.*
latchkey child *n* niño cuyos padres trabajan.
late [leɪt] *a* (*not on time*) tarde, atrasado; (*towards end of period, life*) tardío; (*hour*) avanzado; (*dead*) fallecido ◆ *ad* tarde; (*behind time, schedule*) con retraso; **to be (10 minutes)** ~ llegar con (diez minutos de) retraso; **to be** ~ **with** estar atrasado con; ~ **delivery** entrega tardía; ~ **in life** a una edad avanzada; **of** ~ últimamente; **in** ~ **May** hacia fines de mayo; **the** ~ **Mr X** el difunto Sr X; **to work** ~ trabajar hasta tarde.
latecomer ['leɪtkʌmə*] *n* recién llegado/a.
lately ['leɪtlɪ] *ad* últimamente.
lateness ['leɪtnɪs] *n* (*of person*) demora; (*of event*) tardanza.
latent ['leɪtnt] *a* latente; ~ **defect** defecto latente.
later ['leɪtə*] *a* (*date etc*) posterior; (*version etc*) más reciente ◆ *ad* más tarde, después; ~ **on today** hoy más tarde.
lateral ['lætərl] *a* lateral.
latest ['leɪtɪst] *a* último; **at the** ~ a más tardar.
latex ['leɪtɛks] *n* látex *m.*
lathe [leɪð] *n* torno.
lather ['lɑːðə*] *n* espuma (de jabón) ◆ *vt* enjabonar.
Latin ['lætɪn] *n* latín *m* ◆ *a* latino.
Latin America *n* América Latina, Latinoamérica.
Latin American *a, n* latinoamericano/a *m/f.*
latitude ['lætɪtjuːd] *n* latitud *f;* (*fig: freedom*) latitud *f,* libertad *f.*
latrine [lə'triːn] *n* letrina.
latter ['lætə*] *a* último; (*of two*) segundo ◆ *n:* **the** ~ el último, éste.
latter-day ['lætədeɪ] *a* moderno.
latterly ['lætəlɪ] *ad* últimamente.
lattice ['lætɪs] *n* enrejado.

lattice window *n* ventana enrejada *or* de celosía.
lattice work *n* enrejado.
Latvia ['lætvɪə] *n* Letonia, Latvia.
laudable ['lɔːdəbl] *a* loable.
laugh [lɑːf] *n* risa; (*loud*) carcajada ◆ *vi* reírse, reír; reírse a carcajadas.
laugh at *vt fus* reírse de.
laugh off *vt* tomar a risa.
laughable ['lɑːfəbl] *a* ridículo.
laughing ['lɑːfɪŋ] *a* risueño ◆ *n:* **it's no** ~ **matter** no es cosa de risa.
laughing gas *n* gas *m* hilarante.
laughing stock *n:* **to be the** ~ **of the town** ser el hazmerreír de la ciudad.
laughter ['lɑːftə*] *n* risa.
launch [lɔːntʃ] *n* (*boat*) lancha; *see also* **launching** ◆ *vt* (*ship, rocket, plan*) lanzar.
launch forth *vi:* **to** ~ **forth (into)** lanzarse a *or* en, emprender.
launch out *vi* = **launch forth.**
launching ['lɔːntʃɪŋ] *n* (*of rocket etc*) lanzamiento; (*inauguration*) estreno.
launch(ing) pad *n* plataforma de lanzamiento.
launder ['lɔːndə*] *vt* lavar.
launderette [lɔːn'drɛt], (*US*) **laundromat** ['lɔːndrəmæt] *n* lavandería (automática).
laundry ['lɔːndrɪ] *n* lavandería; (*clothes*) ropa sucia; **to do the** ~ hacer la colada.
laureate ['lɔːrɪət] *a see* **poet.**
laurel ['lɔrl] *n* laurel *m;* **to rest on one's** ~**s** dormirse en *or* sobre los laureles.
lava ['lɑːvə] *n* lava.
lavatory ['lævətrɪ] *n* wáter *m;* **lavatories** *npl* servicios *mpl,* aseos *mpl,* sanitarios *mpl* (*LAm*).
lavatory paper *n* papel *m* higiénico.
lavender ['lævəndə*] *n* lavanda.
lavish ['lævɪʃ] *a* abundante; (*giving freely*): ~ **with** pródigo en ◆ *vt:* **to** ~ **sth on sb** colmar a uno de algo.
lavishly ['lævɪʃlɪ] *ad* (*give, spend*) generosamente, liberalmente; (*furnished*) lujosamente.
law [lɔː] *n* ley *f;* (*study*) derecho; (*of game*) regla; **against the** ~ contra la ley; **to study** ~ estudiar derecho; **to go to** ~ recurrir a la justicia.
law-abiding ['lɔːəbaɪdɪŋ] *a* respetuoso de la ley.
law and order *n* orden *m* público.
lawbreaker ['lɔːbreɪkə*] *n* infractor(a) *m/f* de la ley.
law court *n* tribunal *m* (de justicia).
lawful ['lɔːful] *a* legítimo, lícito.
lawfully ['lɔːfulɪ] *ad* legalmente.
lawless ['lɔːlɪs] *a* (*act*) ilegal; (*person*) rebelde; (*country*) ingobernable.
lawmaker ['lɔːmeɪkə*] *n* legislador(a) *m/f.*
lawn [lɔːn] *n* césped *m.*
lawnmower ['lɔːnməuə*] *n* cortacésped *m.*
lawn tennis *n* tenis *m* sobre hierba.

law school *n* (*US*) facultad *f* de derecho.

law student *n* estudiante *m/f* de derecho.

lawsuit ['lɔːsuːt] *n* pleito; **to bring a ~ against** levantar pleito contra.

lawyer ['lɔːjə*] *n* abogado/a; (*for sales, wills etc*) notario/a.

lax [læks] *a* (*discipline*) relajado; (*person*) negligente.

laxative ['læksətɪv] *n* laxante *m*.

laxity ['læksɪtɪ] *n* flojedad *f*; (*moral*) relajamiento; (*negligence*) negligencia.

lay [leɪ] *pt of* **lie** ◆ *a* laico; (*not expert*) lego ◆ *vt* (*pt, pp* **laid** [leɪd]) (*place*) colocar; (*eggs, table*) poner; (*trap*) tender; **to ~ the facts/one's proposals before sb** presentar los hechos/sus propuestas a uno.

lay aside, lay by *vt* dejar a un lado.

lay down *vt* (*pen etc*) dejar; (*arms*) rendir; (*policy*) asentar; **to ~ down the law** imponer las normas.

lay in *vt* abastecerse de.

lay into *vt fus* (*col: attack, scold*) arremeterse contra.

lay off *vt* (*workers*) despedir.

lay on *vt* (*water, gas*) instalar; (*meal, facilities*) proveer.

lay out *vt* (*plan*) trazar; (*display*) disponer; (*spend*) gastar.

lay up *vt* (*store*) guardar; (*ship*) desarmar; (*subj: illness*) obligar a guardar cama.

layabout ['leɪəbaut] *n* vago/a.

lay-by ['leɪbaɪ] *n* (*Brit AUT*) apartadero.

lay days *npl* días *mpl* de detención *or* inactividad.

layer ['leɪə*] *n* capa.

layette [leɪ'ɛt] *n* ajuar *m* (de niño).

layman ['leɪmən] *n* lego.

lay-off ['leɪɔf] *n* despido, paro forzoso.

layout ['leɪaut] *n* (*design*) plan *m*, trazado; (*disposition*) disposición *f*; (*PRESS*) composición *f*.

laze [leɪz] *vi* no hacer nada; (*pej*) holgazanear.

lazily ['leɪzɪlɪ] *ad* perezosamente.

laziness ['leɪzɪnɪs] *n* pereza.

lazy ['leɪzɪ] *a* perezoso, vago.

LB *abbr* (*Canada*) = Labrador.

lb. *abbr* = **pound** (*weight*).

lbw *abr* (*CRICKET*) = leg before wicket.

LC *n abbr* (*US*) = Library of Congress.

lc *abbr* (*TYP:* = lower case) min.

L/C *abbr* = **letter of credit.**

LCD *n abbr see* **liquid crystal display.**

Ld *abbr* (= Lord) título de nobleza.

LDS *n abbr* (= Licentiate in Dental Surgery) diploma universitario; (= Latter-day Saints) Iglesia de Jesucristo de los Santos del último día.

LEA *n abbr* (*Brit:* = local education authority) organismos locales encargados de la enseñanza.

lead [liːd] *n* (*front position*) delantera; (*distance, time ahead*) ventaja; (*clue*) pista; (*ELEC*) cable *m*; (*for dog*) correa; (*THEATRE*) papel *m* principal; [led] (*metal*) plomo; (*in pencil*) mina ◆ *vb* (*pt, pp* **led** [led]) *vt* conducir; (*life*) llevar; (*be leader of*) dirigir; (*SPORT*) ir en cabeza de; (*orchestra: Brit*) ser el primer violín en; (: *US*) dirigir ◆ *vi* ir primero; **to be in the ~** (*SPORT*) llevar la delantera; (*fig*) ir a la cabeza; **to take the ~** (*SPORT*) tomar la delantera; (*fig*) tomar la iniciativa; **to ~ sb to believe that ...** hacer creer a uno que ...; **to ~ sb to do sth** llevar a uno a hacer algo.

lead astray *vt* llevar por mal camino.

lead away *vt* llevar.

lead back *vt* hacer volver.

lead off *vt* llevar ◆ *vi* (*in game*) abrir.

lead on *vt* (*tease*) engañar; **to ~ sb on to** (*induce*) incitar a uno a.

lead to *vt fus* producir, provocar.

lead up to *vt fus* conducir a.

leaded ['lɛdɪd] *a*: **~ windows** ventanas *fpl* emplomadas.

leaden ['lɛdn] *a* (*sky, sea*) plomizo; (*heavy: footsteps*) pesado.

leader ['liːdə*] *n* jefe/a *m/f*, líder *m*; (*of union etc*) dirigente *m/f*; (*guide*) guía *m/f*; (*of newspaper*) artículo de fondo; **they are ~s in their field** (*fig*) llevan la delantera en su especialidad.

leadership ['liːdəʃɪp] *n* dirección *f*; **qualities of ~** iniciativa *sg*; **under the ~ of ...** bajo la dirección de ..., al mando de ....

lead-free ['lɛdfriː] *a* sin plomo.

leading ['liːdɪŋ] *a* (*main*) principal; (*outstanding*) destacado; (*first*) primero; (*front*) delantero; **a ~ question** una pregunta tendenciosa.

leading lady *n* (*THEATRE*) primera actriz *f*.

leading light *n* (*fig: person*) figura principal.

leading man *n* (*THEATRE*) primer actor *m*.

leading role *n* papel *m* principal.

lead pencil *n* lápiz *m*.

lead poisoning *n* envenenamiento plúmbico.

lead time *n* (*COMM*) plazo de entrega.

lead weight *n* peso de plomo.

leaf, *pl* **leaves** [liːf, liːvz] *n* hoja; **to turn over a new ~** (*fig*) volver la hoja, hacer borrón y cuenta nueva; **to take a ~ out of sb's book** (*fig*) seguir el ejemplo de uno.

leaf through *vt fus* (*book*) hojear.

leaflet ['liːflɪt] *n* folleto.

leafy ['liːfɪ] *a* frondoso.

league [liːg] *n* sociedad *f*; (*FOOTBALL*) liga; **to be in ~ with** estar de manga con.

leak [liːk] *n* (*of liquid, gas*) escape *m*, fuga; (*in pipe*) agujero; (*in roof*) gotera; (*fig: of information, in security*) filtración *f* ◆ *vi* (*shoes, ship*) hacer agua; (*pipe*) tener (un) escape; (*roof*) gotear; (*also*: ~ **out**: *liquid, gas*) escaparse, fugarse; (*fig*: *news*) divulgarse ♦ *vt* (*gen*) dejar escapar; (*fig*: *information*) filtrarse.

leakage ['li:kɪdʒ] *n* (*of water, gas etc*) goteo, filtración *f*.

leaky ['li:kɪ] *a* (*pipe, bucket, roof*) que tiene goteras; (*shoe*) que deja entrar el agua; (*boat*) que hace agua.

lean [li:n] *a* (*thin*) flaco; (*meat*) magro ♦ *vb* (*pt, pp* **leaned** *or* **leant** [lɛnt]) *vt*: **to ~ sth on sth** apoyar algo en algo ♦ *vi* (*slope*) inclinarse; (*rest*): **to ~ against** apoyarse contra; **to ~ on** apoyarse en.

lean back *vi* inclinarse hacia atrás.

lean forward *vi* inclinarse hacia adelante.

lean out *vi*: **to ~ out (of)** asomarse (de).

lean over *vi* inclinarse.

leaning ['li:nɪŋ] *a* inclinado ♦ *n*: ~ **(towards)** inclinación *f* (hacia); **the L~ Tower of Pisa** la Torre Inclinada de Pisa.

leant [lɛnt] *pt, pp of* **lean.**

lean-to ['li:ntu:] *n* (*roof*) tejado de una sola agua; (*building*) cobertizo.

leap [li:p] *n* salto ♦ *vi* (*pt, pp* **leaped** *or* **leapt** [lɛpt]) saltar; **to ~ at an offer** apresurarse a aceptar una oferta.

leap up *vi* (*person*) saltar.

leapfrog ['li:pfrɒg] *n* pídola ♦ *vi*: **to ~ over sb/sth** saltar por encima de uno/algo.

leapt [lɛpt] *pt, pp of* **leap.**

leap year *n* año bisiesto.

learn, *pt, pp* **learned** *or* **learnt** [lɜːn, -t] *vt* (*gen*) aprender; (*come to know of*) enterarse de ♦ *vi* aprender; **to ~ how to do sth** aprender a hacer algo; **to ~ that** ... enterarse *or* informarse de que ...; **to ~ about sth** (*SCOL*) hacer clase de algo; (*hear*) enterarse *or* informarse de algo; **we were sorry to ~ that** ... nos dio tristeza saber que ....

learned ['lɜːnɪd] *a* erudito.

learner ['lɜːnə*] *n* principiante *m/f*; (*Brit*: *also*: ~ **driver**) aprendiz(a) *m/f*.

learning ['lɜːnɪŋ] *n* saber *m*, conocimientos *mpl*.

learnt [lɜːnt] *pp of* **learn.**

lease [li:s] *n* arriendo ♦ *vt* arrendar; **on ~** en arriendo.

lease back *vt* subarrendar.

leaseback ['li:sbæk] *n* subarriendo.

leasehold ['li:shəʊld] *n* (*contract*) derechos *mpl* de arrendamiento ♦ *a* arrendado.

leash [li:ʃ] *n* correa.

least [li:st] *a* (*slightest*) menor, más pequeño; (*smallest amount of*) mínimo ♦ *ad* menos ♦ *n*: **the ~** lo menos; **the ~ expensive car** el coche menos costoso; **at ~** por lo menos, al menos; **not in the ~** en absoluto.

leather ['lɛðə*] *n* cuero ♦ *cpd*: ~ **goods** artículos *mpl* de cuero.

leathery ['lɛðərɪ] *a* (*skin*) curtido.

leave [li:v] *vb* (*pt, pp* **left** [lɛft]) *vt* dejar; (*go away from*) abandonar ♦ *vi* irse; (*train*) salir ♦ *n* permiso; **to ~ school** salir del colegio; ~ **it to me!** ¡yo me encargo!; **he's already left for the airport** ya se ha marchado al aeropuerto; **to be left** quedar, sobrar; **there's some milk left over** sobra *or* queda algo de leche; **on ~** de permiso; **to take one's ~ of** despedirse de; **on ~ of absence** con permiso de ausentarse.

leave behind *vt* (*on purpose*) dejar (atrás); (*accidentally*) olvidar.

leave off *vt* (*lid*) no reemplazar; (*switch*) no encender; (*col*: *stop*): **to ~ off doing sth** dejar de hacer algo.

leave on *vt* (*lid*) dejar puesto; (*light, fire, cooker*) dejar encendido.

leave out *vt* omitir.

leave over *vt* (*postpone*) dejar, aplazar.

leave of absence *n* permiso de ausentarse.

leaves [li:vz] *pl of* **leaf.**

leavetaking ['li:vteɪkɪŋ] *n* despedida.

Lebanon ['lɛbənən] *n*: **the ~** el Líbano.

lecherous ['lɛtʃərəs] *a* lascivo.

lectern ['lɛktən] *n* atril *m*.

lecture ['lɛktʃə*] *n* conferencia; (*SCOL*) clase *f* ♦ *vi* dar una clase ♦ *vt* (*scold*) sermonear; (*reprove*) echar una reprimenda a; **to give a ~ on** dar una conferencia sobre.

lecture hall *n* aula, sala de conferencias.

lecturer ['lɛktʃərə*] *n* conferenciante *m/f*; (*Brit*: *at university*) profesor(a) *m/f*.

lecture theatre *n* = **lecture hall.**

LED *n abbr* (= *light-emitting diode*) LED *m*.

led [lɛd] *pt, pp of* **lead.**

ledge [lɛdʒ] *n* (*of window, on wall*) repisa, reborde *m*; (*of mountain*) saliente *m*.

ledger ['lɛdʒə*] *n* libro mayor.

lee [li:] *n* sotavento; **in the ~ of** al abrigo de.

leech [li:tʃ] *n* sanguijuela.

leek [li:k] *n* puerro.

leer [lɪə*] *vi*: **to ~ at sb** mirar de manera lasciva a uno.

leeward ['li:wəd] *a* (*NAUT*) de sotavento ♦ *n* (*NAUT*) sotavento; **to ~** a sotavento.

leeway ['li:weɪ] *n* (*fig*): **to have some ~** tener cierta libertad de acción.

left [lɛft] *pt, pp of* **leave** ♦ *a* izquierdo ♦ *n* izquierda ♦ *ad* a la izquierda; **on** *or* **to the** ~ a la izquierda; **the L~** (*POL*) la izquierda.

left-hand drive ['lɛfthænd-] *n* conducción *f* a la izquierda.

left-handed [lɛft'hændɪd] *a* zurdo; ~ **scissors** tijeras *fpl* zurdas *or* para zurdos.

left-hand side ['lɛfthænd-] *n* la izquierda.

leftist [lɛftɪst] *a* (*POL*) izquierdista.

left-luggage (office) [lɛft'lʌgɪdʒ(-)] *n* (*Brit*) consigna.

left-overs ['lɛftəuvəz] *npl* sobras *fpl*.

left-wing [lɛft'wɪŋ] *a* (*POL*) de izquierda, izquierdista.

left-winger ['lɛft'wɪŋə*] *n* (*POL*) izquierdista *m/f*.

leg [lɛg] *n* pierna; (*of animal*) pata; (*of chair*) pie *m*; (*CULIN: of meat*) pierna; (*of journey*) etapa; **lst/2nd ~** (*SPORT*) partido de ida/de vuelta; **to pull sb's ~** bromear con uno; **to stretch one's ~s** dar una vuelta.

legacy ['lɛgəsɪ] *n* herencia; (*fig*) herencia, patrimonio.

legal ['liːgl] *a* (*permitted by law*) lícito; (*of law*) legal; (*inquiry etc*) jurídico; **to take ~ action** *or* **proceedings against sb** entablar *or* levantar pleito contra uno.

legal adviser *n* asesor(a) *m/f* jurídico/a.

legal holiday *n* (*US*) fiesta oficial.

legality [lɪ'gælɪtɪ] *n* legalidad *f*.

legalize ['liːgəlaɪz] *vt* legalizar.

legally ['liːgəlɪ] *ad* legalmente; **~ binding** con fuerza legal.

legal tender *n* moneda de curso legal.

legatee [lɛgə'tiː] *n* legatario/a.

legation [lɪ'geɪʃən] *n* legación *f*.

legend ['lɛdʒənd] *n* leyenda.

legendary ['lɛdʒəndərɪ] *a* legendario.

-legged ['lɛgɪd] *suff*: **two-~** (*table etc*) de dos patas.

leggings ['lɛgɪŋz] *npl* polainas *fpl*.

legibility [lɛdʒɪ'bɪlɪtɪ] *n* legibilidad *f*.

legible ['lɛdʒəbl] *a* legible.

legibly ['lɛdʒəblɪ] *ad* legiblemente.

legion ['liːdʒən] *n* legión *f*.

legionnaire [liːdʒə'nɛə*] *n* legionario.

legionnaire's disease *n* enfermedad *f* del legionario.

legislation [lɛdʒɪs'leɪʃən] *n* legislación *f*; **a piece of ~** (*bill*) un proyecto de ley; (*act*) una ley.

legislative ['lɛdʒɪslətɪv] *a* legislativo.

legislator ['lɛdʒɪsleɪtə*] *n* legislador(a) *m/f*.

legislature ['lɛdʒɪslətʃə*] *n* cuerpo legislativo.

legitimacy [lɪ'dʒɪtɪməsɪ] *n* legitimidad *f*.

legitimate [lɪ'dʒɪtɪmət] *a* legítimo.

legitimize [lɪ'dʒɪtɪmaɪz] *vt* legitimar.

leg-room ['lɛgruːm] *n* espacio para las piernas.

Leics *abbr* (*Brit*) = Leicestershire.

leisure ['lɛʒə*] *n* ocio, tiempo libre; **at ~** con tranquilidad.

leisure centre *n* centro de recreo.

leisurely ['lɛʒəlɪ] *a* sin prisa; lento.

leisure suit *n* conjunto tipo chandal.

lemon ['lɛmən] *n* limón *m*.

lemonade [lɛmə'neɪd] *n* (*fruit juice*) limonada; (*fizzy*) gaseosa.

lemon cheese, lemon curd *n* queso de limón.

lemon juice *n* zumo de limón.

lemon tea *n* té *m* con limón.

lend, pt, pp lent [lɛnd, lɛnt] *vt*: **to ~ sth to sb** prestar algo a uno.

lender ['lɛndə*] *n* prestador(a) *m/f*.

lending library ['lɛndɪŋ-] *n* biblioteca circulante.

length [lɛŋθ] *n* (*size*) largo, longitud *f*; (*section: of road, pipe*) tramo; (: *of rope etc*) largo; **at ~** (*at last*) por fin, finalmente; (*lengthily*) largamente; **it is 2 metres in ~** tiene dos metros de largo; **what ~ is it?** ¿cuánto tiene de largo?; **to fall full ~** caer de bruces; **to go to any ~(s) to do sth** ser capaz de hacer cualquier cosa para hacer algo.

lengthen ['lɛŋθn] *vt* alargar ♦ *vi* alargarse.

lengthways ['lɛŋθweɪz] *ad* a lo largo.

lengthy ['lɛŋθɪ] *a* largo, extenso; (*meeting*) prolongado.

lenient ['liːnɪənt] *a* indulgente.

lens [lɛnz] *n* (*of spectacles*) lente *f*; (*of camera*) objetivo.

Lent [lɛnt] *n* Cuaresma.

lent [lɛnt] *pt, pp of* **lend**.

lentil ['lɛntl] *n* lenteja.

Leo ['liːəu] *n* Leo.

leopard ['lɛpəd] *n* leopardo.

leotard ['liːətɑːd] *n* leotardo.

leper ['lɛpə*] *n* leproso/a.

leper colony *n* colonia de leprosos.

leprosy ['lɛprəsɪ] *n* lepra.

lesbian ['lɛzbɪən] *a* lesbiano ♦ *n* lesbiana.

lesion ['liːʒən] *n* (*MED*) lesión *f*.

Lesotho [lɪ'suːtuː] *n* Lesotho.

less [lɛs] *a* (*in size, degree etc*) menor; (*in quantity*) menos ♦ *pron, ad* menos; **~ than half** menos de la mitad; **~ than £1/a kilo/3 metres** menos de una libra/un kilo/tres metros; **~ than ever** menos que nunca; **~ 5%** menos el cinco por ciento; **~ and ~** cada vez menos; **the ~ he works...** cuanto menos trabaja ....

lessee [lɛ'siː] *n* inquilino/a, arrendatario/a.

lessen ['lɛsn] *vi* disminuir, reducirse ♦ *vt* disminuir, reducir.

lesser ['lɛsə*] *a* menor; **to a ~ extent** *or* **degree** en menor grado.

lesson ['lɛsn] *n* clase *f*; **a maths ~** una clase de matemáticas; **to give ~s in** dar clases en; **it taught him a ~** (*fig*) le sirvió de lección.

lessor ['lɛsə*] *n* arrendador(a) *m/f*.

lest [lɛst] *conj*: **~ it happen** para que no pase.

let, pt, pp let [lɛt] *vt* (*allow*) dejar, permitir; (*Brit: lease*) alquilar; **to ~ sb do sth** dejar que uno haga algo; **to ~ sb have sth** dar algo a uno; **to ~ sb know sth** comunicar algo a uno; **~'s go** ¡vamos!; **~ him come** que venga; **"to ~"** "se alquila".

let down *vt* (*lower*) bajar; (*dress*) alargar; (*tyre*) desinflar; (*hair*) soltar;

(*disappoint*) defraudar.
let go *vi* soltar; (*fig*) dejarse ir ♦ *vt* soltar.
let in *vt* dejar entrar; (*visitor etc*) hacer pasar; **what have you ~ yourself in for?** ¿en qué te has metido?
let off *vt* dejar escapar; (*firework etc*) disparar; (*bomb*) accionar; (*passenger*) dejar, bajar; **to ~ off steam** (*fig, col*) desahogarse, desfogarse.
let on *vi*: **to ~ on that ...** revelar que ...
let out *vt* dejar salir; (*dress*) ensanchar; (*rent out*) alquilar.
let up *vi* amainar, disminuir.
let-down ['lɛtdaun] *n* (*disappointment*) decepción *f*.
lethal ['liːθl] *a* (*weapon*) mortífero; (*poison, wound*) mortal.
lethargic [lɛ'θɑːdʒɪk] *a* aletargado.
lethargy ['lɛθədʒɪ] *n* letargo.
letter ['lɛtə*] *n* (*of alphabet*) letra; (*correspondence*) carta; **~s** *npl* (*literature, learning*) letras *fpl*; **small/capital ~** minúscula/mayúscula; **covering ~** carta adjunta.
letter bomb *n* carta-bomba.
letterbox ['lɛtəbɔks] *n* (*Brit*) buzón *m*.
letterhead ['lɛtəhɛd] *n* membrete *m*, encabezamiento.
lettering ['lɛtərɪŋ] *n* letras *fpl*.
letter of credit *n* carta de crédito; **documentary ~** carta de crédito documentaria; **irrevocable ~** carta de crédito irrevocable.
letter-opener ['lɛtərəupnə*] *n* abrecartas *m inv*.
letterpress ['lɛtəprɛs] *n* (*method*) prensa de copiar; (*printed page*) impresión *f* tipográfica.
letter quality *n* calidad *f* de correspondencia.
letters patent *npl* letra *sg* de patente.
lettuce ['lɛtɪs] *n* lechuga.
let-up ['lɛtʌp] *n* descanso, tregua.
leukaemia, (*US*) **leukemia** [luː'kiːmɪə] *n* leucemia.
level ['lɛvl] *a* (*flat*) llano; (*flattened*) nivelado; (*uniform*) igual ♦ *ad* a nivel ♦ *n* nivel *m* ♦ *vt* nivelar, allanar; (*gun*) apuntar; (*accusation*): **to ~ (against)** levantar (contra) ♦ *vi* (*col*): **to ~ with sb** ser franco con uno; **to be ~ with** estar a nivel de; **a ~ spoonful** (*CULIN*) una cucharada rasa; **to draw ~ with** (*team*) igualar; (*runner, car*) alcanzar a; **"A" ~s** *npl* (*Brit*) ≈ Bachillerato Superior *sg*, B.U.P. *msg*; **"O" ~s** *npl* (*Brit*) ≈ bachillerato *sg* elemental, octavo *sg* de básica; **on the ~** (*fig: honest*) en serio; **talks at ministerial ~** charlas *fpl* a nivel ministerial.
level off *or* **out** *vi* (*prices etc*) estabilizarse; (*ground*) nivelarse; (*aircraft*) ponerse en una trayectoria horizontal.

level crossing *n* (*Brit*) paso a nivel.
level-headed [lɛvl'hɛdɪd] *a* sensato.
levelling, (*US*) **leveling** ['lɛvlɪŋ] *a* (*process, effect*) de nivelación ♦ *n* igualación *f*, allanamiento.
lever ['liːvə*] *n* palanca ♦ *vt*: **to ~ up** levantar con palanca.
leverage ['liːvərɪdʒ] *n* (*fig: influence*) influencia.
levity ['lɛvɪtɪ] *n* frivolidad *f*, informalidad *f*.
levy ['lɛvɪ] *n* impuesto ♦ *vt* exigir, recaudar.
lewd [luːd] *a* lascivo; obsceno, colorado (*LAm*).
LI *abbr* (*US*) = *Long Island*.
liabilities [laɪə'bɪlətɪz] *npl* obligaciones *fpl*; pasivo *sg*.
liability [laɪə'bɪlətɪ] *n* responsabilidad *f*; (*handicap*) desventaja.
liable ['laɪəbl] *a* (*subject*): **~ to** sujeto a; (*responsible*): **~ for** responsable de; (*likely*): **~ to do** propenso a hacer; **to be ~ to a fine** ser expuesto a una multa.
liaise [liː'eɪz] *vi*: **to ~ (with)** colaborar (con); **to ~ with sb** mantener informado a uno.
liaison [liː'eɪzɔn] *n* (*coordination*) enlace *m*; (*affair*) relación *f*.
liar ['laɪə*] *n* mentiroso/a.
libel ['laɪbl] *n* calumnia ♦ *vt* calumniar.
libellous ['laɪbləs] *a* difamatorio, calumnioso.
liberal ['lɪbərl] *a* (*gen*) liberal; (*generous*): **~ with** generoso con ♦ *n*: **L~** (*POL*) liberal *m/f*.
liberality [lɪbə'rælɪtɪ] *n* (*generosity*) liberalidad *f*, generosidad *f*.
liberalize ['lɪbərəlaɪz] *vt* liberalizar.
liberally ['lɪbərəlɪ] *ad* liberalmente.
liberal-minded ['lɪbəl'maɪndɪd] *a* de miras anchas.
liberate ['lɪbəreɪt] *vt* liberar.
liberation [lɪbə'reɪʃən] *n* liberación *f*.
Liberia [laɪ'bɪərɪə] *n* Liberia.
Liberian [laɪ'bɪərɪən] *a*, *n* liberiano/a *m/f*.
liberty ['lɪbətɪ] *n* libertad *f*; **to be at ~ to do** estar libre para hacer; **to take the ~ of doing sth** tomarse la libertad de hacer algo.
libido [lɪ'biːdəu] *n* libido.
Libra ['liːbrə] *n* Libra.
librarian [laɪ'brɛərɪən] *n* bibliotecario/a.
library ['laɪbrərɪ] *n* biblioteca.
library book *n* libro de la biblioteca.
libretto [lɪ'brɛtəu] *n* libreto.
Libya ['lɪbɪə] *n* Libia.
Libyan ['lɪbɪən] *a*, *n* libio/a *m/f*.
lice [laɪs] *pl of* **louse**.
licence, (*US*) **license** ['laɪsns] *n* licencia; (*permit*) permiso; (*also*: **driving licence**, (*US*) **driver's license**) carnet *m* de conducir; (*excessive freedom*) libertad *f*; **import ~** licencia *or* permiso de importación; **produced under ~** elaborado bajo licencia.

licence number n matrícula.
licence plate n placa (de matrícula).
license ['laɪsns] n (US) = **licence** ♦ vt autorizar, dar permiso a; (car) sacar la patente or la matrícula de.
licensed ['laɪsnst] a (for alcohol) autorizado para vender bebidas alcohólicas.
licensed trade n comercio or negocio autorizado.
licensee [laɪsən'siː] n (in a pub) concesionario/a, dueño/a de un bar.
licentious [laɪ'sɛnʃəs] a licencioso.
lichen ['laɪkən] n liquen m.
lick [lɪk] vt lamer; (col: defeat) dar una paliza a ♦ n lamedura; **a ~ of paint** una mano de pintura.
licorice ['lɪkərɪs] n = **liquorice**.
lid [lɪd] n (of box, case) tapa; (of pan) cobertera; **to take the ~ off sth** (fig) exponer algo a la luz pública.
lido ['laɪdəu] n (Brit) piscina, alberca (LAm).
lie [laɪ] n mentira ♦ vi mentir; (pt lay, pp lain [leɪ, leɪn]) (rest) estar echado, estar acostado; (of object: be situated) estar, encontrarse; **to tell ~s** mentir; **to ~ low** (fig) mantenerse a escondidas.
lie about, lie around vi (things) estar tirado; (Brit: people) estar acostado or tumbado.
lie back vi recostarse.
lie down vi acostarse.
lie up vi (hide) esconderse.
Liechtenstein ['lɪktənstaɪn] n Liechtenstein m.
lie detector n detector m de mentiras.
lie-down ['laɪdaun] n (Brit): **to have a ~** echarse (una siesta).
lie-in ['laɪɪn] n (Brit): **to have a ~** quedarse en la cama.
lieu [luː]: **in ~ of** prep en lugar de.
Lieut abbr = **lieutenant**.
lieutenant [lɛf'tɛnənt, (US) luː'tɛnənt] n (MIL) teniente m.
lieutenant colonel n teniente m colonel.
life, pl **lives** [laɪf, laɪvz] n vida; (way of ~) modo de vivir; (of licence etc) vigencia; **to be sent to prison for ~** ser condenado a reclusión or cadena perpetua; **country/city ~** la vida del campo/de la ciudad; **true to ~** fiel a la realidad; **to paint from ~** pintar del natural; **to put** or **breathe new ~ into** (person) reanimar; (project, area etc) infundir nueva vida a.
life annuity n anualidad f vitalicia.
life assurance n (Brit) seguro de vida.
lifebelt ['laɪfbɛlt] n (Brit) cinturón m salvavidas.
lifeblood ['laɪfblʌd] n (fig) alma, nervio.
lifeboat ['laɪfbəut] n lancha de socorro.
life-buoy ['laɪfbɔɪ] n boya or guindola salvavidas.
life expectancy n esperanza de vida.

lifeguard ['laɪfgɑːd] n vigilante m/f.
life imprisonment n cadena perpetua.
life insurance n = **life assurance**.
life jacket n chaleco salvavidas.
lifeless ['laɪflɪs] a sin vida; (dull) soso.
lifelike ['laɪflaɪk] a natural.
lifeline ['laɪflaɪn] n (fig) cordón m umbilical.
lifelong ['laɪflɔŋ] a de toda la vida.
life preserver n (US) = **lifebelt**.
life-saver ['laɪfseɪvə*] n socorrista m/f.
life sentence n cadena perpetua.
life-sized ['laɪfsaɪzd] a de tamaño natural.
life span n vida.
lifestyle ['laɪfstaɪl] n estilo de vida.
life support system n (MED) sistema m de respiración asistida.
lifetime ['laɪftaɪm] n: **in his ~** durante su vida; **once in a ~** una vez en la vida; **the chance of a ~** una oportunidad única.
lift [lɪft] vt levantar; (copy) plagiar ♦ vi (fog) disiparse ♦ n (Brit: elevator) ascensor m; **to give sb a ~** (Brit) llevar a uno en el coche.
lift off vt levantar, quitar ♦ vi (rocket, helicopter) despegar.
lift out vt sacar; (troops, evacuees etc) evacuar.
lift up vt levantar.
lift-off ['lɪftɔf] n despegue m.
ligament ['lɪgəmənt] n ligamento.
light [laɪt] n luz f; (flame) lumbre f; (lamp) luz f, lámpara; (daylight) luz f del día; (headlight) faro; (rear ~) luz f trasera; (for cigarette etc): **have you got a ~?** ¿tienes fuego? ♦ vt (pt, pp **lighted** or **lit** [lɪt]) (candle, cigarette, fire) encender; (room) alumbrar ♦ a (colour) claro; (not heavy, also fig) ligero; (room) alumbrado ♦ ad (travel) con poco equipaje; **to turn the ~ on/off** encender/apagar la luz; **in the ~ of** a la luz de; **to come to ~** salir a luz; **to cast** or **shed** or **throw ~ on** arrojar luz sobre; **to make ~ of sth** (fig) hacer poco caso de algo.
light up vi (smoke) encender un cigarrillo; (face) iluminarse ♦ vt (illuminate) iluminar, alumbrar.
light bulb n bombilla, foco (LAm).
lighten ['laɪtn] vi (grow light) clarear ♦ vt (give light to) iluminar; (make lighter) aclarar; (make less heavy) aligerar.
lighter ['laɪtə*] n (also: **cigarette ~**) encendedor m, mechero.
light-fingered [laɪt'fɪŋgəd] a largo de manos.
light-headed [laɪt'hɛdɪd] a (dizzy) mareado; (excited) exaltado; (by nature) casquivano.
light-hearted [laɪt'hɑːtɪd] a alegre.
lighthouse ['laɪthaus] n faro.
lighting ['laɪtɪŋ] n (act) iluminación f; (system) alumbrado.
lighting-up time [laɪtɪŋ'ʌp-] n (Brit) hora

de encendido del alumbrado.

lightly ['laɪtlɪ] *ad* ligeramente; (*not seriously*) con poca seriedad; **to get off** ~ ser castigado con poca severidad.

light meter *n* (*PHOT*) fotómetro.

lightness ['laɪtnɪs] *n* claridad *f*; (*in weight*) ligereza.

lightning ['laɪtnɪŋ] *n* relámpago, rayo.

lightning conductor, (*US*) **lightning rod** *n* pararrayos *m inv*.

lightning strike *n* huelga relámpago.

light pen *n* fotoestilo, lápiz *m* óptico *or* luminoso.

lightweight ['laɪtweɪt] *a* (*suit*) ligero ◆ *n* (*BOXING*) peso ligero.

light year *n* año luz.

like [laɪk] *vt* (*person*) querer a; (*thing*): **I** ~ **swimming/apples** me gusta nadar/me gustan las manzanas ◆ *prep* como ◆ *a* parecido, semejante ◆ *n*: **the** ~ semejante *m/f*; **his** ~**s and dislikes** sus gustos y aversiones; **I would** ~, **I'd** ~ me gustaría; (*for purchase*) quisiera; **would you** ~ **a coffee?** ¿te apetece un café?; **to be** *or* **look** ~ **sb/ sth** parecerse a uno/algo; **that's just** ~ **him** es muy de él, es característico de él; **do it** ~ **this** hazlo así; **it is nothing** ~... no tiene parecido alguno con...; **what's he** ~? ¿cómo es (él)?; **what's the weather** ~? ¿qué tiempo hace?; **something** ~ **that** algo así *or* por el estilo; **I feel** ~ **a drink** me apetece algo de beber; **if you** ~ si quieres.

likeable ['laɪkəbl] *a* simpático, agradable.

likelihood ['laɪklɪhud] *n* probabilidad *f*; **in all** ~ según todas las probabilidades.

likely ['laɪklɪ] *a* probable; **he's** ~ **to leave** es probable que se vaya; **not** ~! ¡ni hablar!

like-minded [laɪk'maɪndɪd] *a* de la misma opinión.

liken ['laɪkən] *vt*: **to** ~ **to** comparar con.

likeness ['laɪknɪs] *n* (*similarity*) semejanza, parecido.

likewise ['laɪkwaɪz] *ad* igualmente.

liking ['laɪkɪŋ] *n*: ~ **(for)** (*person*) cariño (a); (*thing*) afición (a); **to take a** ~ **to sb** tomar cariño a uno; **to be to sb's** ~ ser del gusto de uno.

lilac ['laɪlək] *n* lila ◆ *a* (*colour*) de color lila.

lilt [lɪlt] *n* deje *m*.

lilting ['lɪltɪŋ] *a* melodioso.

lily ['lɪlɪ] *n* lirio, azucena.

lily of the valley *n* lirio de los valles.

Lima ['liːmə] *n* Lima.

limb [lɪm] *n* miembro; (*of tree*) rama; **to be out on a** ~ (*fig*) estar aislado.

limber ['lɪmbə*] *a*: **to** ~ **up** *vi* (*fig*) entrenarse; (*SPORT*) desentumecerse.

limbo ['lɪmbəu] *n*: **to be in** ~ (*fig*) quedar a la expectativa.

lime [laɪm] *n* (*tree*) limero; (*fruit*) lima; (*GEO*) cal *f*.

lime juice *n* zumo (*Sp*) *or* jugo de lima.

limelight ['laɪmlaɪt] *n*: **to be in the** ~ (*fig*) ser el centro de atención.

limerick ['lɪmərɪk] *n* quintilla humorística.

limestone ['laɪmstəun] *n* piedra caliza.

limit ['lɪmɪt] *n* límite *m* ◆ *vt* limitar; **weight/speed** ~ peso máximo/velocidad *f* máxima; **within** ~**s** entre límites.

limitation [lɪmɪ'teɪʃən] *n* limitación *f*.

limited ['lɪmɪtɪd] *a* limitado; **to be** ~ **to** limitarse a; ~ **edition** tirada limitada.

limited (liability) company (Ltd) *n* (*Brit*) sociedad *f* anónima (SA).

limitless ['lɪmɪtlɪs] *a* sin límites.

limousine ['lɪməziːn] *n* limusina.

limp [lɪmp] *n*: **to have a** ~ tener cojera ◆ *vi* cojear ◆ *a* flojo.

limpet ['lɪmpɪt] *n* lapa.

limpid ['lɪmpɪd] *a* (*poetic*) límpido, cristalino.

limply ['lɪmplɪ] *ad* desmayadamente; **to say** ~ decir débilmente.

linchpin ['lɪntʃpɪn] *n* pezonera; (*fig*) eje *m*.

Lincs [lɪŋks] *abbr* (*Brit*) = *Lincolnshire*.

line [laɪn] *n* (*also COMM*) línea; (*straight* ~) raya; (*rope*) cuerda; (*for fishing*) sedal *m*; (*wire*) hilo; (*row, series*) fila, hilera; (*of writing*) renglón *m*; (*on face*) arruga; (*speciality*) rama ◆ *vt* (*SEWING*): **to** ~ **(with)** forrar (de); **to** ~ **the streets** ocupar las aceras; **in** ~ **with** de acuerdo con; **she's in** ~ **for promotion** (*fig*) tiene muchas posibilidades de que la asciendan; **to bring sth into** ~ **with sth** poner algo de acuerdo con algo; ~ **of research/business** campo de investigación/comercio; **to take the** ~ **that** ... ser de la opinión que ...; **hold the** ~ **please** (*TEL*) no cuelgue usted, por favor; **to draw the** ~ **at doing sth** negarse a hacer algo; no permitir que se haga algo; **on the right** ~**s** por buen camino; **a new** ~ **in cosmetics** una nueva línea en cosméticos; *see also* **lines**.

line up *vi* hacer cola ◆ *vt* alinear, poner en fila; **to have sth** ~**d up** tener algo arreglado.

linear ['lɪnɪə*] *a* lineal.

lined [laɪnd] *a* (*face*) arrugado; (*paper*) rayado; (*clothes*) forrado.

line editing *n* (*COMPUT*) corrección *f* por líneas.

line feed *n* (*COMPUT*) avance *m* de línea.

linen ['lɪnɪn] *n* ropa blanca; (*cloth*) lino.

line printer *n* impresora de línea.

liner ['laɪnə*] *n* vapor *m* de línea, transatlántico; **dustbin** ~ bolsa de la basura.

lines [laɪnz] *npl* (*RAIL*) vía *sg*, raíles *mpl*.

linesman ['laɪnzmən] *n* (*SPORT*) juez *m* de línea.

line-up ['laɪnʌp] *n* alineación *f*.

linger ['lɪŋgə*] *vi* retrasarse, tardar en marcharse; (*smell, tradition*) persistir.

lingerie ['lænʒəriː] *n* ropa interior *or* íntima (*LAm*) (de mujer).

lingering ['lɪŋgərɪŋ] *a* persistente; (*death*) lento.

lingo, ~**es** ['lɪŋgəu] *n* (*pej*) jerga.

linguist ['lɪŋgwɪst] *n* lingüista *m/f*.

linguistic [lɪŋ'gwɪstɪk] *a* lingüístico.

linguistics [lɪŋ'gwɪstɪks] *n* lingüística.

liniment ['lɪnɪmənt] *n* linimento.

lining ['laɪnɪŋ] *n* forro; (*TECH*) revestimiento; (*of brake*) guarnición *f*.

link [lɪŋk] *n* (*of a chain*) eslabón *m*; (*connection*) conexión *f*; (*bond*) vínculo, lazo ♦ *vt* vincular, unir; **rail** ~ línea de ferrocarril, servicio de trenes.
link up *vt* acoplar ♦ *vi* unirse.

links [lɪŋks] *npl* (*GOLF*) campo *sg* de golf.

link-up ['lɪŋkʌp] *n* (*gen*) unión *f*; (*meeting*) encuentro, reunión *f*; (*of roads*) empalme *m*; (*of spaceships*) acoplamiento; (*RADIO, TV*) enlace *m*.

lino ['laɪnəu] (*Brit*), **linoleum** [lɪ'nəulɪəm] *n* linóleo.

linseed oil ['lɪnsiːd-] *n* aceite *m* de linaza.

lint [lɪnt] *n* gasa.

lintel ['lɪntl] *n* dintel *m*.

lion ['laɪən] *n* león *m*.

lioness ['laɪənɪs] *n* leona.

lip [lɪp] *n* labio; (*of jug*) pico; (*of cup etc*) borde *m*.

lipread ['lɪpriːd] *vi* leer los labios.

lip salve *n* crema protectora para labios.

lip service *n*: **to pay** ~ **to sth** alabar algo pero sin hacer nada.

lipstick ['lɪpstɪk] *n* lápiz *m* de labios, carmín *m*.

liquefy ['lɪkwɪfaɪ] *vt* licuar ♦ *vi* licuarse.

liqueur [lɪ'kjuə*] *n* licor *m*.

liquid ['lɪkwɪd] *a*, *n* líquido.

liquidate ['lɪkwɪdeɪt] *vt* liquidar.

liquidation [lɪkwɪ'deɪʃən] *n* liquidación *f*; **to go into** ~ entrar en liquidación.

liquid crystal display (LCD) *n* pantalla de cristal líquido.

liquidity [lɪ'kwɪdɪtɪ] *n* (*COMM*) liquidez *f*.

liquidize ['lɪkwɪdaɪz] *vt* (*CULIN*) licuar.

liquidizer ['lɪkwɪdaɪzə*] *n* (*CULIN*) licuadora.

liquor ['lɪkə*] *n* licor *m*, bebidas *fpl* alcohólicas.

liquorice ['lɪkərɪs] *n* regaliz *m*.

liquor store *n* (*US*) bodega, *tienda de vinos y bebidas alcohólicas*.

Lisbon ['lɪzbən] *n* Lisboa.

lisp [lɪsp] *n* ceceo.

lissom ['lɪsəm] *a* ágil.

list [lɪst] *n* lista; (*of ship*) inclinación *f* ♦ *vt* (*write down*) hacer una lista de; (*enumerate*) catalogar; (*COMPUT*) listar ♦ *vi* (*ship*) inclinarse; **shopping** ~ lista de las compras; *see also* **lists**.

listed building ['lɪstɪd-] *n* (*ARCHIT*) edificio protegido.

listed company ['lɪstɪd-] *n* compañía cotizable.

listen ['lɪsn] *vi* escuchar, oír; (*pay attention*) atender.

listener ['lɪsnə*] *n* oyente *m/f*.

listing ['lɪstɪŋ] *n* (*COMPUT*) listado.

listless ['lɪstlɪs] *a* apático, indiferente.

listlessly ['lɪstlɪslɪ] *ad* con indiferencia.

listlessness ['lɪstlɪsnɪs] *n* indiferencia, apatía.

list price *n* precio corriente *or* de tarifa.

lists [lɪsts] *npl* (*HISTORY*) liza *sg*; **to enter the** ~ **(against sb/sth)** salir a la palestra (contra uno/algo).

lit [lɪt] *pt, pp* *of* **light**.

litany ['lɪtənɪ] *n* letanía.

liter ['liːtə*] *n* (*US*) = **litre**.

literacy ['lɪtərəsɪ] *n* capacidad *f* de leer y escribir; ~ **campaign** campaña de alfabetización.

literal ['lɪtərl] *a* literal.

literally ['lɪtrəlɪ] *ad* literalmente.

literary ['lɪtərərɪ] *a* literario.

literate ['lɪtərət] *a* que sabe leer y escribir; (*fig*) culto.

literature ['lɪtərɪtʃə*] *n* literatura; (*brochures etc*) folletos *mpl*.

lithe [laɪð] *a* ágil.

litho(graph) ['lɪθəu(grɑːf)] *n* litografía.

lithography [lɪ'θɒgrəfɪ] *n* litografía.

Lithuania [lɪθju'eɪnɪə] *n* Lituania.

litigate ['lɪtɪgeɪt] *vi* litigar.

litigation [lɪtɪ'geɪʃən] *n* litigio.

litmus paper ['lɪtməs-] *n* papel *m* de tornasol.

litre, (*US*) **liter** ['liːtə*] *n* litro.

litter ['lɪtə*] *n* (*rubbish*) basura; (*paper*) papel *m* tirado; (*young animals*) camada, cría.

litter bin *n* (*Brit*) papelera.

littered ['lɪtəd] *a*: ~ **with** lleno de.

litter lout, (*US*) **litterbug** ['lɪtəbʌg] *n* persona que tira papeles usados en la vía pública.

little ['lɪtl] *a* (*small*) pequeño; (*not much*) poco; (*often translated by suffix, eg*): ~ **house** casita ♦ *ad* poco; **a** ~ un poco (de); ~ **by** ~ poco a poco; ~ **finger** (dedo) meñique *m*; **for a** ~ **while** por un rato; **with** ~ **difficulty** sin problema *or* dificultad; **as** ~ **as possible** lo menos posible.

liturgy ['lɪtədʒɪ] *n* liturgia.

live *vb* [lɪv] *vi* vivir ♦ *vt* (*a life*) llevar; (*experience*) vivir ♦ *a* [laɪv] (*animal*) vivo; (*wire*) conectado; (*broadcast*) en directo; (*issue*) de actualidad; (*unexploded*) sin explotar; **to** ~ **in London** vivir en Londres; **to** ~ **together** vivir juntos.
live down *vt* hacer olvidar.
live off *vt fus* (*land, fish etc*) vivir de; (*pej: parents etc*) vivir a costa de.
live on *vt fus* (*food*) vivirse de, alimentarse de; **to** ~ **on £50 a week** vivir con 50 libras por semana.

live out vi (students) ser externo ♦ vt: **to ~ out one's days** or **life** acabar la vida.

live up vt: **to ~ it up** (col) vivir la gran vida.

live up to vt fus (fulfil) cumplir con; (justify) justificar.

livelihood ['laivlɪhud] n sustento.

liveliness ['laɪvlɪnɪs] n viveza.

lively ['laɪvlɪ] a (gen) vivo; (talk) animado; (pace) rápido; (party, tune) alegre.

liven up ['laɪvn-] vt (discussion, evening) animar.

liver ['lɪvə*] n hígado.

liverish ['lɪvərɪʃ] a: **to feel ~** sentirse or estar mal del hígado.

Liverpudlian [lɪvə'pʌdlɪən] a de Liverpool ♦ n nativo/a (or habitante m/f) de Liverpool.

livery ['lɪvərɪ] n librea.

lives [laɪvz] npl of **life**.

livestock ['laɪvstɔk] n ganado.

livid ['lɪvɪd] a lívido; (furious) furioso.

living ['lɪvɪŋ] a (alive) vivo ♦ n: **to earn** or **make a ~** ganarse la vida; **cost of ~** coste m de la vida; **in ~ memory** que se recuerde or recuerda.

living conditions npl condiciones fpl de vida.

living expenses npl gastos mpl de mantenimiento.

living room n sala (de estar).

living standards npl nivel msg de vida.

living wage n sueldo suficiente para vivir.

lizard ['lɪzəd] n lagartija.

llama ['lɑːmə] n llama.

LLB n abbr (= Bachelor of Laws) Ldo./a. en Dcho.

LLD n abbr (= Doctor of Laws) Dr(a). en Dcho.

LMT n abbr (US: = Local Mean Time) hora local.

load [ləud] n (gen) carga; (weight) peso ♦ vt (COMPUT) cargar; (also: ~ up): **to ~ (with)** cargar (con or de); **a ~ of, ~s of** (fig) (gran) cantidad de, montones de dinero).

loaded ['ləudɪd] a (dice) cargado; (question) intencionado; (col: rich) forrado (de dinero).

loading ['ləudɪŋ] n (COMM) sobreprima.

loading bay n área de carga y descarga.

loaf, pl **loaves** [ləuf, ləuvz] n (barra de) pan m ♦ vi (also: ~ about, ~ around) holgazanear.

loam [ləum] n marga.

loan [ləun] n préstamo; (COMM) empréstito ♦ vt prestar; **on ~** (book, painting) prestado; **to raise a ~** (money) procurar un empréstito.

loan account n cuenta de crédito.

loan capital n empréstito.

loath [ləuθ] a: **to be ~ to do sth** estar poco dispuesto a hacer algo.

loathe [ləuð] vt aborrecer; (person) odiar.

loathing ['ləuðɪŋ] n aversión f; odio.

loathsome ['ləuðsəm] a asqueroso, repugnante; (person) odioso.

loaves [ləuvz] pl of **loaf**.

lob [lɔb] vt (ball) volear por alto.

lobby ['lɔbɪ] n vestíbulo, sala de espera; (POL: pressure group) grupo de presión ♦ vt presionar.

lobbyist ['lɔbɪɪst] n cabildero/a.

lobe [ləub] n lóbulo.

lobster ['lɔbstə*] n langosta.

lobster pot n nasa, langostera.

local ['ləukl] a local ♦ n (pub) bar m; **the ~s** npl los vecinos, los del lugar.

local anaesthetic n (MED) anestesia local.

local authority n municipio, ayuntamiento (Sp).

local call n (TEL) llamada local.

local government n gobierno municipal.

locality [ləu'kælɪtɪ] n localidad f.

localize ['ləukəlaɪz] vt localizar.

locally ['ləukəlɪ] ad en la vecindad.

locate [ləu'keɪt] vt (find) localizar; (situate) colocar.

location [ləu'keɪʃən] n situación f; **on ~** (CINEMA) en exteriores, fuera del estudio.

loch [lɔx] n lago.

lock [lɔk] n (of door, box) cerradura; (of canal) esclusa; (of hair) mechón m ♦ vt (with key) cerrar con llave; (immobilize) inmovilizar ♦ vi (door etc) cerrarse con llave; (wheels) trabarse; **~ stock and barrel** (fig) por completo or entero; **on full ~** (AUT) con el volante girado al máximo.

lock away vt (valuables) guardar bajo llave; (criminal) encerrar.

lock out vt: **the workers were ~ed out** los trabajadores tuvieron que enfrentarse con un cierre patronal.

lock up vi echar la llave.

locker ['lɔkə*] n casillero.

locker-room ['lɔkərum] n (US SPORT) vestuario.

locket ['lɔkɪt] n medallón m.

lockout ['lɔkaut] n (INDUSTRY) paro or cierre m patronal, lockout m.

locksmith ['lɔksmɪθ] n cerrajero/a.

lock-up ['lɔkʌp] n (prison) cárcel f; (cell) jaula; (~ garage) jaula, cochera.

locomotive [ləukə'məutɪv] n locomotora.

locum ['ləukəm] n (MED) (médico/a) interino/a.

locust ['ləukəst] n langosta.

lodge [lɔdʒ] n casa del guarda; (porter's) portería; (FREEMASONRY) logia ♦ vi (person): **to ~ (with)** alojarse (en casa de) ♦ vt (complaint) presentar.

lodger ['lɔdʒə*] n huésped(a) m/f.

lodging house ['lɔdʒɪŋ-] n pensión f, casa de huéspedes.

lodgings ['lɔdʒɪŋz] npl alojamiento sg; (house) casa sg de huéspedes.

loft [lɔft] n desván m.

lofty ['lɔftɪ] a alto; (haughty) orgulloso; (sentiments, aims) elevado, noble.

log [lɔg] n (of wood) leño, tronco; (book) = **logbook** ♦ n abbr (= logarithm) log. ♦ vt anotar, registrar.

log in, log on vi (COMPUT) iniciar la (or una) sesión.

log off, log out vi (COMPUT) finalizar la (or una) sesión.

logarithm ['lɔgərɪðəm] n logaritmo.

logbook ['lɔgbuk] n (NAUT) diario de a bordo; (AVIAT) libro de vuelo; (of car) documentación f (del coche).

log cabin n cabaña de troncos.

log fire n fuego de leña.

loggerheads ['lɔgəhɛdz] npl: **at ~ (with)** de pique (con).

logic ['lɔdʒɪk] n lógica.

logical ['lɔdʒɪkl] a lógico.

logically ['lɔdʒɪkəlɪ] ad lógicamente.

logistics [lɔ'dʒɪstɪks] n logística.

logo ['ləugəu] n logotipo.

loin [lɔɪn] n (CULIN) lomo, solomillo; **~s** npl lomos mpl.

loin cloth n taparrabo.

loiter ['lɔɪtə*] vi vagar; (pej) merodear.

loll [lɔl] vi (also: ~ **about**) repantigarse.

lollipop ['lɔlɪpɔp] n pirulí m; (iced) polo.

lollipop man, lollipop lady n (Brit) persona encargada de ayudar a los niños a cruzar la calle.

lollop ['lɔləp] vi (Brit) moverse desgarbadamente.

Lombardy ['lɔmbədɪ] n Lombardía.

London ['lʌndən] n Londres m.

Londoner ['lʌndənə*] n londinense m/f.

lone [ləun] a solitario.

loneliness ['ləunlɪnɪs] n soledad f, aislamiento.

lonely ['ləunlɪ] a solitario, solo.

loner ['ləunə*] n solitario/a.

lonesome ['ləunsəm] a (esp US) = **lonely**.

long [lɔŋ] a largo ♦ ad mucho tiempo, largamente ♦ vi: **to ~ for sth** anhelar algo ♦ n: **the ~ and the short of it is that ...** (fig) en resumidas cuentas or concretamente, es que ...; **in the ~ run** a la larga; **so** or **as ~ as** mientras, con tal de que; **don't be ~!** ¡no tardes!, ¡vuelve pronto!; **how ~ is the street?** ¿cuánto tiene la calle de largo?; **how ~ is the lesson?** ¿cuánto dura la clase?; **6 metres ~** que mide 6 metros, de 6 metros de largo; **6 months ~** que dura 6 meses, de 6 meses de duración; **all night ~** toda la noche; **~ ago** hace mucho (tiempo); **he no ~er comes** ya no viene; **~ before** mucho antes; **before ~** (+ future) dentro de poco; (+ past) poco tiempo después; **at ~ last** al fin, por fin; **I shan't be ~** termino pronto.

long-distance [lɔŋ'dɪstəns] a (race) de larga distancia; (call) interurbano.

longevity [lɔn'dʒɛvɪtɪ] n longevidad f.

long-haired ['lɔŋ'hɛəd] a de pelo largo.

longhand ['lɔŋhænd] n escritura (corriente).

longing ['lɔŋɪŋ] n anhelo, ansia; (nostalgia) nostalgia ♦ a anhelante.

longingly ['lɔŋɪŋlɪ] ad con ansia.

longitude ['lɔŋgɪtjuːd] n longitud f.

long jump n salto de longitud.

long-lost ['lɔŋlɔst] a desaparecido hace mucho tiempo.

long-playing record (LP) ['lɔŋpleɪŋ-] n elepé m, disco de larga duración.

long-range ['lɔŋ'reɪndʒ] a de gran alcance; (weather forecast) de larga proyección.

longshoreman ['lɔŋʃɔːmən] n (US) estibador m.

long-sighted ['lɔŋ'saɪtɪd] a (Brit) présbita.

long-standing ['lɔŋ'stændɪŋ] a de mucho tiempo.

long-suffering [lɔŋ'sʌfərɪŋ] a sufrido.

long-term ['lɔŋtəːm] a a largo plazo.

long wave n onda larga.

long-winded [lɔŋ'wɪndɪd] a prolijo.

loo [luː] n (Brit: col) wáter m.

loofah ['luːfə] n esponja de lufa.

look [luk] vi mirar; (seem) parecer; (building etc): **to ~ south/on to the sea** dar al sur/al mar ♦ n mirada; (glance) vistazo; (appearance) aire m, aspecto; **~s** npl físico sg, belleza sg; **to ~ ahead** mirar hacia delante; **it ~s about 4 metres long** yo calculo que tiene unos 4 metros de largo; **it ~s all right to me** me parece que está bien; **to have a ~ at sth** echar un vistazo a algo; **to have a ~ for sth** buscar algo.

look after vt fus cuidar.

look around vi echar una mirada alrededor.

look at vt fus mirar; (consider) considerar.

look back vi mirar hacia atrás; **to ~ back at sb/sth** mirar hacia atrás algo/a uno; **to ~ back on** (event, period) recordar.

look down on vt fus (fig) despreciar, mirar con desprecio.

look for vt fus buscar.

look forward to vt fus esperar con ilusión; (in letters): **we ~ forward to hearing from you** quedamos a la espera de sus gratas noticias; **I'm not ~ing forward to it** no tengo ganas de eso, no me hace ilusión.

look in vi: **to ~ in on sb** (visit) pasar por casa de uno.

look into vt fus investigar.

look on vi mirar (como espectador).

look out vi (beware): **to ~ out (for)** tener cuidado (de).

look out for vt fus (seek) buscar; (await) esperar.

look over vt (essay) revisar; (town, building) inspeccionar, registrar; (person) examinar.

look round vi (turn) volver la cabeza; **to ~ round for sth** buscar algo.

look through vt fus (papers, book) hojear; (briefly) echar un vistazo a; (telescope) mirar por.

look to vt fus ocuparse de; (rely on) contar con.

look up vi mirar hacia arriba; (improve) mejorar ♦ vt (word) buscar; (friend) visitar.

look up to vt fus admirar.

look-out ['lukaut] n (tower etc) puesto de observación; (person) vigía m/f; **to be on the ~ for sth** estar al acecho de algo.

look-up table ['lukʌp-] n (COMPUT) tabla de consulta.

LOOM n abbr (US: = Loyal Order of Moose) asociación benéfica.

loom [luːm] n telar m ♦ vi (threaten) amenazar.

loony ['luːnɪ] a, n (col) loco/a m/f.

loop [luːp] n lazo; (bend) vuelta, recodo; (COMPUT) bucle m.

loophole ['luːphəul] n escapatoria.

loose [luːs] a (gen) suelto; (not tight) flojo; (wobbly etc) movedizo; (clothes) ancho; (morals, discipline) relajado ♦ vt (free) soltar; (slacken) aflojar; (also: ~ off: arrow) disparar, soltar; **~ connection** (ELEC) rotura; **to be at a ~ end** or (US) **at ~ ends** no saber qué hacer; **to tie up ~ ends** (fig) no dejar cabo suelto.

loose change n cambio.

loose chippings [-'tʃɪpɪŋz] npl (on road) gravilla sg suelta.

loose-fitting ['luːsfɪtɪŋ] a suelto.

loose-leaf ['luːsliːf] a: **~ binder** or **folder** carpeta de hojas sueltas or insertables.

loose-limbed ['luːslɪmd] a ágil, suelto.

loosely ['luːslɪ] ad libremente, aproximadamente.

loosen ['luːsn] vt (free) soltar; (untie) desatar; (slacken) aflojar.

loosen up vi (before game) desentumecerse; (col: relax) soltarse, relajarse.

looseness ['luːsnɪs] n soltura; flojedad f.

loot [luːt] n botín m ♦ vt saquear.

looter ['luːtə*] n saqueador(a) m/f.

looting ['luːtɪŋ] n pillaje m.

lop [lɔp]: **to ~ off** vt cortar; (branches) podar.

lop-sided ['lɔp'saɪdɪd] a desequilibrado.

lord [lɔːd] n señor m; **L~ Smith** Lord Smith; **the L~** el Señor; **the (House of) L~s** (Brit) la Cámara de los Lores.

lordly ['lɔːdlɪ] a señorial.

Lordship ['lɔːdʃɪp] n: **your ~** su Señoría.

lore [lɔː*] n saber m popular, tradiciones fpl.

lorry ['lɔrɪ] n (Brit) camión m.

lorry driver n camionero/a.

lorry load n carga.

lose, pt, pp **lost** [luːz, lɔst] vt perder ♦ vi perder, ser vencido; **to ~ (time)** (clock) atrasarse; **to ~ no time (in doing sth)** no tardar (en hacer algo); **to get lost** (object) extraviarse; (person) perderse.

lose out vi salir perdiendo.

loser ['luːzə*] n perdedor(a) m/f; **to be a bad ~** no saber perder.

losing ['luːzɪŋ] a (team etc) vencido, perdedor(a).

loss [lɔs] n pérdida; **heavy ~es** (MIL) grandes pérdidas fpl; **to be at a ~** no saber qué hacer; **to be a dead ~** ser completamente inútil; **to cut one's ~es** cortar por lo sano; **to sell sth at a ~** vender algo con pérdida.

loss leader n (COMM) artículo de promoción.

lost [lɔst] pt, pp of **lose** ♦ a perdido; **~ in thought** absorto, ensimismado.

lost and found n (US) = **lost property, lost property office** or **department**.

lost cause n causa perdida.

lost property n (Brit) objetos mpl perdidos.

lost property office or **department** n (Brit) departamento de objetos perdidos.

lot [lɔt] n (at auctions) lote m; (destiny) suerte f; **the ~** el todo, todos mpl, todas fpl; **a ~** mucho, bastante; **a ~ of, ~s of** mucho(s)/a(s) (pl); **I read a ~** leo bastante; **to draw ~s (for sth)** echar suertes (para decidir algo).

lotion ['ləuʃən] n loción f.

lottery ['lɔtərɪ] n lotería.

loud [laud] a (voice, sound) fuerte; (laugh, shout) estrepitoso; (gaudy) chillón/ona ♦ ad (speak etc) fuerte; **out ~** en voz alta.

loudhailer [laud'heɪlə*] n (Brit) megáfono.

loudly ['laudlɪ] ad (noisily) fuerte; (aloud) en alta voz.

loudness ['laudnɪs] n (of sound etc) fuerza.

loudspeaker [laud'spiːkə*] n altavoz m.

lounge [laundʒ] n salón m, sala (de estar); (of hotel) salón m; (of airport) sala (de embarque) ♦ vi (also: ~ about, ~ around) holgazanear, no hacer nada.

lounge bar n salón m.

lounge suit n (Brit) traje m de calle.

louse, pl **lice** [laus, laɪs] n piojo.

louse up vt (col) echar a perder.

lousy ['lauzɪ] a (fig) vil, asqueroso.

lout [laut] n gamberro/a.

louvre, (US) **louver** ['luːvə*] a: **~ door** puerta de rejilla; **~ window** ventana de libro.

lovable ['lʌvəbl] a amable, simpático.

love [lʌv] n amor m ♦ vt amar, querer; **to send one's ~ to sb** dar sus recuerdos a uno; **~ from Anne** (in letter) con cariño de Anne; **I ~ to read** me encanta leer; **to be in ~ with** estar enamorado de; **to make ~** hacer el amor; **for the ~ of** por amor de; **"15 ~"** (TENNIS) "15 a cero"; **I ~ paella**

me encanta la paella; **I'd ~ to come** me gustaría muchísimo venir.
love affair *n* aventura sentimental.
love letter *n* carta de amor.
love life *n* vida sentimental.
lovely ['lʌvlɪ] *a* (*delightful*) precioso, encantador(a); (*beautiful*) hermoso; **we had a ~ time** lo pasamos estupendo.
lovemaking ['lʌvmeɪkɪŋ] *n* relaciones *fpl* sexuales.
lover ['lʌvə*] *n* amante *m/f*; (*amateur*): **a ~ of** un(a) aficionado/a *or* un(a) amante de.
lovesick ['lʌvsɪk] *a* enfermo de amor, amartelado.
lovesong ['lʌvsɔŋ] *n* canción *f* de amor.
loving ['lʌvɪŋ] *a* amoroso, cariñoso.
lovingly ['lʌvɪŋlɪ] *ad* amorosamente, cariñosamente.
low [ləu] *a, ad* bajo ♦ *n* (*METEOROLOGY*) área de baja presión ♦ *vi* (*cow*) mugir; **to feel ~** sentirse deprimido; **to turn (down) ~** bajar; **to reach a new** *or* **an all-time ~** llegar a su punto más bajo.
lowbrow ['ləubrau] *a* (*person*) de poca cultura.
low-calorie ['ləu'kælərɪ] *a* de bajo contenido calorífico.
low-cut ['ləukʌt] *a* (*dress*) escotado.
low-down ['ləudaun] *n* (*col*): **he gave me the ~ on it** me puso al corriente ♦ *a* (*mean*) vil, bajo.
lower ['ləuə*] *vt* bajar; (*reduce: price*) reducir, rebajar; (: *resistance*) debilitar: **to ~ o.s. to** (*fig*) rebajarse a ♦ *vi* ['lauə*]: **to ~ (at sb)** fulminar a uno con la mirada.
lower case *n* (*TYP*) minúscula.
lowering ['lauərɪŋ] *a* (*sky*) amenazador(a).
low-fat ['ləu'fæt] *a* (*milk, yoghurt*) desnatado; (*diet*) bajo en calorías.
low-key ['ləu'ki:] *a* de mínima intensidad; (*operation*) de poco perfil.
lowland ['ləulənd] *n* tierra baja.
low-level ['ləulevl] *a* de bajo nivel; (*flying*) a poca altura.
low-loader ['ləuləudə*] *n* camión *m* de caja a bajo nivel.
lowly ['ləulɪ] *a* humilde.
low-lying [ləu'laɪɪŋ] *a* bajo.
loyal ['lɔɪəl] *a* leal.
loyalist ['lɔɪəlɪst] *n* legitimista *m/f*.
loyally ['lɔɪəlɪ] *ad* lealmente.
loyalty ['lɔɪəltɪ] *n* lealtad *f*.
lozenge ['lɔzɪndʒ] *n* (*MED*) pastilla.
LP *n abbr see* **long-playing record**.
L-plates ['ɛlpleɪts] *npl* (*Brit*) placas *fpl* de aprendiz de conductor.
LPN *n abbr* (*US:* = *Licensed Practical Nurse*) enfermero/a practicante.
LRAM *n abbr* (*Brit*) = *Licentiate of the Royal Academy of Music*.
LSAT *n abbr* (*US*) = *Law School Admissions Test*.
LSD *n abbr* (= *lysergic acid diethylamide*)

LSD *f*; (*Brit:* = *pounds, shillings and pence*) *sistema monetario usado en Gran Bretaña hasta 1971*.
LSE *n abbr* = *London School of Economics*.
Ltd *abbr* (= *limited company*) S.A.
lubricant ['lu:brɪkənt] *n* lubricante *m*.
lubricate ['lu:brɪkeɪt] *vt* lubricar, engrasar.
lubrication [lu:brɪ'keɪʃən] *n* lubricación *f*.
lucid ['lu:sɪd] *a* lúcido.
lucidity [lu:'sɪdɪtɪ] *n* lucidez *f*.
lucidly ['lu:sɪdlɪ] *ad* lúcidamente.
luck [lʌk] *n* suerte *f*; **good/bad ~** buena/mala suerte; **good ~!** ¡(que tengas) suerte!; **to be in ~** estar de *or* con suerte; **to be out of ~** tener mala suerte.
luckily ['lʌkɪlɪ] *ad* afortunadamente.
lucky ['lʌkɪ] *a* afortunado.
lucrative ['lu:krətɪv] *a* lucrativo.
ludicrous ['lu:dɪkrəs] *a* absurdo.
ludo ['lu:dəu] *n* ludo.
lug [lʌg] *vt* (*drag*) arrastrar.
luggage ['lʌgɪdʒ] *n* equipaje *m*.
luggage rack *n* (*in train*) rejilla, redecilla; (*on car*) baca, portaequipajes *m inv*.
luggage van *n* furgón *m or* vagón *m* de equipaje.
lugubrious [lu'gu:brɪəs] *a* lúgubre.
lukewarm ['lu:kwɔ:m] *a* tibio, templado.
lull [lʌl] *n* tregua ♦ *vt* (*child*) acunar; (*person, fear*) calmar.
lullaby ['lʌləbaɪ] *n* nana.
lumbago [lʌm'beɪgəu] *n* lumbago.
lumber ['lʌmbə*] *n* (*junk*) trastos *mpl* viejos; (*wood*) maderos *mpl* ♦ *vt* (*Brit col*): **to ~ sb with sth/sb** hacer que uno cargue con algo/uno ♦ *vi* (*also:* **~ about, ~ along**) moverse pesadamente.
lumberjack ['lʌmbədʒæk] *n* maderero.
lumber room *n* (*Brit*) cuarto trastero.
lumber yard *n* (*US*) almacén *m* de madera.
luminous ['lu:mɪnəs] *a* luminoso.
lump [lʌmp] *n* terrón *m*; (*fragment*) trozo; (*in sauce*) grumo; (*in throat*) nudo; (*swelling*) bulto ♦ *vt* (*also:* **~ together**) juntar.
lump sum *n* suma global.
lumpy ['lʌmpɪ] *a* (*sauce*) lleno de grumos.
lunacy ['lu:nəsɪ] *n* locura.
lunar ['lu:nə*] *a* lunar.
lunatic ['lu:nətɪk] *a, n* loco/a *m/f*.
lunatic asylum *n* manicomio.
lunch [lʌntʃ] *n* almuerzo, comida ♦ *vi* almorzar; **to invite sb to** *or* **for ~** invitar a uno a almorzar.
lunch break, lunch hour *n* hora del almuerzo.
luncheon ['lʌntʃən] *n* almuerzo.
luncheon meat *n* tipo de fiambre.
luncheon voucher *n* vale *m* de comida.
lunchtime ['lʌntʃtaɪm] *n* hora del almuerzo *or* de comer.
lung [lʌŋ] *n* pulmón *m*.
lung cancer *n* cáncer *m* del pulmón.

lunge [lʌndʒ] vi (also: ~ **forward**) abalanzarse; **to ~ at** arremeter contra.
lupin ['lu:pɪn] n altramuz m.
lurch [lə:tʃ] vi dar sacudidas ◆ n sacudida; **to leave sb in the ~** dejar a uno plantado.
lure [luə*] n (bait) cebo; (decoy) señuelo ◆ vt convencer con engaños.
lurid ['luərɪd] a (colour) chillón/ona; (account) sensacional; (detail) horripilante.
lurk [lə:k] vi (hide) esconderse; (wait) estar al acecho.
luscious ['lʌʃəs] a delicioso.
lush [lʌʃ] a exuberante.
lust [lʌst] n lujuria; (greed) codicia.
  lust after vt fus codiciar.
lustful ['lʌstful] a lascivo, lujurioso.
lustre, (US) **luster** ['lʌstə*] n lustre m, brillo.
lustrous ['lʌstrəs] a brillante.
lusty ['lʌstɪ] a robusto, fuerte.
lute [lu:t] n laúd m.
Luxembourg ['lʌksəmbə:g] n Luxemburgo.
luxuriant [lʌg'zjuərɪənt] a exuberante.
luxurious [lʌg'zjuərɪəs] a lujoso.
luxury ['lʌkʃərɪ] n lujo ◆ cpd de lujo.
luxury tax n impuesto de lujo.
LV n abbr (Brit) = **luncheon voucher**.
LW abbr (RADIO) = **long wave**.
lying ['laɪɪŋ] n mentiras fpl ◆ a (statement, story) mentiroso, falso; (person) mentiroso.
lynch [lɪntʃ] vt linchar.
lynx [lɪŋks] n lince m.
Lyons ['laɪənz] n Lyón m.
lyre ['laɪə*] n lira.
lyric ['lɪrɪk] a lírico; ~**s** npl (of song) letra sg.
lyrical ['lɪrɪkl] a lírico.

M

M, m [ɛm] n (letter) M, m f; **M for Mary**, (US) **M for Mike** M de Madrid.
M n abbr = **million(s)**; (= medium) M; (Brit: = motorway): **the M8** ≈ la A8.
m abbr (= metre) m.; = **mile(s)**.
MA n abbr (US) = Military Academy; see **Master of Arts**; (US POST) = Massachusetts.
mac [mæk] n (Brit) impermeable m.
macabre [mə'ka:brə] a macabro.
macaroni [mækə'rəunɪ] n macarrones mpl.
macaroon [mækə'ru:n] n macarrón m, mostachón m.
mace [meɪs] n (weapon, ceremonial) maza; (spice) macis f.
machinations [mæʃɪ'neɪʃənz] npl intrigas fpl, manipulaciones fpl.

machine [mə'ʃi:n] n máquina ◆ vt (dress etc) coser a máquina; (TECH) trabajar a máquina.
machine code n (COMPUT) código máquina.
machine gun n ametralladora.
machine language n (COMPUT) lenguaje m máquina.
machine readable a (COMPUT) legible por máquina.
machinery [mə'ʃi:nərɪ] n maquinaria; (fig) mecanismo.
machine shop n taller m de máquinas.
machine tool n máquina herramienta.
machine translation n traducción f automática.
machine washable a lavable en la lavadora.
machinist [mə'ʃi:nɪst] n operario/a m/f (de máquina).
macho ['mætʃəu] a macho.
mackerel ['mækrl] n, pl inv caballa.
mackintosh ['mækɪntɔʃ] n (Brit) impermeable m.
macro... ['mækrəu] pref macro....
macro-economics ['mækrəui:kə'nɔmɪks] n macroeconomía.
mad [mæd] a loco; (idea) disparatado; (angry) furioso; ~ **(at** or **with sb)** furioso con uno; **to be ~ (keen) about** or **on sth** estar loco por algo; **to go ~** volverse loco, enloquecer(se).
madam ['mædəm] n señora; **can I help you ~?** ¿le puedo ayudar, señora?; **M~ Chairman** señora presidenta.
madden ['mædn] vt volver loco.
maddening ['mædnɪŋ] a enloquecedor(a).
made [meɪd] pt, pp of **make**.
Madeira [mə'dɪərə] n (GEO) Madera; (wine) vino de Madera, madera m.
made-to-measure ['meɪdtəmɛʒə*] a (Brit) hecho a la medida.
made-up ['meɪdʌp] a (story) ficticio.
madly ['mædlɪ] ad locamente.
madman ['mædmən] n loco.
madness ['mædnɪs] n locura.
Madonna [mə'dɔnə] n Virgen f.
Madrid [mə'drɪd] n Madrid m.
madrigal ['mædrɪgəl] n madrigal m.
Mafia ['mæfɪə] n Mafia.
mag [mæg] n abbr (Brit col) = **magazine**.
magazine [mægə'zi:n] n revista; (MIL: store) almacén m; (of firearm) recámara.
maggot ['mægət] n gusano.
magic ['mædʒɪk] n magia ◆ a mágico.
magical ['mædʒɪkəl] a mágico.
magician [mə'dʒɪʃən] n mago/a; (conjurer) prestidigitador(a) m/f.
magistrate ['mædʒɪstreɪt] n juez m/f (municipal).
magnanimity [mægnə'nɪmɪtɪ] n magnanimidad f.
magnanimous [mæg'nænɪməs] a magnáni-

mo.

magnate ['mægneɪt] n magnate m/f.

magnesium [mæg'niːziəm] n magnesio.

magnet ['mægnɪt] n imán m.

magnetic [mæg'nɛtɪk] a magnético.

magnetic disk n (COMPUT) disco magnético.

magnetic tape n cinta magnética.

magnetism ['mægnɪtɪzəm] n magnetismo.

magnification [mægnɪfɪ'keɪʃən] n aumento.

magnificence [mæg'nɪfɪsns] n magnificencia.

magnificent [mæg'nɪfɪsnt] a magnífico.

magnificently [mæg'nɪfɪsntlɪ] ad magníficamente.

magnify ['mægnɪfaɪ] vt aumentar; (fig) exagerar.

magnifying glass ['mægnɪfaɪɪŋ-] n lupa.

magnitude ['mægnɪtjuːd] n magnitud f.

magnolia [mæg'nəʊlɪə] n magnolia.

magpie ['mægpaɪ] n urraca.

maharajah [mɑːhə'rɑːdʒə] n maharajá m.

mahogany [mə'hɔgənɪ] n caoba ♦ cpd de caoba.

maid [meɪd] n criada; **old** ~ (pej) solterona.

maiden ['meɪdn] n doncella ♦ a (aunt etc) solterona; (speech, voyage) inaugural.

maiden name n nombre m de soltera.

mail [meɪl] n correo; (letters) cartas fpl ♦ vt (post) echar al correo; (send) mandar por correo; **by** ~ por correo.

mailbox ['meɪlbɔks] n (US: for letters etc; COMPUT) buzón m.

mailing list ['meɪlɪŋ-] n lista de direcciones.

mailman ['meɪlmæn] n (US) cartero.

mail-order ['meɪlɔːdə*] n pedido postal; (business) venta por correo ♦ a: ~ **firm** or **house** casa de venta por correo.

mailshot ['meɪlʃɔt] n correo instantáneo.

mailtrain ['meɪltreɪn] n tren m correo.

mail van, (US) **mail truck** n (AUT) camioneta de correos or de reparto.

maim [meɪm] vt mutilar, lisiar.

main [meɪn] a principal, mayor ♦ n (pipe) cañería maestra; (US) red f eléctrica; **the** ~**s** (Brit ELEC) la red eléctrica; **in the** ~ en general.

main course n (CULIN) plato principal.

mainframe ['meɪnfreɪm] n (also: ~ **computer**) computador m or ordenador m central.

mainland ['meɪnlənd] n continente m.

main line n línea de largo recorrido.

mainly ['meɪnlɪ] ad principalmente, en su mayoría.

main road n carretera principal.

mainstay ['meɪnsteɪ] n (fig) pilar m.

mainstream ['meɪnstriːm] n (fig) corriente f principal.

main street n calle f mayor.

maintain [meɪn'teɪn] vt mantener; (affirm) sostener; **to** ~ **that** ... mantener or soste-

ner que ... .

maintenance ['meɪntənəns] n mantenimiento; (alimony) pensión f alimenticia.

maintenance contract n contrato de mantenimiento.

maintenance order n (LAW) obligación f de pagar una pensión alimenticia al cónyuge.

maisonette [meɪzə'nɛt] n apartamento de dos pisos.

maize [meɪz] n (Brit) maíz m, choclo (LAm).

Maj. abbr (MIL) = **major**.

majestic [mə'dʒɛstɪk] a majestuoso.

majesty ['mædʒɪstɪ] n majestad f.

major ['meɪdʒə*] n (MIL) comandante m ♦ a principal; (MUS) mayor ♦ vi (US UNIV): **to** ~ (**in**) especializarse en; **a** ~ **operation** una operación or intervención de gran importancia.

Majorca [mə'jɔːkə] n Mallorca.

major general n (MIL) general m de división.

majority [mə'dʒɔrɪtɪ] n mayoría ♦ cpd (verdict) mayoritario.

majority holding n (COMM): **to have a** ~ tener un interés mayoritario.

make [meɪk] vt (pt, pp made [meɪd]) hacer; (manufacture) hacer, fabricar; (cause to be): **to** ~ **sb sad** hacer or poner triste a uno; (force): **to** ~ **sb do sth** obligar a uno a hacer algo; (equal): **2 and 2** ~ **4** 2 y 2 son 4 ♦ n marca; **to** ~ **a fool of sb** poner a uno en ridículo; **to** ~ **a profit/loss** obtener ganancias/sufrir pérdidas; **to** ~ **a profit of £500** sacar una ganancia de 500 libras; **to** ~ **it** (arrive) llegar; (achieve sth) tener éxito; **what time do you** ~ **it?** ¿qué hora tienes?; **to** ~ **do with** contentarse con.

make for vt fus (place) dirigirse a.

make off vi largarse.

make out vt (decipher) descifrar; (understand) entender; (see) distinguir; (write: cheque) extender; **to** ~ **out (that)** (claim, imply) dar a entender (que); **to** ~ **out a case for sth** presentar una defensa de algo.

make over vt (assign): **to** ~ **over (to)** ceder or traspasar (a).

make up vt (invent) inventar; (parcel) hacer ♦ vi reconciliarse; (with cosmetics) maquillarse; **to be made up of** estar compuesto de.

make up for vt fus compensar.

make-believe ['meɪkbɪliːv] n ficción f, invención f.

maker ['meɪkə*] n fabricante m/f.

makeshift ['meɪkʃɪft] a improvisado.

make-up ['meɪkʌp] n maquillaje m.

make-up bag n bolsita del maquillaje or de los cosméticos.

make-up remover n desmaquillador m.

making ['meɪkɪŋ] n (fig): **in the ~** en vías de formación; **to have the ~s of** (person) tener madera de.

maladjusted [mælə'dʒʌstɪd] a inadaptado.

maladroit [maelə'drɔɪt] a torpe.

malaise [mæ'leɪz] n malestar m.

malaria [mə'lɛərɪə] n malaria.

Malawi [mə'lɑːwɪ] n Malawi m.

Malay [mə'leɪ] a malayo ◆ n (person) malayo/a; (LING) malayo.

Malaya [mə'leɪə] n Malaya, Malaca.

Malayan [mə'leɪən] a, n = **Malay**.

Malaysia [mə'leɪzɪə] n Malasia.

Malaysian [mə'leɪzɪən] a, n malasio/a m/f.

Maldive Islands ['mɔːldaɪv-], **Maldives** ['mɔːldaɪvz] npl: **the ~** las Maldivas.

male [meɪl] n (BIOL, ELEC) macho ◆ a (sex, attitude) masculino; (child etc) varón.

male chauvinist (pig) n machista m.

male nurse n enfermero.

malevolence [mə'lɛvələns] n malevolencia.

malevolent [mə'lɛvələnt] a malévolo.

malfunction [mæl'fʌŋkʃən] n mal funcionamiento.

malice ['mælɪs] n (ill will) malicia; (rancour) rencor m.

malicious [mə'lɪʃəs] a malicioso; rencoroso.

maliciously [mə'lɪʃəslɪ] ad con malevolencia, con malicia; rencorosamente.

malign [mə'laɪn] vt difamar, calumniar ◆ a maligno.

malignant [mə'lɪgnənt] a (MED) maligno.

malinger [mə'lɪŋgə*] vi fingirse enfermo.

malingerer [mə'lɪŋgərə*] n enfermo/a fingido/a.

mall [mɔːl] n (US: also: **shopping ~**) centro comercial.

malleable ['mælɪəbl] a maleable.

mallet ['mælɪt] n mazo.

malnutrition [mælnjuː'trɪʃən] n desnutrición f.

malpractice [mæl'præktɪs] n negligencia profesional.

malt [mɔːlt] n malta.

Malta ['mɔːltə] n Malta.

Maltese [mɔːl'tiːz] a maltés/esa ◆ n, pl inv maltés/esa m/f; (LING) maltés m.

maltreat [mæl'triːt] vt maltratar.

mammal ['mæml] n mamífero.

mammoth ['mæməθ] n mamut m ◆ a gigantesco.

man, pl **men** [mæn, mɛn] n hombre m; (CHESS) pieza ◆ vt (NAUT) tripular; (MIL) guarnecer; **an old ~** un viejo; **~ and wife** marido y mujer.

manacle ['mænəkl] n esposa, manilla; **~s** npl grillos mpl.

manage ['mænɪdʒ] vi arreglárselas, ir tirando ◆ vt (be in charge of) dirigir; (person etc) manejar; **to ~ to do sth** alcanzar a or conseguir hacer algo; **to ~ without sth/sb** prescindir de algo/uno.

manageable ['mænɪdʒəbl] a manejable.

management ['mænɪdʒmənt] n dirección f, administración f; **"under new ~"** "bajo nueva dirección".

management accounting n contabilidad f de gestión.

management consultant n consultor(a) m/f en dirección de empresas, asesor(a) m/f administrativo/a.

manager ['mænɪdʒə*] n director m; (SPORT) entrenador m; **sales ~** jefe/a m/f de ventas.

manageress ['mænɪdʒərɛs] n directora; (SPORT) entrenadora.

managerial [mænə'dʒɪərɪəl] a directivo.

managing director ['mænɪdʒɪŋ-] n director(a) m/f general.

Mancunian [mæŋ'kjuːnɪən] a de Manchester ◆ n nativo/a (or habitante m/f) de Manchester.

mandarin ['mændərɪn] n (also: **~ orange**) mandarina; (person) mandarín m.

mandate ['mændeɪt] n mandato.

mandatory ['mændətərɪ] a obligatorio.

mandolin(e) ['mændəlɪn] n mandolina.

mane [meɪn] n (of horse) crin f; (of lion) melena.

maneuver [mə'nuːvə*] (US) = **manoeuvre**.

manful ['mænful] a resuelto.

manfully ['mænfəlɪ] ad resueltamente.

mangle ['mæŋgl] vt mutilar, destrozar ◆ n rodillo.

mango, **~es** ['mæŋgəu] n mango.

mangrove ['mæŋgrəuv] n mangle m.

mangy ['meɪndʒɪ] a roñoso; (MED) sarnoso.

manhandle ['mænhændl] vt maltratar; (move by hand: goods) manipular.

manhole ['mænhəul] n pozo de visita.

manhood ['mænhud] n edad f viril; virilidad f.

man-hour ['mæn'auə*] n hora-hombre f.

manhunt ['mænhʌnt] n caza de hombre.

mania ['meɪnɪə] n manía.

maniac ['meɪnɪæk] n maníaco/a; (fig) maniático.

manic ['mænɪk] a (behaviour, activity) frenético.

manic-depressive ['mænɪkdɪ'presɪv] a, n maniacodepresivo/a m/f.

manicure ['mænɪkjuə*] n manicura.

manicure set n estuche m de manicura.

manifest ['mænɪfest] vt manifestar, mostrar ◆ a manifiesto ◆ n manifiesto.

manifestation [mænɪfɛs'teɪʃən] n manifestación f.

manifestly ['mænɪfestlɪ] ad evidentemente.

manifesto [mænɪ'festəu] n manifiesto.

manifold ['mænɪfəuld] a múltiples ◆ n (AUT etc): **exhaust ~** colector m de escape.

Manila [mə'nɪlə] n Manila.

manil(l)a [mə'nɪlə] n (paper, envelope) manila.

manipulate [mə'nɪpjuleɪt] vt manipular.

manipulation [mənɪpju'leɪʃən] n manipulación f, manejo.

mankind [mæn'kaɪnd] n humanidad f, género humano.

manliness ['mænlɪnɪs] n virilidad f, hombradía.

manly ['mænlɪ] a varonil.

man-made ['mæn'meɪd] a artificial.

manna ['mænə] n maná m.

mannequin ['maenɪkɪn] n (dummy) maniquí m; (fashion model) modelo f.

manner ['mænə*] n manera, modo; (behaviour) conducta, manera de ser; (type) clase f; ~s npl modales mpl, educación fsg; (good) ~s educación fsg, (buenos) modales mpl; **bad** ~s falta sg de educación, pocos modales mpl; **all** ~ **of** toda clase or suerte de.

mannerism ['mænərɪzəm] n hábito, peculiaridad f.

mannerly ['mænəlɪ] a bien educado, formal.

man(o)euvrable [mə'nuːvrəbl] a (car etc) manejable.

manoeuvre, (US) **maneuver** [mə'nuːvə*] vt, vi maniobrar ♦ n maniobra; **to** ~ **sb into doing sth** manipular a uno para que haga algo.

manor ['mænə*] n (also: ~ **house**) casa solariega.

manpower ['mænpauə*] n mano f de obra.

Manpower Services Commission (MSC) n (Brit) comisión para el aprovechamiento de los recursos humanos.

manservant ['mænsəːvənt] n criado.

mansion ['mænʃən] n palacio, casa grande.

manslaughter ['mænslɔːtə*] n homicidio no premeditado.

mantelpiece ['mæntlpiːs] n repisa, chimenea.

mantle ['mæntl] n manto; (fig) capa.

man-to-man ['mæntə'mæn] a entre hombres.

manual ['mænjuəl] a manual ♦ n manual m; ~ **worker** obrero, trabajador m de camisa azul.

manufacture [mænju'fæktʃə*] vt fabricar ♦ n fabricación f.

manufactured goods [mænju'fæktʃəd-] npl manufacturas fpl, bienes mpl manufacturados.

manufacturer [mænju'fæktʃərə*] n fabricante m/f.

manufacturing industries [mænju'fæktʃərɪŋ-] npl industrias fpl de la manufactura.

manure [mə'njuə*] n estiércol m, abono.

manuscript ['mænjuskrɪpt] n manuscrito.

Manx [mæŋks] a de la Isla de Man.

many ['menɪ] a muchos/as ♦ pron muchos/as; **a great** ~ muchísimos, buen número de; ~ **a time** muchas veces; **too** ~ **difficulties** demasiadas dificultades; **twice as** ~ el doble; **how** ~? ¿cuántos?

map [mæp] n mapa m ♦ vt trazar el mapa de.

map out vt (fig: career, holiday, essay) proyectar, planear.

maple ['meɪpl] n arce m, maple m (LAm).

mar [mɑː*] vt estropear.

Mar. abbr (= March) mar.

marathon ['mærəθən] n maratón m ♦ a: **a** ~ **session** una sesión larguísima or interminable.

marathon runner n corredor(a) m/f de maratones.

marauder [mə'rɔːdə*] n merodeador(a) m/f, intruso/a.

marble ['mɑːbl] n mármol m; (toy) canica.

March [mɑːtʃ] n marzo.

march [mɑːtʃ] vi (MIL) marchar; (fig) caminar con resolución ♦ n marcha; (demonstration) manifestación f.

marcher ['mɑːtʃə*] n manifestante m/f.

marching ['mɑːtʃɪŋ] n: **to give sb his** ~ **orders** (fig) mandar a paseo a uno; (employee) poner de patitas en la calle a uno.

march-past ['mɑːtʃpɑːst] n desfile m.

mare [mɛə*] n yegua.

margarine [mɑːdʒə'riːn] n margarina.

marg(e) [mɑːdʒ] n abbr = **margarine**.

margin ['mɑːdʒɪn] n margen m.

marginal ['mɑːdʒɪnl] a marginal.

marginally ['mɑːdʒɪnəlɪ] ad ligeramente.

marginal seat n (POL) circunscripción f políticamente indefinida.

marigold ['mærɪgəuld] n caléndula.

marijuana [mærɪ'wɑːnə] n marijuana.

marina [mə'riːnə] n marina.

marinade [mærɪ'neɪd] n adobo.

marinate ['mærɪneɪt] vt adobar.

marine [mə'riːn] a marino ♦ n soldado de marina.

marine insurance n seguro marítimo.

mariner ['mærɪnə*] n marinero, marino.

marionette [mærɪə'nɛt] marioneta, títere m.

marital ['mærɪtl] a matrimonial; ~ **status** estado civil.

maritime ['mærɪtaɪm] a marítimo.

marjoram ['mɑːdʒərəm] n mejorana.

mark [mɑːk] n marca, señal f; (imprint) huella; (stain) mancha; (Brit SCOL) nota; (currency) marco ♦ vt (also SPORT: player) marcar; (stain) manchar; (Brit SCOL) calificar, corregir; **punctuation** ~s signos mpl de puntuación; **to be quick off the** ~ (fig) ser listo; **up to the** ~ (in efficiency) a la altura de las circunstancias; **to** ~ **time** marcar el paso.

mark down vt (reduce: prices, goods) rebajar.

mark off vt (tick) indicar, señalar.

mark out vt trazar.

mark up vt (price) aumentar.

marked [mɑːkt] a marcado, acusado.

markedly ['mɑːkɪdlɪ] ad marcadamente, apreciablemente.

marker ['mɑːkə*] n (sign) marcador m; (bookmark) registro.

market ['mɑːkɪt] n mercado ♦ vt (COMM) comercializar; (promote) publicitar; **open** ~ mercado libre; **to be on the** ~ estar en venta; **to play the** ~ jugar a la bolsa.

marketable ['mɑːkɪtəbl] a comerciable.

market analysis n análisis m del mercado.

market day n día m de mercado.

market demand n demanda de mercado.

market forces npl tendencias fpl del mercado.

market garden n (Brit) huerto.

marketing ['mɑːkɪtɪŋ] n márketing m, mercadotecnia.

marketing manager n director m de marketing.

market leader n líder m de ventas.

marketplace ['mɑːkɪtpleɪs] n mercado.

market price n precio de mercado.

market research n (COMM) investigación f de mercados.

market value n valor m en el mercado.

marking ['mɑːkɪŋ] n (on animal) pinta; (on road) señal f.

marking ink n tinta indeleble or de marcar.

marksman ['mɑːksmən] n tirador m.

marksmanship ['mɑːksmənʃɪp] n puntería.

mark-up ['mɑːkʌp] n (COMM: margin) margen m de beneficio; (: increase) aumento.

marmalade ['mɑːməleɪd] n mermelada de naranja.

maroon [mə'ruːn] vt: **to be** ~ed (shipwrecked) naufragarse; (fig) quedar abandonado ♦ a marrón inv.

marquee [mɑː'kiː] n entoldado.

marquess, marquis ['mɑːkwɪs] n marqués m.

Marrakech, Marrakesh [mærə'keʃ] n Marrakech m.

marriage ['mærɪdʒ] n (state) matrimonio; (wedding) boda; (act) casamiento.

marriage bureau n agencia matrimonial.

marriage certificate n partida de casamiento.

marriage guidance, (US) marriage counseling n orientación f matrimonial.

married ['mærɪd] a casado; (life, love) conyugal.

marrow ['mærəu] n médula; (vegetable) calabacín m.

marry ['mærɪ] vt casarse con; (subj: father, priest etc) casar ♦ vi (also: **get married**) casarse.

Mars [mɑːz] n Marte m.

Marseilles [mɑː'seɪ] n Marsella.

marsh [mɑːʃ] n pantano; (salt ~) marisma.

marshal ['mɑːʃl] n (MIL) mariscal m; (at sports meeting, demonstration etc) oficial m; (US: of police, fire department) jefe/a m/f ♦ vt (facts) ordenar; (soldiers) formar.

marshalling yard ['mɑːʃəlɪŋ-] n (RAIL) estación f clasificadora.

marshmallow ['mɑːʃmæləu] n (BOT) malvavisco; (sweet) bombón m de merengue blando.

marshy ['mɑːʃɪ] a pantanoso.

marsupial [mɑː'suːpɪəl] a, n marsupial m.

martial ['mɑːʃl] a marcial.

martial law n ley f marcial.

martin ['mɑːtɪn] n (also: **house** ~) avión m.

martyr ['mɑːtə*] n mártir m/f ♦ vt martirizar.

martyrdom ['mɑːtədəm] n martirio.

marvel ['mɑːvl] n maravilla, prodigio ♦ vi: **to** ~ **(at)** maravillarse (de).

marvellous, (US) marvelous ['mɑːvləs] a maravilloso.

marvel(l)ously ['mɑːvləslɪ] ad maravillosamente.

Marxism ['mɑːksɪzəm] n marxismo.

Marxist ['mɑːksɪst] a, n marxista m/f.

marzipan ['mɑːzɪpæn] n mazapán m.

mascara [mæs'kɑːrə] n rímel m.

mascot ['mæskət] n mascota.

masculine ['mæskjulɪn] a masculino.

masculinity [mæskju'lɪnɪtɪ] n masculinidad f.

MASH [mæʃ] n abbr (US) = mobile army surgical hospital.

mash [mæʃ] n (mix) mezcla; (CULIN) puré m; (pulp) amasijo.

mashed potatoes [mæʃt-] npl puré m de patatas or papas (LAm).

mask [mɑːsk] n (also ELEC) máscara ♦ vt enmascarar.

masochism ['mæsəkɪzəm] n masoquismo.

masochist ['mæsəukɪst] n masoquista m/f.

mason ['meɪsn] n (also: **stone**~) albañil m; (also: **free**~) masón m.

masonic [mə'sɔnɪk] a masónico.

masonry ['meɪsnrɪ] n masonería; (building) mampostería.

masquerade [mæskə'reɪd] n baile m de máscaras; (fig) mascarada ♦ vi: **to** ~ **as** disfrazarse de, hacerse pasar por.

mass [mæs] n (people) muchedumbre f; (PHYSICS) masa; (REL) misa; (great quantity) montón m ♦ vi reunirse; (MIL) concentrarse; **the** ~**es** las masas; **to go to** ~ oír misa.

massacre ['mæsəkə*] n masacre f ♦ vt masacrar.

massage ['mæsɑːʒ] n masaje m ♦ vt dar masaje a.

masseur [mæ'sə:*] n masajista m.

masseuse [mæ'sə:z] n masajista f.

massive ['mæsɪv] a enorme; (support, intervention) masivo.

mass media npl medios mpl de comunicación masiva.

mass meeting n (of everyone concerned) reunión f en masa; (huge) mitin m.

mass-produce ['mæsprə'djuːs] *vt* fabricar en serie.

mass-production ['mæsprə'dʌkʃən] *n* fabricación *f or* producción *f* en serie.

mast [mɑːst] *n* (*NAUT*) mástil *m*; (*RADIO etc*) torre *f*, antena.

master ['mɑːstə*] *n* maestro; (*in secondary school*) profesor *m*; (*title for boys*): **M~ X** Señorito X ♦ *vt* dominar; (*learn*) aprender a fondo.

master disk *n* (*COMPUT*) disco maestro.

masterful ['mɑːstəful] *a* magistral, dominante.

master key *n* llave *f* maestra.

masterly ['mɑːstəlɪ] *a* magistral.

mastermind ['mɑːstəmaɪnd] *n* inteligencia superior ♦ *vt* dirigir, planear.

Master of Arts (MA) *n* licenciatura superior en Letras.

Master of Ceremonies *n* encargado de protocolo.

Master of Science (MSc) *n* licenciatura superior en Ciencias.

masterpiece ['mɑːstəpiːs] *n* obra maestra.

master plan *n* plan *m* rector.

master stroke *n* golpe *m* maestro.

mastery ['mɑːstərɪ] *n* maestría.

mastiff ['mæstɪf] *n* mastín *m*.

masturbate ['mæstəbeɪt] *vi* masturbarse.

masturbation [mæstə'beɪʃən] *n* masturbación *f*.

mat [mæt] *n* estera; (*also*: **door~**) felpudo ♦ *a* = **matt**.

match [mætʃ] *n* cerilla, fósforo; (*game*) partido; (*fig*) igual *m/f* ♦ *vt* emparejar; (*go well with*) hacer juego con; (*equal*) igualar ♦ *vi* hacer juego; **to be a good ~** hacer buena pareja.

matchbox ['mætʃbɔks] *n* caja de cerillas.

matching ['mætʃɪŋ] *a* que hace juego.

matchless ['mætʃlɪs] *a* sin par, incomparable.

matchmaker ['mætʃmeɪkə*] *n* casamentero.

mate [meɪt] *n* (*work~*) colega *m/f*; (*col: friend*) amigo/a; (*animal*) macho/hembra; (*in merchant navy*) segundo de a bordo ♦ *vi* acoplarse, parearse ♦ *vt* acoplar, parear.

material [mə'tɪərɪəl] *n* (*substance*) materia; (*equipment*) material *m*; (*cloth*) tela, tejido ♦ *a* material; (*important*) esencial; **~s** *npl* materiales *mpl*; (*equipment etc*) artículos *mpl*.

materialistic [mətɪərɪə'lɪstɪk] *a* materialista.

materialize [mə'tɪərɪəlaɪz] *vi* materializarse.

materially [mə'tɪərɪəlɪ] *ad* materialmente.

maternal [mə'təːnl] *a* maternal; **~ grandmother** abuela materna.

maternity [mə'təːnɪtɪ] *n* maternidad *f*.

maternity benefit *n* subsidio de materni-

dad.

maternity dress *n* vestido premamá.

maternity hospital *n* hospital *m* de maternidad.

maternity leave *n* licencia por maternidad.

math [mæθ] *n abbr* (*US*: = *mathematics*) matemáticas *fpl*.

mathematical [mæθə'mætɪkl] *a* matemático.

mathematically [mæθɪ'mætɪklɪ] *ad* matemáticamente.

mathematician [mæθəmə'tɪʃən] *n* matemático.

mathematics [mæθə'mætɪks] *n* matemáticas *fpl*.

maths [mæθs] *n abbr* (*Brit*: = *mathematics*) matemáticas *fpl*.

matinée ['mætɪneɪ] *n* función *f* de la tarde.

mating ['meɪtɪŋ] *n* aparejamiento.

mating call *n* llamada del macho.

mating season *n* época de celo.

matins ['mætɪnz] *n* maitines *mpl*.

matriarchal [meɪtrɪ'ɑːkl] *a* matriarcal.

matrices ['meɪtrɪsiːz] *pl of* **matrix**.

matriculation [mətrɪkju'leɪʃən] *n* matriculación *f*.

matrimonial [mætrɪ'məunɪəl] *a* matrimonial.

matrimony ['mætrɪmənɪ] *n* matrimonio.

matrix, *pl* **matrices** ['meɪtrɪks, 'meɪtrɪsiːz] *n* matriz *f*.

matron ['meɪtrən] *n* (*in hospital*) enfermera jefe; (*in school*) ama de llaves.

matronly ['meɪtrənlɪ] *a* de matrona; (*fig: figure*) corpulento.

matt [mæt] *a* mate.

matted ['mætɪd] *a* enmarañado.

matter ['mætə*] *n* cuestión *f*, asunto; (*PHYSICS*) sustancia, materia; (*content*) contenido; (*MED: pus*) pus *m* ♦ *vi* importar; **it doesn't ~** no importa; **what's the ~?** ¿qué pasa?; **no ~ what** pase lo que pase; **as a ~ of course** por rutina; **as a ~ of fact** en realidad; **printed ~** impresos *mpl*; **reading ~** algo para leer, libros *mpl*.

matter-of-fact ['mætərəv'fækt] *a* prosaico, práctico.

mattress ['mætrɪs] *n* colchón *m*.

mature [mə'tjuə*] *a* maduro ♦ *vi* madurar.

maturity [mə'tjuərɪtɪ] *n* madurez *f*.

maudlin ['mɔːdlɪn] *a* llorón/ona.

maul [mɔːl] *vt* magullar.

Mauritania [mɔːrɪ'teɪnɪə] *n* Mauritania.

Mauritius [mə'rɪʃəs] *n* Mauricio.

mausoleum [mɔːsə'lɪəm] *n* mausoleo.

mauve [məuv] *a* de color malva *or* guinda (*LAm*).

maverick ['mævrɪk] *n* (*fig*) inconformista *m/f*, persona independiente.

mawkish ['mɔːkɪʃ] *a* empalagoso.

max. *abbr* = **maximum**.

maxim ['mæksɪm] *n* máxima.

maxima ['mæksɪmə] *pl of* **maximum**.
maximize ['mæksɪmaɪz] *vt* (*profits etc*) llevar al máximo; (*chances*) maximizar.
maximum ['mæksɪməm] *a* máximo ♦ *n* (*pl* **maxima** ['mæksɪmə]) máximo.
May [meɪ] *n* mayo.
may [meɪ] *vi* (*conditional*: **might**) (*indicating possibility*): **he ~ come** puede que venga; (*be allowed to*): **~ I smoke?** ¿puedo fumar?; (*wishes*): **~ God bless you!** ¡que Dios le bendiga!; **~ I sit here?** ¿me puedo sentar aquí?
maybe ['meɪbiː] *ad* quizá(s); **~ not** quizás no.
May Day *n* el primero de Mayo.
mayday ['meɪdeɪ] *n* S.O.S. *m*.
mayhem ['meɪhɛm] *n* caos *m* total.
mayonnaise [meɪə'neɪz] *n* mayonesa.
mayor [mɛə*] *n* alcalde *m*.
mayoress ['mɛərɛs] *n* alcaldesa.
maypole ['meɪpəul] *n* mayo.
maze [meɪz] *n* laberinto.
MB *abbr* (*COMPUT*) = **megabyte**; (*Canada*) = *Manitoba*.
MBA *n abbr* (= *Master of Business Administration*) *título universitario*.
MBBS, MBChB *n abbr* (*Brit*: = *Bachelor of Medicine and Surgery*) *título universitario*.
MBE *n abbr* (*Brit*: = *Member of the Order of the British Empire*) *título ceremonial*.
MC *n abbr* (= *master of ceremonies*) e.p.; (*US*: = *Member of Congress*) *diputado del Congreso de los Estados Unidos*.
MCAT *n abbr* (*US*) = *Medical College Admissions Test*.
MCP *n abbr* (*Brit col*) = **male chauvinist pig**.
MD *n abbr* (= *Doctor of Medicine*) *título universitario*; (*COMM*) = **managing director** ♦ *abbr* (*US POST*) = *Maryland*.
MDT *n abbr* (*US*: = *mountain daylight time*) *hora de verano de las Montañas Rocosas*.
ME *abbr* (*US POST*) = *Maine* ♦ *n abbr* (*US MED*) = *medical examiner*.
me [miː] *pron* (*direct*) me; (*stressed, after pronoun*) mí; **can you hear ~?** ¿me oyes?; **he heard ME!** me oyó a mí; **it's ~** soy yo; **give them to ~** dámelos; **with/without ~** conmigo/sin mí; **it's for ~** es para mí.
meadow ['mɛdəu] *n* prado, pradera.
meagre, (*US***) meager** ['miːgə*] *a* escaso, pobre.
meal [miːl] *n* comida; (*flour*) harina; **to go out for a ~** salir a comer.
mealtime ['miːltaɪm] *n* hora de comer.
mealy-mouthed ['miːlɪmauðd] *a*: **to be ~** nunca decir las cosas claras.
mean [miːn] *a* (*with money*) tacaño; (*unkind*) mezquino, malo; (*average*) medio; (*US*: *vicious*: *animal*) resabiado; (: *person*) malicioso ♦ *vt* (*pt, pp* **meant** [mɛnt]) (*signify*) querer decir, significar; (*intend*):

to ~ to do sth pensar *or* pretender hacer algo ♦ *n* medio, término medio; **do you ~ it?** ¿lo dices en serio?; **what do you ~?** ¿qué quiere decir?; **to be meant for sb/sth** ser para uno/algo; *see also* **means**.
meander [mɪ'ændə*] *vi* (*river*) serpentear; (*person*) vagar.
meaning ['miːnɪŋ] *n* significado, sentido.
meaningful ['miːnɪŋful] *a* significativo.
meaningless ['miːnɪŋlɪs] *a* sin sentido.
meanness ['miːnnɪs] *n* (*with money*) tacañería; (*unkindness*) maldad *f*, mezquindad *f*.
means [miːnz] *npl* medio *sg*, manera *sg*; (*resource*) recursos *mpl*, medios *mpl*; **by ~ of** mediante, por medio de; **by all ~!** ¡naturalmente!, ¡claro que sí!
means test *n* control *m* de los recursos económicos.
meant [mɛnt] *pt, pp of* **mean**.
meantime ['miːntaɪm], **meanwhile** ['miːnwaɪl] *ad* (*also*: **in the meantime**) mientras tanto.
measles ['miːzlz] *n* sarampión *m*.
measly ['miːzlɪ] *a* (*col*) miserable.
measurable ['mɛʒərəbl] *a* mensurable, que se puede medir.
measure ['mɛʒə*] *vt* medir; (*for clothes etc*) tomar las medidas a ♦ *vi* medir ♦ *n* medida; (*ruler*) regla; **a litre ~** una medida de un litro; **some ~ of success** cierto éxito; **to take ~s to do sth** tomar medidas para hacer algo.
measure up *vi*: **to ~ up (to)** mostrarse capaz (de).
measured ['mɛʒəd] *a* moderado; (*tone*) mesurado.
measurement ['mɛʒəmənt] *n* (*measure*) medida; (*act*) medición *f*; **to take sb's ~s** tomar las medidas a uno.
meat [miːt] *n* carne *f*; **cold ~s** fiambres *mpl*; **crab ~** carne *f* de cangrejo.
meatball ['miːtbɔːl] *n* albóndiga.
meat pie *n* pastel *m* de carne.
meaty ['miːtɪ] *a* carnoso; (*fig*) sustancioso.
Mecca ['mɛkə] *n* (*city*) la Meca; (*fig*) Meca.
mechanic [mɪ'kænɪk] *n* mecánico/a.
mechanical [mɪ'kænɪkl] *a* mecánico.
mechanical engineering *n* (*science*) ingeniería mecánica; (*industry*) construcción *f* mecánica.
mechanics [mə'kænɪks] *n* mecánica ♦ *npl* mecanismo *sg*.
mechanism ['mɛkənɪzəm] *n* mecanismo.
mechanization [mɛkənaɪ'zeɪʃən] *n* mecanización *f*.
mechanize ['mɛkənaɪz] *vt* mecanizar; (*factory etc*) automatizar, reconvertir.
MEd *n abbr* (= *Master of Education*) *título universitario*.
medal ['mɛdl] *n* medalla.
medallion [mɪ'dælɪən] *n* medallón *m*.
medallist, (*US***) medalist** ['mɛdlɪst] *n*

(*sport*) ganador(a) *m/f*.

meddle ['mɛdl] *vi*: **to ~ in** entrometerse en; **to ~ with sth** manosear algo.

meddlesome ['mɛdlsəm], **meddling** ['mɛdlɪŋ] *a* (*interfering*) entrometido; (*touching things*) curioso.

media ['miːdɪə] *npl* medios *mpl* de comunicación.

mediaeval [mɛdɪ'iːvl] *a* = **medieval**.

median ['miːdɪən] *n* (*US*: also: ~ **strip**) mediana.

media research *n* investigación *f* de los medios de publicidad.

mediate ['miːdɪeɪt] *vi* mediar.

mediation [miːdɪ'eɪʃən] *n* mediación *f*.

mediator ['miːdɪeɪtə*] *n* intermediario/a, mediador(a) *m/f*.

Medicaid ['mɛdɪkeɪd] *n* (*US*) *programa de ayuda médica*.

medical ['mɛdɪkl] *a* médico ◆ *n* (*also*: ~ **examination**) reconocimiento médico.

medical certificate *n* certificado *m* médico.

Medicare ['mɛdɪkɛə*] *n* (*US*) *seguro médico del Estado*.

medicated ['mɛdɪkeɪtɪd] *a* medicinal.

medication [mɛdɪ'keɪʃən] *n* (*drugs etc*) medicación *f*.

medicinal [mɛ'dɪsɪnl] *a* medicinal.

medicine ['mɛdsɪn] *n* medicina; (*drug*) medicamento.

medicine chest *n* botiquín *m*.

medicine man *n* hechicero.

medieval, mediaeval [mɛdɪ'iːvl] *a* medieval.

mediocre [miːdɪ'əukə*] *a* mediocre.

mediocrity [miːdɪ'ɔkrɪtɪ] *n* mediocridad *f*.

meditate ['mɛdɪteɪt] *vi* meditar.

meditation [mɛdɪ'teɪʃən] *n* meditación *f*.

Mediterranean [mɛdɪtə'reɪnɪən] *a* mediterráneo; **the ~ (Sea)** el (Mar *m*) Mediterráneo.

medium ['miːdɪəm] *a* mediano, regular ◆ *n* (*pl* **media**: *means*) medio; (*pl* **mediums**: *person*) médium *m/f*; **happy ~** justo medio.

medium-sized ['miːdɪəm'saɪzd] *a* (*tin etc*) regular; (*clothes*) de tamaño mediano.

medium wave *n* onda media.

medley ['mɛdlɪ] *n* mezcla; (*MUS*) popurrí *m*.

meek [miːk] *a* manso, sumiso.

meekly ['miːklɪ] *ad* mansamente, dócilmente.

meet [miːt] *vb* (*pt, pp* **met** [mɛt]) *vt* encontrar; (*accidentally*) encontrarse con, tropezar con; (*by arrangement*) reunirse con; (*for the first time*) conocer; (*go and fetch*) ir a buscar; (*opponent*) enfrentarse con; (*obligations*) cumplir; (*bill, expenses*) pagar, costear ◆ *vi* encontrarse; (*in session*) reunirse; (*join: objects*) unirse; (*get to know*) conocerse ◆ *n* (Brit: *HUNTING*) cacería; (*US*: *SPORT*) encuentro; **pleased to ~ you!** ¡encantado de conocerle!, ¡mucho gusto!

meet up *vi*: **to ~ up with sb** reunirse con uno.

meet with *vt fus* reunirse con; (*difficulty*) tropezar con.

meeting ['miːtɪŋ] *n* (*also sport*: *rally*) encuentro; (*arranged*) cita, compromiso (*LAm*); (*formal session, business meet*) reunión *f*; (*POL*) mitin *m*; **to call a ~** convocar *or* llamar una reunión.

meeting place *n* lugar *m* de reunión *or* encuentro.

megabyte ['mɛgə'baɪt] *n* (*COMPUT*) megabyte *m*, megaocteto.

megalomaniac [mɛgələu'meɪnɪæk] *a, n* megalómano/a *m/f*.

megaphone ['mɛgəfəun] *n* megáfono.

melancholy ['mɛlənkəlɪ] *n* melancolía ◆ *a* melancólico.

melee ['mɛleɪ] *n* refriega.

mellow ['mɛləu] *a* (*wine*) añejo; (*sound, colour*) suave; (*fruit*) maduro ◆ *vi* (*person*) madurar.

melodious [mɪ'ləudɪəs] *a* melodioso.

melodrama ['mɛləudrɑːmə] *n* melodrama *m*.

melodramatic [mɛləudrə'mætɪk] *a* melodramático.

melody ['mɛlədɪ] *n* melodía.

melon ['mɛlən] *n* melón *m*.

melt [mɛlt] *vi* (*metal*) fundirse; (*snow*) derretirse; (*fig*) ablandarse ◆ *vt* (*also*: ~ **down**) fundir; **~ed butter** mantequilla derretida.

melt away *vi* desvanecerse.

meltdown ['mɛltdaun] *n* (*in nuclear reactor*) fusión *f* (de un reactor nuclear).

melting point ['mɛltɪŋ-] *n* punto de fusión.

melting pot ['mɛltɪŋ-] *n* (*fig*) crisol *m;* **to be in the ~** estar sobre el tapete.

member ['mɛmbə*] *n* (*of political party*) miembro; (*of club*) socio/a; **M~ of Parliament (MP)** (*Brit*) diputado/a; **M~ of the European Parliament (MEP)** (*Brit*) eurodiputado/a; **M~ of the House of Representatives (MHR)** (*US*) diputado/a del Congreso de los Estados Unidos.

membership ['mɛmbəʃɪp] *n* (*members*) número de miembros; **to seek ~ of** pedir el ingreso a.

membership card *n* carnet *m* de socio.

membrane ['mɛmbreɪn] *n* membrana.

memento [mə'mɛntəu] *n* recuerdo.

memo ['mɛməu] *n abbr* (= *memorandum*) memo.

memoirs ['mɛmwɑːz] *npl* memorias *fpl*.

memo pad *n* agenda.

memorable ['mɛmərəbl] *a* memorable.

memorandum, *pl* **memoranda** [mɛmə'rændəm, -də] *n* apunte *m*, nota; (*POL*) memorándum *m*.

memorial [mɪ'mɔːrɪəl] *n* monumento conmemorativo ◆ *a* conmemorativo.

memorize ['mɛmǝraɪz] *vt* aprender de memoria.

memory ['mɛmǝrɪ] *n* memoria; *(recollection)* recuerdo; *(COMPUT)* memoria; **to have a good/bad** ~ tener buena/mala memoria; **loss of** ~ pérdida de memoria.

men [mɛn] *pl of* **man**.

menace ['mɛnǝs] *n* amenaza; *(col: nuisance)* lata ♦ *vt* amenazar; **a public** ~ un peligro para la humanidad.

menacing ['mɛnɪsɪŋ] *a* amenazador(a).

menacingly ['mɛnɪsɪŋlɪ] *ad* amenazadoramente.

menagerie [mɪ'nædʒǝrɪ] *n* casa de fieras.

mend [mɛnd] *vt* reparar, arreglar; *(darn)* zurcir ♦ *vi* reponerse ♦ *n* *(gen)* remiendo; *(darn)* zurcido; **to be on the** ~ ir mejorando.

mending ['mɛndɪŋ] *n* reparación *f*; *(clothes)* ropa por remendar.

menial ['miːnɪǝl] *a* doméstico; *(pej)* bajo.

meningitis [mɛnɪn'dʒaɪtɪs] *n* meningitis *f*.

menopause ['mɛnǝupɔːz] *n* menopausia.

menstrual ['mɛnstruǝl] *a* menstrual.

menstruate ['mɛnstrueɪt] *vi* menstruar.

menstruation [mɛnstru'eɪʃǝn] *n* menstruación *f*.

mental ['mɛntl] *a* mental; ~ **illness** enfermedad *f* mental.

mentality [mɛn'tælɪtɪ] *n* mentalidad *f*.

mentally ['mɛntlɪ] *ad*: **to be** ~ **handicapped** ser un retrasado mental.

menthol ['mɛnθǝl] *n* mentol *m*.

mention ['mɛnʃǝn] *n* mención *f* ♦ *vt* mencionar; *(speak of)* hablar de; **don't** ~ **it!** ¡de nada!; **I need hardly** ~ **that** ... huelga decir que ...; **not to** ~, **without** ~**ing** sin contar.

mentor ['mɛntɔː*] *n* mentor *m*.

menu ['mɛnjuː] *n* *(set* ~) menú *m*; *(printed)* carta; *(COMPUT)* menú *m*.

menu-driven ['mɛnjuːdrɪvn] *a* *(COMPUT)* guiado por menú.

MEP *n abbr see* **Member of the European Parliament**.

mercantile ['mɜːkǝntaɪl] *a* mercantil.

mercenary ['mɜːsɪnǝrɪ] *a, n* mercenario.

merchandise ['mɜːtʃǝndaɪz] *n* mercancías *fpl*.

merchandiser ['mɜːtʃǝndaɪzǝ*] *n* comerciante *m/f*, tratante *m*.

merchant ['mɜːtʃǝnt] *n* comerciante *m/f*.

merchant bank *n* *(Brit)* banco comercial.

merchantman ['mɜːtʃǝntmǝn] *n* buque *m* mercante.

merchant navy, *(US)* **merchant marine** *n* marina mercante.

merciful ['mɜːsɪful] *a* compasivo.

mercifully ['mɜːsɪfulɪ] *ad* con compasión; *(fortunately)* afortunadamente.

merciless ['mɜːsɪlɪs] *a* despiadado.

mercilessly ['mɜːsɪlɪslɪ] *ad* despiadadamente, sin piedad.

mercurial [mǝ:'kjuǝrɪǝl] *a* veleidoso, voluble.

mercury ['mɜːkjurɪ] *n* mercurio.

mercy ['mɜːsɪ] *n* compasión *f*; *(REL)* misericordia; **at the** ~ **of** a la merced de.

mercy killing *n* eutanasia.

mere [mɪǝ*] *a* simple, mero.

merely ['mɪǝlɪ] *ad* simplemente, sólo.

merge [mɜːdʒ] *vt* *(join)* unir; *(mix)* mezclar; *(fuse)* fundir; *(COMPUT: files, text)* intercalar ♦ *vi* unirse; *(COMM)* fusionarse.

merger ['mɜːdʒǝ*] *n* *(COMM)* fusión *f*.

meridian [mǝ'rɪdɪǝn] *n* meridiano.

meringue [mǝ'ræŋ] *n* merengue *m*.

merit ['mɛrɪt] *n* mérito ♦ *vt* merecer.

meritocracy [mɛrɪ'tɔkrǝsɪ] *n* meritocracia.

mermaid ['mɜːmeɪd] *n* sirena.

merrily ['mɛrɪlɪ] *ad* alegremente.

merriment ['mɛrɪmǝnt] *n* alegría.

merry ['mɛrɪ] *a* alegre; **M~ Christmas!** ¡Felices Pascuas!

merry-go-round ['mɛrɪgǝuraund] *n* tiovivo.

mesh [mɛʃ] *n* malla; *(TECH)* engranaje *m* ♦ *vi* *(gears)* engranar; **wire** ~ tela metálica.

mesmerize ['mɛzmǝraɪz] *vt* hipnotizar.

mess [mɛs] *n* confusión *f*; *(of objects)* revoltijo; *(tangle)* lío; *(MIL)* comedor *m*; **to be (in) a** ~ *(room)* estar revuelto; **to be/ get o.s. in a** ~ estar/meterse en un lío.

mess about, mess around *vi* *(col)* perder el tiempo; *(pass the time)* entretenerse.

mess about or around with *vt fus* *(col: play with)* divertirse con; *(: handle)* manosear.

mess up *vt* *(disarrange)* desordenar; *(spoil)* estropear; *(dirty)* ensuciar.

message ['mɛsɪdʒ] *n* recado, mensaje *m;* **to get the** ~ *(fig, col)* caer en la cuenta.

message switching *n* *(COMPUT)* conmutación *f* de mensajes.

messenger ['mɛsɪndʒǝ*] *n* mensajero/a.

Messiah [mɪ'saɪǝ] *n* Mesías *m*.

Messrs *abbr* *(on letters:* = *Messieurs)* Sres.

messy ['mɛsɪ] *a* *(dirty)* sucio; *(untidy)* desordenado; *(confused: situation etc)* confuso.

Met [mɛt] *n abbr* *(US)* = *Metropolitan Opera*.

met [mɛt] *pt, pp of* **meet** ♦ *a abbr* = **meteorological**.

metabolism [mɛ'tæbǝlɪzǝm] *n* metabolismo.

metal ['mɛtl] *n* metal *m*.

metallic [mɛ'tælɪk] *a* metálico.

metallurgy [mɛ'tælǝdʒɪ] *n* metalurgia.

metalwork ['mɛtlwɜːk] *n* *(craft)* metalistería.

metamorphosis, *pl* **metamorphoses** [mɛtǝ'mɔːfǝsɪs, -siːz] *n* metamorfosis *f inv*.

metaphor ['mɛtǝfǝ*] *n* metáfora.

metaphorical [mɛtǝ'fɔrɪkl] *a* metafórico.

metaphysics [mɛtǝ'fɪzɪks] *n* metafísica.

mete [miːt] **to** ~ **out** *vt fus* *(punishment)* imponer.

meteor ['miːtɪə*] n meteoro.
meteoric [miːtɪ'ɔrɪk] a (fig) rápido, meteórico.
meteorite ['miːtɪəraɪt] n meteorito.
meteorological [miːtɪərə'lɔdʒɪkl] a meteorológico.
meteorology [miːtɪə'rɔlədʒɪ] n meteorología.
meter ['miːtə*] n (instrument) contador m; (US: unit) = **metre** ♦ vt (US POST) franquear; **parking** ~ parquímetro.
methane ['miːθeɪn] n metano.
method ['mɛθəd] n método; ~ **of payment** método de pagar.
methodical [mɪ'θɔdɪkl] a metódico.
Methodist ['mɛθədɪst] a, n metodista m/f.
methodology [mɛθə'dɔlədʒɪ] n metodología.
meths [mɛθs], **methylated spirit(s)** ['mɛθɪleɪtɪd-] n (Brit) alcohol m metilado or desnaturalizado.
meticulous [mɛ'tɪkjuləs] a meticuloso.
metre, (US) **meter** ['miːtə*] n metro.
metric ['mɛtrɪk] a métrico; **to go** ~ pasar al sistema métrico.
metrication [mɛtrɪ'keɪʃən] n conversión f al sistema métrico.
metric system n sistema m métrico.
metric ton n tonelada métrica.
metronome ['mɛtrənəum] n metrónomo.
metropolis [mɪ'trɔpəlɪs] n metrópoli f.
metropolitan [mɛtrə'pɔlɪtən] a metropolitano.
Metropolitan Police n (Brit): **the** ~ la policía londinense.
mettle ['mɛtl] n valor m, ánimo.
mew [mjuː] vi (cat) maullar.
mews [mjuːz] (Brit) n: ~ **cottage** casa acondicionada en antiguos establos o cocheras; ~ **flat** piso en antiguos establos o cocheras.
Mexican ['mɛksɪkən] a, n mejicano/a m/f, mexicano/a m/f (LAm).
Mexico ['mɛksɪkəu] n Méjico, México (LAm).
Mexico City n Ciudad f de Méjico or México (LAm).
mezzanine ['mɛtsəniːn] n entresuelo.
MFA n abbr (US: = Master of Fine Arts) título universitario.
mfr abbr (= manufacturer) fab.
mg abbr (= milligram) mg.
Mgr abbr (= Monseigneur, Monsignor) Mons.
mgr abbr = **manager**.
MHR n abbr (US) see **Member of the House of Representatives**.
MHz abbr (= megahertz) MHz.
MI abbr (US POST) = Michigan.
MI5 n abbr (Brit: = Military Intelligence 5) servicio de contraespionaje del gobierno británico.
MI6 n abbr (Brit: = Military Intelligence 6) servicio de inteligencia del gobierno británico.
MIA abbr (= missing in action) desaparecido.
miaow [miː'au] vi maullar.
mice [maɪs] pl of **mouse**.
mickey ['mɪkɪ] n: **to take the** ~ **out of sb** tomar el pelo a uno.
microbe ['maɪkrəub] n microbio.
micro... [maɪkrəu] pref micro....
microbiology [maɪkrəubaɪ'ɔlədʒɪ] n microbiología.
microchip ['maɪkrəutʃɪp] n microplaqueta.
micro(computer) ['maɪkrəu(kəm'pjuːtə*)] n microordenador m, microcomputador m.
microcosm ['maɪkrəukɔzəm] n microcosmo.
microeconomics ['maɪkrəuiːkə'nɔmɪks] n microeconomía.
microfiche ['maɪkrəufiːʃ] n microficha.
microfilm ['maɪkrəufɪlm] n microfilm m.
micrometer [maɪ'krɔmɪtə*] n micrómetro.
microphone ['maɪkrəfəun] n micrófono.
microprocessor ['maɪkrəu'prəusesə*] n microprocesador m.
microscope ['maɪkrəskəup] n microscopio; **under the** ~ bajo el microscopio.
microscopic [maɪkrə'skɔpɪk] a microscópico.
microwave ['maɪkrəuweɪv] n (also: ~ **oven**) horno microondas.
mid [mɪd] a: **in** ~ **May** a mediados de mayo; **in** ~ **afternoon** a media tarde; **in** ~ **air** en el aire; **he's in his** ~ **thirties** tiene unos treinta y cinco años.
midday [mɪd'deɪ] n mediodía m.
middle ['mɪdl] n medio, centro; (waist) cintura ♦ a de en medio; **in the** ~ **of the night** en plena noche; **I'm in the** ~ **of reading it** lo estoy leyendo ahora mismo.
middle-aged [mɪdl'eɪdʒd] a de mediana edad.
Middle Ages npl: **the** ~ la Edad sg Media.
middle class n: **the** ~**(es)** la clase media ♦ a (also: **middle-class**) de clase media.
Middle East n Oriente m Medio.
middleman ['mɪdlmæn] n intermediario.
middle management n dirección f de nivel medio.
middle name n nombre m segundo.
middle-of-the-road ['mɪdləvðə'rəud] a moderado, centrista.
middleweight ['mɪdlweɪt] n (BOXING) peso medio.
middling ['mɪdlɪŋ] a mediano.
Middx abbr (Brit) = **Middlesex**.
midge [mɪdʒ] n mosca.
midget ['mɪdʒɪt] n enano/a.
Midlands ['mɪdləndz] npl región central de Inglaterra.
midnight ['mɪdnaɪt] n medianoche f; **at** ~ a medianoche.
midriff ['mɪdrɪf] n diafragma m.

midst [mɪdst] *n*: **in the ~ of** entre, en medio de.

midsummer [mɪd'sʌmə*] *n*: **a ~ day** un día de pleno verano.

Midsummer's Day *n* Día *m* de San Juan.

midway [mɪd'weɪ] *a*, *ad*: **~ (between)** a mitad de camino *or* a medio camino (entre).

midweek [mɪd'wiːk] *ad* entre semana.

midwife, *pl* **midwives** ['mɪdwaɪf, -waɪvz] *n* comadrona, partera.

midwifery ['mɪdwɪfərɪ] *n* partería.

midwinter [mɪd'wɪntə*] *n*: **in ~** en pleno invierno.

might [maɪt] *vb see* **may** ◆ **he ~ be there** podría estar allí, puede que esté allí; **I ~ as well go** más vale que vaya; **you ~ like to try** podría intentar ◆ *n* fuerza, poder *m*.

mightily ['maɪtɪlɪ] *ad* fuertemente, poderosamente; **I was ~ surprised** me sorprendí enormemente.

mightn't ['maɪtnt] = **might not.**

mighty ['maɪtɪ] *a* fuerte, poderoso.

migraine ['miːgreɪn] *n* jaqueca.

migrant ['maɪgrənt] *a*, *n* (*bird*) migratorio/a *m/f*; (*worker*) emigrante *m/f*.

migrate [maɪ'greɪt] *vi* emigrar.

migration [maɪ'greɪʃən] *n* emigración *f*.

mike [maɪk] *n abbr* (= *microphone*) micro.

Milan [mɪ'læn] *n* Milán *m*.

mild [maɪld] *a* (*person*) apacible; (*climate*) templado; (*slight*) ligero; (*taste*) suave; (*illness*) leve.

mildew ['mɪldjuː] *n* moho.

mildly ['maɪldlɪ] *ad* ligeramente; suavemente; **to put it ~** para no decir más.

mildness ['maɪldnɪs] *n* suavidad *f*; (*of illness*) levedad *f*.

mile [maɪl] *n* milla; **to do 20 ~s per gallon** hacer 20 millas por galón.

mileage ['maɪlɪdʒ] *n* número de millas; (*AUT*) kilometraje *m*.

mileage allowance *n* ≈ asignación *f* por kilometraje.

mileometer [maɪ'lɔmɪtə*] *n* (*Brit*) = **milometer.**

milestone ['maɪlstəun] *n* mojón *m*.

milieu [miːljəː] *n* (medio) ambiente *m*.

militant ['mɪlɪtnt] *a*, *n* militante *m/f*.

militarism ['mɪlɪtərɪzəm] *n* militarismo.

militaristic [mɪlɪtə'rɪstɪk] *a* militarista.

military ['mɪlɪtərɪ] *a* militar.

militate ['mɪlɪteɪt] *vi*: **to ~ against** militar en contra de.

militia [mɪ'lɪʃə] *n* milicia.

milk [mɪlk] *n* leche *f* ◆ *vt* (*cow*) ordeñar; (*fig*) chupar.

milk chocolate *n* chocolate *m* con leche.

milk float *n* (*Brit*) carro de la leche.

milking ['mɪlkɪŋ] *n* ordeño.

milkman ['mɪlkmən] *n* lechero.

milk shake *n* batido, malteada (*LAm*).

milk tooth *n* diente *m* de leche.

milk truck *n* (*US*) = **milk float.**

milky ['mɪlkɪ] *a* lechoso.

Milky Way *n* Vía Láctea.

mill [mɪl] *n* (*windmill etc*) molino; (*coffee* ~) molinillo; (*factory*) fábrica; (*spinning* ~) hilandería ◆ *vt* moler ◆ *vi* (*also*: ~ **about**) arremolinarse.

milled [mɪld] (*grain*) molido; (*coin*, *edge*) acordonado.

millennium, *pl* **~s** *or* **millennia** [mɪ'lenɪəm, 'lenɪə] *n* milenio, milenario.

miller ['mɪlə*] *n* molinero.

millet ['mɪlɪt] *n* mijo.

milli... ['mɪlɪ] *pref* mili... .

milligram(me) ['mɪlɪgraem] *n* miligramo.

millilitre, (*US*) **milliliter** ['mɪlɪliːtə*] *n* mililitro.

millimetre, (*US*) **millimeter** ['mɪlɪmiːtə*] *n* milímetro.

milliner ['mɪlɪnə*] *n* sombrerero/a.

millinery ['mɪlɪnərɪ] *n* sombrerería.

million ['mɪljən] *n* millón *m*; **a ~ times** un millón de veces.

millionaire [mɪljə'neə*] *n* millonario/a.

millipede ['mɪlɪpiːd] *n* milpiés *m inv*.

millstone ['mɪlstəun] *n* piedra de molino.

millwheel ['mɪlwiːl] *n* rueda de molino.

milometer [maɪ'lɔmɪtə*] *n* (*Brit*) cuentakilómetros *m inv*.

mime [maɪm] *n* mímica; (*actor*) mimo/a ◆ *vt* remedar ◆ *vi* actuar de mimo.

mimic ['mɪmɪk] *n* imitador(a) *m/f* ◆ *a* mímico ◆ *vt* remedar, imitar.

mimicry ['mɪmɪkrɪ] *n* imitación *f*.

Min. *abbr* (*Brit POL*: = *Ministry*) Min.

min. *abbr* (= *minute(s)*) m.; = **minimum.**

minaret [mɪnə'ret] *n* alminar *m*.

mince [mɪns] *vt* picar ◆ *vi* (*in walking*) andar con pasos menudos ◆ *n* (*Brit CULIN*) carne *f* picada, picadillo.

mincemeat ['mɪnsmiːt] *n* conserva de fruta picada.

mince pie *n* empanadilla rellena de fruta picada.

mincer ['mɪnsə*] *n* picadora de carne.

mincing ['mɪnsɪŋ] *a* afectado.

mind [maɪnd] *n* (*gen*) mente *f*; (*contrasted with matter*) espíritu *m* ◆ *vt* (*attend to*, *look after*) ocuparse de, cuidar; (*be careful of*) tener cuidado con; (*object to*): **I don't ~ the noise** no me molesta el ruido; **it is on my ~** me preocupa; **to my ~** a mi parecer *or* juicio; **to change one's ~** cambiar de idea *or* de parecer; **to bring** *or* **call sth to ~** recordar algo; **to have sth/ sb in ~** tener algo/a uno en mente; **to be out of one's ~** estar fuera de juicio; **to bear sth in ~** tomar *or* tener algo en cuenta; **to make up one's ~** decidirse; **it went right out of my ~** se me fue por completo (de la cabeza); **to be in two ~s about sth** estar indeciso *or* dudar ante algo; **I don't ~** me es igual; **~ you, ...** te advierto que ...; **never** ~! ¡es igual!, ¡no importa!; (*don't worry*) ¡no te preocupes!; '~ **the step**' 'cuidado con el escalón'.

-minded [-maındıd] *a*: **fair**~ imparcial; **an industrially**~ **nation** una nación que se dedica *or* se orienta a la industria.

minder ['maındə*] *n* guardaespaldas *m inv*.

mindful ['maındful] *a*: ~ **of** consciente de.

mindless ['maındlıs] *a* (*violence, crime*) sin motivo; (*work*) de autómata.

mine [maın] *pron* (el) mío/(la) mía *etc*; **a friend of** ~ un(a) amigo/a mío/mía ◆ *a*: **this book is** ~ este libro es mío ◆ *n* mina ◆ *vt* (*coal*) extraer; (*ship, beach*) minar.

mine detector *n* detector *m* de minas.

minefield ['maınfi:ld] *n* campo de minas.

miner ['maınə*] *n* minero/a.

mineral ['mınərəl] *a* mineral ◆ *n* mineral *m*; ~**s** *npl* (*Brit: soft drinks*) agua *sg* mineral, gaseosa *sg*.

mineral water *n* agua mineral.

minesweeper ['maınswi:pə*] *n* dragaminas *m inv*.

mingle ['mıŋgl] *vi*: **to** ~ **with** mezclarse con.

mingy ['mındʒı] *a* (*col*) tacaño.

mini... [mını] *pref* mini..., micro....

miniature ['mınətʃə*] *a* (en) miniatura ◆ *n* miniatura.

minibus ['mınıbʌs] *n* microbús *m*.

minicab ['mınıkæb] *n* microtaxi *m*.

minicomputer ['mınıkəm'pju:tə*] *n* minicomputador *m*.

minim ['mınım] *n* (*Brit MUS*) blanca.

minimal ['mınıml] *a* mínimo.

minimize ['mınımaız] *vt* minimizar.

minimum ['mınıməm] *n* (*pl* **minima** ['mınımə]) mínimo ◆ *a* mínimo; **to reduce to a** ~ reducir algo al mínimo; ~ **wage** salario mínimo.

minimum lending rate (MLR) *n* tipo de interés mínimo.

mining ['maınıŋ] *n* explotación *f* minera ◆ *a* minero.

minion ['mınjən] *n* secuaz *m*.

miniskirt ['mınıskə:t] *n* minifalda.

minister ['mınıstə*] *n* (*Brit POL*) ministro/a; (*REL*) pastor *m* ◆ *vi*: **to** ~ **to** atender a.

ministerial [mınıs'tıərıəl] *a* (*Brit POL*) ministerial.

ministry ['mınıstrı] *n* (*Brit POL*) ministerio; (*REL*) sacerdocio; **M**~ **of Defence** Ministerio de Defensa.

mink [mıŋk] *n* visón *m*.

mink coat *n* abrigo de visón.

minnow ['mınəu] *n* pececillo (de agua dulce).

minor ['maınə*] *a* (*unimportant*) secundario; (*MUS*) menor ◆ *n* (*LAW*) menor *m/f* de edad.

Minorca [mı'nɔ:kə] *n* Menorca.

minority [maı'nɔrıtı] *n* minoría; **to be in a** ~ estar en la minoría, ser minoría (*LAm*).

minority interest *n* participación *f* minoritaria.

minster ['mınstə*] *n* catedral *f*.

minstrel ['mınstrəl] *n* juglar *m*.

mint [mınt] *n* (*plant*) menta, hierbabuena; (*sweet*) caramelo de menta ◆ *vt* (*coins*) acuñar; **the (Royal) M**~, (*US*) **the (US) M**~ la Casa de la Moneda; **in** ~ **condition** en perfecto estado.

mint sauce *n* salsa de menta.

minuet [mınju'et] *n* minué *m*.

minus ['maınəs] *n* (*also*: ~ **sign**) signo de menos ◆ *prep* menos.

minuscule ['mınəskju:l] *a* minúsculo.

minute *n* ['mınıt] minuto; (*fig*) momento; ~**s** *npl* actas *fpl* ◆ *a* [maı'nju:t] diminuto; (*search*) minucioso; **it is 5** ~**s past 3** son las 3 y 5 (minutos); **at the last** ~ a última hora; **wait a** ~! ¡espera un momento!; **up to the** ~ de última hora; **in** ~ **detail** en detalle minucioso.

minute book *n* libro de actas.

minute hand *n* minutero.

minutely [maı'nju:tlı] *ad* (*by a small amount*) por muy poco; (*in detail*) detalladamente, minuciosamente.

miracle ['mırəkl] *n* milagro.

miracle play *n* auto, milagro.

miraculous [mı'rækjuləs] *a* milagroso.

miraculously [mı'rækjuləslı] *ad* milagrosamente.

mirage ['mıra:ʒ] *n* espejismo.

mire [maıə*] *n* fango, lodo.

mirror ['mırə*] *n* espejo; (*in car*) retrovisor *m* ◆ *vt* reflejar.

mirror image *n* reflejo inverso.

mirth [mə:θ] *n* alegría; (*laughter*) risa, risas *fpl*.

misadventure [mısəd'ventʃə*] *n* desgracia, accidente *m*; **death by** ~ muerte *f* accidental.

misanthropist [mı'zænθrəpıst] *n* misántropo/a.

misapply [mısə'plaı] *vt* emplear mal.

misapprehension ['mısæprı'henʃən] *n* equivocación *f*.

misappropriate [mısə'prəuprıeıt] *vt* (*funds*) malversar.

misappropriation ['mısəprəuprı'eıʃən] *n* malversación *f*, desfalco.

misbehave [mısbı'heıv] *vi* portarse mal.

misbehaviour, (*US*) **misbehavior** [mısbı'heıvjə*] *n* mala conducta.

misc. *abbr* = **miscellaneous**.

miscalculate [mıs'kælkjuleıt] *vt* calcular mal.

miscalculation [mıskælkju'leıʃən] *n* error *m* (de cálculo).

miscarriage ['mıskærıdʒ] *n* (*MED*) aborto; ~ **of justice** error *m* judicial.

miscarry [mıs'kærı] *vi* (*MED*) abortar; (*fail: plans*) fracasar, malograrse.

miscellaneous [mısı'leınıəs] *a* varios/as,

diversos/as; ~ **expenses** diversos gastos.
miscellany [mɪ'sɛlənɪ] n miscelánea.
mischance [mɪs'tʃɑːns] n desgracia, mala suerte f; **by (some)** ~ por (alguna) desgracia.
mischief ['mɪstʃɪf] n (naughtiness) travesura; (harm) mal m, daño; (maliciousness) malicia.
mischievous ['mɪstʃɪvəs] a travieso; dañoso; (playful) malicioso.
mischievously ['mɪstʃɪvəslɪ] ad por travesura; maliciosamente.
misconception ['mɪskən'sɛpʃən] n concepto erróneo; equivocación f.
misconduct [mɪs'kɔndʌkt] n mala conducta; **professional** ~ falta profesional.
miscount [mɪs'kaunt] vt, vi contar mal.
misconstrue [mɪskən'struː] vt interpretar mal.
misdeed [mɪs'diːd] n (old) fechoría, delito.
misdemeanour, (US) **misdemeanor** [mɪsdɪ'miːnə*] n delito, ofensa.
misdirect [mɪsdɪ'rɛkt] vt (person) informar mal; (letter) poner señas incorrectas en.
miser ['maɪzə*] n avaro/a.
miserable ['mɪzərəbl] a (unhappy) triste, desgraciado; (wretched) miserable; **to feel** ~ sentirse triste.
miserably ['mɪzərəblɪ] ad (smile, answer) tristemente; (fail) rotundamente; **to pay** ~ pagar una miseria.
miserly ['maɪzəlɪ] a avariento, tacaño.
misery ['mɪzərɪ] n (unhappiness) tristeza; (wretchedness) miseria, desdicha.
misfire [mɪs'faɪə*] vi fallar.
misfit ['mɪsfɪt] n (person) inadaptado/a.
misfortune [mɪs'fɔːtʃən] n desgracia.
misgiving(s) [mɪs'gɪvɪŋ(z)] n(pl) (mistrust) recelo; (apprehension) presentimiento; **to have ~s about sth** tener dudas sobre algo.
misguided [mɪs'gaɪdɪd] a equivocado.
mishandle [mɪs'hændl] vt (treat roughly) maltratar; (mismanage) manejar mal.
mishap ['mɪshæp] n desgracia, contratiempo.
mishear [mɪs'hɪə*] vt, vi (irg: like hear) oír mal.
mishmash ['mɪʃmæʃ] n (col) revoltijo.
misinform [mɪsɪn'fɔːm] vt informar mal.
misinterpret [mɪsɪn'tɜːprɪt] vt interpretar mal.
misinterpretation ['mɪsɪntəːprɪ'teɪʃən] n mala interpretación f.
misjudge [mɪs'dʒʌdʒ] vt juzgar mal.
mislay [mɪs'leɪ] vt (irg: like lay) extraviar, perder.
mislead [mɪs'liːd] vt (irg: like lead) llevar a conclusiones erróneas.
misleading [mɪs'liːdɪŋ] a engañoso.
misled [mɪs'lɛd] pt, pp of **mislead**.
mismanage [mɪs'mænɪdʒ] vt administrar mal.
mismanagement [mɪs'mænɪdʒmənt] n

mala administración f.
misnomer [mɪs'nəumə*] n término inapropiado o equivocado.
misogynist [mɪ'sɔdʒɪnɪst] n misógino.
misplace [mɪs'pleɪs] vt (lose) extraviar; ~d (trust etc) inmerecido.
misprint ['mɪsprɪnt] n errata, error m de imprenta.
mispronounce [mɪsprə'nauns] vt pronunciar mal.
misquote [mɪs'kwəut] vt citar incorrectamente.
misread [mɪs'riːd] vt (irg: like **read**) leer mal.
misrepresent [mɪsrɛprɪ'zɛnt] vt falsificar.
misrepresentation [mɪsrɛprɪzɛn'teɪʃən] n (LAW) falsa declaración f.
Miss [mɪs] n Señorita; **Dear** ~ **Smith** Estimada Señorita Smith.
miss [mɪs] vt (train etc) perder; (shot) errar, fallar; (appointment, class) faltar a; (escape, avoid) evitar; (notice loss of: money etc) notar la falta de; (regret the absence of): **I ~ him** (yo) le echo de menos or a faltar ◆ vi fallar ◆ n (shot) tiro fallido or perdido; **the bus just ~ed the wall** por poco el autobús se estrelló contra el muro; **you're ~ing the point** no caes, no te entra.
miss out vt (Brit) omitir.
miss out on vt fus (fun, party, opportunity) perder.
missal ['mɪsl] n misal m.
misshapen [mɪs'ʃeɪpən] a deforme.
missile ['mɪsaɪl] n (AVIAT) misil m; (object thrown) proyectil m.
missile base n base f de misiles.
missile launcher n dispositivo de lanzamiento de proyectiles or misiles.
missing ['mɪsɪŋ] a (pupil) ausente; (thing) perdido; (MIL) desaparecido; **to be** ~ faltar; ~ **person** desaparecido/a.
mission ['mɪʃən] n misión f; **on a** ~ **for sb** en una misión para uno.
missionary ['mɪʃənrɪ] n misionero/a.
misspell [mɪs'spɛl] vt (irg: like **spell**) escribir mal.
misspent [mɪs'spɛnt] a: **his** ~ **youth** su juventud disipada.
mist [mɪst] n (light) neblina; (heavy) niebla; (at sea) bruma ◆ vi (also: ~ **over**, ~ **up**: weather) nublarse; (: Brit: windows) empañarse.
mistake [mɪs'teɪk] n error m ◆ vt (irg: like **take**) entender mal; **by** ~ por equivocación; **to make a** ~ (about sb/sth) equivocarse; (in writing, calculating etc) cometer un error; **to** ~ **A for B** confundir A con B.
mistaken [mɪs'teɪkən] pp of **mistake** ◆ a (idea etc) equivocado; **to be** ~ equivocarse, engañarse; ~ **identity** identificación f errónea.
mistakenly [mɪs'teɪkənlɪ] ad erróneamente.

mister ['mɪstə*] n (col) señor m; see **Mr.**

mistletoe ['mɪsltəu] n muérdago.

mistook [mɪs'tuk] pt of **mistake.**

mistranslation [mɪstræns'leɪʃən] n mala traducción f.

mistreat [mɪs'triːt] vt maltratar, tratar mal.

mistress ['mɪstrɪs] n (lover) amante f; (of house) señora (de la casa); (Brit: in primary school) maestra; (in secondary school) profesora; see **Mrs.**

mistrust [mɪs'trʌst] vt desconfiar de ♦ n: ~ (of) desconfianza (de).

mistrustful [mɪs'trʌstful] a: ~ (of) desconfiado (de), receloso (de).

misty ['mɪstɪ] a nebuloso, brumoso; (day) de niebla; (glasses) empañado.

misty-eyed ['mɪstɪ'aɪd] a sentimental.

misunderstand [mɪsʌndə'stænd] vt, vi (irg: like **understand**) entender mal.

misunderstanding [mɪsʌndə'stændɪŋ] n malentendido.

misunderstood [mɪsʌndə'stud] pt, pp of **misunderstand** ♦ a (person) incomprendido.

misuse n [mɪs'juːs] mal uso; (of power) abuso ♦ vt [mɪs'juːz] abusar de; (funds) malversar.

MIT n abbr (US) = Massachusetts Institute of Technology.

mite [maɪt] n (small quantity) pizca; **poor** ~! ¡pobrecito!

mitigate ['mɪtɪgeɪt] vt mitigar; **mitigating circumstances** circunstancias fpl mitigantes.

mitigation [mɪtɪ'geɪʃən] n mitigación f, alivio.

mitre, (US) **miter** ['maɪtə*] n mitra.

mitt(en) ['mɪt(n)] n manopla.

mix [mɪks] vt (gen) mezclar; (combine) unir ♦ vi mezclarse; (people) llevarse bien ♦ n mezcla; **to** ~ **sth with sth** mezclar algo con algo; **to** ~ **business with pleasure** combinar los negocios con el placer; **cake** ~ mezcla de ingredientes de pastelería.

mix in vt (eggs etc) añadir.

mix up vt mezclar; (confuse) confundir; **to be** ~**ed up in sth** estar metido en algo.

mixed [mɪkst] a (assorted) variado, surtido; (school etc) mixto.

mixed doubles n (SPORT) mixtos mpl.

mixed economy n economía mixta.

mixed grill n (Brit) parrillada mixta.

mixed-up [mɪkst'ʌp] a (confused) confuso, revuelto.

mixer ['mɪksə*] n (for food) licuadora; (person): **he's a good** ~ tiene don de gentes.

mixture ['mɪkstʃə*] n mezcla.

mix-up ['mɪksʌp] n confusión f.

Mk abbr (Brit TECH: = mark) Mk.

mk abbr = **mark** (currency).

mkt abbr = **market.**

MLitt n abbr (= Master of Literature, Master of Letters) título universitario.

MLR n abbr (Brit) = **minimum lending rate.**

mm abbr (= millimetre) mm.

MN abbr (Brit) = **Merchant Navy;** (US POST) = Minnesota.

MO n abbr (MED) = medical officer; (US col) = modus operandi ♦ abbr (US POST) = Missouri.

m.o. abbr (= money order) g/.

moan [məun] n gemido ♦ vi gemir; (col: complain): **to** ~ **(about)** quejarse (de).

moaning ['məunɪŋ] n gemidos mpl; quejas fpl, protestas fpl.

moat [məut] n foso.

mob [mɔb] n multitud f; (pej): **the** ~ el populacho ♦ vt acosar.

mobile ['məubaɪl] a móvil ♦ n móvil m; **applicants must be** ~ los candidatos deben ser dispuestos a mudarse de casa.

mobile home n caravana.

mobile shop n (Brit) tienda ambulante.

mobility [məu'bɪlɪtɪ] n movilidad f; (of applicant) disposición f a mudarse de casa; ~ **of labour** or (US) **labor** movilidad f de la mano de obra.

mobilize ['məubɪlaɪz] vt movilizar.

moccasin ['mɔkəsɪn] n mocasín m.

mock [mɔk] vt (make ridiculous) ridiculizar; (laugh at) burlarse de ♦ a fingido.

mockery ['mɔkərɪ] n burla; **to make a** ~ **of** desprestigiar.

mocking ['mɔkɪŋ] a (tone) burlón/ona.

mockingbird ['mɔkɪŋbəːd] n sinsonte m, zenzontle (LAm).

mock-up ['mɔkʌp] n maqueta.

mod cons ['mɔd'kɔnz] npl abbr (= modern conveniences) see **convenience.**

mode [məud] n modo; (of transport) medio; (COMPUT) modo, modalidad f.

model ['mɔdl] n (gen) modelo; (ARCH) maqueta; (person: for fashion, ART) modelo m/f ♦ a modelo inv ♦ vt modelar ♦ vi ser modelo; ~ **railway** ferrocarril m de juguete; **to** ~ **clothes** pasar modelos, ser modelo; **to** ~ **on** crear a imitación de.

modelling, (US) **modeling** ['mɔdlɪŋ] n (modelmaking) modelado.

modem ['məudəm] n modem m.

moderate a, n ['mɔdərət] moderado/a m/f ♦ (vb: ['mɔdəreɪt]) vi moderarse, calmarse ♦ vt moderar.

moderately ['mɔdərətlɪ] ad (act) con moderación; (expensive, difficult) medianamente; (pleased, happy) bastante.

moderation [mɔdə'reɪʃən] n moderación f; **in** ~ con moderación.

modern ['mɔdən] a moderno; ~ **languages** lenguas fpl vivas.

modernity [mə'dɔːnɪtɪ] n modernidad f.

modernization [mɔdənaɪ'zeɪʃən] n modernización f.

modernize ['mɔdənaɪz] vt modernizar.

modest ['mɔdɪst] *a* modesto.
modestly ['mɔdɪstlɪ] *ad* modestamente.
modesty ['mɔdɪstɪ] *n* modestia.
modicum ['mɔdɪkəm] *n*: **a ~ of** un mínimo de.
modification [mɔdɪfɪ'keɪʃən] *n* modificación *f*; **to make ~s** hacer cambios *or* modificaciones.
modify ['mɔdɪfaɪ] *vt* modificar.
Mods [mɔdz] *n abbr* (*Brit*: = *(Honour) Moderations*) *examen de la licenciatura de la universidad de Oxford*.
modular ['mɔdjulə*] *a* (*filing, unit*) modular.
modulate ['mɔdjuleɪt] *vt* modular.
modulation [mɔdju'leɪʃən] *n* modulación *f*.
module ['mɔdjuːl] *n* (*unit, component, SPACE*) módulo.
modus operandi ['mɔudəsɔpə'rændiː] *n* manera de actuar.
Mogadishu [mɔgə'dɪʃuː] *n* Mogadisio.
mogul ['məugəl] *n* (*fig*) magnate *m*.
MOH *n abbr* (*Brit*) = *Medical Officer of Health*.
mohair ['məuhɛə*] *n* mohair *m*.
Mohammed [mə'hæmɛd] *n* Mahoma *m*.
moist [mɔɪst] *a* húmedo.
moisten ['mɔɪsn] *vt* humedecer.
moisture ['mɔɪstʃə*] *n* humedad *f*.
moisturize ['mɔɪstʃəraɪz] *vt* (*skin*) hidratar.
moisturizer ['mɔɪstʃəraɪzə*] *n* crema hidratante.
molar ['məulə*] *n* muela.
molasses [məu'læsɪz] *n* melaza.
mold [məuld] *n*, *vt* (*US*) = **mould**.
mole [məul] *n* (*animal*) topo; (*spot*) lunar *m*.
molecular [mə'lɛkjulə*] *a* molecular.
molecule ['mɔlɪkjuːl] *n* molécula.
molest [məu'lɛst] *vt* importunar.
moll [mɔl] *n* (*slang*) amiga.
mollusc, (*US*) **mollusk** ['mɔləsk] *n* molusco.
mollycoddle ['mɔlɪkɔdl] *vt* mimar.
molt [məult] *vi* (*US*) = **moult**.
molten ['məultən] *a* fundido; (*lava*) líquido.
mom [mɔm] *n* (*US*) = **mum**.
moment ['məumənt] *n* momento; **at** *or* **for the ~** de momento, por el momento, por ahora; **in a ~** dentro de un momento, luego.
momentarily ['məuməntrɪlɪ] *ad* momentáneamente; (*US: very soon*) de un momento a otro.
momentary ['məuməntərɪ] *a* momentáneo.
momentous [məu'mɛntəs] *a* trascendental, importante.
momentum [məu'mɛntəm] *n* momento; (*fig*) ímpetu *m*; **to gather ~** cobrar velocidad.
mommy ['mɔmɪ] *n* (*US*) = **mummy**.
Mon. *abbr* (= *Monday*) lun.
Monaco ['mɔnəkəu] *n* Mónaco.

monarch ['mɔnək] *n* monarca *m/f*.
monarchist ['mɔnəkɪst] *n* monárquico/a.
monarchy ['mɔnəkɪ] *n* monarquía.
monastery ['mɔnəstərɪ] *n* monasterio.
monastic [mə'næstɪk] *a* monástico.
Monday ['mʌndɪ] *n* lunes *m inv*.
Monegasque [mɔnɪ'gæsk] *a, n* monegasco/a *m/f*.
monetarist ['mʌnɪtərɪst] *n* monetarista *m*.
monetary ['mʌnɪtərɪ] *a* monetario.
monetary policy *n* política monetaria.
money ['mʌnɪ] *n* dinero; **to make ~** ganar dinero; **I've got no ~ left** no me queda dinero.
moneyed ['mʌnɪd] *a* adinerado.
moneylender ['mʌnɪlɛndə*] *n* prestamista *m/f*.
moneymaking ['mʌnɪmeɪkɪŋ] *a* rentable.
money market *n* mercado monetario.
money order *n* giro.
money-spinner ['mʌnɪspɪnə*] *n* (*col: person, idea, business*) fuente *f* de ganancias.
money supply *n* oferta monetaria, medio circulante, volumen *m* monetario.
Mongol ['mɔŋgəl] *n* mongol(a) *m/f*; (*LING*) mongol *m*.
mongol ['mɔŋgəl] *a, n* (*MED*) mongólico.
Mongolia [mɔŋ'gəulɪə] *n* Mongolia.
Mongolian [mɔŋ'gəulɪən] *a* mongol(a) ♦ *n* mongol(a) *m/f*; (*LING*) mongol *m*.
mongoose ['mɔŋguːs] *n* mangosta.
mongrel ['mʌŋgrəl] *n* (*dog*) perro mestizo.
monitor ['mɔnɪtə*] *n* (*SCOL*) monitor *m*; (*TV, COMPUT*) monitor *m* ♦ *vt* controlar; (*foreign station*) escuchar, oír.
monk [mʌŋk] *n* monje *m*.
monkey ['mʌŋkɪ] *n* mono.
monkey business *n*, **monkey tricks** *npl* travesuras *fpl*.
monkey nut *n* (*Brit*) cacahuete *m*, maní (*LAm*).
monkey wrench *n* llave *f* inglesa.
mono ['mɔnəu] *a* (*broadcast etc*) mono *inv*.
mono... [mɔnəu] *pref* mono ... .
monochrome ['mɔnəukrəum] *a* monocromo.
monocle ['mɔnəkl] *n* monóculo.
monogram ['mɔnəgræm] *n* monograma *m*.
monolith ['mɔnəlɪθ] *n* monolito.
monolithic [mɔnə'lɪθɪk] *a* monolítico.
monologue ['mɔnəlɔg] *n* monólogo.
monoplane ['mɔnəpleɪn] *n* monoplano.
monopolist [mə'nɔpəlɪst] *n* monopolista *m/f*.
monopolize [mə'nɔpəlaɪz] *vt* monopolizar.
monopoly [mə'nɔpəlɪ] *n* monopolio; **Monopolies and Mergers Commission** (*Brit*) *comisión reguladora de monopolios y fusiones*.
monorail ['mɔnəureɪl] *n* monocarril *m*, monorriel *m*.
monosodium glutamate [mɔnə'səudɪəm'gluːtəmeɪt] *n* glutamato monosódi-

co.

monosyllabic [mɔnɔsɪ'læbɪk] a monosílabo.

monosyllable ['mɔnəsɪləbl] n monosílabo.

monotone ['mɔnətəun] n voz f (or tono) monocorde.

monotonous [mə'nɔtənəs] a monótono.

monotony [mə'nɔtənɪ] n monotonía.

monoxide [mə'nɔksaɪd] n: **carbon** ~ monóxido de carbono.

monseigneur [mɔnsɛn'jə:*], **monsignor** [mɔn'si:njə*] n monseñor m.

monsoon [mɔn'su:n] n monzón m/f.

monster ['mɔnstə*] n monstruo.

monstrosity [mɔns'trɔsɪtɪ] n monstruosidad f.

monstrous ['mɔnstrəs] a (huge) enorme; (atrocious) monstruoso.

montage [mɔn'tɑ:ʒ] n montaje m.

Mont Blanc [mɔ̃'blɑ̃] n el monte Blanco.

month [mʌnθ] n mes m; **300 dollars a** ~ 300 dólares al mes; **every** ~ cada mes.

monthly ['mʌnθlɪ] a mensual ♦ ad mensualmente ♦ n (magazine) revista mensual; **twice** ~ dos veces por mes or mensuales; ~ **instalment** mensualidad f.

monument ['mɔnjumənt] n monumento.

monumental [mɔnju'mɛntl] a monumental.

moo [mu:] vi mugir.

mood [mu:d] n humor m; **to be in a good/bad** ~ estar de buen/mal humor.

moodily ['mu:dɪlɪ] ad malhumoradamente.

moodiness ['mu:dɪnɪs] n humor m cambiante; mal humor m.

moody ['mu:dɪ] a (variable) de humor variable; (sullen) malhumorado.

moon [mu:n] n luna.

moonbeam ['mu:nbi:m] n rayo de luna.

moon landing n alunizaje m.

moonless ['mu:nlɪs] a sin luna.

moonlight ['mu:nlaɪt] n luz f de la luna ♦ vi tener un pluriempleo.

moonlighting ['mu:nlaɪtɪŋ] n pluriempleo.

moonlit ['mu:nlɪt] a: **a** ~ **night** una noche de luna.

moonshot ['mu:nʃɔt] n lanzamiento de una astronave a la luna.

moonstruck ['mu:nstrʌk] a chiflado.

Moor [muə*] n moro/a.

moor [muə*] n páramo ♦ vt (ship) amarrar ♦ vi echar las amarras.

moorings ['muərɪŋz] npl (chains) amarras fpl; (place) amarradero sg.

Moorish ['muərɪʃ] a moro; (architecture) árabe, morisco.

moorland ['muələnd] n páramo, brezal m.

moose [mu:s] n, pl inv alce m.

moot [mu:t] vt proponer para la discusión, sugerir ♦ a: ~ **point** punto discutible.

mop [mɔp] n fregona; (of hair) greña, melena ♦ vt fregar.

mop up vt limpiar.

mope [məup] vi estar deprimido.

mope about, **mope around** vi andar abatido.

moped ['məupɛd] n ciclomotor m.

moquette [mɔ'kɛt] n moqueta.

moral ['mɔrl] a moral ♦ n moraleja; ~**s** npl moralidad f, moral f.

morale [mɔ'rɑ:l] n moral f.

morality [mə'rælɪtɪ] n moralidad f.

moralize ['mɔrəlaɪz] vi: **to** ~ **(about)** moralizar (sobre).

morally ['mɔrəlɪ] ad moralmente.

morass [mə'ræs] n pantano.

moratorium [mɔrə'tɔ:rɪəm] n moratoria.

morbid ['mɔ:bɪd] a (interest) morboso; (MED) mórbido.

more [mɔ:*] a, ad más ♦ pron: **and what's** ~ ... y además ...; **many/much** ~ muchos/mucho más; **is there any** ~? ¿hay más?; **once** ~ otra vez, una vez más; **I want** ~ quiero más; ~ **dangerous than** más peligroso que; ~ **or less** más o menos; ~ **than ever** más que nunca; ~ **and** ~ cada vez más; **no** ~, **not any** ~ ya no.

moreover [mɔ:'rəuvə*] ad además, por otra parte.

morgue [mɔ:g] n depósito de cadáveres.

MORI ['mɔ:rɪ] n abbr (Brit) = Market and Opinion Research Institute.

moribund ['mɔ:rɪbʌnd] a moribundo.

Mormon ['mɔ:mən] n mormón/ona m/f.

morning ['mɔ:nɪŋ] n (gen) mañana; (early ~) madrugada; **in the** ~ por la mañana; **7 o'clock in the** ~ las 7 de la mañana; **this** ~ esta mañana.

morning sickness n (MED) náuseas fpl del embarazo.

Moroccan [mə'rɔkən] a, n marroquí m/f.

Morocco [mə'rɔkəu] n Marruecos m.

moron ['mɔ:rɔn] n imbécil m/f.

morose [mə'rəus] a hosco, malhumorado.

morphine ['mɔ:fi:n] n morfina.

Morse [mɔ:s] n (also: ~ **code**) (código) morse.

morsel ['mɔ:sl] n (of food) bocado.

mortal ['mɔ:tl] a, n mortal m.

mortality [mɔ:'tælɪtɪ] n mortalidad f.

mortality rate n tasa de mortalidad.

mortally ['mɔ:təlɪ] ad mortalmente.

mortar ['mɔ:tə*] n argamasa; (implement) mortero.

mortgage ['mɔ:gɪdʒ] n hipoteca ♦ vt hipotecar; **to take out a** ~ sacar una hipoteca.

mortgage company n (US) ≈ banco hipotecario.

mortgagee [mɔ:gə'dʒi:] n acreedor(a) m/f hipotecario/a.

mortgager ['mɔ:gədʒə*] n deudor(a) m/f hipotecario/a.

mortice ['mɔ:tɪs] = **mortise**.

mortician [mɔ:'tɪʃən] n (US) director(a) m/f de pompas fúnebres.

mortification ['mɔ:tɪfɪ'keɪʃən] n mortificación f, humillación f.

mortified ['mɔ:tɪfaɪd] a: **I was** ~ me dio

muchísima vergüenza.

mortise (lock) ['mɔːtɪs-] *n* cerradura de muesca.

mortuary ['mɔːtjuərɪ] *n* depósito de cadáveres.

mosaic [məu'zeɪɪk] *n* mosaico.

Moscow ['mɔskəu] *n* Moscú *m*.

Moslem ['mɔzləm] *a, n* = **Muslim**.

mosque [mɔsk] *n* mezquita.

mosquito, ~**es** [mɔs'kiːtəu] *n* mosquito.

moss [mɔs] *n* musgo.

mossy ['mɔsɪ] *a* musgoso, cubierto de musgo.

most [məust] *a* la mayor parte de, la mayoría de ♦ *pron* la mayor parte, la mayoría ♦ *ad* el más; (*very*) muy; **the** ~ (*also:* + *adjective*) el más; ~ **of them** la mayor parte de ellos; **I saw the** ~ yo vi el que más; **at the (very)** ~ a lo sumo, todo lo más; **to make the** ~ **of** aprovechar (al máximo); **a** ~ **interesting book** un libro interesantísimo.

mostly ['məustlɪ] *ad* en su mayor parte, principalmente.

MOT *n abbr* (*Brit* = *Ministry of Transport*): **the** ~ (**test**) inspección (*anual*) *obligatoria de coches y camiones*.

motel [məu'tɛl] *n* motel *m*.

moth [mɔθ] *n* mariposa nocturna; (*clothes* ~) polilla.

mothball ['mɔθbɔːl] *n* bola de naftalina.

moth-eaten ['mɔθiːtn] *a* apolillado.

mother ['mʌðə*] *n* madre *f* ♦ *a* materno ♦ *vt* (*care for*) cuidar (como una madre).

mother board *n* (*COMPUT*) placa madre.

motherhood ['mʌðəhud] *n* maternidad *f*.

mother-in-law ['mʌðərɪnlɔː] *n* suegra.

motherly ['mʌðəlɪ] *a* maternal.

mother-of-pearl ['mʌðərəv'pəːl] *n* nácar *m*.

mother's help *n* niñera.

mother-to-be ['mʌðətə'biː] *n* futura madre.

mother tongue *n* lengua materna.

mothproof ['mɔθpruːf] *a* a prueba de polillas.

motif [məu'tiːf] *n* motivo; (*theme*) tema *m*.

motion ['məuʃən] *n* movimiento; (*gesture*) ademán *m*, señal *f*; (*at meeting*) moción *f*; (*Brit: also:* **bowel** ~) evacuación *f* intestinal ♦ *vt, vi*: **to** ~ (**to**) **sb to do sth** hacer señas a uno para que haga algo; **to be in** ~ (*vehicle*) estar en movimiento; **to set in** ~ poner en marcha; **to go through the** ~**s of doing sth** (*fig*) hacer algo mecánicamente *or* sin convicción.

motionless ['məuʃənlɪs] *a* inmóvil.

motion picture *n* película.

motivate ['məutɪveɪt] *vt* (*act, decision*) provocar; (*person*) motivar.

motivated ['məutɪveɪtɪd] *a* motivado.

motivation [məutɪ'veɪʃən] *n* motivación *f*.

motivational research [məutɪ'veɪʃənl-] *n*

estudios *mpl* de motivación.

motive ['məutɪv] *n* motivo; **from the best** ~**s** de los mejores motivos.

motley ['mɔtlɪ] *a* variado.

motor ['məutə*] *n* motor *m*; (*Brit: col: vehicle*) coche *m*, carro (*LAm*), automóvil *m* ♦ *a* motor (*f*: motora, motriz).

motorbike ['məutəbaɪk] *n* moto *f*.

motorboat ['məutəbəut] *n* lancha motora.

motorcar ['məutəkɑː] *n* (*Brit*) coche *m*, carro (*LAm*), automóvil *m*.

motorcoach ['məutəkəutʃ] *n* autocar *m*, autobús *m*, camión *m* (*LAm*).

motorcycle ['məutəsaɪkl] *n* motocicleta.

motorcycle racing *n* motociclismo.

motorcyclist ['məutəsaɪklɪst] *n* motociclista *m/f*.

motoring ['məutərɪŋ] *n* (*Brit*) automovilismo ♦ *a* (*accident*) de tráfico *or* tránsito (*LAm*); (*offence*) de carretera.

motorist ['məutərɪst] *n* conductor(a) *m/f*, automovilista *m/f*.

motorize ['məutəraɪz] *vt* motorizar.

motor oil *n* aceite *m* para motores.

motor racing *n* (*Brit*) carreras *fpl* de coches, automovilismo.

motor scooter *n* moto *f*.

motor vehicle *n* automóvil *m*.

motorway ['məutəweɪ] *n* (*Brit*) autopista.

mottled ['mɔtld] *a* abigarrado, multicolor.

motto, ~**es** ['mɔtəu] *n* lema *m*; (*watchword*) consigna.

mould, (*US*) **mold** [məuld] *n* molde *m*; (*mildew*) moho ♦ *vt* moldear; (*fig*) formar.

mo(u)lder ['məuldə*] *vi* (*decay*) decaer.

mo(u)lding ['məuldɪŋ] *n* (*ARCH*) moldura.

mo(u)ldy ['məuldɪ] *a* enmohecido.

moult, (*US*) **molt** [məult] *vi* mudar (la piel) las plumas).

mound [maund] *n* montón *m*, montículo.

mount [maunt] *n* monte *m*; (*horse*) montura; (*for jewel etc*) engarce *m*; (*for picture*) marco ♦ *vt* montar, subir a; (*stairs*) subir; (*exhibition*) montar; (*attack*) lanzar; (*picture, stamp*) pegar, fijar ♦ *vi* (*also:* ~ **up**) subirse, montarse.

mountain ['mauntɪn] *n* montaña ♦ *cpd* de montaña; **to make a** ~ **out of a molehill** hacerse de todo una montaña.

mountaineer [mauntɪ'nɪə*] *n* alpinista *m/f*, andinista *m/f* (*LAm*).

mountaineering [mauntɪ'nɪərɪŋ] *n* alpinismo, andinismo (*LAm*).

mountainous ['mauntɪnəs] *a* montañoso.

mountain rescue team *n* equipo de rescate de montaña.

mountainside ['mauntɪnsaɪd] *n* ladera de la montaña.

mounted ['mauntɪd] *a* montado.

Mount Everest *n* Monte *m* Everest.

mourn [mɔːn] *vt* llorar, lamentar ♦ *vi*: **to** ~ **for** llorar la muerte de, lamentarse por.

mourner ['mɔːnə*] *n* doliente *m/f*.

mournful ['mɔːnful] a triste, lúgubre.

mourning ['mɔːnɪŋ] n luto ♦ cpd (dress) de luto; **in** ~ de luto.

mouse, pl **mice** [maus, maɪs] n (also COMPUT) ratón m.

mousetrap ['maustræp] n ratonera.

mousse [muːs] n (CULIN) crema batida; (for hair) espuma (moldeadora).

moustache [məs'tɑːʃ], (US) **mustache** ['mʌstæʃ] n bigote m.

mousy ['mausɪ] a (person) tímido; (hair) pardusco.

mouth, pl **mouths** [mauθ, -ðz] n boca; (of river) desembocadura.

mouthful ['mauθful] n bocado.

mouth organ n armónica.

mouthpiece ['mauθpiːs] n (of musical instrument) boquilla; (TEL) micrófono; (spokesman) portavoz m/f.

mouth-to-mouth ['mauθtə'mauθ] a: ~ **resuscitation** boca a boca m.

mouthwash ['mauθwɔʃ] n enjuague m bucal.

mouth-watering ['mauθwɔːtərɪŋ] a apetitoso.

movable ['muːvəbl] a movible.

move [muːv] n (movement) movimiento; (in game) jugada; (: turn to play) turno; (change of house) mudanza ♦ vt mover; (emotionally) conmover; (POL: resolution etc) proponer ♦ vi (gen) moverse; (traffic) circular; (also: Brit: ~ **house**) trasladarse, mudarse; **to** ~ **sb to do sth** mover a uno a hacer algo; **to be** ~**d** estar conmovido; **to get a** ~ **on** darse prisa.

move about or **around** vi moverse; (travel) viajar.

move along vi avanzar, adelantarse.

move away vi alejarse.

move back vi retroceder.

move down vt (demote) degradar.

move forward vi avanzar ♦ vt adelantar.

move in vi (to a house) instalarse.

move off vi ponerse en camino.

move on vi seguir viaje ♦ vt (onlookers) hacer circular.

move out vi (of house) mudarse.

move over vi apartarse.

move up vi subir; (employee) ser ascendido.

movement ['muːvmənt] n movimiento; (TECH) mecanismo; ~ **(of the bowels)** (MED) evacuación f.

mover ['muːvə*] n proponente m/f.

movie ['muːvɪ] n película; **to go to the** ~**s** ir al cine.

movie camera n cámara cinematográfica.

moviegoer ['muːvɪgəuə*] n (US) aficionado/a al cine.

moving ['muːvɪŋ] a (emotional) conmovedor(a); (that moves) móvil; (instigating) motor(a).

mow, pt **mowed**, pp **mowed** or **mown** [məu, -n] vt (grass) cortar; (corn: also: ~ **down**) segar; (shoot) acribillar.

mower ['məuə*] n (also: **lawn**~) cortacéspedes m inv.

Mozambique [məuzæm'biːk] n Mozambique m.

MP n abbr (= Military Police) PM; (Brit: = Member of Parliament) Dip.; (Canada) = Mounted Police.

mpg n abbr (= miles per gallon) millas por galón.

mph abbr = miles per hour (60 mph = 96 km/h.).

MPhil n abbr (= Master of Philosophy) título universitario.

MPS n abbr (Brit) = Member of the Pharmaceutical Society.

Mr, Mr. ['mɪstə*] n: ~ **Smith** (el) Sr. Smith.

MRC n abbr (Brit: = Medical Research Council) departamento estatal que controla la investigación médica.

MRCP n abbr (Brit) = Member of the Royal College of Physicians.

MRCS n abbr (Brit) = Member of the Royal College of Surgeons.

MRCVS n abbr (Brit) = Member of the Royal College of Veterinary Surgeons.

Mrs, Mrs. ['mɪsɪz] n: ~ **Smith** (la) Sra. de Smith.

MS n abbr (= manuscript) MS; = **multiple sclerosis**; (US: = Master of Science) título universitario ♦ abbr (US POST) = Mississippi.

Ms, Ms. [mɪz] n (= Miss or Mrs): ~ **Smith** (la) Sa. Smith.

MSA n abbr (US: = Master of Science in Agriculture) título universitario.

MSC n abbr = **Manpower Services Commission**.

MSc abbr see **Master of Science**.

MSG n abbr = **monosodium glutamate**.

MSS n abbr (= manuscripts) MSS.

MST abbr (US: = Mountain Standard Time) hora de invierno de las Montañas Rocosas.

MSW n abbr (US: = Master of Social Work) título universitario.

MT n abbr (= machine translation) traducción f automática ♦ abbr (US POST) = Montana.

Mt abbr (GEO: = mount) m.

mth abbr (= month) m.

much [mʌtʃ] a mucho ♦ ad, n, pron mucho; (before pp) muy; **how** ~ **is it?** ¿cuánto es?, ¿cuánto cuesta?; **too** ~ demasiado; **so** ~ tanto; **it's not** ~ no es mucho; **as** ~ **as** tanto como; **however** ~ **he tries** por mucho que se esfuerce; **I like it very/so** ~ me gusta mucho/tanto; **thank you very** ~ muchas gracias, muy agradecido.

muck [mʌk] n (dirt) suciedad f; (fig) porquería.

muck about or **around** vi (col) perder

el tiempo; (*enjoy o.s.*) entretenerse; (*tinker*) manosear.

muck in *vi* (*col*) compartir el trabajo.

muck out *vt* (*stable*) limpiar.

muck up *vt* (*col: dirty*) ensuciar; (: *spoil*) echar a perder; (: *ruin*) arruinar, estropear.

muckraking ['mʌkreɪkɪŋ] (*fig col*) *n* amarillismo ◆ *a* especializado en escándalos.

mucky ['mʌkɪ] *a* (*dirty*) sucio.

mucus ['mjuːkəs] *n* moco.

mud [mʌd] *n* barro, lodo.

muddle ['mʌdl] *n* desorden *m*, confusión *f*; (*mix-up*) embrollo, lío ◆ *vt* (*also*: ~ **up**) embrollar, confundir.

muddle along, muddle on *vi* arreglárselas de alguna manera.

muddle through *vi* salir del paso.

muddle-headed [mʌdl'hɛdɪd] *a* (*person*) despistado, confuso.

muddy ['mʌdɪ] *a* fangoso, cubierto de lodo.

mudguard ['mʌdɡɑːd] *n* guardabarros *m inv*.

mudpack ['mʌdpæk] *n* mascarilla.

mud-slinging ['mʌdslɪŋɪŋ] *n* injurias *fpl*, difamación *f*.

muff [mʌf] *n* manguito ◆ *vt* (*chance*) desperdiciar; (*lines*) estropear; (*shot, catch etc*) fallar; **to** ~ **it** fracasar.

muffin ['mʌfɪn] *n* mollete *m*.

muffle ['mʌfl] *vt* (*sound*) amortiguar; (*against cold*) embozar.

muffled ['mʌfld] *a* sordo, apagado.

muffler ['mʌflə*] *n* (*scarf*) bufanda; (*US AUT*) silenciador *m*; (*on motorbike*) silenciador *m*, mofle *m*.

mufti ['mʌftɪ] *n*: **in** ~ (vestido) de paisano.

mug [mʌɡ] *n* (*cup*) taza grande (*sin platillo*); (*for beer*) jarra; (*col: face*) jeta; (: *fool*) bobo ◆ *vt* (*assault*) asaltar; **it's a** ~'s **game** es cosa de bobos.

mug up *vt* (*col: also*: ~ **up on**) empollar.

mugger ['mʌɡə*] *n* asaltador(a) *m/f*.

mugging ['mʌɡɪŋ] *n* ataque *m or* asalto callejero.

muggy ['mʌɡɪ] *a* bochornoso.

mulatto, es [mju:'lætəu] *n* mulato/a.

mulberry ['mʌlbrɪ] *n* (*fruit*) mora; (*tree*) morera, moral *m*.

mule [mjuːl] *n* mula.

mull [mʌl]: **to** ~ **over** *vt* meditar sobre.

mulled [mʌld] *a*: ~ **wine** vino caliente.

mullioned ['mʌliənd] *a* (*windows*) dividido por parteluces.

multi... [mʌltɪ] *pref* multi....

multi-access ['mʌltɪ'ækses] *a* (*COMPUT*) multiacceso, de acceso múltiple.

multicoloured, (*US*) **multicolored** ['mʌltɪkʌləd] *a* multicolor.

multifarious [mʌltɪ'fɛərɪəs] *a* múltiple, vario.

multilateral [mʌltɪ'lætərl] *a* (*POL*) multilateral.

multi-level [mʌltɪ'lɛvl] *a* (*US*) = **multistorey**.

multimillionaire [mʌltɪmɪljə'nɛə*] *n* multimillonario/a.

multinational [mʌltɪ'næʃənl] *n* multinacional *m*, transnacional *m* ◆ *a* multinacional.

multiple ['mʌltɪpl] *a* múltiple ◆ *n* múltiplo; (*Brit: also*: ~ **store**) (cadena de) grandes almacenes *mpl*.

multiple choice *n* examen *m* de tipo test.

multiple crash *n* colisión *f* en cadena.

multiple sclerosis [-sklɪ'rəusɪs] *n* esclerosis *f* múltiple.

multiplication [mʌltɪplɪ'keɪʃən] *n* multiplicación *f*.

multiplication table *n* tabla de multiplicar.

multiplicity [mʌltɪ'plɪsɪtɪ] *n* multiplicidad *f*.

multiply ['mʌltɪplaɪ] *vt* multiplicar ◆ *vi* multiplicarse.

multiracial [mʌltɪ'reɪʃl] *a* multirracial.

multistorey [mʌltɪ'stɔːrɪ] *a* (*Brit: building, car park*) de muchos pisos.

multistrike ribbon ['mʌltɪstraɪk-] *n* (*COMPUT: on printer*) cinta de múltiples impactos.

multi-tasking ['mʌltɪtɑːskɪŋ] *n* (*COMPUT*) ejecución *f* de tareas múltiples, multitarea.

multitude ['mʌltɪtjuːd] *n* multitud *f*.

mum [mʌm] *n* (*Brit*) mamá ◆ *a*: **to keep** ~ (**about sth**) no decir ni mu (de algo).

mumble ['mʌmbl] *vt* decir entre dientes ◆ *vi* hablar entre dientes, musitar.

mummify ['mʌmɪfaɪ] *vt* momificar.

mummy ['mʌmɪ] *n* (*Brit: mother*) mamá; (*embalmed*) momia.

mumps [mʌmps] *n* paperas *fpl*.

munch [mʌntʃ] *vt, vi* mascar.

mundane [mʌn'deɪn] *a* mundano.

municipal [mju:'nɪsɪpl] *a* municipal.

municipality [mju:nɪsɪ'pælɪtɪ] *n* municipio.

munificence [mu:'nɪfɪsns] *n* munificencia.

munitions [mju:'nɪʃənz] *npl* municiones *fpl*.

mural ['mjuərl] *n* (pintura) mural *m*.

murder ['mɜːdə*] *n* asesinato; (*in law*) homicidio ◆ *vt* asesinar, matar; **to commit** ~ cometer un asesinato *or* homicidio.

murderer ['mɜːdərə*] *n* asesino.

murderess ['mɜːdərɪs] *n* asesina.

murderous ['mɜːdərəs] *a* homicida.

murk [mɜːk] *n* oscuridad *f*, tinieblas *fpl*.

murky ['mɜːkɪ] *a* (*water, past*) turbio; (*room*) sombrío.

murmur ['mɜːmə*] *n* murmullo ◆ *vt, vi* murmurar; **heart** ~ soplo cardíaco.

MusB(ac) *n abbr* (= *Bachelor of Music*) título universitario.

muscle ['mʌsl] *n* músculo.

muscle in *vi* entrometerse.

muscular ['mʌskjulə*] *a* muscular; (*person*) musculoso.

MusD(oc) *n abbr* (= *Doctor of Music*)

título universitario.
muse [mju:z] *vi* meditar ◆ *n* musa.
museum [mju:'zɪəm] *n* museo.
mush [mʌʃ] *n* gachas *fpl*.
mushroom ['mʌʃrum] *n* (*gen*) seta, hongo; (*small*) champiñón *m* ◆ *vi* (*fig*) crecer de la noche a la mañana.
mushy ['mʌʃɪ] *a* triturado; (*pej*) sensiblero.
music ['mju:zɪk] *n* música.
musical ['mju:zɪkl] *a* melodioso; (*person*) musical ◆ *n* (*show*) comedia musical.
music(al) box *n* caja de música.
musical instrument *n* instrumento musical.
musically ['mju:zɪklɪ] *ad* melodiosamente, armoniosamente.
music hall *n* teatro de variedades.
musician [mju:'zɪʃən] *n* músico/a.
music stand *n* atril *m*.
musk [mʌsk] *n* (perfume *m* de) almizcle *m*.
musket ['mʌskɪt] *n* mosquete *m*.
musk rat *n* ratón *m* almizclero.
musk rose *n* (*BOT*) rosa almizcleña.
Muslim ['mʌzlɪm] *a*, *n* musulmán/ana *m/f*.
muslin ['mʌzlɪn] *n* muselina.
musquash ['mʌskwɔʃ] *n* (*fur*) piel *f* del ratón almizclero.
muss [mʌs] *vt* (*col: hair*) despeinar; (: *dress*) arrugar.
mussel ['mʌsl] *n* mejillón *m*.
must [mʌst] *auxiliary vb* (*obligation*): **I ~ do it** debo hacerlo, tengo que hacerlo; (*probability*): **he ~ be there by now** ya debe (de) estar allí ◆ *n*: **it's a ~** es imprescindible.
mustache ['mʌstæʃ] *n* (*US*) = **moustache.**
mustard ['mʌstəd] *n* mostaza.
mustard gas *n* gas *m* mostaza.
muster ['mʌstə*] *vt* juntar, reunir; (*also: ~ up: strength, courage*) cobrar.
mustiness ['mʌstɪnɪs] *n* olor *m* a cerrado.
mustn't ['mʌsnt] = **must not.**
musty ['mʌstɪ] *a* mohoso, que huele a humedad.
mutant ['mju:tənt] *a*, *n* mutante *m*.
mutate [mju:'teɪt] *vi* sufrir mutación, transformarse.
mutation [mju:'teɪʃən] *n* mutación *f*.
mute [mju:t] *a*, *n* mudo/a *m/f*.
muted ['mju:tɪd] *a* (*noise*) sordo; (*criticism*) callado.
mutilate ['mju:tɪleɪt] *vt* mutilar.
mutilation [mju:tɪ'leɪʃən] *n* mutilación *f*.
mutinous ['mju:tɪnəs] *a* (*troops*) amotinado; (*attitude*) rebelde.
mutiny ['mju:tɪnɪ] *n* motín *m* ◆ *vi* amotinarse.
mutter ['mʌtə*] *vt*, *vi* murmurar.
mutton ['mʌtn] *n* carne *f* de cordero.
mutual ['mju:tʃuəl] *a* mutuo; (*friend*) común.
mutually ['mju:tʃuəlɪ] *ad* mutuamente.
muzzle ['mʌzl] *n* hocico; (*protective device*)

bozal *m*; (*of gun*) boca ◆ *vt* amordazar; (*dog*) poner un bozal a.
MVP *n abbr* (*US SPORT*) = *most valuable player.*
MW *abbr* (= *medium wave*) onda media.
my [maɪ] *a* mi(s); **~ house/brother/sisters** mi casa/hermano/mis hermanas; **I've washed ~ hair/cut ~ finger** me he lavado el pelo/cortado un dedo; **is this ~ pen or yours?** ¿es este bolígrafo mío o tuyo?
myopic [maɪ'ɔpɪk] *a* miope.
myriad ['mɪrɪəd] *n* (*of people, things*) miríada.
myrrh [mə:*] *n* mirra.
myself [maɪ'sɛlf] *pron* (*reflexive*) me; (*emphatic*) yo mismo; (*after prep*) mí (mismo); *see also* **oneself.**
mysterious [mɪs'tɪərɪəs] *a* misterioso.
mysteriously [mɪs'tɪərɪəslɪ] *ad* misteriosamente.
mystery ['mɪstərɪ] *n* misterio.
mystery play *n* auto, misterio.
mystic ['mɪstɪk] *a*, *n* místico/a *m/f*.
mystical ['mɪstɪkl] *a* místico.
mysticism ['mɪstɪsɪzəm] *n* misticismo.
mystification [mɪstɪfɪ'keɪʃən] *n* perplejidad *f*; desconcierto.
mystify ['mɪstɪfaɪ] *vt* (*perplex*) dejar perplejo; (*disconcert*) desconcertar.
mystique [mɪs'ti:k] *n* misterio.
myth [mɪθ] *n* mito.
mythical ['mɪθɪkl] *a* mítico.
mythological [mɪθə'lɔdʒɪkl] *a* mitológico.
mythology [mɪ'θɔlədʒɪ] *n* mitología.

N

N, n [ɛn] *n* (*letter*) N, n *f;* **N for Nellie,** (*US*) **N for Nan** N de Navarra.
N *abbr* (= *North*) N.
NA *n abbr* (*US*: = *Narcotics Anonymous*) organización de ayuda a los drogadictos; (*US*) = *National Academy.*
n/a *abbr* (= *not applicable*) no interesa; (*COMM etc*) = *no account.*
NAACP *n abbr* (*US*) = *National Association for the Advancement of Colored People.*
NAAFI ['næfɪ] *n abbr* (*Brit*: = *Navy, Army & Air Force Institute*) servicio de cantinas etc para las fuerzas armadas.
nab [næb] *vt* (*col: grab*) coger (*Sp*), agarrar (*LAm*); (: *catch out*) pillar.
NACU *n abbr* (*US*) = *National Association of Colleges and Universities.*
nadir ['neɪdɪə*] *n* (*ASTRO*) nadir *m*; (*fig*) punto más bajo.
nag [næg] *n* (*pej: horse*) rocín *m* ◆ *vt*

(*scold*) regañar; (*annoy*) fastidiar.

nagging ['nægɪŋ] *a* (*doubt*) persistente; (*pain*) continuo ◆ *n* quejas *fpl*.

nail [neɪl] *n* (*human*) uña; (*metal*) clavo ◆ *vt* clavar; (*fig*: *catch*) coger (*Sp*), pillar; **to pay cash on the** ~ pagar al contado; **to** ~ **sb down to a date/price** hacer comprometerse a uno a una fecha.un precio.

nailbrush ['neɪlbrʌʃ] *n* cepillo para las uñas.

nailfile ['neɪlfaɪl] *n* lima para las uñas.

nail polish *n* esmalte *m* or laca para las uñas.

nail polish remover *n* quitaesmalte *m*.

nail scissors *npl* tijeras *fpl* para las uñas.

nail varnish *n* (*Brit*) = **nail polish**.

Nairobi [naɪ'rəʊbɪ] *n* Nairobi *m*.

naïve [naɪ'iːv] *a* ingenuo.

naïvely [naɪ'iːvlɪ] *ad* ingenuamente.

naïveté [naɪ'iːveɪ], **naivety** [naɪ'iːvɪtɪ] *n* ingenuidad *f*, candidez *f*.

naked ['neɪkɪd] *a* (*nude*) desnudo; (*flame*) expuesto al aire; **with the** ~ **eye** a simple vista.

NALGO ['nælgəʊ] *n* abbr (*Brit*: = *National and Local Government Officers' Association*) sindicato de funcionarios.

NAM *n* abbr (*US*) = *National Association of Manufacturers*.

name [neɪm] *n* (*gen*) nombre *m*; (*surname*) apellido; (*reputation*) fama, renombre *m* ◆ *vt* (*child*) poner nombre a; (*appoint*) nombrar; **by** ~ de nombre; **in the** ~ **of** en nombre de; **what's your** ~? ¿cómo se llama usted?; **my** ~ **is Peter** me llamo Pedro; **to give one's** ~ **and address** dar sus señas; **to take sb's** ~ **and address** apuntar las señas de uno; **to make a** ~ **for o.s.** hacerse famoso; **to get (o.s.) a bad** ~ hacerse una mala reputación.

name-drop ['neɪmdrɔp] *vi*: **he's always** ~**ping** siempre está presumiendo de la gente que conoce.

nameless ['neɪmlɪs] *a* anónimo, sin nombre.

namely ['neɪmlɪ] *ad* a saber.

nameplate ['neɪmpleɪt] *n* (*on door etc*) placa.

namesake ['neɪmseɪk] *n* tocayo/a.

nanny ['nænɪ] *n* niñera.

nap [næp] *n* (*sleep*) sueñecito, siesta; **to be caught** ~**ping** estar desprevenido.

NAPA *n* abbr (*US*: = *National Association of Performing Artists*) sindicato de trabajadores del espectáculo.

napalm ['neɪpɑːm] *n* napalm *m*.

nape [neɪp] *n*: ~ **of the neck** nuca, cogote *m*.

napkin ['næpkɪn] *n* (*also*: **table** ~) servilleta.

Naples ['neɪplz] *n* Nápoles.

nappy ['næpɪ] *n* (*Brit*) pañal *m*.

nappy liner *n* gasa.

nappy rash *n* prurito.

narcissism [nɑː'sɪsɪzəm] *n* narcisismo.

narcissus, pl narcissi [nɑː'sɪsəs, -saɪ] *n* narciso.

narcotic [nɑː'kɔtɪk] *a*, *n* narcótico.

narrate [nə'reɪt] *vt* narrar, contar.

narration [nə'reɪʃən] *n* narración *f*, relato.

narrative ['nærətɪv] *n* narrativa ◆ *a* narrativo.

narrator [nə'reɪtə*] *n* narrador(a) *m/f*.

narrow ['nærəʊ] *a* estrecho, angosto; (*resources, means*) escaso ◆ *vi* estrecharse, angostarse; (*diminish*) reducirse; **to have a** ~ **escape** escaparse por los pelos; **to** ~ **sth down** reducir algo.

narrow gauge *a* (*RAIL*) de vía estrecha.

narrowly ['nærəlɪ] *ad* (*miss*) por poco.

narrow-minded [nærəʊ'maɪndɪd] *a* de miras estrechas.

narrow-mindedness ['nærəʊ'maɪndɪdnɪs] *n* estrechez *f* de miras.

NAS *n* abbr (*US*) = *National Academy of Sciences*.

NASA *n* abbr (*US*: = *National Aeronautics and Space Administration*) NASA *f*.

nasal ['neɪzl] *a* nasal.

Nassau ['næsɔː] *n* (*in Bahamas*) Nassau *m*.

nastily ['nɑːstɪlɪ] *ad* (*unpleasantly*) de mala manera; (*spitefully*) con rencor.

nastiness ['nɑːstɪnɪs] *n* (*malice*) malevolencia; (*rudeness*) grosería; (*of person, remark*) maldad *f*; (*spitefulness*) rencor *m*.

nasturtium [nəs'təːʃəm] *n* capuchina.

nasty ['nɑːstɪ] *a* (*remark*) feo; (*person*) antipático; (*revolting*: *taste, smell*) asqueroso; (*wound, disease etc*) peligroso, grave; **to turn** ~ (*situation*) ponerse feo; (*weather*) volverse malo; (*person*) ponerse negro.

NAS/UWT *n* abbr (*Brit*: = *National Association of Schoolmasters/Union of Women Teachers*) sindicato de profesores.

nation ['neɪʃən] *n* nación *f*.

national ['næʃənl] *a*, *n* nacional *m/f*.

national anthem *n* himno nacional.

national debt *n* deuda pública.

national dress *n* vestido nacional.

National Guard *n* (*US*) Guardia Nacional.

National Health Service (NHS) *n* (*Brit*) servicio nacional de sanidad, ≈ INSALUD *m* (*Sp*).

National Insurance *n* (*Brit*) seguro social nacional.

nationalism ['næʃnəlɪzəm] *n* nacionalismo.

nationalist ['næʃnəlɪst] *a*, *n* nacionalista *m/f*.

nationality [næʃə'nælɪtɪ] *n* nacionalidad *f*.

nationalization [næʃnəlaɪ'zeɪʃən] *n* nacionalización *f*.

nationalize ['næʃnəlaɪz] *vt* nacionalizar; ~**d industry** industria nacionalizada.

nationally ['næʃnəlɪ] *ad* (*nationwide*) en escala nacional; (*as a nation*) nacionalmente, como nación.

national press n prensa nacional.
national service n (MIL) servicio militar.
nationwide ['neɪʃənwaɪd] a en escala or a nivel nacional.
native ['neɪtɪv] n (local inhabitant) natural m/f, nacional m/f; (in colonies) indígena m/f, nativo/a ♦ a (indigenous) indígena; (country) natal; (innate) natural, innato; a ~ of Russia un(a) natural de Rusia; ~ language lengua materna; a ~ speaker of French un hablante nativo de francés.
Nativity [nə'tɪvɪtɪ] n: the ~ Navidad f.
NATO ['neɪtəu] n abbr (= North Atlantic Treaty Organization) OTAN f.
NATSOPA [næt'səupə] n abbr (Brit: = National Society of Operative Printers, Graphical and Media Personnel) sindicato de tipógrafos.
natter ['nætə*] vi (Brit) charlar ♦ n: to have a ~ cotillear.
NATTKE n abbr (Brit: = National Association of Television, Theatrical and Kinematographic Employees) sindicato de empleados de televisión, teatro y cine.
natural ['nætʃrəl] a natural; **death from** ~ **causes** (LAW) muerte f de causas naturales.
natural childbirth n parto natural.
natural gas n gas m natural.
naturalist ['nætʃrəlɪst] n naturalista m/f.
naturalization [nætʃrəlaɪ'zeɪʃən] n naturalización f.
naturalize ['nætʃrəlaɪz] vt: **to become** ~d (person) naturalizarse; (plant) aclimatarse.
naturally ['nætʃrəlɪ] ad (speak etc) naturalmente; (of course) desde luego, por supuesto; (instinctively) por instinto, por naturaleza.
naturalness ['nætʃrəlnɪs] n naturalidad f.
natural resources npl recursos mpl naturales.
natural wastage n (INDUSTRY) desgaste natural m.
nature ['neɪtʃə*] n naturaleza; (group, sort) género, clase f; (character) carácter m, genio; **by** ~ por or de naturaleza; **documents of a confidential** ~ documentos mpl de tipo confidencial.
-natured ['neɪtʃəd] suff: **ill**~ malhumorado.
nature reserve n reserva natural.
nature trail n camino forestal educativo.
naturist ['neɪtʃərɪst] n naturista m/f.
naught [nɔːt] = **nought**.
naughtily ['nɔːtɪlɪ] ad (behave) mal; (say) con malicia.
naughtiness ['nɔːtɪnɪs] n travesuras fpl.
naughty ['nɔːtɪ] a (child) travieso; (story, film) verde, escabroso, colorado (LAm).
nausea ['nɔːsɪə] n náusea.
nauseate ['nɔːsɪeɪt] vt dar náuseas a; (fig) dar asco a.
nauseating ['nɔːsɪeɪtɪŋ] a nauseabundo;

(fig) asqueroso, repugnante.
nauseous ['nɔːsɪəs] a (MED, fig) nauseabundo.
nautical ['nɔːtɪkl] a náutico, marítimo; ~ **mile** milla marina.
naval ['neɪvl] a naval, de marina.
naval officer n oficial m/f de marina.
nave [neɪv] n nave f.
navel ['neɪvl] n ombligo.
navigable ['nævɪgəbl] a navegable.
navigate ['nævɪgeɪt] vt gobernar ♦ vi (also AUT) navegar.
navigation [nævɪ'geɪʃən] n (action) navegación f; (science) náutica.
navigator ['nævɪgeɪtə*] n navegador(a) m/f, navegante m/f.
navvy ['nævɪ] n (Brit) peón m caminero.
navy ['neɪvɪ] n marina de guerra; (ships) armada, flota.
navy(-blue) ['neɪvɪ('bluː)] a azul marino.
Nazareth ['næzərɪθ] n Nazaret m.
Nazi ['nɑːtsɪ] a, n nazi m/f.
NB abbr (= nota bene) nótese; (Canada) = New Brunswick.
NBA n abbr (US) = National Basketball Association, National Boxing Association.
NBC n abbr (US: = National Broadcasting Company) cadena de televisión.
NBS n abbr (US: = National Bureau of Standards) ≈ Oficina Nacional de Normas.
NC abbr (COMM etc) = no charge; (US POST) = North Carolina.
NCB n abbr (Brit: old: = National Coal Board) junta nacional británica del carbón.
NCC n abbr (Brit: = Nature Conservancy Council) ≈ ICONA m; (US) = National Council of Churches.
NCCL n abbr (Brit: = National Council for Civil Liberties) asociación para la defensa de las libertades públicas.
NCO n abbr = **non-commissioned officer**.
ND abbr (US POST) = North Dakota.
NE abbr (US POST) = Nebraska, New England.
NEA n abbr US) = National Education Association.
Neapolitan [nɪə'pɔlɪtən] a, n napolitano/a m/f.
neap tide [niːp-] n marea muerta.
near [nɪə*] a (place, relation) cercano; (time) próximo ♦ ad cerca ♦ prep (also: ~ **to**: space) cerca de, junto a; (: time) cerca de ♦ vt acercarse a, aproximarse a; ~ **here/there** cerca de aquí/de allí; **£25,000 or** ~**est offer** 25,000 libras o precio a discutir; **in the** ~ **future** en fecha próxima; **the building is** ~**ing completion** el edificio está por terminarse.
nearby [nɪə'baɪ] a cercano, próximo ♦ ad cerca.
nearly ['nɪəlɪ] ad casi, por poco; **I** ~ **fell** por poco me caigo; **not** ~ ni mucho menos, ni con mucho.

near miss *n* tiro cercano.

nearness ['nɪənɪs] *n* cercanía, proximidad *f*.

nearside ['nɪəsaɪd] *n* (*AUT*: *right-hand drive*) lado izquierdo (: *left-hand drive*) lado derecho.

near-sighted [nɪə'saɪtɪd] *a* miope, corto de vista.

neat [niːt] *a* (*place*) ordenado, bien cuidado; (*person*) pulcro; (*plan*) ingenioso; (*spirits*) solo.

neatly ['niːtlɪ] *ad* (*tidily*) con esmero; (*skilfully*) ingeniosamente.

neatness ['niːtnɪs] *n* (*tidiness*) orden *m*; (*skilfulness*) destreza, habilidad *f*.

nebulous ['nɛbjuləs] *a* (*fig*) vago, confuso.

necessarily ['nɛsɪsrɪlɪ] *ad* necesariamente; **not** ~ no necesariamente.

necessary ['nɛsɪsrɪ] *a* necesario, preciso; **he did all that was** ~ hizo todo lo necesario; **if** ~ si es necesario.

necessitate [nɪ'sɛsɪteɪt] *vt* necesitar, exigir.

necessity [nɪ'sɛsɪtɪ] *n* necesidad *f*; **necessities** *npl* artículos *mpl* de primera necesidad; **in case of** ~ en caso de urgencia.

neck [nɛk] *n* (*ANAT*) cuello; (*of animal*) pescuezo ♦ *vi* besuquearse; ~ **and** ~ parejos; **to stick one's** ~ **out** (*col*) arriesgarse.

necklace ['nɛklɪs] *n* collar *m*.

neckline ['nɛklaɪn] *n* escote *m*.

necktie ['nɛktaɪ] *n* (*US*) corbata.

nectar ['nɛktə*] *n* néctar *m*.

nectarine ['nɛktərɪn] *n* nectarina.

NEDC *n abbr* (*Brit*: = *National Economic Development Council*) ≈ Consejo Económico y Social.

Neddy ['nɛdɪ] *n abbr* (*Brit col*) = **NEDC**.

née [neɪ] *a*: ~ **Scott** de soltera Scott.

need [niːd] *n* (*lack*) escasez *f*, falta; (*necessity*) necesidad *f* ♦ *vt* (*require*) necesitar; **in case of** ~ en caso de necesidad; **there's no** ~ **for ...** no hace(n) falta ...; **to be in** ~ **of, have** ~ **of** necesitar; **10 will meet my immediate** ~**s** 10 satisfacerán mis necesidades más premiantes; **the** ~**s of industry** las necesidades de la industria; **I** ~ **it** lo necesito; **a signature is** ~**ed** se requiere una firma; **I** ~ **to do it** tengo que *or* debo hacerlo; **you don't** ~ **to go** no hace falta que vayas.

needle ['niːdl] *n* aguja ♦ *vt* (*fig: col*) picar, fastidiar.

needless ['niːdlɪs] *a* innecesario, inútil; ~ **to say** huelga decir que.

needlessly ['niːdlɪslɪ] *ad* innecesariamente, inútilmente.

needlework ['niːdlwəːk] *n* (*activity*) costura, labor *f* de aguja.

needn't ['niːdnt] = **need not**.

needy ['niːdɪ] *a* necesitado.

negation [nɪ'geɪʃən] *n* negación *f*.

negative ['nɛgətɪv] *n* (*PHOT*) negativo; (*answer*) negativa; (*LING*) negación *f* ♦ *a* negativo.

negative cash flow *n* flujo negativo de efectivo.

neglect [nɪ'glɛkt] *vt* (*one's duty*) faltar a, no cumplir con; (*child*) descuidar, desatender ♦ *n* (*state*) abandono; (*personal*) dejadez *f*; (*of duty*) incumplimiento; **to** ~ **to do sth** olvidarse de hacer algo.

neglected [nɪ'glɛktɪd] *a* abandonado.

neglectful [nɪ'glɛktful] *a* negligente; **to be** ~ **of sb/sth** descuidarse de algo.

negligee ['nɛglɪʒeɪ] *n* (*nightdress*) salto de cama.

negligence ['nɛglɪdʒəns] *n* negligencia, descuido.

negligent ['nɛglɪdʒənt] *a* (*careless*) descuidado, negligente; (*forgetful*) olvidadizo.

negligently ['nɛglɪdʒəntlɪ] *ad* con descuido, negligentemente.

negligible ['nɛglɪdʒɪbl] *a* insignificante, despreciable.

negotiable [nɪ'gəʊʃɪəbl] *a* (*cheque*) negociable; **not** ~ (*cheque*) no trasmisible.

negotiate [nɪ'gəʊʃɪeɪt] *vt* (*treaty, loan*) negociar; (*obstacle*) franquear; (*bend in road*) tomar ♦ *vi*: **to** ~ **(with)** negociar (con); **to** ~ **with sb for sth** tratar *or* negociar con uno por algo.

negotiation [nɪgəʊʃɪ'eɪʃən] *n* negociación *f*, gestión *f*; **to enter into** ~**s with sb** entrar en negociaciones con uno.

negotiator [nɪ'gəʊʃɪeɪtə*] *n* negociador(a) *m/f*.

Negress ['niːgrɪs] *n* negra.

Negro ['niːgrəʊ] *a*, *n* negro.

neigh [neɪ] *n* relincho ♦ *vi* relinchar.

neighbour, (*US*) **neighbor** ['neɪbə*] *n* vecino/a.

neighbo(u)rhood ['neɪbəhud] *n* (*place*) vecindad *f*, barrio; (*people*) vecindario.

neighbo(u)ring ['neɪbərɪŋ] *a* vecino.

neighbo(u)rly ['neɪbəlɪ] *a* amigable, sociable.

neither ['naɪðə*] *a* ni ♦ *conj*: **I didn't move and** ~ **did John** no me he movido, ni Juan tampoco ♦ *pron* ninguno; ~ **is true** ninguno/a de los/las dos es cierto/a ♦ *ad*: ~ **good nor bad** ni bueno ni malo.

neo... [niːəʊ] *pref* neo....

neolithic [niːəʊ'lɪθɪk] *a* neolítico.

neologism [nɪ'ɔlədʒɪzəm] *n* neologismo.

neon ['niːɔn] *n* neón *m*.

neon light *n* lámpara de neón.

Nepal [nɪ'pɔːl] *n* Nepal *m*.

nephew ['nɛvjuː] *n* sobrino.

nepotism ['nɛpətɪzəm] *n* nepotismo.

nerve [nəːv] *n* (*ANAT*) nervio; (*courage*) valor *m*; (*impudence*) descaro, frescura; **a fit of** ~**s** un ataque de nervios; **to lose one's** ~ (*self-confidence*) perder el valor.

nerve centre *n* (*ANAT*) centro nervioso; (*fig*) punto neurálgico.

nerve gas *n* gas *m* nervino.

nerve-racking ['nə:vrækɪŋ] *a* angustioso.
nervous ['nə:vəs] *a* (*anxious*, ANAT) nervioso; (*timid*) tímido, miedoso.
nervous breakdown *n* crisis *f* nerviosa.
nervously ['nə:vəslɪ] *ad* nerviosamente; tímidamente.
nervousness ['nə:vəsnɪs] *n* nerviosidad *f*, nerviosismo; timidez *f*.
nest [nɛst] *n* (*of bird*) nido ♦ *vi* anidar.
nest egg *n* (*fig*) ahorros *mpl*.
nestle ['nɛsl] *vi*: **to ~ down** acurrucarse.
nestling ['nɛstlɪŋ] *n* pajarito.
net [nɛt] *n* (*gen*) red *f*; (*fabric*) tul *m* ♦ *a* (*COMM*) neto, líquido; (*weight*, *price*, *salary*) neto ♦ *vt* coger (*Sp*) *or* agarrar (*LAm*) con red; (*money*: *subj*: *person*) cobrar; (: *deal*, *sale*) conseguir; (*SPORT*) marcar; **~ of tax** neto; **he earns £10,000 ~ per year** gana 10,000 libras netas por año.
netball ['nɛtbɔ:l] *n* básquet *m*.
net curtain *n* visillo.
Netherlands ['nɛðələndz] *npl*: **the ~** los Países Bajos.
net income *n* renta neta.
net loss *n* pérdida neta.
net profit *n* beneficio neto.
nett [nɛt] *a* = **net**.
netting ['nɛtɪŋ] *n* red *f*, redes *fpl*.
nettle ['nɛtl] *n* ortiga.
network ['nɛtwɔ:k] *n* red *f* ♦ *vt* (*RADIO*, *TV*) difundir por la red de emisores; **local area ~** red local.
neuralgia [njuə'rældʒə] *n* neuralgia.
neurosis, *pl* **-ses** [njuə'rəusɪs, -si:z] *n* neurosis *f inv*.
neurotic [njuə'rɔtɪk] *a*, *n* neurótico/a *m/f*.
neuter ['nju:tə*] *a* (*LING*) neutro ♦ *vt* castrar, capar.
neutral ['nju:trəl] *a* (*person*) neutral; (*colour etc*, *ELEC*) neutro ♦ *n* (*AUT*) punto muerto.
neutrality [nju:'trælɪtɪ] *n* neutralidad *f*.
neutralize ['nju:trəlaɪz] *vt* neutralizar.
neutron ['nju:trɔn] *n* neutrón *m*.
neutron bomb *n* bomba de neutrones.
never ['nɛvə*] *ad* nunca, jamás; **I ~ went** no fui nunca; **~ in my life** jamás en la vida; *see also* **mind**.
never-ending [nɛvər'ɛndɪŋ] *a* interminable, sin fin.
nevertheless [nɛvəðə'lɛs] *ad* sin embargo, no obstante.
new [nju:] *a* nuevo; (*recent*) reciente; **as good as ~** como nuevo/a.
newborn ['nju:bɔ:n] *a* recién nacido.
newcomer ['nju:kʌmə*] *n* recién venido *or* llegado.
new-fangled ['nju:fæŋgld] *a* (*pej*) modernísimo.
new-found ['nju:faund] *a* (*friend*) nuevo; (*enthusiasm*) recién adquirido.
New Guinea *n* Nueva Guinea.

newly ['nju:lɪ] *ad* nuevamente, recién.
newly-weds ['nju:lɪwɛdz] *npl* recién casados.
new moon *n* luna nueva.
newness ['nju:nɪs] *n* novedad *f*; (*fig*) inexperiencia.
news [nju:z] *n* noticias *fpl*; **a piece of ~** una noticia; **the ~** (*RADIO*, *TV*) las noticias *fpl*, telediario; **good/bad ~** buenas/malas noticias *fpl*; **financial ~** noticias *fpl* financieras.
news agency *n* agencia de noticias.
newsagent ['nju:zeɪdʒənt] *n* (*Brit*) vendedor(a) *m/f* de periódicos.
news bulletin *n* (*RADIO*, *TV*) noticiario.
newscaster ['nju:zkɑ:stə*] *n* presentador(a) *m/f*, locutor(a) *m/f*.
news dealer *n* (*US*) = **newsagent**.
news flash *n* noticia de última hora.
newsletter ['nju:zlɛtə*] *n* hoja informativa, boletín *m*.
newspaper ['nju:zpeɪpə*] *n* periódico, diario; **daily ~** diario; **weekly ~** periódico semanal.
newsprint ['nju:zprɪnt] *n* papel *m* de periódico.
newsreader ['nju:zri:də*] *n* = **newscaster**.
newsreel ['nju:zri:l] *n* noticiario.
newsroom ['nju:zru:m] *n* (*PRESS*, *RADIO*, *TV*) sala de redacción.
news stand *n* quiosco *or* puesto de periódicos.
newt [nju:t] *n* tritón *m*.
New Year *n* Año Nuevo; **Happy ~!** ¡Feliz Año Nuevo!; **to wish sb a happy ~** desear a uno un feliz año nuevo.
New Year's Day *n* Día *m* de Año Nuevo.
New Year's Eve *n* Nochevieja.
New York [-'jɔ:k] *n* Nueva York.
New Zealand [-'zi:lənd] *n* Nueva Zelanda(i)a ♦ *a* neozelandés/esa.
New Zealander [-'zi:ləndə*] *n* neozelandés/esa *m/f*.
next [nɛkst] *a* (*house*, *room*) vecino; (*meeting*) próximo; (*page*) siguiente ♦ *ad* después; **the ~ day** el día siguiente; **~ time** la próxima vez; **~ year** el año próximo *or* que viene; **~ month** el mes que viene *or* entrante; **the week after ~** no la semana que viene sino la otra; **"turn to the ~ page"** "vuelva a la página siguiente"; **you're ~** le toca; **~ to** prep junto a, al lado de; **~ to nothing** casi nada.
next door *ad* en la casa de al lado ♦ *a* vecino, de al lado.
next-of-kin ['nɛkstəv'kɪn] *n* pariente(s) *m(pl)* más cercano(s).
NF *n abbr* (*Brit POL*: = *National Front*) partido político de la extrema derecha ♦ *abbr* (*Canada*) = *Newfoundland*.
NFL *n abbr* (*US*) = *National Football League*.
NFU *n abbr* (*Brit*: = *National Farmers'*

Union) sindicato de agricultores.
NG *abbr* (*US*) = **National Guard.**
NGA *n abbr* (*Brit*: = *National Graphical Association*) sindicato de tipógrafos.
NGO *n abbr* (*US*: = *non-governmental organization*) organización no-gubernamental.
NH *abbr* (*US POST*) = *New Hampshire.*
NHL *n abbr* (*US*) = *National Hockey League.*
NHS *n abbr see* **National Health Service.**
NI *abbr* = *Northern Ireland*; (*Brit*) = **National Insurance.**
nib [nɪb] *n* plumilla.
nibble ['nɪbl] *vt* mordisquear, mordiscar.
Nicaragua [nɪkə'ræɡjuə] *n* Nicaragua.
Nicaraguan [nɪkə'ræɡjuən] *a, n* nicaragüense *m/f*, nicaragüeño/a *m/f*.
Nice [niːs] *n* Niza.
nice [naɪs] *a* (*likeable*) simpático; (*kind*) amable; (*pleasant*) agradable; (*attractive*) bonito, mono; (*distinction*) fino; (*taste, smell, meal*) rico.
nice-looking ['naɪslukɪŋ] *a* guapo.
nicely ['naɪslɪ] *ad* amablemente; bien; **that will do ~** perfecto.
niceties ['naɪsɪtɪz] *npl* detalles *mpl*.
niche [niːʃ] *n* (*ARCH*) nicho, hornacina.
nick [nɪk] *n* (*wound*) rasguño; (*cut, indentation*) mella, muesca ♦ *vt* (*cut*) cortar; (*col*) birlar, robar; (: *arrest*) pillar; **in the ~ of time** justo a tiempo; **in good ~** en buenas condiciones; **to ~ o.s.** cortarse.
nickel ['nɪkl] *n* níquel *m*; (*US*) *moneda de 5 centavos*.
nickname ['nɪkneɪm] *n* apodo, mote *m* ♦ *vt* apodar.
Nicosia [nɪkə'siːə] *n* Nicosía.
nicotine ['nɪkətiːn] *n* nicotina.
niece [niːs] *n* sobrina.
nifty ['nɪftɪ] *a* (*col: car, jacket*) elegante; (: *gadget, tool*) diestro.
Niger ['naɪdʒəʳ] *n* (*country, river*) Níger *m*.
Nigeria [naɪ'dʒɪərɪə] *n* Nigeria.
Nigerian [naɪ'dʒɪərɪən] *a, n* nigeriano/a *m/f*.
niggardly ['nɪɡədlɪ] *a* (*person*) avaro, tacaño, avariento; (*allowance, amount*) miserable.
nigger ['nɪɡəʳ] *n* (*col!: highly offensive*) negro/a.
niggle ['nɪɡl] *vt* preocupar ♦ *vi* (*complain*) quejarse; (*fuss*) preocuparse por minucias.
niggling ['nɪɡlɪŋ] *a* (*detail: trifling*) nimio, insignificante; (*annoying*) molesto; (*doubt, pain*) constante.
night [naɪt] *n* (*gen*) noche *f*; (*evening*) tarde *f*; **last ~** anoche; **the ~ before last** antenoche; **at ~, by ~** de noche, por la noche; **in the ~, during the ~** durante la noche.
night-bird ['naɪtbɔːd] *n* pájaro nocturno; (*fig*) trasnochador(a) *m/f*, madrugador(a) *m/f* (*LAm*).
nightcap ['naɪtkæp] *n* (*drink*) *bebida que se toma antes de acostarse.*

night club *n* cabaret *m*.
nightdress ['naɪtdres] *n* (*Brit*) camisón *m*.
nightfall ['naɪtfɔːl] *n* anochecer *m*.
nightgown ['naɪtɡaun], **nightie** ['naɪtɪ] (*Brit*) *n* = **nightdress.**
nightingale ['naɪtɪŋɡeɪl] *n* ruiseñor *m*.
night life *n* vida nocturna.
nightly ['naɪtlɪ] *a* de todas las noches ♦ *ad* todas las noches, cada noche.
nightmare ['naɪtmeəʳ] *n* pesadilla.
night porter *n* guardián *m* nocturno.
night safe *n* caja fuerte.
night school *n* clase(s) *f(pl)* nocturna(s).
nightshade ['naɪtʃeɪd] *n*: **deadly ~** (*BOT*) belladona.
night shift *n* turno nocturno *or* de noche.
night-time ['naɪttaɪm] *n* noche *f*.
night watchman *n* vigilante *m* nocturno, sereno.
nihilism ['naɪɪlɪzəm] *n* nihilismo.
nil [nɪl] *n* (*Brit SPORT*) cero, nada.
Nile [naɪl] *n*: **the ~** el Nilo.
nimble ['nɪmbl] *a* (*agile*) ágil, ligero; (*skilful*) diestro.
nimbly ['nɪmblɪ] *ad* ágilmente; con destreza.
nine [naɪn] *num* nueve.
nineteen ['naɪn'tiːn] *num* diecinueve, diez y nueve.
nineteenth [naɪn'tiːnθ] *num* decimonoveno, decimonono.
ninety ['naɪntɪ] *num* noventa.
ninth [naɪnθ] *num* noveno.
nip [nɪp] *vt* (*pinch*) pellizcar; (*bite*) morder ♦ (*Brit col*): **to ~ out/down/up** salir/bajar/subir un momento ♦ *n* (*drink*) trago.
nipple ['nɪpl] *n* (*ANAT*) pezón *m*; (*of bottle*) tetilla; (*TECH*) boquilla, manguito.
nippy ['nɪpɪ] *a* (*Brit: person*) ágil; (*taste*) picante; **it's a very ~ car** es un coche muy potente para el tamaño que tiene.
nit [nɪt] *n* (*of louse*) liendre *f*; (*col: idiot*) imbécil *m/f*.
nit-pick ['nɪtpɪk] *vi* (*col*) buscar pelos en la sopa.
nitrogen ['naɪtrədʒən] *n* nitrógeno.
nitroglycerin(e) ['naɪtrəu'ɡlɪsəriːn] *n* nitroglicerina.
nitty-gritty ['nɪtɪ'ɡrɪtɪ] *n* (*col*): **to get down to the ~** ir al grano.
nitwit ['nɪtwɪt] *n* cretino/a.
NJ *abbr* (*US POST*) = *New Jersey.*
NLF *n abbr* (= *National Liberation Front*) FLN *m*.
NLQ *abbr* (= *near letter quality*) calidad *f* correspondencia.
NLRB *n abbr* (*US*: = *National Labor Relations Board*) organismo de protección al trabajador.
NM *abbr* (*US POST*) = *New Mexico.*
no [nəu] *ad* no ♦ *a* ninguno, no ... alguno ♦ *n* no; **I won't take ~ for an answer** no hay pero que valga.

no. *abbr* (= *number*) n°., núm.
nobble ['nɒbl] *vt* (*Brit col*: *bribe*) sobornar; (: *catch*) pescar; (: *RACING*) drogar.
Nobel prize [nəu'bɛl-] *n* premio Nobel.
nobility [nəu'bılıtı] *n* nobleza.
noble ['nəubl] *a* (*person*) noble; (*title*) de nobleza.
nobleman ['nəublmən] *n* noble *m*.
nobly ['nəublı] *ad* (*selflessly*) noblemente.
nobody ['nəubədı] *pron* nadie.
no-claims bonus ['nəukleımz-] *n* bonificación *f* por carencia de reclamaciones.
nocturnal [nɔk'tɜːnl] *a* nocturno.
nod [nɒd] *vi* saludar con la cabeza; (*in agreement*) decir que sí con la cabeza ◆ *vt*: **to ~ one's head** inclinar la cabeza ◆ *n* inclinación *f* de cabeza; **they ~ded their agreement** asintieron con la cabeza.
nod off *vi* cabecear.
noise [nɔız] *n* ruido; (*din*) escándalo, estrépito.
noisily ['nɔızılı] *ad* ruidosamente, estrepitosamente.
noisy ['nɔızı] *a* (*gen*) ruidoso; (*child*) escandaloso.
nomad ['nəumæd] *n* nómada *m/f*.
nomadic [nəu'mædık] *a* nómada.
no man's land *n* tierra de nadie.
nominal ['nɒmınl] *a* nominal.
nominate ['nɒmıneıt] *vt* (*propose*) proponer; (*appoint*) nombrar.
nomination [nɒmı'neıʃən] *n* propuesta; nombramiento.
nominee [nɒmı'niː] *n* candidato/a.
non... [nɒn] *pref* no, des..., in....
non-alcoholic [nɒnælkə'hɒlık] *a* no alcohólico.
non-aligned [nɒnə'laınd] *a* no alineado.
non-arrival [nɒnə'raıvl] *n* falta de llegada.
nonce word [nɒns-] *n* hápax *m*.
nonchalant ['nɒnʃələnt] *a* indiferente.
non-commissioned [nɒnkə'mıʃənd] *a*: ~ **officer** suboficial *m/f*.
non-committal ['nɒnkə'mıtl] *a* (*reserved*) reservado; (*uncommitted*) evasivo.
nonconformist [nɒnkən'fɔːmıst] *a* (*attitude*) heterodoxo; (*person*) inconformista *m/f* ◆ *n* inconforme *m/f*; (*Brit REL*) no conformista *m/f*.
non-contributory [nɒnkən'trıbjutərı] *a*: ~ **pension scheme** *or* (*US*) **plan** fondo de pensiones no contributivo.
non-cooperation ['nɒnkəuɔpə'reıʃən] *n* no cooperación *f*.
nondescript ['nɒndıskrıpt] *a* soso.
none [nʌn] *pron* ninguno/a ◆ *ad* de ninguna manera; ~ **of you** ninguno de vosotros; **I've ~ left** no me queda ninguno/a; **he's ~ the worse for it** no le ha hecho ningún mal; **I have ~** no tengo ninguno; ~ **at all** (*not one*) ni uno.
nonentity [nɒ'nɛntıtı] *n* cero a la izquierda, nulidad *f*.

non-essential [nɒnı'sɛnʃl] *a* no esencial ◆ *n*: ~**s** cosas *fpl* secundarias *or* sin importancia.
nonetheless [nʌnðə'lɛs] *ad* sin embargo, no obstante, aún así.
non-executive [nɒnıg'zɛkjutıv] *a*: ~ **director** director *m* no ejecutivo.
non-existent [nɒnıg'zıstənt] *a* inexistente.
non-fiction [nɒn'fıkʃən] *n* literatura no novelesca.
non-intervention [nɒnıntə'vɛnʃən] *n* no intervención *f*.
non obst. *abbr* (= *non obstante*: *notwithstanding*) no obstante.
non-payment [nɒn'peımənt] *n* falta de pago.
nonplussed [nɒn'plʌst] *a* perplejo.
non-profit-making [nɒn'prɔfıtmeıkıŋ] *a* de misión no comercial.
nonsense ['nɒnsəns] *n* tonterías *fpl*, disparates *fpl*; ~**!** ¡qué tonterías!; **it is ~ to say that ...** es absurdo decir que ....
non-shrink [nɒn'ʃrıŋk] *a* inencogible, que no se encoge.
non-skid [nɒn'skıd] *a* antideslizante.
non-smoker ['nɒn'sməukə*] *n* no fumador(a) *m/f*.
non-stick ['nɒn'stık] *a* (*pan*, *surface*) antiadherente.
non-stop ['nɒn'stɔp] *a* continuo; (*RAIL*) directo ◆ *ad* sin parar.
non-taxable [nɒn'tæksəbl] *a*: ~ **income** renta no imponible.
non-U ['nɒnjuː] *a abbr* (*Brit col*: = *non-upper class*) que no pertenece a la clase alta.
non-volatile [nɒn'vɔlətaıl] *a*: ~ **memory** (*COMPUT*) memoria permanente.
non-voting [nɒn'vəutıŋ] *a*: ~ **shares** acciones *fpl* sin derecho a voto.
non-white ['nɒn'waıt] *a* de color ◆ *n* (*person*) persona de color.
noodles ['nuːdlz] *npl* tallarines *mpl*.
nook [nuk] *n* rincón *m*; ~**s and crannies** escondrijos *mpl*.
noon [nuːn] *n* mediodía *m*.
no-one ['nəuwʌn] *pron* = **nobody**.
noose [nuːs] *n* lazo corredizo.
nor [nɔː*] *conj* = **neither** ◆ *ad see* **neither**.
Norf *abbr* (*Brit*) = *Norfolk*.
norm [nɔːm] *n* norma.
normal ['nɔːml] *a* normal; **to return to** ~ volver a la normalidad.
normality [nɔː'mælıtı] *n* normalidad *f*.
normally ['nɔːməlı] *ad* normalmente.
Normandy ['nɔːməndı] *n* Normandía.
north [nɔːθ] *n* norte *m* ◆ *a* del norte, norteño ◆ *ad al or* hacia el norte.
North Africa *n* África del Norte.
North African *a*, *n* norteafricano/a *m/f*.
North America *n* América del Norte.
North American *a*, *n* norteamericano/a

m/f.

Northants *abbr* (*Brit*) = *Northampton-shire.*

northbound ['nɔːθbaʊnd] *a* (*traffic*) que se dirige al norte; (*carriageway*) de dirección norte.

Northd *abbr* (*Brit*) = *Northumberland.*

north-east [nɔːθ'iːst] *n* nor(d)este *m.*

northerly ['nɔːðəlɪ] *a* (*point, direction*) hacia el norte, septentrional; (*wind*) del norte.

northern ['nɔːðən] *a* norteño, del norte.

Northern Ireland *n* Irlanda del Norte.

North Korea *n* Corea del Norte.

North Pole *n*: **the** ~ el Polo Norte.

North Sea *n*: **the** ~ el Mar del Norte.

North Sea oil *n* petróleo del Mar del Norte.

northward(s) ['nɔːθwəd(z)] *ad* hacia el norte.

north-west [nɔːθ'wɛst] *n* nor(d)oeste *m.*

Norway ['nɔːweɪ] *n* Noruega.

Norwegian [nɔː'wiːdʒən] *a*, *n* noruego/a *m/f*; (*LING*) noruego.

nos. *abbr* (= *numbers*) núms.

nose [nəʊz] *n* (*ANAT*) nariz *f*; (*ZOOL*) hocico; (*sense of smell*) olfato ♦ *vi* (*also*: ~ **one's way**) avanzar con cuidado; **to pay through the** ~ (**for sth**) (*col*) pagar un dineral (por algo).
  nose about, nose around *vi* curiosear.

nosebleed ['nəʊzbliːd] *n* hemorragia nasal.

nose-dive ['nəʊzdaɪv] *n* picado vertical.

nose drops *npl* gotas *fpl* para la nariz.

nosey ['nəʊzɪ] *a* curioso, fisgón(ona).

nostalgia [nɔs'tældʒɪə] *n* nostalgia.

nostalgic [nɔs'tældʒɪk] *a* nostálgico.

nostril ['nɔstrɪl] *n* ventana de la nariz.

nosy ['nəʊzɪ] *a* = **nosey.**

not [nɔt] *ad* no; ~ **at all** no ... en absoluto; ~ **that...** no es que...; **it's too late, isn't it?** es demasiado tarde, ¿verdad?; ~ **yet** todavía no; ~ **now** ahora no; **why** ~? ¿por qué no?; **I hope** ~ espero que no; ~ **at all** no ... nada; (*after thanks*) de nada.

notable ['nəʊtəbl] *a* notable.

notably ['nəʊtəblɪ] *ad* especialmente; (*in particular*) sobre todo.

notary ['nəʊtərɪ] *n* (*also*: ~ **public**) notario/a.

notation [nəʊ'teɪʃən] *n* notación *f.*

notch [nɔtʃ] *n* muesca, corte *m.*
  notch up *vt* (*score, victory*) apuntarse.

note [nəʊt] *n* (*MUS, record, letter*) nota; (*banknote*) billete *m*; (*tone*) tono ♦ *vt* (*observe*) notar, observar; (*write down*) apuntar, anotar; **delivery** ~ nota de entrega; **to compare** ~**s** (*fig*) cambiar impresiones; **of** ~ conocido, destacado; **to take** ~ prestar atención a; **just a quick** ~ **to let you know that** ... sólo unas líneas para informarte que ....

notebook ['nəʊtbʊk] *n* libreta, cuaderno; (*for shorthand*) libreta.

notecase ['nəʊtkeɪs] *n* (*Brit*) cartera, billetero.

noted ['nəʊtɪd] *a* célebre, conocido.

notepad ['nəʊtpæd] *n* bloc *m.*

notepaper ['nəʊtpeɪpə*] *n* papel *m* para cartas.

noteworthy ['nəʊtwəːðɪ] *a* notable, digno de atención.

nothing ['nʌθɪŋ] *n* nada; (*zero*) cero; **he does** ~ no hace nada; ~ **new** nada nuevo; **for** ~ (*free*) gratis, sin pago; (*in vain*) en balde; ~ **at all** nada en absoluto.

notice ['nəʊtɪs] *n* (*announcement*) anuncio; (*dismissal*) despido; (*resignation*) dimisión *f*; (*review: of play etc*) reseña ♦ *vt* (*observe*) notar, observar; **to take** ~ **of** tomar nota de, prestar atención a; **at short** ~ a última hora, a corto plazo, con poca anticipación; **without** ~ sin aviso; **advance** ~ previo aviso; **until further** ~ hasta nuevo aviso; **to give sb** ~ **of sth** avisar a uno de algo; **to give** ~, **hand in one's** ~ dimitir, renunciar; **it has come to my** ~ **that** ... he llegado a saber que ...; **to escape** *or* **avoid** ~ pasar inadvertido.

noticeable ['nəʊtɪsəbl] *a* evidente, obvio.

notice board *n* (*Brit*) tablón *m* de anuncios.

notification [nəʊtɪfɪ'keɪʃən] *n* aviso; (*announcement*) anuncio.

notify ['nəʊtɪfaɪ] *vt*: **to** ~ **sb** (**of sth**) comunicar (algo) a uno.

notion ['nəʊʃən] *n* noción *f*, concepto; (*opinion*) opinión *f.*

notions ['nəʊʃənz] *npl* (*US*) mercería.

notoriety [nəʊtə'raɪətɪ] *n* notoriedad *f*, mala fama.

notorious [nəʊ'tɔːrɪəs] *a* notorio, célebre.

notoriously [nəʊ'tɔːrɪəslɪ] *ad* notoriamente.

Notts *abbr* (*Brit*) = *Nottinghamshire.*

notwithstanding [nɔtwɪθ'stændɪŋ] *ad* no obstante, sin embargo; ~ **this** a pesar de esto.

nougat ['nuːgɑː] *n* turrón *m.*

nought [nɔːt] *n* cero.

noun [naʊn] *n* nombre *m*, sustantivo.

nourish ['nʌrɪʃ] *vt* nutrir, alimentar; (*fig*) fomentar, nutrir.

nourishing ['nʌrɪʃɪŋ] *a* nutritivo, rico.

nourishment ['nʌrɪʃmənt] *n* alimento, sustento.

Nov. *abbr* (= *November*) nov.

novel ['nɔvl] *n* novela ♦ *a* (*new*) nuevo, original; (*unexpected*) insólito.

novelist ['nɔvəlɪst] *n* novelista *m/f.*

novelty ['nɔvəltɪ] *n* novedad *f.*

November [nəʊ'vɛmbə*] *n* noviembre *m.*

novice ['nɔvɪs] *n* principiante *m/f*, novato/a; (*REL*) novicio/a.

NOW [naʊ] *n abbr* (*US*) = *National Organization for Women.*

now [nau] *ad* (*at the present time*) ahora; (*these days*) actualmente, hoy día ◆ *conj*: ~ (*that*) ya que, ahora que; **right** ~ ahora mismo; **by** ~ ya; **just** ~: **I'll do it just** ~ ahora mismo lo hago; ~ **and then**, ~ **and again** de vez en cuando; **from** ~ **on** de ahora en adelante; **between** ~ **and Monday** entre hoy y el lunes; **in 3 days from** ~ de hoy en 3 días; **that's all for** ~ eso es todo por ahora.

nowadays ['nauədeɪz] *ad* hoy (en) día, actualmente.

nowhere ['nəuwɛə*] *ad* (*direction*) a ninguna parte; (*location*) en ninguna parte; ~ **else** en *or* a ninguna otra parte.

noxious ['nɔkʃəs] *a* nocivo.

nozzle ['nɔzl] *n* boquilla.

NP *n abbr* = **notary public**.

NS *abbr* (*Canada*) = *Nova Scotia*.

NSC *n abbr* (*US*) = *National Security Council*.

NSF *n abbr* (*US*) = *National Science Foundation*.

NSPCC *n abbr* (*Brit*) = *National Society for the Prevention of Cruelty to Children*.

NSW *abbr* (*Australia*) = *New South Wales*.

NT *n abbr* = *New Testament*.

nth [ɛnθ] *a*: **for the** ~ **time** (*col*) por enésima vez.

NUAAW *n abbr* (*Brit*: = *National Union of Agricultural and Allied Workers*) sindicato de trabajadores del campo.

nuance ['njuːɑːns] *n* matiz *m*.

NUBE *n abbr* (*Brit*: = *National Union of Bank Employees*) sindicato de empleados bancarios.

nubile ['njuːbaɪl] *a* núbil.

nuclear ['njuːklɪə*] *a* nuclear.

nuclear disarmament *n* desarme *m* nuclear.

nucleus, *pl* **nuclei** ['njuːklɪəs, 'njuːklɪaɪ] *n* núcleo.

nude [njuːd] *a*, *n* desnudo/a *m/f*; **in the** ~ desnudo.

nudge [nʌdʒ] *vt* dar un codazo a.

nudist ['njuːdɪst] *n* nudista *m/f*.

nudist colony *n* colonia de desnudistas.

nudity ['njuːdɪtɪ] *n* desnudez *f*.

nugget ['nʌgɪt] *n* pepita.

nuisance ['njuːsns] *n* molestia, fastidio; (*person*) pesado, latoso; **what a** ~! ¡qué lata!

NUJ *n abbr* (*Brit*: = *National Union of Journalists*) sindicato de periodistas.

nuke [njuːk] (*col*) *n* bomba atómica ◆ *vt* atacar con arma nuclear.

null [nʌl] *a*: ~ **and void** nulo y sin efecto.

nullify ['nʌlɪfaɪ] *vt* anular, invalidar.

NUM *n abbr* (*Brit*: = *National Union of Mineworkers*) sindicato de mineros.

numb [nʌm] *a* entumecido; (*fig*) insensible ◆ *vt* quitar la sensación a, entumecer, entorpecer; **to be** ~ **with cold** estar entume-

cido de frío; ~ **with fear** paralizado de miedo; ~ **with grief** paralizado de dolor.

number ['nʌmbə*] *n* número; (*numeral*) número, cifra ◆ *vt* (*pages etc*) numerar, poner número a; (*amount to*) sumar, ascender a; **reference** ~ número de referencia; **telephone** ~ número de teléfono; **wrong** ~ (*TEL*) número equivocado; **opposite** ~ (*person*) homólogo/a; **to be** ~**ed among** figurar entre; **a** ~ **of** varios, algunos; **they were ten in** ~ eran diez.

numbered account *n* (*in bank*) cuenta numerada.

number plate *n* (*Brit*) matrícula, placa.

Number Ten *n* (*Brit*: *10 Downing Street*) residencia del primer ministro.

numbness ['nʌmnɪs] *n* insensibilidad *f*, parálisis *f inv*; (*due to cold*) entumecimiento.

numbskull ['nʌmskʌl] *n* imbécil *m/f*, majadero/a.

numeral ['njuːmərəl] *n* número, cifra.

numerate ['njuːmərɪt] *a* competente en la aritmética.

numerical [njuːˈmɛrɪkl] *a* numérico.

numerous ['njuːmərəs] *a* numeroso, muchos.

nun [nʌn] *n* monja, religiosa.

NUPE ['njuːpɪ] *n abbr* (*Brit*: = *National Union of Public Employees*) sindicato de funcionarios.

nuptial ['nʌpʃəl] *a* nupcial.

NUR *n abbr* (*Brit*: = *National Union of Railwaymen*) sindicato de ferrocarrileros.

nurse [nəːs] *n* enfermero/a; (*nanny*) niñera ◆ *vt* (*patient*) cuidar, atender; (*baby*: *Brit*) mecer; (: *US*) criar, amamantar; **male** ~ enfermero.

nursery ['nəːsərɪ] *n* (*institution*) guardería infantil; (*room*) cuarto de los niños; (*for plants*) criadero, semillero.

nursery rhyme *n* canción *f* infantil.

nursery school *n* parvulario, escuela de párvulos.

nursery slope *n* (*Brit SKI*) cuesta para principiantes.

nursing ['nəːsɪŋ] *n* (*profession*) profesión *f* de enfermera; (*care*) asistencia, cuidado ◆ *a* (*mother*) lactante.

nursing home *n* clínica de reposo.

nurture ['nəːtʃə*] *vt* (*child*, *plant*) alimentar, nutrir.

NUS *n abbr* (*Brit*: = *National Union of Seamen*) sindicato de marineros; (: = *National Union of Students*) sindicato de estudiantes.

NUT *n abbr* (*Brit*: = *National Union of Teachers*) sindicato de profesores.

nut [nʌt] *n* (*TECH*) tuerca; (*BOT*) nuez *f* ◆ *a* (*chocolate etc*) con nueces.

nutcrackers ['nʌtkrækəz] *npl* cascanueces *m inv*.

nutmeg ['nʌtmɛg] *n* nuez *f* moscada.

nutrient ['njuːtrɪənt] *a* nutritivo ◆ *n* nutrimento.

nutrition [nju:'trɪʃən] *n* nutrición *f*, alimentación *f*.

nutritionist [nju:'trɪʃənɪst] *n* dietista *m/f*.

nutritious [nju:'trɪʃəs] *a* nutritivo.

nuts [nʌts] *a* (*col*) chiflado.

nutshell ['nʌtʃel] *n* cáscara de nuez; **in a ~** en resumidas cuentas.

nuzzle ['nʌzl] *vi*: **to ~ up to** arrimarse a.

NV *abbr* (*US POST*) = *Nevada.*

NWT *abbr* (*Canada*) = *Northwest Territories.*

NY *abbr* (*US POST*) = *New York.*

NYC *abbr* (*US POST*) = *New York City.*

nylon ['naɪlɔn] *n* nilón *m* ◆ *a* de nilón.

nymph [nɪmf] *n* ninfa.

nymphomaniac ['nɪmfəu'meɪnɪæk] *a, n* ninfómana.

NYSE *n abbr* (*US*) = *New York Stock Exchange.*

NZ *abbr* = **New Zealand.**

O

O, o [əu] (*letter*) O, o *f*; **O for Oliver**, (*US*) **O for Oboe** O de Oviedo.

oaf [əuf] *n* zoquete *m/f*.

oak [əuk] *n* roble *m* ◆ *a* de roble.

OAP *abbr see* **old-age pensioner.**

oar [ɔ:*] *n* remo; **to put** *or* **shove one's ~ in** (*fig: col*) entrometerse.

OAS *n abbr* (= *Organization of American States*) OEA *f*.

oasis, *pl* **oases** [əu'eɪsɪs, əu'eɪsi:z] *n* oasis *m inv*.

oath [əuθ] *n* juramento; (*swear word*) palabrota; **on** (*Brit*) *or* **under ~** bajo juramento.

oatmeal ['əutmi:l] *n* harina de avena.

oats [əuts] *n* avena.

OAU *n abbr* (= *Organization of African Unity*) OUA *f*.

obdurate ['ɔbdjurɪt] *a* (*stubborn*) terco, obstinado; (*sinner*) empedernido; (*unyielding*) inflexible, firme.

OBE *n abbr* (*Brit*: = *Order of the British Empire*) título ceremonial.

obedience [ə'bi:dɪəns] *n* obediencia; **in ~ to** de acuerdo con.

obedient [ə'bi:dɪənt] *a* obediente.

obelisk ['ɔbɪlɪsk] *n* obelisco.

obesity [əu'bi:sɪtɪ] *n* obesidad *f*.

obey [ə'beɪ] *vt* obedecer; (*instructions, regulations*) cumplir.

obituary [ə'bɪtjuərɪ] *n* necrología.

object ['ɔbdʒɪkt] *n* (*gen*) objeto; (*purpose*) objeto, propósito; (*LING*) complemento ◆ *vi*

[əb'dʒɛkt]: **to ~ to** (*attitude*) protestar contra; (*proposal*) oponerse a; **expense is no ~** no importan los gastos; **I ~!** ¡yo protesto!; **to ~ that** objetar que.

objection [əb'dʒɛkʃən] *n* protesta; **I have no ~ to...** no tengo inconveniente en que....

objectionable [əb'dʒɛkʃənəbl] *a* (*gen*) desagradable; (*conduct*) censurable.

objective [əb'dʒɛktɪv] *a, n* objetivo.

objectively [əb'dʒɛktɪvlɪ] *ad* objetivamente.

objectivity [ɔbdʒɪk'tɪvɪtɪ] *n* objetividad *f*.

object lesson *n* (*fig*) (buen) ejemplo.

objector [əb'dʒɛktə*] *n* objetor(a) *m/f*.

obligation [ɔblɪ'geɪʃən] *n* obligación *f*; (*debt*) deber *m*; **"without ~"** "sin compromiso"; **to be under an ~ to sb/to do sth** estar comprometido con uno/a hacer algo.

obligatory [ə'blɪgətərɪ] *a* obligatorio.

oblige [ə'blaɪdʒ] *vt* (*do a favour for*) complacer, hacer un favor a; **to ~ sb to do sth** forzar *or* obligar a uno a hacer algo; **to be ~d to sb for sth** estarle agradecido a uno por algo; **anything to ~!** (*col*) todo sea por complacerte.

obliging [ə'blaɪdʒɪŋ] *a* servicial, atento.

oblique [ə'bli:k] *a* oblicuo; (*allusion*) indirecto ◆ *n* (*TYP*) oblicua.

obliterate [ə'blɪtəreɪt] *vt* borrar.

oblivion [ə'blɪvɪən] *n* olvido.

oblivious [ə'blɪvɪəs] *a*: **~ of** inconsciente de.

oblong ['ɔblɔŋ] *a* rectangular ◆ *n* rectángulo.

obnoxious [əb'nɔkʃəs] *a* odioso, detestable; (*smell*) nauseabundo.

o.b.o. *abbr* (*US*: = *or best offer*: *in classified ads*) abierto ofertas.

oboe ['əubəu] *n* oboe *m*.

obscene [əb'si:n] *a* obsceno.

obscenity [əb'sɛnɪtɪ] *n* obscenidad *f*.

obscure [əb'skjuə*] *a* oscuro ◆ *vt* oscurecer; (*hide: sun*) esconder.

obscurity [əb'skjuərɪtɪ] *n* oscuridad *f*; (*obscure point*) punto oscuro; **to rise from ~** salir de la nada.

obsequious [əb'si:kwɪəs] *a* obsequioso.

observable [əb'zə:vəbl] *a* observable, perceptible.

observance [əb'zə:vns] *n* observancia, cumplimiento; (*ritual*) práctica; **religious ~s** prácticas *fpl* religiosas.

observant [əb'zə:vnt] *a* observador(a).

observation [ɔbzə'veɪʃən] *n* observación *f*; (*by police etc*) vigilancia; (*MED*) examen *m*.

observation post *n* (*MIL*) puesto de observación.

observatory [əb'zə:vətrɪ] *n* observatorio.

observe [əb'zə:v] *vt* (*gen*) observar; (*rule*) cumplir.

observer [əb'zə:və*] *n* observador(a) *m/f*.

obsess [əb'sɛs] *vt* obsesionar; **to be ~ed by**

or **with sb/sth** estar obsesionado por uno/algo.

obsession [əb'sɛʃən] *n* obsesión *f*, idea fija.

obsessive [əb'sɛsɪv] *a* obsesivo; obsesionante.

obsolescence [ɔbsə'lɛsns] *n* obsolescencia.

obsolescent [ɔbsə'lɛsnt] *a* que está cayendo en desuso.

obsolete ['ɔbsəliːt] *a* (que está) en desuso.

obstacle ['ɔbstəkl] *n* obstáculo; (*nuisance*) estorbo.

obstacle race *n* carrera de obstáculos.

obstetrician [ɔbstə'trɪʃən] *n* obstétrico/a.

obstetrics [ɔb'stɛtrɪks] *n* obstetricia.

obstinacy ['ɔbstɪnəsɪ] *n* obstinación *f*, terquedad *f*; tenacidad *f*.

obstinate ['ɔbstɪnɪt] *a* terco; (*determined*) tenaz.

obstinately ['ɔbstɪnɪtlɪ] *ad* obstinadamente, tercamente.

obstreperous [əb'strɛpərəs] *a* ruidoso; (*unruly*) revoltoso.

obstruct [əb'strʌkt] *vt* (*block*) obstruir; (*hinder*) estorbar, obstaculizar.

obstruction [əb'strʌkʃən] *n* obstrucción *f*; estorbo, obstáculo.

obstructive [əb'strʌktɪv] *a* obstruccionista; **stop being ~!** ¡deja de poner peros!

obtain [əb'teɪn] *vt* (*get*) obtener; (*achieve*) conseguir; **to ~ sth (for o.s.)** conseguir *or* adquirir algo.

obtainable [əb'teɪnəbl] *a* asequible.

obtrusive [əb'truːsɪv] *a* (*person*) importuno, entrometido; (*building etc*) demasiado visible.

obtuse [əb'tjuːs] *a* obtuso.

obverse ['ɔbvəːs] *n* (*of medal*) anverso; (*fig*) complemento.

obviate ['ɔbvɪeɪt] *vt* obviar, evitar.

obvious ['ɔbvɪəs] *a* (*clear*) obvio, evidente; (*unsubtle*) poco sutil; **it's ~ that ...** está claro que ..., es evidente que ....

obviously ['ɔbvɪəslɪ] *ad* evidentemente, naturalmente; **~ not!** ¡por supuesto que no!; **he was ~ not drunk** era evidente que no estaba borracho; **he was not ~ drunk** no se le notaba lo borracho.

OCAS *n abbr* (= *Organization of Central American States*) ODECA *f*.

occasion [ə'keɪʒən] *n* oportunidad *f*, ocasión *f*; (*event*) acontecimiento ♦ *vt* ocasionar, causar; **on that ~** esa vez, en aquella ocasión; **to rise to the ~** ponerse a la altura de las circunstancias.

occasional [ə'keɪʒənl] *a* poco frecuente, ocasional.

occasionally [ə'keɪʒ ə nlɪ] *ad* de vez en cuando; **very ~** muy de tarde en tarde, en muy contadas ocasiones.

occasional table *n* mesita.

occult [ɔ'kʌlt] *a* (*gen*) oculto.

occupancy ['ɔkjupənsɪ] *n* ocupación *f*.

occupant ['ɔkjupənt] *n* (*of house*) inquilino/a; (*of boat, car*) ocupante *m/f*.

occupation [ɔkju'peɪʃən] *n* (*of house*) tenencia; (*job*) trabajo; (: *calling*) oficio.

occupational accident [ɔkju'peɪʃənl] *n* accidente *m* laboral.

occupational guidance *n* orientación *f* profesional.

occupational hazard *n* riesgo profesional.

occupational pension scheme *n* plan *m* profesional de jubilación.

occupational therapy *n* reeducación *f* terapéutica.

occupier ['ɔkjupaɪə*] *n* inquilino/a.

occupy ['ɔkjupaɪ] *vt* (*seat, post, time*) ocupar; (*house*) habitar; **to ~ o.s. with** *or* **by doing** (*as job*) dedicarse a hacer; (*to pass time*) pasar el tiempo haciendo; **to be occupied with sth/in doing sth** estar ocupado con algo/haciendo algo.

occur [ə'kəː*] *vi* pasar, suceder; **to ~ to sb** ocurrírsele a uno.

occurrence [ə'kʌrəns] *n* acontecimiento.

ocean ['əuʃən] *n* océano; **~s of** (*col*) la mar de.

ocean bed *n* fondo del océano.

ocean-going ['əuʃəngəuɪŋ] *a* de alta mar.

Oceania [əuʃɪ'eɪnɪə] *n* Oceanía.

ocean liner *n* buque *m* transoceánico.

ochre, (*US*) **ocher** ['əukə*] *n* ocre *m*.

OCR *n abbr see* **optical character recognition/reader**.

o'clock [ə'klɔk] *ad*: **it is 5 ~** son las 5.

Oct. *abbr* (= *October*) oct.

octagonal [ɔk'tægənl] *a* octagonal.

octane ['ɔkteɪn] *n* octano; **high ~ petrol** *or* (*US*) **gas** gasolina de alto octanaje.

octave ['ɔktɪv] *n* octava.

October [ɔk'təubə*] *n* octubre *m*.

octogenarian ['ɔktəudʒɪ'nɛərɪən] *n* octogenario/a.

octopus ['ɔktəpəs] *n* pulpo.

oculist ['ɔkjulɪst] *n* oculista *m/f*.

odd [ɔd] *a* (*strange*) extraño, raro; (*number*) impar; (*left over*) sobrante, suelto; **60-~** 60 y pico; **at ~ times** de vez en cuando; **to be the ~ one out** estar de más; **if you have the ~ minute** si tienes unos minutos libres; *see also* **odds**.

oddball ['ɔdbɔːl] *n* (*col*) bicho raro.

oddity ['ɔdɪtɪ] *n* rareza; (*person*) excéntrico/a.

odd-job man [ɔd'dʒɔb-] *n* hombre *m* que hace de todo.

odd jobs *npl* bricolaje *m*.

oddly ['ɔdlɪ] *ad* curiosamente, extrañamente.

oddments ['ɔdmənts] *npl* (*Brit COMM*) retales *mpl*.

odds [ɔdz] *npl* (*in betting*) puntos *mpl* de ventaja; **it makes no ~** da lo mismo; **at ~** reñidos/as; **to succeed against all the ~** tener éxito a pesar de todas las desventa-

jas; ~ **and ends** minucias *fpl*.
ode [əud] *n* oda.
odious ['əudɪəs] *a* odioso.
odometer [ɔ'dɔmɪtə*] *n* (*US*) cuentakilómetros *m inv*.
odour, (*US*) **odor** ['əudə*] *n* olor *m*; (*perfume*) perfume *m*.
odo(u)rless ['əudəlɪs] *a* sin olor.
OECD *n abbr* (= *Organization for Economic Co-operation and Development*) OCDE *f*.
oesophagus, (*US*) **esophagus** [iːˈsɔfəgəs] *n* esófago.
oestrogen, (*US*) **estrogen** ['iːstrədʒən] *n* estrógeno.
of [ɔv, əv] *prep* de; **a friend ~ ours** un amigo nuestro; **3 ~ them** 3 de ellos; **the 5th ~ July** el 5 de julio; **a boy ~ 10** un niño de 10 años; **a kilo ~ flour** un kilo de harina; **a quarter ~ 4** (*US*) las 4 menos cuarto; **made ~ wood** hecho de madera; **that was very kind ~ you** fue muy amable de su parte.
off [ɔf] *a, ad* (*engine*) desconectado; (*light*) apagado; (*tap*) cerrado; (*Brit: food: bad*) pasado, malo; (: *milk*) cortado; (*cancelled*) cancelado; (*removed*): **the lid was ~** la tapadera no estaba puesta ♦ *prep* de; **to be ~** (*to leave*) irse, marcharse; **to be ~ sick** estar enfermo *or* de baja; **a day ~** un día libre *or* sin trabajar; **to have an ~ day** tener un día malo; **he had his coat ~** se había quitado el abrigo; **10% ~** (*COMM*) (con el) 10% de descuento; **it's a long way ~** está muy lejos; **5 km ~ (the road)** a 5 km (de la carretera); **~ the coast** frente a la costa; **I'm ~ meat** (*no longer eat/like it*) paso de la carne; **on the ~ chance** por si acaso; **~ and on, on and ~** de vez en cuando; **I must be ~** tengo que irme; **to be well/badly ~** andar bien/mal de dinero; **I'm afraid the chicken is ~** desgraciadamente ya no queda pollo; **that's a bit ~, isn't it!** (*fig, col*) ¡mal hecho!
offal ['ɔfl] *n* (*Brit CULIN*) menudencias *fpl*.
off-centre, (*US*) **off-center** [ɔf'sɛntə*] *a* descentrado, ladeado.
off-colour ['ɔf'kʌlə*] *a* (*Brit: ill*) indispuesto; **to feel ~** sentirse *or* estar mal.
offence, (*US*) **offense** [ə'fɛns] *n* (*crime*) delito; (*insult*) ofensa; **to take ~ at** ofenderse por; **to commit an ~** cometer un delito.
offend [ə'fɛnd] *vt* (*person*) ofender ♦ *vi*: **to ~ against** (*law, rule*) infringir.
offender [ə'fɛndə*] *n* delincuente *m/f*; (*against regulations*) infractor(a) *m/f*.
offense [ə'fɛns] *n* (*US*) = **offence.**
offensive [ə'fɛnsɪv] *a* ofensivo; (*smell etc*) repugnante ♦ *n* (*MIL*) ofensiva.
offer ['ɔfə*] *n* (*gen*) oferta, ofrecimiento; (*proposal*) propuesta ♦ *vt* ofrecer; (*opportunity*) facilitar; **"on ~"** (*COMM*) "en oferta"; **to make an ~ for sth** hacer una

oferta por algo; **to ~ sth to sb, ~ sb sth** ofrecer algo a uno; **to ~ to do sth** ofrecerse *or* brindarse a hacer algo.
offering ['ɔfərɪŋ] *n* ofrenda.
offer price *n* precio de oferta.
offertory ['ɔfətrɪ] *n* (*REL*) ofertorio.
offhand [ɔf'hænd] *a* informal ♦ *ad* de improviso; **I can't tell you ~** no te lo puedo decir así de improviso *or* así nomás.
office ['ɔfɪs] *n* (*place*) oficina; (*room*) despacho; (*position*) cargo, oficio; **doctor's ~** (*US*) consultorio; **to take ~** entrar en funciones; **through his good ~s** gracias a sus buenos oficios; **O~ of Fair Trading** (*Brit*) *oficina de normas comerciales justas*.
office automation *n* ofimática, buromática.
office bearer *n* (*of club etc*) titular *m/f* (de una cartera).
office block, (*US*) **office building** *n* bloque *m* de oficinas.
office boy *n* ordenanza *m*.
office hours *npl* horas *fpl* de oficina; (*US MED*) horas *fpl* de consulta.
office manager *n* jefe/a *m/f* de oficina.
officer ['ɔfɪsə*] *n* (*MIL etc*) oficial *m/f*; (*of organization*) director(a) *m/f*; (*also*: **police ~**) agente *m/f* de policía.
office work *n* trabajo de oficina.
office worker *n* oficinista *m/f*.
official [ə'fɪʃl] *a* (*authorized*) oficial, autorizado; (*strike*) oficial ♦ *n* funcionario, oficial *m*.
officialdom [ə'fɪʃldəm] *n* burocracia.
officially [ə'fɪʃəlɪ] *ad* oficialmente.
official receiver *n* síndico.
officiate [ə'fɪʃɪeɪt] *vi* (*also REL*) oficiar; **to ~ as Mayor** ejercer las funciones de alcalde; **to ~ at a marriage** celebrar una boda.
officious [ə'fɪʃəs] *a* oficioso.
offing ['ɔfɪŋ] *n*: **in the ~** (*fig*) en perspectiva.
off-key [ɔf'kiː] *a* desafinado ♦ *ad* desentonadamente, fuera de tono.
off-licence ['ɔflaɪsns] *n* (*Brit: shop*) bodega, tienda de vinos y bebidas alcohólicas.
off-limits [ɔf'lɪmɪts] *a* (*US MIL*) prohibido al personal militar.
off line *a, ad* (*COMPUT*) fuera de línea; (*switched off*) desconectado.
off-load ['ɔfləud] *vt* descargar, desembarcar.
off-peak ['ɔf'piːk] *a* (*holiday*) de temporada baja; (*electricity*) de banda económica.
off-putting ['ɔfputɪŋ] *a* (*Brit: person*) poco amable, difícil; (*behaviour*) chocante.
off-season ['ɔf'siːzn] *a, ad* fuera de temporada.
offset ['ɔfsɛt] *vt* (*irg: like* set) (*counteract*) contrarrestar, compensar ♦ *n* (*also*: **~ printing**) offset *m*.

offshoot ['ɔfʃuːt] *n* (*BOT*) vástago; (*fig*) ramificación *f*.

offshore [ɔf'ʃɔː*] *a* (*breeze, island*) costero; (*fishing*) de bajura; ~ **oilfield** campo petrolífero submarino.

offside ['ɔf'saɪd] *n* (*AUT*: *with right-hand drive*) lado derecho; (: *with left-hand drive*) lado izquierdo ♦ *a* (*SPORT*) fuera de juego; (*AUT*) del lado derecho; del lado izquierdo.

offspring ['ɔfsprɪŋ] *n* descendencia.

offstage [ɔf'steɪdʒ] *ad* entre bastidores.

off-the-cuff [ɔfðə'kʌf] *a* espontáneo.

off-the-job [ɔfðə'dʒɔb] *a*: ~ **training** formación *f* fuera del trabajo.

off-the-peg [ɔfðə'pɛg], (*US*) **off-the-rack** [ɔfðə'ræk] *ad* confeccionado.

off-white ['ɔfwaɪt] *a* blanco grisáceo.

often ['ɔfn] *ad* a menudo, con frecuencia; **how ~ do you go?** ¿cada cuánto vas?

ogle ['əugl] *vt* comerse con los ojos a.

ogre ['əugə*] *n* ogro.

OH *abbr* (*US POST*) = Ohio.

oh [əu] *excl* ¡ah!

OHMS *abbr* (*Brit*) *On His* (*or Her*) *Majesty's Service*.

oil [ɔɪl] *n* aceite *m*; (*petroleum*) petróleo ♦ *vt* (*machine*) engrasar; **fried in ~** frito en aceite.

oilcan ['ɔɪlkæn] *n* lata de aceite.

oilfield ['ɔɪlfiːld] *n* campo petrolífero.

oil filter *n* (*AUT*) filtro de aceite.

oil-fired ['ɔɪlfaɪəd] *a* que quema aceite combustible.

oil gauge *n* indicador *m* del aceite.

oil industry *n* industria petrolífera.

oil level *n* nivel *m* del aceite.

oil painting *n* pintura al óleo.

oil refinery *n* refinería de petróleo.

oil rig *n* torre *f* de perforación.

oilskins ['ɔɪlskɪnz] *npl* impermeable *msg*, chubasquero *sg*.

oil tanker *n* petrolero.

oil well *n* pozo (de petróleo).

oily ['ɔɪlɪ] *a* aceitoso; (*food*) grasiento.

ointment ['ɔɪntmənt] *n* ungüento.

OK *abbr* (*US POST*) = Oklahoma.

O.K., okay ['əu'keɪ] *excl* O.K., ¡está bien!, ¡vale! ♦ *a* bien ♦ *n*: **to give sth one's ~** dar el visto bueno a *or* aprobar algo ♦ *vt* dar el visto bueno a; **it's ~ with** *or* **by me** estoy de acuerdo, me parece bien; **are you ~ for money?** ¿andas *or* vas bien de dinero?

old [əuld] *a* viejo; (*former*) antiguo; **how ~ are you?** ¿cuántos años tienes?, ¿qué edad tienes?; **he's 10 years ~** tiene 10 años; ~**er brother** hermano mayor; **any ~ thing will do** sirve cualquier cosa.

old age *n* vejez *f*.

old-age pension ['əuldeɪdʒ-] *n* (*Brit*) jubilación *f*, pensión *f*.

old-age pensioner (OAP) ['əuldeɪdʒ-] *n*

(*Brit*) jubilado/a.

olden ['əuldən] *a* antiguo.

old-fashioned ['əuld'fæʃənd] *a* anticuado, pasado de moda.

old maid *n* solterona.

old-time ['əuld'taɪm] *a* antiguo, de antaño.

old-timer [əuld'taɪmə*] *n* veterano/a, anciano/a.

old wives' tale *n* cuento de viejas, patraña.

olive ['ɔlɪv] *n* (*fruit*) aceituna; (*tree*) olivo ♦ *a* (*also*: ~-**green**) verde oliva *inv*.

olive branch *n* (*fig*): **to offer an ~ to sb** ofrecer hacer las paces con uno.

olive oil *n* aceite *m* de oliva.

Olympic [əu'lɪmpɪk] *a* olímpico; **the ~ Games, the ~s** *npl* las Olimpiadas.

OM *n* *abbr* (*Brit*: = *Order of Merit*) título ceremonial.

O & M *n* *abbr* = *organization and method*.

Oman [əu'maːn] *n* Omán *m*.

OMB *n* *abbr* (*US*: = *Office of Management and Budget*) servicio que asesora al presidente en materia presupuestaria.

omelet(te) ['ɔmlɪt] *n* tortilla, tortilla de huevo (*LAm*).

omen ['əumən] *n* presagio.

ominous ['ɔmɪnəs] *a* de mal agüero, amenazador(a).

omission [əu'mɪʃən] *n* omisión *f*; (*error*) descuido.

omit [əu'mɪt] *vt* omitir; (*by mistake*) olvidar, descuidar; **to ~ to do sth** olvidarse *or* dejar de hacer algo.

omnivorous [ɔm'nɪvərəs] *a* omnívoro.

ON *abbr* (*Canada*) = Ontario.

on [ɔn] *prep* en, sobre ♦ *ad* (*machine*) conectado; (*light, radio*) encendido; (*tap*) abierto; **is the meeting still ~?** ¿todavía hay reunión?; **when is this film ~?** ¿cuándo van a poner esta película?; ~ **the wall** en la pared, colgado de la pared; ~ **television** en la televisión; ~ **foot** a pie; ~ **horseback** a caballo; ~ **the Continent** en Europa; ~ **seeing this** al ver esto; ~ **arrival** al llegar; ~ **the left** a la izquierda; ~ **Friday** el viernes; **a week ~ Friday** el viernes en ocho días; **to be ~ holiday** estar de vacaciones; **I haven't any money ~ me** no llevo dinero encima; **we're ~ irregular verbs** estamos con los verbos irregulares; **he's ~ £6000 a year** gana seis mil libras al año; **this round's ~ me** esta ronda la pago yo, invito yo; **a book ~ physics** un libro de *or* sobre física; **to have one's coat ~** tener el abrigo puesto; **to go ~** seguir adelante; **I'm ~ to sth** creo haber encontrado algo; **it's not ~!** (*Brit*) ¡eso no se hace!; **from that day ~** de aquel día en adelante; **it was well ~ in the evening** estaba muy entrada la tarde; **my father's always ~ at me to get a job** (*col*) mi padre siempre me está dando la lata que coja un empleo.

ONC *n abbr* (*Brit*: = *Ordinary National Certificate*) *título escolar.*

once [wʌns] *ad* una vez; (*formerly*) antiguamente ◆ *conj* una vez que; ~ **he had left/it was done** una vez que se había marchado/ se hizo; **at** ~ en seguida, inmediatamente; (*simultaneously*) a la vez; ~ **a week** una vez por semana; ~ **more** otra vez; ~ **and for all** de una vez por todas; ~ **upon a time** érase una vez; **I knew him** ~ le conocía hace tiempo.

oncoming ['ɔnkʌmɪŋ] *a* (*traffic*) que viene de frente.

OND *n abbr* (*Brit*: = *Ordinary National Diploma*) *título escolar.*

one [wʌn] *num* un, uno, una ◆ *pron* uno; (*impersonal*) se ◆ *a* (*sole*) único; (*same*) mismo; **this** ~ éste/a; **that** ~ ése/a, aquél/ aquélla; **which** ~ **do you want?** ¿cuál quieres?; ~ **by** ~ uno por uno; ~ **never knows** nunca se sabe; ~ **another** el uno al otro; **it's** ~ (**o'clock**) es la una; **to be** ~ **up on sb** llevar ventaja a uno; **to be at** ~ (**with sb**) estar completamente de acuerdo (con uno).

one-armed bandit ['wʌnɑːmd-] *n* máquina tragaperras.

one-day excursion ['wʌndeɪ-] *n* (*US*) billete *m* de ida y vuelta en un día.

one-man ['wʌn'mæn] *a* (*business*) individual.

one-man band *n* hombre-orquesta *m.*

one-off [wʌn'ɔf] *n* (*Brit col*) artículo fuera de serie.

one-piece ['wʌnpiːs] *a* (*bathing suit*) de una pieza.

onerous ['ɔnərəs] *a* (*task, duty*) pesado; (*responsibility*) oneroso.

oneself [wʌn'sɛlf] *pron* uno mismo; (*after prep, also emphatic*) sí (mismo/a); **to do sth by** ~ hacer algo solo *or* por sí solo.

one-shot [wʌn'ʃɔt] *n* (*US*) = **one-off.**

one-sided [wʌn'saɪdɪd] *a* (*argument*) parcial; (*decision, view*) unilateral; (*game, contest*) desigual.

one-time ['wʌntaɪm] *a* antiguo, ex-.

one-to-one ['wʌntəwʌn] *a* (*relationship*) de dos.

one-upmanship [wʌn'ʌpmənʃɪp] *n*: **the art of** ~ el arte de quedar siempre por encima.

one-way ['wʌnweɪ] *a* (*street, traffic*) de dirección única; (*ticket*) sencillo.

ongoing ['ɔngəʊɪŋ] *a* continuo.

onion ['ʌnjən] *n* cebolla.

on line *a, ad* (*COMPUT*) en línea; (*switched on*) conectado.

onlooker ['ɔnlʊkə*] *n* espectador(a) *m/f.*

only ['əʊnlɪ] *ad* solamente, sólo ◆ *a* único, solo ◆ *conj* solamente que, pero; **an** ~ **child** un hijo único; **not** ~ **... but also...** no sólo ... sino también...; **I'd be** ~ **too**

pleased to help encantado de servir(les); **I saw her** ~ **yesterday** le vi ayer mismo; **I would come,** ~ **I'm very busy** iría, sólo *or* salvo que estoy muy atareado.

ono *abbr* (= *or nearest offer: in classified ads*) abierto ofertas.

onset ['ɔnsɛt] *n* comienzo.

onshore ['ɔnʃɔ:*] *a* (*wind*) que sopla del mar hacia la tierra.

onslaught ['ɔnslɔ:t] *n* ataque *m*, embestida.

on-the-job ['ɔnðə'dʒɔb] *a*: ~ **training** formación *f* en el trabajo *or* sobre la práctica.

onto ['ɔntʊ] *prep* = **on to.**

onus ['əʊnəs] *n* responsabilidad *f*; **the** ~ **is upon him to prove it** le incumbe a él demostrarlo.

onward(s) ['ɔnwəd(z)] *ad* (*move*) (hacia) adelante.

onyx ['ɔnɪks] *n* ónice *m*, onyx *m.*

ooze [uːz] *vi* rezumar.

opal ['əʊpl] *n* ópalo.

opaque [əʊ'peɪk] *a* opaco.

OPEC ['əʊpɛk] *n abbr* (= *Organization of Petroleum-Exporting Countries*) OPEP *f.*

open ['əʊpn] *a* abierto; (*car*) descubierto; (*road, view*) despejado; (*meeting*) público; (*admiration*) manifiesto ◆ *vt* abrir ◆ *vi* (*flower, eyes, door, debate*) abrirse; (*book etc: commence*) comenzar; **in the** ~ (**air**) al aire libre; ~ **verdict** veredicto inconcluso; ~ **ticket** billete *m* sin fecha; ~ **ground** (*among trees*) claro; (*waste ground*) solar *m;* **to have an** ~ **mind** (**on sth**) estar sin decidirse aún (sobre algo); **to** ~ **a bank account** abrir una cuenta en el banco.

open on to *vt fus* (*subj: room, door*) dar a.

open out *vt* abrir ◆ *vi* (*person*) abrirse.

open up *vt* abrir; (*blocked road*) despejar ◆ *vi* abrirse, empezar.

open-and-shut ['əʊpənən'ʃʌt] *a*: ~ **case** caso claro *or* evidente.

open day *n* (*Brit*) jornada de acceso público.

open-ended [əʊpn'ɛndɪd] *a* (*fig*) indefinido, sin definir.

opener ['əʊpnə*] *n* (*also:* **can** ~, **tin** ~) abrelatas *m inv.*

open-heart surgery [əʊpn'hɑːt-] *n* cirugía a corazón abierto.

opening ['əʊpnɪŋ] *n* abertura, comienzo; (*opportunity*) oportunidad *f*; (*job*) puesto vacante, vacante *f.*

opening night *n* estreno.

openly ['əʊpnlɪ] *ad* abiertamente.

open-minded [əʊpn'maɪndɪd] *a* imparcial.

open-necked ['əʊpnnɛkt] *a* sin corbata.

openness ['əʊpnnɪs] *n* (*frankness*) franqueza.

open-plan ['əʊpn'plæn] *a*: ~ **office** gran oficina sin particiones.

open return *n* vuelta con fecha abierta.

open shop *n* empresa *que contrata a*

mano de obra no afiliada a ningún sindicato.

Open University *n* (*Brit*) ≈ Universidad *f* Nacional de Enseñanza a Distancia, UNED *f*.

opera ['ɔpərə] *n* ópera.

opera glasses *npl* gemelos *mpl*.

opera house *n* teatro de la ópera.

opera singer *n* cantante *m/f* de ópera.

operate ['ɔpəreɪt] *vt* (*machine*) hacer funcionar; (*company*) dirigir ◆ *vi* funcionar; (*drug*) hacer efecto; **to ~ on sb** (*MED*) operar a uno.

operatic [ɔpə'rætɪk] *a* de ópera.

operating costs ['ɔpəreɪtɪŋ-] *npl* gastos *mpl* operacionales.

operating profit *n* beneficio de explotación.

operating table *n* mesa de operaciones.

operating theatre *n* sala de operaciones.

operation [ɔpə'reɪʃən] *n* (*gen*) operación *f*; (*of machine*) funcionamiento; **to be in ~** estar funcionando *or* en funcionamiento; **to have an ~** (*MED*) ser operado; **to have an ~ for** operarse de; **the company's ~s during the year** las actividades de la compañía durante el año.

operational [ɔpə'reɪʃənl] *a* operacional, en buen estado; (*COMM*) en condiciones de servicio; (*ready for use or action*) en condiciones de funcionar; **when the service is fully ~** cuando el servicio esté en pleno funcionamiento.

operative ['ɔpərətɪv] *a* (*measure*) en vigor; **the ~ word** la palabra clave.

operator ['ɔpəreɪtə*] *n* (*of machine*) maquinista *m/f*, operario/a; (*TEL*) operador(a) *m/f*, telefonista *m/f*.

operetta [ɔpə'retə] *n* opereta; (*in Spain*) zarzuela.

ophthalmic [ɔf'θælmɪk] *a* oftálmico.

ophthalmologist [ɔfθæl'mɔlədʒɪst] *n* oftalmólogo/a.

opinion [ə'pɪnjən] *n* (*gen*) opinión *f*; **in my ~** en mi opinión, a mi juicio; **to seek a second ~** pedir una segunda opinión.

opinionated [ə'pɪnjəneɪtɪd] *a* testarudo.

opinion poll *n* encuesta, sondeo.

opium ['əupɪəm] *n* opio.

opponent [ə'pəunənt] *n* adversario/a, contrincante *m/f*.

opportune ['ɔpətjuːn] *a* oportuno.

opportunism [ɔpə'tjuːnɪzm] *n* oportunismo.

opportunist [ɔpə'tjuːnɪst] *n* oportunista *m/f*.

opportunity [ɔpə'tjuːnɪtɪ] *n* oportunidad *f*; **to take the ~ to do** *or* **of doing** aprovechar la ocasión para hacer.

oppose [ə'pəuz] *vt* oponerse a; **to be ~d to sth** oponerse a algo; **as ~d to** a diferencia de.

opposing [ə'pəuzɪŋ] *a* (*side*) opuesto, contrario.

opposite ['ɔpəzɪt] *a* opuesto, contrario a; (*house etc*) de enfrente ◆ *ad* en frente ◆ *prep* en frente de, frente a ◆ *n* lo contrario; **the ~ sex** el otro sexo, el sexo opuesto.

opposite number *n* (*Brit*) homólogo/a.

opposition [ɔpə'zɪʃən] *n* oposición *f*.

oppress [ə'prɛs] *vt* oprimir.

oppression [ə'prɛʃən] *n* opresión *f*.

oppressive [ə'prɛsɪv] *a* opresivo.

opprobrium [ə'prəubrɪəm] *n* (*formal*) oprobio.

opt [ɔpt] *vi*: **to ~ for** optar por; **to ~ to do** optar por hacer; **to ~ out of** optar por no hacer.

optical ['ɔptɪkl] *a* óptico.

optical character recognition/reader (OCR) *n* reconocimiento/lector *m* óptico de caracteres.

optical fibre *n* fibra óptica.

optician [ɔp'tɪʃən] *n* óptico *m/f*.

optics ['ɔptɪks] *n* óptica.

optimism ['ɔptɪmɪzəm] *n* optimismo.

optimist ['ɔptɪmɪst] *n* optimista *m/f*.

optimistic [ɔptɪ'mɪstɪk] *a* optimista.

optimum ['ɔptɪməm] *a* óptimo.

option ['ɔpʃən] *n* opción *f*; **to keep one's ~s open** (*fig*) mantener las opciones abiertas; **I have no ~** no tengo más *or* otro remedio.

optional ['ɔpʃənl] *a* facultativo, discrecional; **~ extras** opciones *fpl* extras.

opulence ['ɔpjuləns] *n* opulencia.

opulent ['ɔpjulənt] *a* opulento.

OR *abbr* (*US POST*) = Oregon.

or [ɔː*] *conj* o; (*before o, ho*) u; (*with negative*): **he hasn't seen ~ heard anything** no ha visto ni oído nada; **~ else** si no; **let me go ~ I'll scream!** ¡suélteme, o me pongo a gritar!

oracle ['ɔrəkl] *n* oráculo.

oral ['ɔːrəl] *a* oral ◆ *n* examen *m* oral.

orange ['ɔrɪndʒ] *n* (*fruit*) naranja ◆ *a* color naranja.

orangeade [ɔrɪndʒ'eɪd] *n* naranjada, refresco de naranja.

orange squash *n* zumo *or* jugo (*LAm*) de naranja.

orang-outang, orang-utan [ɔ'ræŋuː'tæn] *n* orangután *m*.

oration [ɔː'reɪʃən] *n* discurso solemne, **funeral ~** oración *f* fúnebre.

orator ['ɔrətə*] *n* orador(a) *m/f*.

oratorio [ɔrə'tɔːrɪəu] *n* oratorio.

orbit ['ɔːbɪt] *n* órbita ◆ *vt, vi* orbitar; **to be in/go into ~ (round)** estar en/entrar en órbita (alrededor de).

orchard ['ɔːtʃəd] *n* huerto; **apple ~** manzanar *m*, manzanal *m*.

orchestra ['ɔːkɪstrə] *n* orquesta; (*US: seating*) platea.

orchestral [ɔː'kɛstrəl] *a* de orquesta.

orchestrate ['ɔːkɪstreɪt] *vt* (*MUS, fig*) orquestar.

orchid ['ɔːkɪd] *n* orquídea.

ordain [ɔː'deɪn] *vt* (*REL*) ordenar, decretar; (*decide*) mandar.

ordeal [ɔː'diːl] *n* experiencia horrorosa.

order ['ɔːdə*] *n* orden *m*; (*command*) orden *f*; (*type, kind*) clase *f*; (*state*) estado; (*COMM*) pedido, encargo ◆ *vt* (*also*: **put in** ~) arreglar, poner en orden; (*COMM*) encargar, pedir; (*command*) mandar, ordenar; **in** ~ (*gen*) en orden; (*of document*) en regla; **in (working)** ~ en funcionamiento; **a machine in working** ~ una máquina en funcionamiento; **to be out of** ~ (*machine, toilets*) estar estropeado *or* descompuesto (*LAm*); **in** ~ **to do** para hacer; **on** ~ (*COMM*) pedido; **to be on** ~ estar pedido; **to be under** ~s **to do sth** estar bajo órdenes de hacer algo; **a point of** ~ una cuestión de procedimiento; **to place an** ~ **for sth with sb** hacer un pedido de algo a uno; **made to** ~ hecho a la medida; **his income is of the** ~ **of £4000 per year** sus ingresos son del orden de 4 mil libras al año; **to the** ~ **of** (*BANKING*) a la orden de; **to** ~ **sb to do sth** mandar a uno hacer algo.

order book *n* cartera de pedidos.

order form *n* hoja de pedido.

orderly ['ɔːdəlɪ] *n* (*MIL*) ordenanza *m*; (*MED*) enfermero/a (auxiliar) ◆ *a* ordenado.

orderly officer *n* (*MIL*) oficial *m* del día.

order number *n* número de pedido.

ordinal ['ɔːdɪnl] *a* ordinal.

ordinarily ['ɔːdnrɪlɪ] *ad* por lo común.

ordinary ['ɔːdnrɪ] *a* corriente, normal; (*pej*) común y corriente; **out of the** ~ fuera de lo común, extraordinario.

ordinary seaman *n* (*Brit*) marinero.

ordinary shares *npl* acciones *fpl* ordinarias.

ordination [ɔːdɪ'neɪʃən] *n* ordenación *f*.

ordnance ['ɔːdnəns] *n* (*MIL*: *unit*) artillería.

ordnance factory *n* fábrica de artillería.

Ordnance Survey *n* (*Brit*) *servicio oficial de topografía y cartografía*.

ore [ɔː*] *n* mineral *m*.

organ ['ɔːgən] *n* órgano *m*.

organic [ɔː'gænɪk] *a* orgánico.

organism ['ɔːgənɪzəm] *n* organismo.

organist ['ɔːgənɪst] *n* organista *m/f*.

organization [ɔːgənaɪ'zeɪʃən] *n* organización *f*.

organization chart *n* organigrama *m*.

organize ['ɔːgənaɪz] *vt* organizar; **to get** ~**d** organizarse.

organizer ['ɔːgənaɪzə*] *n* organizador(a) *m/f*.

orgasm ['ɔːgæzəm] *n* orgasmo.

orgy ['ɔːdʒɪ] *n* orgía.

Orient ['ɔːrɪənt] *n* Oriente *m*.

oriental [ɔːrɪ'entl] *a* oriental.

orientate ['ɔːrɪənteɪt] *vt* orientar.

origin ['ɔrɪdʒɪn] *n* origen *m*; (*point of departure*) procedencia.

original [ə'rɪdʒɪnl] *a* original; (*first*) primero; (*earlier*) primitivo ◆ *n* original *m*.

originality [ərɪdʒɪ'nælɪtɪ] *n* originalidad *f*.

originally [ə'rɪdʒɪnəlɪ] *ad* (*at first*) al principio; (*with originality*) con originalidad.

originate [ə'rɪdʒɪneɪt] *vi*: **to** ~ **from, to** ~ **in** surgir de, tener su origen en.

originator [ə'rɪdʒɪneɪtə*] *n* inventor(a) *m/f*, autor(a) *m/f*.

Orkneys ['ɔːknɪz] *npl*: **the** ~ (*also*: **the Orkney Islands**) las Orcadas.

ornament ['ɔːnəmənt] *n* adorno; (*trinket*) chuchería.

ornamental [ɔːnə'mentl] *a* decorativo, de adorno.

ornamentation [ɔːnəmen'teɪʃən] *n* ornamentación *f*.

ornate [ɔː'neɪt] *a* muy ornado, vistoso.

ornithologist [ɔːnɪ'θɔlədʒɪst] *n* ornitólogo/a.

ornithology [ɔːnɪ'θɔlədʒɪ] *n* ornitología.

orphan ['ɔːfn] *n* huérfano/a ◆ *vt*: **to be** ~**ed** quedar huérfano/a.

orphanage ['ɔːfənɪdʒ] *n* orfanato.

orthodox ['ɔːθədɔks] *a* ortodoxo.

orthodoxy ['ɔːθədɔksɪ] *n* ortodoxia.

orthopaedic, (US) orthopedic [ɔːθə'piːdɪk] *a* ortopédico.

orthop(a)edics [ɔːθə'piːdɪks] *n* ortopedia.

OS *abbr* (*Brit*: = *Ordnance Survey*) servicio oficial de topografía y cartografía; (: *NAUT*) = **ordinary seaman**; (: *DRESS*) = **outsize**.

O/S *abbr* = **out of stock**.

oscillate ['ɔsɪleɪt] *vi* oscilar; (*person*) vacilar.

oscillation [ɔsɪ'leɪʃən] *n* oscilación *f*; (*of prices*) fluctuación *f*.

OSHA *n abbr* (*US*: = *Occupational Safety and Health Administration*) oficina de la higiene y la seguridad en el trabajo.

Oslo ['ɔzləu] *n* Oslo.

ostensible [ɔs'tensɪbl] *a* aparente, pretendido.

ostensibly [ɔs'tensɪblɪ] *ad* aparentemente.

ostentatious [ɔsten'teɪʃəs] *a* pretencioso, aparatoso; (*person*) ostentativo.

osteopath ['ɔstɪəpæθ] *n* osteópata *m/f*.

ostracize ['ɔstrəsaɪz] *vt* hacer el vacío a.

ostrich ['ɔstrɪtʃ] *n* avestruz *m*.

OT *n abbr* (= *Old Testament*) A.T. *m*.

OTB *n abbr* (*US*: = *off-track betting*) apuestas hechas fuera del hipódromo.

O.T.E. *abbr* (= *on-target earnings*) beneficios según objetivos.

other ['ʌðə*] *a* otro ◆ *pron*: **the** ~ (*one*) el/la otro/a; ~**s** (~ *people*) otros; ~ **than** (*apart from*) aparte de; **the** ~ **day** el otro día; **some** ~ **people have still to arrive** quedan por llegar otros; **some actor or** ~ un actor cualquiera; **somebody or** ~ alguien, alguno; **the car was none** ~ **than Roberta's** fíjate que el coche era de Roberta.

otherwise ['ʌðəwaɪz] *ad, conj* de otra ma-

nera; (*if not*) si no; **an ~ good piece of work** un trabajo que, eso aparte, es bueno.
OTT *abbr* (*col*) = **over the top**; *see* **top**.
otter ['ɔtə*] *n* nutria.
OU *n abbr* (*Brit*) = **Open University**.
ouch [autʃ] *excl* ¡ay!
ought, *pt* **ought** [ɔːt] *auxiliary vb:* **I ~ to do it** debería hacerlo; **this ~ to have been corrected** esto debiera de haberse corregido; **he ~ to win** (*probability*) debe *or* debiera ganar; **you ~ to go and see it** vale la pena ir a verlo.
ounce [auns] *n* onza (*28.35g; 16 in a pound*).
our ['auə*] *a* nuestro; *see also* **my**.
ours ['auəz] *pron* (el) nuestro/(la) nuestra *etc*; *see also* **mine**.
ourselves [auə'sɛlvz] *pron pl* (*reflexive, after prep*) nosotros; (*emphatic*) nosotros mismos; **we did it (all) by ~** lo hicimos nosotros mismos *or* solos; *see also* **oneself**.
oust [aust] *vt* desalojar.
out [aut] *ad* fuera, afuera; (*not at home*) fuera (de casa); (*light, fire*) apagado; (*on strike*) en huelga; **~ there** allí (fuera); **he's ~** (*absent*) no está, ha salido; **to be ~ in one's calculations** equivocarse (en sus cálculos); **to run ~** salir corriendo; **~ loud** en alta voz; **~ of** *prep* (*outside*) fuera de; (*because of: anger etc*) por; **to look ~ of the window** mirar por la ventana; **to drink ~ of a cup** beber de una taza; **made ~ of wood** de madera; **~ of petrol** sin gasolina; **"~ of order"** "no funciona"; **it's ~ of stock** (*COMM*) está agotado; **to be ~ and about again** estar repuesto y levantado; **the journey ~** el viaje de ida; **the boat was 10 km ~** el barco estaba a diez kilómetros de la costa; **before the week was ~** antes del fin de la semana; **he's ~ for all he can get** busca sus propios fines, anda detrás de lo suyo.
out-and-out ['autəndaut] *a* (*liar, thief etc*) redomado, empedernido.
outback ['autbæk] *n* interior *m*.
outbid [aut'bɪd] *vt* pujar más alto que, sobrepujar.
outboard ['autbɔːd] *a:* **~ motor** (motor *m*) fuera borda *m*.
outbreak ['autbreɪk] *n* (*of war*) comienzo; (*of disease*) epidemia; (*of violence etc*) ola.
outbuilding ['autbɪldɪŋ] *n* dependencia; (*shed*) cobertizo.
outburst ['autbəːst] *n* explosión *f*, arranque *m*.
outcast ['autkɑːst] *n* paria *m/f*.
outclass [aut'klɑːs] *vt* aventajar, superar.
outcome ['autkʌm] *n* resultado.
outcrop ['autkrɔp] *n* (*of rock*) afloramiento.
outcry ['autkraɪ] *n* protestas *fpl*.
outdated [aut'deɪtɪd] *a* anticuado, fuera de moda.
outdistance [aut'dɪstəns] *vt* dejar atrás.
outdo [aut'duː] *vt* (*irg: like* **do**) superar.

outdoor [aut'dɔː*] *a* al aire libre.
outdoors [aut'dɔːz] *ad* al aire libre.
outer ['autə*] *a* exterior, externo.
outer space *n* espacio exterior.
outfit ['autfɪt] *n* equipo; (*clothes*) traje *m*; (*col: organization*) grupo, organización *f*.
outfitter's ['autfɪtəz] *n* (*Brit*) sastrería.
outgoing ['autgəuɪŋ] *a* (*president, tenant*) saliente; (*means of transport*) que sale; (*character*) extrovertido.
outgoings ['autgəuɪŋz] *npl* (*Brit*) gastos *mpl*.
outgrow [aut'grəu] *vt:* (*irg: like* **grow**) **he has ~n his clothes** su ropa le queda pequeña ya.
outhouse ['authaus] *n* dependencia.
outing ['autɪŋ] *n* excursión *f*, paseo.
outlandish [aut'lændɪʃ] *a* estrafalario.
outlast [aut'lɑːst] *vt* durar más tiempo que, sobrevivir a.
outlaw ['autlɔː] *n* proscrito/a ♦ *vt* (*person*) declarar fuera de la ley; (*practice*) declarar ilegal.
outlay ['autleɪ] *n* inversión *f*.
outlet ['autlet] *n* salida; (*of pipe*) desagüe *m*; (*US ELEC*) toma de corriente; (*for emotion*) desahogo; (*also:* **retail ~**) punto de venta.
outline ['autlaɪn] *n* (*shape*) contorno, perfil *m*; **in ~** (*fig*) a grandes rasgos.
outlive [aut'lɪv] *vt* sobrevivir a.
outlook ['autluk] *n* perspectiva; (*opinion*) punto de vista.
outlying ['autlaɪɪŋ] *a* remoto, aislado.
outmanoeuvre, (*US*) **outmaneuver** [autmə'nuːvə*] *vt* (*MIL, fig*) superar en la estrategia, superar a.
outmoded [aut'məudɪd] *a* anticuado, pasado de moda.
outnumber [aut'nʌmbə*] *vt* exceder en número.
out of bounds [autəv'baundz] *a:* **it's ~** está prohibido el paso.
out-of-date [autəv'deɪt] *a* (*passport*) caducado, vencido; (*theory, idea*) anticuado; (*clothes, customs*) pasado de moda.
out-of-doors [autəv'dɔːz] *ad* al aire libre.
out-of-the-way [autəvðə'weɪ] *a* (*remote*) apartado; (*unusual*) poco común *or* corriente.
outpatient ['autpeɪʃənt] *n* paciente *m/f* externo/a.
outpost ['autpəust] *n* puesto avanzado.
output ['autput] *n* (volumen *m* de) producción *f*, rendimiento; (*COMPUT*) salida ♦ *vt* (*COMPUT: to power*) imprimir.
outrage ['autreɪdʒ] *n* (*scandal*) escándalo; (*atrocity*) atrocidad *f* ♦ *vt* ultrajar.
outrageous [aut'reɪdʒəs] *a* monstruoso; (*clothes*) extravagante, escandaloso.
outright [aut'raɪt] *ad* (*win*) de manera absoluta; (*be killed*) en el acto; (*completely*) completamente ♦ *a* ['autraɪt] completo.

outrun [aut'rʌn] *vt* (*irg*: *like* **run**) correr más que, dejar atrás.

outset ['autset] *n* principio.

outshine [aut'ʃaɪn] *vt* (irg: *like* **shine**) (*fig*) eclipsar, brillar más que.

outside [aut'saɪd] *n* exterior *m* ♦ *a* exterior, externo ♦ *ad* fuera ♦ *prep* fuera de; (*beyond*) más allá de; **at the** ~ (*fig*) a lo sumo; **an** ~ **chance** una posibilidad remota; ~ **left/right** (*FOOTBALL*) extremo izquierdo/derecho.

outside broadcast *n* (*RADIO*, *TV*) emisión *f* exterior.

outside contractor *n* contratista *m/f* independiente.

outside lane *n* (*AUT*: *in Britain*) carril *m* de la derecha.

outside line *n* (*TEL*) línea (exterior).

outsider [aut'saɪdə*] *n* (*stranger*) extraño, forastero.

outsize ['autsaɪz] *a* (*clothes*) de talla grande.

outskirts ['autskɔːts] *npl* alrededores *mpl*, afueras *fpl*.

outsmart [aut'smɑːt] *vt* ser más listo que.

outspoken [aut'spəukən] *a* muy franco.

outspread [aut'spred] *a* extendido; (*wings*) desplegado.

outstanding [aut'stændɪŋ] *a* excepcional, destacado; (*unfinished*) pendiente.

outstay [aut'steɪ] *vt*: **to** ~ **one's welcome** quedarse más de la cuenta.

outstretched [aut'stretʃt] *a* (*hand*) extendido.

outstrip [aut'strɪp] *vt* (*competitors*, *demand*, *also fig*) dejar atrás, aventajar.

out-tray ['auttreɪ] *n* bandeja de salida.

outvote [aut'vəut] *vt*: **it was** ~**d (by ...)** fue rechazado en el voto (por ...).

outward ['autwəd] *a* (*sign*, *appearances*) externo; (*journey*) de ida.

outwardly ['autwədlɪ] *ad* por fuera.

outweigh [aut'weɪ] *vt* pesar más que.

outwit [aut'wɪt] *vt* ser más listo que.

outworn [aut'wɔːn] *a* (*expression*) cansado.

oval ['əuvl] *a* ovalado ♦ *n* óvalo.

ovary ['əuvərɪ] *n* ovario.

ovation [əu'veɪʃən] *n* ovación *f*.

oven ['ʌvn] *n* horno.

ovenproof ['ʌvnpruːf] *a* resistente al horno.

oven-ready ['ʌvnredɪ] *a* listo para el horno.

ovenware ['ʌvnwɛə*] *n* artículos *mpl* para el horno.

over ['əuvə*] *ad* encima, por encima ♦ *a* (*or ad*) (*finished*) terminado; (*surplus*) de sobra; (*excessively*) demasiado ♦ *prep* (por) encima de; (*above*) sobre; (*on the other side of*) al otro lado de; (*more than*) más de; (*during*) durante; (*about, concerning*): **they fell out** ~ **money** riñeron por una cuestión de dinero; ~ **here** (por) aquí; ~ **there** (por) allí *or* allá; **all** ~ (*everywhere*) por todas partes; ~ **and** ~ (*again*) una y

otra vez; ~ **and above** además de; **to ask sb** ~ invitar a uno a casa; **to bend** ~ inclinarse; **now** ~ **to our Paris correspondent** damos la palabra a nuestro corresponsal de París; **the world** ~ en todo el mundo, en el mundo entero; **she's not** ~ **intelligent** no es muy lista que digamos.

over... [əuvə*] *pref* sobre..., super....

overact [əuvər'ækt] *vi* (*THEATRE*) exagerar el papel.

overall ['əuvərɔːl] *a* (*length*) total; (*study*) de conjunto ♦ *ad* [əuvər'ɔːl] en conjunto ♦ *n* (*Brit*) guardapolvo; ~**s** *npl* mono *sg*, overol *msg* (*LAm*).

overanxious [əuvər'æŋkʃəs] *a* demasiado preocupado *or* ansioso.

overawe [əuvər'ɔː] *vt* impresionar.

overbalance [əuvə'bæləns] *vi* perder el equilibrio.

overbearing [əuvə'bɛərɪŋ] *a* autoritario, imperioso.

overboard ['əuvəbɔːd] *ad* (*NAUT*) por la borda; **to go** ~ **for sth** (*fig*) enloquecerse por algo.

overbook [əuvə'buk] *vt* sobrereservar, reservar con exceso.

overcapitalize [əuvə'kæpɪtəlaɪz] *vi* sobrecapitalizar.

overcast ['əuvəkɑːst] *a* encapotado.

overcharge [əuvə'tʃɑːdʒ] *vt*: **to** ~ **sb** cobrar un precio excesivo a uno.

overcoat ['əuvəkəut] *n* abrigo, sobretodo.

overcome [əuvə'kʌm] *vt* (*irg*: *like* **come**) (*gen*) vencer; (*difficulty*) superar; **she was quite** ~ **by the occasion** la ocasión la conmovió mucho *or* le vino en grande.

overconfident [əuvə'kɔnfɪdənt] *a* demasiado confiado.

overcrowded [əuvə'kraudɪd] *a* atestado de gente; (*city*, *country*) superpoblado.

overcrowding [əuvə'kraudɪŋ] *n* (*in town*, *country*) superpoblación *f*; (*in bus etc*) hacinamiento, apiñamiento.

overdo [əuvə'duː] *vt* (*irg*: *like* **do**) exagerar; (*overcook*) cocer demasiado; **to** ~ **it**, **to** ~ **things** (*work too hard*) trabajar demasiado.

overdose ['əuvədəus] *n* sobredosis *f inv*.

overdraft ['əuvədrɑːft] *n* saldo deudor.

overdrawn [əuvə'drɔːn] *a* (*account*) en descubierto.

overdrive ['əuvədraɪv] *n* (*AUT*) sobremarcha, superdirecta.

overdue [əuvə'djuː] *a* retrasado; (*recognition*) tardío; (*bill*) vencido y no pagado; **that change was long** ~ ese cambio tenía que hacerse hace tiempo.

overenthusiastic ['əuvərənθuːzɪ'æstɪk] *a* demasiado entusiasta.

overestimate [əuvər'estɪmeɪt] *vt* sobreestimar.

overexcited [əuvərɪk'saɪtɪd] *a* sobreexcitado.

overexertion [əuvərɪg'zə:ʃən] n agotamiento, fatiga.

overexpose [əuvərɪk'spəuz] vt (PHOT) sobreexponer.

overflow [əuvə'fləu] vi desbordarse ♦ n ['əuvəfləu] (excess) exceso; (of river) desbordamiento; (also: ~ pipe) (cañería de) desagüe m.

overfly [əuvə'flaɪ] vt (irg: like fly) sobrevolar.

overgenerous [əuvə'dʒɛnərəs] a demasiado generoso.

overgrown [əuvə'grəun] a (garden) cubierto de hierba; **he's just an ~ schoolboy** es un niño en grande.

overhang [əuvə'hæŋ] (irg: like hang) vt sobresalir por encima de ♦ vi sobresalir.

overhaul vt [əuvə'hɔ:l] revisar, repasar ♦ n ['əuvəhɔ:l] revisión f.

overhead ad [əuvə'hɛd] por arriba or encima ♦ a ['əuvəhɛd] (cable) aéreo; (railway) elevado, aéreo ♦ n ['əuvəhɛd] (US) = **overheads**.

overheads ['əuvəhɛdz] npl (Brit) gastos mpl generales.

overhear [əuvə'hɪə*] vt (irg: like hear) oír por casualidad.

overheat [əuvə'hi:t] vi (engine) recalentarse.

overjoyed [əuvə'dʒɔɪd] a encantado, lleno de alegría.

overkill ['əuvəkɪl] n (MIL fig) capacidad f excesiva de destrucción.

overland ['əuvəlænd] a, ad por tierra.

overlap vi [əuvə'læp] traslaparse ♦ n ['əuvəlæp] traslapo.

overleaf [əuvə'li:f] ad al dorso.

overload [əuvə'ləud] vt sobrecargar.

overlook [əuvə'luk] vt (have view of) dar a, tener vistas a; (miss) pasar por alto; (forgive) hacer la vista gorda a.

overlord ['əuvəlɔ:d] n señor m.

overmanning [əuvə'mænɪŋ] n empleo de más personal de lo necesario.

overnight [əuvə'naɪt] ad durante la noche; (fig) de la noche a la mañana ♦ a de noche; **to stay ~** pasar la noche.

overnight bag n fin m de semana, neceser m de viaje.

overnight stay n estancia de una noche.

overpass ['əuvəpɑ:s] vt: n (US) paso superior or a desnivel.

overpay [əuvə'peɪ] vt: **to ~ sb by £50** pagar 50 libras de más a uno.

overpower [əuvə'pauə*] vt dominar; (fig) embargar.

overpowering [əuvə'pauərɪŋ] a (heat) agobiante; (smell) penetrante.

overproduction [əuvəprə'dʌkʃən] n superproducción f.

overrate [əuvə'reɪt] vt sobreestimar.

overreach [əuvə'ri:tʃ] vt: **to ~ o.s.** ir demasiado lejos, pasarse.

override [əuvə'raɪd] vt (irg: like **ride**) (order, objection) no hacer caso de.

overriding [əuvə'raɪdɪŋ] a predominante.

overrule [əuvə'ru:l] vt (decision) anular; (claim) denegar.

overrun [əuvə'rʌn] vt (irg: like **run**) (MIL: country) invadir; (time limit) rebasar, exceder ♦ vi rebasar el límite previsto; **the town is ~ with tourists** el pueblo está inundado de turistas.

overseas [əuvə'si:z] ad en ultramar; (abroad) en el extranjero ♦ a (trade) exterior; (visitor) extranjero.

overseer ['əuvəsɪə*] n (in factory) superintendente m/f; (foreman) capataz m.

overshadow [əuvə'ʃædəu] vt (fig) eclipsar.

overshoot [əuvə'ʃu:t] vt (irg: like **shoot**) excederse.

oversight ['əuvəsaɪt] n descuido; **due to an ~** a causa de un descuido or una equivocación.

oversimplify [əuvə'sɪmplɪfaɪ] vt simplificar demasiado.

oversleep [əuvə'sli:p] vi (irg: like **sleep**) quedarse dormido.

overspend [əuvə'spɛnd] vi gastar más de la cuenta; **we have overspent by 5 dollars** hemos excedido el presupuesto en 5 dólares.

overspill ['əuvəspɪl] n exceso de población.

overstaffed [əuvə'stɑ:ft] a: **to be ~** tener una plantilla excesiva.

overstate [əuvə'steɪt] vt exagerar.

overstatement ['əuvəsteɪtmənt] n exageración f.

overstep [əuvə'stɛp] vt: **to ~ the mark** or **the limits** pasarse de la raya.

overstock [əuvə'stɔk] vt abarrotar.

overstrike n ['əuvəstraɪk] (on printer) superposición f ♦ vt (irg: like **strike**) [əuvə'straɪk] superponer.

oversubscribed [əuvəsəb'skraɪbd] a suscrito en exceso.

overt [əu'vɔ:t] a abierto.

overtake [əuvə'teɪk] vt (irg: like **take**) sobrepasar; (Brit AUT) adelantar.

overtax [əuvə'tæks] vt (ECON) exigir contribuciones fpl excesivas or impuestos mpl excesivos a; (fig: strength, patience) agotar, abusar de; **to ~ o.s.** fatigarse demasiado.

overthrow [əuvə'θrəu] vt (irg: like **throw**) (government) derrocar.

overtime ['əuvətaɪm] n horas fpl extraordinarias; **to do** or **work ~** hacer or trabajar horas extraordinarias or extras.

overtime ban n prohibición f de (hacer) horas extraordinarias.

overtone ['əuvətəun] n (fig) tono.

overture ['əuvətʃuə*] n (MUS) obertura; (fig) propuesta.

overturn [əuvə'tə:n] vt, vi volcar.

overweight [əuvə'weɪt] a demasiado gordo or pesado.

overwhelm [əuvə'wɛlm] vt aplastar.

overwhelming [əuvə'wɛlmɪŋ] *a* (*victory*, *defeat*) arrollador(a); (*desire*) irresistible; **one's ~ impression is of heat** lo que más impresiona es el calor.

overwhelmingly [əuvə'wɛlmɪŋlɪ] *ad* abrumadoramente.

overwork [əuvə'wə:k] *n* trabajo excesivo ♦ *vt* hacer trabajar demasiado ♦ *vi* trabajar demasiado.

overwrite [əuvə'raɪt] *vt* (*irg: like* **write**) (*COMPUT*) sobreescribir.

overwrought [əuvə'rɔ:t] *a* sobreexcitado.

ovulation [ɔvju'leɪʃən] *n* ovulación *f*.

owe [əu] *vt* deber; **to ~ sb sth, to ~ sth to sb** deber algo a uno.

owing to ['əuɪŋtu:] *prep* debido a, por causa de.

owl [aul] *n* búho, lechuza.

own [əun] *vt* tener, poseer ♦ *vi*: **to ~ to sth/to having done sth** confesar *or* reconocer algo/haber hecho algo ♦ *a* propio; **a room of my ~** una habitación propia; **to get one's ~ back** tomar revancha; **on one's ~** solo, a solas; **can I have it for my (very) ~?** ¿puedo quedarme con él?; **to come into one's ~** justificarse.

own up *vi* confesar.

own brand *n* (*COMM*) marca propia.

owner ['əunə*] *n* dueño/a.

owner-occupier ['əunər'ɔkjupaɪə*] *n* ocupante propietario/a *m/f*.

ownership ['əunəʃɪp] *n* posesión *f*; **it's under new ~** está bajo nueva dirección.

ox, *pl* **oxen** [ɔks, 'ɔksn] *n* buey *m*.

Oxfam ['ɔksfæm] *n abbr* (*Brit*: = *Oxford Committee for Famine Relief*) OXFAM.

oxide ['ɔksaɪd] *n* óxido.

Oxon. ['ɔksn] *abbr* (*Brit*: = *Oxoniensis*) = *of Oxford*.

oxtail ['ɔksteɪl] *n*: **~ soup** sopa de rabo de buey.

oxyacetylene ['ɔksɪə'sɛtɪli:n] *a* oxiacetilénico; **~ burner, ~ torch** soplete *m* oxiacetilénico.

oxygen ['ɔksɪdʒən] *n* oxígeno.

oxygen mask *n* máscara de oxígeno.

oxygen tent *n* tienda de oxígeno.

oyster ['ɔɪstə*] *n* ostra.

oz. *abbr* = **ounce(s)**.

ozone ['əuzəun] *n* ozono; **~ layer** capa de ozono.

P

P, p [pi:] *n* (*letter*) P, p *f*; **P for Peter** P de París.

P *abbr* = **president, prince**.

p *abbr* (= *page*) pág.; (*Brit*) = **penny, pence**.

PA *n abbr see* **personal assistant, public address system** ♦ *abbr* (*US POST*) = *Pennsylvania*.

pa [pɑ:] *n* (*col*) papá *m*.

p.a. *abbr* = **per annum**.

PAC *n abbr* (*US*) = *political action committee*.

pace [peɪs] *n* paso; (*rhythm*) ritmo ♦ *vi*: **to ~ up and down** pasearse de un lado a otro; **to keep ~ with** llevar el mismo paso que; (*events*) mantenerse a la altura de *or* al corriente de; **to set the ~** (*running*) marcar el paso; (*fig*) dar la pauta; **to put sb through his ~s** (*fig*) poner a uno a prueba.

pacemaker ['peɪsmeɪkə*] *n* (*MED*) regulador *m* cardíaco, marcapasos *m inv*.

pacific [pə'sɪfɪk] *a* pacífico ♦ *n*: **the P~ (Ocean)** el (Océano) Pacífico.

pacification [pæsɪfɪ'keɪʃən] *n* pacificación *f*.

pacifier ['pæsɪfaɪə*] *n* (*US: dummy*) chupete *m*.

pacifism ['pæsɪfɪzəm] *n* pacifismo.

pacifist ['pæsɪfɪst] *n* pacifista *m/f*.

pacify ['pæsɪfaɪ] *vt* (*soothe*) apaciguar; (*country*) pacificar.

pack [pæk] *n* (*packet*) paquete *m*; (*COMM*) embalaje *m*; (*of hounds*) jauría; (*of wolves*) manada; (*of thieves etc*) manada, bando; (*of cards*) baraja; (*bundle*) fardo; (*US: of cigarettes*) paquete *m*, cajetilla ♦ *vt* (*wrap*) empaquetar; (*fill*) llenar; (*in suitcase etc*) meter, poner; (*cram*) llenar, atestar; (*fig: meeting etc*) llenar de partidarios; (*COMPUT*) comprimir; **to ~ (one's bags)** hacer la maleta; **to ~ sb off** despachar a uno; **the place was ~ed** el local estaba lleno hasta el tope; **to send sb ~ing** (*col*) echar or despedir a uno.

pack in *vi* (*break down: watch, car*) estropearse ♦ *vt* (*col*) dejar; **~ it in!** ¡para!, ¡basta ya!

pack up *vi* (*col: machine*) estropearse; (*person*) irse ♦ *vt* (*belongings, clothes*) recoger; (*goods, presents*) empaquetar, envolver.

package ['pækɪdʒ] *n* paquete *m*; (*bulky*) bulto; (*also*: ~ **deal**) acuerdo global ♦ *vt* (*COMM: goods*) envasar, embalar.

package holiday *n* viaje *m* todo comprendido.

package tour *n* viaje *m* organizado.

packaging ['pækɪdʒɪŋ] *n* envase *m*.

packed lunch [pækt-] *n* almuerzo frío, merienda.

packer ['pækə*] *n* (*person*) empacador(a) *m/f*.

packet ['pækɪt] *n* paquete *m*.

packet switching [-'swɪtʃɪŋ] *n* (*COMPUT*) conmutación *f* por paquetes.

packhorse ['pækhɔ:s] *n* caballo de carga.

pack ice *n* banco de hielo.
packing ['pækɪŋ] *n* embalaje *m*.
packing case *n* cajón *m* de embalaje.
pact [pækt] *n* pacto.
pad [pæd] *n* (*of paper*) bloc *m*; (*cushion*) cojinete *m*; (*launching* ~) plataforma (de lanzamiento); (*col: flat*) casa ◆ *vt* rellenar.
padding ['pædɪŋ] *n* relleno; (*fig*) paja.
paddle ['pædl] *n* (*oar*) canalete *m*; (*US: for table tennis*) raqueta ◆ *vt* impulsar con canalete ◆ *vi* (*with feet*) chapotear.
paddle steamer *n* vapor *m* de ruedas.
paddling pool ['pædlɪŋ-] *n* (*Brit*) estanque *m* de juegos.
paddock ['pædək] *n* corral *m*.
paddy field ['pædɪ-] *n* arrozal *m*.
padlock ['pædlɔk] *n* candado ◆ *vt* cerrar con candado.
padre ['pɑːdrɪ] *n* capellán *m*.
paediatrics, (*US*) **pediatrics** [piːdɪ'ætrɪks] *n* pediatría.
pagan ['peɪgən] *a*, *n* pagano/a *m/f*.
page [peɪdʒ] *n* (*of book*) página; (*of newspaper*) plana; (*also:* ~ **boy**) paje *m* ◆ *vt* (*in hotel etc*) llamar por altavoz a.
pageant ['pædʒənt] *n* (*procession*) desfile *m*; (*show*) espectáculo.
pageantry ['pædʒəntrɪ] *n* pompa.
page break *n* límite *m* de la página.
pager ['peɪdʒə*] *n* localizador *m* personal.
paginate ['pædʒɪneɪt] *vt* paginar.
pagination [pædʒɪ'neɪʃən] *n* paginación *f*.
pagoda [pə'gəudə] *n* pagoda.
paid [peɪd] *pt*, *pp* *of* **pay** ◆ *a* (*work*) remunerado; (*official*) asalariado; **to put** ~ **to** (*Brit*) acabar con.
paid-up ['peɪdʌp], (*US*) **paid-in** ['peɪdɪn] *a* (*member*) con sus cuotas pagadas *or* al día; (*share*) liberado; ~ **capital** capital *m* desembolsado.
pail [peɪl] *n* cubo, balde *m*.
pain [peɪn] *n* dolor *m*; **to be in** ~ sufrir; **on** ~ **of death** so *or* bajo pena de muerte; *see also* **pains**.
pained [peɪnd] *a* (*expression*) afligido.
painful ['peɪnful] *a* doloroso; (*difficult*) penoso; (*disagreeable*) desagradable.
painfully ['peɪnfəlɪ] *ad* (*fig: very*) terriblemente.
painkiller ['peɪnkɪlə*] *n* analgésico.
painless ['peɪnlɪs] *a* que no causa dolor; (*method*) fácil.
pains [peɪnz] *npl* (*efforts*) esfuerzos *mpl*; **to take** ~ **to do sth** tomarse trabajo en hacer algo.
painstaking ['peɪnzteɪkɪŋ] *a* (*person*) concienzudo, esmerado.
paint [peɪnt] *n* pintura ◆ *vt* pintar; **a tin of** ~ una lata de pintura; **to** ~ **the door blue** pintar la puerta de azul.
paintbox ['peɪntbɔks] *n* caja de pinturas.
paintbrush ['peɪntbrʌʃ] *n* (*artist's*) pincel

m; (*decorator's*) brocha.
painter ['peɪntə*] *n* pintor(a) *m/f*.
painting ['peɪntɪŋ] *n* pintura.
paintwork ['peɪntwəːk] *n* pintura.
pair [peə*] *n* (*of shoes, gloves etc*) par *m*; (*of people*) pareja; **a** ~ **of scissors** unas tijeras; **a** ~ **of trousers** unos pantalones, un pantalón.
pair off *vi*: **to** ~ **off (with sb)** hacer pareja (con uno).
pajamas [pɪ'dʒɑːməz] *npl* (*US*) pijama *m*.
Pakistan [pɑːkɪ'stɑːn] *n* Paquistán *m*.
Pakistani [pɑːkɪ'stɑːnɪ] *a*, *n* paquistaní *m/f*.
PAL [pæl] *n* *abbr* (*TV*) = *phase alternation line*.
pal [pæl] *n* (*col*) compinche *m/f*, compañero/a.
palace ['pæləs] *n* palacio.
palatable ['pælɪtəbl] *a* sabroso; (*acceptable*) aceptable.
palate ['pælɪt] *n* paladar *m*.
palatial [pə'leɪʃəl] *a* (*surroundings, residence*) suntuoso, espléndido.
palaver [pə'lɑːvə*] *n* (*fuss*) lío.
pale [peɪl] *a* (*gen*) pálido; (*colour*) claro ◆ *n*: **to be beyond the** ~ pasarse de la raya ◆ *vi* palidecer; **to grow** *or* **turn** ~ palidecer; **to** ~ **into insignificance (beside)** no poderse comparar (con).
paleness ['peɪlnɪs] *n* palidez *f*.
Palestine ['pælɪstaɪn] *n* Palestina.
Palestinian [pælɪs'tɪnɪən] *a*, *n* palestino/a *m/f*.
palette ['pælɪt] *n* paleta.
paling ['peɪlɪŋ] *n* (*stake*) estaca; (*fence*) valla.
palisade [pælɪ'seɪd] *n* palizada.
pall [pɔːl] *n* (*of smoke*) capa (de humo) ◆ *vi* perder el sabor.
pallbearer ['pɔːlbɛərə*] *n* portador *m* del féretro.
pallet ['pælɪt] *n* (*for goods*) paleta.
palletization [pælɪtaɪ'zeɪʃən] *n* paletización *f*.
palliative ['pælɪətɪv] *n* paliativo.
pallid ['pælɪd] *a* pálido.
pallor ['pælə*] *n* palidez *f*.
pally ['pælɪ] *a* (*col*): **to be very** ~ **with sb** ser muy amigo de uno.
palm [pɑːm] *n* (*ANAT*) palma; (*also:* ~ **tree**) palmera, palma ◆ *vt*: **to** ~ **sth off on sb** (*Brit col*) encajar algo a uno.
palmist ['pɑːmɪst] *n* quiromántico/a, palmista *m/f*.
Palm Sunday *n* Domingo de Ramos.
palpable ['pælpəbl] *a* palpable.
palbably ['pælpəblɪ] *ad* obviamente.
palpitation [pælpɪ'teɪʃən] *n* palpitación *f*; **to have** ~**s** tener vahídos *or* palpitaciones.
paltry ['pɔːltrɪ] *a* (*amount etc*) miserable; (*insignificant: person*) insignificante.
pamper ['pæmpə*] *vt* mimar.
pamphlet ['pæmflət] *n* folleto; (*political:*

handed out in street) panfleto.

pan [pæn] *n* (*also*: **sauce**~) cacerola, cazuela, olla; (*also*: **frying** ~) sartén *m*; (*of lavatory*) taza ◆ *vi* (*CINEMA*) tomar panorámicas; **to** ~ **for gold** cribar oro.

pan- [pæn] *pref* pan-.

panacea [pænə'sɪə] *n* panacea.

panache [pə'næʃ] *n* bríos *mpl*, orgullo, brillantez *f*.

Panama ['pænəmɑː] *n* Panamá *m*.

Panama Canal *n* el Canal de Panamá.

pancake ['pænkeɪk] *n* crepe *f*.

Pancake Day *n* martes *m* de carnaval.

pancreas ['pæŋkrɪəs] *n* páncreas *m*.

panda ['pændə] *n* panda *m*.

panda car *n* (*Brit*) coche *m* de la policía.

pandemonium [pændɪ'məunɪəm] *n* (*noise*): **there was** ~ se armó un tremendo jaleo; (*mess*) caos *m*.

pander ['pændə*] *vi*: **to** ~ **to** complacer a.

pane [peɪn] *n* cristal *m*.

panel ['pænl] *n* (*of wood*) panel *m*; (*of cloth*) paño; (*RADIO, TV*) panel *m* de invitados.

panel game *n* (*TV*) programa *m* concurso para equipos.

panelling, (*US*) **paneling** ['pænəlɪŋ] *n* paneles *mpl*.

panellist, (*US*) **panelist** ['pænəlɪst] *n* miembro del jurado.

pang [pæŋ] *n*: ~**s of conscience** remordimiento *sg*; ~**s of hunger** dolores *mpl* del hambre.

panic ['pænɪk] *n* (terror *m*) pánico ◆ *vi* dejarse llevar por el pánico.

panicky ['pænɪkɪ] *a* (*person*) asustadizo.

panic-stricken ['pænɪkstrɪkən] *a* preso de pánico.

pannier ['pænɪə*] *n* (*on bicycle*) cartera; (*on mule etc*) alforja.

panorama [pænə'rɑːmə] *n* panorama *m*.

panoramic [pænə'ræmɪk] *a* panorámico.

pansy ['pænzɪ] *n* (*BOT*) pensamiento; (*col*: *pej*) maricón *m*.

pant [pænt] *vi* jadear.

panther ['pænθə*] *n* pantera.

panties ['pæntɪz] *npl* bragas *fpl*, pantis *mpl*.

pantihose ['pæntɪhəuz] *n* (*US*) pantimedias *fpl*.

pantomime ['pæntəmaɪm] *n* (*Brit*) representación *f* musical navideña.

pantry ['pæntrɪ] *n* despensa.

pants [pænts] *n* (*Brit*: *underwear*: *woman's*) bragas *fpl*; (: *man's*) calzoncillos *mpl*; (*US*: *trousers*) pantalones *mpl*.

pantsuit ['pæntsjuːt] *n* (*US*) traje *m* de chaqueta y pantalón.

papal ['peɪpəl] *a* papal.

paper ['peɪpə*] *n* papel *m*; (*also*: **news**~) periódico, diario; (*study, article*) artículo; (*exam*) examen *m* ◆ *a* de papel ◆ *vt* empapelar; (**identity**) ~**s** *npl* papeles *mpl*, documentos *mpl*; **a piece of** ~ (*odd bit*) un

pedazo de papel (suelto); (*sheet*) una hoja de papel; **to put sth down on** ~ poner algo por escrito.

paper advance *n* (*on printer*) avance *m* de papel.

paperback ['peɪpəbæk] *n* libro de bolsillo.

paper bag *n* bolsa de papel.

paperboy ['peɪpəbɔɪ] *n* (*selling*) vendedor *m* de periódicos; (*delivering*) repartidor *m* de periódicos.

paper clip *n* clip *m*.

paper hankie *n* pañuelo de papel.

paper money *n* papel *m* moneda.

paper profit *n* beneficio no realizado.

paperweight ['peɪpəweɪt] *n* pisapapeles *m inv*.

paperwork ['peɪpəwɔːk] *n* trabajo administrativo; (*pej*) papeleo.

papier-mâché ['pæpɪeɪ'mæʃeɪ] *n* cartón *m* piedra.

paprika ['pæprɪkə] *n* pimienta húngara *or* roja.

Pap test ['pæp-] *n* (*MED*) frotis *m* (cervical).

papyrus [pə'paɪərəs] *n* papiro.

par [pɑː*] *n* par *f*; (*GOLF*) par *m* ◆ *a* a la par; **to be on a** ~ **with** estar a la par con; **at** ~ a la par; **to be above/below** ~ estar sobre/bajo la par; **to feel under** ~ sentirse en baja forma.

parable ['pærəbl] *n* parábola.

parachute ['pærəʃuːt] *n* paracaídas *m inv* ◆ *vi* lanzarse en paracaídas.

parachutist ['pærəʃuːtɪst] *n* paracaidista *m/f*.

parade [pə'reɪd] *n* desfile *m* ◆ *vt* (*gen*) recorrer, desfilar por; (*show off*) hacer alarde de ◆ *vi* desfilar; (*MIL*) pasar revista; **a fashion** ~ un desfile de modelos.

parade ground *n* plaza de armas.

paradise ['pærədaɪs] *n* paraíso.

paradox ['pærədɒks] *n* paradoja.

paradoxical [pærə'dɒksɪkl] *a* paradójico.

paradoxically [pærə'dɒksɪklɪ] *ad* paradójicamente.

paraffin ['pærəfɪn] *n* (*Brit*): ~ (**oil**) parafina.

paraffin heater *n* estufa de parafina.

paraffin lamp *n* quinqué *m*.

paragon ['pærəgən] *n* modelo.

paragraph ['pærəgrɑːf] *n* párrafo; **to begin a new** ~ empezar un nuevo párrafo.

Paraguay ['pærəgwaɪ] *n* Paraguay *m*.

Paraguayan [pærə'gwaɪən] *a, n* paraguayo/a *m/f*, paraguayano/a *m/f*.

parallel ['pærəlel] *a*: ~ (**with/to**) en paralelo (con/a); (*fig*) semejante (a) ◆ *n* (*line*) paralela; (*fig, GEO*) paralelo.

paralysis [pə'rælɪsɪs] *n* parálisis *f inv*.

paralytic [pærə'lɪtɪk] *a* paralítico.

paralyze ['pærəlaɪz] *vt* paralizar.

paramedic [pærə'medɪk] *n* (*US*) ambulanciero/a.

parameter [pə'ræmɪtə*] n parámetro.
paramilitary [pærə'mɪlɪtərɪ] a (organization, operations) paramilitar.
paramount ['pærəmaunt] a: **of ~ importance** de suma importancia.
paranoia [pærə'nɔɪə] n paranoia.
paranoid ['pærənɔɪd] a (person, feeling) paranoico.
paranormal [pærə'nɔːml] a paranormal.
parapet ['pærəpɪt] n parapeto.
paraphernalia [pærəfə'neɪlɪə] n (gear) avíos mpl.
paraphrase ['pærəfreɪz] vt parafrasear.
paraplegic [pærə'pliːdʒɪk] n parapléjico/a.
parapsychology [pærəsaɪ'kɔlədʒɪ] n parasicología.
parasite ['pærəsaɪt] n parásito/a.
parasol ['pærəsɔl] n sombrilla, quitasol m.
paratrooper ['pærətruːpə*] n paracaidista m/f.
parcel ['pɑːsl] n paquete m ♦ vt (also: ~ up) empaquetar, embalar; **to be part and ~ of** ser íntegro a.
parcel out vt parcelar, repartir.
parcel bomb n paquete m bomba.
parcel post n servicio de paquetes postales.
parch [pɑːtʃ] vt secar, resecar.
parched [pɑːtʃt] a (person) muerto de sed.
parchment ['pɑːtʃmənt] n pergamino.
pardon ['pɑːdn] n perdón m; (LAW) indulto ♦ vt perdonar; indultar; **~ me!, I beg your ~!** ¡perdone usted!; **(I beg your) ~?**, (US) **~ me?** ¿cómo?
pare [pɛə*] vt (nails) cortar; (fruit etc) pelar.
parent ['pɛərənt] n: **~s** npl padres mpl.
parentage ['pɛərəntɪdʒ] n familia, linaje m; **of unknown ~** de padres desconocidos.
parental [pə'rɛntl] a paternal/maternal.
parent company n casa matriz.
parenthesis, pl **parentheses** [pə'rɛnθɪsɪs, -θɪsiːz] n paréntesis m inv; **in parentheses** entre paréntesis.
parenthood ['pɛərənthud] n el ser padre o madre.
parent ship n buque m nodriza.
Paris ['pærɪs] n París m.
parish ['pærɪʃ] n parroquia.
parish council n concejo parroquial.
parishioner [pə'rɪʃənə*] n feligrés/esa m/f.
Parisian [pə'rɪzɪən] a, n parisino/a m/f, parisiense m/f.
parity ['pærɪtɪ] n paridad f, igualdad f.
park [pɑːk] n parque m, jardín m público ♦ vt aparcar, estacionar ♦ vi aparcar, estacionarse.
parka ['pɑːkə] n chaquetón acolchado con capucha.
parking ['pɑːkɪŋ] n aparcamiento, estacionamiento; **"no ~"** "prohibido aparcar or estacionarse".
parking lights npl luces fpl de estaciona-

miento.
parking lot n (US) parking m, aparcamiento.
parking meter n parquímetro.
parking offence, (US) **parking violation** n ofensa por aparcamiento indebido.
parking place n sitio para aparcar, aparcamiento.
parking ticket n multa de aparcamiento.
parkway ['pɑːkweɪ] n (US) alameda.
parlance ['pɑːləns] n lenguaje m; **in common/modern ~** en lenguaje corriente/moderno.
parliament ['pɑːləmənt] n parlamento; (Spanish) Cortes fpl.
parliamentary [pɑːlə'mɛntərɪ] a parlamentario.
parlour, (US) **parlor** ['pɑːlə*] n sala de recibo, salón m, living (LAm).
parlous ['pɑːləs] a peligroso, alarmante.
Parmesan [pɑːmɪ'zæn] n (also: ~ **cheese**) queso parmesano.
parochial [pə'rəukɪəl] a parroquial; (pej) de miras estrechas.
parody ['pærədɪ] n parodia ♦ vt parodiar.
parole [pə'rəul] n: **on ~** libre bajo palabra.
paroxysm ['pærəksɪzəm] n (MED) paroxismo, ataque m; (of anger, laughter, coughing) ataque m; (of grief) crisis f.
parquet ['pɑːkeɪ] n: **~ floor(ing)** parquet m.
parrot ['pærət] n loro, papagayo.
parrot fashion ad mecánicamente.
parry ['pærɪ] vt parar.
parsimonious [pɑːsɪ'məunɪəs] a tacaño.
parsley ['pɑːslɪ] n perejil m.
parsnip ['pɑːsnɪp] n chirivía.
parson ['pɑːsn] n cura m.
part [pɑːt] n (gen, MUS) parte f; (bit) trozo; (of machine) pieza; (THEATRE etc) papel m; (of serial) entrega; (US: in hair) raya ♦ ad = **partly** ♦ vt separar; (break) partir ♦ vi (people) separarse; (roads) bifurcarse; (crowd) apartarse; (break) romperse; **to take ~ in** participar or tomar parte en; **to take sb's ~** defender a uno; **for my ~** por mi parte; **for the most ~** en su mayor parte; (people) en su mayoría; **for the better ~ of the day** durante la mayor parte del día; **~ of speech** (LING) parte f de la oración; **to take sth in good/bad ~** aceptar algo bien/tomarse algo a mal.
part with vt fus ceder, entregar; (money) pagar; (get rid of) deshacerse de.
partake [pɑː'teɪk] vi (irg: like **take**) (formal): **to ~ of sth** tomar algo.
part exchange n (Brit): **in ~** como parte del pago.
partial ['pɑːʃl] a parcial; **to be ~ to** ser aficionado a.
partially ['pɑːʃlɪ] ad en parte, parcialmente.

participant [pɑː'tısıpənt] n (in competition) concursante m/f.

participate [pɑː'tısıpeıt] vi: **to ~ in** participar en.

participation [pɑːtısı'peıʃən] n participación f.

participle ['pɑːtısıpl] n participio.

particle ['pɑːtıkl] n partícula; (of dust) grano; (fig) pizca.

particular [pə'tıkjulə*] a (special) particular; (concrete) concreto; (given) determinado; (detailed) detallado, minucioso; (fussy) quisquilloso, exigente; **~s** npl (information) datos mpl, detalles mpl; (details) pormenores mpl; **in ~** en particular; **to be very ~ about** ser muy exigente en cuanto a; **I'm not ~** me es or da igual.

particularly [pə'tıkjuləlı] ad especialmente, en particular.

parting ['pɑːtıŋ] n (act of) separación f; (farewell) despedida; (Brit: in hair) raya ♦ a de despedida; **~ shot** (fig) golpe m final.

partisan [pɑːtı'zæn] a, n partidario/a m/f.

partition [pɑː'tıʃən] n (POL) división f; (wall) tabique m ♦ vt dividir; dividir con tabique.

partly ['pɑːtlı] ad en parte.

partner ['pɑːtnə*] n (COMM) socio/a; (SPORT, at dance) pareja; (spouse) cónyuge m/f; (friend etc) compañero/a ♦ vt acompañar.

partnership ['pɑːtnəʃıp] n (gen) asociación f; (COMM) sociedad f; **to go into ~ (with), form a ~ (with)** asociarse (con).

part payment n pago parcial, abono.

partridge ['pɑːtrıdʒ] n perdiz f.

part-time ['pɑːt'taım] a, ad a tiempo parcial.

part-timer [pɑːt'taımə*] n trabajador(a) m/f a tiempo partido.

party ['pɑːtı] n (POL) partido; (celebration) fiesta; (group) grupo; (LAW) parte f, interesado ♦ a (POL) de partido; (dress etc) de fiesta, de gala; **to have or give or throw a ~** organizar una fiesta; **dinner ~** cena; **to be a ~ to a crime** ser cómplice m/f de un crimen.

party line n (POL) línea política del partido; (TEL) línea compartida.

par value n (of share, bond) valor m a la par.

pass [pɑːs] vt (time, object) pasar; (place) pasar por; (exam, law) aprobar; (overtake, surpass) rebasar; (approve) aprobar ♦ vi pasar; (SCOL) aprobar, ser aprobado ♦ n (permit) permiso; (membership card) carnet m; (in mountains) puerto, desfiladero; (SPORT) pase m; (SCOL: also: **~ mark**): **to get a ~** in aprobar en; **to ~ sth through sth** pasar algo por algo; **to ~ the time of day with sb** pasar el rato con uno; **things have come to a pretty ~!** ¡hasta dónde habremos or hemos llegado!; **to**

make a ~ at sb (col) hacer proposiciones a uno.

pass away vi fallecer.

pass by vi pasar ♦ vt (ignore) pasar por alto.

pass down vt (customs, inheritance) pasar, transmitir.

pass for vt fus pasar por; **she could ~ for twenty-five** se podría creer que sólo tiene 25 años.

pass on vi (die) fallecer, morir ♦ vt (hand on): **to ~ on (to)** transmitir (a); (cold, illness) pegar (a); (benefits) dar (a); (price rises) pasar (a).

pass out vi desmayarse; (MIL) graduarse.

pass over vi (die) fallecer ♦ vt omitir, pasar por alto.

pass up vt (opportunity) dejar pasar, no aprovechar.

passable ['pɑːsəbl] a (road) transitable; (tolerable) pasable.

passably [pɑːsəblı] ad pasablemente (bien).

passage ['pæsıdʒ] n pasillo; (act of passing) tránsito; (fare, in book) pasaje m; (by boat) travesía.

passageway ['pæsıdʒweı] n (in house) pasillo, corredor m; (between buildings etc) pasaje m, pasadizo.

passbook ['pɑːsbuk] n libreta de banco.

passenger ['pæsındʒə*] n pasajero/a, viajero/a.

passer-by [pɑːsə'baı] n transeúnte m/f.

passing ['pɑːsıŋ] a (fleeting) pasajero; **in ~** de paso.

passing place n (AUT) apartadero.

passion ['pæʃən] n pasión f.

passionate ['pæʃənıt] a apasionado.

passionately ['pæʃənıtlı] ad apasionadamente, con pasión.

passive ['pæsıv] a (also LING) pasivo.

passkey ['pɑːskiː] n llave f maestra.

Passover ['pɑːsəuvə*] n Pascua (de los judíos).

passport ['pɑːspɔːt] n pasaporte m.

passport control n control m de pasaporte.

password ['pɑːswəːd] n (also COMPUT) contraseña.

past [pɑːst] prep (further than) más allá de; (later than) después de ♦ a pasado; (president etc) antiguo ♦ n (time) pasado; (of person) antecedentes mpl; **quarter/half ~ four** las cuatro y cuarto/media; **he's ~ forty** tiene más de cuarenta años; **I'm ~ caring** ya no me importa; **to be ~ it** (col: person) ser acabado; **for the ~ few/3 days** durante los últimos días/últimos 3 días; **to run ~** pasar a la carrera por; **in the ~** en el pasado, antes.

pasta ['pæstə] n pasta.

paste [peıst] n (gen) pasta; (glue) engrudo ♦ vt (stick); (glue) engomar;

tomato ~ puré *m* de tomate.
pastel ['pæstl] *a* pastel; *(painting)* al pastel.
pasteurized ['pæstəraızd] *a* pasteurizado.
pastille ['pæstl] *n* pastilla.
pastime ['pɑːstaɪm] *n* pasatiempo.
past master *n*: **to be a ~ at** ser un maestro en.
pastor ['pɑːstə*] *n* pastor *m*.
pastoral ['pɑːstərl] *a* pastoral.
pastry ['peɪstrɪ] *n (dough)* pasta; *(cake)* pastel *m*.
pasture ['pɑːstʃə*] *n (grass)* pasto.
pasty *n* ['pæstɪ] empanada ♦ *a* ['peɪstɪ] pastoso; *(complexion)* pálido.
pat [pæt] *vt* dar una palmadita a; *(dog etc)* acariciar ♦ *n (of butter)* porción *f* ♦ *a*: **he knows it (off)** ~ se lo sabe de memoria *or* al dedillo; **to give sb/o.s. a ~ on the back** *(fig)* felicitar a uno/felicitarse.
patch [pætʃ] *n (of material)* parche *m*; *(mended part)* remiendo; *(of land)* terreno; *(COMPUT)* ajuste *m* ♦ *vt (clothes)* remendar; **(to go through) a bad ~** (pasar por) una mala racha.
patch up *vt (mend temporarily)* reparar; **to ~ up a quarrel** hacer las paces.
patchwork ['pætʃwəːk] *n* labor *f* de retazos.
patchy ['pætʃɪ] *a* desigual.
pate [peɪt] *n*: **bald ~** calva.
pâté ['pæteɪ] *n* paté *m*.
patent ['peɪtnt] *n* patente *f* ♦ *vt* patentar ♦ *a* patente, evidente.
patent leather *n* charol *m*.
patently ['peɪtntlɪ] *ad* evidentemente.
patent medicine *n* medicina de patente.
patent office *n* oficina de patentes y marcas.
patent rights *npl* derechos *mpl* de patente.
paternal [pə'təːnl] *a* paternal; *(relation)* paterno.
paternalistic [pətəːnə'lɪstɪk] *a* paternalista.
paternity [pə'təːnɪtɪ] *n* paternidad *f*.
paternity suit *n (LAW)* caso de paternidad.
path [pɑːθ] *n* camino, sendero; *(trail, track)* pista; *(of missile)* trayectoria.
pathetic [pə'θetɪk] *a (pitiful)* patético, lastimoso; *(very bad)* malísimo; *(moving)* conmovedor(a).
pathetically [pə'θetɪklɪ] *ad* patéticamente; *(very badly)* malísimamente mal.
pathological [pæθə'lɔdʒɪkəl] *a* patológico.
pathologist [pə'θɔlədʒɪst] *n* patólogo/a.
pathology [pə'θɔlədʒɪ] *n* patología.
pathos ['peɪθɔs] *n* patetismo.
pathway ['pɑːθweɪ] *n* sendero, vereda.
patience ['peɪʃns] *n* paciencia; *(Brit CARDS)* solitario; **to lose one's ~** perder la paciencia.
patient ['peɪʃnt] *n* paciente *m/f* ♦ *a* paciente, sufrido; **to be ~ with sb** tener paciencia con uno.

patiently ['peɪʃəntlɪ] *ad* pacientemente, con paciencia.
patio ['pætɪəu] *n* patio.
patriot ['peɪtrɪət] *n* patriota *m/f*.
patriotic [pætrɪ'ɔtɪk] *a* patriótico.
patriotism ['pætrɪətɪzəm] *n* patriotismo.
patrol [pə'trəul] *n* patrulla ♦ *vt* patrullar por; **to be on ~** patrullar, estar de patrulla.
patrol boat *n* patrullero, patrullera.
patrol car *n* coche *m* patrulla.
patrolman [pə'trəulmən] *n (US)* policía *m*.
patron ['peɪtrən] *n (in shop)* cliente *m/f*; *(of charity)* patrocinador(a) *m/f*; **~ of the arts** mecenas *m*.
patronage ['pætrənɪdʒ] *n* patrocinio, protección *f*.
patronize ['pætrənaɪz] *vt (shop)* ser cliente de; *(look down on)* condescender con.
patronizing ['pætrənaɪzɪŋ] *a* condescendiente.
patron saint *n* santo/a patrono/a.
patter ['pætə*] *n* golpeteo; *(sales talk)* labia ♦ *vi (rain)* tamborilear.
pattern ['pætən] *n (SEWING)* patrón *m*; *(design)* dibujo; *(behaviour, events)* esquema; **~ of events** curso de los hechos; **behaviour ~s** modelos *mpl* de comportamiento.
patterned ['pætənd] *a (material)* con diseño *or* dibujo.
paucity ['pɔːsɪtɪ] *n* escasez *f*.
paunch [pɔːntʃ] *n* panza, barriga.
pauper ['pɔːpə*] *n* pobre *m/f*.
pause [pɔːz] *n* pausa; *(interval)* intervalo ♦ *vi* hacer una pausa; **to ~ for breath** detenerse para tomar aliento.
pave [peɪv] *vt* pavimentar; **to ~ the way for** preparar el terreno para.
pavement ['peɪvmənt] *n (Brit)* acera, vereda *(LAm)*; *(US)* calzada, pavimento.
pavilion [pə'vɪlɪən] *n* pabellón *m*; *(SPORT)* vestuarios *mpl*.
paving ['peɪvɪŋ] *n* pavimento, enlosado.
paving stone *n* losa.
paw [pɔː] *n* pata; *(claw)* garra ♦ *vt (animal)* tocar con la pata; *(pej: touch)* tocar, manosear.
pawn [pɔːn] *n (CHESS)* peón *m*; *(fig)* instrumento ♦ *vt* empeñar.
pawnbroker ['pɔːnbrəukə*] *n* prestamista *m/f*.
pawnshop ['pɔːnʃɔp] *n* monte *m* de piedad.
pay [peɪ] *n* paga; *(wage etc)* sueldo, salario ♦ *(vb: pt, pp paid)* *vt* pagar; *(visit)* hacer; *(respect)* ofrecer ♦ *vi* pagar; *(be profitable)* rendir, compensar, ser rentable; **to be in sb's ~** estar al servicio de uno; **to ~ attention (to)** prestar atención (a); **I paid £5 for that record** pagué 5 libras por ese disco; **how much did you ~ for it?** ¿cuánto pagaste por él?; **to ~ one's way** *(contribute one's share)* pagar su parte;

(*remain solvent: company*) ser solvente; **to ~ dividends** (*COMM*) pagar dividendos; (*fig*) compensar; **it won't ~ you to do that** no te merece la pena hacer eso; **to put paid to** (*plan, person*) acabar con.

pay back *vt* (*money*) reembolsar; (*person*) pagar.

pay for *vt fus* pagar.

pay in *vt* ingresar.

pay off *vt* liquidar; (*person*) pagar; (*debts*) liquidar, saldar; (*creditor*) cancelar, redimir; (*workers*) despedir; (*mortgage*) cancelar, redimir ◆ *vi* (*scheme, decision*) dar resultado; **to ~ sth off in instalments** pagar algo a plazos.

pay out *vt* (*rope*) ir dando; (*money*) gastar, desembolsar.

pay up *vt* pagar (de mala gana).

payable ['peɪəbl] *a* pagadero; **to make a cheque ~ to sb** extender un cheque a favor de uno.

pay day *n* día *m* de paga.

PAYE *n abbr* (*Brit*: = *pay as you earn*) sistema de contribuciones personales.

payee [peɪ'iː] *n* portador(a) *m/f*.

pay envelope *n* (*US*) = **pay packet**.

paying ['peɪɪŋ] *a*: **~ guest** huésped(a) *m/f* que paga.

payload ['peɪləud] *n* carga útil.

payment ['peɪmənt] *n* pago; **advance ~** (*part sum*) anticipo, adelanto; (*total sum*) saldo; **monthly ~** mensualidad *f*; **deferred ~, ~ by instalments** pago a plazos *or* diferido; **on ~ of £5** mediante pago de *or* pagando £5; **in ~ for** (*goods, sum owed*) en pago de.

pay packet *n* (*Brit*) sobre *m* (de paga).

pay-phone ['peɪfəun] *n* teléfono público.

payroll ['peɪrəul] *n* nómina; **to be on a firm's ~** estar en la nómina de una compañía.

pay slip *n* recibo de sueldo.

pay station *n* (*US*) teléfono público.

PBS *n abbr* (*US*: = *Public Broadcasting System*) agrupación de ayuda a la realización de emisiones para la TV pública.

PC *n abbr see* **personal computer**; (*Brit*) = **police constable** ◆ *abbr* (*Brit*) = **Privy Councillor**.

pc *abbr* = **per cent, postcard**.

p/c *abbr* = **petty cash**.

PCB *n abbr see* **printed circuit board**.

PD *n abbr* (*US*) = **police department**.

pd *abbr* = **paid**.

PDSA *n abbr* (*Brit*) = *People's Dispensary for Sick Animals*.

PDT *n abbr* (*US*: = *Pacific Daylight Time*) hora de verano del Pacífico.

PE *n abbr* (= *physical education*) ed. física ◆ *abbr* (*Canada*) = *Prince Edward Island*.

pea [piː] *n* guisante *m*, chícharo (*LAm*), arveja (*LAm*).

peace [piːs] *n* paz *f*; (*calm*) paz *f*, tranquili-

dad *f*; **to be at ~ with sb/sth** estar en paz con uno/algo; **to keep the ~** (*policeman*) mantener el orden; (*citizen*) guardar el orden.

peaceable ['piːsəbl] *a* pacífico.

peaceably ['piːsəblɪ] *ad* pacíficamente.

peaceful ['piːsful] *a* (*gentle*) pacífico; (*calm*) tranquilo, sosegado.

peace-keeping ['piːskiːpɪŋ] *a* de pacificación.

peace offering *n* (*fig*) prenda de paz.

peacetime ['piːstaɪm] *n*: **in ~** en tiempo de paz.

peach [piːtʃ] *n* melocotón *m*, durazno (*LAm*).

peacock ['piːkɔk] *n* pavo real.

peak [piːk] *n* (*of mountain: top*) cumbre *f*, cima; (: *point*) pico; (*of cap*) visera; (*fig*) cumbre *f*.

peak-hour ['piːkauə*] *a* (*traffic etc*) de horas punta.

peak hours *npl*, **peak period** *n* horas *fpl* punta.

peaky ['piːkɪ] *a* (*Brit col*) pálido, paliducho; **I'm feeling a bit ~** me encuentro malucho, no me encuentro bien.

peal [piːl] *n* (*of bells*) repique *m*; **~ of laughter** carcajada.

peanut ['piːnʌt] *n* cacahuete *m*, maní *m* (*LAm*).

peanut butter *n* manteca de cacahuete.

pear [pɛə*] *n* pera.

pearl [pəːl] *n* perla.

peasant ['pɛznt] *n* campesino/a.

peat [piːt] *n* turba.

pebble ['pɛbl] *n* guijarro.

peck [pɛk] *vt* (*also*: **~ at**) picotear; (*food*) comer sin ganas ◆ *n* picotazo; (*kiss*) besito.

pecking order ['pɛkɪŋ-] *n* orden *m* de jerarquía.

peckish ['pɛkɪʃ] *a* (*Brit col*): **I feel ~** tengo ganas de picar algo.

peculiar [pɪ'kjuːlɪə*] *a* (*odd*) extraño, raro; (*typical*) propio, característico; (*particular: importance, qualities*) particular; **~ to** propio de.

peculiarity [pɪkjuːlɪ'ærɪtɪ] *n* peculiaridad *f*, característica.

peculiarly [pɪ'kjuːlɪəlɪ] *ad* extrañamente; particularmente.

pedal ['pɛdl] *n* pedal *m* ◆ *vi* pedalear.

pedal bin *n* cubo de la basura con pedal.

pedant ['pɛdənt] *n* pedante *m/f*.

pedantic [pɪ'dæntɪk] *a* pedante.

pedantry ['pɛdəntrɪ] *n* pedantería.

peddle ['pɛdl] *vt* (*goods*) ir vendiendo *or* vender de puerta en puerta; (*drugs*) traficar; (*gossip*) divulgar.

peddler ['pɛdlə*] *n* vendedor(a) *m/f* ambulante.

pedestal ['pɛdəstl] *n* pedestal *m*.

pedestrian [pɪ'dɛstrɪən] *n* peatón/ona *m/f* ◆

a pedestre.

pedestrian crossing *n* (*Brit*) paso de peatones.

pedestrian precinct *n* zona reservada para peatones.

pediatrics [piːdɪ'ætrɪks] *n* (*US*) = **paediatrics**.

pedigree ['pɛdɪɡriː] *n* genealogía; (*of animal*) raza ♦ *cpd* (*animal*) de raza, de casta.

pedlar ['pɛdlə*] *n* (*Brit*) = **peddler**.

pee [piː] *vi* (*col*) mear.

peek [piːk] *vi* mirar a hurtadillas; (*COMPUT*) inspeccionar.

peel [piːl] *n* piel *f*; (*of orange, lemon*) cáscara; (: *removed*) peladuras *fpl* ♦ *vt* pelar ♦ *vi* (*paint etc*) descoвcharse; (*wallpaper*) despegarse, desprenderse.
 peel back *vt* pelar.

peeler ['piːlə*] *n*: **potato ~** mondador *m or* pelador *m* de patatas, pelapatatas *m inv*.

peep [piːp] *n* (*Brit: look*) mirada furtiva; (*sound*) pío ♦ *vi* (*Brit*) piar.
 peep out *vi* asomar la cabeza.

peephole ['piːphəul] *n* mirilla.

peer [pɪə*] *vi*: **to ~ at** escudriñar ♦ *n* (*noble*) par *m*; (*equal*) igual *m*.

peerage ['pɪərɪdʒ] *n* nobleza.

peerless ['pɪəlɪs] *a* sin par, incomparable, sin igual.

peeved [piːvd] *a* enojado.

peevish ['piːvɪʃ] *a* malhumorado.

peevishness ['piːvɪʃnɪs] *n* mal humor *m*.

peg [pɛɡ] *n* clavija; (*for coat etc*) gancho, colgadero; (*Brit: also*: **clothes ~**) pinza; (*tent ~*) estaca ♦ *vt* (*clothes*) tender; (*groundsheet*) enclavijar, fijar con estacas; (*fig: wages, prices*) fijar.

pejorative [pɪ'dʒɔrətɪv] *a* peyorativo.

Pekin [piː'kɪn], **Peking** [piː'kɪŋ] *n* Pekín *m*.

pekinese [piːkɪ'niːz] *n* pequinés/esa *m/f*.

pelican ['pɛlɪkən] *n* pelícano.

pelican crossing *n* (*Brit AUT*) paso de peatones señalizado.

pellet ['pɛlɪt] *n* bolita; (*bullet*) perdigón *m*.

pell-mell ['pɛl'mɛl] *ad* en tropel.

pelmet ['pɛlmɪt] *n* galería.

pelt [pɛlt] *vt*: **to ~ sb with sth** arrojarle algo a uno ♦ *vi* (*rain: also*: **~ down**) llover a cántaros ♦ *n* pellejo.

pelvis ['pɛlvɪs] *n* pelvis *f*.

pen [pɛn] *n* pluma; (*for sheep*) redil *m*; (*US col: prison*) cárcel *f*, chirona; **to put ~ to paper** tomar la pluma.

penal ['piːnl] *a* penal; **~ servitude** trabajos *mpl* forzados.

penalize ['piːnəlaɪz] *vt* (*punish: SPORT*) castigar.

penalty ['pɛnltɪ] *n* (*gen*) pena; (*fine*) multa; (*SPORT*) castigo; **~ (kick)** (*FOOTBALL*) penalty *m*.

penalty area *n* (*Brit SPORT*) área de castigo.

penalty clause *n* cláusula penal.

penance ['pɛnəns] *n* penitencia.

pence [pɛns] *pl of* **penny**.

penchant ['pãːʃãːŋ] *n* predilección *f*, inclinación *f*.

pencil ['pɛnsl] *n* lápiz *m*, lapicero (*LAm*) ♦ *vt* (*also*: **~ in**) escribir con lápiz.

pencil case *n* estuche *m*.

pencil sharpener *n* sacapuntas *m inv*.

pendant ['pɛndnt] *n* pendiente *m*.

pending ['pɛndɪŋ] *prep* antes de ♦ *a* pendiente; **~ the arrival of** ... hasta que llegue ..., hasta llegar ... .

pendulum ['pɛndjuləm] *n* péndulo.

penetrate ['pɛnɪtreɪt] *vt* penetrar.

penetrating ['pɛnɪtreɪtɪŋ] *a* penetrante.

penetration [pɛnɪ'treɪʃən] *n* penetración *f*.

penfriend ['pɛnfrɛnd] *n* (*Brit*) amigo/a por correspondencia.

penguin ['pɛŋgwɪn] *n* pingüino.

penicillin [pɛnɪ'sɪlɪn] *n* penicilina.

peninsula [pə'nɪnsjulə] *n* península.

penis ['piːnɪs] *n* pene *m*.

penitence ['pɛnɪtns] *n* penitencia.

penitent ['pɛnɪtnt] *a* arrepentido; (*REL*) penitente.

penitentiary [pɛnɪ'tɛnʃərɪ] *n* (*US*) cárcel *f*, presidio.

penknife ['pɛnnaɪf] *n* navaja.

pen name *n* seudónimo.

pennant ['pɛnənt] *n* banderola; banderín *m*.

penniless ['pɛnɪlɪs] *a* sin dinero.

Pennines ['pɛnaɪnz] *npl* (Montes *mpl*) Peninos *mpl*.

penny, *pl* **pennies** *or* (*Brit*) **pence** ['pɛnɪ, 'pɛnɪz, pɛns] *n* penique *m*; (*US*) centavo.

penpal ['pɛnpæl] *n* amigo/a por correspondencia.

pension ['pɛnʃən] *n* (*allowance, state payment*) pensión *f*; (*old-age*) jubilación *f*.

pension off *vt* jubilar.

pensioner ['pɛnʃənə*] *n* (*Brit*) jubilado/a.

pension fund *n* fondo de pensiones.

pensive ['pɛnsɪv] *a* pensativo; (*withdrawn*) preocupado.

pentagon ['pɛntəgən] *n* pentágono.

Pentecost ['pɛntɪkɔst] *n* Pentecostés *m*.

penthouse ['pɛnthaus] *n* ático de lujo.

pent-up ['pɛntʌp] *a* (*feelings*) reprimido.

penultimate [pɛ'nʌltɪmət] *a* penúltimo.

penury ['pɛnjurɪ] *n* miseria, pobreza.

people ['piːpl] *npl* gente *f*; (*citizens*) pueblo *sg*, ciudadanos *mpl* ♦ *n* (*nation, race*) pueblo, nación *f* ♦ *vt* poblar; **several ~ came** vinieron varias personas; **~ say that...** dice la gente que...; **old/young ~** los ancianos/jóvenes; **~ at large** la gente en general; **a man of the ~** un hombre del pueblo.

pep [pɛp] *n* (*col*) energía.
 pep up *vt* animar.

pepper ['pɛpə*] *n* (*spice*) pimienta; (*vegetable*) pimiento ♦ *vt* (*fig*) salpicar.

peppermint ['pepəmint] n menta; (sweet) pastilla de menta.

pepperpot ['pepəpɔt] n pimentero.

peptalk ['peptɔːk] n (col): **to give sb a ~** darle a uno una inyección de ánimo.

per [pəː*] prep por; **~ day/person** por día/persona; **as ~ your instructions** de acuerdo con sus instrucciones.

per annum ad al año.

per capita a, ad per capita.

perceive [pə'siːv] vt percibir; (realize) darse cuenta de.

per cent, (US) **percent** [pə'sent] n por ciento; **a 20 ~ discount** un descuento de 20 por ciento.

percentage [pə'sentidʒ] n porcentaje m; **to get a ~ on all sales** percibir un tanto por ciento sobre todas las ventas; **on a ~ basis** sobre una base de porcentaje.

perception [pə'sepʃən] n percepción f; (insight) perspicacia.

perceptible [pə'septəbl] a perceptible; (notable) sensible.

perceptive [pə'septiv] a perspicaz.

perch [pəːtʃ] n (fish) perca; (for bird) percha ◆ vi posarse.

percolate ['pəːkəleit] vt (coffee) filtrar, colar ◆ vi (coffee, fig) filtrarse, colarse.

percolator ['pəːkəleitə*] n cafetera de filtro.

percussion [pə'kʌʃən] n percusión f.

percussionist [pə'kʌʃənist] n percusionista m/f.

peremptory [pə'remptəri] a perentorio.

perennial [pə'reniəl] a perenne.

perfect a ['pəːfikt] perfecto ◆ n (also: **~ tense**) perfecto ◆ vt [pə'fekt] perfeccionar; **he's a ~ stranger to me** no le conozco de nada, me es completamente desconocido.

perfection [pə'fekʃən] n perfección f.

perfectionist [pə'fekʃənist] n perfeccionista m/f.

perfectly ['pəːfiktli] ad perfectamente; **I'm ~ happy with the situation** estoy muy contento con la situación; **you know ~ well** lo sabes muy bien or perfectamente.

perforate ['pəːfəreit] vt perforar.

perforated ulcer n úlcera perforada.

perforation [pəːfə'reiʃən] n perforación f.

perform [pə'fɔːm] vt (carry out) realizar, llevar a cabo; (THEATRE) representar; (piece of music) interpretar ◆ vi (THEATRE) actuar; (TECH) funcionar.

performance [pə'fɔːməns] n (of task) realización f; (of a play) representación f; (of player etc) actuación f; (of car, engine) rendimiento; (of function) desempeño; **the team put up a good ~** el equipo se defendió bien.

performer [pə'fɔːmə*] n (actor) actor m, actriz f; (MUS) intérprete m/f.

performing [pə'fɔːmiŋ] a (animal) amaestrado.

perfume ['pəːfjuːm] n perfume m.

perfunctory [pə'fʌŋktəri] a superficial.

perhaps [pə'hæps] ad quizá(s), tal vez; **~ so/not** puede que sí/no.

peril ['peril] n peligro, riesgo.

perilous ['periləs] a peligroso.

perilously ['periləsli] ad: **they came ~ close to being caught** por poco les cogen or agarran.

perimeter [pə'rimitə*] n perímetro.

period ['piəriəd] n período; (HISTORY) época; (SCOL) clase f; (full stop) punto; (MED) regla; (US SPORT) tiempo ◆ a (costume, furniture) de época; **for a ~ of three weeks** durante (un período de) tres semanas; **the holiday ~** el período de vacaciones.

periodic [piəri'ɔdik] a periódico.

periodical [piəri'ɔdikl] a, n periódico m.

periodically [piəri'ɔdikli] ad de vez en cuando, cada cierto tiempo.

period pains npl dolores mpl de la regla or de la menstruación.

peripatetic [peripə'tetik] a (salesman) ambulante; (teacher) peripatético.

peripheral [pə'rifərəl] a periférico ◆ n (COMPUT) periférico, unidad f periférica.

periphery [pə'rifəri] n periferia.

periscope ['periskəup] n periscopio.

perish ['periʃ] vi perecer; (decay) echarse a perder.

perishable ['periʃəbl] a perecedero.

perishables ['periʃəblz] npl productos mpl perecederos.

peritonitis [peritə'naitis] n peritonitis f.

perjure ['pəːdʒə*] vt: **to ~ o.s.** perjurarse.

perjury ['pəːdʒəri] n (LAW) perjurio.

perk [pəːk] n extra m.

perk up vi (cheer up) animarse.

perky ['pəːki] a alegre, despabilado.

perm [pəːm] n permanente f ◆ vt: **to have one's hair ~ed** hacerse una permanente.

permanence ['pəːmənəns] n permanencia.

permanent ['pəːmənənt] a permanente; (job, position) fijo; (dye, ink) indeleble; **~ address** domicilio permanente; **I'm not ~ here** no trabajo fijo aquí.

permanently ['pəːmənəntli] ad (lastingly) para siempre, de modo definitivo; (all the time) permanentemente.

permeate ['pəːmieit] vi penetrar, trascender ◆ vt penetrar, trascender a.

permissible [pə'misibl] a permisible, lícito.

permission [pə'miʃən] n permiso; **to give sb ~ to do sth** autorizar a uno para que haga algo; **with your ~** con su permiso.

permissive [pə'misiv] a permisivo.

permit n ['pəːmit] permiso, licencia; (entrance pass) pase m ◆ vt [pə'mit] permitir; (accept) tolerar ◆ vi [pə'mit]: **weather ~ting** si el tiempo lo permite; **fishing ~** permiso de pesca; **building/export ~** licencia or permiso de construcción/

exportación.

permutation [pɜ:mju'teɪʃən] n permutación f.

pernicious [pɜː'nɪʃəs] a nocivo; (MED) pernicioso.

pernickety [pə'nɪkɪtɪ] a (col: person) quisquilloso; (: task) delicado.

perpendicular [pɜːpən'dɪkjulə*] a perpendicular.

perpetrate ['pɜ:pɪtreɪt] vt cometer.

perpetual [pə'pɛtjuəl] a perpetuo.

perpetually [pə'pɛtjuəlɪ] ad (eternally) perpetuamente; (continuously) constantemente, continuamente.

perpetuate [pə'pɛtjueɪt] vt perpetuar.

perpetuity [pɜ:pɪ'tjuɪtɪ] n: **in ~** para siempre.

perplex [pə'plɛks] vt dejar perplejo.

perplexed [pə'plɛkst] a perplejo, confuso.

perplexing [pə'plɛksɪŋ] a que causa perplejidad.

perplexity [pə'plɛksɪtɪ] n perplejidad f, confusión f.

perquisites ['pɜ:kwɪzɪts] npl (also: **perks**) gajes y emolumentos mpl.

persecute ['pɜ:sɪkju:t] vt (pursue) perseguir; (harass) acosar.

persecution [pɜ:sɪ'kju:ʃən] n persecución f.

perseverance [pɜ:sɪ'vɪərəns] n perseverancia.

persevere [pɜ:sɪ'vɪə*] vi persistir.

Persia ['pɜ:ʃə] n Persia.

Persian ['pɜ:ʃən] a, n persa m/f ♦ n (LING) persa m; **the ~ Gulf** el Golfo Pérsico.

persist [pə'sɪst] vi: **to ~ (in doing sth)** persistir (en hacer algo).

persistence [pə'sɪstəns] n empeño.

persistent [pə'sɪstənt] a (lateness, rain) persistente; (determined) porfiado; (continuing) constante; **~ offender** (LAW) delincuente m/f reincidente.

persistently [pə'sɪstəntlɪ] ad persistentemente; (continually) constantemente.

persnickety [pə'snɪkətɪ] a (US col) = **pernickety**.

person ['pɜ:sn] n persona; **in ~** en persona; **on** or **about one's ~** (weapon, money) encima; **a ~ to ~ call** (TEL) una llamada (de) persona a persona.

personable ['pɜ:snəbl] a atractivo.

personal ['pɜ:snl] a personal, individual; (visit) en persona; (Brit TEL) persona a persona.

personal allowance n desgravación f personal.

personal assistant (PA) n ayudante m/f personal.

personal belongings npl efectos mpl personales.

personal column n anuncios mpl personales.

personal computer (PC) n computador m personal.

personal effects npl efectos mpl personales.

personal identification number (PIN) n (COMPUT, BANKING) número personal de identificación.

personality [pɜ:sə'nælɪtɪ] n personalidad f.

personal loan n préstamo personal.

personally ['pɜ:snəlɪ] ad personalmente.

personal property n bienes mpl muebles.

personification [pɜ:sɔnɪfɪ'keɪʃən] n personificación f.

personify [pɜː'sɔnɪfaɪ] vt encarnar.

personnel [pɜ:sə'nɛl] n personal m.

personnel department n departamento de personal.

personnel management n gestión f de personal.

personnel manager n jefe m de personal.

perspective [pə'spɛktɪv] n perspectiva; **to get sth into ~** ver algo en perspectiva or como es.

Perspex ® ['pɜ:spɛks] n (Brit) plexiglás m ®.

perspiration [pɜ:spɪ'reɪʃən] n transpiración f, sudor m.

perspire [pə'spaɪə*] vi transpirar, sudar.

persuade [pə'sweɪd] vt: **to ~ sb to do sth** persuadir a uno para que haga algo; **to ~ sb of sth/that** persuadir or convencer a uno de algo/de que; **I am ~d that** ... estoy convencido de que ... .

persuasion [pə'sweɪʒən] n persuasión f; (persuasiveness) persuasiva; (creed) creencia.

persuasive [pə'sweɪsɪv] a persuasivo.

persuasively [pə'sweɪsɪvlɪ] ad de modo persuasivo.

pert [pɜːt] a impertinente, fresco, atrevido.

pertaining [pɜː'teɪnɪŋ]: **~ to** prep relacionado con.

pertinent ['pɜ:tɪnənt] a pertinente, a propósito.

perturb [pə'tɜːb] vt perturbar.

perturbing [pə'tɜːbɪŋ] a inquietante, perturbador(a).

Peru [pə'ru:] n el Perú.

perusal [pə'ru:zəl] n examen m.

peruse [pə'ru:z] vt leer con detención, examinar.

Peruvian [pə'ru:vɪən] a, n peruano/a m/f.

pervade [pə'veɪd] vt impregnar, infundirse en.

pervasive [pə'veɪsɪv] a (smell) penetrante; (influence) muy extendido; (gloom, feelings, ideas) reinante.

perverse [pə'vɜːs] a perverso; (stubborn) terco; (wayward) travieso.

perversely [pə'vɜːslɪ] ad perversamente; tercamente; traviesamente.

perverseness [pə'vɜːsnɪs] n perversidad f; terquedad f; travesura.

perversion [pə'vɜːʃən] n perversión f.

pervert n ['pɜːvɜːt] pervertido/a ◆ vt [pə'vɜːt] pervertir.
pessary ['pesərɪ] n pesario.
pessimism ['pesɪmɪzəm] n pesimismo.
pessimist ['pesɪmɪst] n pesimista m/f.
pessimistic [pesɪ'mɪstɪk] a pesimista.
pest [pest] n (insect) insecto nocivo; (fig) lata, molestia; **~s** npl plaga.
pest control n control m de plagas.
pester ['pestə*] vt molestar, acosar.
pesticide ['pestɪsaɪd] n pesticida m.
pestilent ['pestɪlənt], **pestilential** [pestɪ'lenʃəl] a (col: exasperating) condenado.
pestle ['pesl] n mano f de mortero or de almirez.
pet [pet] n animal m doméstico; (favourite) favorito/a ◆ vt acariciar ◆ vi (col) besuquearse ◆ cpd: **my ~ aversion** mi manía.
petal ['petl] n pétalo.
peter ['piːtə*]: **to ~ out** vi agotarse, acabarse.
petite [pə'tiːt] a chiquita.
petition [pə'tɪʃən] n petición f ◆ vt presentar una petición a ◆ vi: **to ~ for divorce** pedir el divorcio.
pet name n nombre m cariñoso, apodo.
petrified ['petrɪfaɪd] a (fig) pasmado, horrorizado.
petrochemical [petrə'kemɪkl] a petroquímico.
petrodollars ['petrəudɒləz] npl petrodólares mpl.
petrol ['petrəl] (Brit) n gasolina; (for lighter) bencina; **two/four-star ~** gasolina normal/súper.
petrol can n bidón m de gasolina.
petrol engine n (Brit) motor m de gasolina.
petroleum [pə'trəulɪəm] n petróleo.
petroleum jelly n parafina.
petrol pump n (Brit) (in car) bomba de gasolina; (in garage) surtidor m de gasolina.
petrol station n (Brit) gasolinera.
petrol tank n (Brit) depósito (de gasolina).
petticoat ['petɪkəut] n enaguas fpl.
pettifogging ['petɪfɒgɪŋ] a quisquilloso.
pettiness ['petɪnɪs] n mezquindad f.
petty ['petɪ] a (mean) mezquino; (unimportant) insignificante.
petty cash n dinero para gastos menores.
petty cash book n libro de caja auxiliar.
petty officer n contramaestre m.
petulant ['petjulənt] a malhumorado.
pew [pjuː] n banco.
pewter ['pjuːtə*] n peltre m.
Pfc abbr (US MIL) = private first class.
PG n abbr (CINEMA) = parental guidance.
PGA n abbr = Professional Golfers' Association.
PH n abbr (US MIL: = Purple Heart) decoración otorgada a los heridos de guerra.

pH n abbr (= pH value) pH.
p&h abbr (US: = postage and handling) gastos de envío.
PHA n abbr (US) = Public Housing Administration.
phallic ['fælɪk] a fálico.
phantom ['fæntəm] n fantasma m.
Pharaoh ['fɛərəu] n Faraón m.
pharmaceutical [fɑːmə'sjuːtɪkl] a farmacéutico.
pharmacist ['fɑːməsɪst] n farmacéutico.
pharmacy ['fɑːməsɪ] n (US) farmacia.
phase [feɪz] n fase f ◆ vt: **to ~ sth in/out** introducir/retirar algo por etapas; **~ed withdrawal** retirada progresiva.
PhD abbr = **Doctor of Philosophy**.
pheasant ['feznt] n faisán m.
phenomenal [fɪ'nɔmɪnl] a fenomenal.
phenomenally [fɪ'nɔmɪnlɪ] ad fenomenalmente, de modo fenomenal.
phenomenon, pl **phenomena** [fə'nɔmɪnən, -nə] n fenómeno.
phial ['faɪəl] n ampolla.
philanderer [fɪ'lændərə*] n donjuan m.
philanthropic [fɪlən'θrɔpɪk] a filantrópico.
philanthropist [fɪ'lænθrəpɪst] n filántropo/a.
philatelist [fɪ'lætəlɪst] n filatelista m/f.
philately [fɪ'lætəlɪ] n filatelia.
Philippines ['fɪlɪpiːnz] npl: **the ~** las (Islas) Filipinas.
philosopher [fɪ'lɔsəfə*] n filósofo/a.
philosophical [fɪlə'sɔfɪkl] a filosófico.
philosophy [fɪ'lɔsəfɪ] n filosofía.
phlegm [flem] n flema.
phlegmatic [fleg'mætɪk] a flemático.
phobia ['fəubjə] n fobia.
phone [fəun] n teléfono ◆ vt telefonear, llamar por teléfono; **to be on the ~** tener teléfono; (be calling) estar hablando por teléfono.
phone back vt, vi volver a llamar.
phone up vt, vi llamar por teléfono.
phone book n guía telefónica.
phone box, phone booth n cabina telefónica.
phone call n llamada (telefónica).
phone-in ['fəunɪn] n (Brit RADIO, TV) programa m de radio or televisión en el que el público puede llamar por teléfono.
phonetics [fə'netɪks] n fonética.
phon(e)y ['fəunɪ] a falso ◆ n (person) farsante m/f.
phonograph ['fəunəgræf] n (US) fonógrafo, tocadiscos m inv.
phonology [fəu'nɔlədʒɪ] n fonología.
phosphate ['fɔsfeɪt] n fosfato.
phosphorus ['fɔsfərəs] n fósforo.
photo ['fəutəu] n foto f.
photo... ['fəutəu] pref foto... .
photocopier ['fəutəukɔpɪə*] n fotocopiadora.
photocopy ['fəutəukɔpɪ] n fotocopia ◆ vt fotocopiar.

photoelectric [fəutəʊɪ'lɛktrɪk] *a:* ~ **cell** célula fotoeléctrica.

photo finish *n* resultado comprobado por fotocontrol.

photogenic [fəutəʊ'dʒɛnɪk] *a* fotogénico.

photograph ['fəutəgræf] *n* fotografía ♦ *vt* fotografiar; **to take a** ~ **of sb** sacar una foto de uno.

photographer [fə'tɔgrəfə*] *n* fotógrafo.

photographic [fəutə'græfɪk] *a* fotográfico.

photography [fə'tɔgrəfɪ] *n* fotografía.

photostat ® ['fəutəustæt] *n* fotóstato.

photosynthesis [fəutəu'sɪnθəsɪs] *n* fotosíntesis *f*.

phrase [freɪz] *n* frase *f* ♦ *vt* (*letter*) expresar, redactar.

phrase book *n* libro de frases.

physical ['fɪzɪkl] *a* físico; ~ **examination** reconocimiento médico; ~ **exercises** ejercicios *mpl* físicos.

physical education *n* educación *f* física.

physically ['fɪsɪklɪ] *ad* físicamente.

physical training *n* gimnasia.

physician [fɪ'zɪʃən] *n* médico/a.

physicist ['fɪzɪsɪst] *n* físico/a.

physics ['fɪzɪks] *n* física.

physiological [fɪzɪə'lɔdʒɪkl] *a* fisiológico.

physiology [fɪzɪ'ɔlədʒɪ] *n* fisiología.

physiotherapy [fɪzɪəu'θerəpɪ] *n* fisioterapia.

physique [fɪ'ziːk] *n* físico.

pianist ['pɪənɪst] *n* pianista *m/f*.

piano [pɪ'ænəu] *n* piano.

piano accordion *n* (*Brit*) acordeón-piano *m*.

piccolo ['pɪkələu] *n* (*mus*) flautín *m*.

pick [pɪk] *n* (*tool: also:* ~-**axe**) pico, piqueta ♦ *vt* (*select*) elegir, escoger; (*gather*) coger (*Sp*), recoger (*LAm*); (*lock*) abrir con ganzúa; (*scab, spot*) rascar ♦ *vi*: **to** ~ **and choose** ser muy exigente; **take your** ~ escoja lo que quiera; **the** ~ **of** lo mejor de; **to** ~ **one's nose/teeth** hurgarse las narices/limpiarse los dientes; **to** ~ **pockets** ratear, ser carterista; **to** ~ **one's way through** andar a tientas, abrirse camino; **to** ~ **a fight/quarrel with sb** buscar pelea/camorra con uno; **to** ~ **sb's brains** aprovecharse de los conocimientos de uno.

pick at *vt fus*: **to** ~ **at one's food** comer con poco apetito.

pick off *vt* (*kill*) matar de un tiro.

pick on *vt fus* (*person*) meterse con.

pick out *vt* escoger; (*distinguish*) identificar.

pick up *vi* (*improve: sales*) ir mejor; (: *patient*) reponerse; (: *finance*) recobrarse ♦ *vt* (*from floor*) recoger; (*buy*) comprar; (*find*) encontrar; (*learn*) aprender; (*radio, tv, tel*) captar; **to** ~ **up speed** acelerarse; **to** ~ **o.s. up** levantarse; **to** ~ **up where one left off** reempezar algo donde lo había dejado.

pickaxe, (*US*) **pickax** ['pɪkæks] *n* pico, zapapico.

picket ['pɪkɪt] *n* (*in strike*) piquete *m* ♦ *vt* piquetear; **to be on** ~ **duty** estar de piquete.

picketing ['pɪkɪtɪŋ] *n* organización *f* de piquetes.

picket line *n* piquete *m*.

pickings ['pɪkɪŋz] *npl* (*pilferings*): **there are good** ~ **to be had here** se puede sacar buenas ganancias de aquí.

pickle ['pɪkl] *n* (*also:* ~**s:** *as condiment*) escabeche *m*; (*fig: mess*) apuro ♦ *vt* encurtir; (*in vinegar*) envinagrar; **in a** ~ en un lío, en apuros.

pick-me-up ['pɪkmɪʌp] *n* tónico.

pickpocket ['pɪkpɔkɪt] *n* carterista *m/f*.

pickup ['pɪkʌp] *n* (*Brit: on record player*) pickup *m*; (*small truck: also:* ~ **truck,** ~ **van**) furgoneta.

picnic ['pɪknɪk] *n* picnic *m*, merienda ♦ *vi* merendar en el campo.

pictorial [pɪk'tɔːrɪəl] *a* pictórico; (*magazine etc*) ilustrado.

picture ['pɪktʃə*] *n* cuadro; (*painting*) pintura; (*photograph*) fotografía; (*film*) película; (*tv*) imagen *f* ♦ *vt* pintar; **the** ~**s** (*Brit*) el cine; **we get a good** ~ **here** captamos buena imagen aquí; **to take a** ~ **of sb/sth** hacer *or* sacar una foto a uno/de algo; **the garden is a** ~ **in June** el jardín es una preciosidad en junio; **the overall** ~ la impresión en general; **to put sb in the** ~ poner uno al corriente *or* al tanto.

picture book *n* libro de dibujos.

picturesque [pɪktʃə'rɛsk] *a* pintoresco.

piddling ['pɪdlɪŋ] *a* insignificante.

pidgin ['pɪdʒɪn] *a:* ~ **English** el inglés macarrónico.

pie [paɪ] *n* pastel *m*; (*open*) tarta; (*small: of meat*) empanada.

piebald ['paɪbɔːld] *a* pío.

piece [piːs] *n* pedazo, trozo; (*of cake*) trozo; (*draughts etc*) pieza, ficha; (*item*): **a** ~ **of furniture/advice** un mueble/un consejo ♦ *vt*: **to** ~ **together** juntar; (*tech*) armar; **to take to** ~**s** desmontar; **a** ~ **of news** una noticia; **a 10p** ~ una moneda de 10 peniques; **a six-**~ **band** un conjunto de seis (músicos); **in one** ~ (*object*) de una sola pieza; ~ **by** ~ pieza *por* a pieza; **to say one's** ~ decir su parecer.

piecemeal ['piːsmiːl] *ad* poco a poco.

piece rate *n* tarifa a destajo.

piecework ['piːswəːk] *n* trabajo a destajo.

pie chart *n* gráfico de sectores *or* de tarta.

pier [pɪə*] *n* muelle *m*, embarcadero.

pierce [pɪəs] *vt* penetrar en, perforar; **to have one's ears** ~**d** hacerse los agujeros de las orejas.

piercing ['pɪəsɪŋ] *a* (*cry*) penetrante.

piety ['paɪətɪ] *n* piedad *f*.

pig [pɪg] *n* cerdo, puerco; (*fig*) cochino.

pigeon ['pɪdʒən] *n* paloma; (*as food*) pichón *m*.

pigeonhole ['pɪdʒənhəul] *n* casilla.

piggy bank ['pɪgɪbæŋk] *n* hucha (*en forma de cerdito*).

pigheaded ['pɪg'hɛdɪd] *a* terco, testarudo.

piglet ['pɪglɪt] *n* cerdito.

pigment ['pɪgmənt] *n* pigmento.

pigmentation [pɪgmən'teɪʃən] *n* pigmentación *f*.

pigmy ['pɪgmɪ] *n* = **pygmy**.

pigskin ['pɪgskɪn] *n* piel *f* de cerdo.

pigsty ['pɪgstaɪ] *n* pocilga.

pigtail ['pɪgteɪl] *n* (*girl's*) trenza; (*Chinese, TAUR*) coleta.

pike [paɪk] *n* (*spear*) pica; (*fish*) lucio.

pilchard ['pɪltʃəd] *n* sardina.

pile [paɪl] *n* (*heap*) montón *m*; (*of carpet*) pelo ◆ (*vb: also:* ~ **up**) *vt* amontonar; (*fig*) acumular ◆ *vi* amontonarse; **in a** ~ en un montón; **to** ~ **into** (*car*) meterse en.
　pile on *vt:* **to** ~ **it on** (*col*) exagerar.

piles [paɪlz] *npl* (*MED*) almorranas *fpl*, hemorroides *mpl*.

pile-up ['paɪlʌp] *n* (*AUT*) accidente *m* múltiple.

pilfer ['pɪlfə*] *vt, vi* ratear, robar, sisar.

pilfering ['pɪlfərɪŋ] *n* ratería.

pilgrim ['pɪlgrɪm] *n* peregrino/a.

pilgrimage ['pɪlgrɪmɪdʒ] *n* peregrinación *f*, romería.

pill [pɪl] *n* píldora; **the** ~ la píldora; **to be on the** ~ tomar la píldora (anticonceptiva).

pillage ['pɪlɪdʒ] *vt* pillar, saquear.

pillar ['pɪlə*] *n* (*gen*) pilar *m*; (*concrete*) columna.

pillar box *n* (*Brit*) buzón *m*.

pillion ['pɪljən] *n* (*of motorcycle*) asiento trasero; **to ride** ~ ir en el asiento trasero.

pillion passenger *n* pasajero que va detrás.

pillory ['pɪlərɪ] *vt* poner en ridículo.

pillow ['pɪləu] *n* almohada.

pillowcase ['pɪləukeɪs], **pillowslip** ['pɪləuslɪp] *n* funda (de almohada).

pilot ['paɪlət] *n* piloto *inv* ◆ *a* (*scheme etc*) piloto ◆ *vt* pilotar; (*fig*) guiar, conducir.

pilot light *n* piloto.

pimento [pɪ'mɛntəu] *n* pimentón *m*.

pimp [pɪmp] *n* chulo, cafiche *m* (*LAm*).

pimple ['pɪmpl] *n* grano.

pimply ['pɪmplɪ] *a* lleno de granos.

PIN *n abbr see* **personal identification number**.

pin [pɪn] *n* alfiler *m*; (*ELEC: of plug*) clavija; (*TECH*) perno; (: *wooden*) clavija; (*drawing* ~) chincheta; (*in grenade*) percutor *m* ◆ *vt* prender (con alfiler); sujetar con perno; ~**s and needles** hormigueo *sg*; **to** ~ **sth on sb** (*fig*) acusar (falsamente) a uno de algo.
　pin down *vt* (*fig*): **there's something**

strange here, but I can't quite ~ **it down** aquí hay algo raro pero no puedo precisar qué es; **to** ~ **sb down** hacer que uno concrete.

pinafore ['pɪnəfɔː*] *n* delantal *m*.

pinafore dress *n* (*Brit*) mandil *m*.

pinball ['pɪnbɔːl] *n* (*also:* ~ **machine**) millón *m*, fliper *m*.

pincers ['pɪnsəz] *npl* pinzas *fpl*, tenazas *fpl*.

pinch [pɪntʃ] *n* pellizco; (*of salt etc*) pizca ◆ *vt* pellizcar; (*col: steal*) birlar ◆ *vi* (*shoe*) apretar; **at a** ~ en caso de apuro; **to feel the** ~ (*fig*) pasar apuros *or* estrechos.

pinched [pɪntʃt] *a* (*drawn*) cansado; ~ **with cold** transido de frío; ~ **for money/space** mal *or* falto de dinero/espacio *or* sitio.

pincushion ['pɪnkuʃən] *n* acerico.

pine [paɪn] *n* (*also:* ~ **tree**) pino ◆ *vi:* **to** ~ **for** suspirar por.
　pine away *vi* morirse de pena.

pineapple ['paɪnæpl] *n* piña, ananás *m*.

pine nut, (*Brit*) **pine kernel** *n* piña, piñón *m*.

ping [pɪŋ] *n* (*noise*) sonido agudo.

ping-pong ['pɪŋpɒŋ] *n* pingpong *m*.

pink [pɪŋk] *a* rosado, color de rosa ◆ *n* (*colour*) rosa; (*BOT*) clavel *m*, clavellina.

pinking shears, **pinking scissors** ['pɪŋkɪŋ-] *npl* tijeras *fpl* dentadas.

pin money *n* dinero para gastos extra.

pinnacle ['pɪnəkl] *n* cumbre *f*.

pinpoint ['pɪnpɔɪnt] *vt* precisar.

pinstripe ['pɪnstraɪp] *a:* ~ **suit** traje *m* a rayas.

pint [paɪnt] *n* pinta (*Brit* = 0.57 l; *US* = 0.47 l); (*Brit col: of beer*) pinta de cerveza, ≈ jarra (*Sp*).

pin-up ['pɪnʌp] *n* fotografía de mujer desnuda.

pioneer [paɪə'nɪə*] *n* pionero/a ◆ *vt* promover.

pious ['paɪəs] *a* piadoso, devoto.

pip [pɪp] *n* (*seed*) pepita; **the** ~**s** (*Brit TEL*) la señal.

pipe [paɪp] *n* tubo, caño; (*for smoking*) pipa ◆ *vt* conducir en cañerías; ~**s** *npl* (*gen*) cañería *sg*; (*also:* **bag**~**s**) gaita *sg*.
　pipe down *vi* (*col*) callarse.

pipe cleaner *n* limpiapipas *m inv*.

piped music [paɪpt-] *n* música ambiental.

pipe dream *n* sueño imposible.

pipeline ['paɪplaɪn] *n* tubería, cañería; (*for oil*) oleoducto; (*for natural gas*) gasoducto; **it is in the** ~ (*fig*) está en trámite.

piper ['paɪpə*] *n* (*gen*) flautista *m/f*; (*with bagpipes*) gaitero/a.

pipe tobacco *n* tabaco de pipa.

piping ['paɪpɪŋ] *ad:* **to be** ~ **hot** estar que quema.

piquant ['piːkənt] *a* picante.

pique [piːk] *n* pique *m*, resentimiento.

pirate ['paɪərət] *n* pirata *m/f* ◆ *vt* (*record, video, book*) hacer una copia pirata de.

pirated ['paɪərətɪd] *a* (*book, record etc*) pirata *inv*.

pirate radio *n* (*Brit*) emisora pirata.

pirouette [pɪru'ɛt] *n* pirueta ◆ *vi* piruetear.

Pisces ['paɪsiːz] *n* Piscis *m*.

piss [pɪs] *vi* (*col*) mear.

pissed [pɪst] *a* (*col: drunk*) borracho.

pistol ['pɪstl] *n* pistola.

piston ['pɪstən] *n* pistón *m*, émbolo.

pit [pɪt] *n* hoyo; (*also:* **coal** ~) mina; (*in garage*) foso de inspección; (*also:* **orchestra** ~) platea; (*quarry*) cantera ◆ *vt* (*subj: chickenpox*) picar; (: *rust*) comer; **to** ~ **A against B** oponer A a B; ~**s** *npl* (*AUT*) box *msg*; ~**ted with** (*chickenpox*) picado de.

pitapat ['pɪtə'pæt] *ad*: **to go** ~ (*heart*) latir rápidamente; (*rain*) golpetear.

pitch [pɪtʃ] *n* (*throw*) lanzamiento; (*MUS*) tono; (*Brit SPORT*) campo, terreno; (*tar*) brea; (*in market etc*) puesto; (*fig: degree*) nivel *m*, grado ◆ *vt* (*throw*) arrojar, lanzar ◆ *vi* (*fall*) caer(se); (*NAUT*) cabecear; **I can't keep working at this** ~ no puedo seguir trabajando a este ritmo; **at its (highest)** ~ en su punto máximo; **his anger reached such a** ~ **that** ... su ira *or* cólera llegó a tal extremo que ...; **to** ~ **a tent** montar una tienda (de campaña); **to** ~ **one's aspirations too high** tener ambiciones desmesuradas.

pitch-black ['pɪtʃ'blæk] *a* negro como boca de lobo.

pitched battle [pɪtʃt-] *n* batalla campal.

pitcher ['pɪtʃə*] *n* cántaro, jarro.

pitchfork ['pɪtʃfɔːk] *n* horca.

piteous ['pɪtɪəs] *a* lastimoso.

pitfall ['pɪtfɔːl] *n* riesgo.

pith [pɪθ] *n* (*of orange*) médula; (*fig*) meollo.

pithead ['pɪthɛd] *n* (*Brit*) bocamina.

pithy ['pɪθɪ] *a* jugoso.

pitiful ['pɪtɪful] *a* (*touching*) lastimoso, conmovedor(a); (*contemptible*) lamentable, miserable.

pitifully ['pɪtɪfəlɪ] *ad*: **it's** ~ **obvious** es tan evidente que da pena.

pitiless ['pɪtɪlɪs] *a* despiadado, implacable.

pitilessly ['pɪtɪlɪslɪ] *ad* despiadadamente, implacablemente.

pittance ['pɪtns] *n* miseria.

pity ['pɪtɪ] *n* (*compassion*) compasión *f*, piedad *f*; (*shame*) lástima ◆ *vt* compadecer(se de); **to have** *or* **take** ~ **on sb** compadecerse de uno; **what a** ~! ¡qué pena!; **it is a** ~ **that you can't come** ¡qué pena que no puedas venir!

pitying ['pɪtɪɪŋ] *a* compasivo, de lástima.

pivot ['pɪvət] *n* eje *m* ◆ *vi*: **to** ~ **on** girar sobre; (*fig*) depender de.

pixel ['pɪksl] *n* (*COMPUT*) pixel *m*, punto.

pixie ['pɪksɪ] *n* duendecillo.

pizza ['piːtsə] *n* pizza.

P&L *abbr* = *profit and loss.*

placard ['plækɑːd] *n* (*in march etc*) pancarta.

placate [plə'keɪt] *vt* apaciguar.

place [pleɪs] *n* lugar *m*, sitio; (*rank*) rango; (*seat*) plaza, asiento; (*post*) puesto; (*in street names*) plaza; (*home*): **at/to his** ~ en/a su casa ◆ *vt* (*object*) poner, colocar; (*identify*) reconocer; (*find a post for*) dar un puesto a, colocar; (*goods*) vender; **to take** ~ tener lugar; **to be** ~**d** (*in race, exam*) colocarse; **out of** ~ (*not suitable*) fuera de lugar; **in the first** ~ (*first of all*) en primer lugar; **to change** ~**s with sb** cambiarse de sitio con uno; **from** ~ **to** ~ de un sitio a *or* para otro; **all over the** ~ por todas partes; **he's going** ~**s** (*fig, col*) llegará lejos; **I feel rather out of** ~ **here** me encuentro algo desplazado; **to put sb in his** ~ (*fig*) poner a uno en su lugar; **it is not my** ~ **to do it** no me incumbe a mí hacerlo; **to** ~ **an order with sb (for)** hacer un pedido a uno (de); **we are better** ~**d than a month ago** estamos en mejor posición que hace un mes.

placebo [plə'siːbəu] *n* placebo.

place mat *n* (*wooden etc*) salvamanteles *m inv*; (*in linen etc*) mantel *m* individual.

placement ['pleɪsmənt] *n* colocación *f*.

place name *n* topónimo.

placenta [plə'sɛntə] *n* placenta.

placid ['plæsɪd] *a* apacible.

placidity [plæ'sɪdɪtɪ] *n* apacibilidad *f*, placidez *f*.

plagiarism ['pleɪdʒərɪzm] *n* plagio.

plagiarist ['pleɪdʒərɪst] *n* plagiario/a.

plagiarize ['pleɪdʒəraɪz] *vt* plagiar.

plague [pleɪg] *n* plaga; (*MED*) peste *f* ◆ *vt* (*fig*) acosar, atormentar; **to** ~ **sb with questions** acribillar a uno con preguntas.

plaice [pleɪs] *n, pl inv* platija.

plaid [plæd] *n* (*material*) tartán *m*.

plain [pleɪn] *a* (*clear*) claro, evidente; (*simple*) sencillo; (*frank*) franco, abierto; (*not handsome*) poco atractivo; (*pure*) natural, puro ◆ *ad* claramente ◆ *n* llano, llanura; **in** ~ **clothes** (*police*) vestido de paisano; **to make sth** ~ **to sb** poner algo de manifiesto para uno.

plain chocolate *n* chocolate *m* oscuro *or* amargo.

plainly ['pleɪnlɪ] *ad* claramente, evidentemente; (*frankly*) francamente.

plainness ['pleɪnnɪs] *n* (*clarity*) claridad *f*; (*simplicity*) sencillez *f*; (*of face*) falta de atractivo.

plaintiff ['pleɪntɪf] *n* demandante *m/f*.

plaintive ['pleɪntɪv] *a* (*cry, voice*) lastimero, quejumbroso; (*look*) que da lástima.

plait [plæt] *n* trenza ◆ *vt* trenzar.

plan [plæn] *n (drawing)* plano; *(scheme)* plan *m*, proyecto ♦ *vt (think)* pensar; *(prepare)* proyectar, planificar; *(intend)* pensar, tener la intención de ♦ *vi* hacer proyectos; **have you any ~s for today?** ¿piensas hacer algo hoy?; **to ~ to do** pensar hacer; **how long do you ~ to stay?** ¿cuánto tiempo piensas quedarte?; **to ~ (for)** planear, proyectar.
plan out *vt* planear detalladamente.
plane [plein] *n (AVIAT)* avión *m*; *(tree)* plátano; *(tool)* cepillo; *(MATH)* plano.
planet ['plænɪt] *n* planeta *m*.
planetarium [plænɪ'teərɪəm] *n* planetario.
planetary ['plænɪtərɪ] *a* planetario.
plank [plæŋk] *n* tabla.
plankton ['plæŋktən] *n* plancton *m*.
planner ['plænə*] *n* planificador(a) *m/f*; *(chart)* diagrama *m* de planificación; **town ~** urbanista *m/f*.
planning ['plænɪŋ] *n (POL, ECON)* planificación *f*; **family ~** planificación familiar.
planning committee *n (in local government)* comité *m* de planificación.
planning permission *n* permiso para realizar obras.
plant [pla:nt] *n* planta; *(machinery)* maquinaria; *(factory)* fábrica ♦ *vt* plantar; *(field)* sembrar; *(bomb)* colocar.
plantain ['plæntein] *n* llantén *m*.
plantation [plæn'teiʃən] *n* plantación *f*; *(estate)* hacienda.
planter ['pla:ntə*] *n* hacendado.
plant pot *n* maceta, tiesto.
plaque [plæk] *n* placa.
plasma ['plæzmə] *n* plasma *m*.
plaster ['pla:stə*] *n (for walls)* yeso; *(also:* **~ of Paris)** yeso mate; *(Brit: also:* **sticking ~)** tirita, esparadrapo ♦ *vt* enyesar; *(cover)*: **to ~ with** llenar *or* cubrir de; **to be ~ed with mud** estar cubierto de barro.
plaster cast *n (MED)* escayola; *(model, statue)* vaciado de yeso.
plastered ['pla:stəd] *a (col)* borracho.
plasterer ['pla:stərə*] *n* yesero.
plastic ['plæstɪk] *n* plástico ♦ *a* de plástico.
plastic bag *n* bolsa de plástico.
plasticine ® ['plæstɪsi:n] *n (Brit)* plastilina ®.
plastic surgery *n* cirujía plástica.
plate [pleit] *n (dish)* plato; *(metal, in book)* lámina; *(PHOT)* placa; *(on door)* placa; *(AUT: number ~)* matrícula.
plateau, **~s** *or* **~x** ['plætəu, -z] *n* meseta, altiplanicie *f*.
plateful ['pleitful] *n* plato.
plate glass *n* vidrio *or* cristal *m* cilindrado.
platen ['plætən] *n (on typewriter, printer)* rodillo.
plate rack *n* escurreplatos *m inv*.
platform ['plætfɔ:m] *n (RAIL)* andén *m*;

(stage) plataforma; *(at meeting)* tribuna; *(POL)* programa *m* (electoral); **the train leaves from ~ 7** el tren sale del andén número 7.
platform ticket *n (Brit)* billete *m* de andén.
platinum ['plætɪnəm] *n* platino.
platitude ['plætɪtju:d] *n* lugar *m* común, tópico.
platonic [plə'tɔnɪk] *a* platónico.
platoon [plə'tu:n] *n* pelotón *m*.
platter ['plætə*] *n* fuente *f*.
plaudits ['plɔ:dɪts] *npl* aplausos *mpl*.
plausibility [plɔ:zɪ'bɪlɪtɪ] *n* verosimilitud *f*, credibilidad *f*.
plausible ['plɔ:zɪbl] *a* verosímil; *(person)* convincente.
play [plei] *n (gen)* juego; *(THEATRE)* obra, comedia ♦ *vt (game)* jugar; *(instrument)* tocar; *(THEATRE)* representar; (: *part)* hacer el papel de; *(fig)* desempeñar ♦ *vi* jugar; *(frolic)* juguetear; **to ~ safe** ir a lo seguro; **to bring** *or* **call into ~** poner en juego; **to ~ a trick on sb** gastar una broma a uno; **they're ~ing at soldiers** están jugando a (los) soldados; **to ~ for time** *(fig)* tratar de ganar tiempo; **to ~ into sb's hands** *(fig)* hacerle el juego a uno; **a smile ~ed on his lips** una sonrisa le bailaba en los labios.
play about, play around *vi (person)* hacer el tonto; **to ~ about** *or* **around with** *(fiddle with)* juguetear con; *(idea)* darle vueltas a.
play along *vi*: **to ~ along with** *(fig: person)* seguirle el juego a; (: *plan, idea)* seguir el juego a ♦ *vt*: **to ~ sb along** *(fig)* jugar con uno.
play back *vt* repasar.
play down *vt* quitar importancia a.
play on *vt fus (sb's feelings, credulity)* aprovecharse de; **to ~ on sb's nerves** atacarle los nervios a uno.
play up *vi (cause trouble)* dar guerra.
playact ['pleiækt] *vi (fig)* hacer comedia *or* teatro.
play-acting ['pleiæktɪŋ] *n* teatro.
playboy ['pleibɔi] *n* playboy *m*.
player ['pleiə*] *n* jugador(a) *m/f*; *(THEATRE)* actor *m*, actriz *f*; *(MUS)* músico/a.
playful ['pleiful] *a* juguetón/ona.
playground ['pleigraund] *n (in school)* patio de recreo.
playgroup ['pleigru:p] *n* jardín *m* de niños.
playing card ['pleiɪŋ-] *n* naipe *m*, carta.
playing field *n* campo de deportes.
playmate ['pleimeit] *n* compañero/a de juego.
play-off ['pleiɔf] *n (SPORT)* (partido de) desempate *m*.
playpen ['pleipen] *n* corral *m*.
playroom ['pleiru:m] *n* cuarto de juego.
playschool ['pleisku:l] *n* = **playgroup**.

plaything ['pleɪθɪŋ] n juguete m.

playtime ['pleɪtaɪm] n (SCOL) (hora de) recreo.

playwright ['pleɪraɪt] n dramaturgo/a.

plc abbr (= public limited company) S.A.

plea [pliː] n (request) súplica, petición f; (excuse) pretexto, disculpa; (LAW) alegato, defensa.

plead [pliːd] vt (LAW): **to ~ sb's case** defender a alguien; (give as excuse) poner como pretexto ♦ vi (LAW) declararse; (beg): **to ~ with sb** suplicar or rogar a uno; **to ~ guilty/not guilty** (defendant) declararse culpable/inocente; **to ~ for sth** (beg for) suplicar algo.

pleasant ['plɛznt] a agradable.

pleasantly ['plɛzntlɪ] ad agradablemente.

pleasantness ['plɛzntnɪs] n (of person) simpatía, amabilidad f; (of place) lo agradable.

pleasantries ['plɛzntrɪz] npl (polite remarks) cortesías fpl; **to exchange ~** hablar en forma amena.

please [pliːz] vt (give pleasure to) dar gusto a, agradar ♦ vi (think fit): **do as you ~** haz lo que quieras or lo que te dé la gana; **to ~ o.s.** hacer lo que le parezca; **~!** ¡por favor!; **~ yourself!** ¡haz lo que quieras!, ¡como quieras!; **~ don't cry!** ¡no llores! te lo ruego.

pleased [pliːzd] a (happy) alegre, contento; (satisfied): **~ (with)** satisfecho (de); **~ to meet you** (col) ¡encantado!, ¡tanto or mucho gusto!; **to be ~ (about sth)** alegrarse (de algo); **we are ~ to inform you that ...** tenemos el gusto de comunicarle que ....

pleasing ['pliːzɪŋ] a agradable, grato.

pleasurable ['plɛʒərəbl] a agradable, grato.

pleasurably ['plɛʒərəblɪ] ad agradablemente, gratamente.

pleasure ['plɛʒə*] n placer m, gusto; (will) voluntad f ♦ cpd de recreo; **"it's a ~"** "el gusto es mío"; **it's a ~ to see him** da gusto verle; **I have much ~ in informing you that ...** tengo el gran placer de comunicarles que ...; **with ~** con mucho or todo gusto; **is this trip for business or ~?** ¿este viaje es de negocios o de placer?

pleasure ground n parque m de atracciones.

pleasure-seeking ['plɛʒəsɪːkɪŋ] a hedonista.

pleasure steamer n vapor m de recreo.

pleat [pliːt] n pliegue m.

pleb [plɛb] n: **the ~s** la gente baja, la plebe.

plebeian [plɪ'biːən] n plebeyo/a ♦ a plebeyo; (pej) ordinario.

plebiscite ['plɛbɪsɪt] n plebiscito.

plectrum ['plɛktrəm] n plectro.

pledge [plɛdʒ] n (object) prenda; (promise) promesa, voto ♦ vt (pawn) empeñar; (promise) prometer; **to ~ support for sb** pro-

meter su apoyo a uno; **to ~ sb to secrecy** hacer a uno jurar guardar un secreto.

plenary ['pliːnərɪ] a: **in ~ session** en sesión plenaria.

plentiful ['plɛntɪful] a copioso, abundante.

plenty ['plɛntɪ] n abundancia; **~ of** mucho(s)/a(s); **we've got ~ of time to get there** tenemos tiempo de sobra para llegar.

plethora ['plɛθərə] n plétora.

pleurisy ['pluərɪsɪ] n pleuresía.

pliability [plaɪə'bɪlɪtɪ] n flexibilidad f.

pliable ['plaɪəbl] a flexible.

pliers ['plaɪəz] npl alicates mpl, tenazas fpl.

plight [plaɪt] n condición f or situación f difícil.

plimsolls ['plɪmsəlz] npl (Brit) zapatos mpl de tenis.

plinth [plɪnθ] n plinto.

PLO n abbr (= Palestine Liberation Organization) OLP f.

plod [plɔd] vi caminar con paso pesado; (fig) trabajar laboriosamente.

plodder ['plɔdə*] n trabajador(a) m/f diligente pero lento/a.

plodding ['plɔdɪŋ] (student) empollón(ona); (worker) más aplicado que brillante.

plonk [plɔŋk] (col) n (Brit: wine) vino peleón ♦ vt: **to ~ sth down** dejar caer algo.

plot [plɔt] n (scheme) complot m, conjura; (of story, play) argumento; (of land) terreno ♦ vt (mark out) trazar; (conspire) tramar, urdir ♦ vi conspirar; **a vegetable ~** un cuadro de hortalizas.

plotter ['plɔtə*] n (instrument) trazador m (de gráficos); (COMPUT) trazador m.

plotting ['plɔtɪŋ] n conspiración f, intrigas fpl.

plough, (US) **plow** [plau] n arado ♦ vt (earth) arar.

plough back vt (COMM) reinvertir.

plough through vt fus (crowd) abrirse paso a la fuerza por.

ploughing ['plauɪŋ] n labranza.

ploughman ['plaumən] n: **~'s lunch** pan m con queso.

plow [plau] (US) = **plough.**

ploy [plɔɪ] n truco, estratagema.

pluck [plʌk] vt (fruit) coger (Sp), recoger (LAm); (musical instrument) puntear; (bird) desplumar ♦ n valor m, ánimo; **to ~ up courage** hacer de tripas corazón; **to ~ one's eyebrows** depilarse las cejas.

plucky ['plʌkɪ] a valiente.

plug [plʌg] n tapón m; (ELEC) enchufe m, clavija; (AUT: also: **spark(ing) ~**) bujía ♦ vt (hole) tapar; (col: advertise) dar publicidad a; **to give sb/sth a ~** dar publicidad a uno/algo; **to ~ a lead into a socket** enchufar un hilo en una toma.

plug in vt, vi (ELEC) enchufar.

plughole ['plʌghəul] n desagüe m, desaguadero.

plum [plʌm] n (fruit) ciruela ◆ a (col: job) chollo.

plumage ['pluːmɪdʒ] n plumaje m.

plumb [plʌm] a vertical ◆ n plomo ◆ ad (exactly) exactamente, en punto ◆ vt sondar; (fig) sondear.
plumb in vt (washing machine) conectar.

plumber ['plʌmə*] n fontanero/a, plomero/a.

plumbing ['plʌmɪŋ] n (trade) fontanería; (piping) cañería.

plume [pluːm] n (gen) pluma; (on helmet) penacho.

plummet ['plʌmɪt] vi: **to ~ (down)** caer a plomo.

plump [plʌmp] a rechoncho, rollizo ◆ vt: **to ~ sth (down) on** dejar caer algo en.
plump for vt fus (col: choose) optar por.
plump up vt hinchar.

plumpness ['plʌmpnɪs] n gordura.

plunder ['plʌndə*] n pillaje m; (loot) botín m ◆ vt pillar, saquear.

plunge [plʌndʒ] n zambullida ◆ vt sumergir, hundir ◆ vi (fall) caer; (dive) saltar; (person) arrojarse; (sink) hundirse; **to take the ~** lanzarse; **to ~ a room into darkness** dejar una habitación a oscuras.

plunger ['plʌndʒə*] n émbolo; (for drain) desatascador m.

plunging ['plʌndʒɪŋ] a (neckline) escotado.

pluperfect [pluː'pəːfɪkt] n pluscuamperfecto.

plural ['pluərl] n plural m.

plus [plʌs] n (also: ~ sign) signo más; (fig) punto a favor ◆ a: **a ~ factor** (fig) un plus ◆ prep más, y, además de; **ten/twenty ~** más de diez/veinte.

plush [plʌʃ] a de felpa.

plutonium [pluː'təunɪəm] n plutonio.

ply [plaɪ] vt (a trade) ejercer ◆ vi (ship) ir y venir; (for hire) ofrecerse (para alquilar); **three ~** (wool) de tres cabos; **to ~ sb with drink** insistir en ofrecer a alguien muchas copas.

plywood ['plaɪwud] n madera contrachapada.

PM abbr (Brit) see **Prime Minister**.

p.m. ad abbr (= post meridiem) de la tarde or noche.

pneumatic [njuː'mætɪk] a neumático.

pneumatic drill n taladro neumático.

pneumonia [njuː'məunɪə] n pulmonía.

PO n abbr (= Post Office) Correos mpl; (NAUT) = **petty officer**.

po abbr = postal order.

POA n abbr (Brit) = Prison Officers' Association.

poach [pəutʃ] vt (cook) escalfar; (steal) cazar/pescar en vedado ◆ vi cazar/pescar en vedado.

poached [pəutʃt] a (egg) escalfado.

poacher ['pəutʃə*] n cazador(a) m/f furtivo/a.

poaching ['pəutʃɪŋ] n caza/pesca furtiva.

PO Box n abbr see **Post Office Box**.

pocket ['pɔkɪt] n bolsillo; (of air, GEO, fig) bolsa; (BILLIARDS) tronera ◆ vt meter en el bolsillo; (steal) embolsar; (BILLIARDS) entronerar; **breast ~** bolsillo de pecho; **~ of resistance** foco de resistencia; **~ of warm air** bolsa de aire caliente; **to be out of ~** salir perdiendo; **to be £5 in/out of ~** salir ganando/perdiendo 5 libras.

pocketbook ['pɔkɪtbuk] n (US: wallet) cartera; (: handbag) bolso.

pocketful ['pɔkɪtful] n bolsillo.

pocket knife n navaja.

pocket money n asignación f.

pockmarked ['pɔkmaːkt] a (face) picado de viruelas.

pod [pɔd] n vaina.

podgy ['pɔdʒɪ] a gordinflón/ona.

podiatrist [pɔ'diːətrɪst] n (US) pedicuro/a.

podiatry [pɔ'diːətrɪ] n (US) pedicura.

podium ['pəudɪəm] n podio.

POE n abbr = port of embarkation, port of entry.

poem ['pəuɪm] n poema m.

poet ['pəuɪt] n poeta m/f.

poetic [pəu'ctɪk] a poético.

poet laureate [-'lɔːrɪɪt] n poeta m laureado.

poetry ['pəuɪtrɪ] n poesía.

POEU n abbr (Brit: = Post Office Engineering Union) sindicato de trabajadores de correos.

poignant ['pɔɪnjənt] a conmovedor(a).

poignantly ['pɔɪnjəntlɪ] ad de modo conmovedor.

point [pɔɪnt] n punto; (tip) punta; (purpose) fin m, propósito; (Brit ELEC: also: **power ~**) toma de corriente, enchufe m; (use) utilidad f; (significant part) lo significativo; (place) punto, lugar m; (also: **decimal ~**): **2 ~ 3 (2.3)** dos coma tres (2,3) ◆ vt (gun etc): **to ~ sth at sb** apuntar algo a uno ◆ vi señalar con el dedo; **~s** npl (AUT) contactos mpl; (RAIL) agujas fpl; **to be on the ~ of doing sth** estar a punto de hacer algo; **to make a ~ of doing sth** poner empeño en hacer algo; **to get the ~** comprender; **to come to the ~** ir al meollo; **there's no ~ (in doing)** no tiene sentido (hacer); **~ of departure** (also fig) punto de partida; **~ of order** cuestión f de procedimiento; **~ of sale** (COMM) lugar m de venta; **~-of-sale advertising** publicidad f en el punto de venta; **the train stops at Carlisle and all ~s south** el tren para en Carlisle, y en todas las estaciones al sur; **when it comes to the ~** en el momento de la verdad; **in ~ of fact** en realidad; **that's the whole ~!** ¡eso es!, ¡ahí está!; **to be beside the ~** no venir al caso; **you've got a ~ there!** ¡tienes razón!

point out vt señalar.

point to *vt fus* indicar con el dedo; *(fig)* indicar, señalar.

point-blank ['pɔɪnt'blæŋk] *ad (also:* **at ~ range)** a quemarropa.

point duty *n (Brit)* control *m* de circulación.

pointed ['pɔɪntɪd] *a (shape)* puntiagudo, afilado; *(remark)* intencionado.

pointedly ['pɔɪntɪdlɪ] *ad* intencionadamente.

pointer ['pɔɪntə*] *n (stick)* puntero; *(needle)* aguja, indicador *m; (clue)* indicación *f*, pista; *(advice)* consejo.

pointless ['pɔɪntlɪs] *a* sin sentido.

pointlessly ['pɔɪntlɪslɪ] *ad* inútilmente, sin motivo.

point of view *n* punto de vista.

poise [pɔɪz] *n (of head, body)* porte *m; (calmness)* aplomo, elegancia.

poised [pɔɪzd] *a (in temperament)* sereno.

poison ['pɔɪzn] *n* veneno ◆ *vt* envenenar.

poisoning ['pɔɪznɪŋ] *n* envenenamiento.

poisonous ['pɔɪznəs] *a* venenoso; *(fumes etc)* tóxico; *(fig: ideas, literature)* pernicioso; (: *rumours, individual)* nefasto.

poke [pəuk] *vt (fire)* hurgar, atizar; *(jab with finger, stick etc)* empujar; *(COMPUT)* almacenar; *(put):* **to ~ sth in(to)** introducir algo en ◆ *n (jab)* empujón *m; (with elbow)* codazo; **to ~ one's head out of the window** asomar la cabeza por la ventana; **to ~ fun at sb** ridiculizar a uno; **to give the fire a ~** atizar el fuego.

poke about *vi* fisgonear.

poker ['pəukə*] *n* atizador *m; (CARDS)* póker *m*.

poker-faced ['pəukə'feɪst] *a* de cara impasible.

poky ['pəukɪ] *a* estrecho.

Poland ['pəulənd] *n* Polonia.

polar ['pəulə*] *a* polar.

polar bear *n* oso polar.

polarization [pəulərɑɪ'zeɪʃən] *n* polarización *f*.

polarize ['pəulərɑɪz] *vt* polarizar.

Pole [pəul] *n* polaco/a.

pole [pəul] *n* palo; *(GEO)* polo; *(TEL)* poste *m; (flag ~)* asta; *(tent ~)* mástil *m*.

pole bean *n (US)* judía trepadora.

polecat ['pəulkæt] *n (Brit)* turón *m; (US)* mofeta.

Pol. Econ. ['pɔlɪkɔn] *n abbr* = *political economy*.

polemic [pɔ'lɛmɪk] *n* polémica.

polemicist [pɔ'lɛmɪsɪst] *n* polemista *m/f*.

pole star *n* estrella polar.

pole vault *n* salto con pértiga.

police [pə'liːs] *n* policía ◆ *vt (streets, city, frontier)* vigilar.

police car *n* coche-patrulla *m*.

police constable *n (Brit)* guardia *m*, policía *m*.

police department *n (US)* servicios *mpl* de policía.

police force *n* cuerpo de policía.

policeman [pə'liːsmən] *n* guardia *m*, policía *m*.

police officer *n* guardia *m*, policía *m*.

police record *n:* **to have a ~** tener antecedentes penales.

police state *n* estado policial.

police station *n* comisaría.

policewoman [pə'liːswumən] *n* mujer *f* policía.

policy ['pɔlɪsɪ] *n* política; *(also:* **insurance ~)** póliza; *(of newspaper, company)* política; **it is our ~ to do that** tenemos por norma hacer eso; **to take out a ~** sacar una póliza.

policy holder *n* asegurado/a.

polio ['pəulɪəu] *n* polio *f*.

Polish ['pəulɪʃ] *a* polaco ◆ *n (LING)* polaco.

polish ['pɔlɪʃ] *n (for shoes)* betún *m; (for floor)* cera (de lustrar); *(for nails)* esmalte *m; (shine)* brillo, lustre *m; (fig: refinement)* cultura ◆ *vt (shoes)* limpiar; *(make shiny)* pulir, sacar brillo a; *(fig: improve)* perfeccionar.

polish off *vt (work)* terminar; *(food)* despachar.

polish up *vt (shoes, furniture etc)* limpiar, sacar brillo a; *(fig: language)* perfeccionar.

polished ['pɔlɪʃt] *a (fig: person)* elegante.

polite [pə'laɪt] *a* cortés, atento; *(formal)* correcto; **it's not ~ to do that** es de mala educación hacer eso.

politely [pə'laɪtlɪ] *ad* cortésmente.

politeness [pə'laɪtnɪs] *n* cortesía.

politic ['pɔlɪtɪk] *a* prudente.

political [pə'lɪtɪkl] *a* político.

political asylum *n* asilo político.

politically [pə'lɪtɪkəlɪ] *ad* políticamente.

politician [pɔlɪ'tɪʃən] *n* político/a.

politics ['pɔlɪtɪks] *n* política.

polka ['pɔlkə] *n* polca.

polka dot *n* lunar *m*.

poll [pəul] *n (votes)* votación *f*, votos *mpl; (also:* **opinion ~)** sondeo, encuesta ◆ *vt (votes)* obtener; *(in opinion ~)* sondear; **to go to the ~s** *(voters)* votar; *(government)* acudir a las urnas.

pollen ['pɔlən] *n* polen *m*.

pollen count *n* índice *m* de polen.

pollination [pɔlɪ'neɪʃən] *n* polinización *f*.

polling ['pəulɪŋ] *n (Brit POL)* votación *f; (TEL)* interrogación *f*.

polling booth *n* cabina de votar.

polling day *n* día *m* de elecciones.

polling station *n* centro electoral.

pollute [pə'luːt] *vt* contaminar.

pollution [pə'luːʃən] *n* polución *f*, contaminación *f* del medio ambiente.

polo ['pəuləu] *n (sport)* polo.

polo-neck ['pəuləunɛk] *a* de cuello vuelto ◆ *n (sweater)* suéter *m* de cuello vuelto.

poly ['pɔlɪ] *n abbr (Brit)* = **polytechnic**.

poly... [pɔlɪ] *pref* poli....
polyester [pɔlɪ'estə*] *n* poliéster *m*.
polyethylene [pɔlɪ'eθɪliːn] *n* (*US*) politeno.
polygamy [pə'lɪgəmɪ] *n* poligamia.
polymath ['pɔlɪmæθ] *n* erudito/a.
Polynesia [pɔlɪ'niːzɪə] *n* Polinesia.
Polynesian [pɔlɪ'niːzɪən] *a, n* polinesio/a *m/f*.
polyp ['pɔlɪp] *n* (*MED*) pólipo.
polystyrene [pɔlɪ'staɪriːn] *n* poliestireno.
polytechnic [pɔlɪ'tɛknɪk] *n* ≈ escuela de formación profesional.
polythene ['pɔlɪθiːn] *n* (*Brit*) politeno.
polythene bag *n* bolsa de plástico.
polyurethane [pɔlɪ'juərɪθeɪn] *n* poliuretano.
pomegranate ['pɔmɪgrænɪt] *n* granada.
pommel ['pɔml] *n* pomo ♦ *vt* = **pummel**.
pomp [pɔmp] *n* pompa.
pompom ['pɔmpɔm], **pompon** ['pɔmpɔn] *n* borla.
pompous ['pɔmpəs] *a* pomposo; (*person*) presumido.
pond [pɔnd] *n* (*natural*) charca; (*artificial*) estanque *m*.
ponder ['pɔndə*] *vt* meditar.
ponderous ['pɔndərəs] *a* pesado.
pong [pɔŋ] *n* (*Brit col*) mal olor *m* ♦ *vi* (*Brit col*) apestar.
pontiff ['pɔntɪf] *n* pontífice *m*.
pontificate [pɔn'tɪfɪkeɪt] *vi* (*fig*): **to ~ (about)** pontificar (sobre).
pontoon [pɔn'tuːn] *n* pontón *m*; (*Brit: card game*) veintiuna.
pony ['pəʊnɪ] *n* poney *m*, jaca, potro (*LAm*).
ponytail ['pəʊnɪteɪl] *n* cola de caballo.
pony trekking *n* (*Brit*) excursión *f* a caballo.
poodle ['puːdl] *n* caniche *m*.
pooh-pooh [puː'puː] *vt* desdeñar.
pool [puːl] *n* (*natural*) charca; (*pond*) estanque *m*; (*also:* **swimming ~**) piscina, alberca (*LAm*); (*billiards*) chapolín; (*COMM: consortium*) consorcio; (: *US: monopoly trust*) trust *m* ♦ *vt* juntar; **typing ~** servicio de mecanografía; (**football**) **~s** *npl* quinielas *fpl*.
poor [puə*] *a* pobre; (*bad*) de mala calidad ♦ *npl:* **the ~** los pobres.
poorly ['puəlɪ] *a* mal, enfermo.
pop [pɔp] *n* ¡pum!; (*sound*) ruido seco; (*MUS*) (música) pop *m*; (*US col: father*) papá *m*; (*col: drink*) gaseosa ♦ *vt* (*burst*) hacer reventar ♦ *vi* reventar; (*cork*) saltar; **she ~ped her head out (of the window)** asomó de repente la cabeza (por la ventana).
pop in *vi* entrar un momento.
pop out *vi* salir un momento.
pop up *vi* aparecer inesperadamente.
pop concert *n* concierto pop.
popcorn ['pɔpkɔːn] *n* palomitas *fpl*.
pope [pəʊp] *n* papa *m*.

poplar ['pɔplə*] *n* álamo.
poplin ['pɔplɪn] *n* popelina.
popper ['pɔpə*] *n* corchete *m*, botón *m* automático.
poppy ['pɔpɪ] *n* amapola.
poppycock ['pɔpɪkɔk] *n* (*col*) tonterías *fpl*.
popsicle ['pɔpsɪkl] *n* (*US*) polo.
populace ['pɔpjuləs] *n* pueblo, plebe *f*.
popular ['pɔpjulə*] *a* popular; **a ~ song** una canción popular; **to be ~ (with)** (*person*) caer bien (a); (*decision*) ser popular (entre).
popularity [pɔpju'lærɪtɪ] *n* popularidad *f*.
popularize ['pɔpjuləraɪz] *vt* popularizar; (*disseminate*) vulgarizar.
populate ['pɔpjuleɪt] *vt* poblar.
population [pɔpju'leɪʃən] *n* población *f*.
population explosion *n* explosión *f* demográfica.
populous ['pɔpjuləs] *a* populoso.
porcelain ['pɔːslɪn] *n* porcelana.
porch [pɔːtʃ] *n* pórtico, entrada.
porcupine ['pɔːkjupaɪn] *n* puerco *m* espín.
pore [pɔː*] *n* poro ♦ *vi:* **to ~ over** engolfarse en.
pork [pɔːk] *n* carne *f* de cerdo *or* chancho (*LAm*).
pork chop *n* chuleta de cerdo.
pornographic [pɔːnə'græfɪk] *a* pornográfico.
pornography [pɔː'nɔgrəfɪ] *n* pornografía.
porous ['pɔːrəs] *a* poroso.
porpoise ['pɔːpəs] *n* marsopa.
porridge ['pɔrɪdʒ] *n* gachas *fpl* de avena.
port [pɔːt] *n* (*harbour*) puerto; (*NAUT: left side*) babor *m*; (*wine*) vino de Oporto; (*COMPUT*) puerta, puerto, port *m;* **~ of call** puerto de escala.
portable ['pɔːtəbl] *a* portátil.
portal ['pɔːtl] *n* puerta (grande), portalón *m*.
port authorities *npl* autoridades *fpl* portuarias.
portcullis [pɔː'tkʌlɪs] *n* rastrillo.
portend [pɔː'tend] *vt* presagiar, anunciar.
portent ['pɔːtent] *n* presagio, augurio.
porter ['pɔːtə*] *n* (*for luggage*) maletero; (*doorkeeper*) portero/a, conserje *m/f*; (*US RAIL*) mozo de los coches-cama.
portfolio [pɔːt'fəʊlɪəʊ] *n* (*case, of artist*) cartera, carpeta; (*POL, FINANCE*) cartera.
porthole ['pɔːthəʊl] *n* portilla.
portico ['pɔːtɪkəʊ] *n* pórtico.
portion ['pɔːʃən] *n* porción *f*; (*helping*) ración *f*.
portly ['pɔːtlɪ] *a* corpulento.
portrait ['pɔːtreɪt] *n* retrato.
portray [pɔː'treɪ] *vt* retratar; (*in writing*) representar.
portrayal [pɔː'treɪəl] *n* representación *f*.
Portugal ['pɔːtjugl] *n* Portugal *m*.
Portuguese [pɔːtju'giːz] *a* portugués/esa ♦ *n, pl inv* portugués/esa *m/f*; (*LING*) portu-

gués *m*.

Portuguese man-of-war *n* (*jellyfish*) especie *f* de medusa.

pose [pəuz] *n* postura, actitud *f*; (*pej*) afectación *f*, pose *f* ◆ *vi* posar; (*pretend*): **to ~ as** hacerse pasar por ◆ *vt* (*question*) plantear; **to strike a ~** tomar *or* adoptar una pose *or* actitud.

poser ['pəuzə*] *n* problema *m*/pregunta difícil; (*person*) = **poseur**.

poseur [pəu'zə:*] *n* presumido/a, persona afectada.

posh [pɔʃ] *a* (*col*) elegante, de lujo ◆ *ad* (*col*): **to talk ~** hablar con acento afectado.

position [pə'zɪʃən] *n* posición *f*; (*job*) puesto ◆ *vt* colocar; **to be in a ~ to do sth** estar en condiciones de hacer algo.

positive ['pɔzɪtɪv] *a* positivo; (*certain*) seguro; (*definite*) definitivo; **we look forward to a ~ reply** (*COMM*) esperamos ansiosamente su respuesta en firme; **he's a ~ nuisance** es un auténtico pelmazo; **~ cash flow** (*COMM*) flujo positivo de efectivo.

positively ['pɔzɪtɪvlɪ] *ad* (*affirmatively, enthusiastically*) de forma positiva; (*col: really*) absolutamente.

posse ['pɔsɪ] *n* (*US*) pelotón *m*.

possess [pə'zɛs] *vt* poseer; **like one ~ed** como un poseído; **whatever can have ~ed you?** ¿cómo se te ocurrió?

possessed [pə'zɛst] *a* poseso, poseído.

possession [pə'zɛʃən] *n* posesión *f*; **to take ~ of sth** tomar posesión de algo.

possessive [pə'zɛsɪv] *a* posesivo.

possessively [pə'zɛsɪvlɪ] *ad* de modo posesivo.

possessor [pə'zɛsə*] *n* poseedor(a) *m/f*, dueño/a.

possibility [pɔsɪ'bɪlɪtɪ] *n* posibilidad *f*; **he's a ~ for the part** es uno de los posibles para el papel.

possible ['pɔsɪbl] *a* posible; **as big as ~** lo más grande posible; **it is ~ to do it** es posible hacerlo; **as far as ~** en la medida de lo posible; **a ~ candidate** un(a) posible candidato/a.

possibly ['pɔsɪblɪ] *ad* (*perhaps*) posiblemente, tal vez; **I cannot ~ come** me es imposible venir; **could you ~ ...?** ¿podrías ...?

post [pəust] *n* (*Brit: letters, delivery*) correo; (*job, situation*) puesto; (*trading ~*) factoría; (*pole*) poste *m* ◆ *vt* (*Brit: send by ~*) echar al correo; (*MIL*) apostar; (*bills*) fijar, pegar; (*Brit: appoint*): **to ~ to** enviar a; **by ~** por correo; **by return of ~** a vuelta de correo; **to keep sb ~ed** tener a uno al corriente.

post... [pəust] *pref* post..., pos...; **~ 1950** pos(t) 1950.

postage ['pəustɪdʒ] *n* porte *m*, franqueo.

postage stamp *n* sello (de correo).

postal ['pəustl] *a* postal, de correos.

postal order *n* giro postal.

postbag ['pəustbæg] *n* (*Brit*) correspondencia, cartas *fpl*.

postbox ['pəustbɔks] *n* (*Brit*) buzón *m*.

postcard ['pəustkɑːd] *n* tarjeta postal.

postcode ['pəustkəud] *n* (*Brit*) código *or* clave *f* postal.

postdate [pəust'deɪt] *vt* (*cheque*) poner fecha adelantada a.

poster ['pəustə*] *n* cartel *m*.

poste restante [pəust'rɛstɔ̃t] *n* (*Brit*) lista de correos.

posterior [pɔs'tɪərɪə*] *n* (*col*) culo, trasero.

posterity [pɔs'tɛrɪtɪ] *n* posteridad *f*.

poster paint *n* pintura al agua.

post-free [pəust'friː] *a* libre de franqueo.

postgraduate ['pəust'grædjuət] *n* posgraduado/a.

posthumous ['pɔstjuməs] *a* póstumo.

posthumously ['pɔstjuməslɪ] *ad* póstumamente, con carácter póstumo.

posting ['pəustɪŋ] *n* destino.

postman ['pəustmən] *n* cartero.

postmark ['pəustmɑːk] *n* matasellos *m inv*.

postmaster ['pəustmɑːstə*] *n* administrador *m* de correos.

Postmaster General *n* director *m* general de correos.

postmistress ['pəustmɪstrɪs] *n* administradora *f* de correos.

post-mortem [pəust'mɔːtəm] *n* autopsia.

postnatal ['pəust'neɪtl] *a* postnatal, postparto.

post office *n* (*building*) (oficina de) correos *m*; (*organization*): **the P~ O~** Administración *f* General de Correos.

Post Office Box (PO Box) *n* apartado postal, casilla de correos (*LAm*).

post-paid ['pəust'peɪd] *a* porte pagado.

postpone [pəs'pəun] *vt* aplazar.

postponement [pəs'pəunmənt] *n* aplazamiento.

postscript ['pəustskrɪpt] *n* posdata.

postulate ['pɔstjuleɪt] *vt* postular.

posture ['pɔstʃə*] *n* postura, actitud *f*.

postwar [pəust'wɔː*] *a* de la posguerra.

posy ['pəuzɪ] *n* ramillete *m* (de flores).

pot [pɔt] *n* (*for cooking*) olla; (*for flowers*) maceta; (*for jam*) tarro, pote *m*; (*piece of pottery*) cacharro; (*col: marijuana*) costo ◆ *vt* (*plant*) poner en tiesto; (*conserve*) conservar; **~s of** (*col*) montones de; **to go to ~** (*col: work, performance*) irse al traste.

potash ['pɔtæʃ] *n* potasa.

potassium [pə'tæsɪəm] *n* potasio.

potato, ~es [pə'teɪtəu] *n* patata, papa (*LAm*).

potato crisps, (*US*) **potato chips** *npl* patatas *fpl or* papas *fpl* (*LAm*) fritas.

potato peeler *n* pelapatatas *m inv*.

potbellied ['pɔtbɛlɪd] *a* (*from overeating*)

barrigón/ona; (*from malnutrition*) con el vientre hinchado.
potency ['pəutnsɪ] *n* potencia.
potent ['pəutnt] *a* potente, poderoso; (*drink*) fuerte.
potentate ['pəutnteɪt] potentado.
potential [pə'tɛnʃl] *a* potencial, posible ♦ *n* potencial *m*; **to have** ~ mostrar gran potencial.
potentially [pə'tɛnʃəlɪ] *ad* en potencia.
pothole ['pɔthəul] *n* (*in road*) bache *m*; (*Brit: underground*) gruta.
potholer ['pɔthəulə*] *n* (*Brit*) espeleólogo/a.
potholing ['pɔthəulɪŋ] *n* (*Brit*): **to go** ~ dedicarse a la espeleología.
potion ['pəuʃən] *n* poción *f*, pócima.
potluck [pɔt'lʌk] *n*: **to take** ~ tomar lo que haya.
pot roast *n* carne *f* asada.
potshot ['pɔtʃɔt] *n*: **to take a** ~ **at sth** tirar a algo sin apuntar.
potted ['pɔtɪd] *a* (*food*) en conserva; (*plant*) en tiesto *or* maceta; (*fig: shortened*) resumido.
potter ['pɔtə*] *n* alfarero/a ♦ *vi*: **to** ~ **around,** ~ **about** ocuparse en fruslerías; **to** ~ **round the house** ir de aquí para allá sin hacer nada de provecho; ~**'s wheel** torno de alfarero.
pottery ['pɔtərɪ] *n* cerámica, alfarería; **a piece of** ~ un artículo de cerámica.
potty ['pɔtɪ] *a* (*col: mad*) chiflado ♦ *n* orinal *m* de niño.
potty-trained ['pɔtɪtreɪnd] *a* que ya no necesita pañales.
pouch [pautʃ] *n* (*zool*) bolsa; (*for tobacco*) petaca.
pouf(fe) [puːf] *n* (*stool*) pouf *m*.
poultry ['pəultrɪ] *n* aves *fpl* de corral; (*dead*) pollos *mpl*.
poultry farm *n* granja avícola.
poultry farmer *vi*: avicultor(a) *m/f*.
pounce [pauns] *vi*: **to** ~ **on** precipitarse sobre ♦ *n* salto, ataque *m*.
pound [paund] *n* libra; (*for dogs*) corral *m*; (*for cars*) depósito ♦ *vt* (*beat*) golpear; (*crush*) machacar ♦ *vi* (*beat*) dar golpes; **half a** ~ media libra; **a one** ~ **note** un billete de una libra.
pounding ['paundɪŋ] *n*: **to take a** ~ (*team*) sufrir terriblemente.
pound sterling *n* (libra) esterlina.
pour [pɔː*] *vt* echar; (*tea*) servir ♦ *vi* correr, fluir; (*rain*) llover a cántaros.
pour away, pour off *vt* vaciar, verter.
pour in *vi* (*people*) entrar en tropel; **to come** ~**ing in** (*water*) entrar a raudales; (*letters*) llegar a montones; (*cars, people*) llegar en tropel.
pour out *vi* (*people*) salir en tropel ♦ *vt* (*drink*) echar, servir.
pouring ['pɔːrɪŋ] *a*: ~ **rain** lluvia torrencial.

pout [paut] *vi* hacer pucheros.
poverty ['pɔvətɪ] *n* pobreza, miseria; (*fig*) falta, escasez *f*.
poverty-stricken ['pɔvətɪstrɪkn] *a* necesitado.
poverty trap *n* trampa de la pobreza.
POW *n abbr* = **prisoner of war**.
powder ['paudə*] *n* polvo; (*face* ~) polvos *mpl*; (*gun*~) pólvora ♦ *vt* polvorear; **to** ~ **one's face** ponerse polvos; **to** ~ **one's nose** empolvarse la nariz, ponerse polvos; (*euphemism*) ir a los servicios *or* al cuarto de baño.
powder compact *n* polvera.
powdered milk ['paudəd-] *n* leche *f* en polvo.
powder puff *n* borla.
powder room *n* aseos *mpl*.
powdery ['paudərɪ] *a* polvoriento.
power ['pauə*] *n* poder *m*; (*strength*) fuerza; (*nation*) potencia; (*drive*) empuje *m*; (*TECH*) potencia; (*ELEC*) fuerza, energía ♦ *vt* impulsar; **to be in** ~ (*POL*) estar en el poder; **to do all in one's** ~ **to help sb** hacer todo lo posible por ayudar a uno; **the world** ~**s** las potencias mundiales.
powerboat ['pauəbəut] *n* lancha a motor.
power cut *n* (*Brit*) apagón *m*.
power-driven ['pauədrɪvn] *a* mecánico; (*ELEC*) eléctrico.
powered ['pauəd] *a*: ~ **by** impulsado por; **nuclear-**~ **submarine** submarino nuclear.
power failure *n* = **power cut**.
powerful ['pauəful] *a* poderoso; (*engine*) potente; (*strong*) fuerte; (*play, speech*) conmovedor(a).
powerhouse ['pauəhaus] *n* (*fig: person*) fuerza motriz; **a** ~ **of ideas** una cantera de ideas.
powerless ['pauəlɪs] *a* impotente, ineficaz.
power line *n* línea de conducción eléctrica.
power point *n* (*Brit*) enchufe *m*.
power station *n* central *f* eléctrica.
power steering *n* (*AUT*) dirección *f* asistida.
powwow ['pauwau] *n* conferencia ♦ *vi* conferenciar.
pp *abbr* (= *per procurationem*: *by proxy*) p.p.
p & p *abbr* (*Brit*: = *postage and packing*) gastos de envío.
PPE *n abbr* (*Brit SCOL*) = *philosophy, politics and economics*.
PPS *abbr* (= *post postscriptum*) posdata adicional; (*Brit*: = *Parliamentary Private Secretary*) ayudante de un ministro.
PQ *abbr* (*Canada*) = *Province of Quebec*.
PR *n abbr see* **proportional representation**; (= *public relations*) relaciones *fpl* públicas ♦ *abbr* (*US POST*) = *Puerto Rico*.
Pr. *abbr* (= *prince*) P.
practicability [præktɪkə'bɪlɪtɪ] *n* factibilidad *f*.

practicable ['præktɪkəbl] *a* (*scheme*) factible.

practical ['præktɪkl] *a* práctico.

practicality [præktɪ'kælɪtɪ] *n* (*of situation etc*) factibilidad *f*.

practical joke *n* broma pesada.

practically ['præktɪklɪ] *ad* (*almost*) casi.

practice ['præktɪs] *n* (*habit*) costumbre *f*; (*exercise*) práctica, ejercicio; (*training*) adiestramiento; (*MED*) clientela ◆ *vt, vi* (*US*) = **practise**; **in** ~ (*in reality*) en la práctica; **out of** ~ desentrenado; **to put sth into** ~ poner algo en práctica; **it's common** ~ es práctica regular; **target** ~ práctica de tiro; **he has a small** ~ (*doctor*) tiene pocos pacientes; **to set up in** ~ **as** establecerse como.

practise, (*US*) **practice** ['præktɪs] *vt* (*carry out*) practicar; (*profession*) ejercer; (*train at*) practicar ◆ *vi* ejercer; (*train*) practicar.

practised, (*US*) **practiced** ['præktɪst] *a* (*person*) experto; (*performance*) bien ensayado; (*liar*) consumado; **with a** ~ **eye** con ojo experto.

practising, (*US*) **practicing** ['præktɪsɪŋ] *a* (*Christian etc*) practicante; (*lawyer*) que ejerce; (*homosexual*) activo.

practitioner [præk'tɪʃənə*] *n* practicante *m/f*; (*MED*) médico/a.

pragmatic [præg'mætɪk] *a* pragmático.

pragmatism ['prægmətɪzəm] *n* pragmatismo.

pragmatist ['prægmətɪst] *n* pragmatista *m/f*.

Prague [prɑːg] *n* Praga.

prairie ['prɛərɪ] *n* (*US*) pampa.

praise [preɪz] *n* alabanza(s) *f*(*pl*), elogio(s) *m*(*pl*).

praiseworthy ['preɪswɜːðɪ] *a* loable.

pram [præm] *n* (*Brit*) cochecito de niño.

prance [prɑːns] *vi* (*horse*) hacer cabriolas.

prank [præŋk] *n* travesura.

prattle ['prætl] *vi* parlotear; (*child*) balbucear.

prawn [prɔːn] *n* gamba.

pray [preɪ] *vi* rezar; **to** ~ **for forgiveness** pedir perdón.

prayer [prɛə*] *n* oración *f*, rezo; (*entreaty*) ruego, súplica.

prayer book *n* devocionario, misal *m*.

pre- ['priː] *pref* pre..., ante-; **~1970** pre 1970.

preach [priːtʃ] *vi* predicar.

preacher ['priːtʃə*] *n* predicador(a) *m/f*; (*US: minister*) pastor(a) *m/f*.

preamble [prɪ'æmbl] *n* preámbulo.

prearrange [priːə'reɪndʒ] *vt* organizar *or* acordar de antemano.

prearrangement [priːə'reɪndʒmənt] *n*: **by** ~ por previo acuerdo.

precarious [prɪ'kɛərɪəs] *a* precario.

precariously [prɪ'kɛərɪəslɪ] *ad* precariamente.

precaution [prɪ'kɔːʃən] *n* precaución *f*.

precautionary [prɪ'kɔːʃənrɪ] *a* (*measure*) de precaución, precautorio.

precede [prɪ'siːd] *vt, vi* preceder.

precedence ['presɪdəns] *n* precedencia; (*priority*) prioridad *f*.

precedent ['presɪdənt] *n* precedente *m;* **to establish** *or* **set a** ~ sentar un precedente.

preceding [prɪ'siːdɪŋ] *a* precedente.

precept ['priːsept] *n* precepto.

precinct ['priːsɪŋkt] *n* recinto; (*US: district*) distrito, barrio; **~s** *npl* contornos *mpl*; **pedestrian** ~ (*Brit*) zona peatonal; **shopping** ~ (*Brit*) centro comercial.

precious ['preʃəs] *a* precioso; (*stylized*) afectado ◆ *ad* (*col*): ~ **little/few** muy poco/pocos; **your** ~ **dog** (*ironic*) tu bendito perro.

precipice ['presɪpɪs] *n* precipicio.

precipitate *a* [prɪ'sɪpɪtɪt] (*hasty*) precipitado ◆ *vt* [prɪ'sɪpɪteɪt] (*hasten*) acelerar; (*bring about*) provocar.

precipitation [prɪsɪpɪ'teɪʃən] *n* precipitación *f*.

precipitous [prɪ'sɪpɪtəs] *a* (*steep*) escarpado; (*hasty*) precipitado.

précis ['preɪsiː] *n* resumen *m*.

precise [prɪ'saɪs] *a* preciso, exacto; (*person*) escrupuloso.

precisely [prɪ'saɪslɪ] *ad* exactamente, precisamente.

precision [prɪ'sɪʒən] *n* precisión *f*.

preclude [prɪ'kluːd] *vt* excluir.

precocious [prɪ'kəʊʃəs] *a* precoz.

preconceived [priːkən'siːvd] *a* (*idea*) preconcebido.

preconception [priːkən'sepʃn] *n* (*idea*) idea preconcebida.

precondition [priːkən'dɪʃən] *n* condición *f* previa.

precursor [priː'kɜːsə*] *n* precursor(a) *m/f*.

predate ['priː'deɪt] *vt* (*precede*) preceder.

predator ['predətə*] *n* animal *m* de rapiña.

predatory ['predətərɪ] *a* (*animal*) rapaz, de rapiña; (*person*) agresivo, depredador(a).

predecessor ['priːdɪsesə*] *n* antecesor(a) *m/f*.

predestination [priːdestɪ'neɪʃən] *n* predestinación *f*.

predestine [priː'destɪn] *vt* predestinar.

predetermine [priːdɪ'tɜːmɪn] *vt* predeterminar.

predicament [prɪ'dɪkəmənt] *n* apuro.

predicate ['predɪkɪt] *n* predicado.

predict [prɪ'dɪkt] *vt* pronosticar.

predictable [prɪ'dɪktəbl] *a* previsible.

predictably [prɪ'dɪktəblɪ] *ad* (*behave, react*) de forma previsible; ~ **she didn't arrive** como era de esperar, no llegó.

prediction [prɪ'dɪkʃən] *n* pronóstico.

predispose ['priːdɪs'pəʊz] *vt* predisponer.

predominance [prɪ'dɒmɪnəns] *n* predominio.

predominant [prɪ'dɒmɪnənt] *a* predominante.

predominantly [prɪ'dɒmɪnəntlɪ] *ad* en su mayoría.

predominate [prɪ'dɒmɪneɪt] *vi* predominar.

pre-eminent [priː'emɪnənt] *a* preeminente.

pre-empt [priː'emt] *vt* (*Brit*) adelantarse a.

pre-emptive [priː'emtɪv] *a*: ~ **strike** ataque *m* preventivo.

preen [priːn] *vt*: **to** ~ **itself** (*bird*) limpiarse (las plumas); **to** ~ **o.s.** pavonearse.

prefab ['priːfæb] *n* casa prefabricada.

prefabricated [priː'fæbrɪkeɪtɪd] *a* prefabricado.

preface ['prefəs] *n* prefacio.

prefect ['priːfekt] *n* (*Brit: in school*) monitor(a) *m/f*.

prefer [prɪ'fəː*] *vt* preferir; (*LAW: charges, complaint*) presentar; (: *action*) entablar; **to** ~ **coffee to tea** preferir el café al té.

preferable ['prefrəbl] *a* preferible.

preferably ['prefrəblɪ] *ad* de preferencia.

preference ['prefrəns] *n* preferencia; (*priority*) prioridad *f*; **in** ~ **to sth** antes que algo.

preference shares *npl* acciones *fpl* privilegiadas.

preferential [prefə'renʃəl] *a* preferente.

prefix ['priːfɪks] *n* prefijo.

pregnancy ['pregnənsɪ] *n* embarazo.

pregnant ['pregnənt] *a* embarazada; **3 months** ~ tres meses embarazada *or* encinta; ~ **with meaning** cargado de significado.

prehistoric ['priːhɪs'tɒrɪk] *a* prehistórico.

prehistory [priː'hɪstɒrɪ] *n* prehistoria.

prejudge [priː'dʒʌdʒ] *vt* prejuzgar.

prejudice ['predʒudɪs] *n* (*bias*) prejuicio; (*harm*) perjuicio ♦ *vt* (*bias*) predisponer; (*harm*) perjudicar; **to** ~ **sb in favour of/ against** (*bias*) predisponer a uno a favor de/en contra de.

prejudiced ['predʒudɪst] *a* (*person*) predispuesto; (*view*) parcial, interesado; **to be** ~ **against sb/sth** estar predispuesto en contra de uno/algo.

prelate ['prelət] *n* prelado.

preliminaries [prɪ'lɪmɪnərɪz] *npl* preliminares *mpl*, preparativos *mpl*.

preliminary [prɪ'lɪmɪnərɪ] *a* preliminar.

prelude ['preljuːd] *n* preludio.

premarital ['priː'mærɪtl] *a* premarital.

premature ['premətʃuə*] *a* (*arrival etc*) prematuro; **you are being a little** ~ te has adelantado.

prematurely [premə'tʃuəlɪ] *ad* prematuramente, antes de tiempo.

premeditate [priː'medɪteɪt] *vt* premeditar.

premeditated [priː'medɪteɪtɪd] *a* premeditado.

premeditation [priːmedɪ'teɪʃən] *n* premeditación *f*.

premenstrual [priː'menstruəl] *a* premenstrual.

premenstrual tension *n* (*MED*) tensión *f* premenstrual.

premier ['premɪə*] *a* primero, principal ♦ *n* (*POL*) primer(a) ministro/a.

première ['premɪeə*] *n* estreno.

premise ['premɪs] *n* premisa.

premises ['premɪsɪs] *npl* local *msg*; **on the** ~ en el lugar mismo; **business** ~ locales *mpl* comerciales.

premium ['priːmɪəm] *n* premio; (*COMM*) prima; **to be at a** ~ ser muy solicitado; **to sell at a** ~ (*shares*) vender caro.

premium bond *n* (*Brit*) bono del estado que participa en un sorteo nacional.

premium deal *n* (*COMM*) oferta extraordinaria.

premium gasoline *n* (*US*) (gasolina) súper *m*.

premonition [premə'nɪʃən] *n* presentimiento.

preoccupation [priːɒkjuˈpeɪʃən] *n* preocupación *f*.

preoccupied [priː'ɒkjupaɪd] *a* (*worried*) preocupado; (*absorbed*) ensimismado.

prep [prep] *a abbr*: ~ **school** = **preparatory school** ♦ *n abbr* (*SCOL*: = *preparation*) deberes *mpl*.

prepaid [priː'peɪd] *a* porte pagado; ~ **envelope** sobre *m* de porte pagado.

preparation [prepə'reɪʃən] *n* preparación *f*; ~**s** *npl* preparativos *mpl*; **in** ~ **for sth** en preparación para algo.

preparatory [prɪ'pærətɒrɪ] *a* preparatorio, preliminar; ~ **to sth/to doing sth** como preparación para algo/para hacer algo.

preparatory school *n* (*Brit*) escuela preparatoria; (*US*) colegio privado.

prepare [prɪ'peə*] *vt* preparar, disponer ♦ *vi*: **to** ~ **for** prepararse *or* disponerse para; (*make preparations*) hacer preparativos para.

prepared [prɪ'peəd] *a* (*willing*): **to be** ~ **to help sb** estar dispuesto a ayudar a uno.

preponderance [prɪ'pɒndərns] *n* preponderancia, predominio.

preposition [prepə'zɪʃən] *n* preposición *f*.

prepossessing [priːpə'zesɪŋ] *a* agradable, atractivo.

preposterous [prɪ'pɒstərəs] *a* absurdo, ridículo.

prerecorded ['priːrɪ'kɔːdɪd] *a*: ~ **broadcast** programa *m* grabado de antemano; ~ **cassette** cassette *f* pregrabada.

prerequisite [priː'rekwɪzɪt] *n* requisito previo.

prerogative [prɪ'rɒgətɪv] *n* prerrogativa.

Presbyterian [prezbɪ'tɪərɪən] *a, n* presbiteriano/a *m/f*.

presbytery ['prezbɪtərɪ] *n* casa parroquial.

preschool ['priː'skuːl] *a* (*child, age*) preescolar.

prescribe [prɪ'skraɪb] *vt* prescribir; (*MED*)

recetar; ~**d books** (*Brit scol*) libros *mpl* del curso.

prescription [prɪ'skrɪpʃən] *n* (*MED*) receta; **to make up** *or* (*US*) **fill a** ~ preparar una receta; **only available on** ~ se vende solamente con receta (médica).

prescription charges *npl* (*Brit*) precio *sg* de las recetas.

prescriptive [prɪ'skrɪptɪv] *a* normativo.

presence ['prɛzns] *n* presencia; (*attendance*) asistencia.

presence of mind *n* aplomo.

present *a* ['prɛznt] (*in attendance*) presente; (*current*) actual ◆ *n* (*gift*) regalo; (*actuality*) actualidad *f*, presente *m* ◆ *vt* [prɪ'zɛnt] (*introduce*) presentar; (*expound*) exponer; (*give*) presentar, dar, ofrecer; (*THEATRE*) representar; **to be** ~ **at** asistir a, estar presente en; **those** ~ los presentes; **to give sb a** ~, **make sb a** ~ **of sth** regalar algo a uno; **at** ~ actualmente; **to** ~ **o.s. for an interview** presentarse a una entrevista; **may I** ~ **Miss Clark** permítame presentarle *or* le presento a la Srta Clark.

presentable [prɪ'zɛntəbl] *a*: **to make o.s.** ~ arreglarse.

presentation [prɛzn'teɪʃən] *n* presentación *f*; (*gift*) obsequio; (*of case*) exposición *f*; (*THEATRE*) representación *f*; **on** ~ **of the voucher** al presentar el vale.

present-day ['prɛzntdeɪ] *a* actual.

presenter [prɪ'zɛntə*] *n* (*RADIO*, *TV*) locutor(a) *m/f*.

presently ['prɛzntlɪ] *ad* (*soon*) dentro de poco; (*US: now*) ahora.

present participle *n* participio (de) presente.

present tense *n* (tiempo) presente *m*.

preservation [prɛzə'veɪʃən] *n* conservación *f*.

preservative [prɪ'zɜ:vətɪv] *n* preservativo.

preserve [prɪ'zɜ:v] *vt* (*keep safe*) preservar, proteger; (*maintain*) mantener; (*food*) conservar; (*in salt*) salar ◆ *n* (*for game*) coto, vedado; (*often pl: jam*) conserva, confitura.

preshrunk ['pri:'ʃrʌŋk] *a* inencogible.

preside [prɪ'zaɪd] *vi* presidir.

presidency ['prɛzɪdənsɪ] *n* presidencia.

president ['prɛzɪdənt] *n* presidente *m/f*; (*US: of company*) director(a) *m/f*, gerente *m/f*.

presidential [prɛzɪ'dɛnʃl] *a* presidencial.

press [prɛs] *n* (*tool, machine, newspapers*) prensa; (*printer's*) imprenta; (*of hand*) apretón *m* ◆ *vt* (*push*) empujar; (*squeeze*) apretar; (*grapes*) pisar; (*clothes: iron*) planchar; (*pressure*) presionar; (*doorbell*) apretar, pulsar, tocar; (*insist*): **to** ~ **sth on sb** insistir en que uno acepte algo ◆ *vi* (*squeeze*) apretar; (*pressurize*) ejercer presión; **to go to** ~ (*newspaper*) entrar en prensa; **to be in the** ~ (*being printed*)

estar en prensa; (*in the newspapers*) aparecer en la prensa; **we are** ~**ed for time** tenemos poco tiempo; **to** ~ **sb to do** *or* **into doing sth** (*urge, entreat*) presionar a uno para que haga algo; **to** ~ **sb for an answer** insistir a uno para que conteste; **to** ~ **charges against sb** (*LAW*) formular acusaciones contra uno.

press on *vi* avanzar; (*hurry*) apretar el paso.

press agency *n* agencia de prensa.

press clipping *n* = **press cutting**.

press conference *n* rueda de prensa.

press cutting *n* recorte *m* (de periódico).

pressing ['prɛsɪŋ] *a* apremiante.

pressman ['prɛsmæn] *n* periodista *m*.

press release *n* comunicado de prensa.

press stud *n* (*Brit*) botón *m* de presión.

press-up ['prɛsʌp] *n* (*Brit*) plancha.

pressure ['prɛʃə*] *n* presión *f*; (*urgency*) apremio, urgencia; (*influence*) influencia; **high/low** ~ alta/baja presión; **to put** ~ **on sb** presionar a uno, hacer presión sobre uno.

pressure cooker *n* olla a presión.

pressure gauge *n* manómetro.

pressure group *n* grupo de presión.

pressurize ['prɛʃəraɪz] *vt* presurizar; **to** ~ **sb (into doing sth)** presionar a uno (para que haga algo).

pressurized ['prɛʃəraɪzd] *a* (*container*) a presión.

Prestel ® ['prɛstɛl] *n* Prestel *m* ®.

prestige [prɛs'ti:ʒ] *n* prestigio.

prestigious [prɛs'tɪdʒəs] *a* prestigioso.

presumably [prɪ'zju:məblɪ] *ad* es de suponer que, cabe presumir que; ~ **he did it** lo más probable es que lo hiciera.

presume [prɪ'zju:m] *vt* presumir, suponer; **to** ~ **to do** (*dare*) atreverse a hacer.

presumption [prɪ'zʌmpʃən] *n* suposición *f*; (*pretension*) presunción *f*.

presumptuous [prɪ'zʌmptjuəs] *a* presumido.

presuppose [pri:sə'pəuz] *vt* presuponer.

presupposition [pri:sʌpə'zɪʃən] *n* presuposición *f*.

pre-tax [pri:'tæks] *a* anterior al impuesto.

pretence, (*US*) **pretense** [prɪ'tɛns] *n* (*claim*) pretensión *f*; (*pretext*) pretexto; (*make-believe*) fingimiento; **on** *or* **under the** ~ **of doing sth** bajo *or* con el pretexto de hacer algo; **she is devoid of all** ~ es siempre franca.

pretend [prɪ'tɛnd] *vt* (*feign*) fingir ◆ *vi* (*feign*) fingir; (*claim*): **to** ~ **to sth** pretender a algo.

pretense [prɪ'tɛns] *n* (*US*) = **pretence**.

pretension [prɪ'tɪnʃən] *n* (*claim*) pretensión *f*; **to have no** ~**s to sth/to being sth** no engañarse en cuanto a algo/a ser algo.

pretentious [prɪ'tɛnʃəs] *a* presumido; (*ostentatious*) ostenso, aparatoso.

pretext ['priːtɛkst] n pretexto; **on** or **under the ~ of doing sth** so pretexto de hacer algo.

prettily ['prɪtɪlɪ] ad encantadoramente, con gracia.

pretty ['prɪtɪ] a (gen) bonito, lindo (LAm) ♦ ad bastante.

prevail [prɪ'veɪl] vi (gain mastery) prevalecer; (be current) predominar; (persuade): **to ~ (up)on sb to do sth** persuadir a uno para que haga algo.

prevailing [prɪ'veɪlɪŋ] a (dominant) predominante.

prevalent ['prɛvələnt] a (dominant) dominante; (widespread) extendido; (fashionable) de moda.

prevarication [prɪværɪ'keɪʃən] n tergiversación f, evasivas fpl.

prevent [prɪ'vɛnt] vt: **to ~ (sb) from doing sth** impedir (a uno) hacer algo.

preventable [prɪ'vɛntəbl] a evitable.

preventative [prɪ'vɛntətɪv] a preventivo.

prevention [prɪ'vɛnʃən] n prevención f.

preventive [prɪ'vɛntɪv] a preventivo.

preview ['priːvjuː] n (of film) preestreno.

previous ['priːvɪəs] a previo, anterior; **he has no ~ experience in that field** no tiene antecedentes en esa rama; **I have a ~ engagement** tengo un compromiso anterior.

previously ['priːvɪəslɪ] ad antes.

prewar [priː'wɔː*] a antes de la guerra.

prey [preɪ] n presa ♦ vi: **to ~ on** vivir a costa de; (feed on) alimentarse de; **it was ~ing on his mind** se le quitaba el sueño.

price [praɪs] n precio; (BETTING: odds) puntos mpl de ventaja ♦ vt (goods) fijar el precio de; **to go up** or **rise in ~** subir de precio; **what is the ~ of ...?** ¿qué precio tiene ...?; **to put a ~ on sth** poner precio a algo; **what ~ his promises now?** ¿para qué sirven ahora sus promesas?; **he regained his freedom, but at a ~** recobró su libertad, pero le había costado caro; **to be ~d out of the market** (article) no encontrar comprador para ese precio; (nation) no ser competitivo.

price control n control m de precios.

price-cutting ['praɪskʌtɪŋ] n reducción f de precios.

priceless ['praɪslɪs] a que no tiene precio; (col: amusing) divertidísimo.

price list n tarifa.

price range n gama de precios; **it's within my ~** está al alcance de mi bolsillo.

price tag n etiqueta.

price war n guerra de precios.

pricey ['praɪsɪ] a (Brit col) caro.

prick [prɪk] n pinchazo; (with pin) alfilerazo; (sting) picadura ♦ vt pinchar; picar; **to ~ up one's ears** aguzar el oído.

prickle ['prɪkl] n (sensation) picor m; (BOT) espina; (ZOOL) púa.

prickly ['prɪklɪ] a espinoso; (fig: person)

malhumorado; (: touchy) quisquilloso.

prickly heat n sarpullido causado por exceso de calor.

prickly pear n chumbo.

pride [praɪd] n orgullo; (pej) soberbia ♦ vt: **to ~ o.s. on** enorgullecerse de; **to take (a) ~ in** enorgullecerse de; **her ~ and joy** su orgullo; **to have ~ of place** tener prioridad.

priest [priːst] n sacerdote m.

priestess ['priːstɪs] n sacerdotisa.

priesthood ['priːsthud] n (practice) sacerdocio; (priests) clero.

prig [prɪg] n gazmoño/a.

prim [prɪm] a (demure) remilgado; (prudish) gazmoño.

prima donna ['priːmə'dɔnə] n primadonna, diva.

prima facie ['praɪmə'feɪʃɪ] a: **to have a ~ case** (LAW) tener razón a primera vista.

primarily ['praɪmərɪlɪ] ad (above all) ante todo, primordialmente.

primary ['praɪmərɪ] a primario; (first in importance) principal ♦ n (US: also: ~ election) (elección f) primaria.

primary colour, (US) **primary color** n color m primario.

primary education n enseñanza primaria.

primary products npl productos mpl primarios.

primary school n (Brit) escuela primaria.

primate n ['praɪmɪt] (REL) primado ♦ n ['praɪmeɪt] (ZOOL) primate m.

prime [praɪm] a primero, principal; (basic) fundamental; (excellent) selecto, de primera clase ♦ n: **in the ~ of life** en la flor de la vida ♦ vt (gun, pump) cebar; (fig) preparar.

Prime Minister (PM) n primer(a) ministro/a.

primer ['praɪmə*] n (book) texto elemental; (paint) pintura de base, imprimación f.

prime time n (RADIO, TV) tiempo preferencial.

primeval [praɪ'miːvəl] a primitivo.

primitive ['prɪmɪtɪv] a primitivo; (crude) rudimentario; (uncivilized) inculto.

primly ['prɪmlɪ] ad remilgadamente; con gazmoñería.

primrose ['prɪmrəuz] n primavera, prímula.

primus (stove) ® ['praɪməs-] n (Brit) hornillo de camping.

prince [prɪns] n príncipe m.

prince charming n príncipe m azul.

princess [prɪn'sɛs] n princesa.

principal ['prɪnsɪpl] a principal, mayor ♦ n director(a) m/f; (in play) protagonista principal m/f; (COMM) capital m, principal m.

principality [prɪnsɪ'pælɪtɪ] n principado.

principle ['prɪnsɪpl] n principio; **in ~ en** principio; **on ~** por principio.

print [prɪnt] n (*impression*) marca, impresión f; huella; (*letters*) letra de molde; (*fabric*) estampado; (*ART*) grabado; (*PHOT*) impresión f ◆ vt (*gen*) imprimir; (*on mind*) grabar; (*write in capitals*) escribir en letras de molde; **out of** ~ agotado.

print out vt (*COMPUT*) imprimir.

printed circuit ['prɪntɪd-] n circuito impreso.

printed circuit board (PCB) n tarjeta de circuito impreso (TCI).

printed matter n impresos mpl.

printer ['prɪntə*] n (*person*) impresor(a) m/f; (*machine*) impresora.

printhead ['prɪnthɛd] n cabeza impresora.

printing ['prɪntɪŋ] n (*art*) imprenta; (*act*) impresión f; (*quantity*) tirada.

printing press n prensa.

printout ['prɪntaut] n (*COMPUT*) printout m.

print wheel n rueda impresora.

prior ['praɪə*] a anterior, previo ◆ n prior m; ~ **to doing** antes de or hasta hacer; **without** ~ **notice** sin previo aviso; **to have a** ~ **claim to sth** tener prioridad en algo.

prioress [praɪə'rɛs] n priora.

priority [praɪ'ɔrɪtɪ] n prioridad f; **to have** or **take** ~ **over sth** tener prioridad sobre algo.

priory ['praɪərɪ] n priorato.

prise, (*US*) **prize** [praɪz] vt: **to** ~ **open** abrir con palanca.

prism ['prɪzəm] n prisma m.

prison ['prɪzn] n cárcel f, prisión f ◆ cpd carcelario.

prison camp n campamento para prisioneros.

prisoner ['prɪznə*] n (*in prison*) preso/a; (*under arrest*) detenido/a; (*in dock*) acusado/a; **the** ~ **at the bar** el/la acusado/a; **to take sb** ~ hacer or tomar prisionero a uno.

prisoner of war n prisionero/a or preso/a de guerra.

prissy ['prɪsɪ] a remilgado.

pristine ['prɪstiːn] a pristino.

privacy ['prɪvəsɪ] n (*seclusion*) soledad f; (*intimacy*) intimidad f; **in the strictest** ~ de máxima confianza.

private ['praɪvɪt] a (*personal*) particular; (*confidential*) secreto, confidencial; (*intimate*) privado, íntimo; (*sitting etc*) a puertas cerradas ◆ n soldado raso; "~" (*on envelope*) "confidencial"; (*on door*) "privado"; **in** ~ en privado; **in (his)** ~ **life** en su vida privada; **to be in** ~ **practice** tener consultorio particular.

private enterprise n la empresa privada.

private eye n detective m/f privado/a.

private hearing n (*LAW*) vista a puertas cerradas.

private limited company n (*Brit*) sociedad f de responsabilidad limitada.

privately ['praɪvɪtlɪ] ad en privado; (*in o.s.*) en secreto.

private parts npl partes fpl privadas or pudendas.

private practice n: **to be in** ~ ser médico/a (or dentista m/f) particular.

private property n propiedad f privada.

private school n colegio privado.

privation [praɪ'veɪʃən] n (*state*) privación f; (*hardship*) privación f, estrechez f.

privatize ['praɪvɪtaɪz] vt privatizar.

privet ['prɪvɪt] n alheña.

privilege ['prɪvɪlɪdʒ] n privilegio; (*prerogative*) prerrogativa.

privileged ['prɪvɪlɪdʒd] a privilegiado; **to be** ~ **to do sth** gozar del privilegio de hacer algo.

privy ['prɪvɪ] a: **to be** ~ **to** estar enterado de.

privy council n consejo del estado.

prize [praɪz] n premio ◆ a (*first class*) de primera clase ◆ vt apreciar, estimar; (*US*) = **prise**.

prize fighter n boxeador m profesional.

prize fighting n boxeo m profesional.

prize-giving ['praɪzgɪvɪŋ] n distribución f de premios.

prize money n (*SPORT*) bolsa.

prizewinner ['praɪzwɪnə*] n premiado/a.

prizewinning ['praɪzwɪnɪŋ] a (*novel, essay*) premiado.

PRO n abbr = **public relations officer**.

pro [prəu] n (*SPORT*) profesional m/f; **the** ~**s and cons** los pros y los contras.

pro- [prəu] pref (*in favour of*) pro, en pro de; ~**Soviet** pro-soviético.

probability [prɔbə'bɪlɪtɪ] n probabilidad f; **in all** ~ lo más probable.

probable ['prɔbəbl] a probable; **it is** ~/**hardly** ~ **that** es probable/poco probable que.

probably ['prɔbəblɪ] ad probablemente.

probate ['prəubeɪt] n (*LAW*) legalización f de un testamento.

probation [prə'beɪʃən] n: **on** ~ (*employee*) a prueba; (*LAW*) en libertad condicional.

probationary [prə'beɪʃənrɪ] a: ~ **period** período de prueba.

probationer [prə'beɪʃənə*] n (*LAW*) persona en libertad condicional; (*nurse*) ≈ aprendiz m/f de ATS (*Sp*), aprendiz de enfermero.

probation officer n *oficial a cargo de los presos en libertad condicional*.

probe [prəub] n (*MED, SPACE*) sonda; (*enquiry*) encuesta, investigación f ◆ vt sondar; (*investigate*) investigar.

probity ['prəubɪtɪ] n probidad f.

problem ['prɔbləm] n problema m; **what's the** ~? ¿cuál es el problema?, ¿qué pasa?; **no** ~! ¡por supuesto!; **to have** ~**s with the car** tener problemas con el coche.

problematic(al) [prɔblə'mætɪk(l)] a problemático.

procedural [prəu'siːdʒərəl] a de procedimiento; (*law*) procesal.

procedure [prə'siːdʒə*] *n* procedimiento; (*bureaucratic*) trámites *mpl;* **cashing a cheque is a simple ~** cobrar un cheque es un trámite sencillo.

proceed [prə'siːd] *vi* proceder; (*continue*): **to ~ (with)** continuar *or* seguir (con); **to ~ against sb** (*law*) proceder contra uno; **I am not sure how to ~** no sé cómo proceder; *see also* **proceeds.**

proceedings [prə'siːdɪŋz] *npl* acto *sg,* actos *mpl;* (*law*) proceso *sg;* (*meeting*) función *fsg;* (*records*) actas *fpl.*

proceeds ['prəusiːdz] *npl* ganancias *fpl,* ingresos *mpl.*

process ['prəuses] *n* proceso; (*method*) método, sistema *m;* (*proceeding*) procedimiento ◆ *vt* tratar, elaborar ◆ *vi* [prə'sɛs] (*Brit formal: go in procession*): **in ~** en curso; **we are in the ~ of moving to ...** estamos en vías de mudarnos a ....

processed cheese ['prəusɛst-], (*US*) **process cheese** *n* queso procesado.

processing ['prəusesɪŋ] *n* elaboración *f.*

procession [prə'sɛʃən] *n* desfile *m;* **funeral ~** cortejo fúnebre.

proclaim [prə'kleɪm] *vt* proclamar; (*announce*) anunciar.

proclamation [prɔklə'meɪʃən] *n* proclamación *f;* (*written*) proclama.

proclivity [prə'klɪvɪtɪ] *n* propensión *f,* inclinación *f.*

procrastinate [prəu'kræstɪneɪt] *vi* demorarse.

procrastination [prəukræstɪ'neɪʃən] *n* dilación *f.*

procreation [prəukrɪ'eɪʃən] *n* procreación *f.*

procure [prə'kjuə*] *vt* conseguir, obtener.

procurement [prə'kjuəmənt] *n* obtención *f.*

prod [prɔd] *vt* (*push*) empujar; (*with elbow*) dar un codazo a ◆ *n* empuje *m;* codazo.

prodigal ['prɔdɪgl] *a* pródigo.

prodigious [prə'dɪdʒəs] *a* prodigioso.

prodigy ['prɔdɪdʒɪ] *n* prodigio.

produce *n* ['prɔdjuːs] (*agr*) productos *mpl* agrícolas ◆ *vt* [prə'djuːs] producir; (*yield*) rendir; (*bring*) sacar; (*show*) presentar, mostrar; (*proof of identity*) enseñar, presentar; (*theatre*) presentar, poner en escena; (*offspring*) dar a luz.

produce dealer *n* (*US*) verdulero/a.

producer [prə'djuːsə*] *n* (*theatre*) director(a) *m/f;* (*agr, cinema*) productor(a) *m/f.*

product ['prɔdʌkt] *n* producto.

production [prə'dʌkʃən] *n* (*act*) producción *f;* (*theatre*) representación *f,* obra; **to put into ~** lanzar a la producción.

production agreement *n* (*US*) acuerdo de productividad.

production control *n* control *m* de producción.

production line *n* línea de producción.

production manager *n* jefe/jefa *m/f* de producción.

productive [prə'dʌktɪv] *a* productivo.

productivity [prɔdʌk'tɪvɪtɪ] *n* productividad *f.*

productivity agreement *n* (*Brit*) acuerdo de productividad.

productivity bonus *n* bono de productividad.

Prof. [prɔf] *abbr* (= *professor*) Prof.

profane [prə'feɪn] *a* profano.

profess [prə'fɛs] *vt* profesar; **I do not ~ to be an expert** no pretendo ser experto.

professed [prə'fɛst] *a* (*self-declared*) declarado.

profession [prə'fɛʃən] *n* profesión *f.*

professional [prə'fɛʃnl] *n* profesional *m/f* ◆ *a* profesional; (*by profession*) de profesión; **to take ~ advice** buscar un consejo profesional.

professionalism [prə'fɛʃnəlɪzm] *n* profesionalismo.

professionally [prə'fɛʃnəlɪ] *ad:* **I only know him ~** sólo le conozco por nuestra relación de trabajo.

professor [prə'fɛsə*] *n* (*Brit*) catedrático/a; (*US: teacher*) profesor(a) *m/f.*

professorship [prə'fɛsəʃɪp] *n* cátedra.

proffer ['prɔfə*] *vt* ofrecer.

proficiency [prə'fɪʃənsɪ] *n* capacidad *f,* habilidad *f.*

proficiency test *n* prueba de capacitación.

proficient [prə'fɪʃənt] *a* experto, hábil.

profile ['prəufaɪl] *n* perfil *m;* **to keep a high/low ~** tratar de llamar la atención/ pasar inadvertido.

profit ['prɔfɪt] *n* (*comm*) ganancia; (*fig*) provecho ◆ *vi:* **to ~ by** *or* **from** aprovechar *or* sacar provecho de; **~ and loss account** cuenta de ganancias y pérdidas; **with ~s endowment assurance** seguro dotal con beneficios; **to sell sth at a ~** vender algo con ganancia.

profitability [prɔfɪtə'bɪlɪtɪ] *n* rentabilidad *f.*

profitable ['prɔfɪtəbl] *a* (*econ*) rentable; (*beneficial*) provechoso, útil.

profitably ['prɔfɪtəblɪ] *ad* rentablemente; provechosamente.

profit centre, (*US*) **profit center** *n* centro de beneficios.

profiteering [prɔfɪ'tɪərɪŋ] *n* (*pej*) explotación *f.*

profit-making ['prɔfɪtmeɪkɪŋ] *a* rentable.

profit margin *n* margen *m* de ganancia.

profit-sharing ['prɔfɪtʃeərɪŋ] *n* participación *f* de empleados en los beneficios.

profits tax *n* impuesto sobre los beneficios.

profligate ['prɔflɪgɪt] *a* (*dissolute: behaviour, act*) disoluto; (*: person*) libertino; (*extravagant*): **he's very ~ with his money** es muy derrochador.

pro forma ['prəu'fɔːmə] *a:* **~ invoice** factura pro-forma.

profound [prə'faund] *a* profundo.

profoundly [prə'faundlɪ] *ad* profundamente.

profusely [prə'fjuːslɪ] *ad* profusamente.

profusion [prə'fjuːʒən] *n* profusión *f*, abundancia.

progeny ['prɔdʒɪnɪ] *n* progenie *f*.

programme, (*US*) **program** ['prəugræm] *n* programa *m* ♦ *vt* programar.

program(m)er ['prəugræmə*] *n* programador(a) *m/f*.

program(m)ing ['prəugræmɪŋ] *n* programación *f*.

program(m)ing language *n* lenguaje *m* de programación.

progress *n* ['prəugrɛs] progreso; (*development*) desarrollo ♦ *vi* [prə'grɛs] progresar, avanzar; desarrollarse; **in** ~ (*meeting, work etc*) en curso; **as the match** ~ed en el curso del partido.

progression [prə'grɛʃən] *n* progresión *f*.

progressive [prə'grɛsɪv] *a* progresivo; (*person*) progresista.

progressively [prə'grɛsɪvlɪ] *ad* progresivamente, poco a poco.

progress report *n* (*MED*) informe *m* sobre el estado; (*ADMIN*) informe *m* sobre el progreso.

prohibit [prə'hɪbɪt] *vt* prohibir; **to** ~ **sb from doing sth** prohibir a uno hacer algo; **"smoking** ~**ed"** "prohibido fumar".

prohibition [prəuɪ'bɪʃən] *n* (*US*) prohibicionismo.

prohibitive [prə'hɪbɪtɪv] *a* (*price etc*) prohibitivo.

project *n* ['prɔdʒɛkt] proyecto; (*SCOL, UNIV: research*) trabajo, proyecto ♦ (*vb*: [prə'dʒɛkt]) *vt* proyectar ♦ *vi* (*stick out*) salir, sobresalir.

projectile [prə'dʒɛktaɪl] *n* proyectil *m*.

projection [prə'dʒɛkʃən] *n* proyección *f*; (*overhang*) saliente *m*.

projectionist [prə'dʒɛkʃənɪst] *n* (*CINE*) operador(a) *m/f* de cine.

projection room *n* (*CINE*) cabina de proyección.

projector [prə'dʒɛktə*] *n* proyector *m*.

proletarian [prəulɪ'tɛərɪən] *a* proletario.

proletariat [prəulɪ'tɛərɪət] *n* proletariado.

proliferate [prə'lɪfəreɪt] *vi* proliferar, multiplicarse.

proliferation [prəlɪfə'reɪʃən] *n* proliferación *f*.

prolific [prə'lɪfɪk] *a* prolífico.

prologue, (*US*) **prolog** ['prəulɔg] *n* prólogo.

prolong [prə'lɔŋ] *vt* prolongar, extender.

prom [prɔm] *n abbr* = **promenade**, **promenade concert** ♦ *n* (*US: ball*) baile *m* de gala.

promenade [prɔmə'nɑːd] *n* (*by sea*) paseo marítimo ♦ *vi* (*stroll*) pasearse.

promenade concert *n* concierto (en que

parte del público permanece de pie).

promenade deck *n* cubierta de paseo.

prominence ['prɔmɪnəns] *n* (*fig*) importancia.

prominent ['prɔmɪnənt] *a* (*standing out*) saliente; (*important*) eminente, importante; **he is** ~ **in the field of** ... tiene fama en el campo de ....

prominently ['prɔmɪnəntlɪ] *ad* (*display, set*) muy a la vista; **he figured** ~ **in the case** desempeñó un papel importante en el juicio.

promiscuity [prɔmɪs'kjuːɪtɪ] *n* promiscuidad *f*.

promiscuous [prə'mɪskjuəs] *a* (*sexually*) promiscuo.

promise ['prɔmɪs] *n* promesa ♦ *vt, vi* prometer; **to make sb a** ~ prometer algo a uno; **a young man of** ~ un joven con futuro; **to** ~ **(sb) to do sth** prometer (a uno) hacer algo; **to** ~ **well** ser muy prometedor.

promising ['prɔmɪsɪŋ] *a* prometedor(a).

promissory note ['prɔmɪsərɪ-] *n* pagaré *m*.

promontory ['prɔməntrɪ] *n* promontorio.

promote [prə'məut] *vt* promover; (*new product*) dar publicidad a, lanzar; (*MIL*) ascender; **the team was** ~d **to the second division** (*Brit FOOTBALL*) el equipo fue ascendido a la segunda división.

promoter [prə'məutə*] *n* (*of sporting event*) promotor(a) *m/f*; (*of company, business*) patrocinador(a) *m/f*.

promotion [prə'məuʃən] *n* (*gen*) promoción *f*; (*MIL*) ascenso.

prompt [prɔmpt] *a* pronto ♦ *ad*: **at 6 o'clock** ~ a las seis en punto ♦ *n* (*COMPUT*) aviso, guía ♦ *vt* (*urge*) mover, incitar; (*THEATRE*) apuntar; **to** ~ **sb to do sth** instar a uno a hacer algo; **to be** ~ **to do sth** no tardar en hacer algo; **they're very** ~ (*punctual*) son muy puntuales.

prompter ['prɔmptə*] *n* (*THEATRE*) apuntador(a) *m/f*.

promptly ['prɔmptlɪ] *ad* (*punctually*) puntualmente; (*rapidly*) rápidamente.

promptness ['prɔmptnɪs] *n* puntualidad *f*; rapidez *f*.

promulgate ['prɔməlgeɪt] *vt* promulgar.

prone [prəun] *a* (*lying*) postrado; ~ **to** propenso a.

prong [prɔŋ] *n* diente *m*, punta.

pronoun ['prəunaun] *n* pronombre *m*.

pronounce [prə'nauns] *vt* pronunciar; (*declare*) declarar ♦ *vi*: **to** ~ **(up)on** pronunciarse sobre; **they** ~d **him unfit to drive** le declararon incapaz de conducir.

pronounced [prə'naunst] *a* (*marked*) marcado.

pronouncement [prə'naunsmənt] *n* declaración *f*.

pronunciation [prənʌnsɪ'eɪʃən] *n* pronunciación *f*.

proof [pru:f] *n* prueba; **70°** ~ graduación *f* del 70 por 100 ♦ *a:* ~ **against** a prueba de ♦ *vt (tent, anorak)* impermeabilizar.

proofreader ['pru:fri:də*] *n* corrector(a) *m/f* de pruebas.

Prop. *abbr (COMM)* = **proprietor.**

prop [prɔp] *n* apoyo; *(fig)* sostén *m* ♦ *vt (also:* ~ **up)** apoyar; *(lean):* **to** ~ **sth against** apoyar algo contra.

propaganda [prɔpə'gændə] *n* propaganda.

propagate ['prɔpəgeɪt] *vt* propagar.

propagation [prɔpə'geɪʃən] *n* propagación *f*.

propel [prə'pɛl] *vt* impulsar, propulsar.

propeller [prə'pɛlə*] *n* hélice *f*.

propelling pencil [prə'pɛlɪŋ-] *n (Brit)* lapicero.

propensity [prə'pɛnsɪtɪ] *n* propensión *f*.

proper ['prɔpə*] *a (suited, right)* propio; *(exact)* justo; *(apt)* apropiado, conveniente; *(timely)* oportuno; *(seemly)* correcto, decente; *(authentic)* verdadero; *(col: real)* auténtico; **to go through the** ~ **channels** *(ADMIN)* ir por la vía oficial.

properly ['prɔpəlɪ] *ad (adequately)* correctamente; *(decently)* decentemente.

proper noun *n* nombre *m* propio.

properties ['prɔpətɪz] *npl (THEATRE)* accesorios *mpl.*

property ['prɔpətɪ] *n* propiedad *f*; *(estate)* finca; **lost** ~ objetos *mpl* perdidos; **personal** ~ bienes *mpl* muebles.

property developer *n* promotor(a) *m/f* de construcciones.

property owner *n* dueño/a de propiedades.

property tax *n* impuesto sobre la propiedad.

prophecy ['prɔfɪsɪ] *n* profecía.

prophesy ['prɔfɪsaɪ] *vt* profetizar; *(fig)* predecir.

prophet ['prɔfɪt] *n* profeta *m/f.*

prophetic [prə'fɛtɪk] *a* profético.

proportion [prə'pɔ:ʃən] *n* proporción *f*; *(share)* parte *f*; **to be in/out of** ~ **to** *or* **with sth** estar en/no guardar proporción con algo; **to see sth in** ~ *(fig)* ver algo en su justa medida.

proportional [prə'pɔ:ʃənl] *a* proporcional.

proportionally [prəpɔ:ʃnəlɪ] *ad* proporcionalmente, en proporción.

proportional representation (PR) *n (POL)* representación *f* proporcional.

proportional spacing *n (on printer)* espaciado proporcional.

proportionate [prə'pɔ:ʃənɪt] *a* proporcionado.

proportionately [prə'pɔ:ʃnɪtlɪ] *proporcionadamente, en proporción.*

proportioned [prə'pɔ:ʃənd] *a* proporcionado.

proposal [prə'pəuzl] *n* propuesta; *(offer of marriage)* oferta de matrimonio; *(plan)*

proyecto; *(suggestion)* sugerencia.

propose [prə'pəuz] *vt* proponer; *(have in mind):* **to** ~ **sth/to do** *or* **doing sth** proponer algo/proponerse a hacer algo ♦ *vi* declararse.

proposer [prə'pəuzə*] *n (of motion)* proponente *m/f.*

proposition [prɔpə'zɪʃən] *n* propuesta, proposición *f;* **to make sb a** ~ proponer algo a uno.

propound [prə'paund] *vt (theory)* exponer.

proprietary [prə'praɪətərɪ] *a (COMM):* ~ **article** artículo de marca; ~ **brand** marca comercial.

proprietor [prə'praɪətə*] *n* propietario/a, dueño/a.

propriety [prə'praɪətɪ] *n* decoro.

propulsion [prə'pʌlʃən] *n* propulsión *f.*

pro rata [prəu'rɑ:tə] *ad* a prorrata.

prosaic [prəu'zeɪɪk] *a* prosaico.

Pros. Atty. *abbr (US)* = *prosecuting attorney.*

proscribe [prə'skraɪb] *vt* proscribir.

prose [prəuz] *n* prosa; *(SCOL)* traducción *f* inversa.

prosecute ['prɔsɪkju:t] *vt (LAW)* procesar; **"trespassers will be** ~**d"** *(LAW)* "se procesará a los intrusos".

prosecution [prɔsɪ'kju:ʃən] *n* proceso, causa; *(accusing side)* acusación *f.*

prosecutor ['prɔsɪkju:tə*] *n* acusador(a) *m/f;* *(also:* **public** ~**)** fiscal *m.*

prospect *n* ['prɔspɛkt] *(view)* vista; *(chance)* posibilidad *f;* *(outlook)* perspectiva; *(hope)* esperanza ♦ *(vb:* [prə'spɛkt]) *vt* explorar ♦ *vi* buscar; ~**s** *npl (for work etc)* perspectivas *fpl;* **to be faced with the** ~ **of** tener que enfrentarse a la posibilidad de que ...; **we were faced with the** ~ **of leaving early** se nos planteó la posibilidad de marcharnos pronto; **there is every** ~ **of an early victory** hay buenas perspectivas de una pronta victoria.

prospecting [prə'spɛktɪŋ] *n* prospección *f.*

prospective [prə'spɛktɪv] *a (possible)* probable, eventual; *(certain)* futuro; *(buyer)* presunto; *(legislation, son-in-law)* futuro.

prospector [prə'spɛktə*] *n* explorador(a) *m/f;* **gold** ~ buscador *m* de oro.

prospectus [prə'spɛktəs] *n* prospecto.

prosper ['prɔspə*] *vi* prosperar.

prosperity [prɔ'spɛrɪtɪ] *n* prosperidad *f.*

prosperous ['prɔspərəs] *a* próspero.

prostate ['prɔsteɪt] *n (also:* ~ **gland)** próstata.

prostitute ['prɔstɪtju:t] *n* prostituta; **male** ~ prostituto.

prostitution [prɔstɪ'tju:ʃən] *n* prostitución *f.*

prostrate ['prɔstreɪt] *a* postrado; *(fig)* abatido ♦ *vt:* **to** ~ **o.s.** *(before sb)* prosternarse; *(on the floor, fig)* prostrarse.

protagonist [prə'tægənɪst] *n* protagonista *m/f.*

protect [prə'tɛkt] *vt* proteger.
protection [prə'tɛkʃən] *n* protección *f*; **to be under sb's** ~ estar amparado por uno.
protectionism [prə'tɛkʃənizəm] *n* proteccionismo.
protection racket *n* chantaje *m*.
protective [prə'tɛktɪv] *a* protector(a); ~ **custody** (*LAW*) detención *f* preventiva.
protector [prə'tɛktə*] *n* protector(a) *m/f*.
protégé ['prəutɛʒeɪ] *n* protegido/a.
protein ['prəutiːn] *n* proteína.
pro tem [prəu'tɛm] *ad abbr* (= *pro tempore*: *for the time being*) provisionalmente.
protest *n* ['prəutɛst] protesta ♦ (*vb*: [prə'tɛst]) *vi* protestar ♦ *vt* (*affirm*) afirmar, declarar; **to do sth under** ~ hacer algo bajo protesta; **to** ~ **against/about** protestar en contra de/por.
Protestant ['prɒtɪstənt] *a, n* protestante *m/f*.
protester, protestor [prə'tɛstə*] *n* (*in demonstration*) manifestante *m/f*.
protest march *n* manifestación *f or* marcha (de protesta).
protocol ['prəutəkɒl] *n* protocolo.
prototype ['prəutətaɪp] *n* prototipo.
protracted [prə'træktɪd] *a* prolongado.
protractor [prə'træktə*] *n* (*GEOM*) transportador *m*.
protrude [prə'truːd] *vi* salir, sobresalir.
protuberance [prə'tjuːbərəns] *n* protuberancia.
proud [praud] *a* orgulloso; (*pej*) soberbio, altanero ♦ *ad*: **to do sb** ~ tratar a uno a cuerpo de rey; **to do o.s.** ~ no privarse de nada; **to be** ~ **to do sth** estar orgulloso de hacer algo.
proudly ['praudlɪ] *ad* orgullosamente, con orgullo; (*pej*) con soberbia, con altanería.
prove [pruːv] *vt* probar, (*verify*) comprobar; (*show*) demostrar ♦ *vi*: **to** ~ **correct** resultar correcto; **to** ~ **o.s.** ponerse a prueba; **he was** ~**d right in the end** al final *or* por fin se le dio la razón.
proverb ['prɒvəːb] *n* refrán *m*.
proverbial [prə'vəːbɪəl] *a* proverbial.
proverbially [prə'vəːbɪəlɪ] *ad* proverbialmente.
provide [prə'vaɪd] *vt* proporcionar, dar; **to** ~ **sb with sth** proveer a uno de algo; **to be** ~**d with** ser provisto de.
provide for *vt fus* (*person*) mantener a; (*problem etc*) tener en cuenta.
provided [prə'vaɪdɪd] *conj*: ~ **(that)** con tal de que, a condición de que.
Providence ['prɒvɪdəns] *n* Divina Providencia.
providing [prə'vaɪdɪŋ] *conj* a condición de que, con tal de que.
province ['prɒvɪns] *n* provincia; (*fig*) esfera.
provincial [prə'vɪnʃəl] *a* provincial; (*pej*) provinciano.

provision [prə'vɪʒən] *n* provisión *f*; (*supply*) suministro, abastecimiento; ~**s** *npl* provisiones *fpl*, víveres *mpl*; **to make** ~ **for** (*one's family, future*) atender las necesidades de.
provisional [prə'vɪʒənl] *a* provisional; (*temporary*) interino ♦ *n*: **P**~ (*Irish POL*) Provisional *m* (*miembro de la tendencia activista del IRA*).
provisional licence *n* (*Brit AUT*) carnet *m* (de conducir) provisional.
proviso [prə'vaɪzəu] *n* condición *f*, estipulación *f*; **with the** ~ **that** a condición de que.
Provo ['prɒvəu] *n abbr* (*col*) = **Provisional**.
provocation [prɒvə'keɪʃən] *n* provocación *f*.
provocative [prə'vɒkətɪv] *a* provocativo.
provoke [prə'vəuk] *vt* (*arouse*) provocar, incitar; (*cause*) causar, producir; (*anger*) enojar; **to** ~ **sb to sth/to do** *or* **into doing sth** provocar a uno a algo/a hacer algo.
provoking [prə'vəukɪŋ] *a* provocador(a).
provost ['prɒvəst] *n* (*Brit*: *of university*) rector(a) *m/f*; (*Scottish*) alcalde(sa) *m/f*.
prow [prau] *n* proa.
prowess ['prauɪs] *n* (*skill*) destreza, habilidad *f*; (*courage*) valor *m*; **his** ~ **as a footballer** (*skill*) su habilidad como futbolista.
prowl [praul] *vi* (*also*: ~ **about**, ~ **around**) merodear ♦ *n*: **on the** ~ de merodeo, merodeando.
prowler ['praulə*] *n* merodeador(a) *m/f*.
proximity [prɒk'sɪmɪtɪ] *n* proximidad *f*.
proxy ['prɒksɪ] *n* poder *m*; (*person*) apoderado/a; **by** ~ por poderes.
prude [pruːd] *n* gazmoño/a, mojigato/a.
prudence ['pruːdns] *n* prudencia.
prudent ['pruːdnt] *a* prudente.
prudently ['pruːdntlɪ] *ad* prudentemente, con prudencia.
prudish ['pruːdɪʃ] *a* gazmoño.
prudishness [pruː'dɪʃnɪs] *n* gazmoñería, ñoñería.
prune [pruːn] *n* ciruela pasa ♦ *vt* podar.
pry [praɪ] *vi*: **to** ~ **into** entrometerse en.
PS *abbr* (= *postscript*) P.D.
psalm [sɑːm] *n* salmo.
PSAT *n abbr* (*US*) = *Preliminary Scholastic Aptitude Test*.
PSBR *n abbr* (*Brit*: = *public sector borrowing requirement*) necesidades *fpl* de endeudamiento del sector público.
pseud [sjuːd] *n* (*Brit col*: *intellectually*) farsante *m/f*; (: *socially*) pretencioso/a.
pseudo... [sjuːdəu] *pref* seudo....
pseudonym ['sjuːdənɪm] *n* seudónimo.
PST *n abbr* (*US*: = *Pacific Standard Time*) hora de invierno del Pacífico.
PSV *n abbr* (*Brit*) *see* **public service vehicle.**
psyche ['saɪkɪ] *n* psique *f*.
psychiatric [saɪkɪ'ætrɪk] *a* psiquiátrico.

psychiatrist [sai'kaiətrist] *n* psiquiatra *m/f*.
psychiatry [sai'kaiətri] *n* psiquiatría.
psychic ['saikik] *a* (*also*: ~**al**) psíquico.
psychoanalyse, psychoanalyze [saikəu-'ænəlaiz] *vt* psicoanalizar.
psychoanalysis, *pl* **psychoanalyses** [saikəuə'nælisis, -si:z] *n* psicoanálisis *m inv*.
psychoanalyst [saikəu'ænəlist] *n* psicoanalista *m/f*.
psychological [saikə'lɔdʒikl] *a* psicológico.
psychologically [saikə'lɔdʒikli] *ad* psicológicamente.
psychologist [sai'kɔlədʒist] *n* psicólogo/a.
psychology [sai'kɔlədʒi] *n* psicología.
psychopath ['saikəupæθ] *n* psicópata *m/f*.
psychosis, *pl* **psychoses** [sai'kəusis, -si:z] *n* psicosis *f inv*.
psychosomatic ['saikəusə'mætik] *a* psicosomático.
psychotherapy [saikəu'θerəpi] *n* psicoterapia.
psychotic [sai'kɔtik] *a, n* psicótico/a.
PT *n abbr* (*Brit*: = *Physical Training*) Ed. Fís.
pt *abbr* = **pint(s), point(s)**.
Pt. *abbr* (*GEO*: = *Point*) Pta.
PTA *n abbr* (*Brit*: = *Parent-Teacher Association*) ≈ Asociación *f* de Padres de Alumnos.
Pte. *abbr* (*Brit MIL*) = **private**.
PTO *abbr* (= *please turn over*) sigue.
PTV *n abbr* (*US*) = *pay television, public television*.
pub [pʌb] *n abbr* (= *public house*) pub *m*, taberna.
puberty ['pju:bəti] *n* pubertad *f*.
pubic ['pju:bik] *a* púbico.
public ['pʌblik] *a, n* público; **in ~** en público; **to make sth ~** revelar *or* anunciar algo; **to be ~ knowledge** ser del dominio público; **to go ~** (*COMM*) proceder a la venta pública de acciones.
public address system (PA) *n* megafonía, sistema *m* de altavoces.
publican ['pʌblikən] *n* tabernero/a.
publication [pʌbli'keiʃən] *n* publicación *f*.
public company *n* sociedad *f* anónima.
public convenience *n* (*Brit*) aseos *mpl* públicos, sanitarios *mpl* (*LAm*).
public holiday *n* día *m* de fiesta, (día) feriado (*LAm*).
public house *n* (*Brit*) bar *m*, pub *m*.
publicity [pʌb'lisiti] *n* publicidad *f*.
publicize ['pʌblisaiz] *vt* publicitar; (*advertise*) hacer propaganda para.
public limited company (plc) *n* sociedad *f* anónima (S.A.).
publicly ['pʌblikli] *ad* públicamente, en público.
public opinion *n* opinión *f* pública.
public ownership *n* propiedad *f* pública; **to be taken into ~** ser nacionalizado.
Public Prosecutor *n* Fiscal *m* del Estado.

public relations (PR) *n* relaciones *fpl* públicas.
public relations officer *n* encargado/a de relaciones públicas.
public school *n* (*Brit*) colegio privado; (*US*) instituto.
public sector *n* sector *m* público.
public service vehicle (PSV) *n* vehículo de servicio público.
public-spirited [pʌblik'spiritid] *a* cívico.
public transport, (*US*) **public transportation** *n* transporte *m* público.
public utility *n* servicio público.
public works *npl* obras *fpl* públicas.
publish ['pʌbliʃ] *vt* publicar.
publisher ['pʌbliʃə*] *n* (*person*) editor(a) *m/f*; (*firm*) editorial *f*.
publishing ['pʌbliʃiŋ] *n* (*industry*) industria del libro.
publishing company *n* (casa) editorial *f*.
puce [pju:s] *a* de color pardo rojizo.
puck [pʌk] *n* (*ICE HOCKEY*) puck *m*.
pucker ['pʌkə*] *vt* (*pleat*) arrugar; (*brow etc*) fruncir.
pudding ['pudiŋ] *n* pudín *m*; (*Brit*: *sweet*) postre *m*; **black ~** morcilla; **rice ~** arroz *m* con leche.
puddle ['pʌdl] *n* charco.
puerile ['pjuərail] *a* pueril.
Puerto Rican ['pwə:təu'ri:kən] *a,* *n* puertorriqueño/a *m/f*.
Puerto Rico [-'ri:kəu] *n* Puerto Rico.
puff [pʌf] *n* soplo; (*of smoke*) bocanada; (*of breathing, engine*) resoplido; (*powder* ~) borla ♦ *vt*: **to ~ one's pipe** dar chupadas a la pipa; (*also*: ~ **out**: *sails, cheeks*) hinchar, inflar (*LAm*) ♦ *vi* (*gen*) soplar; (*pant*) jadear; **to ~ out smoke** echar humo.
puffed [pʌft] *a* (*col*: *out of breath*) sin aliento.
puffin ['pʌfin] *n* frailecillo.
puff pastry, (*US*) **puff paste** *n* hojaldre *m*.
puffy ['pʌfi] *a* hinchado.
pull [pul] *n* (*tug*): **to give sth a ~** dar un tirón a algo; (*fig*: *advantage*) ventaja; (: *influence*) influencia ♦ *vt* tirar de; (*haul*) tirar, arrastrar; (*strain*): **to ~ a muscle** sufrir un tirón ♦ *vi* tirar; **to ~ to pieces** hacer pedazos; **to ~ one's punches** andarse con bromas; **to ~ one's weight** hacer su parte; **to ~ o.s. together** tranquilizarse; **to ~ sb's leg** tomar el pelo a uno; **to ~ strings (for sb)** enchufar (a uno).
pull about *vt* (*handle roughly*: *object*) manosear; (: *person*) maltratar.
pull apart *vt* (*take apart*) desmontar.
pull down *vt* (*house*) derribar.
pull in *vi* (*AUT*: *at the kerb*) parar (junto a la acera); (*RAIL*) llegar.
pull off *vt* (*deal etc*) cerrar.

pull out *vi* irse, marcharse; (*AUT*: *from kerb*) salir ◆ *vt* sacar, arrancar.
pull over *vi* (*AUT*) hacerse a un lado.
pull round, pull through *vi* salvarse; (*MED*) recobrar la salud.
pull up *vi* (*stop*) parar ◆ *vt* (*uproot*) arrancar, desarraigar; (*stop*) parar.
pulley ['pulɪ] *n* polea.
pull-out ['pulaut] *n* suplemento ◆ *cpd* (*pages, magazine*) separable.
pullover ['puləuvə*] *n* jersey *m*, suéter.
pulp [pʌlp] *n* (*of fruit*) pulpa; (*for paper*) pasta; (*pej*: *also*: ~ **magazines** *etc*) prensa amarilla; **to reduce sth to** ~ hacer algo papilla.
pulpit ['pulpɪt] *n* púlpito.
pulsate [pʌl'seɪt] *vi* pulsar, latir.
pulse [pʌls] *n* (*ANAT*) pulso; (*of music, engine*) pulsación *f*; (*BOT*) legumbre *f*; **to feel** *or* **take sb's** ~ tomar el pulso a uno.
pulverize ['pʌlvəraɪz] *vt* pulverizar; (*fig*) hacer polvo.
puma ['pju:mə] *n* puma.
pumice (stone) ['pʌmɪs-] *n* piedra pómez.
pummel ['pʌml] *vt* aporrear.
pump [pʌmp] *n* bomba; (*shoe*) zapato de tenis ◆ *vt* sacar con una bomba; (*fig*: *col*) (son)sacar; **to** ~ **sb for information** (son)sacarle informes a uno.
pump up *vt* inflar.
pumpkin ['pʌmpkɪn] *n* calabaza.
pun [pʌn] *n* juego de palabras.
punch [pʌntʃ] *n* (*blow*) golpe *m*, puñetazo; (*tool*) punzón *m*; (*for paper*) perforadora; (*for tickets*) taladro; (*drink*) ponche *m* ◆ *vt* (*hit*): **to** ~ **sb/sth** dar un puñetazo *or* golpear a uno/algo; (*make a hole in*) punzar; perforar.
punch-drunk ['pʌntʃdrʌŋk] *a* (*Brit*) grogui, sonado.
punch(ed) card [pʌntʃ(t)-] *n* tarjeta perforada.
punch line *n* (*of joke*) remate *m*.
punch-up ['pʌntʃʌp] *n* (*Brit col*) riña.
punctual ['pʌŋktjuəl] *a* puntual.
punctuality [pʌŋktju'ælɪtɪ] *n* puntualidad *f*.
punctually ['pʌŋktjuəlɪ] *ad*: **it will start** ~ **at 6** empezará a las 6 en punto.
punctuate ['pʌŋktjueɪt] *vt* puntuar; (*fig*) interrumpir.
punctuation [pʌŋktju'eɪʃən] *n* puntuación *f*.
punctuation mark *n* signo de puntuación.
puncture ['pʌŋktʃə*] (*Brit*) *n* pinchazo ◆ *vt* pinchar; **to have a** ~ tener un pinchazo.
pundit ['pʌndɪt] *n* experto/a.
pungent ['pʌndʒənt] *a* acre.
punish ['pʌnɪʃ] *vt* castigar; **to** ~ **sb for sth/for doing sth** castigar a uno por algo/por haber hecho algo.
punishable ['pʌnɪʃəbl] *a* punible, castigable.
punishing ['pʌnɪʃɪŋ] *a* (*fig*: *exhausting*) agotador(a).

punishment ['pʌnɪʃmənt] *n* castigo; (*fig*, *col*): **to take a lot of** ~ (*boxer*) recibir una paliza; (*car*) ser maltratado.
punitive ['pju:nɪtɪv] *a* punitivo.
punk [pʌŋk] *n* (*also*: ~ **rocker**) punki *m/f*; (*also*: ~ **rock**) música punk; (*US col*: *hoodlum*) matón *m*.
punt [pʌnt] *n* (*boat*) batea ◆ *vi* (*bet*) apostar.
punter ['pʌntə*] *n* (*gambler*) jugador(a) *m/f*.
puny ['pju:nɪ] *a* débil.
pup [pʌp] *n* cachorro.
pupil ['pju:pl] *n* alumno/a.
puppet ['pʌpɪt] *n* títere *m*.
puppet government *n* gobierno títere.
puppy ['pʌpɪ] *n* cachorro, perrito.
purchase ['pɜ:tʃɪs] *n* compra; (*grip*) agarre *m*, asidero ◆ *vt* comprar.
purchase order *n* decreto de compra.
purchase price *n* precio de compra.
purchaser ['pɜ:tʃɪsə*] *n* comprador(a) *m/f*.
purchase tax *n* (*Brit*) impuesto sobre la venta.
purchasing power ['pɜ:tʃɪsɪŋ-] *n* poder *m* adquisitivo.
pure [pjuə*] *a* puro; **a** ~ **wool jumper** un jersey de pura lana; **it's laziness,** ~ **and simple** es pura vagancia.
purebred ['pjuəbred] *a* de pura sangre.
purée ['pjuəreɪ] *n* puré *m*.
purely ['pjuəlɪ] *ad* puramente.
purgatory ['pɜ:gətərɪ] *n* purgatorio.
purge [pɜ:dʒ] *n* (*MED*, *POL*) purga ◆ *vt* purgar.
purification [pjuərɪfɪ'keɪʃən] *n* purificación *f*, depuración *f*.
purify ['pjuərɪfaɪ] *vt* purificar, depurar.
purist ['pjuərɪst] *n* purista *m/f*.
puritan ['pjuərɪtən] *n* puritano/a.
puritanical [pjuərɪ'tænɪkl] *a* puritano.
purity ['pjuərɪtɪ] *n* pureza.
purl [pɜ:l] *n* punto del revés.
purloin [pɜ:'lɔɪn] *vt* hurtar, robar.
purple ['pɜ:pl] *a* purpúreo, morado.
purport [pɜ:'pɔ:t] *vi*: **to** ~ **to be/do** dar a entender que es/hace.
purpose ['pɜ:pəs] *n* propósito; **on** ~ a propósito, adrede; **to no** ~ para nada, en vano; **for teaching** ~s con fines pedagógicos; **for the** ~s **of this meeting** para los fines de esta reunión.
purpose-built ['pɜ:pəs'bɪlt] *a* (*Brit*) construido especialmente.
purposeful ['pɜ:pəsful] *a* resuelto, determinado.
purposely ['pɜ:pəslɪ] *ad* a propósito, adrede.
purr [pɜ:*] *n* ronroneo ◆ *vi* ronronear.
purse [pɜ:s] *n* monedero; (*US*: *handbag*) bolso ◆ *vt* fruncir.
purser ['pɜ:sə*] *n* (*NAUT*) comisario/a.
purse snatcher [-snætʃə*] *n* (*US*) tironista

m/f.

pursue [pə'sjuː] *vt* seguir; (*harass*) perseguir; (*profession*) ejercer; (*pleasures*) buscar; (*inquiry, matter*) seguir.

pursuer [pə'sjuːə*] *n* perseguidor(a) *m/f.*

pursuit [pə'sjuːt] *n* (*chase*) caza; (*of pleasure etc*) busca; (*occupation*) actividad *f;* **in (the)** ~ **of sth** en busca de algo.

purveyor [pə'veɪə*] *n* proveedor(a) *m/f.*

pus [pʌs] *n* pus *m.*

push [puʃ] *n* empuje *m*, empujón *m*; (*MIL*) ataque *m*; (*drive*) empuje *m* ♦ *vt* empujar; (*button*) apretar; (*promote*) promover; (*fig: press, advance: views*) avanzar; (*thrust*): **to** ~ **sth (into)** meter algo a la fuerza (en) ♦ *vi* empujar; (*fig*) hacer esfuerzos; **at a** ~ (*col*) a duras penas; **she is** ~**ing 50** (*col*) raya en los 50; **to be** ~**ed for time/money** andar justo de tiempo/ escaso de dinero; **to** ~ **a door open/shut** abrir/cerrar una puerta empujándola; **to** ~ **for** (*better pay, conditions*) reivindicar; "~" (*on door*) "empujar"; (*on bell*) "pulse".

push aside *vt* apartar con la mano.

push in *vi* colarse.

push off *vi* (*col*) largarse.

push on *vi* (*continue*) seguir adelante.

push through *vt* (*measure*) despachar.

push up *vt* (*total, prices*) hacer subir.

push-bike ['puʃbaɪk] *n* (*Brit*) bicicleta.

push-button ['puʃbʌtn] *a* de mando de botón.

pushchair ['puʃtʃɛə*] *n* (*Brit*) sillita de ruedas.

pusher ['puʃə*] *n* (*drug* ~) traficante *m/f* de drogas.

pushover ['puʃəʊvə*] *n* (*col*): **it's a** ~ está tirado.

push-up ['puʃʌp] *n* (*US*) plancha.

pushy ['puʃɪ] *a* (*pej*) agresivo.

puss [pus], **pussy(-cat)** ['pusɪ(kæt)] *n* minino.

put [put], *pt, pp* **put** *vt* (*place*) poner, colocar; (~ *into*) meter; (*express, say*) expresar; (*a question*) hacer; (*estimate*) calcular; (*cause to be*): **to** ~ **sb in a good/bad mood** poner a uno de buen/mal humor; **to** ~ **a lot of time into sth** dedicar mucho tiempo a algo; **to** ~ **money on a horse** jugarse dinero a un caballo; **to** ~ **money into a company** invertir dinero en una compañía; **to** ~ **sb to a lot of trouble** causar mucha molestia a uno; **we** ~ **the children to bed** acostamos a los niños; **how shall I** ~ **it?** ¿cómo puedo explicarlo *or* decirlo?; **I** ~ **it to you that ...** le sugiero que ...; **to stay** ~ no moverse.

put about *vi* (*NAUT*) virar ♦ *vt* (*rumour*) diseminar.

put across *vt* (*ideas etc*) comunicar.

put aside *vt* (*lay down: book etc*) dejar *or* poner a un lado; (*save*) ahorrar; (*in*

shop) guardar.

put away *vt* (*store*) guardar.

put back *vt* (*replace*) devolver a su lugar; (*postpone*) posponer; (*set back: watch, clock*) retrasar; **this will** ~ **us back 10 years** esto nos retrasará 10 años.

put by *vt* (*money*) guardar.

put down *vt* (*on ground*) poner en el suelo; (*animal*) sacrificar; (*in writing*) apuntar; (*suppress: revolt etc*) sofocar; (*attribute*) atribuir; ~ **me down for £15** apúntame por 15 libras; ~ **it down on my account** (*COMM*) póngalo en mi cuenta.

put forward *vt* (*ideas*) presentar, proponer; (*date*) adelantar.

put in *vt* (*application, complaint*) presentar.

put in for *vt fus* (*job*) solicitar; (*promotion*) pedir.

put off *vt* (*postpone*) aplazar; (*discourage*) desanimar.

put on *vt* (*clothes, lipstick etc*) ponerse; (*light etc*) encender; (*play etc*) presentar; (*weight*) ganar; (*brake*) echar; (*assume: accent, manner*) afectar, fingir; (*airs*) adoptar, darse; (*concert, exhibition etc*) montar; (*extra bus, train etc*) poner; (*col: kid, have on: esp US*) tomar el pelo a; (*inform, indicate*): **to** ~ **sb on to sb/sth** informar a uno de uno/algo.

put out *vt* (*fire, light*) apagar; (*one's hand*) alargar; (*news, rumour*) hacer circular; (*tongue etc*) sacar; (*person: inconvenience*) molestar, fastidiar; (*dislocate: shoulder, vertebra, knee*) dislocar(se) ♦ *vi* (*NAUT*): **to** ~ **out to sea** hacerse a la mar; **to** ~ **out from Plymouth** salir de Plymouth.

put through *vt* (*call*) poner; ~ **me through to Miss Blair** póngame *or* comuníqueme con (*LAm*) la Señorita Blair.

put together *vt* unir, reunir; (*assemble: furniture*) armar, montar; (*meal*) confeccionar.

put up *vt* (*raise*) levantar, alzar; (*hang*) colgar; (*build*) construir; (*increase*) aumentar; (*accommodate*) alojar; (*incite*): **to** ~ **sb up to doing sth** instar *or* incitar a uno a hacer algo; **to** ~ **sth up for sale** exponer algo a la venta.

put upon *vt fus*: **to be** ~ **upon** (*imposed upon*) dejarse explotar.

put up with *vt fus* aguantar.

putrid ['pjuːtrɪd] *a* podrido.

putsch [putʃ] *n* golpe *m* de estado.

putt [pʌt] *vt* hacer un putt ♦ *n* putt *m*, golpe *m* corto.

putter ['pʌtə*] *n* putter *m.*

putting green ['pʌtɪŋ-] *n* green *m*, minigolf *m.*

putty ['pʌtɪ] *n* masilla.

put-up ['putʌp] *a*: ~ **job** (*Brit*) estafa.

puzzle ['pʌzl] *n* (*riddle*) acertijo; (*jigsaw*)

rompecabezas *m inv*; (*also*: **crossword** ~) crucigrama *m*; (*mystery*) misterio ◆ *vt* dejar perplejo, confundir ◆ *vi*: **to** ~ **about** quebrar la cabeza por; **to** ~ **over** (*sb's actions*) quebrarse la cabeza por; (*mystery*, *problem*) devanarse los sesos sobre; **to be** ~**d about sth** no llegar a entender algo.

puzzling ['pʌzlɪŋ] *a* (*question*) misterioso, extraño; (*attitude, set of instructions*) extraño.

PVC *n abbr* (= *polyvinyl chloride*) P.V.C. *m*.

Pvt. *abbr* (*US MIL*) = **private.**

PW *n abbr* (*US*) = **prisoner of war.**

pw *abbr* (= *per week*) por semana.

PX *n abbr* (*US*: = *post exchange*) economato militar.

pygmy ['pɪgmɪ] *n* pigmeo/a.

pyjamas, (*US*) **pajamas** [pɪ'dʒɑːməz] *npl* (*Brit*) pijama; **a pair of** ~ un pijama.

pylon ['paɪlən] *n* torre *f* de conducción eléctrica.

pyramid ['pɪrəmɪd] *n* pirámide *f*.

Pyrenean [pɪrə'niːən] *a* pirenaico.

Pyrenees [pɪrə'niːz] *npl*: **the** ~ los Pirineos.

Pyrex ® ['paɪreks] *n* pírex *m* ◆ *cpd*: ~ **casserole** cazuela de pírex.

python ['paɪθən] *n* pitón *m*.

Q

Q, q [kjuː] *n* (*letter*) Q, q *f*; **Q for Queen** Q de Quebec.

Qatar [kæ'tɑː] *n* Qatar *m*.

QC *n abbr* (*Brit*: = *Queen's Council*) *título concedido a determinados abogados*.

QED *abbr* (= *quod erat demonstrandum*) Q.E.D.

QM *n abbr* = **quartermaster.**

q.t. *n abbr* (*col*: = *quiet*): **on the** ~ a hurtadillas.

qty *abbr* (= *quantity*) ctdad.

quack [kwæk] *n* (*of duck*) graznido; (*pej*: *doctor*) curandero/a, matasanos *m inv* ◆ *vi* graznar.

quad [kwɔd] *abbr* = **quadrangle, quadruple, quadruplet.**

quadrangle ['kwɔdræŋgl] *n* (*Brit*: *courtyard*: *abbr*: **quad**) patio.

quadruple [kwɔ'druːpl] *vt*, *vi* cuadruplicar.

quadruplet [kwɔ'druːplɪt] *n* cuatrillizo.

quagmire ['kwægmaɪə*] *n* lodazal *m*, cenegal *m*.

quail [kweɪl] *n* (*bird*) codorniz *f* ◆ *vi* amedrentarse.

quaint [kweɪnt] *a* extraño; (*picturesque*)

pintoresco.

quaintly ['kweɪntlɪ] *ad* extrañamente; pintorescamente.

quaintness ['kweɪntnɪs] *n* lo pintoresco, tipismo.

quake [kweɪk] *vi* temblar ◆ *n abbr* = **earthquake.**

Quaker ['kweɪkə*] *n* cuáquero/a.

qualification [kwɔlɪfɪ'keɪʃən] *n* (*reservation*) reserva; (*modification*) modificación *f*; (*act*) calificación *f*; (*paper* ~) título; **what are your** ~**s?** ¿qué títulos tienes?

qualified ['kwɔlɪfaɪd] *a* (*trained*) cualificado; (*fit*) capacitado; (*limited*) limitado; (*professionally*) titulado; ~ **for/to do sth** capacitado para/para hacer algo; **he's not** ~ **for the job** no está capacitado para ese trabajo; **it was a** ~ **success** fue un éxito relativo.

qualify ['kwɔlɪfaɪ] *vt* (*LING*) calificar a; (*capacitate*) capacitar; (*modify*) modificar; (*limit*) moderar ◆ *vi* (*SPORT*) clasificarse; **to** ~ (**as**) calificarse (de), graduarse (en); **to** ~ (**for**) reunir los requisitos (para); **to** ~ **as an engineer** sacar el título de ingeniero.

qualifying ['kwɔlɪfaɪŋ] *a* (*exam, round*) eliminatorio.

qualitative ['kwɔlɪtətɪv] *a* cualitativo.

quality ['kwɔlɪtɪ] *n* calidad *f*; (*moral*) cualidad *f*; **of good/poor** ~ de buena or alta/ poca calidad.

quality control *n* control *m* de calidad.

qualm [kwɑːm] *n* escrúpulo; **to have** ~**s about sth** sentir escrúpulos por algo.

quandary ['kwɔndrɪ] *n*: **to be in a** ~ tener dudas.

quango ['kwæŋgəu] *n abbr* (*Brit*: = *quasi-autonomous non-governmental organization*) organización no gubernamental casi autónoma.

quantitative ['kwɔntɪtətɪv] *a* cuantitativo.

quantity ['kwɔntɪtɪ] *n* cantidad *f*; **in** ~ en grandes cantidades.

quantity surveyor *n* aparejador(a) *m/f*.

quarantine ['kwɔrntiːn] *n* cuarentena.

quarrel ['kwɔrl] *n* riña, pelea ◆ *vi* reñir, pelearse; **to have a** ~ **with sb** reñir or pelearse con uno; **I can't** ~ **with that** no le encuentro pegas.

quarrelsome ['kwɔrəlsəm] *a* pendenciero.

quarry ['kwɔrɪ] *n* (*for stone*) cantera; (*animal*) presa.

quart [kwɔːt] *n* cuarto de galón = 1.136 *l*.

quarter ['kwɔːtə*] *n* cuarto, cuarta parte *f*; (*of year*) trimestre *m*; (*district*) barrio; (*US, Canada*: 25 *cents*) cuarto de dólar ◆ *vt* dividir en cuartos; (*MIL*: *lodge*) alojar; ~**s** *npl* (*barracks*) cuartel *m*; (*living* ~**s**) alojamiento *sg*; **a** ~ **of an hour** un cuarto de hora; **to pay by the** ~ pagar trimestralmente *or* cada 3 meses; **it's a** ~ **to** *or* (*US*) **of 3** son las 3 menos cuarto; **it's a** ~ **past**

or (*US*) **after 3** son las 3 y cuarto; **from all** ~s de todas partes; **at close** ~s de cerca.

quarter-deck ['kwɔːtədɛk] *n* (*NAUT*) alcázar *m*.

quarter final *n* cuarto de final.

quarterly ['kwɔːtəlɪ] *a* trimestral ◆ *ad* cada 3 meses, trimestralmente.

quartermaster ['kwɔːtəmɑːstə*] *n* (*MIL*) comisario, intendente *m* militar.

quartet(te) [kwɔːˈtɛt] *n* cuarteto.

quarto ['kwɔːtəu] *n* tamaño holandés ◆ *a* de tamaño holandés.

quartz [kwɔːts] *n* cuarzo.

quash [kwɔʃ] *vt* (*verdict*) anular.

quasi- ['kweɪzaɪ] *pref* cuasi.

quaver ['kweɪvə*] *n* (*Brit MUS*) corchea ◆ *vi* temblar.

quay [kiː] *n* (*also:* ~**side**) muelle *m*.

queasiness ['kwiːzɪnɪs] *n* malestar *m*, náuseas *fpl*.

queasy ['kwiːzɪ] *a*: **to feel** ~ tener náuseas.

Quebec [kwɪˈbɛk] *n* Quebec *m*.

queen [kwiːn] *n* reina; (*CARDS etc*) dama.

queen mother *n* reina madre.

queer [kwɪə*] *a* (*odd*) raro, extraño ◆ *n* (*pej: col*) maricón *m*.

quell [kwɛl] *vt* calmar; (*put down*) sofocar.

quench [kwɛntʃ] *vt* (*flames*) apagar; **to** ~ **one's thirst** apagar la sed.

querulous ['kwɛruləs] *a* (*person, voice*) quejumbroso.

query ['kwɪərɪ] *n* (*question*) pregunta; (*doubt*) duda ◆ *vt* preguntar; (*disagree with, dispute*) no estar conforme con, dudar de.

quest [kwɛst] *n* busca, búsqueda.

question ['kwɛstʃən] *n* pregunta; (*matter*) asunto, cuestión *f* ◆ *vt* (*doubt*) dudar de; (*interrogate*) interrogar, hacer preguntas a; **to ask sb a** ~, **put a** ~ **to sb** hacerle una pregunta a uno; **the** ~ **is** ... el asunto es ...; **to bring** *or* **call sth into** ~ poner algo en (tela de) duda; **beyond** ~ fuera de toda duda; **it's out of the** ~ imposible, ni hablar.

questionable ['kwɛstʃənəbl] *a* discutible; (*doubtful*) dudoso.

questioner ['kwɛstʃənə*] *n* interrogador(a) *m/f*.

questioning ['kwɛstʃənɪŋ] *a* interrogativo ◆ *n* preguntas *fpl*; (*by police etc*) interrogatorio.

question mark *n* punto de interrogación.

questionnaire [kwɛstʃəˈnɛə*] *n* cuestionario.

queue [kjuː] (*Brit*) *n* cola ◆ *vi* hacer cola; **to jump the** ~ salirse de su turno, colarse.

quibble ['kwɪbl] *vi* sutilizar.

quick [kwɪk] *a* rápido; (*temper*) vivo; (*agile*) ágil; (*mind*) listo; (*eye*) agudo; (*ear*) fino ◆ *n*: **cut to the** ~ (*fig*) herido en lo vivo; **be** ~! ¡date prisa!; **to be** ~ **to act** obrar con prontitud; **she was** ~ **to see**

that se dio cuenta de eso en seguida.

quicken ['kwɪkən] *vt* apresurar ◆ *vi* apresurarse, darse prisa.

quick-fire ['kwɪkfaɪə*] *a* (*questions etc*) rápido, (*hecho*) a quemarropa.

quickly ['kwɪklɪ] *ad* rápidamente, de prisa; **we must act** ~ tenemos que actuar cuanto antes.

quickness ['kwɪknɪs] *n* rapidez *f*; (*of temper*) viveza; (*agility*) agilidad *f*; (*of mind, eye etc*) agudeza.

quicksand ['kwɪksænd] *n* arenas *fpl* movedizas.

quickstep ['kwɪkstɛp] *n* baile *m* de ritmo rápido.

quick-tempered [kwɪkˈtɛmpəd] *a* de genio vivo.

quick-witted [kwɪkˈwɪtɪd] *a* listo, despabilado.

quid [kwɪd] *n*, *pl inv* (*Brit col*) libra.

quid pro quo ['kwɪdprəuˈkwəu] *n* quid pro quo *m*, compensación *f*.

quiet ['kwaɪət] *a* (*not busy: day*) tranquilo; (*silent*) callado; (*reserved*) reservado; (*discreet*) discreto; (*not noisy: engine*) silencioso ◆ *n* silencio, tranquilidad *f* ◆ *vt*, *vi* (*US*) = **quieten**; **keep** ~! ¡cállate!, ¡silencio!; **business is** ~ **at this time of year** hay poco movimiento en esta época.

quieten ['kwaɪətn] (*also:* ~ **down**) *vi* (*grow calm*) calmarse; (*grow silent*) callarse ◆ *vt* calmar; hacer callar.

quietly ['kwaɪətlɪ] *ad* tranquilamente; (*silently*) silenciosamente.

quietness ['kwaɪətnɪs] *n* (*silence*) silencio; (*calm*) tranquilidad *f*.

quill [kwɪl] *n* (*of porcupine*) púa; (*pen*) pluma.

quilt [kwɪlt] *n* (*Brit*) edredón *m*.

quilting ['kwɪltɪŋ] *n* acolchado, guateado.

quin [kwɪn] *n abbr* = **quintuplet**.

quince [kwɪns] *n* membrillo.

quinine [kwɪˈniːn] *n* quinina.

quintet(te) [kwɪnˈtɛt] *n* quinteto.

quintuplet [kwɪnˈtjuːplɪt] *n* quintillizo.

quip [kwɪp] *n* ocurrencia ◆ *vi* decir sarcásticamente.

quire ['kwaɪə*] *n* mano *f* de papel.

quirk [kwəːk] *n* peculiaridad *f*; **by some** ~ **of fate** por algún capricho del destino.

quit *pt*, *pp* **quit** *or* **quitted** [kwɪt] *vt* dejar, abandonar; (*premises*) desocupar; (*COMPUT*) abandonar ◆ *vi* (*give up*) renunciar; (*go away*) irse; (*resign*) dimitir; ~ **stalling!** (*US col*) ¡déjate de evasivas!

quite [kwaɪt] *ad* (*rather*) bastante; (*entirely*) completamente; ~ **a few of them** un buen número de ellos; ~ **(so)!** ¡así es!, ¡exactamente!; ~ **new** completamente nuevo; **that's not** ~ **right** eso no está del todo bien; **not** ~ **as many as last time** no tantos como la última vez; **she's** ~ **pretty** es bastante guapa.

Quito ['ki:təu] *n* Quito.

quits [kwɪts] *a*: ~ **(with)** en paz (con); **let's call it** ~ dejémoslo en tablas.

quiver ['kwɪvə*] *vi* estremecerse ◆ *n* (*for arrows*) carcaj *m*.

quiz [kwɪz] *n* (*game*) concurso; (: *TV*, *RADIO*) programa-concurso; (*questioning*) interrogatorio ◆ *vt* interrogar.

quizzical ['kwɪzɪkl] *a* burlón(ona).

quoits [kwɔɪts] *npl* juego de aros.

quorum ['kwɔːrəm] *n* quórum *m*.

quota ['kwəutə] *n* cuota.

quotation [kwəu'teɪʃən] *n* cita; (*estimate*) presupuesto.

quotation marks *npl* comillas *fpl*.

quote [kwəut] *n* cita ◆ *vt* (*sentence*) citar; (*COMM*: *sum*, *figure*) cotizar ◆ *vi*: **to** ~ **from** citar de; ~**s** *npl* (*inverted commas*) comillas *fpl*; **in** ~**s** entre comillas; **the figure** ~**d for the repairs** la cifra estimada por las reparaciones; ~ ... **unquote** (*in dictation*) comillas iniciales ... finales.

quotient ['kwəuʃənt] *n* cociente *m*.

qv *n abbr* (= *quod vide*: *which see*) q.v.

qwerty keyboard ['kwɔːtɪ-] *n* teclado QWERTY.

R

R, r [ɑː*] *n* (*letter*) R, r *f*; **R for Robert**, (*US*) **R for Roger** R de Ramón.

R *abbr* (= *right*) dcha.; (= *river*) R.; (= *Réaumur* (*scale*)) R; (*US CINEMA*: = *restricted*) *sólo mayores*; (*US POL*) = **republican**; (*Brit*: = *Rex*, *Regina*) R.

RA *abbr* = *rear admiral* ◆ *n abbr* (*Brit*) = *Royal Academy*, *Royal Academician*.

RAAF *n abbr* = *Royal Australian Air Force*.

Rabat [rə'bɑːt] *n* Rabat *m*.

rabbi ['ræbaɪ] *n* rabino.

rabbit ['ræbɪt] *n* conejo ◆ *vi*: **to** ~ **(on)** (*Brit col*) hablar sin ton ni son.

rabbit hutch *n* conejera.

rabble ['ræbl] *n* (*pej*) chusma, populacho.

rabies ['reɪbiːz] *n* rabia.

RAC *n abbr* (*Brit*: = *Royal Automobile Club*) ≈ RACE *m* (*Sp*).

raccoon [rə'kuːn] *n* mapache *m*.

race [reɪs] *n* carrera; (*species*) raza ◆ *vt* (*horse*) hacer correr; (*person*) competir contra; (*engine*) acelerar ◆ *vi* (*compete*) competir; (*run*) correr; (*pulse*) latir a ritmo acelerado; **the arms** ~ la carrera armamentista; **the human** ~ el género humano; **he** ~**d across the road** cruzó corriendo la carretera; **to** ~ **in/out** entrar/salir corriendo.

race car *n* (*US*) = **racing car**.

race car driver *n* (*US*) = **racing driver**.

racecourse ['reɪskɔːs] *n* hipódromo.

racehorse ['reɪshɔːs] *n* caballo de carreras.

race meeting *n* concurso hípico.

race relations *npl* relaciones *fpl* entre las razas.

racetrack ['reɪstræk] *n* hipódromo; (*for cars*) autódromo.

racial ['reɪʃl] *a* racial.

racial discrimination *n* discriminación *f* racial.

racial integration *n* integración *f* racial.

racialism ['reɪʃəlɪzəm] *n* racismo.

racialist ['reɪʃəlɪst] *a*, *n* racista *m/f*.

racing ['reɪsɪŋ] *n* carreras *fpl*.

racing car *n* (*Brit*) coche *m* de carreras.

racing driver *n* (*Brit*) corredor(a) *m/f* de coches.

racism ['reɪsɪzəm] *n* racismo.

racist ['reɪsɪst] *a*, *n* racista *m/f*.

rack [ræk] *n* (*also*: **luggage** ~) rejilla; (*shelf*) estante *m*; (*also*: **roof** ~) baca, portaequipajes *m inv*; (*clothes* ~) percha ◆ *vt* (*cause pain to*) atormentar; **to go to** ~ **and ruin** (*building*) echarse a perder, venirse abajo; (*business*) arruinarse; **to** ~ **one's brains** devanarse los sesos.

rack up *vt* conseguir, ganar.

rack-and-pinion ['rækənd'pɪnjən] *n* (*TECH*) cremallera y piñón.

racket ['rækɪt] *n* (*for tennis*) raqueta; (*noise*) ruido, estrépito; (*swindle*) estafa, timo.

racketeer [rækɪ'tɪə*] *n* (*esp US*) estafador(a) *m/f*.

racoon [rə'kuːn] *n* = **raccoon**.

racquet ['rækɪt] *n* raqueta.

racy ['reɪsɪ] *a* picante, salado.

RADA ['rɑːdə] *n abbr* (*Brit*) = *Royal Academy of Dramatic Art*.

radar ['reɪdɑː*] *n* radar *m*.

radar trap *n* trampa radar.

radial ['reɪdɪəl] *a* (*tyre*: *also*: ~**-ply**) radial.

radiance ['reɪdɪəns] *n* brillantez *f*, resplandor *m*.

radiant ['reɪdɪənt] *a* brillante, resplandeciente.

radiate ['reɪdɪeɪt] *vt* (*heat*) radiar, irradiar ◆ *vi* (*lines*) extenderse.

radiation [reɪdɪ'eɪʃən] *n* radiación *f*.

radiation sickness *n* enfermedad *f* de radiación.

radiator ['reɪdɪeɪtə*] *n* (*AUT*) radiador *m*.

radiator cap *n* tapón *m* de radiador.

radiator grill *n* (*AUT*) rejilla del radiador.

radical ['rædɪkl] *a* radical.

radically ['rædɪkəlɪ] *ad* radicalmente.

radii ['reɪdɪaɪ] *npl of* **radius**.

radio ['reɪdɪəu] *n* radio *f* ◆ *vi*: **to** ~ **to sb** mandar un mensaje por radio a uno ◆ *vt* (*information*) radiar, transmitir por radio; (*one's position*) indicar por radio; (*person*)

llamar por radio; **on the ~** por radio.
radioactive [reɪdɪəuˈæktɪv] *a* radioactivo.
radioactivity [reɪdɪəuækˈtɪvɪtɪ] *n* radioactividad *f*.
radio announcer *n* locutor(a) *m/f* de radio.
radio-controlled [reɪdɪəukənˈtrəuld] *a* teledirigido.
radiographer [reɪdɪˈɔgrəfə*] *n* radiógrafo/a.
radiography [reɪdɪˈɔgrəfɪ] *n* radiografía.
radiology [reɪdɪˈɔlədʒɪ] *n* radiología.
radio station *n* emisora.
radio taxi *n* radio taxi *m*.
radiotelephone [reɪdɪəuˈtelɪfəun] *n* radioteléfono.
radiotelescope [reɪdɪəuˈtelɪskəup] *n* radiotelescopio.
radiotherapist [reɪdɪəuˈθɛrəpɪst] *n* radioterapeuta *m/f*.
radiotherapy [ˈreɪdɪəuθɛrəpɪ] *n* radioterapia.
radish [ˈrædɪʃ] *n* rábano.
radium [ˈreɪdɪəm] *n* radio.
radius, *pl* **radii** [ˈreɪdɪəs, -ɪaɪ] *n* radio; **within a ~ of 50 miles** en un radio de 50 millas.
RAF *n abbr see* **Royal Air Force**.
raffia [ˈræfɪə] *n* rafia.
raffle [ˈræfl] *n* rifa, sorteo ♦ *vt* (*object*) rifar.
raft [rɑːft] *n* (*craft*) balsa; (*also:* **life ~**) balsa salvavidas.
rafter [ˈrɑːftə*] *n* viga.
rag [ræg] *n* (*piece of cloth*) trapo; (*torn cloth*) harapo; (*pej: newspaper*) periodicucho; (*for charity*) *actividades estudiantiles benéficas* ♦ *vt* (*Brit*) tomar el pelo a; **~s** *npl* harapos *mpl*; **in ~s** en harapos, hecho jirones.
rag-and-bone man [rægənˈbəunmæn] *n* (*Brit*) = **ragman**.
rag doll *n* muñeca de trapo.
rage [reɪdʒ] *n* (*fury*) rabia, furor *m* ♦ *vi* (*person*) rabiar, estar furioso; (*storm*) bramar; **to fly into a ~** montar en cólera; **it's all the ~** es lo último.
ragged [ˈrægɪd] *a* (*edge*) desigual, mellado; (*cuff*) roto; (*appearance*) andrajoso, harapiento; **~ left/right** (*text*) margen *m* izquierdo/derecho irregular.
raging [ˈreɪdʒɪŋ] *a* furioso; **in a ~ temper** de un humor terrible, furioso.
ragman [ˈrægmæn] *n* trapero.
rag trade *n*: **the ~** (*col*) la industria de la confección.
raid [reɪd] *n* (*MIL*) incursión *f*; (*criminal*) asalto; (*by police*) redada ♦ *vt* invadir, atacar; asaltar.
raider [ˈreɪdə*] *n* invasor(a) *m/f*.
rail [reɪl] *n* (*on stair*) barandilla, pasamanos *m inv*; (*on bridge, balcony*) pretil *m*; (*of ship*) barandilla; (*for train*) riel *m*, carril *m*; **~s** *npl* vía *sg*; **by ~** por ferrocarril, en

tren.
railing(s) [ˈreɪlɪŋz] *n(pl)* verja *sg*, enrejado *sg*.
railway [ˈreɪlweɪ], (*US*) **railroad** [ˈreɪlrəud] *n* ferrocarril *m*, vía férrea.
railway engine *n* (*máquina*) locomotora.
railway line *n* (*Brit*) línea (de ferrocarril).
railwayman [ˈreɪlweɪmən] *n* (*Brit*) ferroviario.
railway station *n* (*Brit*) estación *f* de ferrocarril.
rain [reɪn] *n* lluvia ♦ *vi* llover; **in the ~** bajo la lluvia; **it's ~ing** llueve, está lloviendo; **it's ~ing cats and dogs** está lloviendo a cántaros *or* a mares.
rainbow [ˈreɪnbəu] *n* arco iris.
raincoat [ˈreɪnkəut] *n* impermeable *m*.
raindrop [ˈreɪndrɔp] *n* gota de lluvia.
rainfall [ˈreɪnfɔːl] *n* lluvia.
rainproof [ˈreɪnpruːf] *a* impermeable, a prueba de lluvia.
rainstorm [ˈreɪnstɔːm] *n* temporal *m* (de lluvia).
rainwater [ˈreɪnwɔːtə*] *n* agua llovediza *or* de lluvia.
rainy [ˈreɪnɪ] *a* lluvioso.
raise [reɪz] *n* aumento ♦ *vt* (*lift*) levantar; (*build*) erigir, edificar; (*increase*) aumentar; (*doubts*) suscitar; (*a question*) plantear; (*cattle, family*) criar; (*crop*) cultivar; (*army*) reclutar; (*funds*) reunir; (*loan*) obtener; (*end: embargo*) levantar; **to ~ one's voice** alzar la voz; **to ~ one's glass to sb/sth** brindar por uno/algo; **to ~ a laugh/a smile** provocar risa/una sonrisa; **to ~ sb's hopes** dar esperanzas a uno.
raisin [ˈreɪzn] *n* pasa de Corinto.
rake [reɪk] *n* (*tool*) rastrillo; (*person*) libertino ♦ *vt* (*garden*) rastrillar; (*fire*) hurgar; (*with machine gun*) barrer.
rake in, rake together *vt* reunir.
rake-off [ˈreɪkɔf] *n* (*col*) comisión *f*, tajada.
rakish [ˈreɪkɪʃ] *a* (*dissolute*) libertino; **at a ~ angle** (*hat*) echado a un lado, de lado.
rally [ˈrælɪ] *n* (*POL etc*) reunión *f*, mitin *m*; (*AUT*) rallye *m*; (*TENNIS*) peloteo ♦ *vt* reunir ♦ *vi* reunirse; (*sick person, Stock Exchange*) recuperarse.
rally round *vt fus* (*fig*) dar apoyo a.
rallying point [ˈrælɪŋ-] *n* (*POL, MIL*) punto de reunión.
RAM [ræm] *n abbr* (= *random access memory*) RAM *f*.
ram [ræm] *n* carnero; (*TECH*) pisón *m* ♦ *vt* (*crash into*) dar contra, chocar con; (*tread down*) apisonar.
ramble [ˈræmbl] *n* caminata, excursión *f* en el campo ♦ *vi* (*pej: also:* **~ on**) divagar.
rambler [ˈræmblə*] *n* excursionista *m/f*; (*BOT*) trepadora.
rambling [ˈræmblɪŋ] *a* (*speech*) inconexo; (*BOT*) trepador(a); (*house*) laberíntico.
rambunctious [ræmˈbʌŋkʃəs] *a* (*US*) =

rumbustious.

RAMC n abbr (Brit) = Royal Army Medical Corps.

ramification [ræmɪfɪ'keɪʃən] n ramificación f.

ramp [ræmp] n rampa; **on/off** ~ n (US AUT) vía de acceso/salida; "~" (AUT) "rampa".

rampage [ræm'peɪdʒ] n: **to be on the** ~ desmandarse.

rampant ['ræmpənt] a (disease etc): **to be** ~ estar extendiéndose mucho.

rampart ['ræmpɑːt] n terraplén m; (wall) muralla.

ramshackle ['ræmʃækl] a destartalado.

RAN n abbr = Royal Australian Navy.

ran [ræn] pt of **run.**

ranch [rɑːntʃ] n (US) hacienda, estancia.

rancher ['rɑːntʃəʳ] n ganadero.

rancid ['rænsɪd] a rancio.

rancour, (US) **rancor** ['ræŋkəʳ] n rencor m.

random ['rændəm] a fortuito, sin orden; (COMPUT, MATH) aleatorio ♦ n: **at** ~ al azar.

random access n (COMPUT) acceso aleatorio.

randy ['rændɪ] a (Brit col) cachondo.

rang [ræŋ] pt of **ring.**

range [reɪndʒ] n (of mountains) cadena de montañas, cordillera; (of missile) alcance m; (of voice) registro; (series) serie f; (of products) surtido; (MIL: also: **shooting** ~) campo de tiro; (also: **kitchen** ~) fogón m ♦ vt (place) colocar; (arrange) arreglar ♦ vi: **to** ~ **over** (wander) recorrer; (extend) extenderse por; **within** (firing) ~ a tiro; **do you have anything else in this price** ~? ¿tiene algo más de esta gama de precios?; **intermediate-/short-**~ **missile** proyectil m de medio/corto alcance; **to** ~ **from** ... **to...** oscilar entre ... y...; ~**d left/right** (text) alineado a la izquierda/derecha.

ranger [reɪndʒəʳ] n guardabosques m inv.

Rangoon [ræŋ'guːn] n Rangún m.

rangy ['reɪndʒɪ] a alto y delgado.

rank [ræŋk] n (row) fila; (MIL) rango; (status) categoría; (Brit: also: **taxi** ~) parada ♦ vi: **to** ~ **among** figurar entre ♦ a (stinking) fétido, rancio; (hypocrisy, injustice etc) manifiesto; **the** ~ **and file** (fig) la base; **to close** ~**s** (MIL) apretar las filas, cerrar filas; (fig) hacer un frente común; **I** ~ **him 6th** yo le pongo en sexto lugar.

rankle ['ræŋkl] vi (insult) doler.

ransack ['rænsæk] vt (search) registrar; (plunder) saquear.

ransom ['rænsəm] n rescate m; **to hold sb to** ~ (fig) poner a uno entre la espada y la pared.

rant [rænt] vi divagar, desvariar.

ranting ['ræntɪŋ] n desvaríos mpl.

rap [ræp] vt golpear, dar un golpecito en.

rape [reɪp] n violación f; (BOT) colza ♦ vt violar.

rape(seed) oil ['reɪp(siːd)-] n aceite m de colza.

rapid ['ræpɪd] a rápido.

rapidity [rə'pɪdɪtɪ] n rapidez f.

rapidly ['ræpɪdlɪ] ad rápidamente.

rapids ['ræpɪdz] npl (GEO) rápidos mpl.

rapier ['reɪpɪəʳ] n estoque m.

rapist ['reɪpɪst] n violador m.

rapport [ræ'pɔːʳ] n simpatía.

rapprochement [ræ'prɔʃmɑːŋ] n acercamiento.

rapt [ræpt] a (attention) profundo; **to be** ~ **in contemplation** estar ensimismado.

rapture ['ræptʃəʳ] n éxtasis m.

rapturous ['ræptʃərəs] a extático; (applause) entusiasta.

rare [rɛəʳ] a raro, poco común; (CULIN: steak) poco hecho; **it is** ~ **to find that** ... es raro descubrir que ....

rarefied ['rɛərɪfaɪd] a (air, atmosphere) enrarecido.

rarely ['rɛəlɪ] ad rara vez, pocas veces.

raring ['rɛərɪŋ] a: **to be** ~ **to go** (col) tener muchas ganas de empezar.

rarity ['rɛərɪtɪ] n rareza.

rascal ['rɑːskl] n pillo/a, pícaro/a.

rash [ræʃ] a imprudente, precipitado ♦ n (MED) salpullido, erupción f (cutánea); **to come out in a** ~ salirle salpullido a uno.

rasher ['ræʃəʳ] n lonja.

rashly ['ræʃlɪ] ad imprudentemente, precipitadamente.

rashness ['ræʃnɪs] n imprudencia, precipitación f.

rasp [rɑːsp] n (tool) escofina ♦ vt (speak: also: ~ **out**) decir con voz áspera.

raspberry ['rɑːzbərɪ] n frambuesa.

rasping ['rɑːspɪŋ] a: **a** ~ **noise** un ruido áspero.

rat [ræt] n rata.

ratchet ['rætʃɪt] n (TECH) trinquete m.

rate [reɪt] n (ratio) razón f; (percentage) tanto por ciento; (price) precio; (: of hotel) tarifa; (of interest) tipo; (speed) velocidad f ♦ vt (value) tasar; (estimate) estimar; **to** ~ **as** ser considerado como; ~**s** npl (Brit) impuesto sg municipal; (fees) tarifa sg; **failure** ~ porcentaje de fallos; **pulse** ~ pulsaciones fpl por minuto; ~ **of pay** tipos mpl de sueldo; **at a** ~ **of 60 kph** a una velocidad de 60 kph; ~ **of growth** ritmo de crecimiento; ~ **of return** (COMM) tasa de rendimiento; **bank** ~ tipo or tasa de interés bancario; **at any** ~ de todas formas, de todos modos; **to** ~ **sb/sth highly** tener a uno/algo en alta estima; **the house is** ~**d at £84 per annum** (Brit) la casa está tasada en 84 libras al año.

rateable value ['reɪtəbl-] n (Brit) valor m impuesto.

rate-capping ['reɪtkæpɪŋ] n (Brit) fijación f de las contribuciones.

ratepayer ['reɪtpeɪəʳ] n (Brit) contribuyente *m/f*.

rather ['rɑːðə*] *ad* antes, más bien; *(somewhat)* algo, un poco; *(to some extent)* un poco; **it's ~ expensive** es algo caro; *(too much)* es demasiado caro; **there's ~ a lot** hay bastante; **I would** *or* **I'd ~ go** preferiría ir; **I'd ~ not** prefiero que no; **I ~ think he won't come** me inclino a creer que no vendrá; **or ~** *(more accurately)* o mejor dicho.

ratification [rætɪfɪ'keɪʃən] *n* ratificación *f*.

ratify ['rætɪfaɪ] *vt* ratificar.

rating ['reɪtɪŋ] *n* *(valuation)* tasación *f*; *(standing)* posición *f*; *(Brit NAUT: sailor)* marinero; **~s** *npl* *(RADIO, TV)* clasificación *f*.

ratio ['reɪʃɪəu] *n* razón *f*; **in the ~ of 100 to 1** a razón de *or* en la proporción de 100 a 1.

ration ['ræʃən] *n* ración *f*; **~s** *npl* víveres *mpl* ♦ *vt* racionar.

rational ['ræʃənl] *a* racional; *(solution, reasoning)* lógico, razonable; *(person)* cuerdo, sensato.

rationale [ræʃə'nɑːl] *n* razón *f* fundamental.

rationalism ['ræʃnəlɪzəm] *n* racionalismo.

rationalization [ræʃnəlaɪ'zeɪʃən] *n* racionalización *f*.

rationalize ['ræʃnəlaɪz] *vt* *(reorganize: industry)* reconvertir, reorganizar.

rationally ['ræʃnəlɪ] *ad* racionalmente; *(logically)* lógicamente.

rationing ['ræʃnɪŋ] *n* racionamiento.

rat race *n* lucha incesante por la supervivencia.

rattan [ræ'tæn] *n* rota, caña de Indias.

rattle ['rætl] *n* golpeteo; *(of train etc)* traqueteo; *(object: of baby)* sonaja, sonajero; *(: of sports fan)* matraca ♦ *vi* sonar, golpear; traquetear; *(small objects)* castañetear ♦ *vt* hacer sonar agitando; *(col: disconcert)* desconcertar.

rattlesnake ['rætlsneɪk] *n* serpiente *f* de cascabel.

ratty ['rætɪ] *a* *(col)* furioso; **to get ~** ponerse de malas.

raucous ['rɔːkəs] *a* estridente, ronco.

raucously ['rɔːkəslɪ] *ad* de modo estridente, roncamente.

ravage ['rævɪdʒ] *vt* hacer estragos en, destrozar; **~s** *npl* estragos *mpl*.

rave [reɪv] *vi* *(in anger)* encolerizarse; *(with enthusiasm)* entusiasmarse; *(MED)* delirar, desvariar ♦ *cpd*: **~ review** reseña entusiasta.

raven ['reɪvən] *n* cuervo.

ravenous ['rævənəs] *a* famélico.

ravine [rə'viːn] *n* barranco.

raving ['reɪvɪŋ] *a*: **~ lunatic** loco de atar.

ravings ['reɪvɪŋz] *npl* divagaciones *fpl*, desvaríos *mpl*.

ravioli [rævɪ'əulɪ] *n* ravioles *mpl*, ravioli *mpl*.

ravish ['rævɪʃ] *vt* *(charm)* encantar, embe-

lesar; *(rape)* violar.

ravishing ['rævɪʃɪŋ] *a* encantador(a).

raw [rɔː] *a* *(uncooked)* crudo; *(not processed)* bruto; *(sore)* vivo; *(inexperienced)* novato, inexperto.

Rawalpindi [rɔːl'pɪndɪ] *n* Rawalpindi *m*.

raw data *n* *(COMPUT)* datos *mpl* en bruto.

raw deal *n* *(col: bad deal)* mala pasada *or* jugada; *(: harsh treatment)* injusticia.

raw material *n* materia prima.

ray [reɪ] *n* rayo; **~ of hope** (rayo de) esperanza.

rayon ['reɪɔn] *n* rayón *m*.

raze [reɪz] *vt* *(also: ~ to the ground)* arrasar, asolar.

razor ['reɪzə*] *n* *(open)* navaja; *(safety ~)* máquina de afeitar.

razor blade *n* hoja de afeitar.

razzle(-dazzle) ['ræzl('dæzl)] *n* *(Brit col)*: **to be/go on the ~** estar/irse de juerga.

razzmatazz ['ræzmə'tæz] *n* *(col)* animación *f*, bullicio.

R & B *n abbr* = *rhythm and blues*.

RC *abbr* = **Roman Catholic.**

RCAF *n abbr* = *Royal Canadian Air Force.*

RCMP *n abbr* = *Royal Canadian Mounted Police.*

RCN *n abbr* = *Royal Canadian Navy.*

RD *abbr* *(US POST)* = *rural delivery.*

Rd *abbr* = **road.**

R & D *n abbr* *(= research and development)* investigación *f* y desarrollo.

RDC *n abbr* *(Brit)* = *rural district council.*

RE *n abbr* *(Brit)* = *religious education*; *(Brit MIL)* = *Royal Engineers.*

re [riː] *prep* con referencia a.

re... [riː] *pref* re....

reach [riːtʃ] *n* alcance *m*; *(BOXING)* envergadura; *(of river etc)* extensión *f* entre dos recodos ♦ *vt* alcanzar, llegar a; *(achieve)* lograr ♦ *vi* extenderse; *(stretch out hand: also:* **~ down, ~ over, ~ across** *etc)* tender la mano; **within ~** al alcance (de la mano); **out of ~** fuera del alcance; **to ~ out for sth** alargar *or* tender la mano para tomar algo; **can I ~ you at your hotel?** ¿puedo ponerme en contacto contigo en tu hotel?; **to ~ sb by phone** comunicarse con uno por teléfono.

react [riː'ækt] *vi* reaccionar.

reaction [riː'ækʃən] *n* reacción *f*.

reactionary [riː'ækʃənrɪ] *a*, *n* reaccionario/a *m/f*.

reactor [riː'æktə*] *n* reactor *m*.

read, *pt*, *pp* **read** [riːd, rɛd] *vi* leer ♦ *vt* leer; *(understand)* entender; *(study)* estudiar; **to take sth as read** *(fig)* dar algo por sentado; **do you ~ me?** *(TEL)* ¿me escucha?; **to ~ between the lines** leer entre líneas.

read out *vt* leer en alta voz.

read over *vt* repasar.

read through *vt* *(quickly)* leer rápida-

mente, echar un vistazo a; (*thoroughly*) leer con cuidado *or* detenidamente.
read up *vt*, **read up on** *vt fus* estudiar.
readable ['riːdəbl] *a* (*writing*) legible; (*book*) que merece leerse.
reader ['riːdə*] *n* lector(a) *m/f*; (*book*) libro de lecturas; (*Brit*: *at university*) profesor(a) *m/f*.
readership ['riːdəʃɪp] *n* (*of paper etc*) número de lectores.
readily ['rɛdɪlɪ] *ad* (*willingly*) de buena gana; (*easily*) fácilmente; (*quickly*) en seguida.
readiness ['rɛdɪnɪs] *n* buena voluntad; (*preparedness*) preparación *f*; **in ~** (*prepared*) listo, preparado.
reading ['riːdɪŋ] *n* lectura; (*understanding*) comprensión *f*; (*on instrument*) indicación *f*.
reading lamp *n* lámpara portátil.
reading matter *n* lectura.
reading room *n* sala de lectura.
readjust [riːə'dʒʌst] *vt* reajustar ◆ *vi* (*person*): **to ~ to** reajustarse a.
readjustment [riːə'dʒʌstmənt] *n* reajuste *m*.
ready ['rɛdɪ] *a* listo, preparado; (*willing*) dispuesto; (*available*) disponible ◆ *n*: **at the ~** (*MIL*) listo para tirar; **~ for use** listo para usar; **to be ~ to do sth** estar listo para hacer algo; **to get ~** *vi* prepararse ◆ *vt* preparar.
ready cash *n* (dinero) efectivo, dinero contante.
ready-made ['rɛdɪ'meɪd] *a* confeccionado.
ready money *n* dinero contante.
ready reckoner *n* tabla de cálculos hechos.
ready-to-wear ['rɛdɪtə'wɛə*] *a* confeccionado.
reaffirm [riːə'fəːm] *vt* reafirmar.
reagent [riː'eɪdʒənt] *n* reactivo.
real [rɪəl] *a* verdadero, auténtico; **in ~ terms** en términos reales; **in ~ life** en la vida real, en la realidad.
real estate *n* bienes *mpl* raíces.
real estate agency *n* = **estate agency**.
realism ['rɪəlɪzəm] *n* (*also ART*) realismo.
realist ['rɪəlɪst] *n* realista *m/f*.
realistic [rɪə'lɪstɪk] *a* realista.
realistically [rɪə'lɪstɪklɪ] *ad* de modo realista.
reality [riː'ælɪtɪ] *n* realidad *f*; **in ~** en realidad.
realization [rɪəlaɪ'zeɪʃən] *n* comprensión *f*; (*of a project*; *COMM*: *of assets*) realización *f*.
realize ['rɪəlaɪz] *vt* (*understand*) darse cuenta de; (*a project*; *COMM*: *asset*) realizar; **I ~ that** ... comprendo *or* entiendo que ....
really ['rɪəlɪ] *ad* realmente; **~?** ¿de veras?
realm [rɛlm] *n* reino; (*fig*) esfera.
real time *n* (*COMPUT*) tiempo real.

realtor ['rɪəltɔː*] *n* (*US*) corredor(a) *m/f* de bienes raíces.
ream [riːm] *n* resma; **~s** (*fig*, *col*) montones *mpl*.
reap [riːp] *vt* segar; (*fig*) cosechar, recoger.
reaper ['riːpə*] *n* segador(a) *m/f*.
reappear [riːə'pɪə*] *vi* reaparecer.
reappearance [riːə'pɪərəns] *n* reaparición *f*.
reapply [riːə'plaɪ] *vi* volver a presentarse, hacer *or* presentar nueva solicitud.
reappoint [riːə'pɔɪnt] *vt* volver a nombrar.
reappraisal [riːə'preɪzl] *n* revaluación *f*.
rear [rɪə*] *a* trasero ◆ *n* parte *f* trasera ◆ *vt* (*cattle*, *family*) criar ◆ *vi* (*also*: **~ up**) (*animal*) encabritarse.
rear-engined ['rɪər'ɛndʒɪnd] *a* (*AUT*) con motor trasero.
rearguard ['rɪəɡɑːd] *n* retaguardia.
rearm [riː'ɑːm] *vt* rearmar ◆ *vi* rearmarse.
rearmament [riː'ɑːməmənt] *n* rearme *m*.
rearrange [riːə'reɪndʒ] *vt* ordenar *or* arreglar de nuevo.
rear-view ['rɪəvjuː]: **~ mirror** *n* (*AUT*) espejo retrovisor.
reason ['riːzn] *n* razón *f* ◆ *vi*: **to ~ with sb** tratar de que uno entre en razón; **it stands to ~ that** es lógico que; **the ~ for/why** la causa de/la razón por la cual; **she claims with good ~ that she's underpaid** dice con razón que está mal pagada; **all the more ~ why you should not sell it** razón de más para que no lo vendas.
reasonable ['riːznəbl] *a* razonable; (*sensible*) sensato.
reasonably ['riːznəblɪ] *ad* razonablemente; **a ~ accurate report** un informe bastante exacto.
reasoned ['riːznd] *a* (*argument*) razonado.
reasoning ['riːznɪŋ] *n* razonamiento, argumentos *mpl*.
reassemble [riːə'sɛmbl] *vt* volver a reunir; (*machine*) montar de nuevo ◆ *vi* volver a reunirse.
reassert [riːə'səːt] *vt* reafirmar, reiterar.
reassurance [riːə'ʃuərəns] *n* consuelo.
reassure [riːə'ʃuə*] *vt* tranquilizar, alentar; **to ~ sb that** tranquilizar a uno asegurándole que.
reassuring [riːə'ʃuərɪŋ] *a* alentador(a).
reawakening [riːə'weɪknɪŋ] *n* despertar *m*.
rebate ['riːbeɪt] *n* (*on product*) rebaja; (*on tax etc*) descuento; (*repayment*) reembolso.
rebel ['rɛbl] *n* rebelde *m/f* ◆ *vi* [rɪ'bɛl] rebelarse, sublevarse.
rebellion [rɪ'bɛljən] *n* rebelión *f*, sublevación *f*.
rebellious [rɪ'bɛljəs] *a* rebelde; (*child*) revoltoso.
rebirth [riː'bəːθ] *n* renacimiento.
rebound [rɪ'baʊnd] *vi* (*ball*) rebotar ◆ *n* ['riːbaʊnd] rebote *m*.

['riːbaund] rebote *m*.
rebuff [rɪ'bʌf] *n* desaire *m*, rechazo ♦ *vt* rechazar.
rebuild [riː'bɪld] *vt* (*irg: like* build) reconstruir.
rebuilding [riː'bɪldɪŋ] *n* reconstrucción *f*.
rebuke [rɪ'bjuːk] *n* reprimenda ♦ *vt* reprender.
rebut [rɪ'bʌt] *vt* rebatir.
recalcitrant [rɪ'kælsɪtrənt] *a* reacio.
recall [rɪ'kɔːl] *vt* (*remember*) recordar; (*ambassador etc*) retirar; (*comput*) volver a llamar ♦ *n* recuerdo.
recant [rɪ'kænt] *vi* retractarse.
recap ['riːkæp] *vt, vi* recapitular.
recapitulate [riːkə'pɪtjuleɪt] *vt, vi* = **recap**.
recapture [riː'kæptʃə*] *vt* (*town*) reconquistar; (*atmosphere*) hacer revivir.
recd., rec'd *abbr* (= *received*) rbdo.
recede [rɪ'siːd] *vi* retroceder.
receding [rɪ'siːdɪŋ] *a* (*forehead, chin*) huidizo; ~ **hairline** entradas *fpl*.
receipt [rɪ'siːt] *n* (*document*) recibo; (*act of receiving*) recepción *f*; ~**s** *npl* (*comm*) ingresos *mpl*; **to acknowledge** ~ **of** acusar recibo de; **we are in** ~ **of** ... obra en nuestro poder ... .
receivable [rɪ'siːvəbl] *a* (*comm*) a cobrar.
receive [rɪ'siːv] *vt* recibir; (*guest*) acoger; (*wound*) sufrir; "~**ed with thanks**" (*comm*) "recibí".
receiver [rɪ'siːvə*] *n* (*tel*) auricular *m*; (*radio*) receptor *m*; (*of stolen goods*) perista *m/f*; (*law*) administrador *m* jurídico.
recent ['riːsnt] *a* reciente; **in** ~ **years** en los últimos años.
recently ['riːsntlɪ] *ad* recientemente; ~ **arrived** recién llegado; **until** ~ hasta hace poco.
receptacle [rɪ'septɪkl] *n* receptáculo.
reception [rɪ'sepʃən] *n* (*in building, office etc*) recepción *f*; (*welcome*) acogida.
reception centre *n* (*Brit*) centro de recepción.
reception desk *n* recepción *f*.
receptionist [rɪ'sepʃənɪst] *n* recepcionista *m/f*.
receptive [rɪ'septɪv] *a* receptivo.
recess [rɪ'ses] *n* (*in room*) hueco; (*for bed*) nicho; (*secret place*) escondrijo; (*pol etc: holiday*) clausura; (*US law: short break*) descanso; (*scol: esp US*) recreo.
recession [rɪ'seʃən] *n* recesión *f*, depresión *f*.
recharge [riː'tʃɑːdʒ] *vt* (*battery*) recargar.
rechargeable [riː'tʃɑːdʒəbl] *a* recargable.
recipe ['resɪpɪ] *n* receta.
recipient [rɪ'sɪpɪənt] *n* recibidor(a) *m/f*; (*of letter*) destinatario/a.
reciprocal [rɪ'sɪprəkl] *a* recíproco.
reciprocate [rɪ'sɪprəkeɪt] *vt* devolver, corresponder a ♦ *vi* corresponder.
recital [rɪ'saɪtl] *n* (*mus*) recital *m*.

recitation [resɪ'teɪʃən] *n* (*of poetry*) recitado; (*of complaints etc*) enumeración *f*, relación *f*.
recite [rɪ'saɪt] *vt* (*poem*) recitar; (*complaints etc*) enumerar.
reckless ['reklas] *a* temerario, imprudente; (*speed*) peligroso.
recklessly ['rekləslɪ] *ad* imprudentemente; de modo peligroso.
recklessness ['rekləsnɪs] *n* temeridad *f*, imprudencia.
reckon ['rekən] *vt* (*count*) contar; (*consider*) considerar ♦ *vi*: **to** ~ **without sb/sth** dejar de contar con uno/algo; **he is somebody to be** ~**ed with** no se le puede descartar; **I** ~ **that...** me parece que..., creo que .... .
  reckon on *vt fus* contar con.
reckoning ['rekənɪŋ] *n* (*calculation*) cálculo.
reclaim [rɪ'kleɪm] *vt* (*land*) recuperar; (*: from sea*) rescatar; (*demand back*) reclamar.
reclamation [reklə'meɪʃən] *n* recuperación *f*; rescate *m*.
recline [rɪ'klaɪn] *vi* reclinarse.
reclining [rɪ'klaɪnɪŋ] *a* (*seat*) reclinable.
recluse [rɪ'kluːs] *n* recluso/a.
recognition [rekəg'nɪʃən] *n* reconocimiento; **transformed beyond** ~ irreconocible; **in** ~ **of** en reconocimiento de.
recognizable ['rekəgnaɪzəbl] *a*: ~ (**by**) reconocible (por).
recognize ['rekəgnaɪz] *vt* reconocer, conocer; **to** ~ (**by/as**) reconocer (por/como).
recoil [rɪ'kɔɪl] *vi* (*person*): **to** ~ **from doing sth** retraerse de hacer algo ♦ *n* (*of gun*) retroceso.
recollect [rekə'lekt] *vt* recordar, acordarse de.
recollection [rekə'lekʃən] *n* recuerdo; **to the best of my** ~ que yo recuerde.
recommend [rekə'mend] *vt* recomendar; **she has a lot to** ~ **her** tiene mucho a su favor.
recommendation [rekəmen'deɪʃən] *n* recomendación *f*.
recommended retail price (RRP) *n* (*Brit*) precio recomendado de venta al público.
recompense ['rekəmpens] *vt* recompensar ♦ *n* recompensa.
reconcilable ['rekənsaɪləbl] *a* (re)conciliable.
reconcile ['rekənsaɪl] *vt* (*two people*) reconciliar; (*two facts*) compaginar; **to** ~ **o.s. to sth** resignarse *or* conformarse a algo.
reconciliation [rekənsɪlɪ'eɪʃən] *n* reconciliación *f*.
recondite [rɪ'kɒndaɪt] *a* recóndito.
recondition [riːkən'dɪʃən] *vt* (*machine*) reparar, reponer.

reconditioned [riːkən'dɪʃənd] a renovado, reparado.

reconnaissance [rɪ'kɔnɪsns] n (MIL) reconocimiento.

reconnoitre, (US) **reconnoiter** [rɛkə'nɔɪtə*] vt, vi (MIL) reconocer.

reconsider [riːkən'sɪdə*] vt repensar.

reconstitute [riː'kɔnstɪtjuːt] vt reconstituir.

reconstruct [riːkən'strʌkt] vt reconstruir.

reconstruction [riːkən'strʌkʃən] n reconstrucción f.

record n ['rɛkɔːd] (MUS) disco; (of meeting etc) relación f; (register) registro, partida; (file) archivo; (also: **police** or **criminal** ~) antecedentes mpl penales; (written) expediente m; (SPORT) récord m; (COMPUT) registro ◆ vt [rɪ'kɔːd] (set down, also COMPUT) registrar; (relate) hacer constar; (MUS: song etc) grabar; **in ~ time** en un tiempo récord; **public** ~s archivos mpl nacionales; **he is on ~ as saying that ...** hay pruebas de que ha dicho públicamente que ...; **Spain's excellent** ~ el excelente historial de España; **off the** ~ a no oficial ◆ ad confidencialmente.

record card n (in file) ficha.

recorded delivery letter [rɪ'kɔːdɪd-] n (Brit POST) carta de entrega recordada.

recorded music n música grabada.

recorder [rɪ'kɔːdə*] n (MUS) flauta de pico; (TECH) contador m.

record holder n (SPORT) actual poseedor(a) m/f del récord.

recording [rɪ'kɔːdɪŋ] n grabación f.

recording studio n estudio de grabación.

record library n discoteca.

record player n tocadiscos m inv.

recount vt [rɪ'kaunt] contar.

re-count ['riːkaunt] n (POL: of votes) segundo escrutinio, recuento ◆ vt [riː'kaunt] volver a contar.

recoup [rɪ'kuːp] vt: **to ~ one's losses** recuperar las pérdidas.

recourse [rɪ'kɔːs] n recurso; **to have ~ to** recurrir a.

recover [rɪ'kʌvə*] vt recuperar; (rescue) rescatar ◆ vi (from illness, shock) recuperarse; (country) recuperar.

recovery [rɪ'kʌvərɪ] n recuperación f; rescate m; (MED): **to make a** ~ restablecerse.

recreate [riːkrɪ'eɪt] vt recrear.

recreation [rɛkrɪ'eɪʃən] n recreación f; (amusement) recreo.

recreational [rɛkrɪ'eɪʃənl] a de recreo.

recreational vehicle n (US) caravana or roulotte f pequeña.

recrimination [rɪkrɪmɪ'neɪʃən] n recriminación f.

recruit [rɪ'kruːt] n recluta m/f ◆ vt reclutar; (staff) contratar.

recruiting office [rɪ'kruːtɪŋ-] n caja de reclutas.

recruitment [rɪ'kruːtmənt] n reclutamiento.

rectangle ['rɛktæŋgl] n rectángulo.

rectangular [rɛk'tæŋgjulə*] a rectangular.

rectify ['rɛktɪfaɪ] vt rectificar.

rector ['rɛktə*] n (REL) párroco; (SCOL) rector(a) m/f.

rectory ['rɛktərɪ] n casa del párroco.

rectum ['rɛktəm] n (ANAT) recto.

recuperate [rɪ'kuːpəreɪt] vi reponerse, restablecerse.

recur [rɪ'kəː*] vi repetirse; (pain, illness) producirse de nuevo.

recurrence [rɪ'kəːrns] n repetición f.

recurrent [rɪ'kəːrnt] a repetido.

red [rɛd] n rojo ◆ a rojo; **to be in the** ~ (account) estar en números rojos; (business) tener un saldo negativo; **to give sb the** ~ **carpet treatment** recibir a uno con todos los honores.

Red Cross n Cruz f Roja.

redcurrant ['rɛdkʌrənt] n grosella.

redden ['rɛdn] vt enrojecer ◆ vi enrojecerse.

reddish ['rɛdɪʃ] a (hair) rojizo.

redecorate [riː'dɛkəreɪt] pintar de nuevo; volver a decorar.

redecoration [riːdɛkə'reɪʃən] n renovación f.

redeem [rɪ'diːm] vt (sth in pawn) desempeñar; (fig, also REL) rescatar.

redeemable [rɪ'diːməbl] a reembolsable.

redeeming [rɪ'diːmɪŋ] a: ~ **feature** rasgo bueno or favorable.

redeploy [riːdɪ'plɔɪ] vt (resources) disponer de nuevo.

redeployment [riːdɪ'plɔɪmənt] n redistribución f.

redevelop [riːdɪ'vɛləp] vt reorganizar.

redevelopment [riːdɪ'vɛləpmənt] n reorganización f.

red-haired [rɛd'hɛəd] a pelirrojo.

red-handed [rɛd'hændɪd] a: **to be caught** ~ cogerse (Sp) or pillarse (LAm) con las manos en la masa.

redhead ['rɛdhɛd] n pelirrojo/a.

red herring n (fig) pista falsa.

red-hot [rɛd'hɔt] a candente.

redirect [riːdaɪ'rɛkt] vt (mail) reexpedir.

rediscover [riːdɪs'kʌvə*] vt redescubrir.

rediscovery [riːdɪs'kʌvərɪ] n redescubrimiento.

redistribute [riːdɪs'trɪbjuːt] vt redistribuir, hacer una nueva distribución de.

red-letter day [rɛd'lɛtə-] n día m señalado, día m especial.

red light n: **to go through a** ~ (AUT) pasar la luz roja.

red-light district n barrio chino.

redness ['rɛdnɪs] n rojez f.

redo [riː'duː] vt (irg: like do) rehacer.

redolent ['rɛdələnt] a: ~ **of** (smell) oliente or con fragancia a; **to be** ~ **of** (fig) recordar.

redouble [riː'dʌbl] *vt*: **to ~ one's efforts** intensificar los esfuerzos.

redraft [riː'drɑːft] *vt* volver a redactar.

redress [rɪ'drɛs] *n* reparación *f* ♦ *vt* reparar, corregir; **to ~ the balance** restablecer el equilibrio.

Red Sea *n*: **the ~** el mar Rojo.

redskin ['rɛdskɪn] *n* piel roja *m/f*.

red tape *n* (*fig*) trámites *mpl*, papeleo (*col*).

reduce [rɪ'djuːs] *vt* reducir; (*lower*) rebajar; **to ~ sth by/to** reducir algo en/a; **to ~ sb to silence/despair/tears** reducir a uno al silencio/a la desesperación/a las lágrimas; **'~ speed now'** (*AUT*) 'reduzca la velocidad'.

reduced [rɪ'djuːst] *a* (*decreased*) reducido, rebajado; **at a ~ price** con rebaja *or* descuento; **"greatly ~ prices"** "grandes rebajas".

reduction [rɪ'dʌkʃən] *n* reducción *f*; (*of price*) rebaja; (*discount*) descuento.

redundancy [rɪ'dʌndənsɪ] *n* desempleo; **compulsory ~** despido; **voluntary ~** dimisión *f*.

redundancy payment *n* indemnización *f* por desempleo.

redundant [rɪ'dʌndənt] *a* (*Brit*) (*worker*) parado, sin trabajo; (*detail, object*) superfluo; **to be made ~** quedar(se) sin trabajo, perder su empleo.

reed [riːd] *n* (*BOT*) junco, caña; (*MUS: of clarinet etc*) lengüeta.

reedy ['riːdɪ] *a* (*voice, instrument*) aflautado.

reef [riːf] *n* (*at sea*) arrecife *m*.

reek [riːk] *vi*: **to ~ (of)** oler *or* heder (a).

reel [riːl] *n* carrete *m*, bobina; (*of film*) rollo ♦ *vt* (*TECH*) devanar; (*also*: **~ in**) sacar ♦ *vi* (*sway*) tambalear(se); **my head is ~ing** me da vueltas la cabeza.

reel off *vt* recitar de memoria.

re-election [riː'ɪlɛkʃən] *n* reelección *f*.

re-engage [riːɪn'geɪdʒ] *vt* contratar de nuevo.

re-enter [riː'ɛntə*] *vt* reingresar en, volver a entrar en.

re-entry [riː'ɛntrɪ] *n* reingreso, reentrada.

re-examine [riːɪg'zæmɪn] *vt* reexaminar.

re-export *vt* [riːɪks'pɔːt] reexportar ♦ *n* [riː'ɛkspɔːt] reexportación *f*.

ref [rɛf] *n abbr* (*col*) = **referee**.

ref. *abbr* (*COMM*: **= with reference to**) Ref.

refectory [rɪ'fɛktərɪ] *n* comedor *m*.

refer [rɪ'fɜː*] *vt* (*send*) remitir; (*ascribe*) referir a, relacionar con ♦ *vi*: **to ~ to** (*allude to*) referirse a, aludir a; (*apply to*) relacionarse con; (*consult*) remitirse a; **he ~red me to the manager** me envió al gerente.

referee [rɛfə'riː] *n* árbitro; (*Brit: for job application*) persona que recomienda a otro ♦ *vt* (*match*) arbitrar en.

reference ['rɛfrəns] *n* (*mention, in book*) referencia; (*sending*) remisión *f*; (*relevance*) relación *f*; (*for job application: letter*) carta de recomendación; **with ~ to** con referencia a; (*COMM: in letter*) me remito a.

reference book *n* libro de consulta.

reference number *n* número de referencia.

referendum, *pl* **referenda** [rɛfə'rɛndəm, -də] *n* referéndum *m inv*.

refill *vt* [riː'fɪl] rellenar ♦ *n* ['riːfɪl] repuesto, recambio.

refine [rɪ'faɪn] *vt* (*sugar, oil*) refinar.

refined [rɪ'faɪnd] *a* (*person, taste*) refinado, culto.

refinement [rɪ'faɪnmənt] *n* (*of person*) cultura, educación *f*.

refinery [rɪ'faɪnərɪ] *n* refinería.

refit (*NAUT*) *n* ['riːfɪt] equipamiento ♦ *vt* [riː'fɪt] reparar.

reflate [riː'fleɪt] *vt* (*economy*) reflacionar.

reflation [riː'fleɪʃən] *n* reflación *f*.

reflationary [riː'fleɪʃənrɪ] *a* reflacionario.

reflect [rɪ'flɛkt] *vt* (*light, image*) reflejar ♦ *vi* (*think*) reflexionar, pensar; **it ~s badly/well on him** le perjudica/le hace honor.

reflection [rɪ'flɛkʃən] *n* (*act*) reflexión *f*; (*image*) reflejo; (*discredit*) crítica; **on ~** pensándolo bien.

reflector [rɪ'flɛktə*] *n* (*AUT*) captafaros *m inv*; (*telescope*) reflector *m*.

reflex ['riːflɛks] *a, n* reflejo.

reflexive [rɪ'flɛksɪv] *a* (*LING*) reflexivo.

reform [rɪ'fɔːm] *n* reforma ♦ *vt* reformar.

reformat [riː'fɔːmæt] *vt* (*COMPUT*) recomponer.

Reformation [rɛfə'meɪʃən] *n*: **the ~** la Reforma.

reformatory [rɪ'fɔːmətərɪ] *n* (*US*) reformatorio.

reformer [rɪ'fɔːmə*] *n* reformador(a) *m/f*.

refrain [rɪ'freɪn] *vi*: **to ~ from doing** abstenerse de hacer ♦ *n* (*MUS etc*) estribillo.

refresh [rɪ'frɛʃ] *vt* refrescar.

refresher course [rɪ'frɛʃə-] *n* (*Brit*) curso de repaso.

refreshing [rɪ'frɛʃɪŋ] *a* (*drink*) refrescante; (*sleep*) reparador; (*change etc*) estimulante; (*idea, point of view*) estimulante, interesante.

refreshments [rɪ'frɛʃmənts] *npl* (*drinks*) refrescos *mpl*.

refrigeration [rɪfrɪdʒə'reɪʃən] *n* refrigeración *f*.

refrigerator [rɪ'frɪdʒəreɪtə*] *n* nevera, refrigeradora (*LAm*).

refuel [riː'fjuəl] *vi* repostar (combustible).

refuelling, (*US*) **refueling** [riː'fjuəlɪŋ] *n* rebastecimiento de combustible.

refuge ['rɛfjuːdʒ] *n* refugio, asilo; **to take ~ in** refugiarse en.

refugee [rɛfju'dʒiː] *n* refugiado/a.

refugee camp *n* campamento para refugiados.

refund n ['riːfʌnd] reembolso ♦ vt [rɪ'fʌnd] devolver, reembolsar.

refurbish [riː'fɜːbɪʃ] vt restaurar, renovar.

refurnish [riː'fɜːnɪʃ] vt amueblar de nuevo.

refusal [rɪ'fjuːzəl] n negativa; **first** ~ primera opción; **to have first** ~ **on sth** tener la primera opción a algo.

refuse n ['rɛfjuːs] basura ♦ (vb: [rɪ'fjuːz]) vt (reject) rehusar; (say no to) negarse a ♦ vi negarse; (horse) rehusar; **to** ~ **to do sth** negarse a or rehusar hacer algo.

refuse bin n cubo or bote m (LAm) de la basura.

refuse collection n recolección f de basuras.

refuse disposal n eliminación f de basuras.

refuse tip n vertedero.

refute [rɪ'fjuːt] vt refutar, rebatir.

regain [rɪ'geɪn] vt recobrar, recuperar.

regal ['riːgl] a regio, real.

regale [rɪ'geɪl] vt agasajar, entretener.

regalia [rɪ'geɪlɪə] n insignias fpl.

regard [rɪ'gɑːd] n (gaze) mirada; (aspect) respecto; (esteem) respeto, consideración f ♦ vt (consider) considerar; (look at) mirar; **to give one's** ~**s to** saludar de su parte a; **"(kind)** ~**s"** "muy atentamente"; **"with kindest** ~**s"** "con muchos recuerdos"; ~**s to María, please give my** ~**s to María** recuerdos a María, dele recuerdos a María de mi parte; ~**ing, as** ~**s, with** ~ **to** con respecto a, en cuanto a.

regarding [rɪ'gɑːdɪŋ] prep con respecto a, en cuanto a.

regardless [rɪ'gɑːdlɪs] ad a pesar de todo; ~ **of** sin reparar en.

regatta [rɪ'gætə] n regata.

regency ['riːdʒənsɪ] n regencia.

regenerate [rɪ'dʒenəreɪt] vt regenerar.

regent ['riːdʒənt] n regente m/f.

régime [reɪ'ʒiːm] n régimen m.

regiment n ['redʒɪmənt] regimiento ♦ vt ['redʒɪmɛnt] reglamentar.

regimental [redʒɪ'mɛntl] a militar.

regimentation [redʒɪmɛn'teɪʃən] n regimentación f.

region ['riːdʒən] n región f; **in the** ~ **of** (fig) alrededor de.

regional ['riːdʒənl] a regional.

regional development n desarrollo regional.

register ['redʒɪstə*] n registro ♦ vt registrar; (birth) declarar; (letter) certificar; (subj: instrument) marcar, indicar ♦ vi (at hotel) registrarse; (sign on) inscribirse; (make impression) producir impresión; **to** ~ **a protest** presentar una queja; **to** ~ **for a course** matricularse or inscribirse en un curso.

registered ['redʒɪstəd] a (design) registrado; (Brit: letter) certificado; (student) ma-

triculado; (voter) registrado.

registered company n sociedad f legalmente constituida.

registered nurse n (US) enfermero/a calificado/a.

registered office n domicilio social.

registered trademark n marca registrada.

registrar ['redʒɪstrɑː*] n secretario/a (del registro civil).

registration [redʒɪs'treɪʃən] n (act) declaración f; (AUT: also: ~ **number**) matrícula.

registry ['redʒɪstrɪ] n registro.

registry office n (Brit) registro civil; **to get married in a** ~ casarse por lo civil.

regret [rɪ'gret] n sentimiento, pesar m; (remorse) remordimiento ♦ vt sentir, lamentar; (repent of) arrepentirse de; **we** ~ **to inform you that ...** sentimos informarle que ....

regretful [rɪ'gretful] a pesaroso, arrepentido.

regretfully [rɪ'gretfəlɪ] ad con pesar, sentidamente.

regrettable [rɪ'gretəbl] a lamentable; (loss) sensible.

regrettably [rɪ'gretəblɪ] ad desgraciadamente.

regroup [riː'gruːp] vt reagrupar ♦ vi reagruparse.

regt abbr = **regiment**.

regular ['regjulə*] a regular; (soldier) profesional; (col: intensive) verdadero; (listener, reader) asiduo, habitual ♦ n (client etc) cliente/a m/f habitual.

regularity [regju'lærɪtɪ] n regularidad f.

regularly ['regjuləlɪ] ad con regularidad.

regulate ['regjuleɪt] vt (gen) controlar; (TECH) regular, ajustar.

regulation [regju'leɪʃən] n (rule) regla, reglamento; (adjustment) regulación f.

rehabilitation ['riːhəbɪlɪ'teɪʃən] n rehabilitación f.

rehash [riː'hæʃ] vt (col) hacer un refrito de.

rehearsal [rɪ'hɜːsəl] n ensayo; **dress** ~ ensayo general or final.

rehearse [rɪ'hɜːs] vt ensayar.

rehouse [riː'hauz] vt dar nueva vivienda a.

reign [reɪn] n reinado; (fig) predominio ♦ vi reinar; (fig) imperar.

reigning ['reɪnɪŋ] a (monarch) reinante, actual; (predominant) imperante.

reimburse [riːɪm'bɜːs] vt reembolsar.

rein [reɪn] n (for horse) rienda; **to give sb free** ~ dar rienda suelta a uno.

reincarnation [riːɪnkɑː'neɪʃən] n reencarnación f.

reindeer ['reɪndɪə*] n, pl inv reno.

reinforce [riːɪn'fɔːs] vt reforzar.

reinforced concrete [riːɪn'fɔːst-] n hormigón armado.

reinforcement [riːɪn'fɔːsmənt] n (action) refuerzo; ~**s** npl (MIL) refuerzos mpl.

reinstate [riːɪn'steɪt] *vt* (*worker*) reintegrar (a su puesto).

reinstatement [riːɪn'steɪtmənt] *n* reintegración *f*.

reissue [riː'ɪʃuː] *vt* (*record, book*) reeditar.

reiterate [riː'ɪtəreɪt] *vt* reiterar, repetir.

reject *n* ['riːdʒɛkt] (*thing*) desecho ♦ *vt* [rɪ'dʒɛkt] rechazar; (*proposition, offer etc*) descartar.

rejection [rɪ'dʒɛkʃən] *n* rechazo.

rejoice [rɪ'dʒɔɪs] *vi*: **to ~ at** *or* **over** regocijarse *or* alegrarse de.

rejoinder [rɪ'dʒɔɪndə*] *n* (*retort*) réplica.

rejuvenate [rɪ'dʒuːvəneɪt] *vt* rejuvenecer.

rekindle [riː'kɪndl] *vt* reencender; (*fig*) despertar.

relapse [rɪ'læps] *n* (MED) recaída; (*into crime*) reincidencia.

relate [rɪ'leɪt] *vt* (*tell*) contar, relatar; (*connect*) relacionar ♦ *vi* relacionarse; **to ~ to** (*connect*) relacionarse *or* tener que ver con.

related [rɪ'leɪtɪd] *a* afín; (*person*) emparentado; **~ to** con referencia a, relacionado con.

relating [rɪ'leɪtɪŋ]: **~ to** *prep* referente a.

relation [rɪ'leɪʃən] *n* (*person*) pariente *m/f*; (*link*) relación *f*; **in ~ to** en relación con, en lo que se refiere a; **to bear a ~ to** guardar relación con; **diplomatic/international ~s** relaciones *fpl* diplomáticas/internacionales.

relationship [rɪ'leɪʃənʃɪp] *n* relación *f*; (*personal*) relaciones *fpl*; (*also*: **family ~**) parentesco.

relative ['relətɪv] *n* pariente *m/f*, familiar *m/f* ♦ *a* relativo.

relatively ['relətɪvlɪ] *ad* (*fairly, rather*) relativamente.

relative pronoun *n* pronombre *m* relativo.

relax [rɪ'læks] *vi* descansar; (*quieten down*) relajarse ♦ *vt* relajar; (*mind, person*) descansar; **~!** (*calm down*) ¡tranquilo!

relaxation [riːlæk'seɪʃən] *n* (*rest*) descanso; (*easing*) relajación *f*, relajamiento *m*; (*amusement*) recreo; (*entertainment*) diversión *f*.

relaxed [rɪ'lækst] *a* relajado; (*tranquil*) tranquilo.

relaxing [rɪ'læksɪŋ] *a* relajante.

relay *n* ['riːleɪ] (*race*) carrera de relevos ♦ *vt* [rɪ'leɪ] (RADIO, TV, *pass on*) retransmitir.

release [rɪ'liːs] *n* (*liberation*) liberación *f*; (*discharge*) puesta en libertad *f*; (*of gas etc*) escape *m*; (*of film etc*) estreno ♦ *vt* (*prisoner*) poner en libertad; (*film*) estrenar; (*book*) publicar; (*piece of news*) difundir; (*gas etc*) despedir, arrojar; (*free: from wreckage etc*) soltar; (TECH: *catch, spring etc*) desenganchar; (*let go*) soltar, aflojar.

relegate ['reləgeɪt] *vt* relegar; (SPORT): **to**

be ~d to bajar a.

relent [rɪ'lent] *vi* ablandarse; (*let up*) descansar.

relentless [rɪ'lentlɪs] *a* implacable.

relentlessly [rɪ'lentlɪslɪ] *ad* implacablemente.

relevance ['reləvəns] *n* relación *f*.

relevant ['reləvənt] *a* (*fact*) pertinente; **~ to** relacionado con.

reliability [rɪlaɪə'bɪlɪtɪ] *n* fiabilidad *f*; seguridad *f*; veracidad *f*.

reliable [rɪ'laɪəbl] *a* (*person, firm*) de confianza, de fiar; (*method, machine*) seguro; (*source*) fidedigno.

reliably [rɪ'laɪəblɪ] *ad*: **to be ~ informed that...** saber de fuente fidedigna que... .

reliance [rɪ'laɪəns] *n*: **~ (on)** dependencia (de).

reliant [rɪ'laɪənt] *a*: **to be ~ on sth/sb** confiar en algo/uno.

relic ['relɪk] *n* (REL) reliquia; (*of the past*) vestigio.

relief [rɪ'liːf] *n* (*from pain, anxiety*) alivio, desahogo; (*help, supplies*) socorro, ayuda; (ART, GEO) relieve *m*; **by way of light ~** a modo de diversión.

relief road *n* carretera de desgestionamiento.

relieve [rɪ'liːv] *vt* (*pain, patient*) aliviar; (*bring help to*) ayudar, socorrer; (*burden*) aligerar; (*take over from: gen*) sustituir a; (: *guard*) relevar; **to ~ sb of sth** quitar algo a uno; **to ~ sb of his command** (MIL) relevar a uno de su mando; **to ~ o.s.** hacer sus necesidades; **I am ~d to hear you are better** me tranquiliza saber que estás *or* te encuentras mejor.

religion [rɪ'lɪdʒən] *n* religión *f*.

religious [rɪ'lɪdʒəs] *a* religioso.

religiously [rɪ'lɪdʒəslɪ] *ad* religiosamente; (*conscientiously*) puntualmente, fielmente.

reline [riː'laɪn] *vt* (*brakes*) poner nueva guarnición a.

relinquish [rɪ'lɪŋkwɪʃ] *vt* abandonar; (*plan, habit*) renunciar a.

relish ['relɪʃ] *n* (CULIN) salsa; (*enjoyment*) entusiasmo; (*flavour*) sabor *m*, gusto ♦ *vt* (*food etc*) saborear; **to ~ doing** gustar mucho de hacer.

relive [riː'lɪv] *vt* vivir de nuevo, volver a vivir.

relocate [riːləʊ'keɪt] *vt* cambiar de lugar, mudar ♦ *vi* mudarse.

reluctance [rɪ'lʌktəns] *n* renuencia.

reluctant [rɪ'lʌktənt] *a* renuente; **to be ~ to do sth** resistirse a hacer algo.

reluctantly [rɪ'lʌktəntlɪ] *ad* de mala gana.

rely [rɪ'laɪ]: **to ~ on** *vt fus* confiar en, fiarse de; (*be dependent on*) depender de; **you can ~ on my discretion** puedes contar con mi discreción.

remain [rɪ'meɪn] *vi* (*survive*) quedar; (*be left*) sobrar; (*continue*) quedar(se), perma-

necer; **to ~ silent** permanecer callado; **I
~, yours faithfully** (*in letters*) le saluda
atentamente.
remainder [rɪ'meɪndə*] *n* resto.
remaining [rɪ'meɪnɪŋ] *a* sobrante.
remains [rɪ'meɪnz] *npl* restos *mpl*.
remand [rɪ'mɑːnd] *n*: **on ~** detenido (bajo
custodia) ♦ *vt*: **to ~ in custody** mantener
bajo custodia.
remand home *n* (*Brit*) reformatorio.
remark [rɪ'mɑːk] *n* comentario ♦ *vt* comentar; **to ~ on sth** hacer observaciones
sobre algo.
remarkable [rɪ'mɑːkəbl] *a* notable; (*outstanding*) extraordinario.
remarkably [rɪ'mɑːkəblɪ] *ad* extraordinariamente.
remarry [riː'mærɪ] *vi* casarse por segunda
vez, volver a casarse.
remedial [rɪ'miːdɪəl] *a*: **~ education** educación *f* de los niños atrasados.
remedy ['rɛmədɪ] *n* remedio ♦ *vt* remediar,
curar.
remember [rɪ'mɛmbə*] *vt* recordar,
acordarse de; (*bear in mind*) tener presente; **I ~ seeing it, I ~ having seen it** recuerdo haberlo visto; **she ~ed doing it** se
acordó de hacerlo; **~ me to your wife and
children!** ¡déle recuerdos a su familia!
remembrance [rɪ'mɛmbrəns] *n* (*memory,
souvenir*) recuerdo; **in ~ of** en conmemoración de.
remind [rɪ'maɪnd] *vt*: **to ~ sb to do sth** recordar a uno que haga algo; **to ~ sb of sth**
recordar algo a uno; **she ~s me of her
mother** me recuerda a su madre; **that ~s
me!** ¡a propósito!
reminder [rɪ'maɪndə*] *n* notificación *f*; (*memento*) recuerdo.
reminisce [rɛmɪ'nɪs] *vi* recordar (viejas his-
torias).
reminiscences [rɛmɪ'nɪsnsɪz] *npl* remi-
niscencias *fpl*, recuerdos *mpl*.
reminiscent [rɛmɪ'nɪsnt] *a*: **to be ~ of sth**
recordar algo.
remiss [rɪ'mɪs] *a* descuidado; **it was ~ of
me** fue un descuido de mi parte.
remission [rɪ'mɪʃən] *n* remisión *f*; (*of
sentence*) disminución *f* de pena.
remit [rɪ'mɪt] *vt* (*send: money*) remitir, enviar.
remittance [rɪ'mɪtns] *n* remesa, envío.
remnant ['rɛmnənt] *n* resto; (*of cloth*) retazo; **~s** *npl* (*COMM*) restos de serie.
remonstrate ['rɛmənstreɪt] *vi* protestar.
remorse [rɪ'mɔːs] *n* remordimientos *mpl*.
remorseful [rɪ'mɔːsful] *a* arrepentido.
remorseless [rɪ'mɔːslɪs] *a* (*fig*) implacable,
inexorable.
remorselessly [rɪ'mɔːslɪslɪ] *ad* implacablemente, inexorablemente.
remote [rɪ'məut] *a* (*distant*) lejano; (*person*) distante; (*COMPUT*) remoto; **there is a**

~ possibility that ... hay una posibilidad
remota de que ....
remote control *n* telecontrol *m*.
remote-controlled [rɪ'məutkən'trəuld] *a*
teledirigido.
remotely [rɪ'məutlɪ] *ad* remotamente;
(*slightly*) levemente.
remoteness [rɪ'məutnɪs] *n* alejamiento;
distancia.
remould ['riːməuld] *n* (*Brit: tyre*) neumático *or* llanta (*LAm*) recauchutado/a.
removable [rɪ'muːvəbl] *a* (*detachable*) separable.
removal [rɪ'muːvəl] *n* (*taking away*) el quitar; (*Brit: from house*) mudanza; (*from office: dismissal*) destitución *f*; (*MED*) ex-
tirpación *f*.
removal van *n* (*Brit*) camión *m* de mudanzas.
remove [rɪ'muːv] *vt* quitar; (*employee*) destituir; (*name: from list*) tachar, borrar;
(*doubt*) disipar; (*TECH*) retirar, separar;
(*MED*) extirpar; **first cousin once ~d** (*parent's cousin*) tío/a segundo/a; (*cousin's
child*) sobrino/a segundo/a.
remover [rɪ'muːvə*] *n*: **make-up ~** desma-
quilladora; **~s** *npl* (*Brit: company*) agencia de mudanzas.
remunerate [rɪ'mjuːnəreɪt] *vt* remunerar.
remuneration [rɪmjuːnə'reɪʃən] *n* remuneración *f*.
Renaissance [rɪ'neɪsɔ̃s] *n*: **the ~** el Renacimiento.
rename [riː'neɪm] *vt* poner nuevo nombre a.
render ['rɛndə*] *vt* (*thanks*) dar; (*aid*) proporcionar; (*honour*) dar, conceder; (*assistance*) dar, prestar; **to ~ sth + a** volver
algo + *a*.
rendering ['rɛndərɪŋ] *n* (*MUS etc*) interpretación *f*.
rendez-vous ['rɔndɪvuː] *n* cita ♦ *vi* reunirse, encontrarse; (*spaceship*) efectuar
una reunión espacial.
rendition [rɛn'dɪʃən] *n* (*MUS*) interpretación
f.
renegade ['rɛnɪɡeɪd] *n* renegado/a.
renew [rɪ'njuː] *vt* renovar; (*resume*) reanudar; (*extend date*) prorrogar; (*negotiations*) volver a.
renewal [rɪ'njuːəl] *n* renovación *f*; reanudación *f*; prórroga.
renounce [rɪ'nauns] *vt* renunciar a; (*right,
inheritance*) renunciar.
renovate ['rɛnəveɪt] *vt* renovar.
renovation [rɛnə'veɪʃən] *n* renovación *f*.
renown [rɪ'naun] *n* renombre *m*.
renowned [rɪ'naund] *a* renombrado.
rent [rɛnt] *n* alquiler *m*; (*for house*)
arriendo, renta ♦ *vt* (*also: ~ out*) alquilar.
rental ['rɛntl] *n* (*for television, car*) alquiler
m.
renunciation [rɪnʌnsɪ'eɪʃən] *n* renuncia.
reopen [riː'əupən] *vt* volver a abrir, reabrir.

reorder [ri:'ɔːdə*] vt volver a pedir, repetir el pedido de; (rearrange) volver a ordenar or arreglar.

reorganization [riːɔːgənaɪ'zeɪʃən] n reorganización f.

reorganize [riː'ɔːgənaɪz] vt reorganizar.

rep [rɛp] n abbr (COMM) = **representative**; (THEATRE) = **repertory**.

Rep. abbr (US POL) = **representative, republican**.

repair [rɪ'pɛə*] n reparación f, compostura; (patch) remiendo ♦ vt reparar, componer; (shoes) remendar; **in good/bad** ~ en buen/mal estado; **under** ~ en obras.

repair kit n caja de herramientas.

repair man n mecánico.

repair shop n taller m de reparaciones.

repartee [rɛpɑː'tiː] n réplicas fpl agudas.

repast [rɪ'pɑːst] n (formal) comida.

repatriate [riː'pætrɪeɪt] vt repatriar.

repay [riː'peɪ] vt (irg: like **pay**) (money) devolver, reembolsar; (person) pagar; (debt) liquidar; (sb's efforts) devolver, corresponder a.

repayment [riː'peɪmənt] n reembolso, devolución f; (sum of money) recompensa.

repeal [rɪ'piːl] n revocación f ♦ vt revocar.

repeat [rɪ'piːt] n (RADIO, TV) reposición f ♦ vt repetir ♦ vi repetirse.

repeatedly [rɪ'piːtɪdlɪ] ad repetidas veces.

repeat order n (COMM): **to place a** ~ **for** renovar un pedido de.

repel [rɪ'pɛl] vt repugnar.

repellent [rɪ'pɛlənt] a repugnante ♦ n: **insect** ~ crema/loción f anti-insectos.

repent [rɪ'pɛnt] vi: **to** ~ **(of)** arrepentirse (de).

repentance [rɪ'pɛntəns] n arrepentimiento.

repercussion [riːpə'kʌʃən] n (consequence) repercusión f; **to have** ~**s** repercutir.

repertoire ['rɛpətwɑː*] n repertorio.

repertory ['rɛpətərɪ] n (also: ~ **theatre**) teatro de repertorio.

repertory company n compañía de repertorio.

repetition [rɛpɪ'tɪʃən] n repetición f.

repetitious [rɛpɪ'tɪʃəs] a repetidor(a), que se repite.

repetitive [rɪ'pɛtɪtɪv] a (movement, work) reiterativo; (speech) lleno de repeticiones.

rephrase [riː'freɪz] vt decir or formular de otro modo.

replace [rɪ'pleɪs] vt (put back) devolver a su sitio; (take the place of) reemplazar, sustituir.

replacement [rɪ'pleɪsmənt] n reemplazo; (act) reposición f; (thing) recambio; (person) suplente m/f.

replacement cost n costo de sustitución.

replacement part n repuesto.

replacement value n valor m de sustitución.

replay ['riːpleɪ] n (SPORT) desempate m; (TV: playback) repetición f.

replenish [rɪ'plɛnɪʃ] vt (tank etc) rellenar; (stock etc) reponer; (with fuel) repostar.

replete [rɪ'pliːt] a repleto, lleno.

replica ['rɛplɪkə] n copia, reproducción f.

reply [rɪ'plaɪ] n respuesta, contestación f ♦ vi contestar, responder; **in** ~ en respuesta; **there's no** ~ (TEL) no contestan.

reply coupon n cupón-respuesta m.

reply-paid [rɪ'plaɪ'peɪd] a: ~ **postcard** tarjeta postal con respuesta pagada.

report [rɪ'pɔːt] n informe m; (PRESS etc) reportaje m; (Brit: also: **school** ~) nota; (of gun) estallido ♦ vt informar sobre; (PRESS etc) hacer un reportaje sobre; (notify: accident, culprit) denunciar ♦ vi (make a report) presentar un informe; (present o.s.): **to** ~ **(to sb)** presentarse (ante uno); **annual** ~ (COMM) informe m anual; **to** ~ **(on)** hacer un informe (sobre); **it is** ~**ed from Berlin that** ... se informa desde Berlín que ....

report card n (US, Scottish) cartilla escolar.

reportedly [rɪ'pɔːtɪdlɪ] ad según se dice, según se informe.

reporter [rɪ'pɔːtə*] n (PRESS) periodista m/f; (RADIO, TV) locutor(a) m/f.

repose [rɪ'pəuz] n: **in** ~ (face, mouth) en reposo.

repossess [riːpə'zɛs] vt recobrar.

reprehensible [rɛprɪ'hɛnsɪbl] a reprensible, censurable.

represent [rɛprɪ'zɛnt] vt representar; (COMM) ser agente de.

representation [rɛprɪzɛn'teɪʃən] n representación f; (petition) petición f; ~**s** npl (protest) quejas fpl.

representative [rɛprɪ'zɛntətɪv] n (US POL) representante m/f, diputado/a; (COMM) representante m/f ♦ a: ~ **(of)** representativo (de).

repress [rɪ'prɛs] vt reprimir.

repression [rɪ'prɛʃən] n represión f.

repressive [rɪ'prɛsɪv] a represivo.

reprieve [rɪ'priːv] n (LAW) indulto; (fig) alivio ♦ vt indultar; (fig) salvar.

reprimand ['rɛprɪmɑːnd] n reprimenda ♦ vt reprender.

reprint ['riːprɪnt] n reimpresión f, reedición f ♦ vt [riː'prɪnt] reimprimir.

reprisal [rɪ'praɪzl] n represalia; **to take** ~**s** tomar represalias.

reproach [rɪ'prəutʃ] n reproche m ♦ vt: ~ **sb with sth** reprochar algo a uno; **beyond** ~ intachable.

reproachful [rɪ'prəutʃful] a de reproche, de acusación.

reproduce [riːprə'djuːs] vt reproducir ♦ vi reproducirse.

reproduction [riːprə'dʌkʃən] n reproducción f.

reproductive [riːprə'dʌktɪv] a reproductor(a).

reproof [rɪ'pruːf] n reproche m.

reprove [rɪ'pruːv] vt: **to ~ sb for sth** reprochar algo a uno.

reptile ['reptaɪl] n reptil m.

republic [rɪ'pʌblɪk] n república.

republican [rɪ'pʌblɪkən] a, n republicano/a m/f.

repudiate [rɪ'pjuːdɪeɪt] vt (accusation) rechazar; (obligation) desconocer.

repudiation [rɪpjuːdɪ'eɪʃən] n incumplimiento.

repugnance [rɪ'pʌgnəns] n repugnancia.

repugnant [rɪ'pʌgnənt] a repugnante.

repulse [rɪ'pʌls] vt rechazar.

repulsion [rɪ'pʌlʃən] n repulsión f, repugnancia.

repulsive [rɪ'pʌlsɪv] a repulsivo.

repurchase [riː'pəːtʃəs] vt volver a comprar, readquirir.

reputable ['repjutəbl] a (make etc) de renombre.

reputation [repju'teɪʃən] n reputación f; **he has a ~ for being awkward** tiene fama de difícil.

repute [rɪ'pjuːt] n reputación f, fama.

reputed [rɪ'pjuːtɪd] a supuesto; **to be ~ to be rich/intelligent** etc tener fama de rico/inteligente etc.

reputedly [rɪ'pjuːtɪdlɪ] ad según dicen or se dice.

request [rɪ'kwest] n solicitud f, petición f ♦ vt: **to ~ sth of** or **from sb** solicitar algo a uno; **at the ~ of** a petición de; **"you are ~ed not to smoke"** "se ruega no fumar".

request stop n (Brit) parada a petición.

requiem ['rekwɪəm] n réquiem m.

require [rɪ'kwaɪə*] vt (need: subj: person) necesitar, tener necesidad de; (: thing, situation) exigir; (want) pedir; (demand) insistir en que; **to ~ sb to do sth/sth of sb** exigir que uno haga algo; **what qualifications are ~d?** ¿qué títulos se requieren?; **~d by law** requerido por la ley.

requirement [rɪ'kwaɪəmənt] n requisito; (need) necesidad f.

requisite ['rekwɪzɪt] n requisito ♦ a necesario, requerido.

requisition [rekwɪ'zɪʃən] n: **~ (for)** solicitud f (de) ♦ vt (MIL) requisar.

reroute [riː'ruːt] vt desviar.

resale ['riːseɪl] n reventa.

resale price maintenance n mantenimiento del precio de venta.

rescind [rɪ'sɪnd] vt (LAW) abrogar; (contract, order etc) anular.

rescue ['reskjuː] n rescate m ♦ vt rescatar; **to come/go to sb's ~** ir en auxilio de uno, socorrer a uno; **to ~ from** librar de.

rescue party n expedición f de salvamento.

rescuer ['reskjuə*] n salvador(a) m/f.

research [rɪ'səːtʃ] n investigaciones fpl ♦ vt investigar; **a piece of ~** un trabajo de investigación; **to ~ (into sth)** investigar (algo).

research and development (R & D) n investigación f y desarrollo.

researcher [rɪ'səːtʃə*] n investigador(a) m/f.

research work n investigación f.

resell [riː'sel] vt revender.

resemblance [rɪ'zembləns] n parecido; **to bear a strong ~ to** parecerse mucho a.

resemble [rɪ'zembl] vt parecerse a.

resent [rɪ'zent] vt resentirse de.

resentful [rɪ'zentful] a resentido.

resentment [rɪ'zentmənt] n resentimiento.

reservation [rezə'veɪʃən] n reserva; (booking) reservación f; (Brit: also: **central ~**) mediana; **with ~s** con reservas.

reservation desk n (US: in hotel) recepción f.

reserve [rɪ'zəːv] n reserva; (SPORT) suplente m/f ♦ vt (seats etc) reservar; **~s** npl (MIL) reserva sg; **in ~** en reserva.

reserve currency n divisa de reserva.

reserved [rɪ'zəːvd] a reservado.

reserve price n (Brit) precio mínimo.

reserve team n (SPORT) equipo de reserva.

reservist [rɪ'zəːvɪst] n (MIL) reservista m.

reservoir ['rezəvwaː*] n (artificial lake) embalse m, represa (LAm); (small) depósito.

reset [riː'set] vt (COMPUT) reinicializar.

reshape [riː'ʃeɪp] vt (policy) reformar, rehacer.

reshuffle [riː'ʃʌfl] n: **Cabinet ~** (POL) remodelación f del gabinete.

reside [rɪ'zaɪd] vi residir, vivir.

residence ['rezɪdəns] n residencia; (formal: home) domicilio; (length of stay) permanencia; **in ~** (queen etc) en residencia; (doctor) residente; **to take up ~** instalarse.

residence permit n (Brit) permiso de permanencia.

resident ['rezɪdənt] n vecino/a; (in hotel) huésped/a m/f ♦ a (population) permanente; (COMPUT) residente.

residential [rezɪ'denʃəl] a residencial.

residue ['rezɪdjuː] n resto, residuo.

resign [rɪ'zaɪn] vt (gen) renunciar a ♦ vi: **to ~ (from)** dimitir (de), renunciar (a); **to ~ o.s.** (endure) resignarse a.

resignation [rezɪg'neɪʃən] n dimisión f; (state of mind) resignación f; **to tender one's ~** presentar la dimisión.

resigned [rɪ'zaɪnd] a resignado.

resilience [rɪ'zɪlɪəns] n (of material) elasticidad f; (of person) resistencia.

resilient [rɪ'zɪlɪənt] a (person) resistente.

resin ['rezɪn] n resina.

resist [rɪ'zɪst] vt resistir, oponerse a.

resistance [rɪ'zɪstəns] n resistencia.

resistant [rɪ'zɪstənt] a: **~ (to)** resistente

(a).

resolute ['rezəlu:t] a resuelto.

resolutely ['rezəlu:tlɪ] ad resueltamente.

resolution [rezə'lu:ʃən] n (gen) resolución f; (purpose) propósito; (comput) definición f; **to make a ~** tomar una resolución.

resolve [rɪ'zɔlv] n (determination) resolución f; (purpose) propósito ◆ vt resolver ◆ vi resolverse; **to ~ to do** resolver hacer.

resolved [rɪ'zɔlvd] a resuelto.

resonance ['rezənəns] n resonancia.

resonant ['rezənənt] a resonante.

resort [rɪ'zɔ:t] n (town) centro turístico; (recourse) recurso ◆ vi: **to ~ to** recurrir a; **in the last ~** como último recurso; **seaside/winter sports ~** playa, estación f balnearia/centro de deportes de invierno.

resound [rɪ'zaund] vi: **to ~ (with)** resonar (con).

resounding [rɪ'zaundɪŋ] a sonoro; (fig) clamoroso.

resource [rɪ'sɔ:s] n recurso; **~s** npl recursos mpl; **natural ~s** recursos mpl naturales; **to leave sb to his/her own ~s** (fig) abandonar a uno/a a sus propios recursos.

resourceful [rɪ'sɔ:sful] a despabilado, ingenioso.

resourcefulness [rɪ'sɔ:sfulnɪs] n inventiva, iniciativa.

respect [rɪs'pekt] n (consideration) respeto; (relation) respecto; **~s** npl recuerdos mpl, saludos mpl ◆ vt respetar; **with ~ to** con respecto a; **in this ~** en cuanto a eso; **to have** or **show ~ for** tener or mostrar respeto a; **out of ~ for** por respeto a; **in some ~s** en algunos aspectos; **with due ~ I still think you're wrong** con el respeto debido, sigo creyendo que está equivocado.

respectability [rɪspektə'bɪlɪtɪ] n respetabilidad f.

respectable [rɪs'pektəbl] a respetable; (quite big: amount etc) apreciable; (passable) tolerable; (quite good: player, result etc) bastante bueno.

respected [rɪs'pektɪd] a respetado, estimado.

respectful [rɪs'pektful] a respetuoso.

respectfully [rɪs'pektfulɪ] ad respetuosamente; **Yours ~** Le saluda atentamente.

respecting [rɪs'pektɪŋ] prep (con) respecto a, en cuanto a.

respective [rɪs'pektɪv] a respectivo.

respectively [rɪs'pektɪvlɪ] ad respectivamente.

respiration [respɪ'reɪʃən] n respiración f.

respiratory [res'pɪrətərɪ] a respiratorio.

respite ['respaɪt] n respiro; (LAW) prórroga.

resplendent [rɪs'plendənt] a resplandeciente.

respond [rɪs'pɔnd] vi responder; (react) reaccionar.

respondent [rɪs'pɔndənt] n (LAW) acusado/a.

response [rɪs'pɔns] n respuesta; (reaction) reacción f; **in ~ to** como respuesta a.

responsibility [rɪspɔnsɪ'bɪlɪtɪ] n responsabilidad f; **to take ~ for sth/sb** admitir responsabilidad por algo/uno.

responsible [rɪs'pɔnsɪbl] a (liable): **~ (for)** responsable (de); (character) serio, formal; (job) de confianza; **to be ~ to sb (for sth)** ser responsable ante uno (de algo).

responsibly [rɪs'pɔnsɪblɪ] ad con seriedad.

responsive [rɪs'pɔnsɪv] a sensible.

rest [rest] n descanso, reposo; (MUS) pausa, silencio; (support) apoyo; (remainder) resto ◆ vi descansar; (be supported): **to ~ on** posar(se) en ◆ vt (lean): **to ~ sth on/ against** apoyar algo en or sobre/contra; **the ~ of them** (people, objects) los demás; **to set sb's mind at ~** tranquilizar a uno; **to ~ one's eyes** or **gaze on** fijar la mirada en; **it ~s with him** depende de él; **~ assured that ...** téngalo por seguro que ....

restaurant ['restərɔŋ] n restorán m, restaurante m.

restaurant car n (Brit) coche-comedor m.

restaurant owner n dueño/a or propietario/a de un restaurante.

rest cure n cura de reposa.

restful ['restful] a descansado, tranquilo.

rest home n residencia para jubilados.

restitution [restɪ'tju:ʃən] n: **to make ~ to sb for sth** indemnizar a uno por algo.

restive ['restɪv] a inquieto; (horse) rebelón/ona.

restless ['restlɪs] a inquieto; **to get ~** impacientarse.

restlessly ['restlɪslɪ] ad inquietamente, con inquietud f.

restlessness ['restlɪsnɪs] n inquietud f.

restock [ri:'stɔk] vr reaprovisionar.

restoration [restə'reɪʃən] n restauración f.

restorative [rɪ'stɔ:rətɪv] a reconstituyente, fortalecedor(a) ◆ n reconstituyente m.

restore [rɪ'stɔ:*] vt (building) restaurar; (sth stolen) devolver; (health) restablecer.

restorer [rɪ'stɔ:rə*] n (ART etc) restaurador(a) m/f.

restrain [rɪs'treɪn] vt (feeling) contener, refrenar; (person): **to ~ (from doing)** disuadir (de hacer).

restrained [rɪs'treɪnd] a (style) reservado.

restraint [rɪs'treɪnt] n (restriction) freno, control m; (of style) reserva; **wage ~** control m de sueldos.

restrict [rɪs'trɪkt] vt restringir, limitar.

restricted [rɪs'trɪktɪd] a restringido, limitado.

restriction [rɪs'trɪkʃən] n restricción f, limitación f.

restrictive [rɪs'trɪktɪv] a restrictivo.

restrictive practices n (INDUSTRY) prácticas fpl restrictivas.

rest room n (US) aseos mpl.

restructure [riː'strʌktʃə*] *vt* reestructurar.

result [rɪ'zʌlt] *n* resultado ♦ *vi*: **to ~ in** terminar en, tener por resultado; **as a ~ of** a *or* como consecuencia de; **to ~ (from)** resultar (de).

resultant [rɪ'zʌltənt] *a* resultante.

resume [rɪ'zjuːm] *vt* (*work, journey*) reanudar; (*sum up*) resumir ♦ *vi* (*meeting*) continuar.

résumé ['reɪzjuːmeɪ] *n* resumen *m*.

resumption [rɪ'zʌmpʃən] *n* reanudación *f*.

resurgence [rɪ'sɜːdʒəns] *n* resurgimiento.

resurrection [rezə'rekʃən] *n* resurrección *f*.

resuscitate [rɪ'sʌsɪteɪt] *vt* (*MED*) resucitar.

resuscitation [rɪsʌsɪ'teɪʃn] *n* resucitación *f*.

retail ['riːteɪl] *n* venta al por menor ♦ *cpd* al por menor ♦ *vt* vender al por menor *or* al detalle ♦ *vi*: **to ~ at** (*COMM*) tener precio al público de.

retailer ['riːteɪlə*] *n* detallista *m/f*.

retail outlet *n* punto de venta.

retail price *n* precio de venta al público, precio al detalle *or* al por menor.

retail price index *n* índice *m* de precios al por menor.

retain [rɪ'teɪn] *vt* (*keep*) retener, conservar; (*employ*) contratar.

retainer [rɪ'teɪnə*] *n* (*servant*) criado; (*fee*) anticipo.

retaliate [rɪ'tælieɪt] *vi*: **to ~ (against)** tomar represalias (contra).

retaliation [rɪtælɪ'eɪʃən] *n* represalias *fpl;* **in ~ for** como represalia por.

retaliatory [rɪ'tælɪətərɪ] *a* de represalia.

retarded [rɪ'tɑːdɪd] *a* retrasado.

retch [retʃ] *vi* darle a uno arcadas.

retentive [rɪ'tentɪv] *a* (*memory*) retentivo.

rethink [riː'θɪŋk] *vt* repensar.

reticence ['retɪsns] *n* reticencia, reserva.

reticent ['retɪsnt] *a* reservado.

retina ['retɪnə] *n* retina.

retinue ['retɪnjuː] *n* séquito, comitiva.

retire [rɪ'taɪə*] *vi* (*give up work*) jubilarse; (*withdraw*) retirarse; (*go to bed*) acostarse.

retired [rɪ'taɪəd] *a* (*person*) jubilado.

retirement [rɪ'taɪəmənt] *n* (*state*) retiro; (*act*) jubilación *f;* **early ~** jubilación *f* temprana.

retiring [rɪ'taɪərɪŋ] *a* (*departing*: *chairman*) saliente; (*shy*) retraído.

retort [rɪ'tɔːt] *n* (*reply*) réplica ♦ *vi* contestar.

retrace [riː'treɪs] *vt*: **to ~ one's steps** volver sobre sus pasos, desandar lo andado.

retract [rɪ'trækt] *vt* (*statement*) retirar; (*claws*) retraer; (*undercarriage, aerial*) replegar ♦ *vi* retractarse.

retractable [rɪ'træktəbl] *a* replegable.

retrain [riː'treɪn] *vt* reciclar.

retraining [riː'treɪnɪŋ] *n* readaptación *f* profesional.

retread ['riːtred] *n* neumático *or* llanta

(*LAm*) recauchutado/a.

retreat [rɪ'triːt] *n* (*place*) retiro; (*MIL*) retirada ♦ *vi* retirarse; (*flood*) bajar; **to beat a hasty ~** (*fig*) retirarse en desorden.

retrial ['riːtraɪəl] *n* nuevo proceso.

retribution [retrɪ'bjuːʃən] *n* desquite *m*.

retrieval [rɪ'triːvəl] *n* recuperación *f*; **information ~** recuperación *f* de datos.

retrieve [rɪ'triːv] *vt* recobrar; (*situation, honour*) salvar; (*COMPUT*) recuperar; (*error*) reparar.

retriever [rɪ'triːvə*] *n* perro cobrador.

retroactive [retrəu'æktɪv] *a* retroactivo.

retrograde ['retrəgreɪd] *a* retrógrado.

retrospect ['retrəspekt] *n*: **in ~** retrospectivamente.

retrospective [retrə'spektɪv] *a* retrospectivo; (*law*) retroactivo ♦ *n* exposición *f* retrospectiva.

return [rɪ'tɜːn] *n* (*going or coming back*) vuelta, regreso; (*of sth stolen etc*) devolución *f*; (*recompense*) recompensa; (*FINANCE: from land, shares*) ganancia, ingresos *mpl*; (*COMM: of merchandise*) devolución *f* ♦ *cpd* (*journey*) de regreso; (*Brit: ticket*) de ida y vuelta; (*match*) de desquite ♦ *vi* (*person etc: come or go back*) volver, regresar; (*symptoms etc*) reaparecer ♦ *vt* devolver; (*favour, love etc*) corresponder a; (*verdict*) pronunciar; (*POL: candidate*) elegir; **~s** *npl* (*COMM*) ingresos *mpl*; **tax ~** declaración *f* sobre la renta; **in ~ (for)** en cambio (de); **by ~ of post** a vuelta de correo; **many happy ~s (of the day)!** ¡feliz cumpleaños!

returnable [rɪ'tɜːnəbl] *a*: **~ bottle** envase *m* retornable.

return key *n* (*COMPUT*) tecla de retorno.

reunion [riː'juːnɪən] *n* reunión *f*.

reunite [riːjuː'naɪt] *vt* reunir; (*reconcile*) reconciliar.

rev [rev] *n abbr* (*AUT*: = *revolution*) revolución *f* ♦ (*vb: also*: **~ up**) *vt* girar ♦ *vi* (*engine*) girarse; (*driver*) girar el motor.

revaluation [riːvæljuː'eɪʃən] *n* revalorización *f*.

revamp [riː'væmp] *vt* (*house, company*) renovar.

Rev(d). *abbr* (= *reverend*) R., Rvdo.

reveal [rɪ'viːl] *vt* (*make known*) revelar.

revealing [rɪ'viːlɪŋ] *a* revelador(a).

reveille [rɪ'vælɪ] *n* (*MIL*) diana.

revel ['revl] *vi*: **to ~ in sth/in doing sth** gozar de algo/con hacer algo.

revelation [revə'leɪʃən] *n* revelación *f*.

reveller, (*US*) **reveler** ['revlə*] *n* jaranero, juergista *m/f*.

revelry ['revlrɪ] *n* jarana, juerga.

revenge [rɪ'vendʒ] *n* venganza; (*in sport*) revancha; **to take ~ on** vengarse de; **to get one's ~ (for sth)** vengarse (de algo).

revengeful [rɪ'vendʒful] *a* vengativo.

revenue ['revənjuː] *n* ingresos *mpl*, rentas

fpl.

revenue account *n* cuenta de ingresos presupuestarios.

revenue expenditure *n* gasto corriente.

reverberate [rɪ'vɜːbəreɪt] *vi* (*sound*) resonar, retumbar.

reverberation [rɪvɜːbə'reɪʃən] *n* retumbo, eco.

revere [rɪ'vɪə*] *vt* reverenciar, venerar.

reverence ['rɛvərəns] *n* reverencia.

Reverend ['rɛvərənd] *a* (*in titles*): **the** ~ **John Smith** (*Anglican*) el Reverendo John Smith; (*Catholic*) el Padre John Smith; (*Protestant*) el Pastor John Smith.

reverent ['rɛvərənt] *a* reverente.

reverie ['rɛvərɪ] *n* ensueño.

reversal [rɪ'vɜːsl] *n* (*of order*) inversión *f*; (*of policy*) cambio de rumbo; (*of decision*) revocación *f*.

reverse [rɪ'vɜːs] *n* (*opposite*) contrario; (*back*: *of cloth*) revés *m*; (: *of coin*) reverso; (: *of paper*) dorso; (*AUT*: *also*: ~ **gear**) marcha atrás ♦ *a* (*order*) inverso; (*direction*) contrario ♦ *vt* (*decision*, *AUT*) dar marcha atrás a; (*position*, *function*) invertir ♦ *vi* (*Brit AUT*) poner en marcha atrás; **in** ~ **order** en orden inverso; **the** ~ lo contrario; **to go into** ~ dar marcha atrás.

reverse-charge call [rɪ'vɜːstʃɑːdʒ-] *n* (*Brit*) llamada a cobro revertido.

reverse video *n* vídeo inverso.

reversible [rɪ'vɜːsəbl] *a* (*garment*, *procedure*) reversible.

reversing lights [rɪ'vɜːsɪŋ-] *npl* (*Brit AUT*) luces *fpl* de marcha atrás.

revert [rɪ'vɜːt] *vi*: **to** ~ **to** volver *or* revertir a.

review [rɪ'vjuː] *n* (*magazine*, *MIL*) revista; (*of book*, *film*) reseña; (*US*: *examination*) repaso, examen *m* ♦ *vt* repasar, examinar; (*MIL*) pasar revista a; (*book*, *film*) reseñar; **to come under** ~ ser examinado.

reviewer [rɪ'vjuːə*] *n* crítico/a.

revile [rɪ'vaɪl] *vt* injuriar, vilipendiar.

revise [rɪ'vaɪz] *vt* (*manuscript*) corregir; (*opinion*) modificar; (*Brit*: *study*: *subject*) repasar; (*look over*) revisar; ~**d edition** edición *f* corregida.

revision [rɪ'vɪʒən] *n* corrección *f*; modificación *f*; (*revised version*) repaso, revisión *f*.

revisit [riː'vɪzɪt] *vt* volver a visitar.

revitalize [riː'vaɪtəlaɪz] *vt* revivificar.

revival [rɪ'vaɪvəl] *n* (*recovery*) reanimación *f*; (*POL*) resurgimiento; (*of interest*) renacimiento; (*THEATRE*) reestreno; (*of faith*) despertar *m*.

revive [rɪ'vaɪv] *vt* resucitar; (*custom*) restablecer; (*hope*, *courage*) reanimar; (*play*) reestrenar ♦ *vi* (*person*) volver en sí; (*from tiredness*) reponerse; (*business*) reactivarse.

revoke [rɪ'vəuk] *vt* revocar.

revolt [rɪ'vəult] *n* rebelión *f* ♦ *vi* rebelarse,

sublevarse ♦ *vt* dar asco a, repugnar; **to** ~ (**against sb/sth**) rebelarse (contra uno/algo).

revolting [rɪ'vəultɪŋ] *a* asqueroso, repugnante.

revolution [rɛvə'luːʃən] *n* revolución *f*.

revolutionary [rɛvə'luːʃənrɪ] *a*, *n* revolucionario/a *m/f*.

revolutionize [rɛvə'luːʃənaɪz] *vt* revolucionar.

revolve [rɪ'vɔlv] *vi* dar vueltas, girar.

revolver [rɪ'vɔlvə*] *n* revólver *m*.

revolving [rɪ'vɔlvɪŋ] *a* (*chair*, *door etc*) giratorio.

revolving credit *n* crédito rotativo *or* renovable.

revue [rɪ'vjuː] *n* (*THEATRE*) revista.

revulsion [rɪ'vʌlʃən] *n* asco, repugnancia.

reward [rɪ'wɔːd] *n* premio, recompensa ♦ *vt*: **to** ~ (**for**) recompensar *or* premiar (por).

rewarding [rɪ'wɔːdɪŋ] *a* (*fig*) valioso; **financially** ~ económicamente provechoso.

rewind [riː'waɪnd] *vt* (*watch*) dar cuerda a; (*wool etc*) devanar.

rewire [riː'waɪə*] *vt* (*house*) renovar la instalación eléctrica de.

reword [riː'wɜːd] *vt* expresar en otras palabras.

rewrite [riː'raɪt] *vt* (*irg*: *like* **write**) reescribir.

Reykjavik ['reɪkjəviːk] *n* Reykjavik *m*.

RFD *abbr* (*US POST*) = *rural free delivery*.

Rh *abbr* (= *rhesus*) Rh *m*.

rhapsody ['ræpsədɪ] *n* (*MUS*) rapsodia; (*fig*): **to go into rhapsodies over** extasiarse por.

rhesus factor ['riːsəs-] *n* (*MED*) factor *m* rhesus.

rhetoric ['rɛtərɪk] *n* retórica.

rhetorical [rɪ'tɔrɪkˌ] *a* retórico.

rheumatic [ruː'mætɪk] *a* reumático.

rheumatism ['ruːmətɪzəm] *n* reumatismo, reúma.

rheumatoid arthritis ['ruːmətɔɪd-] *n* reúma *m* articular.

Rhine [raɪn] *n*: **the** ~ el (río) Rin.

rhinestone ['raɪnstəun] *n* diamante *m* de imitación.

rhinoceros [raɪ'nɔsərəs] *n* rinoceronte *m*.

Rhodes [rəudz] *n* Rodas *f*.

rhododendron [rəudə'dɛndrn] *n* rododendro.

Rhone [rəun] *n*: **the** ~ el (río) Ródano.

rhubarb ['ruːbɑːb] *n* ruibarbo.

rhyme [raɪm] *n* rima; (*verse*) poesía ♦ *vi*: **to** ~ (**with**) rimar (con); **without** ~ **or reason** sin ton ni son.

rhythm ['rɪðm] *n* ritmo.

rhythmic(al) ['rɪðmɪk(l)] *a* rítmico.

rhythmically ['rɪðmɪklɪ] *ad* rítmicamente.

RI *n abbr* (*Brit*: = *religious instruction*) ed. religiosa ♦ *abbr* (*US POST*) = *Rhode Island*.

rib [rɪb] n (ANAT) costilla ♦ vt (mock) tomar el pelo a.

ribald ['rɪbəld] a escabroso.

ribbon ['rɪbən] n cinta; **in ~s** (torn) hecho trizas.

rice [raɪs] n arroz m.

ricefield ['raɪsfiːld] n arrozal m.

rice pudding n arroz m con leche.

rich [rɪtʃ] a rico; (soil) fértil; (food) pesado; (: sweet) empalagoso; **the ~** npl los ricos; **~es** npl riqueza sg; **to be ~ in sth** abundar en algo.

richly ['rɪtʃlɪ] ad ricamente.

richness ['rɪtʃnɪs] n riqueza; fertilidad f.

rickets ['rɪkɪts] n raquitismo.

rickety ['rɪkɪtɪ] a (old) desvencijado; (shaky) tambaleante.

rickshaw ['rɪkʃɔː] n carro de culi.

ricochet ['rɪkəʃeɪ] n rebote m ♦ vi rebotar.

rid, pt, pp **rid** [rɪd] vt: **to ~ sb of sth** librar a uno de algo; **to get ~ of** deshacerse or desembarazarse de.

riddance ['rɪdns] n: **good ~!** ¡y adiós muy buenas!

ridden ['rɪdn] pp of **ride**.

-ridden ['rɪdn] suff: **disease~** plagado de enfermedades; **inflation~** minado por la inflación.

riddle ['rɪdl] n (conundrum) acertijo; (mystery) enigma m, misterio ♦ vt: **to be ~d with** ser lleno or plagado de.

ride [raɪd] n paseo; (distance covered) viaje m, recorrido ♦ vb (pt **rode**, pp **ridden**) vi (horse: as sport) montar; (go somewhere: on horse, bicycle) dar un paseo, pasearse; (journey: on bicycle, motor cycle, bus) viajar ♦ vt (a horse) montar a; (distance) viajar; **to ~ a bicycle** andar en bicicleta; **to ~ at anchor** (NAUT) estar fondeado; **can you ~ a bike?** ¿sabes montar en bici(cleta)?; **to go for a ~** dar un paseo; **to take sb for a ~** (fig) engañar a uno.

ride out vt: **to ~ out the storm** (fig) capear el temporal.

rider ['raɪdə*] n (on horse) jinete m; (on bicycle) ciclista m/f; (on motorcycle) motociclista m/f.

ridge [rɪdʒ] n (of hill) cresta; (of roof) caballete m; (wrinkle) arruga.

ridicule ['rɪdɪkjuːl] n irrisión f, burla ♦ vt poner en ridículo, burlarse de; **to hold sth/sb up to ~** poner algo/a uno en ridículo.

ridiculous [rɪ'dɪkjuləs] a ridículo.

ridiculously [rɪ'dɪkjuləslɪ] ad ridículamente, de modo ridículo.

riding ['raɪdɪŋ] n equitación f; **I like ~** me gusta montar a caballo.

riding habit n traje m de montar.

riding school n escuela de equitación.

rife [raɪf] a: **to be ~** ser muy común; **to be ~ with** abundar en.

riffraff ['rɪfræf] n chusma, gentuza.

rifle ['raɪfl] n rifle m, fusil m ♦ vt saquear.

rifle through vt fus saquear.

rifle range n campo de tiro; (at fair) tiro al blanco.

rift [rɪft] n (fig: between friends) desavenencia; (: in party) escisión f.

rig [rɪg] n (also: **oil ~**: on land) torre f de perforación; (: at sea) plataforma petrolera ♦ vt (election etc) amañar los resultados de.

rig out vt (Brit) ataviar.

rig up vt improvisar.

rigging ['rɪgɪŋ] n (NAUT) aparejo.

right [raɪt] a (true, correct) correcto, exacto; (suitable) indicado, debido; (proper) apropiado, propio; (just) justo; (morally good) bueno; (not left) derecho ♦ n (title, claim) derecho; (not left) derecha ♦ ad (correctly) bien, correctamente; (straight) derecho, directamente; (not on the left) a la derecha; (to the ~) hacia la derecha ♦ vt enderezar ♦ excl ¡bueno!, ¡está bien!; **to be ~** (person) tener razón; **to get sth ~** acertar en algo; **you did the ~ thing** hiciste bien; **let's get it ~ this time!** ¡a ver si esta vez nos sale bien!; **to put a mistake ~** corregir un error; **the ~ time** la hora exacta; (fig) el momento oportuno; **by ~s** en justicia; **~ and wrong** el bien y el mal; **film ~s** derechos mpl de la película; **on the ~** a la derecha; **to be in the ~** tener razón; **~ now** ahora mismo; **~ before/after** inmediatamente antes/después; **~ in the middle** exactamente en el centro; **~ away** en seguida; **to go ~ to the end of sth** llegar hasta el final de algo; **~, who's next?** bueno, ¿quién sigue?; **all ~!** ¡vale!; **I'm/I feel all ~ now** ya estoy bien.

right angle n ángulo recto.

righteous ['raɪtʃəs] a justado, honrado; (anger) justificado.

righteousness ['raɪtʃəsnɪs] n justicia.

rightful ['raɪtful] a (heir) legítimo.

right-hand ['raɪthænd] a (drive, turn) por la derecha.

right-handed [raɪt'hændɪd] a (person) que usa la mano derecha.

right-hand man n brazo derecho.

right-hand side n derecha.

rightly ['raɪtlɪ] ad correctamente, debidamente; (with reason) con razón; **if I remember ~** si me acuerdo bien.

right-minded ['raɪt'maɪndɪd] a (sensible) sensato; (decent) honrado.

right of way n (on path etc) derecho de paso; (AUT) prioridad f de paso.

rights issue n (STOCK EXCHANGE) emisión f gratuita de acciones.

right-wing [raɪt'wɪŋ] a (POL) derechista.

right-winger [raɪt'wɪŋə*] n (POL) derechista m/f; (SPORT) extremo derecha.

rigid ['rɪdʒɪd] a rígido; (person, ideas) inflexible.

rigidity [rı'dʒıdıtı] *n* rigidez *f*; inflexibilidad *f*.

rigidly ['rıdʒıdlı] *ad* rígidamente; (*inflexibly*) inflexiblemente.

rigmarole ['rıgmərəʊl] *n* galimatías *m inv*.

rigor mortis ['rıgə'mɔːtıs] *n* rigidez *f* cadavérica.

rigorous ['rıgərəs] *a* riguroso.

rigorously ['rıgərəslı] *ad* rigurosamente.

rigour, (US) rigor ['rıgə*] *n* rigor *m*, severidad *f*.

rig-out ['rıgaut] *n* (*Brit col*) atuendo.

rile [raıl] *vt* irritar.

rim [rım] *n* borde *m*; (*of spectacles*) montura, aro; (*of wheel*) llanta.

rimless ['rımlıs] *a* (*spectacles*) sin aros.

rimmed [rımd] *a*: ~ **with** con un borde de, bordeado de.

rind [raınd] *n* (*of bacon*) corteza; (*of lemon etc*) cáscara; (*of cheese*) costra.

ring [rıŋ] *n* (*of metal*) aro; (*on finger*) anillo; (*of people*) corro; (*of objects*) círculo; (*gang*) banda; (*for boxing*) cuadrilátero; (*of circus*) pista; (*bull* ~) ruedo, plaza; (*sound of bell*) toque *m*; (*telephone call*) llamada ♦ *vb* (*pt* **rang**, *pp* **rung** [ræŋ, rʌŋ]) *vi* (*on telephone*) llamar por teléfono; (*large bell*) repicar; (*also*: ~ **out**: *voice, words*) sonar; (*ears*) zumbar ♦ *vt* (*Brit TEL*: *also*: ~ **up**) llamar; (*bell etc*) hacer sonar; (*doorbell*) tocar; **that has the ~ of truth about it** eso suena a verdad; **to give sb a ~** (*Brit TEL*) llamar por teléfono a uno, dar un telefonazo a uno; **the name doesn't ~ a bell (with me)** el nombre no me suena; **to ~ sb (up)** llamar a uno.

ring back *vt, vi* (*TEL*) devolver la llamada.

ring off *vi* (*Brit TEL*) colgar, cortar la comunicación.

ring binder *n* carpeta.

ring finger *n* (dedo) anular *m*.

ringing ['rıŋıŋ] *n* (*of bell*) toque *m*, tañido; (*louder: of large bell*) repique *m*; (*of telephone*) sonar *m*; (*in ears*) zumbido.

ringing tone *n* (*TEL*) tono de llamada.

ringleader ['rıŋliːdə*] *n* (*of gang*) cabecilla *m/f*.

ringlets ['rıŋlıts] *npl* rizos *mpl*, bucles *mpl*.

ring road *n* (*Brit*) carretera periférica *or* de circunvalación.

rink [rıŋk] *n* (*also*: **ice** ~) pista de hielo; (*for roller-skating*) pista de patinaje.

rinse [rıns] *n* (*of dishes*) enjuague *m*; (*of clothes*) aclarado; (*of hair*) reflejo ♦ *vt* enjuagar; aclarar; dar reflejos a.

Rio (de Janeiro) ['riːəʊ(dədʒə'nıərəʊ)] *n* Río de Janeiro.

riot ['raıət] *n* motín *m*, disturbio ♦ *vi* amotinarse; **to run ~** desmandarse.

rioter ['raıətə*] *n* amotinado/a.

riotous ['raıətəs] *a* alborotado/a; (*party*) bullicioso; (*uncontrolled*) desenfrenado.

riotously ['raıətəslı] *ad* bulliciosamente.

riot police *n* policía antidisturbios.

RIP *abbr* (= *rest in peace*) q.e.p.d.

rip [rıp] *n* rasgón *m*, rasgadura ♦ *vt* rasgar, desgarrar ♦ *vi* correr.

rip up *vt* hacer pedazos.

ripcord ['rıpkɔːd] *n* cabo de desgarre.

ripe [raıp] *a* (*fruit*) maduro.

ripen ['raıpən] *vt* madurar ♦ *vi* madurarse.

ripeness ['raıpnıs] *n* madurez *f*.

rip-off ['rıpɔf] *n* (*col*): **it's a ~!** ¡es una estafa!, ¡es un timo!

riposte [rı'pɔst] *n* respuesta aguda, réplica.

ripple ['rıpl] *n* onda, rizo; (*sound*) murmullo ♦ *vi* rizarse ♦ *vt* rizar.

rise [raız] *n* (*slope*) cuesta, pendiente *f*; (*hill*) altura; (*increase: in wages: Brit*) aumento; (: *in prices, temperature*) subida, alza; (*fig: to power etc*) ascenso; (: *ascendancy*) auge *m* ♦ *vi* (*pt* **rose**, *pp* **risen** [rəuz, 'rızn]) (*gen*) elevarse; (*prices*) subir; (*waters*) crecer; (*river*) nacer; (*sun*) salir; (*person: from bed etc*) levantarse; (*also*: ~ **up**: *rebel*) sublevarse; (*in rank*) ascender; ~ **to power** ascenso al poder; **to give ~ to** dar lugar *or* origen a; **to ~ to the occasion** ponerse a la altura de las circunstancias.

rising ['raızıŋ] *a* (*increasing: number*) creciente; (: *prices*) en aumento *or* alza; (*tide*) creciente; (*sun, moon*) naciente ♦ *n* (*uprising*) sublevación *f*.

rising damp *n* humedad *f* de paredes.

risk [rısk] *n* riesgo, peligro ♦ *vt* (*gen*) arriesgar; (*dare*) atreverse a; **to take** *or* **run the ~ of doing** correr el riesgo de hacer; **at ~** en peligro; **at one's own ~** bajo su propia responsabilidad; **fire/health/ security ~** peligro de incendio/para la salud/para la seguridad.

risk capital *n* capital *m* de riesgo.

risky ['rıskı] *a* arriesgado, peligroso.

risqué ['riːskeı] *a* (*joke*) subido de color.

rissole ['rısəʊl] *n* croqueta.

rite [raıt] *n* rito; **last ~s** últimos sacramentos *mpl*.

ritual ['rıtjʊəl] *a* ritual ♦ *n* ritual *m*, rito.

rival ['raıvl] *n* rival *m/f*; (*in business*) competidor(a) *m/f* ♦ *a* rival, opuesto ♦ *vt* competir con.

rivalry ['raıvlrı] *n* rivalidad *f*, competencia.

river ['rıvə*] *n* río ♦ *cpd* (*port, traffic*) de río, del río; **up/down** ~ río arriba/abajo.

riverbank ['rıvəbæŋk] *n* orilla (del río).

riverbed ['rıvəbed] *n* lecho, cauce *m*.

rivet ['rıvıt] *n* roblón *m*, remache *m* ♦ *vt* remachar; (*fig*) captar.

riveting ['rıvıtıŋ] *a* (*fig*) fascinante.

Riviera [rıvı'eərə] *n*: **the (French) ~** la Costa Azul (francesa), la Riviera (francesa); **the Italian ~** la Riviera italiana.

Riyadh [rı'jɑːd] *n* Riyadh *m*.

RN *n abbr* (*Brit*) see **Royal Navy**; (*US*) =

registered nurse.
RNA n abbr (= ribonucleic acid) ARN m, RNA m.
RNLI n abbr (Brit: = Royal National Lifeboat Institution) organización benéfica que proporciona un servicio de lanchas de socorro.
RNZAF n abbr = Royal New Zealand Air Force.
RNZN n abbr = Royal New Zealand Navy.
road [rəud] n (gen) camino; (motorway etc) carretera; (in town) calle f; **major/minor** ~ carretera general/secundaria; **main** ~ carretera; **it takes 4 hours by** ~ se tarda 4 horas por carretera; **on the** ~ **to success** en camino del éxito.
roadblock ['rəudblɔk] n barricada.
road haulage n transporte m por carretera.
roadhog ['rəudhɔg] n loco/a del volante.
road map n mapa m de carreteras.
road safety n seguridad f vial.
roadside ['rəudsaɪd] n borde m (del camino) ◆ cpd al lado de la carretera; **by the** ~ al borde del camino.
roadsign ['rəudsaɪn] n señal f de tráfico.
roadsweeper ['rəudswiːpə*] n (Brit: person) barrendero/a.
road transport n = **road haulage.**
road user n usuario/a de la vía pública.
roadway ['rəudweɪ] n calzada.
roadworks ['rəudwə:ks] npl obras fpl.
roadworthy ['rəudwə:ðɪ] a (car) en buen estado para circular.
roam [rəum] vi vagar ◆ vt vagar por.
roar [rɔ:*] n (of animal) rugido, bramido; (of crowd) rugido; (of vehicle, storm) estruendo; (of laughter) carcajada ◆ vi rugir, bramar; hacer estruendo; **to** ~ **with laughter** reírse a carcajadas.
roaring ['rɔ:rɪŋ] a: **a** ~ **success** un tremendo éxito; **to do a** ~ **trade** hacer buen negocio.
roast [rəust] n carne f asada, asado ◆ vt (meat) asar; (coffee) tostar.
roast beef n rosbif m.
rob [rɔb] vt robar; **to** ~ **sb of sth** robar algo a uno; (fig: deprive) quitar algo a uno.
robber ['rɔbə*] n ladrón/ona m/f.
robbery ['rɔbərɪ] n robo.
robe [rəub] n (for ceremony etc) toga; (also: **bath** ~) bata.
robin ['rɔbɪn] n petirrojo.
robot ['rəubɔt] n robot m.
robotics [rəu'bɔtɪks] n robótica.
robust [rəu'bʌst] a robusto, fuerte.
rock [rɔk] n (gen) roca; (boulder) peña, peñasco; (Brit: sweet) ≈ pirulí m ◆ vt (swing gently: cradle) balancear, mecer; (: child) arrullar; (shake) sacudir ◆ vi mecerse, balancearse; sacudirse; **on the** ~**s** (drink) con hielo; (marriage etc) en ruinas; **to** ~ **the boat** (fig) causar

perturbaciones.
rock and roll n rocanrol m.
rock-bottom ['rɔk'bɔtəm] a (fig) por los suelos; **to reach** or **touch** ~ (price) estar por los suelos; (person) tocar fondo.
rock cake n (Brit) bollito de pasas con superficie rugosa.
rock climber n escalador(a) m/f.
rock climbing n (SPORT) escalada.
rockery ['rɔkərɪ] n cuadro alpino.
rocket ['rɔkɪt] n cohete m ◆ vi (prices) ir por las nubes.
rocket launcher n lanzacohetes m inv.
rock face n pared f de roca.
rocking chair ['rɔkɪŋ-] n mecedora.
rocking horse n caballo de balancín.
rocky ['rɔkɪ] a (gen) rocoso; (unsteady: table) débil.
Rocky Mountains npl: **the** ~ las Montañas Rocosas.
rococo [rə'kəukəu] a rococó inv ◆ n rococó.
rod [rɔd] n vara, varilla; (TECH) barra; (also: **fishing** ~) caña.
rode [rəud] pt of **ride.**
rodent ['rəudnt] n roedor m.
rodeo ['rəudɪəu] n rodeo.
roe [rəu] n (species: also: ~ **deer**) corzo; (of fish): **hard/soft** ~ hueva/lecha.
rogue [rəug] n pícaro, pillo.
roguish ['rəugɪʃ] a (child) travieso; (smile etc) pícaro.
role [rəul] n papel m, rol m.
roll [rəul] n rollo; (of bank notes) fajo; (also: **bread** ~) panecillo; (register) lista, nómina; (sound: of drums etc) redoble m; (movement: of ship) balanceo ◆ vt hacer rodar; (also: ~ **up:** string) enrollar; (: sleeves) arremangar; (cigarettes) liar; (also: ~ **out:** pastry) aplanar ◆ vi (gen) rodar; (drum) redoblar; (in walking) bambolearse; (ship) balancearse; **cheese** ~ panecillo de queso.
roll about, roll around vi (person) revolcarse.
roll by vi (time) pasar.
roll in vi (mail, cash) entrar a raudales.
roll over vi dar una vuelta.
roll up vi (col: arrive) presentarse, aparecer ◆ vt (carpet, cloth, map) arrollar; (sleeves) arremangar; **to** ~ **o.s. up into a ball** acurrucarse, hacerse un ovillo.
roll call n: **to take a** ~ pasar lista.
rolled [rəuld] a (umbrella) plegado.
roller ['rəulə*] n rodillo; (wheel) rueda.
roller blind n (Brit) persiana (enrollable).
roller coaster n montaña rusa.
roller skates npl patines mpl de rueda.
rollicking ['rɔlɪkɪŋ] a: **we had a** ~ **time** nos divertimos una barbaridad.
rolling ['rəulɪŋ] a (landscape) ondulado.
rolling mill n taller m de laminación.
rolling pin n rodillo (de cocina).
rolling stock n (RAIL) material m rodante.

ROM [rɔm] *n abbr* (= *read only memory*) (memoria) ROM *f*.
Roman ['rəumən] *a, n* romano/a *m/f*.
Roman Catholic *a, n* católico/a *m/f* (romano/a).
romance [rə'mæns] *n* (*love affair*) amor *m*; (*charm*) lo romántico; (*novel*) novela de amor.
romanesque [rəumə'nɛsk] *a* románico.
Romania [ruː'meɪnɪə] *n* = **Rumania**.
Romanian [ruː'meɪnɪən] *a, n* = **Rumanian**.
Roman numeral *n* número romano.
romantic [rə'mæntɪk] *a* romántico.
romanticism [rə'mæntɪsɪzəm] *n* romanticismo.
Romany ['rəumənɪ] *a* gitano ◆ *n* (*person*) gitano/a; (*LING*) lengua gitana, caló (*Sp*).
Rome [rəum] *n* Roma.
romp [rɔmp] *n* retozo, juego ◆ *vi* (*also*: ~ **about**) jugar, brincar; **to** ~ **home** (*horse*) ganar fácilmente.
rompers ['rɔmpəz] *npl* pelele *m*.
roof [ruːf] *n* (*gen*) techo; (*of house*) techo, tejado; (*of car*) baca ◆ *vt* techar, poner techo a; ~ **of the mouth** paladar *m*.
roofing ['ruːfɪŋ] *n* techumbre *f*.
roof rack *n* (*AUT*) baca, portaequipajes *m inv*.
rook [ruk] *n* (*bird*) graja; (*CHESS*) torre *f*.
room [ruːm] *n* (*in house*) cuarto, habitación *f*, pieza (*esp LAm*); (*also*: **bed~**) dormitorio; (*in school etc*) sala; (*space*) sitio, cabida; ~**s** *npl* (*lodging*) alojamiento *sg*; "~**s to let**", (*US*) "~**s for rent**" "se alquilan pisos *or* cuartos"; **single/double** ~ habitación individual/doble *or* para dos personas; **is there** ~ **for this?** ¿cabe esto?; **to make** ~ **for sb** hacer lugar para uno; **there is** ~ **for improvement** podría mejorarse.
roominess ['ruːmɪnɪs] *n* amplitud *f*, espaciosidad *f*.
rooming house ['ruːmɪŋ-] *n* (*US*) pensión *f*.
roommate ['ruːmmeɪt] *n* compañero/a de cuarto.
room service *n* servicio de habitaciones.
room temperature *n* temperatura ambiente.
roomy ['ruːmɪ] *a* espacioso.
roost [ruːst] *n* percha ◆ *vi* pasar la noche.
rooster ['ruːstə*] *n* gallo.
root [ruːt] *n* (*BOT, MATH*) raíz *f* ◆ *vi* (*plant, belief*) arriesgarse; **to take** ~ (*plant*) echar raíces; (*idea*) arraigar(se); **the** ~ **of the problem is that** ... el fondo *or* lo fundamental del problema es que ....
root about *vi* (*fig*) andar buscando.
root for *vt fus* apoyar a.
root out *vt* desarraigar.
rooted ['ruːtɪd] *a* enraizado; (*opinions etc*) arraigado.
rope [rəup] *n* cuerda; (*NAUT*) cable *m* ◆ *vt* (*box*) atar *or* amarrar con (una) cuerda;

(*climbers*: *also*: ~ **together**) encordarse; **to** ~ **sb in** (*fig*) persuadir a uno a tomar parte; **to know the** ~**s** (*fig*) conocer los trucos (del oficio).
rope ladder *n* escala de cuerda.
rosary ['rəuzərɪ] *n* rosario.
rose [rəuz] *pt of* **rise** ◆ *n* rosa; (*also*: ~**bush**) rosal *m*; (*on watering can*) roseta ◆ *a* color de rosa.
rosé ['rəuzeɪ] *n* vino rosado, clarete *m*.
rosebed ['rəuzbɛd] *n* rosaleda.
rosebud ['rəuzbʌd] *n* capullo de rosa.
rosebush ['rəuzbuʃ] *n* rosal *m*.
rosemary ['rəuzmərɪ] *n* romero.
rosette [rəu'zɛt] *n* rosetón *m*.
ROSPA ['rɔspə] *n abbr* (*Brit*) = *Royal Society for the Prevention of Accidents*.
roster ['rɔstə*] *n*: **duty** ~ lista de deberes.
rostrum ['rɔstrəm] *n* tribuna.
rosy ['rəuzɪ] *a* rosado, sonrosado; **the future looks** ~ el futuro parece prometedor.
rot [rɔt] *n* (*decay*) putrefacción *f*, podredumbre *f*; (*fig*: *pej*) tonterías *fpl* ◆ *vt, vi* pudrirse, corromperse; **it has** ~**ted** está podrido; **to stop the** ~ (*fig*) poner fin a las pérdidas.
rota ['rəutə] *n* lista (de tandas).
rotary ['rəutərɪ] *a* rotativo.
rotate [rəu'teɪt] *vt* (*revolve*) hacer girar, dar vueltas a; (*change round*: *crops*) cultivar en rotación; (: *jobs*) alternar ◆ *vi* (*revolve*) girar, dar vueltas.
rotating [rəu'teɪtɪŋ] *a* (*movement*) rotativo.
rotation [rəu'teɪʃən] *n* rotación *f*; **in** ~ por turno.
rote [rəut] *n*: **by** ~ de memoria.
rotor ['rəutə*] *n* rotor *m*.
rotten ['rɔtn] *a* (*decayed*) podrido; (: *wood*) carcomido; (*fig*) corrompido; (*col*: *bad*) pésimo; **to feel** ~ (*ill*) sentirse muy mal; ~ **to the core** completamente podrido.
rotund [rəu'tʌnd] *a* rotundo.
rouble, (*US*) **ruble** ['ruːbl] *n* rublo.
rouge [ruːʒ] *n* colorete *m*.
rough [rʌf] *a* (*skin, surface*) áspero; (*terrain*) quebrado; (*road*) desigual; (*voice*) bronco; (*person, manner*: *coarse*) tosco, grosero; (*weather*) borrascoso; (*treatment*) brutal; (*sea*) bravo; (*cloth*) basto; (*plan*) preliminar; (*guess*) aproximado; (*violent*) violento ◆ *n* (*GOLF*): **in the** ~ en las hierbas altas; **to** ~ **it** vivir sin comodidades; **to sleep** ~ (*Brit*) pasar la noche al raso; **the sea is** ~ **today** el mar está agitado hoy; **to have a** ~ **time (of it)** pasar una mala temporada; ~ **estimate** cálculo aproximado.
roughage ['rʌfɪdʒ] *n* fibra(s) *f(pl)*, forraje *m*.
rough-and-ready ['rʌfən'rɛdɪ] *a* improvisado, tosco.
rough-and-tumble ['rʌfən'tʌmbl] *n* pelea.
roughcast ['rʌfkɑːst] *n* mezcla gruesa.

rough copy *n*, **rough draft** *n* borrador *m*.

roughen ['rʌfn] *vt* (*a surface*) poner áspero.

roughly ['rʌflɪ] *ad* (*handle*) torpemente; (*make*) toscamente; (*approximately*) aproximadamente; ~ **speaking** más o menos.

roughness ['rʌfnɪs] *n* aspereza; tosquedad *f*; brutalidad *f*.

roughshod ['rʌfʃɔd] *ad*: **to ride** ~ **over** (*person*) pisotear a; (*objections*) hacer caso omiso de.

rough work *n* (*SCOL etc*) borrador *m*.

roulette [ruː'lɛt] *n* ruleta.

Roumania [ruː'meɪnɪə] *n* = **Rumania**.

round [raund] *a* redondo ♦ *n* círculo; (*Brit: of toast*) rodaja; (*of policeman*) ronda; (*of milkman*) recorrido; (*of doctor*) visitas *fpl*; (*game: of cards, in competition*) partida; (*of ammunition*) cartucho; (*BOXING*) asalto; (*of talks*) ronda ♦ *vt* (*corner*) doblar ♦ *prep* alrededor de ♦ *ad*: **all** ~ por todos lados; **the long way** ~ por el camino menos directo; **all the year** ~ durante todo el año; **it's just** ~ **the corner** (*fig*) está a la vuelta de la esquina; **to ask sb** ~ invitar a uno a casa; **I'll be** ~ **at 6 o'clock** llegaré a eso de las 6; **she arrived** ~ (**about**) **noon** llegó alrededor del mediodía; ~ **the clock** *ad* las 24 horas; **to go** ~ **to sb's** (**house**) ir a casa de uno; **to go** ~ **the back** pasar por atrás; **to go** ~ **a house** visitar una casa; **enough to go** ~ bastante (para todos); **in** ~ **figures** en cifras redondas; **to go the** ~**s** (*story*) divulgarse; **a** ~ **of applause** una salva de aplausos; **a** ~ **of drinks/ sandwiches** una ronda de bebidas/ bocadillos; **the daily** ~ la rutina cotidiana.

round off *vt* (*speech etc*) acabar, poner término a.

round up *vt* (*cattle*) acorralar; (*people*) reunir; (*prices*) redondear.

roundabout ['raundəbaut] *n* (*Brit: AUT*) glorieta, redondel *m*; (: *at fair*) tiovivo ♦ *a* (*route, means*) indirecto.

rounded ['raundɪd] *a* redondeado, redondo.

rounders ['raundəz] *n* (*Brit: game*) *juego similar al béisbol*.

roundly ['raundlɪ] *ad* (*fig*) rotundamente.

round-shouldered ['raund'ʃəuldəd] *a* cargado de espaldas.

round trip *n* viaje *m* de ida y vuelta.

roundup ['raundʌp] *n* rodeo; (*of criminals*) redada; **a** ~ **of the latest news** un resumen de las últimas noticias.

rouse [rauz] *vt* (*wake up*) despertar; (*stir up*) suscitar.

rousing ['rauzɪŋ] *a* (*applause*) caluroso; (*speech*) conmovedor(a).

rout [raut] *n* (*MIL*) derrota; (*flight*) fuga ♦ *vt* derrotar.

route [ruːt] *n* ruta, camino; (*of bus*) recorrido; (*of shipping*) rumbo, derrota; **the best** ~ **to London** el mejor camino *or* la mejor ruta para ir a Londres; **en** ~ **from** ... **to** en el viaje de ... a; **en** ~ **for** rumbo a, con destino en.

route map *n* (*Brit: for journey*) mapa *m* de carreteras.

routine [ruː'tiːn] *a* (*work*) rutinario ♦ *n* rutina; (*THEATRE*) número; (*COMPUT*) rutina; ~ **procedure** trámite *m* rutinario.

rover ['rəuvə*] *n* vagabundo/a.

roving ['rəuvɪŋ] *a* (*wandering*) errante; (*salesman*) ambulante; (*reporter*) volante.

row [rəu] *n* (*line*) fila, hilera; (*KNITTING*) pasada; [rau] (*noise*) escándalo; (*dispute*) bronca, pelea; (*fuss*) jaleo; (*scolding*) regaño ♦ *vi* (*in boat*) remar; [rau] reñir(se) ♦ *vt* (*boat*) conducir remando; **4 days in a** ~ 4 días seguidos; **to make a** ~ armar un lío; **to have a** ~ pelearse, reñir.

rowboat ['rəubəut] *n* (*US*) bote *m* de remos.

rowdy ['raudɪ] *a* (*person: noisy*) ruidoso; (: *quarrelsome*) pendenciero; (*occasion*) alborotado ♦ *n* pendenciero.

rowdyism ['raudɪɪzəm] *n* pendencias *fpl*.

row houses (*US*) casas *fpl* adosadas.

rowing ['rəuɪŋ] *n* remo.

rowing boat *n* (*Brit*) bote *m or* barco de remos.

rowlock ['rɔlək] *n* (*Brit*) chumacera.

royal ['rɔɪəl] *a* real.

Royal Air Force (RAF) *n* Fuerzas Aéreas Británicas *fpl*.

royal blue *n* azul *m* marino.

royalist ['rɔɪəlɪst] *a*, *n* monárquico/a *m/f*.

Royal Navy (RN) *n* (*Brit*) Marina Británica.

royalty ['rɔɪəltɪ] *n* (*royal persons*) (miembros *mpl* de la) familia real; (*payment to author*) derechos *mpl* de autor.

RP *n abbr* (*Brit*: = *received pronunciation*) *pronunciación f estándar de inglés*.

rpm *abbr* (= *revs per minute*) r.p.m.

RR *abbr* (*US*) = **railroad**.

R & R *n abbr* (*US MIL*) = *rest and recreation*.

RSA *n abbr* (*Brit*) = *Royal Society of Arts, Royal Scottish Academy*.

RSPB *n abbr* (*Brit*) = *Royal Society for the Protection of Birds*.

RSPCA *n abbr* (*Brit*) = *Royal Society for the Prevention of Cruelty to Animals*.

R.S.V.P. *abbr* (= *répondez s'il vous plaît*) SRC.

Rt. Hon. *abbr* (*Brit*: = *Right Honourable*) *título honorífico de diputado*.

Rt. Rev. *abbr* (= *Right Reverend*) Rvdo.

rub [rʌb] *vt* (*gen*) frotar; (*hard*) restregar ♦ *n* (*gen*) frotamiento; (*touch*) roce *m;* **to** ~ **sb up** *or* (*US*) ~ **sb the wrong way** entrarle uno por mal ojo.

rub down *vt* (*body*) secar frotando; (*horse*) almohazar.

rub in vt (*ointment*) frotar.
rub off vt borrarse ♦ vi quitarse (frotando); **to ~ off on sb** influir en uno, pegársele a uno.
rub out vt borrar ♦ vi borrarse.
rubber ['rʌbə*] n caucho, goma; (*Brit*: *eraser*) goma de borrar.
rubber band n goma, gomita.
rubber plant n ficus m.
rubber ring n (*for swimming*) flotador m.
rubber stamp n sello (de caucho) ♦ vt: **rubber-stamp** (*fig*) aprobar maquinalmente.
rubbery ['rʌbəri] a elástico, parecido a la goma.
rubbish ['rʌbɪʃ] (*Brit*) n (*from household*) basura; (*waste*) desperdicios mpl; (*fig*: *pej*) tonterías fpl; (*trash*) pacotilla ♦ vt (*col*) poner por los suelos; **what you've just said is ~** lo que acabas de decir es una tontería.
rubbish bin n cubo or bote m (*LAm*) de la basura.
rubbish dump n (*in town*) vertedero, basurero.
rubbishy ['rʌbɪʃɪ] a de mala calidad, de pacotilla.
rubble ['rʌbl] n escombros mpl.
ruby ['ru:bɪ] n rubí m.
RUC n abbr (= *Royal Ulster Constabulary*) fuerza de policía en Irlanda del Norte.
rucksack ['rʌksæk] n mochila.
ructions ['rʌkʃənz] npl: **there will be ~** se va a armar la gorda.
rudder ['rʌdə*] n timón m.
ruddy ['rʌdɪ] a (*face*) rubicundo; (*col*: *damned*) condenado.
rude [ru:d] a (*impolite*: *person*) grosero; (: *word, manners*) rudo, grosero; (*indecent*) indecente; **to be ~ to sb** ser grosero con uno.
rudeness ['ru:dnɪs] n grosería, tosquedad f.
rudiment ['ru:dɪmənt] n rudimento.
rudimentary [ru:dɪ'mɛntərɪ] a rudimentario.
rueful ['ru:ful] a arrepentido.
ruffian ['rʌfɪən] n matón m, criminal m.
ruffle ['rʌfl] vt (*hair*) despeinar; (*clothes*) arrugar; (*fig*: *person*) agitar.
rug [rʌg] n alfombra; (*Brit*: *for knees*) manta.
rugby ['rʌgbɪ] n (*also*: ~ **football**) rugby m.
rugged ['rʌgɪd] a (*landscape*) accidentado; (*features*) robusto.
rugger ['rʌgə*] n (*Brit col*) rugby m.
ruin ['ru:ɪn] n ruina ♦ vt arruinar; (*spoil*) estropear; **~s** npl ruinas fpl, restos mpl; **in ~s** en ruinas.
ruinous ['ru:ɪnəs] a ruinoso.
rule [ru:l] n (*norm*) norma, costumbre f; (*regulation*) regla; (*government*) dominio; (*ruler*) metro; (*dominion etc*): **under British ~** bajo el dominio británico ♦ vt (*coun-*

try, person) gobernar; (*decide*) disponer; (*draw lines*) trazar ♦ vi gobernar; (*LAW*) fallar; **to ~ against/in favour of/on** fallar en contra de/a favor de/sobre; **to ~ that** (*umpire, judge*) fallar que ...; **it's against the ~s** está prohibido; **as a ~** por regla general, generalmente; **by ~ of thumb** por experiencia; **majority ~** (*POL*) gobierno mayoritario.
rule out vt excluir.
ruled [ru:ld] a (*paper*) rayado.
ruler ['ru:lə*] n (*sovereign*) soberano; (*for measuring*) regla.
ruling ['ru:lɪŋ] a (*party*) gobernante; (*class*) dirigente ♦ n (*LAW*) fallo, decisión f.
rum [rʌm] n ron m.
Rumania [ru:'meɪnɪə] n Rumanía.
Rumanian [ru:'meɪnɪən] a, n rumano/a m/f.
rumble ['rʌmbl] n retumbo, ruido sordo; (*of thunder*) redoble m ♦ vi retumbar, hacer un ruido sordo; (*stomach, pipe*) sonar.
rumbustious [rʌm'bʌstʃəs] a (*person*) bullicioso.
rummage ['rʌmɪdʒ] vi revolverlo todo.
rumour, (*US*) **rumor** ['ru:mə*] n rumor m ♦ vt: **it is ~ed that...** se rumorea que... .
rump [rʌmp] n (*of animal*) ancas fpl, grupa.
rumple ['rʌmpl] vt (*clothes*) arrugar; (*hair*) despeinar.
rump steak n filete m de lomo.
rumpus ['rʌmpəs] n (*col*) lío, jaleo; (*quarrel*) pelea, riña; **to kick up a ~** armar un follón or armar bronca.
run [rʌn] n (*SPORT*) carrera; (*outing*) paseo, excursión f; (*distance travelled*) trayecto; (*series*) serie f; (*THEATRE*) temporada; (*SKI*) pista; (*in tights, stockings*) carrera; ♦ vb (*pt* **ran**, *pp* **run**) [ræn, rʌn] vt (*operate*: *business*) dirigir; (: *competition, course*) organizar; (: *hotel, house*) administrar, llevar; (*COMPUT*: *program*) ejecutar; (*to pass*: *hand*) pasar; (*bath*): **to ~ a bath** llenar la bañera ♦ vi (*gen*) correr; (*work*: *machine*) funcionar, marchar; (*bus, train*: *operate*) circular, ir; (: *travel*) ir; (*continue*: *play*) seguir; (: *contract*) ser válido; (*flow*: *river, bath*) fluir; (*colours, washing*) desteñirse; (*in election*) ser candidato; **to go for a ~** dar una vuelta; **to make a ~ for it** echar(se) a correr, escapar(se), huir; **to have the ~ of sb's house** tener el libre uso de la casa de uno; **a ~ of luck** una racha de suerte; **there was a ~ on** (*meat, tickets*) hubo mucha demanda de; **in the long ~** a la larga; **on the ~** en fuga; **I'll ~ you to the station** te llevaré a la estación en coche; **to ~ a risk** correr un riesgo; **to ~ errands** hacer or llevar recados; **it's very cheap to ~** es muy económico; **to be ~ off one's feet** estar ocupadísimo; **to ~ for the bus** correr tras el autobús; **we shall have to ~ for it** tendremos que escapar; **the train ~s between Gatwick and**

Victoria el tren circula entre Gatwick y Victoria; **the bus ~s every 20 minutes** hay salidas de bus cada 20 minutos; **to ~ on petrol/on diesel/off batteries** funcionar con gasolina/gasoil/baterías; **my salary won't ~ to a car** mi sueldo no me da para comprarme un coche; **the car ran into the lamppost** el coche chocó contra el farol.

run about, run around vi (children) correr por todos lados.

run across vt fus (find) dar or topar con.

run away vi huir.

run down vi (clock) parar ♦ vt (reduce: production) ir reduciendo; (factory) restringir la producción de; (AUT) atropellar; (criticize) criticar; **to be ~ down** (person: tired) encontrarse agotado.

run in vt (Brit: car) rodar.

run into vt fus (meet: person, trouble) tropezar con; (collide with) chocar con; **to ~ into debt** contraer deudas, endeudarse.

run off vt (water) dejar correr ♦ vi huir corriendo.

run out vi (person) salir corriendo; (liquid) irse; (lease) caducar, vencer; (money) acabarse.

run out of vt fus quedar sin; **I've ~ out of petrol** se me acabó la gasolina.

run over vt (AUT) atropellar ♦ vt fus (revise) repasar.

run through vt fus (instructions) repasar.

run up vt (debt) incurrir en; **to ~ up against** (difficulties) tropezar con.

runaway ['rʌnəweɪ] a (horse) desbocado; (truck) sin frenos; (person) fugitivo.

rundown ['rʌndaun] n (Brit: of industry etc) cierre m gradual.

rung [rʌŋ] pp of **ring** ♦ n (of ladder) escalón m, peldaño.

run-in ['rʌnɪn] n (col) altercado.

runner ['rʌnə*] n (in race: person) corredor(a) m/f; (: horse) caballo; (on sledge) patín m; (wheel) ruedecilla.

runner bean n (Brit) judía escarlata.

runner-up [rʌnər'ʌp] n subcampeón/ona m/f.

running ['rʌnɪŋ] n (sport) atletismo; (race) carrera ♦ a (costs, water) corriente; (commentary) continuo; **to be in/out of the ~ for sth** tener/no tener posibilidades de ganar algo; **6 days ~** 6 días seguidos.

running costs npl (of business) gastos mpl (de operación); (of car) gastos mpl corrientes.

running head n (TYP, WORD PROCESSING) encabezamiento normal.

running mate n (US POL) candidato/a a la vice-presidencia.

runny ['rʌnɪ] a derretido.

run-off ['rʌnɔf] n (in contest, election) desempate m; (extra race) carrera de desempate.

run-of-the-mill ['rʌnəvðə'mɪl] a común y corriente.

runt [rʌnt] n (also pej) redrojo, enano.

run-up ['rʌnʌp] n: ~ **to** (election etc) período previo a.

runway ['rʌnweɪ] n (AVIAT) pista de aterrizaje.

rupee [ruː'piː] n rupia.

rupture ['rʌptʃə*] n (MED) hernia ♦ vt: **to ~ o.s.** causarse una hernia.

rural ['ruərl] a rural.

ruse [ruːz] n ardid m.

rush [rʌʃ] n ímpetu m; (hurry) prisa, apuro (LAm); (COMM) demanda repentina; (BOT) junco; (current) corriente f fuerte, ráfaga ♦ vt apresurar; (work) hacer de prisa; (attack: town etc) asaltar ♦ vi correr, precipitarse; **gold ~** fiebre f del oro; **we've had a ~ of orders** ha habido una gran demanda; **I'm in a ~ (to do)** tengo prisa or apuro (LAm) (por hacer); **is there any ~ for this?** ¿te corre prisa esto?; **to ~ sth off** hacer algo de prisa.

rush through vt fus (meal) comer de prisa; (book) leer de prisa; (work) hacer de prisa; (town) atravesar a toda velocidad; (COMM: order) despachar rápidamente.

rush hour n horas fpl punta.

rush job n (urgent) trabajo urgente.

rusk [rʌsk] n bizcocho tostado.

Russia ['rʌʃə] n Rusia.

Russian ['rʌʃən] a ruso ♦ n ruso/a; (LING) ruso.

rust [rʌst] n herrumbre f, moho ♦ vi oxidarse.

rustic ['rʌstɪk] a rústico.

rustle ['rʌsl] vi susurrar ♦ vt (paper) hacer crujir; (US: cattle) hurtar, robar.

rustproof ['rʌstpruːf] a inoxidable.

rusty ['rʌstɪ] a oxidado, mohoso.

rut [rʌt] n surco; (ZOOL) celo; **to be in a ~** ser esclavo de la rutina.

ruthless ['ruːθlɪs] a despiadado.

RV abbr (= revised version) traducción inglesa de la Biblia de 1855 ♦ n abbr (US) = **recreational vehicle.**

rye [raɪ] n centeno.

rye bread n pan de centeno.

S

S, s [ɛs] n (letter) S, s f; **S for Sugar** S de sábado.

S abbr (= Saint) Sto./a.; (US SCOL: mark: = satisfactory) suficiente; (= south) S; = **small.**

SA *n abbr* = **South Africa, South America.**

sabbath ['sæbəθ] *n* domingo; (*Jewish*) sábado.

sabbatical [sə'bætɪkl] *a*: ~ **year** año de licencia.

sabotage ['sæbətɑːʒ] *n* sabotaje *m* ♦ *vt* sabotear.

sabre, (*US*) **saber** ['seɪbə*] *n* sable *m*.

saccharin(e) ['sækərɪn] *n* sacarina.

sachet ['sæʃeɪ] *n* sobrecito.

sack [sæk] *n* (*bag*) saco, costal *m* ♦ *vt* (*dismiss*) despedir; (*plunder*) saquear; **to get the** ~ ser despedido; **to give sb the** ~ despedir *or* echar a uno.

sackful ['sækful] *n* saco.

sacking ['sækɪŋ] *n* (*material*) arpillera.

sacrament ['sækrəmənt] *n* sacramento.

sacred ['seɪkrɪd] *a* sagrado, santo.

sacrifice ['sækrɪfaɪs] *n* sacrificio ♦ *vt* sacrificar; **to make** ~**s (for sb)** sacrificarse (a favor de uno), privarse (para uno).

sacrilege ['sækrɪlɪdʒ] *n* sacrilegio.

sacrosanct ['sækrəusæŋkt] *a* sacrosanto.

sad [sæd] *a* (*unhappy*) triste; (*deplorable*) lamentable.

sadden ['sædn] *vt* entristecer.

saddle ['sædl] *n* silla (de montar); (*of cycle*) sillín *m* ♦ *vt* (*horse*) ensillar; **to** ~ **sb with sth** (*col: task, bill, name*) cargar a uno con algo; (: *responsibility*) gravar a uno con algo; **to be** ~**d with sth** (*col*) quedar cargado con algo.

saddlebag ['sædlbæg] *n* alforja.

sadism ['seɪdɪzm] *n* sadismo.

sadist ['seɪdɪst] *n* sádico/a.

sadistic [sə'dɪstɪk] *a* sádico.

sadly ['sædlɪ] *ad* tristemente; (*regrettably*) desgraciadamente; ~ **lacking (in)** muy deficiente (en).

sadness ['sædnɪs] *n* tristeza.

sae *abbr* (*Brit*: = *stamped addressed envelope*) *sobre con las propias señas de uno y con sello.*

safari [sə'fɑːrɪ] *n* safari *m*.

safari park *n* parque *m* aventura.

safe [seɪf] *a* (*out of danger*) fuera de peligro; (*not dangerous, sure*) seguro; (*unharmed*) ileso; (*trustworthy*) digno de confianza ♦ *n* caja de caudales, caja fuerte; ~ **and sound** sano y salvo; **(just) to be on the** ~ **side** para mayor seguridad; ~ **journey!** ¡buen viaje!; **it is** ~ **to say that ...** se puede decir con confianza que ....

safe-breaker ['seɪfbreɪkə*] *n* (*Brit*) ladrón/ona *m/f* de cajas fuertes.

safe-conduct [seɪf'kɔndʌkt] *n* salvoconducto.

safe-cracker ['seɪfkrækə*] *n* (*US*) = **safe-breaker.**

safe-deposit ['seɪfdɪpɔzɪt] *n* (*vault*) cámara acorazada; (*box*) caja de seguridad *or* de caudales.

safeguard ['seɪfgɑːd] *n* protección *f*, garantía ♦ *vt* proteger, defender.

safekeeping ['seɪf'kiːpɪŋ] *n* custodia.

safely ['seɪflɪ] *ad* seguramente, con seguridad; (*without mishap*) sin peligro; **I can** ~ **say** puedo decir *or* afirmar con toda seguridad.

safeness ['seɪfnɪs] *n* seguridad *f*.

safety ['seɪftɪ] *n* seguridad *f* ♦ *cpd* de seguridad; **road** ~ seguridad *f* en carretera; ~ **first!** ¡precaución!

safety belt *n* cinturón *m* (de seguridad).

safety curtain *n* telón *m* de seguridad.

safety net *n* red *f* (de seguridad).

safety pin *n* imperdible *m*, seguro (*LAm*).

safety valve *n* válvula de seguridad *or* de escape.

saffron ['sæfrən] *n* azafrán *m*.

sag [sæg] *vi* aflojarse.

saga ['sɑːgə] *n* (*HISTORY*) saga; (*fig*) epopeya.

sage [seɪdʒ] *n* (*herb*) salvia; (*man*) sabio.

Sagittarius [sædʒɪ'tɛərɪəs] *n* Sagitario.

sago ['seɪgəu] *n* sagú *m*.

Sahara [sə'hɑːrə] *n*: **the** ~ **(Desert)** el Sáhara.

Sahel [sæ'hɛl] *n* Sahel *m*.

said [sɛd] *pt, pp of* **say.**

Saigon [saɪ'gɔn] *n* Saigón *m*.

sail [seɪl] *n* (*on boat*) vela ♦ *vt* (*boat*) gobernar ♦ *vi* (*travel: ship*) navegar; (: *passenger*) pasear en barco; (*set off: also*: **to set** ~) zarpar; **to go for a** ~ dar un paseo en barco; **they** ~**ed into Copenhagen** arribaron a Copenhague.

sail through *vt fus* (*exam*) aprobar fácilmente.

sailboat ['seɪlbəut] *n* (*US*) velero, barco de vela.

sailing ['seɪlɪŋ] *n* (*SPORT*) balandrismo; **to go** ~ salir en balandro.

sailing ship *n* barco de vela.

sailor ['seɪlə*] *n* marinero, marino.

saint [seɪnt] *n* santo; **S**~ **John** San Juan.

saintliness ['seɪntlɪnɪs] *n* santidad *f*.

saintly ['seɪntlɪ] *a* santo.

sake [seɪk] *n*: **for the** ~ **of** por; **for the** ~ **of argument** digamos, es un decir; **art for art's** ~ el arte por el arte.

salad ['sæləd] *n* ensalada; **tomato** ~ ensalada de tomate.

salad bowl *n* ensaladera.

salad cream *n* (*Brit*) mayonesa.

salad dressing *n* aliño.

salad oil *n* aceite *m* para ensalada.

salami [sə'lɑːmɪ] *n* salami *m*, salchichón *m*.

salaried ['sælərɪd] *a* asalariado.

salary ['sælərɪ] *n* sueldo.

salary earner *n* asalariado/a.

salary scale *n* escala salarial.

sale [seɪl] *n* venta; (*at reduced prices*) liquidación *f*, saldo; **"for** ~**"** "se vende"; **on** ~ en venta; **on** ~ **or return** (*goods*) venta por

reposición; **closing-down** *or* (*US*) **liquidation** ~ liquidación *f;* ~ **and lease back** venta y arrendamiento al vendedor.
saleroom ['seɪlruːm] *n* sala de subastas.
sales assistant *n* (*Brit*) dependiente/a *m/f.*
sales campaign *n* campaña de venta.
sales clerk *n* (*US*) dependiente/a *m/f.*
sales conference *n* conferencia de ventas.
sales drive *n* promoción *f* de ventas.
sales figures *npl* cifras *fpl* de ventas.
sales force *n* personal *m* de ventas.
salesman ['seɪlzmən] *n* vendedor *m;* (*in shop*) dependiente *m;* (*representative*) viajante *m.*
sales manager *n* gerente *m/f* de ventas.
salesmanship ['seɪlzmənʃɪp] *n* arte *m* de vender.
sales meeting *n* reunión *f* de ventas.
sales tax *n* (*US*) = **purchase tax.**
saleswoman ['seɪlzwumən] *n* vendedora; (*in shop*) dependienta; (*representative*) viajante *f.*
salient ['seɪlɪənt] *a* (*features, points*) sobresaliente.
saline ['seɪlaɪn] *a* salino.
saliva [sə'laɪvə] *n* saliva.
sallow ['sæləu] *a* cetrino.
sally forth, sally out *vi* salir, ponerse en marcha.
salmon ['sæmən] *n* (*pl inv*) salmón *m.*
salon ['sælɒn] *n* (*hairdressing ~, beauty ~*) salón *m.*
saloon [sə'luːn] *n* (*US*) bar *m,* taberna; (*Brit* AUT) (coche *m* de) turismo; (*ship's lounge*) cámara, salón *m.*
Salop ['sæləp] *n abbr* (*Brit*) = **Shropshire.**
SALT [sɔːlt] *n abbr* (= *Strategic Arms Limitation Treaty*) tratado SALT.
salt [sɔːlt] *n* sal *f* ♦ *vt* salar; (*put ~ on*) poner sal en; **an old** ~ un lobo de mar.
salt away *vt* (*col: money*) ahorrar.
salt cellar *n* salero.
salt mine *n* mina de sal.
saltwater ['sɔːlt'wɔːtə*] *a* (*fish etc*) de agua salada, de mar.
salty ['sɔːltɪ] *a* salado.
salubrious [sə'luːbrɪəs] *a* sano; (*fig: district etc*) atractivo.
salutary ['sæljutərɪ] *a* saludable.
salute [sə'luːt] *n* saludo; (*of guns*) salva ♦ *vt* saludar.
salvage ['sælvɪdʒ] *n* (*saving*) salvamento, recuperación *f;* (*things saved*) objetos *mpl* salvados ♦ *vt* salvar.
salvage vessel *n* buque *m* de salvamento.
salvation [sæl'veɪʃən] *n* salvación *f.*
Salvation Army *n* Ejército de Salvación.
salve [sælv] *n* (*cream etc*) ungüento, bálsamo.
salver ['sælvə*] *n* bandeja.
salvo ['sælvəu] *n* (MIL) salva.

Samaritan [sə'mærɪtən] *n:* **to call the ~s** llamar al teléfono de la esperanza.
same [seɪm] *a* mismo ♦ *pron:* **the** ~ **el** mismo/la misma; **the** ~ **book as** el mismo libro que; **on the** ~ **day** el mismo día; **at the** ~ **time** (*at the ~ moment*) al mismo tiempo; (*yet*) sin embargo; **all** *or* **just the** ~ sin embargo, aun así; **they're one and the** ~ (*person*) son la misma persona; (*thing*) son iguales; **to do the** ~ **(as sb)** hacer lo mismo (que otro); **and the** ~ **to you!** ¡igualmente!; ~ **here!** ¡yo también!; **the** ~ **again** (*in bar etc*) otro igual.
sampan ['sæmpæn] *n* sampán *m.*
sample ['saːmpl] *n* muestra ♦ *vt* (*food, wine*) probar; **to take a** ~ tomar una muestra; **free** ~ muestra gratuita.
sanatorium, *pl* **-ria** [sænə'tɔːrɪəm, -rɪə] *n* (*Brit*) sanatorio.
sanctify ['sæŋktɪfaɪ] *vt* santificar.
sanctimonious [sæŋktɪ'məunɪəs] *a* santurrón/ona.
sanction ['sæŋkʃən] *n* sanción *f* ♦ *vt* sancionar; **to impose economic** ~**s on** *or* **against** imponer sanciones económicas a *or* contra.
sanctity ['sæŋktɪtɪ] *n* (*gen*) santidad *f;* (*inviolability*) inviolabilidad *f.*
sanctuary ['sæŋktjuərɪ] *n* (*gen*) santuario; (*refuge*) asilo, refugio.
sand [sænd] *n* arena; (*beach*) playa ♦ *vt* (*also:* ~ **down**: *wood etc*) lijar.
sandal ['sændl] *n* sandalia.
sandalwood ['sændlwud] *n* sándalo.
sandbag ['sændbæg] *n* saco de arena.
sandblast ['sændblaːst] *vt* limpiar con chorro de arena.
sandbox ['sændbɔks] *n* (*US*) = **sandpit.**
sandcastle ['sændkaːsl] *n* castillo de arena.
sand dune *n* duna.
sandpaper ['sændpeɪpə*] *n* papel *m* de lija.
sandpit ['sændpɪt] *n* (*for children*) cajón *m* de arena.
sands [sændz] *npl* playa *sg* de arena.
sandstone ['sændstəun] *n* piedra arenisca.
sandstorm ['sændstɔːm] *n* tormenta de arena.
sandwich ['sændwɪtʃ] *n* bocadillo (*Sp*), sandwich *m* (*LAm*) ♦ *vt* (*also:* ~ **in**) intercalar; **to be** ~**ed between** estar apretujado entre; **cheese/ham** ~ sandwich de queso/jamón.
sandwich board *n* cartelón *m.*
sandwich course *n* (*Brit*) curso de medio tiempo.
sandy ['sændɪ] *a* arenoso; (*colour*) rojizo.
sane [seɪn] *a* cuerdo, sensato.
sang [sæŋ] *pt of* **sing.**
sanitarium [sænɪ'tɛərɪəm] *n* (*US*) = **sanatorium.**
sanitary ['sænɪtərɪ] *a* (*system, arrangements*) sanitario; (*clean*) higiénico.
sanitary towel, (*US*) **sanitary napkin** *n*

paño higiénico, compresa.

sanitation [sænɪ'teɪʃən] n (in house) servicios mpl higiénicos; (in town) servicio de desinfección.

sanitation department n (US) departamento de limpieza y recogida de basuras.

sanity ['sænɪtɪ] n cordura; (of judgment) sensatez f.

sank [sæŋk] pt of **sink**.

San Marino ['sænmə'riːnəu] n San Marino.

Santa Claus [sæntə'klɔːz] n San Nicolás m, Papá Noel m.

Santiago [sæntɪ'ɑːgəu] n (also: ~ **de Chile**) Santiago (de Chile).

sap [sæp] n (of plants) savia ◆ vt (strength) minar, agotar.

sapling ['sæplɪŋ] n árbol nuevo or joven.

sapphire ['sæfaɪə*] n zafiro.

Saragossa [særə'gɔsə] n Zaragoza.

sarcasm ['sɑːkæzm] n sarcasmo.

sarcastic [sɑː'kæstɪk] a sarcástico; **to be ~** ser sarcástico.

sarcophagus, pl sacrophagi [sɑː'kɔfəgəs, -gaɪ] n sarcófago.

sardine [sɑː'diːn] n sardina.

Sardinia [sɑː'dɪnɪə] n Cerdeña.

Sardinian [sɑː'dɪnɪən] a, n sardo/a m/f.

sardonic [sɑː'dɔnɪk] a sardónico.

sari ['sɑːrɪ] n sari m.

SAS n abbr (Brit MIL: = Special Air Service) cuerpo del ejército británico encargado de misiones clandestinas.

SASE n abbr (US: = self-addressed stamped envelope) sobre con las propias señas de uno y con sello.

sash [sæʃ] n faja.

SAT n abbr (US) = Scholastic Aptitude Test.

sat [sæt] pt, pp of **sit**.

Sat. abbr (= Saturday) sáb.

Satan ['seɪtn] n Satanás m.

satanic [sə'tænɪk] a satánico.

satchel ['sætʃl] n bolsa; (child's) cartera, mochila (LAm).

sated ['seɪtɪd] a (appetite, person) saciado.

satellite ['sætəlaɪt] n satélite m.

satiate ['seɪʃɪeɪt] vt saciar, hartar.

satin ['sætɪn] n raso ◆ a de raso; **with a ~ finish** satinado.

satire ['sætaɪə*] n sátira.

satirical [sə'tɪrɪkl] a satírico.

satirist ['sætɪrɪst] n (writer etc) escritor(a) m/f satírico/a; (cartoonist) caricaturista m/f.

satirize ['sætɪraɪz] vt satirizar.

satisfaction [sætɪs'fækʃən] n satisfacción f; **it gives me great ~** es para mí una gran satisfacción; **has it been done to your ~?** ¿se ha hecho a su satisfacción?

satisfactorily [sætɪs'fæktərɪlɪ] ad satisfactoriamente, de modo satisfactorio.

satisfactory [sætɪs'fæktərɪ] a satisfactorio.

satisfy ['sætɪsfaɪ] vt satisfacer; (pay) liqui-

dar; (convince) convencer; **to ~ the requirements** llenar los requisitos; **to ~ sb that** convencer a uno de que; **to ~ o.s. of sth** convencerse de algo.

satisfying ['sætɪsfaɪɪŋ] a satisfactorio.

saturate ['sætʃəreɪt] vt: **to ~ (with)** empapar or saturar (de).

saturation [sætʃə'reɪʃən] n saturación f.

Saturday ['sætədɪ] n sábado.

sauce [sɔːs] n salsa; (sweet) crema; (fig: cheek) frescura.

saucepan ['sɔːspən] n cacerola, olla.

saucer ['sɔːsə*] n platillo.

saucily ['sɔːsɪlɪ] ad con frescura, descaradamente.

sauciness ['sɔːsɪnɪs] n frescura, descaro.

saucy ['sɔːsɪ] a fresco, descarado.

Saudi Arabia ['saudɪ-] n Arabia Saudí or Saudita.

Saudi (Arabian) ['saudɪ-] a, n saudí m/f, saudita m/f.

sauna ['sɔːnə] n sauna.

saunter ['sɔːntə*] vi deambular.

sausage ['sɔsɪdʒ] n salchicha; (salami etc) salchichón m.

sausage roll n empanadilla.

sauté ['səuteɪ] a (CULIN: potatoes) salteado; (: onions) dorado, rehogado ◆ vt saltear; dorar.

savage ['sævɪdʒ] a (cruel, fierce) feroz, furioso; (primitive) salvaje ◆ n salvaje m/f ◆ vt (attack) embestir.

savagely ['sævɪdʒlɪ] ad con ferocidad, furiosamente; de modo salvaje.

savagery ['sævɪdʒrɪ] n ferocidad f; salvajismo.

save [seɪv] vt (rescue) salvar, rescatar; (money, time) ahorrar; (put by) guardar; (COMPUT) salvar (y guardar); (avoid: trouble) evitar ◆ vi (also: ~ **up**) ahorrar ◆ n (SPORT) parada ◆ prep salvo, excepto; **to ~ face** salvar las apariencias; **God ~ the Queen!** ¡Dios guarde a la Reina!, ¡Viva la Reina!; **I ~d you a piece of cake** te he guardado un trozo de tarta; **it will ~ me an hour** con ello ganaré una hora.

saving ['seɪvɪŋ] n (on price etc) economía ◆ a: **the ~ grace of** el único mérito de; **~s** npl ahorros mpl; **to make ~s** economizar.

savings account n cuenta de ahorros.

savings bank n caja de ahorros.

saviour, (US) savior ['seɪvjə*] n salvador(a) m/f.

savoir-faire ['sævwɑː'fɛə*] n don m de gentes.

savour, (US) savor ['seɪvə*] n sabor m, gusto ◆ vt saborear.

savo(u)ry ['seɪvərɪ] a sabroso; (dish: not sweet) salado.

savvy ['sævɪ] n (col) conocimiento, experiencia.

saw [sɔː] pt of **see** ◆ n (tool) sierra ◆ vt (pt **sawed**, pp **sawed** or **sawn** [sɔːn])

serrar; **to ~ sth up** (a)serrar algo.
sawdust ['sɔːdʌst] n (a)serrín m.
sawmill ['sɔːmɪl] n aserradero.
sawn [sɔːn] pp of **saw**.
sawn-off ['sɔːnɔf], (US) **sawed-off** ['sɔːdɔf] a: **~ shotgun** escopeta de cañones recortados.
saxophone ['sæksəfəun] n saxófono.
say [seɪ] n: **to have one's ~** expresar su opinión; **to have a or some ~ in sth** tener voz or tener que ver en algo ◆ vt, vi (pt, pp **said** [sɛd]) decir; **to ~ yes/no** decir que sí/no; **my watch ~s 3 o'clock** mi reloj marca las tres; **that is to ~** es decir; **that goes without ~ing** ni que decir tiene; **she said (that) I was to give you this** me pidió que te diera esto; **I should ~ it's worth about £100** yo diría que vale unas 100 libras; **~ after me** repite lo que yo diga; **shall we ~ Tuesday?** ¿quedamos en el martes?; **that doesn't ~ much for him** eso no dice nada a su favor; **when all is said and done** al fin y al cabo, a fin de cuentas; **there is something or a lot to be said for it** hay algo or mucho que decir a su favor.
saying ['seɪɪŋ] n dicho, refrán m.
say-so ['seɪsəu] n (col) autorización f.
SBA n abbr (US) = Small Business Administration.
SC n abbr (US) = **Supreme Court** ◆ abbr (US POST) = South Carolina.
s/c abbr = **self-contained**.
scab [skæb] n costra; (pej) esquirol(a) m/f.
scaffold ['skæfəld] n (for execution) cadalso.
scaffolding ['skæfəldɪŋ] n andamio, andamiaje m.
scald [skɔːld] n escaldadura ◆ vt escaldar.
scalding ['skɔːldɪŋ] a (also: **~ hot**) hirviendo, que arde.
scale [skeɪl] n (gen, MUS) escala; (of fish) escama; (of salaries, fees etc) escalafón m ◆ vt (mountain) escalar; (tree) trepar; **~s** npl (small) balanza sg; (large) báscula sg; **on a large ~** en gran escala; **~ of charges** tarifa, lista de precios; **pay ~** escala salarial; **to draw sth to ~** dibujar algo a escala.
scale down vt reducir.
scale model n modelo a escala.
scallop ['skɔləp] n (ZOOL) venera; (SEWING) festón m.
scalp [skælp] n cabellera ◆ vt escalpar.
scalpel ['skælpl] n bisturí m.
scamper ['skæmpə*] vi: **to ~ away, ~ off** irse corriendo.
scampi ['skæmpɪ] npl gambas fpl.
scan [skæn] vt (examine) escudriñar; (glance at quickly) dar un vistazo a; (TV, RADAR) explorar, registrar ◆ n (MED) examen m ultrasónico.
scandal ['skændl] n escándalo; (gossip) chismes mpl.

scandalize ['skændəlaɪz] vt escandalizar.
scandalous ['skændələs] a escandaloso.
Scandinavia [skændɪ'neɪvɪə] n Escandinavia.
Scandinavian [skændɪ'neɪvɪən] a, n escandinavo/a m/f.
scanner ['skænə*] n (RADAR, MED) escáner m.
scant [skænt] a escaso.
scantily ['skæntɪlɪ] ad: **~ clad or dressed** ligeramente vestido.
scantiness ['skæntɪnɪs] n escasez f, insuficiencia.
scanty ['skæntɪ] a (meal) insuficiente; (clothes) ligero.
scapegoat ['skeɪpgəut] n cabeza de turco, chivo expiatorio.
scar [skɑː] n cicatriz f ◆ vt marcar con una cicatriz ◆ vi cicatrizarse.
scarce [skɛəs] a escaso.
scarcely ['skɛəslɪ] ad apenas; **~ anybody** casi nadie; **I can ~ believe it** casi no puedo creerlo.
scarceness ['skɛəsnɪs], **scarcity** ['skɛəsɪtɪ] n escasez f.
scarcity value n valor m de escasez.
scare [skɛə*] n susto, sobresalto; (panic) pánico ◆ vt asustar, espantar; **to ~ sb stiff** dar a uno un susto de muerte; **bomb ~** amenaza de bomba.
scare away, scare off vt espantar, ahuyentar.
scarecrow ['skɛəkrəu] n espantapájaros m inv.
scared [skɛəd] a: **to be ~** asustarse, estar asustado.
scaremonger ['skɛəmʌŋgə*] n alarmista m/f.
scarf, pl **scarves** [skɑːf, skɑːvz] n (long) bufanda; (square) pañuelo.
scarlet ['skɑːlɪt] a escarlata.
scarlet fever n escarlatina.
scarred [skɑːd] a lleno de cicatrices.
scarves [skɑːvz] npl of **scarf**.
scary ['skɛərɪ] a (col) de miedo.
scathing ['skeɪðɪŋ] a mordaz; **to be ~ about sth** criticar algo duramente.
scatter ['skætə*] vt (spread) esparcir, desparramar; (put to flight) dispersar ◆ vi desparramarse; dispersarse.
scatterbrained ['skætəbreɪnd] a ligero de cascos.
scavenge ['skævɪndʒ] vi: **to ~ (for)** (person) revolver entre la basura (para encontrar); **to ~ for food** (hyenas etc) nutrirse de carroña.
scavenger ['skævɪndʒə*] n (person) basurero/a; (ZOOL: animal) animal m de carroña; (: bird) ave f de carroña.
SCE n abbr = Scottish Certificate of Education.
scenario [sɪ'nɑːrɪəu] n (THEATRE) argumento; (CINEMA) guión m; (fig) escenario.

scene [siːn] *n* (*THEATRE, fig etc*) escena; (*of crime, accident*) escenario; (*sight, view*) vista, perspectiva; (*fuss*) escándalo; **the political ~ in Spain** el panorama político español; **behind the ~s** (*also fig*) entre bastidores; **to appear** *or* **come on the ~** (*also fig*) aparecer, presentarse; **to make a ~** (*col: fuss*) armar un escándalo.

scenery ['siːnərɪ] *n* (*THEATRE*) decorado; (*landscape*) paisaje *m*.

scenic ['siːnɪk] *a* (*picturesque*) pintoresco.

scent [sɛnt] *n* perfume *m*, olor *m*; (*fig: track*) rastro, pista; (*sense of smell*) olfato ◆ *vt* perfumar; (*suspect*) presentir; **to put** *or* **throw sb off the ~** (*fig*) despistar a uno.

sceptic, (*US*) **skeptic** ['skɛptɪk] *n* escéptico/a.

sceptical, (*US*) **skeptical** ['skɛptɪkl] *a* escéptico.

scepticism, (*US*) **skepticism** ['skɛptɪsɪzm] *n* escepticismo.

sceptre, (*US*) **scepter** ['sɛptə*] *n* cetro.

schedule ['ʃɛdjuːl, (*US*) 'skɛdjuːl] *n* (*of trains*) horario; (*of events*) programa *m*; (*list*) lista ◆ *vt* (*timetable*) establecer el horario de; (*list*) catalogar; (*visit*) fijar la hora de; **on ~** a la hora, sin retraso; **to be ahead of/behind ~** estar adelantado/en retraso; **we are working to a very tight ~** tenemos un programa de trabajo muy exigente; **everything went according to ~** todo sucedió según se había previsto; **the meeting is ~d for 7** *or* **to begin at 7** la reunión está fijada para las 7.

scheduled ['ʃɛdjuːld, (*US*) 'skɛdjuːld] *a* (*date, time*) fijado; (*visit, event, bus, train*) programado; (*stop*) previsto; **~ flight** vuelo regular.

schematic [skɪ'mætɪk] *a* (*diagram etc*) esquemático.

scheme [skiːm] *n* (*plan*) plan *m*, proyecto; (*method*) esquema *m*; (*plot*) intriga; (*trick*) ardid *m*; (*arrangement*) disposición *f*; (*pension ~ etc*) sistema *m* ◆ *vt* proyectar ◆ *vi* (*plan*) hacer proyectos; (*intrigue*) intrigar; **colour ~** combinación *f* de colores.

scheming ['skiːmɪŋ] *a* intrigante.

schism ['skɪzəm] *n* cisma *m*.

schizophrenia [skɪtsə'friːnɪə] *n* esquizofrenia.

schizophrenic [skɪtsə'frɛnɪk] *a* esquizofrénico.

scholar ['skɔlə*] *n* (*pupil*) alumno/a, estudiante *m/f*; (*learned person*) sabio/a, erudito/a.

scholarly ['skɔləlɪ] *a* erudito.

scholarship ['skɔləʃɪp] *n* erudición *f*; (*grant*) beca.

school [skuːl] *n* (*gen*) escuela, colegio; (*in university*) facultad *f*; (*of fish*) banco ◆ *vt* (*animal*) amaestrar; **to be at** *or* **go to ~**

ir al colegio *or* a la escuela.

school age *n* edad *f* escolar.

schoolbook ['skuːlbuk] *n* libro de texto.

schoolboy ['skuːlbɔɪ] *n* alumno.

schoolchild, *pl* **-children** ['skuːltʃaɪld, -tʃɪldrən] *n* alumno/a.

schooldays ['skuːldeɪz] *npl* años *mpl* del colegio.

schoolgirl ['skuːlgɜːl] *n* alumna.

schooling ['skuːlɪŋ] *n* enseñanza.

schoolmaster ['skuːlmɑːstə*] *n* (*primary*) maestro; (*secondary*) profesor *m*.

schoolmistress ['skuːlmɪstrɪs] *n* (*primary*) maestra; (*secondary*) profesora.

schoolroom ['skuːlrum] *n* clase *f*.

schoolteacher ['skuːltiːtʃə*] *n* (*primary*) maestro/a; (*secondary*) profesor(a) *m/f*.

schooner ['skuːnə*] *n* (*ship*) goleta.

sciatica [saɪ'ætɪkə] *n* ciática.

science ['saɪəns] *n* ciencia; **the ~s** las ciencias.

science fiction *n* ciencia-ficción *f*.

scientific [saɪən'tɪfɪk] *a* científico.

scientist ['saɪəntɪst] *n* científico/a.

sci-fi ['saɪfaɪ] *n* *abbr* (*col*) = **science fiction**.

Scilly Isles ['sɪlɪ-], **Scillies** ['sɪlɪz] *npl*: **the ~** las Islas Sorlingas.

scintillating ['sɪntɪleɪtɪŋ] *a* (*wit, conversation, company*) brillante, chispeante, ingenioso.

scissors ['sɪzəz] *npl* tijeras *fpl*; **a pair of ~** unas tijeras.

scoff [skɔf] *vt* (*Brit col: eat*) engullir ◆ *vi*: **to ~ (at)** (*mock*) mofarse (de).

scold [skəuld] *vt* regañar.

scolding ['skəuldɪŋ] *n* riña, reprimenda.

scone [skɔn] *n* pastel de pan.

scoop [skuːp] *n* cucharón *m*; (*for flour etc*) pala; (*PRESS*) exclusiva ◆ *vt* (*COMM: market*) adelantarse a; (: *profit*) sacar; (*COMM, PRESS: competitors*) adelantarse a.

scoop out *vt* excavar.

scoop up *vt* recoger.

scooter ['skuːtə*] *n* (*motor cycle*) moto *f*; (*toy*) patinete *m*.

scope [skəup] *n* (*of plan, undertaking*) ámbito; (*reach*) alcance *m*; (*of person*) competencia; (*opportunity*) libertad *f* (de acción); **there is plenty of ~ for improvement** hay bastante campo para efectuar mejoras.

scorch [skɔːtʃ] *vt* (*clothes*) chamuscar; (*earth, grass*) quemar, secar.

scorcher ['skɔːtʃə*] *n* (*col: hot day*) día *m* abrasador.

scorching ['skɔːtʃɪŋ] *a* abrasador(a).

score [skɔː*] *n* (*points etc*) puntuación *f*; (*MUS*) partitura; (*reckoning*) cuenta; (*twenty*) veintena ◆ *vt* (*goal, point*) ganar; (*mark, cut*) rayar ◆ *vi* marcar un tanto; (*FOOTBALL*) marcar un gol; (*keep score*) llevar el tanteo; **to keep (the) ~** tantear, llevar la cuenta (*LAm*); **to have an old ~ to settle with sb** (*fig*) tener cuentas pendientes con uno; **on that ~** en lo que se refiere a eso; **~s of people** (*fig*) muchísima gente, cantidad de gente; **to ~ 6 out of 10** obtener una puntuación de 6 sobre 10.

score out *vt* tachar.

scoreboard ['skɔːbɔːd] *n* marcador *m*.

scorer ['skɔːrə*] *n* marcador *m*; (*keeping score*) tanteador(a) *m/f*.

scorn [skɔːn] *n* desprecio ♦ *vt* despreciar.

scornful ['skɔːnful] *a* desdeñoso, despreciativo.

scornfully ['skɔːnfulɪ] *ad* desdeñosamente, con desprecio.

Scorpio ['skɔːpɪəu] *n* Escorpión *m*.

scorpion ['skɔːpɪən] *n* alacrán *m*.

Scot [skɔt] *n* escocés/esa *m/f*.

Scotch [skɔtʃ] *n* whisky *m* escocés.

scotch [skɔtʃ] *vt* (*rumour*) desmentir; (*plan*) abandonar.

Scotch tape ® *n* (*US*) cinta adhesiva, celo, scotch ® *m* (*LAm*).

scot-free [skɔt'friː] *ad*: **to get off ~** (*unpunished*) salir impune; (*unhurt*) salir ileso.

Scotland ['skɔtlənd] *n* Escocia.

Scots [skɔts] *a* escocés/esa.

Scotsman ['skɔtsmən] *n* escocés *m*.

Scotswoman ['skɔtswumən] *n* escocesa.

Scottish ['skɔtɪʃ] *a* escocés/esa.

scoundrel ['skaundrəl] *n* canalla *m/f*, sinvergüenza *m/f*.

scour ['skauə*] *vt* (*clean*) fregar, estregar; (*search*) recorrer, registrar.

scourer ['skauərə*] *n* (*pad*) estropajo; (*powder*) limpiador *m*, desgrasador *m*.

scourge [skɔːdʒ] *n* azote *m*.

scout [skaut] *n* (*MIL*, *also*: **boy ~**) explorador *m*.

scout around *vi* reconocer el terreno.

scowl [skaul] *vi* fruncir el ceño; **to ~ at sb** mirar con ceño a uno.

scrabble ['skræbl] *vi* (*claw*): **to ~ (at)** arañar ♦ *n*: **S~** ® Scrabble *m* ®; **to ~ about** *or* **around for sth** revolver todo buscando algo.

scraggy ['skrægɪ] *a* flaco, descarnado.

scram [skræm] *vi* (*col*) largarse.

scramble ['skræmbl] *n* (*climb*) subida (difícil); (*struggle*) pelea ♦ *vi*: **to ~ out/ through** salir/abrirse paso con dificultad; **to ~ for** pelear por; **to go scrambling** (*SPORT*) hacer motocrós.

scrambled eggs ['skræmbld-] *npl* huevos *mpl* revueltos.

scrap [skræp] *n* (*bit*) pedacito; (*fig*) pizca; (*fight*) riña, bronca; (*also*: **~ iron**) chatarra, hierro viejo ♦ *vt* (*discard*) desechar, descartar ♦ *vi* reñir, armar (una) bronca; **~s** *npl* (*waste*) sobras *fpl*, desperdicios *mpl*; **to sell sth for ~** vender algo como chatarra.

scrapbook ['skræpbuk] *n* álbum *m* de recortes.

scrap dealer *n* chatarrero/a.

scrape [skreɪp] *n* (*fig*) lío, apuro ♦ *vt* raspar; (*skin etc*) rasguñar; (~ *against*) rozar.

scrape through *vi* (*succeed*) apenas lograr hacer algo; (*exam*) aprobar por los pelos.

scraper ['skreɪpə*] *n* raspador *m*.

scrap heap *n* (*fig*): **on the ~** desperdiciado; **to throw sth on the ~** desechar *or* descartar algo.

scrap iron *n* chatarra.

scrap merchant *n* (*Brit*) chatarrero/a.

scrap metal *n* chatarra, desecho de metal.

scrap paper *n* pedazos *mpl* de papel.

scrappy ['skræpɪ] *a* (*poor*) pobre; (*bitty*) fragmentario.

scrap yard *n* depósito de chatarra; (*for cars*) cementerio de coches.

scratch [skrætʃ] *n* rasguño; (*from claw*) arañazo ♦ *a*: **~ team** equipo improvisado ♦ *vt* (*record*) rayar; (*with claw, nail*) rasguñar, arañar; (*COMPUT*) borrar ♦ *vi* rascarse; **to start from ~** partir de cero; **to be up to ~** cumplir con los requisitos.

scratchpad ['skrætʃpæd] *n* (*US*) bloc *m*.

scrawl [skrɔːl] *n* garabatos *mpl* ♦ *vi* hacer garabatos.

scrawny ['skrɔːnɪ] *a* (*person, neck*) flaco.

scream [skriːm] *n* chillido ♦ *vi* chillar; **it was a ~** (*fig, col*) fue para morirse de risa *or* muy divertido; **he's a ~** (*fig, col*) es muy divertido *or* de lo más gracioso; **to ~ at sb (to do sth)** gritarle a uno (para que haga algo).

scree [skriː] *n* cono de desmoronamiento.

screech [skriːtʃ] *vi* chirriar.

screen [skriːn] *n* (*CINEMA, TV*) pantalla; (*movable*) biombo; (*wall*) tabique *m*; (*also*: **wind~**) parabrisas *m inv* ♦ *vt* (*conceal*) tapar; (*from the wind etc*) proteger; (*film*) proyectar; (*fig: person: for security*) investigar a; (*: for illness*) hacer una exploración a.

screen editing *n* (*COMPUT*) corrección *f* en pantalla.

screening ['skriːnɪŋ] *n* (*of film*) proyección *f*; (*for security*) investigación *f*; (*MED*) exploración *f*.

screen memory *n* (*COMPUT*) memoria de la pantalla.

screenplay ['skriːnpleɪ] *n* guión *m*.

screen test *n* prueba de pantalla.

screw [skruː] *n* tornillo; (*propeller*) hélice *f* ♦ *vt* atornillar; **to ~ sth to the wall** fijar algo a la pared con tornillos.

screw up *vt* (*paper, material etc*) arrugar; (*col: ruin*) fastidiar; **to ~ up one's eyes** cerrar el entrecejo; **to ~ up one's face** torcer *or* arrugar la cara.

screwdriver ['skruːdraɪvə*] *n* destornillador

m.

screwy ['skru:ı] *a* (*col*) chiflado.

scribble ['skrıbl] *n* garabatos *mpl* ◆ *vt* escribir con prisa; **to ~ sth down** garabatear algo.

script [skrıpt] *n* (*CINEMA etc*) guión *m*; (*writing*) escritura, letra.

scripted ['skrıptıd] *a* (*RADIO, TV*) escrito.

Scripture ['skrıptʃə*] *n* Sagrada Escritura.

scriptwriter ['skrıptraıtə*] *n* guionista *m/f*.

scroll [skrəul] *n* rollo ◆ *vt* (*COMPUT*) desplazar.

scrotum ['skrəutəm] *n* escroto.

scrounge [skraund3] (*col*) *vt*: **to ~ sth off** *or* **from sb** obtener algo de uno de gorra ◆ *vi*: **to ~ on sb** vivir a costa de uno.

scrounger ['skraund3ə*] *n* gorrón/ona *m/f*.

scrub [skrʌb] *n* (*clean*) fregado; (*land*) maleza ◆ *vt* fregar, restregar; (*reject*) cancelar, anular.

scrubbing brush ['skrʌbıŋ-] *n* cepillo de fregar.

scruff [skrʌf] *n*: **by the ~ of the neck** por el pescuezo.

scruffy ['skrʌfı] *a* desaliñado, piojoso.

scrum(mage) ['skrʌm(mıd3)] *n* (*RUGBY*) meleé *f*.

scruple ['skru:pl] *n* escrúpulo; **to have no ~s about doing sth** no tener reparos en *or* escrúpulos acerca de hacer algo.

scrupulous ['skru:pjuləs] *a* escrupuloso.

scrupulously ['skru:pjuləslı] *ad* escrupulosamente; **to be ~ fair/honest** ser sumamente justo/honesto.

scrutinize ['skru:tınaız] *vt* escudriñar; (*votes*) escrutar.

scrutiny ['skru:tını] *n* escrutinio, examen *m*; **under the ~ of sb** bajo la mirada *or* el escrutinio de uno.

scuba ['sku:bə] *n* escafandra autónoma.

scuba diving *n* buceo con escafandra autónoma.

scuff [skʌf] *vt* (*shoes, floor*) rayar.

scuffle ['skʌfl] *n* refriega.

scullery ['skʌlərı] *n* trascocina.

sculptor ['skʌlptə*] *n* escultor(a) *m/f*.

sculpture ['skʌlptʃə*] *n* escultura.

scum [skʌm] *n* (*on liquid*) nata; (*pej: people*) canalla; (*fig*) heces *fpl*.

scupper ['skʌpə*] *vt* (*Brit: boat*) hundir; (*: fig: plans etc*) acabar con.

scurrilous ['skʌrıləs] *a* difamatorio, calumnioso.

scurry ['skʌrı] *vi*: **to ~ off** escabullirse.

scurvy ['skə:vı] *n* escorbuto.

scuttle ['skʌtl] *n* (*also:* **coal ~**) cubo, carbonera ◆ *vt* (*ship*) barrenar ◆ *vi* (*scamper*): **to ~ away, ~ off** escabullirse.

scythe [saıð] *n* guadaña.

SD *abbr* (*US POST*) = South Dakota.

SDI *n abbr* (= *Strategic Defense Initiative*) IDE *f*.

SDLP *n abbr* (*Brit POL*) = Social Democratic and Labour Party.

SDP *n abbr* (*Brit POL*) = Social Democratic Party.

sea [si:] *n* mar *m/f*; **by ~** (*travel*) en barco; **on the ~** (*boat*) en el mar; (*town*) junto al mar; **to be all at ~** (*fig*) estar despistado; **out to** *or* **at ~** en alta mar; **to go by ~** ir en barco; **heavy** *or* **rough ~s** mar *msg* agitado *or* picado; **by** *or* **beside the ~** (*holiday*) en la playa; (*village*) a orillas del mar; **a ~ of faces** una multitud *f* de caras.

sea bed *n* fondo del mar.

sea bird *n* ave *f* marina.

seaboard ['si:bɔ:d] *n* litoral *m*.

sea breeze *n* brisa de mar.

seadog ['si:dɔg] *n* lobo de mar.

seafarer ['si:fɛərə*] *n* marinero.

seafaring ['si:fɛərıŋ] *a* (*community*) marinero; (*life*) de marinero.

seafood ['si:fu:d] *n* mariscos *mpl*.

sea front *n* (*beach*) playa; (*prom*) paseo marítimo.

seagoing ['si:gəuıŋ] *a* (*ship*) de alta mar.

seagull ['si:gʌl] *n* gaviota.

seal [si:l] *n* (*animal*) foca; (*stamp*) sello ◆ *vt* (*close*) cerrar; (*: with ~*) sellar; (*decide: sb's fate*) decidir; (*: bargain*) cerrar; **~ of approval** sello de aprobación.

seal off *vt* obturar.

seal cull *n* matanza de crías de foca.

sea level *n* nivel *m* del mar.

sealing wax ['si:lıŋ-] *n* lacre *m*.

sea lion *n* león *m* marino.

sealskin ['si:lskın] *n* piel *f* de foca.

seam [si:m] *n* costura; (*of metal*) juntura; (*of coal*) veta, filón *m*; **the hall was bursting at the ~s** la sala rebosaba de gente.

seaman ['si:mən] *n* marinero.

seamanship ['si:mənʃıp] *n* náutica.

seamless ['si:mlıs] *a* sin costura(s).

seamy ['si:mı] *a* sórdido.

seance ['seıɔns] *n* sesión *f* de espiritismo.

seaplane ['si:pleın] *n* hidroavión *m*.

seaport ['si:pɔ:t] *n* puerto de mar.

search [sə:tʃ] *n* (*for person, thing*) busca, búsqueda; (*of drawer, pockets*) registro; (*inspection*) reconocimiento ◆ *vt* (*look in*) buscar en; (*examine*) examinar; (*person, place*) registrar; (*COMPUT*) buscar ◆ *vi*: **to ~ for** buscar; **in ~ of** en busca de; **"~ and replace"** (*COMPUT*) "buscar y reemplazar".

search through *vt fus* registrar.

searcher ['sə:tʃə*] *n* buscador(a) *m/f*.

searching ['sə:tʃıŋ] *a* (*question*) penetrante.

searchlight ['sə:tʃlaıt] *n* reflector *m*.

search party *n* pelotón *m* de salvamento.

search warrant *n* mandamiento (judicial).

searing ['sıərıŋ] *a* (*heat*) abrasador(a); (*pain*) agudo.

seashore ['si:ʃɔ*] *n* playa, orilla del mar; **on the ~** a la orilla del mar.

seasick ['si:sık] *a* mareado; **to be ~** marearse.

seaside ['siːsaɪd] n playa, orilla del mar; **to go to the ~** ir a la playa.

seaside resort n playa.

season ['siːzn] n (of year) estación f; (sporting etc) temporada; (gen) época, período ◆ vt (food) sazonar; **to be in/out of ~** estar en sazón/fuera de temporada; **the busy ~** (for shops, hotels etc) la temporada alta; **the open ~** (HUNTING) la temporada de caza or de pesca.

seasonal ['siːznl] a estacional.

seasoned ['siːznd] a (wood) curado; (fig: worker, actor) experimentado; (troops) aguerrido; **~ campaigner** veterano/a.

seasoning ['siːznɪŋ] n condimento, aderezo.

season ticket n abono.

seat [siːt] n (in bus, train: place) asiento; (chair) silla; (PARLIAMENT) escaño; (buttocks) culo, trasero; (centre: of government etc) sede f ◆ vt sentar; (have room for) tener cabida para; **are there any ~s left?** ¿quedan plazas?; **to take one's ~** sentarse, tomar asiento; **to be ~ed** estar sentado, sentarse.

seat belt n cinturón m de seguridad.

seating ['siːtɪŋ] n asientos mpl.

seating arrangements npl arreglo sg de los asientos.

seating capacity n cabida, número de asientos.

SEATO ['siːtəu] n abbr (= Southeast Asia Treaty Organization) OTASE f.

sea water n agua m del mar.

seaweed ['siːwiːd] n alga marina.

seaworthy ['siːwəːðɪ] a en condiciones de navegar.

SEC n abbr (US: = Securities and Exchange Commission) comisión de operaciones bursátiles.

sec. abbr = **second(s)**.

secateurs [sɛkə'təːz] npl podadera sg.

secede [sɪ'siːd] vi: **to ~ (from)** separarse (de).

secluded [sɪ'kluːdɪd] a retirado.

seclusion [sɪ'kluːʒən] n retiro.

second ['sɛkənd] a segundo ◆ ad (in race etc) en segundo lugar ◆ n (gen) segundo; (AUT: also: **~ gear**) segunda; (COMM) artículo con algún desperfecto; (Brit SCOL: degree) título universitario de segunda clase ◆ vt (motion) apoyar; [sɪ'kɔnd] (employee) trasladar temporalmente; **~ floor** (Brit) segundo piso; (US) primer piso; **Charles the S~** Carlos Segundo; **to ask for a ~ opinion** (MED) pedir una segunda opinión; **just a ~!** ¡un momento!; **to have ~ thoughts** cambiar de opinión; **on ~ thoughts** or (US) **thought** pensándolo bien; **~ mortgage** segunda hipoteca.

secondary ['sɛkəndərɪ] a secundario.

secondary education n segunda enseñanza.

secondary picket n piquete m secundario.

secondary school n escuela secundaria.

second-best [sɛkənd'bɛst] n segundo.

second-class ['sɛkənd'klɑːs] a de segunda clase ◆ ad: **to send sth ~** enviar algo por segunda clase; **to travel ~** viajar en segunda; **~ citizen** ciudadano/a de segunda clase.

second cousin n primo/a segundo/a.

seconder ['sɛkəndə*] n el/la que apoya una moción.

secondhand ['sɛkənd'hænd] a de segunda mano, usado ◆ ad: **to buy sth ~** comprar algo de segunda mano; **to hear sth ~** oír algo indirectamente.

second hand n (on clock) segundero.

second-in-command ['sɛkəndɪnkə'mɑːnd] n (MIL) segundo jefe m; (ADMIN) segundo/a, ayudante m/f.

secondly ['sɛkəndlɪ] ad en segundo lugar.

secondment [sɪ'kɔndmənt] n (Brit) traslado temporal.

second-rate ['sɛkənd'reɪt] a de segunda categoría.

secrecy ['siːkrəsɪ] n secreto.

secret ['siːkrɪt] a, n secreto; **in ~** ad en secreto; **to keep sth ~ (from sb)** ocultarle algo (a uno); **to make no ~ of sth** no ocultar algo.

secret agent n agente m/f secreto/a, espía m/f.

secretarial [sɛkrɪ'tɛərɪəl] a (course) de secretariado; (staff) de secretaría; (work, duties) de secretaria.

secretariat [sɛkrɪ'tɛərɪət] n secretaría.

secretary ['sɛkrətərɪ] n secretario/a; **S~ of State** (Brit POL) Ministro (con cartera).

secretary pool n (US) = **typing pool**.

secrete [sɪ'kriːt] vt (MED, ANAT, BIO) secretar; (hide) ocultar, esconder.

secretion [sɪ'kriːʃən] n secreción f.

secretive ['siːkrətɪv] a reservado, sigiloso.

secretly ['siːkrɪtlɪ] ad en secreto.

sect [sɛkt] n secta.

sectarian [sɛk'tɛərɪən] a sectario.

section ['sɛkʃən] n sección f; (part) parte f; (of document) artículo; (of opinion) sector m; **business ~** (PRESS) sección f de economía.

sectional ['sɛkʃənl] a (regional) regional, local.

sector ['sɛktə*] n (gen, COMPUT) sector m.

secular ['sɛkjulə*] a secular, seglar.

secure [sɪ'kjuə*] a (free from anxiety) seguro; (firmly fixed) firme, fijo ◆ vt (fix) asegurar, afianzar; (get) conseguir; (COMM: loan) garantizar; **to make sth ~** afianzar algo; **to ~ sth for sb** conseguir algo para uno.

secured creditor [sɪ'kjuəd-] n acreedor(a) m/f con garantía.

securely [sɪ'kjuəlɪ] ad firmemente; **it is ~**

fastened está bien sujetado.

security [sɪˈkjuərɪtɪ] n seguridad f; (for loan) fianza; (: object) prenda; **securities** npl (COMM) valores mpl, títulos mpl; ~ **of tenure** tenencia asegurada; **to increase/tighten** ~ aumentar/estrechar las medidas de seguridad; **job** ~ trabajo asegurado.

security forces npl fuerzas fpl de seguridad.

security guard n guardia m/f de seguridad.

security risk n riesgo para la seguridad.

secy. abbr (= secretary) Srio/a.

sedan [sɪˈdæn] n (US AUT) sedán m.

sedate [sɪˈdeɪt] a tranquilo ♦ vt tratar con sedantes.

sedation [sɪˈdeɪʃən] n (MED) sedación f; **to be under** ~ estar bajo sedación.

sedative [ˈsɛdɪtɪv] n sedante m, sedativo.

sedentary [ˈsɛdntrɪ] a sedentario.

sediment [ˈsɛdɪmənt] n sedimento.

sedimentary [sɛdɪˈmɛntərɪ] a (GEO) sedimentario.

sedition [sɪˈdɪʃən] n sedición f.

seduce [sɪˈdjuːs] vt (gen) seducir.

seduction [sɪˈdʌkʃən] n seducción f.

seductive [sɪˈdʌktɪv] a seductor(a).

see [siː] vb (pt **saw**, pp **seen** [sɔː, siːn]) vt (gen) ver; (understand) ver, comprender; (look at) mirar ♦ vi ver ♦ n sede f; **to** ~ **sb to the door** acompañar a uno a la puerta; **to** ~ **that** (ensure) asegurar que; ~ **you soon/later/tomorrow!** ¡hasta pronto/luego/mañana!; **as far as I can** ~ por lo visto or por lo que yo veo; **there was nobody to be** ~n no se veía a nadie; **let me** ~ (show me) a ver; (let me think) vamos a ver; **to go and** ~ **sb** ir a ver a uno; ~ **for yourself** míralo tú mismo; **I don't know what she** ~s **in him** no sé qué le encuentra.

see about vt fus atender a, encargarse de.

see off vt despedir.

see through vt fus penetrar (con la vista) ♦ vt llevar a cabo.

see to vt fus atender a, encargarse de.

seed [siːd] n semilla; (in fruit) pepita; (fig) germen m; (TENNIS) preseleccionado/a; **to go to** ~ (plant) granar; (fig) descuidarse.

seedless [ˈsiːdlɪs] a sin semillas or pepitas.

seedling [ˈsiːdlɪŋ] n planta de semillero.

seedy [ˈsiːdɪ] a (shabby) desaseado, raído.

seeing [ˈsiːɪŋ] conj: ~ **(that)** visto que, en vista de que.

seek, pt, pp **sought** [siːk, sɔːt] vt (gen) buscar; (post) solicitar; **to** ~ **advice/help from sb** pedir consejos/solicitar ayuda a uno.

seek out vt (person) buscar.

seem [siːm] vi parecer; **there** ~s **to be...** parece que hay ...; **it** ~s **(that)** ... parece que ...; **what** ~s **to be the trouble?** ¿qué

pasa?; **I did what** ~ed **best** hice lo que parecía mejor.

seemingly [ˈsiːmɪŋlɪ] ad aparentemente, según parece.

seen [siːn] pp of **see**.

seep [siːp] vi filtrarse.

seer [sɪə*] n vidente m/f, profeta m/f.

seersucker [ˈsɪəsʌkə*] n sirsaca.

seesaw [ˈsiːsɔː] n balancín m, columpio.

seethe [siːð] vi hervir; **to** ~ **with anger** enfurecerse.

see-through [ˈsiːθruː] a transparente.

segment [ˈsɛgmənt] n segmento.

segregate [ˈsɛgrɪgeɪt] vt segregar.

segregation [sɛgrɪˈgeɪʃən] n segregación f.

Seine [seɪn] n Sena m.

seismic [ˈsaɪzmɪk] a sísmico.

seize [siːz] vt (grasp) agarrar, asir; (take possession of) secuestrar; (: territory) apoderarse de; (opportunity) aprovecharse de.

seize up vi (TECH) agarrotarse.

seize (up)on vt fus valerse de.

seizure [ˈsiːʒə*] n (MED) ataque m; (LAW) incautación f.

seldom [ˈsɛldəm] ad rara vez.

select [sɪˈlɛkt] a selecto, escogido; (hotel, restaurant, clubs) exclusivo ♦ vt escoger, elegir; (SPORT) seleccionar; **a** ~ **few** una minoría privilegiada.

selection [sɪˈlɛkʃən] n selección f, elección f; (COMM) surtido.

selection committee n comisión f de nombramiento.

selective [sɪˈlɛktɪv] a selectivo.

self [sɛlf] n (pl **selves** [sɛlvz]) uno mismo ♦ pref auto ...; **the** ~ el yo.

self-addressed [ˈsɛlfəˈdrɛst] a: ~ **envelope** sobre m con dirección propia.

self-adhesive [sɛlfədˈhiːzɪv] a autoadhesivo, autoadherente.

self-appointed [sɛlfəˈpɔɪntɪd] a autonombrado.

self-assurance [sɛlfəˈʃuərəns] n confianza en sí mismo.

self-assured [sɛlfəˈʃuəd] a seguro de sí mismo.

self-catering [sɛlfˈkeɪtərɪŋ] a (Brit) sin pensión; ~ **apartment** piso sin pensión.

self-centred, (US) **self-centered** [sɛlfˈsɛntəd] a egocéntrico.

self-cleaning [sɛlfˈkliːnɪŋ] a autolimpiador.

self-coloured, (US) **self-colored** [sɛlfˈkʌləd] a de un color.

self-confessed [sɛlfkənˈfɛst] a (alcoholic etc) confeso.

self-confidence [sɛlfˈkɒnfɪdns] n confianza en sí mismo.

self-confident [sɛlfˈkɒnfɪdnt] a seguro de sí (mismo), lleno de confianza en sí mismo.

self-conscious [sɛlfˈkɒnʃəs] a cohibido.

self-contained [sɛlfkənˈteɪnd] a (gen) independiente; (Brit: flat) con entrada particular.

self-control [sɛlfkən'trəul] n autodominio.
self-defeating [sɛlfdɪ'fiːtɪŋ] a contraproducente.
self-defence, (US) **self-defense** [sɛlfdɪ'fɛns] n defensa propia.
self-discipline [sɛlf'dɪsɪplɪn] n autodisciplina.
self-employed [sɛlfɪm'plɔɪd] a que trabaja por cuenta propia.
self-esteem [sɛlfɪ'stiːm] n amor m propio.
self-evident [sɛlf'ɛvɪdnt] a patente.
self-explanatory [sɛlfɪks'plænətərɪ] a que no necesita explicación.
self-financing [sɛlffaɪ'nænsɪŋ] a autofinanziado.
self-governing [sɛlf'gʌvənɪŋ] a autónomo.
self-help ['sɛlf'hɛlp] n autosuficiencia, ayuda propia.
self-importance [sɛlfɪm'pɔːtns] n presunción f, vanidad f.
self-important [sɛlfɪm'pɔːtnt] a presumido.
self-indulgent [sɛlfɪn'dʌldʒənt] a inmoderado.
self-inflicted [sɛlfɪn'flɪktɪd] a infligido a sí mismo.
self-interest [sɛlf'ɪntrɪst] n egoísmo.
selfish ['sɛlfɪʃ] a egoísta.
selfishly ['sɛlfɪʃlɪ] ad con egoísmo, de modo egoísta.
selfishness ['sɛlfɪʃnɪs] n egoísmo.
selflessly ['sɛlfləslɪ] ad desinteresadamente.
selfless ['sɛlfləs] a desinteresado.
self-made man ['sɛlfmeɪd-] n hombre m que ha triunfado por sus propios esfuerzos.
self-pity [sɛlf'pɪtɪ] n lástima de sí mismo.
self-portrait [sɛlf'pɔːtreɪt] n autorretrato.
self-possessed [sɛlfpə'zɛst] a sereno, dueño de sí mismo.
self-preservation ['sɛlfprɛzə'veɪʃən] n propia conservación f.
self-propelled [sɛlfprə'pɛld] a autopropulsado, automotor/triz.
self-raising [sɛlf'reɪzɪŋ], (US) **self-rising** [sɛlf'raɪzɪŋ] a: ~ **flour** harina con levadura.
self-reliant [sɛlfrɪ'laɪənt] a independiente, autosuficiente.
self-respect [sɛlfrɪ'spɛkt] n amor m propio.
self-respecting [sɛlfrɪ'spɛktɪŋ] a que tiene amor propio.
self-righteous [sɛlf'raɪtʃəs] a santurrón/ona.
self-rising [sɛlf'raɪzɪŋ] a (US) = **selfraising**.
self-sacrifice [sɛlf'sækrɪfaɪs] n abnegación f.
self-same [sɛlfseɪm] a mismo, mismísimo.
self-satisfied [sɛlf'sætɪsfaɪd] a satisfecho de sí mismo.
self-service [sɛlf'səːvɪs] a de autoservicio.
self-styled ['sɛlfstaɪld] a supuesto, sedicente.
self-sufficient [sɛlfsə'fɪʃənt] a autosuficiente.
self-supporting [sɛlfsə'pɔːtɪŋ] a económicamente independiente.
self-taught [sɛlf'tɔːt] a autodidacta.
self-test ['sɛlftɛst] n (COMPUT) autocomprobación f.
sell, pt, pp **sold** [sɛl, səuld] vt vender ♦ vi venderse; **to ~ at** or **for £10** venderse a 10 libras; **to ~ sb an idea** (fig) convencer a uno de una idea.
sell off vt liquidar.
sell out vi transigir, transar (LAm); **to ~ out (to sb/sth)** (COMM) vender su negocio (a uno/algo) ♦ vt agotar las existencias de, venderlo todo; **the tickets are all sold out** los billetes están agotados.
sell up vi (COMM) liquidarse.
sell-by date ['sɛlbaɪ-] n fecha de caducidad.
seller ['sɛlə*] n vendedor(a) m/f; ~**'s market** mercado de demanda.
selling price ['sɛlɪŋ-] n precio de venta.
sellotape ® ['sɛləuteɪp] n (Brit) cinta adhesiva, celo, scotch m ® (LAm).
sellout ['sɛlaut] n traición f; **it was a ~** (THEATRE etc) fue un éxito de taquilla.
selves [sɛlvz] npl of **self**.
semantic [sɪ'mæntɪk] a semántico.
semaphore ['sɛməfɔː*] n semáforo.
semblance ['sɛmbləns] n apariencia.
semen ['siːmən] n semen m.
semester [sɪ'mɛstə*] n (US) semestre m.
semi... [sɛmɪ] pref semi..., medio....
semicircle ['sɛmɪsəːkl] n semicírculo.
semicircular ['sɛmɪ'səːkjulə*] a semicircular.
semicolon [sɛmɪ'kəulən] n punto y coma.
semiconductor [sɛmɪkən'dʌktə*] n semiconductor m.
semiconscious [sɛmɪ'kɒnʃəs] a semiconsciente.
semidetached (house) [sɛmɪdɪ'tætʃt-] n (casa) semiseparada.
semi-final [sɛmɪ'faɪnl] n semi-final m.
seminar ['sɛmɪnɑː*] n seminario.
seminary ['sɛmɪnərɪ] n (REL) seminario.
semiprecious stone [sɛmɪ'prɛʃəs-] a piedra semipreciosa.
semiquaver ['sɛmɪkweɪvə*] n (Brit) semicorchea.
semiskilled ['sɛmɪskɪld] a (work, worker) semicalificado.
semitone ['sɛmɪtəun] n semitono.
semolina [sɛmə'liːnə] n sémola.
SEN n abbr (Brit) = State Enrolled Nurse.
Sen., sen. abbr = **senator, senior**.
senate ['sɛnɪt] n senado.
senator ['sɛnɪtə*] n senador(a) m/f.
send, pt, pp **sent** [sɛnd, sɛnt] vt mandar, enviar; **to ~ by post** mandar por correo; **to ~ sb for sth** mandar a uno a buscar algo; **to ~ word that** ... avisar or mandar decir que ...; **she ~s (you) her love** te manda or envía cariñosos recuerdos; **to ~ sb to**

sleep/into fits of laughter dormir/hacer reír a uno; **to ~ sth flying** echar a uno; **to ~ sb flying** tirar algo.

send away vt (letter, goods) despachar.

send away for vt fus pedir.

send back vt devolver.

send for vt fus mandar traer; (by post) escribir pidiendo algo.

send in vt (report, application, resignation) mandar.

send off vt (goods) despachar; (Brit SPORT: player) expulsar.

send on vt (letter) mandar, expedir; (luggage etc: in advance) facturar.

send out vt (invitation) mandar; (emit: light, heat) emitir, difundir; (: signal) emitir.

send round vt (letter, document etc) hacer circular.

send up vt (person, price) hacer subir; (Brit: parody) parodiar.

sender ['sɛndə*] n remitente m/f.

send-off ['sɛndɔf] n: **a good ~** una buena despedida.

send-up ['sɛndʌp] n (col) parodia, sátira.

Senegal [sɛnɪ'gɔːl] n Senegal m.

Senegalese [sɛnɪgə'liːz] a, n senegalés/esa m/f.

senile ['siːnaɪl] a senil.

senility [sɪ'nɪlɪtɪ] n senilidad f.

senior ['siːnɪə*] a (older) mayor, más viejo; (: on staff) más antiguo; (of higher rank) superior ◆ n mayor m; **P. Jones ~** P. Jones padre.

senior citizen n jubilado/a, anciano/a.

senior high school n (US) ≈ instituto de enseñanza media or de BUP (Sp).

seniority [siːnɪ'ɔrɪtɪ] n antigüedad f; (in rank) rango superior.

sensation [sɛn'seɪʃən] n (physical feeling, impression) sensación f.

sensational [sɛn'seɪʃənl] a sensacional.

sense [sɛns] n (faculty, meaning) sentido; (feeling) sensación f; (good ~) sentido común, juicio ◆ vt sentir, percibir; **~ of humour** sentido del humor; **it makes ~** tiene sentido; **there is no ~ in (doing) that** no hay sentido en (hacer) eso; **to come to one's ~s** (regain consciousness) volver en sí, recobrar el sentido; **to take leave of one's ~s** perder el juicio.

senseless ['sɛnslɪs] a estúpido, insensato; (unconscious) sin conocimiento.

senselessly ['sɛnslɪslɪ] ad estúpidamente, insensatamente.

sensibility [sɛnsɪ'bɪlɪtɪ] n sensibilidad f; **sensibilities** npl delicadeza sg.

sensible ['sɛnsɪbl] a sensato; (reasonable) razonable, lógico.

sensibly ['sɛnsɪblɪ] ad sensatamente; razonablemente, de modo lógico.

sensitive ['sɛnsɪtɪv] a sensible; (touchy) susceptible; **he is very ~ about it** es muy susceptible acerca de eso.

sensitivity [sɛnsɪ'tɪvɪtɪ] nr sensibilidad f; susceptibilidad f.

sensual ['sɛnsjuəl] a sensual.

sensuous ['sɛnsjuəs] a sensual.

sent [sɛnt] pt, pp of **send**.

sentence ['sɛntəns] n (LING) frase f, oración f; (LAW) sentencia, fallo ◆ vt: **to ~ sb to death/to 5 years** condenar a uno a muerte/a 5 años de cárcel; **to pass ~ on sb** (also fig) sentenciar or condenar a uno.

sentiment ['sɛntɪmənt] n sentimiento; (opinion) opinión f.

sentimental [sɛntɪ'mɛntl] a sentimental.

sentimentality [sɛntɪmɛn'tælɪtɪ] n sentimentalismo, sensiblería.

sentinel ['sɛntɪnl] n centinela m.

sentry ['sɛntrɪ] n centinela m.

sentry duty n: **to be on ~** estar de guardia, hacer guardia.

Seoul [səʊl] n Seúl m.

separable ['sɛpərəbl] a separable.

separate a ['sɛprɪt] separado; (distinct) distinto ◆ (vb: ['sɛpəreɪt]) vt separar; (part) dividir ◆ vi separarse; **~ from** separado or distinto de; **under ~ cover** (COMM) por separado; **to ~ into** dividir or separar en; **he is ~d from his wife, but not divorced** está separado de su mujer, pero no (está) divorciado.

separately ['sɛprɪtlɪ] ad por separado.

separates ['sɛprɪts] npl (clothes) coordinados mpl.

separation [sɛpə'reɪʃən] n separación f.

sepia ['siːpɪə] a color sepia inv.

Sept. abbr (= September) sep.

September [sɛp'tɛmbə*] n se(p)tiembre m.

septic ['sɛptɪk] a séptico; **to go ~** ponerse séptico.

septicaemia, (US) **septicemia** [sɛptɪ'siːmɪə] n septicemia.

septic tank n fosa séptica.

sequel ['siːkwl] n consecuencia, resultado; (of story) continuación f.

sequence ['siːkwəns] n sucesión f, serie f; (CINEMA) secuencia; **in ~** en orden or serie.

sequential [sɪ'kwɛnʃəl] a: **~ access** (COMPUT) acceso en serie.

sequin ['siːkwɪn] n lentejuela.

Serbo-Croat ['səːbəʊ'krəʊæt] n (LING) serbocroata m.

serenade [sɛrə'neɪd] n serenata ◆ vt dar serenata a.

serene [sɪ'riːn] a sereno, tranquilo.

serenely [sɪ'riːnlɪ] ad serenamente, tranquilamente.

serenity [sə'rɛnɪtɪ] n serenidad f, tranquilidad f.

sergeant ['sɑːdʒənt] n sargento.

sergeant major n sargento mayor.

serial ['sɪərɪəl] n novela por entregas; (TV) telenovela.

serial access n (COMPUT) acceso en serie.

serial interface n (COMPUT) interface m en serie.

serialize ['sɪərɪəlaɪz] vt publicar/televisar por entregas.

serial number n número de serie.

serial printer n (COMPUT) impresora en serie.

series ['sɪəriːz] n, pl inv serie f.

serious ['sɪərɪəs] a serio; (grave) grave; **are you ~ (about it)?** ¿lo dices en serio?

seriously ['sɪərɪəslɪ] ad en serio; (ill, wounded etc) gravemente; **to take sth/sb ~** tomar algo/a uno en serio.

seriousness ['sɪərɪəsnɪs] n seriedad f; gravedad f.

sermon ['sɜːmən] n sermón m.

serpent ['sɜːpənt] n serpiente f.

serrated [sɪ'reɪtɪd] a serrado, dentellado.

serum ['sɪərəm] n suero m.

servant ['sɜːvənt] n (gen) servidor(a) m/f; (house ~) criado/a.

serve [sɜːv] vt servir; (customer) atender; (subj: train) pasar por; (apprenticeship) hacer; (prison term) cumplir ♦ vi (servant, soldier etc) servir; (TENNIS) sacar ♦ n (TENNIS) saque m; **it ~s him right** se lo merece, se lo tiene merecido; **to ~ a summons on sb** entregar una citación a uno; **it ~s my purpose** me viene al caso; **are you being ~d?** ¿le atienden?; **the power station ~s the entire region** la central eléctrica abastece a toda la región; **to ~ as/for/to do** servir de/para/para hacer; **to ~ on a committee/a jury** ser miembro de una comisión/un jurado.

serve out, serve up vt (food) servir.

service ['sɜːvɪs] n (gen) servicio; (REL: Catholic) misa; (: other) oficio (religioso); (AUT) mantenimiento; (of dishes) juego ♦ vt (car, washing machine) mantener; (: repair) reparar; **the S~s** las fuerzas armadas; **funeral ~** exequias fpl; **to hold a ~** celebrar un oficio religioso; **the essential ~s** los servicios esenciales; **medical/social ~s** servicios mpl médicos/sociales; **the train ~ to London** el servicio de tren para Londres; **to be of ~ to sb** ser útil a uno.

serviceable ['sɜːvɪsəbl] a servible, utilizable.

service area n (on motorway) servicios mpl.

service charge n (Brit) servicio.

service industries npl industrias fpl del servicio.

serviceman ['sɜːvɪsmən] n militar m.

service station n estación f de servicio.

servicing ['sɜːvɪsɪŋ] n (of car) revisión f; (of washing machine etc) servicio de reparaciones.

serviette [sɜːvɪ'et] n (Brit) servilleta.

servile ['sɜːvaɪl] a servil.

session ['seʃən] n (sitting) sesión f; **to be in ~** estar en sesión.

set [set] n juego; (RADIO) aparato; (TV) televisor m; (of utensils) batería; (of cutlery) cubierto; (of books) colección f; (TENNIS) set m; (group of people) grupo; (CINEMA) plató m; (THEATRE) decorado; (HAIRDRESSING) marcado ♦ a (fixed) fijo; (ready) listo; (resolved) resuelto, decidido ♦ (vb: pt, pp set) vt (place) poner, colocar; (fix) fijar; (adjust) ajustar, arreglar; (decide: rules etc) establecer, decidir; (assign: task) asignar; (: homework) poner ♦ vi (sun) ponerse; (jam, jelly) cuajarse; (concrete) fraguar; **a ~ of false teeth** una dentadura postiza; **a ~ of dining-room furniture** muebles mpl de comedor; **~ in one's ways** con costumbres arraigadas; **a ~ phrase** una frase hecha; **to be all ~ to do sth** estar listo para hacer algo; **to be ~ on doing sth** estar empeñado en hacer algo; **a novel ~ in Valencia** una novela ambientada en Valencia; **to ~ to music** poner música a; **to ~ on fire** incendiar, poner fuego a; **to ~ free** poner en libertad; **to ~ sth going** poner algo en marcha; **to ~ sail** zarpar, hacerse a la vela.

set about vt fus: **to ~ about doing sth** ponerse a hacer algo.

set aside vt poner aparte, dejar de lado.

set back vt (progress): **to ~ back (by)** retrasar (por); **a house ~ back from the road** una casa apartada de la carretera.

set down vt (subj: bus, train) dejar; (record) poner por escrito.

set in vi (infection) declararse; (complications) comenzar; **the rain has ~ in for the day** parece que va a llover todo el día.

set off vi partir ♦ vt (bomb) hacer estallar; (cause to start) poner en marcha; (show up well) hacer resaltar.

set out vi: **to ~ out to do sth** proponerse hacer algo ♦ vt (arrange) disponer; (state) exponer; **to ~ out (from)** salir (de).

set up vt (organization) establecer.

setback ['setbæk] n (hitch) revés m, contratiempo; (in health) recaída.

set menu n menú m.

set phrase n frase f hecha.

set square n cartabón m.

settee [se'tiː] n sofá m.

setting ['setɪŋ] n (scenery) marco; (of jewel) engaste m, montadura.

setting lotion n fijador m (para el pelo).

settle ['setl] vt (argument, matter) resolver; (pay: bill, accounts) pagar, ajustar, liquidar; (colonize: land) colonizar; (MED: calm) calmar, sosegar ♦ vi (dust etc) depositarse; (weather) serenarse; (also: ~ down) instalarse; (calm down) tranquilizarse; **to ~ for sth** convenir en aceptar algo; **to ~ on sth** decidirse por algo; **that's ~d then** bueno, está arreglado; **to ~ one's stomach** asentar el estómago.

settle in vi instalarse.

settle up *vi*: **to ~ up with sb** ajustar cuentas con uno.

settlement ['sɛtlmənt] *n* (*payment*) liquidación *f*; (*agreement*) acuerdo, convenio; (*village etc*) pueblo; **in ~ of our account** (*COMM*) en pago or liquidación de nuestra cuenta.

settler ['sɛtlə*] *n* colono/a, colonizador(a) *m/f*.

setup ['sɛtʌp] *n* sistema *m*.

seven ['sɛvn] *num* siete.

seventeen [sɛvn'tiːn] *num* diez y siete, diecisiete.

seventh ['sɛvnθ] *a* séptimo.

seventy ['sɛvntɪ] *num* setenta.

sever ['sɛvə*] *vt* cortar; (*relations*) romper.

several ['sɛvərl] *a*, *pron* varios/as *m/fpl*, algunos/as *m/fpl*; **~ of us** varios de nosotros; **~ times** varias veces.

severance ['sɛvərəns] *n* (*of relations*) ruptura.

severance pay *n* pago or indemnización *f* de despedida.

severe [sɪ'vɪə*] *a* severo; (*serious*) grave; (*hard*) duro; (*pain*) intenso.

severely [sɪ'vɪəlɪ] *ad* severamente; (*wounded, ill*) de gravedad, gravemente.

severity [sɪ'vɛrɪtɪ] *n* severidad *f*; gravedad *f*; intensidad *f*.

Seville [sə'vɪl] *n* Sevilla.

sew, *pt* **sewed**, *pp* **sewn** [səu, səud, səun] *vt*, *vi* coser.

sew up *vt* coser, zurcir.

sewage ['suːɪdʒ] *n* (*effluence*) aguas *fpl* residuales; (*system*) alcantarillado.

sewer ['suːə*] *n* alcantarilla, cloaca.

sewing ['səuɪŋ] *n* costura.

sewing machine *n* máquina de coser.

sewn [səun] *pp of* **sew**.

sex [sɛks] *n* sexo; **the opposite ~** el sexo opuesto; **to have ~ with sb** tener relaciones (sexuales) con uno.

sex act *n* acto sexual, coito.

sexism ['sɛksɪzəm] *n* sexismo

sexist ['sɛksɪst] *a*, *n* sexista *m/f*.

sextant ['sɛkstənt] *n* sextante *m*.

sextet [sɛks'tɛt] *n* sexteto.

sexual ['sɛksjuəl] *a* sexual; **~ assault** atentado contra el pudor; **~ intercourse** relaciones *fpl* sexuales.

sexually ['sɛksjuəlɪ] *ad* sexualmente.

sexy ['sɛksɪ] *a* sexy.

Seychelles [seɪ'ʃɛlz] *npl*: **the ~** las Seychelles.

SF *n abbr* = **science fiction.**

SG *n abbr* (*US*: = *Surgeon General*) jefe del servicio federal de sanidad.

Sgt *abbr* (= *sergeant*) sgto.

shabbily ['ʃæbɪlɪ] *ad* (*treat*) muy mal; (*dressed*) pobremente.

shabbiness ['ʃæbɪnɪs] *n* (*of dress, person*) aspecto desharrapado; (*of building*) mal estado.

shabby ['ʃæbɪ] *a* (*person*) desharrapado; (*clothes*) raído, gastado.

shack [ʃæk] *n* choza, chabola.

shackle ['ʃækl] *vt* encadenar; (*fig*): **to be ~d by sth** verse obstaculizado por algo.

shackles ['ʃæklz] *npl* grillos *mpl*, grilletes *mpl*.

shade [ʃeɪd] *n* sombra; (*for lamp*) pantalla; (*for eyes*) visera; (*of colour*) matiz *m*, tonalidad *f*; (*US*: *window ~*) persiana ♦ *vt* dar sombra a; **~s** *npl* (*US*: *sunglasses*) gafas *fpl* de sol; **in the ~** a la sombra; (*small quantity*): **a ~ of** un poquito de; **a ~ smaller** un poquito menor.

shadow ['ʃædəu] *n* sombra ♦ *vt* (*follow*) seguir y vigilar; **without** or **beyond a ~ of doubt** sin lugar a dudas.

shadow cabinet *n* (*Brit POL*) gabinete paralelo formado por el partido de oposición.

shadowy ['ʃædəuɪ] *a* oscuro; (*dim*) indistinto.

shady ['ʃeɪdɪ] *a* sombreado; (*fig*: *dishonest*) sospechoso; (: *deal*) turbio.

shaft [ʃɑːft] *n* (*of arrow, spear*) astil *m*; (*AUT, TECH*) eje *m*, árbol *m*; (*of mine*) pozo; (*of lift*) hueco, caja; (*of light*) rayo; **ventilator ~** chimenea de ventilación.

shaggy ['ʃægɪ] *a* peludo.

shake [ʃeɪk] *vb* (*pt* **shook**, *pp* **shaken** [ʃuk, 'ʃeɪkn]) *vt* sacudir; (*building*) hacer temblar; (*perturb*) inquietar, perturbar; (*weaken*) debilitar; (*alarm*) trastornar ♦ *vi* estremecerse; (*tremble*) temblar ♦ *n* (*movement*) sacudida; **to ~ one's head** (*in refusal*) negar con la cabeza; (*in dismay*) mover or menear la cabeza, incrédulo; **to ~ hands with sb** estrechar la mano a uno; **to ~ in one's shoes** (*fig*) temblar de aprensión, tener mieditis.

shake off *vt* sacudirse; (*fig*) deshacerse de.

shake up *vt* agitar.

shake-up ['ʃeɪkʌp] *n* reorganización *f*.

shakily ['ʃeɪkɪlɪ] *ad* (*reply*) con voz temblorosa or trémula; (*walk*) con paso vacilante; (*write*) con mano temblorosa.

shaky ['ʃeɪkɪ] *a* (*unstable*) inestable, poco firme; (*trembling*) tembloroso; (*health*) delicado; (*memory*) defectuoso; (*person*: *from illness*) temblando; (*premise etc*) incierto.

shale [ʃeɪl] *n* esquisto.

shall [ʃæl] *auxiliary vb*: **I ~ go** iré.

shallot [ʃə'lɔt] *n* (*Brit*) cebollita, chalote *m*.

shallow ['ʃæləu] *a* poco profundo; (*fig*) superficial.

shallows ['ʃæləuz] *npl* bajío *sg*, bajos *mpl*.

sham [ʃæm] *n* fraude *m*, engaño ♦ *a* falso, fingido ♦ *vt* fingir, simular.

shambles ['ʃæmblz] *n* desorden *m*, confusión *f*; **the economy is (in) a complete ~** la economía está en ruinas.

shame [ʃeɪm] *n* vergüenza; (*pity*) lástima ♦ *vt* avergonzar; **it is a ~ that/to do** es una lástima que/hacer; **what a ~!** ¡qué lástima!; **to put sth/sb to ~** (*fig*) ridiculizar algo/a uno.

shamefaced ['ʃeɪmfeɪst] *a* avergonzado.

shameful ['ʃeɪmful] *a* vergonzoso.

shamefully ['ʃeɪmfulɪ] *ad* vergonzosamente.

shameless ['ʃeɪmlɪs] *a* descarado.

shampoo [ʃæm'pu:] *n* champú *m* ♦ *vt* lavar con champú.

shampoo and set *n* lavado y marcado.

shamrock ['ʃæmrɔk] *n* trébol *m*.

shandy ['ʃændɪ], (*US*) **shandygaff** ['ʃændɪgæf] *n* mezcla de cerveza con gaseosa.

shan't [ʃɑːnt] = **shall not**.

shanty town ['ʃæntɪ-] *n* barrio de chabolas.

SHAPE [ʃeɪp] *n abbr* (= *Supreme Headquarters Allied Powers, Europe*) cuartel general de las fuerzas aliadas en Europa.

shape [ʃeɪp] *n* forma ♦ *vt* formar, dar forma a; (*clay*) modelar; (*stone*) labrar; (*sb's ideas*) formar; (*sb's life*) determinar ♦ *vi* (*also:* ~ **up**) (*events*) desarrollarse; (*person*) formarse; **to take ~** tomar forma; **to get s.o.s. into** ~ ponerse en forma *or* en condiciones; **in the ~ of a heart** en forma de corazón; **I can't bear gardening in any ~ or form** no aguanto la jardinería de ningún modo.

-shaped *suff*: **heart~** en forma de corazón.

shapeless ['ʃeɪplɪs] *a* informe, sin forma definida.

shapely ['ʃeɪplɪ] *a* bien formado *or* proporcionado.

share [ʃɛə*] *n* (*part*) parte *f*, porción *f*; (*contribution*) cuota; (*COMM*) acción *f* ♦ *vt* dividir; (*fig: have in common*) compartir; **to have a ~ in the profits** tener una proporción de las ganancias; **he has a 50% ~ in a new business venture** tiene una participación del 50% en un nuevo negocio; **to ~ in** participar en; **to ~ out (among** *or* **between)** repartir (entre).

share capital *n* (*COMM*) capital *m* en acciones *or* accionario.

share certificate *n* certificado *or* título de una acción.

shareholder ['ʃɛəhəʊldə*] *n* (*Brit*) accionista *m/f*.

share index *n* (*COMM*) índice *m* de la bolsa.

share issue *n* emisión *f* de acciones.

share price *n* (*COMM*) cotización *f*.

shark [ʃɑːk] *n* tiburón *m*.

sharp [ʃɑːp] *a* (*razor, knife*) afilado; (*point*) puntiagudo; (*outline*) definido; (*pain*) intenso; (*MUS*) desafinado; (*contrast*) marcado; (*voice*) agudo; (*curve, bend*) cerrado; (*person: quick-witted*) astuto; (*: dishonest*) poco escrupuloso ♦ *n* (*MUS*) sostenido ♦

ad: **at 2 o'clock ~** a las 2 en punto; **to be ~ with sb** hablar a uno con voz tajante; **turn ~ left** dobla fuertemente a la izquierda.

sharpen ['ʃɑːpn] *vt* afilar; (*pencil*) sacar punta a; (*fig*) agudizar.

sharpener ['ʃɑːpnə*] *n* (*gen*) afilador *m*; (*pencil* ~) sacapuntas *m inv*.

sharp-eyed [ʃɑːp'aɪd] *a* de vista aguda.

sharply ['ʃɑːplɪ] *ad* (*abruptly*) bruscamente; (*clearly*) claramente; (*harshly*) severamente.

sharp-tempered [ʃɑːp'tempəd] *a* de genio arisco.

sharp-witted [ʃɑːp'wɪtɪd] *a* listo, despabilado.

shatter ['ʃætə*] *vt* hacer añicos *or* pedazos; (*fig: ruin*) destruir, acabar con ♦ *vi* hacerse añicos.

shattered ['ʃætəd] *a* (*grief-stricken*) destrozado, deshecho; (*exhausted*) agotado, hecho polvo.

shattering ['ʃætərɪŋ] *a* (*experience*) devastador(a), anonadante.

shatterproof ['ʃætəpruːf] *a* inastillable.

shave [ʃeɪv] *vt* afeitar, rasurar ♦ *vi* afeitarse ♦ *n*: **to have a ~** afeitarse.

shaven ['ʃeɪvn] *a* (*head*) rapado.

shaver ['ʃeɪvə*] *n* (*also:* **electric ~**) máquina de afeitar (eléctrica).

shaving ['ʃeɪvɪŋ] *n* (*action*) el afeitarse, rasurado; **~s** *npl* (*of wood etc*) virutas *fpl*.

shaving brush *n* brocha (de afeitar).

shaving cream *n* crema (de afeitar).

shaving point *n* enchufe *m* para máquinas de afeitar.

shaving soap *n* jabón *m* de afeitar.

shawl [ʃɔːl] *n* chal *m*.

she [ʃiː] *pron* ella; **there ~ is** allí está; **~-cat** gata; *NB: for ships, countries follow the gender of your translation*.

sheaf, *pl* **sheaves** [ʃiːf, ʃiːvz] *n* (*of corn*) gavilla; (*of arrows*) haz *m*; (*of papers*) fajo.

shear [ʃɪə*] *vt* (*pt* ~**ed**, *pp* ~**ed** *or* **shorn** [ʃɔːn]) (*sheep*) esquilar, trasquilar.

shear off *vi* romperse.

shears ['ʃɪəz] *npl* (*for hedge*) tijeras *fpl* de jardín.

sheath [ʃiːθ] *n* vaina; (*contraceptive*) preservativo.

sheath knife *n* cuchillo de monte.

sheaves [ʃiːvz] *npl of* **sheaf**.

shed [ʃed] *n* cobertizo; (*INDUSTRY, RAIL*) nave *f* ♦ *vt* (*pt, pp* **shed**) (*skin*) mudar; (*tears*) derramar; **to ~ light on** (*problem, mystery*) aclarar, arrojar luz sobre.

she'd [ʃiːd] = **she had**, **she would**.

sheen [ʃiːn] *n* brillo, lustre *m*.

sheep [ʃiːp] *n* (*pl inv*) oveja.

sheepdog ['ʃiːpdɔg] *n* perro pastor.

sheep farmer *n* ganadero.

sheepish ['ʃiːpɪʃ] *a* tímido, vergonzoso.

sheepskin ['ʃiːpskɪn] *n* piel *f* de carnero.

sheepskin jacket n zamarra.
sheer [ʃɪə*] a (utter) puro; completo; (steep) escarpado; (material) diáfano ◆ ad verticalmente; **by ~ chance** de pura casualidad.
sheet [ʃiːt] n (on bed) sábana; (of paper) hoja; (of glass, metal) lámina.
sheet feed n (on printer) alimentador m de papel.
sheet lightning n relámpago (difuso).
sheet metal n metal m en lámina.
sheet music n hojas fpl de partitura.
sheik(h) [ʃeɪk] n jeque m.
shelf, pl **shelves** [ʃelf, ʃelvz] n estante m.
shelf life n (COMM) periodo de conservación antes de la venta.
shell [ʃel] n (on beach) concha; (of egg, nut etc) cáscara; (explosive) proyectil m, obús m; (of building) armazón m ◆ vt (peas) desenvainar; (MIL) bombardear.
shell out vi (col): **to ~ out (for)** soltar el dinero (para), desembolsar (para).
she'll [ʃiːl] = **she will, she shall**.
shellfish [ʃelfɪʃ] n (pl inv) crustáceo; (pl: as food) mariscos mpl.
shelter [ʃeltə*] n abrigo, refugio ◆ vt (aid) amparar, proteger; (give lodging to) abrigar; (hide) esconder ◆ vi abrigarse, refugiarse; **to take ~ (from)** refugiarse or asilarse (de); **bus ~** parada de autobús cubierta.
sheltered [ʃeltəd] a (life) protegido; (spot) abrigado.
shelve [ʃelv] vt (fig) dar carpetazo a.
shelves [ʃelvz] npl of **shelf**.
shelving [ʃelvɪŋ] n estantería.
shepherd [ʃepəd] n pastor m ◆ vt (guide) guiar, conducir.
shepherdess [ʃepədɪs] n pastora.
shepherd's pie n pastel de carne y patatas.
sherbert [ʃɔːbət] n (Brit: powder) polvos mpl azucarados; (US: water ice) sorbete m.
sheriff [ʃerɪf] n (US) sheriff m.
sherry [ʃerɪ] n jerez m.
she's [ʃiːz] = **she is, she has**.
Shetland [ʃetlənd] n (also: **the ~s, the ~ Isles**) las Islas fpl de Zetlandia.
shield [ʃiːld] n escudo; (TECH) blindaje m ◆ vt: **to ~ (from)** proteger (de).
shift [ʃɪft] n (change) cambio; (at work) turno ◆ vt trasladar; (remove) quitar ◆ vi moverse; (change place) cambiar de sitio; **the wind has ~ed** el viento ha virado al sur; **a ~ in demand** (COMM) un desplazamiento de la demanda.
shift key n (on typewriter) tecla de mayúsculas.
shiftless [ʃɪftlɪs] a (person) vago.
shift work n (Brit) trabajo por turno; **to do ~** trabajar por turno.
shifty [ʃɪftɪ] a tramposo; (eyes) furtivo.

shilling [ʃɪlɪŋ] n (Brit) chelín m (= 12 old pence; 20 in a pound).
shilly-shally [ʃɪlɪʃælɪ] vi titubear, vacilar.
shimmer [ʃɪmə*] n reflejo trémulo ◆ vi relucir.
shimmering [ʃɪmərɪŋ] a reluciente; (haze) trémulo; (satin etc) lustroso.
shin [ʃɪn] n espinilla ◆ vi: **to ~ up/down a tree** trepar/bajar de un árbol.
shindig [ʃɪndɪg] n (col) fiesta, juerga.
shine [ʃaɪn] n brillo, lustre m ◆ (vb: pt, pp **shone** [ʃɔn]) vi brillar, relucir ◆ vt (shoes) lustrar, sacar brillo a; **to ~ a torch on sth** dirigir una linterna hacia algo.
shingle [ʃɪŋgl] n (on beach) guijarras fpl.
shingles [ʃɪŋglz] n (MED) herpes mpl or fpl.
shining [ʃaɪnɪŋ] a (surface, hair) lustroso; (light) brillante.
shiny [ʃaɪnɪ] a brillante, lustroso.
ship [ʃɪp] n buque m, barco ◆ vt (goods) embarcar; (oars) desarmar; (send) transportar or enviar por vía marítima; **~'s manifest** manifiesto del buque; **on board ~** a bordo.
shipbuilder [ʃɪpbɪldə*] n constructor(a) m/f de buques.
shipbuilding [ʃɪpbɪldɪŋ] n construcción f de barcos.
ship canal n canal m de navegación.
ship chandler [-ˈtʃɑːndlə*] n proveedor m de efectos navales.
shipment [ʃɪpmənt] n (act) embarque m; (goods) envío.
shipowner [ʃɪpəunə*] n naviero, armador m.
shipper [ʃɪpə*] n exportador(a) m/f, empresa naviera.
shipping [ʃɪpɪŋ] n (act) embarque m; (traffic) buques mpl.
shipping agent n agente m/f marítimo/a.
shipping company n compañía naviera.
shipping lane n ruta de navegación.
shipping line n = **shipping company**.
shipshape [ʃɪpʃeɪp] a en buen orden.
shipwreck [ʃɪprek] n naufragio ◆ vt: **to be ~ed** naufragar.
shipyard [ʃɪpjɑːd] n astillero.
shire [ʃaɪə*] n (Brit) condado.
shirk [ʃɔːk] vt eludir, esquivar; (obligations) faltar a.
shirt [ʃɔːt] n camisa; **in ~ sleeves** en mangas de camisa.
shirty [ʃɔːtɪ] a (Brit col): **to be ~** estar de malas pulgas.
shit [ʃɪt] excl (col!) ¡mierda! (!).
shiver [ʃɪvə*] vi temblar, estremecerse; (with cold) tiritar.
shoal [ʃəul] n (of fish) banco.
shock [ʃɔk] n (impact) choque m; (ELEC) descarga (eléctrica); (emotional) conmoción f; (start) sobresalto, susto; (MED) postración f nerviosa ◆ vt dar un susto a; (of-

fend) escandalizar; **to get a** ~ (*ELEC*) sentir una sacudida eléctrica; **to give sb a** ~ dar un susto a uno; **to be suffering from** ~ padecer una postración nerviosa; **it came as a** ~ **to hear that ...** me (*etc*) asombró descubrir que ....

shock absorber [-əbsɔ:bə*] *n* amortiguador *m*.

shocking ['ʃɔkɪŋ] *a* (*awful: weather, handwriting*) espantoso, horrible; (*improper*) escandaloso; (*result*) inesperado.

shock therapy, shock treatment *n* (*MED*) tratamiento por electrochoque.

shod [ʃɔd] *pt, pp of* **shoe** ♦ *a* calzado.

shoddiness ['ʃɔdɪnɪs] *n* baja calidad *f*.

shoddy ['ʃɔdɪ] *a* de pacotilla.

shoe [ʃu:] *n* zapato; (*for horse*) herradura; (*brake* ~) zapata ♦ *vt* (*pt, pp* **shod** [ʃɔd]) (*horse*) herrar.

shoebrush ['ʃu:brʌʃ] *n* cepillo para zapatos.

shoehorn ['ʃu:hɔ:n] *n* calzador *m*.

shoelace ['ʃu:leɪs] *n* cordón *m*.

shoemaker ['ʃu:meɪkə*] *n* zapatero/a.

shoe polish *n* betún *m*.

shoeshop ['ʃu:ʃɔp] *n* zapatería.

shoestring ['ʃu:strɪŋ] *n* (*shoelace*) cordón *m*; (*fig*): **on a** ~ con muy poco dinero, a lo barato.

shone [ʃɔn] *pt, pp of* **shine**.

shoo [ʃu:] *excl* ¡fuera!; (*to animals*) ¡zape! ♦ *vt* (*also:* ~ **away**, ~ **off**) ahuyentar.

shook [ʃuk] *pt of* **shake**.

shoot [ʃu:t] *n* (*on branch, seedling*) retoño, vástago; (*shooting party*) cacería; (*competition*) concurso de tiro; (*preserve*) coto de caza ♦ (*vb: pt, pp* **shot** [ʃɔt]) *vt* disparar; (*kill*) matar a tiros; (*execute*) fusilar; (*CINE: film, scene*) rodar, filmar ♦ *vi* (*FOOTBALL*) chutar; **to** ~ **(at)** tirar (a); **to** ~ **past sb** pasar a uno como un rayo; **to shoot in/out** *vi* entrar corriendo/salir disparado.

shoot down *vt* (*plane*) derribar.

shoot up *vi* (*prices*) dispararse.

shooting ['ʃu:tɪŋ] *n* (*shots*) tiros *mpl*, tiroteo; (*HUNTING*) caza con escopeta; (*act: murder*) asesinato (a tiros); (*CINE*) rodaje *m*.

shooting star *n* estrella fugaz.

shop [ʃɔp] *n* tienda; (*workshop*) taller *m* ♦ *vi* (*also:* **go** ~**ping**) ir de compras; **to talk** ~ (*fig*) hablar del trabajo; **repair** ~ taller *m* de reparaciones.

shop around *vi* comparar precios.

shop assistant *n* (*Brit*) dependiente/a *m/f*.

shop floor *n* (*Brit fig*) taller *m*, fábrica.

shopkeeper ['ʃɔpki:pə*] *n* (*Brit*) tendero/a.

shoplift ['ʃɔplɪft] *vi* robar en las tiendas.

shoplifter ['ʃɔplɪftə*] *n* ratero/a.

shoplifting ['ʃɔplɪftɪŋ] *n* mechería.

shopper ['ʃɔpə*] *n* comprador(a) *m/f*.

shopping ['ʃɔpɪŋ] *n* (*goods*) compras *fpl*.

shopping bag *n* bolsa (de compras).

shopping centre, (*US*) **shopping center** *n* centro comercial.

shopping mall *n* (*US*) galería comercial.

shop-soiled ['ʃɔpsɔɪld] *a* (*Brit*) usado.

shop steward *n* (*Brit INDUSTRY*) enlace *m/f*.

shop window *n* escaparate *m*, vidriera (*LAm*).

shopworn ['ʃɔpwɔ:n] *a* (*US*) usado.

shore [ʃɔ:*] *n* (*of sea, lake*) orilla ♦ *vt*: **to** ~ **(up)** reforzar; **on** ~ en tierra.

shore leave *n* (*NAUT*) permiso para bajar a tierra.

shorn [ʃɔ:n] *pp of* **shear**.

short [ʃɔ:t] *a* (*not long*) corto; (*in time*) breve, de corta duración; (*person*) bajo; (*curt*) brusco, seco ♦ *vi* (*ELEC*) ponerse en cortocircuito ♦ *n* (*also:* ~ **film**) cortometraje *m*; (**a pair of**) ~**s** (unos) pantalones *mpl* cortos; **to be** ~ **of sth** estar falto de algo; **in** ~ en pocas palabras; **a** ~ **time ago** hace poco (tiempo); **in the** ~ **term** a corto plazo; **to be in** ~ **supply** escasear, haber escasez de; **I'm** ~ **of time** me falta tiempo; ~ **of doing...** fuera de hacer...; **everything** ~ **of...** todo menos...; **it is** ~ **for** es la forma abreviada de; **to cut** ~ (*speech, visit*) interrumpir, terminar inesperadamente; **to fall** ~ **of** no alcanzar; **to run** ~ **of sth** acabársele algo; **to stop** ~ parar en seco; **to stop** ~ **of** detenerse antes de.

shortage ['ʃɔ:tɪdʒ] *n* escasez *f*, falta.

shortbread ['ʃɔ:tbrɛd] *n* torta seca y quebradiza.

short-change [ʃɔ:t'tʃeɪndʒ] *vt*: **to** ~ **sb** no dar el cambio completo a uno.

short-circuit [ʃɔ:t'sə:kɪt] *n* cortocircuito ♦ *vt* poner en cortocircuito ♦ *vi* ponerse en cortocircuito.

shortcoming ['ʃɔ:tkʌmɪŋ] *n* defecto, deficiencia.

short(crust) pastry ['ʃɔ:t(krʌst)-] *n* (*Brit*) pasta quebradiza.

shortcut ['ʃɔ:tkʌt] *n* atajo.

shorten ['ʃɔ:tn] *vt* acortar; (*visit*) interrumpir.

shortfall ['ʃɔ:tfɔ:l] *n* déficit *m*, deficiencia.

shorthand ['ʃɔ:thænd] *n* (*Brit*) taquigrafía; **to take sth down in** ~ escribir algo taquigráficamente.

shorthand notebook *n* cuaderno de taquigrafía.

shorthand typist *n* (*Brit*) taquimecanógrafo/a.

short list *n* (*Brit: for job*) lista de candidatos escogidos.

short-lived ['ʃɔ:t'lɪvd] *a* efímero.

shortly ['ʃɔ:tlɪ] *ad* en breve, dentro de poco.

shortness ['ʃɔ:tnɪs] *n* (*of distance*) cortedad *f*; (*of time*) brevedad *f*; (*manner*)

brusquedad *f*.
short-sighted [ʃɔːt'saɪtɪd] *a* (*Brit*) corto de vista, miope; (*fig*) imprudente.
short-sightedness [ʃɔːt'saɪtɪdnɪs] *n* miopía, cortedad *f* de vista; (*fig*) falta de previsión, imprudencia.
short-staffed [ʃɔːt'stɑːft] *a* falto de personal.
short story *n* cuento.
short-tempered [ʃɔːt'tɛmpəd] *a* enojadizo.
short-term ['ʃɔːttəːm] *a* (*effect*) a corto plazo.
short time *n*: **to work ~, be on ~** (*INDUSTRY*) trabajar con sistema de horario reducido.
short-time working ['ʃɔːttaɪm-] *n* trabajo de horario reducido.
short wave *n* (*RADIO*) onda corta.
shot [ʃɔt] *pt, pp of* **shoot ♦** *n* (*sound*) tiro, disparo; (*person*) tirador(a) *m/f*; (*try*) tentativa; (*injection*) inyección *f*; (*PHOT*) toma, fotografía; (*shotgun pellets*) perdigones *mpl*; **to fire a ~ at sb/sth** tirar *or* disparar contra uno/algo; **to have a ~ at (doing) sth** probar suerte con algo; **like a ~** (*without any delay*) como un rayo; **a big ~** (*col*) un pez gordo; **to get ~ of sth/sb** (*col*) deshacerse de algo/uno, quitarse algo/ a uno de encima.
shotgun ['ʃɔtgʌn] *n* escopeta.
should [ʃud] *auxiliary vb*: **I ~ go now** debo irme ahora; **he ~ be there now** debe de haber llegado (ya); **I ~ go if I were you** yo en tu lugar me iría; **I ~ like to** me gustaría; **~ he phone** ... si llamara ..., en caso de que llamase ....
shoulder ['ʃəuldə*] *n* hombro; (*Brit: of road*): **hard ~** andén *m* ♦ *vt* (*fig*) cargar con; **to look over one's ~** mirar hacia atrás; **to rub ~s with sb** (*fig*) codearse con uno; **to give sb the cold ~** (*fig*) dar de lado a uno.
shoulder blade *n* omóplato.
shoulder bag *n* bolso de bandolera.
shoulder strap *n* tirante *m*.
shouldn't ['ʃudnt] = **should not**.
shout [ʃaut] *n* grito ♦ *vt* gritar ♦ *vi* gritar, dar voces.
shout down *vt* hundir a gritos.
shouting ['ʃautɪŋ] *n* griterío.
shove [ʃʌv] *n* empujón *m* ♦ *vt* empujar; (*col: put*): **to ~ sth in** meter algo a empellones; **he ~d me out of the way** me quitó de en medio de un empujón.
shove off *vi* (*NAUT*) alejarse del muelle; (*fig: col*) largarse.
shovel ['ʃʌvl] *n* pala; (*mechanical*) excavadora ♦ *vt* mover con pala.
show [ʃəu] *n* (*of emotion*) demostración *f*; (*semblance*) apariencia; (*COMM, TECH: exhibition*) exhibición *f*, exposición *f*; (*THEATRE*) función *f*, espectáculo; (*organization*) negocio, empresa ♦ *vb* (*pt* **showed,**

pp **shown** [ʃəun]) *vt* mostrar, enseñar; (*courage etc*) mostrar, manifestar; (*exhibit*) exponer; (*film*) proyectar ♦ *vi* mostrarse; (*appear*) aparecer; **on ~** (*exhibits etc*) expuesto; **to be on ~** estar expuesto; **it's just for ~** es para lucir nada más; **to ask for a ~ of hands** pedir una votación a mano alzada; **who's running the ~ here?** ¿quién manda aquí?; **to ~ a profit/loss** (*COMM*) arrojar un saldo positivo/negativo; **I have nothing to ~ for it** no saqué ningún provecho (de ello); **to ~ sb to his seat/to the door** acompañar a uno a su asiento/a la puerta; **as ~n in the illustration** como se ve en el grabado; **it just goes to ~ that ...** queda demostrado que ...; **it doesn't ~** no se ve *or* nota.
show in *vt* (*person*) hacer pasar.
show off *vi* (*pej*) presumir ♦ *vt* (*display*) lucir; (*pej*) hacer gala de.
show out *vt*: **to ~ sb out** acompañar a uno a la puerta.
show up *vi* (*stand out*) destacar; (*col: turn up*) presentarse ♦ *vt* descubrir; (*unmask*) desenmascarar.
show business *n* el mundo del espectáculo.
showcase ['ʃəukeɪs] *n* vitrina; (*fig*) escaparate *m*.
showdown ['ʃəudaun] *n* crisis *f*, momento decisivo.
shower ['ʃauə*] *n* (*rain*) chaparrón *m*, chubasco; (*of stones etc*) lluvia; (*also: ~ bath*) ducha ♦ *vi* llover ♦ *vt*: **to ~ sb with sth** colmar a uno de algo; **to have *or* take a ~** ducharse.
shower cap *n* gorro de baño.
showerproof ['ʃauəpruːf] *a* impermeable.
showery ['ʃauərɪ] *a* (*weather*) lluvioso.
showground ['ʃəugraund] *n* ferial *m*, real *m* (de la feria).
showing ['ʃəuɪŋ] *n* (*of film*) proyección *f*.
show jumping *n* hipismo.
showman ['ʃəumən] *n* (*at fair, circus*) empresario; (*fig*) persona extrovertida, exhibicionista *m/f*.
showmanship ['ʃəumənʃɪp] *n* dotes *fpl* teatrales.
shown [ʃəun] *pp of* **show**.
show-off ['ʃəuɔf] *n* (*col: person*) presumido/a.
showpiece ['ʃəupiːs] *n* (*of exhibition etc*) objeto cumbre; **that hospital is a ~** ese hospital es un modelo del género.
showroom ['ʃəuruːm] *n* sala de muestras.
showy ['ʃəuɪ] *a* ostentoso.
shrank [ʃræŋk] *pt of* **shrink**.
shrapnel ['ʃræpnl] *n* metralla.
shred [ʃrɛd] *n* (*gen pl*) triza, jirón *m*; (*fig: of truth, evidence*) pizca, chispa ♦ *vt* hacer trizas; (*documents*) triturar; (*CULIN*) desmenuzar.
shredder ['ʃrɛdə*] *n* (*vegetable shredder*)

picadora; (*document shredder*) trituradora (de papel).

shrewd [ʃruːd] *a* astuto.

shrewdly ['ʃruːdlɪ] *ad* astutamente.

shrewdness ['ʃruːdnɪs] *n* astucia.

shriek [ʃriːk] *n* chillido ♦ *vt, vi* chillar.

shrill [ʃrɪl] *a* agudo, estridente.

shrimp [ʃrɪmp] *n* camarón *m*.

shrine [ʃraɪn] *n* santuario, sepulcro.

shrink, *pt* **shrank**, *pp* **shrunk** [ʃrɪŋk, ʃræŋk, ʃrʌŋk] *vi* encogerse; (*be reduced*) reducirse ♦ *vt* encoger; **to ~ from (doing) sth** no atreverse a hacer algo.

shrink away *vi* retroceder, retirarse.

shrinkage ['ʃrɪŋkɪdʒ] *n* encogimiento; reducción *f*; (*COMM: in shops*) pérdidas *fpl.*

shrink-wrap ['ʃrɪŋkræp] *vt* empaquetar en envase termoretráctil.

shrivel ['ʃrɪvl] (*also:* **~ up**) *vt* (*dry*) secar; (*crease*) arrugar ♦ *vi* secarse; arrugarse.

shroud [ʃraud] *n* sudario ♦ *vt*: **~ed in mystery** envuelto en el misterio.

Shrove Tuesday ['ʃrəuv-] *n* martes *m* de carnaval.

shrub [ʃrʌb] *n* arbusto.

shrubbery ['ʃrʌbərɪ] *n* arbustos *mpl.*

shrug [ʃrʌg] *n* encogimiento de hombros ♦ *vt, vi*: **to ~ (one's shoulders)** encogerse de hombros.

shrug off *vt* negar importancia a; (*cold, illness*) deshacerse de.

shrunk [ʃrʌŋk] *pp of* **shrink**.

shrunken ['ʃrʌŋkn] *a* encogido.

shudder ['ʃʌdə*] *n* estremecimiento, escalofrío ♦ *vi* estremecerse.

shuffle ['ʃʌfl] *vt* (*cards*) barajar; **to ~ (one's feet)** arrastrar los pies.

shun [ʃʌn] *vt* rehuir, esquivar.

shunt [ʃʌnt] *vt* (*RAIL*) maniobrar.

shunting yard ['ʃʌntɪŋ-] *n* estación *f* de maniobras.

shut, *pt, pp* **shut** [ʃʌt] *vt* cerrar ♦ *vi* cerrarse.

shut down *vt, vi* cerrarse, parar; (*machine*) apagar.

shut off *vt* (*stop: power, water supply etc*) interrumpir, cortar; (: *engine*) parar.

shut out *vt* (*person*) excluir, dejar fuera; (*noise, cold*) no dejar entrar; (*block: view*) tapar; (: *memory*) tratar de olvidar.

shut up *vi* (*col: keep quiet*) callarse ♦ *vt* (*close*) cerrar; (*silence*) callar.

shutdown ['ʃʌtdaun] *n* cierre *m*.

shutter ['ʃʌtə*] *n* contraventana; (*PHOT*) obturador *m*.

shuttle ['ʃʌtl] *n* lanzadera; (*also:* **~ service**: *AVIAT*) puente *m* aéreo ♦ *vi* (*subj: vehicle, person*) ir y venir ♦ *vt* (*passengers*) transportar, trasladar (*LAm*).

shuttlecock ['ʃʌtlkɔk] *n* volante *m*.

shy [ʃaɪ] *a* tímido ♦ *vi*: **to ~ away from doing sth** (*fig*) rehusar hacer algo; **to be ~ of doing sth** esquivar hacer algo.

shyly ['ʃaɪlɪ] *ad* tímidamente.

shyness ['ʃaɪnɪs] *n* timidez *f*.

Siam [saɪ'æm] *n* Siam *m*.

Siamese [saɪə'miːz] *a* siamés/esa ♦ *n* (*person*) siamés/esa *m/f*; (*LING*) siamés *m*; **~ cat** gato siamés; **~ twins** gemelos/as *m/fpl* siameses/as.

Siberia [saɪ'bɪərɪə] *n* Siberia.

sibling ['sɪblɪŋ] *n* (*formal*) hermano/a.

Sicilian [sɪ'sɪlɪən] *a, n* siciliano/a *m/f.*

Sicily ['sɪsɪlɪ] *n* Sicilia.

sick [sɪk] *a* (*ill*) enfermo; (*nauseated*) mareado; (*humour*) negro; **to be ~** (*Brit*) vomitar; **to feel ~** estar mareado; **to be ~ of** (*fig*) estar harto de; **a ~ person** un(a) enfermo/a; **to be (off) ~** estar ausente por enfermedad; **to fall** *or* **take ~** ponerse enfermo.

sick bay *n* enfermería.

sickbed ['sɪkbɛd] *n* lecho de enfermo.

sicken ['sɪkn] *vt* dar asco a ♦ *vi* enfermar; **to be ~ing for** (*cold, flu etc*) mostrar síntomas de.

sickening ['sɪknɪŋ] *a* (*fig*) asqueroso.

sickle ['sɪkl] *n* hoz *f.*

sick leave *n* baja por enfermedad.

sick list *n*: **to be on the ~** estar de baja.

sickly ['sɪklɪ] *a* enfermizo; (*taste*) empalagoso.

sickness ['sɪknɪs] *n* enfermedad *f*, mal *m*; (*vomiting*) náuseas *fpl.*

sickness benefit *n* subsidio de enfermedad.

sick pay *n* subsidio de enfermedad.

sickroom ['sɪkruːm] *n* cuarto del enfermo.

side [saɪd] *n* (*gen*) lado; (*face, surface*) cara; (*of paper*) cara; (*slice of bread*) rebanada; (*of body*) costado; (*of animal*) ijar *m*, ijada; (*of lake*) orilla; (*part*) lado; (*aspect*) aspecto; (*team: SPORT*) equipo; (: *POL etc*) partido; (*of hill*) ladera ♦ *a* (*door, entrance*) de al lado ♦ *vi*: **to ~ with sb** tomar el partido de uno; **by the ~ of** al lado de; **~ by ~** juntos/as; **from all ~s** de todos lados; **to take ~s (with)** tomar partido (con); **~ of beef** flanco de vaca; **the right/wrong ~** el derecho/revés; **from ~ to ~** de un lado a otro.

sideboard ['saɪdbɔːd] *n* aparador *m*.

sideboards ['saɪdbɔːdz] (*Brit*), **sideburns** ['saɪdbəːnz] *npl* patillas *fpl.*

sidecar ['saɪdkɑː*] *n* sidecar *m*.

side dish *n* entremés *m*.

side drum *n* (*MUS*) tamboril *m*.

side effect *n* efecto secundario.

sidekick ['saɪdkɪk] *n* compinche *m*.

sidelight ['saɪdlaɪt] *n* (*AUT*) luz *f* lateral.

sideline ['saɪdlaɪn] *n* (*SPORT*) línea lateral; (*fig*) empleo suplementario.

sidelong ['saɪdlɔŋ] *a* de soslayo; **to give a ~ glance at sth** mirar algo de reojo.

side plate *n* platito.

side road *n* (*Brit*) calle *f* lateral.

sidesaddle ['saɪdsædl] *ad* a mujeriegas, a la inglesa.

side show *n* (*stall*) caseta; (*fig*) atracción *f* secundaria.

sidestep ['saɪdstɛp] *vt* (*question*) eludir; (*problem*) esquivar ♦ *vi* (*BOXING etc*) dar un quiebro.

side street *n* calle *f* lateral.

sidetrack ['saɪdtræk] *vt* (*fig*) desviar (de su propósito).

sidewalk ['saɪdwɔːk] *n* (*US*) acera.

sideways ['saɪdweɪz] *ad* de lado.

siding ['saɪdɪŋ] *n* (*RAIL*) apartadero, vía muerta.

sidle ['saɪdl] *vi*: **to ~ up (to)** acercarse furtivamente (a).

SIDS [sɪdz] *n abbr* (= *sudden infant death syndrome*) muerte *f* en la cuna.

siege [siːdʒ] *n* cerco, sitio; **to lay ~ to** cercar, sitiar.

siege economy *n* economía de sitio *or* de asedio.

Sierra Leone [sɪ'ɛrəlɪ'əun] *n* Sierra Leona.

siesta [sɪ'ɛstə] *n* siesta.

sieve [sɪv] *n* colador *m* ♦ *vt* cribar.

sift [sɪft] *vt* cribar; (*fig: information*) escudriñar ♦ *vi*: **to ~ through** pasar por una criba; (*of information*) llegar a saberse.

sigh [saɪ] *n* suspiro ♦ *vi* suspirar.

sight [saɪt] *n* (*faculty*) vista; (*spectacle*) espectáculo; (*on gun*) mira, alza ♦ *vt* ver, divisar; **in ~** a la vista; **out of ~** fuera de (la) vista; **at ~** a la vista; **at first ~** a primera vista; **to lose ~ of sth/sb** perder algo/a uno de vista; **to catch ~ of sth/sb** divisar algo/a uno; **I know her by ~** la conozco de vista; **to set one's ~s on (doing) sth** aspirar a *or* ambicionar (hacer) algo.

sighted ['saɪtɪd] *a* que ve, de vista normal; **partially ~** de vista limitada.

sightseer ['saɪtsiːə*] *n* excursionista *m/f*, turista *m/f*.

sightseeing ['saɪtsiːŋ] *n* excursionismo, turismo; **to go ~** visitar monumentos.

sign [saɪn] *n* (*with hand*) señal *f*, seña; (*trace*) huella, rastro; (*notice*) letrero; (*written*) signo; (*road ~*) indicador *m*; (: *with instructions*) señal *f* de tráfico ♦ *vt* firmar; **as a ~ of** en señal de; **it's a good/bad ~** es buena/mala señal; **plus/minus ~** signo de más/de menos; **to ~ one's name** firmar.

sign away *vt* (*rights etc*) ceder.

sign off *vi* (*RADIO, TV*) cerrar el programa.

sign on *vi* (*MIL*) alistarse; (*as unemployed*) registrarse como desempleado; (*employee*) firmar un contrato ♦ *vt* (*MIL*) alistar; (*employee*) contratar; **to ~ on for a course** matricularse en un curso.

sign out *vi* firmar el registro (al salir).

sign over *vt*: **to ~ sth over to sb** traspasar algo a uno.

sign up *vi* (*MIL*) alistarse ♦ *vt* (*contract*) contratar.

signal ['sɪgnl] *n* señal *f* ♦ *vi* (*AUT*) señalizar ♦ *vt* (*person*) hacer señas a uno; (*message*) transmitir; **the engaged ~** (*TEL*) la señal de comunicando; **the ~ is very weak** (*TV*) no captamos bien la sintonía; **to ~ a left/right turn** (*AUT*) indicar que se va a doblar a la izquierda/derecha; **to ~ to sb (to do sth)** hacer señas a uno (para que haga algo).

signal box *n* (*RAIL*) garita de señales.

signalman ['sɪgnlmən] *n* (*RAIL*) guardavía *m*.

signatory ['sɪgnətərɪ] *n* firmante *m/f*.

signature ['sɪgnətʃə*] *n* firma.

signature tune *n* sintonía de apertura de un programa.

signet ring ['sɪgnət-] *n* anillo de sello.

significance [sɪg'nɪfɪkəns] *n* significado; (*importance*) trascendencia; **that is of no ~** eso no tiene importancia.

significant [sɪg'nɪfɪkənt] *a* significativo; trascendente; **it is ~ that ...** es significativo que ....

significantly [sɪg'nɪfɪkəntlɪ] *ad* (*smile*) expresivamente; (*improve, increase*) sensiblemente; **and, ~ ...** y debe notarse que ....

signify ['sɪgnɪfaɪ] *vt* significar.

sign language *n* mímica, lenguaje *m* por *or* de señas.

signpost ['saɪnpəust] *n* indicador *m*.

silage ['saɪlɪdʒ] *n* ensilaje *m*.

silence ['saɪlns] *n* silencio ♦ *vt* hacer callar; (*guns*) reducir al silencio.

silencer ['saɪlnsə*] *n* (*on gun, Brit AUT*) silenciador *m*.

silent ['saɪlnt] *a* (*gen*) silencioso; (*not speaking*) callado; (*film*) mudo; **to keep** *or* **remain ~** guardar silencio.

silently ['saɪlntlɪ] *ad* silenciosamente, en silencio.

silent partner *n* (*COMM*) socio/a comanditario/a.

silhouette [sɪlu'ɛt] *n* silueta; **~d against** destacado sobre *or* contra.

silicon ['sɪlɪkən] *n* silicio.

silicon chip *n* plaqueta de silicio.

silicone ['sɪlɪkəun] *n* silicona.

silk [sɪlk] *n* seda ♦ *cpd* de seda.

silky ['sɪlkɪ] *a* sedoso.

sill [sɪl] *n* (*also:* **window~**) alféizar *m*; (*AUT*) umbral *m*.

silliness ['sɪlɪnɪs] *n* (*of person*) necedad *f*; (*of idea*) lo absurdo.

silly ['sɪlɪ] *a* (*person*) tonto; (*idea*) absurdo; **to do sth ~** hacer una tontería.

silo ['saɪləu] *n* silo.

silt [sɪlt] *n* sedimento.

silver ['sɪlvə*] *n* plata; (*money*) moneda suelta ♦ *a* de plata, plateado.

silver paper (*Brit*), **silver foil** *n* papel *m* de plata.

silver plate *n* vajilla de plata.
silver-plated [sɪlvə'pleɪtɪd] *a* plateado.
silversmith ['sɪlvəsmɪθ] *n* platero/a.
silverware ['sɪlvəwɛə*] *n* plata.
silver wedding (anniversary) *n* (*Brit*) bodas *fpl* de plata.
silvery ['sɪlvrɪ] *a* plateado.
similar ['sɪmɪlə*] *a*: ~ **to** parecido *or* semejante a.
similarity [sɪmɪ'lærɪtɪ] *n* parecido, semejanza.
similarly ['sɪmɪləlɪ] *ad* del mismo modo; (*in a similar way*) de manera parecida; (*equally*) igualmente.
simile ['sɪmɪlɪ] *n* símil *m*.
simmer ['sɪmə*] *vi* hervir a fuego lento.
  simmer down *vi* (*fig, col*) calmarse, tranquilizarse.
simpering ['sɪmpərɪŋ] *a* afectado; (*foolish*) bobo.
simple ['sɪmpl] *a* (*easy*) sencillo; (*foolish, COMM*) simple; **the ~ truth** la pura verdad.
simple interest *n* (*COMM*) interés *m* simple.
simple-minded [sɪmpl'maɪndɪd] *a* simple, ingenuo.
simpleton ['sɪmpltən] *n* inocentón/ona *m/f*.
simplicity [sɪm'plɪsɪtɪ] *n* sencillez *f*; (*foolishness*) ingenuidad *f*.
simplification [sɪmplɪfɪ'keɪʃən] *n* simplificación *f*.
simplify ['sɪmplɪfaɪ] *vt* simplificar.
simply ['sɪmplɪ] *ad* (*in a simple way*: *live, talk*) sencillamente; (*just, merely*) sólo.
simulate ['sɪmjuleɪt] *vt* simular.
simulation [sɪmju'leɪʃən] *n* simulación *f*.
simultaneous [sɪməl'teɪnɪəs] *a* simultáneo.
simultaneously [sɪməl'teɪnɪəslɪ] *ad* simultáneamente, a la vez.
sin [sɪn] *n* pecado ♦ *vi* pecar.
since [sɪns] *ad* desde entonces, después ♦ *prep* desde ♦ *conj* (*time*) desde que; (*because*) ya que, puesto que; ~ **then** desde entonces; ~ **Monday** desde el lunes; (**ever**) ~ **I arrived** desde que llegué.
sincere [sɪn'sɪə*] *a* sincero.
sincerely [sɪn'sɪəlɪ] *ad* sinceramente; **yours** ~ (*in letters*) le saluda (afectuosamente); ~ **yours** (*US*: *in letters*) le saluda atentamente.
sincerity [sɪn'sɛrɪtɪ] *n* sinceridad *f*.
sinecure ['saɪnɪkjuə*] *n* chollo.
sinew ['sɪnjuː] *n* tendón *m*.
sinful ['sɪnful] *a* (*thought*) pecaminoso; (*person*) pecador(a).
sing, *pt* **sang**, *pp* **sung** [sɪŋ, sæŋ, sʌŋ] *vt* cantar ♦ *vi* (*gen*) cantar; (*bird*) trinar; (*ears*) zumbar.
Singapore [sɪŋə'pɔː*] *n* Singapur *m*.
singe [sɪndʒ] *vt* chamuscar.
singer ['sɪŋə*] *n* cantante *m/f*.
Singhalese [sɪŋə'liːz] *a* = **Sinhalese**.
singing ['sɪŋɪŋ] *n* (*of person, bird*) canto;

(*songs*) canciones *fpl*; (*in the ears*) zumbido; (*of kettle*) silbido.
single ['sɪŋgl] *a* único, solo; (*unmarried*) soltero; (*not double*) simple, sencillo ♦ *n* (*Brit*: *also*: ~ **ticket**) billete *m* sencillo; (*record*) sencillo, single *m*; ~**s** *npl* (*TENNIS*) individual *msg*; **not a ~ one was left** no quedaba ni uno; **every ~ day** todos los días (sin excepción).
  single out *vt* (*choose*) escoger; (*point out*) singularizar.
single bed *n* cama individual.
single-breasted [sɪŋgl'brɛstɪd] *a* (*jacket, suit*) recto.
single-density ['sɪŋgldɛnsɪtɪ] *a* (*COMPUT*: *disk*) de densidad sencilla.
single-entry book-keeping ['sɪŋglɛntrɪ-] *n* contabilidad *f* por partida simple.
single file *n*: **in** ~ en fila de uno.
single-handed [sɪŋgl'hændɪd] *ad* sin ayuda.
single-minded [sɪŋgl'maɪndɪd] *a* resuelto, firme.
single parent *n* (*mother*) madre *f* soltera; (*father*) padre *m* soltero.
single room *n* cuarto individual.
single-sided [sɪŋgl'saɪdɪd] *a* (*COMPUT*: *disk*) de una cara.
single spacing *n* (*TYP*) interlineado simple.
singlet ['sɪŋglɪt] *n* camiseta.
singly ['sɪŋglɪ] *ad* uno por uno.
singsong ['sɪŋsɒŋ] *a* (*tone*) cantarín/ina ♦ *n* (*songs*): **to have a** ~ tener un concierto improvisado.
singular ['sɪŋgjulə*] *a* (*odd*) raro, extraño; (*LING*) singular ♦ *n* (*LING*) singular *m*; **in the feminine** ~ en femenino singular.
singularly ['sɪŋgjuləlɪ] *ad* singularmente, extraordinariamente.
Sinhalese [sɪnhə'liːz] *a* singhalese.
sinister ['sɪnɪstə*] *a* siniestro.
sink [sɪŋk] *n* fregadero ♦ *vb* (*pt* **sank**, *pp* **sunk** [sæŋk, sʌŋk]) *vt* (*ship*) hundir, echar a pique; (*foundations*) excavar; (*piles etc*): **to** ~ **sth into** hundir algo en ♦ *vi* (*gen*) hundirse; **he sank into a chair/the mud** se dejó caer en una silla/se hundió en el barro; **the shares** *or* **share prices have sunk to 3 dollars** las acciones han bajado a 3 dólares.
  sink in *vi* (*fig*) penetrar, calar; **the news took a long time to** ~ **in** la noticia tardó mucho en hacerle (*or* hacerme *etc*) mella.
sinking fund ['sɪŋkɪŋ-] *n* fondo de amortización.
sink unit *n* fregadero.
sinner ['sɪnə*] *n* pecador(a) *m/f*.
sinuous ['sɪnjuəs] *a* sinuoso.
sinus ['saɪnəs] *n* (*ANAT*) seno.
sip [sɪp] *n* sorbo ♦ *vt* sorber, beber a sorbitos.
siphon ['saɪfən] *n* sifón *m* ♦ *vt* (*also*: ~ **off**) (*funds*) desviar.

sir [sɔ:*] n señor m; **S~ John Smith** el Señor John Smith; **yes ~** sí, señor; **Dear S~** (in letter) Muy señor mío, Estimado Señor; **Dear S~s** Muy señores nuestros, Estimados Señores.

siren ['saɪərn] n sirena.

sirloin ['sɔ:lɔɪn] n solomillo; **~ steak** filete m de solomillo.

sisal ['saɪsəl] n pita, henequén m (LAm).

sissy ['sɪsɪ] n (col) marica m.

sister ['sɪstə*] n hermana; (Brit: nurse) enfermera jefe.

sister-in-law ['sɪstərɪnlɔ:] n cuñada.

sister organization n organización f hermana.

sister ship n barco gemelo.

sit, pt, pp **sat** [sɪt, sæt] vi sentarse; (be sitting) estar sentado; (assembly) reunirse; (dress etc) caer, sentar ♦ vt (exam) presentarse a; **that jacket ~s well** esa chaqueta sienta bien; **to ~ on a committee** ser miembro de una comisión or un comité.

sit about, sit around vi holgazanear.

sit back vi (in seat) recostarse.

sit down vi sentarse; **to be ~ting down** estar sentado.

sit in on vt fus: **to ~ in on a discussion** asistir a una discusión.

sit up vi incorporarse; (not go to bed) velar.

sitcom ['sɪtkɔm] n abbr (= situation comedy) serie f cómica.

sit-down ['sɪtdaun] a: **~ strike** huelga de brazos caídos; **a ~ meal** una comida sentada.

site [saɪt] n sitio; (also: **building ~**) solar m ♦ vt situar.

sit-in ['sɪtɪn] n (demonstration) ocupación f.

siting ['saɪtɪŋ] n (location) situación f, emplazamiento.

sitter ['sɪtə*] n (ART) modelo m/f; (baby~) canguro m/f.

sitting ['sɪtɪŋ] n (of assembly etc) sesión f; (in canteen) turno.

sitting member n (POL) titular m/f de un escaño.

sitting room n sala de estar.

sitting tenant n inquilino con derechos de estancia ilimitada.

situate ['sɪtjueɪt] vt situar.

situated ['sɪtjueɪtɪd] a situado.

situation [sɪtju'eɪʃən] n situación f; **"~s vacant"** (Brit) "bolsa del trabajo".

situation comedy n (TV, RADIO) serie f cómica.

six [sɪks] num seis.

sixteen [sɪks'ti:n] num diez y seis, dieciséis.

sixth [sɪksθ] a sexto; **the upper/lower ~** (SCOL) el séptimo/sexto año.

sixty ['sɪkstɪ] num sesenta.

size [saɪz] n (gen) tamaño; (extent) extensión f; (of clothing) talla; (of shoes) número; **I take ~ 5 shoes** calzo el número

cinco; **I take ~ 14** mi talla es la 42; **I'd like the small/large ~** (of soap powder etc) quisiera el tamaño pequeño/grande.

size up vt formarse una idea de.

sizeable ['saɪzəbl] a importante, considerable.

sizzle ['sɪzl] vi crepitar.

SK abbr (Canada) = Saskatchewan.

skate [skeɪt] n patín m; (fish: pl inv) raya ♦ vi patinar.

skate over, skate round vt fus (problem, issue) pasar por alto.

skateboard ['skeɪtbɔ:d] n monopatín m.

skater ['skeɪtə*] n patinador(a) m/f.

skating ['skeɪtɪŋ] n patinaje m; **figure ~** patinaje m de figuras.

skating rink n pista de patinaje.

skeleton ['skɛlɪtn] n esqueleto; (TECH) armazón m; (outline) esquema m.

skeleton key n llave f maestra.

skeleton staff n personal m reducido.

skeptic ['skɛptɪk] etc (US) = **sceptic**.

sketch [skɛtʃ] n (drawing) dibujo; (outline) esbozo, bosquejo; (THEATRE) pieza corta ♦ vt dibujar; esbozar.

sketch book n libro de dibujos.

sketching ['skɛtʃɪŋ] n dibujo.

sketch pad n bloc m de dibujo.

sketchy ['skɛtʃɪ] a incompleto.

skewer ['skju:ə*] n broqueta.

ski [ski:] n esquí m ♦ vi esquiar.

ski boot n bota de esquí.

skid [skɪd] n patinazo ♦ vi patinar; **to go into a ~** comenzar a patinar.

skid mark n señal f de patinazo.

skier ['ski:ə*] n esquiador(a) m/f.

skiing ['ski:ɪŋ] n esquí m; **to go ~** practicar el esquí, (ir a) esquiar.

ski instructor n instructor(a) m/f de esquí.

ski jump n pista para salto de esquí.

skilful, (US) **skillful** ['skɪlful] a diestro, experto.

ski lift n telesilla m, telesquí m.

skill [skɪl] n destreza, pericia; (technique) arte m, técnica; **there's a certain ~ to doing it** se necesita cierta habilidad para hacerlo.

skilled [skɪld] a hábil, diestro; (worker) cualificado.

skillet ['skɪlɪt] n sartén f pequeña.

skillful ['skɪlful] etc (US) = **skilful** etc.

skil(l)fully ['skɪlfulɪ] ad hábilmente, con destreza.

skim [skɪm] vt (milk) desnatar; (glide over) rozar, rasar ♦ vi: **to ~ through** (book) hojear.

skimmed milk [skɪmd-] n leche f desnatada or descremada.

skimp [skɪmp] vt (work) chapucear; (cloth etc) escatimar; **to ~ on** (material etc) economizar; (work) escatimar.

skimpy ['skɪmpɪ] a (meagre) escaso; (skirt)

muy corto.

skin [skɪn] *n* (*gen*) piel *f*; (*complexion*) cutis *m*; (*of fruit, vegetable*) piel *f*, cáscara, pellejo; (*crust: on pudding, paint*) nata ♦ *vt* (*fruit etc*) pelar; (*animal*) despellejar; **wet** *or* **soaked to the** ~ calado hasta los huesos.

skin-deep ['skɪn'diːp] *a* superficial.

skin diver *n* buceador(a) *m/f*.

skin diving *n* buceo.

skinflint ['skɪnflɪnt] *n* tacaño/a, roñoso/a.

skinny ['skɪnɪ] *a* flaco, magro.

skintight ['skɪntaɪt] *a* (*dress etc*) muy ajustado.

skip [skɪp] *n* brinco, salto; (*container*) cuba ♦ *vi* brincar; (*with rope*) saltar a la comba ♦ *vt* (*pass over*) omitir, saltar.

ski pants *npl* pantalones *mpl* de esquí.

ski pole *n* bastón *m* de esquiar.

skipper ['skɪpə*] *n* (*NAUT, SPORT*) capitán *m*.

skipping rope ['skɪpɪŋ-] *n* (*Brit*) cuerda (de saltar).

ski resort *n* estación *f* de esquí.

skirmish ['skɜːmɪʃ] *n* escaramuza.

skirt [skɜːt] *n* falda, pollera (*LAm*) ♦ *vt* (*surround*) ceñir, rodear; (*go round*) ladear.

skirting board ['skɜːtɪŋ-] *n* (*Brit*) rodapié *m*.

ski run *n* pista de esquí.

ski suit *n* traje *m* de esquiar.

skit [skɪt] *n* sátira, parodia.

ski tow *n* arrastre *m* (de esquí).

skittle ['skɪtl] *n* bolo; ~**s** (*game*) boliche *m*.

skive [skaɪv] *vi* (*Brit col*) gandulear.

skulk [skʌlk] *vi* esconderse.

skull [skʌl] *n* calavera; (*ANAT*) cráneo.

skullcap ['skʌlkæp] *n* (*worn by Jews*) casquete *m*; (*worn by Pope*) solideo.

skunk [skʌŋk] *n* mofeta.

sky [skaɪ] *n* cielo; **to praise sb to the skies** poner a uno por las nubes.

sky-blue [skaɪ'bluː] *a* (azul) celeste.

sky-high ['skaɪ'haɪ] *ad* (*throw*) muy alto; **prices have gone** ~ los precios están por las nubes.

skylark ['skaɪlɑːk] *n* (*bird*) alondra.

skylight ['skaɪlaɪt] *n* tragaluz *m*, claraboya.

skyline ['skaɪlaɪn] *n* (*horizon*) horizonte *m*; (*of city*) perfil *m*.

skyscraper ['skaɪskreɪpə*] *n* rascacielos *m inv*.

slab [slæb] *n* (*stone*) bloque *m*; (*of wood*) tabla, plancha; (*flat*) losa; (*of cake*) trozo; (*of meat, cheese*) tajada, trozo.

slack [slæk] *a* (*loose*) flojo; (*slow*) de poca actividad; (*careless*) descuidado; (*COMM: market*) poco activo; (: *demand*) débil; (*period*) bajo; **business is** ~ hay poco movimiento en el negocio.

slacken ['slækn] (*also:* ~ **off**) *vi* aflojarse ♦ *vt* aflojar; (*speed*) disminuir.

slackness ['slæknɪs] *n* flojedad *f*; negligencia.

slacks [slæks] *npl* pantalones *mpl*.

slag [slæg] *n* escoria, escombros *mpl*.

slag heap *n* escorial *m*, escombrera.

slain [sleɪn] *pp of* **slay**.

slake [sleɪk] *vt* (*one's thirst*) apagar.

slalom ['slɑːləm] *n* eslálom *m*.

slam [slæm] *vt* (*door*) cerrar de golpe; (*throw*) arrojar (violentamente); (*criticize*) vapulear, vituperar ♦ *vi* cerrarse de golpe.

slander ['slɑːndə*] *n* calumnia, difamación *f* ♦ *vt* calumniar, difamar.

slanderous ['slɑːndərəs] *a* calumnioso, difamatorio.

slang [slæŋ] *n* argot *m*; (*jargon*) jerga.

slant [slɑːnt] *n* sesgo, inclinación *f*; (*fig*) punto de vista; **to get a new** ~ **on sth** obtener un nuevo punto de vista sobre algo.

slanted ['slɑːntɪd], **slanting** ['slɑːntɪŋ] *a* inclinado.

slap [slæp] *n* palmada; (*in face*) bofetada ♦ *vt* dar una palmada/bofetada a ♦ *ad* (*directly*) exactamente, directamente.

slapdash ['slæpdæʃ] *a* descuidado.

slapstick ['slæpstɪk] *n*: ~ **comedy** comedia de golpe y porrazo.

slap-up ['slæpʌp] *a*: **a** ~ **meal** (*Brit*) un banquetazo, una comilona.

slash [slæʃ] *vt* acuchillar; (*fig: prices*) quemar.

slat [slæt] *n* (*of wood, plastic*) tablilla, listón *m*.

slate [sleɪt] *n* pizarra ♦ *vt* (*Brit: fig: criticize*) criticar duramente, dar una paliza a.

slaughter ['slɔːtə*] *n* (*of animals*) matanza; (*of people*) carnicería ♦ *vt* matar.

slaughterhouse ['slɔːtəhaus] *n* matadero.

Slav [slɑːv] *a* eslavo.

slave [sleɪv] *n* esclavo/a ♦ *vi* (*also:* ~ **away**) sudar tinta; **to** ~ (**away**) **at (doing)** **sth** sudar tinta en (hacer) algo.

slave labour, (*US*) **slave labor** *n* trabajo de esclavos.

slaver ['slævə*] *vi* (*dribble*) babear.

slavery ['sleɪvərɪ] *n* esclavitud *f*.

slavish ['sleɪvɪʃ] *a* (*devotion*) de esclavo; (*imitation*) servil.

slay, *pt* **slew**, *pp* **slain** [sleɪ, sluː, sleɪn] *vt* (*literary*) matar.

SLD *n abbr* (*Brit POL*) = *Social and Liberal Democrats.*

sleazy ['sliːzɪ] *a* (*fig: place*) de mala fama.

sledge [sledʒ], (*US*) **sled** [sled] *n* trineo.

sledgehammer ['sledʒhæmə*] *n* mazo.

sleek [sliːk] *a* (*shiny*) lustroso.

sleep [sliːp] *n* sueño ♦ *vb* (*pt, pp* **slept** [slept]) *vi* dormir ♦ *vt*: **we can** ~ **4** podemos alojar a 4, tenemos cabida para 4; **to go to** ~ quedarse dormido; **to have a good night's** ~ dormir toda la noche; **to put to** ~ (*patient*) dormir; (*animal: euphemism: kill*) sacrificar; **to** ~ **lightly** tener el

sueño ligero; **to ~ with sb** (*euphemism*) acostarse con uno.
sleep in *vi* (*oversleep*) dormir tarde.
sleeper ['sli:pə*] *n* (*person*) durmiente *m/f*; (*Brit RAIL: on track*) traviesa; (: *train*) coche-cama *m*.
sleepiness ['sli:pɪnɪs] *n* somnolencia.
sleeping bag ['sli:pɪŋ-] *n* saco de dormir.
sleeping car ['sli:pɪŋ-] *n* coche-cama *m*.
sleeping partner ['sli:pɪŋ-] *n* (*COMM*) socio/a comanditario/a.
sleeping pill ['sli:pɪŋ-] *n* somnífero.
sleepless ['sli:plɪs] *a*: **a ~ night** una noche en blanco.
sleeplessness ['sli:plɪsnɪs] *n* insomnio.
sleepwalker ['sli:pwɔ:kə*] *n* sonámbulo/a.
sleepy ['sli:pɪ] *a* soñoliento; **to be** *or* **feel ~** tener sueño.
sleet [sli:t] *n* nevisca.
sleeve [sli:v] *n* manga; (*TECH*) manguito; (*of record*) funda.
sleeveless ['sli:vlɪs] *a* (*garment*) sin mangas.
sleigh [sleɪ] *n* trineo.
sleight [slaɪt] *n*: **~ of hand** escamoteo.
slender ['slɛndə*] *a* delgado; (*means*) escaso.
slept [slɛpt] *pt, pp* of **sleep**.
sleuth [slu:θ] *n* (*col*) detective *m/f*.
slew [slu:] *vi* (*veer*) torcerse ♦ *pt* of **slay**.
slice [slaɪs] *n* (*of meat*) tajada; (*of bread*) rebanada; (*of lemon*) rodaja; (*utensil*) pala ♦ *vt* cortar, tajar; rebanar; **~d bread** pan *m* de molde.
slick [slɪk] *a* (*skilful*) hábil, diestro ♦ *n* (*also:* **oil ~**) capa de aceite.
slid [slɪd] *pt, pp* of **slide**.
slide [slaɪd] *n* (*in playground*) tobogán *m*; (*PHOT*) diapositiva; (*microscope* **~**) portaobjetos *m inv*, plaquilla de vidrio; (*Brit: also:* **hair ~**) pasador *m* ♦ (*vb: pt, pp* **slid** [slɪd]) *vt* correr, deslizar ♦ *vi* (*slip*) resbalarse; (*glide*) deslizarse; **to let things ~** (*fig*) dejar que ruede la bola.
slide projector *n* (*PHOT*) proyector *m* de diapositivas.
slide rule *n* regla de cálculo.
sliding ['slaɪdɪŋ] *a* (*door*) corredizo; **~ roof** (*AUT*) techo de corredera.
sliding scale *n* escala móvil.
slight [slaɪt] *a* (*slim*) delgado; (*frail*) delicado; (*pain etc*) leve; (*trifling*) insignificante; (*small*) pequeño ♦ *n* desaire *m* ♦ *vt* (*offend*) ofender, desairar; **a ~ improvement** una ligera mejora; **not in the ~est** en absoluto; **there's not the ~est possibility** no hay la menor *or* más mínima posibilidad.
slightly ['slaɪtlɪ] *ad* ligeramente, un poco; **~ built** delgado, fino.
slim [slɪm] *a* delgado, esbelto ♦ *vi* adelgazar.
slime [slaɪm] *n* limo, cieno.
slimness ['slɪmnɪs] *n* delgadez *f*.

slimy ['slaɪmɪ] *a* limoso; (*covered with mud*) fangoso; (*also fig: person*) adulón, zalamero.
slimming ['slɪmɪŋ] *n* adelgazamiento ♦ *a* (*diet, pills*) adelgazador(a), adelgazante.
sling [slɪŋ] *n* (*MED*) cabestrillo; (*weapon*) honda ♦ *vt* (*pt, pp* **slung** [slʌŋ]) tirar, arrojar; **to have one's arm in a ~** llevar el brazo en cabestrillo.
slink, pt, pp slunk [slɪŋk, slʌŋk] *vi*: **to ~ away, ~ off** escabullirse.
slip [slɪp] *n* (*slide*) resbalón *m*; (*mistake*) descuido; (*underskirt*) combinación *f*; (*of paper*) papelito ♦ *vt* (*slide*) deslizar ♦ *vi* (*slide*) deslizarse; (*stumble*) resbalar(se); (*decline*) decaer; (*move smoothly*): **to ~ into/out of** (*room etc*) introducirse en/salirse de; **to let a chance ~ by** escapársele la oportunidad; **to ~ sth on/off** ponerse/quitarse algo; **to ~ on a jumper** ponerse un jersey *or* un suéter; **it ~ped from her hand** se la cayó de la mano; **to give sb the ~** eludir a uno; **wages ~** (*Brit*) hoja de paga; **a ~ of the tongue** un lapsus.
slip away *vi* escabullirse.
slip in *vt* meter ♦ *vi* meterse.
slip out *vi* (*go out*) salir (un momento).
slip-on ['slɪpɔn] *a* de quitaipón; (*shoes*) sin cordones.
slipped disc [slɪpt-] *n* vértebra dislocada.
slipper ['slɪpə*] *n* zapatilla, pantufla.
slippery ['slɪpərɪ] *a* resbaladizo.
slip road *n* (*Brit*) carretera de acceso.
slipshod ['slɪpʃɔd] *a* descuidado.
slipstream ['slɪpstri:m] *n* viento de la hélice.
slip-up ['slɪpʌp] *n* (*error*) desliz *m*.
slipway ['slɪpweɪ] *n* grada, gradas *fpl*.
slit [slɪt] *n* raja; (*cut*) corte *m* ♦ *vt* (*pt, pp* **slit**) rajar, cortar; **to ~ sb's throat** cortarle el pescuezo a uno.
slither ['slɪðə*] *vi* deslizarse.
sliver ['slɪvə*] *n* (*of glass, wood*) astilla; (*of cheese, sausage*) lonja, loncha.
slob [slɔb] *n* (*col*) patán/ana *m/f*, palurdo/a.
slog [slɔg] (*Brit*) *vi* sudar tinta ♦ *n*: **it was a ~** costó trabajo (hacerlo).
slogan ['sləʊgən] *n* eslogan *m*, lema *m*.
slop [slɔp] *vi* (*also:* **~ over**) derramarse, desbordarse ♦ *vt* derramar, verter.
slope [sləʊp] *n* (*up*) cuesta, pendiente *f*; (*down*) declive *m*; (*side of mountain*) falda, vertiente *f* ♦ *vi*: **to ~ down** estar en declive; **to ~ up** inclinarse.
sloping ['sləʊpɪŋ] *a* en pendiente; en declive.
sloppily ['slɔpɪlɪ] *ad* descuidadamente; con descuido *or* desaliño.
sloppiness ['slɔpɪnɪs] *n* descuido; desaliño.
sloppy ['slɔpɪ] *a* (*work*) descuidado; (*appearance*) desaliñado.
slosh [slɔʃ] *vi*: **to ~ about** *or* **around** chapotear.

sloshed [slɔʃt] *a* (*col*: *drunk*): **to get ~** agarrar una trompa.

slot [slɔt] *n* ranura; (*fig*: *in timetable, RADIO, TV*) hueco ♦ *vt*: **to ~ into** encajar en.

sloth [sləuθ] *n* (*vice*) pereza; (*ZOOL*) oso perezoso.

slot machine *n* (*Brit*: *vending machine*) aparato vendedor, distribuidor *m* automático; (*for gambling*) máquina tragaperras.

slot meter *n* contador *m*.

slouch [slautʃ] *vi*: **to ~ about, ~ around** (*laze*) gandulear.

slovenly [ˈslʌvənlɪ] *a* (*dirty*) desaliñado, desaseado; (*careless*) descuidado.

slow [sləu] *a* lento; (*watch*): **to be ~** estar atrasado ♦ *ad* lentamente, despacio ♦ *vt, vi* (*also*: **~ down, ~ up**) retardar; **"~"** (*road sign*) "disminuir velocidad"; **at a ~ speed** a una velocidad lenta; **the ~ lane** el carril derecho; **business is ~** (*COMM*) hay poca actividad; **my watch is 20 minutes ~** mi reloj lleva 20 minutos de retraso; **bake for two hours in a ~ oven** cocer *or* asar 2 horas en el horno a fuego lento; **to be ~ to act/decide** tardar en obrar/decidir; **to go ~** (*driver*) conducir despacio; (*in industrial dispute*) trabajar a ritmo lento.

slow-acting [sləuˈæktɪŋ] *a* de efecto retardado.

slowdown [ˈsləudaun] *n* (*US*) huelga de manos caídas.

slowly [ˈsləulɪ] *ad* lentamente, despacio; **to drive ~** conducir despacio; **~ but surely** paso a paso.

slow motion *n*: **in ~** a cámara lenta.

slow-moving [ˈsləuˈmuːvɪŋ] *a* lento.

sludge [slʌdʒ] *n* lodo, fango.

slug [slʌg] *n* babosa; (*bullet*) posta.

sluggish [ˈslʌgɪʃ] *a* (*slow*) lento; (*lazy*) perezoso; (*business, market, sales*) inactivo, moroso.

sluggishly [ˈslʌgɪʃlɪ] *ad* lentamente.

sluggishness [ˈslʌgɪʃnɪs] *n* lentitud *f*.

sluice [sluːs] *n* (*gate*) esclusa; (*channel*) canal *m* ♦ *vt*: **to ~ down** *or* **out** regar.

slum [slʌm] *n* (*area*) barrio bajo, tugurios *mpl*; (*house*) casucha.

slumber [ˈslʌmbə*] *n* sueño.

slum clearance (programme) *n* (programa *m* de) deschabolización *f*.

slump [slʌmp] *n* (*economic*) depresión *f* ♦ *vi* hundirse; **the ~ in the price of copper** la baja repentina del precio del cobre; **he was ~ed over the wheel** se había desplomado encima del volante.

slung [slʌŋ] *pt, pp of* **sling**.

slunk [slʌŋk] *pt, pp of* **slink**.

slur [sləː*] *n* calumnia ♦ *vt* calumniar, difamar; (*word*) pronunciar indistintamente; **to cast a ~ on sb** manchar la reputación de uno, difamar a uno.

slurred [sləːd] *a* (*pronunciation*) mal articu-

lado, borroso.

slush [slʌʃ] *n* nieve *f* a medio derretir.

slush fund *n* fondos *mpl* para sobornar.

slushy [ˈslʌʃɪ] *a* (*col*: *poetry etc*) sentimentaloide.

slut [slʌt] *n* marrana.

sly [slaɪ] *a* (*clever*) astuto; (*nasty*) malicioso.

slyly [ˈslaɪlɪ] *ad* astutamente; taimadamente.

slyness [ˈslaɪnɪs] *n* astucia.

smack [smæk] *n* (*slap*) manotada; (*blow*) golpe *m* ♦ *vt* dar una manotada a; golpear con la mano ♦ *vi*: **to ~ of** saber a, oler a ♦ *ad*: **it fell ~ in the middle** (*col*) cayó justo en medio.

smacker [ˈsmækə*] *n* (*col*: *kiss*) beso sonoro; (: *Brit*: *pound note*) billete *m* de una libra; (: *US*: *dollar bill*) billete *m* de un dólar.

small [smɔːl] *a* pequeño; (*in height*) bajo, chaparro (*LAm*); (*letter*) en minúscula ♦ *n*: **~ of the back** región *f* lumbar; **~ shopkeeper** pequeño/a comerciante *m/f*; **to get** *or* **grow ~er** (*stain, town*) empequeñecer; (*debt, organization, numbers*) reducir, disminuir; **to make ~er** (*amount, income*) reducir; (*garden, object, garment*) achicar.

small ads *npl* (*Brit*) anuncios *mpl* por palabras.

small arms *npl* armas *fpl* cortas.

small change *n* suelto, cambio.

smallholder [ˈsmɔːlhəuldə*] *n* (*Brit*) granjero/a, parcelero/a.

smallholding [ˈsmɔːlhəuldɪŋ] *n* parcela, minifundio.

small hours *npl*: **in the ~** en las altas horas (de la noche).

smallish [ˈsmɔːlɪʃ] *a* más bien pequeño.

small-minded [smɔːlˈmaɪndɪd] *a* mezquino, de miras estrechas.

smallness [ˈsmɔːlnɪs] *n* pequeñez *f*.

smallpox [ˈsmɔːlpɔks] *n* viruela.

small print *n* letra pequeña *or* menuda.

small-scale [ˈsmɔːlskeɪl] *a* (*map, model*) en escala reducida; (*business, farming*) en pequeña escala.

small talk *n* cháchara.

small-time [ˈsmɔːltaɪm] *a* (*col*) de poca categoría *or* monta; **a ~ thief** un(a) ratero/a.

smarmy [ˈsmɑːmɪ] *a* (*Brit pej*) pelotillero (*fam*).

smart [smɑːt] *a* elegante; (*clever*) listo, inteligente; (*quick*) rápido, vivo ♦ *vi* escocer, picar; **the ~ set** la gente de buen tono; **to look ~** estar elegante; **my eyes are ~ing** me pican los ojos.

smarten up [ˈsmɑːtn-] *vi* arreglarse ♦ *vt* arreglar.

smartness [ˈsmɑːtnɪs] *n* elegancia; (*cleverness*) inteligencia.

smash [smæʃ] *n* (*also*: **~-up**) choque *m*; (*sound*) estrépito ♦ *vt* (*break*) hacer pedazos; (*car etc*) estrellar; (*SPORT*: *record*)

batir ♦ *vi* hacerse pedazos; (*against wall etc*) estrellarse.
smash up *vt* (*car*) hacer pedazos; (*room*) destrozar.
smash hit *n* exitazo.
smashing ['smæʃɪŋ] *a* (*col*) cojonudo.
smattering ['smætərɪŋ] *n*: **a ~ of Spanish** algo de español.
smear [smɪə*] *n* mancha; (*MED*) frotis *m inv* (cervical); (*insult*) calumnia ♦ *vt* untar; (*fig*) calumniar, difamar; **his hands were ~ed with oil/ink** tenía las manos manchadas de aceite/tinta.
smear campaign *n* campaña de calumnias.
smear test *n* (*MED*) citología, frotis *m inv* (cervical).
smell [smɛl] *n* olor *m*; (*sense*) olfato ♦ (*vb*: *pt*, *pp* **smelt** *or* **~ed** [smɛlt, smɛld]) *vt*, *vi* oler; **it ~s good/of garlic** huele bien/a ajo.
smelly ['smɛlɪ] *a* maloliente.
smelt [smɛlt] *vt* (*ore*) fundir ♦ *pt*, *pp of* **smell**.
smile [smaɪl] *n* sonrisa ♦ *vi* sonreír.
smiling ['smaɪlɪŋ] *a* sonriente, risueño.
smirk [smə:k] *n* sonrisa falsa *or* afectada.
smith [smɪθ] *n* herrero.
smithy ['smɪðɪ] *n* herrería.
smitten ['smɪtn] *a*: **he's really ~ with her** está totalmente loco por ella.
smock [smɔk] *n* blusa; (*children's*) delantal *m*; (*US*: *overall*) guardapolvo.
smog [smɔg] *n* esmog *m*.
smoke [sməuk] *n* humo ♦ *vi* fumar; (*chimney*) echar humo ♦ *vt* (*cigarettes*) fumar; **to go up in ~** (*house etc*) quemarse; (*fig*) irse todo en humo, fracasar; **do you ~?** ¿fumas?
smoked [sməukt] *a* (*bacon*, *glass*) ahumado.
smokeless fuel ['sməuklɪs-] *n* combustible *m* sin humo.
smokeless zone ['sməuklɪs-] *n* zona libre de humo.
smoker ['sməukə*] *n* (*person*) fumador(a) *m/f*; (*RAIL*) coche *m* fumador.
smoke screen *n* cortina de humo.
smoke shop *n* (*US*) estanco, tabaquería (*LAm*).
smoking ['sməukɪŋ] *n*: "**no ~**" "prohibido fumar"; **he's given up ~** ha dejado de fumar.
smoking compartment, (*US*) **smoking car** *n* departamento de fumadores.
smoky ['sməukɪ] *a* (*room*) lleno de humo.
smolder ['sməuldə*] *vi* (*US*) = **smoulder**.
smooth [smu:ð] *a* liso; (*sea*) tranquilo; (*flavour*, *movement*) suave; (*person*: *pej*) meloso ♦ *vt* alisar; (*also*: **~ out**) (*creases*, *difficulties*) allanar.
　smooth over *vt*: **to ~ things over** (*fig*) limar las asperezas.
smoothly ['smu:ðlɪ] *ad* (*easily*) fácilmente;

everything went ~ todo pasó sin novedad.
smoothness ['smu:ðnɪs] *n* (*of skin*, *cloth*) tersura; (*of surface*, *flavour*, *movement*) suavidad *f*.
smother ['smʌðə*] *vt* sofocar; (*repress*) contener.
smoulder, (*US*) **smolder** ['sməuldə*] *vi* arder sin llama.
smudge [smʌdʒ] *n* mancha ♦ *vt* manchar.
smug [smʌg] *a* presumido.
smuggle ['smʌgl] *vt* pasar de contrabando; **to ~ in/out** (*goods etc*) meter/sacar de contrabando.
smuggler ['smʌglə*] *n* contrabandista *m/f*.
smuggling ['smʌglɪŋ] *n* contrabando.
smugly ['smʌglɪ] *ad* con suficiencia.
smugness ['smʌgnɪs] *n* suficiencia.
smut [smʌt] *n* (*grain of soot*) carbonilla, hollín *m*; (*mark*) tizne *m*; (*in conversation etc*) obscenidades *fpl*.
smutty ['smʌtɪ] *a* (*fig*) verde, obsceno.
snack [snæk] *n* bocado; **to have a ~** probarse un bocado.
snack bar *n* cafetería.
snag [snæg] *n* problema *m*; **to run into** *or* **hit a ~** encontrar inconvenientes, dar con un obstáculo.
snail [sneɪl] *n* caracol *m*.
snake [sneɪk] *n* (*gen*) serpiente *f*; (*harmless*) culebra; (*poisonous*) víbora.
snap [snæp] *n* (*sound*) chasquido; golpe *m* seco; (*photograph*) foto *f* ♦ *a* (*decision*) instantáneo ♦ *vt* (*fingers etc*) castañetear; (*break*) quebrar; (*photograph*) tomar una foto de ♦ *vi* (*break*) quebrarse; (*fig*: *person*) contestar bruscamente; **to ~ (at sb)** (*subj*: *person*) hablar con brusquedad (a uno); (: *dog*) intentar morder (a uno); **to ~ shut** cerrarse de golpe; **to ~ one's fingers at sth/sb** (*fig*) burlarse de algo/uno; **a cold ~** (*of weather*) una ola de frío.
　snap off *vi* (*break*) partirse.
　snap up *vt* agarrar.
snap fastener *n* (*US*) botón *m* de presión.
snappy ['snæpɪ] *a* (*col*: *answer*) instantáneo; (*slogan*) conciso; **make it ~!** (*hurry up*) ¡date prisa!
snapshot ['snæpʃɔt] *n* foto *f* (instantánea).
snare [snɛə*] *n* trampa ♦ *vt* cazar con trampa; (*fig*) engañar.
snarl [snɑ:l] *n* gruñido ♦ *vi* gruñir; **to get ~ed up** (*wool*, *plans*) enmarañarse, enredarse; (*traffic*) quedar atascado.
snatch [snætʃ] *n* (*fig*) robo; **~es of** trocitos *mpl* de ♦ *vt* (~ *away*) arrebatar; (*grasp*) coger (*Sp*), agarrar; **~es of conversation** fragmentos *mpl* de conversación; **to ~ a sandwich** comer un bocadillo a prisa; **to ~ some sleep** buscar tiempo para dormir; **don't ~!** ¡no me lo quites!
　snatch up *vt* agarrar.
sneak [sni:k] *vi*: **to ~ in/out** entrar/salir a hurtadillas ♦ *vt*: **to ~ a look at sth** mirar

algo de reojo ◆ *n* (*fam*) soplón/ona *m/f*.

sneakers ['sni:kəz] *npl* (*US*) zapatos *mpl* de lona, zapatillas *fpl*.

sneaking ['sni:kɪŋ] *a*: **to have a ~ feeling/ suspicion that** ... tener la (horrible) sensación/sospecha de que ....

sneaky ['sni:kɪ] *a* furtivo.

sneer [snɪə*] *n* sonrisa de desprecio ◆ *vi* sonreír con desprecio; **to ~ at sth/sb** burlarse *or* mofarse de algo/uno.

sneeze [sni:z] *n* estornudo ◆ *vi* estornudar.

snide [snaɪd] *a* (*col*: *sarcastic*) sarcástico.

sniff [snɪf] *vi* sorber (por la nariz) ◆ *vt* husmear, oler; (*glue, drug*) esnifar.

sniff at *vt fus*: **it's not to be ~ed at** no es de despreciar.

snigger ['snɪgə*] *n* risa disimulada ◆ *vi* reírse con disimulo.

snip [snɪp] *n* (*piece*) recorte *m*; (*bargain*) ganga ◆ *vt* tijeretear.

sniper ['snaɪpə*] *n* francotirador(a) *m/f*.

snippet ['snɪpɪt] *n* retazo.

snivelling, (*US*) **sniveling** ['snɪvlɪŋ] *a* llorón/ona.

snob [snɔb] *n* (e)snob *m/f*.

snobbery ['snɔbərɪ] *n* (e)snobismo.

snobbish ['snɔbɪʃ] *a* (e)snob.

snobbishness ['snɔbɪʃnɪs] *n* (e)snobismo.

snooker ['snu:kə*] *n* especie de billar.

snoop [snu:p] *vi*: **to ~ about** fisgonear.

snooper ['snu:pə*] *n* fisgón/ona *m/f*.

snooty ['snu:tɪ] *a* (e)snob.

snooze [snu:z] *n* siesta ◆ *vi* echar una siesta.

snore [snɔ:*] *vi* roncar ◆ *n* ronquido.

snoring ['snɔ:rɪŋ] *n* ronquidos *mpl*.

snorkel ['snɔ:kl] *n* (tubo) respirador *m*.

snort [snɔ:t] *n* bufido ◆ *vi* bufar ◆ *vt* (*col*: *drugs*) esnifar.

snotty ['snɔtɪ] *a* (*col*) engreído.

snout [snaut] *n* hocico, morro.

snow [snəu] *n* nieve *f* ◆ *vi* nevar ◆ *vt*: **to be ~ed under with work** estar agobiado de trabajo.

snowball ['snəubɔ:l] *n* bola de nieve ◆ *vi* ir aumentándose.

snow-blind ['snəublaɪnd] *a* cegado por la nieve.

snowbound ['snəubaund] *a* bloqueado por la nieve.

snow-capped ['snəukæpt] *a* (*peak*) cubierto de nieve, nevado.

snowdrift ['snəudrɪft] *n* ventisquero.

snowdrop ['snəudrɔp] *n* campanilla.

snowfall ['snəufɔ:l] *n* nevada.

snowflake ['snəufleɪk] *n* copo de nieve.

snowline ['snəulaɪn] *n* límite de las nieves perpetuas.

snowman ['snəumæn] *n* figura de nieve.

snowplough ['snəuplau] (*US*) **snowplow** ['snəuplau] *n* quitanieves *m inv*.

snowshoe ['snəuʃu:] *n* raqueta (de nieve).

snowstorm ['snəustɔ:m] *n* nevada, nevasca.

Snow White *n* Blancanieves *f*.

snowy ['snəuɪ] *a* de (mucha) nieve.

SNP *n abbr* (*Brit POL*) = *Scottish National Party*.

snub [snʌb] *vt*: **to ~ sb** desairar a uno ◆ *n* desaire *m*, repulsa.

snub-nosed [snʌb'nəuzd] *a* chato.

snuff [snʌf] *n* rapé *m* ◆ *vt* (*also*: **~ out**: *candle*) apagar.

snuffbox ['snʌfbɔks] *n* caja de rapé.

snug [snʌg] *a* (*cosy*) cómodo; (*fitted*) ajustado.

snuggle ['snʌgl] *vi*: **to ~ down in bed** hacerse un ovillo en la cama; **to ~ up to sb** arrimarse *or* abrazarse a uno.

snugly ['snʌglɪ] *ad* cómodamente; **it fits ~** (*object in pocket etc*) cabe perfectamente; (*garment*) ajusta perfectamente.

SO *abbr* (*BANKING*) = **standing order**.

so [səu] *ad* (*degree*) tan; (*manner: thus*) así, de este modo ◆ *conj* así que, por tanto; **~ that** (*purpose*) para que, a fin de que; (*result*) de modo que; **~ do I** yo también; **if ~** de ser así, si es así; **I hope ~** espero que sí; **10 or ~** 10 más o menos; **~ far** hasta aquí; **~ quickly** (*early*) tan pronto; (*fast*) tan rápidamente; **quite ~!** ¡así es!, ¡exacto!; **even ~** sin embargo; **~ to speak** por decirlo así, es un decir; **~ it is!**, **~ it does!** ¡es verdad!, ¡es cierto!; **~ long!** ¡hasta luego!; **~ many** tantos/as; **~ much** *a*, *ad* tanto; **she didn't ~ much as send me a birthday card** no me mandó ni una tarjeta siquiera por mi cumpleaños; **~ that's the reason!** ¡así que es por eso *or* por eso es!; **~ (what)?** (*col*) ¿y (qué)?

soak [səuk] *vt* (*drench*) empapar; (*put in water*) remojar ◆ *vi* remojarse, estar a remojo.

soak in *vi* penetrar.

soak up *vt* absorber.

soaking ['səukɪŋ] *a* (*also*: **~ wet**) calado *or* empapado (hasta los huesos *or* el tuétano).

so-and-so ['səuənsəu] *n* (*somebody*) fulano/a de tal.

soap [səup] *n* jabón *m*.

soapflakes ['səupfleɪks] *npl* jabón *msg* en escamas.

soap opera *n* (*TV*) telenovela; (*RADIO*) radionovela.

soap powder *n* jabón en polvo.

soapsuds ['səupsʌdz] *npl* espuma *sg*.

soapy ['səupɪ] *a* jabonoso.

soar [sɔ:*] *vi* (*on wings*) remontarse; (*building etc*) elevarse; (*price*) subir vertiginosamente; (*morale*) renacer.

soaring ['sɔ:rɪŋ] *a* (*flight*) planeador(a), que vuela; (*prices*) en alza *or* aumento; **~ inflation** inflación *f* altísima *or* en aumento.

sob [sɔb] *n* sollozo ◆ *vi* sollozar.

s.o.b. *n abbr* (*US col!* = *son of a bitch*) hijo de puta (*!*).

sober ['səubə*] a (moderate) moderado; (not drunk) sobrio; (colour, style) discreto.
sober up vi pasársele a uno la borrachera.
soberly ['səubəlı] ad sobriamente.
sobriety [sə'braiəti] n (not being drunk) sobriedad f; (seriousness, sedateness) seriedad f, sensatez f.
Soc. abbr (= society) S.
so-called ['səu'kɔːld] a presunto, supuesto.
soccer ['sɔkə*] n fútbol m.
soccer pitch n campo or cancha (LAm) de fútbol.
soccer player n jugador(a) m/f de fútbol.
sociability [səuʃə'bılıtı] n sociabilidad f.
sociable ['səuʃəbl] a sociable.
social ['səuʃl] a social ♦ n velada, fiesta.
social class n clase f social.
social climber n arribista m/f.
social club n club m.
Social Democrat n socialdemócrata m/f.
social insurance n (US) seguro social.
socialism ['səuʃəlızəm] n socialismo.
socialist ['səuʃəlıst] a, n socialista m/f.
socialite ['səuʃəlaıt] n vividor(a) m/f.
socialize ['səuʃəlaız] vi hacer vida social; **to ~ with** (colleagues) salir con.
socially ['səuʃəlı] ad socialmente.
social science(s) n ciencias fpl sociales.
social security n seguridad f social.
social welfare n asistencia social.
social work n asistencia social.
social worker n asistente/a m/f social.
socio-economic ['səusıəui:kə'nɔmık] a socioeconómico.
society [sə'saıətı] n sociedad f; (club) asociación f; (also: **high ~**) buena sociedad ♦ cpd (party, column) social, de sociedad.
sociological [səusıə'lɔdʒıkəl] a sociológico.
sociologist [səusı'ɔlədʒıst] n sociólogo/a.
sociology [səusı'ɔlədʒı] n sociología.
sock [sɔk] n calcetín m, media (LAm); **to pull one's ~s up** (fig) hacer esfuerzos, despabilarse.
socket ['sɔkıt] n (ELEC) enchufe m.
sod [sɔd] n (of earth) césped m; (col!) cabrón/ona m/f (!).
soda ['səudə] n (CHEM) sosa; (also: **~ water**) soda; (US: also: **~ pop**) gaseosa.
sodden ['sɔdn] a empapado.
sodium ['səudıəm] n sodio.
sodium chloride n cloruro sódico or de sodio.
sofa ['səufə] n sofá m.
Sofia ['səufıə] n Sofía.
soft [sɔft] a (teacher, parent) blando; (gentle, not loud) suave; (stupid) bobo; **~ currency** divisa blanda or débil.
soft-boiled ['sɔftbɔıld] a (egg) pasado (por agua).
soft copy n (COMPUT) copia transitoria.
soft drink n bebida no alcohólica.
soft drugs npl drogas fpl blandas.

soften ['sɔfn] vt ablandar; suavizar ♦ vi ablandarse; suavizarse.
softener ['sɔfnə*] n suavizador m.
soft fruit n frutas fpl blandas.
soft furnishings npl textiles mpl.
soft-hearted [sɔft'hɑːtıd] a bondadoso.
softly ['sɔftlı] ad suavemente; (gently) delicadamente, con delicadeza.
softness ['sɔftnıs] n blandura; suavidad f.
soft sell n venta suave.
soft toy n juguete m de peluche.
software ['sɔftwɛə*] n (COMPUT) software m.
soft water n agua blanda.
SOGAT ['səugæt] n abbr (Brit: = Society of Graphical and Allied Trades) sindicato de tipógrafos.
soggy ['sɔgı] a empapado.
soil [sɔıl] n (earth) tierra, suelo ♦ vt ensuciar.
soiled [sɔıld] a sucio, manchado.
sojourn ['sɔdʒɔːn] n (formal) estancia.
solace ['sɔlıs] n consuelo.
solar ['səulə*] a solar.
solarium, pl **solaria** [sə'lɛərıəm, -rıə] n solario.
solar plexus [-'plɛksəs] n (ANAT) plexo solar.
solar system n sistema m solar.
sold [səuld] pt, pp of **sell**.
solder ['səuldə*] vt soldar ♦ n soldadura.
soldier ['səuldʒə*] n (gen) soldado; (army man) militar m ♦ vi: **to ~ on** seguir adelante; **toy ~** soldadito de plomo.
sold out a (COMM) agotado.
sole [səul] n (of foot) planta; (of shoe) suela; (fish: pl inv) lenguado ♦ a único; **the ~ reason** la única razón.
solely ['səullı] ad únicamente, sólo, solamente; **I will hold you ~ responsible** le daré toda la responsabilidad.
solemn ['sɔləm] a solemne.
sole trader n (COMM) comerciante m/f exclusivo/a.
solicit [sə'lısıt] vt (request) solicitar ♦ vi (prostitute) abordar, importunar.
solicitor [sə'lısıtə*] n (Brit: for wills etc) notario/a; (: in court) abogado/a.
solid ['sɔlıd] a sólido; (gold etc) macizo; (line) continuo; (vote) unánime ♦ n sólido; **we waited 2 ~ hours** esperamos 2 horas enteras; **to be on ~ ground** estar en tierra firme; (fig) estar seguro.
solidarity [sɔlı'dærıtı] n solidaridad f.
solidify [sə'lıdıfaı] vi solidificarse.
solidity [sə'lıdıtı] n solidez f.
solidly ['sɔlıdlı] ad sólidamente; (fig) unánimemente.
solid-state ['sɔlıdsteıt] a (ELEC) estado sólido.
soliloquy [sə'lıləkwı] n soliloquio.
solitaire [sɔlı'tɛə*] n (game, gem) solitario.
solitary ['sɔlıtərı] a solitario, solo; (iso-

lated) apartado, aislado; (*only*) único.
solitary confinement *n* incomunicación
f; **to be in ~** estar incomunicado.
solitude ['sɔlɪtjuːd] *n* soledad *f*.
solo ['səuləu] *n* solo.
soloist ['səuləuɪst] *n* solista *m/f*.
Solomon Islands ['sɔləmən-] *npl*: **the ~**
las Islas Salomón.
solstice ['sɔlstɪs] *n* solsticio.
soluble ['sɔljubl] *a* soluble.
solution [sə'luːʃən] *n* solución *f*.
solve [sɔlv] *vt* resolver, solucionar.
solvency ['sɔlvənsɪ] *n* (*COMM*) solvencia.
solvent ['sɔlvənt] *a* (*COMM*) solvente ◆ *n*
(*CHEM*) solvente *m*.
solvent abuse *n* abuso de los solventes.
Som. *abbr* (*Brit*) = *Somerset*.
Somali [sə'mɑːlɪ] *a*, *n* somalí *m/f*.
Somalia [sə'mɑːlɪə] *n* Somalia.
sombre, (*US*) **somber** ['sɔmbə*] *a* sombrío.
some [sʌm] *a* (*a few*) algunos/as; (*certain*)
algún/una; (*a certain number or amount*)
see phrases below; (*unspecified*) algo de ◆
pron algunos/as; (*a bit*) algo ◆ *ad*: **~ 10
people** unas 10 personas; **~ children came**
vinieron algunos niños; **~ people say that
...** hay quien dice que ...; **have ~ tea** tome
té; **there's ~ milk in the fridge** hay leche
en la nevera (*Sp*) *or* el frigo; **~ (of it) was
left** quedaba algo; **could I have ~ of that
cheese?** ¿me sirve un poco del queso
aquel?; **I've got ~** (*books etc*) tengo algunos; (*milk, money etc*) tengo algo *or* un
poco; **would you like ~?** ¿quieres algunos
(*or* un poco)?; **after ~ time** pasado algún
tiempo; **at ~ length** con mucho detalle; **in
~ form or other** en alguna que otra manera.
somebody ['sʌmbədɪ] *pron* alguien; **~ or
other** alguien.
someday ['sʌmdeɪ] *ad* algún día.
somehow ['sʌmhau] *ad* de alguna manera;
(*for some reason*) por una u otra razón.
someone ['sʌmwʌn] *pron* = **somebody**.
someplace ['sʌmpleɪs] *ad* (*US*) = **somewhere**.
somersault ['sʌməsɔːlt] *n* (*deliberate*) salto
mortal; (*accidental*) vuelco ◆ *vi* dar un
salto mortal; dar vuelcos.
something ['sʌmθɪŋ] *pron* algo ◆ *ad*: **he's
~ like me** es un poco como yo; **~ to do**
algo que hacer; **it's ~ of a problem** es bastante problemático.
sometime ['sʌmtaɪm] *ad* (*in future*) algún
día, en algún momento; **~ last month** durante el mes pasado; **I'll finish it ~** lo
terminaré un día de éstos.
sometimes ['sʌmtaɪmz] *ad* a veces.
somewhat ['sʌmwɔt] *ad* algo.
somewhere ['sʌmweə*] *ad* (*be*) en alguna
parte; (*go*) a alguna parte; **~ else** (*be*) en
otra parte; (*go*) a otra parte.

son [sʌn] *n* hijo.
sonar ['səunɑː*] *n* sonar *m*.
sonata [sə'nɑːtə] *n* sonata.
song [sɔŋ] *n* canción *f*.
songwriter ['sɔŋraɪtə*] *n* compositor(a) *m/f*
de canciones.
sonic ['sɔnɪk] *a* (*boom*) sónico.
son-in-law ['sʌnɪnlɔː] *n* yerno.
sonnet ['sɔnɪt] *n* soneto.
sonny ['sʌnɪ] *n* (*col*) hijo.
soon [suːn] *ad* pronto, dentro de poco; **~
afterwards** poco después; **very/quite ~**
muy/bastante pronto; **how ~ can you be
ready?** ¿cuánto tardas en prepararte?; **it's
too ~ to tell** es demasiado pronto para saber; **see you ~!** ¡hasta pronto!; *see also*
as.
sooner ['suːnə*] *ad* (*time*) antes, más temprano; **I would ~ do that** preferiría hacer
eso; **~ or later** tarde o temprano; **no ~
said than done** dicho y hecho; **the ~ the
better** cuanto antes mejor; **no ~ had we
left than ...** apenas nos habíamos marchado
cuando ....
soot [sut] *n* hollín *m*.
soothe [suːð] *vt* tranquilizar; (*pain*) aliviar.
soothing ['suːðɪŋ] *a* (*ointment etc*) sedante; (*tone, words etc*) calmante, tranquilizante.
SOP *n* *abbr* = *standard operating
procedure*.
sophisticated [sə'fɪstɪkeɪtɪd] *a* sofisticado.
sophistication [səfɪstɪ'keɪʃən] *n* sofisticación *f*.
sophomore ['sɔfəmɔː*] *n* (*US*) estudiante
m/f de segundo año.
soporific [sɔpə'rɪfɪk] *a* soporífero.
sopping ['sɔpɪŋ] *a*: **~ (wet)** empapado.
soppy ['sɔpɪ] *a* (*pej*) bobo, tonto.
soprano [sə'prɑːnəu] *n* soprano *f*.
sorbet ['sɔːbeɪ] *n* sorbete *m*.
sorcerer ['sɔːsərə*] *n* hechicero.
sordid ['sɔːdɪd] *a* (*place etc*) sórdido;
(*motive etc*) mezquino.
sore [sɔː*] *a* (*painful*) doloroso, que duele;
(*offended*) resentido ◆ *n* llaga; **~ throat**
dolor *m* de garganta; **my eyes are ~, I
have ~ eyes** me duelen los ojos; **it's a ~
point** es un asunto delicado *or* espinoso.
sorely *ad*: **I am ~ tempted to (do it)** estoy
muy tentado a (hacerlo).
soreness ['sɔːnɪs] *n* dolor *m*.
sorrel ['sɔrəl] *n* (*BOT*) acedera.
sorrow ['sɔrəu] *n* pena, dolor *m*.
sorrowful ['sɔrəuful] *a* afligido, triste.
sorrowfully ['sɔrəufulɪ] *ad* tristemente.
sorry ['sɔrɪ] *a* (*regretful*) arrepentido;
(*condition, excuse*) lastimoso; (*sight, failure*) triste; **~!** ¡perdón!, ¡perdone!; **to
feel ~ for sb** tener lástima a uno; **I feel ~
for him** me da lástima; **I'm ~ to hear that
...** me da pena *or* tristeza saber que ...; **to
be ~ about sth** lamentar algo.

sort [sɔːt] n clase f, género, tipo; (make: of coffee, car etc) marca ♦ vt (also: ~ out: papers) clasificar; (: problems) arreglar, solucionar; (COMPUT) clasificar; **what ~ do you want?** (make) ¿qué marca quieres?; **what ~ of car?** ¿qué tipo de coche?; **I shall do nothing of the ~** no haré eso bajo ningún concepto; **it's ~ of awkward** (col) es bastante difícil.

sortie ['sɔːtɪ] n salida.

sorting office ['sɔːtɪŋ-] n sala de batalla.

SOS n SOS m.

so-so ['səusəu] ad regular, así así.

soufflé ['suːfleɪ] n suflé m.

sought [sɔːt] pt, pp of **seek**.

sought-after ['sɔːtɑːftə*] a solicitado, codiciado.

soul [səul] n alma f; **God rest his ~** Dios le reciba en su seno or en su gloria; **I didn't see a ~** no vi a nadie; **the poor ~ had nowhere to sleep** el pobre no tenía dónde dormir.

soul-destroying ['səuldɪstrɔɪɪŋ] a (work) deprimente.

soulful ['səulful] a lleno de sentimiento.

soulmate ['səulmeɪt] n compañero/a del alma.

soul-searching ['səulsɜːtʃɪŋ] n: **after much ~** después de pensarlo mucho, después de darle muchas vueltas.

sound [saund] a (healthy) sano; (safe, not damaged) en buen estado; (valid: argument, policy, claim) válido; (: move) acertado; (dependable: person) de fiar; (sensible) sensato, razonable ♦ ad: **~ asleep** profundamente dormido ♦ n (noise) sonido, ruido; (GEO) estrecho ♦ vt (alarm) sonar; (also: ~ out: opinions) consultar, sondear ♦ vi sonar, resonar; (fig: seem) parecer; **to ~ like** sonar a; **to be of ~ mind** estar en su cabal juicio; **I don't like the ~ of it** no me gusta nada; **it ~s as if** ... parece que ....

sound off vi (col): **to ~ off (about)** (give one's opinions) despotricar (contra).

sound barrier n barrera del sonido.

sound effects npl efectos mpl sonoros.

sound engineer n ingeniero/a del sonido.

sounding ['saundɪŋ] n (NAUT etc) sondeo.

sounding board n (MUS) tablero sonoro; (fig) piedra de toque.

soundly ['saundlɪ] ad (sleep) profundamente; (beat) completamente.

soundproof ['saundpruːf] a insonorizado.

soundtrack ['saundtræk] n (of film) banda sonora.

sound wave n (PHYSICS) onda sonora.

soup [suːp] n (thick) sopa; (thin) caldo; **in the ~** (fig) en apuros.

soup kitchen n comedor m de beneficencia.

soup plate n plato sopero.

soupspoon ['suːpspuːn] n cuchara sopera.

sour ['sauə*] a agrio; (milk) cortado; **it's just ~ grapes!** (fig) ¡están verdes!; **to go or turn ~** (milk) cortarse; (wine) agriarse; (fig: relationship, plans) agriarse.

source [sɔːs] n fuente f; **I have it from a reliable ~ that** ... sé de fuente fidedigna que ....

source language n (COMPUT) lenguage m original.

south [sauθ] n sur m ♦ a del sur ♦ ad al sur, hacia el sur; **(to the) ~ of** al sur de; **the S~ of France** el Sur de Francia; **to travel ~** viajar hacia el sur.

South Africa n África del Sur.

South African a, n sudafricano/a m/f.

South America n América del Sur, Sudamérica.

South American a, n sudamericano/a m/f.

southbound ['sauθbaund] a (con) rumbo al sur.

south-east [sauθ'iːst] n sudeste m ♦ a (counties etc) (del) sudeste.

Southeast Asia n Sudeste m asiático.

southerly ['sʌðəlɪ] a sur; (from the south) del sur.

southern ['sʌðən] a del sur, meridional; **the ~ hemisphere** el hemisferio sur.

South Korea n Corea del Sur.

South Pole n Polo Sur.

South Sea Islands npl: **the ~** Oceania.

South Seas npl: **the ~** los Mares del Sur.

southward(s) ['sauθwəd(z)] ad hacia el sur.

south-west [sauθ'west] n suroeste m.

souvenir [suːvə'nɪə*] n recuerdo.

sovereign ['sɔvrɪn] a, n soberano/a m/f.

sovereignty ['sɔvrɪntɪ] n soberanía.

soviet ['səuvɪət] a soviético.

Soviet Union n: **the ~** la Unión Soviética.

sow [sau] n cerda, puerca ♦ vt [səu] (pt ~ed, pp ~n [səun]) (gen) sembrar; (spread) esparcir.

soya ['sɔɪə], (US) **soy** [sɔɪ] n soja.

soy(a) bean n semilla de soja.

soy(a) sauce n salsa de soja.

spa [spɑː] n balneario.

space [speɪs] n espacio; (room) sitio ♦ vt (also: ~ out) espaciar; **to clear a ~ for sth** hacer sitio para algo; **in a confined ~** en un espacio restringido; **in a short ~ of time** en poco or un corto espacio de tiempo; **(with)in the ~ of an hour/three generations** en el espacio de una hora/tres generaciones.

space bar n (on typewriter) barra espaciadora.

spacecraft ['speɪskrɑːft] n nave f espacial, astronave f.

spaceman ['speɪsmæn] n astronauta m, cosmonauta m.

spaceship ['speɪsʃɪp] n = **spacecraft**.

space shuttle n transportador m espacial.

spacesuit ['speɪssuːt] n traje m espacial.
spacewoman ['speɪswumən] n astronauta, cosmonauta.
spacing ['speɪsɪŋ] n espaciamiento.
spacious ['speɪʃəs] a amplio.
spade [speɪd] n (tool) pala, laya; ~s npl (CARDS: British) picos mpl; (: Spanish) espadas fpl.
spadework ['speɪdwəːk] n (fig) trabajo preliminar.
spaghetti [spə'getɪ] n espaguetis mpl, fideos mpl.
Spain [speɪn] n España.
span [spæn] pt of **spin** ♦ n (of bird, plane) envergadura; (of hand) palmo; (of arch) luz f; (in time) lapso ♦ vt extenderse sobre, cruzar; (fig) abarcar.
Spaniard ['spænjəd] n español(a) m/f.
spaniel ['spænjəl] n perro de aguas.
Spanish ['spænɪʃ] a español(a) ♦ n (LING) español m, castellano; **the** ~ npl (people) los españoles; ~ **omelette** tortilla española.
spank [spæŋk] vt zurrar.
spanner ['spænə*] n (Brit) llave f (inglesa).
spar [spɑː*] n palo, verga ♦ vi (BOXING) entrenarse (en el boxeo).
spare [speə*] a de reserva; (surplus) sobrante, de más ♦ n (part) pieza de repuesto ♦ vt (do without) pasarse sin; (afford to give) tener de sobra; (refrain from hurting) perdonar; (details etc) ahorrar; **to** ~ (surplus) sobrante, de sobra; **there are 2 going** ~ sobran or quedan 2; **to** ~ **no expense** no escatimar gastos; **can you** ~ **(me) £10?** ¿puedes prestarme or darme 10 libras?; **can you** ~ **the time?** ¿tienes tiempo?; **I've a few minutes to** ~ tengo unos minutos libres; **there is no time to** ~ no hay tiempo que perder.
spare part n pieza de repuesto.
spare room n cuarto para visitas.
spare time n ratos mpl de ocio, tiempo libre.
spare tyre, (US) **spare tire** n (AUT) neumático or llanta (LAm) de recambio.
spare wheel n (AUT) rueda de recambio.
sparing ['speərɪŋ] a: **to be** ~ **with** ser parco en.
sparingly ['speərɪŋlɪ] ad escasamente.
spark [spɑːk] n chispa; (fig) chispazo.
spark(ing) plug ['spɑːk(ɪŋ)-] n bujía.
sparkle ['spɑːkl] n centelleo, destello ♦ vi centellear; (shine) relucir, brillar.
sparkling ['spɑːklɪŋ] a centelleante; (wine) espumoso.
sparrow ['spærəu] n gorrión m.
sparse [spɑːs] a esparcido, escaso.
sparsely ['spɑːslɪ] ad escasamente; **a** ~ **furnished room** un cuarto con pocos muebles.
spartan ['spɑːtən] a (fig) espartano.
spasm ['spæzəm] n (MED) espasmo; (fig) arranque m, ataque m.

spasmodic [spæz'mɔdɪk] a espasmódico.
spastic ['spæstɪk] n espástico/a.
spat [spæt] pt, pp of **spit** ♦ n (US) riña.
spate [speɪt] n (fig): ~ **of** torrente m de; **in** ~ (river) crecido.
spatial ['speɪʃl] a espacial.
spatter ['spætə*] vt: **to** ~ **with** salpicar de.
spatula ['spætjulə] n espátula.
spawn [spɔːn] vt (pej) engendrar ♦ vi desovar, frezar ♦ n huevas fpl.
SPCA n abbr (US) = Society for the Prevention of Cruelty to Animals.
SPCC n abbr (US) = Society for the Prevention of Cruelty to Children.
speak, pt **spoke**, pp **spoken** [spiːk, spəuk, 'spəukn] vt (language) hablar; (truth) decir ♦ vi hablar; (make a speech) intervenir; **to** ~ **one's mind** hablar claro or con franqueza; **to** ~ **to sb/of** or **about sth** hablar con uno/de or sobre algo; **to** ~ **at a conference/in a debate** hablar en un congreso/un debate; **he has no money to** ~ **of** no tiene mucho dinero que digamos; ~**ing!** ¡al habla!; ~ **up!** ¡habla más alto!
speak for vt fus: **to** ~ **for sb** hablar por or en nombre de uno; **that picture is already spoken for** (in shop) ese cuadro está reservado.
speaker ['spiːkə*] n (in public) orador(a) m/f; (also: **loud**~) altavoz m; (for stereo etc) bafle m; (POL): **the S**~ (Brit) el Presidente de la Cámara de los Comunes; (US) el Presidente del Congreso; **are you a Welsh** ~? ¿habla Ud galés?
speaking ['spiːkɪŋ] a hablante.
-speaking ['spiːkɪŋ] suff -hablante; **Spanish**~ **people** los hispanoparlantes.
spear [spɪə*] n lanza; (for fishing) arpón m ♦ vt alancear; arponear.
spearhead ['spɪəhed] vt (attack etc) encabezar ♦ n (MIL) punta de lanza; (fig) vanguardia.
spearmint ['spɪəmɪnt] n (BOT etc) menta verde.
spec [spek] n (col): **on** ~ como especulación; **to buy on** ~ comprar como especulación.
special ['speʃl] a especial; (edition etc) extraordinario; (delivery) urgente ♦ n (train) tren m especial; **nothing** ~ nada de particular, nada extraordinario.
special agent n agente m/f especial.
special correspondent n corresponsal m/f especial.
special delivery n (POST): **by** ~ por entrega urgente.
specialist ['speʃəlɪst] n especialista m/f; **a heart** ~ (MED) un(a) especialista del corazón.
speciality [speʃɪ'ælɪtɪ], (US) **specialty** ['speʃəltɪ] n especialidad f.
specialize ['speʃəlaɪz] vi: **to** ~ **(in)** especializarse en.

specially ['speʃlı] *ad* sobre todo, en particular.

special offer *n* (*COMM*) oferta especial, ganga.

special train *n* tren *m* especial.

specialty ['speʃəltı] *n* (*US*) = **speciality**.

species ['spiːʃiːz] *n* especie *f*.

specific [spə'sıfık] *a* específico.

specifically [spə'sıfıklı] *ad* (*explicitly*: *state*, *warn*) específicamente, expresamente; (*especially*: *design*, *intend*) especialmente.

specification [spesıfı'keıʃən] *n* especificación *f*; ~**s** *npl* (*plan*) presupuesto *sg*; (*of car*, *machine*) especificación *fsg*; (*for building*) plan *msg* detallado.

specify ['spesıfaı] *vt*, *vi* especificar, precisar; **unless otherwise specified** salvo indicaciones contrarias.

specimen ['spesımən] *n* ejemplar *m*; (*MED*: *of urine*) espécimen *m*; (*: of blood*) muestra.

specimen copy *n* ejemplar *m* de muestra.

specimen signature *n* muestra de firma.

speck [spek] *n* grano, mota.

speckled ['spekld] *a* moteado.

specs [speks] *npl* (*col*) gafas *fpl* (*Sp*), anteojos *mpl*.

spectacle ['spektəkl] *n* espectáculo.

spectacle case *n* estuche *m* (de gafas).

spectacles ['spektəklz] *npl* (*Brit*) gafas *fpl* (*Sp*), anteojos *mpl*.

spectacular [spek'tækjuˠlə*] *a* espectacular; (*success*) impresionante.

spectator [spek'teıtə*] *n* espectador(a) *m/f*.

spectra ['spektrə] *npl* of **spectrum**.

spectre, (*US*) **specter** ['spektə*] *n* espectro, fantasma *m*.

spectrum, *pl* **spectra** ['spektrəm, -trə] *n* espectro.

speculate ['spekjuleıt] *vi* especular; (*try to guess*): **to ~ about** especular sobre.

speculation [spekju'leıʃən] *n* especulación *f*.

speculative ['spekjuˠlətıv] *a* especulativo.

speculator ['spekjuleıtə*] *n* especulador(a) *m/f*.

sped [sped] *pt*, *pp of* **speed**.

speech [spiːtʃ] *n* (*faculty*) habla; (*formal talk*) discurso; (*words*) palabras *fpl*; (*manner of speaking*) forma de hablar; (*language*) idioma *m*, lenguaje *m*.

speech day *n* (*Brit SCOL*) ≈ reparto de premios.

speech impediment *n* defecto del habla.

speechless ['spiːtʃlıs] *a* mudo, estupefacto.

speech therapy *n* logopedia.

speed [spiːd] *n* (*also: AUT, TECH: gear*) velocidad *f*; (*haste*) prisa; (*promptness*) rapidez *f* ◆ *vi* (*pt*, *pp* **sped** [sped]) (*AUT*: *exceed ~ limit*) conducir con exceso de velocidad; **at full** *or* **top ~** a máxima veloci-

dad; **at a ~ of 70 km/h** a una velocidad de 70 km por hora; **at ~** a gran velocidad; **a five-~ gearbox** una caja de cambios de 5 velocidades; **shorthand/typing ~** rapidez *f* en taquigrafía/mecanografía; **the years sped by** los años volando pasaron.

speed up *vi* acelerarse ◆ *vt* acelerar.

speedboat ['spiːdbəut] *n* lancha motora.

speedily ['spiːdılı] *ad* rápido, rápidamente.

speeding ['spiːdıŋ] *n* (*AUT*) exceso de velocidad.

speed limit *n* límite *m* de velocidad, velocidad *f* máxima.

speedometer [spı'dɔmıtə*] *n* velocímetro.

speed trap *n* (*AUT*) control *m* de velocidades.

speedway ['spiːdweı] *n* (*SPORT*) pista de carrera.

speedy ['spiːdı] *a* (*fast*) veloz, rápido; (*prompt*) pronto.

spell [spel] *n* (*also*: **magic ~**) encanto, hechizo; (*period of time*) rato, período; (*turn*) turno ◆ *vt* (*pt*, *pp* **spelt** *or* **~ed** [spelt, speld]) (*also*: **~ out**) deletrear; (*fig*) anunciar, presagiar; **to cast a ~ on sb** hechizar a uno; **he can't ~** no sabe escribir bien, sabe poco de ortografía; **can you ~ it for me?** ¿cómo se deletrea *or* se escribe?; **how do you ~ your name?** ¿cómo se escribe tu nombre?

spellbound ['spelbaund] *a* embelesado, hechizado.

spelling ['spelıŋ] *n* ortografía.

spelling mistake *n* falta de ortografía.

spelt [spelt] *pt*, *pp of* **spell**.

spend, *pt*, *pp* **spent** [spend, spent] *vt* (*money*) gastar; (*time*) pasar; (*life*) dedicar; **to ~ time/money/effort on sth** gastar tiempo/dinero/energías en algo.

spending ['spendıŋ] *n*: **government ~** gastos *mpl* del gobierno.

spending money *n* dinero para gastos.

spending power *n* poder *m* de compra *or* adquisitivo.

spendthrift ['spendθrıft] *n* derrochador(a) *m/f*, pródigo/a.

spent [spent] *pt*, *pp of* **spend** ◆ *a* (*cartridge*, *bullets*, *match*) usado.

sperm [spəːm] *n* esperma.

sperm whale *n* cachalote *m*.

spew [spjuː] *vt* vomitar, arrojar.

sphere [sfıə*] *n* esfera.

spherical ['sferıkl] *a* esférico.

sphinx [sfıŋks] *n* esfinge *f*.

spice [spaıs] *n* especia ◆ *vt* especiar.

spiciness ['spaısınıs] *n* el picante.

spicy ['spaısı] *a* picante.

spick-and-span ['spıkən'spæn] *a* aseado, (bien) arreglado.

spider ['spaıdə*] *n* araña.

spider's web *n* telaraña.

spiel [ʃpiːl] *n* (*col*) rollo.

spike [spaık] *n* (*point*) punta; (*ZOOL*) pincho, púa; (*BOT*) espiga; (*ELEC*) pico parásito ◆ *vt*: **to ~ a quote** cancelar una cita; **~s** *npl* (*SPORT*) zapatillas *fpl* con clavos.

spiky ['spaɪkɪ] *a* (*bush, branch*) cubierto de púas; (*animal*) erizado.

spill, *pt, pp* **spilt** *or* **~ed** [spɪl, spɪlt, spɪld] *vt* derramar, verter; (*blood*) derramar ◆ *vi* derramarse; **to ~ the beans** (*col*) descubrir el pastel.
spill out *vi* derramarse, desparramarse.
spill over *vi* desbordarse.

spin [spɪn] *n* (*revolution of wheel*) vuelta, revolución *f*; (*AVIAT*) barrena; (*trip in car*) paseo (en coche) ◆ *vb* (*pt* **spun, span**, *pp* **spun** [spʌn, spæn]) *vt* (*wool etc*) hilar; (*wheel*) girar ◆ *vi* girar, dar vueltas; **the car spun out of control** el coche se descontroló dando vueltas.
spin out *vt* alargar, prolongar.

spinach ['spɪnɪtʃ] *n* espinaca; (*as food*) espinacas *fpl*.

spinal ['spaɪnl] *a* espinal.

spinal column *n* columna vertebral.

spinal cord *n* médula espinal.

spindly ['spɪndlɪ] *a* (*leg*) zanquivano.

spin-dry ['spɪn'draɪ] *vt* centrifugar.

spin-dryer [spɪn'draɪə*] *n* (*Brit*) secador *m* centrífugo.

spine [spaɪn] *n* espinazo, columna vertebral; (*thorn*) espina.

spine-chilling ['spaɪntʃɪlɪŋ] *a* de terror.

spineless ['spaɪnlɪs] *a* (*fig*) débil, flojo.

spinet [spɪ'nɛt] *n* espineta.

spinning ['spɪnɪŋ] *n* (*of thread*) hilado; (*art*) hilandería.

spinning top *n* peonza.

spinning wheel *n* rueca, torno de hilar.

spin-off ['spɪnɔf] *n* derivado, producto secundario.

spinster ['spɪnstə*] *n* soltera; (*pej*) solterona.

spiral ['spaɪərl] *n* espiral *m* ◆ *a* en espiral ◆ *vi* (*prices*) dispararse; **the inflationary ~** la espiral inflacionista.

spiral staircase *n* escalera de caracol.

spire ['spaɪə*] *n* aguja, chapitel *m*.

spirit ['spɪrɪt] *n* (*soul*) alma *f*; (*ghost*) fantasma *m*; (*attitude*) espíritu *m*; (*courage*) valor *m*, ánimo; **~s** *npl* (*drink*) alcohol *msg*, bebidas *fpl* alcohólicas; **in good ~s** alegre, de buen ánimo; **Holy S~** Espíritu *m* Santo; **community ~, public ~** civismo.

spirit duplicator *n* copiadora al alcohol.

spirited ['spɪrɪtɪd] *a* enérgico, vigoroso.

spirit level *n* nivel *m* de aire.

spiritual ['spɪrɪtjuəl] *a* espiritual ◆ *n* (*also*: **Negro ~**) canción *f* religiosa, espiritual *m*.

spiritualism ['spɪrɪtjuəlɪzəm] *n* espiritualismo.

spit [spɪt] *n* (*for roasting*) asador *m*, espetón *m*; (*spittle*) esputo, escupitajo; (*saliva*) saliva ◆ *vi* (*pt, pp* **spat** [spæt]) escupir;

(*sound*) chisporrotear.

spite [spaɪt] *n* rencor *m*, ojeriza ◆ *vt* causar pena a, mortificar; **in ~ of** a pesar de, pese a.

spiteful ['spaɪtful] *a* rencoroso, malévolo.

spitting ['spɪtɪŋ] *n*: "**~ prohibited**" "se prohíbe escupir" ◆ *a*: **to be the ~ image of sb** ser la viva imagen de uno.

spittle ['spɪtl] *n* saliva, baba.

splash [splæʃ] *n* (*sound*) chapoteo; (*of colour*) mancha ◆ *vt* salpicar de ◆ *vi* (*also*: **~ about**) chapotear; **to ~ paint on the floor** manchar el suelo de pintura.

splashdown ['splæʃdaun] *n* amaraje *m*, amerizaje *m*.

spleen [spliːn] *n* (*ANAT*) bazo.

splendid ['splɛndɪd] *a* espléndido.

splendidly ['splɛndɪdlɪ] *ad* espléndidamente; **everything went ~** todo fue a las mil maravillas.

splendour, (*US*) **splendor** ['splɛndə*] *n* esplendor *m*; (*of achievement*) brillo, gloria.

splice [splaɪs] *vt* empalmar.

splint [splɪnt] *n* tablilla.

splinter ['splɪntə*] *n* (*of wood*) astilla; (*in finger*) espigón *m* ◆ *vi* astillarse, hacer astillas.

splinter group *n* grupo disidente, facción *f*.

split [splɪt] *n* hendedura, raja; (*fig*) división *f*; (*POL*) escisión *f* ◆ (*vb*: *pt, pp* **split**) *vt* partir, rajar; (*party*) dividir; (*work, profits*) repartir ◆ *vi* (*divide*) dividirse, escindirse; **to ~ the difference** partir la diferencia; **to do the ~s** esparrancarse; **to ~ sth down the middle** (*also fig*) dividir algo en dos.
split up *vi* (*couple*) separarse; (*meeting*) acabarse.

split-level ['splɪtlɛvl] *a* (*house*) dúplex.

split peas *npl* guisantes *mpl* secos.

split personality *n* personalidad *f* desdoblada.

split second *n* fracción *f* de segundo.

splitting ['splɪtɪŋ] *a* (*headache*) horrible.

splutter ['splʌtə*] *vi* chisporrotear; (*person*) balbucear.

spoil, *pt, pp* **spoilt** *or* **~ed** [spɔɪl, spɔɪlt, spɔɪld] *vt* (*damage*) dañar; (*ruin*) estropear, echar a perder; (*child*) mimar, consentir; (*ballot paper*) invalidar ◆ *vi*: **to be ~ing for a fight** estar con ganas de lucha, andar con ganas de pelea.

spoiled [spɔɪld] *a* (*US*: *food*: *bad*) pasado, malo; (: *milk*) cortado.

spoils [spɔɪlz] *npl* despojo *sg*, botín *msg*.

spoilsport ['spɔɪlspɔːt] *n* aguafiestas *m inv*.

spoilt [spɔɪlt] *pt, pp* de **spoil** ◆ *a* (*child*) mimado, consentido; (*ballot paper*) invalidado.

spoke [spəuk] *pt* de **speak** ◆ *n* rayo, radio.

spoken ['spəukn] *pp* de **speak**.

spokesman ['spəuksmən] *n*, **spokeswoman** ['spəukswumən] *n* vocero *m/f*, portavoz *m/f*.

sponge [spʌndʒ] *n* esponja; (*CULIN: also*: ~ **cake**) bizcocho ◆ *vt* (*wash*) lavar con esponja ◆ *vi*: **to** ~ **on** *or* (*US*) **off sb** vivir a costa de uno.

sponge bag *n* (*Brit*) esponjera.

sponge cake *n* bizcocho, pastel *m*.

sponger ['spʌndʒə*] *n* gorrón/ona *m/f*.

spongy ['spʌndʒɪ] *a* esponjoso.

sponsor ['spɔnsə*] *n* (*RADIO*, *TV*) patrocinador(a) *m/f*; (*for membership*) padrino/madrina; (*COMM*) fiador(a) *m/f* ◆ *vt* patrocinar; apadrinar; (*parliamentary bill*) apoyar, respaldar; (*idea etc*) presentar, promover; **I** ~**ed him at 3p a mile** (*in fund-raising race*) me suscribí a darle 3 peniques la milla.

sponsorship ['spɔnsəʃɪp] *n* patrocinio.

spontaneity [spɔntə'neɪɪtɪ] *n* espontaneidad *f*.

spontaneous [spɔn'teɪnɪəs] *a* espontáneo.

spontaneously [spɔn'teɪnɪəslɪ] *ad* espontáneamente.

spooky ['spuːkɪ] *a* (*col: place, atmosphere*) espeluznante, horripilante.

spool [spuːl] *n* carrete *m*; (*of sewing machine*) canilla.

spoon [spuːn] *n* cuchara.

spoon-feed ['spuːnfiːd] *vt* dar de comer con cuchara a; (*fig*) tratar como a un niño a.

spoonful ['spuːnful] *n* cucharada.

sporadic [spə'rædɪk] *a* esporádico.

sport [spɔːt] *n* deporte *m*; (*person*) buen(a) perdedor(a) *m/f*; (*amusement*) juego, diversión *f*; **indoor/outdoor** ~**s** deportes *mpl* en sala cubierta/al aire libre; **to say sth in** ~ decir algo en broma.

sport coat *n* (*US*) = **sports jacket**.

sporting ['spɔːtɪŋ] *a* deportivo; **to give sb a** ~ **chance** darle a uno su oportunidad.

sports car *n* coche *m* sport.

sports coat *n* (*US*) = **sports jacket**.

sports ground *n* campo de deportes, centro deportivo (*LAm*).

sports jacket, (*US*) **sport jacket** *n* chaqueta deportiva.

sportsman ['spɔːtsmən] *n* deportista *m*.

sportsmanship ['spɔːtsmənʃɪp] *n* deportividad *f*.

sports pages *npl* páginas *fpl* deportivas.

sportswear ['spɔːtswɛə*] *n* trajes *mpl* de deporte *or* sport.

sportswoman ['spɔːtswumən] *n* deportista.

sporty ['spɔːtɪ] *a* deportivo.

spot [spɔt] *n* sitio, lugar *m*; (*dot: on pattern*) punto, mancha; (*pimple*) grano; (*also*: **advertising** ~) spot *m*; (*small amount*): **a** ~ **of** un poquito de ◆ *vt* (*notice*) notar, observar ◆ *a* (*COMM*) inmediatamente efectivo; **on the** ~ en el acto, acto seguido; (*in difficulty*) en un aprieto;

to do sth on the ~ hacer algo en el acto; **to put sb on the** ~ poner a uno en un apuro.

spot check *n* reconocimiento rápido.

spotless ['spɔtlɪs] *a* nítido, perfectamente limpio.

spotlessly ['spɔtlɪslɪ] *ad*: ~ **clean** limpísimo.

spotlight ['spɔtlaɪt] *n* foco, reflector *m*; (*AUT*) faro auxiliar.

spot-on [spɔt'ɔn] *a* (*Brit col*) exacto.

spot price *n* precio de entrega inmediata.

spotted ['spɔtɪd] *a* (*pattern*) de puntos.

spotty ['spɔtɪ] *a* (*face*) con granos.

spouse [spauz] *n* cónyuge *m/f*.

spout [spaut] *n* (*of jug*) pico; (*pipe*) caño ◆ *vi* chorrear.

sprain [spreɪn] *n* torcedura ◆ *vt*: **to** ~ **one's ankle** torcerse el tobillo.

sprang [spræŋ] *pt of* **spring**.

sprawl [sprɔːl] *vi* tumbarse ◆ *n*: **urban** ~ crecimiento urbano descontrolado; **to send sb** ~**ing** tirar a uno al suelo.

sprawling ['sprɔːlɪŋ] *a* (*town*) desparramado.

spray [spreɪ] *n* rociada; (*of sea*) espuma; (*container*) atomizador *m*; (*of paint*) pistola rociadora; (*of flowers*) ramita ◆ *vt* rociar; (*crops*) regar ◆ *cpd* (*deodorant*) en atomizador.

spread [sprɛd] *n* extensión *f*; (*of idea*) diseminación *f*; (*col: food*) comilona; (*PRESS, TYP: two pages*) plana ◆ *vb* (*pt, pp* **spread**) *vt* extender; diseminar; (*butter*) untar; (*wings, sails*) desplegar; (*scatter*) esparcir ◆ *vi* extenderse; diseminarse; untarse; desplegarse; esparcirse; **middle-age** ~ gordura de la mediana edad; **repayments will be** ~ **over 18 months** los pagos se harán a lo largo de 18 meses.

spread-eagled ['sprɛdiːgld] *a*: **to be** ~ estar despatarrado.

spreadsheet ['sprɛdʃiːt] *n* (*COMPUT*) hoja de cálculo.

spree [spriː] *n*: **to go on a** ~ ir de juerga.

sprightly ['spraɪtlɪ] *a* vivo, enérgico.

spring [sprɪŋ] *n* (*season*) primavera; (*leap*) salto, brinco; (*coiled metal*) resorte *m*; (*of water*) fuente *f*, manantial *m*; (*bounciness*) elasticidad *f* ◆ *vb* (*pt* **sprang**, *pp* **sprung** [spræŋ, sprʌŋ]) *vi* (*arise*) brotar, nacer; (*leap*) saltar, brincar ◆ *vt*: **to** ~ **a leak** (*pipe etc*) empezar a hacer agua; **he sprang the news on me** de repente me soltó la noticia; **in (the)** ~ en (la) primavera; **to walk with a** ~ **in one's step** andar dando saltos *or* brincos; **to** ~ **into action** lanzarse a la acción.

spring up *vi* (*problem*) surgir.

springboard ['sprɪŋbɔːd] *n* trampolín *m*.

spring-clean [sprɪŋ'kliːn] *n* (*also*: ~**ing**) limpieza general.

spring onion *n* cebolleta.

springtime ['sprɪŋtaɪm] *n* primavera.

springy ['sprɪŋɪ] *a* elástico; (*grass*) muelle.

sprinkle ['sprɪŋkl] *vt* (*pour*) rociar; **to ~ water on, ~ with water** rociar *or* salpicar de agua.

sprinkler ['sprɪŋklə*] *n* (*for lawn*) rociadera; (*to put out fire*) aparato de rociadura automática.

sprinkling ['sprɪŋklɪŋ] *n* (*of water*) rociada; (*of salt, sugar*) un poco de.

sprint [sprɪnt] *n* esprint *m* ◆ *vi* (*gen*) correr a toda velocidad; (*SPORT*) esprintar; **the 200 metres ~** el esprint de 200 metros.

sprinter ['sprɪntə*] *n* esprínter *m/f*, corredor(a) *m/f*.

sprocket ['sprɔkɪt] *n* (*on printer etc*) rueda de espigas.

sprocket feed *n* avance *m* por rueda de espigas.

sprout [spraut] *vi* brotar, retoñar ◆ *n*: **(Brussels) ~s** *npl* coles *mpl* de Bruselas.

spruce [spru:s] *n* (*BOT*) pícea ◆ *a* aseado, pulcro.

spruce up *vt* (*tidy*) arreglar, acicalar; (*smarten up: room etc*) ordenar; **to ~ o.s up** arreglarse.

sprung [sprʌŋ] *pp of* **spring**.

spry [spraɪ] *a* ágil, activo.

SPUC *n abbr* (= *Society for the Protection of Unborn Children*) ≈ Federación *f* Española de Asociaciones Pro-vida.

spun [spʌn] *pt, pp of* **spin**.

spur [spə:*] *n* espuela; (*fig*) estímulo, aguijón *m* ◆ *vt* (*also*: **~ on**) estimular, incitar; **on the ~ of the moment** de improviso.

spurious ['spjuərɪəs] *a* falso.

spurn [spə:n] *vt* desdeñar, rechazar.

spurt [spə:t] *n* chorro; (*of energy*) arrebato ◆ *vi* chorrear; **to put in** *or* **on a ~** (*runner*) acelerar; (*fig: in work etc*) hacer un gran esfuerzo.

sputter ['spʌtə*] *vi* = **splutter**.

spy [spaɪ] *n* espía *m/f* ◆ *vi*: **to ~ on** espiar a ◆ *vt* (*see*) divisar, lograr ver ◆ *cpd* (*film, story*) de espionaje.

spying ['spaɪɪŋ] *n* espionaje *m*.

Sq. *abbr* (*in address*: = *Square*) Plza.

sq. *abbr* (*MATH etc*) = **square**.

squabble ['skwɔbl] *n* riña, pelea ◆ *vi* reñir, pelear.

squad [skwɔd] *n* (*MIL*) pelotón *m*; (*POLICE*) brigada; (*SPORT*) equipo; **flying ~** (*POLICE*) brigada móvil.

squad car *n* (*POLICE*) coche-patrulla *m*.

squadron ['skwɔdrn] *n* (*MIL*) escuadrón *m*; (*AVIAT, NAUT*) escuadra.

squalid ['skwɔlɪd] *a* vil, miserable.

squall [skwɔ:l] *n* (*storm*) chubasco; (*wind*) ráfaga.

squalor ['skwɔlə*] *n* miseria.

squander ['skwɔndə*] *vt* (*money*) derrochar, despilfarrar; (*chances*) desperdiciar.

square [skwɛə*] *n* cuadro; (*in town*) plaza;

(*US: block of houses*) manzana, cuadra (*LAm*) ◆ *a* cuadrado ◆ *vt* (*arrange*) arreglar; (*MATH*) cuadrar; (*reconcile*): **can you ~ it with your conscience?** ¿cómo lo justifica? ◆ *vi* cuadrar, conformarse; **all ~** igual(es); **a ~ meal** una comida decente; **2 metres ~** 2 metros en cuadro; **1 ~ metre** un metro cuadrado; **to get one's accounts ~** dejar las cuentas claras; **I'll ~ it with him** (*col*) yo lo arreglo con él; **we're back to ~ one** (*fig*) hemos vuelto al principio.

square up *vi* (*settle*): **to ~ up (with sb)** ajustar cuentas (con uno).

square bracket *n* (*TYP*) corchete *m*.

squarely ['skwɛəlɪ] *ad* (*fully*) de lleno; (*honestly, fairly*) honradamente, justamente.

square root *n* raíz *f* cuadrada.

squash [skwɔʃ] *n* (*vegetable*) calabaza; (*SPORT*) squash *m*, frontenis *m*; (*Brit: drink*): **lemon/orange ~** zumo (*Sp*) *or* jugo (*LAm*) de limón/naranja ◆ *vt* aplastar.

squat [skwɔt] *a* achaparrado ◆ *vi* agacharse, sentarse en cuclillas; (*on property*) ocupar ilegalmente.

squatter ['skwɔtə*] *n* persona que ocupa ilegalmente una casa.

squawk [skwɔ:k] *vi* graznar.

squeak [skwi:k] *vi* (*hinge, wheel*) chirriar, rechinar; (*shoe, wood*) crujir ◆ *n* (*of hinge, wheel etc*) chirrido, rechinamiento; (*of shoes*) crujir *m*; (*of mouse etc*) chillido.

squeal [skwi:l] *vi* chillar, dar gritos agudos.

squeamish ['skwi:mɪʃ] *a* delicado, remilgado.

squeeze [skwi:z] *n* presión *f*; (*of hand*) apretón *m*; (*COMM: credit ~*) restricción *f* ◆ *vt* (*lemon etc*) exprimir; (*hand, arm*) apretar; **a ~ of lemon** unas gotas de limón; **to ~ past/under sth** colarse al lado de/por debajo de algo.

squeeze out *vt* exprimir; (*fig*) excluir.

squeeze through *vi* abrirse paso con esfuerzos.

squelch [skwɛltʃ] *vi* chapotear.

squid [skwɪd] *n* calamar *m*.

squiggle ['skwɪgl] *n* garabato.

squint [skwɪnt] *vi* guiñar los ojos ◆ *n* (*MED*) estrabismo; **to ~ at sth** mirar algo entornando los ojos.

squire ['skwaɪə*] *n* (*Brit*) terrateniente *m*.

squirm [skwə:m] *vi* retorcerse, revolverse.

squirrel ['skwɪrəl] *n* ardilla.

squirt [skwə:t] *vi* salir a chorros.

Sr *abbr* = **senior**, **sister** (*REL*).

SRC *n abbr* (*Brit*: = *Students' Representative Council*) consejo de estudiantes.

Sri Lanka [srɪ'læŋkə] *n* Sri Lanka *m*.

SRN *n abbr* (*Brit*) = *State Registered Nurse*.

SRO *abbr* (*US*) = *standing room only*.

SS *abbr* (= *steamship*) M.V.

SSA *n abbr* (*US*: = *Social Security Adminis-*

tration) ≈ Seguro Social.

SST *n abbr* (*US*) = *supersonic transport.*

ST *abbr* (*US*: = *Standard Time*) hora oficial.

St *abbr* (= *saint*) Sto./a.; (= *street*) c/.

stab [stæb] *n* (*with knife etc*) puñalada; (*of pain*) pinchazo; **to have a ~ at (doing) sth** (*col*) intentar (hacer) algo ♦ *vt* apuñalar; **to ~ sb to death** matar a uno a puñaladas.

stabbing ['stæbɪŋ] *n*: **there's been a ~** han apuñalado a alguien ♦ *a* (*pain*) punzante.

stability [stə'bɪlɪtɪ] *n* estabilidad *f*.

stabilization [steɪbəlaɪ'zeɪʃən] *n* estabilización *f*.

stabilize ['steɪbəlaɪz] *vt* estabilizar ♦ *vi* estabilizarse.

stabilizer ['steɪbəlaɪzə*] *n* (*AVIAT*, *NAUT*) estabilizador *m*.

stable ['steɪbl] *a* estable ♦ *n* cuadra, caballeriza; **riding ~s** escuela hípica.

staccato [stə'kɑːtəu] *a*, *ad* staccato.

stack [stæk] *n* montón *m*, pila; (*col*) mar *f* ♦ *vt* amontonar, apilar; **there's ~s of time to finish it** hay cantidad de tiempo para acabarlo.

stacker ['stækə*] *n* (*for printer*) apiladora.

stadium ['steɪdɪəm] *n* estadio.

staff [stɑːf] *n* (*work force*) personal *m*, plantilla; (*Brit SCOL*: *also*: **teaching ~**) cuerpo docente; (*stick*) bastón *m* ♦ *vt* proveer de personal; **to be ~ed by Asians/ women** tener una plantilla asiática/ femenina.

staffroom ['stɑːfruːm] *n* sala de profesores.

Staffs *abbr* (*Brit*) = *Staffordshire.*

stag [stæg] *n* ciervo, venado; (*Brit STOCK EX-CHANGE*) especulador *m* con nuevas emisiones.

stage [steɪdʒ] *n* escena; (*point*) etapa; (*platform*) plataforma; **the ~** el escenario, el teatro ♦ *vt* (*play*) poner en escena, representar; (*organize*) montar, organizar; (*fig*: *perform*: *recovery etc*) efectuar; **in ~s** por etapas; **in the early/final ~s** en las primeras/últimas etapas; **to go through a difficult ~** pasar una fase *or* etapa mala.

stagecoach ['steɪdʒkəutʃ] *n* diligencia.

stage door *n* entrada de artistas.

stagehand ['steɪdʒhænd] *n* tramoyista *m/f*.

stage-manage ['steɪdʒmænɪdʒ] *vt* (*fig*) manipular.

stage manager *n* director(a) *m/f* de escena.

stagger ['stægə*] *vi* tambalear ♦ *vt* (*amaze*) asombrar; (*hours*, *holidays*) escalonar.

staggering ['stægərɪŋ] *a* (*amazing*) asombroso, pasmoso.

stagnant ['stægnənt] *a* estancado.

stagnate [stæg'neɪt] *vi* estancarse; (*fig*: *economy*, *mind*) quedarse estancado.

stagnation [stæg'neɪʃən] *n* estancamiento.

stag night, **stag party** *n* despedida de soltero.

staid [steɪd] *a* (*clothes*) serio, formal.

stain [steɪn] *n* mancha; (*colouring*) tintura ♦ *vt* manchar; (*wood*) teñir.

stained glass window [steɪnd-] *n* vidriera de colores.

stainless ['steɪnlɪs] *a* (*steel*) inoxidable.

stain remover *n* quitamanchas *m inv*.

stair [stɛə*] *n* (*step*) peldaño, escalón *m*; **~s** *npl* escaleras *fpl*.

staircase ['stɛəkeɪs], **stairway** ['stɛəweɪ] *n* escalera.

stairwell ['stɛəwɛl] *n* hueco *or* caja de la escalera.

stake [steɪk] *n* estaca, poste *m*; (*BETTING*) apuesta ♦ *vt* (*bet*) apostar; (*also*: **~ out**: *area*) estacar, cercar con estacas; **to be at ~** estar en juego; **to have a ~ in sth** tener interés en algo; **to ~ a claim to (sth)** presentar reclamación por *or* reclamar (algo).

stalactite ['stæləktaɪt] *n* estalactita.

stalagmite ['stæləgmaɪt] *n* estalagmita.

stale [steɪl] *a* (*bread*) duro; (*food*) pasado.

stalemate ['steɪlmeɪt] *n* tablas *fpl* (por ahogado); **to reach ~** (*fig*) estancarse.

stalk [stɔːk] *n* tallo, caña ♦ *vt* acechar, cazar al acecho; **to ~ off** irse airado.

stall [stɔːl] *n* (*in market*) puesto; (*in stable*) casilla (de establo) ♦ *vt* (*AUT*) parar ♦ *vi* (*AUT*) pararse; (*fig*) buscar evasivas; **~s** *npl* (*Brit*: *in cinema*, *theatre*) butacas *fpl*; **a newspaper ~** un quiosco de (periódicos); **a flower ~** un puesto de flores.

stallholder ['stɔːlhəuldə*] *n* dueño/a de un puesto.

stallion ['stælɪən] *n* semental *m*, garañón *m*.

stalwart ['stɔːlwət] *n* partidario/a incondicional.

stamen ['steɪmən] *n* estambre *m*.

stamina ['stæmɪnə] *n* resistencia.

stammer ['stæmə*] *n* tartamudeo, balbuceo ♦ *vi* tartamudear, balbucir.

stamp [stæmp] *n* sello, estampilla (*LAm*); (*mark*, *also fig*) marca, huella; (*on document*) timbre *m* ♦ *vi* (*also*: **~ one's foot**) patear ♦ *vt* patear, golpear con el pie; (*letter*) poner sellos en; (*with rubber ~*) marcar con sello; **~ed addressed envelope (sae)** sobre *m* sellado con las señas propias.

stamp out *vt* (*fire*) apagar con el pie; (*crime*, *opposition*) acabar con.

stamp album *n* álbum *m* para sellos.

stamp collecting *n* filatelia.

stamp duty *n* (*Brit*) derecho de timbre.

stampede [stæm'piːd] *n* (*of cattle*) estampida.

stamp machine *n* máquina (expendedora) de sellos.

stance [stæns] *n* postura.

stand [stænd] *n* (*attitude*) posición *f*, postura; (*for taxis*) parada; (*music ~*) atril *m*; (*SPORT*) tribuna; (*at exhibition*) stand *m* ♦ *vb* (*pt*, *pp* **stood** [stud]) *vi* (*be*) estar, encontrarse; (*be on foot*) estar de pie; (*rise*) levantarse; (*remain*) quedar en pie ♦ *vt* (*place*) poner, colocar; (*tolerate, withstand*) aguantar, soportar; **to make a ~** resistir; (*fig*) mantener una postura firme; **to take a ~ on an. issue** adoptar una actitud hacia una cuestión; **to ~ for parliament** (*Brit*) presentarse (como candidato) a las elecciones; **nothing ~s in our way** nada nos lo impide; **to ~ still** quedarse inmóvil; **to let sth ~ as it is** dejar algo como está; **as things ~** tal como están las cosas; **to ~ sb a drink/meal** invitar a uno a una copa/a comer; **the company will have to ~ the loss** la empresa tendrá que encargarse de las pérdidas; **I can't ~ him** no le aguanto, no le puedo ver; **to ~ guard** *or* **watch** (*MIL*) hacer guardia.

stand aside *vi* apartarse, mantenerse aparte.

stand by *vi* (*be ready*) estar listo ♦ *vt fus* (*opinion*) aferrarse a.

stand down *vi* (*withdraw*) ceder el puesto; (*MIL, LAW*) retirarse.

stand for *vt fus* (*signify*) significar; (*tolerate*) aguantar, permitir.

stand in for *vt fus* suplir a.

stand out *vi* (*be prominent*) destacarse.

stand up *vi* (*rise*) levantarse, ponerse de pie.

stand up for *vt fus* defender.

stand up to *vt fus* hacer frente a.

stand-alone ['stændələʊn] *a* (*COMPUT*) autónomo.

standard ['stændəd] *n* patrón *m*, norma; (*flag*) estandarte *m* ♦ *a* (*size etc*) normal, corriente, estándar; **~s** *npl* (*morals*) valores *mpl* morales; **the gold ~** (*COMM*) el patrón oro; **high/low ~** de alto/bajo nivel; **below** *or* **not up to ~** (*work*) de calidad inferior; **to be** *or* **come up to ~** satisfacer los requisitos; **to apply a double ~** aplicar un doble criterio.

standardization [stændədaɪ'zeɪʃən] *n* normalización *f*.

standardize ['stændədaɪz] *vt* estandarizar.

standard lamp *n* (*Brit*) lámpara de pie.

standard model *n* modelo estándar.

standard of living *n* nivel *m* de vida.

standard practice *n* norma, práctica común.

standard rate *n* tasa de imposición.

standard time *n* hora legal.

stand-by ['stændbaɪ] *n* (*alert*) alerta, aviso; **to be on ~** estar sobre aviso, estar preparado para salir; (*doctor*) estar listo para acudir.

stand-by generator *n* generador *m* de reserva.

stand-by passenger *n* (*AVIAT*) pasajero/a que está en la lista de espera.

stand-by ticket *n* (*AVIAT*) (billete *m*) standby *m*.

stand-in ['stændɪn] *n* suplente *m/f*; (*CINEMA*)

doble *m/f*.

standing ['stændɪŋ] *a* (*upright*) derecho; (*on foot*) de pie, en pie; (*permanent*: *committee*) permanente; (: *rule*) fijo; (: *army*) permanente, regular; (*grievance*) constante, viejo ♦ *n* reputación *f*; (*duration*): **of 6 months' ~** que lleva 6 meses; **of many years' ~** que lleva muchos años; **he was given a ~ ovation** le aplaudieron mucho (de a pie); **~ joke** motivo constante de broma; **a man of some ~** un hombre de posición *or* categoría.

standing order *n* (*Brit*: *at bank*) giro bancario; **~ orders** *npl* (*MIL*) reglamento *sg* general.

standing room *n* sitio para estar de pie.

stand-offish [stænd'ɔfɪʃ] *a* reservado, poco afable.

standpat ['stændpæt] *a* (*US*) inmovilista.

standpipe ['stændpaɪp] *n* tubo vertical.

standpoint ['stændpɔɪnt] *n* punto de vista.

standstill ['stændstɪl] *n*: **at a ~** paralizado, en paro; **to come to a ~** pararse, quedar paralizado.

stank [stæŋk] *pt of* **stink**.

staple ['steɪpl] *n* (*for papers*) grapa; (*product*) producto *or* artículo de primera necesidad ♦ *a* (*crop, industry, food etc*) básico ♦ *vt* engrapar.

stapler ['steɪplə*] *n* grapadora.

star [stɑː*] *n* estrella; (*celebrity*) estrella, astro ♦ *vi*: **to ~ in** ser la estrella *or* el astro de; **four-~ hotel** hotel *m* de cuatro estrellas; **4-~ petrol** gasolina extra.

star attraction *n* atracción *f* principal.

starboard ['stɑːbəd] *n* estribor *m*.

starch [stɑːtʃ] *n* almidón *m*.

starchy ['stɑːtʃɪ] *a* (*food*) feculento.

stardom ['stɑːdəm] *n* estrellato.

stare [stɛə*] *n* mirada fija ♦ *vi*: **to ~ at** mirar fijo.

starfish ['stɑːfɪʃ] *n* estrella de mar.

stark [stɑːk] *a* (*bleak*) severo, escueto; (*simplicity, colour*) austero; (*reality, poverty, truth*) absoluto, puro ♦ *ad*: **~ naked** en cueros, en pelotas.

starlet ['stɑːlɪt] *n* (*CINEMA*) actriz *f* principiante.

starling ['stɑːlɪŋ] *n* estornino.

starry ['stɑːrɪ] *a* estrellado.

starry-eyed [stɑːrɪ'aɪd] *a* (*gullible, innocent*) inocentón/ona, ingenuo; (*idealistic*) idealista; (*from wonder*) asombrado; (*from love*) enamoradísimo.

star-studded ['stɑːstʌdɪd] *a*: **a ~ cast** un elenco estelar.

start [stɑːt] *n* (*beginning*) principio, comienzo; (*departure*) salida; (*sudden movement*) salto, sobresalto; (*advantage*) ventaja ♦ *vt* empezar, comenzar; (*cause*) causar; (*found*: *business, newspaper*) establecer; fundar; (*engine*) poner en marcha ♦ *vi* (*begin*) comenzar, empezar; (*with fright*)

asustarse, sobresaltarse; (*train etc*) salir; **to give sb a** ~ dar un susto a uno; **at the** ~ al principio; **for a** ~ en primer lugar; **to make an early** ~ ponerse en camino temprano; **the thieves had 3 hours'** ~ los ladrones llevaban 3 horas de ventaja; **to** ~ **a fire** provocar un incendio; **to** ~ **doing** *or* **to do sth** empezar a hacer algo; **to** ~ **(off) with ...** (*firstly*) para empezar; (*at the beginning*) al principio.
start off *vi* empezar, comenzar; (*leave*) salir, ponerse en camino.
start over *vi* (*US*) volver a empezar.
start up *vi* comenzar; (*car*) ponerse en marcha ♦ *vt* comenzar; (*car*) poner en marcha.
starter ['stɑːtə*] *n* (*AUT*) botón *m* de arranque; (*SPORT*: *official*) juez *m/f* de salida; (: *runner*) corredor(a) *m/f*; (*Brit CULIN*) entrada.
starting price ['stɑː-tɪŋ-] *n* (*COMM*) precio inicial.
starting point ['stɑː-tɪŋ-] *n* punto de partida.
startle ['stɑːtl] *vt* asustar, sobrecoger.
startling ['stɑːtlɪŋ] *a* alarmante.
star turn *n* (*Brit*) atracción *f* principal.
starvation [stɑːˈveɪʃən] *n* hambre *f*; (*MED*) inanición *f*.
starvation wages *npl* sueldo *sg* de hambre.
starve [stɑːv] *vi* pasar hambre; (*to death*) morir de hambre ♦ *vt* hacer pasar hambre; (*fig*) privar; **I'm starving** estoy muerto de hambre.
state [steɪt] *n* estado; (*pomp*): **in** ~ con mucha ceremonia ♦ *vt* (*say, declare*) afirmar; (*a case*) presentar, exponer; ~ **of emergency** estado de excepción *or* emergencia; ~ **of mind** estado de ánimo; **to lie in** ~ (*corpse*) estar de cuerpo presente; **to be in a** ~ estar agitado.
State Department *n* (*US*) Ministerio de Asuntos Exteriores.
state education *n* (*Brit*) enseñanza pública.
stateless ['steɪtlɪs] *a* desnacionalizado.
stately ['steɪtlɪ] *a* majestuoso, imponente.
statement ['steɪtmənt] *n* afirmación *f*; (*LAW*) declaración *f*; (*COMM*) estado; **official** ~ informe *m* oficial; ~ **of account, bank** ~ estado de cuenta.
state-of-the-art ['steɪtəvðɪ'ɑːt] *a* (*technology etc*) de punta.
state-owned ['steɪtəund] *a* estatal, del estado.
States [steɪts] *npl*: **the** ~ los Estados Unidos.
statesman ['steɪtsmən] *n* estadista *m*.
statesmanship ['steɪtsmənʃɪp] *n* habilidad *f* política, arte *m* de gobernar.
static ['stætɪk] *n* (*RADIO*) parásitos *mpl* ♦ *a* estático.

static electricity *n* estática.
station ['steɪʃən] *n* (*gen*) estación *f*; (*place*) puesto, sitio; (*RADIO*) emisora; (*rank*) posición *f* social ♦ *vt* colocar, situar; (*MIL*) apostar; **action** ~**s!** ¡a los puestos de combate!; **to be** ~**ed in** (*MIL*) estar estacionado en.
stationary ['steɪʃnərɪ] *a* estacionario, fijo.
stationer ['steɪʃənə*] *n* papelero/a.
stationer's (shop) *n* (*Brit*) papelería.
stationery ['steɪʃənərɪ] *n* (*writing paper*) papel *m* de escribir; (*writing materials*) artículos *mpl* de escritorio.
station master *n* (*RAIL*) jefe *m* de estación.
station wagon *n* (*US*) furgoneta.
statistic [stəˈtɪstɪk] *n* estadística.
statistical [stəˈtɪstɪkl] *a* estadístico.
statistics [stəˈtɪstɪks] *n* (*science*) estadística.
statue ['stætjuː] *n* estatua.
statuette [stætjuˈet] *n* figurilla.
stature ['stætʃə*] *n* estatura; (*fig*) talla.
status ['steɪtəs] *n* condición *f*, estado; (*reputation*) reputación *f*, estatus *m*; **the** ~ **quo** el statu quo.
status line *n* (*COMPUT*) línea de situación *or* de estado.
status symbol *n* símbolo de prestigio.
statute ['stætjuːt] *n* estatuto, ley *f*.
statute book *n* código de leyes.
statutory ['stætjutrɪ] *a* estatutario; ~ **meeting** junta ordinaria.
staunch [stɔːntʃ] *a* leal, incondicional ♦ *vt* (*flow, blood*) restañar.
stave [steɪv] *vt*: **to** ~ **off** (*attack*) rechazar; (*threat*) evitar.
stay [steɪ] *n* (*period of time*) estancia; (*LAW*): ~ **of execution** aplazamiento de una sentencia ♦ *vi* (*remain*) quedar(se); (*as guest*) hospedarse; **to** ~ **put** seguir en el mismo sitio; **to** ~ **the night/5 days** pasar la noche/estar 5 días.
stay behind *vi* quedar atrás.
stay in *vi* (*at home*) quedarse en casa.
stay on *vi* quedarse.
stay out *vi* (*of house*) no volver a casa; (*strikers*) no volver al trabajo.
stay up *vi* (*at night*) velar, no acostarse.
staying power ['steɪɪŋ-] *n* resistencia, aguante *m*.
STD *n abbr* (*Brit*: = *subscriber trunk dialling*) servicio de conferencias automáticas; (= *sexually transmitted disease*) enfermedad *f* venérea.
stead [sted] *n*: **in sb's** ~ en lugar de uno; **to stand sb in good** ~ ser muy útil a uno.
steadfast ['stedfɑːst] *a* firme, resuelto.
steadily ['stedɪlɪ] *ad* (*firmly*) firmemente; (*unceasingly*) sin parar; (*fixedly*) fijamente; (*walk*) normalmente; (*drive*) a velocidad constante.
steady ['stedɪ] *a* (*fixed*) firme, fijo; (*regu-*

lar) regular; (*boyfriend etc*) formal, fijo; (*person, character*) sensato, juicioso ♦ *vt* (*hold*) mantener firme; (*stabilize*) estabilizar; (*nerves*) calmar; **to ~ o.s. on** *or* **against sth** afirmarse en algo.

steak [steɪk] *n* (*gen*) filete *m*; (*beef*) bistec *m*.

steal, *pt* **stole,** *pp* **stolen** [stiːl, stəul, 'stəuln] *vt, vi* robar.

steal away, steal off *vi* marcharse furtivamente, escabullirse.

stealth [stɛlθ] *n*: **by ~** a escondidas, sigilosamente.

stealthy ['stɛlθɪ] *a* cauteloso, sigiloso.

steam [stiːm] *n* vapor *m*; (*mist*) vaho, humo ♦ *vt* (*CULIN*) cocer al vapor ♦ *vi* echar vapor; (*ship*): **to ~ along** avanzar, ir avanzando; **under one's own ~** (*fig*) por sus propios medios *or* propias fuerzas; **to run out of ~** (*fig: person*) quedar(se) agotado; **to let off ~** (*fig*) desahogarse.

steam up *vi* (*window*) empañarse; **to get ~ed up about sth** (*fig*) volverse loco por algo.

steam engine *n* máquina de vapor.

steamer ['stiːmə*] *n* (buque *m* de) vapor *m*; (*CULIN*) vaporera.

steam iron *n* plancha de vapor.

steamroller ['stiːmrəulə*] *n* apisonadora.

steamship ['stiːmʃɪp] *n* = **steamer**.

steamy ['stiːmɪ] *a* (*room*) lleno de vapor; (*window*) empañado.

steel [stiːl] *n* acero ♦ *a* de acero.

steel band *n* banda de percusión del Caribe.

steel industry *n* industria siderúrgica.

steel mill *n* fábrica de acero.

steelworks ['stiːlwəːks] *n* acería.

steely ['stiːlɪ] *a* (*determination*) inflexible; (*gaze*) duro; (*eyes*) penetrante; **~ grey** gris *m* metálico.

steelyard ['stiːljɑːd] *n* romana.

steep [stiːp] *a* escarpado, abrupto; (*stair*) empinado; (*price*) exorbitante, excesivo ♦ *vt* empapar, remojar.

steeple ['stiːpl] *n* aguja, campanario.

steeplechase ['stiːplʧeɪs] *n* carrera de obstáculos.

steeplejack ['stiːplʤæk] *n* reparador(a) *m/f* de chimeneas *or* de campanarios.

steer [stɪə*] *vt* (*car*) conducir (*Sp*), manejar (*LAm*); (*person*) dirigir ♦ *vi* conducir; **to ~ clear of sb/sth** (*fig*) esquivar a uno/evadir algo.

steering ['stɪərɪŋ] *n* (*AUT*) dirección *f*.

steering committee *n* comisión *f* directiva.

steering wheel *n* volante *m*.

stellar ['stɛlə*] *a* estelar.

stem [stɛm] *n* (*of plant*) tallo; (*of glass*) pie *m*; (*of pipe*) cañón *m* ♦ *vt* detener; (*blood*) restañar.

stem from *vt fus* ser consecuencia de.

stench [stɛntʃ] *n* hedor *m*.

stencil ['stɛnsl] *n* (*typed*) cliché *m*, clisé *m*; (*lettering*) plantilla ♦ *vt* hacer un cliché de.

stenographer [stɛ'nɔgrəfə*] *n* (*US*) taquígrafo/a.

step [stɛp] *n* paso; (*sound*) paso, pisada; (*stair*) peldaño, escalón *m* ♦ *vi*: **to ~ forward** dar un paso adelante; **~s** *npl* (*Brit*) = **~ladder**; **~ by ~** paso a paso; (*fig*) poco a poco; **to keep in ~ (with)** llevar el paso de; (*fig*) llevar el paso de, estar de acuerdo con; **to be in/out of ~ with** estar acorde con/estar en disonancia con; **to take ~s to solve a problem** tomar medidas para resolver un problema.

step down *vi* (*fig*) retirarse.

step in *vi* entrar; (*fig*) intervenir.

step off *vt fus* bajar de.

step on *vt fus* pisar.

step over *vt fus* pasar por encima de.

step up *vt* (*increase*) aumentar.

stepbrother ['stɛpbrʌðə*] *n* hermanastro.

stepdaughter ['stɛpdɔːtə*] *n* hijastra.

stepfather ['stɛpfɑːðə*] *n* padrastro.

stepladder ['stɛplædə*] *n* escalera doble *or* de tijera.

stepmother ['stɛpmʌðə*] *n* madrastra.

stepping stone ['stɛpɪŋ-] *n* pasadera.

stepsister ['stɛpsɪstə*] *n* hermanastra.

stepson ['stɛpsʌn] *n* hijastro.

stereo ['stɛrɪəu] *n* estéreo ♦ *a* (*also:* **~phonic**) estéreo, estereofónico; **in ~** en estéreo.

stereotype ['stɪərɪətaɪp] *n* estereotipo ♦ *vt* estereotipar.

sterile ['stɛraɪl] *a* estéril.

sterilization [stɛrɪlaɪ'zeɪʃən] *n* esterilización *f*.

sterilize ['stɛrɪlaɪz] *vt* esterilizar.

sterling ['stəːlɪŋ] *a* (*silver*) de ley ♦ *n* (*ECON*) (libras *fpl*) esterlinas *fpl*; **a pound ~** una libra esterlina; **he is of ~ character** tiene un carácter excelente.

stern [stəːn] *a* severo, austero ♦ *n* (*NAUT*) popa.

sternum ['stəːnəm] *n* esternón *m*.

steroid ['stɪərɔɪd] *n* esteroide *m*.

stethoscope ['stɛθəskəup] *n* estetoscopio.

stevedore ['stiːvədɔː*] *n* estibador *m*.

stew [stjuː] *n* cocido, estofado, guisado (*LAm*) ♦ *vt, vi* estofar, guisar; (*fruit*) cocer; **~ed fruit** compota de fruta.

steward ['stjuːəd] *n* (*Brit: gen*) camarero; (*shop* ~) enlace *m/f* sindical.

stewardess ['stjuːədɛs] *n* azafata.

stewing steak ['stjuː ɪŋ-], (*US*) **stew meat** *n* carne *f* de vaca.

St. Ex. *abbr* = **stock exchange**.

stg *abbr* (= *sterling*) ester.

stick [stɪk] *n* palo; (*as weapon*) porra; (*walking* ~) bastón *m* ♦ *vb* (*pt, pp* **stuck** [stʌk]) *vt* (*glue*) pegar; (*col: put*) meter; (:

tolerate) aguantar, soportar ◆ *vi* pegarse; (*come to a stop*) quedarse parado; (*get jammed*: *door, lift*) atascarse; **to get hold of the wrong end of the** ~ entender al revés; **to** ~ **to** (*word, principles*) atenerse a, ser fiel a; (*promise*) cumplir; **it stuck in my mind** se me quedó grabado; **to** ~ **sth into** clavar *or* hincar algo en.
stick around *vi* (*col*) quedarse.
stick out *vi* sobresalir ◆ *vt*: **to** ~ **it out** (*col*) aguantar.
stick up *vi* sobresalir.
stick up for *vt fus* defender.
sticker ['stɪkə*] *n* (*label*) etiqueta engomada; (*with slogan*) pegatina.
sticking plaster ['stɪkɪŋ-] *n* (*Brit*) esparadrapo.
stickler ['stɪklə*] *n*: **to be a** ~ **for** insistir mucho en.
stick-up ['stɪkʌp] *n* asalto, atraco.
sticky ['stɪkɪ] *a* pegajoso; (*label*) engomado; (*fig*) difícil.
stiff [stɪf] *a* rígido, tieso; (*hard*) duro; (*difficult*) difícil; (*person*) inflexible; (*price*) exorbitante; **to have a** ~ **neck/ back** tener tortícolis/dolor de espalda; **the door's** ~ la puerta está atrancada.
stiffen ['stɪfn] *vt* hacer más rígido; (*limb*) entumecer ◆ *vi* endurecerse; (*grow stronger*) fortalecerse.
stiffness ['stɪfnɪs] *n* rigidez *f*, tiesura.
stifle ['staɪfl] *vt* ahogar, sofocar.
stifling ['staɪflɪŋ] *a* (*heat*) sofocante, bochornoso.
stigma, *pl* (*BOT, MED, REL*) ~**ta**, (*fig*) ~**s** ['stɪgmə, stɪg'mɑːtə] *n* estigma *m*.
stile [staɪl] *n* escalera (*para pasar una cerca*).
stiletto [stɪ'letəu] *n* (*Brit*: *also*: ~ **heel**) tacón *m* de aguja.
still [stɪl] *a* inmóvil, quieto; (*orange juice etc*) sin gas ◆ *ad* (*up to this time*) todavía; (*even*) aún; (*nonetheless*) sin embargo, aun así ◆ *n* (*CINEMA*) foto *f* fija; **keep** ~! ¡estate quieto!, ¡no te muevas!; **he** ~ **hasn't arrived** todavía no ha llegado.
stillborn ['stɪlbɔːn] *a* nacido muerto.
still life *n* naturaleza muerta.
stilt [stɪlt] *n* zanco; (*pile*) pilar *m*, soporte *m*.
stilted ['stɪltɪd] *a* afectado.
stimulant ['stɪmjulənt] *n* estimulante *m*.
stimulate ['stɪmjuleɪt] *vt* estimular.
stimulating ['stɪmjuleɪtɪŋ] *a* estimulante.
stimulation [stɪmju'leɪʃən] *n* estímulo.
stimulus, *pl* **-li** ['stɪmjuləs, -laɪ] *n* estímulo, incentivo.
sting [stɪŋ] *n* (*wound*) picadura; (*pain*) escozor *m*, picazón *m*; (*organ*) aguijón *m*; (*col*: *confidence trick*) timo ◆ *vb* (*pt, pp* **stung** [stʌŋ]) *vt* picar ◆ *vi* picar, escocer; **my eyes are** ~**ing** los ojos me pican *or* escuecen.

stingy ['stɪndʒɪ] *a* tacaño.
stink [stɪŋk] *n* hedor *m*, tufo ◆ *vi* (*pt* **stank**, *pp* **stunk** [stæŋk, stʌŋk]) heder, apestar.
stinking ['stɪŋkɪŋ] *a* hediondo, fétido; (*fig*: *col*) horrible.
stint [stɪnt] *n* tarea, destajo; **to do one's** ~ **at sth** hacer su parte (de algo), hacer lo que corresponde (de algo) ◆ *vi*: **to** ~ **on** escatimar.
stipend ['staɪpend] *n* salario, remuneración *f*.
stipendiary [staɪ'pendɪərɪ] *a*: ~ **magistrate** magistrado/a estipendiario/a.
stipulate ['stɪpjuleɪt] *vt* estipular.
stipulation [stɪpju'leɪʃən] *n* estipulación *f*.
stir [stə:*] *n* (*fig*: *agitation*) conmoción *f* ◆ *vt* (*tea etc*) remover; (*fire*) atizar; (*move*) agitar; (*fig*: *emotions*) conmover ◆ *vi* moverse; **to give sth a** ~ remover algo; **to cause a** ~ causar conmoción *or* sensación.
stir up *vt* excitar; (*trouble*) fomentar.
stirrup ['stɪrəp] *n* estribo.
stitch [stɪtʃ] *n* (*SEWING*) puntada; (*KNITTING*) punto; (*MED*) punto (de sutura); (*pain*) punzada ◆ *vt* coser; (*MED*) suturar.
stoat [stəut] *n* armiño.
stock [stɔk] *n* (*COMM*: *reserves*) existencias *fpl*, stock *m*; (: *selection*) surtido; (*AGR*) ganado, ganadería; (*CULIN*) caldo; (*fig*: *lineage*) estirpe *f*, cepa; (*FINANCE*) capital *m*; (: *shares*) acciones *fpl*; (*RAIL*: *rolling* ~) material *m* rodante ◆ *a* (*COMM*: *goods, size*) normal, de serie; (*fig*: *reply etc*) clásico, trillado; (: *greeting*) acostumbrado ◆ *vt* (*have in* ~) tener existencias de; (*supply*) proveer, abastecer; **in** ~ en existencia *or* almacén; **to have sth in** ~ tener existencias de algo; **out of** ~ agotado; **to take** ~ **of** (*fig*) asesorar, examinar; ~**s** *npl* (*HISTORY*: *punishment*) cepo *sg*; ~**s and shares** acciones y valores; **government** ~ papel *m* del Estado.
stock up with *vt fus* abastecerse de.
stockbroker ['stɔkbrəukə*] *n* agente *m/f or* corredor(a) *m/f* de bolsa.
stock control *n* (*COMM*) control *m* de existencias.
stock cube *n* pastilla *or* cubito de caldo.
stock exchange *n* bolsa.
stockholder ['stɔkhəuldə*] *n* (*US*) accionista *m/f*.
Stockholm ['stɔkhəum] *n* Estocolmo.
stocking ['stɔkɪŋ] *n* media.
stock-in-trade ['stɔkɪn'treɪd] *n* (*tools etc*) herramientas *fpl*; (*stock*) existencia de mercancías; (*fig*): **it's his** ~ es su especialidad.
stockist ['stɔkɪst] *n* (*Brit*) distribuidor(a) *m/f*.
stock market *n* bolsa (de valores).
stock phrase *n* vieja frase *f*.
stockpile ['stɔkpaɪl] *n* reserva ◆ *vt* acumular, almacenar.

stockroom ['stɔkruːm] n almacén m, depósito.

stocktaking ['stɔkteɪkɪŋ] n (Brit COMM) inventario, balance m.

stocky ['stɔkɪ] a (strong) robusto; (short) achaparrado.

stodgy ['stɔdʒɪ] a indigesto, pesado.

stoical ['stəʊɪkəl] a estoico.

stoke [stəʊk] vt atizar.

stole [stəʊl] pt of **steal** ♦ n estola.

stolen ['stəʊln] pp of **steal**.

stolid ['stɔlɪd] a (person) imperturbable, impasible.

stomach ['stʌmək] n (ANAT) estómago; (belly) vientre m ♦ vt tragar, aguantar.

stomach ache n dolor m de estómago.

stomach pump n bomba gástrica.

stomach ulcer n úlcera de estómago.

stomp [stɔmp] vi: **to ~ in/out** entrar/salir con pasos ruidosos.

stone [stəʊn] n piedra; (in fruit) hueso; (Brit: weight) = 6.348kg; 14 pounds ♦ a de piedra ♦ vt apedrear; **within a ~'s throw of the station** a tiro de piedra or a dos pasos de la estación.

Stone Age n: **the ~** le Edad de Piedra.

stone-cold ['stəʊn'kəʊld] a helado.

stoned [stəʊnd] a (col: drunk) trompa, borracho, colocado.

stone-deaf ['stəʊn'dɛf] a sordo como una tapia.

stonemason ['stəʊnmeɪsən] n albañil m.

stonework ['stəʊnwɜːk] n (art) cantería.

stony ['stəʊnɪ] a pedregoso; (glance) glacial.

stood [stud] pt, pp of **stand**.

stool [stuːl] n taburete m.

stoop [stuːp] vi (also: **have a ~**) ser cargado de espaldas; (bend) inclinarse, encorvarse; **to ~ to (doing) sth** rebajarse a (hacer) algo.

stop [stɔp] n parada, alto; (in punctuation) punto ♦ vt parar, detener; (break off) suspender; (block) tapar, cerrar; (prevent) impedir; (also: **put a ~ to**) poner término a ♦ vi pararse, detenerse; (end) acabarse; **to ~ doing sth** dejar de hacer algo; **to ~ sb (from) doing sth** impedir a uno hacer algo; **to ~ dead** pararse en seco; **~ it!** ¡basta ya!, ¡párate! (LAm).

stop by vi pasar por.

stop off vi interrumpir el viaje.

stop up vt (hole) tapar.

stopcock ['stɔpkɔk] n llave f de paso.

stopgap ['stɔpgæp] n interino; (person) sustituto/a; (measure) medida provisoria ♦ cpd (situation) provisional.

stoplights ['stɔplaɪts] npl (AUT) luces fpl de detención.

stopover ['stɔpəʊvə*] n parada intermedia; (AVIAT) escala.

stoppage ['stɔpɪdʒ] n (strike) paro; (temporary stop) interrupción f; (of pay)

suspensión f; (blockage) obstrucción f.

stopper ['stɔpə*] n tapón m.

stop press n noticias fpl de última hora.

stopwatch ['stɔpwɔtʃ] n cronómetro.

storage ['stɔːrɪdʒ] n almacenaje m; (COMPUT) almacenamiento.

storage capacity n espacio de almacenaje.

storage heater n calentador m, acumulador m.

store [stɔː*] n (stock) provisión f; (depot; Brit: large shop) almacén m; (US) tienda; (reserve) reserva, repuesto ♦ vt (gen, COMPUT) almacenar; (keep) guardar; (in filing system) archivar; **~s** npl víveres mpl; **who knows what is in ~ for us** quién sabe lo que nos espera; **to set great/little ~ by sth** dar mucha/poca importancia a algo, valorar mucho/poco algo.

store up vt acumular.

storehouse ['stɔːhaʊs] n almacén m, depósito.

storekeeper ['stɔːkiːpə*] n (US) tendero/a.

storeroom ['stɔːruːm] n despensa.

storey, (US) **story** ['stɔːrɪ] n piso.

stork [stɔːk] n cigüeña.

storm [stɔːm] n tormenta; (wind) vendaval m; (fig) tempestad f ♦ vi (fig) rabiar ♦ vt tomar por asalto, asaltar; **to take a town by ~** (MIL) tomar una ciudad por asalto.

storm cloud n nubarrón m.

storm door n contrapuerta.

stormy ['stɔːmɪ] a tempestuoso.

story ['stɔːrɪ] n historia; (PRESS) artículo; (joke) cuento, chiste m; (plot) argumento; (lie) cuento; (US) = **storey**.

storybook ['stɔːrɪbuk] n libro de cuentos.

storyteller ['stɔːrɪtɛlə*] n cuentista m/f.

stout [staut] a (strong) sólido; (fat) gordo, corpulento ♦ n cerveza negra.

stove [stəʊv] n (for cooking) cocina; (for heating) estufa; **gas/electric ~** cocina de gas/eléctrica.

stow [stəʊ] vt meter, poner; (NAUT) estibar.

stowaway ['stəʊəweɪ] n polizón/ona m/f.

straddle ['strædl] vt montar a horcajadas.

straggle ['strægl] vi (wander) vagar en desorden; (lag behind) rezagarse.

straggler ['stræglə*] n rezagado/a.

straggling ['stræglɪŋ], **straggly** ['stræglɪ] a (hair) desordenado.

straight [streɪt] a (direct) recto, derecho; (plain, uncomplicated) sencillo; (frank) franco, directo; (in order) en orden; (continuous) continuo; (THEATRE: part, play) serio; (person: conventional) recto, convencional; (: heterosexual) heterosexual ♦ ad derecho, directamente; (drink) sin mezcla; **to put or get sth ~** dejar algo en claro; **10 ~ wins** 10 victorias seguidas; **to be (all) ~** (tidy) estar en orden; (clarified) estar claro; **I went ~ home** (me) fui directamente a casa; **~ away, ~ off** (at *once*) en seguida.

straighten ['streitn] *vt* (*also*: ~ **out**) enderezar, poner derecho; **to ~ things out** poner las cosas en orden.

straight-faced [streit'feist] *a* serio ◆ *ad* sin mostrar emoción, impávido.

straightforward [streit'fɔ:wəd] *a* (*simple*) sencillo; (*honest*) honrado, franco.

strain [strein] *n* (*gen*) tensión *f*; (*TECH*) esfuerzo; (*MED*) torcedura; (*breed*) raza; (*lineage*) linaje *m*; (*of virus*) variedad *f* ◆ *vt* (*back etc*) torcerse; (*tire*) cansar; (*stretch*) estirar; (*filter*) filtrar; (*meaning*) tergiversar ◆ *vi* esforzarse; **~s** *npl* (*MUS*) son *m*; **she's under a lot of** ~ está bajo mucha tensión.

strained [streind] *a* (*muscle*) torcido; (*laugh*) forzado; (*relations*) tenso.

strainer ['streinə*] *n* colador *m*.

strait [streit] *n* (*GEO*) estrecho; **to be in dire ~s** (*fig*) estar en un gran aprieto.

straitjacket ['streitdʒækit] *n* camisa de fuerza.

strait-laced [streit'leist] *a* mojigato, gazmoño.

strand [strænd] *n* (*of thread*) hebra; (*of hair*) trenza; (*of rope*) ramal *m*.

stranded ['strændid] *a* (*person: without money*) desamparado; (: *without transport*) colgado.

strange [streindʒ] *a* (*not known*) desconocido; (*odd*) extraño, raro.

stranger ['streindʒə*] *n* desconocido/a; (*from another area*) forastero/a; **I'm a ~ here** no soy de aquí.

strangle ['stræŋgl] *vt* estrangular.

stranglehold ['stræŋglhəuld] *n* (*fig*) dominio completo.

strangulation [stræŋgju'leiʃən] *n* estrangulación *f*.

strap [stræp] *n* correa; (*of slip, dress*) tirante *m* ◆ *vt* atar con correa.

straphanging ['stræphæŋiŋ] *n* viajar *m* de pie *or* parado (*LAm*).

strapless ['stræplis] *a* (*bra, dress*) sin tirantes.

strapping ['stræpiŋ] *a* robusto, fornido.

Strasbourg ['stræzbə:g] *n* Estrasburgo.

strata ['strɑ:tə] *npl of* **stratum**.

stratagem ['strætidʒəm] *n* estratagema.

strategic [strə'ti:dʒik] *a* estratégico.

strategy ['strætidʒi] *n* estrategia.

stratum, *pl* **strata** ['strɑ:təm, 'strɑ:tə] *n* estrato.

straw [strɔ:] *n* paja; (*drinking* ~) caña, pajita; **that's the last ~!** ¡eso es el colmo!

strawberry ['strɔ:bəri] *n* fresa, frutilla (*LAm*).

stray [strei] *a* (*animal*) extraviado; (*bullet*) perdido; (*scattered*) disperso ◆ *vi* extraviarse, perderse; (*wander: walker*) vagar, ir sin rumbo fijo; (: *speaker*) desvariar.

streak [stri:k] *n* raya; (*fig: of madness etc*)

vena ◆ *vt* rayar ◆ *vi*: **to ~ past** pasar como un rayo; **to have ~s in one's hair** tener vetas en el pelo; **a winning/losing** ~ una racha de buena/mala suerte.

streaky ['stri:ki] *a* rayado.

stream [stri:m] *n* riachuelo, arroyo; (*jet*) chorro; (*flow*) corriente *f*; (*of people*) oleada ◆ *vt* (*SCOL*) dividir en grupos por habilidad ◆ *vi* correr, fluir; **to ~ in/out** (*people*) entrar/salir en tropel; **against the** ~ a contracorriente; **on** ~ (*new power plant etc*) en funcionamiento.

streamer ['stri:mə*] *n* serpentina.

stream feed *n* (*on photocopier etc*) alimentación *f* continua.

streamline ['stri:mlain] *vt* aerodinamizar; (*fig*) racionalizar.

streamlined ['stri:mlaind] *a* aerodinámico.

street [stri:t] *n* calle *f* ◆ *a* callejero; **the back** ~s las callejuelas; **to be on the** ~s (*homeless*) estar sin vivienda; (*as prostitute*) ser de la vida.

streetcar ['stri:tkɑ:] *n* (*US*) tranvía *m*.

street lamp *n* farol *m*.

street lighting *n* alumbrado público.

street market *n* mercado callejero.

street plan *n* plano callejero.

streetwise ['stri:twaiz] *a* (*col*) pícaro.

strength [streŋθ] *n* fuerza; (*of girder, knot etc*) resistencia; (*of chemical solution*) potencia, proporción *f*; (*of wine*) graduación *f* de alcohol; **on the** ~ **of** a base de, en base a; **to be at full/below** ~ tener/no tener todo su complemento.

strengthen ['streŋθən] *vt* fortalecer, reforzar.

strenuous ['strenjuəs] *a* (*tough*) arduo; (*energetic*) enérgico; (*opposition*) firme, tenaz; (*efforts*) intensivo.

stress [stres] *n* (*force, pressure*) presión *f*; (*mental strain*) estrés *m*; (*accent, emphasis*) énfasis *m*, acento; (*LING, POETRY*) acento; (*TECH*) tensión *f*, carga ◆ *vt* subrayar, recalcar; **to be under** ~ sufrir una tensión nerviosa; **to lay great** ~ **on sth** hacer hincapié en algo.

stressful ['stresful] *a* (*job*) que produce tensión nerviosa.

stretch [stretʃ] *n* (*of sand etc*) trecho; (*of road*) tramo; (*of time*) período, tiempo ◆ *vi* estirarse; (*extend*): **to ~ to** *or* **as far as** extenderse hasta; (*be enough: money, food*): **to ~ to** alcanzar para, dar de sí para ◆ *vt* extender, estirar; (*make demands of*) exigir el máximo esfuerzo a; **to ~ one's legs** estirar las piernas.

stretch out *vi* tenderse ◆ *vt* (*arm etc*) extender; (*spread*) estirar.

stretcher ['stretʃə*] *n* camilla.

stretcher-bearer ['stretʃəbɛərə*] *n* camillero/a.

stretch marks *npl* estrillas *fpl*.

strewn [stru:n] *a*: ~ **with** cubierto *or* sembrado de.

stricken ['strɪkən] a (*person*) herido; (*city, industry etc*) condenado; ~ **with** (*arthritis, disease*) afligido por; **grief-~** destrozado por el dolor.

strict [strɪkt] a (*order, rule etc*) estricto; (*discipline, ban*) severo; **in ~ confidence** en la más absoluta confianza.

strictly ['strɪktlɪ] ad estrictamente; (*totally*) terminantemente; ~ **confidential** estrictamente confidencial; ~ **speaking** en (el) sentido estricto (de la palabra); ~ **between ourselves** ... entre nosotros ... .

stridden ['strɪdn] pp of **stride**.

stride [straɪd] n zancada, tranco ♦ vi (*pt* **strode**, *pp* **stridden** [strəud, 'strɪdn]) dar zancadas, andar a trancos; **to take in one's ~** (*fig: changes etc*) tomar con calma.

strident ['straɪdnt] a estridente; (*colour*) chillón/ona.

strife [straɪf] n lucha.

strike [straɪk] n huelga; (*of oil etc*) descubrimiento; (*attack*) ataque m; (*SPORT*) golpe m ♦ vb (*pt, pp* **struck** [strʌk]) vt golpear, pegar; (*oil etc*) descubrir; (*obstacle*) topar con; (*produce: coin, medal*) acuñar; (: *agreement, deal*) concertar ♦ vi declarar la huelga; (*attack: MIL etc*) atacar; (*clock*) dar la hora; **on ~** (*workers*) en huelga; **to call a ~** declarar una huelga; **to go on** or **come out on ~** ponerse or declararse en huelga; **to ~ a match** encender un fósforo; **to ~ a balance** (*fig*) encontrar un equilibrio; **to ~ a bargain** cerrar un trato; **the clock struck 9 o'clock** el reloj dio las nueve.

strike back vi (*MIL*) contraatacar; (*fig*) devolver el golpe.

strike down vt derribar.

strike off vt (*from list*) tachar; (*doctor etc*) suspender.

strike out vt borrar, tachar.

strike up vt (*MUS*) empezar a tocar; (*conversation*) entablar; (*friendship*) trabar.

strikebreaker ['straɪkbreɪkə*] n rompehuelgas m/f inv.

striker ['straɪkə*] n huelgista m/f; (*SPORT*) delantero.

striking ['straɪkɪŋ] a (*colour*) llamativo; (*obvious*) notorio.

string [strɪŋ] n (*gen*) cuerda; (*row*) hilera; (*COMPUT*) cadena ♦ vt (*pt, pp* **strung** [strʌŋ]): **to ~ together** ensartar; **to ~ out** extenderse; **the ~s** npl (*MUS*) los instrumentos de cuerda; **to pull ~s** (*fig*) mover palancas; **to get a job by pulling ~s** conseguir un trabajo por enchufe; **with no ~s attached** (*fig*) sin compromiso.

string bean n judía verde, habichuela.

string(ed) instrument [strɪŋ(d)-] n (*MUS*) instrumento de cuerda.

stringent ['strɪndʒənt] a riguroso, severo.

string quartet n cuarteto de cuerdas.

strip [strɪp] n tira; (*of land*) franja; (*of metal*) cinta, lámina ♦ vt desnudar; (*also*: ~ **down**: *machine*) desmontar ♦ vi desnudarse.

strip cartoon n tira cómica, historieta (*LAm*).

stripe [straɪp] n raya; (*MIL*) galón m; **white with green ~s** blanco con rayas verdes.

striped ['straɪpt] a a rayas, rayado.

strip lighting n alumbrado fluorescente.

stripper ['strɪpə*] n artista m/f de striptease.

striptease ['strɪptiːz] n striptease m.

strive, *pt* **strove**, *pp* **striven** [straɪv, strəuv, 'strɪvn] vi: **to ~ to do sth** esforzarse or luchar por hacer algo.

strode [strəud] pt of **stride**.

stroke [strəuk] n (*blow*) golpe m; (*MED*) apoplejía; (*caress*) caricia; (*of pen*) trazo; (*SWIMMING: style*) estilo; (*of piston*) carrera ♦ vt acariciar; **at a ~** de golpe; **a ~ of luck** un golpe de suerte; **two-~ engine** motor m de dos tiempos.

stroll [strəul] n paseo, vuelta ♦ vi dar un paseo or una vuelta; **to go for a ~, have** or **take a ~** dar un paseo.

stroller ['strəulə*] n (*US: pushchair*) cochecito.

strong [strɔŋ] a fuerte; (*bleach, acid*) concentrado ♦ ad: **to be going ~** (*company*) marchar bien; (*person*) conservarse bien; **they are 50 ~** son 50.

strong-arm ['strɔŋɑːm] a (*tactics, methods*) represivo.

strongbox ['strɔŋbɔks] n caja fuerte.

strong drink n bebida cargada or fuerte.

stronghold ['strɔŋhəuld] n fortaleza; (*fig*) baluarte m.

strong language n lenguaje m fuerte.

strongly ['strɔŋlɪ] ad fuertemente, con fuerza; (*believe*) firmemente; **to feel ~ about sth** tener una opinión decidida de algo.

strongman ['strɔŋmæn] n forzudo; (*fig*) hombre m robusto.

strongroom ['strɔŋruːm] n cámara acorazada.

strove [strəuv] pt of **strive**.

struck [strʌk] pt, pp of **strike**.

structural ['strʌktʃərəl] a estructural.

structure ['strʌktʃə*] n estructura; (*building*) construcción f.

struggle ['strʌgl] n lucha ♦ vi luchar; **to have a ~ to do sth** esforzarse por hacer algo.

strum [strʌm] vt (*guitar*) rasguear.

strung [strʌŋ] pt, pp of **string**.

strut [strʌt] n puntal m ♦ vi pavonearse.

strychnine ['strɪkniːn] n estricnina.

stub [stʌb] n (*of ticket etc*) talón m; (*of cigarette*) colilla ♦ vt: **to ~ one's toe on sth**

dar con el dedo del pie contra algo.

stub out *vt* (*cigarette*) apagar.

stubble ['stʌbl] *n* rastrojo; (*on chin*) barba (incipiente).

stubborn ['stʌbən] *a* terco, testarudo.

stucco ['stʌkəu] *n* estuco.

stuck [stʌk] *pt, pp of* **stick** ♦ *a* (*jammed*) atascado.

stuck-up [stʌk'ʌp] *a* engreído, presumido.

stud [stʌd] *n* (*shirt* ~) corchete *m*; (*of boot*) taco; (*of horses*) caballeriza; (*also:* ~ **horse**) caballo semental ♦ *vt* (*fig*): ~**ded with** salpicado de.

student ['stju:dənt] *n* estudiante *m/f* ♦ *a* estudiantil; **a law/medical** ~ un(a) estudiante de derecho/medicina.

student driver *n* (*US AUT*) aprendiz(a) *m/f*.

students' union *n* (*Brit: association*) federación *f* de estudiantes; (: *building*) centro estudiantil.

studio ['stju:diəu] *n* estudio; (*artist's*) taller *m*.

studio flat, (*US*) **studio apartment** *n* estudio.

studious ['stju:diəs] *a* estudioso; (*studied*) calculado.

studiously ['stju:diəslı] *ad* (*carefully*) con esmero.

study ['stʌdı] *n* estudio ♦ *vt* estudiar; (*examine*) examinar, investigar ♦ *vi* estudiar; **to make a** ~ **of sth** realizar una investigación de algo; **to** ~ **for an exam** preparar un examen.

stuff [stʌf] *n* materia; (*cloth*) tela; (*substance*) material *m*, sustancia; (*things, belongings*) cosas *fpl* ♦ *vt* llenar; (*CULIN*) rellenar; (*animal: for exhibition*) disecar; **my nose is** ~**ed up** tengo la nariz tapada; ~**ed toy** juguete *m* or muñeco de trapo.

stuffing ['stʌfɪŋ] *n* relleno.

stuffy ['stʌfɪ] *a* (*room*) mal ventilado; (*person*) de miras estrechas.

stumble ['stʌmbl] *vi* tropezar, dar un traspié.

stumble across *vt fus* (*fig*) tropezar con.

stumbling block ['stʌmblɪŋ-] *n* tropiezo, obstáculo.

stump [stʌmp] *n* (*of tree*) tocón *m*; (*of limb*) muñón *m* ♦ *vt*: **to be** ~**ed** quedar perplejo; **to be** ~**ed for an answer** no tener respuesta.

stun [stʌn] *vt* dejar sin sentido.

stung [stʌŋ] *pt, pp of* **sting**.

stunk [stʌŋk] *pp of* **stink**.

stunning ['stʌnɪŋ] *a* (*fig*) pasmoso.

stunt [stʌnt] *n* (*AVIAT*) vuelo acrobático; (*publicity* ~) truco publicitario.

stunted ['stʌntɪd] *a* enano, achaparrado.

stuntman ['stʌntmæn] *n* especialista *m*.

stupefaction [stju:pɪ'fækʃən] *n* estupefacción *f*.

stupefy ['stju:pɪfaɪ] *vt* dejar estupefacto.

stupendous [stju:'pɛndəs] *a* estupendo, asombroso.

stupid ['stju:pɪd] *a* estúpido, tonto.

stupidity [stju:'pɪdɪtɪ] *n* estupidez *f*.

stupor ['stju:pə*] *n* estupor *m*.

sturdy ['stɜ:dɪ] *a* robusto, fuerte.

stutter ['stʌtə*] *n* tartamudeo ♦ *vi* tartamudear.

sty [staɪ] *n* (*for pigs*) pocilga.

stye [staɪ] *n* (*MED*) orzuelo.

style [staɪl] *n* estilo; (*fashion*) moda; (*of dress etc*) hechura; (*hair* ~) corte *m*; **in the latest** ~ en el último modelo.

stylish ['staɪlɪʃ] *a* elegante, a la moda.

stylist ['staɪlɪst] *n* (*hair* ~) peluquero/a.

stylus, *pl* **styli** *or* **styluses** ['staɪləs, -laɪ] *n* (*of record player*) aguja.

suave [swɑ:v] *a* cortés, fino.

sub [sʌb] *n abbr* = **submarine, subscription.**

sub... [sʌb] *pref* sub....

subcommittee ['sʌbkəmɪtɪ] *n* subcomisión *f*.

subconscious [sʌb'kɒnʃəs] *a* subconsciente ♦ *n* subconsciente *m*.

subcontinent [sʌb'kɒntɪnənt] *n*: **the Indian** ~ el subcontinente (de la India).

subcontract *n* ['sʌb'kɒntrækt] subcontrato ♦ *vt* ['sʌbkən'trækt] subcontratar.

subcontractor ['sʌbkən'træktə*] *n* subcontratista *m/f*.

subdivide [sʌbdɪ'vaɪd] *vt* subdividir.

subdue [səb'dju:] *vt* sojuzgar; (*passions*) dominar.

subdued [səb'dju:d] *a* (*light*) tenue; (*person*) sumiso, manso.

sub-editor ['sʌb'edɪtə*] *n* (*Brit*) redactor(a) *m/f*.

subject *n* ['sʌbdʒɪkt] súbdito; (*SCOL*) tema *m*, materia ♦ *vt* [səb'dʒɛkt]: **to** ~ **sb to sth** someter a uno a algo ♦ *a* ['sʌbdʒɪkt]: **to be** ~ **to** (*law*) estar sujeto a; ~ **to confirmation in writing** sujeto a confirmación por escrito; **to change the** ~ cambiar de tema.

subjective [səb'dʒɛktɪv] *a* subjetivo.

subject matter *n* materia; (*content*) contenido.

sub judice [sʌb'dju:dɪsɪ] *a* (*LAW*) pendiente de resolución.

subjugate ['sʌbdʒugeɪt] *vt* subyugar, sojuzgar.

subjunctive [səb'dʒʌŋktɪv] *a, n* subjuntivo.

sublet [sʌb'lɛt] *vt, vi* subarrendar, realquilar.

sublime [sə'blaɪm] *a* sublime.

subliminal [sʌb'lɪmɪnl] *a* subliminal.

submachine gun ['sʌbmə'ʃi:n-] *n* metralleta.

submarine [sʌbmə'ri:n] *n* submarino.

submerge [səb'mɜ:dʒ] *vt* sumergir; (*flood*) inundar ♦ *vi* sumergirse.

submersion [səb'mɜ:ʃən] *n* submersión *f*.

submission [səb'mɪʃən] *n* sumisión *f*; (*to committee etc*) ponencia.
submissive [səb'mɪsɪv] *a* sumiso.
submit [səb'mɪt] *vt* someter; (*proposal, claim*) presentar ♦ *vi* someterse; **I ~ that ... me permito sugerir que ....**
subnormal [sʌb'nɔːməl] *a* subnormal.
subordinate [sə'bɔːdɪnət] *a*, *n* subordinado/a *m/f*.
subpoena [səb'piːnə] (*LAW*) *n* citación *f* ♦ *vt* citar.
subroutine [sʌbruː'tiːn] *n* (*COMPUT*) subrutina.
subscribe [səb'skraɪb] *vi* suscribir; **to ~ to** (*opinion*, *fund*) suscribir, aprobar; (*newspaper*) suscribirse a.
subscribed capital [səb'skraɪbd-] *n* capital *m* suscrito.
subscriber [səb'skraɪbə*] *n* (*to periodical*, *telephone*) abonado/a.
subscript ['sʌbskrɪpt] *n* (*TYP*) subíndice *m*.
subscription [səb'skrɪpʃən] *n* (*to club*) abono; (*to magazine*) suscripción *f*; **to take out a ~ to** suscribir a, abonarse a.
subsequent ['sʌbsɪkwənt] *a* subsiguiente, posterior; **~ to** posterior a.
subsequently ['sʌbsɪkwəntlɪ] *ad* posteriormente, más tarde.
subservient [səb'sɜːvɪənt] *a*: **~ (to)** servil (a).
subside [səb'saɪd] *vi* hundirse; (*flood*) bajar; (*wind*) amainar.
subsidence [səb'saɪdns] *n* hundimiento; (*in road*) socavón *m*.
subsidiary [səb'sɪdɪərɪ] *n* sucursal *f*, filial *f* ♦ *a* (*UNIV: subject*) secundario.
subsidize ['sʌbsɪdaɪz] *vt* subvencionar.
subsidy ['sʌbsɪdɪ] *n* subvención *f*.
subsist [səb'sɪst] *vi*: **to ~ on sth** sustentarse con algo.
subsistence [səb'sɪstəns] *n* subsistencia.
subsistence allowance *n* dietas *fpl*.
subsistence level *n* nivel *m* de subsistencia.
subsistence wage *n* sueldo de subsistencia.
substance ['sʌbstəns] *n* sustancia; (*fig*) esencia; **to lack ~** (*argument*) ser poco convincente; (*accusation*) no tener fundamento; (*film, book*) tener poca profundidad.
substandard [sʌb'stændəd] *a* (*goods*) inferior; (*housing*) deficiente.
substantial [səb'stænʃl] *a* sustancial, sustancioso; (*fig*) importante.
substantially [səb'stænʃəlɪ] *ad* sustancialmente; **~ bigger** bastante más grande.
substantiate [səb'stænʃɪeɪt] *vt* comprobar.
substitute ['sʌbstɪtjuːt] *n* (*person*) suplente *m/f*; (*thing*) sustituto ♦ *vt*: **to ~ A for B** sustituir B por A, reemplazar A por B.
substitution [sʌbstɪ'tjuːʃən] *n* sustitución *f*.
subterfuge ['sʌbtəfjuːdʒ] *n* subterfugio.

subterranean [sʌbtə'reɪnɪən] *a* subterráneo.
subtitle ['sʌbtaɪtl] *n* subtítulo.
subtle ['sʌtl] *a* sutil.
subtlety ['sʌtltɪ] *n* sutileza.
subtly ['sʌtlɪ] *ad* sutilmente.
subtotal [sʌb'təutl] *n* subtotal *m*.
subtract [səb'trækt] *vt* restar; sustraer.
subtraction [səb'trækʃən] *n* resta; sustracción *f*.
suburb ['sʌbəːb] *n* suburbio; **the ~s** las afueras (de la ciudad).
suburban [sə'bəːbən] *a* suburbano; (*train etc*) de cercanías.
suburbia [sə'bəːbɪə] *n* barrios *mpl* residenciales *or* satélites.
subversion [səb'vəːʃən] *n* subversión *f*.
subversive [səb'vəːsɪv] *a* subversivo.
subway ['sʌbweɪ] *n* (*Brit*) paso subterráneo *or* inferior; (*US*) metro.
sub-zero [sʌb'zɪərəu] *a*: **~ temperatures** temperaturas *fpl* por debajo del cero.
succeed [sək'siːd] *vi* (*person*) tener éxito; (*plan*) salir bien ♦ *vt* suceder a; **to ~ in doing** lograr hacer.
succeeding [sək'siːdɪŋ] *a* (*following*) sucesivo; **~ generations** generaciones *fpl* futuras.
success [sək'sɛs] *n* éxito; (*gain*) triunfo.
successful [sək'sɛsful] *a* (*venture*) de éxito; **to be ~ (in doing)** lograr (hacer).
successfully [sək'sɛsfulɪ] *ad* con éxito.
succession [sək'sɛʃən] *n* (*series*) sucesión *f*, serie *f*; (*descendants*) descendencia; **in ~ sucesivamente.**
successive [sək'sɛsɪv] *a* sucesivo, consecutivo; **on 3 ~ days** tres días seguidos.
successor [sək'sɛsə*] *n* sucesor(a) *m/f*.
succinct [sək'sɪŋkt] *a* sucinto.
succulent ['sʌkjulənt] *a* suculento ♦ *n* (*BOT*): **~s** plantas *fpl* carnosas.
succumb [sə'kʌm] *vi* sucumbir.
such [sʌtʃ] *a* tal, semejante; (*of that kind*): **~ a** book tal libro; **~ books** tales libros; (*so much*): **~ courage** tanto valor ♦ *ad* tan; **~ a long trip** un viaje tan largo; **~ a lot of** tanto; **~ as** (*like*) tal como; **a noise ~ as** to un ruido tal que; **~ books as I have** cuantos libros tengo; **I said no ~ thing** no dije tal cosa; **it's ~ a long time since we saw each other** hace tanto tiempo que no nos vemos; **~ a long time ago** hace tantísimo tiempo; **as ~** *ad* como tal.
such-and-such ['sʌtʃənsʌtʃ] *a* tal o cual.
suchlike ['sʌtʃlaɪk] *pron* (*col*): **and ~** y cosas por el estilo.
suck [sʌk] *vt* chupar; (*bottle*) sorber; (*breast*) mamar; (*subj: pump, machine*) aspirar.
sucker ['sʌkə*] *n* (*BOT*) serpollo; (*ZOOL*) ventosa; (*col*) bobo, primo.
sucrose ['suːkrəuz] *n* sucrosa.

suction ['sʌkʃən] n succión f.
suction pump n bomba aspirante or de succión.
Sudan [su'dæn] n Sudán m.
Sudanese [suːdə'niːz] a, n sudanés/esa m/f.
sudden ['sʌdn] a (rapid) repentino, súbito; (unexpected) imprevisto; **all of a ~** de repente.
suddenly ['sʌdnlɪ] ad de repente.
suds [sʌdz] npl espuma sg de jabón.
sue [suː] vt demandar; **to ~ (for)** demandar (por); **to ~ for divorce** solicitar or pedir el divorcio; **to ~ for damages** demandar por daños y perjuicios.
suede [sweɪd] n ante m, gamuza (LAm).
suet ['suɪt] n sebo.
Suez Canal ['suːɪz-] n Canal m de Suez.
Suff. abbr (Brit) = Suffolk.
suffer ['sʌfə*] vt sufrir, padecer; (tolerate) aguantar, soportar; (undergo: loss, setback) experimentar ♦ vi sufrir, padecer; **to ~ from** sufrir, tener; **to ~ from the effects of alcohol/a fall** resentirse del alcohol/de una caída.
sufferance ['sʌfərns] n: **he was only there on ~** estuvo allí sólo por tolerancia.
sufferer ['sʌfərə*] n víctima f; (MED) **~ from** enfermo/a de.
suffering ['sʌfərɪŋ] n (hardship, deprivation) sufrimiento; (pain) dolor m.
suffice [sə'faɪs] vi bastar, ser suficiente.
sufficient [sə'fɪʃənt] a suficiente, bastante.
sufficiently [sə'fɪʃəntlɪ] ad suficientemente, bastante.
suffix ['sʌfɪks] n sufijo.
suffocate ['sʌfəkeɪt] vi ahogarse, asfixiarse.
suffocation [sʌfə'keɪʃən] n sofocación f, asfixia.
suffrage ['sʌfrɪdʒ] n sufragio.
suffuse [sə'fjuːz] vt: **to ~ (with)** (colour) bañar (de); **her face was ~d with joy** su cara estaba llena de alegría.
sugar ['ʃugə*] n azúcar m ♦ vt echar azúcar a, azucarar.
sugar basin n (Brit) = **sugar bowl**.
sugar beet n remolacha.
sugar bowl n azucarero.
sugar cane n caña de azúcar.
sugar-coated [ʃugə'kəutɪd] a azucarado, garapiñado.
sugar lump n terrón m de azúcar.
sugar refinery n ingenio azucarero.
sugary ['ʃugərɪ] a azucarado.
suggest [sə'dʒɛst] vt sugerir; (recommend) aconsejar; **what do you ~ I do?** ¿qué sugieres que haga?; **this ~s that ...** esto hace pensar que ....
suggestion [sə'dʒɛstʃən] n sugerencia; **there's no ~ of ...** no hay indicación or evidencia de ....
suggestive [sə'dʒɛstɪv] a sugestivo; (pej: indecent) indecente.
suicidal ['suɪsaɪdl] a suicida; (fig) suicida,
peligroso.
suicide ['suɪsaɪd] n suicidio; (person) suicida m/f; **to commit ~** suicidarse.
suicide attempt, suicide bid n intento de suicidio.
suit [suːt] n (man's) traje m; (woman's) conjunto; (LAW) pleito; (CARDS) palo ♦ vt convenir; (clothes) sentar a, ir bien a; (adapt): **to ~ sth to** adaptar or ajustar algo a; **to be ~ed to sth** (suitable for) ser apto para algo; **well ~ed** (couple) hechos el uno para el otro; **to bring a ~ against sb** entablar demanda contra uno; **to follow ~** (CARDS) seguir el palo; (fig) seguir el ejemplo (de uno); **that ~s me** me va bien.
suitable ['suːtəbl] a conveniente; (apt) indicado.
suitably ['suːtəblɪ] ad convenientemente; (appropriately) en forma debida.
suitcase ['suːtkeɪs] n maleta, valija (LAm).
suite [swiːt] n (of rooms, MUS) suite f; (furniture): **bedroom/dining room ~** (juego de) dormitorio/comedor m; **a three-piece ~** un tresillo.
suitor ['suːtə*] n pretendiente m.
sulfate ['sʌlfeɪt] n (US) = **sulphate**.
sulfur ['sʌlfə*] n (US) = **sulphur**.
sulk [sʌlk] vi estar de mal humor.
sulky ['sʌlkɪ] a malhumorado.
sullen ['sʌlən] a hosco, malhumorado.
sulphate, (US) sulfate ['sʌlfeɪt] n sulfato; **copper ~** sulfato de cobre.
sulphur, (US) sulfur ['sʌlfə*] n azufre m.
sultan ['sʌltən] n sultán m.
sultana [sʌl'tɑːnə] n (fruit) pasa de Esmirna.
sultry ['sʌltrɪ] a (weather) bochornoso; (seductive) seductor(a).
sum [sʌm] n suma; (total) total m.
sum up vt resumir; (evaluate rapidly) evaluar ♦ vi hacer un resumen.
Sumatra [su'mɑːtrə] n Sumatra.
summarize ['sʌməraɪz] vt resumir.
summary ['sʌmərɪ] n resumen m ♦ a (justice) sumario.
summer ['sʌmə*] n verano ♦ a de verano; **in (the) ~** en (el) verano.
summerhouse ['sʌməhaus] n (in garden) cenador m, glorieta.
summertime ['sʌmətaɪm] n (season) verano.
summer time n (by clock) hora de verano.
summery ['sʌmərɪ] a veraniego.
summing-up [sʌmɪŋ'ʌp] n (LAW) resumen m.
summit ['sʌmɪt] n cima, cumbre f.
summit (conference) n (conferencia) cumbre f.
summon ['sʌmən] vt (person) llamar; (meeting) convocar; **to ~ a witness** citar a un testigo.
summon up vt (courage) armarse de.

summons ['sʌmənz] *n* llamamiento, llamada ◆ *vt* citar, emplazar; **to serve a ~ on sb** citar a uno ante el juicio.
sump [sʌmp] *n* (*Brit AUT*) cárter *m*.
sumptuous ['sʌmptjuəs] *a* suntuoso.
sun [sʌn] *n* sol *m*; **they have everything under the ~** no les falta nada, tienen de todo.
Sun. *abbr* (= *Sunday*) dom.
sunbathe ['sʌnbeɪð] *vi* tomar el sol.
sunbeam ['sʌnbiːm] *n* rayo de sol.
sunbed ['sʌnbɛd] *n* cama solar.
sunburn ['sʌnbəːn] *n* (*painful*) quemadura del sol; (*tan*) bronceado.
sunburnt ['sʌnbəːnt], **sunburned** ['sʌnbəːnd] *a* (*tanned*) bronceado; (*painfully*) quemado por el sol.
sundae ['sʌndeɪ] *n* helado con frutas y nueces.
Sunday ['sʌndɪ] *n* domingo.
Sunday school *n* catequesis *f*.
sundial ['sʌndaɪəl] *n* reloj *m* de sol.
sundown ['sʌndaun] *n* anochecer *m*, puesta de sol.
sundries ['sʌndrɪz] *npl* géneros *mpl* diversos.
sundry ['sʌndrɪ] *a* varios, diversos; **all and ~** todos sin excepción.
sunflower ['sʌnflauə*] *n* girasol *m*.
sung [sʌŋ] *pp of* **sing**.
sunglasses ['sʌnglɑːsɪz] *npl* gafas *fpl or* anteojos *mpl* de sol.
sunk [sʌŋk] *pp of* **sink**.
sunken ['sʌŋkn] *a* (*bath*) hundido.
sunlamp ['sʌnlæmp] *n* lámpara solar ultravioleta.
sunlight ['sʌnlaɪt] *n* luz *f* del sol.
sunlit ['sʌnlɪt] *a* iluminado por el sol.
sunny ['sʌnɪ] *a* soleado; (*day*) de sol; (*fig*) alegre; **it is ~** hace sol.
sunrise ['sʌnraɪz] *n* salida del sol.
sun roof *n* (*AUT*) techo corredizo; (*on building*) azotea, terraza.
sunset ['sʌnsɛt] *n* puesta del sol.
sunshade ['sʌnʃeɪd] *n* (*over table*) sombrilla.
sunshine ['sʌnʃaɪn] *n* sol *m*.
sunstroke ['sʌnstrəuk] *n* insolación *f*.
suntan ['sʌntæn] *n* bronceado.
suntanned ['sʌntænd] *a* bronceado.
suntan oil *n* aceite *m* bronceador.
super ['suːpə*] *a* (*col*) bárbaro.
superannuation [suːpərænju'eɪʃən] *n* jubilación *f*.
superb [suːˈpəːb] *a* magnífico, espléndido.
supercilious [suːpəˈsɪlɪəs] *a* (*disdainful*) desdeñoso; (*haughty*) altanero.
superficial [suːpəˈfɪʃəl] *a* superficial.
superfluous [suˈpəːfluəs] *a* superfluo, de sobra.
superhuman [suːpəˈhjuːmən] *a* sobrehumano.
superimpose ['suːpərɪm'pəuz] *vt* sobreponer.
superintend [suːpərɪn'tɛnd] *vt* supervisar.
superintendent [suːpərɪn'tɛndənt] *n* director(a) *m/f*; (*police* ~) subjefe/a *m/f*.
superior [suˈpɪərɪə*] *a* superior; (*smug: person*) presumido, desdeñoso; (: *smile, air*) de suficiencia; (: *remark*) desdeñoso ◆ *n* superior *m*; **Mother S~** (*REL*) madre *f* superiora.
superiority [supɪərɪ'ɔrɪtɪ] *n* superioridad *f*; desdén *m*.
superlative [suˈpəːlətɪv] *a*, *n* superlativo.
superman ['suːpəmæn] *n* superhombre *m*.
supermarket ['suːpəmɑːkɪt] *n* supermercado.
supernatural [suːpəˈnætʃərəl] *a* sobrenatural.
superpower ['suːpəpauə*] *n* (*POL*) superpotencia.
supersede [suːpəˈsiːd] *vt* suplantar.
supersonic ['suːpə'sɔnɪk] *a* supersónico.
superstition [suːpəˈstɪʃən] *n* superstición *f*.
superstitious [suːpəˈstɪʃəs] *a* supersticioso.
superstore ['suːpəstɔː*] *n* (*Brit*) hipermercado.
supertanker ['suːpətæŋkə*] *n* superpetrolero.
supertax ['suːpətæks] *n* sobretasa, sobreimpuesto.
supervise ['suːpəvaɪz] *vt* supervisar.
supervision [suːpəˈvɪʒən] *n* supervisión *f*.
supervisor ['suːpəvaɪzə*] *n* (*gen, UNIV*) supervisor(a) *m/f*.
supervisory ['suːpəvaɪzərɪ] *a* de supervisión.
supine ['suːpaɪn] *a* supino.
supper ['sʌpə*] *n* cena; **to have ~** cenar.
supplant [səˈplɑːnt] *vt* suplantar, reemplazar.
supple ['sʌpl] *a* flexible.
supplement *n* ['sʌplɪmənt] suplemento ◆ *vt* [sʌplɪ'mɛnt] suplir.
supplementary [sʌplɪ'mɛntərɪ] *a* suplementario.
supplementary benefit *n* (*Brit*) subsidio adicional de la seguridad social.
supplier [səˈplaɪə*] *n* suministrador(a) *m/f*; (*COMM*) distribuidor(a) *m/f*.
supply [səˈplaɪ] *vt* (*provide*) suministrar; (*information*) facilitar; (*fill: need, want*) suplir, satisfacer; (*equip*): **to ~ (with)** proveer (de) ◆ *n* provisión *f*; (*of gas, water etc*) suministro ◆ *a* (*Brit: teacher etc*) suplente; **supplies** *npl* (*food*) víveres *mpl*; (*MIL*) pertrechos *mpl*; **office supplies** materiales *mpl* para oficina; **to be in short ~** escasear, haber escasez de; **the electricity/water/gas ~** el suministro de electricidad/agua/gas; **~ and demand** la oferta y la demanda.
support [səˈpɔːt] *n* (*moral, financial etc*) apoyo; (*TECH*) soporte *m* ◆ *vt* apoyar; (*financially*) mantener; (*uphold*) sostener;

(SPORT: team) seguir; **they stopped work in ~ (of)** pararon de trabajar en apoyo (de); **to ~ o.s.** (financially) ganarse la vida.

support buying [-'baɪɪŋ] n compra proteccionista.

supporter [sə'pɔːtə*] n (POL etc) partidario/a; (SPORT) aficionado/a.

supporting [sə'pɔːtɪŋ] a (THEATRE: role, actor) secundario.

suppose [sə'pəuz] vt, vi suponer; (imagine) imaginarse; **to be ~d to do sth** deber hacer algo; **I don't ~ she'll come** no creo que venga; **he's ~d to be an expert** se le supone un experto.

supposedly [sə'pəuzɪdlɪ] ad según cabe suponer.

supposing [sə'pəuzɪŋ] conj en caso de que; **always ~ (that) he comes** suponiendo que venga.

supposition [sʌpə'zɪʃən] n suposición f.

suppository [sə'pɔzɪtrɪ] n supositorio.

suppress [sə'prɛs] vt suprimir; (yawn) ahogar.

suppression [sə'prɛʃən] n represión f.

supremacy [su'prɛməsɪ] n supremacía.

supreme [su'priːm] a supremo.

Supreme Court n (US) Tribunal m Supremo, Corte f Suprema (LAm).

Supt. abbr (POLICE) = **superintendent**.

surcharge ['sɔːtʃɑːdʒ] n sobretasa, recargo.

sure [ʃuə*] a seguro; (definite, convinced) cierto; (aim) certero ♦ ad: **that ~ is pretty, that's ~ pretty** (US) ¡qué bonito es!; **to be ~ of sth** estar seguro de algo; **to be ~ of o.s.** estar seguro de sí mismo; **to make ~ of sth/that** asegurarse de algo/asegurar que; **I'm not ~ how/why/when** no estoy seguro de cómo/por qué/cuándo; **~!** (of course) ¡claro!, ¡por supuesto!; **~ enough** efectivamente.

sure-footed [ʃuə'futɪd] a de pie firme.

surely ['ʃuəlɪ] ad (certainly) seguramente; **~ you don't mean that!** ¡no lo dices en serio!

surety ['ʃuərətɪ] n fianza; (person) fiador(a) m/f; **to go or stand ~ for sb** ser fiador de uno, salir garante por uno.

surf [sɔːf] n olas fpl.

surface ['sɔːfɪs] n superficie f ♦ vt (road) revestir ♦ vi salir a la superficie ♦ cpd (MIL, NAUT) de (la) superficie; **on the ~ it seems that ...** (fig) a primera vista parece que ... .

surface area n área de la superficie.

surface mail n vía terrestre.

surface-to-air missile ['sɔːfɪstə'ɛə-] n proyectil m tierra-aire.

surfboard ['sɔːfbɔːd] n plancha (de surf).

surfeit ['sɔːfɪt] n: **a ~ of** un exceso de.

surfer ['sɔːfə*] n súrfer m/f.

surfing ['sɔːfɪŋ] n surf m.

surge [sɔːdʒ] n oleada, oleaje m; (ELEC) so-

bretensión f transitoria ♦ vi avanzar a tropel; **to ~ forward** avanzar rápidamente.

surgeon ['sɔːdʒən] n cirujano/a.

surgery ['sɔːdʒərɪ] n cirugía; (Brit: room) consultorio; **to undergo ~** operarse.

surgery hours npl (Brit) horas fpl de consulta.

surgical ['sɔːdʒɪkl] a quirúrgico.

surgical spirit n (Brit) alcohol m.

surly ['sɔːlɪ] a hosco, malhumorado.

surmount [sɔː'maunt] vt superar, vencer.

surname ['sɔːneɪm] n apellido.

surpass [sɔː'pɑːs] vt superar, exceder.

surplus ['sɔːpləs] n excedente m; (COMM) superávit m ♦ a (COMM) excedente, sobrante; **to have a ~ of sth** tener un excedente de algo; **it is ~ to our requirements** nos sobra; **~ stock** saldos mpl.

surprise [sə'praɪz] n sorpresa ♦ vt sorprender; **to take by ~** (person) coger a uno desprevenido, sorprender a uno; (MIL: town, fort) atacar por sorpresa.

surprising [sə'praɪzɪŋ] a sorprendente.

surprisingly [sə'praɪzɪŋlɪ] ad (easy, helpful) de modo sorprendente; **(somewhat) ~, he agreed** para sorpresa de todos, aceptó.

surrealism [sə'rɪəlɪzəm] n surrealismo.

surrealist [sə'rɪəlɪst] a, n surrealista m/f.

surrender [sə'rɛndə*] n rendición f, entrega ♦ vi rendirse, entregarse ♦ vt (claim, right) renunciar.

surrender value n valor m de rescate.

surreptitious [sʌrəp'tɪʃəs] a subrepticio.

surrogate ['sʌrəgɪt] n (Brit: substitute) sustituto/a ♦ a: **~ coffee** sucedáneo de café.

surrogate mother n madre f portadora.

surround [sə'raund] vt rodear, circundar; (MIL etc) cercar.

surrounding [sə'raundɪŋ] a circundante.

surroundings [sə'raundɪŋz] npl alrededores mpl, cercanías fpl.

surtax ['sɔːtæks] n sobretasa, sobreimpuesto.

surveillance [sɔː'veɪləns] n vigilancia.

survey n ['sɔːveɪ] inspección f, reconocimiento; (inquiry) encuesta; (comprehensive view: of situation etc) vista de conjunto ♦ vt [sɔː'veɪ] examinar, inspeccionar; (SURVEYING: building) inspeccionar; (: land) hacer un reconocimiento de, reconocer; (look at) mirar, contemplar; (make inquiries about) hacer una encuesta de; **to carry out a ~ of** inspeccionar, examinar.

surveyor [sə'veɪə*] n (Brit) agrimensor(a) m/f.

survival [sə'vaɪvl] n supervivencia.

survival course n curso de supervivencia.

survival kit n equipo de emergencia.

survive [sə'vaɪv] vi sobrevivir; (custom etc) perdurar ♦ vt sobrevivir a.

survivor [sə'vaɪvə*] n superviviente m/f.

susceptibility [səsɛptə'bɪlɪtɪ] *n* (*to illness*) propensión *f*.

susceptible [sə'sɛptəbl] *a* (*easily influenced*) influenciable; (*to disease, illness*): ~ **to** propenso a.

suspect *a, n* ['sʌspɛkt] sospechoso/a *m/f* ◆ *vt* [səs'pɛkt] sospechar.

suspend [səs'pɛnd] *vt* suspender.

suspended sentence [səs'pɛndəd-] *n* (*LAW*) libertad *f* condicional.

suspender belt [səs'pɛndə*-] *n* (*Brit*) portaligas *m inv*.

suspenders [səs'pɛndəz] *npl* (*Brit*) ligas *fpl*; (*US*) tirantes *mpl*.

suspense [səs'pɛns] *n* incertidumbre *f*, duda; (*in film etc*) suspense *m*.

suspense account *n* cuenta en suspenso.

suspension [səs'pɛnʃən] *n* (*gen, AUT*) suspensión *f*; (*of driving licence*) privación *f*.

suspension bridge *n* puente *m* colgante.

suspension file *n* archivador *m* colgante.

suspicion [səs'pɪʃən] *n* sospecha; (*distrust*) recelo; (*trace*) traza; **to be under** ~ estar bajo sospecha; **arrested on** ~ **of murder** detenido bajo sospecha de asesinato.

suspicious [səs'pɪʃəs] *a* (*suspecting*) receloso; (*causing suspicion*) sospechoso; **to be** ~ **of** *or* **about sb/sth** tener sospechas de uno/algo.

suss out [sʌs-] *vt* (*Brit col*) explorar.

sustain [səs'teɪn] *vt* sostener, apoyar; (*suffer*) sufrir, padecer.

sustained [səs'teɪnd] *a* (*effort*) sostenido.

sustenance ['sʌstɪnəns] *n* sustento.

suture ['suːtʃə*] *n* sutura.

SW *abbr* = **short wave**.

swab [swɔb] *n* (*MED*) algodón *m*, frotis *m inv* ◆ *vt* (*NAUT: also:* ~ **down**) limpiar, fregar.

swagger ['swægə*] *vi* pavonearse.

swallow ['swɔləu] *n* (*bird*) golondrina; (*of food*) bocado; (*of drink*) trago ◆ *vt* tragar.

swallow up *vt* (*savings etc*) consumir.

swam [swæm] *pt of* **swim**.

swamp [swɔmp] *n* pantano, ciénaga ◆ *vt* abrumar, agobiar.

swampy ['swɔmpɪ] *a* pantanoso.

swan [swɔn] *n* cisne *m*.

swank [swæŋk] (*col*) *n* (*vanity, boastfulness*) fanfarronada ◆ *vi* fanfarronear, presumir.

swan song *n* (*fig*) canto del cisne.

swap [swɔp] *n* canje *m*, trueque *m* ◆ *vt*: **to** ~ **(for)** canjear (por).

SWAPO ['swaːpəu] *n abbr* (= *South-West Africa People's Organization*) SWAPO *m*.

swarm [swɔːm] *n* (*of bees*) enjambre *m*; (*fig*) multitud *f* ◆ *vi* (*fig*) hormiguear, pulular.

swarthy ['swɔːðɪ] *a* moreno.

swashbuckling ['swɔʃbʌklɪŋ] *a* (*person*) aventurero; (*film*) de capa y espada.

swastika ['swɔstɪkə] *n* esvástica, cruz *f* gamada.

swat [swɔt] *vt* aplastar ◆ *n* (*also:* **fly** ~) matamoscas *m inv*.

swathe [sweɪð] *vt*: **to** ~ **in** (*blankets*) envolver en; (*bandages*) vendar en.

sway [sweɪ] *vi* mecerse, balancearse ◆ *vt* (*influence*) mover, influir en ◆ *n* (*rule, power*): ~ **(over)** dominio (sobre); **to hold** ~ **over sb** dominar a uno, mantener el dominio sobre uno.

Swaziland ['swɑːzɪlænd] *n* Swazilandia.

swear, *pt* **swore**, *pp* **sworn** [swɛə*, swɔː*, swɔːn] *vi* jurar ◆ *vt*: **to** ~ **an oath** prestar juramento, jurar; **to** ~ **to sth** declarar algo bajo juramento.

swear in *vt* tomar juramento (a).

swearword ['swɛəwɔːd] *n* taco, palabrota.

sweat [swɛt] *n* sudor *m* ◆ *vi* sudar.

sweatband ['swɛtbænd] *n* (*SPORT: on head*) venda, banda; (: *on wrist*) muñequera.

sweater ['swɛtə*] *n* suéter *m*.

sweatshirt ['swɛtʃɔːt] *n* sudadera.

sweatshop ['swɛtʃɔp] *n* fábrica donde se explota al obrero.

sweaty ['swɛtɪ] *a* sudoroso.

Swede [swiːd] *n* sueco/a.

swede [swiːd] *n* (*Brit*) nabo.

Sweden ['swiːdn] *n* Suecia.

Swedish ['swiːdɪʃ] *a, n* (*LING*) sueco.

sweep [swiːp] *n* (*act*) barrida; (*of arm*) manotazo *m*; (*curve*) curva, alcance *m*; (*also:* **chimney** ~) deshollinador(a) *m/f* ◆ *vb* (*pt, pp* **swept** [swɛpt]) *vt* barrer; (*disease, fashion*) recorrer ◆ *vi* barrer.

sweep away *vt* barrer; (*rub out*) borrar.

sweep past *vi* pasar rápidamente; (*brush by*) rozar.

sweep up *vi* barrer.

sweeping ['swiːpɪŋ] *a* (*gesture*) dramático; (*generalized*) generalizado; (*changes, reforms*) radical.

sweepstake ['swiːpsteɪk] *n* lotería.

sweet [swiːt] *n* (*candy*) dulce *m*, caramelo; (*Brit: pudding*) postre *m* ◆ *a* dulce; (*sugary*) azucarado; (*charming: person*) encantador(a); (: *smile, character*) dulce, amable, agradable ◆ *ad*: **to smell/taste** ~ oler/saber dulce.

sweet and sour *a* agridulce.

sweetcorn ['swiːtkɔːn] *n* maíz *m*.

sweeten ['swiːtn] *vt* (*person*) endulzar; (*add sugar to*) poner azúcar a.

sweetener ['swiːtnə*] *n* (*CULIN*) dulcificante *m*.

sweetheart ['swiːthɑːt] *n* novio/a; (*in speech*) amor.

sweetness ['swiːtnɪs] *n* (*gen*) dulzura.

sweet pea *n* guisante *m* de olor.

sweet potato *n* batata, camote *m* (*LAm*).

sweetshop ['swiːtʃɔp] *n* (*Brit*) confitería, bombonería.

swell [swɛl] *n* (*of sea*) marejada, oleaje *m*

◆ *a* (*US*: *col*: *excellent*) estupendo, fenomenal ◆ *vb* (*pt* ~**ed**, *pp* **swollen** *or* ~**ed** ['swəulən]) *vt* hinchar, inflar ◆ *vi* hincharse, inflarse.

swelling ['swɛlɪŋ] *n* (*MED*) hinchazón *f*.

sweltering ['swɛltərɪŋ] *a* sofocante, de mucho calor.

swept [swɛpt] *pt, pp of* **sweep**.

swerve [swəːv] *n* esguince *m*; (*in car*) desvío brusco ◆ *vi* desviarse bruscamente.

swift [swɪft] *n* (*bird*) vencejo ◆ *a* rápido, veloz.

swiftly ['swɪftlɪ] *ad* rápidamente.

swiftness ['swɪftnɪs] *n* rapidez *f*, velocidad *f*.

swig [swɪg] *n* (*col*: *drink*) trago.

swill [swɪl] *n* bazofia ◆ *vt* (*also*: ~ **out**, ~ **down**) lavar, limpiar con agua.

swim [swɪm] *n*: **to go for a** ~ ir a nadar *or* a bañarse ◆ *vb* (*pt* **swam**, *pp* **swum** [swæm, swʌm]) *vi* nadar; (*head, room*) dar vueltas ◆ *vt* pasar a nado; **to go** ~**ming** ir a nadar(se); **to** ~ **a length** nadar *or* hacer un largo.

swimmer ['swɪmə*] *n* nadador(a) *m/f*.

swimming ['swɪmɪŋ] *n* natación *f*.

swimming cap *n* gorro de baño.

swimming costume *n* bañador *m*, traje *m* de baño.

swimming pool *n* piscina, alberca (*LAm*).

swimming trunks *npl* bañador *msg*.

swimsuit ['swɪmsuːt] *n* = **swimming costume**.

swindle ['swɪndl] *n* estafa ◆ *vt* estafar.

swine [swaɪn] *n, pl inv* cerdos *mpl*, puercos *mpl*; (*col!*) canalla *m* (*!*).

swing [swɪŋ] *n* (*in playground*) columpio; (*movement*) balanceo, vaivén *m*; (*change of direction*) viraje *m*; (*rhythm*) ritmo; (*POL*: *in votes etc*): **there has been a** ~ **towards/away from Labour** ha habido un viraje en favor/en contra del Partido Laborista ◆ *vb* (*pt, pp* **swung** [swʌŋ]) *vt* balancear; (*on a* ~) columpiar; (*also*: ~ **round**) voltear, girar ◆ *vi* balancearse, columpiarse; (*also*: ~ **round**) dar media vuelta; **a** ~ **to the left** un movimiento hacia la izquierda; **to be in full** ~ estar en plena marcha; **to get into the** ~ **of things** ponerse al corriente de las cosas *or* de la situación; **the road** ~**s south** la carretera gira hacia el sur.

swing bridge *n* puente *m* giratorio.

swing door, (*US*) **swinging door** ['swɪŋɪŋ-] *n* puerta giratoria.

swingeing ['swɪndʒɪŋ] *a* (*Brit*) abrumador(a).

swipe [swaɪp] *n* golpe *m* fuerte ◆ *vt* (*hit*) golpear fuerte; (*col*: *steal*) guindar.

swirl [swəːl] *vi* arremolinarse.

swish [swɪʃ] *n* (*sound*: *of whip*) chasquido; (: *of skirts*) frufrú *m*; (: *of grass*) crujido

◆ *a* (*col*: *smart*) elegante ◆ *vi* chasquear.

Swiss [swɪs] *a, n* (*pl inv*) suizo/a *m/f*.

switch [swɪtʃ] *n* (*for light, radio etc*) interruptor *m*; (*change*) cambio ◆ *vt* (*change*) cambiar de; (*invert*: *also*: ~ **round**, ~ **over**) intercambiar.

switch off *vt* apagar; (*engine*) parar.

switch on *vt* (*AUT*: *ignition*) encender, prender (*LAm*); (*engine, machine*) arrancar; (*water supply*) conectar.

switchboard ['swɪtʃbɔːd] *n* (*TEL*) centralita (de teléfonos), conmutador *m* (*LAm*).

Switzerland ['swɪtsələnd] *n* Suiza.

swivel ['swɪvl] *vi* (*also*: ~ **round**) girar.

swollen ['swəulən] *pp of* **swell**.

swoon [swuːn] *vi* desmayarse.

swoop [swuːp] *n* (*by police etc*) redada; (*of bird etc*) calada ◆ *vi* (*also*: ~ **down**) calarse.

swop [swɔp] = **swap**.

sword [sɔːd] *n* espada.

swordfish ['sɔːdfɪʃ] *n* pez *m* espada.

swore [swɔː*] *pt of* **swear**.

sworn [swɔːn] *pp of* **swear**.

swot [swɔt] (*Brit*) *vt, vi* empollar ◆ *n* empollón/ona *m/f*.

swum [swʌm] *pp of* **swim**.

swung [swʌŋ] *pt, pp of* **swing**.

sycamore ['sɪkəmɔː*] *n* sicomoro.

sycophant ['sɪkəfænt] *n* adulador(a), pelotillero/a.

Sydney ['sɪdnɪ] *n* Sidney *m*.

syllable ['sɪləbl] *n* sílaba.

syllabus ['sɪləbəs] *n* programa *m* de estudios; **on the** ~ en el programa de estudios.

symbol ['sɪmbl] *n* símbolo.

symbolic(al) [sɪm'bɔlɪk(l)] *a* simbólico; **to be** ~ **of sth** simbolizar algo.

symbolism ['sɪmbəlɪzəm] *n* simbolismo.

symbolize ['sɪmbəlaɪz] *vt* simbolizar.

symmetrical [sɪ'mɛtrɪkl] *a* simétrico.

symmetry ['sɪmɪtrɪ] *n* simetría.

sympathetic [sɪmpə'θɛtɪk] *a* compasivo; (*understanding*) comprensivo; **to be** ~ **to a cause** (*well-disposed*) apoyar una causa; **to be** ~ **towards** (*person*) ser comprensivo con.

sympathize ['sɪmpəθaɪz] *vi*: **to** ~ **with sb** compadecerse de uno; (*understand*) comprender a uno.

sympathizer ['sɪmpəθaɪzə*] *n* (*POL*) simpatizante *m/f*.

sympathy ['sɪmpəθɪ] *n* (*pity*) compasión *f*; (*understanding*) comprensión *f*; **a letter of** ~ un pésame; **with our deepest** ~ nuestro más sentido pésame.

symphony ['sɪmfənɪ] *n* sinfonía.

symposium [sɪm'pəuzɪəm] *n* simposio.

symptom ['sɪmptəm] *n* síntoma *m*, indicio.

symptomatic [sɪmptə'mætɪk] *a*: ~ (**of**) sintomático (de).

synagogue ['sɪnəgɔg] *n* sinagoga.

synchromesh ['sɪŋkrəumɛʃ] *n* cambio sincronizado de velocidades.

synchronize ['sɪŋkrənaɪz] *vt* sincronizar ♦ *vi*: **to ~ with** sincronizarse con.

syncopated ['sɪŋkəpeɪtɪd] *a* sincopado.

syndicate ['sɪndɪkɪt] *n* (*gen*) sindicato; (*PRESS*) agencia (de noticias).

syndrome ['sɪndrəum] *n* síndrome *m*.

synonym ['sɪnənɪm] *n* sinónimo.

synonymous [sɪ'nɔnɪməs] *a*: **~ (with)** sinónimo (con).

synopsis, *pl* **synopses** [sɪ'nɔpsɪs, -siːz] *n* sinopsis *f inv*.

syntax ['sɪntæks] *n* sintaxis *f*.

syntax error *n* (*COMPUT*) error *m* sintáctico.

synthesis, *pl* **syntheses** ['sɪnθəsɪs, -siːz] *n* síntesis *f inv*.

synthesizer ['sɪnθəsaɪzə*] *n* sintetizador *m*.

synthetic [sɪn'θetɪk] *a* sintético ♦ *n* sintético.

syphilis ['sɪfɪlɪs] *n* sífilis *f*.

syphon ['saɪfən] = **siphon.**

Syria ['sɪrɪə] *n* Siria.

Syrian ['sɪrɪən] *a*, *n* sirio/a *m/f*.

syringe [sɪ'rɪndʒ] *n* jeringa.

syrup ['sɪrəp] *n* jarabe *m*, almíbar *m*.

system ['sɪstəm] *n* sistema *m*; (*ANAT*) organismo; **it was quite a shock to his ~** fue un golpe para el organismo.

systematic [sɪstə'mætɪk] *a* sistemático; metódico.

system disk *n* (*COMPUT*) disco del sistema.

systems analyst *n* analista *m/f* de sistemas.

T

T, t [tiː] *n* (*letter*) T, t *f;* **T for Tommy** T de Tarragona.

TA *n abbr* (*Brit*) = *Territorial Army.*

ta [tɑː] *excl* (*Brit col*) ¡gracias!

tab [tæb] *n abbr* = **tabulator** ♦ *n* lengüeta; (*label*) etiqueta; **to keep ~s on** (*fig*) vigilar.

tabby ['tæbɪ] *n* (*also:* **~ cat**) gato atigrado.

tabernacle ['tæbənækl] *n* tabernáculo.

table ['teɪbl] *n* mesa; (*chart: of statistics etc*) cuadro, gráfica, tabla ♦ *vt* (*Brit: motion etc*) presentar; **to lay** *or* **set the ~** poner la mesa; **to clear the ~** quitar *or* levantar la mesa; **league ~** (*FOOTBALL, RUGBY*) clasificación *f* del campeonato; **~ of contents** índice *m* de materias.

tablecloth ['teɪblklɔθ] *n* mantel *m*.

table d'hôte [tɑːbl'dəut] *n* menú *m*.

table lamp *n* lámpara de mesa.

tableland ['teɪbllænd] *n* meseta, altiplano (*LAm*).

tablemat ['teɪblmæt] *n* salvamanteles *m inv*.

tablespoon ['teɪblspuːn] *n* cuchara grande; (*also:* **~ful:** *as measurement*) cucharada.

tablet ['tæblɪt] *n* (*MED*) pastilla, comprimido; (*for writing*) bloc *m*; (*of stone*) lápida; **~ of soap** pastilla de jabón.

table talk *n* conversación *f* de sobremesa.

table tennis *n* ping-pong *m*, tenis *m* de mesa.

table wine *n* vino de mesa.

tabloid ['tæblɔɪd] *n* (*newspaper*) periódico popular sensacionalista; **the ~s** la prensa amarilla.

taboo [tə'buː] *a*, *n* tabú *m*.

tabulate ['tæbjuleɪt] *vt* disponer en tablas.

tabulator ['tæbjuleɪtə*] *n* tabulador *m*.

tachograph ['tækəgrɑːf] *n* tacógrafo.

tachometer [tæ'kɔmɪtə*] *n* taquímetro.

tacit ['tæsɪt] *a* tácito.

tacitly ['tæsɪtlɪ] *ad* tácitamente.

taciturn ['tæsɪtɜːn] *a* taciturno.

tack [tæk] *n* (*nail*) tachuela; (*stitch*) hilván *m*; (*NAUT*) bordada ♦ *vt* (*nail*) clavar con tachuelas; (*stitch*) hilvanar ♦ *vi* virar; **to ~ sth on to (the end of) sth** (*of letter, book*) añadir algo a(l final de) algo.

tackle ['tækl] *n* (*gear*) equipo; (*fishing ~, for lifting*) aparejo; (*FOOTBALL*) entrada, tackle *m*; (*RUGBY*) placaje *m* ♦ *vt* (*difficulty*) enfrentar; (*grapple with*) agarrar; (*FOOTBALL*) entrar; (*RUGBY*) placar.

tacky ['tækɪ] *a* pegajoso; (*US: shabby*) destartalado.

tact [tækt] *n* tacto, discreción *f*.

tactful ['tæktful] *a* discreto, diplomático; **to be ~** tener tacto, actuar discretamente.

tactfully ['tæktfulɪ] *ad* diplomáticamente, con tacto.

tactical ['tæktɪkl] *a* táctico.

tactics ['tæktɪks] *n*, *npl* táctica *sg*.

tactless ['tæktlɪs] *a* indiscreto.

tactlessly ['tæktlɪslɪ] *ad* indiscretamente, sin tacto.

tadpole ['tædpəul] *n* renacuajo.

taffy ['tæfɪ] *n* (*US*) melcocha.

tag [tæg] *n* (*label*) etiqueta; **price/name ~** etiqueta con el precio/con el nombre.

tag along *vi*: **to ~ along with sb** acompañar a uno.

tag question *n* pregunta coletilla.

Tahiti [tɑː'hiːtɪ] *n* Tahití *m*.

tail [teɪl] *n* cola; (*ZOOL*) rabo; (*of shirt, coat*) faldón *m* ♦ *vt* (*follow*) vigilar a; **heads or ~s** cara o cruz; **to turn ~** volver la espalda.

tail away, tail off *vi* (*in size, quality etc*) ir disminuyendo.

tailback ['teɪlbæk] *n* (*Brit AUT*) cola.

tail coat *n* frac *m*.

tail end n cola, parte f final.
tailgate ['teɪlgeɪt] n (AUT) puerta trasera.
tail light n (AUT) luz f trasera.
tailor ['teɪlə*] n sastre m ♦ vt: **to ~ sth (to)** confeccionar algo a medida (para); **~'s (shop)** sastrería.
tailoring ['teɪlərɪŋ] n (cut) corte m; (craft) sastrería.
tailor-made ['teɪlə'meɪd] a (also fig) hecho a la medida.
tailwind ['teɪlwɪnd] n viento de cola.
taint [teɪnt] vt (meat, food) contaminar; (fig: reputation) manchar, tachar (LAm).
tainted ['teɪntɪd] a (water, air) contaminado; (fig) manchado.
Taiwan [taɪ'wɑːn] n Taiwán m.
take [teɪk] vb (pt **took**, pp **taken** [tuk, 'teɪkn]) vt tomar; (grab) coger (Sp), agarrar (LAm); (gain: prize) ganar; (require: effort, courage) exigir; (support weight of) aguantar; (hold: passengers etc) tener cabida para; (accompany, bring, carry) llevar; (exam) presentarse a; (conduct: meeting) presidir ♦ vi (fire) prender; (dye) agarrar, tomar ♦ n (CINEMA) toma; **to ~ sth from** (drawer etc) sacar algo de; (person) coger (Sp) algo a; **to ~ sb's hand** tomar de la mano a uno; **to ~ notes** tomar apuntes; **to be ~n ill** ponerse enfermo; **~ the first on the left** toma la primera a la izquierda; **I only took Russian for one year** sólo estudié el ruso un año; **I took him for a doctor** le tenía por médico; **it won't ~ long** durará poco; **it will ~ at least 5 litres** tiene cabida para 5 litros como mínimo; **to be ~n with sb/ sth** (attracted) tomarle cariño a uno/ tomarle gusto a algo; **I ~ it that...** supongo que....
take after vt fus parecerse a.
take apart vt desmontar.
take away vt (remove) quitar; (carry off) llevar vi: **to ~ away from** quitar mérito a.
take back vt (return) devolver; (one's words) retractar.
take down vt (building) derribar; (dismantle: scaffolding) desmantelar; (letter etc) apuntar.
take in vt (Brit: deceive) engañar; (understand) entender; (include) abarcar; (lodger) acoger, recibir; (orphan, stray dog) recoger; (SEWING) achicar.
take off vi (AVIAT) despegar ♦ vt (remove) quitar; (imitate) imitar.
take on vt (work) emprender; (employee) contratar; (opponent) desafiar.
take out vt sacar; (remove) quitar; **don't ~ it out on me!** ¡no te desquites conmigo!
take over vt (business) tomar posesión de ♦ vi: **to ~ over from sb** reemplazar a uno.

take to vt fus (person) coger cariño a (Sp), encariñarse con (LAm); (activity) aficionarse a; **to ~ to doing sth** entregarse a (hacer) algo.
take up vt (a dress) acortar; (occupy: time, space) ocupar; (engage in: hobby etc) dedicarse a; (absorb: liquids) absorber; (accept: offer, challenge) aceptar ♦ vi: **to ~ up with sb** hacerse amigo de uno.
take upon vt: **to ~ it upon o.s. to do sth** encargarse de hacer algo.
takeaway ['teɪkəweɪ] a (Brit: food) para llevar.
take-home pay ['teɪkhəum-] n salario neto.
taken ['teɪkən] pp of **take**.
takeoff ['teɪkɔf] n (AVIAT) despegue m.
takeover ['teɪkəuvə*] n (COMM) absorción f.
takeover bid n oferta pública de compra.
takings ['teɪkɪŋz] npl (COMM) ingresos mpl.
talc [tælk] n (also: **~um powder**) talco.
tale [teɪl] n (story) cuento; (account) relación f; **to tell ~s** (fig) chismear.
talent ['tælnt] n talento.
talented ['tæləntɪd] a talentoso, de talento.
talk [tɔːk] n charla; (gossip) habladurías fpl, chismes mpl; (conversation) conversación f ♦ vi (speak) hablar; (chatter) charlar; **~s** npl (POL etc) conversaciones fpl; **to give a ~** dar una charla or conferencia; **to ~ about** hablar de; **to ~ sb into doing sth** convencer a uno para que haga algo; **to ~ sb out of doing sth** disuadir a uno de que haga algo; **to ~ shop** hablar del trabajo; **~ing of films, have you seen ...?** hablando de películas, ¿has visto ...?
talk over vt discutir.
talkative ['tɔːkətɪv] a hablador(a).
talker ['tɔːkə*] n hablador(a) m/f.
talking point ['tɔːkɪŋ-] n tema m de conversación.
talking-to ['tɔːkɪŋtuː] n: **to give sb a good ~** echar una buena bronca a uno.
talk show n programa m magazine.
tall [tɔːl] a alto; (tree) grande; **to be 6 feet ~** ≈ medir 1 metro 80, tener 1 metro 80 de alto; **how ~ are you?** ¿cuánto mides?
tallboy ['tɔːlbɔɪ] n (Brit) cómoda alta.
tallness ['tɔːlnɪs] n altura.
tall story n cuento chino.
tally ['tælɪ] n cuenta ♦ vi: **to ~ (with)** corresponder (con); **to keep a ~ of sth** llevar la cuenta de algo.
talon ['tælən] n garra.
tambourine [tæmbə'riːn] n pandereta.
tame [teɪm] a (mild) manso; (tamed) domesticado; (fig: story, style) mediocre; (: person) soso.
tameness ['teɪmnɪs] n mansedumbre f.
tamper ['tæmpə*] vi: **to ~ with** entrometerse en.
tampon ['tæmpən] n tampón m.

tan [tæn] *n* (*also:* **sun~**) bronceado ◆ *vt* broncear ◆ *vi* ponerse moreno ◆ *a* (*colour*) marrón; **to get a ~** broncearse, ponerse moreno.

tandem ['tændəm] *n* tándem *m*.

tang [tæŋ] *n* sabor *m* fuerte.

tangent ['tændʒənt] *n* (*MATH*) tangente *f*; **to go off at a ~** (*fig*) salirse por la tangente.

tangerine [tændʒə'riːn] *n* mandarina.

tangible ['tændʒəbl] *a* tangible; **~ assets** bienes *mpl* tangibles.

Tangier [tæn'dʒiə*] *n* Tánger *m*.

tangle ['tæŋgl] *n* enredo; **to get in(to) a ~** enredarse.

tango ['tæŋgəu] *n* tango.

tank [tæŋk] *n* (*water* ~) depósito, tanque *m*; (*for fish*) acuario; (*MIL*) tanque *m*.

tankard ['tæŋkəd] *n* bock *m*.

tanker ['tæŋkə*] *n* (*ship*) petrolero; (*truck*) camión *m* cisterna.

tankful ['tæŋkful] *n*: **to get a ~ of petrol** llenar el depósito de gasolina.

tanned [tænd] *a* (*skin*) moreno, bronceado.

tannin ['tænɪn] *n* tanino.

tanning ['tænɪŋ] *n* (*of leather*) curtido.

tannoy ® ['tænɔɪ] *n*: **over the ~** por el altavoz.

tantalizing ['tæntəlaɪzɪŋ] *a* tentador(a).

tantamount ['tæntəmaunt] *a*: **~ to** equivalente a.

tantrum ['tæntrəm] *n* rabieta; **to throw a ~** coger una rabieta.

Tanzania [tænzə'nɪə] *n* Tanzanía.

Tanzanian [tænzə'nɪən] *a*, *n* tanzano/a *m*/*f*.

tap [tæp] *n* (*Brit: on sink etc*) grifo, canilla (*LAm*); (*gentle blow*) golpecito; (*gas* ~) llave *f* ◆ *vt* (*table etc*) tamborilear; (*shoulder etc*) palmear; (*resources*) utilizar, explotar; (*telephone conversation*) interceptar, escuchar clandestinamente; **on ~** (*fig: resources*) a mano; **beer on ~** cerveza de barril.

tap-dancing ['tæpdɑ:nsɪŋ] *n* claqué *m*.

tape [teɪp] *n* cinta; (*also: magnetic* ~) cinta magnética; (*sticky* ~) cinta adhesiva ◆ *vt* (*record*) grabar (en cinta); **on ~** (*song etc*) grabado (en cinta).

tape deck *n* tocacassettes *m inv*.

tape measure *n* cinta métrica, metro.

taper ['teɪpə*] *n* cirio ◆ *vi* afilarse.

tape-record ['teɪprɪkɔ:d] *vt* grabar (en cinta).

tape recorder *n* grabadora.

tape recording *n* grabación *f*.

tapered ['teɪpəd], **tapering** ['teɪpərɪŋ] *a* terminado en punta.

tapestry ['tæpɪstrɪ] *n* (*object*) tapiz *m*; (*art*) tapicería.

tape-worm ['teɪpwə:m] *n* solitaria, tenia.

tapioca [tæpɪ'əukə] *n* tapioca *m*.

tappet ['tæpɪt] *n* varilla de levantamiento.

tar [tɑ:] *n* alquitrán *m*, brea; **low/middle ~ cigarettes** cigarrillos con contenido bajo/ medio de alquitrán.

tarantula [tə'ræntjulə] *n* tarántula.

tardy ['tɑ:dɪ] *a* (*late*) tardío; (*slow*) lento.

tare [tɛə*] *n* (*COMM*) tara.

target ['tɑ:gɪt] *n* (*gen*) blanco; **to be on ~** (*project*) seguir el curso previsto.

target audience *n* público objetivo.

target market *n* (*COMM*) mercado objetivo.

target practice *n* tiro al blanco.

tariff ['tærɪf] *n* tarifa.

tariff barrier *n* (*COMM*) barrera arancelaria.

tarmac ['tɑ:mæk] *n* (*Brit: on road*) alquitranado; (*AVIAT*) pista (de aterrizaje).

tarn [tɑ:n] *n* lago pequeño de montaña.

tarnish ['tɑ:nɪʃ] *vt* deslustrar.

tarpaulin [tɑ:'pɔ:lɪn] *n* alquitranado.

tarragon ['tærəgən] *n* estragón *m*.

tarry ['tærɪ] *vi* entretenerse, quedarse atrás.

tart [tɑ:t] *n* (*CULIN*) tarta; (*Brit col: pej: woman*) fulana ◆ *a* (*flavour*) agrio, ácido.

tart up *vt* (*room, building*) dar tono a.

tartan ['tɑ:tn] *n* tartán *m*, escocés *m* ◆ *a* de tartán.

tartar ['tɑ:tə*] *n* (*on teeth*) sarro.

tartar sauce *n* salsa tártara.

tartly ['tɑ:tlɪ] *ad* (*answer*) ásperamente.

task [tɑ:sk] *n* tarea; **to take to ~** reprender.

task force *n* (*MIL, POLICE*) grupo de operaciones.

taskmaster ['tɑ:skmɑ:stə*] *n*: **he's a hard ~** es muy exigente.

Tasmania [tæz'meɪnɪə] *n* Tasmania.

tassel ['tæsl] *n* borla.

taste [teɪst] *n* sabor *m*, gusto; (*also: after~*) dejo; (*sip*) sorbo; (*fig: glimpse, idea*) muestra, idea ◆ *vt* probar ◆ *vi*: **to ~ of or like** (*fish etc*) saber a; **you can ~ the garlic (in it)** se nota el sabor a ajo; **can I have a ~ of this wine?** ¿puedo probar este vino?; **to have a ~ for sth** ser aficionado a algo; **in good/bad ~** de buen/mal gusto; **to be in bad or poor ~** ser de mal gusto.

taste bud *n* papila gustativa *or* del gusto.

tasteful ['teɪstful] *a* de buen gusto.

tastefully ['teɪstfulɪ] *ad* elegantemente, con buen gusto.

tasteless ['teɪstlɪs] *a* (*food*) soso; (*remark*) de mal gusto.

tastelessly ['teɪstlɪslɪ] *ad* con mal gusto.

tastily ['teɪstɪlɪ] *ad* sabrosamente.

tastiness ['teɪstɪnɪs] *n* (buen) sabor *m*, lo sabroso.

tasty ['teɪstɪ] *a* sabroso, rico.

ta-ta ['tæ'tɑ:] *interj* (*Brit col*) hasta luego, adiós.

tatters ['tætəz] *npl*: **in ~** (*also:* **tattered**) hecho jirones.

tattoo [tə'tu:] *n* tatuaje *m*; (*spectacle*) espectáculo militar ◆ *vt* tatuar.

tatty ['tætɪ] *a* (*Brit col*) raído.

taught [tɔ:t] *pt, pp of* **teach**.

taunt [tɔ:nt] *n* burla ♦ *vt* burlarse de.

Taurus ['tɔ:rəs] *n* Tauro.

taut [tɔ:t] *a* tirante, tenso.

tavern ['tævən] *n* (*old*) posada, fonda.

tawdry ['tɔ:drɪ] *a* de mal gusto.

tawny ['tɔ:nɪ] *a* leonado.

tax [tæks] *n* impuesto ♦ *vt* gravar (con un impuesto); (*fig*: *test*) poner a prueba; (: *patience*) agotar; **before/after** ~ impuestos excluidos/incluidos; **free of** ~ libre de impuestos.

taxable ['tæksəbl] *a* (*income*) imponible, sujeto a impuestos.

tax allowance *n* desgravación *f* fiscal.

taxation [tæk'seɪʃən] *n* impuestos *mpl*; **system of** ~ sistema *m* tributario.

tax avoidance *n* evasión *f* de impuestos.

tax collector *n* recaudador(a) *m/f*.

tax disc *n* (*Brit AUT*) pegatina del impuesto de circulación.

tax evasion *n* evasión *f* fiscal.

tax exemption *n* exención *f* de impuestos.

tax-free ['tæksfri:] *a* libre de impuestos.

tax haven *n* paraíso fiscal.

taxi ['tæksɪ] *n* taxi *m* ♦ *vi* (*AVIAT*) rodar por la pista.

taxidermist ['tæksɪdə:mɪst] *n* taxidermista *m/f*.

taxi driver *n* taxista *m/f*.

taximeter ['tæksɪmi:tə*] *n* taxímetro *m*.

tax inspector *n* tasador(a) *m/f* de impuestos.

taxi rank (*Brit*), **taxi stand** *n* parada de taxis.

tax payer *n* contribuyente *m/f*.

tax rebate *n* devolución *f* de impuestos, reembolso fiscal.

tax relief *n* desgravación *f* fiscal.

tax return *n* declaración *f* de ingresos.

tax shelter *n* protección *f* fiscal.

tax year *n* año fiscal.

TB *n abbr* = **tuberculosis**.

TD *n abbr* (*US*) (: **Treasury Department**; (: *FOOTBALL*) = **touchdown**.

tea [ti:] *n* té *m*; (*Brit*: *snack*) merienda; **high** ~ (*Brit*) merienda-cena.

tea bag *n* bolsita de té.

tea break *n* (*Brit*) descanso para el té.

teacake ['ti:keɪk] *n* bollito, queque *m* (*LAm*).

teach, *pt, pp* **taught** [ti:tʃ, tɔ:t] *vt*: **to** ~ **sb sth**, ~ **sth to sb** enseñar algo a uno ♦ *vi* enseñar; (*be a teacher*) ser profesor(a); **it taught him a lesson** (eso) le sirvió de escarmiento.

teacher ['ti:tʃə*] *n* (*in secondary school*) profesor(a) *m/f*; (*in primary school*) maestro/a; **Spanish** ~ profesor(a) *m/f* de español.

teacher training college *n* (*for primary schools*) escuela normal; (*for secondary schools*) centro de formación profesoral.

teach-in ['ti:tʃɪn] *n* reunión tipo seminario con *fines formativos o didácticos.

teaching ['ti:tʃɪŋ] *n* enseñanza.

teaching aids *npl* ayudas *fpl* pedagógicas.

teaching hospital *n* hospital *m* con facultad de medicina.

tea cosy *n* cubretetera *m*.

teacup ['ti:kʌp] *n* taza para el té.

teak [ti:k] *n* (madera de) teca.

tea leaves *npl* hojas *fpl* de té.

team [ti:m] *n* equipo; (*of animals*) pareja.

team up *vi* asociarse.

team spirit *n* espíritu *m* de equipo.

teamwork ['ti:mwə:k] *n* trabajo en equipo.

tea party *n* té *m*.

teapot ['ti:pɔt] *n* tetera.

tear [tɛə*] *n* rasgón *m*, desgarrón *m*; [tɪə*] lágrima ♦ *vb* [tɛə*] (*pt* **tore,** *pp* **torn** [tɔ:*, tɔ:n]) *vt* romper, rasgar ♦ *vi* rasgarse; **in** ~**s** llorando; **to burst into** ~**s** deshacerse en lágrimas; **to** ~ **to pieces** *or* **to bits** *or* **to shreds** (*also fig*) hacer pedazos, destrozar.

tear along *vi* (*rush*) precipitarse.

tear apart *vt* (*also fig*) hacer pedazos.

tear away *vt*: **to** ~ **o.s. away (from sth)** arrancarse (de algo), dejar (algo).

tear out *vt* (*sheet of paper, cheque*) arrancar.

tear up *vt* (*sheet of paper etc*) romper.

tearaway ['tɛərəweɪ] *n* (*col*) gamberro/a.

teardrop ['tɪədrɔp] *n* lágrima.

tearful ['tɪəful] *a* lloroso.

tear gas *n* gas *m* lacrimógeno.

tearing ['tɛərɪŋ] *a*: **to be in a** ~ **hurry** tener muchísima prisa.

tearoom ['ti:ru:m] *n* salón *m* de té, cafetería.

tease [ti:z] *n* bromista *m/f* ♦ *vt* tomar el pelo a.

tea set *n* servicio de té.

teashop ['ti:ʃɔp] *n* café *m*, cafetería.

teaspoon ['ti:spu:n] *n* cucharita; (*also*: ~**ful**: *as measurement*) cucharadita.

tea strainer *n* colador *m* de té.

teat [ti:t] *n* (*of bottle*) boquilla, tetilla.

teatime ['ti:taɪm] *n* hora del té.

tea towel *n* (*Brit*) paño de cocina.

tea urn *n* tetera grande.

tech [tɛk] *n abbr* (*col*) = **technology, technical college**.

technical ['tɛknɪkl] *a* técnico.

technical college *n* centro de formación profesional.

technicality [tɛknɪ'kælɪtɪ] *n* detalle *m* técnico; **on a legal** ~ por una cuestión formal.

technically ['tɛknɪklɪ] *ad* técnicamente.

technician [tɛk'nɪʃn] *n* técnico/a.

technique [tɛk'ni:k] *n* técnica.

technocrat ['tɛknəkræt] *n* tecnócrata *m/f*.

technological [tɛknə'lɔdʒɪkl] *a* tecnológico.

technologist [tɛk'nɔlədʒɪst] *n* tecnólogo/a.

technology [tɛk'nɔlədʒɪ] *n* tecnología.

teddy (bear) ['tɛdɪ-] *n* osito de felpa.
tedious ['tiːdɪəs] *a* pesado, aburrido.
tediously ['tiːdɪəslɪ] *ad* aburridamente, de modo pesado.
tedium ['tiːdɪəm] *n* tedio.
tee [tiː] *n* (*GOLF*) tee *m*.
teem [tiːm] *vi*: **to ~ with** rebosar de; **it is ~ing (with rain)** llueve a mares.
teenage ['tiːneɪdʒ] *a* (*fashions etc*) juvenil.
teenager ['tiːneɪdʒə*] *n* joven *m/f* (de 13 a 19 años).
teens [tiːnz] *npl*: **to be in one's ~** ser adolescente.
tee-shirt ['tiːʃəːt] *n* = **T-shirt.**
teeter ['tiːtə*] *vi* balancearse.
teeth [tiːθ] *npl of* **tooth.**
teethe [tiːð] *vi* echar los dientes.
teething ring ['tiːðɪŋ-] *n* mordedor *m*.
teething troubles ['tiːðɪŋ-] *npl* (*fig*) dificultades *fpl* iniciales.
teetotal ['tiː'təutl] *a* (*person*) abstemio.
teetotaller, (*US*) **teetotaler** ['tiː'təutlə*] *n* (*person*) abstemio/a.
TEFL ['tɛfl] *n abbr* = *Teaching of English as a Foreign Language.*
Teheran [tɛə'rɑːn] *n* Teherán *m*.
tel. *abbr* (= *telephone*) tel.
Tel Aviv ['tɛlə'viːv] *n* Tel Aviv *m*.
telecast ['tɛlɪkɑːst] *vt, vi* transmitir por televisión.
telecommunications ['tɛlɪkəmjuːnɪ'keɪʃənz] *n* telecomunicaciones *fpl*.
telefax ['tɛlɪfæks] *n* telefax *m*.
telegram ['tɛlɪgræm] *n* telegrama *m*.
telegraph ['tɛlɪgrɑːf] *n* telégrafo.
telegraphic [tɛlɪ'græfɪk] *a* telegráfico.
telegraph pole *n* poste *m* telegráfico.
telegraph wire *n* hilo telegráfico.
telepathic [tɛlɪ'pæθɪk] *a* telepático.
telepathy [tə'lɛpəθɪ] *n* telepatía.
telephone ['tɛlɪfəun] *n* teléfono ♦ *vt* llamar por teléfono, telefonear; **to be on the ~** (*subscriber*) tener teléfono; (*be speaking*) estar hablando por teléfono.
telephone booth, (*Brit*) **telephone box** *n* cabina telefónica.
telephone call *n* llamada (telefónica).
telephone directory *n* guía (telefónica).
telephone exchange *n* central *f* telefónica.
telephone kiosk *n* (*Brit*) cabina telefónica.
telephone number *n* número de teléfono.
telephonist [tə'lɛfənɪst] *n* (*Brit*) telefonista *m/f*.
telephoto ['tɛlɪ'fəutəu] *a*: **~ lens** teleobjetivo.
teleprinter ['tɛlɪprɪntə*] *n* teletipo, teleimpresora.
teleprompter ® ['tɛlɪprɔmptə*] *n* teleapuntador *m*.
telescope ['tɛlɪskəup] *n* telescopio.
telescopic [tɛlɪ'skɔpɪk] *a* telescópico; (*um-*

brella) plegable.
Teletex ® ['tɛlɪtɛks] *n* (*TEL*) Teletex(to) *m* ®.
televise ['tɛlɪvaɪz] *vt* televisar.
television ['tɛlɪvɪʒən] *n* televisión *f*; **to watch ~** mirar la televisión.
television licence *n* impuesto de televisor.
television set *n* televisor *m*.
telex ['tɛlɛks] *n* télex *m*; (*machine*) máquina télex ♦ *vt* (*message*) enviar por télex; (*person*) enviar un télex a ♦ *vi* enviar un télex.
tell *pt, pp* **told** [tɛl, təuld] *vt* decir; (*relate: story*) contar; (*distinguish*): **to ~ sth from** distinguir algo de ♦ *vi* (*talk*): **to ~ (of)** contar; (*have effect*) tener efecto; **to ~ sb to do sth** mandar a uno hacer algo; **to ~ sb about sth** explicar algo a uno; **to ~ the time** dar *or* decir la hora; **can you ~ me the time?** ¿me puedes decir la hora?; **(I) ~ you what ...** fíjate ...; **I couldn't ~ them apart** no podía distinguirlos.
tell off *vt*: **to ~ sb off** regañar a uno.
tell on *vt fus*: **to ~ on sb** chivarse de uno.
teller ['tɛlə*] *n* (*in bank*) cajero/a.
telling ['tɛlɪŋ] *a* (*remark, detail*) revelador(a).
telltale ['tɛlteɪl] *a* (*sign*) indicador(a).
telly ['tɛlɪ] *n* (*Brit col*) tele *f*.
temerity [tə'mɛrɪtɪ] *n* temeridad *f*.
temp [tɛmp] *n abbr* (*Brit: = temporary office worker*) temporero/a ♦ *vi* trabajar de interino/a.
temper ['tɛmpə*] *n* (*mood*) humor *m*; (*bad ~*) (mal) genio; (*fit of anger*) ira; (*of child*) rabieta ♦ *vt* (*moderate*) moderar; **to be in a ~** estar furioso; **to lose one's ~** enfadarse, enojarse (*LAm*); **to keep one's ~** contenerse, no alterarse.
temperament ['tɛmprəmənt] *n* (*nature*) temperamento.
temperamental [tɛmprə'mɛntl] *a* temperamental.
temperance ['tɛmpərns] *n* moderación *f*; (*in drinking*) sobriedad *f*.
temperate ['tɛmprət] *a* moderado; (*climate*) templado.
temperature ['tɛmprətʃə*] *n* temperatura; **to have** *or* **run a ~** tener fiebre.
tempered ['tɛmpəd] *a* (*steel*) templado.
tempest ['tɛmpɪst] *n* tempestad *f*.
tempestuous [tɛm'pɛstjuəs] *a* (*relationship, meeting*) tempestuoso.
tempi ['tɛmpiː] *npl of* **tempo.**
template ['tɛmplɪt] *n* plantilla.
temple ['tɛmpl] *n* (*building*) templo; (*ANAT*) sien *f*.
templet ['tɛmplɪt] *n* = **template.**
tempo, **~s** *or* **tempi** ['tɛmpəu, 'tɛmpiː] *n* tempo; (*fig: of life etc*) ritmo.
temporal ['tɛmpərl] *a* temporal.

temporarily ['tɛmpərərɪlɪ] *ad* temporalmente.

temporary ['tɛmpərərɪ] *a* provisional, temporal; (*passing*) transitorio; (*worker*) temporero; ~ **teacher** maestro/a interino/a.

tempt [tɛmpt] *vt* tentar; **to ~ sb into doing sth** tentar *or* inducir a uno a hacer algo; **to be ~ed to do sth** (*person*) sentirse tentado de hacer algo.

temptation [tɛmp'teɪʃən] *n* tentación *f*.

tempting ['tɛmptɪŋ] *a* tentador(a).

ten [tɛn] *num* diez; **~s of thousands** decenas *fpl* de miles.

tenable ['tɛnəbl] *a* sostenible.

tenacious [tə'neɪʃəs] *a* tenaz.

tenaciously [tə'neɪʃəslɪ] *ad* tenazmente.

tenacity [tə'næsɪtɪ] *n* tenacidad *f*.

tenancy ['tɛnənsɪ] *n* alquiler *m*; (*of house*) inquilinato.

tenant ['tɛnənt] *n* (*rent-payer*) inquilino/a; (*occupant*) habitante *m/f*.

tend [tɛnd] *vt* (*sick etc*) cuidar, atender; (*cattle, machine*) vigilar, cuidar ♦ *vi*: **to ~ to do sth** tener tendencia a hacer algo.

tendency ['tɛndənsɪ] *n* tendencia.

tender ['tɛndə*] *a* tierno, blando; (*delicate*) delicado; (*sore*) sensible; (*affectionate*) tierno, cariñoso ♦ *n* (*comm: offer*) oferta; (*money*): **legal ~** moneda de curso legal ♦ *vt* ofrecer; **to put in a ~ (for)** hacer una oferta (para); **to put work out to ~** ofrecer un trabajo a contrata; **to ~ one's resignation** presentar la dimisión.

tenderize ['tɛndəraɪz] *vt* (*culin*) ablandar.

tenderly ['tɛndəlɪ] *ad* tiernamente.

tenderness ['tɛndənɪs] *n* ternura; (*of meat*) blandura.

tendon ['tɛndən] *n* tendón *m*.

tendril ['tɛndrɪl] *n* zarcillo.

tenement ['tɛnəmənt] *n* casa *or* bloque *m* de pisos *or* vecinos (*Sp*).

Tenerife [tɛnə'riːf] *n* Tenerife *m*.

tenet ['tɛnət] *n* principio.

tenner ['tɛnə*] *n* (billete *m* de) diez libras *fpl*.

tennis ['tɛnɪs] *n* tenis *m*.

tennis ball *n* pelota de tenis.

tennis club *n* club *m* de tenis.

tennis court *n* cancha de tenis.

tennis elbow *n* (*med*) sinovitis *f* del codo.

tennis match *n* partido de tenis.

tennis player *n* tenista *m/f*.

tennis racket *n* raqueta de tenis.

tennis shoes *npl* zapatillas *fpl* de tenis.

tenor ['tɛnə*] *n* (*mus*) tenor *m*.

tenpin bowling ['tɛnpɪn-] *n* bolos *mpl*, bolera.

tense [tɛns] *a* tenso; (*stretched*) tirante; (*stiff*) rígido, tieso; (*person*) nervioso ♦ *n* (*ling*) tiempo ♦ *vt* (*tighten: muscles*) tensar.

tensely ['tɛnslɪ] *ad* tensamente.

tenseness ['tɛnsnɪs] *n* tirantez *f*, tensión *f*.

tension ['tɛnʃən] *n* tensión *f*.

tent [tɛnt] *n* tienda (de campaña), carpa (*LAm*).

tentacle ['tɛntəkl] *n* tentáculo.

tentative ['tɛntətɪv] *a* (*person*) indeciso; (*provisional*) provisional.

tentatively ['tɛntətɪvlɪ] *ad* con indesición; (*provisionally*) provisionalmente.

tenterhooks ['tɛntəhuks] *npl*: **on ~** sobre ascuas.

tenth [tɛnθ] *a* décimo.

tent peg *n* clavija, estaca.

tent pole *n* mástil *m*.

tenuous ['tɛnjuəs] *a* tenue.

tenure ['tɛnjuə*] *n* posesión *f*, tenencia; **to have ~** tener posesión *or* título de propiedad.

tepid ['tɛpɪd] *a* tibio.

term [təːm] *n* (*limit*) límite *m*; (*comm*) plazo; (*word*) término; (*period*) período; (*scol*) trimestre *m* ♦ *vt* llamar; **~s** *npl* (*conditions*) condiciones *fpl*; (*comm*) precio, tarifa; **in the short/long ~** a corto/largo plazo; **during his ~ of office** bajo su mandato; **to be on good ~s with sb** llevarse bien con uno; **to come to ~s with** (*problem*) adaptarse a; **in ~s of ...** en cuanto a ..., en términos de ....

terminal ['təːmɪnl] *a* terminal; (*disease*) mortal ♦ *n* (*elec*) borne *m*; (*comput*) terminal *m*; (*also:* **air ~**) terminal *f*; (*Brit: also:* **coach ~**) (estación *f*) terminal *f*.

terminate ['təːmɪneɪt] *vt* terminar ♦ *vi*: **to ~ in** acabar por.

termination [təːmɪ'neɪʃən] *n* fin *m*; (*of contract*) terminación *f*; **~ of pregnancy** aborto.

termini ['təːmɪnaɪ] *npl of* **terminus.**

terminology [təːmɪ'nɔlədʒɪ] *n* terminología.

terminus, *pl* **termini** ['təːmɪnəs, 'təːmɪnaɪ] *n* término, (estación *f*) terminal *f*.

termite ['təːmaɪt] *n* termita.

Ter(r). *abbr* = **terrace.**

terrace ['tɛrəs] *n* terraza; (*Brit: row of houses*) hilera de casas adosadas; **the ~s** (*Brit sport*) las gradas *fpl*.

terraced ['tɛrəst] *a* (*garden*) escalonado; (*house*) alineado, adosado.

terracotta ['tɛrə'kɔtə] *n* terracota.

terrain [tɛ'reɪn] *n* terreno.

terrible ['tɛrɪbl] *a* terrible, horrible; (*fam*) malísimo.

terribly ['tɛrɪblɪ] *ad* terriblemente; (*very badly*) malísimamente.

terrier ['tɛrɪə*] *n* terrier *m*.

terrific [tə'rɪfɪk] *a* fantástico, fenomenal; (*wonderful*) maravilloso.

terrify ['tɛrɪfaɪ] *vt* aterrorizar; **to be terrified** estar aterrado *or* aterrorizado.

terrifying ['tɛrɪfaɪŋ] *a* aterrador(a).

territorial [tɛrɪ'tɔːrɪəl] *a* territorial.

territorial waters *npl* aguas *fpl* jurisdiccionales.

territory ['tɛrɪtərɪ] *n* territorio.

terror ['tɛrə*] *n* terror *m*.

terrorism ['tɛrərɪzəm] *n* terrorismo.

terrorist ['tɛrərɪst] *n* terrorista *m/f*.

terrorize ['tɛrəraɪz] *vt* aterrorizar.

terse [tɜːs] *a* (*style*) conciso; (*reply*) brusco.

tertiary ['tɜːʃərɪ] *a* terciario; ~ **education** enseñanza superior.

Terylene ® ['tɛrəliːn] *n* (*Brit*) terylene *m* ®.

TESL [tɛsl] *n abbr* = *Teaching of English as a Second Language*.

test [tɛst] *n* (*trial, check*) prueba, ensayo; (: *of goods in factory*) control *m*; (*of courage etc, CHEM*) prueba; (*MED*) examen *m*; (*exam*) examen *m*, test *m*; (*also:* **driving** ~) examen *m* de conducir ♦ *vt* probar, poner a prueba; (*MED*) examinar; **to put sth to the** ~ someter algo a prueba; **to** ~ **sth for sth** analizar algo en busca de algo.

testament ['tɛstəmənt] *n* testamento; **the Old/New T**~ el Antiguo/Nuevo Testamento.

test ban *n* (*also:* **nuclear** ~) suspensión *f* de pruebas nucleares.

test card *n* (*TV*) carta de ajuste.

test case *n* (*JUR*) juicio que sienta precedente.

test flight *n* vuelo de ensayo.

testicle ['tɛstɪkl] *n* testículo.

testify ['tɛstɪfaɪ] *vi* (*LAW*) prestar declaración; **to** ~ **to sth** atestiguar algo.

testimonial [tɛstɪ'məunɪəl] *n* (*of character*) (carta de) recomendación *f*, testimonial *m*.

testimony ['tɛstɪmənɪ] *n* (*LAW*) testimonio, declaración *f*.

testing ['tɛstɪŋ] *a* (*difficult: time*) duro.

testing ground *n* zona de pruebas.

test match *n* (*CRICKET, RUGBY*) partido internacional.

test paper *n* examen *m*, test *m*.

test pilot *n* piloto/mujer piloto *m/f* de pruebas.

test tube *n* probeta.

test-tube baby *n* bebé *m* (de) probeta.

testy ['tɛstɪ] *a* irritable.

tetanus ['tɛtənəs] *n* tétano.

tetchy ['tɛtʃɪ] *a* malhumorado, irritable.

tether ['tɛðə*] *vt* atar (con una cuerda) ♦ *n*: **to be at the end of one's** ~ no aguantar más.

text [tɛkst] *n* texto.

textbook ['tɛkstbuk] *n* libro de texto.

textiles ['tɛkstaɪlz] *npl* textiles *mpl*, tejidos *mpl*.

texture ['tɛkstʃə*] *n* textura.

TGWU *n abbr* (*Brit*: = *Transport and General Workers' Union*) *sindicato de transportistas*.

Thai [taɪ] *a, n* tailandés/esa *m/f*.

Thailand ['taɪlænd] *n* Tailandia.

thalidomide ® [θə'lɪdəmaɪd] *n* talidomida ®.

Thames [tɛmz] *n*: **the** ~ el (río) Támesis.

than [ðæn, ðən] *conj* que; (*with numerals*): **more** ~ **10/once** más de 10/una vez; **I have more/less** ~ **you** tengo más/menos que tú; **it is better to phone** ~ **to write** es mejor llamar por teléfono que escribir; **no sooner did he leave** ~ **the phone rang** en cuanto se marchó, sonó el teléfono.

thank [θæŋk] *vt* dar las gracias a, agradecer; ~ **you (very much)** muchas gracias; ~ **heavens,** ~ **God!** ¡gracias a Dios!, ¡menos mal!

thankful ['θæŋkful] *a*: ~ **for** agradecido (por).

thankfully ['θæŋkfəlɪ] *ad* (*gratefully*) con agradecimiento; (*with relief*) por suerte; ~ **there were few victims** afortunadamente hubo pocas víctimas.

thankless ['θæŋklɪs] *a* ingrato.

thanks [θæŋks] *npl* gracias *fpl* ♦ *excl* ¡gracias!; ~ **to** *prep* gracias a.

Thanksgiving (Day) ['θæŋksgɪvɪŋ-] *n* día *m* de Acción de Gracias.

that [ðæt, ðət] *conj* que ♦ *a* ese/esa; (*more remote*) aquel/aquella ♦ *pron* ése/ésa; aquél/aquélla; (*neuter*) eso; aquello; (*relative: subject*) que; (: *object*) que, el cual/la cual *etc*; (*with time*): **on the day** ~ **he came** el día que vino ♦ *ad*: ~ **high** tan alto, así de alto; **it's about** ~ **high** es más o menos así de alto; ~ **one** ése/ésa; aquél/aquélla; ~ **one over there** aquél/aquélla; **what's** ~**?** ¿qué es eso?; **who's** ~**?** ¿quién es?; **is** ~ **you?** ¿eres tú?; (*formal*) ¿es usted?; ~**'s what he said** eso es lo que dijo; **all** ~ todo eso; **I can't work** ~ **much** no puedo trabajar tanto; **at** *or* **with** ~ **she** ... **con eso, ella** ...; **do it like** ~ hazlo así; **not** ~ **I know of** que yo sepa, no; **so** ~**, in order** ~ para que + *subjun*.

thatched [θætʃt] *a* (*roof*) de paja; ~ **cottage** casita con tejado de paja.

thaw [θɔː] *n* deshielo ♦ *vi* (*ice*) derretirse; (*food*) descongelarse ♦ *vt* (*food*) descongelar.

the [ðiː, ðə] *def art* el/la; (*pl*) los/las; (*neuter*) lo; (*in titles*): **Richard** ~ **Second** Ricardo Segundo; ~ **sooner** ~ **better** cuanto antes mejor; ~ **more he works,** ~ **more he earns** cuanto más trabaja, más gana; **I haven't** ~ **time/money** no tengo tiempo/dinero; **100 pesetas to** ~ **dollar** 100 pesetas por dólar; **paid by** ~ **hour** pagado por hora; **do you know** ~ **Smiths?** ¿conoce a los Smith?

theatre, (*US*) **theater** ['θɪətə*] *n* teatro.

theatre-goer, (*US*) **theater-goer** ['θɪətə-gəuə*] *n* aficionado/a al teatro.

theatrical [θɪ'ætrɪkl] *a* teatral.

theft [θɛft] *n* robo.

their [ðɛə*] *a* su.

theirs [ðɛəz] *pron* (el) suyo/(la) suya *etc*; *see also* **my, mine**.

them [ðɛm, ðəm] *pron* (*direct*) los/las; (*in-*

direct) les; (*stressed, after prep*) ellos/ ellas; **I see** ~ los veo; **both of** ~ ambos/ as, los/las dos; **give me a few of** ~ dame algunos/as; *see also* **me.**

theme [θiːm] *n* tema *m.*

theme song *n* tema *m* (musical).

themselves [ðəmˈsɛlvz] *pl pron* (*subject*) ellos mismos/ellas mismas; (*complement*) se; (*after prep*) sí (mismos/as); *see also* **oneself.**

then [ðɛn] *ad* (*at that time*) entonces; (*next*) pues; (*later*) luego, después; (*and also*) además ◆ *conj* (*therefore*) en ese caso, entonces ◆ *a*: **the** ~ **president** el entonces presidente; **from** ~ **on** desde entonces; **until** ~ hasta entonces; **and** ~ **what?** y luego, ¿qué?; **what do you want me to do,** ~**?** ¿qué quiere que haga, entonces?

theologian [θɪəˈləudʒən] teólogo/a.

theological [θɪəˈlɒdʒɪkl] *a* teológico.

theology [θɪˈɒlədʒɪ] *n* teología.

theorem [ˈθɪərəm] *n* teorema *m.*

theoretical [θɪəˈrɛtɪkl] *a* teórico.

theoretically [θɪəˈrɛtɪklɪ] *ad* teóricamente, en teoría.

theorize [ˈθɪəraɪz] *vi* teorizar.

theory [ˈθɪərɪ] *n* teoría.

therapeutic(al) [θɛrəˈpjuːtɪk(l)] *a* terapéutico.

therapist [ˈθɛrəpɪst] *n* terapeuta *m/f.*

therapy [ˈθɛrəpɪ] *n* terapia.

there [ðɛə*] *ad* allí, allá, ahí; ~, ~! ¡cálmate!; **it's** ~ está ahí; ~**s the bus** ahí *or* ya viene el autobús; ~ **is,** ~ **are** hay; ~ **he is** ahí está; **on/in** ~ allí encima/dentro; **back/down** ~ allá *or* allí atrás/abajo; **over** ~, **through** ~ por allí.

thereabouts [ˈðɛərəˈbauts] *ad* por ahí.

thereafter [ðɛərˈɑːftə*] *ad* después.

thereby [ˈðɛəbaɪ] *ad* así, de ese modo.

therefore [ˈðɛəfɔː*] *ad* por lo tanto.

there's [ðɛəz] = **there is, there has.**

thereupon [ðɛərəˈpɒn] *ad* (*at that point*) en eso, en seguida.

thermal [ˈθəːml] *a* termal.

thermal paper *n* papel *m* térmico.

thermal printer *n* termoimpresora.

thermodynamics [ˈθəːmədaɪnæmɪks] *n* termodinámica.

thermometer [θəˈmɒmɪtə*] *n* termómetro.

thermonuclear [θəːməuˈnjuːklɪə*] *a* termonuclear.

Thermos ® [ˈθəːməs] *n* (*also:* ~ **flask)** termo ®.

thermostat [ˈθəːməustæt] *n* termostato.

thesaurus [θɪˈsɔːrəs] *n* tesoro.

these [ðiːz] *pl a* estos/as ◆ *pl pron* éstos/as.

thesis, *pl* **theses** [θiːsɪs, -siːz] *n* tesis *f inv.*

they [ðeɪ] *pl pron* ellos/ellas; (*stressed*) ellos (mismos)/ellas (mismas); ~ **say that...** (*it is said that*) se dice que....

they'd [ðeɪd] = **they had, they would.**

they'll [ðeɪl] = **they shall, they will.**

they're [ðɛə*] = **they are.**

they've [ðeɪv] = **they have.**

thick [θɪk] *a* (*wall, slice*) grueso; (*dense:* *liquid, smoke etc*) espeso; (*vegetation, beard*) tupido; (*stupid*) torpe ◆ *n*: **in the** ~ **of the battle** en lo más reñido de la batalla; **it's 20 cm** ~ tiene 20 cm de espesor.

thicken [ˈθɪkn] *vi* espesarse ◆ *vt* (*sauce etc*) espesar.

thicket [ˈθɪkɪt] *n* espesura.

thickly [ˈθɪklɪ] *ad* (*spread*) en capa espesa; (*cut*) en rebanada gruesa; (*populated*) densamente.

thickness [ˈθɪknɪs] *n* espesor *m*, grueso.

thickset [θɪkˈsɛt] *a* fornido.

thickskinned [θɪkˈskɪnd] *a* (*fig*) insensible.

thief, *pl* **thieves** [θiːf, θiːvz] *n* ladrón/ona *m/f.*

thieving [ˈθiːvɪŋ] *n* tobo, hurto ◆ *a* ladrón/ona.

thigh [θaɪ] *n* muslo.

thighbone [ˈθaɪbəun] *n* fémur *m.*

thimble [ˈθɪmbl] *n* dedal *m.*

thin [θɪn] *a* delgado; (*watery*) aguado; (*light*) tenue; (*hair*) escaso; (*fog*) ligero; (*crowd*) disperso ◆ *vt*: **to** ~ **(down)** (*sauce, paint*) diluir ◆ *vi* (*fog*) aclararse; (*also:* ~ **out:** *crowd*) dispersarse; **his hair is** ~**ning** está perdiendo (el) pelo.

thing [θɪŋ] *n* cosa; (*object*) objeto, artículo; (*contraption*) chisme *m*; (*mania*) manía; ~**s** *npl* (*belongings*) efectos *mpl* (personales); **the best** ~ **would be to**... lo mejor sería...; **the main** ~ **is to**... lo principal que hay que hacer es ...; **first** ~ **(in the morning)** a primera hora (de la mañana); **last** ~ **(at night)** a última hora (de la noche); **the** ~ **is**... lo que pasa es que ...; **how are** ~**s?** ¿qué tal?; **she's got a** ~ **about mice** le da no sé qué de los ratones; **poor** ~! ¡pobre! *m/f*, ¡pobrecito/a!

think, *pt, pp* **thought** [θɪŋk, θɔːt] *vi* pensar ◆ *vt* pensar, creer; (*imagine*) imaginar; **what did you** ~ **of it?** ¿qué te parece?; **what did you** ~ **of them?** ¿qué te parecieron?; **to** ~ **about sth/sb** pensar en algo/ uno; **I'll** ~ **about it** lo pensaré; **to** ~ **of doing sth** pensar en hacer algo; **I** ~ **so/not** creo que sí/no; ~ **again!** ¡piénsalo bien!; **to** ~ **aloud** pensar en voz alta; **to** ~ **well of sb** tener buen concepto de uno.

think out *vt* (*plan*) elaborar, tramar; (*solution*) encontrar.

think over *vt* reflexionar sobre, meditar; **I'd like to** ~ **things over** me gustaría examinarlo detenidamente.

think through *vt* pensar bien.

think up *vt* imaginar.

thinking [ˈθɪŋkɪŋ] *n*: **to my (way of)** ~ a mi parecer.

think tank *n* gabinete *m* de estrategia.

thinly [ˈθɪnlɪ] *ad* (*cut*) en lonchas finas;

(spread) en una ligera capa.

thinness ['θɪnnɪs] *n* delgadez *f.*

third [θəːd] *a (before nmsg:* **tercer**) tercero ♦ *n* tercero/a; *(fraction)* tercio; *(Brit SCOL: degree)* título universitario de tercera clase.

third degree *a (burns)* de tercer grado.

thirdly ['θəːdlɪ] *ad* en tercer lugar.

third party insurance *n (Brit)* seguro contra terceros.

third-rate ['θəːd'reɪt] *a* (de calidad) mediocre.

Third World *n:* **the** ~ el Tercer Mundo ♦ *cpd* tercermundista.

thirst [θəːst] *n* sed *f.*

thirsty ['θəːstɪ] *a (person)* sediento; **to be** ~ tener sed.

thirteen [θəː'tiːn] *num* trece.

thirteenth [θəː'tiːnθ] *a* decimotercero ♦ *n (in series)* decimotercero/a; *(fraction)* decimotercio.

thirtieth ['θəːtɪəθ] *a* trigésimo ♦ *n (in series)* trigésimo/a; *(fraction)* treintavo.

thirty ['θəːtɪ] *num* treinta.

this [ðɪs] *a* este/esta ♦ *pron* éste/ésta; *(neuter)* esto; ~ **is what he said** esto es lo que dijo; ~ **high** así de alto; ~ **way** por aquí; ~ **time** esta vez; ~ **time last year** hoy hace un año; **who is** ~? ¿quién es éste/ésta? **what is** ~? ¿qué es esto?; ~ **is Mr Brown** *(in introductions)* le presento al Sr Brown; *(in photo)* éste es el Sr Brown; *(on telephone)* el Sr Brown al habla; **they were talking of** ~ **and that** hablaban de esto y aquello.

thistle ['θɪsl] *n* cardo.

thong [θɒŋ] *n* correa.

thorn [θɔːn] *n* espina.

thorny ['θɔːnɪ] *a* espinoso.

thorough ['θʌrə] *a (search)* minucioso; *(knowledge, research)* profundo.

thoroughbred ['θʌrəbred] *a (horse)* de pura sangre.

thoroughfare ['θʌrəfɛə*] *n* calle *f;* "**no** ~" "prohibido el paso".

thoroughly ['θʌrəlɪ] *ad* minuciosamente; profundamente, a fondo.

thoroughness ['θʌrənɪs] *n* minuciosidad *f.*

those [ðəuz] *pl pron* ésos/ésas; *(more remote)* aquéllos/as ♦ *pl a* esos/esas; aquellos/as.

though [ðəu] *conj* aunque ♦ *ad* sin embargo, aún así; **even** ~ aunque; **it's not so easy,** ~ sin embargo no es tan fácil.

thought [θɔːt] *pt, pp* of **think** ♦ *n* pensamiento; *(opinion)* opinión *f; (intention)* intención *f;* **to give sth some** ~ pensar algo detenidamente; **after much** ~ pensándolo bien; **I've just had a** ~ se me acaba de ocurrir una idea.

thoughtful ['θɔːtful] *a* pensativo; *(considerate)* atento.

thoughtfully ['θɔːtfəlɪ] *ad* pensativamente;

atentamente.

thoughtless ['θɔːtlɪs] *a* desconsiderado.

thoughtlessly ['θɔːtlɪslɪ] *ad* impensadamente, insensatamente.

thousand ['θauzənd] *num* mil; **two** ~ dos mil; ~**s of** miles de.

thousandth ['θauzəntθ] *num* milésimo.

thrash [θræʃ] *vt* apalear; *(defeat)* derrotar.
thrash about *vi* revolcarse.
thrash out *vt* discutir a fondo.

thrashing ['θræʃɪŋ] *n:* **to give sb a** ~ dar una paliza a uno.

thread [θred] *n* hilo; *(of screw)* rosca ♦ *vt (needle)* enhebrar.

threadbare ['θredbɛə*] *a* raído.

threat [θret] *n* amenaza; **to be under** ~ **of** estar amenazado de.

threaten ['θretn] *vi* amenazar ♦ *vt:* **to** ~ **sb with sth/to do** amenazar a uno con algo/con hacer.

threatening ['θretnɪŋ] *a* amenazador(a), amenazante.

three [θriː] *num* tres.

three-dimensional [θriːdɪ'menʃənl] *a* tridimensional.

threefold ['θriːfəuld] *ad:* **to increase** ~ triplicar.

three-piece ['θriːpiːs]: ~ **suit** *n* traje *m* de tres piezas; ~ **suite** *n* tresillo.

three-ply [θriː'plaɪ] *a (wood)* de tres capas; *(wool)* triple.

three-quarter [θriː'kwɔːtə*] *a:* ~ **length sleeves** mangas *fpl* tres cuartos.

three-quarters [θriː'kwɔːtəz] *npl* tres cuartas partes; ~ **full** tres cuartas partes lleno.

three-wheeler [θriː'wiːlə*] *n (car)* coche *m* cabina.

thresh [θreʃ] *vt (AGR)* trillar.

threshing machine ['θreʃɪŋ-] *n* trilladora.

threshold ['θreʃhəuld] *n* umbral *m;* **to be on the** ~ **of** *(fig)* estar al borde de.

threshold agreement *n* convenio de nivel crítico.

threw [θruː] *pt of* **throw.**

thrift [θrɪft] *n* economía.

thrifty ['θrɪftɪ] *a* económico.

thrill [θrɪl] *n (excitement)* emoción *f* ♦ *vt* emocionar; **to be** ~**ed** *(with gift etc)* estar encantado.

thriller ['θrɪlə*] *n* película/novela de suspense.

thrilling ['θrɪlɪŋ] *a* emocionante.

thrive, *pt* **thrived, throve,** *pp* **thrived, thriven** [θraɪv, θrəuv, 'θrɪvn] *vi (grow)* crecer; *(do well)* prosperar.

thriving ['θraɪvɪŋ] *a* próspero.

throat [θrəut] *n* garganta; **to have a sore** ~ tener dolor de garganta.

throb [θrɒb] *n (of heart)* latido; *(of engine)* vibración *f* ♦ *vi* latir; vibrar; *(with pain)* dar punzadas; **my head is** ~**bing** la cabeza me da punzadas.

throes [θrəuz] *npl:* **in the** ~ **of** en medio de.

thrombosis [θrɔm'bəʊsɪs] n trombosis f.

throne [θrəʊn] n trono.

throng [θrɒŋ] n multitud f, muchedumbre f ♦ vt, vi apiñarse, agolparse.

throttle ['θrɔtl] n (AUT) acelerador m ♦ vt estrangular.

through [θruː] prep por, a través de; (time) durante; (by means of) por medio de, mediante; (owing to) gracias a ♦ a (ticket, train) directo ♦ ad completamente, de parte a parte; de principio a fin; **(from) Monday ~ Friday** (US) de lunes a viernes; **to go ~ sb's papers** mirar entre los papeles de uno; **I am halfway ~ the book** voy por la mitad del libro; **the soldiers didn't let us ~** los soldados no nos dejaron pasar; **to put sb ~ to sb** (TEL) poner or pasar a uno con uno; **to be ~** (TEL) tener comunicación; (have finished) haber terminado; **"no ~ road"** (Brit) "calle sin salida".

throughout [θruː'aʊt] prep (place) por todas partes de, por todo; (time) durante todo ♦ ad por or en todas partes.

throughput ['θruːpʊt] n (of goods, materials) producción f; (COMPUT) capacidad f de procesamiento.

throve [θrəʊv] pt of **thrive**.

throw [θrəʊ] n tiro, (SPORT) lanzamiento ♦ vt (pt **threw**, pp **thrown** [θruː, θrəʊn]) tirar, echar; (SPORT) lanzar; (rider) derribar; (fig) desconcertar; **to ~ a party** dar una fiesta.

throw about, throw around vt (litter etc) tirar, esparcir.

throw away vt tirar.

throw off vt deshacerse de.

throw open vt (doors, windows) abrir de par en par; (house, gardens etc) abrir al público; (competition, race) abrir a todos.

throw out vt tirar.

throw together vt (clothes) amontonar; (meal) preparar a la carrera; (essay) hacer sin cuidado.

throw up vi vomitar.

throwaway ['θrəʊəweɪ] a para tirar, desechable.

throwback ['θrəʊbæk] n: **it's a ~ to** (fig) eso nos lleva de nuevo a.

throw-in ['θrəʊɪn] n (SPORT) saque m.

thrown [θrəʊn] pp of **throw**.

thru [θruː] (US) = **through**.

thrush [θrʌʃ] n zorzal m, tordo; (MED) afta.

thrust [θrʌst] n (TECH) empuje m ♦ vt (pt, pp **thrust**) empujar; (push in) introducir.

thrusting ['θrʌstɪŋ] a (person) dinámico, con empuje.

thud [θʌd] n golpe m sordo.

thug [θʌg] n gamberro/a.

thumb [θʌm] n (ANAT) pulgar m ♦ vt: **to ~ a lift** hacer autostop; **to give sth/sb the ~s up** aprobar algo/a uno.

thumb through vt fus (book) hojear.

thumb index n índice m recortado.

thumbnail ['θʌmneɪl] n uña del pulgar.

thumbnail sketch n esbozo.

thumbtack ['θʌmtæk] n (US) chincheta, chinche m (LAm).

thump [θʌmp] n golpe m; (sound) ruido seco or sordo ♦ vt, vi golpear.

thumping ['θʌmpɪŋ] a (col: huge) descomunal.

thunder ['θʌndə*] n trueno; (of applause etc) estruendo ♦ vi tronar; (train etc): **to ~ past** pasar como un trueno.

thunderbolt ['θʌndəbəʊlt] n rayo.

thunderclap ['θʌndəklæp] n trueno.

thunderous ['θʌndərəs] a ensordecedor(a), estruendoso.

thunderstorm ['θʌndəstɔːm] n tormenta.

thunderstruck ['θʌndəstrʌk] a pasmado.

thundery ['θʌndərɪ] a tormentoso.

Thur(s). abbr (= Thursday) juev.

Thursday ['θəːzdɪ] n jueves m inv.

thus [ðʌs] ad así, de este modo.

thwart [θwɔːt] vt frustrar.

thyme [taɪm] n tomillo.

thyroid ['θaɪrɔɪd] n tiroides m inv.

tiara [tɪ'ɑːrə] n tiara, diadema.

Tiber ['taɪbə*] n Tíber m.

Tibet [tɪ'bet] n el Tibet.

Tibetan [tɪ'betən] a tibetano/a; (LING) tibetano.

tibia ['tɪbɪə] n tibia.

tic [tɪk] n tic m.

tick [tɪk] n (sound: of clock) tictac m; (mark) palomita; (ZOOL) garrapata; (Brit col): **in a ~** en un instante; (Brit col: credit): **to buy sth on ~** comprar algo a crédito ♦ vi hacer tictac ♦ vt marcar; **to put a ~ against sth** marcar algo (con palmita).

tick off vt marcar; (person) reñir.

tick over vi (Brit: engine) girar en marcha lenta; (: fig) ir tirando.

ticker tape ['tɪkə-] n cinta perforada.

ticket ['tɪkɪt] n billete m, tíquet m, boleto (LAm); (for cinema etc) entrada, boleto (LAm); (in shop: on goods) etiqueta; (for library) tarjeta; (US POL) lista (de candidatos); **to get a parking ~** (AUT) ser multado por estacionamiento ilegal.

ticket agency n (THEATRE) agencia de billetes.

ticket collector n revisor(a) m/f.

ticket holder n poseedor(a) m/f de billete.

ticket inspector n revisor(a) m/f, inspector(a) m/f de boletos (LAm).

ticket office n (THEATRE) taquilla, boletería (LAm); (RAIL) despacho de billetes or boletos (LAm).

ticking-off ['tɪkɪŋ'ɔf] n (col): **to give sb a ~** echarle una bronca a uno.

tickle ['tɪkl] n: **to give sb a ~** hacer cosquillas a uno ♦ vt hacer cosquillas a.

ticklish ['tɪklɪʃ] a (person) cosquilloso; (which tickles: blanket) que pica; (:

cough) irritante.
tidal ['taɪdl] *a* de marea.
tidal wave *n* maremoto.
tidbit ['tɪdbɪt] (*US*) = **titbit**.
tiddlywinks ['tɪdlɪwɪŋks] *n juego infantil de habilidad con fichas de plástico.*
tide [taɪd] *n* marea; (*fig: of events*) curso, marcha ◆ *vt*: **to ~ sb over** *or* **through (until)** ayudarle a uno con medios (hasta); **high/low ~** marea alta/baja; **the ~ of public opinion** la tendencia de la opinión pública.
tidily ['taɪdɪlɪ] *ad* bien, ordenadamente; **to arrange ~** ordenar; **to dress ~** vestir bien.
tidiness ['taɪdɪnɪs] *n* (*order*) orden *m*; (*cleanliness*) aseo.
tidy ['taɪdɪ] *a* (*room*) ordenado; (*drawing, work*) limpio; (*person*) (bien) arreglado; (: *in character*) metódico; (*mind*) claro, metódico ◆ *vt* (*also:* **~ up**) poner en orden.
tie [taɪ] *n* (*string etc*) atadura; (*Brit: neck~*) corbata; (*fig: link*) vínculo, lazo; (*SPORT: draw*) empate *m* ◆ *vt* atar ◆ *vi* (*SPORT*) empatar; **family ~s** obligaciones *fpl* familiares; **cup ~** (*SPORT: match*) partido de copa; **to ~ in a bow** hacer un lazo; **to ~ a knot in sth** hacer un nudo en algo.
tie down *vt* atar; (*fig*): **to ~ sb down to** obligar a uno a.
tie in *vi*: **to ~ in (with)** (*correspond*) concordar (con).
tie on *vt* (*Brit: label etc*) atar.
tie up *vt* (*parcel*) envolver; (*dog*) atar; (*boat*) amarrar; (*arrangements*) concluir; **to be ~d up** (*busy*) estar ocupado.
tie-break(er) ['taɪbreɪk(əʳ)] *n* (*TENNIS*) tie-break *m*, muerte *f* rápida; (*in quiz*) punto decisivo.
tie-on ['taɪɔn] *a* (*Brit: label*) para atar.
tie-pin ['taɪpɪn] *n* (*Brit*) alfiler *m* de corbata.
tier [tɪəʳ] *n* grada; (*of cake*) piso.
tie tack *n* (*US*) alfiler *m* de corbata.
tiff [tɪf] *n* (*col*) pelea, riña.
tiger ['taɪgəʳ] *n* tigre *m*.
tight [taɪt] *a* (*rope*) tirante; (*money*) escaso; (*clothes, budget*) ajustado; (*programme*) apretado; (*col: drunk*) borracho ◆ *ad* (*squeeze*) muy fuerte; (*shut*) herméticamente; **to be packed ~** (*suitcase*) estar completamente lleno; (*people*) estar apretados; **everybody hold ~!** ¡agárrense bien!
tighten ['taɪtn] *vt* (*rope*) estirar; (*screw*) apretar ◆ *vi* estirarse; apretarse.
tight-fisted ['taɪt'fɪstɪd] *a* tacaño.
tightly ['taɪtlɪ] *ad* (*grasp*) muy fuerte.
tightness ['taɪtnɪs] *n* (*of rope*) tirantez *f*; (*of clothes, budget*) estrechez *f*, lo ajustado.
tightrope ['taɪtrəup] *n* cuerda floja.
tightrope walker *n* equilibrista *m/f*, funambulista *m/f*.
tights [taɪts] *npl* (*Brit*) pantimedias *fpl*.

tigress ['taɪgrɪs] *n* tigresa.
tilde ['tɪldə] *n* tilde *f*.
tile [taɪl] *n* (*on roof*) teja; (*on floor*) baldosa; (*on wall*) azulejo ◆ *vt* (*floor*) poner baldosas en; (*wall*) poner azulejos en.
tiled [taɪld] *a* (*floor*) embaldosado; (*wall, bathroom*) cubierto de azulejos; (*roof*) tejado.
till [tɪl] *n* caja (registradora) ◆ *vt* (*land*) cultivar ◆ *prep, conj* = **until**.
tiller ['tɪləʳ] *n* (*NAUT*) caña del timón.
tilt [tɪlt] *vt* inclinar ◆ *vi* inclinarse ◆ *n* (*slope*) inclinación *f*; **to wear one's hat at a ~** llevar el sombrero echado a un lado *or* terciado; **(at) full ~** a toda velocidad *or* carrera.
timber ['tɪmbəʳ] *n* (*material*) madera; (*trees*) árboles *mpl*.
time [taɪm] *n* tiempo; (*epoch: often pl*) época; (*by clock*) hora; (*moment*) momento; (*occasion*) vez *f*; (*MUS*) compás *m* ◆ *vt* calcular *or* medir el tiempo de; (*race*) cronometrar; (*remark etc*) elegir el momento para; **a long ~** mucho tiempo; **4 at a ~** 4 a la vez; **for the ~ being** de momento, por ahora; **at ~s** a veces, a ratos; **~ after ~, ~ and again** repetidas veces, una y otra vez; **from ~ to ~** de vez en cuando; **in ~** (*soon enough*) a tiempo; (*after some time*) con el tiempo; (*MUS*) al compás; **in a week's ~** dentro de una semana; **in no ~** en un abrir y cerrar de ojos; **any ~** cuando sea; **on ~** a la hora; **to be 30 minutes behind/ahead of ~** llevar media hora de retraso/adelanto; **to take one's ~** hacer las cosas con calma; **he'll do it in his own ~** (*without being hurried*) lo hará sin prisa; (*out of working hours*) lo hará en su tiempo libre; **by the ~ he arrived** cuando llegó; **5 ~s 5** 5 por 5; **what ~ is it?** ¿qué hora es?; **what ~ do you make it?** ¿qué hora es *or* tiene?; **to be behind the ~s** estar atrasado; **to carry 3 boxes at a ~** llevar 3 cajas a la vez; **to keep ~** llevar el ritmo *or* el compás; **to have a good ~** pasarlo bien, divertirse; **to ~ sth well/badly** poner algo en vigor en un momento oportuno/ inoportuno; **the bomb was ~d to explode 5 minutes later** la bomba estaba sincronizada para explotar 5 minutos más tarde.
time-and-motion expert ['taɪmənd'mɔuʃən-] *n* experto/a en la ciencia de la producción.
time-and-motion study ['taɪmənd'mɔuʃən-] *n* estudio de desplazamientos y tiempos.
time bomb *n* bomba de efecto retardado.
time card *n* tarjeta de registro horario.
time clock *n* reloj *m* registrador.
time-consuming ['taɪmkənsjuːmɪŋ] *a* que requiere mucho tiempo.
time-honoured, (*US*) **time-honored** ['taɪmɔnəd] *a* consagrado.

timekeeper ['taɪmkiːpə*] n (SPORT) cronómetro.

time lag n desfase m.

timeless ['taɪmlɪs] a eterno.

time limit n (gen) limitación f de tiempo; (COMM) plazo.

timely ['taɪmlɪ] a oportuno.

time off n tiempo libre.

timer ['taɪmə*] n (~ switch) interruptor m; (in kitchen, TECH) reloj m automático.

time-saving ['taɪmseɪvɪŋ] a que ahorra tiempo.

time scale n escala de tiempo.

time sharing n (COMPUT) tiempo compartido.

time sheet n = **time card**.

time signal n señal f horaria.

time switch n (Brit) interruptor m (horario).

timetable ['taɪmteɪbl] n horario; (programme of events etc) programa m, itinerario.

time zone n huso horario.

timid ['tɪmɪd] a tímido.

timidity [tɪ'mɪdɪtɪ] n timidez f.

timidly ['tɪmɪdlɪ] ad tímidamente.

timing ['taɪmɪŋ] n (SPORT) cronometraje m; **the ~ of his resignation** el momento que eligió para dimitir.

timpani ['tɪmpənɪ] npl tímpanos mpl.

tin [tɪn] n estaño; (also: ~ plate) hojalata; (Brit: can) lata.

tinfoil ['tɪnfɔɪl] n papel m de estaño.

tinge [tɪndʒ] n matiz m ♦ vt: **~d with** teñido de.

tingle ['tɪŋgl] n hormigueo ♦ vi (cheeks, skin: from cold) sentir comezón; (: from bad circulation) sentir hormigueo.

tinker ['tɪŋkə*] n calderero/a; (gipsy) gitano/a.

tinker with vt fus jugar con, tocar.

tinkle ['tɪŋkl] vi tintinear.

tin mine n mina de estaño.

tinned [tɪnd] a (Brit: food) en lata, en conserva.

tinny ['tɪnɪ] a (sound, taste) metálico; (pej: car) poco sólido, de pacotilla.

tin opener [-əupnə*] n (Brit) abrelatas m inv.

tinsel ['tɪnsl] n oropel m.

tint [tɪnt] n matiz m; (for hair) tinte m ♦ vt (hair) teñir.

tinted ['tɪntɪd] a (hair) teñido; (glass, spectacles) ahumado.

tiny ['taɪnɪ] a minúsculo, pequeñito.

tip [tɪp] n (end) punta; (gratuity) propina; (Brit: for rubbish) vertedero; (advice) consejo ♦ vt (waiter) dar una propina a; (tilt) inclinar; (empty: also ~ out) vaciar, echar; (predict: winner) pronosticar; (: horse) recomendar; **he ~ped out the contents of the box** volcó el contenido de la caja.

tip off vt avisar, notificar.

tip over vt volcar ♦ vi volcarse.

tip-off ['tɪpɔf] n (hint) advertencia.

tipped [tɪpt] a (Brit: cigarette) con filtro.

Tipp-Ex ® ['tɪpɛks] n Tipp-Ex m ®.

tipple ['tɪpl] n (Brit): **his ~ is Cointreau** bebe Cointreau.

tipsy ['tɪpsɪ] a alegre, mareado.

tiptoe ['tɪptəu] n (Brit): **on ~** de puntillas.

tiptop ['tɪptɔp] a: **in ~ condition** en perfectas condiciones.

tire ['taɪə*] n (US) = **tyre** ♦ vt cansar ♦ vi (gen) cansarse; (become bored) aburrirse.

tire out vt agotar, rendir (LAm).

tired ['taɪəd] a cansado; **to be ~ of sth** estar harto de algo; **to be/feel/look ~** estar/sentirse/parecer cansado.

tiredness ['taɪədnɪs] n cansancio.

tireless ['taɪəlɪs] a incansable.

tirelessly ['taɪəlɪslɪ] ad incansablemente.

tiresome ['taɪəsəm] a aburrido.

tiring ['taɪrɪŋ] a cansado.

tissue ['tɪʃuː] n tejido; (paper handkerchief) pañuelo de papel, kleenex m ®.

tissue paper n papel m de seda.

tit [tɪt] n (bird) herrerillo común; **to give ~ for tat** dar ojo por ojo.

titbit ['tɪtbɪt], (US) **tidbit** ['tɪdbɪt] n (food) golosina; (news) pedazo.

titillate ['tɪtɪleɪt] vt estimular, excitar.

titillation [tɪtɪ'leɪʃən] n estimulación f, excitación f.

titivate ['tɪtɪveɪt] vt emperejilar.

title ['taɪtl] n título; (LAW: right): **~ (to)** derecho (a).

title deed n (LAW) título de propiedad.

title page n portada.

title role n papel m principal.

titter ['tɪtə*] vi reírse entre dientes.

tittle-tattle ['tɪtltætl] n chismes mpl.

titular ['tɪtjulə*] a (in name only) nominal.

T-junction ['tiːdʒʌŋkʃən] n cruce m en T.

TM abbr (= trademark) marca de fábrica; = **transcendental meditation**.

TN abbr (US POST) = Tennessee.

TNT n abbr (= trinitrotoluene) TNT m.

to [tuː, tə] prep a; (towards) hacia; (of time) a, hasta; (of hour) menos; (with vb: purpose, result) para; (of) de; (following another vb): **to want/try ~ do** querer/intentar hacer; **the road ~ Edinburgh** la carretera de Edimburgo; **to count ~ 10** contar hasta diez; **~ the left/right** a la izquierda/derecha; **to give sth ~ sb** darle algo a uno; **give it ~ me** dámelo; **the key ~ the door** la llave de la puerta; **the main thing is ~...** lo importante es...; **to go ~ France/school** ir a Francia/al colegio; **a quarter ~ 5** las 5 menos cuarto; **it's twenty-five ~ 3** son las 3 menos veinticinco; **it belongs ~ him** le pertenece a él; **superior ~ the others** superior a los otros; **8 apples ~ the kilo** 8 manzanas por kilo;

pull/push the door ~ tirar/empujar la puerta; **to go** ~ **and fro** ir y venir; **I don't want** ~ no quiero; **I have things** ~ **do** tengo cosas que hacer; **ready** ~ **go** listo para salir; **he did it** ~ **help you** lo hizo para ayudarte.

toad [təud] *n* sapo.

toadstool ['təudstuːl] *n* hongo venenoso.

toady ['təudɪ] *n* pelotillero/a, lameculos *m/f inv* ◆ *vi*: **to** ~ **to sb** hacer la pelotilla a uno.

toast [təust] *n* (*CULIN: also:* **piece of** ~) tostada; (*drink, speech*) brindis *m inv* ◆ *vt* (*CULIN*) tostar; (*drink to*) brindar.

toaster ['təustə*] *n* tostadora.

toastmaster ['təustmɑːstə*] *n* persona que propone brindis y anuncia a los oradores en un banquete.

toast rack *n* rejilla para tostadas.

tobacco [tə'bækəu] *n* tabaco; **pipe** ~ tabaco de pipa.

tobacconist [tə'bækənɪst] *n* estanquero/a, tabaquero/a (*LAm*); ~**'s (shop)** (*Brit*) estanco, tabaquería (*LAm*).

tobacco plantation *n* plantación *f* de tabaco, tabacal *m*.

Tobago [tə'beɪgəu] *n see* **Trinidad and Tobago.**

toboggan [tə'bɔgən] *n* tobogán *m*.

today [tə'deɪ] *ad*, *n* (*also fig*) hoy *m;* **what day is it** ~**?** ¿qué día es hoy?; **what date is it** ~**?** ¿cuál es la fecha de hoy?; ~ **is the 4th of March** hoy es el 4 de marzo; ~**'s paper** el periódico de hoy; **a fortnight** ~ de hoy en 15 días, dentro de 15 días.

toddle ['tɔdl] *vi* empezar a andar, dar los primeros pasos.

toddler ['tɔdlə*] *n* niño/a (que empieza a andar).

toddy ['tɔdɪ] *n* ponche *m*.

to-do [tə'duː] *n* (*fuss*) lío.

toe [təu] *n* dedo (del pie); (*of shoe*) punta ◆ *vt*: **to** ~ **the line** (*fig*) conformarse; **big/ little** ~ dedo gordo/pequeño del pie.

toehold ['təuhəuld] *n* punto de apoyo (para el pie).

toenail ['təuneɪl] *n* uña del pie.

toffee ['tɔfɪ] *n* caramelo.

toffee apple *n* (*Brit*) pirulí *m*.

toga ['təugə] *n* toga.

together [tə'geðə*] *ad* juntos; (*at same time*) al mismo tiempo, a la vez; ~ **with** *prep* junto con.

togetherness [tə'geðənɪs] *n* compañerismo.

toggle switch ['tɔgl-] *n* (*COMPUT*) conmutador *m* de palanca.

Togo ['təugəu] *n* Togo.

togs [tɔgz] *npl* (*col: clothes*) atuendo, ropa.

toil [tɔɪl] *n* trabajo duro, labor *f* ◆ *vi* esforzarse.

toilet ['tɔɪlət] *n* (*Brit: lavatory*) servicios *mpl*, wáter *m*, sanitario (*LAm*) ◆ *cpd*

(*bag, soap etc*) de aseo; **to go to the** ~ ir al excusado *or* al baño; *see also* **toilets.**

toilet bag *n* neceser *m*, bolsa de aseo.

toilet bowl *n* taza (de retrete).

toilet paper *n* papel *m* higiénico.

toiletries ['tɔɪlətrɪz] *npl* artículos *mpl* de aseo; (*make-up etc*) artículos *mpl* de tocador.

toilet roll *n* rollo de papel higiénico.

toilets ['tɔɪləts] *npl* (*Brit*) servicios *mpl*.

toilet soap *n* jabón *m* de tocador.

toilet water *n* (agua de) colonia.

to-ing and fro-ing ['tuɪŋən'frəuɪŋ] *n* vaivén *m*.

token ['təukən] *n* (*sign*) señal *f*, muestra; (*souvenir*) recuerdo; (*voucher*) vale *m*; (*disc*) ficha ◆ *cpd* (*fee, strike*) nominal, simbólico; **book/record** ~ (*Brit*) vale *m* para comprar libros/discos; **by the same** ~ (*fig*) por la misma razón.

Tokyo ['təukjəu] *n* Tokio, Tokío.

told [təuld] *pt, pp of* **tell.**

tolerable ['tɔlərəbl] *a* (*bearable*) soportable; (*fairly good*) pasable.

tolerably ['tɔlərəblɪ] *ad* (*good, comfortable*) medianamente.

tolerance ['tɔlərns] *n* (*also: TECH*) tolerancia.

tolerant ['tɔlərnt] *a*: ~ **of** tolerante con.

tolerantly ['tɔlərntlɪ] *ad* con tolerancia.

tolerate ['tɔləreɪt] *vt* tolerar.

toleration [tɔlə'reɪʃən] *n* tolerancia.

toll [təul] *n* (*of casualties*) número de víctimas; (*tax, charge*) peaje *m* ◆ *vi* (*bell*) doblar.

toll bridge *n* puente *m* de peaje.

toll road *n* carretera de peaje.

tomato, ~**es** [tə'mɑːtəu] *n* tomate *m*.

tomato puree *n* puré *m* de tomate.

tomb [tuːm] *n* tumba.

tombola [tɔm'bəulə] *n* tómbola.

tomboy ['tɔmbɔɪ] *n* marimacho.

tombstone ['tuːmstəun] *n* lápida.

tomcat ['tɔmkæt] *n* gato.

tomorrow [tə'mɔrəu] *ad*, *n* (*also fig*) mañana; **the day after** ~ pasado mañana; ~ **morning** mañana por la mañana; **a week** ~ de mañana en ocho (días).

ton [tʌn] *n* tonelada (*Brit* = 1016 *kg; US: also* **short** ~ = 907,18 *kg*) tonelada; ~**s of** (*col*) montones de.

tonal ['təunl] *a* tonal.

tone [təun] *n* tono ◆ *vi* armonizar; **dialling** ~ (*TEL*) señal *f* para marcar.

tone down *vt* (*criticism*) suavizar; (*colour*) atenuar.

tone up *vt* (*muscles*) tonificar.

tone-deaf [təun'dɛf] *a* que no tiene oído musical.

toner ['təunə*] *n* (*for photocopier*) virador *m*.

Tonga ['tɔŋə] *n* Islas *fpl* Tonga.

tongs [tɔŋz] *npl* (*for coal*) tenazas *fpl*; (*for*

hair) tenacillas *fpl*.

tongue [tʌŋ] *n* lengua; ~ **in cheek** *ad* irónicamente.

tongue-tied ['tʌŋtaɪd] *a* (*fig*) mudo.

tongue-twister ['tʌŋtwɪstə*] *n* trabalenguas *m inv*.

tonic ['tɔnɪk] *n* (*MED*) tónico; (*MUS*) tónica; (*also:* ~ **water**) (agua) tónica.

tonight [tə'naɪt] *ad*, *n* esta noche; **I'll see you** ~ nos vemos esta noche.

tonnage ['tʌnɪdʒ] *n* (*NAUT*) tonelaje *m*.

tonsil ['tɔnsl] *n* amígdala; **to have one's** ~**s out** sacarse las amígdalas *or* anginas.

tonsillitis [tɔnsɪ'laɪtɪs] *n* amigdalitis *f*; **to have** ~ tener amigdalitis.

too [tuː] *ad* (*excessively*) demasiado; (*very*) muy; (*also*) también; **it's** ~ **sweet** está demasiado dulce; **I'm not** ~ **sure about that** no estoy muy seguro de eso; **I went** ~ yo fui también; ~ **much** *ad*, *a* demasiado; ~ **many** *a* demasiados/as; ~ **bad!** ¡mala suerte!

took [tuk] *pt of* **take**.

tool [tuːl] *n* herramienta; (*fig: person*) instrumento.

tool box *n* caja de herramientas.

tool kit *n* juego de herramientas.

tool shed *n* cobertizo (para herramientas).

toot [tuːt] *n* (*of horn*) bocinazo; (*of whistle*) silbido ♦ *vi* (*with car horn*) tocar la bocina.

tooth, *pl* **teeth** [tuːθ, tiːθ] *n* (*ANAT*, *TECH*) diente *m*; (*molar*) muela; **to clean one's teeth** lavarse los dientes; **to have a** ~ **out** sacarse una muela; **by the skin of one's teeth** por un pelo.

toothache ['tuːθeɪk] *n* dolor *m* de muelas.

toothbrush ['tuːθbrʌʃ] *n* cepillo de dientes.

toothpaste ['tuːθpeɪst] *n* pasta de dientes.

toothpick ['tuːθpɪk] *n* palillo.

tooth powder *n* polvos *mpl* dentífricos.

top [tɔp] *n* (*of mountain*) cumbre *f*, cima; (*of head*) coronilla; (*of ladder*) lo alto; (*of cupboard*, *table*) superficie *f*; (*lid: of box, jar*) tapa; (*: of bottle*) tapón *m*; (*of list, table, queue, page*) cabeza; (*toy*) peonza; (*DRESS: blouse etc*) blusa; (*: of pyjamas*) chaqueta ♦ *a* de arriba; (*in rank*) principal, primero; (*best*) mejor ♦ *vt* (*exceed*) exceder; (*be first in*) encabezar; **on** ~ **of** sobre, encima de; **from** ~ **to bottom** de pies a cabeza; **the** ~ **of the milk** la nata; **at the** ~ **of the stairs** en lo alto de la escalera; **at the** ~ **of the street** al final de la calle; **at the** ~ **of one's voice** (*fig*) a voz en grito; **at** ~ **speed** a máxima velocidad; **a** ~ **surgeon** un cirujano eminente; **over the** ~ (*col*) excesivo, desmesurado; **to go over the** ~ pasarse.

top up, (*US*) **top off** *vt* llenar.

topaz ['təupæz] *n* topacio.

topcoat ['tɔpkəut] *n* sobretodo, abrigo.

topflight ['tɔpflaɪt] *a* de primera (categoría

or clase).

top floor *n* último piso.

top hat *n* sombrero de copa.

top-heavy [tɔp'hɛvɪ] *a* (*object*) descompensado en la parte superior.

topic ['tɔpɪk] *n* tema *m*.

topical ['tɔpɪkl] *a* actual.

topless ['tɔplɪs] *a* (*bather etc*) topless.

top-level ['tɔplɛvl] *a* (*talks*) al más alto nivel.

topmost ['tɔpməust] *a* más alto.

topography [tə'pɔgrəfɪ] *n* topografía.

topping ['tɔpɪŋ] *n* (*CULIN*) cubierta.

topple ['tɔpl] *vt* volcar, derribar ♦ *vi* caerse.

top-ranking ['tɔpræŋkɪŋ] *a* de alto rango.

TOPS [tɔps] *n abbr* (*Brit*: = *Training Opportunities Scheme*) plan de promoción de empleo.

top-secret [tɔp'siːkrɪt] *a* de alto secreto.

top-security ['tɔpsɪ'kjuərɪtɪ] *a* (*Brit*) de máxima seguridad.

topsy-turvy ['tɔpsɪ'təːvɪ] *a*, *ad* patas arriba.

top-up ['tɔpʌp] *n*: **would you like a** ~? ¿quiere que se llene?

torch [tɔːtʃ] *n* antorcha; (*Brit: electric*) linterna.

tore [tɔː*] *pt of* **tear**.

torment *n* ['tɔːmɛnt] tormento ♦ *vt* [tɔː'mɛnt] atormentar; (*fig: annoy*) fastidiar.

torn [tɔːn] *pp of* **tear**.

tornado, ~**es** [tɔː'neɪdəu] *n* tornado.

torpedo, ~**es** [tɔː'piːdəu] *n* torpedo.

torpedo boat *n* torpedero, lancha torpedera.

torpor ['tɔːpə*] *n* letargo.

torrent ['tɔrnt] *n* torrente *m*.

torrential [tɔ'rɛnʃl] *a* torrencial.

torrid ['tɔrɪd] *a* tórrido; (*fig*) apasionado.

torso ['tɔːsəu] *n* torso.

tortoise ['tɔːtəs] *n* tortuga.

tortoiseshell ['tɔːtəʃɛl] *a* de carey.

tortuous ['tɔːtjuəs] *a* tortuoso.

torture ['tɔːtʃə*] *n* tortura ♦ *vt* torturar; (*fig*) atormentar.

torturer ['tɔːtʃərə*] *n* torturador(a) *m/f*.

Tory ['tɔːrɪ] *a*, *n* (*Brit POL*) conservador(a) *m/f*.

toss [tɔs] *vt* tirar, echar; (*head*) sacudir ♦ *n* (*movement: of head etc*) sacudida; (*of coin*) tirada, echada (*LAm*); **to** ~ **a coin** echar a cara o cruz; **to** ~ **up for sth** jugar algo a cara o cruz; **to** ~ **and turn** (*in bed*) dar vueltas (en la cama); **to win/lose the** ~ (*also SPORT*) ganar/perder (a cara o cruz).

tot [tɔt] *n* (*Brit: drink*) copita; (*child*) nene/a *m/f*.

tot up *vt* sumar.

total ['təutl] *a* total, entero ♦ *n* total *m*, suma ♦ *vt* (*add up*) sumar; (*amount to*) ascender a; **grand** ~ importe *m* total; **in** ~ en total, en suma.

totalitarian [təutælɪ'tɛərɪən] *a* totalitario.

totality [təu'tælɪtɪ] *n* totalidad *f*.

total loss *n* siniestra total.

totally ['təutəlɪ] *ad* totalmente.

tote [təut] *vt* (*col*) acarrear, cargar con.

tote bag *n* bolsa, bolso.

totem pole ['təutəm-] *n* poste *m* totémico.

totter ['tɔtə*] *vi* tambalearse.

touch [tʌtʃ] *n* tacto; (*contact*) contacto; (*FOOTBALL*) fuera de juego ♦ *vt* tocar; (*emotionally*) conmover; **a** ~ **of** (*fig*) una pizca *or* un poquito de; **to get in** ~ **with sb** ponerse en contacto con uno; **I'll be in** ~ le llamaré/escribiré; **to lose** ~ (*friends*) perder contacto; **to be out of** ~ **with events** no estar al corriente (de los acontecimientos); **the personal** ~ el toque personal; **to put the finishing** ~**es to sth** dar el último toque a algo; **no artist in the country can** ~ **him** no hay artista en todo el país que le iguale.

touch on *vt fus* (*topic*) aludir (brevemente) a.

touch up *vt* (*paint*) retocar.

touch-and-go ['tʌtʃən'gəu] *a* arriesgado.

touchdown ['tʌtʃdəun] *n* aterrizaje *m*; (*US FOOTBALL*) ensayo.

touched [tʌtʃt] *a* conmovido; (*col*) chiflado.

touchiness ['tʌtʃɪnɪs] *n* susceptibilidad *f*.

touching ['tʌtʃɪŋ] *a* conmovedor(a).

touchline ['tʌtʃlaɪn] *n* (*SPORT*) línea de banda.

touch-type ['tʌtʃtaɪp] *vi* mecanografiar al tacto.

touchy ['tʌtʃɪ] *a* (*person*) quisquilloso.

tough [tʌf] *a* (*meat*) duro; (*journey*) penoso; (*task, problem, situation*) difícil; (*resistant*) resistente; (*person*) fuerte; (: *pej*) bruto ♦ *n* (*gangster etc*) gorila *m*; **they got** ~ **with the workers** fueron muy duros con los trabajadores.

toughen ['tʌfn] *vt* endurecer.

toughness ['tʌfnɪs] *n* dureza; (*resistance*) resistencia; (*strictness*) inflexibilidad *f*.

toupée ['tuːpeɪ] *n* peluca.

tour ['tuə*] *n* viaje *m*, vuelta; (*also:* **package** ~) viaje *m* todo comprendido; (*of town, museum*) visita ♦ *vt* viajar por; **to go on a** ~ **of** (*region, country*) ir de viaje por; (*museum, castle*) dar una vuelta de; **to go on** ~ partir *or* ir de gira.

touring ['tuərɪŋ] *n* viajes *mpl* turísticos, turismo.

tourism ['tuərɪzm] *n* turismo.

tourist ['tuərɪst] *n* turista *m/f* ♦ *cpd* turístico; **the** ~ **trade** el turismo.

tourist office *n* oficina de turismo.

tournament ['tuənəmənt] *n* torneo.

tourniquet ['tuənɪkeɪ] *n* (*MED*) torniquete *m*.

tour operator *n* agente *m/f or* agencia de viajes.

tousled ['tauzld] *a* (*hair*) despeinado.

tout [taut] *vi*: **to** ~ **for business** solicitar clientes ♦ *n*: **ticket** ~ revendedor(a) *m/f*.

tow [təu] *n*: **to give sb a** ~ (*AUT*) darle remolque *or* remolcar a uno ♦ *vt* remolcar; **"on** *or* (*US*) **in** ~**"** (*AUT*) "a remolque".

toward(s) [tə'wɔːd(z)] *prep* hacia; (*of attitude*) respecto a, con; (*of purpose*) para; ~ **noon** alrededor de mediodía; ~ **the end of the year** hacia finales de año; **to feel friendly** ~ **sb** sentir amistad hacia uno.

towel ['tauəl] *n* toalla; **to throw in the** ~ (*fig*) darse por vencido, renunciar.

towelling ['tauəlɪŋ] *n* (*fabric*) felpa.

towel rail, (*US*) **towel rack** *n* toallero.

tower ['tauə*] *n* torre *f* ♦ *vi* (*building, mountain*) elevarse; **to** ~ **above** *or* **over sth/sb** dominar algo/destacarse sobre uno.

tower block *n* (*Brit*) rascacielos *m inv*.

towering ['tauərɪŋ] *a* muy alto, imponente.

town [taun] *n* ciudad *f*; **to go to** ~ ir a la ciudad; (*fig*) echar los bofes; **in the** ~ en la ciudad; **to be out of** ~ estar fuera de la ciudad.

town centre *n* centro de la ciudad.

town clerk *n* secretario/a del Ayuntamiento.

town council *n* Ayuntamiento, consejo municipal.

town hall *n* ayuntamiento.

town plan *n* plano de la ciudad.

town planner *n* urbanista *m/f*.

town planning *n* urbanismo.

townspeople ['taunzpiːpl] *npl* gente *f* de ciudad.

towpath ['təupɑːθ] *n* camino de sirga.

towrope ['təurəup] *n* cable *m* de remolque.

tow truck *n* (*US*) camión *m* grúa.

toxic ['tɔksɪk] *a* tóxico.

toxin ['tɔksɪn] *n* toxina.

toy [tɔɪ] *n* juguete *m*.

toy with *vt fus* jugar con; (*idea*) acariciar.

toyshop ['tɔɪʃɔp] *n* juguetería.

toy train *n* tren *m* de juguete.

trace [treɪs] *n* rastro ♦ *vt* (*draw*) trazar, delinear; (*locate*) encontrar; **there was no** ~ **of it** no había ningún indicio de eso.

trace element *n* oligoelemento.

trachea [trə'kɪə] *n* (*ANAT*) tráquea.

tracing paper ['treɪsɪŋ-] *n* papel *m* de calco.

track [træk] *n* (*mark*) huella, pista; (*path: gen*) camino, senda; (: *of bullet etc*) trayectoria; (: *of suspect, animal*) pista, rastro; (*RAIL*) vía; (*COMPUT, SPORT*) pista; (*on record*) canción *f* ♦ *vt* seguir la pista de; **to keep** ~ **of** mantenerse al tanto de, seguir; **a 4-**~ **tape** una cinta de 4 pistas; **the first** ~ **on the record/tape** la primera canción en el disco/cassette; **to be on the**

right ~ (fig) ir por buen camino.
track down vt (person) localizar; (sth lost) encontrar.
tracker dog ['trækə*-] n (Brit) perro rastreador.
track events npl (SPORT) pruebas fpl en pista.
tracking station ['trækɪŋ-] n (SPACE) estación f de seguimiento.
track record n: **to have a good** ~ (fig) tener (buenos) antecedentes.
tracksuit ['træksuːt] n chandal m.
tract [trækt] n (GEO) región f; (pamphlet) folleto.
traction ['trækʃən] n (AUT, power) tracción f; **in** ~ (MED) en tracción.
traction engine n locomotora de tracción.
tractor ['træktə*] n tractor m.
tractor feed n (on printer) arrastre m de papel por tracción.
trade [treɪd] n comercio, negocio; (skill, job) oficio, empleo; (industry) industria ♦ vi negociar, comerciar; **foreign** ~ comercio exterior.
 trade in vt (old car etc) ofrecer como parte del pago.
trade barrier n barrera comercial.
trade deficit n déficit m comercial.
Trade Descriptions Act n (Brit) ley sobre descripciones comerciales.
trade discount n descuento comercial.
trade fair n feria de muestras.
trade-in ['treɪdɪn] a: ~ **price/value** precio/valor m de entrega or a cuenta.
trademark ['treɪdmaːk] n marca de fábrica.
trade mission n misión f comercial.
trade name n marca registrada.
trade price n precio al detallista.
trader ['treɪdə*] n comerciante m/f.
trade reference n referencia comercial.
trade secret n secreto profesional.
tradesman ['treɪdzmən] n (shopkeeper) tendero.
trade union n sindicato.
trade unionist [-'juːnjənɪst] n sindicalista m/f.
trade wind n viento alisio.
trading ['treɪdɪŋ] n comercio.
trading account n cuenta de compra-venta.
trading estate n (Brit) zona comercial.
trading stamp n cupón m, sello de prima.
tradition [trə'dɪʃən] n tradición f.
traditional [trə'dɪʃənl] a tradicional.
traditionally [trə'dɪʃənlɪ] ad tradicionalmente.
traffic ['træfɪk] n (gen, AUT) tráfico, circulación f, tránsito (LAm); **air** ~ tránsito aéreo ♦ vi: **to** ~ **in** (pej: liquor, drugs) traficar en.
traffic circle n (US) glorieta de tráfico.
traffic island n refugio, isleta.
traffic jam n embotellamiento, atasco.

trafficker ['træfɪkə*] n traficante m/f.
traffic lights npl semáforo sg.
traffic offence, (US) **traffic violation** n infracción f de tránsito.
traffic warden n guardia m/f de tráfico.
tragedy ['trædʒədɪ] n tragedia.
tragic ['trædʒɪk] a trágico.
tragically ['trædʒɪkəlɪ] ad trágicamente.
trail [treɪl] n (tracks) rastro, pista; (path) camino, sendero; (dust, smoke) estela ♦ vt (drag) arrastrar; (follow) seguir la pista de; (follow closely) vigilar ♦ vi arrastrarse; **to be on sb's** ~ seguir la pista de uno.
 trail away, trail off vi (sound) desvanecerse; (interest, voice) desaparecer.
 trail behind vi quedar a la zaga.
trailer ['treɪlə*] n (AUT) remolque m; (caravan) caravana f; (CINEMA) trailer m, avance m.
trail truck n (US) trailer m.
train [treɪn] n tren m; (of dress) cola; (series): ~ **of events** curso de los acontecimientos ♦ vt (educate) formar; (teach skills to) adiestrar; (sportsman) entrenar; (dog) amaestrar; (point: gun etc): **to** ~ **on** apuntar a ♦ vi (SPORT) entrenarse; (be educated, learn a skill) formarse; **to go by** ~ ir en tren; **one's** ~ **of thought** el razonamiento de uno; **to** ~ **sb to do sth** entrenar a uno a hacer algo.
train attendant n (US RAIL) empleado/a de coches-cama.
trained [treɪnd] a (worker) cualificado; (animal) amaestrado.
trainee [treɪ'niː] n aprendiz(a) m/f ♦ cpd: **he's a** ~ **teacher** (primary) es estudiante de magisterio; (secondary) está haciendo las prácticas del I.C.E.
trainer ['treɪnə*] n (SPORT) entrenador(a) m/f; (of animals) domador(a) m/f; ~**s** npl (shoes) zapatillas fpl (de deporte).
training ['treɪnɪŋ] n formación f; entrenamiento; **to be in** ~ (SPORT) estar entrenando; (: fit) estar en forma.
training college n (gen) colegio de formación profesional; (for teachers) escuela normal.
training course n curso de formación.
training shoes npl zapatillas fpl (de deporte).
traipse [treɪps] vi andar penosamente.
trait [treɪt] n rasgo.
traitor ['treɪtə*] n traidor(a) m/f.
trajectory [trə'dʒɛktərɪ] n trayectoria, curso.
tram [træm] n (Brit: also: ~**car**) tranvía m.
tramline ['træmlaɪn] n carril m de tranvía.
tramp [træmp] n (person) vagabundo/a; (col: offensive: woman) puta ♦ vi andar con pasos pesados.
trample ['træmpl] vt: **to** ~ **(underfoot)** pisotear.

trampoline ['træmpəli:n] n trampolín m.

trance [trɑ:ns] n trance m; **to go into a ~** entrar en trance.

tranquil ['træŋkwɪl] a tranquilo.

tranquillity, (US) **tranquility** [træŋ'kwɪlɪtɪ] n tranquilidad f.

tranquillizer, (US) **tranquilizer** ['træŋkwɪlaɪzə*] n (MED) tranquilizante m.

trans- [trænz] pref trans-, tras-.

transact [træn'zækt] vt (business) tramitar.

transaction [træn'zækʃən] n transacción f, operación f; **cash ~s** comercio al contado.

transatlantic ['trænzət'læntɪk] a transatlántico.

transcend [træn'sɛnd] vt rebasar.

transcendent [træn'sɛndənt] a trascendente.

transcendental [trænsɛn'dɛntl] a: **~ meditation** meditación f transcendental.

transcribe [træn'skraɪb] vt transcribir, copiar.

transcript ['trænskrɪpt] n copia.

transcription [træn'skrɪpʃən] n transcripción f.

transept ['trænsɛpt] n crucero.

transfer n ['trænsfə*] transferencia; (SPORT) traspaso; (picture, design) calcomanía ◆ vt [træns'fə:*] trasladar, pasar; **to ~ the charges** (Brit TEL) llamar a cobro revertido; **by bank ~** por transferencia bancaria or giro bancario; **to ~ money from one account to another** transferir dinero de una cuenta a otra; **to ~ sth to sb's name** transferir algo al nombre de uno.

transferable [træns'fə:rəbl] a: **not ~** intransferible.

transfix [træns'fɪks] vt traspasar; (fig): **~ed with fear** paralizado por el miedo.

transform [træns'fɔ:m] vt transformar.

transformation [trænsfə'meɪʃən] n transformación f.

transformer [træns'fɔ:mə*] n (ELEC) transformador m.

transfusion [træns'fju:ʒən] n transfusión f.

transgress [træns'grɛs] vt (go beyond) traspasar; (violate) violar, infringir.

tranship [træn'ʃɪp] vt trasbordar.

transient ['trænzɪənt] a transitorio.

transistor [træn'zɪstə*] n (ELEC) transistor m.

transistorized [træn'zɪstəraɪzd] a (circuit) transistorizado.

transistor radio n transistor m.

transit ['trænzɪt] n: **in ~** en tránsito.

transit camp n campo de tránsito.

transition [træn'zɪʃən] n transición f.

transitional [træn'zɪʃənl] a transitorio.

transition period n período de transición.

transitive ['trænzɪtɪv] a (LING) transitivo.

transitively ['trænsɪtɪvlɪ] ad transitivamente.

transitory ['trænzɪtərɪ] a transitorio.

transit visa n visado de tránsito.

translate [trænz'leɪt] vt: **to ~ (from/into)** traducir (de/a).

translation [trænz'leɪʃən] n traducción f.

translator [trænz'leɪtə*] n traductor(a) m/f.

translucent [trænz'lu:snt] a traslúcido.

transmission [trænz'mɪʃən] n transmisión f.

transmit [trænz'mɪt] vt transmitir.

transmitter [trænz'mɪtə*] n transmisor m; (station) emisora.

transparency [træns'pɛərnsɪ] n (Brit PHOT) diapositiva.

transparent [træns'pærnt] a transparente.

transpire [træns'paɪə*] vi (turn out) resultar (ser); (happen) ocurrir, suceder; (become known): **it finally ~d that ...** por fin se supo que ....

transplant vt [træns'plɑ:nt] transplantar ◆ n ['trænsplɑ:nt] (MED) transplante m; **to have a heart ~** hacerse un transplante de corazón.

transport n ['trænspɔ:t] transporte m ◆ vt [træns'pɔ:t] transportar; **public ~** transporte m público.

transportable [træns'pɔ:təbl] a transportable.

transportation [trænspɔ:'teɪʃən] n transporte m; (of prisoners) deportación f.

transport café n (Brit) bar-restaurante m de carretera.

transpose [træns'pəuz] vt transponer.

transship [træns'ʃɪp] vt trasbordar.

transverse ['trænzvɜ:s] a transverso, transversal.

transvestite [trænz'vɛstaɪt] n travesti m/f.

trap [træp] n (snare, trick) trampa; (carriage) cabriolé m ◆ vt coger (Sp) or agarrar (LAm) en una trampa; (immobilize) bloquear; (jam) atascar; **to set** or **lay a ~ (for sb)** poner(le) una trampa (a uno); **to ~ one's finger in the door** cogerse el dedo en la puerta.

trap door n escotilla.

trapeze [trə'pi:z] n trapecio.

trapper ['træpə*] n trampero, cazador m.

trappings ['træpɪŋz] npl adornos mpl.

trash [træʃ] n (pej: goods) pacotilla; (: nonsense) tonterías fpl; (US: rubbish) basura.

trash can n (US) cubo or balde m (LAm) de la basura.

trash can liner n (US) bolsa de basura.

trashy ['træʃɪ] a malísimo.

trauma ['trɔ:mə] n trauma m.

traumatic [trɔ:'mætɪk] a (PSYCH, fig) traumático.

travel ['trævl] n viaje m ◆ vi viajar ◆ vt (distance) recorrer; **this wine doesn't ~ well** este vino no se transporta bien.

travel agency n agencia de viajes.

travel agent n agente m/f de viajes.

travel brochure n folleto turístico.

traveller, (US) **traveler** ['trævlə*] n viajero/

a; (*COMM*) viajante *m/f*.

traveller's cheque, (*US*) **traveler's check** *n* cheque *m* de viajero.

travelling, (*US*) **traveling** ['trævlɪŋ] *n* los viajes, el viajar ♦ *a* (*circus, exhibition*) ambulante ♦ *cpd* (*bag, clock*) de viaje.

travel(l)ing expenses *npl* dietas *fpl*.

travel(l)ing salesman *n* viajante *m*.

travelogue ['trævəlɔg] *n* (*book*) relación *f* de viajes; (*film*) documental *m* de viajes; (*talk*) recuento de viajes.

travel sickness *n* mareo.

traverse ['trævəs] *vt* atravesar.

travesty ['trævəstɪ] *n* parodia.

trawler ['trɔːlə*] *n* pesquero de arrastre.

tray [treɪ] *n* (*for carrying*) bandeja; (*on desk*) cajón *m*.

treacherous ['trɛtʃərəs] *a* traidor(a); **road conditions are ~** el estado de las carreteras es peligroso.

treachery ['trɛtʃərɪ] *n* traición *f*.

treacle ['triːkl] *n* (*Brit*) melaza.

tread [trɛd] *n* (*step*) paso, pisada; (*sound*) ruido de pasos; (*of tyre*) banda de rodadura ♦ *vi* (*pt* **trod**, *pp* **trodden** [trɔd, 'trɔdn]) pisar.

tread on *vt fus* pisar.

treas. *abbr* = **treasurer**.

treason ['triːzn] *n* traición *f*.

treasure ['trɛʒə*] *n* tesoro ♦ *vt* (*value*) apreciar, valorar.

treasure hunt *n* caza al tesoro.

treasurer ['trɛʒərə*] *n* tesorero/a.

treasury ['trɛʒərɪ] *n*: **the T~**, (*US*) **the T~ Department** ≈ el Ministerio *or* la Secretaría de Hacienda.

treasury bill *n* bono del Tesoro.

treat [triːt] *n* (*present*) regalo; (*pleasure*) placer *m* ♦ *vt* tratar; (*consider*) considerar; **to give sb a ~** hacer un regalo a uno; **to ~ sb to sth** invitar a uno a algo; **to ~ sth as a joke** tomar algo a broma.

treatise ['triːtɪz] *n* tratado.

treatment ['triːtmənt] *n* tratamiento; **to have ~ for sth** recibir tratamiento por algo.

treaty ['triːtɪ] *n* tratado.

treble ['trɛbl] *a* triple ♦ *vt* triplicar ♦ *vi* triplicarse.

treble clef *n* (*MUS*) clave *f* de sol.

tree [triː] *n* árbol *m*.

tree-lined ['triːlaɪnd] *a* bordeado de árboles.

tree trunk *n* tronco de árbol.

trek [trɛk] *n* (*long journey*) expedición *f*; (*tiring walk*) caminata.

trellis ['trɛlɪs] *n* enrejado.

tremble ['trɛmbl] *vi* temblar.

trembling ['trɛmblɪŋ] *n* temblor *m* ♦ *a* tembloroso.

tremendous [trɪ'mɛndəs] *a* tremendo; (*enormous*) enorme; (*excellent*) estupendo.

tremendously [trɪ'mɛndəslɪ] *ad* enormemente, sobremanera; **he enjoyed it ~** lo

disfrutó de lo lindo.

tremor ['trɛmə*] *n* temblor *m*; (*also:* **earth ~**) temblor *m* de tierra.

trench [trɛntʃ] *n* zanja; (*MIL*) trinchera.

trench coat *n* trinchera.

trench warfare *n* guerra de trincheras.

trend [trɛnd] *n* (*tendency*) tendencia; (*of events*) curso; (*fashion*) moda; **~ towards/away from sth** tendencia hacia/en contra de algo; **to set the ~** marcar la pauta.

trendy ['trɛndɪ] *a* de moda.

trepidation [trɛpɪ'deɪʃən] *n* inquietud *f*.

trespass ['trɛspəs] *vi*: **to ~ on** entrar sin permiso en; **"no ~ing"** "prohibido el paso".

trespasser ['trɛspəsə*] *n* intruso/a *m/f*; **"~s will be prosecuted"** "se procesará a los intrusos".

tress [trɛs] *n* trenza.

trestle ['trɛsl] *n* caballete *m*.

trestle table *n* mesa de caballete.

tri- [traɪ] *pref* tri-.

trial ['traɪəl] *n* (*LAW*) juicio, proceso; (*test: of machine etc*) prueba; (*hardship*) desgracia; **~s** *npl* (*ATHLETICS, of horses*) pruebas *fpl*; **to bring sb to ~ (for a crime)** llevar a uno a juicio (por un delito); **~ by jury** juicio ante jurado; **to be sent for ~** ser remitido al tribunal; **by ~ and error** a fuerza de probar.

trial balance *n* balance *m* de comprobación.

trial basis *n*: **on a ~** en concepto de prueba.

trial offer *n* oferta de prueba.

trial run *n* prueba.

triangle ['traɪæŋgl] *n* (*MATH, MUS*) triángulo.

triangular [traɪ'æŋgjulə*] *a* triangular.

tribal ['traɪbəl] *a* tribal.

tribe [traɪb] *n* tribu *f*.

tribesman ['traɪbzmən] *n* miembro de una tribu.

tribulation [trɪbju'leɪʃən] *n* tribulación *f*.

tribunal [traɪ'bjuːnl] *n* tribunal *m*.

tributary ['trɪbjuːtərɪ] *n* (*river*) afluente *m*.

tribute ['trɪbjuːt] *n* homenaje *m*, tributo; **to pay ~ to** rendir homenaje a.

trice [traɪs] *n*: **in a ~** en un santiamén.

trick [trɪk] *n* trampa; (*conjuring ~, deceit*) truco; (*joke*) broma; (*CARDS*) baza ♦ *vt* engañar; **it's a ~ of the light** es una ilusión óptica; **to play a ~ on sb** gastar una broma a uno; **that should do the ~** eso servirá; **to ~ sb out of sth** quitarle algo a uno con engaños; **to ~ sb into doing sth** hacer que uno haga algo con engaños.

trickery ['trɪkərɪ] *n* engaño.

trickle ['trɪkl] *n* (*of water etc*) chorrito ♦ *vi* gotear.

trick question *n* pega.

trickster ['trɪkstə*] *n* estafador(a) *m/f*.

tricky ['trɪkɪ] *a* difícil; (*problem*) delicado.

tricycle ['traɪsɪkl] *n* triciclo.

tried [traɪd] *a* probado.

trifle ['traɪfl] *n* bagatela; (*CULIN*) *dulce de bizcocho, gelatina, fruta y natillas* ♦ *ad*: **a ~ long** un poquito largo ♦ *vi*: **to ~ with** jugar con.

trifling ['traɪflɪŋ] *a* insignificante.

trigger ['trɪgə*] *n* (*of gun*) gatillo.

   trigger off *vt* desencadenar.

trigonometry [trɪgə'nɔmətrɪ] *n* trigonometría.

trilby ['trɪlbɪ] *n* (*also*: **~ hat**) sombrero flexible *or* tirolés.

trill [trɪl] *n* (*of bird*) gorjeo; (*MUS*) trino.

trilogy ['trɪlədʒɪ] *n* trilogía.

trim [trɪm] *a* (*elegant*) aseado; (*house, garden*) en buen estado; (*figure*): **to be ~** tener buen talle ♦ *n* (*haircut etc*) recorte *m* ♦ *vt* (*neaten*) arreglar; (*cut*) recortar; (*decorate*) adornar; (*NAUT*: *a sail*) orientar; **to keep in (good) ~** mantener en buen estado.

trimmings ['trɪmɪŋz] *npl* (*extras*) accesorios *mpl*; (*cuttings*) recortes *mpl*.

Trinidad and Tobago ['trɪnɪdæd-] *n* Trinidad *f* y Tobago.

Trinity ['trɪnɪtɪ] *n*: **the ~** la Trinidad.

trinket ['trɪŋkɪt] *n* chuchería, baratija.

trio ['triːəu] *n* trío.

trip [trɪp] *n* viaje *m*; (*excursion*) excursión *f*; (*stumble*) traspié *m* ♦ *vi* (*stumble*) tropezar; (*go lightly*) andar a paso ligero; **on a ~** de viaje.

   trip over *vt fus* tropezar con.

   trip up *vi* tropezar, caerse ♦ *vt* hacer tropezar *or* caer.

tripartite [traɪ'pɑːtaɪt] *a* (*agreement, talks*) tripartito.

tripe [traɪp] *n* (*CULIN*) callos *mpl*; (*pej*: *rubbish*) bobadas *fpl*.

triple ['trɪpl] *a* triple ♦ *ad*: **~ the distance/ the speed** 3 veces la distancia/la velocidad.

triplets ['trɪplɪts] *npl* trillizos/as *m/fpl*.

triplicate ['trɪplɪkət] *n*: **in ~** por triplicado.

tripod ['traɪpɔd] *n* trípode *m*.

Tripoli ['trɪpəlɪ] *n* Trípoli *m*.

tripper ['trɪpə*] *n* turista *m/f*, excursionista *m/f*.

tripwire ['trɪpwaɪə*] *n* cuerda de trampa.

trite [traɪt] *a* trillado.

triumph ['traɪʌmf] *n* triunfo ♦ *vi*: **to ~ (over)** vencer.

triumphal [traɪ'ʌmfl] *a* triunfal.

triumphant [traɪ'ʌmfənt] *a* triunfante.

triumphantly [traɪ'ʌmfəntlɪ] *ad* triunfalmente, en tono triunfal.

trivia ['trɪvɪə] *npl* trivialidades *fpl*.

trivial ['trɪvɪəl] *a* insignificante, trivial.

triviality [trɪvɪ'ælɪtɪ] *n* insignificancia, trivialidad *f*.

trivialize ['trɪvɪəlaɪz] *vt* minimizar, tratar con desprecio.

trod [trɔd] *pt of* **tread**.

trodden ['trɔdn] *pp of* **tread**.

trolley ['trɔlɪ] *n* carrito; (*in hospital*) camilla.

trolley bus *n* trolebús *m*.

trombone [trɔm'bəun] *n* trombón *m*.

troop [truːp] *n* grupo, banda; *see also* **troops**.

   troop in *vi* entrar en tropel.

   troop out *vi* salir en tropel.

troop carrier *n* (*plane*) transporte *n* (militar); (*NAUT*: *also*: **troopship**) (buque *m* de) transporte *m*.

trooper ['truːpə*] *n* (*MIL*) soldado (de caballería); (*US*: *policeman*) policía *m/f* montado/a.

trooping the colour ['truːpɪŋ-] *n* (*ceremony*) presentación *f* de la bandera.

troopship ['truːpʃɪp] *n* (buque *m* de) transporte *m*.

trophy ['trəufɪ] *n* trofeo.

tropic ['trɔpɪk] *n* trópico; **the ~s** los trópicos, la zona tropical; **T~ of Cancer/ Capricorn** trópico de Cáncer/Capricornio.

tropical ['trɔpɪkl] *a* tropical.

trot [trɔt] *n* trote *m* ♦ *vi* trotar; **on the ~** (*Brit fig*) seguidos/as.

   trot out *vt* (*excuse, reason*) sacar a luz; (*names, facts*) sacar a relucir.

trouble ['trʌbl] *n* problema *m*, dificultad *f*; (*worry*) preocupación *f*; (*bother, effort*) molestia, esfuerzo; (*unrest*) inquietud *f*; (*with machine etc*) fallo, avería; (*MED*): **stomach ~** problemas *mpl* gástricos ♦ *vt* molestar; (*worry*) preocupar, inquietar ♦ *vi*: **to ~ to do sth** molestarse en hacer algo; **~s** *npl* (*POL etc*) conflictos *mpl*; **to be in ~** estar en un apuro; (*for doing wrong*) tener problemas; **to have ~ doing sth** tener dificultad en *or* para hacer algo; **to go to the ~ of doing sth** tomarse la molestia de hacer algo; **what's the ~?** ¿qué pasa?; **the ~ is ...** el problema es ..., lo que pasa es ...; **please don't ~ yourself** por favor no se moleste.

troubled ['trʌbld] *a* (*person*) preocupado; (*epoch, life*) agitado.

trouble-free ['trʌblfriː] *a* sin problemas *or* dificultades.

troublemaker ['trʌblmeɪkə*] *n* agitador(a) *m/f*.

troubleshooter ['trʌblʃuːtə*] *n* (*in conflict*) conciliador(a) *m/f*.

troublesome ['trʌblsəm] *a* molesto, inoportuno.

trouble spot *n* centro de fricción, punto caliente.

trough [trɔf] *n* (*also*: **drinking ~**) abrevadero; (*also*: **feeding ~**) comedero; (*channel*) canal *m*.

trounce [trauns] *vt* derrotar.

troupe [truːp] *n* grupo.

trouser press *n* prensa para pantalones.

trousers ['trauzəz] *npl* pantalones *mpl*;

short ~ pantalones *mpl* cortos.
trouser suit *n* traje *m* de chaqueta y pantalón.
trousseau, *pl* ~**x** *or* ~**s** ['tru:səu, -z] *n* ajuar *m*.
trout [traut] *n* (*pl inv*) trucha.
trowel ['trauəl] *n* paleta.
truant ['truənt] *n*: **to play** ~ (*Brit*) hacer novillos.
truce [tru:s] *n* tregua.
truck [trʌk] *n* (*US*) camión *m*; (*RAIL*) vagón *m*.
truck driver *n* camionero/a.
trucker ['trʌkə*] *n* (*esp US*) camionero/a, camionista *m/f*.
truck farm *n* (*US*) huerto de hortalizas.
trucking ['trʌkɪŋ] *n* (*esp US*) acarreo, transporte *m* en camión.
trucking company *n* (*US*) compañía de transporte por carretera.
truckload ['trʌkləud] *n* camión *m* lleno.
truculent ['trʌkjulənt] *a* agresivo.
trudge [trʌdʒ] *vi* caminar penosamente.
true [tru:] *a* verdadero; (*accurate*) exacto; (*genuine*) auténtico; (*faithful*) fiel; (*wheel*) centrado; (*wall*) a plomo; (*beam*) alineado; ~ **to life** verídico; **to come** ~ realizarse, cumplirse.
truffle ['trʌfl] *n* trufa.
truly ['tru:lɪ] *ad* realmente; (*faithfully*) fielmente; **yours** ~ (*in letter-writing*) atentamente.
trump [trʌmp] *n* (*CARDS*) triunfo; **to turn up** ~**s** (*fig*) salir *or* resultar bien.
trump card *n* triunfo; (*fig*) baza.
trumped-up ['trʌmptʌp] *a* inventado.
trumpet ['trʌmpɪt] *n* trompeta.
truncated [trʌŋ'keɪtɪd] *a* truncado.
truncheon ['trʌntʃən] *n* (*Brit*) porra.
trundle ['trʌndl] *vt*, *vi*: **to** ~ **along** rodar haciendo ruido.
trunk [trʌŋk] *n* (*of tree, person*) tronco; (*of elephant*) trompa; (*case*) baúl *m*; (*US AUT*) maletero; *see also* **trunks**.
trunk call *n* (*Brit TEL*) llamada interurbana.
trunk road *n* carretera principal.
trunks [trʌŋks] *npl* (*also*: **swimming** ~**s**) bañador *m*.
truss [trʌs] *n* (*MED*) braguero ♦ *vt*: **to** ~ (**up**) atar; (*CULIN*) espetar.
trust [trʌst] *n* confianza; (*COMM*) trust *m*; (*LAW*) fideicomiso ♦ *vt* (*rely on*) tener confianza en; (*entrust*): **to** ~ **sth to sb** confiar algo a uno; (*hope*): **to** ~ (**that**) esperar (que); **in** ~ en fideicomiso; **you'll have to take it on** ~ tienes que aceptarlo a ojos cerrados.
trust company *n* empresa de fideicomiso.
trusted ['trʌstɪd] *a* de confianza, fiable, de fiar.
trustee [trʌs'ti:] *n* (*LAW*) fideicomisario.
trustful ['trʌstful] *a* confiado.

trust fund *n* fondo fiduciario *or* de fideicomiso.
trusting ['trʌstɪŋ] *a* confiado.
trustworthy ['trʌstwə:ðɪ] *a* digno de confianza, fiable, de fiar.
trusty ['trʌstɪ] *a* fiel.
truth, ~**s** [tru:θ, tru:ðz] *n* verdad *f*.
truthful ['tru:θful] *a* (*person*) sincero; (*account*) fidedigno.
truthfully ['tru:θfulɪ] *ad* (*answer*) con sinceridad.
truthfulness ['tru:θfulnɪs] *n* (*of account*) verdad *f*; (*of person*) sinceridad *f*.
try [traɪ] *n* tentativa, intento; (*RUGBY*) ensayo ♦ *vt* (*LAW*) juzgar, procesar; (*test: sth new*) probar, someter a prueba; (*attempt*) intentar; (*strain: patience*) hacer perder ♦ *vi* probar; **to give sth a** ~ intentar hacer algo; **to** ~ **one's (very) best** *or* **hardest** poner todo su empeño, esmerarse; **to** ~ **to do sth** intentar hacer algo.
try on *vt* (*clothes*) probarse.
try out *vt* probar, poner a prueba.
trying ['traɪɪŋ] *a* cansado; (*person*) pesado.
tsar [za:*] *n* zar *m*.
T-shirt ['ti:ʃə:t] *n* camiseta.
T-square ['ti:skwɛə*] *n* regla en T.
TT *a abbr* (*Brit col*) = **teetotal** ♦ *abbr* (*US POST*) = *Trust Territory*.
tub [tʌb] *n* cubo (*Sp*), balde *m* (*LAm*); (*bath*) tina, bañera.
tuba ['tju:bə] *n* tuba.
tubby ['tʌbɪ] *a* regordete.
tube [tju:b] *n* tubo; (*Brit: underground*) metro; (*US col: television*) tele *f*.
tubeless ['tju:blɪs] *a* (*tyre*) sin cámara.
tuber ['tju:bə*] *n* (*BOT*) tubérculo.
tuberculosis [tjubə:kju'ləusɪs] *n* tuberculosis *f inv*.
tube station *n* (*Brit*) estación *f* de metro.
tubing ['tju:bɪŋ] *n* tubería (*Sp*), cañería; **a piece of** ~ un trozo de tubo.
tubular ['tju:bjulə*] *a* tubular.
TUC *n abbr* (*Brit*: = *Trades Union Congress*) federación nacional de sindicatos.
tuck [tʌk] *n* (*SEWING*) pliegue *m* ♦ *vt* (*put*) poner.
tuck away *vt* esconder.
tuck in *vt* meter dentro; (*child*) arropar ♦ *vi* (*eat*) comer con apetito.
tuck up *vt* (*child*) arropar.
tuck shop *n* (*SCOL*) tienda de golosinas.
Tue(s). *abbr* (= *Tuesday*) mart.
Tuesday ['tju:zdɪ] *n* martes *m inv*; **on** ~ el martes; **on** ~**s** los martes; **every** ~ todos los martes; **every other** ~ cada dos martes; **last/next** ~ el martes pasado/próximo; **a week/fortnight on** ~, ~**week/fortnight** del martes en 8/15 días, del martes en una semana/dos semanas.
tuft [tʌft] *n* mechón *m*; (*of grass etc*) manojo.
tug [tʌg] *n* (*ship*) remolcador *m* ♦ *vt* re-

molcar.

tug-of-war [tʌgəv'wɔː*] *n* lucha de tiro de cuerda.

tuition [tjuː'ɪʃən] *n* (*Brit*) enseñanza; (: *private* ~) clases *fpl* particulares; (*US*: *school fees*) matrícula.

tulip ['tjuːlɪp] *n* tulipán *m*.

tumble ['tʌmbl] *n* (*fall*) caída ♦ *vi* caerse, tropezar; **to ~ to sth** (*col*) caer en la cuenta de algo.

tumbledown ['tʌmbldaun] *a* destartalado.

tumble dryer *n* (*Brit*) secadora.

tumbler ['tʌmblə*] *n* vaso.

tummy ['tʌmɪ] *n* (*col*) barriga, vientre *m*.

tumour, (*US*) **tumor** ['tjuːmə*] *n* tumor *m*.

tumult ['tjuːmʌlt] *n* tumulto.

tumultuous [tjuː'mʌltjuəs] *a* tumultuoso.

tuna ['tjuːnə] *n* (*pl inv*) (*also*: ~ **fish**) atún *m*.

tundra ['tʌndrə] *n* tundra.

tune [tjuːn] *n* (*melody*) melodía ♦ *vt* (*MUS*) afinar; (*RADIO, TV, AUT*) sintonizar; **to be in/out of** ~ (*instrument*) estar afinado/ desafinado; (*singer*) cantar afinadamente/ desafinar; **to be in/out of** ~ **with** (*fig*) armonizar/desentonar con; **to the** ~ **of** (*fig: amount*) por (la) cantidad de.

tune in *vi* (*RADIO, TV*): **to** ~ **in (to)** sintonizar (con).

tune up *vi* (*musician*) afinar (su instrumento).

tuneful ['tjuːnful] *a* melodioso.

tuner ['tjuːnə*] *n* (*radio set*) sintonizador *m*; **piano** ~ afinador(a) *m/f* de pianos.

tungsten ['tʌŋstn] *n* tungsteno.

tunic ['tjuːnɪk] *n* túnica.

tuning ['tjuːnɪŋ] *n* sintonización *f*; (*MUS*) afinación *f*.

tuning fork *n* diapasón *m*.

Tunis ['tjuːnɪs] *n* Túnez *m*.

Tunisia [tjuː'nɪzɪə] *n* Túnez *m*.

Tunisian [tjuː'nɪzɪən] *a, n* tunecino/a *m/f*.

tunnel ['tʌnl] *n* túnel *m*; (*in mine*) galería ♦ *vi* construir un túnel/una galería.

tunny ['tʌnɪ] *n* atún *m*.

turban ['tɜːbən] *n* turbante *m*.

turbine ['tɜːbaɪn] *n* turbina.

turbid ['tɜːbɪd] *a* turbio.

turboprop ['tɜːbəuprɔp] *n* turbohélice *m*.

turbot ['tɜːbət] *n* (*pl inv*) rodaballo.

turbulence ['tɜːbjuləns] *n* (*AVIAT*) turbulencia.

turbulent ['tɜːbjulənt] *a* turbulento.

tureen [tə'riːn] *n* sopera.

turf [tɜːf] *n* césped *m*; (*clod*) tepe *m* ♦ *vt* cubrir con césped.

turf out *vt* (*col*) echar a la calle.

turf accountant *n* corredor(a) *m/f* de apuestas.

turgid ['tɜːdʒɪd] *a* (*prose*) pesado.

Turin [tjuə'rɪn] *n* Turín *m*.

Turk [tɜːk] *n* turco/a.

Turkey ['tɜːkɪ] *n* Turquía.

turkey ['tɜːkɪ] *n* pavo.

Turkish ['tɜːkɪʃ] *a* turco ♦ *n* (*LING*) turco.

Turkish bath *n* baño turco.

turmeric ['tɜːmərɪk] *n* cúrcuma.

turmoil ['tɜːmɔɪl] *n* desorden *m*, alboroto.

turn [tɜːn] *n* turno; (*in road*) curva; (*THEATRE*) número; (*MED*) ataque *m* ♦ *vt* girar, volver; (*collar, steak*) dar la vuelta a; (*shape: wood, metal*) tornear; (*change*): **to** ~ **sth into** convertir algo en ♦ *vi* volver; (*person: look back*) volverse; (*reverse direction*) dar la vuelta; (*milk*) cortarse; (*change*) cambiar; (*become*): **to** ~ **into sth** convertirse *or* transformarse en algo; **a good** ~ un favor; **it gave me quite a** ~ me dio un susto; **"no left** ~**"** (*AUT*) "prohibido girar a la izquierda"; **it's your** ~ te toca a ti; **in** ~ por turnos; **to take** ~**s** turnarse; **at the** ~ **of the year/century** a fin de año/a finales de siglo; **to take a** ~ **for the worse** (*situation, patient*) empeorar; **they** ~**ed him against us** le pusieron en contra nuestra; **the car** ~**ed the corner** el coche dobló la esquina; **to** ~ **left** (*AUT*) torcer *or* girar a la izquierda; **she has no-one to** ~ **to** no tiene a quién recurrir.

turn away *vi* apartar la vista ♦ *vt* (*reject: person, business*) rechazar.

turn back *vi* volverse atrás.

turn down *vt* (*refuse*) rechazar; (*reduce*) bajar; (*fold*) doblar.

turn in *vi* (*col: go to bed*) acostarse ♦ *vt* (*fold*) doblar hacia dentro.

turn off *vi* (*from road*) desviarse ♦ *vt* (*light, radio etc*) apagar; (*engine*) parar.

turn on *vt* (*light, radio etc*) encender, prender (*LAm*); (*engine*) poner en marcha.

turn out *vt* (*light, gas*) apagar; (*produce: goods, novel etc*) producir ♦ *vi* (*attend: troops*) presentarse; (: *doctor*) atender; **to** ~ **out to be ...** resultar ser ... .

turn over *vi* (*person*) volverse ♦ *vt* (*mattress, card*) dar la vuelta a; (*page*) volver.

turn round *vi* volverse; (*rotate*) girar.

turn to *vt fus*: **to** ~ **to sb** acudir a uno.

turn up *vi* (*person*) llegar, presentarse; (*lost object*) aparecer ♦ *vt* (*radio*) subir, poner más alto; (*heat, gas*) poner más fuerte.

turnabout ['tɜːnəbaut], **turnaround** ['tɜːnəraund] *n* (*fig*) giro total.

turncoat ['tɜːnkəut] *n* renegado/a.

turned-up ['tɜːndʌp] *a* (*nose*) respingón/ ona.

turning ['tɜːnɪŋ] *n* (*side road*) bocacalle *f*; (*bend*) curva; **the first** ~ **on the right** la primera bocacalle a la derecha.

turning point *n* (*fig*) momento decisivo.

turnip ['tɜːnɪp] *n* nabo.

turnkey system ['tɜːnkiː-] *n* (*COMPUT*) sistema *m* de seguridad.

turnout ['tɜːnaut] *n* asistencia, número de asistentes, público.

turnover ['tɜːnəuvə*] *n* (*COMM*: *amount of money*) facturación *f*; (: *of goods*) movimiento; **there is a rapid ~ in staff** hay una rápida rotación de personal.

turnpike ['tɜːnpaɪk] *n* (*US*) autopista de peaje.

turnstile ['tɜːnstaɪl] *n* torniquete *m*.

turntable ['tɜːnteɪbl] *n* plato.

turn-up ['tɜːnʌp] *n* (*Brit*: *on trousers*) vuelta.

turpentine ['tɜːpəntaɪn] *n* (*also*: **turps**) trementina.

turquoise ['tɜːkwɔɪz] *n* (*stone*) turquesa ♦ *a* color turquesa.

turret ['tʌrɪt] *n* torreón *m*.

turtle ['tɜːtl] *n* galápago.

turtleneck (sweater) ['tɜːtlnɛk-] *n* (jersey *m* de) cuello cisne.

Tuscany ['tʌskənɪ] *n* Toscana.

tusk [tʌsk] *n* colmillo.

tussle ['tʌsl] *n* lucha, pelea.

tutor ['tjuːtə*] *n* profesor(a) *m/f*.

tutorial [tjuː'tɔːrɪəl] *n* (*SCOL*) seminario.

tuxedo [tʌk'siːdəu] *n* (*US*) smóking *m*, esmoquin *m*.

TV [tiː'viː] *n abbr* (= *television*) tele *f*.

twaddle ['twɔdl] *n* (*col*) tonterías *fpl*.

twang [twæŋ] *n* (*of instrument*) punteado; (*of voice*) timbre *m* nasal.

tweak [twiːk] *vt* (*nose, ear*) pellizcar; (*hair*) tirar.

tweed [twiːd] *n* tweed *m*.

tweezers ['twiːzəz] *npl* pinzas *fpl* (de depilar).

twelfth [twɛlfθ] *num* duodécimo.

Twelfth Night *n* (Día *m* de) Reyes *mpl*.

twelve [twɛlv] *num* doce; **at ~ o'clock** (*midday*) a mediodía; (*midnight*) a medianoche.

twentieth ['twɛntɪɪθ] *num* vigésimo.

twenty ['twɛntɪ] *num* veinte.

twerp [twəːp] *n* (*col*) idiota *m/f*.

twice [twaɪs] *ad* dos veces; **~ as much** dos veces más; **she is ~ your age** ella tiene dos veces tu edad; **~ a week** dos veces a la *or* por semana.

twiddle ['twɪdl] *vt, vi*: **to ~ (with) sth** dar vueltas a algo; **to ~ one's thumbs** (*fig*) estar mano sobre mano.

twig [twɪg] *n* ramita ♦ *vi* (*col*) caer en la cuenta.

twilight ['twaɪlaɪt] *n* crepúsculo; (*morning*) madrugada; **in the ~** en la media luz.

twill [twɪl] *n* sarga, estameña.

twin [twɪn] *a, n* gemelo/a *m/f* ♦ *vt* hermanar.

twin(-bedded) room ['twɪn('bɛdɪd)-] *n* habitación *f* con camas gemelas.

twin beds *npl* camas *fpl* gemelas.

twin-carburettor ['twɪnkɑːbjuː'rɛtə*] *a* de dos carburadores.

twine [twaɪn] *n* bramante *m* ♦ *vi* (*plant*) enroscarse.

twin-engined [twɪn'ɛndʒɪnd] *a* bimotor; **~ aircraft** avión *m* bimotor.

twinge [twɪndʒ] *n* (*of pain*) punzada; (*of conscience*) remordimiento.

twinkle ['twɪŋkl] *n* centelleo ♦ *vi* centellear; (*eyes*) parpadear.

twin town *n* ciudad *f* hermanada *or* gemela.

twirl [twəːl] *n* giro ♦ *vt* dar vueltas a ♦ *vi* piruetear.

twist [twɪst] *n* (*action*) torsión *f*; (*in road, coil*) vuelta; (*in wire, flex*) doblez *f*; (*in story*) giro ♦ *vt* torcer, retorcer; (*roll around*) enrollar; (*fig*) deformar ♦ *vi* serpentear; **to ~ one's ankle/wrist** (*MED*) torcerse el tobillo/la muñeca.

twisted ['twɪstɪd] *a* (*wire, rope*) trenzado, enroscado; (*ankle, wrist*) torcido; (*fig*: *logic, mind*) retorcido.

twit [twɪt] *n* (*col*) tonto.

twitch [twɪtʃ] *n* sacudida; (*nervous*) tic *m* nervioso ♦ *vi* moverse nerviosamente.

two [tuː] *num* dos; **~ by ~, in ~s** de dos en dos; **to put ~ and ~ together** (*fig*) atar cabos.

two-door [tuː'dɔː*] *a* (*AUT*) de dos puertas.

two-faced [tuː'feɪst] *a* (*pej*: *person*) falso.

twofold ['tuːfəuld] *ad*: **to increase ~** duplicarse ♦ *a* (*increase*) doble; (*reply*) en dos partes.

two-piece [tuː'piːs] *n* (*also*: **~ suit**) traje *m* de dos piezas; (*also*: **~ swimsuit**) dos piezas *m inv*, bikini *m*.

two-seater [tuː'siːtə*] *n* (*plane, car*) avión *m*/coche *m* de dos plazas.

two-stroke ['tuːstrəuk] *n* (*also*: **~ engine**) motor *m* de dos tiempos ♦ *a* de dos tiempos.

twosome ['tuːsəm] *n* (*people*) pareja.

two-tone ['tuː'təun] *a* (*colour*) bicolor, de dos tonos.

two-way ['tuːweɪ] *a*: **~ traffic** circulación *f* de dos sentidos; **~ radio** radio *f* emisora y receptora.

TX *abbr* (*US POST*) = *Texas*.

tycoon [taɪ'kuːn] *n*: **(business) ~** magnate *m/f*.

type [taɪp] *n* (*category*) tipo, género; (*model*) modelo; (*TYP*) tipo, letra ♦ *vt* (*letter etc*) escribir a máquina; **what ~ do you want?** ¿qué tipo quieres?; **in bold/italic** en negrita/cursiva.

type-cast ['taɪpkɑːst] *a* (*actor*) encasillado.

typeface ['taɪpfeɪs] *n* tipo de letra.

typescript ['taɪpskrɪpt] *n* texto mecanografiado.

typeset ['taɪpsɛt] *vt* (*irg*: *like* **set**) componer.

typesetter ['taɪpsɛtə*] *n* cajista *m/f*, compositor(a) *m/f*.

typewriter ['taɪpraɪtə*] *n* máquina de escribir.

typewritten ['taɪprɪtn] a mecanografiado.

typhoid ['taɪfɔɪd] n tifoidea.

typhoon [taɪ'fuːn] n tifón m.

typhus ['taɪfəs] n tifus m.

typical ['tɪpɪkl] a típico.

typically ['tɪpɪklɪ] ad típicamente.

typify ['tɪpɪfaɪ] vt tipificar.

typing ['taɪpɪŋ] n mecanografía.

typing pool n (Brit) servicio de mecanógrafos.

typist ['taɪpɪst] n mecanógrafo/a.

typography [tɪ'pɔgrəfɪ] n tipografía.

tyranny ['tɪrənɪ] n tiranía.

tyrant ['taɪərənt] n tirano/a.

tyre, (US) **tire** ['taɪə*] n neumático, llanta (LAm).

tyre pressure n presión f de los neumáticos.

Tyrol [tɪ'rəul] n Tirol m.

Tyrolean [tɪrə'lɪən], **Tyrolese** [tɪrə'liːz] a tirolés/esa.

Tyrrhenian Sea [tɪ'riːnɪən-] n Mar m Tirreno.

tzar [zɑː*] n = **tsar**.

U

U, u [juː] n (letter) U, u f; **U for Uncle** U de Uruguay.

U n abbr (Brit CINEMA: = universal) todos los públicos.

UB40 n abbr (Brit: = unemployment benefit form 40) número de referencia en la solicitud de inscripción en la lista de parados; por extensión, el beneficiario.

U-bend ['juːbend] n (AUT, in pipe) recodo.

ubiquitous [juː'bɪkwɪtəs] a ubicuo.

UCCA ['ʌkə] n abbr Brit: = Universities Central Council on Admissions.

UDA n abbr (Brit: = Ulster Defence Association) organización paramilitar protestante en Irlanda del Norte.

UDC n abbr (Brit) = Urban District Council.

udder ['ʌdə*] n ubre f.

UDI n abbr (Brit POL) = unilateral declaration of independence.

UDR n abbr (Brit: = Ulster Defence Regiment) fuerza de seguridad de Irlanda del Norte.

UEFA [juː'eɪfə] n abbr (= Union of European Football Associations) U.E.F.A. f.

UFO ['juːfəu] n abbr (= unidentified flying object) OVNI m.

Uganda [juː'gændə] n Uganda.

Ugandan [juː'gændən] a de Uganda.

UGC n abbr (Brit: = University Grants Committee) entidad gubernamental que controla las finanzas de las universidades.

ugh [əːh] excl ¡uf!

ugliness ['ʌglɪnɪs] n fealdad f.

ugly ['ʌglɪ] a feo; (dangerous) peligroso.

UHF abbr (= ultra-high frequency) UHF m.

UHT a abbr (= ultra heat treated): ~ **milk** leche f uperizada.

UK n abbr (= United Kingdom) R.U.

ulcer ['ʌlsə*] n úlcera; **mouth** ~ úlcera oral.

Ulster ['ʌlstə*] n Úlster m.

ulterior [ʌl'tɪərɪə*] a ulterior; ~ **motive** segundas intenciones fpl.

ultimate ['ʌltɪmət] a último, final; (greatest) mayor ◆ n: **the** ~ **in luxury** el colmo del lujo.

ultimately ['ʌltɪmətlɪ] ad (in the end) por último, al final; (fundamentally) a or en fin de cuentas.

ultimatum, pl ~**s** or **ultimata** [ʌltɪ'meɪtəm, -tə] n ultimátum m.

ultra- ['ʌltrə] pref ultra-.

ultrasonic [ʌltrə'sɔnɪk] a ultrasónico.

ultrasound [ʌltrə'saund] n (MED) ultrasonido.

ultraviolet ['ʌltrə'vaɪəlɪt] a ultravioleta.

umbilical cord [ʌmbɪ'laɪkl-] n cordón m umbilical.

umbrage ['ʌmbrɪdʒ] n: **to take** ~ **(at)** ofenderse por.

umbrella [ʌm'brelə] n paraguas m inv; **under the** ~ **of** (fig) bajo la protección de.

umpire ['ʌmpaɪə*] n árbitro ◆ vt arbitrar.

umpteen [ʌmp'tiːn] num enésimos/as; **for the** ~**th time** por enésima vez.

UMW n abbr (= United Mineworkers of America) sindicato de mineros.

UN n abbr (= United Nations) N.U. fpl, NN.UU. fpl.

un- [ʌn] pref in-; des-; no ...; poco ...; nada ...

unabashed [ʌnə'bæʃt] a nada avergonzado.

unabated [ʌnə'beɪtɪd] a: **to continue** ~ seguir sin disminuir.

unable [ʌn'eɪbl] a: **to be** ~ **to do sth** no poder hacer algo; (not know how to) ser incapaz de hacer algo, no saber hacer algo.

unabridged [ʌnə'brɪdʒd] a íntegro.

unacceptable [ʌnək'septəbl] a (proposal, behaviour, price) inaceptable; **it's** ~ **that** no se puede aceptar que.

unaccompanied [ʌnə'kʌmpənɪd] a no acompañado; (singing, song) sin acompañamiento.

unaccountably [ʌnə'kauntəblɪ] ad inexplicablemente.

unaccounted [ʌnə'kauntɪd] a: **two passengers are** ~ **for** faltan dos pasajeros.

unaccustomed [ʌnə'kʌstəmd] a: **to be** ~ **to** no estar acostumbrado a.

unacquainted [ʌnə'kweɪntɪd] *a*: **to be ~ with** (*facts*) desconocer, ignorar.

unadulterated [ʌnə'dʌltəreɪtɪd] *a* (*gen*) puro; (*wine*) sin mezcla.

unaffected [ʌnə'fɛktɪd] *a* (*person, behaviour*) sin afectación, sencillo; (*emotionally*): **to be ~ by** no estar afectado por.

unafraid [ʌnə'freɪd] *a*: **to be ~** no tener miedo.

unaided [ʌn'eɪdɪd] *a* sin ayuda, por sí solo.

unanimity [ju:nə'nɪmɪtɪ] *n* unanimidad *f*.

unanimous [ju:'nænɪməs] *a* unánime.

unanimously [ju:'nænɪməslɪ] *ad* unánimemente.

unanswered [ʌn'ɑ:nsəd] *a* (*question, letter*) sin contestar; (*criticism*) incontestado.

unappetizing [ʌn'æpɪtaɪzɪŋ] *a* poco apetitoso.

unappreciative [ʌnə'pri:ʃɪətɪv] *a* desagradecido.

unarmed [ʌn'ɑ:md] *a* (*person*) desarmado; (*combat*) sin armas.

unashamed [ʌnə'ʃeɪmd] *a* desvergonzado.

unassisted [ʌnə'sɪstɪd] *a, ad* sin ayuda.

unassuming [ʌnə'sju:mɪŋ] *a* modesto, sin pretensiones.

unattached [ʌnə'tætʃt] *a* (*person*) soltero; (*part etc*) suelto.

unattended [ʌnə'tɛndɪd] *a* (*car, luggage*) sin atender.

unattractive [ʌnə'træktɪv] *a* poco atractivo.

unauthorized [ʌn'ɔ:θəraɪzd] *a* no autorizado.

unavailable [ʌnə'veɪləbl] *a* (*article, room, book*) indisponible; (*person*) ocupado.

unavoidable [ʌnə'vɔɪdəbl] *a* inevitable.

unavoidably [ʌnə'vɔɪdəblɪ] *ad* (*detained*) por causas ajenas a su voluntad.

unaware [ʌnə'weə*] *a*: **to be ~ of** ignorar.

unawares [ʌnə'weəz] *ad* de improviso.

unbalanced [ʌn'bælənst] *a* desequilibrado; (*mentally*) trastornado.

unbearable [ʌn'bɛərəbl] *a* insoportable.

unbeatable [ʌn'bi:təbl] *a* (*gen*) invencible; (*price*) inmejorable.

unbeaten [ʌn'bi:tn] *a* imbatido; (*team, army*) invicto; (*record*) no batido.

unbecoming [ʌnbɪ'kʌmɪŋ] *a* (*unseemly: language, behaviour*) indecoroso, impropio; (*unflattering: garment*) poco favorecedor(a).

unbeknown(st) [ʌnbɪ'nəun(st)] *ad*: **~ to me** sin saberlo yo.

unbelief [ʌnbɪ'li:f] *n* incredulidad *f*.

unbelievable [ʌnbɪ'li:vəbl] *a* increíble.

unbelievingly [ʌnbɪ'li:vɪŋlɪ] *ad* sin creer.

unbend [ʌn'bɛnd] (*irg: like bend*) *vi* (*fig: person*) relajarse ♦ *vt* (*wire*) enderezar.

unbending [ʌn'bɛndɪŋ] *a* (*fig*) inflexible.

unbias(s)ed [ʌn'baɪəst] *a* imparcial.

unblemished [ʌn'blɛmɪʃt] *a* sin mancha.

unblock [ʌn'blɔk] *vt* (*pipe*) desatascar; (*road*) despejar.

unborn [ʌn'bɔ:n] *a* que va a nacer.

unbounded [ʌn'baundɪd] *a* ilimitado, sin límite.

unbreakable [ʌn'breɪkəbl] *a* irrompible.

unbridled [ʌn'braɪdld] *a* (*fig*) desenfrenado.

unbroken [ʌn'brəukən] *a* (*seal*) intacto; (*series*) continuo; (*record*) no batido; (*spirit*) indómito.

unbuckle [ʌn'bʌkl] *vt* desabrochar.

unburden [ʌn'bə:dn] *vr*: **to ~ o.s.** desahogarse.

unbusinesslike [ʌn'bɪznɪslaɪk] *a* (*trader*) poco metódico; (*transaction*) incorrecto; (*fig: person*) poco práctico.

unbutton [ʌn'bʌtn] *vt* desabrochar.

uncalled-for [ʌn'kɔ:ldfɔ:*] *a* gratuito, inmerecido.

uncanny [ʌn'kænɪ] *a* extraño, extraordinario.

unceasing [ʌn'si:sɪŋ] *a* incesante.

unceremonious ['ʌnsɛrɪ'məunɪəs] *a* (*abrupt, rude*) brusco, hosco.

uncertain [ʌn'sə:tn] *a* incierto; (*indecisive*) indeciso; **it's ~ whether** no se sabe si; **in no ~ terms** sin dejar lugar a dudas.

uncertainty [ʌn'sə:tntɪ] *n* incertidumbre *f*.

unchallenged [ʌn'tʃælɪndʒd] *a* (*LAW etc*) incontestado; **to go ~** no encontrar respuesta.

unchanged [ʌn'tʃeɪndʒd] *a* sin cambiar *or* alterar.

uncharitable [ʌn'tʃærɪtəbl] *a* (*remark, behaviour*) demasiado duro.

uncharted [ʌn'tʃɑ:tɪd] *a* inexplorado.

unchecked [ʌn'tʃɛkt] *a* desenfrenado.

uncivil [ʌn'sɪvɪl] *a* grosero.

uncivilized [ʌn'sɪvɪlaɪzd] *a* (*gen*) inculto, poco civilizado; (*fig: behaviour etc*) bárbaro.

uncle ['ʌŋkl] *n* tío.

unclear [ʌn'klɪə*] *a* poco claro; **I'm still ~ about what I'm supposed to do** todavía no estoy muy seguro de lo que tengo que hacer.

uncoil [ʌn'kɔɪl] *vt* desenrollar ♦ *vi* desenrollarse.

uncomfortable [ʌn'kʌmfətəbl] *a* incómodo; (*uneasy*) inquieto.

uncomfortably [ʌn'kʌmfətəblɪ] *ad* (*uneasily: say*) con inquietud; (: *think*) con remordimiento *or* nerviosismo.

uncommitted [ʌnkə'mɪtɪd] *a* (*attitude, country*) no comprometido; **to remain ~ to** (*policy, party*) no comprometerse a.

uncommon [ʌn'kɔmən] *a* poco común, raro.

uncommunicative [ʌnkə'mju:nɪkətɪv] *a* poco comunicativo, reservado.

uncomplicated [ʌn'kɔmplɪkeɪtɪd] *a* sin complicaciones.

uncompromising [ʌn'kɔmprəmaɪzɪŋ] *a* intransigente.

unconcerned [ʌnkən'sɜːnd] *a* indiferente, despreocupado; **to be ~ about** ser indiferente a, no preocuparse de.

unconditional [ʌnkən'dɪʃənl] *a* incondicional.

uncongenial [ʌnkən'dʒiːnɪəl] *a* desagradable.

unconnected [ʌnkə'nɛktɪd] *a* (*unrelated*): **to be ~ with** no estar relacionado con.

unconscious [ʌn'kɒnʃəs] *a* sin sentido; (*unaware*) inconsciente ◆ *n*: **the ~** el inconsciente; **to knock sb ~** dejar a uno sin sentido.

unconsciously [ʌn'kɒnʃəslɪ] *ad* inconscientemente.

unconsciousness [ʌn'kɒnʃəsnɪs] *n* inconsciencia.

unconstitutional [ʌnkɒnstɪ'tjuːʃənl] *a* anti-constitucional.

uncontested [ʌnkən'tɛstɪd] *a* (*champion*) incontestado; (*PARLIAMENT: seat*) ganado sin oposición.

uncontrollable [ʌnkən'trəuləbl] *a* (*temper*) indomable; (*laughter*) incontenible.

uncontrolled [ʌnkən'trəuld] (*child, dog, emotion*) incontrolado; (*inflation, price rises*) desenfrenado.

unconventional [ʌnkən'vɛnʃənl] *a* poco convencional.

unconvinced [ʌnkən'vɪnst] *a*: **to be** *or* **remain ~** seguir sin convencerse.

unconvincing [ʌnkən'vɪnsɪŋ] *a* poco convincente.

uncork [ʌn'kɔːk] *vt* descorchar, destapar.

uncorroborated [ʌnkə'rɒbəreɪtɪd] *a* no confirmado.

uncouth [ʌn'kuːθ] *a* grosero, inculto.

uncover [ʌn'kʌvə*] *vt* (*gen*) descubrir; (*take lid off*) destapar.

undamaged [ʌn'dæmɪdʒd] *a* (*goods*) en buen estado; (*fig: reputation*) intacto, indemne.

undaunted [ʌn'dɔːntɪd] *a*: **~ by** nada desanimado por.

undecided [ʌndɪ'saɪdɪd] *a* (*character*) indeciso; (*question*) no resuelto, pendiente.

undelivered [ʌndɪ'lɪvəd] *a* no entregado al destinatario; **if ~ return to sender** en caso de no llegar a su destino devolver al remitente.

undeniable [ʌndɪ'naɪəbl] *a* innegable.

undeniably [ʌndɪ'naɪəblɪ] *ad* innegablemente.

under ['ʌndə*] *prep* debajo de; (*less than*) menos de; (*according to*) según, de acuerdo con ◆ *ad* debajo, abajo; **~ there** allí abajo; **~ construction** en construcción; en obras; **~ the circumstances** dadas las circunstancias; **in ~ 2 hours** en menos de dos horas; **~ anaesthetic** bajo los efectos de la anestesia; **~ discussion** en discusión, sobre el tapete.

under... [ʌndə*] *pref* sub....

under-age [ʌndər'eɪdʒ] *a* menor de edad.

underarm ['ʌndərɑːm] *n* axila, sobaco ◆ *cpd*: **~ deodorant** desodorante *m* corporal.

undercapitalised [ʌndə'kæpɪtəlaɪzd] *a* descapitalizado.

undercarriage ['ʌndəkærɪdʒ] *n* (*Brit AVIAT*) tren *m* de aterrizaje.

undercharge [ʌndə'tʃɑːdʒ] *vt* cobrar de menos.

underclothes ['ʌndəkləuðz] *npl* ropa *sg* interior *or* íntima (*LAm*).

undercoat ['ʌndəkəut] *n* (*paint*) primera mano.

undercover [ʌndə'kʌvə*] *a* clandestino.

undercurrent ['ʌndəkʌrnt] *n* corriente *f* submarina; (*fig*) tendencia oculta.

undercut ['ʌndəkʌt] *vt* (*irg: like* cut) vender más barato que; fijar un precio más barato que.

underdeveloped [ʌndədɪ'vɛləpt] *a* subdesarrollado.

underdog ['ʌndədɒg] *n* desvalido/a.

underdone [ʌndə'dʌn] *a* (*CULIN*) poco hecho.

underemployment [ʌndərɪm'plɔɪmənt] *n* subempleo.

underestimate [ʌndər'ɛstɪmeɪt] *vt* subestimar.

underexposed [ʌndərɪks'pəuzd] *a* (*PHOT*) subexpuesto.

underfed [ʌndə'fɛd] *a* subalimentado.

underfoot [ʌndə'fut] *ad*: **it's wet ~** el suelo está mojado.

undergo [ʌndə'gəu] *vt* (*irg: like* go) sufrir; (*treatment*) recibir; **the car is ~ing repairs** están reparando el coche.

undergraduate ['ʌndə'grædjuət] *n* estudiante *m/f* ◆ *cpd*: **~ courses** cursos *mpl* de licenciatura.

underground ['ʌndəgraund] *n* (*Brit: railway*) metro; (*POL*) movimiento clandestino ◆ *a* subterráneo.

undergrowth ['ʌndəgrəuθ] *n* maleza.

underhand(ed) [ʌndə'hænd(ɪd)] *a* (*fig*) socarrón.

underinsured [ʌndərɪn'ʃuəd] *a* insuficientemente asegurado.

underlie [ʌndəlaɪ] *vt* (*irg: like* lie) (*fig*) ser la razón fundamental de; **the underlying cause** la causa fundamental.

underline [ʌndə'laɪn] *vt* subrayar.

underling ['ʌndəlɪŋ] *n* (*pej*) subalterno/a.

undermanning [ʌndə'mænɪŋ] *n* falta de personal.

undermentioned [ʌndə'mɛnʃənd] *a* abajo citado.

undermine [ʌndə'maɪn] *vt* socavar, minar.

underneath [ʌndə'niːθ] *ad* debajo ◆ *prep* debajo de, bajo.

undernourished [ʌndə'nʌrɪʃt] *a* desnutrido.

underpaid [ʌndə'peɪd] *a* mal pagado.

underpants ['ʌndəpænts] *npl* calzoncillos

mpl.

underpass ['ʌndəpɑːs] *n* (*Brit*) paso subterráneo.

underpin [ʌndə'pɪn] *vt* (*argument, case*) secundar, sostener.

underplay [ʌndə'pleɪ] *vt* (*Brit*) minimizar.

underpopulated [ʌndə'pɔpjuleɪtɪd] *a* despoblado.

underprice [ʌndə'praɪs] *vt* vender demasiado barato.

underpriced [ʌndə'praɪst] *a* con precio demasiado bajo.

underprivileged [ʌndə'prɪvɪlɪdʒd] *a* desvalido.

underrate [ʌndə'reɪt] *vt* menospreciar, subestimar.

underscore ['ʌndəskɔː*] *vt* subrayar, sostener.

underseal [ʌndə'siːl] *vt* (*AUT*) proteger contra la corrosión.

undersecretary [ʌndə'sɛkrətrɪ] *n* subsecretario/a.

undersell [ʌndə'sɛl] *vt* (*competitors*) vender más barato que.

undershirt ['ʌndəʃəːt] *n* (*US*) camiseta.

undershorts ['ʌndəʃɔːts] *npl* (*US*) calzoncillos *mpl.*

underside ['ʌndəsaɪd] *n* parte *f* inferior, revés *m.*

undersigned ['ʌndəsaɪnd] *a, n*: **the** ~ el/la *etc* abajo firmante.

underskirt ['ʌndəskəːt] *n* (*Brit*) enaguas *fpl.*

understaffed [ʌndə'stɑːft] *a* falto de personal.

understand [ʌndə'stænd] (*irg: like* **stand**) *vt, vi* entender, comprender; (*assume*) tener entendido; **to make o.s. understood** hacerse entender; **I ~ you have been absent** tengo entendido que (usted) ha estado ausente.

understandable [ʌndə'stændəbl] *a* comprensible.

understanding [ʌndə'stændɪŋ] *a* comprensivo ◆ *n* comprensión *f*, entendimiento; (*agreement*) acuerdo; **to come to an ~ with sb** llegar a un acuerdo con uno; **on the ~ that** a condición de que (+ *subjun*).

understate [ʌndə'steɪt] *vt* minimizar.

understatement [ʌndə'steɪtmənt] *n* subestimación *f*; (*modesty*) modestia (excesiva).

understood [ʌndə'stud] *pt, pp of* **understand** ◆ *a* entendido; (*implied*): **it is ~ that** se sobreentiende que.

understudy ['ʌndəstʌdɪ] *n* suplente *m/f.*

undertake [ʌndə'teɪk] (*irg: like* **take**) *vt* emprender; **to ~ to do sth** comprometerse a hacer algo.

undertaker ['ʌndəteɪkə*] *n* director(a) *m/f* de pompas fúnebres.

undertaking ['ʌndəteɪkɪŋ] *n* empresa; (*promise*) promesa.

undertone ['ʌndətəun] *n* (*of criticism*) connotación *f*; (*low voice*): **in an ~** en voz baja.

undervalue [ʌndə'væljuː] (*fig*) subestimar, menospreciar; (*COMM etc*) valorizar por debajo de su precio.

underwater [ʌndə'wɔːtə*] *ad* bajo el agua ◆ *a* submarino.

underwear ['ʌndəwɛə*] *n* ropa interior *or* íntima (*LAm*).

underweight [ʌndə'weɪt] *a* de peso insuficiente; (*person*) demasiado delgado.

underworld ['ʌndəwɔːld] *n* (*of crime*) hampa, inframundo.

underwrite [ʌndə'raɪt] (*irg: like* **write**) *vt* (*COMM*) suscribir; (*INSURANCE*) asegurar (*contra riesgos*).

underwriter ['ʌndəraɪtə*] *n* (*INSURANCE*) asegurador/a *m/f.*

undeserving [ʌndɪ'zəːvɪŋ] *a*: **to be ~ of** no ser digno de.

undesirable [ʌndɪ'zaɪərəbl] *a* indeseable.

undeveloped [ʌndədɪ'vɛləpt] *a* (*land, resources*) sin explotar.

undies ['ʌndɪz] *npl* (*col*) ropa *sg* interior *or* íntima (*LAm*).

undiluted [ʌndaɪ'luːtɪd] *a* (*concentrate*) concentrado.

undiplomatic [ʌndɪplə'mætɪk] *a* poco diplomático.

undischarged [ʌndɪs'tʃɑːdʒd] *a*: ~ **bankrupt** quebrado/a no rehabilitado/a.

undisciplined [ʌn'dɪsɪplɪnd] *a* indisciplinado.

undiscovered [ʌndɪs'kʌvəd] *a* no descubierto; (*unknown*) desconocido.

undisguised [ʌndɪs'gaɪzd] *a* (*dislike*) no disfrazado; (*amusement etc*) franco, abierto.

undisputed [ʌndɪ'spjuːtɪd] *a* incontestable.

undistinguished [ʌndɪs'tɪŋgwɪʃt] *a* mediocre.

undisturbed [ʌndɪs'təːbd] *a* (*sleep*) ininterrumpido; **to leave sth ~** dejar algo tranquilo.

undivided [ʌndɪ'vaɪdɪd] *a*: **I want your ~ attention** quiero su completa atención.

undo [ʌn'duː] *vt* (*irg: like* **do**) deshacer.

undoing [ʌn'duːɪŋ] *n* ruina, perdición *f.*

undone [ʌn'dʌn] *pp of* **undo** ◆ *a*: **to come ~** (*clothes*) desabrocharse; (*parcel*) desatarse.

undoubted [ʌn'dautɪd] *a* indudable.

undoubtedly [ʌn'dautɪdlɪ] *ad* indudablemente, sin duda.

undress [ʌn'drɛs] *vi* desnudarse.

undrinkable [ʌn'drɪŋkəbl] *a* (*unpalatable*) que no se puede beber; (*poisonous*) no potable.

undue [ʌn'djuː] *a* indebido, excesivo.

undulating ['ʌndjuleɪtɪŋ] *a* ondulante.

unduly [ʌn'djuːlɪ] *ad* excesivamente, demasiado.

undying [ʌn'daɪɪŋ] a eterno.

unearned [ʌn'ɜːnd] a (praise, respect) inmerecido; ~ **income** ingresos mpl no ganados, renta no ganada or salarial.

unearth [ʌn'ɜːθ] vt desenterrar.

unearthly [ʌn'ɜːθlɪ] a: ~ **hour** (col) hora inverosímil or intempestiva.

unease [ʌn'iːz] n malestar m.

uneasy [ʌn'iːzɪ] a intranquilo; (worried) preocupado; **to feel** ~ **about doing sth** sentirse incómodo con la idea de hacer algo.

uneconomic(al) ['ʌniːkə'nɔmɪk(l)] a no económico.

uneducated [ʌn'ɛdjukeɪtɪd] a ignorante, inculto.

unemployed [ʌnɪm'plɔɪd] a parado, sin trabajo ♦ n: **the** ~ los parados.

unemployment [ʌnɪm'plɔɪmənt] n paro, desempleo.

unemployment benefit n (Brit) subsidio de paro.

unending [ʌn'ɛndɪŋ] a interminable.

unenviable [ʌn'ɛnvɪəbl] a poco envidiable.

unequal [ʌn'iːkwəl] a (length, objects etc) desigual; (amounts) distinto; (division of labour) poco justo.

unequalled, (US) **unequaled** [ʌn'iːkwəld] a inigualado, sin par.

unequivocal [ʌnɪ'kwɪvəkəl] a (answer) inequívoco, claro; (person) claro.

unerring [ʌn'ɜːrɪŋ] a infalible.

UNESCO [juː'nɛskəu] n abbr (= United Nations Educational, Scientific and Cultural Organization) UNESCO f.

unethical [ʌn'ɛθɪkəl] a (methods) inmoral; (doctor's behaviour) que infringe la ética profesional.

uneven [ʌn'iːvn] a desigual; (road etc) quebrado.

uneventful [ʌnɪ'vɛntful] a sin novedad.

unexceptional [ʌnɪk'sɛpʃənl] a sin nada de extraordinario, corriente.

unexciting [ʌnɪk'saɪtɪŋ] a (news) sin interés; (film, evening) aburrido.

unexpected [ʌnɪk'spɛktɪd] a inesperado.

unexpectedly [ʌnɪk'spɛktɪdlɪ] ad inesperadamente.

unexplained [ʌnɪks'pleɪnd] a inexplicado.

unexploded [ʌnɪks'pləudɪd] a sin explotar.

unfailing [ʌn'feɪlɪŋ] a (support) indefectible; (energy) inagotable.

unfair [ʌn'fɛə*] a: ~ **(to sb)** injusto (con uno); **it's** ~ **that** ... es injusto que ..., no es justo que ....

unfair dismissal n despido improcedente.

unfairly [ʌn'fɛəlɪ] ad injustamente.

unfaithful [ʌn'feɪθful] a infiel.

unfamiliar [ʌnfə'mɪlɪə*] a extraño, desconocido; **to be** ~ **with sth** desconocer or ignorar algo.

unfashionable [ʌn'fæʃnəbl] a (clothes) pasado or fuera de moda; (district) poco elegante.

unfasten [ʌn'fɑːsn] vt desatar.

unfathomable [ʌn'fæðəməbl] a insondable.

unfavourable, (US) **unfavorable** [ʌn'feɪvərəbl] a desfavorable.

unfavo(u)rably [ʌn'feɪvrəblɪ] ad: **to look** ~ **upon** ver desfavorablemente.

unfeeling [ʌn'fiːlɪŋ] a insensible.

unfinished [ʌn'fɪnɪʃt] a inacabado, sin terminar.

unfit [ʌn'fɪt] a (ill) indispuesto, enfermo; (incompetent) incapaz; ~ **for work** no apto para trabajar.

unflagging [ʌn'flægɪŋ] a incansable.

unflappable [ʌn'flæpəbl] a imperturbable.

unflattering [ʌn'flætərɪŋ] a (dress, hairstyle) poco halagüeño.

unflinching [ʌn'flɪntʃɪŋ] a impávido, resuelto.

unfold [ʌn'fəuld] vt desdoblar; (fig) revelar ♦ vi abrirse; revelarse.

unforeseeable [ʌnfɔː'siːəbl] a imprevisible.

unforeseen ['ʌnfɔː'siːn] a imprevisto.

unforgettable [ʌnfə'gɛtəbl] a inolvidable.

unforgivable [ʌnfə'gɪvəbl] a imperdonable.

unformatted [ʌn'fɔːmætɪd] a (disk, text) sin formato.

unfortunate [ʌn'fɔːtʃnət] a desgraciado; (event, remark) inoportuno.

unfortunately [ʌn'fɔːtʃnətlɪ] ad desgraciadamente, por desgracia.

unfounded [ʌn'faundɪd] a infundado.

unfriendly [ʌn'frɛndlɪ] a antipático.

unfulfilled [ʌnful'fɪld] a (ambition) sin realizar; (prophecy, promise, terms of contract) incumplido; (desire, person) insatisfecho.

unfurl [ʌn'fɜːl] vt desplegar.

unfurnished [ʌn'fɜːnɪʃt] a desamueblado.

ungainly [ʌn'geɪnlɪ] a (walk) desgarbado.

ungodly [ʌn'gɔdlɪ] a: **at an** ~ **hour** a una hora inverosímil.

ungrateful [ʌn'greɪtful] a ingrato.

unguarded [ʌn'gɑːdɪd] a (moment) de descuido.

unhappily [ʌn'hæpɪlɪ] ad (unfortunately) desgraciadamente.

unhappiness [ʌn'hæpɪnɪs] n tristeza.

unhappy [ʌn'hæpɪ] a (sad) triste; (unfortunate) desgraciado; (childhood) infeliz; ~ **with** (arrangements etc) poco contento con, descontento de.

unharmed [ʌn'hɑːmd] a (person) ileso.

unhealthy [ʌn'hɛlθɪ] a (gen) malsano; (person) enfermizo; (interest) morboso.

unheard-of [ʌn'hɜːdɔv] a inaudito, sin precedente.

unhelpful [ʌn'hɛlpful] a (person) poco servicial; (advice) inútil.

unhesitating [ʌn'hɛzɪteɪtɪŋ] a (loyalty) automático; (reply, offer) resuelto, inmediato.

unhook [ʌn'huk] vt desenganchar; (from wall) descolgar; (undo) desabrochar.

unhurt [ʌn'hɜːt] a ileso.

unhygienic [ʌnhaɪ'dʒiːnɪk] a antihigiénico.

UNICEF ['juːnɪsef] n abbr (= United Nations International Children's Emergency Fund) UNICEF m.

unidentified [ʌnaɪ'dentɪfaɪd] a no identificado; ~ **flying object (UFO)** objeto volante no identificado.

unification [juːnɪfɪ'keɪʃən] n unificación f.

uniform ['juːnɪfɔːm] n uniforme m ♦ a uniforme.

uniformity [juːnɪ'fɔːmɪtɪ] n uniformidad f.

unify ['juːnɪfaɪ] vt unificar, unir.

unilateral [juːnɪ'lætərəl] a unilateral.

unimaginable [ʌnɪ'mædʒɪnəbl] a inconcebible, inimaginable.

unimaginative [ʌnɪ'mædʒɪnətɪv] a falto de imaginación.

unimpaired [ʌnɪm'peəd] a (unharmed) intacto; (not lessened) no disminuido; (unaltered) inalterado.

unimportant [ʌnɪm'pɔːtənt] a sin importancia.

unimpressed [ʌnɪm'prest] a poco impresionado.

uninhabited [ʌnɪn'hæbɪtɪd] a desierto; (country) despoblado; (house) deshabitado, desocupado.

uninhibited [ʌnɪn'hɪbɪtɪd] a nada cohibido, desinhibido.

uninjured [ʌn'ɪndʒəd] a (person) ileso.

unintelligent [ʌnɪn'telɪdʒənt] a poco inteligente.

unintentional [ʌnɪn'tenʃənəl] a involuntario.

unintentionally [ʌnɪn'tenʃnəlɪ] ad sin querer.

uninvited [ʌnɪn'vaɪtɪd] a (guest) sin invitación.

uninviting [ʌnɪn'vaɪtɪŋ] a (place, offer) poco atractivo; (food) poco apetitoso.

union ['juːnjən] n unión f; (also: **trade** ~) sindicato ♦ cpd sindical; **the U**~ (US) la Unión.

union card n carnet m de sindicato.

unionize ['juːnjənaɪz] vt sindicalizar.

Union Jack n bandera del Reino Unido.

Union of Soviet Socialist Republics (USSR) n Unión f de Repúblicas Socialistas Soviéticas.

union shop n (US) taller de afiliación sindical obligatoria.

unique [juː'niːk] a único.

unisex ['juːnɪseks] a unisex.

unison ['juːnɪsn] n: **in** ~ en armonía.

unissued capital [ʌn'ɪʃuːd-] n capital m no emitido.

unit ['juːnɪt] n unidad f; (team, squad) grupo; **kitchen** ~ módulo de cocina; **production** ~ taller m de fabricación; **sink** ~ fregadero.

unit cost n costo unitario.

unite [juː'naɪt] vt unir ♦ vi unirse.

united [juː'naɪtɪd] a unido.

United Arab Emirates npl Emiratos mpl Árabes Unidos.

United Kingdom (UK) n Reino Unido.

United Nations (Organization) (UN, UNO) n Naciones Unidas fpl (ONU f).

United States (of America) (US, USA) n Estados Unidos mpl (de América) (EE.UU. mpl).

unit price n precio unitario.

unit trust n (Brit) bono fiduciario.

unity ['juːnɪtɪ] n unidad f.

Univ. abbr = **university**.

universal [juːnɪ'vɜːsl] a universal.

universally [juːnɪ'vɜːsəlɪ] ad universalmente.

universe ['juːnɪvɜːs] n universo.

university [juːnɪ'vɜːsɪtɪ] n universidad f ♦ cpd (student, professor, education, degree) universitario; (year) académico, universitario; **to be at/go to** ~ estudiar en/ir a la universidad.

unjust [ʌn'dʒʌst] a injusto.

unjustifiable [ʌndʒʌstɪ'faɪəbl] a injustificable.

unjustified [ʌn'dʒʌstɪfaɪd] a (text) no alineado or justificado.

unkempt [ʌn'kempt] a descuidado; (hair) despeinado.

unkind [ʌn'kaɪnd] a poco amable; (comment etc) cruel.

unkindly [ʌn'kaɪndlɪ] ad (speak) severamente; (treat) cruelmente, mal.

unknown [ʌn'nəun] a desconocido ♦ ad: ~ **to me** sin saberlo yo; ~ **quantity** (MATH, fig) incógnita.

unladen [ʌn'leɪdən] a (weight) vacío, sin cargamento.

unlawful [ʌn'lɔːful] a ilegal, ilícito.

unleash [ʌn'liːʃ] vt desatar.

unleavened [ʌn'levənd] a ácimo, sin levadura.

unless [ʌn'les] conj a menos que; ~ **he comes** a menos que venga; ~ **otherwise stated** salvo indicación contraria; ~ **I am mistaken** si no mi equivoco.

unlicensed [ʌn'laɪsənst] a (Brit: to sell alcohol) no autorizado.

unlike [ʌn'laɪk] a distinto ♦ prep a diferencia de.

unlikelihood [ʌn'laɪklɪhud] n improbabilidad f.

unlikely [ʌn'laɪklɪ] a improbable.

unlimited [ʌn'lɪmɪtɪd] a ilimitado; ~ **liability** responsabilidad f ilimitada.

unlisted [ʌn'lɪstɪd] a (US TEL) que no consta en la guía; ~ **company** empresa sin cotización en bolsa.

unlit [ʌn'lɪt] a (room) oscuro, sin luz.

unload [ʌn'ləud] vt descargar.

unlock [ʌn'lɔk] vt abrir (con llave).

unlucky [ʌn'lʌkɪ] a desgraciado; (object, number) que da mala suerte; **to be** ~

(person) tener mala suerte.
unmanageable [ʌn'mænɪdzəbl] *a* *(unwieldy: tool, vehicle)* difícil de manejar; *(: situation)* incontrolable.
unmanned [ʌn'mænd] *a* *(spacecraft)* sin tripulación.
unmannerly [ʌn'mænəlɪ] *a* mal educado, descortés.
unmarked [ʌn'mɑːkt] *a* *(unstained)* sin mancha; ~ **police car** vehículo policial camuflado.
unmarried [ʌn'mærɪd] *a* soltero.
unmask [ʌn'mɑːsk] *vt* desenmascarar.
unmatched [ʌn'mætʃt] *a* incomparable.
unmentionable [ʌn'menʃnəbl] *a* *(topic, vice)* indecible; *(word)* que no se debe decir.
unmerciful [ʌn'mɜːsɪful] *a* despiadado.
unmistakable [ʌnmɪs'teɪkəbl] *a* inconfundible.
unmistakably [ʌnmɪs'teɪkəblɪ] *ad* de modo inconfundible.
unmitigated [ʌn'mɪtɪgeɪtɪd] *a* rematado, absoluto.
unnamed [ʌn'neɪmd] *a* *(nameless)* sin nombre; *(anonymous)* anónimo.
unnatural [ʌn'nætʃrəl] *a* *(gen)* antinatural; *(manner)* afectado; *(habit)* perverso.
unnecessary [ʌn'nɛsəsərɪ] *a* innecesario, inútil.
unnerve [ʌn'nɜːv] *vt* *(subj: accident)* poner nervioso; *(: hostile attitude)* acobardar; *(: long wait, interview)* intimidar.
unnoticed [ʌn'nəʊtɪst] *a*: **to go** *or* **pass** ~ pasar desapercibido.
UNO ['juːnəu] *n abbr* = *(United Nations Organization)* ONU *f*.
unobservant [ʌnəb'zɜːvnt] *a*: **to be** ~ ser poco observador, ser distraído.
unobtainable [ʌnəb'teɪnəbl] *a* inconseguible; *(TEL)* inexistente.
unobtrusive [ʌnəb'truːsɪv] *a* discreto.
unoccupied [ʌn'ɔkjupaɪd] *a* *(house etc)* libre, desocupado.
unofficial [ʌnə'fɪʃl] *a* no oficial; ~ **strike** huelga no oficial.
unopened [ʌn'əupənd] *a* *(letter, present)* sin abrir.
unopposed [ʌnə'pəuzd] *a* *(enter, be elected)* sin oposición.
unorthodox [ʌn'ɔːθədɔks] *a* poco ortodoxo.
unpack [ʌn'pæk] *vi* deshacer las maletas, desempacar *(LAm)*.
unpaid [ʌn'peɪd] *a* *(bill, debt)* sin pagar, impagado; *(COMM)* pendiente; *(holiday)* sin sueldo; *(work)* sin pago, voluntario.
unpalatable [ʌn'pælətəbl] *a* *(truth)* desagradable.
unparalleled [ʌn'pærəleld] *a* *(unequalled)* sin par; *(unique)* sin precedentes.
unpatriotic [ʌnpætrɪ'ɔtɪk] *a* *(person)* poco patriota; *(speech, attitude)* antipatriótico.
unplanned [ʌn'plænd] *a* *(visit)* imprevisto;

(baby) no planeado.
unpleasant [ʌn'plɛznt] *a* *(disagreeable)* desagradable; *(person, manner)* antipático.
unplug [ʌn'plʌg] *vt* desenchufar, desconectar.
unpolluted [ʌnpə'luːtɪd] *a* impoluto, no contaminado.
unpopular [ʌn'pɔpjulə*] *a* poco popular; **to be** ~ **with sb** *(person, law)* no ser popular con uno; **to make o.s.** ~ **(with)** hacerse impopular (con).
unprecedented [ʌn'prɛsɪdəntɪd] *a* sin precedentes.
unpredictable [ʌnprɪ'dɪktəbl] *a* imprevisible.
unprejudiced [ʌn'prɛdʒudɪst] *a* *(not biased)* imparcial; *(having no prejudices)* sin prejuicio.
unprepared [ʌnprɪ'pɛəd] *a* *(person)* desprevenido; *(speech)* improvisado.
unprepossessing [ʌnpriːpə'zɛsɪŋ] *a* poco atractivo.
unprincipled [ʌn'prɪnsɪpld] *a* sin escrúpulos.
unproductive [ʌnprə'dʌktɪv] *a* improductivo; *(discussion)* infructuoso.
unprofessional [ʌnprə'fɛʃənl] *a* indigno de su profesión; ~ **conduct** negligencia.
unprofitable [ʌn'prɔfɪtəbl] *a* poco provechoso, no rentable.
unprovoked [ʌnprə'vəukt] *a* no provocado.
unpunished [ʌn'pʌnɪʃt] *a*: **to go** ~ quedar sin castigo, salir impune.
unqualified [ʌn'kwɔlɪfaɪd] *a* sin título, no cualificado; *(success)* total, incondicional.
unquestionably [ʌn'kwɛstʃənəblɪ] *ad* indiscutiblemente.
unquestioning [ʌn'kwɛstʃənɪŋ] *a* *(obedience, acceptance)* incondicional.
unravel [ʌn'rævl] *vt* desenmarañar.
unreal [ʌn'rɪəl] *a* irreal.
unrealistic [ʌnrɪə'lɪstɪk] *a* poco realista.
unreasonable [ʌn'riːznəbl] *a* irrazonable; **to make** ~ **demands on sb** hacer demandas excesivas a uno.
unrecognizable [ʌn'rɛkəgnaɪzəbl] *a* irreconocible.
unrecognized [ʌn'rɛkəgnəɪzd] *a* *(talent, genius)* desapercibido; *(POL: regime)* no reconocido.
unrecorded [ʌnrɪ'kɔːdɪd] *a* no registrado.
unrefined [ʌnrɪ'faɪnd] *a* *(sugar, petroleum)* sin refinar.
unrehearsed [ʌnrɪ'hɜːst] *a* *(THEATRE etc)* improvisado; *(spontaneous)* espontáneo.
unrelated [ʌnrɪ'leɪtɪd] *a* sin relación; *(family)* no emparentado.
unrelenting [ʌnrɪ'lɛntɪŋ] *a* implacable.
unreliable [ʌnrɪ'laɪəbl] *a* *(person)* informal; *(machine)* poco fiable.
unrelieved [ʌnrɪ'liːvd] *a* *(monotony)* constante.
unremitting [ʌnrɪ'mɪtɪŋ] *a* constante.

unrepeatable [ʌnrɪ'piːtəbl] *a* irrepetible.
unrepentant [ʌnrɪ'pɛntənt] *a* (*smoker, sinner*) impenitente; **to be ~ about sth** no arrepentirse de algo.
unrepresentative [ʌnrɛprɪ'zɛntətɪv] *a* (*untypical*) poco representativo.
unreserved [ʌnrɪ'zɜːvd] *a* (*seat*) no reservado; (*approval, admiration*) total.
unreservedly [ʌnrɪ'zɜːvɪdlɪ] *ad* sin reserva.
unresponsive [ʌnrɪ'spɒnsɪv] *a* insensible.
unrest [ʌn'rɛst] *n* inquietud *f*, malestar *m*; (*POL*) disturbios *mpl*.
unrestricted [ʌnrɪ'strɪktɪd] *a* (*power, time*) sin restricción; (*access*) libre.
unrewarded [ʌnrɪ'wɔːdɪd] *a* sin recompensa.
unripe [ʌn'raɪp] *a* verde, inmaduro.
unrivalled, (*US*) **unrivaled** [ʌn'raɪvəld] *a* incomparable, sin par.
unroll [ʌn'rəʊl] *vt* desenrollar.
unruffled [ʌn'rʌfld] *a* (*person*) imperturbable, ecuánime; (*hair*) liso.
unruly [ʌn'ruːlɪ] *a* indisciplinado.
unsafe [ʌn'seɪf] *a* (*journey*) peligroso; (*car etc*) inseguro; (*method*) arriesgado; **~ to drink/eat** no apto para el consumo humano.
unsaid [ʌn'sɛd] *a*: **to leave sth ~** dejar algo sin decir.
unsaleable, (*US*) **unsalable** [ʌn'seɪləbl] *a* invendible.
unsatisfactory ['ʌnsætɪs'fæktərɪ] *a* poco satisfactorio.
unsatisfied [ʌn'sætɪsfaɪd] *a* (*desire, need etc*) insatisfecho.
unsavoury, (*US*) **unsavory** [ʌn'seɪvərɪ] *a* (*fig*) repugnante.
unscathed [ʌn'skeɪðd] *a* ileso.
unscientific [ʌnsaɪən'tɪfɪk] *a* poco científico.
unscrew [ʌn'skruː] *vt* destornillar.
unscrupulous [ʌn'skruːpjuləs] *a* sin escrúpulos.
unsecured [ʌnsɪ'kjuəd] *a*: **~ creditor** acreedor(a) *m/f* común.
unseen [ʌn'siːn] *a* (*person, danger*) oculto.
unselfish [ʌn'sɛlfɪʃ] *a* generoso, poco egoísta; (*act*) desinteresado.
unsettled [ʌn'sɛtld] *a* inquieto; (*situation*) inestable; (*weather*) variable.
unsettling [ʌn'sɛtlɪŋ] *a* perturbador(a), inquietante.
unshak(e)able [ʌn'ʃeɪkəbl] *a* inquebrantable.
unshaven [ʌn'ʃeɪvn] *a* sin afeitar.
unsightly [ʌn'saɪtlɪ] *a* feo.
unskilled [ʌn'skɪld] *a*: **~ workers** mano *f* de obra no cualificada.
unsociable [ʌn'səʊʃəbl] *a* (*person*) poco sociable, huraño; (*behaviour*) insociable.
unsocial [ʌn'səʊʃl] *a*: **~ hours** horario nocturno.
unsold [ʌn'səʊld] *a* sin vender.
unsolicited [ʌnsə'lɪsɪtɪd] *a* no solicitado.
unsophisticated [ʌnsə'fɪstɪkeɪtɪd] *a* (*per-*

son) sencillo, ingenuo; (*method*) poco sofisticado.
unsound [ʌn'saʊnd] *a* (*health*) malo; (*in construction: floor, foundations*) defectuoso; (*policy, advice, judgment*) erróneo; (*investment*) poco seguro.
unspeakable [ʌn'spiːkəbl] *a* indecible; (*awful*) incalificable.
unspoken [ʌn'spəʊkn] *a* (*words*) sobreentendido; (*agreement, approval*) tácito.
unstable [ʌn'steɪbl] *a* inestable.
unsteady [ʌn'stɛdɪ] *a* inestable.
unstinting [ʌn'stɪntɪŋ] *a* (*support etc*) pródigo.
unstuck [ʌn'stʌk] *a*: **to come ~** despegarse; (*fig*) fracasar.
unsubstantiated [ʌnsəb'stænʃɪeɪtɪd] *a* (*rumour, accusation*) no comprobado.
unsuccessful [ʌnsək'sɛsful] *a* (*attempt*) infructuoso; (*writer, proposal*) sin éxito; **to be ~** (*in attempting sth*) no tener éxito, fracasar.
unsuccessfully [ʌnsək'sɛsfulɪ] *ad* en vano, sin éxito.
unsuitable [ʌn'suːtəbl] *a* inconveniente, inapropiado; (*time*) inoportuno.
unsuited [ʌn'suːtɪd] *a*: **to be ~ for** *or* **to** ser poco apto para.
unsupported [ʌnsə'pɔːtɪd] *a* (*claim*) sin fundamento; (*theory*) sin base firme.
unsure [ʌn'ʃuə*] *a* inseguro, poco seguro; **to be ~ of o.s.** estar poco seguro de sí mismo.
unsuspecting [ʌnsə'spɛktɪŋ] *a* confiado.
unsweetened [ʌn'swiːtnd] *a* sin azúcar.
unsympathetic [ʌnsɪmpə'θɛtɪk] *a* (*attitude*) poco comprensivo; (*person*) sin compasión; **~ (to)** indiferente(a).
untangle [ʌn'tæŋgl] *vt* desenredar.
untapped [ʌn'tæpt] *a* (*resources*) sin explotar.
untaxed [ʌn'tækst] *a* (*goods*) libre de impuestos; (*income*) antes de impuestos.
unthinkable [ʌn'θɪŋkəbl] *a* inconcebible, impensable.
untidy [ʌn'taɪdɪ] *a* (*room*) desordenado, en desorden; (*appearance*) desaliñado.
untie [ʌn'taɪ] *vt* desatar.
until [ən'tɪl] *prep* hasta ♦ *conj* hasta que; **~ he comes** hasta que venga; **~ now** hasta ahora; **~ then** hasta entonces; **from morning ~ night** de la mañana a la noche.
untimely [ʌn'taɪmlɪ] *a* inoportuno; (*death*) prematuro.
untold [ʌn'təʊld] *a* (*story*) nunca contado; (*suffering*) indecible; (*wealth*) incalculable.
untouched [ʌn'tʌtʃt] *a* (*not used etc*) intacto, sin tocar; (*safe: person*) indemne, ileso; (*unaffected*): **~ by** insensible a.
untoward [ʌntə'wɔːd] *a* (*behaviour*) impropio; (*event*) adverso.
untrammelled, (*US*) **untrammeled** [ʌn'træməld] *a* ilimitado.

untranslatable [ʌn'trænz'leɪtəbl] *a* intraducible.
untried [ʌn'traɪd] *a* (*plan*) no probado.
untrue [ʌn'truː] *a* (*statement*) falso.
untrustworthy [ʌn'trʌstwɜːðɪ] *a* (*person*) poco fiable.
unusable [ʌn'juːzəbl] *a* inservible.
unused [ʌn'juːzd] *a* sin usar, nuevo; **to be ~ to (doing) sth** no estar acostumbrado a (hacer) algo.
unusual [ʌn'juːʒuəl] *a* insólito, poco común.
unusually [ʌn'juːʒuəlɪ] *ad*: **he arrived ~ early** llegó más temprano que de costumbre.
unveil [ʌn'veɪl] *vt* (*statue*) descubrir.
unwanted [ʌn'wɒntɪd] *a* (*person, effect*) no deseado.
unwarranted [ʌn'wɒrəntɪd] *a* injustificado.
unwary [ʌn'weərɪ] *a* imprudente, incauto.
unwavering [ʌn'weɪvərɪŋ] *a* inquebrantable.
unwelcome [ʌn'wɛlkəm] *a* (*at a bad time*) inoportuno, molesto; **to feel ~** sentirse incómodo.
unwell [ʌn'wɛl] *a*: **to feel ~** estar indispuesto, sentirse mal.
unwieldy [ʌn'wiːldɪ] *a* difícil de manejar.
unwilling [ʌn'wɪlɪŋ] *a*: **to be ~ to do sth** estar poco dispuesto a hacer algo.
unwillingly [ʌn'wɪlɪŋlɪ] *ad* de mala gana.
unwind [ʌn'waɪnd] (*irg: like* **wind**) *vt* desenvolver ♦ *vi* (*relax*) relajarse.
unwise [ʌn'waɪz] *a* imprudente.
unwitting [ʌn'wɪtɪŋ] *a* inconsciente.
unworkable [ʌn'wɜːkəbl] *a* (*plan*) impráctico.
unworthy [ʌn'wɜːðɪ] *a* indigno; **to be ~ of sth/to do sth** ser indigno de algo/de hacer algo.
unwrap [ʌn'ræp] *vt* deshacer.
unwritten [ʌn'rɪtn] *a* (*agreement*) tácito; (*rules, law*) no escrito.
unzip [ʌn'zɪp] *vt* abrir la cremallera de.
up [ʌp] *prep*: **to go/be ~ sth** subir/estar encima de algo ♦ *ad* hacia arriba, arriba ♦ *vi* (*col*): **she ~ped and left** se levantó y se marchó ♦ *vt* (*col: price*) subir, aumentar; **when the year was ~** (*finished*) al terminarse el año; **he's well ~ in** *or* **on politics** (*Brit: knowledgeable*) está muy al día en política; **what's ~?** (*col: wrong*) ¿qué pasa?; **~ there** allí arriba; **~ above** encima, allí arriba; **"this side ~"** "este lado hacia arriba''; **to be ~** (*out of bed*) estar levantado; (*installed, built etc*) estar construido; (*tent*) estar levantado; (*curtains, paper etc*) estar colocado; **to be ~ (by)** (*in price, value*) haber alzado (en); **prices are ~ on last year** los precios han subido desde el año pasado; **it is ~ to you** usted decide/ tú decides; **what is he ~ to?** ¿qué es lo que quiere?, ¿qué está tramando?; **he is not ~ to it** no es capaz de hacerlo; **I don't**

feel ~ to it no me encuentro con ánimos para ello; **to stop halfway ~** pararse a mitad del camino *or* de la subida; **time's ~** se acabó el tiempo; **~ the Celtic!** ¡arriba el Celtic!; **what's ~ with him?** ¿qué le pasa (a él)?; **to live/go ~ North** vivir en el norte/ir al norte; **~s and downs** *npl* (*fig*) altibajos *mpl*.
up-and-coming [ʌpənd'kʌmɪŋ] *a* prometedor(a).
upbeat ['ʌpbiːt] *n* (*MUS*) tiempo no acentuado; (*in economy, prosperity*) aumento ♦ *a* (*col*) optimista, animado.
upbraid [ʌp'breɪd] *vt* censurar, reprender.
upbringing ['ʌpbrɪŋɪŋ] *n* educación *f*.
update [ʌp'deɪt] *vt* poner al día.
upend [ʌp'ɛnd] *vt* poner vertical.
upgrade [ʌp'greɪd] *vt* ascender; (*COMPUT*) modernizar.
upheaval [ʌp'hiːvl] *n* trastornos *mpl*; (*POL*) agitación *f*.
uphill [ʌp'hɪl] *a* cuesta arriba; (*fig: task*) penoso, difícil ♦ *ad*: **to go ~** ir cuesta arriba.
uphold [ʌp'həuld] (*irg: like* **hold**) *vt* sostener.
upholstery [ʌp'həulstərɪ] *n* tapicería.
upkeep ['ʌpkiːp] *n* mantenimiento.
upmarket [ʌp'mɑːkɪt] *a* (*product*) de primera calidad.
upon [ə'pɒn] *prep* sobre.
upper ['ʌpə*] *a* superior, de arriba ♦ *n* (*of shoe: also:* **~s**) pala.
upper case *n* (*TYP*) mayúsculas *fpl*.
upper-class [ʌpə'klɑːs] *a* (*district, people, accent*) de clase alta; (*attitude*) altivo.
upper hand *n*: **to have the ~** tener la sartén por el mango, llevar la delantera.
uppermost ['ʌpəməust] *a* el más alto; **what was ~ in my mind** lo que me preocupaba más.
Upper Volta [-'vəultə] *n* Alto Volta *m*.
upright ['ʌpraɪt] *a* vertical; (*fig*) honrado.
uprising ['ʌpraɪzɪŋ] *n* sublevación *f*.
uproar ['ʌprɔː*] *n* tumulto, escándalo.
uproot [ʌp'ruːt] *vt* desarraigar.
upset *n* ['ʌpsɛt] (*to plan etc*) revés *m*, contratiempo; (*MED*) trastorno ♦ *vt* [ʌp'sɛt] (*irg: like* **set**) (*glass etc*) volcar; (*spill*) derramar; (*plan*) alterar; (*person*) molestar, perturbar ♦ *a* [ʌp'sɛt] preocupado, perturbado; (*stomach*) revuelto; **to have a stomach ~** (*Brit*) tener el estómago revuelto; **to get ~** ofenderse, llevarse un disgusto.
upset price *n* (*US, Scottish*) precio mínimo *or* de reserva.
upsetting [ʌp'sɛtɪŋ] *a* (*worrying*) inquietante; (*offending*) ofensivo; (*annoying*) molesto.
upshot ['ʌpʃɒt] *n* resultado.
upside-down ['ʌpsaɪd'daun] *ad* al revés.
upstairs [ʌp'stɛəz] *ad* arriba ♦ *a* (*room*) de

arriba ♦ *n* el piso superior.
upstart ['ʌpstɑːt] *n* advenedizo.
upstream [ʌp'striːm] *ad* río arriba.
upsurge ['ʌpsəːdʒ] *n* (*of enthusiasm etc*) arrebato.
uptake ['ʌpteɪk] *n*: **he is quick/slow on the** ~ es muy listo/torpe.
uptight [ʌp'taɪt] *a* tenso, nervioso.
up-to-date ['ʌptə'deɪt] *a* moderno, actual; **to bring sb** ~ **(on sth)** poner a uno al corriente/tanto (de algo).
upturn ['ʌptəːn] *n* (*in luck*) mejora; (*COMM*: *in market*) resurgimiento económico; (: *in value of currency*) aumento.
upturned ['ʌptəːnd] *a*: ~ **nose** nariz *f* respingona.
upward ['ʌpwəd] *a* ascendente.
upward(s) ['ʌpwəd(z)] *ad* hacia arriba.
URA *n abbr* (*US*) = *Urban Renewal Administration*.
Ural Mountains ['juərəl-] *npl*: **the** ~ (*also*: **the Urals**) los Montes Urales.
uranium [juə'reɪnɪəm] *n* uranio.
Uranus [juə'reɪnəs] *n* (*ASTRO*) Urano.
urban ['əːbən] *a* urbano.
urbane [əː'beɪn] *a* cortés, urbano.
urbanization ['əːbənəɪ'zeɪʃən] *n* urbanización *f*.
urchin ['əːtʃɪn] *n* pilluelo, golfillo.
urge [əːdʒ] *n* (*force*) impulso; (*desire*) deseo ♦ *vt*: **to** ~ **sb to do sth** animar a uno a hacer algo.
urge on *vt* animar.
urgency ['əːdʒənsɪ] *n* urgencia.
urgent ['əːdʒənt] *a* (*earnest, persistent*: *plea*) insistente; (: *tone*) urgente.
urgently ['əːdʒəntlɪ] *ad* con urgencia, urgentemente.
urinal ['juərɪnl] *n* (*building*) urinario; (*vessel*) orinal *m*.
urinate ['juərɪneɪt] *vi* orinar.
urine ['juərɪn] *n* orina, orines *mpl*.
urn [əːn] *n* urna; (*also*: **tea** ~) cacharro metálico grande para hacer té.
Uruguay ['juerəgwaɪ] *n* el Uruguay.
Uruguayan [juərə'gwaɪən] *a, n* uruguayo/a *m/f*.
US *n abbr* (= *United States*) EE.UU.
us [ʌs] *pron* nos; (*after prep*) nosotros/as; (*col: me*): **give** ~ **a kiss** dame un beso; *see also* **me**.
USA *n abbr see* **United States of America**; (*MIL*) = *United States Army*.
usable ['juːzəbl] *a* utilizable.
USAF *n abbr* = *United States Air Force*.
usage ['juːzɪdʒ] *n* (*LING*) uso; (*utilization*) utilización *f*.
USCG *n abbr* = *United States Coast Guard*.
USDA *n abbr* = *United States Department of Agriculture*.
USDAW ['ʌzdɔː] *n abbr* (*Brit*: = *Union of Shop, Distributive and Allied Workers*) sindicato de empleados de comercio.

USDI *n abbr* = *United States Department of the Interior*.
use *n* [juːs] uso, empleo; (*usefulness*) utilidad *f* ♦ *vt* [juːz] usar, emplear; **in** ~ en uso; **out of** ~ en desuso; **to be of** ~ servir; **ready for** ~ listo (para ser usado); **to make** ~ **of sth** aprovecharse *or* servirse de algo; **it's no** ~ (*pointless*) es inútil; (*not useful*) no sirve; **what's this** ~**d for?** ¿para qué sirve esto?; **to be** ~**d to** estar acostumbrado a (*Sp*), acostumbrar; **to get** ~**d to acostumbrarse a; she** ~**d to do it** (ella) solía *or* acostumbraba hacerlo.
use up *vt* agotar.
used [juːzd] *a* (*car*) usado.
useful ['juːsful] *a* útil; **to come in** ~ ser útil.
usefulness ['juːsfəlnɪs] *n* utilidad *f*.
useless ['juːslɪs] *a* inútil; (*unusable: object*) inservible.
uselessly ['juːslɪslɪ] *ad* inútilmente, en vano.
uselessness ['juːslɪsnɪs] *n* inutilidad *f*.
user ['juːzə*] *n* usuario(a); (*of petrol, gas etc*) consumidor(a) *m/f*.
user-friendly ['juːzə'frendlɪ] *a* (*COMPUT*) amistoso, fácil de utilizar.
USES *n abbr* = *United States Employment Service*.
usher ['ʌʃə*] *n* (*at wedding*) ujier *m*; (*in cinema etc*) acomodador *m* ♦ *vt*: **to** ~ **sb in** (*into room*) hacer pasar a uno; **it** ~**ed in a new era** (*fig*) anunció una nueva era.
usherette [ʌʃə'rɛt] *n* (*in cinema*) acomodadora.
USIA *n abbr* = *United States Information Agency*.
USM *n abbr* = *United States Mail, United States Mint*.
USN *n abbr* = *United States Navy*.
USPHS *n abbr* = *United States Public Health Service*.
USPO *n abbr* = *United States Post Office*.
USS *abbr* = *United States Ship* (*or Steamer*).
USSR *n abbr*: **the** ~ la U.R.S.S.
usu. *abbr* = **usually**.
usual ['juːʒuəl] *a* normal, corriente; **as** ~ como de costumbre, como siempre.
usually ['juːʒuəlɪ] *ad* normalmente.
usurer ['juːʒərə*] *n* usurero.
usurp [juː'zəːp] *vt* usurpar.
usury ['juːʒərɪ] *n* usura.
UT *abbr* (*US POST*) = *Utah*.
utensil [juː'tɛnsl] *n* utensilio; **kitchen** ~**s** batería de cocina.
uterus ['juːtərəs] *n* útero.
utilitarian [juːtɪlɪ'tɛərɪən] *a* utilitario.
utility [juː'tɪlɪtɪ] *n* utilidad *f*.
utility room *n* office *m*.
utilization [juːtɪlaɪ'zeɪʃən] *n* utilización *f*.
utilize ['juːtɪlaɪz] *vt* utilizar.
utmost ['ʌtməust] *a* mayor ♦ *n*: **to do one's** ~ hacer todo lo posible; **it is of the**

~ **importance that** ... es de la mayor importancia que ... .

utter [ˈʌtə*] a total, completo ◆ vt pronunciar, proferir.

utterance [ˈʌtərns] n palabras fpl, declaración f.

utterly [ˈʌtəlɪ] ad completamente, totalmente.

U-turn [ˈjuːˈtəːn] n viraje m or vuelta en U.

V

V, v [viː] (letter) V, v f; **V for Victor** V de Valencia.

v. abbr (= verse) vers.º (= vide: see) V, vid., vide; (= versus) vs.; = **volt**.

VA abbr (US POST) = Virginia.

vac [væk] n abbr (Brit col) = **vacation**.

vacancy [ˈveɪkənsɪ] n (Brit: job) vacante f; (room) cuarto libro; **have you any vacancies?** ¿tiene or hay alguna habitación or algún cuarto libre?

vacant [ˈveɪkənt] a desocupado, libre; (expression) distraído.

vacant lot n (US) solar m.

vacate [vəˈkeɪt] vt (house) desocupar; (job) dejar (vacante).

vacation [vəˈkeɪʃən] n vacaciones fpl ; **on ~** de vacaciones; **to take a ~** (esp US) tomarse unas vacaciones.

vacation course n curso de vacaciones.

vacationer [vəˈkeɪʃənə*], **vacationist** [vəˈkeɪʃənɪst] n (US) turista m/f.

vaccinate [ˈvæksɪneɪt] vt vacunar.

vaccination [væksɪˈneɪʃən] n vacunación f.

vaccine [ˈvæksiːn] n vacuna.

vacuum [ˈvækjum] n vacío.

vacuum bottle n (US) = **vacuum flask**.

vacuum cleaner n aspiradora.

vacuum flask n (Brit) termo.

vacuum-packed [ˈvækjumˈpækt] a envasado al vacío.

vagabond [ˈvægəbɔnd] n vagabundo/a.

vagary [ˈveɪgərɪ] n capricho.

vagina [vəˈdʒaɪnə] n vagina.

vagrancy [ˈveɪgrənsɪ] n vagabundeo.

vagrant [ˈveɪgrənt] n vagabundo/a.

vague [veɪg] a vago; (blurred: memory) borroso; (uncertain) incierto, impreciso; (person) distraído; **I haven't the ~st idea** no tengo la más remota idea.

vaguely [ˈveɪglɪ] ad vagamente.

vagueness [ˈveɪgnɪs] n vaguedad f; imprecisión f; (absent-mindedness) despiste m.

vain [veɪn] a (conceited) presumido; (useless) vano, inútil; **in ~** en vano.

vainly [ˈveɪnlɪ] ad (to no effect) en vano;

(conceitedly) vanidosamente.

valance [ˈvælɔns] n (for bed) volante alrededor de la colcha que cuelga hasta el suelo.

valedictory [vælɪˈdɪktərɪ] a de despedida.

valentine [ˈvæləntaɪn] n (also: ~ **card**) tarjeta del Día de los Enamorados.

valet [ˈvæleɪ] n ayuda m de cámara.

valet service n (for clothes) planchado.

valiant [ˈvæljənt] a valiente.

valiantly [ˈvæljəntlɪ] ad valientemente, con valor.

valid [ˈvælɪd] a válido; (ticket) valedero; (law) vigente.

validate [ˈvælɪdeɪt] vt (contract, document) convalidar; (argument, claim) dar validez a.

validity [vəˈlɪdɪtɪ] n validez f; vigencia.

valise [vəˈliːz] n maletín m.

valley [ˈvælɪ] n valle m.

valour, (US) **valor** [ˈvælə*] n valor m, valentía.

valuable [ˈvæljuəbl] a (jewel) de valor; (time) valioso; **~s** npl objetos mpl de valor.

valuation [væljuˈeɪʃən] n tasación f, valuación f.

value [ˈvæljuː] n valor m; (importance) importancia ◆ vt (fix price of) tasar, valorar; (esteem) apreciar; **~s** npl (moral) valores mpl morales; **to lose (in) ~** (currency) bajar; (property) desvalorizarse; **to gain (in) ~** (currency) subir; (property) valorizarse; **you get good ~ (for money) in that shop** los precios son muy buenos en esa tienda; **to be of great ~ to sb** ser de gran valor para uno; **it is ~d at £8** está valorado en ocho libras.

value added tax (VAT) n (Brit) impuesto sobre el valor añadido (IVA m).

valued [ˈvæljuːd] a (appreciated) apreciado.

valueless [ˈvæljuːlɪs] a sin valor.

valuer [ˈvæljuːə*] n tasador(a) m/f.

valve [vælv] n (ANAT, TECH) válvula.

vampire [ˈvæmpaɪə*] n vampiro/vampiresa m/f.

van [væn] n (AUT) furgoneta, camioneta (LAm); (Brit RAIL) furgón m (de equipajes).

V and A n abbr (Brit) = Victoria and Albert Museum.

vandal [ˈvændl] n vándalo/a.

vandalism [ˈvændəlɪzəm] n vandalismo.

vandalize [ˈvændəlaɪz] vt dañar, destruir, destrozar.

vanguard [ˈvænɡɑːd] n vanguardia.

vanilla [vəˈnɪlə] n vainilla.

vanish [ˈvænɪʃ] vi desaparecer, esfumarse.

vanity [ˈvænɪtɪ] n vanidad f.

vanity case n neceser m.

vantage point [ˈvɑːntɪdʒ-] n posición f ventajosa.

vaporize [ˈveɪpəraɪz] vt vaporizar ◆ vi va-

porizarse.
vapour, (*US*) **vapor** ['veɪpə*] *n* vapor *m*; (*on breath, window*) vaho.
vapo(u)r trail *n* (*AVIAT*) estela.
variable ['veərɪəbl] *a* variable ♦ *n* variable *f*.
variance ['veərɪəns] *n*: **to be at ~ (with)** estar en desacuerdo (con), no cuadrar (con).
variant ['veərɪənt] *n* variante *f*.
variation [veərɪ'eɪʃən] *n* variación *f*.
varicose ['værɪkəus] *a*: **~ veins** varices *fpl*.
varied ['veərɪd] *a* variado.
variety [və'raɪətɪ] *n* variedad *f*, diversidad *f*; (*quantity*) surtido; **for a ~ of reasons** por varias *or* diversas razones.
variety show *n* espectáculo de variedades.
various ['veərɪəs] *a* varios/as, diversos/as; **at ~ times** (*different*) en distintos momentos; (*several*) varias veces.
varnish ['vɑːnɪʃ] *n* (*gen*) barniz *m*; (*nail ~*) esmalte *m* ♦ *vt* (*gen*) barnizar; (*nails*) pintar (con esmalte).
vary ['veərɪ] *vt* variar; (*change*) cambiar ♦ *vi* variar; (*disagree*) discrepar; **to ~ with** *or* **according to** variar según *or* de acuerdo con.
varying ['veərɪŋ] *a* diversos/as.
vase [vɑːz] *n* florero.
vasectomy [və'sɛktəmɪ] *n* vasectomía.
Vaseline ® ['væsɪliːn] *n* vaselina ®.
vast [vɑːst] *a* enorme; (*success*) abrumador(a), arrollador(a).
vastly ['vɑːstlɪ] *ad* enormemente.
vastness ['vɑːstnɪs] *n* inmensidad *f*.
VAT [væt] *n abbr* (*Brit*: = *value added tax*) IVA *m*.
vat [væt] *n* tina, tinaja.
Vatican ['vætɪkən] *n*: **the ~** el Vaticano.
vaudeville ['vɔːdəvɪl] *n* (*US*) vodevil *m*, vaudeville *m*.
vault [vɔːlt] *n* (*of roof*) bóveda; (*tomb*) tumba; (*in bank*) cámara acorazada ♦ *vt* (*also*: **~ over**) saltar (por encima de).
vaunted ['vɔːntɪd] *a*: **much ~** cacarreado, alardeado.
VC *n abbr* = **vice-chairman, vice-chancellor**; (*Brit*: = *Victoria Cross*) *condecoración militar*.
VCR *n abbr* = **video cassette recorder**.
VD *n abbr see* **venereal disease**.
VDU *n abbr see* **visual display unit**.
veal [viːl] *n* ternera.
veer [vɪə*] *vi* (*ship*) virar.
veg. [vedz] *n abbr* (*Brit col*) = **vegetable(s)**.
vegetable ['vedʒtəbl] *n* (*BOT*) vegetal *m*; (*edible plant*) legumbre *f*, hortaliza ♦ *a* vegetal; **~s** *npl* (*cooked*) verduras *fpl*.
vegetable garden *n* huerta, huerto.
vegetarian [vedʒɪ'teərɪən] *a*, *n* vegetariano/a *m/f*.

vegetate ['vedʒɪteɪt] *vi* vegetar.
vegetation [vedʒɪ'teɪʃən] *n* vegetación *f*.
vehemence ['viːɪməns] *n* vehemencia; violencia.
vehement ['viːɪmənt] *a* vehemente, apasionado; (*dislike, hatred*) violento.
vehicle ['viːɪkl] *n* vehículo; (*fig*) vehículo, medio.
vehicular [vɪ'hɪkjulə*] *a*: **~ traffic** circulación *f* rodada.
veil [veɪl] *n* velo ♦ *vt* velar; **under a ~ of secrecy** (*fig*) en el mayor secreto.
veiled [veɪld] *a* (*also fig*) disimulado, velado.
vein [veɪn] *n* vena; (*of ore etc*) veta.
vellum ['veləm] *n* (*writing paper*) papel *m* vitela.
velocity [vɪ'lɒsɪtɪ] *n* velocidad *f*.
velvet ['vɛlvɪt] *n* terciopelo ♦ *a* aterciopelado.
vendetta [vɛn'dɛtə] *n* vendetta.
vending machine ['vɛndɪŋ-] *n* distribuidor *m* automático.
vendor ['vɛndə*] *n* vendedor(a) *m/f*; **street ~** vendedor(a) *m/f* callejero/a.
veneer [və'nɪə*] *n* chapa, enchapado; (*fig*) barniz *m*.
venereal [vɪ'nɪərɪəl] *a*: **~ disease (VD)** enfermedad *f* venérea.
Venetian blind [vɪ'niːʃən-] *n* persiana.
Venezuela [vɛnɛ'zweɪlə] *n* Venezuela.
Venezuelan [vɛnɛ'zweɪlən] *a*, *n* venezolano/a *m/f*.
vengeance ['vɛndʒəns] *n* venganza; **with a ~** (*fig*) con creces.
vengeful ['vɛndʒful] *a* vengativo.
Venice ['vɛnɪs] *n* Venecia.
venison ['vɛnɪsn] *n* carne *f* de venado.
venom ['vɛnəm] *n* veneno.
venomous ['vɛnəməs] *a* venenoso.
venomously ['vɛnəməslɪ] *ad* con odio.
vent [vɛnt] *n* (*opening*) abertura; (*air-hole*) respiradero; (*in wall*) rejilla (de ventilación) ♦ *vt* (*fig: feelings*) desahogar.
ventilate ['vɛntɪleɪt] *vt* ventilar.
ventilation [vɛntɪ'leɪʃən] *n* ventilación *f*.
ventilation shaft *n* pozo de ventilación.
ventilator ['vɛntɪleɪtə*] *n* ventilador *m*.
ventriloquist [vɛn'trɪləkwɪst] *n* ventrílocuo/a.
venture ['vɛntʃə*] *n* empresa ♦ *vt* arriesgar; (*opinion*) ofrecer ♦ *vi* arriesgarse, lanzarse; **a business ~** una empresa comercial; **to ~ to do sth** aventurarse a hacer algo.
venture capital *n* capital *m* arriesgado.
venue ['vɛnjuː] *n* lugar *m*; (*meeting place*) lugar *m* de reunión.
Venus ['viːnəs] *n* (*ASTRO*) Venus *m*.
veracity [və'ræsɪtɪ] *n* veracidad *f*.
veranda(h) [və'rændə] *n* terraza; (*with glass*) galería.
verb [vəːb] *n* verbo.

verbal ['vɜːbl] a verbal.
verbally ['vɜːbəlɪ] ad verbalmente, de palabra.
verbatim [vɜːˈbeɪtɪm] a, ad al pie de la letra, palabra por palabra.
verbose [vɜːˈbəʊs] a prolijo.
verdict ['vɜːdɪkt] n veredicto, fallo; (fig: opinion) opinión f, juicio; ~ **of guilty/not guilty** veredicto de culpabilidad/inocencia.
verge [vɜːdʒ] n (Brit) borde m; **to be on the ~ of doing sth** estar a punto de hacer algo.
  verge on vt fus rayar en.
verger ['vɜːdʒə*] n sacristán m.
verification [vɛrɪfɪˈkeɪʃən] n comprobación f, verificación f.
verify ['vɛrɪfaɪ] vt comprobar, verificar; (COMPUT) verificar; (prove the truth of) confirmar.
veritable ['vɛrɪtəbl] a verdadero, auténtico.
vermin ['vɜːmɪn] npl (animals) bichos mpl; (insects, fig) sabandijas fpl.
vermouth ['vɜːməθ] n vermut m.
vernacular [vəˈnækjʊlə*] n vernáculo.
versatile ['vɜːsətaɪl] a (person) polifacético; (machine, tool etc) versátil.
versatility [vɜːsəˈtɪlɪtɪ] n versatilidad f.
verse [vɜːs] n versos mpl, poesía; (stanza) estrofa; (in bible) versículo; **in ~** en verso.
versed [vɜːst] a: **(well-)~ in** versado en.
version ['vɜːʃən] n versión f.
versus ['vɜːsəs] prep contra.
vertebra, pl **~e** ['vɜːtɪbrə, briː] n vértebra.
vertebrate ['vɜːtɪbrɪt] n vertebrado.
vertical ['vɜːtɪkl] a vertical.
vertically ['vɜːtɪkəlɪ] ad verticalmente.
vertigo ['vɜːtɪgəʊ] n vértigo; **to suffer from ~** tener vértigo.
verve [vɜːv] n brío.
very ['vɛrɪ] ad muy ♦ a: **the ~ book which** el mismo libro que; **the ~ last** el último (de todos); **at the ~ least** al menos; **~ much** muchísimo; **~ well/little** muy bien/poco; **~ high frequency** (RADIO) frecuencia muy alta; **it's ~ cold** hace mucho frío; **the ~ thought (of it) alarms me** con sólo pensarlo me entra miedo.
vespers ['vɛspəz] npl vísperas fpl.
vessel ['vɛsl] n (ANAT) vaso; (ship) barco; (container) vasija.
vest [vɛst] n (Brit) camiseta; (US: waistcoat) chaleco.
vested interests ['vɛstɪd-] npl (COMM) intereses mpl creados.
vestibule ['vɛstɪbjuːl] n vestíbulo.
vestige ['vɛstɪdʒ] n vestigio, rastro.
vestry ['vɛstrɪ] n sacristía.
Vesuvius [vɪˈsuːvɪəs] n Vesubio.
vet [vɛt] n abbr = **veterinary surgeon** ♦ vt repasar, revisar; **to ~ sb for a job** investigar a uno para un trabajo.
veteran ['vɛtərn] n veterano/a ♦ a: **she is a ~ campaigner for ...** es una veterana de la

campaña de ... .
veteran car n coche m antiguo.
veterinarian [vɛtrɪˈnɛərɪən] n (US) = **veterinary surgeon**.
veterinary ['vɛtrɪnərɪ] a veterinario.
veterinary surgeon n (Brit) veterinario/a.
veto ['viːtəʊ] n (pl ~es) veto ♦ vt prohibir, vedar; **to put a ~ on** vetar.
vex [vɛks] vt (irritate) fastidiar; (make impatient) impacientar.
vexed [vɛkst] a (question) controvertido.
vexing ['vɛksɪŋ] a molesto, engorroso.
VFD n abbr (US) = voluntary fire department.
VG n abbr (Brit SCOL etc: = very good) S (= sobresaliente).
VHF abbr (= very high frequency) VHF m.
VI abbr (US POST) = Virgin Islands.
via ['vaɪə] prep por, por vía de.
viability [vaɪəˈbɪlɪtɪ] n viabilidad f.
viable ['vaɪəbl] a viable.
viaduct ['vaɪədʌkt] n viaducto.
vibrant ['vaɪbrənt] a (lively, bright) vivo; (full of emotion: voice) vibrante; (colour) fuerte.
vibrate [vaɪˈbreɪt] vi vibrar.
vibration [vaɪˈbreɪʃən] n vibración f.
vicar ['vɪkə*] n párroco.
vicarage ['vɪkərɪdʒ] n parroquia.
vicarious [vɪˈkɛərɪəs] a indirecto; (responsibility) delegado.
vice [vaɪs] n (evil) vicio; (TECH) torno de banco.
vice- [vaɪs] pref vice-... .
vice-chairman ['vaɪsˈtʃɛəmən] n vicepresidente m.
vice-chancellor [vaɪsˈtʃɑːnsələ*] n (Brit UNIV) rector(a) m/f.
vice-president [vaɪsˈprɛzɪdənt] n vicepresidente/a m/f.
vice versa ['vaɪsɪˈvɜːsə] ad viceversa.
vicinity [vɪˈsɪnɪtɪ] n (area) vecindad f; (nearness) proximidad f; **in the ~ (of)** cercano (a).
vicious ['vɪʃəs] a (remark) malicioso; (blow) fuerte; **a ~ circle** un círculo vicioso.
viciousness ['vɪʃənɪs] n brutalidad f.
vicissitudes [vɪˈsɪsɪtjuːdz] npl vicisitudes fpl, peripecias fpl.
victim ['vɪktɪm] n víctima; **to be the ~ of** ser víctima de.
victimization [vɪktɪmaɪˈzeɪʃən] n persecución f; (of striker etc) represalias fpl.
victimize ['vɪktɪmaɪz] vt (strikers etc) tomar represalias contra.
victor ['vɪktə*] n vencedor(a) m/f.
Victorian [vɪkˈtɔːrɪən] a victoriano.
victorious [vɪkˈtɔːrɪəs] a vencedor(a).
victory ['vɪktərɪ] n victoria; **to win a ~ over sb** obtener una victoria sobre uno.
video ['vɪdɪəʊ] cpd vídeo ♦ n (~ film) videofilm m; (also: ~ cassette) video-

cassette *f*; (*also*: ~ **cassette recorder**) videograbadora, vídeo.
video cassette *n* videocassette *f*.
video cassette recorder *n* videograbadora, vídeo.
video recording *n* videograbación *f*.
video tape *n* cinta de vídeo.
vie [vaɪ] *vi*: **to** ~ **with** competir con.
Vienna [vɪ'enə] *n* Viena.
Viennese [vɪə'niːz] *a*, *n* vienés/esa *m/f*.
Vietnam, Viet Nam [vjɛt'næm] *n* Vietnam *m*.
Vietnamese [vjɛtnə'miːz] *a* vietnamita ♦ *n* (*pl inv*) vietnamita *m/f*; (*LING*) vietnamita *m*.
view [vjuː] *n* vista, perspectiva; (*landscape*) paisaje *m*; (*opinion*) opinión *f*, criterio ♦ *vt* (*look at*) mirar; (*examine*) examinar; **on** ~ (*in museum etc*) expuesto; **in full** ~ **of sb** a la vista *or* a plena vista de uno; **to be within** ~ (**of sth**) estar a la vista (de algo); **an overall** ~ **of the situation** una visión de conjunto de la situación; **in** ~ **of the fact that** en vista del hecho de que; **to take** *or* **hold the** ~ **that** ... opinar *or* pensar que ...; **with a** ~ **to doing sth** con miras *or* vistas a hacer algo.
viewdata ['vjuːdeɪtə] *n* (*Brit*) vídeodatos *mpl*.
viewer ['vjuːə*] *n* (*small projector*) visionadora; (*TV*) televidente *m/f*.
viewfinder ['vjuːfaɪndə*] *n* visor *m* de imagen.
viewpoint ['vjuːpɔɪnt] *n* punto de vista.
vigil ['vɪdʒɪl] *n* vigilia; **to keep** ~ velar.
vigilance ['vɪdʒɪləns] *n* vigilancia.
vigilance committee *n* (*US*) comité *m* de autodefensa.
vigilant ['vɪdʒɪlənt] *a* vigilante.
vigilantly ['vɪdʒɪləntlɪ] *ad* vigilantemente.
vigorous ['vɪgərəs] *a* enérgico, vigoroso.
vigorously ['vɪgərəslɪ] *ad* enérgicamente, vigorosamente.
vigour, (*US*) **vigor** ['vɪgə*] *n* energía, vigor *m*.
vile [vaɪl] *a* (*action*) vil, infame; (*smell*) asqueroso.
vilify ['vɪlɪfaɪ] *vt* denigrar, vilipendiar.
villa ['vɪlə] *n* (*country house*) casa de campo; (*suburban house*) chalet *m*.
village ['vɪlɪdʒ] *n* aldea.
villager ['vɪlɪdʒə*] *n* aldeano/a.
villain ['vɪlən] *n* (*scoundrel*) malvado/a; (*criminal*) maleante *m/f*.
VIN *n abbr* (*US*) = *vehicle identification number*.
vindicate ['vɪndɪkeɪt] *vt* vindicar, justificar.
vindication [vɪndɪ'keɪʃən] *n*: **in** ~ **of** en justificación de.
vindictive [vɪn'dɪktɪv] *a* vengativo.
vine [vaɪn] *n* vid *f*.
vinegar ['vɪnɪgə*] *n* vinagre *m*.
vine-growing ['vaɪngrəʊɪŋ] *a* (*region*) viti-

cultor(a).
vineyard ['vɪnjɑːd] *n* viña, viñedo.
vintage ['vɪntɪdʒ] *n* (*year*) vendimia, cosecha; **the 1970** ~ la cosecha de 1970.
vintage car *n* coche *m* antiguo *or* de época.
vintage wine *n* vino añejo.
vintage year *n*: **it's been a** ~ **for plays** ha sido un año destacado en lo que a teatro se refiere.
vinyl ['vaɪnl] *n* vinilo.
viola [vɪ'əʊlə] *n* (*MUS*) viola.
violate ['vaɪəleɪt] *vt* violar.
violation [vaɪə'leɪʃən] *n* violación *f*; **in** ~ **of sth** en violación de algo.
violence ['vaɪələns] *n* violencia; **acts of** ~ actos *mpl* de violencia.
violent ['vaɪələnt] *a* (*gen*) violento; (*pain*) intenso; **a** ~ **dislike of sb/sth** una profunda antipatía *or* manía a uno/algo.
violently ['vaɪələntlɪ] *ad* (*severely*: *ill*, *angry*) muy.
violet ['vaɪələt] *a* violado, violeta ♦ *n* (*plant*) violeta.
violin [vaɪə'lɪn] *n* violín *m*.
violinist [vaɪə'lɪnɪst] *n* violinista *m/f*.
VIP *n abbr* (= *very important person*) VIP *m*.
viper ['vaɪpə*] *n* víbora.
virgin ['vɜːdʒɪn] *n* virgen *m/f* ♦ *a* virgen; **the Blessed V**~ la Santísima Virgen.
virginity [vɜː'dʒɪnɪtɪ] *n* virginidad *f*.
Virgo ['vɜːgəʊ] *n* Virgo.
virile ['vɪraɪl] *a* viril.
virility [vɪ'rɪlɪtɪ] *n* virilidad *f*.
virtual ['vɜːtjʊəl] *a* virtual.
virtually ['vɜːtjʊəlɪ] *ad* (*almost*) virtualmente; **it is** ~ **impossible** es prácticamente imposible.
virtue ['vɜːtjuː] *n* virtud *f*; **by** ~ **of** en virtud de.
virtuoso [vɜː'tjuːəʊsəʊ] *n* virtuoso.
virtuous ['vɜːtjuəs] *a* virtuoso.
virulence ['vɪrʊləns] *n* virulencia.
virulent ['vɪrʊlənt] *a* virulento, violento.
virus ['vaɪərəs] *n* virus *m*.
visa ['viːzə] *n* visado, visa (*LAm*).
vis-à-vis [viːzə'viː] *prep* con respecto a.
viscount ['vaɪkaunt] *n* vizconde *m*.
viscous ['vɪskəs] *a* viscoso.
vise [vaɪs] *n* (*US TECH*) = **vice**.
visibility [vɪzɪ'bɪlɪtɪ] *n* visibilidad *f*.
visible ['vɪzəbl] *a* visible; ~ **exports/imports** exportaciones *fpl*/importaciones *fpl* visibles.
visibly ['vɪzɪblɪ] *ad* visiblemente.
vision ['vɪʒən] *n* (*sight*) vista; (*foresight*, *in dream*) visión *f*.
visionary ['vɪʒənrɪ] *n* visionario/a.
visit ['vɪzɪt] *n* visita ♦ *vt* (*person*) visitar, hacer una visita a; (*place*) ir a, (ir a) conocer; **to pay a** ~ **to** (*person*) visitar a; **on a private/official** ~ en visita privada/

oficial.
visiting ['vɪzɪtɪŋ] *a* (*speaker, professor*) invitado; (*team*) visitante.
visiting card *n* tarjeta de visita.
visiting hours *npl* (*in hospital etc*) horas *fpl* de visita.
visitor *n* (*gen*) visitante *m/f*; (*to one's house*) invitado/a; (*tourist*) turista *m/f*; (*tripper*) excursionista *m/f*; **to have ~s** (*at home*) tener visita.
visitors' book *n* libro de visitas.
visor ['vaɪzə*] *n* visera.
VISTA ['vɪstə] *n abbr* (= *Volunteers In Service to America*) *programa de ayuda voluntaria a los necesitados.*
vista ['vɪstə] *n* vista, panorama.
visual ['vɪzjuəl] *a* visual.
visual aid *n* medio visual.
visual display unit (VDU) *n* unidad *f* de despliegue visual, monitor *m*.
visualize ['vɪzjuəlaɪz] *vt* imaginarse; (*foresee*) prever.
visually ['vɪzjuəlɪ] *ad*: **~ handicapped** con visión deficiente.
vital ['vaɪtl] *a* (*essential*) esencial, imprescindible; (*crucial*) crítico; (*person*) enérgico, vivo; (*of life*) vital; **of ~ importance (to sb/sth)** de suma importancia (para uno/algo).
vitality [vaɪ'tælɪtɪ] *n* energía, vitalidad *f*.
vitally ['vaɪtəlɪ] *ad*: **~ important** de primera importancia.
vital statistics *npl* (*of population*) estadísticas *fpl* demográficas; (*col: woman's*) medidas *fpl* vitales.
vitamin ['vɪtəmɪn] *n* vitamina.
vitamin pill *n* pastilla de vitaminas.
vitreous ['vɪtrɪəs] *a* (*china, enamel*) vítreo.
vitriolic [vɪtrɪ'ɔlɪk] *n* mordaz.
viva ['vaɪvə] *n* (*also*: **~ voce**) examen *m* oral.
vivacious [vɪ'veɪʃəs] *a* vivaz, alegre.
vivacity [vɪ'væsɪtɪ] *n* vivacidad *f*.
vivid ['vɪvɪd] *a* (*account*) gráfico; (*light*) intenso; (*imagination*) vivo.
vividly ['vɪvɪdlɪ] *ad* (*describe*) gráficamente; (*remember*) como si fuera hoy.
vivisection [vɪvɪ'sekʃən] *n* vivisección *f*.
vixen ['vɪksn] *n* (*zool*) zorra, raposa; (*pej: woman*) arpía, bruja.
viz *abbr* (= *videlicet: namely*) v.gr.
VLF *abbr* = *very low frequency.*
V-neck ['viːnek] *n* cuello de pico.
VOA *n abbr* (= *Voice of America*) Voz *f* de América.
vocabulary [vəu'kæbjulərɪ] *n* vocabulario.
vocal ['vəukl] *a* vocal; (*articulate*) elocuente.
vocal cords *npl* cuerdas *fpl* vocales.
vocalist ['vəukəlɪst] *n* cantante *m/f*.
vocation [vəu'keɪʃən] *n* vocación *f*.
vocational [vəu'keɪʃənl] *a* vocacional; **~ guidance** orientación *f* profesional; **~ train-**

ing formación *f* profesional.
vociferous [və'sɪfərəs] *a* vociferante.
vociferously [və'sɪfərəslɪ] *ad* a gritos, clamorosamente.
vodka ['vɔdkə] *n* vodka *m*.
vogue [vəug] *n* boga, moda; **to be in ~, be the ~** estar de moda *or* en boga.
voice [vɔɪs] *n* voz *f* ♦ *vt* (*opinion*) expresar; **in a loud/soft ~** en voz alta/baja; **to give ~ to** expresar.
void [vɔɪd] *n* vacío; (*hole*) hueco ♦ *a* (*invalid*) nulo, inválido; (*empty*): **~ of** carente *or* desprovisto de.
voile [vɔɪl] *n* gasa.
vol. *abbr* (= *volume*) t.
volatile ['vɔlətaɪl] *a* volátil; (*comput: memory*) no permanente.
volcanic [vɔl'kænɪk] *a* volcánico.
volcano, ~es [vɔl'keɪnəu] *n* volcán *m*.
volition [və'lɪʃən] *n*: **of one's own ~** de su propia voluntad.
volley ['vɔlɪ] *n* (*of gunfire*) descarga; (*of stones etc*) lluvia; (*tennis etc*) volea.
volleyball *n* vol(e)ibol *m*.
volt [vəult] *n* voltio.
voltage ['vəultɪdʒ] *n* voltaje *m*; **high/low ~** alto/bajo voltaje, alta/baja tensión.
volte-face ['vɔlt'fɑːs] *n* viraje *m*.
voluble ['vɔljubl] *a* locuaz, hablador(a).
volume ['vɔljuːm] *n* (*of tank*) volumen *m*; (*book*) tomo; **~ one/two** (*of book*) tomo primero/segundo; **~s** *npl* (*great quantities*) cantidad *fsg*; **his expression spoke ~s** su expresión (lo) decía todo.
volume control *n* (*radio, tv*) (botón *m* del) volumen *m*.
volume discount *n* (*comm*) descuento por volumen de compras.
voluminous [və'luːmɪnəs] *a* (*large*) voluminoso; (*prolific*) prolífico.
voluntarily ['vɔləntrɪlɪ] *ad* libremente, voluntariamente.
voluntary ['vɔləntərɪ] *a* voluntario, espontáneo.
voluntary liquidation *n* (*comm*) liquidación *f* voluntaria.
voluntary redundancy *n* (*Brit*) despido voluntario.
volunteer [vɔlən'tɪə*] *n* voluntario/a ♦ *vi* ofrecerse (de voluntario); **to ~ to do** ofrecerse a hacer.
voluptuous [və'lʌptjuəs] *a* voluptuoso.
vomit ['vɔmɪt] *n* vómito ♦ *vt, vi* vomitar.
vote [vəut] *n* (*votes cast*) votación *f*; (*right to ~*) derecho de votar; (*franchise*) sufragio ♦ *vt* (*chairman*) elegir ♦ *vi* votar, ir a votar; **~ of thanks** voto de gracias; **to put sth to the ~, take a ~ on sth** someter algo a voto; **~ for** *or* **in favour of/ against** voto a favor de/en contra de; **to ~ to do sth** votar por hacer algo; **he was ~d secretary** fue elegido secretario por votación; **to pass a ~ of confidence/no con-**

fidence aprobar un voto de confianza/de censura.

voter ['vəʊtə*] n votante m/f.

voting ['vəʊtɪŋ] n votación f.

voting paper n (Brit) papeleta de votación.

voting right n derecho a voto.

vouch [vaʊtʃ]: **to ~ for** vt fus garantizar, responder de.

voucher ['vaʊtʃə*] n (for meal, petrol) vale m; **luncheon/travel ~** vale m de comida/de viaje.

vow [vaʊ] n voto ◆ vi hacer voto; **to take or make a ~ to do sth** jurar hacer algo, comprometerse a hacer algo.

vowel ['vaʊəl] n vocal f.

voyage ['vɔɪɪdʒ] n (journey) viaje m; (crossing) travesía.

VP n abbr (= vice-president) V.P.

vs abbr (= versus) vs.

VSO n abbr (Brit: = Voluntary Service Overseas) organización que envía jóvenes voluntarios a trabajar y enseñar en los países del Tercer Mundo.

VT abbr (US POST) = Vermont.

vulgar ['vʌlgə*] a (rude) ordinario, grosero; (in bad taste) de mal gusto.

vulgarity [vʌl'gærɪtɪ] n grosería; mal gusto.

vulnerability [vʌlnərə'bɪlɪtɪ] n vulnerabilidad f.

vulnerable ['vʌlnərəbl] a vulnerable.

vulture ['vʌltʃə*] n buitre m.

W

W, w ['dʌbljuː] n (letter) W, w f; **W for William** W de Washington.

W abbr (= west) O; (ELEC: = watt) v.

WA abbr (US POST) = Washington.

wad [wɔd] n (of cotton wool, paper) bolita; (of banknotes etc) fajo.

wadding ['wɔdɪŋ] n relleno.

waddle ['wɔdl] vi anadear.

wade [weɪd] vi: **to ~ through** caminar por el agua; (fig: a book) leer con dificultad.

wading pool ['weɪdɪŋ-] n (US) piscina para niños.

wafer ['weɪfə*] n (biscuit) galleta, barquillo; (REL) oblea; (COMPUT) oblea, microplaqueta.

wafer-thin ['weɪfə'θɪn] a finísimo.

waffle ['wɔfl] n (CULIN) gofre m ◆ vi dar el rollo.

waffle iron n molde m para hacer gofres.

waft [wɔft] vt llevar por el aire ◆ vi flotar.

wag [wæg] vt menear, agitar ◆ vi moverse, menearse; **the dog ~ged its tail** el perro

meneó la cola.

wage [weɪdʒ] n (also: **~s**) sueldo, salario ◆ vt: **to ~ war** hacer la guerra; **a day's ~** un día de salario.

wage claim n reivindicación f salarial.

wage differential n diferencia salarial.

wage earner n asalariado/a.

wage freeze n congelación f de los salarios.

wage packet n sobre m de paga.

wager ['weɪdʒə*] n apuesta ◆ vt apostar.

waggle ['wægl] vt menear, mover.

wag(g)on ['wægən] n (horse-drawn) carro; (Brit RAIL) vagón m.

wail [weɪl] n gemido ◆ vi gemir.

waist [weɪst] n cintura, talle m.

waistcoat ['weɪstkəʊt] n (Brit) chaleco.

waistline ['weɪstlaɪn] n talle m.

wait [weɪt] n espera; (interval) pausa ◆ vi esperar; **to lie in ~ for** acechar a; **I can't ~ to** (fig) estoy deseando; **to ~ for** esperar (a); **to keep sb ~ing** hacer esperar a uno; **~ a moment!** ¡un momento!, ¡un momentito! (LAm); **"repairs while you ~"** "reparaciones en el acto".

wait behind vi quedarse.

wait on vt fus servir a.

wait up vi quedarse levantado.

waiter ['weɪtə*] n camarero.

waiting ['weɪtɪŋ] n: **"no ~"** (Brit AUT) "prohibido estacionarse".

waiting list n lista de espera.

waiting room n sala de espera.

waitress ['weɪtrɪs] n camarera.

waive [weɪv] vt suspender.

waiver ['weɪvə*] n renuncia.

wake [weɪk] vb (pt **woke** or **waked**, pp **woken** or **waked**) [wəʊk, 'wəʊkn] vt (also: **~ up**) despertar ◆ vi (also: **~ up**) despertarse ◆ n (for dead person) vela, velatorio; (NAUT) estela; **to ~ up to sth** (fig) darse cuenta de algo; **in the ~ of** tras, después de; **to follow in sb's ~** (fig) seguir las huellas de uno.

waken ['weɪkn] vt, vi = **wake**.

Wales [weɪlz] n País m de Gales.

walk [wɔːk] n (stroll) paseo; (hike) excursión f a pie, caminata; (gait) paso, andar m; (in park etc) paseo, alameda ◆ vi andar, caminar; (for pleasure, exercise) pasearse ◆ vt (distance) recorrer a pie, andar; (dog) pasear; **to go for a ~** ir de paseo; **10 minutes' ~ from here** a 10 minutos de aquí andando; **people from all ~s of life** gente de todas las esferas; **to ~ in one's sleep** ser sonámbulo/a; **I'll ~ you home** te acompañaré a casa.

walk out vi (go out) salir; (as protest) salirse; (strike) declararse en huelga; **to ~ out on sb** abandonar a uno.

walker ['wɔːkə*] n (person) paseante m/f, caminante m/f.

walkie-talkie ['wɔːkɪ'tɔːkɪ] n walkie-talkie

m.

walking ['wɔːkɪŋ] *n* el andar; **it's within ~ distance** se puede ir andando *or* a pie.

walking shoes *npl* zapatos *mpl* para andar.

walking stick *n* bastón *m*.

walk-on ['wɔːkɔn] *a* (*THEATRE*: *part*) de comparsa.

walkout ['wɔːkaut] *n* (*of workers*) huelga.

walkover ['wɔːkəuvə*] *n* (*col*) pan *m* comido.

walkway ['wɔːkweɪ] *n* paseo.

wall [wɔːl] *n* pared *f*; (*exterior*) muro; (*city ~ etc*) muralla; **to go to the ~** (*fig*: *firm etc*) quebrar, ir a la bancarrota.

wall in *vt* (*garden etc*) cercar con una tapia.

walled [wɔːld] *a* (*city*) amurallado; (*garden*) con tapia.

wallet ['wɔlɪt] *n* cartera, billetera (*LAm*).

wallflower ['wɔːlflauə*] *n* alhelí *m*; **to be a ~** (*fig*) comer pavo.

wall hanging *n* tapiz *m*.

wallop ['wɔləp] *vt* (*col*) zurrar.

wallow ['wɔləu] *vi* revolcarse; **to ~ in one's grief** sumirse en su pena.

wallpaper ['wɔːlpeɪpə*] *n* papel *m* pintado.

wall-to-wall ['wɔːltə'wɔːl] *a*: **~ carpeting** moqueta.

wally ['wɔlɪ] *n* (*col*) palurdo/a, majadero/a.

walnut ['wɔːlnʌt] *n* nuez *f*; (*tree*) nogal *m*.

walrus, *pl* **~** *or* **~es**, ['wɔːlrəs] *n* morsa.

waltz [wɔːlts] *n* vals *m* ♦ *vi* bailar el vals.

wan [wɔn] *a* pálido.

wand [wɔnd] *n* (*also*: **magic ~**) varita (mágica).

wander ['wɔndə*] *vi* (*person*) vagar; deambular; (*thoughts*) divagar; (*get lost*) extraviarse ♦ *vt* recorrer, vagar por.

wanderer ['wɔndərə*] *n* vagabundo/a.

wandering ['wɔndərɪŋ] *a* (*tribe*) nómada; (*minstrel, actor*) ambulante; (*path, river*) sinuoso; (*glance, mind*) distraído.

wane [weɪn] *vi* menguar.

wangle ['wæŋgl] (*Brit col*) *vt*: **to ~ sth** agenciarse *or* conseguir algo ♦ *n* chanchullo.

want [wɔnt] *vt* (*wish for*) querer, desear; (*need*) necesitar; (*lack*) carecer de ♦ *n* (*poverty*) pobreza; **for ~ of** por falta de; **~s** *npl* (*needs*) necesidades *fpl*; **to ~ to do** querer hacer; **to ~ sb to do sth** querer que uno haga algo; **you're ~ed on the phone** te llaman al teléfono; **to be in ~** estar necesitado; **"cook ~ed"** "se busca cocinero/a".

want ads *npl* (*US*) anuncios *mpl* por palabras.

wanting ['wɔntɪŋ] *a*: **to be ~ (in)** estar falto (de); **to be found ~** no estar a la altura de las circunstancias.

wanton ['wɔntn] *a* (*playful*) juguetón/ona; (*licentious*) lascivo.

war [wɔː*] *n* guerra; **to make ~** hacer la guerra.

warble ['wɔːbl] *n* (*of bird*) trino, gorjeo ♦ *vi* (*bird*) trinar.

war cry *n* grito de guerra.

ward [wɔːd] *n* (*in hospital*) sala; (*POL*) distrito electoral; (*LAW*: *child*) pupilo/a.

ward off *vt* desviar, parar; (*attack*) rechazar.

warden ['wɔːdn] *n* (*Brit*: *of institution*) director(a) *m/f*; (*of park, game reserve*) guardián/ana *m/f*; (*Brit*: *also*: **traffic ~**) guardia *m/f*.

warder ['wɔːdə*] *n* (*Brit*) guardián/ana *m/f*, carcelero/a.

wardrobe ['wɔːdrəub] *n* armario, guardarropa, ropero (*esp LAm*).

warehouse ['wɛəhaus] *n* almacén *m*, depósito.

wares [wɛəz] *npl* mercancías *fpl*.

warfare ['wɔːfɛə*] *n* guerra.

war game *n* juego de estrategia militar.

warhead ['wɔːhed] *n* cabeza armada; **nuclear ~s** cabezas *fpl* armadas.

warily ['wɛərɪlɪ] *ad* con cautela, cautelosamente.

warlike ['wɔːlaɪk] *a* guerrero.

warm [wɔːm] *a* caliente; (*person, greeting, heart*) afectuoso, cariñoso; (*supporter*) entusiasta; (*thanks, congratulations, apologies*) efusivo; (*clothes etc*) que abriga; (*welcome, day*) caluroso; **it's ~** hace calor; **I'm ~** tengo calor; **to keep sth ~** mantener algo caliente.

warm up *vi* (*room*) calentarse; (*person*) entrar en calor; (*athlete*) hacer ejercicios de calentamiento; (*discussion*) acalorarse ♦ *vt* calentar.

warm-blooded ['wɔːm'blʌdɪd] *a* de sangre caliente.

war memorial *n* monumento a los caídos.

warm-hearted [wɔːm'hɑːtɪd] *a* afectuoso.

warmly ['wɔːmlɪ] *ad* afectuosamente.

warmonger ['wɔːmʌŋgə*] *n* belicista *m/f*.

warmongering ['wɔːmʌŋgrɪŋ] *n* belicismo.

warmth [wɔːmθ] *n* calor *m*.

warm-up ['wɔːmʌp] *n* (*SPORT*) ejercicios *mpl* de calentamiento.

warn [wɔːn] *vt* avisar, advertir; **to ~ sb not to do sth** *or* **against doing sth** aconsejar a uno que no haga algo.

warning ['wɔːnɪŋ] *n* aviso, advertencia; **gale ~** (*METEOROLOGY*) aviso de vendaval; **without (any) ~** sin aviso *or* avisar.

warning light *n* luz *f* de advertencia.

warning triangle *n* (*AUT*) triángulo señalizador.

warp [wɔːp] *vi* (*wood*) combarse.

warpath ['wɔːpɑːθ] *n*: **to be on the ~** (*fig*) estar en pie de guerra.

warped [wɔːpt] *a* (*wood*) alabeado; (*fig*: *character, sense of humour etc*) pervertido.

warrant ['wɔrnt] *n* (*LAW*: *to arrest*) orden *f*

de detención; (: *to search*) mandamiento de registro ◆ *vt* (*justify*, *merit*) merecer.

warrant officer *n* (*MIL*) brigada *m*; (*NAUT*) contramaestre *m*.

warranty ['wɔrəntɪ] *n* garantía; **under** ~ (*COMM*) bajo garantía.

warren ['wɔrən] *n* (*of rabbits*) madriguera; (*fig*) laberinto.

warring ['wɔːrɪŋ] *a* (*interests etc*) opuesto; (*nations*) en guerra.

warrior ['wɔrɪə*] *n* guerrero/a.

Warsaw ['wɔːsɔː] *n* Varsovia.

warship ['wɔːʃɪp] *n* buque *m* o barco de guerra.

wart [wɔːt] *n* verruga.

wartime ['wɔːtaɪm] *n*: **in** ~ en tiempos de guerra, en la guerra.

wary ['wɛərɪ] *a* cauteloso; **to be** ~ **about** *or* **of doing sth** tener cuidado con hacer algo.

was [wɔz] *pt of* **be.**

wash [wɔʃ] *vt* lavar; (*sweep, carry*: *sea etc*) llevar ◆ *vi* lavarse ◆ *n* (*clothes etc*) lavado; (*bath*) baño; (*of ship*) estela; **he was** ~**ed overboard** fue arrastrado del barco por las olas; **to have a** ~ lavarse.

wash away *vt* (*stain*) quitar lavando; (*subj*: *river etc*) llevarse; (*fig*) limpiar.

wash down *vt* lavar.

wash off *vt* quitar lavando.

wash up *vi* (*Brit*) fregar los platos; (*US*) *have a wash*) lavarse.

washable ['wɔʃəbl] *a* lavable.

washbasin ['wɔʃbeɪsn], (*US*) **washbowl** ['wɔʃbəul] *n* lavabo.

washcloth ['wɔʃklɔθ] *n* (*US*) manopla.

washer ['wɔʃə*] *n* (*TECH*) arandela.

wash-hand basin ['wɔʃhænd-] *n* (*Brit*) lavabo.

washing ['wɔʃɪŋ] *n* (*dirty*) ropa sucia; (*clean*) colada.

washing line *n* cuerda de (colgar) la ropa.

washing machine *n* lavadora.

washing powder *n* (*Brit*) detergente *m* (en polvo).

Washington ['wɔʃɪŋtən] *n* (*city, state*) Washington *m*.

washing-up [wɔʃɪŋ'ʌp] *n* fregado, platos *mpl* (para fregar).

washing-up liquid *n* (detergente *m*) lavavajillas *m inv*.

wash leather *n* gamuza.

wash-out ['wɔʃaut] *n* (*col*) fracaso.

washroom ['wɔʃrum] *n* servicios *mpl*.

wasn't ['wɔznt] = **was not.**

Wasp, WASP [wɔsp] *n* *abbr* (*US col*: = *White Anglo-Saxon Protestant*) *sobrenombre, en general peyorativo, que se da a los americanos de origen anglosajón, acomodados y de tendencia conservadora.*

wasp [wɔsp] *n* avispa.

waspish ['wɔspɪʃ] *a* (*character*) irascible; (*comment*) mordaz, punzante.

wastage ['weɪstɪdʒ] *n* desgaste *m*; (*loss*) pérdida; **natural** ~ desgaste natural.

waste [weɪst] *n* derroche *m*, despilfarro; (*misuse*) desgaste *m*; (*of time*) pérdida; (*food*) sobras *fpl*; (*rubbish*) basura, desperdicios *mpl* ◆ *a* (*material*) de desecho; (*left over*) sobrante; (*energy, heat*) desperdiciado; (*land, ground*: *in city*) sin construir; (: *in country*) baldío ◆ *vt* (*squander*) malgastar, derrochar; (*time*) perder; (*opportunity*) desperdiciar; ~**s** *npl* (*area of land*) tierras *fpl* baldías; **to lay** ~ devastar, arrasar; **it's a** ~ **of money** es dinero perdido; **to go to** ~ desperdiciarse.

waste away *vi* consumirse.

wastebin ['weɪstbɪn] *n* cubo *or* bote *m* (*LAm*) de la basura.

waste disposal (unit) *n* (*Brit*) triturador *m* de basura.

wasteful ['weɪstful] *a* derrochador(a); (*process*) antieconómico.

wastefully ['weɪstfulɪ] *ad* derrochadoramente; antieconómicamente.

waste ground *n* (*Brit*) terreno baldío.

wasteland ['weɪstlənd] *n* (*urban*) descampados *mpl*.

wastepaper basket ['weɪstpeɪpə-] *n* papelera.

waste pipe *n* tubo de desagüe.

waste products *npl* (*INDUSTRY*) residuos *mpl*.

watch [wɔtʃ] *n* reloj *m*; (*vigil*) vigilia; (*vigilance*) vigilancia; (*MIL*: *guard*) centinela *m*; (*NAUT*: *spell of duty*) guardia ◆ *vt* (*look at*) mirar, observar; (: *match, programme*) ver; (*spy on, guard*) vigilar; (*be careful of*) cuidarse de, tener cuidado de ◆ *vi* ver, mirar; (*keep guard*) montar guardia; **to keep a close** ~ **on sth/sb** vigilar algo/a uno de cerca; ~ **how you drive/ what you're doing** ten cuidado al conducir/con lo que haces.

watch out *vi* cuidarse, tener cuidado.

watch band *n* (*US*) pulsera (de reloj).

watchdog ['wɔtʃdɔg] *n* perro guardián; (*fig*) autoridad *f* protectora.

watchful ['wɔtʃful] *a* vigilante, sobre aviso.

watchfully ['wɔtʃfulɪ] *ad* vigilantemente.

watchmaker ['wɔtʃmeɪkə*] *n* relojero/a.

watchman *n* guardián *m*; (*also*: **night** ~) sereno, vigilante *m* (*LAm*); (*in factory*) vigilante *m* nocturno.

watch stem *n* (*US*) cuerda.

watch strap *n* pulsera (de reloj).

watchword ['wɔtʃwəːd] *n* consigna, contraseña.

water ['wɔːtə*] *n* agua ◆ *vt* (*plant*) regar ◆ *vi* (*eyes*) llorar; **I'd like a drink of** ~ quisiera un vaso de agua; **in British** ~**s** en aguas británicas; **to pass** ~ hacer aguas; **to make sb's mouth** ~ hacerle la boca agua a uno.

water down *vt* (*milk etc*) aguar.

water closet *n* wáter *m*.

watercolour, (*US*) **watercolor** ['wɔːtə-kʌlə*] *n* acuarela.

water-cooled ['wɔːtəkuːld] *a* refrigerado (por agua).

watercress ['wɔːtəkrɛs] *n* berro.

waterfall ['wɔːtəfɔːl] *n* cascada, salto de agua.

waterfront ['wɔːtəfrʌnt] *n* (*seafront*) parte *f* que da al mar; (*at docks*) muelles *mpl*.

water heater *n* calentador *m* de agua.

water hole *n* abrevadero.

watering can ['wɔːtərɪŋ-] *n* regadera.

water level *n* nivel *m* del agua.

water lily *n* nenúfar *m*.

waterline ['wɔːtəlaɪn] *n* (*NAUT*) línea de flotación.

waterlogged ['wɔːtəlɔgd] *a* (*boat*) anegado; (*ground*) inundado.

water main *n* cañería del agua.

watermark ['wɔːtəmɑːk] *n* (*on paper*) filigrana.

watermelon ['wɔːtəmɛlən] *n* sandía.

water polo *n* polo acuático.

waterproof ['wɔːtəpruːf] *a* impermeable.

water-repellent ['wɔːtərɪ'pɛlənt] *a* hidrófugo.

watershed ['wɔːtəʃɛd] *n* (*GEO*) cuenca; (*fig*) momento crítico.

water-skiing ['wɔːtəskiːɪŋ] *n* esquí *m* acuático.

water softener *n* ablandador *m* de agua.

water tank *n* depósito de agua.

watertight ['wɔːtətaɪt] *a* hermético.

water vapour, (*US*) **water vapor** *n* vapor *m* de agua.

waterway ['wɔːtəweɪ] *n* vía fluvial *or* navegable.

waterworks ['wɔːtəwɔːks] *npl* central *fsg* depuradora.

watery ['wɔːtərɪ] *a* (*colour*) desvaído; (*coffee*) aguado; (*eyes*) lloroso.

watt [wɔt] *n* vatio.

wattage ['wɔtɪdʒ] *n* potencia en vatios.

wattle ['wɔtl] *n* zarzo.

wave [weɪv] *n* ola; (*of hand*) señal *f* con la mano; (*RADIO, in hair*) onda; (*fig: of enthusiasm, strikes*) oleada ♦ *vi* agitar la mano; (*flag*) ondear ♦ *vt* (*handkerchief, gun*) agitar; **short/medium/long ~** (*RADIO*) onda corta/media/larga; **the new ~** (*CINEMA, MUS*) la nueva ola; **to ~ goodbye to sb** decir adiós a uno con la mano; **he ~d us over to his table** nos hizo señas (con la mano) para que fuéramos a su mesa.

wave aside, wave away *vt* (*person*): **to ~ sb aside** apartar a uno con la mano; (*fig: suggestion, objection*) rechazar; (*doubts*) desechar.

waveband ['weɪvbænd] *n* banda de ondas.

wavelength ['weɪvlɛŋθ] *n* longitud *f* de onda.

waver ['weɪvə*] *vi* oscilar; (*confidence*) disminuir; (*faith*) flaquear.

wavy ['weɪvɪ] *a* ondulado.

wax [wæks] *n* cera ♦ *vt* encerar ♦ *vi* (*moon*) crecer.

waxen ['wæksn] *a* (*fig: pale*) blanco como la cera.

waxworks ['wækswɔːks] *npl* museo *sg* de cera.

way [weɪ] *n* camino; (*distance*) trayecto, recorrido; (*direction*) dirección *f*, sentido; (*manner*) modo, manera; (*habit*) costumbre *f*; **which ~? — this ~** ¿por dónde? *or* ¿en qué dirección? — por aquí; **on the ~** (*en route*) en (el) camino; (*expected*) en camino; **you pass it on your ~ home** está en el camino a tu casa; **to be in the ~** bloquear el camino; (*fig*) estorbar; **to keep out of sb's ~** esquivar a uno; **to make ~ (for sb/sth)** dejar paso (a uno/algo); (*fig*) abrir camino (a uno/algo); **to go out of one's ~ to do sth** desvivirse por hacer algo; **to lose one's ~** perderse, extraviarse; **to be the wrong ~ round** estar del *or* al revés; **in a ~** en cierto modo *or* sentido; **by the ~** a propósito; **by ~ of** (*via*) pasando por; (*as a sort of*) como, a modo de; **"~ in"** (*Brit*) "entrada"; **"~ out"** (*Brit*) "salida"; **the ~ back** el camino de vuelta; **the village is rather out of the ~** el pueblo está un poco apartado *or* retirado; **it's a long ~ away** está muy lejos; **to get one's own ~** salirse con la suya; **"give ~"** (*Brit AUT*) "ceda el paso"; **no ~!** (*col*) ¡ni pensarlo!; **put it the right ~ up** ponlo boca arriba; **he's in a bad ~** está grave; **to be under ~** (*work, project*) estar en marcha.

waybill ['weɪbɪl] *n* (*COMM*) hoja de ruta, carta de porte.

waylay [weɪ'leɪ] *vt* (*irg: like* lay) atacar.

wayside ['weɪsaɪd] *n* borde *m* del camino; **to fall by the ~** (*fig*) fracasar.

way station *n* (*US RAIL*) apeadero; (*fig*) paso intermedio.

wayward ['weɪwəd] *a* díscolo, caprichoso.

WC ['dʌblju'siː] *n* abbr (*Brit:* = *water closet*) wáter *m*.

WCC *n* abbr = World Council of Churches.

we [wiː] *pl* pron nosotros/as; **~ understand** (nosotros) entendemos; **here ~ are** aquí estamos.

weak [wiːk] *a* débil, flojo; (*tea, coffee*) flojo, aguado; **to grow ~(er)** debilitarse.

weaken ['wiːkən] *vi* debilitarse; (*give way*) ceder ♦ *vt* debilitar.

weak-kneed [wiːk'niːd] *a* (*fig*) sin voluntad *or* carácter.

weakling ['wiːklɪŋ] *n* debilucho/a.

weakly ['wiːklɪ] *a* enfermizo, débil ♦ *ad* débilmente.

weakness ['wiːknɪs] *n* debilidad *f*; (*fault*) punto débil.

wealth [wɛlθ] *n* (*money*, *resources*) riqueza; (*of details*) abundancia.
wealth tax *n* impuesto sobre el patrimonio.
wealthy ['wɛlθɪ] *a* rico.
wean [wiːn] *vt* destetar.
weapon ['wɛpən] *n* arma.
wear [wɛə*] *n* (*use*) uso; (*deterioration
through use*) desgaste *m*; (*clothing*):
sports/baby~ ropa de deportes/de niños ♦
vb (*pt* **wore**, *pp* **worn** [wɔ:*, wɔ:n]) *vt*
(*clothes*, *beard*) llevar; (*shoes*) calzar;
(*look*, *smile*) tener; (*damage: through use*)
gastar, usar ♦ *vi* (*last*) durar; (*rub
through etc*) desgastarse; **evening** ~
(*man's*) traje *m* de etiqueta; (*woman's*)
traje *m* de noche; **to** ~ **a hole in sth** hacer
un agujero en algo.
wear away *vt* gastar ♦ *vi* desgastarse.
wear down *vt* gastar; (*strength*)
agotar.
wear off *vi* (*pain*, *excitement etc*) pasar,
desaparecer.
wear out *vt* desgastar; (*person*,
strength) agotar.
wearable ['wɛərəbl] *a* que se puede llevar.
wear and tear *n* desgaste *m*.
wearer ['wɛərə*] *n*: **the** ~ **of this jacket** el/
la que lleva puesta esta chaqueta.
wearily ['wɪərɪlɪ] *ad* con cansancio.
weariness ['wɪərɪnɪs] *n* cansancio; abatimiento.
wearisome ['wɪərɪsəm] *a* (*tiring*) cansado,
pesado; (*boring*) aburrido.
weary ['wɪərɪ] *a* (*tired*) cansado; (*dispirited*) abatido ♦ *vt* cansar ♦ *vi*: **to** ~ **of**
cansarse de, aburrirse de.
weasel ['wiːzl] *n* (*ZOOL*) comadreja.
weather ['wɛðə*] *n* tiempo ♦ *vt* (*storm*,
crisis) hacer frente a; **under the** ~ (*fig:
ill*) mal, indispuesto; **what's the** ~ **like?**
¿qué tiempo hace?
weather-beaten ['wɛðəbiːtn] *a* curtido.
weathercock ['wɛðəkɔk] *n* veleta.
weather forecast *n* boletín *m* meteorológico.
weatherman ['wɛðəmæn] *n* hombre *m* del
tiempo.
weatherproof ['wɛðəpruːf] *a* (*garment*)
impermeable.
weather report *n* parte *m* meteorológico.
weather vane *n* = **weathercock**.
weave, *pt* **wove**, *pp* **woven** [wiːv, wəuv,
'wəuvn] *vt* (*cloth*) tejer; (*fig*) entretejer ♦
vi (*fig: pt*, *pp* ~**d**: *move in and out*) zigzaguear.
weaver ['wiːvə*] *n* tejedor(a) *m/f*.
weaving ['wiːvɪŋ] *n* tejeduría.
web [wɛb] *n* (*of spider*) telaraña; (*on foot*)
membrana; (*network*) red *f*.
webbed [wɛbd] *a* (*foot*) palmeado.
webbing ['wɛbɪŋ] *n* (*on chair*) cinchas *fpl*.
wed [wɛd] *vt* (*pt*, *pp* **wedded**) casar ♦ *n*:

the newly-~**s** los recién casados.
Wed. *abbr* (= *Wednesday*) miérc.
we'd [wiːd] = **we had, we would**.
wedded ['wɛdɪd] *pt*, *pp* of **wed**.
wedding ['wɛdɪŋ] *n* boda, casamiento.
wedding anniversary *a* aniversario de
boda; **silver/golden** ~ bodas *fpl* de plata/de
oro.
wedding day *n* día *m* de la boda.
wedding dress *n* traje *m* de novia.
wedding present *n* regalo de boda.
wedding ring *n* alianza.
wedge [wɛdʒ] *n* (*of wood etc*) cuña; (*of
cake*) trozo ♦ *vt* acuñar; (*push*) apretar.
wedge-heeled ['wɛdʒ'hiːld] *a* con suela de
cuña.
wedlock ['wɛdlɔk] *n* matrimonio.
Wednesday ['wɛdnzdɪ] *n* miércoles *m inv*.
wee [wiː] *a* (*Scottish*) pequeñito.
weed [wiːd] *n* mala hierba, maleza ♦ *vt*
escardar, desherbar.
weedkiller ['wiːdkɪlə*] *n* herbicida *m*.
weedy ['wiːdɪ] *a* (*person*) debilucho.
week [wiːk] *n* semana; **a** ~ **today** de hoy en
ocho días; **Tuesday** ~, **a** ~ **on Tuesday** de
martes en una semana; **once/twice a** ~
una vez/dos veces a la semana; **this** ~ esta
semana; **in 2** ~**s'** **time** dentro de 2 semanas; **every other** ~ cada 2 semanas.
weekday ['wiːkdeɪ] *n* día *m* laborable; **on**
~**s** entre semana, en días laborables.
weekend [wiːk'ɛnd] *n* fin *m* de semana.
weekend case *n* neceser *m*.
weekly ['wiːklɪ] *ad* semanalmente, cada semana ♦ *a* semanal ♦ *n* semanario; ~
newspaper semanario.
weep, *pt*, *pp* **wept** [wiːp, wɛpt] *vi*, *vt* llorar;
(*MED: wound etc*) supurar.
weeping willow ['wiːpɪŋ-] *n* sauce *m* llorón.
weft [wɛft] *n* (*TEXTILES*) trama.
weigh [weɪ] *vt*, *vi* pesar; **to** ~ **anchor** levar
anclas; **to** ~ **the pros and cons** pesar el
pro y el contra.
weigh down *vt* sobrecargar; (*fig: with
worry*) agobiar.
weigh out *vt* (*goods*) pesar.
weigh up *vt* pesar.
weighbridge ['weɪbrɪdʒ] *n* báscula para
camiones.
weighing machine ['weɪɪŋ-] *n* báscula,
peso.
weight [weɪt] *n* peso; (*on scale*) pesa; **to
lose/put on** ~ adelgazar/engordar; ~**s and
measures** pesas y medidas.
weighting ['weɪtɪŋ] *n* (*allowance*):
(London) ~ dietas *fpl* (por residir en
Londres).
weightlessness ['weɪtlɪsnɪs] *n* ingravidez
f.
weight lifter *n* levantador(a) *m/f* de
pesas.
weight limit *n* límite *m* de peso.

weighty ['weɪtɪ] *a* pesado.
weir [wɪə*] *n* presa.
weird [wɪəd] *a* raro, extraño.
welcome ['welkəm] *a* bienvenido ◆ *n*
bienvenida ◆ *vt* dar la bienvenida a; (*be
glad of*) alegrarse de; **to make sb** ~ recibir *or* acoger bien a uno; **thank you —
you're** ~ gracias — de nada; **you're** ~ **to
try** puede intentar cuando quiera; **we** ~
this step celebramos esta medida.
weld [weld] *n* soldadura ◆ *vt* soldar.
welding ['weldɪŋ] *n* soldadura.
welfare ['welfeə*] *n* bienestar *m*; (*social
aid*) asistencia social; **W~** (*US*) subsidio de
paro; **to look after sb's** ~ cuidar del
bienestar de uno.
welfare state *n* estado benefactor.
welfare work *n* asistencia social.
well [wel] *n* fuente *f*, pozo ◆ *ad* bien ◆ *a*:
to be ~ estar bien (de salud) ◆ *excl*
¡vaya!, ¡bueno!; **as** ~ (*in addition*) además, también; **as** ~ **as** además de; **you
might as** ~ **tell me** más vale decírmelo; **it
would be as** ~ **to ask** más valdría preguntar; ~ **done!** ¡bien hecho!; **get** ~
soon! ¡que te mejores pronto!; **to do** ~
(*business*) ir bien; (*in exam*) salir bien; **to
be doing** ~ ir bien; **to think** ~ **of sb**
pensar bien de uno; **I don't feel** ~ no me
encuentro *or* siento bien; ~, **as I was saying** ... bueno, como decía ... .
well up *vi* brotar.
we'll [wiːl] = **we will, we shall**.
well-behaved ['welbɪ'heɪvd] *a* modoso.
well-being ['wel'biːɪŋ] *n* bienestar *m*.
well-bred ['wel'bred] *a* bien educado.
well-built ['wel'bɪlt] *a* (*person*) fornido.
well-chosen ['wel'tʃəuzn] *a* (*remarks,
words*) acertado.
well-deserved ['weldɪ'zɜːvd] *a* merecido.
well-developed ['weldɪ'veləpt] *a* (*arm,
muscle etc*) bien desarrollado; (*sense*)
agudo, fino.
well-disposed ['weldɪs'pəuzd] *a*: ~
to(wards) bien dispuesto a.
well-dressed ['wel'drest] *a* bien vestido.
well-earned ['welɜːnd] *a* (*rest*) merecido.
well-groomed ['wel'gruːmd] *a* de apariencia cuidada.
well-heeled ['wel'hiːld] *a* (*col*: *wealthy*)
rico.
well-informed ['welɪn'fɔːmd] *a* (*having
knowledge of sth*) enterado, al corriente.
Wellington ['welɪŋtən] *n* Wellington *m*.
wellingtons ['welɪŋtənz] *npl* (*also*: **Wellington boots**) botas *fpl* de goma.
well-kept ['wel'kept] *a* (*secret*) bien
guardado; (*hair, hands, house, grounds*)
bien cuidado.
well-known ['wel'nəun] *a* (*person*) conocido.
well-mannered ['wel'mænəd] *a* educado.
well-meaning ['wel'miːnɪŋ] *a* bienintencio-

nado.
well-nigh ['wel'naɪ] *ad*: ~ **impossible** casi
imposible.
well-off ['wel'ɔf] *a* acomodado.
well-read ['wel'red] *a* culto.
well-spoken ['wel'spəukən] *a* bienhablado.
well-stocked ['wel'stɔkt] *a* (*shop, larder*)
bien surtido.
well-timed ['wel'taɪmd] *a* oportuno.
well-to-do ['weltə'duː] *a* acomodado.
well-wisher ['welwɪʃə*] *n* admirador(a)
m/f.
Welsh [welʃ] *a* galés/esa ◆ *n* (*LING*) galés
m; **the** ~ *npl* los galeses.
Welshman ['welʃmən] *n* galés *m*.
Welsh rarebit [-'reəbɪt] *n* pan *m* con queso
tostado.
Welshwoman ['welʃwumən] *n* galesa.
welter ['weltə*] *n* mescolanza, revoltijo.
went [went] *pt of* **go**.
wept [wept] *pt, pp of* **weep**.
were [wɜː*] *pt of* **be**.
we're [wɪə*] = **we are**.
weren't [wɜːnt] = **were not**.
werewolf, *pl* **-wolves** ['wɪəwulf, -wulvz] *n*
hombre *m* lobo.
west [west] *n* oeste *m* ◆ *a* occidental, del
oeste ◆ *ad* al *or* hacia el oeste; **the W~** el
Oeste, el Occidente.
westbound ['westbaund] *a* (*traffic,
carriageway*) con rumbo al oeste.
West Country *n*: **the** ~ el suroeste de Inglaterra.
westerly ['westəlɪ] *a* (*wind*) del oeste.
western ['westən] *a* occidental ◆ *n* (*CINE-
MA*) película del oeste.
westernized ['westənaɪzd] *a* occidentaliza-
do.
West German *a* de Alemania Occidental
◆ *n* alemán/ana *m/f* (de Alemania Occidental.
West Germany *n* Alemania Occidental.
West Indian *a, n* antillano/a *m/f*.
West Indies [-'ɪndɪz] *npl*: **the** ~ las Antillas, las Islas Occidentales.
westward(s) ['westwəd(z)] *ad* hacia el oeste.
wet [wet] *a* (*damp*) húmedo; (~ *through*)
mojado; (*rainy*) lluvioso ◆ *vt*: **to** ~ **one's
pants** *or* **o.s.** mojarse; **to get** ~ mojarse;
"~ **paint**" 'recién pintado'.
wet blanket *n*: **to be a** ~ (*fig*) ser un/una
aguafiestas.
wetness ['wetnɪs] *n* humedad *f*.
wet rot *n* putrefacción *f* húmeda.
wet suit *n* traje *m* de buzo.
we've [wiːv] = **we have**.
whack [wæk] *vt* dar un buen golpe a.
whale [weɪl] *n* (*ZOOL*) ballena.
whaler ['weɪlə*] *n* (*ship*) ballenero.
wharf, *pl* **wharves** [wɔːf, wɔːvz] *n* muelle
m.
what [wɔt] *excl* ¡qué!, ¡cómo! ◆ *a* que ◆

pron (*interrogative*) qué, cómo; (*relative*, *indirect*: *object*) lo que; (: *subject*) el/la que; **for ~ reason?** ¿por qué (razón)?; **~ are you doing?** ¿qué haces?; **~'s happening?** ¿qué pasa?; **I don't know ~ to do** no sé qué hacer; **I saw ~ you did** he visto lo que hiciste; **~ a mess!** ¡qué lío!; **~ is it called?** ¿cómo se llama?; **~ is his address?** ¿cuáles son sus señas?; **~ will it cost?** ¿cuánto costará?; **~ about me?** ¿y yo?; **~ I want is a cup of tea** lo que quiero es una taza de té.

whatever [wɔt'ɛvə*] *a*: **~ book you choose** cualquier libro que elijas ♦ *pron*: **do ~ is necessary** haga lo que sea necesario; **no reason ~** ninguna razón sea la que sea; **nothing ~** nada en absoluto; **~ it costs** cueste lo que cueste.

wheat [wi:t] *n* trigo.

wheatgerm ['wi:tdʒə:m] *n* germen *m* de trigo.

wheatmeal ['wi:tmi:l] *n* harina integral.

wheedle ['wi:dl] *vt*: **to ~ sb into doing sth** engatusar a uno para que haga algo *or* para hacer algo; **to ~ sth out of sb** sonsacar algo a uno.

wheel [wi:l] *n* rueda; (*AUT*: *also*: **steering ~**) volante *m*; (*NAUT*) timón *m* ♦ *vt* (*pram etc*) empujar ♦ *vi* (*also*: **~ round**) dar la vuelta, girar; **four-~ drive** tracción *f* en las cuatro ruedas; **front-/rear-~ drive** tracción *f* delantera/trasera.

wheelbarrow ['wi:lbærəu] *n* carretilla.

wheelbase ['wi:lbeɪs] *n* batalla.

wheelchair ['wi:ltʃɛə*] *n* silla de ruedas.

wheel clamp *n* (*AUT*) cepo.

wheeler-dealer ['wi:lə'di:lə*] *n* negociante *m/f* muy astuto/a.

wheeling ['wi:lɪŋ] *n*: **~ and dealing** (*col*) intrigas *fpl*.

wheeze [wi:z] *vi* resollar.

when [wɛn] *ad* cuándo ♦ *conj* cuando; (*whereas*) mientras; **on the day ~ I met him** el día que le conocí; **that's ~ the train arrives** eso es cuando llega el tren.

whenever [wɛn'ɛvə*] *conj* cuando; (*every time*) cada vez que; **I go ~ I can** voy siempre *or* todas las veces que puedo.

where [wɛə*] *ad* dónde ♦ *conj* donde; **this is ~** aquí es donde; **~ possible** donde sea posible; **~ are you from?** ¿de dónde es usted?

whereabouts ['wɛərəbauts] *ad* dónde ♦ *n*: **nobody knows his ~** nadie conoce su paradero.

whereas [wɛər'æz] *conj* visto que, mientras.

whereby [wɛə'baɪ] *ad* mediante el/la cual *etc*.

whereupon [wɛərə'pɔn] *conj* con lo cual, después de lo cual.

wherever [wɛər'ɛvə*] *ad* dondequiera que; (*interrogative*) dónde; **sit ~ you like** siéntese donde quiera.

wherewithal ['wɛəwɪðɔ:l] *n* recursos *mpl*; **the ~ (to do sth)** los medios (para hacer algo).

whet [wɛt] *vt* estimular.

whether ['wɛðə*] *conj* si; **I don't know ~ to accept or not** no sé si aceptar o no; **~ you go or not** vayas o no vayas.

whey [weɪ] *n* suero.

which [wɪtʃ] *a* (*interrogative*) qué, cuál; **~ one of you?** ¿cuál de vosotros?; **~ picture do you want?** ¿qué cuadro quieres? ♦ *pron* (*interrogative*) ¿cuál?; (*relative*: *subject*) que, lo que; (: *object*) el que *etc*, el cual *etc*, lo cual; **after ~** después de lo cual; **~ do you want?** ¿cuál quieres?; **I don't mind ~** no me importa cuál; **the apple ~ is on the table** la manzana que está sobre la mesa; **the chair on ~ you are sitting** la silla sobre la que estás sentado; **he said he knew, ~ is true** el dijo que sabía, lo cual es cierto; **by ~ time** a esas alturas, para entonces; **in ~ case** en cuyo caso.

whichever [wɪtʃ'ɛvə*] *a*: **take ~ book you prefer** coja el libro que prefiera; **~ book you take** cualquier libro que coja.

whiff [wɪf] *n* bocanada; **to catch a ~ of sth** oler algo.

while [waɪl] *n* rato, momento ♦ *conj* durante; (*whereas*) mientras; (*although*) aunque ♦ *vt*: **to ~ away the time** pasar el rato; **for a ~** durante algún tiempo; **in a ~** dentro de poco; **all the ~** todo el tiempo; **we'll make it worth your ~** te lo compensaremos generosamente.

whilst [waɪlst] *conj* = **while**.

whim [wɪm] *n* capricho.

whimper ['wɪmpə*] *n* (*weeping*) lloriqueo; (*moan*) quejido ♦ *vi* lloriquear; quejarse.

whimsical ['wɪmzɪkl] *a* (*person*) caprichoso.

whine [waɪn] *n* (*of pain*) gemido; (*of engine*) zumbido ♦ *vi* gemir; zumbar.

whip [wɪp] *n* látigo; (*POL*: *person*) encargado/a de la disciplina partidaria en el parlamento ♦ *vt* azotar; (*snatch*) arrebatar; (*US CULIN*) batir.

whip up *vt* (*cream etc*) batir (rápidamente); (*col*: *meal*) preparar rápidamente; (: *stir up*: *support*, *feeling*) avivar.

whiplash ['wɪplæʃ] *n* (*MED*: *also*: **~ injury**) latigazo.

whipped cream [wɪpt-] *n* nata *or* crema montada.

whipping boy ['wɪpɪŋ-] *n* (*fig*) cabeza de turco.

whip-round ['wɪpraund] *n* (*Brit*) colecta.

whirl [wə:l] *n* remolino ♦ *vt* hacer girar, dar vueltas a ♦ *vi* (*dancers*) girar, dar vueltas; (*leaves*, *dust*, *water etc*) arremolinarse.

whirlpool ['wə:lpu:l] *n* remolino.

whirlwind ['wə:lwɪnd] *n* torbellino.

whirr [wə:*] *vi* zumbar.

whisk [wɪsk] *n* (*Brit CULIN*) batidor *m* ◆ *vt* (*Brit CULIN*) batir; **to ~ sb away** *or* **off** llevar volando a uno.

whiskers [wɪskəz] *npl* (*of animal*) bigotes *mpl*; (*of man*) patillas *fpl*.

whisky, (*US*, *Ireland*) **whiskey** [wɪskɪ] *n* whisky *m*.

whisper [wɪspə*] *n* cuchicheo; (*rumour*) rumor *m*; (*fig*) susurro, murmullo ◆ *vi* cuchichear, hablar bajo; (*fig*) susurrar ◆ *vt* decir en voz muy baja; **to ~ sth to sb** decirle algo al oído a uno.

whispering [wɪspərɪŋ] *n* cuchicheo.

whist [wɪst] *n* (*Brit*) whist *m*.

whistle [wɪsl] *n* (*sound*) silbido; (*object*) silbato ◆ *vi* silbar; **to ~ a tune** silbar una melodía.

whistle-stop [wɪslstɒp] *a*: **~ tour** (*US POL*) gira electoral rápida; (*fig*) recorrido rápido.

Whit [wɪt] *n* Pentecostés *m*.

white [waɪt] *a* blanco; (*pale*) pálido ◆ *n* blanco; (*of egg*) clara; **to turn** *or* **go ~** (*person*) palidecer, ponerse blanco; (*hair*) encanecer; **the ~s** (*washing*) la ropa blanca; **tennis ~s** ropa *f* de tenis.

whitebait [waɪtbeɪt] *n* morralla.

white coffee *n* (*Brit*) café *m* con leche.

white-collar worker [waɪtkɒlə-] *n* oficinista *m/f*.

white elephant *n* (*fig*) maula.

white goods *npl* (*appliances*) electrodomésticos *mpl* de línea blanca; (*linen etc*) lencería, ropa blanca.

white-hot [waɪthɒt] *a* (*metal*) calentado al (rojo) blanco.

white lie *n* mentirilla.

whiteness [waɪtnɪs] *n* blancura.

white noise *n* sonido blanco.

whiteout [waɪtaʊt] *n* resplandor *m* sin sombras; (*fig*) masa confusa.

white paper *n* (*POL*) libro rojo.

whitewash [waɪtwɒʃ] *n* (*paint*) jalbegue *m*, cal *f* ◆ *vt* (*also fig*) encubrir.

whiting [waɪtɪŋ] *n* (*pl inv*) (*fish*) pescadilla.

Whit Monday *n* lunes *m* de Pentecostés.

Whitsun [wɪtsn] *n* (*Brit*) Pentecostés *m*.

whittle [wɪtl] *vt*: **to ~ away**, **~ down** ir reduciendo.

whizz [wɪz] *vi*: **to ~ past** *or* **by** pasar a toda velocidad.

whizz kid *n* (*col*) prodigio/a.

WHO *n abbr* (= *World Health Organization*) OMS *f*.

who [hu:] *pron* (*relative*) que, el que *etc*, quien; (*interrogative*) quién; (*pl*) quiénes.

whodun(n)it [hu:dʌnɪt] *n* (*col*) novela policíaca.

whoever [hu:evə*] *pron*: **~ finds it** cualquiera *or* quienquiera que lo encuentre; **ask ~ you like** pregunta a quién quieras;

~ he marries no importa con quién se case.

whole [həʊl] *a* (*complete*) todo, entero; (*not broken*) intacto ◆ *n* (*total*) total *m*; (*sum*) conjunto; **~ villages were destroyed** pueblos enteros fueron destruídos; **the ~ of the town** toda la ciudad, la ciudad entera; **on the ~, as a ~** en general.

wholehearted [həʊlhɑːtɪd] *a* (*support, approval*) total; (*sympathy*) todo.

wholeheartedly [həʊlhɑːtɪdlɪ] *ad* con entusiasmo.

wholemeal [həʊlmiːl] *a* (*Brit*: *flour, bread*) integral.

wholesale [həʊlseɪl] *n* venta al por mayor ◆ *a* al por mayor; (*destruction*) sistemático.

wholesaler [həʊlseɪlə*] *n* mayorista *m/f*.

wholesome [həʊlsəm] *a* sano.

wholewheat [həʊlwiːt] *a* = **wholemeal**.

wholly [həʊlɪ] *ad* totalmente, enteramente.

whom [huːm] *pron* que, a quien; (*interrogative*) ¿a quién?; **those to ~ I spoke** aquéllos a *or* con los que hablé.

whooping cough [huːpɪŋ-] *n* tos *f* ferina.

whoosh [wuʃ] *n*: **it came out with a ~** (*sauce etc*) salió todo de repente; (*air*) salió con mucho ruido.

whopper [wɒpə*] *n* (*col*: *lie*) embuste *m*; (: *large thing*): **a ~** uno/a enorme.

whopping [wɒpɪŋ] *a* (*col*) enorme.

whore [hɔ:*] *n* (*col*: *pej*) puta.

whose [huːz] *a*: **~ book is this?** ¿de quién es este libro?; **the man ~ son you rescued** el hombre cuyo hijo salvaste; **the girl ~ sister you were speaking to** la chica con cuya hermana estabas hablando ◆ *pron*: **~ is this?** ¿de quién es esto?; **I know ~ it is** yo sé de quien es.

why [waɪ] *ad* por qué; (*interrogative*) por qué, para qué ◆ *excl* ¡toma!, ¡cómo!; **tell me ~** dime por qué, dime la razón; **~ is he late?** ¿por qué lleva retraso?

whyever [waɪevə*] *ad* por qué.

WI *n abbr* (*Brit*: = *Women's Institute*) ≈ Asociacion *f* de Amas de casa ◆ *abbr* (*GEO*) = **West Indies**; (*US POST*) = *Wisconsin*.

wick [wɪk] *n* mecha.

wicked [wɪkɪd] *a* malvado, cruel.

wickedness [wɪkɪdnɪs] *n* maldad *f*, crueldad *f*.

wicker [wɪkə*] *n* (*also:* **~work**) artículos *mpl* de mimbre.

wicket [wɪkɪt] *n* (*CRICKET*) palos *mpl*.

wicket keeper *n* guardameta *m*.

wide [waɪd] *a* ancho; (*area, knowledge*) vasto, grande; (*choice*) grande ◆ *ad*: **to open ~** abrir de par en par; **to shoot ~** errar el tiro; **it is 3 metres ~** tiene 3 metros de ancho.

wide-angle lens [waɪdæŋgl-] *n* objetivo gran angular.

wide-awake [waɪdə'weɪk] *a* bien despierto.
wide-eyed [waɪd'aɪd] *a* con los ojos muy abiertos; *(fig)* ingenuo.
widely ['waɪdlɪ] *ad (differing)* muy; **it is ~ believed that ...** hay una convicción general de que ...; **to be ~ read** *(author)* ser muy leído; *(reader)* haber leído mucho.
widen ['waɪdn] *vt* ensanchar.
wideness ['waɪdnɪs] *n* anchura; amplitud *f*.
wide open *a* abierto de par en par.
wide-ranging [waɪd'reɪndʒɪŋ] *a (survey, report)* de gran alcance; *(interests)* muy diversos.
widespread ['waɪdsprɛd] *a (belief etc)* extendido, general.
widow ['wɪdəu] *n* viuda.
widowed ['wɪdəud] *a* viudo.
widower ['wɪdəuə*] *n* viudo.
width [wɪdθ] *n* anchura; *(of cloth)* ancho; **it's 7 metres in ~** tiene 7 metros de ancho.
widthways ['wɪdθweɪz] *ad* a lo ancho.
wield [wiːld] *vt (sword)* manejar; *(power)* ejercer.
wife, *pl* **wives** [waɪf, waɪvz] *n* mujer *f*, esposa.
wig [wɪg] *n* peluca.
wigging ['wɪgɪŋ] *n (Brit col)* rapapolvo, bronca.
wiggle ['wɪgl] *vt* menear ♦ *vi* menearse.
wiggly ['wɪglɪ] *a (line)* ondulado.
wigwam ['wɪgwæm] *n* tipí *m*, tienda india.
wild [waɪld] *a (animal)* salvaje; *(plant)* silvestre; *(rough)* furioso, violento; *(idea)* descabellado; *(col: angry)* furioso ♦ *n:* **the ~** la naturaleza; **~s** *npl* regiones *fpl* salvajes, tierras *fpl* vírgenes; **to be ~ about** *(enthusiastic)* estar *or* andar *(LAm)* loco por; **in its ~ state** en su estado natural.
wild card *n (COMPUT)* comodín *m.*
wildcat ['waɪldkæt] *n* gato montés.
wildcat strike *n* huelga espontánea *or* salvaje.
wilderness ['wɪldənɪs] *n* desierto.
wildfire [waɪldfaɪə*] *n:* **to spread like ~** correr como la pólvora (en reguero).
wild-goose chase [waɪld'guːs-] *n (fig)* búsqueda inútil.
wildlife ['waɪldlaɪf] *n* fauna.
wildly ['waɪldlɪ] *ad (roughly)* violentamente; *(foolishly)* locamente; *(rashly)* descabelladamente.
wiles [waɪlz] *npl* artimañas *fpl*, ardides *mpl.*
wilful, *(US)* **willful** ['wɪlful] *a (action)* deliberado; *(obstinate)* testarudo.
will [wɪl] *auxiliary vb:* **he ~ come** vendrá; **you won't lose it, ~ you?** no lo vayas a perder *or* no lo perderás ¿verdad?; *(in conjectures):* **that ~ be the postman** debe ser el cartero; **~ you sit down** *(politely)* ¿quiere (usted) sentarse?; *(angrily)* ¡siéntate!; **the car won't start** el coche no arranca ♦ *vt (pt, pp* **willed**): **to ~ sb to do sth** desear que uno haga algo; **he ~ed**

himself to go on con gran fuerza de voluntad, continuó ♦ *n* voluntad *f*; *(testament)* testamento; **against sb's ~** contra la voluntad de uno; **to do sth of one's own free ~** hacer algo por voluntad propia.
willful ['wɪlful] *a (US)* = **wilful.**
willing ['wɪlɪŋ] *a (with goodwill)* de buena voluntad; complaciente; **he's ~ to do it** está dispuesto a hacerlo; **to show ~** mostrarse dispuesto.
willingly ['wɪlɪŋlɪ] *ad* con mucho gusto.
willingness ['wɪlɪŋnɪs] *n* buena voluntad.
will-o'-the-wisp ['wɪləðə'wɪsp] *n* fuego fatuo; *(fig)* quimera.
willow ['wɪləu] *n* sauce *m.*
willpower ['wɪlpauə*] *n* fuerza de voluntad.
willy-nilly [wɪlɪ'nɪlɪ] *ad* quiérase o no.
wilt [wɪlt] *vi* marchitarse.
Wilts *abbr (Brit)* = Wiltshire.
wily ['waɪlɪ] *a* astuto.
wimp [wɪmp] *n (col)* endeble *m/f*, enclenque *m/f.*
win [wɪn] *n (in sports etc)* victoria, triunfo ♦ *vb (pt, pp* **won** [wʌn]) *vt* ganar; *(obtain: contract etc)* conseguir, lograr ♦ *vi* ganar, tener éxito.
win over, *(Brit)* **win round** *vt* convencer a.
wince [wɪns] *vi* encogerse.
winch [wɪntʃ] *n* torno.
Winchester disk ® ['wɪntʃɪstə-] *n (COMPUT)* disco Winchester ®.
wind *n* [wɪnd] viento; *(MED)* gases *mpl*; *(breath)* aliento ♦ *vb* [waɪnd] *(pt, pp* **wound** [waund]) *vt* enrollar; *(wrap)* envolver; *(clock, toy)* dar cuerda a; [wɪnd] *(take breath away from)* dejar sin aliento a ♦ *vi (road, river)* serpentear; **into** *or* **against the ~** contra el viento; **to get ~ of sth** enterarse de algo; **to break ~** ventosear.
wind down *vt (car window)* bajar; *(fig: production, business)* disminuir, bajar.
wind up *vt (clock)* dar cuerda a; *(debate)* concluir, terminar.
windbreak ['wɪndbreɪk] *n* barrera contra el viento.
windcheater ['wɪndtʃiːtə*], *(US)* **windbreaker** ['wɪndbreɪkə*] *n* cazadora.
winder ['waɪndə*] *n (on watch)* cuerda.
wind erosion *n* erosión *f* del viento.
windfall ['wɪndfɔːl] *n* golpe *m* de suerte.
winding ['waɪndɪŋ] *a (road)* tortuoso.
wind instrument *n (MUS)* instrumento de viento.
windmill ['wɪndmɪl] *n* molino de viento.
window ['wɪndəu] *n* ventana; *(in car, train)* ventanilla; *(in shop etc)* escaparate *m*, vitrina *(LAm)*, vidriera *(LAm)*; *(COMPUT)* ventanilla.
window box *n* jardinera (de ventana).
window cleaner *n (person)* limpiacristales *m inv.*
window dressing *n* decoración *f* de esca-

parates.

window envelope n sobre m de ventanilla.

window frame n marco de ventana.

window ledge n alféizar m, repisa (LAm).

window pane n cristal m.

window-shopping [wɪndəu'ʃɔpɪŋ] n: **to go ~** ir a ver or mirar escaparates.

windowsill ['wɪndəusɪl] n alféizar m, repisa (LAm).

windpipe ['wɪndpaɪp] n tráquea.

windscreen ['wɪndskriːn], (US) **windshield** ['wɪndʃiːld] n parabrisas m inv.

windscreen washer, (US) **windshield washer** n lavaparabrisas m inv.

windscreen wiper, (US) **windshield wiper** n limpiaparabrisas m inv.

windswept ['wɪndswɛpt] a azotado por el viento.

wind tunnel n túnel m aerodinámico.

windy ['wɪndɪ] a de mucho viento; **it's ~** hace viento.

wine [waɪn] n vino ◆ vt: **to ~ and dine sb** agasajar or festejar a uno.

wine cellar n bodega.

wine glass n copa (para vino).

wine-growing ['waɪngrəuɪŋ] a viticultor(a).

wine list n lista de vinos.

wine merchant n vinatero.

wine tasting n degustación f de vinos.

wine waiter n escanciador m.

wing [wɪŋ] n ala; (Brit AUT) aleta; **~s** npl (THEATRE) bastidores mpl.

winger ['wɪŋə*] n (SPORT) extremo.

wing mirror n (espejo) retrovisor m.

wing nut n tuerca (de) mariposa.

wingspan ['wɪŋspaen], **wingspread** ['wɪŋsprɛd] n envergadura.

wink [wɪŋk] n guiño, pestañeo ◆ vi guiñar, pestañear; (light etc) parpadear.

winkle ['wɪŋkl] n bígaro, bigarro.

winner ['wɪnə*] n ganador(a) m/f.

winning ['wɪnɪŋ] a (team) ganador(a); (goal) decisivo; (charming) encantador(a).

winning post n meta.

winnings ['wɪnɪŋz] npl ganancias fpl.

winsome ['wɪnsəm] a atractivo.

winter ['wɪntə*] n invierno ◆ vi invernar.

winter sports npl deportes mpl de invierno.

wintry ['wɪntrɪ] a invernal.

wipe [waɪp] n: **to give sth a ~** pasar un trapo sobre algo ◆ vt limpiar; **to ~ one's nose** limpiarse la nariz.

wipe off vt limpiar con un trapo.

wipe out vt (debt) liquidar; (memory) borrar; (destroy) destruir.

wipe up vt limpiar.

wire ['waɪə*] n alambre m; (ELEC) cable m (eléctrico); (TEL) telegrama m ◆ vt (house) poner la instalación eléctrica en;

(also: **~ up**) conectar.

wire cutters npl cortaalambres msg inv.

wireless ['waɪəlɪs] n (Brit) radio f.

wire mesh, wire netting n tela metálica.

wire-tapping ['waɪə'tæpɪŋ] n intervención f telefónica.

wiring ['waɪərɪŋ] n instalación f eléctrica.

wiry ['waɪərɪ] a enjuto y fuerte.

wisdom ['wɪzdəm] n sabiduría, saber m; (good sense) cordura.

wisdom tooth n muela del juicio.

wise [waɪz] a sabio; (sensible) juicioso; **I'm none the ~r** sigo sin entender.

wise up vi (col): **to ~ up (to sth)** enterarse (de algo).

...wise [waɪz] suff: **time~** en cuanto a or respecto al tiempo.

wisecrack ['waɪzkræk] n broma.

wish [wɪʃ] n (desire) deseo ◆ vt desear; (want) querer; **best ~es** (on birthday etc) felicidades fpl; **with best ~es** (in letter) saludos mpl, recuerdos mpl; **to ~ sb goodbye** despedirse de uno; **he ~ed me well** me deseó mucha suerte; **to ~ sth on sb** imponer algo a uno; **to ~ to do/sb to do sth** querer hacer/que uno haga algo; **to ~ for** desear.

wishful ['wɪʃful] n: **it's ~ thinking** eso sería soñar.

wishy-washy ['wɪʃɪwɔʃɪ] a (col: colour) desvaído; (: ideas, thinking) insípido.

wisp [wɪsp] n mechón m; (of smoke) voluta.

wistful ['wɪstful] a pensativo; (nostalgic) nostálgico.

wit [wɪt] n (wittiness) ingenio, gracia; (intelligence: also: **~s**) inteligencia; (person) chistoso/a; **to have** or **keep one's ~s about one** no perder la cabeza.

witch [wɪtʃ] n bruja.

witchcraft ['wɪtʃkrɑːft] n brujería.

witch doctor n hechicero.

witch-hunt ['wɪtʃhʌnt] n (POL) caza de brujas.

with [wɪð, wɪθ] prep con; (manner, means, cause): **she's gone down ~ flu** está con gripe; **red ~ anger** rojo de cólera; **to shake ~ fear** temblar de miedo; **to stay ~ friends** estar en casa de amigos; **the man ~ the grey hat** el hombre del sombrero gris; **I am ~ you** (I understand) te entiendo.

withdraw [wɪθ'drɔː] vb (irg: like draw) vt retirar, sacar ◆ vi retirarse; (go back on promise) retractarse; **to ~ money (from the bank)** retirar fondos (del banco); **to ~ into o.s.** ensimismarse.

withdrawal [wɪθ'drɔːəl] n retirada.

withdrawal symptoms npl síndrome m de abstinencia.

withdrawn [wɪθ'drɔːn] a (person) reservado, introvertido, apartado (LAm) ◆ pp of **withdraw**.

wither ['wɪðə*] *vi* marchitarse.
withered ['wɪðəd] *a* marchito, seco.
withhold [wɪθ'həuld] *vt* (*irg*: *like* **hold**) (*money*) retener; (*decision*) aplazar; (*permission*) negar; (*information*) ocultar.
within [wɪð'ɪn] *prep* dentro de ♦ *ad* dentro; ~ **reach** al alcance de la mano; ~ **sight of** a la vista de; ~ **the week** antes de acabar la semana; **to be** ~ **the law** estar dentro de la ley; ~ **an hour from now** dentro de una hora.
without [wɪð'aut] *prep* sin; **to go** *or* **do** ~ **sth** prescindir de algo; ~ **anybody knowing** sin saberlo nadie.
withstand [wɪθ'stænd] *vt* (*irg*: *like* **stand**) resistir a.
witness ['wɪtnɪs] *n* (*person*) testigo *m/f*; (*evidence*) testimonio ♦ *vt* (*event*) presenciar; (*document*) atestiguar la veracidad de; ~ **for the prosecution/defence** testigo de cargo/descargo; **to** ~ **to (having seen) sth** dar testimonio de (haber visto) algo.
witness box, (*US*) **witness stand** *n* tribuna de los testigos.
witticism ['wɪtɪsɪzm] *n* dicho ingenioso.
wittily ['wɪtɪlɪ] *ad* ingeniosamente.
witty ['wɪtɪ] *a* ingenioso.
wives [waɪvz] *npl of* **wife**.
wizard ['wɪzəd] *n* hechicero.
wizened ['wɪznd] *a* arrugado, marchito.
wk *abbr* = **week**.
Wm. *abbr* = **William**.
WO *n abbr* = **warrant officer**.
wobble ['wɔbl] *vi* tambalearse; (*chair*) ser poco firme.
wobbly ['wɔblɪ] *a* (*hand, voice*) tembloroso; (*table, chair*) tambaleante, cojo.
woe [wəu] *n* desgracia.
woke [wəuk] *pt of* **wake**.
woken ['wəukn] *pp of* **wake**.
wolf, *pl* **wolves** [wulf, wulvz] *n* lobo.
woman, *pl* **women** ['wumən, 'wɪmɪn] *n* mujer *f*; **young** ~ (mujer *f*) joven *f*; **women's page** (*PRESS*) sección *f* de la mujer.
woman doctor *n* doctora.
woman friend *n* amiga.
womanize ['wumənaɪz] *vi* ser un mujeriego.
womanly ['wumənlɪ] *a* femenino.
womb [wu:m] *n* (*ANAT*) matriz *f*, útero.
women ['wɪmɪn] *npl of* **woman**.
Women's (Liberation) Movement *n* (*also*: **women's lib**) Movimiento de Liberación de la Mujer.
won [wʌn] *pt*, *pp of* **win**.
wonder ['wʌndə*] *n* maravilla, prodigio; (*feeling*) asombro ♦ *vi*: **to** ~ **whether** preguntarse si; **to** ~ **at** asombrarse de; **to** ~ **about** pensar sobre *or* en; **it's no** ~ **that** no es de extrañarse que.
wonderful ['wʌndəful] *a* maravilloso.
wonderfully ['wʌndəfəlɪ] *ad* maravillosamente, estupendamente.

wonky ['wɔŋkɪ] *a* (*Brit col*: *unsteady*) poco seguro, cojo; (: *broken down*) estropeado.
won't [wəunt] = **will not**.
woo [wu:] *vt* (*woman*) cortejar.
wood [wud] *n* (*timber*) madera; (*forest*) bosque *m* ♦ *cpd* de madera.
wood alcohol *n* (*US*) alcohol *m* desnaturalizado.
wood carving *n* tallado en madera.
wooded ['wudɪd] *a* arbolado.
wooden ['wudn] *a* de madera; (*fig*) inexpresivo.
woodland ['wudlənd] *n* bosque *m*.
woodpecker ['wudpɛkə*] *n* pájaro carpintero.
wood pigeon *n* paloma torcaz.
woodwind ['wudwɪnd] *n* (*MUS*) instrumentos *mpl* de viento de madera.
woodwork ['wudwə:k] *n* carpintería.
woodworm ['wudwə:m] *n* carcoma.
woof [wuf] *n* (*of dog*) ladrido ♦ *vi* ladrar; ~, ~! ¡guau, guau!
wool [wul] *n* lana; **knitting** ~ lana (de hacer punto); **to pull the** ~ **over sb's eyes** (*fig*) dar a uno gato por liebre.
woollen, (*US*) **woolen** ['wulən] *a* de lana ♦ *n*: ~s géneros *mpl* de lana.
woolly, (*US*) **wooly** ['wulɪ] *a* lanudo, de lana; (*fig*: *ideas*) confuso.
word [wə:d] *n* palabra; (*news*) noticia; (*promise*) palabra (de honor) ♦ *vt* redactar; ~ **for** ~ palabra por palabra; **what's the** ~ **for "pen" in Spanish?** ¿cómo se dice "pen" en español?; **to put sth into** ~s expresar algo en palabras; **to have a** ~ **with sb** hablar (dos palabras) con uno; **in other** ~s en otras palabras; **to break/keep one's** ~ faltar a la palabra/ cumplir la promesa; **to leave** ~ **(with/for sb) that ...** dejar recado (con/para uno) de que ...; **to have** ~s **with sb** (*quarrel with*) discutir *or* reñir con uno.
wording ['wə:dɪŋ] *n* redacción *f*.
word-perfect ['wə:d'pə:fɪkt] *a* (*speech etc*) sin falta de expresión.
word processing *n* procesamiento de textos.
word processor [-'prəusɛsə*] *n* procesador *m* de textos.
wordwrap ['wə:dræp] *n* (*COMPUT*) salto de línea automático.
wordy ['wə:dɪ] *a* verboso, prolijo.
wore [wɔ:*] *pt of* **wear**.
work [wə:k] *n* trabajo; (*job*) empleo, trabajo; (*ART, LIT*) obra ♦ *vi* trabajar; (*mechanism*) funcionar, marchar; (*medicine*) ser eficaz, surtir efecto ♦ *vt* (*shape*) trabajar; (*stone etc*) tallar; (*mine etc*) explotar; (*machine*) manejar, hacer funcionar; (*cause*) producir; **to go to** ~ ir a trabajar *or* al trabajo; **to be at** ~ **(on sth)** estar trabajando (sobre algo); **to set to** ~, **start** ~ ponerse a trabajar; **to be out of** ~ estar

parado, no tener trabajo; **his life's** ~ el trabajo de su vida; **to** ~ **hard** trabajar mucho *or* duro; **to** ~ **to rule** (*INDUSTRY*) estar en huelga de brazos caídos; **to** ~ **loose** (*part*) desprenderse; (*knot*) aflojarse; *see also* **works**.

work off *vt*: **to** ~ **off one's feelings** desahogarse.

work on *vt fus* trabajar en, dedicarse a; (*principle*) basarse en; **he's** ~**ing on the car** está reparando el coche.

work out *vi* (*plans etc*) salir bien, funcionar; (*SPORT*) hacer ejercicios ♦ *vt* (*problem*) resolver; (*plan*) elaborar; **it** ~**s out at £100** suma 100 libras.

work up *vt*: **he** ~**ed his way up in the company** ascendió en la compañía mediante sus propios esfuerzos.

workable ['wɔːkəbl] *a* (*solution*) práctico, factible.

workaholic [wɔːkə'hɔlɪk] *n* curroadicto/a.

workbench ['wɔːkbɛntʃ] *n* banco *or* mesa de trabajo.

worked up [wɔːkt-] *a*: **to get** ~ excitarse.

worker ['wɔːkə*] *n* trabajador(a) *m/f*, obrero/a; **office** ~ oficinista *m/f*.

work force *n* mano *f* de obra.

work-in ['wɔːkɪn] *n* (*Brit*) ocupación *f* (de la empresa) sin interrupción del trabajo.

working ['wɔːkɪŋ] *a* (*day, week*) laborable; (*tools, conditions, clothes*) de trabajo; (*wife*) que trabaja; (*partner*) activo.

working capital *n* (*COMM*) capital *m* circulante.

working class *n* clase *f* obrera ♦ *a*: **working-class** obrero.

working knowledge *n* conocimientos *mpl* básicos.

working man *n* obrero.

working model *n* modelo operacional.

working order *n*: **in** ~ en funcionamiento.

working party *n* comisión *f* de investigación, grupo de trabajo.

working week *n* semana laboral.

work-in-progress ['wɔːkɪn'prəugrɛs] *n* (*COMM*) trabajo en proceso.

workload ['wɔːkləud] *n* carga de trabajo.

workman ['wɔːkmən] *n* obrero.

workmanship ['wɔːkmənʃɪp] *n* (*art*) hechura, arte *m*; (*skill*) habilidad *f*, trabajo.

workmate ['wɔːkmeɪt] *n* compañero/a de trabajo.

workout ['wɔːkaut] *n* (*SPORT*) sesión *f* de ejercicios.

work permit *n* permiso de trabajo.

works [wɔːks] *nsg* (*Brit: factory*) fábrica ♦ *npl* (*of clock, machine*) mecanismo; **road** ~ obras *fpl*.

works council *n* comité *m* de empresa.

worksheet ['wɔːkʃiːt] *n* (*COMPUT*) hoja de trabajo.

workshop ['wɔːkʃɔp] *n* taller *m*.

work station *n* puesto *or* estación *f* de trabajo.

work study *n* estudio del trabajo.

work-to-rule ['wɔːktə'ruːl] *n* (*Brit*) huelga de brazos caídos.

world [wɔːld] *n* mundo ♦ *cpd* (*champion*) del mundo; (*power, war*) mundial; **all over the** ~ por todo el mundo, en el mundo entero; **the business** ~ el mundo de los negocios; **what in the** ~ **is he doing?** ¿qué diablos está haciendo?; **to think the** ~ **of sb** (*fig*) tener un concepto muy alto de uno; **to do sb a** ~ **of good** sentar muy bien a uno; **W**~ **War One/Two** la primera/segunda Guerra Mundial.

World Cup *n* (*FOOTBALL*) Copa Mundial.

world-famous [wɔːld'feɪməs] *a* de fama mundial, mundialmente famoso.

worldly ['wɔːldlɪ] *a* mundano.

world-wide ['wɔːldwaɪd] *a* mundial, universal.

worm [wɔːm] *n* gusano; (*earth*~) lombriz *f*.

worn [wɔːn] *pp of* **wear** ♦ *a* usado.

worn-out ['wɔːnaut] *a* (*object*) gastado; (*person*) rendido, agotado.

worried ['wʌrɪd] *a* preocupado; **to be** ~ **about sth** estar preocupado por algo.

worrisome ['wʌrɪsəm] *a* preocupante, inquietante.

worry ['wʌrɪ] *n* preocupación *f* ♦ *vt* preocupar, inquietar ♦ *vi* preocuparse; **to** ~ **about** *or* **over sth/sb** preocuparse por algo/uno.

worrying ['wʌrɪɪŋ] *a* inquietante.

worse [wɔːs] *a, ad* peor ♦ *n* el peor, lo peor; **a change for the** ~ un empeoramiento; **so much the** ~ **for you** tanto peor para ti; **he is none the** ~ **for it** se ha quedado tan fresco *or* tan tranquilo; **to get** ~, **to grow** ~ empeorar.

worsen ['wɔːsn] *vt, vi* empeorar.

worse off *a* (*fig*): **you'll be** ~ **this way** de esta forma estarás peor que nunca; **he is now** ~ **than before** ha quedado aun peor que antes.

worship ['wɔːʃɪp] *n* (*organized* ~) culto; (*act*) adoración *f* ♦ *vt* adorar; **Your W**~ (*Brit: to mayor*) señor alcalde; (: *to judge*) señor juez.

worshipper, (*US*) **worshiper** ['wɔːʃɪpə*] *n* devoto/a.

worst [wɔːst] *a* (el/la) peor ♦ *ad* peor ♦ *n* lo peor; **at** ~ en el peor de los casos; **to come off** ~ llevar la peor parte; **if the** ~ **comes to the** ~ en último caso.

worsted ['wustɪd] *n*: (**wool**) ~ estambre *m*.

worth [wɔːθ] *n* valor *m* ♦ *a*: **to be** ~ valer; **how much is it** ~? ¿cuánto vale?; **it's** ~ **it** vale *or* merece la pena; **to be** ~ **one's while (to do)** merecer la pena (hacer); **it's not** ~ **the trouble** no vale *or* merece la pena.

worthless ['wɔːθlɪs] *a* sin valor; (*useless*)

inútil.

worthwhile ['wəːθwaɪl] a (activity) que merece la pena; (cause) loable.

worthy [wəːðɪ] a (person) respetable; (motive) honesto; ~ **of** digno de.

would [wʊd] auxiliary vb: **she** ~ **come** (ella) vendría; (emphatic): **you WOULD say that,** ~**n't you!** ¡ ¡qué otra cosa ibas a decir!; (insistence): **she** ~**n't behave** no hubo forma de que se portara bien; **he** ~ **have come** él hubiera venido; ~ **you like a biscuit?** ¿quieres una galleta?; ~ **you close the door please?** ¿quiere hacer el favor de cerrar la puerta?; **he** ~ **go on Mondays** solía ir los lunes.

would-be ['wʊdbiː] a (pej) presunto.

wouldn't ['wʊdnt] = **would not.**

wound vb [waʊnd] pt, pp of **wind** ♦ n, vt [wuːnd] n herida ♦ vt herir.

wove [wəʊv] pt of **weave.**

woven ['wəʊvən] pp of **weave.**

WP n abbr = **word processing, word processor** ♦ abbr (Brit col: = **weather permitting**) si lo permite el tiempo.

WPC n abbr (Brit) = **woman police constable.**

wpm abbr (= **words per minute**) p.p.m.

WRAC n abbr (Brit: = **Women's Royal Army Corps**) cuerpo auxiliar femenino del ejército de tierra.

WRAF n abbr (Brit: = **Women's Royal Air Force**) cuerpo auxiliar femenino del ejército del aire.

wrangle ['ræŋgl] n riña ♦ vi reñir.

wrap [ræp] n (stole) chal m ♦ vt (also: ~ up) envolver; **under** ~**s** (fig: plan, scheme) escondido; (LAm) tapado.

wrapper ['ræpə*] n (Brit: of book) sobrecubierta; (on chocolate etc) envoltura.

wrapping paper ['ræpɪŋ-] n papel m de envolver.

wrath [rɔθ] n cólera.

wreak [riːk] vt (destruction) causar; **to** ~ **havoc (on)** hacer or causar estragos (en); **to** ~ **vengeance (on)** vengarse (en).

wreath, ~**s** [riːθ, riːðz] n (funeral ~) corona; (of flowers) guirnalda.

wreck [rɛk] n (ship: destruction) naufragio; (: remains) restos mpl del barco; (pej: person) ruina ♦ vt destruir, hundir; (fig) arruinar.

wreckage ['rɛkɪdʒ] n (remains) restos mpl; (of building) escombros mpl.

wrecker ['rɛkə*] n (US: breakdown van) camión-grúa m.

WREN [rɛn] n abbr (Brit) miembro del WRNS.

wren [rɛn] n (zool) reyezuelo.

wrench [rɛntʃ] n (tech) llave f inglesa; (tug) tirón m ♦ vt arrancar; **to** ~ **sth from sb** arrebatar algo violentamente a uno.

wrest [rɛst] vt: **to** ~ **sth from sb** arrebatar

or arrancar algo a uno.

wrestle ['rɛsl] vi: **to** ~ **(with sb)** luchar (con or contra uno).

wrestler ['rɛslə*] n luchador(a) m/f (de lucha libre).

wrestling ['rɛslɪŋ] n lucha libre.

wrestling match n partido de lucha libre.

wretch [rɛtʃ] n desgraciado/a, miserable m/f; **little** ~! (often humorous) ¡pillo!; ¡pícaro!

wretched ['rɛtʃɪd] a miserable.

wriggle ['rɪgl] vi serpentear.

wring pt, pp **wrung** [rɪŋ, rʌŋ] vt torcer, retorcer; (wet clothes) escurrir; (fig): **to** ~ **sth out of sb** sacar algo por la fuerza a uno.

wringer ['rɪŋə*] n escurridor m.

wringing ['rɪŋɪŋ] a (also: ~ **wet**) ·empapado.

wrinkle ['rɪŋkl] n arruga ♦ vt arrugar ♦ vi arrugarse.

wrinkled ['rɪŋkld], **wrinkly** ['rɪŋklɪ] a (fabric, paper, etc) arrugado.

wrist [rɪst] n muñeca.

wristband ['rɪstbænd] n (Brit: of shirt) puño; (: of watch) correa.

wrist watch n reloj m de pulsera.

writ [rɪt] n mandato judicial; **to serve a** ~ **on sb** notificar un mandato judicial a uno.

write, pt **wrote,** pp **written** [raɪt, rəʊt, 'rɪtn] vt, vi escribir; **to** ~ **sb a letter** escribir una carta a uno.

write away vi: **to** ~ **away for** (information, goods) pedir por escrito or carta.

write down vt escribir; (note) apuntar.

write off vt (debt) borrar (como incobrable); (fig) desechar por inútil; (smash up: car) destrozar.

write out vt escribir.

write up vt redactar.

write-off ['raɪtɔf] n pérdida total; **the car is a** ~ el coche es pura chatarra.

write-protect ['raɪtprə'tɛkt] vt (comput) proteger contra escritura.

writer ['raɪtə*] n escritor(a) m/f.

write-up ['raɪtʌp] n (review) crítica, reseña.

writhe [raɪð] vi retorcerse.

writing ['raɪtɪŋ] n escritura; (hand~) letra; (of author) obras; **in** ~ por escrito; **to put sth in** ~ poner algo por escrito; **in my own** ~ escrito por mí.

writing case n estuche m de papel de escribir.

writing desk n escritorio.

writing paper n papel m de escribir.

writings npl obras fpl.

written ['rɪtn] pp of **write.**

WRNS n abbr (Brit: = **Women's Royal Naval Service**) cuerpo auxiliar femenino de la armada.

wrong [rɔŋ] a (wicked) malo; (unfair) injusto; (incorrect) equivocado, incorrecto;

(*not suitable*) inoportuno, inconveniente ◆ *ad* mal; equivocadamente ◆ *n* mal *m*; (*injustice*) injusticia ◆ *vt* ser injusto con; (*hurt*) agraviar; **to be** ~ (*answer*) estar equivocado; (*in doing, saying*) equivocarse; **it's** ~ **to steal, stealing is** ~ es malo robar; **you are** ~ **to do it** estás equivocado en hacerlo, cometes un error al hacerlo; **you are** ~ **about that, you've got it** ~ en eso estás equivocado; **to be in the** ~ no tener razón, tener la culpa; **what's** ~? ¿qué pasa?; **what's** ~ **with the car?** ¿qué le pasa al coche?; **there's nothing** ~ no pasa nada; **you have the** ~ **number** (*TEL*) se ha equivocado (usted) de número; **to go** ~ (*person*) equivocarse; (*plan*) salir mal; (*machine*) estropearse.

wrongful [ˈrɔŋful] *a* injusto; ~ **dismissal** (*INDUSTRY*) despido improcedente *or* injustificado.

wrongly [ˈrɔŋlɪ] *ad* (*answer, do, count*) incorrectamente; (*treat*) injustamente.

wrote [rəut] *pt of* **write**.

wrought [rɔːt] *a:* ~ **iron** hierro forjado.

wrung [rʌŋ] *pt, pp of* **wring**.

WRVS *n abbr* (*Brit:* = *Women's Royal Voluntary Service*) cuerpo de voluntarias al servicio de la comunidad.

wry [raɪ] *a* irónico.

wt. *abbr* = **weight**.

WV *abbr* (*US POST*) = *West Virginia*.

WY *abbr* (*US POST*) = *Wyoming*.

WYSIWYG [ˈwɪzɪwɪg] *abbr* (*COMPUT*: = *what you see is what you get*) tipo de presentación en un procesador de textos.

X

X, x [eks] *n* (*letter*) X, x *f*: (*Brit CINEMA*: *formerly*) no apto para menores de 18 años; **X for Xmas** X de Xiquena; **if you earn X dollars a year** si ganas X dólares al año.

X-certificate [ˈɛksəˈtɪfɪkɪt] *a* (*Brit: film: formerly*) no apto para menores de 18 años.

Xerox ® [ˈzɪərɔks] *n* (*also:* ~ **machine**) fotocopiadora; (*photocopy*) fotocopia ◆ *vt* fotocopiar.

XL *abbr* (= *extra large*) E.

Xmas [ˈɛksməs] *n abbr* = **Christmas**.

X-rated [ˈeksˈreɪtɪd] *a* (*US: film*) no apto para menores de 18 años.

X-ray [eksˈreɪ] *n* radiografía; ~**s** *npl* rayos *mpl* X ◆ *vt* radiografiar a.

xylophone [ˈzaɪləfəun] *n* xilófono.

Y

Y, y [waɪ] *n* (*letter*) Y, y *f*; **Y for Yellow**, (*US*) **Y for Yoke** Y de Yegua.

yacht [jɔt] *n* yate *m*.

yachting [ˈjɔtɪŋ] *n* (*sport*) balandrismo.

yachtsman [ˈjɔtsmən] *n* balandrista *m*.

yachtswoman [ˈjɔtswumən] balandrista.

yam [jæm] *n* ñame *m*; (*sweet potato*) batata, (*LAm*) camote *m*.

Yank [jæŋk], **Yankee** [ˈjæŋkɪ] *n* (*pej*) yanqui *m/f*.

yank [jæŋk] *vt* tirar de, (*LAm*) jalar de ◆ *n* tirón *m*.

yap [jæp] *vi* (*dog*) aullar.

yard [jɑːd] *n* patio; (*US: garden*) jardín *m*; (*measure*) yarda; **builder's** ~ depósito.

yardstick [ˈjɑːdstɪk] *n* (*fig*) criterio, norma.

yarn [jɑːn] *n* hilo; (*tale*) cuento (chino), historia.

yawn [jɔːn] *n* bostezo ◆ *vi* bostezar.

yawning [ˈjɔːnɪŋ] *a* (*gap*) muy abierto.

yd. *abbr* (= *yard*) yda.

yeah [jɛə] *ad* (*col*) sí.

year [jɪə*] *n* año; (*SCOL, UNIV*) curso, clase *f*; **this** ~ este año; ~ **in,** ~ **out** año tras año; **a** *or* **per** ~ al año; **to be 8** ~**s old** tener 8 años; **she's three** ~**s old** tiene tres años; **an eight-**~**-old child** un niño de ocho años (de edad).

yearbook [ˈjɪəbuk] *n* anuario.

yearling [ˈjɪəlɪŋ] *n* (*racehorse*) potro de un año.

yearly [ˈjɪəlɪ] *a* anual ◆ *ad* anualmente, cada año; **twice** ~ dos veces al año.

yearn [jəːn] *vi:* **to** ~ **for sth** añorar algo, suspirar por algo.

yearning [ˈjəːnɪŋ] *n* ansia, añoranza.

yeast [jiːst] *n* levadura.

yell [jɛl] *n* grito, alarido ◆ *vi* gritar.

yellow [ˈjɛləu] *a, n* amarillo.

yellow fever *n* fiebre *f* amarilla.

yellowish [ˈjɛləuʃ] *a* amarillento.

Yellow Sea *n:* **the** ~ el Mar Amarillo.

yelp [jɛlp] *n* aullido ◆ *vi* aullar.

Yemen [ˈjɛmən] *n* el Yemen.

Yemeni [ˈjɛmənɪ] *a, n* yemenita *m/f*.

yen [jɛn] *n* (*currency*) yen *m*.

yeoman [ˈjəumən] *n:* **Y**~ **of the Guard** alabardero de la Casa Real.

yes [jɛs] *ad, n* sí *m*; **to say/answer** ~ decir/contestar que sí; **to say** ~ **(to)** decir que sí (a), conformarse (con).

yes man *n* pelotillero.

yesterday [ˈjɛstədɪ] *ad, n* ayer *m*; ~ **morning/evening** ayer por la mañana/

tarde; **all day** ~ todo el día de ayer; **the day before** ~ antes de ayer, anteayer.

yet [jɛt] *ad* todavía ♦ *conj* sin embargo, a pesar de todo; ~ **again** de nuevo; **it is not finished** ~ todavía no está acabado; **the best** ~ el/la mejor hasta ahora; **as** ~ hasta ahora, todavía.

yew [juː] *n* tejo.

YHA *n abbr* (*Brit*: = *Youth Hostel Association*) ≈ Red *f* Española de Albergues Juveniles.

Yiddish ['jɪdɪʃ] *n* yiddish *m*.

yield [jiːld] *n* producción *f*; (*AGR*) cosecha; (*COMM*) rendimiento ♦ *vt* producir, dar; (*profit*) rendir ♦ *vi* rendirse, ceder; (*US AUT*) ceder el paso; **a** ~ **of 5%** un rédito del 5 por ciento.

YMCA *n abbr* (= *Young Men's Christian Association*) Asociación *f* de Jóvenes Cristianos.

yob(bo) ['jɔb(bəu)] *n* (*Brit col*) gamberro.

yodel ['jəudl] *vi* cantar a la tirolesa.

yoga ['jəugə] *n* yoga *m*.

yog(h)ourt, yog(h)urt ['jəugət] *n* yogur *m*.

yoke [jəuk] *n* (*of oxen*) yunta; (*on shoulders*) balancín *m*; (*fig*) yugo ♦ *vt* (*also:* ~ **together**: *oxen*) uncir, acoplar.

yolk [jəuk] *n* yema (de huevo).

yonder ['jɔndə*] *ad* allá (a lo lejos).

Yorks *abbr* (*Brit*) = *Yorkshire*.

you [juː] *pron* tú; (*pl*) vosotros; (*polite form*) usted; (: *pl*) ustedes; (*complement*) te; (: *pl*) os; (*after prep*) tí; (: *pl*) vosotros; (: *formal*) le/la; (: *pl*) les; (*after prep*) usted; (: *pl*) ustedes; (*one*): ~ **never know** nunca se sabe; (*impersonal*) uno; **fresh air does** ~ **good** el aire fresco te hace bien; ~ **can't do that** eso no se hace; **I'll see** ~ **tomorrow** hasta mañana; **if I was or were** ~ yo que tú, yo en tu lugar.

you'd [juːd] = **you had, you would**.

you'll [juːl] = **you will, you shall**.

young [jʌŋ] *a* joven ♦ *npl* (*of animal*) cría; (*people*): **the** ~ los jóvenes, la juventud; **a** ~ **man/lady** un(a) joven; **my** ~**er brother** mi hermano menor; **the** ~**er generation** la nueva generación.

youngster ['jʌŋstə*] *n* joven *m/f*.

your [jɔː*] *a* tu; (*pl*) vuestro; (*formal*) su; ~ **house** tu *etc* casa; *see also* **my**.

you're [juə*] = **you are**.

yours [jɔːz] *pron* tuyo; (: *pl*) vuestro; (*formal*) suyo; **a friend of** ~ un amigo tuyo *etc*; *see also* **faithfully, mine, sincerely**.

yourself [jɔː'sɛlf] *pron* (*reflexive*) tú mismo; (*complement*) te; (*after prep*) tí (mismo); (*formal*) usted mismo; (: *complement*) se; (: *after prep*) sí (mismo); **you** ~ **told me** me lo dijiste tú mismo; **(all) by** ~ sin ayuda de nadie, solo; *see also* **oneself**.

yourselves [jɔː'sɛlvz] *pl pron* vosotros mismos; (*after prep*) vosotros (mismos);

(*formal*) ustedes (mismos); (: *complement*) se; (: *after prep*) sí mismos.

youth [juːθ] *n* juventud *f*; (*young man*) (*pl* ~**s** [juːðz]) joven *m*; **in my** ~ en mi juventud.

youth club *n* club *m* juvenil.

youthful ['juːθful] *a* juvenil.

youthfulness ['juːθfəlnɪs] *n* juventud *f*.

youth hostel *n* albergue *m* de juventud.

youth movement *n* movimiento juvenil.

you've [juːv] = **you have**.

yowl [jaul] *n* (*of animal, person*) aullido ♦ *vi* aullar.

yr. *abbr* (= *year*) a.

YT *abbr* (*Canada*) = *Yukon Territory*.

YTS *n abbr* (*Brit*: = *Youth Training Scheme*) *plan de inserción profesional juvenil*.

Yugoslav ['juːgəuslɑːv] *a, n* yugoslavo/a *m/f*.

Yugoslavia [juːgəu'slɑːvɪə] *n* Yugoslavia.

Yugoslavian [juːgəu'slɑːvɪən] *a* yugoslavo/a.

yuppie ['jʌpɪ] (*col*) *a, n* yuppie *m/f*.

YWCA *n abbr* (= *Young Women's Christian Association*) Asociación *f* de Jóvenes Cristianas.

Z

Z, z [zɛd, (*US*) ziː] *n* (*letter*) Z, z *f*; **Z for Zebra** Z de Zaragoza.

Zaire [zɑː'iːə*] *n* Zaire *m*.

Zambia ['zæmbɪə] *n* Zambia.

Zambian ['zæmbɪən] *a, n* zambiano/a *m/f*.

zany ['zeɪnɪ] *a* estrafalario.

zap [zæp] *vt* (*COMPUT*) borrar.

zeal [ziːl] *n* celo, entusiasmo.

zealot ['zɛlət] *n* fanático/a.

zealous ['zɛləs] *a* celoso, entusiasta.

zebra ['ziːbrə] *n* cebra.

zebra crossing *n* (*Brit*) paso de peatones.

zenith ['zɛnɪθ] *n* (*ASTRO*) cénit *m*; (*fig*) apogeo.

zero ['zɪərəu] *n* cero; **5 degrees below** ~ 5 grados bajo cero.

zero hour *n* hora cero.

zero-rated ['zɪərəureɪtɪd] *a* (*Brit*) de tasa cero.

zest [zɛst] *n* ánimo, vivacidad *f*; ~ **for living** brío.

zigzag ['zɪgzæg] *n* zigzag *m* ♦ *vi* zigzaguear.

Zimbabwe [zɪm'bɑːbwɪ] *n* Zimbabwe *m*.

Zimbabwean [zɪm'bɑːbwɪən] *a, n* zimbabuo/a *m/f*.

zinc [zɪŋk] *n* cinc *m*, zinc *m*.

Zionism ['zaɪənɪzm] *n* sionismo.

Zionist ['zaɪənɪst] *a, n* sionista *m/f*.
zip [zɪp] *n* (*also:* ~ **fastener**, (*US*) ~**per**) cremallera, cierre *m* (*LAm*); (*energy*) energía, vigor *m* ◆ *vt* (*also:* ~ **up**) cerrar la cremallera de ◆ *vi*: **to** ~ **along to the shops** ir de compras volando.
zip code *n* (*US*) código postal.
zither ['zɪðə*] *n* cítara.
zodiac ['zəudɪæk] *n* zodíaco.
zombie ['zɔmbɪ] *n* (*fig*): **like a** ~ como un autómata.
zone [zəun] *n* zona.

zoo [zuː] *n* (jardín *m*) zoológico.
zoological [zuːəˈlɔdʒɪkəl] *a* zoológico.
zoologist [zuˈɔlədʒɪst] *n* zoólogo/a.
zoology [zuːˈɔlədʒɪ] *n* zoología.
zoom [zuːm] *vi*: **to** ~ **past** pasar zumbando; **to** ~ **in (on sth/sb)** (*PHOT, CINEMA*) enfocar (algo/a uno) con el zoom.
zoom lens *n* zoom *m*.
zucchini [zuːˈkiːnɪ] *n*(*pl*) (*US*) calabacín(ines) *m*(*pl*).
Zulu ['zuːluː] *a, n* zulú *m/f*.

THE COLLINS
PAPERBACK SPANISH DICTIONARY

★ Over 70,000 references and 100,000 translations

★ Fully up-to-date with emphasis on current usage

★ Thousands of constructions and idioms

★ Extensive vocabulary to help the general reader
understand Spanish newspapers, magazines and
contemporary literature

★ Wide coverage in areas relevant to business and office
automation

★ Hundreds of common abbreviations and acronyms
explained and translated

★ Clear signposting of meanings and style level, to guide
the user to the most appropriate translation

★ Pronunciation clearly shown using the International
Phonetic Alphabet

★ The most useful and comprehensive Spanish paperback
dictionary available for home, office and study use

Price in the U.K.
£5.99 net
Canada $11.95

ISBN 0-00-433335-7

00599